## IN BRIEF

## THE RESPONSIBLE MANAGER

## INSIDE STORY

# Managers and the Legal Environment

## STRATEGIES FOR THE 21ST CENTURY

CONSTANCE E. BAGLEY
*Harvard Business School*

DIANE W. SAVAGE
*Stanford Graduate School of Business*
*Cooley Godward LLP*

Australia · Canada · Mexico · Singapore · Spain · United Kingdom · United States

***Managers and the Legal Environment: Strategies for the 21st Century, Fifth Edition***

Constance E. Bagley, Diane W. Savage

**VP/Editorial Director:**
Jack W. Calhoun

**Publisher:**
Rob Dewey

**Acquisitions Editor:**
Steve Silverstein, Esq.

**Senior Developmental Editor:**
Jan Lamar

**Executive Marketing Manager:**
Lisa Lysne

**Production Editor:**
Tamborah E. Moore

**Manager of Technology, Editorial:**
Vicky True

**Technology Project Editor:**
Christine Wittmer

**Web Coordinator:**
Scott Cook

**Senior Manufacturing Coordinator:**
Charlene Taylor

**Production House:**
LEAP Publishing Services

**Compositor:**
Parkwood Composition

**Printer:**
Transcontinental Printing

**Art Director:**
Michelle Kunkler

**Cover and Internal Designer:**
Grannan Graphic Design,
Cincinnati, OH

**Cover Images:**
© Solveig Stibbe/Alamy and Getty Images, Inc.



Printed in Canada

3 4 5 08 07 06

Student Edition:
ISBN 13: 978-0-324-26951-2
ISBN 10: 0-324-26951-X



Library of Congress Control Number:
2005925692

For more information about our products, contact us at:

Thomson Learning Academic Resource Center 1-800-423-0563

**Thomson Higher Education**
5191 Natorp Boulevard
Mason, Ohio 45040
USA

# DEDICATION

*To my son*
*Christoph Alexei.*
*You're the best.*
*C.E.B.*

*To my family*
*John, Brandon, Shannon, and Caitlin.*
*D.W.S.*

# CONTENTS IN BRIEF

# TABLE OF CONTENTS

## UNIT V
## Corporate Governance, Ownership, and Control 707



## UNIT VI
## Securities and Financial Transactions 817

# TABLE OF CASES

The principal cases are in bold type. Cases cited or discussed are in light type.

## A



## B

# C

# D

# H



# I

# J



# K



# L

# M

# N



# O



# P

# Q



# R



# S

# T



# U

# V



# W

# X



# Y



# Z

# PREFACE

It is hard to imagine a time when law was more important to managers. The demise of Arthur Andersen, Enron, and WorldCom; the convictions of top executives at ImClone Systems, Adelphia Communications, Rite Aid, WorldCom, and Enron; the payment of record fines by Wall Street firms and drug companies; and the scandals at Tyco, Boeing, Marsh McLellan, and other companies all graphically demonstrate the consequences of failing to comply with the letter and spirit of the law. An unprecedented series of accounting scandals in the late 1990s shook public confidence in the U.S. capital markets. In the case of WorldCom alone, $200 billion of shareholder value was lost in less than 12 months, making it the largest corporate fraud in history. Clearly, no business curriculum today would be complete without an overview of the legal environment in which business takes place.

Yet, staying out of trouble is only part of the picture. Law not only regulates, it also enables and facilitates.[1] From the outset, *Managers and the Legal Environment: Strategies for the 21st Century* has sought to reframe the relationship of law to business by addressing topics not traditionally covered, such as intellectual property and corporate governance. Rather than viewing law and ethics purely as constraints to be complied with and reacted to, we believe that managers can be proactive and exploit opportunities to use the law and the legal system to increase both the total value created and the share of that value captured by the firm.

A key objective of the fifth edition of *Managers and the Legal Environment: Strategies for the 21st Century,* co-authored by the new team of Constance E. Bagley from the Harvard Business School and Diane W. Savage from the Stanford Graduate School of Business and the law firm of Cooley Goward LLP, is to help future managers develop a managerial competency we call "legal astuteness," which enables them to use the law to manage the business enterprise more effectively. To achieve legal astuteness, managers must learn to bridge the communications gaps that can occur when they work with attorneys. They need to develop a common language. *Managers and the Legal Environment: Strategies for the 21st Century* will help future managers develop such a common language and an appreciation of the role of law in management.

As its title implies, the text is designed as a "hands-on" transactional guide for future and current business managers and leaders, including entrepreneurs. It provides a broad and detailed understanding of how law impacts daily management decisions and business strategies and offers tools managers can use to manage more effectively. The text also highlights traps for the unwary so managers can both spot legal issues before they become legal problems and effectively handle the inevitable legal disputes that will arise in the course of doing business. No manager operating in the complex and ever-changing global business environment of the early twenty-first century can compete successfully without such knowledge.

The text tightly integrates the treatment of law and management. Law is not presented in a vacuum. Instead, its relevance to management is made explicit at the beginning of every chapter. Court cases are chosen for their managerial relevance. Each chapter ends not with a summary of black-letter law but with a discussion of ways managers can use the laws and legal tools discussed in the chapter to create value, marshal resources, and manage risk.

The text provides practical examples of how managers can use the law strategically and tactically to craft solutions that make it possible to attain the core business objectives without incurring undue legal risk or

1. M. C. Suchman, D. J. Steward & C. A. Westfall, *The Legal Environment of Entrepreneurship: Observations on the Legitimization of Venture Finance in Silicon Valley,* in C. B. Schoonhoven & E. Romanell (eds.), The Entrepreneurship Dynamic: Origins of Entrepreneurship and the Evolution of Industries (2001).

forgoing the capture of value. For example, the chapter on intellectual property explains how firms can use copyrights, patents, and trade-secret protection to capture the value of the intellectual capital they create. It also discusses the use of trademarks to protect brand equity.

The topics covered in *Managers and the Legal Environment: Strategies for the 21st Century* demonstrate its focus on meeting the needs of business managers and leaders. The text covers not only such essential legal topics as agency, contracts, torts, criminal law, antitrust, and employment law, but also others of vital concern to business managers, such as intellectual property, corporate governance, securities regulation, bankruptcy, and environmental law. The chapter on international business transactions illustrates the overall approach in the text: It includes not only such key legal concepts as sovereign immunity and extraterritorial application of national law, but also a detailed discussion of the blend of legal, financial, operational, and logistical issues that often will determine the success or failure of an international investment transaction or joint venture.

The legal topics discussed in the text are on the leading edge of business regulation. They include corporate governance and executive compensation; the requirements of the Sarbanes–Oxley Act of 2002; consumer privacy, identity theft, and the Internet; copyright law in cyberspace; the patentability of business processes and genetically modified organisms; mandatory arbitration of employment disputes; employer liability for sexual harassment; selective disclosure of inside information to securities analysts; and product liability for product design defects.

This text is suitable for classes in the legal environment of business at the undergraduate, M.B.A., executive M.B.A., or executive education levels. It is a comprehensive and challenging, yet approachable and understandable, text that will work for those with substantial work experience as well as those who are studying business at the undergraduate level for the first time.

## Pedagogical Features

Each chapter of *Managers and the Legal Environment: Strategies for the 21st Century* employs a wide array of effective teaching devices that reinforce the goals of the text.

### NEW CONCEPTUAL FRAMEWORKS

The fifth edition presents several new conceptual frameworks to help students better understand the intersection of law, management, and ethics. Based on Professor Bagley's analysis of literally thousands of cases, statutes, and regulations, she has created a typology of the underlying rationales of the U.S. public law governing businesses, which is presented in Exhibits 1.1 through 1.5. As the chapter points out, other countries tend to have laws that further many of these same objectives, albeit with varying degrees of emphasis on the different objectives and varying ways of furthering them. Exhibit 1.6 illustrates the role of law in the value chain, and Exhibit 1.7 presents a systems approach to business regulation and the pursuit of opportunity. The model explains that public laws affect the firm's ability to create realizable value and to manage risk by helping shape the firm's competitive environment and its resources and capabilities. It also shows how firm action prompts changes in the public rules and how managers can use the law and the tools it offers to pursue opportunity and capture value while managing the attendant risks.

Exhibit 1.8 summarizes a variety of legal tools available during various stages of business development (ranging from evaluating the opportunity and defining the value proposition to harvest) to further the managerial objectives of creating realizable value and managing risk. By mapping legal tools against these key managerial objectives, Exhibit 1.8 seeks to frame the legal aspects of management in terms more readily accessible to students of business. Exhibit 1.10 presents the Ethical Business Leader's Decision Tree[2], which is a tool managers and their counsel can use to evaluate the legal and ethical aspects of their strategy and its implementation. Exhibit 20.1 presents a revised decision tree for understanding how the business judgment rule is applied to board decisions.

### A CASE IN POINT

Each chapter presents two to six cases, set off from the body of the text, as examples of business law in action. These cases represent crucial court decisions that have shaped important business law concepts or that present key legal conflicts that managers will address in their careers. Included are many modern cases that represent the most current statement of the law. These cases include, for example, the U.S. Supreme Court's 2005 decision in *United States v. Booker* (Case 14.2), which struck down the mandatory character of the Federal Sentencing Guidelines; the U.S. District Court's 2004 antitrust ruling permitting the merger of Oracle Corporation and PeopleSoft, two of the largest software

2. This first appeared in Constance E. Bagley, *The Ethical Leader's Decision Tree,* 81 HARV. BUS. REV. 18 (Feb. 2003).

manufacturers in the world (*United States v. Oracle*) (Case 16.5); and the Delaware Court of Chancery's 2003 decision holding that the directors of the Disney Company could be personally liable for breach of the duty of good faith for supinely acquiescing in CEO Michael Eisner's selection, compensation, and termination of his long-time friend Michael Ovitz (*In re The Walt Disney Company Derivative Litigation*) (Case 21.1). Other traditional cases, such as *Meinhard v. Salmon* (Case 1.2) and *MacPherson v. Buick Motor Co.* (Case 10.1), are used to show early developments in the law that remain applicable today. The selection and approach to cases is guided by the authors' goals of teaching students how to use the law strategically and how to identify legal issues before they become legal problems.

The format of each Case in Point is designed to convey a detailed understanding of the cases while covering a large range of material. The case citation and facts are followed by a statement of the issue presented, which reinforces the legal principle being illustrated by the case. Each case discussion then proceeds with a presentation of the court's decision and a description of the result.

The opinions in at least two cases in each chapter are presented in the language of the court, edited for clarity and brevity. Excerpts from dissenting opinions are used occasionally to demonstrate how reasonable people can come to different conclusions about the same facts. This is important for two reasons. First, today's dissent may be tomorrow's majority opinion. Second, comparing the arguments raised in the opinion with those of the dissent requires—and strengthens the student's ability to engage in—critical analysis. Each edited case is followed by two thought-provoking critical thinking questions that challenge the student's understanding of the court's language and reasoning and encourage the student to consider the ramifications of the decision for future cases and managerial decisions.

The opinions in the remaining cases in each chapter are summarized, thereby permitting the coverage of more cases and concepts than would be feasible if all cases were in the language of the court. The authors believe that students benefit from reading a more rigorous treatment of cases than is provided by the short briefs found in many texts. Thus, students are provided with a detailed recitation of the facts, the issues, the court's reasoning, and the result.

Many cases also include comments. The comments place the case in its proper legal perspective and offer commentary on why the case is important, why the court decided it a certain way, or what the ramifications of the decision are for businesses. This helps students understand how an individual case impacts the legal environment as a whole. In addition, the comments encourage students to think critically about court decisions and the conduct of the managers involved.

## Ethical Considerations

This text places great emphasis on ethical concerns, stimulating students to understand how their actions as managers and business leaders must incorporate considerations of ethics and social responsibility. Ethical considerations are emphasized in four ways. First, the opening chapter, "Ethics, Value Creation, and Risk Management," includes topics such as rampant accounting fraud by companies intent on managing their earnings to meet analyst expectations, exploitation of foreign workers, the marketing of tobacco and beer to children, and conflicts of interest in the securities, insurance brokerage, and mutual fund industries. Second, the text includes relevant excerpts from the *Dun & Bradstreet Code of Business Conduct* and the *American Express Company Code of Conduct.* Third, ethical considerations are highlighted throughout the text in separate boxed sections entitled "Ethical Considerations" and are raised in many of the end-of-chapter Questions and Case Problems. Finally, the Manager's Dilemma question at the end of each chapter requires students to consider how ethics factor into a managerial decision.

These ethical considerations are commentaries on how standards of ethics and social responsibility do (and sometimes do not) inform the process of lawmaking. The text discusses the ethical implications of business decisions made in response to legal rules, as well as the moral boundaries of the legal regime.

## International Coverage, the Global View and International Snapshots

The text addresses the international aspects of the legal environment in three ways. The chapter on international business (Chapter 25) provides a transactional, integrated discussion of international business transactions, including the use of letters of credit, sovereign immunity, and complying with local labor laws. Many chapters also include a boxed section entitled the "Global View" that discusses key differences between U.S. law and the laws applied in the European Union, Japan, Canada, and other countries. For example, both the product liability and the securities fraud and insider trading chapters (Chapters 10 and 23) describe the relevant European

Union Directives. The chapter on civil rights and employment discrimination (Chapter 13) discusses European, Japanese, and Indian discrimination law. Finally, a number of chapters also highlight international considerations in short boxed features called "International Snapshots." Taiwanese law is discussed in International Snapshots in the environmental law and consumer protection chapters (Chapters 16 and 17).

## Economic, Historical, and Political Perspectives

Most chapters have a separate boxed section that puts the law in that chapter into economic, historical, or political perspective. For example, the criminal law chapter (Chapter 14) traces the history of white-collar crime; the new executive compensation chapter (Chapter 21) discusses the effect of tax policy on stock options; and the torts chapter (Chapter 9) describes the politics behind efforts at tort reform.

These perspectives add a real-world dimension to the material. Too often law is presented in a vacuum, divorced from the larger political and economic context in which the law is created. The goal of these sections is to heighten students' awareness of these larger forces. In addition, business managers should be made aware of the complicated interplay between economics and the law. That interplay is crucial to the operation of a business, but it is often less than predictable.

## View from Cyberspace

Almost every chapter includes the boxed discussion "View from Cyberspace" of how the laws addressed in the chapter apply to electronic commerce, the Internet, and cyberspace in general. For example, the chapter on public and private offerings of securities (Chapter 22) discusses direct initial public offerings on the World Wide Web. The constitutional law chapter (Chapter 2) discusses pornography and free speech on the Internet, and the chapter on alternate dispute resolution (Chapter 3) describes the use of ADR for online disputes. The consumer protection chapter (Chapter 17) discusses the difficulty of protecting privacy on the Internet.

## In Brief

To provide a visual aid for the student, each chapter contains a boxed summary, the "In Brief," that breaks down into digestible pieces the key elements of material presented in that chapter. In some cases, this may be presented in the form of a flow chart; in others, it may appear in the form of a decision tree or matrix.

## Inside Story

Each chapter contains mini-cases that present fascinating and detailed descriptions of real-world business situations. A strong effort has been made to include up-to-the-minute, cutting-edge business situations. The Inside Stories include the conviction of Bernard J. Ebbers, former CEO of WorldCom; the regulation of Voice over Internet Protocol telephone service; gender discrimination at Merrill Lynch and Wal-Mart; and litigation against Jack Grasso, former head of the New York Stock Exchange, to recover allegedly excessive executive compensation. The Inside Stories bring the legal conflicts and developments to life and reinforce the students' appreciation for how such conflicts are played out in the real world.

## The Responsible Manager

Each chapter concludes with a section entitled "The Responsible Manager." This section is an in-depth discussion of the crucial legal considerations that the successful manager must take into account. The Responsible Manager sections summarize each chapter, but they are far more than a mere summary. In a concise yet sophisticated manner, they alert managers to the legal issues they must spot in order to avoid violating the law or plunging the company into expensive, time-consuming litigation. In addition, these sections highlight the ethical concerns managers need to confront to adequately serve their company and community.

These sections play a vital role in establishing this text as a "must-have" for upcoming and practicing business managers. In The Responsible Manager section for a particular area of the law, managers will find a wealth of practical information that will bring them up to speed on the key legal issues in that area. These sections are not merely checklists—they contain a depth of analysis that is demanded by the complex, real-life nature of the problems at hand.

As examples, The Responsible Manager section for the chapter on alternative dispute resolution (Chapter 3) provides a step-by-step guide to setting up an effective alternative dispute resolution procedure. The torts chapter (Chapter 9) provides a manager's guide to reducing risks of exposure for tort liability. The international business transactions chapter (Chapter 25) highlights the issues likely to arise in transactions involving more than one country and suggests strategies for managing successfully in a global setting.

### Defined Terms, Key Words and Phrases, and Glossary

Throughout the text, all crucial legal terms appear in italics and are defined immediately. A list of key terms used in a chapter appears immediately before the end-of-chapter Questions and Case Problems, with a page reference to the place where that term is defined.

In addition to the references to defined terms contained in Key Words and Phrases, there is also a comprehensive glossary at the end of the text. The Glossary defines each term that has been set in italics anywhere in the text. The definition of terms in the Glossary and the Key Words and Phrases helps convey the concepts and improves the students' legal and business vocabulary.

### End-of-Chapter Questions and Case Problems and the Manager's Dilemma

Each chapter is followed by ten sophisticated and thought-provoking questions and case problems that require students to synthesize and review the material. The questions are diverse. Some are mini-cases that require students to figure out the legal and business issues and make a managerial decision. Others are based directly on specific cases, presenting real-world legal conflicts or decisions as opportunities for students to apply the appropriate law. For example, the bankruptcy chapter includes a question based on the attempts of a failed dot-com to transfer a below-market retail lease to another firm. In most chapters, more than half of the questions are based on actual cases, and citations are provided for enterprising students who want to look up the cases in preparation for class. The questions that are based on actual cases often raise issues at the cutting edge of law and management. The last question in each chapter, "Manager's Dilemma," requires students to analyze the legal, business, and ethical aspects of a managerial decision and make a recommendation for action.

### Internet Sources

Each chapter contains a list of World Wide Web sites (including their electronic addresses or URLs) relevant to the chapter. These sites give students a starting point for on-line legal research. The URLs are current as of January 1, 2005. Although every attempt was made to identify Internet sites that are maintained and updated regularly, the Internet is highly dynamic, and a "hot" site today may be gone in six months.

## Changes in the Fifth Edition

The Fifth Edition represents a major revision of the text. First, as noted earlier, it presents new conceptual frameworks to show the interplay between law and management and the role of law in competitive strategy. It strengthens the text's coverage of corporate governance by adding a new chapter on executive compensation. The fifth edition provides more in-depth coverage of international business and the laws of the European Union, Japan, and certain other countries in new sections entitled the "Global View."

It updates and strengthens the features that worked well in previous editions, such as the Perspectives and Inside Stories. It consolidates discussions of topics that have become more settled since the last edition or are of less general interest. For example, labor regulation under the National Labor Relations Act is now folded into the employment agreement chapter (Chapter 12). The criminal law chapter now focuses less on criminal procedure and more on white-collar crime and the mitigating and aggravating factors that affect sentencing recommendations under the Federal Sentencing Guidelines.

The chapter on sales and e-commerce discusses Article 2 of the Uniform Commercial Code, both as currently enacted by the states and as amended by the American Law Institute and the National Conference of Commissioners on Uniform State Laws in 2003.

The chapter on civil rights and employment discrimination has been reworked to highlight same-gender harassment and disabilities based on mental conditions such as depression. The chapter on forms of business organization includes an expanded discussion of franchises. Because it builds on many of the earlier chapters, the chapter on international business now concludes the text.

Finally, consistent with the text's reputation as a cutting-edge discussion of the intersection of law and management, the text discusses the latest cases, such as the first federal case to apply U.S. environmental law extraterritorially to a Canadian smelter (Case 15.3) and regulatory developments, such as the requirements imposed by the Sarbanes–Oxley Act of 2002.

More than half of the cases presented as A Case in Point and many of the end-of-chapter Questions and Case Problems are new. The text includes many cases decided in 2004 and even a few decided in 2005. Most of the Inside Stories and the Economic, Historical, and Political Perspectives are also new or have been substantially revised to reflect the latest developments.

## Ancillary Components

### Answers to End-of-Chapter Questions and Case Problems

A complete and separate Answer Manual, prepared by the authors, identifies the issues presented in each of the end-of-chapter Questions and Case Problems and provides thorough, cogent model answers to facilitate teaching by the Socratic and case method.

### Text Web Site

Adopters can access the text Web site directly at http://bagley.westbuslaw.com.

### Instructor's Manual

The Instructor's Manual was developed by Joseph A. Zavaletta, Jr. (University of Texas at Brownsville). This manual includes chapter outlines, case summaries, and teaching suggestions.

### PowerPoint Presentation Slides

A set of PowerPoint slides prepared by Joseph A. Zavaletta, Jr. (University of Texas at Brownsville) provides outlines of topics covered in each chapter, which can be used for lecture or review.

### Test Bank

The Test Bank was developed by Vonda Laughlin from Carson Newman College. It contains true/false, multiple-choice, and essay test questions. Suggested answers for the essay questions are provided. The Test Bank also includes multi-subject final exam essay questions prepared by Constance E. Bagley.

The test bank is available on *ExamView* ™, which is a computerized testing software program containing all of the questions in the printed test bank. This program is an easy-to-use test creation software package compatible with Microsoft Windows. Instructors can add or edit questions and provide customized instructions

### Study Guide

The Study Guide was prepared by Joseph A. Zavaletta, Jr. (University of Texas at Brownsville). It includes chapter objectives, chapter outlines, study questions (fill-in-the-blank, true/false, multiple choice, and essay). Answers are provided in a separate answer key.

### *Pennzoil v. Texaco* Case Study and Accompanying Video

The *Pennzoil v. Texaco* case study is the Inside Story for the contracts chapter (Chapter 7). It includes excerpts from the court's opinion and the legal documents so students can experience seeing such material first hand. This case study can serve as the basis for discussion or for the staging of a mock trial in which students can play the lawyers, executives, investment bankers, and jury. An edited videotape of the mock trial conducted by students in Professor Bagley's class at the Graduate School of Business at Stanford University is also available.

## Other Teaching Aids

West Legal Studies in Business offers qualified adopters of this text a wide range of other teaching aids.

### West Legal Studies in Business Resource Center

The http://www.westbuslaw.com website offers a unique, rich, and robust online resource for instructors and students. It provides customer service and product information, a link to the text Web site, and other cutting-edge resources, such as *NewsEdge* (live legal news and company data from the world's leading news sources) and *Court Case Updates* (summaries, updated and augmented monthly, of the most important recent developments in legal cases from around the United States, all organized by topic for easy syllabus integration).

### Student Guide to the Sarbanes–Oxley Act

A brief overview of the Sarbanes–Oxley Act for undergraduate business students that explains the Sarbanes–Oxley Act, what is required of whom, and how it might affect students in their business life is available free in a bundle with a new text.

### West's Digital Video Library

Featuring 60+ segments on the most important topics in legal environment and business law, *West's Digital Video Library* helps students make the connection between their textbook and the business world. Four types of clips are represented: (1) "Legal Conflicts in Business," which feature modern business scenarios; (2) "Ask the

Instructor" clips, which offer concept review; (3) "Drama of the Law," which present classic legal situations; and (4) the newest addition to the Digital Video Library, *LawFlix,* which features segments from widely recognized, modern-day movies. Together these clips bring the legal environment and business law to life. Access to West's Digital Video Library is free when bundled with a new text. For more information about this product, visit http://digitalvideolibrary.westbuslaw.com.

### WEST'S LEGAL STUDIES IN BUSINESS VHS VIDEO LIBRARY

Videos on many business law and legal environment issues are available (with some restrictions) to qualified adopters of this text. For more detailed information about the videos, please visit http://video.westbuslaw.com.

### *THE WALL STREET JOURNAL*

For a nominal additional cost, any new West Legal Studies in Business text can be packaged with a card entitling students to a 15-week subscription to both the print and online versions of *The Wall Street Journal.* Instructors who have at least seven students activate their subscriptions will automatically receive their own subscription free.

### THE BUSINESS & COMPANY RESOURCE CENTER

The Business & Company Resource Center (BCRC) is a premier online business research tool that allows one to seamlessly search thousands of periodicals, journals, references, financial information, industry reports, company histories, and much more. Visit http://bcrc.swlearning.com to learn more about this powerful tool. BCRC is available as an optional package with a new text.

### LEGALTRAC

An excellent resource for research and writing assignments, LegalTrac ™ provides indexing for approximately 875 titles, including major law reviews, legal newspapers, bar association journals, and international legal journals. It also contains law-related articles from over 1,000 additional business and general interest titles. LegalTrac™ is available as an optional package with a new text.

### WESTLAW

Westlaw®, West Group's vast online source of value-added legal and business information, contains over 15,000 databases of information spanning a variety of jurisdictions, practice areas, and disciplines. Qualified adopters may receive ten complimentary hours of Westlaw for their course (certain restrictions apply).

### CUTTING-EDGE CASES IN THE LEGAL ENVIRONMENT OF BUSINESS (2ND ED.)

A collection of seventeen legal environment of business edited cases from 1995 to 1998, using the court's own language in an expanded format, may be purchased separately.

## Acknowledgments

A number of academics and practitioners reviewed portions of this manuscript and the first four editions, and provided valuable guidance, correction, and helpful commentary. We thank each of them.

Reviewers and others who provided insight for this edition include:

Teresa M. Amabile, Harvard Business School
Lynda M. Applegate, Harvard Business School
Steven Arsenault, College of Charleston
Joseph L. Badaracco, Harvard Business School
Carliss Y. Baldwin, Harvard Business School
Frederick Baron, partner, Cooley Godward LLP
Todd Bontemps, special counsel, Cooley Godward LLP
Susan Boyd, University of Tulsa
Tom Cary, City University
Thomas Cavenagh, North Central College
Patrick Costello, partner, Bialson, Bergen & Schwab
Larry Alan Di Matteo, University of Florida
Steve Fackler, partner, Simson, Thacher & Bartlett
Ian Feinberg, partner Mayer Brown Rowe & Maw
Stephen Friedlander, partner, Cooley Godward LLP
William E. Fruhan, Jr., Harvard Business School
Bill Galliani, partner, Cooley Godward LLP
Robert Gebhard, special counsel, Sedgwick Detert, Moran & Arnold
Ernest W. King, University of Southern Mississippi
Virginia Maurer, University of Florida
Ellwood F. Oakley, III, Georgia State University
David A. Redle, The University of Akron
William A. Sahlman, Harvard Business School
Cindy A. Schipani, University of Michigan
Lillian Stenfeld, partner, Cooley Godward LLP
Anita Stork, partner, Cooley Godward LLP
Lois Voelz, partner, Cooley Godward LLP
Mark Webber, associate, Osborne Clarke

Reviewers and others who provided insight for the fourth edition include:

Robert W. Emerson, University of Florida, Gainesville
Joan T. A. Gabel, University of Georgia
Steven J. Green, University of California, Berkeley and Davis
Laurie A. Lucas, Arkansas Technical University
Claude Mosseri-Marlio, Schiller University and American Business School in Paris
Arthur Segel, Harvard Business School
Lynn Sharp Paine, Harvard Business School
John A. Wrieden, Florida International University

Reviewers for the third edition include:

Royce de R. Barondes, Louisiana State University
Susan M. Denbo, Rider College
Joan T. A. Gabel, Georgia State University
Ernest W King, University of Southern Mississippi
Eugene P. O'Connor, Canisius College
Lou Ann Simpson, Drake University

Reviewers for the second edition include:

Barbara Ahna, Pacific Lutheran University
Rodolfo Camacho, Oregon State University
Kenneth D. Crews, Indiana University
James G. Frierson, East Tennessee State University
John P. Geary, Appalachian State University
David G. Jaeger, Case Western Reserve University
Arthur Levine, California State University-Long Beach
Susan L. Martin, Hofstra University
William F. Miller, Stanford University
Alan R Thiele, University of Houston

Reviewers for the first edition include:

Thomas M. Apke, California State University, Fullerton
Dawn Bennett-Alexander, University of Georgia
Robert L. Cherry, Appalachian State University
Frank B. Cross, University of Texas, Austin
Charles J. Cunningham, University of Tampa
Michael Engber, Ball State University
Andrea Giampetro-Meyer, Loyola College, Maryland
James P. Hill, Central Michigan University
Tom Jackson, University of Vermont
Roger J. Johns, Jr., Eastern New Mexico University
Jack E. Karns, East Carolina University
Mary C. Keifer, Ohio University
Nancy Kubasek, Bowling Green University
Paul Lansing, University of Iowa
Nancy R Mansfield, Georgia State University
Arthur J. Marinelli, Ohio University
John McMahon, Stanford University
Gregory C. Mosier, Oklahoma State University
Patricia H. Nunley, Baylor University
Mark M. Phelps, University of Oregon
Michael W. Pustay, Texas A&M University
Roger Richman, University of Hartford
John C. Ruhnka, University of Colorado at Denver
Linda B. Samuels, George Mason University
Susan Samuelson, Boston University
Rudy Sandoval, University of Texas, San Antonio
John E. H. Sherry, Cornell University
S. Jay Sklar, Temple University
Larry D. Strate, University of Nevada, Las Vegas
Gary L. Tidwell, College of Charleston
William V. Vetter, Wayne State University
William H. Walker, Indiana-Purdue University, Ft. Wayne
Darryl Webb, University of Alabama

Any mistakes or inadequacies are our own.

Professor Bagley thanks Jeff Crudup and J. P. Traue, students at the Boston College School of Law, and Trevor Bloom for their invaluable assistance. Anna Harrington, a Research Associate at the Harvard Business School, took the laboring oar for Chapter 14—Criminal Law. Professor Bagley thanks each of them for their hard work, creativity, and good cheer. She would also like to acknowledge the amazing productivity, endurance, hard work, and grace under pressure of her faculty assistant Mark Lamoureux.

Professor Savage would like to thank the following Cooley Godward attorneys: David Herman, who assisted with the Constitutional Bases for Business Regulation chapter; Jill Green, who assisted with the Intellectual Property chapter ; Mindy Shore Laponis, who assisted in the revision of the Antitrust, Employment Agreement, and Civil Rights and Employment Discrimination chapters; Katherine Loo (now at Google), who assisted with the Executive Compensation chapter; and Oliver Breme, who assisted with the International Law and Transactions chapter. Professor Savage would also like to thank her assistant, J. Chandler Werline, who provided invaluable assistance every step of the way.

Thanks to Publisher Rob Dewey, Acquisition Editor Steve Silverstein, and Senior Developmental Editor Jan Lamar of West Legal Studies in Business for their insightful and creative suggestions for this fifth edition. Thanks also to Production Editors Kara ZumBahlen and Tammy Moore for their even tempers while meeting a seemingly impossible production schedule, their tolerance of multiple missed author deadlines, and their wise decision to bring in the pros at Parkwood Composition to get the book into type. Best wishes to Kara as she pursues her studies in art history. We will miss you.

Finally, thanks to the Division of Research at the Harvard Business School and the law firm of Cooley Godward LLP for their generous support of this edition.

Constance E. Bagley
Harvard Business School

Diane W. Savage
Stanford Graduate School of Business
Cooley Godward LLP

# ABOUT THE AUTHORS

## CONSTANCE E. BAGLEY

Constance E. Bagley is an Associate Professor of Business Administration at the Harvard Business School. Before joining the HBS faculty in 2000, she taught for more than ten years at the Stanford University Graduate School of Business, where she received Honorable Mention (first runner-up) for the Distinguished Teaching Award and was a GSB Trust Faculty Fellow. Before teaching at Stanford, she was a corporate securities law partner in the San Francisco office of Bingham McCutchen. Professor Bagley is the co-author of *The Entrepreneur's Guide to Business Law* (West Legal Studies in Business, 2d ed., 2003) and the author of *Winning Legally: Using Law to Create Value, Marshal Resources, and Manage Risk* (Harvard Business School Press, 2005). She is a member of the National Adjudicatory Council of the National Association of Securities Dealers and the Editorial Board of the *Journal of Internet Law*. Professor Bagley is also a staff editor of the *American Business Law Journal* and a member of the Advisory Board for the Bureau of National Affairs Corporate Practice Series. She received her J.D., *magna cum laude*, from the Harvard Law School and was invited to join the *Harvard Law Review*. She received her A.B., with Honors and Distinction, from Stanford University, where she was elected Phi Beta Kappa her junior year. Professor Bagley is a member of the State Bar of California and the State Bar of New York, and she is delighted to have co-authored this fifth edition with Diane W. Savage, her long-time friend and successor at Stanford.

## DIANE W. SAVAGE

Diane W. Savage has been Lecturer on Business Law at the Stanford Graduate School of Business since 2000. She is also of counsel to Cooley Godward LLP, a 450-lawyer firm with offices in California, Colorado, and Virginia. Cooley Godward is a recognized leader in the practice of corporate law. From 1994 to 2000, Professor Savage was a partner at Cooley Godward, where she headed the firm's Technology Transactions group. Prior to that time, she served as General Counsel of Adobe Systems. Professor Savage is on the Editorial Board of the *Boalt Hall Law Review* and a member of the American Law Institute. She received her J.D. from Georgetown International Law Center and was invited to join the *Georgetown Law Review*. She received her B.A. from Emory University, where she was elected to Phi Beta Kappa and the Women's Honorary Organization. She is a member of the State Bar of California.

# UNIT I

# FOUNDATIONS OF THE LEGAL AND REGULATORY ENVIRONMENT

CHAPTER 1

# Ethics, Value Creation, and Risk Management

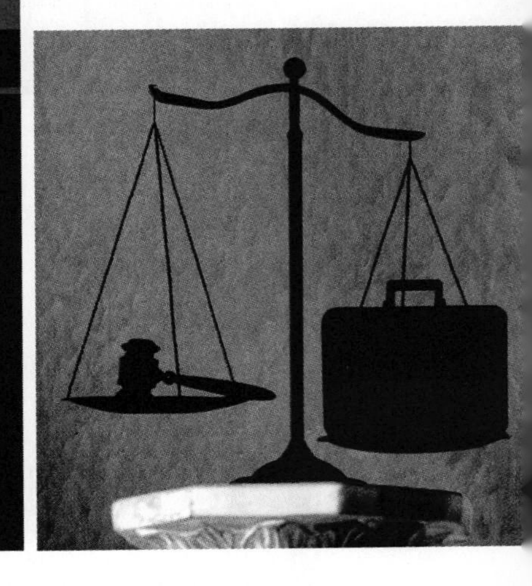

## INTRODUCTION

The spectacle of corporate executives doing the perp walk in handcuffs after the collapse of Enron, WorldCom, and Adelphia Communications, the criminal conviction and demise of Arthur Andersen, the payment of record fines by Wall Street firms and other companies, and the sentencing of the founder and former chief executive officer (CEO) of ImClone Systems to more than seven years in prison for insider trading all serve as stark reminders of the consequences of failing to comply with the law. An unprecedented series of accounting scandals has shaken public confidence in the U.S. capital markets and led to the passage of the Sarbanes-Oxley Act of 2002, the most sweeping federal securities legislation since the Securities Exchange Act of 1934.

In a widely publicized speech before the National Press Club in 2002, Henry M. Paulson, Jr., CEO of Goldman, Sachs & Co., declared, "In my lifetime, American business has never been under such scrutiny. To be blunt, much of it is deserved."[1] Paul A. Volcker, former chair of the Federal Reserve Board, remarked, "People now don't have faith and reasonable confidence in financial reporting. That affects the flow of capital, and ultimately it could affect the amount of capital that's available to business. In a capitalist system, that's not good."[2]

Complying with the law is only the baseline for appropriate managerial action. Just because something is legal does not mean that it makes good business sense to do it or that an individual of conscience should do it. Enduring success in the modern global marketplace requires attention not just to complying with the laws on the books today, but also to meeting society's evolving expectations of what constitutes ethical and socially responsible corporate behavior. Failures to meet society's expectations tend to spawn more onerous government regulation, making it all the more important for managers to conduct business in an ethical manner.

Yet staying out of trouble is only part of the picture. Managers who view the law and ethics purely as constraints to be complied with and reacted to, rather than something to be used proactively, will miss opportunities to use the law and the legal system to increase both the total value created and the share of that value captured by the firm. For example, companies can use patents, copyrights, trademarks, and trade secrets to differentiate their products, command premium prices, erect barriers to entry, sustain first-mover advantage, and reduce costs. In addition, the law offers a variety of tools that can help managers assess and manage risk. These range from insurance contracts to indemnification provisions and limitations on liability.

## CHAPTER OVERVIEW

The purpose of this chapter is to provide a framework for analyzing how ethics, business, and law interact. It begins with a discussion of the four primary public policies furthered by business regulation in the United States. The chapter continues with a brief overview of the relationship between law and strategy. Then it explains the business leader's role in setting the ethical tone of the firm and provides several examples of executives who failed to fill that role. Next it presents the Ethical Business Leader's Decision Tree, which

1. John A. Byrne, *Restoring Trust in Corporate America: Business Must Lead the Way to Real Reform,* BUS.WK., June 24, 2002, at 31, 32.
2. *Volcker on the Crisis of Faith,* BUS.WK., June 24, 2002, at 42.

managers can use to evaluate the legality and the appropriateness of various courses of action. After comparing short-term and long-term perspectives on ethics, it gives examples of social responsibility and irresponsibility on the part of corporations. Finally, the chapter concludes by comparing the standards imposed by law with those mandated as a matter of ethics.

## Law and Public Policy

Law—which we are defining to encompass policy and government as well as constitutions, statutes, regulations, and judicial decisions[3]—provides "the rules of the game" within which firms compete to create and capture value.[4] Managers can also make their own "private law" by, for example, entering into contracts and crafting certain governance structures.

The laws and regulations applicable to U.S. business in the early twenty-first century further four primary public policy objectives: promoting economic growth, protecting workers, promoting consumer welfare, and promoting public welfare. This typology is depicted in Exhibit 1.1.

- *Promoting Economic Growth.* The first objective is to promote economic growth. As shown in Exhibit 1.2, this is done by protecting private property rights; enforcing private agreements; allocating risks;[5] facilitating the raising of capital; creating incentives to

3. Following the lead of James Willard Hurst, we use the term "law" to refer to "all formal and informal aspects of political organized power," including "the functions of all legal agencies (legislative, executive, administrative, or judicial)." James Willard Hurst, *Problems of Legitimacy in the Contemporary Legal Order*, 24 Okla. L. Rev. 224 (1971) ("In deciding what to include as 'law' I do not find it profitable to distinguish 'law' from 'government' or from 'policy.'").

4. Douglass C. North, Institutions, Institutional Change and Economic Performance 3–4 (1990).

5. For an excellent discussion of government's role in allocating risk, see David A. Moss, When All Else Fails: Government as the Ultimate Risk Manager (2001).

EXHIBIT 1.1 Underlying Rationales of U.S. Public Law Governing Business

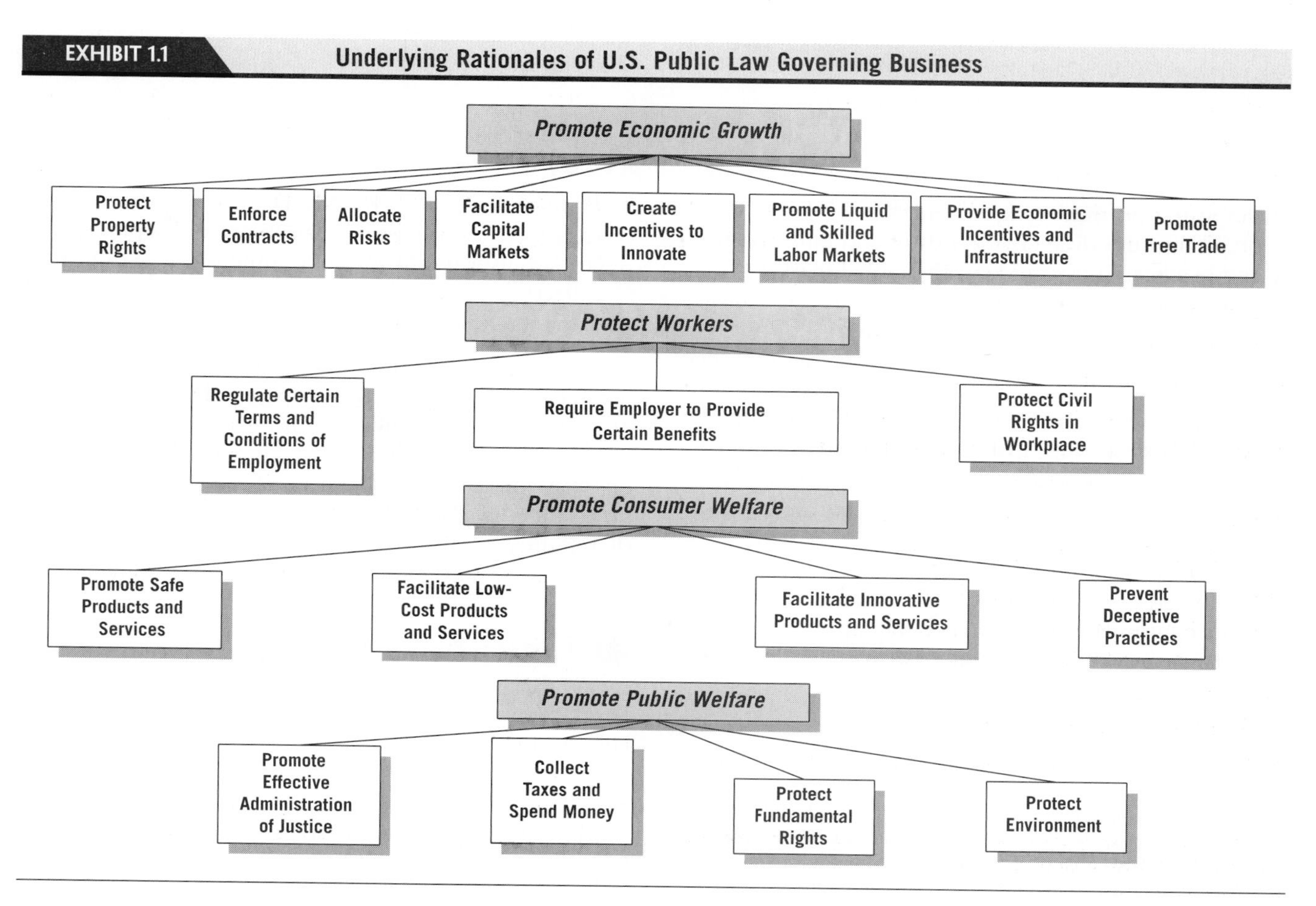

EXHIBIT 1.2 How U.S. Law Promotes Economic Growth

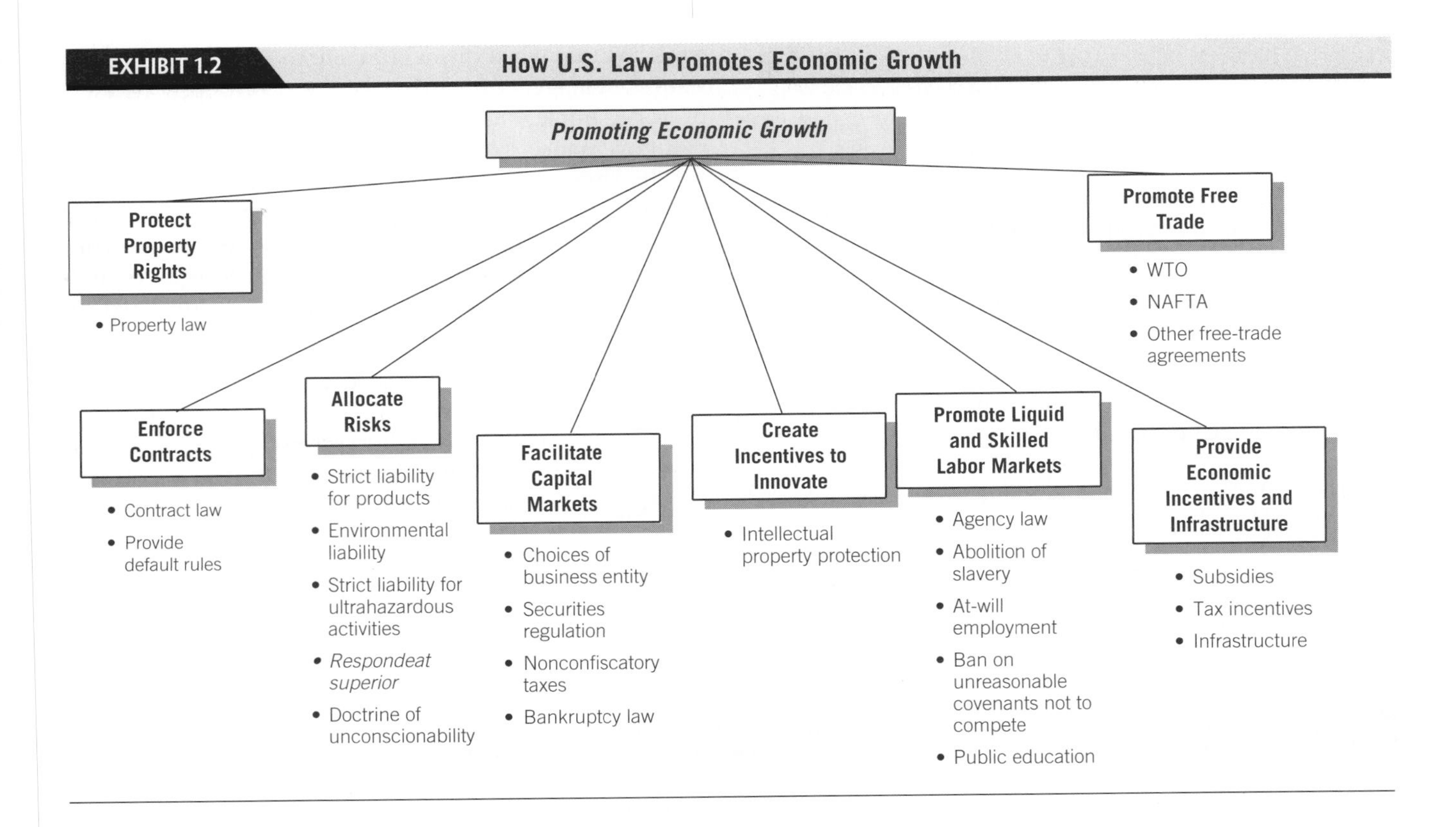


innovate;[6] promoting liquid and skilled labor markets; providing subsidies, tax incentives, and infrastructure; and promoting free trade in the global markets.

- *Protecting Workers.* Worker protection constitutes a second major public policy underlying U.S. business law. As depicted in Exhibit 1.3, this is accomplished by regulating certain terms and conditions of employment, requiring the employer to provide certain benefits, and protecting workers' civil rights. Complying with these requirements imposes costs on employers that society, acting through the legislature, has deemed it appropriate for employers to bear.
- *Promoting Consumer Welfare.* Third, as shown in Exhibit 1.4, business regulation is designed to promote consumer welfare by encouraging the sale of safe and innovative products and services at a fair price.
- *Promoting Public Welfare.* Fourth, as depicted in Exhibit 1.5, business regulation promotes public welfare by ensuring the effective administration of justice, collecting taxes and spending money, protecting fundamental rights, and protecting the environment.

Other major economic powers tend to have laws that further these same objectives, albeit with varying degrees of emphasis on the different objectives and varying ways of furthering them.[7] Indeed, much of the current debate on what constitutes good corporate governance turns on how much weight each country gives to the interests of shareholders, debtholders, employees, customers, and suppliers and to the protection of the environment.

## Law and Strategy

Part of every manager's job is the formulation and execution of firm strategy.

6. Although policymakers often equate greater intellectual property protection with more innovation, economist Josh Lerner argues that this is an overly simplistic view. Amy Harmon, *Suddenly, 'Idea Wars' Take on a New Global Urgency,* N.Y. TIMES, Nov. 11, 2001. Professor Lerner studied sixty developing countries and found no statistically significant relationship between the amount of innovation and the strength of patent protection provided in the different countries.

7. For example, Germany seeks to promote economic growth by facilitating the capital markets, but its goal of protecting workers has led to the system of codetermination whereby half the members of the supervisory boards of large German corporations are elected by the workers and unions, and half are elected by the shareholders.

EXHIBIT 1.3 How U.S. Law Protects Workers

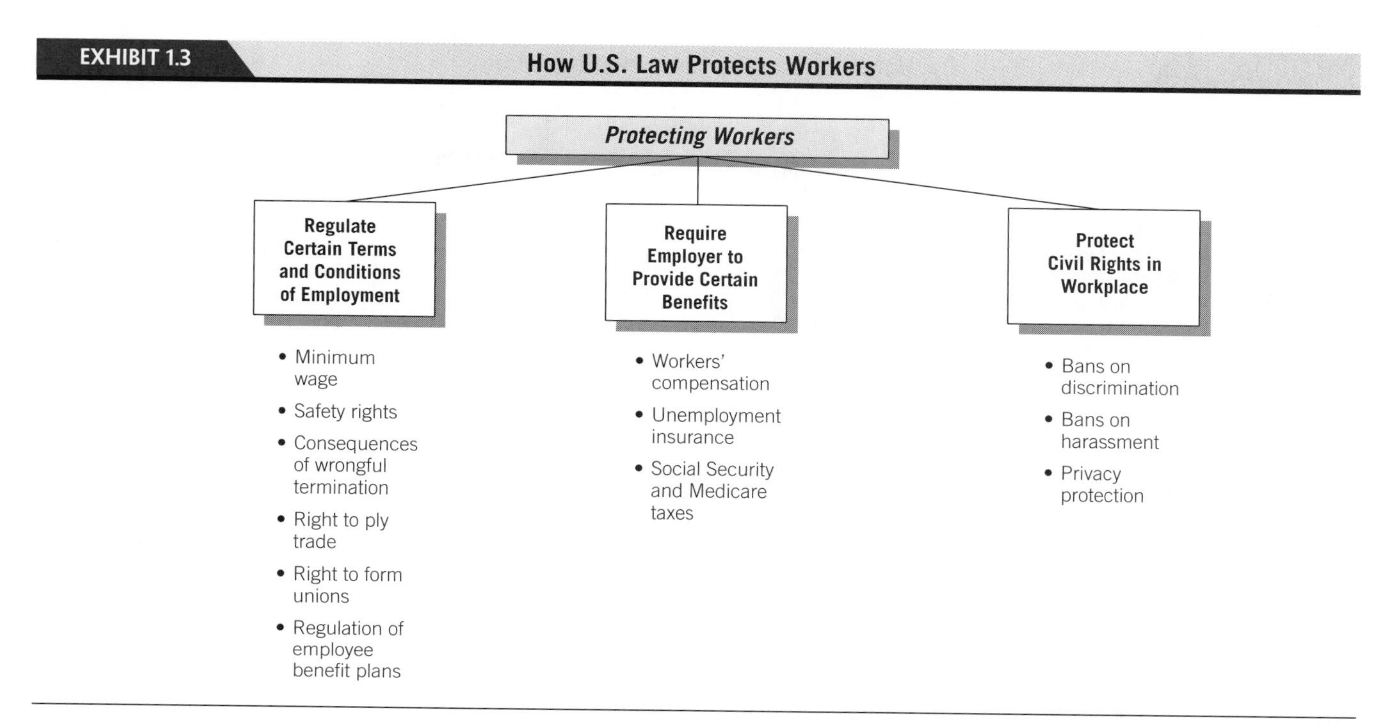
Protecting Workers
Regulate Certain Terms and Conditions of Employment
• Minimum wage
• Safety rights
• Consequences of wrongful termination
• Right to ply trade
• Right to form unions
• Regulation of employee benefit plans
Require Employer to Provide Certain Benefits
• Workers' compensation
• Unemployment insurance
• Social Security and Medicare taxes
Protect Civil Rights in Workplace
• Bans on discrimination
• Bans on harassment
• Privacy protection

## A Systems Approach to Business Regulation

Law helps shape the competitive environment and affects each of the five forces that Professor Michael E. Porter has identified as determining the attractiveness of an industry: buyer power, supplier power, the competitive threat posed by current rivals, the availability of substitutes, and the threat of new entrants.[8] Law affects the

8. Michael E. Porter, *How Competitive Forces Shape Strategy, in* On Competition 21–22 (1996). *See also* Richard G. Shell, Make the Rules or Your Competitors Will (2004).

EXHIBIT 1.4 How U.S. Law Promotes Consumer Welfare

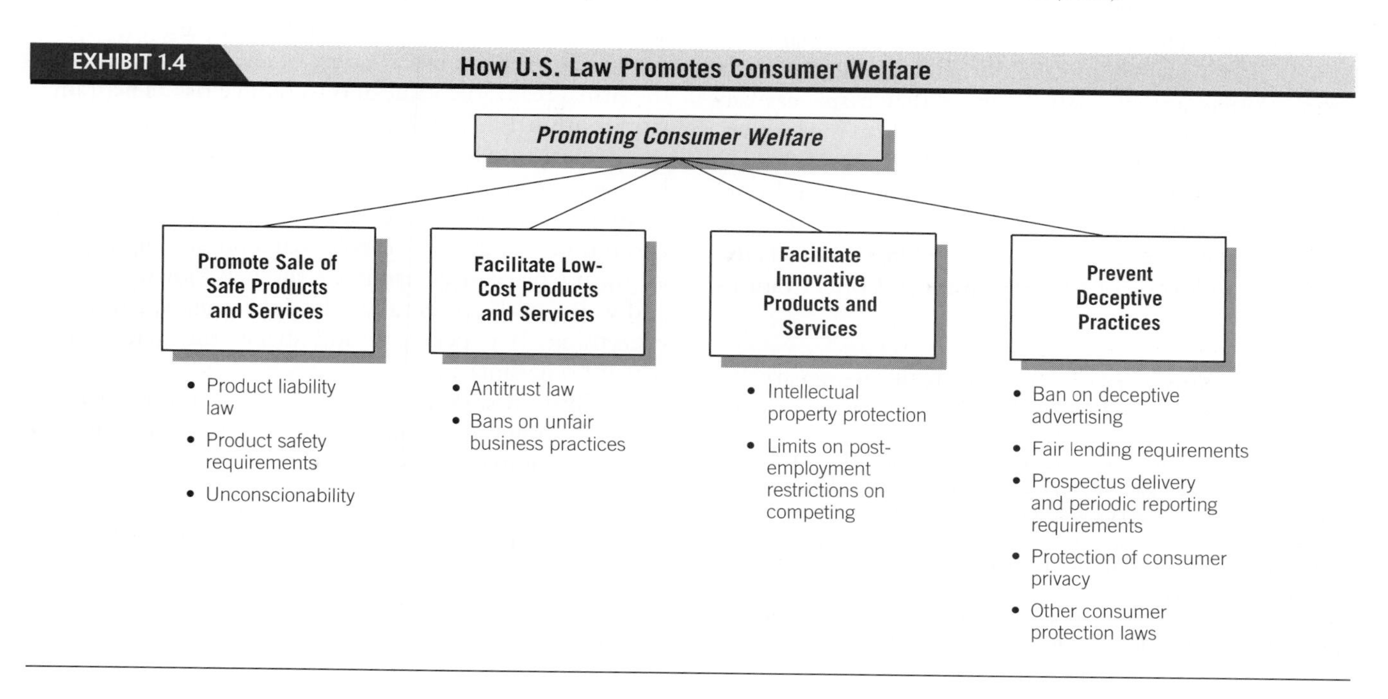
Promoting Consumer Welfare
Promote Sale of Safe Products and Services
• Product liability law
• Product safety requirements
• Unconscionability
Facilitate Low-Cost Products and Services
• Antitrust law
• Bans on unfair business practices
Facilitate Innovative Products and Services
• Intellectual property protection
• Limits on post-employment restrictions on competing
Prevent Deceptive Practices
• Ban on deceptive advertising
• Fair lending requirements
• Prospectus delivery and periodic reporting requirements
• Protection of consumer privacy
• Other consumer protection laws

EXHIBIT 1.5 How U.S. Law Promotes Public Welfare

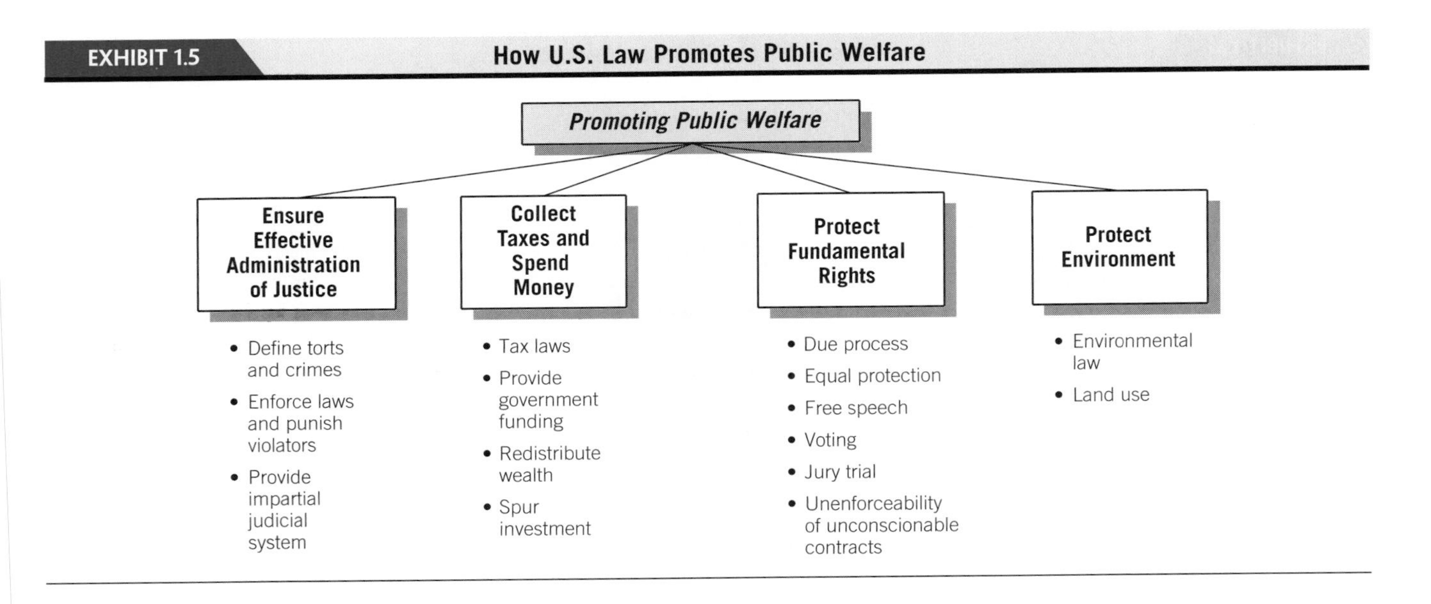


*internal* organization of the firm,[9] including the choice of business entity, and its resources and capabilities. Law also affects the firm's *external* relationships with customers, suppliers, competitors, and complementors, that is, those players who cause customers to value another firm's products and services more.[10] As Exhibit 1.6 depicts, law affects each activity in the value chain.

Law and business form a system, in which law affects the market and market players, but market players also affect the law. Thus, law is not just a static external force acting upon managers and their firms. Law and the other tools it offers are an enabling force that managers can help to shape and can use to manage the firm more effectively. This system is depicted in Exhibit 1.7.

At the center is the manager who evaluates and pursues opportunities and seeks to create and capture value while managing the attendant risks. Public law affects the allocation and value of firm resources and offers various organizational structures for the firm including a choice of governance models. It also helps shape the competitive environment by providing the rules of the game. Courts enforce the private rules embodied in contracts between the firm and its employees, customers, investors, suppliers, and others, as long as they do not conflict with the public policies embodied in the public law.

Given the public law's constraints and the firm's strategic position within the competitive environment and its internal organization and resources, the legally astute manager can use a variety of legal tools to increase the firm's realizable value and to reduce risk. The framework outlined in Exhibit 1.7 can be used both by managers of existing lines of business in established firms and by managers pursuing new opportunities.

In some respects, the law's impact on competition and business is akin to the role that a physical force, such as gravity, plays in determining the behavior of particles and waves in the physical world. Like gravity, law affects everything. It is pervasive and shapes the space within which bodies interact.

Exhibit 1.8 shows how managers can use law to create and capture value and to manage risk during the five stages of business development:

- Evaluating the opportunity and defining the value proposition, which includes developing the business concept for exploiting the opportunity.
- Assembling the team.
- Raising capital.

9. See GARTH SALONER ET AL., STRATEGIC MANAGEMENT (2002), for a more complete discussion of the internal organization and context of firms.

10. ADAM M. BRANDENBURGER & BARRY J. NALEBUFF, CO-OPETITION viii (1996). For example, although American Airlines and Delta are competitors for passengers and landing slots and gates at airports, they are complementors with respect to Boeing, a key supplier of aircraft. It is much cheaper for Boeing to design a new plane for both airlines together than to design one for each of them separately. Design and development costs can be shared, and the demand for more units helps Boeing move along the learning curve more quickly.

**EXHIBIT 1.6** Law's Role in the Value Chain[a]

**Support Activities**

| | |
|---|---|
| **Firm Infrastructure** | *Limited liability, corporate governance, choice of business entity, tax planning* |
| **Human Resource Management** | *Employment contracts, at-will employment, wrongful termination, bans on discrimination, equity compensation, Fair Labor Practices Act* |
| **Technology Development** | *Intellectual property protection, nondisclosure agreements, assignments of inventions, convenants not to compete, licensing agreements* |
| **Procurement** | *Contracts, Uniform Commerical Code, Convention on the International Sale of Goods, bankruptcy, securities regulation* |

**Primary Activities**

| Inbound Logistics | Operations | Outbound Logistics | Marketing and Sales | Service |
|---|---|---|---|---|
| *Contracts*<br>*Antitrust limits on exclusive dealing contracts*<br>*Environmental compliance* | *Workplace safety*<br>*Environmental compliance* | *Contracts*<br>*Environmental compliance* | *Contracts*<br>*UCC and CISG*<br>*Consumer protection laws*<br>*Bans on deceptive or misleading advertising or sales practices*<br>*Antitrust limits on vertical and horizontal market division, tying, and predatory pricing*<br>*Import/export*<br>*World Trade Organization* | *Strict product liability*<br>*Warranties*<br>*Waivers*<br>*Doctrine of unconscionability* |

**Margin**

a. This framework (including the text in roman) is from Michael E. Porter, *How Competitive Forces Shape Strategy,* in ON COMPETITION 77 (1996). The words in italics have been added by these authors to Porter's framework.

EXHIBIT 1.7 A Systems Approach to Business Regulation

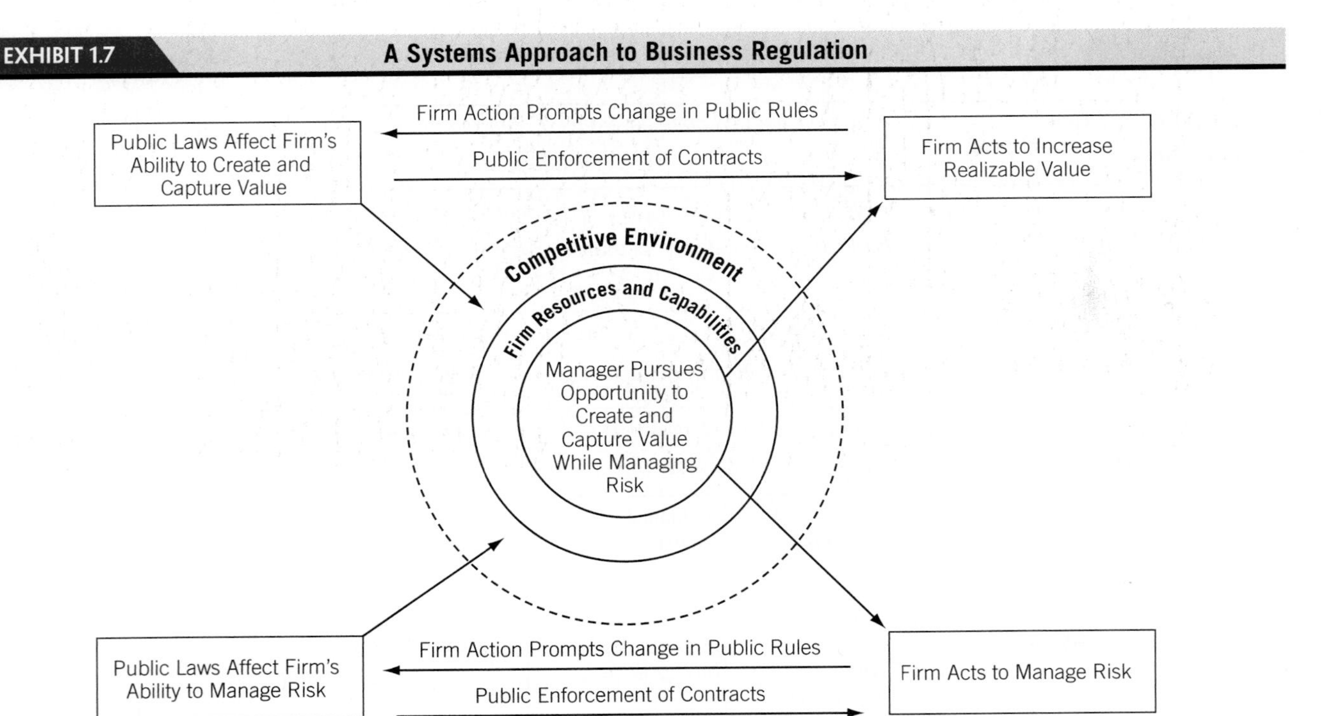


- Developing, producing, and marketing the product or service.
- Harvesting the opportunity, through sale of the venture, an initial public offering of stock, or reinvestment and renewal.[11]

Exhibit 1.8 does not purport to be an all-inclusive list of techniques for using the law to increase realizable value while managing risk. Rather, it is intended to suggest both the variety and the pervasive nature of the tools available.

## NONCOMPLIANCE IS NOT AN OPTION

At first blush, legal compliance might appear to be a nonstrategic issue. Yet strategies of noncompliance can threaten the very existence and continued viability of a firm. Consider the demise of Drexel Burnham in the wake of the insider trading scandals of the 1980s; the collapse of the savings and loan industry as a result of massive fraud; the implosion of Barings, England's oldest merchant bank after illegal trades by Nick Leeson; and the disintegration of the once venerable accounting powerhouse Arthur Andersen. Violation of the criminal laws can also land an executive in prison, as happened to Andrew Fastow, former chief financial officer (CFO) of Enron, who was convicted of fraud and sentenced to ten years in prison.

If legal requirements are not met, the law can also impose a very negative monetary return. This can be in the form of fines for criminal violations (such as the $875 million TAP Pharmaceuticals paid for Medicare fraud), civil judgments (such as the $3 billion Texaco paid Pennzoil for interfering with its agreement to buy Getty Oil), or a court-ordered termination of an entire line of business (such as Kodak's instant picture business, which was shut down after Kodak was found to have violated Polaroid's patents).

Even if the firm survives, noncompliance destroys value. In 2000, Cendant paid $3.19 billion to settle securities fraud cases against it arising out of its fraudulent financial reporting. The market capitalization of the firm had dropped $14 billion in one day after the

11. Professors Stevenson, Roberts, and Grousbeck break down the entrepreneurial process into five steps: (1) evaluating the opportunity, (2) developing the business concept, (3) assessing required resources both human and capital, (4) acquiring needed resources, and (5) managing and harvesting the venture. HOWARD H. STEVENSON, MICHAEL J. ROBERTS & H. IRVING GROUSBECK, NEW BUSINESS VENTURES AND THE ENTREPRENEUR 17–21 (2d ed. 1985). The five steps in Exhibit 1.8 are based on this model with modifications to reflect the fact that very different but significant legal issues arise in the course of marshaling human resources and raising money and in the course of managing the development, production, marketing, and sale of the product or service and in harvesting the venture.

**EXHIBIT 1.8 Legal Tools for Increasing Realizable Value While Managing Risk**

**Stages of Business Development**

| Managerial Objectives | Evaluating Opportunity and Defining Value Proposition | Assembling Team | Raising Capital | Development, Production, Marketing, and Sale of Product or Service | Harvest |
|---|---|---|---|---|---|
| **Create and Capture Value** | • Ask whether idea is patentable or otherwise protectable.<br>• Examine branding possibilities. | • Choose appropriate form of business entity and issue equity to founders early.<br>• Structure appropriate equity incentives for employees.<br>• Enter into nondisclosure agreements and assignments of inventions.<br>• Secure intellectual property protection. | • Be prepared to negotiate downside and sideways protection and upside rights for preferred stock.<br>• Be prepared to subject at least some founder stock to vesting.<br>• Sell stock in exempt transaction. | • Implement trade secret policy.<br>• Consider patent protection for new business processes and other inventions. Select a strong trademark and protect it. Register copyrights.<br>• Enter into licensing agreements.<br>• Create options to buy and sell.<br>• Secure distribution rights.<br>• Decide whether to buy or build, then enter into contracts. | • If investor, exercise demand registration rights or board control to force IPO or sale of company. Rely on exemptions for sale of restricted stock. Ask whether employee vesting accelerates on an initial public offering or sale.<br>• Negotiate and document arrangements with underwriter or investment banker. |
| **Manage Risk** | • Ask whether anyone else has rights to opportunity. | • Document founder arrangements and subject founders' shares to vesting.<br>• Analyze any covenants not to compete or trade-secret issues.<br>• Require arbitration or mediation of disputes.<br>• Comply with antidiscrimination laws in hiring and firing. Institute harassment policy.<br>• Avoid wrongful termination by documenting performance issues.<br>• Caution employees on discoverability of e-mail.<br>• Provide whistle-blower protection. | • Be prepared to make representations and warranties in stock-purchase agreement with or without knowledge qualifiers.<br>• Choose business entity wtih limited liability.<br>• Respect corporate form to avoid piercing of corporate veil. | • Enter into purchase and sale contracts.<br>• Impose limitations on liability and use releases. Buy insurance for product liabilities. Recall unsafe products.<br>• Create safe workplace.<br>• Install compliance system.<br>• Do due diligence before buying or leasing property to avoid environmental problems. No tying or horizontal price-fixing. Integrate products; no bolting.<br>• Be active in finding business solutions to legal disputes.<br>• Avoid misleading advertising.<br>• File tax returns on time and pay taxes when due. Do tax planning. | • Be mindful of difference between letter of intent and contract of sale.<br>• Consider entering into no-shop agreements if buyer. Negotiate fiduciary out if seller.<br>• Disclose fully in prospectus or acquisition agreement. Secure indemnity rights.<br>• Perform due diligence.<br>• Allocate risk of unknown.<br>• Make sure board of directors is informed and disinterested.<br>• Ban insider trading and police trades. |

fraud came to light. In the case of WorldCom, $200 billion of shareholder value was lost in fewer than twelve months, making it the largest corporate fraud in history.[12]

## "WHAT SHOULD THE FIRM DO?"

The law does not forbid all "bad" behavior. Indeed, the law often permits an array of behavior, ranging from the ethically questionable to the downright shameful. Thus, an action that is unethical may nonetheless be legal.

As C. Roland Christensen and his Harvard Business School colleagues pointed out in their seminal work on business policy and strategic management, the business leaders responsible for formulating the firm's strategy must consider not only what the firm *can* do but also what it *should* do.[13] They were writing in 1987, in the wake of the Watergate break-in that led to the resignation of President Richard Nixon; the payment of bribes

12. See Richard Breeden, *Restoring Trust,* filed with the WorldCom bankruptcy court on August 26, 2003.

13. C. ROLAND CHRISTENSEN ET AL., BUSINESS POLICY 121 (6th ed. 1987).

by Gulf Oil, Lockheed Aircraft, and others that led to passage of the Foreign Corrupt Practices Act of 1977; overcharges by General Dynamic and other government defense contractors; and check kiting fraud by E.F. Hutton. Accordingly, they argued that "determining strategy must take into account—as part of [the firm's] social environment—steadily rising moral and ethical standards."[14] Similarly, Robert S. Kaplan and David P. Norton, creators of the Balanced Scorecard strategic management system, call on business leaders to manage and report their regulatory and social performance as it relates to the environment, safety and health, employment practices, and community investment.[15] Kaplan and Norton "recognize companies' responsibilities to employees, citizens, and their communities because failure to perform adequately on regulatory and social processes puts at risk the company's ability to operate, grow, and deliver future value to shareholders."[16]

Patterns of unethical behavior tend to result in illegal behavior over time. Therefore, Harvard Business School Professor Lynn Sharp Paine argues that creating an organization that encompasses exemplary conduct may be the best way to prevent damaging misconduct.[17] Nevertheless, what is unethical may not necessarily be illegal. When a manager breaks a law, he or she can expect to be punished. The same may not be true for those who engage in unethical conduct. In finding that former executives of General Development Corporation had not violated a criminal law even though they "behaved badly," the U.S. Court of Appeals for the Eleventh Circuit explained:

> Construing the evidence at its worst against defendants, it is true that these men behaved badly. We live in a fallen world. But "bad men, like good men, are entitled to be tried and sentenced in accordance with law." And, the fraud statutes, do not cover all behavior which strays from the ideal; Congress has not yet criminalized all sharp conduct, manipulative acts, or unethical transactions.
>
> We might prefer that [the defendants] would have told these customers to shop around before buying. But, "there are . . . things . . . which we wish that people should do, which we like or admire them for doing, perhaps dislike or despise them for not doing, but yet admit that they are not bound to do."[18]

Another court stated, "We do not hold that the mail fraud statute criminalizes sleazy sales tactics, which abound in a free commercial society."[19]

The following case exemplifies the failure of the law to address all unethical conduct.

14. *Id.* at 460–61.
15. Robert S. Kaplan and David P. Norton, Strategy Maps: Converting Intangible Assets into Tangible Outcomes 167–68 (2004).
16. *Id.* at 165.
17. Lynn Sharp Paine, *Managing for Organizational Integrity*, Harv. Bus. Rev., Mar.–Apr. 1994, at 106, 117.
18. United States v. Brown, 79 F.3d 1550 (11th Cir. 1996).
19. Emery v. Am. Gen. Fin., Inc., 71 F.3d 1343, 1348 (7th Cir. 1995).

**A Case in Point**

**CASE 1.1**
**Bammert v. Don's Super Valu, Inc.**
*Supreme Court of Wisconsin*
*646 N.W.2d 365 (Wis. 2002).*

## Summary

**› FACTS** For some twenty-six years, Karen Bammert worked at Don's Super Valu, Inc. in Menomonie, Wisconsin. Her husband was a sergeant in the Menomonie police department. On one occasion, Bammert's husband administered a breathalyzer test to Nona Williams, the wife of Don Williams, owner of Don's Super Valu. Nona failed the test and was arrested for drunk driving. Don's Super Valu then fired Karen Bammert, allegedly in retaliation for her husband's participation in the arrest.

Karen Bammert was an at-will employee. Although at-will employees can generally be fired at will for any reason or for no reason at all without risk of judicial action, there is a public policy exception to this rule in Wisconsin. An at-will employee can recover for wrongful termination "when the discharge is contrary to a fundamental and well-defined public policy as evidenced by existing law."[20] Bammert sued Don's Super Valu for wrongful discharge, claiming that her firing was contrary to both the public policy against drunk driving and the public policy promoting marriage, both of which were reflected in existing Wisconsin law.

20. Brockmeyer v. Dun & Bradstreet, 335 N.W.2d 834, 834 (Wis. 1983).

*(Continued)*

(Case 1.1 *continued*)

The trial court rejected Bammert's argument and dismissed the complaint for failure to state a claim. The court of appeals affirmed, and the Supreme Court of Wisconsin accepted review.

› **ISSUE PRESENTED** Does the public policy exception to the employment-at-will doctrine apply when an at-will employee is fired in retaliation for the lawful actions of her nonemployee spouse?

› **SUMMARY OF OPINION** The Supreme Court of Wisconsin began by pointing out that the public policy exception was intended to be a narrow one. For purposes of this exception, a public policy must be "clearly articulate[d]," "fundamental and well-defined." The court went on to stress the value and importance of the employment-at-will doctrine and advised that employment contracts are the best way to protect against unjust firings.

After acknowledging that the policies implicated in this case were "clearly articulate[d]," "fundamental and well-defined," the court noted that previous cases had not addressed the vindication of a public policy by a third party: "Bammert was not fired for her participation in the enforcement of the laws against drunk driving; she was fired for her husband's participation." Previous cases had dealt with behavior only within the context of employment.

Viewing the expansion of the exception as a slippery slope, the Wisconsin Supreme Court concluded that "[e]xtending [the public policy exception] to discharges for fulfillment of an affirmative obligation which the law places on a relative would go too far, and have no logical stopping point." The court feared that the exception, once expanded to include "police officers' spouses fired in retaliation for the officers' conduct in the line of duty," might expand to "spouses of prosecutors, judges, . . . or IRS agents." The court questioned whether "discharges in retaliation for the conduct of nonemployee parents, children, and siblings" would be included in such an exception. The court concluded that the public policy exception to the employment-at-will doctrine should not be expanded to protect an at-will employee from firing in retaliation for the actions of his or her nonemployee spouse.

› **RESULT** The Supreme Court of Wisconsin declined to expand the public policy exception to the employment-at-will doctrine and affirmed the dismissal of Bammert's complaint, leaving her with no legal recourse.

› **COMMENTS** The Wisconsin Supreme Court acknowledged that Bammert's firing was retaliatory and "reprehensible." The dissenting judge lamented that "society owes its police officers a duty not to put them in the no-win position that Bammert's husband was placed in." Some would argue that courts and lawmakers should expand the law to punish all unethical behavior. But, even though courts can and do retroactively expand or contract the law when they elect to interpret it broadly or narrowly, such judicial alteration of the law can lead to inconsistent outcomes when today's case becomes tomorrow's precedent. The fear of starting down a slippery slope (also commonly known as opening Pandora's box or generating a snowball effect) is one reason courts hesitate to expand existing law in order to right an apparent wrong. The firing in this case is a perfect example of an action that was unethical, but nonetheless legal.

## The Ethical Tone Is Set at the Top

The chief executive officer plays the most significant role in instilling a sense of ethics throughout the organization. William F. May, chair of the Trinity Center for Ethics and Corporate Policy, described this role: "The CEO has a unique responsibility; he's a role model. What he does, how he lives, and the principles under which he operates become pretty much those the rest of the corporation emulate."[21] This is not to downplay the role of middle management. An employee's immediate supervisor often has the most direct effect on the employee. Nevertheless, direction from the top makes middle management aware that the CEO has a serious commitment to ethics. Ethics cannot be made a high priority of the corporation overnight, but it can be achieved through strong leadership and support from the CEO and the board of directors. In 1998, Terry Taylor, then chair and CEO of The Dun & Bradstreet Corporation (a global credit-rating agency), introduced his company's policy on business conduct with the letter shown in Exhibit 1.9.

21. Alden Lank, *The Ethical Criterion in Business Decision Making: Operational or Imperative?*, in TOUCHE ROSS AND CO., ETHICS IN AMERICAN BUSINESS: A SPECIAL REPORT 28 (1998) (the TOUCHE REPORT).

John J. Mackowski, chair and CEO of the Atlantic Mutual Companies, explained how strong leadership can affect a company:

> I think the CEO's responsibility is to view ethics within the corporate culture, understand how its values—good or bad—come to bear upon the company, its business, and its employees. In well-run corporations, for example, the great thing is the sense the staff has of fairness. And for most things, they know enough so that they really need not go to a supervisor to find out what is right or wrong. It's there in specific statements about how they are supposed to deal with customers or one another. And that direction has to come from the top.[22]

As we have seen in the first few years of the twenty-first century, upper-level management sometimes fails to provide that direction, often with catastrophic results.

### EXECUTIVES ON TRIAL

Between 1985 and 2001, CEO pay rose by 866 percent, but worker pay rose by only 63 percent.[23] This disparity reflected a widening gap between upper-level managers and their subordinates. Critics of overly generous executive compensation packages argue that putting CEOs on

22. *Dun & Bradstreet Corporation Policy on Business Conduct* (1998).
23. Alan Webber, *Above-It-All CEOs Forget Workers,* USA TODAY, Nov. 11, 2002, at 13A.

**EXHIBIT 1.9 A CEO's Message on Ethics**

Dear Associate:

For more than 155 years, The Dun & Bradstreet Corporation has carefully nurtured a reputation for integrity. As associates of this great company, we are stewards of that reputation and must act in keeping with the highest standards of fairness, honesty and integrity in all our dealings with our fellow associates, customers, suppliers, and investors around the world. . . .

Please familiarize yourself with this document and refer to it frequently when you are presented with a complex issue or predicament in your work for the Dun & Bradstreet Corporation. If you ever have a question about proper business conduct, please consult with your manager, a Human Resources representative or a member of your unit's Legal Department before taking any action. The Dun & Bradstreet Corporation's Office of Business Protection is also available to assist you. . . .

. . .

Each and every day, it is imperative that all of our actions work to preserve and strengthen our commitment to integrity. That commitment has been a cornerstone of The Dun & Bradstreet Corporation's success for more than 155 years, and it will be a key to our success for the next 155 years and beyond.

Sincerely,
Terry Taylor
Chairman and Chief Executive Officer

Source: *Dun & Bradstreet Corporation Policy on Business Conduct* (1998). Used by permission.

*"Don't get me wrong. Legality has its place."*



a compensatory pedestal can often lead to greedy and unethical behavior and reinforces narcissistic tendencies. Indeed, some even argue that narcissistic personality disorder (recognized and classified by the American Psychiatric Association) is prevalent within the corporate world for exactly this reason.[24] Sam Vaknin, former director of an Israeli investment firm, who was himself diagnosed with narcissistic personality disorder while imprisoned for engaging in stock manipulation, described the disorder in an e-mail, writing, "The narcissist lacks empathy—the ability to put himself in other people's shoes. . . . He does not recognize boundaries—personal, corporate or legal."[25] Consider Vaknin's description while reading the following examples.

### Dennis Kozlowski

Leo Dennis Kozlowski took over as CEO of Tyco International in 1992 and became chair in 1993. In May 2001, at the pinnacle of his career, Kozlowski appeared on the cover of *BusinessWeek*. But his fall was quick. Kozlowski was forced to resign in 2002 when he was charged with tax evasion after allegedly having art he had bought in New York shipped out of state to avoid paying $1 million in New York sales tax. Soon thereafter, Kozlowski and Mark H. Swartz, Tyco's former CFO, were charged with stealing $600 million from the company.

At trial, uncontested testimony revealed that Kozlowski had had sexual affairs with at least two Tyco employees and spent tens of millions of Tyco's money to purchase and outfit apartments in New York.[26] Kozlowski allegedly once spent $2 million on his wife's birthday party and billed half of the cost to Tyco. Among other items paid for as corporate expenses were a $6,000 shower curtain, a $15,000 poodle-shaped umbrella stand, a $6,300 sewing basket, two sets of sheets for $5,960, a $2,200 wastebasket, coat hangers totaling $2,900, and a $445 pincushion.[27]

Ironically, about a month before prosecutors announced the tax evasion charges, Kozlowski had cautioned graduating students at St. Anselm's College:

> As you go forward in life, you will become leaders of families, communities and even companies. . . . You will be confronted with questions every day that test your morals. The questions will get tougher and the consequences will become more severe. Think carefully, and for your sake, do the right thing, not the easy thing.[28]

A mistrial in the New York state criminal fraud case against Kozlowski was declared on April 2, 2004, and a second trial date was set for early 2005.

### The Rigas Family

John J. Rigas, founder and former CEO of Adelphia Communications Corporation, and his son, Timothy, the company's former CFO, were convicted in 2004 of defrauding investors out of billions of dollars by looting Adelphia, the nation's fifth-largest cable company. The case against the other son, Michael, the former chief operating officer, resulted in a hung jury.

The family had used the company as their personal piggy bank and engaged in extensive, undisclosed self-dealing. They misappropriated Adelphia money to cover margin calls on their personal portfolios, purchase timber rights to land in Pennsylvania, construct a golf course on private land, pay off personal loans and family debts, and purchase luxury condominiums for the family in Colorado, Mexico, and New York City.[29] Financial data were fabricated through what James R. Brown, Adelphia's former vice president of finance and the prosecution's star witness, called "aggressive accounting."[30] In March 2002, Adelphia reported its fourth quarter

24. Tim Race, *Like Narcissus, Executives Are Smitten, and Undone, by Their Own Images,* N.Y. TIMES, July 29, 2002, at C4.
25. *Id.*

26. Alex Berenson, *Tyco Chief and His Deputy Avoid Convictions, but Not Tattered Reputations,* N.Y. TIMES, Apr. 3, 2004, at C5.
27. Linda Hales, *The Curtain That Just Won't Wash,* WASH. POST, Apr. 3, 2004, at C1.
28. Berenson, *supra* note 26.
29. SEC v. Adelphia Communications Corp., Litigation Release No. 17627, *available at* http://www.sec.gov/litigation/litreleases/lr17627.htm.
30. Christine Nuzum, *Star Witness in Adelphia Case Felt 'Relief' When Fraud Got By,* WALL ST. J., May 18, 2004, at C6.

earnings, revealing that it had understated its debt and overstated the number of subscribers to its services.[31] In June 2002, Adelphia filed for bankruptcy protection.

### *Phil Condit*

On December 1, 2003, Philip M. Condit resigned from his position as CEO of Boeing Company. His resignation came in the wake of investigations regarding deals with the Air Force and NASA (discussed later in this chapter), but some argue that the end of Condit's tenure had been a long time coming.[32] Boeing's stock fell 6.5 percent during Condit's seven-year tenure, while the Standard & Poor's 500 stock index rose 61.8 percent. *BusinessWeek* reported:

> He developed a reputation as a womanizer, often with Boeing employees, and an appetite for the high life. In a hiatus between one of his four marriages, Condit took up residence in the Boeing suite at Seattle's Four Seasons Olympic Hotel, where he had the suite remodeled at company expense to add a bedroom. . . . Said one Boeing lawyer to another senior Boeing executive [regarding the womanizing]: "We have another Bill Clinton on our hands."[33]

When Condit became CEO, Boeing had three small corporate jets, but in an effort to keep in touch with customers, senior executives were required to fly commercial airlines. By the end of Condit's tenure, Boeing had a fleet of corporate jets and a 737 decorated especially for Condit.

### *Dick Grasso*

Dick Grasso, former chair of the New York Stock Exchange (NYSE), a not-for-profit organization, left his position in September 2003 amidst a firestorm of controversy over his compensation. Apparently, in 1996, a salary consultant firm had urged the NYSE to use the pay at large companies as benchmarks for figuring its officials' pay packages. In August 2003, the NYSE announced that Grasso would receive $139.5 million in deferred pay and retirement benefits. Shortly thereafter, the NYSE announced that Grasso was entitled to another $48 million, which Grasso said he would forgo.

On May 24, 2004, New York's Attorney General, Eliot Spitzer, filed a suit alleging that Grasso's payment violated New York state laws governing not-for-profit organizations and demanding the return of more than $100 million. The complaint accused Grasso and others of presenting the exchange's board with inaccurate and misleading information regarding the level and nature of his compensation. Grasso insisted that he would not return any of the money and said that he anticipated "complete vindication" in the matter.[34] Even if Grasso ultimately prevails in the lawsuit, his reputation (and that of the NYSE members who served on the compensation committee) has been besmirched by the apparent lack of self-restraint.

## The Ethical Business Leader's Decision Tree

As noted earlier, compliance with the law is just the baseline for effective and responsible managerial action. As Edmund Burke declared almost 200 years ago, "All it takes for evil to prevail is for good men to do nothing." Successful managers go beyond what the law requires to ensure that the firm conducts business in an ethical manner with due regard not just for shareholders but also for other stakeholders, such as employees, customers, suppliers, the community, and the environment.[35] Put another way, successful managers work hard to ensure that their firms behave in a socially responsible manner. This entails more than mere legal compliance coupled with a narrow-minded focus on maximizing shareholder value. Socially responsible firms consider all stakeholders, not just shareholders.

The *Ethical Business Leader's Decision Tree* in Exhibit 1.10 provides a tool business leaders and their counsel can use to evaluate the legal and ethical aspects of their strategy and its implementation.

### Is the Action Legal?

Managers should first ask themselves whether the proposed action is legal. Legality is addressed first to reinforce the notion that legal compliance is the baseline standard. If an action is not in accordance with the letter and the spirit of the law, then, regardless of the likely effect on shareholder value, the action should not be taken.

31. Peter Grant, *Adelphia Insider Tells of Culture of Lies at Firm,* WALL ST. J., May 19, 2004, at C1.
32. Stanley Holmes, *Boeing: What Really Happened,* BUS.WK., Dec. 15, 2003, at 33.
33. *Id.* at 33–34, 36.

34. Kara Scannell, *Spitzer's Winning Streak Heads for Court,* WALL ST. J., May 25, 2004, at C6.
35. As Professor Lynn Sharp Paine demonstrates in VALUE SHIFT: WHY COMPANIES MUST MERGE SOCIAL AND FINANCIAL IMPERATIVES TO ACHIEVE SUPERIOR PERFORMANCE (2003), greatness in the global marketplace requires attention to ethics and social responsibility as well as to the financial return to shareholders. *See also* Constance E. Bagley & Karen L. Page, *The Devil Made Me Do It: Replacing Corporate Director's Veil of Secrecy with the Mantle of Stewardship,* 33 SAN DIEGO L. REV. 897 (Fall 1999).

EXHIBIT 1.10 The Ethical Business Leader's Decision Tree

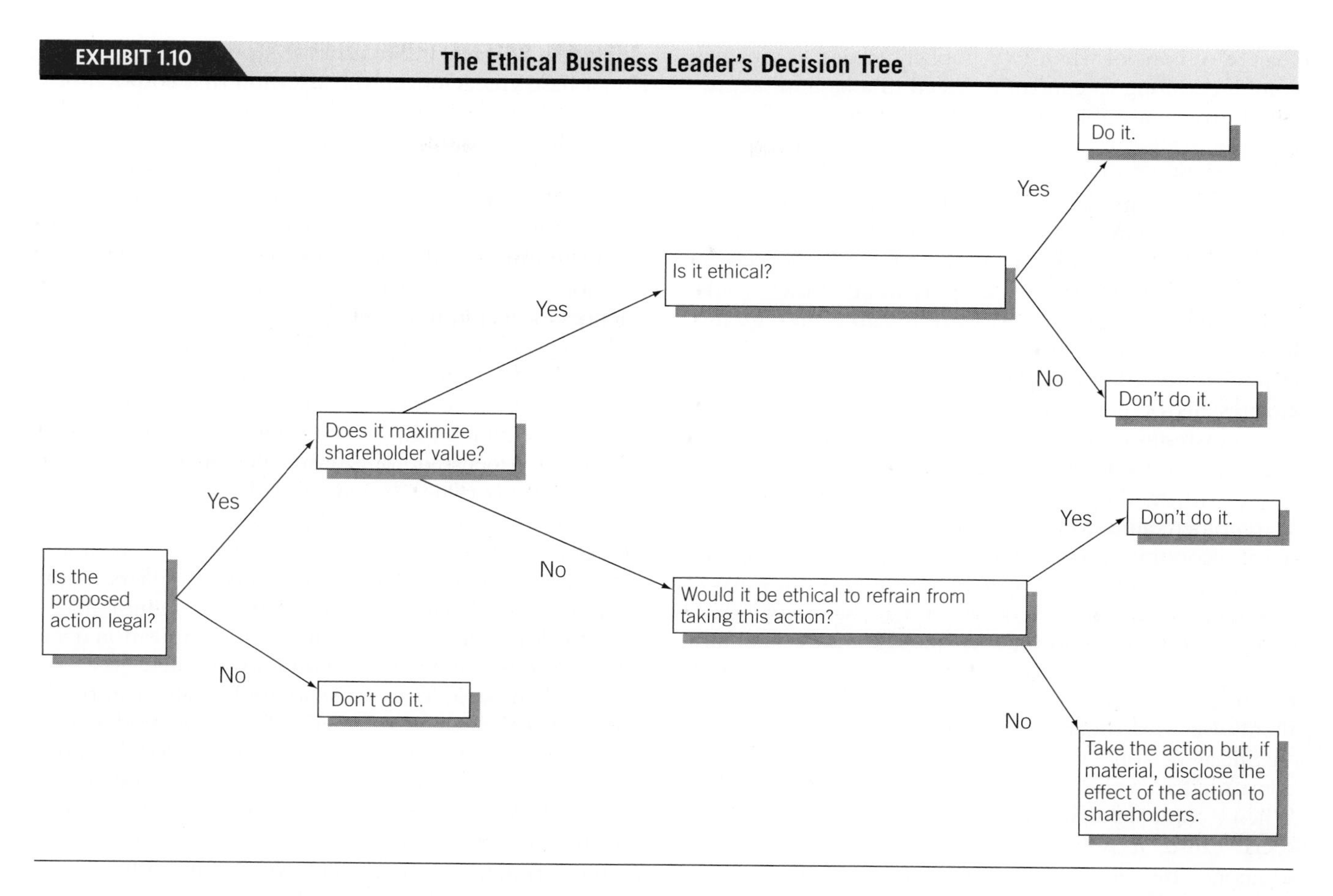


## Would It Maximize Shareholder Value?

The filter for shareholder value is intended to require managers to consider early on whether the interests of the shareholders—the group given the ultimate legal authority to change management—are being served by the proposed action. Yet the inquiry need not stop there.

Contrary to popular belief, maximization of shareholder wealth, so-called *shareholder primacy*, is not legally mandated, except in very narrow circumstances.[36] The courts and many state legislatures have made it abundantly clear that the directors' obligation is to manage the corporation "for the best interest of the corporation." In deciding what is in the best interest of the corporation, the board may legitimately consider not only the effect a decision might have on the shareholders, but also the effect it might have on employees, customers, suppliers, and the community where the corporation does business.[37] Legislatures in a majority of the states have enacted so-called constituency statutes, which expressly authorize the boards of corporations incorporated there to take into account all stakeholders and constituencies even when a change in control or breakup of the corporation has become inevitable.[38]

Although Delaware, where a majority of the Fortune 500 companies are incorporated, has not enacted a constituency statute, the Delaware Supreme Court has made it clear that the role of the director shifts from "being a protector of the corporate bastion" to being an "auctioneer" charged with obtaining the highest realizable short-term value for the shareholders only when the breakup of the corporation has become inevitable or there has been a change of control.[39] Further, the Delaware Supreme Court narrowly defines what constitutes a change of control. In Delaware, there is no

36. *See* Bagley & Page, *supra* note 35.
37. Unocal Corp. v. Mesa Petroleum Co., 493 A.2d 946 (Del. 1985).
38. *See,* e.g., Steven M.H. Wallman, *The Proper Interpretation of Corporate Constituency Statutes and Formulations of Director Duties,* 21 Stetson L. Rev. 1 (1991).
39. Revlon, Inc. v. MacAndrews & Forbes Holdings, Inc., 506 A.2d 173 (Del. 1986).

change of control when two publicly traded companies combine as long as control is vested in a large disaggregated group of public shareholders before and after the transaction.[40]

Thus, the CEO who asserted, "I have a duty to maximize value for my shareholders. I can't let my own sense of right and wrong get in the way," is just plain wrong as a matter of law. A CEO or board member may *choose* to do things in the name of the corporation that they would feel wrong doing in their personal lives, but they are not legally *required* to do so. In the same way that medical ethics do not compel a physician to do something that violates his or her own personal ethics, corporate law does not require managers to check their sense of right and wrong outside the executive suite.

Notwithstanding the lack of a legal duty to maximize shareholder value, Milton Friedman, a Nobel Prize winner in economics, would have the inquiry stop here. In his seminal article, *The Social Responsibility of Business Is to Increase Its Profits,*[41] he asserted that the only guiding criterion for the corporation should be profitability within the confines of the law. He argued that it is not the role of business to promote social ends in and of themselves. Friedman asserted that a corporation is an "artificial person" with no true responsibilities to any constituencies other than its owners, the shareholders. When a company makes a decision to spend money for a social cause, it is in essence making the decision for someone else and spending someone else's money for a general social interest.

Friedman argued that spending money in ways that are not consistent with shareholder wishes is tantamount to imposing a tax and unilaterally deciding where the money will be spent. Because taxation is a governmental function, and only the government has sufficient legislative and judicial protections to ensure that taxation and expenditures fairly reflect the desires of the public, a corporation making taxation decisions on its own would render the executive "simultaneously legislator, executive and jurist."

Friedman concluded his landmark article by asserting that "social responsibility" is an inherently collectivist attitude and a "fundamentally subversive doctrine." In a free society, "there is one and only one social responsibility of business—to use its resources and engage in activities designed to increase its profits so long as it stays within the rules of the game, which is to say, engages in open and free competition without deception or fraud."

Professors Henry Mintzberg, Robert Simons, and Kunal Basu characterized the assertion that corporations exist solely to maximize shareholder value as a "half-truth" that contributed significantly to the "syndrome of selfishness" that took hold of our corporations and society in the late twentieth and early twenty-first century.[42] They argued that focusing on shareholder value without taking account of other stakeholders' interests "reflects a fallacious separation of the economic and social consequences of decisionmaking."[43]

Even economist Michael C. Jensen, a staunch believer in shareholder primacy, acknowledged in a 2001 article the importance of focusing on long-term, not short-term, shareholder value: "Short-term profit maximization at the expense of long-term value creation is a sure way to destroy value."[44] Jensen explained, "In order to maximize value, corporate managers must not only satisfy, but enlist the support of, all corporate stakeholders—customers, employees, managers, suppliers, local communities."[45] He cautioned that "we cannot maximize the long-term market value of an organization if we ignore or mistreat any important constituency."[46]

Thus, a myopic focus on shareholder value can result not only in the unfair treatment of nonshareholder constituencies, but also in harm to the shareholders.[47] In the age of the Internet and 24/7 cable networks dedicated exclusively to news, misdeeds in faraway places are often featured on the evening news at home the same day. Nongovernment organizations (NGOs) and other interest groups track and report on the working conditions in overseas factories, the dumping of hazardous waste and spoliation of forests and rivers, the exploitation of indigenous peoples, and the sale of shoddy and dangerous products. Maintaining a reputation for integrity and honesty is more important than ever as customers vote with their feet and boycott clothing made in sweat shops in the Mauritius Islands or gasoline made from oil transported in pipelines built with slave labor in Myanmar.

Edward Simon, president of Herman Miller, goes even further and encourages managers to focus not just on avoiding harm but on doing good: "Why can't we do good works at work? . . . Business is the only institution

40. Paramount Communications, Inc. v. QVC Network, Inc., 637 A.2d 34 (Del. 1994).

41. MILTON FRIEDMAN, AN ECONOMIST'S PROTEST 177–84 (1972).

42. Henry Mintzberg et al., *Beyond Selfishness,* SLOAN MGMT. REV., Fall 2002, at 67.

43. *Id.* at 69.

44. Michael C. Jensen, *Value Maximization, Stakeholder Theory, and the Corporate Objective Function,* 14 J. APPLIED CORP. FIN. 8, 16 (2001).

45. *Id.* at 8, 9.

46. *Id.*

47. Bagley & Page, *supra* note 35.

that has a chance, as far as I can see, to fundamentally improve the injustice that exists in the world."[48]

## Is the Action Ethical? What Is Ethical?

The next question to consider is whether the proposed action would be ethical. But how does one define what constitutes good ethical behavior? This is sometimes difficult, due in part to the fact that there are numerous and diverse ethical theories. People, consciously or not, employ ethical theories in their decision-making processes. The important thing for a manager to remember is that there may be different "ethically correct" ways of looking at a decision. As a result, a manager's constituencies may not always reach a similar decision and hence may not be as willing to accept the implications and consequences of the manager's decision.

### Teleological and Deontological Schools

The two main schools of ethical thought are teleological and deontological. *Teleological theory* is concerned with consequences. The ethical good of an action is to be judged by the effect of the action on others. *Deontological theory* focuses more on the motivation and principle behind an action than on the consequences.

For example, suppose that a construction company donates materials to build shelters for the homeless. In judging this action within the teleological framework, the fact that some homeless people are given housing is the important issue. Within a deontological framework, one would want to know why the company was motivated to supply the materials for the shelters. As another example, suppose that an employer promises to throw a party if the firm reaches profitability and then breaks the promise. Under teleological theory, as long as the consequences of breaking the promise are insignificant, the action of breaking the promise is not in and of itself bad. Deontological theory, however, would suggest that there is something intrinsically wrong with breaking a promise, no matter what the consequences. Thus, a particular action can be evaluated differently, depending on the system under which it is examined.

A brief examination of several theories within these two schools further illustrates their differences. *Utilitarianism* is a major teleological system that operates under the proposition that the ideal is to maximize the total benefit for everyone involved. Under a utilitarian theory, no one person's particular interest is given more weight than another's, but rather the utility of everyone as a group is maximized.

For example, suppose that a $10,000 bonus pool is to be divided among three project managers and that their marginal benefits from receiving a portion of the money can be quantified. Imagine that the money can be allocated in either of two ways: Under Distribution 1, the three persons benefit 6, 12, and 24 units, respectively. Under Distribution 2, the three persons benefit 8, 12, and 16 units, respectively. A utilitarian would want Distribution 1 because the total benefit (6 + 12 + 24 = 42) is greater than under Distribution 2 (8 + 12 + 16 = 36). The utilitarian would not be concerned that the other distribution seems more equal and fair or that under the benefit-maximizing utility distribution, the worst-off person has considerably less than the worst-off person in Distribution 2.

In contrast, *Rawlsian moral theory,* a deontological theory, aims to maximize the plight of the worst-off person in society by developing principles behind a "veil of ignorance." Each person in society is to imagine that he or she does not know what his or her allotment of society's resources will be and then to decide which principles should govern society's interactions. John Rawls believed that behind the veil of ignorance individuals would create a system that benefited the least-well-off people most. According to this theory, Distribution 2 should be favored because it is the one that would be preferred by the person who faced the possibility of getting the worst share.

*Kantian theory* is another important deontological line of thought. Immanuel Kant's categorical imperative looks to the form of an action, rather than the intended result, in examining the ethical worth. The form of an action can be delineated into universalizability and reversibility. *Universalizability* asks whether one would want everyone to act in this manner; *reversibility* looks to whether one would want such a rule applied to oneself.

For example, suppose that a manager is deciding how long a break to give the workers on an assembly line. In choosing between a system allowing a ten-minute break every three hours with bathroom breaks whenever necessary versus a longer lunch break, the manager might ask—under universalizability—whether he or she would like a world in which all companies applied a similar system. Under reversibility, the manager would decide whether he or she would want to be subjected to a particular break system as an employee.

### Comparative Justice

The consequences of an action motivated by a certain ethical system can also be evaluated within a comparative justice framework. This framework allows the rights-based

48. Quoted in Peter M. Senge, The Fifth Discipline: The Art and Practice of the Learning Organization 5 (1990).

## HISTORICAL PERSPECTIVE

# AQUINAS ON LAW AND ETHICS

Saint Thomas Aquinas (1225?–1274), a theologian and philosopher, believed that an unjust law could not properly be considered a law at all. The only true laws were those that followed eternal law—as far as eternal law could be discovered by the use of human reason and revelation. Eternal law is the orderly governance of the acts and movements of all creatures by God as the divine governor of the universe. Because not every individual follows a natural inclination to do good—that is, to act virtuously in order to achieve happiness and to avoid evil—human laws are framed to train, and sometimes compel, a person to do what is right, as well as to restrain the person from doing harm to others. According to Aquinas, for human law to be considered law, that is, binding on human conscience, it must be just. To be just, a human law must be (1) consonant with a reasoned determination of the universal good; (2) within the power of individuals to fulfill; (3) clearly expressed by legitimate authority; (4) approved by custom, that is, the declaration of right reason by a community; and (5) widely promulgated. To the extent that human law is just, it is in concert with eternal law, as discerned through human reason, and it is binding on individuals. Human laws that promote private benefit over the common good are unjust, and individuals are bound not to obey them. Instead individuals should "disregard them, oppose them, and do what [they] can to revoke them."[a]

Most modern legal theorists separate the question of a law's status as law from the question of its inherent morality. They argue that a law may help to resolve moral issues, punish immoral action, and serve a moral purpose (as, for example, when laws permit participation in government); but a law need not be inherently moral to be a real law. In this so-called positive-law view, any law counts as a real law if it has been created according to recognized procedures by someone with the recognized authority to do so—for instance, a king in a monarchy or, in the U.S. system, a legislature, judge, or administrative agency. A properly created law may, of course, be criticized as immoral. Some people may even wish to disobey it. But they do so in the full knowledge that they are disobeying a valid law.

In the United States, the split between legal and moral debate has always been less clear than positive-law theorists might wish. Americans have always given their moral debates a peculiarly legal flavor, mainly because certain important but ambiguous phrases in the U.S. and state constitutions invite a person to "constitutionalize" moral questions. Moral questions are readily translatable into questions about the meaning and scope of the constitutional doctrines of due process of law, liberty, equal protection under the laws, or cruel and unusual punishment. For example, in upholding a woman's right to have an abortion, the U.S. Supreme Court stated: "At the heart of liberty is the right to define one's own concept of existence, of meaning, of the universe, and of the mystery of human life."[b]

It has become a national trait of Americans to expect their constitutions to support their moral convictions. Just as Aquinas believed that unjust laws could not accord with eternal law, many Americans believe that unjust laws cannot be constitutional. Perhaps it is for this reason that many of the most controversial American moral debates, such as those on slavery, segregation, affirmative action, same-sex marriage, abortion, student-led prayer in public school, capital punishment, and the right to die, have focused on the interpretation of constitutions or have been framed in terms of possible constitutional amendments. In some ways, the tendency in the United States to look to constitutions for substantiation of the just quality of law is akin to the use by theologians of the Judeo-Christian scriptures as supernatural revelation of knowledge of the universal good that is eternal law.

As this comparison of present-day constitutional analysis to thirteenth-century theology indicates, the past is often a valuable pointer to the future. At the same time, one must be able to distinguish differences between doctrines that prevailed in the past and those that should prevail in the future. In this regard, it is important to recall the positivists' distinction between law and morals. If people confuse what's "allowed" with what's "right," they risk cutting their ethical discussions short and missing opportunities both for the encouragement of morality by law and for the reform of law in the light of society's morals.

a. P. Glenn, A Tour of the Summa 170 (1978).

b. Planned Parenthood v. Casey, 505 U.S. 833 (1992).

moral theories of Kant or Rawls to be compared to, for example, a utilitarian framework. Distributive, compensatory, and retributive theories of justice are the three main categories within this framework.

*Distributive justice* focuses on how the burden and benefits of a particular system are distributed. An ideal system maximizes the overall pie by dividing it such that incentives are enough to entice persons to produce more. The system also concerns itself with a fair distribution of these goods—compensating those who contributed while still upholding a certain minimum standard. For example, the use of progressively higher income tax rates for those with more income and earned income tax credits for those earning the least can be understood within a distributive justice framework.

*Compensatory justice* aims at compensating people for the harm done by others. For example, if someone is found to be responsible for making another person miss five days of work, a compensatory system of justice would demand that the victim be somehow compensated for the lost wages.

*Retributive justice* is also concerned with the harm people do to others, but here the focus is more on how to deter them from inflicting further harm. For example, suppose that X steals an idea from Y and makes $10,000. If the idea had not been stolen, Y would have made $5,000. Under a compensatory framework, X would compensate Y for the thievery by paying Y $5,000. Under a retributive framework, X should be taught that stealing an idea is wrong. Thus, X would be required to give up any benefit and pay Y $10,000.

### *How Do Business Leaders Define Ethics?*

Many business leaders associate ethics with such concepts as integrity, fairness, and honesty. For more than seventy-five years, the J.C. Penney Company has considered ethical business behavior to be that which conforms to the Golden Rule: Do unto others as you would have them do unto you.

The CEO of a highly successful Scandinavian multinational tells his managers to conjure up the following scenario: Assume that the decision you are about to make in Timbuktu becomes public knowledge in our home country, the host country, and significant developing countries where our company is operating. Assume further that you, as the decision maker, are called upon to defend the decision on television both at home and abroad. If you think you can defend it successfully in these public forums, the probability is high that your decision is ethical.[49]

49. TOUCHE REPORT, *supra* note 21, at 48.

Taking a simpler approach, Carly Fiorina, former chair and CEO of Hewlett-Packard, remarked, "Good leadership means doing the right thing when no one's watching."[50]

## FINDING THE "SWEET SPOT"

Ideal courses of action are ethically sound and maximize shareholder value. Great managers reframe issues and work hard to create such solutions. Ralph Larsen, CEO of Johnson & Johnson, rejected what he termed the "tyranny of the 'or'" and refused to treat social responsibility and profit maximization as mutually exclusive. When asked whether he would rather be a good corporate citizen or maximize profits, Larsen replied, "Yes."[51]

Some proponents of the deontological school would argue that courses of action that confer incidental benefits on stakeholders are not truly ethical if they were motivated primarily by the desire to maximize shareholder value. This appears to elevate form over function. An action that confers a benefit (incidentally or otherwise) on stakeholders in addition to maximizing shareholder value is clearly more ethical than two alternatives: maximizing shareholder value without conferring any benefit on other stakeholders or maximizing shareholder value while harming other stakeholders.

## ACTIONS THAT MIGHT MAXIMIZE SHAREHOLDER VALUE BUT WOULD BE UNETHICAL

Some actions might maximize at least short-term shareholder value but are nonetheless unethical. Because there is generally no legal obligation to undertake actions solely because they maximize shareholder value (see the discussion above), an ethical business leader will not take such actions. Joseph Neubauer, CEO of Aramark Worldwide Corporation, walked away from two well-priced and fully negotiated overseas acquisitions that were perfectly suited to Aramark's goal of international expansion after a closer look at their operations and books revealed unsavory business practices. He justified the loss of time and money, stating, "It takes a lifetime to build a reputation, and only a short time to lose it all."[52]

50. Stephen Overell, *Blowing Your Own Credibility,* PERSONNEL TODAY, May 27, 2003, at 13.

51. *Quoted in* Ira M. Millstein, *The Responsible Board,* 52 BUS. LAW. 407, 408–09 (1997).

52. Nannette Byrnes et al., *The Good CEO,* BUS.WK., Sept. 23, 2002, at 80.

### ANOTHER "EASY" CATEGORY

If an action does not maximize shareholder value and the firm has no ethical reason to act, the action should not be taken. Indeed, taking actions that will not maximize shareholder value without any other justification might result in liability for waste of corporate assets.

### ACTIONS THAT DO NOT MAXIMIZE SHAREHOLDER VALUE BUT ARE ETHICALLY REQUIRED

Sometimes firms will have an ethical reason to act, even though acting will not maximize shareholder value (at least not in the short term). These situations can present the most difficult issues for ethical business decision making. Because the firm is under no legal duty to maximize shareholder value at the expense of all other stakeholders, and because good ethics and social responsibility usually make good business sense (at least in the long term), when shareholder value and ethics are truly at odds, managers should follow the ethical high road and disclose the reasons for taking the action to the shareholders. Disclosure is important to prevent managers from using social responsibility as a fig leaf to cover up mediocre performance or self-dealing.

Consider a company establishing a manufacturing facility overseas in a country that has much less stringent environmental laws than the United States. The managers legally may and should consider not only the possibility that those laws might later be tightened and applied retroactively to require costly cleanups that will adversely affect shareholder value, but also evaluate the cost of installing pollution-control equipment and the potential harm that would result if the equipment were not installed. Thus, top management might feel ethically compelled to install $5 million worth of pollution-control equipment in a country that does not require such equipment if a failure to do so would cause $100 million worth of damage or certain loss of life or serious physical injury. Spending that money may even provide a source of competitive advantage over firms that wait until more costly "tail-pipe" regulations are put into effect. If the company elects to spend a material amount of the shareholders' money to install such equipment, the board should disclose its decision and the reasons for it in the periodic reports to shareholders.

Conoco (one of the largest U.S. oil companies) took the high road in the wake of the environmental disaster created in 1989 when the *Exxon Valdez* ran aground, spilling 10.1 million gallons of crude oil into the waters of Prince William Sound in Alaska. Experts believe double-hulled tankers can prevent or limit spills, but they were not required even after the *Valdez* spill. Notwithstanding the lack of a legal requirement to install double hulls, Conoco announced in April 1990 that it was ordering two new oil tankers with double hulls. Conoco president and CEO Constantine S. Nicandros explained the decision to incur the extra cost: "We are in the business by the public's consent. We are sincere in our concern for the air, water and land of our planet as a matter of enlightened self-interest."[53]

## Resolving the Tension Between Long-Term and Short-Term Values

This is not to suggest that ethics always pay. Depending on the timeframe, sometimes good guys do come in last.

### IN THE LONG TERM, GOOD ETHICS ARE SIMPLY GOOD BUSINESS

At least in the long term, good ethics are simply good business. As the Business Roundtable, the leading association of CEOs in the United States, proclaimed, "[Long-term] stockholder value is enhanced when a corporation treats its employees well, serves its customers well, maintains good relationships with suppliers, and has a reputation for civic responsibility and legal compliance."[54]

A 1997 study of sixty-seven companies rated in every corporate survey conducted by *Fortune* magazine from 1982 to 1992 found "a positive correlation between social and financial performance in large U.S. corporations," regardless of the financial performance measure (i.e., return on assets, return on equity, or return on investment).[55] A 1999 Arthur D. Little survey of 481 executives worldwide found that 95 percent of the managers believed that sustainable development (combining environmental protection and social responsibility with business strategy) offered real business value.[56] Clearly,

53. *Conoco Says It Will Order Oil Tankers with Double Hulls,* L.A. TIMES, Apr. 11, 1990, at D1.

54. THE BUSINESS ROUNDTABLE, PRINCIPLES OF CORPORATE GOVERNANCE 30 (2002).

55. *See* Lee E. Preston & Douglas P. O'Bannon, *The Corporate Social-Financial Performance Relationship,* 36 BUS. & SOC'Y 419 (1997).

56. Kantantin Richter, *Managers & Managing: Sustainable Development Teases Consultants—Potential Looks Big, but Field Has Taken Off Slowly,* WALL ST. J. Eur, Dec. 14, 1999, at 4.

customers care about ethical issues, so managers should care as well.

Current and prospective employees also care. Through postings on websites and Internet message boards, questions in job interviews, and contacts between present and past employees, job hunters search for clues of ethical values when evaluating a potential employer. The mere existence of a code of conduct or a toothless ethics program is not enough to attract these individuals, who seek not only employment, but also to protect their personal integrity, retirement savings, and future employability by working only for upstanding organizations. For many of the same reasons, the ethical reputation of an employer makes a difference to its current employees as well.

Jurors, as members of the public and arbiters of guilt and damages, also care about a corporation's ethical reputation. In a study conducted partially by the Los Angeles jury consulting firm DecisionQuest, support from even white males—the category of jurors that has historically been most supportive of large corporations—has eroded dramatically in light of recent scandals.[57] According to Arthur Patterson, a psychologist with DecisionQuest, "For years, our jury research has shown an increasing distrust of corporate America. Now jurors have validation for their distrust."[58]

Finally, as demonstrated most graphically by the passage of the Sarbanes–Oxley Act of 2002, corporate conduct that violates society's expectations can also result in "[n]ew forms of regulation or effective enforcement . . . without regard for feasibility or cost."[59] This insight prompted Professor Christensen and his business policy colleagues to caution students of management fifteen years before the passage of Sarbanes–Oxley that "government regulation is not a good substitute for knowledgeable self-restraint."[60]

## The Tension: Costco, Stride Rite, and IBM

Nonetheless, the reality is that, at least in the short term, there can be tension between ethics and maximizing economic returns. Although Costco Wholesale Corporation, the nation's top warehouse retailer, is well known for having the best benefits in retail, it has come under attack from investors for that very reason.[61] In early 2004, Costco employees started at $10 an hour; within three and a half years, a full-time hourly worker could make $40,000 per year. In early 2004, Costco paid 92 pecent of its employees' health-care premiums, compared to Wal-Mart's 66.6 percent; further, 82 percent of Costco employees were covered by company health insurance, compared to 48 percent of Wal-Mart employees.

But Costco's employee benefits come at a cost. In early 2004, Costco's shares traded at around twenty times projected per-share earnings, while Wal-Mart's traded at around twenty-four. Bill Dreher, a retailing analyst with Deutsche Bank Securities, Inc., said, "From the perspective of investors, Costco's benefits are overly generous." He continued, "Public companies need to care for shareholders first. Costco runs its business like it is a private company." On a previous occasion, Dreher criticized Costco's strict markup ceiling because it "place[d] club member interests too far ahead of shareholder interests."[62] Costco's CEO James Sinegal reaffirmed his belief "that in order to reward the shareholder in the long term, you have to please your customers and workers."[63]

This tension also arises in situations involving plant closings and outsourcing. In 1993, Stride Rite, renowned for its focus on social responsibility, announced that it was closing its plant in New Bedford, Massachusetts. Facing an unemployment rate of about 14 percent, residents of New Bedford criticized the firm's decision; two suspicious fires caused damage estimated at $750,000. Chair Ervin Shames defended the shoe company's seemingly split personality: "Putting jobs into places where it doesn't make economic sense is a dilution of corporate and community wealth. . . . It was a difficult decision. Our hearts said, 'Stay,' but our heads said 'Move.'"[64] A former chair of the company, Arnold Hiatt, acknowledges the inherent difficulty in this situation: "To the extent that you can stay in the city, I think you have to, [but] if it's at the expense of your business, I think you can't forget that your primary responsibility is to your stockholders."[65]

Many corporations now stand to save large amounts of money by outsourcing upscale jobs. Accenture, Microsoft, Conseco, Delta Air Lines, General Electric,

57. Tamara Loomis, *Business Scandals Rock Juror Attitudes,* 228 N.Y.L.J. 1, 1 (2002).
58. *Id.*
59. Christensen et al., *supra* note 13, at 461.
60. *Id.*
61. Ann Zimmerman, *Costco's Dilemma: Be Kind to Its Workers, or Wall Street?,* Wall St. J., Mar. 26, 2004, at B1.
62. Byrnes et al., *supra* note 52, at 82–83.
63. Zimmerman, *supra* note 61, at B1.
64. Joseph Pereira, *Social Responsibility and Need for Low Cost Clash at Stride Rite,* Wall St. J., May 28, 1993, at A1.
65. *Id.*

Intel, Oracle, and Boeing are among the firms that have expanded their overseas employment in recent years in an effort to utilize inexpensive, but well-educated, workforces in other countries.[66] Aerospace engineering work that would cost $6,000 a month in the United States costs $650 a month in Russia; chip design work that would cost $7,000 a month in the United States costs $1,000 a month in India and China; architectural work, $3,000 a month in the United States versus $250 in the Philippines; equity research and industry reports prepared by finance specialists, $7,000 in the United States versus $1,000 in India; and bookkeeping, taxes, and financial reports, $5,000 a month in the United States versus $300 in the Philippines.[67]

Critics of outsourcing claim that these companies are shipping valuable jobs overseas and often simultaneously laying off loyal, white-collar American workers. Proponents of the practice maintain that better jobs will be created in the United States with the money saved by the outsourcing. At a minimum, companies should be honest about what they are doing. After an employee leaked a memo that called on managers to hide the decision to outsource more programming jobs to India, IBM came under fire and subsequently reduced the number of planned layoffs.[68] Meanwhile, economic experts struggle to understand the implications of this rapidly growing trend.

## APPROACHES TO RECONCILING THE TENSION

Firms and individuals can take affirmative steps to help resolve the tension between short-term results and long-term value.

### *Softening the Edges*

To avoid or reduce layoffs, many companies soften the edges of difficult economic times by cutting personnel costs through different means. These less draconian measures include hiring freezes, shortening the workweek, reducing pay and bonuses, eliminating bonuses altogether, reducing salary increases, reassignments, and offering buyout packages to employees who might be considering leaving anyway.[69]

66. Pete Engardio et al., *The New Global Job Shift*, BUS.WK., Feb. 3, 2003, at 50.
67. *Id.*
68. William M. Bulkeley, *IBM Now Plans Fewer Layoffs from Offshoring*, WALL ST. J., July 29, 2004, at B1.
69. Karen F. Lehr, *Smart Companies Use Alternatives Instead of Layoffs*, WASH. BUS. J., Nov. 9. 2001, *available at* http://www.bizjournals.com/washington/stories/2001/11/12/editorial4.html.

### *Lobbying for Changes in the Law or the Enactment of Codes of Conduct*

In many instances, corporations or coalitions of corporations have the economic and political power to lobby for changes in applicable law. In 1976, the Organisation of Economic Co-operation and Development (OECD) promulgated a generalized code of business conduct for multinationals reflecting the views of government, business, labor, and consumer groups. The OECD comprises thirty nations from North America, Europe, and Asia–Pacific representing more than half of the goods and services produced worldwide. Its members are committed to an open-market economy, pluralistic democracy, and respect for human rights.

The OECD code of business conduct has had a significant impact on international business practice. It requires multinational corporations (1) to act in accordance with the economic, commercial, and social goals and priorities of the host country; (2) to abstain from bribery and other corrupt practices seeking favorable treatment from the host government; (3) to abstain from political intervention in the host country; (4) to make a positive contribution to the balance of payments of the host country; (5) to abstain from borrowing from local financial institutions so that they can reserve their capital for local enterprises; (6) to monitor the multinational's impact on employment, wages, labor standards, working conditions, and industrial relations; (7) to protect the environment of the host country; and (8) to disclose information on the multinational's activities so that the home country and the host country can formulate government policy.

In 1999, the OECD adopted a convention committing the OECD countries and other nonmember countries to adopt rules outlawing bribery.[70] The United States had lobbied for such an agreement since enacting the Foreign Corrupt Practices Act (FCPA) in 1977 in response to the bribery scandals of the mid-1970s. The FCPA prohibits U.S. companies from paying bribes to government officials. The OECD convention criminalizes bribes to government officials, and a related recommendation prohibits the tax deductibility of bribes. Also in 1999, the OECD agreed to work with the World Bank to persuade nations to reject bribery and corrupt practices.[71] As part of that agreement, the OECD agreed to monitor closely nations' compliance with the antibribery convention and to publicize that information.

70. G. Pascal Zachary, *Industrialized Countries Agree to Adopt Rules to Curb Bribery*, WALL ST. J., Feb. 16, 1999, at A18.
71. Harry Dunphy, *OECD Will Scrutinize Compliance with Anti-Bribery Treaty*, ASSOCIATED PRESS NEWSWIRES, June 23, 1999.

Unfortunately, the OECD convention may have little effect on the business climate of the worst offenders. In Transparency International's 2002 Bribe Payers Index, Russia, China, Taiwan, and South Korea were among the countries where companies were considered most likely to pay bribes.[72] (Transparency International is a German NGO that fights corruption.) It is imperative for developing countries to curtail corruption because research has established a correlation between corruption and lower annual capital inflows and lower productivity.[73]

## *Adopt an Ethics Program*

Corporations that set an ethical tone at the top make it clear to employees that ethics are a priority within the firm and are not to be sacrificed to obtain short-term gains. This can be accomplished by enacting a code of conduct, establishing an ethics training program, arranging a formal system for reporting misconduct, and setting up an ethics advice line or office. According to the 2003 National Business Ethics Survey by the Ethics Resource Center, employees were more likely to report misconduct they observed if their employer had such ethics program elements in place.[74] The survey also showed that the more ethics program elements an organization had, the more likely employees were to report misconduct. Perhaps more importantly, employees who worked for organizations with more comprehensive ethics programs were more satisfied with their organizations than those with less comprehensive programs.[75] Furthermore, the survey found that the reasons employees cited most often for not reporting misconduct were a lack of confidence that corrective action would be taken and a lack of trust that the report would be kept confidential.[76] Thus, an ethical program may not sufficiently encourage ethical behavior unless management takes appropriate corrective action and protects those who report unethical conduct.

**Walk the Walk** An organization should be consistently ethical both in principle and in practice. Employees are more likely to report misconduct when they feel that they can count on the support of their coworkers and their supervisor or manager, when they believe that corrective action will be taken, and when they believe that the report will be kept confidential.[77]

Top management should resist the temptation to settle for "the appearance of a compliant reputation."[78] As Richard S. Gruner warned, "Compliance programs that are treated by management as a sham tend to encourage cynicism by employees. Such cynicism, in turn, tends to cause employees to pay less attention to legal requirements and to be more willing to commit offenses."[79] It takes discipline for management to maintain this kind of commitment to ethical standards, but many firms are already exemplifying that discipline. For example, in order to maintain a more ethical focus on the creation of long-term shareholder value, as opposed to short term, many corporations are restructuring their corporate governance, accounting, and reporting practices.

**Google** Sergey Brin and Larry Page, cofounders of Google, Inc., began developing the Google Internet search engine in 1996. On April 29, 2004, they officially announced their intention to raise as much as $2.7 billion in an unorthodox initial public offering of the company's stock by auction.[80] Google has long been heralded as an unconventional company, offering medical services, washing machines, and free meals as employee benefits. In a letter entitled "An Owner's Manual," included in the registration statement for the offering, Brin and Page suggested that atypical benefits and "high-risk, high-reward projects" reflected their dedication to long-term value. To sustain that long-term focus and a commensurate commitment to its employees, Google announced that it had structured the corporation with two classes of stock and offered the weaker class—the Series A shares—to the public. The founders, executive officers, directors, and employees retained control of the corporation because their Class B shares had ten times the voting power of the publicly held Class A shares. The auction style of the offering was designed to discourage short-term speculation and to ensure that the company realized the full value of the stock being sold to the public.

72. *2002 Transparency International Bribe Payers Index,* http://www.transparency.org/surveys/index.html#bpi (last visited June 25, 2004).
73. *2003 Transparency International Corruption Perceptions Index,* http://www.transparency.org/surveys/index.html (last visited June 25, 2004).
74. Ethics Resource Center, National Business Ethics Survey 42 (2003).
75. *Id.* at 58.
76. *Id.* at 43.
77. *Id.* at 42, 44.
78. *Quoted in* William S. Laufer, *Corporate Liability, Risk Shifting, and the Paradox of Compliance,* 52 Vand. L. Rev. 1343, 1372 n.127 (1999).
79. *Id.*
80. Chris Gaither, *Google's Initial Stock Sale Is a Truly Public Offering,* N.Y. Times, Apr. 30, 2004, at A1.

**Coca-Cola** In December 2002, the Coca-Cola Company announced that it would no longer provide quarterly or annual earnings estimates. Coke's chair and CEO explained, "We believe that establishing short-term guidance prevents a more meaningful focus on the strategic initiatives that a company is taking to build its business and succeed over the long run." Warren Buffett, billionaire investor and Coke board member, was thought to be behind the decision. Buffett, Coke's largest single shareholder, is also chair of Berkshire Hathaway, Inc. and a member of Gillette's board. Neither Berkshire Hathaway nor Gillette offers earnings guidance.

### *Individual Action*

Individual employees, particularly those without substantial authority, are faced with a more daunting task when they see their company acting in an unethical manner or are asked to engage in unethical behavior themselves. First, an individual should determine whether the activity is illegal. Supervisors and managers cannot legally require subordinates to engage in illegal behavior. Even at-will employees are generally protected from discharge in retaliation for refusing to commit an illegal act. Furthermore, if an employee chooses to follow orders (and breaks the law), the fact that the employee was ordered to do so by a superior is no defense in a criminal trial. Thus, if asked to engage in illegal behavior, an employee is fully justified in "just saying 'no'" and well advised to do so.

If an employee is asked to engage in legal, but unethical, behavior, the course of action is often less clear. First, the employee should review the company's code of conduct for guidance. Often consulting an ombudsperson or calling an ethics hotline, if available, is a good idea. Sometimes, it might be worthwhile to make others (coworkers, managers, supervisors, or even the board of directors) aware of the ethical implications of the situation because those implications might not be apparent to persons who are not intimately involved in the specific case. If no other parties take interest, a careful appraisal of one's own personal beliefs, an assessment of the social, environmental, or other ethical consequences of the action, and a realistic understanding of the consequences of refusing to take the action are all essential to deciding how to proceed.

Sometimes, managers have conflicting responsibilities and must decide, "What to do when one clear right thing must be left undone in order to do another or when doing the right thing requires doing something wrong?"[81] When trying to resolve problems that raise questions of personal integrity and moral identity, Professor Joe Badaracco calls on managers to ask, "Who am I?" and "What is my moral center?"[82] Managers with power over others faced with organizational challenges should ask, "Who are we? What do we stand for? What norms and values guide how we work together and treat each other? How do we define ourselves as a human institution?"[83] Faced with problems involving responsibilities a company shares with other groups in society, senior executives must negotiate with stakeholders to define the firm's role in society and its relationship with its stakeholders.[84]

## Social Responsibility

Companies have suffered severe financial setbacks as a result of decisions that, in hindsight, were perceived by the public as unethical. Consumer products companies are particularly sensitive to public perception, given their reliance on individual retail sales. As William D. Smithburg, chair and CEO of the Quaker Oats Company, wrote: "[I] know ethical behavior is sound business practice because every day at the Quaker Oats Company I am reminded that we succeed or fail according to the trust consumers have in us."[85] Issues of social responsibility arise in many areas including product safety, advertising campaigns, client conflicts of interest, anticompetitive practices, customer service, sweatshops and child labor, workplace conditions, pensions and employee benefits, and the environment.

### Customers and Clients

### *Product Safety*

Socially responsible businesses place a heavy emphasis on the safety of their products. Huge costs have been associated with failure to meet the public's perception of what is safe.

**Bridgestone/Firestone, Ford, and Tire Failures** In 2000 and 2001, Firestone announced three recalls of more than 6.5 million tires, many of which were installed on Ford Explorers. More than 200 people had died when

81. Joseph Badaracco, Jr., Defining Moments: When Managers Must Choose Between Right and Right 6 (1997).
82. *Id.* at 13.
83. *Id.* at 18.
84. *Id.* at 22–23.
85. Touche Report, *supra* note 21, at 45.

the tread on their Firestone tires separated from the rest of the tire. The Firestone unit of Bridgestone/Firestone, which had previously accounted for 40 percent of the parent company's revenue, posted a net loss of $510 million for the fiscal year ending December 2000, after taking a $750 million one-time charge for legal expenses. In testimony before Congress, Ford's CEO Jacques Nassar asserted, "This is a tire issue and only a tire issue."[86] John Lampe, Firestone's CEO, dubbed Ford's call for the replacement of an additional 13 million more Firestone tires "an attempt to scapegoat our tires by falsely alarming consumers about some very real safety problems of [Ford's] vehicle which should be addressed honestly and seriously."[87]

**General Motors and the Chevrolet Malibu's Exploding Fuel Tank** In 1999, General Motors Corporation was ordered to pay $4.8 billion in punitive damages and $107.89 million in compensatory damages to six people who were burned when their 1979 Chevrolet Malibu exploded after its fuel tank was ruptured in a crash. Internal GM memos introduced during the trial suggested that GM executives had decided that redesigning the fuel system to reduce fire risk at a cost of $8.59 per car would impose a greater cost than paying claims for fuel-fire deaths. A key memo written by a GM engineer estimated that each death from burns from a fuel-related fire would cost the company $200,000. Based on that amount, the memo calculated that such deaths would cost $2.40 for every one of the potentially dangerous vehicles that had been sold. The memo cautioned, however, that "a human fatality is really beyond value, subjectively."[88] Subsequent to the case, the GM lawyer stated that the company had no plans to notify owners of cars with the same fuel system as the Malibu that the system was dangerous.

The GM case is reminiscent of Ford Motor Company's ultimately very costly decision to produce the Ford Pinto without safety modifications to keep the gas tank from rupturing when rear-ended at low speeds. Ford managers relied on a classic cost-benefit analysis, which compared the $4 to $8 cost of the alterations with the cost of defending the lawsuits stemming from injuries or deaths caused by the exploding gas tanks.[89]

86. Frank Swoboda & Caroline E. Mayer, *Firestone, Ford CEOs Duel at Hearing; Safety Agency Says It Will Test Tires,* WASH. POST, June 20, 2001, at A1.
87. *Id.*
88. Jeffrey Ball & Milo Geyelin, *GM Ordered by Jury to Pay $4.9 Billion—Auto Maker Plans to Appeal Huge California Verdict in Fuel-Tank-Fire Case,* WALL ST. J., July 12, 1999, at A3.
89. *See* Grimshaw v. Ford Motor Co., 174 Cal. Rptr. 348, 361–62 (Cal. Ct. App. 1981).

## *Advertising*

**Marketing Tobacco and Beer to Children** Parents and public health officials sharply criticized RJR Nabisco (the maker of Camel cigarettes) for its advertisements featuring a cartoon figure, Old Joe Camel. A number of studies showed that ads showing this sharply dressed camel, who frequents pool halls and pickup bars, were tremendously successful in targeting children. In a study involving 229 children ages three to six, more than half were familiar with the figure and associated him with cigarettes. Six-year-olds were nearly as familiar with Joe Camel as they were with the Mickey Mouse logo for the Disney Channel.[90]

Faced with the Food and Drug Administration's threat to regulate nicotine as a drug and increasingly hostile public opinion, RJR voluntarily agreed in 1997 to abandon the Joe Camel ad campaign in the United States. Nevertheless, Joe Camel continues to thrive outside the United States. He started showing up in other countries in 1996. Argentinian antismoking activists became incensed when Joe Camel and friends began appearing in smoking advertisements and promotional gimmicks primarily targeted at teenagers and young adults in that country.[91]

After surveying the eight largest alcoholic beverage companies in the United States (including Anheuser-Busch, Inc.; Bacardi-Martini U.S.A., Inc.; Miller Brewing Company; and Joseph E. Seagram & Sons, Inc.), the Federal Trade Commission (FTC) concluded that they were targeting children.[92] The companies placed products on eight of the fifteen TV programs most popular with teenagers and in movies targeted at young audiences, including PG and PG-13 movies. The FTC recommended that companies impose stricter voluntary rules and establish a third-party review to ensure that they are following these codes. Nevertheless, the FTC did not recommend government regulation of the $1 billion alcohol advertising market.

**NBC and Liquor Advertising** In 2001, NBC, a unit of General Electric Company, began working with Diageo PLC, the world's biggest spirits marketer, to prepare advertising guidelines for hard liquor. After airing "responsibility" ads for one of Diageo's clients, Smirnoff vodka, NBC announced that it would be the first broadcast network in more than fifty years to run liquor ads in the

90. Kathleen Deveny, *Joe Camel Is Also Pied Piper, Research Finds,* WALL ST. J., Dec. 11, 1991, at B1, B6.
91. Jonathan Friedland, *Under Siege in the U.S., Joe Camel Pops Up Alive, Well in Argentina,* WALL ST. J., Sept. 10, 1996, at B1.
92. Denise Gellene, *Leave Alcohol Ad Curbs to Industry, FTC Report Says,* L.A. TIMES, Sept. 11, 1999, at C1.

United States. This plan sparked sharp opposition. The House Energy and Commerce Committee began considering holding hearings on the issue, and Mothers Against Drunk Driving planned a press conference to encourage such hearings. Meanwhile, the Harvard School of Public Health prepared to release the results of an eight-year study analyzing binge drinking on college campuses.

Three months after the announcement, NBC called off the deal. The Distilled Spirits Council, a major trade organization, was predictably disappointed. The council president, Peter Cressy, called the move "a disservice to the American public because it blocks responsible advertising while reinforcing the dangerous misperception that beer is 'soft' alcohol and spirits are 'hard' alcohol."[93]

**Pfizer and Off-label Drug Promotion** Although it is illegal for a drug company to market a medicine for uses the Food and Drug Administration has not approved, physicians are allowed to prescribe drugs in any manner that they think will help their patients. Pfizer, Inc.'s Warner-Lambert division crossed this line when marketing an epilepsy drug, Neurontin, for unapproved uses. Doctors were paid thousands of dollars apiece to speak to other physicians about how Neurontin could be prescribed for more than a dozen other medical uses and to write reports and articles on the topic. One doctor received more than $300,000 for speeches; another received $71,477 for talking to other doctors; and yet another received $49,250, plus an additional $303,764 that Warner-Lambert paid to publish that doctor's textbook on epilepsy.[94] Warner-Lambert also flew doctors to Hawaii and to the 1996 Olympics, paid them consulting fees, and sponsored expensive dinners at which unapproved uses of Neurontin were discussed.[95] On May 13, 2004, Pfizer settled criminal charges that it had failed to provide adequate directions for Neurontin's use and had engaged in the interstate sale of an unapproved drug.[96] Pfizer agreed to pay a $430 million fine to settle all civil and criminal liability to state and federal governments.

## *Conflicts of Interest*

**Merrill Lynch and Other Brokerage Firms** In 2001, a pediatrician named Debases Kanjilal filed an arbitration claim alleging that Henry Blodgett, a broker at Merrill Lynch & Co., had urged him not to sell his Infospace, Inc. stock when it was trading at $60 a share. Kanjilal took the advice and lost $500,000 when he later sold the stock for $11 a share. The complaint claimed that Blodgett had been fraudulently promoting low-quality stocks to curry favor with Merrill's investment banking clients. In the wake of this lawsuit, Eliot Spitzer, the New York State Attorney General, launched an investigation that ultimately unearthed and made public hundreds of documents, including analyst-written e-mails that privately disparaged the same stocks the analysts were publicly promoting, calling them "crap" and "junk."[97] On May 21, 2002, to end the criminal investigation, Merrill agreed to pay $100 million to New York and other states and to substantially change the way it paid analysts. Merrill apologized for the behavior of its analysts but did not admit to any wrongdoing. Nevertheless, Spitzer commented, "You don't pay a $100 million fine if you didn't do anything wrong."[98]

In the fall of 2003, a group of brokerage firms agreed to pay $1.3 billion to settle similar state and federal charges of analyst conflicts of interest. Citigroup's Salomon Smith Barney paid the largest fine of $324 million.

In February 2003, the Securities and Exchange Commission (SEC) adopted Regulation Analyst Certification, or Regulation AC. Regulation AC requires analysts to certify that their reports "accurately reflect their personal views" and to indicate if any of their compensation is tied to the report.[99] Regulation AC was a direct consequence of the failure of Merrill and other investment banks to protect their clients from analyst conflicts of interest and is yet another example of unethical behavior leading to increased regulation.

**Citigroup** In June 1996, Citigroup's Salomon Smith Barney allocated Bernard J. Ebbers, the founder and CEO of WorldCom, 200,000 shares of McLeodUSA's initial public offering.[100] Prior to that month, Salomon had done no brokerage work for WorldCom, but shortly after the allocation, Salomon got its first WorldCom brokerage assignment. Ebbers made around $12 million in profits over the next four years from more than a million "hot" initial offering shares allocated to him by Salomon Smith Barney and Citigroup.

93. Joe Flint & Shelly Branch, *In Face of Widening Backlash, NBC Gives Up Plan to Run Liquor Ads,* WALL ST. J., Mar. 21, 2002, at B1.
94. Melody Petersen, *Court Papers Suggest Scale of Drug's Use,* N.Y. TIMES, May 20, 2003, at C1.
95. Gardiner Harris, *Pfizer to Pay $430 Million over Promoting Drug to Doctors,* N.Y. TIMES, May 14, 2004, at C1.
96. *Id.*
97. Marcia Vickers et al., *How Corrupt Is Wall Street?,* BUS.WK., May 13, 2002, at 37.
98. Patrick McGeehan, *$100 Million Fine for Merrill Lynch,* N.Y. TIMES, May 22, 2002, at A1.
99. Andrew Countryman, *SEC Adopts New Rule on Analyst Assurance,* CHI. TRIB., Feb. 7, 2003, at N3.
100. The allegations contained in this paragraph are all drawn from Gretchen Morgenson & Timothy L. O'Brien, *When Citigroup Met WorldCom,* N.Y. TIMES, May 16, 2004, § 3, at 1.

In a report submitted to the bankruptcy court, Richard Thornburgh, a former U.S. Attorney General appointed by the court to examine WorldCom's history, wrote:

> [Salomon Smith Barney] provided personal financial assistance to Mr. Ebbers as a means of enhancing the probability that S.S.B. would keep a preferred position in receipt of WorldCom business, including investment banking and stock-option business, and also as a means of avoiding sales of Mr. Ebbers's stock, which would adversely affect WorldCom's stock price.[101]

In 2004, Citigroup paid $2.65 billion to settle a fraud class-action suit filed by investors who lost money in WorldCom bonds and stock underwritten by Salomon Smith Barney. It was also fined another $1 million for failing to supervise WorldCom's stock option program.

In 2004, Citigroup also paid $70 million in fines to the Federal Reserve Board to settle claims of predatory lending practices by its subprime mortgage lending unit, CitiFinancial Credit Company. The Fed also claimed that CitiFinancial employees had misled bank examiners.[102] This is the largest penalty ever imposed by the Federal Reserve for consumer lending violations.[103] Citigroup announced that it expected to pay at least $30 million more in restitution.

As of 2004, Citigroup had reserved $6.7 billion for settlements and fines related to financial abuses since 2002. Citigroup's CEO, Charles Prince, promised to "move forward with standards that define best practices in our business."[104]

## *Anticompetitive Tactics: Boeing*

In June 2003, Boeing Company alerted the U.S. Air Force and Lockheed Martin Corporation, one of Boeing's competitors, that a former Lockheed Martin official, Richard Hora, had "retained several [Lockheed Martin] proprietary or competition sensitive documents" after being employed by Boeing.[105] Boeing later acknowledged that data produced by Hora were utilized in the pricing calculations for a successful bid on a 1999 Air Force rocket. Matt Jew, the mid-level Boeing manager responsible for preparing computer models for costs, voluntarily walked into the U.S. attorney's office and began cooperating with investigators. Jew resigned in April 2004 and recanted previous statements that the Lockheed Martin documents had had no impact on Boeing's bids.

The Pentagon suspended Boeing from bidding on rocket contracts indefinitely, costing it billions of dollars of business. The investigation was subsequently expanded to determine whether another former Lockheed Martin employee brought other sensitive documents to Boeing from Lockheed Martin and whether Boeing made use of those data in decisions concerning rocket-launch contracts with NASA. In late 2003, another government contract with Boeing, this one for the acquisition of 100 Boeing 767 tankers, was placed on hold for a similar ethical inquiry.[106]

## *Discriminatory Customer Service: Denny's*

When the Civil Rights Act of 1964 was promulgated, the laws prohibiting discrimination in public accommodations, such as restaurants, were designed with the lunch counters of Birmingham, Alabama, in mind. Some thirty years later, in the largest settlement under the federal public accommodation laws, Denny's Restaurants agreed to pay more than $54 million to settle two class-action lawsuits filed by African-American customers. The customers received $46 million, and another $8.7 million was paid to their attorneys.[107]

African-American customers of Denny's had filed more than 4,300 claims of discrimination, which included not being served, having to pay a cover charge, and having to prepay for meals. Among the claims were those of six African-American Secret Service agents assigned to President Bill Clinton's detail. In a Denny's in Annapolis, Maryland, fifteen white Secret Service agents were seated and served, while the African-American agents were refused a table. In another incident an African-American federal judge from Houston and his wife, who had been traveling for eighteen hours, were forced to wait for almost an hour at a Denny's in California, while white teenagers taunted them, calling them "niggers."[108] The company denied that it had a policy of discrimination.

Rachel Thomas, the thirty-three-year-old vice president of a skin-care company, recalled how she, her husband, and their three children waited for an hour and

101. *Id.*
102. Erick Bergquist, *Citi-Fed Pact on Subprime: Opening Act?*, AM. BANKER, May 28, 2004, at 1.
103. Timothy L. O'Brien, *Fed Assesses Citigroup Client $70 Million in Loan Abuse*, N.Y. TIMES, May 28, 2004.
104. *Id.*
105. Andy Pasztor & Jonathan Karp, *As Boeing Tries to Put Scandals to Rest, Prosecutors Widen Probe*, WALL ST. J., Apr. 27, 2004, at A1.
106. Holmes, *supra* note 32, at 38.
107. Stephen Labaton, *Denny's Restaurants to Pay $54 Million in Race Bias Suit*, N.Y. TIMES, May 25, 1994, at A1.
108. Timothy Ziegler, *Denny's Victims Discuss Harassment*, S.F. CHRON., May 25, 1994, at A3.

twenty minutes after a waitress took their order and never returned. About her children, she said, "Those babies don't have anything to do with this racism, and they were the ones put out by it. . . . You can't explain it to them; they don't understand."[109]

John Relman, a lawyer for the Washington Lawyers' Committee for Civil Rights, blamed management for failing to lead by example:

> We believe that there was, at the company, an attitude that went into the management level, but we don't know exactly how high. This attitude at the company, at the management level and working its way down, had the effect of causing discriminatory attitudes going down to the lowest levels of the company.[110]

In 1999, Denny's corporate parent, Advantica Restaurant Group, spent millions of dollars on a publicity campaign designed to persuade minorities that Denny's had changed its policies. The corporation published statistics showing that it did $125 million worth of business (approximately 18 percent of its business) with minority-owned companies and that one-half of Denny's workforce and one-third of Advantica's management team was African American. In 1993, only one Denny's franchise was owned by African Americans; in 1999, more than a dozen African Americans and other minorities owned 36 percent of Denny's franchise restaurants. In 2000, in a dramatic demonstration of how a company can radically alter its culture, the Council on Economic Priorities (a New York–based nonprofit promoting corporate social responsibility) named Denny's the winner of its diversity award and declared it "one of the most successfully diverse places to work in America."[111]

## EMPLOYEES

### *Sweatshops and Child Labor*

**Nike** In 1996, critics claimed that Nike was exploiting labor in developing countries in Asia by working with subcontractors that used child labor, paid substandard wages, and provided hazardous working conditions.[112] One factory producing Nike shoes had only seven toilets available for 10,000 employees. Other factories were cited for having blocked fire exits and permitting only one bathroom break and two water breaks in an eight-hour day. Reports of abuse, both physical and verbal, were common, as were accounts of sexual harassment and corporal punishment. At one Vietnamese factory, fifty-six women were made to run laps around the building because they had not worn regulation shoes to work. They were forced to continue running even after women started to collapse; eventually, twelve of the women had to be hospitalized. Activists also reported that Nike's subcontractors paid their workers a regular average wage well below the livable wage in Indonesia and that Nike forced its employees to work overtime. Nike denied the allegations.

Nike and others initially maintained that the company has done more good than harm in Indonesia and other Asian countries by improving working conditions, raising the standard of living, and moving people from farming jobs to factory jobs (purportedly a key step in industrialization). Yet Nike's CEO Phil Knight eventually concluded that the buying public expected Nike to do more to ensure fair treatment of its contract workers and the payment of a living wage. Accordingly, Nike enlisted third parties to conduct inspections of its contract factories and publicly report their findings. As of 2004, Nike employed more than eighty people who focus exclusively on compliance issues in the supply chain.

**Child Labor at Wal-Mart** In 1992, the press revealed that some of the products Wal-Mart labeled "Made in the U.S.A." were actually made in Bangladesh by child laborers working for pennies a day. Rosalene Costa, a human rights worker in Bangladesh interviewed by *NBC Dateline,* said the children working at the factory were about twelve years old. The children told her their real ages when the supervisor was not around.[113] The head of Wal-Mart's Bangladesh operation denied that they were children, saying, "The workers just look young because they are malnourished adults."[114] As of late 2003, Wal-Mart refused to allow independent inspections of its suppliers' factories.[115]

### *Danger in the Workplace: McWane, Inc.*

McWane, Inc., a privately held company based in Birmingham, Alabama, is one of the world's largest manufacturers of cast-iron sewer and water pipe. A regular on *Fortune* magazine's list of the 500 largest private compa-

109. *Id.*
110. Labaton, *supra* note 107.
111. *Business Bulletin,* WALL ST. J., Apr. 27, 2000, at A1.
112. Keith Richburg & Anne Swardson, *US Industry Overseas: Sweatshop or Job Source?,* WASH. POST, July 28, 1996, at A1.
113. *Id.*
114. *NBC Questions Wal-Mart's "Buy America" Campaign,* UNITED PRESS INT'L, Dec. 22, 1992.
115. Evelyn Iritani & Nancy Cleeland, *The Wal-Mart Effect,* L.A. TIMES, Nov. 24, 2003, at A19.

nies, McWane employs around 5,000 workers. At least 4,600 injuries were reported in McWane foundries between 1992 and 2002, and nine workers died. Upon inspection, more than 400 health and safety violations were identified—four times as many as the violations at McWane's six largest competitors combined. When inspectors from the federal Occupational Safety and Health Administration (OSHA) investigated one of the deaths, McWane employees said the company policy was "not to correct anything until OSHA found it."[116] Although McWane employed "safety professionals," they were said to divide their time between dealing with safety issues and attempting to reduce workers' compensation costs by investigating the credibility of injury claims, placing injured workers under surveillance, and challenging doctors on expensive treatment plans. Reportedly, workers who protested the dangerous working conditions were marked for termination.[117] In addition to the health and safety violations, McWane has violated pollution rules and emission limits at least 450 times since 1995.

## *Jobs and Pensions: Enron*

Once the nation's seventh-largest company by revenue, Enron Corporation filed for Chapter 11 bankruptcy in late 2001 in the wake of an accounting scandal described in the "Inside Story" for this chapter. While encouraging employees to hold on to or purchase more Enron stock, former CEO Jeffrey Skilling allegedly netted $89 million in profit from selling around $200 million worth of Enron stock and options between 1998 and 2001.[118] Former chair Kenneth L. Lay collected more than $209 million from selling the stock over the same period.[119] The accounting fraud that eventually led to the energy giant's collapse led predictably to the layoffs of some 6,000 employees[120] and to the decimation of employees' pensions, a substantial portion of which was invested in Enron stock. Almost 21,000 Enron employees held $2.1 billion of securities in the company's 401(k) plans at the end of 2000; 63 percent consisted of Enron stock. Another 7,600 employees held an additional $1 billion worth of stock in the employee stock ownership plan.[121] Former directors of Enron agreed to pay up to $86.5 million to settle part of the $3 billion in employee pension-fund claims related to the company's collapse.[122] In 2004, Skilling and Lay were indicted for fraud, insider trading, and conspiracy.

## *Bonuses for Layoffs: AT&T*

In 2003, AT&T eliminated 9,400 jobs, a 13 percent reduction in employees in the course of one year. The company's profit in 2003 was only $3.7 billion, down 16 percent from the prior year. That same year, David W. Dornan, AT&T's chair and CEO, received a larger salary, a bigger bonus, and more grants of stock and options than he received in 2002. Dornan's 2003 package, which was valued at $18.3 million,[123] was worth more than the package his predecessor, C. Michael Armstrong, received in 1999, when AT&T's operating profit exceeded $12 billion. A spokesman for AT&T pointed out that Dornan's 2003 pay was "certainly not out of line with what the leaders of Verizon, BellSouth, SBC or Sprint [we]re being paid."[124]

## *Contingent Workers*

Many large companies not only substantially reduced their full-time workforce in the early to mid-1990s, but they also hired part-time, temporary, or contract workers for many of the jobs that remained. According to the Bureau of Labor Statistics, 7.8 percent of the American workforce (approximately 10.2 million workers) were employed in temporary or contract jobs or as independent contractors in 1999.[125] They earned on average 35 percent less than regular workers; only 7 percent received health-care insurance benefits from their employer; and just 4 percent were given a pension.[126]

In lawsuits against Microsoft and Time Warner, contingent workers claimed that they had been unfairly denied benefits. A federal appeals court required Microsoft to pay workers who worked at least half-time the money they had lost by not being offered company

116. David Barstow & Lowell Bergman, *A Family's Fortune, a Legacy of Blood and Tears,* N.Y. TIMES, Jan. 9, 2003, at 1.
117. *Id.*
118. Kurt Eichenwald, *Enron's Skilling Is Indicted by U.S. in Fraud Inquiry,* N.Y. TIMES, Feb. 20, 2004, at A1.
119. Carrie Johnson, *Prosecutors to Seek Charges Against Lay,* WASH. POST, June 20, 2004, at A8.
120. David Streitfeld & Dana Calvo, *Ex-CEO Arraigned in Fraud at Enron,* L.A. TIMES, Feb. 20, 2004, at A1.
121. Jo Thomas, *Enron's Collapse: Fading Nest Eggs,* N.Y. TIMES, Jan. 24, 2002, at C6.
122. *Deal Reached on Enron Pensions,* N.Y. TIMES, May 13, 2004, at C4.
123. Patrick McGeehan, *Is CEO Pay Up or Down? Both,* N.Y. TIMES, Apr. 4, 2004, § 3, at 1.
124. *Id.*
125. Kirstin Downey Grimskey, *Revenge of the Temps: Independent Contractors' Victory in Microsoft Case May Have Wide Impact,* WASH. POST, Jan. 16, 2000, at H1.
126. Aaron Bernstein, *A Leg Up for the Lowly Temp: Advocates Are Lobbying for Better Benefits and an Employer's Code of Conduct,* BUS. WK., June 21, 1999, at 102.

stock at a discount as full-time workers were.[127] Supporters of the trend to use temporary workers argue that it is necessary to give U.S. companies the flexibility to adjust the workforce to reflect changing and seasonal needs for labor. Critics claim that the practice saps worker morale and ultimately adversely affects worker productivity.[128] For example, Edward Hennessy, Jr., former chair and CEO of Allied-Signal, Inc., asserted:

> If we choose to deny the larger human and social impact of the corporation, if we try to reduce the company to the bare essentials of a commercial transaction, we will end up with a work force that is less capable and less dedicated over the long run. We will also cause society to be indifferent—if not completely hostile—to the interests of corporations and their shareholders.[129]

### *Discrimination*

**Coca-Cola** In 2000, the Coca-Cola Company paid $192.5 million to settle charges of racial bias. Allegedly, black workers at Coke made an average of $26,000 less per year than white workers—the black employees sometimes made even less than the white subordinates they trained or supervised.[130] The allegations also charged that African-American employees were routinely denied promotions. Under the settlement, more than 2,000 former and current black employees of the company were made eligible to receive around $40,000 each.

**Texaco** In 1996, Texaco lost $1 billion in market capitalization the day after a group of its African-American employees filed a Title VII class-action suit alleging racial discrimination. The complaint included racist comments made by a member of top management who had been secretly recorded by a disgruntled employee. The Reverend Jesse Jackson organized a consumer boycott, and in 1997, Texaco agreed to pay more than $100 million to settle the charges of racial discrimination in hiring and promotion. Discrimination costs more than money. It also saps employee morale. After the lawsuit, employee morale hit lows not seen since the $10.5 billion verdict rendered against Texaco when it was sued by Pennzoil over the acquisition of Getty Oil. One executive, who had suffered through the Pennzoil ordeal, said that friends called and asked how she could work at a "place like that." She commented, "It's one thing to be called stupid; it's another to be called a bigot."[131]

Texaco's newly elected CEO, Peter Bijur, responded to the lawsuit by summoning the managers who reported to him directly and telling them to get the word out to all managers that there would be zero tolerance of racial epithets, taunts, and joking on the job. When one officer asked whether Bijur thought this was realistic, given the somewhat rowdy atmosphere on oil rigs and the like, Bijur responded, "Tell the local managers, that if they can't enforce this policy, then you will replace them." He went on to say, "And if you can't find managers who can enforce this policy, I'll replace you."[132] Although Bijur's predecessor, Al deCrane, had circulated memos about Texaco's policies against discrimination, Bijur went a step further and instituted a policy requiring an African American and a woman to be present at each human resources meeting to ensure that there would be no repeat of the odious comments that triggered the lawsuit.[133]

## INVESTORS

### *Managed Earnings*

In an effort to meet securities analysts' earnings expectations and thereby avoid the punishing drop in stock price that usually follows a company's announcement that its earnings were below Wall Street's estimates, a number of public companies have been managing earnings.[134] They have used what Arthur Leavitt, former chair of the SEC, called "accounting hocus-pocus" to recognize revenue improperly, take unjustified restructuring charges, and create "cookie-jar reserves" that can be used to smooth out earnings by making up earnings shortfalls in later periods.

SEC investigations in 1998 and 1999 found misappropriation of unclaimed money from security holders that should have escheated (been forfeited) to the state (Bankers Trust); improper inflation of operating income and other accounting irregularities, which, when made known, caused the company's stock to drop by more than $14 billion in a single day (Cendant); and intentional underreporting of earnings with the excess above analysts' expectations being stuffed in a cookie-jar reserve and then fed back into earnings when needed to

127. Vizcaino v. Microsoft Corp., 120 F.3d 1006 (9th Cir. 1997).
128. *See* JEFFREY PFEFFER, THE HUMAN EQUATION: BUILDING PROFITS BY PUTTING PEOPLE FIRST 161–94 (1998).
129. TOUCHE REPORT, *supra* note 21, at 44.
130. Greg Winter, *Coca-Cola Still Faces Suits in Race Discrimination Case*, N.Y. TIMES, July 7, 2001, at C3.
131. Interview with Elizabeth P. Smith by Constance E. Bagley, Boston, Mass. (Nov. 9, 2003).
132. Peter Bijur, Keynote Address at the Stanford Law School General Counsel Institute, Palo Alto, Cal. (Jan. 14, 1998).
133. Smith, *supra* note 131.
134. *See* Carol J. Loomis, *Lies, Damned Lies, and Managed Earnings*, FORTUNE, Aug. 2, 1999, at 74.

meet expectations (W.R. Grace). Questionable conduct ranged from making off-price deals at the end of a quarter to increase revenues (dumb but probably legal) to engaging in bill-and-hold scams, whereby sales of goods are recorded but the goods are held in the seller's warehouse (probably illegal), to creating false invoices to book fictitious sales (clearly illegal).[135]

**Rite Aid** In 1999, Martin L. Grass was ousted from his position as CEO of Rite Aid, the corporation that his father had co-founded. Under Grass, the company grew rapidly through a series of takeovers. Following his departure, he orchestrated a two-year conspiracy to cover up his fraudulent inflation of financial results and self-dealing. In 2000, Rite Aid restated its earnings downward by $1.6 billion. Grass was prosecuted and sentenced to eight years in prison—longer than the seven years recommended by prosecutors. The judge also fined him $500,000 and gave him three years' probation. Prior to his sentencing, Grass addressed the judge, saying, "In early 1999, when things started to go wrong financially, I did some things to try to hide that fact. Those things were wrong. They were illegal. I did not do it to line my own pockets."[136]

### *Mutual Fund Scandals*

Richard S. Strong founded Strong Financial Corporation in 1974. The mutual fund manager had warned investors since 1997 against market timing, also known as rapid trading, whereby investors buy and sell fund shares in the course of days or even hours. Beginning in 1999, the firm repeatedly told its own employees that its funds were not to be used as short-term trading vehicles. Rapid trading is not illegal, but it is discouraged because it can hurt the performance of the fund.

While the corporation was publicly advocating this stance, Richard Strong was doing the opposite.[137] According to the SEC, Mr. Strong traded rapidly in and out of the company's funds and allowed one hedge fund, Canary Capital Partners LLC, both to engage in market timing and to make illegal trades after the market had closed. Over the course of one year, alleged the SEC, Strong made over 500 trades in the company's funds, with the value of one of his short-term trades exceeding $1 million. In a written apology, Strong admitted:

> Throughout my career, I have considered it to be my sacred duty to protect my investors; and yet in a particular and persistent way I let them down. In previous years, I frequently traded the shares of the Strong funds, at the same time that the advice which we gave our investors was to do the opposite and to hold their shares for the long term. My personal behavior in this regard was wrong and at odds with the obligations I owed my shareholders, and for this I am deeply sorry.[138]

Strong agreed to pay $60 million and issued the written apology to settle state and federal claims against him. He was banned from the investment industry for life. Strong Financial agreed to pay another $80 million and to reduce its fees by at least $35 million over five years.

Strong Financial was just one of a number of mutual fund operators implicated in the largest scandal to rock the $3 trillion mutual fund industry. Putnam Investors paid a $100 million fine and suffered a 9 percent decline in funds under management after being investigated for market timing and illegal after-hours trading.

## ENVIRONMENT

### *Shell Oil*

In 1995, Royal Dutch/Shell planned to dispose of its Brent Spar oil platform (an old offshore rig) by towing it from the North Sea and sinking it in the North Atlantic. Shell represented that it had complied with environmental regulations and that dumping was the "best practicable environmental option."[139] In April 1995, Greenpeace activists boarded the platform in protest and began a publicity campaign that resulted in consumer boycotts throughout Europe. In June 1995, Shell backed down and agreed to spend as much as $42 million to salvage the oil rig, more than twice what the company had planned to spend to dump the rig at sea.[140]

In March 1997, as a result of the media backlash from the Brent Spar incident and Shell's failure to try to stop the hanging of the Ogoni activists in Nigeria (where Shell has a major presence), Shell released a new operating charter reflecting a commitment to the environment, health, safety, and human rights. Shell executives reasoned that the company's investment in sustainable

135. *Id.*
136. Mark Maremont, *Rite Aid's Ex-CEO Sentenced to 8 Years for Accounting Fraud,* WALL ST. J., May 28, 2004, at A3.
137. Christopher Oster, *A Fund Mogul's Costly Apology,* WALL ST. J., May 21, 2004, at C1.
138. *A Statement of Apology,* N.Y. Times, May 21, 2004, at C2.
139. Rubin Grove-White, *Brent Spar Rewrote the Rules (Shell Oil Co.'s Decision to Dispose of the Brent Spar Oil Platform in the North Sea),* NEW STATESMAN, June 20, 1997, at 17.
140. *Shell Makes Move to End Dispute over Oil Platform—Plan to Cut up Brent Spar to Make a Pier in Norway Pleases Environmentalists,* WALL ST. J., Jan. 30, 1998, at B7E.

development will give it a competitive edge over other companies facing similar challenges. Mark Wade, a manager on Shell's sustainable development team, said, "Brent Spar was our wake-up call telling us that there are heightened expectations towards corporate behavior that we hadn't recognized."[141]

In line with this new charter, Shell took special care to avoid harming the vulnerable Amazon rain forest while it proceeds with its $3 billion, forty-year natural-gas project in Camisea, Peru.[142] The area is accessible only by air or river and is unusually rich in plant and animal life. Shell is also trying to ensure that local villagers directly affected by its operations actually benefit from them. According to Thomas Lovejoy, a Smithsonian scientist and rain forest expert, big companies are finally realizing "that if you do things right from the start, it will save you a lot of money and a lot of grief in the long run."[143]

Shell has voluntarily reported on environmental and social issues since 1998, in accordance with the Global Reporting Initiative and the United Nations Global Compact principles. Parts of each report are supported by reports from external auditors.

### *Disposal of Electronics*

According to environmental groups, high-tech garbage is causing substantial health and safety risks in China, India, Pakistan, and other developing countries. Businesses in the United States that offer to recycle retired electronics are often not recycling them responsibly, perhaps because dismantling and reusing the waste here in America is substantially more expensive than the alternatives. It costs ten times more to dismantle and reuse the materials in a computer monitor in the United States, for instance, than to ship it to China for recycling.[144] Reportedly, up to 80 percent of electronics waste collected in America for recycling ends up in developing countries where laborers tear the waste apart, often by hand, to extract traces of copper, small amounts of gold, and other valuable minerals.[145] The health and environmental risks are substantial because the waste includes many toxic materials. An average fourteen-inch monitor contains five to eight pounds of lead, which can seep into ground water or disperse into the air if the monitor is crushed and burned. Semiconductor chips contain cadmium; computer exteriors contain chromium; batteries and switches contain mercury; and circuit boards contain brominated flame retardants.[146] As workers pick apart the waste and its toxic ingredients disperse into the soil and air, people in China are suffering high incidences of birth defects, infant mortality, tuberculosis, blood diseases, and severe respiratory problems.[147] Recently, several U.S. computer companies started offering more responsible recycling services (discussed later in this chapter).

## COMMUNITIES

### *Union Carbide and Bhopal*

On December 3, 1984, in the most lethal industrial accident ever, forty tons of methyl isocyanate gas were emitted from a Union Carbide Corporation pesticide factory outside Bhopal, India. More than 3,000 people died at the time of the accident; nearly 11,000 more died in the following years due to related illnesses.[148] Estimates of the number of individuals who were injured and still suffer from damage to their lungs and immune system vary, but the number of victims is at least 200,000.

Prior to the accident, a team of experts had warned Union Carbide that the plant had "serious potential for sizable releases of toxic materials."[149] In addition, six serious accidents had occurred at the Bhopal facility during the six years that preceded the disaster. Evidently, Union Carbide had reason to believe the facility was at risk.

In a settlement with the Indian government, Union Carbide—which had $5 billion in equity—agreed to pay $470 million to settle all present and future claims. As of 2002, about half of the settlement had been dispersed. More than 95 percent of the victims who have received payments were given approximately $600 in the case of injuries or approximately $3,000 in the case of death.[150] These amounts are low even by Indian standards.[151]

141. Konstantin Richter, *Managers & Managing: Sustainable Development Teases Consultants—Potential Looks Big, but Field Has Taken Off Slowly,* WALL ST. J., Dec. 14, 1999, at 4.
142. Jonathan Friedland, *Oil Companies Strive to Turn a New Leaf to Save Rain Forest,* WALL ST. J., July 17, 1997, at A1.
143. *Id.*
144. Peter S. Goodman, *China Serves as Dump Site for Computers,* WASH. POST, Feb. 24, 2003, at A1.
145. *Id.*
146. *Id.;* P.J. Huffstutter, *Recycled Electronics Pose a Health Hazard in Asia,* L.A. TIMES, Feb. 26, 2002, pt. 3, at 1.
147. Goodman, *supra* note 144.
148. *Faulty Design Blamed for Union Carbide Plant '84 Gas Leak,* DOW JONES BUS. NEWS, Jan. 12, 2000.
149. Robert Sherrill, *Corporate Crime and Violence: Big Business Power and the Abuse of the Public Trust,* NATION, Nov. 28, 1988, at 568.
150. Anthony Spaeth, *Court Settlement Stuns Bhopal Survivors,* WALL ST. J., Feb. 22, 1989, at A12.
151. Chris Hedges, *A Key Figure Proves Elusive in a U.S. Suit over Bhopal,* N.Y. TIMES, Mar. 5, 2000, at 4.

In late 1999, individual survivors and victims' organizations sued Union Carbide and its former CEO, Warren Anderson, in the U.S. District Court for the Southern District of New York for violating international law and the fundamental human rights of the victims and survivors.[152] Union Carbide argued that it was not required to provide further compensation after the 1988 settlement. Anderson disappeared and could not be served with a summons to appear in the New York federal court. The company accepted it on his behalf. Union Carbide and Anderson were also placed on trial as criminal defendants in India, but Anderson and other company officials refused to subject themselves to the jurisdiction of the Bhopal district court. The Indian government issued an arrest warrant for Anderson in 1992 and finally asked the United States for extradition in 2003.[153] As of May 2004, Washington had not honored the request.[154] Union Carbide has long claimed the leak was a result of sabotage. The bulk of the federal case was dismissed, but smaller claims were still pending as of March 2004.[155]

### *Unocal in Myanmar*

Energy giant Unocal Corporation has been sharply criticized for its continuous involvement with the $1.2 billion Yadana pipeline in the country of Myanmar, formerly known as Burma. Rather than ceding power after a free election won by an opposing party, Myanmar's military leaders took control in 1990. The government has since established a reputation as one of the most oppressive in the world. Myanmar's state-owned oil company, Unocal's partner on the pipeline, has allegedly been involved in rapes, murders, and slavery.[156] President Clinton banned any new American investments in Myanmar in April 1997.[157] In May 2004, President George W. Bush labeled the military government an "extraordinary threat" to U.S. interests and renewed an import ban against the country.[158]

Unocal is the largest U.S. investor remaining in Myanmar. Between 1996 and 2004, numerous lawsuits were filed in the United States by various parties, but with no real success. Unocal chair and CEO, Charles Williamson, defended the company's involvement in Myanmar, calling it "good for stockholders . . . and the country."[159]

## POSITIVE ACTION

Although examples of corporate misdeeds abound, there are also encouraging examples of responsible corporate behavior.

### *Customers and Product Safety: Johnson & Johnson and Tylenol*

Johnson & Johnson's Tylenol success story is a classic illustration of socially responsible behavior. In September 1982, several Tylenol capsules were tampered with and laced with cyanide poison. As soon as the first deaths were reported, the company recalled 31 million bottles of Tylenol at a cost of approximately $100 million. Although the short-term economic costs were enormous, within a matter of months Johnson & Johnson was able to regain the market share it had lost. By living up to its reputation for integrity and social responsibility, Johnson & Johnson enhanced both its public image and its long-term profitability. That image was later tarnished, however, by claims that Johnson & Johnson had been slow to warn consumers that Tylenol can cause liver damage—a demonstration of the importance of being ever vigilant to protect the firm's reputation.[160]

### *Employees*

**Auditing of Supplier Work Conditions** For many years, American companies claimed that their foreign factories were not stereotypical sweatshops, but they stubbornly refused to release the reports detailing the audits they used to substantiate those claims. Some companies, however, now go public with the audit reports. Adidas-Salomon, Nike, Reebok, and other companies post the results of their factory audits on the Fair Labor Association (FLA) website, http://www.fairlabor.org. Consequently, other companies, particularly those with less than stellar human rights reputations, are feeling pressure to publicize their

152. Frederick Noronha, *Union Carbide Sued in U.S. for 1984 Bhopal Gas Release,* ENV'T NEWS SERVICE, Nov. 16, 1999.
153. Saritha Rai, *Bhopal Extradition Sought,* N.Y. TIMES, July 3, 2003, at W3.
154. Mark Hertsgaard, *Bhopal's Legacy,* NATION, May 24, 2004, at 6.
155. *See* Bano v. Union Carbide Corp., 361 F.3d 696 (2d Cir. 2004).
156. Steven Erlanger, *Clinton Approves New U.S. Sanctions Against Burmese,* N.Y. TIMES, April 22, 1997, at A1.
157. The U.S. Supreme Court struck down a Massachusetts statute barring state entities from buying goods or services from companies doing business with Myanmar. Cosby v. Nat'l Foreign Trade Council, 530 U.S. 363 (2000).
158. *Shareholders Reject Bid for Dissidents' Access to Board,* L.A. TIMES, May 25, 2004, at C2.
159. *Id.*
160. See Thomas Easton, *Medicine, J&J's Dirty Little Secret: Despite Bad Publicity and Costly Legal Settlements, Johnson & Johnson Refuses to Put Ample Warnings on Its Tylenol Labels,* FORBES, Jan. 12, 1998, at 42.

audits as well. Some critics, however, maintain that the posted audit reports do not evaluate whether the factories pay a living wage and claim that the inspection regime is "watered down."[161] Nonetheless, some accountability is better than none at all.

**Levi's Layoffs** Even the best of companies may have to reduce their workforce. Some employers choose to reward employee loyalty by going about layoffs in a gracious, respectful manner. In 1999, when Levi Strauss & Co. announced the closing of eleven U.S. plants and layoffs of 5,900 employees because of decreased demand for its goods and its decision to move more of its manufacturing offshore, the company committed to providing a $245 million employee package. Employees were given eight months' notice, as much as three weeks of severance pay for every year of service, up to eighteen months of medical coverage, an enhanced early retirement program, and a flexible allowance of up to $6,000 for training and start-up expenses.[162]

## *Environment*

**Honda** Most automakers are members of the Alliance of Automobile Manufacturers, the trade group leading the fight against tougher fuel and emissions standards. Honda Motor Company stands out as a notable exception.

In 2002, Honda shocked other automakers by telling regulators that most sport utility vehicles, pickup trucks, and minivans should meet the same fuel standards as passenger cars.[163] New Hondas in 2000 averaged nearly 30 miles per gallon, about 6 miles per gallon higher than the average American-made automobile and higher than any other automaker's average.

In 1999, Honda released America's first gasoline-electric hybrid vehicle, the Insight. In 2002, Honda released a hybrid version of its popular Civic, becoming the first to mass-produce the hybrid powertrain for the consumer market. Honda also opened a "green" facility in 2002. The warehouse was designed, constructed, and will continue to operate using environmentally friendly products and practices. James Olson, the top lobbyist for Toyota, said of Honda generally, "Honda is a superb technical company, they have very strong principles, and they're very honest."[164]

**Ford** In late 1999, Ford Motor Company announced plans to spend $2 billion for a complete "green" renovation of the company's 1,200-acre Rouge manufacturing complex.[165] Under the aegis of environmental architect William McDonough (one of *Time* magazine's "Heroes for the Planet"), Ford transformed the complex into "a very visible testament to Ford's commitment to environmental leadership and social responsibility."[166] Among other features, the site includes the world's largest "living roof"—a 10.4-acre roof covered with drought-resistant ground cover that helps to filter rainwater, catch airborne dust and dirt, and provide a habitat for wildlife. The overhaul included not only the site, its buildings, and the surrounding ecosystem, but also the methods by which Ford designs, manufactures, and scraps its cars and trucks. Ford's chair, William Clay Ford, Jr., the driving force behind the new commitment to the environment, said that he hoped the renovated Rouge site would be "the icon of 21st-century sustainable manufacturing."[167] The redesigned plant began producing the F-150 in April 2004.

Ford also announced plans to release a gasoline-electric hybrid sport utility vehicle, the Escape Hybrid. Ford projected that the Escape Hybrid will get 35 miles per gallon in the city and around 30 on the highway, or 400 miles on one tank of gas.

## *Community*

**Dell, Hewlett-Packard, and Computer Recycling** Dell and Hewlett-Packard, the nation's two largest personal computer makers, both offer computer waste recycling programs.[168] Environmentalists favor Dell's program because it uses state of the art practices and helps to build the recycling infrastructure. Hewlett-Packard's

161. Aaron Bernstein, *Sweatshops: Finally, Airing the Dirty Linen,* BUS.WK., June 23, 2003, at 100. In addition, Nike has an in-house staff of 97 that inspected 600 factories in the two-year period ending in 2004 and graded them on later standards. Maria S. Eitel, the Nike vice president for corporate responsibility, commented, "You haven't heard about us recently because we had our head down doing it the hard way. Now we have a system to deal with the labor issue, not a crisis mentality." Quoted in Stanley Holmes, *The New Nike,* BUS.WK. Sept. 20, 2004, at 78, 84.
162. Miles Socha, *Bad Day at Levi's! 11 Plants to Close, Costing 5,900 Jobs,* WOMEN'S WEAR DAILY, Feb. 23, 1999, at 1.
163. Danny Hakim, *Honda Takes Up Case in U.S. for Green Energy,* N.Y. TIMES, June 12, 2002.
164. *Id.*
165. Jim Motavalli, *Harnessing Hydrogen,* E THE ENV'T MAG., March/April 2000, at 34.
166. Jane Morley, *Former Green Dean Works for 'Eco-Effectiveness,'* WASH. BUS. J., Feb. 11, 2000, at 101.
167. Martha Hamilton, *Irresistibly Drawn Toward a More Hopeful Future: Architect William McDonough Tries to Combine Life's Lessons with the Designs That Are His Life's Work,* WASH. POST, Feb. 21, 2000, at F16.
168. This discussion is drawn from John Markoff, *2 PC Makers Given Credit and Blame in Recycling,* N.Y. TIMES, June 27, 2003, at C3.

program utilizes labor in the prison system through Unicor, an industrial prison system operator. Although Hewlett-Packard's methods are less advanced than Dell's, the inmates who participate in the voluntary program have a 24 percent lower recidivism rate than inmates who do not. Critics complain that the Hewlett-Packard system is "primitive" and that it interferes with the creation of a profitable recycling industry. Nevertheless, either option seems preferable to the exportation of computer waste to developing countries (discussed earlier in this chapter).

**Poultry and Antibiotics** For years, poultry farmers have used chicken feed containing antibiotics, which critics claim contributes to the growing antibiotic resistance in bacteria. Drug-resistant strains of bacteria grow and spread more quickly when bacteria susceptible to antibiotics are killed off. But three major poultry companies have voluntarily changed their ways: Tyson Foods cut back on antibiotics similar to those used in humans; Perdue Farms began using only antibiotics that are not the same as or similar to those used in human medicine; and Foster Farms stopped using antibiotics altogether, except to treat sick birds.[169] As of 2002, these three companies accounted for the production of a third of all chicken consumed in the United States annually.

## Socially Responsible Investment

Individual and institutional investors continue to promote more environmentally responsible behavior. In 1989, the Coalition for Environmentally Responsible Economies (CERES) promulgated investor guidelines that focus on environmental awareness and corporate activities, such as using and preserving natural resources, safely disposing of pollutants, marketing safe products, and reducing environmental risks. CERES is a diverse network of investors, environmentalists, labor unions, and community advocates, collectively representing more than $400 billion in invested capital. More than seventy companies (including General Motors, American Airlines, Polaroid, and Sunoco) had endorsed the principles by 2004.

American investors are investing in ethically or environmentally responsible funds in increasing numbers. In the first three months of 2003, Americans pulled $13 billion out of conventional mutual funds while investing $185 million in ethically or environmentally responsible funds.[170] Many such funds consistently offer returns comparable to or better than those of the Standard & Poor's 500. In 2003, there were more than 200 socially responsible funds; 18 had more than $100 million in assets, and 4 had assets of more than $1 billion.[171]

Europe has seen a similar growth in socially responsible funds.[172] Moreover, pursuant to a regulation that went into effect in July 2000, pension-fund trustees in the United Kingdom must disclose in their statement of investment principles the extent, if any, to which they consider social, environmental, or ethical factors when deciding in which companies to invest. Although the regulation does not require trustees to have a policy on these issues, they must disclose the lack of one. Experts have called for the SEC to adopt similar requirements in the United States.[173]

Besides expressing concern about product and environmental safety, the public has put pressure on corporations and institutional investors to invest responsibly, that is, in a way that does not lend support to unjust, oppressive regimes. For instance, many companies with direct or indirect economic ties to South Africa were the subject of consumer boycotts and shareholder resolutions prohibiting investment in South Africa. South Africa's policy of racial segregation (called *apartheid*) relegated its black citizens to second-class status in employment, housing, and opportunity. The boycotts and shareholder resolutions were critical in helping end apartheid in South Africa, a result for which Nelson Mandela and F. W. de Klerk won the Nobel Peace Prize in 1993. As discussed earlier, Unocal has been sharply criticized for its continued involvement in Myanmar.

## Promoting Ethical Behavior

While remembering that there is no substitute for leading by example, that is, that the CEO and upper-level management set the tone of an organization, many companies use the following techniques to promote ethical behavior.

169. Marian Burros, *Poultry Industry Quietly Cuts Back on Antibiotic Use*, N.Y. TIMES, Feb. 10, 2002.

170. James K. Glassman, *Good for the Soul, Works for the Wallet*, WASH. POST, May 25, 2003, at F1.

171. *Id.*

172. Sara Calian & Tamzin Booth, *Ethical-Investment Practices Expand in U.K. in Response to New Legislation*, WALL ST. J., June 19, 2000, at A15B.

173. Bagley & Page, *supra* note 35.

## MISSION STATEMENTS

Corporations sometimes include ethical language in their corporate mission statements. This language may not mention ethics by name but may stress that the corporation has responsibilities in addition to profit maximization and that it has obligations to both employees and customers. For example, Toyo Glass Company, a Japanese supplier of glass products, includes the following statement:

1. Our objective is to contribute our share of work towards the happiness of the public at large.
2. Profit is not our first aim to attain, it is a natural outgrowth of successful business activities.
3. Everybody is expected to do his duty as a service to the public, individually and collectively, and thus to benefit the property of his own as well as others.[174]

## CODES OF ETHICS AND ETHICS TRAINING

Codes of ethics are the most widespread means by which companies communicate their ethical standards to their employees. A code of ethics is a written set of rules or standards that states the company's principles and clarifies its expectations of employee conduct in various situations. Although these codes vary from company to company, they govern such areas as selling and marketing practices, conflicts of interest, political activities, and product safety and quality.

The 2003 *National Business Ethics Survey* published by the Ethics Resource Center reported that approximately 87 percent of large for-profit organizations surveyed had adopted a code of conduct or other written standard of ethical conduct.[175] In addition, 49 percent of the for-profit organizations surveyed provided ethics training.[176]

Business leaders consider a code of ethics to be one of the most effective measures for encouraging ethical business behavior. James Burke, chair of Johnson & Johnson during the Tylenol scare, believes that Johnson & Johnson's code of ethics helped the company out of the crisis. Johnson & Johnson's code begins: "We believe that our first responsibility is to the doctors, nurses and patients, to mothers and fathers, and all others who use our products and services. In meeting their need, everything we do must be of high quality."[177] As described earlier, when it discovered that Tylenol capsules had been tampered with, the company acted swiftly to remove the product from the shelves. "Dozens of people had to make hundreds of decisions on the fly," says Burke. "There was no doubt in their minds that the public was going to come first in this issue because we had spelled it out [in our credo] as their responsibility."[178]

Having a code in place before a crisis strikes is essential. Bowen H. "Buzz" McCoy, one of *National Real Estate Investor Magazine's* 100 real estate "icons" of the twentieth century, observed that "if a common sense of values has not been discussed and articulated before an ethical issue intrudes unexpectedly, it is too late."[179]

It is important to note that a company code of ethics is ineffective without proper implementation. Enron had a great policy on paper. It is not enough simply to state general rules; the code must give employees an understanding of principles to guide them in making practical decisions. The code should be a living document that is reviewed periodically to meet new circumstances. Managers should go over the code with personnel to ensure that they understand the company's values. The company should supplement the written code with ethics education programs conducted by professional trainers. The company should also pay increased attention to ethical standards in recruiting and hiring. Exhibit 1.11 contains excerpts from the American Express Company Code of Conduct (2002).

Many companies hold workshops and courses in ethics for their employees or hire ethics consultants to run training sessions. Good programs are also available on the Internet. Sixty percent of the companies that provide ethics training do so during the orientation process for new employees. Companies cite two primary goals of ethics training: (1) developing a general awareness of ethics in business and (2) drawing attention to practical ethical issues.

Some companies have developed innovative methods for educating their employees in ethics. Aircraft manufacturer Boeing offers an online quiz (with answers) to try to guide its staff through the whole gamut of moral quandaries from how to deal with employees who fiddle their expenses to suppliers who ask for kickbacks. Exhibit

174. ROBERT E. ALLINSON, GLOBAL DISASTERS: INQUIRIES INTO MANAGEMENT ETHICS (1997).
175. ETHICS RESOURCE CENTER, *supra* note 74 at 7.
176. *Id.* at 8.
177. *Quoted in* PATRICK E. MURPHY, EIGHTY EXEMPLARY ETHICS STATEMENTS 123 (1998).
178. Stanley J. Modic, *Corporate Ethics: From Commandments to Commitment*, INDUSTRY WK., Dec. 14, 1987, at 33.
179. Bowen H. McCoy, *Real Estate Ethics*, 4 REAL EST. REV. 27, 31 (2000).

**EXHIBIT 1.11** **Excerpts from the American Express Company Code of Conduct**

**Business Ethics and Compliance with the Law**

**You are expected to protect and enhance the assets and reputation of American Express Company.**
Our business is based on a strong tradition of trust. It is the reason our customers come to us. Honesty and integrity are cornerstones of ethical behavior. Trustworthiness and dependability are essential to lasting relationships. Our continued success depends on doing what we promise—promptly, competently and fairly.

. . .

The Code of Conduct provides guidelines for a variety of business situations. It does not try to anticipate every ethical dilemma you may face. American Express, therefore, relies on your good judgment.

. . .

Leaders, by virtue of their positions of authority, must be ethical role models for all employees.
An important part of a leader's responsibility is to exhibit the highest standards of integrity in all dealings with fellow employees, customers, suppliers and the community at large.

Source: All excerpts from the *American Express Company Code of Conduct* (2002). Used by permission.

1.12 provides several sample questions from one of Boeing's past quizzes.

Ethics training may be particularly important for business managers. Research indicates that students planning a career in business are more likely to cheat than students planning to pursue other disciplines (76 percent of business students admitted that they have cheated on at least one test).[180] Other research supports the assertion that business students are more tolerant of unethical behavior than other students.[181] Nonetheless, business schools are trying to increase the scope and quality of their ethics coverage. Many business schools offer stand-alone courses in ethics or corporate responsibility and business law, and most try to integrate such topics into strategy, and accounting/auditing courses, among others. To preserve the reputation of tomorrow's business leaders and to prevent unethical behavior in the future, there must be a renewed focus on trustworthiness and personal responsibility in business schools.[182]

## OVERSIGHT

In an effort to enforce ethical standards, some companies have set up oversight committees, and many large firms employ at least one full-time ethics officer. The Ethics Officer Association has grown from a dozen members in 1992 to more than 950 members in 2004. The association's member companies include more than half of the *Fortune* 100. As of 2004, defense and engineering giant United Technologies had an international network of 215 "business practice officers," who were responsible for distributing and reinforcing a code of ethics in twenty-seven languages to its employees around the world.[183]

In general, ethics committees are responsible for setting standards and policy and for handling employee complaints or infractions. The membership of these committees often includes executive officers or directors of the company. Ombudspersons investigate employee complaints. Judiciary boards usually decide cases of ethics code violations.

Another method of oversight is the social audit. Increasingly, companies have been performing social audits of their activities in sensitive or controversial areas. For example, a semiconductor company might conduct an internal audit of its disposal of chemical waste, or a bank might audit the reporting practices of its securities trading division. The Body Shop retained ethics expert Kirk Hanson to audit the effect of its activities on the environment and the communities where it operates.

A 2000 study of social auditing revealed that corporate financial performance typically improves with increased social responsibility. The companies studied increased their efficiency and productivity, lowered legal exposure and risk to the company's reputation, and reduced direct and overhead costs as a result of adopting

180. Donald L. McCabe & Linda Klebe Trevino, *Cheating Among Business Students,* 19 J. MGMT. EDUC. 205 (1995).
181. M. Lynette Smyth & James R. Davis, *An Examination of Student Cheating in the Two-Year College,* 31 COMMUNITY C. REV. 17 (2003).
182. Carolyn Y. Woo, *Personally Responsible,* BIZED, May/June 2003, at 22.
183. This information was gleaned from the United Technologies website, *at* http://www.utc.com/social/ethics/index.htm (last visited March 2004).

**EXHIBIT 1.12** **Sample Questions from Boeing's Online Ethics Challenge**

**The Minister Drops a Hint**

You are working on an important new joint venture overseas. You are asked by your boss, a vice president, to accompany him on a series of crucial meetings with the country's Minister of Transportation. During the first meeting, the Minister, who is a technology buff, admires your expensive brand new laptop computer. After the meeting, your boss tells you to have a new computer exactly like yours air shipped from the United States for presentation to the minister during the next meeting, remarking that "this is a small price to pay for landing this deal." What should you do?

**POTENTIAL ANSWERS**

**A** Arrange to have the computer given, record it as a business expense.
**B** Substitute a less expensive electronic gift, like the Boeing logo watch, for the Minister.
**C** Tell your boss that you believe such a gift is inappropriate, and do not arrange to have the computer sent over.
**D** Ignore your boss's instructions and hope he forgets the matter.

**Graffiti**

While washing your hands in the rest room at a company facility, you notice that a variety of abusive racial words and phrases have been written on the wall. Upon closer scrutiny, you notice that the graffiti is not targeted at just one race. It appears to have been written by different people, targeting different ethnic groups. What should you do?

**POTENTIAL ANSWERS**

**A** Do nothing, it's not your problem.
**B** Try to cover up the graffiti on your own.
**C** Contact the Facilities Department and ask that the graffiti be removed.
**D** Contact your manager, the EEO People representative or your Ethics Advisor.

**Recycling**

Your machine shop shift has ended and you are no longer on company time. No night shift follows yours. You have saved some scrap materials that would otherwise be discarded. Using the large machine tools in the shop, you plan to make a few spare parts in a matter of minutes that could be used in your home bicycle shop, a side business that you run. Can you use the scrap materials to make parts, and can you use the tools?

**POTENTIAL ANSWERS**

**A** You can use the scrap to make parts, but cannot use the tools.
**B** You can use the scrap to make parts, and you can use the tools.
**C** You cannot use the scrap to make the parts, and cannot use the tools.

**Quality Quandary**

While working on the assembly line, you notice that a fellow employee, who is also a close friend, has deliberately bypassed a required procedure because of schedule pressures. You have a lot of loyalty to your friend, and certainly don't want to get him in trouble. At the same time, you are concerned about the quality of the product and the possibility that safety might be compromised. What should you do?

**POTENTIAL ANSWERS**

**A** Let it go. Friendship is the most important thing.
**B** Report the problem to your manager or the regulatory expert in your area.
**C** You are an empowered employee: use your expertise. Evaluate the procedure yourself to determine if it is really necessary. If in your judgment it is not, forget about the incident.
**D** Mention your concern to your friend, and ask him to follow the procedure.

Source: ETHICS CHALLENGE, *at* http://active.boeing.com/company offices/ethics challenge/ (last visited in 2001). For a current version of the quiz, visit the URL above.

socially responsible practices.[184] The financial payback to the company was between six and twenty times the audit cost over periods of six months to three years.[185]

## Making It Easier to Blow the Whistle

Many employees are reluctant to "blow the whistle"—to report illegal or unethical conduct that they observe at work—for fear of being considered a troublemaker or of being fired. A number of federal, state, and local laws prohibit reprisals against employees who report activities that they believe violate a law, rule, or regulation. These whistle-blowing laws are discussed in Chapter 12.

Even with legislative and judicial protections, whistle-blowers do suffer. For example, on the eve of the space shuttle *Challenger's* takeoff in January 1986, two senior engineers from Morton Thiokol warned that the shuttle's O-ring gaskets (manufactured by Morton Thiokol) might be affected by the forecasted cold weather. The launch was not canceled, and seven astronauts died when the shuttle exploded in a ball of flame. According to the *Economist,* even though the two Morton Thiokol employees were praised for their actions, their careers suffered.[186]

Edna Ottney, a quality assurance engineer who has investigated employee concerns in the nuclear power industry since 1985, reported that 90 percent of the 1,700 whistle-blowers she interviewed had experienced negative reactions. A person who reported violations at the Comanche Peak nuclear plant in Glen Rose, Texas, warns: "Be prepared for old friends to suddenly become distant. Be prepared to change your type of job and lifestyle. Be prepared to wait years for blind justice to prevail."[187]

184. Sandra Waddock & Neil Smith, *Corporate Responsibility Audits: Doing Well by Doing Good,* SLOAN MGMT. REV., Winter 2000, at 75.
185. *Id.* at 82.
186. *Good Takes on Greed,* ECONOMIST, Feb. 17, 1990, at 72.
187. *Quoted in* Joel Chineson, *Bureaucrats with Conscience,* LEGAL TIMES, Apr. 17, 1989, at 50.

A study published in the September 1993 issue of the *British Medical Journal* shows that this problem transcends national borders. Of thirty-five Australian whistle-blowers surveyed, eight lost their jobs as a result of whistle-blowing, ten were demoted, ten resigned or retired early because of ill health related to victimization, fifteen were taking prescribed medication to deal with stress, and seventeen had considered suicide.[188]

A manager can make it easier for employees to blow the whistle by protecting them from retaliation by their immediate supervisor and coworkers. A manager provides moral and psychological support by emphasizing to coworkers the courage shown by the whistle-blower and by providing free counseling to deal with any victimization by coworkers.

The Sarbanes–Oxley Act made it illegal to fire, demote, or harass employees of publicly traded companies who attempt to report suspected financial fraud.[189] Further, the law requires companies to find a way for employees to confidentially inform directors of problematic accounting. It remains to be seen whether the Act's provisions will make whistle-blowing any more common or whether those provisions truly will mitigate the attendant risks.

# The Law and the "Unethical"

## Role of the Law

As explained earlier, the line separating the legal from the illegal and the line separating the ethical from the unethical are not always congruent. Courts are particularly intolerant of unethical conduct when a relationship of confidence and trust exists between the parties, as seen in the following case.

188. Marcy Mason, *The Curse of Whistle-Blowing,* WALL ST. J., Mar. 14, 1994, at A14.
189. Tom Petruno & Thomas S. Mulligan, *Corporate Reform's Baby Steps,* L.A. TIMES, July 27, 2003, at 1.

A CASE IN POINT

## In the Language of the Court

**CASE 1.2**
**Meinhard v. Salmon**
*Court of Appeals of New York*
*164 N.E. 545 (N.Y. 1928).*

**› FACTS** In 1902, Louisa Gerry leased the Bristol Hotel in New York City to the defendant, Walter Salmon. The lease was for a term of twenty years, beginning in 1902 and ending in 1922. The lessee, Salmon, was to renovate the hotel building for use as shops and offices at a cost of $200,000. Salmon needed funds to complete his proposed renovations to the building, and he persuaded Morton Meinhard to act as a financial backer. Salmon and Meinhard entered into a joint venture agreement with the following terms: Meinhard agreed to pay to Salmon half of the moneys necessary to reconstruct,

(Continued)

(Case 1.2 *continued*)

alter, manage, and operate the property, and Salmon agreed to pay to Meinhard 40 percent of the net profits for the first five years of the lease and 50 percent for the years thereafter. If there were losses, each party was to bear them equally. Salmon, however, was to have sole power to "manage, lease, underlet and operate" the building.

In January 1922, with less than four months of the lease to run, Elbridge Gerry, who had become the owner of the property, approached the defendant, Salmon. Salmon and Gerry agreed to enter into a new twenty-year lease for not only the Bristol Hotel but also an entire tract of property surrounding it. The new lessor (the entity leasing the property) was the Midpoint Realty Company, which was owned and controlled by Salmon. Under the new lease, the Bristol Hotel would eventually be torn down, and new buildings would be built on the old Bristol site and adjacent lots at a cost of $3 million.

The lease between Gerry and the Midpoint Realty Company was signed and delivered on January 25, 1922. Salmon had not told Meinhard anything about it. Meinhard was not informed even of the existence of a new project until February, when the new lease was a done deal.

Meinhard demanded to be included in the new lease. The defendants, Salmon and Gerry, refused to do so.

Meinhard sued. A referee found in favor of Meinhard but limited his interest in (and corresponding obligations under) the lease to 25 percent. Both the plaintiff and the defendant cross-appealed to the Appellate Division of the New York court. On appeal, Meinhard was awarded one-half of the interest in (and corresponding obligations under) the lease. Salmon appealed to the New York Court of Appeals, the highest state court in New York.

**› ISSUE PRESENTED** Did Salmon, as Meinhard's joint venturer, have a relationship of trust (or *fiduciary duty*) to Meinhard that obligated him to give Meinhard the opportunity to be included in a new lease covering property that was originally leased by Salmon on behalf of the joint venture?

**› OPINION** CARDOZO, C.J. (later a justice of the U.S. Supreme Court), writing for the New York Court of Appeals:

Joint adventurers, like copartners, owe to one another, while the enterprise continues, the duty of the finest loyalty. Many forms of conduct permissible in a workaday world for those acting at arm's length are forbidden to those bound by fiduciary ties. A trustee is held to something stricter than the morals of the market place. Not honesty alone, but the punctilio of an honor the most sensitive, is then the standard of behavior. As to this there has developed a tradition that is unbending and inveterate. Uncompromising rigidity has been the attitude of courts of equity when petitioned to undermine the rule of undivided loyalty by the "disintegrating erosion" of particular exceptions. Only thus has the level of conduct for fiduciaries been kept at a level higher than that trodden by the crowd. It will not consciously be lowered by any judgment of this court.

The owner of the [property], Mr. Gerry, had vainly striven to find a tenant who would favor his ambitious scheme of demolition and construction. Baffled in the search, he turned to the defendant Salmon [who was] in possession of the Bristol, the keystone of the project. . . . To the eye of an observer, Salmon held the lease as owner in his own right, for himself and no one else. In fact he held it as a fiduciary, for himself and another, sharers in a common venture. If this fact had been proclaimed, if the lease by its terms had run in favor of a partnership, Mr. Gerry, we may fairly assume, would have laid before the partners, and not merely before one of them, his plan for reconstruction. . . . The trouble about [Salmon's] conduct is that he excluded his coadventurer from any chance to

*(Continued)*

(Case 1.2 *continued*)

compete, from any chance to enjoy the opportunity for benefit that had come to him alone by virtue of his agency. This chance, if nothing more, he was under a duty to concede. . . .

We have no thought to hold that Salmon was guilty of a conscious purpose to defraud. Very likely he assumed in all good faith that with the approaching end of the venture he might ignore his coadventurer and take the extension for himself. He had given to the enterprise time and labor as well as money. He had made it a success. Meinhard, who had given money, but neither time nor labor, had already been richly paid. There might seem to be something grasping in his insistence upon more. Such recriminations are not unusual when coadventurers fall out. They are not without their force if conduct is to be judged by the common standards of competitors. That is not to say that they have pertinency here. Salmon had put himself in a position in which thought of self was to be renounced, however hard the abnegation. He was much more than a coadventurer. He was a managing coadventurer. For him and for those like him the rule of undivided loyalty is relentless and supreme. . . .

**› RESULT** The judgment for the plaintiff, Meinhard, was affirmed. He was granted one-half of the interest in (and corresponding obligations under) the new lease between Salmon and Gerry.

**› COMMENTS** In *Meinhard v. Salmon,* the court seemed to assume without explanation that joint venturers had a fiduciary duty to one another. Judges can disagree on what types of business relations give rise to a standard that is "higher than the morals of the market place." Furthermore, there is even disagreement as to what constitutes proper morals of the marketplace. In a 1993 case, decided by the New York Court of Appeals, the same court that decided *Meinhard v. Salmon,* a majority of the judges concluded that a finder of a buyer for a business did not have a fiduciary duty to disclose to the seller the unsavory reputation of the potential buyer.[190] The dissenting judge disagreed. He argued that there was a fiduciary relationship between the parties and, even if there were not, that the morals of the marketplace would require disclosure. Fiduciary duty is discussed more fully in Chapter 5.

**› CRITICAL THINKING QUESTIONS**

1. Would the result in this case have been different if Gerry had offered Salmon a lease on property far removed from the Bristol property that was the subject of the Salmon-Meinhard joint venture?
2. What, if any, provisions could Salmon have included in a written joint venture agreement with Meinhard that would have relieved Salmon of any obligation to Meinhard once the initial twenty-year lease ended?

190. Northeastern Gen. Corp. v. Wellington Advert., 624 N.E.2d 129 (N.Y. 1993).

## *The Law Is Dynamic*

As explained earlier, lawmakers will adopt more onerous regulation in response to companies' failure to meet societal expectations of what constitutes acceptable behavior. Courts will also impose new duties to reflect changing societal expectations. Consider, for example, the liability an employer might have for injury caused by an intoxicated employee sent home from work.

In *Otis Engineering Corp. v. Clark,*[191] a supervisor at Otis Engineering sent an employee home because he was drunk. The employee had a history of drinking at work and was intoxicated on the evening in question. Unfortunately, the employee was involved in a fatal automobile accident on his way home from work—the

191. 668 S.W.2d 307 (Tex. 1983).

## Global View

### "When Ethics Travel"

With the rapid globalization of the marketplace, many corporations face complex ethical challenges abroad.[a] Sometimes, practices regarded as ethically unacceptable in the United States are common practice in foreign countries. How should managers deal with such differences? Corporations take diverse approaches. One method is simply to conform to host-country customs; another is to apply home-country customs uniformly and ignore host-country customs. Both of these extreme approaches present problems. Universally conforming to host-country customs places no limits on the potential abuses that take place in developing countries. On the other hand, the opposite approach amounts to ethical imperialism and leaves no room for legitimate local norms.

Professors Dunfee and Donaldson, of the Wharton School at the University of Pennsylvania, argue that the better option is to balance the opportunity for local identity with the acknowledgment that certain values transcend individual communities. They call these transcendent values "hypernorms." One such hypernorm, known as the efficiency hypernorm, requires that economic agents efficiently utilize resources when their society has a stake. Another hypernorm, at least in democratic or quasi-democratic states, values citizen participation in political affairs. Both of these hypernorms relate to the controversial international business ethics issue of bribery.

Although bribery is prevalent in many countries, it is overwhelmingly regarded as ethically (and legally) wrong, even in those countries where it is widespread. Thus, for that reason alone, bribery should not be viewed as an acceptable norm, even where it is common. But bribery often also interferes with the two hypernorms described above. The efficiency hypernorm frequently proscribes bribery in business dealings because bribe recipients make decisions based on bribes rather than price and quality. Business decisions based on bribery, therefore, undermine the market mechanism. Bribery of high-level government officials in democratic and quasi-democratic states violates the hypernorm that values citizen participation in political affairs. This is because such bribery undercuts accountability to the citizenry in favor of an official's personal gain.

Managers must make other, far more subtle, ethical judgments in international management. Although many legitimate cultural norms that are not proscribed by hypernorms are consistent from culture to culture, others fall into an area known as moral free space. Consider the following value matrix shown to 567 managers in twelve nations.

1. Clean, obedient, polite, responsible, and self-controlled
2. Forgiving, helpful, loving, and cheerful
3. Broad-minded, capable, and courageous
4. Imaginative, independent, and intellectual

Japanese managers assigned a significantly high priority to the first value dimension (i.e., clean, obedient, polite, responsible, and self-controlled). In contrast, Swedish and Brazilian managers assigned a significantly high priority to the third (i.e., broad-minded, capable, and courageous). Thus, managers in different countries value different characteristics. Many managers in Hong Kong, for instance, view taking credit for the work of another as more unethical than bribery or gaining competitor information.

An international manager would be well advised to understand and respect such cultural differences, rather than trample them with moral imperialism. In the end, a manager unprepared to balance moral tensions is unprepared for the international business realm where subtle, and not so subtle, cultural differences abound.

a. This discussion is based on Thomas Donaldson & Thomas W. Dunfee, *When Ethics Travel: The Promise and Peril of Global Business Ethics,* 41 CAL. MGMT. REV. 45 (1999).

employee was killed as were two women traveling in another automobile. The husbands of the two women brought a wrongful death action against Otis. Historically, employers were not responsible for accidents caused by employees traveling to and from work. The Texas Supreme Court broke new ground and held that the corporation had a duty to prevent the intoxicated employee from causing an unreasonable risk of harm to others. The court explained that "changing social conditions led constantly to the recognition of new duties. . . . [T]he courts will find a duty where, in general reasonable men would recognize it and agree that it exists."

In *Riddle v. Arizona Oncology Services,*[192] the Arizona Court of Appeals came to a different conclusion on an extremely similar fact pattern. In *Riddle,* an Arizona Oncology Services (AOS) supervisor sent home an employee because she was high on cocaine. The employee had a history of drug abuse and had consumed cocaine

192. 924 P.2d 468 (Ariz. Ct. App. 1996).

while at work on the date in question. On her way home, the employee drove her vehicle across the centerline and collided with Steven Riddle's vehicle, seriously injuring Riddle. Riddle brought a personal-injury action against AOS. The Arizona Court of Appeals expressly declined to follow the Texas Supreme Court's decision in *Otis Engineering* and held that AOS had no duty to protect a third party from injury allegedly caused by the employee.

*Otis* and *Riddle* make clear that standards of duty are not always consistent between jurisdictions. Moreover, prior to *Otis*, no case in Texas had established a duty for employers in such a situation, making employers like Otis oblivious to the possibility that they might be held to such a standard. *Otis* proves that the law can be changed, in a sense retroactively, to hold parties to a higher standard than they might have previously expected. Because courts and lawmakers generally push the law toward higher standards, rather than lower ones, managers should make sure that they constantly reach for higher, more ethical standards.

Similarly, over time, courts have been more willing to hold employers vicariously liable for the misdeeds of their employees under the doctrine of ***respondeat superior*** (discussed further in Chapter 9) and to hold supervisors vicariously liable for the misdeeds of their subordinates under the responsible corporate officer doctrine (discussed further in Chapter 14). Because these standards vary between jurisdictions and over time, prudent managers strive for the higher standard.

## THE RESPONSIBLE MANAGER

### ENSURING ETHICAL CONDUCT

Ethical behavior is reinforced when (1) top management exemplifies the company's values and takes a leadership role in programs to promote ethics, (2) the company creates an atmosphere of openness and trust in which employees feel comfortable in reporting violations, and (3) activities to enhance and reward ethics are part of every operational level of the company.

At the outset, a business must accept the proposition that high ethical standards and business success go hand in hand. Although ethics alone may not ensure long-term success, unethical behavior often leads to illegal activity and can result in business failure. Members of top management cannot just pay lip service to this notion. Rather, they should show a dedication and commitment to ethics.

The manager should recognize the critical importance of self-esteem at both the individual and the organizational levels. In the same way that a woman cannot be a little bit pregnant, a manager cannot be a little bit unethical. Once a person starts breaking the little rules, he or she is destined to fall into bigger ethical lapses, often culminating in illegal behavior. If a manager will cheat on the little stuff, imagine what he or she will do when the stakes really matter.

This is not to say that even the best of managers will not sometimes fail to be true to their ethical resolutions. But it is critical not to let such lapses go unnoticed. Instead, ethical managers pick themselves up from the ground and reorient their sights to the high ground. Managers who set their sights on the stars are far more likely to reach the top of the mountain than those who aim for the foothills.

Managers should strive to strike a proper balance between economic performance and ethics and demonstrate that a strong ethical culture is a prerequisite to long-term profitability. In doing so, top management must look at the firm honestly and objectively. They should ask themselves what factors, either because of its industry or its internal corporate structure, inhibit the firm from being ethical.

A corporation needs a clearly written policy, such as a code of ethics. This policy must be legitimized and reinforced through formal and informal interaction with the entire management, beginning with the board of directors and the CEO. It should include procedural steps for reporting violations of the code of ethics and enforcing the code. The company should include a reference to the code of ethics in its employment agreements.

A company should institute ethics training, including setting up a forum to discuss ethical dilemmas. In deciding whether a decision is ethically right, managers should ask whether a decision is fair or unfair to the firm's personnel, customers, suppliers, and the communities where it does business. Managers should consider the direct and indirect results of a particular decision, including the impact on public image. They should ask themselves

*(Continued)*

(The Responsible Manager *continued*)

how much short-term benefit they are willing to forgo for long-term gain.

Ethics are related to laws, but they are not identical. The legal thing to do is usually the right thing to do—but managers often have to go beyond their legal obligations to act ethically.

The law acknowledges that in a business deal, misunderstandings may arise, unforeseen events may occur, expected gains may disappear, or dislikes may develop that tempt one party to act in bad faith. The law, by requiring each party to act in good faith, significantly reduces the risk of a party breaking faith.[193] When reading the chapters that follow, consider whether the courts, in applying the law, are doing anything more than requiring businesspersons to do what they knew or suspected they really should have been doing all along.

193. *See* Robert S. Summers, "Good Faith," *in General Contract Law and the Sales Provisions of the Uniform Commercial Code,* 54 VA. L. REV. 195 (1968).

INSIDE STORY

## ENRON IMPLODES

Enron Corporation began as a modest gas pipeline company but evolved into an energy giant and a Wall Street favorite over the course of the 1990s. At its pinnacle, the corporation was the nation's seventh-largest public company by revenue with 32,000 employees worldwide. But the company's increasingly aggressive accounting, which began as clever tricks and grew into complex and illegal schemes, led to the energy giant's demise in 2001.[194]

Largely due to the brilliance and foresight of Harvard MBA Jeffrey K. Skilling, who eventually took the reins as CEO for a short period, Enron was among the vanguard corporations in the field of energy trading. Skilling was the de facto leader of Enron—insiders say that Kenneth Lay was largely a figurehead even before officially naming Skilling CEO. By all accounts, Skilling was a genius, but he was reportedly also shrewd and hypercompetitive. Enron was a dog-eat-dog world where short-term shareholder value was paramount. The "deal" was everything.

Upon joining Enron to lead the gas trading business, Skilling insisted that the business use mark-to-market accounting. In mark-to-market accounting, a business books the entire value of a contract on the day it is signed, rather than as cash is collected. Enron estimated the value of natural gas a decade in advance and booked the profits of a ten-year contract at once. This system led to a tremendous drive for growth at Enron, and a huge difference between its reported profits and its cash flow.

194. The discussion that follows is based on BETHANY MCLEAN & PETER ELKIND, THE SMARTEST GUYS IN THE ROOM: THE AMAZING RISE AND SCANDALOUS FALL OF ENRON (2003) and other public sources.

Even when Enron was trading profitably, Skilling and Lay avoided calling Enron a trading corporation because Wall Streeters understood the extraordinary volatility of trading. Instead, Skilling and Lay dubbed Enron a logistics company. After the corporation reaped a sizable windfall through speculative (and perhaps illegal) trading during the energy crisis in California, the profits were moved into reserve accounts and saved for subsequent quarters. This was but one of many dubious accounting strategies that Enron utilized to manipulate its books.

Andrew S. Fastow, former CFO at Enron, was long touted as a wunderkind. He employed a number of structured finance tools, such as special-purpose entities to hide debt, manufacture profits, and fabricate capital. He personally profited by millions of dollars from some of the transactions.

According to the felony charges filed against Richard A. Causey, the company's former chief accounting officer, the value of one Enron asset known as Mariner Energy was simply increased by $100 million in 2000. This accounting sleight of hand translated into profits Enron needed to reach its projected earnings for the quarter—the same quarter in which Enron had collected, but not reported, profits from the California energy crisis. Enron reported profits from sham sales of assets to an investment partnership called LJM2, which Fastow controlled. The profits were not legitimate because Enron had agreed to bear any losses after the

*(Continued)*

(Inside Story *continued*)

sales. To make matters worse, Enron used its own stock to hedge and secure its obligations.

LJM2 also acted as an "independent" investor in Enron's off-the-books partnerships. The law requires such partnerships to have at least 3 percent of their capital from an independent investor. This requirement is intended to ensure the legitimacy of off-the-books deals. At least one set of off-the-books partnerships, called the Raptors, received the 3 percent from LJM2. Fastow went so far as to arrange for LJM2 to retrieve its 3 percent (plus a substantial profit) before the Raptors engaged in any hedging. This guaranteed Enron compensation if one of its assets lost value. Thus, LJM2, the "independent" investor, did not have any true interest in the Raptors or the legitimacy of their dealings.

Because Enron had used its own stock to hedge its obligations, the scheme depended on the maintenance of Enron's high stock price to achieve its purpose. After the stock price began to fall, a few of Enron's faults surfaced, causing the stock to fall farther, exposing more problems. Enron's myopic focus on short-term shareholder value blinded those with the power to prevent this inevitable and foreseeable cycle. Fastow and other decision makers at Enron apparently believed that as long as an action maximized short-term shareholder value and was even arguably legal, it had to be taken. The pressure to meet earnings projections and hide instability increased as time went on until desperate measures were required to meet those pressures. At some point, executives at Enron began taking illegal actions to avoid exposing the corporation's frail state.

Arthur Andersen LLP, the accounting firm responsible for auditing Enron's financial statements, was sentenced the maximum fine and five years' probation for obstruction of justice after shredding documents related to the Enron audit. The real damage had already occurred before sentencing—the firm's payroll was already down to 1,000 employees, compared to the 28,000 it employed before the obstruction charge. Andersen no longer does accounting in the United States.[195]

Enron filed for Chapter 11 bankruptcy in late 2001. Many of Enron's assets were sold to raise money for creditors. The energy trading business was sold to an investment bank. Enron expected to close a sale on its original natural-gas pipeline business by September 2004.

By the summer of 2004, Enron employed only 10,300 employees worldwide.[196] Employees and investors alike lost substantial portions of their retirement accounts. As of July 2004, thirty-one individuals had been charged with crimes surrounding the Enron debacle, and eleven had been convicted by plea or jury.[197] It was estimated that Enron's creditors would receive around 18 cents on the dollar for the $67 billion still owed, and there was some question as to whether Enron's pension plans would be able to cover future benefits, although they are legally required to do so.[198] In the end, Enron's stockholders may receive nothing for stock once valued at $90 a share.[199]

195. Lianne Hart & Jeff Leeds, *Andersen Sentenced to $500,000 Fine, 5 Years of Probation*, L.A. TIMES, Oct. 17, 2002, pt. 3, at 3.
196. Simon Romero, *Once a Corporate Hunter, Enron Is Now Just Leftovers*, N.Y. TIMES, July 8, 2004, at C1.
197. *Id.*
198. *Id.*
199. *Id.*

## KEY WORDS AND PHRASES

apartheid 35
compensatory justice 19
deontological theory of ethics 17
distributive justice 19
Ethical Business Leader's Decision Tree 14
fiduciary duty 40
Kantian theory 17
Rawlsian moral theory 17
retributive justice 19
reversibility 17
shareholder primacy 15
teleological theory of ethics 17
universalizability 17
utilitarianism 17

## QUESTIONS AND CASE PROBLEMS

1. Christine Bancroft is a twenty-five-year-old blonde with a face and a figure that some of her male colleagues thought seemed better suited to the cover of the *Sports Illustrated* swimsuit issue than *Advertising Age*. After spending her first three months as an analyst at the privately held advertising boutique Scot Wayne More sitting in her cubicle doing research on the Hispanic market, she looked forward to the day

she would have a chance to wow clients with the finely honed marketing skills she had acquired while pursuing her MBA at Northwestern University.

Christine knew that Allen Scot and Bart Wayne had a reputation for entertaining clients from out of town at San Francisco's all-male Pacific Union Club, so she was pleasantly surprised when Allen asked her to join him and Bart for lunch with Andrew Wise at the World Trade Club. Wise was an account executive from the Cincinnati headquarters of Quinn & Inder, the second largest consumer products firm in the United States. At first, Christine thought that she'd been invited to discuss their plans to extend their reach into the Hispanic youth market. But when she asked Bart how she might best prepare for the meeting, he just smiled and said, "Just wear that little black dress you wore at the firm's holiday party and leave the talking to Allen and me. Andrew asked for California, so we're giving him California."

What should Christine do? What would you do if you were head of human resources for Scot Wayne More and overheard the conversation between Bart and Christine while waiting in Allen's office to go over an offer letter for a new hire? [Adapted from JOSEPH L. BADARACCO, JR., DEFINING MOMENTS: WHEN MANAGERS MUST CHOOSE BETWEEN RIGHT AND RIGHT (1997).]

2. In 2005, shops began selling a line of clothes and other items depicting Charles Manson, the mass murderer whose followers killed seven persons, including actress Sharon Tate, in two Los Angeles homes in August 1969. Manson has been denied parole repeatedly and remains in prison for the gruesome murders that he and members of his cult committed. In 1993, the rock band Guns 'N' Roses had included in its new release a song written and sung by Manson.

   Cesar Turner is in charge of ordering policies for Mammoth Records, a large national retail chain of stores selling compact discs, tapes, videos, and T-shirts. He has received a flood of letters and faxes from angry parent groups, church leaders, politicians, and others demanding that Mammoth pull the Guns 'N' Roses CD and tape and stop selling the Manson T-shirts. Turner knows that these are very popular items at the retail stores. If Mammoth stops selling them, its competitors will pick up the extra business, thereby reducing Mammoth's profits. What should Turner do?

   Mammoth has also come under fire from local right-to-life groups because it sells directories of physicians and clinics that will perform abortions. Should Turner stop selling the directories? Does it matter whether Turner personally views abortion as legalized murder or as a choice every woman should have?

   Finally, local police and Broad Based Apprehension Suppression Treatment and Alternatives (an antigang coalition) are pressuring record stores to stop carrying the CD "G.U.N. Generations of United Norteños . . . XIV Till Eternity," which includes songs exhorting members of the Norteños (a northern California gang) to kill members of the southern California gang Sureños. Lyrics include the lines, "It's up to Norteños to kill the beast. All Sureños must cease." In what ways, if any, should Turner's analysis of this request differ from his analysis of the controversies over the Guns 'N' Roses CD and tapes, the Manson T-shirts, and the abortion directories?

3. Zandra Quartney is a manager/buyer in charge of purchasing children's shoes for a large retail store chain. She is also a die-hard football fan. This year, the Super Bowl will be played in the Georgia Dome in Atlanta, Georgia, her hometown. Quartney's favorite team, the Steelers, is expected to reach the Super Bowl.

   Currently, the store chain carries four brands of children's rain boots. In an effort to streamline its product line, the CEO has decided to cut back to three brands of rain boots, leaving to Quartney the decision of which brand to cut. Assume that all four brands are equally profitable. If the makers of Brand One send Quartney a pair of Super Bowl tickets, should she accept them? Does it matter whether the maker of Brand One is also a close friend of hers?

4. Assume the same facts as in Question 3, except that Brand One underperforms the other three brands. How, if at all, should that affect Quartney's decision? What if it is mid-January and the Steelers are definitely in the Super Bowl? Quartney has waited her entire life to watch the Steelers play in the Super Bowl. Even if she would not accept the tickets before, should she accept them now? Can she get out of her dilemma by offering to pay the face value of the tickets? Should she accept the tickets if she has already decided to discontinue Brand One?

5. Antonio Rossati is one of two partners who own a chain of twenty-four family-style restaurants in the Northeast. The restaurants have a reputation for serving quality food at bargain prices. Since the opening of the first restaurant thirty-four years ago, the restaurants have generated a loyal clientele. Now, however, many of their customers are older.

Because the restaurant business recently took a turn for the worse, Rossati and his partner decided to revamp the restaurants' image so that they will appeal to the younger generation. Consequently, Rossati and his partner have taken on a significant amount of debt to remodel and renovate.

Five of the twenty-four restaurants are in Boston. In the last few days, Rossati has received seven phone calls from people who claim that they have gotten sick after eating at his restaurant in the North End. After investigating, Rossati discovers that a shipment of frozen sausage was contaminated with *Salmonella ohio,* a rare form of food poisoning. How should Rossati respond to the seven customers who have already called? How should he respond to any further complaints? If Rossati denies that the contamination was caused by his restaurants, it is possible that no one will find out. After all, there are hundreds of restaurants and grocery stores in Boston that could have poisoned the customers.

Should Rossati pull all of the shipments of sausage from his freezers? What if he wants to compensate the victims but his partner disagrees? What if both Rossati and his partner agree to compensate the poisoned victims, but because of the recent debt this is not financially feasible? How should Rossati balance the ethical considerations with the economic implications? Should his response vary depending on whether the restaurants are covered by liability insurance?

6. Virginia Pocock, a recent graduate of New York University, is a first-year associate with the McBain Consulting Group. The partner in charge of a major strategy study for an important new client in the shipping business has asked Pocock to call low-level employees in competing shipping companies to gather competitive data to be used to devise a winning strategy for the client. She was instructed not to identify the client but to introduce herself as a consultant doing an analysis of the shipping industry.

   Assume that Pocock knows that senior managers in the competing firms would consider the data she is collecting proprietary and would not talk with her at all if they knew that she worked for a direct competitor. Is it ethical for Pocock to question the lower-level employees without revealing that she is working for a direct competitor? What should she do if after telling the partner that she considers it unethical to make the calls, she is told that consultants do this all the time and that refusal to do it would be a career-limiting move?

7. Indra Wu, a sales rep at Rite Engineering, attended a trade show and conference at company expense. Many exhibitors donated prizes, which were awarded to attendees based on a drawing of free tickets given to all attendees upon registration. Wu won a $12,000 plasma television in one of the drawings. The winner's certificate included the winner's name with no mention of the company.

   What should Wu do? What should Wu's supervisor do if she learns of the prize from someone other than Wu?

8. Jody Hunter and Jim Boling, two managers at Georgia-Pacific Corporation, a paper manufacturer, disagree about continuing the company's membership in Business for Affordable Medicine (BAM), a coalition of state governors and corporations supporting a U.S. Senate bill that would bring generic versions of brand-name drugs to market more quickly. Experts predict that the bill, if adopted by Congress, will reduce total spending on prescription drugs by $60 billion over the next ten years. Hunter, Georgia-Pacific's director of health and welfare, strongly supports the bill. Georgia-Pacific's prescription drug costs for employees increased by 21 percent in the last year alone. If the bill becomes law, the resultant drop in health-care costs will save Georgia-Pacific large amounts of money (in addition to saving money for other people across the country who need prescriptions).

   Eli Lilly & Co., a large, name-brand pharmaceutical firm for which Georgia-Pacific is the leading supplier of paper goods and packaging, has been pressuring the paper company to withdraw from BAM. Boling, a Georgia-Pacific sales manager, fears that "we may lose our business position if this is not managed correctly." Boling points out that Lilly plans to launch six new compounds next year, "which could mean millions of dollars in paper business for us." In one e-mail, Boling mentioned that a three-year agreement with Lilly "is sitting on the Procurement Managers [sic] desk now to be signed." Should Georgia-Pacific withdraw from BAM? Is it ethical for Lilly to use their business relationship to try to force Georgia-Pacific to withdraw? [This question is drawn largely from Laurie McGinley, *Georgia-Pacific Curbs Push to Speed Generic Drugs,* WALL ST. J., Sept. 4, 2002, at 2.]

9. In April 1999, Tim Rudolph left the Stanford Graduate School of Business to become the founder and CEO of IPO.com, a securities brokerage firm specializing in helping young companies use the Internet

to raise money from the public. IPO.com went public on March 2, 2000. On September 5, 2000, Rudolph personally sold one million shares of stock for $75 million. He used $10 million of the proceeds to buy a large house in Atherton, California, an easy commute to the company's Silicon Valley offices. Rudolph still owns another four million shares.

IPO.com employs thirty senior computer programmers who are paid a starting salary of $125,000 and given stock options potentially worth millions. The company also employs five janitors who empty the trash, clean the latrines, and vacuum the senior programmers' work areas. These janitors are paid approximately $15,000 a year. Due to the astronomical cost of living in Silicon Valley, several janitors with children have second jobs and rent out space in their one-bedroom apartments to make additional money to support their families. Four of the company's janitors are non-English-speaking immigrants from Mexico who are desperate for employment and, as a result, are willing to work for the low salary.

Although there is a large pool of unskilled workers willing to work as janitors for $15,000 a year, the market for skilled programmers is so tight that IPO.com has had to institute special incentives to keep the programmers happy. Most recently, the senior programmer was given a Hummer, the civilian version of the U.S. Army's Humvee vehicle, to celebrate the completion of an important piece of code.

What ethical and business considerations should a corporation and its CEO consider when setting the salaries for the different types of workers it employs?

## MANAGER'S DILEMMA

**10.** André Gastaux is the CEO of Euro Air, a large international airline with an excellent safety record, having had only two fatal crashes in its fifty years of operations. Unfortunately, a flight from New York to Paris with 350 passengers crashed off the coast of Canada killing all of the passengers on board.

Gastaux has tentatively decided to compensate all of the victims' families immediately by giving them a $150,000 check. Euro Air's insurers have complained that this payment would be overly generous and premature, and they have advised Euro Air not to make any payments until the claims are litigated in court, a process that could take several years. Euro Air's lawyers and its insurers have also advised Gastaux to offer to pay non-American passengers a smaller sum than that offered to the American passengers because the non-American passengers earned substantially less than the American passengers and only U.S. courts award large damages to the families of airplane crash victims. Should Gastaux delay making payments to the families of victims? Should he offer every family the same amount of money even though he knows that the courts in many of the countries with citizens on the doomed plane would award far less if the case were litigated? What factors should Gastaux consider in making these decisions?

## INTERNET SOURCES

| | |
|---|---|
| The Business Roundtable's page offers information about its efforts to affect public policy. The Business Roundtable is an association of CEOs from leading U.S. corporations committed to taking an increased role in debates about public policy. | http://www.businessroundtable.org |
| The International Business Ethics Institute's page provides information about assisting corporations in establishing international ethics programs. | http://www.business-ethics.org |
| The Organisation for Economic Co-operation and Development provides various types of information about ethics, both in and out of business, through its searchable home page. | http://www.oecd.org |
| The Novartis Foundation for Sustainable Development's page provides access to a large collection of ethics articles and links to other sites addressing ethics. | http://www.novartisfoundation.com |
| The Center for Business Ethics at Bentley College provides information about research and other activities focusing on ethics. The site has a searchable business ethics online library with books and journal articles on business ethics. | http://ecampus.bentley.edu/dept/cbe/index.html |
| The Stanford University page contains its official *University Code of Conduct.* | http://adminguide.stanford.edu/1.pdf |
| The Better Business Bureau's searchable page offers information about ethics in business. | http://www.bbb.org |
| The Institute for Business and Professional Ethics at DePaul University provides many resources regarding ethics and includes articles from the magazine *Business Ethics: Insider's Report on Corporate Responsibility.* | http://www.depaul.edu/ethics |
| The Ethics Officer Association's page provides links to major corporations' ethics-related websites and other ethics-related sites. | http://www.eoa.org |
| The Ethics Resource Center's site provides information regarding its *National Business Ethics Survey* measuring business ethics at the national level. | http://www.ethics.org |
| The site of the Markkula Center for Applied Ethics at Santa Clara University provides decision-making resources, articles from the publication *Issues in Ethics,* case studies, and transcripts from presentations and lectures. | http://www.scu.edu/ethics/ |

CHAPTER 2

# Constitutional Bases for Business Regulation

## INTRODUCTION

### Effect of the U.S. Constitution on Business

The U.S. Constitution gives the federal and state governments the power to regulate many business activities, but it also provides that certain rights cannot be taken away from individuals and organizations. Responsibility for regulating business at the federal level is allocated to the three branches of government: the legislative (the Congress, which consists of the House of Representatives and the Senate), the executive (which includes the president), and the judicial (which includes the U.S. Supreme Court).

The Constitution became effective in 1789. The first ten amendments, called the *Bill of Rights,* were added in 1791. Seventeen other amendments have subsequently been added. The most recent, the Twenty-seventh Amendment, was adopted in 1992; it prohibits changes in congressional pay from taking effect until after an intervening election of representatives.

Although this chapter focuses on the U.S. Constitution, many of the legal and policy issues discussed have analogues in the constitutions of other countries. For example, many jurisdictions afford a certain degree of protection for commercial speech and prescribe the procedures that must be followed before a person can be deprived of life, liberty, or property.

### Chapter Overview

This chapter first discusses the structure of the government of the United States as established by the Constitution and the allocation of different responsibilities to the three branches of government. The scope of powers of the federal courts and the concept of judicial review are outlined, as is the Supremacy Clause. Next, the chapter details the scope of executive and legislative power. This is followed by an analysis of conflicts that can arise among the three branches.

The chapter then discusses the doctrine of *federalism,* which serves to allocate power between the federal government and the various state governments. The central importance of the Constitution's Commerce Clause to this doctrine is explored. Finally, the chapter outlines the individual rights established by the Constitution and the various methods of protecting those rights. Among the various constitutional issues discussed are the rights to free speech, freedom of association and religion, and due process guaranteed under the Bill of Rights, and the concepts of substantive due process, eminent domain, and equal protection.

## Structure of Government

The Constitution divides governmental power between the federal government and the state governments, giving the federal government certain specified powers. Without a grant of power from the Constitution, the federal government cannot act. All powers not expressly given to the federal government in the Constitution rest with either the states or the people.

Often both the states and the federal government can regulate the same business activity. For example, there are both federal and state laws governing environmental protection, antitrust, and retail banking. If a state law conflicts with federal law, however, then the federal law takes precedence or *preempts* the state law.

# Separation of Powers

Within the federal government, power is divided among the judicial branch (the courts), the executive branch (the president and cabinet departments), and the legislative branch (the Congress). This division of power among the three branches is typically referred to as the *separation of powers.*

## THE JUDICIAL POWER

The power of the judiciary is established in various parts of the Constitution. Articles I and III give Congress the authority to establish federal courts. Article III provides the basis for the judicial power of federal courts.

### *Article III*

Article III of the Constitution vests judicial power in the Supreme Court of the United States and such other lower courts as Congress may from time to time establish. Federal judicial power extends to all cases or controversies:

- Arising under the Constitution, laws, or treaties of the United States.
- Of admiralty and maritime jurisdiction.
- In which the United States is a party.
- Between two or more states.
- Between a state and citizens of another state.
- Between citizens of different states.
- Between citizens of the same state claiming lands under grants of different states.
- Between a state or citizens thereof and foreign states, citizens, or subjects.

In other words, the federal courts have *subject matter jurisdiction* to decide such cases.

Article III gives the Supreme Court *appellate jurisdiction* in all such cases. A lower court tries the case, and the Supreme Court hears appeals from the lower court's decision. The Supreme Court also has *original jurisdiction* over cases affecting ambassadors and cases in which a state is a party. This means that such cases are tried in the Supreme Court, not in a lower court. Today, the Supreme Court's original jurisdiction is used mainly to decide controversies between states.

Congress has used its authority under Article III to establish federal district courts and courts of appeals. The structure of the federal court system is discussed in Chapter 3. All cases that fall under one of the categories listed above, except those in which the Supreme Court has original jurisdiction, are tried in federal district courts or, in some instances, in state courts with a right to remove them to federal court.

### *Article I*

Article I allows Congress to establish special courts other than the federal district courts and courts of appeals established under Article III. These specialized courts are often granted administrative as well as judicial powers. Examples of such courts include the U.S. Tax Court, the U.S. Bankruptcy Court, and the courts of the District of Columbia.

### *Judicial Review*

The federal courts also have the power to review acts of the other two branches of the federal government to determine whether they violate the Constitution. This power of *judicial review* makes the federal judiciary a watchdog over the government.

Though the Constitution does not explicitly state that the federal courts have this power of review, the power was established by a landmark decision of the U.S. Supreme Court in 1803. In *Marbury v. Madison,*[1] the Supreme Court stated that one of its functions is to determine what the law is. The Court held that the written Constitution must be the fundamental and paramount law of the land. Therefore, any law enacted by Congress that conflicts with the Constitution is void. More recently, the Supreme Court reiterated its ultimate authority to determine the law of the land in *City of Boerne v. Flores,*[2] when it struck down the Religious Freedom Restoration Act of 1993 (RFRA). Congress had adopted the RFRA in an effort to codify a strict scrutiny standard for restrictions on religion, but the Court rejected the RFRA standard in favor of a new, lower standard that corresponded with the Constitution. The strict scrutiny test is discussed later in this chapter.

## THE EXECUTIVE POWER

The executive power of the president is defined in Article II, Section 1, of the Constitution. Various executive functions may be delegated within the executive branch by the president or by Congress.

Article II, Section 2, enables the president, with the advice and consent of the Senate, to appoint the justices of the U.S. Supreme Court. It also allows the president to appoint all ambassadors and consuls and all other offi-

1. 5 U.S. (1 Cranch) 137 (1803).
2. 521 U.S. 507 (1997).

cers of the United States whose appointments are not provided for elsewhere in the Constitution.

Article II, Section 2, also empowers the president to grant reprieves and pardons for offenses against the United States, except in cases of impeachment. President Gerald Ford invoked this section when he pardoned Richard Nixon after Nixon resigned from the presidency following the Watergate burglary scandal in the early 1970s.

Article I, Section 7, grants the president the power either to approve or to disapprove acts of Congress before they take effect. The president thus has *veto power* over laws that do not meet his or her approval. Congress can *override* a president's veto by a two-thirds vote of both the House of Representatives and the Senate.

The president has extensive power over foreign affairs. Although only Congress can formally declare war, the president may take other military action through the president's power as commander-in-chief of the armed forces under Article II, Section 2. President George Bush used this power in 1991 to drive Iraqi forces from Kuwait during Operation Desert Storm, and President George W. Bush used this power in 2003 to invade Iraq and overthrow Saddam Hussein during Operation Iraqi Freedom.

The president also has the power to make treaties with the advice and consent of the Senate—that is, with two-thirds of the senators voting to ratify the treaty. The president may also make executive agreements, which do not require the advice and consent of the Senate. These agreements are superior to state law but not to federal law. Treaties and executive agreements are discussed further in Chapter 25.

## The Legislative Power

Article I, Section 8, of the Constitution enumerates the powers of the Congress, which consists of the House of Representatives and the Senate. Among other things, Congress has the power to (1) regulate commerce with foreign nations and among the states, (2) spend to provide for the common defense and general welfare, (3) coin money, (4) establish post offices, (5) levy and collect taxes, (6) issue patents and copyrights, (7) declare war, and (8) raise and support armies. Congress also has the power to make such laws as are "necessary and proper" to carry out any power vested in the government of the United States.

## Conflicts Between the Branches

Inherent in this system of checks and balances is the potential for conflict between the three branches of government. At times, the power of one branch of the government must be curbed to ensure the integrity of another branch.

For example, it has been inferred from the extensive impeachment proceedings outlined in the Constitution that the president is immune from criminal prosecution prior to impeachment. The president also has a type of immunity known as *executive privilege*, which protects against the forced disclosure of presidential communications made in the exercise of executive power. Yet sometimes executive privilege must give way to the judicial branch's need to obtain evidence in a criminal trial.[3] Courts are more likely to override the privilege when the president's claim of privilege is based only on a generalized interest in confidentiality and not on the need to protect military or diplomatic secrets.

Executive privilege also provides the president "absolute immunity from damages liability predicated on his official acts."[4] However, such immunity does not protect the president during his or her term of office from civil litigation over events that occurred before he or she took office. In *Clinton v. Jones*,[5] the Supreme Court held that President Bill Clinton could be sued while still in office by Paula Jones, formerly an Arkansas state employee, for sexual harassment and tort claims arising from acts that allegedly took place in 1991, when Clinton was governor of Arkansas. Although conceding that the litigation would subject the president to the power of the judiciary, the Court concluded that it would not violate the separation of powers. After concluding that the litigation was "highly unlikely" to occupy a "substantial amount" of Clinton's time, the Court rejected the argument that the litigation would impose an unacceptable burden on the president's time and energy and thereby impair the effective performance of his office. In fact, the case triggered special prosecutor Kenneth Starr's investigation of Clinton's sexual relations with White House intern Monica Lewinsky, and it culminated in Clinton's impeachment by the House of Representatives for perjury and obstruction of justice. Clinton was not convicted by the Senate, but the proceedings proved a major distraction.

3. United States v. Nixon, 418 U.S. 683 (1974) (holding that President Nixon was required to produce tape recordings and documents relating to confidential conversations with his advisers in a criminal case involving seven advisers charged with obstruction of justice and other offenses related to the 1972 burglary of the Democratic National Headquarters in the Watergate Hotel in Washington, D.C.).

4. Nixon v. Fitzgerald, 457 U.S. 731 (1982).

5. 520 U.S. 681 (1997).

The principle of separation of powers has also been invoked to invalidate certain legislation. In *Clinton v. City of New York*,[6] the Supreme Court struck down the *line item veto* given to the president by Congress. The line item veto allowed the president to sign a bill into law, then cancel any dollar amounts that he or she believed to be fiscally irresponsible.[7] Essentially, the veto gave the president the power to strike specific provisions from tax and spending bills, which usually include thousands of separate, discrete provisions. This made it possible for the president to shape budgetary policy without having to make the stark choice to accept or reject an entire package of provisions. Congress could effectively override any particular line item veto by adopting a disapproval bill by a two-thirds vote of both houses.

The U.S. Supreme Court, by a vote of six to three, declared the line item veto unconstitutional.[8] The Court said that the veto impermissibly altered the "single, finely wrought and exhaustively considered, procedure" in Article I, Section 7, of the U.S. Constitution, which requires that laws be approved by both houses of Congress (*bicameralism*) and then presented to the president. The Court stated that the president must approve all parts of a bill or reject it in toto. The amendment and repeal of statutes must meet these same requirements. If the act were valid, it would authorize the president to create a different law—one whose text was not voted on by either house of Congress or presented to the president for signature. The Court concluded that if there is to be a new procedure in which the president will play a different role in determining the final text of what may become a law, "such change must come not by legislation but through the amendment procedures set forth in Article V of the Constitution." President Clinton called the decision "a defeat for all Americans," which "deprives the president of a valuable tool for eliminating waste in the federal budget and for enlivening the public debate over how to make the best use of public funds."

## Supremacy Clause and Preemption

The Supremacy Clause of Article VI states that the Constitution, laws, and treaties of the United States take precedence over state laws and that the judges of the state courts must follow federal law. Any federal or state laws enacted in violation of the Constitution or ratified treaties are void. State law is preempted when it directly conflicts with federal law or when Congress has manifested an intention to regulate the entire area without state participation.

For example, in *Crosby v. National Foreign Trade Council*,[9] the U.S. Supreme Court struck down a Massachusetts statute enacted as a protest against human rights violations by Burma (now known as Myanmar) that restricted the ability of the state of Massachusetts and its agencies to purchase goods and services from individuals or companies doing business in Burma. Subsequently, Congress imposed mandatory and conditional sanctions on Burma but authorized the president to terminate the measures upon certifying that Burma had made progress in human rights and democracy, to impose new sanctions upon findings of repression, and to suspend sanctions in the interest of national security. The Court concluded that the Massachusetts statute posed an obstacle to the accomplishment and execution of Congress's full purposes and objectives in at least three respects: (1) the statute interfered with Congress's delegation of discretion to the president to control economic sanctions against Burma; (2) it interfered with Congress's intention to limit economic pressure against the Burmese government to a specific range by prohibiting some contracts and investments permitted under the federal act; and (3) it was at odds with the president's authority to speak for the United States among the world's nations to develop a comprehensive, multilateral Burma strategy. Accordingly, even though the federal act did not expressly preempt state legislation, the Court ruled that the Massachusetts law was preempted by the federal act and was therefore invalid.

In *Geier v. American Honda Motor Co.*,[10] the U.S. Supreme Court held that the National Traffic and Motor Vehicle Safety Act of 1996 (the Safety Act) preempted state product liability claims based upon a manufacturer's failure to equip a vehicle with air bags. Whereas the Safety Act deliberately provided the manufacturers of cars with a range of choices among different passive restraint devices and sought a gradual phase-in of passive restraints to allow more time for manufacturers to develop better systems, the state law imposed a duty to install an airbag. This presented an obstacle to the variety and mix of devices that the federal statute sought.

In an earlier case, *Medtronic, Inc. v. Lohr*,[11] the U.S. Supreme Court considered the issue of preemption with

6. 524 U.S. 417 (1998).
7. 2 U.S.C. § 691 *et seq.* (Supp. 1997).
8. Clinton v. City of New York, 524 U.S. 417 (1998).
9. 530 U.S. 363 (2000).
10. 529 U.S. 861 (2000).
11. 518 U.S. 470 (1996).

regard to claims of defective design, negligent manufacture, and failure to warn in the area of medical devices. The Medical Device Amendments (MDA) to the Food, Drug and Cosmetic Act specifically forbid states from establishing "any requirement" that is different from or in addition to those of the MDA. In *Medtronic*, a pacemaker recipient sued the device's manufacturer under state product liability law. The manufacturer argued that the state law was preempted by the MDA. Reasoning that the MDA's requirements for pacemakers were too general to preempt state law, the Court rejected the manufacturer's challenge.

Similarly, in *Duncan v. Northwest Airlines, Inc.*,[12] the U.S. Court of Appeals for the Ninth Circuit found that the Airline Deregulation Act (ADA) did not preempt a class action by flight attendants under state tort law against the airline for exposure to secondhand tobacco smoke on certain flights. Under the terms of the ADA, no state can enact or enforce any law relating to the rates, routes, or service of any carrier. Northwest argued that allowing smoking on its international flights constituted or related to a "service" and was covered by the ADA. The court of appeals rejected this argument on the grounds that a "service" concerns "the frequency and scheduling of transportation, [or] the selection of markets to or from which transportation is provided," whereas a rule permitting or prohibiting smoke concerned "amenities."

Ultimately, preemption depends on the specificity of federal regulation, any statutory language addressing preemption, and the nature of the conflict between the federal and state approaches. Federal preemption of state law claims related to tobacco is discussed in Chapter 10.

# Federalism

The federal government's powers are limited to those expressly granted in the Constitution. Its powers are also subject to specific restrictions, such as those in the Bill of Rights. State governments, on the other hand, have general powers not specified in the Constitution. These general powers, sometimes termed the *police power*, include the power to protect the health, safety, welfare, and morals of state residents.

Some powers are exclusively federal because the Constitution expressly limits the states' exercise of those powers. Exclusive federal powers include the power to make treaties, to coin money, and to impose duties on imports. Other powers are inherently in the states' domain, such as the power to structure state and local governments.

## The Eleventh Amendment

To further protect this division of power between the federal and state governments, the Eleventh Amendment was added to the Constitution in 1798. It immunizes states from lawsuits in federal court brought by citizens of another state or of another nation. Although a state may waive this sovereign immunity, it must do so voluntarily, explicitly, and in accordance with its own law.

In a variety of contexts, Congress has adopted legislation that purports to abrogate the states' Eleventh Amendment immunity. In reviewing the constitutionality of such legislation, the Supreme Court has held that a state cannot be required to litigate a case involving a person from another state in federal court unless Congress (1) unequivocally expressed its intent to abrogate that immunity and (2) acted pursuant to a valid grant of constitutional authority.

The Supreme Court surprised many when it ruled in 1999 that nonconsenting states cannot be sued in federal court for patent infringement under the Patent Remedy Act even though Article I gives Congress the power to issue patents.[13] The Court held that Congress's powers under Article I of the Constitution do not include the power to subject states to suit at the hands of private individuals. The Court also ruled that Congress had not enacted the Patent Remedy Act pursuant to a valid exercise of power under Section 5 of the Fourteenth Amendment. Section 5 gives Congress the power to enforce the states' compliance with the Fourteenth Amendment, which bars states from denying any person due process or equal protection under the law. To invoke Section 5, Congress must identify conduct transgressing the Fourteenth Amendment and tailor legislation to remedy or prevent that conduct. In this case, Congress had identified neither a pattern of unremedied patent infringement by the states nor a pattern of constitutional violations. In addition, the Court found that Congress had barely considered the availability of state remedies for patent infringement even though under the Fourteenth Amendment's Due Process Clause, a state's infringement of a patent violates the Constitution only when the state provides no adequate remedy to injured patent owners.

In the following case, the Court considered whether a state employer could be sued in federal court for violating the federal Family and Medical Leave Act of 1993.

12. 208 F.3d 1112 (9th Cir. 2000), *cert. denied*, 531 U.S. 1058 (2000).

13. Florida Prepaid Postsecondary Educ. Expense Bd. v. Coll. Sav. Bank & United States, 527 U.S. 627 (1999).

A CASE IN POINT

**CASE 2.1**

**Nevada Department of Human Resources v. Hibbs**

*Supreme Court of the United States 538 U.S. 721 (2003).*

## In the Language of the Court

› **FACTS** William Hibbs worked for the Nevada Department of Human Resources. In 1997, he sought leave under the Family and Medical Leave Act of 1993 (FMLA), which entitles eligible employees to take up to twelve weeks of unpaid leave annually for any of several reasons, to care for his wife, who was recovering from a car accident and neck surgery. Although the Department initially granted his request, it later told him that he would be terminated unless he returned to work. When he failed to do so, the Department terminated his employment. Hibbs sued the State of Nevada for violation of the FMLA. The district court awarded the State summary judgment on the ground that the FMLA claim was barred by the Eleventh Amendment. Hibbs appealed, and the United States intervened to defend the validity of the FMLA's application to the states. The U.S. Court of Appeals for the Ninth Circuit reversed the district court's decision, and the U.S. Supreme Court granted certiorari to resolve a split among the courts of appeals on the question whether an individual may sue a state for violation of the FMLA.

› **ISSUE PRESENTED** Does the FMLA validly abrogate a state's Eleventh Amendment immunity from suits in federal court?

› **OPINION** REHNQUIST, C.J., writing for the U.S. Supreme Court:
[*Ed.:* The Court first concluded that the language of the statute made it unmistakably clear that Congress intended to subject the states to suits for money damages by individual employees and that Congress had acted within its constitutional authority through a valid exercise of its power under Section 5 of the Fourteenth Amendment when it sought to abrogate the states' immunity for purposes of the FMLA. The Court explained:

> [T]he Eleventh Amendment, and the principle of state sovereignty which it embodies, are necessarily limited by the enforcement provisions of § 5 of the Fourteenth Amendment.
>
> . . . Section 5 grants Congress the power "to enforce" the substantive guarantees of § 1 [of the Fourteenth Amendment]—among them, equal protection of the laws—by enacting "appropriate legislation."

The Court then distinguished this case from *Board of Trustees of University of Alabama. v. Garrett*[14] and *Kimel v. Florida Board of Regents,*[15] in which it found that Congress had not acted within its constitutional authority when it sought to abrogate the states' immunity for purposes of the Americans with Disabilities Act (ADA) and the Age Discrimination in Employment Act (ADEA), respectively.]

In [*Garrett* and *Kimel*], the § 5 legislation under review responded to a purported tendency of state officials to make age- or disability-based distinctions. Under our equal protection case law, discrimination on the basis of such characteristics is not judged under a heightened review standard, and passes muster if there is "a rational basis for doing so at a class-based level, even if it 'is probably not true' that those reasons are valid in the majority of cases." Thus, in order to impugn the constitutionality of state discrimination against the disabled or the elderly, Congress must identify not just the existence of age- or disability-based state decisions, but a "widespread pattern" of irrational reliance on such criteria. We found no such showing with respect to the ADEA and Title I of the Americans with Disabilities Act of 1990 (ADA).

14. 531 U.S. 356 (2001).
15. 528 U.S. 62 (2000).

*(Continued)*

(Case 2.1 *continued*)

Here, however, Congress directed its attention to state gender discrimination, which triggers a heightened level of scrutiny. Because the standard for demonstrating the constitutionality of a gender-based classification is more difficult to meet than our rational-basis test—it must "serv[e] important governmental objectives" and be "substantially related to the achievement of those objectives,"—it was easier for Congress to show a pattern of state constitutional violations. . . .

The impact of the discrimination targeted by the FMLA is significant. . . . Stereotypes about women's domestic roles are reinforced by parallel stereotypes presuming a lack of domestic responsibilities for men. Because employers continued to regard the family as the woman's domain, they often denied men similar accommodations or discouraged them from taking leave. . . . Those perceptions, in turn, Congress reasoned, led to subtle discrimination that may be difficult to detect on a case-by-case basis.

. . .

By creating an across-the-board, routine employment benefit for all eligible employees, Congress sought to ensure that family-care leave would no longer be stigmatized as an inordinate drain on the workplace caused by female employees, and that employers could not evade leave obligations simply by hiring men. By setting a minimum standard of family leave for all eligible employees, irrespective of gender, the FMLA attacks the formerly state-sanctioned stereotype that only women are responsible for family caregiving, thereby reducing employers' incentives to engage in discrimination by basing hiring and promotion decisions on stereotypes.

**› RESULT** The Court concluded that Congress acted within its authority under Section 5 of the Fourteenth Amendment when it sought to abrogate a state's immunity for purposes of the FMLA. Hibbs's suit against the State of Nevada could proceed.

**› CRITICAL THINKING QUESTIONS**

1. Based on the reasoning in *Hibbs,* would a private individual be allowed to sue a state in federal court for race discrimination in violation of Title VII of the Civil Rights Act of 1964?
2. What congressional findings might have supported the application of the Americans with Disabilities Act or the Age Discrimination in Employment Act to the states?

---

In *Alden v. Maine*,[16] the U.S. Supreme Court held that the State of Maine could not be sued in *state* court by a group of employees seeking private damages for violating the overtime provisions of the Fair Labor Standards Act, a federal statute. Although the literal wording of the Eleventh Amendment refers to cases against states brought in federal court, the Court ruled that "the sovereign immunity of the States neither derives from nor is limited by the terms of the Eleventh Amendment." Due to the constitutional system recognizing the essential sovereignty of the states, nonconsenting states cannot be subject to suits in their own courts without their consent.

16. 527 U.S. 706 (1999).

## Dual Sovereignty

The Supreme Court reaffirmed the system of dual sovereignty when it struck down provisions of the Brady Handgun Violence Prevention Act that required state law enforcement officers to receive reports from gun dealers regarding prospective handgun sales and to conduct background checks on prospective handgun purchasers.[17] The Court stated that "[t]he power of the Federal Government would be augmented immeasurably if it were able to impress into its service—and at no cost to itself—the police officers of the 50 States."

17. Printz v. United States, 521 U.S. 898 (1997).

In *Reno v. Condon,*[18] however, the Supreme Court upheld the Driver's Privacy Protection Act of 1994, which restricts a state's ability to disclose without the driver's consent personal information contained in the records of the state department of motor vehicles. The Supreme Court rejected the contention that the Act violated the Tenth Amendment's federalism principles, and it ruled that the Act was a proper exercise of Congress's authority to regulate interstate commerce under the Commerce Clause. The Court explained:

> The motor vehicle information, which the States have historically sold, is used by insurers, manufacturers, direct marketers, and others engaged in interstate commerce to contact drivers with customized solicitations. The information is also used in the stream of interstate commerce by various public and private entities for matters related to interstate motoring. Because drivers' personal, identifying information is, in this context, an article of commerce, its sale or release into the interstate stream of business is sufficient to support congressional regulation.

## The Commerce Clause

Another boundary between federal and state powers is the Constitution's Commerce Clause. The *Commerce Clause,* contained in Article I, Section 8, gives Congress the power to regulate commerce with other nations, with Indian tribes, and between states. It is both a restraint on state action and a source of federal authority. The commerce power has been interpreted to allow federal regulation of such areas as interstate travel, labor relations, and discrimination in accommodations. As explained below, the U.S. Supreme Court has over time changed its view regarding what commerce is subject to federal regulation.

### 1824 TO 1887

The first Supreme Court discussion of the Commerce Clause was by Chief Justice John Marshall in the 1824 case *Gibbons v. Ogden.*[19] A state-granted steamboat monopoly affecting navigation between New York and New Jersey violated a federal statute regulating interstate commerce. The Court held that under the Supremacy Clause, the federal statute prevailed. In the decision, Justice Marshall discussed in detail his view that interstate commerce—which he defined as "commerce which concerns more states than one"—included every activity having any interstate impact. Therefore, Congress could regulate all such activities.

### 1887 TO 1937

From 1887 to 1937, the Supreme Court viewed the Commerce Clause quite differently than Justice Marshall. During this period, the Court interpreted "commerce" narrowly, holding that activities such as mining and manufacturing were not commerce and therefore could not be regulated by Congress under the Commerce Clause. The Supreme Court was not persuaded by the fact that the products of these activities would later enter interstate commerce. Toward the end of this period, the Court struck down various pieces of New Deal legislation, arguing that the Commerce Clause did not grant Congress the power to regulate such activities.

### 1937 TO 1995

A turning point in the Supreme Court's attitude came in *NLRB v. Jones & Laughlin Steel Corp.*[20] The Court held that Congress could regulate labor relations in a manufacturing plant because a work stoppage at such a plant would have a serious effect on interstate commerce; the steel manufactured by the plant was shipped across state lines.

From 1937 until 1995, virtually all federal regulation of commerce was upheld under the Commerce Clause. If legislation had a "substantial economic effect" on interstate commerce, it was held to be a valid exercise of the commerce power.

For example, in *Heart of Atlanta Motel, Inc. v. United States,*[21] the Supreme Court upheld Title II of the Civil Rights Act of 1964, which prohibits discrimination or segregation on the grounds of race, color, religion, or national origin in any inn, hotel, motel, or other establishment of more than five rooms that provides lodging to transient guests. The party challenging the act—the Heart of Atlanta Motel—had followed a practice of refusing to rent rooms to African Americans, and it alleged that it intended to continue to do so. The operator of the motel solicited patronage from both inside and outside the state of Georgia through billboards, signs, and various national advertising media, including

18. 528 U.S. 141 (2000).
19. 22 U.S. (1 Wheat) 1 (1824).
20. 301 U.S. 1 (1937).
21. 379 U.S. 241 (1964).

magazines of national circulation. Approximately 75 percent of its registered guests were from out of state.

The Court noted that the population had become increasingly mobile, with millions of people of all races traveling from state to state. African Americans in particular were subjected to discrimination in transient accommodations, which forced them to travel great distances to secure lodging. This impaired their ability to travel to other states.

In *Katzenbach v. McClung*,[22] the Supreme Court upheld the application of the Civil Rights Act to a restaurant because a substantial portion of the food that it served had previously moved in interstate commerce. The Court reasoned that the restaurant's discrimination against African Americans, who were potential customers, resulted in its selling less food that had traveled in interstate commerce. Thus, the discrimination had a substantial effect on interstate commerce.

## 1995 to Present

In 1995, in *United States v. Lopez*,[23] the Supreme Court again changed course when it struck down a federal law banning guns near schools as being beyond Congress's power under the Commerce Clause. The Court found that the statute was neither a regulation of the use of the channels of interstate commerce, nor an attempt to prohibit the interstate transportation of a commodity through the channels of interstate commerce, nor an attempt to protect an instrumentality of interstate commerce or a thing in interstate commerce. The Court ruled that the law was not sustainable as a regulation of an activity that substantially affects interstate commerce because its terms had nothing to do with commerce or any sort of economic enterprise.

22. 379 U.S. 294 (1964).
23. 514 U.S. 549 (1995).

The Court rejected the government's argument that the statute was constitutional because possession of a firearm at school might result in violent crime, which in turn would (1) affect the functioning of the national economy by increasing costs and reducing people's willingness to travel to parts of the country deemed unsafe and (2) reduce national productivity by threatening the learning environment. The Court reasoned that the "cost of crime" argument would give Congress the power to regulate not only all violent crime but also all activities that might lead to violent crime. The "national productivity" argument would empower Congress to regulate any activity related to the economic productivity of individual citizens, including family law governing marriage, child support, and divorce. As a result, there would be virtually no limitation on federal power, even in areas such as criminal law and education where the states historically have been sovereign, a result unacceptable to five members of the Court.

Congress had not stated any factual findings justifying its adoption of the Gun-Free School Zones Act at issue in *Lopez*. In the following case, the Court struck down the Violent Crimes Against Women Act notwithstanding Congress's express findings about the effect of violence on the economy.

**A Case in Point**

**CASE 2.2**
**United States v. Morrison**
*Supreme Court of the United States*
*529 U.S. 598 (2000).*

### In the Language of the Court

**› FACTS** Christy Brzonkala enrolled at Virginia Polytechnic Institute where she met fellow students Antonio Morrison and James Crawford. Brzonkala claimed that within thirty minutes of meeting the two men, they assaulted and repeatedly raped her. In the ensuing months, Morrison continued to harass Brzonkala with offensive and vulgar comments. Brzonkala became severely emotionally disturbed and depressed, then stopped attending classes, and finally withdrew from the university. Although Morrison was found guilty of sexual assault and using abusive language on two separate occasions under Virginia Tech's Assault Policy, Virginia Tech's senior vice president set aside Morrison's punishment on his appeal.

Brzonkala then sued Morrison, Crawford, and Virginia Tech under Section 13981 of the Violence Against Women Act of 1994, which states that "persons within the United States shall have the right to be free from crimes of violence motivated by gender."[24] After both the district court and the appeals court held that Congress lacked authority to enact Section 13981, Brzonkala appealed.

24. 42 U.S.C. § 13981.

*(Continued)*

(Case 2.2 *continued*)

**› ISSUE PRESENTED** Did Congress have constitutional authority to enact Section 13981 of the Violence Against Women Act of 1994, which provides a private federal civil remedy for the victims of gender-motivated violence?

**› OPINION** REHNQUIST, C.J., writing for the U.S. Supreme Court:

". . . Congress' commerce authority includes the power to regulate those activities having a substantial relation to interstate commerce. . . ."

. . .

. . . Gender-motivated crimes of violence are not, in any sense of the phrase, economic activity. While we need not adopt a categorical rule against aggregating the effects of any noneconomic activity in order to decide these cases, thus far in our Nation's history our cases have upheld Commerce Clause regulation of interstate activity only where that activity is economic in nature.

Like the Gun-Free School Zones Act at issue in *Lopez*, section 13981 contains no jurisdictional element establishing that the federal cause of action is in pursuance of Congress' power to regulate interstate commerce. Although *Lopez* makes clear that such a jurisdictional element would lend support to the argument that section 13981 is sufficiently tied to interstate commerce, Congress elected to cast section 13981's remedy over a wider, and more purely intrastate, body of violent crime.

. . .

In contrast with the lack of congressional findings that we faced in *Lopez*, section 13981 is supported by numerous findings regarding the serious impact that gender-motivated violence has on victims and their families. But the existence of congressional findings is not sufficient, by itself, to sustain the constitutionality of Commerce Clause legislation. As we stated in *Lopez*, "Simply because Congress may conclude that a particular activity substantially affects interstate commerce does not necessarily make it so." Rather, "whether particular operations affect interstate commerce sufficiently to come under the constitutional power of Congress to regulate them is ultimately a judicial rather than a legislative question, and can be settled finally only by this Court."

. . .

. . . [T]he concern that we expressed in *Lopez* that Congress might use the Commerce Clause to completely obliterate the Constitution's distribution between national and local authority seems well founded. . . . If accepted, petitioners' reasoning would allow Congress to regulate any crime as long as the nationwide, aggregated impact of that crime has substantial effects on employment, production, transit, or consumption. . . .

. . .

We accordingly reject the argument that Congress may regulate noneconomic violent criminal conduct based solely on that conduct's aggregate effect on interstate commerce.

[*Ed.:* The Court also rejected the argument that the Act should be upheld as an exercise of Congress's remedial power under Section 5 of the Fourteenth Amendment. Because the Fourteenth Amendment prohibits only state action, it cannot be the basis for a statute aimed at individuals.]

**› RESULT** Section 13981 was struck down, and the case was dismissed.

**› DISSENT** SOUTER, J., dissenting from the majority opinion:

*(Continued)*

(Case 2.2 *continued*)

Congress has the power to legislate with regard to activity that, in the aggregate, has a substantial effect on interstate commerce. The fact of such a substantial effect is not an issue for the courts in the first instance, but for the Congress, whose institutional capacity for gathering evidence and taking testimony far exceeds ours. . . .

One obvious difference from *United States v. Lopez* is the mountain of data assembled by Congress, here showing the effects of violence against women on interstate commerce. . . .

. . .

Three out of four American women will be victims of violent crimes sometime during their life. Violence is the leading cause of injuries to women ages 15 to 44. As many as 50 percent of homeless women and children are fleeing domestic violence. Since 1974, the assault rate against women has outstripped the rate for men by at least twice for some age groups and far more for others. Battering is the single largest cause of injury to women in the United States. An estimated 4 million American women are battered each year by their husbands or partners.

. . .

Arrest rates may be as low as 1 for every 100 domestic assaults. Partial estimates show that violent crime against women costs this country at least 3 billion—not million, but billion—dollars a year. Estimates suggest that we spend $5 to $10 billion a year on health care, criminal justice, and other social costs of domestic violence.

. . .

[The incidence of] rape rose four times as fast as the total national crime rate over the past 10 years. According to one study, close to half a million girls now in high school will be raped before they graduate. [One hundred twenty-five thousand] college women can expect to be raped during this—or any—year. Three-quarters of women never go to the movies alone after dark because of the fear of rape and nearly 50 percent do not use public transit alone after dark for the same reason. [Forty-one] percent of judges surveyed believed that juries give sexual assault victims less credibility than other crime victims. Less than 1 percent of all [rape] victims have collected damages. An individual who commits rape has only about 4 chances in 100 of being arrested, prosecuted, and found guilty of any offense. Almost one-quarter of convicted rapists never go to prison and another quarter received sentences in local jails where the average sentence is 11 months. Almost 50 percent of rape victims lose their jobs or are forced to quit because of the crime's severity.

. . .

Congress . . . explicitly stated the predicate for the exercise of its Commerce Clause power. Is its conclusion irrational in view of the data amassed?

. . .

Indeed, the legislative record here is far more voluminous than the record compiled by Congress and found sufficient in two prior cases upholding Title II of the Civil Rights Act of 1964 against Commerce Clause challenges [*Heart of Atlanta Motel, Inc. v. United States* and *Katzenbach v. McClung*]. . . .

. . .

. . . [G]ender-based violence in the 1990's was shown to operate in a manner similar to racial discrimination in the 1960's in reducing the mobility of employees and their production and consumption of goods shipped in interstate commerce. Like racial discrimination, gender-based violence bars its most likely targets—women—from full participation in the national economy.

In 2000, the Supreme Court also ruled that Congress could not extend a federal arson statute to the burning of a private home.[25] The statute made it a federal crime for any person to damage or destroy "by means of fire or an explosive, any . . . property used in interstate or foreign commerce or in any activity affecting interstate or foreign commerce." The government argued that the burned Indiana home was used in at least three activities affecting commerce: (1) the homeowner used the house as collateral to obtain a mortgage from an Oklahoma lender; (2) the house was used to obtain an insurance policy from a Wisconsin insurer; and (3) the house received natural gas from outside Indiana. The Court rejected this argument, finding that "hardly a building in the land would fall outside the federal statute's domain. Practically every building in our cities, towns, and rural areas is constructed with supplies that have moved in interstate commerce, served by utilities that have an interstate connection, financed or insured by enterprises that do business across state lines, or bears some other trace of interstate commerce."[26] Because the private residence was used for everyday family living, not commerce or any activity affecting commerce, the federal arson law did not apply to arson of the home. Unlike the *Morrison* decision, however, the Court did not strike down the federal arson statute because it found that Congress could legitimately regulate damage or destruction to property that was in fact used in interstate or foreign commerce or in activities affecting such commerce.

## Limits on State Powers

Federal powers enumerated in the Constitution impose many limits on state action. This chapter discusses only the limits on state power resulting from the commerce power, but the principles apply to other federal powers as well.

As mentioned earlier, when Congress has indicated a policy by acting, its action preempts state action because the Supremacy Clause makes federal laws supreme over state laws. Even when Congress has not taken action, the *"dormant"* or *"negative" Commerce Clause* may impose restrictions on state action.

### Dormant or Negative Commerce Clause

Since the mid-1930s, the U.S. Supreme Court has tried to clarify when state regulation affecting interstate commerce is valid in the absence of preempting federal regulation. The principle the Court now follows is that such state regulation will be upheld if the regulation (1) is rationally related to a legitimate state end and (2) does not create an ***undue burden*** on interstate commerce. A regulation creates an undue burden when the regulatory burden on interstate commerce outweighs the state's interest in the legislation.

The Supreme Court is hostile toward state protectionism and discrimination against out-of-state interests. However, not all state regulations found invalid under the Commerce Clause are protectionist or discriminatory. The problem lies in determining the purpose of the legislation. Protectionist regulations may be explicitly discriminatory; they may be enacted for a discriminatory purpose; or they may simply have the effect of favoring local interests at the expense of out-of-state concerns.

For example, the Supreme Court invalidated a North Carolina statute that prohibited the sale of apples that bore a grade other than the applicable U.S. grade. Washington State apples bore their own state's grade on the container, a grade that was equal to or more stringent than the U.S. grade. Although neutral on its face, the effect of the statute was to discriminate against Washington apples.[27] On the other hand, a Minnesota statute banning plastic, nonreturnable milk containers was upheld in the face of claims that it discriminated against interstate commerce.[28] The statute was not "simple protectionism"; it "regulate[d] evenhandedly" by prohibiting all milk retailers from selling their products in the plastic containers. The regulation applied regardless of whether the milk, the containers, or the sellers were from inside or outside the state.

The Supreme Court struck down a Massachusetts law that required every milk dealer who sold milk in Massachusetts to contribute to a state fund based on the volume of milk that the dealer had sold within the state, regardless of the price the dealer paid for the milk or its point of origin.[29] Massachusetts dairy farmers received a form of subsidy because they, but not the out-of-state producers, were entitled to disbursements from the fund, based on the volume of milk they produced. In part, because most of the milk sold in Massachusetts is produced by out-of-state entities, the Massachusetts law had the effect of enabling higher-cost Massachusetts dairy farmers to compete unfairly with lower-cost dairy farmers in other states. This "violates the principle of the unitary national market by handicapping out-of-state competitors, thus artificially encouraging in-state pro-

25. Jones v. United States, 529 U.S. 848 (2000).
26. *Id.* at 857.

27. Hunt v. Wash. State Apple Adver. Comm'n, 432 U.S. 333 (1977).
28. Minnesota v. Clover Leaf Creamery Co., 449 U.S. 456 (1981).
29. West Lynn Creamery Inc. v. Healy, 512 U.S. 186 (1994).

duction even when the same goods could be produced at lower cost in other States."[30]

##  Federal Fiscal Powers

Two other federal powers, the taxing and spending powers, have been invoked to regulate traditionally local "police problems" as well as purely economic problems.

The Constitution grants a broad taxing power to the federal government. The only specific limitations imposed are that (1) direct taxes on anything but income and capitation (per head) taxes must be allocated among the states in proportion to population, and (2) all custom duties and excise taxes must be uniform throughout the United States. The single prohibition is that no duty shall be levied upon exports from any state. The Fifth Amendment's Due Process Clause is also a general limitation on Congress's taxing power.

Taxes have an economic impact on business. The federal government has imposed taxes in order to affect the behavior of business as well as to raise revenues. The Supreme Court has upheld both of these types of taxes under the government's power to tax without regard to the purpose behind the tax.

Congress has the power to spend in order to provide for the common defense and general welfare. An exercise of the spending power will be upheld as long as it does not violate a specific check on the federal power.

##  Protection of Individual Liberties

The Constitution and the Bill of Rights guarantee certain individual rights, including freedom of speech, association, and religion; due process; compensation for takings; equal protection; and the right to a jury trial.

### THE CONSTITUTION

Although most explicit guarantees of individual liberty are found in the amendments to the Constitution, the original Constitution contains three specific guarantees of individual rights: the Contracts Clause, a ban on *ex post facto* laws, and a prohibition against bills of attainder.

#### *The Contracts Clause*

Article I, Section 10, of the Constitution specifically prohibits a state legislature from impairing the obligation of existing contracts. The Fifth Amendment imposes a similar bar on federal legislation that would retroactively impair the obligations of a contract. In *Calfarm Insurance Co. v. Deukmejian*,[31] insurance companies raised issues under the Contracts Clause in connection with insurance law changes mandated by California Proposition 103. Proposition 103, a voter initiative that made fundamental changes to the regulation of automobile and other types of insurance, included new restrictions on an insurance company's ability to refuse to renew an automobile insurance policy entered into prior to enactment of the new initiative. Seven insurers and the Association of California Insurance Companies sued to invalidate the initiative as an unconstitutional law impairing the obligations of contracts because the restrictions on renewal applied to policies issued before enactment of Proposition 103.

The California Supreme Court upheld the nonrenewal restrictions, finding that California could legally change the nonrenewal provisions applicable to existing auto insurance policies without violating the U.S. or state constitution. The decision rested in part on the fact that insurance is a highly regulated industry in which further regulation can reasonably be anticipated. In addition, the court found that the public interest in making insurance available to all Californians and the fear that insurance companies would refuse to renew in California, leaving drivers without the car insurance required by law, was sufficient, when measured against the relatively low degree of impairment of contract rights involved, to justify the nonrenewal. The court explained:

> Although the language of the Contracts Clause is facially absolute, its prohibition must be accommodated to the inherent police power of the State "to safeguard the vital interests of its people." This Court has long recognized that a statute does not violate the Contracts Clause simply because it has the effect of restricting, or even barring altogether, the performance of duties created by contracts entered into prior to its enactment. Thus, a state prohibition law may be applied to contracts for the sale of beer that were valid when entered into, a law barring lotteries may be applied to lottery tickets that were valid when issued, and workmen's compensation law may be applied to employers and employees operating under pre-existing contracts of employment that made no provision for work-related injuries.

#### *Ex Post Facto Laws*

Article I, Section 9, and Article I, Section 10, prohibit *ex post facto* laws. These are laws that punish actions that were not illegal when performed. *Ex post facto* laws are discussed in greater deal in Chapter 14.

30. *Id.*

31. 771 P.2d 1247 (Cal. 1989).

### *Bills of Attainder*

Article I, Section 9, prohibits the federal government from enacting laws to punish specific individuals. Such laws are termed *bills of attainder.*

## THE BILL OF RIGHTS

The first ten amendments of the Constitution constitute the Bill of Rights. The first eight amendments contain specific guarantees of individual liberties that limit the power of the federal government. Importantly, the last two make clear that the federal government's powers are limited and enumerated, whereas the rights of the people go beyond those listed in the Constitution.

The First Amendment guarantees freedom of religion, speech, press, and assembly. The Second Amendment grants persons the right to bear arms. The Third Amendment provides that no soldier shall be quartered in any house. The Fourth Amendment prohibits unreasonable searches and seizures and requires that warrants shall be issued only upon probable cause. The Fifth Amendment (1) contains the grand jury requirements; (2) forbids double jeopardy (that is, being tried twice for the same crime); (3) prohibits forcing a person to be a witness against himself or herself; (4) prohibits the deprivation of life, liberty, or property without due process of law; and (5) requires just compensation when private property is taken for public use. The Sixth Amendment guarantees a speedy and public jury trial in all criminal prosecutions. The Seventh Amendment gives the right to a jury trial in all civil (that is, noncriminal) cases when the value in dispute is greater than $20. The Eighth Amendment prohibits excessive bails or fines as well as cruel and unusual punishment. Aspects of the Fourth, Fifth, and Sixth Amendments relevant to criminal cases are discussed in Chapter 14.

### *Applicability to the States*

The Fourteenth Amendment provides that no state shall "deprive any person of life, liberty, or property, without due process of law" (the *Due Process Clause*) and that

## IN BRIEF

### Outline of the Bill of Rights

**Amendment I**
Establishment Clause
Free Exercise Clause
Freedom of speech
Freedom of press
Right to assembly and petition

**Amendment II**
Well-regulated militia and right to keep and bear arms

**Amendment III**
Restrictions on quartering soldiers

**Amendment IV**
No unreasonable search and seizure
Requirements for warrants

**Amendment V**
Presentment or indictment of a grand jury required for capital or otherwise infamous crime
Prohibition on double jeopardy
Prohibition on compulsory self-incrimination
Due process required before taking life, liberty, or property
Just compensation for taking of private property

**Amendment VI**
In criminal prosecutions:
Right to a speedy and public trial
Right to a jury trial
Right to confront witnesses
Right to counsel

**Amendment VII**
Right to a jury trial in civil cases

**Amendment VIII**
No excessive bail
No excessive fines
No cruel and unusual punishment

**Amendment IX**
Rights of the people not limited to those listed in the Constitution

**Amendment X**
Powers not delegated to the United States in the Constitution are reserved to the states or the people, except for those powers prohibited to the states by the Constitution, which are reserved to the people

"[n]o State shall make or enforce any law which shall abridge the privileges or immunities of citizens of the United States" (the *Privileges and Immunities Clause*). After the Fourteenth Amendment was passed, it was argued that the Due Process Clause and the Privileges and Immunities Clause made the entire Bill of Rights applicable to state governments.

The Supreme Court has rejected this theory. It has held that the provisions of the Bill of Rights are incorporated (selectively) into the Fourteenth Amendment only if they are fundamental to the American system of law or are safeguards "essential to liberty in the American scheme of justice."[32]

Many provisions of the Bill of Rights have been held to limit the actions of state governments as well as the federal government. For example, if a state government were to abridge the freedom of speech, it would violate the First Amendment as applied to state governments through the Fourteenth Amendment.

The provisions that have been held not to apply to the states are the Second Amendment right to bear arms, the Fifth Amendment requirement of a grand jury indictment before any criminal prosecution, and the Seventh Amendment guarantee of a jury trial in civil cases.

Although the Eighth Amendment prohibition against the imposition of excessive bail has not been explicitly applied to the states, the Supreme Court has assumed that it applied in a number of state cases. The Fifth Amendment's prohibition against the taking of property without just compensation has not been incorporated into the Fourteenth Amendment, but the due process guarantee in the Fourteenth Amendment has been interpreted to provide the same protection.

The Supreme Court has not yet determined whether the Third Amendment, which prohibits the quartering of soldiers in private houses, and the excessive-fine provision of the Eighth Amendment are applicable to state governments.

Article IV, Section 2, of the Constitution and Section 1 of the Fourteenth Amendment both guarantee the privileges and immunities of citizens of the United States, that is, the rights that go with being a citizen of the federal government, such as the right to vote in a federal election and the right to travel. Article IV provides that citizens of each state shall receive all the privileges and immunities of citizens of other states. These provisions prohibit any unreasonable discrimination between the citizens of different states. Any such discrimination must reasonably relate to legitimate state or local purposes.

32. Duncan v. Louisiana, 391 U.S. 145 (1968).

## Freedom of Speech and Press

The First Amendment states that "Congress shall make no law . . . abridging the freedom of speech, or of the press." However, the U.S. Supreme Court has not applied the First Amendment to protect all speech to the same degree. The type of speech most clearly protected is political speech, including speech critical of governmental policies and officials. Some types of expression—bribery, perjury, and obscenity—are not protected by the First Amendment at all.

A government may violate the right to free speech not only by forbidding speech but by commanding it as well. For example, the U.S. Supreme Court ruled that Massachusetts had violated the First Amendment when it ordered organizers of South Boston's St. Patrick's Day Parade to include a group of gay and lesbian Bostonians of Irish ancestry.[33] Such compulsory inclusion of a group imparting a message the organizers did not wish to convey was forbidden by the Free Speech Clause.

Determining whether a type of speech is protected by the First Amendment is only the first step of the analysis. If it is determined that a certain expression is protected, it must then be determined to what extent the expression may be regulated without violating the First Amendment.

### "Clear and Present Danger" Test

Throughout most of the nineteenth and early twentieth centuries, Congress followed the mandate of the First Amendment literally and made "no law" restricting freedom of speech, assembly, or the press. In response to vocal resistance to World War I, Congress passed the Espionage Act of 1917 and the Sedition Act of 1918. Charles Schenck, a dissident, was convicted under the Espionage Act for circulating to men who had been called and accepted for military service a document that stated that the draft violated the Thirteenth Amendment, which prohibits slavery or involuntary servitude. In 1919, the Supreme Court, in an opinion by Justice Oliver Wendell Holmes, first articulated the *"clear and present danger" test* and affirmed Schenck's conviction.[34]

The Supreme Court explained that many things that might be said in peacetime cannot be allowed in time of war:

> [T]he character of every act depends upon the circumstances in which it is done. The most stringent protection of

33. Hurley v. Irish-American Gay, Lesbian & Bisexual Group of Boston, 515 U.S. 557 (1995).
34. Schenck v. United States, 249 U.S. 47 (1919).

free speech would not protect a man in falsely shouting fire in a theatre and causing a panic. [The] question in every case is whether the words used are used in such circumstances and are of such a nature as to create a *clear and present danger* that they will bring about the substantive evils that Congress has a right to prevent. (Emphasis added.)

Later, during the height of the Cold War, the clear and present danger doctrine was applied in a manner restricting First Amendment freedoms even more severely. But, in the 1960s, the test became stricter and more protective of free speech. In *Brandenburg v. Ohio,* the Supreme Court held that "the constitutional guarantees of free speech and free press do not permit a State to forbid or proscribe advocacy of the use of force or of law violation except where such advocacy is directed to inciting or producing imminent lawless action and is likely to incite or produce such action." [35]

In 1997, the U.S. Court of Appeals for the Fourth Circuit ruled that the First Amendment did not bar a wrongful-death action against the publisher of *Hit Man: A Technical Manual for Independent Contractors,* a 130-page manual of detailed factual instructions on how to become a professional killer.[36] A convicted murderer had used the book to commit a triple homicide. The publisher stipulated that it had targeted the market of murderers, would-be murderers, and other criminals and that it knew and intended that criminals would immediately use the book to solicit, plan, and commit murder. The court rejected the publisher's claim that this was abstract advocacy protected under *Brandenburg v. Ohio,* stating: "[T]his book constitutes the archetypal example of speech which, because it methodically and comprehensively prepares and steels its audience to specific criminal conduct through exhaustively detailed instructions on the planning, commission, and concealment of criminal conduct, finds no preserve in the First Amendment."

## Defamation of Public Figures by Media

Defamatory words—words that harm a person's reputation—are protected by the First Amendment, even when they are false, if they are made by a media defendant (such as a newspaper or television network) about a public figure without knowledge they were false, that is, without actual malice. Defamation is discussed further in Chapter 9.

35. 395 U.S. 444 (1969).
36. Rice v. Paladin Enter., Inc., 128 F.3d 233 (4th Cir. 1997), *cert. denied,* 523 U.S. 1074 (1998).

## Obscenity

Obscene material does not enjoy any protection under the First Amendment. Material is obscene if it (1) appeals to a prurient or sordid and perverted interest in sex; (2) has no serious literary, artistic, political, or scientific merit; and (3) is on the whole offensive to the average person in the community.[37] Applying this test, the U.S. Court of Appeals for the Second Circuit held that the label for Bad Frog Beer, which depicts a frog with its middle finger raised, was perhaps in bad taste, but not obscene.[38]

## Academic Research

The First Amendment also protects academic research. During the U.S. government's antitrust suit against Microsoft Corporation (the "Inside Story" in Chapter 16), Microsoft sought to compel two university professors to produce notes and tape recordings of the interviews they conducted with Netscape Communications employees while researching their book *Competing on Internet Time: Lessons from Netscape and the Battle with Microsoft.* The First Circuit denied access, reasoning that the academics, in gathering and disseminating information, were acting almost as journalists. Compelling disclosure of their research materials would "infrigidate the free flow of information to the public, thus denigrating a fundamental First Amendment value."[39] In addition, the court noted that the Netscape nondisclosure agreements signed by the authors made the information confidential and not discoverable.

## Commercial Speech

Unlike political speech, commercial speech, especially advertising, has always been subject to substantial regulation. The government cannot suppress commercial speech, but it can make reasonable regulations regarding the time, place, and manner of such speech.

To determine whether content-based regulation of commercial speech violates the First Amendment, the Supreme Court has formulated an intermediate scrutiny test. For commercial speech to come within this provision, it must concern lawful activity and not be misleading.

37. Miller v. California, 413 U.S. 15, 24 (1973).
38. Bad Frog Brewery v. New York State Liquor Auth., 134 F.3d 87 (2d Cir. 1998). The Bad Frog label can be seen at http://www.badfrog.com/about.html (last visited Feb. 11, 2004).
39. Cusamano v. Microsoft Corp., 162 F.3d 708, 717 (1st Cir. 1998).

## View from Cyberspace

### Pornography and Free Speech on the Internet

Since 1995 Congress has struggled with how to regulate pornography on the Internet. Most attempts to date have not withstood judicial scrutiny. In 1995, Congress enacted the Communications Decency Act (CDA) to protect children from sexually explicit materials in cyberspace.[a] The CDA required that material considered "indecent"—including pornography—be outlawed in public forums accessible by children, most notably the Internet. In 1997, however, the U.S. Supreme Court held that the CDA's "indecent transmission" and "patently offensive display" provisions violated the First Amendment.[b] The Court rejected the government's analogy to broadcast media, which have traditionally enjoyed less First Amendment protection, noting that unlike other media, the Internet does not have an extensive history of government regulation, is not a scarce resource in need of monitored allocation, and is not intrusive into individuals' homes. Instead, the Court viewed the Internet as analogous to a public square, a place where speech is given heightened protection. Although it struck down much of the CDA, the Court left in place its prohibition of online transmission of obscene speech.

In 1996, Congress enacted the Child Pornography Prevention Act (CPPA), which criminalized the transmission of "child pornography," defined as any image that "appears to be" or "conveys the impression" of a minor engaging in sex, including computer-generated images or "virtual" child pornography.[c]

In *Ashcroft v. Free Speech Coalition,* the U.S. Supreme Court found that two provisions of the CPPA were overly broad and violated the First Amendment: the provision that prohibited various depictions of child pornography, including computer-generated or "virtual" child pornography that "appears to be of a minor engaging in sexually explicit conduct," and the provision that prohibited depictions promoted or distributed "in such a manner that conveys the impression" that they depict minors.[d] The Court noted that the CPPA prohibited "speech that records no crime and no victims by its production," whether or not the speech was "patently offensive." Expressing concern that certain popular works of artistic and literary value, such as *Traffic* and *American Beauty,* in which adult actors represent minors engaged in sexual conduct, might be deemed child pornography under the CPPA, the Court concluded that when images do not involve real children, the First Amendment protects speech unless it is obscene or the product of sexual abuse.

Almost immediately, a new bill (the Child Obscenity and Pornography Prevention Act) was introduced in Congress in an attempt to circumvent the Supreme Court's decision in *Ashcroft v. Free Speech Coalition.* A modified version of this bill was included in the Prosecutorial Remedies and Tools Against the Exploitation of Children Today Act (PROTECT), which was enacted in 2003.[e] Among many other provisions, PROTECT outlaws digitally "morphed" images made to appear as if children are having sex or being used in pornographic images. Morphed child porn is illegal if prosecutors can prove beyond a reasonable doubt that the maker intended others to believe that the images depicted actual children. PROTECT also requires pornographers to show that children were not involved in their products.

In 1998, Congress passed the Child Online Protection Act (COPA).[f] To address the concerns raised by the Supreme Court when it invalidated the CDA, COPA's scope was restricted to material on the Web rather than the Internet as a whole; it targeted only Web communications for "commercial purposes"; and limited its scope to material "deemed harmful to minors." Under COPA, courts are instructed to consider contemporary community standards in determining whether material is "harmful to minors."

In a case challenging COPA, the U.S. Court of Appeals for the Third Circuit found that COPA's reliance on "contemporary community standards" to identify material that was harmful to minors was overbroad and would probably lead to a finding that COPA was unconstitutional.[g] The court argued that due to the "geography-free" nature of the Internet, a community standards test would require every Web communication to comply with the most restrictive community's standards. The Supreme Court vacated the Third Circuit's decision, finding that "COPA's reliance on 'community standards' to identify what material 'is harmful to minors' does not by

a. Pub. L. No. 104–104, 110 Stat. 133 (1996).
b. Reno v. American Civil Liberties Union, 521 U.S. 844 (1997).
c. Pub. L. No. 104–208, 110 Stat. 3009-26 (1996).
d. 535 U.S. 234 (2002).
e. Pub. L. No. 108–21, 117 Stat. 650 (2003).
f. Pub. L. No. 105–277, 112 Stat. 2681-736 (1998).
g. American Civil Liberties Union v. Reno, 217 F.3d 162 (3d Cir. 2000). The Third Circuit affirmed a preliminary injunction issued by the district court to prevent enforcement of COPA. To receive a preliminary injunction, a plaintiff must show a "substantial likelihood" of prevailing on the merits of the case.

(Continued)

(View from Cyberspace *continued*)

itself render the statute substantially overbroad for First Amendment purposes," but a majority of the Court could not agree on how to measure "community standards" for the Internet.[h] The Court also did not "express any view as to whether . . . the statute is unconstitutionally vague, or whether the District Court correctly concluded that the statute likely will not survive strict scrutiny analysis once adjudication of the case is completed below."

On remand, the Third Circuit once again held that COPA was likely unconstitutional.[i] The court held that the plaintiffs had established a substantial likelihood of prevailing on two claims: (1) the statute fails the strict scrutiny test because it was not narrowly tailored (and the least restrictive means) to serve a necessary state interest, and (2) the statute is unconstitutionally overbroad. In October 2003, the Supreme Court granted certiorari in the case for yet another time,[j] and in June 2004 the Court sent the case back to the trial court, stating that the government would have to show why the voluntary use of filters would not work as well as the law's criminal penalties. Although the opinion strongly suggested that the government would not be able to meet this burden, Justice Anthony Kennedy left open the possibility that COPA might ultimately be upheld: "This opinion does not hold that Congress is incapable of enacting any regulation of the Internet designed to prevent minors from gaining access to harmful materials."[k]

In 2000, Congress passed the Children's Internet Protection Act (CIPA), which requires public schools and libraries to install Internet filters on their computers so that children cannot view depictions that are harmful, obscene, or child pornography.[l] In 2003, for the first time, the Supreme Court upheld a congressional attempt to regulate Internet pornography when it upheld CIPA in a six-to-three decision.[m]

**h.** Ashcroft v. American Civil Liberties Union, 535 U.S. 564 (3d Cir. 2002).
**i.** American Civil Liberties Union v. Ashcroft, 322 F.3d 240 (2003).
**j.** Ashcroft v. American Civil Liberties Union, 540 U.S. 944 (2003) (mem).
**k.** Ashcroft v. American Civil Liberties Union, 124 S. Ct. 2783, 2795 (2004).
**l.** Pub. L. No. 106–554, 114 Stat. 2763 (2000).
**m.** United States. v. American Library Ass'n, Inc., 539 U.S. 194 (2003).

Next, the Court asks whether the asserted governmental interest is substantial. If the answer to both questions is yes, the Court determines whether the regulation directly advances the governmental interest asserted and whether it is no more extensive than is necessary to serve that interest.[40] Determining whether the regulation is no more extensive than necessary only requires a "reasonable fit" between the government's purpose and the means chosen to achieve it. It does not require that the government adopt the least restrictive means.[41] The Supreme Court treats actually or inherently misleading commercial speech the same as false commercial speech, which the state may prohibit entirely.[42]

In the following case, the California Supreme Court considered how to distinguish commercial speech from protected noncommercial speech.

40. Central Hudson Gas & Elec. v. Public Serv. Comm'n, 447 U.S. 557 (1980).
41. Board of Trustees, State Univ. of N.Y. v. Fox, 492 U.S. 469 (1989).
42. *In re* R.M.J., 455 U.S. 191 (1982).

A CASE IN POINT

**CASE 2.3**

**Kasky v. Nike, Inc.**

*California Supreme Court 45 P.3d 243 (Cal. 2002), cert. granted, 537 U.S. 1099 (2003), cert. dismissed as improvidently granted, 539 U.S. 654 (2003).*

## Summary

**› FACTS** Nike, Inc. manufactures and sells athletic shoes and apparel. Most of its products are manufactured by subcontractors in China, Vietnam, and Indonesia by female workers under the age of twenty-four. Commencing in March 1993, Nike assumed responsibility for its subcontractors' compliance with applicable local laws and regulations regarding minimum wages, overtime, safety and health, and environmental protection.

In 1996, the television news program *48 Hours* reported that Nike products were made in factories where workers were paid less than the applicable minimum wage; were required to work overtime and encouraged to work more than the legal overtime

*(Continued)*

(Case 2.3 *continued*)

limits; were subjected to physical, verbal, and sexual abuse; and were exposed to toxic chemicals, noise, heat, and dust in violation of applicable occupational health and safety laws. These allegations were repeated in articles published in a variety of media.

In response to this adverse publicity, Nike made statements to the public in press releases, letters to newspapers, letters to university presidents and athletic directors, and other documents (including full-page advertisements in leading newspapers) that the allegations were false and misleading. Nike stated that its workers were paid in accordance with local minimum-wage and overtime laws, that they received free meals and medical care, and that their working conditions complied with safety and health rules.

Plaintiff Marc Kasky sued Nike on behalf of the general public under California Business and Professions Code Sections 17204 and 17535, claiming that Nike's statements were false and misleading and were made "with knowledge or reckless disregard of the laws of California prohibiting false and misleading statements." Nike moved to dismiss the complaint on grounds, among others, that the relief the plaintiff sought was barred by the First Amendment to the U.S. Constitution. The trial court found that Nike's allegedly false and misleading statements constituted noncommercial speech entitled to full First Amendment protection and granted Nike's motion to dismiss without leave to amend. The California Court of Appeal affirmed the trial court's judgment, and the California Supreme Court granted the plaintiff's petition for review.

**› ISSUE** Can a corporation participating in a public debate be subjected to liability for factual inaccuracies on the theory that its statements are "commercial speech"?

**› SUMMARY OF OPINION** The California Supreme Court noted that the U.S. Supreme Court has not adopted an all-purpose test to distinguish commercial from noncommercial speech under the First Amendment. However, it found that a close reading of the Supreme Court's decisions suggests that "when a court must decide whether particular speech may be subjected to laws aimed at preventing false advertising or other forms of commercial deception, categorizing a particular statement as commercial or noncommercial speech requires consideration of three elements." The three elements a court must consider are the speaker, the intended audience, and the message's content.

Applying this limited purpose test, the California Supreme Court found that the first element—a commercial speaker—was satisfied because Nike was engaged in commerce. The second element—an intended commercial audience—was also satisfied because Nike's various communications were directed to actual and potential purchasers of Nike's products. The court also found that the third element—representations of fact of a commercial nature—was also present even though Nike argued that its allegedly false and misleading statements were not commercial speech because they were part of "an international media debate on issues of intense public interest." The court stated:

> Here, Nike's speech is not removed from the category of commercial speech because it is intermingled with noncommercial speech. To the extent Nike's press releases and letters discuss policy questions such as the degree to which domestic companies should be responsible for working conditions in factories located in other countries, or what standards domestic companies ought to observe in such factories, or the merits and effects of economic "globalization" generally, Nike's statements are noncommercial speech. Any content-based regulation of these noncommercial messages would be subject to the strict scrutiny test for fully protected speech. But Nike may not "immunize false or misleading product information

*(Continued)*

(Case 2.3 *continued*)

> from government regulation simply by including references to public issues." Here, the alleged false and misleading statements all relate to the commercial portions of the speech in question—the description of actual conditions and practices in factories that produce Nike's products—and thus the proposed regulations reach only that commercial portion.

The court also rejected Nike's argument that regulating its speech would restrict or disfavor its point of view and not the point of view of its critics. The court stated that differential treatment of speech about products and services based on the identity of the speaker is inherent in the commercial speech doctrine because a noncommercial speaker's statements about a product are protected while a commercial speaker's statements may be prohibited entirely to the extent they are either false or actually or inherently misleading.

**› RESULT** The California Supreme Court reversed the judgment of the California Court of Appeal and remanded the matter to it for further proceedings consistent with this opinion. In September 2003, the parties settled the case. Without admitting fault or liability, Nike agreed to make a $1.5 million donation to the Fair Labor Association's program operations and worker development programs and to maintain minimum funding of its footwear factory after-hours worker education programs for two years.

---

## *Liquor and Cigarette Advertising*

In 1995, Coors Brewing Company successfully challenged a provision of the 1935 Federal Alcohol Administration Act that prohibited statements of alcohol content on malt beverage labels unless state law required disclosure.[43] The government's asserted goal of preventing competition based on high alcoholic strength was legitimate, but the Supreme Court found no evidence that the labeling restriction served the goal.

In 1996, the Court struck down a forty-year-old Rhode Island statute that prohibited the advertisement of liquor prices except at the point of sale.[44] Rhode Island asserted its interest in promoting temperance and argued that the law prevented retailers from competing on price and thereby encouraging alcohol consumption. The Court accepted that interest as legitimate but found the statute too restrictive to meet Free Speech Clause standards. Although commercial speech generally receives less protection than political speech under the First Amendment, the Court recognized a limit to that diminished standard: "[W]hen a State entirely prohibits the dissemination of truthful, nonmisleading commercial messages for reasons unrelated to the preservation of a fair bargaining process, there is far less reason to depart from the rigorous review that the First Amendment generally demands."

43. Rubin v. Coors Brewing Co., 514 U.S. 476 (1995).
44. Liquormart, Inc. v. Rhode Island, 517 U.S. 484 (1996).

## *Nonspeech Business*

The First Amendment also protects seemingly nonspeech business. The U.S. Court of Appeals for the Ninth Circuit affirmed a lower court's decision enjoining California's Santa Clara County from enforcing its ban on gun sales at the county's fairgrounds.[45] The county argued that rather than regulating speech, the ban regulated the unprotected conduct of selling guns. The trial court had found that "some type of speech is necessarily involved in the sale of any gun,"[46] and the appeals court ruled that the offer to buy constituted commercial speech. Although the county asserted an interest in curtailing gun possession, the court ruled that the ban did not directly advance that interest.

## *Encryption*

In *Junger v. Daley,* a professor challenged the Export Administration Regulations insofar as they attempted to restrict him from posting on his website the human readable source code of an encryption software program that he had written to demonstrate how computers work. The professor claimed that the regulations were vague, overly broad, and an impermissible prior restraint in violation of the First and Fifth Amendments to the Constitution. In 2000, the U.S. Court of Appeals for the Sixth Circuit

45. Nordyke v. Santa Clara County, Cal., 110 F.3d 707 (9th Cir. 1997).
46. Nordyke v. Santa Clara County, Cal., 933 F. Supp. 903 (N.D. Cal. 1996).

ruled that the source code was entitled to the First Amendment protection.[47] The court reasoned: "Because computer source code is an expressive means for the exchange of information and ideas about computer programming, we hold that it is protected by the First Amendment." As such, the appeals court determined that the regulations should be subjected to intermediate scrutiny, or the *substantially related test,* which requires the government to prove that regulations further a governmental interest that is "important" or "substantial" and that they prevent real, not conjectural, harm "in a direct and material way." The court noted that subsequent to the district court's decision upholding the Export Administration Regulations and oral arguments before the court on appeal, the Bureau of Export Control had issued an interim final rule amending the regulations to allow most encryption software to be exported without a license to nongovernmental entities. Having concluded that the First Amendment protects computer source code, the court returned the case to the district court for further consideration of the professor's constitutional claims in light of the amended regulations.

47. Junger v. Daley, 209 F.3d 481 (6th Cir. 2000).

## INTERNATIONAL SNAPSHOT

The legal limits of free speech are different in the United States and Europe. Racist speech is the most controversial example of these differences. In the United States, racist speech is regarded as a variety of political opinion and is protected by the Constitution's First Amendment. The European approach, set forth in Article 10 of the Convention for the Protection of Human Rights and Fundamental Freedoms, imposes restrictions and penalties on racist speech. Conflicts have arisen as the United States and Europe have attempted to apply their own free speech standards to Internet communications.[a]

In May 2000, a French court ordered Yahoo! to prevent Internet users in France from accessing auction sites with Nazi paraphernalia.[b] A French law prohibits the sale or display of symbols that incite racism. In response to Yahoo!'s arguments that it was technologically impossible to block French users from the auction sites, the judge ordered three technology experts—one American, one French, and one other European—to study the issue and present their findings to the court. Based on their report indicating that Yahoo! could achieve a significant filtering success rate, the court gave Yahoo! three months to find a way to prevent users based in France from accessing pages on Yahoo! that featured Nazi-related objects.

Under pressure from U.S. organizations, Yahoo! banned hate-related goods from its auction site and removed numerous pro-Nazi Web pages from Geocities, although it said that these actions had nothing to do with the French judge's decision. At the same time, Yahoo! filed a suit in a federal district court in California, asking that the French decision be declared void on the ground that it violates the First Amendment. In November 2001, the district court voided the French court's decision.[c] The U.S. Court of Appeals for the Ninth Circuit reversed this decision, however, finding that it had no personal jurisdiction over the French plaintiffs.[d]

Attempts to establish international standards for the Internet have made some progress. In November 2002, the Council of Europe approved an Additional Protocol to the Cybercrime Convention that would make it illegal to distribute or publish anything online that "advocates, promotes or incites hatred [or] discrimination." Although the United States is a signatory to the Cybercrime Convention, which is designed to encourage other countries to enact computer crime and intellectual property laws, it has stated that it will not support the addition to the Convention. "The important thing to realize is that the U.S. can't be a party to any convention that abridges a constitutional protection," said Drew Wade, a spokesman for the U.S. Justice Department.[e]

**a.** Benoît Frydman & Isabelle Rorive, *Regulating Internet Content through Intermediaries in Europe and the USA,* 23 Zeitschrift fur Rechtssoziologie 41 (2002), *available at* http://www.philodroit.be/uploaded/regulating%20internet%20through%20intermediaries.pdf (last visited Feb. 20, 2004).
**b.** Kevin J. Delany, *Law & Technology: Ruling in France Could Be Landmark of Internet Law—Yahoo Tests Boundaries of Cyberspace Regulations,* WALL ST. J., Aug. 11, 2000, at 21.
**c.** Yahoo, Inc. v. La Ligue Contre Le Racisme et L'Antisemitisme, 145 F. Supp. 2d 1168 (N.D. Cal. 2001). Under the principle of comity, courts will respect and enforce judgments of foreign tribunals. However, Judge Jeremy Fogel noted that the principle of comity is not without exceptions. Generally, U.S. courts will not enforce foreign judgments that are inconsistent with fundamental U.S. public policies. Here, the French court decision ran counter to the First Amendment's free speech protections.
**d.** Yahoo! Inc. v. La Ligue Contre Le Racisme et L'Antisemitisme 379 F.3d 1120 (9th Cir. 2004).
**e.** Declan McCullagh, *U.S. Won't Support Net "Hate Speech" Ban,* CNET NEWS.COM, Nov. 15, 2002, *at* http://news.com.com/2100-1023-965983.html (last visited Feb. 23, 2004).

### *English-Only Laws*

Freedom of speech issues also arise in connection with "English-only" laws, requiring that all government business be conducted in English. This is discussed in Chapter 14.

## PRIOR RESTRAINTS

*Prior restraints* of speech, such as prohibiting in advance a demonstration in a public area, are considered a more drastic infringement on free speech than permitting the speech to occur but punishing it afterwards. Restrictions concerning the time, place, and manner of speech are usually acceptable under the First Amendment, but regulations that restrict speech in traditional public forums are scrutinized closely.

In 1986, the city of Dallas adopted an ordinance regulating "sexually oriented businesses," defined as any "adult arcade, adult bookstore or adult video store, adult cabaret, adult motel, adult motion picture theater, adult theater, escort agency, nude model studio, or sexual encounter center." The ordinance regulated such businesses through zoning, licensing, and inspections. The ordinance also banned motels that rented rooms for fewer than ten hours. The Supreme Court struck down all of the ordinance, except the ban on ten-hour motels, as a prior restraint on speech that did not comply with the procedural safeguards for that type of regulation. The Supreme Court upheld the provision prohibiting motels from renting rooms for less than ten hours. (Such rooms are often used for prostitution.) Dismissing the argument that the ordinance unconstitutionally interfered with the right of association, Justice Sandra Day O'Connor stated: "Any 'personal bonds' that are formed from the use of a motel room for less than 10 hours are not those that have 'played a critical role in the culture and traditions of the nation by cultivating and transmitting shared ideals and beliefs.'"[48] Similarly, in 2000, the Supreme Court upheld a ban on nude dancing.[49]

Prior restraints can be particularly problematic for members of the media, who may need to publish immediately or not at all. For example, during a suit by Procter & Gamble against Bankers Trust for negligent sale of financial derivative products, *BusinessWeek* obtained confidential documents about both parties that had emerged from their court-approved secret discovery process. The trial court granted the litigants' request for a temporary restraining order (TRO) to immediately keep *BusinessWeek* from publishing the information and later enjoined the magazine from ever publishing it. The U.S. Court of Appeals for the Sixth Circuit struck down the injunction as a violation of the First Amendment.[50] Noting that "[a] prior restraint comes to a court 'with a heavy presumption against its constitutional validity,'" the appeals court found the trial court's grounds for granting the TRO insufficient to meet the high standard required for prior restraint.

48. FW/PBS, Inc. v. City of Dallas, 493 U.S. 215 (1990).
49. City of Erie v. Pap's A.M., 529 U.S. 277 (2000).

# Right of Association

Closely related to the right to free speech and freedom of the press is the constitutional right of association. As with protection of free speech, this right is most protected when an association is formed for political ends. In 2000, the Supreme Court struck down California's law requiring political parties to hold open primaries that allowed any registered voter to vote to select that party's candidate for elected office.[51] The Court reasoned:

> Proposition 198 forces petitioners to adulterate their candidate-selection process—the "basic function of a political party"—by opening it up to persons wholly unaffiliated with the party. Such forced association has the likely outcome—indeed, in this case the intended outcome—of changing the parties' message. We can think of no heavier burden on a political party's associational freedom.

Similar issues arise when city or state governments enact laws banning discriminatory clubs. The courts will balance the First Amendment rights of association and free speech against the government's social policy against discrimination. To increase the likelihood that such laws will be upheld, most antidiscrimination statutes apply only to clubs of a certain size where business is conducted.

In *Warfield v. Peninsula Golf Country Club*,[52] the California Supreme Court held that a private country club that allowed nonmembers, for a fee, to use its golf course, tennis courts, or dining areas was a "business establishment" and therefore subject to the state law prohibiting discrimination against women and minorities. It will generally be assumed that business is conducted in a private club if the member's employer pays for club dues, meals, or drinks or if it is the site of company-sponsored events.

In the following case, the Supreme Court considered whether a New Jersey ban on discrimination based on sexual orientation could be constitutionally applied to the Boy Scouts.

50. Procter & Gamble v. Bankers Trust, 78 F.3d 219 (6th Cir. 1996).
51. California Democratic Party v. Jones, 530 U.S. 567 (2000).
52. 896 P.2d 776 (Cal. 1995).

A CASE IN POINT

**CASE 2.4**

**Boy Scouts of America v. Dale**

*Supreme Court of the United States 530 U.S. (2000).*

## In the Language of the Court

› **FACTS** The Boy Scouts of America is a private, nonprofit organization engaged in instilling values in young people. James Dale became a Boy Scout when he was eight years old and remained a Scout until he turned eighteen in 1989. He was an exemplary Scout and achieved the rank of Eagle Scout, one of the organization's highest honors. In 1989, Dale was approved for adult membership with the position of assistant scoutmaster.

Around that time, he left home to attend Rutgers University and acknowledged to himself and others that he was gay. After he was interviewed about the psychological and health needs of gay and lesbian teenagers and his picture appeared in the paper, Dale received a letter from the Boy Scouts revoking his adult membership because the group forbids membership to homosexuals.

Dale filed a complaint against the Boy Scouts in New Jersey Superior Court, alleging that the Boy Scouts had violated New Jersey's public accommodations statute, which prohibits discrimination on the basis of sexual orientation in places of public accommodation. After the New Jersey Supreme Court ruled that the public accommodations statute applied to the Boy Scouts and that the First Amendment did not provide protection, the Boy Scouts appealed.

› **ISSUE PRESENTED** Does application of New Jersey's public accommodations law prohibiting discrimination on the basis of sexual orientation violate the Boy Scouts' First Amendment right of association?

› **OPINION** REHNQUIST, C.J., writing for the U.S. Supreme Court:

"[I]mplicit in the right to engage in activities protected by the First Amendment" is "a corresponding right to association with others in pursuit of a wide variety of political, social, economic, educational, religious, and cultural ends." This right is crucial in preventing the majority from imposing its views on groups that would rather express other, perhaps unpopular, ideas.

. . .

The forced inclusion of an unwanted person in a group infringes the group's freedom of expressive association if the presence of that person affects in a significant way the group's ability to advocate public or private viewpoints. But the freedom of expressive association, like many freedoms, is not absolute. We have held that the freedom could be overridden "by regulations adopted to serve compelling state interests, unrelated to the suppression of ideas, that cannot be achieved through means significantly less restrictive of associational freedoms."

. . .

[T]he general mission of the Boy Scouts is clear: "To instill values in young people." The Boy Scouts seeks to instill these values by having its adult leaders spend time with the youth members, instructing and engaging them in activities like camping, archery, and fishing. During the time spent with the youth members, the scoutmasters and assistant scoutmasters inculcate them with the Boy Scouts' values—both expressly and by example. It seems indisputable that an association that seeks to transmit such a system of values engages in expressive activity.

. . .

The Boy Scouts asserts that it "teaches that homosexual conduct is not morally straight," and that it does "not want to promote homosexual conduct as a legitimate form of behavior." We accept the Boy Scouts' assertion. We need not inquire further to determine the nature of the Boy Scouts' expression with respect to homosexuality.

*(Continued)*

(Case 2.4 *continued*)

. . .

We must then determine whether Dale's presence as an assistant scoutmaster would significantly burden the Boy Scouts' desire to not "promote homosexual conduct as a legitimate form of behavior." As we give deference to an association's assertion regarding the nature of its expression, we must also give deference to an association's view of what would impair its expression. That is not to say that an expressive association can erect a shield against antidiscrimination laws simply by asserting that mere acceptance of a member from a particular group would impair its message. But here Dale, by his own admission, is one of a group of gay Scouts who have "become leaders in their community and are open and honest about their sexual orientation."

. . .

Having determined that the Boy Scouts is an expressive association and that the forced inclusion of Dale would significantly affect its expression, we inquire whether the application of New Jersey's public accommodations law to require that the Boy Scouts accept Dale as an assistant scoutmaster runs afoul of the Scouts' freedom of expressive association. We conclude that it does.

. . .

We have already concluded that a state requirement that the Boy Scouts retain Dale as an assistant scoutmaster would significantly burden the organization's right to oppose or disfavor homosexual conduct. The state interests embodied in New Jersey's public accommodations law do not justify such a severe intrusion on the Boy Scouts' rights to freedom of expressive association.

**› RESULT** The Supreme Court reversed the New Jersey Supreme Court. The Boy Scouts were not required to admit homosexuals as members or scoutmasters.

**› DISSENT** STEVENS, J., dissenting from the majority opinion:

Unfavorable opinions about homosexuals "have ancient roots." Like equally atavistic opinions about certain racial groups, those roots have been nourished by sectarian doctrine. Over the years, however, interaction with real people, rather than mere adherence to traditional ways of thinking about members of unfamiliar classes, have modified those opinions. A few examples: The American Psychiatric Association's and the American Psychological Association's removal of "homosexuality" from their lists of mental disorders; a move toward greater understanding within some religious communities; . . . and New Jersey's enactment of the provision at issue in this case. Indeed, the past month alone has witnessed some remarkable changes in attitudes about homosexuals [with observance of Gay Pride Day by sixty CIA workers, car manufacturers' extension of benefits to gay couples, and the acceptance of gay couples as role models at Exeter].

That such prejudices are still prevalent and that they have caused serious and tangible harm to countless members of the class New Jersey seeks to protect are established matters of fact neither the Boy Scouts nor the Court disputes. That harm can only be aggravated by the creation of a constitutional shield for a policy that is itself the product of a habitual way of thinking about strangers. As Justice Brandeis has wisely advised, "we must be ever on our guard, lest we erect our prejudices into legal principles."

If we would guide by the light of reason, we must let our minds be bold. I respectfully dissent. [*Ed.*: Consider also Case 3.4.]

## Freedom of Religion

Two clauses of the First Amendment deal with religion. The *Establishment Clause* prohibits the establishment of a religion by the federal government. The same ban applies to state government through the Due Process Clause of the Fourteenth Amendment. The *Free Exercise Clause* prohibits certain, but not all, restrictions on the practice of religion.

The Establishment Clause requires that the government remain neutral in matters of religion. The U.S. Supreme Court has prohibited teacher- or student-led prayer (including benedictions at football games and graduations) in public schools,[53] although it has permitted the federal government to provide secular books and other teaching materials and supplies to parochial schools on the same basis that they are given to public schools.[54] In 2002, the Supreme Court held that an Ohio school voucher program that allows parents to use public money to pay for tuitions at private schools, including religious schools, does not violate the Establishment Clause.[55] As Chief Justice William Rehnquist explained, "[t]hat the program was one of true private choice, with no evidence that the State deliberately skewed incentives toward religious schools, was sufficient for the program to survive scrutiny under the Establishment Clause."

In *Jimmy Swaggart Ministries v. Board of Equalization*,[56] the Supreme Court held that the imposition of general taxes on the sale of religious materials does not contravene the Free Exercise Clause of the First Amendment. The tax was only a small fraction of any sale, and it applied neutrally to all relevant sales regardless of the nature of the seller or purchaser. The Court also held that the tax did not violate the Establishment Clause. There was little evidence of administrative entanglement between religion and the government; the government was not involved in the organization's day-to-day activities. The imposition of the tax did not require the state to inquire into the religious content of the items sold or the religious motivation behind selling or purchasing them.

In *Employment Division, Oregon Department of Human Resources v. Smith*,[57] the Supreme Court upheld an Oregon statute that made criminal the use of peyote, an hallucinogenic drug, even though peyote is used in Native American religious ceremonies. In deciding *Smith*, the Court overturned precedent that required courts hearing Free Exercise Clause challenges to apply the stricter compelling-state-interest test. Instead, the Court ruled that generally applicable laws that burden but do not target religion need not be justified by a compelling state interest to pass muster under the Free Exercise Clause. Congress responded by passing the Religious Freedom Restoration Act of 1993 (RFRA), which attempted to strengthen religious freedom by codifying the prior strict scrutiny standard. As described earlier, the Supreme Court subsequently struck down the RFRA as an unconstitutional encroachment by Congress on the powers of the judiciary to interpret the Constitution.[58]

Religion in government offices is a difficult issue that may bring the Establishment and Free Exercise Clauses into conflict. In 1996, the U.S. Court of Appeals for the Ninth Circuit ruled unconstitutional a near total ban on religious activity in the workplace imposed by the California Department of Education's Child Nutrition and Food Distribution Division.[59] Tensions arose in the division between computer analyst Monte Tucker and his supervisor after Tucker refused to stop signing office memos with his name and the acronym "SOTLJC," which stood for "Servant of the Lord Jesus Christ." After several warnings, the supervisor suspended Tucker and prohibited all employees from displaying religious materials outside their cubicles, engaging in any religious advocacy, and putting any acronym or other symbol on office communications. Although the state argued its interests in avoiding workplace disruption and the appearance of religious endorsement (which would constitute a violation of the Establishment Clause), the appeals court found such interests outweighed by Tucker's constitutional right to talk about religion. Such issues also come up in the private sector, which is regulated by various statutes barring discrimination based on religion.

## Due Process

The Due Process Clauses of the Fifth Amendment (which applies to the federal government) and the Fourteenth Amendment (which applies to the states) prohibit depriving any person of life, liberty, or property without due process of law. *Procedural due process*

53. Santa Fe Independent School Dist. v. Doe, 530 U.S. 290 (2000).
54. Mitchell v. Helms, 530 U.S. 1296 (2000).
55. Zelman v. Simmons-Harris, 536 U.S. 639 (2002).
56. 493 U.S. 378 (1990).
57. 494 U.S. 872 (1990).
58. City of Boerne v. Flores, 521 U.S. 507 (1997).
59. Tucker v. Cal. Dep't of Educ., 97 F.3d 1204 (9th Cir. 1996).

focuses on the fairness of the legal proceeding. *Substantive due process* focuses on the fundamental rights protected by the Due Process Clauses.

## Procedural Due Process

Whenever a governmental action affects a person's life, liberty, or property, the due process requirement applies, and some form of notice and hearing is required. Explaining the notice requirement, the Supreme Court stated:

> An elementary and fundamental requirement of due process in any proceeding which is to be accorded finality is notice, reasonably calculated, under all the circumstances, to apprise interested parties of the pendency of the action and afford them an opportunity to present their objections. . . . The notice must be of such nature as reasonably to convey the required information, and it must afford a reasonable time for those interested to make their appearance. [60]

The type of hearing varies depending on the nature of the action, but some opportunity to be heard must be provided. In general, greater procedural protections are afforded to criminal defendants because the possibility of imprisonment and even death in capital cases is at stake.

The Due Process Clause of the Fourteenth Amendment has been interpreted to make virtually all of the procedural requirements in the Bill of Rights applicable to state criminal proceedings. These rights are discussed in Chapter 14.

## Substantive Due Process

Disputes have raged over the years as to what are the fundamental rights—rights with which the government may not interfere—possessed by people in our society. It has been argued that such rights and liberty interests, including the right to privacy, are guaranteed by the Due Process Clauses of the Fifth and Fourteenth Amendments. This protection of fundamental rights is known as substantive due process. The notion of substantive due process was not wholeheartedly accepted by the Supreme Court until the end of the nineteenth century, mainly because substantive due process rights are not specifically listed in the Constitution.

60. Mullane v. Cent. Hanover Bank & Trust Co., 339 U.S. 306 (1950).

### *Limit on Economic Regulation*

The Supreme Court first invalidated a state law on substantive due process grounds in 1897.[61] A Louisiana law prohibited anyone from obtaining insurance on Louisiana property from any marine insurance company that had not complied in all respects with Louisiana law. The Court held that the statute violated the fundamental right to make contracts.

Early in the twentieth century, the concept was applied to more controversial areas, such as state statutes limiting working hours. In *Lochner v. New York*,[62] the Supreme Court struck down a New York statute that prohibited the employment of bakery employees for more than ten hours a day or sixty hours a week. The Court held that the statute interfered with the employers' and employees' fundamental right to contract with each other.

In the period from 1905 to 1937, the Supreme Court invoked the doctrine of substantive due process to invalidate a number of laws relating to regulation of prices, labor relations, and conditions for entry into business.

In 1937, the Supreme Court reversed direction. After President Franklin Delano Roosevelt threatened to "pack" the Court (discussed in the "Inside Story"), the justices upheld a minimum-wage law for women in Washington,[63] overruling an earlier decision striking down a similar statute. In 1938, the Court upheld a statute that prohibited the interstate shipment of "filled" milk (milk to which any fat or oil other than milk fat has been added).[64] The Court made clear that if any set of facts, either known or imaginable, provides a rational basis for the legislation, the legislation will not be held to violate substantive due process. Under this test, economic regulation is rarely constrained by economic liberty.

### *Protection of Fundamental Rights*

Substantive due process challenges are given more weight when fundamental rights other than the right to make contracts are at issue. Fundamental rights and liberty interests protected by the Due Process Clause include the guarantees of the Bill of Rights, the right to marry and to have children, the right to raise children, the right to travel, the right to vote, and the right to associate with other people. The Supreme Court has made clear that the fundamental rights protected by substantive due process are not limited to those specifically

61. Allegeyer v. Louisiana, 165 U.S. 578 (1897).
62. 198 U.S. 45 (1905).
63. West Coast Hotel Co. v. Parrish, 300 U.S. 379 (1937).
64. United States v. Carolene Products Co., 304 U.S. 144 (1938).

enumerated in the Constitution or the Bill of Rights. Legislation that limits fundamental rights violates substantive due process unless it can be shown to promote a compelling or overriding governmental interest.

**Right to Privacy** Substantive due process was extended to the right to privacy in *Griswold v. Connecticut*.[65] The executive director of the Planned Parenthood League of Connecticut and a physician who served as medical director for the league at its center in New Haven were arrested. They were charged with giving birth control advice in violation of a Connecticut statute that prohibited the use of any drug, medicinal article, or instrument for the purpose of preventing conception.

In finding that the Connecticut statute was an unconstitutional invasion of individuals' right to privacy, the Supreme Court discussed the penumbra of rights surrounding each guarantee in the Bill of Rights. The Court defined *penumbra* as the peripheral rights that are implied by the specifically enumerated rights. For example, the Court noted that the First Amendment's freedom of the press necessarily includes the right to distribute, the right to receive, the right to read, freedom of inquiry, freedom of thought, freedom to teach, and freedom of association. The Fourth Amendment, which prohibits unreasonable searches and seizures, similarly includes a "right to privacy, no less important than any other right carefully and particularly reserved to the people." The Supreme Court found that the Connecticut statute encroached on the right to privacy in marriage.

The right to privacy is an essential element in the debate between pro-choice and pro-life groups concerning a woman's right to an abortion. It is relevant in other areas as well. For example, the Supreme Court has upheld a person's right to refuse life-sustaining treatment (such as lifesaving hydration and nutrition)[66] but declined to recognize a right to physician-assisted suicide.[67] In another case,[68] a schoolteacher successfully sued a board of education, alleging that her teaching contract was not renewed because she was an unwed mother and her pregnancy had been by means of artificial insemination. The district court held that a woman has a constitutional privacy right to become pregnant by means of artificial insemination. In 2003, the Supreme Court, overruling an earlier decision, held that a Texas statute criminalizing the act of sodomy performed by consenting adults in private infringed upon their constitutionally protected right of privacy.[69]

Mandatory drug testing also presents privacy issues. The Supreme Court has upheld certain regulations concerning drug testing for public employees. This issue is discussed in Chapter 12.

### *Limit on Punitive Damages*

In certain cases involving torts, or civil wrongs, the jury is entitled to award the plaintiff not only compensatory damages equal to the plaintiff's actual loss but also *punitive* or *exemplary damages*, designed to punish and make an example of the defendant. Usually, the size of the punitive damages bears some relationship to the size of the compensatory damages and the degree of reprehensibility. The following case addressed the issue of whether an award of punitive damages that was 145 times the amount of compensatory damages was so excessive as to violate substantive due process.

65. 381 U.S. 479 (1965).

66. Cruzan v. Dir., Mo. Dep't of Health, 497 U.S. 261 (1990).
67. Washington v. Glucksberg, 521 U.S. 702 (1997).
68. Cameron v. Bd. of Educ., 795 F. Supp. 228 (S.D. Ohio 1991).
69. Lawrence v. Texas, 123 S. Ct. 2472 (2003).

A CASE IN POINT

## In the Language of the Court

**CASE 2.5**
**State Farm Mutual Automobile Insurance Co. v. Campbell et al.**
*Supreme Court of the United States*
*538 U.S. 408 (2003).*

**› FACTS** Although investigators and witnesses concluded that Curtis Campbell caused an accident in which one person was killed and another was permanently disabled, Campbell's insurer, State Farm, declined offers by the plaintiffs to settle their claims within Campbell's policy limits ($25,000 per claimant or $50,000) and took the case to trial. State Farm assured Campbell and his wife that "their assets were safe, and that they had no liability for the accident, that [the insurance company] would represent their interests, and that they did not need to procure separate counsel." However, a jury subsequently determined that Campbell was 100 percent at fault and that he was liable for $185,849. State Farm refused to cover the excess liability over the policy limit. Its counsel made this clear when he advised the Campbells, "[y]ou may want to put for sale signs on your property to get things moving."

*(Continued)*

(Case 2.5 *continued*)

The plaintiffs made an agreement with Campbell that they would not seek satisfaction of their claims against him if he agreed to use their lawyer to sue State Farm for bad faith and give them 90 percent of any award. Even though State Farm ultimately paid the entire judgment, including the amounts in excess of the policy limits, Campbell sued State Farm for bad faith, fraud, and intentional infliction of emotional distress. The trial court granted State Farm's motion for summary judgment, but the court of appeals reversed and sent the case back for trial, which was divided into two phases conducted before two different juries. In the first phase, the jury found that State Farm's refusal to settle was unreasonable because there was a substantial likelihood of a jury award in excess of the policy limits. The second part addressed State Farm's liability for fraud and intentional infliction of emotional distress, as well as damages.

State Farm claimed that it had made an honest mistake, but the Campbells introduced evidence (1) showing that the company had a national policy of meeting fiscal goals by capping payouts on claims and (2) describing fraudulent practices by State Farm outside Utah, which bore no relationship to third-party automobile claims. The jury awarded Campbell $2.6 million in compensatory damages and $145 million in punitive damages, but the trial court reduced the award to $1 million and $25 million, respectively. Both sides appealed. The Utah Supreme Court said it was applying guidelines from the 1996 U.S. Supreme Court ruling in *BMW of North America v. Gore*[70] (which overturned an award of $2 million in punitive damages where the compensatory award was only $4,000) and reinstated the $145 million punitive award, noting State Farm's massive wealth and the clandestine nature of its actions.

**› ISSUE PRESENTED** Is a $145 million punitive damages award, where full compensatory damages are $1 million, so excessive as to violate the Fourteenth Amendment's Due Process Clause?

**› OPINION** KENNEDY, J., writing for the U.S. Supreme Court:

[I]n *Gore* we instructed courts reviewing punitive damages to consider three guideposts: (1) the degree of reprehensibility of the defendant's misconduct; (2) the disparity between the actual or potential harm suffered by the plaintiff and the punitive damages award; and (3) the difference between the punitive damages awarded by the jury and the civil penalties authorized or imposed in comparable cases. . . .

Under the principles outlined in [*Gore*] this case is neither close nor difficult. It was error to reinstate the jury's $145 million punitive damages award. We address each guidepost of *Gore* in some detail.

**A**

"[T]he most important indicium of the reasonableness of a punitive damages award is the degree of reprehensibility of the defendant's conduct." We have instructed courts to determine the reprehensibility of a defendant by considering whether: the harm caused was physical as opposed to economic; the tortious conduct evinced an indifference to or a reckless disregard of the health or safety of others; the target of the conduct had financial vulnerability; the conduct involved repeated actions or was an isolated incident; and the harm was the result of intentional malice, trickery, or deceit, or mere accident. . . .

Applying these factors . . . , we must acknowledge that State Farm's handling of the claims against the Campbells merits no praise. . . .

70. 517 U.S. 559 (1996).

*(Continued)*

(Case 2.5 *continued*)

. . .

[However, a] State cannot punish a defendant for conduct that may have been lawful where it occurred. . . .

. . . A jury must be instructed, furthermore, that it may not use evidence of out-of-state conduct to punish a defendant for action that was lawful in the jurisdiction where it occurred. . . .

For a more fundamental reason, however, the Utah courts erred in relying upon this and other evidence. . . . A defendant's dissimilar acts, independent from the acts upon which liability was premised, may not serve as the basis for punitive damages. . . .

. . .

**B**

Turning to the second *Gore* guidepost, we have been reluctant to identify concrete constitutional limits on the ratio between harm, or potential harm, to the plaintiff and the punitive damages award. We decline again to impose a bright-line ratio which a punitive damages award cannot exceed. Our jurisprudence and the principles it has now established demonstrate, however, that, in practice, few awards exceeding a single-digit ratio between punitive and compensatory damages, to a significant degree, will satisfy due process. . . .

. . .

**C**

The third guidepost in *Gore* is the disparity between the punitive damages award and the "civil penalties authorized or imposed in comparable cases." . . .

Here, we need not dwell long on this guidepost. The most relevant civil sanction under Utah state law for the wrong done to the Campbells appears to be a $10,000 fine for an act of fraud. . . .

**› RESULT** The Supreme Court reversed the judgment of the Utah Supreme Court, finding that the $145 million award was "neither reasonable nor proportionate to the wrong committed, and it was an irrational and arbitrary deprivation of the property of the defendant." The Court remanded the case for reconsideration of the punitive damages award.

**› CRITICAL THINKING QUESTIONS**

1. The Supreme Court left open the possibility of higher ratios in punitive to compensatory damages in instances where "a particularly egregious act has resulted in only a small amount of economic damages." Would the rules applied by the Court in *State Farm* apply to a product liability case in which $6.2 million in compensatory damages and $290 million in punitive damages were awarded for an accident involving a Ford Bronco that killed three people?[71]
2. Should the rule applied by the Court in *State Farm* apply to a lawsuit for breach of contract and fraud for an allegedly false promise to sell property in downtown Los Angeles in which the jurors awarded the plaintiff $5,000 in compensatory damages and $1.7 million in punitive damages?[72]

71. See Ramon Romo v. Ford Motor Co., 6 Cal. Rptr. 3d 793 (Cal. Ct. App. 2003).
72. See Simon v. San Paolo U.S. Holding Co., 7 Cal. Rptr. 3d 367 (Cal. Ct. App. 2003).

Another due process concern in awarding punitive damages is the availability of judicial review of the amount. Along with the substantive due process requirement illustrated in *State Farm,* there is a procedural due process requirement that such awards be subject to appellate review. In *Honda Motor Co. v. Oberg,*[73] an Oregon jury had awarded $5 million in punitive damages to a plaintiff injured in a three-wheel all-terrain vehicle accident. Although Honda wished to appeal the penalty, Oregon's constitution barred review of punitive awards unless there was no evidence to support the jury's decision. The U.S. Supreme Court found that the Oregon rule violated due process and was insufficient to protect Honda's constitutional rights.

## Compensation for Takings

One of the first provisions of the Bill of Rights incorporated into the Fourteenth Amendment was the Fifth Amendment provision that private property may not be taken for public use without just compensation. State and federal governments have the power of *eminent domain,* which is the power to take property for public uses such as building a school, park, or airport. If property is taken from a private owner for such a purpose, the owner is entitled to just compensation. A more complex situation arises when the government does not physically take the property but imposes regulations that restrict its use. If the regulation amounts to a taking of the property, the owner is entitled to just compensation. In a sense, all regulation takes some aspect of property away from the owner. The question is when does a regulation constitute a taking that requires compensation.

In one instance, the Supreme Court held that there was a taking when a homeowner was required to grant a public right-of-way through his property in order to obtain a building permit to replace his oceanfront house with a larger one.[74] Another case involved the Federal Communications Commission's regulation of the rates a utility company could charge for the attachment of television cables to the utility company's poles. The Supreme Court held that the regulation was not a taking, as long as the rates were not set so low as to be unjust and confiscatory.[75]

In another case, Penn Central Transportation Company, the owner of Grand Central Station in midtown Manhattan, was prohibited from constructing an office building above the station. The prohibition was ordered by the Landmarks Preservation Commission, which had designated the station a landmark. Under New York City law, the commission could prevent any alteration of the fundamental character of such buildings. A high-rise would arguably have altered the fundamental character of Grand Central Station. The Supreme Court found that the prohibition was not a taking.[76] This case, as well as other land-use taking cases, is discussed in Chapter 18.

In *Eastern Enterprises v. Apfel,*[77] the Supreme Court invalidated the Coal Industry Retiree Health Benefits Act of 1992 under which a former coal mine operator, Eastern Enterprises, was required to contribute an annual premium of $5 million to a health fund for coal workers. Eastern Enterprises had ceased its mine operations in 1987. The Act was enacted to remedy the shortfalls in the preexisting multi-employer benefits plans the coal industry had negotiated with the United Mine Workers union. It required all companies that had signed onto the union plans to contribute to a new health fund and to pay for their former employees even if the amount exceeded a company's obligation under the negotiated plan. The Supreme Court held that the Act was an unconstitutional "taking" of private property without compensation. The Court stated that a law violates the Fifth Amendment if "[1] it imposes a severe retroactive liability [2] on a limited class of parties that could not have anticipated the liability, and [3] the extent of the liability is substantially disproportionate to the parties' experience." Chapter 15 discusses environmental cases in which the defendants argued that, in light of *Eastern Enterprises v. Apfel,* environmental statutes imposing cleanup costs could not be applied to activities that predated the statutes' enactment.

## Equal Protection

The Equal Protection Clause of the Fourteenth Amendment places another limitation on the power of state governments to regulate. A comparable limitation is imposed on the federal government by the Due Process Clause of the Fifth Amendment. The Equal Protection Clause provides that no state shall "deny to any person within its jurisdiction the equal protection of the laws." The Supreme Court's interpretation of this clause continues to be the subject of much debate.

73. 512 U.S. 415 (1994).
74. Nollan v. Cal. Coastal Comm'n, 483 U.S. 825 (1987).
75. FCC v. Fla. Power Corp., 480 U.S. 245 (1987).
76. Penn Cent. Transp. Co. v. New York City, 438 U.S. 104 (1978).
77. 524 U.S. 498 (1998).

## Establishing Discrimination

In order to challenge a statute on equal protection grounds, it is first necessary to establish that the statute discriminates against a class of persons. Discrimination may be found on the face of the statute, in its application, or in its purpose. The statute may (1) explicitly (on its face) treat different classes of persons differently; (2) contain no classification, but government officials may apply it differently to different classes of people; or (3) be neutral on its face and in its application but have the purpose of creating different burdens for different classes of persons.

In determining whether a facially neutral law is a device to discriminate against certain classes of people, the Supreme Court looks at three things: (1) the practical or statistical impact of the statute on different classes of persons, (2) the history of the problems that the statute seeks to solve, and (3) the legislative history of the statute. Even if a government action has a disproportionate effect on a racial minority group, it will be upheld if there was no racially discriminatory purpose or intent.[78]

## Validity of Discrimination

The Supreme Court uses three tests to determine the constitutionality of various types of discrimination, depending on how the statute classifies the persons concerned.

### Rational Basis Test

The *rational basis test* applies to all classifications that relate to matters of economics or social welfare. Under this test, a classification will be held valid if there is any conceivable basis on which the classification might relate to a legitimate governmental interest. It is a rare regulation that cannot meet this minimal standard. For example, a system of progressive taxation, in which persons with higher income are required to pay taxes at a higher marginal rate, passes muster under this test.

### Strict Scrutiny Test

A classification that determines who may exercise a fundamental right or a classification based on a suspect trait, such as race, is subject to strict scrutiny. Under the *strict scrutiny test,* a classification will be held valid only if it is necessary to promote a compelling state interest and is narrowly tailored to achieve that interest. The right to privacy, the right to vote, the right to travel, and certain other guarantees in the Bill of Rights are fundamental rights. Rights such as welfare payments, housing, education, and government employment are not fundamental rights.

### Substantially Related Test

The Supreme Court occasionally applies a third test, which is stricter than the rational basis test but less strict than strict scrutiny. This intermediate-level (substantially related) test applies to classifications such as gender and legitimacy of birth. Under this test, a classification will be upheld if it is substantially related to an important governmental interest.

## Racial Discrimination

Racial discrimination was the major target of the Fourteenth Amendment, so it is clear that racial classifications are suspect. Nonetheless, from 1896 to 1954, the "separate but equal" doctrine allowed governments to provide separate services for minorities as long as they were equal to the services provided for whites. For example, in *Plessy v. Ferguson,*[79] the U.S. Supreme Court upheld a law requiring all railway companies to provide separate but equal accommodations for African-American and white passengers. Fifty-eight years later, the Supreme Court held in *Brown v. Board of Education*[80] that the separate but equal doctrine had no place in education. The justices unanimously held that the "segregation of children in public schools solely on the basis of race, even though the physical facilities and other 'tangible' factors may be equal, deprives the children of the minority group of equal educational opportunities." Supreme Court rulings following *Brown* made it clear that no governmental entity may segregate people because of their race or national origin.

Complications concerning racial classifications have arisen more recently in the area of affirmative action programs intended to benefit racial or ethnic minorities. A debate raged over whether strict scrutiny should be applied only to legislation that discriminates against a minority or to any legislation that generally discriminates based on race. The Supreme Court resolved that issue in *Adarand Constructors, Inc. v. Peña,*[81] when it held that all racial classifications—whether imposed by federal,

78. Arlington Heights v. Metro. Hous. Dev. Corp., 429 U.S. 252 (1977) (upholding a largely white suburb's refusal to rezone to permit multifamily dwellings for low- and moderate-income tenants, including members of racial minorities).

79. 163 U.S. 537 (1896).
80. 347 U.S. 483 (1954).
81. 515 U.S. 200 (1995).

state, or local government—are subject to strict scrutiny. In *Adarand,* the white owner of a construction company successfully challenged regulations adopted by the U.S. Department of Transportation that made use of race-based presumptions in awarding lucrative federal highway project contracts to economically disadvantaged businesses. The Court rejected the argument it had accepted in an earlier case[82] that because the Equal Protection Clause was adopted after the Civil War to protect African Americans, it permits "benign" (or protective) racial classifications as long as there is a rational basis for the classification.

A number of cases have raised the question of whether universities and schools can consider an applicant's race when deciding whether to admit the student. In the following case, the U.S. Supreme Court considered the University of Michigan Law School's admissions policy, which allows officials to consider diversity as a factor in evaluating potential students.

82. Metro Broad., Inc. v. FCC, 497 U.S. 547 (1990) (upholding two minority-preference policies mandated by Congress to achieve broadcast diversity).

A CASE IN POINT

**CASE 2.6**
**Grutter v. Bollinger**
*Supreme Court of the United States*
*539 U.S. 306 (2003).*

## Summary

**› FACTS** The highly ranked University of Michigan Law School follows an admissions policy that focuses on a student's academic ability, coupled with a flexible appraisal of his or her talents, experiences, and potential. The policy requires admissions officials to evaluate each applicant based on all information in his or her file, including a personal statement, letters of recommendation, an essay describing how the student will contribute to law school life and diversity, the student's undergraduate performance, and Law School Admissions Test (LSAT) score. Officials must also consider "soft variables," such as recommenders' enthusiasm, the quality of the undergraduate school and the student's essay, and the student's course selection. Although the admissions policy does not define diversity solely in terms of race and ethnicity and does not restrict the types of diversity eligible for consideration, it affirms the school's commitment to diversity, with specific references to African-American, Hispanic, and Native American students.

After the law school denied admission to Ms. Grutter, a white Michigan resident with a 3.8 GPA and a high LSAT score, she filed suit, alleging, among other things, that the law school had discriminated against her on the basis of race in violation of the Fourteenth Amendment. The district court found that the University of Michigan's use of race as an admissions factor was unlawful, but the U.S. Court of Appeals for the Sixth Circuit reversed,[83] holding that Supreme Court Justice Lewis Powell's opinion in *Regents of University of California v. Bakke*[84] was binding precedent that established diversity as a compelling state interest. The appeals court found that the law school's use of race was narrowly tailored because race was merely a "potential 'plus factor'" and because the policy was "virtually identical" to the Harvard admissions program described by Justice Powell and appended to the *Bakke* opinion.

**› ISSUE PRESENTED** Does the Equal Protection Clause of the Fourteenth Amendment permit a public university's narrowly tailored use of race in its admissions policy?

**› SUMMARY OF OPINION** The U.S. Supreme Court began by noting that the Court had last addressed the use of race in public higher education twenty-five years earlier in the landmark *Bakke* case, which produced six separate opinions, none of which commanded a majority. In *Bakke,* the Court struck down a racial set-aside program that reserved 16 out of 100 seats in a medical school class for members of certain minority groups as violating the Fourteenth Amendment, but the only holding for the Court was

83. Grutter v. Bollinger, 288 F.3d 732 (2002).
84. 438 U.S. 265 (1978).

*(Continued)*

(Case 2.6 *continued*)

that a "State has a substantial interest that legitimately may be served by a properly devised admissions program involving the competitive consideration of race and ethnic origin." In *Bakke,* Justice Powell approved the university's use of race to further only one interest: "the attainment of a diverse student body," noting that nothing less than the "'nation's future depends upon leaders trained through wide exposure' to the ideas and mores of students as diverse as this Nation of many peoples."

Turning to the case before it, the Court noted that "[w]e have held that all racial classifications imposed by government 'must be analyzed by a reviewing court under strict scrutiny.' This means that such classifications are constitutional only if they are narrowly tailored to further compelling governmental interests."

Applying these principles, the Court found that the law school's use of race was justified by a compelling state interest.

> We are mindful, however, that "[a] core purpose of the Fourteenth Amendment was to do away with all governmentally imposed discrimination based on race." Accordingly race-conscious admissions policies must be limited in time. This requirement reflects that racial classifications, however compelling their goals, are potentially so dangerous that they may be employed no more broadly than the interest demands.

Observing that it had been twenty-five years since Justice Powell first approved the use of race to further an interest in student body diversity, the Court stated that "[w]e expect that 25 years from now, the use of racial preferences will no longer be necessary to further the interest approved today."

The Court also found that the law school's admissions program bore the hallmarks of a narrowly tailored plan:

> As Justice Powell made clear in *Bakke,* truly individualized consideration demands that race be used in a flexible, nonmechanical way. It follows from this mandate that universities cannot establish quotas for members of certain racial groups or put members of those groups on separate admissions tracks. Nor can universities insulate applicants who belong to certain racial or ethnic groups from the competition for admission. Universities can, however, consider race or ethnicity more flexibly as a "plus" factor in the context of individualized consideration of each and every applicant.

**› RESULT** The Supreme Court affirmed the judgment of the U.S. Court of Appeals for the Sixth Circuit, holding that the Equal Protection Clause did not prohibit the law school's narrowly tailored use of race in admissions decisions to further a compelling interest in obtaining the educational benefits that flow from a diverse student body.

**› COMMENTS** Although the Supreme Court voted five to four to uphold the use of race by the University of Michigan Law School in *Grutter v. Bollinger,* it struck down the University of Michigan's undergraduate admissions policy, which awarded points to African Americans, Hispanics, and Native Americans on an admissions rating scale. The Court found that this use of race was not "narrowly tailored" to achieve the university's diversity goals. [85]

85. Gratz v. Bollinger, 539 U.S. 244 (2003).

In *Eisenberg v. Montgomery County Public Schools*,[86] the U.S. Court of Appeals for the Fourth Circuit held that a public school district with racially imbalanced schools could not use race or ethnicity as a factor in determining whether to allow transfers from one school to another. The court found that this policy was not narrowly tailored to remedy past discrimination.

Private employers are not limited by the Equal Protection Clause, which applies only to governmental actors, such as state and local governments, schools, and police departments. However, as explained in Chapter 13, private entities are subject to the Civil Rights Act and other regulations imposed by federal and state antidiscrimination statutes.

## OTHER FORMS OF DISCRIMINATION

The U.S. Supreme Court has applied the substantially related test to laws that classify on the basis of gender, illegitimacy, and alienage.

### *Gender*

In *United States v. Virginia*,[87] the Supreme Court ruled that the Virginia Military Institute, an all-male, state-supported military college, violated the Equal Protection Clause by excluding women. The Court held that classifications based on gender must (1) serve important governmental objectives, (2) be substantially related to achieving those objectives, and (3) rest on an "exceedingly persuasive justification." Justice Ruth Bader Ginsburg's majority opinion can be read to require gender classifications to meet a standard somewhere between intermediate and strict scrutiny. In prior cases, the Court (1) invalidated statutory provisions that gave female workers fewer benefits for their families than male workers; (2) upheld differential treatment for women when it was compensatory for past discrimination, but not when it unreasonably denied benefits to men; (3) upheld a statutory rape law that applied only to male offenders; (4) upheld exempting women from the draft; and (5) upheld disability insurance policies that excluded insurance benefits for costs relating to pregnancy, but not other disabilities. Gender discrimination is discussed further in Chapter 13.

### *Illegitimacy*

Classifications based on the legitimacy of children will be held invalid unless substantially related to a proper state interest. The Supreme Court will usually look at the purpose behind the classification and will not uphold any law intended to punish children born out of wedlock.

### *Alienage*

Aliens, that is, persons who are not citizens of the United States, do not receive the protection of all constitutional guarantees, many of which apply only to citizens. For example, in 1990, the Supreme Court held that the Fourth Amendment prohibition of search and seizure without a warrant did not apply to a drug raid of an alien's premises in Mexico.[88] Because of Congress's *plenary* (or absolute) power to regulate aliens and immigration, classifications imposed by the federal government based on alienage are valid if they are not arbitrary and unreasonable. State and local laws that classify on the basis of alienage are subject to strict scrutiny, however, except for state laws discriminating against alien participation in certain state government positions, which are evaluated under the rational basis test. Foreign organizations without property or presence in the United States also have no constitutional rights.[89]

# Right to Jury Trial

The Seventh Amendment provides that "[i]n Suits at common law, where the value in controversy shall exceed twenty dollars, the right of trial by jury shall be preserved." The phrase "suits at common law" refers to suits in which legal rights are to be ascertained and monetary damages awarded, in contrast to suits where only equitable rights and remedies (such as injunctions) are recognized. To determine whether a particular action will resolve legal rights, a court must analyze both the nature of the issues involved and the remedy sought. In particular, a court will (1) compare the statutory actions to eighteenth-century actions brought before the American Revolution in the courts of England prior to the merger of the courts of law and equity and (2) examine the remedy sought to determine whether it is legal or equitable in nature.[90] In this two-part analysis, the second inquiry is more important than the first. However, as previously discussed, the Seventh Amendment has not been incorporated to apply to the states; thus, when state law is involved, the matter becomes more complicated.

86. 197 F.3d 123 (4th Cir. 1999), *cert denied*, 529 U.S. 1019 (2000).
87. 518 U.S. 515 (1996).
88. United States v. Verdugo-Urquidez, 494 U.S. 259 (1990).
89. People's Mojahedin Org. of Iran v. Dep't of State, 182 F.3d 17 (D.C. Cir. 1999), *cert. denied*, 529 U.S. 1104 (2000).
90. Chauffers, Teamsters & Helpers Local No. 391 v. Terry, 494 U.S. 558 (1990).

HISTORICAL PERSPECTIVE

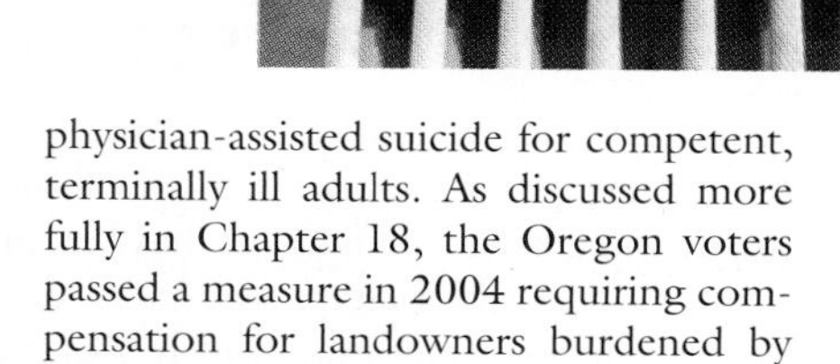

## THE INITIATIVE PROCESS

In 1898, South Dakota became the first state to establish a procedure whereby citizens could initiate change on their own without going through their elected representatives. During the next twenty years, eighteen other states adopted initiative processes; by 2004, the number had grown to twenty-four. Unlike representative democracy, initiatives give direct legislative power to voters by allowing them to make new laws, either by amending the state constitution or by enacting legislation. Some states, such as California, do not allow an executive veto of initiatives (unlike legislation passed by the state legislature) and forbid repeal except by subsequent voter initiative. The initiative process has been used by citizens seeking to change governmental policy on a wide range of topics including child labor, women's suffrage, gambling, alcohol, prostitution, civil rights, the death penalty, environmental protection, and property taxes.

Although it has been in existence in states for over a century, the initiative has seen most of its use in recent years. For example, in the 1950s, California circulated only 17 initiatives and only 10 qualified for the ballot. Compare that to the 1980s, when citizens proposed more than 200 initiatives and voted on more than 40. In the 1990s, Californians voted on over 130 initiatives, approving almost half of them.

In recent years, a number of major public policy battles have moved out of the state capitols and into the land of initiatives. In 1996, voters in California and Arizona legalized medical use of marijuana by ballot initiative. That same year, Californians also approved Proposition 209, which sought to end racial preferences by state and local governments. One year later, voters in Houston turned down an initiative to end that city's affirmative action program. In 1994 and again in 1997, Oregon voters authorized physician-assisted suicide for competent, terminally ill adults. As discussed more fully in Chapter 18, the Oregon voters passed a measure in 2004 requiring compensation for landowners burdened by new land use restrictions.

Voters have even used initiative-type processes to remove elected officials from office. In 2003, groups opposed to newly reelected California Governor Gray Davis gathered enough signatures to force a recall election. In October 2003, Governor Davis was recalled by California voters, who replaced him with Arnold Schwarzenegger.

Sources: This discussion is based in part on K. K. DuVivier, *By Going Wrong All Things Come Right*, 63 U. CIN. L. REV. 1185 (1995); P. K. Jameson & Marsha Hosack, *Citizen Initiatives in Florida*, 23 FLA. ST. U. L. REV. 417 (1995); and David L. Callies et al., *Ballot Box Zoning*, 39 WASH. U. J. URB. & CONTEMP. L. 53 (1991).

For example, in *GTFM, LLC v. TKN Sales, Inc.*,[91] GTFM, an apparel manufacturer in New York, challenged the constitutionality of a Minnesota statute that required a non-Minnesota corporation to submit disputes with distributors in Minnesota to binding arbitration, even in the absence of an agreement or consent to arbitrate. The district court analyzed the claims and the remedies sought by TKN, the Minnesota distributor, to determine whether they were legal or equitable. The court found that TKN's claims for breach of contract and for unpaid commissions sought clearly legal damages, which entitled GTFM to a jury trial. The fact that TKN also sought an equitable remedy, through its claim for reinstatement of the contract, did not defeat GTFM's right to a jury trial on the legal claims and issues. The U.S. Court of Appeals for the Second Circuit, however, disagreed with any application of the Seventh Amendment to this case, concluding that there is no federal constitutional requirement that jury trials be held in state court civil cases. Because this case did not involve a federal law but was in federal court solely because the parties were from different states, the federal court was basically acting like a state court.

91. 2000 WL 364871 (S.D.N.Y. 2000), *rev'd*, 257 F.3d 235 (2d Cir. 2001).

THE RESPONSIBLE MANAGER

## PRESERVING CONSTITUTIONAL RIGHTS

Although the Constitution is directed primarily at establishing and limiting the powers of the federal and state governments, its provisions have a profound effect on private actors in society. The costs are usually high, but at times a company may find it worthwhile to challenge a regulation on constitutional grounds. This was true for the insurance companies that successfully challenged California's Proposition 103's freeze on rate increases for one year,[92] and for Eastern Enterprises, the former coal company that successfully challenged the $5 million assessment to fund health plans for former employees.[93] It was also true for State Farm, the insurance company that successfully challenged the $145 million punitive damages award against it.[94] Companies engaged in advertising their products and services or in broadcasting such ads have been particularly successful in recent years in persuading the Supreme Court that the restrictions violate their free speech rights.

92. Calfarm Ins. Co. v. Deukmejian, 771 P.2d 1247 (Cal. 1989).
93. Eastern Enter. v. Apfel, 524 U.S. 498 (1998).
94. State Farm Mut. Auto. Ins. Co. v. Campbell et al., 538 U.S. 408 (2003).

Managers often have an interest in influencing legislation or other government action through direct lobbying or political action committees. When pursuing change, it is useful to know the constitutional limitations placed on different government segments.

Although the Constitution refers only to government actions, managers of private organizations should be aware of the societal values reflected in the Constitution. These include the right to fair and equal treatment and respect for the individual.

It may seem at times that constitutional law is far removed from the world of business. This is a misconception. Constitutional law is as close as the nearest private club that does not admit African Americans, Jews, women, or homosexuals. Such clubs may be important places for conducting business and for general networking. A manager invited to become a member of such a club or to accompany his or her boss or client as a guest may face a tough choice between his or her personal values and the perceived need to get along and not challenge an important business colleague.

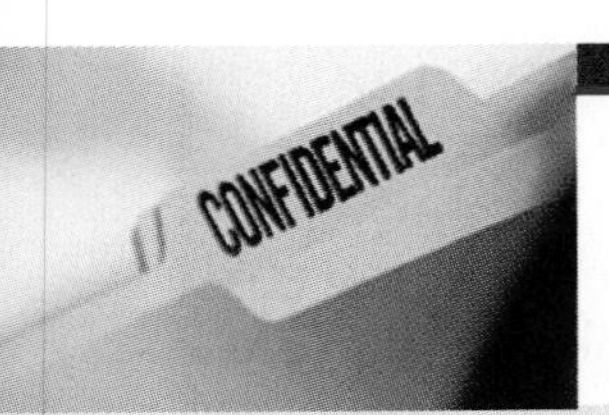


INSIDE STORY

## EFFECT OF POLITICS ON SUPREME COURT APPOINTMENTS

The nomination process for the U.S. Supreme Court has grown increasingly politicized and controversial over time. Nomination to the Supreme Court now brings along with it a process of public scrutiny akin to running for national political office. Politics, however, is not new to the process of selecting Supreme Court justices.

Franklin Delano Roosevelt was probably the first president to attempt explicitly and publicly to use the power of judicial appointment to change the Court's position on the key political issues of the day. Frustrated because the Supreme Court was invalidating much of his New Deal legislation, Roosevelt introduced his now-famous Court-packing bill. The bill would have added one justice to the Court for every sitting justice who had reached the age of seventy, thereby increasing the Court's membership to fifteen. Roosevelt hoped that by appointing additional justices, he would soon gain a majority sympathetic to his programs.

Although the bill was never passed by the Senate, the threat was clear. The Court quickly capitulated and abandoned its commitment to limited government, especially regarding economic liberty. By the time of his death during his fourth term, Roosevelt had com-

*(Continued)*

(Inside Story *continued*)

pletely revamped the Court, secured passage of his New Deal legislation, and ushered in a new era of constitutional law.

Other presidents have made considerations of diversity and representation key to their selection of nominees. President Lyndon Johnson's appointment of Thurgood Marshall took into consideration the need for African Americans to be represented on the Court for the first time. Similarly, the appointments of Justices Sandra Day O'Connor (the first female member of the Court) and Clarence Thomas by Presidents Ronald Reagan and the elder George Bush, respectively, served to expand and maintain the Court's gender and racial diversity.

Still other presidents have used the appointment power to reward political allies. When President Dwight Eisenhower appointed Earl Warren as the Chief Justice in 1953, Warren was the Republican governor of California and had been an important supporter of Eisenhower's successful 1952 bid for the presidency. Eisenhower repaid the political debt with the nomination, despite misgivings by powerful Republicans, such as Vice President Richard Nixon, about Warren's progressive stance on certain issues.

Another pivotal nomination in the recent past was that of Robert Bork, a well-known conservative constitutional scholar, by President Reagan in 1987. Bork was the last nominee to the Supreme Court to have an extensive "paper trail" of opinions and writings on constitutional matters. The nightmare Senate hearings, in which Bork was forced to attempt to explain to the senators and the general public the reasoning behind some of his more radical statements over the years—of which there were many—have apparently convinced subsequent presidents that it would be nearly impossible to successfully nominate someone with that kind of record. In the end, Bork's views and the resultant political uproar across the nation led the Senate to deny him confirmation to the Court.

Subsequent presidents have tended to nominate individuals who have produced few or no legal opinions on critical issues. Illustrative is the elder President Bush's successful nomination of David Souter, often referred to as a "stealth candidate" due to his anonymity prior to nomination.

The 1991 nomination of Clarence Thomas to the "black seat" on the Supreme Court, vacated by Justice Thurgood Marshall's resignation, was supposed to be similarly quiet but resulted in another Bork-like public spectacle. Thomas seemed to be a safe bet: his writings and opinions were sparse and generally without controversy. Thomas even went so far as to deny ever having engaged in a debate on the issue of abortion:

> **Senator Leahy:** Have you [Judge Thomas] ever had discussion of *Roe v. Wade*[95] other than in this room, in the 17 or 18 years it's been there?
>
> **Judge Thomas:** Only, I guess, Senator, in the fact in the most general sense that other individuals express concerns one way or the other, and you listen and you try to be thoughtful. If you are asking me whether or not I have ever debated the contents of it, the answer to that is no, Senator.[96]

Even this denial, preposterous as it seemed to some, could not derail Thomas's quest for a seat on this nation's highest court. Without extensive writings to defend, Thomas gained wide support in the Senate.

After completing an initial hearing, however, Thomas was called back before the Judiciary Committee to face allegations of sexual harassment put forward by African-American law professor and former colleague, Anita Hill. The ensuing melee became a circus in which actors on both sides paraded before the committee, asserting their versions of the truth. Thomas, undaunted by the allegations, charged the committee with conducting a "high-tech lynching of uppity Blacks." This aggressive challenge to the senators dulled the edge of their remaining questions.

In the end, only three senators, all Democrats, admitted to changing their votes. Thomas was approved by a vote of fifty-two to forty-eight. Many members of the Senate sought to avoid the political fallout on both sides of the issue.

Though public opinion polls following the hearings found that more Americans believed Judge Thomas than Professor Hill, the image of twelve white men grilling an African-American woman about her charges of sexual harassment set in motion a political movement that resulted in the election of historic numbers of women and African Americans to both the House of Representatives and the Senate.

Two years later, in 1993, President Bill Clinton nominated Ruth Bader Ginsburg to the Court. The politics

95. 410 U.S. 113 (1973).

96. *Nomination of Judge Clarence Thomas to Be Associate Justice of the Supreme Court of the United States: Hearings Before the Senate Comm. on the Judiciary,* 102d Cong., 1st. Sess. 222 (1991).

*(Continued)*

(Inside Story *continued*)

of that nomination swirled around the question of whether the Senate should apply an abortion "litmus test" to her appointment in light of the changing Supreme Court position on the pivotal issue of whether a woman has a constitutional right to an abortion. Any indication of a controversial hearing was immediately dispelled by Judge Ginsburg's opening remarks. In an effort to preempt potential litmus test–type questions, she hinted at the inappropriateness of deciding a case in advance and promised to impartially hear each case before the Court "without reaching out to cover cases not yet seen." She stated:

> You are well aware that I come to this proceeding to be judged as a judge not an advocate. . . . A judge sworn to decide impartially can offer no forecasts, no hints, for that would show not only disregard for the specifics of a particular case; it would display disdain for the entire judicial process.[97]

Judge Ginsburg's thirteen years of judicial experience on the U.S. Court of Appeals for the District of Columbia, coupled with her impressive credentials, won her nearly unanimous support from the public as well as the Judiciary Committee. She was easily confirmed by a vote of ninety-six to three, and her hearing served as an opportunity to reduce hostility in the nomination process.

One year later, President Clinton had another opportunity to nominate a justice to the Court. Having learned from his success with Justice Ginsburg and the difficulties of his predecessors, he avoided controversy and nominated "technocrat" Stephen Breyer, a judge on the U.S. Court of Appeals for the First Circuit known for his academic writings on regulatory economics. One reporter covering Breyer's nomination hearing characterized it this way:

> The most unlikely story of the moment is that the Senate Judiciary Committee's hearings on Stephen Breyer's appointment to the Supreme Court unexpectedly became a bore, albeit a pleasant bore. That is to Breyer's advantage, for it signals an overdue cooling of the passions superheated by earlier Supreme Court confirmation fights.[98]

Whether these nominations demonstrate a return to the earlier practice of polite and deliberative advice and consent by the Senate or a temporary respite from raging political winds remains to be seen. Court watchers expect to know soon, however, as Chief Justice William Rehnquist and Justices O'Connor and John Paul Stevens are all thought likely to leave the Court in the near future.

97. *Nomination of Judge Ruth Bader Ginsburg to Be Associate Justice of the Supreme Court of the United States: Hearings Before the Senate Comm. on the Judiciary*, 103d Cong., 1st. Sess. 222 (1993).

98. Edwin M. Yoder, *Breyer's Hearings Lack Passion of Bork's*, DENVER POST, July 18, 1994, at B7.

## KEY WORDS AND PHRASES

appellate jurisdiction 52
bicameralism 54
bill of attainder 64
Bill of Rights 51
clear and present danger test 65
Commerce Clause 58
dormant Commerce Clause 62
Due Process Clause (Fifth and Fourteenth Amendments) 64
eminent domain 80
Establishment Clause 75
executive privilege 53
exemplary damages 77
*ex post facto* laws 63
federalism 51
Free Exercise Clause 75
judicial review 52
line item veto 54
negative Commerce Clause 62
original jurisdiction 52
override (of a president's veto) 53
penumbra 77
plenary 84
police power 55
preempt 51
prior restraints 72
Privileges and Immunities Clause (Fourteenth Amendment) 65
procedural due process 75
punitive damages 77
rational basis test 81
separation of powers 52
strict scrutiny test 81
subject matter jurisdiction 52
substantially related test 71
substantive due process 76
tender offer 90
trespass to chattels 90
undue burden 62
veto power 53

## QUESTIONS AND CASE PROBLEMS

1. Congress enacted legislation making carjacking a federal crime. Its stated justification included stopping transportation of carjacked vehicles across state lines, either in parts or intact, and the adverse effect of car theft on insurance rates. Does Congress have the power to make carjacking a federal crime? [*United States v. Oliver,* 60 F.3d 547 (9th Cir. 1995).]

2. The Connecticut State Employee Campaign raises funds for 900 charities through voluntary contributions by state employees; the employees can designate which of the participating organizations will receive their contributions. The Boy Scouts have a policy against employing known or avowed homosexuals as commissioned, professional Scouters or in other capacities (including adult volunteer leaders or youth members) in which such employment or position would interfere with the Boy Scouts' mission of transmitting values to youth. The Boy Scouts received about $10,000 annually from the Campaign until 2000, when the state dropped them from the Campaign after the state Human Rights Commission asserted that including the Boy Scouts would violate Connecticut's gay rights law, which prohibits the state from "becoming a party to any agreement, arrangement or plan which has the effect of sanctioning discrimination." The Boy Scouts sued on the basis that they were "singled out and excluded" from the Campaign based on their First Amendment right of association, a right that the U.S. Supreme Court recognized in *Boy Scouts of America v. Dale,* 530 U.S. 640 (2000). What will each side argue? Who will win? [*Boy Scouts of America v. Wyman,* 335 F.3d 80 (2d Cir. 2003), *cert. denied,* 124 S. Ct. 1602 (2004).]

3. Most wine in the United States is distributed through a three-tier network that developed after the repeal of Prohibition. First, the winery obtains a permit to sell wine. Next, the winery sells its wine to a licensed wholesaler, who pays excise taxes and delivers the wine to a retailer. The retailer then sells the wine to consumers. As demand for wine has increased over the last two decades, the number of wineries has grown to more than 2,000, including many small wineries. Meanwhile, the number of wholesalers has declined from several thousand to a few hundred. As a result, many small wineries are unable to find wholesalers to carry their wine and are trying to market their wine directly to consumers.

   Juanita Swedenburg runs the Swedenburg Estate Vineyard in Middleburg, Virginia. People from all over the United States visit her winery and purchase wine to take home with them. Once they get home, many call the winery or use its website to order more bottles. However, the laws in twenty-six states prohibit the direct shipment of wine to consumers across state lines. The states claim that the Twenty-first Amendment, which repealed Prohibition, gives them the authority to regulate the importation of alcohol. Their claim is based on Section 2 of the amendment, which states that "[t]he transportation or importation into any state, territory, or possession of the United States for delivery or use therein of intoxicating liquors, in violation of the laws thereof, is hereby prohibited."

   Swedenburg, other winery owners, and wine lovers are challenging direct-shipment laws in suits around the country. What arguments can they make against the direct-shipment laws? What arguments can the states make in favor of the laws? [*Dickerson v. Bailey,* 336 F.3d 388 (5th Cir. 2003); *Swedenburg v. Kelly,* 358 F.3d 223 (2d Cir. 2004), *cert. granted in part,* 124 S. Ct. 2391 (2004).]

4. A Wisconsin law permitted creditors to freeze the wages of a debtor (in legal terms, to garnish the wages) until the completion of a trial to determine the debtor's liability. Under the law, creditors' lawyers could effect a garnishment by requesting a summons from a court and serving it on the debtor's employer. No notice to the debtor was required until ten days after the summons was served. Is this procedure constitutional? Explain why or why not. [*Sniadach v. Family Fin. Corp. of Bay View,* 395 U.S. 337 (1969).]

5. Kouresh Hamidi, a former Intel engineer, together with others, formed Former and Current Employees of Intel (FACE-Intel) to distribute information and views critical of Intel's employment policies and practices. FACE-Intel maintained a website containing such material. In addition, over a two-year period Hamidi, on behalf of FACE-Intel, sent six mass e-mails criticizing Intel's employment practices to as many as 35,000 employee addresses in Intel's e-mail system. The e-mails warned employees of the danger these

practices posed for their careers, suggested that employees seek employment at other companies, solicited their participation in FACE-Intel, and urged them to visit FACE-Intel's website. Intel sued Hamidi for *trespass to chattels,* a tort action that is available when personal property is interfered with but not taken, destroyed, or substantially altered. Does Hamidi have a defense based on the Constitution? Explain why or why not. [*Intel Corp. v. Hamidi,* 71 P.3d 296 (Cal. 2003).]

6. In an effort to protect local corporations from hostile takeover bids, a number of states have adopted antitakeover regulations.
   a. MITE Corporation, an Illinois company, initiated a *tender offer* (an offer to shareholders to buy their shares) for all the outstanding shares of Chicago River & Machine Company by filing with the Securities and Exchange Commission the schedule required by the Williams Act, which is the part of the federal Securities Exchange Act of 1934 governing tender offers. A basic purpose of the Williams Act is to place investors on an equal footing with the takeover bidder. It is based on the assumption that independent shareholders faced with tender offers are at a disadvantage. MITE did not comply with the Illinois Business Take-Over Act, which required any person or company intending to make a tender offer to notify the secretary of state and the target company of the offer twenty days before it was to become effective. During that time, the offeror could not communicate its offer to the shareholders, but the target company was free to disseminate information to its shareholders concerning the impending offer. Additionally, any takeover offer had to be registered with the Illinois secretary of state, who was authorized to hold a hearing on the fairness of the offer. Is the Illinois Business Take-Over Act constitutional? [*Edgar v. MITE Corp.,* 457 U.S. 624 (1982).]
   b. Indiana's Control Share Acquisition Act provided that a "control share acquisition" that would otherwise have given an acquirer the power to vote more than specified percentages of the stock of that target (that is, 20, 33.3, or 50 percent) would not in fact result in acquisition of the commensurate voting rights unless they were conferred by a majority of the disinterested shareholders at a meeting to be held within not more than fifty days. Is the Indiana Control Share Acquisition Act constitutional? [*CTS Corp. v. Dynamics Corp. of America,* 481 U.S. 69 (1987).]

7. Terry Mitchell is a chronic alcoholic who has been unable to keep a job because of his addiction. He applied for disability insurance benefits (DIB) and supplemental security income (SSI) under the Social Security Act. Benefits were denied on the basis of Section 105 of the Contract with America Advancement Act, which prohibits the award of DIB and SSI to individuals disabled by alcoholism or drug addiction. Mitchell filed a suit alleging that Section 105 singles out alcoholics and drug addicts for unequal treatment and denies him the equal protection of the law in violation of the Fifth Amendment. What arguments can be made for striking down Section 105? What arguments can be made to justify denying DIB and SSI benefits to alcoholics and drug addicts? [*Mitchell v. Comm'r of SSA,* 182 F.3d 272 (4th Cir. 1999), *cert. denied,* 528 U.S. 944 (1999).]

8. In 1999, the State of Washington created a new college scholarship program, pursuant to which it awarded Promise Scholarships to low- and middle-income students who had achieved an excellent academic record in high school. Joshua Davey was awarded one of the Promise Scholarships. When he met with the director of financial aid at Northwest College, however, the director determined that Davey did not meet the enrollment requirements for the Promise Scholarship because he was pursuing a degree in pastoral ministries. Davey filed a lawsuit, alleging that the provision of the Washington law that denied Promise Scholarships to students pursuing a degree in theology is unconstitutional. What arguments will Davey make? What arguments will the state make? Who wins? [*Davey v. Locke,* 540 U.S. 712 (2004).]

9. The U.S. Congress enacted the Controlled Substances Act (CSA) as part of the Comprehensive Drug Abuse Prevention and Control Act of 1970. The CSA establishes that marijuana is a controlled substance and makes it unlawful to knowingly or intentionally manufacture, distribute, dispense, or possess with intent to manufacture, distribute, or dis-

pense a controlled substance, including marijuana. The CSA was enacted pursuant to Congress's authority under the Commerce Clause and includes findings that controlled substances have a substantial detrimental effect on the health and general welfare of Americans, that controlled substances manufactured and distributed intrastate cannot be differentiated from controlled substances manufactured and distributed interstate, and that federal control of the intrastate incidents of traffic in controlled substances is essential to the effective control of the interstate incidents of such traffic.

In 1996, California voters passed Proposition 215, codified as the Compassionate Use Act of 1996, to ensure that patients and their primary caregivers who obtain and use marijuana for medical purposes upon the recommendation of a physician are not subject to criminal prosecution. Angel McClary Raich and Diane Monson are California citizens who use marijuana as a medical treatment. Raich has been diagnosed with more than ten serious medical conditions, including an inoperable brain tumor, and Monson suffers from severe chronic back pain caused by a degenerative disease of the spine. In April 2002, deputies from the Butte County Sheriff's Department and agents from the U.S. Drug Enforcement Administration (DEA) came to Monson's home. The sheriff's deputies concluded that Monson's use of marijuana was legal under the Compassionate Use Act. Nonetheless, after a three-hour standoff involving the Butte County District Attorney and the U.S. Attorney for the Eastern District of California, the DEA agents seized and destroyed Monson's six cannabis plants. Fearing raids in the future and the prospect of being deprived of medicinal marijuana, Raich and Monson filed suit against the U.S. Attorney General and the Administrator of the DEA, alleging that the CSA is unconstitutional. What arguments will the plaintiffs make to try to show that the CSA is unconstitutional? What arguments will the U.S. government make in favor of the CSA? [*Raich v. Ashcroft,* 352 F.3d 1222 (9th Cir. 2003), *cert. granted,* 124 S. Ct. 2909 (2004).]

## MANAGER'S DILEMMA

**10.** The federal election laws prohibit corporate contributions to political candidates but allow corporations to establish separate segregated funds known as political action committees (PACs). PACs are permitted to collect contributions from supervisory employees and management and to distribute this money to candidates. A corporation can solicit contributions from its stockholders and administrative and executive personnel and their families, the "restricted class" for its PAC. A member of a restrictive class can contribute a maximum of $5,000 to a federal PAC. Although corporations may also solicit other employees, this solicitation is highly restricted and regulated. A corporation is prohibited from giving annual bonuses to its executives with the understanding that they will contribute part of the bonus to the corporation's PAC or to a candidate.

The CEO of Techno Corporation, Sunil Zamba, is a friend and supporter of Senator Wood from Idaho, where Techno is headquartered. He has sent memos to all of the executives and managers in the company reminding them that legislation is pending in the Senate that could negatively affect Techno's business and that Senator Wood is an opponent of the bill. Although he has not instituted a formal company policy, Zamba has strongly suggested that all of the executives and managers attend a fundraising dinner for Senator Wood and persuade at least one other business associate outside Techno to attend. Attendance at the dinner requires a donation of $6,000 per person. Zamba has made it clear that Techno will reimburse the cost of the dinner for the Techno employees and their business associate guests; he claims that this dinner is an opportunity for Techno managers and executives to network with potential clients. Have Zamba and Techno Corporation violated the federal election laws? Have they acted ethically? Would your answer be different if the dinner cost only $500 per person? Should the Techno executives attend the event?

## INTERNET SOURCES

| | |
|---|---|
| The website for the U.S. Supreme Court offers a searchable full-text database of Supreme Court opinions. New opinions are usually posted the same day they are issued. | http://www.supremecourtus.gov/ |
| The Legal Information Institute page at Cornell University Law School offers a wide variety of resources related to the U.S. Constitution, including its various articles and amendments and related historical documents; state constitutions; and international constitutional law. | http://www.law.cornell.edu/topics/constitutional.html |
| The International Constitutional Law Project at the University of Bern in Switzerland addresses constitutional law around the world and contains numerous national constitutions and related materials and links. | http://www.oefre.unibe.ch/law/icl/ |
| The Library of Congress's Broadside Collection offers a collection of materials concerning the framing of the U.S. Constitution. | http://lcweb2.loc.gov/ammem/bdsds/bdsdhome.html |
| The Constitution Society's home page offers a variety of materials about the U.S. constitutional republic, including discussions of various constitutional principles, founding documents, and related sources. | http://www.constitution.org/ |
| Yahoo!'s Constitutional Law page offers links to related sites and the opportunity to search for specific items. | http://www.yahoo.com/law/constitutional |
| White House | http://www.whitehouse.gov |
| U.S. House of Representatives | http://www.house.gov |
| U.S. Senate | http://www.senate.gov |

CHAPTER 3

# Courts, Sources of Law, and Litigation

## INTRODUCTION

### EQUAL JUSTICE UNDER THE LAW

"Equal justice under the law" is the inscription on the front of the U.S. Supreme Court building in Washington, D.C. It is a reminder that the judicial system is intended to protect the legal rights of those who come before a court. In a litigation-prone society, it is important for managers to understand the judicial system and be prepared to use it, when appropriate, to protect their rights and the rights of their companies.

### CHAPTER OVERVIEW

This chapter begins with a discussion of the federal and state court systems, including subject matter and personal jurisdiction and choice of law. It continues with a description of the sources of law, including constitutions, statutes, regulations, and common law. The chapter outlines the litigation process, including discovery, the attorney–client privilege, class actions, various trial strategies for companies involved in a lawsuit, and document-retention programs. Alternatives to litigation, such as mediation and arbitration, are discussed in Chapter 4.

## How to Read a Case Citation

When an appellate court decides a case, the court writes an opinion, which is published in one or more *reporters*—collections of court opinions. Some trial courts also publish opinions. The citation of a case (the *cite*) includes the following information:

1. The plaintiff's name
2. The defendant's name
3. The volume number and title of the reporter in which the case is reported
4. The page number at which the case report begins
5. The court that decided the case (if the court is not indicated, it is understood to be the state supreme court or the U.S. Supreme Court, depending on the reporter in which the case appears)
6. The year in which the case was decided

For example, *Callahan v. First Congregational Church of Haverhill,* 808 N.E.2d 301 (Mass. 2004), indicates that in 2004 an opinion was issued in a case involving Callahan as the plaintiff with the First Congregational Church of Haverhill as the defendant. The case was decided by the Massachusetts Supreme Judicial Court. The case is reported in volume 808 of the second series of the North Eastern Reporter, beginning on page 301. *In re WorldCom, Inc. Securities Litigation,* 293 B.R. 308 (Bankr. S.D.N.Y. 2003), refers to the bankruptcy proceedings of the communications giant WorldCom, now known as MCI. The case is reported in the Bankruptcy Reporter, volume 293, beginning on page 308. The parenthetical information indicates that this is a U.S. Bankruptcy Court sitting in the Southern District of New York.

Some cases are reported in more than one reporter. For example, the famous New York taxicab case discussed in Chapter 19, *Walkovszky v. Carlton,* is cited as 18 N.Y.2d 414, 223 N.E.2d 6, 276 N.Y.S.2d 585 (1966). One may locate this case in volume 18 of the second series of New York Reports, in volume 223 of the second series of the North Eastern Reporter, or in volume 276 of the second series of the New York Supplement.

Opinions are also available online from Westlaw at Westlaw.com and from LexisNexis. An opinion that has not yet been placed into a printed reporter receives an alphanumeric designation until it is given a published cite of the type described above. For example, *Robb v. Hungerbeeler*, 2004 WL 1208516 (8th Cir. June 3, 2004), is available online at Westlaw.com, and WL1208516 is its temporary number until it is written into the third edition of the Federal Reporter. The same case in the LexisNexis database has the cite U.S. App. LEXIS 10786 (8th Cir. June 3, 2004). Once the case is in print, the citation will change from WL1208516 or U.S. App. LEXIS 10786 to a citation with the volume and page number in "F.3d."

When quoting a particular passage from an opinion, one should include the page number on which the information is found after the page number at which the case report begins. A comma should separate the two numbers. For example, suppose one wanted to quote language from the part of the opinion where the Supreme Court of Delaware considered a class action brought by stockholders challenging the board of directors' decision to delay a company merger. The cite would read *Tooley v. Donaldson, Lufkin, Jenrette, Inc.*, 845 A.2d 1031, 1040 (Del. 2004). Thus, the case report begins on page 1031 of volume 845 of the second series of the Atlantic Reporter, and the quoted material is on page 1040. The parenthetical information identifies the adjudicating body as the Supreme Court of Delaware and the year of the opinion as 2004.

When a lawsuit is originally filed, the case name appears as *plaintiff v. defendant*. If the case is appealed, the case name usually appears as *appellant* or *petitioner* (the person who is appealing the case or seeking a writ of certiorari) *v. appellee* or *respondent* (the other party). So, if the defendant loses at the trial level and appeals the decision to a higher court, the name of the defendant (now the appellant) will appear first in the case citation.

## The U.S. and State Court Systems

The United States has two judicial systems: federal and state. Federal and state courts have different subject matter jurisdiction, meaning that they hear different kinds of cases. In general, federal courts are courts of limited subject matter jurisdiction, meaning they can adjudicate only certain types of cases. The jurisdiction of the federal courts arises from the U.S. Constitution and statutes enacted by Congress. By contrast, state courts have general subject matter jurisdiction and can therefore hear any type of dispute. The jurisdiction of a state's courts arises from that state's constitution and statutes. The two coexisting judicial systems are a result of the federalism created by the U.S. Constitution, which gives certain powers to the federal government while other powers remain with the states.

The basic structure of the federal and state court systems is diagrammed in Exhibit 3.1. In practice, this structure is more complex than the diagram indicates. For example, an applicant may appeal an adverse decision from the U.S. Patent and Trademark Office to the Board of Patent Appeals and Interferences. The person may then appeal an unfavorable ruling from this court to the Court of Appeals for the Federal Circuit. Alternatively, the applicant may appeal the unfavorable ruling of the Board of Patent Appeals and Interferences by filing a civil action, in the U.S. District Court for the District of Columbia, against the Commissioner of the U.S. Patent and Trademark Office.

## Federal Jurisdiction

Federal courts derive their legal power to hear civil cases from three sources: federal question jurisdiction, diversity jurisdiction, and jurisdiction when the United States is a party. As explained in Chapter 2, the Eleventh Amendment to the U.S. Constitution protects a state (or an agency thereof) from being sued without its consent in a federal court by a citizen of another state. Congress can abrogate this immunity only if it unequivocally expresses its intention to do so and acts pursuant to a constitutional grant of authority, such as Section 5 of the Fourteenth Amendment.

### Federal Question Jurisdiction

A *federal question* exists when the dispute concerns federal law, namely a legal right arising under the U.S. Constitution, a federal statute, federal common law, a treaty of the United States, or an administrative regulation issued by a federal government agency. There is no minimum monetary requirement for lawsuits involving a federal question.

### Diversity Jurisdiction

*Diversity jurisdiction* exists when a lawsuit is between citizens of two different states and the amount in controversy, exclusive of interest and all costs, exceeds $75,000. The purpose of the monetary requirement is to prevent trivial cases from overwhelming the federal judicial system.

EXHIBIT 3.1 Structure of the U.S. Court System

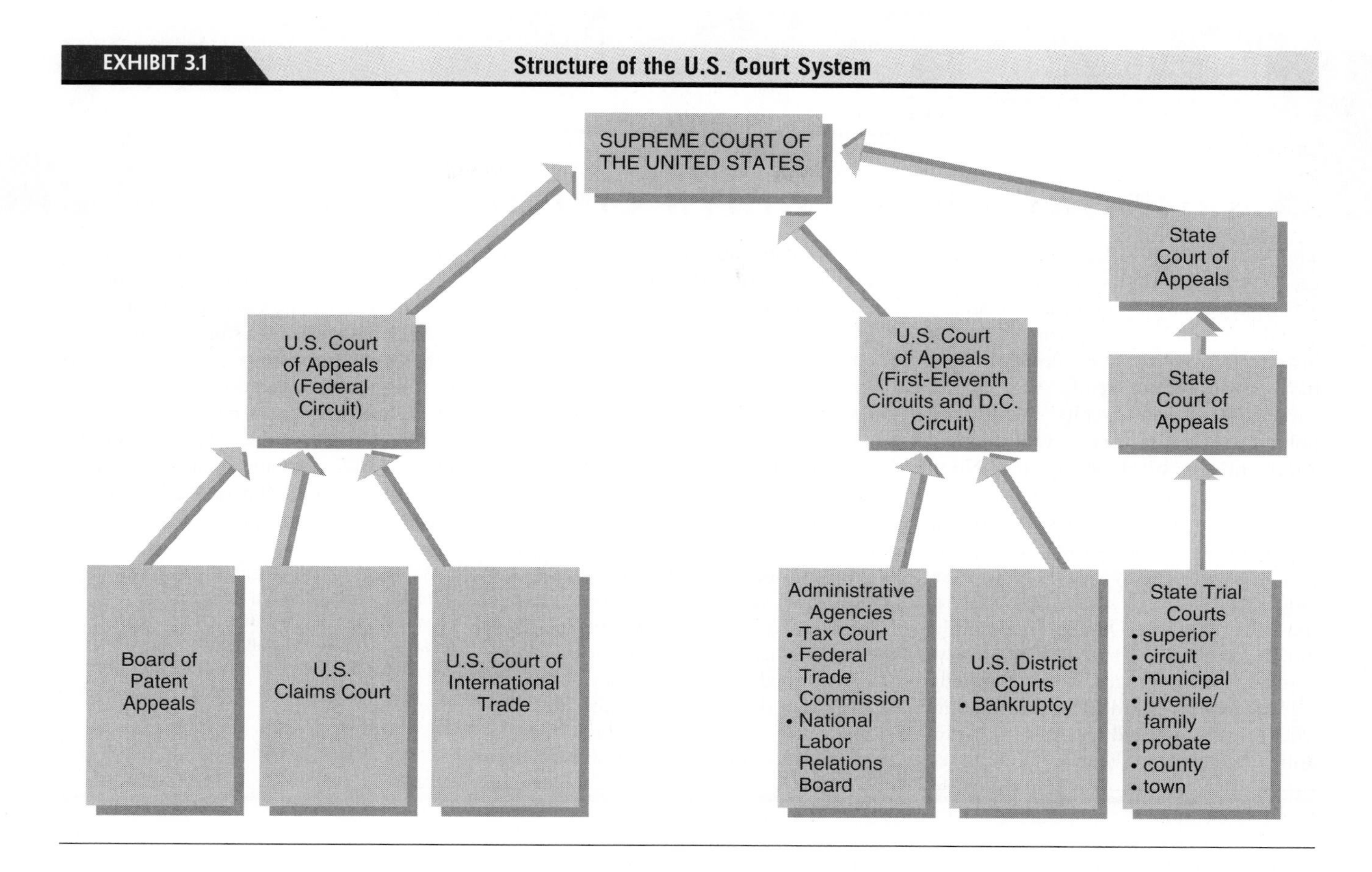


Diversity jurisdiction was traditionally justified by the fear that state courts might be biased against the out-of-state party. In federal district court, all litigants are in a neutral forum, and there should be no local prejudice for the home team.

Most diversity cases do not involve federal statutes or the U.S. Constitution and thus could also be resolved in state court. In a landmark case, *Erie Railroad Co. v. Tompkins,*[1] the U.S. Supreme Court addressed the question of whether state or federal law should apply to a suit brought in a federal court exercising its diversity jurisdiction. The Court held that a federal court must apply state law unless the lawsuit concerns the U.S. Constitution or a federal statute. In essence, the Supreme Court abolished the notion of federal common law in diversity cases.

The *Erie doctrine,* as the holding of this case is known, serves an important purpose. It ensures that the outcome of a diversity case in federal court will be similar to the outcome in a state court because the same law will govern either adjudication. This prevents litigants (the parties to a lawsuit) from *forum shopping* between federal and state courts in an attempt to have the more favorable law govern their dispute.

When litigants are in federal court due to diversity jurisdiction, they cannot choose which state's law will govern the dispute. The court itself makes this decision, applying well-established *conflict-of-law rules,* which prescribe which state's law should apply to a particular kind of case. For example, a case involving a tort, such as negligent operation of a motor vehicle, is often governed by the laws of the state where the accident occurred.

## DETERMINING CITIZENSHIP

An individual is a citizen of the state where that person has his or her legal residence or domicile. A person may have a house in more than one state. A person is a citizen, however, only of the state that he or she considers home.

1. 304 U.S. 64 (1983).

POLITICAL PERSPECTIVE

## SPLITTING UP THE NINTH CIRCUIT

The Ninth Circuit is the largest circuit in the country, with twenty-six full-time active judges and two on inactive status. Republicans in the U.S. Senate, known historically to favor less activist judges, have proposed splitting the Ninth Circuit into several circuits. Republicans point to several factors to validate their argument for breaking up the Ninth Circuit. First, the Ninth Circuit has a significant backlog of cases waiting to be heard. Even judges on the circuit admit that it has too many cases and too few judges. Secondly, its sheer size dwarfs all the other circuits. Due to its size, the judges rarely sit for en banc review. Instead, eleven judges, who, ironically, may not even include the three judges who originally heard the case, are randomly selected to hear a "limited en banc." Finally, and most controversially, Republicans argue that the Ninth Circuit is particularly liberal and activist compared to other circuits. They point out that the Ninth Circuit has been overturned more than any other circuit and that seventeen of the twenty-eight judges were appointed by Democrats.

Democrats counter that five of the judges appointed by Democrats are solidly conservative, leaving sixteen conservative judges as a counterweight to their more active colleagues. As to the number of overturned verdicts, the Democrats say that it is a function of the sheer number of verdicts handed down. The percentage of overturned verdicts is actually not much higher than that of other circuits. Still, the Republicans maintain that this circuit is unacceptably activist. They point to controversial decisions that have subsequently been overturned such as *Newdow v. United States Congress.*[a] In that case, the Ninth Circuit upheld a suit brought by the father of an elementary school student to ban teacher-led recitations of the Pledge of Allegiance in school because the Pledge contains the phrase "under God." Democrats maintain that the Ninth Circuit's perceived "liberal bias" is illusory and that its size is manageable.

a. 328 F.3d 466 (9th Cir. 2003), *rev'd* sub nom Elk Grove Unified Sch. Dist. v. Newdow, 124 S. Ct. 2301 (2004) (parent had no standing to challenge Pledge of Allegiance on behalf of minor child).

A corporation, on the other hand, may have dual citizenship. A corporation is deemed a citizen of the state in which it has been incorporated and of the state where the company has its principal place of business. Federal courts usually apply one of three tests in determining where a company engaged in multistate operations has its principal place of business.

The first is the nerve-center test. To find the corporation's nerve center, courts consider where (1) the executive and administrative offices are located, (2) the income tax return is filed, and (3) the directors and shareholders meet. The second test focuses on the place of operations. This test requires locating the majority of the corporation's physical operations, such as its manufacturing facilities or offices. The *total-activity test,* a combination of the first two tests, considers all aspects of the corporate entity, including the nature and scope of the company's activities. The total-activity test is gaining popularity among the courts.

### UNITED STATES IS A PARTY

Federal courts have jurisdiction over all lawsuits in which the U.S. government, or an officer or agency thereof, is the plaintiff or the defendant. As with federal question jurisdiction, there is no minimum monetary requirement for lawsuits where the United States is a party.

## Federal Courts

The main function of the federal courts is to interpret the Constitution and laws of the United States. President George Washington told the Supreme Court in 1790, "I have always been persuaded that the stability and success of the National Government, and consequently the happiness of the American people, would depend in a considerable degree on the interpretation and execution of its laws."

President Washington signed into law the U.S. Congress's first piece of legislation, entitled "An Act to Establish the Judicial Courts of the United States." This act created federal trial courts. Two years later, Congress created the federal courts of appeals. The three-tiered system of district courts, courts of appeals, and the U.S. Supreme Court remains today.

The president of the United States nominates each judge who serves on these federal courts. The U.S. Senate, pursuant to its "advice and consent" power, then votes to approve or reject the judicial nominees. The

Constitution does not impose any age or citizenship requirements on judicial candidates. Once confirmed by the Senate, federal judges have a lifetime appointment to the bench. They may be removed from office only by legislative impeachment if they violate the law. Lifetime tenure protects federal judges from public reprisal for making unpopular or difficult decisions. As a result, the federal judiciary is more independent than either the executive or the legislative branch.

## U.S. District Courts

The U.S. district courts are the trial courts of the federal system. Currently, the country is divided into ninety-four judicial districts. Each state has at least one district, and the more populous states have as many as four. Exhibit 3.2 shows the various districts. Many districts have two or more divisions. For example, the main location for the U.S. District Court for the Southern District of Florida is Miami, but that district also has courts in Key West, Miami/Ft. Lauderdale, West Palm Beach, and Fort Pierce. Thus, a plaintiff may file its lawsuit with the nearest federal district court, provided, of course, that the court has jurisdiction over the particular controversy.

## U.S. Courts of Appeals

The primary functions of a court of appeals are (1) to review decisions of the trial courts within its territory; (2) to review decisions of certain administrative agencies and commissions; and (3) to issue *writs,* or orders, to lower courts or to litigants. Only final decisions of lower courts are appealable. A decision is final if it conclusively resolves an issue in a dispute or the entire controversy.

Cases before the courts of appeals are usually presented to a panel of three judges. Occasionally, all the judges of a court of appeals will sit together to hear and decide a particularly important or close case. This is called an *en banc* (or *in banc*) *hearing.* The court of appeals can either affirm or reverse the decision of the lower court. It may also *vacate,* or nullify, the previous

**EXHIBIT 3.2** **Map of Federal Judicial Districts and Circuits**

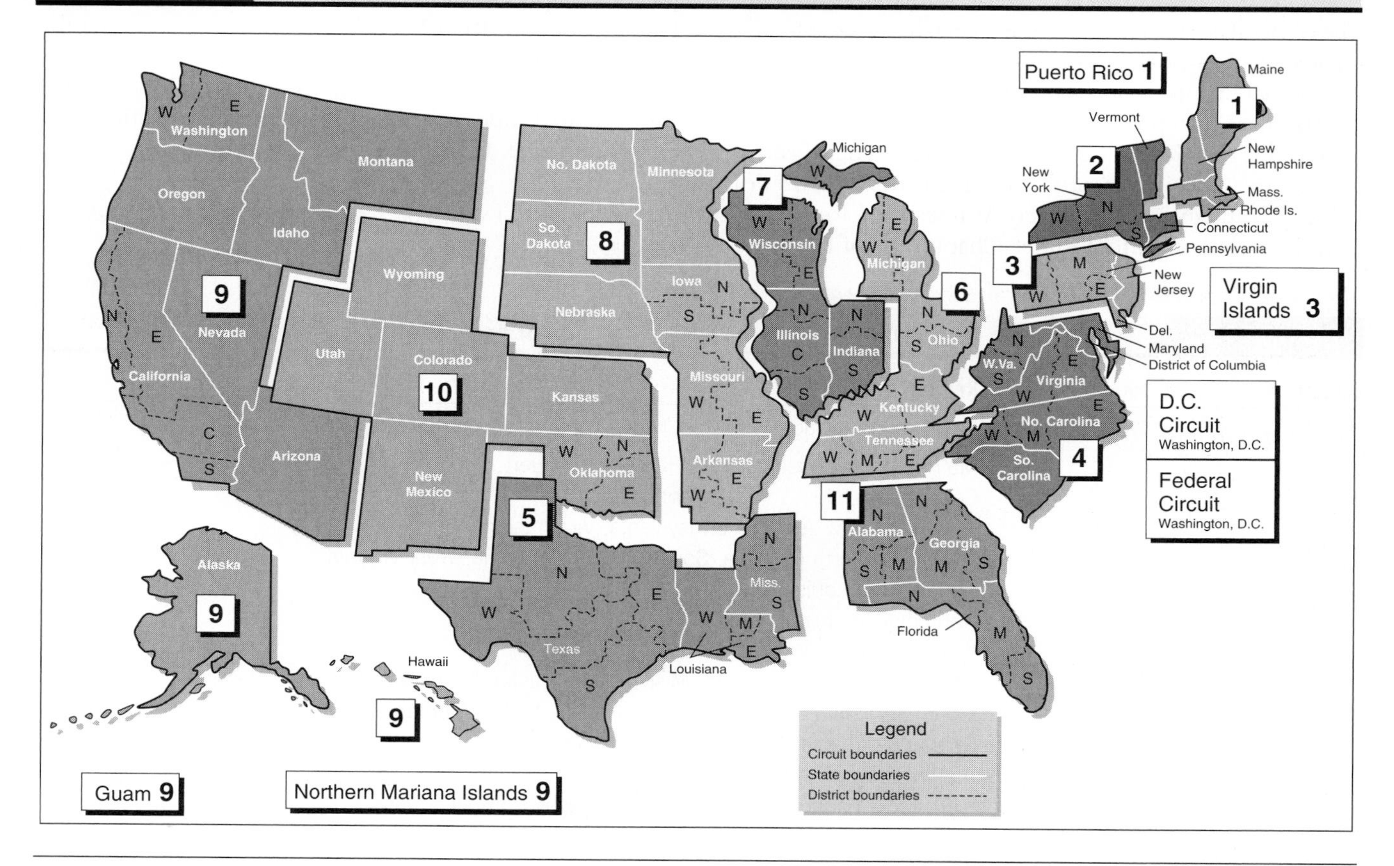

court's ruling and *remand* the case—send it back to the lower court for reconsideration. Frequently, the panel of judges will decide an appeal based upon the legal briefs, or written memoranda, submitted to the court, rather than hearing oral arguments presented by the lawyers.

There are thirteen courts of appeals, one for each of the twelve regional circuits in the United States and one for the federal circuit. The Ninth Circuit, encompassing ten states and Guam, is the largest circuit, with twenty-six active judges and two with inactive status. The Court of Appeals for the First Circuit has only six active judges. Exhibit 3.2 shows the geographic boundaries of the circuits.

The Court of Appeals for the Federal Circuit, created in 1982, does not have jurisdiction over a specific geographic region but rather hears appeals from various specialized federal courts, including the Claims Court, the Court of International Trade, and the International Trade Commission, which handles disputes involving unfair practices in import trade. The Federal Circuit also hears all cases involving patents. Exhibit 3.3 lists the states and territories included within each circuit.

## SPECIALIZED FEDERAL COURTS

The federal system has several specialized courts that resolve legal disputes within particular subject areas.

The bankruptcy courts are units of the federal district courts that hear proceedings involving the bankruptcy laws and regulations of the United States. When Fruit of the Loom (clothing manufacturer), Enron Corporation (energy company), and United Airlines filed for protection from their creditors under Chapter 11 of the bankruptcy laws, they did so in federal bankruptcy court. (The law of bankruptcy is discussed in Chapter 24.)

The tax courts hear taxpayer petitions or appeals regarding federal income, estate, and gift taxes. The Court of International Trade has jurisdiction over disputes involving tariffs, or import taxes, and trade laws. This court also hears cases on appeal from the U.S. International Trade Commission. The U.S. Court of Military Appeals hears cases from the lower courts and tribunals within the armed services.

## U.S. SUPREME COURT

The Supreme Court consists of one chief justice and eight associate justices. At least six justices must be present to hear a case. A majority of the cases heard by the Supreme Court are on appeal from the U.S. courts of appeals. A decision by a state supreme court is also appealable to the U.S. Supreme Court, but only when the case concerns the U.S. Constitution or some other federal law. The Supreme Court may hear direct appeals from a federal district court decision if the court declared an act of the U.S. Congress unconstitutional. For example, the Supreme Court directly reviewed the invalidation of the Line Item Veto Act by the District Court for the District of Columbia.[2]

The Supreme Court has discretionary review, meaning that it decides which cases within its jurisdiction it will adjudicate. When it decides to hear a case, the

2. City of New York v. Clinton, 985 F. Supp. 168 (D.D.C. 1998), *aff'd*, 524 U.S. 417 (1998).

**EXHIBIT 3.3 Geographic Regions of the U.S. Courts of Appeal**

| Circuit | Region |
|---|---|
| *District of Columbia* | District of Columbia |
| *First* | Maine, Massachusetts, New Hampshire, Puerto Rico, Rhode Island |
| *Second* | Connecticut, New York, Vermont |
| *Third* | Delaware, New Jersey, Pennsylvania, Virgin Islands |
| *Fourth* | Maryland, North Carolina, South Carolina, Virginia, West Virginia |
| *Fifth* | Canal Zone, Louisiana, Mississippi, Texas |
| *Sixth* | Kentucky, Michigan, Ohio, Tennessee |
| *Seventh* | Illinois, Indiana, Wisconsin |
| *Eighth* | Arkansas, Iowa, Minnesota, Missouri, Nebraska, North Dakota, South Dakota |
| *Ninth* | Alaska, Arizona, California, Guam, Hawaii, Idaho, Montana, Nevada, Oregon, Washington |
| *Tenth* | Colorado, Kansas, New Mexico, Oklahoma, Utah, Wyoming |
| *Eleventh* | Alabama, Florida, Georgia |
| *Federal* | Based in Washington D.C., but hears cases from all regions |

Supreme Court issues a *writ of certiorari* ordering the lower court to certify the record of proceedings below and send it up to the Supreme Court. Four justices must vote to hear a case before a writ can be issued. If a writ was sought but denied by the Supreme Court, the citation for the case will indicate *"cert. denied."*

The Supreme Court will not decide cases that involve a political question. A *political question* is a conflict that should be decided by either the executive or the legislative branch of government. Under the political question doctrine, the Supreme Court identifies those disputes that are more appropriately decided by democratically elected officials. Nonetheless, the Court effectively decided the 2000 U.S. presidential election when it prohibited Florida from doing a manual recount of the ballots in *Bush v. Gore,* 531 U.S. 98 (2000).

## STANDING

Courts will not hear an appeal unless a real and substantial controversy is involved and resolving the lawsuit will provide actual relief to one party.[3] Further, the party pursuing the appeal must have standing to sue. *Standing* means that the party seeking relief (1) is the proper party to advance the litigation, (2) has a personal interest in the outcome of the suit, and (3) will benefit from a favorable ruling. The following case addressed the issue of whether commercial banks have standing to challenge the National Credit Union Administration's interpretation of the Federal Credit Union Act.

3. United States v. Hays, 515 U.S. 737 (1995).

A CASE IN POINT

### In the Language of the Court

**CASE 3.1**

**National Credit Union Administration v. First National Bank & Trust Co.**

*Supreme Court of the United States*
*522 U.S. 479 (1998).*

**› FACTS** Section 109 of the Federal Credit Union Act (FCUA) provides that "federal credit union membership shall be limited to groups having a common bond of occupation or association, or to groups within a well-defined neighborhood, community, or rural district." The National Credit Union Administration (NCUA), the agency responsible for administering the FCUA, interpreted Section 109 to permit federal credit unions to be composed of multiple unrelated employer groups. The NCUA later approved a series of amendments to the charter of a federal credit union that added several unrelated employer groups.

As competitors to the credit unions, five commercial banks and the American Bankers Association brought an action alleging that the new employer groups did not share the "common bond of occupation" required under Section 109. They brought their claim under Section 10 of the Administrative Procedure Act (APA), which provides that "[a] person suffering legal wrong because of agency action, or adversely affected or aggrieved by agency action within the meaning of the statute, is entitled to judicial review thereof." The district court dismissed the complaint on grounds of lack of standing. The appeals court reversed, and the defendants raised the issue again before the Supreme Court.

**› ISSUE PRESENTED** Do commercial banks have standing to seek federal court review of the NCUA's interpretation of Section 109 of the FCUA?

**› OPINION** THOMAS, J., writing for the U.S. Supreme Court:

For a plaintiff to have prudential standing under the APA, "the interest sought to be protected by the complainant [must be] arguably within the zone of interests to be protected or regulated by the statute . . . in question."

. . .

Our prior cases . . . have consistently held that for a plaintiff's interests to be arguably within the "zone of interests" to be protected by a statute, there does not have to be an "indication of congressional purpose to benefit the would-be plaintiff." The proper inquiry is simply "whether the interest sought to be protected by the complainant is arguably within the zone of interests to be protected . . . by the statute."

*(Continued)*

(Case 3.1 *continued*)

. . .

. . . By its express terms, §109 limits membership in every federal credit union to members of definable "groups." Because federal credit unions may, as a general matter, offer banking services only to members, §109 also restricts the markets that every federal credit union can serve. . . . [E]ven if it cannot be said that Congress had the specific purpose of benefiting commercial banks, one of the interests "arguably . . . to be protected" by §109 is an interest in limiting the markets that federal credit unions can serve. . . . [T]he NCUA's interpretation has affected that interest by allowing federal credit unions to increase their customer base.

**› RESULT** Commercial banks had standing to challenge the NCUA's interpretation of the Federal Credit Union Act.

**› COMMENTS** Justice O'Connor stated in a brief dissent, joined by Justices Stevens, Souter, and Breyer, that the decision of the Court "all but eviscerates the zone-of-interests requirements." Congress responded by passing legislation that expressly adopted the NCUA's interpretation.

**› CRITICAL THINKING QUESTIONS**

1. Why would commercial banks favor a narrower definition of "common bond of occupation"?
2. Should commercial banks be permitted to challenge the NCUA's interpretation of the Federal Credit Union Act?

## State Courts

State courts handle the bulk of legal disputes in the United States. Each state's constitution creates the judicial branch of government for that state. For example, the Constitution of Texas provides:

> [T]he judicial power of this State shall be vested in one Supreme Court, in one Court of Criminal Appeals, in Courts of Appeals, in District Courts, in County Courts, in Commissioners Courts, in Courts of Justices of the Peace, and in such other courts as may be provided by law.[4]

The various sections then provide the details of the state judicial system. These include the number of justices sitting on the state's supreme court, the jurisdiction of the state courts, the geographic districts of the various courts of appeal, the way in which justices and judges are selected or appointed, and the tenure of the justices and judges.

### State Trial Courts

At the lowest level of the state trial court system are several courts of limited jurisdiction. These courts decide minor criminal matters, small civil suits, and other specialized legal disputes. Examples include traffic courts, small claims courts, juvenile courts, and family courts. In these courts, the procedures can be informal. Parties may appear without lawyers, the court may not keep a complete transcript or recording of the proceedings, and the technical rules of evidence and formal courtroom procedures may not apply. The jurisdiction of a small claims court is usually limited to disputes involving less than, for example, $5,000. Any dispute involving more than this amount must be heard by a higher-level trial court.

The second level of state trial courts consists of courts of general or unlimited jurisdiction. These courts have formal courtroom procedures, apply the standard rules of evidence, and record all proceedings.

In 2002, the State of Michigan created the first "cybercourt" to hear business-related litigation. Circuit court judges preside over the court, which uses videoconferencing, digital record keeping, and other online tools. All filings and briefs are filed online. The court's goal is to expedite business litigation involving more than $25,000 and significantly lower its cost. The success of the Michigan cybercourt has prompted several other states to consider starting their own cybercourts.

State court actions cover a broad spectrum of business activities. For example, in Vermont an employee of a ski lodge filed a claim for workers' compensation benefits

4. Tex. Const., art. V, § 1.

for an injury sustained while he was skiing in his position as a "ski bum."[5] In Louisiana, a plant worker sued the chemical company Monsanto because she suffered an anxiety attack after a supervisor violently berated her for not working.[6] In a class action brought by smokers in state court in Florida against five top tobacco companies, including Philip Morris and R.J. Reynolds, the jury awarded $6.9 million in compensatory damages and $145 billion in punitive damages.[7]

### STATE APPELLATE COURTS

A state appellate court is similar to its counterpart in the federal system. It usually consists of a panel of three judges who review the lower court ruling for errors in application of the law or procedures. The appellate court usually accepts the findings of fact of the trial judge or jury, unless a particular finding is clearly unsupported by the evidence presented at trial. The appellate court is not required to accept the lower court's conclusions of law but may consider legal issues *de novo,* or anew, as if the trial court had not made any conclusions of law. An appellate court may affirm, reverse, or vacate and remand any final decision of a lower court.

### STATE SUPREME COURT

Each state has one court that acts as the highest judicial authority in that state. Most states call that court the supreme court. (In New York, however, the highest state court is called the Court of Appeals; the intermediate appellate court is called the Supreme Court, Appellate Division; and the state trial courts are called supreme courts.) The number of justices on a state supreme court varies from three to nine. A state supreme court usually has discretionary jurisdiction over all decisions of a court of appeals. Further, a state supreme court may have jurisdiction over cases where a statute of the state or the United States has been ruled unconstitutional in whole or in part. A state supreme court also resolves appeals in criminal cases in which a sentence of death has been imposed.

## Personal Jurisdiction

For a state court to hear a civil case, the court must have personal jurisdiction. *Personal jurisdiction* means that the court has legal authority over the parties to the lawsuit. Personal jurisdiction may be based upon the residence or activities of the person being sued (called *in personam jurisdiction*) or upon the location of the property at issue in the lawsuit (called *in rem jurisdiction*). For example, if an individual does any business in the state, then he or she is properly within the jurisdiction of that state's courts. Owning property in a state, causing a personal injury or property damage within the state, or even paying alimony or child support to someone living within the state might justify the exercise of personal jurisdiction by that state's courts.

The Anticybersquatting Consumer Protection Act (ACPA)[8] was enacted in November 1999 to give trademark owners the ability to bring an *in rem* suit to invalidate a domain name registration by a cybersquatter when personal jurisdiction is not attainable. *In rem* jurisdiction is available only in situations where the plaintiff has "disproved" the existence of personal jurisdiction.[9]

Most states have *long-arm statutes,* which can subject an out-of-state defendant to jurisdiction in the state, as long as due process requirements are met. The Due Process Clause exists, in part, to give "a degree of predictability to the legal system that allows potential defendants to structure their primary conduct with some minimum assurance as to where that conduct will and will not render them liable to suit."[10] The critical test is whether the defendant has certain *minimum contacts* with the state "such that the maintenance of the suit does not offend 'traditional notions of fair play and substantial justice.'"[11]

The courts generally require that the nonresident defendant (1) have done some act or consummated some transaction in the forum in which it is being sued or (2) have purposefully availed itself of the privilege of conducting activities in the forum, thereby invoking the benefits and protections of the forum. Courts have held that negotiating business contracts by means of telephone calls, the mail, or even a fax machine is sufficient to provide a state court with personal jurisdiction over an individual or corporation. Personal jurisdiction may also be proper over a nonresident defendant who committed an intentional tort outside the forum when the tortious conduct was aimed at the forum and the brunt of the harm was felt by the plaintiff in the forum.[12]

5. Grather v. Gables Inn, Ltd., 751 A.2d 762 (Vt. 2000).
6. Proyer v. Monsanto Co., 606 So. 2d 1307 (La. Cir. 1992).
7. Marc Kaufman, *Tobacco Suit Award: $145 Billion; Fla. Jury Hands Industry Major Setback,* WASH. POST, July 15, 2000.
8. 15 U.S.C. § 1125(d) (1999).
9. Heathmont A.E. Corp. v. Technodome.com, 106 F. Supp. 2d 860 (E.D. Va. 2000).
10. World-Wide Volkswagen Corp. v. Woodson, 444 U.S. 286 (1980).
11. International Shoe Co. v. Washington, 326 U.S. 310, 316 (1945) (quoting Milliken v. Meyer, 311 U.S. 457, 463 (1940)).
12. IMO Indus., Inc. v. Kiekert AG, 155 F.3d 254 (3d Cir. 1999).

# View from Cyberspace

## PERSONAL JURISDICTION AND THE WEB

The global reach of the Internet, enabling businesses to sell goods and services throughout the world, has raised new issues about the permissible scope of personal jurisdiction based on use of the Internet. In general, "the likelihood that personal jurisdiction can be constitutionally exercised is directly proportionate to the nature and quality of commercial activity that an entity conducts over the Internet."[a] The U.S. District Court for the Western District of Pennsylvania adopted a sliding scale, stating:

> At one end of the spectrum are situations where a defendant clearly does business over the Internet. If the defendant enters into contracts with residents of a foreign jurisdiction that involved the knowing and repeated transmission of computer files over the Internet, personal jurisdiction is proper. At the opposite end are situations where a defendant has simply posted information on an Internet Web site that is accessible to users in foreign jurisdictions. A passive Web site that does little more than make information available to those who are interested in it is not grounds for the exercise of personal jurisdiction. The middle ground is occupied by interactive Web sites where a user can exchange information with the host computer. In these cases, the exercise of jurisdiction is determined by examining the level of interactivity and commercial nature of the exchange of information that occurs on the Web site.[b]

On one end of that spectrum lies *Pavlovich v. Superior Court,*[c] the first case involving jurisdiction based on Internet postings to reach the California Supreme Court. In this case, Pavlovich, a Texas resident, was sued in California for posting on the Internet decryption codes that could be used to decode and copy DVDs. The plaintiff, DVD Copy Control Association, Inc., claimed that Pavlovich, the president of Media Driver, LLC, facilitated the illegal copying of DVDs and thereby reduced sales for motion picture companies based in California. The court ruled that posting the codes merely provided information that was accessible to users in foreign jurisdictions. It did not subject the defendants to personal jurisdiction in California because the website did not, in itself, have any particular contact with California.

On the other end of the spectrum lies *Gator.com v. L.L. Bean, Inc.,*[d] a case involving retailer L.L. Bean whose website generates millions of dollars annually for the company. Gator.com, a software company based in California, distributed a computer program that displayed coupons for a competitor's websites when a user accessed the L.L. Bean website. L.L. Bean, which is based in Maine and has no place of business in California, sent a letter to Gator.com requesting that it cease distributing the program. Gator.com responded by filing an action in California asking for a court order against L.L. Bean and affirming the legality of its program. L.L. Bean sought to have the case dismissed for lack of jurisdiction. A three-judge panel of the Ninth Circuit ruled that L.L. Bean could be sued in California. Its interactive website generated almost $11 million in sales, a substantial portion of which were to customers in California.

The panel distinguished *Pavlovich,* reasoning that L.L. Bean's website did more than post information on the Internet—it effected interactive exchanges with residents in California. The Ninth Circuit agreed to rehear the case *en banc* in 2004, effectively vacating the three-judge panel opinion.

To date, most courts have been unwilling to extend personal jurisdiction to out-of-state defendants who have posted defamatory articles about an in-state resident on a passive website. In *Revell v. Lidov,*[e] an out-of-state individual posted an article alleging that a former FBI agent, now a resident of Texas, had acted to cover up information regarding the famous Pan Am jetliner bombing over Lockerbie, Scotland. The Fifth Circuit, looking for "something more" than just universal accessibility of the article, found that the article did not make direct or indirect reference to Texas and ruled that the harm suffered by the plaintiff was incidental to his residence in Texas. Similarly, in *Young v. New Haven Advocate,*[f] the Fourth Circuit was unwilling to grant jurisdiction in Virginia over a Connecticut-based newspaper based solely on the fact that Virginia residents had default access to the Internet and therefore, by default, had access to an article about a Virginia resident.

In contrast, the High Court of Australia exercised personal jurisdiction over Dow Jones & Co. after it published allegedly defamatory statements about an Australian citizen.[g] The Court based jurisdiction solely on the accessibility of the company's website in Australia.

a. Zippo Mfg. Co. v. Zippo Dot Com, 952 F. Supp. 1119, 1124 (W.D. Pa. 1997).
b. *Id.*
c. 58 P.3d 2, 31 (Cal. 2002).
d. 341 F.3d 1072 (9th Cir. 2003), *reh'g en banc granted,* 366 F.3d 789 (9th Cir. 2004).
e. 317 F.3d 467 (5th Cir. 2002).
f. 315 F.3d 256 (4th Cir. 2002), *cert. denied,* 538 U.S. 1035 (2003).
g. Dow Jones & Co. v. Gutnick (2002) HCA 56, 194 A.L.R. 433.

*Service of process* (notifying the defendant of a claim) has traditionally been accomplished either by mail or by personally handing a prospective defendant papers notifying him or her of the claim. If a party happens to be physically present in the forum, personal service will always be considered proper regardless of the party's contact with the forum. The Supreme Court has gone as far as to allow someone merely vacationing in a state to be served and then forced to answer to charges in that state.[13] Recently, the U.S. Court of Appeals for the Ninth Circuit ruled that service via e-mail was acceptable for an "elusive" Costa Rican–based entity.[14]

**INTERNATIONAL SNAPSHOT**

In 2002, the European Union (EU) adopted the Brussels Conventions to standardize the rules for determining where suits involving e-commerce may be brought. A person may bring suit (1) in the EU state where he or she is domiciled; (2) in the EU state where the defendant is domiciled; (3) in the place of performance when the case involves a contract dispute; or (4) where the harmful act occurred in the event of a tortious (that is, wrongful) act. In effect, the Brussels Conventions are attempting to instruct European courts to use the same standards for e-commerce as for standard commerce.

## Choice of Law, Choice of Forum, and the Doctrine of *Forum Conveniens*

The question of which jurisdiction's law to apply comes up not only in the context of diversity cases heard in federal court but also in state court actions involving the citizens of more than one state. This question is governed by a complicated set of conflict-of-law rules. In general, the state that has the greatest governmental interest in a case will provide the governing law. Put another way, selecting the governing law is guided by a grouping of contacts: the state with the strongest contacts with the litigants and the subject matter of the litigation has the greatest interest in the application of its law.

Sometimes a state will use formalistic rules. Some states look only to where a contract was entered into when deciding which state's contract law should govern a dispute. For example, because Pennzoil and Getty Oil Company entered into their contract in New York, the lens of New York's contract law was used to evaluate whether there was a binding contract. (Texaco's intentional interference with this contract, and the related litigation, is discussed in the "Inside Story" in Chapter 7.)

Sometimes more than one state or country has an interest in the outcome of a case. When that happens, the court is permitted to apply the laws of different states or countries to different issues, under the doctrine of *depeçage*. For example, *Calhoun v. Yamaha Motor Corp.*[15] involved a suit for the wrongful death of a twelve-year-old child from Pennsylvania in a jet-ski accident in the territorial waters of Puerto Rico. The court held that Pennsylvania had an interest in securing remedies for its citizens; thus, Pennsylvania law should govern compensating damages. Because Puerto Rico had an equally strong interest in punishing wrongdoing in its territory, the court used Puerto Rican law to determine the availability of punitive damages.

The parties to a contract may agree in advance which law will govern their dispute in the event that one develops. This section is usually entitled "Governing Law" or "Choice of Law." Parties can also decide in advance where any disputes will be litigated. This is done by including a *choice-of-forum clause*. A contract may also provide that disputes will be decided by a method other than litigation. A common choice is arbitration, which is discussed in Chapter 4.

A court will usually uphold the contracting parties' choice of law and forum. In particular, U.S. courts will honor clauses in a valid contract requiring disputes to be resolved in another country under its laws unless (1) the clause was fraudulently included in the contract, (2) enforcement would deprive a party "of his day in court," or (3) enforcement would contravene a strong

**INTERNATIONAL SNAPSHOT**

Although issues of choice of law and choice of forum often arise in cases involving parties from different jurisdictions within the United States, similar issues arise when parties are from different countries. In either context, the court adjudicating the dispute must balance the competing interests of different sovereignties and resolve the conflict according to one jurisdiction's conflict-of-laws rules. To avoid confusion, it is customary for a contract involving parties from different jurisdictions to specify which country's laws will govern and where the dispute will be tried.

13. Burnham v. Superior Court of Cal., 495 U.S. 604 (1990).
14. Rio Props., Inc. v. Rio Int'l Interlink, 284 F.3d 1007 (9th Cir. 2002).
15. 216 F.3d 338 (3d Cir. 2000), *cert. denied*, 531 U.S. 1037 (2004).

public policy of the forum in which suit is brought.[16] For example, the Ninth Circuit enforced a contract between U.S. citizens and the English insurance company Lloyd's of London that stipulated that any dispute would be resolved by English law in an English court.[17] The court rejected the plaintiffs' assertion that they should have the protections afforded by the U.S. securities laws. To mandate that American standards govern such controversies would demean the standards elsewhere and place U.S. law over that of other countries. Furthermore, the court explained, it is simply not possible for the United States to trade in world markets and across international waters exclusively on its terms, governed by its laws, and resolved in its courts.

The doctrine of *forum non conveniens* may be invoked by a defendant to require a change of forum when there is no choice-of-forum clause to enforce. The following case highlights some of the factors a court will consider in determining whether it is the proper forum.

16. The Bremen v. Zapata Off Shore Co., 407 U.S. 1 (1972).
17. Richards v. Lloyd's of London, 135 F.3d 1289 (9th Cir. 1998), *cert. denied,* 525 U.S. 943 (1998).

A CASE IN POINT

**CASE 3.2**
**Dawdy v. Union Pacific Railroad Co.**
*Supreme Court of Illinois*
*797 N.E.2d 687 (Ill. 2003).*

## Summary

**› FACTS** In May 1997, William Dawdy was driving a tractor on a highway in Macoupin County, Illinois, when he was struck by a truck driven by an employee of the Union Pacific Railroad. The Union Pacific employee was acting within the scope of employment when the accident occurred, thereby exposing Union Pacific to liability as well.

Dawdy filed two complaints in Madison County, Illinois. Union Pacific then filed a motion to transfer the case to Macoupin County under the doctrine of *forum non conveniens.* Union Pacific pointed out that Dawdy did not reside in Madison County; the accident did not occur there; most of the witnesses did not reside there; and Union Pacific was based in Omaha, Nebraska, and incorporated in Delaware. Dawdy claimed that Madison was just as convenient as Macoupin or only negligibly less convenient. Most of the witnesses identified in Union Pacific's motion lived outside both Madison and Macoupin counties but conducted business regularly in Madison County. In addition, both Union Pacific's and Dawdy's lawyers lived closer to Madison County. After an appeals court denied the motion to change forums, Union Pacific appealed to the Supreme Court of Illinois.

**› ISSUE PRESENTED** Under what circumstances should a court require a plaintiff to litigate a case in the forum preferred by the defendant?

**› SUMMARY OF OPINION** The Illinois Supreme Court began by acknowledging that Illinois, like virtually all states, has a statute governing forum selection. Yet its statute was so broad as to permit suit in either county. The court invoked the equitable doctrine of *forum non conveniens* to determine which forum was more appropriate. Relying on the analytical framework set out by the U.S. Supreme Court in *Gulf Oil Corp. v. Gilbert,*[18] the Illinois Supreme Court laid out the private and public factors to be considered when determining the most fundamentally fair and judicially efficient decision.

First, the court looked at private interest factors, such as (1) ease of access to and for witnesses; (2) ability to view the actual accident site; (3) and "other practical considerations" that would make the trial easy, expeditious, and inexpensive. The court found that access to witnesses, ability to view the accident site, and, for the most part, the general ease of trial favored moving the case to Macoupin County.

The court then analyzed the public interest factors, including court congestion, the burden of jury duty on a community with no relationship to the incident, and any local interest in the given controversy. Again, the court concluded that these factors supported a finding of *forum non conveniens.*

18. 330 U.S. 301 (1947).

*(Continued)*

(Case 3.2 *continued*)

**› RESULT** The Illinois Supreme Court reversed the lower court and ordered the trial moved to Macoupin County.

**› COMMENTS** Justice Kilbride dissented from the majority opinion, arguing that the doctrine of *forum non conveniens* should be invoked only in exceptional circumstances when the interests of justice *require* a more convenient forum.

---

## Sources of Law

In applying the law, federal and state courts look to constitutions, statutes, regulations, and common (or case) law.

### CONSTITUTIONS

Courts may be called upon to interpret the U.S. or state constitutions. For example, the First Amendment provides that Congress shall make no law abridging the freedom of speech. Incidents of flag burning have required courts to interpret just what type of conduct constitutes speech protected by the First Amendment. Lawsuits concerning random drug testing of employees have centered on whether this testing violates the Fourth Amendment ban on unreasonable searches and/or the right to privacy.

The U.S. Constitution does not expressly set forth a right to privacy. As explained in Chapter 2, such a right is found in the penumbra of other articulated rights. The following case considered whether it was constitutional to require random drug testing of student athletes.

A CASE IN POINT

### In the Language of the Court

**CASE 3.3**

**Board of Education of Independent School District No. 92 of Pottawatomie County v. Earls**

*Supreme Court of the United States*
*536 U.S. 822 (2002).*

**› FACTS** The Tecumseh, Oklahoma school district adopted a policy requiring all student-athletes to consent to urinalysis drug testing as a condition of participating in extracurricular activities. In effect, this gave schools the right to test athletes without any suspicion of drug use. Earls, along with another student and their parents, claimed that this policy violated the Fourth Amendment to the U.S. Constitution's ban on unreasonable searches.

**› ISSUE PRESENTED** Does requiring a drug test without any suspicion of drug use violate the Fourth Amendment?

**› OPINION** THOMAS, J., writing for the U.S. Supreme Court:

The Fourth Amendment to the United States Constitution protects "[t]he right of the people to be secure in their persons, houses, papers, and effects, against unreasonable searches and seizures." Searches by public school officials, such as the collection of urine samples, implicate Fourth Amendment interests. . . . We must therefore review the School District's Policy for "reasonableness," which is the touchstone of the constitutionality of a governmental search.

Respondents argue that drug testing must be based at least on some level of individualized suspicion. It is true that we generally determine the reasonableness of a search by balancing the nature of the intrusion on the individual's privacy against the promotion of legitimate governmental interests. But we have long held that "the Fourth Amendment imposes no irreducible requirement of [individualized] suspicion.". . . "[I]n certain limited circumstances, the Government's need to discover such latent or hidden conditions, or to prevent their development, is sufficiently compelling to justify the intrusion on privacy entailed by conducting such searches without any measure of individualized suspicion." Therefore, in the context of safety

*(Continued)*

(Case 3.3 *continued*)

and administrative regulations, a search unsupported by probable cause may be reasonable "when 'special needs, beyond the normal need for law enforcement, make the warrant and probable-cause requirement impracticable.'"

In *Vernonia*,[19] this Court held that the suspicionless drug testing of athletes was constitutional. The Court, however, did not simply authorize all school drug testing, but rather conducted a fact-specific balancing of the intrusion on the children's Fourth Amendment rights against the promotion of legitimate governmental interests. Applying the principles of *Vernonia* to the somewhat different facts of this case, we conclude that Tecumseh's Policy is also constitutional.

[Justice Thomas went on to identify and examine several factors influencing the Court's decision, including the nature of the students' privacy being compromised by the drug testing, the degree to which a urinalysis is intrusive to the students, and the urgency of a school's need to obtain results quickly. After discussing and weighing these factors, the Court ruled that the policy was tailored to further the school district's goal of lower drug use among its student-athletes.]

**› RESULT** In a five-to-four decision, the Supreme Court ruled that the random drug testing of student-athletes was constitutional.

**› COMMENTS** In her dissent from the judgment of the Court, Justice Ginsburg (with whom Justices O'Connor, Stevens and Souter joined) stated:

> "[T]he legality of a search of a student," this Court has instructed, "should depend simply on the reasonableness, under all the circumstances, of the search.". . . The particular testing program upheld today is not reasonable; it is capricious, even perverse: [Tecumseh's] policy targets for testing a student population least likely to be at risk from illicit drugs and their damaging effects. I therefore dissent. . . .
>
> Concern for student health and safety is basic to the school's caretaking, and it is undeniable that "drug use carries a variety of health risks for children, including death from overdose."
>
> Those risks, however, are present for all schoolchildren. *Vernonia* cannot be read to endorse invasive and suspicionless drug testing of all students upon any evidence of drug use, solely on the ground that drugs jeopardize the life and health of those who use them.

**› CRITICAL THINKING QUESTIONS**

1. Do you find the argument of the majority or the dissent more persuasive?
2. Several very famous American professional athletes, primarily baseball players, have recently been subpoenaed in connection with an investigation of a lab that allegedly provided them with "designer steroids" to enhance physical performance.[20] These drugs are not illegal under state or federal law and are not prohibited by the rules of Major League Baseball. The only thing stopping some baseball players from openly taking these drugs is the public outrage occasioned by these revelations. What, if any, impact do you think this decision will have on Major League Baseball's ongoing discussions to reach an agreement with the players to randomly test for steroids?

19. Vernonia Sch. Dist. 47J v. Acton, 515 U.S. 646 (1995).
20. Harvey Araton, *Sports of the Times; Proof Is Needed Before Athletes Are Disciplined,* N.Y. Times, May 29, 2004, at D1.

## STATUTES

Congress enacts statutes in such areas as public assistance, food and drugs, patents and copyrights, labor relations, and civil rights. For example, Title 42 of the United States Code, Section 2000(a), provides that "all persons shall be entitled to the full and equal enjoyment of the goods, services, facilities, privileges, advantages, and accommodations of any place of public accommodation . . . without discrimination or segregation on the grounds of race, color, religion or national origin." State legislatures also adopt statutes covering a broad range of topics, from requirements for a will to the formation and governance of corporations to rights of employers. For example, Section 16600[21] of the California Business and Professions Code generally invalidates employee covenants not to compete except in connection with the sale of an employee's stock in a transaction involving the sale of the corporation as a going concern.

## REGULATIONS

Courts sometimes hear cases arising under regulations issued by administrative agencies and executive departments. Federal regulations and rules are printed in the multivolume *Code of Federal Regulations (CFR),* which is revised and updated every year.

The CFR covers such varied topics as the regulations applying to federal highways issued by the Department of Transportation; the Internal Revenue Service regulations issued by the Department of the Treasury; the immigration and naturalization rules and procedures issued by the Bureau of Citizenship and Immigration Services in the Department of Homeland Security; the regulations governing the sale of securities issued by the Securities and Exchange Commission; and the regulations governing television, radio, and telecommunications issued by the Federal Communications Commission. Administrative rules and regulations, and the various agencies, are discussed in Chapter 6.

## COMMON LAW

*Common law* is case law—the legal rules made by judges when they decide a case where no constitution, statute, or regulation exists to resolve the dispute. Common law originated in England, and in the United States it includes all of the case law of England and the American colonies before the American Revolution, as well as American case law since the colonial period.

### *Stare Decisis*

Common law is developed through the doctrine of *stare decisis,* which means "to abide by decided cases." Once a court resolves a particular issue, other courts addressing a similar legal problem will generally follow that court's decision.

A legal rule established by a court's decision may be either persuasive or authoritative. A decision is *persuasive* if it reasonably and fairly resolved the dispute. Another court confronting a similar dispute will probably choose to apply the same reasoning.

An *authoritative decision,* by contrast, is one that must be followed, regardless of its persuasive power. The U.S. Court of Appeals for the Seventh Circuit explained:

> Whether a decision is authoritative depends on a variety of factors, of which the most important is the relationship between the court that decided it and the court to which it is cited later as a precedent. The simplest relationship is hierarchical: the decisions of a superior court in a unitary system bind the inferior courts. The most complex relationship is between a court and its own previous decisions.
>
> A court must give considerable weight to its own decisions unless and until they have been overruled or undermined by the decisions of a higher court, or other supervening developments, such as a statutory overruling. But [a court] is not absolutely bound by [its previous rulings], and must give fair consideration to any substantial argument that a litigant makes for overruling a previous decision.[22]

Federal courts interpreting state law must follow that state's courts—this was the principle established in *Erie Railroad Co. v. Tompkins,* discussed earlier in this chapter. Every court must follow a decision of the U.S. Supreme Court, unless powerfully convinced that the Supreme Court itself would change its decision at the first possible opportunity.

The U.S. Supreme Court rarely overrules its previous decisions, but it does do so on occasion. The Court has articulated four primary questions to be considered when deciding whether an earlier decision should be overruled:

1. Has the prior decision's central rule proved unworkable?
2. Can the rule be changed without serious inequity to those who have relied upon it, or would such a

21. CAL. BUS. & PROF. CODE § 16600 (2000).

22. Colby v. J.C. Penney Co., 811 F.2d 1119, 1123 (7th Cir. 1987).

change significantly damage the stability of the society governed by the rule in question?

3. Has the law's growth in the intervening years left the prior decision's central rule a doctrinal anachronism discounted by society?
4. Have the prior decision's premises of fact so greatly changed since the decision was issued as to render its central holding somehow irrelevant or unjustifiable in dealing with the issue it addressed?

Consider the Supreme Court's explanation in *Casey*[23] of why the "separate but equal" rule for applying the Fourteenth Amendment's equal protection guarantee test, first adopted in *Plessy v. Ferguson*,[24] was appropriately overruled in *Brown v. Board of Education*,[25] the 1954 school-desegregation case:

> In *Plessy v. Ferguson* the Court held that legislatively mandated racial segregation in public transportation was no denial of equal protection and rejected the argument that racial separation enforced by the legal machinery of American society treats the black race as inferior. The *Plessy* Court considered "the underlying fallacy of the plaintiff's argument to consist in the assumption that the enforced separation of the two races stamps the colored race with a badge of inferiority. If this be so, it is not by reason of anything found in the act, but solely because the colored race chooses to put that construction upon it." Whether, as a matter of historical fact, the Justices in the *Plessy* majority believed this or not, this understanding of the implication of segregation was the stated justification for the Court's opinion. But this understanding of the facts and the rule it was stated to justify were repudiated in *Brown v. Board of Education*. . . .
>
> The Court in *Brown* addressed these facts of life by observing that whatever may have been the understanding in *Plessy's* time of the power of segregation to stigmatize those who were segregated with a "badge of inferiority," it was clear by 1954 that legally sanctioned segregation had just such an effect, to the point that racially separate public educational facilities were deemed inherently unequal. Society's understanding of the facts upon which a constitutional ruling was sought in 1954 was thus fundamentally different from the basis claimed for the decision in 1896. While we think *Plessy* was wrong the day it was decided, . . . we must also recognize that the *Plessy* Court's explanation for its decision was so clearly at odds with the facts apparent to the Court in 1954 that the decision to reexamine *Plessy* was on this ground alone not only justified but required.

In *Casey*, the Supreme Court declined the invitation by right-to-life groups to overrule its decision in *Roe v. Wade*[26] upholding the right of a woman to have an abortion before the fetus becomes viable. In the following case, the majority and dissenters sharply disagreed on whether the ban on sodomy upheld in *Bowers v. Hardwick*[27] should be retained or overruled.

23. Planned Parenthood of Southeastern Pa. v. Casey, 505 U.S. 833 (1992).
24. 163 U.S. 537 (1896).
25. 347 U.S. 483 (1954).
26. 410 U.S. 113 (1973).
27. 478 U.S. 186 (1986).

A CASE IN POINT

## In the Language of the Court

**CASE 3.4**
**Lawrence v. Texas**
*Supreme Court of the United States*
*539 U.S. 558 (2003).*

**› FACTS** A Texas statute forbids persons of the same sex from engaging in "certain intimate sexual acts," including sodomy. Police officers responding to an unrelated call entered the home of John Lawrence and found him and Tyron Garner engaging in conduct that violated this statute. After they were convicted, they challenged the Texas statute, claiming that it violated their constitutional right to privacy. After hearing the case *en banc,* the Texas Court of Appeals, in a divided opinion, rejected the constitutional arguments and affirmed the convictions. The majority opinion indicated that the court considered the U.S. Supreme Court decision in *Bowers v. Hardwick* to be controlling on the federal due process aspect of the case. *Bowers,* therefore, was authoritative at the time, and the Texas court's ruling was proper.

Petitioners Lawrence and Garner appealed, asking the U.S. Supreme Court to invalidate the Texas statute on the ground that it violated their federal constitutional rights.

**› ISSUE PRESENTED** In light of the holding in *Bowers v. Hardwick* that the U.S. Constitution does not confer a fundamental right to engage in sodomy and the doctrine of *stare decisis,* is the Texas statute constitutional?

*(Continued)*

(Case 3.4 *continued*)

**› OPINION** KENNEDY, J., joined by STEVENS, SOUTER, GINSBURG, and BREYER, JJ., writing for a plurality of the U.S. Supreme Court:

Liberty protects the person from unwarranted government intrusions into a dwelling or other private places. In our tradition the State is not omnipresent in the home. And there are other spheres of our lives and existence, outside the home, where the State should not be a dominant presence. Freedom extends beyond spatial bounds. Liberty presumes an autonomy of self that includes freedom of thought, belief, expression, and certain intimate conduct. The instant case involves liberty of the person both in its spatial and more transcendent dimensions.

We conclude the case should be resolved by determining whether the petitioners were free as adults to engage in the private conduct in the exercise of their liberty under the Due Process Clause of the Fourteenth Amendment to the Constitution. For this inquiry we deem it necessary to reconsider the Court's holding in *Bowers*.

The Court began its substantive discussion in *Bowers* as follows: "The issue presented is whether the Federal Constitution confers a fundamental right upon homosexuals to engage in sodomy and hence invalidates the laws of the many States that still make such conduct illegal and have done so for a very long time." That statement, we now conclude, discloses the Court's own failure to appreciate the extent of the liberty at stake. To say that the issue in *Bowers* was simply the right to engage in certain sexual conduct demeans the claim the individual put forward, just as it would demean a married couple were it to be said marriage is simply about the right to have sexual intercourse. . . .

Almost five years before *Bowers* was decided, the European Court of Human Rights considered a case with parallels to *Bowers* and to today's case. An adult male resident in Northern Ireland alleged he was a practicing homosexual who desired to engage in consensual homosexual conduct. The laws of Northern Ireland forbade him that right. He alleged that he had been questioned, his home had been searched, and he feared criminal prosecution. The court held that the laws proscribing the conduct were invalid under the European Convention on Human Rights. *Dudgeon v. United Kingdom*.[28] Authoritative in all countries that are members of the Council of Europe (21 nations then, 45 nations now), the decision is at odds with the premise in *Bowers* that the claim put forward was insubstantial in our Western civilization. . . .

The doctrine of stare decisis is essential to the respect accorded to the judgments of the Court and to the stability of the law. It is not, however, an inexorable command. . . . In *Casey* we noted that when a Court is asked to overrule a precedent recognizing a constitutional liberty interest, individual or societal reliance on the existence of that liberty cautions with particular strength against reversing course. ("Liberty finds no refuge in a jurisprudence of doubt.") The holding in *Bowers*, however, has not induced detrimental reliance comparable to some instances where recognized individual rights are involved. . . .

*Bowers* was not correct when it was decided, and it is not correct today. It ought not to remain binding precedent. *Bowers v. Hardwick* should be and now is overruled.

**› RESULT** The conviction was reversed.

28. 45 Eur. Ct. H.R. P52 (1981).

*(Continued)*

(Case 3.4 *continued*)

**› COMMENTS** In a biting dissent, Justice Scalia questioned "the Court's surprising readiness to reconsider a decision rendered a mere 17 years ago in *Bowers v. Hardwick.*"

> I do not myself believe in rigid adherence to *stare decisis* in constitutional cases; but I do believe that we should be consistent rather than manipulative in invoking the doctrine.
>
> In any event, an "emerging awareness" is by definition not "deeply rooted in this Nation's history and tradition[s]," as we have said "fundamental right" status requires. Constitutional entitlements do not spring into existence because some States choose to lessen or eliminate criminal sanctions on certain behavior. Much less do they spring into existence, as the Court seems to believe, because *foreign nations* decriminalize conduct.

The majority responded that its reference to decisions by European and Canadian courts did not imply deference to foreign courts, but rather pointed to evidence of changing societal norms that warranted a departure from *stare decisis*.

In his dissent, Justice Scalia predicted that the Court's determination that the state had no compelling interest in preserving the morals of its citizens would lead to same-sex marriage as well as the legalization of prostitution, pornography, and polygamy. In 2003, relying in part on the decision in *Lawrence v. Texas,* the Massachusetts Supreme Judicial Court struck down the Massachusetts statute that permitted a man and a woman but not a same-sex couple to marry.[29]

Justice O'Connor concurred in the decision to invalidate the Texas statute but based her concurrence on the fact that the state prohibited sodomy between homosexuals but not heterosexuals. She concluded that the Texas sodomy law would not pass scrutiny under the Equal Protection Clause, regardless of the standard of review applied.

**› CRITICAL THINKING QUESTIONS**

1. Does this decision change the standards set forth in *Casey?*
2. What impact, if any, will this decision have on the efforts to overturn *Roe v. Wade?*

29. Goodridge v. Dep't of Pub. Health, 798 N.E.2d 941 (Mass. 2003).

One court of appeals does not have to follow another court of appeals. One trial court does not have to follow another trial court. It must follow the court of appeals above it but need not follow other appellate courts. Thus, if the U.S. Court of Appeals for the Tenth Circuit (based in Denver) interprets a federal air pollution regulation in a certain way, the U.S. Court of Appeals for the Sixth Circuit (based in Cincinnati) may follow that interpretation, but it is not compelled to do so. The authority of the Tenth Circuit does not reach beyond its own geographic boundaries. However, a federal district court in Tulsa, which is within the Tenth Circuit, would be compelled to interpret the regulation in accordance with the decision of the Court of Appeals for the Tenth Circuit.

### *Restatements*

Today, many rules that originated as common law have been collected into *restatements* compiled by legal scholars, practicing attorneys, and judges. There are restatements of various areas of the law, such as torts, contracts, property, and trusts. The restatements do not compel a judge to make a particular decision unless the rule has been adopted by the state's legislature or its highest court. They are persuasive rather than authoritative.

## Civil Procedure

*Civil procedure* refers to the methods, procedures, and practices that govern the processing of a civil lawsuit from start to finish. The Federal Rules of Civil Procedure (FRCP) control the trial practices in all of the U.S. district courts. Each federal district court may also adopt its own local rules, applicable only within that district, to supplement the federal rules. Individual judges may even have particular rules as to how certain procedures operate in their own courts.

Each state has a set of rules governing the procedures in the state trial court system. Often, the state rules are similar in many respects to the federal rules. Separate sets of rules govern practice before the various courts of appeals and supreme courts. These rules address every requirement, from the time deadline for filing an appeal, to the contents of the notice of appeal, to the paper size, line spacing, and type style for briefs filed with the court. Each court system has its own rules or guidelines to ensure the orderly processing of the lawsuit.

## FILING AND PROSECUTING A CLAIM

Exhibit 3.4 provides a typical timeline for a suit filed in federal court.

### *Complaint*

The *complaint* briefly states a grievance and makes allegations of (1) the particular facts giving rise to the dispute; (2) the legal reason why the plaintiff is entitled to a remedy; and (3) the *prayer*, or request for relief. The complaint should also explain why this particular court has jurisdiction over the alleged dispute and indicate whether the plaintiff requests a jury trial. If the plaintiff does not request a jury trial within the time limit, that right is deemed to be waived.

### *Summons*

After the plaintiff files the complaint, the clerk of the court prepares a summons. The *summons* officially notifies the defendant that a lawsuit is pending against it in a particular court and that it must file a response to the complaint within a certain number of days. The clerk then stamps the official seal of the court on the summons. Next, the plaintiff or the clerk will serve the official summons and complaint on the defendant. Service is usually completed by sending the documents to the defendant by mail.

### *Answer*

The defendant's *answer* may admit or deny the various allegations in the complaint. If the defendant believes that it lacks sufficient information to assess the truth of an allegation, it should state this. Such a statement has

EXHIBIT 3.4 Typical Timeline for Suit Filed in Federal Court

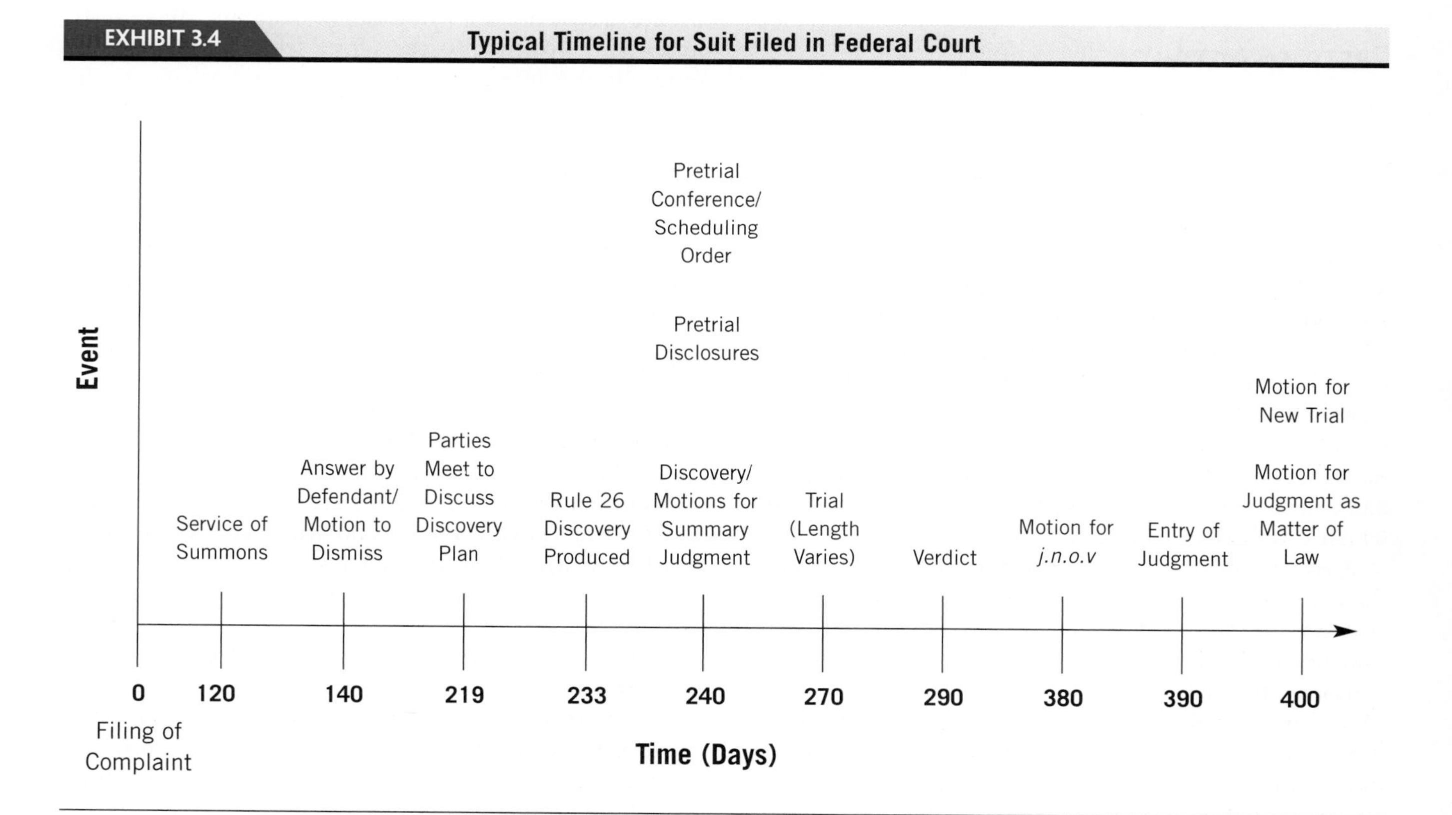

the effect of a denial. The answer may also deny that the law provides relief for the plaintiff's claim regardless of whether the plaintiff's factual allegations are true.

The answer may put forth affirmative defenses to the allegations in the complaint. An *affirmative defense* admits that the defendant has acted in a certain way but claims that the defendant's conduct was not the real or legal cause of harm to the plaintiff or that the defendant's conduct is excused for some reason. An example of an affirmative defense in a contract case is the requirement under the statute of frauds (discussed in Chapter 7) that certain agreements must be in writing to be enforceable.

An answer may also include a *counterclaim,* a legal claim by the defendant against the plaintiff. The counterclaim need not be related to the plaintiff's claim.

The complaint, the answer, and any reply to the answer filed by the plaintiff are referred to as the *pleadings.*

If the defendant does not file an answer within the time required, a *default judgment* may be entered in favor of the plaintiff. The defendant may, however, ask the court to set aside the default judgment if there were extenuating circumstances for not filing the answer to the complaint on time.

## PRETRIAL ACTIVITY

Before the trial begins, the attorneys and the judge usually meet to discuss certain issues.

### *Motion to Dismiss*

The lawsuit may be resolved before trial by the judge granting a motion to dismiss. A motion formally requests the court to take some action. A *motion to dismiss* seeks to terminate the lawsuit on the ground that the plaintiff's claim is technically inadequate. A judge will grant a motion to dismiss if (1) the court lacks jurisdiction over the subject matter or the parties involved, (2) the plaintiff failed to properly serve the complaint on the defendant, or (3) the plaintiff has failed to state a claim on which relief can be granted.

A party may file a motion to dismiss immediately after the complaint and answer have been filed. This is known as a *motion for judgment on the pleadings.* One party, usually the defendant, argues that the complaint alone demonstrates that the action is futile.

The moving party may file *affidavits,* that is, sworn statements, or other written evidence in an attempt to show that the cause of action is without merit. When information or documents other than the pleadings are involved, the motion becomes a *motion for summary judgment.*

### *Summary Judgment*

A judge will grant *summary judgment* only if all of the written evidence before the court clearly establishes that there are no disputed issues of material fact and that the party who requested the summary judgment is entitled to recover as a matter of law. If there is even a scintilla, that is, even the slightest bit, of evidence that casts doubt on an important fact in the lawsuit, the judge must not grant summary judgment. A judge may, however, grant summary judgment on some issues of the case and let the other issues proceed to trial. This is called a *partial summary judgment.*

### *Pretrial Conference*

Pretrial or status conferences may be held either in open court or in the judge's chambers. During these conferences, the attorneys for the litigants meet with the judge to discuss the progress of their case. Topics discussed may include (1) the issues as stated in the pleadings; (2) any amendments to the pleadings; (3) the scheduling of future discovery and a plan for the timely completion of discovery; (4) the status of pending motions or prospective motions that a party may file; (5) a schedule of the disclosure of witnesses or exhibits; and—most important—(6) the prospects for a settlement of the dispute. In the interests of promoting a settlement, the judge will often use this occasion to give each side a candid assessment of the strengths and weaknesses of its case and the likely outcome if the case goes to trial. If a settlement clearly is not feasible, then the pretrial conference will focus on formulating an efficient plan for the trial.

## TRIAL

A trial usually goes through the following stages:

1. Selection of the jury (if the trial is before a jury). The judge or attorneys may question the potential jurors.
2. Opening statements, first by the plaintiff's attorney and then by the defendant's attorney.
3. Presentation of evidence and witnesses by the plaintiff's attorney. This consists of:
   a. Direct examination of witnesses by the plaintiff's attorney.
   b. Cross-examination of witnesses by the defendant's attorney.
   c. Redirect examination by the plaintiff's attorney.
   d. Recross-examination by the defendant's attorney.
   e. Redirect and recross-examination until both sides have no further questions to ask.

4. Presentation of evidence and witnesses by the defendant's attorney. This consists of:
   a. Direct examination of witnesses by the defendant's attorney
   b. Cross-examination of witnesses by the plaintiff's attorney
   c. Redirect and recross-examination until both sides have no further questions to ask.
5. Motion for a directed verdict by either attorney.
6. Closing arguments, first by the plaintiff's attorney, then by the defendant's attorney, and then rebuttal by the plaintiff's attorney.
7. The judge's instructions to the jury.
8. Jury deliberations.
9. Announcement of the jury verdict.

### Selection of Jury

Each side can challenge any number of jurors for cause during the questioning of potential jurors, which is called *voir dire*. Cause includes any relationship between the juror and any of the parties or their counsel. Most jurisdictions also permit a limited number of preemptory challenges. These can be used by counsel to remove potential jurors who counsel thinks might be inclined to decide for the other side. It is unconstitutional to use a preemptory challenge to remove a potential juror due to race or gender.[30]

*"When the Court questions a witness, the witness is not permitted to reply, 'Let's not go there.'"*



### Motion for a Directed Verdict

At the close of the presentation of all the evidence, either attorney may ask the judge to grant a motion for a *directed verdict*. The moving party asserts that the other side has not produced enough evidence to support the legal claim or defense alleged. The motion requests that the judge take the case away from the jury and direct that a verdict be entered in favor of the party making the motion. Should the judge agree that there is not even an iota of evidence to support one party's claim or defense, the judge will issue a directed verdict. This does not happen very frequently.

### Jury Verdict

After both sides have presented their closing arguments, the judge instructs the jury on applicable rules of law. After deliberating in private, the jury delivers its verdict, specifying both the prevailing party and the relief to which that party is entitled. In federal court, the six-person jury verdict must be unanimous. In state courts, a unanimous jury verdict is not always required. Frequently, nine out of twelve votes is sufficient.

## Posttrial Motions

The announcement of the jury verdict does not necessarily conclude the case. Either party may make a motion to set aside the verdict or to have the case retried.

### Judgment Notwithstanding the Verdict

Immediately after the jury has rendered its verdict and the jury has been excused from the courtroom, the attorney for the losing party may make a motion for a *judgment notwithstanding the verdict*. Such a judgment, also known as a *judgment n.o.v.*, from the Latin *non obstante veredicto*, or *j.n.o.v.*, reverses the jury verdict on the ground that the evidence of the prevailing party was so weak that no reasonable jury could have resolved the dispute in that party's favor. If there is any reasonable possibility that the evidence could support the jury verdict, however, the judge will deny the motion.

### New Trial

The judge may order a new trial if there were serious errors in the trial process. Examples of such errors include misconduct on the part of the attorneys or the

30. *See* Batson v. Kentucky, 476 U.S. 79 (1986) (race); J.E.B. v. Alabama, 511 U.S. 127 (1994) (gender).

jurors and the improper admission of evidence that severely prejudiced one party's chances for a fair trial.

### Appeal

If the trial judge does not grant the motion for a *j.n.o.v.* or a new trial, the losing party can appeal the decision. The appellate court will review the manner in which the trial judge applied the law to the case and conducted the trial. The appeals court can review the presentation of evidence at trial, the denial of a motion for a directed verdict, the jury instructions, and even the jury award of damages. The appellate court will not review the facts *de novo* and will reverse a judge's findings of fact only if they are clearly erroneous.

If the appellant loses before the court of appeals, it may want to have the supreme court consider the decision. Appeals are expensive, however, so the losing party should seriously consider the likelihood of success at the higher court before pursuing an appeal.

## Discovery

Before a trial is held, the parties collect evidence to support their claims through a process called *discovery.* In general, parties may obtain discovery regarding any matter relevant to the lawsuit. Discovery includes *depositions,* which are written or oral questions asked of any person who may have helpful information about the facts of the case; *interrogatories,* which are written questions to the parties in the case and their attorneys; and *requests for production of documents,* such as medical records and personal files. In addition, computer files, including electronic mail (e-mail) correspondence, are also subject to discovery and are often the source of crucial evidence.

Electronic mail has become crucial evidence in corporate litigation; parties routinely demand access to company e-mail dating back ten to twenty years.[31] The Justice Department relied upon e-mail to build its antitrust suit against Microsoft (discussed in the "Inside Story" in Chapter 16). Among these damaging e-mails were Microsoft e-mails about rival Netscape calling for "choking off Netscape's air supply" and "knifing the baby" and an internal e-mail from AOL recounting a meeting with Microsoft CEO Bill Gates during which Gates allegedly said, "How much do we need to pay you to screw Netscape?" Most corporate executives would never write damaging statements in official company correspondence, yet they often are candid or impolitic in e-mail without realizing that e-mails are evidence subject to discovery in a lawsuit. As one commentator noted, "E-mail is a truth serum."[32] Parties are frequently able to obtain e-mail messages even if they have been deleted because backup tapes and information on hard drives are also frequently subject to discovery. In fact, computer specialists can restore e-mail messages from magnetic tapes even if they have been overwritten several times.[33]

The basic purpose of discovery is to eliminate the "game" elements in a trial. If all the parties to the lawsuit have all the evidence before trial, everyone benefits. By revealing the strengths and weaknesses of the various claims, discovery frequently allows the lawsuit to be *settled*—resolved by agreement without a trial. At the least, discovery helps prevent any major surprises from occurring at trial because each side has already learned about the other's case.

Discovery serves other useful functions. First, it can preserve evidence. For example, depositions preserve the

#### Ethical Consideration

You are a top manager at a major corporation. The corporation has recently been sued in federal district court by an individual who was injured by one of its widgets. Your in-house counsel tells you that the plaintiff's counsel is competent but a sole practitioner specializing in family law. You discuss litigation strategy with your attorney. One possible tactic is to overwhelm opposing counsel through the discovery process. Your counsel provides several options: (1) delivering forty boxes of corporate documents a day for four days, of which perhaps sixty pages are relevant to the suit, then moving for dismissal on the fifth day; (2) actively mislabeling or hiding documents in the above "document dump"; (3) not providing any relevant information to opposing counsel but sending box after box of useless material; (4) stalling and delaying document requests because the corporation "is unable to locate them"; (5) accurately labeling the relevant material, but including it in a "document dump"; (6) declaring that only through extensive travel would opposing counsel be able to access the relevant information (sending individuals likely to be deposed all over the world on "important projects"); (7) continuously delaying and extending the number of depositions, interrogatories, and other materials needed in order to "effectively prepare for trial"; (8) promptly providing only the relevant information in a way the opposing counsel may easily access it; and (9) lying and destroying all relevant documents. Which option should you select and why?

31. David S. Bennahum, *Old E-mail Never Dies,* WIRED, May 1999, at 100.

32. *Id.* at 102.

33. *Id.* at 109.

testimony of important witnesses who may otherwise be unavailable at trial. Second, discovery reduces the number of legal issues to be presented at trial because the parties can see beforehand which claims they have evidence to support and which ones are not worth pursuing.

Discovery has its drawbacks, however. The process is labor-intensive and therefore very expensive. Frequently, hours and days of depositions and hundreds of interrogatories will be undertaken. The strategy behind such a plan can be twofold: to wear down the opposing party by making the lawsuit more expensive than a victory would be worth, or to keep the papers flowing at such a rate that the other side cannot discern what all the documents really state. Such tactics often lead to discovery disputes that end up before the court. Taken too far, these strategies can lead to discovery abuse, which reduces the already slow pace of litigation, significantly increases costs, and can anger judges.

As discussed further in Chapter 23, the Private Securities Litigation Reform Act of 1995 severely cut back on a plaintiff's right to discovery in a securities fraud case prior to the court's ruling on the defendant's motion to dismiss. Congress intended thereby to deter plaintiffs with no evidence of wrongdoing from going on "fishing expeditions," which often proved very expensive and burdensome for the defendant and made it more likely that a defendant would settle an otherwise frivolous claim just to avoid the costs of discovery and litigation.

Rule 26 of the Federal Rules of Civil Procedure imposes certain mandatory disclosure requirements on parties. Prior to a discovery request, parties must produce (1) the names of individuals likely to have discoverable information relevant to disputed facts at issue in the case, (2) documents relating to the facts alleged in the complaint, (3) documents relating to the calculation of damages, (4) insurance agreements that may cover the claims at issue in the case, and (5) the names of expert witnesses who may testify at trial.

Courts may impose penalties upon companies and their counsel for discovery abuses. In 1996, a woman was abducted from a Wal-Mart parking lot and raped. She sued Wal-Mart and requested, through the discovery process, any studies Wal-Mart might have undertaken to determine any inherent dangers that might exist in its parking lots. Wal-Mart's attorneys denied having any such surveys. It turned out, however, that Wal-Mart had completed such a study and that it showed a clear danger in parking lots with no security. Wal-Mart had engaged in similar evasions in the past, having been sanctioned for abusing discovery twenty-four times in the year and a half preceding the case. This time the judge threatened to fine Wal-Mart $18 million for its obvious disregard of the discovery rules. Clearly, such sanctions in the past had not affected Wal-Mart's actions. This time, however, Wal-Mart's assistant general counsel made a public apology and vowed to change Wal-Mart's practices. In the past, Wal-Mart had taken a "hard-nosed" stance on litigation to avoid appearing to be an easy corporate target. But the company began to realize that even though monetary sanctions were not a major issue, a deteriorating public image was. Wal-Mart's new goal is to find a balanced approach to litigation that is tough enough to deter lawsuits, but not so tough as to tarnish its public image.[34]

**INTERNATIONAL SNAPSHOT**

Discovery rules in foreign countries are not as liberal as American discovery rules and frequently allow the parties to obtain relatively little information or none at all. As a result, if litigation in an American court concerns either an American corporation's foreign subsidiary or one of its offices located in a foreign country, it may prove difficult to obtain documents or take depositions of the employees located in the foreign country. Although litigants can obtain an order from the U.S. court that permits them to petition the court of the foreign country to obtain discovery to be used in the United States, the process is lengthy, and many countries will allow either no or very limited discovery. Even the United Kingdom, which has a legal system similar to the U.S. system, permits only limited discovery. In addition, the process for taking discovery in foreign countries is frequently different from the U.S. practice. For example, countries often require a judge to be present at depositions, making the procedure more formal and controlled than it is in the United States where only lawyers and witnesses are present.

## Attorney–Client Privilege, the Attorney Work-Product Doctrine, and Other Privileges

Although generally any person with knowledge of facts relevant to a case can be required to testify in depositions or at trial, the attorney–client privilege and other privileges designed to protect certain relationships limit the introduction of certain types of evidence.

34. Richard Willing, *Lawsuits a Volume Business at Wal-Mart*, USA TODAY, Aug. 13, 2001.

## ATTORNEY–CLIENT PRIVILEGE

Perhaps the most important limitation on discovery and testimony at trial is the *attorney–client privilege*. It dates back to the sixteenth century and provides that a court cannot force the disclosure of confidential communications between a client and his or her attorney. The privilege survives after the client is no longer represented by the attorney and even after the death of the client.

The attorney–client privilege is intended to promote the administration of justice. Clients are more likely to make a full and frank disclosure of the facts to an attorney if they know that the attorney cannot be compelled to pass the information on to adverse parties. An attorney is better able to advise and represent a client if the client discloses the complete facts. The privilege may also help to prevent unnecessary litigation because an attorney who knows all the facts should be better able to assess whether litigation is justified.

To be protected by the privilege, a communication must occur between the attorney and the client. The communication must also be intended to be confidential. If the client plans to relay the information to others or makes the communication in the presence of other individuals not involved in the lawsuit, there is no confidentiality.

The attorney–client privilege belongs to the client alone. The attorney, however, has an obligation to alert the client to the existence of the privilege and, if necessary, to invoke it on the client's behalf. The client can waive the privilege over the attorney's objection if the client so desires.

### *Limitations*

The attorney to whom the communication is made must be a practicing attorney at the time of the communication, and the person making the communication must be a current or prospective client seeking legal advice. A conversation between the client and the attorney about nonlegal matters is not protected. In *United States v. Frederick*,[35] the U.S. Court of Appeals for the Seventh Circuit held that neither the attorney–client privilege nor the work-product doctrine (discussed below) protected documents created by or communications with a lawyer who was acting as both an attorney and a tax preparer in preparing a client's tax returns. The court reasoned that a taxpayer "must not be allowed, by hiring a lawyer to do the work that an accountant, or other tax preparer, or the taxpayer himself, normally would do, to obtain greater protection from government investigations than a taxpayer who did not use a lawyer as his tax preparer."

In *Satcom International Group PLC v. Orbcomm International Partners LP*,[36] the district court held that Virginia's attorney–client privilege protected discussions between corporate executives and the company's lawyer at a meeting called for the purpose of making a legal decision, even though this decision had commercial ramifications, as long as the corporation's counsel was present to provide legal advice and all discussion concerned the legal decision. In contrast, in *United States v. Ackert*,[37] the U.S. Court of Appeals for the Second Circuit ruled that the attorney–client privilege did not protect a corporate counsel's discussion with an investment banker for the purpose of learning information to help advise the corporation on an investment decision.

The attorney–client privilege does not protect client communications that are made to further a crime or other illegal act. Thus, if an executive asks his or her attorney about the best way to embezzle money, that conversation is not privileged.

In July 1997, the Florida Court of Appeal rejected the tobacco companies' claim of attorney–client privilege for eight confidential documents, including attorneys' notes from in-house meetings on legal strategy.[38] The court concluded that because the documents contained evidence that tobacco attorneys participated in an industry-wide conspiracy to defraud the public about the danger of smoking, they came within the exception for communications to further commission of fraud or a crime.

### *Corporate Clients*

With communications between a corporate client and an attorney, it is often difficult to define what element of the corporation can be considered the client. The corporation does not fit the common definition of a client because the corporation itself is unable to communicate with the attorney except through its officers, directors, agents, or employees. In *Upjohn Co. v. United States*,[39] the Supreme Court adopted a subject matter test to determine when the attorney–client privilege is available to a corporation. Under this test, the privilege protects the communications or discussions of any company employee with counsel as long as the subject matter of the communication relates to that employee's duties and the communication is made at the direction of a corpo-

35. 182 F.3d 496 (7th Cir. 1999), *cert. denied*, 528 U.S. 1154 (2000).

36. 1999 WL 76847 (S.D.N.Y. Feb. 16, 1999).

37. 169 F.3d 136 (2d Cir. 1999).

38. 66 U.S.L.W. 1112 (Aug. 19, 1997).

39. 449 U.S. 383 (1981).

rate superior. Thus, communications between a corporation's attorneys and any of its employees, not just a small, upper-level group, are protected under the attorney–client privilege as long as those communications pass the subject matter test. The Court also ruled that the attorney–client privilege extends to communications made to both in-house and outside counsel as long as the attorneys are acting in a legal capacity.

The attorney–client privilege may also extend to communications between a consultant hired by a corporation and an attorney, although courts will examine the specific facts of each situation to determine whether the privilege applies. In *In re Bieter Co.*,[40] the U.S. Court of Appeals for the Eighth Circuit held that the attorney–client privilege extended to communications between a partnership's attorney and a consultant to the partnership who was the functional equivalent of an employee. Even though the consultant was an independent contractor, not an employee, he was still a representative of the client partnership. He had daily contact with the partnership's principals, had acted as the partnership's sole representative in critical meetings, and had worked with the partnership's attorneys on the lawsuit.

The decision in *Upjohn* did not resolve all of the uncertainties regarding the application of attorney–client privilege to corporations. The Supreme Court did not decide whether the attorney–client privilege applies to communications with former employees. Nor did it resolve the issue of what exactly constitutes a voluntary waiver of the attorney–client privilege by a corporation. Finally, there is still uncertainty about the protection the privilege gives corporations in suits brought against them by shareholders.

**Guidelines** Following the Supreme Court's decision in *Upjohn*, a few guidelines can be suggested for attorneys and corporations concerning the best way to keep communications within the scope of the attorney–client privilege:[41]

1. Communication between an attorney and a corporation is protected only when a client is seeking or receiving legal advice, not business advice. Thus, corporations should request legal advice in writing and assign communication with the attorney to a specific employee who has responsibility over the subject matter at issue. Experts say that the way the interactions of an attorney and client are characterized can determine whether a court will find them to be protected or not. Even documents that appear to be business in nature may fall under the privilege if they are created in connection with impending litigation.
2. Corporations should make sure that all communication between employees and corporate counsel is directed by senior management and that the employees know they must keep all communications confidential.
3. Corporations should deal directly with counsel (not through intermediaries) and maintain confidential files and documentation.
4. When a corporation gives a government agency access to its communications or files, the corporation should negotiate a written agreement of confidentiality with the agency. A California appellate court ruled that documents disclosed to the government are no longer protected by attorney–client privilege and are therefore discoverable in civil and class-action suits brought by private parties.[42]

## Attorney–Client Privilege under Siege?

Recently, the attorney–client privilege has come under attack on four different fronts. First, Section 307 of the Sarbanes–Oxley Act of 2002 greatly expanded the responsibility of attorneys to report "up the ladder" evidence of material violations of securities laws, breaches of fiduciary duty, and "similar" violations of Securities and Exchange Commission (SEC) rules by their corporate clients. The goal is to promote better corporate responsibility by requiring lower-level lawyers to report wrongdoing to the supervising attorney. If nothing is done to remedy the situation, then the supervising attorney must report to the CEO. If the situation remains unresolved, then the supervising attorney must report to the board of directors.

Second, in conjunction with Sarbanes–Oxley, the SEC has proposed regulations that would require lawyers to make a "noisy withdrawal" if nothing is done to remedy the wrongdoing after the board becomes aware of it; here a *noisy withdrawal* means to withdraw from representation and inform the SEC of the withdrawal. The SEC is currently soliciting opinions on its

40. 16 F.3d 929 (8th Cir. 1994).

41. This discussion is based in large part on Block & Remz, *After "Upjohn": The Uncertain Confidentiality of Corporate Internal Investigative Files*, 1983. A.B.A. Sec. Litig.: Recent Developments in Attorney–Client Privilege, Work-Product Doctrine and Confidentiality of Communications between Counsel and Client.

42. McKesson HBOC, Inc. v. Superior Court of San Francisco County, 9 Cal. Rptr. 3d 812 (Cal. Ct. App. 2004). McKesson HBOC, Inc. had agreed to cooperate with a government investigation and disclosed internal findings showing improper revenue recognition.

newest proposals to implement Section 307 of Sarbanes-Oxley.[43]

Third, recent changes to Rule 1.13 of the American Bar Association's (ABA's) Model Rules of Professional Conduct direct an attorney representing a corporation to "report up the ladder" any actions by employees that the attorney feels will significantly injure the corporation. [44] Attorneys are permitted (but not required) to reveal client confidences if doing so is necessary to prevent serious financial harm.[45] Attorneys face possible disbarment if their conduct is inconsistent with their state rules of professional conduct, which are usually patterned after the ABA's model rules.

Fourth, the U.S. Attorney General has indicated that to be deemed "cooperative" and therefore eligible for a reduced corporate sentence under the Federal Sentencing Guidelines, companies under government investigation must, if necessary, agree to waive attorney–client privilege and disclose any reports of internal investigations.[46]

## ATTORNEY WORK PRODUCT

The attorney *work-product doctrine* protects information that an attorney prepares in the course of his or her work. This information includes the private memoranda created by the attorney and his or her personal thoughts while preparing a case for trial. The rationale behind the work-product rule is that lawyers, while performing their duties, must "work with a certain degree of privacy, free from unnecessary intrusion by opposing parties and their counsel."[47] Work-product materials may be obtained only with a showing of extreme necessity, such that the failure to obtain the materials would unduly prejudice an attorney's case or create hardship and injustice. The work-product doctrine is broader than the attorney–client privilege and may thus protect materials that are not protected by the privilege. For example, in *National Education Training Group, Inc. v. SkillSoft Corp.*,[48] the court found that a corporation had waived the attorney–client privilege regarding notes summarizing its counsel's legal advice at board meetings by permitting an assistant to one of the directors to attend the meetings. However, the assistant's notes were protected by the work-product doctrine because they summarized the lawyer's advice regarding litigation against the corporation.

## OTHER PRIVILEGES

In addition to the attorney–client privilege and the attorney work-product doctrine, there are other privileges a party may assert to protect information the opposing party seeks to discover. Discussions between a physician and patient are privileged unless the patient has made his or her medical condition an issue at trial. For example, a person claiming damages for a back injury resulting from an automobile accident will be deemed to have waived the privilege at least as to any medical history relating to his or her back. The U.S. Supreme Court has recognized a privilege protecting discussions between a psychologist or licensed social worker and a patient.[49] The priest–penitent privilege protects disclosures made to a priest during confession. The Fifth Amendment to the U.S. Constitution gives any person the right to refuse to testify if it would tend to incriminate him or her.

Several courts have recognized a privilege for corporate "self-critical analysis," on the grounds that the forced disclosure of such potentially negative information could deter socially beneficial investigation and evaluation. For instance, in *Tice v. American Airlines, Inc.*,[50] the plaintiffs sought to obtain American Airlines' "top-to-bottom" safety reports in connection with their claim that the forced retirement of airline pilots over the age of sixty constituted age discrimination. The court upheld American Airlines' claim of privilege, emphasizing that "the public has a strong interest in preserving the free flow of airline safety [monitoring- and improvement-] related information."

# Class Actions

If the conduct of the defendant affected numerous persons in a common way, the case may be brought as a *class action* by a representative of the class of persons affected. This was done in the asbestos personal-injury cases brought against asbestos manufacturers such as GAF Corporation and Pfizer, Inc.; the silicone-breast-implant

43. Patrick McGeehan, *Lawyers Take Suspicions on TV Azteca to Its Board*, N.Y. TIMES, Dec. 24, 2003, at C1; see also Final Rule: Disclosure Required by Sections 406 and 407 of the Sarbanes-Oxley Act of 2002, Release No. 33-8177 (Jan. 24, 2003), *available at* http://www.sec.gov/rules/final/33-8177.htm.
44. MODEL RULES OF PROF'L CONDUCT R. 1.13 (2002).
45. *Id.*
46. This is discussed further in Chapter 14.
47. Hickman v. Taylor, 329 U.S. 495, 510 (1947).
48. 1999 WL 378337 (S.D.N.Y. June 9, 1999).

49. Jaffee v. Redmond, 518 U.S. 1 (1996).
50. 192 F.R.D. 270 (N.D. Ill. 2000).

### ETHICAL CONSIDERATION

Is it ethical for a manufacturer of a product that caused harm to persons who will not discover the injury until a future date to enter into a class-action settlement that provides limited funds for future claimants?

cases involving Dow Corning and others; and the smoking cases brought against the tobacco companies. Class actions are the norm in actions alleging securities fraud.

Written notice of the formation of the class must be mailed to all potential class members. Until recently, doing this could be very difficult, and many people who were possible class members never received notice of the suit. Now, however, the Internet and websites, such as Findlaw.com, Classactiononline.com, Classactionamerica.com, and numerous small sites, have made finding and joining these suits much easier.[51]

Anyone who wants to litigate separately can opt out of the class. *BusinessWeek* estimated that 260,000 out of millions of potential claimants for asbestos-related injury elected to opt out of a $1 billion settlement reached in 1993 with twenty of the largest asbestos manufacturers.[52] If a person does not opt out, he or she is a member of the class and will be bound by any decision or settlement reached in the class action.

Although historically corporate defendants have condemned class actions as an easy way for an eager plaintiff and his or her lawyer to get to court, this is changing. Some companies view class actions as a "strategic management tool" that can end litigation nightmares and work to their advantage by avoiding potentially devastating jury awards, reducing litigation costs, and limiting long-term liability.[53] A class action can have the following advantages in a major product liability case: (1) the settlement can bind not only present class members but also future claimants; (2) standardized payment schedules avoid the risk of widely divergent jury awards; (3) some claimants who suffered less harm than others can be excluded from the settlement; and (4) the filing of suits and the settlement can occur on the same day.[54]

Any settlement of a class action requires approval by the court hearing the case. Until recently, courts were hesitant to reject a mutually agreed upon settlement. In *Amchem Products, Inc. v. Windsor*,[55] however, the U.S. Supreme Court tightened the requirements for class certification, making settlement more difficult. The named plaintiffs, nine individuals who were exposed to asbestos, filed a class-action complaint, answer, and settlement proposal with the defendant, Amchem Products, Inc. They purported to represent the class of individuals who had not previously sued asbestos manufacturers and either (1) had been exposed to asbestos attributable to the petitioner through their occupations or the occupations of a household member or (2) had a spouse or family member who had been exposed to asbestos. The size of the class was indeterminate but was estimated to include hundreds of thousands, perhaps millions, of individuals. Only half of the named plaintiffs currently manifested medical conditions as a result of exposure, while others had not yet developed any asbestos-related medical condition.

The Supreme Court held that the proposed class did not satisfy Federal Rules of Civil Procedure Rule 23(b)(3)'s mandate that common questions "predominate over any question affecting only individual members." The class members' shared experience of exposure to asbestos was not sufficient, because there were different categories of class members (different medical problems and the existence or absence of asbestos-related symptoms) and multiple individual differences (different medical histories, different levels and types of exposure, and varying degrees of severity of asbestos-related medical conditions). Characterizing the class as "sprawling," the Court concluded that the differences between the class members were greater than their commonalties. Therefore, the predominance requirement of Rule 23(b)(3) was not fulfilled.

The Court also found that the class failed to satisfy the Rule 23(a)(4) requirement for adequate representation. Essentially, Rule 23(a)(4) requires that the representatives of a class be part of the class and have the same interests as the class members. In this case, however, the class members had different interests. Those currently injured would seek immediate payment while exposure-only plaintiffs would seek a generous, protected fund for future compensation. Thus, it was impossible to ensure that the class representatives could adequately represent their interests.

The *Amchem* decision was handed down as the Supreme Court's Advisory Committee on Civil Rules

51. Dina Temple-Raston, *Class-Action Lawsuits Gain Strength on the Web*, N.Y. TIMES, July 28, 2002, at 10.
52. Catherine Yan, *Look Who's Talking Settlement*, BUS.WK., July 18, 1994, at 72.
53. Richard B. Schmitt, *The Deal Makers: Some Firms Embrace the Widely Dreaded Class-Action Lawsuit*, WALL ST. J., July 18, 1996, at A1.
54. Yan, *supra* note 52.

55. 521 U.S. 591 (1997).

was considering a proposal to make settlements easier in class-action lawsuits.[56] The decision was a signal to both the Advisory Committee and the lower courts to evaluate petitions for class certification and class-action settlements more carefully. Indeed, lawyers working on lawsuits involving the so-called fen-phen diet pill (*ex post,* diet pills were linked to heart valve damage and a rare form of lung disease) indicated that class-action lawsuits "are in a new era"[57] with courts less likely to accept class certifications and settlements.

## Litigation Strategies for Plaintiffs

When planning to file a lawsuit, the plaintiff must decide which legal claim is most likely to succeed. The plaintiff must also decide in which court to pursue the lawsuit.

### The Decision to Sue

Parties frequently file a lawsuit without giving sufficient thought to the various consequences. Before filing a lawsuit, one should consider (1) whether the likelihood of recovery and the amount of recovery are enough to justify the cost and disruption of litigation; (2) whether the defendant will be able to satisfy a judgment against it; (3) whether the defendant is likely to raise a counterclaim; (4) whether suing will cause any ill will among customers, suppliers, or other sources of corporate financing; (5) whether the suit will result in any harmful publicity; and (6) the impact of the litigation on the company's relationship with the defendant.

For example, Texaco, Inc. had contracted to supply oil to a particular plant at a below-market price. The owner of the plant kept it running despite its inefficiencies to take advantage of the favorable supply contract. After the owner of the plant sued Texaco for breach of contract and various business torts, the heads of the two companies conferred and negotiated a settlement. The plant owner agreed to drop its lawsuit (which could have resulted in hundreds of millions of dollars in damages) in exchange for Texaco's agreement to permit the plant owner to transfer the contract to a more efficient plant. The relationship was salvaged, and both companies declared victory.

56. Richard B. Schmitt, *High Court Upsets Class-Action Proposal,* WALL ST. J., July 10, 1997, at B10.

57. Richard B. Schmitt, *Thinning the Ranks: Diet-Pill Litigation Finds Courts Frowning on Mass Settlements,* WALL ST. J., Jan. 8, 1998, at A1.

The win–lose nature of lawsuits usually makes it impossible for both parties to claim satisfaction, save face, or forgive-and-forget. After a lawsuit, at best one party feels vindicated and the other feels wronged. Even the ostensible winner often feels angry about the time and money spent getting what it felt was its due to begin with.

If a company ends up in court, it has already lost, regardless of the ultimate verdict. Or, as Jay Walker, founder of Priceline.com, put it, "It's not a matter of who wins. It's a matter of who loses less."

Sometimes, though, litigation cannot be avoided. If a lawsuit appears inevitable, there may be some advantage to filing a claim first. The plaintiff's claim determines in which court the case will be heard. The defendant, however, may be able to remove an action from state court to federal court if there is diversity of citizenship or a federal question. Alternatively, it may be able to remove the action to a more appropriate *venue,* or location.

Sometimes the managers or employees intimately involved in a dispute lack the perspective and objectivity to determine the merits of a particular litigation decision and the impact it will have on the company as a whole. As a result, it is important for members of higher management and, in some cases, the full board of directors to become involved in the decisions of when to sue, when to settle or dismiss, and how vigorously to defend.

Some attorneys recommend that companies construct a prelitigation "decision tree," which determines at each step of the proceeding the chances of prevailing or losing, the costs of going forward, and the potential amount of recovery. Developing a decision tree forces a company to conduct a substantial factual and legal analysis of its claim. This is in everyone's interest, as courts are inclined to impose monetary penalties or "sanctions" on companies, individuals, and attorneys who file lawsuits without sufficient facts or the legal basis to support their claims.

Initiation and prosecution of a meritless and frivolous claim may result in an award of attorneys' fees. In *Kirby v. General Electric Co.,*[58] the court granted General Electric's motion for attorneys' fees after determining that a class of employees initiated a claim alleging that GE interfered with their rights under the Employee Retirement Income Security Act without inquiring into the factual or legal justification of the claim and continued to prosecute it even after it was clear that the claim was meritless and flawed. The court ordered that one-half of the attorneys' fees be assessed against the plain-

58. No. 5:98CV70-V (W.D.N.C. Mar. 22, 2000) (order awarding attorneys' fees).

tiffs' counsel personally. Similarly, in *Jandrt v. Jerome Foods, Inc.*,[59] the Wisconsin Supreme Court imposed sanctions against a law firm that pursued a toxic torts case without taking any steps to investigate a critical element of the case, namely, whether the plaintiff's exposure to chemicals while working at her employer's plant was the cause of her children's birth defects. Instead, the law firm had simply waited for the results of formal discovery. The court found that the law firm was not justified in rushing to file the lawsuit before consulting an expert about causation. The law firm's motivation for its haste appeared to be an imminent statutory change in the law that could have negatively affected the plaintiff's case before the investigation was completed.

The Private Securities Reform Act of 1995, enacted for the purpose of making it more difficult to initiate securities class actions, includes a provision that awards to the opposing party the cost of attorneys' fees if the court finds that a party filed a complaint, pleading, or motion that does not comply with Rule 11 of the Federal Rules of Civil Procedure. To deter frivolous actions, Rule 11 requires motions and complaints to be filed in good faith and substantiated by facts.

## The Decision to Settle

Parties should always consider settling the suit. Recent figures show that more than 90 percent of cases settle out of court, saving all parties the time, cost, and ill will of a trial. Filing a lawsuit can be a tactic to encourage settlement of a dispute that neither party really wishes to bring to trial. Settlement discussions usually occur during the pretrial stages. Alternative dispute resolution (ADR) techniques, such as negotiation, mediation, arbitration, med-arb, arb-med, minitrials, and summary jury trials, can save valuable management time by avoiding litigation. ADR techniques are discussed in Chapter 4.

Some lawsuits, however, are unlikely to settle; for example, (1) cases presenting legal questions—such as the meaning of an ambiguous term in a contract—that the court should clarify to avoid future disputes between the same parties; (2) cases that could bring a large recovery if the plaintiff wins and no great harm if it loses; and (3) cases where one side has acted so unreasonably that settlement is impossible.

Sometimes a lawsuit is worth pursuing simply to establish a company's credibility as one that will fight to support a legitimate business position. If applied too rigidly, though, such a philosophy can be expensive and may do more harm than good. Sometimes what the other party really wants is just an apology, a strategy Mike France of *BusinessWeek* dubbed the "mea culpa defense."[60] He calls on executives to acknowledge their mistakes and apologize instead of stonewalling.

Settlement is likely in a case when pursuing the lawsuit all the way to trial is not cost efficient. For example, if a plaintiff alleges that a product is defective and caused him or her a loss of $4,500, the legal expenses will far exceed the original loss. Discovery alone is likely to cost more than $4,500. In such a case, it is in both parties' interest to settle the dispute if at all possible. However, if the plaintiff's claim is similar to many other identical claims that may be brought against the company, settling the first claim could appear to commit the defendant to paying all the other claims, too.

## Pretrial Preparation

Having decided to file a lawsuit, the company should carefully select the personnel who will act as the contacts for the attorneys. These individuals should make sure that the necessary information and documents are gathered for the attorneys. They should have substantial authority in the company.

Executives or senior management who will be involved in the lawsuit or with the corporate attorneys should not handle public relations. This could lead to disputes regarding waiver of the attorney–client privilege.

The company should instruct all employees not to destroy any documents that may be relevant to the lawsuit. Destruction of these documents, particularly after the claim is filed, can be harmful and even illegal. Document-retention policies are discussed in greater detail later in this chapter.

The company should instruct employees not to discuss the lawsuit with anyone, including family or close friends. Casual comments about bankrupting the opposing party or teaching an opponent a lesson may turn up as testimony at trial, with undesirable consequences.

The company and its attorney should develop a budget for the lawsuit. Then, at each step of the case, strategic options can be discussed on the basis of cost-benefit analysis. The budget should include not only the lawyer's fees but also (1) the cost of employee time, (2) damage to company morale, (3) disruption of business, and (4) other hidden expenses. A budget will help the company manager

59. 597 N.W.2d 744 (Wis. 1999).

60. Mike France, *Mea Culpa Defense*, BUS.WK., Aug. 26, 2002, at 77.

POLITICAL PERSPECTIVE

## SHOULD THE UNITED STATES ADOPT THE BRITISH RULE THAT THE LOSER PAYS THE WINNER'S ATTORNEYS' FEES?

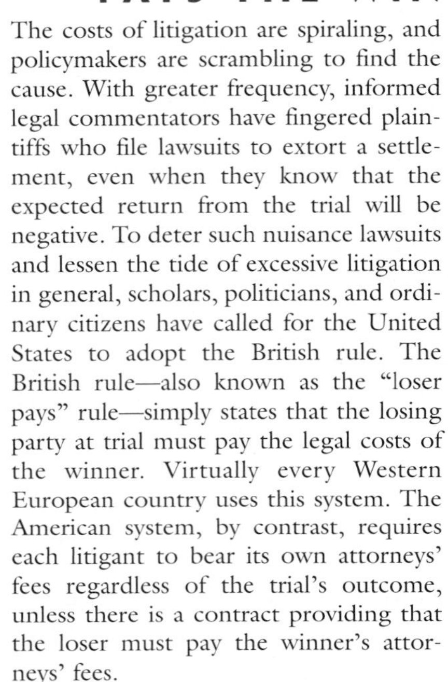

The costs of litigation are spiraling, and policymakers are scrambling to find the cause. With greater frequency, informed legal commentators have fingered plaintiffs who file lawsuits to extort a settlement, even when they know that the expected return from the trial will be negative. To deter such nuisance lawsuits and lessen the tide of excessive litigation in general, scholars, politicians, and ordinary citizens have called for the United States to adopt the British rule. The British rule—also known as the "loser pays" rule—simply states that the losing party at trial must pay the legal costs of the winner. Virtually every Western European country uses this system. The American system, by contrast, requires each litigant to bear its own attorneys' fees regardless of the trial's outcome, unless there is a contract providing that the loser must pay the winner's attorneys' fees.

In the early 1990s, these calls for legal reform entered mainstream politics. President George Bush's Council on Competitiveness established a working group on Federal Civil Justice Reform, which recommended adoption of a modified "loser pays" rule in cases involving state law brought under the federal courts' diversity jurisdiction. The loser would pay the winner's costs of vindicating its prevailing position, but fee shifting would be limited to the amount in fees that the loser incurred, which could be further limited by judicial discretion. The council explained:

> Adopting a "loser pays" rule for payment of attorney's fees will provide those bringing suit with a choice of methods to finance their litigation. The rule would help fund meritorious claims not currently initiated because the cost of pursuing the claim would have exceeded the expected recovery. . . . Because the losing party will be obligated to pay the winner's fees, this approach will encourage litigants to evaluate carefully the merits of their cases before initiating a frivolous claim or adopting a spurious defense.[a]

The proposal aroused considerable opposition, however, and was rejected by the American Bar Association (ABA). John Curtin, a former ABA president, said that the rule was rejected because it would have a "chilling effect" on the legal rights of certain individuals. He explained that the "loser pays" rule would discourage potential litigants with bona fide claims from bringing suit due to trepidation over monetary ruin.[b]

Both consumer groups and civil libertarians also attacked the proposal. Public Citizen, a consumer advocate organization led by Ralph Nader, criticized the council's recommendations, calling the report an "anti-worker, anti-consumer, pro-corporate-wrongdoer blueprint for undermining America's system of common law."[c] Other critics contended that the fee-shifting rule would limit access to the judiciary for the indigent and would inhibit the bringing of novel or untested legal theories. Efforts by the Republican majority in Congress in the mid-1990s to adopt the British rule as part of the "Contract With America" failed.[d]

a. *Less Litigation, More Justice,* WALL ST. J., Aug. 14, 1991.

b. *Agenda for Civil Justice Reform in America,* 24 (1991).

c. Herbert M. Kritzer, *The English Rule,* A.B.A.J., Nov. 1992, at 55.

d. This part of the "Contract With America" was proposed by Jim Ramstad (R-Min.) in the 104th Congress in a bill entitled "The Common Sense Legal Reforms Act" (H.R. 956). It failed to pass the House of Representatives.

---

and lawyer decide whether to pursue the lawsuit or attempt to settle.

The attorney and client should then select a court in which to file the lawsuit. Federal courts may be more accustomed to handling complex business litigation, such as that involving federal securities law or employment-discrimination laws. State courts are usually skilled in handling business disputes ranging from contract matters to personal-injury lawsuits. Other considerations about where to file include (1) the convenience and location of necessary witnesses and documents, (2) the location of trial counsel, (3) the reputation and size of the company and its opponent in a particular area, and (4) the possibility of favorable or unfavorable publicity.

All courts urge the parties to confer and settle the case if possible. The judge will act as a settlement mediator and objectively assist counsel in recognizing the strengths and weaknesses of their cases. Some state courts require a settlement conference before a specially designated settlement judge. The parties may also hire retired judges, professional mediators, law school professors, or mediators who are part of a bar association settlement program to facilitate settlement.

## Litigation Strategies for Defendants

A defendant receiving a complaint and summons should never let the lawsuit go unattended. The defendant should plan a defense strategy and follow it step by step. Factual and legal preparation should be done promptly so that important evidence—such as the memory of key witnesses—is not lost.

When a company receives a complaint, efforts should be made to determine why the plaintiff felt it necessary to sue. Some of the factors may include (1) whether prior bargaining or negotiations with the plaintiff broke down, and why; (2) whether the company's negotiator was pursuing the wrong tactics or following an agenda inconsistent with the company's best interests; and (3) whether the lawsuit resulted from bad personnel practices that the company still needs to correct. Senior executives should also get together and decide whether it would be beneficial to discuss the lawsuit with the plaintiff.

A defendant should also promptly consider the possibility of a settlement and review the ways in which amicable negotiations could be commenced or resumed. The defendant may also want to consider mediation or arbitration as alternatives to an expensive trial. Sometimes an apology can be more important than a vigorous defense in a case where the plaintiff feels unjustly wronged.

Increasingly, employers, residential lessors, banks, lenders, and other firms are requiring employees and customers to agree in advance to waive their right to a jury trial.[61] Although courts in New York, Massachusetts, and Florida have generally upheld these prelitigation waivers, courts in California and Georgia have refused to enforce them.

If the lawsuit cannot be settled, then the defendant should proceed with the same steps required of the plaintiff—plan a strategy, prepare a budget for the action, and so on. If the suit was filed in a state court, the defendant must decide whether it is possible and desirable to move the action to federal court.

Courts have imposed sanctions upon defendants for pursuing litigation in bad faith. In *Johnston v. Vendel*,[62] the Delaware Supreme Court concluded that the defendants' bad faith in prolonging litigation justified invoking an exception to the "American Rule" that each side pays its own attorneys' fees and awarded the plaintiff $1.6 million in attorneys' fees and disbursements. The court found that the defendants misled the court in compelling unnecessary discovery, falsified evidence, and tried to justify violating a standstill agreement with the plaintiff based on changed sworn testimony.

If the plaintiff has sued in a place that is greatly inconvenient for the defendant and its witnesses, the defendant may file a motion for a change of venue. A federal district court may transfer the case to a federal district court in another state. A state court, however, can only transfer the case to another location within the state.

61. Jane Spencer, *Waiving Your Right to a Jury Trial*, WALL ST. J., Aug. 17, 2003, at D1.
62. 720 A.2d 542 (Del. 1998).

### ETHICAL CONSIDERATION

You are a manager of Dow Chemical Company, overseeing the silicone-breast-implant litigation across the United States. Your market research tells you that most individuals distrust Big Business and that most consumers cannot identify many products of your company, except those involved in the litigation. With an upcoming trial in Louisiana, you are considering conducting a full-scale advertising campaign to boost Dow Chemical's public image. The goal is to influence public opinion in the jurisdiction of the suit, thereby creating a positive image in the minds of potential jurors. You have several options for the campaign:

1. Emphasize Dow Chemical's citizenship: employee volunteers, donations to charities, and the improvement of society as a result of Dow's products.
2. Describe the benefits of silicone products. Without mentioning the breast-implant issue, tell numerous heart-wrenching tales about how silicone products have saved the lives of children.
3. Begin the final campaign the week before jury selection. Highlight the greed of attorneys who represent plaintiffs in such cases and lament the growing litigiousness of our society. The final slogan: "You can stop the greedy lawyers!"
4. Same as 3, but also argue that silicone breast implants do no harm.[a]

What should you do? If you were the plaintiff, how would you respond to these tactics?

a. *See* Richard B. Schmitt, *Can Corporate Advertising Sway Juries?*, WALL ST. J., Mar. 3, 1997, at B1.

## Document Retention and Destruction

When a company is a defendant in a lawsuit, company documents, including computer files, may be used to prove liability in court. Nearly any corporate document can become a powerful weapon in court in the hands of opposing counsel.

A well-known example is the memorandum that was found in the files of Ford Motor Company during discovery for a 1972 trial arising out of a death caused by a Ford Pinto's allegedly defectively designed fuel tank. The memo, prepared in compliance with the regulations of a federal agency, compared the cost of design modifications to the Pinto fuel tank with the potential loss of life that might be caused by the existing design. During the trial, the plaintiff's counsel convinced the jury that the memo was proof that Ford decided to defer redesign of the fuel tanks on the basis of this cost study. The jury awarded compensatory damages of $3.5 million and punitive damages of $125 million against Ford. (Compensatory damages compensate the injured party for the harm suffered; punitive damages are intended to punish the wrongdoer for conduct that is outrageous, willful, or malicious.)

Most companies do not have established policies regarding document retention and destruction. They practice what some professionals call the "search and destroy" technique of file management: arbitrarily cleaning out file cabinets when storage space is running low. Yet, as Arthur Andersen learned the hard way when it was convicted of obstruction of justice after shredding documents related to its audit of Enron Corporation (see the "Inside Story"), it is illegal to destroy potentially relevant documents in the face of a threatened or pending lawsuit or government investigation. The Sarbanes-Oxley Act made it a felony punishable by up to twenty years in prison.

Federal and state regulations require companies to retain certain records. The Code of Federal Regulations contains more than 2,400 regulations requiring that certain types of business records be maintained for specific periods of time. Many regulatory agencies have increased their retention requirements, forcing some companies to increase their file capacities by more than 15 percent a year.

A well-designed and well-executed document-management program can (1) reduce corporate liability, (2) protect trade secrets and other confidential information, and, most important, (3) save on litigation costs.[63] Time and money are wasted when corporate staff and lawyers are forced to search for documents during discovery. With an organized document-management program, a company knows exactly what documents are in its possession and where these documents are located.

63. Much of the discussion of document retention that follows is based on the work of John Ruhnka, Associate Professor at the Graduate School of Business Administration, University of Colorado at Denver, and Robert B. Austin, CRM, CSP, of Austin Associates, Denver. See John Ruhnka & Robert Austin, *Design Considerations for Document Retention/Destruction Programs,* 1 CORP. CONFIDENTIALITY & DISCLOSURE LETTER 2 (1988).

## DESIGNING A POLICY

In general, documents that a company is not required to retain for any business or legal purpose should be eliminated from company files. Documents that are kept may be obtained by opposing counsel during discovery, and they may be harmful to the company in court. However, it is important to note throughout the discussion that follows that a duty to preserve any document either by law or court order will always override a document-management program, no matter how well planned.

In July 2004, a federal judge ordered Philip Morris USA Inc. to pay sanctions of $2.75 million for deleting e-mails sought by the U.S. Justice Department in its fraud-and-racketeering lawsuit in "reckless disregard and gross indifference" to a court order requiring the preservation of documents and other records containing potentially relevant information. Philip Morris and its parent, Altria Group, had deleted e-mails that were more than sixty days old pursuant to its routine document-retention program. The judge also banned Philip Morris from using at trial testimony from any of its top eleven executives, including its director of corporate responsibility, who permitted the destruction of the e-mails over a two-and-one-half-year period. The judge characterized the mishandling of the e-mails as "astounding" for such "a particularly sophisticated litigant"[64] but refused to instruct the jury that it could assume that the deleted e-mails would have been damaging to Philip Morris. The judge concluded that "such a far reaching sanction is simply inappropriate" because it would violate the concept of proportionality.

Even if a company has been careful to destroy records, duplicates may exist in an employee's personal files, where they are still subject to discovery. For example, in the mid-1970s, the Weyerhaeuser Company paid $200 million in a case after company documents were found through discovery in personal files in the home of a retired company administrative assistant.

An employee's private diaries, calendars, and notebooks are also subject to discovery. Opposing counsel could glean from them a great deal about a company's

64. United States v. Philip Morris USA Inc., No. 99–2496 (D.C.C. July 21, 2004); *Destroyed E-Mails Result in Sanctions of $2.75 Million Against Philip Morris,* 19 CORP. COUNSEL WKLY. 225–26 (July 28, 2004).

operations. Companies should therefore include this type of record in their document-management programs.

## Corporate Privacy

Besides protecting a company in the event of litigation, a document-management program protects corporate privacy and trade secrets. A company should destroy confidential or proprietary materials as soon as possible. It should also preserve the confidentiality of employee records and destroy these records when they are no longer necessary. If an employee sues a company for wrongful termination, the employee's file is subject to discovery, and careless or unsubstantiated information in the file may be persuasive evidence at trial. Further, corporations can be liable for damages if confidential information in an employee's file, such as a medical record indicating past drug use, is made public.

## Dangerous Electronic Communications

Unlike official documents that employees are likely to treat as formal communications, electronic communications are often seen as a much less formal medium. Careless e-mails have led to the downfall of more than one company, so building an e-mail policy into a document-management system is imperative.

Five major securities firms, Goldman Sachs, Morgan Stanley, Citigroup, U.S. Bancorp, and Deutsche Bank, agreed to pay almost $8.3 million between them for failing to keep e-mails that had become pertinent in regulatory investigations.[65] Walt Disney CEO Michael Eisner commented that he has "come to believe that if anything will bring about the downfall of a company, or maybe even a country, it is blind copies of email that should never have been sent in the first place."[66] Having a clear policy on the proper use of corporate e-mail and standard policies for deleting old e-mails are essential to limiting potential liability.

Another even less formal form of communication that has yet to be a major component in litigation is instant messaging, or IM. The system falls somewhere between a telephone call and an e-mail because a sender can type messages that are immediately received by another user when the sender hits "return." Many businesses use IM as a cheap, efficient way for employees to communicate in real time with other employees without having to use a telephone or leave their work area. But many users and managers are not aware that virtually all IM programs automatically save all conversations in log files. Conversations conducted over IM are rarely as formal as those conducted via interoffice memo or even e-mail, yet these files are almost certainly discoverable.[67]

But incriminating e-mails and instant messages are not the only peril confronting companies. The method by which electronic data are destroyed is just as important as whether they are destroyed at all. A plaintiff used a program called "Evidence Eliminator" to clean files from a hard drive on the night before it was to be turned over during discovery. Even though there was no conclusive evidence that any relevant files were deleted by Evidence Eliminator, the magistrate was not amused. He called the erasure a blatant disregard for the litigation process and recommended that the plaintiff's case be dismissed with prejudice.

With the proliferation of electronic documents, e-mails, text messaging, and instant messaging, electronic communications are quickly becoming the most voluminous files that must be dealt with by a document-management system. In late 2003, office workers exchanged an estimated 2.8 billion e-mails a day; 99.997 percent of all documents were created and stored electronically; and by the middle of the decade, corporations will generate a whopping 17.5 trillion electronic documents annually.[68] Hence, managing electronic files is a primary concern for any document-management system.

## Necessary Elements of a Document-Retention Program

### *Well Planned and Systematic*

To stand up in court, a document-retention program must be well planned and systematic. Companies usually appoint a senior officer of the organization to be responsible for supervising and auditing the document-management program. Policies should be established as to the types of documents to be destroyed, including documents stored on computer or word-processing disks. The documents should then be systematically destroyed according to an established time frame (for example, when they reach a certain age).

65. Randall Smith, *Securities Firms Agree to Pay $8.3 Million in Message Dispute,* WALL ST. J., Nov. 18, 2002, at C1.
66. Michael Overly, *Dealing with Risky Emails,* CAL. LAW., Oct. 2001, at 27.
67. Deborah H. Juhnke & David P. Stenhouse, *Instant Messaging: What You Can't See Can Hurt You (In Court), at* http://www.discoveryresources.org/pdfFiles/TL_InstantMessaging.pdf.
68. Ronald Raether, *Email Maelstrom: Electronic Documents Must Be Managed,* BUS. L. TODAY, Sept.–Oct. 2003, at 57–59.

### *No Destruction in the Face of a Potential Lawsuit*

It is illegal to destroy documents when the company has notice of a potential lawsuit. A company cannot wait until a suit is formally filed against it to stop destroying relevant documents. A company must halt destruction as soon as it has good reason to believe that a suit is likely to be filed or an investigation started. Companies that did not halt destruction of documents have been forced to pay damages even when they acted accidentally. For example, in *Carlucci v. Piper Aircraft Corp.*,[69] flight data information essential to the case was missing. The judge did not believe Piper Aircraft's claim that it had not deliberately destroyed the relevant document. The judge issued a directed verdict for the plaintiff and rendered a $10 million judgment against Piper.

The recent Enron affair has become a cautionary example of what a corporation should not do in anticipation of a lawsuit or investigation. In the storm of litigation that accompanied the company's collapse, numerous documents were destroyed that would likely have been requested during the discovery phases of the trials. This violated the general rule that a company should maintain a consistent document-management system and never destroy documents in anticipation of litigation.

69. 102 F.R.D. 472 (S.D. Fla. 1984).

### *No Selective Destruction*

The importance of a systematic document-management program cannot be emphasized enough. The court will scrutinize whether document destruction was done in the ordinary course of business. Any hint of selective destruction jeopardizes the defensibility of a document-management program. If a court does determine that document destruction was improper, the court may remedy the situation by instructing the jury that it may infer that whatever documents were destroyed would have had a negative impact on the party that destroyed them. This is known as a ***spoliation inference***.

For example, a former employee sued UBS Warburg for employment discrimination and asked for the recovery and production of a number of e-mails and other records. The court ordered that one quarter of the costs of producing the non-e-mail records, approximately $40,000, be shifted to the former employee. However, the entire cost of producing the e-mails, approximately $106,000, was held to be the responsibility of the employer. When UBS Warburg could not produce some of these e-mails, the judge instructed the jury that it could assume that the e-mails not produced were damaging to UBS Warburg's case.[70]

70. Zubulake v. UBS Warburg LLC, 216 F.R.D. 280 (S.D.N.Y. 2004).

THE RESPONSIBLE MANAGER

## REDUCING LITIGATION EXPENSES

Legal disputes often arise in the normal course of business operations. Some may be resolved amicably, but others may require a third party to adjudicate the dispute. Although the courts do provide one venue, a corporate manager should not rush to trial. The costs of effective counsel, the protracted nature of most commercial disputes, and the resultant opportunity costs can be significant. The allocation of corporate funds is one concern, but so is the distraction of corporate managers who must spend time on litigation-related activities, such as depositions, interrogatories, document searches, and trial. And although most cases are settled, the settlement generally occurs only after hundreds of hours of pretrial activities.

To avoid these predictable pitfalls, a responsible manager seeks alternatives that maximize corporate value and interests. One solution is to engage in a continuing conversation with counsel to find ways to reduce litigation costs.[71] In other words, find ways to settle cases cheaply and quickly. This requires identifying and overcoming litigious working assumptions of both the corporation and the lawyer. Emotions, a desire to pass the buck, and partisan bias can create a litigation trap that prevents some conflicts from being settled in a timely manner. Egos must be set aside—by both managers and lawyers—and optimal solutions to the *problem* of litigation must be pursued.

One option is for a manager to instruct counsel to develop a settlement strategy in addition to a litigation strategy. In other words, while litigators are searching for ways to overcome a potential adversary, counsel should also seek ways to resolve the conflict as soon as possible.

71. This discussion is based on Roger Fisher, *He Who Pays the Piper*, HARV. BUS. REV., Mar.–Apr. 1985, at 150.

*(Continued)*

(The Responsible Manager *continued*)

Such an organized approach enables the manager to keep the conflict in perspective by comparing the costs, advantages, and disadvantages of litigation and settlement. This approach also assists a manager in identifying those situations in which it is worthwhile to go to court, whether to establish a beneficial precedent or limit (or overturn) a disadvantageous one. Delineating specific settlement options and reviewing the results of settlement or litigation and the accuracy of cost predictions may also help reduce legal fees.

Frequent contact with counsel is also critical to reducing litigation expenses. Lack of good communication is often cited as a key problem by both managers and attorneys. Law firms often wrongly assume that they call the shots and spend more time and money on a case than the client may have intended.[72] A manager often needs legal advice to make an informed decision but should resist the temptation to just "leave it to the lawyers." Instead, the responsible manager treats legal disputes like any other business problem that requires a business solution.

72. Ann Davis, *Businesses' Poor Communications with Law Firms Is Found Costly*, WALL ST. J., July 17, 1997, at B5.

INSIDE STORY

## ARTHUR ANDERSEN AND FRANK QUATTRONE SHRED THEIR CREDIBILITY

Accounting firms are said to have a policy of retaining documents that may be relevant to an audit for at least six to seven years.[73] In the wake of the collapse of Enron Corporation, however, Arthur Andersen, formerly one of the "big five" accounting firms, seems to have deviated from this rule of thumb. Ultimately, this led to the demise of the firm.

Andersen publicly admitted to destroying a "significant" amount of correspondence and papers relating to the audit of Enron, their client. The "smoking gun" was an e-mail in which Nancy Temple, Andersen's top attorney, encouraged auditors in the Houston office to abide by Andersen's document-retention policy. The prosecution contended that the e-mail directed employees to destroy evidence. Although Temple claimed that it was not intended to ellicit such a response, the damage had already been done.

Without some crucial documents, Andersen had the difficult, if not impossible, task of proving that the firm was not involved in the fraud and cover-up that had haunted Enron. The claims of spoliation of evidence had more force because the evidence had been destroyed in an unusual way. Mark Cheffers, a Massachusetts accountant, called this "the most extraordinary accounting malpractice case ever" and characterized Andersen's destruction of Enron-related documents as "an extraordinary example of bad judgment."[74]

73. *Accounting Firms Check Their Document-Destruction Policies*, U.S.L.W., Jan. 1, 2002, at 36–37.
74. *Id.*

Errors in document management have wreaked havoc on other major corporations as well. Frank Quattrone, a highly successful technology banker, was embroiled in litigation for several years regarding the intent of e-mail that he sent at a time when his First Boston Bank was about to be investigated by the SEC. The prosecution contended that Quattrone had learned of the impending subpoenas through an e-mail communication sent by David Brodsky, former lead counsel for First Boston. Shortly thereafter and before a holiday, Quattrone endorsed a message via the "reply to all" button that directed employees to "catch up on file cleaning" before the holiday break. If he was not aware of the subpoenas, Quattrone's e-mail can be interpreted as an innocent reminder by a responsible executive; if he was aware of them, it was an illegal instruction to destroy material evidence.

Quattrone's first trial ended in a deadlocked jury, but at the second trial, Quattrone was convicted of obstruction of justice. Judge Richard Owen sentenced him to eighteen months in prison after concluding that it was "crystal clear" that Quattrone had committed perjury.[75]

These cases make it clear that managers must be extremely careful when instructing employees to destroy documents. Every firm needs a consistent, well-reasoned document-management program to avoid such inferences of impropriety.

75. *In Biz this Week*, BUS.WK., Sept. 20, 2004, at 46.

## KEY WORDS AND PHRASES

affidavit 112
affirmative defense 112
answer 111
appellant 94
appellee 94
attorney–client privilege 116
authoritative decision 107
*cert. denied* 99
choice-of-forum clause 103
civil procedure 110
class action 118
Code of Federal Regulations (CFR) 107
common law 107
complaint 111
conflict-of-law rules 95
counterclaim 112
*de novo* 101
declaratory judgment 130
default judgment 112
depeçage 103
deposition 114
directed verdict 113
discovery 114
diversity jurisdiction 94
*en banc* hearing 97
*Erie* doctrine 95
federal question 94
*forum non conveniens* 104
forum shopping 95
*in personam* jurisdiction 101
*in rem* jurisdiction 101
interrogatory 114
judgment notwithstanding the verdict 113
judgment n.o.v (*j.n.o.v.*) 113
long-arm statute 101
minimum contacts 101
motion for judgment on the pleadings 112
motion for summary judgment 112
motion to dismiss 112
*non obstante veredicto* 113
partial summary judgment 112
personal jurisdiction 101
persuasive 107
petitioner 94
pleadings 112
political question 99
prayer 111
remand 98
reporter 93
request for production of documents 114
respondent 94
restatement 110
service of process 103
settled 114
spoliation inference 126
standing 99
*stare decisis* 107
summary judgment 112
summons 111
total-activity test 96
vacate 97
venue 120
*voir dire* 113
work-product doctrine 118
writ 97
writ of certiorari 99

## QUESTIONS AND CASE PROBLEMS

1. Answer the following questions with regard to the case *Bush v. Gore*, 531 U.S. 98 (2000):
   a. In what year was the case decided?
   b. Which court decided the case?
   c. Can you tell from the cite which party originally brought the lawsuit or which party brought the appeal?
   d. Suppose you want to cite the following passage that appeared on page 111:

      None are more conscious of the vital limits on judicial authority than are the members of this Court, and none stand more in admiration of the Constitution's design to leave the selection of the President to the people, through their legislatures, and to the political sphere. When contending parties invoke the process of the courts, however, it becomes our unsought responsibility to resolve the federal and constitutional issues the judicial system has been forced to confront.

   Where would the page designation go?

2. Trouver Capital Partners contracted with Healthcare Acquisition, Inc. to provide financial advisory and investment banking services relating to Healthcare's efforts to secure funding for several projects. Trouver's principal place of business is in Pennsylvania; Healthcare is headquartered in Florida. The parties had a dispute about the services performed under the contract, and Trouver sued Healthcare in federal court in Pennsylvania. Healthcare has filed a motion to dismiss the case for lack of jurisdiction. Trouver argues that the Pennsylvania court has jurisdiction over Healthcare because its president, Elizabeth Fago, visited Pennsylvania on a number of occasions for business meetings regarding the contract. In addition, Fago and an executive at Trouver communicated by telephone and fax on several occasions. Are these actions by Fago sufficient to establish jurisdiction in Pennsylvania over Healthcare? [*Trouver Capital Partners v. Healthcare Acquisition, Inc.*, Civil Action No. 99-3535 (E.D. Pa. Mar. 24, 2000).]

3. FC Schaffer & Associates, Inc. is an engineering firm based in Louisiana that did business with ODA Trading Agency, an Ethiopian entity that represents businesses wanting to do business in Ethiopia. Endrias, the founder and owner of ODA, employs Mesfin Gebreyes and an independent contractor, Kifle Gebre. Endrias left Ethiopia to live in the United States for five years. Shortly after Endrias's departure, Kifle learned that the Ethiopian Sugar Corporation was going to build a sugar mill and ethanol plant in Ethiopia. Kifle then contacted Schaffer about bidding for the project. Schaffer was interested and entered into a contract with ODA that provided that Schaffer would pay a commission to ODA if it was the successful bidder on the project. Schaffer was the low bidder and was chosen to build the mill and plant.

   Two months after Schaffer was awarded the contract, Endrias returned to Ethiopia and contacted Schaffer to introduce himself as the owner of ODA. Schaffer had never worked with or heard of Endrias and decided to enter into a new agreement with Mesfin and Kifle. This agreement purported to supersede the prior agreement between Schaffer and ODA. Schaffer refused to pay any commission to ODA under the first agreement, and Endrias sued Schaffer for breach of contract in the U.S. District Court for the Middle District of Louisiana. Can Endrias sue Schaffer in federal court? What law will apply to the breach-of-contract claim—federal law, the state law of Louisiana, or the law of Ethiopia? [*ODA v. FC Schaffer & Associates, Inc.*, 204 F.3d 639 (5th Cir. 2000).]

4. Spalding Sports Worldwide, Inc. sued Wilson Sporting Goods Company for infringement of U.S. Patent 5,310,178 pertaining to its basketball with a polyurethane cover. During discovery, Wilson asked Spalding to produce its invention record. Invention records are standard forms used by corporations as a means for inventors to disclose to the corporation's patent attorneys that an invention has been made and to initiate patent action. They usually contain such information as the names of the inventors, descriptions and scope of the invention, closest prior art, first date of conception, and disclosure to others and dates of publications. Spalding refused to produce its invention record, asserting that the record was protected by the attorney–client privilege because it was prepared for the purpose of securing legal advice concerning the patentability of the invention and served as an aid in completing the patent application. Wilson argues that even if the invention record was submitted to Spalding's patent committee, there was no evidence that the committee "acted as a lawyer" by rendering legal advice, as opposed to making business decisions. Wilson also contends that even if a portion of the invention record was submitted for the purpose of obtaining legal advice, the portion that contains technical information and does not ask for legal advice is not protected by the attorney–client privilege and should be produced.
   a. Should Spalding be forced to produce the invention record or part of it? Explain your reasoning. Would your answer be different if the invention record was the only record that contained the technical information at issue in the case?
   b. Wilson also argues that Spalding committed "fraud on the patent office" by making a material misrepresentation to the office and that, as a result, the attorney–client privilege was abrogated by the crime-fraud exception. Under the crime-fraud exception, the attorney–client privilege will be waived if the party made a communication "in furtherance of" a crime or fraud. Wilson has alleged that Spalding made a material misrepresentation but has submitted no evidence in support of this claim. Should the court find that the crime-fraud exception applies here and that Spalding has waived the attorney–client privilege? If not, what evidence would Wilson have to present to substantiate its claim that the crime-fraud exception applies in this case? [*In re Spalding Sports Worldwide, Inc.*, 203 F.3d 800 (Fed. Cir. 2000).]

5. DuLac Corporation, a leading U.S. manufacturer of chemicals and synthetic fabrics, is incorporated in the state of Blue Waters. All of DuLac's business is conducted within Blue Waters, and all its offices are located within the state. Blue Waters is under the federal jurisdiction of the U.S. Court of Appeals for the Fourth Circuit. The Environmental Protection Agency (EPA) commenced an investigation of DuLac's disposal procedures for DRT, a mixture of the toxic compound DNGR and the neutralizing agent HRMLS. Upon discovering that DuLac had disposed of DRT in dump sites not approved for toxic-waste disposal, the EPA filed suit against DuLac for cleanup costs and punitive damages under a federal statute forbidding the disposal of

DNGR or any derivative thereof except in approved toxic-waste-dump sites. The action was brought in a federal district court sitting in Blue Waters. DuLac's only defense to the action is that because the DNGR in DRT is fully neutralized, DRT should not be considered a derivative of DNGR for purposes of the statute. A month later, the lawyer for the EPA offers to settle the case for cleanup costs only.

**a.** Assume that the U.S. Court of Appeals for the Sixth Circuit recently interpreted the statute literally, upholding an award of punitive damages against a company that had disposed of fully neutralized DNGR. As DuLac's manager, would you recommend that the company accept the settlement offer?

**b.** Assume that another district court within the Fourth Circuit recently reached the same result as the Sixth Circuit. How would you advise DuLac regarding the settlement offer?

**c.** Assume that the U.S. Supreme Court recently reached the same result as the Sixth Circuit. Would your advice to DuLac remain the same?

**6.** AltoCom, a small software company with only twelve employees, is incorporated in California and headquartered in Silicon Valley. It develops software that is incorporated into computers, fax machines, video telephones, personal digital assistants, and other communication devices to make them run more efficiently. AltoCom licenses these softmodems to companies that manufacture these electronic devices. Its softmodems are integrated into a variety of electronic products manufactured by corporations such as Hewlett-Packard, Philips, Samsung, Sharp, and Sony. These goods are then put into worldwide distribution networks that place them for sale in retail stores such as Circuit City, OfficeMax, Service Merchandise, CompUSA, and Sears, all of which have outlets in Delaware. Motorola has sued AltoCom for patent infringement in the U.S. District Court of Delaware. AltoCom has filed a motion to dismiss for lack of personal jurisdiction on the grounds that it has never had any contact with Delaware. The company ships its software code for its softmodems to its licensees' principal place of business, and none of its eleven U.S.-based licensees is headquartered in Delaware, so it has never shipped its product there. In addition, AltoCom has never advertised its softmodems, conducted any of its business, or maintained any of its assets in Delaware. Does the Delaware court have jurisdiction over AltoCom because its product is a component in products that are sold there? [*Motorola, Inc. v. AltoCom, Inc.,* 58 F. Supp. 2d 349 (D. Del. 1999).]

**7.** Three same-sex couples who are residents of Vermont have lived together in committed relationships for a period ranging from four to twenty-five years. Two of the couples have raised children together. All three couples applied for marriage licenses and were refused a license on the grounds that they were ineligible under the state marriage laws. Plaintiffs filed a lawsuit against the State of Vermont and the towns where they lived, seeking a *declaratory judgment* that the refusal to issue them a license violated the marriage statutes and the Vermont Constitution. Specifically, they argued that it violated the Common Benefits Clause of the Vermont Constitution, which provides "[t]hat government is, or ought to be, instituted for the common benefit, protection, and security of the people, nation, or community, and not for the particular emolument or advantage of any single person, family, or set of persons, who are part of that community." They argued that in not having access to a civil marriage license, they are denied many legal benefits and protections incident to marriage, including coverage under a spouse's medical, life, and disability insurance, hospital visitation and other medical decision-making privileges, and spousal support.

**a.** Does Vermont's marriage license law violate same-sex couples' rights under the Vermont Constitution?

**b.** Vermont claims that the state marriage laws reasonably serve the state's interest in promoting the "link between procreation and child rearing." Is this a reasonable justification for the marriage laws? Would your answer change if Vermont had a law that guarantees the right to adopt and raise children regardless of the sex or marital status of the prospective parents? [*Baker v. State,* 744 A.2d 864 (Vt. 1999).]

**8.** Sterling, Inc. is a manufacturer of state-of-the-art computers. For the past ten years, Sterling has acquired all of its microchips from NoBugs Corporation, the only producer of chips meeting Sterling's high specifications. The relationship has been mutually profitable. Sterling could not have built its reputation as an industry leader without NoBugs's reliable and consistently high-quality products; Sterling's business has enabled NoBugs to grow rapidly while providing its investors with an attractive rate of return.

Some months ago, several of Sterling's computers exploded shortly after installation. Upon investigation, Sterling discovered that tiny imperfections in NoBugs's microchips had aggravated a dormant design defect in the computers, causing the explosions. Analysis of the chips indicated that they were indeed below specifications and that the imperfections were caused by a slight miscalibration of NoBugs's encoding equipment. NoBugs recalibrated the equipment and promptly resumed production of perfect chips. Sterling's losses from the explosions—lost profits, out-of-pocket costs associated with compensating customers for the explosions, and injury to business reputation—are estimated to exceed $20 million. Sterling and NoBugs disagree on the amount of the loss for which NoBugs should be responsible. Sterling's CEO is considering a lawsuit. She asks you to prepare a memo outlining the advantages and disadvantages of litigation and proposing a litigation strategy. Draft that memo.

9. In a securities case, the plaintiff sought to compel documents regarding a merger between EdgeMark Financial Corporation and Old Kent Financial Corporation. EdgeMark retained David Olson of Donaldson, Lufkin & Jenrette (DLJ) to act as its investment banker in connection with the merger. EdgeMark sent a number of documents to Olson that it claims are protected by the attorney–client privilege. The plaintiff argues that these documents are no longer protected by the privilege because disclosure to Olson resulted in waiver of the privilege. EdgeMark argues that after the plaintiff's counsel threatened to sue it, EdgeMark's and DLJ's interests became "inextricably linked" because the litigation jeopardized the merger. As a result, EdgeMark argues, the documents are protected under the "common interest" rule, which is an exception to the general rule under the attorney–client privilege that the privilege is waived when a document is disclosed to a third party. The common interest rule protects from disclosure communications between one party and an attorney for another party where the parties are engaged in a joint defense effort. DLJ is not a party to the lawsuit and has not been asked to assist in the defense. Has the attorney–client privilege been waived, or does the common interest rule preserve the privilege? [*Blanchard v. EdgeMark Financial Corp.*, 192 F.R.D. 233 (N.D. Ill. 2000).]

### MANAGER'S DILEMMA

10. One way to avoid future claims is to settle via a confidentiality agreement. Such settlements may delay future lawsuits or even save the company from liability because the public may never hear about the settled claim. Also, in the event that future claims are filed, the plaintiffs will not know the economic particulars associated with the settlement, so they may settle for less than the original claim. Such settlements are a mainstay in conflict resolution and litigation in the United States, but in 2002, ten federal judges in South Carolina voted to ban all secret settlements on the ground that they often hide information that could be valuable to the public. The judges cited the Ford–Firestone tire tread separation cases in which secret settlements deprived the public of the knowledge that some Firestone tires were dangerously defective. Had consumers been aware, lives might have been saved. Change seems to be in the wind, and that wind is blowing against confidential settlements. Nevertheless, for now they remain an indispensable tool in minimizing exposure for companies. If you were a manager responsible for major litigation, what factors would you take into account in insisting on a confidentiality clause in an agreement? What factors might lead you *not* to insist on confidentiality? [See Adam Liptak, *South Carolina Judges Seek to Ban Secret Settlements*, N.Y. TIMES, Sept. 2, 2002, at A1.]

## INTERNET SOURCES

| | |
|---|---|
| Courts.net provides directory listing for courts throughout the nation on a state-by-state basis. | http://www.courts.net |
| The state of California's judicial system has its own home page with information about its court system, including structure and recent decisions. | http://www.courtinfo.ca.gov |

| | |
|---|---|
| The National Center for State Courts' home page offers a variety of information pertaining to state courts, including information about court technology and administration. | http://www.ncsconline.org/ |
| The Cornell University Law School offers access to all U.S. Supreme Court decisions since 1990, as well as more than 600 of the most important decisions before 1990. It also includes the Court calendar, schedule of oral arguments, summary of questions presented in cases the Court will consider, and information about Supreme Court justices. | http://supct.law.cornell.edu/supct/ |
| Under the direction of the U.S. Department of Commerce, this site offers access to more than 7,000 U.S. Supreme Court opinions from 1937 to 1975, as well as to a wide range of information related to the federal government. | http://www.fedworld.gov/ |
| FindLaw allows users to search for state and federal statutes, cases, and regulations. | http://www.findlaw.com/casecode |
| The *Congressional Record* website contains the full text of the *Congressional Record* from 1995 to the present. It can be searched by date or keyword. | http://www.gpoaccess.gov/crecord/index.html |
| The Federal Judiciary home page has information about the federal court system including information from the Administrative Office of the U.S. Courts about courts with vacancies. | http://www.uscourts.gov |
| The California Judiciary website is designed to ask and answer common litigation and business law questions in "plain English." It is based on the writings of Edwin Chemerinsky, a well-known law professor. | http://www.calbar.ca.gov/calbar/pdfs/publications/legalliteracy2001.pdf |
| The Michigan State Cybercourt site allows all kinds of business litigation to take place via the Internet. | http://www.michigancybercourt.net/ |

CHAPTER 4

# Alternative Dispute Resolution

## INTRODUCTION

### WHY NOT JUST SUE?

Why would a manager consider alternative methods for resolving disputes when the manager has access to a judicial system provided by the government and financed through taxation? For anyone who has used litigation and the courts to resolve a business dispute, the answer is obvious. Litigation is expensive and takes a toll on management and employees. In addition to generating legal fees, lawsuits distract management from the company's business, risk damaging the firm's public image, and jeopardize relationships with the opposing party.

Instead of automatically taking legal conflicts to the courthouse, more firms than ever are using alternatives to formal litigation to settle conflicts with customers, suppliers, and employees. A survey of the 1,000 largest U.S. corporations found that 88 percent have used mediation and 70 percent have used arbitration; 84 percent indicated that they were likely or very likely (46 percent) to use mediation in the future, and 71 percent were likely or very likely to use arbitration.[1]

### CHAPTER OVERVIEW

This chapter explains the manager's nonlitigation options for the resolution of business disputes. Alternative dispute resolution (ADR) methods include negotiation, mediation, and arbitration, as well as hybrids, such as minitrials, med-arb, and summary jury trials. The chapter suggests various strategies for resolving disputes out of court. Finally, the chapter explains how the law views these alternatives to litigation.

## Thinking About ADR

To select the best alternative to litigation, managers must be aware of their own needs and constraints. Like other business decisions, choosing a dispute resolution mechanism—including litigation—involves many tradeoffs: Is the right decision more important than quick resolution, or is time of the essence? Will public attention help in resolving the conflict, or does the matter require confidentiality? Does the company need to preserve its relationship with the other party, or is this conflict the last interaction with that party? Will mutual resolution of the conflict make the company a desirable business partner, or will potential disputants seek conflict because the company appears weak and unwilling to defend itself vigorously?

To distinguish among the alternatives, a manager should consider the following questions about dispute settlement and the possible answers:[2]

1. How are the disputants represented?
   - By lawyers
   - By persons without formal legal training
   - By themselves without any outside representation
2. Who makes the final decision?
   - A judge or other government employee with formal legal training

1. DAVID LIPSKY & RONALD SEEBER, THE APPROPRIATE RESOLUTION OF CORPORATE DISPUTES: A REPORT ON THE GROWING USE OF ADR BY U.S. CORPORATIONS (1998).

2. These questions and answers are based on JOHN J. COUND ET AL., CIVIL PROCEDURE: CASES AND MATERIALS 1311–13 (6th ed. 1993).

- An attorney or other legal professional
- An expert in the industry
- A representative of the community in which the company operates
- The disputants with the help of a neutral third party
- The disputants themselves

3. How are facts found and standards of judgment set?
   - The disputants or their representatives are responsible for presenting evidence of the facts and arguments to establish the standard for resolution.
   - The dispute resolver, or final decision maker, can aid the disputants in performing any of these tasks.
   - The dispute resolver alone establishes the standards and finds the facts.
4. What is the source of the standard for resolution?
   - Rules already established by legislatures and courts
   - Evolving rules and standards
   - Prior practice of those whose disputes were resolved before this one
   - Prevailing values and notions of fairness
   - The disputants themselves, as determined either before or after the dispute arises
   - A delegated third party, such as the American Arbitration Association (AAA)
5. How will any decision be enforced?
   - By a court or threat of legal action
   - By the good faith of the disputants
   - By concern for reputation and future relationships
6. Who will pay for the dispute resolution procedure?
   - The losing party
   - All parties on an equal basis
   - The parties, as allocated by the dispute resolver
   - The employer (in the case of conflicts with employees) or the supplier (in the case of conflicts with customers)
   - The party bringing the dispute for resolution

Different answers to these questions will suggest different alternatives, and parties can often mix and match to suit their circumstances. Before attempting to resolve any dispute, good managers should think carefully about their own goals and the nature of dispute resolution alternatives.

## Varieties of ADR

There are three basic varieties of ADR: negotiation, mediation, and arbitration. By mixing these with each other and the formal judicial system, a manager has four more options: minitrials, med-arb, arb-med, and summary jury trials.

## Negotiation

*Negotiation* is the give-and-take people engage in when coming to terms with each other. One can view negotiation along several different dimensions. Negotiation can be either forward looking with concern for desired relationships—*transactional negotiation*—or backward looking to address past events that have caused disagreement—*dispute negotiation*. For example, two firms involved in a joint venture might engage in a transactional negotiation, whereas a steel manufacturer that failed to deliver I-beams and the construction company that has already paid for them would engage in a dispute negotiation. In the former, both parties are looking to the future with positive expectations; in the latter, the parties are looking to the past and apportioning blame. Conflicts need not be simply one or the other. Labor negotiations often have elements of both transactions and disputes. The parties must work together in the future but may also feel the need to apportion blame for the event that precipitated the crisis.

Negotiation can be viewed as involving a fixed or a growing pie. In *distributive* or *zero-sum negotiations*, the only issue is the distribution of a fixed pie. In contrast, in *integrative* or *variable-sum negotiations*, mutual gains are possible as parties trade lower-valued resources for higher-valued ones.

For example, consider a dispute between the manufacturer of a telecommunications device and the supplier of one of the device's critical components. Although the supplier delivered the component as scheduled, the component failed to work properly in the device, causing significant friction between the manufacturer and the supplier. It is unclear which party caused the problem. In distributive negotiations, the parties would merely battle over who should absorb the resulting loss, a process that could irreversibly injure the manufacturer–supplier relationship and lead to litigation. By looking beyond the boundaries of the original transaction and dispute, however, the parties may be able to create value between them. For instance, the supplier may have the capacity to expedite delivery of a modified component at very little cost in a short period of time. The manufacturer, in turn, might highly value the ability to secure this modified component. Thus, the parties could strike a deal in which the manufacturer agrees to pay the original amount owed plus a premium for replacement in exchange for the supplier's agreement to expedite a modified component. Both parties receive more than was originally due and preserve their relationship.

In the employment context, parties often expand a distributive discussion about salary to integrate issues of medical benefits, vacation days, formal titles, and other perquisites, such as parking spaces, first-class air travel, and corporate credit cards. For example, it may not cost a company anything to call a prospective employee "administrative assistant" instead of "secretary," but the title might mean enough to the employee to make up for a slightly lower cash salary.

**INTERNATIONAL SNAPSHOT**

In negotiating across cultures or in international settings, cultural myopia is a serious barrier to success. For instance, eye contact implies dramatically different attitudes in Japan and the United States. In the United States, a negotiator who avoids eye contact will be perceived as being intimidated or shifty. In Japan, that same behavior is taken as a sign of respect. When signals are misinterpreted, complex negotiations become even more difficult. Consider the Tokyo conference room where respectful officials of Mitsubishi avoid eye contact as they begin discussions with the aggressive owners of a Texas car dealership who rarely avert their eyes. What of teetotalling in Moscow? Bare heads in Jerusalem? Shoed feet in Beijing?[a]

The following excerpt from an essay written by an anonymous Japanese negotiator provides insight into how the Japanese view the American style of negotiation:

> Often they [the Americans] argue among themselves in public, so it is safe to assume that they argue even more in private. This is part of their idea of adversary proceedings and they seem to feel no shame about such embarrassing behavior.
>
> . . .
>
> Americans like to concentrate on one problem at a time. They seem not to understand that the whole picture is more important, and they spend little time on developing a general understanding of the views and interests of both sides. Since their habit of focusing on one issue often forces a direct disagreement, they often propose setting the issue aside, but they come back to it later with the same attitude and concentration. A negotiation with them may therefore become a series of small conflicts and we must always make a special effort to give proper attention to the large areas of agreement and common interest.[b]

**a.** For discussions of issues in cross-cultural negotiation, see Frank E. A. Sader & Jeffrey Z. Rubin, *Culture, Negotiation, and Eye of the Beholder,* 7 NEGOTIATION J. 249 (1991); Stephen E. Weiss, *Negotiating with "Romans"—Part 1,* SLOAN MGMT. REV. 51 (Winter 1994); John L. Graham, *The Japanese Negotiation Style: Characteristics of a Distinct Approach,* 9 NEGOTIATION J. 123 (1993).

**b.** YUKO YANAGIDA ET AL., LAW AND INVESTMENT IN JAPAN 219–20 (1994).

Unsurprisingly, distributive negotiations can easily become adversarial and strain even the closest relationships. With nothing to do but fight over the pie, the parties inevitably do fight. Integrating other issues into the discussion creates the possibility of trade-offs that allow both parties to gain relative to their distributive starting point.

## PLANNING AND PREPARATION

Professors Max Bazerman and Margaret Neale, authors of the popular book *Negotiating Rationally,* recommend asking and answering three questions before entering a negotiation (or at least before entering a negotiation you wish to win): First, ask what is your *reservation price,* that is, the price at which you are indifferent between the success and failure of the negotiation. In their framework, a negotiator should first establish his or her *Best Alternative to a Negotiated Agreement (BATNA)*. This is the outcome a person will choose if the negotiation fails. By definition, it is the best outcome available outside the negotiation. Consequently, any settlement higher than one's BATNA is preferable to a failed negotiation. Although reservation price and BATNA are not the same, they are closely related. The transaction costs of executing the BATNA are the essential difference.

By understanding their BATNA, managers can determine the highest price they should be willing to pay. If a manager makes an offer close to his or her reservation price and the opponent refuses, the manager knows that further concessions are not in his or her interest. As Bazerman and Neale remind us, "[T]he goal of negotiating is not to reach just any agreement, but to reach an agreement that is better for you than what you would get without one."[3] Well-intentioned managers can easily get caught up in the heat of an important negotiation and mistake agreement for success.

Second, ask what are your interests, as opposed to your positions. Positions are the stated requirements that one negotiator demands of his or her opponent. Interests are what he or she actually desires, whether revealed or withheld. Knowing one's interests allows a person to fashion integrative solutions.

Third, ask how important, comparatively, each negotiation issue is to you. Establishing priorities and distinguishing between positions and interests enable a manager to think systematically about trade-offs that

3. MAX H. BAZERMAN & MARGARET A. NEALE, NEGOTIATING RATIONALLY 173 (1992).

create mutual gain. Prudent negotiators ask these three questions about their opponents as well as about themselves.

Exhibit 4.1 summarizes the steps to take in preparation for a negotiation. An unprepared negotiator is a manager's favorite opponent.

**EXHIBIT 4.1 Negotiation Preparation**

Before embarking on a negotiation, a manager should do the following:

1. Analyze the nature of the dispute:
   - Ask why this particular constellation of actors is at the negotiating table now.
2. Specify superordinate goals and objectives:
   - Figure out what you want.
3. Outline the scope of the negotiation:
   - Identify the issues to be negotiated, both tangible and intangible.
   - Determine your reservation price.
   - Consider your alternatives to this negotiation.
   - Analyze the priorities for each issue to be negotiated.
   - Consider alternative proposals you could offer or accept.
4. Understand your opponent by asking:
   - What issues will be of concern to him or her?
   - What are his or her priorities on those issues?
   - What is his or her reservation price?
   - What are his or her alternatives to this negotiation?
   - What is the history of negotiations between you and your opponent?
   - What is your opponent's reputation?
   - Is the opponent monolithic or a group with members having differing views?
5. Understand the particular negotiation situation and ask:
   - What are the deadlines or other time constraints?
   - Who has the authority to ratify any agreement, and is that person at the negotiation?
   - Will this negotiation affect future negotiations and, if so, how?
   - How important is your relationship with the other party going forward?

Source: Based on Professor Margaret Neale's course "Conflict and Negotiation" at the Stanford Graduate School of Business.

Exhibit 4.2 summarizes a number of mistakes that can create barriers to a satisfactory negotiated resolution.

**EXHIBIT 4.2 Common Negotiation Mistakes**

Common negotiation mistakes include:

- Pursuing a negotiated course of action only to justify an earlier decision
- Assuming that what is good for you is necessarily bad for your opponent and vice versa
- Being irrationally affected by an initial anchor price, that is, a price that was suggested early in the negotiations and may now be an unnatural standard for evaluating other offers
- Failing to look for another frame or characterization of the issues that would put a different perspective on the negotiation
- Being affected by readily available information (such as personal experience or recent events) and ignoring other valid, but less accessible, data
- Placing too much confidence in your own fallible judgment

Source: Adapted from NEGOTIATING RATIONALLY by Max H. Bazerman & Margaret A. Neale. Copyright © 1992 by Max H. Bazerman and Margaret A. Neale.

## LIABILITY FOR FAILED NEGOTIATIONS

In the United States, it is difficult to establish legal liability on the grounds that a party did not finalize a contract after a series of negotiations. As explained more fully in Chapter 7, in the United States a party is generally free to terminate negotiations for any or no reason at any time prior to contract formation. For example, in *Apothekernes Laboratorium for Special Praeparater v. IMC Chemical Group, Inc.*,[4] IMC's board of directors rejected a negotiated deal with Apothekernes after a letter of intent had been signed and IMC's negotiator had assured Apothekernes that the board would approve the deal. Even though the negotiators had a meeting of the minds, the U.S. appeals court held that there was no contract because the letter of intent expressly stated that the terms were "subject to our concluding an Agreement of Sale which shall be acceptable to the Boards of Directors of our respective corporations, whose discretion shall in no way be limited by this letter."

In some jurisdictions, however, a covenant of good faith and trust applies to negotiations even if they do not ripen into a contract. The following case from Japan provides an example.[5]

4. 873 F.2d 155 (7th Cir. 1989).
5. Excerpted from YUKO YANAGIDA ET AL., LAW AND INVESTMENT IN JAPAN 223–29 (1994).

A CASE IN POINT

**CASE 4.1**
**D. James Wan Kim Min v. Mitsui Bussan K.K.**
*Tokyo High Court (1987).*

## Summary

› **FACTS** D. James Wan Kim Min, a Malaysian politician and businessman, negotiated with Mitsui Bussan (Mitsui), a Japanese general trading company, to enter into a joint venture to log and develop a forested area in Indonesia. In January 1974, Min and the manager of the lumber division of Mitsui agreed upon the principal terms of the agreement, whereby Mitsui would pay $4 million by April 30, 1974, to purchase from Min 50 percent of the shares of a Brunei corporation that held a majority of the shares in the Indonesian corporation with the lumbering rights in Indonesia. The parties continued to negotiate, but by the April 30 deadline, Mitsui had neither signed the draft contract nor paid the purchase price to Min. In July, Mitsui offered to loan $4 million to Min rather than purchase the shares in the Brunei corporation. Mitsui suspended this offer in October 1974 when Min was arrested and detained by Malaysian authorities allegedly for political reasons.

While imprisoned, Min maintained communication with Mitsui. In July 1975, Mitsui agreed by letter to use its best efforts to execute the loan after Min was released. When Min was released in January 1976, however, Mitsui refused to proceed with the loan. In May 1976, Mitsui told Min that it had no legal obligations to him. Min brought suit against Mitsui for breach of contract and violation of the principle of good faith. The trial court rejected Min's contract claim but held in his favor with respect to the principle of good faith. Both Min and Mitsui appealed.

› **ISSUE PRESENTED** May negotiations give rise to an expectation that a contract will be formed so that if the contract is not formed, a party may recover damages from the other party?

› **SUMMARY OF OPINION** The Tokyo High Court affirmed the trial court's rejection of Min's contract claims after finding that Mitsui had not made a final and definite offer to purchase the shares. However, the High Court ruled that Mitsui was obligated under the principles of trust and good faith to conclude the contract in order not to injure Min's expectations:

> [I]n the modern world, the principles of good faith and trust govern not only contractual relationships, but also all relationships under private law, and such principles thus apply not only after conclusion of an agreement but also at the stage of preparations toward conclusion of an agreement. In the event that preparation between two parties progresses towards conclusion of an agreement and the first party comes to expect that the agreement will surely be concluded, the second party becomes obligated under the principles of good faith and trust to try to conclude the agreement, in order not to injure the expectation of the first party. Therefore, if the second party, in violation of its obligation, concludes that the agreement is undesirable, then absent certain circumstances it is liable for damages incurred by the first party as the results of its illegal acts.
>
> . . .
>
> [T]he Letter sent by the [Mitsui] manager and Min's response, to which Mitsui offered no subsequent objection, caused Min to expect that the agreement would be concluded. Mitsui, therefore, should be considered to have become obligated from that time to make good-faith efforts, under the principles of good-faith and trust, to conclude the agreements. Absent special circumstances that justified suspension of efforts to conclude the agreements, Mitsui should not have been allowed unilaterally and unconditionally to suspend conclusion.

*(Continued)*

(Case 4.1 *continued*)

**› RESULT** Mitsui had violated the principle of good faith and trust. The Tokyo High Court awarded damages for Min's expenses in preparing for the joint venture, including expenses relating to transportation, accommodations, correspondence, compensation paid to representatives of the joint venture, rent for office space, expenditures for investigating lumber forests, and attorneys' fees. However, the High Court held that Min's damages resulting from depreciation in the market price of the shares, mental distress, and lost profits did not reasonably relate to Mitsui's breach.

**› COMMENTS** As explained in Chapter 7, in the United States, the doctrine of promissory estoppel can provide limited relief when a party makes promises during the course of negotiations on which the other party reasonably relies to his or her detriment.

## Mediation

As Chapter 3 pointed out, the win–lose nature of litigation can turn business colleagues into bitter enemies. Mediation can be a less hostile alternative to a lawsuit. Like negotiation, mediation can lead to joint gains. It can also help preserve relationships that might otherwise break under the strain of conflict. In a survey of 1,000 large U.S. corporations, 81 percent of the respondents said they used mediation because it provided "a more satisfactory process" than litigation; 66 percent said it provided more "satisfactory settlements"; and 59 percent asserted that it "preserves good relationships."[6]

In *mediation,* the parties agree to try to reach a solution themselves with the assistance of a neutral third party who helps them find a mutually satisfactory resolution. This third party is the *mediator.*

In many ways, mediation is an extension of the negotiation process. One can view mediation as a facilitated negotiation. The mediator/facilitator guides the parties in a structured set of discussions about the issues and alternatives. He or she confers with both parties, together and in private, and points out the elements in dispute and the areas of agreement. Sometimes the mediator helps the parties identify their own goals.

As in negotiation, parties often confuse their positions with their interests, especially after publicly stating a commitment to a position. In this situation, a neutral mediator is better positioned to ask questions and offer suggestions without creating the suspicion of ulterior motives. Parties to mediation are less likely to ask of a good mediator, "What is she really trying to do?" Unlike the parties, a mediator can offer compromises without fear of appearing weak or too eager to settle.

A mediator's role is to suggest ways to resolve the dispute fairly and to guide the parties toward resolution. Unlike a judge, a mediator cannot enforce a solution; the parties must come to a resolution themselves and then agree to abide by it. Once agreement is reached, the parties may formalize the arrangement with contracts, public statements, or letters of understanding.

### History

The formal use of mediation is hardly a recent phenomenon. Early immigrant groups, including Quaker, Chinese, and Jewish communities, used mediation to resolve intragroup conflict and to avoid the American judicial system's foreign legal culture. Organized labor has used mediation since the nineteenth century. In 1926, Congress established the National Mediation Board, and in 1947 it created the Federal Mediation and Conciliation Service. These two entities remain active in dispute resolution.

Because mediators can allow parties to vent their feelings and encourage them to at least acknowledge each other's perspectives, mediation can diffuse difficult interpersonal tensions. Courts often mandate mediation before allowing disputes to go to trial. The Equal Employment Opportunity Commission has successfully used mediation to reduce its case backlog.[7]

Insurance companies are using mediation to save money, time, and other resources. The Travelers Insurance Company found that more than 85 percent of the cases it submitted to mediation were settled. Even when a settlement could not be reached, the mediation process helped the litigants focus on the most important issues, which allowed for a quicker resolution at trial. Recently, thirty-

6. Lipsky & Seeber, *supra* note 1.

7. Aurora Mackey, *Close Calls,* Cal. Law., June 1999, at 36.

seven insurance companies entered into pacts to mediate their claims against each other. Chubb & Son, Inc., a participating insurance company, has resolved nearly a dozen disputes under mediation pacts and saved between $150,000 and $200,000 per case.[8]

In recent years, several companies have successfully settled class-action lawsuits through mediation. In 2000, an antitrust class action against the toy company Toys 'R' Us was settled following mediation for approximately $57 million in toys and cash.[9] The same year, a class action against Toshiba America Information Systems, Inc., which involved allegations that the company manufactured and distributed faulty floppy-diskette controllers, was settled through mediation.[10] Toshiba agreed to pay approximately $2.1 billion in cash, warranty remedies, hardware replacements, and coupons to repair the allegedly defective equipment.

## SELECTING A MEDIATOR

Although not pronouncing final judgment, a mediator can powerfully affect the outcome of the mediation. By asking some questions but not others, the mediator can move the discussion to or away from an issue. By suggesting solutions and reacting to proposals, the mediator can influence both parties' attitudes toward fairness, risk aversion, and trust. A skilled mediator knows how to bring disputing parties to genuine settlement; an unskilled mediator can push parties into agreements they later regret or, worse, can inflame the situation. Mediation agreements may or may not specify how a mediator will be selected.

In the 1980s, the Society of Professionals in Dispute Resolution (SPDR) formed a commission to study the qualifications of mediators. After concluding that performance rather than credentials should be the central qualification criterion, it determined that qualified mediators should be able to (1) understand the negotiating process and the role of advocacy, (2) earn trust and maintain acceptability, (3) convert the parties' positions into needs and interests, (4) screen out nonmediable issues, (5) help the parties invent creative options, (6) help the parties identify principles and criteria that will guide their decision making, (7) help the parties assess their nonsettlement alternatives, (8) help the parties make their own informed choices, and (9) help the parties assess whether their agreement can be implemented.[11]

The CPR Institute for Dispute Resolution (CPR), a nonprofit alliance of 500 major corporations and law firms, offers a standard mediation clause for parties to incorporate into their contracts: "The parties shall endeavor to resolve any dispute arising out of or relating to this Agreement by mediation under the CPR Mediation Procedure. Unless otherwise agreed, the parties will select a mediator from the CPR Panels of Distinguished Neutrals." The Panels of Distinguished Neutrals are the CPR's rosters of 700 attorneys, former judges, legally trained executives, and academics who can mediate disputes. The CPR is a strong proponent of self-administered ADR, in which the parties and the mediator manage the process themselves, because it provides the parties with optimum control over the dispute resolution process and is cheaper and more efficient.

## CONFIDENTIALITY

The issue of confidentiality is central to negotiation and mediation. If parties do not feel comfortable revealing important, sensitive information, they are less likely to identify opportunities for mutual gain. Unlike negotiation, mediation allows disputants to confide in a third party without fear of being exploited. Whether the mediation process involves caucusing or shuttle diplomacy, confiding in a mediator can allow the mediator to identify potential gains and point them out to the

8. Margaret A. Jacobs, *Industry Giants Join Movement to Mediate,* WALL ST. J., July 21, 1997, at B1.

9. *In re* Toys 'R' Us Antitrust Litig., 191 F.R.D. 347 (E.D.N.Y. 2000).

10. Shaw v. Toshiba Am. Info. Sys., Inc., 91 F. Supp. 2d 942 (E.D. Tex. 2000).

11. National Institute of Dispute Resolution, *Dispute Resolution Forum,* May 9, 1989.

### ETHICAL CONSIDERATION

During a dispute with a competitor over copyrighted software that is similar to the competitor's products, you ask a mediator friend about his work in ADR. In the course of a few nameless anecdotes about his recent clients, you are shocked to learn how much sensitive information a skilled mediator can induce parties to share. At the same time, your attorneys tell you that without more evidence against your competitor, a lawsuit is not justified or economically prudent at this time. Should you propose mediation to the other company in the hope of learning enough information to justify legal action? If such a proposal is accepted, should you send as your representative a new employee who has no sensitive information to reveal? Should you hire a professional investigator as your representative to elicit as much damaging information as possible from your competitor?

parties. If that confidentiality is doubted, the parties will withhold useful but potentially damaging information. Even worse, if the promise of confidentiality is not honored, the parties will come to regret their decision to mediate.

To protect such confidences, many states extend legal privileges to mediators; others do so only if the parties have agreed to keep communications with the mediator confidential. In an effort to provide some consistency in states' treatment of mediation communications, the National Conference of Commissioners on Uniform State Laws has proposed a Uniform Mediation Act that is still under consideration.[12] The revised interim draft, dated August 2000, would entitle a mediator to refuse to disclose, and prevent any other person from disclosing, a communication with the mediator in a civil proceeding before a judicial, administrative, arbitration, or juvenile court or tribunal, or in a criminal misdemeanor proceeding. Although federal law does not directly address the question, federal courts have shown a willingness to recognize a mediation privilege, even if doing so deprives a party of truthful probative evidence.[13]

## When to Use Mediation

Mediation, like other forms of ADR, is better suited to some conflicts than to others. For mediation to be appropriate, the parties must sincerely desire to settle their dispute. If they are unwilling to compromise or seek to harm their opponents, mediation will be a frustrating waste of time. Conversely, parties who wish to preserve their relationship may find that mediation is their best option. Litigation is adversarial by nature and often leaves hard feelings in its wake. Arbitration can also pit one party against another such that future interactions are filled with animosity.

Mediation is often attractive because it offers resolutions that are speedy, inexpensive, and logistically simple when compared to litigation. Mediation can also be therapeutic for the parties involved if they can express their pent-up feelings of anger, frustration, or betrayal.

Legal uncertainty also makes mediation an attractive alternative. If the law is clear and one party's rights are clearly being violated, mediation will seem unnecessary. The less black-and-white the situation, the more risky legal action is. Mediation allows parties to resolve their differences more quickly and without appeal to undeveloped, ill-formed, or uncertain legal doctrine.

The need for privacy may also make some disputes more appropriate for mediation. Lawsuits require the filing of public documents and can alert the media to sensitive areas of business. A company may wish to keep trade secrets, embryonic research, organizational structures, and internal training documents from the front pages of newspapers. Suppliers and customers may also become nervous if problems that could have been kept confidential are reported in the press. "Keeping it between ourselves" is much more realistic if few outsiders are involved.

## The Mediation Process

By definition, mediation is a flexible process that allows for many different structures, rules, and procedures. Because parties are less likely to agree to anything once a dispute has arisen, mediation organizations have evolved sets of default rules to which disputants can subscribe in advance of a specific conflict or to which they can defer once a conflict has arisen. However, disputants may also agree to alternative ground rules that are specifically tailored to their particular conflict and needs.

## Dangers

Critics of mediation point to the lack of procedural protections. Some parties may be surprised to find that legal rights that would be protected in litigation are not protected in mediation. Parties with equal bargaining power may wisely agree to trade such rights for expediency. An unequal bargainer, however, may unfairly take advantage of the other side. For example, in a conflict between a landlord and rent-controlled tenants over a rat infestation, the tenants might accept the placing of rat traps instead of the full-scale extermination that the housing code and a court would mandate.

Mediation may also effect changes in the distribution of power in a relationship. For example, introducing mediation into a nonunion plant may effectively defuse tensions and hinder efforts to unionize the plant.[14] Before agreeing to mediation, parties should consider the possibility of such consequences, including possible effects on continued adjudication of the dispute, future dealings with the opponent, and the firm's reputation with internal and external constituencies.

12. The revised interim draft of the Uniform Mediation Act can be found *at* http://www.pon.harvard.edu/guests/uma.

13. *See, e.g.*, Dell v. Dep't of Commerce, 618 F.2d 51 (9th Cir. 1980).

14. William L. Ury et al., Getting Disputes Resolved 52 (1988).

# View from Cyberspace

## ADR FOR ONLINE DISPUTES

The Internet's electronic marketplace poses new challenges for resolving disputes. A survey of online shoppers conducted by the National Consumers League found that one in five consumers had experienced a problem with online transactions in the previous year.[a]

In 1999, the Organisation for Economic Cooperation and Development (OECD) approved Guidelines on Consumer Protection in the Context of Electronic Commerce.[b] The section on dispute resolution and redress states that "[c]onsumers should be provided meaningful access to fair and timely alternative dispute resolution and redress without undue cost or burden." The Guidelines encourage businesses, consumer representatives, and governments to "work together to continue to provide consumers with the option of alternative dispute resolution mechanisms that provide effective resolution of the dispute in a fair and timely manner and without undue cost or burden to the consumer." Similarly, the Federal Trade Commission issued a report in 2000 that recognized the importance of ADR to consumer protection: "[T]he same technology that enables e-commerce can provide consumers with practical access to redress without unduly burdening business."[c]

The Internet Corporation for Assigned Names and Numbers (ICANN) approved a Uniform Domain Name Dispute Resolution Policy (UDRP) and Rules for the Uniform Domain Name Dispute Resolution Policy in 1999.[d] The ICANN is a quasi-governmental Internet regulating body. Its policy provides for an administrative proceeding for the resolution of disputes between domain name owners and trademark owners. The UDRP applies to every domain name registrant that registers its domain names through an ICANN-accredited registrar. The filings, communications, and much of the panelists' deliberations take place online, and there are no in-person hearings.

In 2000, the World Intellectual Property Organization (WIPO), a United Nations agency, signed an agreement with the Application Service Provider Industry Consortium to create an international arbitration and mediation center for the application service provider (ASP) industry. The center allows parties to resolve their disputes quickly by filing claims and supporting documents online. In addition, WIPO selects arbitrators who have the technological expertise to understand the issues in dispute.

a. Michael Liedtke, *Mediators See Profit in Online Discontent/Buyer Complaints Create Opportunity,* SAN DIEGO UNION-TRIB., May 1, 2000, at A-3.

b. The text of the Guidelines can be found at the OECD website: http://www.oecd.org/dsti/sti/it/consumer/prod/ guidelines.htm.

c. FEDERAL TRADE COMMISSION, CONSUMER PROTECTION IN THE GLOBAL ELECTRONIC MARKETPLACE (2000).

d. M. Scott Donahey, *Mandatory Resolution of Domain Name Disputes,* J. INTERNET L., Jan. 2000, at 1.

## Arbitration

*Arbitration* is the resolution of a dispute by a neutral third party, called an *arbitrator*. The process is consensual and created by a contract. The number of business disputes submitted to arbitration increased 14 percent from 2002 to 2003.[15]

In July 1999, Jeffrey Katzenberg, former chairman of Walt Disney Studios, sued the company for breach of contract, alleging that he was owed at least 2 percent of studio profits created during the ten years that he worked at Disney. The parties settled the salary portion of the case for $117 million and agreed to determine through arbitration the additional amount of money he was owed for his bonus. Although the terms of the agreement worked out in arbitration are confidential, insiders estimated that Katzenberg received an additional $150 million along with the $117 million Disney agreed to pay him.[16]

Although *nonbinding arbitration* is certainly an option, most parties enter binding arbitration. In *final-offer arbitration,* used most notably in baseball salary disputes, each side submits its "best and final" offer to the arbitrator, who must choose one of the two proposals. Such a structure strongly encourages the parties to submit fair and reasonable offers. Otherwise, the less reasonable party is likely to lose with no chance for further

15. Gary Weiss, *Walled Off from Justice,* BUS.WK., Mar. 22, 2004, at 90–92.

16. Janet Shprintz, *Jeff & Mickey's Odd Courtship,* VARIETY, July 12, 1999, at 1.

concessions. Without its binding nature, such an exercise would be pointless. Still, some parties value the result of nonbinding arbitration as a guide to what is fair. If a neutral third party has heard the strongest evidence and best arguments of both sides in a dispute, his or her opinion can serve as a baseline for what a court might decide.

## Arbitration Process

Arbitration is the most formal of the ADR methods. It is unlike both negotiation, in which there is no structure unless the parties first negotiate one, and mediation, in which the mediator focuses more on creating dialogue than on enforcing a technical format. In some ways, arbitration is like a trial. The first stage is usually a *prehearing*, in which parties may submit trial-like briefs, supporting documents, and other written statements making their case. Because neither federal nor state statutes grant arbitrators the authority to use discovery devices at this stage, prehearing discovery is usually limited to what the parties voluntarily disclose unless the parties agreed to greater discovery when they agreed to arbitrate the dispute.

Because the *hearing* itself is adversarial (like a trial), the hearing is more structured than the prehearing. The precise structure varies from arbitration to arbitration, but Rule 32 of the Commercial Arbitration Rules, Conduct of Proceedings, promulgated by the American Arbitration Association (AAA), provides an illustration:

> The claimant shall present evidence to support its claim. The respondent shall then present evidence to support its defense. Witnesses for each party shall also submit to questions from the arbitrator and the adverse party. The arbitrator has the discretion to vary this procedure, provided that the parties are treated with equality and that each party has the right to be heard and is given a fair opportunity to present its case.

Although no detailed rules of evidence or procedure need apply—unlike in state and federal court, where much statutory and case law addresses fine points in exacting detail—many arbitrators believe that compliance with some of these rules is useful and necessary. Arbitrators may also subpoena documents and witnesses for the hearing.

In the final, *posthearing* phase, the arbitrator makes his or her award after considering all the evidence presented in the prehearing and the hearing itself. Often the award is not accompanied by any discussion or explanation of the decision. "Written opinions can be dangerous because they identify targets for the losing party to attack," warns one arbitration scholar.[17] In a profession neither subject to appeal nor constrained by precedent, arbitrators may be reluctant to give extra grist to the loser's mill. On the other hand, the U.S. Supreme Court has noted that "a well reasoned opinion tends to engender confidence in the integrity of the process and aids in clarifying the underlying agreement."[18] In some settings, such as federal labor arbitrations under the auspices of the National Labor Relations Board (NLRB), arbitrators are required to write an opinion. Also, parties can insist on an opinion as part of their contract with the arbitrator.

## Choice of Arbitrator

The arbitrator is usually chosen by the parties to the dispute or by a third-party delegate, such as the AAA, which represents 18,000 arbitrators. As at a trial, each side can strike any panelist it feels uncomfortable with, but unlike a trial there is no limit to the number of "peremptory challenges" allowed. The choice of an arbitrator is crucial. Unlike a judge's decision, which can be set aside if erroneous, an arbitrator's ruling generally is binding.

An arbitration clause may list the names of potential arbitrators. If so, the parties should check the availability of these candidates before enlisting them. Like judges and their courts, particular arbitrators may be too busy to provide speedy resolution. Alternatively, the arbitration clause may refer the selection of an arbitrator to the

17. R. Coulson, Business Arbitration—What You Need to Know 29 (3d ed. 1986).
18. United Steelworkers of Am. v. Enter. Wheel & Car Corp., 363 U.S. 593, 598 (1960).

### Ethical Consideration

In many businesses, volume discounts are standard practice, and large customers reasonably expect to receive favorable treatment. How should a large, international corporation with a steady stream of disputes screen prospective arbitrators or mediators? Statistics have shown that companies using a particular arbitration service more than once are five times more likely to win in a repeat use than a first-time user. Even when repeat users do lose, they pay only 20 percent of the usual award.[a] Is it appropriate for a manager to point out to prospective arbitrators or mediators the potential for future lucrative business "if this one goes well"?

a. *Panelists Say Ethics, Neutrality Challenges Create Vulnerability for Arbitration Providers,* 70 U.S.L.W. 2616 (Apr. 2, 2002).

HISTORICAL PERSPECTIVE

## EARLY BINDING ARBITRATION

In one of the earliest examples of ADR, two women brought their dispute over the maternity of an infant boy to a leading official:

> Then the king [Solomon] said, "The one says, 'This is my son, who is living, and your son is the dead one'; and the other says, 'No! For your son is the dead one, and my son is the living one.'"
>
> And the king said, "Get me a sword." So they brought a sword before the king. And the king said, "Divide the living child in two, and give half to the one and half to the other."
>
> Then the woman whose child was the living one spoke to the king for she was deeply stirred over her son and said, "Oh my lord, give her the living child and by no means kill him."
>
> But the other said, "He shall be neither mine nor yours; divide him!"
>
> Then the king answered and said, "Give the first woman the living child and by no means kill him. She is his mother."
>
> When all Israel heard of the judgment which the king had handed down, they feared the king; for they saw that the wisdom of God was in him to administer justice.[a]

a. 1 *Kings* 3:23–28.

AAA or another dispute resolution organization. Arbitrators from the AAA are skilled, and the association makes special efforts to identify arbitrators experienced in handling particular types of disputes. The AAA decides how many arbitrators to appoint (usually from one to three) and may include arbitrators from different professions, unless the arbitration clause specifies the number and kind of arbitrators desired. Arbitration clauses often provide that each party will choose its own arbitrator and that these two will pick a third. In some states, the government itself is willing to intervene. In New York, for instance, a court may name the arbitrator upon application by either party.[19] The Federal Arbitration Act has a similar provision.[20]

The ability to select an arbitrator familiar with the industry or form of dispute further distinguishes arbitration from much of the judicial system. Judges tend to be experts in judicial procedure. Consequently, they hear cases touching on many substantive areas of the law. A federal district judge, for instance, could in a single day preside over cases ranging from felony narcotic sales to toxic tort class actions; the judge's docket might include price-fixing cases, contract disputes between financial institutions, and racially motivated employment discrimination. Arbitrators tend to focus on business sectors or conflict types, such as labor relations or landlord–tenant disputes. To the extent one is more concerned with substance than procedure, arbitration can be an attractive alternative to litigation.

### ARBITRATION CLAUSES

Parties commonly enter into arbitration through the inclusion of an arbitration clause in a contract. An *arbitration clause* specifies that in the event of a dispute arising out of the contract, the parties will arbitrate specific issues in a stated manner. It is important that parties negotiate arbitration agreements that clearly state the types of disputes to be resolved by arbitration as well as the procedure and rules, such as discovery and the types of damages to be awarded, to be used at the arbitration. The agreement should expressly state whether the arbitration will be binding or nonbinding. It is far easier for parties to negotiate these terms at the beginning of their relationship than at the time a dispute arises. Arbitration clauses are especially important in international contracts when each party wishes to avoid the labyrinth of a foreign legal system and the many pitfalls awaiting a novice litigant.

A well-drafted arbitration clause can help the parties avoid the lengthy, complicated process of trial. The more standard and reasonable the clause, the less likely it is to spawn derivative litigation questioning the arbitration itself. All issues arising from a claim can be settled by an arbitrator. When there is a challenge to the

19. N.Y. C.P.L.R. 7504 (1999).
20. 9 U.S.C. § 5.

**INTERNATIONAL SNAPSHOT**

When parties to a contract are from different nations, a dispute between the parties can lead to a collision between at least one party's expectations and a foreign legal regime. To avoid such difficulties, it is often helpful to include arbitration clauses in these contracts. After all, few managers would appreciate being haled into a foreign-language court 5,000 miles from their home office and being held to unfamiliar legal standards. Many European and Asian business leaders, for example, are uncomfortable with the U.S. legal system's discovery procedures for obtaining evidence prior to trial through depositions, written interrogatories, and document production. Often the parties can draft an arbitration clause to their mutual satisfaction, but once litigation has begun, the parties cannot "negotiate around" many rules of a legal system, even if both are willing to do so.

entire agreement itself, however, a claimant may be able to bring suit in a court of law.[21]

When drafting a contract, managers should consider the scope of any arbitration clause. In *mandatory arbitration,* one party will not do business with the other unless he or she agrees to arbitrate any future claims. Usually, the parties to the contract are the parties to the arbitration. Sometimes, however, a dispute may arise between parties to several different contracts. For example, there may be a dispute between a construction subcontractor and an architect. The parties should ensure that each contract contains an arbitration clause and that each party agrees to a consolidated arbitration with other parties on related issues.

Foreseeing which disputes are better arbitrated than litigated is more difficult than foreseeing which parties might come into conflict. Most arbitration clauses simply state that the parties will arbitrate all disputes relating to or arising out of their contract—leaving the parties to fight over the specifics of arbitration after a dispute arises. Instead, parties should specify in the agreement the types of issues and disputes that they want to arbitrate rather than litigate.

Unfortunately, arbitration clauses often do not include details of how arbitration will proceed, when and where it will take place, and who will preside. Once again, it is better to agree upon these details before a dispute arises. Parties should agree upon a location close to their businesses and a reasonable timetable by which to settle their disputes. The arbitration clause may provide that the arbitration will commence with a prehearing conference. To minimize the conflict over such specifics, parties often designate that arbitrations will be conducted according to the rules of a third-party organization, such as the American Arbitration Association. As in mediation, such organizations have evolved rules and procedures that may serve as defaults for disputing parties. However, these rules rarely include provisions concerning the scope of discovery and limits on punitive damages. Parties are better served by including specific provisions concerning these matters. In some states, such as Illinois, an arbitrator cannot award punitive damages unless the parties expressly authorize it.

## Judicial Enforcement of Arbitration Clauses: Federal Arbitration Act

In 1920, New York enacted the first arbitration statute in the United States, giving parties the right to settle current disputes and control future ones through private arbitration. The New York act served as a model for the Uniform Arbitration Act enacted thirty-five years later. Today, most states have amended their laws to conform to the Uniform Arbitration Act, making agreements to arbitrate and arbitration awards judicially enforceable.

Five years after New York blazed the trail, Congress passed what is now known as the *Federal Arbitration Act (FAA).* Many years later, the Supreme Court proclaimed that in enacting the law, "Congress declared a national policy favoring arbitration and withdrew the power of the states to require a judicial forum for the resolution of claims which the contracting parties agreed to resolve by arbitration."[22]

**ETHICAL CONSIDERATION**

A common premise underlying advocacy of ADR is that the parties have consented to the dispute resolution mechanism as opposed to the judicial system. Should the manager of a local appliance store whose sales contracts call for binding arbitration—in barely legible typeface buried in the middle of five pages of legalese—be able to enforce those arbitration clauses? Does it matter that this is the only refrigerator distributor for miles in a poor urban area? If the store serves a neighborhood where most residents speak only Chinese, should the agreement be in Chinese?

21. Spahr v. Secco, 330 F.3d 1266 (10th Cir. 2003).

22. Southland Corp. v. Keating, 465 U.S. 1, 2 (1984).

### *Arbitration of Statutory Claims*

The U.S. Supreme Court has enforced arbitration clauses, even when the rights at issue were protected by federal law. For example, in *Rodriguez de Quijas v. Shearson/American Express, Inc.*,[23] the Supreme Court held that a predispute agreement to submit to compulsory arbitration any controversy relating to a securities investment was enforceable even though the plaintiff alleged claims under the Securities Act of 1933. The Court noted that in recent years it had upheld agreements to arbitrate claims under the Securities Exchange Act of 1934,[24] the Racketeer Influenced and Corrupt Organizations Act (RICO),[25] and the antitrust laws.[26] By agreeing to arbitrate a statutory claim, the Court reasoned, a party does not forgo the substantive rights afforded by the statute. The agreement means only that the resolution of the dispute will be in an arbitral, rather than judicial, forum. The Supreme Court strongly endorsed statutes, such as the FAA, that favor this method of resolving disputes.

Section 2 of the FAA provides that arbitration agreements in contracts concerning interstate commerce are "valid, irrevocable, and enforceable, save upon such grounds as exist at law or in equity for the revocation of any contract." By placing arbitration agreements on the same footing as contracts, Congress precluded the states from "singling out arbitration agreements for suspect status."[27] For example, the Supreme Court struck down a Montana law that rendered an arbitration clause unenforceable unless "[n]otice that [the] contract is subject to arbitration" was "typed in underlined capital letters on the first page of the contract."[28] Montana's first-page notice requirement conflicted with the FAA in that it applied specifically to arbitration agreements and not to all contracts.

23. 490 U.S. 477 (1989).
24. Shearson/Am. Express v. McMahon, 482 U.S. 220 (1987), *reh'g denied*, 483 U.S. 1056 (1987).
25. *Id.*
26. Mitsubishi Motors Corp. v. Soler Chrysler-Plymouth, Inc., 473 U.S. 614 (1985).
27. Doctor's Assoc., Inc. v. Casarotto, 517 U.S. 681, 687 (1996).

### *Arbitration of Employment Disputes*

Employees are increasingly being asked to sign applications or employment agreements that contain mandatory arbitration clauses. This means that a firm will not hire an individual unless he or she agrees at the outset to arbitrate all future claims.

Exhibit 4.3 contains an excerpt from an arbitration agreement used by a national professional services firm. All employees were required to sign it as a condition of their employment with the firm.

Agreement to arbitrate is clear when an employee signs an application form or agreement requiring arbitration. Some jurisdictions will infer an employee's agreement to arbitrate if the employee continues to work for the firm after receiving notice of the company's policy requiring all employees to arbitrate their claims. In *Howard v. Oakwood Homes Corp.*,[29] a North Carolina court found that an employee's continued employment with the company after she received a written notice of the employer's required program of dispute resolution reflected her assent to the terms of the agreement. As a result, she was compelled to arbitrate her claims of wrongful termination pursuant to the terms of the dispute resolution program.

28. *Id.*
29. 516 S.E.2d 879 (N.C. App. 1999), *cert. denied*, 528 U.S. 1155 (2000).

**EXHIBIT 4.3** **Sample Arbitration Clause in Employment Context**

The Firm and I mutually consent to the resolution by final and binding arbitration of all claims or controversies, whether or not arising out of my employment (or its termination), that the Firm may have against me or that I may have against the Firm or its partners, employees or agents in their capacity as such, including, but not limited to, claims for compensation due; claims for breach of any contract or covenant (express or implied); tort claims; claims of discrimination (including, but not limited to, claims based on race, sex, sexual preference, religion, national origin, age, marital status, medical condition, handicap or disability); claims for benefits (except as set forth in paragraph 3, below [which excludes workers' compensation and unemployment benefits]); and claims alleging a violation of any federal, state or other governmental law, statute, regulation or ordinance (collectively, "Claims"), *provided however* that Claims shall not include claims excluded in [paragraph 3]. All Claims shall be arbitrated in accordance with the attached Arbitration Rules and Procedures, which are expressly incorporated herein and made part of this Agreement.

In contrast, in *Rosenberg v. Merrill Lynch, Pierce, Fenner & Smith, Inc.*,[30] the First Circuit ruled that Merrill Lynch could not compel Rosenberg, a financial consultant who filed a suit against the company alleging age and gender discrimination, to arbitrate these claims because the company had not provided her with proper notice of its policy regarding arbitration. Although Rosenberg had signed a standard securities industry form agreeing to arbitrate certain claims, Merrill Lynch never provided her with a copy of the relevant arbitration rules.

Today, most major collective bargaining agreements include arbitration clauses. The Supreme Court has upheld provisions for mandatory arbitration of contract claims arising under a collective bargaining agreement,[31] but it struck down a collective bargaining agreement's provisions for mandatory arbitration of statutory Title VII claims in 1974.[32] This decision may not stand in the face of subsequent Supreme Court decisions upholding mandatory arbitration of statutory claims, as discussed below.

In *Gilmer v. Interstate/Johnson Lane Corp.*,[33] the Court ruled that employees who had signed individual agreements to arbitrate could be required to arbitrate age discrimination claims under the Age Discrimination in Employment Act. The Court also upheld a predispute agreement to arbitrate statutory claims under the Employment Retirement Income Security Act (ERISA), which governs pensions and other benefits.[34]

In the following case, the Supreme Court made it clear that the FAA compels judicial enforcement of agreements to arbitrate employment disputes even when the employee is asserting discrimination claims under Title VII of the Civil Rights Act of 1964.

30. 170 F.3d 1 (1st Cir. 1999).
31. AT&T Tech., Inc. v. Communication Workers of Am., 475 U.S. 643 (1986).
32. Alexander v. Gardner-Denver Co., 415 U.S. 36 (1974).
33. 500 U.S. 20 (1991).
34. Shearson Lehman/Am. Express v. Bird, 493 U.S. 884 (1989).

A CASE IN POINT

**CASE 4.2**
**Circuit City Stores, Inc. v. Adams**
*Supreme Court of the United States*
*532 U.S. 105 (2001).*

## In the Language of the Court

**› FACTS** In October 1995, Saint Clair Adams applied for a job at a Circuit City retail electronics store. All Circuit City applications contained the following clause: "I agree that I will settle any and all previously unasserted claims, disputes or controversies arising out of or relating to my application or candidacy for employment, employment and/or cessation of employment with Circuit City, exclusively by final and binding arbitration before a neutral Arbitrator." Two years later, Adams filed an employment-discrimination suit in California state court against Circuit City. Circuit City sought to enjoin the court from hearing the case and force Adams to arbitrate. The district court agreed with Circuit City, but the U.S. Court of Appeals for the Ninth Circuit reversed. Circuit City appealed.

**› ISSUE PRESENTED** Is a court compelled to enforce an agreement requiring employees to arbitrate all employment claims, including those under Title VII?

**› OPINION** KENNEDY, J., writing for the U.S. Supreme Court:

Section 1 of the Federal Arbitration Act (FAA) excludes from the Act's coverage "contracts of employment of seamen, railroad engineers, or any other class of workers engaged in foreign or interstate commerce." *9 U.S.C. § 1.* All but one of the Courts of Appeals which have addressed the issue interpret this provision as exempting contracts of employment of transportation workers, but not other employment contracts, from the FAA's coverage. A different interpretation has been adopted by the Court of Appeals for the Ninth Circuit, which construes the exemption so that all contracts of employment are beyond the FAA's reach, whether or not the worker is engaged in transportation. It applied the rule to the instant case. We now decide that the better interpretation is to construe the statute, as most of the Courts of Appeals have done, to confine the exemption to transportation workers. . . .

*(Continued)*

(Case 4.2 *continued*)

The FAA's coverage provision, § 2, provides that "[a] written provision in any maritime transaction or a contract evidencing a transaction involving commerce to settle by arbitration a controversy thereafter arising out of such contract or transaction, or the refusal to perform the whole or any part thereof, or an agreement in writing to submit to arbitration an existing controversy arising out of such a contract, transaction, or refusal, shall be valid, irrevocable, and enforceable, save upon such grounds as exist at law or in equity for the revocation of any contract." *9 U.S.C. § 2.* . . . [In *Allied-Bruce*[35]], the Court interpreted § 2 as implementing Congress' intent "to exercise [its] commerce power to the full."

The instant case, of course, involves not the basic coverage authorization under § 2 of the Act, but the exemption from coverage under § 1. . . .

Respondent Adams, at the outset, contends that we need not address the meaning of the § 1 exclusion provision to decide the case in his favor. In his view, an employment contract is not a "contract evidencing a transaction involving interstate commerce" at all, since the word "transaction" in § 2 extends only to commercial contracts. This line of reasoning proves too much, for it would make the § 1 exclusion provision superfluous. If all contracts of employment are beyond the scope of the Act under the § 2 coverage provision, the separate exemption for "contracts of employment of seamen, railroad employees, or any other class of workers engaged in . . . interstate commerce" would be pointless. . . . If, then, there is an argument to be made that arbitration agreements in employment contracts are not covered by the Act, it must be premised on the language of the § 1 exclusion provision itself. . . .

The two provisions [Sections 1 and 2], it is argued, are coterminous; under this view the "involving commerce" provision brings within the FAA's scope all contracts within the Congress' commerce power, and the "engaged in . . . commerce" language in § 1 in turn exempts from the FAA all employment contracts falling within that authority.

This reading of § 1, however, runs into an immediate and, in our view, insurmountable textual obstacle. Unlike the "involving commerce" language in § 2, the words "any other class of workers engaged in . . . commerce" constitute a residual phrase, following, in the same sentence, explicit reference to "seamen" and "railroad employees." Constructing the residual phrase to exclude all employment contracts fails to give independent effect to the statute's enumeration of the specific categories of workers which precedes it; there would be no need for Congress to use the phrases "seamen" and "railroad employees" if those same classes of workers were subsumed within the meaning of the "engaged in . . . commerce" residual clause. The wording of § 1 calls for the application of the maxim ejusdem generic, the statutory canon that "where general words follow specific words in a statutory enumeration, the general words are construed to embrace only objects similar in nature to those objects enumerated by the preceding specific words." Under this rule of construction the residual clause should be read to give effect to the terms "seamen" and "railroad employees," and should itself be controlled and defined by reference to the enumerated categories of workers which are recited just before it; the interpretation of the clause pressed by respondent fails to produce these results.

Furthermore, for parties to employment contracts not involving the specific exempted categories set forth in § 1, it is true here, just as it was for the parties to

35. Allied-Bruce Terminix Cos. v. Dobson, 513 U.S. 265 (1995).

*(Continued)*

(Case 4.2 *continued*)

the contract at issue in Allied-Bruce [in which the Court upheld a contract to arbitrate disputes], that there are real benefits to the enforcement of arbitration provisions. We have been clear in rejecting the supposition that the advantages of the arbitration process somehow disappear when transferred to the employment context. Arbitration agreements allow parties to avoid the costs of litigation, a benefit that may be of particular importance in employment litigation, which often involves smaller sums of money than disputes concerning commercial contracts. . . .

The considerable complexity and uncertainty that the construction of § 1 urged by respondent would introduce into the enforceability of arbitration agreements in employment contracts would call into doubt the efficacy of alternative dispute resolution procedures adopted by many of the Nation's employers, in the process undermining the FAA's pro-arbitration purposes and "breeding litigation from a statute that seeks to avoid it."

**› RESULT** The Federal Arbitration Act applied to Adams's claims and required arbitration unless the arbitration agreement was invalid on grounds that would allow the revocation of any contract. The case was remanded to the Ninth Circuit.

**› COMMENTS** Following the Supreme Court's reversal of *Circuit City,* a bill was introduced in the California Senate that would have made mandatory arbitration clauses in employment contracts automatically unenforceable. This bill was later withdrawn by its author. In 2002, the Ninth Circuit ruled that mandatory employment arbitration agreements were enforceable.[36]

**› DISSENT** STEVENS, J., with whom GINSBURG and BREYER, JJ., join:

Section 2 of the FAA makes enforceable written agreements to arbitrate "in any maritime transaction or a contract evidencing a transaction involving commerce." *9 U.S.C. § 2.* If we were writing on a clean slate, there would be good reason to conclude that neither the phrase "maritime transaction" nor the phrase "contract evidencing a transaction involving commerce" was intended to encompass employment contracts.

The history of the Act, which is extensive and well-documented, makes clear that the FAA was a response to the refusal of courts to enforce commercial arbitration agreements, which were commonly used in the maritime context. . . .

Nevertheless, the original bill was opposed by representatives of organized labor, most notably the president of the International Seamen's Union of America because of their concern that the legislation might authorize federal judicial enforcement of arbitration clauses in employment contracts and collective-bargaining agreements. In response to those objections, the chairman of the ABA committee that drafted the legislation emphasized at a Senate Judiciary Subcommittee hearing that "it is not intended that this shall be an act referring to labor disputes at all," but he also observed that "if your honorable committee should feel that there is any danger of that, they should add to the bill the following language, 'but nothing herein contained shall apply to seamen or any class of workers in interstate and foreign commerce.'" Similarly, another supporter of the bill, then Secretary of Commerce Herbert Hoover, suggested that "if objection appears to the inclusion of workers' contracts in the law's scheme, it might be well amended by stating 'but nothing herein contained shall apply to contracts of employment of seamen, railroad employees, or any other class of workers engaged in interstate or foreign commerce.'"

36. EEOC v. Luce Forward, Hamilton, & Scripps, 345 F.3d 742 (9th Cir. 2002).

*(Continued)*

(Case 4.2 *continued*)

The legislation was reintroduced in the next session of Congress with Secretary Hoover's exclusionary language added to § 1, and the amendment eliminated organized labor's opposition to the proposed law.

That amendment is what the Court construes today. History amply supports the proposition that it was an uncontroversial provision that merely confirmed the fact that no one interested in the enactment of the FAA ever intended or expected that § 2 would apply to employment contracts. It is particularly ironic, therefore, that the amendment has provided the Court with its sole justification for refusing to give the text of § 2 a natural reading. Playing ostrich to the substantial history behind the amendment, the Court reasons in a vacuum that "if all contracts of employment are beyond the scope of the Act under the § 2 coverage provision, the separate exemption" in § 1 "would be pointless." But contrary to the Court's suggestion, it is not "pointless" to adopt a clarifying amendment in order to eliminate opposition to a bill. . . .

The irony of the Court's reading of § 2 to include contracts of employment is compounded by its cramped interpretation of the exclusion inserted into § 1. As proposed and enacted, the exclusion fully responded to the concerns of the Seamen's Union and other labor organizations that § 2 might encompass employment contracts by expressly exempting not only the labor agreements of "seamen" and "railroad employees," but also of "any other class of workers engaged in foreign or interstate commerce." Today, however, the Court fulfills the original—and originally unfounded—fears of organized labor by essentially rewriting the text of § 1 to exclude the employment contracts solely of "seamen, railroad employees, or any other class of transportation workers engaged in foreign or interstate commerce." In contrast, whether one views the legislation before or after the amendment to § 1, it is clear that it was not intended to apply to employment contracts at all.

**› CRITICAL THINKING QUESTIONS**

1. Is there any reasoned basis for treating an arbitration agreement required as a condition of employment any differently from an arbitration agreement required as a condition to buying goods? As a condition to receiving medical treatment in the emergency room? Having elective surgery?
2. Who has the better argument, the majority or the dissent?

The Equal Employment Opportunity Commission (EEOC) may file a claim in court on its own behalf against an employer, even if the employee involved had entered into an enforceable arbitration agreement, if the EEOC is either (1) seeking a permanent injunction enjoining an employer from engaging in discriminatory practices or (2) enforcing the individual rights of the employee. The employee's agreement to arbitrate in no way limits the relief, including damages, that the EEOC is entitled to recover on the employee's behalf in a court of law.[37]

37. EEOC v. Waffle House, Inc., 534 U.S. 279 (2002).

### *Unconscionable Arbitration Agreements*

Parties constrained by an arbitration clause may claim that the contract itself (including its arbitration clause) is void due to force, fraud, or the like. As with other unconscionable contracts, courts will not enforce an arbitration agreement if it operates in a harsh and one-sided manner without any justification.

The U.S. Supreme Court appeared to have validated mandatory employment arbitration clauses in *Circuit City,* but the Ninth Circuit found other reasons to give Adams his day in court when the case was remanded to it for reconsideration in light of the Supreme Court's ruling.

A CASE IN POINT

**CASE 4.3**

**Circuit City Stores, Inc. v. Adams**

*United States Court of Appeals for the Ninth Circuit 279 F.3d 889 (9th Cir. 2002), cert. denied, 535 U.S. 1112 (2002).*

## Summary

**› FACTS** Once again we visit Mr. Adams and his dispute with Circuit City Stores, Inc. After the U.S. Supreme Court ruled that the arbitration clause at issue was subject to the Federal Arbitration Act, it remanded the case back to the Ninth Circuit for reconsideration.

**› ISSUE PRESENTED** Is an arbitration contract unconscionable if it is required as a condition of employment, requires arbitration of only employee claims, and limits the employee's damages?

**› SUMMARY OF OPINION** The U.S. Court of Appeals for the Ninth Circuit began by characterizing Circuit City's arbitration policy as "a thumb on Circuit City's side of the scale should an employment dispute ever arise between the company and one of its employees." Nonetheless, the Ninth Circuit acknowledged that it was bound by the Supreme Court's ruling that the FAA was applicable. Having lost its attempt to exclude all employment agreements from the reach of the FAA, the Ninth Circuit seized on the language in Section 2 of the FAA, which permits judges to invalidate an arbitration contract if the contract as a whole would be invalid under principles of state law applicable to contracts generally. The Ninth Circuit reasoned that this language permits a court to apply all applicable California state law to decide whether the contract as a whole was valid.

Although the arbitration clause itself was valid, the court concluded that the contract as a whole was still unenforceable because it was procedurally and substantively unconscionable. It was a *contract of adhesion,* that is, a standard-form contract that is drafted by the party with superior bargaining power, which relegates to the other party the option of either adhering to the contract's terms without modification or rejecting it entirely. Under California state law, contracts of adhesion are not enforceable and are thus voidable in their entirety.

**› RESULT** The Ninth Circuit held that the contract was substantively and procedurally unconscionable and voided it. Adams was entitled to his day in court.

**› COMMENTS** California courts clearly do not approve of mandatory employment arbitration agreements. Indeed, to support its decision, the Ninth Circuit cited a California Supreme Court ruling[38] that preceded the U.S. Supreme Court's decision in *Circuit City.*

**› CRITICAL THINKING QUESTIONS**

1. What would have happened if Circuit City had again persuaded the Supreme Court to hear the case?
2. Would the Ninth Circuit have reached the same result if the arbitration clause had required the arbitration of both employee *and* employer claims and did not limit the recoverable damages?

38. Armendariz v. Found. Health Psychcare Servs., Inc., 6 P.3d 669 (Cal. 2000).

As discussed further in Chapter 3, some employers are using mandatory waivers of the right to have a jury hear an employment dispute instead of arbitration clauses to try to achieve more consistent and less generous awards of damages to employees. The dispute is still litigated, but it is decided by a judge, not a jury. Studies suggest that judges find in favor of employees in roughly the same proportion of cases as juries, but judges tend to award substantially lower damages than juries.

## JUDICIAL REVIEW OF AWARDS

The FAA lists only four circumstances in which an arbitration award may be set aside by a court: (1) the award was procured by corruption, fraud, or undue means; (2) the arbitrator was demonstrably impartial or corrupt; (3) the arbitrator engaged in misconduct by refusing to postpone the hearing when given sufficient reason or by refusing to hear pertinent evidence; and (4) the arbitrator exceeded his or her powers or executed them so badly that a final award on the issue put to arbitration was not made. Acknowledging the rights of parties to arbitration to agree to tailor-made procedural rules, one court held that the parties could agree to give a court the power to overturn an arbitration award if the court concluded that it was not supported by substantial evidence.[39]

Although courts tend to look favorably on arbitration and favor its results, case law suggests that awards may be reversed for reasons beyond those enumerated in the FAA or provided for in the arbitration agreement itself. A court may strike down an arbitration award if it would "violate some explicit public policy that is well defined and dominant."[40] This has been construed narrowly. The Supreme Court determined that an arbitration award that reinstated an employee who had been fired for drug use should not and could not be set aside by a court for public policy reasons even though the employee was involved in the "safety sensitive" job of operating heavy machinery.[41]

Similarly, the Connecticut Supreme Court upheld an arbitration award that reinstated an employee who was fired after pleading nolo contendere to embezzling his employer's money.[42] A defendant making such a plea does not deny or admit guilt but agrees not to contest the charges. The collective bargaining agreement required termination of any employee convicted of an offense involving job duties but was silent on the effect of a nolo contendere plea. The arbitrator decided that the employee should not have been terminated and ordered the town to reinstate him. The town went to court to try to vacate the arbitrator's decision on the grounds that it violated public policy, but the Supreme Court of Connecticut upheld the award after concluding that it could not use the employee's nolo contendere plea as an admission of guilt. In a dissent, Chief Justice McDonald stated that "[u]nder the majority's reasoning, a dishonest employee very simply avoids the application of the personnel rule [requiring termination for conviction of an offense involving job duties] by pleading nolo contendere."

A court might set aside an arbitrator's decision if it was "arbitrary and capricious,"[43] or if the arbitrator manifestly disregarded the law.[44] However, courts tend to act only in egregious cases. As New York's highest court stated more than two decades ago, "An arbitrator's paramount responsibility is to reach an equitable result, and the courts will not assume the role of overseers to mold the award to conform to their sense of justice. Thus, an arbitrator's award will not be vacated for errors of law and fact committed by the arbitrator."[45]

In fact, courts have consistently ruled that once arbitrators are chosen, their rulings are final even if they lack professional training or are actually incompetent. Thus,

### INTERNATIONAL SNAPSHOT

Throughout the 1990s, India undertook significant reforms to liberalize its economy. As part of its effort to attract international business, India enacted its Arbitration and Conciliation Act of 1996. Although India had been a signatory to the United Nations Convention on the Recognition and Enforcement of Foreign Arbitral Awards since 1958, arbitration in India had been viewed abroad with distrust. Indian courts had intervened during and after arbitrations, thereby preventing parties from reliably avoiding local courts and enjoying closure to any specific dispute. The 1996 law, based on the United Nations Model Arbitration Law, brought international standards to both domestic and international arbitrations in India. Court interference during arbitration has been nearly eliminated, and the bases for judicial review of awards have been severely limited.

### INTERNATIONAL SNAPSHOT

The United Nations Convention on the Recognition and Enforcement of Foreign Arbitral Awards, Article III, implemented in the United States by Chapter 2 of the Federal Arbitration Act,[a] provides: "Each Contracting State shall recognize arbitral awards as binding and enforce them in accordance with the rules of procedure of the territory where the award is relied upon, under the conditions laid down in the following articles." As of 2004, more than 115 countries were signatories to the Convention.[b]

**a.** 9 U.S.C. § 201 (West Elec. Update 1997).
**b.** For the full text of the Convention and a list of signatories, see the International Alternative Dispute Resolutions website at http://www.internationaladr.com.

39. LaPine Tech. Corp. v. Kyocera Corp., 130 F.3d 884 (9th Cir. 1997).
40. United Paperworkers Int'l Union v. Misco, Inc., 484 U.S. 29 (1987).
41. Eastern Associated Coal Corp. v. United Mine Workers, 531 U.S. 57 (2000).
42. Town of Groton v. United Steelworkers of America, 757 A.2d 501 (Conn. 2000).
43. Wilko v. Swan, 346 U.S. 427 (1953), *overturned by* Rodriquez de Quijas v. Shearson/Am. Express, Inc., 490 U.S. 477 (1989), on other grounds.
44. Greenberg v. Bear, Stearns & Co., 220 F.3d 22 (2d Cir. 2000), *cert. denied*, 531 U.S. 1075 (2001).
45. Sprinzen v. Nomberg, 389 N.E. 2d 456, 458 (N.Y. 1979).

it is very much in the interest of counsel to learn as much as they can about potential arbitrators because all parties involved will be bound regardless of "however bad [the arbitrators'] choices appear to be."[46]

46. IDS Ins. Co. v. Royal Alliance Assocs., 266 F.3d 645 (7th Cir. 2001). American Express accused the arbitrators of incompetence and not addressing the issues, but the court found that to be immaterial because all parties agreed to be bound by the arbitrator's decision.

Recently, decisions such as the one that follows have given arbitrators increasing power to make determinations that are not directly related to the issue the parties agreed to arbitrate.

A CASE IN POINT

**CASE 4.4**

**Green Tree Financial Corp. v. Bazzle**

*Supreme Court of the United States*

*539 U.S. 444 (2003).*

## In the Language of the Court

**› FACTS** Several families, including the Bazzles, entered into lending agreements with Green Tree Financial Corporation that included an arbitration clause. Later, these parties separately decided to bring a claim against Green Tree for violating South Carolina state law by failing to provide forms informing them of their right to name their own lawyers and insurance agents. Green Tree moved for arbitration and then agreed to an arbitrator. The Bazzles, after several arbitration decisions were rendered for other parties, moved to be certified as a class, a designation that allows one group of persons to seek judgment on behalf of all other people of that class. The contract the Bazzles and the other Green Tree clients had signed was silent on the availability of class arbitration as opposed to individual arbitration. The same arbitrator who had decided other claims arbitrated the Bazzle case as a class arbitration after a trial court granted the Bazzles' request for class certification. Green Tree moved in court to overturn the award. The Supreme Court of South Carolina ruled that because the contract was silent on the issue of class arbitration, the contract tacitly allowed it. Green Tree appealed.

**› ISSUE PRESENTED** Is it for the court or an arbitrator to decide whether class certification is available when the arbitration clause is silent on a matter?

**› OPINION** BREYER, J., writing for a plurality of the U.S. Supreme Court, joined by SCALIA, SOUTER, and GINSBURG, JJ.:

Green Tree argues that the contracts are not silent—that they forbid class arbitration. If the contracts are not silent, then the state court's holding is flawed on its own terms; that court neither said nor implied that it would have authorized class arbitration had the parties' arbitration agreement forbidden it. . . . The question here does not fall into the limited circumstances where courts assume that the parties intended courts, not arbitrators, to decide a particular arbitration-related matter, as it concerns neither the arbitration clause's validity nor its applicability to the underlying dispute. . . .

[Chief Justice Rehnquist] believes that Green Tree is right; indeed, that Green Tree is so clearly right that we should ignore the fact that state law, not federal law, normally governs such matters. . . .

With respect to this underlying question—whether the arbitration contracts forbid class arbitration—the parties have not yet obtained the arbitration decision that their contracts foresee. As far as concerns the Bazzle plaintiffs, the South Carolina Supreme Court wrote that the "trial court" issued "an order granting class certification" and the arbitrator subsequently "administered" class arbitration proceedings "without further involvement of the trial court.". . .

*(Continued)*

(Case 4.4 *continued*)

On balance, there is at least a strong likelihood . . . that the arbitrator's decision reflected a court's interpretation of the contracts rather than an arbitrator's interpretation. That being so, we remand the case so that the arbitrator may decide the question of contract interpretation—thereby enforcing the parties' arbitration agreements according to their terms.

**› RESULT** The Supreme Court remanded the case to the arbitrator who was given the authority to decide whether the contract allowed for class arbitration.

**› COMMENTS** This decision gave the arbitrator the power to define its own level of jurisdiction within the confines of a vague clause.

**› CRITICAL THINKING QUESTIONS**

1. Should it matter whether the court or the arbitrator decides what the arbitration contract means?
2. Should an arbitrator be allowed to make awards that can affect public policy?

## Hybrids

Various hybrid forms of ADR are available, including med-arb, arb-med, minitrials, summary jury trials, and collaborative law.

### MED-ARB

In *med-arb* the parties to a dispute enter mediation with the commitment to submit to binding arbitration if mediation fails to resolve the conflict. Often, the same person serves as mediator and arbitrator. Delay and expense are reduced if the arbitrator is already familiar with the situation from mediation. A danger of med-arb is that honesty in mediation could become damaging revelation in arbitration, especially if the mediator then acts as arbitrator. A decision-making arbitrator cannot forget what he or she has learned confidentially in mediation caucuses with a party. Looking ahead to such a possibility, parties in the "med" stage of med-arb may be reluctant to participate openly and in good faith, thus ensuring the final "arb" stage from the beginning. In such a scenario, time and money are wasted by the doomed mediation phase. For this reason, it is usually preferable to specify that a different person will act as arbitrator if mediation fails to resolve the conflict.

### ARB-MED

Parties using arbitration/mediation *(arb-med)* present their case to an arbitrator who makes an award but keeps it secret while the parties try to resolve the dispute through mediation. If the mediation fails, then the arbitrator's award is unsealed and becomes binding on the parties.

### MINITRIAL

In a *minitrial,* lawyers conduct discovery for a limited period, usually a few weeks. They then exchange legal briefs or memoranda of law. At this point, the top managers of the two businesses hear the lawyers from each side present their case in a trial format. The presentations are moderated by a neutral third party, often an attorney or a judge.

After the minitrial, the managers of the two businesses meet to settle the case. If they are unable to reach a settlement, the presiding third party can issue a nonbinding opinion. The managers can then meet again to try to settle on the basis of the third-party opinion. For this reason, minitrials are a cross between arbitration and negotiation.

Minitrials have several advantages. Like litigation, they allow a thorough investigation and presentation of the parties' claims, but they give the managers the opportunity to work out their differences directly rather than through their attorneys. By shortening the time for discovery and presentation of the case, minitrials can reduce the possibility of the two sides becoming locked into opposing positions. The presence of a neutral third party gives the process an added element of discipline. Should the managers come to an impasse in their discussions, the third party can offer suggestions about a settlement. Finally, minitrials have the advantage of remaining relatively private. This is important to parties in disputes over confidential information or trade secrets.

An example of a successful minitrial is the 1986 settlement of the dispute between Telecredit and TRW. This minitrial took place in a hotel conference room. After brief presentations by both sides, Telecredit's cofounder conferred with a vice president of TRW. Within half an hour, the two parties had agreed on the outlines of a settlement, which was negotiated over the next eleven weeks. The two companies estimated that the minitrial saved them at least $1 million in combined legal fees.

Because minitrials involve discovery, the production of briefs, oral argument, and the hiring of a third party, they can still be fairly expensive. Only when disputes are expected to involve large damage awards or protracted litigation do minitrials make economic sense.

### SUMMARY JURY TRIAL

In a *summary jury trial (SJT),* parties to a dispute put their cases before a real jury, which renders a nonbinding decision. Like nonbinding arbitration, this allows the parties to assess how a decision maker might decide the case in a real trial. The result is often the basis for a negotiated settlement. Like minitrials, SJTs offer disputants the opportunity to present their best case in a trial-like setting. Because the SJT makes use of abbreviated procedures, the result is achieved more quickly and with less expense.

A unique feature of SJTs is their focus-group opportunity. Disputants often debrief jurors after the trial to find out how and why they reached their decision. Like discovery, this helps align the parties' information and expectations so there is less reason to go through the expense of a formal trial. For example, a car accident victim suing for $5 million may balk at the insurance company's offer of $50,000 to settle the claim. If the jury in an SJT renders an award of only $75,000, the plaintiff will be more willing to consider settlement. On the other hand, if the jury awards $3 million, the defendant insurance company will wish to revise its settlement offer. Either way, the parties' expectations will be brought closer together, making settlement more likely.

### COLLABORATIVE LAW AND OTHER TECHNIQUES

*Collaborative law* is a quickly expanding breed of law that attempts to combine mediation and negotiation into a more efficient, more satisfying, and ultimately more successful form of dispute resolution. Currently, it is practiced in twenty-five states by about 3,000 attorneys and is used widely in Canada.[47] Attorneys who practice collaborative law attempt to work out disputes, either business or family, without going to court. Of course, all negotiators purport to try and avoid lengthy and expensive litigation, but collaborative lawyers take their promises a bit more seriously. They voluntarily sign a contract with their clients requiring the clients to seek other attorneys if the negotiations break down and the dispute goes to court. In effect, the contracts remove any incentive the attorneys might have to go to trial, allowing them to focus on successful conflict resolution.[48]

Typically, these negotiations are four-way meetings with attorneys and clients present. Attorneys who practice this unorthodox style insist that it allows them to practice law in an ethical, rewarding, yet still effective manner. The greatest indicator of its effectiveness, however, lies in the average costs. The typical courtroom divorce takes about twenty months and costs from $10,000 to $25,000 per spouse. The typical collaborative law divorce takes about three months and costs about $3,000 per spouse. See "Internet Sources" for more on collaborative law.

*Ombudspersons* are also used to help parties in conflict. Such a person hears complaints, engages in fact-finding, and generally promotes dispute resolution through information methods such as counseling or mediation. An ombudsperson allows aggrieved parties to vent their concerns and alert *related* parties to problems before they become *opposing* parties.

The "In Brief" summarizes the most common ADR techniques in use today.

## Other Laws Favoring Settlement over Litigation

The government promotes alternatives to litigation in a variety of ways, including requiring courts and administrative agencies to use ADR, mandating pretrial settlement conferences, providing liberal discovery, penalizing plaintiffs who reject favorable settlement offers, limiting the ability of a party to introduce willingness to negotiate as evidence of fault, and generally enforcing agreements to arbitrate.

47. Bette A. Winik, *Breakthrough in Law Practice,* NEWTON MAG., Sept. 4, 2002, at 21–22.
48. Steven Keeva, *Working It Out Amicably,* 89 A.B.A. J. 66–67 (June 2003).

## IN BRIEF

### Models of Alternative Dispute Resolution

| | Negotiation | Mediation | Arbitration | Med-Arb/ Arb-Med | Minitrial | Summary Jury Trial |
|---|---|---|---|---|---|---|
| *How are the disputants represented?* | Disputants represent themselves, or legal counsel negotiates on their behalf | By themselves | By legal counsel | By legal counsel | By legal counsel | By legal counsel |
| *Who makes the final decision?* | Disputants mutually decide | Disputants mutually decide | If binding arbitration, arbitrator(s) decides | Arbitrator(s) if parties can't agree | Disputants mutually decide | Disputants mutually decide |
| *How are the facts found and standards of judgment set?* | Parties decide ad hoc | Parties decide ad hoc | Arbitrator(s) decides based on preset rules, e.g., those of the AAA | Parties and arbitrator(s) decide | Parties decide ad hoc | Rules of court |
| *What is the source for the standard of resolution?* | Mutual agreement | Mutual agreement | Arbitrator's sense of fairness | Arbitrator's sense of fairness | Mutual agreement | Mutual agreement |
| *How will the resolution be enforced?* | Agreement usually turned into a contract that is enforceable by the courts | Agreement usually turned into a contract that is enforceable by the courts | By courts, according to the agreement to arbitrate the dispute | By courts, according to the agreement to arbitrate the dispute | Agreement usually turned into a contract that is enforceable by the courts | Agreement usually turned into a contract that is enforceable by the courts |
| *Who will pay the dispute resolution fees?* | Parties decide ad hoc | Parties decide ad hoc | Parties decide before entering arbitration, often in arbitration clause | Parties decide in advance | Parties decide ad hoc | Parties decide ad hoc |

The Civil Justice Reform Act of 1990[49] required every federal district court to develop a civil justice expense and delay reduction plan (EDRP). The purpose of such plans is "to facilitate deliberate adjudication of civil cases on the merits, monitor discovery, improve litigation management, and ensure just, speedy, and inexpensive resolution of civil disputes." The Act recommends six methods for courts to use in developing EDRPs, one of which is referring appropriate cases "to alternative dispute resolution programs . . . including mediation, minitrial, and summary jury trial." The Alternative Dispute Resolution Act of 1998[50] required federal trial courts to establish at least one ADR program and requires parties in federal litigation to consider using ADR. Courts are encouraged to offer several choices.

*Early Neutral Evaluation (ENE)* was created by the U.S. District Court for the Northern District of California in 1985 to help litigants honestly appreciate their positions. In ENE, a neutral attorney familiar with the law in the area reviews the case and offers each side his or her evaluation of the strengths and weaknesses. Such early feedback by a disinterested expert can assist parties before they become engrossed in the adversarial process.

49. *Id. See also* First Options of Chicago, Inc. v. Kaplan, 514 U.S. 938, 942 (1995).

50. 28 U.S.C. 652 (1998).

Federal agencies must also use ADR to resolve administrative cases. The Administrative Dispute Resolution Act of 1996[51] requires federal agencies to look at their mission to see where ADR might be effective.

The states also have supported efforts to use ADR rather than courts to resolve disputes. The court systems in more than half of the states now either require or encourage resolving cases through ADR in order to reduce case backlogs and provide a quicker resolution of disputes.[52]

These efforts appear to be working. Although Americans are filing cases in court at a record pace, partly due to the growing population in the United States, the percentage of trials that actually go to a jury or the bench (a trial where a judge, not a jury, decides all issues) has seen a steady decrease in the last thirty years. These trends are shown in Exhibit 4.4.

## PRETRIAL CONFERENCES

The *Federal Rules of Civil Procedure (FRCP)* in the federal system and their counterparts in the state systems allow judges to require disputants to meet and explore settlement before beginning a trial. As in mediation, the judge may be able to bridge differences and propose solutions that the parties could not negotiate on their own. In fact, the official advisory committee on the FRCP observed:

> Empirical studies reveal that when a trial judge intervenes personally at an early stage to assume judicial control over a case and to schedule dates for completion by the parties of the principal pretrial steps, the case is disposed of by settlement or trial more efficiently and with less cost and delay than when the parties are left to their own devices.[53]

For example, the judge assigned to ten of the suits brought by twenty-seven utility companies against Westinghouse Corporation in 1975 forced the chief executives concerned to meet in his office to try to settle the case. Westinghouse had breached its contracts to deliver about 70 million pounds of uranium after the price of uranium had more than doubled. The judge thought that a business solution to the lawsuits, rather than a legal one, might be more advantageous to all parties. If the court forced Westinghouse to pay damages, Westinghouse would be crippled financially. It might not have been able to complete the construction of certain nuclear power plants that it was building for the same utility companies. Inventive and mutually beneficial settlements were reached in many of the cases.

51. 5 U.S.C. §§ 571–585.
52. Legal Information Institute, *Alternative Dispute Resolution: An Overview, at* http://www.law.cornell.edu/topics/adr.html. For actual state statutes governing ADR, see http://www.law.cornell.edu/topics/state_statutes.html#alternate_dispute_resolution.

53. 28 U.S.C. § 471.

**EXHIBIT 4.4 Resolution of Cases in Federal Courts**

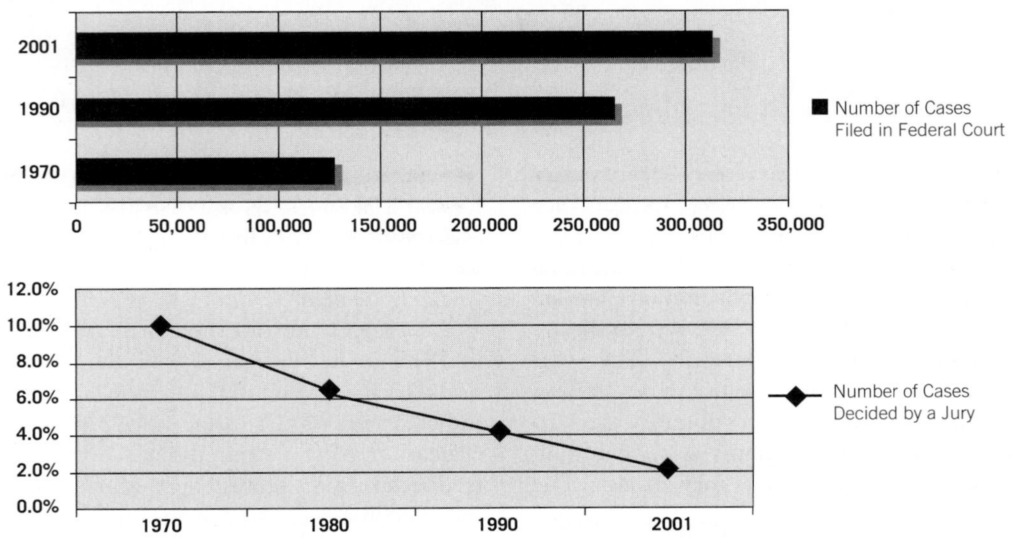

Number of Cases Filed in Federal Court

Number of Cases Decided by a Jury

Source: Data drawn from Hope Viner Samborn, *The Vanishing Trial,* A.B.A. J. (Oct. 2002), at 27.

## Liberal Discovery

As explained in Chapter 3, the entire discovery process is aimed at increasing both parties' access to information. If both plaintiff and defendant have similar information—through interrogatories, depositions, and production of documents—they are more likely to expect the same outcome at trial. With less uncertainty to resolve by a lengthy and expensive trial, parties are more likely to settle. The discovery process aims to reduce the *asymetric information* problem, which arises because each party has information not possessed by the other party, and to align the parties' expectations about continued litigation. This makes settlement more likely.

## Rejected-Offer Sanctions

In addition to the carrot of discovery, the rules of civil procedure provide a stick for plaintiffs unwilling to entertain settlement seriously. Rule 68 of the FRCP allows a defendant to offer to accept judgment against it for a specific amount of money no fewer than ten days before the trial begins. If the plaintiff accepts the offer, the case concludes, and the court enters judgment per the agreement. If the plaintiff refuses and the case goes to trial, then the plaintiff must pay the defendant's legal expenses incurred subsequent to the offer if the final judgment is not more favorable than the rejected offer. Looking forward to such an unpleasant sanction, plaintiffs will think carefully before rejecting settlement proposals. This not only encourages defendants to make serious settlement offers as early as possible but also encourages plaintiffs to consider those offers just as seriously.

## Negotiation as Evidence of Fault

Whereas the FRCP govern procedure in litigation before federal courts, the *Federal Rules of Evidence (FRE)* govern the use of evidence in such litigation. Individual states have similar sets of rules, which, along with related case law, determine what evidence is admissible in court and, therefore, the evidence on which a fact finder may rely. For a party exploring solutions or attempting to integrate issues, these rules are most important.

For example, a manager faced with a highly dubious claim of product defect may be willing to replace the item to preserve customer goodwill. At the same time, the manager may be unwilling to pay the customer for the profits it lost because of the alleged defect in the product. At a trial, the customer might want to introduce the manager's offer to replace the product as evidence of the defect and the validity of its case against the supplier: "After all, ladies and gentlemen of the jury, why would a company give my client a new product if there was nothing wrong with the old one?" Looking ahead to such a possibility, the manager will be reluctant to negotiate at all for fear that sincere efforts to preserve goodwill could appear later as admissions of fault. At a minimum, the manager will use exceedingly circumspect language. Both results make settlement more difficult and less likely.

To exclude that trial scenario and its chilling effect on negotiations beforehand, Rule 408 prohibits the use of settlement offers as evidence of liability. The protection extends to conduct and statements made in such negotiations, as well as formal offers of settlement. The goal is to insulate the entire negotiation process from the threat of exposure at trial. As Congress observed when enacting the restriction, "The purpose of [the] rule is to encourage settlements which would be discouraged if such evidence were admissible."[54]

Managers should not take too much comfort in Rule 408, however, because if damaging revelations made in negotiations are otherwise discoverable, they are admissible. Similarly, although offers to settle may not be used as evidence of liability, such offers may be used to show witness bias or obstruction of criminal investigation or to disprove a suggestion of undue delay. In short, a clever lawyer can often find a way to introduce some evidence concerning negotiations.

## Tortious Dispute Resolution

Although the law supports settlements through ADR, managers are not immune from the law simply because they pursue alternative mechanisms to resolve their disputes. The applicability of tort law is a good example.

The law of torts, which is discussed in Chapter 9, deals with civil wrongs causing injury to a person or his or her property. A claim of fraudulent misrepresentation requires proof that the defendant intentionally misled the plaintiff by making a material misrepresentation of fact upon which the plaintiff relied to his or her detriment. It is not difficult to imagine a negotiation in which one might be tempted to so mislead an opponent. Still, the law of fraud will apply, and managers may be liable for the injury they cause. Furthermore, an overly aggressive manager attempting to "resolve" a dispute by force or threats may be found liable for assault, intentional infliction of emotional distress, defamation, invasion of privacy, disparagement, injurious falsehood, interference with contractual obligations, or interference with prospective business advantage. Attempting to settle a conflict outside of court does not exempt managers from the law.

54. Fed. R. Civ. P. 16, Notes of Advisory Committee on Rules.

## THE RESPONSIBLE MANAGER

# STAYING OUT OF COURT

Legal problems or disputes often arise in business, and an amicable solution to them is not always possible. Some form of dispute resolution then becomes the next step.

The courts exist to assist litigants in working out a fair solution to their dispute. But litigation is expensive, time-consuming, and disruptive to everyone involved. Consequently, all parties benefit when the courts are used as the last step in the legal process, rather than as the starting point.

Often communication, or the lack thereof, can make the difference between a minor disagreement and protracted litigation. Apologizing may be just as crucial as filing or defending a lawsuit.

In a case that has become the poster child for tort reform, an elderly woman named Stella Liebeck received third-degree burns on her legs when she spilled a cup of McDonald's coffee she had just bought on her lap. Contrary to many press reports of this incident, she was not driving the car at the time this happened. The car was parked, and she spilled the coffee while trying to remove the lid to put in cream and sugar. There had been some 700 other instances of people scalded by McDonald's coffee, which was served at a temperature approximately twenty degrees hotter than that of its competitors. Indeed, McDonald's own expert testified that its coffee was not fit for human consumption at the temperature served. Noting that McDonald's sold millions of cups of coffee a day, managers testified at trial that they had dismissed those prior incidents as meaningless.

When Liebeck asked McDonald's to reimburse her for the $2,600 she had spent on out-of-pocket medical expenses, McDonald's gave her a take-it-or-leave-it offer of $800. A jury awarded Liebeck $2.7 million, which represented the profits McDonald's made on an average day from its coffee sales. The judge reduced the award to $400,000. Although this case is often cited as an example of a tort system run amok, the *Wall Street Journal* faulted McDonald's not only for failing to respond to prior scalding incidents but also for mishandling the injured woman's complaints by not apologizing.[55]

55. Andrea Gerlin, *A Matter of Degree: How a Jury Decided That a Coffee Spill Is Worth $2.7 Million*, WALL ST. J., Sept. 1, 1994.

Even though insurers and hospital lawyers have historically discouraged physicians from apologizing for fear of fueling lawsuits, prestigious hospitals (such as Johns Hopkins) and major insurers (such as General Electric's Medical Protective unit) now encourage doctors to be candid about their errors and to apologize to injured parties. In fact, the managing attorney for claims and litigation at Johns Hopkins attributed the hospital's 30 percent reduction in expense payments for malpractice in 2003 at least in part to the new policy adopted in 2001.[56] As Andrew Meyer, a prominent Boston plaintiff lawyer who represents victims of malpractice, explained: "The hardest case for me to bring is the case where the defense has admitted error [and apologized to the injured patient]. If you have no conflict, you have no story, no debate. And it doesn't play well."[57]

A manager should decide when litigation, as opposed to a settlement or another method of resolving the dispute, is the company's best strategic move. If the problem is a recurring one, or if the opposing party is clearly making a frivolous claim or attempting to use the lawsuit as a way to extort money from the company, then the courtroom becomes the most practical alternative. Similarly, if the adverse publicity that attends a trial would be more damaging to one party than another, the party better positioned to endure the publicity may prefer to retain the right to threaten to take the dispute to court. In many cases, however, negotiation, mediation, a minitrial, or arbitration will enable the parties to conclude their dispute more quickly and with less expense and hardship.

The first step in implementing an ADR program is generating enthusiasm within the company for the program.[58] The general counsel or other appropriate person should explain to company officers and executives the benefits of an ADR program, including the savings of

56. Rachel Zimmerman, *Doctors' New Tool to Fight Lawsuits: Saying "I'm Sorry,"* WALL ST. J., May 18, 2004.

57. *Quoted in id.*

58. This discussion is based in part on CENTER FOR PUBLIC RESOURCES, MAINSTREAMING: CORPORATE STRATEGIES FOR SYSTEMATIC ADR USE (1989).

*(Continued)*

(The Responsible Manager *continued*)

time and money, the decrease in disruption to employees and management, and the fact that more business-oriented solutions generally are reached. High-level management should demonstrate a commitment to an ADR program and explain its benefits to other executives, who may be unfamiliar with such a program. The company needs to involve (1) in-house counsel; (2) the executives and corporate managers; (3) outside counsel; (4) the company's adversaries; and (5) certain field personnel, such as insurance industry claims personnel. Training of these various players is also essential. The company also needs to make clear that management's early and personal involvement in disputes resolved through the ADR program is crucial. Frequently, involvement by both executives and the disputants at early stages of the conflict is critical to an effective resolution of the matter.

Once a company establishes a formal program, the next step is for the general counsel and company manager to ensure that the ADR procedures are employed. Some companies negotiate ADR clauses into all of their standard business agreements or contracts. Other companies leave it to their attorneys to decide which disputes are better resolved by ADR than by litigation.

After deciding that an ADR method will be the best way to achieve its goal, the company must persuade the opposing party to participate in the procedure. Certain forms of ADR, such as mediation, are usually accepted readily—the proceeding is informal and can be terminated at any time, and a mediator can also protect the confidentiality of sensitive data, which might be made public during litigation.

Once a company has developed an ADR program, continuous feedback from all participants is required in order to monitor, refine, and improve the program. Constructive criticism is vital. Frequently, corporate managers or executives are in a position to discover a weakness in a particular ADR procedure that could harm the company. The company may wish to designate one employee as the ADR "point person" who monitors the program to ensure that flaws are corrected and strengths are further refined.

Establishing an ADR program has cost-benefit advantages. Valuable management time is saved by avoiding litigation. Equally important, ADR procedures can help the company maintain a relationship with the opposing party and allow flexibility in resolving legal disputes.

INSIDE STORY

## ARBITRATING THE DOT-COM BUST

At the close of the last century, the severe downturn of the technology market caused many small investors to lose a considerable amount of money. Many of these investors brought claims against their brokers. The National Association of Securities Dealers (NASD) is the arbitration forum all investors are required to use when bringing claims against brokers. As a condition to opening a brokerage account, an investor must agree to arbitrate rather than bringing a claim in a state or federal court. Many investors, already feeling betrayed by their brokers, began to feel that the NASD was not the impartial forum it purported to be.[59]

For example, one investor who brought an $800,000 claim against Prudential Securities was awarded just $25,000 even though the NASD arbitrators ruled in his favor. The investor asked the arbitrators for an explanation of their decision but received none. Finally, the investor appealed to a U.S. district court. Despite the courts' historical reluctance to overturn arbitration decisions, the court considered this decision to be so "incomprehensible" that it "shocked the conscience of the court." As a result, the judge demanded an explanation of the decision and vacated the award.[60]

Although arbitration does lower costs, attorneys for investors have begun to say that there is such an "overwhelming industry bias" that financial investment groups are simply not paying what they should.

59. Much of the discussion that follows is based on Gary Weiss, *Walled Off from Justice*, BUS.WK., Mar. 22, 2004, at 90–92.

60. Tripi v. Prudential Sec., Inc., 303 F. Supp. 2d 349 (S.D.N.Y. 2003), *recon. denied*, 2003 WL 22339467 (S.D.N.Y. Oct 14, 2003).

*(Continued)*

(Inside Story *continued*)

Although 54 percent of claims are decided against the large firms, the NASD does not release figures as to how much each claimant is awarded per case. In fact, some lawyers have accused the NASD of adhering to an unwritten rule of awarding no more than half the money sought by the claimant. One ex-panelist insinuated that because his panel criticized the NASD, he was pulled from the roster of available arbitrators.

The questions raised about the impartiality of the system concern many legal experts. Arbitrators are still paid by a private company, and they are not as insulated as a judge with a lifetime appointment. Furthermore, and perhaps even more worrisome, there is virtually no appeal process to rectify a wrong or faulty judgment. For example, the U.S. Supreme Court recently ruled that NASD arbitrators could decide whether a statute of limitation has run or not.[61] Critics of the arbitration process argue that arbitrators are asked to be infallible judges in a system that has no balances built in to check their limitless power.

61. Howsam v. Dean Witter Reynolds, Inc., 537 U.S. 79 (2002).

These fears may be unfounded. In October 2004, a three-person National Association of Securities Dealers panel awarded $75,000 in damages to Linda Naples, a former WorldCom employee who claimed that she lost $600,000 as a result of a breach of fiduciary duty by Salomon Smith Barney (since renamed Citigroup Global Markets). The firm had served as both WorldCom's investment banker and the administrator of the WorldCom employee stock-option program. The panel explained, "Salomon Smith Barney's continuing pursuit of its own interests, without any regard to the contrary interests of those for which SSB owes its fiduciary duty, leads this panel to find that such conflict directly caused the plaintiff's damages."[62] In short, the panel concluded, Ms. Naples "was participating in a rigged game to begin with."[63] Although arbitration awards do not set precedents binding on other panels, arbitrators deciding similar cases may look to them for guidance.

62. Susanne Craig, *Ruling Offers Hope to WorldCom Ex-Employees*, WALL ST. J., Nov. 3, 2004, at C1.
63. *Id.*

## KEY WORDS AND PHRASES

arbitration 141
arbitration clause 143
arbitrator 141
arb-med 153
asymmetric information 157
Best Alternative to a Negotiated Agreement (BATNA) 135
collaborative law 154
contract of adhesion 150
dispute negotiation 134
distributive negotiations 134
Early Neutral Evaluation (ENE) 155
Federal Arbitration Act (FAA) 144
Federal Rules of Civil Procedure (FRCP) 156
Federal Rules of Evidence (FRE) 157
final-offer arbitration 141
hearing 142
integrative negotiations 134
mandatory arbitration 144
med-arb 153
mediation 138
mediator 138
minitrial 153
negotiation 134
nonbinding arbitration 141
ombudsperson 154
posthearing 142
prehearing 142
reservation price 135
summary jury trial (SJT) 154
transactional negotiation 134
variable-sum negotiations 134
zero-sum negotiations 134

## QUESTIONS AND CASE PROBLEMS

1. As a manager, how would you design and implement a policy to limit litigation costs by taking advantage of ADR mechanisms? Be specific in your answer.

2. Mary Martindale and Scott Lauer both applied to become administrative assistants for Widget Company. After the interviewing process, both were hired and asked to sign contracts that contained the same provision: "If there is any dispute as to employment practices or employee/employer actions, this dispute will be decided via binding arbitration." Both signed the contract after being given ample time to review it and to consult an attorney. Several months later, Scott became addicted to cocaine, and Mary became pregnant with her first child. When Mary experienced complications during her pregnancy, Widget initially agreed to grant her medical leave, but shortly thereafter the company informed Mary

that her position had been eliminated due to a "reorganization." Fearing that Scott might have trouble picking up the slack for the recently released Mary, Widget asked him to take a surprise drug test. Scott, confused and alarmed, refused to take one. Widget informed him that because of his refusal, he was also fired. Mary decided to file a lawsuit in state court under the state and federal Family and Medical Leave Acts that guarantee pregnant women a set number of weeks off for pregnancy. Scott, on the other hand, submitted his case to an arbitrator. Will either of their grievances be heard? What will the results of each be?

3. Frank Boomer received a contract in the mail from his long-distance carrier, AT&T, that stated in unambiguous language that his rates were changing and that he should contact AT&T immediately if this was not acceptable. The agreement also contained a clause stating that any dispute concerning the contract would be settled by binding arbitration. Boomer did nothing initially and continued to make long-distance calls. Later, he decided to file a class-action suit against AT&T for overcharging him and other customers. Will Boomer be successful in getting his case heard by a court instead of an arbitrator? [*Boomer v. AT&T Corp.*, 309 F.3d 404 (7th Cir. 2002).]

4. Two commercial fisherman, Gill and Brook, live on the edge of a lake teeming with 10,000 pounds of fish. Each depends on the fish catch for his livelihood and has equipment to harvest immediately the lake's entire 10,000 pounds of fish, worth $10 per pound. For the fish population to sustain itself and offer both fishermen a lifetime of catch, no more than 4,000 pounds can be harvested in any one year. If less than 6,000 pounds are left behind to reproduce, the lake will be empty forever. But if at least 6,000 pounds are left to reproduce, a perpetual supply of 4,000 pounds, worth $40,000 now, will remain available each year.

   If alone on the lake, Gill or Brook would happily harvest only 4,000 pounds per year and ensure a continual supply of fish. In competition with each other, however, both Gill and Brook are deeply suspicious of each other. Gill fears that Brook will harvest any fish Gill leaves behind, and Brook fears Gill will do the same if he limits his catch.

   Without any additional information, what are the incentives for Gill and Brook to fish at various rates? What could Gill and Brook do to ensure the optimal outcome? What barriers would they face in such an attempt?

5. During her second year of business school at the University of Wisconsin, Ursula learned that Freedom Consulting wanted to hire an MBA with her experience, skills, and interests to come on board as a consultant in its Boston office. After discussing Freedom with some of her classmates, Ursula discovered that the firm offered few benefits: two weeks of vacation and basic health maintenance coverage by Kaiser Permanente. To her delight, she also learned that Freedom has an office in warm and sunny San Diego, although the firm was not recruiting for that office.

   After interviewing with Freedom and feeling good about the position and the company overall, Ursula asked about compensation. Because she had a similar offer from Decisions Forever with a salary of $95,000, Ursula would not accept less than $95,000 in salary. Freedom had another candidate nearly as qualified as Ursula who was willing to work for $90,000. Freedom saw no reason to increase its offer to Ursula.

   During their discussions, Freedom explained that it was considering switching medical insurance providers to a preferred provider plan with Blue Cross and had an immediate and pressing need for MBAs to join its Chicago office. After an unusually open and honest discussion, both parties learned the value the other placed on the following issues.

| Issue | Ursula's Value | | Freedom's Value | |
|---|---|---|---|---|
| Official title | Analyst | −$1,000 | Analyst | $ 0 |
| | Consultant | 0 | Consultant | 0 |
| | Manager | 2,600 | Manager | −500 |
| Number of vacation days | 10 | 2,000 | 10 | 0 |
| | 20 | 4,000 | 20 | −2,500 |
| Medical insurance provider | Blue Cross | 500 | Blue Cross | −3,000 |
| | Kaiser | 0 | Kaiser | 0 |
| Geographic location | Boston | 0 | Boston | 0 |
| | Chicago | −300 | Chicago | 2,500 |
| | San Diego | 1,000 | San Diego | −5,000 |
| Matching 401(k) retirement plan | Yes | 2,000 | Yes | −1,600 |
| | No | 0 | No | 0 |
| Start date | Immediately | −1,000 | Immediately | 5,000 |
| | In 3 months | 1,000 | In 3 months | −1,000 |
| Signing bonus of $5,000 | Yes | 5,000 | Yes | −5,000 |
| | No | 0 | No | 0 |

Why might Ursula and Freedom place differing values on these issues? How easy would it really be for Ursula to learn fully about Freedom's values and vice versa?

Given the information above, what should a manager at Freedom who wants to hire Ursula now offer her? What should Ursula be willing to accept? How much value has been created by integration? How much value remains to be distributed?

6. Dana Bexley signed an agreement with Powertel, Inc. to purchase a cellular telephone service plan. Several months after signing the agreement, Powertel included in an envelope with Bexley's bill a pamphlet describing the terms and conditions of its service. The pamphlet restated many of the same terms and conditions outlined in the pamphlet accompanying the original service contract but included a new provision that stated that all disputes would be resolved through arbitration. Nothing on the pamphlet indicated that it was a revision of the original contract except the date printed in small print below the title "Terms and Conditions of Service." The arbitration clause limited Powertel's liability to actual damages and precluded recovery of punitive damages against the company. The clause also stated that customers could not pursue a class action against Powertel or file claims under several statutory remedies.

   Dana Bexley filed a lawsuit, alleging that Powertel had wrongfully billed her and that the arbitration clause was unconscionable. Florida courts may decline to enforce a contract on the ground that it is unconscionable, but the court must find that the contract is both procedurally and substantively unconscionable. How should the court rule? Would the result be the same if Powertel had included the arbitration clause in the original agreement so that Bexley could have read it at the time she purchased the service? Would it matter if the revised agreement did not limit Bexley's rights with respect to recovery of damages, class-action relief, or types of claims? [*Powertel, Inc. v. Bexley*, 743 So. 2d 570 (Fla. 1999).]

7. Weavers Galore, Inc., a Virginia textile manufacturer, instituted a just-in-time (JIT) inventory system to tighten its operations, reduce its working capital, and increase its lackluster profits. In such a system, the timing of supply deliveries is critical because inventories are not kept on hand but are delivered immediately prior to the time they are needed. In anticipation of the new JIT system, Weavers negotiated a supply contract with a cotton farming syndicate headquartered in Birmingham, Alabama.

   In the contract, the syndicate agreed to supply Weavers with 1.25 tons of top quality cotton on the Tuesday morning of each week for the next eighteen months. In return, Weavers agreed to pay $.65 per pound, one month in advance of each shipment. For instance, on March 15, Weavers would pay $1,625 for 1.25 tons of cotton to be delivered by the syndicate on the morning of Tuesday, April 15. Strict adherence to the delivery schedule was of paramount importance to Weavers, the first textile manufacturer in the region and the only customer of the syndicate to implement JIT.

   On October 15, six months into the agreement, the syndicate announced that it would be unable to deliver the next few shipments to Weavers on time and complete. Poor harvests and equipment failures had disrupted the syndicate's operations, and its contracts with other customers were already straining its operations. Many of them would also have to receive late and/or incomplete shipments. For the time being, the syndicate announced, Weavers would have to make do with a single ton of cotton delivered on Wednesday evenings, at best.

   Christina Snow, Weavers' CEO, was livid. Without the next few shipments of cotton on time, she might well lose customers, market share, and profits. Snow's first instinct was to have Weavers' general counsel fire off a terse letter to the syndicate reminding it of its contractual obligations and Weavers' willingness to enforce its rights in court. After that, she might file a lawsuit.

   Should Snow turn this matter over to Weavers' general counsel? What else could Snow do to protect and further Weavers' interests? What are the pros and cons of these courses of action?

8. Delfina Montes went to work for Shearson Lehman Brothers and signed an agreement to arbitrate any disputes arising from her employment. After the termination of her employment, Montes filed suit for allegedly unpaid overtime under the Fair Labor Standards Act (FLSA), which mandates overtime pay for certain workers. Honoring the arbitration agreement, the trial court referred the dispute to arbitration. The arbitration panel ruled that Shearson did not owe Montes any overtime pay. Montes petitioned the trial court to vacate the arbitration panel's ruling as arbitrary and capricious

because the panel heeded Shearson's urging that it disregard the FLSA. In support of her claims, Montes has highlights from the transcript of arbitration in which Shearson's attorneys try to persuade the arbitrator not to follow the black letter statute. Can a plea to deliberately disregard the relevant law provide a basis for overturning the result of an arbitration? [*Montes v. Shearson Lehman Brothers, Inc.*, 128 F.3d 1456 (11th Cir. 1997).]

9. PacifiCare Health Systems sells health insurance to individuals as well as companies. José Cruz was enrolled in one such plan but found PacifiCare's advertising to be false. He could not get the healthcare services PacifiCare had advertised. He has brought a suit seeking to enjoin PacifiCare from advertising in what he feels is a deceptive and fraudulent manner. He is seeking a public injunction to protect the welfare of the public as a whole. As a member of PacifiCare's system, however, Cruz was required to sign an agreement to arbitrate all claims he has against the company. Because of the likelihood that the arbitrators' decisions may affect many people who were not party to Cruz's arbitration clause, the California Supreme Court has allowed this suit to proceed. Do you think this decision is consistent with *Circuit City, Waffle House,* and *Green Tree?* [*Cruz v. PacifiCare Health Systems,* 66 P.3d 1157 (Cal. 2003).]

### MANAGER'S DILEMMA

10. The New Jersey Supreme Court ruled that an employee who continues to work after being given a revised employee handbook containing a waiver clause calling for binding arbitration does not tacitly consent to that new waiver clause. On the other hand, the Texas Supreme Court ruled that if an employee continues to work after the date specified in a notice informing the employee of a new arbitration resolution program, then the employee is tacitly consenting to the new arbitration program. With which court ruling do you agree? If you were a manager, which policy would you adopt and why? [*Leodori v. CIGNA Corp.,* 814 A.2d 1098 (N.J. 2003); *In re Halliburton Co.,* 80 S.W.3d 566 (Tex. 2002); *Nelson v. Cyprus Bagdad Copper Corp.,* 119 F.3d 756 (9th Cir. 1997), *cert. denied,* 523 U.S. 1072 (1998).]

## INTERNET SOURCES

| | |
|---|---|
| The American Arbitration Association's home page offers avenues into its many services. | http://www.adr.org |
| The Dispute Resolution Section of the American Bar Association offers information about the law of ADR. | http://www.abanet.org/dispute/home.html |
| The Mediation Information Research Center offers articles and other information about mediation as well as resources concerning professional mediators. | http://www.mediate.com |
| JAMS/Endispute's page offers information about its many dispute resolution services. | http://www.jams-endispute.com |
| The CPR Institute for Dispute Resolution website has information about its roster of 700 attorneys, former judges, executives, and academics who can mediate disputes and a standard mediation clause for parties to incorporate into their contracts. | http://www.cpradr.org |
| The Organisation for Economic Co-operation and Development's website has Guidelines on Consumer Protection in the Context of Electronic Commerce and information regarding a forum on electronic commerce. | http://www.oecd.org |
| The World Intellectual Property Organization Electronic Commerce and Intellectual Property site provides information about WIPO's program and activities concerning intellectual property and electronic commerce, including the WIPO Arbitration and Mediation Center for the resolution of domain name disputes. | http://arbiter.wipo.int/domains<br>http://www.wipo.int/copyright/ecommerce/en/index.html |
| icourthouse | http://www.icourthouse.com |
| SquareTrade | http://www.squaretrade.com |
| Cybersettle | http://www.cybersettle.com |
| National Arbitration and Mediation | http://www.clicknsettle.com |
| This is the Kluwer Law International Alternative Dispute Resolutions website | http://www.internationaladr.com |
| International Academy of Collaborative Professionals website. This is an umbrella organization that encompasses collaborative practitioners and groups. | http://www.collabgroup.com |
| Operating rules for the Tokyo Center for Arbitration | http://www.niben.or.jp/chusai/e_chusai/e_gaiyo/e_gaiyo.htm |

CHAPTER 5

# Agency

## INTRODUCTION

### AGENCY AND THE CONDUCT OF BUSINESS

In an *agency* relationship, one person—the *agent*—acts for or represents another person—the *principal.* The principal delegates a portion of his or her power to the agent. The agent then manages the assigned task and exercises the discretion given by the principal. The agency relationship can be created by an express or implied agreement or by law.

Agency is perhaps the most pervasive legal relationship in the business world. Businesses of all kinds require the assistance of agents in order to conduct multiple operations in various locations. Indeed, without the law of agency, corporations could not function at all. Only through its human agents can the legal fiction of a corporation enter into any kind of binding agreement.

### CHAPTER OVERVIEW

This chapter defines and discusses the central principles of agency law. First, it describes the different methods by which an agency relationship can be formed. The chapter identifies the different types of agency relationships (employer–employee and principal–independent contractor) and the consequences that flow from each. It examines the duties an agent owes to the principal, and an agent's authority to enter into agreements that are binding upon the principal. Finally, the chapter discusses the extent to which a principal may be liable for the tortious or illegal conduct of an agent.

## Formation of an Agency Relationship

The agency relationship is consensual in nature and is typically created by agreement of the parties. This agreement can be either written or oral. However, if the agent enters into an agreement of a type that must be in writing to be enforceable (such as an agreement for the sale of real property), then the agent's signature on the agreement will not be binding on the principal unless the agency relationship itself is evidenced by some signed writing.

An agency agreement can also be implied from conduct. For example, suppose that computer maker C agrees that sales representative R will sell C's computers to retailers and end users. R solicits sales for C, and C pays R a commission for each sale. An agency relationship exists between C and R, even if they have not entered into a formal agreement.

Agency relationships can also be formed without agreement—by ratification or by estoppel. If a principal approves or accepts the benefits of the actions of an otherwise unauthorized agent, he or she has formed an *agency by ratification*. An *agency by estoppel* occurs when a person leads another to believe that someone else is his or her agent and is thereafter estopped (prevented) from denying it. For example, suppose that Jack causes Kendra to believe that Lori is his agent, and Kendra, relying on this misrepresentation, proceeds to deal with Lori. Even if Lori is not in fact Jack's agent, Kendra's reliance creates an agency by estoppel. As a result, Lori's dealings with Kendra will be binding upon Jack.

# Types of Agency Relationships

An agent may be either an employee of the principal or an independent contractor.

## Employee

The most common form of agency relationship is the employer–employee relationship, sometimes still referred to as the master–servant relationship. The basic characteristic of this relationship is that the employer has the right to control the conduct of the employee. The employee may have the authority to bind the employer to a contract under theories of actual or apparent authority.

## Independent Contractor

An *independent contractor*, such as a lawyer working for a client or a plumber working for a house builder, is not an employee of the person paying for his or her services because the independent contractor's conduct is not fully subject to that person's control. The person hiring an independent contractor bargains only for results.

An independent contractor may or may not be an agent. Generally, an agency relationship exists when the hiring person gives the independent contractor authority to enter into contracts on his or her behalf. For example, suppose that a builder contracts to build a house for Ken for $200,000. Ken has no control over the builder's manner of doing the work because the house is one of a large group of houses that the builder is constructing in a housing subdivision. The builder is not Ken's agent. On the other hand, suppose that Ken expressly authorized the builder to buy redwood siding from a lumber company on his behalf. Here, the independent contractor is Ken's agent for purposes of buying the siding.

# Distinguishing Between Employees and Independent Contractors

Determining whether a worker is an employee or an independent contractor is a legal issue with several important consequences, including the liability of the principal for the worker's torts, as well as the principal's duty to deduct and pay certain taxes on behalf of the worker and to permit the worker to participate in employee benefit plans.

Employers are liable for the torts of their employees, as long as the employee was acting within the scope of employment. In contrast, persons hiring independent contractors are generally not liable for torts committed by the independent contractor.

Employers are required to deduct or pay income, Social Security, and unemployment taxes for employees but not for independent contractors, who are responsible for paying their own self-employment taxes. Moreover, independent contractors are generally not eligible for the same fringe benefits provided to employees, such as medical insurance, stock options, and 401(k) retirement plans. This was a crucial factor in the *Microsoft* case discussed in the "Inside Story" in this chapter. Because an employer does not pay employment taxes and may not provide fringe benefits for independent contractors, hiring an independent contractor may be less costly than hiring an employee to do the same work.

Although the distinction between employees and independent contractors is an important one, there is no bright-line test to distinguish one from the other. Significantly, the label used in an employment contract does not determine the employment status of a worker. The outcome turns on what one does, not on how the relationship has been characterized by the parties. The law looks at a variety of factors, including the following:

1. How much control can the employer exercise over the details of the work?
2. Is the employed person engaged in an occupation distinct from that of the employer?
3. Is the kind of work being done usually performed under the direction of an employer or by a specialist without supervision?
4. What degree of skill does the work require?
5. Does the employer provide the worker with tools and a place of work?
6. For how long is the worker employed?
7. Is the worker paid on the basis of time or by the job?
8. Does the worker offer his or her services to the public at large?

Employee status is more likely to be found for workers who are lower paid and less skilled, lack bargaining power, and have a high degree of economic dependence on their employers.

### ETHICAL CONSIDERATION

Is it ethical for an employer to create artificial differences between its regular employees and workers whom it characterizes as "contractors" in order to avoid providing the "contractors" with insurance and other benefits? Should individuals who work side by side, on the same project or job, under the same supervisor, always receive the same benefits?

## Fiduciary Duty

In agreeing to act on behalf of the principal, the agent becomes a *fiduciary*. Loyalty, obedience, and care are the hallmarks of the fiduciary relationship. An agent has a duty to act solely for the benefit of his or her principal in all matters directly connected with the agency undertaking. This is the *duty of loyalty*. For example, if Adrienne is entrusted with the power to buy a piece of land for Pierre, she cannot buy the best piece of land for herself instead. An agent is also obligated to obey all reasonable orders of his or her principal. For example, if Adrienne refuses to follow Pierre's order to purchase a particular parcel of property, her insubordination would violate the *duty of obedience*.

An agent also has a duty to act with due care. This *duty of care* includes a duty to avoid mistakes, whether through negligence, recklessness, or intentional misconduct. Some states require an agent to use the same level of care a person would use in the conduct of his or her own affairs. Others use a comparative approach: an agent must exercise the same level of care that a reasonable person in a like situation would use. Application of these duties to officers, directors, and controlling shareholders is discussed in Chapter 20.

The following case examines the contours of the duty of loyalty. Specifically, it considers the propriety of the actions of directors and employees who made arrangements to resign and work for a direct competitor while still employed by their current employer.

### A CASE IN POINT

**CASE 5.1**

**Feddeman & Co. v. Langan Associates**

*Supreme Court of Virginia*
*530 S.E.2d 668 (Va. 2000).*

### Summary

**› FACTS** In August 1996, Kent Feddeman, the 95 percent shareholder and president of Feddeman & Co. (F&C), a certified public accounting firm, initiated discussions with John Langan, president of Langan Associates (LA), a rival accounting firm. In early 1997, Feddeman asked Joseph Kotwicki, a director and employee of F&C, to take over the negotiations. In the summer of 1997, the American Express Company offered to purchase both LA and F&C. On August 31, a number of directors and officers of F&C, including Kotwicki, met with Langan at the offices of LA's attorney, Tenenbaum, and decided to refuse the American Express offer. A group of five F&C employees (including three directors) decided to form a "Buying Group" to purchase Feddeman's 95 percent interest in F&C and then merge the company with LA. Feddeman was aware of and did not oppose the two-step merger process.

When it became clear that the Buying Group and Feddeman might not be able to reach agreement on purchase terms related to Feddeman's interest, Tenenbaum advised the members of the Buying Group that to avoid liability to F&C, they should not solicit F&C clients or employees until after their resignation, use company resources in preparing their resignations, make negative statements about F&C, or remove any company property. When representatives of the Buying Group met with other F&C senior employees to report on the status of the merger negotiations, they informed the employees that there was a possibility that the Buying Group would resign on December 1 if negotiations with Feddeman did not improve. The Buying Group also indicated that they believed that LA would hire them if they resigned and that the Buying Group "would take care" of the senior employees.

When Feddeman became aware of the proposed walkout, he contacted a national accounting firm to see if it could provide assistance and to discuss possible merger options. On December 1, Feddeman announced the alternative merger proposal to some of his employees. The Buying Group also met with Feddeman on December 1, but they subsequently decided to resign during a lunch meeting. After lunch Kotwicki called Langan

*(Continued)*

(Case 5.1 *continued*)

to inform him of their decision, and Langan agreed to hire the Buying Group and any other F&C employees who decided to resign. The next morning Kotwicki delivered eleven letters of resignation to Feddeman. That evening LA held a reception for the Feddeman employees who had not yet resigned. Eventually, twenty-five of the thirty-one F&C employees began working for LA. By December 3, all of F&C's clients had been contacted by employees of LA, and 50 percent of these clients ultimately transferred their business to LA.

**› ISSUE PRESENTED** Are directors and employees of a company liable for breach of fiduciary duty if they make arrangements to resign and compete while still employed by that company?

**› SUMMARY OF OPINION** The Virginia Supreme Court began by noting that directors and employees owe a fiduciary duty to their employer. Prior to resignation, however, directors and employees are entitled to make arrangements to resign, including plans to compete, and such conduct does not ordinarily result in liability for breach of fiduciary duty. The court noted that "[t]his right, based on a policy of free competition, must be balanced with the importance of the integrity and fairness attaching to the relationship between employer and employee or corporation and corporate director." Specific conduct taken prior to resignation will be evaluated on a case-by-case basis to determine whether it breaches the agent's fiduciary duty to his or her employer.

The court held that the directors' and officers' conduct in this case had crossed the line and breached their fiduciary obligations to F&C. The defendants did more than prepare to leave and advise others of their plan. They met and formulated a plan to resign en masse if Feddeman rejected their buyout offer, "knowing that a resignation or walk out by all of them would 'be devastating to' the corporation." The plan included anticipation of future employment with a key competitor and soliciting F&C's clients and employees. The record showed that the defendants not only informed other F&C employees of their plan to resign, but also supplied them with resignation letters for their use and assurances that they would be employed by LA.

**› RESULT** The defendant directors and employees had violated their duty of loyalty to their existing employer.

**› CRITICAL THINKING QUESTIONS**

1. What could the Buying Group have done differently to avoid breaching their fiduciary duty to F&C?
2. Assuming that it was legal for the Buying Group to solicit F&C's clients once they had resigned, was it ethical?

Sometimes it is not clear whether a person acting on behalf of another has a fiduciary duty to the other person. This was the issue in the following case dealing with a tax preparation and refund service.

A CASE IN POINT

## In the Language of the Court

**CASE 5.2**
**Green v. H&R Block**
*Court of Appeals of Maryland*
*735 A.2d 1039 (Md. 1999).*

**› FACTS** H&R Block is a tax preparation and filing service. H&R Block's tax filing service allows customers to obtain faster tax refunds in two ways: (1) the customer can pay $25 for H&R Block to file the return with the Internal Revenue Service electronically, in which case the customer will receive the refund in two weeks, or (2) if the customer

*(Continued)*

(Case 5.2 *continued*)

wants the funds even faster, H&R Block can arrange a loan from a third-party bank in the amount of the customer's refund through its Rapid Anticipation Loan (RAL) program. Loans arranged through the RAL program are secured by the customer's anticipated refund.

H&R Block benefited financially in at least one way, and potentially in as many as three ways, from each loan arranged through the RAL program. First, H&R Block received a "license fee" of $3 to $9 for every RAL referred to a lending bank. Second, H&R Block's affiliate, H&R Block Financial, purchased about one-half of the RALs from lender banks. Third, under an arrangement with Sears Roebuck, H&R Block encouraged RAL customers to cash their checks at Sears and received a fee equal to 15 percent of the check-cashing fee that Sears charged for cashing the loan checks. H&R Block did not disclose its financial participation in the RAL program to its customers.

Joyce Green filed a class-action suit on behalf of all Maryland customers who obtained RAL bank loans, claiming, among other things, that H&R Block had breached its fiduciary duty to these customers by failing to disclose the benefits it received from the lending institutions to which it referred them.

**› ISSUE PRESENTED** Does a tax preparation and filing service owe a fiduciary duty to its customers?

**› OPINION** CHASANOW, J., writing for the Maryland Court of Appeals:

According to the . . . complaint, for consumers who contract with H&R Block for tax preparation and filing, H&R Block undertakes a fiduciary duty in the form of an agency relationship "to both explain and/or prepare . . . the various options, elections, forms and documents involved with the taxpayer obtaining back any tax refund he or she was owed by the government." This duty pertains to all matters within the scope of the taxpayer/tax preparer relationship, including assuring that the amount of the refund a customer receives is the maximum amount or the additional taxes required to be paid is the minimal amount. As evidence of the agency relationship, Green points out that H&R Block agrees to accompany the taxpayer to any IRS audit should one be required. Further H&R Block's tax preparers offer general tax advice for retirement and for the sale of residences. Regarding the RAL program, Green alleges that H&R Block acts as the customer's agent in preparing and explaining the loan application and forwarding the application to the lender bank.

. . . Green emphasizes the context in which H&R Block offers and provides its services, particularly its promotional activities. H&R Block's advertising campaigns create "the impression that [H&R] Block and its tax preparation offices and personnel are trustworthy," Green alleges. These advertisements tell consumers to "[d]o what millions of Americans do. Trust H&R Block."

. . .

The trial court determined that no agency relationship had been created between H&R Block and its customers as a matter of law. . . . [T]he trial court's written order stated that "three essential elements must be satisfied" in order to determine the existence of an agency relationship, including (1) the principal's right of control over the agent, (2) the agent's duty to act primarily for the benefit of the principal, and (3) the agent's power to alter the legal relationships of the principal. . . . [T]he trial court held that Green failed to demonstrate the first and third elements. . . .

. . .

. . . [W]e conclude that the evidence alleged concerning the "control" and "legal relations" factors supports a finding of agency. . . .

*(Continued)*

(Case 5.2 *continued*)

. . .

Similar to the client who is represented by an attorney in settlement negotiations, the H&R Block customer may be unknowledgeable in tax and financial matters, trusting H&R Block to further his or her interests. . . . It is not dispositive, as the trial court implied, that H&R Block's customers do not generally exercise control over the manner in which H&R Block prepares the tax filings. Indeed, H&R Block conceded . . . that it serves as its customers' agent for the purpose of filing the tax return and transmitting the loan application to the lender. Thus, H&R Block's customers retain enough control over H&R Block to support a finding of an agency relationship. . . .

We also disagree with the trial court's analysis regarding H&R Block's ability to alter the legal relations of its customers. . . . Because H&R Block's customers actually sign the loan application, and not H&R Block, the trial court concluded that Green "fail[ed] to demonstrate that [H&R Block] had the authority to represent Plaintiff in her transactions with RAL lenders. . . ."

When the facts otherwise demonstrate an agency relationship, that relationship cannot be negated simply because the principal's and not the agent's signature appears on a document otherwise prepared and negotiated by the agent. Such a result would create a legal fiction contrary to the substantive reality. . . .

. . .

. . . [A]n agent is under a strict duty to avoid any conflict between his or her self-interest and that of the principal. . . . As Professor Mechem has observed:

> "It is the duty of the agent to conduct himself with the utmost loyalty and fidelity to the interests of his principal, and not to place himself or voluntarily permit himself to be placed in a position where his own interests or those of any other person whom he has undertaken to represent may conflict with the interests of his principal."

**› RESULT** The Maryland Court of Appeals reversed the trial court's summary judgment in favor of H&R Block on the ground that there were genuine issues of material fact regarding the existence of an agency relationship between H&R Block and its customers.

**› CRITICAL THINKING QUESTIONS**

1. Could H&R Block have added language to its customer contracts to ensure that it would not owe any fiduciary obligations to its customers?
2. Even if H&R Block were ultimately found not to have a fiduciary obligation to its customers, was it ethical for H&R Block to receive undisclosed fees from the RAL program?

## Agent's Ability to Bind the Principal to Contracts Entered into by the Agent

An agent has the ability to bind the principal in legal relations with third parties if the agent has actual or apparent authority to do so. Even in the absence of such authority, the principal may be bound by the unauthorized acts of the agent if the principal subsequently ratifies those acts. A principal can be bound even if his or her identity is undisclosed to the third party.

### ACTUAL AUTHORITY

The principal may give the agent *actual authority* to enter into agreements on his or her behalf; that is, the principal may give consent for the agent to act for and bind the principal. This consent (or authority) may be express or implied.

## View from Cyberspace

### INTELLIGENT AGENTS AND CLICK-WRAP AGREEMENTS

*Intelligent agents* are semi-autonomous computer programs that can be dispatched by the user to execute certain tasks. An important type of intelligent agent can search the Internet and retrieve relevant information or serve as a "personal shopping agent" that makes purchases on behalf of its user.[a]

A prominent feature of electronic commerce is the *click-wrap agreement*,[b] whereby computer users assent to the terms of an online contract by clicking on an acceptance box. The convergence of these two forms of cyberspace technology raises an interesting legal question: What happens when an intelligent agent comes across a click-wrap agreement?

Intelligent agents may someday have the natural language abilities to parse through contract provisions and accept only those terms their users have preprogrammed. But at least for the near term, these agents will likely be able only to accept or to reject online contracts in full. Because click-wrap agreements are so prevalent, the value of an agent that completely avoids them will be significantly reduced. The problem, however, is that traditional agency law does not offer clear guidance as to whether an electronic device can bind an individual to a contract.

At the urging of Microsoft, the Electronic Signatures in Global and National Commerce Act, enacted in 2000, specifically recognizes the validity of contracts executed by electronic agents. Section 101(h) provides that a contract in or affecting interstate or foreign commerce may not be denied legal effect, validity, or enforceability solely because it involved the action of an electronic agent, as long as the action is "legally attributable to the person to be bound."

The Uniform Computer Information Transactions Act (UCITA), a proposed uniform commercial code for software licenses and other computer information transactions, seems to place the onus on the user of an intelligent agent. Section 107 provides that a person who uses an electronic agent is bound by its operations "even if no individual was aware of or reviewed the agent's operations or the results of the operations."[c] The Official Comment to Section 107 states:

> [T]he concept stated here embodies principles like those in agency law, but it does not depend on agency law. The electronic agent must be operating within its intended purpose. For human agents, this is often described in terms of acting within the scope of authority. Here, the focus is on whether the agent was used for the relevant purpose.

See Chapter 8 for more information about UCITA.

a. This discussion is based in part on Stuart D. Levi & Robert Sporn, *Can Programs Bind Humans to Contracts?*, NAT'L L.J., Jan. 13, 1997, at B9.

b. The term *click-wrap agreement* is derived from shrink-wrap license. Under a *shrink-wrap license*, users are deemed to have assented to a licensing agreement with a software manufacturer by their act of tearing open the shrink wrap covering the software package. The U.S. Court of Appeals for the Seventh Circuit held that shrink-wrap licenses are generally enforceable. *See* ProCD, Inc. v. Zeidenberg, 86 F.3d 1447 (7th Cir. 1996).

c. *The Uniform Computer Information Transactions Act (UCITA): A Firestorm of Controversy*, ONLINE LIBR. & MICROCOMPUTERS, May 1, 2000.

One purpose of keeping minutes of meetings of the board of directors of a corporation is to answer agency questions that may arise from corporate transactions. Board minutes, when read in conjunction with corporate bylaws, enable a manager to determine whether an officer had actual authority to execute an agreement or to take other actions on behalf of the corporation.

### Express Authority

*Express authority* may be given by the principal's actual words, for example, a request that the agent hire an architect to design a new office. Express authority may also be given by an action that indicates the principal's consent, for example, by sending the agent a check for the architect's retainer. An agent has express authority if the agent has a justifiable belief that the principal has authorized the agent to do what he or she is doing.

### Implied Authority

Once an agent is given express authority, he or she also has *implied authority* to do whatever is reasonable to complete the task he or she has been instructed to undertake. For example, if a principal instructs an agent to purchase a truck costing up to $20,000, the agent has implied authority to select the appropriate make and model, negotiate the purchase price, and finalize the sale.

Persons in certain positions or offices have implied authority to do what is reasonable for someone in that position. For example, the vice president of purchasing for a trucking business, because of his or her position, has the implied authority to engage in the activities described in the preceding paragraph. There are limits to such implied authority, however. For example, the vice president of purchasing for a trucking division does not have the implied authority to buy an office building. Similarly, an officer of a corporation does not have the authority to bind the corporation to sell or grant rights to purchase shares of its stock; stock issuances must be approved by the corporation's board of directors.

## APPARENT AUTHORITY

*Apparent authority* is created when a third party reasonably believes that the agent has authority to act for and bind the principal. This belief may be based on the words or acts of the principal or on knowledge that the principal has allowed its agent to engage in certain activities on its behalf over an extended period of time.

In *Aeroquip Corp. v. Adams*,[1] Aeroquip Corporation sued two of its former distributors, alleging that they had breached their contracts with Aeroquip by improperly requesting rebates. The distributors claimed that they requested the rebates in good faith reliance on representations by Aeroquip's field agents who appeared to have apparent authority to modify the terms of the company's rebate program when they realized that their competitors were offering the product at a lower price. The U.S. Court of Appeals for the Ninth Circuit concluded that there was sufficient evidence for the jury to find that the sales engineers had apparent authority to modify the rebate program. The evidence showed that Aeroquip intended the sales engineers to explain the terms of the rebate programs to the distributors; the manual the company provided to its distributors contained little information so they had to learn about the program from the sales engineers. From the distributors' perspective, the sales engineers appeared to have authority to modify the terms of the program in order to compete in the local market.

In the following case, the court considered whether the president of a corporation had apparent authority to enter into a contract to redeem a terminated employee's stock.

1. 203 F.3d 830 (9th Cir. 1999).

A CASE IN POINT

**CASE 5.3**

**Powell v. MVE Holdings, Inc.**

*Court of Appeals of Minnesota*

*626 N.W.2d 451 (Minn. App. 2001).*

## In the Language of the Court

**› FACTS** From 1993 until January 1997, R. Edwin Powell was the CEO and president of CAIRE, Inc., a Delaware company that manufactured home health-care products. Powell had worked for CAIRE, a subsidiary of MVE Holdings, Inc. (Holdings), for the preceding thirteen years as an at-will employee. Powell also held 11.9 percent of Holdings.

In 1996, a group of investors formed MVE Investors LLC (Investors) to acquire a majority interest in Holdings. Investors purchased the shares of three Holdings shareholders at $125.456 per share, for a total of $47 million, in June 1996. Powell declined Investors' offer to sell his stock and retire with the other Holdings' shareholders and instead continued as CAIRE's president and CEO.

Subsequently, CAIRE suffered a series of financial setbacks. In early 1998, an independent company valued Powell's shares in Holdings at $5.37 per share. In response to CAIRE's financial setbacks, David O'Halleran, Holdings' CEO and president, met with Powell on January 23, 1997, to fire him. O'Halleran gave Powell the option to resign in lieu of termination, and Powell chose to resign. O'Halleran and Powell also agreed on the terms of Powell's separation agreement. After the meeting, however, a dispute arose over the terms for the purchase of Powell's stock in Holdings. Powell brought an action against Holdings, claiming, among other things, that O'Halleran, on behalf of Holdings, had contracted to buy back Powell's shares during the January 23 meeting and that Holdings had breached that contract.

At the trial, Powell testified that O'Halleran agreed, on behalf of Holdings, to buy Powell's stock at the same price that the retiring shareholders had received in 1996. Following a nine-day bench trial, the trial court found that Holdings had breached its

*(Continued)*

(Case 5.3 *continued*)

contract to buy Powell's stock and awarded Powell $3,456,000. Holdings appealed, claiming O'Halleran did not have authority to agree to buy Powell's stock on its behalf.

› **ISSUE PRESENTED** Does the president and CEO of a company have apparent authority to enter into a stock-redemption agreement with a former employee?

› **OPINION** LANSING, J., writing for the Court of Appeals of Minnesota:

A principal is bound not only by an agent's actual authority, but also by authority that the principal has apparently delegated to the agent. Apparent authority is authority that a principal "holds an agent out as possessing, or knowingly permits an agent to assume." To find apparent authority, (1) "the principal must have held the agent out as having authority, or must have knowingly permitted the agent to act on its behalf," (2) third parties "must have [had] actual knowledge that the agent was held out by the principal as having such authority or been permitted by the principal to act on its behalf," and (3) "proof of the agent's apparent authority must be found in the conduct of the principal, not the agent."

Whether an agent is clothed with apparent authority is a question of fact. . . . [T]he court may consider any statements, conduct, lack of ordinary care or manifestation of the principal's consent, such that a third party might be justified in concluding that the agent acted with apparent authority.

. . . [B]ecause corporate presidents usually control and supervise a corporation's business, unless there is contrary evidence, contracts made by a corporation's president in the ordinary course of business are presumed to be made within the president's authority. Holdings argues that the stock-redemption agreement was so extraordinary that, as a matter of law, Powell could not reasonably have believed that O'Halleran was authorized to agree to it. The evidence, however, does not support this argument.

. . .

Because corporations are engaged in many different transactions and because the pace of corporate business is too swift to insist on express approval by a corporation's board of directors for every transaction labeled as "unusual," third parties commonly rely on the authority bestowed on corporate officials. . . .

It is significant that O'Halleran's appearance of authority resulted from Holdings' conduct. Holdings placed O'Halleran in the position to ask Powell to resign or be fired and to offer Powell a severance package. Holdings also invested authority in O'Halleran to buy shares from the retiring shareholders at the time of the recapitalization, leading to Powell's reasonable belief that O'Halleran had authority to buy Powell's stock as well.

› **RESULT** The court of appeals affirmed the trial court's judgment for Powell, finding that O'Halleran had apparent authority to bind Holdings to the stock repurchase.

› **CRITICAL THINKING QUESTIONS**

1. Holdings fired O'Halleran from his position as CEO and president of Holdings in August 1997. As a part of his severance agreement, O'Halleran agreed to represent that he did not make any written or oral statement that could reasonably be construed to constitute any agreement concerning the redemption or other disposition of Powell's stock. Was it ethical for Holdings to condition O'Halleran's severance package on his agreement to support Holdings' position in the litigation filed by Powell?
2. Should a third party dealing with an agent have an obligation to ascertain whether the agent has the authority to complete the proposed act? What types of actions can a third party take to determine whether the agent has such authority?

## RATIFICATION

The principal can bind himself or herself to an agent's unauthorized acts through *ratification,* that is, affirmation, of the prior acts. When an act has been ratified, it is then treated as if the principal had originally authorized it.

Ratification, like authorization, can be either express or implied. *Express ratification* occurs when the principal, through words or behavior, manifests an intent to be bound by the agent's act. For example, a principal could ratify an agent's unauthorized purchase of a truck by saying "OK" or simply by paying the bill for the vehicle. *Implied ratification* occurs when the principal, by silence or failure to repudiate the agent's act, acquiesces in it.

## UNDISCLOSED PRINCIPAL

An agent may lawfully conceal the principal's identity or even his or her existence. This may be desirable if, for instance, the principal is trying to buy up adjacent properties in an area before news of a business venture is made public, or if the principal's wealth would cause the seller to demand a higher price. If there is an *undisclosed principal,* that is, if the third party does not know the agent is acting for the principal, the principal will nonetheless be bound by any contract the agent enters into with actual authority. In some states, an agent who negotiates a contract with a third party can be sued for breach of the contract unless the agent discloses both the fact that he or she is acting on behalf of a principal and the identity of the principal. If the agent acts without authority, the principal will not be bound; however, the agent may be personally liable on such a contract.

### ETHICAL CONSIDERATION

Is it ethical to use an agent to enter into a contract with a third party who has made it clear that he or she is unwilling to enter into a deal with the undisclosed principal?

### IN BRIEF

**Agent's Authority to Bind the Principal**

| | | |
|---|---|---|
| **Actual Authority** (express and implied) | P → A | Principal communicates authority directly to Agent either by expressly authorizing certain acts (express) or by expressly authorizing certain acts that naturally suggest the power to do related collateral acts (implied). |
| **Apparent Authority** | P → TP | Principal, by words, actions, or the position it puts the Agent in, leads Third Party to reasonably believe that the Agent has authority. |
| **Ratification** | P → TP | Principal leads Third Party to believe that Agent has authority (ratification by estoppel), or Principal agrees to be bound by the Agent's act even though it was not authorized at the time the Agent acted (either by words or by accepting the benefits of the act). |

# Liability for Torts of Agents

A principal may be liable for not only the contracts but also the torts of its agents. According to the doctrine of *respondeat superior,* an agent's employer will be liable for any injuries or damage to the property of another that the agent causes while acting within the scope of his or her employment. As stated in *Jones v. Hart,* decided in England in 1798:

> If the servants of A with his cart run against another cart, wherein is a pipe of wine, and overturn the cart and spoil the wine, an action lieth against A. For whoever employs another is answerable for him, and undertakes for his care to all that make use of him. The act of the servant is the act of his master, where he acts by authority of the master.

If the principal is required to pay damages to a third party because of an agent's negligence, the principal has the right to demand reimbursement from the agent.

## SCOPE OF EMPLOYMENT

Many cases in this area turn on whether the employee was acting within the scope of employment. (Torts of independent contractors are discussed in a later section.) What constitutes scope of employment? Some of the relevant factors include (1) whether the employee's act was authorized by the employer, (2) the extent to which the employer's interests were advanced by the act, (3) whether the employer furnished the instrumentality (for example, truck or machine) that caused the injury, and (4) whether the employer had reason to know the employee would perform the act. Even an action that is a violation of the law may be within the scope of employment if the employee performed the act to serve the employer. For example, when a salesperson lies to a customer to make a sale, the tortious conduct is within the scope of employment because it benefits the employer by increasing sales, even though it may also violate the employer's policy as well as the law.

It is often not clear whether the agent is acting within the scope of employment. Courts tend to use the term "detour" to refer to a slight deviation from the employer's business and "frolic" to refer to conduct that in no way serves the interests of the employer. Detours are deemed to be within the scope of employment, but frolics are not. The following classic case is an illustration of how hard it can be to decide whether a deviation is a detour or a frolic.

**A CASE IN POINT**

**CASE 5.4**
**Riley v. Standard Oil Co. of New York**
*Court of Appeals of New York*
*132 N.E. 97 (N.Y. 1921).*

## Summary

**› FACTS** Arthur Riley, a child, was hit and severely injured by Million, a truck driver employed by the Standard Oil Company of New York, a large corporation even in the 1920s. Riley's mother, acting as a guardian *ad litem* (a person authorized to bring suit on behalf of a minor), sued Standard Oil. She sought to recover damages for personal injury from Standard Oil on the ground that the company was responsible for the tortious act of its truck driver.

Million had been instructed by his supervisor to drive a company truck from the Standard Oil mill to the freight yard of the Long Island Railroad, which was about two-and-a-half miles away. Million was supposed to pick up several barrels of paint at the freight yard and bring them back to the mill. Before leaving the mill, Million found some pieces of scrap wood and loaded them in the truck. As he pulled out of the mill, he did not turn in the direction of the freight yard. Instead, he drove to his sister's house, which was about four blocks in the opposite direction. After unloading the wood for his sister, he headed back toward the mill on his way to the freight yard. En route to the freight yard, but before he passed the mill, Million hit Riley. The only issue on appeal was whether Million was in fact acting as an agent for the company—that is, whether he was acting within the scope of his employment—when he hit Riley.

Standard Oil claimed that Million was not acting as an authorized agent of the company at the moment he hit Riley. His supervisor had told him to go to the freight yard, and he had no express or implied actual authority to go in the opposite direction to deliver the wood to his sister. The defendant argued that, at least until Million returned to his initial point of departure (the entrance to the mill), he was not acting as an agent for Standard Oil and therefore the company could not be held liable for his actions.

**› ISSUE PRESENTED** For the purpose of determining a principal's liability for the conduct of its agent, does the scope of employment include returning to work after a diversion for a personal errand?

**› SUMMARY OF OPINION** The New York Court of Appeals rejected Standard Oil's argument. It held that if Million had hit Riley while on the way to his sister's house, it would have been up to the jury to decide whether this side trip was a separate journey on his own business, distinct from that of his master, or a mere deviation from the general route. If the jury found it to be a new journey, Million would not have been acting as Standard Oil's agent, and the company would not be liable for his negligence. In fact, the accident occurred when Million had already completed his personal errand and was headed back in the direction of his assigned destination. The court concluded that "at some point in the route Million again engaged in the defendant's business. That point, in view of all the circumstances, we think he had reached."

*(Continued)*

(Case 5.4 *continued*)

**› RESULT** Standard Oil was liable for employee Million's negligence. Million was deemed to be acting within the scope of his employment when returning from his errand.

**› COMMENTS** Courts apply various standards in determining whether an agent is acting within the scope of his or her employment for purposes of tort liability. Most courts, however, consider such factors as when and where the tort occurred, what the employee was doing when the tort occurred, and why the employee was doing what he or she was doing.

Before the *Riley* case, there was much precedent for not holding an employer responsible for accidents caused by an employee–driver who was using the employer's vehicle for his own purposes. The three-out-of-seven judges who dissented in *Riley* were able to cite a long list of such cases. The court could have held that Million, like the drivers in the previous cases, was still on his errand and not an agent when he hit Riley.

Several of the judges, however, were concerned with improving the tort system for victims of accidents. Standard Oil, as a large company, was in the best financial position to pay the damages for the serious injury caused by one of its drivers. To decide this close call the other way would have placed the financial burden on those least able to cover the loss.

## Liability for Torts of Employees Acting Outside the Scope of Employment

Under certain circumstances, an employer may be liable for an employee's action even if the employee was acting outside the scope of employment. The employer will be liable if (1) it intended the employee's conduct or its consequences; (2) the employee's high rank in the company makes him or her the employer's alter ego; (3) the employee's action can be attributed to the employer's own negligence or recklessness; (4) the employee uses apparent authority to act or to speak on behalf of the employer and there was reliance upon apparent authority; or (5) the employee was aided in accomplishing the tort by the existence of the agency relationship (the ***aided-in-the-agency relation theory***). For example, the California Supreme Court used the aided-in-the-agency relation theory to hold a city liable for a uniformed police officer who used his badge of authority to persuade a woman to get into his car and then raped her.[2] In another case, however, the U.S. Court of Appeals for the First Circuit, applying Maine law, found that a trucking company was not liable for the actions of its driver, who attacked and stabbed a motorist in an incident of "road rage" that occurred while the driver was driving a tractor-trailer for the company, because his attack was not actuated by a purpose to serve the trucking company.[3]

In the following case, the U.S. Supreme Court considered whether an employer can be vicariously liable for sexual harassment by a supervisor that led to an employee's constructive discharge.

2. Mary M. v. City of Los Angeles, 814 P.2d 1341 (Cal. 1991).
3. Nichols v. Land Transp. Corp., 223 F.3d 21 (1st Cir. 2000).

**A Case in Point**

### In the Language of the Court

**CASE 5.5**
**Pennsylvania State Police v. Suders**
*Supreme Court of the United States*
*124 S. Ct. 2342 (2004).*

**› FACTS** In March 1998, the Pennsylvania State Police (PSP) hired Nancy Drew Suders as a police communications operator. Her supervisors were Sergeant Easton, who was the Station Commander, Patrol Corporal Baker, and Corporal Eric Prendergast. These three supervisors subjected Suders to continuous harassment during her employment. For example, Easton told Prendergast, in front of Suders, that young girls should be given instructions on how to gratify men with oral sex. Easton, wearing spandex shorts, would also sit down near Suders and spread his legs wide apart. Baker made an obscene gesture in Suders's presence by grabbing his genitals and shouting out a vulgar comment. Prendergast told Suders that "the village idiot could do her job" and pounded on furniture to intimidate her.

*(Continued)*

(Case 5.5 *continued*)

In June 1998, Suders informed the PSP Equal Employment Opportunity Officer, Virginia Smith-Elliott, that she "might need some help." Smith-Elliott gave Suders her phone number, but never followed up on the conversation. Suders contacted Smith-Elliott again in August to tell her that she was being harassed and that she was afraid. Smith-Elliott told her how to file a complaint but did not tell her how to obtain the necessary form. Suders felt that Smith-Elliott was insensitive and unhelpful, and she never filed a formal complaint with the PSP.

Several times during her employment Suders had taken a computer-skills exam to satisfy a PSP job requirement. Each time she asked her supervisors about the results, they told her she had failed. One day she found her exams in a drawer in the women's locker room. Suspecting that her supervisors had never turned her tests in for grading, she removed them from the drawer. Suders's supervisors discovered that the exams had been removed and dusted the drawer where they had been stored with a theft-detection powder that turns hands blue when touched. As they expected, Suders attempted to return the exams to the drawer, and her hands turned blue. Her supervisors confronted her, handcuffed her, photographed her hands, and began to question her. Suders had prepared a letter of resignation, which she gave them soon after they detained her, but the supervisors initially refused to release her. Instead, they took her to an interrogation room, gave her a *Miranda* warning, and continued to question her. When Suders reiterated her desire to resign, they let her leave. The PSP never brought theft charges against her.

Suders sued the PSP, alleging that she had been subjected to sexual harassment and constructively discharged in violation of Title VII of the Civil Rights Act. At the close of discovery, the district court granted PSP's motion for summary judgment.

› **ISSUE PRESENTED** Is an employer strictly liable for a supervisor's sexual harassment that results in the constructive discharge of the harassed employee?

› **OPINION** GINSBURG, J., writing for the U.S. Supreme Court:

. . . At the close of discovery, the District Court granted PSP's motion for summary judgment. Suders' testimony, the District Court recognized, sufficed to permit a trier of fact to conclude that the supervisors had created a hostile work environment. The court nevertheless held that the PSP was not vicariously liable for the supervisors' conduct.

In so concluding, the District Court referred to our 1998 decision in *Faragher v. Boca Raton*.[4] In *Faragher*, along with *Burlington Industries, Inc. v. Ellerth*,[5] decided the same day, the Court distinguished between supervisor harassment unaccompanied by an adverse official act and supervisor harassment attended by "a tangible employment action." Both decisions held that an employer is strictly liable for supervisor harassment that "culminates in a tangible employment action, such as discharge, demotion, or undesirable reassignment." But when no tangible employment action is taken, both decisions also hold, the employer may raise an affirmative defense to liability, subject to proof by a preponderance of the evidence: "The defense comprises two necessary elements: (a) that the employer exercised reasonable care to prevent and correct promptly any sexually harassing behavior, and (b) that the plaintiff employee unreasonably failed to take advantage of any preventive or corrective opportunities provided by the employer or to avoid harm otherwise."

. . .

Under the constructive discharge doctrine, an employee's reasonable decision to resign because of unendurable working conditions is assimilated to a formal discharge for remedial purposes. . . .

4. 524 U.S. 775 (1998).
5. 524 U.S. 742 (1998).

*(Continued)*

(Case 5.5 *continued*)

. . .

This case concerns an employer's liability for one subset of Title VII constructive discharge claims: constructive discharge resulting from sexual harassment, or "hostile work environment," attributable to a supervisor. Our starting point is the framework *Ellerth* and *Faragher* established to govern employer liability for sexual harassment by supervisors. . . . With the background set out above in mind, we turn to the key issues here at stake: Into which *Ellerth/Faragher* category do hostile environment constructive discharge claims fall—and what proof burdens do the parties bear in such cases.

. . .

The constructive discharge here at issue stems from, and can be regarded as an aggravated case of, sexual harassment or hostile work environment. For an atmosphere of sexual harassment or hostility to be actionable, we reiterate, the offending behavior "must be sufficiently severe or pervasive to alter the conditions of the victim's employment and create an abusive working environment." A hostile-environment constructive discharge claim entails something more: A plaintiff who advances such a compound claim must show working conditions so intolerable that a reasonable person would have felt compelled to resign. . . .

. . .

To be sure, a constructive discharge is functionally the same as an actual termination in damages-enhancing respects. . . . But when an official act does not underlie the constructive discharge, the *Ellerth* and *Faragher* analysis, we here hold, calls for extension of the affirmative defense to the employer. . . . Absent "an official act of the enterprise," as the last straw, the employer ordinarily would have no particular reason to suspect that a resignation is not the typical kind daily occurring in the workforce. . . . Absent such an official act, the extent to which the supervisor's misconduct has been aided by the agency relation . . . is less certain. That uncertainty . . . justifies affording the employer the chance to establish, through the *Ellerth/Faragher* affirmative defense, that it should not be held vicariously liable.

**› RESULT** The Supreme Court vacated the judgment of the court of appeals and remanded the case to the district court to determine whether an official act of the PSP gave rise to Suders's constructive discharge.

**› COMMENTS** The Supreme Court acknowledged that the facts alleged by Suders, if true, created a sexually hostile environment. As a result of this decision, however, in order for an employer to be held liable for sexual harassment by its supervisors that results in a constructive discharge of the harassed employee, the trial court will also have to find that an official act resulted in the constructive discharge.

**› CRITICAL THINKING QUESTIONS**

1. Based on the Supreme Court's decision, will Suders win her constructive discharge case now if the facts she has alleged are true? What act by the employer will satisfy the "official act" requirement?
2. Title VII, the federal antidiscrimination statute under which this case was filed, does not permit individual harassers—even if they are supervisors—to be held liable for their actions. Is it fair that sexual harassment by a supervisor that forces an employee to leave his or her job also does not result in employer liability unless some "official act" underlies the decision to quit?

### TORTS OF INDEPENDENT CONTRACTORS

The *respondeat superior* doctrine typically applies only to the actions of employees. Principals may be held liable for the torts of independent contractors only in extraordinary circumstances, usually involving highly dangerous acts or nondelegable duties. For instance, if a principal hires an independent contractor to blast boulders off its land, the principal will be liable for any injuries or damages resulting from the blast. In other words, a principal cannot avoid liability for damages resulting from ultrahazardous activities simply by contracting out the work. Similarly, the South Carolina Supreme Court ruled that a hospital could not escape liability for the medical care provided by hiring physicians as independent contractors.[6]

6. Simmons v. Tuomey Reg'l Med. Ctr., 533 S.E.2d 312 (S.C. 2000).

## Liability of the Principal for Violations of Law by the Agent

Under the theory of *vicarious liability,* a company can be held liable for violations of law by its employee even if a manager told the employee not to violate the law. The following case considers whether a corporation can be held vicariously liable under the Fair Credit Reporting Act for its employee's illegal use of credit records for an improper purpose.

A CASE IN POINT

**CASE 5.6**

**Del Amora v. Metro Ford Sales & Service**

*United States District Court for the Northern District of Illinois*
*206 F. Supp. 2d 947 (N.D. Ill. 2002).*

### In the Language of the Court

**› FACTS** In early 2001, Mike Del Amora was in the process of getting a divorce. His estranged wife's brother, Jesus Roman, worked as a salesman for Metro Ford Sales & Service. Although Roman knew that he was only authorized by Metro Ford to obtain credit reports of customers who were interested in purchasing cars from Metro Ford and who had given him permission to check their credit histories, he used his position at the company to obtain credit reports on Del Amora. Roman's motivation was solely to obtain information for his sister, not to further Metro Ford's business, and he obtained the credit reports without Metro Ford's knowledge or consent. When Del Amora learned that Roman had obtained his credit reports, he sued Metro Ford, alleging that it had willfully violated the Fair Credit Reporting Act (FCRA), which prohibits any person from using or obtaining a consumer credit report for other than permissible purposes.

**› ISSUE PRESENTED** Is an employer liable under the Fair Credit Reporting Act for its employee's actions in obtaining a consumer credit report for an improper purpose?

**› OPINION** KENNELLY, J., writing for the U.S. District Court of the Northern District of Illinois:

In this case, the parties agree that Roman, a non-supervisory employee, obtained Del Amora's credit reports for an improper purpose under false pretenses. . . . The only question is whether Metro Ford can be vicariously liable for Roman's willful misconduct. . . .

The FCRA does not specifically provide for vicarious liability. . . .

. . .

. . . [I]mposing vicarious liability under the FCRA is consistent with Congress's intent to protect consumers from improper use of credit reports and to deter statutory violations. . . .

. . .

Where, as here, an employee cannot be considered an employer's "alter ego," we look to the common law of agency to determine the circumstances in which the employer may be liable under the FCRA for its employee's willful misconduct. . . .

*(Continued)*

(Case 5.6 *continued*)

Under general agency rules, an employer may be vicariously liable for the acts of its employees under one of two theories. Under the respondeat superior doctrine, an employer is strictly liable for its employee's acts committed within the scope of employment. Intentional torts generally do not fall within the scope of this doctrine "unless the employee or agent is acting in furtherance (however misguidedly) of his principal's business.". . .

An employer may also be subject to vicarious liability if an employee had apparent authority to act on behalf of the employer or was aided in accomplishing the wrongful act by the existence of the agency relation. The apparent authority doctrine addresses the situation where an employee purports to exercise a power which he or she does not have; the "aided in the agency relation" doctrine applies where an employee threatens to misuse actual power. . . .

If an employer cannot be vicariously liable under one of these theories, liability may attach only where the employer expressly or implicitly authorized the conduct; the employer was negligent or reckless in allowing the conduct to occur; or the conduct violated a non-delegable duty of the employer.

. . .

Neither party addresses the "aided in the agency relation" standard; instead, both debate whether Roman had apparent authority as set forth in [*Jones v. Federated Financial Reserve Corp.*[7]]. However, the apparent agency theory does not encompass the situation presented here, which involves an employee's misuse of actual authority, as opposed to the exercise of authority the employee did not rightly have. The aided in the agency relation doctrine requires a showing that the violation was "accomplished by an instrumentality, or through conduct associated with the agency status." In this case, it is undisputed that Roman was able to obtain Del Amora's credit report solely by virtue of his position with Metro Ford and his resultant access to Metro Ford's consumer reporting facilities. Metro Ford is in the best position to prevent future FCRA violations through employee training and screening programs, and it is therefore liable for Roman's actions.

**› RESULT** The court granted Del Amora's cross-motion for summary judgment on the claim of Metro Ford's vicarious liability. Metro Ford was liable for Roman's violation of the Fair Credit Reporting Act.

**› CRITICAL THINKING QUESTIONS**

1. What can Metro Ford do now to avoid liability in the future for its employees' violations of the FCRA?
2. Under the court's reasoning, would Metro Ford still be liable if it had had adequate procedures in place to prevent violations and Roman still managed to circumvent them?

7. 144 F.3d 961 (6th Cir. 1998).

## THE RESPONSIBLE MANAGER

## WORKING WITH AGENTS

The relationship between a manager and his or her employer is one of trust. As an agent, a manager owes the employer fiduciary duties, which are most often summarized as the duty of care, the duty of obedience, and the duty of loyalty. The duty of care typically requires a manager to avoid grossly negligent, reckless, or intentional behavior that would harm the company. Rarely will an act of simple negligence be treated as a breach of fiduciary duty. The duty of obedience requires the agent to follow his or her employer's reasonable orders. The duty of loyalty imposes more complex obligations. It requires a manager to avoid self-dealing or for-profit activity that competes with the employer's business. In other words, a manager has a duty to act solely for the benefit of his or her employer in all matters related to its business. This duty includes an obligation to notify the employer of all relevant facts—all that the agent knows, the principal should know.

A manager must be concerned with the scope of authority granted to the company's workers and the company's potential liability for the actions of those workers. Perhaps the most determinable aspect of this relationship is whether the worker is deemed an employee or an independent contractor. A manager may prefer to label workers as independent contractors rather than employees for several reasons—for instance, lower tax and benefits costs or reduced exposure to liability. The manager should be aware, however, that legally the status of workers will be determined by the manner in which they are used, not by the label written into the employment agreements.

Once a manager has hired an agent, the manager must be careful to leave little doubt about the scope of the agent's authority. If the manager does not do this, he or she may find, for example, that a purchasing agent has inadvertently been given the apparent authority to bind the business to a large purchase of supplies, above the actual needs of the business. A manager can help avoid scope-of-authority problems by making explicit, unambiguous statements to third parties that specify the limits on an employee's ability to enter into a binding contract. When using an employee or other agent to deal with third parties, a manager must also monitor transactions to avoid conduct that might legally ratify an otherwise unauthorized agreement entered into by the agent.

The manager should ensure that the work environment and the machines and other equipment used in the business are safe. He or she should also stress to the employees the importance not only of complying with the law but also of being concerned about safety and ethical behavior. These concerns pertain mostly to the duties owed by employers to their employees. But employers may owe similar duties even to workers properly termed independent contractors, depending on where the independent contractor works and how much control the employer exerts over that work.

Finally, an employer must be concerned about liability for the wrongdoing of its workers. Because the employer will be liable for those torts of employees that are committed within the scope of employment, a manager should attempt to decrease the risk of such vicarious liability by defining the employees' scope of employment as narrowly as possible. In light of an employer's potential liability under the aided-in-the-agency relation theory for acts outside the scope of employment, managers should exercise particular care when giving an employee authority that could be misused. The managers should ensure both that the employee is trustworthy and that any persons under the employee's control have the ability to complain to someone other than the supervisor. Because a company cannot avoid liability for injuries caused while it is engaged in an ultrahazardous activity, even if it is working through an independent contractor, managers should ensure that the company has adequate liability insurance. Finally, as discussed in Chapter 14, employers may be responsible for the criminal acts of employees. For example, if an employee violates an industry-related regulation during the normal course of employment, the employer could be held vicariously liable. In some situations, the supervising manager may be liable as well.

Although having a policy against illegal practices may not insulate the employer and its owner from civil liability for criminal acts of its lower-level employees, it reduces the chance the employees will break the law to begin with. It also reduces the likelihood that punitive damages will be asserted against the employer and its owner.

INSIDE STORY

## WHEN ARE "TEMPORARY" WORKERS EMPLOYEES?

In an economy that has seen many employers attempt to reduce labor costs and increase staffing flexibility by hiring temporary workers and independent contractors, the classification of workers has risen to new importance. The U.S. Court of Appeals for the Ninth Circuit caused a stir when it ordered Microsoft Corporation, the world's largest computer software company, to provide fringe benefits to certain freelance workers even though they had signed agreements expressly stating that they were independent contractors and were not eligible for such benefits.[8]

Although hired to work as freelancers on specific projects, seven of the eight named plaintiffs (who sued on their own behalf and as representatives of a class of workers) had worked on successive projects for a minimum of two years prior to the time the action was filed, while the eighth had worked for more than a year. During that time, they performed services as software testers, production editors, proofreaders, formatters, and indexers. They often worked on teams with regular employees, sharing the same supervisors, performing identical functions, and working the same core hours. However, they were not permitted to assign their work to others, were not invited to official company functions, and were not paid overtime wages. In addition, they were not paid through Microsoft's payroll department. Instead, they submitted invoices for their services, documenting their hours and the projects on which they worked, and were paid through the accounts receivable department.

Even though the freelancers had agreed to be responsible for all federal and state taxes, withholding, and Social Security, the Internal Revenue Service (IRS) concluded that they were employees, not independent contractors, for withholding and employment tax purposes. Microsoft therefore agreed to (1) pay overdue employer withholding taxes, (2) issue retroactive W-2 forms to allow the freelancers to recover Microsoft's share of Social Security taxes (which they had been required to pay), and (3) pay the freelancers retroactively for any overtime they had worked.

After learning of the IRS rulings, the plaintiffs sought various employee benefits, including benefits under Microsoft's Employee Stock Purchase Plan (ESPP) and Savings Plus Plan (SPP). The ESPP permitted Microsoft employees to purchase company stock at 85 percent of the fair market value on either the first or the last day of each six-month offering period, whichever was lower. The SPP was a retirement plan under Section 401(k) of the Internal Revenue Code, which permitted Microsoft's employees to save and invest up to 15 percent of their income through tax-deferred payroll deductions. Microsoft matched 50 percent of the employee's contribution in any year, with a maximum matching contribution of 3 percent of the employee's yearly compensation. Microsoft rejected the plaintiffs' demand for benefits on the ground that they were independent contractors who were personally responsible for all their own benefits.

A three-judge panel of the U.S. Court of Appeals for the Ninth Circuit addressed the ESPP and SPP claims separately. With respect to the ESPP claim, because Microsoft stated in the ESPP document that the plan was intended to comply with provisions of the Internal Revenue Code, Microsoft was deemed to have adopted the IRS's definition of common law employee. As a result, the ESPP expressly extended eligibility to all of the workers in the plaintiffs' class. As for the SPP claims, the court ruled that it should not address issues of plan interpretation until the plan administrator had determined whether the workers were "on the U.S. payroll" of Microsoft within the meaning of the plan.

Many companies responded to the *Microsoft* decision by leasing workers from temporary employment agencies instead of hiring them directly. This arrangement may not be fail-safe, however. The fact that leased workers are on the payroll of an employment agency does not preclude them from being considered employees of the company—the agency and company could be considered joint employers.[9]

To determine whether a company is a joint employer of leased workers, a manager should consider such factors as whether the company (1) supervises the workers,

8. Vizcaino v. Microsoft Corp., 97 F.3d 1187 (9th Cir. 1996), *aff'd on reh'g*, 120 F.3d 1006 (9th Cir. 1997), *cert. denied*, 522 U.S. 1099 (1998). The statement of facts that follows is excerpted from this opinion.

9. Vizcaino v. Microsoft, 173 F.3d 713, 723 (9th Cir. 1999), *cert. denied*, 528 U.S. 1105 (2000).

*(Continued)*

(Inside Story *continued*)

(2) has the ability to hire and fire, (3) is involved in day-to-day labor relations, (4) establishes wage rates, or (5) has the power to promote or discipline the worker. As with questions surrounding the independent contractor label, the bottom line is that if leased employees are treated the same as regular employees, they may be treated as common law employees of the company.

In January 2000, the Ninth Circuit ruled that approximately 10,000 current and former independent contractors and longtime "temporary" employees at Microsoft who worked at least half-time, or five months a year, had become "common-law" employees of the company and thus were entitled to compensation for their exclusion from the ESPP. At the time of the decision, analysts estimated that Microsoft would have to pay approximately $100 million to the workers.

More recently, the California Court of Appeal cited the *Vizcaino* case when it overruled a trial court's dismissal of a complaint by an attorney who was hired as a legal consultant in MGM's legal department. The attorney claimed that he was entitled to severance benefits that MGM had extended to all employees affected by a reduction in force. MGM defended on the basis that the attorney was an independent contractor, not an employee. Citing *Vizcaino,* the appellate court noted that in determining whether a worker is an "employee," the classification by the parties, while significant, is not conclusive and in the usual situation, employers cannot deprive workers of substantial benefits simply by not calling them employees.[10]

10. Walker v. Metro Goldwyn Mayer Studios, 2002 WL 194203 (Cal. App. 2002).

## KEY WORDS AND PHRASES

actual authority 170
agency 165
agency by estoppel 165
agency by ratification 165
agent 165
aided-in-the-agency relation theory 176
apparent authority 172
click-wrap agreement 171
duty of care 167
duty of loyalty 167
duty of obedience 167
express authority 171
express ratification 174
fiduciary 167
implied authority 171
implied ratification 174
independent contractor 166
intelligent agents 171
principal 165
ratification 174
*respondeat superior* 174
undisclosed principal 174
vicarious liability 179

## QUESTIONS AND CASE PROBLEMS

1. Singer was employed by General Automotive Manufacturing Company (GAMC) as its general manager from 1953 until 1959. He had worked in the machine-shop field for more than thirty years and enjoyed a fine reputation in machine-shop circles.

   GAMC was a small concern with only five employees and a low credit rating. Singer attracted a large volume of business to GAMC and was invaluable in bolstering the company's credit rating. At times, when collections were slow, Singer paid the customer's bill to GAMC and waited for his own reimbursement until the customer remitted. Also, when work was slack, Singer would finance the manufacture of unordered parts and wait for recoupment until the stockpiled parts were sold. Some parts were never sold, and Singer personally absorbed the loss on them.

   While working for GAMC, Singer set up his own sideline operation, in which he acted as a machinist–consultant. As orders came in to GAMC through him, Singer would decide that some of them required equipment GAMC lacked or that GAMC could not do the job at a competitive price. For such orders, Singer would give the customer a price, then deal with another machine shop to do the work at a lower price, and pocket the difference. Singer conducted his operation without notifying GAMC of the orders that it (through Singer) did not accept.

   Contending that Singer's sideline business was in direct competition with its business, GAMC sued

Singer for breach of fiduciary duty. What result? What were Singer's duties to GAMC as its agent? Was Singer's operation of a sideline business ethical? Would it have been ethical had he disclosed it to his GAMC superiors? [*General Automotive Manufacturing Co. v. Singer,* 120 N.W.2d 659 (Wis. 1963).]

2. NTG Telecommunications, which was interested in purchasing a computer network for its office, received a promotional letter from IBM regarding IBM's PC Server 310, Small Business Solution, a computer network server designed for and marketed to small businesses. The letter stated: "When you're ready to get down to business, give us a call. . . . We'll give you the name of the IBM business partner nearest you, as well as answer any questions you might have." The Small Business Solution was available only through an IBM business partner, which is an entity authorized to resell IBM products.

   Jud Berkowitz, president of NTG, contacted Frank Cubbage of Sun Data Services, an IBM business partner, regarding the Small Business Solution. Berkowitz decided to purchase the Small Business Solution after being informed by Cubbage that it was compatible with Windows 95, the operating system installed on each of the networked computers. After he installed the server, NTG started having serious computer problems, which were not resolved until NTG replaced PerfectOffice (which was sold as part of the Small Business Solution) with Lotus Smart Suite. Berkowitz sued IBM for fraud based in part on Cubbage's representation that the Small Business Solution was compatible with Windows 95. IBM argued that Cubbage's statement could not be attributed to it because a formal licensing or dealership agreement does not create an agency relationship. How should the court rule? [*NTG Telecommunications, Inc. v. IBM, Inc.,* 2000 U.S. Dist. LEXIS 6279 (E.D. Pa. May 8, 2000).]

3. Foley Company was the general contractor on a construction site, and All Temp was a subcontractor on the site. Foley and All Temp entered into a construction contract pursuant to which All Temp agreed to name Foley as an additional insured on its liability insurance policy with Scottsdale Insurance Company, its carrier. At the time Foley was added to the Scottsdale policy, Scottsdale's general agent, MCI, was authorized to issue certificates of insurance with binding authority for Scottsdale, but Scottsdale prohibited MCI from delegating this authority without Scottsdale's written consent. Despite this prohibition, MCI informed its agent, CLC, that CLC could issue certificates naming general contractors, like Foley, on the All Temp policy, subject to MCI's approval, as long as doing so did not increase Scottsdale's risk. CLC subsequently issued a certificate of insurance to Foley. Scottsdale did not learn that CLC had issued the certificate until after Bryant was fatally injured at the Foley construction site. Rather than canceling All Temp's policy when it learned about the certificate, Scottsdale continued to renew the policy for three years. Subsequently, Bryant's heirs successfully recovered damages in an action against All Temp and Foley. Foley then sued Scottsdale for indemnification, and Scottsdale sought indemnification from MCI and CLC on the basis that MCI had breached the agency agreement between Scottsdale and MCI when it allowed CLC to issue a certificate of insurance to Foley. MCI and CLC moved for summary judgment against Scottsdale. Will MCI and CLC be required to indemnify Scottsdale? On what basis? [*Foley Co. v. Scottsdale Insurance Co.,* 15 P.3d 353 (Kan. App. 2000).]

4. In 1988, Northeast General Corporation entered into an agreement with Wellington Advertising, Inc. relating to the sale of Wellington Advertising. The agreement provided that (1) Northeast was to act "as a non-exclusive independent investment banker and business consultant for the purposes of finding and presenting candidates for purchase, sale, merger or other business combination" and (2) would be entitled to a finder's fee, based on the size of the transaction, if a transaction was completed within three years of when Wellington was introduced to the "found" buying party.

   An unidentified investment banker informed Northeast's president, Dunton, that Sternau, a potential purchaser, had a reputation for buying companies, removing assets, rendering the companies borderline insolvent, and leaving minority investors unprotected. Despite this information, Margolis, one of Northeast's agents, introduced Sternau to Wellington's president, Arpadi, and did not disclose the information about Sternau to him. After the introduction but before Sternau and Arpadi signed an acquisition agreement, Dunton called Arpadi to offer further help with the transaction. Arpadi declined that help and discouraged Dunton from further involvement. After the merger agreement was signed, companies controlled by

Sternau purchased the controlling stock of Wellington, leaving Wellington's principals, including Arpadi, as minority investors. Ultimately, Wellington was rendered insolvent, and Arpadi and other minority investors suffered financial losses. Wellington had delivered a check to Northeast for its services but stopped payment before the check was cashed. Northeast then sued Wellington to recover its finder's fee. Does a finder–seller agreement create a relationship of trust with a "fiduciary-like" obligation on the finder to share information with the seller regarding the potential buyer's bad reputation? Assuming it does not, was it ethical for Northeast not to disclose information about Sternau to its client? [*Northeast General Corp. v. Wellington Advertising, Inc.*, 624 N.E.2d 129 (N.Y. 1993).]

5. Holabird & Root (Holabird) hired the Chicago law firm Sabo & Zahn (Sabo) to bring a collection action against a local real estate developer, Horwitz Matthews, Inc., (HM). Sabo won a $150,000 judgment against HM on behalf of Holabird and then began enforcement proceedings to collect on it. Responding to a citation to discover assets, HM provided Sabo with tax returns that were subject to a confidentiality agreement barring the attorneys from disclosing information derived from the returns to anyone outside the firm. Despite the agreement, the Sabo attorneys told about forty of HM's associates and investors by mail that HM had apportioned to itself a greater percentage of some partnership business than it was entitled to and that investors' losses had been underreported. HM sued Sabo & Zahn and Holabird, claiming it was vicariously liable. Is a law firm an agent of its clients, or is it an independent contractor? Should a client be liable for torts committed by its law firm? [*Horwitz v. Holabird & Root,* 2004 WL 1118511 (Ill. Sup. Ct. 2004).]

6. The president of a corporation hired an assistant to be responsible for both his personal and business affairs, including review of vendor invoices and credit card statements for the American Express corporate account. Without the knowledge of the president, the assistant obtained an additional credit card for the corporate account in her own name. The corporation alleged that the assistant stole $412,000 via unauthorized credit card charges. The corporation sued American Express, seeking to recover $276,000 in unauthorized charges and a declaration that it was not liable for the $51,000 outstanding balance on one of the cards. The applicable federal law limits the liability of cardholders from "unauthorized" charges to $50.

   American Express argued that the corporation, because of its negligence in failing to examine the credit card statements that would have revealed the assistant's fraudulent charges, had given the assistant apparent authority to make the charges. Therefore, American Express contended, the charges were not unauthorized under the meaning of the statute and the corporation was fully liable for those charges. What result? [*Minskoff v. American Express Travel Related Services Co.*, 98 F.3d 703 (2d Cir. 1996).]

7. Frederick Richmond agreed to sell UForma Shelby Business Forms, Inc., a business forms printing business, to Samuel Peters pursuant to a stock-purchase agreement at a price of $3.6 million to be paid in annual installments. The amount of each installment was one-half the amount by which the profits of UForma and Miami Systems, Inc., another company owned by Peters, exceeded the 1988 and 1989 average annual profits of Miami Systems alone. The agreement stated that this formula might result in no payment being made in some years. At the time of the sale, UForma was operating at a loss. The sales agreement also stated that Peters should operate UForma according to "sound business practices." Peters paid Richmond $496,057 for 1990 and $147,368 for 1991. Because the earnings of UForma and Miami Systems were insufficient to trigger a payment under the formula in the agreement, Peters paid Richmond nothing for the years 1992 through 1995. Richmond sued Peters for breach of contract and breach of fiduciary duty, alleging that he was entitled to additional payments and that Peters had not operated UForma in accordance with sound business practices. How should the court rule? [*Richmond v. Peters,* No. 97-3647 (6th Cir. Nov. 20, 1998), *reh'g. denied,* 173 F.3d 429 (6th Cir. 1999).]

8. Johnson was the sole general partner of a large office building in Austin, Texas, along with several limited partners. The limited partners were also lessees of space in the office building. Each tenant of the building (including the limited partners/lessees) was responsible for the "finish-out" construction of that tenant's office space. Most of these tenants hired one of two contractors to finish out their office spaces. On most of these finish-out jobs, the contractors paid Johnson, the sole general partner, a 15 percent fee. Each contractor simply added this fee to

the sum charged to the tenant. Some tenants knew about the fee and others did not. Did Johnson owe a fiduciary duty to his limited partners (who were also his tenants) to disclose the fee? [*Johnson v. J. Hiram Moore, Ltd.*, 763 S.W.2d 496 (Tex. Ct. App. 1988), *writ denied* (Sept. 20, 1989).]

9. The plaintiffs were models in a "fitness fashion show," featured as part of the Working Women's Survival Show exhibition at a convention center in St. Louis. B.P.S., doing business as Wells Fargo Guard Service, had contracted with the city to provide guards at the center. Security arrangements at the convention center included a number of television surveillance cameras scattered around the center, which were monitored on small screens in a central control room. The direction in which each camera was pointing could be adjusted manually or automatically in the control room. The control room also had a large screen that the guards could use to view the images from the cameras or to monitor what was being taped on the VCR. The purpose of having the VCR was to enable the guards to videotape suspicious activities. The Wells Fargo guards were told to practice taping on the VCR.

   Promoters for the Working Women's Survival Show had a makeshift curtained dressing area set up near the stage for the models in the fashion show. Unbeknownst to the models, the dressing area was in a location that could be monitored by one of the surveillance cameras. That fortuity was discovered by two Wells Fargo guards, Rook and Smith. Rook had the rank of captain at Wells Fargo, denoting supervisory capacity, though there was testimony that when he worked in the control room, he had no supervisory authority. Another supervisor with disputed supervisory authority, Ramey, walked by the control room and saw the guards using the large screen to view women in a state of undress. Ramey said that he thought the guards were watching pornographic tapes that they had brought to work. (There was testimony that the guards watched their own pornographic tapes in the control room.) Either Smith or Rook (each accused the other) focused the camera on the plaintiffs and taped them as they were changing clothes for the fashion show.

   Is Wells Fargo Guard Service liable for the unauthorized actions of its agents, even if those actions were done for reasons of personal pleasure rather than for work? [*Does v. B.P.S. Guard Service, Inc., d/b/a Wells Fargo Guard Service*, 945 F.2d 1422 (8th Cir. 1991).]

**MANAGER'S DILEMMA**

10. Peter Pierce was the president of Pierce Leahy Corporation, the chief competitor of records storage company, Iron Mountain. When Pierce Leahy merged with Iron Mountain in 2000, Pierce became president of Iron Mountain's main operating unit and was elected to its board of directors. Pierce also signed a noncompete agreement in which he agreed not to "own, manage, engage in, participate in, provide advice to, be employed by [or] have a financial interest in" any records storage business for five years after termination of his employment with Iron Mountain. Four months after the merger, Iron Mountain fired Pierce, but he remained on the board of directors. After Pierce's departure, Iron Mountain heard rumors that Pierce was competing; at the same time, several Pierce Leahy managers left Iron Mountain without disclosing their future plans. Iron Mountain hired a private investigator, who staked out Pierce. A consultant to Iron Mountain reported that Pierce's sister and his son had provided funding for Sequedex, a competitive start-up records storage business.

   At about the same time, Thomas Carr, an unhappy business partner of Pierce in Logisteq, a trucking and warehouse business, contacted Iron Mountain shortly after Pierce removed him as CEO (apparently, Carr had been indicted on federal fraud charges of aiding a money-laundering scheme). Carr informed Iron Mountain that three of Logisteq's employees were secretly working at Sequedex (these employees subsequently denied in depositions that they worked for Sequedex). With Iron Mountain's knowledge, Carr began recording his conversations with Pierce to get documentation for his claims, and Iron Mountain's lawyers arranged to give Carr $50,000 to help him fund a lawsuit he had filed against Pierce. In March 2002, Iron Mountain sued Pierce and Sequedex, alleging that Pierce had violated his noncompete, breached his duty as an Iron Mountain director, and misappropriated trade secrets. Although Sequedex managed to sign contracts with some of Iron Mountain's customers, Iron Mountain fought back, and Sequedex received no revenue from these contracts.

   In August 2002, Sequedex closed its doors. At about the same time, Logisteq filed for bankruptcy protection and loaded its records onto a truck trailer at a storage lot. Six months later, Carr's lawyer found out where the trailer was. Days later, a trucking company operator who was informally helping Carr and Iron Mountain phoned Iron Mountain's law firm to say he had the trailer. After Iron Mountain's lawyer traveled to New Jersey to inspect the trailer's contents and arrange to have them copied, the trucking company operator sent the trailer back to the lot. Although Pierce claimed at the arbitration that the trailer had been stolen and broken into, the operator said it was all a mistake. Did Pierce's activities subsequent to his termination constitute a breach of the fiduciary duty he owed to Iron Mountain as its director? Was Iron Mountain's response to these activities legal? Was it ethical? [David Armstrong, *What Does a Noncompete Pact Truly Bar? Nasty Row Sorts It Out,* WALL ST. J., June 14, 2004, at A1.]

## INTERNET SOURCES

| | |
|---|---|
| The Independent Contractor Report provides frequent updates on rulings and other issues relevant to users of independent contractors. | http://www.workerstatus.com |
| The Internet Revenue Service site provides information concerning the proper classification of workers. | http://www.irs.gov |

CHAPTER 6

# Administrative Law

## INTRODUCTION

### Importance of Administrative Agencies

Administrative law concerns the powers and procedures of administrative agencies, such as the Internal Revenue Service (IRS), which collects taxes, and the Securities and Exchange Commission (SEC), which regulates the securities markets. The activities of administrative agencies affect nearly everyone, frequently on a daily basis. Administrative agencies set limits on pollution and emissions and regulate disposal of hazardous waste. They regulate radio and television, food and drugs, and health and safety.

Federal and state administrative agencies solve practical problems that cannot be handled effectively by the courts or legislatures. Agencies make rules to effectuate legislative enactments; they resolve conflicts by formal adjudication, a courtlike proceeding; they carry out informal discretionary actions; and they conduct investigations regarding compliance with specific laws and regulations. Although usually part of the executive branch, administrative agencies can rightly be called a fourth branch of government.

Failure to comply with applicable regulations can result in the revocation of licenses and permits and in the imposition of stiff fines. In 2002, Schering-Plough Corporation agreed to pay the government $500 million for repeated violations of Food and Drug Administration (FDA) regulations regarding its factory practices.[1] Even the President of the United States is not immune from regulatory constraints. A Department of the Interior's ruling that three large methane bed leases were illegal could halt President Bush's push for increased methane gas production.

1. Melody Peterson, *Drug Maker to Pay $500 Million Fine for Factory Lapses,* N.Y. Times, May 18, 2002, at 1.

### Chapter Overview

This chapter discusses the various ways in which administrative agencies operate and addresses the key principles of administrative law. Constitutional issues include separation of powers, delegation of authority, and the protections afforded by the Bill of Rights. Issues arising from the judicial review of agency actions include the doctrines of ripeness and exhaustion of administrative remedies. Doctrines that limit the decision-making power of agencies include the principles that agencies are bound by their own rules and that they must explain the basis for their decisions. The chapter also describes how to find the rules of a particular agency and how to obtain documents from the government.

## How Administrative Agencies Act

An administrative agency functions in four primary ways: making rules, conducting formal adjudications, taking informal discretionary actions, and conducting investigations.

### Making Rules

Congress and the state legislatures frequently lack the time, human resources, and expertise to enact detailed regulations. Sometimes issues are so politically sensitive that elected officials lack the will to make the tough decisions. In such cases, the legislature will often pass a law setting forth general principles and guidelines and will delegate authority to an administrative agency to carry out this legislative intent. The agency will then follow a three-step procedure to promulgate appropriate rules or regulations.

### *Notice to the Public*

First, the administrative agency gives notice to the public of its intent to propose a rule. Generally, the agency publishes the proposed rule and gives the public an opportunity to submit written comments. A comment letter usually (1) identifies the company that is concerned, (2) describes why it is concerned, (3) suggests a specific change in the language of the proposed rule, and (4) provides factual information to support its position. For example, the SEC's proposed "noisy withdrawal" rule would have required attorneys to withdraw from representing a public company if they uncovered financial fraud and then to inform the SEC of the withdrawal. The proposal prompted hundreds of adverse comment letters. Comment letters are very helpful to an agency and can influence the final rule.

For example, the Mercatus Center, an independent think tank associated with George Mason University that receives funding from many sources, has been particularly successful in promoting less rigorous business regulation. Mercatus provides formal comment letters that analyze whether the costs of a proposed rule exceed the benefits, whether the rule disadvantages consumers or small businesses, and whether there are less burdensome alternatives.[2]

2. Bob Davis, *In Washington, Tiny Think Tank Wields Big Stick on Regulation*, WALL ST. J., July 16, 2004, at A1.

Agencies may, but are not always required to, hold a formal public hearing. They always allow people to comment on proposed rules by meeting informally or telephoning the agency personnel. If a company is particularly concerned about a proposed rule, it should both call and meet with the proposing agency about its concerns.

### *Evaluation*

Second, the administrative agency evaluates the comments, responds to them, and decides on the scope and extent of the final rule. If the comments prompt the agency to make substantial changes in the proposed rule, the agency may publish a revised proposed rule for public comment.

### *Adoption*

Third, the agency will formally adopt the rule by publishing it in the *Federal Register* along with an explanation of the changes. The *Federal Register* is published daily by the U.S. Government Printing Office. Rules that are not properly published there are void. The final rule will also be *codified,* that is, added to the *Code of Federal Regulations* (CFR). The CFR contains more than fifty titles and includes the regulations of approximately 400 federal agencies and bureaus.

The Administrative Procedure Act (APA) requires notice to the public and an opportunity to comment before an agency can promulgate a rule. There is an exception for rules of agency procedure and general statements of policy. In the following case, the court considered whether a directive issued by the Occupational Safety and Health Administration (OSHA), part of the U.S. Department of Labor, fell into either category.

A CASE IN POINT

## In the Language of the Court

**CASE 6.1**
**Chamber of Commerce of the United States v. U.S. Department of Labor**
*United States Court of Appeals for the District of Columbia Circuit*
*174 F.3d 206*
*(D.C. Cir. 1999).*

**› FACTS** OSHA issued a directive (the Directive) establishing the OSHA High Injury/Illness Rate Targeting and Cooperative Compliance Program, a new approach to the problem of work safety at dangerous workplaces. The Directive set up a procedure whereby dangerous workplaces would be placed on a "primary inspection list" and subjected to a comprehensive inspection. OSHA would remove a workplace from the list only if the employer participated in the agency's Cooperative Compliance Program (CCP), which obligated the employer to satisfy eight requirements designed to reduce dangerous conditions at the sites. The Chamber of Commerce challenged the Directive for failure to provide notice and an opportunity to comment.

**› ISSUE PRESENTED** Was OSHA required to provide notice and an opportunity to comment?

**› OPINION** GINSBURG, J., writing for the U.S. Court of Appeals for the District of Columbia Circuit:

*(Continued)*

(Case 6.1 *continued*)

In defense of its position that the Directive is a procedural rule, the OSHA advances two arguments. First, minimizing the significance of the CCP, it asserts that the Directive is merely an inspection plan that does not put its "stamp of approval or disapproval" on any particular behavior. Then, ignoring the inspection plan, it maintains that the Directive has no "substantial impact" upon covered employers because of the voluntary nature of the CCP. But the inspection plan and the CCP are two elements of the same rule; in determining whether notice and comment were required before it could be promulgated, we must view the rule as a whole.

So viewed, it is apparent that the Directive cannot be considered procedural. If the function of the CCP were simply to provide each employer with the option of substituting self-inspection for an equivalent inspection conducted by the OSHA, then the agency could make a creditable argument that the Directive does not represent the kind of normative judgment characteristic of a substantive rule. . . . The OSHA may not, however, tell employers in one breath that participation in the CCP requires more than mere compliance with the OSH Act—which clearly ups the substantive ante—and tell us in the next that the sole purpose of the CCP is to make unnecessary the inspections it performs in order to uncover violations of the Act. At least to the extent that participation in the CCP requires more than adherence to existing law, the Directive imposes upon employers more than "the incidental inconveniences of complying with an enforcement scheme. . . ." [I]t has a substantive component.

A general statement of policy "does not establish a binding norm. It is not finally determinative of the issues or rights to which it is addressed. The agency cannot apply or rely upon [such a] policy as law because a general statement of policy only announces what the agency seeks to establish as policy." . . . The OSHA argues that the Directive meets this definition, raising once more the point that the rule imposes no formal legal obligation upon an employer that chooses not to participate in the CCP.

In this context, the agency's contention has some intuitive appeal: At first glance, one might think that a rule could not be considered a "binding norm" unless it is backed by a threat of legal sanction. Beyond that first glance, however, its appeal is fleeting.

In *American Bus Association v. United States,*[3] we held that the question whether a rule is a policy statement is to be determined by whether it (1) has only a prospective effect, and (2) leaves agency decisionmakers free to exercise their informed discretion in individual cases. Both criteria lead us here to the conclusion that the Directive is a substantive rule rather than a policy statement. First, the Directive provides that every employer that does not participate in the CCP will be searched. The effect of the rule is therefore not to "announce[ ] the agency's tentative intentions for the future,". . . but to inform employers of a decision already made. . . . Indeed, the OSHA admits in its brief that the inspection plan "leave[s] no room for discretionary choices by inspectors in the field." And the Directive itself suggests that the agency will not remove an employer from the CCP unless the employer fails to abide by the terms of the program. Therefore, although the Directive does not impose a binding norm in the sense that it gives rise to a legally enforceable duty, neither can it be shoehorned into the exception for policy statements.

**› RESULT** The court held that the Directive was neither a procedural rule nor a policy statement. As a result, OSHA was required to provide notice and an opportunity to

3. 627 F.2d 525 (D.C. Cir. 1980).

*(Continued)*

(Case 6.1 *continued*)

comment before issuing it. The court vacated the Directive without prejudice to OSHA to repromulgate it using the proper procedures.

**› CRITICAL THINKING QUESTIONS**

1. Why should procedural rules and policy statements be exempt from the notice and comment requirements?
2. How might OHSA have modified its rule to bring it within the exceptions for procedural rules and policy statements?

The federal government has attempted to make the regulatory process less cumbersome and time-consuming, more informal, and less vulnerable to judicial review by applying the Japanese style of negotiating with the major affected groups in an effort to obtain a concensus on the substance of new regulations. This process is known as *regulatory negotiations* or "reg. neg." Congress facilitated this process by adopting amendments to the APA entitled Negotiated Rulemaking Procedure.[4]

4. 5 U.S.C. §§ 561 *et seq.*

## CONDUCTING FORMAL ADJUDICATIONS

Courts do not have the time, money, or personnel to hear all cases that might arise in the course of regulating individual and corporate behavior. Consequently, legislatures frequently give administrative agencies the responsibility for solving specific types of legal disputes, such as who is entitled to government benefits or whether civil penalties should be imposed on regulated industries.

Formal agency adjudications are courtlike proceedings that can be presided over by one or more members of the agency or by an *administrative law judge (ALJ)*. The pre-

## HISTORICAL PERSPECTIVE

### FROM REVOLUTIONARY WAR VETS TO THE ENVIRONMENT

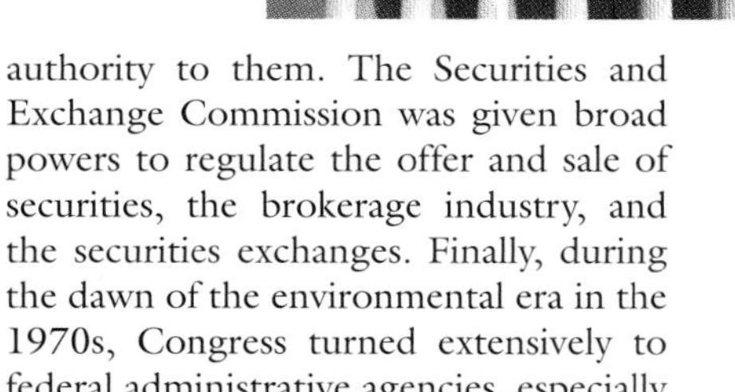

Administrative agencies date back to the country's earliest days. The first Congress established three administrative agencies, including one for the payment of benefits to Revolutionary War veterans. The Patent Office was created in 1790, and ten other federal administrative agencies were established before the Civil War.

At three critical junctures in U.S. history, Congress has made extensive use of administrative agencies. During the Progressive Era, from 1885 until 1914, Congress turned to agencies such as the Interstate Commerce Commission, the Federal Reserve Board, the Federal Trade Commission, and the Food and Drug Administration to solve problems involving railroads and shipping, banks, trade, and food and drugs. In response to the stock market crash in 1929 and the Great Depression that followed, Congress created many agencies to deal with the crisis and delegated broad authority to them. The Securities and Exchange Commission was given broad powers to regulate the offer and sale of securities, the brokerage industry, and the securities exchanges. Finally, during the dawn of the environmental era in the 1970s, Congress turned extensively to federal administrative agencies, especially the Environmental Protection Agency (EPA), to regulate hazardous waste disposal and restrict pollution.

siding official is entitled to administer oaths, issue subpoenas, rule on offers of proof and relevant evidence, authorize depositions, and decide the case at hand.

These formal adjudications typically include a prehearing discovery phase. The hearing itself is conducted like a trial. Each side presents its evidence under oath, and testimony is subject to cross-examination. The main difference between administrative adjudications and courtroom trials is that there is never a jury at the administrative level.

An administrative agency's decision in a formal adjudication can be appealed to a court. Agency actions setting rates for natural gas prices or providing licenses for dams are examples of the types of cases that regularly go to court. In most instances, judicial review of an agency action is based on the *record,* that is, the oral and written evidence presented at the administrative hearing. The court's review is limited to determining whether the administrative agency acted properly based on the evidence reflected in the record. In some cases, the laws governing the administrative adjudication provide for a *de novo* (i.e., new) proceeding in court, where the entire matter is litigated from the beginning.

## TAKING INFORMAL DISCRETIONARY ACTIONS

The basic role of administrative agencies is to provide a practical decision-making process for repetitive, frequent actions that are inappropriate to litigate in the courts. These *informal discretionary actions* have been called the lifeblood of administrative agencies. Common examples are the awarding of governmental grants and loans, the resolution of workers' compensation claims, the administration of welfare benefits, the informal resolution of tax disputes, and the determination of Social Security claims. Informal discretionary action also governs most applications to governmental agencies for licenses, leases, and permits, such as leases of federal lands and the registration of securities offerings.

Informal discretionary actions also include contracting, planning, and negotiation. Thus, the process of negotiating a contract with a governmental agency to supply military parts or to build bridges or highways is within the realm of administrative law. In fact, most of what governmental agencies do falls within the category of informal discretionary action.

The most noteworthy aspect of these informal actions is their lack of clear procedural rules. In court, there is a strict set of rules and procedures to be followed, and a specific person (the judge) is assigned to hear the case. In informal discretionary actions, the agency frequently has no formal procedures, such as notice to the public, opportunity to file briefs, or opportunity to submit oral testimony. Informal agency actions can lead to quick and practical problem resolution, but they can also lead to seemingly endless administrative paper shuffling.

### ETHICAL CONSIDERATION

The National Highway Traffic Safety Administration (NHTSA) estimates that 20 to 30 percent of fatal accidents are due to distractions.[a] According to the Network of Employers for Traffic Safety, distracted drivers cause at least 4,000, and perhaps as many as 8,000, accidents a day. Cellular phones and other computerized gadgets used by drivers are among the distractions that are contributing to car accidents. According to the *New England Journal of Medicine,* a driver talking on a cell phone is approximately four times as likely to get into a crash as an undistracted driver—making talking on the phone as dangerous as driving while drunk.[b]

Most states have considered cracking down on cellphone use; some cities, including New York City, have already imposed restrictions. Some foreign countries, including Italy and Japan, have imposed regulations, but most still allow drivers to use hands-free phones, even though studies show that the conversation, rather than holding the phone, is the greatest source of distraction.

Certainly, large numbers of consumers purchase cell phones to use in their cars.[c] One NHTSA survey found that more than 44 percent of drivers have cell phones in their cars. General Motors Corporation claims that 70 percent of wireless calls are made from cars.

Should the companies that produce cellular phones and other computer gadgets warn consumers about the dangers associated with driving while talking on the phone or using other devices? Should they take other measures, such as designing phones that are safer? What are their obligations in light of the studies that indicate that driving while using a cell phone is as dangerous as driving when drunk? Do car manufacturers have any ethical obligations here? Or should cellular phone companies and car manufacturers wait until the government adopts regulations addressing these safety concerns?

a. Nedra Pickler, *Transportation Officials Hear About Distracted Drivers,* ASSOCIATED PRESS, July 18, 2000.
b. Jeffrey Ball, *New Road Hazard—Driving While Cell-Phoning—Gets Federal Scrutiny,* WALL ST. J., July 14, 2000, at B1.
c. Ricardo Alonso-Zaldiver, *High-Tech Users Told Not to Be Driven to Distraction,* L.A. TIMES, July 19, 2000, at A-1.

## CONDUCTING INVESTIGATIONS

Many administrative agencies have the responsibility to determine whether a regulated company or person is complying with the laws and regulations. They can use their subpoena power to make mandatory requests for information, conduct interviews, and perform searches. Based on these investigations, the agencies may file administrative suits seeking civil penalty assessments, or they may go to court and seek civil and criminal penalties.

Since 1970, governmental agencies have increasingly relied on their investigatory and prosecutorial powers. The indictment and conviction of arbitrageur Ivan Boesky and numerous other financial figures for insider trading in the 1980s resulted from administrative investigations and the exercise of administrative prosecutorial powers.

The investigatory powers possessed by administrative agencies can lead to fines ranging from thousands of dollars to hundreds of millions of dollars. For example, the SEC settled its three-year securities fraud investigation of junk bond king Michael Milken in 1990 for $600 million.

## Administrative Agencies and the Constitution

Constitutional issues raised by the creation of administrative agencies concern separation of powers, proper delegation of authority, and the limits imposed on agency actions by the Bill of Rights.

### Separation of Powers

The U.S. Constitution provides for a legislature, an executive, and a judiciary. This division of power created a system of checks and balances to preserve liberty. It does not specifically provide for administrative agencies, thus raising the question of whether the delegation of legislative and judicial powers to an administrative agency is constitutional.

The few cases addressing this issue have upheld the constitutionality of this "fourth branch" of government. In 1856, the U.S. Supreme Court upheld the authority of the Department of the Treasury to audit accounts for money owed to the United States by customs collectors and to issue a warrant for the money owed. The Court rejected the argument that only the courts of the United States were empowered to perform such activities.[5]

In 1935, in a case involving the Federal Trade Commission (FTC), the Supreme Court explained with approval that the FTC was an administrative body created by Congress to carry out legislative policies in accordance with a prescribed legislative standard and to act as a legislative or judicial aide by performing rulemaking and adjudicatory functions. It found no constitutional violation in allowing an administrative agency to perform judicial and legislative functions. It did not, however, provide much explanation as to why this was permissible.[6] Justice Jackson subsequently stated:

> [Administrative bodies] have become a veritable fourth branch of the Government which has deranged our three-branch legal theories as much as the concept of a fourth dimension unsettles our three dimensional thinking. . . . Administrative agencies have been called quasi-legislative, quasi-executive and quasi-judicial, as the occasion required. . . . The mere retreat to the qualifying "quasi". . . is a smooth cover which we draw over our confusion as we might use a counterpane to conceal a disordered bed.[7]

In *INS v. Chadha*,[8] the Supreme Court struck down a statute that gave either house of Congress the right to pass a resolution overturning a decision by the Immigration and Naturalization Service (INS) suspending the deportation of a deportable alien. The Supreme Court reasoned that the resolution passed by the House of Representatives revising the INS decision was essentially legislative. As such, it required passage by both houses of Congress and presentment to the president for signature or veto.

#### *The Patriot Act*

Libertarians claim that the greatest threat to the separation-of-powers doctrine in American history is embodied in the Patriot Act.[9] Passed by Congress soon after the terrorist attacks on the World Trade Center and the Pentagon on September 11, 2001, the Patriot Act gave the executive branch broad new powers in the name of fighting terrorism. For example, in the past if a federal agent wanted to conduct a search, he or she had to obtain a search warrant from a judge who was responsible for determining whether the reasons proffered by the government warranted the invasion of personal privacy. Now, under Section 215 of the Patriot Act, if a federal agent investigating a terrorist threat wants to search personal belongings, then, "upon an application made pursuant to [Section 215], the judge *shall* enter [the

5. Den ex dem. Murray v. Hoboken Land & Improvement Co., 59 U.S. 272 (1856). *See also* Noriega-Perez v. United States, 179 F.3d 1166 (9th Cir. 1999) (upholding the authority of an administrative law judge to impose a civil fine for violations of the Immigration and Nationality Act).

6. Humphrey's Ex'r v. United States, 295 U.S. 602 (1935).

7. FTC v. Ruberoid Co., 343 U.S. 470, 487–88 (1952).

8. 462 U.S. 919 (1983).

9. Adam Cohen, *Rough Justice*, TIME, Dec. 10, 2001.

order]." This all but removes judicial review of the proposed search.

Conservatives argue that this legislation does not expand any powers but merely streamlines the process to cut through bureaucratic red tape that can cause dangerous delays in the fight against terrorism. The libertarian Cato Institute calls the Act an insidious, reactionary piece of legislation capable of completely destroying the separation-of-powers doctrine that has served as one of the bedrocks of American government.[10]

## Delegation of Authority

The delegation-of-authority issue concerns the nature and degree of direction the legislature must give to administrative agencies. Because Article I of the Constitution vests all legislative powers in the Congress, "when Congress confers decisionmaking authority upon agencies, *Congress* must 'lay down by legislative act an intelligible principle to which the person or body authorized to [act] is directed to conform.'"[11] The Supreme Court has refused to uphold the delegation of power to administrative agencies in only two cases. One case concerned delegation of power regarding shipments of oil between states in excess of government-set quotas.[12] The second case concerned the delegation of authority to the president to determine codes of fair competition for various trades and industries.[13] In both cases, the Supreme Court held that although Congress was free to allow agencies to make rules within prescribed limits, Congress itself must lay down the policies and establish the standards. Both before and after these two cases, however, the Supreme Court has upheld vague standards, such as those requiring rules to be set "in the public interest," "for the public convenience, interest or necessity," or "to prevent unfair methods of competition."

## Limits Imposed by the Bill of Rights

There is very little limit to the investigatory powers of administrative agencies. They must, of course, comply with constitutional principles protecting freedom from self-incrimination and from unreasonable search and seizure. Over the years, however, these principles have been severely eroded.

10. Timothy Lynch, Cato Institute, *More Surveillance Equals Less Liberty*, *at* http://www.cato.org/dailys/10-03-03.html (Oct. 3, 2003).
11. Whitman v. Am. Trucking Ass'ns, Inc., 531 U.S. 457 (2001) (emphasis in original).
12. Panama Ref. Co. v. Ryan, 293 U.S. 388 (1935).
13. Schechter Poultry Corp. v. United States, 295 U.S. 495 (1935).

### *Self-Incrimination*

The Fifth Amendment's protection against self-incrimination does not apply to records that the government requires to be kept. Specifically, the Fifth Amendment protections do not apply to records that are regulatory in nature, are of a kind that the party has customarily kept, and have at least some public aspect to them. In addition, the Fifth Amendment's protection against self-incrimination does not apply to corporations.

### *Probable Cause*

In carrying out their investigatory powers, administrative agencies are not required to have probable cause—that is, reason to suspect a violation—before beginning an investigation. An agency may inquire into regulated behavior merely to satisfy itself that the law is being upheld. For example, the IRS needs no specific cause to audit a company's tax returns.

### *Search and Seizure*

In the administrative arena, the courts have largely obliterated the protection of the Fourth Amendment against unreasonable searches and seizures. Particularly for highly regulated industries, such as liquor and firearms, government regulators can conduct full inspections of property and records almost without restriction.

### *Right to Jury Trial*

The Seventh Amendment right to a jury trial extends only to cases for which a right to trial by jury existed in common law before the enactment of the Seventh Amendment. Because administrative agencies adjudicate statutory rights that were unknown at the time the Seventh Amendment was enacted, the Supreme Court has held that there is no constitutional right to a jury in a formal adjudication before an administrative agency.[14]

# Principles of Administrative Law

## Choice of Approach

In some cases, Congress will require the agency to enact a regulatory program and will provide a deadline for the issuance of final regulations (for an example, see Appendix N). In the absence of congressional direction, administrative agencies have a fundamental right to decide whether

14. *See* Wickmire v. Reinecke, 275 U.S. 101 (1927); NLRB v. Jones & Laughlin Steel Corp., 301 U.S. 1 (1937).

to promulgate regulations or to proceed on a case-by-case basis.[15] The right to proceed on a case-by-case basis is necessary because an administrative agency cannot anticipate every problem it might encounter. Problems could arise that are so specialized and varying in nature as to be impossible to capture within the boundaries of a general rule.

### Authority to Act

Administrative agencies can be compared to large corporations in size, structure, and, to some extent, function. Agencies provide benefits, sign contracts, and produce products. In the private arena, a person acting on behalf of an organization may bind the organization in accordance with not only the person's actual authority but also his or her apparent authority (concepts discussed in Chapter 5). Under the rules for government agencies, there is only actual authority.

The Supreme Court has repeatedly upheld the fundamental principle that government employees acting beyond their authority cannot bind the government. For example, in 1917, the Supreme Court held that the United States was not bound by acts of its officials who, on behalf of the government, entered into an agreement that was not permitted by law.[16] The Court rejected the argument that the neglect of duty by officers of the government was a defense to the suit by the United States to enforce a public right to protect a public interest.

The uninitiated naturally rely on the word of a government employee as to the scope of his or her authority. This is a mistake. In fact, it is incumbent upon anyone dealing with governmental agencies to make sure that the person he or she is dealing with is authorized to act and that the proposed actions are permitted by law.

This rule is intended to prevent personal actions from circumventing congressional intent and the formal process of law. Unfortunately, the rule also takes away the incentive for the government to make sure that its officials know the law and administer it properly.

## Judicial Review of Agency Actions

If the courts control agency action with too heavy a hand, an agency can grind to a halt. If too little oversight is exercised, agencies can run roughshod over individual rights.

Congress or the appropriate state legislature sets the standards for judicial review of agency actions. Some agency actions are not reviewable because they are taken at the discretion of the agency. Most agency actions, however, are reviewable by the courts, but the basic standard of review is highly deferential to the agency. Once it has been determined that an agency has the authority to act, its actions will be given the "highest deference possible."[17]

### Review of Rulemaking and Informal Discretionary Actions

Courts will generally uphold an agency's action unless it is arbitrary and capricious. Under the *arbitrary and capricious standard,* if the agency chose from among several courses of action, the court will presume the validity of the chosen course unless it is shown to lack any rational basis.

Nonetheless, courts will invalidate any regulation that is inconsistent with the statute pursuant to which the agency was acting. In *Ragsdale v. Wolverine World Wide,*[18] the U.S. Supreme Court invalidated a regulation promulgated by the Department of Labor (DOL) that gave an employee the right to an additional twelve weeks of family or medical leave if the employer failed to notify the employee that the twelve weeks of leave provided by the Family and Medical Leave Act ran concurrently with the thirty weeks of paid disability leave provided by the employer. The Court ruled that DOL regulations may not grant entitlements that extend beyond those set forth in the statute and are inconsistent with the statute's purpose. In this case, the statute's purpose was to encourage more generous employer policies, which was exactly what this employer provided.

Courts also will not defer to an agency action when Congress has not expressly delegated rulemaking authority to the agency. In *Food and Drug Administration v. Brown & Williamson Tobacco Corp.,*[19] the Supreme Court looked to the congressional history of regulating tobacco in order to determine whether the FDA had the authority to regulate tobacco products. Because Congress had consistently acted to regulate tobacco on its own, this implied that it had not granted the FDA the authority to do so. The Court struck down the FDA regulations regarding tobacco.

15. SEC v. Chenery Corp., 332 U.S. 194 (1947).
16. Utah Power Light Co. v. United States, 243 U.S. 389 (1917).
17. United States v. Mead Corp., 533 U.S. 218 (2001).
18. 535 U.S. 81 (2002).
19. 529 U.S. 120 (2000).

Although positive actions by agencies often grab headlines, sometimes not acting at all can have just as lasting and powerful an effect. An appeals court invalidated a Federal Communications Commission (FCC) rule requiring larger national telephone companies to lease their networks to regional networks and to long-distance carriers at a discounted rate.[20] Rather than appealing that ruling to the Supreme Court, the Bush administration let it stand, thereby abandoning the existing FCC rule.[21]

## REVIEW OF FACTUAL FINDINGS

An agency's factual findings are determinations that can be made without reference to the relevant law or regulation. The arbitrary and capricious standard of judicial review is not applied to the agency's factual findings. Instead, courts use a *substantial evidence standard* to review factual findings in formal adjudications. Under this standard, courts determine whether the evidence in the record could reasonably support the agency's conclusion.[22] Courts will defer to an agency's reasonable factual determinations, even if the record would support other factual conclusions. This standard of review is similar to an appellate court's review of jury verdicts. Courts acknowledge that the agency's fact finder is generally in a better position to judge the credibility of witnesses and to evaluate evidence, especially if the evidence is highly technical or scientific.

## REVIEW OF STATUTORY INTERPRETATIONS

Courts will generally defer to an agency's *construction* (i.e., interpretation) of a statute within its area of expertise. This permits those with relevant practical experience to have the greatest influence in deciding how to implement a particular law. Although the Supreme Court's position on this issue has varied somewhat, its most recent cases have reinforced the rule of deference to any "reasonable" administrative interpretation of law.[23] However, if "the agency's interpretation goes beyond the limits of what is ambiguous and contradicts [language that in the Court's] view is quite clear," then the Court will invalidate the agency's policy.[24]

In the following case, the appeals court considered whether the Federal Communications Commission had properly construed provisions in the Telecommunications Act of 1996 entitling carriers to a permanent forbearance from FCC regulations under certain circumstances.

20. United States Telecom Ass'n v. FCC, 359 F.3d 554 (D.C. Cir. 2004).
21. For a more in-depth review of this policy decision, see the "Inside Story" for this chapter.
22. Consol. Edison Co. v. NLRB, 305 U.S. 197 (1938).
23. *See, e.g.,* Chevron U.S.A. Inc. v. Natural Res. Defense Council, Inc., 467 U.S. 837 (1984).
24. Whitman v. Am. Trucking Ass'ns, Inc., 531 U.S. 457 (2001). ("The EPA may not construe the statute in a way that completely nullifies textually applicable provisions meant to limit its discretion.")

A CASE IN POINT

**CASE 6.2**
**Cellular Telecommunications & Internet Association v. Federal Communications Commission**
*United States Court of Appeals for the District of Columbia Circuit*
*330 F.3d 502 (D.C. Cir. 2003).*

## Summary

**› FACTS** In 1996, the Federal Communications Commission enacted regulations to require cellular phone companies to implement "number portability" by June 1999. Under such a system, customers are permitted to change carriers without having to change their cell-phone numbers. The FCC reasoned that this would promote competition and improve overall quality in the industry. The major cellular companies, acting through the Cellular Telecommunications and Internet Association (Cellular), petitioned the FCC for a forbearance on the 1999 deadline, claiming they did not have the infrastructure or technology to implement such a regulation at that time. The FCC gave them an additional two years, until November 2002, to implement the 1996 regulations. When this deadline approached, Cellular petitioned for a permanent forbearance but was given only another year. Cellular then brought this suit, seeking a permanent forbearance.

**› ISSUE PRESENTED** Did the FCC's denial of a permanent forbearance for number portability meet the standards set forth in the Telecommunications Act?

**› SUMMARY OF OPINION** The U.S. Court of Appeals for the District of Columbia Circuit began by reviewing the three-pronged test laid out in the Telecommuncations Act for a permanent forbearance. A forbearance should be granted when (1) enforcement of the regulation is not necessary to ensure that the charges, practices, or classifications

*(Continued)*

(Case 6.2 *continued*)

are just and reasonable and are not unjustly or unreasonably discriminatory; (2) enforcement of the regulation is not necessary for the protection of consumers; and (3) forbearance from applying the regulation is consistent with the public interest. The FCC had concluded that Cellular had not satisfied this test.

The court noted that the earlier requests for a temporary forbearance were justified because the need for number portability was low. Competition was high in the wireless industry, and most people were not using wireless phones as substitutes for landline phones. However, the agency recognized that eventually number portability would become important, so it granted only temporary forbearances.

The court explained that agencies should be relied upon to interpret the language of their own enabling statutes and regulations. If the intent of Congress is clear, then the agency must give effect to the unambiguously expressed intent of Congress. If Congress has not directly addressed the precise question at issue, and the agency has acted pursuant to an express or implicit delegation of authority, then the agency's interpretation of the statute is entitled to deference as long as it is reasonable and not otherwise "arbitrary, capricious, or manifestly contrary to the statute." The court ruled that the FCC's interpretation was reasonable and entitled to deference.

Cellular also challenged the authority of the FCC to pass any regulation requiring number portability. The court ruled that Cellular had not raised this objection in a timely manner because it had failed to raise any objections within sixty days from the time the portability regulations were enacted. As a result, the cellular companies had to wait until the FCC enforced the regulations to challenge them.

› **RESULT** The cellular companies were required to comply with the regulations and offer number portability to the general public by November 2003.

› **COMMENTS** The cellular companies argued that number portability did not foster competition and that customers did not consider it a burden to switch numbers. Many cell-phone customers would disagree. In 2003, Verizon became the first major carrier to offer number portability. Its ads invited consumers to join the Verizon network while keeping their existing numbers. In essence, Verizon developed a strategy to attract customers by working *with* the new regulations rather than against them.

Not all cell-phone companies were as eager to comply. AT&T Wireless experienced serious problems in the first few months it implemented portability, sparking more than 322 complaints to the FCC. The FCC launched two investigations to find out why AT&T customers were being told it would take weeks to switch their numbers to another carrier. AT&T blamed its problems on an outside technology company, but several industry analysts said implementing the technology presented "minimal" difficulties. Others wondered aloud whether AT&T was attempting to discourage customers from changing carriers. Soon after rumors of a subpoena directed at AT&T's records surfaced, AT&T fell into line with the other major carriers and complied with the number portability regulations, which had been eight years in the making.

## Review of Procedures

Absent extremely compelling circumstances, administrative agencies are free to fashion their own rules of procedure and to pursue their own methods of inquiry to discharge their broad and varied duties. A court is not free to impose on an agency its view as to what procedures the agency must follow; the court may only require the agency to comply with its own procedural rules and to conform to the requirements of the Due Process Clause. [25]

25. Vt. Yankee Nuclear Power Corp. v. Natural Res. Defense Council, Inc., 435 U.S. 519 (1978).

The reason for these highly deferential review standards is evident: the role of administrative agencies is to relieve the burden on the courts by having the agencies make their own adjudications. If the courts engage in a searching inquiry of all factual questions and exercise their own judgment on policy or procedural issues, then the effectiveness of administrative agencies would be greatly diminished.

## No Right to Probe the Mental Processes of the Agency

One of the most critical points of administrative law concerns the extent to which a court can inquire into the process by which an administrative agency makes its decision. This issue was one of the first decided in the administrative law arena. It was resolved in a case involving a decision of the Secretary of Agriculture that made news headlines at the end of the New Deal era.[26]

The Packers and Stockyards Act authorized the Secretary of Agriculture to determine reasonable rates for services rendered by cattle-marketing agencies. The marketing agencies of the Kansas Stockyards challenged the ultimate price set as too low. The federal district court had allowed the marketing agents to require the Secretary to appear in person at the trial. He was questioned at length regarding the process by which he had reached his decision about the rates. The interrogation included questions as to what documents he had studied and the nature of his consultations with subordinates. The Supreme Court held that this questioning into the mental processes of the Secretary was improper.

Today, formal federal review procedures limit judicial review of agency actions to the record compiled before the agency. Thus, once an administrative process is complete, there is generally no judicial opportunity to inquire into the whys and wherefores of the decision-making process. Without this shield from judicial review, agency actions would be tied up in court.

Although a court may not inquire into the decision-making process, the legislature may. Congress regularly holds oversight hearings on how agencies are administering the law. Criticism from a key member of Congress or a congressional committee can lead to newspaper headlines and changed agency policies. Congress can also use the appropriation process to withhold funds from disfavored programs and to fund favored ones.

26. United States v. Morgan, 313 U.S. 409 (1941).

## Timing of Review

Two judicial doctrines are intended to prevent cases from being prematurely transferred from the administrative arena to the courts: the doctrines of exhaustion of administrative remedies and of ripeness.

### *Exhaustion*

*Exhaustion of administrative remedies* concerns the timing and substance of the administrative review process. The general rule is that a court will not entertain an appeal to review the administrative process until the agency has had the chance to act and all possible avenues of relief before the agency have been fully pursued. The purpose is to conserve judicial resources. A party is not required to exhaust all administrative avenues when that would be futile, however.

In *Harline v. Drug Enforcement Administration*,[27] the U.S. Court of Appeals for the Tenth Circuit considered when the exhaustion of remedies requirement may properly be waived. Harline brought suit in federal district court before satisfying the exhaustion of remedies requirement. Because he believed that the Drug Enforcement Administration's (DEA's) use of an administrative law judge employed by the DEA violated his procedural due process rights to a fair and impartial tribunal, Harline argued that the exhaustion requirement should be waived. The court stated that exhaustion is waivable either by the agency or at the court's discretion where the plaintiff's interest in prompt resolution is so great that it renders the doctrine of exhaustion inappropriate. This occurs when (1) the plaintiff asserts a colorable constitutional claim collateral to the substantive issues of the administrative law proceeding, (2) exhaustion would result in irreparable harm, and (3) exhaustion would be futile. The court concluded that Harline's general claims of due process violations were insufficient to justify waiver of the exhaustion requirement.

In reviewing an administrative agency's action, courts typically will not rule on issues that a party has failed to raise with the agency. In *Sims v. Apfel*,[28] however, the Supreme Court held that an individual pursuing judicial review of denial of benefits by the Social Security Administration had not waived issues she had failed to raise in administrative proceedings. Juatassa Sims had applied for disability and supplemental security income benefits under the Social Security Act. An administrative

27. 148 F.3d 1199 (10th Cir. 1998), *cert. denied*, 525 U.S. 1068 (1999).
28. 530 U.S. 103 (2000).

law judge denied her claim, and the Social Security Appeals Council denied her request for a review of that decision. Sims filed suit in district court, contending that the ALJ (1) made selective use of the record, (2) posed defective questions to a vocational expert, and (3) should have ordered a consultative examination. The district court rejected all of these arguments. The appeals court affirmed but held that it could not consider the second and third contentions because Sims had not raised them in her request for review by the Appeals Council.

The Supreme Court reversed on the grounds that the reasons for requiring issue exhaustion were not present in Social Security proceedings. Although many administrative proceedings are adversarial, Social Security proceedings are primarily inquisitorial. The ALJ has the duty to investigate the facts and develop the arguments both for and against granting benefits. As a result, the Court ruled, the adversarial development of issues by the parties was not essential. Therefore, a party who exhausted administrative remedies available from the Social Security Appeals Council need not also exhaust issues in order to preserve judicial review of them.

### *Ripeness*

The *ripeness* doctrine helps ensure that courts are not forced to decide hypothetical questions. Courts will not hear cases until they are "ripe" for decision. The issue of ripeness most frequently arises in pre-enforcement review of statutes and ordinances; this occurs when review is sought after a rule is adopted but before the agency seeks to apply the rule in a particular case. The general rule is that agency action is ripe for judicial review when the impact of the action is sufficiently direct and immediate as to make review appropriate.[29]

## Standing to Sue

To obtain judicial review of a federal agency's action, the plaintiff must have *standing* to sue. Standing involves three elements. First, the plaintiff must have suffered an injury in fact, that is, an invasion of a legally protectable interest that is (1) concrete and particularized and (2) actual or imminent, not conjectural or hypothetical. Second, the injury must be fairly traceable to the challenged action. Third, it must be "likely," as opposed to merely "speculative," that the injury will be redressed by a favorable decision.[30]

In the following case, the court considered whether an "average" U.S. citizen had standing to sue the Secretary of Agriculture for policies he felt might be exposing him and the rest of the country to added health risks.

29. *See* Abbott Lab. v. Gardner, 387 U.S. 136 (1967) (pre-enforcement review of FDA generic drug-labeling rule was appropriate because the issue was purely legal, the regulations represented final agency action, and the impact of the rules was direct and immediate).

30. Lujan v. Defenders of Wildlife, 504 U.S. 555 (1992).

**A Case in Point**

## In the Language of the Court

**CASE 6.3**

**Baur v. Veneman**

*United States Court of Appeals for the Second Circuit*

*352 F.3d 625 (2d Cir. 2003).*

**› FACTS** Michael Baur is an American who eats beef and other meat. Baur became very concerned with Secretary of Agriculture Ann Veneman's policy of allowing "downed" cattle to be used for human consumption after they have passed a postmortem inspection by a veterinary officer. Downed cattle are animals that collapse for unknown reasons or are too sick to stand at the time of slaughter. Baur contended that these cattle are more likely to have a potentially lethal bovine spongiform encephalopathy (BSE), also known as mad cow disease. Humans who consume meat products from BSE-infected cattle may contract mad cow disease. There is no effective treatment or cure for the disease.

Baur sued Veneman in her capacity as Secretary of the Department of Agriculture (USDA) in an attempt to ban the use of downed livestock. Baur claimed that the British outbreak of mad cow disease had already demonstrated the very real threat of human disease through exposure to BSE—a threat made all the more serious by scientific research suggesting that downed cattle in the United States might already be infected with an unidentified variant of BSE. He also argued that preventing the human consumption of downed cattle was necessary because "current [BSE] surveillance efforts, including slaughterhouse inspection procedures," could provide only limited screening.

*(Continued)*

(Case 6.3 *continued*)

**› ISSUE PRESENTED** Does mere exposure to BSE give a private citizen standing to challenge the USDA's policy on the human consumption of downed cows?

**› OPINION** STRAUB, J., writing for the U.S. Court of Appeals for the Second Circuit:

On appeal, the parties frame a narrow question for us to consider: whether Baur's allegation that he faces an increased risk of contracting a food-borne illness from the consumption of downed livestock constitutes a cognizable injury-in-fact for Article III standing purposes. . . . To establish Article III standing, a plaintiff must . . . allege, and ultimately prove, that he has suffered an injury-in-fact that is fairly traceable to the challenged action of the defendant, and which is likely to be redressed by the requested relief.

The government does not contest causation and redressibility, and it seems clear that if the alleged risk of disease transmission from downed livestock qualifies as a cognizable injury-in-fact then Baur's injury is fairly traceable to the USDA's decision to permit the use of such livestock for human consumption and could be redressed if the court granted Baur's request for equitable relief.

In this case, only the injury-in-fact requirement of Article III standing is at issue. To qualify as a constitutionally sufficient injury-in-fact, the asserted injury must be "concrete and particularized" as well as "actual or imminent, not 'conjectural' or 'hypothetical,' [and] in evaluating whether the alleged injury is concrete and particularized, we assess whether the injury 'affect[s] the plaintiff in a personal and individual way'. . . ."

Here, the government largely concedes, at least for the purposes of this type of administrative action, that relevant injury-in-fact may be the increased risk of disease transmission caused by exposure to a potentially dangerous food product. . . . In the specific context of food and drug safety suits, however, we conclude that such injuries are cognizable for standing purposes, where the plaintiff alleges exposure to potentially harmful products.

. . . Like threatened environmental harm, the potential harm from exposure to dangerous food products or drugs "is by nature probabilistic," yet an unreasonable exposure to risk may itself cause cognizable injury. Significantly, the very purpose of the Federal Meat Inspection Act and the Federal Food, Drug and Cosmetic Act, the statutes which Baur alleges the USDA has violated, is to ensure the safety of the nation's food supply and to minimize the risk to public health from potentially dangerous food and drug products.

Baur must allege that he faces a direct risk of harm which rises above mere conjecture. While the standard for reviewing standing at the pleading stage is lenient, a plaintiff cannot rely solely on conclusory allegations of injury or ask the court to draw unwarranted inferences in order to find standing. Given the potentially expansive and nebulous nature of enhanced risk claims, we agree that plaintiffs like Baur must allege a "credible threat of harm" to establish injury-in-fact based on exposure to enhanced risk. In evaluating the degree of risk sufficient to support standing, however, we are mindful that "Supreme Court precedent teaches us that the injury in fact requirement . . . is qualitative, not quantitative, in nature.". . .

There are two critical factors that weigh in favor of concluding that standing exists in this case: (1) the fact that government studies and statements confirm several of Baur's key allegations, and (2) that Baur's alleged risk of harm arises from an established government policy. Significantly, the USDA itself as well as other government

*(Continued)*

(Case 6.3 *continued*)

agencies have recognized that downed cattle are especially susceptible to BSE infection. . . . Based on Baur's complaint and the accompanying materials submitted by the parties, we believe that Baur has successfully alleged a credible threat of harm from downed cattle.

**› RESULT** The court vacated the earlier judgment against Baur and remanded the case back to the lower court to be heard. Baur had standing to challenge the USDA's policy on downed cows.

**› COMMENTS** The dissent argued that Baur did not have standing because he had asserted only a generalized grievance and could not distinguish himself from the millions of other Americans who regularly consume beef.

**› CRITICAL THINKING QUESTIONS**

1. Should it matter that Baur could not distinguish himself from any other American who eats beef?
2. Ordinarily, a harm must have already occurred or be imminent for a court to hear a case. Baur could not demonstrate such an injury or the immediacy of an injury to him. Nonetheless, the court permitted his case to proceed. Why did the court not require Baur to demonstrate that he had contracted BSE or had almost eaten a product infected with it?

## Decision-Making Power of Agencies

There are a number of doctrines that limit administrative agencies' decision-making powers.

### Only Delegated Powers

The general rule is that an administrative agency may do only what Congress or the state legislature has authorized it to do. Agency action contrary to or in excess of its delegated authority is void.

### Obligation to Follow Own Rules

Not only are agencies required to act within the authority delegated to them, they are also required to follow their own rules and regulations. When an administrative agency adopts a regulation, it becomes binding on the public. It also binds the agency. For example, in *Service v. Dulles*,[31] the Supreme Court held that a State Department employee could not be discharged without being provided reasons because that would be contrary to the State Department's own regulations regarding discharges under its Loyalty Security Program.

At the federal level, one of the most prominent procedural obligations is the requirement to prepare an environmental impact statement before approving major federal actions. The National Environmental Policy Act (NEPA), passed in 1969, dramatically changed the way all federal agencies conduct their business.

Before 1969, an agency could focus exclusively on its substantive legal obligations (the legal rules that define the rights and duties of the agency and of persons dealing with it) and on its own duly adopted procedural obligations (the rules that define the manner in which these rights and duties are enforced). With the NEPA's passage, each federal agency assumed a new procedural obligation to consider the environmental impacts of its proposed actions and the alternatives to those impacts. Each of the hundreds of thousands of federal actions must comply with the NEPA. As a result, each agency attempts to document its compliance as a routine part of its procedures. The agencies have not found it easy to meet these procedural requirements. Hundreds of cases have invalidated agency actions as a result of the failure to meet this obligation.

31. 354 U.S. 363 (1957).

## EXPLANATION OF DECISIONS

As discussed earlier in this chapter, courts will not inquire into the mental processes of the decision maker. The corollary to this principle is that an agency must explain the basis for its decisions and show that it has taken into account all relevant considerations as required by the statute. If an agency makes a decision and fails to provide an adequate explanation of why it acted, then the courts will invalidate the agency's action.[32] In some instances, however, the court may permit the agency to explain deficiencies in the record and to add supplementary explanations of why it acted. The judiciary's insistence that an agency make a reasoned decision, supported by an explanation of why it acted, is a major restraint on improper agency action.

# Finding an Agency's Rules and Procedures

In addition to rules and regulations set forth in officially published documents such as the *Federal Register* and the *Code of Federal Regulations,* federal agencies maintain internal guidance documents. For example, the U.S. Forest Service controls millions of acres of timber land. Its formal rules are sparse, but it publishes a manual and a handbook that contain thousands of pages of guidance on such topics as how to conduct timber sales. The Forest Service's manual and handbook are not generally available and may be difficult to find, but they are an important source of law, agency practice, and policy. Reports of court cases provide equivalent information, but cases decided by agency adjudication usually are not reported.

Finding the rules is just a small part of the difficult task of complying with administrative rules and regulations. A small business typically must comply with more than two dozen regulatory procedures at the local, state, and federal levels in order to open.[33] This task is made even more difficult by the fact that relatively few places provide help to a small business trying to figure out the many regulations with which it must comply. Although the Small Business Administration, neighborhood economic development organizations, and banks may provide some guidance, few private small-business consultants specialize in the regulatory aspect of opening a business.

32. *See, e.g.,* Motor Vehicle Mfr. Ass'n v. State Farm Mut. Auto. Ins. Co., 463 U.S. 29 (1983).

33. Kenneth Howe, *Maze of Regulations,* SAN FRANCISCO CHRON., Oct. 29, 1997, at D1.

# Obtaining Documents from an Agency

In court proceedings and in formal agency adjudications, documents may be obtained by discovery. In other situations, individuals are entitled to obtain copies of government records pursuant to federal and state statutes. The federal statute authorizing this procedure is the Freedom of Information Act (FOIA).[34] Under the FOIA, any citizen may request records of the government on any subject of interest. Unlike discovery, a FOIA request need not show the relevance of the documents to any particular legal proceeding or that the requester has any specific interest in the documents. It is sufficient that the requester seeks the documents.

In theory, the FOIA provides an easy way to obtain documents from a government agency. The agency is required to respond to a document request within ten days. In practice, months, weeks, or even years may pass before the government responds to an FOIA request. Moreover, requesters are required to pay the cost of locating and copying the records. However, these costs are waived for public interest groups, newspaper reporters, and certain other requesters.

Not all documents in the government's possession are available for public inspection. The FOIA exempts:

1. Records required by an executive order to be kept secret in the interest of national defense or foreign policy.
2. Records related solely to the internal personnel rules and practice of an agency.
3. Records exempted from disclosure by another statute.
4. Trade secrets or confidential commercial and financial information.
5. Interagency memorandums or decisions that reflect the deliberative process.
6. Personnel files and other files that, if disclosed, would constitute a clearly unwarranted invasion of personal privacy.
7. Information compiled for law enforcement purposes.
8. Reports prepared on behalf of an agency responsible for the regulation of financial institutions.
9. Geological information concerning wells.

The government is not required to withhold information under any of these exemptions. It may do so or not at its discretion.

From the perspective of those doing business with the government, the FOIA provides an excellent opportunity

34. 5 U.S.C. § 552.

## Global View

### THE BRITISH FINANCIAL SERVICES AUTHORITY

In the United Kingdom, the Financial Services Authority (FSA) regulates the banking, securities, commodities futures, and insurance industries. The FSA is an independent, nongovernmental body whose board of directors is nominally appointed by the Crown. In contrast, in the United States, banks are regulated by the Federal Reserve Board, the Comptroller of the Currency, and state bank regulators; securities firms are regulated by the SEC, state securities commissions, and the National Association of Securities Dealers; commodities futures are regulated by the Commodities Futures Trading Commission; and insurance is regulated by state insurance commissions.

The FSA's self-avowed goals are to (1) maintain confidence in the British financial system, (2) promote public understanding of that system, (3) secure the right degree of protection for customers, and (4) help reduce financial crime.[a] Like its American counterparts, the FSA oversees transactions, demands ethical and legal conduct from firms, and sets standards. Unlike the American system, which utilizes government funding, the FSA charges all firms it regulates annual licensing fees and is thus privately funded. The idea is to remove all subjectivity, such as governmental wishes, to allow the FSA to act independently. The concentration of power in the FSA theoretically allows it to better regulate the country's banking and trading exchanges because it does not have to coordinate with other bodies that may have diverging goals and interests.

a. For more on the FSA, see its official website at http://www.fsa.gov.uk/what/.

to learn who is communicating with the agency and what the agency is thinking about a particular matter. The FOIA can also be useful in obtaining government studies and learning generally about government activities.

Frequently, regulated companies are required to submit confidential information to the government. From the perspective of a company submitting such information, the FOIA presents a danger of disclosure to competitors. To protect information from disclosure, the company should mark each document as privileged and confidential so that government officials reviewing FOIA requests will not inadvertently disclose it.

Each federal agency has its own set of regulations relating to FOIA requests. These regulations must be complied with strictly, or consideration of the request may be greatly delayed.

## IN BRIEF

**Seven Basic Steps for Working Successfully with an Administrative Agency**

STEP 1
Investigate the applicable standards that will govern the agency's actions.

STEP 2
Identify and evaluate the agency's formal structure.

STEP 3
Determine what facts are before the agency.

STEP 4
Identify the interests of others who may be involved in the decision-making process.

STEP 5
Adopt a strategy to achieve the desired goal.

STEP 6
Eliminate any adverse impact on other interested parties.

STEP 7
Get involved in the administrative process early and stay involved.

THE RESPONSIBLE MANAGER

## WORKING WITH ADMINISTRATIVE AGENCIES

It is important for managers to be active, rather than reactive or passive, participants in administrative decision making and processes. Indeed, the ability to help shape the regulatory environment can be a source of competitive advantage. American Express and MCI both adopted corporate political strategies that allowed them to help shape the rules for financial service firms and telecommunications.[35] In contrast, the major U.S. automakers missed opportunities to work with the Environmental Protection Agency to create livable rules on fleet gasoline mileage requirements.[36]

Seven basic recommendations for working successfully with an administrative agency were offered in the "In Brief" above. As recommended in Step 1, a manager working with an agency should first investigate the basic legal standards that will govern the agency's actions in the matter at hand. These include the agency's laws, its regulations, and its internal manuals and procedures. It is also important to investigate how the agency's administration of its laws and regulations is affected by its past history and by current political influences. Agencies, like any other bureaucracy, tend to have biases in how they carry out the applicable laws and regulations.

These investigations are important for three reasons. First, a manager needs to know what facts must be presented in order to prevail on a claim. Second, it is possible that the agency personnel may not know the applicable legal standard. Many administrative agencies have little access to legal advice and find it helpful to have a clear presentation of the law under which a person is proceeding. Third, it is important to know the law at the outset of an administrative proceeding because, under the doctrine of exhaustion of administrative remedies, issues not raised before the agency are generally deemed to be waived if the matter is later brought before a court.

The second step is for the manager to learn how the agency operates by identifying and evaluating its formal structure. Administrative agencies can have complicated structures. Because the power to make decisions may be vested in more than one official, it is important to know all of the decision maker's options before proceeding. A person can start at the top, the middle, or the bottom. The important point is to start at the right place. Finding out where that is takes some effort.

Next, the manager needs to determine what facts the agency already has (Step 3). In a judicial proceeding, the parties create the record by filing documents with the court. All parties have access to those documents and share the same factual record. The same is not true in an administrative agency proceeding. The factual record may be scattered about the agency in different files and offices. To function effectively before the agency, a manager must identify and locate this record.

Step 4 recommends that the manager identify the interests of other agencies or parties who may be involved in the decision-making process. In a court proceeding, all the parties to a case are known; in an administrative matter, the parties may not be designated formally. It helps to identify the people concerned at the outset and to determine how the proposed action will affect them.

Upon completing this background information, the manager should adopt a strategy to achieve the desired goal (Step 5). Investigation of an administrative matter could show that the agency lacks the authority to do what is proposed. In that case, the manager must persuade the agency to adopt new rules or go to the legislature to have new laws adopted. The most significant task, however, is to decide whether additional factual information should be gathered and presented to the agency. The record before the agency will normally be the record in court. The use of experts during the administrative process and the submission of key documents are important.

In reviewing a proposed action, the manager may find that the action would have undesirable impacts on other interested parties (Step 6). Elimination of those impacts is an effective way to avoid costly disputes.

Finally, as recommended in Step 7, the manager needs to participate in the administrative process at the earliest

*(Continued)*

35. David B. Yoffie & Sigrid Bergenstein, *Creating Political Advantage: The Rise of the Corporate Political Entrepreneur,* 28 CAL. MGMT. REV. 124 (1985). See also David B. Yoffie, *Corporate Strategy for Political Action: A Rational Model, in* BUSINESS STRATEGY AND PUBLIC POLICY 92–111 (A. Marcus et al. eds., 1987).

36. PAUL R. LAWRENCE & NITIN NOHRIA, DRIVEN: HOW HUMAN NATURE SHAPES OUR CHOICES 234–39 (2001).

(The Responsible Manager *continued*)
possible time and to continue participating throughout the proceedings. Once set in motion, agencies tend to stay in motion unless they are deflected by an outside force. The greater the momentum that has gathered, the harder it is to move the agency off the path it is pursuing. Therefore, it is important to participate early in the process in an effort to influence the agency before it makes up its mind rather than after.

## INSIDE STORY

## REGULATION OF VOICE OVER INTERNET PROTOCOL PHONE SERVICE

Voice over Internet Protocol (VoIP) phone service transmits voice signals via the Internet or a data network rather than by traditional circuit switch telephone technology. VoIP technology, which has only recently become a practical alternative to land-based telephones, is cheaper and offers more features than traditional phone service.

Unlike telephone companies, which have been heavily regulated by the Federal Communications Commission for decades, VoIP providers use a nascent technology that does not fit neatly into the regulatory scheme created by the Telecommunications Act of 1996, which distinguished telephone service from cable and satellite television service and from Internet access. The convergence of telecommunications with cable television service and Internet access has resulted in telephone companies offering Internet access and discounted satellite television service and in cable companies offering telephone and Internet access. The Yankee Group estimates that by 2008, cable companies will be selling phone service to 17.5 million subscribers, up from 2.8 million at the end of 2003.[37]

As its name implies, the FCC enacts most of the regulations that govern the telecommunications industry, from cable companies to national networks like Fox and NBC. There are five commissioners appointed by the President. Traditionally, three of the five seats are held by members of the President's party.

VoIP service offers a firsthand look at the fine line between too much government regulation, which stifles innovation, and too little regulation, which can harm the public and result in less consumer choice and higher prices. Private companies, state and federal governments, public interest groups, and private collaborative groups like the United States Telecom Association (USTA) are all vying for policies that favor their various interests or what they perceive to be the best interests of consumers.

Experts anticipate a battle between the states and the federal government for the right to regulate VoIP. State governments have historically overseen telecom providers and relied on billions in fees levied on these firms to fund their own universal service plans, which subsidize rural phone service and Internet to schools. The winner will hinge on whether this technology is classified as interstate or intrastate. If, as many expect, the federal government ultimately wins the right to regulate VoIP, then the FCC is likely to play the leading role.

FCC Chairman Michael Powell went on record in 2004 as being in favor of a light regulatory framework so as not to stifle innovation. Ironically, the FCC's first major move was a decision not to move at all. In a decision the USTA says will stabilize the telecommuncations industry, the Bush administration acquiesced in the District of Columbia Circuit's invalidation of the rules that had forced phone giants like AT&T to lease bandwidth to competitors.[38] The theory behind abandoning mandatory access is that regional "long distance" will no longer be marketable if consumers can use VoIP-based systems to call anywhere for one low local rate. Therefore, the Bush administration argued that large national phone companies should be allowed to consolidate their networks without being forced to lease bandwidth to other companies. Experts, including FCC Commissioner Michael Copps, a Democrat, are concerned that the Bush policy will result in fewer phone choices and therefore even higher phone rates.

Walter McCormick, president and CEO of the USTA, argued that monopoly legislation should not be applied to

37. Peter Grant, *Here Comes Cable . . . and It Wants a Big Piece of the Residential Phone Market,* WALL ST. J., Sept. 13, 2004, at R4.

38. Anne Marie Squeo & Almar Latour, *U.S. Sides with Bells in Battle over Local Calling,* WALL ST. J., June 10, 2004, at A1.

*(Continued)*

(Inside Story *continued*)

VoIP because users are free to choose any number of different means of receiving Internet voice messaging, including cable, DSL, dial-up, and satellite. However, a subtle, but no less important, effect of this approach would be to leave some regulators without a field to regulate, putting them out of business. Therefore, regulators at governmental agencies may attempt to subject these new companies to monopoly rules in order to preserve their own jobs.

In November 2004, the FCC unanimously approved a petition by Vonage Holdings Inc., a start-up offering Internet phone plans to consumers, and declared the plans an interstate service. This exempted Vonage from numerous state telephone regulations, including contributing to state phone-subsidy programs and service-quality and reporting requirements. FCC Chair Michael K. Powell declared, "This landmark order recognizes that a revolution has occurred. Internet voice services have cracked the 19-century mold to the great benefit of consumers."[39] The Eighth Circuit upheld an injunction prohibiting Minnesota from imposing common carrier telecommunications regulations upon Vonage.[40]

As of 2004, the House of Representatives was considering a number of bills that could materially affect VoIP.[41] The European Commission was also in the process of transforming its regulation of both traditional telecommunications services and the new interactive information services.

39. Yuki Noguchi, *FCC Asserts Role as Internet Phone Regulator,* WASH. POST, Nov. 10, 2004, at EI.
40. Vonage Holdings Corp. v. Minn. PUC, 394 F.3d 568 (8th Cir. 2004).
41. Cherly Bolen, *Voice Over Internet Technology Promises to Occupy Lawmakers in 2004,* 9 U.S.L.W. 86–91 (2004).

## KEY WORDS AND PHRASES

administrative law judge (ALJ) 192
arbitrary and capricious standard 196
codified 190
construction 197
*de novo* 193
exhaustion of administrative remedies 199
informal discretionary actions 193
record 193
regulatory negotiations (reg. neg.) 192
ripeness 200
sequestration order 208
standing 200
substantial evidence standard 197

## QUESTIONS AND CASE PROBLEMS

1. A statute gives the Department of the Interior the power to allow or to curtail mining within the national forests "as the best interests of all users of the national forest shall dictate." Is this a valid delegation of legislative power to the agency, or is it too broad a delegation of power?

2. Congress recently decided to set stricter limits on harmful car emissions. As part of the crackdown, the Environmental Protection Agency (EPA) was directed to devise a test for all automobiles to determine if they were in compliance with the stringent new emissions standard. The EPA, already stretched thin by many preexisting projects, enacted the CAP 2000 regulation, which requires all automobile manufacturers to devise their own tests for their automobiles. The EPA hopes this will do three things: cut down on the cost of producing its own test, force automobile manufacturers to share in the cost of producing cleaner cars, and result in an even more effective test for emissions.

   Ethyl Corporation produces gasoline additives, but because these tests will now be devised behind closed doors at automobile companies, it will have a more difficult time producing additives that will pass emission standards. Ethyl sued the EPA, challenging the CAP regulation. What arguments should Ethyl advance to persuade the court to strike down the EPA regulations? How else might Ethyl affect the EPA's rulemaking? [*Ethyl Corp. v. EPA,* 306 F.3d 1144 (D.C. Cir. 2002).]

3. In January 1998, the Occupational Safety and Health Administration (OSHA) issued a new regulatory standard for respiratory protection in the workplace. This represented a comprehensive revision of the portions of the old standard concerning the manner and condition of respirator use. The old standard reflected a preference for engineering controls over respirators in controlling employees' exposure to hazardous materials in the air (Hierarchy-of-Controls Policy). Although there were a number of changes, the new standard

retained the Hierarchy-of-Controls Policy. After OSHA published its proposed new regulatory standard, it allowed a thirty-day comment period and held a public hearing regarding the new standard.

The American Steel and Iron Institute (Steel) objected to the new standard because OSHA excluded the Hierarchy-of-Controls Policy from the rulemaking proceeding so that this policy was not open to comment or scrutiny. OSHA claimed that it did not have to expose this policy to public commentary because the policy had not changed since it first came into effect in 1971. Steel argued that OSHA should not be permitted to selectively insulate favored aspects of the standard from public scrutiny and judicial review. In addition, Steel claimed that the facts had changed dramatically since the Hierarchy-of-Controls Policy was adopted in 1971; now respirators might be as effective as engineering controls. Should the public be allowed to comment on the Hierarchy-of-Controls Policy, or should OSHA's decision be upheld? [*American Iron & Steel Institute v. OSHA,* 182 F.3d 1261 (11th Cir. 1999).]

4. The Federal Aviation Administration (FAA) issued an enforcement order to Captain Richard Merrell, a Northwest Airlines pilot who the FAA determined had violated airline safety regulations. While Merrell was pilot-in-command of a commercial plane, the air traffic controller (ATC) instructed him to climb to an altitude of 17,000 feet. Merrell correctly repeated this instruction to the ATC, a standard procedure referred to as "readback." A minute later, the ATC transmitted an altitude clearance to another plane, directing it to climb to an altitude of 23,000 feet. Merrell mistakenly thought that this instruction was for him and repeated the instruction to the ATC. The ATC did not hear Merrell's readback, however, because it overlapped with another pilot's message sent at the same time. The ATC radio system can handle only one transmission at a time; if two transmissions overlap completely, the ATC will neither receive the pilot's readback nor be alerted by a noise that sounds when instructions somewhat, but not completely, overlap. Merrell, unaware that ATC had not received his transmission, began to climb to the higher altitude. Before the ATC controller noticed Merrell was off course and alerted him to change his direction, he had lost the standard safety separation required between commercial flights.

   FAA safety regulations obligate pilots to listen to, hear, and comply with all ATC instructions except in an emergency. Under FAA regulations, inattention, carelessness, or an unexplained misunderstanding, including an error of perception, do not excuse a deviation from a clearly transmitted instruction. In response to claims that the FAA's interpretation of this regulation was arbitrary and capricious, the FAA stated that its apparently harsh regulation was justified in "the unforgiving environment of aviation, in which even good-faith error can lead to tragedy." Should a court reviewing the FAA's regulation uphold it? What is the applicable standard for review? [*FAA v. National Transportation Safety Board,* 190 F.3d 571 (D.C. Cir. 1999).]

5. The Food and Drug Administration (FDA), charged with implementation of the Federal Food, Drug and Cosmetic Act, refused to approve the cancer-treatment drug Laetrile on the ground that it failed to meet the statute's safety and effectiveness standards. Terminally ill cancer patients sued, claiming that the safety and effectiveness standards implemented by the FDA could have no reasonable application to drugs used by the terminally ill. The statute contained no explicit exemption for drugs used by the terminally ill. The U.S. court of appeals reviewing the case agreed with the plaintiffs and approved intravenous injections of Laetrile for terminally ill cancer patients. The United States appealed to the Supreme Court. Under what standard should the Supreme Court review the FDA's determination that an exemption from the Federal Food, Drug and Cosmetic Act should not be implied for drugs used by the terminally ill? [*United States v. Rutherford,* 442 U.S. 544 (1979).]

6. In 1985, President Ronald Reagan signed into law the Gramm-Rudman-Hollings Act. The purpose of the Act was to reduce the federal deficit by setting a maximum deficit amount for fiscal years 1986 to 1991, progressively reducing the budget deficit to zero by 1991.

   If the federal budget deficit failed to be reduced as the Act required, an automatic budget process was to take effect. The Comptroller would calculate, on a program-by-program basis, the amount of reductions needed to meet the target. He or she would then report that amount to the President, who was required to issue a sequestration order mandating these reductions. (A *sequestration order* directs spending levels to be reduced below the levels authorized in the original budget.) Unless Congress then acted to modify the budget to reduce the deficit to the required level, the sequestrations would go into effect.

   The Comptroller, unlike the employees of the executive branch and agency officials, does not serve at the pleasure of the President. He or she can be removed from office only by Congress.

Opponents of the Gramm-Rudman-Hollings Act argued that the Comptroller's role in the automatic budget process was an exercise of executive functions. Because the Comptroller was controlled by Congress, they argued that this role violated the constitutional requirement of separation of powers. Were they right? [*Bowsher v. Synar,* 478 U.S. 714 (1986).]

7. The Supreme Court has recognized that administrative inspections may be conducted without warrants in some situations when a company's business concerns an industry that has a history of government oversight and, as a result, has a reduced expectation of privacy. The Court held that a warrantless search would be held reasonable in the context of a pervasively regulated business if (1) there is a "substantial" government interest that underlies the regulatory scheme pursuant to which the search is made; (2) the warrantless inspection is necessary to further the regulatory scheme; and (3) the inspection program, in terms of the certainty and regularity of its application, provides a constitutionally adequate substitute for a warrant. Based on this standard, would the Court allow warrantless administrative inspections to occur in the following industries: (a) firearms, (b) mining, (c) pharmaceutical, and (d) computer software design? [*In re Subpoenas Duces Tecum,* 51 F. Supp. 2d 726 (W.D. Va. 1999).]

8. James O'Hagan was a partner in the law firm of Dorsey & Whitney in Minneapolis, Minnesota. In July 1988, the London-based company Grand Metropolitan PLC (Grand Met) retained Dorsey & Whitney as local counsel for a potential tender offer for the common stock of the Pillsbury Company, headquartered in Minneapolis. Both Grand Met and Dorsey & Whitney took precautions to protect the confidentiality of Grand Met's tender offer plans. O'Hagan, who was not working on the deal, began purchasing Pillsbury stock and call options for Pillsbury stock. When Grand Met announced its tender offer in October, the price of Pillsbury stock rose to $60 per share. O'Hagan sold his Pillsbury call options and stock, making a profit of more than $4.3 million.

   The Securities and Exchange Commission (SEC) initiated an investigation into O'Hagan's transactions that culminated in a fifty-seven-count indictment, charging O'Hagan with, among other counts, violation of Rule 14e-3(a). Rule 14e-3(a) was adopted by the SEC pursuant to Section 14(e) of the Securities Exchange Act of 1934. Section 14(e) reads in relevant part:

   > It shall be unlawful for any person . . . to engage in fraudulent, deceptive, or manipulative acts or practices, in connection with any tender offer. . . . The [SEC] shall, for the purposes of this subsection, by rules and regulations define, and prescribe means reasonably designed to prevent, such acts and practices as are fraudulent, deceptive, or manipulative.

   Relying on Section 14(e)'s rulemaking authorization, the SEC promulgated Rule 14e-3(a) in 1980. Traders violate Rule 14e-3(a) if they trade on the basis of material nonpublic information concerning a pending tender offer that they know or have reason to know has been acquired "directly or indirectly" from an insider of the offeror or the target, or someone working on their behalf. Rule 14e-3(a) requires traders who fall within its ambit to abstain from trading or to disclose the nonpublic information, without regard to whether the trader owes a preexisting fiduciary duty to respect the confidentiality of the information. In contrast, courts have interpreted Section 14(e) to apply only to situations in which the person trading violated a fiduciary duty by trading. Did the SEC exceed its rulemaking authority by adopting Rule 14e-3(a) without requiring a showing that the trading at issue entailed a breach of fiduciary duty? [*United States v. O'Hagan,* 521 U.S. 642 (1997).]

9. Section 7(a)(2) of the Endangered Species Act of 1973 (ESA) is intended to protect species of animals against threats to their continuing existence caused by humans. The ESA instructs the Secretary of the Interior to promulgate a list of those endangered or threatened species and requires each federal agency, in consultation with the Secretary of the Interior, to ensure that any action authorized, funded, or carried out by such agency is not likely to jeopardize the continued existence of any endangered or threatened species.

   In 1978, the Department of the Interior and the Department of Commerce promulgated a joint regulation stating that the obligations imposed by Section 7(a)(2) extended to actions taken in foreign nations. Thus, any actions taken by the United States would require consultation with the Department of the Interior. The Secretary of the Interior, however, reinterpreted the section to require consultation only for actions taken in the United States or on the high seas.

   Almost immediately, organizations dedicated to wildlife conservation and other environmental causes sued Manuel Lujan, the Secretary of the Interior, and sought an injunction requiring the Secretary to promulgate a new regulation restoring the initial interpretation of the geographic scope. They claimed that U.S.-funded projects in Egypt and Sri Lanka would significantly reduce endangered and threatened species in the areas. Two members of Defenders of Wildlife, Joyce Kelly and Amy Skilbred, submitted affidavits indicating that they had traveled to foreign countries to observe endangered species (the Nile crocodile in Egypt, the Asian elephant and leopard in Sri Lanka) and that they planned to do so in the future. The U.S. Supreme Court ruled that Kelly and Skilbred did not have standing to challenge the new interpretation.

In *Bennett v. Spear*, however, the Court held that ranchers in irrigation districts that would be directly affected economically by a Fish and Wildlife Service finding regarding two endangered species of fish had standing to challenge it. Why did they have standing when Kelly and Skilbred did not? [*Lujan v. Defenders of Wildlife*, 504 U.S. 555 (1992); *Bennett v. Spear*, 520 U.S. 154 (1997).]

**MANAGER'S DILEMMA**

10. Dora Reilly is the executive vice president of DNA in Combat, Inc., a genetic-engineering company based in Cambridge, Massachusetts. Eighteen months ago she filed an application for FDA approval of a promising anticancer drug, DBL. Two months ago she met Gene Splice at an après-ski party and invited him to her room at the ski lodge to listen to her CD collection. After that night, Splice returned to his job as a senior specialist in the division of the FDA responsible for approving new drugs based on recombinant DNA, and Reilly returned to Cambridge. Two weeks after her return, Splice wrote Reilly a letter on FDA letterhead, saying, "It was nice to see your name cross my desk on your company's petition for approval of DBL. I'd really like to see you again—why don't you fly down this weekend?"

Reilly considered requesting that the petition be referred to another specialist at the FDA. However, she is concerned that that would delay the approval process by at least eighteen months. Her chief scientist has advised her that a key competitor is expected to have a similar drug on the market in four months. What should she do? What would you advise her to do if you were head of human resources for Combat, Inc.?

## INTERNET SOURCES

| | |
|---|---|
| The Federal Web Locator, a service of the Center for Information Law and Policy, offers users a chance to search for materials from and about the federal government, including its many agencies and their Web pages. | http://www.infoctr.edu/fwl/ |
| The National Archives and Records Administration's page allows users to search the entire *Code of Federal Regulations.* | http://www.access.gpo.gov/nara/cfr/cfr-table-search.html |
| This page of the National Archives and Records Administration allows users to search the entire *Federal Register.* | http://www.gpoaccess.gov/fr/index.html |
| Cornell University's Legal Information Institute page provides the text of the entire U.S. Code, including the Administrative Procedure Act. | http://www.law.cornell.edu/uscode |
| Federal Communications Commission | http://www.fcc.gov |
| Equal Employment Opportunity Commission | http://www.eeoc.gov |
| Securities and Exchange Commission | http://www.sec.gov |
| Occupational Safety and Health Administration | http://www.osha.gov |
| The Mercatus Center website posts tips about new regulations on its Reg. Radar page. | http://www.mercatus.org |
| The European Commission's website has information regarding the Green Paper on the Convergence of the Telecommunications, Media, and Information Technology Sectors. | http://www.itb.hu/dokumentumok/green_paper/ |

# UNIT II

# THE LEGAL ENVIRONMENT

CHAPTER 7

# Contracts

## INTRODUCTION

### WHY CONTRACT LAW IS IMPORTANT

Contracts are central to the conduct of business both in the United States and internationally. Contract law determines which agreements will be enforced by the courts and which will not. Without contract law, a company could not make plans to move its offices into a new building knowing that the lease gives it an enforceable right to exclusive use of the space for the term of the lease at the specified rent. Similarly, an owner could not rent space knowing that the tenant must pay rent and comply with the other terms of the lease. Employees could not leave their current employers and begin work for a start-up company knowing that the new firm will grant the stock options promised by the start-up when they were recruited. Each of these transactions is based on the parties' expectation that the promises made will be enforceable.

Contract law comes from case law, statutes, and tradition. It varies slightly from state to state. Many states follow the Restatement (Second) of Contracts, which is the basis for much of the discussion in this chapter. Common law contracts include employment agreements and other contracts involving services, leases and sales of real property, loan agreements, stock-purchase agreements, settlement agreements, and joint venture agreements. Commercial transactions involving the sale of goods, that is, movable personal property, are governed by Article 2 of the Uniform Commercial Code (UCC). Article 2, as well as the laws governing the sale of goods internationally and contracts for the sale and licensing of software, are discussed in Chapter 8.

### CHAPTER OVERVIEW

This chapter discusses the elements necessary for a valid contract: agreement (formed by an offer and acceptance), consideration, contractual capacity, and legality. It explains the equitable doctrines of promissory estoppel and unconscionability. Promissory estoppel can, in certain circumstances, result in limited relief for a party who has relied on a promise even though it lacks one or more of the elements required for a contract. The doctrine of unconscionability, on the other hand, allows a court to elect not to enforce all or a portion of an otherwise enforceable contract. The need for genuine assent and the effects of fraud and duress are discussed, as are issues concerning misunderstanding or mistake about the meaning of a contract or the facts underlying the contract. The chapter explains the requirement that certain contracts be in writing and the rules for looking beyond the written terms of an agreement to discern the parties' intentions. It discusses damages for breach of contract and court orders for specific performance. The chapter then addresses precontractual liability, including the enforcement of an agreement to negotiate. It concludes with a look at the conflicts that may arise between a party's contractual obligations and its obligations to others and at liability for interference with a contract.

## Basic Requirements of a Contract

A *contract* is a legally enforceable promise or set of promises. If the promise is broken, the person to whom the promise was made—the *promisee*—has certain legal rights against the person who made the promise—the *promisor.* If the promisor fails to carry out its promise, the promisee may be able to recover money damages, or it may be able to get an injunction or a court order forcing the promisor to perform the promise.

Formation of a valid contract requires four basic elements: (1) there must be an agreement between the parties, formed by an offer and acceptance; (2) the parties' promises must be supported by something of value, known as consideration; (3) both parties must have the capacity to enter into a contract; and (4) the contract must have a legal purpose.

In addition, courts may invalidate contracts that do not reflect a true "meeting of the minds." For instance, if one party is induced to enter into a contract by fraud, duress, or misrepresentation, courts may refuse to enforce the contract because both parties did not genuinely assent to its terms.

# Agreement

A valid contract requires an offer and acceptance resulting in agreement between the two parties. Contract law has traditionally treated offer and acceptance as a rather sterile, step-by-step process. Despite its incongruity with the fluid nature of business deal making today, this narrow view continues to give the rules governing contract formation a formalistic flavor.

## OFFER

An *offer* is a manifestation of willingness to enter into a bargain that justifies another person in understanding that his or her assent to that bargain is invited and will conclude it. An offer is effective if (1) the *offeror* (the person making the offer) has an intention to be bound by the offer, (2) the terms of the offer are reasonably definite, and (3) the offer is communicated to the *offeree* (the intended recipient).

### *Intention*

Courts will evaluate the offeror's outward expression of intent, not his or her secret intentions. Thus, if a reasonable person would consider an offeror's statement to be a serious offer, an offer has been made. This means that offers made in obvious jest or in the heat of anger do not meet the intention requirement because a reasonable person would know the offer was not serious. This objective standard of contract interpretation makes it possible to plan one's business based on reasonable expectations of what the other party's words mean.

Most advertisements are treated not as offers but as invitations to negotiate. Sellers do not have an unlimited ability to provide services or an unlimited supply of goods. If advertisements were offers, then everyone who "accepted" could sue the seller for breach of contract if the seller's supply ran out. An advertisement will be treated as an offer only in the rare case where a seller makes a promise so definite that it is clearly binding itself to the conditions stated. This can arise, for example, when the advertisement calls for some performance by the offeree, such as providing information that leads to the recovery of a lost or stolen article.

### *Definiteness*

An offer will form the basis for a contract if it is definite, meaning that essential terms are not left open. If essential terms (such as price, subject matter, duration of the contract, and manner of payment) are left open, then there is no contract.

### *Communication*

The offeror must communicate the offer to the offeree. For instance, a good Samaritan who returns a lost pet cannot claim a reward offered by the owner if he or she did not know about the reward beforehand.

### *Termination of Offer*

An offer can be terminated either by operation of law or by action of the parties.

**Termination by Operation of Law** An offer terminates when the time of acceptance specified by the offeror has elapsed or at the end of a reasonable period if the offeror did not specify a time. Death or incapacitation of either party terminates an offer, as does destruction of the subject matter.

**Termination by Action of the Parties** The offeror can *revoke* the offer—that is, cancel it—at any time before the offeree accepts. An offer is also terminated if the offeree rejects it. Merely inquiring into the terms of an offer, however, is not a rejection. For example, suppose Cassandra offers Misha a managerial position at $105,000 per year, and Misha responds, "Does that include a five-week paid vacation?" This is an inquiry into terms, as distinguished from a counteroffer, and does not terminate the original offer.

A *counteroffer* is a new offer by the original offeree. A counteroffer constitutes a rejection of the original offer and has the effect of reversing the roles of the original offeror and offeree. Had Misha replied, "That salary is too low, but I'll take the job at $120,000 per year," he would have terminated the offer by making a counteroffer.

### *Irrevocable Offers*

An *irrevocable offer* cannot be terminated by the offeror. Irrevocable offers arise in two circumstances: (1) when an option contract has been created, and (2) when an offeree has relied on an offer to his or her detriment.

**Option Contracts** An *option contract* is created when an offeror agrees to hold an offer open for a certain amount of time in exchange for some consideration from the other party. Under such an agreement, the offeror cannot revoke the offer until the time for acceptance has expired. For example, in exchange for a $200 payment by the offeree, a company might agree to keep the position of general manager open for ten days while the person offered the position decides whether to take the job.

**Detrimental Reliance** Another type of irrevocable offer can occur when an offeree has changed his or her position because of justifiable reliance on the offer. Sometimes courts will hold that such *detrimental reliance* makes the offer irrevocable.

Suppose Aunt Leila offers the use of her Maui condo to her niece Jaye during spring break in exchange for Jaye's promise to fix a hole in the condo roof during her stay. Under traditional contract law, Aunt Leila could revoke this offer at any time before Jaye accepts. But suppose Jaye relies on this offer, purchases a nonrefundable plane ticket to Maui, and passes up the opportunity to rent other condos for her stay. The modern view of this situation is quite different from traditional contract law. If Aunt Leila should reasonably have known Jaye would act to her detriment in reliance on her aunt's offer, then the doctrine of promissory estoppel would make the offer irrevocable. In other words, Aunt Leila would be estopped—or barred—from revoking her offer. The doctrine of promissory estoppel is described in more detail below.

## ACCEPTANCE

*Acceptance* is a response by the person receiving the offer that indicates willingness to enter into the agreement proposed in the offer. A typical example of an offer and acceptance is something like this: Nanci says to Jim, "I'll give you $100 to install my new computer software package and explain how it works," and Jim says, "OK." A contract has been made. Nanci is now legally obliged to give Jim the money, and Jim is obliged to install the software and show Nanci how to use it.

Both offer and acceptance can be oral, written, or implied by conduct. For example, a manager offers a consultant $5,000 to develop a business plan for her company. The consultant begins interviewing key executives and drafting a business plan. By starting work on the business plan, the consultant has accepted the offer. The acceptance is implied by his action, even though he did not actually say, "I accept your offer."

### *Mode of Acceptance*

The offeror is the "master of his offer" in that he or she can specify authorized and unauthorized means of acceptance. For example, the offeror could specify that the offer can be accepted only by a facsimile (fax) to a stated fax number and that the acceptance is not effective until actually received. In the absence of such a provision, acceptance is effective upon dispatch. Thus, if a person drops into the mailbox a properly addressed envelope with adequate postage containing a letter accepting an offer, a contract is formed when the letter is put in the mailbox; the offeror cannot thereafter revoke the offer.

### *Mirror Image Rule*

The traditional concept of contract formation requires that acceptance be unequivocal. In other words, what the offeree accepts must be exactly the same as what the offeror has offered. If it is not, the *mirror image rule* dictates that no contract has been formed.

For example, suppose Alyssa offers to rent to Victor 6,000 square feet of office space in Houston for $60 per square foot. Victor accepts the offer of 6,000 square feet of office space but says he wants ten free underground parking spaces as well. The requirements of the mirror image rule have not been met because Victor's acceptance is not unequivocal. Victor's request for the parking spaces is considered a counteroffer rather than an acceptance. Accordingly, there is no contract.

### *Intent to Be Bound*

Formalistic rules of contract formation often do not reflect the realities of how businesses enter into agreements. A joint venture agreement between contractors to build a hydroelectric dam, for example, can involve months of negotiations and a series of letters, memorandums, and draft contracts. As a result, it is sometimes difficult to determine at exactly what point the parties have entered into a valid legally binding contract.

At some point in the negotiations, the parties will usually manifest an intention, either orally or in writing, to enter into a contract. Such *intent to be bound* can create an enforceable contract even if nonessential terms must still be hammered out or a more definitive agreement is contemplated. The courts will look at the specific facts of each case when determining whether the parties regarded themselves as having completed a bargain.

In general, to determine the enforceability of preliminary agreements, courts examine (1) the intent of the parties to be bound and (2) the definiteness of the terms of the agreement. The great bulk of litigation concerning the enforceability of preliminary agreements with open terms has involved the problem of intent, as in the landmark case of *Pennzoil v. Texaco,* discussed in the "Inside Story" for this chapter. In that case, the court ruled that Getty Oil, the Getty Trust, and the Getty Museum intended to be bound by a four-page "memorandum of agreement" calling for the sale of Getty Oil to Pennzoil, even though the memorandum was not expressly made binding, and the consummation of the multibillion dollar deal was subject to execution of a definitive agreement.

In deciding whether the parties to a preliminary agreement intended to be bound, courts look to a variety of factors, including (1) the degree to which the terms of the agreement are spelled out; (2) the circumstances of the parties (e.g., the importance of the deal to them); (3) the parties' prior course of dealing with each other, if any; and (4) the parties' behavior subsequent to the execution of the agreement (for example, issuing a press release may demonstrate intent).

The parties can make a preliminary agreement nonbinding by stating their intention not to be bound. However, courts will honor such an intent only if it is expressed in the clearest language. For example, titling an agreement a "letter of intent" or using the phrase "formal agreement to follow" might not be enough to prove to a court that the parties did not intend to be bound.

## Consideration

In addition to an offer and acceptance, formation of a valid contract requires that each side provide something of value. The thing of value, known as *consideration,* can be money, an object, a promise, a service, or a giving up of the right to do something. For instance, an adult's promise to quit smoking for five years constitutes consideration because the promisor is giving up something he or she is legally entitled to do. A promise to take property off the market for thirty days constitutes consideration. So does a promise to do a midyear audit.

A promise to do something illegal, however, such as to pay for sexual favors in a state where prostitution is prohibited, does not constitute valid consideration. Likewise, a promise to fulfill a preexisting legal obligation, that is, to do something the promisor is already obligated to do—either by law or by contract—is not consideration.

For example, suppose Brett's Builders Corporation (BBC) has a contract to build a production facility for Hardware, Inc. for $15 million. Halfway through the project, BBC demands an additional $3 million to finish the project. Because it wants the project done as quickly as possible, Hardware promises to pay the additional $3 million. Hardware's promise is not enforceable by BBC because BBC's promise to "finish the project" did not constitute consideration. BBC was already contractually obligated to build the facility in its entirety. This type of situation is explored further in the discussion of contract modification below.

### Adequacy of Consideration

Generally, courts will not scrutinize the value of the consideration or the fairness of a contract. This means that a court will deem consideration adequate—and thus hold the parties to their bargain—unless it feels the purported consideration is nothing more than a sham. Hence, the adage that even a peppercorn can be adequate consideration. The rare exception to this rule is the unconscionability doctrine discussed below.

### Bilateral and Unilateral Contracts

Consideration can be either a promise to do a certain act or the performance of the act itself.

A *bilateral contract* is a promise given in exchange for another promise. One party agrees to do one thing, and the other party agrees to do something in return. For example, Ibrahim promises to give Mercedes $10 if she promises to drive him to business school. The exchange of promises represents consideration and makes the promises binding.

A *unilateral contract* is a promise given in exchange for an act. A unilateral contract is accepted by performing the specified act. For example, Ibrahim promises to give Mercedes $10 if she drives him to business school. Mercedes can accept the contract only by driving Ibrahim to business school, and no contract is performed until she does so.

## Mutuality of Obligation in Bilateral Contracts

The corollary of consideration in the case of bilateral contracts is the concept of *mutuality of obligation.* Unless both parties are obligated to perform their side of the bargain, neither will be. In other words, to be enforceable, a bilateral contract must limit the behavior of both parties in some fashion. If one party has full freedom of action, there is no contract.

Mutuality of obligation applies only to bilateral contracts. In the case of a unilateral contract, the promisor becomes bound only after the promisee has performed the required act. Thus, in the example above, Ibrahim has no obligation to pay Mercedes $10 until she drives him to school.

## Illusory Promise

A promise that neither confers any benefit on the promisee nor subjects the promisor to any detriment is an *illusory promise.* Because there is no mutuality of obligation in such a case, the resulting agreement is unenforceable. For example, a classic case[1] involved a coal company, Wickham, that agreed to sell at a certain price all the coal that Farmers' Lumber, a lumber company, wanted to purchase from Wickham. The Iowa Supreme Court held that Farmers' Lumber's promise to purchase only what it wanted to purchase, which could be nothing at all, was illusory. Because there was no consideration flowing from Farmers' Lumber to Wickham, there was no contract. Farmers' Lumber could have avoided the finding of an illusory contract by agreeing to purchase all the coal it needed from Wickham. Such an agreement is called a requirements contract, which is discussed further below.

Sometimes a party may mischaracterize a unilateral contract as an illusory promise, as happened in the following case.

1. Wickham & Burton Coal Co. v. Farmers' Lumber Co., 179 N.W. 417 (Iowa 1920).

A Case in Point

### In the Language of the Court

**CASE 7.1**
**Dahl v. Hem Pharmaceuticals Corp.**
*United States Court of Appeals for the Ninth Circuit*
*7 F.3d 1399 (9th Cir. 1993).*

**› FACTS** HEM Pharmaceuticals Corporation designed a new drug, Ampligen, to fight chronic fatigue syndrome. Typically, new medicines go through several phases of clinical evaluation before approval by the Food and Drug Administration (FDA) and general release onto the market. As part of that process, HEM began a clinical trial with ninety-two patients to evaluate the effectiveness, side effects, and risks of Ampligen.

Dahl and the other patients signed consent forms that warned them of the experimental nature of Ampligen and its possible side effects. Although the patients were free to withdraw from the clinical trial at any time, if they remained in the study they were required to accept the risks of treatment, to forgo other drugs, to not become pregnant, and to submit to intrusive and uncomfortable testing for one year. In return, after the testing ended, they would be entitled to receive Ampligen for a full year at no charge.

At the end of the year-long study, HEM refused to provide the year's supply of the drug to the patients free of charge. The patients sued HEM for breach of contract.

**› ISSUE PRESENTED** Is voluntary participation in a clinical trial sufficient consideration to form a contract when the participants could have dropped out of the trial at any time?

**› OPINION** KLEINFELD, J., writing for the U.S. Court of Appeals for the Ninth Circuit:

The arrangement with the experimental subjects was that they would participate in the double-blind study for a year. This was to facilitate evaluation of the safety and effectiveness of Ampligen. After the double-blind phase of testing ended, they would be entitled to receive Ampligen for a full year at no charge. . . .

. . .

*(Continued)*

(Case 7.1 *continued*)

HEM argues that as a matter of contract law, petitioners' probability of success on the merits was low, because its promise was not supported by consideration. This argument is without merit. The patients submitted themselves to months of periodic injections with an experimental drug or, unbeknownst to them, mere saline solution, combined with intrusive and necessarily uncomfortable testing to determine their condition as the tests proceeded. HEM sought to have them participate in its study so that it could obtain FDA approval for its new drug.

HEM argues that because petitioners participated voluntarily and were free to withdraw, they had no binding obligation and so gave no consideration. Somehow the category of unilateral contracts appears to have escaped HEM's notice. The deal was, "if you submit to our experiment, we will give you a year's supply of Ampligen at no charge." This form of agreement resembles that in the case taught in the first year of law school.[2] There, an uncle promised his nephew that if he would refrain from drinking, using tobacco, or playing cards and billiards until age 21, he would receive $5,000. The court held that consideration had been given because the nephew had refrained from the prohibited [but legally permissible] activities during the requisite period on the faith of his uncle's promise. He had accepted the offer by completing performance.

In this case, the petitioners performed by submitting to the double-blind tests. They incurred the detriment of being tested upon for HEM's studies in exchange for the promise of a year's treatment of Ampligen. Upon completion of the double-blind tests, there was a binding contract.

**› RESULT** A binding contract was formed when the patients completed the trials, and the court ordered HEM to provide Ampligen to the participants who wanted it.

**› CRITICAL THINKING QUESTIONS**

1. Given that a unilateral contract can be accepted only by performing the requested act, what would have been the result if HEM had unilaterally terminated the trials two days before the first anniversary of their commencement and thereby made it impossible for the participants to complete the one-year trial?
2. Was it ethical for HEM to refuse to supply the drug or to require the participants to litigate?

2. Hammer v. Sidway, 27 N.E. 256 (N.Y. 1891).

## Conditional Promises

Conditional promises often look illusory, but they are enforceable as long as the promisor is bound by conditions beyond his or her control. For example, Xerox promises to hire Diane as an inventor on condition that the Patent and Trademark Office issues a patent on her new photocopying process. Although the likelihood of obtaining a patent may be remote, the decision is out of the parties' hands. If the patent is issued, Xerox will be obligated to hire Diane. The contract is valid at the time it is agreed upon, but performance is not required until the condition is satisfied.

There are three types of conditions: (1) conditions precedent, (2) conditions concurrent, and (3) conditions subsequent. A *condition precedent* must be satisfied before performance under a contract is due. For example, if Martin agrees to buy Josie's house, provided that he can obtain financing at less than 8 percent for thirty years within sixty days of signing the contract, then Martin's obtaining the specified financing is a condition precedent to his duty to buy the house. If the condition is satisfied, he must buy the house; if it is not, the contract will fail, and Martin will not be required to buy the house. When a condition is partially within the control of one party, that party will often have an implied-in-law duty to use its best efforts to cause the condition to be satisfied.

*Conditions concurrent* occur when the mutual duties of performance are to take place simultaneously. For example, a buyer's obligation to pay for stock often does not become absolute until the seller tenders or delivers the stock certificates. Similarly, the seller's obligation to deliver the stock certificates does not become absolute until the buyer tenders or actually makes payment.

A *condition subsequent* is a contract term that operates to terminate an existing contractual obligation if that condition occurs. For example, a partner agrees to sell his share of the partnership for ten times the partnership's earnings unless an audit of the partnership's books shows earnings of less than $5 million. The parties have entered into a contract, but if the earnings of the partnership are less than $5 million (that is, if the condition subsequent occurs), then the partner will not be obligated to sell his share.

Conditional clauses must not be illusory promises. For example, courts usually disallow clauses that condition an agreement on the approval of a party's own lawyer.

### Requirements and Output Contracts

In a *requirements contract,* the buyer agrees to buy all its requirements of a specified commodity, such as steel, from the seller, and the seller agrees to meet those requirements. The parties do not know how much steel the buyer will actually need, but whatever that amount is, the buyer will buy it all from that seller. The buyer is constrained from buying steel from another supplier.

In an *output contract,* the buyer promises to buy all the output that the seller produces. Again, the parties do not how know many units that will be, but the seller must sell all its output to that buyer. The seller cannot sell any of its product to another buyer.

These types of contracts are not enforceable if the requirement or output is unreasonable or out of proportion to prior requirements or outputs. For example, the buyer cannot take advantage of the seller by increasing its requirement to triple the usual amount. The seller will not be required to sell anything over the reasonable or usual amount required by the buyer.

## Capacity

A valid contract also requires that both parties possess the capacity to enter into an agreement. *Capacity* to contract is a legal term of art that refers to a person's ability to understand the nature and effect of an agreement. The widely accepted rule is that minors and mentally incompetent persons lack capacity.

The law's concern is that one party may take advantage of someone who is unable to protect his or her interests. As a result, the law generally gives minors or incompetent persons the power to repudiate their obligations under the contract. In other words, such contracts are *voidable* at the option of the person lacking capacity: that person can enforce the contract if it is favorable to him or her or avoid the contract if it is not. Moreover, in some states minors have the right to avoid their contract obligations and at the same time retain any property they acquired under the voidable contract.

These voidability rules are subject to certain limitations. Both minors and mentally incompetent persons will be held to contracts for necessaries, such as food, clothing, and shelter. Otherwise, no one would be willing to provide the necessaries a minor or mentally incompetent person needs to survive. Both minors and mentally incompetent persons can ratify (agree to be bound by) contracts after they reach majority or gain competency. In many states, minors cannot repudiate their contractual obligations if they misrepresented their age to the other party.

Finally, it should be noted that contracts entered into by incompetent persons have the potential to be either void, voidable (at the option of the incompetent person), or valid. If the party has been legally adjudged incompetent and a guardian has been appointed for him or her, the contract is void. If the party simply lacked the mental capacity to comprehend the subject matter, the contract is voidable. If the party was able to understand the nature and effect of the agreement, however, then even if he or she lacked capacity to engage in other activities, the contract is valid, and the incompetent person cannot avoid it.

## Legality

Contracts must have a legal purpose. Contracts that are either contrary to a statute or contrary to public policy are illegal and are generally considered void—that is, they are not valid contracts at all.

### Licensing Statutes

Many states require licenses for the conduct of particular kinds of business, ranging from real estate and securities broker licenses to chauffeur and contractor licenses. Many statutes provide that if a party fails to have a required license, the other party to the contract does not have to fulfill its side of the bargain, usually payment. This is true even if the unlicensed party performed the work perfectly and the other party knew that the person doing the work was unlicensed.

### OTHER CONTRACTS CONTRARY TO STATUTE

Sometimes a statute will expressly make a contract illegal. For example, *usury statutes*, which limit the interest rate on loans, usually provide that any loan agreement in violation of the statute is unenforceable. In some jurisdictions, this means that no amount of interest can be collected; in some states, the principal amount of the loan is not collectible either. Loans that violate the usury statutes also violate criminal law.

Other examples of *illegal contracts* include price-fixing agreements in violation of the antitrust laws, bribes, wagering contracts or bets in violation of applicable gambling laws, and unreasonable covenants not to compete. To be reasonable, a *covenant not to compete* entered into in connection with the sale of a business must be reasonable as to scope of activities, length of time, and geographic area and must be necessary to protect trade secrets or goodwill. The enforceability of covenants not to compete in the employment context is discussed in Chapter 12.

##  Promissory Estoppel

The primary exception to the rule that only promises supported by consideration will be enforced is the doctrine of promissory estoppel. *Promissory estoppel* (sometimes referred to as detrimental reliance or *unjust enrichment*) provides an exception to this rule only if four requirements are met: (1) a promise, (2) justifiable reliance, (3) forseeability, and (4) injustice.

### PROMISE

There must be a promise. A statement of future intent is not sufficient; neither is an estimate or a misstatement of fact. For example, Hank asks Bart the time, and Bart mistakenly tells Hank it is two o'clock when it is actually three o'clock. As a result, Hank misses an important appointment. Hank relied on the information to his detriment, but there was no promise.

### JUSTIFIABLE RELIANCE

The promise must cause the promisee to take an action that he or she would not otherwise have taken. In the earlier example, when the niece Jaye bought the plane ticket to Hawaii, she was relying on Aunt Leila's promise. If Jaye had not bought the ticket, there would be no reliance, and her aunt would be free to withdraw her promise.

### FORESEEABILITY

The action taken in reliance on the promise must be reasonably foreseeable by the promisor. It is foreseeable that the niece would buy a plane ticket as a result of her aunt's promise. It is not foreseeable that she would quit her job to take a six-month vacation in Hawaii. Therefore, the aunt would probably have to pay for the plane ticket but not for the niece's lost wages.

### INJUSTICE

A promise that has been reasonably relied on will give rise to relief only if the failure to do so would cause injustice. The exact meaning of "injustice" has been debated in a variety of legal tracts, but a good rule of thumb is to ask whether the promisee has been harmed by his or her reliance on the promise. If the niece had made a plane reservation that could be canceled without penalty, there would be no injustice in letting the aunt take back her promise; thus, promissory estoppel would not apply.

The original interpretation of promissory estoppel was that it applied only to gifts, not to bilateral exchanges. A series of cases in the mid-1960s extended the doctrine of promissory estoppel to promises made in the course of contract negotiations. The following case addresses whether a rejected tenant could seek damages from a prospective lessor that backed out of negotiations.

A CASE IN POINT

## In the Language of the Court

**CASE 7.2**
**Pop's Cones, Inc. v. Resorts International Hotel, Inc.**
*New Jersey Superior Court*
*704 A.2d 1321*
*(N.J. Super. Ct. 1998).*

**› FACTS** Pop's Cones (Pop's) was a franchisee of TCBY Systems (TCBY), a national franchisor of frozen yoghurt products. From June 1991 through September 1994, Pop's operated its franchise in Margate, New Jersey. About that time, Brenda Taube, the president of Pop's, had a number of meetings with Marlon Phoenix, the executive director of business development and sales for Resorts International (Resorts), a casino hotel in Atlantic City that leased retail space along prime boardwalk frontage. Taube and Phoenix

*(Continued)*

(Case 7.2 *continued*)

discussed the possibility of Pop's leasing a Resorts boardwalk property. When Taube expressed concerns about the rental fees, Phoenix assured her that Resorts management was anxious to have Pop's as a tenant and that "financial issues . . . could be easily resolved, such as through a percentage of gross revenue." In late July 1994, Taube drafted a written proposal to lease the location, which offered Resorts "7 percent of net monthly sales (gross less sales tax) for the duration of the lease . . . [and] if this proposal is acceptable, . . . a six year lease, and a renewable option for another six years." In mid-September, Taube asked Phoenix about the status of her lease proposal, noting that Pop's had an option to renew the lease for its Margate location and needed to notify its landlord whether it would be staying at that location by no later than October 1, 1994. Another conversation occurred in late September during which Taube asked Phoenix if the proposal was "in the ballpark" of what Resorts was looking for. Phoenix responded, "[W]e are 95 percent there, we just need [Phoenix's boss's] signature on the deal." Phoenix told Taube that he expected that his boss would follow his recommendation and approve the deal, and he advised Taube to give notice that Pop's would not extend its Margate lease.

Taube subsequently gave notice that Pop's would not renew its lease and moved its equipment out of the Margate location and into storage while she began site preparations, including sending designs for the new store to TCBY and retaining an attorney to represent Pop's in finalizing the lease with Resorts. The general counsel for Resorts sent a proposed lease form to Pop's attorney and offered to lease the space for an initial three-year term for the greater of 7 percent of gross revenues or $50,000 in year one, $60,000 in year two, and $70,000 in year three, with a three-year option to renew after the initial term. The letter concluded with the following statement:

> This letter is not intended to be binding upon Resorts. It is intended to set forth the basic terms and conditions upon which Resorts would be willing to negotiate a lease and is subject to those negotiations and the execution of a definitive agreement. . . . We think TCBY will be successful at the Boardwalk location based upon the terms we propose. We look forward to having your client as part of . . . Resorts family of customer service providers and believe TCBY will benefit greatly from some of the dynamic changes we plan. . . . We would be pleased . . . to discuss this proposal in greater detail.

Later in December, however, the Resorts general counsel told Taube that Resorts wanted to postpone finalizing the lease until after the first of the year because of a public announcement it intended to make about an unrelated business venture. In January 1995, the Resorts general counsel advised Pop's attorney that Resorts was withdrawing its offer, orally and in a letter stating, "This letter is to confirm our conversation of this date wherein I advised that Resorts is withdrawing its December 1, 1994 offer to lease space to your client, TCBY." As soon as Taube heard of the withdrawal, she undertook extensive efforts to reopen the franchise at a different location, but she was unable to reopen for business until July 1996.

**› ISSUE PRESENTED** Can a party to failed lease negotiations successfully assert a claim for promissory estoppel based on precontractual negotiations and acts taken in reliance thereon?

**› OPINION** KLEINER, J., writing for the New Jersey Superior Court:

It seems quite clear from plaintiff's complaint that plaintiff was not seeking damages relating to a lease of the boardwalk property, but rather was seeking damages

*(Continued)*

(Case 7.2 *continued*)

flowing from its reliance upon promises made to it prior to October 1, 1994, when it failed to renew its lease for its Margate location. Thus, plaintiff's claim was predicated upon the concept of promissory estoppel and was not a traditional breach of contract claim.

The doctrine of promissory estoppel is well-established in New Jersey. A promissory estoppel claim will be justified if the plaintiff satisfies its burden of demonstrating the existence of, or for purposes of summary judgment, a dispute as to material fact with regard to, four separate elements which include:

> (1) a clear and definite promise by the promisor; (2) the promise must be made with the expectation that the promisee will rely thereon; (3) the promisee must in fact reasonably rely on the promise, and (4) detriment of a definite and substantial nature must be incurred in reliance on the promise.

The essential justification for the promissory estoppel doctrine is to avoid the substantial hardship or injustice which would result if such a promise were not enforced.

. . .

The facts as presented by plaintiff . . . clearly show that when Taube informed Phoenix that Pop's option to renew its lease at its Margate location had to be exercised by October 1, 1994, Phoenix instructed Taube to give notice that it would not be extending the lease. . . .

. . .

It is also uncontradicted that based upon those representations that Pop's, in fact, did not renew its lease. It vacated its Margate location, placed its equipment and personalty into temporary storage, retained the services of an attorney to finalize the lease with defendant, and engaged in planning the relocation to defendant's property. . . . That plaintiff . . . relied to its detriment on defendant's assurances seems unquestionable, the facts clearly at least raise a jury question. Additionally, whether plaintiff's reliance upon defendant's assurances was reasonable is also a question for the jury.

**› RESULT** The New Jersey Superior Court reversed the trial court's summary judgment in favor of Resorts and remanded the case for appropriate proceedings.

**› CRITICAL THINKING QUESTIONS**

1. What damages should Pop's be able to recover?
2. Assuming Taube relocated her family to be near the new store site, should the personal moving expenses of her family be reimbursed by Resorts?
3. Should Taube be able to recover her opportunity costs, that is, the profits Pop's would have earned had she been able to move into the Resorts location in January 1995?

## Unconscionability

A contract term is *unconscionable* if it is oppressive or fundamentally unfair. This concept is applied most often to consumer contracts where the consumer may have little or no bargaining power. The seller dictates the terms of the contract, and the buyer can take it or leave it.

A recent case presents the issue vividly. In August 1997, the State of Florida settled a suit against the tobacco industry for more than $11 billion. The State had hired a group of outside attorneys to represent it in the case, in exchange for a 25 percent contingency fee. The settlement agreement with the tobacco industry called for attorneys' fees to be determined by an independent arbitrator. Several of the State's outside attorneys then went to

### Ethical Consideration

Envelopes for the processing of photographic film typically contain printed language on the outside of the envelope stating that in the event of loss, defect, or negligence in the processing, the purchaser's damages are limited to the replacement of the film and processing. Shortly before Mr. Sam Smoke died of a heart attack, his wife, Sara Smoke, took pictures of him playing with his new granddaughter. After his death, Mrs. Smoke took the film to Photo-Finish for processing. She gave the company her name but did not sign anything. Photo-Finish lost the film. Mrs. Smoke sued for negligence and claimed damages to compensate her for the emotional distress caused by the loss of the invaluable pictures. What is Photo-Finish legally required to do? What should it do?

court in an effort to enforce their 25 percent contingency-fee contract.

A Florida state judge denied their claim on unconscionability grounds. The court stated that a fee of tens of millions of dollars or perhaps even hundreds of millions could be reasonable, "but a fee of 2.8 *billion* dollars simply shocks the conscience of the court." The court calculated that if the twelve principal lawyers had worked around the clock from the outset of negotiations in mid-1994 through the end of 1997, they would be paid the equivalent of $7,716 per hour if the contingency-fee agreement were upheld. The court found these figures to be "patently ridiculous" and "per se unreasonable."[3]

Courts usually refuse to enforce contract terms that they find unconscionable. Unconscionability has both a procedural and a substantive element. When the term is central to the contract, the court can either rewrite the term (for example, by substituting a fair market price) or void the contract. As the "Historical Perspective" in this chapter describes further, the doctrine of unconscionability had its origins in Roman law.

3. John McKinnon, *Florida Judge Blocks Lawyers' Bid to Collect Tobacco-Accord Fee,* WALL ST. J., Nov. 13, 1997, at B3.

## Procedural Element

The procedural element of unconscionability focuses on two factors: oppression and surprise. *Oppression* arises from an inequality of bargaining power that results in no real negotiation and an absence of meaningful choice for one party to the contract. *Surprise* arises when the terms of the contract are hidden in a densely printed form drafted by the party seeking to enforce these terms. Form contracts are usually drafted by the party with the superior bargaining position.

## Substantive Element

Substantive unconscionability cannot be defined precisely. Courts have talked in terms of "overly harsh" or "one-sided" results. One commentator has pointed out that unconscionability turns not only on a "one-sided" result but also on an absence of justification for it. The most detailed and specific commentaries observe that a contract is largely an allocation of risk between the parties; therefore, a contractual term is substantively suspect if it reallocates the risk of the bargain in an objectively unreasonable or unexpected manner. But not all unreasonable risk allocations are unconscionable. The greater the unfair surprise or the inequality of bargaining power, the less likely the courts will tolerate an unreasonable risk allocation.

## Releases

The user of a facility is sometimes asked to sign a general release, especially before embarking on a dangerous activity such as skydiving or race car driving. A *general release* purports to relieve the owner of the facility of any liability for injuries suffered by the person using the facility, including liability for negligence. A number of earlier cases held that the exculpatory language in a general release agreement was invalid because the agreement was unconscionable. There appears to be a trend toward honoring these releases, however, as demonstrated in the following case.

A Case in Point

**CASE 7.3**

**Schmidt v. United States**

*Oklahoma Supreme Court*

*912 P.2d 871 (Okla. 1996).*

## In the Language of the Court

**FACTS** Elizabeth Schmidt went to the Artillery Hunt Riding Stables at Fort Sill, Oklahoma, to engage in horseback riding. Before her ride, she signed a Rental Riding Agreement that included the following exculpatory clause:

> In consideration for being allowed to participate in Horse Rental, I hereby release the Artillery Hunt Center and its employees and/or ride leaders . . . and the United States

*(Continued)*

(Case 7.3 *continued*)

> Government from any liabilities or claims arising from my participation. I agree that I will never prosecute or in any way aid in prosecuting any demand, claim or suit against the United States Government for any loss, damages or injury to my person or property that may occur from any cause whatsoever as a result of taking part in this activity.

Schmidt claimed that during her ride, a ride leader employed by the Stables negligently rode up behind her and frightened her horse, causing it to throw her on the ground and then fall on and injure her. Schmidt brought a lawsuit against the U.S. Government, alleging that it was vicariously liable for the ride leader's action and culpable for its own negligence in selecting and keeping an unfit ride leader. The United States sought a summary judgment on the ground that the exculpatory clause prevented Schmidt's lawsuit.

**› ISSUE PRESENTED** Was the exculpatory provision in the Rental Riding Agreement valid and enforceable, and did it operate to bar the plaintiff's negligent entrustment and negligence claims?

**› OPINION** OPALA, J., writing for the Oklahoma Supreme Court:

By entering into an exculpatory agreement of the type dealt with here the promisor *assumes the risks* that are waived. While these exculpatory promise-based obligations are *generally enforceable,* they are *distasteful* to the law. For a validity test the exculpatory clause must pass a gauntlet of judicially-crafted hurdles: (1) their language must evidence a *clear and unambiguous* intent to exonerate the would-be defendant from liability for the sought-to-be-recovered damages; (2) at the time the contract (containing the clause) was executed there must have been *no vast differences* in bargaining power between the parties; and (3) enforcement of these clauses must never (a) be injurious to public health, public morals or confidence in administration of the law *or* (b) so undermine the security of individual rights vis-à-vis personal safety or private property as to *violate public policy.*

The clause will *never* avail to relieve a party from liability for intentional, willful or fraudulent acts or gross, wanton negligence.

. . .

Courts consider two factors when called upon to ascertain the quality of the parties' bargaining power, vis-à-vis each other, in the setting of a promissory risk assumption: (1) the importance of the subject matter to the physical or economic well-being of the party agreeing to the release and (2) the amount of free choice that party could have exercised when seeking alternative services.

. . .

While courts *may declare void* those provisions of private contracts which contradict public policy, they must do so *only with great caution.* Two classes of exculpating agreements may be said to violate public policy: (1) those which—if enforced—patently would tend to injure public morals, public health or confidence in the administration of the law and (2) those which would destroy the security of individuals' rights to personal safety or private property.

. . .

National jurisprudence teaches that parties *may* contractually allocate the risk of future harm. The exercise of this power is conditional; . . . . The parties must have bargained for their exchange on a level playing field—the level to be measured by the seriousness of the contract's subject matter and the options available to the person giving up the right to sue. If the clause is to pass the test's muster, the assumed

*(Continued)*

(Case 7.3 *continued*)

obligation cannot be deemed to have brought about a result perceived as harmful to the principles of public policy.

› **RESULT** The court determined that the validity of the Rental Riding Agreement exculpatory clause would depend on the outcome of the fact-finding investigation to be conducted in the trial court.

› **CRITICAL THINKING QUESTIONS**

1. Applying the test articulated by the Oklahoma Supreme Court, will the trial court find the exculpatory clause to be enforceable?
2. Would it make a difference if the exculpatory clause had been hidden in a printed form? What if it had been included in boldface type on the front page of the agreement?
3. What types of services would "so undermine the security of individual rights vis-à-vis personal safety or private property as to violate public policy"? Bus services? Those provided by a cosmetic surgery clinic? Camping at a public park that charges a small fee?

## Genuineness of Assent

Even if a contract meets all the requirements of validity (agreement, consideration, capacity, and legality), it may not be enforceable if there was no true "meeting of the minds" between the two parties. In other words, a court will refuse to enforce a contract if it feels one or both of the parties did not genuinely assent to the terms of the contract. The discussion below examines a variety of problems that could prevent a true meeting of the minds, including fraud, duress, ambiguity, and mistake.

### FRAUD

A contract is voidable if it is tainted with fraud. There are two types of fraud: fraud in the factum and fraud in the inducement. *Fraud in the factum* occurs when, because of a *misrepresentation*, or untrue statement of material fact, one party does not understand that he or she is entering into a contract or does not understand one or more essential terms of the contract. For example, if a person was given a deed to sign for the transfer of real property, after being told that the document was an employment agreement, the deed could be voided by the defrauded party.

The second type of fraud, *fraud in the inducement*, occurs when a party makes a false statement to persuade the other party to enter into an agreement. For example, if a jeweler told a customer that the stone in a ring was a diamond, when the jeweler knew it was zirconium, an agreement to purchase the ring would be fraudulent, and the purchaser would have the right to rescind, that is, cancel, the contract. A contract is not voidable due to fraudulent misrepresentation unless the misrepresentation was material to the bargain and was relied on by the party seeking to void the contract.

Another variation of fraud in the inducement occurs when a party has a duty to disclose information to the other party but fails to do so. For example, a partner who knows the true value of a piece of property cannot sell it to a fellow partner without disclosing the true value. The duty to disclose often arises out of a special relationship between the parties (that is, a fiduciary relationship), such as between an officer and a corporation or between a trustee and a beneficiary. Parties engaged in arm's-length transactions cannot affirmatively misrepresent a fact, but as a general rule, they do not have a duty to disclose every fact that might be material to the other party.

*Promissory fraud* occurs when one party makes a promise without any intention of carrying it out. This is a misrepresentation of intent, rather than a misrepresentation of fact. Because a promise to do something necessarily implies the intention to perform, when a promise is made without such an intention, there is an implied misrepresentation of fact that can give the other party the right to rescind the contract. Promissory fraud is a tort as well as a defense to a contract action, and punitive damages may be available if the injured party can prove malice.

### DURESS

A contract is also voidable if one party was forced to enter into it through fear created by threats. Thus, inducing someone to sign a contract by blackmail or extortion is

HISTORICAL PERSPECTIVE

## UNCONSCIONABILITY AND FREEDOM OF CONTRACT

The principle of freedom of contract embodies the idea that the judicial system should give effect to the expressed intention of the parties to an agreement. It is difficult for a court to evaluate the fairness of a contract and to figure out the relative values of a business deal to the parties. Accordingly, courts observe the general principle that they should not substitute their judgment about the fairness of a contract for that of the parties.

Freedom of contract ensures that the law does not unduly restrict the ability of the competitive market to bring about productive and allocative efficiency. Productive efficiency exists when competition among parties seeking to earn profits results in resources flowing to the lowest-cost producers of a good. Allocative efficiency exists when goods and services are produced up to the point at which their cost of production equals their price; at this point, scarce societal resources are efficiently allocated to the production of various goods.

Leaving the parties to define the contract terms as they see fit will result in greater maximization of profit, provided that three conditions are met: (1) the parties to the contract are better informed than the courts about the conditions under which the benefits of the deal can be maximized; (2) the parties are equally well informed and enjoy roughly equal bargaining power; and (3) the legislature is unable to provide rules detailed enough to govern the particular business situations in which the contract was negotiated.

Naturally, these conditions are met more fully in some contexts than in others. Also, public policy concerns must be respected. Contracts that produce results contrary to public policy should not be enforced, even if they enhance economic efficiency. Courts have therefore created exceptions to the principle of freedom of contract and will void contracts in two types of cases: (1) when the three conditions mentioned above are not met, and (2) when the purpose or result of the contract violates public policy.

The first type, in which the conditions necessary for freedom of contract to maximize economic efficiency are not met, may be characterized as involving procedural unconscionability. The second type, in which the contract leads to a result that is against public policy, may be characterized as involving substantive unconscionability.

These concepts date back to Aristotelian theory and Roman law.[a] Under Roman law, each party to an exchange had to give something equal in value to what he or she received. Unequal exchanges were considered fundamentally unjust. In extreme cases, the law remedied the injustice through the doctrine of *laesio enormis*. This doctrine developed from language in the Code of Justinian that provided a remedy for those who sold land for less than half its "just price." *Laesio enormis* expanded this provision to cover contracts for goods whose contract price deviated by at least half from the just price. Under the Roman system, the just price was the market price for similar goods under similar circumstances. The German and French laws that relieve a party from its obligations under a contract that is not for the just price have their roots in the Roman doctrine of *laesio enormis*.

In the United States and England, the general principle of freedom of contract, embodied in the common law rule that the judiciary will not examine the fairness of an exchange, has always been limited by the doctrine of unconscionability. In the eighteenth century, unequal exchanges were considered evidence of fraud in the making of the contract. Courts would refuse to enforce unconscionable contracts, which were generally defined as those involving harsh or oppressive terms of exchange.

The coming of the Industrial Revolution and the emergence of large corporations in the mid-1800s brought about fundamental changes in the mode of analysis of contract law. As goods became more complex, the seller typically had greater knowledge of them than the buyer, and the bargaining power of large corporations often greatly exceeded that of the individuals with whom they contracted. Thus, a greater number of contracts failed to satisfy the "equal footing" condition necessary to make freedom of contract efficiency enhancing. Consequently, courts became less hesitant to intervene to protect the party to a contract who was perceived to be weaker. The doctrine of unconscionability was expanded to cover situations where the parties were not on an equal footing.

**a.** This discussion of Roman, French, German, and English law and certain aspects of the discussion of U.S. law are based upon James Gordley, *Equality in Exchange*, 69 CAL. L. REV. 1587 (1981), and the authorities cited therein.

*duress.* Duress is present only if the threatened act is wrongful or illegal. Therefore, more subtle forms of pressure, such as an implied threat that at-will employees will lose their jobs unless they sign agreements waiving certain rights to employee benefits, do not constitute duress.

Historically, economic duress was usually not enough to invalidate a contract. Early common law provided that a contract could be avoided only if the party claiming economic duress could show that the agreement was entered into for fear of loss of life or limb, mayhem, or imprisonment. Today, however, the courts are increasingly recognizing the law's role in protecting parties from unfair or unequal exchanges and are refusing to enforce contracts entered into under coercive circumstances. As a result, courts are now willing to set aside contracts on the basis of economic duress where (1) the party alleging economic duress involuntarily accepted the terms of another, (2) the circumstances permitted no other alternative, and (3) the circumstances resulted from the other party's wrongful and oppressive conduct. For example, a court found economic duress where a company deliberately withheld payment of an acknowledged debt of $260,000 knowing that the other party had no choice but to accept its offer of $97,500 in settlement of the debt because of that party's pressing debts.[4]

Under the related doctrine of *undue influence,* a court may invalidate an agreement if one party exercised improper persuasion on the other that made genuine assent impossible. Improper persuasion may result from such factors as constant pressure, a need for the victim to act quickly, unavailability of independent advice, or the weakness or infirmity of the victim. For example, if an invalid living alone, with few contacts with the outside world and dependent on a caregiver, agreed to sell her house to the caregiver at a bargain price, a court might set aside that agreement based on undue influence.

## AMBIGUITY

Misunderstandings may arise from ambiguous language in a contract or from a mistake as to the facts. If the terms of a contract are subject to differing interpretations, some courts will construe the ambiguity against the party who drafted the agreement. More often, courts will apply the following rule: The party who would be adversely affected by a particular interpretation can void the contract when (1) both interpretations are reasonable, and (2) the parties either both knew or both did not know of the different interpretations. If only one party knew or had reason to know of the other's interpretation, the court will find for the party who did not know or did not have reason to know of the difference.

For example, in a case involving Mark Suwyn, an executive vice president of International Paper Company (the world's largest paper company), a federal court refused to prevent Suwyn from joining Louisiana-Pacific, a producer of wood products.[5] Suwyn had signed a broad covenant not to compete with International Paper after allegedly being assured by International Paper's chairman and chief executive officer John Georges that the covenant was aimed at preventing Suwyn from going to one of the big paper companies. Suwyn had attached to the signed agreement a note indicating that it was meant to prevent him from joining a major paper company such as Georgia-Pacific, Champion, or Weyerhauser. Because Louisiana-Pacific did not make paper and was not on the list, Suwyn argued that he was free to join the company. Georges responded that the noncompete agreement was broad and included wood products, such as plywood and lumber, that both companies produced. The judge ruled that Suwyn and Georges had such different meanings in mind that there had been no real agreement on the noncompete pact. As a result, there was no contract.

4. Totem Marine Tug & Barge, Inc. v. Alyeska Pipeline Serv. Co., 584 P.2d 15 (Alaska 1978).

### ETHICAL CONSIDERATION

Is it unethical, or just good business, to take advantage of someone's financial hardship to drive a hard bargain?

## MISTAKE OF FACT

As a general rule, a unilateral mistake of fact by one party does not make the contract voidable. This rule has two narrow exceptions, however: (1) where the mistaken party has made an unintentional mistake in preparing its offer that makes the offer too good to be true, or (2) where the nonmistaken party is guilty of blameworthy conduct, such as fraud or misrepresentation.

Like misunderstanding due to ambiguity, a *mistake of fact* by both parties can make a contract voidable. A court's willingness to undo a contract based on a mistaken assumption of fact depends heavily on the particular circumstances. The court will look at three factors to determine if a mistake has been made: (l) the substantiality of the mistake, (2) whether the risks were allocated, and (3) timing.

5. William M. Carley, *CEO Gets Hard Lesson in How Not to Keep His Top Lieutenants,* WALL ST. J., Feb. 11, 1998, at A1.

### *Substantiality of the Mistake*

A court is more likely to void the contract when the mistake has a material effect on one of the parties. For example, in the classic case *Raffles v. Wichelhaus*,[6] two parties had signed a contract in which Wichelhaus agreed to buy 125 bales of cotton to be brought by Raffles from India on a ship named *Peerless*. There were, however, two ships named *Peerless*, both sailing out of Bombay during the same year. Raffles meant the *Peerless* that was sailing in December, and Wichelhaus meant the *Peerless* that was sailing in October. When the cotton arrived in the later ship, Wichelhaus refused to complete the purchase, and Raffles sued for breach of contract. The English court held that the contract was voidable due to the mutual mistake of fact. The court described the situation as one of "latent ambiguity" and declared that there was no meeting of the minds and therefore no contract.

Note that the three-month delay made the cotton worthless to the buyer and thus the mistake was substantial. What if the delay had been only a few days? In that case, the court would probably have enforced the contract. On the other hand, even if the delay had been only a few days, if the buyer had planned to resell the cotton on the open market and the price of cotton had dropped sharply during that period, then the mistake would probably have been substantial enough to make the contract voidable.

### *Allocation of the Risks*

If one party accepts a risk, then, even if it is doubtful that the risk will materialize, this allocation of risk becomes part of the bargain, and that party must bear the consequences. For example, suppose Gerald wants to sell Brandee a house. He says he is uncertain whether the house needs a retaining wall to bolster the foundation. Brandee does not want to pay for a report by a structural engineer. She says she doesn't think the house needs a retaining wall and that she is willing to take the risk of being wrong about that if Gerald will lower the selling price. They sign a contract to this effect. Structural damage is subsequently discovered. The parties have allocated the risk of a mistake about the need for a retaining wall, and the contract is valid.

If the parties have not expressly allocated a risk, sometimes a court will place the risk on the party who had access to the most information. In other cases, the court might impose the risk on the party better able to bear it.

### *Timing*

The party alleging a mistake of fact must give prompt notice when the mistake is discovered. If too much time passes before the other party is notified, undoing the contract might create more problems than letting it stand.

## MISTAKE OF JUDGMENT

A *mistake of judgment* occurs when the parties make an erroneous assessment about some aspect of what is bargained for. For example, in a futures contract a seller agrees to sell a buyer a crop of sugar in three months at a price of fifty cents per pound. The seller is betting that the market price in three months will be less than fifty cents. The buyer is betting that the market price will be higher. One of them will be mistaken, but the futures contract will still be valid. This is a mistake of judgment. Such a mistake is not a valid defense to enforcement of the contract.

The line between judgment and fact can sometimes be unclear. In two recent cases, the courts found that parties had made mistakes of judgment despite their attempts to characterize their actions as mistakes of fact. In *CTA, Inc. v. United States*,[7] a company that entered into a contract to provide technical support services to the government included labor rates for its workers that were substantially lower than the market rates. After realizing this discrepancy, the company argued that it had made a mistake in the numbers contained in the labor rates set forth in its bid. The court rejected this argument and found that the company had made an error in business judgment, not a mistake of fact. Similarly, in *Bissell Homecare, Inc. v. Oreck Corp.*,[8] the court rejected the plaintiff's argument that a settlement agreement had to be reformed because Bissell had made a mistake in the amount of equipment that Oreck had to purchase under the terms of the contract. The court found that the company had made a business judgment, not a mistake of fact, in providing an estimate rather than a more precise calculation of the amount of inventory to be purchased.

In a classic case, a seller agreed to sell a barren cow for a low price, but before the sale closed, the seller discovered the cow was pregnant and therefore was worth about ten times the agreed-on price. As a result, the seller refused to proceed with the sale, and the buyer sued for breach of contract. The Michigan Supreme Court held that the contract was based on a mutual mistake of fact that made the contract unenforceable.[9] The court reasoned:

> If there is a difference or misapprehension as to the substance of the thing bargained for; if the thing actually delivered or received is different in substance from the

6. 159 Eng. Rep. 375 (Exch. 1864).

7. 44 Fed. Cl. 684 (Fed. 1999).

8. 243 F.3d 563 (Fed. Cir. 2000).

9. Sherwood v. Walker, 33 N.W. 919 (Mich. 1887).

> thing bargained for, and intended to be sold, then there is no contract. . . . A barren cow is substantially a different creature than a breeding one.

A dissenting judge pointed out that the buyer had believed the cow could be made to breed, in spite of the seller's statements to the contrary, and had decided to take a chance on the purchase. He reasoned:

> There was no mistake of any material fact by either of the parties in the case as would license the vendors to rescind. . . . As to the quality of the animal, subsequently developed, both parties were equally ignorant, and as to this each party took his chances. If this were not the law, there would be no safety in purchasing this kind of stock.

It is unclear whether the assumption that the cow was barren was an assumption of fact or of judgment. As the majority and dissenting opinions in the Michigan case demonstrate, different judges reach different conclusions.

Much of contract law comes down to the expectations of the parties involved. In the cow case, the seller did not consider the possibility that the cow was fertile. The buyer did not make known his secret belief that the cow could be made to breed. From the seller's point of view, the transaction was for a barren cow with no chance of breeding. However, the buyer did not see the transaction that way. The case might have come out differently if the buyer had explicitly said to the seller, "I know you believe the cow is barren, but I believe she can be made to breed, and I'm willing to take the chance in buying her."

Disclosing all expectations may make for firm contracts, but it is not the most effective negotiating technique. If the seller believes a cow is fertile, he or she will demand a higher price. Why pay the higher price when the vast majority of business transactions are completed without any need to do battle in the courtroom? One of the challenges of business is balancing the slim (but expensive) chances of litigation against the desire to capture value not apparent to the other party.

## Statute of Frauds

Although most oral contracts are enforceable, many states have statutes requiring certain types of contracts to be evidenced by some form of written communication. Such a statute is called a *statute of frauds.* If a contract covered by the statute is oral, it is still valid, but the courts will not enforce it if the statute of frauds is raised as a defense. Therefore, if neither party raises the issue, the contract will be enforced. Similarly, even if the party seeking to enforce the contract has not signed anything, it can still enforce the contract against a party who has signed a writing embodying the essential terms of the deal.

There are four traditional justifications for requiring certain contracts to be evidenced by writing. First, requiring a written document avoids fraudulent claims that an oral contract was made. Second, the existence of a written document avoids fraudulent claims as to the terms of the contract. Third, the statute encourages persons to put their agreements in writing, thereby reducing the risk of future misunderstandings. Fourth, the writing required by the statute has the psychological effect of reinforcing the importance of the parties' decision to enter into a contract.

### Transactions Subject to the Statute of Frauds

Contracts that must be evidenced by some writing include (1) a contract for the transfer of any interest in real property (such as a deed, lease, or option to buy); (2) a promise to pay the debt of another person; (3) an agreement that by its terms cannot be performed within a year; and (4) a *prenuptial agreement* (that is, an agreement entered into before marriage that sets forth the manner in which the parties' assets will be distributed and the support to which each party will be entitled in the event of divorce).

The statute-of-frauds issue that arises most often in litigation is whether a contract can by its terms be performed in one year. If it cannot—that is, if the contract is longer than one year in duration—then it must be put in writing to be enforceable.

A typical "performed within one year" case involves an oral promise of "lifetime employment." For example, *McInerney v. Charter Golf, Inc.*[10] involved a golf-apparel sales representative who received an offer to join a rival company, which promised to pay him an 8 percent commission. When notified of this offer, his employer orally promised to guarantee the sales rep a 10 percent commission "for the remainder of his life," subject to discharge only for dishonesty or disability. The sales rep accepted this offer and passed up the rival's offer. When he was fired three years later, he sued for breach of contract.

The Illinois Supreme Court ruled that a lifetime employment contract is intended to be permanent. It inherently anticipates a relationship of long duration—certainly longer than one year. Thus, the court found that the contract was subject to the statute of frauds and unenforceable because it was not put in writing.

Other courts have taken a contrasting approach and construe the words "cannot be performed" to mean "not

10. 680 N.E.2d 1347 (Ill. 1997).

### ETHICAL CONSIDERATION

Is it ethical for a manager to raise the defense of failure to comply with the statute of frauds to avoid enforcement of an oral promise that the manager knows he or she made?

capable of being performed within one year." Because, theoretically, an employee can die at any time, these courts reason that lifetime employment contracts are *capable* of being performed within one year. As a result, they deem such contracts to be outside the scope of the statute of frauds and valid even if not put in writing.

The statute of frauds does not require the agreement to be embodied in a formal, legal-looking document. An agreement can be represented by an exchange of letters that refer to each other, even if no single letter is sufficient to reflect all essential terms. Details or particulars can be omitted; only the essential terms must be stated. A writing may satisfy the statute of frauds even if the party never delivers or communicates it to the other party. What is essential depends on the agreement, its context, and the subsequent conduct of the parties. Under the *equal dignities rule,* if an agent acts on behalf of another (the principal) in signing an agreement of the type that must, under the statute of frauds, be in writing, the authority of the agent to act on behalf of the principal must also be in writing. Thus, an individual signs a written *power of attorney* to authorize a person, called an attorney-in-fact (who need not be a lawyer), to sign documents on the individual's behalf. Corporations authorize officers to sign through a combination of written authority specified in the bylaws of the corporation and the minutes of the governing body, the board of directors.

If there is clear evidence that a person made an oral promise, a court will strain to recharacterize the nature of the agreement so that it does not come within the statute of frauds.[11] One cannot count on such leniency, however, so the prudent manager will put any and all agreements that might fall within the statute of frauds in writing.

## The Parol Evidence Rule

If a contract is in writing, when will a court go beyond the words of the contract and look to other evidence to ascertain the intent of the parties? Under the *parol evidence rule,* when there is a written contract that the parties intended would encompass their entire agreement, parol (that is, oral) evidence of prior or contemporaneous statements will not be permitted to alter the terms of the contract. Such extrinsic evidence is inadmissible in court and cannot be used to interpret, vary, or add to the terms of an unambiguous written contract that purports to be the entire agreement of the parties. A court will usually not look beyond the "four corners" of the document to discern the intentions of the parties.

For example, in *White v. Security Pacific Financial Services, Inc.,*[12] the borrower plaintiffs tried to introduce evidence that the lender defendant had fraudulently induced them to execute a promissory note by assuring them that its sole recourse upon default would be under a deed of trust that collateralized the loan. The court found that this evidence could not be admitted because it contradicted the parties' written agreement.

### CLARIFYING AMBIGUOUS LANGUAGE

The parol evidence rule does not prohibit presenting evidence to show what the contract means. Thus, courts are willing to look beyond the written agreement if its language is ambiguous. For example, if the contract stated that a party was to purchase a carload of tomatoes, it would not violate the parol evidence rule to present evidence showing that "carload" in the relevant commercial setting means a train carload, not a Chevy truckload. This evidence merely explains the ambiguous term "carload"; it does not vary the term. Parol evidence is also admissible to show mistake, fraud, or duress.

## Changed Circumstances

Contracts often contain provisions for a variety of future events so that the parties involved can allocate the risks of different outcomes. It is not always possible to anticipate every occurrence, however. Three theories are used to address this situation: impossibility, impracticability, and frustration of purpose.

### IMPOSSIBILITY

Suppose that Antonio signs a contract to sell Trevor computer chips of a special type manufactured only in Antonio's factory. Before he can manufacture the computer chips, however, the factory burns down

11. *See, e.g.,* Wilson Floors Co. v. Sciota Park, Ltd., 377 N.E.2d 514 (Ohio 1978) (oral promise by construction lender to pay subcontractor if he returned to work served lender's own pecuniary interest, so the agreement did not have to be in writing to be enforceable).

12. No. 5079754 (Cal. July 21, 1999), *cert. denied,* 528 U.S. 1160 (2000).

# View from Cyberspace

## Electronic Contracts: The Uniform Electronic Transactions Act and the E-Sign Act

With the rise of e-commerce, more and more transactions are taking place electronically. Until recently, however, many states did not give contracts executed electronically the same legal effect as physical paper contracts. Moreover, laws governing electronic transactions varied widely from state to state.

In 1999, the National Conference of Commissioners on Uniform State Laws (NCCUSL) adopted the Uniform Electronic Transactions Act (UETA) to address the issue of whether electronic contracts and signatures are legal contracts. The UETA serves as a model for state legislatures seeking to implement laws relating to electronic transactions. Adoption is not mandatory, however. As of May 2004, over forty states had enacted the UETA.

The UETA sets forth four basic rules regarding contracts entered into by parties that agree to conduct business electronically: (1) a record or signature may not be denied legal effect or enforceability solely because it is in electronic form; (2) a contract may not be denied legal effect or enforceability solely because an electronic record was used in its formation; (3) an electronic record satisfies a law that requires a record to be in writing; and (4) an electronic signature satisfies a law that requires a signature.[a]

Under the UETA, almost any mark or process intended to sign an electronic record will constitute an electronic signature, including a typed name at the bottom of an e-mail message, a faxed signature, and a "click-through" process on a computer screen whereby a person clicks "I agree" on a Web page. The essential element necessary to determine the validity of an electronic signature is whether the person intended the process or mark provided to act as a signature and whether it can be attributed to that person.

In an effort to ensure more uniform treatment of electronic transactions across the United States, Congress enacted the Electronic Signatures in Global and National Commerce Act, more commonly known as the E-Sign Act, effective October 1, 2000. Consistent with the UETA, the E-Sign Act provides that a signature, contract, or other record "may not be denied legal effect, validity, or enforceability solely because it is in electronic form."[b] The provisions of the E-Sign Act are very similar to those of the UETA, except that the UETA, where enacted, applies to intrastate transactions, where the E-Sign Act governs only transactions in interstate and foreign commerce. Moreover, the provisions of the E-Sign Act are mandatory.

The E-Sign Act resolves the problem of inconsistency among states that have and have not enacted the UETA by expressly preempting all state laws inconsistent with its provisions. The E-Sign Act does, however, demonstrate some flexibility toward those states that have adopted the UETA by allowing state law "to modify, limit, or supersede" the provisions of the E-Sign Act to the extent that such variations are not inconsistent with the E-Sign Act. What variations will ultimately be considered "inconsistent" is not entirely clear and may have to be determined by the courts.

To protect those individuals or companies that choose not to conduct business electronically or do not have access to computers, the E-Sign Act and the UETA require that the use or acceptance of electronic records or electronic signatures be voluntary. Moreover, under the E-Sign Act, if a business is legally bound to produce information to a consumer in writing, electronic records may be used only if the business first secures the consumer's informed consent.

Notwithstanding the broad scope of the E-Sign Act and the UETA, several classes of documents are not covered by their provisions and thus may not be considered fully enforceable if transacted electronically. Both the UETA and the E-Sign Act exclude:

- Wills, codicils, and trusts.
- Contracts or records relating to adoption, divorce, or other matters of family law.
- Contracts governed by certain provisions of the Uniform Commercial Code in effect in each state.

Unlike the UETA, the E-Sign Act also excludes:

- Court orders and notices and other official court documents.
- Notices of cancellation or termination of utility services.
- Notices regarding credit agreements secured by, or rental agreements for, a primary residence (for example, eviction notices).
- Notices of cancellation or termination of health or life insurance benefits.
- Notices of recall.
- Documents required to accompany the transport of hazardous materials, pesticides, or other toxic materials.

Of course, a national standard governing electronic transactions does not

a. David Schumacher, *U.S. Addresses Legal Issues Raised by Electronic Trading,* INT'L FIN. L. REV., Apr. 1, 2000, at 19.

b. Electronic Signatures in Global and National Commerce Act, 15 U.S.C. § 7101(a)(2) (2000).

*(Continued)*

(View from Cyberspace *continued*)
resolve inconsistencies in laws of other countries. Some form of international coordination will be necessary to ensure that electronic transactions are consistently enforced across national borders. Toward that end, an effort is under way to encourage other countries to adopt similar standards.[c] The European Electronic Signature Directive, which became effective in January 2001, requires member states to adopt laws and regulations similar to the E-Sign/UETA approach (although it also contains some special rules applicable to certification services). Some Asian countries, including Japan, have enacted digital signature laws, but to date Latin American, Middle Eastern and African countries have generally been silent on the issue.

c. Office of the Press Secretary, the White House, "Statement by the President," June 30, 2000.

through no fault of Antonio's, making it impossible for him to perform the contract. The destruction of Antonio's factory is a changed circumstance that neither party contemplated when they made the contract.

Is Trevor entitled to money damages for Antonio's nonperformance? No, because Antonio's performance has become impossible, he is discharged from his obligations under the contract due to *impossibility,* and Trevor is not entitled to damages. If, however, the computer chips could be manufactured in another factory, Antonio would have an obligation to have them manufactured there after his factory burned down. This would be the case even if it costs Antonio more money to manufacture them at another facility.

## Impracticability

Closely related to impossibility is the concept of *impracticability,* where performance is possible but commercially impractical. As a rule, impracticability is difficult to prove.

Impracticability was invoked by several shipping companies in 1967 when political turmoil in the Middle East gave rise to the temporary closing of the Suez Canal. A number of merchant ships had to detour around the Cape of Good Hope at the southern tip of Africa. The detour increased shipping costs so much that the shipping companies suffered substantial losses. Several of these companies sued to nullify the contracts they had entered into before the Suez Canal was closed. They claimed performance was impractical and sought to recover the full costs of sailing the longer route around the Cape of Good Hope. In only one case did the court grant relief. The other courts found that the added costs were not so great as to make performance impracticable. (Chapter 8 addresses impracticability in contracts for the sale of goods.)

When changed circumstances make performance of a contract more difficult, a party to the contract may wish to seek assurances that the other party can still perform despite the new difficulties. In the following case, the New York Court of Appeals considered whether one party can demand adequate assurances from the other party if there is reason to be concerned that the party may breach the contract.

A Case in Point

### In the Language of the Court

**CASE 7.4**

**Norcon Power Partners, L.P. v. Niagara Mohawk Power Corp.**

*New York Court of Appeals*
*705 N.E.2d 656*
*(N.Y. 1998).*

› **FACTS** In 1989, Norcon Power Partners, L.P., an independent power producer, entered into a contract with Niagara Mohawk Power Corporation, a public utility provider, whereby Niagara Mohawk agreed to purchase electricity generated at Norcon's Pennsylvania facility for a period of twenty-five years. There were three pricing periods under the contract. In the first period, Niagara Mohawk paid six cents per kilowatt-hour for electricity. In the second and third periods, the price paid by Niagara Mohawk was based on "avoided cost," which was calculated using the cost that Niagara Mohawk would incur to generate electricity itself or to purchase it from other sources. In the second period, Niagara Mohawk's payments were capped by a ceiling price. In the third period, the price paid by Niagara Mohawk was not subject to a cap or a floor. Payments made by Niagara Mohawk in the third period were adjusted to account for any balance existing in the adjustment account that operated in the second period.

*(Continued)*

(Case 7.4 *continued*)

In February 1994, Niagara Mohawk wrote to Norcon stating that, based on revised avoided cost estimates, substantial credits in Niagara Mohawk's favor would occur in the adjustment account during the second pricing period. As a result, the company's analysis reflected that the cumulative avoided cost account would reach over $610 million by the end of the second period. Concerned that Norcon would be unable to satisfy the escalating credits in the third period, Niagara Mohawk demanded that Norcon provide adequate assurance to Niagara Mohawk that it would duly perform all of its future repayment obligations. Norcon sued Niagara Mohawk, seeking a declaration that Niagara Mohawk had no contractual right to demand adequate assurance.

The district court found that New York common law recognizes the doctrine of demand for adequate assurance only when a promisor becomes insolvent or when the contract involves a sale of goods and is therefore governed by the Uniform Commercial Code. The decision was appealed to the U.S. Court of Appeals for the Second Circuit, which certified the question to the New York Court of Appeals for assistance in the correct application of New York law.

**› ISSUE PRESENTED** Can a party demand adequate assurance of future performance when reasonable grounds arise to believe that the other party will commit a breach by nonperformance of a contract governed by New York law, when the other party is solvent and the contract is not governed by the Uniform Commercial Code?

**› OPINION** BELLACOSA, J., writing for the New York Court of Appeals:

This Court is . . . persuaded that the policies underlying the UCC 2–609 counterpart should apply with similar cogency for the resolution of this kind of controversy. [*Ed.:* Section 2-609 of the UCC provides that a party to a contract for the sale of goods has the right to demand assurances of future performance from the other party when grounds for insecurity exist. If no such assurances are provided, the party may assume that a repudiation has occurred.] A useful analogy can be drawn between the contract at issue and a contract for the sale of goods. If the contract here was in all respects the same, except that it was for the sale of oil or some other tangible commodity instead of the sale of electricity, the parties would unquestionably be governed by the demand for adequate assurance of performance factors in UCC 2–609. We are convinced to take this prudent step because it puts commercial parties in these kinds of disputes at relatively arms length equilibrium in terms of reliability and uniformity of governing legal rubrics. The availability of the doctrine may even provide an incentive and tool for parties to resolve their own differences, perhaps without the necessity of judicial intervention. Open, serious re-negotiation of dramatic developments and changes in unusual contractual expectations and qualifying circumstances would occur because of and with an eye to the doctrine's application.

The various authorities, factors and concerns, in sum, prompt the prudence and awareness of the usefulness of recognizing the extension of the doctrine of demand for adequate assurance, as a common law analogue. It should apply to the type of long-term commercial contract between corporate entities entered into by Norcon and Niagara Mohawk here, which is complex and not reasonably susceptible of all security features being anticipated, bargained for and incorporated in the original contract. Norcon's performance, in terms of reimbursing Niagara Mohawk for credits, is still years away. In the meantime, potential quantifiable damages are accumulating and Niagara Mohawk must weigh the hard choices and serious consequences that the doctrine of demand for adequate assurance is designed to mitigate.

*(Continued)*

(Case 7.4 *continued*)

**› RESULT** The New York Court of Appeals found that the doctrine of adequate assurance of future performance should be incorporated into New York common law and applied to long-term commercial contracts between corporate entities.

**› CRITICAL THINKING QUESTIONS**

1. Are there circumstances in which it would be appropriate to permit a party to demand adequate assurance of future performance under a contract for sale of goods but not under a contract for services?
2. Why did the court limit its holding to long-term commercial contracts between corporate entities?

### FRUSTRATION OF PURPOSE

*Frustration of purpose* occurs when performance is possible, but changed circumstances have made the contract useless to one or both of the parties. A famous example is the King Edward VII coronation case.[13] Henry contracted to rent a room in London from Krell for the acknowledged purpose of viewing King Edward VII's coronation procession. Krell had advertised the room as one that would be good for viewing the coronation. When the King became ill with appendicitis and the coronation was postponed, Henry refused to pay for the apartment. Krell sued. The English court ruled that Henry did not have to pay because the entire reason for the contract had been "frustrated."

Note that performance of the contract was not impossible: Henry could still have rented the room. The outcome of the case would have been different if the room had not been rented for the express purpose of viewing the coronation. In that case, Krell would have won because the purpose of the contract would have been for just the rental of the room, not for the viewing of the coronation.

The contract defense of frustration requires that (1) the parties' principal purpose in making the contract is frustrated, (2) without that party's fault, (3) by the occurrence of an event, the nonoccurrence of which was a basic assumption on which the contract was made. For performance to be excused, this frustration of purpose must have occurred without the defendant's fault. The defense of frustration is unavailable if the defendant helped cause the frustrating event or if the parties were aware of the possibility of the frustrating event when they entered into the contract.

13. Krell v. Henry, 2 K.B. 740 (C.A. 1903).

### CONTRACTS WITH THE GOVERNMENT AND THE SOVEREIGN ACTS DOCTRINE

Changes in the law can also affect contracts. When a party's performance is made illegal or impossible because of a new law, performance of the contract is usually discharged, and damages are not awarded. But what happens when a party contracts with the government, and the government then promulgates a new law making its own performance impossible? If it no longer wishes to follow a contract, can the government simply change the law to make performance illegal, thereby discharging its obligations?

According to the *sovereign acts doctrine*, the government cannot be held liable for breach of contract due to legislative or executive acts. Because one Congress cannot bind a later Congress, the general rule is that subsequent acts of the government can discharge the government's preexisting contractual obligations.

This doctrine has limits, however. If Congress passes legislation deliberately targeting its extant contractual obligations, the defense otherwise provided by the sovereign acts doctrine is unavailable.[14] In that situation, the government is not prevented from changing the law, but must pay damages for its legislatively chosen breach. On the other hand, if a new law of general application indirectly affects a government contract and makes the government's performance impossible, the sovereign acts doctrine will protect the government in a subsequent suit for breach of the contract.

## Contract Modification

Traditional contract law does not allow a contract to be modified if the modification would change the obligations of only one party. Under this view, no consideration has

14. United States v. Winstar, 518 U.S. 839 (1996).

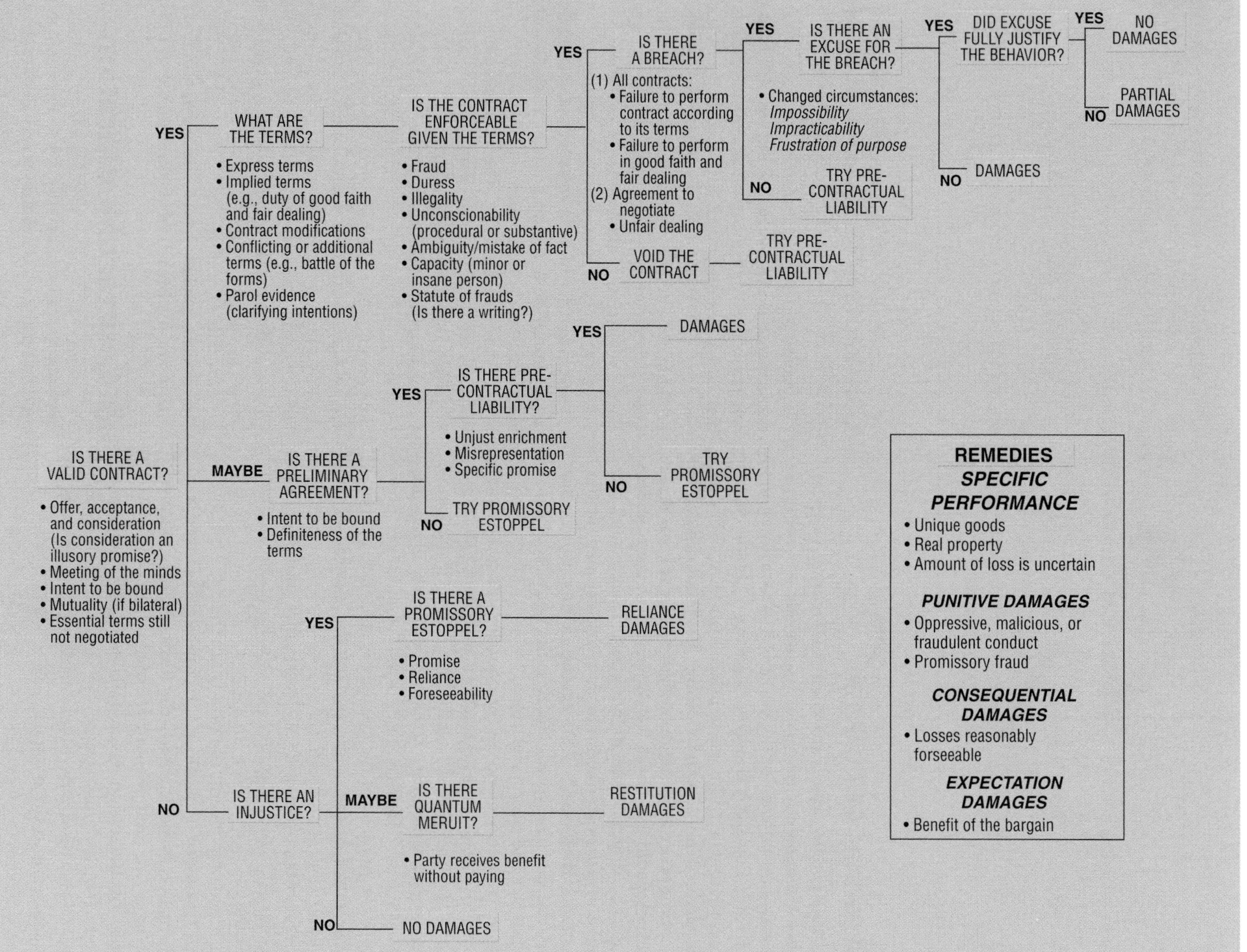


**Source:** This was prepared by Sheila Bonini with information and input from Constance E. Bagley. Used by permission.

been given for the change. Over time, lawyers developed a variety of techniques to meet the formal requirements of consideration. One technique was *novation*, by which a new party is substituted for one of the old parties, and a new contract is written (with the consent of all old and new parties) effecting the desired change. Another technique was formal change, where the consideration for the desired modification is a formal but meaningless change, such as making the payment in cash rather than with a bank check. Similarly, if both parties agree to terminate the contract and enter into a new one, the new one will be valid.

## Discharge of Contract

Once a manager has entered into a legally enforceable contract, his or her next concern is determining when the contractual obligations have been terminated or *discharged*. Most commonly discharge of contracts occurs when both parties have fully performed their obligations toward one another. But what happens when one party performs and the other does not? Or when one party performs only some of its obligations under the contract? These questions are answered under the rules on discharging contracts.

If one party fails to perform a contract according to its essential terms, such as by not performing a service after receiving payment, that party has *materially breached* the contract. Any material breach of a contract discharges the nonbreaching party from its obligations and provides grounds to sue for damages. A breach is minor if the essential terms and purpose of the contract have been fulfilled. In the case of a minor breach, the nonbreaching party still retains its contractual obligations but may suspend performance or sue for damages.

An *anticipatory repudiation* of a contract occurs when one party knows ahead of time (before performance is due) that the other party will breach the contract. Such a repudiation is treated as a material breach of the contract. By treating an anticipatory repudiation as a breach, the nonbreaching party can avoid having to wait to take action until an actual breach occurs.

Contracts may also be discharged by the failure or occurrence of certain conditions stipulated in the contract, such as a condition precedent or a condition subsequent, as discussed above. If both parties agree, they may terminate the contract by *mutual rescission*. A mutual rescission is itself a type of contract and, as such, requires a valid offer, acceptance, and consideration. Often the consideration is simply the agreement by both parties not to enforce their legal obligations.

If one party prefers to retain the original contract but wants to contract with someone else, a third party may be substituted for one of the original parties. The third party will assume the original party's rights and responsibilities. All parties must agree to the substitution. Formally, a new contract is formed, with the same terms but with different parties.

An *accord and satisfaction* is any agreement to accept performance that is different from what is called for in the contract. For example, a contract involving a debt subject to a good faith dispute can be discharged by accord and satisfaction. Assume a creditor believes he is owed $100,000, but the debtor feels she owes only $75,000. An *accord* is formed when the creditor accepts the debtor's offer to settle the dispute for an amount less than the creditor claims is due (say, by cashing the debtor's check for $80,000 with "Full Payment" written on it). *Satisfaction* is the discharge of the debt.

Parties may sometimes have a valid contract that is discharged by operation of law. Certain types of changed circumstances, such as impossibility, impracticability, or frustration of purpose (described above), may discharge the contractual obligations of both parties. A bankruptcy proceeding by one party can also discharge its contractual obligations. Similarly, failing to file suit for breach of contract before the time specified in the statute of limitations has passed effectively discharges a contract because the courts will no longer enforce it. In many states, an action for breach of a written contract must be filed within four years after the breach occurs.

## Duty of Good Faith and Fair Dealing

Every contract contains an implied covenant of good faith and fair dealing in its performance. This implied covenant imposes on each party a duty not to do anything that will deprive the other party of the benefits of the agreement. One court defined a lack of good faith as "some type of affirmative action consisting of at least . . . a design to mislead or to deceive another."[15] The covenant has been implied and enforced in a variety of contexts, including insurance contracts, agreements to make mutual wills, agreements to sell real property, employment agreements, and leases. (Its application in the employment context is discussed in Chapter 12.)

15. Bunge Corp. v. Recker, 519 F.2d 449, 452 (8th Cir. 1975).

Courts have long deemed the relationship between an insurance company and its insured a special relationship that calls for a careful examination of the faithfulness of contractual dealings. For example, suppose Reese is looking for an apartment. He comes upon Tara's apartment building and proceeds up the stairs to speak with the manager. Reese trips on a broken step, falls, and breaks his arm and leg. It is clear that the steps had not been maintained properly. Tara has insurance of $125,000 to cover this type of liability claim. Reese's lawyer originally demands $120,000, which includes a claim for punitive damages. Tara's insurance company refuses to pay the claim; the company does not believe that Tara was negligent and takes the case to trial. The jury awards Reese $180,000. Tara is liable for the full amount, although she was insured for only $125,000. Tara then brings an action against her insurance company for not settling the claim within the policy limits. Under the implied covenant of good faith and fair dealing, the insurance company will be obliged to pay the full $180,000 judgment. An insurance company can refuse to settle within the policy limits. But once an insurance company refuses an offer to settle within the policy limits and instead goes to trial, the company becomes contractually responsible for paying whatever amount is awarded at trial.

In addition, claims that a party has complied with the letter of the contract may not be sufficient to satisfy the duty of good faith and fair dealing. In *Marsu B.V. v. Walt Disney Co.*,[16] Disney entered into an agreement with Marsu B.V. regarding a cartoon character "Marsupilami" owned by Marsu. Under the terms of the agreement, Disney was to create half-hour animated films for broadcast on television and to coordinate a merchandising campaign that would provide broad exposure for Marsupilami. Although Disney did some merchandising, the company's effort was halfhearted; among other things, it assigned junior employees to the project and failed to coordinate the merchandising campaign with the television broadcast. A memo written by a Disney executive that was introduced as evidence of Disney's attitude toward the campaign stated that "we have neither the time nor the resources to do Marsu right" and "we have lots of other Disney priorities, more important both financially and strategically." The U.S. Court of Appeals for the Ninth Circuit rejected Disney's argument that it had fulfilled its express obligations under the terms of the contract and affirmed the district court's determination that Disney had breached the implied covenant of good faith and fair dealing.

16. 185 F.3d 932 (9th Cir. 1999).

### ETHICAL CONSIDERATION

Alejandro purchased a forty-foot-wide strip of land from a homeowner for a small sum of money. He then sold most of the land to the county, which constructed a road on the land. Alejandro kept a two-foot-wide strip of the land between the homeowner's property and the new road. When the homeowner crossed over this two-foot strip to get to the road, Alejandro threatened to sue for trespass. He then offered to sell back the two-foot strip for an extravagant sum. Should a court rescind the contract? On what theory? Was Alejandro's conduct ethical?

The precise meanings of "good faith" and "fair dealing" are the subject of extended debate among legal scholars. The terms themselves are ambiguous, and the practical meanings may vary over time. What was considered fair dealing twenty years ago may be considered unfair today, and vice versa.

Two commonly used rules of thumb, though not precise, do offer guidance. Managers in doubt should ask themselves whether an action would embarrass them or their company if it became public. They can also consider whether they would follow the same course of action if they were dealing with a friend or relative. Although these questions address moral rather than legal issues, they can be useful in evaluating whether a contemplated action would meet the legal test of good faith. (Good faith in the context of negotiations is discussed more fully later in this chapter.)

## Third-Party Beneficiaries

A person who is not a party to a contract can sometimes enforce the contract between the contracting parties. For example, suppose Sheila agrees to sell to Fernando a piece of real property in exchange for a $100,000 payment by Fernando to Jack. Fernando is the promisor, Sheila is the promisee, and Jack is the *third-party beneficiary* or intended beneficiary. A person is not a third-party beneficiary with legal rights to enforce the contract unless the contracting parties intended to benefit that party.

### CREDITOR BENEFICIARY

If the promisee entered into the contract in order to discharge a duty he or she owed to the third party, then the third party is a *creditor beneficiary* and has the right to enforce the contract between the promisor and promisee. The third party must prove, however, that the promisee intended the contract to satisfy his or her obligation to the third party. For example, if Sheila owes Jack $100,000 and she and Fernando agree that she will sell land to Fernando in order to pay off that debt, Jack has enforceable rights under the contract as a creditor beneficiary. Jack can sue Fernando directly to compel performance. If the contract is not carried out, Jack also has the option of suing Sheila for the $100,000 she owes him.

### DONEE BENEFICIARY

A *donee beneficiary* is created when the promisee does not owe an obligation to the third party but rather wishes to confer a gift. For example, if Sheila agreed to sell her property to Fernando for $100,000 in order to make a $100,000 gift to Jack, Jack would be a donee beneficiary and could enforce the contract in most jurisdictions, but only against Fernando. Some jurisdictions, such as New York, require a family relationship between the donee beneficiary and the promisee before allowing the beneficiary to sue under the contract.

## Remedies

If one party breaches a contract, the other party is entitled to monetary damages or, in some instances, a court order requiring performance. The purpose of damages is to give the plaintiff the benefit of the bargain it contracted for, that is, to put the plaintiff in the position it would have been in had the contract been performed. A secondary purpose of damages is to discourage breaches of contract. Sometimes, however, it is economically efficient to breach a contract, so the legal system, recognizing this, generally does not punish a party for breach of contract alone. As a result, the courts generally do not allow punitive damages, traditionally a tort remedy, in contract cases. However, the courts have developed several exceptions that allow for the award of punitive damages in cases involving (1) a breach of a promise to marry; (2) a breach of a fiduciary duty; or (3) a breach of a contract the performance of which involves a public duty or is regulated by public authorities, such as contracts involving public utilities, common carriers, or insurance companies.

Over the years, a variety of methods have been developed to measure appropriate monetary damages in contract cases. The three standard measures are (1) expectation, (2) reliance, and (3) restitution. The interest to be compensated determines which of these measures is most appropriate in a particular case. These measures may seem similar, but the resulting damage awards can be very different, as discussed below. In certain situations, a court may also order the equitable remedies of specific performance or injunctive relief.

### EXPECTATION DAMAGES

*Expectation damages* give the plaintiff the benefit of its bargain, putting the plaintiff in the cash position it would have been in if the contract had been fulfilled. The general formula for expectation damages is Compensatory Damages + Consequential Damages + Incidental Damages – Avoidable Losses.

#### Compensatory Damages

*Compensatory damages* are the amount necessary to make up for the economic loss caused by the breach of contract. For example, suppose an independent contractor agrees to work for AAA Manufacturing Company for $15 per hour. When the time comes to start working, the contractor reneges. AAA can find another independent contractor elsewhere, but the market price is now $20 per hour. This extra cost will cut into the profit margin on the product that the contractor was helping to manufacture. Instead of spending $600 for a forty-hour workweek, AAA must now pay $800. AAA's compensatory damages are the difference between the two expenditures, or $200.

#### Consequential Damages

In addition to damages that compensate for the breach itself, the plaintiff is entitled to *consequential damages*, that is, compensation for losses that occur as a foreseeable result of the breach. For example, suppose AAA contracts with another person at $20 per hour, but the new contractor cannot start working immediately. As a result, AAA has to use a temporary employee who charges $21 per hour for two weeks. Thus, AAA incurs an additional cost of $1 more per hour for two weeks, which results in $80 additional damages. This $80 is added to the $200 in compensatory damages. If the two-week delay causes AAA to be late in delivering its product to one of its customers, any late fees that AAA pays will also be added to the damages.

Two principles operate to limit consequential damages: (1) the damages must be reasonably foreseeable, and (2) they must be reasonably certain.

**Foreseeability** Consequential damages will be awarded only if the breaching party knew, or should have known, that the loss would result from a breach of the contract.

For example, in *Hadley v. Baxendale,*[17] the plaintiff was a mill owner who sent a broken crankshaft by carrier to be repaired. Because this was the only crankshaft the mill owned, the mill was completely shut down until the carrier returned with the repaired crankshaft. The carrier did not deliver the shaft as quickly as promised. The mill owner sued the carrier for profits lost during the time the mill was closed. The English appellate court did not award damages for lost profits. The court observed that most mills had more than one crankshaft, so the carrier had no way of knowing that the nondelivery of the crankshaft would mean the closure of the mill. In order for lost profits to have been awarded, the lost profits would have had to be reasonably foreseeable or a natural consequence of the breach. Neither was the case here.

In another case, a stove manufacturer paid a carrier $50 to ship a new model of stove to a major exhibition.[18] The stove did not arrive until the exhibition was over. The manufacturer sued for the value of all the lost business it had expected to get at the exhibition. The court found that the $50 was too small an amount to serve as insurance for the entire business. Moreover, the value of the lost business was too speculative to calculate with any certainty. Damages were limited to the shipping expenses of $50.

**Uncertainty of Damages** In the stove case just described, it was impossible to measure the consequential damages (the stove manufacturer's lost business). Sometimes it is not even possible to know what the benefit of the bargain would have been. For example, Publisher & Sons signs a contract to publish a book Rachel Author has written. It is her first book. Publisher later decides not to publish the book. To what damages is Rachel entitled? The benefit of her bargain would be the royalties from a published book, but the parties have no way to measure how much those royalties would have been. Because Rachel has the burden of proving the amount of her loss, she may collect very little in damages.

Similarly, new businesses have no record of past profits by which to estimate the loss caused by a breach. Traditionally, this prevented start-ups from collecting anything for lost profits. Today, however, with more sophisticated methods for projecting future profits, new businesses are having more success recovering damages.

17. 156 Eng. Rep. 145 (1854).

18. Sec. Stove & Mfg. Co. v. Am. Ry. Express Co., 51 S.W.2d 572 (Mo. App. Ct. 1932).

## Incidental Damages

*Incidental damages* are the lesser and relatively minor damages that a nonbreaching party incurs. Examples of incidental damages include the charges, expenses, and commissions incurred in stopping delivery; the cost of the transportation, care, and custody of goods after a buyer's default; or the expenses incurred in connection with the return or subsequent disposition of goods that are the subject of a contract.

## Mitigation of Damages

When one party breaches a contract, the other party has a duty to use reasonable efforts to *mitigate,* or lessen, the amount of damages that flow from the breach. As a general rule, the nonbreaching party cannot recover damages that it could have reasonably avoided. This gives the nonbreaching party an incentive to make the best of a bad situation.

For example, suppose AAA Manufacturing Company and Hazmat, a hazardous-waste collection company, enter into a contract whereby Hazmat agrees to pick up AAA's hazardous-waste for a fee of $500 per pickup. If Hazmat fails to pick up the hazardous waste, AAA should *cover*—find another hazardous-waste collection company at the current market price, say, $625 per pickup, at the time of the breach. AAA will still be entitled to compensatory damages, measured by the difference between the market price at the time it learned of the breach ($625 per pickup) and the contract price ($500 per pickup), plus any consequential damages, such as extra storage fees, late fees, and incidental damages incurred in finding a substitute hazardous-waste collection company.

AAA could also elect not to cover. If it does not cover, however, the company is limited to compensatory damages (as measured above) and cannot recover any consequential damages that could have been prevented by covering, such as late fees. If no cover is available, AAA is entitled to foreseeable consequential damages resulting from the breach.

Additionally, AAA must avoid compounding damages from the breach. If hazardous-waste collection services are available at both $625 and $650 per pickup and the quality is the same, then AAA is required to purchase at the lower price. Thus, its expectation damages are limited to $125 per pickup. Any expenses incurred by AAA in reasonably attempting to mitigate damages, such as the costs of finding another collection company, are also recoverable under consequential damages, regardless of whether the efforts were successful.

From the seller's perspective, the duty to mitigate damages works similarly. For example, suppose Best Software

Company contracts to develop a customized program for Smith Architects, LLC, a small architecture firm. Best learns midway through the development process that Smith plans to breach the contract. Best should cover by finding another buyer for the software, then charge Smith for the difference between the contract price and the resale price (compensatory damages), plus any consequential damages. If no other buyer is available, perhaps because the program is too customized, Best should immediately stop its work and charge Smith for expenses incurred plus the expected net profit.

## Reliance Damages

*Reliance damages* compensate the plaintiff for any expenditures it made in reliance on a contract that was subsequently breached. Instead of giving the plaintiff the benefit of the bargain, reliance damages return it to the position it was in before the contract was formed. For example, a seller agrees to sell a buyer a heavy drill press. The buyer invests in renovation work to strengthen the floor where the drill press will be installed. The buyer tells the seller about this work. The seller then sells the drill press to someone else. Reliance damages will require the seller to reimburse the buyer for the renovation expenses. Reliance damages are an alternative to expectation damages when it is not possible to determine the expectation damages. Reliance damages are also awarded in promissory estoppel cases, where expectation damages are generally not allowed.

## Restitution and *Quantum Meruit*

Restitution is similar to reliance damages, but whereas reliance damages look at what the plaintiff has lost, *restitution* looks at what the other party has gained from the transaction. The usual measure of restitution is the amount it would cost the receiver of the benefit to buy that benefit elsewhere.

A court will order restitution under the doctrine of *quantum meruit* if one party has received a benefit for which it has not paid and there was no contract between the parties. The obligation to give restitution is implied as a matter of law. For example, suppose that an entrepreneur asks an advertising agency to place an advertisement. The advertising agency contracts with an industry publication to place the advertisement but fails to pay for it. Under the doctrine of *quantum meruit,* the agency's default on payment renders the entrepreneur liable to the publication for the value of the benefit the entrepreneur received (the advertisement). The entrepreneur must pay the publication even though there was no contract between the entrepreneur and the publication.

A court may also order restitution in cases where a plaintiff seeks to rescind, or cancel, a contract that it entered into based on fraud or mutual mistake, or where the defendant has breached an executory contract (i.e., a contract under which the parties have continuing obligations to perform). Rescission terminates the parties' rights under the contract, and restitution restores the parties to the position they were in prior to entering the contract by requiring them to return any benefits they received under the contract.

In the following case, the U.S. Court of Appeals for the Federal Circuit considered whether to award Glendale Federal Bank expectation, reliance, or restitution damages as a result of the federal government's breach of contract. The bank suffered losses when the government passed the Financial Institutions Reform, Recovery and Enforcement Act.

A Case in Point

**CASE 7.5**

**Glendale Federal Bank, FSB v. United States**

*United States Court of Appeals for the Federal Circuit*
*239 F.3d 1374*
*(Fed. Cir. 2001).*

## In the Language of the Court

**› FACTS** In 1981, Glendale Federal Bank, a savings and loan institution in California, entered into a supervisory merger with First Federal Savings and Loan Association of Broward County in Florida. At the time of the merger, the market value of First Federal's liabilities exceeded the market value of its assets by $734 million. Pursuant to its contract with the government, Glendale was permitted to treat First Federal's negative net worth as goodwill for regulatory capital purposes and to amortize it over a forty-year period. Otherwise, Glendale would have immediately become insolvent.

In 1989, eight years into the contract, Congress passed the Financial Institutions Reform, Recovery and Enforcement Act (FIRREA). The FIRREA eliminated Glendale's ability to count goodwill as regulatory capital by requiring an accelerated amortization schedule. The FIRREA also established new capital requirements. Glendale initially failed to meet these new requirements and was forced to engineer a massive recapitalization to satisfy them.

*(Continued)*

(Case 7.5 *continued*)

The Supreme Court had previously ruled in *United States v. Winstar*[19] that banks such as Glendale had an enforceable contract with the government to treat negative net worth in supervisory mergers as goodwill and to count such goodwill toward capital requirements. Because the government breached this contract, Glendale filed suit seeking damages. After trial on damages, the U.S. Court of Federal Claims denied Glendale's claim for expectancy (expectation) damages; awarded Glendale $528 million in restitution damages, which was the amount by which First Federal's liabilities exceeded its assets on the date of the merger, less the value of the benefits Glendale received from the contract; and found that Glendale was entitled to $381,000 in nonoverlapping reliance damages, or "wounded bank damages," caused by its failure to maintain capital compliance after the breach. The U.S. Government appealed the court's award of restitution damages.

**› ISSUE PRESENTED** Under what contract measure of relief—expectancy, reliance, or restitution—is Glendale entitled to recover damages?

**› OPINION** PLAGER, J., writing for the U.S. Court of Appeals for the Federal Circuit:

When proof of expectancy damages fails, the law provides a fall-back position for the injured party—he can sue for restitution. The idea behind the restitution is to . . . restore the nonbreaching party to the position he would have been in had there never been a contract to breach. . . .

. . . [I]t is clear that the Government's promise that was breached had substantial value. . . .

At the same time, the action taken by [Glendale] in acquiring [First Federal] did not result in the Government . . . saving the dollar value of the net obligations of the thrift. . . .

This case, then, presents an illustration of the problem in granting restitution based on an assumption that the non-breaching party is entitled to the supposed gains received by the breaching party, when those gains are both speculative and indeterminate. We do not see how the restitution award granted by the trial court, measured in terms of a liability that never came to pass, and based on a speculative assessment of what might have been, can be upheld; accordingly we vacate the trial court's damage award on this theory.

This does not mean that Glendale is without remedy. Glendale recognized the problems in the restitution award, and cross-appealed, arguing that, should the court reject the award, Glendale nevertheless would be entitled to damages on a reliance theory. Indeed, the trial court recognized this third category of damages, known as reliance damages, and added specified reliance damages to the total award it granted plaintiff.

**› RESULT** The court vacated the trial court's damages award and remanded the case with instructions for further proceedings to determine the amount of Glendale's reliance damages for prebreach or postbreach activities from which ascertainable losses as a result of the breach could be shown.

**› CRITICAL THINKING QUESTIONS**

1. Why didn't Glendale receive expectation damages?
2. Given that the plaintiff bears the burden of proving damages, why should Glendale be able to recover anything?

19. 518 U.S. 839 (1996).

### LIQUIDATED DAMAGES

The parties to a contract may include a clause that specifies the amount of money to be paid if one of them should later breach the agreement. Such *liquidated damages* clauses are frequently used in real estate and construction contracts. The amount of the liquidated damages should be the parties' best estimate of what the expectation damages would be. Courts will not enforce penalties. Thus, clauses that provide for damages that are substantially higher than the losses will not be enforced. The purpose of contract damages is to restore the aggrieved party to the position it would have been in had the contract been performed, not to punish the party who has committed the breach.

### SPECIFIC PERFORMANCE AND INJUNCTIVE RELIEF

Instead of awarding monetary damages, a court may order the breaching party to complete the contract as promised. *Specific performance* is ordered only when (1) the goods are unique (for example, an antique car or a painting), (2) the subject of the contract is real property, or (3) the amount of the loss is so uncertain that there is no fair way to calculate damages.

Courts never force an employee to provide services under an employment contract because that would constitute involuntary servitude in violation of the Thirteenth Amendment to the U.S. Constitution. For example, suppose a chief executive officer agrees to work for a corporation for five years. If she walks out after three years, the court will not force her to continue her employment. The court may, however, issue an injunction barring her from working for someone else. Similarly, if a professional baseball player with a seven-year contract with the Boston Red Sox breaches his contract and starts playing for the Houston Astros, an injunction may be granted to prevent him from playing for the Astros.

## Precontractual Liability

Under traditional contract law, the offeror is free to back out and revoke an offer at any time before a contract is made without risk of *precontractual liability*. A party entering negotiations does so at the risk of the negotiations breaking off. Courts typically will impose a duty to negotiate in good faith only if a letter of intent between the two parties specifically includes that duty. For example, in *Venture Associates Corp. v. Zenith Data Systems Corp.*,[20] a U.S. district court held that two parties had entered into a preliminary agreement to negotiate in good faith on the basis of a letter of intent that Venture sent to Zenith Data stating, "this letter is intended to evidence the preliminary understanding which we have reached . . . and our mutual intent to negotiate in good faith to enter into a definitive Purchase Agreement." Similarly, in *Channel Home Centers v. Frank Grossman*,[21] the U.S. Court of Appeals for the Third Circuit found that Grossman had a duty to negotiate in good faith to complete a leasing transaction with Channel because the letter of intent signed by both parties expressly provided for their good faith negotiation.

In the following case, the court considered whether Baskin Robbins had a good faith duty to negotiate even though there was no written agreement that required the parties to negotiate in good faith.

20. 887 F. Supp. 1014 (N.D. Ill. 1995).
21. 795 F.2d 291 (3d Cir. 1986).

A CASE IN POINT

**In the Language of the Court**

**CASE 7.6**
**Copeland v. Baskin Robbins**
*Court of Appeal of California*
*117 Cal. Rptr. 2d 875*
*(Cal. Ct. App. 2002).*

**› FACTS** Baskin Robbins operated an ice cream manufacturing plant in the city of Vernon. When the company announced its intention to close the plant, Copeland expressed an interest in acquiring it but made clear that his agreement to purchase the plant was contingent on the execution of a co-packing agreement in which Baskin Robbins would agree to purchase the ice cream that he manufactured in the plant. In May 1999, Baskin Robbins sent Copeland a letter that stated:

> This letter details the terms which our . . . executives have approved for subletting and sale of our Vernon manufacturing facility/equipment and a product supply

*(Continued)*

(Case 7.6 *continued*)

> agreement. . . . (1) Baskin Robbins will sell [Copeland] Vernon's ice cream manufacturing equipment . . . for $1,300,000 cash. . . . (2) Baskin Robbins would agree, subject to a separate co-packaging agreement and negotiated pricing, to provide [Copeland] a three year co-packing agreement for 3,000,000 gallons in year 1, 2,000,000 gallons in year 2 and 2,000,000 in year 3. . . . If the above is acceptable please acknowledge by returning a copy of this letter with a non-refundable check for three thousand dollars. . . . We should be able to coordinate a closing [within] thirty days thereafter.

Copeland signed a statement at the bottom of the letter agreeing that "[t]he above terms are acceptable" and returned the letter to Baskin Robbins along with the $3,000 deposit.

Thereafter, however, the negotiations broke down with regard to several items, and in July 1999, Baskin Robbins broke off negotiations over the co-packing arrangement and returned Copeland's $3,000 deposit. Although Baskin Robbins offered to proceed with the agreement for the sale and lease of the Vernon plant assets, Copeland was not interested.

Copeland filed a lawsuit for breach of contract. He alleged that he had entered into a contract with Baskin Robbins pursuant to which Baskin Robbins had agreed to enter into a co-packing agreement under the terms of the May 1999 letter and additional terms to be negotiated and that Baskin Robbins had breached this contract by "unreasonably and wrongfully refusing to enter into any co-packing agreement with [Copeland]." The trial court granted Baskin Robbins' motion for summary judgment on the ground that the May 1999 letter failed as a contract because the essential terms of the co-packing deal were never agreed to and there was no reasonable basis on which to determine them.

**› ISSUE PRESENTED** Can a party to failed contract negotiations sue for breach of contract to negotiate an agreement or is such a "contract" merely an unenforceable "agreement to agree"?

**› OPINION** JOHNSON, Acting P.J., writing for the California Court of Appeal:

When Baskin Robbins refused to continue negotiating the terms of the co-packing agreement, Copeland faced a dilemma. "Many millions of dollars" in anticipated profits had melted away like so much banana ripple ice cream on a hot summer day. . . . [H]e could proceed with the contract for the purchase and lease of the Vernon plant's assets and use those assets to produce ice cream for other retailers. But . . . without the Baskin Robbins co-packing agreement he could not afford to purchase the assets and pay on-going costs of operating the plant while he searched for other business. Alternatively he could attempt to sue Baskin Robbins for breach of the co-packing agreement on the theory the terms of the agreement set out in the May 1999 letter plus additional terms supplied by the court constituted an enforceable contract. Such a suit, however, had a slim prospect of success. . . . It is still the general rule that where any of the essential elements of a promise are reserved for the future agreement of both parties, no legal obligation arises until such "future agreement is made." . . .

Copeland chose a third course. Rather than insist the parties had formed a co-packing contract and Baskin Robbins had breached it, he claimed the May 1999 letter constituted a contract to negotiate the remaining terms of the co-packing agreement and Baskin Robbins breached this contract by refusing without excuse to continue negotiations or, alternatively, by failing to negotiate in good faith. This path too has its difficulties. No reported California case has held breach of a contract to negotiate an agreement gives rise to a cause of action for damages. . . . We believe, however, these difficulties could be overcome in an appropriate case.

*(Continued)*

(Case 7.6 *continued*)

Initially, we see no reason why in principle the parties could not enter into a valid, enforceable contract to negotiate the terms of the co-packing agreement. A contract, after all, is "an agreement to do or not to do a certain thing." Persons are free to contract to do just about anything that is not illegal or immoral. Conducting negotiations to buy and sell ice cream is neither.

A contract to negotiate the terms of an agreement is not, in form or substance, an "agreement to agree." If, despite their good faith efforts, the parties fail to reach ultimate agreement on the terms in issue the contract to negotiate is deemed performed and the parties are discharged from their obligations. Failure to agree is not, itself, a breach of the contract to negotiate. A party will be liable only if a failure to reach ultimate agreement results from a breach of the party's obligation to negotiate or to negotiate in good faith. . . .

. . .

Baskin Robbins maintains that there are sound public policy reasons for not enforcing a contract to negotiate an agreement. In doing so, we would be injecting a covenant of good faith and fair dealing into the negotiation process whether or not the parties specifically agreed to such a term. . . . Most parties, Baskin Robbins suggests, would prefer to risk losing their out-of-pocket costs if the negotiation fails rather than risk losing perhaps millions of dollars in expectation damages if their disappointed negotiating partner can prove bad faith. Finally, Baskin Robbins argues, any precontractual wrong-doing can be adequately remedied by existing causes of action for unjust enrichment, promissory fraud and promissory estoppel. . . .

. . .

. . . [W]e believe there are sound public policy reasons for protecting parties to a business negotiation from bad faith practices by their negotiating partners. Gone are the days when our ancestors sat around a fire and bargained for the exchange of stones axes for bear hides. Today the stakes are much higher and negotiations are much more complex. Deals are rarely made in a single negotiating session. Rather, they are the product of a gradual process in which agreements are reached piecemeal on a variety of issues in a series of face-to-face meetings, telephone calls, e-mails and letters involving corporate officers, lawyers, bankers, accountants, architects, engineers and others. . . . [C]ontracts today are not formed by discrete offers, counter-offers and acceptances. Instead they result from a gradual flow of information between the parties followed by a series of compromises and tentative agreements on major points which are finally refined into contract terms. These slow contracts are not only time consuming but costly. For these reasons, the parties should have some assurance "their investments in time and money and effort will not be wiped out by the other party's footdragging or change of heart or taking advantage of a vulnerable position created by the negotiation." . . .

For obvious reasons, damages for breach of a contract to negotiate an agreement are measured by the injury the plaintiff suffered in relying on the defendant to negotiate in good faith. This measure encompasses the plaintiff's out-of-pocket costs in conducting the negotiations and may or may not include lost opportunity costs. The plaintiff cannot recover for lost expectations (profits) because there is no way of knowing what the ultimate terms of the agreement would have been or even if there would have been an ultimate agreement.

**› RESULT** The court found that Baskin Robbins was entitled to summary judgment because Copeland failed to establish any reliance damages.

*(Continued)*

(Case 7.6 *continued*)

**› CRITICAL THINKING QUESTIONS**

1. What other causes of action might Copeland have been able to allege against Baskin Robbins?
2. How could Baskin Robbins have structured the negotiations to avoid any potential liability when it elected to break off negotiations related to the co-packing agreement?

In addition to imposing liability for a breach of the duty to negotiate, in narrow circumstances, American courts will impose precontractual liability on theories of misrepresentation, promissory estoppel, or restitution.[22] For example, the Supreme Court of Washington found misrepresentation when the owner of a warehouse told the lessee that he intended to renew the lease for three years, when in fact the owner was negotiating the sale of the facility.[23]

## Mergers and Acquisitions

A corporation can acquire control of another corporation (the *target*) by merger, a sale of stock by the target's shareholders, or a sale of substantially all the assets of the target. A *merger agreement* is an agreement between two companies to combine into a single entity. Mergers and sales of substantially all the assets generally cannot be completed until the transaction is approved by the shareholders of both the acquiring and the target company.

Mergers and acquisitions are usually highly negotiated transactions that are governed by detailed acquisition agreements containing representations and warranties (statements about the entity being sold), covenants (promises to do or refrain from doing something), and conditions (events that must occur before either party has a duty to *close*, or consummate, the transaction, as well as events that will terminate a party's obligation to close). The seller's representations and warranties typically cover such matters as the proper organization of the entity as a corporation, the accuracy of its financial statements, title to its assets, the absence of undisclosed liabilities, the absence of undisclosed legal proceedings, and its compliance with all laws and contractual obligations by which it is bound. Covenants typically include promises to (1) conduct the business in the ordinary course until the closing date, (2) refrain from entering into any new major contracts, and (3) permit access to the business to enable the buyer to conduct due diligence.

22. For an excellent summary of the law in this area, see E. Allen Farnsworth, *Precontractual Liability and Preliminary Agreements: Fair Dealing and Failed Negotiations,* 87 COLUM. L. REV. 217 (1987).
23. Markov v. ABC Transfer & Storage Co., 457 P.2d 535 (Wash. 1969).

Acquisition agreements in transactions involving private companies typically provide for indemnification by the seller for breaches of its representations, warranties, and covenants. The seller may also require the buyer to include indemnification provisions if the buyer is purchasing the company with shares of its stock. Public company acquisition agreements typically do not include indemnification clauses because the sellers consist of public shareholders and collecting indemnification from them would be virtually impossible.

The indemnification provisions often limit the seller's or buyer's exposure to some percentage of the total purchase price. In some agreements, different ceilings apply to different types of liabilities. In addition, the provisions may stipulate that breaches of representations, warranties, or covenants must be material before indemnification will be available. For example, the parties might agree that a claim must be worth at least $100,000 before the seller has an obligation to pay any damages to the buyer. If the parties decide to establish a dollar threshold, they must also decide whether the threshold should be a deductible amount or whether the indemnifying party should provide "dollar one" coverage. For example, under an agreement that uses the deductible approach, if the claim is $150,000 and the threshold is $100,000, the indemnifying party would be liable for only $50,000, the excess over $100,000. In contrast, if the agreement uses the dollar one coverage approach, the party would be liable for the full amount of $150,000.

The issue of time limits on indemnification obligations is frequently one of the most controversial negotiating points in an acquisition agreement. The indemnifying party usually wants a shorter period than the applicable statute of limitations, and many acquisition agreements will place some time limit on indemnification obligations. The seller typically argues that the buyer, as the owner and operator of the business, should discover any misstatements within a certain period of time. The buyer, however, often argues for longer time limits for tax claims, environmental claims, and capitalization matters as these problems may not surface for years.

# Global View

## CONTRACTING WITH FOREIGN ENTITIES

When entering into contracts with companies in other nations, it is important to remember that whereas the law in the United States and England stems from a common law tradition, most non-English-speaking countries follow the civil law tradition. This system of jurisprudence was originally used in the Roman Empire. Civil law countries rely primarily on civil codes, or statutes, rather than case-by-case common law to develop rules for behavior.

Most civil law countries do not recognize certain common law principles. One is the doctrine of consideration, which means that no consideration is required to make a contract binding in a civil law country. Another is *privity of contract,* which means that third parties who are not signatories to a contract may be entitled to enforce its terms. In addition, whereas common law countries generally treat contracts with the government in the same way as contracts with private entities, civil law counties have different rules for private and public entities.

The concept of nonperformance and the remedies for it also differ. In the United States, damages are the standard remedy for breach of contract, and specific performance or injunctive relief is left to the court's discretion. A court will enter an order for specific performance or injunctive relief only if it finds that damages would not be an adequate remedy. In civil law countries, however, specific performance will generally be awarded in contract cases. For example, a German court will attempt to put the parties back into the position that they would have been in if they had never entered into the contract. As a result, the nonbreaching party cannot claim damages for breach of contract. In France, on the other hand, a court may grant a defaulting party a grace period during which it will be allowed to perform the contract.

In general, other common law countries, such as the United Kingdom, do not recognize a common law duty to negotiate in good faith and thus do not impose liability for its breach. However, civil law countries, including France, Germany, the Netherlands, and Japan, have been more willing to impose a good faith obligation during the negotiation of a contract.[a] In 1994, the International Institute for the Unification of Private Law (Unidroit) published its Principles of International Commercial Contracts (Unidroit Principles), which set forth general rules for international commercial contracts for services. Article 2.15(2) provides that one who "breaks off negotiations in bad faith is liable for the losses caused to the other party." The Unidroit Principles, like the American Law Institute's Restatement of the Law, are not designed for legislative enactment and are used primarily in international arbitration. As a result, in many international agreements, there may be the expectation that parties have a duty to negotiate in good faith and can be held liable if they fail to do so.

Since 1982 the Commission on European Contract Law, a nongovernmental body of lawyers from the European Union member states, has been working to establish Principles of European Contract Law. The Principles include comments that explain the purpose of the rules and illustrations and notes that give an account of the sources and compare the rules with those of the member states. Part I of the Principles deals with the performance of contracts, nonperformance, and remedies for nonperformance; Part II contains rules on the formation of contracts, validity, interpretation, and contents. The main purpose of the Principles is to serve as a draft European Code of Private Law. The Commission on European Contract law, better known as the Lando Commission, has produced a draft version of a complete code of European Contract Law. However, even before the Code is enacted, the parties to an international contract may adopt the Principles. If a dispute arises, a court or arbitrator will then apply the Principles instead of national rules of law. Although the parties are free to exclude or vary most of the Principles, certain provisions are considered to be of such importance as to be mandatory. These include the provisions requiring each party to act in accordance with good faith and fair dealing, beginning with contract negotiations, and those dealing with invalidity caused by mistake, fraud, threat, undue influence, and unfair contract terms.

Because of the differences in each country's laws regarding contract interpretation, performance, and remedies, it is generally appropriate to include a provision that specifies which country's laws will govern (a *choice-of-law provision*) in every multinational contract. It may also be appropriate to include a provision that specifies which country's courts will have exclusive jurisdiction over any dispute involving the contract (a *choice-of-forum provision*). Finally, many contracts involving parties located in different countries will also include an agreement that any disputes will be arbitrated, rather than tried in court, because arbitration awards are enforceable in every country that is a participant in the Paris Convention. These provisions are discussed in more detail in Chapter 25.

**a.** See D. James Wan Kim Min v. Mitsui Bussan K.K. (Tokyo High Court 1987), cited in YUKO YANAGIDA, ET AL., LAW AND INVESTMENT IN JAPAN 223–29 (1994).

## THE RESPONSIBLE MANAGER

## ACTING IN GOOD FAITH AND DEALING FAIRLY

Managers should deal fairly in negotiations. The standard of fair dealing ordinarily requires at least three things. First, each party must actually negotiate and refrain from imposing improper conditions on the negotiation. Second, each party must disclose enough about parallel negotiations to allow the other party to make a counterproposal. Third, each party must continue to negotiate until an impasse or an agreement has been reached.

In general, managers who are parties to a negotiation should describe as specifically as possible the duty of fair dealing to which they have agreed. Instead of simply pledging to use their "best efforts" to negotiate fairly, the parties should specify whether the negotiations are to be exclusive, how long they must continue, and what must be held in confidence. Given the uncertain state of the law on these matters, no drafter should leave these items to be filled in by a court.

Managers should avoid signing a letter of intent unless they intend to be bound by its proposed terms. Many courts will let a jury decide whether there was intent to be bound, even when the letter of intent states that it is not meant to be binding. If a letter of intent is necessary to obtain financing or to begin due diligence, then the manager not intending to be bound if negotiations of the definitive agreement break down should consider doing the following: First, insert clear language into the letter stating that it is not binding, that there is no contract unless and until the parties execute a definitive written contract, and that the letter creates no obligation to negotiate in good faith and cannot be reasonably relied upon. Second, label the document "tentative proposal" or "status letter." Third, do not sign the document.[24]

24. See William G. Schopf et al., *When a Letter of Intent Goes Wrong,* 5 BUS. L. TODAY 31 (Jan.–Feb. 1996).

It is almost always preferable to put the terms of an agreement or deal in writing. Memories of even the most well-intentioned parties fade over time. A manager should review any contract before signing it. If the terms are unfamiliar or unclear, the manager should consult with an attorney. A manager should never sign a contract he or she does not understand.

It is rarely to a manager's advantage to try to slip a provision by the other party that the manager knows would be unacceptable if it were pointed out. It is far preferable to hash out any ambiguities at the negotiation stage while the parties are on good terms and in the mood to make a deal. Positions tend to polarize once the agreement is signed and a dispute arises.

Similarly, it is inappropriate and often unethical to bury offensive terms in a preprinted form contract in the hope that the other party will not spot them. Courts will sometimes refuse to enforce such terms, especially when they conflict with the position taken in the negotiations or are contrary to the spirit of the deal. It makes both legal and ethical sense to abide by the covenant of good faith and fair dealing in negotiating a contract. It is also good business. Contract litigation is expensive and time-consuming.

Managers should also ensure that they are not tortiously interfering with the contract of another. As *Pennzoil v. Texaco,* discussed in the "Inside Story" below, demonstrates, even a very large company can be driven into bankruptcy if its executives guess wrong on either the question of whether there is a contract or the question of whether their deal tortiously interferes with it.

It is sometimes tempting to view the drafting and review of contracts as a necessary evil. However, astute managers realize that contract drafting and negotiation can provide opportunities to strengthen business relationships and to protect key assets such as trade secrets, which give a firm a competitive edge.

INSIDE STORY

## PENNZOIL v. TEXACO

In 1983, Pennzoil Company and Getty Oil Company negotiated a memorandum of agreement for a merger. While their lawyers drafted the final documents, Texaco, Inc. offered a better price for Getty. Getty accepted Texaco's offer, and Pennzoil subsequently sued Texaco for tortious interference with a contract. To win, Getty had to prove (1) the existence of a contract, (2) Texaco's knowledge of the contract, (3) Texaco's intentional inducement of a breach of the contract, and (4) damages.[25] Texaco asserted that Pennzoil never had a contract because the parties had not yet agreed on every essential term of the deal.

It took the two parties four and a half months to present all the facts and arguments to the jury. The published opinion of the Texas Court of Appeals summarizes the events in question.[26]

**Excerpts from the Opinion of the Court of Appeals: Facts**

> . . . Pennzoil had followed with interest the well-publicized dissension between the board of directors of Getty Oil Company and Gordon Getty, who was a director of Getty Oil and also the owner, as trustee, of approximately 40.2% of the outstanding shares of Getty Oil. On December 28, 1983, Pennzoil announced an unsolicited, public tender offer for 16 million shares of Getty Oil at $100 each.
>
> Soon afterwards, Pennzoil contacted both Gordon Getty and a representative of the J. Paul Getty Museum, which held approximately 11.8% of the shares of Getty Oil, to discuss the tender offer and the possible purchase of Getty Oil. In the first two days of January 1984, a "Memorandum of Agreement" was drafted to reflect the terms that had been reached in conversations between representatives of Pennzoil, Gordon Getty, and the Museum.
>
> Under the . . . Memorandum of Agreement, Pennzoil and the Trust (with Gordon Getty as trustee) were to become partners on a 3/7ths to 4/7ths basis, respectively, in owning and operating Getty Oil. Gordon Getty was to become chairman of the board, and Hugh Liedtke, the chief executive officer of Pennzoil, was to become chief executive officer of the new company. The plan also provided that Pennzoil and the Trust were to try in good faith to agree upon a plan to restructure Getty Oil within a year, but if they could not reach an agreement, the assets of Getty Oil were to be divided between them, 3/7ths to Pennzoil and 4/7ths to the Trust.
>
> The Memorandum of Agreement stated that it was subject to approval of the board of Getty Oil, and it was to expire by its own terms if not approved at the board meeting that was to begin on January 2. Pennzoil's CEO, Liedtke, and Gordon Getty, for the Trust, signed the Memorandum of Agreement before the Getty Oil board meeting on January 2, and Harold Williams, the president of the Museum, signed it shortly after the board meeting began. Thus, before it was submitted to the Getty Oil board, the Memorandum of Agreement had been executed by parties who together controlled a majority of the outstanding shares of Getty Oil.
>
> The Memorandum of Agreement was then presented to the Getty Oil board, which had previously held discussions on how the company should respond to Pennzoil's public tender offer.
>
> The board voted to reject recommending Pennzoil's tender offer to Getty's shareholders, then later also rejected the Memorandum of Agreement price of $110 per share as too low. On the morning of January 3, Getty Oil's investment banker, Geoffrey Boisi, began calling other companies, seeking a higher bid than Pennzoil's for the Getty Oil shares.
>
> When the board reconvened at 3 P.M. on January 3, a revised Pennzoil proposal was presented, offering $110 per share plus a $3 "stub" that was to be paid after the sale of a Getty Oil subsidiary ("ERC"), from the excess proceeds over $1 billion. Each shareholder was to receive a pro rata share of these excess proceeds, but in any case, a minimum of $3 per share at the end of five years. During the meeting, Boisi briefly informed the board of the status of his inquiries of other companies that might be interested in bidding for the company. He reported some preliminary indications of interest, but no definite bid yet.
>
> The Museum's lawyer told the board that, based on his discussions with Pennzoil, he believed that if the board went back "firm" with an offer of $110 plus a $5 stub, Pennzoil would accept it. After a recess, the Museum's president (also a director of Getty Oil) moved that the Getty

*(Continued)*

25. *See, e.g.,* Kronos, Inc. v. AVX Corp., 612 N.E.2d 289 (N.Y. 1993).
26. Texaco, Inc. v. Pennzoil Co., 729 S.W.2d 768 (Tex. Ct. App. 1987), *cert. dismissed,* 485 U.S. 994 (1988).

(Inside Story *continued*)

board should accept Pennzoil's proposal provided that the stub be raised to $5, and the board voted 15 to 1 to approve this counterproposal to Pennzoil. The board then voted themselves and Getty's officers and advisors indemnity for any liability arising from the events of the past few months. There was evidence that during another brief recess of the board meeting, the counter-offer of $110 plus a $5 stub was presented to and accepted by Pennzoil. After Pennzoil's acceptance was conveyed to the Getty board, the meeting was adjourned, and most board members left town for their respective homes.

That evening, the lawyers and public relations staff of Getty Oil and the Museum drafted a press release describing the transaction between Pennzoil and the Getty entities. The press release, announcing an agreement in principle on the terms of the Memorandum of Agreement but with a price of $110 plus a $5 stub, was issued on Getty Oil letterhead the next morning, January 4, and later that day, Pennzoil issued an identical press release.

On January 4, Boisi continued to contact other companies, looking for a higher price than Pennzoil had offered. After talking briefly with Boisi, Texaco management called several meetings with its in-house financial planning group. . . .

On January 5, the *Wall Street Journal* reported on an agreement reached between Pennzoil and the Getty entities, describing essentially the terms contained in the Memorandum of Agreement. The Pennzoil board met to ratify the actions of its officers in negotiating an agreement with the Getty entities, and Pennzoil's attorneys periodically attempted to contact the other parties' advisors and attorneys to continue work on the transaction agreement.

The board of Texaco also met on January 5, authorizing its officers to make an offer for 100% of Getty Oil and to take any necessary action in connection therewith. Texaco first contacted the Museum's lawyer, Marty Lipton, and arranged a meeting to discuss the sale of the Museum's shares of Getty Oil to Texaco. Lipton instructed his associate, on her way to the meeting in progress of the lawyers drafting merger documents for the Pennzoil/Getty transaction, not to attend that meeting, because he needed her at his meeting with Texaco. At the meeting with Texaco, the Museum outlined various issues it wanted resolved in any transaction with Texaco, and then agreed to sell its 11.8% ownership in Getty Oil [for $125 per share].

At noon on January 6, Getty Oil held a telephone board meeting to discuss the Texaco offer. The board voted to withdraw its previous counterproposal to Pennzoil and unanimously voted to accept Texaco's offer. Texaco immediately issued a press release announcing that Getty Oil and Texaco would merge.

Soon after the Texaco press release appeared, Pennzoil telexed the Getty entities, demanding that they honor their agreement with Pennzoil. Later that day, prompted by the telex, Getty Oil filed a suit in Delaware for declaratory judgment that it was not bound to any contract with Pennzoil. The merger agreement between Texaco and Getty Oil was signed on January 6; the stock purchase agreement with the Museum was signed on January 6; and the stock exchange agreement with the Trust was signed on January 8, 1984.

In addition to the facts described in the excerpts from the opinion of the court of appeals, the Pennzoil lawyers emphasized several other events as evidence that both Pennzoil and Getty intended to be bound by the five-page memorandum of agreement.

At the conclusion of the January 3 Getty board meeting approving the Pennzoil merger, congratulations were exchanged, and many of the individuals present, including several Pennzoil representatives, shook hands. At trial, Pennzoil made this an issue of honor and the value of a man's word, asserting that a handshake could and often did seal a bargain.

Texaco pointed out that, handshakes notwithstanding, the Getty board of directors left the meeting without signing the memorandum of agreement. Texaco also noted that it had not made an offer until it was invited to do so by Getty. John McKinley, chairman of Texaco, repeatedly asked if Getty Oil was free to deal and was assured by Gordon Getty and by the Getty Museum that there was no contract with Pennzoil. In addition, under the law of New York, where all the deals were made, a contract does not exist until the parties have agreed on all the essential terms of the deal. Texaco argued that a five-page memorandum could not possibly cover all the essential terms in a $5 billion deal involving four parties (Pennzoil, Getty Oil Company, the Sarah Getty Trust, and the Getty Museum).

Before going further into the many legal arguments involved, it is useful to look more closely at the memorandum of agreement reproduced in Exhibit 7.1.

Getty and Pennzoil had an agreement in principle, but did they have a contract? As soon as the board meeting adjourned on the evening of January 3, some thirty lawyers began working around the clock to draw up the merger documents and the press release to announce the deal. Both were supposed to be completed by the next morning, but only the press release was ready. Typed on Getty Oil letterhead and dated January 4, 1984, it announced that Getty Oil and Pennzoil had "agreed in principle" to a merger. It further stated: "The transaction

*(Continued)*

EXHIBIT 7.1 **The Pennzoil–Getty Memorandum of Agreement**

**Memorandum of Agreement**

January 2, 1984

The following plan (the "Plan") has been developed and approved by (i) Gordon P. Getty, as Trustee (the "Trustee") of the Sarah C. Getty Trust dated December 31, 1934 (the "Trust"), which Trustee owns 31,805,800 shares (40.2% of the total outstanding shares) of Common Stock, without par value, of Getty Oil Company (the "Company"), which shares as well as all other outstanding shares of such Common Stock are hereinafter referred to as the "Shares", (ii) The J. Paul Getty Museum (the "Museum"), which Museum owns 9,320,340 Shares (11.8% of the total outstanding Shares) and (iii) Pennzoil Company ("Pennzoil"), which owns 593,900 Shares through a subsidiary, Holdings Incorporated, a Delaware corporation (the "Purchaser"). The Plan is intended to assure that the public shareholders of the Company and the Museum will receive $110 per Share for all their Shares, a price which is approximately 40% above the price at which the Company's Shares were trading before Pennzoil's subsidiary announced its Offer (hereinafter described) and 10% more than the price which Pennzoil's subsidiary offered in its Offer for 20% of the Shares. The Trustee recommends that the Board of Directors of the Company approve the Plan. The Museum desires that the Plan be considered by the Board of Directors and has executed the Plan for that purpose.

**1.** Pennzoil agreement. Subject to the approval of the Plan by the Board of Directors of the Company as provided in paragraph 6 hereof, Pennzoil agrees to cause the Purchaser promptly to amend its Offer to Purchase dated December 28, 1983 (the "Offer") for up to 16,000,000 Shares so as:
   **(a)** to increase the Offer price to $110 per Share, net to the Seller in cash and
   **(b)** to increase the number of Shares subject to the Offer to 23,406,100 (being 24,000,000 Shares less 593,900 now owned by the Purchaser).

**2.** Company agreement. Subject to approval of the Plan by the Board of Directors of the Company as provided in paragraph 6 hereof, the Company agrees:
   **(a)** to purchase forthwith all 9,320,340 Shares owned by the Museum at a purchase price of $110 per Share (subject to adjustment before or after closing in the event of any increase in the Offer price or in the event any higher price is paid by any person who hereafter acquires 10 percent or more of the outstanding Shares) payable either (at the election of the Company) in cash or by means of a promissory note of the Company, dated as of the closing date, payable to the order of the Museum, due on or before thirty days from the date of issuance, bearing interest at a rate equivalent to the prime rate as in effect at Citibank, N.A. and backed by an irrevocable letter of credit (the "Company Note")
   **(b)** to proceed promptly upon completion of the Offer by the Purchaser with a cash merger transaction whereby all remaining holders of Shares (other than the Trustee and Pennzoil and its subsidiaries) will receive $110 per Share in cash, and
   **(c)** in consideration of Pennzoil's agreement provided for in paragraph 1 hereof and in order to provide additional assurance that the Plan will be consummated in accordance with its terms, to grant to Pennzoil hereby the option, exercisable at Pennzoil's election at any time on or before the later of consummation of the Offer referred to in paragraph 1 and the purchase referred to in (a) of this paragraph 2, to purchase from the Company up to 8,000,000 Shares of Common Stock of the Company held in the treasury of the Company at a purchase price of $110 per share in cash.

**3.** Museum agreement. Subject to approval of the Plan by the Board of Directors of the Company as provided in paragraph 6 hereof, the Museum agrees to sell to the Company forthwith all 9,320,340 Shares owned by the Museum at a purchase price of $110 per Share (subject to adjustment before or after closing as provided in paragraph 2(a)) payable either (at the election of the Company) in cash or by means of the Company Note referred to in paragraph 2(c).

**4.** Trustee and Pennzoil agreement. The Trustee and Pennzoil hereby agree with each other as follows:
   **(a)** Ratio of Ownership of Shares. The Trustee may increase its holdings to up to 32,000,000 Shares and Pennzoil may increase its holdings to up to 24,000,000 Shares of the approximately 79,132,000 outstanding Shares. Neither the Trustee nor Pennzoil will acquire in excess of such respective amounts without the prior written agreement of the other, it being the agreement between the Trustee and Pennzoil to maintain a relative Share ratio of 4 (for the Trustee) to 3 (for Pennzoil). In connection with the Offer in the event that more than 23,406,100 Shares are duly tendered to the Purchaser, the Purchaser may (if it chooses) purchase any excess over 23,406,000; provided, however, (i) the Purchaser agrees to sell any such excess Shares to the Company (and the company shall agree to purchase) forthwith

(Exhibit 7.1 *continues*)

(Exhibit 7.1 *continued*)

at $110 per Share and (ii) pending consummation of such sale to the Company the Purchaser shall grant to the Trustee the irrevocable proxy to vote such excess Shares.

**(b)** Restructuring plan. Upon completion of the transactions provided for in paragraphs 1, 2 and 3 hereof, the Trustee and Pennzoil shall endeavor in good faith to agree upon a plan for the restructuring of the Company. In the event that for any reason the Trustee and Pennzoil are unable to agree upon a mutually acceptable plan on or before December 31, 1984, then the Trustee and Pennzoil hereby agree to cause the Company to adopt a plan of complete liquidation of the Company pursuant to which (i) any assets which are mutually agreed to be sold shall be sold and the net proceeds therefrom shall be used to reduce liabilities of the Company and (ii) individual interests in all remaining assets and liabilities shall be distributed to the shareholders pro rata in accordance with their actual ownership interest in the Company. In connection with the plan of distribution, Pennzoil agrees (if requested by the Trustee) that it will enter into customary joint operating agreements to operate any properties so distributed and otherwise to agree to provide operating management for any business and operations requested by the Trustee on customary terms and conditions.

**(c)** Board of Directors and Management. Upon completion of the transactions provided for in paragraphs 1, 2 and 3 hereof, the Trustee and Pennzoil agree that the Board of Directors of the Company shall be composed of approximately fourteen Directors who shall be mutually agreeable to the Trustee and Pennzoil (which Directors may include certain present Directors) and who shall be nominated by the Trustee and Pennzoil, respectively, in the ratio of 4 to 3. The Trustee and Pennzoil agree that the senior management of the Company shall include Gordon P. Getty as Chairman of the Board, J. Hugh Liedtke as President and Chief Executive Officer and Blaine P. Kerr as Chairman of the Executive Committee.

**(d)** Access to Information. Pennzoil, the Trustee and their representatives will have access to all information concerning the Company necessary or pertinent to accomplish the transactions contemplated by the Plan.

**(e)** Press releases. The Trustee and Pennzoil (and the Company upon approval of the Plan) will coordinate any press releases or public announcements concerning the Plan and any transactions contemplated hereby.

**5.** Compliance with regulatory requirements. The Plan shall be implemented in compliance with applicable regulatory requirements.

**6.** Approval by the Board of Directors. This Plan is subject to approval by the Board of Directors of the Company at the meeting of the Board being held on January 2, 1984, and will expire if not approved by the Board. Upon such approval the Company shall execute three or more counterparts of the "Joinder by the Company" attached to the Plan and deliver one such counterpart to each of the Trustee, the Museum and Pennzoil.

IN WITNESS WHEREOF, this Plan, or a counterpart hereof, has been signed by the following officials thereunto duly authorized this January 2, 1984.

/s/ GORDON P. GETTY
Gordon P. Getty as Trustee of the Sarah C. Getty Trust

The J. Paul Getty Museum
By /s/ HAROLD WILLIAMS
Harold Williams, President

Pennzoil Company
By ______________________
J. Hugh Liedtke, Chairman of the Board and
Chief Executive Officer

**Joinder by the Company**

The foregoing Plan has been approved by the Board of Directors.

Getty Oil Company
By ______________________

January 2, 1984

(Inside Story *continued*)

is subject to execution of a definitive merger agreement, approval by the stockholders of Getty Oil and completion of various governmental filing and waiting period requirements."

The Texaco deal was much simpler than the Pennzoil deal. Texaco simply bought out everyone at $125 a share. By 8 A.M. on January 6, a news release on Texaco letterhead had gone out. At 9 A.M., the Getty board of directors held another board meeting and approved the deal with Texaco. Texaco acquired Getty Oil, and Pennzoil was left out in the cold.

No one on Wall Street saw anything wrong with the deal, but the attitude in the Texas oil business was different. At the 1984 Pennzoil stockholder meeting, Hugh Liedtke described the decision to sue Texaco:

> It's one thing to play hardball. It's quite another thing to play foul ball. Conduct such as Texaco's is not made legal simply by protestations that the acts involved were, in fact, legal. All too often such assertions go unchallenged, and so slip into some sort of legal limbo, and become accepted as the norm by default. In this way, actions previously considered amoral somehow become clothed in respectability.[27]

On January 10, 1984, Pennzoil filed suit in Delaware against Getty Oil, Gordon Getty, the Getty Museum, and Texaco. Pennzoil wanted specific performance—that is, a court order that would give it back its deal with Getty. A few days later, Pennzoil discovered the indemnity clauses and added tortious interference with contract to its claims against Texaco.

The Delaware case was to be tried before a judge, not a jury. Through some legal maneuvering on Pennzoil's part and Texaco's failure to file an answer in the Delaware case right away, the case against Texaco ended up in a Texas court before a jury. (The suits against Getty, the Trust, and the Museum continued in Delaware.) For four and a half months, the two sides presented their evidence. Before the jury retired to the jury room, the judge instructed them how to apply the law to the facts they had heard. The word "contract" never appeared in the jury instructions. Instead, the judge used the word "agreement."

On the issue of damages, Pennzoil presented a single witness, who testified that the jury should award "replacement" damages, rather than expectation damages. He asserted that it would have cost Pennzoil $3.4 billion, or $3.40 per barrel, for the one billion barrels that it would have owned through its three-sevenths ownership of Getty Oil's reserves. With the deal destroyed, however, Pennzoil would have to drill from scratch at a cost of $10.87 per barrel: $10.87 per barrel minus $3.40 per barrel times one billion barrels equaled $7.47 billion in replacement costs—three times the price that Pennzoil had agreed to pay to purchase its three-sevenths interest in Getty Oil. Under a benefit of the bargain analysis, Pennzoil had lost the opportunity to buy 32 million shares of Getty Oil at $112.50 each—shares that Texaco subsequently purchased for $128 each—or a total of $496 million ($15.50 per share times 32 million shares). Despite convincing arguments by Texaco's counsel that the replacement damages claimed by Pennzoil were inappropriate, Texaco presented no witnesses or other evidence on the issue of damages.

As the jury considered the question of punitive damages during its deliberations, the jurors asked the judge, "To what extent is Texaco liable for the actions of [Gordon Getty's lawyer and Getty Oil's lawyer and investment banker]?" The Texaco lawyer thought that the jury instructions had included a charge that a party is accountable only for its own agents, so he agreed that no response to this question was required. As a result, the jury decided to award punitive damages against Texaco because it found that the actions of the indemnitees were outrageous (even though the indemnitees were not Texaco's agents and were not themselves parties to the action because the lawsuit against them was proceeding in Delaware).

The jury returned a verdict in favor of Pennzoil. For Texaco's interference with a contract, the jury awarded Pennzoil $7.53 billion compensatory damages and $3 billion punitive damages, or $1 billion for each indemnity given—$1 billion for the indemnity to Gordon Getty, $1 billion for the indemnity to Getty Oil, and $1 billion for the indemnity to the Getty Museum. (The punitive damages were eventually reduced to $1 billion. The compensatory damages were not changed.)

What did the judges for the Court of Appeals for the First Supreme Judicial District of Texas think of all this? In a lengthy opinion, excerpted below, they upheld the jury's verdict.

**Excerpts from the Opinion of the Court of Appeals: Legal Analysis**

> Under New York law, if parties do not intend to be bound to an agreement until it is reduced to writing and signed by both parties, then there is no contract until that event occurs. If there is no understanding that a signed

*(Continued)*

27. THOMAS PETZINGER, JR., OIL AND HONOR: THE TEXACO–PENNZOIL WARS 275–76 (1987).

(Inside Story *continued*)

writing is necessary before the parties will be bound, and the parties have agreed upon all substantial terms, then an informal agreement can be binding, even though the parties contemplate evidencing their agreement in a formal document later.

Thus, under New York law, the parties are given the power to obligate themselves informally or only by a formal signed writing, as they wish. The emphasis in deciding when a binding contract exists is on intent rather than on form.

To determine intent, a court must examine the words and deeds of the parties, because these constitute the objective signs of such intent. Only the outward expressions of intent are considered—secret or subjective intent is immaterial to the question of whether the parties were bound.

. . .

Although the magnitude of the transaction here was such that normally a signed writing would be expected, there was sufficient evidence to support an inference by the jury that the expectation was satisfied here initially by the Memorandum of Agreement, signed by a majority of shareholders of Getty Oil and approved by the board with a higher price, and by the transaction agreement in progress that had been intended to memorialize the agreement previously reached.

. . .

Texaco claims that even if the parties intended to bind themselves before a definitive document was signed, no binding contract could result because the terms that they intended to include in their agreement were too vague and incomplete to be enforceable as a matter of law. . . . The question of whether the agreement is sufficiently definite to be enforceable is a difficult one. The facts of the individual case are decisively important. . . .

Texaco's attempts to create additional "essential" terms from the mechanics of implementing the agreement's existing provisions are unpersuasive. The terms of the agreement found by the jury are supported by the evidence, and the promises of the parties are clear enough for a court to recognize a breach and to determine the damages resulting from that breach.

Burdened by the largest damages award in U.S. history, Texaco filed for bankruptcy in 1987 after its appeals in the Texas courts failed. As part of its reorganization plan, Texaco agreed to settle the case with Pennzoil for $3 billion.

This case had a tremendous impact on Wall Street, which the *Wall Street Journal* dubbed "the Texaco chill." Investment banker Alan Rothenberg summarized the new attitude: "No longer can we say, 'We stole a deal fair and square.'"[28] In legal circles, the arguments still continue as to whether the Texas judges properly understood New York contract law and the jury reached the correct verdict.

*Pennzoil v. Texaco* is still on the books and can be cited as precedent in similar cases. Note, however, that the Texas Supreme Court's recent decision in *Wal-Mart Stores, Inc. v. Sturges*[29] has made it more difficult to recover damages in an action claiming interference with a prospective contractual relationship. In this case, Sturges had sued Wal-Mart, claiming that it had tortiously interfered with its prospective lease. A trial court found Wal-Mart liable and awarded Sturges $1 million in actual damages and $500,000 in punitive damages, but the Texas Supreme Court reversed the trial court's decision. The supreme court found that where a case involves a prospective business relationship as opposed to a signed contract, "aggressive but legal interference" cannot be attacked as tortious interference.

28. *Id.* at 459–60.
29. 52 S.W.3d 711 (Tex. 2001).

## KEY WORDS AND PHRASES

acceptance 214
accord 235
accord and satisfaction 235
anticipatory repudiation 235
bilateral contract 215
capacity 218
choice-of-forum provision 245
choice-of-law provision 245
close 244
compensatory damages 237
condition precedent 217
condition subsequent 218
conditions concurrent 217
consequential damages 237
consideration 215
contract 212
counteroffer 213
covenant not to compete 219
cover 238
creditor beneficiary 236
detrimental reliance 214
discharge 235
donee beneficiary 237
duress 226
equal dignities rule 229
expectation damages 237
fraud in the factum 224

## QUESTIONS AND CASE PROBLEMS

1. Leslie Landlord agreed to rent Ted Tenant an office for $3,000 per month for three years. Tenant encountered financial difficulties. Landlord agreed to reduce the rent to $2,200 per month, and Tenant agreed not to file for bankruptcy. Tenant had no plans to file for bankruptcy. Unbeknownst to both Landlord and Tenant, a promise not to file for bankruptcy is unenforceable under the Bankruptcy Code. Was the agreement to reduce the rent binding? Would it make a difference if Tenant had planned to file for bankruptcy if he couldn't get the rent reduction? Was Tenant's conduct ethical?

2. Factors, a company in the business of purchasing accounts receivable and lending money to other businesses, asked Unisearch to conduct a Uniform Commercial Code (UCC) search on its behalf for liens against The Benefit Group, Inc. Unisearch completed the search and sent Factors an invoice along with a search report showing no security interests. The invoice was identical to forty-seven others that Unisearch had previously sent to Factors. Upon receiving the report, Factors lent $100,000 to The Benefit Group, secured by its existing and future accounts receivable and other business assets. A year later, The Benefit Group defaulted, and when Factors tried to foreclose on the collateral, it discovered a prior UCC filing under the name of "The Benefits Group, Inc." Factors sued Unisearch, alleging breach of contract and negligence. Prior to trial, Unisearch brought a motion for summary judgment on damages, claiming that its liability was limited to $25 because a clause in its invoice limited liability for any action arising out of or related to the contract to that amount. The limitation of liability was printed on the front of the one-page invoice in the upper right-hand corner in a shaded box. Factors argued that the limitation of liability was unenforceable. Is the limitation of liability unenforceable? On what basis? [*Puget Sound Financial, L.L.C. v. Unisearch, Inc.*, 47 P.3d 940 (Wash. 2002).]

3. Andy Barstow, the owner of a store, entered into a detailed letter of intent to negotiate in good faith the lease of the store with Zandra Ingalls, a prospective tenant. The letter included an outline of the terms that needed to be negotiated, including rent. Barstow promised to withdraw the store from the marketplace during the negotiations. Ingalls, during the time of the negotiations, spent money developing a marketing plan for her business. She also brought in a carpenter, who started building some furniture and cabinets specially designed for the new store. Barstow called Ingalls the following week, saying that he had decided to lease the store to his friend, Bob Burke. What damages, if any, can Ingalls recover?

4. Lanci was involved in an automobile accident with an uninsured motorist. Lanci and Metropolitan Insurance Company entered settlement negotiations and ultimately agreed to settle all claims for $15,000. Lanci's correspondence accepting the settlement offer clearly indicated his belief that his policy limit was $15,000. However, Lanci did not have a copy of his policy, and, in fact, his policy limit was $250,000. When Lanci learned the correct policy limit, he refused to accept the settlement proceeds of $15,000. Should Lanci be able to void the contract? On what basis? [*Lanci v. Metropolitan Insurance Co.*, 564 A.2d 972 (Pa. Super. Ct. 1989).]

5. Oracle Corporation unveiled new versions of its flagship database software and Web application at its annual Oracle OpenWorld in October 2000. Oracle said the new enhancements made the Oracle9i software faster, more reliable, and better able to handle the heavy duty computing needs of application service providers (ASPs)—companies that deliver software services over the Web. In a speech at OpenWorld, Oracle Chairman Larry Ellison offered to give any Microsoft or IBM database customers $1 million if they weren't able to triple their performance on the Oracle9i products. If an ASP attended the OpenWorld conference, heard Ellison speak, and purchased the Oracle9i software shortly thereafter to replace its existing Microsoft database, would it have a cause of action against Oracle if it could show, six months later, that the Oracle9i software had only doubled its performance? What arguments would the ASP make? What defenses might Oracle assert? Who will win? [See Cecelia Kang, *Ellison: We'll Guarantee It,* SAN JOSE MERCURY NEWS, Oct. 4, 2000, *available at* http://www.mercurycenter.com/premium/business/docs/oracle04.html.]

6. Hydrotech Systems, Ltd., a New York corporation, agreed to sell wave-pool equipment to Oasis Waterpark, an amusement park in Palm Springs, California. Although Hydrotech was not licensed to install such equipment in California, it agreed to install the wave-pool equipment after Oasis promised to arrange for a California-licensed contractor to "work with" Hydrotech on any construction.

   The contract between Hydrotech and Oasis called for Oasis to withhold a specific portion of the contract price pending satisfactory operation of the wave pool. Although the pool functioned properly after installation, Oasis continued to withhold payment for both the equipment and the installation services.

   Section 7031 of the California Business and Professions Code states that a suit may not be brought in a California court to recover compensation for any act or contract that requires a California contractor's license unless the plaintiff alleges and proves that he or she was duly licensed at all times during the performance.

   Can Hydrotech recover its compensation due under the contract? Does Hydrotech have a valid action against Oasis for fraud? Is it ethical for Oasis to use the California law to defend itself? [*Hydrotech Systems, Ltd. v. Oasis Waterpark,* 803 P.2d 370 (Cal. 1991).]

7. Emmett Employer called Sally Denoco and offered her a two-year employment contract. Denoco said, "Great, I accept," then quit her present job, forfeiting unvested stock options. After Denoco had worked for Employer for six months for a cash salary of $8,000 a month, Employer fired Denoco. She then sued. Who should win? Does it matter that Employer made a note to himself after the phone call: "Sally Denoco—two-year contract. Salary to be negotiated"? If Denoco were to win, what would be her damages? Would she be entitled to anything if she quit her old job but never started work for Employer? What should Employer and Denoco each have done to protect their rights?

8. Bruce Gardner took his Porsche to be repaired at Downtown Porsche Audi in downtown Los Angeles. Gardner signed Downtown's repair order form contract, which contained the following exculpatory clause: "NOT RESPONSIBLE FOR LOSS OR DAMAGE TO CARS OR ARTICLES LEFT IN CARS IN CASE OF FIRE, THEFT, OR ANY OTHER CAUSE BEYOND OUR CIRCUMSTANCES." Someone stole Gardner's Porsche while it was parked at the garage. Gardner sued Downtown for damages. Did Gardner win? If so, on what basis? [*Gardner v. Downtown Porsche Audi,* 225 Cal. Rptr. 757 (Cal. App. 1986).]

9. Adobe Systems, Inc. is a leading software publishing company. SoftMan Products Company distributes computer software products primarily through its website, http://www.buycheapsoftware.com. Adobe distributes its products, including certain collections of products (Collections), through license agreements with distributors. Each Adobe Collection is also accompanied by an End User License Agreement (EULA) that sets forth the terms of the license between Adobe and the end user for that specific product. The EULA is electronically recorded

on the computer disk, and customers are asked to agree to its terms when they attempt to install the software. The EULA includes a provision that prohibits licensees from transferring or assigning any individual Adobe product that was originally distributed as part of a Collection unless it is transferred with all the software in the original Collection. Adobe filed a lawsuit seeking a preliminary injunction against SoftMan on the ground that SoftMan had violated the terms of Adobe's EULA by breaking apart various Adobe Collection packages and distributing the individual pieces of them as single products. SoftMan defended on the ground that it was not subject to the EULA terms because it did not install the software before reselling it to end users. Who will prevail? [*SoftMan Products Co., L.L.C. v. Adobe Systems, Inc.*, 171 F. Supp. 2d 1075 (C.D. Cal. 2001); contra *Adobe Systems, Inc. v. Stargate Software, Inc.*, 216 F. Supp. 2d 1051 (N.D. Cal. 2002).]

## MANAGER'S DILEMMA

**10.** When Circuit City hired Paul Mantor in 1992, it did not have an arbitration program. In 1995, Circuit City adopted an arbitration program called the "Associate Issue Resolution Program" (AIRP). The AIRP provided that:

> . . . except as otherwise limited herein, any and all employment-related legal disputes, controversies or claims of an [employee] arising out of, or related to, an [employee's] application or candidacy for employment or cessation of employment with Circuit City . . . shall be settled exclusively by final and binding arbitration before a neutral, third-party Arbitrator selected in accordance with these Dispute Resolution Rules and Procedures. Arbitration shall apply to any and all such disputes, controversies or claims whether asserted against the Company and/or against any employee, officer, alleged agent, director or affiliate company.

The AIRP also (1) required an employee to pay a $75 filing fee to Circuit City to begin an arbitration, (2) provided that Circuit City had sole discretion to decide whether to waive the filing fee and other costs of arbitration (in a court action, an indigent plaintiff is exempt from having to pay court fees), and (3) prohibited arbitrators from hearing an arbitration as a class action.

Circuit City emphasized to its managers the importance of full participation in the AIRP, claiming that the company had been losing money because of lawsuits filed by employees. Although Circuit City circulated the forms regarding the AIRP in 1995, Mantor avoided signing them for three years. In 1998, however, Circuit City management met with him to discuss his participation in the program. When Mantor asked them what would happen if he declined to participate, they told him he would have no future with Circuit City. Soon thereafter, Mantor agreed to participate, acknowledging in writing his receipt of the program and an opt-out form by which employees could ostensibly elect not to participate in the AIRP.

In 2000, Circuit City terminated Mantor's employment. When Mantor brought a civil action against Circuit City in state court, the court granted Circuit City's motion to compel arbitration. The Federal Arbitration Act provides that arbitration agreements generally "shall be valid, irrevocable, and enforceable," but when grounds "exist at law or in equity for the revocation of any contract," courts may decline to enforce such agreements. On appeal Mantor argued that the district court erred in granting the order to compel arbitration. If you had been the manager at Circuit City who spoke with Mantor, what would you have said when he asked what would happen if he declined to participate in the AIRP? Was it ethical for Circuit City to distribute an opt-out form while informing employees orally that they would be terminated if they refused to participate in the AIRP? What arguments could Mantor make to support his position that he was not bound by the AIRP's mandatory arbitration provision? [*Circuit City Stores, Inc. v. Mantor*, 335 F.3d 1101 (9th Cir. 2003), *cert. denied*, 540 U.S. 1160 (2004).]

## INTERNET SOURCES

| | |
|---|---|
| Contract-Law.com provides answers to the most commonly asked questions about contracts and contract law. | http://www.contract-law.com |
| The 'Lectric Law Library page offers a variety of business contract forms. | http://www.lectlaw.com/formb.html |
| The website of the National Conference of Commissioners on Uniform State Laws contains information about the Uniform Acts including their organization and legislative status. | http://www.nccusl.org |

CHAPTER 8

# Sales and E-Commerce

## INTRODUCTION

### Managers, Sales of Goods, Licensing of Software, and Electronic Commerce

Virtually all commercial enterprises engage in the purchase or sale of goods. Sales of goods within the United States are governed by Article 2 of the Uniform Commercial Code (UCC); most international sales are governed by the Convention on Contracts for the International Sale of Goods. The UCC does not govern the rendering of services or the sale of land. Contracts for selling services or land are governed by common law contract principles, which are discussed in Chapter 7. The UCC has attempted to eliminate some of the legal formalities of traditional contract law to meet the needs and realities of the business world. Many provisions of the UCC can be changed by the express agreement of the parties. To the extent that the UCC is silent on a subject, the common law contract provisions described in Chapter 7 apply.

The Internet has transformed the way businesses and individuals conduct business in the United States and throughout the world. According to the Census Bureau, e-commerce transactions by manufacturers, wholesalers, service providers, and retailers amounted to $1.16 trillion in 2002 and are expected to continue to grow in coming years.[1] Due to the speed at which technology is developing and the range of novel issues it presents, state and national governments are scrambling to enact laws that both protect consumers and businesses and facilitate electronic sales transactions using the Internet. In addition, the international reach of the Internet is forcing countries throughout the world to engage in legal cooperation and collaboration.

1. Census numbers are available *at* http://www.census.gov/eos/www/2002tables.html. The most recent e-commerce forecast was obtained from Carrie Johnson, Senior Analyst, Forrester Research Inc., *The Growth of Multichannel Retailing* (July 2004) (unpublished report prepared for the National Governors Association and the National Conference of State Legislatures), *at* http://www.nga.org/cda/files/0407MULTICHANNEL.PDF.

### Chapter Overview

This chapter begins by addressing contract formation under the UCC and the UCC approach to the *battle of the forms,* which occurs when the form accepting an offer contains terms different from those on the form that constitutes the offer. The special warranty provisions of the UCC are discussed, including express warranties and implied warranties of merchantability and fitness for a particular purpose. The chapter explains how the risk of loss is allocated and a buyer's right to reject nonconforming goods. The chapter then reviews excuses for nonperformance, including unconscionability and commercial impracticability, and remedies for unexcused nonperformance. Rules applicable to the international sale of goods are described and compared with those applicable to domestic sales transactions governed by the UCC.

The chapter also addresses laws regulating e-commerce such as the Uniform Computer Information Transactions Act, which provides a uniform commercial contract code for the licensing of computer software and other computer information transactions, and the Uniform Electronic Transactions Act. The chapter also discusses the issue of taxing e-commerce, in particular, the imposition of sales taxes on purchases made over the Internet. The "Inside Story" addresses the increasing problem of fraud at online auction houses and efforts by law enforcement agencies to regulate crime on the Internet where it is often difficult to identify the criminals.

# When Does Article 2 of the UCC Apply?

The Uniform Commercial Code deals with a broad range of commercial transactions, from the use of negotiable instruments to secured transactions. It was promulgated in the early 1940s under the joint authority of the American Law Institute (ALI) and the National Conference of Commissioners on Uniform State Laws (NCCUSL) to bring greater certainty and predictability to an increasingly national commercial system. The ALI, a national organization of 4,000 lawyers, judges, and academics from all areas of the United States and some foreign countries, was organized in 1923 to address uncertainty in the law, in part by generating restatements of basic legal subjects to assist judges and lawyers in understanding the law in that area. The NCCUSL, a national organization of 350 lawyers, judges, and academics from the fifty states, the District of Columbia, Puerto Rico, and the U.S. Virgin Islands, was organized in the late nineteenth century to provide states with nonpartisan model legislation to help bring stability and clarity to critical areas of state statutory law.

The UCC is a model law, meaning that it must be enacted into law by a state legislature to become effective in that state. Because the UCC is approved by both the ALI and the NCCUSL, however, it has generally been accepted by the states more readily than model laws promulgated only by the NCCUSL.

Article 2 of the UCC deals with contracts for the sale of goods. The original version of Article 2 was first enacted in Pennsylvania in 1953 and was eventually adopted in every state except Louisiana. Although other articles of the UCC have been revised since the early 1950s (some more than once), efforts to revise Article 2 did not begin until the late 1980s. During most of the 1990s, the plan was to divide Article 2 into three sections: Article 2, which would continue to deal with the sale of goods; Article 2A, which would deal with certain lease transactions and is outside the scope of this chapter; and Article 2B, which would deal with licensing, including licensing arrangements for software. In 1999, however, the ALI rejected the final version of Article 2B, and the NCCUSL elected instead to adopt it as a model state law, the Uniform Computer Information Transactions Act (UCITA).

Both the NCCUSL and the ALI did, however, approve the final version of the amendments to Article 2 in 2003, paving the way for their introduction in state legislatures. Because most states adopt amendments to the UCC within three to four years after their final approval by the NCCUSL and ALI, this chapter will reference the changes to Article 2 that will occur if and when the 2003 amendments are adopted by the states.

## Uniform Computer Information Transactions Act

Like the UCC, model laws such as UCITA become effective only when enacted by individual state legislatures. Although many sectors of the software industry strongly supported UCITA, many others opposed it, including consumer advocates, technology trade associations, law professors, the American Library Association, the Consumers Union, the Institute of Electrical and Electronics Engineers, and a long list of state attorneys general. Critics complained that UCITA provided too much protection to companies and not enough to consumers. They strongly opposed giving software vendors the right to monitor the use of their products by accessing computers remotely, and they argued that UCITA would weaken the warranty protection consumers receive under software licenses and make it more difficult to sue software vendors that sold faulty programs. As of August 2004, only two states (Maryland and Virginia) have adopted UCITA, while at least five states have adopted anti-UCITA laws that limit the power of their courts to apply UCITA by virtue of a choice-of-law determination. In 2003, the NCCUSL attempted to persuade the American Bar Association (ABA) to approve UCITA but withdrew its request in the face of opposition by several ABA sections. As a result, the NCCUSL decided to forgo, at least for the time being, any further efforts to convince the states to enact UCITA.[2]

## What Types of Contracts Are Governed by Article 2?

Section 2-105 of the UCC defines *goods* as "all things (including specially manufactured goods) which are movable at the time of identification to the contract for sale." *Identification to the contract* means the designation—by marking, setting aside, or other means—of the particular goods that are to be supplied under the contract. Sometimes it is not clear whether an activity should

2. *UCITA Update*, COM. L. REP., Oct. 2003, at 146–48.

be characterized as a sale of goods or a sale of services. For example, when a hospital performs a blood transfusion, is it selling blood or rendering medical services? This distinction can be critical for purposes of both the UCC warranties and product liability in tort (discussed in Chapter 10). Many states have addressed precisely this issue by passing special amendments to their versions of the UCC. These so-called blood shield statutes define blood transfusions as the provision of services, rather than the sale of goods, in order to limit hospital and blood bank liability for reasons of public policy.[3] In other states, the common law has led to the conclusion that such sales are incidental to the provision of medical services and are therefore outside the scope of the UCC.[4]

Similarly, there can be an issue as to whether something attached to land is considered goods or land. This gray area includes *fixtures,* which are items of personal property that are attached to real property and cannot be removed without substantial damage. Fixtures are not considered goods under Article 2. They are generally subject to the rules governing real property.

Most cases addressing the subject have held, either directly or by analogy, that Article 2 applies to most transactions involving software.[5] Under the proposed amendments to Article 2, this case law will be subject to question because the amendments exclude "information" from the definition of "goods." Although the amendments do not define the term "information," the official comments state that "this article does not directly apply to an electronic transfer of information, such as the transaction involved in Specht v. Netscape." Because the transaction in *Specht,* which appears as Case 8.1 in this chapter, involved downloading of copies of a computer program to computers, "information" presumably excludes electronic transfers of computer software. The comments continue:

> However, transactions often include both goods and information: some are transactions in goods as that term is used in Section 2-107 and some are not. For example, the sale of "smart goods" such as an automobile is a transaction in goods fully within this article even though the automobile contains many computer products.

3. *See, e.g.*, Zichichi v. Middlesex Mem'l Hosp., 528 A.2d 805 (Conn. 1987); Garcia v. Edgewater Hosp., 613 N.E.2d 1243 (Ill. App. Ct. 1993).

4. *See, e.g.*, Lovett v. Emory Univ., Inc., 156 S.E.2d 923 (Ga. Ct. App. 1967).

5. Restatement (Third) of Torts, § 19, cmt. d (1997) (stating "[u]nder the [UCC] software that is mass-marketed is considered a good" and citing numerous cases).

These comments to the proposed amendments seem to invite case-by-case, product-by-product determination of the application of Article 2 to software.

The UCC regulates sales of goods by both merchants and nonmerchants, but different rules may apply to them. Thus, for example, if Navrov sells a car to Jay, the UCC dictates both parties' rights and obligations under the sales contract, whether Navrov is employed as a car dealer or is simply selling his personal possessions on his own behalf. Section 2-104 of the UCC defines a *merchant* as "a person who deals in goods of the kind or otherwise by his occupation holds himself out as having knowledge or skill peculiar to the practices or goods involved in the transaction."

# Contract Formation

The UCC permits a contract to be enforced if the parties intended a binding contract, even though important terms may have been left open for later agreement. If a dispute later arises over a missing term, the court may simply use a "gap-filler" as provided by the UCC. The court will fill in missing terms, however, only if the party attempting to enforce the contract can prove that there was a genuine agreement, not a mere proposal or intention to continue negotiations. It must be apparent that there has been an offer, acceptance, and consideration.

## Offer

*Offer* is not defined by the UCC, although it is used in several important sections. Therefore, traditional common law principles (discussed in Chapter 7) determine whether an offer has been made. Under the UCC, neither an invitation for bids nor a price quotation is an offer. Similarly, a proposal by a sales representative that is subject to approval by the home office is not an offer.

## Acceptance

The UCC does not define *acceptance* either, except to state that an acceptance may contain terms additional to or different from those in the offer. This is different from the common law *mirror image rule,* which requires the acceptance to contain the exact same terms as the offer. Unless the offeror indicates unambiguously that his or her offer can be accepted only in a particular way, an offer may be accepted in any manner and by any medium that is reasonable in the circumstances.

The sale of software, in stores, by mail, and over the Internet, has resulted in several specialized forms of licenses that have raised new issues about what constitutes acceptance. In *ProCD, Inc. v. Zeidenberg*,[6] the U.S. Court of Appeals for the Seventh Circuit upheld the enforceability of a software license agreement that was "encoded on the CD-ROM disks, as well as printed on the manual, and which appear[ed] on a user's screen every time the software [ran]." The court acknowledged that use of a *shrink-wrap license,* which places the license terms on the outside of the box containing the software, was not practical. The court held, though, that a notice on the box stating that the software was purchased subject to an enclosed license was sufficient, in part because the software could not be used unless and until the purchaser was shown the license and manifested his or her acceptance by using the software after having an opportunity to read the license.

6. 86 F.3d 1447 (7th Cir. 1996).

A second type of license, a *click-wrap,* is frequently used for software that is distributed over the Internet. A click-wrap license presents the user with a notice on his or her computer screen that requires the user to agree to the terms of the license by clicking on an icon. The software cannot be obtained or used until the icon is clicked. The few cases that have considered click-wrap licenses have generally found them to be enforceable.[7]

Some websites use a third type of software license, a browse-wrap. A *browse-wrap license* is an online agreement that appears on a website but does not require the user to take any action to express his or her consent to the agreement. In the following case, the court considered whether a user was bound by the terms of a browse-wrap license.

7. *See, e.g., In re* RealNetworks, Inc. Privacy Litig., 2000 WL 631341 (N.D. Ill. 2000); Hotmail Corp. v. Van$ Money Pie, Inc., 1998 WL 388389 (N.D. Cal. 1998).

A CASE IN POINT

## In the Language of the Court

**CASE 8.1**

**Specht v. Netscape**

*United States Court of Appeals for the Second Circuit*

*306 F.3d 17 (2d Cir. 2002).*

› **FACTS** SmartDownload is a program that makes it easier for users to download files from the Internet without losing their interim progress when they pause to engage in some other task or if their Internet connection is severed. Netscape, a provider of computer software programs that enable and facilitate use of the Internet, offered SmartDownload free of charge on its website to all those who visited the site and indicated, by clicking their mouse in a designated box, that they wished to obtain it. The sole reference on this page to the license agreement appeared in text that was visible only if the visitor scrolled down through the page to the next screen. If a visitor did so, he or she saw the following invitation to review the license agreement: "Please review and agree to the terms of the *Netscape SmartDownload software license agreement* before downloading and using the software."

Visitors were not required to indicate their assent to the license agreement, or even to view it, before proceeding to download the software. However, if a visitor chose to click on the underlined text in the invitation, a hypertext link took the visitor to a Web page entitled "License and Support Agreements," which began as follows:

> The use of each Netscape software product is governed by a license agreement. You must read and agree to the license agreement terms BEFORE acquiring a product. Please click on the appropriate link below to review the current license agreement for the product of interest to you before acquisition. For products available for download, you must read and agree to the license agreement terms BEFORE you install the software. If you do not agree to the license terms, do not download, install or use the software.

The plaintiffs alleged that their use of the software transmitted to Netscape private information about their file transfer activity on the Internet, thereby effecting an electronic surveillance of their activity in violation of two federal statutes, the Electronic Communications Privacy Act and the Computer Fraud and Abuse Act. Netscape moved

*(Continued)*

(Case 8.1 *continued*)

to compel arbitration and stay the proceedings, arguing that the disputes reflected in the complaint were subject to a binding arbitration clause in the license agreement for the SmartDownload software.

**› ISSUE PRESENTED** Did Netscape give the plaintiffs sufficient notice of the existence and terms of the license agreement, and did the act of downloading the software sufficiently manifest their agreement to be bound by the license agreement?

**› OPINION** SOTOMAYOR, J., writing for the U.S. Court of Appeals for the Second Circuit:

Whether governed by the common law or by Article 2 of the Uniform Commercial Code ("UCC"), a transaction, in order to be a contract, requires a manifestation of agreement between the parties. . . . Although an onlooker observing the disputed transactions in this case would have seen each of the user plaintiffs click on the SmartDownload "Download" button, a consumer's clicking on a download button does not communicate assent to contractual terms if the offer did not make clear to the consumer that clicking on the download button would signify assent to those terms. . . .

. . .

We conclude that in circumstances such as these, where consumers are urged to download free software at the immediate click of a button, a reference to the existence of license terms on a submerged screen is not sufficient to place consumers on inquiry or constructive notice of those terms. . . . Internet users may have, as defendants put it, "as much time as they need" to scroll through multiple screens on a webpage, but there is no reason to assume that viewers will scroll down to subsequent screens simply because screens are there. When products are "free" and users are invited to download them in the absence of reasonably conspicuous notice that they are about to bind themselves to contract terms, the transactional circumstances cannot be fully analogized to those in the paper world of arm's length bargaining. . . .

. . .

Cases in which courts have found contracts arising from Internet use do not assist defendants, because in those circumstances there was much clearer notice than in the present case that a user's act would manifest assent to contract terms. . . .

. . .

. . . Reasonably conspicuous notice of the existence of contract terms and unambiguous manifestation of assent to these terms by consumers are essential if electronic bargaining is to have integrity and credibility. We hold that a reasonably prudent offeree in plaintiffs' position would not have known or learned, prior to acting on the invitation to download, of the reference to SmartDownload's license terms hidden below the "Download" button on the next screen.

**› RESULT** The user plaintiffs were not bound by the arbitration clause contained in the license agreement.

**› CRITICAL THINKING QUESTIONS**

1. Would the outcome have been different if the plaintiffs had been aware of the terms of the end user license agreement at the time they downloaded the SmartDownload software?
2. Would the outcome have been different if the plaintiffs had received a copy of the end user license agreement when they downloaded the SmartDownload software and then purchased additional copies of the software?

In a subsequent case, the U.S. Court of Appeals for the Second Circuit took what may be a significant step toward enforcing browse-wrap agreements.[8] Register.com, an Internet registrar authorized to sell Internet domain names, accused Verio of using an automated software program to submit daily queries to Register.com to collect information about new domain name registrants from whom it would then solicit business. Register.com complained that Verio's actions violated its Terms of Use, which were provided to Verio when it received the query results. Verio argued that the Terms of Use were not binding because it never manifested its assent to the terms, but Register.com countered that Verio's conduct—repeatedly submitting queries even after it became aware of Register.com's Terms of Use—demonstrated Verio's assent to be bound by them. The court ruled in favor of Register.com, comparing the situation to a roadside fruit stand displaying a bin of apples. If a visitor, D, took an apple and bit into it before he saw a sign posted by the owner, P, that stated that the apples were for sale, D might not be obligated to pay for that apple. However, if D returned to the stand and took another apple without paying for it, the situation would be different.

> In our view, . . . D cannot continue on a daily basis to take apples for free, knowing full well that P is offering them only in exchange for . . . compensation, merely because the sign demanding payment is so placed that on each occasion D does not see it until he has bitten into the apple.

### CONSIDERATION

Contracts for the sale of goods ordinarily must have consideration to be enforceable. However, a *firm offer*, that is, a signed offer by a merchant that indicates that the offer will be kept open, is not revocable for lack of consideration. The offer must be kept open during the time stated or, if none is stated, for a reasonable period of time, up to a maximum of three months. This rule is just one example of how the UCC provides more stringent standards for merchants than for nonmerchants.

Under the UCC, an agreement to modify a contract is binding even if there is no consideration for the modification as long as the modification was made in good faith. However, if the original contract was required to be in writing to satisfy the statute of frauds (discussed later in this chapter), then the agreement to modify the contract must be in writing also.

8. Register.com v. Verio, 356 F.3d 393 (2d Cir. 2004).

### ETHICAL CONSIDERATION

Devon Cartagena, an antique dealer, sees a desk for sale for $50 at a garage sale that he recognizes as a Louis XV desk worth $15,000. Does he have a legal or ethical obligation to disclose the true value to the person holding the garage sale? Should it matter that difficult financial circumstances made it necessary for the homeowner to sell the desk? Should Cartagena get some reward for the effort he has spent in becoming an expert in antiques and for the time he has spent pawing through junk at countless garage sales?

A person recently sold a map for $3 that later turned out to be worth more than $19 million. Does the buyer have a moral duty to share the windfall with the seller? Would the seller have a moral duty to share the loss if the buyer paid $19 million for a map worth only $3?

What if a framed picture sold for $25 turns out to have an original copy of the U.S. Constitution behind the picture? Is this a mistake of judgment or of fact? What, if anything, is the buyer's ethical responsibility to the seller in such a case?

## Battle of the Forms

In a battle of the forms, the parties negotiate the essential terms of the contract (for example, quantity, quality, and delivery date) but neglect to bargain over items that are less immediately important (for example, whether disputes will be subject to arbitration, for how long a period after delivery the buyer may assert complaints of defects, or on whom the risk of loss during shipment falls). The parties then exchange standard printed forms, each of which is filled with fine print listing all kinds of terms advantageous to the party that drew up the form. Often goods are shipped, received, and paid for before both parties have expressly accepted the same document as their contract. As a result of these exchanges, two questions arise: (1) Is there a contract? (2) If so, what are its terms?

The UCC calls a truce in the battle of the forms by effectively abolishing the mirror image rule. It is not necessary for an offer and acceptance to match exactly in order for a contract for the sale of goods to exist. Adding to or modifying terms in the offer does not make the acceptance a counteroffer, as is true under common law.

### DEFINITE RESPONSE

A definite and timely assent to an offer constitutes an acceptance. The presence of additional or different terms is not a bar to contract formation. The crucial inquiry is whether the parties intended to close a deal. Under Section 2-207, a contract exists whenever the parties act as if there is a contract between them. It is not necessary to determine which document constitutes the offer and which the acceptance. If the offeree's response manifests the intent to enter into a deal, the offer has been accepted. For example, if additional or different terms merely appear in the standard printed language of a form contract, it is likely that the offeree intended to close a deal. Once the contract is formed, the only issue to be decided is what are its terms.

If, however, the response indicates only a willingness to continue negotiations, it is not an acceptance but a counteroffer. For example, an additional or different term that directly pertains to one of the negotiated terms, such as price or quantity, is evidence that the parties are still negotiating and have not reached an agreement.

## CONDITIONAL RESPONSE

If the offeree wants to make a counteroffer rather than an acceptance, he or she should state clearly that acceptance is conditioned on the offeror's agreement to the additional or different terms. The safest course is to use the language of the UCC: "This acceptance is expressly made conditional on offeror's assent to all additional or different terms contained herein. Should offeror not give assent to said terms, there is no contract between the parties." Less direct language (such as "The acceptance of your order is subject to the conditions set forth herein" or "Acceptance of this order is expressly limited to the conditions of purchase printed on the reverse side") has been held to be an acceptance rather than a counteroffer.

## ACCEPTANCE WITH MISSING TERMS

What happens when the parties ship, receive, and pay for goods without first agreeing on all material terms? In that case, Section 2-207(3) provides that the terms of the contract will be those on which the writings exchanged by the parties agree, supplemented by the UCC's gap-fillers where needed.

## ACCEPTANCE WITH ADDITIONAL TERMS

What is the effect of additional terms in an acceptance when the contract is not expressly made subject to the offeror's agreeing to those terms? The answer depends on whether the parties are merchants. Under Section 2-207(2), if either of the parties is not a merchant, additional terms are construed as proposals for additions to the contract that the acceptance has created. Unless the offeror expressly agrees to the added provisions, they do not become part of the contract. If all parties are merchants, on the other hand, the additional provisions in the acceptance automatically become part of the contract, unless (1) the offer expressly limits acceptance to the terms of the offer, (2) the new terms materially alter the original offer, or (3) the party making the original offer notifies the other party within a reasonable time that it objects to the new terms. If any one of these exceptions applies, the additional terms serve as proposals requiring the express consent of the offeror to become part of the contract.

## ACCEPTANCE WITH DIFFERENT TERMS

What is the effect of different—as opposed to additional—terms in an acceptance when the acceptance is not expressly made subject to the offeror's agreeing to those terms? As in the case of additional terms in a response to an offer, different terms neither defeat the acceptance nor impede the formation of the contract. But do the different terms become part of the contract? Surprisingly, the language of Section 2-207 does not address this situation. Under common law, the courts usually found that an offeree's response to an offer that contained different terms was a counteroffer that the offeror accepted by continuing its performance.

The following case illustrates how most courts applying the UCC deal with the situation in which the parties have sent conflicting forms, transacted their business, and then realized that they disagree about the terms of their contract.

**A CASE IN POINT**

**CASE 8.2**
**Richardson v. Union Carbide Industrial Gases, Inc.**
*Superior Court of New Jersey, Appellate Division*
*790 A.2d 962*
*(N.J. Super. Ct. 2002).*

## Summary

**› FACTS** Prior to 1988, Hoeganaes Corporation operated furnace 2S, which it used for annealing iron powders. In 1988, Hoeganaes undertook to convert furnace 2S to a distalloy furnace. As part of the conversion, Hoeganaes had to buy a powder transporter system to transport iron to the input end of the furnace. Hoeganaes purchased the system from Rage Engineering, Inc.

*(Continued)*

(Case 8.2 *continued*)

The Rage proposal included the following language, in all capital letters, at the bottom of each page:

> ANY PURCHASE ORDER ISSUED AS A RESULT OF THIS QUOTE IS MADE EXPRESSLY SUBJECT TO THE TERMS AND CONDITIONS ATTACHED HERETO IN LIEU OF ANY CONFLICTING TERMS PROPOSED BY THE PURCHASER.

The terms and conditions attached to the proposal were standard, boilerplate terms that were never discussed by Rage and Hoeganaes. They included the following provisions:

> LIMITATION OF ACCEPTANCE. This sale (including all services) is limited to and expressly made conditional on Purchaser's assent to these Terms and Conditions as well as all other provisions contained in any other document to which these terms or conditions are attached. . . .
>
> . . .
>
> INDEMNITY. Purchaser shall indemnify and hold Seller harmless against and in respect of any loss, claim or damage (including costs of suit and attorneys' fees) or other expense incident to or in connection with: the goods/equipment . . . unless such loss, claim or damage is due solely and directly to the negligence or willful misconduct of Seller.

The following language was included in bold face type at the bottom of the purchase order issued by Hoeganaes: "THIS ORDER IS ALSO SUBJECT TO THE TERMS AND CONDITIONS ON THE REVERSE SIDE OF THIS PAGE[.]" The reverse side of the Hoeganaes purchase order included the following terms and conditions:

> 1. Compliance with Terms and Conditions of Order—The terms and conditions set forth below, along with the provisions set forth on the front page hereof, constitute the entire contract of purchase and sale between Buyer and Seller. Any provisions in the Seller's acceptance, acknowledgment or other response to this Order which are different from or in addition to any of the terms and conditions and other provisions of this Order . . . shall not become a part of Buyer's contract of purchase and sale. . . .
>
> . . .
>
> 14. Indemnification—Seller agrees to indemnify and hold harmless Buyer, . . . from and against all losses, damages, liabilities, claims, demands (including attorneys' fees), and suits at law or equity that arise out of . . . any act of omission or commission, negligent or otherwise, of Seller, . . . or otherwise out of the performance or attempted performance by Seller of this purchase order. . . .

Except as expressed in the boilerplate forms they exchanged, neither side objected to the language in the documents and the contract was performed.

Jeffrey Richardson, an employee of Hoeganaes who was injured when the furnace exploded, filed suit against numerous defendants, including Hoeganaes and Rage. In its answer, Rage cross-complained against Hoeganaes for contractual indemnification. Hoeganaes answered Rage's cross-complaint, denying that Rage had any right to indemnification arising out of the contract. Rage filed a motion for summary judgment seeking contractual indemnification from Hoeganaes, and Hoeganaes cross-moved for summary judgment seeking dismissal of Rage's cross-claim for indemnification. The trial court granted Hoeganaes's motion and dismissed Rage's claim for indemnification. Rage

*(Continued)*

(Case 8.2 *continued*)

appealed from the summary judgment granted to Hoeganaes, dismissing Rage's contractual indemnification claim.

**› ISSUE PRESENTED** If the parties have performed, but the buyer's and seller's preprinted forms contain contradictory terms, is there a contract, and if so, what are its terms?

**› SUMMARY OF OPINION** The Appellate Division of the New Jersey Superior Court began by noting that Hoeganaes had taken the position that Rage's proposal was an offer and that Hoeganaes's response to the offer was an acceptance. The court next stated that the relevant statutory provision was Section 2-207, which addresses additional terms made on acceptance or confirmation of an order. The court noted that Section 2-207(1) addresses "additional terms in acceptance" and also uses the language "different" terms. But Section 2-207(2), which provides the standard to determine whether additional terms become part of the contract, does not include the word "different."

The court observed that when faced with conflicting terms in contracts in similar circumstances, courts had used three approaches:

> . . . The majority view is that the conflicting terms fall out and, if necessary, are replaced by suitable UCC gap-filler provisions.
>
> The minority view is that the offeror's terms control because the offeree's different terms cannot be saved by . . . 2-207(2), because that section applies only to additional terms.
>
> The third view assimilates "different" to "additional" so that the terms of the offer prevail over the different terms in the acceptance only if the latter are materially different. This is the least adopted approach.

The court then concluded that the majority approach, the "knockout" rule, is preferable and should be adopted. The court explained that it reached this conclusion "because other approaches are inequitable and unjust and run counter to the policy behind" Section 2-207, which jettisoned the common law "mirror image" rule by recognizing the existence of a contract even though certain terms remain in conflict or are unresolved.

The court quoted the motion judge who stated:

> The truth is, and this really is the truth, what's happening is some little person some place writing these little—trying to plan it out, trying to conflict these things out, but the business people are out there delivering and taking money. And if the people really want to really get into all of this, then they should have taken their stuff away and they should have said, ooh, you know, we—you know, this is real here and, sorry, I'm not going to be able to take your check and, sorry, you're not going to be able to keep the stuff, but they're not doing that. They're just playing a little game with forms.

As a result, the court found that even though Rage's offer had specifically limited acceptance to its terms, Rage's indemnity did not become part of the contract because the terms of the parties' writings had conflicting indemnification provisions.

**› RESULT** The appeals court affirmed the trial court's decision to strike the contradictory indemnity provisions.

**› COMMENTS** By formally adopting the knockout rule instead of the common law approach, the appeals court made it much harder to game the system by exchanging preprinted forms with boilerplate rejection of the other party's terms. Because conflicting terms may simply be thrown out and replaced by UCC gap-fillers, managers using such forms should be aware of which UCC provisions might replace their standard terms.

### 2003 Revisions to Section 2-207

Section 2-206(c) of the 2003 amendments to Article 2 states that unless otherwise unambiguously indicated by the language or circumstances, "[a] definite and seasonable expression of acceptance in a record operates as an acceptance even if it contains terms additional to or different from the offer." This language was adapted from Section 2-207(1) of the original UCC. The 2003 amendment to Section 2-207 specifies the terms of all contracts of sale, regardless of whether there was a "battle of the forms." Under the amended Section 2-207, the terms of the contract are "(1) terms that appear in the records of both parties; (2) terms, whether in a record or not, to which both parties agree; and (3) terms supplied or incorporated under any provision of [the Uniform Commercial Code]." Critics of the amendments argue that revised Section 2-207 downgrades the standard of assent by requiring only agreement, rather than "express" agreement, to such additional terms and also appears to apply this standard even to material additional terms. They are also concerned that in some instances, two of the above provisions could apply but be in conflict, making the lack of an explicit hierarchy confusing. For example, terms might appear in the records of both parties, but the parties might have orally agreed to different terms. In such a case, the court will have to decide whether to use provision (1) or (2) of revised Section 2-207.

## Statute of Frauds

Section 2-201 of the UCC is a *statute of frauds*. It provides that a contract for the sale of goods for $500 or more is unenforceable unless it is at least partly in writing. It states:

1. There must be some writing evidencing the sale of goods.
2. The writing must be signed by the party against whom enforcement is sought.
3. The writing must specify the quantity of the goods sold.

The 2003 amendments to Section 2-201 raise the amount that triggers the statute of frauds to $5,000.

### "Some Writing"

Statutes of fraud generally require all the essential terms of the contract to be in writing; the UCC's requirement for "some writing" is relatively lenient. The official comments to Section 2-201 state: "All that is required is that the writing afford a basis for believing that the offered oral evidence rests on a real transaction. It may be written in lead pencil on a scratch pad." The comments go on to state: "The price, time and place of payment or delivery, the general quality of the goods, or any particular warranties may all be omitted."

The only term that must appear in the writing is the quantity of goods to be sold. This term is necessary to provide a basis for awarding monetary damages in the case of a breach. The contract is not enforceable beyond the quantity of goods shown in the writing. If no quantity is specified, the contract is unenforceable unless (1) the goods were specially manufactured for the buyer and are not suitable for resale to others in the ordinary course of the seller's business, (2) the defendant admits in a judicial proceeding that there was an agreement, or (3) payment for the goods was made and accepted or the goods were received and accepted.

### Signature

The writing must be signed by the party against whom enforcement is sought, unless the sale is between merchants and (1) a confirmation of the contract has been received, (2) the party receiving it has reason to know its contents, and (3) that party has not made a written objection within ten days after the confirmation was received. For example, an invoice that a seller sent to a buyer would be a contract enforceable against the buyer if the buyer did not respond within ten days after receiving the invoice.

#### *The E-Sign Act and Uniform Electronic Transactions Act*

As more business is being conducted electronically, state and federal statutes recognizing electronic signatures are being enacted. On June 30, 2000, President Bill Clinton signed the Electronic Signatures in Global and National Commerce Act (the E-Sign Act), which validates many transactions that take place electronically. The E-Sign Act states that "a signature, contract, or other record relating to such transaction may not be denied legal effect, validity, or enforceability solely because it is in electronic form."[9] Similarly, the Uniform Electronic Transactions Act (UETA), which had been adopted by forty-eight states by November 2004, provides that an

9. Electronic Signatures in Global and National Commerce Act, 15 U.S.C. § 7001(a)(1).

electronic contract may not be denied legal effect simply because it is in electronic form. Under the E-Sign Act and UETA, almost any mark or process intended to sign an electronic contract or record (including a name typed at the bottom of an e-mail message and a "click-through" process on a computer screen whereby a person clicks "I agree" on a Web page) will constitute a valid electronic signature. (The E-Sign Act and UETA are discussed more fully in Chapter 7.)

The 2003 amendments to Article 2 of the UCC replace the word "writing" with "record" throughout Article 2. The words "sign" and "conspicuous" have also been defined to apply to electronic media in addition to tangible media. The new electronic commerce provisions in the amendments generally repeat UETA. They also add one new regulatory provision concerning Internet transactions. Amended Section 2-211(4) provides that the operator of an electronic agent is not subject to terms sent by an individual "if the individual had reason to know that the agent could not react." In addition, the amendments state that Article 2 is intended to modify, limit, and supersede the E-Sign Act. As a result, the E-Sign Act will not apply in states that adopt the 2003 amendments, but it will continue to apply in states that do not.

Although the terms are frequently used interchangeably, there is a distinction between "electronic signatures" and "digital signatures."[10] A "digital signature" refers to a type of electronic signature that uses an information security measure, typically cryptography, to authenticate the identity of the person providing the electronic signature and to ensure the integrity and authenticity of the information.[11]

Digital signature technology provides a variety of options: a signature can be a smart card, thumbprint, retinal scan, or voice-recognition test.[12] This range of options provides companies with varying levels of security for their transactions. The E-Sign Act does not require the use of any particular technology, and a number of companies have developed technology to capitalize on the growing market created by the Act.[13]

10. Tom Melling, *Digital Signatures v. Electronic Signatures,* E-BUSINESS ADVISOR, Apr. 1, 2000, at 48.

11. Robert G. Ballen & Thomas A. Fox, *Sign of the Times: Electronic Disclosures, Contracts and Signatures,* J. INTERNET L., Sept. 1998, at 12.

12. Dan Briody, *Digital Signatures Create Market Potential: How Will Companies Make Consumers Feel Secure Enough to Sign on the Digital Line?,* INFOWORLD, July 24, 2000.

13. Lizette Alvarez & Jeri Clausing, *Senate Approves Bill That Allows Online Contracts,* N.Y. TIMES, June 17, 2000, at 1.

## Duty of Good Faith Under the UCC

Section 1-203 of the UCC states that "every contract or duty within this Act imposes an obligation of good faith in its performance and enforcement." This section imposes on each party a duty not to do anything that will deprive the other party of the benefits of the agreement. One court defined "good faith" as "a compact reference to an implied undertaking not to take opportunistic advantage in a way that could not have been contemplated at the time of drafting, and which therefore was not resolved explicitly by the parties."[14] Good faith in the case of a merchant has been interpreted as the observance of reasonable commercial standards of fair dealing in the trade.

The UCC applies to the enforcement, performance, or modification of a contract for the sale of goods, but not to the formation or procurement of a contract. For example, the Texas Supreme Court refused to invalidate a mutual release of liabilities for violation of good faith after characterizing the mutual release as the formation, not the modification, of a contract.[15]

## Warranties

Goods delivered pursuant to a contract may not live up to the buyer's expectations. In many such cases, the buyer can sue the seller for breaching an express or implied warranty that the goods sold would have certain qualities or would perform in a certain way.

The UCC's warranty provisions attempt to determine which attributes of the goods the parties have agreed on. The UCC allows a great deal of flexibility in determining which warranties apply, permitting consideration of the description of the goods, the seller's words, common uses in the trade, the price paid, and the extent to which the buyer communicated particular needs to the seller. As a result, the seller of goods may find itself bound, perhaps unintentionally, by one of the three warranties provided by the UCC: express warranty, implied warranty of merchantability, and implied warranty of fitness for a particular purpose.

14. Brooklyn Bagel Boys, Inc. v. Earthgrains Refrigerated Dough Prods., Inc., 212 F.3d 373 (7th Cir. 2000).

15. El Paso Natural Gas Co. v. Minco Oil & Gas, Inc., 8 S.W.3d 309 (Tex. 1999).

## HISTORICAL PERSPECTIVE

# FROM MEDIEVAL GUILDS TO ONLINE ARBITRATION

The increased use of the Internet by businesses and individuals, combined with the lack of established legal rules, has resulted in the development of private legal institutions.[a] For example, individuals doing business on the Internet are devising ways to ensure that the information they transmit to each other will remain confidential and be used only in an authorized manner. In addition, as noted in Chapter 4, Internet companies have established online mediation and dispute resolution sites that allow consumers to resolve their disputes without filing claims in courts. Although these private legal regimes may be revolutionary in that they are being used in connection with a new technology, private legal regimes have developed at other times in history when individuals needed to protect their rights and the existing legal regime was unable to do so.

In medieval Europe, the nation-state had not yet developed, so merchants and traders could not rely on a central government to enforce laws or contracts to protect their trading activities. As long-distance trade became more common, traders and merchants began to venture beyond the protection of a local ruler or entrusted agents to carry and deliver their goods to fairs and markets in other countries and collect payment for these goods. As a result, the merchants needed a mechanism to protect their interests. Accordingly, they developed private organizations, or guilds, and courts enforced by groups of merchants. To determine whether an unknown trader or agent was trustworthy, merchants turned to each other for information about the stranger's reputation. Merchants refused to trade with parties who breached commitments to pay or to perform services, and they organized guildwide embargoes to freeze out members of the guild who violated its rules.

Similarly, in modern society, members of private organizations often agree to be governed by a legal regime created and enforced by the organization. For example, a number of trade associations have rules that govern relationships among their members and establish procedures for resolving disputes arising from breaches of these rules. Although these associations' rules are based upon public law, such as contract law, these legal regimes typically rely upon simple rules, which they interpret and apply literally.

Stock exchanges, such as the New York Stock Exchange and Nasdaq, also operate under quasi-private legal regimes. Members of an exchange must comply with its rules and are subject to its monitoring, investigation, and enforcement mechanisms. These exchanges are not subject just to a set of private rules, however. Their private rules are subject to review by the Securities and Exchange Commission and the courts, and they also incorporate public laws.

The Digital Revolution and the rapid development of e-commerce are also driving the development of a private legal regime. Not only is the Internet essentially unregulated, but with its innovative technology and ability to reach billions of consumers in countries all over the world, it presents enormous challenges for legal regulation. Some early efforts to regulate the Internet reflect the introduction of privatization into this new electronic market. In addition to the domain-name dispute procedures described in the "View from Cyberspace" for Chapter 4, companies are using private law regimes to deal with consumer concerns about privacy on the Internet and secure transmissions of sensitive data (such as credit card numbers) by establishing "Seal" programs. For example, TRUSTe, a nonprofit corporation founded by the Online Privacy Alliance (a group of leading Internet firms), the Electronic Frontier Foundation (a public interest group), and the Boston Consulting Group (a management consulting firm), has established a set of practices regarding user privacy to which a company wishing to display the TRUSTe seal must adhere. TRUSTe enforces its policies by several methods including a dispute resolution process.

In 1999, leading companies in the Internet, online, and e-commerce industries, including America Online, Microsoft, and AT&T, formed the E-Commerce Group to establish industry best practices for business conducted over the Internet and a global jurisdictional framework for e-commerce. The E-Commerce Group published "Guidelines for Merchant-to-Consumer Transactions" to help create an effective global framework that will reduce the need for compliance with the laws of various countries. It also issued a "Statement on Global Jurisdiction Framework for Electronic Commerce" that addresses the difficulty of applying traditional concepts of jurisdiction to global transactions conducted over the Internet and encourages merchants to resolve their disputes through online dispute resolution mechanisms.[b]

a. This discussion is based on Gillian K. Hadfield, *Privatizing Commercial Law: Lessons from the Middle and Digital Ages* (Mar. 2000), *at* http://aei-brookings.org/publications/related/hadfield.htm.

b. *Internet and E-Commerce Group Proposes Guidelines for Consumer Protection Online*, PR Newswire, June 6, 2000.

## EXPRESS WARRANTY

An *express warranty* is an explicit guarantee by the seller that the goods will have certain qualities. Section 2-313 of the UCC has two requirements for the creation of an express warranty. First, the seller must (1) make a statement or promise relating to the goods, (2) provide a description of the goods, or (3) furnish a sample or model of the goods. Second, this statement, promise, description, sample, or model must become a "part of the basis of the bargain" between the seller and the buyer. This second requirement is intended to ensure that the buyer actually relied on the seller's statement when making a purchasing decision. For example, if a car dealer asserts that a car will reach 130 mph and the buyer responds, "I'm never going to take it above 55," it is unlikely that the buyer could claim breach of warranty if the car failed to go over 70 mph. The seller has the burden of proving that the buyer did not rely on his or her representations.

### *Puffing*

Section 2-313(2) provides that a warranty may be found even though the seller never used the word "warranty" or "guarantee" and had no intention of making a warranty. However, if a seller is merely *puffing*—that is, expressing an opinion about the quality of the goods—he or she has not made a warranty. For example, a car salesperson's statement that "this is a top-notch car" is puffing, whereas a factual statement such as "it will get twenty-five miles to the gallon" is an express warranty.

Unfortunately, the line between opinion and fact is not always easy to draw. Much turns on the circumstances surrounding the representation, including the identities and relative knowledge of the parties involved.

A number of courts employ a two-prong test to distinguish warranty language from opinion. The first prong is whether the seller asserted a fact of which the buyer was ignorant. If so, the assertion may be a warranty. The second prong is whether the seller merely stated a view on something about which the buyer could be expected to have formed his or her own opinion and whether the buyer could judge the validity of the seller's statement. In this second instance, the seller's statement is an opinion, not a warranty. The following case illustrates the distinction between sales talk and a warranty.

A CASE IN POINT

## In the Language of the Court

**CASE 8.3**

**Connor, Inc. v. Proto-Grind, Inc.**

*Court of Appeal of Florida*
*761 So.2d 426*
*(Fla. App. 2000).*

› **FACTS** Doug Connor, the president of Connor, Inc., a land-clearing business, became interested in purchasing a large commercial grinding machine manufactured by Proto-Grind, Inc., called the Proto-Grind 1200. Proto-Grind's brochure described the machine as the toughest grinder on the market and stated that the machine could grind timber, stumps, and railroad ties into mulch. Connor attended a demonstration of the machine during which a large log was reduced to mulch. During the demonstration, he spoke to Protos, the president of Proto-Grind, and told him that he needed a machine that would grind palmettos, palm trees, oak trees, and other trees. Protos assured him that the machine was capable of doing this work.

Connor purchased a Proto-Grind 1200 for $226,000 pursuant to a contract that provided for a two-week trial period during which he could use the machine and, only if satisfied, be committed to purchase it. However, Protos also offered an incentive that eliminated Connor's first installment payment of $5,500 in exchange for elimination of the trial period. Connor accepted this offer and gave up the two-week trial period.

Connor experienced problems with the new machine, including its inability to discharge mulch from cabbage palm trees and palmettos. Connor wrote several letters to Protos complaining about the deficiencies. After Proto-Grind failed to resolve the problem, Connor sued for breach of express oral warranties that the machine would grind organic materials effectively, that the machine would be free from defects for a period of six months, and that Proto-Grind would fix the machine. The case went to trial, and the trial court granted Proto-Grind's motion for a directed verdict at the conclusion of Connor's case on the grounds that Connor had waived the express warranty in exchange for elimination of the first installment payment of $5,500. Connor appealed.

*(Continued)*

(Case 8.3 *continued*)

**› ISSUE PRESENTED** When do oral statements by a seller about the capability of a commercial grinding machine constitute an express warranty? Is a warranty claim waived if the buyer agrees to eliminate a trial period?

**› OPINION** PETERSON, J., writing for the Florida Court of Appeal:

[*Ed:* The Florida Court of Appeal first found that only implied warranties, not express warranties, are waived when the buyer refuses an opportunity to inspect the product prior to purchase.]

Proto-Grind argues that the oral affirmations made by the Proto-Grind agents merely constituted puffing, sales talk, or otherwise non-actionable opinion and that in order to satisfy the threshold of an affirmation of fact, the statement must be detailed and specific. In *Miles,*[16] the court found that a seller of an airplane, by reference to his logbook, had warranted the accuracy of the information contained in the book. Proto-Grind states that the principle of that case is that the threshold of making a factual affirmation is that the statement be specific and detailed. Contrarily, *Miles* seems to support the opposite conclusion by providing a broad definition of an express warranty. The Court wrote: "An express warranty need not be by words, but can be by conduct as well, such as the showing of a blueprint or other description of the goods sold to the buyer."

We believe that the statements made by Proto-Grind could amount to more than puffing or sales talk. Proto-Grind specifically understood the buyer's needs and represented to Connor that the Proto-Grind 1200 would meet those needs.

Proto-Grind further argues that an express warranty generally arises only where the seller asserts a fact of which the buyer is ignorant prior to the beginning of the transaction, and on which the buyer reasonably relies as part of the basis of the bargain. It is not clear from the record, however, that when Connor purchased the Proto-Grind 1200 he was aware that it was ill-equipped to mulch palm trees and palmetto brush.

On a similar note, Proto-Grind argues that because Doug knew that a competitor was, at times, quite dissatisfied with his Proto-Grind 1200, Connor was on equal footing with Proto-Grind with respect to knowledge of the machine's capability. Doug testified that the Proto-Grind was the first grinder that Connor ever purchased. Even if Doug was more savvy than he acknowledged, the manufacturer of an expensive product should be well aware of the product's attributes and deficiencies before it offers it to the public. We conclude that the relative knowledge of the parties is a matter for the jury to consider, not a complete bar to recovery by Connor. . . . [T]he finder of fact could reasonably conclude that the alleged oral promises made were more than mere puffing, that the product failed to meet the promise that it would sufficiently grind palm trees and palmettos, that Connor relied on these affirmations, and that because the deficiency of the product was not cured, Proto-Grind breached this express warranty.

**› RESULT** The Florida Court of Appeal vacated the directed verdict in favor of Proto-Grind and remanded the case to the trial court for further proceedings.

**› COMMENTS** Whether a statement about a product is an express warranty or merely an opinion depends on the context in which it is made, the degree to which the buyer is

16. Miles v. Kavanaugh, 350 So. 2d 1090 (Fla. App. Ct. 1977).

*(Continued)*

(Case 8.3 *continued*)

ignorant of the subject matter of the statement, the extent to which the seller was merely puffing, the time when the statement was made, and other factors concerning the relationship between the two parties.

**› CRITICAL THINKING QUESTIONS**

1. Why doesn't elimination of a trial period waive any express warranties?
2. How could Connor have relied on Proto-Grind's statements when he knew that a competitor was quite dissatisfied with his Proto-Grind 1200?

---

## Obligations for Statements to Remote Purchasers

Generally, the doctrine of privity has limited actions for breach of warranty to a buyer who purchased the product directly from the seller/manufacturer and the members of the buyer's immediate family. However, the 2003 amendments to Article 2 of the UCC extend certain warranty-like rights to indirect purchasers of goods. Revised Sections 2-313A and 2-313B are both limited to "new goods and goods sold or leased as new goods in a transaction of purchase in the normal course of distribution." Each section addresses representations made to a *remote purchaser,* defined as "a person that buys or leases goods from an immediate buyer or other person in the normal chain of distribution." Section 2-313A creates obligations for records that are packaged with or accompany the goods if they contain an affirmation of fact or promise that relates to the goods, provide a description that relates to the goods, or make a *remedial promise,* which is defined as a promise by the seller to repair or replace the goods or to refund all or part of the price of the goods upon the happening of a specified event. Section 2-313B creates obligations for similar statements made in advertisements or other communications to the public.

Amended Sections 2-313A and 2-313B apply only if a reasonable person in the position of the remote buyer would believe that the statements created an obligation and if certain other conditions apply. In the case of Section 2-313A, the manufacturer must also have reasonably expected such statements would be furnished to the remote buyer. In the case of Section 2-313B, the remote buyer must have had knowledge of the statements at the time of purchase and must have expected that the goods would conform to the statements. In both instances, the seller may modify or limit remedies, but only if the remote buyer receives the modification or limitation before the time of purchase. If the remedy is not limited, the seller is liable for the remote buyer's incidental and consequential damages, but not for his or her lost profits.

## Implied Warranty of Merchantability

The ***implied warranty of merchantability*** guarantees that the goods are reasonably fit for the general purpose for which they are sold and that they are properly packaged and labeled. The warranty applies to all goods sold by merchants in the normal course of business. It does not depend on the seller's statements or use of a sample or model. Rather, it depends on the identity of the seller as a merchant who deals in goods of a certain kind.

To be merchantable under Section 2-314(2) of the UCC, goods must (1) pass without objection in the trade under the contract description; (2) be fit for the ordinary purposes for which such goods are used; (3) be within the variations permitted by the agreement and be of even kind, quality, and quantity within each unit and among all units involved; (4) be adequately contained, packaged, and labeled as the agreement may require; and (5) conform to the promises or affirmations of fact made on the container or label, if any. Fungible goods, such as grain, must be of average quality within the contract description.

### *Reasonable Expectations*

The key issue in determining merchantability is whether the goods do what a reasonable person would expect of them. The contract description is crucial. Goods considered merchantable under one contract may be considered not merchantable under another. A bicycle with a cracked frame and bent wheels is not fit for the ordinary purpose for which bicycles are used, but it will pass under a contract for the sale of scrap metal.

When no contract description exists, the most frequent claim on which breach is based is that the goods are not fit "for the ordinary purposes for which such goods are used." Proof that the goods are imperfect or

> **ETHICAL CONSIDERATION**
>
> What investigations should a seller make before putting goods on the market? Should a bookstore test every recipe in every cookbook it sells? If not, should a bookstore buy cookbooks only from well-regarded publishers that have test kitchens?

flawed is often insufficient to succeed on this claim. Even imperfect goods can be fit for their ordinary purposes.

In *Lescs v. William R. Hughes, Inc.*,[17] a homeowner filed a claim against Dow Chemical Company when she became ill after moving into a home that had been sprayed with insecticide manufactured by Dow. The homeowner argued that Dow had breached the implied warranty of merchantability by marketing an unreasonably dangerous product. The U.S. Court of Appeals for the Fourth Circuit rejected her claim that the insecticide failed to meet consumer expectations because the warning label on the pesticide had been approved by the Environmental Protection Agency. The court reasoned that "it would be anomalous to hold 'that a consumer is entitled to expect a product to perform more safely than its government mandated warnings indicate.'"

## IMPLIED WARRANTY OF FITNESS FOR A PARTICULAR PURPOSE

The *implied warranty of fitness for a particular purpose* is set forth in Section 2-315 of the UCC. It guarantees that the goods are fit for the particular purpose for which the seller recommended them. Broad in scope, it may apply to merchants and nonmerchants alike. A "particular purpose" differs from the ordinary purpose for which a good is used in that a "particular purpose" contemplates a specific use by the buyer that is peculiar to that buyer or that buyer's business. By contrast, the ordinary purpose is that contemplated by the concept of merchantability. For example, dress shoes are generally used for the purpose of walking on ordinary ground and are not warranted for mountain climbing, but a seller may know that a particular pair was selected for mountain climbing.

Unlike the implied warranty of merchantability, the implied warranty of fitness for a particular purpose does not arise in every sale of goods. It will be implied only if four elements are present: (1) the buyer had a particular purpose for the goods, (2) the seller knew or had reason to know of that purpose, (3) the buyer relied on the seller's expertise, and (4) the seller knew or had reason to know of the buyer's reliance. Although the warranty usually arises when the seller is a merchant with some level of skill or judgment, it is not restricted to such circumstances.

17. 168 F.3d 482 (4th Cir. 1999), *cert. denied*, 528 U.S. 1119 (2000).

### *Reliance*

To prove that the buyer did not rely on the seller's expertise, the seller may try to show that (1) the buyer's expertise was equal to or superior to the seller's, (2) the buyer relied on the skill and judgment of persons hired by the buyer, or (3) the buyer supplied the seller with detailed specifications or designs that the seller was to follow.

Identifiable patents and trademarks can play an interesting role in this area of the law. If the buyer insists on a particular brand and style, he or she cannot be relying on the seller's skill or judgment. Hence, no warranty results. The mere fact that a good has an identifiable patent or trademark, however, does not prove nonreliance, especially if the seller recommended the product to the buyer.

## PROVIDING ADEQUATE TRAINING

Managers must provide adequate instruction and training to salespersons and agents about express and implied warranties. Aggressive salespersons willing to say what it takes to close a deal may unwittingly cause their company to be held liable under an implied warranty of fitness for a particular purpose when it never intended to make any such warranty at all.

## LIMITING LIABILITY

The seller can avoid responsibility for the quality of the goods under any of these warranties. First, the seller need not make any express warranties. This may be difficult to do, however, because even a simple description of the goods may constitute a warranty. Second, a seller may disclaim any warranties of quality if it follows specifically delineated rules in the UCC designed to ensure that the buyer is aware of, and assents to, the disclaimers. Section 2-316(2) requires that (1) a disclaimer of the implied warranty of merchantability must mention merchantability and, if in writing, must be conspicuous, and (2) a disclaimer of the implied warranty of fitness must be in writing and conspicuous. Language to exclude all implied warranties (for example, "AS IS" or "WITH ALL FAULTS") is also sufficient if it makes plain that there is no implied warranty. Third, the seller can refrain from professing expertise with respect to the goods and leave the selection to the buyer.

More commonly, the seller limits its responsibility for the quality of the goods by limiting the remedies available to the buyer in the event of a breach of warranty. A typical method is to include a provision limiting the seller's responsibility for defective goods to repair or replacement. Unless this remedy is clearly identified as exclusive, however, it will be interpreted as additional to all other remedies set forth in the UCC. In addition, a limited or exclusive remedy will not be enforced if the remedy fails in its purpose or operates to deprive either party of the substantial value of the bargain. In that case, the remedies in the UCC will govern as if the parties had not agreed on any remedies of their own.[18] In addition, some states limit a seller's right to limit liability, especially for personal injury.

Sellers may also limit their liability by including disclaimers of liability for special or consequential damages and by capping their liability for direct damages to the amounts received under the contract.

The 2003 amendments to Article 2 create different standards for disclaimers of implied warranties in a *consumer contract,* which is defined as a contract between a merchant seller and a natural person who enters into the contract primarily for personal, family, or household purposes. A disclaimer of the warranties of merchantability or fitness in a consumer contract must be in a record, be conspicuous, and either include specially prescribed language or use language that in common understanding calls the buyer's attention to the exclusion of warranties.

Finally, under the UCC, a seller is not an absolute insurer of the quality of goods sold. To recover for breach of warranty, a buyer must prove that (1) the seller made an express or implied warranty under the UCC; (2) the goods were defective at the time of the sale; (3) the loss or injury was caused by the defect rather than the buyer's negligent or inappropriate use of the goods; and (4) the seller has no affirmative defenses, such as a disclaimer of warranty.

As an alternative to suing for breach of warranty, the plaintiff may sue in tort for strict product liability. A product liability claim may succeed where a breach-of-warranty claim would not. This may happen when there is no contractual relationship between the buyer and the seller. However, product liability actions generally only permit recovery for bodily injury or property damage caused by a defective product, while warranty actions permit recovery of economic damage suffered by the purchaser who has purchased an inferior or defective product. Chapter 10 discusses this issue.

18. U.C.C. § 2-719(2), cmt. 1, 1962.

## Magnuson-Moss Warranty Act

The Magnuson-Moss Warranty Act[19] is a federal law that protects consumers against deception in warranties. It gives a consumer purchaser of a product the right to sue a manufacturer or retailer for failing to comply with the Act or the terms of a written or implied warranty arising from the Act. The Act was adopted "to improve the adequacy of information available to consumers, to prevent deception, and to improve competition in the marketing of consumer products."[20]

Nothing in the Act requires a supplier of consumer products to give a written warranty; the Act applies only when a seller chooses to do so. If the seller does make a written promise or affirmation of fact, however, then it must also state whether the warranty is a full or a limited warranty. A *full warranty* gives the consumer the right to free repair or replacement of a defective product. A *limited warranty* might restrict the availability of free repair or replacement. These designations inform the average consumer about the level of protection provided by the warranty. To earn the designation of "full warranty," a warranty must meet minimum standards provided in the Act. The Magnuson-Moss Warranty Act is discussed further in Chapter 17.

## Right to Reject Nonconforming Goods

Generally, a buyer that has contracted to purchase goods from a seller must fulfill its obligation and pay for those goods. A buyer has the right to reject nonconforming goods, however. Under Section 2-601 of the UCC, if the goods or the tender of delivery fails to conform to the contract in any respect, the buyer may reject any or all of the goods. Section 2-602 requires that any rejection be made within a reasonable time after the goods are delivered. After such a rejection, the buyer may not treat the goods as if it owned them. To the contrary, if the buyer has taken possession of the goods before rejecting them, then it must hold the goods with reasonable care for a time sufficient to permit the seller to remove them. As the following case illustrates, the right to reject can be waived inadvertently by a buyer who accepts goods with knowledge of their nonconformity.

19. 15 U.S.C. §§ 2301–12.
20. 15 U.S.C. § 2302(a).

# View from Cyberspace

## TAXING E-COMMERCE

The issue of whether to tax electronic commerce has generated great controversy at the state and federal level. In 1998, Congress enacted the Internet Tax Freedom Act (ITFA), which declared a moratorium on new taxes on Internet access and e-commerce (if such e-commerce taxes are "multiple or discriminatory") but allowed states to enforce existing tax laws. At the same time Congress created the Advisory Commission on Electronic Commerce to study federal, state, local, and international taxation of transactions using the Internet. The commission included executives of America Online, AT&T, Charles Schwab, Gateway, MCI WorldCom, and Time Warner as well as representatives of government at various levels.[a]

In March 2000, the Advisory Commission narrowly approved a report to Congress on continuing the tax moratorium, but the group was too divided to reach the two-thirds majority required for any "findings and recommendations" to Congress. Under the report, activities not triggering an obligation to collect state sales and use taxes included the solicitation of orders, the presence of websites, the use of the Internet to create a website, the use of an Internet service provider, and the use of a telecommunications carrier.[b]

Certainly, the existing maze of state sales tax regimes presents some difficulties in taxing Internet sales transactions. In *Quill v. North Dakota*,[c] the U.S. Supreme Court ruled that, given the complexity of state sales and use taxes, a business selling goods through catalogs is required to collect sales taxes only on purchases made by consumers within the states where the business has a physical presence. The Court acknowledged, however, that Congress could pass a law compelling the collection of sales and use tax on interstate sales.

Under the ruling in *Quill*, an Internet company that sells to customers in states all over the country has no obligation to collect sales tax on sales to persons in states where it is not physically located. Forty-five states require their citizens to pay sales taxes on their purchases, including those made online or in another state, but few online businesses collect these taxes and consumers buying goods from outside their state of residence rarely pay this tax either. As a result, many Internet purchases by individuals escape sales and use tax altogether. Many online retailers have even gone so far as to locate their sale operations in the five U.S. states that do not levy a sales tax so that they have no obligation to collect sales taxes from any of their customers. Recently, though, some online retailers including Wal-Mart, Target, and Amazon, which initially opposed the collection of taxes on online sales transactions, have started to support it.

States are heavily dependent on sales taxes, which on average account for one-third of state tax revenues and one-quarter of the total state and local take. In some states, such as Texas, which has no income tax, the sales tax accounts for more than half of all revenues.[d] In the early years of the Internet, online transactions represented only a small percentage of retail sales. As of March 2000, for example, retail sales on the Internet amounted to less than 1 percent of all retail sales; according to Forrester Research, Inc., in 1999, states lost only $525 million, or 0.3 percent of all sales tax revenue, as a result of the Internet.[e] This situation is changing, however. More recent studies have predicted that, by 2008, state and local governments could lose between $21.5 billion and $33.7 billion a year in revenues if taxes are not collected on Internet sales.[f]

Opponents of taxes on Internet sales argue that the growth of Internet businesses should not be slowed down by the imposition of taxes. According to a study by an economist at the University of Chicago, Internet sales in 1998 would have been 25 to 30 percent lower if sales taxes had been charged.[g] Proponents of taxing Internet transactions point out that e-commerce has grown tremendously since 1998. Contending that it no longer needs to be protected from taxation, they cite more recent studies such as a Jupiter Research report from February 2003 that concluded that collection of sales tax on Internet purchases would "not be a significant impediment to the growth of the online retail channel."[h]

The degree to which Internet sales will be taxed in the future remains

a. David Cay Johnson, *Agreement on Internet Taxes Eludes Deeply Divided Commission*, N.Y. TIMES, Mar. 21, 2000, at 1.
b. *Panel Passes E-Commerce Report 10-8, Administration Officials All Vote Against Plan*, 68 U.S.L.W. 2601 (2000).
c. 504 U.S. 298 (1992).
d. Howard Gleckman, *The Great Internet Tax Debate: Should the States Get a Slice of Every E-Commerce Dollar or Should Cyber-Sales Be Free of Any Tax Burden?*, BUS.WK., Mar. 27, 2000, at 228.
e. *Id.*
f. Donald Bruce & William Fox, *State and Local Sales Tax Revenue Losses from E-Commerce: Estimates as of July 2004* (July 2004) (unpublished report prepared for the National Governors Association and the National Conference of State Legislatures), *at* http://www.nga.org/cda/files/0407ecommerce.PDF.
g. *The Happy E-Shopper: How Feasible Is It to Tax Internet Spending?*, ECONOMIST, Jan. 29, 2000.
h. Beth Cox, *Online Sales Tax? No Big Deal*, Feb. 5, 2003, *at* http://www.clickz.com/stats/markets/retailing/print.php/1579891.

*(Continued)*

(View from Cyberspace *continued*)

unclear. ITFA was extended until November 1, 2007.[i]

Should the existing state tax regime be amended to address Internet sales? Regular "brick and mortar" retailers are opposed to the current system on the grounds that it gives Internet retailers an unfair advantage by allowing them to charge lower prices. As Governor John Engler of Michigan, testifying before Congress for the National Governors Association in February 2000, stated, "It is, in essence, a two-tiered system: good for clicks, bad for bricks."[j]

Forty-two states and the District of Columbia (all but three of the states that have a sales tax) are participating in the Streamlined Sales Tax Project (SSTP), which has developed uniform rules and improved technology to simplify the collection of sales tax. States that have passed some version of the SSTP also participate in the Streamlined Sale Tax Implementing States (SSTIS), which recommends legislative changes by the states. In November 2002, the SSTIS proposed rules that states must adopt if they want to participate in the streamlined sales tax system. The goal of the SSTP is to persuade Congress to grant participating states the authority to compel retailers to collect taxes on remote sales.

**i.** Grant Gross, *Bush Signs Internet Tax Moratorium*, INFOWORLD, Dec. 3, 2004.

**j.** Ann Scott Tyson, *Should World Wide Web Be a Tax-Free Zone? E-Commerce Boosters Argue a Ban on Internet Taxes Is Critical for Growth, but States Worry They'll Lose Revenues*, CHRISTIAN SCI. MONITOR, Feb. 28, 2000, at 3.

## INTERNATIONAL SNAPSHOT

On July 1, 2003, European Union Council Directive 2002/38/EC, which applies to sales by businesses to individual consumers (B2C), became effective. VAT is a consumption tax that each EU member levies on the sale of goods and services within its jurisdiction. As a result of this legislation, companies based outside the EU must collect and remit value-added tax on Internet sales of software, music, films, games, and other digital products and services to EU consumers. The VAT provides 44 percent of the EU's budget.[a] Prior to July 1, 2003, U.S. businesses selling online services to European consumers were not required to collect VAT. The EU believed that this gave U.S. businesses an advantage over their European competitors, who were required to charge VAT on sales of digital products and services delivered to locations both within and without the EU. To eliminate this competitive advantage, the Directive treats the service, i.e., the electronic delivery of digital products and services, as occurring at the place where the consumer resides. As a consequence, non-EU companies are now required to charge VAT on B2C sales of digital products and services delivered to locations within the EU. Under the Directive, EU companies are no longer required to charge VAT on B2C sales of digital products and services delivered to locations outside the EU.

**a.** James Graff, *Brussels Decrees on E-VAT; The European Commission Wants to Tax Content Sold by Foreign Firms on the Web—But Can It?*, TIME INT'L, June 19, 2000, at 119.

The Directive created a special registration regime that allows non-EU businesses to register and pay VAT in only one EU member country if the non-EU business (1) registers and obtains a tax number from the country of registration, (2) distinguishes between B2C and business to business sales, (3) identifies the country of consumption for B2C sales, (4) charges and collects VAT at the applicable rate in the country of consumption, (5) pays the VAT due in a euro-denominated account in the country of registration, and (6) maintains transaction records for ten years that are sufficient to allow each state of consumption to determine the VAT that was due and paid. A non-EU business that qualifies for the special regime is entitled to claim a credit for VAT paid, if any, on its purchases of goods and services.

Prior to its enactment, U.S. companies opposed the Directive, characterizing it as "e-protectionism." The president of the U.S. Software and Information Industry Association commented: "U.S. vendors should not be tax collectors for european governments. It is also doubtful, under public international law, whether the EU has any authority to impose such a legal obligation on U.S. entities."[b]

**b.** Geoff Winestock, *EU Plans Rule for Web Tax; U.S. Companies Protest Proposal*, WALL ST. J., June 8, 2000, at A19.

A CASE IN POINT

**CASE 8.4**

**Moore & Moore General Contractors, Inc. v. Basepoint, Inc.**

*Supreme Court of Virginia*
*485 S.E.2d 131 (Va. 1997).*

## Summary

**› FACTS** In late 1990, General Mills Restaurants, Inc. made plans to build a Red Lobster restaurant in Spotsylvania, Virginia. After requesting bids from various subcontractors for the elements of the project, general contractor Moore & Moore awarded a millwork subcontract to Basepoint. The subcontract called for Basepoint to provide custom-made cabinets of "melamine" for use throughout the restaurant. Even in the industry, the meaning of that term was unclear. Some evidence suggested that "melamine" referred to a composite product with a particular type of hard finish; other evidence suggested that it referred only to a finish and did not imply use of composite material.

In March and April of 1991, Basepoint delivered its cabinets to the job site, where they were received by Moore & Moore. Allen Lyle, Moore & Moore's field superintendent, and Donnie Hall, Lyle's subordinate, inspected the cabinets and noticed they were made of particle board instead of sturdier plywood, as called for in the master plans prepared by the project's architects. Believing that General Mills Restaurants would not know the difference and that he would be saving money by accepting delivery of the particle-board cabinets, Lyle directed the installation of all the cabinets.

On May 1, an inspector from General Mills Restaurants examined the installed millwork and rejected the cabinets as not conforming to the plans and specifications. The next day, Moore & Moore sent Basepoint a letter stating, "On Wednesday, May 1, 1991, it was discovered that most of your casework is constructed of particle board. Since the plans . . . we provided you for the above referenced job . . . call for plywood, all of the casework that has particle board does not conform and must be replaced." In the letter, Moore & Moore set the following Tuesday as the deadline for delivery of the replacement material, noting that Basepoint had already notified Lyle that it could not meet the deadline. Upon removal of the cabinets made of particle board, Moore & Moore immediately procured plywood replacements from another subcontractor. The new cabinets were installed promptly, and the project was completed nearly on time.

Subsequently, Moore & Moore refused to pay Basepoint for the cabinets it had delivered. Basepoint then sued Moore & Moore for the $28,080 price of the cabinets. Moore & Moore denied any indebtedness to Basepoint, claiming that the materials supplied were defective. In addition, Moore & Moore filed a cross-complaint against Basepoint for the $47,000 cost of removing the particle-board casework, rebuilding the casework with plywood, and finishing the remaining work under the contract.

The trial court found for Basepoint and rejected Moore & Moore's cross-claim. Moore & Moore appealed.

**› ISSUE PRESENTED** Can a buyer's acceptance of goods be revoked because of their nonconformity? If not, is the buyer entitled to recover from the seller the cost of substitute goods?

**› SUMMARY OF OPINION** The Virginia Supreme Court first noted that as a sale of goods between merchants, the dispute was controlled by the UCC. Section 2-601 provides that if goods fail to conform to the contract, the buyer may (1) reject the whole, (2) accept the whole, or (3) accept any commercial unit or units and reject the rest. Section 2-606(1)(c) provides that acceptance of goods occurs when the buyer performs any act that is inconsistent with the seller's ownership of the goods. Because Moore & Moore's installation of the cabinets was an act inconsistent with Basepoint's ownership, the court found that Moore & Moore had accepted the goods. Even though Moore & Moore could have rejected any or all of the cabinets at delivery, its installation of them served as its acceptance.

*(Continued)*

(Case 8.4 *continued*)

Moore & Moore did not dispute this conclusion but instead contended that it had revoked its acceptance of the cabinets because of their nonconformity. The court, however, turned to Section 2-607(2), which provides that a buyer's acceptance of goods precludes their rejection and that acceptance cannot be revoked if it was given with knowledge of the nonconformity. Lyle and Hall's awareness that the cabinets were made of particle board amounted to such knowledge. Therefore, Moore & Moore could not revoke its acceptance.

Regardless of its liability to Basepoint for the cost of the cabinets, Moore & Moore pointed to Section 2-607(2), which provides that acceptance by a buyer "does not of itself impair any other remedy provided by this title for nonconformity." By its argument, Moore & Moore was entitled to an award based on the cover remedy of Sections 2-711 and 2-712, which allow a buyer to recover for procurement of substitute goods. The court noted, however, that under Section 2-711, the cover remedy is available in only four situations: (1) when the seller fails to make delivery, (2) when the seller repudiates the contract, (3) when the buyer rightfully rejects the goods, and (4) when the buyer justifiably revokes its acceptance of the goods. Here, Basepoint did make delivery and did not repudiate the contract. Moreover, Moore & Moore accepted the goods, thereby precluding rejection, and accepted with knowledge of nonconformity, making any revocation unjustified. With none of the four situations applicable, the court rejected Moore & Moore's cross-claim.

› **RESULT** The trial court's decision was affirmed. Moore & Moore was required to pay for the cabinets.

---

Under the preexisting Article 2 it was not clear whether a buyer can make an effective, but wrongful, rejection of goods. The 2003 amendments to Article 2 clarify that a buyer can effectively reject goods, even when the rejection constitutes a breach of contract. Under the unamended version of Article 2, a buyer's postrejection or postrevocation use of goods could be treated as a violation of the buyer's obligation of reasonable care, as a reasonable use for which the buyer must compensate the seller, or, as in *Moore & Moore,* as an acceptance. The 2003 amendments to Section 2-603 take the approach that a buyer's postrejection or postrevocation use of goods will be treated as a use for which the seller must be compensated. If the use is reasonable under the circumstances, the buyer no longer needs to be concerned that its actions might be treated as an acceptance of the goods.

## Allocation of Risk of Loss

Goods can be lost in transit due to such events as fire, earthquake, flood, and theft. In the absence of an agreement to the contrary, Section 2-509 of the UCC places the risk of loss on the party controlling the goods at the time loss occurs because that party is better able to insure against loss and to take precautions to protect the goods. Section 2-319 expressly authorizes the buyer and seller to allocate risk of loss between them as they see fit and provides shorthand symbols, such as "FOB" (free on board), with defined meanings to facilitate the expression of such an agreement between the parties.

The 2003 amendments to Article 2 delete Sections 2-319 through 2-324, which defined FOB, FAS, CIF, C&F, and Delivery Ex Ship. According to the official comments, the definitions have been deleted because they are inconsistent with modern commercial practices. The comments direct parties to define these terms in their contracts or to refer to INCOTERMS, a set of definitions of the most important trade terms now in use, created by the international mercantile community acting through the International Chamber of Commerce. Traders of all countries are incorporating INCOTERMS into their international sales contracts. The terms are revised every ten years; the latest edition is INCOTERMS 2000.

INCOTERMS 2000 contains thirteen main trade terms, including FAS, FOB, CTF, and CIF, as well as several secondary terms. CIF, for example, requires a seller to procure, at its own cost and in a transferable form, a marine insurance policy against the risk of carriage involved in the contract.

## GOODS SHIPPED BY CARRIER

If a sales contract requires or authorizes the seller to ship the goods by carrier, the risk of loss passes to the buyer (1) at the time the goods are properly delivered to the carrier, if the contract does not require delivery at a particular destination; or (2) at the time the carrier tenders the goods to the buyer at the specified destination, if the contract specifies one. If nothing is said about delivery, the contract is not a delivery contract and does not require delivery to the destination.

If the parties indicate that shipment is to be made "FOB seller's place of business" (or "FCA seller's place of business" if INCOTERMS are used), delivery at a particular place is not required, so the risk of loss shifts to the buyer once the goods are properly placed in the possession of the carrier. An indication in the contract that shipment is to be made "FOB buyer's place of business" (or "FCA buyer's place of business" if INCOTERMS are used) means that delivery at a particular place is required, so the risk of loss will not shift to the buyer until the goods are tendered to the buyer at its place of business. The parties' selection of an FOB (or FCA) term in a sales contract controls the allocation of the risk of loss even if contrary language exists elsewhere in the contract.

## GOODS HELD BY INDEPENDENT WAREHOUSE

When the goods are in the possession of an independent warehouse and the seller provides the buyer with a document enabling it to pick up the goods at the warehouse, the risk of loss passes to the buyer when the buyer receives the document entitling it to pick up the goods.

## ALL OTHER CASES

When the goods are neither to be shipped by carrier nor held by an independent warehouse, the allocation of the risk of loss in transit depends on whether the seller is a merchant. (As mentioned earlier, a seller is a merchant if he or she possesses experience and special knowledge relating to the goods in question.) If the seller is a merchant, the risk of loss passes to the buyer only when the buyer receives physical possession of the goods. If the seller is not a merchant, the risk passes to the buyer when tender of delivery is made. *Tender of delivery* is made when the seller notifies the buyer that it has the goods ready for delivery.

The 2003 amendments to Article 2 eliminate the distinction between merchant and nonmerchant sellers. In all such cases, risk of loss passes to the buyer upon the buyer's receipt of the goods, and receipt requires taking physical possession of the goods.

The following case deals with the question of when a buyer has physical possession of the goods and thus bears the risk of loss.

A CASE IN POINT

**CASE 8.5**

**Lynch Imports, Ltd. v. Frey**

*Appellate Court of Illinois*

*558 N.E.2d 484*

*(Ill. App. Ct. 1990).*

## Summary

› **FACTS** On October 22, 1987, the buyers agreed to purchase a 1987 Volkswagen automobile from the seller for the price of $8,706. The agreement was set forth in a purchase order in which the following phrases were handwritten on the purchase contract: "Car to be in totally acceptable condition or money will be refunded to the customer" and "Acceptance subject to inspection."

On October 24, the buyers took possession of the vehicle and paid the seller $4,706 as partial payment of the purchase price. The balance of the purchase price was to be financed. It was understood that the car was to come with air-conditioning, but at the time of delivery it was not yet installed. One of two riders attached to the purchase contract provided that the buyer was responsible for having the vehicle fully covered under liability and collision automobile insurance from the instant the buyer took possession. The rider also stated that the buyer was not authorized to return the vehicle without the seller's authorization and that no vehicle was to be sold with the condition that the buyer might later return it.

*(Continued)*

(Case 8.5 *continued*)

Two to three days thereafter, the buyers brought the vehicle to the seller to have the air conditioner installed. When they returned in the evening to pick up the vehicle, the buyers were informed that the air conditioner had been installed but that the vehicle had sustained body damage in an accident. The buyers refused to take delivery of the automobile because of the damage and demanded that a new, undamaged car be substituted. When the seller refused, the buyers stopped payment on the check and canceled their application for financing the balance of the purchase price.

The car dealership sued the automobile purchasers for damages of $8,706 for breaching the sales contract and $4,706 for wrongfully stopping the check. The buyers filed a counterclaim for the seller's breach of contract in failing to deliver an acceptable car and sought damages of $1,330.35, representing the difference between the price paid by the buyers when they subsequently purchased a similar automobile and the contract price of the Volkswagen. The trial court granted summary judgment to the seller. The buyers appealed.

› **ISSUE PRESENTED** When a buyer takes possession of a car, but it is understood that the buyer will return the car to have air-conditioning installed per the purchase order, has the buyer fully accepted the car and assumed complete responsibility for it?

› **SUMMARY OF OPINION** The Illinois Appellate Court stated that there was an issue of material fact as to whether the buyers "accepted" the vehicle on October 24. The buyers argued that they did not accept the vehicle and therefore had the right to reject it, which they properly did, when it was damaged upon its return to the seller to install the air conditioner.

Under the provisions of Section 2-606 of the UCC, acceptance is deemed to have occurred when the buyer either signifies that the vehicle is conforming or "takes or retains" the vehicle in spite of its nonconformity. It was unclear to the court what the agreement was on October 24, 1987, just prior to the buyers' taking the vehicle. This uncertainty as to what transpired between the parties when the buyers took possession of the vehicle was of particular significance because the original purchase order contained the handwritten phrases: "Car to be in totally acceptable condition or money will be refunded to customer" and "Acceptance subject to inspection."

Section 1-202 of the UCC provides that the effect of the provisions of the UCC may be varied by agreement. The court concluded that the handwritten notations in the purchase agreement were sufficient to raise an inference that the buyers did not intend to waive their right to defer acceptance until the vehicle was brought to full conformity, even though they took interim possession of the vehicle.

Under Section 2-509 of the UCC, the risk of loss does not pass to the buyer until the buyer accepts the goods, even though the buyer obtains an insurable interest under Section 2-501 after the goods are identified to the purchase contract. Thus, Rider 2, which required the buyer to obtain insurance, was not conclusive on its face to pass the risk of loss to the buyer.

› **RESULT** The Illinois Appellate Court reversed the lower court's grant of summary judgment for the seller. There were material issues of disputed fact precluding summary judgment. The case was remanded to determine whether the buyers had accepted the vehicle on October 24 and whether they had the right to reject it when they later discovered that it had been damaged during its return to the seller for the installation of air-conditioning.

# Unconscionability

A party is normally bound by the terms of a contract he or she enters into. However, if the contract is so unfair as to shock the conscience of the court, the judge may decline to enforce the offending terms or the entire contract.

Section 2-302(1) of the UCC provides procedural guidelines for judicial review of unconscionable clauses in contracts for the sale of goods, but it does not define "unconscionable." The official comments, however, do provide some guidance. For example, comment 1 to Section 2-302 states:

> The basic test is whether, in the light of the general background and the commercial needs of the particular trade or case, the clauses involved are so one sided as to be unconscionable under the circumstances existing at the time of the making of the contract. . . . The principle is one of the prevention of oppression and unfair surprise . . . and not of disturbance of allocation of risks because of superior bargaining power.

In deciding whether a contract is unconscionable, the court considers evidence in addition to the contractual language, particularly (1) whether the contractual obligation was bargained for and (2) whether the parties understood and accepted the obligation. As under common law (discussed in Chapter 7), unconscionability can be either procedural (relating to the bargaining process) or substantive (relating to the provisions of the contract).

## Procedural Unconscionability

A contract is procedurally unconscionable when one party is induced to enter the contract without having any meaningful choice. For example, in highly concentrated industries with few competitors, all the sellers may offer the same unfair contracts on a "take it or leave it" basis. Such contracts are known as *adhesion contracts*. They are most prevalent in consumer transactions where bargaining power is unequal.

It is also procedurally unconscionable for a seller to tuck oppressive clauses into the fine print or for high-pressure salespersons to mislead illiterate consumers. In commercial transactions, however, it is presumed that the parties have the sophistication to bargain knowledgeably. Hence, procedural unconscionability is more difficult to prove in a commercial setting.

## Substantive Unconscionability

A contract is substantively unconscionable if its terms are unduly harsh or oppressive or unreasonably favorable to one side, such as when the price is excessive or one party's rights and remedies are unreasonably limited. The courts have not agreed on any well-defined test for determining when a price is so excessive as to be unconscionable. However, prices that were two to three times the price of similar goods sold in the same area have been held unconscionable.

Similarly, parties to a contract are allowed to limit the remedies available for breach but only to a certain extent. If, for example, consumer goods are involved, a provision that limits the purchaser's ability to recover monetary damages for personal injury is *prima facie* (or on its face) evidence of unconscionability. In the following case, the Superior Court of New Jersey considered whether a limitation of liability provision in a fur storage bailment contract was unconscionable.

**A Case in Point**

## In the Language of the Court

**CASE 8.6**
**Jasphy v. Osinsky**
*Superior Court of New Jersey*
*834 A.2d 426*
*(N.J. Super. Ct. 2003).*

**› FACTS** In 2001, Felice Jasphy brought a ranch mink coat, a shearling coat, and a blush mink coat to Cedar Lane Furs for storage and cleaning. Jasphy signed a written contract, titled "fur storage sales receipt," which included the following preprinted provision limiting the furrier's liability:

> [T]his receipt is a storage contract, articles listed are accepted for storage until December 31, of dated year, subject to the terms and conditions hereof, in accepting this receipt, the depositor agrees to be bound by all its terms and conditions and acknowledges that this receipt is the entire agreement with the furrier, which cannot be changed except by endorsement herein signed by the furrier. If no value is specified, or if no separate insurance covering the garment is declared at the time of issuance of the receipt, insurance in the amount of $1.00 will be placed on the garment. . . .

*(Continued)*

(Case 8.6 *continued*)

Immediately above the signature on the receipt, the following was printed: "I understand and agree that Cedar Lane Furs' liability for loss or damage from any cause whatsoever, including their own negligence or that of employees and others, is limited to the declared valuation." Jasphy signed and dated this receipt, although she did not state the value of the coats or declare whether she had separate insurance coverage; the form included no identifiable place to record such information.

The next day, Jasphy's three coats were completely destroyed by a fire caused by a hot iron that the furrier failed to unplug overnight. Jasphy demanded full replacement value for the coats. Ultimately, she filed a lawsuit against the furrier to recover the value of her lost coats.

The furrier moved for summary judgment based on the contract provision limiting liability to $1 per garment, but the trial court dismissed the motion. The furrier appealed.

**› ISSUE PRESENTED** Is a clause in a fur storage agreement, limiting liability of the furrier to $1 per garment, unconscionable?

**› OPINION** NEWMAN, J., writing for the Superior Court of New Jersey:

The undisputed facts show that the contract was a standard contract pre-printed before plaintiff even entered the store. Plaintiff was given no opportunity to negotiate its terms with defendant. Plaintiff was a member of the public, not a business person possessing knowledge of the fur industry. As such, plaintiff was in an inferior bargaining position compared to the defendant.

There is no indication that plaintiff read the terms of the agreement or knew of the limitation of liability at the time of the transaction. Defendant did not highlight or bring to plaintiff's attention the limitation of liability clause. Nor did defendant inquire as to plaintiff's valuation of each fur piece or provide a space on its preprinted form to include valuation figures. Plaintiff had no economic incentive to sign this agreement; it was simply a prerequisite to having her furs stored and cleaned. Defendants failed to secure plaintiff's furs in their vault overnight. In fact, it appears the fire itself was a result of defendant's negligent failure to unplug a hot iron. Yet, defendants still seek to limit their liability for plaintiff's furs, which were destroyed as a result of their negligence and are valued at approximately $18,000, to $3. Such a result would be unconscionable.

Under the circumstances presented, we do not hesitate to hold the limitations of liability clause unenforceable and properly stricken from the contract by the trial court.

**› RESULT** The court affirmed the trial court's dismissal of defendant's motion for summary judgment. The $1 per garment limitation of liability was invalid.

**› CRITICAL THINKING QUESTIONS**

1. Is it ethical for a company to limit its liability to a token amount?
2. What could the furrier have done to create an enforceable limitation of liability?

## Commercial Impracticability Under the UCC

The UCC has adopted the doctrine of *commercial impracticability* rather than the common law doctrine of strict impossibility discussed in Chapter 7. Section 2-615 states that unless the contract provides otherwise, a failure to perform is not a breach if performance is made impractical by an event unforeseen by the contract. Section 2-615, the associated official comments, and the cases that have arisen under Section 2-615 establish certain criteria that a party seeking discharge from performance must show.

### Ethical Consideration

Merchants selling goods on credit to low-income customers often charge a very high rate of interest. How should a manager balance the need for low-income persons to have credit to buy goods with the need for businesses to make a profit? Some businesspeople suggest that because low-income persons are statistically more likely to default on loans, creditors must charge a higher interest rate to cover themselves for the increased risk of default. They argue that if sellers are not allowed to charge higher interest rates or prices, low-income buyers will not be able to buy goods on credit. Are such higher rates and prices ethical? Should there be any limit to what a seller can charge for credit?

## Underlying Condition

First, a party must show that there was a failure of an underlying condition of the contract, that is, a condition that was not included in the parties' bargain. Contracts provide fully for certain occurrences, and the seller is assumed to have included an appropriate "insurance premium" when setting the contract price. Other risks are deemed too remote and uncertain to be included in the contract price. The function of the court in applying the doctrine of commercial impracticability is to determine which risks were, or properly should have been, allocated to the buyer and which to the seller.

## Unforeseen Contingency

In addition to showing that a condition was not reflected in the contract price, a seller seeking discharge must prove that the contingency that prevents performance was both unforeseen and unforeseeable. To some extent every occurrence is foreseeable—there is always some probability that a fire will destroy the anticipated source of supply, that a key person will die, or that various acts of God will occur. Legally, however, a foreseeable contingency is one that the parties should have contemplated in the circumstances surrounding the contracting. If there is a standard trade custom for allocating the risk, it is assumed that a particular contract follows that custom, unless it specifies differently.

Official Comment 4 provides an illustrative, but not exhaustive, list of contingencies that are considered unforeseeable. Wars and embargoes are considered unforeseeable; market fluctuations are not.

## Impracticable Performance

Even if a party is able to show that there was a failure of an underlying condition of the contract and that it did not implicitly assume the risk of this occurrence, the party must still prove that performance was impracticable. Increased cost alone is not sufficient reason to excuse performance unless it is a marked increase. In one case, a ten- to twelvefold increase was considered sufficient. In another case, the court observed: "We are not aware of any cases where something less than a 100% cost increase has been held to make a seller's performance impracticable."[21] Transactions that have merely become unprofitable will not be excused. Sellers cannot rely on Section 2-615 to get them out of a bad bargain.

Some of the most famous cases dealing with the issue of impracticability involved Westinghouse Electric Corporation, which argued unsuccessfully that the doctrines of impracticability and impossibility should relieve it of its obligation to supply uranium at a fixed price to utilities after a sharp increase in uranium prices.[22] On September 8, 1975, Westinghouse surprised and shocked the business and legal communities when it announced that it would not deliver about seventy million pounds of uranium under fixed-price contracts to twenty-seven utility companies. Westinghouse claimed that the potential loss of $2 billion made it commercially impractical to meet its obligations. In 1976, Westinghouse brought suit against its uranium suppliers, claiming that an international cartel had caused an unforeseen and precipitous increase in the price of uranium.

The judges involved in the ensuing litigation between Westinghouse and the utilities saw the conflict as primarily a business issue and pushed for settlement. Judge I. Marting Wickselman of the Court of Common Pleas in Pennsylvania stated:

> I am tired of pussyfooting and, more than that, I am tired of talking to lawyers when other, more powerful men, who have the ultimate power of decision, have not been here. The fiscal well-being, possibly the survival of one of the world's corporate giants is in jeopardy. Any decision I hand down will hurt someone and, because of the potential damage, I want to make it clear that it will happen only because certain captains of industry could not

21. Publicker Indus., Inc. v. Union Carbide Corp., 17 U.C.C. Rep. Serv. 989 (E.D. Pa. 1975).
22. This discussion is based on William Eagan, *The Westinghouse Uranium Contracts: Commercial Impracticability and Related Matters,* 18 AM. BUS. L.J. 281 (1980).

together work out their problems so that the hurt might have been held to a minimum.

On October 27, 1978, the U.S. District Court for the Eastern District of Virginia found that Westinghouse had not met its burden of establishing that it was entitled to be excused from its contractual obligations under Section 2-615 of the UCC. The court did not issue its supporting findings of facts and conclusions of law at the time, however; instead, the court urged the parties to settle as it was reluctant for the case to serve as legal precedent.

## IN BRIEF

### Comparison of the UCC, 2003 Amendments to the UCC, Common Law, UCITA, and CISG

| | Scope | Battle of the Forms | Warranties | Statute of Frauds |
|---|---|---|---|---|
| **UCC** | Sale of goods | If both parties are merchants, additional terms are generally incorporated; if not, mirror image rule applies. For different terms, "knockout" rule applies. | 1. Implied warranties of merchantability and fitness for a particular purpose<br>2. Any express warranties made | Sales of $500 or more |
| **2003 Amendments to UCC** | Sale of goods (excludes information) | In all cases, the contract terms are (1) terms that appear in both parties' records, (2) terms to which the parties agree, and (3) terms supplied or incorporated under the UCC. | 1. Implied warranties of merchantability and fitness for a particular purpose<br>2. Any express warranties made<br>3. Certain obligations to remote purchasers | Sales of $5,000 or more |
| **Common Law** | 1. Provision of services<br>2. Contracts for sale of land or securities<br>3. Loan agreements | Mirror image rule | Any express warranties made | 1. Transfer of real estate<br>2. Contract can't be performed within one year<br>3. Prenuptial agreement<br>4. Agreement to pay debt of another |
| **UCITA** | Computer information (including software, computer games, and online access) | Contract even if acceptance has additional or different terms, unless acceptance materially alters the offer | 1. Warranty of noninterference and noninfringement<br>2. Implied warranties of merchantability of computer program, informational content, fitness for licensee's particular purpose, and fitness for system integration<br>3. Any express warranties made | Contracts for $5,000 or more |
| **CISG** | Sale of goods by merchants in different countries unless parties opt out | In practice, mirror image rule | 1. Implied warranties of merchantability and fitness for a particular use<br>2. Any express warranties made | None |

## Damages

The UCC generally tries to put the nonbreaching party in the same position it would have been in if the contract had been performed. This is usually done through the award of monetary damages.

### SELLER'S REMEDIES

If a buyer wrongfully cancels a contract or refuses to accept delivery of the goods covered by the contract, the seller is entitled to damages under Section 2-708 of the UCC. The measure of direct damages is the difference between the market price at the time and place for delivery and the unpaid contract price, less expenses saved because of the buyer's breach. If this measure of damages is inadequate to put the seller in as good a position as performance would have, then the seller is entitled to recover the profit (including reasonable overhead) that it would have made from full performance by the buyer. Such a seller is called a *lost volume seller*.

Under the unamended Article 2, the courts split on whether to allow sellers to recover consequential damages. The 2003 revisions to Article 2 resolve this split by stating that an aggrieved seller is entitled to recover consequential damages if the seller's loss results from general or particular requirements that the buyer had reason to know at the time the contract was entered into. The seller's right to consequential damages is subject to two restrictions: (1) the buyer is not liable for losses that could have been mitigated by the seller, and (2) the seller cannot recover consequential damages from a consumer.

### BUYER'S REMEDIES

If a seller wrongfully fails to deliver the goods or repudiates the contract, or if the buyer justifiably rejects the tendered goods, then under Section 2-711 of the UCC the buyer has several choices. The buyer may cancel the contract and recover as much of the price as has been paid and then either (1) *cover*, that is, buy the goods elsewhere and be reimbursed for the extra cost of the substitute goods, or (2) recover damages for nondelivery.

If the buyer elects to cover under Section 2-712, it must make, in good faith and without unreasonable delay, a reasonable purchase of substitute goods. The buyer may then recover from the seller the difference between the cost of cover and the contract price.

If the buyer elects not to cover, then under Section 2-713 the buyer is entitled to direct damages. The measure of these damages is the difference between the market price at the time the buyer learned of the breach and the contract price. Section 2-715 of the UCC also permits the buyer to recover consequential damages for (1) any loss resulting from general or particular requirements and needs of the buyer that the seller at the time of contracting had reason to know and that could not reasonably be prevented by cover or otherwise and (2) injury to person or property proximately resulting from any breach of warranty.

## Specific Performance

If the promised goods are unique, then under Section 2-716 of the UCC a court may order the seller to deliver them to the buyer. For example, if there is only one antique Mercedes-Benz of a certain vintage, then damages alone will not be adequate to remedy the loss suffered by the disappointed buyer. Only delivery of the promised car will suffice. On the other hand, if the car is one of thousands, monetary damages will suffice because an equivalent car can be purchased elsewhere.

The 2003 amendments make several changes to Section 2-716. First, the right to specific performance is extended to sellers as well as buyers. Second, in a nonconsumer contract, a contractual agreement to specific performance (other than for payment of money) will be enforced.

# Global View

## THE CONVENTION ON CONTRACTS FOR THE INTERNATIONAL SALE OF GOODS

The UCC's Article 2 largely unified the laws of the separate states in the United States governing the domestic sale of goods. International sales of goods, however, remain outside its scope. As international trade and the global economy grew throughout the twentieth century, the need for more uniform laws throughout the world became apparent. The Convention on Contracts for the International Sale of Goods (CISG), promulgated under the auspices of the United Nations, became effective in 1988. More than fifty countries have ratified the Convention, including many of the world's largest economies: Canada, China, France, Germany, Russia, Singapore, and the United States. Today, the signatories to CISG account for nearly two-thirds of the world's imports and exports.

### Scope of the Convention

CISG sets out substantive provisions of law to govern the formation of international sales contracts between merchants and the rights and obligations of buyers and sellers.[a] It applies to (1) sales contracts between parties with places of business in different countries if those countries are bound by the Convention (member countries) and (2) sales contracts between parties with places of business in different countries if the application of choice-of-law rules would apply the law of a member country to the transaction. Parties located in member countries may elect to have CISG govern their sales contracts, or they may expressly opt out of CISG. A provision that calls for the application of the laws of a member country is not construed as an "opt-out" provision, however.

CISG does not apply to sales (1) of goods bought for personal, family, or household use, unless the seller neither knew nor should have known that the goods were bought for such use; (2) by auction; (3) on execution of a judgment or otherwise by authority of law; (4) of stocks, shares, investment securities, negotiable instruments, or money; (5) of ships, vessels, hovercraft, or aircraft; and (6) of electricity. As for the distinction between goods and services, CISG does not apply to contracts in which goods are sold in conjunction with services unless the preponderance of the obligations of the seller consists of the supply of goods. Neither does it apply to liability of the seller for death or personal injury to any person caused by its goods.

CISG applies to oral as well as written contracts of sale. CISG contains no statute of frauds requiring certain contracts to be in writing, unless one party has its place of business in a country that has made a reservation to the Convention in this regard. The United States did not make this reservation.

### Offer and Acceptance

Under CISG, an offer becomes effective when it reaches the offeree, and it may be withdrawn if the withdrawal reaches the offeree before or at the same time as the offer. Until a contract is concluded, an offeror may revoke its offer if the revocation reaches the offeree before the offeree has dispatched its acceptance. An offer cannot be revoked, however, if the offer indicates that it is irrevocable or if the offeree reasonably relied on its irrevocability. Even if irrevocable, an offer is terminated when the offeree's rejection reaches the offeror.

A contract is concluded at the moment acceptance of an offer becomes effective. A statement made by the offeree indicating its assent is an acceptance. Conduct indicating assent is also acceptance, but silence or inactivity does not in itself amount to acceptance. An acceptance becomes effective when it reaches the offeror, although an acceptance is not effective if it fails to reach the offeror within the time the offeror has specified. If the offeror has specified no time, then the acceptance must reach the offeror within a reasonable time. If the offer is oral, however, it must be accepted immediately unless circumstances indicate otherwise.

Recognizing the importance of custom and practice, CISG also provides that if the parties have established practices between themselves, the offeree may accept the offer by performing an appropriate act, such as sending the goods or paying the price, without notifying the offeror. In such a case, acceptance is effective as soon as the act is performed. Such acceptance by performance without notification differs from the UCC, which allows for acceptance by performance but requires notification.

### Battle of the Forms

An important difference between the UCC and CISG is the approach to the battle of the forms. Under CISG, a reply to an offer that purports to be an acceptance but contains additional terms or other modifications that materially alter the terms of the offer is a rejection of the offer and constitutes a counteroffer. Thus, there is no contract. If the modifications do not materially alter the terms of the offer and the offeror fails to object in a timely fashion, then there is a contract, which will include the terms of the offer with the modifications stated in the acceptance. CISG lists categories of differences that are presumed to alter the terms of the offer materially: price, payment, quality and quantity of the

*(Continued)*

a. For extensive materials relating to CISG, including international cases and commentary, *see* the Pace University School of Law's website on the Convention *at* http://www.cisg.law.pace.edu/cisg/guide.html.

(Global View *continued*)

goods, place and time of delivery, extent of one party's liability to the other, and settlement of disputes. The list leaves little for the sphere of "immateriality" and largely effects the old mirror image rule. As explained earlier, under the UCC, an acceptance with additional or conflicting terms may still result in a contract unless the offeree clearly specifies that there will not be a contract unless the offeror accepts the additions or modifications.

### Good Faith

CISG provides that in interpreting the Convention there shall be regard for promoting "the observance of good faith in international trade." As noted earlier, Section 1-203 of the UCC provides that "[e]very contract or duty within this Act imposes a duty of good faith in its performance or enforcement." At the most superficial level, the UCC provision is broader than the CISG principle, which literally applies only to the interpretation of the Convention rather than the conduct of merchants under it. Throughout CISG, however, are numerous requirements of "reasonableness," such as those for giving notice, making substitutions, relying, measuring inconvenience and expense, delaying performance, examining goods, incurring expenses, and making excuses.

Some commentators have suggested that the combination of CISG's requirements of good faith in interpretation and of reasonableness in so many areas of merchant behavior makes for a broad, albeit uncertain, duty for merchants to conduct themselves with good faith.[b] If that interpretation is correct, then, for example, if a seller requests additional time to deliver goods, a buyer would be required to act in good faith in deciding whether to grant that request. The buyer could not whimsically decide to enforce the letter of the contract to the seller's detriment. This contrasts with the UCC's *perfect tender rule,* which gives the buyer an absolute right to reject any goods not meeting all the contract requirements, including time of delivery. Nonetheless, managers are well advised to act in good faith rather than arbitrarily, both to protect their own long-term interests and reputation and to enhance their ability to attain a sympathetic hearing by possible legal decision makers.

### Implied Warranties

Under CISG, the seller must deliver goods that are of the quantity, quality, and description required by the contract, and such goods must be packaged as specified by the contract. Like the UCC, the Convention holds sellers liable for implied warranties of merchantability and fitness for particular use and for any express warranties they make. Under CISG:

> Unless the parties agree otherwise, goods do not conform unless they (a) are fit for the purposes for which goods of the same description would ordinarily be used; (b) are fit for any particular purpose expressly or impliedly made known to the seller at the time of the conclusion of the contract, except where the circumstances show that the buyer did not rely, or that it was unreasonable for him to rely, on the seller's skill and judgment; (c) possess the qualities of goods which the seller has held out to the buyer as a sample or model.[c]

CISG makes clear, however, that the implied warranty of merchantability does not attach if the buyer knew that the goods were not fit for ordinary use.

b. *See, e.g.,* Phanesh Koneru, *The International Interpretation of the UN Convention on Contracts for the International Sale of Goods: An Approach Based on General Principles,* 6 MINN. J. GLOBAL TRADE 105 (1997).

c. 15 U.S.C. app. (1997), Convention on Contracts for the Sale of International Goods, art. 35.

## THE RESPONSIBLE MANAGER

## OPERATING UNDER VARYING LEGAL REGIMES

Any manager who enters into contracts on behalf of a business should know which body of contract law will govern the transaction. In particular, the manager should determine whether the transaction is governed by Article 2 of the UCC (and if so, whether the 2003 amendments to Article 2 have been enacted in the relevant jurisdiction), the common law rules concerning contracts, CISG, or UCITA. Article 2 applies only to the sale of goods, not services or land. Although some things are clearly goods, others may be more difficult to categorize. CISG will apply to most international sales of goods unless the parties affirmatively opt out of its provisions. In states that have enacted the Uniform Computer Information Transactions Act, UCITA governs contracts to license or buy software, computer programs, multimedia products, computer games, and online access. A manager should obtain legal advice if there is any doubt as to which body of law controls in a particular situation.

(Continued)

(The Responsible Manager *continued*)

Managers should be aware of the requirements that must be met for the valid formation of a contract under the different regimes. In particular, managers should focus on one of the key elements in creating a valid contract: the process of offer and acceptance. This knowledge is crucial to ensuring that the company can enforce the contracts it has entered into and wishes to uphold. In addition, a manager may have a valid reason to attempt to avoid an agreement that was not formed in the correct manner. Only if the manager knows the rules of contract formation can he or she assess whether a contract was validly created.

The manner of making an appropriate offer is the same under the UCC as it is under common law. However, a manager should note that Article 2 allows an offeree to accept an offer even if the offeree's acceptance contains terms additional to or different from those in the offer. In contrast, CISG in practice generally imposes the mirror image rule applied by the common law. The rules in this area and the corresponding case law are both complex and fact specific. Nonetheless, it is crucial that managers understand these rules before they engage in negotiations. Failure to develop this understanding can lead to adverse results. A manager or company may be legally bound to a contract even when there was no intention to be bound. Or a manager may inadvertently extinguish an offer by proposing modifications that ultimately the offeree might have been willing to forgo.

Article 2 of the UCC, CISG, and UCITA establish three types of warranties that buyers may rely on when purchasing goods or computer information. Managers should be aware of how each warranty is created, how the warranties are applied, and how liability for products can be limited. These warranties also provide guidelines for managers as to what is expected from a product in terms of quality and suitability for its intended use. It is essential that managers obtain legal advice in this area because lawsuits for breach of warranty can lead to large awards of damages that are far in excess of the purchase price. In addition, the 2003 amendments to Article 2 create new obligations for certain kinds of statements made to remote purchasers of goods, either in records that accompany the goods or in advertisements or other public communications made by the seller concerning the goods.

Managers should also be familiar with the legal doctrines that allow parties legally to back out of contracts. The doctrine of impracticability can protect a party when unexpected changes in circumstances make performance commercially ruinous, though not literally impossible. The doctrine of unconscionability provides guidelines on the legal limits to one-sided contracts. Managers should keep in mind that sometimes more is less; extracting onerous concessions from a weaker party may backfire and cause a judge to declare a set of provisions invalid *in toto* when less onerous provisions might have passed judicial muster.

Both the UCC and CISG require the parties to act in good faith and in a commercially reasonable manner. Managers should avoid acting in an arbitrary manner and try to accommodate the reasonable requests of the other side (e.g., a seller's request to delay delivery when the delay would not have an adverse effect on the buyer's business).

INSIDE STORY

## CAUGHT IN THE WEB OF INTERNET AUCTION FRAUD

According to the National Fraud Information Center, a project of the National Consumers League, a nonprofit consumer organization, businesses and individuals lost $14,648,000 in 2002 as a result of Internet fraud of all kinds. Fraud in Internet auctions constituted 90 percent of these losses.[23] The opportunity to defraud bidders has increased as the dollar value of online auction sales has grown, from $3 billion in 1999, to approximately $13 billion in 2002; it continues to grow at a rate of 33 percent per year.[24]

23. National Fraud Information Center, *Internet Fraud Statistics*, *at* http://www.fraud.org/2002intstats.htm.

24. Eiichiro Kazumori & John McMillan, *Selling Online Versus Live* (Jan. 29, 2003) (unpublished report), *at* http://www.gsb.stanford.edu/CEBC/pdfs/sothebysmc0129.pdf.

*(Continued)*

(Inside Story *continued*)

As the use of Internet auctions has grown, the schemes to defraud bidders have become more sophisticated than the early more straightforward schemes in which Internet buyers who "won" the bid simply failed to receive their merchandise. In one case, the defendants combined auction fraud with serial identity theft to conceal their identities. Starting in 1999, one operator constantly changed his name to conceal the fact that he was not delivering the goods for which he was accepting payment. In 2001, he began to direct the payments to bank accounts and post office boxes that he had set up in the names of people whose identity information he had stolen. As a result, buyers and law enforcement officials believed that the identity theft victims had defrauded the purchasers in the Internet auctions he had run.[25]

In another case, the defendants acted as both buyers and sellers of merchandise in Internet auctions, but regardless of whether they "bought" or "sold," they insisted that the transaction be processed through premier-escrow.com, a bogus escrow service that they had set up to provide their victims with a false sense of security about the transactions. When victims sold merchandise to the defendants, premier-escrow.com assured them it would not release the items until the funds were received, and when they bought items from the defendants, premier-escrow.com assured them it would not release the funds until it had received and inspected the goods. In both cases, of course, the defendants wound up with the merchandise and the money, and the victims never heard from them or from premier-escrow.com again.[26]

Online auction site fraud has not been limited to the United States. In May 2000, a twenty-three-year-old resident of Tokyo was arrested for fraudulently acquiring seven million yen by posting a bogus advertisement for a popular game machine on an Internet auction site.[27] Even the National Police Agency in Japan became a victim of cyber-auction fraud when allegedly authentic police uniforms and badges were offered on Yahoo!Auction, a site opened in September 1999 by Yahoo!Japan Corporation.[28]

Online auction sites claim that they are under no legal obligation to determine whether goods auctioned on their sites are stolen. EBay's user agreement states:

> We are not involved in the actual transaction between buyers and sellers. As a result, we have no control over the quality, safety or legality of the items advertised, the truth or accuracy of the listings, the ability of sellers to sell items, or the ability of buyers to buy them.[29]

The company also claims that fraud affects only a tiny percentage of the sales at its site—one in 25,000.[30]

Although eBay has been criticized for failing to take enough steps to protect its customers, the company has made some effort to protect online bidders and sellers. EBay runs a Fraud Automated Detection Engine that screens and analyzes its databases for fraud patterns and compares transactions with reported fraud. It also offers an escrow service that allows a bidder to inspect the auctioned item before the seller is paid. The company also operates a standard purchase protection program that provides buyers with coverage of up to $200, with a $25 deductible fee to cover its processing costs. In October 2002, eBay acquired PayPal, one of the biggest e-payment companies, which offers eBay buyers coverage of up to $500 for claims of nondelivery or significant misrepresentations on listings that are paid for through PayPal. PayPal also offers a Seller Protection Policy that protects against chargebacks due to fraud. The policy is available to U.S. and Canadian sellers transacting business with U.S. buyers and to British sellers transacting business with U.S. or British buyers.[31]

In large part, eBay relies upon its customers to police its auction house website. EBay has implemented a feedback ratings system that enables a potential buyer to check the reputation of the seller through his or her feedback rating, which is accessible from the page advertising any item he or she is selling. EBay also encourages buyers to report questionable sellers to the site-sponsored Community Watch, and it supports the use of trustmarks to boost consumer confidence by ensuring that the seller is committed to good selling standards. The PowerSeller trustmark assures buyers that the seller is experienced and reputable, has consistently sold a high volume of items, and has maintained a 98 percent posi-

25. Federal Trade Commission, *Internet Auction Fraud Targeted by Law Enforcers,* Apr. 30, 2003, *at* http://www.ftc.gov/opa/2003/04/bidderbeware.htm.
26. *Id.*
27. *Suspected Net Auction Bilker Bagged,* YOMIURI SHIMBUN/DAILY YOMIURI, May 5, 2000.
28. *Police Goods Hawked on Internet Irks NPA,* YOMIURI SHIMBUN/DAILY YOMIURI, Apr. 15, 2000.
29. Marcella Bombardierei & John Ellement, *Stolen Goods Making Way to Internet: Fencing Schemes Use Online Auction Sites,* BOSTON GLOBE, June 1, 2000, at A1.
30. Jim Carlton & Ken Besinger, *CEO Seeks to Reassure Public, but Use of Multiple Names by Bidders Poses Problems,* WALL ST. J., May 24, 2000, at B1.
31. Mohamed S. Wahab, *Ecommerce and Internet Auction Fraud: The E-Bay Community Model,* Apr. 29, 2004, *at* http://www.crime-research.org/articles/wahab1.

*(Continued)*

(Inside Story *continued*)

tive feedback rating. The SquareTrade seal means that the seller's identity and contact information have been verified and that the seller has agreed to mediate disputes and has adhered to good selling practices. SquareTrade also offers buyers who buy from holders of the SquareTrade seal up to $250 in coverage against fraud.

Despite these efforts, eBay is not immune to fraud. For example, from April 2001 through October 2002, Teresa Smith sold hundreds of computers to individual buyers through eBay's auction site. She required the purchasers to pay in advance and then failed to send the computers and refused all refund requests. Each time eBay received a complaint about Smith, it would suspend her auctions on the site, but Smith would simply change her identity and begin selling on the site again. Ultimately, more than 300 defrauded buyers filed complaints with the Internet Fraud Complaint Center about Smith. In April 2003, she was sentenced to four years, nine months in federal prison for her actions.[32]

Various agencies have set up websites where consumers can learn about cybercrime and file complaints in an effort to combat fraud. In February 2000, the Federal Trade Commission (FTC) launched Project Safebid, an effort to get local, state, and federal law enforcement to address the problem of auction fraud cases.[33] The agency also created the Computer Sentinel database, a database of online auction complaints, which logged more than 51,000 complaints in 2002. In April 2003, the FTC, in conjunction with the National Association of Attorneys General, launched Operation Bidder Beware, a law enforcement crackdown targeting Internet auction scams, which resulted in fifty-seven criminal and civil law enforcement actions and a consumer education campaign to alert consumers about Internet auction fraud and provide tips for how to avoid it.[34]

Due to the global reach of the Internet, regulation of Internet auction sites requires international cooperation. On April 27, 2000, the Council of Europe approved the final version of the Convention on Cybercrime, the first international treaty to address various types of criminal behavior directed against computer systems, networks, or data, including computer-related fraud and forgery. The Convention calls for countries to harmonize their laws on cybercrime, including hacking, fraud, and child pornography, and to cooperate in cross-border investigations. Thirty countries, including the United States, signed the Convention in November 2001, when it was opened for signature at a signing ceremony in Budapest, Hungary. Since that time, additional countries have signed. The Convention entered into force on July 1, 2004. On November 17, 2003, President Bush submitted the Convention to the Senate, promising to receive its advice and consent to ratification.[35]

32. The Internet Fraud Complaint Center was created in 2000 by the Federal Bureau of Investigation, the Department of Justice, and the National White Collar Crime Center as a place where victims of Internet crime could file a crime report online.
33. Daniel Roth, *Fraud's Booming in Online Auctions, but Help Is Here Bidding Adieu,* FORTUNE, May 29, 2000, at 276.
34. Federal Trade Commission, *supra* note 25.
35. A current list of signatories and ratifying states is available *at* http://conventions.coe.int/Treaty/Commun/QueVoulezVous.asp?CL=ENG.

## KEY WORDS AND PHRASES

acceptance 259
adhesion contracts 280
battle of the forms 257
browse-wrap license 260
click-wrap license 260
commercial impracticability 281
consumer contract 273
Convention on Cybercrime 289
cover 284
express warranty 269
firm offer 262
fixtures 259
full warranty 273
goods 258
identification to the contract 258
implied warranty of fitness for a particular purpose 272
implied warranty of merchantability 271
limited warranty 273
lost volume seller 284
merchant 259
mirror image rule 259
offer 259
perfect tender rule 286
*prima facie* 280
puffing 269
remedial promise 271
remote purchaser 271
shrink-wrap license 260
statute of frauds 266
tender of delivery 278

## QUESTIONS AND CASE PROBLEMS

**1.** James Moore was interested in purchasing a used Mack truck from Worldwide, but he was concerned about the eighteen-speed transmission. Worldwide's sales representative assured Moore that the transmission had been completely rebuilt and that the truck would suit his needs because it had a large rear differential and a larger motor, allowing it to get up and down hills. Moore decided to purchase the truck. Mack's warranty stated:

THIS WARRANTY IS MADE EXPRESSLY IN LIEU OF ANY OTHER WARRANTIES OR CONDITIONS, EXPRESSED OR IMPLIED, INCLUDING ANY IMPLIED WARRANTY OR CONDITION OF MERCHANTABILITY OR FITNESS FOR A PARTICULAR PURPOSE, AND OF ANY OTHER OBLIGATION OR LIABILITY ON THE PART OF THE MANUFACTURER INCLUDING, WITHOUT LIMITATION OF THE FOREGOING, CONSEQUENTIAL AND INCIDENTAL DAMAGES.

Worldwide's sales agreement, which Moore signed, contained the following:

SELLER MAKES NO WARRANTIES AS TO THE PROPERTY, EXPRESS, IMPLIED OR IMPLIED BY LAW EXCEPT, AS TO NEW VEHICLES ONLY, THE MANUFACTURER'S STANDARD VEHICLE WARRANTY, WHICH IS INCORPORATED HEREIN BY REFERENCE. SELLER SPECIFICALLY DISCLAIMS ANY IMPLIED WARRANTY OF MERCHANTABILITY FOR CONSEQUENTIAL DAMAGES FOR ANY BREACH OF WARRANTY. ALL USED VEHICLES ARE SOLD "AS IS."

Moore brought the truck in for repairs on two occasions, four months apart, and the truck was operational after the first repair. Worldwide repossessed it five months after the second repair, and Moore sued Mack and Worldwide for breach of express and implied warranty. He also alleged that he could claim consequential and incidental damages because the defendants' exclusive remedy had failed of its essential purpose. How will the defendants respond? Will the court find in favor of Moore or the defendants? On what basis? [*Moore v. Mack Trucks, Inc.*, 40 S.W.3d 888 (Ky. Ct. App. 2001).]

**2.** Hardie-Tynes Manufacturing Company subcontracted with Hunger United States Special Hydraulic Cylinders Corporation to manufacture two hydraulic cylinders to be used in construction of the Jordanelle Dam in Utah. After Hardie-Tynes sent a request for quotations for Hunger's best price for the two cylinders, Hunger responded with a letter providing specific quantity, price, delivery, and payment terms. Both parties agreed that this constituted an offer to contract. A copy of Hunger's standard terms and conditions, which included a provision attempting to specify a mode of acceptance and limiting acceptance to Hunger's terms, accompanied the offer. None of the terms related to payment of attorneys' fees in the event of a contract dispute.

Hardie-Tynes accepted Hunger's offer by sending a purchase order, which required payment of attorneys' fees in the event that Hardie-Tynes commenced litigation upon Hunger's default. Like Hunger, Hardie-Tynes limited the agreement to its own terms.

The cylinders manufactured by Hunger did not comply with government standards. Hardie-Tynes sued Hunger for breach of contract and claimed that it was entitled to recover attorneys' fees. Did Hunger and Hardie-Tynes enter into a contract? If so, what were its terms? Would your answer differ if the 2003 revisions to Article 2 were enacted? What if the transaction was governed by CISG? [*Hunger United States Special Hydraulic Cylinders Corp. v. Hardie-Tynes Manufacturing Co.*, 41 U.C.C. Rep. Serv. 2d 165 (10th Cir. 2000).]

**3.** On February 15, 2001, Rohm & Haas Company (R&H) and Crompton Corporation entered into a contract pursuant to which Crompton agreed to satisfy all of its needs for 2-Mercaptoethanol (product) with product purchased from R&H, and R&H agreed to supply Crompton with all of the product it required during a three-year term. The contract obligated R&H to maintain a minimum of 150,000 pounds of product at its facility in Moss Point, Mississippi, and to have available to Crompton, onsite at a North American location, not less than 150,000 pounds of product from an approved source. The contract contained a *force majeure* provision that stated: "Deliveries may be reduced or suspended by either party upon the occurrence of any event beyond the reasonable control of such party."

One month prior to execution of the contract, a U.S. district court entered a consent decree that resolved a suit brought by the federal and Mississippi governments on account of certain operational practices at the Moss Point facility. R&H alleged that it was forced to close the facility in December 2001 as a result of the dramatic costs associated with bringing it into compliance with the consent decree. R&H sought a declaratory judgment to determine whether it was relieved of its contractual duties to Crompton, and Crompton filed a counterclaim for damages. What arguments will R&H make in support of its claim that its performance should be excused? Who will prevail? [*Rohm & Haas Co. v. Crompton Corp.*, 2002 WL 1023435 (Pa. Com. Pl. 2002).]

4. Before deciding what remedies are available under Article 2 of the UCC, one must first determine whether the transaction involved the sale of goods. Consider the following cases.
   a. True North and Trinity entered into a carbodies supply agreement pursuant to which (1) True North agreed to produce composite carbodies for railcars; (2) Trinity agreed to separately manufacture steel undercarriages, with wheels and a platform; (3) True North agreed to mount its carbodies to Trinity's undercarriages to create complete railcars; and (4) after assembly, Trinity agreed to market and sell the railcars. Following cost overruns and difficulties in agreeing on final specifications for the carbodies, True North filed suit, alleging that Trinity had breached the agreement and its duty of good faith and fair dealing. Does the claim involve a contract action for goods or for services? [*True North Composites, L.L.C. v. Trinity Industries*, 2003 WL 21206154 (Fed. Cir. 2003).]
   b. Lockheed Martin Idaho Technical Company (LMITCO) requested bids for a comprehensive fire alarm system for its twelve buildings located in Idaho Falls. Mountain West Electric, Inc. (MWE), an electrical contractor, and Rodney Fox, a fire alarm supplier, decided that MWE would bid on the contract and Fox would work under MWE. When MWE won the contract (in which the goods comprised one-half of the contract price), Fox began performing various services related to the LMITCO project. A dispute arose between Fox and MWE, and Fox left the project after delivering the remaining equipment and materials to MWE. Fox filed a complaint seeking damages representing money due and owing for materials and services he had provided. Does the claim involve the sale of goods or services? [*Fox v. Mountain West Electric, Inc.*, 52 P.3d 848 (Idaho 2002).]
   c. Micro Data Base Systems (MDBS) entered into a contract with Dharma Systems, Inc., which provided that Dharma would customize its existing software program for use in a system that MDBS would provide to Unisys. The contract was for the program itself and the work of customizing the program. Was this a contract for the sale of a good or services? Would UCITA apply to such a contract? Would the result be different in a state that had enacted the 2003 amendments to UCC Article 2? [*Micro Data Base Systems, Inc. v. Dharma Systems, Inc.*, 148 F.3d 649 (7th Cir. 1998).]
5. In connection with upgrading its computer system, Cablescope entered into a contract with ASK Technologies to install a new computer system. The bugs in the system surfaced almost immediately after ASK installed the system, and Cablescope made its dissatisfaction clear. ASK was either unwilling or unable to perform the necessary fine-tuning required to integrate the new system with the existing system. In July, Cablescope sent a letter to ASK, claiming that the installation had not been adequately performed, followed by a letter informing ASK that it would not pay for services and equipment already supplied. ASK subsequently sued to recover payments plus interest for the computer hardware and service. Who will prevail? On what basis? [*ASK Technologies, Inc. v. Cablescope, Inc.*, 51 U.C.C. Rep. Serv. 2d 1028 (D.D.N.Y. 2003).]
6. In 1991, Brian Yarusso catapulted over the handlebars of his off-road motorcycle while traveling over a series of dirt moguls at a dirt motocross track in Newark, Delaware. He landed on his head, flipped over, and came to rest face down in the dirt. As a result of the accident, Yarusso was rendered a quadriplegic. Yarusso was wearing a full complement of safety equipment, including a Bell Moto-5 helmet, a full-face motocross helmet that was designed for off-road use. The Bell Moto-5 helmet complied with the U.S. Department of Transportation standards and was also certified by the Snell Foundation, a leading worldwide helmet research and testing laboratory. The owner's manual for the helmet included the following:

> Five Year Limited Warranty: Any Bell helmet found by the factory to be defective in materials or workmanship within five years from the date of purchase will be repaired or replaced at the option of the manufacturer. . . . This warranty is expressly in lieu of all other warranties, and any implied warranties of merchantability or fitness for a particular purpose created hereby, are limited in duration to the same duration of the express warranty herein. Bell shall not be liable for any incidental or consequential damages. . . .
>
> Introduction: Your new Moto-5 helmet is another in the long line of innovative off-road helmets from Bell. . . . [T]he primary function of a helmet is to reduce the harmful effects of a blow to the head. However, it is important to recognize that the wearing of a helmet is not an assurance of absolute protection. NO HELMET CAN PROTECT THE WEARER AGAINST ALL FORESEEABLE IMPACTS.

Yarusso filed suit against Bell. He testified at trial that he had purchased the helmet based on Bell's assertion that the helmet's primary function was to reduce the harmful effects of a blow to the head. On what grounds could Yarusso sue Bell? What will Bell argue in its defense? Who will prevail? [*Bell Sports, Inc. v. Yarusso,* 759 A.2d 582 (Del. 2000).]

7. Jordan Panel Systems Corporation is a construction subcontractor that contracted to install windows at an air cargo facility at John F. Kennedy Airport in New York City. Jordan entered into a contract to purchase custom-made windows from Windows, Inc., a fabricator and seller of windows located in South Dakota. The contract specified that the windows were to be shipped properly packaged and delivered to New York City. Windows, Inc. arranged to have the windows shipped to Jordan by common carrier and delivered the windows to the common carrier properly packaged. During the course of the shipment, however, much of the glass was broken, and many of the window frames were gouged and twisted. Jordan refused to pay for the damaged windows, and Windows, Inc. sued to recover the full purchase price. Which company should win? [*Windows, Inc. v. Jordan Panel Systems Corp.,* 177 F.3d 114 (2d Cir. 1999).]

8. Sandy Singlefather has two children and lives in a subsidized housing development in New City. He receives federal assistance to help raise his two children. Singlefather recently read an advertisement for household appliances. The advertisement stated that he could "rent to own" appliances with no credit. Singlefather was in need of a washing machine but had a poor credit history, so he answered the advertisement. The appliance store was more than delighted to accommodate him. Singlefather now pays $30 a week for his washing machine and will own it after he makes seventy-eight payments. That model of washing machine usually sells for $350.

   Has Singlefather entered into an unconscionable bargain? Should the manager of the rent-to-own business repossess the washing machine if Singlefather fails to pay the $30 weekly rent after possessing the machine and paying rent for fifty weeks?

   Suppose that a rent-to-own business rents a large-screen television that retails for $3,000 for $100 a week with the right to own it after eighty weeks. The renter defaults after possessing the television and paying the $100 weekly rent for fifty weeks. Should the manager treat the transaction differently from the rental of the washing machine? How could the manager structure the pricing to permit the transactions to withstand legal challenge yet still be profitable for the rent-to-own company? [*Murphy v. McNamara,* 416 A.2d 170 (Conn. Sup. Ct. 1979).]

9. When the Darbys purchased a male horse, the seller and the horse's trainer told them that the horse was not physically sound enough to be a show horse (even though the horse had successfully competed in two horse shows). As a result, they were able to purchase the horse for $1,000. A year later, the Darbys entered the horse in a horse show where it competed successfully (placing four times).

   After watching the horse at the show, Ashley Sheffield contacted the Darbys about buying the horse. The Darbys assured her that the horse had no problems and would make a good show horse for use in competition. In the presence of her father (who raised horses for a living), Sheffield rode the horse and decided to buy him for $8,500. At Sheffield's request, a veterinarian cursorily examined the horse prior to the sale and opined that it was not lame, although it had a limiting condition known as "straight in the pasterns." Within three weeks, however, Sheffield and her trainer determined that the horse was lame. Sheffield sued the Darbys for fraud and breach of express and implied warranties, alleging that they had falsely informed her that the horse had no problems and would make a good show horse. How will the Darbys respond? Who will prevail? [*Sheffield v. Darby,* 535 S.E.2d 776 (Ga. Ct. App. 2000).]

MANAGER'S DILEMMA

10. Mortenson, a nationwide construction contractor, had used Timberline's Bid Analysis software to assist with its preparation of bids for several years. In 1993, Mortenson issued a purchase order to Softworks, an authorized Timberline dealer, for eight copies of a new version of Bid Analysis. The purchase order did not include a clause stating that the order constituted the entire agreement of the parties. Softworks signed the purchase order and ordered the software from Timberline. The full text of the Timberline license agreement was set forth on the outside of each diskette pouch and in the inside cover of the instruction manuals delivered to Mortenson. The license agreement included the following warning:

    CAREFULLY READ THE FOLLOWING TERMS AND CONDITIONS BEFORE USING THE PROGRAMS. USE OF THE PROGRAMS INDICATES YOUR ACKNOWLEDGEMENT THAT YOU HAVE READ THIS LICENSE, UNDERSTAND IT, AND AGREE TO BE BOUND BY ITS TERMS AND CONDITIONS. IF YOU DO NOT AGREE TO THESE TERMS AND CONDITIONS, PROMPTLY RETURN THE PROGRAMS AND USER MANUALS TO THE PLACE OF PURCHASE AND YOUR PURCHASE PRICE WILL BE REFUNDED. YOU AGREE THAT YOUR USE OF THE PROGRAM ACKNOWLEDGES THAT YOU HAVE READ THIS LICENSE, UNDERSTAND IT, AND AGREE TO BE BOUND BY ITS TERMS AND CONDITIONS.

    Mortenson's chief estimator claimed that Mortenson never saw any of the licensing information or any of the manuals because the software was installed by Softworks.

    Mortenson subsequently used the Precision Bid Analysis software to prepare a bid for a project. On the day of the bid, the software allegedly malfunctioned many times and gave the following message: "Abort: Cannot find alternate." Nevertheless, Mortenson submitted a bid generated by the software. After Mortenson was awarded the project, it learned that the bid was approximately $1.95 million lower than it had intended. Mortenson sued Timberline and Softworks for breach of express and implied warranties. After the suit was filed, a Timberline internal memorandum surfaced stating that "[a] bug has been found . . . that results in two rather obscure problems." The memo explained that "[t]hese problems only happen if the following [four] conditions are met." Apparently, other Timberline customers had encountered the same problem, and a new version of the software had been sent to some of these customers. After extensive investigation, Timberline's lead programmer acknowledged that Mortenson's error message appeared when the four conditions were met.

    Did Timberline have an ethical obligation to notify all of its customers when it became aware of the defect in its software that could result in significant errors in the calculation of bids? Is Timberline's disclaimer of consequential damages enforceable? Is it unconscionable to allow Timberline to use the disclaimer of consequential damages to avoid liability to its customers for a known product defect? [*Mortenson Co. v. Timberline Software Corp.*, 998 P.2d 305 (Wash. 2000).]

## INTERNET SOURCES

| | |
|---|---|
| The Uniform Law Commissioners, who draft the UCC, have a website at the University of Pennsylvania Law School that contains the entire UCC, including Article 2, and its history and proposed changes, as well as other uniform laws. | http://www.law.upenn.edu/library/ulc/ulc.htm |
| This site provides a daily summary of Internet and technology law news stories, with links to the full-text stories. | http://www.GigaLaw.com |
| Pace University's Institute for International Consumer Law sponsors a page about the U.N. Convention on Contracts for the International Sale of Goods. | http://www.cisg.law.pace.edu |
| The Justice Department sponsors this site, which provides information about computer crime and how to report it. | http://www.cybercrime.gov |
| These sites, maintained by international publisher Cameron May, provide information about international commercial law and useful links to other sites related to international trade and commerce. | http://www.lexmercatoria.org<br>http://www.lexmercatoria.com |

CHAPTER 9

# Torts

## INTRODUCTION

### WHAT IS A TORT?

A *tort* is a civil wrong resulting in injury to a person or property. A tort case is brought by the injured party to obtain compensation for the wrong done. A crime, by contrast, is a wrong to society that is prosecuted by the state. (Criminal law is discussed in Chapter 14.) Even though a crime may be perpetrated against an individual, the victim is not a party to a criminal action. Criminal law generally is concerned with protecting society and punishing the criminal, not with compensating the victim.

The distinctions between tort and criminal law are not always as clear as they first appear, however. A criminal statute might call for the criminal to compensate the victim. The victim might sue the perpetrator of the crime in tort, using the violation of a criminal statute as a basis for the tort claim. In some instances, tort law, like criminal law, purports to protect society through the award of punitive damages.

### CHAPTER OVERVIEW

This chapter first discusses intentional torts, which fall into three general categories: (1) torts that protect individuals from physical and mental harm, (2) torts that protect interests in property, and (3) torts that protect certain economic interests and business relationships. The chapter then addresses negligence (including an accountant's liability to third parties) and strict liability. Tortious activity by more than one individual or entity raises the issues of vicarious liability and apportioned responsibility. The chapter applies these various theories to the evolving law of toxic torts.

## Elements of an Intentional Tort

To prevail in a tort action, the plaintiff must prove all elements of a claim. Intentional torts require the plaintiff to prove (1) actual or implied intent, (2) a voluntary act by the defendant, (3) causation, and (4) injury or harm. The act must be the actual and legal cause of the injury. The act required depends on the specific intentional tort.

### INTENT

*Intent* is the subjective desire to cause the consequences of an act. *Actual intent* can be shown by evidence that the defendant intended a specific consequence to a particular individual. Intent is implied if the defendant knew that the consequences of the act were certain or substantially certain even if he or she did not actually intend any consequence at all.

As the degree of certainty of the result decreases, the defendant's conduct loses the character of intent and becomes recklessness. As the result becomes even less certain, the act becomes negligence, which is treated later in this chapter. For example, if Metro Corporation's custodian, Teddy, dumped garbage out of Metro's third-floor office window onto a busy sidewalk and hit Alexa, the law would likely imply intent to hit Alexa. Even though Teddy may have had no subjective intention of hitting Alexa with the garbage, throwing it onto a busy sidewalk was substantially certain to result in at least one pedestrian being hit. However, if late one night Teddy put garbage in the middle of the sidewalk in front of the office building for morning pickup and Alexa tripped over it, the intent to cause harm is not so clear. If intent is not established, Teddy will not be liable for the intentional tort of battery, which requires intent to bring about a harmful or offensive contact. Alexa might be able to establish negligence, however, if she can show that a reasonable person would not have left the garbage on the sidewalk.

Intent may be transferred. If the defendant intended to hit one person but instead hit the plaintiff, the intent requirement is met as to the plaintiff.

## Types of Intentional Torts and Defenses

The intentional torts of battery, assault, false imprisonment, intentional infliction of emotional distress, defamation, and invasion of privacy are designed to protect individuals from physical and mental harm. The torts of trespass to land, nuisance, conversion, and trespass to personal property protect interests in property. Certain economic interests and business relationships are protected by the torts of disparagement, injurious falsehood, fraudulent misrepresentation, malicious prosecution, interference with contractual relations, interference with prospective business advantage, and bad faith. A single set of facts may give rise to claims under more than one theory.

Even if a plaintiff has proved all the elements of an intentional tort, the defendant may raise a legal defense to absolve himself or herself of liability. The most frequently raised defense is consent. If the plaintiff consented to the defendant's act, there is no tort. Even if the plaintiff did not explicitly consent, the law may imply consent. For example, a professional athlete injured during practice is deemed to have consented to the physical contact attendant to practice. The defendant may also be absolved of liability by a claim of self-defense or defense of others.

## Intentional Torts to Protect Persons

### Battery

Tort law recognizes a basic right to have one's body be free from harmful or offensive contact. Battery is the violation of that right.

*Battery* is intentional, nonconsensual, harmful or offensive contact with the plaintiff's body or with something in contact with it. Offensive contact, such as dousing a person with water or spitting in his or her face, may be a battery, even though the plaintiff has suffered no physical harm. The contact may be by the defendant directly or by something the defendant has set in motion. For example, putting poison in someone's food is a battery.

A company president committed battery when he spanked an employee with a carpenter's level in a hazing ritual while other employees watched.[1] The jury awarded $6,000 for pain and suffering and loss of consortium and $1 million in punitive damages. The trial court reduced the punitive damages award to $130,000 after finding the original award excessive.

### Assault

The tort of assault also protects the right to have one's body be left alone. Unlike battery, however, it does not require contact. *Assault* is an intentional, nonconsensual act that gives rise to the apprehension (though not necessarily the fear) that a harmful or offensive contact is imminent.

Generally, assault requires some act, such as a threatening gesture, and the ability to follow through immediately with a battery. A punch thrown from close range that misses its target may be an assault, but a threat to punch someone out of punching range is not. For example, if a defendant makes a threatening gesture and says, "I would hit you if I weren't behind this desk," and the defendant is in fact behind the desk, there is no assault. The immediacy requirement has not been met. Similarly, the threat "I'll beat you up if you come to class next week" is not immediate enough to be an assault.

### False Imprisonment

The tort of false imprisonment protects the right to be free from restraint of movement. *False imprisonment* is intentional, nonconsensual confinement by physical barriers or by physical force or threats of force. It requires that the plaintiff either knew he or she was confined or suffered harm as a result of the confinement.

False imprisonment has been found when the plaintiff's freedom of movement was restricted because of force applied to the plaintiff's valuable property. For example, if a store clerk grabs a package from a customer

1. Smith v. Phillips Getschow Co., 616 N.W.2d 526 (Wis. 2000).

walking out the door, this is false imprisonment because the customer cannot be expected to abandon the package to leave the store.

Shopkeepers who detain and later release a person mistakenly suspected of shoplifting are sometimes sued for false imprisonment. Most states have legislation exempting shopkeepers from such claims if the shopkeeper acted in good faith and the detention was made in a reasonable manner, for a reasonable time, and was based on reasonable cause.

## Intentional Infliction of Emotional Distress

The tort of intentional infliction of emotional distress protects the right to peace of mind. The law has been slow to provide redress for purely mental injuries and is still evolving in this area. Jurisdictions differ sharply in their acceptance of this tort. In most jurisdictions, to prove *intentional infliction of emotional distress,* a plaintiff must show (1) outrageous conduct by the defendant; (2) intent to cause, or reckless disregard of the probability of causing, emotional distress; (3) severe emotional suffering; and (4) actual and proximate (or legal) causation of the emotional distress. The reluctance of the courts to accept intentional infliction of emotional distress as an independent tort most likely stems from the fear that plaintiffs will file false claims. Therefore, some jurisdictions also require a physical manifestation of the emotional distress.

The mental distress must be foreseeable. The defendant is liable only to the extent that the plaintiff's response is reasonably within the range of normal human emotions.

The acts of the defendant must be outrageous or intolerable. Insulting, abusive, threatening, profane, or annoying conduct is not in itself a tort. Everyone is expected to be hardened to a certain amount of abuse. In determining outrageousness, courts will consider both the context of the conduct and the relationship of the parties. For example, an employee can expect to be subjected to evaluation and criticism in the workplace, and neither criticism nor discharge is in itself outrageous. On the other hand, sexual harassment by a supervisor in the workplace is less tolerated than it might be, for example, if done by a patron in a nightclub.

In *Ford v. Revlon, Inc.,*[2] the Supreme Court of Arizona found that Revlon was liable for intentional infliction of emotional distress after a Revlon employee, Leta Fay Ford, was harassed by her supervisor, the manager for the purchasing department. In addition to making vulgar and threatening remarks to Ford, the manager held her in a chokehold and fondled her at a company picnic. Ford repeatedly complained to management, but Revlon did not confront the supervisor for nine months. Indeed, one manager to whom Ford complained told her that her complaint was too hot to handle and encouraged her to try not to think about her predicament. Ford not only suffered emotional distress but also developed physical complications, including high blood pressure and chest pains, as a result of her stressful work environment. Revlon had a specific policy and several guidelines for handling sexual harassment claims but recklessly disregarded them.

## Defamation

*Defamation* is the communication (often termed *publication*) to a third party of an untrue statement, asserted as fact, that injures the plaintiff's reputation by exposing him or her to "hatred, ridicule or contempt." *Libel* is written defamation, and *slander* is spoken defamation. The distinction between libel and slander is sometimes blurred with respect to modern communications.

Special rules apply to the requirement of injury to reputation. In an action for slander (spoken defamation), the plaintiff must prove that he or she has suffered actual harm, such as the loss of credit, a job, or customers, unless the statement is so obviously damaging that it falls into the category of slander *per se. Slander per se* means that the words are slanderous in and of themselves, for example, a statement that a person has committed a serious crime, is guilty of sexual misconduct, or is not fit to conduct business. In an action for libel (written defamation), the law presumes injury; that is, no actual harm need be shown unless the statement on its face is not damaging.

An opinion is defamation only if it implies a statement of objective fact. In *Sagan v. Apple Computer, Inc.,*[3] noted astronomer Carl Sagan sued Apple Computer for libel when Apple changed its code name for a new personal computer from "Carl Sagan" to "Butt-Head Astronomer" after Sagan demanded that the company cease using his name. The court ruled that the dispositive question in determining whether a statement of opinion can form the basis of a libel action is whether a reasonable fact finder could conclude that the statement implies an assertion of fact. The court found that a

2. 734 P.2d 580 (Ariz. 1987).

3. 874 F. Supp. 1072 (C.D. Cal. 1994).

reasonable fact finder would conclude that Apple Computer was not making a statement of fact about Sagan's competency as an astronomer in using the figurative term "Butt-Head" and would understand that the company was using the figurative term to retaliate in a humorous and satirical way for Sagan's reaction to Apple's use of his name. In addition, the court found that the statement that Sagan was a "Butt-Head Astronomer" could not rest on a core of objective evidence, so it could not be proved true or false.

In contrast, in *Flamm v. American Ass'n of University Women*,[4] the U.S. Court of Appeals for the Second Circuit found that a lawyer's libel claim against the American Association of University Women's Legal Advocacy Fund (AAUW) was based on a statement of fact, not opinion. The AAUW compiles a directory of attorneys who are willing to consult with women involved in higher education who are considering bringing gender discrimination claims. The directory's entry on Mr. Flamm stated: "At least one plaintiff has described Flamm as an 'ambulance chaser' with interest only in 'slam dunk cases.'" The appeals court found that this statement contained in a "fact-laden" directory did not simply express an opinion but could reasonably be interpreted to imply a factual statement that Flamm engaged in the unethical solicitation of clients and took only easy cases.

The requirement of publication generally means that the statement must be made in the presence of a third person. Thus, the statement "You are a thief" made in a one-on-one conversation is not defamation. However, some courts have adopted the doctrine of *self-publication* to give an employee a claim for defamation when an employer, in firing an employee, makes a false assertion that the employer could reasonably expect the employee would be required to repeat to a prospective employer.

## Defenses

Defenses to defamation actions are framed in terms of privilege and may be asserted in a number of circumstances. An *absolute privilege* cannot be lost. A *qualified privilege* can be lost under certain conditions. If the defendant has an absolute privilege, he or she can publish with impunity a statement he or she knows to be false. The defendant can even do so with the most evil intention. Absolute privilege is limited to situations in which (1) the defendant has consented to the publication, (2) the statement is a political broadcast made under the federal "equal time" statute, (3) the statement is made by a government official in the performance of governmental duties, (4) the statement is made by participants in judicial proceedings, or (5) the statement is made between spouses.

In most jurisdictions, truth is an absolute defense to a defamation claim. The law will not protect a reputation the plaintiff does not deserve. However, the burden is on the defendant to prove that the derogatory statements are true. The law in most jurisdictions presumes that the plaintiff has a pristine reputation unless the defendant proves otherwise.

There is a qualified privilege to make statements to protect one's own personal interests, including statements to a peer review committee. There is also a qualified privilege to make statements to protect legitimate business interests, such as statements to a prospective employer, or to provide information for the public interest, such as credit reports. A qualified privilege can be lost if the person making the statement abuses the privilege.

4. 201 F.3d 144 (2d Cir. 2000).

### Ethical Consideration

The damage done to a person's reputation by defamation can be instantaneous because the false statements frequently receive attention in electronic and print media. The public, quick to latch on to the initial defamatory statements, is less likely to notice a court decision some years later that holds that the statements were, in fact, false.

Because of this phenomenon, someone determined to cast doubt on another person's reputation has a good chance of success. Once the damage is done, it is largely irreversible. Therefore, ethical restraint must sometimes take the place of legal restraint.

### INTERNATIONAL SNAPSHOT

The Australian High Court exercised jurisdiction over a defamation lawsuit arising out of an article published in the United States that was accessible on the Internet in Australia.[a] The Court rejected the single publication rule, which states that, regardless of accessibility, a piece of writing has a single time and place of publication and only the place of publication will have legal authority over the writing. The Internet has given publishers the ability to reach global markets and removed their ability to block access to their publications. International policymakers are scrambling to come up with an international convention on defamation and other publication-related litigation.

a. Dow Jones & Co. v. Gutnick (Austl. 2002) H.C.A. 56.

In addition to common law privileges, statutory devices may protect speakers. For instance, under the Communications Decency Act of 1996, an Internet service provider will not be treated as the publisher of information provided by a third party.[5] Applying this statute, the U.S. Court of Appeals for the Fourth Circuit refused to hold America Online (AOL) liable for defamation when an unidentified user posted offensive (and false) messages related to the Oklahoma City bombing and attributed these messages to the plaintiff.[6]

Similarly, in *Ben Ezra, Weinstein, & Co. v. America Online, Inc.*,[7] AOL was sued for defamation for allegedly publishing inaccurate information about the price and share volume of a company's publicly traded stock. Because AOL did not create or develop the information, the U.S. Court of Appeals for the Tenth Circuit held that AOL was not the publisher of the stock information and was protected under the Communications Decency Act.

### Public Figures and Media Defendants

The media, such as newspapers, television, or radio, have a qualified privilege that is almost absolute when they are commenting on a public official or a public figure. The U.S. Supreme Court, in applying the First Amendment right of freedom of the press, has held that for a public official or public figure to recover damages for defamation by a media defendant, there must be a showing of *actual malice*. That means the statement must have been made with the knowledge that it was false or with a reckless disregard as to whether it was false. (Other aspects of the First Amendment are discussed in Chapter 2.)

*Public officials* include legislators, judges, and police officers. *Public figures* are those who, by reason of the notoriety of their achievements or the vigor and success with which they seek the public's attention, are injected into the public eye. In *Wells v. Liddy*,[8] the U.S. Court of Appeals for the Fourth Circuit made it clear that a private individual does not automatically become a public figure simply because he or she is involved in a public event. The event at issue in *Wells* was the 1972 Watergate burglary scandal, which ultimately resulted in President Richard Nixon's resignation. The defendant was G. Gordon Liddy, the former self-described "political intelligence chieftain" and general counsel of the Committee to Reelect the President. Liddy publicly offered an alternative theory to explain the purpose of the Watergate break-in. He claimed that the burglars' objective was to determine whether the Democrats had information embarrassing to John Dean, former legal counsel to President Nixon. Specifically, Liddy claimed that the burglars were searching the desk of Ida Wells, secretary of the Democratic National Committee, to find a compromising photograph of Dean's fiancée among other photographs of women hired to offer prostitution services to out-of-town guests. After Liddy claimed that Wells was involved in setting up these guests with prostitutes, Wells sued for defamation. The court found that Wells was a private figure even though she had become involved in a public matter. As the court commented:

> There is a great temptation when evaluating a controversy as longstanding and significant as Watergate to allow the controversy itself to take precedence in the analysis and let it convert all individuals in its path into public figures. The Supreme Court has admonished us strongly against allowing the public event with which the individual is connected to be the determinative factor governing an individual's public figure designation.[9]

A publicly traded corporation is generally considered a public figure, however, and thus must prove actual malice. Because proving actual malice can be difficult, a corporation that anticipates that the press may publish an unfavorable story about its business may take proactive steps to counteract the negative publicity rather than try to initiate a defamation action after the fact in court. In October 1999, the diet product company Metabolife International, Inc. became concerned that ABC would broadcast an unfair report on the medical risks of a dietary supplement sold by Metabolife. The company therefore posted on the Internet a complete, unedited videotaped interview between an ABC News correspondent and the company's chief executive. Although ABC said that Metabolife's decision to post the interview on the Internet would not affect the interview that it broadcast, television executives indicated that in the future networks might ask interviewees to agree not to make public material from the interview until after it is broadcast on television.

If the plaintiff suing a media defendant is not a public figure, he or she need not prove malice. A private plaintiff can recover for defamation if the defendant acted with knowledge, acted in reckless disregard of the facts, or was negligent in failing to ascertain the facts. If the plaintiff proceeds on a negligence theory, he or she must

5. 47 U.S.C. § 230.

6. Zeran v. America Online, Inc., 129 F.3d 327 (4th Cir. 1997), *cert. denied*, 524 U.S. 937 (1998).

7. 206 F.3d 980 (10th Cir. 2000), *cert. denied*, 531 U.S. 824 (2000).

8. 186 F.3d 505 (4th Cir. 1999), *cert. denied*, 528 U.S. 1118 (2000).

9. *Id.*

prove actual damages, such as loss of business or out-of-pocket costs. If the plaintiff proves malice, damages are presumed, meaning no proof of damages is required.

## Invasion of Privacy

*Invasion of privacy* is a violation of the right to keep personal matters to oneself. It can take several forms.

*Intrusion* is objectionable prying, such as eavesdropping or unauthorized rifling through files. Injunctions or court orders are usually available to prevent further intrusion. There must be a reasonable expectation of privacy in the thing into which there is intrusion. For example, courts have held there is no legitimate expectation of privacy in conversations in a public restaurant. The tort of intrusion does not require publication of the information obtained.

In the following case, the Minnesota Supreme Court considered whether employees could recover for invasion of privacy when their employer distributed their names and Social Security numbers in a manner that could allow a third party to steal and misuse the numbers.

**A Case in Point**

**CASE 9.1**

**Bodah v. Lakeville Motor Express Inc.**

*Minnesota Supreme Court*
*663 N.W.2d 550*
*(Minn. 2003).*

### Summary

**› FACTS** Lakeville Motor Express Inc. (LME) is a trucking company operating primarily in Minnesota. LME sent a facsimile containing the names and Social Security numbers of 204 LME employees to its sixteen terminals across six states with a coversheet that was addressed simply to "Terminal Managers." The purpose of the fax was to allow LME to keep better records of accidents and injuries throughout its trucking network. Four months later, after being advised of the potential for identity theft, Peter Martin, president of LME, sent a letter of apology to all employees informing them of the mistake. The letter also notified them that the information was not shared with anyone other than the terminal managers and that Martin had instructed all terminal managers to destroy or return the list. Despite the president's apology and assurances, several employees filed a class-action suit on behalf of all 204 employees alleging invasion of privacy. The trial court dismissed the case in favor of LME, but the court of appeals reversed and found for the plaintiffs. The defendants appealed this judgment.

**› ISSUE PRESENTED** Does a company violate its employees' right to privacy by transmitting their names and Social Security numbers in an unsecured manner that could lead to identity theft?

**› SUMMARY OF OPINION** After concluding that it had the authority to review the earlier findings of the lower courts, the Minnesota Supreme Court explained the rationale behind recognizing the tort of invasion of privacy: "The right to privacy is an integral part of our humanity; one has a public persona, exposed and active, and a private persona, guarded and reserved. The heart of our liberty is choosing which parts of our lives shall become public and which parts we shall hold close."

In order to find invasion of privacy, (1) the defendant must have publicized some aspect of the plaintiff's life, (2) that information must not be a legitimate concern of the public, and (3) disclosure must be offensive to a reasonable person. The employees' Social Security numbers qualified under the second and third prongs of the test because the public would have no reason to know the numbers and many found their distribution offensive and potentially dangerous. Therefore, the case turned on the meaning of publication in the first prong.

LME maintained that faxing numbers to its terminal managers did not constitute publication because the general public never saw the numbers. The employees argued that it did constitute publication because (1) the names and corresponding Social Security numbers were sent to sixteen terminals in six states with no warning of the confidential nature of the information; (2) no corrective action was taken for at least four months;

*(Continued)*

(Case 9.1 *continued*)

and (3) most importantly, there was no guarantee that the numbers were ever destroyed. As a result, they could still be used maliciously.

The court ruled that "publicized" means that "the matter is made public, by communicating it to the public at large, or to so many persons that the matter must be regarded as substantially certain to become one of public knowledge."

› **RESULT** Distribution of the facsimile did not constitute publication so there was no invasion of privacy. The lawsuit was dismissed.

› **COMMENTS** The court characterized the fax as a private transmission but did not completely absolve LME of any potential liability simply because the fax was not *intended* to be made public. The court addressed the employees' fears of identity theft directly:

> If an unauthorized transmission of private data actually resulted in pecuniary loss due to identity theft, a plaintiff may be able to bring a negligence action. Likewise, a plaintiff may have a cause of action for negligent infliction of emotional distress if, because private information was shared, the plaintiff suffered severe emotional distress with accompanying physical manifestations.

---

*Public disclosure of private facts* requires publication, for example, by stating in a newspaper that the plaintiff does not pay debts or posting such a notice in a public place. The matter made public must not be newsworthy. The matter must be private, such that a reasonable person would find publication objectionable. Unlike in a defamation case, truth is not a defense.

*Appropriation of a person's name or likeness* may be an invasion of privacy. Often this tort is committed for financial gain. For example, using a fictitious testimonial in an advertisement would be a tort, as would using a person's picture in an advertisement or article with which he or she has no connection. In *Brown v. Ames*,[10] a group of blues musicians, songwriters, and music producers sued a music producer and record label for distributing cassettes, CDs, posters, and other products using the names and likenesses of the performers. The U.S. Court of Appeals for the Fifth Circuit ruled in the plaintiffs' favor by applying Texas state law, which allows recovery for unauthorized appropriation of names or likenesses if the plaintiff can prove that (1) the defendant misappropriated the plaintiff's name or likeness for the value associated with it and not in an incidental manner or for a newsworthy purpose, (2) the plaintiff can be identified from the publication, and (3) the defendant derived some advantage or benefit.

Public figures from John F. Kennedy to Nicole Kidman have required employees to sign confidentiality agreements, which prohibit them from talking about their famous employers, even after their employment has been terminated. Oprah Winfrey, who also requires employees to sign nondisclosure agreements, won her case against a former employee who had planned on writing a book about her time with Oprah. Courts enforce these agreements to protect celebrities' privacy.[11]

## Intentional Torts That Protect Property

### Trespass to Land

The previously described torts involved interference with personal rights. *Trespass to land* is an interference with a property right. It is an invasion of real property (that is, land) without the consent of the owner. The land need not be injured by the trespass. The intent required is the intent to enter the property, not the intent to trespass. Thus, a mistake as to ownership is irrelevant.

Trespass may occur both below the surface and in the airspace above the land. Throwing something, such as trash, on the land and shooting bullets over it may be trespasses, even though the perpetrator was not standing on the plaintiff's land.

Refusing to move something that at one time the plaintiff permitted the defendant to place on the land

10. 201 F.3d 654 (5th Cir. 2000), *cert. denied*, 531 U.S. 925 (2000).

11. Coady v. Harpo Inc., 719 N.E.2d 244 (N.Y. 1999); Margaret Graham Tebo, *Zipped Lips*, A.B.A. J., Sept. 2000, at 16.

may be a trespass. For example, if the plaintiff gave the defendant permission to leave a forklift on the plaintiff's land for one month, and it was left for two, the defendant may be liable for trespass.

Trespass may also occur if an individual permitted access to property does a wrongful act in excess of and in abuse of the authorized entry. In *Food Lion Inc. v. Capital Cities/ABC Inc.*,[12] two ABC reporters used false résumés to obtain jobs at Food Lion supermarkets in order to videotape unsanitary meat-handling practices at the markets. Food Lion sued, alleging that the reporters had committed trespass by secretly videotaping while working at the supermarkets. The U.S. Court of Appeals for the Fourth Circuit found that the two reporters had breached their duty of loyalty to the company as employees by videotaping in nonpublic areas, thereby nullifying Food Lion's consent for them to enter the property. Accordingly, the court found that the reporters had committed trespass. The court rejected, however, Food Lion's argument that misrepresentation on a job application nullifies the consent given to an employee to enter the employer's property and thereby turns the employee into a trespasser.

## NUISANCE

*Nuisance* is a nontrespassory interference with the use and enjoyment of real property, for example, by an annoying odor or noise.

*Public nuisance* is unreasonable and substantial interference with the public health, safety, peace, comfort, convenience, or utilization of land. An action for public nuisance is usually brought by the government. As discussed in the "Inside Story" for this chapter, cities have used the tort of public nuisance to sue gun manufacturers for gun violence. A suit for public nuisance may also be brought by a private citizen who experiences special harm different from that of the general public.

In July 2004, eight states (including California, New Jersey, and New York) and New York City filed a lawsuit against five of the largest U.S. energy providers under the federal common law of nuisance in hopes of obtaining an order requiring reductions in carbon dioxide emissions.[13] This is the first time governmental officials have sued private power companies to reduce greenhouse gases. The five defendants are among the worst polluters in the industry. They own or operate 174 fossil-fuel-burning power plants in twenty states and emit almost 25 percent of the U.S. utility sector's annual emissions of carbon dioxide.

*Private nuisance* is interference with an individual's use and enjoyment of his or her land. Destruction of crops by flooding, the pollution of a stream, or playing loud music late at night in a residential neighborhood can constitute a private nuisance.

For example, the Wisconsin Supreme Court held that stray voltage that reduced a dairy herd's milk production was actionable on a private nuisance theory.[14] The court noted that the common law doctrine of private nuisance was broad enough to meet a wide variety of possible invasions and flexible enough to adapt to changing social values and conditions.

The focus of both public and private nuisance claims is on the plaintiff's harm, not on the degree of the defendant's fault. Therefore, even innocent behavior on the part of the defendant is actionable—that is, it may be the basis for a claim—if that behavior resulted in unreasonable and substantial interference with the use and enjoyment of the plaintiff's property. To determine whether the defendant's conduct is unreasonable, the court will balance the utility of the activity creating the harm and the burden of preventing it against the nature and the gravity of the harm. For example, hammering noise during the remodeling of a house may be easier to justify than playing loud music purely for recreation.

## CONVERSION

*Conversion* is the exercise of dominion and control over the personal property, rather than the real property, of another. This tort protects the right to have personal property left alone. It prevents the defendant from treating the plaintiff's property as if it were his or her own. It is the tort claim a plaintiff would assert to recover the value of property stolen, destroyed, or substantially altered by the defendant.

The intent element for conversion does not include a wrongful motive. It merely requires the intent to exercise dominion or control over goods, inconsistent with the plaintiff's rights. The defendant need not know that the goods belonged to the plaintiff.

12. 194 F.3d 505 (4th Cir. 1999).

13. Connecticut v. Am. Power Co., No. 1:04-cv-05669-LAP (S.D.N.Y. July 21, 2004), 73 U.S.L.W. 2056 (Aug. 3, 2004). See also J. Kevin Healy & Jeffrey M. Tapick, *Climate Change: It's Not Just a Policy Issue for Corporate Counsel—It's a Legal Problem*, 29 COLUM. J. ENVTL. L. 1 (2004).

14. Vogel v. Grant-LaFayette Elec. Coop., 548 N.W.2d 829 (Wis. 1996).

## View from Cyberspace

### SUING TO STAMP OUT SPAM

Frustrated by the proliferation of unsolicited e-mail advertisements (known as "spam") clogging their servers, online service providers EarthLink and America Online (AOL) sued a number of prominent Internet junk mailers in 2004 to prevent them from sending unsolicited e-mail to the providers' subscribers.[a] In an earlier case brought by EarthLink, the court ruled that EarthLink had a viable claim of trespass to personal property against one Khan C. Smith and was entitled to a broad injunction preventing him from sending e-mail advertisements to EarthLink subscribers as well as all other Internet users. The court commented that Smith "has engaged in a massive scheme of illegal acts, including credit card and identity theft, password theft, theft of EarthLink's computer resources and accounts, fraud, spamming and spoofing." Moreover, the messages were largely unwanted by EarthLink's customers, many of whom terminated their accounts specifically because of the unabated receipt of bulk e-mail messages. Thus, insofar as Smith's mailings diminished the capacity of EarthLink's equipment and harmed EarthLink's business reputation and goodwill with its customers, those mailings were actionable as a common law trespass to chattels. EarthLink said that the $25 million damages award was the largest the company has ever received from this type of suit.[b]

Similarly, AOL sued several Florida-based companies for conspiring to set up a number of computer servers that sent close to 1 billion unsolicited e-mail messages to AOL members. This case is still pending, but a similar result is likely.

In 2004, President Bush signed the Controlling the Assault of Non-Solicited Pornography and Marketing (CAN-SPAM) Act. This Act is discussed in Chapter 17.

a. Grant Gross, AOL, *EarthLink Sue Spammers,* PCWorld.com, Feb. 18, 2004, *at* http://www.pcworld.com/news/article/0,aid,114841,00.asp.

b. *EarthLink Wins $25 Million Judgment Against Tennessee-Based Spammer,* 7 U.S.L.W. 781 (July 31, 2002).

## TRESPASS TO PERSONAL PROPERTY

When personal property is interfered with but not converted—that is, taken, destroyed, or substantially altered—there is a *trespass to personal property* (sometimes referred to as *trespass to chattels*). No wrongful motive need be shown. The intent required is the intent to exercise control over the plaintiff's personal property. For example, an employer who took an employee's car on a short errand without the employee's permission would be liable for trespass to personal property. However, if the employer damaged the car or drove it for several thousand miles, thereby lowering its value, then the employer would be liable for conversion.

The tort of trespass to chattels can include demonstrations that involve private property on private land. For example, a logging company successfully sued six members of an environmental group who climbed on and chained themselves to the company's logging equipment.[15] The members of the environmental group were required to pay punitive damages for demonstrating against government policies while on private property. The court ruled that the assessment of punitive damages did not violate the protesters' First Amendment rights.

Internet auction powerhouse eBay, Inc. sued Bidder's Edge, Inc. when it discovered that Bidder's Edge had used an automated system to pull information off of eBay's website. All eBay users must agree to the eBay User Agreement, which specifically forbids such data mining. Bidder's Edge argued that eBay's website is public and that it had a right to use that public information. The court disagreed and ruled that Bidder's Edge's actions constituted a trespass to chattels. Even though eBay's website is public, eBay's servers are private property, and the unauthorized use of even a small portion of a server's capacity deprived eBay of its ability to use its personal property in the way it saw fit.[16]

In the following case, the court considered whether Intel, under the theory of trespass to chattels, could prevent a former employee from sending e-mails to thousands of Intel employees.

15. Huffman & Wright Logging Co. v. Wade, 857 P.2d 101 (Or. 1993).

16. 100 F. Supp. 2d 1058 (N.D. Cal. 2000).

A CASE IN POINT

**CASE 9.2**
**Intel Corp. v. Hamidi**
*Supreme Court of California*
*71 P.3d 296 (Cal. 2003).*

## In the Language of the Court

**› FACTS** Kourosh Kenneth Hamidi, a former Intel employee, sent six e-mail messages to about 35,000 Intel e-mail addresses over a twenty-one-month span. Hamidi gained access to the e-mail addresses through a floppy disk that was sent to him anonymously. The e-mails criticized the company and its policies. Intel sued him for trespass to chattels. The trial court granted Intel's motion for summary judgment and enjoined Hamidi from sending any further e-mails. Hamidi then appealed.

**› ISSUE PRESENTED** Does sending tens of thousands of e-mails constitute a trespass to chattels?

**› OPINION** WERDEGAR, J., writing for the Supreme Court of California:

Our conclusion does not rest on any special immunity for communications by electronic mail; we do not hold that messages transmitted through the Internet are exempt from the ordinary rules of tort liability. To the contrary, e-mail, like other forms of communication, may in some circumstances cause legally cognizable injury to the recipient or to third parties and may be actionable under various common law or statutory theories.

. . .

Intel's claim fails not because e-mail transmitted through the Internet enjoys unique immunity, but because the trespass to chattels tort . . . may not, in California, be proved without evidence of an injury to the plaintiff's personal property or legal interest therein.

. . .

A series of federal district court decisions ha[ve] approved the use of trespass to chattels as a theory of spammers' liability to ISPs, based upon evidence that the vast quantities of mail sent by spammers both overburdened the ISP's own computers and made the entire computer system harder to use for recipients, the ISP's customers. In those cases . . . the underlying complaint was that the extraordinary quantity of UCE [unsolicited commercial e-mail] impaired the computer system's functioning. In the present case, the claimed injury is located in the disruption or distraction caused to recipients by the contents of the e-mail messages, an injury entirely separate from, and not directly affecting, the possession or value of personal property.

. . .

[T]he defendant's interference must, to be actionable, have caused some injury to the chattel or to the plaintiff's rights in it. Under California law, trespass to chattels "lies where an intentional interference with the possession of personal property has proximately caused injury." In cases of interference with possession of personal property not amounting to conversion, the owner may recover only the actual damages suffered by reason of the impairment of the property or the loss of its use.

. . .

The Restatement [Second of Torts § 218], too, makes clear that some actual injury must have occurred in order for a trespass to chattels to be actionable. . . . In order that an actor who interferes with another's chattel may be liable, his conduct must affect some other and more important interest of the possessor. Therefore, one who intentionally intermeddles with another's chattel is subject to liability only if his intermeddling is harmful to the possessor's materially valuable interest in the physical

*(Continued)*

(Case 9.2 *continued*)

condition, quality, or value of the chattel, or if the possessor is deprived of the use of the chattel for a substantial time, or some other legally protected interest of the possessor is affected. . . .

**› RESULT** The California Supreme Court overruled the trial court and dismissed the lawsuit. Because he did not cause Intel any harm, Hamidi did not commit trespass to chattels under California law.

**› CRITICAL THINKING QUESTIONS**

1. Would Hamidi have committed trespass to chattels if he had hacked into the Intel database to find the e-mail addresses he used?
2. What alternative legal theories might Intel use against Hamidi to stop the unwanted e-mails? What nonlegal strategies might Intel use to accomplish the same goal?

---

## Intentional Torts That Protect Certain Economic Interests and Business Relationships

### DISPARAGEMENT

*Disparagement* is the publication of statements derogatory to the quality of the plaintiff's business, to the business in general, or even to the plaintiff's personal affairs, in order to discourage others from dealing with him or her. To prove disparagement, the plaintiff must show that the defendant made false statements about the quality or ownership of the plaintiff's goods or services, knowing that the statements were false or with conscious indifference as to their truth. The plaintiff must also prove that the statements caused him or her actual harm; damages will not be presumed.

### INJURIOUS FALSEHOOD

Knowingly making false statements may give rise to a claim for *injurious falsehood*. For example, a false statement that the plaintiff has gone out of business or does not carry certain goods is a tort if it results in economic loss to the plaintiff.

The range of damages available for injurious falsehood is more restricted than for defamation. Injurious falsehood permits recovery of only pecuniary (that is, monetary) losses related to business operations, whereas defamation permits recovery for loss of reputation, including emotional damages, as well.

#### *Defenses*

The defenses available to the defendant in a defamation action also apply to injurious falsehood. When the statement involves a comparison of goods, the privilege in an injurious falsehood case is even broader than the privilege available in defamation. For example, a defendant who favorably compares his or her own goods to those of a competitor is privileged, even though the defendant may not honestly believe in the superiority of his or her own goods.

### FRAUDULENT MISREPRESENTATION

The tort of *fraudulent misrepresentation,* also called *fraud* or *deceit,* protects economic interests and the right to be treated fairly and honestly. Fraud requires proof that the defendant either (1) intentionally misled the plaintiff by making a material misrepresentation of fact upon which the plaintiff relied or (2) omitted to state a material fact when the defendant had a duty to speak because of a special relationship with the plaintiff. Intent can be constructive—in other words, a court will sometimes impute a fraudulent intent to the defendant if the defendant showed reckless disregard for the truth. For example, a shareholder who has relied to his or her

**ETHICAL CONSIDERATION**

If a person knows that his or her goods are inferior, is it ethical to claim that they are better than a competitor's?

detriment upon an intentionally misleading accountant's opinion regarding the company's financial statements might sue the accountant for fraud.

Everyone has a duty to refrain from affirmatively misrepresenting the facts, that is, lying. But, as explained in Chapter 5, as a general rule, parties dealing at arm's length are not required to disclose all facts that might be relevant to the other party's decision. If, however, one party is a fiduciary (a person entrusted to protect the interests of another), then he or she has a *fiduciary duty* to act with integrity and in the best interests of the other party. In this instance, that duty means that the fiduciary must disclose all relevant facts to the other party even if that party has not asked any questions. For example, if an executive is negotiating to buy a piece of property from the corporation, the executive must volunteer all information known to him or her that might affect the terms (such as the price) on which the corporation would be willing to sell the property.

Occasionally, a court will impose a duty to disclose even if the party required to disclose is not a fiduciary. For example, in *Brass v. American Film Technologies, Inc.*,[17] the defendant American Film Technologies (AFT) convinced Brass and other plaintiffs to buy warrants that could be used to acquire common stock, but AFT failed to reveal that the underlying stock was restricted and could not be freely traded for a period of two years. Upon discovering the omission, the plaintiffs sued for fraud. The court held that because AFT had superior knowledge about the restrictions on its securities, it had a duty to reveal those restrictions. Its failure to do so amounted to fraudulent concealment.

In contrast, the Supreme Court of Georgia held that physicians do not have a common law or statutory duty to disclose to a patient personal factors that might adversely affect their professional performance.[18] Cleveland sued his urologist for negligently performing unnecessary surgery on him and for fraudulently concealing his illegal use and abuse of cocaine. The court held that although a doctor has a common law duty to answer a patient's questions regarding medical or procedural risks, the doctor does not have the duty to disclose personal factors such as illicit drug use. The court ruled that the patient could sue the doctor for professional negligence but could not base a claim of fraud on the physician's failure to disclose his drug use.

A mere expression of opinion generally is not a valid basis for a fraud claim. Although statements as to future actions are generally deemed opinions and therefore not actionable, they can constitute fraud when (1) the defendant held itself out to be specially qualified and the plaintiff acted reasonably in relying upon the defendant's superior knowledge, (2) the opinion is that of a fiduciary or other trusted person, or (3) the defendant stated its opinion as an existing fact or as implying facts that justify a belief in its truth.

To state a claim of fraud, a plaintiff must establish that he or she suffered damages as a result of the fraud. In *Maio v. Aetna, Inc.*,[19] a class of persons enrolled in Aetna's health maintenance organization (HMO) plan filed a claim alleging that the company had engaged in a fraudulent scheme to induce individuals to enroll in the HMO plan by representing that Aetna's primary commitment was to maintain and improve the quality of health care given to its members. The class alleged that, in fact, Aetna was driven primarily by financial and administrative considerations. The U.S. District Court for the Eastern District of Pennsylvania ruled that the plaintiffs' vague allegation that "quality of care" might suffer in the future was too hypothetical an injury to confer standing. The court also found that Aetna's general assertions about its commitment to "quality of care" were "mere puffery" and could not serve as the basis for a fraud claim.

## MALICIOUS PROSECUTION AND DEFENSE

A plaintiff can successfully sue for *malicious prosecution* by showing that a prior proceeding was instituted against him or her maliciously and without probable cause or factual basis. In addition, the earlier case must have been resolved in the plaintiff's favor. This tort originated from the misuse of the criminal process but has been adapted to redress malicious civil prosecution as well. A victorious plaintiff can recover damages for attorneys' fees paid in connection with the prior action, injury to reputation, and psychological distress.

Courts frequently state that the malicious prosecution action is disfavored under the law. Because the action has the potential to produce a chilling effect that discourages legitimate claims, courts have been reluctant to expand its reach.

Nevertheless, one state expanded the doctrine to recognize an action for *malicious defense*. In *Aronson v. Schroeder*,[20] the defendant allegedly created false material evidence while serving as defense counsel in a prior case

17. 987 F.2d 142 (2d Cir. 1993).
18. Albany Urology Clinic PC v. Cleveland, 528 S.E.2d 777 (Ga. 2000).
19. 1999 WL 800315 (E.D. Pa. Sept. 29, 1999), *aff'd*, 221 F.3d 472 (3d Cir. 2000).
20. 671 A.2d 1023 (N.H. 1995).

and then gave false testimony concerning the evidence. In a ruling for the plaintiff, the New Hampshire Supreme Court stated:

> [W]hen a defense is based upon false evidence and perjury or is raised for an improper purpose, the litigant is not made whole if the only remedy is reimbursement of counsel fees. It follows that upon proving malicious defense, the aggrieved party is entitled to the same damages as are recoverable in a malicious prosecution claim.

## Interference with Contractual Relations and Participation in a Breach of Fiduciary Duty

The tort of *interference with contractual relations* protects the right to enjoy the benefits of legally binding agreements. It provides a remedy when the defendant intentionally induces another person to breach a contract with the plaintiff. The defendant must know of the existence of the contract between the plaintiff and the other person, or there must be sufficient facts that a reasonable person would be led to believe that such a contract existed. Interference with contractual relations requires intent to interfere. Thus, courts usually require that the defendant induce the contracting party to breach, rather than merely create the opportunity for the breach. Similarly, a defendant who knowingly participates in or induces a breach of fiduciary duty by another commits the tort of *participation in a breach of fiduciary duty.*

In some jurisdictions, interference with contractual relations also requires an unacceptable purpose. If good grounds exist for the interference, the defendant is not liable. For example, if a manager of a corporation is incompetent, then a stockholder of the corporation may be entitled to induce a breach of the employment agreement between the manager and the corporation. The stockholder's motive would be to protect his or her investment. On the other hand, a defendant may not interfere with another person's contract in order to attract customers or employees away from that person.

Perhaps the most famous case involving tortious interference with contract was *Pennzoil v. Texaco,* discussed in the "Inside Story" in Chapter 7. In 1983, Pennzoil and Getty Oil Company negotiated an agreement for a merger. During the process of drafting the final merger documents, Texaco offered a better price for Getty and agreed to indemnify Getty for any claims that might be asserted by Pennzoil. After Getty accepted Texaco's offer, Pennzoil sued Texaco for tortious interference with contract. Under New York law, Pennzoil had to prove (1) the existence of a valid contract, (2) Texaco's knowledge of the existence of the contract, (3) Texaco's intentional inducement of breach of that contract, and (4) damages incurred by Pennzoil as a result of the breach of contract. A jury decided against Texaco and awarded $10.5 billion to Pennzoil. The case was ultimately settled for $3 billion.

### *Defense*

As in defamation, truth is a defense to a claim for interference with contractual relations. There is no liability if a true statement was made to induce another to break off relations with the plaintiff.

## Interference with Prospective Business Advantage

Courts are less willing to award damages for interference with prospective contracts than they are to protect existing contracts. To prove *interference with prospective business advantage,* the plaintiff must prove that the defendant interfered with a relationship the plaintiff sought to develop and that the interference caused the plaintiff's loss. The interference must be intentional. In rare cases, however, courts have permitted recovery when the defendant was merely negligent.

In one case,[21] Baum Research and Development Company, a manufacturer of wooden baseball bats, filed a claim of tortious interference with prospective economic advantage against several manufacturers of aluminum baseball bats, a trade association of bat manufacturers, and the National Collegiate Athletic Association. Baum claimed that the defendants had prevented the company from establishing relationships with amateur baseball teams and had disrupted its sale of bats to these teams by, among other things, disseminating false information about the Baum Hitting Machine manufactured by Baum, inducing baseball teams to terminate arrangements with Baum for the use of its wooden bats, and removing and destroying Baum bats and replacing them with aluminum bats. The court stated that the necessary elements of tortious interference with economic relations are (1) the existence of a valid business relationship or expectancy, (2) knowledge of the relationship or expectancy on the part of the interferor, (3) intentional interference inducing or causing a breach or termination of a relationship or expectancy, and (4) damages. Concluding that the company "had more than a mere hope for business opportunities or the innate optimism of

21. *In re* Baseball Bat Antitrust Litig., 75 F. Supp. 2d 1189 (D. Kan. 1999).

a salesman,"[22] the court ruled that Baum had a valid claim of tortious interference with economic relations.

### *Defenses*

Most jurisdictions recognize a privilege to act for one's own financial gain. In some jurisdictions, the plaintiff has the burden of showing that the defendant acted from a motive other than financial gain, such as revenge. In others, the defendant has the burden of proving that he or she acted only for financial gain. Any purpose sufficient to create a privilege to disturb existing contractual relations will also justify interference with prospective business advantage.

As in defamation and interference with contractual relations, truth is a defense. Some jurisdictions have also applied the First Amendment defenses available in defamation cases.

Interference with prospective business advantage is usually done by a competitor or at least by one who stands to benefit from the interference. Competing fairly is not a tort, however. For the purposes of competition, a defendant may attempt to increase its business by cutting prices, offering rebates, refusing to deal with the plaintiff, secretly negotiating with the plaintiff's customers, or refusing to deal with third parties unless they agree not to deal with the plaintiff.

## BAD FAITH

Bad faith conduct by one party to a contract to the other party may serve as the basis for a claim of bad faith. This tort claim is separate and independent from a breach-of-contract claim. Typically, a claim of bad faith is brought by an insured against an insurance company for breaching its duty to act in good faith in the handling and payment of claims. The plaintiff must show that the insurer failed to exercise good faith in processing a claim and that there was no reasonable justification for the insurer's refusal to pay it.

22. *Id.*

### ETHICAL CONSIDERATION

Is it ethical to refuse to deal with the plaintiff, to secretly negotiate with the plaintiff's customers, or to refuse to deal with third parties unless they agree not to deal with the plaintiff?

# Negligence

An essential element of every intentional tort is the mental element of intent. Negligence does not include a mental element. Rather, the focus is on the defendant's conduct. The law of negligence requires that all people take appropriate care in any given situation. It does not require that the defendant intended, or even knew, that his or her actions would harm the plaintiff. In fact, even if the defendant was full of concern for the safety of the plaintiff, the defendant's conduct might still be negligent. It is enough that the defendant acted carelessly or, in other words, that his or her conduct created an unreasonable risk of harm.

*Negligence* is defined as conduct that involves an unreasonably great risk of causing injury to another person or damage to property. To establish liability under a negligence theory, the plaintiff must show that (1) the defendant owed a duty to the plaintiff to act in conformity with a certain standard of conduct, that is, to act reasonably under the circumstances; (2) the defendant breached that duty by failing to conform to the standard; (3) a reasonably close causal connection exists between the plaintiff's injury and the defendant's breach; and (4) the plaintiff suffered an actual loss or injury.

## DUTY

A person with a *legal duty* to another is required to act reasonably under the circumstances to avoid harming the other person. The required standard of care is what a reasonable person of ordinary prudence would do in the circumstances. It is not graduated to include the reasonably slow person, the reasonably forgetful person, or the reasonable person of low intelligence. In determining duty, the law allows reasonable mistakes of judgment in some circumstances. In emergency situations, the duty is to act as a reasonable person would act in the circumstances. The defendant is expected to anticipate emergencies. Drivers must drive defensively. Innkeepers must anticipate fires and install smoke alarms and, in some cases, sprinkler systems and must provide fire escapes and other fire-safety features. Owners of swimming pools in subdivisions with children must fence their property.

As explained further below, most states take a formalistic approach to duty and alter the scope of the defendant's liability depending on the court's characterization of the injured party (e.g., trespasser versus business guest). In 1993, the New Jersey Supreme Court articulated a more general framework: "Whether a person owes a duty of reasonable care toward another turns on whether the imposition of such a duty satisfies an abiding sense of basic fairness under all of the circumstances in light of considerations of public policy."[23] For that court, the analysis involves balancing many factors, including the relationship between the parties, the nature of the attendant risk, the opportunity and ability to exercise care, and the public interest in the proposed solution.

## *Duty to Rescue*

The law does not impose a general duty to rescue. However, once one undertakes a rescue, the law imposes a duty to act as a reasonable person and not to abandon the rescue effort unreasonably. Thus, if Ciril Wyatt sat on a riverbank and watched Edward Donnelly drown, she would not be liable in negligence for Donnelly's death. However, if Wyatt saw Donnelly drowning, jumped in her boat, sped to him, tried to pull him into the boat and then changed her mind and let him drown, she would be liable.

A special relationship between two people may create a duty to rescue. If Donnelly were Wyatt's husband or child or parent, Wyatt would have a duty to rescue him. Other relationships that create a duty to rescue are employer and employee; innkeeper and guest; teacher and student; employee of a bus, train, or other common carrier and passenger; and possibly team members, hunting partners, and hiking partners.

There is a duty to rescue those whom one has placed in peril. For example, if Wyatt had been driving her boat in a negligent manner, thereby causing Donnelly to fall overboard, she would have a duty to rescue him.

## *Duty of Landowner or Tenant*

A possessor of land (such as a tenant) or its owner has a legal duty to keep the property reasonably safe. Such a person may be liable for injury that occurs outside the premises as well as on them. For example, a landowner may be liable for harm caused when water from a cooling tower covers the highway; when sparks from a railroad engine, which is not properly maintained, start a fire on adjacent property; or when a roof sheds snow onto the highway.

23. Hopkins v. Fox & Lazo Realtors, 625 A.2d 1110 (N.J. 1993).

**INTERNATIONAL SNAPSHOT**

Some countries do impose a general duty to rescue. For example, France and Brazil require bystanders to try and help those in danger if trying to help will not put the bystanders at risk.

A landowner must exercise care in the demolition or construction of buildings on his or her property and in the excavation of his or her land. Landowners have been held liable when a pole on a landowner's property collapsed and injured a pedestrian after being hit by a car and when a landowner erected a sign that obstructed the view and caused an accident.

A landowner has a general duty to inspect his or her property and keep it in repair, and he or she may be liable if a showroom window, a downspout, a screen, or a loose sign falls and injures someone. In a few jurisdictions, landowners have a duty to maintain sidewalks that abut (are right next to) their property.

**Traditional Approach to Liability for Injuries on Premises** Traditionally, the liability associated with injury on the premises of another has hinged on the distinctions between trespassers, licensees, and invitees. The landowner's duty is least for the trespasser and greatest for the invitee.

**Duty to Trespassers** In general, a landowner owes no duty to an undiscovered trespasser. If a substantial number of trespassers are in the habit of entering at a particular place, however, then the possessor of the property has a duty to take reasonable care to discover and to protect the trespassers from activities he or she carries on. Some courts have also established a duty to protect such trespassers from dangerous conditions, such as concealed high-tension wires, that do not result from the possessor's activities. Some jurisdictions require the possessor to exercise reasonable care once he or she knows of the trespasser's presence.

Trespassing children are owed a higher level of duty. The *attractive nuisance* doctrine imposes liability for physical injury to child trespassers caused by artificial conditions on the land if (1) the landowner knew or should have known that children were likely to trespass; (2) the condition is one the landowner would reasonably know involved an unreasonable risk of injury to such children; (3) the children because of their youth did not discover the condition or realize the risk involved; (4) the utility to the landowner of maintaining the condition is not great; (5) the burden of eliminating the risk is slight compared with the magnitude of the risk to the children; and (6) the landowner fails to exercise reasonable care to protect the children.

**Duty to Licensees** A *licensee* is anyone who is on the land of another person with the possessor's express or implied consent. The licensee enters for his or her own purposes, not for those of the possessor. Social guests and uninvited sales representatives are licensees.

The possessor must exercise reasonable care for the protection of the licensee. This duty differs from that owed to a trespasser because the possessor is required to look out for licensees before they enter the land. The possessor is not required to inspect for unknown dangers, however. The duty arises only when the possessor has actual knowledge of a risk.

**Duty to Invitees** An *invitee*, or business visitor, is someone who enters the premises for purposes of the possessor's business. The possessor owes a higher duty to an invitee than to a licensee. The possessor must protect invitees against known dangers and also against those dangers that the possessor might discover with reasonable care.

A customer is clearly an invitee and is accordingly owed a higher duty of care than a licensee such as a social guest. Managers thus have particular reason to be concerned about invitees. Every year businesses must deal with thousands of "slip and fall" cases brought by customers who have fallen due to wet floors, icy sidewalks, or broken steps.

Invitees of a landowner, such as contractors, may also have a duty to other persons admitted onto the property by the owner. Contractors that create a dangerous condition while working at a construction site may be held liable for an injury caused by the dangerous condition after the contractor leaves the site and turns its work over to the property owner. In *Brent v. Unocal*,[24] ARCO Alaska, Inc. hired Unocal, Inc., an independent contractor, to perform excavation and install sheet piling as part of a bridge construction project. After Unocal had finished its work and turned the property over to ARCO, construction worker William Brent was injured while working on the site when he fell into a hole created by Unocal. The Supreme Court of Alaska found that Unocal was liable under Section 385 of the Restatement (Second) of Torts, which states that "a contractor is held to the standard of reasonable care for the protection of third parties who may foreseeably be endangered by his negligence, even after acceptance of the work by the contractor." Section 385 reflects the majority rule adopted by courts that have considered this issue.

A business's duty to invitees may even include an obligation to protect invitees from criminal conduct by third parties. States have been mixed in their application of this standard. The New Jersey Supreme Court held a supermarket liable when a seventy-nine-year-old woman was abducted from its parking lot and later killed.[25] Even though there had never been an abduction or similar incident on the property, the court ruled that Food Circus was negligent in failing to provide any security or warning signs in its parking lot. Employing an analysis that considered the "totality of the circumstances," the court concluded that it was foreseeable that an individual would over the course of time enter the supermarket's parking lot and assault a customer.

The Washington Supreme Court also held that businesses have a duty to take reasonable steps to protect invitees from criminal conduct by third parties, but it indicated that this general duty does not necessarily include a duty to provide security personnel. The court denied a claim by an assaulted convenience store patron.[26] It reasoned that imposing a requirement that businesses provide guards in all cases would unfairly shift responsibility for policing from the government to the private sector. In *dicta*, the court said that a duty to provide security guards may arise if "the construction or maintenance of the premises brings about a . . . peculiar temptation . . . for criminal misconduct" by third parties, but such facts were not present in that case.

**Reasonable Care Approach** The traditional approach of classifying one who enters a tenant or landowner's property as a trespasser, licensee, or invitee has fallen into disfavor in several jurisdictions. Determining the proper classification of an injured plaintiff is often difficult and may require courts and juries to sift through hundreds of pages of testimony. Moreover, a person's status could change over the course of a day or a transaction. For example, an intruder would be deemed a trespasser, but if the landowner spotted the intruder and permitted him or her to remain, then the trespasser's status could shift to licensee. The New York Court of Appeals put it this way: "[I]t remains a curiosity of the law that the duty owed to a plaintiff on exit may have been many times greater than that owed him on his entrance, though he and the premises all the while remained the same."[27]

To eliminate this potential for confusion, several jurisdictions have opted to abandon the traditional "trichotomy" in favor of a standard of *reasonable care under the circumstances*. Under this standard, courts require all

24. 969 P.2d 627 (Alaska 1998).

25. Clohesy v. Food Circus Supermarkets, Inc., 694 A.2d 1017 (N.J. 1997).

26. Nivens v. 7-11 Hoagy's Corner, 943 P.2d 286 (Wash. 1997).

27. Basso v. Miller, 352 N.E.2d 868 (N.Y. 1976).

landowners to act in a reasonable manner with respect to entrants on their land, with liability hinging on the foreseeability of harm. Some jurisdictions, such as New York, have collapsed all three of the old standards into a single reasonable care standard. The New York Court of Appeals explained that "this standard of reasonable care should be no different that that applied in the usual negligence action."[28] Other jurisdictions, such as North Carolina, have eliminated the distinction between licensees and invitees but continue to treat trespassers differently because they had no right to enter the land. In determining whether the landowner has exercised reasonable care, courts will consider the identity of the person entering the property and the reasons why that person entered.

### *Duty of Landlord to Tenant*

In general, a landlord has a duty to provide adequate security to protect tenants from foreseeable criminal acts of a third party. Relevant issues are whether (1) the area was a high crime area, (2) there had been earlier criminal acts, (3) there was a failure to maintain locks, and (4) the landlord had knowledge of prior criminal acts.

In *Sharon P. v. Arman Ltd.*,[29] the plaintiff was sexually assaulted in an underground commercial parking garage below her office building. She sued the garage owner for failing to take measures to prevent criminal acts in the garage. The California Supreme Court ruled that a commercial landlord owes a duty to take reasonable steps to secure common areas against *foreseeable* criminal acts of third parties that are likely to occur in the absence of such precautionary measures. Under this standard, a court must balance the foreseeability of the harm against the burden imposed on the landlord if required to take precautionary measures. The court found that the garage had a ten-year history with no assaults and stated that "absent any prior similar incidents or other indications of a reasonably foreseeable risk of violent criminal assaults in that location, we cannot conclude defendants were required to secure the area against such crime."

## BREACH OF DUTY

Once it is determined that the defendant owed the plaintiff a duty, the next issue in a negligence case is whether the defendant breached that duty. In many cases, the required standard of conduct will be that of a reasonable person. However, a person who is specially trained to practice in a profession or trade will be held to the higher standard of care of a reasonably skilled member of that profession or trade. For example, the professional conduct of a doctor, architect, pilot, attorney, or accountant will be measured against the standard of the profession. A specialist within a profession will be held to the standard of specialists.

The court will also look to statutes and regulations to determine whether the defendant's conduct amounted to a breach of duty. Some jurisdictions merely allow the statute to be introduced into evidence to establish the standard of care. In other jurisdictions, however, once the plaintiff shows that the defendant violated a statute and the violation caused the injury, the burden shifts to the defendant to prove that he or she was not negligent. This is often an impossible burden to satisfy. This rule, sometimes referred to as *negligence per se*, applies only when the statute or regulation was designed to protect a class of persons from the type of harm suffered by the plaintiff and the plaintiff is a member of the class to be protected.

Courts will also look to the custom or practice of others under similar circumstances to determine the standard of care. Although the custom in the industry may be given great weight, it is ordinarily not dispositive or conclusive.

### *Res Ipsa Loquitur*

The doctrine of *res ipsa loquitur* ("the thing speaks for itself") allows the plaintiff to prove breach of duty and causation (discussed below) indirectly. *Res ipsa loquitur* applies when an accident has occurred, and it is obvious, although there is no direct proof, that the accident would not have happened without someone's negligence. For example, if a postoperative X-ray shows a surgical clamp in the plaintiff's abdomen, even if no one testifies as to how the clamp got there, it can reasonably be inferred that the surgeon negligently left it there.

*Res ipsa loquitur* has three requirements. First, the plaintiff's injury must have been caused by a condition or instrumentality that was within the exclusive control of the defendant. This requirement eliminates the possibility that other persons, not named as defendants, were responsible for the condition that gave rise to the injury. Second, the accident must be of such a nature that it ordinarily would not occur in the absence of negligence by the defendant. Third, the accident must not be due to the plaintiff's own negligence.

Once *res ipsa loquitur* is established, jurisdictions vary as to its effect. In some jurisdictions, it creates a presumption of negligence, and the plaintiff is entitled to a directed verdict (whereby the judge directs the jury to find in favor of

28. *Id.*
29. 989 P.2d 121 (Cal. 1999), *cert. denied*, 530 U.S. 1243 (2000).

the plaintiff), unless the defendant can prove he or she was not responsible. This rule has the effect of shifting the burden of proof, normally with the plaintiff, to the defendant. Other jurisdictions leave the burden of proof with the plaintiff, requiring the jury to weigh the inference of negligence and to find the defendant negligent only if the preponderance of the evidence (including the *res ipsa* inference) favors such a finding.

## CAUSAL CONNECTION

In addition to establishing duty and breach, a plaintiff claiming negligence must prove that the defendant's breach of duty caused the injury. The causation requirement has two parts: actual cause and proximate (or legal) cause.

### *Actual Cause*

To establish *actual cause,* the plaintiff must prove that he or she would not have been harmed but for the defendant's negligent conduct. The defendant is not liable if the plaintiff's injury would have occurred in the absence of the defendant's conduct. For example, if George Broussard put a garbage can out on the sidewalk for morning pickup and Anna Chang came along and broke her ankle, Broussard's conduct would not be the actual cause of Chang's injury if it were established that Chang had caught her heel in the sidewalk, turned her ankle, and then bumped into Broussard's garbage can.

When the plaintiff names more than one defendant, the actual-cause test may become a substantial-factor test: Was the defendant's conduct a substantial factor in bringing about the plaintiff's injury?

A further problem may arise if more than one individual could possibly have been the negligent party. A classic case involved two hunters shooting quail on an open range.[30] Both shot at exactly the same time, using identical shotguns. A shot from one of the guns accidentally hit another hunter. Clearly, only one of the two defendants caused the injury, but there was no way to determine which one it was. The court imposed the burden on each defendant to prove that he had not caused the injury. Because neither could do so, both were held liable for the whole injury.

### *Proximate Cause*

Once the plaintiff has proved that the defendant's conduct is an actual cause of the plaintiff's injury, he or she must also prove that it is the *proximate cause,* that is, that the defendant had a duty to protect the particular plaintiff against the particular conduct that injured him or her. Through the requirement of proximate cause, the law places limits on the defendant's liability.

In the following case involving the highly publicized bombing of a federal building in Oklahoma City in 1995, the court considered whether the negligence of the manufacturer of the fertilizer used to manufacture the bomb was the proximate cause of the injuries suffered by the bombing victims.

30. Summers v. Tice, 199 P.2d 1 (Cal. 1948).

**A CASE IN POINT**

**Summary**

**CASE 9.3**
**Gaines-Tabb v. ICI Explosives USA, Inc.**
*United States Court of Appeals for the Tenth Circuit*
*160 F.3d 613*
*(10th Cir. 1998).*

**› FACTS** On April 19, 1995, a bomb exploded in a federal building in Oklahoma City killing 168 people and injuring hundreds of others. Individuals injured by the bomb filed a suit for negligence against ICI Explosives (ICI), its parent company Imperial Chemical Industries, and a subsidiary of the parent. ICI manufactures ammonium nitrate that can be either "explosive grade" or "fertilizer grade." "Explosive-grade" ammonium nitrate can absorb sufficient amounts of fuel to allow detonation.

The plaintiffs alleged that ICI sold explosive-grade ammonium nitrate mislabeled as fertilizer-grade ammonium nitrate to Farmland Industries, which then sold it to Mid-Kansas Cooperative Association. Either Timothy McVeigh or Terry Nichols purchased eighty-five-pound bags of the mislabeled ammonium nitrate from Mid-Kansas and used it to make a bomb. The plaintiffs claimed, among other things, that ICI was negligent in making explosive-grade ammonium nitrate available to the men who bombed the federal building.

The district court dismissed the plaintiffs' claims against ICI, finding that ICI did not have a duty to protect the plaintiffs and that ICI's actions were not the proximate cause of their injuries. The plaintiffs appealed.

*(Continued)*

(Case 9.3 *continued*)

**› ISSUE PRESENTED** Was ICI's sale of explosive-grade ammonium nitrate mislabeled as fertilizer-grade ammonium nitrate the proximate cause of injuries to the Oklahoma bombing victims?

**› SUMMARY OF OPINION** The U.S. Court of Appeals for the Tenth Circuit began its analysis by stating that under Oklahoma law, "the causal nexus between an act of negligence and the resulting injury will be deemed broken with the intervention of a new, independent and efficient cause which was neither anticipated nor reasonably foreseeable." This intervening cause (known as a *supervening cause*) must (1) be independent of the original act, (2) be adequate to bring about the injury, and (3) not be reasonably foreseeable. If the intervening act is intentionally tortious or criminal, then the court must determine whether the negligent party realized or should have realized that his or her negligent conduct created a situation that afforded an opportunity to the third party to commit the tort or crime. The court looked to Section 448 of the Restatement (Second) of Torts for assistance in determining whether the criminal acts at issue in the case constituted a supervening cause of harm: "[U]nder comment b, the criminal acts of a third party may be foreseeable if (1) the situation provides a temptation to which a 'recognizable percentage' of persons would yield, or (2) the temptation is created at a place where 'persons of a peculiarly vicious type are likely to be.'" The court found no indication that a peculiarly vicious type of person was likely to frequent the Mid-Kansas Co-op; then the court considered the first alternative.

After finding no guidance as to the meaning of the term "recognizable percentage" as used in Section 448, comment b, the court held that:

> [T]he term does not require a showing that the mainstream population or the majority would yield to a particular temptation; a lesser number will do. Equally, it does not include merely the law-abiding population. In contrast, we also believe that the term is not satisfied by pointing to the existence of a small fringe group or the occasional irrational individual, even though it is foreseeable generally that such groups and individuals will exist.

The plaintiffs were able to identify only two successful terrorist attacks using ammonium nitrate in the last twenty-eight years—a 1970 bombing at the University of Wisconsin–Madison and the Oklahoma City bombing at issue in this case. Due to the apparent complexity of manufacturing an ammonium nitrate bomb, including the difficulty of acquiring the correct ingredients (many of which are not widely available), mixing them properly, and triggering the resulting bomb, only a small number of persons would be able to create a bomb using ammonium nitrate. The court concluded that this group did not rise to the level of a "recognizable percentage" of the population.

**› RESULT** The appeals court ruled as a matter of law that it was not foreseeable to the defendants that the ammonium nitrate that they distributed to the Mid-Kansas Co-op would be used to blow up the federal building. The criminal activities of the bombers were a supervening cause of the plaintiffs' injuries. Because ICI's negligence was not the proximate cause of the victims' injuries, the case was dismissed.

---

The defendant is not required to compensate the plaintiff for injuries that were unforeseeable, even if the defendant's conduct was careless. Courts apply the foreseeability requirement in two different ways. Some courts limit the defendant's liability to those consequences that were foreseeable. Others look to whether the plaintiff was a foreseeable plaintiff, that is, whether the plaintiff was within the *zone of danger* caused by the defendant's careless conduct.

A classic case involved a woman, Mrs. Palsgraf, who was injured when scales on a railroad platform fell on her.[31] Two railroad employees were helping a man carrying a bulky package climb onto a moving train. Unbeknownst to the employees, the package contained fireworks. The man dropped the package and the fireworks exploded, causing the scales, which were located many feet away, to fall on the unfortunate Mrs. Palsgraf. She sued the railroad for negligence. The New York Court of Appeals ruled that even if the employees failed to use due care, Mrs. Palsgraf's injury was not foreseeable. As a result, the employees' actions were not the proximate cause of her injury. The railroad was not liable for negligence.

### INJURY

Finally, the plaintiff must prove that he or she or his or her property was injured. Even if a defendant is negligent, the plaintiff cannot recover unless he or she can show that some harm was suffered as a result of the defendant's conduct.

This requirement is often the controlling factor in actions for *negligent infliction of emotional distress*. The traditional rule is that a plaintiff cannot recover for negligent infliction of emotional distress unless he or she can show some form of physical injury. However, in recent cases involving exposure to the human immunodeficiency virus (HIV), courts have permitted plaintiffs to recover for emotional distress (over the fear of contracting HIV) without requiring that they actually have contracted the virus. Courts have set forth objective standards that prevent someone from basing an action on an irrational fear that he or she contracted HIV. In *Bain v. Wells*,[32] the Tennessee Supreme Court ruled that a plaintiff must actually have been exposed to HIV in order to recover for emotional distress. Presumably, this means the plaintiff must demonstrate some medically sound channel of transmission. In *Williamson v. Waldman*,[33] the New Jersey Supreme Court held that a plaintiff can recover if a reasonable person would have experienced emotional distress over the prospect of contracting HIV under the circumstances. However, this hypothetical reasonable person would be presumed to have "then-current, accurate, and generally available" knowledge concerning the transmission of HIV. Again, an irrational fear of catching the virus would not be a valid basis for an emotional distress suit. Fears arising out of exposure to toxic materials are discussed toward the end of this chapter.

31. Palsgraf v. Long Island R.R., 162 N.E. 99 (N.Y. 1928).
32. 936 S.W.2d 618 (Tenn. 1997).
33. 696 A.2d 14 (N.J. 1997).

##  Defenses to Negligence

In some jurisdictions, the defendant may absolve itself of part or all of the liability for negligence by proving that the plaintiff was also negligent.

### CONTRIBUTORY NEGLIGENCE

Under the doctrine of *contributory negligence*, if the plaintiff was also negligent in any manner, he or she cannot recover any damages from the defendant. Thus, if a plaintiff was 5 percent negligent and the defendant was 95 percent negligent, the plaintiff's injury would go unredressed. To address this inequity, most courts have replaced the doctrine of contributory negligence with that of comparative negligence.

### COMPARATIVE NEGLIGENCE

Under the doctrine of *comparative negligence*, the plaintiff may recover the proportion of his or her loss attributable to the defendant's negligence. For example, if the plaintiff was 5 percent negligent and the defendant 95 percent, the plaintiff can recover 95 percent of the loss. Comparative negligence may take two forms: ordinary and pure. In an *ordinary comparative negligence* jurisdiction, the plaintiff may recover only if he or she is less culpable than the defendant. Thus, if the plaintiff is found 51 percent negligent and the defendant 49 percent negligent, the plaintiff cannot recover. In a *pure comparative negligence* state, the plaintiff may recover for any amount of the defendant's negligence, even if the plaintiff was the more negligent party. For example, if the plaintiff was 80 percent negligent and the defendant was 20 percent negligent, the plaintiff may recover 20 percent of his or her loss.

### ASSUMPTION OF RISK

The *assumption of risk* defense requires that the plaintiff (1) knew the risk was present and understood its nature and (2) voluntarily chose to incur the risk. It applies when the plaintiff, in advance of the defendant's wrongdoing, expressly or impliedly consented to take his or her chances of injury from the defendant's actions. Such consent, like consent to an intentional tort, relieves the defendant of any liability. For example, the plaintiff assumes the risk if he or she, knowing that a car has faulty brakes, consents to take the chance of injury by riding in the car, or if he or she voluntarily chooses to walk where the defendant has negligently scattered broken glass.

In those jurisdictions that have adopted the comparative negligence doctrine, there is a strong trend to abolish assumption of risk as a defense. Sometimes courts use duty to determine the viability of the defense of assumption of risk. In *Mosca v. Lichtenwalter*,[34] a man who went ocean fishing and was accidentally struck in the eye by the sinker of another man's fishing pole sued the other fisherman for negligence. The California Court of Appeal found that the injury arose from a risk inherent in the activity of sportfishing and that imposing a duty on the other fisherman would alter the fundamental nature of the sport. Similarly, a Boston court dismissed a lawsuit brought by a Red Sox baseball fan who was hit by a fly ball.

In *Cheong v. Antablin*,[35] the California Supreme Court extended the doctrine of assumption of risk to skiing when it held that a skier is not liable for injury to a fellow skier unless the defendant intentionally caused the injury or engaged in conduct so reckless as to be totally outside the range of ordinary activity involved in the sport.

## Liability of Accountants and Other Professionals to Third Parties

### Intentional Misrepresentation

If an accountant, attorney, or other professional commits fraud, he or she is liable not only to the client but also to any other person whom the accountant (or other professional) reasonably should have foreseen would rely upon the intentional misrepresentation. For example, suppose that an auditor issued an audit opinion to a company's board of directors stating that its financial statements were prepared in accordance with generally accepted accounting principles, even though he or she knew that they contained material misstatements. In this case, the auditor could be sued for fraud by not only the company but also its shareholders. If the auditor knew that the company would be giving the audited financial statements to a bank, then the auditor could also be liable to the bank if it relied upon the audit letter when extending credit.

**INTERNATIONAL SNAPSHOT**

Americans have gained an international reputation as being eager to sue whenever they are physically or emotionally injured. When asked to explain why the Japanese Bar Association has half as many members in all of Japan as the American Bar Association has in the greater Washington, D.C. area alone, Koji Yanase replied, "If an American is hit on the head by a ball at the ballpark, he sues. If a Japanese person is hit on the head he says, 'It's my honor. It's my fault. I shouldn't have been standing there.'"[a]

a. *Perspectives '96*, NEWSWEEK, Dec. 30, 1996, at 110.

**INTERNATIONAL SNAPSHOT**

In *Hercules Managements Ltd. v. Ernst & Young*,[a] the shareholders of Northguard Acceptance Ltd. and Northguard Holdings Ltd. sued Ernst & Young, claiming that the accountants had negligently prepared audit reports that the shareholders relied upon in making their personal investment decisions. In its analysis, the Supreme Court of Canada focused on whether the shareholders used the audit reports for the specific purpose for which they were prepared. The Court found that the accountants had prepared the audit reports to help the shareholders in overseeing the management of the companies, not to assist the shareholders in making personal investment decisions. In reaching its decision that Ernst & Young was not liable, the Court stated: "The only purpose for which the reports could have been used so as to give rise to a duty of care on the part of the respondents, therefore, is as a guide for the shareholders, as a group, in supervising or overseeing management."

a. 2 S.C.R. 165 (1997).

### Negligent Misrepresentation

If the claim is for professional negligence, or *malpractice*, however, rather than for fraud, the class of parties eligible to sue is more limited. Thus, the greater the defendant's degree of fault, the wider the scope of potential plaintiffs.

Clearly, a professional owes a duty of due care to the client, and the client can sue for malpractice if the professional fails to satisfy that duty. But a professional may not have a duty to a third party with whom he or she does not have a contractual relationship.

#### *Accountants*

Courts have developed three main approaches to the duty of care owed by a public accountant to third parties who rely on the accountant's reports. New York's "near privity" approach, which several states have followed, is the

34. 68 Cal. Rptr. 2d 58 (Cal. Ct. App. 1997).
35. 946 P.2d 817 (Cal. 1997).

most restrictive. In New York, a plaintiff claiming negligent misrepresentation against an accountant with whom the plaintiff had no contractual relationship must establish three elements: (1) the accountant must have been aware that the reports would be used for a particular purpose, (2) a known party must have been intended to rely on the reports to further that purpose, and (3) there must be some conduct by the accountant "linking" him or her to that known party. This strict limitation on the class of potential plaintiffs represents a policy determination by the New York courts that accountants will not, merely by contracting with a particular client, expose themselves to a liability in an indeterminate amount for an indeterminate time to an indeterminate class.[36]

The most liberal approach, which few jurisdictions have adopted, extends an accountant's liability to all persons whom the accountant should reasonably foresee might obtain and rely on the accountant's report. States adopting the foreseeability approach compare defective audits with defective products and refuse to insulate auditors with a privity requirement when manufacturers of defective products are strictly liable regardless of their relationship with the end user.[37]

The majority view is set forth in Section 552 of the Restatement (Second) of Torts (1977):

> [U]nder the Restatement, an accountant's duty is limited to the client and third parties whom the accountant or client intends the information to benefit. The Restatement approach recognizes that an accountant's duty should extend beyond those in privity or near-privity with the accountant, but is not so expansive as to impose liability where the accountant knows only the possibility of distribution to anyone, and their subsequent reliance.[38]

### *Attorneys*

In the following case, the court considered a corporate lawyer's obligation to the investors and directors of a corporation he represented.

36. *See, e.g.*, White v. Guarantee, 372 N.E.2d 315 (N.Y. 1977).

37. ML–Lee Acquisition Fund, L.P. v. Deloitte & Touche, 463 S.E.2d 618 (S.C. Ct. App. 1995).

38. *Id.*

**A CASE IN POINT**

**CASE 9.4**
**Chem-Age Industries, Inc. v. Glover**
*Supreme Court of South Dakota*
*652 N.W.2d 756 (S.D. 2002).*

## In the Language of the Court

**› FACTS** Alan Glover represented Byron Dahl, an entrepreneur, in a number of business transactions. At some point, Glover, acting on behalf of Dahl, approached Roger Pederson and Garry Shepard about investing in a start-up company called Chem-Age Industries. Pederson and Shepard agreed to invest in the company in exchange for stock and became members of the board of directors. Soon thereafter, both investors became suspicious when the credit cards in the company's name began to accrue large balances due to charges by Dahl for what appeared to be personal items. Pederson and Shepard asked Dahl and Glover about the charges and were informed that Chem-Age Industries was in negotiations with another company to be bought out and that the charges would be paid with the proceeds from that sale. During this meeting, Glover stated that he "represented Chem-Age Industries" and that Chem-Age was owned by Dahl. Shortly after this meeting, Chem-Age failed to pay its taxes and was dissolved entirely. Pederson and Shepard sued both Dahl and Glover for negligent misrepresentation and Glover for legal malpractice.

**› ISSUE PRESENTED** Does a company's corporate counsel have a duty to the company's investors and directors such that the counsel can be held liable to them for legal malpractice?

**› OPINION** KONENKAMP, J., writing for the Supreme Court of South Dakota:

To prevail in a legal malpractice claim, a plaintiff must prove: (1) the existence of an attorney–client relationship giving rise to a duty; (2) the attorney, either by an act or a failure to act, breached that duty; (3) the attorney's breach of duty proximately caused injury to the client; and (4) the client sustained actual damage. Whether an

*(Continued)*

(Case 9.4 *continued*)

attorney–client relationship existed is ordinarily a question of fact. Here, we will examine the elements for an attorney–client relationship regarding, first, the corporation and, next, the individual plaintiffs.

. . .

Dahl hired Glover to organize the business as a corporation. By his own admission, Glover's involvement with Dahl was directly related to that incorporation, notwithstanding Dahl's earlier engagement of Glover on personal matters before and independent of the events at issue here. . . . Glover contends nonetheless that he did not represent the corporation. This is clearly a question of material fact. In the absence of some indication otherwise, Glover can be deemed the attorney for the corporation, even if he was also representing Dahl personally. An attorney may represent both a corporation and individuals in the corporation. . . . If it is shown that he represented the corporation, then it follows that Glover had a duty to the client corporation.

. . .

South Dakota recognizes that an attorney–client relationship may arise expressly or impliedly from the parties' conduct. Such a relationship is created when: (1) a person seeks advice or assistance from an attorney; (2) the advice or assistance sought pertains to matters within the attorney's professional competence; and (3) the attorney expressly or impliedly agrees to give or indeed gives the advice or assistance. . . . Here, the individual plaintiffs sought no advice from Glover. Correspondingly, Glover never agreed to advise or assist them. Glover had no personal consultation with Pederson and Shepard in creating the corporation. [Therefore, although Glover did owe a duty to the corporation, and the corporation may in turn have owed the plaintiffs a duty, Glover did not directly owe them a duty as individual shareholders or directors of the corporation.]

. . .

We earlier found that no attorney–client relationship existed between Glover and the two investor-directors, Pederson and Shepard. We now turn to the question whether Glover may have owed a fiduciary duty to them or to the corporation, even in the absence of an attorney–client relationship. To ascertain a fiduciary duty, we must find three things: (1) plaintiffs reposed "faith, confidence and trust" in Glover; (2) plaintiffs were in a position of "inequality, dependence, weakness, or lack of knowledge;" and (3) Glover exercised "dominion, control or influence" over plaintiffs' affairs.

. . .

Plaintiffs Pederson and Shepard have submitted no evidence to show how they were in a confidential relationship with Glover, where they depended on him specifically to protect their investment interests, and where Glover exercised dominance and influence over their business affairs. On the contrary, they never consulted with Glover during the time he is alleged to have breached a fiduciary duty to them.

. . .

Holding attorneys liable for aiding and abetting the breach of a fiduciary duty in rendering professional services poses both a hazard and a quandary for the legal profession. On the one hand, overbroad liability might diminish the quality of legal services, since it would impose "self protective reservations" in the attorney–client relationship. Attorneys acting in a professional capacity should be free to render advice without fear of personal liability to third persons if the advice later goes awry. On the other hand, the privilege of rendering professional services not being absolute, lawyers should not be free to substantially assist their clients in committing

*(Continued)*

(Case 9.4 *continued*)

tortious acts. To protect lawyers from meritless claims, many courts strictly interpret the common law elements of aiding and abetting the breach of a fiduciary duty.

The substantial assistance requirement carries with it a condition that the lawyer must actively participate in the breach of a fiduciary duty. Merely acting as a scrivener for a client is insufficient. A plaintiff must show that the attorney defendant rendered "substantial assistance" to the breach of duty, not merely to the person committing the breach. In *Granewich*,[39] the lawyers facilitated the squeeze-out, not just by providing legal advice and drafting documents, but by sending letters containing misrepresentations and helping to amend by-laws eliminating voting requirements that protected the minority shareholder's interest.

Another condition to finding liability for assisting in the breach of a fiduciary duty is the requirement that the assistance be "knowing." Knowing participation in a fiduciary's breach of duty requires both knowledge of the fiduciary's status as a fiduciary and knowledge that the fiduciary's conduct contravenes a fiduciary duty.

Although Glover may not have taken any active role in defrauding the investor-directors and may not have owed any direct fiduciary duty to them, Dahl did owe such a duty, and a material question of fact exists on whether Glover substantially assisted Dahl in breaching that duty. It may be that Glover, as much as Pederson and Shepard, was duped by Dahl's conniving business dealings, but that is for a jury to decide.

**› RESULT** Although Pederson and Shepard could not sue Glover for legal malpractice or breach of fiduciary duty, they could sue him for aiding and abetting a breach of fiduciary duty by Dahl. To prevail, they had to show that Glover was aware of Dahl's breach and substantially assisted him in breaching his duty.

**› CRITICAL THINKING QUESTIONS**

1. Why shouldn't corporate lawyers be liable to the shareholders for malpractice?
2. Should a corporate attorney who discovers a breach of fiduciary duty by an officer and director be required to disclose that breach to all of the other directors?

39. Granewich v. Harding, 985 P.2d 788 (Or. 1999).

In contrast, in 1995, the New Jersey Supreme Court held a property seller's attorney liable to the buyer for providing incomplete inspection reports in the course of a sale of land.[40] Although the attorney claimed that he had no duty to the purchaser and therefore could not be liable, the court disagreed. The court ruled that when an attorney knows or should know that a nonclient buyer will rely on his or her professional capacity, then the attorney owes a duty to the third party and may be liable for breaching that duty.

### *Investment Bankers*

The issues surrounding attorney and auditor liability to third parties closely parallel those surrounding the liability of investment bankers who issue fairness opinions in leveraged buyouts. Should shareholders be able to sue the investment bankers directly for negligent misrepresentation? Do investment bankers owe shareholders a duty? The actual client of the investment banker is the board of directors of the target company. Nevertheless, some courts have upheld negligent misrepresentation actions by shareholders against investment bankers on a foreseeability basis.[41]

40. Petrillo v. Bachenberg, 655 A.2d 1354 (N.J. 1995).

41. For an excellent discussion of the potential liability of investment bankers to shareholders, see Bill Shaw & Edward J. Gac, *Fairness Opinions in Leveraged Buy Outs: Should Investment Bankers Be Directly Liable to Shareholders?* 23 SEC. REG. L.J. 293 (1995).

# Negligent Hiring and Liability for Letters of Recommendation

Employers face potential liability for negligently hiring incompetent employees and for harm caused by former employees for whom the prior employer wrote a favorable letter of recommendation.

## Negligent Hiring

An employer may be held liable for the negligent or tortious conduct of its employee if the employer breached its duty to use care in hiring competent employees. Under the theory of negligent hiring, the proximate cause of the plaintiff's injury is the employer's negligence in hiring the employee, rather than the employee's wrongful act. A plaintiff must prove that (1) the employer was required to make an investigation of the employee and failed to do so, (2) an investigation would have revealed the unsuitability of the employee for the job, and (3) it was unreasonable for the employer to hire the employee in light of the information the employer knew or should have known. In addition, the plaintiff must prove that (1) the employee was "unfit" for the employment position, (2) the employer knew or should have known that the employee was unfit for the position, and (3) the employee's particular unfitness proximately caused the plaintiff's injury.

In *Van Horne v. Evergreen Media Corp.*,[42] the Supreme Court of Illinois considered whether a radio station and its owner could be held liable for negligently hiring a disc jockey who allegedly made defamatory remarks during his radio show. The plaintiff argued that the defendants knew or should have known that the disc jockey was likely to make defamatory comments because of his prior outrageous conduct. The court rejected this argument, reasoning that the fact the disc jockey had engaged in offensive and outrageous conduct did not establish that he had a propensity to make false and defamatory statements. The court cautioned that adopting the defendant's argument as its holding would have a "chilling effect on free speech, as media employers would be reluctant to hire controversial broadcasters or reporters." The court declined, however, to decide whether First Amendment concerns would preclude all attempts to state a cause of action for negligent hiring of media employees based on an employee's prior defamatory statement.

42. 705 N.E.2d 898 (Ill. 1998), *cert. denied*, 528 U.S. 811 (1999).

## Duty of Employers to Third Parties Based on Letters of Recommendation

In recent years, employers have backed away from providing letters of recommendation, primarily because of the fear of lawsuits.[43] Employers have chosen to issue "no comment" or "name, rank, and serial number" reference letters largely because writing a substantive reference may put them in a "damned if you do, damned if you don't" legal conundrum. Employers who disclose "too much" negative information may be subject to a defamation suit by the former employee. Employers who disclose "too little" negative information may be held liable to injured third parties for negligent misrepresentation.[44] Some states have enacted statutes offering some protection to employers who make recommendations in good faith.

# Strict Liability

*Strict liability* is liability without fault, that is, without either intent or negligence. Strict liability is imposed in two circumstances: (1) in product liability cases (the subject of Chapter 10) and (2) in cases involving abnormally dangerous, that is, ultrahazardous activities.

## Ultrahazardous Activities

If the defendant's activity is ultrahazardous, the defendant is strictly liable for any injuries that result. An activity is *ultrahazardous* if it (1) necessarily involves a risk of serious harm to persons or property that cannot be eliminated by the exercise of utmost care and (2) is not a matter of common usage.

Courts have found the following activities ultrahazardous: (1) storing flammable liquids in quantity in an urban area, (2) pile driving, (3) blasting, (4) crop dusting,

43. *Note: Addressing the Cloud over Employee References: A Survey of Recently Enacted State Legislation*, 39 WM. & MARY L. REV. 177 (1997).

44. *See, e.g.*, Randi W. v. Muroc Joint Unified Sch. Dist., 929 P.2d 582 (Cal. 1997). For a clever way a prospective employer may be able to finesse this issue, see PIERRE MORNELL, HIRING SMART (1999). Dr. Mornell recommends that the prospective employer call the former employer at a time when the supervisor is unlikely to be in the office and leave a voice message asking the supervisor to return the call only if the supervisor considers the former employee to be an excellent candidate.

(5) fumigating with cyanide gas, (6) constructing a roof so as to shed snow onto a highway, (7) emission of noxious fumes by a manufacturing plant located in a settled area, (8) locating oil wells or refineries in populated communities, and (9) test-firing solid-fuel rocket motors. In contrast, courts have considered parachuting, drunk driving, maintaining power lines, and letting water escape from an irrigation ditch not to be ultrahazardous. Discharging fireworks is not ultrahazardous because the risk of serious harm could be eliminated by proper manufacture. In most jurisdictions, liability does not attach until a court determines that the dangerous activity is inappropriate to the particular location.

Under strict liability, once the court determines that the activity is abnormally dangerous, it is irrelevant that the defendant observed a high standard of care. For example, if the defendant's blasting injured the plaintiff, it is irrelevant that the defendant took every precaution available. Although evidence of such precautions might prevent the plaintiff from recovering under a theory of negligence, it does not affect strict liability. Evidence of due care would, however, prevent an award of punitive damages. Adequate liability insurance is particularly important for companies engaged in ultrahazardous activities.

## *Respondeat Superior* and Vicarious Liability

Under certain circumstances, a person can be held vicariously liable for the negligent, or in some cases the intentional, conduct of another.

### *RESPONDEAT SUPERIOR*

Under the doctrine of *respondeat superior*—"let the master answer"—a "master" or employer is vicariously liable for the torts of the "servant" or employee if the employee was acting within the scope of his or her employment. The doctrine of *respondeat superior* may also apply when the person is not paid but acts on behalf of another out of friendship or loyalty or as a volunteer.

Underlying the doctrine of *respondeat superior* is the policy of allocating the risk of doing business to those who stand to profit from the undertaking. Because the employer benefits from the business, it is deemed more appropriate for the employer to bear the risk of loss than for the innocent customer or bystander to do so. The employer is in a better position to absorb such losses or to shift them, through liability insurance or price increases, to insurers and customers and, thus, to the community in general.

#### *Liability for Torts Committed Within the Scope of Employment*

An employer is directly liable for its own negligence in hiring or supervising an employee. In addition, the employer may be vicariously liable for an employee's wrongful acts, even though the employer had no knowledge of them and in no way directed them, if the acts were committed while the employee was acting within the scope of employment. To be within the scope of employment, activities must be closely connected to what the employee is employed to do or reasonably incidental to it. Whether an act was in the scope of employment is an issue for the jury to decide. (Scope of employment is discussed in greater detail in Chapter 5.)

Courts have held employers vicariously liable for an accident caused by an employee's negligence in driving while intoxicated after drinking alcohol at a company function on the grounds that the injury-producing event—the consumption of alcohol—occurred while the employee was acting within the scope of his employment by attending a company function.[45] In *Dickinson v. Edwards*,[46] the Washington Supreme Court ruled that an employer hosting a banquet may be sued under *respondeat superior* if the plaintiff establishes that (1) the employee consumed alcohol at a party hosted by the employer at which the employee's presence was requested or required by the employer, (2) the employee caused the accident while driving from the banquet, and (3) the proximate cause of the accident (the intoxication) occurred at the time the employee negligently consumed the alcohol. Because the banquet was beneficial to the employer who required the employee's attendance, the employee negligently consumed the alcohol during the scope of his employment. The Rhode Island Supreme Court went so far as to find an employer responsible for workers' compensation benefits when an employee got drunk at a Christmas party and fell from a third-floor window.[47]

If intentional conduct caused the plaintiff's injury, courts will look to the nexus, or connection, between the conduct and the employment. In general, an employer is liable for his or her employee's intentional torts if the

45. *See, e.g.*, Chastain v. Litton Sys., Inc., 694 F.2d 957 (4th Cir. 1982), *cert. denied*, 462 U.S. 1006 (1983); Wong-Leong v. Hawaiian Indep. Refinery, 879 P.2d 538 (Haw. 1994).
46. 716 P.2d 814 (Wash. 1986).
47. Beauchesne v. David London & Co., 375 A.2d 920 (R.I. 1977).

wrongful act in any way furthered the employer's purpose, however misguided the manner of furthering that purpose. Often intentional torts do not further the employer's business and are therefore outside the scope of employment. For example, a security company was found not liable when one of its security guards raped a worker in a client's building, even though the guard used his position to create the circumstances for the rape.[48]

### *Employer Liability Based on the Aided-in-the-Agency Doctrine*

Other courts will apply the *aided-in-the-agency doctrine* (discussed in Chapter 5) and look beyond the scope of employment to determine whether the employee exercised authority conferred by, or used assets provided by, the employer. Thus, one court held a county vicariously liable for battery, among other things, when one of its law enforcement officers stopped a woman, placed her in his patrol car, drove to an isolated place, and threatened to rape and murder her.[49]

In the following case, the Supreme Court of Oregon held that an employer could be vicariously liable for intentional torts outside of the scope of employment that resulted from acts within the scope of employment.

48. Rabon v. Guardsmark, Inc., 571 F.2d 1277 (4th Cir. 1978), *cert. denied*, 439 U.S. 866 (1978).

49. White v. County of Orange, 212 Cal. Rptr. 493 (Cal. Ct. App. 1985).

A CASE IN POINT

## In the Language of the Court

**CASE 9.5**

**Fearing v. Bucher**

*Supreme Court of Oregon*

*977 P.2d 1163 (Or. 1998).*

**› FACTS** From 1970 through 1972, Bucher, a priest employed by the Franciscan Friars of California, Inc. and the Archdiocese of Portland in Oregon, acted as youth pastor, friend, confessor, and priest to Fearing (then a minor) and his family. Bucher gained the trust and confidence of Fearing's family and was a frequent guest in their home. Bucher began to spend substantial periods of time alone with Fearing and committed a series of sexual assaults upon him.

Many years later, Fearing filed claims against the Archdiocese on theories of vicarious liability through application of the doctrine of *respondeat superior* and of negligent retention, supervision, and training of Bucher. The court of appeals affirmed the trial court's dismissal, and Fearing appealed.

**› ISSUE PRESENTED** Can an employer be held vicariously liable for an employee's sexual assault on a minor based on the doctrine of *respondeat superior?*

**› OPINION** GILLETTE, J., writing for the Supreme Court of Oregon:

Bucher's alleged sexual assaults on plaintiff clearly were outside the scope of his employment, but our inquiry does not end there. The Archdiocese still could be found vicariously liable, if acts that were within Bucher's scope of employment "resulted in the acts which led to injury to plaintiff."

. . .

Bucher used his position as youth pastor, spiritual guide, confessor, and priest to plaintiff and his family to gain their trust and confidence, and thereby to gain the permission of plaintiff's family to spend large periods of time alone with plaintiff. By virtue of that relationship, Bucher gained the opportunity to be alone with plaintiff, to touch him physically, and then to assault him sexually. . . . [T]hose activities were committed in connection with Bucher's employment as youth pastor and priest, . . . they were committed within the time and space limitations of Bucher's employment, . . . they were committed out of a desire, at least partially and initially, to fulfill Bucher's employment duties as youth pastor and priest, and

*(Continued)*

(Case 9.5 *continued*)

. . . they generally were of a kind and nature that was required to perform as youth pastor and priest.

. . .

This is not a case . . . in which the *only* nexus alleged between the employment and the assault was that the employment brought the tortfeasor and the victim together in time and place and, therefore, gave the tortfeasor the "opportunity" to commit the assaults. . . . A jury reasonably could infer that Bucher's performance of his pastoral duties with respect to plaintiff and his family were a necessary precursor to the sexual abuse and that the assaults thus were a direct outgrowth of and were engendered by conduct that was within the scope of Bucher's employment.

**› RESULT** The Supreme Court of Oregon held that the allegations of the amended complaint were sufficient to state a claim of vicarious liability against the Archdiocese based on the doctrine of *respondeat superior.* The plaintiff was permitted to proceed with his lawsuit.

**› COMMENTS** On the same day, the Supreme Court of Oregon ruled in *Lourim v. Swensen*[50] that the Boy Scouts of America could be vicariously liable for the actions of a volunteer leader who sexually assaulted a Boy Scout. The court stated: "[A] jury could infer that [the leader's] contact with the plaintiff was the direct result of the relationship sponsored and encouraged by the Boy Scouts, which invested [the Boy Scout leader] with authority to decide how to supervise minor boys under his care." Rejecting the Boy Scouts' argument that the organization could not be held liable because the Boy Scout leader was a volunteer, not an employee, the court found that a master–servant relationship may exist even if the servant is doing work gratuitously; the relevant inquiry is whether the master has the right to control the actions of the servant.

In 2004, the Archdiocese of Portland, Oregon, declared bankruptcy due to its inability to pay the awards of damages for childhood sexual abuse by its priests.

**› CRITICAL THINKING QUESTIONS**

1. What, if anything, could the Archdiocese have done to avoid liability for the priest's sexual assault?
2. Based on the Oregon Supreme Court's reasoning in *Fearing,* would the owner of an appliance store be liable if one of its repairmen raped a customer while in her house for a service call?

50. 977 P.2d 1157 (Or. 1998).

## VICARIOUS LIABILITY

Under certain circumstances, an employer may be vicariously, or indirectly, liable for harm caused by an employee even when the employee was not acting within the scope of employment and did not exercise authority conferred by, or use assets provided by, the employer. Courts are most likely to impose vicarious liability when the employer took an action (or failed to act) and thereby increased the likelihood that an employee would commit a tort.

For example, the employer may be responsible for the safe passage home of an employee who was not intoxicated but was tired from working too many consecutive hours. In *Robertson v. LeMaster,*[51] LeMaster was an employee of the Norfolk and Western Railway Company. He was doing heavy manual labor, including lifting railroad ties and shoveling coal. After thirteen hours at work, he told his supervisor that he was tired and wanted to go home. The supervisor told him to continue working. This happened several times, until finally LeMaster said that he could no longer work because he was too tired. His supervisor told him that if he would not work,

51. 301 S.E.2d 563 (W. Va. 1983).

he should get his bucket and go home. LeMaster had been at work a total of twenty-seven consecutive hours. On his way home, he fell asleep at the wheel and was involved in an accident, causing injuries to Robertson. Robertson sued the railroad.

The Supreme Court of Appeals of West Virginia concluded that requiring LeMaster to work such long hours and then setting him loose on the highway in an obviously exhausted condition was sufficient to sustain a claim against the railroad. The court found that the issue in this case was not whether the railway failed to control LeMaster while he was driving on the highway but rather whether the railroad's conduct prior to the accident created a foreseeable risk of harm. The court concluded that the railway's actions created such a foreseeable risk.

As explained in Chapter 5, courts are split on whether to impose liability on an employer who sends home an intoxicated employee who then injures a third party en route. The Court of Appeals of Arizona refused to impose vicarious liability for injury caused by an employee who had been using cocaine before and during work and had been ordered to leave the premises.[52] In contrast, the Supreme Court of Texas imposed a duty on employers to act with the degree of care a reasonably prudent employer would use to prevent injury to third parties when sending an intoxicated employee home.[53] In Texas, the failure to use due care would make the employer vicariously liable for the injury caused by the intoxicated employee.

## Successor Liability

As explained further in Chapter 10, under the doctrine of *successor liability*, individuals or entities that purchase a business may be held liable for product defects and certain other tortious acts of the previous owner. For example, if a company buys the assets of a ladder manufacturer and continues in the same line of business, the acquiring company may be liable for defective ladders manufactured and sold before the acquisition. Successor liability may also apply in the area of toxic torts, discussed later in this chapter.

## Damages

Tort damages generally attempt to restore the plaintiff to the same position he or she was in before the tort occurred. (In contrast, contract damages try to place the plaintiff in the position he or she would have been in had the contract been performed, as explained in Chapter 7.) Tort damages may include punitive as well as compensatory damages.

### Actual (or Compensatory) Damages

*Actual damages,* also known as *compensatory damages,* measure the cost to repair or replace an item or the decrease in market value caused by the tortious conduct. Actual damages may also include compensation for medical expenses, lost wages, and pain and suffering.

### Punitive Damages

*Punitive damages,* also known as *exemplary damages,* may be awarded to punish the defendant and deter others from engaging in similar conduct. Punitive damages are awarded only in cases of outrageous misconduct.

The amount of punitive damages may properly be based on the defendant's degree of culpability and wealth. But, as discussed in Chapter 2, the U.S. Supreme Court has indicated that, except in egregious cases, the ratio of punitive damages to actual damages should be "in the single digits."[54]

As discussed in the "Political Perspective," business leaders have called for legislative reform to cap or eliminate punitive damages as part of more general tort reform. Indeed, the head of the American Manufacturers Association declared, "[Trial lawyers are] the pariahs of the business community, which is more frightened by them than terrorists, China, or high energy prices."[55] Several states have limited punitive damages awards to situations in which the plaintiff can prove by clear and convincing evidence that the defendant was guilty of oppression, fraud, or malice.

The desire to curb punitive damages seems, however, to be largely limited to product liability cases, where businesses are defendants but rarely plaintiffs. In other areas, where businesses tend to be plaintiffs as well as defendants (such as contracts, unfair competition, and misleading advertising), reform of punitive damages appears to be less of a priority.[56]

52. Riddle v. Ariz. Oncology Servs., Inc., 924 P.2d 468 (Ariz. Ct. App. 1996).
53. Otis Eng'g Corp. v. Clark, 668 S.W.2d 307 (Tex. 1983).
54. State Farm Mut. Auto. Ins. Co. v. Campbell, 538 U.S. 408 (2003).
55. Richard A. Oppel Jr. & Glen Justice, *The 2004 Election: The Response: Kerry Gains Campaign Ace, Risking Anti-Lawyer Anger,* N.Y. TIMES, July 7, 2004.
56. Richard B. Schmitt, *Why Businesses Sometimes Like Punitive Awards,* WALL ST. J., Dec. 11, 1995, at B1.

## POLITICAL PERSPECTIVE

# THE CHANGING TIDE OF TORT REFORM

For years, critics and supporters of the U.S. tort system have advanced largely unchanged arguments about the perceived need for tort reform.[a] The topic became an election-year issue in 2004 when Vice President Dick Cheney called on challenger, Senator John Edwards, to defend his record as a trial lawyer and his approach to tort reform in the vice presidential debate.

Critics assert that the tort system has a random, Russian roulette flavor to it. To buttress this claim, they point to several cases where juries granted multimillion-dollar punitive damages awards to injured plaintiffs. These well-publicized horror stories include a $2.9 million award to an elderly woman, Stella Liebeck, who received third-degree burns after spilling McDonald's coffee on her lap;[b] a $4 million award against BMW for selling as new a car that had been damaged by acid rain and repainted;[c] and a $150 million award against General Motors in a case where the plaintiff who was injured in a single-car accident had admittedly consumed at least one beer and was not wearing a seatbelt.[d]

The critics argue that large and unpredictable jury awards have resulted in sharply higher liability insurance rates, which in turn may (1) increase the cost of vital products and services, (2) stifle innovation in valuable but potentially dangerous products, and (3) render U.S. firms less equipped to compete with rivals abroad. Moreover, claim the critics, attorneys' fees and administrative costs are so extensive that less than half of the amount awarded by verdict or settlement is paid to the injured plaintiffs.

Supporters of the present tort system respond that it is the one place where the average citizen can battle the powerful on nearly equal terms. They claim that without the threat of lawsuits and their accompanying discovery process, large corporations would have every incentive to conceal harmful information about the effects of their products. The supporters believe that if any reform of the system is necessary, judicial review and self-policing would be more effective tools than legislation at either the state or federal level.[e]

The U.S. Chamber of Commerce has singled out Mississippi as the "jackpot justice" state and the perfect example of tort lawyers run amok.[f] Statistical studies claim to show a connection between so-called frivolous lawsuits and the impediment of economic growth in the area. The basic premise, as it has played out in Mississippi, is that jurors assume that by awarding large settlements against businesses in favor of the ordinary person, they can force big business to be more responsible. For better or worse, however, businesses are leaving Mississippi and other similar states in droves. Instead of effecting change, citizens are driving business and economic development out of their states and thereby helping to depress their economies.

Other studies, however, have found that punitive damages awards are both extremely rare and are usually closely related to the size of compensatory damages. In a survey of the country's seventy-five most populous counties, the U.S. Department of Justice found that only 2 percent of the 762,000 cases filed even reached a jury. Plaintiffs won just over half of the cases that went to a jury, but juries awarded punitive damages in just 6 percent of these cases. Half of the punitive damages awards were for less than $50,000.[g] Of course, fear of large punitive damages awards may cause businesses to settle cases for larger amounts than they would otherwise have agreed to pay. Furthermore, large awards make headlines, but when they are reduced on appeal, as often happens, the reduction receives much less attention. Even the $2.9 million award in the notorious McDonald's coffee case, for example, was reduced to $400,000.[h]

Because getting broad federal legislation passed to limit tort damages has been unsuccessful, tort reformists and lobbyists have turned to inserting smaller, more specific acts, such the Securities Litigation Uniform Standards Act and the Biomaterials Access Assurance Act, as rid-

**a.** *See, e.g.,* George Melloan, *Rule of Law or Rule of Lawyers?,* WALL ST. J., Nov. 21, 2000, at A27.
**b.** Andrea Gerlin, *A Matter of Degree: How a Jury Decided That a Coffee Spill Is Worth $2.9 Million,* WALL ST. J., Sept. 1, 1994.
**c.** The Alabama Supreme Court subsequently reduced this award to $2 million. BMW of North Am., Inc. v. Gore, 646 So. 2d 619 (Ala. 1994). The U.S. Supreme Court then declared the $2 million award void as "grossly excessive" and unconstitutional. BMW of North Am., Inc. v. Gore, 517 U.S. 559 (1996). On remand, the Alabama Supreme Court further reduced the award to $50,000. BMW of North Am., Inc. v. Gore, 701 So. 2d 507 (Ala. 1997).
**d.** Eric Peters, *Captious Spin on the Wheel of Misfortune,* WASH. POST, June 10, 1996, at A17.
**e.** Philip Shuchman, *It Isn't That the Tort Lawyers Are So Right, It's Just That the Tort Reformers Are So Wrong,* 49 RUTGERS L. REV. 485 (1995).
**f.** Todd Buchholz, *The High Cost of "Jackpot Justice,"* WALL ST. J., July 8, 2002, at A23. See also the information published by the American Tort Reform Association at http://atra.org/atra/atri2c.htm.
**g.** Richard C. Reuben, *Plaintiffs Rarely Win Punitives, Study Says,* 81 A.B.A. J. 26 (1995). See also the information published by the Association of Trial Lawyers of America at http://www.atla.org.
**h.** Gerlin, *supra* note b.

*(Continued)*

(Political Perspective *continued*)

ers to other congressional bills.[i] A recent example is the rider attached to the Homeland Security Act, which sought to shield pharmaceutical giant Eli Lilly from billions in potential litigation awards arising out of certain of its drugs. Other tactics being employed are (1) contributing to the election campaigns of business-friendly judges (a practice long employed by trial lawyers seeking favorable judges); (2) lobbying the writers of the Federal Rules of Civil Procedure to restrict access to e-mails, which are currently said to be given less protection than traditional business documents; and (3) insisting on mandatory jury service in an attempt to get more representative and possibly business-friendly juries.[j]

i. Terry Carter, *Piecemeal Tort Reform,* A.B.A. J., Dec. 2001, at 51.

j. Lorraine Woellert, *Tort Reform: A Little Here, A Little There,* BUS.WK., Jan. 20, 2003, at 60–64.

## Equitable Relief

If a monetary award cannot adequately compensate for the plaintiff's loss, courts may give *equitable relief.* For example, the court may issue an *injunction,* that is, a court order, to prohibit the defendant from continuing a certain course of activity. This remedy is particularly appropriate for torts such as trespass or nuisance, when the plaintiff does not want the defendant's conduct to continue. The court may also issue an injunction ordering the defendant to take certain action. For example, a newspaper could be ordered to publish a retraction. In determining whether to grant injunctive relief, the courts will balance the hardship to the defendant against the benefit to the plaintiff.

## Liability of Multiple Defendants

A plaintiff may name numerous defendants. In some cases, the defendants may ask the court to join, or add, other defendants. As a result, when a court determines liability and damages, it must grapple with the problem of allocating the damages among multiple defendants.

### JOINT AND SEVERAL LIABILITY

Under the doctrine of *joint and several liability,* multiple defendants are jointly (that is, collectively) liable and also severally (that is, individually) liable. This means that once the court determines that multiple defendants are at fault, the plaintiff may collect the entire judgment from any one of them, regardless of the degree of that defendant's fault. Thus, it is possible that a defendant who played a minor role in causing the plaintiff's injury might have to pay all the damages. This is particularly likely when only one defendant is solvent, that is, when only one has money to pay the damages.

Many states have adopted statutes to limit the doctrine of joint and several liability for tort defendants. Most states that have abolished joint and several liability have moved to a contributory regime. Under a joint and several liability regime, a defendant can be liable for all of a plaintiff's damages, even if the defendant was only 1 percent responsible for causing the plaintiff's injuries. This would be the result if the other defendants (those 99 percent responsible for causing the injuries) lacked funds to pay the judgment. Under contributory rules, the same defendant would under no circumstances be liable for more than 1 percent of the total damages award.

### CONTRIBUTION AND INDEMNIFICATION

The doctrines of contribution and indemnification can mitigate the harsh effects of joint and several liability. *Contribution* distributes the loss among several defendants by requiring each to pay its proportionate share to one defendant; by doing so, they discharge their joint liability. *Indemnification* allows a defendant to shift its individual loss to other defendants whose relative blame is greater. The other defendants can be ordered to reimburse the one that has discharged a joint liability. It is important to keep in mind, however, that the rights to contribution and indemnification are worthless to a defendant if all the other defendants are insolvent or lack sufficient assets to contribute their share.

## Toxic Torts

Since the 1970s, tort law has been evolving in response to sustained social and political concern over toxic substances and their potential for personal injury and environmental and property damage. When courts have been asked to adjudicate the disputes arising from the widespread use of toxic substances, the traditional tort rules for determining liability, measuring damages, and allocating them among the parties have not always provided ready answers. The resulting pressure for change has caused some courts to modify these rules and even to recognize new categories of damages.

## DEFINITION

A *toxic tort* is a wrongful act that causes injury by exposure to a harmful, hazardous, or poisonous substance. Modern industrial and consumer societies utilize these substances in a variety of ways, creating countless opportunities for toxic tort claims.

Potential toxic tort defendants include those manufacturers (1) that utilize substances that may injure an employee, a consumer, or a bystander; (2) whose processes emit hazardous by-products into the air or discharge them into a river; (3) whose waste material goes to a disposal site where it may migrate to the groundwater and contaminate nearby wells; or (4) whose product itself contains or creates substances that can injure. Liability is not limited to manufacturers, however. Everyday activities of governmental agencies, distribution services, and consumers may provide a basis for toxic tort claims. Some substances once thought safe, such as asbestos, have resulted in ruinous litigation when it was later established that they were harmful. Even financial institutions can be caught in the toxic tort net by becoming involved in the operations of a business handling hazardous materials or by buying contaminated land at a foreclosure sale.

## EXPENSIVE TO DEFEND

Toxic tort claims are among the most difficult and expensive lawsuits to defend or prosecute. Expert witness costs alone can run into the millions of dollars for a single case. Toxic tort claims are also difficult to evaluate and, as a consequence, often cannot be insured against at a reasonable cost. Cause-and-effect relationships are difficult to establish because of disagreement within the medical and scientific community. Often illness or injury does not occur until years after the exposure began. Because exposures causing the injury can accumulate from a multitude of sources, including food, air, water, and skin contact, it is difficult to allocate blame among the various possible sources. Open-ended claims for punitive damages are commonplace in toxic tort cases.

## STRICT LIABILITY

Some courts have held hazardous-waste disposal to be an ultrahazardous activity and have imposed strict liability for injuries resulting from it. For instance, in *Sterling v. Velsicol Chemical Corp.*,[57] the U.S. Court of Appeals for the Sixth Circuit held that the operator of a waste-burial site for toxic material was responsible for all resulting contamination under the doctrine of strict liability for ultrahazardous activities.

The federal Comprehensive Environmental Response, Compensation and Liability Act of 1980 (CERCLA) embodies this strict liability doctrine, as do many state statutes that largely mirror its provisions. CERCLA imposes strict liability for cleanup costs on (1) the owner or operator of the property at the time the hazardous substance was discharged and (2) the parties responsible for transporting and disposing of the waste. The current owner or operator of the property may also be liable if it was aware of the waste at the time of purchase or failed to use proper care to investigate the site. (The exception for brownfield sites is discussed in the "Inside Story" in Chapter 18.)

In *Farm Bureau Mutual Insurance Co. v. Porter & Heckman, Inc.*,[58] the Court of Appeals of Michigan considered whether Porter & Heckman, which serviced an outdoor, aboveground heating-oil tank, was liable for the water and soil contamination caused by oil leaking from the tank. The plaintiff argued that because Porter & Heckman was in the business of servicing equipment containing a hazardous substance (the heating oil), it should be strictly liable for any damage attributable to the oil.

The Michigan Court of Appeals analyzed Farm Bureau's claim under Michigan's Environmental Response Act, which states that a defendant will be held strictly liable for contamination damage if (1) it is an operator of a facility that deals in hazardous substances or (2) it otherwise arranges for the disposal of a hazardous substance. As for the "operator" claim, the court ruled that a defendant is an operator only if it has authority to control the area where the hazardous substances were located. One who services a system does not automatically control the operation of the system. Thus, Porter & Heckman was not liable as an "operator" merely because it serviced the heating-oil tank. Nor was it liable as an "arranger for disposal." The court ruled that this portion of the statute required an intent to dispose of the hazardous substance, as well as some ownership of or authority to control the actual substance. Here, Porter & Heckman had the intent and authority only to repair the heating-oil tank, not to dispose of or control the oil itself.

57. 855 F.2d 1188 (6th Cir. 1988).
58. 560 N.W.2d 367 (Mich. Ct. App. 1996).

## THEORIES OF DAMAGES

Under traditional tort principles, toxic tort plaintiffs who prove exposure to a toxic substance and a defendant's liability for that exposure may still not receive damages if there is no proof of an actual injury. The plaintiffs may be at risk of developing cancer or some other disease in the future, but tort law generally has not allowed recovery for risk of future disease unless some precursor symptom is present or the plaintiffs prove that they are more likely than not to get the disease. In the face of these limitations on damages, courts are being asked to allow awards for emotional distress in the absence of either physical symptoms or an intentional tort. Another remedy being urged is damages to cover the future cost of medical monitoring so that the disease can be detected at the onset, when treatment may be more effective.

In a series of cases brought under the Federal Employers' Liability Act,[59] the U.S. Supreme Court has adapted the common law zone-of-danger test for determining when a plaintiff exposed to hazardous substances can recover for the negligent infliction of emotional distress. The Court stated:

> [This test] confines recovery for stand-alone emotional distress claims to plaintiffs who: (1) sustain a physical impact as a result of a defendant's negligent conduct; (2) are placed in immediate risk of physical harm by that conduct—that is, those who escaped instant physical harm, but were within the zone of danger of physical impact.[60]

59. 45 U.S.C.S. §§ 51 *et seq.*
60. Consol. Rail Corp. v. Gottshall, 512 U.S. 532, 547–548 (1994) (internal quotation marks omitted).

Applying this test, the Court has distinguished claims for stand-alone negligently inflicted emotional distress (such as fear of cancer) not provoked by any physical injury from "parasitic" claims for negligently inflicted emotional distress brought on by a physical injury for which pain and suffering recovery is permitted. The Court ruled that mere exposure to asbestos or another carcinogenic substance is insufficient to show "physical impact" under the common law zone-of-danger test.[61]

Thus, it dismissed claims for damages for fear of cancer as a result of exposure to asbestos brought by a pipefitter who had a clean bill of health at the time of the lawsuit. But in a subsequent case dealing with railroad workers who had developed the disease of asbestosis as a result of the railroad's negligence, the Court ruled that the workers could include in their recovery for their asbestosis-related pain and suffering damages for fear of developing cancer.[62] Such damages were recoverable even though the workers had not proved an actual likelihood of developing cancer or physical manifestations of the fear of cancer. Although the Court was applying federal common law principles developed under the Federal Employers' Liability Act, the ruling, which permitted recovery for "future harm genuinely feared," is expected to have broad effect.

61. Metro-North Commuter R.R. Co. v. Buckley, 521 U.S. 424 (1994).
62. Norfolk & Western Ry. Co. v. Ayers, 538 U.S. 135 (2003).

THE RESPONSIBLE MANAGER

## REDUCING TORT RISKS

Managers should implement ongoing programs of education and monitoring to reduce the risks of tort liability. Because torts can be committed in numerous ways, the programs should cover all possible sources of liability. For example, the management of a company that does not respond satisfactorily to an allegation of sexual harassment may be liable for intentional infliction of emotional distress. Statements made by company representatives about an individual or product can constitute defamation.

In addition to preventing intentional torts, managers should work to prevent their employees from committing acts of negligence, which can lead to large damages awards against the company. Any tort-prevention program must recognize that under the principle of *respondeat superior,* employers will be held liable for any torts their employees commit in the scope of their employment. It is crucial, therefore, to define the scope of employment clearly.

Managers should use care to avoid committing torts that are related to contractual relations and competition with other firms. For example, a company may be held

*(Continued)*

(The Responsible Manager *continued*)

liable for interference with contractual relations if a court finds that the company intentionally tried to induce a party to breach a contract. Also, although competition itself is permissible, intentionally seeking to sabotage the efforts of another firm is not. Managers may need to consult counsel when they are unsure whether their activity has crossed the line from permissible competition to tortious interference with a prospective business advantage.

Prudent managers should keep abreast of developments in the emerging area of toxic tort law and strive to reduce the risk of liability for toxic substances used or distributed in their enterprise. Managers should adopt a long-term policy to protect employees, customers, and the environment from excess toxic exposure. They should identify any hazardous toxic substances used in their business activities or products or released into the environment. Where appropriate, managers should test and monitor to determine levels of exposure. Often it is necessary to obtain an expert assessment of the hazards of toxicity of these substances. Managers should develop a plan to control and reduce toxic exposure. This can be done by reducing the quantity of toxic substances used, by recycling, by seeking less toxic alternatives, and by educating and training employees. Managers should implement a plan by assigning responsibilities, allocating resources, and auditing compliance. The waste-management plan should include criteria for choosing third-party contractors. Insurance should be obtained, if available, and coverage should be reviewed periodically. Management should adopt a contingency plan for responding to toxic accidents and develop a public relations plan both for routine (that is, safe) use of toxic substances and for possible toxic accidents.

A program of overall risk management and reduction is essential to limit the potential of tort liability. It is often desirable to designate one person to be in charge of risk management. That person should keep track of all claims and determine what areas of the business merit special attention. The head of risk management should be free to report incidents and problems to the chief executive officer and the board of directors, in much the same way as an internal auditor reports directly to the independent directors on the audit committee. This enhances independence and reduces the fear of reprisals if the risk manager blows the whistle on high-ranking managers.

INSIDE STORY

## TAKING AIM AT THE GUN INDUSTRY

In 2001, an Illinois court ruled that gun dealers as well as gun makers could be held responsible under a theory of public nuisance for distributing firearms in a way that would make them more accessible to juveniles and criminals.[63] A number of other states have brought similar public nuisance suits against gun manufacturers.[64] In 2002, the Ohio Supreme Court ruled that prosecutors could proceed with public nuisance claims against gun makers after two lower courts dismissed the cases.[65] Chicago filed a similar suit against Beretta USA at around the same time.[66] The theory is that the companies that reap profits from producing dangerous products should also be liable for the injuries they cause.

63. Young v. Bryco Arms, 765 N.E.2d 1 (Ill. App. Ct. 2001).
64. Molly McDonough, *Lawyers, Guns, and Lead,* A.B.A. J., Feb. 2003, at 22–23.
65. Cincinnati v. Beretta USA Corp., 768 N.E.2d 1136 (Ohio 2002).
66. City of Chicago v. Beretta USA Corp., 785 N.E.2d 16 (Ill. App. Ct. 2002).

Notwithstanding these successes, plaintiffs seem to be meeting with more failures than successes in proceeding under a nuisance theory.[67] A Florida jury initially ordered gun distributor Valor Corporation to pay $1.2 million for its role in the death of a teacher shot by one of his thirteen-year-old students.[68] Although the vast majority of the blame was placed on the gun owner (from whom the gun was stolen) and on school officials, 5 percent of the blame was apportioned to Valor Corporation for producing the small, inexpensive pistol used in the killing. The prosecution contended that criminals often use this type of handgun because it is cheap and that children often mistake it for a toy because it is so small.

67. McDonough, *supra* note 64.
68. Associated Press, *Jury Allots Blame in Teacher's Death,* WASH. POST, Nov. 15, 2002, at A12.

*(Continued)*

(Inside Story *continued*)

Nevertheless, a Florida appellate court completely vacated the judgment.[69] The appeals court found a "total absence of facts or reasonable inferences therefrom which would support the jury's verdict" and granted Valor's motion for judgment notwithstanding the verdict. In such a motion, a defendant asks that a judgment be set aside because the jury had no rational basis for making its decision.

Perhaps even more ominous for gun-control advocates is the growing number of state laws shielding gun makers from suit. Since 1998 thirty states have passed legislation granting gun makers immunity. One notable exception is California, which recently repealed an act that had protected gun manufacturers in the state.[70] It remains to be seen whether the federal and state governments will jump on the gun bandwagon the way they did when they decided to sue the tobacco companies for the costs associated with smoking.

69. Grunow v. Valor (Fla. Cir. Ct. 2003).

70. Fox Butterfield, *Gun Industry Is Gaining Immunity from Suits*, N.Y. TIMES, Sept. 1, 2002, at 19.

## KEY WORDS AND PHRASES



## QUESTIONS AND CASE PROBLEMS

1. Linda was the sole proprietor of Clowntown USA, a successful amusement park. The park's main attraction was a very steep, fast roller coaster. Although Linda maintained the roller coaster meticulously, she knew that it was unsafe for riders under four feet tall. Accordingly, she instructed her employee, Oliver, not to permit anyone less than four feet tall to ride on the roller coaster. On a particularly busy day in

June, Oliver forgot his instructions and allowed several children below four feet tall to ride on the roller coaster. The children were thrown from the ride and suffered serious bodily injury.

**a.** Under what doctrine could the children's parents sue Linda for damages? What would Linda's lawyer assert as a defense? Who would be likely to prevail?

**b.** Would your answer change if Linda had merely told Oliver to be careful in operating the roller coaster, without specifically telling him not to permit anyone under four feet tall to ride it?

**c.** What additional defense could Linda assert if she could prove that the children's parents had read and understood a conspicuous sign posted at the roller coaster ticket booth stating that the ride was dangerous for those under four feet tall and that any persons under that height rode at their own risk?

**d.** What steps, if any, could Linda have taken to reduce exposure for this type of accident?

**2.** Joe, Alice, and their baby, Pearl, live in a house next to a closed city dump. Since they moved in five years ago, their only source of water for drinking, cooking, and bathing has been a well under the house. Last month, Joe discovered that the well was contaminated by small amounts of waste solvents leaking from the dump. Joe and Alice show no symptoms but worry that the contamination will eventually make them sick. Baby Pearl has a condition that may become leukemia, and Joe and Alice are concerned that future children may be harmed as well. As a result of stress caused by worrying about the effects of the contamination on themselves and their family, Joe and Alice begin to smoke and do so even while Alice is nursing Pearl. Joe and Alice learn that Big Corporation sent 5 percent of the solvents to the dump. Big has $10 million in insurance. Last year, Big shut down its local plant, laying off 2,000 employees. Ten percent of the solvents came to the dump from Small Company, which dissolved last year. Its former owner, Bill Small, is worth $3 million. The other 85 percent of the solvents came from thousands of separate households and small businesses throughout the city, all of which paid the city trash-collection fees.

Joe and Alice's lawyer discovers that ten years ago Big Corporation and Small Company received copies of federal regulations classifying the solvent wastes as hazardous. No one at Small Company bothered to read the regulations, and the company continued to dispose of the solvents at the city dump. At Big Corporation, however, the environmental engineer issued orders that the solvents be sent to a hazardous-waste site instead of the city dump. No one was assigned to police the order, though, and about once a month some solvents went to the city dump by mistake. The environmental engineer reissued the orders twice after hearing of the mistakes, but occasional violations continued until the plant closed.

**a.** What claims are likely to prevail in a suit against the city? Big Corporation? Small Company? Bill Small? The local dry cleaner?

**b.** What torts can Pearl claim if she develops leukemia and lung cancer thirty years later? Against whom?

**c.** Can Joe and his family recover punitive damages against any of the defendants?

**d.** What additional facts would improve the family's chances of securing a large punitive damages award?

**e.** If you had been the CEO of Big Corporation or Small Company, what steps would you have taken to ensure that hazardous waste was disposed of properly?

**3.** A group of eBay customers successfully bid for twelve autographed baseballs at an eBay auction. When the balls arrived, the purchasers discovered that they were cheap forgeries. When the seller was nowhere to be found, the purchasers brought a lawsuit against eBay for selling forgeries. EBay never claimed to be anything other than an open marketplace. It did not hold itself out as a purveyor of collectibles. Is eBay liable for the forgeries? Even if eBay is found not liable, how should the company respond to this incident from a business point of view? What would be the ethical thing to do? [*Gentry v. eBay Inc.,* 121 Cal. Rptr. 2d 703 (Cal. Ct. App. 2002).]

**4.** De Angelo Bailey sued Marshall Bruce Mathers III, the rapper better known as Eminem, for defamation, claiming that Eminem falsely depicted him as a bully in a song entitled "Brain Damage" on Eminem's 1999 debut CD "The Slim Shady LP." The verses at issue were:

"Way before my baby daughter Hailey/

I was harassed daily by this fat kid named D'Angelo Bailey/

An eight grader who acted obnoxious, cause his father boxes/

So everyday he'd shove me in the lockers/

One day he came in the bathroom while I was p---/

And had me in the position and beat me into submission/

He banged my head against the urinal till he broke my nose/

Soaked my clothes in blood, grabbed me and choked my throat."

Bailey claimed that he only bumped into Mathers. Is Mathers liable for defamation? Would the result be the same if Mathers had been Bailey's employer and inserted the same verses into his personnel file? [Chad Halcom, *Rhymin' Ruling*, MACOMB DAILY ONLINE, Oct. 18, 2003).]

5. The Republic of Korea wished to purchase military radar systems and solicited competing bids from manufacturers, including Loral Corporation and MacDonald, Dettwiler, and Associates Ltd. The Korea Supply Company represented MacDonald, Dettwiler in the negotiations for the contract and stood to receive a commission of over $30 million if MacDonald, Dettwiler's bid was accepted. Ultimately, the contract was awarded to Loral (now Lockheed Martin Tactical Systems, Inc.) even though MacDonald, Dettwiler's bid was $50 million lower and its equipment was superior. MacDonald, Dettwiler claimed that it was not awarded the contract because Loral and its agent, Linda Kim, had offered bribes and sexual favors to key Korean officials. Does Korea Supply Company have any legal basis for suing Lockheed Martin (formerly Loral) or its agent, Linda Kim? If so, what damages would be available? Is there any criminal exposure? [*Korea Supply Co. v. Lockheed Martin Corp.*, 63 P.3d 937 (Cal. 2003).]

6. After two years of negotiations, the four shareholders and founders of Access Inc. sold their health-care start-up to a subsidiary of Res-Care, Inc. and agreed to stay on as employees based on assurances from the buyer that Res-Care would not merge with VOCA of North Carolina. The Access shareholders had explained to Res-Care that they were all former employees of VOCA and had left and formed Access because of differences over the way VOCA was run. They made it clear to Res-Care that they would not sell their shares without assurances that they would never be affiliated with VOCA or their former supervisor.

   Res-Care's chief development officer told the shareholders that his company was not interested in buying VOCA because it had poor profits and was poorly managed. Res-Care's vice president of the central region made similar assurances in a later meeting.

   A week after the Access shareholders signed the deal, Res-Care announced that it had signed a letter of intent to buy VOCA. The Access shareholders' former boss at VOCA was given the job of statewide director, thereby becoming the Access shareholders' new supervisor.

   Do the former Access shareholders have any legal basis for suing Res-Care? Assume that the acquisition agreement between the Access shareholders and Res-Care contained no representation or warranty by Res-Care regarding a possible merger with VOCA and that it contained a standard merger clause stating that the written acquisition agreement superseded any and all prior negotiations and oral statements. What could the Access shareholders have done to avoid this dispute? [*Godfrey v. Res-Care Inc.*, N.C. App. No. COA 03-790 (N.C. July 6, 2004).]

7. Street Clash Games, Inc. is a software company that produces a popular video game featuring a number of highly violent scenes. Gamettimee.com is a website that shows its members home videos of street fights caught on tape. Both of these companies adhere to all laws requiring warnings as to the content of their products. A high school student who was a member of the website and an owner of the video game shot and killed five of his fellow students and wounded several others during the lunch hour at his high school. Could the companies be found negligent for their products' content? Should they be? What moral responsibility, if any, do you believe the two companies bear for the shooting? [*James v. Meow Media, Inc.*, 300 F.3d 683 (6th Cir. 2002), *cert. denied*, 537 U.S. 1159 (2003).]

8. Bruce Marecki, an employee of Crystal Rock Spring Water Company, attended a seminar sponsored by the company at a Ramada Inn. At the seminar, he drank several beers. After the seminar ended, he was planning to go to happy hour at the hotel but at a separate location from the seminar room. Instead, he left the hotel to purchase cigarettes after discovering that the cigarette machine in the hotel was broken. While he was driving to a store to buy cigarettes, he rear-ended another car and caused injuries to the driver. The driver sued Crystal Rock Spring

Water Company under the doctrine of *respondeat superior.* Should the company be liable for the injuries the driver suffered? What if Crystal Rock Spring Water had not supplied the liquor at the seminar but had allowed it to be served? What if Marecki had nothing to drink at the seminar but then drank at the happy hour with his coworkers and had an accident when he was driving home after socializing with them? What if the seminar was optional and Marecki had no obligation to attend? [*Sheftic v. Marecki,* 1999 Conn. Super. LEXIS 2953 (Conn. Oct. 22, 1999).]

9. Harold Tod Parrot was employed as vice president of sales by Capital Corporation, a privately held investment adviser. Parrot purchased 40,500 shares of Capital stock pursuant to a stock-purchase agreement that provided that upon termination of Parrot's employment, the company would repurchase his shares at fair market value. The fair market value was to be determined by the accounting firm Coopers & Lybrand, which had been retained by Capital Corporation for that purpose. Several years after the stock purchase, Parrot was terminated. He then sought to sell his shares back to Capital Corporation at fair market value. Parrot objected to the price of the shares established by Coopers & Lybrand in the company's most recent biannual report and sued both Capital Corporation and Coopers & Lybrand. His complaint against Coopers & Lybrand alleged professional negligence and negligent misrepresentation. He argued that the accountants had changed the valuation methodology, at Capital's request, in order to reduce the price of the shares and, as a result, Parrot was induced to accept a lesser value for his stock. Does Parrot's suit against Coopers & Lybrand have merit? [*Parrot v. Coopers & Lybrand, LLP,* 702 N.Y.S.2d 40 (2000), *aff'd,* 95 N.Y.2d 479 (2000).]

### MANAGER'S DILEMMA

10. A number of overweight Americans brought a class-action suit for deceptive trade practices and negligence against McDonald's Corporation, a "fast-food" chain famous for its hamburgers, french fries, and chicken nuggets. The class claimed that McDonald's food is fatty and addictive and that the general public has no idea how bad McDonald's food is for their health. The attorneys for the class obtained copies of McDonald's food studies, which showed that McDonald's was aware of the fat content of its food but did not look any further into the possible health consequences of eating fatty foods. Can McDonald's be held responsible for its customers' obesity? Would it matter if McDonald's had added certain fats to its food after conducting another study that showed that adding those fats would make its products more addictive? What if the amount of fat needed to make the products highly addictive was so small that it would not be detected by the average consumer? If you were the CEO of McDonald's, what changes, if any, would you make in your menu and marketing strategy in response to these lawsuits? What, if anything, would you do about the obesity epidemic if you were the CEO of PepsiCo, which sells Frito Lay potato chips and other salted snacks, Pepsi cola, Tropicana orange juice, and Gatorade sports drink? [*Pelman v. McDonald's Corp.,* 237 F. Supp. 2d 512 (S.D.N.Y. 2003).]

## INTERNET SOURCES

| | |
|---|---|
| The Worldwide Legal Information Association page provides information about tort law around the world. | http://www.hg.org/torts.html |
| The British law firm of Sweet & Maxwell provides a collection of reports on professional negligence. | http://www.sweetandmaxwell.co.uk/online/index.html |
| The New York law firm of Queller & Fisher maintains a page dedicated to issues of negligence, including recent decisions and publications, descriptions of legislation, and links to other websites. | http://www.quellerfisher.com/verdicts.htm |
| The Alexander Law Firm of San Jose, California, maintains the Consumer Law Page to disseminate information about torts, especially personal injury. | http://consumerlawpage.com |

*(Continued)*

(Internet Sources *continued*)

| | |
|---|---|
| The American Tort Reform Association hosts a page addressing various issues about tort reform, including information about states that have enacted tort reform measures and facts about the impact of tort liability on the economy. | http://www.atra.org |
| The Association of Trial Lawyers of America, a group of attorneys who represent plaintiffs in tort and consumer protection lawsuits, maintains a site with articles and news clippings regarding recent developments in tort litigation and reform. | http://www.atla.org |

CHAPTER 10

# Product Liability

## INTRODUCTION

### DEFINITION OF PRODUCT LIABILITY

*Product liability* is the legal liability manufacturers and sellers have for defective products that cause injury to the purchaser, a user or bystander, or their property. Liability extends to anyone in the chain of distribution: manufacturers, distributors, wholesalers, and retailers.

Today, most states in the United States have adopted strict product liability, whereby an injured person may recover damages without showing that the defendant was negligent or otherwise at fault. No contractual relationship between the defendant and the injured person is necessary. The injured person merely needs to show that the defendant sold the product in a defective or dangerous condition and that the defect caused his or her injury.

### CHAPTER OVERVIEW

This chapter discusses the evolution of the strict liability doctrine, beginning with its origin in warranty and negligence theories. It then focuses on the bases for strict liability, including manufacturing defect, design defect, and failure to warn. The chapter examines who may be held liable for defective products and the allocation of liability among multiple defendants. Defenses to a product liability claim are discussed, along with legislative reforms designed to correct perceived abuses in the system. Finally, the chapter describes the law of product liability in the European Union.

## Theories of Recovery

The primary theories on which a product liability claim can be brought are breach of warranty, negligence, and strict liability.

### BREACH OF WARRANTY

In a warranty action, the reasonableness of the manufacturer's actions is not at issue. Rather, the question is whether the quality, characteristics, and safety of the product were consistent with the implied or express representations made by the seller. A buyer may bring a warranty action whenever the product fails to meet the standards that the seller represents to the buyer at the time of purchase.

#### *UCC Warranties*

As explained in Chapter 8, a warranty may be either express or implied. An express warranty is an affirmation made by the seller relating to the quality of the goods sold. An implied warranty is created by law and guarantees the merchantability of the goods sold and, in some circumstances, their fitness for a particular purpose.

#### *Privity of Contract*

A breach-of-warranty action is based on principles of contract law. To recover, an injured person must be in a contractual relationship with the seller. This requirement is known as *privity of contract*. It necessarily precludes recovery by those persons, such as bystanders, who are not in privity with the seller.

### NEGLIGENCE

*MacPherson*, which follows, is the landmark case in which the defendant manufacturer was found liable for negligence even though there was no contractual relationship between the manufacturer and the plaintiff. Thus, one of the obstacles posed in breach-of-warranty actions—the requirement of privity of contract—was removed. Although liability was still based on the negligence principles of reasonableness and due care, *MacPherson's* abandonment of the privity requirement made it an important forerunner to the doctrine of strict product liability.

A CASE IN POINT

## Summary

**CASE 10.1**

**MacPherson v. Buick Motor Co.**

*Court of Appeals of New York*
*111 N.E. 1050 (N.Y. 1916).*

› **FACTS** MacPherson purchased a new Buick car with wooden wheels from a Buick Motor Company dealer who had previously purchased the car from its manufacturer, Buick Motor Company. MacPherson was injured when the car ran into a ditch. The accident was caused by the collapse of one of the car's wheels due to defective wood used for the spokes. The wheel had been made by a manufacturer other than Buick.

MacPherson sued Buick Motor Company directly. He proved that Buick could have discovered the defect by reasonable inspection and that such an inspection had not been conducted. No claim was made that the manufacturer knew of the defect and willfully concealed it. After the trial court found in favor of MacPherson, Buick appealed.

› **ISSUE PRESENTED** May a consumer who purchases a product from a retailer sue the manufacturer directly for negligent manufacture of the product even though there is no contract *per se* between the consumer and the manufacturer?

› **SUMMARY OF OPINION** The New York Court of Appeals held that Buick could be held liable for negligence. As a manufacturer, it owed a duty to any person who could foreseeably be injured as a result of a defect in an automobile it manufactured. The court stated that a manufacturer's duty to inspect varies with the nature of the thing to be inspected. The more probable the danger, the greater the need for caution. Because the action was one in tort for negligence, no contract between the plaintiff and the defendant was required.

› **RESULT** The court of appeals affirmed the lower court's finding that the manufacturer, Buick Motor Company, was liable for the injuries sustained by the plaintiff. Buick was found negligent for not inspecting the wheels and was responsible for the finished product.

› **COMMENTS** This case established the rule, still applicable today, that a manufacturer can be liable for failure to exercise reasonable care in the manufacture of a product when such failure involves an unreasonable risk of bodily harm to users of the product. This rule is embodied in Sections 1 and 2(a) of the Restatement (Third) of Torts: Product Liability (1997).[1]

1. This rule also appeared in the RESTATEMENT (SECOND) OF TORTS § 395 (1977).

To prove negligence in a products case, the injured party must show that the defendant did not use reasonable care in designing or manufacturing its product or in providing adequate warnings. This can be quite difficult to prove. Moreover, injured persons have often been negligent themselves in their use or misuse of the product. This precludes recovery in a contributory negligence state and reduces recovery in a comparative negligence state.

A manufacturer can be found negligent even if the product met all regulatory requirements because, under some circumstances, a reasonably prudent manufacturer would have taken additional precautions.[2] As discussed later in this chapter, the only exception is when a feder-

2. *See, e.g.*, Hasson v. Ford Motor Co., 650 P.2d 1171 (Cal. 1982).

ally mandated standard is deemed to have preempted state product liability law.[3]

Courts will not permit a plaintiff to prove negligence by introducing evidence of subsequent remedial measures taken by a defendant to improve a product.[4] The public policy behind this rule is to encourage companies to continually strive to improve the safety of their products. If such safety measures could be used to establish legal liability, companies would be deterred from improving their products.

## STRICT LIABILITY IN TORT

Strict liability in tort allows a person injured by an unreasonably dangerous product to recover damages from the manufacturer or seller of the product. Negligent conduct on the part of the manufacturer or seller is not required. Because the defect in the product is the basis for liability, the injured person may recover damages even if the seller has exercised all possible care in the manufacture and sale of the product.

In 1963, in *Greenman v. Yuba Power Products, Inc.*,[5] the California Supreme Court became the first state supreme court to adopt strict product liability. The case involved a consumer who was injured while using a Shopsmith combination power tool that could be used as a saw, drill, and wood lathe. Claiming that the tool was defective and not suitable to perform the work for which it was intended, Greenman sued the manufacturer and the retailer who had sold the power tool to his wife for breach of express and implied warranties and for negligent construction of the tool. The California Supreme Court ruled that a manufacturer is strictly liable in tort when it places an article on the market, knowing that the product is to be used without inspection for defects, and it proves to have a defect that causes injury to a human being.

### *Rationale*

The legal principle of strict product liability is grounded in considerations of public policy. The rationale has four basic parts: (1) the law should protect consumers against unsafe products; (2) manufacturers should not escape liability simply because they typically do not sign a formal contract with the end user of their product (or with nonusers who might be injured by their product); (3) manufacturers and sellers of products are in the best position to bear the costs of injuries caused by their products, because they can pass these costs on to all consumers in the form of higher prices; and (4) the law should give sellers an incentive to deal only with reputable manufacturers. In short, the goal of strict product liability is to force companies to internalize the costs of product-caused injuries. The crafters of the doctrine recognized that it would give manufacturers an incentive to improve the safety of their products.

### *Elements of a Strict Liability Claim*

For a defendant to be held strictly liable, the plaintiff must prove that (1) the plaintiff, or his or her property, was harmed by the product; (2) the injury was caused by a defect in the product; and (3) the defect existed at the time the product left the defendant and did not substantially change along the way. Most states have followed the formulation of Section 402A of the Restatement (Second) of Torts, which states:

1. One who sells any product in a defective condition unreasonably dangerous to the user or consumer or to his property is subject to liability for physical harm thereby caused to the ultimate user or consumer, or to his property, if
   a. the seller is engaged in the business of selling such a product, and
   b. it is expected to and does reach the user or consumer without substantial change in the condition in which it is sold.
2. The rule stated in Subsection (1) applies although
   a. the seller has exercised all possible care in the preparation and sale of his product, and the user or consumer has not bought the product from or entered into any contractual relation with the seller.

As discussed later in this chapter, the American Law Institute (ALI) promulgated the Restatement (Third) of Torts: Product Liability in 1997. The ALI is a body of lawyers and law professionals that periodically produces a restatement of various areas of the law (such as agency, contracts, and property). These restatements provide judges and lawyers with a comprehensive view of the status of American case law (drawn from a survey of courts throughout the country) and the rationale behind it. The restatements are, of course, infused with their drafters' vision of the way that a particular area of the law should evolve.

The Restatement (Third) imposes strict liability for manufacturing defects, but for design defects and defects based on inadequate instructions or warnings, it opts instead for a standard predicated on negligence.

3. *See, e.g.*, Kemp v. Medtronic, Inc., 231 F.3d 216 (6th Cir. 2000), *cert. denied*, 534 U.S. 818 (2001).

4. For more on subsequent remedial measures, see "The Responsible Manager" in this chapter.

5. 377 P.2d 897 (Cal. 1963).

Although judges often regard the most recent restatement as persuasive authority and an accurate depiction of present case law, courts are free either to follow or to ignore the restatement's formulation. Because a majority of states still follow the Restatement (Second), the discussion that follows is, except as otherwise noted, based on that restatement. It remains to be seen whether in the future courts will broadly adopt the Restatement (Third) standard for defects in design, instructions, and warnings.

### *Strategy and Punitive Damages*

Although negligence and breach of warranty are alleged in most product liability cases, they play a secondary role compared to strict liability. Under strict liability, the injured person does not have the burden of proving negligence and does not have to be in privity with the seller. Thus, strict liability is easier to prove than either negligence or breach of warranty.

Nonetheless, plaintiffs' attorneys usually try to prove negligence as well as strict liability. Proof of negligence will often stir the jury's emotions, leading to higher damages awards and, in some cases, to punitive damages.[6] For example, in August 1999, the Florida Supreme Court upheld a $31 million punitive damages award against Owens-Corning Fiberglass Corporation, the manufacturer of an asbestos-containing product, after finding that the company showed "blatant disregard for human safety."[7] The plaintiff suffered from a rare lung disease following asbestos exposure. The trial court found that Owens-Corning had intentionally and knowingly misrepresented and concealed the dangers of asbestos for more than thirty years. The company had intentionally contaminated a new product with asbestos, even though it knew that slight exposure to asbestos could cause the lung disease. Similarly, in May 2000, an Illinois jury found Shell Oil liable for asbestos exposure and awarded $34.1 million in compensatory and punitive damages to a former union worker who contracted lung disease after exposure.[8]

On the other hand, once the plaintiff has raised the issue of negligence, the defense can introduce evidence that its products were "state-of-the-art" and manufactured with due care. Such evidence would be irrelevant to the issue of strict liability and hence inadmissible.

In some cases, the defendant's own internal memos have been the basis of large awards. In a product liability case against General Motors Corporation, internal documents written by a GM engineer in 1973 were key to the jury's award of $4.9 billion, one of the largest ever in a product liability case. Six people were burned when their 1979 Chevrolet Malibu exploded after its fuel tank was ruptured in an accident, and they sued GM. The plaintiffs introduced evidence revealing that GM had been aware of problems with the fuel tank but chose not to redesign it due to economic considerations. In one GM memo, an engineer estimated that each death from burns from a fuel-related fire in a GM vehicle would cost the company $200,000. Using that figure, the memo calculated that fuel tank–related deaths would cost GM $2.40 for every vehicle on the road. The memo concluded that "a human fatality is really beyond value, subjectively." The company also calculated that it would cost an additional $8.95 to redesign the car to reduce the fire risk, a greater cost than paying claims for deaths. Thus, the internal memos reflected that GM had made a business decision to put people at risk rather than correct the design problem at a higher cost to the company. GM tried to prevent the memo from being introduced at trial and, when it was produced, argued that it was irrelevant.

6. Punitive damages are discussed further in Chapters 2 and 9.

7. *$31 Million Punitive Award Upheld in Asbestos Case,* CORP. COUNS. WKLY., Oct. 6, 1999, at 7.

8. *Illinois Jury Awards Former Roofer $34 Million,* MEALEY'S LITIG. REP.: INSURANCE, May 23, 2000.

## Definition of Product

Strict liability in tort applies only to products, not services. What qualifies as a *product* is sometimes not clear. In some cases, it is unclear whether an injury was caused by a defective product or a negligently performed service. For example, a person may be injured by a needle used by a dentist or the hair solution used by a beautician. Some courts apply strict liability in these situations. Other courts will not go so far down the chain of distribution.

Courts that have addressed the definition-of-product question have required that the thing giving rise to liability be a tangible item. In *Winter v. G.P. Putnam's Sons,*[9] the plaintiffs were mushroom enthusiasts who purchased a book entitled *The Encyclopedia of Mushrooms,* which was published by the defendant. The plaintiffs, who relied on descriptions in the book to determine which wild mushrooms were safe to eat, became critically ill after eating a poisonous variety. The court rejected the plaintiffs' strict

9. 938 F.2d 1033 (9th Cir. 1991).

### ETHICAL CONSIDERATION

Do publishers have an ethical obligation to warn readers that information in a book is not complete and should not be relied on?

product liability claim because the "product" involved was a collection of ideas and expressions, not a tangible item. The court reasoned that a high value should be placed on the unfettered exchange of ideas and that the threat of imposing strict liability on the contents of books could seriously inhibit that exchange.

Massachusetts extended this "tangible item" requirement to the promotion of a sport or game. The plaintiff in *Garcia v. Kusan, Inc.*[10] was an elementary school student who was hit in the eye by a wayward stick in a floor hockey game in a physical education class. He claimed that Kusan marketed the sport of floor hockey to elementary schools and then sold them the equipment necessary to play. Garcia did not argue that the stick was defective; instead he argued that the game of floor hockey itself (as marketed by Kusan) was defective. Garcia referred the court to an old Kusan floor hockey instruction manual, which stated that the game required no protective equipment. The court, citing the rationale of *Winter*, entered summary judgment for Kusan. It reasoned that a game—the concept and instructions—could not constitute a "product" that would give rise to product liability; the necessary "tangible item" was lacking.

A similar issue arises when a telephone pole or other product installed in the ground is defective. Some courts take the position that fixtures of this type are structural improvements of real property and, as such, are not products for purposes of product liability actions.

Others have treated certain structural improvements as products. For example, the Supreme Court of Alabama ruled that all of the following were products: (1) a conveyor belt installed in a grain-storage facility;[11] (2) a gas water heater in a home;[12] (3) a cylindrical rotary soybean conditioner located in a soybean extraction facility;[13] (4) a diving board that had been installed with an in-ground, vinyl-lined swimming pool;[14] (5) a telephone pole installed in the ground;[15] and (6) an exterior installation attached to a house.[16] The Alabama Supreme Court reasoned that the policies underlying the application of strict product liability have little relation to the policies underlying the fixtures doctrine.[17] As a result, the application of product liability law should not be totally dependent upon the intricacies of real property law.

10. 655 N.E.2d 1290 (Mass. App. 1995).
11. Beam v. Tramco, Inc., 655 So. 2d. 979 (Ala. 1995).
12. Sears, Roebuck & Co. v. Harris, 630 So. 2d. 1018 (Ala. 1993).
13. McDaniel v. French Oil Mill Mach. Co., 623 So. 2d 1146 (Ala. 1993).
14. King v. S.R. Smith, Inc., 578 So. 2d 1285 (Ala. 1991).
15. Bell v. T.R. Miller Mill Co., 768 So. 2d 953 (Ala. 2000).
16. Keck v. Dryvit Sys., 830 So. 2d 1 (Ala. 2002).
17. Bell v. T.R. Miller Co., 768 So. 2d 953 (Ala. 2000).

## What Makes a Product Defective?

An essential element for recovery in strict liability is proof of a defect in the product. The injured party must show that (1) the product was defective when it left the hands of the manufacturer or seller and (2) the defect made the product unreasonably dangerous. Typically, a product is dangerous if its characteristics do not meet the consumer's expectations. For example, a consumer expects that a stepladder will not break when someone stands on the bottom step. Not all situations are so clear-cut, however.

John Wade, a noted American jurist whose articles are frequently cited by courts,[18] set forth the following factors for determining whether a product is defective:

1. The usefulness and desirability of the product—its utility to the user and to the public as a whole.
2. The safety aspects of the product—the likelihood that it will cause injury and the probable seriousness of the injury.
3. The availability of a substitute product that would meet the same need and not be as unsafe.
4. The manufacturer's ability to eliminate the unsafe character of the product without impairing its usefulness or making it too expensive to maintain its utility.
5. The user's ability to avoid danger by the exercise of care in the use of the product.
6. The user's anticipated awareness of the dangers inherent in the product and their avoidability, because of general public knowledge of the obvious condition of the product or of the existence of suitable warnings or instructions.
7. The feasibility, on the part of the manufacturer, of spreading the loss by setting the price of the product or carrying liability insurance.[19]

### Manufacturing Defect

A *manufacturing defect* is a flaw in a product that occurs during production, such as a failure to meet the design specifications. A product with a manufacturing defect is not like the others rolling off the production line. For example, suppose the driver's seat in an automobile is designed to be bolted to the frame. If a worker forgets to tighten the bolts, the loose seat will be a manufacturing defect.

18. *See, e.g.*, Larsen v. Pacesetter Sys., Inc., 837 P.2d 1273 (Haw. 1992).
19. *Id.*

## View from Cyberspace

### Jurisdictional Disputes

By their very nature, jurisdictional battles tend to lead to an expansive view of the disputes over which a body can exercise jurisdiction. This tendency stems from the fact that a local tribunal will often seek to protect the interests of those living within its jurisdiction. Consequently, any action that even remotely affects its citizens will likely be treated as bringing the dispute within the jurisdiction of the court. When two tribunals' jurisdictions overlap, a battle often ensues over which one will be allowed to resolve the dispute and whose law will be applied. The inherently international character of e-commerce makes such battles more common. The president and CEO of the Electronic Retailing Association, a group of online retailers, predicted that as "international transactions increase, this is going to become a much larger issue."[a] She appears to be correct.

A fierce debate raged in the European Union (EU) as to whether and under what circumstances consumers could bring suit in their national courts against companies based in another country but selling products through websites powered by computers located outside the consumer's home country.[b] Some argued that the ability to sue in national court would promote e-commerce growth by increasing consumer confidence. Others argued that fear of suit in other countries would discourage small and medium-sized businesses from setting up websites, thereby hindering growth in e-commerce. The European Parliament voted in September 2000 to grant jurisdiction in disputes between online buyers and sellers to the country of destination rather than the country of origin. In November 2000, the European Commission approved the plan, making it EU policy to try e-commerce cases in the country of the purchaser.[c] Although consumer activists welcomed the action, one critic complained that the ruling "means we will still have 15 separate markets in the EU rather than one unified internal market, which I thought was the aim."[d]

More generally, there appears to be a growing consensus on the need for the international harmonization of laws regarding jurisdiction over e-commerce disputes. The American Bar Assocation's Cyberspace Law Committee undertook a yearlong study of the problem and suggested, among other things, a global online standards association.[e] But a representative from the U.S. Undersecretary of State questioned whether an international bureaucracy was the best way to reach harmonization. Everyone does seem to agree, however, that subjecting every U.S.-based website to the contradictions inherent in the laws of 195 different countries could cause e-commerce to grind to a halt.[f]

a. *Industry Lobbyists Say Jurisdiction Issues Threaten E-Business if Not Addressed Soon,* 6 U.S.L.W. 215 (Feb. 2001).

b. Paul Meller, *Jurisdiction Dispute Heats Up in Europe,* STANDARD, Nov. 22, 2000.

c. Paul Meller, *Buyers Gain Online Rights in Europe; Effort Made to Lift Confidence in Web,* N.Y. TIMES, Dec. 1, 2000.

d. *Id.*

e. *Industry Lobbyists Say Jurisdiction Issues Threaten E-Business if Not Addressed Soon, supra* note a.

f. *Id.*

## Design Defect

A *design defect* occurs when, even though the product is manufactured according to specifications, its inadequate design or poor choice of materials makes it dangerous to users. Typically, there is a finding of defective design if the product is not safe for its intended or reasonably foreseeable use. A highly publicized example was the Ford Pinto, which a jury found to be defectively designed because the car's fuel tank was too close to the rear axle, causing the tank to rupture when the car was struck from behind.

### Ethical Consideration

You are a manager of a major manufacturing corporation. An interview with a low-level engineer leads you to believe that the design specifications for your model PaZazz-4 are, in fact, the cause of numerous deaths. You are facing a wrongful-death and product liability suit for defective design. The plaintiffs have not deposed this engineer, though his name was provided as one of the hundreds who worked on this project. Thus, although you believe the design for PaZazz-4 was defective, it will be extremely difficult—if not impossible—for the plaintiffs to prove this. What should you do?

## INADEQUATE WARNINGS, LABELING, OR INSTRUCTIONS

To avoid charges of *failure to warn,* a product must carry adequate warnings of the risks involved in its normal use. For example, the manufacturer of a ladder must warn the user not to stand on the top step. A product must also be accompanied by instructions for its safe use. For example, sellers have been found liable for failing to provide adequate instructions about the proper use and capacity of a hook and the assembly and use of a telescope and sun filter.

Although a warning can shield a manufacturer from liability for a properly manufactured and designed product, it cannot shield the manufacturer from liability for a *defectively* manufactured or designed product. For example, an automobile manufacturer cannot escape liability for defectively designed brakes merely by warning that "under certain conditions this car's brakes may fail." As will be explained later, however, some products, such as certain prescription drugs, are unavoidably unsafe. In cases involving such products, the adequacy of the warning determines whether the product, known to be dangerous, is also "defective."

### *Causation Requirement*

To prevail on a failure-to-warn claim, a plaintiff must show both that the defendant breached a duty to warn and that the defendant's failure to warn was the proximate cause (or legal cause) of the plaintiff's injuries. The question of proximate cause is one for the jury to determine. As a result, the vast majority of courts will not disturb jury findings that a failure to warn was the proximate cause of an injury. However, in an extreme case—one in which the court believes no reasonable person could have deemed the failure to warn a proximate cause of the plaintiff's injury—the court may set aside a verdict on causation grounds.

### *Bilingual Warnings*

The United States is a heterogeneous country. Diversity is one of its great strengths. With diversity can come challenges, however. Misunderstandings may arise due to differences in culture or language. Legislatures in states with substantial non-English-speaking populations have recognized the need for bilingual or multilingual documents in such areas as voting and public services. The following case addresses the need for bilingual warnings on nonprescription drugs.

A CASE IN POINT

**CASE 10.2**

**Ramirez v. Plough, Inc.**

*Supreme Court of California*
*863 P.2d 167 (Cal. 1993).*

## Summary

**› FACTS** In March 1986, when he was less than four months old, plaintiff Jorge Ramirez exhibited symptoms of a cold or similar upper respiratory infection. To relieve these symptoms, Ramirez's mother gave him St. Joseph's Aspirin for Children (SJAC), a nonprescription drug manufactured and distributed by Plough, Inc. The product label stated that the dosage for a child under two years old was "as directed by doctor." Moreover, the package displayed this warning:

> Warning: Reye Syndrome is a rare but serious disease which can follow flu or chicken pox in children and teenagers. While the cause of Reye Syndrome is unknown, some reports claim aspirin may increase the risk of developing this disease. Consult doctor before use in children or teenagers with flu or chicken pox.

The warnings were provided in English, although Plough was aware that non-English-speaking Hispanics purchased the product. Ramirez's mother, who could read only Spanish, did not consult a doctor before using SJAC to treat Ramirez's condition. After two days, Ramirez's mother took him to a hospital, where the doctor advised her to administer Dimetapp or Pedialyte (nonprescription medications that do not contain aspirin); she disregarded the advice and continued to treat Ramirez with SJAC. He thereafter developed the potentially fatal Reye syndrome, resulting in severe neurological damage, including cortical blindness, spastic quadriplegia, and mental retardation.

Ramirez sued Plough, alleging that he contracted Reye syndrome as a result of ingesting SJAC. He sought compensatory and punitive damages on, among other things, a theory of product liability. The complaint alleged that SJAC was defective when it left the

*(Continued)*

(Case 10.2 *continued*)

defendant's control and that the product's reasonably foreseeable use involved a substantial and not readily apparent danger of which the defendant failed to warn adequately.

Finding no duty to warn and no causal relation between the defendant's actions and the plaintiff's illness, the trial court granted summary judgment for the defendant. On appeal, the appellate court reversed because it found a duty to warn and concluded that a jury should decide whether the warnings were adequate. The defendant appealed.

**› ISSUE PRESENTED** May a manufacturer of nonprescription drugs that can lead to a deadly illness when taken as normally expected incur tort liability for distributing its products with warnings only in English when the manufacturer knows that there are non-English-reading users?

**› SUMMARY OF OPINION** The California Supreme Court began by noting that a manufacturer of nonprescription drugs has a duty to warn purchasers about dangers of its products. The issue under consideration was whether the defendant's duty to warn required it to provide label or package warnings in Spanish.

The court acknowledged that although the Food and Drug Administration (FDA) encourages labeling that meets the needs of non-English speakers, it only requires manufacturers to provide full labeling in English for all nonprescription drugs except those distributed solely in Puerto Rico or another territory where the predominant language is not English.

Although the California legislature has enacted laws to protect non-English speakers in certain circumstances, the court noted that California does not have a law requiring labeling in a foreign language. Because the state and federal statutes expressly require only English labeling, the court decided not to intrude upon a matter it deemed best handled by the legislature.

**› RESULT** Because both state and federal law require warnings in English but not in any other language, a manufacturer is not liable in tort for failing to label a nonprescription drug with warnings in a language other than English. Ramirez's case was dismissed.

**› COMMENTS** The California Supreme Court was influenced by the experience of FDA-mandated Spanish inserts for prescription drugs. Recognizing that "the United States is too heterogeneous to enable manufacturers, at reasonable cost and with reasonable simplicity, to determine exactly where to provide alternative language inserts," the FDA for a time required manufacturers, as an alternative to multilingual or bilingual inserts, to provide Spanish-language translations of their patient package inserts on request to doctors and pharmacists. The FDA later concluded that manufacturers were having difficulty obtaining accurate translations, and eventually it abandoned altogether the patient package insert requirement for prescription drugs.

**› CRITICAL THINKING QUESTIONS**

1. Would the result have been different if the nonprescription medicine had been for an illness particular to a certain non-English-speaking group residing in the United States?
2. Should it matter whether the drug company advertises a particular medicine in a language other than English?

## UNAVOIDABLY UNSAFE PRODUCTS

If the societal value of using an inherently dangerous product outweighs the risk of harm from its use, the manufacturer may be exonerated from liability for sale of such an *unavoidably unsafe product*. For example, certain drugs are generally beneficial but are known to have harmful side effects in some situations. The authors of the Restatement (Second) of Torts recognized that there should be a separate concept of product liability for manufacturers of prescription drugs. Nearly every jurisdiction in the United States has fol-

**"Great little product, but liability could eat you up."**



lowed the reasoning of the Restatement (Second) in some form or another.[20]

For example, in a 1986 case, the plaintiff had contracted polio from the Sabin oral polio vaccine. The odds of contracting polio from the vaccine are one in a million. The Kansas Supreme Court held that harm resulting from the use of a drug would not give rise to strict liability if it was "unavoidably unsafe," that is, if the drug's benefits outweighed its dangers and if proper warnings were given.[21]

Comment b to Section 6 of the Restatement (Third) of Torts reflects a similar view of product liability for manufacturers of prescription drugs:

> The traditional refusal by courts to impose tort liability for defective designs of prescription drugs and medical devices is based on the fact that a prescription drug or medical device entails a unique set of risks and benefits. What may be harmful to one patient may be beneficial to another. Under Subsection (c) [of Section 6] a drug is defectively designed only when it provides no net benefit to any class of patients. . . . [M]anufacturers must have ample discretion to develop useful drugs and devices without subjecting their design decisions to the ordinary test applied to products generally.[22]

## Who May Be Liable

In theory, each party in the chain of distribution may be liable: manufacturers, distributors, wholesalers, and retailers. In addition, the courts have developed the concepts of successor, market-share, and premises liability, which are used to allocate liability among defendants in certain cases.

### Manufacturers of Products and Component Parts

A manufacturer will be held strictly liable for its defective products regardless of how remote the manufacturer is from the final user of the product. The only requirement for strict liability is that the manufacturer be in the business of selling the injury-causing product. The manufacturer may be held liable even when the distributor makes final inspections, corrections, and adjustments of the product.

Manufacturers of component parts are frequently sued as well. In the following case, the court considered whether a manufacturer of component parts for a prefabricated home could be held liable if the parts failed.

20. *See* Restatement (Second) of Torts § 402A cmt. k (1997).
21. Johnson v. Am. Cyanamid Co., 718 P.2d 1318 (Kan. 1986).
22. Restatement (Third) of Torts: Product Liability § 6 cmt. b (1997).

**A Case in Point**

## In the Language of the Court

**CASE 10.3**

**Jimenez v. Superior Court of San Diego County**

*Supreme Court of California*
*58 P.3d 450 (Cal. 2002).*

**› FACTS** The Jimenez family purchased a mass-produced home in a newly completed housing development. Soon after they moved in, their house and the houses of many of their neighbors developed damage to the stucco, insulation, framing, drywall, paint, wall coverings, floor coverings, and baseboards. Later investigation confirmed that all of this damage stemmed from defective windows produced by T.M. Cobb Company. The Jimenez family, along with their fellow homeowners, sued Cobb. Cobb argued that because its windows were only a part of the whole house and Cobb was not in control of the products when they were installed in the house, Cobb could not be held liable.

*(Continued)*

(Case 10.3 *continued*)

**› ISSUE PRESENTED** May a manufacturer of a component for mass-produced homes be held liable for damage suffered by the homeowners if the homes are ultimately defective because of the defective component?

**› OPINION** KENNARD, J., writing for the California Supreme Court:

Nearly 60 years ago Justice Roger Traynor expressed his view that a manufacturer should be liable in tort for placing on the market a defective product that causes personal injury. Such liability, Justice Traynor reasoned, was justified because of a consumer's inability to prove that a defect was caused by a flaw in the manufacturing process, because the manufacturer is best able to reduce the risks of injury caused by product defects, and because a manufacturer can equitably distribute the loss broadly among the buying public as a cost of doing business. . . . Such liability was necessary to protect injured consumers "who are powerless to protect themselves" because the law of contractual warranties developed for commercial transactions offered no protection to those harmed by defective products.

In 1969, the Court of Appeal applied strict products liability to mass-produced homes. . . .

[But] the Court of Appeal in *La Jolla Village Homeowners' Assn. v. Superior Court*[23] held that a subcontractor hired by a developer cannot be strictly liable for defects in mass-produced homes, unless it also owns or controls the housing development.

Citing *La Jolla Village,* Defendant contends that because they merely supplied component parts (the windows) of mass-produced homes, not the completed homes themselves, they should not be subject to strict products liability. They argue that extending strict products liability to component manufacturers would not serve the purposes of strict products liability.

The policies underlying strict products liability in tort are equally applicable to component manufacturers and suppliers. Like manufacturers, suppliers, and retailers of complete products, component manufacturers and suppliers are "an integral part of the overall producing and marketing enterprise," may in a particular case "be the only member of that enterprise reasonably available to the injured plaintiff," and may be in the best position to ensure product safety. . . . For purposes of strict products liability, there are "no meaningful distinctions" between, on the one hand, component manufacturers and suppliers and, on the other hand, manufacturers and distributors of complete products; for both groups, the "overriding policy considerations are the same."

. . .

Insisting that they should not be held strictly liable, defendant window manufacturers point out that their windows are shipped in parts, assembled by others, and installed by others. They rely on language in Restatement Second of Torts.[24] [The Restatement (Second)] says that the seller of a defective product "is subject to liability for physical harm thereby caused to the ultimate user or consumer, or to his property, if 'it is expected to and does reach the user or consumer without substantial change in the condition in which it is sold.'" The mere assembly of a product that is sold in parts is not a "substantial change" in the product within the meaning of the Restatement.

**› RESULT** The window manufacturer was strictly liable for the damage caused by the defective windows.

23. 212 Cal. App. 3d 1131 (Cal. App. 1989).
24. *See* RESTATEMENT (SECOND) OF TORTS § 402A cmt. a (1997).

*(Continued)*

(Case 10.3 *continued*)

**› COMMENTS** The defendant relied upon language in the Second Restatement of Torts, but the court disagreed with the defendant's interpretation. A concurring opinion in the case cited the Third Restatement of Torts, discussed later in this chapter, which explicitly imposes tort liability on manufacturers of component parts:

> The manufacturer of a component part may be strictly liable in tort for physical injuries caused by defects in the component. As the Restatement Third of Torts[25] recognizes: "One engaged in the business of selling or otherwise distributing product components who sells or distributes a component is subject to liability for harm to persons or property caused by a product into which the component is integrated if: (a) the component is defective in itself . . . and the defect causes the harm."[26]

**› CRITICAL THINKING QUESTIONS**

1. A supercomputer is made up of several thousand microchips. If one chip, supplied to the computer company by a third-party manufacturer, fails, destroying the whole computer, can the third party be held liable by the owner of the computer?
2. At what point does a component cease to be a component and merely become part of the whole? From a public policy standpoint, should such a distinction exist at all?

25. *See* RESTATEMENT (THIRD) OF TORTS § 5 (1997).
26. *Id.*

---

A maker of component parts to a manufacturer's specifications is not liable for a defective design if the specifications for the entire product are questioned; such a shortcoming is considered to be the manufacturer's design defect. For example, the maker of a car's fuel-injection system will not be liable if the automaker's specifications for the fuel-injection system turn out to be defective and the engine provides insufficient power to change lanes safely on a freeway. Makers of component parts are liable for manufacturing defects, however.

## WHOLESALERS

Wholesalers are usually held strictly liable for defects in the products they sell. In some jurisdictions, however, a wholesaler is not liable for latent or hidden defects if the wholesaler sells the products in exactly the same condition it received them.

## RETAILERS

A retailer may also be held strictly liable. For example, in the automobile industry, retailers have a duty to inspect and care for the products. In several jurisdictions, however, a retailer will not be liable if it did not contribute to the defect and played no part in the manufacturing process.

## SELLERS OF USED GOODS AND OCCASIONAL SELLERS

Sellers of used goods are usually not held strictly liable because they are not within the original chain of distribution of the product.[27] In addition, the custom in the used-goods market is that there are no warranties or expectations relating to the quality of the products (although some jurisdictions have adopted rules requiring warranties for used cars). A seller of used goods is, however, strictly liable for any defective repairs or replacements he or she makes. Occasional sellers, such as people who host garage sales, are not strictly liable.

## SUCCESSOR LIABILITY

A corporation purchasing or acquiring the assets of another is liable for its debts if there is (1) a consolidation or merger[28] of the two corporations or (2) an express or implied agreement to assume such obligations. Many jurisdictions will also impose successor liability when (1) the purchasing corporation is merely a

27. Allenberg v. Bentley Hedges Travel Serv., Inc., 22 P.3d 223 (Okla. 2001).
28. The de facto merger doctrine is discussed in Chapter 19.

continuation of the selling corporation or (2) the transaction was entered into to escape liability.[29]

Thus, the acquiring corporation can be liable to a party injured by a defect in the transferor corporation's product. For example, a corporation that acquired all of a truck manufacturing company's assets was held liable for an injury caused by a defect in one of that company's trucks.[30] The court reasoned that the new company was essentially a continuation of the predecessor corporation and that the acquiring corporation was in a better position to bear and allocate the risk than the consumer.

## MARKET-SHARE LIABILITY

When there are multiple manufacturers of identical products, the injured party may not be able to prove which of the defendant manufacturers sold the product that caused the injury. In certain cases, particularly those involving prescription drugs, the court may allocate liability on the basis of each defendant's share of the market. This doctrine of *market-share liability* was developed by the California Supreme Court in *Sindell v. Abbott Laboratories*[31] to address the specific problem of DES litigation.

Women whose mothers took the drug diethylstilbestrol (DES) during pregnancy alleged that they were injured by the DES, which, among other things, increased their likelihood of developing cancer. They sought damages from a number of DES manufacturers. Many of the plaintiffs could not pinpoint which manufacturer was directly responsible for their injuries.

A number of factors made it difficult to identify particular DES manufacturers. All manufacturers made DES from an identical chemical formula. Druggists typically filled prescriptions from whatever stock they had on hand. During the twenty-four years that DES was sold for use during pregnancy, more than three hundred companies entered and left the market. The harmful effects of DES were not discovered until many years after the plaintiffs' mothers had used the drug.

By the time the lawsuit was filed, memories had faded, records had been lost, and witnesses had died. Given the difficulty of identifying the defendant responsible for each plaintiff, the court held that the fairest approach was to apportion liability based on each manufacturer's national market share. The court reasoned that it was more appropriate that the loss be borne by those who produced the drug than by those who suffered injury.

Although the New York Court of Appeals applied market-share liability in DES cases,[32] it characterized the DES situation as "a singular case." The Appellate Division of the Supreme Court of New York (New York's intermediate appeals court) refused to extend the doctrine to lead-based paints because (1) 20 percent of the lead pigments could have been manufactured by defendants not named in the litigation; (2) the plaintiffs were unable to identify the years in which the house was painted, making it impossible to determine which defendants manufactured paint during the relevant period; (3) lead-based paints were not uniform, fungible products; and (4) there was no signature injury in lead poisoning cases.[33]

In *Doe v. Baxter Healthcare Corp.*,[34] the U.S. Court of Appeals for the Eighth Circuit refused to apply market-share liability when a young boy became infected with HIV (human immunodeficiency virus) after using Factor VII, a drug for hemophiliacs. The parents of the boy claimed that one of several companies that produced Factor VII placed it on the market despite knowing of the risk of infection. The court determined that the plaintiffs did not present enough evidence to sustain the charges against any one defendant and therefore could not hold all of them responsible. In addition to finding that the plaintiffs had presented an insufficient factual case, the court generally rejected the theory of market-share liability on "broad policy grounds." Thus, market-share liability was considered an inappropriate basis for recovery.

Many jurisdictions have rejected market-share liability outright. It has been criticized for being a simplistic response to a complex problem and for implying that manufacturers must be the insurers of all their industry's products. Market-share liability has also been challenged on the constitutional ground that it violates a defendant's right to due process of law because it denies a defendant the opportunity to prove that its individual products did not cause the plaintiff's injury.

## PREMISES LIABILITY

Recently, courts have recognized liability for asbestos-related diseases on a *premises liability* theory. Under this theory, a building owner may be found liable for violating its general duty to manage the premises and warn of

29. Conway *ex rel.* Roadway Express, Inc. v. White Trucks, 639 F. Supp. 160 (M.D. Pa. 1986).
30. *Id.*
31. 607 P.2d 924 (Cal. 1980), *cert. denied*, 449 U.S. 912 (1980).
32. Hymowitz v. Eli Lilly & Co., 539 N.E.2d 1069 (N.Y. 1989), *cert. denied*, 493 U.S. 944 (1989).
33. Brenner v. Am. Cyanamid Co., 263 A.D.2d 165 (N.Y. App. 1999).
34. 380 F.3d 399 (8th Cir. 2004).

HISTORICAL PERSPECTIVE

## ASBESTOS LITIGATION

Asbestos litigation has been a high-profile topic for decades. As the timeline in Exhibit 10.1 shows, the targets of these suits have changed over the years as money and liability insurance have been depleted and companies, such as Johns Manville, have discharged their liability in bankruptcy. At least 90,000 new suits were filed in 2001 alone. Today, more than a quarter century after the first suits were filed, more asbestos-based suits are pending than ever before. The notes to the timeline indicate typical examples of the cases being brought during each period.[a]

**EXHIBIT 10.1** **Types of Asbestos Cases Over Time**

| 1970s | 1980s | 1990s→ |
|---|---|---|
| Asbestos manufacturers are sued directly in federal court by those who handled asbestos products.[b] | Owners of property where asbestos is located are sued by those who installed the asbestos or by workers exposed to asbestos.[c] | Small-business owners and businesses that incorporated asbestos products, even small ones, into other larger products are sued in state court.[d] |

a. This chart is based on data in Richard O. Faulk, *Asbestos Litigation in State Court,* 71 U.S.L.W. 2323 (Nov. 2002).
b. Borel v. Fibreboard Paper Prods. Corp., 493 F.2d 1076 (5th Cir. 1973) (upholding an insulation worker's successful suit against certain manufacturers of insulation materials containing asbestos to recover for injuries caused by defendants' alleged breach of duty in failing to warn of dangers involved in handling asbestos).
c. Cox v. Alloyd Insulation Co., Inc., WL 13621 (Ohio Ct. App. 1987). The Occupational Safety and Health Administration (OSHA) was created in part to regulate asbestos use and immediately passed regulations limiting asbestos exposure. But property owners who installed the material prior to the adoption of the regulations were still held liable for the damage they might have caused. *See* 36 Fed. Reg. 10,466, 10,506 (1971).
d. John Crane, Inc. v. Jones, WL 2495019 (Ga. 2004).

asbestos dangers.[35] Exhibit 10.1 illustrates how asbestos litigation has changed over the years.

# Defenses

The defendant in a product liability case may raise the traditional tort defenses of assumption of risk and, in some jurisdictions, a variation of comparative negligence known as comparative fault. Other defenses, such as obvious risk, unforeseeable misuse of the product, the statute of limitations, the government-contractor defense, and the state-of-the-art defense, may apply only to product liability cases. Acceptance of these defenses varies from state to state. Finally, under certain circumstances, state product liability law is preempted by federal law.

35. *CA App. Ct. Reverses Exxon Nonsuit Ruling*, ASBESTOS LITIG. REP., July 16, 1999.

## ASSUMPTION OF RISK

Under the doctrine of *assumption of risk,* when a person voluntarily and unreasonably assumes the risk of a known danger, the manufacturer is not liable for any resulting injury. For example, under Ohio law, if the claimant's express or implied assumption of risk is the direct and proximate cause of harm, then recovery is completely barred.[36] Thus, if a ladder bears a conspicuous warning not to stand on the top step, but a person steps on it anyway and falls, the ladder manufacturer will not be liable for any injuries caused by the fall.

In a leading case in this area, a Washington appellate court found no assumption of risk when a grinding disc

36. OHIO REV. CODE ANN. § 2315.42 (Anderson 2004).

exploded and hit a person in the eye.[37] The court reasoned that although the injured person should have been wearing goggles, he could not have anticipated that a hidden defect in the disc would cause it to explode. By not wearing goggles, the injured person assumed only the risk that dust or small particles of wood or metal would lodge in his eyes.

## Comparative Fault

Contributory negligence by the plaintiff is not a defense in a strict liability action. Nevertheless, in some states, the plaintiff's damages may be reduced by the degree to which his or her own negligence contributed to the injury. This doctrine is known as *comparative fault.*

For example, Michigan law provides that the negligence of the plaintiff does not bar recovery, but damages are reduced by his or her degree of fault—that is, the negligence attributed to the plaintiff.[38] Under Illinois law, if the jury finds that the degree of the plaintiff's fault exceeds 50 percent, then the plaintiff cannot recover damages. If the jury finds that the degree of the plaintiff's fault is less than 50 percent, the plaintiff can recover damages, but the damages will be reduced in proportion to the plaintiff's fault.[39]

## Obvious Risk

If the use of a product carries an *obvious risk,* the manufacturer will not be held liable for injuries that result from ignoring the risk. Although a plaintiff will argue that the manufacturer had a duty to warn of the dangers of a foreseeable use of the product, courts often apply the standard that a manufacturer need not warn of a certain danger if that danger is generally known and recognized.

For example, in *Maneely v. General Motors Corp.,*[40] two men who rode in the cargo bed of a pickup truck sued GM after sustaining serious injuries in a collision. The men argued that GM failed to warn of the dangers of riding in a cargo bed. The court rejected their claims, noting that a manufacturer should not bear the paternalistic responsibility of warning users of every possible risk that could arise from use of its product. As the public generally recognizes the dangers of riding unrestrained in the cargo bed of a moving pickup truck, GM had no duty to warn of those dangers.

## Unforeseeable Misuse of the Product

A manufacturer or seller is entitled to assume that its product will be used in a normal manner. The manufacturer or seller will not be held liable for injuries resulting from abnormal use of its product. For example, unforeseeable misuse of a product is a defense under Indiana law if it is the proximate cause of the harm and the misuse is not reasonably expected by the seller at the time the seller conveyed the product to another party.[41] An unusual use that is reasonably foreseeable may be considered a normal use.

For example, operating a lawn mower with the grass bag removed was held to be a foreseeable use, and the manufacturer was liable to a bystander injured by an object that shot out of the unguarded mower.[42] The alteration and misuse of fertilizer to create a bomb was not considered to be an "objectively foreseeable" result, however.[43] Thus, the owner of the World Trade Center could not hold fertilizer manufacturers liable for damages resulting from the 1993 terrorist bombing on grounds that they failed to use additives to make it more difficult to turn their products into explosives.

In the following case, the court considered whether a video game manufacturer was strictly liable for a teenager's shooting spree.

37. Haugen v. Minn. Mining & Mfg. Co., 550 P.2d 71 (Wash. App. 1976).
38. MICH. COMP. LAWS § 600.2959 (2004).
39. 735 ILL. COMP. STAT. ANN. 5/2-1116 (2004).
40. 108 F.3d 1176 (9th Cir. 1997).
41. IND. CODE ANN. § 34-20-6-4 (West 2004).
42. LaPaglia v. Sears Roebuck & Co., 531 N.Y.S.2d 623 (N.Y. App. Div. 1988).
43. Port Auth. of New York & New Jersey v. Arcadian Corp., 991 F. Supp. 309 (D.N.J. 1998), *aff'd,* 189 F.3d 305 (3d Cir. 1999).

A CASE IN POINT

**CASE 10.4**

**James v. Meow Media Inc.**

*United States Court of Appeals for the Sixth Circuit 300 F.3d 683 (6th Cir. 2002), cert. denied, 537 U.S. 1159 (2003).*

## Summary

**› FACTS** In 2002, a teenager in Kentucky went on a shooting spree, killing a number of his classmates at the high school he attended. The families of the victims brought this suit against Meow Media, Inc., a video game distributor that makes and sells video games. The families claimed that the defendant's games desensitized the shooter to violence, thereby leading to the tragedy.

*(Continued)*

(Case 10.4 *continued*)

› **ISSUE PRESENTED** Is the creator of a video game, movie, or Internet site that contains violent images and themes liable under either a theory of negligence or a strict product liability claim when children who view these images act violently?

› **SUMMARY OF OPINION** The U.S. Court of Appeals for the Sixth Circuit first addressed the negligence claim. In order to prove negligence, the plaintiffs needed to prove three separate elements: (1) the defendants owed a duty of care to the victims, (2) they breached that duty of care, and (3) that breach was the proximate cause of the injury.

To find a duty of care, the plaintiffs had to show that the shooter's actions were reasonably foreseeable by the defendant. After a lengthy discussion, the court concluded that the shooting was so aberrant as to be unforeseeable by the video game producer. Furthermore, there is a general rule, with few exceptions, that no one is responsible for the "intentional criminal acts of a third party." In this case, the shooter's intentional act of murder, regardless of the situation, made his act unforeseeable to the defendant. Since there was no duty of care, the defendant could not have breached a duty of care to the victims.

The court then considered whether the plaintiffs had proved proximate cause. Proximate cause is the establishment of a direct connection between the action (the shooting) and the defendant's conduct (distributing video games). The court returned to the fact that the shooter's actions were intentional criminal acts and found, in keeping with a century of precedent, that a third party's criminal act functions as an intervening act, rendering all actions before that act not the proximate cause of the injury.

The court also addressed the defendant's actions in light of the First Amendment guarantees of free speech and expression. Like virtually all U.S. courts, the Sixth Circuit was "loathe to attach tort liability to the dissemination of ideas."

Finally, the court characterized the plaintiffs' theory that the defendant's works were defective products as "deeply flawed." In a prior case decided more than a decade before, the court had ruled that the "words and pictures" contained in the board game *Dungeons and Dragons* were not products. In light of the changing times and rash of school shootings, the court revisited the issue rather than flatly rejecting the claim based on its earlier ruling. Nonetheless, it concluded that the same logic should apply in this case.

› **RESULT** The plaintiffs had no valid product liability claim. Their suit was dismissed.

## Government-Contractor Defense

Under the *government-contractor defense*, a manufacturer of products under contract to the government can avoid product liability if (1) the product was produced according to government specifications, (2) the manufacturer possessed less knowledge about the specifications than did the government agency, (3) the manufacturer exercised proper skill and care in production, and (4) the manufacturer did not deviate from the specifications. The rationale for this immunity is that the manufacturer is acting merely as an agent of the government; to hold the manufacturer liable would unfairly shift the insurance burden from the government to the manufacturer. As discussed below, the Homeland Security Act extended this defense to certain products designed to thwart terrorists.

## State-of-the-Art Defense

In some states, the *state-of-the-art defense* shields a manufacturer from liability for a defective design if no safer product design is generally recognized as being possible. As discussed further below, the Restatement (Third) would require plaintiffs in defective design cases to prove the existence of an alternative design.

The contours of the state-of-the-art defense are often first laid down by judges, then codified by state legislatures. For example, an Arizona statute provides a defense "if the plans or designs for the product or the methods and techniques of manufacturing, inspecting, testing and labeling the product conformed with the state of the art at the time the product was first sold by defendant."[44]

State courts have split over how to analyze this defense on two grounds. First, states have defined "state of the art" differently. Some states have defined state-of-the-art evidence either in terms of industry custom (e.g., Alaska and New Jersey) or in terms of compliance with existing governmental regulations (e.g., Illinois).[45] A majority of the states that accept the state-of-the-art defense, however, deem "state-of-the-art" to refer to what is technologically feasible at the time of design. Accordingly, a manufacturer may have a duty to use a safer design even if the custom of the industry is to use a less safe alternative.[46]

Second, the states have also split on whether to even allow the defense in defective design cases. Some courts have ruled that state-of-the-art evidence is irrelevant in strict product liability cases because it improperly focuses the jury's attention on the reasonableness of the manufacturer's conduct. The overwhelming majority of the states, however, hold that state-of-the-art evidence is relevant simply to determining the adequacy of the product's design. As the Connecticut Supreme Court concluded, "state of the art is a relevant factor in considering the adequacy of the design of a product and whether it is in a defective condition unreasonably dangerous to the ordinary consumer."[47]

The state-of-the art defense has also been applied in failure-to-warn cases. For example, a Missouri statute provides that if the defendant can prove that the dangerous nature of the product was not known and could not reasonably have been discovered at the time the product was placed in the stream of commerce, then the defendant will not be held liable for failure to warn.[48]

## Preemption Defense

Perhaps the most significant and controversial of the defenses to product liability is the *preemption defense.* Certain federal laws and regulations set minimum safety standards for products. For example, the National Traffic and Motor Vehicle Safety Act sets standards for auto manufacturers, and the Safe Medical Devices Act sets standards for the manufacture of medical devices. Manufacturers that meet those standards will sometimes be granted immunity from product liability claims based on state law on the grounds of federal preemption. The rationale for deferring to the federal regulatory scheme is that allowing states to impose fifty different sets of requirements would frustrate the purpose of a uniform federal scheme.

Unable to obtain sweeping tort reform, U.S. firms are increasingly lobbying for riders to congressional bills to exempt particular products and industries from product liability claims brought under state law. For example, Eli Lilly persuaded Congress to add a rider to the Homeland Security Act of 2002[49] to protect drug companies from certain liability suits.

The SAFETY Act[50] (1) grants exclusive federal jurisdiction over sellers of "qualified anti-terrorism technology"; (2) limits the liability of sellers of qualified anti-terrorism technologies to an amount of liability insurance coverage specified for each individual technology; (3) prohibits joint and several liability for noneconomic damages, so sellers are liable only for the percentage of noneconomic damages that is proportionate to their responsibility for the harm; (4) bars punitive damages and prejudgment interest; and (5) creates a

### IN BRIEF
**Bases for Product Liability and Defenses**

| Theory of Liability | Defenses |
|---|---|
| Breach of warranty | No privity of contract |
| Negligence | Defendant used reasonable care |
| | Contributory or comparative negligence |
| Strict liability in tort | Unavoidably unsafe product |
| | Comparative fault (only reduces damages) |
| | Assumption of risk |
| | Obvious risk |
| | Abnormal misuse |
| | Government contractor |
| | State of the art |
| | Preemption |

44. Ariz. Rev. Stat. § 12-683(1) (2000).
45. *See* Potter v. Chicago Pneumatic Tool Co., 694 A.2d 1319 (Conn. 1997).
46. *Id.* at 1347.
47. *Id.*
48. Mo. Rev. Stat. § 537.764 (1999).
49. Pub. L. 107–296, 116 Stat. 2229.
50. Support Antiterrorism by Fostering Effective Technologies Act, Pub. L. 107–296, 116 Stat. 2238, §§ 861–865. *See also* 6 C.F.R. Pt. 25.3.

rebuttable presumption that the seller is entitled to the "government-contractor defense," provided that its "qualified anti-terrorism technology" is certified by the Department of Homeland Security as an "Approved Product for Homeland Security."

Manufacturing groups want preemption to serve as a "silver bullet" defense, effectively eliminating the possibility of state law product liability claims in any sphere governed by federal safety law and regulation. Commenting on a medical-device case before the U.S. Supreme Court, one of the manufacturers' most vocal representatives put the argument this way: "What it boils down to is whether we want to have the experts at the FDA tell us what is a safe pacemaker, or do we want each jury designing its own pacemaker—one doing it one way in Brooklyn and one doing it another way in Missouri?"[51]

In practice, the availability of the preemption defense depends largely on the language and context of the federal statute at issue. In recent years, courts have struggled to determine whether federal safety statutes preempt state product liability claims involving tobacco, faulty medical devices, and automobiles without air bags.

In *Cipollone v. Liggett Group, Inc.* (a 1992 decision), the Supreme Court concluded that Congress intended the Public Health Cigarette Smoking Act of 1969 to have a broad preemptive effect.[52] In particular, the Court held that the Act preempted claims based on a failure to warn and the neutralization of federally mandated warnings to the extent that those claims relied on omissions or inclusions in a tobacco company's advertising or promotions. The Court ruled that the Act did not preempt claims based on express warranty, intentional fraud and misrepresentation, or conspiracy, however.

Four years later, in *Medtronic, Inc. v. Lohr*,[53] the Court examined similar statutory language in the Medical Device Amendments of 1976 and found no preemption. *Medtronic* involved a pacemaker that the Food and Drug Administration (FDA) had cleared for distribution under a statutory provision requiring premarket notification for some types of medical devices. *Medtronic* makes it clear that compliance with a regulatory scheme is not always a valid defense. In general, however, the more rigorous the regulatory process, the more likely that product liability claims will be preempted. In *Medtronic*, the FDA had not closely scrutinized the pacemaker: the device had received an exemption from thorough review because it was deemed "substantially equivalent" to pacemakers already on the market. The fact that the pacemaker had not undergone rigorous regulatory examination was an important factor in the Court's decision not to preempt product liability claims against Medtronic.[54]

In the following case, the Supreme Court resolved the question of whether state product liability "no air bag" claims were preempted by federal requirements for passive restraints in automobiles.

51. Paul M. Barrett, *Lora Lohr's Pacemaker May Alter Liability Law*, WALL ST. J., Apr. 9, 1996, at B1 (quoting Victor Schwartz).
52. 505 U.S. 504 (1992).
53. 518 U.S. 470 (1996).
54. This interpretation is supported by the FDA's proposal of regulations that serve to clarify its position.

A CASE IN POINT

## In the Language of the Court

**CASE 10.5**
**Geier v. American Honda Motor Co.**
*Supreme Court of the United States*
*529 U.S. 861 (2000).*

**› FACTS** While driving a 1987 Honda Accord, Alexis Geier crashed into a tree and was seriously injured. Although the car had manual shoulder and lap belts that Geier was using at the time of the accident, it had no air bags or other passive restraint devices. Geier and her parents sued American Honda under state law for failing to include a driver's side air bag.

Federal Motor Vehicle Safety Standard (FMVSS) 208, promulgated pursuant to the National Traffic and Motor Vehicle Safety Act, required auto manufacturers to equip 10 percent of their national fleet of cars with passive restraints but did not require air bags. The district court dismissed the plaintiff's claim on the grounds that it was preempted by federal law. The U.S. court of appeals affirmed, and the Geiers appealed.

**› ISSUE PRESENTED** Does the Safety Act preempt state tort claims based upon a manufacturer's failure to equip a vehicle with air bags?

**› OPINION** BREYER, J., writing for the U.S. Supreme Court:

*(Continued)*

(Case 10.5 *continued*)

The basic question . . . is whether a common-law "no airbag" action like the one before us actually conflicts with FMVSS 208. We hold that it does.

[The Department of Transportation's] comments, which accompanied the promulgation of FMVSS 208, make clear that the standard deliberately provided the manufacturer with a range of choices among different passive restraint devices. Those choices would bring about a mix of different devices introduced gradually over time; and FMVSS 208 would thereby lower costs, overcome technical safety problems, encourage technological development, and win widespread consumer acceptance—all of which would promote FMVSS 208's safety objectives. . . .

. . .

[P]etitioners' tort action depends upon its claim that manufacturers had a duty to install an airbag when they manufactured the 1987 Honda Accord. Such a state law—i.e., a rule of state tort law imposing such a duty—by its terms would have required manufacturers of all similar cars to install airbags rather than other passive restraint systems, such as automatic belts or passive interiors. It thereby would have presented an obstacle to the variety and mix of devices that the federal regulation sought. It would have required all manufacturers to have installed airbags in respect to the entire District-of-Columbia-related portion of their 1987 new car fleet, even though FMVSS 208 at that time required only that 10% of a manufacturer's nationwide fleet be equipped with any passive restraint device at all. It thereby also would have stood as an obstacle to the gradual passive restraint phase-in that the federal regulation deliberately imposed. In addition, it could have made less likely the adoption of a state mandatory buckle-up law. Because the rule of law for which petitioners contend would have stood "as an obstacle to the accomplishment and execution of" the important means-related federal objectives that we have just discussed, it is preempted.

**› RESULT** The Supreme Court held that the state product liability claims asserted by the Geiers conflicted with the objectives of FMVSS 208 and were preempted by the Safety Act. The claims were dismissed.

**› CRITICAL THINKING QUESTIONS**

1. Why were state mandatory buckle-up laws not preempted by federal standards?
2. Must a conflict between state and federal law exist for preemption to occur?

## Other Legislative Limits on Liability

Legislative reforms continue in response to large jury awards, perceived inconsistent treatment of litigants, and the insurance crisis of the 1980s, which made it prohibitively expensive or impossible to obtain product liability insurance in some industries. For example, states have enacted legislation to limit nonmanufacturers' and joint liability and to cap punitive damages.

### Limitations on Nonmanufacturers' Liability

Rather than holding all companies in the chain of distribution liable, many states limit the liability of nonmanufacturers. For example, a Minnesota statute provides that once an injured person files a claim against the manufacturer of the product, the court must dismiss the strict liability claim against any other defendants. A nonmanufacturer can be held strictly liable, however, if it was involved in the design or manufacture of the product or provided instructions or warnings about the defect, or if it knew of or created the defect. The nonmanufacturer may also be held strictly liable if the manufacturer is no longer in business or if it cannot satisfy a judgment against it.[55]

An Illinois statute provides that an action against a defendant other than the manufacturer will be dismissed unless the plaintiff can show that (1) the defendant had some control over the design or manufacture of the product, or instructed or warned the manufacturer about the alleged defect; (2) the defendant actually knew of the defect; or (3) the defendant created the defect.[56]

### LIMITATIONS ON JOINT LIABILITY

Traditionally, all defendants in a strict liability action were held jointly and severally liable. Each defendant was held liable not only for the injuries it severally—that is, individually—caused, but also for all of the injuries caused by all of the defendants jointly.

At least thirty-eight states have placed limits on joint and several liability, and many have abolished joint liability altogether.[57] For example, an Oregon statute limits joint and several liability as follows:

> Liability of each defendant for non-economic damages is several, not joint. Liability of a defendant who is less than 15% at fault for economic damages is several only. Liability of a defendant who is 15% or more at fault for the economic damages is joint and several, except that a defendant whose fault is less than the plaintiff's is liable only for that percentage of the recoverable economic damages.[58]

### CAPS ON PUNITIVE DAMAGES

Large awards of punitive damages have been criticized for providing windfalls to injured parties far in excess of their actual losses and for motivating plaintiffs and their lawyers to engage in expensive and wasteful litigation rather than settling the case.

More than thirty states have enacted legislation limiting punitive damages awards. These reforms have typically taken three basic forms. Some states have placed limits on when punitive damages are available or require a higher standard of evidence (such as clear and convincing evidence rather than a mere preponderance of evidence) before punitives will be awarded. For example, North Dakota requires plaintiffs to prove oppression, fraud, or actual malice before claiming punitive damages. Other states have placed outright caps on punitive damages (Georgia, for instance, caps punitives at $250,000) or have tied punitive damages to compensatory damages (in Florida, for example, punitives cannot exceed three times compensatory damages). Finally, a few states (such as New Hampshire) have banned punitive awards altogether.

As explained in Chapter 2, the U.S. Supreme Court ruled, in *State Farm Mutual Automobile Insurance Co. v. Campbell*,[59] that punitive damages should be less than ten times the award of compensatory damages. In December 2004, President George W. Bush announced a plan to pass federal legislation to cap punitive damages in many cases.[60] For the foreseeable future, however, the United States will remain one of the few countries that allows juries to award punitive damages.[61]

### PENALTIES FOR FRIVOLOUS SUITS

Some states have enacted penalties to deter frivolous lawsuits. For example, a Wisconsin statute provides that if a claim or defense is found to be frivolous, the prevailing party can be awarded its legal costs and attorneys' fees.[62] Minnesota and South Dakota passed similar legislation in 1997.

##  Statutes of Limitations, Revival Statutes, and Statutes of Repose

Statutes of limitations, revival statutes, and statutes of repose affect the time within which a product liability suit must be brought.

### STATUTES OF LIMITATIONS

A *statute of limitations* is a time limit, defined by the statute, within which a lawsuit must be brought. Ordinarily, the statute of limitations starts to run at the time a person is injured. There are exceptions, however. In many cases involving exposure to asbestos, for example, the plaintiff did not become aware of the injury until

55. MINN. STAT. § 544.41 (2003).
56. 735 ILL. COMP. STAT. ANN. 5/2-621 (2004).
57. David Olsen, *Minnesota: Key Reform Bills Head for State Senate*, METROPOLITAN CORP. COUNS., Feb. 2000.
58. OR. REV. STAT. § 18.485 (2003).
59. 538 U.S. 1028 (2003).
60. Peter H. Stone, *Putting a Price Tag on Pain and Suffering*, NAT'L L. J. (Jan. 8, 2005).
61. *See, generally*, KIP VISCUSI & CASS SUNSTEIN, PUNITIVE DAMAGES: HOW JURIES DECIDE (2002).
62. WIS. STAT. § 814.025 (2003).

after the statute of limitations had run out. This situation led to the adoption of *discovery-of-injury statutes,* which generally provide that the statute of limitations for asbestos claims does not begin to run until the person discovers the injury from exposure to asbestos.

## Revival Statutes

When information about the prenatal injuries caused by the drug DES emerged, state legislatures passed *revival statutes* permitting plaintiffs to file lawsuits that had previously been barred by the running of the statute of limitations. DES manufacturers argued that the revival statutes violated their rights to due process of law and to equal protection of the laws because the statutes typically apply to only a few substances, such as DES or asbestos, and not to other dangerous chemical substances. The manufacturers claimed that this categorization was without sufficient basis and that it was the result of political compromise. Most courts rejected these arguments and held that state revival statutes have a rational basis and that legislatures enacting such statutes are acting within their broad discretion.[63] More recently, revival statutes have been enacted to extend the time in which women may sue for injuries caused by silicone breast implants.

As injuries are increasingly being discovered long after exposure, many states have amended their statutes of limitations to define more precisely when a cause of action arises. For example, the Ohio statute provides that:

- An asbestos cause of action arises when the claimant learns or should have realized that he or she was injured by exposure to asbestos, whichever is earlier.
- An Agent Orange cause of action involving exposure of a veteran to chemical defoliants or herbicides arises when the claimant learns that he or she was injured by the exposure.
- A DES cause of action arises when the claimant learns from a physician that her injury might be related to DES exposure or when she should have realized that she had such an injury, whichever is earlier.[64]

## Statutes of Repose

A *statute of repose* cuts off the right to assert a cause of action after a specified period of time from the delivery of the product or the completion of the work. A statute of repose is different from a statute of limitations, which measures the time period from the time when the injury occurred. Thus, under a statute of repose, if the repose period is ten years, a person injured eleven years after the product was delivered would be time-barred from suing by the statute of repose, though not by the statute of limitations.

For example, Cessna and other light airplane manufacturers lobbied hard for the General Aviation Revitalization Act, which was enacted in 1994. The Act created an eighteen-year statute of repose limiting an aircraft manufacturer's liability for performance of an aircraft after the first eighteen years of the aircraft's life. Because the average aircraft was thirty years old in 1994, the Act significantly limited the product liability exposure of aircraft manufacturers.[65]

Statutes of repose have usually been upheld on the ground that they serve some legitimate state purpose, such as encouraging manufacturers to upgrade their products. Absent a statute of repose, a manufacturer might not upgrade, out of fear that upgrading might be seen as an admission that the earlier version was inadequate.

# Tobacco and Guns

One of the most dramatic applications of product liability law has been the lawsuits against tobacco companies for illness, death, and medical expenses resulting from the use of tobacco or from secondhand smoke. In November 1998, forty-six states that had filed claims to recover billions they had spent on health-care costs related to smoking settled with the tobacco industry for $206 billion—the largest civil settlement in U.S. history.[66] Four other states had previously entered into settlements with tobacco companies totaling $40 billion. In September 1999, the federal government filed a similar suit to recover the more than $20 billion that the government spends every year to care for individuals who have health problems caused by smoking and use of tobacco.[67]

Litigation against the tobacco industry is not limited to the United States. The governments of Guatemala, Venezuela, Bolivia, and Nicaragua filed claims in the federal district court in Washington, D.C., in an effort to

63. *See, e.g.,* Hymowitz v. Eli Lilly & Co., 539 N.E.2d 1069 (N.Y. 1989), *cert. denied,* 493 U.S. 944 (1989).
64. Ohio Rev. Code Ann. § 2305.10 (Anderson 2000).

65. Allen Michel et al., *Protecting Future Product Liability Claimants,* Am. Bankr. Inst. J., Dec. 1999, at 3–4.
66. Milo Geyelin, *States Agree to $206 Billion Tobacco Deal,* Wall St. J., Nov. 23, 1998, at B13.
67. *Tobacco Industry Hits Home on Federal Lawsuit,* Dow Jones Int'l, June 24, 2000.

recover health-care expenses related to smoking.[68] Similar suits have been filed in the courts of other countries as well. In addition, individual suits have been brought against the tobacco industry in a number of countries including Argentina, Canada, Germany, Ireland, Israel, Japan, Sri Lanka, Thailand, and Turkey.

After the enormous success of the litigation against the tobacco industry, cities and counties launched a similar attack against the gun industry. Unlike the tobacco industry, however, which has companies with deep pockets and many assets to satisfy damage claims, the gun industry is composed of generally small, mostly privately held companies with annual sales of only $2.5 billion.[69] Nuisance suits against gun manufacturers are discussed in Chapter 9.

In early 2000, two Clinton administration lawyers—the deputy general counsel of Housing and Urban Development and the general counsel at the Treasury Department, which helped oversee the Bureau of Alcohol, Tobacco and Firearms—presented a list of gun-control demands to Ed Schultz, the CEO of Smith & Wesson Corporation. Smith & Wesson, a unit of Britain's Tomkins PLC, is America's largest maker of handguns. Schultz initially answered by asking one of the lawyers how old he was. When the lawyer answered that he was thirty-four years old, Schultz said, "If you live a good long life, you will not live to see this proposal happen." Two months later, however, Smith & Wesson agreed to a settlement based upon that initial proposal.

Smith & Wesson agreed to make a number of changes, including the following:

- All guns would be shipped with external child safety locks.
- Within two years, all pistols would be manufactured with internal safety locks.
- Within one year, all firearms would be made child-proof.
- Handguns would have to pass a stringent performance test.
- The company would devote 2 percent of its gross revenues to developing a "smart" gun that can be fired only by its owner.

The company also agreed to develop a code of conduct for its dealers and distributors that would require background checks on purchases and would forbid sales to anyone who had not passed a safety exam or taken a training class.

Commentators have compared Smith & Wesson's settlement to Liggett Group's decision to break ranks with the other tobacco companies and settle its tobacco cases. But whereas Liggett was a small tobacco company, Smith & Wesson is one of the most powerful companies in the gun industry. Eliot Spitzer, the New York attorney general who was involved in designing the Smith & Wesson settlement, commented, "The idea all along was that one responsible company would break away from the rest of the industry and that would be leverage to use against the rest."[70]

The gun industry sharply criticized Smith & Wesson. The head of the National Shooting Sports Foundation, which represents all major gun makers, stated that Smith & Wesson's decision to settle "violated a trust with their consumers and with the entire domestic firearms industry." He also charged that the company had "run off and cut their own deal" in a manner that "fractures the unity we had since the first lawsuit was filed in October 1998."[71] Some claimed that Smith & Wesson's settlement amounts to an admission that guns can be made safer, thus undermining the industry's long-held position that companies have no obligation to make naturally dangerous products safer.

Commentators outside the gun industry also criticized the Smith & Wesson deal as an undemocratic way of making public policy.[72] They argued that the Clinton administration, frustrated with the partisan gridlock in Congress preventing the enactment of gun-control legislation, used litigation to establish new regulations for the gun industry.[73] "This is backdoor gun control through coercion and through threat of litigation," said one member of Congress.[74] Indeed, Representative Bob Barr of Georgia, who is also a member of the National Rifle Association's board of directors, introduced legislation in Congress to ban lawsuits against the gun industry. Others, however, applauded the ability of private

68. Richard A. Daynard, *Litigants Worldwide Blaming then Branding Big Tobacco in Court,* WORLDPAPER, June 1, 2000.

69. Paul Barret, *As Lawsuits Loom, Gun Industry Presents a Fragmented Front,* WALL ST. J., Dec. 9, 1998, at A1.

70. Paul M. Barrett, Vanessa O'Connell, & Joe Mathews, *Glock May Accept Handgun Restrictions—Austrian Firm May Follow Lead of Smith & Wesson to Avoid U.S. Sanctions,* WALL ST. J., Mar. 20, 2000, at A3.

71. Sharon Walsh, *Gun Industry Views Pact as Threat to Its Unity,* WASH. POST, Mar. 18, 2000, at A10.

72. Stuart Taylor, *Guns and Tobacco: Government by Litigation,* NAT'L L. J., Mar. 25, 2000.

73. Walter K. Olson, *Plaintiffs' Lawyers Take Aim at Democracy,* WALL ST. J., Mar. 21, 2000, at A26.

74. Alan Fram, *House Kills Effort to Scuttle Safety Pact with Smith & Wesson,* ASSOC. PRESS NEWSWIRE, June 27, 2000.

litigation to succeed in an area where Congress, locked in partisan gridlock, had failed.[75]

Recently, however, gun-control advocates have experienced setbacks. In 2003, the City of Cincinnati dropped its product liability and nuisance suit against gun makers.[76] The controversial suit had been ongoing for four years and managed to survive motions to dismiss, but ultimately the City determined that the litigation was simply too expensive and wasteful of public funds.

## Product Liability Class Actions

Product liability cases are frequently resolved through class actions, a procedural device that allows a large number of plaintiffs to recover against a defendant in a single case. Lawsuits involving the tobacco industry, asbestos, silicone breast implants, and harmful diet drugs were all resolved through class actions.

In *Amchem Products, Inc. v. Windsor*,[77] the U.S. Supreme Court tightened the requirements for certification of a class of plaintiffs suing asbestos manufacturers. The proposed class included individuals who had not previously sued asbestos manufacturers and either (1) had been exposed to asbestos by the asbestos manufacturers through their occupations or the occupation of a household member or (2) had a spouse or family member who had been exposed to asbestos. The Court denied the class certification because the class members had differing interests. For example, those individuals who were currently injured would seek immediate payment, whereas those who had been exposed and were anticipating future injury would seek a fund for future compensation. The Court identified additional differences as well to support its denial of class certification.

Rule 23(b)(1)(B) of the Federal Rules of Civil Procedure provides a mechanism to resolve class actions in which the total of the aggregated liquidated claims exceeds the fund available to satisfy them (*limited fund class actions*). In *Ortiz v. Fibreboard Corp.*,[78] another asbestos class action, the Supreme Court made it clear that the trial court itself must determine whether the fund is limited. Thus, it was improper for the trial court to simply accept an agreement among the lead plaintiffs, the insurance companies, and the manufacturer as to the maximum amount the insurance companies could be required to pay tort victims.

In some class actions, the class may base its suit on the anticipation of illness or physical injury resulting from drug ingestion or exposure to a toxic product. In other words, no actual injury or illness has yet emerged. In *Petito v. A.H. Robins Co.*,[79] the Florida Court of Appeal recognized a cause of action for "medical monitoring" for plaintiffs who had been prescribed the weight-loss drugs Fenfluramine and Phentermine. Although they had no physical injuries, the class members argued that taking the drugs had placed them at a substantially increased risk of developing serious cardiac and circulatory damage, including heart valve damage. Therefore, the class sought to require the drug manufacturers and sellers to pay for a court-supervised medical monitoring program. The program would provide for medical testing, monitoring, and study of the class. The court found for the plaintiffs and commented, "[O]ne can hardly dispute that an individual has just as great an interest in avoiding expensive diagnostic examinations as in avoiding physical injury."[80]

But the Ohio Supreme Court refused to certify a class of more than 4,000 workers exposed to beryllium at an Ohio job site who were seeking the creation of a medical monitoring program.[81] The court concluded that "lack of cohesiveness is fatal." The members of the proposed class spanned forty-six years, multiple contractors, and multiple locations within the plant. As a result, the individual questions outweighed the questions common to the class.

## Problems with the Product Liability System and the Restatement (Third) Approach to Design Defects

The product liability scheme that has evolved has increasingly been criticized because of the financial burden it imposes on industry. The cornerstone of the scheme is the assumption that manufacturers are in the best position to insure against loss or to spread the risk of loss among their customers. Nevertheless, the costs to manufacturers—huge jury awards and high insurance premiums—have been enormous. Moreover, manufacturers often find it difficult to obtain an insurance policy

75. *Id.*
76. 71 U.S.L.W. 2750 (May 27, 2003).
77. 521 U.S. 591 (1997).
78. 527 U.S. 815 (1999).
79. 750 So. 2d 103 (Fla. App. 1999).
80. *Id.* at 105.
81. Wilson v. Brush Wellman Inc., No. 2003-0048 (Ohio Nov. 17, 2004).

### ETHICAL CONSIDERATION

In September 2004, the pharmaceutical giant Merck & Co. recalled one of its most profitable and widely used drugs, Vioxx, after finding that the arthritis drug increased the risk of heart attacks and strokes in patients who took it for more than eighteen months. Merck's stock dropped from around $45 before the Vioxx fiasco to less than $26 after the company disclosed that as of October 31, 2004, it was the defendant in about 375 Vioxx personal-injury lawsuits, involving about 1,000 plaintiff groups.[a] Merck has about $630 million in product liability insurance, far less than the potential product liability exposure of $12 billion estimated by Richard Evans, a drug industry analyst with Sanford Bernstein. In early November 2004, the *Wall Street Journal* described Merck documents and e-mails that raised the possibility that Merck may have known more about the risks of Vioxx than it had previously acknowledged.[b] Merck also announced that the U.S. Justice Department had launched a criminal probe into its handling of Vioxx and that the Securities and Exchange Commission had begun an informal inquiry into whether Merck fully informed investors about the risks identified in the research on Vioxx.

Individuals who took Vioxx and were either demonstrably injured or now must spend money on medical monitoring must decide whether to join in a single class-action lawsuit against the company to recover their medical costs. Plaintiffs' lawyers began running advertisements to encourage potential plaintiffs to sue Merck individually and settle before a class-action suit can be brought.[c] The theory is that individuals suing the company will end up with much larger cash settlements. Is it ethical for attorneys or other groups to try to persuade former Vioxx users to attempt to settle separately? Is it ethical for Merck to pay money to individual claimants without first ascertaining its full exposure?

a. Scott Hensley, *Merck Faces Twin Vioxx Inquiries,* WALL ST. J., Nov. 9, 2004, at A3.
b. *Id.*
c. For examples of such advertising, see http://vioxxnews.x.yi.org and http://www.lawyervioxx.com/.

that does not include a substantial deductible, which the manufacturer must pay. Sometimes insurance is not available at all, and companies have to pay all claims themselves. This leads to higher manufacturing costs.

The product liability scheme also takes its toll on industry efficiency and competitiveness. Companies have become unwilling to invest in product creation or modification because this may be seen as an admission of guilt. In most jurisdictions, product modification is admissible as evidence of the product's prior defective condition. Companies find themselves in a no-win situation: failure to remedy a defect may expose the company to punitive damages, but remedying the defect may expose the company to compensatory damages in subsequent suits.

## RESTATEMENT (THIRD) OF TORTS: PRODUCT LIABILITY

Informed by these concerns, the American Law Institute (ALI) completed its five-year effort to synthesize the current case law of product liability and approved the Restatement (Third) of Torts: Product Liability in 1997. The new Restatement proposes bold changes in the doctrine of product liability. Most importantly, it requires that any claim of design defect be supported by a showing of a reasonable alternative design. The effect of this change is to move away from strict liability for defectively designed products. (The new Restatement avoids using the term *strict liability* altogether.) Instead, the reasonable-alternative-design requirement forces plaintiffs to prove that defendants acted wrongly or negligently in choosing an improper design.

In many respects, those who failed in their ardent attempts to push tort and product liability reform through Congress saw their ideas embodied in the new Restatement. Indeed, the most vocal critics of the Restatement (Third) charged that the effort had been captured by defense attorneys seeking to accomplish through the ALI what they could not achieve on Capitol Hill.

As noted earlier, no court is bound by the Restatement's formulation of product liability law. As of late 2004, only a minority of states had adopted the Restatement (Third) approach, either in whole or in part. In the following case, the Supreme Court of Iowa considered whether to accept the Restatement (Third)'s reasonable-alternative-design test.

A CASE IN POINT

### In the Language of the Court

**CASE 10.6**
**Wright v. Brooke Group Ltd.**
*Supreme Court of Iowa*
*652 N.W.2d 159 (Iowa 2002).*

› **FACTS** Robert and DeAnn Wright filed a lawsuit against all cigarette manufacturers alleging, among other things, a design defect in cigarettes that made them unreasonably dangerous. The defendants asked the Iowa Supreme Court to rule on the elements necessary to establish liability for a design defect.

*(Continued)*

(Case 10.6 *continued*)

**› ISSUE PRESENTED** Under Iowa law, may defendants rely on Comment 1 of Section 402A of the Restatement (Second) of Torts to show that cigarettes are unreasonably dangerous, or should the court adopt the Restatement (Third) approach, which requires the plaintiff to show the existence of a reasonable alternative design before a product will be deemed unreasonably dangerous?

**› OPINION** TERNUS, J., writing for the Iowa Supreme Court:

The Iowa Supreme Court first applied strict liability in tort for a product defect in 1970, adopting Restatement (Second) of Torts. Section 402A of the Restatement (Second) provides:

> Special Liability of Seller of Product for Physical Harm to User or Consumer:
>
> (1) one who sells any product in a defective condition unreasonably dangerous to the user or consumer or to his property is subject to liability for physical harm thereby caused to the ultimate user or consumer, or to his property. . . .

Our purpose in adopting this provision was to relieve injured plaintiffs of the burden of proving the elements of warranty or negligence theories, thereby insuring that the costs of injuries resulting from defective products are borne by the manufacturers that put such products on the market.

. . .

[The defendant] suggests this case presents an appropriate opportunity for the court to adopt the principles of law set forth in § 2 of Restatement (Third) of Torts.

In determining what test should be applied in assessing whether cigarettes are unreasonably dangerous, we are confronted with the anomaly of using a risk/benefit analysis for purposes of strict liability based on defective design that is identical to the test employed in proving negligence in product design. This incongruity has drawn our attention once again to the debate over whether the distinction between strict liability and negligence theories should be maintained when applied to a design defect case. We are convinced such a distinction is illusory. . . . Because the Products Restatement [Third] is consistent with our conclusion, we think it sets forth an intellectually sound set of legal principles for product defect cases.

The Products Restatement demonstrates a recognition that strict liability is appropriate in manufacturing defect cases, but negligence principles are more suitable for other defective product cases. . . . Accordingly, it establish[es] separate standards of liability for manufacturing defects, design defects, and defects based on inadequate instructions or warnings.

One engaged in the business of selling or otherwise distributing products who sells or distributes a defective product is subject to liability for harm to persons or property caused by the defect. . . . The "unreasonably dangerous" element of Restatement (Second) section 402A has been eliminated and has been replaced with a multifaceted definition of defective product. This definition is set out in section 2 of the Restatement (Third):

> A product is defective when, at the time of sale or distribution, it contains a manufacturing defect, is defective in design, or is defective because of inadequate instructions or warning.

[Note that the unreasonably dangerous requirement no longer exists.]

. . .

*(Continued)*

(Case 10.6 *continued*)

In summary, we now adopt Restatement (Third) of Torts sections 1 and 2 for product defect cases. Under these sections, a plaintiff seeking to recover damages on the basis of a design defect must prove the foreseeable risks of harm posed by the product could have been reduced or avoided by the adoption of a reasonable alternative design by the seller or other distributor, or a predecessor in the commercial chain of distribution, and the omission of the alternative design renders the product not reasonably safe.

**› RESULT** The court adopted Sections 1 and 2 of the Restatement (Third). To establish liability, the plaintiffs had to produce evidence of a reasonable alternative design.

**› COMMENTS** In essence, the Restatement (Third) replaces the requirement that a product be "unreasonably dangerous" with a showing that there was a "reasonable alternative design." Considerable legal writing asserts that alternative design and unreasonably dangerous tests are really the same test, but some lawyers concede that the alternative design test is more easily understood and applied by the courts.[82]

**› CRITICAL THINKING QUESTIONS**

1. How do the approaches of the Restatement (Second) and the Restatement (Third) differ?
2. Should the plaintiff or the defendant have the burden of proving the existence of a reasonable alternative design?

82. Opinions of several large law firms are available at http://www.nmmlaw.com/articles/designdef.html and http://www.cliffordlaw.com/press/detail.aspx?sctnID=389&pgID=36003&prssrmID=000000268100.

## Global View

### Product Liability in the European Union

Differences among the product liability laws of the various countries within the European Union (EU) created two major problems. First, there was uncertainty as to what law would apply to cross-border disputes. This uncertainty was harmful to both the consumer and the manufacturer of the product. Second, competition was distorted within the EU because liability and the severity of financial repercussions varied from one nation to another. Thus, the need for a uniform product liability directive was recognized.

In July 1985, after nearly a decade of debate, the Council of Ministers of the EU adopted a product liability directive. The directive was intended to provide increased consumer protection and to harmonize competitive conditions within the EU.[a] In 1995, the European Commission decided to leave the directive unchanged, rejecting the urging of consumer groups to strengthen the liability provisions.[b]

The directive's basic purpose is to hold manufacturers strictly liable for injuries caused by defects in their products. This represents a fundamental change for manufacturers of products marketed in Europe. Traditionally, in most of the member states, an injured consumer had to prove both negligence and privity of contract in order to recover damages from the producer of a defective product. Only France had previously imposed strict product liability.

a. 1985 O.J. (L 210) 29.

b. Robert Rice, *Business and the Law: A Question of Safety—The European Union's Product Liability Legislation*, FIN. TIMES, Jan. 16, 1996, at 13.

*(Continued)*

(Global View *continued)*

**Comparison with U.S. Strict Liability**

The EU product liability directive is quite similar to the strict liability doctrine prevalent in the United States. To recover damages, an injured party has to prove the existence of a defect, an injury, and a causal relationship between the defect and the injury. (Plaintiffs may also sue under the traditional negligence and contract laws of the EU member states.) In determining whether a product is defective, the courts in the EU countries, like those in the United States, consider such factors as the product's foreseeable uses and the instructions and warnings provided by the manufacturer.

In June 1999, in light of separate outbreaks of mad cow disease, *E. coli,* and salmonella, the Commission adopted an amendment to the 1985 directive that extended product liability to cover agricultural products.[c] The directive does not apply to services, which are still governed solely by national law.

The available defenses are similar to those available in the United States. For example, a manufacturer will not be liable if (1) the manufacturer did not put the product into circulation, (2) the defect did not exist when the product went into circulation, (3) the product was a component that was neither manufactured nor distributed by the manufacturer of the overall product, or (4) the defect was due to compliance of the product with mandatory regulations. The manufacturer of a component part will not be liable if the defect was attributable to the design of the product into which the component was fitted.

The directive includes a statute of limitations and a statute of repose. An injured person must sue within three years of when he or she knew, or should have known, of the injury, the defect, and the manufacturer's identity. A manufacturer's liability will be extinguished ten years after the product was put into circulation, unless the injured party has commenced proceedings in the meantime. Thus, as in some states in the United States, a defect that does not become apparent until eleven years after the product went into circulation may leave the injured person without a remedy. Most EU member states previously had statutes of repose with a thirty-year period.

Unlike in the United States, a supplier or wholesaler is not strictly liable unless the injured party is unable to identify the manufacturer. In such an instance, the supplier can escape liability by informing the injured person of the manufacturer's identity.

The directive provides for a "development risks" or state-of-the-art defense. A producer can escape liability by proving that the state of scientific knowledge when the product went into circulation was insufficient to allow it to discover the defect.

Importers of products into the EU are strictly liable under the directive. Thus, U.S. exporters may be required to indemnify overseas importers. U.S. exporters should carry product liability insurance and adhere to EU safety standards.

c. John R. Schmertz, Jr. & Mike Meier, *EU Amends Product Liability Directive to Include Agricultural Products,* INT'L L. UPDATE, June 1999.

THE RESPONSIBLE MANAGER

## REDUCING PRODUCT LIABILITY RISK

Managers have the responsibility to minimize their company's exposure to liability in the design, manufacture, assembly, and use of its products. They should implement a product safety program to ensure that products are sold in a legally safe condition. They also have an obligation to discover and correct any defects in the product. The goal should be to prevent accidents. If an accident does occur, evidence of a product safety program is crucial for limiting the manufacturer's liability for punitive damages. To protect against potential liabilities, managers should implement internal loss-control procedures, obtain insurance protection, and seek the advice of product liability counsel from the earliest stages of product development.

Managers should have a thorough understanding of all statutes, regulations, and administrative rulings to which a product must conform. Failure of the product to comply with any of these rules will typically be deemed a product defect. Mere conformance with these rules is considered a minimum requirement, however, and does not automatically release a manufacturer from liability.

Managers should ensure that their products are performing as intended over the lives of the products and that the products have as little adverse effect on the environment as possible under current technology. It is helpful to establish a product safety committee and to conduct regular safety audits to identify and correct problems. The advice of experienced counsel can be helpful in this area.

Nonetheless, accidents and product defects will occur. One of the most difficult, and ethically challenging, deci-

*(Continued)*

(The Responsible Manager *continued*)

sions a manager must make is whether to undertake *subsequent remedial measures.* When a product is found to be inherently defective, it is in society's best interest for the manufacturer to fix the dangerous condition or to improve the design; nevertheless, manufacturers may fear that such remedies will be used as evidence against them in subsequent proceedings. For this reason, courts often refuse to allow plaintiffs to submit evidence of subsequent remedial measures as proof that the original design was defective.

INSIDE STORY

## BIG FOOD FACING BIG LAWSUITS

In the 1970s, it was asbestos. In the 1980s, it was tobacco. In the 1990s, it was breast implants and guns. The next round of high-profile product litigation could be developing on an unlikely front: fast food.[83] Unlike several lawsuits brought in the late 1990s over coffee spillage and objects found in sandwiches, this litigation is aimed directly at the sellers of Big Macs, supersized fries, and other fat- and sugar-laden fast foods.

In July 2002, Caesar Barber, a clinically obese man, sued McDonald's, KFC, and Wendy's International for selling unhealthful foods. Barber alleged that the food sold in these "fast-food" establishments caused his weight to balloon to 270 pounds and caused him to have two heart attacks and to develop diabetes. A spokesperson for McDonald's, the largest of the named corporations, disagreed, asserting that its food could easily fit into a balanced diet.[84]

This and other litigation has prompted an intense lobbying effort by the restaurant industry and the introduction of legislation in nineteen state legislatures and the U.S. House of Representatives to eliminate Big Food's liability for obesity. The federal bill has been nicknamed the "cheeseburger bill," while the state-level bills have been dubbed "Baby McBills." The bills would bar obese individuals from suing restaurants for causing them to gain weight.

Despite this legislative movement to the contrary, many experienced lawyers predict ultimate victory for the plaintiffs. "Conditions are ripe," remarked Alice Johnson, an attorney in Pittsburgh, while advising representatives from many major food chains. Joseph Price, a veteran lawyer who defended breast implantation companies in past litigation, remarked, "I'm old enough to remember when they first started talking about suing the cigarette companies and everyone thought it was a joke. [The plaintiff's bar] said they're going to make this the next tobacco. If you go blithely along and ignore it, sooner or later it'll turn around and bite you."

Unlike the tobacco litigation, which began before smoking was recognized as a major public health threat, obesity and healthy eating are already at the forefront of public awareness. The U.S. government has called obesity an epidemic in the United States.

Although Caesar Barber's lawsuit seemed destined for dismissal, the second-generation suits may be more likely to succeed. Suits asserting personal injury or tort lend themselves to the natural defense that no one burger, cookie, or milkshake leads to obesity. With a healthier regimen, eating those foods need not lead to poor health. Consequently, rather than arguing about personal versus corporate responsibility, future suits are likely to focus on the advertising used by the fast-food chains. Ad campaigns that are directed at children and those that are misleading or fudge nutritional facts are particularly vulnerable to attack.

McDonald's sales of Happy Meals with toys are reminiscent of Joe Camel, the smooth-talking well-dressed camel who smoked while playing pool and was as readily recognized by many children as Mickey Mouse. Ronald McDonald might suffer the same indignity of being banned from advertising aimed at children.

Plaintiffs' lawyers have already had several moderate successes. McDonald's paid $12 million for not disclosing that there was beef fat in its fries.[85] In a similar case,

83. The following discussion is based heavily on Kate Zernike's article *Lawyers Shift Focus from Big Tobacco to Big Food,* N.Y. TIMES, Apr. 9, 2002, at A15.

84. CNN interview *at* http://money.cnn.com/2003/01/22/news/companies/mcdonalds/.

85. Herbert McCann, *McDonald's Apologizes for Fry Labeling,* CHICAGO ASSOC. PRESS, June 6, 2002. McDonald's official apology is available at http://www.mcdonalds.com/countries/usa/whatsnew/pressrelease/2002/06012002/index.html.

*(Continued)*

(Inside Story *continued*)

the makers of the snack food "Pirate's Booty" paid $4 million for underestimating the product's fat content.[86]

In September 2002, Ashley Pelman brought just such a second-generation lawsuit.[87] Pelman's suit attacked the McDonald's advertisements that tout the nutritional value of its products, particularly the ad directed at younger people. Pelman, a teenager, argued that young people are more likely to be susceptible to misleading advertising, especially advertising directed at them. Even if laws were passed exempting Big Food from liability for making people obese, the companies could still be held responsible for their advertising and tactics.

In addition to attacking McDonald's advertising claims, the Pelman suit also utilized the "Frankenfood" argument that "McDonald's failed adequately to disclose the fact that certain of its foods were substantially less healthier, as a result of processing and ingredient additives, than represented by McDonald's in its advertising campaigns and other publicity."[88] The case was dismissed but others are pending. Meanwhile, Subway is using the obesity epidemic as a marketing opportunity to distinguish its more healthful food from the burgers and fries sold by its competitors.

Restaurants have reacted swiftly to this new litigation by pushing for Baby McBills and other legislative relief, settling claims out of court, and holding massive strategy sessions with representatives from the various corporations. Most lawyers have recommended that their clients label ingredients correctly and avoid any health claims. Time will tell whether Big Food learned anything from Big Tobacco.

86. Ann Romano, *The Week in Review,* PORTLAND MERCURY, Apr. 18, 2002.

87. Pelman *ex rel.* Pelman v. McDonald's Corp., WL 22052778 (S.D.N.Y. Sept. 4, 2003).

88. *Id.*

## KEY WORDS AND PHRASES

assumption of risk 347
comparative fault 348
design defect 340
discovery-of-injury statute 354
failure to warn 341
government-contractor defense 349
limited fund class action 356
manufacturing defect 339
market-share liability 346
obvious risk 348
preemption defense 350
premises liability 346
privity of contract 335
product 338
product liability 335
revival statute 354
state-of-the-art defense 349
statute of limitations 353
statute of repose 354
subsequent remedial measures 361
unavoidably unsafe product 342

## QUESTIONS AND CASE PROBLEMS

1. Lee James Crews had been the chief of Maryland Gas Company's "Dangerous Gas Response Team" for twelve years. After an excavation accident contaminated an area with flammable gas, Crews was called out to repair the leak. While Crews was employing his proven system to neutralize the threat, the gas ignited and then exploded, seriously injuring him. Crews sued the excavation company that created the gas leak in the first place, claiming negligence and strict liability. Does the excavation company have any defenses? [*Crews v. Hollenbach*, 751 A.2d 481 (Md. 2000).]

2. Roy Mercurio drove his Nissan Altima into a tree in the middle of the night at a speed of approximately thirty-five miles per hour. When the car struck the tree, the passenger compartment collapsed, and Mercurio was seriously injured. He was driving while intoxicated with a blood alcohol content of at least .18 percent. Mercurio brought a product liability action against Nissan on the grounds that the car was not crashworthy. Nissan argued that the claim should be dismissed, asserting as defenses assumption of risk and unforeseeable misuse of the car in that Mercurio was driving while intoxicated. Mercurio argued that evidence of his blood alcohol level at the time of the accident was irrelevant and should be excluded. How should the court rule? [*Mercurio v. Nissan Motor Corp.*, 81 F. Supp. 2d 859 (N.D. Ohio 2000).]

3. Pamela Murray had spinal fusion surgery to treat severe back pain. Her physician used two stainless steel dynamic compression plates to stabilize her

spine and also used six screws during the surgery to secure the plates to her spine. The plates and four of the screws were manufactured by Synthes (U.S.A.), Inc. The other two screws were manufactured by two other companies. At the time of the surgery, the Food and Drug Administration had not approved the use of bone screws to attach an internal fixation device. When Murray learned that the process had not been approved by the FDA, she filed suit in U.S. district court in Pennsylvania, alleging design defect and manufacturing defect against the manufacturers.

Under Pennsylvania state law, strict liability is imposed on manufacturers of products sold "in a defective condition unreasonably dangerous to the user or consumer." However, state law denies the application of strict liability to "unavoidably unsafe products," such as prescription drugs. Should Murray be entitled to sue the manufacturers in strict liability? Are there other theories under which she could recover against the companies? [*Murray v. Synthes (U.S.A.), Inc.*, WL 672937 (E.D. Pa. Aug. 23, 1999).]

4. Terrell Redman, a senior vice president of Alligator Corporation, is evaluating a potential acquisition for the company. The entity he wishes to acquire has several divisions, two of which manufacture chemicals and industrial tools.
   - **a.** What risks does the acquisition present to Alligator Corporation under product liability law?
   - **b.** Are there ways to limit the company's exposure?
   - **c.** To the extent that product liability law will expose Alligator to liability for the acquired company's prior conduct, what steps must be taken at the time of the acquisition to ensure Alligator's ability to defend potential claims? [*Tolo v. Wexco*, 993 F.2d 884 (9th Cir. 1993).]

5. Rochelle Black's husband worked as an auto mechanic in the Air Force from 1971 to 1986. When he died of lung cancer in 1991, Mrs. Black sued forty-eight asbestos manufacturers, alleging that her husband's death had been caused by his exposure to asbestos-containing products while working as an auto mechanic. She based her claims on market-share liability. Although she conceded that market-share liability would be inappropriate if she were alleging injury from exposure to many different types of asbestos products, she argued that she should be allowed to proceed in her market-share claims against four manufacturers of asbestos-containing "friction products," including brake and clutch products. These four companies produced friction products, which contained between 7 and 75 percent asbestos fibers. How should the court rule? What if the range of asbestos fibers in the products produced by the four companies was 40 to 60 percent? [*Black v. Abex Corp.*, 603 N.W.2d 182 (N.D. 1999).]

6. Laura Hollister was a business student at Northwestern University. She attended a business school party and then returned to her apartment with a friend. When Hollister left the party, she was intoxicated. She woke the next morning with no memory of subsequent events after she had returned to her apartment, but she had third-degree burns over 55 percent of her body. From the evidence, police determined that she had been cooking; when she reached for the cupboard over the stove, her shirt brushed against the hot burner and caught fire. Hollister brought an action against the department store where her mother purchased the shirt on the grounds that it was defective because it lacked a warning regarding its extreme flammability. The department store argued that the danger inherent in having clothing come into contact with a hot stove is "open and obvious." How should the court rule? [*Hollister v. Dayton Hudson Corp.*, 201 F.3d 731 (6th Cir. 2000), *cert. denied*, 531 U.S. 819 (2000).]

7. Jeanne Sprietsma was riding on a motorboat in the Gulf of Mexico when the boat hit a sudden wave and threw her overboard. She was struck by the propeller and killed instantly. Jeanne's widower brought suit against Mercury Marine, a leading manufacturer of boat engines and maker of the engine that killed Jeanne. The lawsuit alleged that Mercury's design was "unreasonably dangerous" because the engine did not have a propeller guard. Mercury contended that the Federal Boat Safety Act and the Coast Guard's decision not to amend its regulations to require guards preempted a suit brought in state court under state product liability law. By purposefully omitting any mention of propeller guards, the defendant argued, federal law allowed manufacturers to build engines without guards and not worry about being sued in state courts. Should the federal government's silence be construed as tacit affirmation that engines need not have guards or be seen as an opportunity for individual states to regulate that aspect of motor construction as they see fit? [*Sprietsma v. Mercury Marine*, 537 U.S. 51 (2002).]

**8.** Richard Welge loves to sprinkle peanuts on his ice cream sundaes. One day Karen Godfrey, with whom Welge boards, bought a 24-ounce vacuum-sealed plastic-capped glass jar of peanuts at a convenience store in Chicago. To obtain a $2 rebate that the manufacturer was offering to anyone who bought a "party" item, such as peanuts, Godfrey needed proof of her purchase from the jar of peanuts. Using an Exacto knife, she removed the part of the label that contained the bar code. She then placed the jar on top of the refrigerator. About a week later, Welge removed the plastic seal from the jar, uncapped it, took some peanuts, replaced the cap, and returned the jar to the top of the refrigerator, all without incident.

A week later, Welge took down the jar, removed the plastic cap, spilled some peanuts into his left hand to put on his sundae, and replaced the cap with his right hand. But as he pushed the cap down on the open jar, the jar shattered. His hand was severely cut and is now, he claims, permanently impaired.

Welge has brought suit and has named three defendants: the convenience store, the manufacturer of the peanuts, and the manufacturer of the jar itself. From whom will Welge be able to recover? What defenses, if any, are available to the defendants? [*Welge v. Planters Lifesavers Co.*, 17 F.3d 209 (7th Cir. 1994).]

**9.** Darleen Johnson was driving her Ford car under rainy conditions on a two-lane highway through Missouri. The car's front tires had a reasonable amount of tread remaining on them, but the back tires were nearly bald. For an undetermined reason, Johnson lost control of the car, spun into the other lane, and collided with a pickup truck driven by Kathyleen Sammons. Johnson was killed instantly.

Johnson's father claimed that the inboard C.V. joint boot on the front axle was torn, which allowed debris to contaminate the joint. (The boot is a covering that contains the grease that lubricates the joint.) This contamination allegedly made the joint act like a brake on the left front wheel and caused Johnson's car to pivot around that wheel and into the path of the oncoming pickup truck. Ford admits that the joint boot can become torn, which will allow contamination of the joint. In its manuals, Ford recommends periodic inspection of the boots. However, Ford contends that the joint on Johnson's car was contaminated during or after the accident. Ford also contends that contamination of the joint could not result in the joint seizing and creating a loss of steering control, and that the worst that could result from contamination would be some vibration and noise. According to Ford, Johnson's accident was caused by road conditions and driving error. The case is submitted to the jury on theories of strict liability and negligent design and manufacture. Is Ford liable for Johnson's death? Are there any additional arguments that Ford can raise in its defense? Who will prevail in this case? [*Johnson v. Ford Motor Co.*, 988 F.2d 573 (9th Cir. 1993).]

## MANAGER'S DILEMMA

**10.** In the early 1990s, Pacesetter Systems, Inc. became aware that its pacemakers—devices that regulate the heartbeat within the body—were failing at any temperature above normal body temperature. Pacesetter asked hospitals with unused units to return them for credit and advised doctors to remove any that had been implanted in patients.

Larsen required several major open chest surgeries to remedy problems stemming from the faulty pacemaker. After settlement negotiations broke down, Larsen sued Pacesetter for breach of the implied warranty of merchantability. Larsen claimed that Pacesetter's pacemaker could easily have been made safer through inexpensive tests and use of an alternative design. Will Larsen be able to recover from Pacesetter? On what theory? What defenses can Pacesetter assert? Are they likely to prevail? Is it ethical to both recall a product and fight a lawsuit regarding its viability at the same time? Should Pacesetter offer to pay the out-of-pocket expenses Larsen incurred for the operations necessitated by the need to remove the faulty pacemaker? [*Larsen v. Pacesetter Systems, Inc.*, 837 P.2d 1273 (Haw. 1992).]

## INTERNET SOURCES

| | |
|---|---|
| The U.S. Consumer Product Safety Commission's website provides information about recent recalls and other agency activity. | http://www.cpsc.gov |
| The Federal Trade Commission's website provides information about its enforcement actions, consumer protection efforts, and regional offices. | http://www.ftc.gov |
| The Better Business Bureau's website provides consumers with information about its private regulation of business, including recent warnings and local offices. | http://www.bbb.org |
| The International Organization for Standardization's website provides information about its attempt to create various technical and product standards for business and government. | http://www.iso.ch |
| This site, maintained by the tobacco industry, links to various tobacco companies' websites regarding tobacco litigation. | http://tobaccoresolution.com/ |
| The Association of Trial Lawyers of America, a group of attorneys who represent plaintiffs in tort and consumer protection lawsuits, maintains a site with articles and news clippings regarding recent product liability cases and developments. | http://www.atla.org |

CHAPTER 11

# Intellectual Property

## INTRODUCTION

### Strategic Importance of Intellectual Property

Today's legally astute managers recognize that intellectual property is an essential part of their business. *Intellectual property* is any product or result of a mental process that is given legal protection against unauthorized use. Representing somewhere in the range of 87 percent of an average firm's value (up from 62 percent in 1992 and 38 percent in 1982),[1] intellectual property now constitutes one of a company's most important assets. According to Nathan Myhrvold, the multimillionaire former chief technologist at Microsoft who has raised $350 million from some of the largest high-tech companies to buy patents from all over the world, "Intellectual property is the next software." In other words, he expects that his company, Intellectual Ventures, will be a model for future companies that deal exclusively in the licensing of intellectual property.[2]

There are four basic types of intellectual property: patents, copyrights, trademarks, and trade secrets. The Semiconductor Chip Protection Act of 1984 created a fifth, highly specialized form of intellectual property, the registered mask work. Different types of intellectual property are protected in different ways and protect different aspects of a product.

1. Richard Lee, *Don't Underestimate the Value of Intellectual Property, Expert Says,* GREENWICH TIME, June 24, 2004, *at* http://www.usa-canada.les.org/chapters/fairfield/6.24_Newspaper_Article.pdf.
2. Brad Stone, *Next Frontier—Factory of the Future?,* NEWSWEEK, Nov. 22, 2004, at 60.

A *patent* is a government-granted right to exclude others from making, using, or selling an invention. The patent holder need not personally make use of the invention. After a period of time (twenty years from the application date for utility patents and fourteen years for design patents in the United States), the patent expires and the invention is dedicated to the public.

A *copyright* is the legal right to prevent others from copying an original expression embodied in any original work of authorship fixed in a tangible medium. The protection also extends to derivative works, that is, works based upon the protected work. Copyright protects the expression, not the underlying ideas in the work. The owner also has exclusive rights to distribute, display, and perform the work. Copyright protection lasts for at least seventy years. The Semiconductor Chip Protection Act of 1984 provides copyright-like protection for the layout or topography of an integrated circuit.

*Trademarks*—words or symbols (such as brand names) that identify the source of goods or services—are also legally protected. Because trademarks tend to embody or represent the goodwill of the business, they are not legally transferable without that goodwill. Trademarks are protected for an indefinite time and can be valuable marketing and business assets. The packaging or dressing of a product may also be protected under the trademark laws as *trade dress.*

A *trade secret* is information that gives a business an advantage over its competitors that do not know the information. The classic example of a trade secret is the formula for Coca-Cola. Trade secrets are protected for an indefinite time.

*Know-how*—detailed information on how to make or do something—can be a trade secret, or it can be show-how. *Show-how* is nonsecret information used to teach someone how to make or do something; it is generally not protectable.

Since 1991 when the U.S. Supreme Court declared in *Feist Publications v. Rural Telephone Service Co.*[3] that copyright protection did not extend to collections of factual information, database publishers have pressured Congress to pass new legislation that would strengthen the protection of databases in the United States, but to date these efforts have been unsuccessful.

International piracy, or the unauthorized reproduction and distribution of patented, copyrighted, or trademarked goods, is a major issue today.[4] In its 2004 annual report, the U.S. Trade Representative noted that piracy losses to U.S. industries alone "are estimated at $200–$250 billion per year," and more than fifty-two countries have ineffective patent or copyright protection. Increasingly, private companies are forming alliances to work with government officials to combat worldwide piracy. For example, sixty companies doing business in Mexico (including Levi Strauss, Reebok, Hard Rock Café, Walt Disney, and Tequila Herradura) banded together in 1998 to fight piracy there.

## CHAPTER OVERVIEW

This chapter describes the law of patents, copyrights, mask work rights, trademarks, and trade secrets in detail. It also discusses efforts to enact new federal legislation protecting databases of non-copyrightable information. It then addresses technology licensing, that is, the selling of permission to use a patented invention, a copyrighted work, a trade secret, or a trademark. The chapter concludes with a discussion of international intellectual property protection and the growing trend towards harmonization of national laws.

# Patents

Patents are one of the oldest recognized forms of intellectual property. Their importance has increased as our society has become more technologically advanced. Patents have formed the basis for whole businesses, such as the production of instant cameras, high-engineering plastics, and biotechnology.

3. 499 U.S. 340 (1991).
4. *U.S. Urges Global Action on Copyright Theft*, USATODAY.COM, May 3, 2004, *at* http://www.usatoday.com/tech/news/techpolicy/2004-05-03-piracy-pitch_x.htm.

Article I of the U.S. Constitution specifically grants Congress the power "to promote the Progress of Science and useful Arts, by securing for limited times to . . . Inventors the exclusive Right to their . . . Discoveries." The Patent and Trademark Office (PTO), an agency of the U.S. Department of Commerce, is responsible for issuing patents.

The PTO issued its first patent in 1790.[5] Since that time, the PTO has issued over six million patents. It issued 187,017 patents in 2003 alone, a 51 percent increase from the number issued in 1997. The types of patents issued by the PTO have varied dramatically over the years, particularly in the last century. The first patent issued in 1900 was for an early version of the washing machine. The first patent issued in 2000 was for a sun visor/eye shield for athletes participating in "extreme" sports. The top ten private-sector patent recipients for the 2004 calendar year (based on a preliminary count) are identified in Exhibit 11.1.

## TYPES OF PATENTS

U.S. patent law provides for three types of patents: utility, design, and plant patents.

### Utility Patents

*Utility patents,* the most frequently issued type, protect any novel, useful, and nonobvious process, machine, manufacture, or composition of matter, or any novel, useful, and nonobvious improvement thereof. To be approved, an application for a utility patent must satisfy the *utility requirement;* that is, the invention must have a practical or real-world benefit. If the PTO issues a utility patent, the patent owner has the exclusive right to make, use, sell, and import for use the invention for a nonrenewable period of twenty years from the date on which the patent application was filed.

An invention is *novel* if it was not anticipated, that is, if it was not previously known or used by others in the United States and was not previously patented or described in a printed publication in any country. Even if the invention is novel, it will be denied patent protection if its novelty merely represents an obvious development over *prior art,* that is, existing technology. This novelty requirement concerned two New Yorkers applying for a patent for their device to remove garbage bags blown into tree branches. Although similar to the fruit picker,

5. Press Release, Patent & Trademark Office, PTO Announces First Patent and Trademark of New Millennium (Jan. 13, 2000), *available at* http://www.uspto.gov/web/offices/com/speeches/00-05.htm.

EXHIBIT 11.1 **Top Ten Private-Sector Patent Recipients for the 2004 Calendar Year**

| Preliminary Rank in 2004 | Preliminary Number of Patents in 2004 | Organization | Final Rank in 2003 | Final Number of Patents in 2003 |
|---|---|---|---|---|
| 1 | 3,248 | International Business Machines Corp. | 1 | 3,415 |
| 2 | 1,934 | Matsushita Electric Industrial Co., Ltd. | 4 | 1,774 |
| 3 | 1,805 | Canon Kabushiki Kaisha | 2 | 1,992 |
| 4 | 1,775 | Hewlett-Packard Development Co., L.P. | 5 | 1,759 |
| 5 | 1,760 | Micron Technology, Inc. | 6 | 1,707 |
| 6 | 1,604 | Samsung Electronics Co., Ltd. | 9 | 1,313 |
| 7 | 1,601 | Intel Corp. | 7 | 1,592 |
| 8 | 1,514 | Hitachi, Ltd. | 3 | 1,893 |
| 9 | 1,310 | Toshiba Corp. | 13 | 1,184 |
| 10 | 1,305 | Sony Corp. | 10 | 1,311 |

Source: Press Release, Patent & Trademark Office, USPTO Releases Annual List of Top 10 Organizations Receiving Most U.S. Patents (Jan. 11, 2005), *available at* http://www.uspto.gov/web/offices/com/speeches/05-03.htm.

invented in 1869, their "bag-snagger" was found sufficiently different to warrant a separate patent.

The inventor must be diligent in his or her effort to file for patent protection. A *statutory bar* precludes protection in the United States if, prior to one year before the inventor's filing, the invention was either described in a printed publication in the United States or a foreign country or was publicly used or sold in the United States. In most other countries, a patent application must be filed *before* the invention is described in a publication, publicly used, or sold.

Even when the inventor files promptly for protection of a novel, useful, and nonobvious invention, he or she may still be denied a patent. There is no protection for nonstatutory subject matter, such as abstract ideas (rather than specific applications of ideas), mental processes, naturally occurring substances, arrangements of printed matter, scientific principles, or laws of nature.

**Biotechnology** In *Diamond v. Chakrabarty*,[6] a microbiologist sought patent protection for his invention of a live human-made, genetically engineered bacterium capable of breaking down crude oil. The patent examiner rejected the application. On appeal, the U.S. Supreme Court held that living organisms can be patented if they are human-made. The Supreme Court stated that patent statutes should include "anything under the sun that is *made* by man." Thus, patent protection was extended to the new organism.

6. 447 U.S. 303 (1980).

The Supreme Court prophetically noted that its decision in *Chakrabarty* might determine whether research efforts would be accelerated by the hope of reward or slowed by the want of incentives. In fact, the *Chakrabarty* decision allowed small biotechnology firms to attract venture capitalists and other investors and spawned a whole new industry.

In 1987, the PTO confirmed that nonnaturally occurring, nonhuman multicellular living organisms (including animals) are patentable subject matter. The PTO issued a patent in 1988 on a transgenic mouse that was engineered to be susceptible to cancer. It issued three more mouse patents in 1993.

More recently, patent laws have been applied even more broadly to include patents on human and other genes. According to the PTO, gene sequences are patentable subject matter. Specifically, a gene patent covers "the genetic composition isolated from its natural state and processed through purifying steps that separate the gene from other molecules naturally associated with it."[7] As of January 2005, over 36,000 DNA-based patents have been issued.[8] Many gene patents have been associated with research leading to the treatment of disease.

Gene patenting (which has always been controversial) sparked new controversy when a patent was issued to Human Genome Sciences, Inc. for a gene found to serve

7. 66 Fed. Reg. 4 (Jan. 5, 2001).

8. DNA Patent Database, *at* http://dnapatents.georgetown.edu/ (accessed Jan. 11, 2005).

## ETHICAL CONSIDERATION

What legal and ethical issues are raised by efforts to patent the process for creating a chimera, a two-species mixture created by combining human and animal embryo cells? Should an inventor be allowed to patent the process for making human clones?

as a platform from which the AIDS virus can infect cells of the body. Questions arose as to the legal and moral right to own a human gene. Perhaps more significantly, concerns arose over the effect of giving one company the ability to control medical research related to a life-threatening disease, especially when that company may not appreciate the medical value of the gene.[9] In response to these concerns, on December 29, 2000, the PTO issued new guidelines for examination of gene applications for compliance with the utility requirement. The PTO had been faulted for issuing patents on genes before the inventors had ascertained the gene's function. The new guidelines were designed to make it more difficult for genes to be patented by requiring a stronger showing of utility. These guidelines have had great impact; by 2003 the explosive growth of the biotech industry had leveled off. The strategy of many U.S. biotech firms seems to have shifted from acquiring new patents to vigorously defending their existing patents.

**Computer Software** The law's embrace of software patents began in 1981, when the Supreme Court held, in *Diamond v. Diehr,* that if a "claim containing a mathematical formula implements or applies that formula in a structure or process, which when considered as a whole, is performing a function which the patent laws were designed to protect (e.g., transforming or reducing an article to a different state or thing), then the claim [may be patentable]."[10] After this decision, developers successfully acquired software patents at a quickening pace.

Most software code is not published, so much of the relevant prior art is not accessible to the PTO examiners. In addition, until recently, U.S. patent applications were not published until and unless a patent was issued. As a result, many experts believed that the PTO was issuing patents for computer programs that were not novel or were merely obvious improvements of existing programs.

In 1994, partly in response to charges from intellectual property lawyers that the patent was overly broad, the PTO took the unusual step of reversing a patent granted to Compton's New Media and Encyclopedia Britannica. The patent (which covered virtually all ways of storing and retrieving text, sound, and images stored on compact discs) appeared to give Compton's a dominant position in the fast-growing multimedia market. The fact that the patent was issued in the first place was cited by the Interactive Multimedia Association as evidence of the need to improve the training of the PTO's software examiners.

**Business Method Patents** In recent years, some of the most criticized patents have been patents on "business method" inventions, particularly in connection with the Internet and electronic commerce. Until 1998 the courts had held that business methods were not patentable, but in *State Street Bank & Trust Co. v. Signature Financial Group,* the U.S. Court of Appeals for the Federal Circuit upheld the validity of a patent on a mutual fund investment method.[11] The court determined that business methods, like all processes, are patentable if they meet all the usual requirements for patentability.

The case spurred a wave of applications; in 2000 alone, 7,800 inventors filed business method applications and 899 patents were issued.[12] In response to criticism that these patents were granted too readily, with an inadequate review of prior art, the PTO announced in March 2000 that it was adding a second layer of review for applications seeking protection for e-commerce-based business methods. These efforts have had an impact; in 2003, 6,000 business method applications were filed, but only 495 patents were issued.

Some of the most notorious e-commerce business method patents are well known. Amazon.com's patent for the "one-click" shopping system, Priceline.com's patent for the online reverse auction, and Microsoft's patent on "e-commerce" all pushed the boundaries of the novelty requirement. Other industries are also taking advantage of business method patents, however. The insurance industry has seen a wave of patents covering computerized risk management for disasters, methods of shared life insurance, and ways to insure against gambling losses.[13] NetFlix, the popular movie delivery ser-

9. For an excellent collection of articles on the pros and cons of gene patents, see MIT TECH. REV. (Sept.–Oct. 2000).
10. 450 U.S. 175, 176 (1981).

11. 149 F.3d 1368 (Fed. Cir. 1998).
12. Patent & Trademark Office, *at* http://www.uspto.gov/web/menu/pbmethod/applicationfiling.htm (accessed Nov. 2, 2004).
13. Sabra Chartrand, *Protecting Ideas in the Insurance Business,* N.Y. TIMES, June 30, 2003, at C4.

vice, received a patent covering the technology and mailing methods that are the core of its business.

### *Design Patents*

A *design patent* protects any novel, original (rather than nonobvious), and ornamental (rather than useful) design for an article of manufacture. Design patents protect against the copying of the appearance or shape of an article such as a computer terminal cabinet, a perfume bottle, a typeface, or the icons and screen displays used in computer programs. A design dictated by function rather than aesthetic concerns cannot be protected by a design patent, but it may be protectable by a utility patent. A design patent has a duration of fourteen years from the date on which the patent application was filed, compared to twenty years for utility and plant patents.

Traditionally, design patents have rarely been used in the United States; other forms of protection, such as unfair competition law, have been relied on instead. Recently, however, the use of design patents has been increasing because the application process is simpler and less expensive than for utility patents.

### *Plant Patents*

*Plant patents* protect any distinct and new variety of plant that is asexually reproduced (that is, not reproduced by means of seeds). The variety must not exist naturally. Thus, a plant patent will not be issued to someone who merely discovers a wild plant not previously known to exist. Once a plant patent is granted, the patent owner will have the exclusive right to exclude others from asexually reproducing, using, or selling the plant. In *J.E.M. AG Supply v. Pioneer Hi-Bred International*[14] in 2001, the Supreme Court affirmed that plant patents do not foreclose utility patent protection for the same plants.

## FILING FOR PATENT PROTECTION

To obtain patent protection in the United States, the inventor must file a patent application with the PTO. Each patent application contains four parts: the specifications, the claims, the drawings (except in chemical cases), and a declaration by the inventor.

The *specifications* must describe the invention (as defined by the claims) in its best mode and the manner and process of making and using the invention so that a person skilled in the relevant field could make and use it. The description of the *best mode* must be the best way the inventor knows to make the invention at the time of filing the application. All descriptions must be clear, concise, and exact.

The *claims* (the numbered paragraphs at the end of the patent) describe the elements of the invention that the patent will protect. Any element not specifically set forth in the claims is unprotected by the patent. Thus, drafting the claims is crucial to obtaining adequate protection.

The *drawings* must show the claimed invention. The *declaration by the inventor* must state that the inventor has reviewed the application and believes that he or she is the first inventor of the invention. The inventor must also make full disclosure of any known relevant prior art. Knowing the prior developments assists the patent attorney in drafting the claims to avoid the prior art; it also permits the patent examiner to determine whether the patent is novel or whether it would have been obvious to those familiar with the relevant field.

The patent examiner may initially reject the application as being precluded by prior inventions or otherwise failing to meet the statutory requirements (the PTO initially rejects 99 percent of all patent applications). The inventor may then either present arguments (and in extreme cases, evidence) to contest the rejection or seek to amend the application to overcome the examiner's objections. If the application is finally rejected, the inventor can either refile the application as a *continuation application* or appeal to the PTO's Board of Appeals and subsequently to either the U.S. District Court for the District of Columbia or the U.S. Court of Appeals for the Federal Circuit. Once the examiner agrees that a patent should be issued, and the examiner and applicant agree on the precise language of the claims, a patent will be issued.

Since 1995 inventors have been able to file provisional patent applications, which can be filed without formal patent claims; a provisional application must be followed by a nonprovisional application within twelve months. The provisional application provides a low-cost way to establish an early filing date for the later, nonprovisional patent application.

# Patent Infringement

## TYPES OF INFRINGEMENT

A patent may be infringed in three ways: directly, indirectly, or contributorily. *Direct patent infringement* is the making, use, or sale of any patented invention within the United States during the term of the patent. When an accused device or process does not have precisely each

14. 534 U.S. 124 (2001).

element of a particular claim of a patent (that is, the patent is not literally infringed), but the patented invention is replicated in a product or process that works in substantially the same way and accomplishes substantially the same result, a direct infringement can be found under the *doctrine of equivalents*. In 2002, the U.S. Supreme Court narrowed the reach of this doctrine so that it is now effectively available only to inventors who did not amend their patent applications in order to satisfy patentability requirements.[15] As the patent examiner asks the majority of patent applicants to amend their applications to satisfy these requirements, the doctrine of equivalents now provides patent owners with considerably less recourse against competitors who design around their patents.

*Indirect patent infringement* is a party's active inducement of another party to infringe a patent. *Contributory patent infringement* occurs when one party knowingly sells an item with one specific use that will result in the infringement of another's patent. For example, if a company sells a computer add-on card for a specific use that will infringe another's patent, the sale is a contributory infringement even though the add-on card itself does not infringe any patent. Direct infringement can be committed innocently and unintentionally; indirect and contributory infringement require some knowledge or intent that a patent will be infringed.

## DEFENSES

A defendant to a patent-infringement action may claim a variety of defenses, including (1) noninfringement of the patent, (2) invalidity of the patent, (3) misuse of the patent, or (4) innocent infringement.

### Noninfringement

The defense of *noninfringement* asserts that the allegedly infringing matter does not fall within the claims of the issued patent. Under this defense, the specific language of the patent claims is compared with the allegedly infringing matter. If the allegedly infringing matter is not described by the patent claims, the defense of noninfringement is successful. The doctrine of *file-wrapper estoppel* prevents a patent owner from asserting any claim interpretation at odds with the application on file with the PTO. Because the patent holder has previously negotiated the scope of his or her invention with the PTO, the patent holder may not renegotiate that scope in a subsequent court proceeding.

In 1996, the U.S. Supreme Court held that the construction of the words in patent claims is a matter of law for the court, not the jury, to decide.[16] The Court reasoned that "[t]he construction of written instruments is one of those things that judges often do and are likely to do better than jurors unburdened by training in exegesis."

### Invalidity

A patent is presumed to be valid, but a court may find it invalid if (1) the invention was not novel, useful, or nonobvious when the patent was issued; (2) the patent covers nonstatutory subject matter such as an abstract idea, a scientific principle, or a mental process; (3) a statutory bar was created by a publication or sale of the invention more than one year prior to the filing of the patent application; or (4) any other requirement of the patent law was not met.

### Patent Misuse

A *patent misuse* defense asserts that although the defendant has infringed a valid patent, the patent holder has abused its patent rights and therefore has lost, at least temporarily, its right to enforce them. Courts have found misuse when a patent holder has conditioned the granting of a patent license upon the purchase of other, unrelated goods or technologies. The patent holder will be barred from recovering for any infringement of its patent during the period of misuse. If the patent holder later "purges" itself of the misuse, it may recover for any subsequent infringement.

### Innocent Infringement

A defendant may claim innocent infringement if the patented item did not carry adequate notice of its patent status. Although this is not a complete defense to patent infringement, a patent owner cannot sue for damages until the defendant receives actual notice of infringement. Filing an infringement suit constitutes notice but does not allow the patent owner to recover damages for any infringement that occurred before the notice.

## REMEDIES

If a valid patent has been infringed, the patent holder may seek preliminary and permanent injunctive relief and damages, as well as court costs and attorneys' fees.

### Injunctive Relief

A patent holder may use a preliminary injunction to prevent any further infringement of the patent pending the court's ultimate decision. Most courts, however, are reluctant to grant injunctive relief before they have determined that a valid patent has actually been infringed. Once such a determination has been made, the patent holder is entitled to permanent injunctive relief.

15. Festo Corp. v. Shoketsu Kinzoku Kogyo Kabushiki Co., 535 U.S. 722 (2002).

16. Markman v. Westview Instruments, Inc., 517 U.S. 370 (1996).

### ETHICAL CONSIDERATION

Some inventors have made fortunes by turning out a steady stream of blueprints and drawings for new or improved devices without bothering to develop them into commercial products or even to create prototypes. Instead, they design their claims on top of existing products in order to create infringements by current manufacturers; then they delay filing their applications as long as possible to maximize their patents' value and longevity.[a] Is it ethical to use the patent system simply to collect revenue rather than to spur innovation?

**a.** For an example of such a controversy, see Bernard Wysocki, Jr., *How Patent Lawsuits Make a Quiet Engineer Rich and Controversial,* WALL ST. J., Apr. 9, 1997, at A1.

### *Damages*

Damages may also be awarded, based on a reasonable royalty for the infringer's use of the invention. Court costs, as fixed by the court, may be added. The court also has discretion to increase the damages award by up to three times for intentional or willful infringement and to award attorneys' fees in exceptional cases.

The instant-camera litigation between Polaroid Corporation and Eastman Kodak Company illustrates the potential for large damages awards for patent infringement. In the 1970s, Kodak sought a license from Polaroid to produce instant cameras and film, but the parties never reached an agreement. When Kodak nonetheless introduced an instant camera and film in 1976, Polaroid sued for patent infringement. A federal district court held that Kodak had infringed twenty claims of seven Polaroid patents and enjoined Kodak from any further infringements. The injunction terminated Kodak's instant-camera business and left it with $200 million worth of useless manufacturing equipment and $600 million in losses.[17] Kodak was later ordered to pay Polaroid $910 million for infringing its patents, including $454.2 million in lost profits and royalties and $455.3 million in interest. Even though this was the largest award ever granted in a patent-infringement suit, it "disappointed Polaroid and heartened Kodak, for it was less than Polaroid originally sought."[18]

Patent litigation is a high stakes game for both established market participants and small companies. In 2004, Hewlett-Packard filed a patent-infringement suit against Gateway, claiming that Gateway refused to pay license fees on six of HP's PC-related patented designs.[19] Although HP refused to state the magnitude of Gateway's alleged liability—which could be tens of millions of dollars—it asked the court for triple damages and attorneys' fees. HP also filed a complaint with the U.S. International Trade Commission, seeking to ban Gateway from importing infringing computers and components. In response, Gateway countersued HP, claiming that HP had violated five Gateway patents related to multimedia functions and alleging that HP's patents were invalid. Gateway also filed a complaint with the International Trade Commission, seeking to ban HP from importing infringing computers, monitors, and components. Both sides claimed they were ready for a long fight, although they also appeared to be open to settling the dispute.

It can be much more difficult for small companies to recover damages from larger firms because of the prohibitive cost of patent litigation. One analyst says that "seventy-six percent of patent suits settle, but not before each side incurs more than $1 million in direct legal fees and indirect expenses."[20] Some corporations purposely lengthen and complicate the discovery process in order to strain the resources of their smaller challengers. Nevertheless, patent rights can provide a David with an effective means to strike down a Goliath. For example, Stac Electronics sued Microsoft for patent infringement in 1994, and a jury awarded Stac $120 million.[21] More recently, SPX Corporation successfully sued Microsoft for willful infringement of SPX's real-time conferencing technology, and a jury awarded SPX $62.3 million.[22]

## Copyrights

Best-selling novels, award-winning films, off-the-shelf software packages, and compact discs are all copyrightable works. So are restaurant menus, digital

17. Polaroid Corp. v. Eastman Kodak Co., 789 F.2d 1556 (Fed. Cir. 1986).
18. Lawrence Ingrassia & James S. Hirsch, *Polaroid's Patent-Case Award, Smaller than Anticipated, Is a Relief for Kodak,* WALL ST. J., Oct. 15, 1990, at A3.
19. Rachel Konrad, *HP Sues Gateway for Patent Infringement,* BOSTON.COM, *at* http://www.boston.com/business/technology/articles/2004/03/26/hp_sues_gateway_for_patent_infringement.
20. Kimberly Moore, *Judges, Juries, and Patent Cases—An Empirical Peek Inside the Black Box,* 99 MICH. L. REV. 365, 367 (2000).
21. Morgan Chu, *A Giant-Killer Should Limit Scope of Attack,* NAT'L L.J., Mar. 13, 1995, at C10. This litigation was settled when Microsoft agreed to pay Stac $43 million and buy $40 million of Stac stock.
22. Press Release, SPX, SPX Corporation and Microsoft Research Settlement in Patent Infringement Suit (Dec. 24, 2003), *available at* http://investors.spx.com/releasedetail.cfm?releaseid=125325. This litigation was settled a month later for $60 million. Christopher Sanders, *Microsoft Settles NetMeeting Suit,* Dec. 29, 2003, *at* http://www.instantmessagingplanet.com/enterprise/article.php/3293651.

videodiscs, designer linens, plush toy animals, and cereal boxes. The United States Copyright Act of 1976 requires that the material for which copyright protection is sought be original (not copied) and fall within one of the following categories: (1) literary works; (2) musical works; (3) dramatic works; (4) pantomimes and choreographic works; (5) pictorial, graphic, and sculptural works; (6) motion pictures and other audiovisual works; and (7) sound recordings.

The Act requires that the works be fixed in a tangible medium from which they can be perceived, reproduced, or communicated. For example, stories may be fixed in written manuscripts, computer software on floppy disks, recordings of songs on compact discs, and the staging of a play recorded on videotape. Copyright does not extend to names, familiar phrases, government publications, standardized information, or facts. Copyright protects expression; it does not protect the underlying ideas.

In addition to being fixed, the works must be sufficiently original—have some degree of creativity—to qualify for protection. As mentioned, facts are not copyrightable. A compilation of facts may be eligible for copyright protection, but only to the extent that the selection, coordination, or arrangement of the facts is original. As the U.S. Supreme Court explained in *Feist Publications,* "[t]he sine qua non of copyright is originality."[23] In that case, Feist, a publisher of a rural telephone directory, sued Rural Telephone for copying its listings in its rival telephone directory. Feist argued that because it had invested substantial time and effort in compiling and arranging the factual listings, the data were copyrightable. The Supreme Court rejected this "sweat of the brow" argument, holding that originality is the critical element of copyright protection and that the alphabetical arrangement of the phone listings was not sufficiently original to entitle it to copyright protection.

If an author can establish the fixity and originality of a work, copyright protection is automatic and entitles the author to the exclusive economic rights to (1) reproduce the copyrighted work, (2) prepare derivative works based on the copyrighted work, (3) distribute copies or phonorecords of the copyrighted work to the public, (4) perform the copyrighted work publicly, and (5) display the copyrighted work publicly.

## Ownership and Scope of Protection

The creator of the work or, in the case of a work made for hire, the party for whom the work was prepared, is the author of the copyrighted work. A *work made for hire* is either (1) a work created by an employee within the scope of his or her employment or (2) a work in one of nine listed categories that is specially commissioned through a signed writing that states that the work is a "work made for hire."

The author of a copyrighted work can transfer ownership by an assignment of copyright. Parties that commission independent contractors to produce works that fall outside the nine listed categories, such as computer programs, often seek copyright assignments.

The advent of nonprint media, such as CD-ROMs and electronic databases, has led to disputes between freelance writers and photographers on one side, and the newspapers and magazines that buy their work on the other, about who owns the electronic or digital rights. For example, a group of freelance writers sued the newspapers to which they sold their stories, alleging that the newspapers' publishing of their work in nonprint media exceeded the newspapers' rights to the material. The U.S. Court of Appeals for the Second Circuit agreed. Although the owner of a copyright for a collective work (in this case, the publisher of the newspaper or magazine) has the right to revise the individual works, it does not have the right to republish them in an electronic database.[24] The publishers appealed, but the U.S. Supreme Court affirmed the Second Circuit's ruling, underscoring the importance of negotiating an assignment of rights that clearly applies to any known or future media.[25]

### *Expression Versus Idea*

The Copyright Act prohibits unauthorized copying of the *protected expression* of a work, but the underlying ideas embodied in the work remain freely usable by others. Section 102 of the Act excludes from copyright protection any "idea, procedure, process, system, method of operation, concept, principle or discovery, regardless of the form in which it is described, explained, illustrated, or embodied."

The U.S. Court of Appeals for the First Circuit held that the menu-command structure of the Lotus 1-2-3 computer spreadsheet program, taken as a whole—including the choice of command terms; the structure, sequence, and organization of these terms; their presentation on the screen; and the long prompts—was a method of operation and therefore not protectable.[26] The court reasoned that Lotus 1-2-3's use of commands

23. 499 U.S. 340, 345 (1991).

24. Tasini v. New York Times, 206 F.3d 161 (2d Cir. 2000), *cert. granted,* 531 U.S. 978 (2000).

25. Tasini v. New York Times, 533 U.S. 483 (2001).

26. Lotus Dev. Corp. v. Borland Int'l, Inc., 49 F.3d 807 (1st Cir. 1995), *aff'd,* 516 U.S. 233 (1996).

labeled "Print" and "Copy" was no different from buttons on a videocassette recorder (VCR) labeled "Play" and "Fast Forward." Labeling and arranging the VCR buttons does not make them an expression of the abstract method of operating a VCR. Rather, the buttons *are* the method of operating the VCR. To the extent there was expression in Lotus 1-2-3's choice of terms such as "Exit" or "Save," the court deemed it part of the method of operation and therefore not copyrightable. Quoting the U.S. Supreme Court's *Feist* decision,[27] the court noted that "copyright assures authors the right to their original expression, but encourages others to build freely upon the ideas and information conveyed by that work." An evenly divided U.S. Supreme Court affirmed.

When an idea and its expression are inseparable, the *merger doctrine* dictates that the expression is not copyrightable. If it were, the copyright would confer a monopoly over the idea. Thus, a manufacturer of a karate video game cannot keep a competitor from producing another video game based on standard karate moves and rules. The idea of a karate game (including game procedures, karate moves, background scenes, a referee, and the use of computer graphics) is not protected expression. The manufacturer can, however, keep a competitor from copying any original graphics it has used in the game so long as they are not inseparable from the idea of karate or of a karate video game.

### *Useful Article Doctrine*

The *useful article doctrine* provides that copyright protection does not extend to the useful application of an idea. The Copyright Act defines pictorial, graphic, and sculptural works to include "works of artistic craftsmanship insofar as their form but not their mechanical or utilitarian aspects are concerned." For example, blank forms used to record, rather than convey, information are considered noncopyrightable useful articles.

If the expression of a pictorial, graphic, or sculptural work cannot be identified separately from and exist independently of such utilitarian aspects, courts will deny copyright protection to the whole work. An example of an article whose expression is separable from its utilitarian aspects would be a lamp that incorporates a statue of a woman in its base. An example of an article whose expression is not separable from its utilitarian aspects is the layout of an integrated circuit. Although a drawing of the circuit is copyrightable, the actual circuitry is not copyrightable because it is impossible to separate the utilitarian aspect of the circuit from its expression or layout. It is the layout of the circuit that enables the circuit to operate correctly. The circuit may be patentable, however. In addition, the layout or topography of the circuit may be protectable as a registered mask work under the Semiconductor Chip Protection Act of 1984.

## PREEMPTION OF STATE LAW

Because the Copyright Act is a federal statute, it preempts any state law that enforces rights "equivalent" to one of the exclusive rights in federal copyright. Nonetheless, copyright law does not preempt a state law if the state-protected rights are qualitatively different from those protected under federal copyright.

For example, in *National Basketball Ass'n v. Motorola, Inc.*,[28] the National Basketball Association (NBA) sued Motorola and STATS for federal copyright infringement and for unfair competition under state law when Motorola began marketing the SportsTrax paging device, which displayed information on NBA games in progress with only a two- to three-minute lag. STATS reporters, who watched the games on television or listened to them on the radio, provided the data feed for SportsTrax.

The U.S. Court of Appeals for the Second Circuit noted that although a live event itself is not an "original [work] of authorship," a simultaneously recorded broadcast of the event is entitled to protection under the Copyright Act.[29] The court recognized that the *hot-news exception* applies in cases where (1) the plaintiff generates or gathers the information at a cost; (2) the information is time-sensitive; (3) the defendant's use of the information amounts to free riding on the plaintiff's efforts; (4) the defendant is in direct competition with the plaintiff; and (5) the availability of other parties to free ride on the plaintiff's efforts would so reduce the plaintiff's incentive to provide the product or service that its existence or quality would be threatened. The court concluded, however, that the hot-news exception did not apply in this case because the NBA failed to show that SportsTrax's free riding had any competitive effect on the NBA's incentive to provide a high-quality product; therefore, federal copyright law preempted the state misappropriation claim. Nonetheless, federal copyright law did not preclude STATS from collecting its data from television or radio broadcasts, and therefore the NBA's case was dismissed.

27. 499 U.S. 340 (1991).

28. 105 F.3d 841 (2d Cir. 1997).

29. 17 U.S.C. § 101.

In contrast, in *Brown v. Ames*,[30] the U.S. Court of Appeals for the Fifth Circuit ruled that state tort claims for misappropriation of the names and likenesses of music artists were not preempted by federal copyright law. The defendants had allegedly marketed CDs and cassettes of musical performances by the plaintiff artists without obtaining copyright permission and had used the artists' names and likenesses to assist in the illegal marketing effort. The artists sued for copyright infringement and for misappropriation. In deciding that the misappropriation claim was not preempted, the court emphasized that names and likenesses are not copyrightable and therefore could not be the subject of a federal copyright claim.

### TERM OF PROTECTION

The Sonny Bono Term Extension Act of 1998 extended the duration of U.S. copyrights by twenty years.[31] If the author is a known individual, the term is now the life of the author plus seventy years. For a work made for hire or for an anonymous or pseudonymous work, the term is the lesser of ninety-five years after first publication or one hundred and twenty years after creation of the work. Publishers and librarians, among others who opposed the Bono Act, brought an action to obtain an injunction on its enforcement, challenging the constitutionality of the Act on the basis that it was not "necessary and proper" to achieve the purpose of "promoting the progress of science and useful arts." In 2003, however, the Supreme Court upheld the extension, citing congressional authority to determine the scope and duration of copyright protection.[32]

### COPYRIGHT FORMALITIES: REGISTRATION AND NOTICE

U.S. copyright law traditionally required authors to both register their works with the Copyright Office and affix a notice to the work itself. Although neither formality is now required, U.S. copyright law still encourages authors to comply by conferring substantial benefits on those who do.

#### *Copyright Notice*

Copyright notices are not mandatory for works first published after March 1, 1989, but use of a notice will preclude an infringer from claiming innocent infringement in mitigation of actual or statutory damages.[33] Proper U.S. copyright notice for works distributed within the United States includes these elements: "Copyright" or "Copr." or "©," the year of first publication, and the name of the copyright owner.

#### *Copyright Registration*

For U.S. copyright owners, registration with the Copyright Office is a prerequisite to filing any infringement suit. Statutory damages and attorneys' fees are available only if either (1) the work was registered prior to the infringement at issue or (2) the owner registered the work within ninety days after first publication. Availability of statutory damages (up to $30,000 per infringement or up to $150,000 per willful infringement) can be particularly important for a start-up—or a more established company selling a new product—because the absence of historical sales can make it very difficult to prove actual damages (discussed later under Remedies). Registration also creates a legal presumption of ownership and copyright validity, which can be extremely helpful to a plaintiff in a copyright-infringement suit.

## Copyright Infringement

Copyright infringement occurs when a party copies, modifies, displays, performs, or distributes a copyrighted work without the owner's permission. The plaintiff in a copyright-infringement suit must show (1) substantial similarity of the protected expression, not merely substantial similarity of the ideas contained in the work; and (2) that the alleged infringer had access to the plaintiff's work.

### TYPES OF INFRINGEMENT

Copyright infringement may take three forms: direct, contributory, or vicarious.

#### *Direct Infringement*

*Direct copyright infringement* occurs when the copyright owner alleges that the defendant violated at least one of the five exclusive rights of the copyright holder. For example, the publishers in *Princeton University Press v. Michigan Document Service*[34] successfully sued a Michigan copy shop for direct infringement when the copy shop reproduced and sold excerpts of a variety of copyrighted works selected by professors without obtaining the publishers' permission to do so.

30. 201 F.3d 654 (5th Cir. 2000).
31. Sonny Bono Term Extension Act of 1998, Pub. L. No. 105-298, 11 Stat. 2827 (1998).
32. Eldred v. Ashcroft, 537 U.S. 186 (2003).
33. For works published before March 1, 1989, most copyright authorities agree that owners should continue to use a copyright notice to avoid the risk of releasing the work into the public domain.
34. 99 F.3d 1381 (6th Cir. 1996).

## *Contributory Infringement*

A party may also be liable for *contributory copyright infringement*—inducing, causing, or materially contributing to the infringing conduct of another with knowledge of the infringing activity. Recent case law on contributory infringement is based on the seminal Supreme Court decision in *Sony Corp. of America v. Universal City Studios.*[35] In 1984, Universal City Studios alleged that Sony, by manufacturing and selling the Betamax videocassette recorder, contributed to the infringement of Universal's copyrights on programs broadcast over the public airwaves, which viewers could copy using their VCRs. The Court held that the sale of copying equipment does not constitute contributory infringement if the product has substantial noninfringing uses. In Sony's case, the trial court had found that time-shifting of television programs by private, noncommercial viewers so that the programs could be viewed later was such a substantial noninfringing use. As a result, the Court held that Sony's manufacture and sale of VCRs did not contributorily infringe on Universal's copyrights.[36]

## *Vicarious Infringement*

A defendant may face *vicarious copyright liability* for a direct infringer's actions if the defendant (1) has the right and ability to control the infringer's acts and (2) receives a direct financial benefit from the infringement. Unlike contributory infringement, vicarious infringement does not require that the defendant know of the primary infringement. Although "direct financial benefit" certainly includes a percentage of the value of each illegal sale, it is not limited to such per-unit arrangements.

The *Napster* case illustrates how the Sony-Betamax principle of "substantial nonfringing use" and vicarious liability principles apply to peer-to-peer networks. In Napster's original system, users downloaded free file-sharing software from the Napster website that enabled them to (1) make MP3 files stored on their hard drives available to other Napster users, (2) search for MP3 files stored on other users' computers, and (3) transfer exact copies of those files from one computer to another. By uploading MP3 file names to Napster network servers, users added to the collective library of files available for transfer to any user logged into Napster. The music industry soon brought suit, claiming that Napster had engaged in contributory and vicarious copyright infringement.

In 2001, the U.S. Court of Appeals for the Ninth Circuit reviewed the case.[37] Because there can be no contributory or vicarious liability without direct infringement by a third party, the court first considered whether Napster's users engaged in direct infringement. Napster argued that its users did not directly infringe because they were engaged in a fair use of the material ("fair use" is discussed in the next section). The Ninth Circuit disagreed, holding that the users were engaged in wholesale, commercial copying of copyright-protected works. The court then found Napster liable under both contributory infringement and vicarious liability. Napster contributorially infringed because it knowingly encouraged and assisted its users' direct infringement. Napster met the two-prong vicarious liability test as well; the availability of the infringing material attracted customers, thereby increasing the user base on which Napster's future revenues depended. Napster's ability to control access to its servers and its software was sufficient to give it the requisite right and ability to supervise the infringing activity.

This and subsequent court decisions contributed to Napster's demise and its resurrection as a paid subscription service, but the file-sharing seed had been planted. Grokster, StreamCast, Aimster, KaZaa, and other systems arose to take Napster's place, and new litigation has tested the boundaries of the *Napster* decision. In 2004, the U.S. Court of Appeals for the Ninth Circuit considered whether Grokster and StreamCast were liable for contributory or vicarious copyright infringement.

35. 464 U.S. 417 (1984).

36. Courts have also applied this concept of contributory infringement to trademark law. *See* Hard Rock Café Licensing Corp. v. Concession Serv., Inc., 955 F.2d 1143 (7th Cir. 1992).

37. A & M Records, Inc. v. Napster, 239 F.3d 1004 (9th Cir. 2001).

A CASE IN POINT

**CASE 11.1**

**Metro-Goldwyn-Mayer Studios v. Grokster**

*United States Court of Appeals for the Ninth Circuit*
*380 F.3d 1154*
*(9th Cir. 2004), cert. granted, 125 S. Ct. 686 (2004).*

## In the Language of the Court

**› FACTS** In their continuing battle against all peer-to-peer file-sharing software, music publishers and motion picture studios (the copyright owners) sued Grokster and StreamCast Networks (the software distributors) for contributory and vicarious liability. The copyright owners claimed that the software distributors enabled users of their software to illegally copy and transmit copyrighted material.

*(Continued)*

(Case 11.1 *continued*)

Unlike previous peer-to-peer systems, Grokster and StreamCast provided free software that enabled users to connect to a decentralized file-sharing network of computers. There was no centralized server, and any computer on the network could function as a server if it met the technical requirements. Neither Grokster nor StreamCast maintained control over entry to the network. The district court held that neither software distributor was liable for copyright infringement. The copyright owners appealed.

**› ISSUE PRESENTED** Are distributors of peer-to-peer file-sharing software contributorily or vicariously liable for copyright infringements by users?

**› OPINION** THOMAS, J., writing for the U.S. Court of Appeals for the Ninth Circuit:

The question of direct copyright infringement is not at issue in this case. Rather, the Copyright Owners contend that the Software Distributors are liable for the copyright infringement of the software users. The Copyright Owners rely on the two recognized theories of secondary copyright liability: contributory copyright infringement and vicarious copyright infringement. . . .

**A. Contributory Copyright Infringement**

The three elements required to prove a defendant liable under the theory of contributory copyright infringement are: (1) direct infringement by a primary infringer, (2) knowledge of the infringement, and (3) material contribution to the infringement. . . .

**1. Knowledge**

. . .

In *Napster I,* we construed Sony-Betamax to apply to the knowledge element of contributory copyright infringement. *Napster I* held that if a defendant could show that its product was capable of substantial or commercially significant noninfringing uses, then constructive knowledge of the infringement could not be imputed. Rather, if substantial noninfringing use was shown, the copyright owner would be required to show that the defendant had reasonable knowledge of specific infringing files.

Thus, in order to analyze the required element of knowledge . . . , we must first determine what level of knowledge to require. If the product at issue is not capable of substantial or commercially significant noninfringing uses, then the copyright owner need only show that the defendant had constructive knowledge of the infringement. On the other hand, if the product at issue is capable of substantial or commercially significant noninfringing uses, then the copyright owner must demonstrate that the defendant had reasonable knowledge of specific infringing files and failed to act on that knowledge to prevent infringement.

In this case, . . . the software distributed by each defendant was capable of substantial noninfringing uses. . . .

. . .

. . . [T]he Copyright Owners argue that the evidence establishes that the vast majority of the software use is for copyright infringement. This argument misapprehends the *Sony* standard as construed in *Napster I,* which emphasized that in order for limitations imposed by *Sony* to apply, a product need only be *capable* of substantial noninfringing uses.

. . .

*(Continued)*

(Case 11.1 *continued*)

Having determined that the "reasonable knowledge of specific infringement" requirement applies here, we must then decide whether the Copyright Owners have raised sufficient genuine issues of material fact to satisfy that higher standard. . . .

. . . [A]t present, neither StreamCast nor Grokster maintains control over index files. As the district court observed, even if the Software Distributors "closed their doors and deactivated all computers within their control, users of their products could continue sharing files with little or no interruption.". . .

. . .

**2. Material Contribution**

. . .

. . . [T]he Software Distributors do not provide the "site and facilities" for infringement, and do not otherwise materially contribute to direct infringement. Infringing messages or file indices do not reside on defendants' computers, nor do defendants have the ability to suspend user accounts. . . .

. . .

The Copyright Owners have not provided evidence that defendants materially contribute in any other manner. . . . Both defendants . . . communicate with users incidentally, but not to facilitate infringement. All of these activities are too incidental to any direct copyright infringement to constitute material contribution.

. . .

**B. Vicarious Copyright Infringement**

Three elements are required to prove a defendant vicariously liable for copyright infringement: (1) direct infringement by a primary party, (2) a direct financial benefit to the defendant, and (3) the right and ability to supervise the infringers. . . .

The elements of direct infringement and a direct financial benefit, via advertising revenue, are undisputed in this case.

**1. Right and Ability to Supervise**

We agree with the district court that there is no issue of material fact as to whether defendants have the right and ability to supervise the direct infringers in this case. . . .

. . .

In *Cherry Auction*,[38] we held that the right and ability to supervise existed where a swap meet operator reserved the right to terminate vendors for any reason, promoted the swap meet, controlled access by customers, patrolled the meet, and could control direct infringers through its rules and regulations. . . .

It does not appear from any evidence in the record that either of the defendants has the ability to block access to individual users. Grokster nominally reserves the right to terminate access, while StreamCast does not maintain a licensing agreement with persons who download [its program]. However, given the lack of a registration and log-in process, even Grokster has no ability to actually terminate access to file sharing functions. . . .

. . .

The district court here found that unlike Napster, Grokster and StreamCast do not operate and design an "integrated service," which they monitor and control. We agree.

. . .

38. Fonovisa, Inc. v. Cherry Auction, Inc., 76 F.3d 259 (9th Cir. 1996).

*(Continued)*

(Case 11.1 *continued*)

### C. Turning a "Blind Eye" to Infringement

The Copyright Owners finally argue that Grokster and StreamCast should not be able to escape vicarious liability by turning a "blind eye" to the infringement of their users, and that "[t]urning a blind eye to detectable acts of infringement for the sake of profit gives rise to liability." If the Software Distributors had a right and ability to control and supervise that they proactively refused to exercise, such refusal would not absolve them of liability. However, although that rhetoric has occasionally been employed in describing vicarious copyright infringement, there is no separate "blind eye" theory or element of vicarious liability that exists independently of the traditional elements of liability. . . .

› **RESULT** The district court's grant of summary judgment for the defendants was affirmed. In December 2004, the U.S. Supreme Court agreed to hear the case.[39]

› **CRITICAL THINKING QUESTIONS**

1. Do you agree that Grokster's and StreamCast's file-sharing systems were sufficiently different from Napster's system to warrant this result?
2. What recourse do copyright owners have if they wish to prevent the sharing of copyrighted music files?

39. 125 S. Ct. 686 (2004).

## Defenses to Copyright Infringement

Defenses to copyright-infringement claims include the doctrines of fair use, first sale, and copyright misuse.

### *Fair Use Doctrine*

The *fair use doctrine,* embodied in Section 107 of the Copyright Act, provides that a person may infringe the copyright owner's exclusive rights without liability if he or she engages in such activities as literary criticism, social comment, news reporting, education, scholarship, or research. To decide what constitutes fair use, courts balance the public benefit of the defendant's use against any detrimental effect on the copyright owner's interests. In doing so, they consider (1) the purpose and character of the use (including whether it was for profit), (2) the economic effect of the use on the copyright owner, (3) the nature of the work used, and (4) the amount of the work used.

In *Campbell v. Acuff-Rose Music, Inc.,*[40] the U.S. Supreme Court held that a parody that uses no more than necessary of the lyrics and music of the original work to make it recognizable constitutes a fair use, even if the copied part is the heart of the original work. In a more recent case, the owners of the copyright for *Gone with the Wind* tried to enjoin publication of the parodic novel *The Wind Done Gone.*[41] The U.S. Court of Appeals for the Eleventh Circuit held that the copyright owners would be unlikely to defeat a claim of fair use because of the transformative nature of the latter novel, as well as the low risk that it would serve as a market substitute for the original work.

Fair use arguments are common in the academic environment. As mentioned earlier, a publisher sued a Michigan copy shop that was in the business of preparing course readers for university professors.[42] The professors excerpted a variety of copyrighted works, which the copy shop then compiled and sold to students without the permission of the copyright owners. The U.S. Court of Appeals for the Sixth Circuit noted that the copy shop's motivation was commercial profit, not education; the "transformative value" was slight, at best; the excerpts were substantial; and the market value of the original works was indeed harmed. As a result, the court found that the copy shop was liable for copyright infringement and enjoined it from further infringement.

Courts often find that all four factors in the fair use test tilt in favor of one party or the other. In the following case, the court weighed the various factors but found that they did not all point to the same result.

40. 510 U.S. 569 (1994).

41. Suntrust Bank v. Houghton Mifflin Co., 268 F.3d 1257 (11th Cir. 2001).

42. Princeton Univ. Press v. Michigan Document Serv., 99 F.3d 1381 (6th Cir. 1996).

A CASE IN POINT

**CASE 11.2**

**NXIVM Corp. v. The Ross Institute**

*United States Court of Appeals for the Second Circuit*
*364 F.3d 471*
*(2d Cir. 2004).*

## Summary

**› FACTS** NXIVM Corporation conducts executive training seminars for participants who pay for its proprietary materials and techniques. All participants sign a nondisclosure agreement regarding the materials. Rick Ross, a website operator of a database about cults, controversial groups, and "mind-control" organizations, acquired a NXIVM manual from a past seminar participant and posted excerpts from the manual on his website as part of his critical analysis of it. NXIVM sued Ross for copyright infringement and requested a preliminary injunction to require Ross to remove NXIVM's materials from the website. The district court denied the preliminary injunction, and NXIVM appealed.

**› ISSUE PRESENTED** Does criticism of proprietary seminar materials constitute fair use by a website operator with a commercial interest?

**› SUMMARY OF OPINION** The U.S. Court of Appeals for the Second Circuit applied the four-factor fair use test to the case, noting that all factors are considered together. With respect to the first factor, the purpose and character of the use, the court determined that the defendant had acted with bad faith in acquiring the materials through a breach of the nondisclosure agreement. Nevertheless, the court held that bad faith alone is not dispositive. Given the transformative nature of the defendant's criticism, the court found that the first factor weighed in favor of the defendant. The defendant's use of only minor amounts of material (given the size of the original manual) tilted the amount and substantiality factor to the defendant. In addition, the defendant's use was not a market substitute for the executive seminars, which tilted the economic effect factor in the defendant's favor as well. On the other hand, given the secretive and unpublished nature of the seminar manual, the nature of the work factor weighed in favor of the plaintiff.

**› RESULT** The defendant's quotations of seminar materials for purposes of criticism constituted fair use. The court affirmed the district court's denial of the preliminary injunction.

**› COMMENT** In a concurring opinion, one judge agreed with the majority's ultimate conclusion but viewed the defendant's bad faith as completely irrelevant to the fair use inquiry.

---

### *First Sale Doctrine*

Under the *first sale doctrine*, codified in Section 109(a) of the Copyright Act, a copyright owner has exhausted his or her statutory right to control distribution of a copyrighted item once the owner sells the item and thereby puts it in the stream of commerce. In 1998, the U.S. Supreme Court held that the first sale doctrine applies even when the product is sold outside the United States with the expectation that it will not be resold in the United States.[43] This decision dealt a blow to U.S. companies trying to combat the *gray market*, in which products are sold outside the normal channel of distribution, often at a discounted price.[44]

According to sellers of so-called premium brands, consumers are less willing to pay higher prices for high-quality products if they are sold by discounters. Thus, companies, such as high-end hair-product manufacturer L'anza, try to maintain a list of authorized retailers. By contrast, big retailers, such as Costco and Wal-Mart, favor application of the first sale doctrine to imports so that their consumers can buy brand name products at discounted prices.

43. Quality King Distrib., Inc. v. L'anza Research Int'l, Inc., 523 U.S. 135 (1998).

44. See Edward Felsenthan, *Copyright Scope Limited for Some Firms*, WALL ST. J., Mar. 10, 1998, at B5.

### *Copyright Misuse*

Modeled after the patent misuse doctrine, copyright misuse exists when a copyright owner leverages his or her statutory copyright to gain control over areas outside the copyright's intended scope. For example, if a copyright owner licenses its software on the condition that the licensee may not use its competitors' products or develop complementary products, that action will constitute copyright misuse. If a court finds misuse, the copyright owner cannot enforce its copyright against infringers until the misuse has been purged.

## PIRACY AND CURRENT RESPONSES

Piracy is a problem for many companies, but especially for software companies, which lose billions of dollars each year because of illegal copying or pirating of their software. According to a recent study by International Planning and Research, the software piracy rate in the United States is about 25 percent. The rapid growth of the Internet and file-sharing technology has facilitated such piracy and created new problems for copyright holders. The Business Software Alliance estimated that worldwide losses from all software piracy in 2003 amounted to nearly $29 billion.[45]

As discussed earlier, music publishers are being challenged by the file-sharing technologies that help evaders become ever more elusive. To identify illegal copying, the Recording Industry Association of America (RIAA) is using *web robots;* these programs search and index the Internet for specific content by visiting websites, requesting documents based on certain criteria, and following up with requests for documents referenced in the documents already retrieved. Companies are also using encryption, watermarking, and mandatory online activation. The RIAA focuses at least three-fourths of its antipiracy resources on the Internet and new technology.[46] Those resources include lawsuits against online music servers and against downloaders themselves, as in the RIAA's high-profile suits against college students, elementary and high school students, and many other casual music downloaders in 2003 and 2004.

## REMEDIES

Under the Copyright Act, a plaintiff can recover both its actual damages and the defendant's profits attributable to the infringements, to the extent that these are not duplicative. Alternatively, if the copyright is registered within three months of first publication or prior to the alleged infringement, a plaintiff may elect to recover statutory damages (which can be up to $30,000 for infringement and up to $150,000 for willful infringement), as well as attorneys' fees under certain circumstances. Injunctive relief, the seizure of infringing copies, and exclusion of infringing copies from import into the United States may also be available.

Although the Copyright Act does not provide a statutory right to a jury trial, a defendant in a copyright-infringement suit in which the copyright owner seeks statutory damages is entitled to a jury trial under the Seventh Amendment to the U.S. Constitution.[47] The defendant also has the right to have the jury determine the amount of statutory damages.

The Digital Millennium Copyright Act (DMCA) may apply to copyright violations as well. In a civil action, a court may impose injunctions and award damages, costs, and attorneys' fees. It may also order impounding, modification, or destruction of any devices or products involved in the violation. The court may punish repeat offenders by awarding treble damages.

## CRIMINAL LIABILITY

Willful infringers may face criminal penalties as well as civil remedies. Before 1997, criminal penalties applied only to willful copyright violations for commercial gain; those who stole copyrighted works and gave them away were immune from criminal prosecution. In December 1997, President Bill Clinton signed the No Electronic Theft Act, which punishes with fines and prison time those who copy compact discs, videocassettes, or software worth more than $1,000 without permission of the copyright holder. The law requires no proof that the defendant commercially gained from the infringement.[48] It is also a crime to fraudulently use or remove a copyright notice or to make false representations in connection with a copyright application.

The DMCA also imposes criminal penalties. Criminal sanctions include fines up to $500,000 and imprisonment up to five years for violators whom a court finds to be willful or motivated by financial gain. Repeat offenders face increased fines (up to $1 million) and up to ten years in prison. (See the "Inside Story" for more details on the DMCA.)

45. Business Software Alliance, *Major Study Finds 36 Percent of the Software in Use Worldwide Is Pirated,* July 7, 2004, *at* http://www.bsa.org/usa/press/newsreleases/Major-Study-Finds-36-Perent-of-Software-in-Use-Worldwide-is-Pirated.cfm.

46. *Copyright Owners Learning to Police Online Sales, Performance of Musical Works,* 66 U.S.L.W. 2483 (Feb. 17, 1998).

47. Feltner v. Columbia Pictures Television, Inc., 523 U.S. 340 (1998).

48. No Electronic Theft Act of 1997, Pub. L. No. 105-147, 111 Stat. 2687 (1997).

ECONOMIC PERSPECTIVE

## INTELLECTUAL PROPERTY RIGHTS AND INCENTIVES TO INNOVATE

A basic tenet of neoclassical economic theory is that productive efficiency and allocative efficiency will be achieved through free competition by private parties interested in maximizing their own welfare. Productive efficiency exists when competition among individual producers drives all but the lowest-cost producers of goods or services out of the market. Allocative efficiency exists when scarce societal resources are allocated to the production of various goods and services up to the point at which the cost of producing each good or service equals the benefit society reaps from its use.

In general, U.S. economic policy is to foster the functioning of free markets in which individuals may compete. For example, the antitrust laws, discussed in Chapter 16, are designed to protect competition by prohibiting any individual entity or group of entities from monopolizing an industry.

The area of intellectual property is a seeming exception to the general free-market orientation of the U.S. economy. Patent laws provide inventors with the opportunity to gain a legally enforceable monopoly to prevent the manufacture, use, and sale of their inventions for a limited time.

The economic rationale for granting monopolies to inventors is based on the high value of innovation to society and the need to provide incentives to inventors. Without legal rules protecting the ownership of inventions, once a valuable new product or cost-saving technique is introduced, others could immediately copy and profit from it, even though they bore none of the cost of its creation. Technological advances are crucial to a growing economy. Development of new techniques increases productive efficiency, thereby expanding the quantity of goods and services that can be produced with a given level of societal resources. Development of new products meeting previously unfulfilled needs increases the welfare of society as a whole. Such innovation has taken on increasing importance for the United States in the international context. Although countries with lower-cost labor have a competitive advantage in the manufacture of goods with established production techniques, the United States' competitive advantage lies in its ability to develop new technologies.

Individuals will produce innovations only up to the point at which the rewards they reap equal their costs. To ensure that innovations are produced fully up to the point at which the social cost equals the social benefit (that is, to ensure allocative efficiency), the law must guarantee to innovators a significant part of the benefit from their innovations. The U.S. solution to this problem is to provide inventors whose inventions meet the requirements for a patent with a limited monopoly to exclude others from the manufacture, use, and sale of those inventions. This system ensures that inventors will be able to capture the full benefit of their inventions during the period of their monopoly and that the innovation will be freely available to others thereafter. The stringent requirements for patents are designed to prevent unnecessary restrictions on free competition. In fact, overly broad patents can actually hamper innovation.[a]

An important secondary objective is to give the scientific community access to state-of-the-art technology. Without a legal monopoly, innovators would keep their advances secret to prevent others from copying them. Such secrecy would result in waste of scarce societal resources, as other researchers would struggle to discover what is already known.

The World Bank has identified property rights, including intellectual property rights, as one of the keys to energizing countries in transition to market-based economies. Many developing and transitioning economies have already adopted intellectual property laws similar to those of the developed nations, but, as the World Bank acknowledges, these laws are difficult to enforce. Nevertheless, enforcement of these laws will encourage development of intellectual property and the foreign investment needed to spur growth.

**a.** Adam B. Jaffe & Josh Lerner, Innovation and Its Discontents: How Our Broken Patent System Is Endangering Innovation and Progress, and What to Do About It 56–77 (2004).

## Registered Mask Work

The Semiconductor Chip Protection Act of 1984 created a highly specialized form of intellectual property, the *registered mask work*. Semiconductor masks are detailed transparencies representing the topological layout of semiconductor chips. The mask work was the first significant new intellectual property right introduced in the United States in nearly one hundred years. The Act gives the owner copyright-like exclusive rights in the registered mask work for a period of ten years and prohibits its copying or use by others. The Act specifically allows reverse engineering, however. The law was aimed primarily at counterfeiters who replicate the semiconductor masks for a chip already on the market and produce the chips without having to expend their own resources on development. Remedies for infringement include injunctive relief, damages, and impoundment of the infringing mask and chips.

## Trademarks

Most people associate a particular trademark with the product to which it is applied without considering how this association has been generated. For example, when consumers purchase Apple computers, they usually do not think about how the word for a type of fruit has become representative of that particular brand of personal computer. Trademark law concerns itself with just such questions: how trademarks are created, how trademark rights arise, how such rights are preserved, and why certain marks are given greater protection than others.

### Ownership and Scope of Protection

The federal trademark act, known as the Lanham Act, and the 1988 Trademark Law Revision Act[49] define a trademark as "any word, name, symbol, or device or any combination thereof adopted and used by a manufacturer or merchant to identify and distinguish his goods, including a unique product, from those manufactured or sold by others, and to indicate the source of the goods, even if that source is unknown."

49. 15 U.S.C. §§ 1051–1072.

This definition has been interpreted as recognizing four different purposes of a trademark: (1) to provide an identification symbol for a particular merchant's goods, (2) to indicate that the goods to which the trademark has been applied are from a single source, (3) to guarantee that all goods to which the trademark has been applied are of a constant quality, and (4) to advertise the goods.

A trademark tells a consumer where a product comes from and who is responsible for its creation. A trademark also implies that all goods sold under the mark are of a consistent level of quality. A consumer purchasing french fries at a McDonald's restaurant, for instance, can reasonably expect them to taste as good as those sold at any other McDonald's. The trademark does not necessarily reveal the product's manufacturer. For example, the trademark Sanka identifies a brand of decaffeinated coffee. We may not know whether the manufacturer is a company called Sanka, but we know that all coffee products bearing the Sanka mark are sponsored by a single company (or its licensees).

For producers, a trademark represents the goodwill of a business, that is, an accumulation of satisfied customers who will continue buying from that business. Trademark rights are largely determined by the perceptions and associations in the minds of the buying public, so maintaining a strong trademark is essential to preserving the success of a business. The top brand names for 2004 are listed in Exhibit 11.2.

The first trademark issued in 1900 was for Cream of Wheat and its design, which is still in use. The first trademark registered in the new millennium was issued to a cosmetic company, Origins Natural Resources, Inc., for its name and design. The PTO registered over 220,000 trademarks in 2003 alone.

**EXHIBIT 11.2** **Most Valuable Brand Names in 2004**

| 2004 Rank | 2004 Brand Value (in millions) | 2003 Brand Value (in millions) | Percentage Change (from prior year) |
|---|---|---|---|
| 1. Coca-Cola | $67,394 | $70,453 | −4% |
| 2. Microsoft | 61,372 | 65,174 | −6 |
| 3. IBM | 53,791 | 51,767 | +4 |
| 4. GE | 44,111 | 42,340 | +4 |
| 5. Intel | 33,499 | 31,112 | +8 |
| 6. Disney | 27,113 | 28,036 | −3 |
| 7. McDonald's | 25,001 | 24,699 | +1 |
| 8. Nokia | 24,041 | 29,440 | −18 |
| 9. Toyota | 22,673 | 20,784 | +9 |
| 10. Marlboro | 22,128 | 22,183 | 0 |

Source: *Cult Brands,* BUS.WK. ONLINE, Aug. 2, 2004, *at* http://www.businessweek.com/magazine/content/04_31/b3894096.htm.

Although most trademarks are verbal or graphic, trademark law also protects distinctive shapes, odors, packaging, and sounds. For instance, there is trademark protection for the unique shape of the Coca-Cola bottle and the sound of NBC's three chimes. Color may also qualify as a trademark. In *Qualitex Co. v. Jacobson Products Co.*,[50] the Supreme Court articulated two principal criteria for determining whether trademark protection is available for a color: (1) the color must have attained secondary meaning and thus identifies and distinguishes a particular brand, and (2) the color must not serve a useful function because granting trademark protection in this circumstance would amount to the grant of monopoly control.

## OTHER MARKS

Trademarks should not be confused with other forms of legally protected identifying marks, such as service marks, trade names, and certification marks.

### *Service Marks*

A trademark is used in connection with a tangible product; a *service mark* is used in connection with services. The law concerning service marks is almost identical to that of trademarks.

### *Trade Names*

Whereas a trademark is used to identify and distinguish products, a *trade name* or a corporate name identifies a company, partnership, or business. Trade names cannot be registered under federal law unless they are also used as trademarks or service marks. The use of a trade name—evidenced by the filing of articles of incorporation or a fictitious business name statement—gives the company using the name certain common law rights, however.

### *Certification Marks*

A *certification mark* placed on a product indicates that the product has met the certifier's standards of safety or quality. An example is the "Good Housekeeping" seal of approval placed on certain consumer goods.

# Choosing a Trademark

To get a sense of how one chooses a trademark, consider a hypothetical entrepreneur who has developed a new form of computer software. This entrepreneur's program takes personal information—such as place and date of birth and daily biorhythms—and processes it to give the user predictions as to what may happen in the future based on "the past" (the inserted information). He has chosen three possible names for his software: Viron, Venus, and Gypsy in a Disc.

The entrepreneur wants to be certain that the trademark he chooses for his software is protectable. Under trademark law, the degree of protection is determined by where a trademark can be classified on a continuum of distinctiveness. The more distinctive a mark is, the less likelihood of confusion with other marks. Hence, fanciful and arbitrary marks, which are the most distinctive, are given, at least initially, the greatest legal protection, and descriptive marks, which are the least distinctive, receive no initial protection. The policy is to reward originality in the creation of a mark. Exhibit 11.3 shows where different types of marks fall on the distinctiveness continuum.

## FANCIFUL AND ARBITRARY MARKS

Fanciful or arbitrary marks are often called strong marks because they are immediately protectable.

### *Fanciful Marks*

A *fanciful mark* is a coined term having no prior meaning until used as a trademark in connection with a particular product. Fanciful marks are usually made-up words, such as Kodak for camera products and Exxon for gasoline. In the hypothetical, "Viron" is an example of a fanciful, made-up mark.

### *Arbitrary Marks*

*Arbitrary marks* are real words whose ordinary meaning has nothing to do with the trademarked product, for example, Camel for cigarettes and Shell for gasoline. In the hypothetical, "Venus" is an example of an arbitrary mark.

## SUGGESTIVE MARKS

A *suggestive mark* suggests something about the product without directly describing it. After seeing the mark, a consumer must use his or her imagination to determine the nature of the goods. For instance, Chicken of the Sea does not immediately create an association with tuna fish; it merely suggests some type of seafood. In the hypothetical, "Gypsy in a Disc" is an example of a suggestive mark. It merely suggests a future-predicting software program.

50. 514 U.S. 159 (1995).

EXHIBIT 11.3 **The Varying Distinctiveness of Trademarks**

The same word can be arbitrary, suggestive, descriptive, or generic, depending on the product on which it is used.

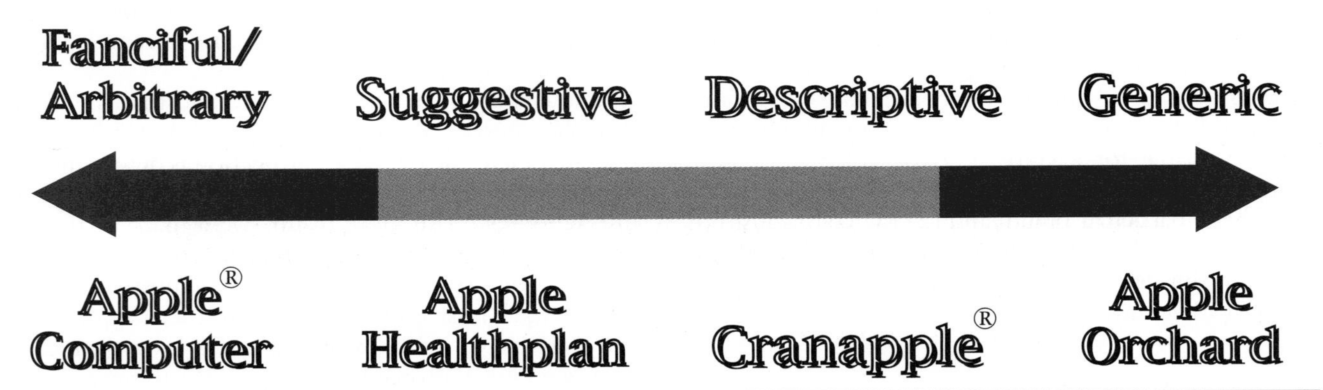


## Descriptive Marks

*Descriptive marks* specify certain characteristics of the goods, such as size or color, proposed uses, the intended consumers of the goods, or the effect of using the goods. Laudatory terms, such as First Rate or Gold Medal, are also considered descriptive marks.

### *Geographic Terms*

Geographic descriptive terms are usually considered nondistinctive unless secondary meaning (discussed below) has been established. Geographic terms used in an arbitrary manner are distinctive, however, for example, Salem for cigarettes and North Pole for bananas.

### *Personal Names*

Personal first names and surnames are not distinctive. But an arbitrary use of a historical name, such as Lincoln for a savings bank, does not require secondary meaning to be protectable.

Often even judges do not agree on whether a proposed trademark is distinctive or not. For example, in 1998, AOL Time Warner registered "Buddy List" as a trademark for its Buddy Chat function, which let Internet users know when friends and family were online, thereby permitting real-time instant exchange of e-mails. After AOL sued AT&T to prevent it from using the term "Buddy List" on its WorldNet online service, the trial court held that the mark was not distinctive enough to warrant protection and dismissed the suit. The U.S. Court of Appeals for the Fourth Circuit reversed, concluding that the trial judge had failed to give proper weight to the PTO's finding that the "Buddy List" phrase was sufficiently distinctive.[51] It remanded the case for a trial to determine whether "Buddy List" was a protectable trademark.

### *Secondary Meaning*

Descriptive marks are initially unprotectable, but they can still become protectable if they acquire *secondary meaning*, that is, a mental association by the buyer that links the mark with a single source of the product. Through secondary meaning, a mark obtains distinctiveness. Once this occurs, the mark is granted trademark protection. Secondary meaning is necessary to establish trademark protection for descriptive marks, including geographic terms and personal names.

Establishment of secondary meaning depends on a number of factors, such as the amount of advertising, the type of market, the number of sales, and consumer recognition and response. The testimony of random buyers or of product dealers may be required to prove that a mark has acquired secondary meaning.

## Generic Terms

Trademark law grants no protection to generic terms, such as "spoon" or "software," because doing so would permit a producer to monopolize a term that all producers should be able to use equally. It would be ridiculous to permit one manufacturer to obtain the exclusive right to use the word "computer," for example, and thereby force all competitors to come up with a new word, rather

51. America Online, Inc. v. AT&T Corp., 243 F.3d 812 (4th Cir. 2001).

than a brand name, for the same type of product. Generic terms are not protected even when they acquire secondary meaning.

Many terms that were once enforceable trademarks have become generic. For example, "escalator" was once the brand name of a moving staircase, and "cellophane" was a plastic wrap developed by DuPont. Due to misuse or negligence by the owners, these marks lost their connection with particular brands and became ordinary words (see Exhibit 11.4). That is the reason Xerox

**EXHIBIT 11.4** **Attempts to Preserve a Trademark**

Used by permission.

Corporation engages in substantial advertising to explain that you don't "Xerox" a document, you "copy" it on a Xerox copier.

For terms that describe products made by only one company, the problem of *genericism*—the use of the product name as a generic name—is acute. Without competitive products, buyers may begin to think of the trademark as indicative of what the product is rather than where the product comes from. Manufacturers can try to avoid this problem by always using the trademark as an adjective in conjunction with a generic noun. It is all right to say "Kleenex tissue" or "I'm going to use the Google search engine for research," but not "a Kleenex" or "I'm going to Google that research topic." Once the buying public starts using the mark as a synonym for the product, rather than as a means of distinguishing its source, loss of the trademark is imminent.

Microsoft battled genericism in its suit against Lindows.com, in which it claimed that the "Lindows.com" name infringed its Windows trademark. Lindows.com argued that Windows was a generic term used to describe general user interfaces at the time Microsoft launched its product. In response, Microsoft presented studies demonstrating that users subsequently came to associate the Windows term with Microsoft's operating system. The district court rejected Microsoft's argument, stating:

> [T]he Court declares it will instruct the jury to consider whether the Windows mark was generic during the period before Microsoft Windows 1.0 entered the marketplace in November 1985. Furthermore, the Court will *not* instruct the jury that even if Windows were generic prior to November 1985, the trademark would nonetheless be valued today so long as the primary significance of the term today is generic.[52]

The U.S. Court of Appeals for the Ninth Circuit denied Microsoft's appeal of the district court decision. Subsequent to the Ninth Circuit's decision, Microsoft reached an unusual settlement in which it agreed to pay Lindows.com $20 million to phase out the use of the Lindows.com name. Although Microsoft was unsuccessful in its trademark action against Lindows.com in the United States, several European courts proved more sympathetic to its arguments and forced Lindows.com to change its name and trademark in their countries.

52. Microsoft Corp. v. Lindows.com, Inc., 2004 WL 329250 (W.D. Wash. Feb. 10, 2004), *appeal denied*, Microsoft Corp. v. Lindows.com, Inc., 2004 WL 1208044 (9th Cir. 2004).

## Creating Rights in a Trademark

U.S. trademark owners initially obtain rights by using the mark in commerce or filing an "intent to use" application with the PTO. Following use in interstate commerce, owners may obtain additional rights by federal registration. State registration requires only intrastate use.

### Trademark Searches

A company about to use a new trademark needs first to conduct a trademark search to determine whether use of the proposed mark will constitute an infringement. The time, money, and effort spent on promotion and advertising will be wasted if use of the mark is ultimately prohibited.

There are various ways to search a mark. The records of the PTO provide information on federally registered marks; the office of the secretary of state can usually provide relevant data for that state's registered marks. Both state and federal registrations describe the mark and the goods it identifies, the owners of the mark, the date of registration, and the date on which the mark was first used. Most of this registration material has been computerized and can be accessed online.

Searching for unregistered common law marks is more difficult. Trade and telephone directories are often a good source of common law uses of marks. Some searches can be done by anyone using the Internet. There are also professional trademark search firms that search databases for customers. Although there is always the risk that a new mark or a common law user may be untraceable, any search is better than no search. Searching is evidence of a good faith effort to determine whether any other entity has preexisting rights in a mark.

### Common Law Rights of Use

A trademark is used in commerce if it is physically attached to goods that are then sold or distributed. Each subsequent use of a trademark creates greater rights because increased sales and advertising generate greater customer awareness of the mark as representing the product. Use is also necessary to establish secondary meaning for descriptive marks.

In the United States, the first person to sell the goods under a mark becomes the owner and senior user of the mark. The mark is protected immediately, provided the adoption and use of the mark are done in good faith and without actual or constructive knowledge of any superior rights in the mark.

There is an exception to the rule of first use. If a subsequent, or junior, user establishes a strong consumer identification with its mark in a separate geographic area, the junior user may be granted superior rights for that area. By failing to expand its business to other parts of the country, the senior user takes the risk that a junior user may be permitted to use the same or a confusingly similar mark in a distant area. The junior user's use must be in good faith; that is, the junior user must take reasonable steps to determine whether any preexisting mark is confusingly similar to the one it plans to use.

This geographic rule is inapplicable, however, if the senior user has applied for or obtained federal registration (see the next section). Once the senior user has filed an application or has obtained federal registration, it is permitted to claim nationwide constructive notice of the mark. This precludes any use of the mark—even a good faith use—by a junior user. Even with an application pending or registration, however, the senior user may not take any action against the junior user in a geographically removed area until the senior user is likely to expand into that area.

### FEDERAL REGISTRATION

Although not a requirement for obtaining U.S. rights in a mark, registration on the federal Principal Register provides (1) constructive notice of a claim of ownership in all fifty states, which makes it easier to enjoin subsequent users; (2) *prima facie* evidence of ownership; (3) the "incontestable" right (subject to certain defenses) to use the mark, obtainable after five years of continuous use following registration; and (4) the right to prevent importation into the United States of articles bearing an infringing mark.

Trademarks are grouped into different classes, covering over forty different industries and goods. When a trademark is registered, the holder of the mark must specify the particular class to which the mark belongs. Although a single trademark may be registered in more than one classification, it is also possible for the same mark to be registered by different holders for different types of products.

Certain marks that do not qualify for registration on the Principal Register may be registered on the Supplemental Register. Such registration does not afford the owner any of the above benefits, however, and should be pursued only upon the advice of counsel.

The PTO conducts federal registration of trademarks. An applicant may file either an "actual use" application or an "intent to use" application. For the latter, the applicant must state a bona fide intent to use the mark and must then commence use and provide the PTO with a statement of use within six months of receiving notice that its application is entitled to registration. The six-month period can be extended for up to thirty months, giving applicants a total of three years from the date of the notice of allowance in which to file the statement of use. Registration is postponed until the applicant actually uses the mark. The applicant has priority rights, however, against any party who did not use the same mark or file an application for it before the filing date of the intent to use application.

### STATE REGISTRATION

Although state registration does not provide as much protection as federal registration, it does offer certain benefits. In most states, registration can be obtained within a few weeks of filing and is proof of ownership of the mark. For marks that are not eligible for federal registration, state registration usually provides at least some protection as long as there has been sufficient use of the mark.

State registration cannot preempt or narrow the rights granted by federal registration. For example, a junior user with a state registration predating a senior user's federal registration gains exclusive rights in the mark only in the geographic area of continuous usage preceding the federal registration, and not the entire state. A state trademark law that purported to reserve the entire state for the junior user would be preempted by the Lanham Act.

## Loss of Trademark Rights

Failure to use one's mark—known as *abandonment*—may result in the loss of rights. A federally registered mark that has been abandoned can be used by a junior user. Trademark searches can reveal whether a previously registered trademark has lost its enforceability. There are two types of abandonment: actual and constructive.

### ACTUAL ABANDONMENT

*Actual abandonment* occurs when an owner discontinues use of the mark with the intent not to resume use. Mere nonuse for a limited period does not result in loss of protection. There is, however, a presumption of abandonment after two years of nonuse. Because protection for federally registered marks is nationwide, the abandonment must be nationwide for loss of rights to result.

### CONSTRUCTIVE ABANDONMENT

*Constructive abandonment* results when the owner does something, or fails to do something, that causes the mark to lose its distinctiveness. Constructive abandonment can result from a mark lapsing into genericism through improper use. It can also result from the failure of an owner to adequately control companies licensed to use its mark. Thus, a licensor should carefully exercise quality controls and approval procedures for its licensees' products in order to ensure a consistent quality level.

## Trademark Infringement

To establish direct trademark infringement, a trademark owner must prove (1) the validity of the mark (note that a federally registered mark is *prima facie* valid), (2) priority of usage of the mark, and (3) a likelihood of confusion in the minds of the purchasers of the products in question. A trademark owner may also allege vicarious and/or contributory infringement of his or her marks.

Proving validity and priority of usage is fairly straightforward if the mark is registered. If the mark is not registered, such proof is a factual matter. Establishing likelihood of confusion, on the other hand, involves subjectively weighing a variety of factors. These may include (1) the similarity of the two marks with respect to appearance, sound, connotation, and commercial impression; (2) the similarity of the goods; (3) the similarity of the channels of trade in which the goods are sold; (4) the strength of the marks, as evidenced by the amount of sales and advertising and the length of use; (5) the use of similar marks by third parties with respect to related goods and services; (6) the length of time of concurrent use without actual confusion; and (7) the extent and nature of any actual confusion of the two marks in the marketplace.[53]

Taking advantage of trademark confusion does not necessarily amount to infringement. In 1996, the U.S. Court of Appeals for the Sixth Circuit ruled that a travel agency had not infringed Holiday Inns' trademark in its vanity toll-free telephone number by using a similar number.[54] To promote itself, Holiday Inns had widely publicized its toll-free reservation line as 1-800-HOLIDAY, which translates to 1-800-465-4329 on a numeric keypad. Perhaps anticipating that dialers would mistake Holiday Inns' letter "O" for the number zero, the travel agency reserved the toll-free number 1-800-405-4329 for its own use. Though acknowledging the potential for confusion, the court rejected Holiday Inns' claim of trademark infringement. The travel agency did not create the confusion; it merely took advantage of it.

In 1996, Congress enacted the Federal Trademark Dilution Act of 1995,[55] which allows the owner of a famous mark to sue for injunctive relief from a party whose commercial use of a mark "begins after the mark has become famous and causes dilution of the distinctive quality of the mark." Dilution can result from "blurring" or "tarnishment." *Blurring* occurs when the nonfamous mark reduces the strong association between the owner of the famous mark and its products. *Tarnishment* occurs when use of the famous mark in connection with a particular category of goods or goods of an inferior quality reduces the positive image associated with the products bearing the famous mark.

To prevail in an action under the Federal Trademark Dilution Act, the trademark owner must prove actual dilution, not just the potential for dilution.[56] Damages are available only if the defendant willfully intended to trade on the reputation of the famous mark owner or to cause dilution of the famous mark; in this event, the trademark owner is entitled to recover its damages, the dilutor's profits, and costs. Unlike in an action for trademark infringement, relief is available even if the other mark does not cause consumer confusion as to the source of the product. In one dilution case, a court found that use of candyland.com for a child pornography website tarnished the value of Hasbro's popular trademarked "Candy Land" children's game.[57]

### DEFENSES

Possible defenses in trademark-infringement cases include the first sale and fair use doctrines, nominative use, genericity, and the First Amendment.

53. *See, e.g.,* Interstellar Starship Servs., Ltd. v. Epix, Inc., 304 F.3d 936 (9th Cir. 2002).

54. Holiday Inns, Inc. v. 800 Reservation, Inc., 86 F.3d 619 (6th Cir. 1996).

55. 15 U.S.C. §§ 1125, 1127.

56. Moseley v. V. Secret Catalogue, Inc., 537 U.S. 418 (2003).

57. Hasbro, Inc. v. Internet Entm't Group, Ltd., 1996 WL 84853 (W.D. Wash. Feb. 9, 1996).

### First Sale Doctrine

The first sale doctrine provides that a trademark owner cannot act against resellers of products after the first sale of the product. The idea behind the first sale doctrine is that the trademark owner had the chance to control the quality of the product and to make money on the first sale of the trademarked product. The first sale doctrine attempts to strike a balance among (1) trademark law's goal of allowing producers to reap the benefits of their reputation, (2) consumers' desire to receive what they bargain for, and (3) the public interest in maintaining competitive markets by limiting a producer's control of resale.

In 2003, Taylor Made Golf, a manufacturer of trademarked golf clubs, sued MJT Consulting, a company that sold Taylor Made clubs without authorization.[58] The court found that MJT had taken defective club heads that Taylor Made had rejected and discarded, affixed alternative shafts and grips, and sold the "new" clubs under the Taylor Made trademark. MJT's defense was that it had bought the club heads from a middleman (that represented that it had bought the club heads from another middleman), and Taylor Made's infringement claim was therefore invalid under the first sale doctrine. Pointing to factual evidence that the club heads were originally Taylor Made club heads, and that Taylor Made did not intend them to be sold, the court rejected MJT's defense on the basis that the first sale doctrine applies only where the seller is legally selling genuine trademarked goods.

58. Taylor Made Golf Co. v. MJT Consulting Group, LLC, 265 F. Supp. 2d 732 (N.D. Tex. 2003).

### Fair Use

The defense of fair use is available when a trademark user truthfully uses a competitor's mark to identify the competitor's product for the user's own purposes. The user must use the competitor's mark in its descriptive sense (for example, use of the mark in an index or catalog, or to describe the user's relationship to the mark's owner) and in good faith (the user must not intend to capitalize on the mark's goodwill or reputation). The Supreme Court has held that defendants relying on the fair use doctrine do not have to prove a lack of consumer confusion, noting that "some possibility of consumer confusion must be compatible with fair use."[59]

### Nominative Use

A defendant is not liable for trademark infringement if his or her use is *nominative use,* where the defendant uses the mark to talk about the mark itself. Courts employ a three-prong test in evaluating this defense: (1) there must be no descriptive substitute available, (2) the defendant must use no more of the mark than necessary, and (3) the use of the mark must not suggest sponsorship of the defendant by the mark's owner.[60] The distinction between a fair use defense and a nominative use defense is subtle, but important. The following case discusses this difference and illustrates when a nominative use defense is appropriate.

59. KP Permanent Make-Up, Inc. v. Lasting Impression, Inc., 125 S. Ct. 542, 550 (2004).

60. New Kids on the Block v. News Am. Publ'g, Inc., 971 F.2d 302 (9th Cir. 1992).

A CASE IN POINT

## In the Language of the Court

**CASE 11.3**

**Playboy Enterprises v. Welles**

*United States Court of Appeals for the Ninth Circuit 279 F.3d 796 (9th Cir. 2001).*

**› FACTS** Terri Welles was on the cover of *Playboy* in 1981 and was chosen to be the Playboy Playmate of the Year for 1981. Welles's website offered information about and free photos of Welles, advertised photos for sale, advertised memberships in her photo club, and promoted her services as a spokesperson. A biographical section described Welles's selection as Playmate of the Year in 1981 and her years modeling for Playboy Enterprises, Inc. (PEI).

Welles used (1) the terms "Playboy" and "Playmate" in the metatags of her website, (2) the phrase "Playmate of the Year 1981" on the masthead of the website, and (3) the phrases "Playboy Playmate of the Year 1981" and "Playmate of the Year 1981" on various banner ads. She also repeatedly used the abbreviation "PMOY '81" as the watermark on the pages of her website. PEI filed a lawsuit claiming that these uses of its marks constituted trademark infringement, dilution, false designation of origin, and unfair competition. After the lawsuit began, Welles included discussions of the suit and criticism of PEI on her website, in addition to a note disclaiming any association with PEI.

*(Continued)*

(Case 11.3 *continued*)

**› ISSUE PRESENTED** Did a former Playboy bunny's use of the terms "Playboy" and "Playmate" in the metatags of her website, the use of "Playboy Playmate of the Year 1981" on various banner ads and on the masthead of the website, and the repeated use of "PMOY '81" as the wallpaper of the website infringe PEI's trademarks?

**› OPINION** NELSON, J., writing for the U.S. Court of Appeals for the Ninth Circuit:

### A. Trademark Infringement

Except for the use of PEI's protected terms in the wallpaper of Welles' website, we conclude that Welles' uses of PEI's trademarks are permissible, nominative uses. They imply no current sponsorship or endorsement by PEI. Instead, they serve to identify Welles as a past PEI "Playmate of the Year."

We articulated the test for a permissible, nominative use in *New Kids on the Block v. New America Publishing, Inc.* The band . . . claimed trademark infringement arising from the use of their trademarked names by several newspapers. The newspapers had conducted polls asking which member of the band . . . was the best and most popular. The papers' use of the trademarked term did not fall within the traditional fair use doctrine. Unlike a traditional fair use scenario, the defendant newspaper was using the trademarked term to describe not its own product, but the plaintiff's. Thus, the factors used to evaluate fair use were inapplicable. . . .

We adopted the following test for nominative use:

> First, the product or service in question must be one not readily identifiable without use of the trademark; second, only so much of the mark or marks may be used as is reasonably necessary to identify the product or service; and third, the user must do nothing that would, in conjunction with the mark, suggest sponsorship or endorsement by the trademark holder.

. . .

We group the uses of PEI's trademarked terms into three for the purpose of applying the test for nominative use.

### 1. Headlines and banner advertisements.

. . .

The district court properly identified Welles' situation as one which must . . . be excepted. No descriptive substitute exists for PEI's trademarks in this context. . . . Just as the newspapers in *New Kids* could only identify the band clearly by using its trademarked name, so can Welles only identify herself clearly by using PEI's trademarked title.

The second part of the nominative use test requires that "only so much of the mark or marks may be used as is reasonably necessary to identify the product or service." . . . Welles' banner advertisements and headlines satisfy this element because they use only the trademarked words, not the font or symbols associated with the trademarks. . . .

The third element requires that the use do "nothing that would, in conjunction with the mark, suggest sponsorship or endorsement by the trademark holder." As to this element, we conclude that aside from the wallpaper, which we address separately, Welles does nothing in conjunction with her use of the marks to suggest sponsorship or endorsement by PEI. The marks are clearly used to describe the title she received from PEI in 1981, a title that helps describe who she is. . . .

. . .

*(Continued)*

(Case 11.3 *continued*)

For the foregoing reasons, we conclude that Welles' use of PEI's marks in her headlines and banner advertisements is a nominative use excepted from the law of trademark infringement.

**2. Metatags.**

Welles includes the terms "playboy" and "playmate" in her metatags. Metatags describe the contents of a website using keywords. Some search engines search metatags to identify websites relevant to a search. . . . Because Welles' metatags do not repeat the terms extensively, her site will not be at the top of the list of search results. Applying the three-factor test for nominative use, we conclude that the use of the trademarked terms in Welles' metatags is nominative.

As we discussed above with regard to the headlines and banner advertisements, Welles has no practical way of describing herself without using trademarked terms. . . .

Precluding their use would have the unwanted effect of hindering the free flow of information on the internet, something which is certainly not a goal of trademark law. . . .

We conclude that the metatags satisfy the second and third elements of the test as well. . . . We note that our decision might differ if the metatags listed the trademarked terms so repeatedly that Welles' site would regularly appear above PEI's in searches for one of the trademarked terms.

**3. Wallpaper/watermark.**

The background, or wallpaper, of Welles' site consists of the repeated abbreviations "PMOY '81," which stands for "Playmate of the Year 1981." . . . Accepting, for the purposes of this appeal, that the abbreviation "PMOY" is indeed entitled to protection, we conclude that the repeated, stylized use of this abbreviation fails the nominative use test.

The repeated depiction of "PMOY '81" is not necessary to describe Welles. "Playboy Playmate of the Year 1981" is quite adequate. Moreover, the term does not even appear to describe Welles—her name or likeness do not appear before or after each "PMOY '81." Because the use of the abbreviation fails the first prong of the nominative use test, we need not apply the next two prongs of the test.

[*Eds.:* The court then addressed the trademark dilution claims, concluding that nominative uses, by definition, do not dilute the trademark.]

**› RESULT** The court affirmed the district court's grant of summary judgment to Welles as to PEI's claims for trademark infringement and trademark dilution, but it remanded the case to the district court to determine whether trademark law protects the abbreviation "PMOY '81" as used in the wallpaper.

**› CRITICAL THINKING QUESTIONS**

1. Do you agree with the court's decision that Welles's repetition of "PMOY '81" on her wallpaper was not a nominative use?
2. Do you agree with the court's dismissal of fair use as a potential defense? Does the fair use doctrine also apply to Welles' uses of Playboys' marks? Why or why not?

### *Genericity*

As seen in the *Microsoft v. Lindows.com* litigation, genericity can be a defense when a trademark owner brings suit over a trademark that is arguably a generic term. Trademark owners must take appropriate measures to ensure that their marks are not, and do not become, generic.

### *First Amendment*

Defendants may claim a First Amendment defense when their use of another's trademark is part of their communicative or expressive message and thus is protected as free speech. For example, courts have upheld consumers' rights to criticize corporations or service providers through websites that use the corporation's trademarked name. Courts have protected these so-called gripe sites as protected speech even though the corporations often allege that the sites confuse other consumers, hurt their business, and dilute their trademarks.[61]

## REMEDIES

One of the most common remedies for trademark infringement is injunctive relief. Courts may also award damages, measured either by the owner's lost sales and profits due to the infringement or by economic injury to the owner's goodwill and reputation. To the extent they are not duplicative, courts may award the trademark owner the profits that the infringer earned through its use of the mark. In cases of flagrant infringement, a court may take the unusual step of awarding attorneys' fees to the trademark owner. Finally, in the particular case of trafficking in goods or services that knowingly use a *counterfeit mark,* the Lanham Act imposes substantial fines and/or imprisonment.[62]

# Trade Dress

In addition to protecting registered marks, courts interpret the Lanham Act to include protection for trade dress, that is, the packaging or dressing of a product. Trade dress includes all elements making up the total visual image by which a product is presented to customers as defined by its overall composition and design.

The elements of trade dress infringement parallel those of trademark infringement, with the likelihood of consumer confusion as the core issue. In one case, Best Cellars sued Grape Finds for copying the style and arrangement of its retail wine shops.[63] Best Cellars' business model was predicated on demystifying wine purchases for unsophisticated shoppers by using a "wall of wine" racking system and other distinctive visual displays. Grape Finds started using the same system. The court ruled that Best Cellars' store arrangements were arbitrary and therefore protectable and granted a preliminary injunction to prevent Grape Finds from using the same system in its stores.

The Supreme Court recently held that trade dress protection may not be claimed for functional product features.[64] In general, a product feature is functional if it is essential to the use or purpose of the article or if it affects the cost or quality of the article.

# Trade Secrets

In our free-market system, the demand for modern technologies and innovation may lead to unauthorized disclosure of sensitive information. Trade secret law is necessary to protect the owners of such information.

## SCOPE OF PROTECTION

The growing emphasis on the value of trade secrets has been accompanied by increasingly high stakes litigation. In 2000, a jury awarded $240 million to All Pro Sports Camps in its trade secret suit against Walt Disney Company.[65] All Pro had met with Disney to pitch its idea for a year-round sports complex. After declining to invest, Disney soon announced its own Wide World of Sports complex in Orlando. All Pro sued, citing architectural and design similarities between its idea and the new complex. After All Pro obtained a favorable jury award, Disney announced that it would appeal, but two years later, the parties settled for an undisclosed amount.[66]

61. Tresa Baldas, *The Cost of Griping on the Web: Lawsuits,* NAT'L L.J., Nov. 29, 2004, *at* http://www.law.com/jsp/nlj/PubArticleNLJ.jsp?id=1101136524084.

62. The Lanham Act defines a "counterfeit mark" as "(a) a spurious mark (i) that is used in connection with trafficking in goods or services; (ii) that is identical with, or substantially indistinguishable from, a registered trademark, and (iii) the use of which is likely to cause confusion or mistake or to deceive, or (b) a spurious designation that is identical with, or substantially indistinguishable from, the holder of the right to use the designation." 18 U.S.C. § 2320(e).

63. Best Cellars, Inc. v. Grape Finds at Dupont, Inc., 90 F. Supp. 2d 431 (S.D.N.Y. 2000).

64. Traffix Devices, Inc. v. Mktg. Displays, Inc., 532 U.S. 23 (2001).

65. *Disney Must Pay $240 Million in Sports Park Lawsuit,* CNN.COM, Aug. 11, 2000, *at* http://archives.cnn.com/2000/LAW/08/11/disney.lawsuit.01/.

66. *Disney Settles Sports Complex Case,* ST. PETERSBURG TIMES ONLINE, Sept. 26, 2002, *at* http://www.sptimes.com/2002/09/26/Business/Disney_settles_sports.shtml.

# View from Cyberspace

## DOMAIN NAMES AND CYBERSQUATTING

Internet addresses are called *domain names.* The top-level domain is the domain name's suffix, which characterizes the type of organization. For example, ".edu" is used by educational organizations, and ".com" is used by commercial organizations. Country codes, such as ".fr" for France, also serve as top-level domain names. The secondary domain identifies the specific organization. For example, in the domain name "cnn.com," the "cnn" identifies Cable News Network. As the Internet increasingly is used to conduct business, companies seek domain names that easily identify their Web locations. Disputes have arisen when entities have registered domain names that are confusingly similar to another business's trademark. Unlike the trademark system, where more than one company can register the same mark for noncompetitive products or services, only one entity can own the right to each domain name.

The Internet Corporation for Assigned Names and Numbers (ICANN) is the regulatory body that oversees the Internet's address system. Until 2000, only a limited number of top-level domain names were available through ICANN, forcing companies to compete for the treasured .com address. In November 2000, ICANN approved the use of seven new top-level domain names, thereby increasing the list of possible Internet addresses available. These new domain names included .aero, .biz, .info, .museum, .name, and .pro. In 2004, ICANN preliminarily approved four additional domain names: .mobi, for use in the cell-phone industry; .jobs, for human resources; .post, for postal services; and .travel, for the travel industry. Nevertheless, .com continues to be the most popular and most sought-after top-level domain name by far.

Domain names are registered on a first-come, first-served basis. Because the registrar does not check whether use of the name by the person seeking registration would violate someone else's trademark, the practice of *cybersquatting*, developed: an individual would register famous trademarks as domain names and then offer to sell them to the trademark owner for a "ransom."[a]

To combat this practice, ICANN developed a worldwide, fast-track online domain name dispute resolution policy (UDRP), which became effective in 1999; under the UDRP, a trademark owner who proves cybersquatting can receive an order from an arbitration panel that the domain name be canceled or transferred to the trademark owner. To prove cybersquatting under the UDRP, the complainant must prove that (1) the disputed domain name is identical or misleadingly similar to a trademark to which the complainant has rights, (2) the respondent has no legitimate rights in the domain name, and (3) the domain name is being held and used in bad faith. A successful complainant is not entitled to money damages under the UDRP. Supporters applauded the ICANN process, saying that it would "benefit small-business defendants who do not have the financial resources to battle major corporations in court."[b]

Even though the U.S. Department of Commerce had designated ICANN to set up a globally based system for Internet management, including trademark issues, Congress passed the Anticybersquatting Consumer Protection Act (ACPA) before it was clear whether ICANN's process would be able to solve the cybersquatting problem. The ACPA, which became effective on November 29, 1999, created a separate, federal remedy, applicable only to domestic name registrations. Under the ACPA, a complainant must prove that (1) the defendant has a bad faith intent to profit from a mark, including a defendant name that is protected as a mark, and (2) registers, traffics in, or uses a domain name that (a) in the case of a mark that is distinctive at the time of registration of the domain name, is identical or confusingly similar to that mark, or (b) in the case of a famous mark that is famous at the time of registration of the domain name, is identical or confusingly similar to or dilutive of that mark. The ACPA's definition of cybersquatting is broader than ICANN's definition in that it makes bad faith alone actionable, regardless of use. In addition to authorizing a court to order the forfeiture or cancellation of a domain name or the transfer of the domain name to the owner of the mark, the ACPA also authorizes the award of actual or statutory damages of not less than $1,000 and not more than $100,000 per domain name.

Critics of the ACPA expressed concern that Congress had undermined the ICANN's worldwide dispute resolution process: "In acting unilaterally, Congress has set a bad precedent. It[s action] encourages every nation to pass its own laws, creating a fragmented approach to resolving cross-border disputes over domain names."[c] Opponents also claimed that the ACPA infringed free

a *See, e.g.,* Panavision Int'l, L.P. v. Toeppen, 141 F.3d 1316 (9th Cir. 1998).

b. Aaron L. Melville, *New Cybersquatting Law Brings Mixed Reactions from Trademark Owners, at* http://www.bu.edu/law/scitech/volume6/Melville.htm (accessed Jan. 14, 2005).

c. Editorial, *What's in a (Domain) Name?,* SAN JOSE MERCURY NEWS, Nov. 1, 1999, at 6B.

*(Continued)*

(View from Cyberspace *continued*)

speech rights and overlooked small business and individual interests. Calling the ACPA "massive overkill," Michael Froomkin, a law professor at the University of Miami, predicted that its $100,000 in statutory penalties would allow large companies, like the Hollywood studios that pushed for its passage, to threaten small businesses and individuals. The first lawsuits based on the ACPA were filed just weeks after it was enacted. Harvard University filed a complaint on December 6, 1999, seeking an injunction against a defendant who registered sixty-five domain names related to Harvard and Radcliffe, and the New York Yankees brought an action against a fan who registered the name www.newyorkyankees.com in 1997.[d]

From the institution of the ICANN arbitration system through 2003, 5,845 arbitration decisions involving more than 9,722 domain names were issued. Of the 5,845 decisions, 4,595 resulted in domain name transfers or cancellations. From November 1999 through 2003, more than 700 lawsuits seeking injunctions or damages were filed.[e] At least one court has awarded $500,000 ($100,000 per domain) under the ACPA to deter a known cybersquatter from further squatting and to put him out of business.[f]

**d.** Melville, *supra* note b.

**e.** Judith Silver, *Cybersquatting Ain't What It Used To Be: Trademark Holders and the Future, at* http://library.lp.findlaw.com/articles/file/00982/008852/title/Subject/topic/Intellectual%20Property-Cybersquating/filename/intellectualproperty_1_745 (accessed Jan. 5, 2005).

**f.** Elecs. Boutique Holdings Corp. v. Zuccarini, 2000 U.S. Dist. LEXIS 15719 (E.D. Pa. 2000), 56 U.S.P.Q. 1705 (BNA).

Trade secret law is primarily the province of the states. Until recently, courts developed the law of trade secrets on a case-by-case basis, applying the laws of the relevant state. Courts based their decisions on tort theories in cases involving theft or misappropriation of trade secrets and on contract theories when a special relationship or duty was present. Many trade secret cases involved a combination of the two theories. Now courts also consider new federal legislation that intersects with these traditional state law approaches.

## COMMON LAW

The most widely accepted definition of "trade secret" is contained in the Restatement (Second) of Torts. Section 757(b) provides:

> A trade secret may consist of any formula, pattern, device, or compilation of information which is used in one's business, and which gives him an opportunity to obtain an advantage over competitors who do not know or use it. It may be a formula for a chemical compound, a process of manufacturing, treating or preserving materials, a pattern for a machine or other device, or a list of customers.

The courts have developed a number of factors to determine whether specific information qualifies as a trade secret. These factors include (1) the extent to which the information is known outside the business, (2) the extent to which measures are taken to protect the information, (3) the value of the information, (4) the amount of money or time spent to develop the information, and (5) the ease of duplicating the information.

Unfortunately, even with this formal definition and set of factors, a certain amount of guesswork is still required to determine whether a particular type of information qualifies as a trade secret under the common law. The courts have classified identical types of information differently when the factual settings were only slightly different.

## THE UNIFORM TRADE SECRETS ACT

In 1979, the National Conference of Commissioners on Uniform State Laws (NCCUSL) promulgated the Uniform Trade Secrets Act (UTSA) in an attempt to provide a coherent framework for trade secret protection. The NCCUSL hoped to eliminate the unpredictability of the common law by providing a more comprehensive definition of trade secrets. In particular, the NCCUSL expanded the common law definition by adding the terms "method," "program," and "technique" to the Restatement's list of types of protected information. The intention was to specifically include know-how (technical knowledge, methods, and experience). In addition, the NCCUSL broadened the common law definition by deleting the requirement that the secret be continuously used in a business. Accordingly, the UTSA defines a trade secret as:

> Information, including a formula, pattern, compilation, program, device, method, technique, or process, that (1) derives independent economic value, actual or potential, from not being generally known to, and not being readily ascertainable by proper means by, other persons who can obtain economic value from its disclosure or use, and (2) is the subject of efforts that are reasonable under the circumstances to maintain its secrecy.

Although the common law does not protect information unless it is in use, the UTSA definition is broad enough to include (1) information that has potential value from being secret; (2) information regarding one-time events; and (3) negative information, such as test results showing what will not work for a particular process or product.

The most significant difference between the UTSA and the common law definitions is in the overall approach to determining whether information is protectable as a trade secret. As discussed above, at common law a fairly objective five- or six-part test was developed. Although many courts adopted a reasonableness standard when interpreting the individual factors of the test, the focus was on objectivity, as delineated in this test. The UTSA uses a more flexible test, indicating that the steps taken to preserve the information as a trade secret must be reasonable and that the owner must derive independent economic value from secrecy. Although the "independent economic value" factor is subjective, a number of courts now use it as part of their trade secret test.

Adopted, at least in part, in forty-five states, the UTSA has only partially fulfilled its goal of standardizing trade secret law. States have tended to enact only those parts of the UTSA that embody the existing common law of the particular state. Consequently, in states that have adopted the UTSA, the courts rely on a combination of the common law and the UTSA. Although the UTSA seems to have fallen short of its goal of establishing consistent protection for trade secrets, it may provide broader protection to owners of trade secrets in states that have adopted it. Its definition of the term "trade secret" is broader than the common law definition, so the burden of proof on the owner is reduced. In addition, the UTSA provides more effective remedies.

### CRIMINAL LIABILITY UNDER THE ECONOMIC ESPIONAGE ACT

The federal Economic Espionage Act,[67] enacted in 1996, imposes criminal liability (including fines and prison sentences) on any person who intentionally or knowingly steals a trade secret or knowingly receives or purchases a wrongfully obtained trade secret. The Act's definition of trade secret is substantially similar to the definition in the Uniform Trade Secrets Act.

Although the Economic Espionage Act was prompted by a desire to remedy perceived problems created by foreign thefts of trade secrets from U.S. businesses, it applies to any trade secret related to or included in products placed in interstate commerce. Organizations (other than foreign instrumentalities) can be fined up to $5 million (or two times the greater of the defendant's gain or the trade secret owner's loss). Foreign instrumentalities, defined as entities substantially owned or controlled by a foreign government, can be fined up to $10 million; individuals knowingly benefiting a foreign instrumentality can be fined up to $500,000 and imprisoned up to fifteen years.

The Act has extraterritorial application: it applies to any violation outside the United States by a U.S. citizen, a resident alien, or an organization organized in the United States. It also applies to violations outside the United States if any act in furtherance of the offense was committed in the United States.

The government has moved swiftly to add violations of the Economic Espionage Act to its arsenal of potential actions against white-collar criminals. A nineteen-year-old student in Los Angeles was sentenced to five years probation, six months home detention, and restitutionary fees when he stole trade secrets relating to smart card technology during his work as a contractor for a law firm defending a smart card client.[68] In *United States v. Lange*,[69] a disgruntled former employee of Replacement Aircraft Parts offered to sell secret manufacturing details to competitors. Even though he pled guilty to criminal violation of the Economic Espionage Act, Lange received a fairly substantial thirty-month prison sentence.

## Creating Rights in a Trade Secret

In contrast to the formal process required for patent and copyright protection, no lengthy application and filing procedures are needed for trade secret protection. No review or approval by a governmental agency is required. To create and protect a trade secret, one need only develop and maintain a trade secret protection program. When the information being protected has a short shelf life, trade secret protection may be a more practical solution than copyright or patent protection.

Trade secrets are immediately protectable and will continue to be protectable as long as the protected information remains confidential and is not developed independently by someone else. Material that would not qualify for patent or copyright protection is often protectable as a trade secret. A

67. Economic Espionage Act of 1996, Pub. L. No. 104-294, 110 Stat. 3488.

68. Press Release, *U.S. Dept. of Justice, L.A. Man Sentenced for Stealing Trade Secrets Pertaining to "Smart Card" Technology* (Sept. 8, 2003), *available at* http://www.cybercrime.gove/serebryanysent.htm.

69. 312 F.2d 263 (7th Cir. 2002).

trade secret need not be as unique as a patentable invention or as original as a copyrightable work. It only needs to provide a competitive advantage. It may be merely an idea that has been kept secret, such as a way to organize common machines in an efficient manner, a marketing plan, or a formula for mixing the ingredients of a product. Trade secrets can also consist of a compilation of information, even though each component part of the compilation is generally known.

In addition, obtaining patent and copyright protection usually requires the disclosure of valuable information. There is always a risk that after the sensitive information has been revealed, the reviewing agency will not grant the protection. To avoid this risk, trade secret protection may be the safest course of action.

There are two disadvantages to utilizing trade secret protection, however. First, maintaining a full-fledged protection program can be expensive because confidentiality procedures must be continuously and rigidly followed to preserve trade secret status. Second, trade secret protection provides no protection against reverse engineering or independent discovery, and the uncertainty of protection may limit the productive uses of the trade secret.

## Protecting a Trade Secret

Misappropriation of trade secrets most commonly occurs as a result of inadvertent disclosures or employee disclosures. To properly protect trade secret information, the owner must develop a program to preserve its confidentiality. In almost every jurisdiction, the test of a trade secret program's adequacy may be reduced to the question of whether the owner has taken reasonable precautions to preserve the confidentiality of his or her trade secrets.

A trade secret program should cover the following four areas: (1) notification, (2) identification, (3) security, and (4) exit interviews.

### *Notification*

The first critical element is a written indication that all employees are aware of the trade secret program. A written notice should be posted. Ideally, the company's trade secret policy should be explained to each new employee during orientation, and each new employee should sign a confidentiality agreement. The agreement should specify how long confidentiality will be required.[70]

70. Many confidentiality agreements do not include a fixed term. Instead, they require an employee to maintain confidentiality as long as the information remains confidential and is not otherwise publicly released by the employer.

Labeling is another means of notification. A rubber stamp denoting confidential material and the posting of signs in areas containing sensitive materials will in most cases satisfy the reasonableness requirement. Some authorities, however, believe that labeling may actually hurt the trade secret status of information because in practice it can be difficult to ensure consistent and continuous labeling procedures. These authorities claim that failure to label some of the documents may be seen as evidence that the information in those documents should not be afforded trade secret status. More advanced kinds of labeling, such as passwords, lend additional support for a finding of reasonableness.

The company should also provide written notice to any consultant, vendor, joint venturer, or other party to whom a trade secret must be revealed. This notice should take the form of a confidentiality agreement that describes the protected information and limits the receiving party's rights to use it. Without such notice, the receiving party may be unaware of the nature of the information and unwittingly release it into the public domain.

A nondisclosure agreement (NDA) can serve as the basis of recovery if a court later determines that the party who gained access to trade secrets used or disclosed them in violation of the agreement. For example, in *Celeritas Technologies, Ltd. v. Rockwell*,[71] the parties entered into negotiations for licensing Celeritas's "de-emphasis technology," a method for reducing high-frequency noise in cellular communications. Prior to allowing access to the information, Celeritas asked Rockwell to sign an NDA. The licensing negotiations ultimately failed, and Rockwell subsequently developed its own modem chips that incorporated de-emphasis technology. The same engineers who had access to Celeritas's technology under the NDA worked on Rockwell's de-emphasis technology project. Celeritas brought suit claiming, among other things, breach of the NDA. Because the technology was not readily ascertainable in the public domain and was found to have come directly from Celeritas, the court concluded that Rockwell had breached the NDA and that Celeritas was entitled to damages.

Sometimes an NDA may contain a "residuals" provision, which permits either party to use and exploit any information retained in the minds of the representatives of the nondisclosing party that they learned in the course of the subject negotiations or engagement. This can create a very large loophole in the restrictions on nondisclosure.

71. 150 F.3d 1354 (Fed. Cir. 1998).

### *Identification*

There is some controversy about the appropriate method of identifying trade secrets. One view is that everything in the workplace, or pertaining to the business, is a trade secret, but a court will most likely deem this umbrella approach to be overly restrictive of commerce and therefore against public policy. Such a finding could undermine the company's trade secret program, exposing all of its trade secrets to unrecoverable misappropriation.

At the other extreme is a program that attempts to specify every one of the company's trade secrets. This approach may be too narrow because any legitimate trade secrets that are not specified will not be protected. Also, it is often difficult to pinpoint all of a company's potential trade secrets. For example, although it may be easy to designate all research and development projects as trade secrets, gray areas such as sales data, customer lists, or marketing surveys may cause problems. The best solution may be a program that specifies as much information as possible while also including a limited number of catchall categories.

### *Security*

Measures must be taken to ensure that trade secret information remains secret, at least from the public. The disclosure of a trade secret, whether intentional (for example, as part of a sale) or by mistake, destroys any legal protection. Access to trade secret information should therefore be limited to those who truly have a need to know. Hard copies of trade secret information should be locked in secure filing cabinets or a secure room. Photocopying machines should be placed as far as possible from trade secret files. Digital confidential information should be encrypted.

A company should also guard against unintentional disclosure of a trade secret during a public tour of the facility. An offhand remark in the hall overheard by a visitor, or a formula left written on a chalkboard in plain view of a tour group, is all that is needed. The best way to avoid this situation is to keep all trade secrets in areas restricted from public access. If such physical barriers are not possible, visitors' access should be controlled through a system that logs in all visitors, identifies them with badges, and keeps track of them while they are on the premises.

Employees may inadvertently disclose trade secrets when participating in trade groups, conferences, and conventions and through publication of articles in trade journals and other periodicals. To avoid this problem, an employer should consistently remind its employees and contractors of when and how to talk about the company's business activities.

### *Exit Interviews*

When an employee who has had access to trade secrets leaves the company, he or she should be given an exit interview. The exit interview provides an opportunity to reinforce the confidentiality agreement that the employee signed on joining the company. If no confidentiality agreement exists, the exit interview is even more important. It will provide the notice and possibly the identification necessary to legally protect the employer's trade secrets. The exit interview also lets the departing employee know that the company is serious about protecting its trade secrets and that any breach of confidentiality could result in legal proceedings against him or her. After such a warning, any misappropriation would be deliberate and could therefore result in punitive damages.

In some states, posttermination restrictions on competition imposed on a departing employee may be unenforceable. In California, for example, a provision in an employment contract that prohibits an employee based in California from later working for a competitor is void as an unlawful business restraint, except to the extent necessary to prevent the misappropriation of trade secrets. It is therefore important to consult with local counsel concerning the permissible scope of posttermination restrictions.

## Misappropriation of Trade Secrets

An individual misappropriates a trade secret when he or she (1) uses or discloses the trade secret of another or (2) learns of a trade secret through improper means. The UTSA defines "improper means" by a list of deceitful actions. The list, however, is not exclusive, and anything that strikes a court as improper would probably qualify as an improper means.

In one recent misappropriation case, Wyeth, a large pharmaceutical company, sued Natural Biologics for misappropriating its secret manufacturing process for Premarin, a highly profitable hormone replacement therapy drug.[72] Pretrial discovery uncovered a series of phone calls between Natural Biologics and a retired Wyeth scientist who had been instrumental in developing the

72. Wyeth v. Natural Biologics, Inc., 2003 WL 22282371 (D. Minn. 2003).

Premarin manufacturing process. The court determined that these calls gave the fledgling company all the knowledge it needed to copy the process. Because Natural Biologics had improperly obtained this information, the court issued a permanent injunction forbidding it from using the information or in any way engaging in drug development processes.

## Inevitable Disclosure Doctrine

Courts have begun to recognize a form of employee misappropriation under the *inevitable disclosure doctrine,* which recognizes that former employees who go to work for a competitor in a similar capacity will inevitably rely on and disclose the trade secrets gained in their former employment.

The inevitable disclosure doctrine was first recognized by a federal appeals court in *PepsiCo, Inc. v. Redmond.*[73] William Redmond, Jr. worked as a senior marketing manager for PepsiCo in its Pepsi-Cola North America division. Redmond had just completed work on the strategic marketing plans for AllSport (a sports drink that competed against Gatorade) and PepsiCo.'s powdered teas (which competed against Snapple, among others). In November 1994, Redmond accepted an offer by Quaker Oats to work as the vice president of field operations in Quaker's combined Gatorade and Snapple drinks subsidiary. PepsiCo sued to enjoin Redmond from working at Quaker Oats on grounds of threatened misappropriation.

The U.S. Court of Appeals for the Seventh Circuit held that a company may prove trade secret misappropriation by demonstrating that the employee's new position will inevitably lead him to rely on his ex-employer's trade secrets. Because of the competition between AllSport and Gatorade, the court concluded that Redmond could not help but rely on PepsiCo trade secrets as he plotted Gatorade's course. Specifically, Quaker Oats would have a substantial advantage by knowing how PepsiCo would price, distribute, and market its sports drinks. The court likened the situation to that faced by a football team whose key player leaves to play for the other team and takes the play book with him.

By recognizing the notion of inevitable disclosure as being within the UTSA's provision of "threatened disclosure," the *PepsiCo* case gives employers greater leverage over departing employees and a powerful weapon against competitors who would lure away valuable employees. Nevertheless, situations that spark the risk of inevitable disclosure have continued to arise. After initiating a lawsuit, Campbell Soup Company agreed to let the former head of its U.S. soup business join the tuna and pet-food businesses of H.J. Heinz on the condition that he stay out of the soup business at Heinz for one year. When one of Intel's chief software architects left to work on a competing semiconductor chip at Intel's rival, Broadcom, Intel sued to block his move based on the inevitable disclosure doctrine. Ultimately, however, a court found little risk of trade secret disclosure.[74]

Although a number of courts have accepted the inevitable disclosure doctrine in some form, other courts have hesitated to apply the doctrine. For example, in *Earthweb, Inc. v. Schlack,*[75] the U.S. District Court for the Southern District of New York refused to apply the inevitable disclosure doctrine in circumstances where a noncompete agreement was considered overbroad and thus unenforceable. The court reasoned that the inevitable disclosure doctrine "treads an exceedingly narrow path through judicially disfavored territory. Absent evidence of actual misappropriation by an employee, the doctrine should be applied in only the rarest of cases." A California district court went further, holding that the inevitable disclosure doctrine created a "de facto covenant not to compete," which was contrary to California law and public policy.[76]

## Remedies

Once a trade secret has been misappropriated, the law provides a choice of remedies, which are not mutually exclusive.

### *Injunctions*

A court may issue an injunction ordering the misappropriator to refrain from disclosing or using the stolen trade secret. An injunction is available only to prevent irreparable harm, however. If the secret has already been disclosed, an injunction may no longer be appropriate to protect the secret. The court may, however, still enjoin the misappropriator from using the information in order to deny the misappropriator the benefits of his or her wrongful act. In this situation, the injunction is often combined with an award of damages.

73. 54 F.3d 1262 (7th Cir. 1995).

74. Intel Corp. v. Broadcom Corp., 2000 WL 33260713 (Cal. Super. Ct. June 20, 2000).

75. 71 F. Supp. 2d 299 (S.D.N.Y. 1999), *aff'd,* 205 F.3d 1322 (2d Cir. 2000).

76. Whyte v. Schlage Lock Co., 101 Cal. App. 4th 1443 (Cal. App. Ct. 2002).

The owner may also be able to seek an injunction or damages from anyone receiving the misappropriated trade secret or anyone hiring the individual who misappropriated it. For example, as mentioned earlier, the court issued a permanent injunction against Natural Biologics forbidding it from any drug development because its entire drug manufacturing business was based on information stolen from Wyeth. Finally, an injunction may also be appropriate when an individual threatens to use or disclose a trade secret, although the real damage has not yet occurred. In the *PepsiCo* case, the former PepsiCo employee was not permitted to work for Quaker Oats until the information he had in his head about PepsiCo's marketing strategy was stale and lacked competitive value.

### *Damages*

When the owner of the trade secret has suffered financial harm, courts often award monetary damages, based on either a contract or a tort theory. Under the tort theory of trade secrets, the purpose of the damages is not only to make the owner whole but also to disgorge any profits the misappropriator may have made due to his or her wrongful act. The key to the tort measure of damages is that there was either a harm or an unjust gain, or both. The contract theory of trade secrets, on the other hand, measures damages by the loss of value of the trade secret to the owner as a result of a breach of contract. Courts determine the loss of value by adding the general loss to any special losses resulting from the breach and subtracting any costs avoided by the owner as a result of the breach.

The technical differences between the two measures of damages make little practical difference. Most courts will attempt to fairly compensate the owner of a misappropriated trade secret regardless of how the case is characterized.

### *Punitive Damages*

Punitive damages are available when the misappropriation was willful and wanton. Under the UTSA, the court may award double the ordinary damages if it finds willful and malicious misappropriation; in some states, courts may award attorneys' fees as well.

## Criminal Liability

As described earlier, the Economic Espionage Act criminalizes the theft of trade secrets and imposes fines and imprisonment on those convicted under it. In addition, many state statutes also impose criminal liability for theft of trade secrets. Although criminal charges are less common than civil charges, in part due to the higher standard of proof for a criminal conviction, they still occur.

# Database Protection

After the *Feist* decision (see the earlier discussion under Copyrights),[77] owners of factual databases could no longer rely on copyright protection. As a result, database publishers began pressuring Congress to pass legislation that would strengthen database protection in the United States. Databases are already afforded greater protection in the European Union (EU) as a result of the EU Directive on the Legal Protection of Databases, adopted by the EU Parliament in 1996. Numerous bills have been proposed in Congress, but none have passed. In 2003, Congress considered the Database and Collections of Information Misappropriation Act, which would have protected databases from uses leading to material harm to the database owner's economic market. This proposed act would have allowed database owners to sue for triple damages and to enjoin any unauthorized use, although scientific study, research, or private use would still have been allowed.

Some of the pressure to pass new legislation to protect factual databases may have been removed by the emergence of a tort cause of action to protect factual databases. In 2000, eBay sued Bidder's Edge, an online auction aggregating site, for trespass to chattel, based on Bidder's Edge's repeated access to the eBay site to troll for pricing information.[78] A U.S. district court in California agreed that the actions of Bidder's Edge had the potential to overload eBay's servers, and thus eBay was likely to prevail on its trespass to chattel claim. Other courts have affirmed that the tort of trespass to chattel can be used to protect proprietary databases.[79]

# Technology Licensing

In today's business environment, technology licensing is a key element in every industry. The volume of commercial technology transfers has increased dramatically since World War II and is accelerating. Whereas revenues from patent licensing amounted to approximately $15 billion in 1990, they exceeded $100 billion by 2000 and were still increasing. International technology transfer is

77. 499 U.S. 340 (1991).

78. eBay v. Bidder's Edge, 100 F. Supp. 2d 1058 (N.D. Cal. 2000).

79. Register.com v. Verio, Inc., 356 F.3d 393 (2d Cir. 2004); Intel Corp. v. Hamidi, 71 P.3d 296 (Cal. 2003). *But see* Ticketmaster Corp. v. Tickets.com, 2003 WL 21406289 (C.D. Cal. Mar. 7, 2003) (holding that a trespass to chattels claim could be used in an online context).

## IN BRIEF

### Intellectual Property Protection: Comparative Advantages

| | Trade Secret | Copyright | Patent | Trademark |
|---|---|---|---|---|
| **Benefits** | Very broad protection for sensitive, competitive information; very inexpensive | Prevents copying of a wide array of artistic and literary expressions, including software; very inexpensive | Very strong protection; provides exclusive right to exclude others from making, using, and selling an invention; protects the idea itself | Protects marks that customers use to identify a business; prevents others from using confusingly similar identifying marks |
| **Duration** | As long as the information remains valuable and is kept confidential | Life of author plus 70 years; for corporations, 95 years from date of first publication or 120 years from date of creation, whichever is shorter | 20 years from date of filing utility or plant patent application; 14 years from date of filing design patent application | As long as the mark is not abandoned and steps are taken to police its use |
| **Weaknesses** | No protection from accidental disclosure, independent creation by a competitor, or disclosure by someone without a duty to maintain confidentiality | Protects only particular way an idea is expressed, not the idea itself; hard to detect copying in digital age | Must meet high standards of novelty, utility, and nonobviousness; often expensive and time consuming to pursue (especially when overseas patents are needed); must disclose invention to public | Limited scope; protects corporate image and identity but little else; can be costly if multiple overseas registrations are needed |
| **Required Steps** | Take reasonable steps to protect—generally a trade secret protection program | None required; however, notice and filing can strengthen rights, and filing is required before an action for infringement can be filed | Detailed filing with U.S. Patent and Trademark Office that requires search for prior art and hefty fees | Only need to use mark in commerce; however, filing with U.S. Patent and Trademark Office is usually desirable to gain stronger protections |
| **International Validity of U.S. Rights?** | No. Trade secret laws vary significantly by country, and some countries have no trade secret laws. | Generally, yes | No. Separate patent examinations and filings are required in each country unless an international patent application is filed under Patent Cooperation Treaty; can file a single filing in the European Patent Office for the EU countries | No. Separate filings are required in foreign jurisdictions, and a mark available in the U.S. may not be available overseas |

Source: Adapted from CONSTANCE E. BAGLEY & CRAIG E. DAUCHY, THE ENTREPRENEUR'S GUIDE TO BUSINESS LAW 471–72 (1998).

accelerating as well. U.S. businesses currently earn licensing revenues in excess of $30 billion each year from global transactions; Japanese and British firms rank second and third, respectively, with businesses in each country earning between $5 billion and 10 billion from licensing annually.[80]

Until very recently, the market for intellectual property was highly fragmented and inefficient. Sales and licensing occurred infrequently and often took place between parties that already had a preexisting relationship, whether formal or informal. Finding an interested and qualified buyer or seller of intellectual property was a time-consuming and difficult task. As a result, many potential revenue sources remained untapped. Indeed, according to *Fortune,* only 2 percent of the worldwide market for new intellectual property (estimated at $5 trillion) was licensed in 1998.[81] Recognizing the inadequacies of the current market for intellectual property, several companies have emerged to offer a solution.

One such company, Yet2.com, was founded in 1999 to promote technology licensing and transfer, with joint investment from Siemens, Honeywell, DuPont, Procter & Gamble, Caterpillar, and NTT Leasing. The exchange focuses on patents. According to Bob Dupont, Yet2com's president, protecting a company's intellectual property through elusively written patents is "going the way of the dinosaur." Dupont says that "[a]t this time of significant interest and growth in the intellectual property marketplace, our clients are as excited as we are with the opportunities to create substantial value through licensing technology."[82]

Nathan Myhrvold, the former chief technologist at Microsoft, is the cofounder of Intellectual Ventures, a firm based on the idea that intellectual property can be bought, sold, and treated like any other product. Intellectual Ventures plans to accumulate patent rights either by buying existing rights or by developing its own new patents. Funded by some of the largest high-tech companies, including Microsoft, Intel, Sony, Nokia, Apple, Google, and eBay, the firm can also protect the interests of its investors by buying up patents that could threaten those companies and by deploying its patent portfolio against their competitors.[83]

80. Barry Quest, *The Growing Importance of Licensing,* Nov. 2000, *at* http://suentific.thomson.com/knowtrend/ipmatters/ipmanage/8204381/.
81. Tyler Maroney, *The New Online Marketplace for Ideas,* FORTUNE, Apr. 17, 2000, at 521.
82. Yet2.com, *at* http://www.yet2.com/app/about/about/press?page=press42 (accessed Jan. 8, 2005).
83. Stone, *supra* note 2.

## Global View

### The Move Toward Harmonization of Intellectual Property Regimes

Several multinational treaties are attempting to harmonize the application of intellectual property laws across jurisdictions. Although they do not alter the substantive criteria that each jurisdiction applies to determine whether patent, trademark, or copyright protection is available, the treaties seek to coordinate the registration and recognition process among signatory countries.

In most countries, if two entities file for protection of the same invention or trademark, the entity that filed first receives protection. This can be a problem for an inventor or trademark owner who files for protection in one country and later discovers that someone else has subsequently filed for protection of the same invention or trademark in another country. The International Convention for the Protection of Industrial Property Rights (known as the Paris Convention) addresses this problem by encouraging reciprocal recognition of patents, trademarks, service marks, and similar forms of intellectual property rights among its eighty-plus signatory nations. Each signatory nation grants nationals of other signatory nations a grace period after filing in their home country within which to file corresponding patent or trademark applications. Patent applicants have one year, and trademark owners have six months.

The Paris Convention does not alter the substantive requirements of the laws of each nation, so patent or trademark protection in one country does not necessarily translate into

*(Continued)*

(Global View *continued*)

protection in another country. Differing rules governing eligibility may mean that actions in one's home country that do not compromise protection there may forfeit protection abroad (for example, disclosure or sale of inventions prior to filing for a patent).

## PATENTS

The Patent Cooperation Treaty (PCT) allows an inventor to file a single international patent application to preserve the right to seek patent protection in each contracting country, rather than having to initially apply for separate patents in many different countries. The inventor may file this application either with the national patent office (e.g., the PTO for U.S. inventors) or the International Bureau of the World Intellectual Property Organization (WIPO).

Every international patent application is subject to an "international search" by an International Searching Authority. The search results include a list of citations of prior art relevant to the international patent application claims and information regarding possible relevance of the citations to questions of novelty and inventiveness (nonobviousness). This information enables the applicant to evaluate its chances of obtaining patents in the countries designated. An applicant may also have an international preliminary examination of the patent, which provides even more information about the invention's patentability. This information helps an applicant decide whether to file applications in individually designated countries.

The patent practice of other countries is often different from that of the United States. For example, foreign laws regarding statutory bars are radically different from U.S. patent law. A rule of thumb is that any public disclosure of an invention prior to filing the patent application will prevent an inventor from obtaining foreign patent protection. Also, some jurisdictions are more receptive to certain types of patents than others. In Europe, there are significant obstacles to obtaining patents on certain types of software innovations, including business methods. Some countries do not permit composition patents for pharmaceuticals, although they may receive some protection under process patents. Given these differences, managers should discuss the rules that apply in foreign jurisdictions with an attorney prior to disclosure or sale of any patentable invention.

## COPYRIGHTS

International copyright protection has also begun to harmonize. For decades, the United States was the lone holdout from the two key international copyright treaties: the Berne Convention and the Universal Copyright Convention. Realizing the importance of international standards, the United States has slowly adjusted its copyright law to comply with treaty standards (e.g., removing formality requirements, extending the term of protection, and enacting the DMCA). Under these treaties, American works receive the same protection that is afforded to the works of a national in foreign countries that are signatories of the same treaty.

In May 2001, the European Union approved a Copyright Directive that would update and harmonize member state copyright laws to bring them into conformity with the WIPO Treaty and the WIPO Performances and Phonograms Treaty. The Copyright Directive identified four areas that require legislative action if the EU is to achieve harmony in its copyright laws: (1) a reproduction right, (2) a communication to the public right, (3) a distribution right, and (4) protection against circumvention of abuse and protection systems.

The directive outlaws the manufacture of devices that facilitate the circumvention of technology used for copyright protection. The directive also provides authors with the exclusive right to authorize or prohibit communication of their work to the public by wire or wireless means, including interactive Internet sites that offer such works without the author's permission. In contrast to the DMCA in the United States, however, the directive contains several different, yet still compliant, implementation methods regarding exceptions, penalties, and remedies that allow each country to modify the proposal as needed.

All EU member countries were required to ratify the directive by December 2002; however, implementing the lengthy directive has proved difficult because of the controversies surrounding the balance between copyright owners' rights and the public's right of use. As of January 2005, many EU countries were still drafting the legislation required for compliance with the directive.

## TRADEMARKS

Every country has its own methods for determining what is a protectable trademark, how to obtain and maintain trademarks, and the scope of protection available for trademarks. In contrast to the United States, in most countries, use of a mark confers no rights; the first person to register the mark owns the rights to use it. In addition, registration of a trademark in the United States confers no rights in foreign countries, although a U.S. registration can provide an easy basis for registration of corresponding trademarks in countries that participate in multilateral trademark conventions with the United States.

Currently, several overlapping international regimes govern trademark applications, reflecting the trend toward increased global harmonization. As noted earlier, the Paris Convention provides a six-month grace period from the date an owner files a trademark registration application in his or her home country to file in other signatory countries. As long as the foreign filing is made within that grace period, it is treated as if it were filed in the foreign jurisdiction on the date the home country filing occurred.

The Madrid Protocol allows for centralized international registration of trademarks. The United States joined the Madrid Protocol in 2003, bringing the number of signatory countries to sixty-one. A U.S. trademark owner can now file a single application at WIPO's International Bureau in Geneva or at the

*(Continued)*

(Global View *continued*)

U.S. PTO to register the trademark in all signatory countries. Many lawyers see this process as beneficial and believe that it will substantially reduce the time and expense associated with trademark application filings. Others, however, point to differences in protection between national trademark regimes that may prove disadvantageous to U.S. trademark holders who use the WIPO registration process. For example, the PTO application requires narrower descriptions of goods and services than are required in other countries. As a result, a U.S. trademark holder may be better off filing separate, broader applications in each relevant foreign country.

The Pan American Convention recognizes the right of a trademark owner in one signatory country to successfully challenge the registration or use of that same trademark in another country. The key issue is whether persons using or applying to register the mark had knowledge of the existence and continuous use of the mark in any of the member states on goods of the same category.

For EU members, the Community Trade mark (CTM) can confer protection in the entire EU. The CTM does not replace national rights or Madrid Protocol rights but coexists with them. A CTM can only be registered, assigned, or canceled with respect to the entire EU.

Several foreign nations have enacted laws to harmonize their trademark procedures with the international community in an effort to attract foreign investment and trade. In 1997, Japan enacted a trademark law to address the accumulation of unused registered trademarks by allowing anyone to petition for the cancellation of a mark that has gone unused and by making it more difficult to defend against such petitions. The law also shortened the time required to approve trademark applications. Observers expected the new trademark regime would make it easier for non-Japanese businesses to register and protect their marks in Japan. Among its many provisions, the law allowed for the registration of three-dimensional marks for the first time.

As part of the normalization of trade relations with the United States in 1996, Cambodia signed a bilateral treaty with the United States. In exchange for formally receiving most favored nation status in the United States and the lower tariffs that accompany such status, Cambodia agreed to allow U.S. trademark holders to take legal action against companies using their already established and popular names. For instance, one company in Phnom Penh had been selling pizza under the name "Pizza Hot" and using the familiar red triangle roof of PepsiCo's Pizza Hut. The new law allowed PepsiCo to petition to have the imitator's mark canceled.

## TRADE SECRETS

International trade secret protection is perhaps the least codified and harmonized aspect of intellectual property; thus, this area is the riskiest for U.S. companies doing business abroad. A primary concern is that countries differ in their interpretation of what constitutes a trade secret. For example, in the EU, trade secrets must be fixed in a tangible medium to be legally recognized. Japan does not recognize trade secrets as protectable property in and of themselves; instead, Japanese law forbids unfair acts of acquiring, disclosing, or using information in a manner that harms the trade secret owner. Other countries, like the Philippines, provide no legal protection at all for trade secrets.

Some countries recognize the importance of trade secrets but have legislation that forces their exposure. For example, at one time, India required foreign companies to create joint venture arrangements that result in compulsory technology transfers to Indian companies. In 1977, Coca-Cola abandoned its Indian operations, rather than divulge the trade secret for its secret formula. And in China, government approval is required for any licensing agreement involving trade secrets; if the parties fail to comply, the trade secret owner forfeits the trade secret after ten years.

Most foreign countries will enforce reasonable nondisclosure restrictions in contracts, at least against parties to the contract; however, most countries do not recognize the tort law aspect of trade secrets that is recognized in the United States. In some countries, the judicial process itself may destroy the confidential character of the misappropriated information. For example, the Japanese and German judicial systems do not have a procedure equivalent to the U.S. *in camera* (confidentiality) procedure for review of trade secret information.

## THE RESPONSIBLE MANAGER

## PROTECTING INTELLECTUAL PROPERTY RIGHTS

Some of a company's most important assets may be intangible forms of intellectual property. Consider the formula for Coke, never registered as a patent but kept as a trade secret by generations of executives at the Coca-Cola Company. An effective trade secret policy is essential to almost all forms of business today. This chapter has provided suggestions regarding the implementation of such a policy.

*(Continued)*

(The Responsible Manager *continued*)

Problems can arise when a manager leaves the employment of one company to assume a position at another. During the exit interview, employees should be reminded of their obligations, and materials and computers being removed from the employer's premises should be inspected. It is critical that the manager and the new employer ensure that no confidential information, including trade secrets, is conveyed to the new employer, either in the form of documents or information in the manager's head. At the time of hire, the employer should determine whether the potential employee is bound by a restrictive covenant. Moreover, a company should provide written notice to all employees that it has a policy against receiving, using, or purchasing any trade secrets belonging to third parties. Misappropriation of trade secrets is a civil and criminal offense.

If the manager cannot fulfill all the duties of his or her new job without using the prior employer's trade secrets, the new employer should scale back the manager's activities and responsibilities. This can be accomplished by having the former employer and the new employer agree that the manager will not assume responsibility for certain product lines that compete with his or her former employer's until a date when the strategic and other confidential information known by the manager is stale. If possible, the departing manager should negotiate this issue as part of his or her severance arrangements, rather than wait for a costly lawsuit to be brought by the former employer.

Because international trade secret protection is the least codified and least harmonized aspect of intellectual property, a manager should consult with local counsel before making trade secrets available, by license or otherwise, in a foreign country. Patents, copyrights, and trademarks also provide legal protection for different aspects of a company's intellectual property. Patents are extremely important to high-technology companies and some e-commerce firms. Royalties from patents can add tens or even hundreds of millions of dollars to a company's revenues.

Patents also have an important strategic use as a defensive measure in the event that another company claims patent infringement. In such a case, it is very helpful for a manager to have patents that can be used as bargaining chips to negotiate a settlement, which often takes the form of a cross-license.

A manager should develop a global patent strategy because 180 different jurisdictions grant patents, each of which gives the holder exclusive rights only in the granting jurisdiction. The United States is the only country that uses a "first-to-invent," instead of "first-to-file," approach in issuing patents.

Copyrights prevent others from copying literary works, musical works, sound recordings, computer software, and other forms of expression fixed in a tangible medium. A manager should consult with an experienced copyright attorney to ensure that his or her company obtains copyright ownership when it commissions, or contracts with, a third party to prepare a copyrighted work. A manager should also discuss with an attorney what, if any, copyright protection is available for a work in any foreign jurisdiction in which the company wants to distribute the work, and what steps are necessary to obtain such protection. A manager should be aware that copyright registration with the U.S. Copyright Office is a prerequisite for filing an infringement suit for a work of U.S. origin. Statutory damages and attorneys' fees are available only to owners who have registered the work within ninety days of first publication or prior to the infringement that forms the basis of the suit. Because the timing of the registration is critical, a manager should consult with a copyright attorney before publication of an important copyrighted work.

Trademarks that identify brands of goods or services are protected for an indefinite time. Managers must work to preserve trademarks, however. Once the buying public starts using the trademark as a synonym for the product, rather than as a means of distinguishing its source, loss of the trademark is imminent. The trademark registration process can be complex and confusing. It can also take up to eighteen months after an application is filed for a federal registration to be issued. Early consultation with legal counsel is therefore strongly advised.

In addition to protecting his or her company's own intellectual property, a manager should also ensure that the company does not infringe the intellectual property rights of others, whether they be patents, copyrights, trademarks, or trade secrets.

A company may benefit from technology licensing. Such arrangements offer advantages and disadvantages for both the licensor and licensee.

Finally, managers should evaluate the adequacy of the company's insurance coverage for losses and claims related to electronic commerce and intellectual property. In light of the importance of computers, it is important to ensure that policies for property damage and business interruption cover damage to hardware and software,

*(Continued)*

(The Responsible Manager *continued*)

loss of data, and business disruptions caused by a virus, hacker attack, or other electronic assault. Commercial general liability policies, which provide coverage for liability a company may face for harm to third parties, usually cover bodily injury, property damage, personal injury, and advertising injury. Emerging issues include whether data are tangible property, whether the insertion of a defective computer part or software into a larger system causes property damages, and whether any company with a website is in the business of advertising and therefore not covered by the usual advertising injury provisions, which can cover intellectual property infringement and defamation claims.

Some insurance companies are attempting to eliminate coverage for cyberspace and e-commerce claims from traditional policies, often with the hope of selling specialty policies to cover cyber-risks. Although the new specialty policies are potentially valuable, policyholders must be careful to assess the gaps in coverage that can result if traditional "all-risk" liability coverage is replaced with a patchwork of specialty policies. Also, the language of the new policies can vary widely, so managers need to ensure that the coverage chosen matches the risks. Finally, managers should be aware that the new language used in these policies will inevitably result in disputes about its meaning.

INSIDE STORY

## DIGITAL MILLENNIUM COPYRIGHT ACT

In October 1998, President Clinton signed the Digital Millennium Copyright Act (DMCA) into law. The DMCA implemented two digital copyright treaties to which the United States was a signatory: the World Intellectual Property Organization (WIPO) Copyright Treaty and the WIPO Performances and Phonograms Treaty. The DMCA provides copyright protection for all creative works transmitted in digital form over the Internet. Generally, it outlaws the manufacture, sale, or distribution of devices that may be used to illegally copy software and makes it a crime to circumvent antipiracy measures that are part of most commercial software.

### THE DMCA'S PROVISIONS AND EARLY CRITIQUES

Each of the subsections of Section 1201 of the DMCA has a distinct purpose and goal. Section 1201(a)(1)(a) makes it illegal to circumvent technology that controls access to a work protected under the Copyright Act. For example, Section 1201(a)(1)(a) makes it illegal for a user to attempt to decrypt a copy-protected digital video disc (DVD), that is, a DVD with antipiracy measures to protect against copying.

Section 1201(a)(2) makes it illegal to traffic in, or sell, tools or technologies that are primarily designed to circumvent, or have only limited commercial purposes other than to circumvent, technology that controls access to a copyrightable work. A company that sells a tool designed to decrypt a copy-protected DVD violates Section 1201(a)(2).

Section 1201(b)(1) makes it illegal to traffic in, or sell, tools or technologies that are primarily designed (or have only limited commercial purposes other than) to circumvent the uses and rights of copyright owners. For example, a company that sells a program that interferes with a copyright owner's streaming media program, in which a certain level of access is permitted (e.g., watching a video once) but other kinds of access are prohibited (e.g., downloading the video file), violates Section 1201(b)(1).

Scientists, technology companies, librarians, and university professors opposed the passage of the DMCA for many reasons. One of the most salient was that it criminalized the use of copyrighted works in digitized research papers and classroom materials because it outlawed the circumvention of technological protections for any purpose, thus eroding the fair use doctrine. The language of the DMCA implies that there is no fair use defense to a Section 1201 violation, a change that cuts against years of copyright tradition. Some scholars consider fair use akin to a constitutional right, one that the DMCA violated. In response to these concerns,

*(Continued)*

(Inside Story *continued*)

Congress added exemptions for fair use, particularly for libraries and educational institutions.

A second criticism was that Sections 1201(a)(2) and 1201(b)(1) broke with long-standing U.S. legal tradition. In the U.S. system, the government typically regulates unlawful acts, not potentially unlawful tools. For example, photocopiers are not illegal, but making illegal photocopies is; similarly, it is not unlawful to own a gun, but it is illegal to use a gun improperly. When tools have multiple uses, U.S. law typically does not eliminate legitimate uses. The DMCA breaks with this tradition by making it illegal to traffic in tools that may be used to circumvent access or use restrictions, even if the tools have other legitimate uses.

In addition, some scholars argued that the DMCA went further than the WIPO Treaty required.[84] Still others argued that the DMCA would create a "pay-to-play" Internet that would prohibit users from making legal copies of material for private use.

**THE DMCA AS APPLIED**

Since its enactment, the DMCA has been used in several cases that validate some of these scholarly concerns. In 2000, Edward Felten, a professor of computer science at Princeton, entered a challenge issued by the Secure Digital Music Initiative (SDMI). SDMI offered $10,000 to anyone who could break its antipiracy systems, designed to protect audio files. Felten and his colleagues easily cracked the software and prepared to present a research paper about their work at a related conference. Two weeks before the conference, SDMI sent a letter to Felten warning that the publication of the research paper could expose the research team "to actions under the [DMCA]."[85] Although SDMI ultimately decided not to bring suit, at least one of the researchers involved in the project decided to abandon further research in the field.[86]

Another prominent case involved Dmitry Skylarov, a Russian programmer who created software that allowed owners of Adobe e-books to convert the files into Adobe pdf files. This program removed restrictions embedded in the e-book programs by the e-book publishers, thus subjecting Skylarov to liability under the DMCA. In July 2001, Skylarov was jailed for several weeks in Las Vegas after speaking at a programming conference there. Eventually, the Department of Justice allowed him to return home but charged his employer with violations of the DMCA. Because of this extraterritorial reach of the DMCA, several foreign scientists and scholars have avoided the United States entirely or have chosen to present their research abroad instead of in the United States as planned. Critics point to such behavior as yet another example of how the DMCA stifles innovation, competition, and basic research.

Though neither Felten nor Skylarov ultimately faced personal civil or criminal liability, U.S. companies are using the DMCA to pressure competitors with the threat of litigation. For example, Lexmark, a major printer manufacturer, sought to eliminate its competitors in the printer-cartridge aftermarket by adding an "authentication" step to its printer-cartridge recognition process to ensure that only Lexmark toner cartridges would be usable in Lexmark printers. In 2003, Lexmark sued its competitor, Static Control Components (SCC), alleging that SCC violated the DMCA when it included a chip in its toner cartridges to make them compatible with Lexmark printers. The trial court granted Lexmark a preliminary injunction. On appeal, however, the U.S. Court of Appeals for the Sixth Circuit found that the purchase of the printer, not the authentication step, granted "access" to the computer; therefore, the chip that SCC made to ensure compatibility did not contravene the DMCA's prohibitions. After dismissing Lexmark's other allegations, the appellate court vacated the injunction and remanded the case for further proceedings.[87]

The intersection of the DMCA and principles of fair use remains an issue. Several cases have tested the DMCA's application to the publication of software code, specifications, and fixes that copyright owners did not want publicly available. Courts generally decided the cases in favor of the copyright owners. Another current debate is whether consumers have a right of fair use to make an MP3 copy of a copy-protected CD for their personal, noncommercial use.

**PROPOSALS FOR REFORM**

Critics of the DMCA contend that the rights of copyright owners were already protected by existing legal regimes. The Computer Fraud and Abuse Act, the Wiretap Act, and the Electronic Communications Privacy Act, as well as the tort of trespass of chattels, all balance the rights of property owners with the rights of

84. Electronic Frontier Foundation, *Unintended Consequences: Five Years Under the DMCA*, vol. 3, Sept. 24, 2003, *at* http://www.eff.org/IP/DMCA/unintended_consequences.pdf.

85. Benny Evangelista, *Judges' Rulings Boost Strength of Digital Copyright Law*, SAN FRANCISCO CHRON., Nov. 29, 2001, at B3.

86. *Id.*

87. Lexmark Int'l, Inc. v. Static Control Components, Inc., 387 F.3d 522 (6th Cir. 2004).

*(Continued)*

(Inside Story *continued*)

the public. Arguably, the DMCA disrupts the regimes set in place by these laws, as well as the Copyright Act itself. Still, support for the DMCA from content providers like the movie and music industries suggests that the DMCA will not disappear but may instead be modified. New proposals in Congress attempt to rectify the perceived excesses of the DMCA while retaining its original goals.

One such bill, titled the Digital Media Consumers' Rights Act, would allow decryption software to be created and used to circumvent copy protections, so long as no copyright infringement took place. In addition, it would require any copy-protected consumer goods, such as DVDs or CDs, to be labeled as such, giving consumers fair warning that the goods might not be copyable or play in certain devices. Many technology companies, including Sun Microsystems, Verizon, and Philips Consumer Electronics, have announced their support for this proposal.

Another proposed solution is to amend the DMCA to explicitly allow a fair use defense, thereby shifting the burden of proof to the copyright owner to prove copyright infringement. Any legislative change, however, will have to balance the competing interests of content providers such as record labels and software publishers, which heavily support the DMCA; technology companies, which find the DMCA too restrictive as to the potential uses of basic tools; and consumers and others interested in fair use and free access to information, who worry that the DMCA restricts information and public use far beyond what the copyright regime intended.

## KEY WORDS AND PHRASES



## QUESTIONS AND CASE PROBLEMS

1. When Gerald Banks, an optical engineering expert, was hired to work for Burroughs Corporation in 1987, he was not asked to sign an agreement to assign inventive rights to the company's parent, Unisys, although such agreements were standard procedure. Two years later, Unisys filed a number of patent applications derived from Banks's engineering work. Banks was listed as co-inventor on only three of them. Banks was asked to sign assignment agreements for these three applications in return for

payment. Banks later discovered that three other patent applications were based on his work, although his name was not listed as co-inventor. Unisys refused to pay Banks for assignment rights to these applications, and Banks sued. At the time of the suit, who had the right to the inventions? [*Banks v. Unisys Corp.*, 228 F.3d 1357 (Fed. Cir. 2000).]

2. In its *Grokster* decision, the Ninth Circuit stated:

   > The introduction of new technology is always disruptive to old markets, and particularly to those copyright owners whose works are sold through well-established distribution mechanisms. Yet, history has shown that time and market forces often provide equilibrium in balancing interests, whether the new technology be a player piano, . . . a tape recorder, . . . a personal computer . . . , or an MP3 player.

   Do you agree? Does government have a role to play in determining the balance between established copyright interests and new, potentially infringing technology? [*MGM Studios v. Grokster*, 380 F.3d 1154 (9th Cir. 2004), *cert. granted,* 125 S. Ct. 686 (2004) (Case 11.1).]

3. Virgil Richards conceived a way to regulate the translation of heterologous DNA in bacteria. He worked on this invention with three other people. Richards conceived of the idea in May 2003, reduced it to practice on May 14, 2004, and filed a patent application on June 1, 2005. Richards was sued by the co-inventors for not including their names on the application. On May 3, 2004, Richards published an article in Japan that explained his idea in detail. Clyde Taylor reduced this idea to practice on May 14, 2004, making only minor changes to the procedure disclosed in the article. He applied for a patent on June 1, 2004.

   Can Richards or Taylor obtain a patent for the technology? The process includes some basic scientific principles. Does that mean that both patent applications will be rejected? [*In re O'Farrell,* 853 F.2d 894 (Fed. Cir. 1988).]

4. A hypothetical new communications product is described below. After reading the product description, think up three trademarks for this product: one that is fanciful, arbitrary, or suggestive; one that is geographic, descriptive, or a personal name; and one that is nondistinctive.

   **New Product Description**

   This new product incorporates global positioning technology into a multifunctional device that is worn like a watch. Not only does the device provide the time, but it also allows others to determine the location of the device and thus the location of the person. Moreover, the device is equipped to send and receive simple e-mail messages. The device may be especially suited for parents hoping to track remotely the whereabouts of their children. The location of the device can be determined through an online site that requires input of an identifying password.

5. Louis Vuitton filed a lawsuit against Google relating to its keyword-linked advertising model. When a Google user typed in search terms, including trademarked brand names such as Louis Vuitton, the Google results page included banner advertisements paid for by any company that wanted its advertisement to be linked to a Louis Vuitton search term. Vuitton claimed that the practice of selling advertising linked to such trademarks constitutes unauthorized commercial use and thus trademark infringement. Vuitton also argued that when other companies paid to be associated with Vuitton's trademarked terms, the posting of these advertisements constituted trademark dilution of the Vuitton brand. Does the Google advertising system infringe on Vuitton's trademarks? If so, does Google have any defenses? If you were running Vuitton, do you think it would be important to prevent Google from selling your brand name as a search term, or could it be beneficial to your business? [*Government Employees Insurance Co. v. Google,* 330 F. Supp. 2d 700 (E.D. Va. 2004).]

6. Gerald Hsu, a vice president at Cadence Design Systems, a maker of integrated circuit design software, resigned to work for Avant!, a direct competitor. Cadence told Hsu that because of its concern that he would share proprietary information and trade secrets with Avant!, it was planning to sue him and Avant! for trade secret misappropriation. Hsu was able to negotiate a mutual general release with Cadence that released all parties from claims against each other concerning any trade secret misappropriation or other unfair competition at the time of the settlement. One year later, a Cadence engineer discovered line-by-line copying of Cadence code in an Avant! software product. It turned out the copying occurred four years earlier—three years before the general release—and was continuing through the present day. Cadence argued that it could still bring a trade secret misappropriation against Avant! because the misappropriation continued to occur after the general release. Hsu and Avant! argued that

the general release precluded any suit for misappropriation occurring before the date of the release. Who wins? [*Cadence Design Systems v. Avant! Corp.*, 253 F.3d 1147 (9th Cir. 2001).]

7. WhenU.com is a software distributor that bundles sales of software to consumers with pop-up advertising on consumers' computers. WhenU.com's system recognizes the URL that the consumer's computer is visiting and matches related advertisements to it; the ads are frequently those of competitors to the destination site. U-Haul, the international moving company, sued WhenU.com, alleging that WhenU.com's pop-up ads that occurred when consumers visited U-Haul's website constituted copyright infringement, trademark infringement, and dilution of U-Haul's website. Does U-Haul have actionable claims against WhenU.com? [*U-Haul International, Inc. v. WhenU.com, Inc.*, 279 F. Supp. 2d 723 (E.D. Va. 2003).]
8. FairTest, a nonprofit organization dedicated to improving standardization tests, posted data on its website that demonstrated that minorities and low-income students score lower on the SAT and ACT than white and upper-class students. The College Board, the nonprofit that administers the SAT, demanded that FairTest remove the data, claiming that it was using College Board copyrighted data without permission. The College Board has a formal process by which it grants permission to organizations wishing to use its data; FairTest did not use this process. In reply, FairTest alleged that the data were not owned by the College Board and that even if they were, the data are widely available in the public domain, thus removing them from copyright protection. Does FairTest's defense have merit? [See http://www.fairtest.org/univ/FT_Response_to_CB.html.]
9. Martha Graham, one of the founders of modern dance, created the nonprofit Martha Graham Center of Contemporary Dance to support her work and the work of other artists. She was its artistic director and created much of her choreography while employed by the center; after 1966, her primary duty was to create new dances. At her death in 1991, Graham left her estate, including rights and interests in her work, to a friend, Ronald Portas, who opened a rival dance group, the Martha Graham School and Dance Foundation. Portas claimed the copyrights to all Graham's choreography. The Graham Center, however, claimed ownership under the "work for hire" doctrine. In arguments before the court, Portas claimed that the Center's lack of direct control over Graham's creative endeavors exempts Graham's choreography from the "work for hire" doctrine. Should the court accept this exemption? What result? [*Martha Graham School and Dance Foundation v. Martha Graham Center of Contemporary Dance*, 380 F.3d 624 (2d Cir. 2004).]

## MANAGER'S DILEMMA

10. You are the director of business development at a Silicon Valley semiconductor tools company. In order to use your hardware, customers usually buy the accompanying software installation package. Your job is to cut costs and improve the quality of that software package. Your company currently ships a copy of Microsoft Windows with its end-user software package. One effective way to cut costs while not compromising on quality might be to switch to Linux as the operating system for your hardware, an area in which you have some experience. (Linux is an open-source alternative to Microsoft Windows that can be used without charge as long as the licensee complies with the terms of the GPL, the Linux open-source license. See http://www.gnu.org/copyleft/gpl.html for the terms of the license.)

    You are eager to make the switch, but your in-house counsel warns you of rumors and lawsuits relating to SCO, a one-time Linux distributor that alleges that most current versions of Linux infringe its intellectual property rights in its own proprietary, non-open-source code. SCO has sued IBM for releasing SCO's proprietary code into the Linux kernel. It also has sued AutoZone and DaimlerChrysler for the unauthorized use of the SCO code included in the Linux kernel. SCO has announced that all commercial users of Linux must buy an SCO IP License to avoid the risk of infringement (and, presumably, an SCO lawsuit against them).

    The SCO license costs are comparable to the royalties your company is already paying Microsoft, so the advantages to switching to Linux would be nullified if your company is forced to buy an SCO license. Your in-house counsel, as well as many industry observers, says SCO's legal case seems weak; it could lose the lawsuits it launched against IBM and others. On the other hand, if SCO's claims have merit, then any commercial user of Linux is directly infringing SCO's intellectual property rights.

In response to the SCO suits, several companies, including Hewlett-Packard, Novell, and Sun Microsystems, offered their Linux customers indemnification programs and assistance through legal defense funds should SCO sue them. Your company's customers might expect a similar indemnity, which could prove costly.

Will you switch to Linux, given this tumultuous legal environment? Do you consider the legal or ethical risks prohibitive? Or does the need for a low-cost, high-quality software product override the risk of being sued?

## INTERNET SOURCES

| | |
|---|---|
| Registration of Internet domain names | http://www.uspto.gov/web/offices/tac/tmep/1200.htm#_Toc2666059 |
| Japanese Patent Office | http://www.jpo.go.jp |
| Foreign and International Law Resources on the Internet: Annotated from Cornell Law Library (International) | http://www.lawschool.cornell.edu/library/guides/foreign2/ |
| The Internet Law Library site, published by LawMoose, contains a variety of links to useful intellectual property articles and resources on the Web. | http://www.lawmoose.com/internetlawlib/ |
| "Thomas," the U.S. Congress's Official Legislative Information Page, is an extremely well-organized page describing pending bills, committee information, and Internet sources. | http://thomas.loc.gov |
| Franklin Pierce Law Center's Intellectual Property "Mall" | http://www.ipmall.info/ |
| American Bar Association Section of Intellectual Property Law | http://www.aipla.org |
| Intellectual Property Owners Association | http://www.ipo.org |
| The GigaLaw.com site provides legal information for Internet professionals, including a free daily e-mail update on breaking developments and articles of interest. | http://www.gigalaw.com |
| Emory Law Library Federal Courts Finder | http://www.law.emory.edu/FEDCTS/ |
| FindLaw Cyberspace Law News | http://news.findlaw.com/legalnews/scitech/cyber/ |
| Internet Law Wire from the University of Pittsburgh Law School | http://jurist.law.pitt.edu/internet_law.htm |
| The Filter is operated by the Berkman Center for Internet and Society at Harvard Law School and offers free monthly newsletters. | http://cyber.law.harvard.edu/filter/intro.html |
| New York Times Cyber Law Journal | http://www.nytimes.com/library/tech/reference/indexcyberlaw.html |
| Tech Law Journal | http://www.techlawjournal.com/ |
| KuesterLaw—The Technology Resource Center | http://www.kuesterlaw.com/ |
| Law.com—Tech Law Practice Center | http://www.law.com/professionals/techlaw.html |
| BNA's Internet Law News provides free daily e-mail updates. | http://www.bna.com/ilaw/ |

*(Continued)*

(Internet Sources *continued*)

| | |
|---|---|
| The law firm of Baker & McKenzie provides a free weekly e-mail on developments in electronic commerce and cyberlaw throughout the world. | http://www.lawincontext.com/elaw/ |
| Yahoo!—Copyright Law | http://dir.yahoo.com/Government/Law/Intellectual_Property/Copyrights/ |
| U.S. Copyright Office | http://www.copyright.gov/ |
| Legal Information Institute: Copyright Law | http://www.law.cornell.edu/topics/copyright.html |
| FindLaw Copyright Index | http://www.findlaw.com/01topics/23intellectprop/01copyright/index.html |
| Yahoo!—Patent Law | http://dir.yahoo.com/Government/Law/Intellectual_Property/Patents/ |
| Legal Information Institute: Patent Law | http://www.law.cornell.edu/topics/patent.html |
| FindLaw Patent Index | http://www.findlaw.com/01topics/23intellectprop/02patent/index.html |
| Yahoo!—Trademark Law | http://dir.yahoo.com/Government/Law/Intellectual_Property/Trademarks/ |
| Legal Information Institute: Trademark Law | http://www.law.cornell.edu/topics/trademark.html |
| FindLaw Trademark Index | http://www.findlaw.com/01topics/23intellectprop/03trademark/index.html |
| The Trade Secrets Home Page | http://www.execpc.com/~mhallign/index.html |
| Recording Industry of America | http://www.riaa.com |
| World Intellectual Property Organization's Arbitration and Mediation Center | http://arbiter.wipo.int/center/index.html |
| Syracuse University's Digital Convergence Center | http://dcc.syr.edu/ |
| The Internet Corporation for Assigned Names and Numbers (ICANN) | http://www.icann.org |
| National Telecommunications and Information Administration | http://www.ntia.doc.gov |
| The European Union Online | http://www.europa.eu.int |
| Electronic Frontier Foundation | http://www.eff.org |
| Stanford Law School Center for Internet and Society | http://cyberlaw.stanford.edu/index.shtml |

# UNIT III

# HUMAN RESOURCES IN THE LEGAL AND REGULATORY ENVIRONMENT

CHAPTER 12

# The Employment Agreement

## INTRODUCTION

### Employee Rights, Powers, and Protection

Over the past seventy-five years, there has been an explosion in laws regulating the employment relationship. As a result of the union movement, employees acquired economic and political power in their dealings with employers. With the emergence of the civil rights movement and the antidiscrimination legislation of the 1960s, employers began to examine their hiring and other employment practices more closely with respect to the treatment of women, minorities, and other protected groups. New laws concerning worker safety challenged employers to make the workplace safer. Federal and state whistle-blower statutes prohibited retaliation against employees who complained to a governmental agency about working conditions that they believed violated the law.

The courts developed new doctrines that limit a U.S. employer's traditional right to discharge an employee for any reason. These judicial decisions moved U.S. employment law closer to the European model, which requires an employer to show just cause for a discharge. Indeed, under the current law, an employer may be bound by contracts with its employees without even knowing it. Managers must devote an ever-increasing amount of attention and resources to complying with the sometimes bewildering array of statutes, regulations, and common law principles that bear upon their relations with their employees.

### Chapter Overview

This chapter discusses the traditional U.S. rule that employees can be terminated at will and the exceptions to this rule that have developed in recent years, including wrongful termination based on a violation of public policy, breach of an implied contract, and breach of the implied covenant of good faith and fair dealing. It also examines the common law doctrine of fair procedure, the tort of fraudulent inducement, and the enforceability of covenants not to compete. The laws relating to drug testing, genetic testing, lie detector tests, and certain hiring practices are also addressed. The chapter explains the employer's responsibility for worker safety and the system of workers' compensation, including the minimum wage and overtime payments. It also briefly discusses the coverage and application of the National Labor Relations Act (NLRA), which governs union activities in the United States. In addition, the chapter examines how U.S. immigration law affects domestic employment of foreign citizens and how foreign employment laws generally require just cause for the termination of workers.

## At-Will Employment

Most nonunionized American workers have no written employment contract. They are hired for a job without any express agreement as to how long the job will last. For at least the last hundred years, the American rule has been that an employment agreement of indefinite duration is an *at-will contract;* that is, the employee can quit at any time, and the employer can discharge the employee at any time, for any or no reason, with or without advance notice. Whether by statute or judicial decision, all states originally followed this rule. The courts reasoned that denying the employer the right to discharge its employee, while the employee was at liberty to quit at any time for any reason, would deprive the employer of property without due process of law.

Today, however, in many states, the at-will rule has been largely buried under its exceptions. Although some courts have declined to recognize these exceptions to the at-will doctrine, the trend is toward some level of protection against discharge in certain circumstances. Employers are well advised to consider whether the reasons for any termination will pass muster as "good" or "just" cause.

## EMPLOYEES NOT SUBJECT TO THE AT-WILL RULE

Public employees, employees who negotiated express contracts for a fixed term with their employers, and unionized workers have generally not been subject to the at-will rule.

### *Public Employees*

Most employees of federal, state, and local government agencies have long worked under civil service or merit systems that provide for tenure, require just cause for discharge, and guarantee administrative procedures to determine whether there is just cause for discharge.

### *Employees with Individual Contracts*

A private-sector employee can avoid at-will status by negotiating a contract that provides for a specific term of employment and defines how the contract can be terminated. Employers will almost always reserve the right to fire an employee, but the employment contract will usually require the employer to provide some level of severance pay if the termination was without cause. For example, a contract might give an employee with a three-year contract, who is fired without cause at the end of the first year, the right to salary and benefits for the remaining two years. In some cases, but not all, the amount due is reduced by any monies the employee receives from another employer. Negotiated contracts requiring just cause for termination by the employer may also provide some level of payment and benefits if the employee quits "for good reason." This is often defined to include being required to move more than fifty miles from the original place of employment or having one's duties and responsibilities substantially changed or reduced. Persons in professional or managerial positions are more likely to be able to negotiate individual contracts with such provisions.

### *Union Contracts*

Other employees rely on union contracts, which almost universally require just cause for termination and establish grievance procedures whereby an employee can challenge his or her discharge.

## WRONGFUL DISCHARGE

Beginning in the early 1970s, courts in a number of states began to recognize exceptions to the at-will doctrine in new causes of action for *wrongful discharge,* that is, termination of employment without good cause. Wrongful discharge is a common-law-based claim supported by three theories: public policy, implied contract, and implied covenant of good faith and fair dealing.

These causes of action are based on both contract and tort law. Although the line between wrongful discharge and fraud is not always clear, each claim receives different damages. Wrongful discharge gives rise only to contract damages, whereas fraud gives rise to personal-injury and punitive damages. Even this distinction is hazy, however. Thus, some wrongful-discharge plaintiffs may be able to collect damages for emotional distress and punitive damages, not simply lost wages.

### *The Public Policy Exception*

One of the earliest exceptions to the at-will rule was the *public policy exception.* Even if an individual is an at-will employee, in most states the employer is prohibited from discharging the employee for a reason that violates public policy. The greatest protection is given to an employee discharged due to a refusal to commit an unlawful act, such as perjury or price-fixing, at the employer's request. Indeed, an employer's request that an employee violate a criminal statute—or even a noncriminal regulation—is almost always deemed to be against public policy and would give rise to damages for discharge.

Although most states recognize a public policy exception to at-will employment, several states do not.[1]

**Remedies** In *Tameny v. Atlantic Richfield,*[2] the California Supreme Court held that an employee may maintain both tort and contract actions if the employee's discharge violated fundamental principles of public policy. As a result, damages for pain and suffering and possibly punitive damages were available.

**Sources of Public Policy** Different jurisdictions recognize different sources of public policy.

**State Sources** Jurisdictions are split as to whether to recognize an exception to the at-will rule for nonlegislative sources of public policy. Some jurisdictions, including

1. Alabama, Florida, Georgia, Louisiana, Maine, New York, Rhode Island. *See, e.g.,* Kiddler v. AmSouth Bank, N.A., 639 So. 2d 1361 (Ala. 1994); Smith v. AVSC Inking, Inc., 148 F. Supp. 2d 302 (S.D.N.Y. 2001).
2. 610 P.2d 1330 (Cal. 1980).

California and Georgia, limit the sources of public policy to statutory or constitutional provisions designed to protect society at large.[3] For example, the Georgia Supreme Court held in *Reilly v. Alcan Aluminum Corp.*[4] that an at-will employee could not sue in tort for wrongful discharge based on age discrimination because only the state legislature can create a public policy exception to the at-will doctrine. The court ruled that since the Georgia age discrimination law provided no civil remedy and another state statute merely set forth general principles of tort law, the court had no authority to create an exception to the state's at-will doctrine.

Other jurisdictions permit courts to find that a termination violates public policy even where no state statute prohibits the discharge. For example, an employee claimed she was discharged by the Central Indiana Gas Company for filing a workers' compensation claim. Although no state statute prohibiting such a discharge existed, the Indiana Supreme Court recognized that employees should be able to sue an employer in tort because "retaliatory discharge for filing a workmen's compensation claim is a wrongful, unconscionable act and should be actionable in a court of law."[5] The court further stated that an employee must be able to exercise his or her right under the Indiana workers' compensation statute without fear of reprisal in order for the public policy of the statute to be actualized.

The Oregon Supreme Court created a public policy exception for termination of an employee for performing jury duty.[6] The court reasoned that jury duty was an important civic duty and that the will of the community and the effectiveness of the jury system would be thwarted if employers were allowed to discharge employees for fulfilling such an obligation.

**Federal Sources** Many federal statutes expressly prohibit termination of employees who report violations of, or exercise rights under, the statutes. For example, the National Labor Relations Act prohibits discharge for union or other concerted activities or for filing charges under the Act.[7] In addition, the Occupational Health and Safety Act prohibits discharge of employees in retaliation for exercising rights under the Act, such as complaining about work procedures or about health and safety violations in the workplace.[8] Many state statutes contain similar provisions.

The Fair Labor Standards Act (FLSA) prohibits discharge for exercising rights guaranteed by its minimum-wage and overtime provisions.[9] In *Valerio v. Putnam Associates,*[10] the U.S. Court of Appeals for the First Circuit extended the antiretaliation provisions of the FLSA to retaliatory discharge as a result of internal complaints lodged by employees with employers as well as legal proceedings commenced by an employee. In that case, the court held that a worker, who was fired after complaining to her employer that it was not properly paying her overtime pursuant to the FLSA, could sue under the antiretaliation provisions of the FLSA. The U.S. courts of appeals are split on this issue, however: the majority allow employees to sue if they are discharged after filing internal complaints with their employers, but a minority of the courts require the employee to have initiated a formal, legal proceeding.

**Nongovernmental Sources** Some jurisdictions have recognized that nongovernmental sources of public policy, including professional ethical codes, may provide the basis for a public policy exception to the at-will doctrine.[11] For example, in *General Dynamics Corp. v. Rose,*[12] the California Supreme Court held that an attorney could base a claim of retaliatory discharge on allegations that he was terminated for refusing to violate a mandatory ethical duty embodied in the rules of attorney professional conduct. Andrew Rose, former in-house counsel at General Dynamics, had filed a claim for retaliatory discharge, alleging that he had been fired because he had (1) spearheaded an investigation of drug use at the company that resulted in the termination of more than sixty employees; (2) protested the company's failure to investigate the bugging of the office of the chief of security, a criminal offense; and (3) advised company officials that General Dynamics' salary policy might be in violation of the FLSA, which could potentially expose the company to several hundred million dollars in backpay claims.

In contrast, in *Jacobson v. Knepper & Moga,*[13] the Illinois Supreme Court held that an attorney, who had

3. *See, e.g.,* Phillips v. St. Mary's Reg'l Med. Ctr., 96 Cal. App. 4th 218 (2002); Reilly v. Alcan Aluminum Corp., 528 S.E.2d 238 (Ga. 2000).
4. 528 S.E.2d 238 (Ga. 2000).
5. Frampton v. Cent. Ind. Gas Co., 297 N.E.2d 425 (Ind. 1973).
6. Nees v. Hocks, 536 P.2d 512 (Or. 1975).
7. 29 U.S.C. §§ 158(a) (1), (3), and (4).
8. 29 U.S.C. § 660(c).
9. 29 U.S.C. §§ 215(a) (3), 216(b).
10. 173 F.3d 35 (1st Cir. 1999).
11. *See, e.g.,* Winkelman v. Beloit Mem'l Hosp., 483 N.W.2d 211 (Wis. 1992) (administrative rules); Pierce v. Ortho Pharm. Corp., 417 A.2d 505 (N.J. 1980) (legislation; administrative rules, regulations, or decisions; judicial decisions; and, in certain instances, a professional code of ethics).
12. 876 P.2d 487 (Cal. 1994).
13. 706 N.E.2d 491 (Ill. 1998).

been fired by his firm after complaining that it was violating federal law, could not recover for retaliatory discharge. Alan Jacobson, an associate at the law firm, Knepper & Moga, discovered that the firm was filing consumer debt collection actions in violation of the Fair Debt Collection Practices Act. He was terminated after he complained about these activities several times to one of the principal partners of the firm. Jacobson filed a claim against the firm, alleging that he had been discharged in retaliation for his insistence that the firm comply with the rules of attorney professional conduct and cease violating the federal law. The court found that the public policy to be protected by the Fair Debt Collection Practices Act (protecting debtors' property and ensuring them due process) was already adequately safeguarded by the ethical obligations imposed by the rules of attorney professional conduct, making it unnecessary to expand the tort of retaliatory discharge to protect discharged employee attorneys.

**Whistleblower Statutes** A more recent development has been the adoption of *whistleblower statutes* that protect employees who report illegal activities going on within their company. The rationale behind protecting whistleblowers is that it is in the public interest to promote compliance with the law. It would be irresponsible to blindly protect all employee disclosures, however, because some disclosures may be intended merely to harass the employer. Hence, courts must balance the public interest in the enforcement of laws, the whistleblower's interest in being protected from reprisal, and the employer's interest in managing its workforce.

A number of states have statutes that provide whistleblower protection for terminated employees. For example, the New York state statute[14] protecting private-sector whistleblowers provides:

> An employer shall not take any retaliatory personnel action against an employee because such employee does any of the following:
>
> (a) discloses, or threatens to disclose to a supervisor or to a public body an activity, policy or practice of the employer that is in violation of law, rule or regulation which violation creates and presents a substantial and specific danger to the public health or safety;
> (b) provides information to, or testifies before, any public body conducting an investigation, hearing or inquiry into any such violation of a law, rule or regulation by such employer; or
> (c) objects to, or refuses to participate in any such activity, policy or practice in violation of a law, rule or regulation.

California's whistleblower statute is similar to New York's but is broader in that it does not limit its protection to violations of law that create a danger to public health or safety.[15] In addition, the California attorney general maintains a "whistleblower" hotline to receive telephone reports of violations of laws by corporations.[16]

In addition to state whistleblower provisions, there are a number of federal whistleblower statutes, many of which apply only to federal employees who report violations by governmental agencies or employees. The Sarbanes-Oxley Act of 2002 (SOX)[17] includes several whistleblower provisions that apply to all public companies and one that applies to private companies as well.[18] In the following case, the U.S. District Court for the Northern District of Georgia considered whether an employee of a public company was terminated in violation of the whistleblower provision set forth in Section 806 of SOX.

14. N.Y. LAB. LAW § 740 (McKinney 2002).

15. CAL. LAB. CODE § 1102.5 (West 2004).

16. CAL. LAB. CODE § 1102.7 (West 2004).

17. 18 U.S.C. § 1514A.

18. The SOX whistleblower provision provides criminal penalties for public and private company employers who retaliate against a person who provides truthful information relating to the commission of a federal offense to a law enforcement officer. 18 U.S.C. § 1514A.

A CASE IN POINT

**CASE 12.1**
**Collins v. Beazer Homes USA, Inc.**
*United States District Court for the Northern District of Georgia 334 F. Supp. 2d 1365 (N.D. Ga. 2004).*

## Summary

**› FACTS** Judy Collins was offered and accepted a position as director of marketing for the Jacksonville, Florida division of Beazer Homes Corporation. According to the offer, Collins would be subject to a ninety-day assessment review period during which "either [Collins] or the Company may decide to terminate employment without giving a reason."

Soon after starting with Beazer, Collins began having conflicts with her manager, Bill Mazar, and another coworker stemming from Collins's disagreement with Mazar's use of the Montello Advertising Agency for advertising services. Collins found Montello's

*(Continued)*

(Case 12.1 *continued*)

services to be unsatisfactory and terminated the agency's contract with Beazer's Jacksonville division. Collins alleged that Mazar continued to use and pay Montello behind her back simply because the president of Montello and the Jacksonville division president, Marty Schaffer, were friends. Collins also suspected that employees in the Jacksonville division were providing kickbacks on lumber purchases and that marketing costs were being categorized incorrectly in an attempt to hide certain information. In addition, Collins believed that the director of sales was providing more favorable sales commissions to her friends.

In early August 2002, Collins raised her concerns to Beazer's vice president of sales and marketing, the vice president of human resources, and the company's CEO. In a subsequent meeting between Schaffer and Collins on August 19, 2002, Schaffer terminated Collins's employment.

Collins filed a complaint in the U.S. District Court for the Northern District of Georgia, alleging that Beazer retaliated against her in violation of SOX because she was terminated soon after she raised concerns about violations of securities laws. Beazer moved for summary judgment, arguing that the court should dismiss the case because no genuine issue of material fact existed regarding whether Collins's termination was retaliatory. Beazer also contended that Collins had not engaged in a protected activity and that she was terminated during her ninety-day probationary period because of personality conflicts with her coworkers.

**› ISSUE PRESENTED** Does a genuine issue of material fact exist regarding whether Beazer violated SOX by terminating Collins soon after she raised concerns about violations of securities laws?

**› SUMMARY OF OPINION** The court noted that Section 806 of SOX provides "whistleblower" protection to employees of publicly traded companies. Pursuant to that section, an employer may not discriminate against any employee in the terms and conditions of employment because of any lawful act done by the employee "to provide information . . . regarding any conduct which the employee reasonably believes constitutes a violation of section 1341, 1343, 1344, or 1348, any rule or regulation of the Securities and Exchange Commission, or any provision of Federal law relating to fraud against shareholders."[19]

The court found that the evidentiary framework for a claim under SOX required that Collins show by a preponderance of the evidence that (1) she had engaged in a protected activity, (2) Beazer knew of the protected activity, (3) she suffered an unfavorable personnel action, and (4) circumstances exist to suggest that the protected activity was a contributing factor to the unfavorable action. Assuming that Collins met her burden of proof, Beazer could still avoid liability if it could demonstrate by clear and convincing evidence that it "would have taken the same unfavorable personnel action in the absence of [the protected] behavior."

Applying the above framework, the court found that Collins had engaged in a protected activity despite Beazer's assertions that she never specifically alleged securities or accounting fraud and that her complaints were too vague to constitute protected activity. Comparing Collins with Sherron Watkins, the former Enron vice president, Beazer argued that Watkins had outlined specific accounting procedures and transactions about which she was concerned and had expressed concerns that specific securities laws were being violated whereas Collins expressed only vague concerns that amounted to "nothing more than personality conflicts and differences in marketing strategies." The court concluded:

> Though this is a close case, . . . the Court finds that there is a genuine issue of material fact whether Plaintiff engaged in protected activity. It is evident that Plaintiff's complaints

19. 18 U.S.C. § 1514A(a)(1).

*(Continued)*

(Case 12.1 *continued*)

> do not rise to the level of complaints that were raised by Sherron Watkins. . . . However, the mere fact that the severity or specificity of her complaints does not rise to the level of action that would spur Congress to draft legislation does not mean that the legislation it did draft was not meant to protect her. In short if Congress had intended to limit the protection of Sarbanes-Oxley to accountants, or to have required complainants to specifically identify the code section they believe was being violated, it could have done so. It did not.

The court also found that Beazer knew of Collins's protected activity and that she suffered an unfavorable personnel action when she was terminated. Finally, the court found that the fact that Collins was fired fourteen days after making her complaint established circumstances sufficient to demonstrate causation.

Because Collins had met her burden of proof, the court found that Beazer would be entitled to summary judgment only if it could establish by clear and convincing evidence that it would have fired her even if she had not participated in the protected activity. The court concluded that Beazer had not met this burden of proof. Although Beazer contended that Schaffer fired Collins based on her personality conflicts with her coworkers and Mazar's dissatisfaction with her performance, Mazar testified that he did not believe he had a personality conflict with Collins. In addition, none of Collins's superiors had ever met with her to discuss the alleged personality conflicts or her job performance. Finally, Collins's short employment history with Beazer made it more difficult to determine whether the alleged problems would have ultimately resulted in her termination without her participation in the protected activity or whether they could have been addressed and resolved.

› **RESULT** The court found that there was a genuine issue of material fact as to whether Beazer terminated Collins in violation of SOX and therefore denied Beazer's motion for summary judgment.

---

## *Implied Contracts*

The second judicial exception to the at-will rule arises out of the willingness of courts to interpret the parties' conduct as implying a contract that limits the employer's right to discharge, even though no written or express oral contract exists. Such a contract is known as an *implied contract*. Some factors that can give rise to an implied obligation to discharge the employee only for good cause are that the person (1) has been a long-term employee; (2) has never been formally criticized or warned about his or her conduct; (3) has received raises, bonuses, and promotions throughout his or her career; (4) has been assured that his or her employment would continue if he or she did a good job or that the company did not terminate employees at his or her level except for good cause; and (5) has been assured by the company's management that he or she was doing a good job. Other relevant factors include the personnel policies or practices of the employer and the practices of the industry in which the employee is engaged.

A personnel manual stating that it was the employer's policy to release employees for just cause only, together with oral assurances that the employee would be with the company as long as he or she did his or her job properly, can give rise to a reasonable expectation that an employee will not be terminated except for good cause. In so holding in *Toussaint v. Blue Cross & Blue Shield of Michigan*,[20] the Michigan Supreme Court stated that there could be a contractual obligation binding on the employer without negotiations or any meeting of the minds, or even any communication of the policies to the employee:

> No pre-employment negotiations need take place and the parties' minds need not meet on the subject; nor does it matter that the employee knows nothing of the particulars of the employer's policies and practices or that the employer may change them unilaterally. It is enough that the employer chooses, presumably in its own interest, to create an

20. 292 N.W.2d 880 (Mich. 1980).

environment in which the employee believes that, whatever the personnel policies and practices, they are established and official at any given time, purport to be fair, and are applied consistently and uniformly to each employee. The employer has then created a situation "instinct with an obligation."

Although few courts have been willing to go as far as the Michigan Supreme Court went in *Toussaint,* some courts have agreed that a personnel manual given to employees may give rise to contractual obligations. For example, the Oklahoma Court of Appeals held that a manual constitutes an offer of terms and conditions and that the employee's continuing to work is deemed an acceptance of the offer.[21]

In *Havill v. Woodstock Soapstone Co.,*[22] the Vermont Supreme Court ruled that Woodstock's failure to follow the discipline policy set forth in its personnel manual amounted to a breach of its implied contract with its employee, Lois Havill. Woodstock's personnel policy stated that an employee was entitled to two written warnings in a twelve-month period prior to termination for "willful or repeated violations, or exaggerated behavior not in the best interest of the company or its employees." Prior to her termination, Havill continually clashed with a corporate reorganization consultant hired by Woodstock to redefine employment duties. The consultant complained to Woodstock's management about Havill's "rude" and "insubordinate" behavior. Forty-one days after the consultant's initial complaint, Woodstock fired Havill without providing her with any formal written warning. The court ruled that the personnel manual required Woodstock to provide Havill with two written warnings before terminating her; thus, Woodstock was liable for damages arising out of its breach of the implied promise of "just cause" termination and progressive discipline.

Other courts have been unwilling to treat written personnel policies as contracts. For example, an employee of Citibank based his claim that he was entitled not to be discharged except for cause on provisions of a personnel manual. A New York appellate court rejected this argument and held that the manual did not create any legal obligation upon the employer because the employee was still free to terminate the relationship at will.[23] Similarly, in a case involving Westinghouse Electrical Corporation, the North Carolina Court of Appeals held that unilaterally implemented employment policies are not part of the employment contract unless expressly included in it.[24]

21. Langdon v. Saga Corp., 569 P.2d 524 (Okla. Ct. App. 1976).
22. 2004 WL 1801776 (Vt. 2004).
23. Edwards v. Citibank, N.A., 74 A.D.2d 553 (N.Y. App. Div. 1980).
24. Walker v. Westinghouse Elec. Corp., 335 S.E.2d 79 (N.C. Ct. App. 1985).

Even when there is an implied contract not to terminate except for good cause, an employer may legally terminate an employee suspected of misconduct if, acting in good faith and following an investigation that is appropriate under the circumstances, the employer has reasonable grounds for believing that the employee did engage in misconduct. For example, in one case,[25] a male manager was terminated following charges of sexual harassment by two female employees. The employer conducted a thorough investigation, which included interviews with the manager, the two accusers, and twenty-one other people who had worked with the manager. The investigation was inconclusive, however; the employer could not determine with certainty whether the acts of harassment had actually taken place. The company felt that the accusers were credible, and its investigator concluded that, more likely than not, the harassment had occurred. Fearing a suit by the two women, the company terminated the male manager. He sued for wrongful termination; the jury awarded him $1.78 million, after apparently finding that the charges against him were false. The California Supreme Court reversed and sent the case back for retrial so that the jury could determine whether the company had a good faith belief, following a reasonable investigation, that the manager had engaged in sexual harassment. If so, the company would not be liable for wrongful termination.

### Implied Covenant of Good Faith and Fair Dealing

The third prong in the developing law of wrongful discharge is the recognition of an *implied covenant of good faith and fair dealing* in the employment relationship. For example, the Supreme Judicial Court of Massachusetts held that a twenty-five-year employee of National Cash Register Company, with a written contract providing for at-will employment, could sue for wrongful termination when the employer discharged him to deprive him of $46,000 in commissions.[26]

Courts in Texas, New Mexico, Florida, and Wisconsin have expressly declined to recognize an implied covenant of good faith and fair dealing in employment cases. About a dozen states[27] have recognized the covenant in the employment context. California, like Massachusetts,

25. Cotran v. Rollins Hudig Hall Int'l, 948 P.2d. 412 (Cal. 1998).
26. Fortune v. Nat'l Cash Register Co., 364 N.E.2d 1251 (Mass. 1977).
27. Alaska, Arizona, California, Connecticut, Delaware, Idaho, Massachusetts, Montana, New Hampshire, New Jersey, Utah, and Wyoming.

recognizes such an implied covenant but provides only contract remedies for breach of the implied covenant; tort remedies, such as damages for pain and suffering and punitive damages, are not available.[28]

## Right to Fair Procedure

The California courts have acknowledged the common law right of fair procedure, a right that is related to the doctrine of wrongful discharge. *Fair procedure* protects individuals from arbitrary exclusion or expulsion from private organizations that control important economic interests. Individuals having this right must be given notice of the charges against them and an opportunity to respond to those charges. They cannot be expelled from membership for reasons that are arbitrary, capricious, or contrary to public policy, even though the organization's bylaws contain provisions to the contrary. Organizations can exercise their sound business judgment when establishing standards for membership, but any removal must be "both substantively rational and procedurally fair."[30] This right has become increasingly important for healthcare providers belonging to managed care networks.

For example, the California Supreme Court applied the doctrine of fair procedure to an insurance company's decision to remove a physician from its preferred provider lists even though the contract between the physician and the insurer provided that the listing could be terminated by either party at any time with or without cause.[31] The court declined to extend its holding to every insurer wishing to remove a doctor from one of its preferred provider lists, however: "The [fair procedure] obligation . . . arises only when the insurer possesses power so substantial that the removal significantly impairs the ability of an ordinary, competent physician to practice medicine or a medical specialty in a particular geographic area, thereby affecting an important, substantial economic interest."[32]

28. Foley v. Interactive Data Corp., 765 P.2d 373 (Cal. 1988).

### IN BRIEF

**Limits on At-Will Employment**

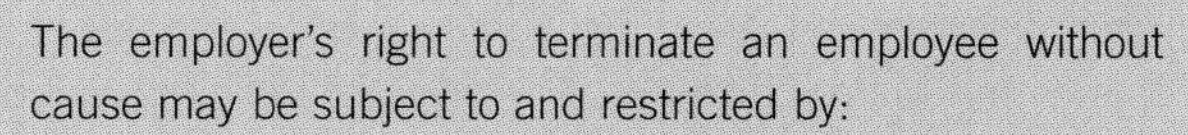

The employer's right to terminate an employee without cause may be subject to and restricted by:

- Express statutory abrogation of terminable at-will employment[29]
- Statutory prohibition of discrimination on specified characteristic (e.g., race, sex, age)
- Statutory prohibition of discrimination for protected activity (e.g., NLRA, protected leaves of absence, off-duty lawful conduct)
- Civil service systems
- Union contracts
- Express employment contracts (oral or written)
- The public policy exception
- Whistleblower statutes
- Implied contracts
- The implied covenant of good faith and fair dealing

29. *See, e.g.*, MONT. CODE ANN. §§ 39-2-901 to 39-2-915, as amended.

## Fraudulent Inducement

During difficult economic times, a business may engage in puffery and exaggeration to keep and attract highly qualified personnel. The following case serves as a warning that a company may be held liable for overzealous sales pitches under a theory of fraudulent inducement.

30. Pinsker v. Pacific Coast Soc'y. of Orthodontists, 526 P.2d 253 (Cal. 1974).
31. Potvin v. Metro. Life Ins. Co., 997 P.2d 1153 (Cal. 2000). *See also* Harper v. Healthsource New Hampshire, Inc., 674 A.2d 962, 966 (N.H. 1996) ("The public has a substantial interest in the relationship between health maintenance organizations and their preferred provider physicians.").
32. *Potvin.*

A CASE IN POINT

**CASE 12.2**
**Lazar v. Rykoff-Sexton, Inc.**
*Supreme Court of California*
*909 P.2d 981 (Cal. 1996).*

## In the Language of the Court

**› FACTS** Andrew Lazar was employed as president of a family-owned restaurant equipment company in New York where he lived with his wife and two children. In September 1989, a vice president of Rykoff-Sexton, Inc. (Rykoff) contacted Lazar and asked him to move to Los Angeles to work as Rykoff's West Coast general manager for contract design. The company intensively recruited Lazar through February 1990. During this

*(Continued)*

(Case 12.2 *continued*)

process, Lazar expressed concern to Rykoff about relinquishing a secure job with a family business, moving his children far away from their friends, and leaving his home of forty years. As a condition of agreeing to relocate, Lazar required Rykoff's assurance that his job would be secure and would involve significant pay increases.

Rykoff represented that Lazar would become part of Rykoff's "family," would enjoy continued advancement, and would have security and a long-term relationship with the company. The company told Lazar that it would employ him as long as he performed his job and achieved goals. Rykoff also implied that the current head of the department in which Lazar would work had plans to retire and that Lazar would be groomed for that position. In addition, Rykoff represented that the company was very strong financially and anticipated profits and growth in the future. Lazar was assured that he would receive annual reviews and raises.

In fact, Rykoff's representations were false, as the company had just experienced its worst economic performance in recent history and its financial outlook was pessimistic. Rykoff was planning an operational merger that would eliminate Lazar's position, and the company had no intention of retaining him. The company also knew that the promised compensation increases would not be forthcoming as company policy limited increases to only 3 percent a year.

Based on Rykoff's false representations, in May 1990, Lazar resigned from his job in New York, relocated his family to Los Angeles, and commenced employment at Rykoff. He performed his job in an exemplary manner, obtaining sales increases for his assigned regions and lowering operating costs within his department. In April 1992, Rykoff failed to pay Lazar bonus compensation to which he was entitled. Several months later, Rykoff told Lazar his job was being eliminated owing to management reorganization. After being terminated, Lazar was unable to find comparable employment.

Lazar sued Rykoff on a number of theories, including fraudulent inducement, for inducing his relocation to Los Angeles by making false representations. The trial court dismissed most of Lazar's claims, but the appeals court vacated this order. Rykoff appealed.

› **ISSUE PRESENTED** Can an employer be held liable to an employee for promissory fraud for statements that it made to induce the employee to come to work for it?

› **OPINION** WERDEGAR, J., writing for the California Supreme Court:

An action for promissory fraud may lie where a defendant fraudulently induces the plaintiff to enter into a contract. . . . In such cases, the plaintiff's claim does not depend upon whether the defendant's promise is ultimately enforceable as a contract. "If it is enforceable, the [plaintiff] . . . has a cause of action in tort as an alternative at least, and perhaps in some instances in addition to his cause of action on the contract.". . . Recovery, however, may be limited by the rule against double recovery of tort and contract compensatory damages. . . .

Lazar's allegations, if true, would establish all the elements of promissory fraud. As detailed above, Lazar alleges that, in order to induce him to come to work in California, Rykoff intentionally represented to him that he would be employed by the company so long as he performed his job, he would receive significant increases in salary, and the company was strong financially. Lazar further alleges that Rykoff's representations were false, and he justifiably relied on them in leaving secure New York employment, severing his connections with the New York employment market, uprooting his family, purchasing a California home and moving here.

. . .

*(Continued)*

(Case 12.2 *continued*)

. . . Lazar's reliance on Rykoff's misrepresentations was truly detrimental, such that he may plead all the elements of fraud. Lazar's employer, Rykoff, did not have the power to compel Lazar to leave his former employment. Rykoff's misrepresentations were made before the employment relationship was formed, when Rykoff had no coercive power over Lazar and Lazar was free to decline the offered position. Rykoff used misrepresentations to induce Lazar to change employment, a result Rykoff presumably could not have achieved truthfully (because Lazar had required assurances the Rykoff position would be secure and would involve significant increases in pay). Moreover, Lazar's decision to join Rykoff left Lazar in worse circumstances than those in which he would have found himself had Rykoff not lied to him. (Allegedly, Lazar's secure living and working circumstances were disrupted, and Lazar became the employee of a financially troubled company, which intended to treat him as an at-will employee.)

. . .

. . . Because of the extra measure of blameworthiness inhering in fraud, and because in fraud cases we are not concerned about the need for "predictability about the cost of contractual relationships," fraud plaintiffs may recover "out-of-pocket" damages. . . .

. . .

Consistent with the foregoing, as to his fraud claim Lazar may properly seek damages for the costs of uprooting his family, expenses incurred in relocation, and the loss of security and income associated with his former employment in New York. On the facts as pled, however, Lazar must rely on his contract claim for recovery of any loss of income allegedly caused by wrongful termination of his employment with Rykoff. Moreover, any overlap between damages recoverable in tort and damages recoverable in contract would be limited by the rule against double recovery.

**› RESULT** The court affirmed the appeals court's decision, finding that Lazar had stated a cause of action for fraudulent inducement.

**› COMMENTS** In reaching its decision, the court distinguished *Hunter v. Up-Right, Inc.,*[33] an earlier case in which the California Supreme Court had held that an at-will employee who was induced to resign by being falsely told that his job was being eliminated could not state a valid tort claim for fraud. The *Lazar* court reasoned that the employer in *Hunter* had used deception when it could have directly fired the employee. In contrast, the employer in *Lazar* did not have the power to force the executive to leave his company in New York. As a result, the executive's reliance on the employer's representations was truly detrimental.

**› CRITICAL THINKING QUESTIONS**

1. What is the difference between breach of contract and fraudulent inducement?
2. Why was it necessary for the plaintiff to couch his claim in terms of fraudulent inducement?

33. 864 P.2d 88 (Cal. 1993).

In *Rodowicz v. Massachusetts Mutual Life Insurance Co.,*[34] certain retired MassMutual employees sued the company, alleging that it had failed to reveal that a more favorable retirement option was forthcoming at the time they were considering retiring. As a result, they retired under terms that were less favorable than those in a special offer made to employees shortly after they retired. Under Massachusetts fraud law, the plaintiffs had to

34. 192 F.3d 162 (1st Cir. 1999).

**ETHICAL CONSIDERATION**

What role, if any, should the law play in penalizing an employer who lies to its employee about the reason for termination in order to persuade the employee to resign? What role do ethics play in this situation?

demonstrate that (1) MassMutual made false statements of material fact to induce them to retire when they did and (2) they reasonably relied on those statements to their detriment. In contrast, the Employee Retirement Income Security Act (ERISA) requires employers to disclose information to employees about possible changes in benefits only if those changes reach a level of "serious consideration." The U.S. Court of Appeals for the First Circuit ruled that the retired employees could sue for fraudulent inducement under state law based upon MassMutual's misrepresentation that its board of directors was not considering changing its retirement package.

##  Noncompete Agreements

A *covenant not to compete* is a device, ancillary to another agreement (such as an employment contract), that is designed to protect a company's interests by limiting a former employee's ability to use trade secrets in working for a competitor or setting up a competing business. Enforcing a noncompete agreement can be difficult because rules vary by jurisdiction. For example, California, Texas, and Georgia severely limit the enforceability of noncompetes.

Due to these differences in state laws, disputes can arise regarding which law to apply to noncompete agreements. In a recent case, an employee working in Ohio signed a noncompete with his employer, Convergys, which included an Ohio choice-of-law provision. When the employee resigned to work for a competitor in Georgia, he filed a lawsuit in Georgia seeking a declaration that the noncompete was unenforceable and an injunction restraining Convergys from enforcing the noncompete. The district court concluded that it could not follow "a contractual selection of law of a foreign state where such chosen law would contravene the public policy of Georgia," declared the noncompete void, and granted an injunction against Convergys that prohibited the company from seeking to enforce the noncompete in any court nationwide. On appeal, the U.S. Court of Appeals for the Eleventh Circuit found that although Georgia was entitled to enforce its public policy interests within its borders, "Georgia cannot in effect apply its public policy decisions nationwide—the public policy of Georgia is not that everywhere [sic]. To permit a nationwide injunction would in effect interfere both with parties' ability to contract and their ability to enforce appropriately derived expectations." As a result, the court modified the injunction to preclude Convergys only from enforcing the noncompete in Georgia.[35]

Even if an employment agreement does not contain an express noncompetition clause, any provisions having a similar effect will be unenforceable in a jurisdiction banning noncompetes. For example, Dean Witter's employment agreement forced brokers in Los Angeles to repay training costs if they left the company within two years. In a settlement of a class-action suit in October 1997, Dean Witter agreed to return $540,000 collected from thirty-four former brokers and to pay another $1.2 million in legal fees for "involuntary servitude" in violation of California's ban on noncompetes unrelated to the sale of a business.[36]

Even in states permitting noncompete agreements, courts will enforce only reasonable restrictions on competition. Unreasonableness can be found on many grounds, including duration of limitation, geographic extent, scope of activities prohibited, and the employer's relation to the interests being protected. For example, the Nevada Supreme Court invalidated a noncompete agreement that restricted a lighting-retrofitting employee from competing with his former employer within a 100-mile radius of the former employer's site for five years.[37] The duration placed a great hardship on the employee and was not necessary to protect the former employer's interests.

Thus, care must be taken when drafting noncompete agreements to ensure that they are not unduly restrictive. Corporate managers should keep the following guidelines in mind:[38]

- Know the relevant state laws. Given that different states apply different standards for reviewing noncompetes, be sure to structure each agreement in a way that courts will recognize and uphold.

35. Keener v. Convergys Corp., 342 F.3d 1264 (11th Cir. 2003).
36. Patrick McGeehan, *Attempting to Dun a Former Broker Costs Dean Witter $1.8 Million,* WALL ST. J., Oct. 23, 1997, at B12.
37. Jones v. Deeter, 913 P.2d 1272 (Nev. 1996). See also Rollins Burdick Hunter of Wis., Inc. v. Hamilton, 304 N.W.2d 752 (Wis. 1981).
38. See Christopher Caggiano, *Think All Noncompetes Stink? Think Again,* INC., Oct. 1997, at 114.

- Be specific. Clarify the specific roles and responsibilities of a given employee so that the noncompete is not overly restrictive, thereby reducing the risk of judicial invalidation.
- Provide consideration for the noncompete. The noncompete may be a condition of employment; but for existing employees, be sure to provide something in exchange, such as a bonus or a promotion.[39]

To protect trade secrets, a New York court imposed noncompete obligations in the absence of a written agreement. Former employees of DoubleClick, Inc. who had not signed noncompete agreements were enjoined from working in the same industry for six months.[40] The court reasoned that the similarity in the two businesses and positions made it inevitable that the employees would use the former employer's trade secrets in their work for the new company. Trade secret protection and the inevitable disclosure doctrine are discussed further in Chapter 11.

The majority of states recognize an employer's investment of time and money to develop customer and client relationships as a legitimate employer interest that can justify a noncompete agreement. In the following case, the New York Court of Appeals considered whether the protection of customer and client relationships was a justification for enforcing a noncompete agreement.

39. Some jurisdictions state that a continued at-will employment relationship amounts to consideration for a noncompetition agreement. *See* Lake Land Employment Group of Akron v. Columber, 804 N.E.2d 27 (Ohio 2004).

40. Frances A. McMorris, *Judge Restricts Two Executives Despite Lack of Noncompete Pacts,* WALL ST. J., Nov. 25, 1997, at B10.

A CASE IN POINT

## In the Language of the Court

**CASE 12.3**

**BDO Seidman v. Hirshberg**

*Court of Appeals of New York*
*712 N.E.2d 1220*
*(N.Y. 1999).*

**› FACTS** Jeffrey Hirshberg was employed in the Buffalo, New York office of BDO Seidman, a national accounting firm. As a condition of receiving a promotion to the position of manager, Hirshberg was required to sign a "Manager's Agreement." Paragraph SIXTH of the agreement provided that if, within eighteen months following the termination of his employment, Hirshberg served any former client of BDO Seidman's Buffalo office, he would be required to compensate BDO Seidman "for the loss and damages suffered" in an amount equal to one-and-a-half times the fees BDO Seidman had charged that client over the last fiscal year of the client's patronage.

After Hirshberg resigned from BDO Seidman, the accounting firm claimed that it lost to Hirshberg 100 former clients who were billed a total of $138,000 in the year he left the firm. Hirshberg denied serving some of the clients; claimed that a substantial number of them were personal clients he had brought to the firm through his own contacts; and claimed, with respect to some clients, that he had not been the primary BDO Seidman employee working on their accounts.

The trial court invalidated the reimbursement clause on the grounds that it constituted an overbroad and unenforceable anticompetitive agreement. BDO Seidman appealed.

**› ISSUE PRESENTED** Is an agreement requiring a former employee to reimburse the employer for any loss sustained by losing clients to the employee enforceable?

**› OPINION** LEVINE, J., writing for the New York Court of Appeals:

The modern, prevailing common-law standard of reasonableness for employee agreements not to compete applies a three-pronged test. A restraint is reasonable only if it: (1) is no greater than is required for the protection of the legitimate interest of the employer, (2) does not impose undue hardship on the employee, and (3) is not injurious to the public. . . . A violation of any prong renders the covenant invalid.

. . .

. . . Close analysis of paragraph SIXTH of the agreement under the first prong of the common-law rule, to identify the legitimate interest of BDO and determine

*(Continued)*

(Case 12.3 *continued*)

whether the covenant is no more restrictive than is necessary to protect that interest, leads us to conclude that the covenant as written is overbroad in some respects. BDO claims that the legitimate interest it is entitled to protect is its entire client base, which it asserts a modern, large accounting firm expends considerable time and money building and maintaining. However, the only justification for imposing an employee agreement not to compete is to forestall unfair competition. . . . If the employee abstains from unfair means in competing for those clients, the employer's interest in preserving its client base against the competition of the former employee is no more legitimate and worthy of contractual protection than when it vies with unrelated competitors for those clients.

. . . Protection of customer relationships the employee acquired in the course of employment may indeed be a legitimate interest. . . . "The risk to the employer reaches a maximum in situations in which the employee must work closely with the client or customer over a long period of time, especially when his services are a significant part of the total transaction.". . . The employer has a legitimate interest in preventing former employees from exploiting or appropriating the goodwill of a client or customer, which had been created and maintained at the employer's expense, to the employer's competitive detriment. . . .

. . .

To the extent, then that paragraph SIXTH of the Manager's Agreement requires defendant to compensate BDO for lost patronage of clients with whom he never acquired a relationship through the direct provision of substantive accounting services during his employment, the covenant is invalid and unenforceable. . . . Indeed, enforcement of the restrictive covenant as to defendant's personal clients would permit BDO to appropriate goodwill created and maintained through defendant's efforts, essentially turning on its head the principal justification to uphold any employee agreement not to compete based on protection of customer or client relationships.

Except for the overbreadth in the foregoing two respects, the restrictions in paragraph SIXTH do not violate the tripartite common-law test for reasonableness. The restraint on serving BDO clients is limited to eighteen months, and to clients of BDO's Buffalo office. The time constraint appears to represent a reasonably brief interlude to enable the firm to replace the client relationship and goodwill defendant was permitted to acquire with some of its clients. Defendant is free to compete immediately for new business in any market and, if the overbroad provisions of the covenant are struck, to retain his personal clients and those clients of BDO's that he had not served to any significant extent while employed at the firm. . . .

Moreover, given the likely broad array of accounting services available in the greater Buffalo area, and the limited remaining class of BDO clientele affected by the covenant, it cannot be said that the restraint, as narrowed, would seriously impinge on the availability of accounting services in the Buffalo area from which the public may draw, or cause any significant dislocation in the market or create a monopoly in accounting services in that locale. These factors militate against a conclusion that a reformed paragraph SIXTH would violate the third prong of the common-law test, injury to the public interest.

**› RESULT** The New York Court of Appeals found that the agreement was reasonable and enforceable except to the extent that it required Hirshberg to compensate BDO Seidman for fees paid by his personal clients or by clients with whom he had never acquired a relationship through his employment at BDO Seidman.

*(Continued)*

(Case 12.3 *continued*)

**› COMMENTS** Six weeks before *BDO Seidman v. Hirshberg* was decided, the U.S. Court of Appeals for the Second Circuit reached a similar conclusion on the issue of recognizing relationships with customers as a basis to enforce a noncompete agreement. In *Ticor Title Insurance Co. v. Cohen,*[41] the Court of Appeals for the Second Circuit affirmed the enforcement of a noncompete agreement between a title insurance company and one of its most successful salespeople. The noncompete agreement prohibited the salesman from competing for six months after leaving Ticor to afford the company an opportunity to fairly compete to retain the business of the customers with whom the former employee had maintained relationships on Ticor's behalf. The salesman's relationships with Ticor clients qualified as unique services because competition for title insurance business relied heavily on personal relationships with salespeople. In addition, because Ticor's potential clients were limited and well known throughout the industry, maintaining current clients from this established group was crucial to the company.

**› CRITICAL THINKING QUESTIONS**

1. Could Hirshberg be required to reimburse BDO for fees paid by a client for whom he had not worked while at BDO if the firm could prove that he was aware of the client only because the name was on BDO's client list?
2. Should Hirshberg be excused from paying fees to BDO in connection with a client that testifies that it was dissatisfied with BDO's services and had planned to move its account elsewhere even before knowing that Hirshberg had left?

41. 173 F.3d 63 (2d Cir. 1999).

Employers may attempt to prevent other companies from poaching employees. In *Reeves v. Hanlon,*[42] the California Supreme Court held that although competition between companies for at-will employees is encouraged, inducing the termination of an at-will employment relationship may be tortious intentional interference with prospective economic advantage if the new employer engages in "independently wrongful acts" when inducing the employee to join its ranks. The court defined "independently wrongful acts" as acts "proscribed by constitutional, statutory, regulatory, common law, or other determinable legal standard." When the defendants in *Reeves* left their former employer, an immigration law firm, they induced six other employees to leave to join their new law practice. The court found that the defendants were liable for damages suffered by Reeves because they had also mounted "a campaign to deliberately disrupt plaintiff's business," including having employees resign without notice, leaving no status reports of outstanding matters or deadlines, destroying the firm's computer files and forms, taking confidential information, and improperly soliciting Reeves's clients.

42. 33 Cal. 4th 1140 (2004).

## ETHICAL CONSIDERATION

Companies can require their employees to sign a noncompete agreement as a condition of employment. In *Tatge v. Chambers & Owen, Inc.,*[43] a company asked an at-will employee to sign a noncompete agreement that provided that he would not work for one of the company's competitors for a period of six months after termination of his employment. Tatge refused to sign the agreement, and the company terminated him. He sued the company, alleging several claims including wrongful discharge. The Supreme Court of Wisconsin dismissed his claim, after concluding that the company's requirement that he sign the noncompete agreement was not a violation of public policy. The court noted that signing the agreement would not have prevented Tatge from arguing that its terms were unreasonable if the company had tried to enforce it. California law reaches a different outcome. An employer's termination of an employee for refusing to sign an unenforceable noncompete agreement constitutes a wrongful termination in violation of public policy.[44] Although it was legal for the employer to fire Tatge for failing to sign the noncompete agreement, was it ethical? Does it matter whether the employer knows the agreement is overbroad?

43. 579 N.W.2d 217 (Wis. 1998).
44. D'sa v. Playhut, 85 Cal. App. 4th 927, 929 (2000).

## Preserving At-Will Employment Status

In deciding whether there is an express or implied contractual right not to be fired except for cause, a court may consider statements made during preemployment interviews or performance review meetings, or language on application forms or in offer letters, bonus plans, or policy manuals. Consequently, if an employer wants to preserve the traditional legal right to discharge employees at will, it should take steps to ensure that it does not inadvertently limit this right.

To illustrate, an application form might include the following language above the employee signature line: "I understand that, if hired, my employment can be terminated at any time, with or without cause, at either my employer's or my option." Inclusion of such language reminds the employee that his or her employment is at will—and verifies that he or she was so informed—and lessens the likelihood that the employee will be able to establish an implied contractual right to be discharged only for cause. Additionally, no statements should be made during interviews that could create an impression that the applicant will not be fired without good cause. "Employees are never fired from here without good reason," "Your job will be secure, as long as you do your work," and "We treat our employees like family" are examples of such statements. In short, the employer should not mislead an applicant about the security of the job offered.

In some states, it may be difficult to maintain an at-will relationship except by an express contract or by a disclaimer in the employment application or the personnel manual stating that nothing in the employment relationship and no personnel policy or benefit shall create a right to continued employment or to employment for a specified duration. If such a disclaimer is plainly contrary to the company's stated policy, however, it may be rejected by a court. For example, a statement on an application form that employment is at will probably will not be upheld if the company's written personnel policy expressly provides that employees will be given progressive discipline and will not be fired without just cause.

Employers should also have a system of checks and balances in place to ensure that the company's policies and managers do not promise more job security than the company intends. Appropriate policies should be properly communicated and followed. To avoid disputes, discharges should be well documented whenever possible, handled in accordance with these policies, and employees should be treated in a fair and consistent manner. Nevertheless, a written policy requiring extensive documentation for termination, or promising fairness and consistency, may undermine at-will employment and invite second-guessing by a court and jury.

These guidelines can help to avoid suits for wrongful discharge:

- If an employer chooses to have a written personnel policy, care should be taken to see that the language expressly reserves those rights that the employer wishes to maintain, especially with respect to discharge. Also, if employees are given handbooks that purport to summarize the official personnel manuals, the handbook and the manuals must be consistent. Otherwise, courts and juries are likely to uphold the policy that is most favorable to the employee.
- If an employer chooses to have a policy of progressive discipline, it is essential that the policy explain that the policy does not alter at-will employment, and that all decisions on progressive discipline—whether to apply it, what steps to take or skip—are within the sole discretion of the company. If specific rules of conduct are listed, the manual should describe them as examples, not an exhaustive list, and inform employees that violation of a stated rule is not required for termination because employment remains terminable at will. Supervisors and managers, as well as the human resources staff, must be trained to administer the policy. In particular, they should be trained to document performance problems and to counsel employees about the need to improve, but not to portray the policy as an entitlement.
- An employer can enter into an agreement with the employee that any dispute shall be subject to arbitration. Most courts will enforce an evenhanded arbitration clause in a fairly negotiated written contract; however, a *boilerplate clause*—that is, standardized, nonnegotiable language—in an employment application form may be found invalid. As discussed in Chapter 4, mandatory arbitration of discrimination claims can pose special concerns.
- An employer should decide whether to establish an internal grievance procedure. Such a procedure can result in fewer lawsuits. If established, however, a grievance procedure must be followed. Otherwise, the employer may face claims for failure to follow its own procedure, especially when the procedure is elaborate.

## Recommendations for Former Employees

Employers are often asked to give references regarding former employees to prospective employers. An employee always hopes that a reference will be favorable, but that is not always the case. At any rate, the employee expects the reference to be fair. If the reference is not fair and the employer has impugned the individual's reputation, he or she can sue the employer for defamation.

In *Deutsch v. Chesapeake Center*,[45] a reverend, who was hired as director of an overnight lodging and meeting facility for church groups, was terminated as a result of accusations of racism and sexual harassment. When he applied for a position as a church pastor in another community, his former employer told the prospective employer of the charges that had resulted in termination of his employment. The reverend sued his former employer for defamation, but the U.S. District Court for the District of Maryland dismissed his claim, finding that the former employer's statements were protected by a conditional privilege to communicate information concerning a former employee to a prospective employer.

In contrast, in *MacCord v. Christian Academy*,[46] the U.S. District Court for the Eastern District of Pennsylvania concluded that a principal's comments regarding a teacher's poor performance during a faculty meeting were not protected by the privilege. The principal had abused the privilege by publishing the defamatory statements to the entire faculty and including allegedly defamatory matter not reasonably believed to be necessary for the purpose of informing the faculty that some teachers' contracts would not be renewed.

Traditionally, defamation law requires publication, meaning that the communicator of the defamatory information tells the information to a third party, such as a prospective employer. A few jurisdictions, however, recognize an exception in the employment context. Under the *doctrine of self-publication,* a defamatory communication by an employer to an employee may constitute publication if the employer could foresee that the employee would be required to repeat the communication, for instance, to a prospective employer. The doctrine is designed to provide a cause of action to the job-seeking employee who is forced to self-publicize a former employer's defamatory statement. Although as many as seven state appellate courts have adopted the doctrine of self-publication, the highest courts of only two states, Colorado and Minnesota, have adopted it, and the legislatures of both these states responded by eliminating or restricting it. The majority of the other states have concluded that public policy concerns favor the rejection of the doctrine. As the Connecticut Supreme Court stated in a recent decision rejecting the doctrine:

> The most compelling public policy consideration against recognition of the doctrine is that acceptance of the doctrine would have a chilling effect on communication in the workplace, thereby contradicting society's fundamental interest in encouraging the free flow of information. . . . Recognition of compelled self-publication defamation . . . would encourage employers to curtail communications with employees, and the employees' prospective employers, for fear of liability. As one commentator noted, recognition of the doctrine could create a perpetual "culture of silence," negatively affecting not only employers, but employees in numerous ways.[47]

An employer may be protected against liability for defamation claims by a former employee if the employee signs a waiver and release form releasing potential claims. In *Bardin v. Lockheed Aeronautical Systems Co.*,[48] Bethany Bardin had worked for Lockheed from 1987 until 1993. After she was laid off by the company, she applied for a job as a police officer with the Los Angeles Police Department. As part of the application process, she signed a "Release and Waiver" form, which authorized a background investigation and provided that former employers were cleared "from any and all liability for damage of whatever kind." The police department notified Bardin that her application was suspended because she had failed to disclose employment problems at Lockheed, including a complaint related to her drinking. Bardin sued Lockheed, but the court found the language in the waiver and release form sufficiently broad to protect Lockheed from liability.

In general, employers should be cautious when giving recommendations for former employees. A growing number of job applicants are hiring third-party companies to investigate what their former employers are saying about them.[49] Companies should have a written policy outlining who may provide references and what

45. 27 F. Supp. 2d 642 (Md. 1998).
46. 1998 U.S. Dist. LEXIS 19412 (E.D. Pa. Dec. 4, 1998).
47. Cweklinksy v. Mobil Chem. Co., 837 A.2d 759 (Conn. 2004).
48. 82 Cal. Rptr. 2d 726 (Cal. Ct. App. 1999).
49. Marci Alboher Nusbaum, *When a Reference Is a Tool for Snooping*, N.Y. TIMES, Oct. 19, 2003, BU12.

information can be provided to companies seeking a reference. Although fear of a defamation claim may tempt an employer to give an overly positive recommendation, this is not prudent. As explained in Chapter 9, an employer giving an untrue assessment of a former employee may be liable not only to the new employer who relies on the recommendation but also to third parties physically harmed as a foreseeable result of the recommendation.

# Employer Testing and Surveillance

Employers often administer tests to employees in an effort to increase productivity, manage legal risks, and cut costs. However, such testing and surveillance activities may conflict with an employee's right to privacy.

## DRUG TESTING

Many employers have adopted drug-screening programs for their employees and applicants to avoid the decreased productivity, quality control problems, absenteeism, on the job accidents, and employee theft that can result from drug and alcohol abuse. According to the American Management Association, 62 percent of companies in the United States test their employees for drugs.[50] Some employers use drug testing in conjunction with a comprehensive drug program that provides education and assistance to an employee with a drug or an alcohol problem.

The issue of drug testing generally comes before the courts in the context of discipline or discharge of an employee for refusing to take a test. An employee may challenge a drug test in many ways. The employee may claim that (1) the test breached his or her employment contract; (2) there was no justification for the test; (3) it violated the public policy that protects privacy; (4) he or she was defamed by false accusations of drug use based on an erroneous test; (5) he or she suffered emotional distress, especially if the test result was in error; or (6) the testing disproportionately affected employees of one race or gender and therefore was discriminatory.

Whether testing will be deemed permissible in a particular situation depends on four factors: (1) the scope of the testing program, (2) whether the employer is a public or private employer, (3) any state constitutional guarantees of a right to privacy, and (4) any state statutes regulating drug testing.

The first major factor, scope, concerns who is being tested: all employees (random testing); only employees in a specific job where the employer believes there is a legitimate job-related need (for example, nuclear power plant employees); groups of employees (for example, all employees in one facility because there is a general suspicion of drug use within that group); or specific individuals who are believed to be using drugs. The smaller the group to be tested and the more specific the reason for testing, the more likely a court will uphold the test. Random testing is the most difficult to defend. The final three factors are discussed in more detail below.

### *Public Employees*

Because public employees are protected by the U.S. Constitution's Fourth Amendment prohibition against unreasonable searches and seizures and by the right to privacy, there are greater limitations on testing public employees than on testing private-sector employees. It has long been recognized that urine tests and blood tests are a substantial intrusion upon bodily privacy and are therefore searches subject to regulation. With some exceptions, there is no federal constitutional limitation on drug testing in the private sector.

In *Skinner v. Railway Labor Executives' Ass'n,*[51] the U.S. Supreme Court held that railroads can be required to test public employees involved in a major train accident and have the authority to test employees who violate certain safety rules. The Court reasoned that any intrusion upon individual privacy rights in the railroad context was outweighed by the government's compelling interest in public and employee safety.

The Supreme Court also upheld mandatory drug testing of U.S. Customs Service employees in line for transfer or promotion to certain sensitive positions involving drug interdiction or the handling of firearms.[52] Although there was no perceived drug problem among Customs employees, the Court held that the program was justified by the need for national security and by the extraordinary safety hazards attendant to the positions involved.

In *Knox County Education Ass'n v. Knox County Board of Education,*[53] the U.S. Court of Appeals for the Sixth Circuit held that subjecting public school teachers

50. American Management Association, *2004 Workplace Testing Survey: Medical Testing* (2004), *at* http://www.amanet.org/research/pdfs/Medical_testing_04.pdf.

51. 489 U.S. 602 (1989).
52. Nat'l Treasury Employees Union v. Von Raab, 489 U.S. 656 (1989).
53. 158 F.3d 361 (6th Cir. 1998).

to drug and alcohol testing was not an unconstitutional violation of their right to privacy. Of primary importance in the court's decision was the unique role teachers play by accepting *in loco parentis* (in place of the parents) obligations to ensure the safety of children and to serve as role models. The court commented that "teachers must expect with this extraordinary responsibility, they will be subject to scrutiny to which other civil servants or professionals might not be subjected, including drug testing."[54]

### Constitutional Protection

The right to privacy guaranteed by the U.S. Constitution protects against invasions of privacy by public actors (i.e, state and federal governments or agencies) but does not protect against invasions by private (i.e., nongovernmental) actors. Similarly, the Fourth Amendment ban on unreasonable searches and seizures applies only to governmental activity. Many state constitutions also guarantee the right to privacy, however, and some states extend this right to private invasions of privacy.

In *Luddtke v. Nabors Alaska Drilling, Inc.*,[55] the Alaska Supreme Court held that the right to privacy in the state constitution applied only to governmental intrusions, not to alleged violations by private entities. Therefore, the state constitution did not shield its citizens from drug tests by a private employer. Moreover, even if there was a right to privacy, the company's interest in maintaining the health, safety, and welfare of its workers would outweigh any privacy interest.

In contrast, the California Court of Appeal held that a pupillary-reaction test given to all employees of Kerr–McGee Corporation at its chemical plant in Trono, California, might violate the California Constitution's right to privacy, depending on the intrusiveness of the test and the employer's safety needs.[56] The test consisted of shining a light in the person's eye and observing how much the pupil contracted. Although the court acknowledged that the pupillary test was less intrusive than urine, blood, or breath tests, it held that the trial court needed more facts to determine just how intrusive the test was.

### Statutory Regulation

A number of states have enacted legislation regarding drug testing of private employees. Such legislation often sets forth the notice procedures an employer must follow before asking an employee to submit to a drug test. In Vermont, for example, before administering the test, the employer must give the employee a copy of a written policy setting forth the circumstances under which persons may be tested, the drugs that will be screened, the procedures involved, and the consequences of a positive result.

A number of states have comprehensive drug- and alcohol-testing laws that require reasonable suspicion or probable cause before an employer may test. The requirements for establishing reasonable suspicion or probable cause vary from state to state. For instance, Connecticut's law permits testing when "the employer has reasonable suspicion that the employee is under the influence of drugs or alcohol which adversely affects or could adversely affect such employee's job performance."[57] Other states take the opposite approach and encourage fair and consistent testing in order to promote drug-free workplaces. For example, Alabama permits discounted workers' compensation insurance premiums for employers that follow fair testing procedures, including random testing.[58]

Although private employers, as well as public employers, may face some limits on implementing a drug-testing program, it should be noted that employers have the right to make and enforce rules prohibiting drug use or possession on work premises, as well as rules prohibiting employees from being under the influence of drugs while at work. When an employee exhibits visible signs of intoxication or impairment or inadequate performance, the employer may take disciplinary action. Because of the inadequacy of drug tests and the uncertainty about the scope of employees' rights, the employer may wish instead to develop programs that provide assistance and drug education and to counsel employees about the performance problems that drug abuse can cause.

## Health Screening and Genetic Testing

Health screening and genetic testing have become important issues and raise many of the same questions that arise in the context of drug testing. Genetic testing predicts whether a person has a genetic predisposition for developing a certain disease, although the accuracy of such tests is unproven.[59] Employers may be motivated to perform

54. *Id.* at 384.
55. 768 P.2d 1123 (Alaska 1989).
56. Semore v. Pool, 217 Cal. App. 3d 1087 (Cal. Ct. App. 1990).
57. Conn. Gen. Stat. Ann. § 31-51x (West 1993).
58. Alabama seeks to maximize productivity, enhance competitive positions of its companies in the marketplace, and reach companies' "desired levels of success without experiencing the costs, delays, and tragedies associated with work related accidents resulting from substance abuse by employees." Ala. Code § 25–5–330 *et seq.*
59. American Civil Liberties Union, *Genetic Discrimination in the Workplace Fact Sheet* (Mar. 12, 2002), *at* http://www.aclu.org/workplacerights/workplacerights.cfm?ID=9918&c=34.

genetic tests to (1) decrease exposure to tort liability for negligent hiring of an employee who, for example, has a propensity toward dangerous behavior or (2) reduce costs by lowering absenteeism rates and health insurance premiums kept high by unhealthy workers.[60]

A survey of U.S. companies in 2004 found that 15 percent of the surveyed companies inquired into their employees' family medical history.[61]

In February 2000, President Bill Clinton signed an executive order prohibiting the federal government from using genetic testing in hiring or promotion decisions.[62] As of January 2005, no federal legislation had passed relating to genetic discrimination in the workplace, although several bills were introduced in Congress during the past decade.[63] However, at least thirty-one states have enacted laws outlawing genetic discrimination in the workplace.[64] These state laws generally fit within one of three types of legislation: (1) laws prohibiting discrimination in employment based on genetic characteristics, (2) laws prohibiting employers from requiring applicants or employees to undergo genetic testing, and (3) laws banning discrimination based on genetic test results or the refusal to take a genetic test.[65] Private employers may also have liability under state constitutions that provide protection from private invasions of privacy.

Although no federal statute regulates genetic testing, employees may be able to sue for violation of their constitutional right to privacy if a public employer tests them for medical conditions without their knowledge or consent. In *Norman-Bloodsaw v. Lawrence Berkeley Laboratory*,[66] employees sued their government employer when they discovered that it had tested them for syphilis, sickle-cell anemia, and pregnancy without their knowledge or consent. The district court granted the laboratory's motion for summary judgment, but the U.S. Court of Appeals for the Ninth Circuit reversed, stating:

> The constitutionally protected privacy interest in avoiding disclosure of personal matters clearly encompasses medical information and its confidentiality. Although cases defining the privacy interest in medical information have typically involved its disclosure to "third" parties, rather than the collection of information by illicit means, it goes without saying that the most basic violation possible involves the performance of unauthorized tests—that is, the non-consensual retrieval of previously unrevealed medical information that may be unknown even to plaintiffs. These tests may also be viewed as searches in violation of Fourth Amendment rights that require Fourth Amendment scrutiny. The tests at issue in this case thus implicate rights protected under both the Fourth Amendment and the Due Process Clause of the Fifth or Fourteenth Amendments.

The court also found that genetic testing may violate Title VII when employees or applicants are singled out for testing based on race or gender. For example, the laboratory singled out black and female employees for additional nonconsensual testing and thus selectively invaded the privacy of certain employees on the basis of race, gender, or pregnancy. As a result, the Ninth Circuit found that the district court had erred in dismissing the plaintiffs' Title VII claims because "it was error to rule that as a matter of law no 'adverse effect' could arise from a classification that singled out particular groups for unconstitutionally invasive, non-consensual medical testing."

The Americans with Disabilities Act (ADA) may also provide employees with a cause of action for genetic testing. A person is protected by the ADA only if he or she is disabled. The ADA defines "disability" as "(A) a physical or mental impairment that substantially limits one or more of the major life activities . . . (B) a record of such an impairment; or (C) being regarded as having such an impairment."[67] Since 1995 the Equal Employment Opportunity Commission (EEOC) has argued that genetically predisposed individuals possess an "impairment" under section C and thereby qualify for ADA protection. In 2002, the EEOC brought suit against the Burlington Northern Santa Fe Railroad on behalf of Burlington employees who were secretly tested after they complained of carpal tunnel syndrome (CTS) stemming from work-related activities. The EEOC attempted to include the employees under its definition of those suffering from an "impairment" under section C, although it conceded that Burlington had taken no action to discriminate against the employees based on the results of the genetic testing and that no employees tested were

60. Human Genome Project Information, *Genetics Privacy and Legislation* (Sept. 16, 2004), *at* http://www.ornl.gov/sci/techresources/Human_Genome/elsi/lesislat.shtml.
61. American Management Association, *supra* note 50.
62. Francine Kiefer, *Amid Genetic Discoveries, a Nod to Privacy. As Science Advances, Clinton Bars Use of Genetic Information in Hiring for Federal Jobs*, CHRISTIAN SCI. MONITOR, Feb. 10, 2000, at 2.
63. Human Genome Project Information, *supra* note 60.
64. Public Broadcast System, *Bloodlines* (Apr. 2003), http://www.pbs.org/bloodlines/mapping_the_future/map.html.
65. Samantha French, *Genetic Testing in the Workplace: The Employer's Coin Toss*, 2002 DUKE L. & TECH. REV. 15 (Sept. 5, 2002).
66. 135 F.3d 1260 (9th Cir. 1998).

67. 42 U.S.C. § 12102(2).

found to possess the CTS genetic disorder. Nevertheless, Burlington agreed to pay $2.2 million to settle the case.[68]

Although efforts to conduct genetic testing may lead to suits for invasion of privacy, an employer may also be concerned that its failure to use genetic testing could result in possible tort liability under theories of employer negligence. Because employers have a duty of good faith and due care to prevent unnecessary work-related injuries, an employer could be sued by a third party who is injured by an employee with an undiscovered genetic condition that caused a lapse of consciousness or incapacity. An employee who is injured as a result of an undiscovered genetic condition might also sue his or her employer for failure to implement genetic testing.

Where employees are exposed to dangerous chemicals or conditions as part of their jobs, regular health monitoring is encouraged and in some instances required in standards adopted by the Occupational Safety and Health Administration.[69] Presumably, even where regulations do not require monitoring, an employer may choose to require participation in the health monitoring program as a condition of employment in positions affected by hazardous exposure.

## Polygraph Testing of Employees

Polygraph testing is another area where an employee's right to privacy may limit an employer's investigative rights. The Employee Polygraph Protection Act of 1988 (EPPA)[70] generally makes it unlawful for employers to (1) ask an applicant or employee to take a polygraph exam or other lie detector test; (2) rely on or inquire about the results of a lie detector test that an applicant or employee has taken; (3) take or threaten to take any adverse action against an applicant or employee because of a refusal to take a lie detector test or on the basis of the results of such a test; or (4) take or threaten to take any adverse action against an employee or applicant who has filed a complaint or participated in a proceeding relating to the polygraph law.

These rights cannot be waived by the employee in advance. For example, a federal district court held that a bartender could still sue for violation of the EPPA even though she had signed a release form stating that her employer had reasonable suspicion of theft before the employer requested that she take a polygraph test.[71] The court held that an employee can waive rights or procedures under the EPPA only pursuant to a written settlement of a pending lawsuit.

The EPPA does not completely ban the use of polygraph exams. Employers may test employees who are reasonably suspected of conduct injurious to the business, as well as applicants or employees in certain businesses involving security services or the handling of drugs. In addition, the EPPA does not restrict federal, state, or local government employers from administering polygraph exams.

Several states have laws that restrict or prohibit the use of polygraph examinations, however. For example, in Massachusetts, an employer cannot request that an applicant or employee take a lie detector test as a condition of employment.[72] Rhode Island,[73] Delaware,[74] and Pennsylvania[75] have similar statutes. Even when lie detector tests are permitted, no question should be asked during the test that could not lawfully be asked on an application form or during an interview.

## Employee Surveillance

According to a 2001 survey by the American Management Association, 82 percent of surveyed businesses in the United States check up on their employees by using various strategies such as listening in on employees' phone calls, inspecting their computer files, and conducting video surveillance. Of those companies, 12 percent indicated that they conducted these activities without the consent or awareness of employees.

Companies engage in employee surveillance for several reasons. Regulated industries, such as telemarketing, may conduct surveillance to show their compliance with regulations; other industries may do so to satisfy due diligence requirements. Another reason is to limit legal liability; for example, employees unwittingly exposed to offensive material on a colleague's computer may sue the employer for allowing a hostile workplace environment. Surveillance is also used to gain information for performance reviews and productivity measures and to promote security, including the protection of trade secrets and other confidential information.[76]

68. French, *supra* note 65.
69. *See, e.g.*, 29 C.F.R. § 1910.1450 & Apps. A and B.
70. 29 U.S.C. §§ 2001–2009.
71. Long v. Mango's Tropical Cafe, Inc., 958 F. Supp. 612 (S.D. Fla. 1997).
72. Mass. Gen. Laws Ann. ch. 149, § 19B (West 1996).
73. R.I. Gen. Laws § 28-6.1-1 (1996).
74. Del. Code Ann. tit. 19, § 704 (1997).
75. 18 Pa. Cons. Stat. Ann. § 7321 (West 1998).
76. American Management Association, *2001 AMA Survey: Workplace Monitoring & Surveillance* (2001), *at* http://www.amanet.org/research/pdfs/ems_short2001.pdf.

Employers have a legitimate interest in observing their employees, but under certain circumstances surveillance may transgress the employees' privacy rights. The watershed case in this area was *O'Connor v. Ortega*.[77] In that case, the U.S. Supreme Court ruled that a public employee may, in certain circumstances, enjoy a reasonable expectation of privacy in the workplace. However, the employee's privacy interest is to be balanced by the "operational realities" of the workplace. Since *Ortega*, lower courts have looked to (1) whether the employee was provided exclusive working space, (2) the nature of the employment, and (3) whether the employee was on notice that parts of the workplace were subject to employer intrusions. For example, in *Vega-Rodriguez v. Puerto Rico Telephone Co.*,[78] the U.S. Court of Appeals for the First Circuit held that governmental security operators, sitting in an open, undifferentiated work area, who monitored computer banks to detect alarm-system signals, had no reasonable expectation of privacy. As a result, the public employer's soundless video surveillance of the workplace did not violate the employees' Fourth Amendment rights.

The following case examines whether an employee has a legitimate expectation of privacy in personal information stored on an employer's computer.

77. 480 U.S. 709 (1987).

78. 110 F.3d 174 (1st Cir. 1997).

**A CASE IN POINT**

**CASE 12.4**

**TBG Insurance Services Corp. v. Superior Court of Los Angeles County**

*Court of Appeal of California*
*96 Cal. App. 4th 443*
*(Cal. Ct. App. 2002).*

## Summary

**› FACTS** Robert Zieminski worked as a senior executive for TBG Insurance Services Corporation. In the course of his employment, Zieminski used two computers owned by TBG, one at the office, the other at his residence. Zieminski signed TBG's "electronic and telephone equipment policy statement" in which he agreed, among other things, that he would use the computers "for business purposes only and not for personal benefit or non-company purposes, unless such use [was] expressly approved. Under no circumstances [could the] equipment or systems be used for improper, derogatory, defamatory, obscene or other inappropriate purposes." Zieminski consented to have his computer use "monitored by authorized company personnel" on an "as needed" basis and agreed that communications transmitted by computer were not private. He acknowledged that he understood that his improper use of the computers could result in disciplinary action, including discharge.

Zieminski was terminated when TBG discovered that he had "violated TBG's electronic policies by repeatedly accessing pornographic sites on the Internet while he was at work." According to Zieminski, the pornographic websites were not accessed intentionally but simply "popped up" on his computer. Zieminski sued TBG for wrongful termination. In its answer, TBG asked Zieminski to return his home computer so that TBG could corroborate evidence that Zieminski accessed sexually explicit websites using its computers. Zieminski objected, claiming an invasion of his constitutional right to privacy. Zieminski and his entire family had used the home computer for personal purposes, and it contained details of his personal finances and his family's personal correspondence. Zieminski stated that he had a privacy interest in the information stored on the computer and that TBG had no right to access such information because it was "universally accepted and understood by all that the home computers would also be used for personal purposes as well."

The trial court denied TBG's demand that Zieminski return its computer. It concluded that TBG already had extensive evidence supporting its claim that Zieminski accessed sexually explicit material from his TBG office computer, and "any additional evidence that the home computer may disclose does not outweigh the fact that the computer contains personal information." TBG then filed a petition for a writ of mandate, asking the California Court of Appeal to intervene.

*(Continued)*

(Case 12.4 *continued*)

**› ISSUE PRESENTED** Does an employee have a protectable privacy interest in the information stored on a computer owned by his employer?

**› SUMMARY OF OPINION** The California Court of Appeal began by defining what constitutes a reasonable expectation of privacy. The court concluded that "[a] 'reasonable' expectation of privacy is an objective entitlement founded on broadly based and widely accepted community norms," and "the presence or absence of opportunities to consent voluntarily to activities impacting privacy interests obviously affects the expectations of the participant."

The court then noted that a party who seeks affirmative relief to prevent a constitutionally prohibited invasion of privacy must establish "(1) a legally protected privacy interest; (2) a reasonable expectation of privacy in the circumstances; and (3) conduct by [the other party] constituting a serious invasion of privacy." The court stated:

> We are concerned in this case with the "community norm" within 21st Century computer-dependent businesses. In 2001, the 700,000 member American Management Association (AMA) reported that more than three-quarters of this country's major firms monitor, record, and review employee communications and activities on the job, including their telephone calls, e-mails, Internet connections, and computer files.

The court concluded that the evidence was "insufficient to support the trial court's implied finding that Zieminksi had a reasonable expectation of privacy." The court stated that TBG's electronic and telephone equipment policy statement gave Zieminski the opportunity to consent to or reject use of the home computer. No one at TBG compelled Zieminski or his family to use the home computer for personal matters, and no one prevented Zieminski from purchasing his own computer for personal use. As a result of signing the equipment policy, Zieminski was aware that TBG would monitor the files and messages stored on the employer-owned computers that he used at home and at the office. Thus, Zieminski fully and voluntarily relinquished his privacy rights in the information he stored on his employer-owned home computer.

**› RESULT** The court granted TBG's petition and commanded the trial court to vacate its order denying TBG's demand that Zieminski return the employer-owned home computer. The court stated that on remand, it would be up to Zieminski to identify with particularity the information that should be excluded from TBG's inspection and up to the trial court to determine whether to issue a protective order excluding such information from TBG's inspection.

## Responsibility for Worker Safety

Both federal and state laws require employers to provide a reasonably safe workplace.

### Occupational Safety and Health Act

The Occupational Safety and Health Act of 1970 (OSHA)[79] was enacted to require employers to establish safe and healthful working environments. The federal agency responsible for enforcing the provisions of OSHA is the Occupational Safety and Health Administration (also called OSHA). This agency is authorized by Congress to govern additional workplace issues, including exposure to hazardous chemicals, protective gear, fire protection, and workplace temperatures and ventilation. About half of the states have enacted similar legislation and established enforcement agencies at the state level. Typically, in states with approved employment health and safety programs, federal OSHA defers to the state agency for enforcement activities.

An employer governed by OSHA has a general duty to provide a safe workplace, which includes the obligation to abate workplace hazards that are causing or are

79. Pub. L. No. 91-596, 84 Stat. 1590 (1970) (codified as amended at 29 U.S.C. §§ 651–678).

## View from Cyberspace

### BIG BROTHER IS READING YOUR E-MAIL

A 2000 survey of over a thousand U.S. employees by The Vault.com found that electronic mail had become the primary business communication tool: 80 percent of respondents used e-mail as their primary form of business correspondence.[a] By 2004, instant messaging (IM) had also become an important tool of communication. According to another survey, 31 percent of employees surveyed were using IM at work.[b] Employee use of the Internet, e-mail, and IM has raised a number of new issues in the workplace. Employers are increasingly concerned that employees are wasting company time by using the Internet for personal reasons during working hours. In addition, employees' improper use of the Internet, e-mail, and IM could (1) subject their employers to various forms of liability, such as potential discrimination claims due to inappropriate e-mails or liability for copyright and trademark violations due to unauthorized downloading of materials, and (2) disrupt business by allowing viruses to enter the employer's computer systems or disclosing the employer's confidential information and trade secrets.[c] Despite employers' concerns, a survey by the American Management Association (AMA) revealed that 46 percent of surveyed companies do not train their employees on the proper and improper use of e-mail (although 78 percent have formal written policies addressing its use)[d] and only 20 percent have a written policy governing use of IM.

Nearly three-quarters of employers monitored employee e-mail in 2004, up from 27 percent in 1999, but only 10 percent monitored employee IMs.[e] In 1999, the New York Times Company fired more than twenty employees for sending e-mail that was "inappropriate and offensive"; Xerox Corporation fired forty workers, including those who visited pornographic websites from office computers, for violating its company policy on Internet use; and investment firm Edward Jones & Co. terminated nineteen employees when it discovered they were using the company's e-mail system to send inappropriate material.[f] Despite such incidents, the 2004 AMA survey revealed that most companies have never terminated an employee for violating an e-mail policy.[g]

Most courts have upheld the right of employers to monitor and regulate workplace e-mail and use of computers on the grounds that the employees could not prove that they had a reasonable expectation of privacy in workplace e-mails or computer use.[h] In 2004, the U.S. Court of Appeals for the Third Circuit ruled that an employer may read and access employees' e-mails without violating the Electronic Communications Privacy Act, which bars the interception of any electronic communication or the unauthorized access of stored communications, as long as the employer reads only e-mail messages that were already sent and stored on the company's own e-mail system.[i] Because the Internet and e-mail can be used for union-organizing and other protected concerted activities, the General Counsel of the National Labor Relations Board has imposed more restrictions than the courts on employers' monitoring and regulation of employee use of the Internet and e-mail.[j]

An employer's control of its e-mail systems may not extend to former employees, however. In 2003, the Supreme Court of California ruled that a former employee of Intel Corporation, Kenneth Hamidi, did not trespass on Intel property when he sent seven mass e-mailings criticizing the company to as many as 30,000 Intel employees.[k] After Hamidi was fired by Intel, he began a campaign of criticizing its human resource policies; in addition to his mass e-mailings, he established a website critical of the company. The court stated that Hamidi's e-mails neither damaged Intel's computer system nor impaired its functioning, as was required by Intel's trespass claim. The court ultimately rejected Intel's plea for a permanent injunction against Hamidi.

To avoid problems and resolve conflicts with employees, companies should draft Internet, e-mail, IM, and computer use policies.[l] These policies should prohibit the sending of unlawful, offensive, or defamatory statements, or unauthorized disclosures of trade secrets, via the corporate e-mail system. They should also eliminate employees' expectations of privacy in use of the electronic resources, and advise employees of the company's right to monitor use and contents without notice. In addition, companies should establish security measures and educate their employees about the policies and the manner in which the employer will enforce them.

**a.** The Vault.com, *Email Behavior in the Workplace*, THE VAULT (May 2000), *at* http://www.vault.com/surveys/email_behavior/email_behavior.jsp.
**b.** American Management Association, *2004 Workplace E-mail & Instant Messaging Survey Summary, (2004), at* http://www.amanet.org/research/pdfs/IM_2004_Summary.pdf.
**c.** Lou Licata, *An Employer's Right to Read an Employee's Email,* CLEV. B.J. (Apr. 2004), http://www.clevelandbar.org/new/right_to_email.php.
**d.** American Management Association, *supra* note b.
**e.** *Id.;* Nick Wingfield, *More Companies Monitor Employees' E-Mail,* WALL ST. J., Dec. 2, 1999, at B8.
**f.** Wingfield, *supra* note e.
**g.** American Management Association, *supra* note b.
**h.** Susan E. Gindin, *Employee E-Mail and Internet Use Raises Many Legal Issues,* CORP. COUNS. WKLY., Sept. 15, 1999, at 8.
**i.** *See* Fraser v. Nationwide Mut. Ins. Co., 352 F.3d 107 (3d Cir. 2004).
**j.** Gindin, *supra* note h.
**k.** *See* Intel v. Hamidi, 30 Cal. 4th 1342 (Cal. 2003).
**l.** Gindin, *supra* note h.

likely to cause death or serious physical harm to employees.[80] Conditions that are obviously dangerous or are regarded by the employer or other employers in the industry as dangerous are considered to be *recognized hazards*. What constitutes a recognized hazard is not entirely clear. However, its reach is broad and includes anything from sharp objects to radiation to repetitive stress injuries.[81]

In February 2004, OSHA announced that approximately 13,000 employers needed to correct workplace safety and health hazards or face comprehensive safety and health inspections.[82] OSHA identified the employers based on data reported in a 2002 OSHA survey of injuries resulting in lost workdays and illness rates at 80,000 workplaces. The identified employers had seven or more injuries and illnesses resulting in lost workdays for every 100 workers, substantially higher than the national average of 2.8 incidents per 100 workers.

OSHA inspectors are allowed to conduct surprise inspections at work sites when (1) OSHA believes an imminent danger is present, (2) an employee has filed a complaint, or (3) a fatality or catastrophe has occurred. During the inspection, the OSHA investigator may review company records, check for compliance with the relevant OSHA standards, inspect fire-protection and other safety equipment, examine the company's safety and health-management programs, interview employees, and walk through the facility.

When the inspection has been completed, the inspector meets with the employer and the employee representative, if any. The inspector discusses the results of the inspection and, if appropriate, issues a written citation for violations. There are five types of violations: (1) *de minimis* (that is, unimportant) violations, for which no notice is posted and no penalty is imposed; (2) nonserious violations, which present hazards that are not likely to cause death or serious bodily harm, for which a fine of up to $7,000 for each violation may be imposed; (3) serious violations, which have a substantial likelihood of resulting in death or serious bodily harm, for which a fine of up to $7,000 for each violation may be imposed; (4) willful violations, which are deliberate or intentional, for which a fine of at least $5,000 and up to $70,000 may be imposed for each violation; and (5) repeated violations, which occur within three years of a previously cited violation, for which a fine of up to $70,000 for each violation may be imposed. Failure to correct a prior violation may result in civil penalties of up to $7,000 per day for each day the violation continues beyond the prescribed abatement date. Inspectors may also decide to criminally prosecute employers for misdemeanors for "willful violations" by sending the case to the Department of Justice (see Chapter 14).

For purposes of sanctioning violations, the U.S. Court of Appeals for the Fifth Circuit held that the hazardous condition is the proper unit of prosecution, rather than the number of employees exposed to the hazardous condition.[83] Thus, if eighty-seven employees are threatened by a chemical explosion, then one violation (the explosion), rather than eighty-seven (the number of individuals exposed to the risk of heat, burns, and flying debris as a result of the explosion), may be cited.

If OSHA finds a violation, the employer is required to remedy the problem immediately. If remedial action is not taken, OSHA will seek a court order to ensure compliance. The employer may either settle the violation or seek review of the OSHA decision by the Occupational Safety and Health Review Commission. OSHA may penalize egregious violations by imposing a separate fine for each violation rather than an overall fine for a group of violations. Additionally, punitive damages are available, and the courts have upheld their application in extreme cases. For example, a federal district court permitted punitive damages in a suit against a nursing home that "blatantly" retaliated against a nurse for filing a complaint with OSHA regarding the lack of latex gloves at the site.[84]

In September 2000, OSHA imposed a fine of $2.5 million—its largest in recent years—on Chevron Phillips Chemical Company, a Texas petrochemical company, for an explosion that killed one plant worker and injured sixty-nine others.[85] The company had failed to properly train workers to recognize when certain chemical reactions amount to a hazard. OSHA issued citations alleging thirty willful violations for failure to train plant

80. Reich v. Pepperidge Farm, 66 U.S.L.W. 2095 (1997).

81. In 2001 President Bush signed legislation that repealed OSHA's controversial ergonomics rule, which was aimed at repetitive stress injuries. It would have compensated employees who suffered such injuries on the job and required employers to fix workplace hazards after receiving a report of a repetitive stress injury. Businesses and labor groups opposed the rules on the basis that they were too onerous and expensive. President Bush said that the administration would pursue a comprehensive approach to ergonomics that addressed the concerns surrounding the repealed rule.

82. Occupational Safety and Health Administration, *13,000 High Rate Workplaces Receiving OSHA Letters* (Feb. 2004), *at* http://www.osha.gov/as/opa/foia/hot_10.html.

83. Reich v. Arcadian Corp., 110 F.3d 1192 (5th Cir. 1997).

84. Reich v. Skyline Terrace, Inc., 977 F. Supp. 1141 (N.D. Okla. 1997).

85. Ruth Rendon, *Phillips Facing Fine for Fatal Plant Blast,* CNN.COM, Sept. 22, 2000, *at* http://archives.cnn.com/2000/LOCAL/southwest/09/22/hci.phillips.blast/ (last visited Dec. 8, 2004).

operators and four willful violations of process safety management. OSHA records revealed that it had inspected the facility forty-six times since 1974, including three inspections in 1999. Three of the inspections occurred after explosions. Chevron Phillips had previously been fined in both 1989 and 1999 for blasts that killed a total of twenty-five people.

OSHA also requires employers to maintain certain records, including the OSHA Form 300, which lists and summarizes all work-related injuries and illnesses. (Certain industries, such as retail, finance, and insurance, are exempt from this record-keeping requirement.) A summary of these records must be posted annually at the job site. In addition, employers must post in a conspicuous place (1) OSHA's official Job Safety Poster; (2) any OSHA citations for violations; and (3) notices of imminent danger to employees, including exposure to toxic substances.

A 1999 OSHA survey revealed that more than 85 percent of employers conduct voluntary self-audits of safety and health conditions at their work sites as part of an effort to reduce workplace injury and illness rates, to ensure compliance with OSHA regulations, and because it is the "right thing" to do.[86] California requires employers of at least ten employees to maintain a written Injury and Illness Prevention Program, calling for regular safety inspections, safety training for employees, and hazard abatement provisions.[87]

### *Criminal Prosecutions*

OSHA makes it a misdemeanor to cause the death of a worker by willfully violating safety laws. The maximum penalty is six months in jail and a $500,000 fine. By law, a willful violation means the employer demonstrated either "intentional disregard" or "plain indifference" toward safety laws. Safety violations that result in workplace deaths may also be prosecuted under state manslaughter and reckless homicide statutes.

An eight-month examination of workplace deaths by the *New York Times,* however, found that such deaths seldom result in prosecution, conviction, or jail time because state and federal OSHA inspectors rarely refer cases to law enforcement authorities. "A company official who willfully and recklessly violates federal OSHA laws stands a greater chance of winning a state lottery than being criminally charged," according to a 1988 congressional report.

Since 1982, more than 170,000 American workers have been killed on the job, but federal and state workplace safety regulators investigated less than 25 percent of these cases. Of those they examined, they found that 2,197 were caused by "willful" safety violations. The 2,197 deaths were the result of 1,798 different incidents, more than two-thirds of which were investigated by OSHA (the rest were investigated by states that administer their own versions of OSHA). Of these 2,197 deaths, 1,798 cases were eligible for prosecution, but only 104 were prosecuted. In 2003, OSHA's former administrator, John L. Henshaw, acknowledged that the agency had referred few cases to prosecutors, but he insisted that OSHA sought criminal sanctions "to the fullest extent that the law provides." According to Henshaw, OSHA did not seek more prosecutions because officials concluded that most cases lacked enough evidence for conviction.[88]

### *State Analogues to OSHA*

Many states have enacted laws similar to OSHA to ensure employees' safety in the workplace. In 2002, after two workers drowned in sewage while repairing a sewer line, the state of Iowa fined Insituform Technologies, Inc. $808,250 for safety violations under Iowa's OSHA.[89] The workers were not wearing or using the required protective equipment. The fine was the largest monetary sanction ever levied by the state of Iowa under its OSHA statute. California has one of the strongest safety violation penalties in the nation, with a maximum penalty of up to three years in prison and a $1.5 million fine for worker deaths.[90]

## STATE CRIMINAL PROSECUTIONS

Many states enforce workplace safety laws independently of OSHA by empowering state prosecutors to charge employers for crimes ranging from assault and battery to reckless homicide for ignoring warnings to correct workplace safety hazards.[91] In addition, Maine and California

86. *More Than 85 Percent of Employers Do Self-Audits of Work Site Safety, Health Conditions, OSHA Says,* CORP. COUNS. WKLY., Dec. 1, 1999, at 4, *available at* http://pubs.bna.com/ip/BNA/CCW.NSF/0fe6b3166851874585256d0c004c4ca3/dfe30577a91bf0d9852568390005c5b4?OpenDocument.
87. CAL. LAB. CODE § 6401.7.
88. David Barstow, *U.S. Rarely Seeks Charges for Deaths in Workplace,* N.Y. TIMES, Dec. 22, 2003, at A1.
89. Sandy Smith, *Iowa OSHA Issues $808,000 Fine Following Des Moines Drownings,* OCCUPATIONAL HAZARDS, Sept. 12, 2002, *at* http://www.occupationalhazards.com/articles/4646.
90. David Barstow, *California Leads in Making Employers Pay for Job Deaths,* N.Y. TIMES, Dec. 23, 2003, at A1.
91. Ann Davis, *Treating On-the-Job Injuries as True Crimes,* WALL ST. J., Feb. 26, 1997, at B1.

have enacted laws specifically providing for criminal penalties for employers who endanger their employees.

Prosecutors have criminally charged a number of managers and officers of corporations in connection with serious violations that led to the death of employees. These prosecutions have had mixed results. For example, in 1990, the Michigan Court of Appeals held that a supervisor was not guilty of involuntary manslaughter because he did not own the equipment that caused the accident.[92] In 1992, after twenty-five workers died in a fire at a chicken plant in North Carolina because fire-exit doors were locked, allegedly to prevent employees from stealing chickens, the plant owner pled guilty to involuntary manslaughter and was sentenced to nearly twenty years, the stiffest prison term to date.[93]

In 2004, a New York district attorney charged the owner of Tri-State Scaffolding & Equipment Supplies with five counts of manslaughter in the second degree and five counts of assault in the second degree when the scaffolding he designed collapsed on five workers who were attempting to erect it.[94] New York law requires that scaffolding over seventy-five feet high be designed and built by a licensed architect or engineer; the defendant was neither. The defendant, who admitted the scaffolding was dangerous, was sentenced to three-and-a-half to ten-and-a-half years in prison. The New York State Supreme Court Justice who heard the cases stated: "This sentence will, I trust, serve as a warning to others who, in pursuit of their own economic interests, care to be cavalier about the lives of others."

## LIABILITY FOR TERRORIST ATTACKS

As a result of the terrorist attack on the World Trade Center on September 11, 2001, OSHA has encouraged employers to implement emergency action plans to ensure employee safety in the event of another terrorist attack.[95] OSHA recommends that employers have plans for evacuation, anthrax risk management, and tightened security at building entrances and exits. As of 2004, 43 percent of the businesses surveyed by the American Management Association had implemented such a plan.[96] Some employers, such as the U.S. military, have terminated employees for refusing to cooperate with such plans.[97]

## TORT LIABILITY FOR VIOLENCE IN THE WORKPLACE

Employers also face potential liability for violence in the workplace perpetrated by employees or their former lovers or spouses. A survey of security professionals for Fortune 1000 companies, released in June 2002, revealed that workplace violence was the most significant security concern for U.S. businesses.[98] Workplace violence is the third leading cause of fatal occupational injuries in the United States,[99] resulting in three deaths daily and thousands of injuries yearly, as well as costing employers $36 billion annually.[100]

According to a survey conducted in 2004 regarding crisis management and security issues by the American Management Association, 50 percent of businesses surveyed have a crisis prevention and management plan addressing workplace violence.[101] To help prevent domestic violence from spilling over into the workplace, some companies hold seminars on domestic-violence issues on company time, provide a twenty-four-hour telephone counseling service for employees and their partners, and tap the phones of women who fear an attack and provide them with escorts to and from parking lots. Sometimes, the employer seeks restraining orders in its name to keep alleged abusers from potential victims' work sites.[102]

Once an employer is informed about the risk of violence or takes an interest in the case, it exposes itself to liability for negligence if it fails to take reasonable steps to prevent injury. For example, in 1995, both the employer of a woman killed in her Houston office by a former

92. Michigan v. Hegedus, 451 N.W.2d 861 (Mich. Ct. App. 1990).
93. Davis, *supra* note 91.
94. Karen Freifeld, *Punishment for "Cavalier" Act: Prison Time in Scaffold Deaths*, NEWSDAY, Jan. 15, 2004, *available at* http://www.nynewsday.com/news/local/manhattan/nyc-nysent153637070jsn25,0,3773583.story?coll=nyc-topheadlines-left.
95. OSHA, *How Should I Prepare if My Company Has a Credible Risk of Anthrax Exposure?* (2001), http://www.osha.gov/SLTC/etools/anthrax/credible_risk.html.
96. American Management Association, *2004 AMA Survey: Crisis Management and Security Issues* (2004), http://www.amanet.org/research/pdfs/CMSI_04.pdf.
97. *See* Mazares v. Dep't of the Navy, 302 F.3d 1382 (Fed. Cir. 2002).
98. Press Release, Pinkerton Consulting & Investigations, Fortune 1000 Rate Workplace Violence Top Security Threat, (June 4, 2002), http://www.ci-pinkterton.com/news/prTST6.4.html.
99. OSHA, *Workplace Violence* (Mar. 15, 2004), http://www.osha.gov/SLTC/workplaceviolence/.
100. Pinkerton Consulting & Investigations, *supra* note 98.
101. American Management Association, *supra* note 96.
102. U.S. FEDERAL BUREAU OF INVESTIGATION, WORKPLACE VIOLENCE: ISSUES IN RESPONSE 44–45 (Mar. 1, 2004), http://www.fbi.gov/page2/march04/violence030104.htm.

boyfriend and the office-building manager agreed to pay more than $350,000 to settle a case brought by the woman's family. The woman had told them that the former boyfriend was subject to a restraining order and that she feared he would kill her. According to her mother, "They didn't believe her story."[103]

In contrast, in *Jarrell v. Englefield*,[104] the Ohio Court of Appeals did not hold a gas station/convenience store operator responsible when a cashier was murdered at one of its stores. The court found that the company did not know of the existence of a dangerous condition or of a high probability that an employee would be injured there because there was no history of violence at the store. In addition, the store contained security devices (including a closed-circuit camera, a silent alarm, and signs indicating there was a camera), and the employee had been trained in handling himself during a robbery. Thus, the court concluded that the employer had taken adequate measures to protect its employees.

## Workers' Compensation

State workers' compensation statutes provide for coverage of income and medical expenses for employees[105] who suffer work-related accidents or illnesses.[106] The statutes are based on the principle that the risks of injury in the workplace should be borne by industry. The system is no-fault, and an employee is entitled to monetary benefits from the employer regardless of the level of safety in the work environment and the degree to which the employee's carelessness contributed to the incident. Workers receive medical treatment and benefits sooner and with more certainty, as a trade-off for receiving smaller total compensation than civil litigation might bring.

Monetary awards paid through the workers' compensation system are generally lower than those that might be awarded in lawsuits for negligence or other torts. The amount of workers' compensation received by an employee is determined by a definite schedule, based on the employee's loss of earning power. The usual provision is for payment of a specified amount at regular intervals over a definite period of time. In most cases, benefits include medical, surgical, hospital, nursing, and burial services in addition to payment of compensation.[107] Workers' compensation can be provided through (1) self-insurance, (2) insurance purchased through a state fund, or (3) insurance purchased through a private company.

Generally, workers' compensation benefits paid by the employer are the employee's sole remedy for workplace injuries. Some courts have recognized exceptions to this general rule, however, and allow employees to sue employers in tort for their injuries, in addition to collecting workers' compensation, for the following: (1) nonphysical injuries resulting from the tort of intentional infliction of emotional distress; (2) mental distress, indignity, or loss of wages or promotion opportunities due to sexual harassment; (3) injury to reputation caused by an employer's defamatory statements; and (4) both physical and nonphysical injuries as a result of an employer's intentional tort or misconduct.[108]

For example, the Washington Supreme Court held that a suit involving employee exposure to toxic chemicals in a fiberglass cloth used in airplane construction was not barred by the workers' compensation remedy because the employer's conduct amounted to deliberate intent to injure.[109] On the other hand, the California Supreme Court ruled that a firefighter's claim of intentional infliction of emotional distress was barred by the workers' compensation statutes.[110]

## Minimum Wage, Overtime, and Child Labor

The federal Fair Labor Standards Act (FLSA),[111] enacted in 1938 and amended many times thereafter, was established primarily to regulate the minimum wage, overtime pay, and the use of child labor. Many, if not all, states have established wage and hour regulations as well. In general, when the federal and state laws vary, employers must abide by the stricter law. Because of the wide variance in state laws, this discussion focuses on the federal law.

### Who Is Covered

The FLSA applies to employees who individually are engaged in interstate commerce or in the production of goods for interstate commerce, or who are employed by

103. *As Reports of Workplace Violence Rise, Employers Step Up Security Measures, Training*, Corp. Couns. Wkly., Nov. 24, 1999.
104. 2000 Ohio App. LEXIS 1076 (Ohio Ct. App. Mar. 17, 2000).
105. Independent contractors are generally excluded from workers' compensation.
106. See Constance E. Bagley & Craig E. Dauchy, The Entrepreneur's Guide to Business Law 291–92 (2d ed. 2003).
107. 82 Am. Jur. 2d *Workers' Compensation* § 6 (2004).
108. 82 Am. Jur. 2d *Workers' Compensation* §§ 62, 58, 73, 74 (2004).
109. Birklid v. Boeing Co., 904 P.2d 278 (Wash. 1995).
110. Cole v. Fair Oaks Fire Prot. Dist., 729 P.2d 743 (Cal. 1987).
111. 29 U.S.C. §§ 201–219.

employers that engage in interstate commerce. In other words, employers of any size that participate in interstate commerce or in the production of goods for interstate commerce are covered by the FLSA.

The FLSA does not apply to independent contractors. Proper characterization of workers as employees or independent contractors can be hotly contested. Chapter 5 outlines the factors courts use in deciding whether a worker is an employee or an independent contractor.

### *Who Is Liable for Violations*

Individuals as well as corporations may be held liable for violations under the FLSA. In *Herman v. RSR Security Services,*[112] the U.S. Court of Appeals for the Second Circuit ruled that Murray Portnoy, a principal in a labor relations firm, exercised enough control over a security company's employees to be held liable as an employer for violations of the FLSA's minimum-wage, overtime, and record-keeping requirements. Portnoy partially owned the security company, funded its start-up costs, and chaired its board of directors. The appeals court affirmed a judgment of $160,000 against Portnoy.

In contrast, in *Luder v. Endicott,*[113] the U.S. Court of Appeals for the Seventh Circuit held that individual employees of a state government could not be liable under the FLSA. In this case, hourly employees at a Wisconsin state penitentiary brought a claim alleging that the warden and other supervisors violated the FLSA by altering time sheets and not compensating them for their work. The court ruled that the plaintiffs, who were suing the supervisors in their individual capacities because a suit against the state of Wisconsin was barred by the Eleventh Amendment, could not bring a suit against the supervisors because the effect of suing the supervisors was the same as suing the state.

112. 172 F.3d 132 (2d Cir. 1999).
113. 253 F.3d 1020 (7th Cir. 2001).

## Hours Worked

The FLSA does not limit the number of hours that an employee may work in a workweek or workday, as long as the employee is paid appropriate overtime. (But, as noted in Chapter 9, if an employer forces an employee to work too many hours, the employer may be liable under common law negligence for injury to a third party resulting from the employee's fatigue.) The FLSA requires that, with some exceptions, every employee be paid one and one-half times the regular rate of pay for hours worked in excess of forty in a workweek. The "regular rate" is not necessarily the hourly wage, but includes all cash compensation for the workweek. In most cases, employers can exclude profits from certain employer-provided stock options, stock appreciation rights, and bona fide stock purchases from the calculation of regular pay rates when calculating overtime pay.[114]

In 1985, Congress amended the FLSA to permit state and local governments to comply with the statute's overtime provisions by giving employees compensatory time (comp time) in lieu of overtime pay. *Comp time* is extra paid vacation time granted instead of extra pay for overtime work.

In the following case, the U.S. Supreme Court considered whether public employers can require employees to use their accrued comp time when the amount reaches a certain level.

114. Simon J. Nadel, *FLSA: The Law Employers Love to Hate Is Scrutinized in Light of the New Economy,* 68 U.S.L.W. 49, June 27, 2000, at 2771.

**A CASE IN POINT** | **Summary**

**CASE 12.5**
**Christensen v. Harris County**
*Supreme Court of the United States*
*529 U.S. 576 (2000).*

**› FACTS** Sheriff Tommy B. Thomas of Harris County, Texas, and 127 deputy sheriffs agreed to accept compensatory time, instead of cash, as compensation for overtime. As they accumulated comp time, Harris County became concerned that it lacked the financial resources to pay employees who (1) worked overtime after reaching the statutory cap on comp time accrual or (2) left their jobs with large amounts of accrued time.

To address these concerns, Harris County implemented a policy setting the maximum number of hours of comp time that could be accumulated. After an employee's hours had reached the maximum, the employee was asked to reduce his or her comp time; if the employee did not do so, a supervisor could order the employee to use the comp time at specified times. The sheriffs sued, claiming that the policy violated the FLSA.

*(Continued)*

(Case 12.5 *continued*)

› **ISSUE PRESENTED** Can a state or its subdivision require employees to use accrued comp time?

› **SUMMARY OF OPINION** The U.S. Supreme Court began its analysis by noting that both parties conceded that nothing in the FLSA expressly prohibits a state or subdivision thereof from compelling employees to use accrued comp time. The sheriffs argued, however, that the FLSA implicitly prohibits this practice in the absence of an agreement authorizing compelled use, because the statute requires an employer to reasonably accommodate employee requests to use comp time. The Court found this argument unpersuasive. The Court read this provision as a safeguard to ensure that an employee will receive timely compensation for working overtime rather than as setting forth the exclusive method by which compensatory time can be used. Thus, the statute imposes a restriction upon an employer's efforts to prohibit the use of comp time when employees request to do so, but it says nothing about restricting an employer's efforts to require employees to use comp time.

› **RESULT** The Supreme Court upheld Harris County's policy requiring use of comp time.

## COMPENSATION

The FLSA requires that employees be compensated for all hours worked. In general, the hours that an employer knows or has reason to know that an employee has worked, even though the employee has not been requested to work, are deemed hours worked. If an employee is asked to be on standby—that is, available to return to work while off duty—the hours spent on standby will not be counted as hours worked if the employee is generally free to use the time for his or her own purposes.

Workers will also not be compensated for their time spent traveling to or from the job. In *Kavanagh v. Grand Union Co.,*[115] a supermarket employee who worked as a mechanic traveling to different job sites sought overtime compensation for his commute. Although the U.S. Court of Appeals for the Second Circuit held that he was entitled to compensation for travel between the different sites during his workday between 8:00 A.M. and 4:30 P.M., he was not entitled to overtime compensation for time spent traveling between his home and the first job of the day or the time between the last job of the day and home.

## MINIMUM WAGE

In 1938, the FLSA established the first minimum wage at 25 cents per hour. The federal minimum wage in December 2004 was $5.15 per hour. States often impose higher minimum wages. For example, the California minimum wage in December 2004 was $6.75 per hour. During the 1990s, as many full-time, minimum-wage workers were unable to support their families' basic needs, various localities around the country began requiring employers to provide wages and employee benefits higher than either federal or state minimum wages.[116] Called *living wage ordinances,* these programs require employers to pay their employees wages approximating the real cost of living in the locality, which is often significantly higher than the applicable state or federal minimum wage.

Such living wage ordinances, unlike their state and federal counterparts, often target only certain businesses, such as recipients of city contracts or lessees of city property, or larger businesses with more employees and higher earnings. For example, RUI One Corporation, which owned and operated a restaurant located on an open space preserve held in public trust by the City of Berkeley, California, challenged Berkeley's living wage ordinance, arguing that it violated the Equal Protection Clause of the U.S. and California Constitutions. The ordinance applied only to five employers that (1) were located on the open space preserve, (2) had a minimum number of employees, and (3) earned an annual revenue of more than $350,000.[117] The U.S. Court of Appeals

115. 192 F.3d 269 (2d Cir. 1999).

116. RUI One Corp. v. City of Berkeley, 371 F.3d 1137 (9th Cir. 2004).

117. *Id.*

for the Ninth Circuit determined that RUI was not unfairly targeted by the ordinance because RUI operated its restaurant on the highly desirable open space preserve under a privilege granted by the City. The court also stated that, ultimately, cities should be allowed leeway to approach the problem of their working poor by implementing their living wage ordinances incrementally.

## OVERTIME

Certain types of employees are exempt from the minimum-wage and overtime requirements of the FLSA, including employees classified as executive, administrative, professional, computer, and outside sales employees. The regulations of the Wage and Hour Division of the Department of Labor define the characteristics of these exempt employees in terms of salary and work duties. These regulations were updated for the first time in decades in August 2004 to more accurately reflect the realities of the contemporary workplace.[118]

To qualify as an *exempt employee,* generally three requirements must be met. First, the employee must be paid a minimum salary amount. Second, the employee must be paid on a "salary basis." Third, the employee must meet the "duties test" for the particular exemption. All other employees are *nonexempt employees* and must be paid both minimum wage and overtime as required by the FLSA. The regulations also provide that certain types of jobs do not qualify for the exemptions from the FLSA minimum-wage and overtime requirements; these workers include manual laborers and other blue-collar workers, as well as police officers, firefighters, paramedics, and other public safety "first responders."

### *Minimum Salary*

Employees who earn less than $455 per week ($23,660 annualized) are automatically considered nonexempt. The Labor Department has also adopted a "bright-line" test for highly paid employees—those employees who earn an annual salary of at least $100,000 per year (including commissions and nondiscretionary bonuses). Highly paid employees are considered exempt as long as the employer can show that they regularly perform at least one of the exempt duties or responsibilities of an executive, administrative, or professional employee. For employees earning between $23,660 and $100,000, the FLSA provides a test based on the types of duties the employee performs to determine whether the employee will be classified as exempt or nonexempt.

118. *See generally* 29 C.F.R. pt. 541 (2004).

### *Salary Basis Test*

The salary basis test requires that an employee regularly receive a predetermined amount of compensation for each pay period in which work is performed, without reduction because of variations in the quality or quantity of work performed. Thus, an employee must be paid his or her full weekly salary for any week within which he or she performs work and is ready, willing, and able to perform additional work, subject to certain exceptions. Employers may, however, make deductions from an exempt employee's pay for personal or sick days off, or for certain disciplinary suspensions, without violating the salary basis test. Also, certain computer employees paid on an hourly basis will still qualify for exemption if he or she is paid at a rate not less than $27.63 per hour.

If an employer is found to have an actual practice of making improper deductions, it will lose the exemption during the time period in which the deductions were made for all employees in the same job classification who are working for the manager responsible for the improper deductions. Inadvertent or isolated improper deductions will not result in a loss of the exemption, however, if the employer reimburses the employee for the improper deductions. The regulations also provide a safe harbor that allows an employer to retain the exemption despite improper deductions if the employer complies with the safe harbor requirements.

### *Duties Test*

For each exemption category, the FLSA sets forth the "primary duty", the performance of which will qualify the employee as exempt. Although the FLSA notes that the amount of time spent performing exempt duties may indicate whether the exempt work is the employee's primary duty, there is no requirement that the employee spend more than 50 percent of his or her time in exempt work.

To qualify as an *executive,* an employee must (1) have the primary duty of management of the enterprise or a customarily recognized department or subdivision; (2) customarily and regularly direct the work of two or more other employees, and (3) have authority to hire or fire other employees or be an employee whose suggestions and recommendations as to the hiring, firing, advancement, promotion, or any other change of status of other employees are given particular weight. The executive exemption also includes an employee who owns at least a 20 percent interest in the business, so long as the employee is actively engaged in the management of the company.

To qualify as an *administrative employee,* an employee must (1) have the primary duty of the performance of office or nonmanual work directly related to the management or general business operations of the employer or the employer's customers and (2) have a primary duty that includes the exercise of discretion and independent judgment with respect to matters of significance. For example, the U.S. Court of Appeals for the First Circuit held that insurance company marketing representatives qualify as administrative employees. The court rejected the Department of Labor's argument that the representatives were not given discretion in "matters of consequence."[119] Instead, the court looked to the nature of the work and held that the discretion and independent judgment involved, in addition to its substantial economic consequences, satisfied the requirements of an administrative employee.

For a person to qualify as a *professional employee,* he or she must be either a "learned" professional or a "creative" professional. The test for the *learned professional* requires that the employee's primary duty be the performance of work requiring advanced knowledge in a field of science or learning customarily acquired by a prolonged course of specialized intellectual instruction; "work requiring advanced knowledge" is defined as work that (1) is predominantly intellectual in character and (2) includes work requiring the consistent exercise of discretion and judgment. The FLSA permits some of the advanced knowledge to be acquired through a combination of work experience and intellectual instruction. *Creative professionals,* on the other hand, must have the primary duty of performance of work requiring invention, imagination, originality, or talent in a recognized field of artistic or creative endeavor.

The *computer employee* exemption is available to computer systems analysts, computer programmers, software engineers, and other similarly skilled workers in the computer field. This exemption does not cover employees who are engaged in the manufacture or repair of computer hardware or related equipment, nor does it cover employees whose work is highly dependent upon computers or computer software (such as engineers, drafters, and employees who work with computer-aided design), but who are not primarily engaged in systems analysis and programming or similarly skilled jobs.

The *outside sales employee* exemption requires that the employee have the primary duty of either making sales or obtaining orders or contracts for services or for the use of facilities. In addition, the employee must be customarily and regularly engaged away from the employer's place of business in performing such duty.

119. Reich v. John Alden Life Ins. Co., 126 F.3d 1 (1st Cir. 1997).

### Ethical Consideration

In November 2003, lawyers representing a group of thousands of immigrant janitors filed a lawsuit in federal court accusing Wal-Mart of violating federal racketeering laws by conspiring with cleaning contractors to cheat the janitors out of overtime wages.[a] According to the suit, the janitors, who were hired by the cleaning contractors, generally earned $325 to $500 per week for waxing and washing floors seven nights a week in Wal-Mart department stores, usually for 56 hours or more each week. The contractors did not pay the janitors the required overtime of time and a half for hours worked over a forty-hour workweek. Wal-Mart allegedly shielded itself from liability for paying overtime by hiring the corporate contractors, to whom Wal-Mart was not required to pay overtime; the contractors in turn hired the janitors to work at Wal-Mart stores. The plaintiff janitors, however, say that they were actually supervised and controlled by Wal-Mart managers; thus, Wal-Mart should be responsible for the overtime payments because the contractors and Wal-Mart were acting as joint employers. Is it ethical for a company to shield itself from liability for violations of the Fair Labor Standards Act by employing workers indirectly through contractors rather than directly?

**a.** Steven Greenhouse, *Suit by Wal-Mart Cleaners Asserts Rackets Violation,* N.Y. Times, Nov. 11, 2003, at A12.

## Child Labor

The FLSA child-labor provisions were enacted to stop the early twentieth-century abuses of many employers who employed children at minimal wages. Under federal law, it is illegal to employ anyone under the age of fourteen, except in specified agricultural occupations. Children aged fourteen or fifteen may work in some occupations, but only if the employment occurs outside school hours and does not exceed daily and weekly hour limits. Individuals aged sixteen to eighteen may work in manufacturing occupations, but they may not work in jobs that the secretary of labor has declared to be particularly hazardous, such as operating a power-driven woodworking machine, a hoisting apparatus, a metal-forming machine, or a circular or band saw. Jobs entailing exposure to radioactive materials are also deemed to be hazardous.

## Modern-Day Slavery

Trafficking in persons, which often involves the recruitment and smuggling of foreign nationals into the United States to force them to work in factories, fields, or homes, amounts to "modern-day slavery." In one case, Mexican farm workers were smuggled into the United States and then forced to work for their captors to pay their smuggling fees. In another case, Russian women, who were recruited and transported to the United States as folk dancers, were subsequently forced to work as exotic dancers and turn their earnings over to their captors. The Victims of Trafficking and Violence Protection Act of 2000, which became effective October 28, 2000, amended the slavery statute to make prosecutions more effective and to increase the statutory maximum sentences that traffickers faced. From January 2001 to July 2001, the Criminal Section of the Civil Rights Division of the U.S. Department of Justice, working with the U.S. Attorneys' offices, charged 150 human traffickers, more than triple the number charged during the preceding three-year period, and achieved a 100 percent conviction rate.[120]

## Immigration Law

On October 23, 2003, Immigration and Customs Enforcement officials arrested approximately 250 to 300 alien workers at sixty-one Wal-Mart stores across the country and searched the office of one of the retail chain's corporate executives.[121] The workers were arrested for working without proper authorization and were threatened with immediate deportation.[122] Wal-Mart was also threatened with fines for employing such workers. In March 2005 Wal-Mart agreed to pay $11 million, the largest fine ever imposed for employing illegal immigrants, to settle the federal charges.

Under the Immigration and Reform and Control Act of 1986,[123] employers may hire only persons who may legally work in the United States, that is, citizens and nationals of the United States and aliens authorized to work in the United States. Employers that violate this rule are subject to penalties.

### Obtaining Authorization

The primary way by which aliens become authorized to work in the United States is by obtaining a work visa. The U.S. government offers a number of visas based on different classifications including, for example, as (1) a student, (2) an educational or cultural exchange visitor, (3) a professional worker from Canada or Mexico authorized to work in the United States under the North American Free Trade Agreement, or (4) a foreign employee of an overseas company who is temporarily transferred to the United States.

Many U.S. employers, especially those in Silicon Valley, rely on the employment of foreign workers with an *H-1B visa,* which is available only for workers in professional and specialty occupations (generally those requiring a bachelor's degree or its equivalent), such as computer programmers, engineers, doctors, or fashion models,[124] where the employer can show an inability to recruit qualified workers in the United States. Employers generally apply for the visa on behalf of the foreign worker; it authorizes the worker to work in the United States for up to six years (with some exceptions). During a worker's tenure, he or she is entitled to the same wages, benefits, and working conditions as other similarly situated employees. The U.S. government caps the number of H1-B visas granted each year in the United States. As of January 2005, this cap was set at 65,000 workers, with an exemption from the cap for up to 20,000 master's and Ph.D. graduates from U.S. universities.

### Verifying Authorization

To ensure that only authorized workers are hired, the U.S. government requires that all employers verify the identity and employment eligibility of all persons they hire.[125] This includes completing the Employment Eligibility Verification Form, also called the *I-9,* which must be kept on file by the employer for at least three years for purposes of government audits. Employers may also ask a potential employee questions regarding his or her work status. The questions should not identify a candidate by his or her national origin or citizenship status, however, because doing so could expose the employer to an employment-discrimination claim.[126] Questions that may be asked include "Can you, if hired, show that you are legally authorized to work in the United States?"

120. AAG R. Alexander Costa, Keynote Address at National Conference on Trafficking in Persons (July 15, 2004), *at* http://www.usdoj.gov/crt/crim/acosta_tp_071504.htm.

121. CBS News, *INS Agents Raid Wal-Mart Stores,* CBSNEWS.COM, Oct. 23, 2003 *at* http://www.cbsnews.com/stories/2003/10/24/national/printable579798.shtml.

122. Press Release, U.S. Immigration and Customs Enforcement, ICE Employment Investigation Yields Hundreds of Arrests (Oct. 23, 2003), *at* http://www.ice.gov/graphics/news/newsreleases/articles/arrests102303.htm.

123. 8 U.S.C. § 1101.

124. U.S. Department of Labor, *Employment Law Guide: Workers in Professional and Specialty Occupations (H-1B Visas)* (Jan. 5, 2005), http://www.dol.gov/asp/programs/guide/h1b.htm.

125. U.S. Department of Labor, *Employment Law Guide: Authorized Workers* (Jan. 4, 2005), http://www.dol.gov/asp/programs/guide/aw.htm.

126. Letter from Nguyen Van Hanh, Director of the Office of Refugee Resettlement, and Juan Carlos Benitez, Special Counsel to the Office of Special Counsel for Immigration-Related Unfair Employment Practices, Civil Rights Division, U.S. Department of Justice, to State Refugee Coordinators, National Voluntary Agencies and Other Interested Parties (Nov. 21, 2001), *at* http://www.acf.dhhs.gov/programs/orr/policy/oscj_lt.htm.

## AMNESTY PROPOSAL

As of January 2005, approximately ten million illegal aliens were working in the United States,[127] even though an employer can be fined up to $11,000 and imprisoned for up to six months for each illegal alien it has knowingly hired.[128] In 2004, President George W. Bush proposed a plan that would grant amnesty to all illegal alien workers. Under Bush's plan, illegal aliens would be allowed to apply for a three-year temporary-worker permit, renewable for at least another three years. They could also apply for a green card to obtain permanent residency status. Bush said that his proposal would allow illegal workers to live without constant fear of deportation. Many employers applauded the proposal because they would no longer have to worry about federal raids and lawsuits alleging that they hire undocumented workers. Companies would also have a more stable supply of low-wage labor, with fewer hiring problems and less turnover.

Opponents of the proposal argued that bringing ten million illegal residents into the mainstream would increase labor costs by raising wages and benefits for formerly illegal

127. Aaron Bernstein, et al., *This Plan May Not Get a Green Card*, BUS. WK. ONLINE, Jan. 8, 2004, http://www.businessweek.com:/pring/bwdaily/dnflash/jan2004/nf2004018_7637_db038.html.

128. Memorandum from the U.S. Citizenship and Immigration Services Office of Business Liaison, Employer Sanctions (Dec. 7, 2004), http://uscis.gov/graphics/services/employerinfo/EIB111.pdf.

ECONOMIC PERSPECTIVE

## OUTSOURCING

Between 1987 and 1997, the share of imported components used in U.S. manufacturing increased from 10.5 percent to 16.2 percent overall and from 26 percent to 38 percent in high-tech manufacturing, such as computers and electronics. As these statistics demonstrate, in its early years, foreign outsourcing largely affected U.S. manufacturing and was associated with the loss of blue-collar jobs in many industrial sectors. The outsourcing of manufactured parts resulted in a shift of demand, and hence jobs, from blue-collar to white-collar workers and from manufacturing to services. It also increased wage inequality between blue-collar and white collar workers and increased the profitability of U.S. firms.

Since the late 1990s, however, white-collar jobs have been moving overseas as well. Nonmanufacturing sectors, such as information technology, telecommunications, retail trade, and finance (including banking and insurance), have seen the most outsourcing to countries such as India, Malaysia, the Philippines, South Africa, Russia, and Israel. Companies find outsourcing an attractive cost-cutting measure because wages and health-care costs for employees are generally lower overseas.

White-collar outsourcing has become a viable option for many companies due to (1) the rapid dissemination of the Internet; (2) the liberalization of emerging market economies; (3) the widespread acceptance of English as a medium of education, business, and communication; (4) the emergence of a common legal and accounting system (at least in some countries); (5) the 24/7 capability and overnight turnaround time made possible by the time differential between the United States and other geographic locations; and (6) the abundant supply of technically savvy graduates in other countries.

Data on the number of U.S. jobs moving overseas are generally scattered and unreliable. The U.S. Chamber of Commerce claims that 200,000 jobs a year are going abroad, whereas a bipartisan congressional commission found that 406,000 U.S. jobs are migrating overseas each year. Although outsourcing may cause pain and dislocation for many U.S. workers, most economists believe that it should not lead to job losses in the long run. Instead, it will result in a reshuffling of jobs and a new composition of occupations in the economy.

Many managers may feel the need to outsource jobs to foreign countries as a result of their perceived duty to maximize profits for shareholders. At the same time, however, these managers may also have an obligation to provide U.S. workers terminated as a result of outsourcing with transparency regarding the layoffs and access to retraining programs.

**Sources:** This discussion is based on (1) Ashok Deo Bardhan & Cynthia A. Kroll, *The New Wave of Outsourcing*, RESEARCH REPORT OF THE FISHER CENTER FOR REAL ESTATE AND URBAN ECONOMICS AT THE UNIVERSITY OF CALIFORNIA, BERKELEY (Fall 2003), *at* http://repositories.cdlib.org/iber/fcreue/reports/1103/; (2) Kimberly Blanton, *Outsourcing of Jobs Is Accelerating in U.S.*, INT'L HERALD TRIB. ONLINE, Nov. 18, 2004, *at* http://www.iht.com/bin/print/ipub.php?file=/articles/2004/11/17/business/jobs.html.

workers. In addition, they claimed it would cause an influx of illegal immigrants. As of January 2005, Congress was debating the issue, which was viewed by many as a key step in the reform of U.S. immigration policy that the Bush administration had started prior to September 11, 2001.[129]

# Labor–Management Relations

Before the mid-1930s, attempts by employees to band together and demand better wages and working conditions were largely ineffective. Organized economic actions, such as strikes and picketing, were enjoined as unlawful conspiracies. Employers squelched attempts to organize by lawfully discharging union organizers. Starting in the 1930s, Congress has attempted to equitably balance the economic power of employers, individual employees, and unions by comprehensively regulating labor–management relations.

## National Labor Relations Act

Since 1932, Congress has enacted a series of legislation aimed at both providing employees with greater economic bargaining power and curbing union excess and corruption.[130] The central statute governing labor relations in most private industries is the National Labor Relations Act (NLRA). An earlier similar law governing railroads, and later airlines, is the Railway Labor Act.[131] Pubic sector employees have since been granted similar rights under both federal and state laws.

Section 7 of the NLRA grants rights only to employees. It does not grant rights to independent contractors or to supervisors. The NLRA defines *supervisor* to mean:

> Any individual having authority, in the interest of the employer, to hire, transfer, suspend, lay off, recall, promote, discharge, assign, reward or discipline other employees, or responsibility to direct them, or to adjust their grievances, or effectively to recommend such action, if in connection with the foregoing the exercise of such authority is not of a merely routine or clerical nature, but requires the use of independent judgment.

## Union Representation

The five-member National Labor Relations Board (NLRB) oversees *representation elections,* that is, elections among employees to decide whether they want a union to represent them for collective bargaining. The procedure for conducting a representation election is initiated by filing a petition with a regional office of the NLRB. The NLRB will hold an election only in an *appropriate collective bargaining unit* of employees. To form such a unit, the group of employees must share a community of interest, meaning that they have similar compensation, working conditions, and supervision and work under the same general employer policies.

Following an agreement between the parties for an election or a decision from the regional director over disputed unit issues, the regional office of the NLRB will conduct an election. The party losing the election may file objections to it. If the objections are deemed to be without merit, the NLRB will certify the election. If the objections are meritorious, the NLRB will conduct a new election. Once a union is elected, it is the employees' exclusive bargaining representative and has a statutory duty under Section 8(b)(1) of the NLRA to represent all employees fairly when engaging in collective bargaining (without regard to their union affiliation) and when enforcing the collective bargaining agreement.[132]

## Unfair Labor Practices by Employers

Section 8(a) of the NLRA prohibits employers from engaging in specified activities against employees or their unions. Such activities, known as *unfair labor practices,* are investigated and prosecuted by the general counsel of the NLRB and his or her representatives.

Section 8(a)(1) of the NLRA makes it illegal for an employer to interfere with, restrain, or coerce employees in the exercise of their Section 7 rights to organize and bargain collectively and to engage in other protected, concerted activities. This prohibition covers a wide range of employer conduct, including (1) threatening employees with any adverse action for organizing or supporting a union, (2) promising employees any benefits if they abandon support for a union, (3) interrogating employees about union sentiment or activity, and (4) engaging in surveillance of employees' union activities.

Section 8(a)(1) also prohibits an employer from enforcing an overly broad rule against soliciting other employees (perhaps for union support) or distributing

129. Tom Raum, *Bush Faces GOP Fight over Guest Workers,* ABCNEWS.COM, Dec. 27, 2004, *at* http://abcnews.go.com/Politics/print?id=362524.
130. *See generally* Norris–La Guardia Act, 29 U.S.C. §§ 101–115; Wagner Act, 29 U.S.C. §§ 151–169; Taft–Hartley Act, 29 U.S.C. §§ 141–144.
131. 45 U.S.C. §§ 151 *et seq.* (enacted 1926).

132. Vaca v. Sipes, 386 U.S. 171 (1967).

literature on company premises and protects employees who engage in concerted activities for mutual aid and protection. For example, an employer may not retaliate against a group of employees who approach management and complain about some aspect of their working conditions, such as poor lighting or uncomfortable temperatures in the workplace. For an activity to be a *concerted activity,* it must be "engaged in with or on the authority of other employees, and not solely by and on behalf of the employee himself."[133]

Under Section 8(a)(2) of the NLRA, an employer may not dominate or assist a labor organization. The employer may not instigate, encourage, or directly participate in the formation of a labor organization, nor may it give financial support to a labor organization. These provisions were enacted to prevent employers from assisting compliant organizations in becoming representatives of their employees and then imposing "sweetheart" collective bargaining contracts—that is, contracts unduly favorable to the employer.

Section 8(a)(3) prohibits employers from discriminating against any employee to encourage or discourage membership in any labor organization. If an employee has been unlawfully discharged, the NLRB may order that the employee be reinstated and given full back pay.

Under Section 8(a)(4) of the NLRA, it is an unfair labor practice for an employer to discharge or otherwise discriminate against an employee because he or she has filed charges with, or given testimony to, the NLRB, either in a representation proceeding or pursuant to an unfair labor practice charge.

Section 8(a)(5) of the NLRA imposes upon unionized employers a duty to bargain collectively. A related provision, Section 8(d), requires employers to bargain in good faith, that is, to approach negotiations with an honest and serious intent to engage in give-and-take bargaining in an attempt to reach an agreement. The obligation to bargain in good faith does not, however, compel either party to agree to a proposal or to make concessions. If an employer does not bargain in good faith, a union may seek redress through the NLRB. Remedies may include damages payable to employees, or injunctive relief.

## Lawful and Unlawful Strikes and Economic Action

Labor law permits both employers and labor organizations to engage in certain tactics against each other, known as "economic action," to influence the other party to reach agreement in collective bargaining. Strikes and related publicity tactics such as picketing form an important part of the economic actions available to labor organizations.

Lawful strikes are of two kinds: economic strikes and unfair labor practice strikes. An *economic strike* occurs when a union is unable to extract acceptable terms and conditions of employment through collective bargaining. An employer subjected to an economic strike is permitted to hire permanent replacements for the positions vacated by the striking employees. If it does so, the employer is not required to reinstate striking employees who offer to return to work unless the departure of replacements creates vacancies. An *unfair labor practice strike* occurs when workers strike an employer wholly or partly to protest an unfair labor practice and the employer's conduct is in fact found to violate the NLRA. For example, a union may strike to protest the employer's bad faith bargaining. Workers who engage in an unfair labor practice strike have a right to be reinstated upon an unconditional offer to return to work.

Striking employees may have no legal protection or reinstatement rights if they conduct a "wildcat" strike by violating a "no-strike" provision in their collective bargaining agreements. Slowdowns, intermittent strikes, and work stoppages likewise are unprotected activity. Strikes otherwise lawful under the labor laws may incur liability for employees if striker tactics violate local safety or public peace ordinances or the state penal code (e.g., assault and battery).

The NLRA prohibits unduly lengthy *recognitional* picketing (whose purpose is to force the employer to recognize the union as a collective bargaining agent for its employees). It also outlaws *secondary boycotts,* which are certain threats or tactics against an outside company to induce the third party to put pressure (usually by withholding business) on the employer with whom the union has a dispute.

## Non-Strike-Related Unfair Labor Practices by Unions

Section 8(b)(1)(A) of the NLRA prohibits unions from coercing employees to join the union or to support its activities. A union is also prohibited from coercing employees to join, or refrain from abandoning, a strike. Unions are prohibited from discriminating against represented employees on the basis of race, sex, national origin, union membership, or internal union political affiliations.

Under Section 8(b)(2) of the NLRA, a union may not cause or attempt to cause an employer to discriminate against an employee on the basis of union affiliation or activities. Section 8(b)(3) requires the union to bargain in good faith with the employer.

133. Meyers Indus., Inc., 268 N.L.R.B. 493, 497 (1984).

# Global View

## THE RIGHT TO CONTINUED EMPLOYMENT

Most foreign countries do not share the U.S. concept of "employment at will" and instead provide employees with certain rights to continued employment.

### THE EUROPEAN UNION

Although the European Union (EU) has worked on harmonizing many employment laws of its member states, it has not attempted to harmonize the laws related to termination of employment.[a] No member states recognize the U.S. concept of employment at will. Instead, each country has specific laws on unfair dismissal and/or general civil code provisions that apply to the termination of employment contracts. Although the specifics of these laws vary, they all provide employees with a basis for challenging a dismissal on the grounds that it is unfair and a mechanism for adjudicating such claims. The laws of the United Kingdom and France are summarized here to demonstrate how individual EU members differ in terms of the right to vested employment.

***United Kingdom*** The employment laws of the United Kingdom are largely based on contract law and thus have more similarities with U.S. law than the employment laws of other EU countries.[b] The employee's contract of employment governs his or her contract rights, whether these are contained in an express, written or oral agreement or by terms that are implied by common law, custom, or practice.

In general, employers are free to agree with their employees to whatever employment relationship suits them both, subject to certain statutory restrictions. These restrictions are set forth in various statutes, the most important of which is the Employee Rights Agreement 1996 (ERA 1996). The restrictions are superimposed on the contract rights and are generally enforced by a claim for unfair dismissal.

A fixed-term employment contract ends on the expiration of that term. Unless a contract specifies a fixed term, it is considered to be for an indefinite term and can be terminated in accordance with the contract's notice and termination provisions. In addition, the Fixed Term Employees (Prevention of Less Favorable Treatment) Regulations 2002 place a four-year limit on the use of successive fixed-term contracts and provide that an employment contract becomes a permanent contract after four years unless the employer can objectively justify continued employment on a fixed-term basis.

a. *See generally* INTERNATIONAL LABOR AND EMPLOYMENT LAWS 1-1–1-187 (Timothy J. Dorby & William L. Keller eds., 2003).
b. *Id.*

Section 86 of the ERA 1996 provides that an employee who is employed for an indefinite term, or pursuant to a permanent contract, and who has been continuously employed for one month or more is entitled to one week's notice of termination. This is the applicable notice period until the employee has two years of continuous service; from that time, he or she is entitled to one week's notice for each completed year of service up to a maximum of twelve weeks' notice. Subject to these statutory requirements, the notice period may be expressly stated in the contract. If the notice period is not stated in the contract, termination is subject to an implied requirement of "reasonable notice," although no notice is required if the employee is terminated for gross misconduct. An employer can pay the employee an amount in lieu of notice only if the employment contract contains an express provision that allows the employer to do so. If an employer provides a terminated employee with the correct notice, no claim for wrongful termination arises.

Wrongful dismissal occurs when an employer dismisses an employee in breach of its contractual obligations. An employee's normal remedy for breach of contract is to sue for damages, which are limited to the amount required to put the employee in the position he or she would have been in had the contract been performed.

Unfair dismissal is a statutory concept embodied in the ERA 1996. To bring a claim for unfair dismissal, an employee must show that his or her dismissal was for a reason listed in Section 95 of the ERA 1996, which applies to terminations for, among others, a union-related reason, the assertion of a statutory right, a health- and safety-related reason, a reason related to working time or the assertion of rights under the national minimum-wage law, a reason connected with trade union recognition or bargaining arrangements, and taking part in protected industrial action in certain circumstances. The three remedies for unfair dismissal are reinstatement (which treats the employee as if he or she had never been dismissed); reengagement (which involves returning to the same or a similar job); or compensation (which consists of a basic award calculated on a strict formula and a compensatory award, which is based on what the tribunal considers just and equitable according to the loss sustained by the employee as a result of the dismissal).

***France*** French workers are entitled to significantly more benefits and legal protection than their counterparts in the United States or the United Kingdom. French law recognizes the concept of "just cause" dismissal, in that an employer must

*(Continued)*

(Global View *continued*)

justify an employee's dismissal and will be subject to legal sanctions if it is unable to do so.[c] During any agreed-on trial period, a French employee can be dismissed without formalities or particular reasons. Once the trial period has elapsed, however, the employer must prove that any dismissal is for legitimate reasons (either for cause or as a result of a reduction in force due to economic factors). Case law has accepted that "just cause" includes professional incompetence, insufficient results, professional shortcomings, loss of confidence in the employee, and sexual harassment.

Regardless of the reason, the employer must provide the employee with a written notice of a conciliatory meeting before confirming any termination decision. Only after the meeting is the employer entitled to notify the employee of his or her dismissal. The employer must also provide notice to French labor authorities. After notice of dismissal is given, the employment still remains in force during the notice period. The length of the notice period depends on the seniority of the employee and the position he or she held, but it generally ranges from one to three months. An employee is not entitled to any notice period if he or she is terminated for "gross negligence" (which has been defined as behavior that makes it impossible for the employer to keep the employee performing his or her functions, such as unauthorized and unjustified absence, damage caused to the employer, or assault and battery) or "willful misconduct" (which requires an intentional element similar to that involved in theft).

Unless terminated for gross negligence or willful misconduct, the employee is entitled to a payment, or indemnity, set by statute, if he or she has at least two years of uninterrupted seniority and any accrued, but unused vacation pay and if the employer wants to pay the employee, in lieu of providing the required notice, an indemnity equal to the salary he or she would have received during the notice period. In addition, if the employee is dismissed without legitimate reason, he or she is entitled to receive compensation and damages for abusive breach of the employment contract. Although this indemnity is based on the prejudice suffered by the employee, French labor courts have tended to grant a minimum of six months' salary if the employee has two years of seniority. An employer's failure to comply with the statutory dismissal procedure also gives rise to damages even if the dismissal was justified.

c. *See generally id.* at 3-1–3-78.

### JAPAN

Employers in Japan must give a minimum of either thirty days' prior notice of dismissal or thirty days' wages in lieu of notice.[d] An employer may apply to the Labor Standards' Inspection Office for prior recognition that the employee's dismissal is for cause based on the employee's conduct or is due to natural calamity. If this recognition is granted, neither prior notice of dismissal nor payment of wages in lieu of notice is required.

Although Japanese law contains no statutory provision requiring cause for the termination of employees, an employer's freedom to dismiss is restricted by its work rules and by established case law that requires just cause. If an employee challenges a termination on these grounds, the employer must demonstrate just cause. A wrongfully terminated employee may recover his or her wages for the period of dismissal plus 5 percent interest and may also seek reinstatement and reimbursement of the costs of litigation (exclusive of attorneys' fees). Generally, no further penalties or compensation will be awarded.

### INDIA

India views the employment relationship as a contract that is subject to judicial intervention. Thus, the courts have implemented procedural safeguards shielding employees from indiscriminate termination by employers.[e] According to Indian law, termination is to be used solely as punishment for employee misconduct, which must be proved under very stringent procedural and evidentiary requirements. In addition, employers are required to provide some form of compensation to a terminated employee, and most employers with more than 100 employees must seek permission from the labor department of the government before dismissing or laying off a worker, or shutting down, irrespective of financial condition. Such approval is very hard to obtain.

d. *See generally id.* at 32-1–32-57.

e. Jaivir Singh, The Law, Labour and Development in India, paper presented at the Annual World Bank Conference on Development Economics in Oslo, Norway (June 24–26, 2002), *at* http://wbln0018.worldbank.org/eurup/web.nsf/pages/paper+by+Jaivir+Singh/$File/SINGH.PDF.

## THE RESPONSIBLE MANAGER

## AVOIDING WRONGFUL-DISCHARGE SUITS AND OTHER EMPLOYEE PROBLEMS

Many courts appear to be moving toward providing all employees the protection against discharge without good cause that traditionally was offered only by union contracts or by individually negotiated contracts. As a result, employers often find themselves in costly litigation, attempting to convince a jury that a discharge was justified. A survey released by Chubb Group of Insurance

*(Continued)*

(The Responsible Manager *continued*)

Companies in 2004 revealed that 26 percent of Chubb insureds were named as a defendant in at least one employment-related suit during the past few years.[134]

An employer needs to develop a human resource approach that takes into account its own business needs and the laws of the state or country in which its employees are located.[135] This need is particularly acute in the new economy where busy employers, under pressure from rapidly changing conditions and intense competition, may neglect to devote sufficient attention to compliance with employment laws and regulations.

An employer can do many things to limit its exposure to unwanted contractual obligations.[136] First, the employer should articulate the kind of contractual relationship it wishes to have with its employees. That relationship may not be the same for every employee or job classification. In some instances, it may be appropriate to maintain an at-will relationship documented in a simple offer letter and clear policy statements. For other employees, the employer may prefer to have a more elaborate written contract that specifies the circumstances under which the employment relationship may be terminated, including a definition of "Cause", and a specific severance agreement in the event of termination without cause. Restrictive covenants may be available and desired by the employer as a fair exchange for the severance obligation.

If the company has a code of conduct (as discussed in Chapter 1), violations of the code may be good cause for termination, particularly if the employee has signed an agreement to comply with it. For example, American Express Company requires each of its approximately 15,000 managers to sign an agreement to abide by the policies set forth in the company's code of conduct.

Recently, companies have been exploring the viability of peer review of employment conflicts rather than judicial review. For example, Darden Restaurants (the company that owns the Red Lobster and Olive Garden chains of restaurants) has been using peer review of employee complaints since 1994.[137] The company has found that peer review (1) reduces the quantity, and therefore the costs, of litigation; (2) reduces tensions in the workplace; and (3) often avoids the costs of hiring and training a new person by facilitating reconciliation rather than conflict. Red Lobster takes peer review seriously. Employees who have been fired or disciplined may seek a peer review. The decision of the peer review panel is binding and can overturn management's decision. The panels can even award damages. The program has reduced annual legal fees by $1 million.

There are numerous issues that employers should consider with respect to the FLSA.[138] Most importantly, an employer must carefully classify its employees as exempt or nonexempt to ensure that it is paying overtime to all employees who do not qualify for one of the FLSA exemptions. Employers should make sure that nonexempt employees required to work through lunch are compensated. Employers cannot dock salary for late arrivals or partial-day absences of exempt employees. Employers should factor in bonus payments, prorated to a weekly rate of pay, when calculating overtime payments to nonexempt employees. Although commuting time to and from work is not compensable, employers must consider whether they should compensate for commuting time if the employee travels from home directly to a client's site rather than to the employer's site. Although outside salespeople are exempt, salespeople who work at the employer's place of business are not exempt. Perhaps the best defense against a lawsuit is to create a corporate culture where employees feel appreciated, which includes compensating them fairly and providing honest feedback about job requirements and performance.

Most managers in the United States have a visceral negative reaction to attempts to unionize their workers, believing that unions interfere with management control in the workplace and hinder efforts to achieve competitive levels of costs, quality, and productivity. Nevertheless, some academics argue that there is systemic empirical evidence indicating that unions are positively associated with higher training expenditures, successful employee involvement, and successful quality-improvement programs and organizational innovation. Indeed, many of the best-known examples of high-performance production systems occur at unionized plants, such as those at Saturn, Xerox, Corning, Levi-Strauss, NUMMI, and AT&T.[139] These and other benefits of a well-regulated workforce—and the assistance of a labor organization to achieve that objective—may become apparent to management faced with organizing desires in its workforce.

134. Press Release, Chubb Group of Insurance Companies, Employment Practices Liability Survey Findings (May 25, 2004), *at* http://www.chubb.com/news/pr20040525.html.

135. See Jeffrey Pfeffer, COMPETITIVE ADVANTAGE THROUGH PEOPLE 137–48 (1994).

136. See Bagley & Dauchy, *supra* note 106, at 321–24.

137. Margaret A. Jacobs, *Red Lobster Tale: Peers Decide Fired Waitress's Fate,* WALL ST. J., Jan. 20, 1998, at B1.

138. Nadel, *supra* note 114.

139. JEFFREY PFEFFER, THE HUMAN EQUATION: BUILDING PROFITS BY PUTTING PEOPLE FIRST 226 (1998).

## INSIDE STORY

## WORKING "OFF THE CLOCK"

The FLSA requires all nonexempt employees working more than forty hours per week to receive overtime, that is, pay for one and one-half times the hours worked. Many businesses, however, are finding ways to avoid this requirement by having their employees work "off the clock" so that they will not be compensated for the time they put in. Companies avoid paying overtime by (1) not marking the hours employees work on their time cards, (2) having employees come to work at different hours, (3) rolling one week's overtime to another week, (4) encouraging a work atmosphere where everyone puts in extra time, and (5) even making promotions and social acceptance dependent upon working the extra hours without pay.

The practice is surprisingly pervasive. The Department of Labor estimated that 288,296 workers were owed more than $196 million in overtime pay in 2004.[140] Off-the-clock work is most often found at workplaces that employ immigrants, like farms and poultry-processing plants, but the phenomenon has spread, especially among low-wage companies in the service sector. Analysts attribute the rise in off-the-clock work to middle managers facing greater pressure to lower labor costs and workers' ignorance and fear that they will lose their jobs if they complain. But as workers learn their rights and news about the practice spreads, more lawsuits are appearing.

For example, the U.S. Court of Appeals for the Second Circuit held that workers required to remain at outdoor work sites over their lunch break were providing a valuable service and were entitled to compensation for that time.[141] The court upheld the lower court's award of $5 million in overtime pay and almost $10 million in damages for 1,500 telecommunications employees. Similarly, Wal-Mart has been sued in a class-action lawsuit brought on behalf of 100,000 California employees, who allege that Wal-Mart routinely asked workers to work "off the clock" without pay. The work allegedly included times when workers were told to shorten, skip, or interrupt lunch and other breaks.[142]

Many other cases have been settled. In November 2003, the Labor Department announced a $4.8 million back-wages settlement with T-Mobile, the wireless telephone company, after finding that it had forced 20,500 call-center employees to work off the clock by making them show up ten to fifteen minutes before their scheduled clock-in time.[143] Nordstrom's department stores also settled a suit that alleged that the company required employees to deliver packages to customers' homes off the clock. The Department of Labor settled a case with Kinko's Copies, a chain of photocopy centers, after finding that store managers in Ithaca, New York, and Hyannis, Massachusetts, had erased time on thirteen employees' time cards.[144]

Not all claims of off-the-clock work have been successful, however. The U.S. Court of Appeals for the Eleventh Circuit rejected a claim by police officers that physical training necessary to pass mandatory physical fitness tests constitutes work under the FLSA.[145] The court reasoned that the officers' exercise time was not compensable because it was undertaken outside regular working hours and was neither compulsory nor productive work. Moreover, the court found that the exercise provided benefits that transcended the employment requirements and, as a result, the exercise was not directly related to the police officers' jobs. Thus, although claims of off-the-clock work are increasingly brought by disgruntled employees, courts do not blindly accept the plaintiffs' charges.

140. Department of Labor, *Wage and Hour Maintains High Enforcement Levels in Fiscal Year 2004* (2004), *at* http://www.dol.gov/esa/whd/statistics/200411.htm.

141. Reich v. Southern New Eng. Telecomm. Corp., 121 F.3d 58 (2d Cir. 1997).

142. Savaglio v. Wal-Mart Stores, Inc., 2004 WL 20434092 (Cal. Super. Ct. 2004).

143. Steven Greenhouse, *Forced to Work Off the Clock, Some Fight Back*, N.Y. TIMES, Nov. 19, 2004, at A1.

144. Steven Greenhouse, *Altering of Worker Time Cards Spurs Growing Number of Suits,* N.Y. TIMES, Apr. 4, 2004, http://www.nytimes.com/2004/04/04/national/04WAGE.html?th=&pagewanted=print&posi.

145. Dade County v. Alvarez, 124 F.3d 1380 (11th Cir. 1997), *cert. denied,* 523 U.S. 1122 (1998).

## KEY WORDS AND PHRASES

administrative employee 445
appropriate collective bargaining unit 449
at-will contract 416
boilerplate clause 430
comp time 443
computer employee 446
concerted activity 450
covenant not to compete 426
creative professional 446
doctrine of self-publication 431
economic strike 450
executive 445
exempt employee 445
fair procedure 423
H-1B visa 447
I-9 447
implied contract 421
implied covenant of good faith and fair dealing 422
*in loco parentis* 433
learned professional 446
living wage ordinances 444
nonexempt employees 445
outside sales employee 446
professional employee 446
public policy exception 417
recognitional strikes 450
recognized hazard 439
representation elections 449
secondary boycotts 450
supervisor 449
unfair labor practice strike 450
unfair labor practices 449
whistleblower statutes 419
wrongful discharge 417

## QUESTIONS AND CASE PROBLEMS

**1.** Terry Spence, a computer trainer at Compuware Corporation, was discharged after he threatened to tell Compuware's client about work-related problems. Although Spence was the only employee who threatened to complain, he had consulted with other employees before threatening to speak out. Did Spence's discharge violate the NRLA? Does it matter whether Compuware knew that Spence had consulted with other employees? [*Compuware v. NLRB,* 134 F.3d 1285 (6th Cir. 1998), *cert. denied,* 523 U.S. 1123 (1998).]

**2.** In March 1994, 43-year-old Peter Barnes read an ad in the *Chicago Tribune* that Pentrix was seeking experienced word processors to work in its Chicago office. Pentrix is a national corporation specializing in the design and manufacture of hand-held computers. The ad stated that Pentrix was looking for "experienced word processors seeking a career in a stable and growing company." On March 8, 1994, Barnes interviewed with Renee Thompson, the head of Pentrix's word processing department in Chicago. Thompson was impressed with Barnes's prior experience and reassured him that although Pentrix is a national corporation, the employees in Pentrix are like a family and look after one another. Thompson offered Barnes a job at the end of the interview, and Barnes began work on March 15, 1994.

Barnes received an updated policy manual from the personnel department every year that he worked for Pentrix. In addition to discussing such things as vacation, salary, and benefits, the policy manual described Pentrix's progressive discipline system.

Pentrix's progressive discipline system consisted of three basic steps. First, an employee's supervisor must discuss the employee's deficiencies with the employee and suggest ways for the employee to improve his or her work performance. Second, the employee must receive written notice of his or her poor performance with suggestions of how the performance can improve. Third, the employee must receive a written warning that if the employee's performance does not improve, he or she will be terminated.

The manual provided that in cases of "material misconduct" a supervisor had the discretion to decide whether to follow the progressive discipline procedures. The policy manual also provided that Pentrix had complete discretion to decide who would be discharged in the event of a company layoff.

In 1996, the following language was added to the policy manual:

> These policies are simply guidelines to management. Pentrix reserves the right to terminate or change them at any time or to elect not to follow them in any case. Nothing in these policies is intended or should be understood as creating a contract of employment or a guarantee of continued employment with Pentrix. Employment at Pentrix remains terminable at the will of either the employee or Pentrix at any time for any reason or for no reason.

Barnes signed an acknowledgment of receipt of the 1996 policy manual.

Barnes received several good performance reviews during the time he worked at Pentrix. On a few occasions, Thompson discussed with Barnes the importance of arriving at work on time, but no record was kept of the times that Barnes was late. Thompson noted in Barnes's 2001 and 2002 performance evaluations that Barnes should proofread his work more carefully.

In October 2003, Barnes received an offer to work as a word processor for Lintog, another computer manufacturing corporation in Chicago. Barnes discussed this offer with Thompson. Thompson persuaded Barnes to remain at Pentrix by suggesting that he might be promoted to day-shift word processing supervisor when the current day-shift supervisor resigned. The day-shift supervisor has yet to resign from Pentrix.

Barnes was discharged from Pentrix on July 1, 2004. Thompson told Barnes that he was being fired because Pentrix was experiencing a slowdown and that two word processors were being let go in each of Pentrix's twenty offices across the country. Thompson wrote on the separation notice placed in Barnes's personnel file that Barnes was being discharged as a result of a workforce reduction. Before leaving on July 1, Barnes saw Olga Svetlana, Pentrix's vice president of computer design, getting into her car. Svetlana said to Barnes, "Too bad about your job, but maybe this will teach you to stop leaking our computer designs to other companies."

Barnes had trouble sleeping and felt depressed after being fired from Pentrix. He waited three weeks before he began looking for another job. He then submitted an application to Lintog, the company that had offered him a job in 2003. Rob Grey, the head of the word processing department at Lintog, called Renee Thompson at Pentrix to find out why Barnes had left. Thompson responded that Barnes had worked in Pentrix's word processing department for more than ten years and was discharged as a result of a slowdown. Barnes interviewed with Grey on July 26, 2004. During the interview, Grey asked Barnes why he had left his job at Pentrix. Barnes responded that although he was officially told that he was being discharged because of a reduction in force, he was fired because he was wrongly suspected of leaking the corporation's computer designs. Barnes was not hired by Lintog.

**a.** What claims might Barnes bring against Pentrix, Inc.?

**b.** If you were investigating whether Barnes could successfully sue Pentrix, what information would you want to know?

**c.** What damages might Barnes be entitled to recover?

**3.** In the following cases, should the court find that the employee was an exempt employee who received a salary or an hourly employee entitled to overtime pay?

**a.** Heather Hagadorn joined M.F. Smith & Associates, Inc. as a human resources consultant in August 1994 and worked thirteen months on a project. A month after the project ended, she was furloughed for lack of work. Hagadorn sued under the FLSA, claiming that she was an hourly employee and seeking pay for approximately 500 hours for which she was not paid overtime. M.F. Smith contends that she was a salaried employee paid a predetermined amount each pay period, but paid straight time on an hourly basis for time she worked that exceeded the minimum 37.5 hours required each pay period. Documents produced during the litigation include pay statements that reflect the number of hours for which Hagadorn was paid; these statements do not separate the regular minimum required hours (37.5 hours per week) from any overtime hours. A memorandum indicating a base annual salary of $48,500 contains the handwritten notation "$24.88/hr." M.F. Smith argues that it computed this hourly amount by dividing the annual salary by fifty-two weeks and then by 37.5 hours to determine Hagadorn's regular salary rate on an hourly basis. It claims it used this rate to pay Hagadorn for hours worked that exceeded the standard 37.5-hour workweek. [*Hagadorn v. M.F. Smith & Associates, Inc.*, 172 F.3d 878 (10th Cir. 1999).]

**b.** Anthony Piscione worked as a consultant at Ernst & Young LLP from 1991 until September 1996. During that time, he was promoted from staff consultant to senior staff consultant and then to manager. He was paid straight overtime for the hours he worked in excess of forty hours per week during the first eight months of his employment, but after that he did not receive any overtime pay. After resigning from the firm in 1996, Piscione filed a claim, alleging that Ernst & Young violated the FLSA by classifying him as an exempt employee and not paying him overtime. Ernst & Young argued that Piscione fell within the FLSA's administrative or professional exemption and thus was not entitled to overtime pay. The firm contended that he was a salaried employee and that his duties required the exercise of discretion and independent judgment and related to the general business operations of the firm. Piscione argued that his work did not require independent thought or creativity, as he was simply plugging numbers into formulas; that his supervision of employees involved only a small amount of his time; and that his work was more similar to the work of a cashier in a retail store than that of a professional or administrative employee. In addition, he claimed that Ernst & Young docked his pay if he did not work for eight hours each day. [*Piscione v. Ernst & Young, LLP,* 171 F.3d 527 (7th Cir. 1999).]

4. Robinson was the branch manager of one of Smith Barney's brokerage offices. One of his most important duties was to recruit experienced brokers. He contracted annually with Smith Barney in 1991, 1992, and 1993 under three separate but identical agreements. The 1993 agreement provided that:

> [I]n consideration of payment of the 1993 Incentive Compensation to me, I agree that should my employment with Smith Barney terminate for any reason and I become employed at a competitor organization, I will not for a one-year period directly or indirectly solicit or induce any Smith Barney employee to resign from either (a) the Smith Barney branch office at which I worked; or (b) any other Smith Barney office within a 50-mile radius of the competitor organization's office at which I work in order for that employee to accept employment at the competitor organization at which I work.

Robinson made this promise in return for a promise from Smith Barney to allow him to participate in the firm's 1993 incentive compensation program. The exact amount of Robinson's incentive compensation was to be calculated after Smith Barney's 1993 profits were determined. He was to receive quarterly advances toward the compensation that he would ultimately be paid. In the event that Robinson were to resign or be terminated for cause during 1993, he would be required to return any advances received in that year. In April 1993, Robinson received a $7,000 advance, which he did not repay after he voluntarily left Smith Barney's employ on June 17, 1993.

Robinson conceded that during 1993 he left Smith Barney's employ, began to work for a competitor organization, and, having been advised that the nonsolicitation agreement was unenforceable, knowingly breached the agreement by actively recruiting Smith Barney's employees. Will Robinson succeed in challenging the validity of the nonsolicitation agreement? [*Smith, Barney, Harris Upham & Co. v. Robinson,* 12 F.3d 515 (5th Cir. 1994).]

5. In October 2002, Weyerhaeuser Corporation hired a security company to bring in four dogs to search for drugs and guns in its parking lot. The dogs did not find any drugs but focused on several vehicles containing guns. The company then ordered the owners of the vehicles to open their cars so that they could be hand searched. Weyerhaeuser said the weapons violated a new company policy that extended a longtime workplace gun ban to the parking area, and it terminated four Weyerhaeuser employees and eight others who worked for subcontractors, all of whom had stored guns in their vehicles in violation of the policy. The company claimed that it had told workers about the new policy in writing and at team meetings, but the terminated workers claimed they were never told about the rule. The employees immediately sued for wrongful termination. What arguments can the employees make in their wrongful-termination suit? What arguments will Weyerhaeuser make in response? Will the employees succeed?

The firings outraged many in the rural community in the foothills of the Ouachita Mountains, where carrying a firearm in one's car is commonplace, especially during deer hunting season. As a result, the Oklahoma legislature overwhelmingly passed a law stating that "no person, property owner, tenant, employer, or business entity shall be permitted to establish any policy or rule that has the effect of prohibiting any person, except a convicted felon, from transporting or storing firearms in a locked vehicle on any property set aside for any vehicle." Before the law became effective, however, several prominent companies with Oklahoma operations, including the Williams Companies and ConocoPhillips, sued to stop it. A federal judge has put the law on hold pending a hearing. The plaintiffs assert that the statute violates their property rights and due process rights, is unconstitutionally vague, and is inconsistent with federal laws regulating firearms. They also argue that the statute will impair their ability to guarantee workplace safety by prohibiting weapons on their property. What arguments will the state of Oklahoma make in response? Which party should prevail? [Susan Warren, *In Oklahoma, a Ban on Guns Pits State Against Big Firms,* WALL ST. J., Nov. 26, 2004, at A1.]

6. Lisa Mull was a line operator at Zeta Consumer Products' plastic-bag manufacturing facility in New Jersey. One of Mull's duties was to work with a machine known as a "winder," which winds plastic bags onto spools for packaging and delivery. The machine's frequent malfunctions required Mull to clear the jam and replace the nylon ropes that turned the machine's cylinders. On one occasion, after Mull had turned off the machine by pressing the stop button on the control panel, the winder suddenly began to operate, pulling Mull's left hand into the machine and causing serious injuries, including amputation of two fingers.

   Several months before the accident, OSHA had cited Zeta for failing to provide its employees with so-called lockout/tagout procedures, which are required by federal law and are designed to control the release of hazardous energy when a worker is servicing or performing maintenance on equipment or machinery. Also prior to the date of Mull's injury, another line operator had sustained injuries similar to Mull's; Zeta was aware of the injuries. In addition, other line operators indicated that Zeta, motivated by a desire to enhance productivity, had altered the original design of the winder by removing safety interlock switches (which prevent the machine from operating when the access cover is open). Line operators had also complained to management that Zeta failed to post warnings on the winder to inform workers of its "sudden start-up" capabilities or that the safety interlock switches had been removed.

   Mull sued the employer for damages, and Zeta moved for summary judgment on the basis that Mull's sole remedy was recovery under New Jersey's Workers' Compensation Act. What, if any, OSHA liability does Zeta face based on these facts? How should the court rule? Should Zeta be concerned about any other potential liability arising out of these facts? [*Mull v. Zeta Consumer Products,* 176 N.J. 385 (2003).]

7. Luellen Datar married Roger Salt in 2002 while he was finishing his Ph.D. in electrical engineering at Rensselaer Polytechnic Institute. Upon graduation, Salt started a new company to develop a device that could be used both as a wireless telephone and as a means of accessing the Internet. He used money he had inherited from his great-aunt to finance the company until his first round of venture-capital financing. When the company went public in 2004, he owned 30 percent of the outstanding stock.

   Luellen did not own any stock in her own name but served as vice president of business development. She had never gotten around to negotiating an employment contract and thus served as an at-will employee. Roger was CEO and chair of the board. After a series of nasty fights regarding the state of their marriage, Roger asked his wife to sign a postnuptial agreement confirming that, in the event of a divorce, she would have no right to any of Roger's stock in the company. When she refused to sign, Roger fired her. She sued the company for wrongful termination. How should the court rule?

8. Elizabeth M. Stewart was a highly talented salesperson for Cendant Mobility Services Corporation. Stewart's husband was also employed by Cendant as an executive in the operations department. During a major corporate reorganization, Cendant terminated Stewart's husband. Shortly thereafter, Stewart spoke with James Simon, Cendant's executive vice president of sales, regarding her concerns about how her employment with Cendant might be affected if her husband ultimately found employment with a competitor. Simon told Stewart that her husband's employment would have no bearing on her employment with Cendant and that she had no reason to be concerned about her status at Cendant because she was a highly valued employee. On the basis of these assurances, Stewart continued in her position with Cendant and did not pursue other employment opportunities.

   Nearly one year after Cendant's reorganization, Cendant learned that Stewart's husband was working for a competitor and subsequently reduced her duties and limited her interaction with clients. Cendant also requested that Stewart verbally agree to a document that purported to delineate her obligations to Cendant in relation to her husband's work on behalf of any competitor of Cendant. When

Stewart declined to agree to this document, Cendant terminated her employment. Stewart sued Cendant claiming that she had relied to her detriment on Simon's promise that her employment with Cendant would not be affected adversely by her husband's probable future employment with a competitor. How should the court rule? [*Stewart v. Cendant Mobility Services Corp.,* 836 A.2d 736 (Conn. 2003).]

9. Have any of the employers in the following cases terminated an employee in violation of public policy? Has the employer acted ethically?
   **a.** An at-will employee accountant was fired by her supervisor after she refused to violate the Colorado State Board of Accountancy Rules of Professional Conduct following the discovery of numerous improper accounting practices at the private company. [*Rocky Mountain Hospital and Medical Service v. Mariani,* 916 P.2d (Colo. 1996).]
   **b.** An at-will employee of a lumber company was terminated for attending meetings of a group opposed to the company's stance on logging in a nearby national forest. [*Edmonson v. Shearer Lumber Products,* 75 P.3d 733 (Idaho 2003).]
   **c.** A doctor employed at the *New York Times* who was responsible for examining employees who were seeking workers' compensation benefits claimed that she was fired after she refused to follow the instructions of the vice president of human resources to misinform employees about the work-related nature of their injuries in order to limit the company's workers' compensation liability. [*Horn v. New York Times,* 760 N.Y.S.2d 378 (N.Y. 2003).]
   **d.** An employee whose complaint led to governmental safety inspections that, in turn, led to eight safety citations for the employer was fired two weeks after the inspections. [*Gabel Stone Co. v. Federal Mine Safety and Health Review Commission,* 307 F.3d 691 (8th Cir. 2002).]

## MANAGER'S DILEMMA

10. Gita Bhandari joins your high-tech start-up in 2002, immediately after graduating from Carnegie-Mellon University. She forgoes better-paying consulting and investment banking opportunities to get in on the ground floor of a young, fast-growing company. As compensation, Bhandari receives a nominal salary and stock options. Because the company's product will require three years to bring to market, the options do not vest for three years. This means that Bhandari forfeits all of the stock options if she leaves the company before 2005.

    In 2004, the company begins having serious problems. Even though the project is on schedule and is anticipated to be a huge success, costs are skyrocketing, and your investors demand a significant reduction in operating expenses.

    You are considering firing Bhandari. Although she has performed well, Bhandari was the most recent person hired. She is an at-will employee, but, considering that she has less than one year to go until she can exercise her stock options, you fear a lawsuit, especially given the company's close-knit character. At this critical stage, the legal fees alone from a wrongful-termination lawsuit could bankrupt the company.
    **a.** Should you fire Bhandari to reduce operating expenses?
    **b.** If Bhandari is terminated, on what basis could she sue the company? Would she prevail?
    **c.** How could you have structured the relationship to avoid this potential lawsuit?

## INTERNET SOURCES

| | |
|---|---|
| The Department of Labor site includes information about Bureau of Labor statistics, OSHA data on occupational injuries, and laws and regulations administered and enforced by DOL agencies. | http://www.dol.gov |
| This site provides an index of laws and articles on employment law and the Labor and Employment Law Web Guide. | http://www.findlaw.com/01topics/27labor |
| The United Food and Commercial Workers International site provides news and information about employment cases and issues, particularly workers' rights. | http://www.ufcw.org |
| The AFL–CIO site includes information regarding safety on the job, workers' rights, and unequal pay. | http://www.aflcio.org |
| OSHA | http://www.osha.gov |

CHAPTER 13

# Civil Rights and Employment Discrimination

## INTRODUCTION

### Laws Designed to Eliminate Employment Discrimination

The abolition of slavery after the Civil War and the civil rights movement of the 1960s were two great forces behind modern civil rights legislation. From the Civil Rights Act of 1866 to that of 1991, the law has been moving in a direction to eliminate discrimination based on race, gender, color, religion, national origin, age, or disability. Civil rights laws help ensure that every member of society has the opportunity to reach his or her full potential.

Managers who fail to enact and enforce policies to ensure compliance with federal legislation prohibiting employment discrimination put their companies at risk of being penalized by large fines and judgments. In 2003 and 2004, corporations paid millions of dollars in settlements or judgments as a result of discrimination lawsuits brought by their employees: as described further in the "Inside Story" for this chapter, Merrill Lynch agreed to pay more than $100 million to settle charges that it paid women employees less than men and did not promote them as often; Abercrombie & Fitch paid $50 million to a class of job applicants claiming that Abercrombie's recruitment program excluded women and minorities; Home Depot paid $5.5 million for a suit alleging a hostile work environment based on gender, race, and national origin; and Foot Locker settled a class-action age discrimination lawsuit brought by hundreds of workers terminated in a nationwide layoff for $3.5 million.[1]

1. EEOC, *EEOC Litigation Settlements Monthly Reports,* at http://www.eeoc.gov/litigation/settlements/index.html (last modified Jan. 10, 2005).

### Chapter Overview

This chapter provides an overview of federal legislation barring employment discrimination, with special attention to Title VII, the Age Discrimination in Employment Act, the Americans with Disabilities Act, and the Family and Medical Leave Act. It illustrates the various legal theories pursued under each piece of legislation and shows how those theories relate to legal and appropriate behavior by managers in a business environment. It also discusses how discrimination laws apply to affirmative action and the hiring of contingent or temporary workers. The chapter concludes with an overview of the ways that other countries approach workplace discrimination and diversity.

## Overview of Civil Rights Legislation

The federal statutes that forbid various kinds of discrimination in employment are summarized in Exhibit 13.1. Many states have passed their own fair employment acts, which in some instances provide greater protection than their federal counterparts. The federal statutes apply only to employees, not independent contractors (see Chapter 5 for a discussion of the difference between employees and contractors).

Although the statutes described in Exhibit 13.1 have created a far more level playing field for all workers, progress can be slow. For example, the Equal Pay Act was enacted in 1963, but as of 2000, women earned 80 percent of what men earned annually.[2]

2. U.S. General Accounting Office, *U.S. General Accounting Office Report to Congressional Requestors, Women's Earnings* (Oct. 2003), http://www.gao.gov/new.items/d0435.pdf.

**EXHIBIT 13.1 Major Pieces of Federal Civil Rights Legislation**

| Statute | Major Provisions | Employers Subject to Statute | Comments |
|---|---|---|---|
| Civil Rights Act of 1866[a] (Section 1981) | Prohibits racial discrimination by employers of any size in the making and enforcement of contracts, including employment contracts. | All public and private employers. | The bar against racial discrimination applies not only to hiring, promotion, and termination but also to working conditions, such as racial harassment, and to breaches of contract occurring during the term of the contract. |
| Equal Pay Act of 1963[b] | Mandates equal pay for equal work without regard to gender. | All public and private employers with twenty or more employees (including federal, state, and local governments). | |
| Title VII of the Civil Rights Act of 1964[c] (Title VII) | Prohibits discrimination in employment on the basis of race, color, religion, national origin, or sex. Later amended to provide that discrimination on the basis of sex includes discrimination on the basis of pregnancy, childbirth, or related medical conditions. | All public and private employers with fifteen or more employees (including federal, state, and local governments). | |
| Age Discrimination in Employment Act of 1967[d] (ADEA) | Protects persons forty years and older from discrimination on the basis of age. The ADEA was amended in 1990 by the Older Workers' Benefit Protection Act, which prohibits age discrimination in providing employee benefits and establishes minimum standards for waiver of one's rights under the ADEA. | All public and private employers with twenty or more employees (including federal, state, and local governments). | |
| Vietnam Era Veterans' Readjustment Assistance Acts of 1972 and 1974[e] | Require affirmative action to employ disabled Vietnam-era veterans. | Employers holding federal contracts of $10,000 or more. | Enforced by U.S. Department of Labor. |
| Vocational Rehabilitation Act of 1973[f] | Prohibits discrimination against the physically and mentally disabled. Imposes affirmative-action obligations on employers having contracts with the federal government in excess of $2,500. | Employers receiving federal financial assistance of any amount. | Enforced by U.S. Department of Labor. This legislation was the precursor to and guided the development of the Americans with Disabilities Act. |

a. 42 U.S.C. § 1981.
b. 29 U.S.C. § 206(d).
c. 42 U.S.C. §§ 2000e–2000e-17.
d. 29 U.S.C. §§ 621–634.
e. 38 U.S.C. §§ 4100 *et seq.*
f. 29 U.S.C. §§ 701–797.

*(Continued)*

EXHIBIT 13.1 **Major Pieces of Federal Civil Rights Legislation—continued**

| Statute | Major Provisions | Employers Subject to Statute | Comments |
|---|---|---|---|
| Veterans Re-Employment Act of 1974[g] | Gives employees who served in the military at any time the right to be reinstated in employment without loss of benefits and the right not to be discharged without cause for one year following such reinstatement. | All public and private employers. | |
| Immigration Reform and Control Act of 1986[h] (IRCA) | Prohibits discrimination against applicants or employees based on national origin or citizenship status. | All private employers with four or more employees. | If employer has fifteen or more employees, plaintiff must file national origin discrimination claims under Title VII. |
| Americans with Disabilities Act of 1990[i] (ADA) | Prohibits discrimination in employment on the basis of a person's disability. Also requires businesses to provide "reasonable accommodation" to the disabled, unless such an accommodation would result in "undue hardship" on business operations. | All private employers with fifteen or more employees. | The ADA is the most sweeping civil rights measure since the Civil Rights Act of 1964. |
| Civil Rights Act of 1991[j] | Legislatively overruled several parts of recent Supreme Court rulings that were unfavorable to the rights of plaintiffs in employment-discrimination cases. Also extended coverage of the major civil rights statutes to the staffs of the president and the Senate. | Varies. | |
| Family and Medical Leave Act of 1993[k] | Designed to allow employees to take time off from work to handle domestic responsibilities, such as the birth or adoption of a child or the care of an elderly parent. Employees are guaranteed job security despite familial responsibilities. | Private employers with fifty or more employees at work sites within seventy-five miles of each other. | Part-time employees are excluded from the Act's coverage and are not to be counted in calculating the fifty employees necessary for an employer to be covered by the Act. |

g. 38 U.S.C. §§ 4301–4307.
h. Pub. L. No. 99-603, 100 Stat. 3359 (codified as amended in scattered sections of the U.S.C.) (1986).
i. 42 U.S.C. §§ 12101–12213.
j. Pub. L. No. 102–106, 105 Stat. 1071 (codified in scattered sections of the U.S.C.) (1991).
k. 29 U.S.C. §§ 2601–2654.

### Definition of Adverse Employment Action

In most discrimination and retaliation cases, the employee must establish that his or her employer subjected him or her to an adverse employment action. The federal appeals courts are split as to what constitutes an adverse employment action. Seven of the circuits have taken an expansive view.[3] Under this interpretation, demotions, refusals to hire or promote, unwarranted negative job evaluations, disadvantageous transfers or assignments, depriving an employee of support services, cutting off challenging assignments, moving an employee from a spacious office to a dingy closet, forcing an employee to jump through hoops in order to obtain severance benefits, making and soliciting from coworkers negative comments about an employee, needlessly delaying authorization for medical treatment, requiring an employee to work without a lunch break, and changing an employee's schedule without notification have all been characterized as adverse employment actions.[4] Two circuits have held that an adverse action is something that materially affects the terms and conditions of employment, such as employee compensation or privileges.[5] The remaining two circuits have adopted the most restrictive test, holding that only actions affecting hiring, firing, promoting, and demoting are adverse employment actions.[6]

## Enforcement

The Equal Employment Opportunity Commission (EEOC) is the primary enforcer of civil rights legislation in the United States. A part of the Department of Justice, the EEOC processes hundreds of complaints, investigating and evaluating their merit. If a claim is unfounded, it is dismissed. If the claim withstands initial inquiry and the EEOC is unable to pursue the case due to staff and resource constraints, the agency will provide a right-to-sue letter to the private party. Without this administrative permission, private litigants cannot initiate suits under various statutes, including Title VII and the ADA.

The EEOC has become more proactive in its approach to enforcing antidiscrimination laws. In early 1998, the EEOC began contracting with private organizations to use "testers" to identify employers that discriminate.[7] In employment-discrimination testing, pairs of individuals who are equally qualified are sent to apply for entry-level positions in an effort to determine whether impermissible factors such as race, gender, national origin, or disability influence employment decisions. In 2000, the U.S. Court of Appeals for the Seventh Circuit held that testers had standing to bring employment-discrimination cases under Title VII even though they had no real desire to work for the companies to which they applied.[8]

Although an individual employee can be required to agree to arbitrate civil rights' disputes, this does not preclude the EEOC from suing the employer in a court of law for damages payable to the aggrieved employee. See Chapter 4 for further information on the arbitration of discrimination claims.

## Title VII

### Scope

Title VII bans discrimination based on an individual's race, color, religion, national origin, or sex. Title VII claims generally fall within one of four broad categories: traditional discrimination, harassment, failure to accommodate religious beliefs, and retaliation.

### Traditional Discrimination Claims

Litigation in traditional Title VII actions has produced two distinct legal theories of discrimination: (1) disparate treatment and (2) disparate impact.

#### *Disparate Treatment*

A plaintiff claiming *disparate treatment* must prove that the employer intentionally discriminated against him or her by denying a benefit or privilege of employment (such as a promotion or pay raise) because of his or her race, color, religion, sex, or national origin. The U.S.

3. The U.S. Courts of Appeals for the First, Fourth, Seventh, Ninth, Tenth, Eleventh, and D.C. Circuits have defined adverse employment action broadly. *See, e.g.*, Ray v. Henderson, 217 F.3d 1234 (9th Cir. 2000); Von Gunten v. Maryland, 243 F.3d 858 (4th Cir. 2001).
4. *E.g., Ray.*
5. The U.S. Courts of Appeals for the Second and Third Circuits have adopted this intermediate test.
6. The U.S. Courts of Appeals for the Fifth and Eighth Circuits have adopted the most restrictive test. *But see* Fierros v. Tex. Dep't of Health, 274 F.3d 187 (5th Cir. 2001) (upholding a narrow standard of adverse employment action while applying a broader standard).

7. *EEOC Contracts with Private Testers to Uncover Employers' Discriminatory Hiring*, 66 U.S.L.W. 2391–92 (Jan. 8, 1998).
8. Kyles v. J.K. Guardian Sec. Servs., Inc., 222 F.3d 289 (7th Cir. 2000).

Supreme Court has established a systematic approach for proving these claims.[9] First, the employee must prove a *prima facie* case, which entails proving that (1) he or she is a member of a class of persons protected by Title VII and (2) he or she was denied a position or benefit that he or she sought, for which he or she was qualified, and that was available. If the employee proves the *prima facie* case, the employer then must present evidence, but need not prove, that it had legitimate, nondiscriminatory grounds for its decision, such as the employee's lack of qualifications or poor job performance. If the employer meets this burden of producing evidence, the employee then must prove that the grounds offered by the employer were merely a pretext for the employer's actions and that intentional discrimination was the true reason.

In a disparate treatment case, for example, an African-American employee might claim that he was fired because of his race. To prove his *prima facie* case, he might introduce evidence that he is an African American, was fired, and possessed at least the minimum qualifications for the job. Some courts may require that he also show that his job was not eliminated but was filled by someone else after his termination. Once he proves this, his employer must present evidence that the employee was terminated for a legitimate, nondiscriminatory reason, for example, excessive absenteeism. The employer might produce the employee's attendance records and a supervisor's testimony that his attendance was unacceptable. The employee could attempt to prove pretext in a number of ways. He might show that his employer's attendance policy requires a written warning about poor attendance before the employee can be terminated on that ground, and that he received no such warning. He might show that white employees with similar attendance records were not fired. He might show that his supervisor uttered racial slurs from time to time. In any event, the employee has the burden of proving that his employer fired him because of his race.

In *Frank v. United Airlines, Inc.*,[10] the U.S. Court of Appeals for the Ninth Circuit held that United Airlines' use of different weight policies for male and female flight attendants was illegal disparate treatment on the basis of sex. The airline required female flight attendants to meet weight limits based on suggested weights for medium body frames but permitted male flight attendants to meet weight limits based on large body frames. The court held that United failed to show that having thinner female than male flight attendants affected the flight attendants' ability to greet passengers, move luggage, push carts, or provide physical assistance in emergencies. The court found that the plaintiffs had successfully established that United's reasons were a pretext and that the different weight limits for male and female flight attendants constituted illegal discrimination. In fact, the court concluded, the discriminatory weight requirement may have actually hindered female employees' job performance.

## Disparate Impact

The *disparate impact* theory arose out of Title VII class actions brought in the 1970s against large employers. These suits challenged testing and other selection procedures, claiming that they systematically excluded women or particular ethnic groups from certain types of jobs. It is not necessary to prove intentional discrimination to prevail in a disparate impact case. Discrimination can be established by proving that an employment practice, although neutral on its face, disproportionately affected a protected group in a negative way.

For example, suppose an employer has a policy of hiring for security guard positions only persons who are at least 5 feet 8 inches tall, weigh at least 150 pounds, and can pass certain agility tests. This policy would seem to be neutral, in that it does not expressly exclude women or some Asian males. However, if the number of qualified women or Asian males who are refused employment is proportionately greater than the number of white males refused employment, then that policy has a disparate impact.

To prove disparate impact, the plaintiff must demonstrate that the specific employment practice, policy, or rule being challenged has caused a statistically significant disproportion between the racial or other composition of the persons holding the jobs at issue and the racial or other composition of the *qualified* persons in the relevant labor market.[11] The employer then has the burden of demonstrating that the challenged practice is job related for the position in question and consistent with business necessity.

If a job requires no special skills, then all members of the labor pool are considered when doing the statistical analysis necessary to determine whether a facially neutral policy has a disparate impact. For example, in *EEOC v. Steamship Clerks Union, Local 1066*,[12] a labor union representing the individuals who check cargo passing through the port of Boston against inventory lists had adopted a membership sponsorship policy (MSP) that

9. *See* McDonnell Douglas Corp. v. Green, 411 U.S. 792 (1973).
10. 216 F.3d 845 (9th Cir. 2000).
11. Wards Cove Packing Co. v. Atonio, 490 U.S. 642 (1989).
12. 48 F.3d 594 (1st Cir. 1995).

required union applicants to be sponsored by an existing member. When the union adopted the MSP, it had no African-American or Hispanic members. Over the next six years, the union accepted thirty new members, all of whom were Caucasian. After 1986, the union closed its membership rolls.

In 1991, the EEOC sued the union for disparate impact discrimination. Although African Americans and Hispanics constituted between 8 and 27 percent of the relevant labor pool in the Boston area, none had been hired by the union. Because the jobs required no special skills, all members of the labor pool were deemed qualified and therefore included in the calculation of qualified applicants. The union claimed that its MSP was merely a form of nepotism, not racial discrimination, because every member admitted between 1980 and 1986 was closely related to an existing member of the union. The U.S. Court of Appeals for the First Circuit disagreed, holding that the union's membership policy was discriminatory: by its very nature, it created a strong likelihood that no nonwhite face would ever appear in the union's ranks.

Historically, disparate impact analysis has been limited to objective selection criteria, such as tests and degree requirements. This analysis may also apply to subjective bases for decisions, such as interviews and supervisor evaluations.[13]

The business justification offered by the employer to justify the disparate impact must relate to job performance. Inconvenience, annoyance, or expense to the employer will not suffice. For example, a Latina applicant who is denied employment because she failed an English-language test might challenge the language requirement. If she has applied for a sales job, the employer might be able to justify the requirement on the ground that ability to communicate with customers is an indispensable qualification. On the other hand, if she has applied for a job on the production line, that justification would probably not suffice unless her duties included communicating with others in English. As under disparate treatment analysis, the ultimate burden of persuasion rests with the plaintiff.

## HARASSMENT

Employees can bring claims for harassment in violation of Title VII on the basis of sex, race, color, religion, or national origin. The most prevalent type of harassment claim is sexual harassment, and thus the law regarding harassment has been developed in the context of sexual harassment claims.[14] Nevertheless, the analysis used in sexual harassment cases is applied to claims of harassment on the basis of race, color, religion, and national origin as well.

### Sexual Harassment

As more women have entered the workforce and risen to positions previously dominated by men, courts have recognized sexual harassment as a form of sexual discrimination. Sexual harassment, which can be asserted by male or female employees, is one of the more complex and emotional issues in antidiscrimination law. Sexual harassment law is based on language in Title VII that prohibits discrimination "because of sex."

**_Quid Pro Quo_ Harassment** Early on, the courts recognized that a specific, job-related adverse action, such as denial of a promotion, in retaliation for a person's refusal to respond to his or her supervisor's sexual advances is a violation of Title VII. Such retaliation, which is referred to as *quid pro quo harassment,* is a theory unique to sexual harassment claims.

**Hostile Environment Harassment** A threat of adverse job action in retaliation for rebuffing sexual advances does not constitute *quid pro quo* harassment, however, if the threat is not carried out. Instead, it is a form of ***hostile environment harassment.***[15] Claims for hostile environment harassment can be brought under Title VII on the basis of race, religion, and national origin as well.

In *Meritor Savings Bank v. Vinson,*[16] the U.S. Supreme Court first ruled that creation of a hostile environment by sexual harassment is a form of sex discrimination barred by Title VII, even if the employee cannot show a concrete economic effect on employment, such as discharge or denial of a raise or promotion, to establish a violation. Not every sexually offensive comment or act constitutes actionable sexual harassment; there must be sufficient offensive conduct to give rise to a pervasively hostile atmosphere. This determination should be based upon the totality of the circumstances.

In *Harris v. Forklift Systems, Inc.,* [17] the U.S. Supreme Court held that a showing of a serious effect on an employee's psychological well-being, or other injury, is not necessary for a hostile work environment claim under Title VII, reasoning that "Title VII comes into

13. *See* Allen v. City of Chicago, 351 F.3d 306 (7th Cir. 2003).

14. EMPLOYMENT DISCRIMINATION LAW 749 (Barbara Lindemann and Paul Grossman eds., 1996).
15. Burlington Indus. v. Ellerth, 524 U.S. 742 (1998).
16. 477 U.S. 51 (1986).
17. 510 U.S. 17 (1993).

play before the harassing conduct leads to a nervous breakdown." The Court ruled in favor of a female manager of an equipment-rental company who was harassed for two years by its president. In the presence of other employees, the president said such things as, "You're a woman, what do you know?" and "We need a man as the rental manager," and called her "a dumb-ass woman." The president also made sexual innuendos, suggesting that they "go to the Holiday Inn to negotiate her raise," and occasionally asked female employees to get coins from his front pants pocket. Despite the employee's complaints, the sexual comments continued.

**Defining a Hostile Work Environment** To determine whether there is a hostile or abusive environment, courts must look at all the circumstances, including (1) the frequency and severity of the discriminatory conduct; (2) whether it is physically threatening or humiliating, or merely an offensive utterance; and (3) whether it unreasonably interferes with an employee's work performance.

To be actionable under Title VII, sexual harassment must be so severe or pervasive as to alter the conditions of the victim's employment and create an abusive work environment. The U.S. Supreme Court has ruled that "'simple teasing,' offhand comments, and isolated incidents (unless extremely serious) will not amount to discriminatory changes in the terms and conditions of employment.'"[18] The conduct must be "extreme." The standards for judging hostility are sufficiently demanding to prevent plaintiffs from converting Title VII into a "general civility code"; they are intended to filter out "complaints attacking 'the ordinary tribulations of the workplace, such as the sporadic use of abusive language, gender-related jokes, and occasional teasing.'"

For example, the U.S. Court of Appeals for the Seventh Circuit ruled that a supervisor's multiple and direct propositions for sex during a business meeting were sufficiently severe to create a hostile work environment.[19] In *Duncan v. General Motors*,[20] however, the U.S. Court of Appeals for the Eighth Circuit concluded that a male supervisor did not create a hostile work environment when he showed three-dimensional models of sexual organs and a picture of a naked woman to a female subordinate. The court stated that such action, while "boorish, chauvinistic, and decidedly immature," did not create an objectively hostile work environment where the plaintiff's employment had been altered. Similarly, in *Brooks v. San Mateo, California*,[21] the U.S. Court of Appeals for the Ninth Circuit held that a single incident in which a male coworker touched a female employee's breast and stomach while she was answering a 911 emergency call was not sufficient to establish a hostile work environment. The employee suffered no physical injury, and the employer took prompt steps to remove the male employee from the workplace. The court noted that a single incident involving a supervisor was more likely to result in employer liability for hostile environment than comparable conduct by a coworker.

In *Schmitz v. ING Securities, Futures & Options, Inc.*,[22] however, the court considered whether repeated comments made by the employer's chief financial officer to the receptionist regarding her risqué clothing constituted sexual harassment. The CFO told her that her skirts and blouses were too tight, too short, and too revealing. He called her an "exhibitionist" and once summoned her into his office to reprimand her for dressing so provocatively that any "hot-blooded male" in the office would be aroused and distracted from his work. After she complained to ING's director of human resources, her workload increased, and the CFO became openly hostile to her. Six weeks later, she was terminated for inadequate work performance. The court dismissed her claim for sexual discrimination and retaliation, and the U.S. Court of Appeals for the Seventh Circuit affirmed on the grounds that the receptionist failed to establish that she was subject to sexual advances or requests for sexual favors. The court also held that the receptionist had failed to show that her work environment was hostile or abusive. Commenting on the CFO's behavior, the court said that "[his] failings 'to treat a female employee with sensitivity, tact, and delicacy'" are "too commonplace . . . to be classified as discriminatory."[23]

A majority of the federal courts of appeals have struck down claims for hostile work environment in so-called paramour cases where coworkers have claimed that an employee has received preferential treatment by a supervisor as a result of having sexual relations with the supervisor.[24] For example, in *Ackel v. National Communications, Inc.*,[25] the plaintiff complained that she was replaced by her supervisor's paramour as a result of favoritism based on their sexual relationship. The U.S. Court of Appeals for the Fifth Circuit stated that "'courts have held that when an employer discriminates in favor of a paramour, such an

18. Faragher v. City of Boca Raton, 524 U.S. 775 (1998).
19. Quantock v. Shared Mktg. Servs., 32 F.3d 899 (7th Cir. 2002).
20. 300 F.3d 928 (8th Cir. 2002).
21. 229 F.3d 917 (9th Cir. 2000).
22. 191 F.3d 456 (7th Cir. 1999).
23. *Id.* (quoting Minor v. Ivy Tech State Coll., 174 F.3d 855, 858 (7th Cir. 1999)).
24. Riggs v. County of Banner, 159 F. Supp. 2d 1158 (D. Neb. 2001).
25. 339 F.3d 376 (5th Cir. 2003).

action is not sex-based discrimination, as the favoritism, while unfair, disadvantages both sexes alike for reasons other than gender.'"[26]

**Same-Sex Sexual Harassment** In 1988, in *Oncale v. Sundowner Offshore Services, Inc.*, the U.S. Supreme Court held that Title VII prohibits same-sex harassment; in other words, it prohibits harassment where the harasser is the same sex as the employee being harassed.[27] Acknowledging that same-sex harassment was not the evil Congress sought to remedy when it passed Title VII, the Court nevertheless saw "no justification in the statutory language or our precedents for a categorical rule excluding same-sex harassment claims from the coverage of Title VII." However, the Court was careful to explain that to be actionable, the harassment must be tied to some type of gender discrimination: it must be "discrimination because of sex." "The critical issue is whether members of one sex are exposed to disadvantageous terms or conditions of employment to which members of the other sex are not exposed." The Supreme Court called on courts and juries to use "common sense" to differentiate sex discrimination from horseplay, saying that a pat on the bottom by a football coach to a player running onto the field may not constitute sex discrimination, but similar touching of a secretary might.[28]

Applying the standard set forth in *Oncale*, the U.S. Court of Appeals for the Fifth Circuit found that obnoxious comments by a male supervisor about a male employee's sexuality, inappropriate touching of the employee's private body parts, and spitting tobacco juice on him could constitute sex discrimination if the plaintiff could show that the same-sex harasser's actions were "explicit or implicit proposals of sexual activity" and that there was "credible evidence that the harasser was homosexual."[29] Such evidence would prove that the same-sex employee would not have been harassed if he had been a member of the opposite sex.

The EEOC reported that sexual harassment charges brought by men accounted for 13.5 percent of all sexual harassment charges brought to the commission in 2003, up from 9.1 percent in 1992.[30] The vast majority of such charges involve harassment by other men.

26. *Id.* (quoting Green v. Adm'rs of the Tulane Educ. Fund, 284 F.3d 642 (5th Cir. 2002)).
27. 523 U.S. 75 (1988).
28. *Id.*
29. La Day v. Catalyst Technology, 302 F.3d 474 (5th Cir. 2002).
30. EEOC, *Sexual Harassment Charges, at* http://www.eeoc.gov/stats/harass.html (last modified Mar. 8, 2004); see also Reed Abelson, *Men Are Claiming Harassment by Men*, N.Y. TIMES, June 10, 2001, *available at* http://www.nytimes.com/2001/06/10/business/10SAME.html?pagewanted=print.

**Sexual Orientation Harassment** The *Oncale* decision did not extend Title VII protection to harassment based on a person's sexual orientation. Although legislation to amend Title VII to include sexual orientation has been introduced in every term of Congress since 1975, it has not been enacted.

As a result, lower courts have had to decide (1) whether claims are based on sex or sexual orientation and (2) whether sexual orientation claims are actionable under Title VII. In *Simonton v. Runyan*[31] the U.S. Court of Appeals for the Second Circuit held that harassment on the basis of sexual orientation is not actionable under Title VII. Dwayne Simonton sued the U.S. Postal Service for abuse and harassment he suffered because of his sexual orientation. The court noted that the abuse that Simonton allegedly incurred—which included repeated verbal assaults, notes, pornographic photographs, demeaning posters, and repeated statements that he was a "f—— faggot"—was "morally reprehensible whenever and in whatever context it occurs, particularly in the modern workplace." However, the court concluded that "[w]hen interpreting a statute, the role of a court is limited to discerning and adhering to legislative meaning. The law is well settled in this circuit . . . that Simonton has no cause of action under Title VII because Title VII does not prohibit harassment or discrimination because of sexual orientation."

In contrast, the U.S. Court of Appeals for the Ninth Circuit's broad definition of what constitutes harassment "because of sex" appears to permit claims based on sexual orientation to be brought under Title VII. In *Rene v. MGM Grand Hotel*[32] a gay male alleged that his harassers grabbed and poked at his genitals, but there was no evidence that any of his harassers had expressed any interest in engaging in sexual activity with Rene. The court found that harassment that included touching body parts was "inescapably [harassment] because of sex." The court held that an employee's sexual orientation is irrelevant for purposes of Title VII and neither provides nor precludes a cause of action for sexual harassment. "That the harasser is, or may be, motivated by hostility based on sexual orientation is similarly irrelevant. . . . It is enough that the harasser engaged in severe or pervasive unwelcome physical conduct of a sexual nature."

More recently, the U.S. Court of Appeals for the Sixth Circuit held that a self-identified transsexual could sue for sex discrimination under Title VII on the basis of discrimination due to nonstereotypical behavior and

31. 232 F.3d 33 (2d Cir. 2000).
32. 305 F.3d 1061 (9th Cir. 2002).

appearance. Smith, a biological male, was employed by the City of Salem, Ohio, as a lieutenant in the fire department. After he informed his supervisor that he had been diagnosed as a transsexual and began treatment, which involved expressing a more feminine appearance, a plan was devised to require Smith to undergo a series of psychological evaluations in the hope that he would either resign or refuse to comply and be terminated for insubordination. The court held that Title VII's protection is available for transsexuals because its prohibition against sex discrimination applies to males as well as females and Smith had sufficiently stated a claim of sexual stereotyping and sex discrimination.[33] Several courts have also allowed homosexual employees to state sexual stereotyping claims under Title VII against employers who discriminated against them because they were not "manly" enough men or "womanly" enough women.

### *Racial, National Origin, and Religious Harassment*

Similar to claims of hostile environment harassment on the basis of sex, claims of racial, national origin, or religious harassment are evaluated according to the rule in *Harris v. Forklift Systems, Inc.*[34] Courts examine the totality of the circumstances to determine whether an employee was exposed to a hostile environment. In *Bowen v. Missouri Department of Social Services,*[35] the U.S. Court of Appeals for the Eighth Circuit found that Bowen's exposure to racial epithets, such as "white bitch," coupled with physically threatening behavior by her supervisor were sufficiently severe and pervasive to constitute a racially hostile work atmosphere.

Although some courts have held that a onetime incident is not enough to create a hostile environment, the trend in both sexual harassment suits and other claims of harassment appears to be to find a hostile environment if the incident is severe enough and involves a supervisor. For example, in *Taylor v. Metzger,*[36] an African-American female county employee alleged that while she was training at a police academy firing range, her direct supervisor turned to a deputy and said, "There's the jungle bunny." The New Jersey Supreme Court identified several factors that made the incident severe enough to create actionable hostile environment discrimination under the New Jersey Law Against Discrimination (patterned after Title VII): (1) the derogatory term used by the sheriff was "patently a racial slur, and [was] ugly, stark and raw in its opprobrious connotation"; (2) the sheriff was the plaintiff's ranking supervisor, effectively closing her avenue for redress; (3) the sheriff was a chief law enforcement officer; and (4) the remark was made not only in the plaintiff's presence but in front of the deputy.

33. Smith v. City of Salem, 378 F.3d 566 (6th Cir. 2004).

## IN BRIEF

**Elements of a Sexual Harassment Claim**

Unwelcome sexual advances, requests for sexual favors, and other verbal or physical conduct of a sexual nature constitute sexual harassment when:

1. An individual's employment depends on submission to such conduct;
2. Submission to or rejection of such conduct is used as the basis of employment decisions; or
3. Such conduct unreasonably interferes with the individual's work performance or creates an intimidating, hostile, or offensive working environment.

To establish a claim of hostile environment sexual harassment under Title VII, the plaintiff must show that:

1. The harassment created an abusive working environment;
2. The harassment was based on sex; and
3. The harassment was so severe or pervasive as to alter the conditions of the victim's employment.

### *Liability for Hostile Environment*

As explained in Chapter 5, employers are vicariously liable under the doctrine of *respondeat superior* for all torts committed by employees acting within the scope of employment. As a result, if a supervisor fails to promote an employee because of his or her national origin, the employer is liable for discrimination because the supervisor was acting within the scope of employment when deciding whom to promote. But when a supervisor harasses an employee (either by demanding sexual favors or by creating a hostile environment), the supervisor is rarely acting within the scope of his or her employment.

The U.S. Supreme Court reviewed general principles of agency law to determine when an employer is liable for the creation of a hostile environment. Under Section 219(2) of the Restatement (Second) of Agency, an

34. 510 U.S. 17 (1993).
35. 311 F.3d 878 (8th Cir. 2002).
36. 706 A.2d 685 (N.J. 1998).

employer is liable for torts of employees not acting in the scope of employment if (1) the employer intended the conduct, (2) the employee's high rank makes him or her the employer's alter ego, (3) the employer was negligent, or (4) the employee was aided in accomplishing the tort by the existence of the agency relation.[37]

**Negligence** The employer is negligent with respect to harassment if it knew or should have known of the harassment but failed to stop it by taking appropriate corrective measures. This negligence standard governs hostile environment by coworkers (and probably customers with whom the employee must deal as part of his or her job). For example, in *Ferris v. Delta Air Lines,*[38] the U.S. Court of Appeals for the Second Circuit found that Delta was responsible for a sexually hostile work environment that allowed the plaintiff flight attendant to be raped by a male coworker. Delta was on notice that the male employee had previously raped three other flight attendants, yet it failed to take any action against him. The court stated that Delta had a "responsibility to warn or protect likely future victims."

37. *See* Burlington Indus. v. Ellerth, 524 U.S. 742 (1998).

38. 277 F.3d 128 (2d. Cir. 2001).

## *View from Cyberspace*

### Harassment in the Virtual Office

In December 1989, Tammy Blakey became the first female captain at Continental to fly an Airbus 300 widebody jet.[a] Soon thereafter, she began complaining to Continental about a hostile working environment, based on conduct and comments directed at her by male coworkers. Among other things, they placed pornographic photographs in her plane's cockpit and other work areas and directed vulgar gender-based comments at her. After she sued Continental for sexual discrimination in 1993, a number of Continental's male pilots posted derogatory and insulting remarks about Blakey on the Crew Members Forum, the pilots' online computer bulletin board. Although employees using the Forum, not Continental, paid the Internet service provider (CompuServe) an hourly fee to access the Forum, the Forum was an option on the Continental Airlines Home Access program, which crew members were required to access to learn their flight schedules.

In analyzing Continental's potential liability for the retaliatory comments posted on the Forum, the New Jersey Supreme Court began by stating that if a bulletin board in an airport lounge used exclusively by the pilots and crew members of an airline contained similar comments by the pilots, there would be "little doubt" that if management had notice of the messages that created a hostile environment, the airline would be liable for hostile environment harassment, if it failed to take prompt corrective action. Similarly, if senior management, pilots, and crew members frequented some nearby place where one of the crew was subjected to sexually offensive insults that continued a pattern of harassment in the workplace, then an employer with notice of the harassment "would not be entirely free to ignore it." The court then reasoned that the fact that an electronic bulletin board is located outside the workplace does not mean that the employer has no duty to correct off-site harassment by coworkers.[b] The court noted the importance of extensions of the workplace where "the relations among employees are cemented or sometimes sundered" and asked "what exactly is the outsider (whether black, Latino, or woman) to do" when the belittling conduct continues in an after-hours setting: "Keep swallowing the abuse or give up the chance to make the team?"

The court was careful to explain that employers have no duty to monitor employees' mail, given the "[g]rave privacy concerns" implicated. But, the court suggested, employers may not disregard the posting of offensive messages on company or state agency e-mail systems when the employer knows or has reason to know that this is part of a pattern of harassment that is taking place in the workplace and in settings related to the workplace. Otherwise, the employer "sends the harassed employee the message that the harassment is acceptable and that the management supports the harasser."

**a.** Blakey v. Cont'l Airlines, Inc., 751 A.2d 538 (2000).

**b.** *See, generally,* Diana J.P. McKenzie, *Information Technology Policies: Practical Protection in Cyberspace,* 3 STAN. J. L. BUS. & FIN. 84 (1997).

**Aided-in-the-Agency Relation and Supervisor Harassment** In *quid pro quo* sexual harassment cases and hostile environment cases, the employer is always vicariously liable under the aided-in-the-agency-relation standard when a supervisor takes a tangible employment action against a subordinate (such as firing, failing to promote, reassigning with significantly different responsibilities, or reducing benefits). Thus, in such cases, the employer is vicariously liable for the hostile environment created by a supervisor with immediate (or successively higher) authority over the victimized employee regardless of whether the employer knew or should have known about the supervisor's conduct.

In *Faragher v. City of Boca Raton,*[39] the U.S. Supreme Court applied the aided-in-the-agency-relation standard to a case involving the creation of a hostile environment by a supervisor who threatened to take tangible adverse employment action but did not do so. The Court acknowledged that in a sense a harassing supervisor is always assisted in his or her conduct by the supervisory relationship: "When a fellow employee harasses, the victim can walk away or tell the offender where to go, but it may be difficult to offer such responses to a supervisor" with the power to hire, fire, and set work schedules and pay raises.

Even so, the Court felt constrained by its prior holding in *Meritor* that the employer is not automatically liable for harassment by a supervisor. It also noted that the primary objective of Title VII is to avoid harm. To implement that statutory policy, the Court considered it appropriate "to recognize the employer's affirmative obligation to prevent violations and give credit here to employers who make the reasonable efforts to discharge their duty." At the same time, the Court acknowledged an employee's duty to avoid or mitigate harm. If the employee unreasonably failed to avail himself or herself of the employer's preventive or remedial apparatus, the employee should not recover damages that could have been avoided if he or she had done so.

Accordingly, the Court held that if the supervisor's harassment does not culminate in a tangible employment action, then the employer may raise an affirmative defense to liability or damages. To establish the defense, the employer must prove two things: (1) it exercised reasonable care to prevent and correct promptly any harassing behavior, and (2) the employee unreasonably failed to take advantage of any preventive or corrective opportunities provided by the employer or to avoid harm otherwise. For example, if an employer has provided a proven, effective mechanism for reporting and resolving complaints of sexual harassment that is available to the employee without undue risk or expense, then the employee's unreasonable failure to use that complaint procedure will normally suffice to satisfy the employer's burden under the second element of the defense.

In the following case, the court considered whether the employer had taken adequate steps to prevent and correct harassing behavior and was, therefore, able to establish the affirmative defense provided in *Faragher.*

39. 524 U.S. 775 (1998).

A CASE IN POINT

**CASE 13.1**

**Hill v. American General Finance, Inc.**

*United States Court of Appeals for the Seventh Circuit 218 F.3d 639 (7th Cir. 2000).*

## Summary

**› FACTS** Louise Hill worked as a lending/collection administrator in the Alton, Illinois office of American General Finance, Inc. (AGF). She was the only African American working in the office. Within a month of her arrival, her supervisor Darin Brandt started to racially and sexually harass her. For example, he said, "I like a woman with a big ass, like Louise's," and he made reference to the size of his penis. On one occasion, he rubbed his pelvis against her buttocks and said, "Boy that feels good." He also said, "Once you go black, you never go back." In addition to the sexual comments, he made offensive racial comments such as, "Don't come into this office talking black, because this ain't no Aunt Jemima office." He also told her that he was "sick of black people getting food stamps and having those black babies."

On two separate occasions, Hill wrote a letter to AGF's chief executive officer complaining about Brandt's behavior. Rather than signing her own name, she signed the letters with a pseudonym, pretending to be a customer. AGF's human resources officer conducted an investigation, including an interview with Hill. Although no other employees confirmed the harassment, some said that conversations of a sexual nature did occur in the office. Gary English, the director of operations, issued Brandt a letter warning him for allowing these conversations to occur.

*(Continued)*

(Case 13.1 *continued*)

Subsequently, Hill wrote a letter to English describing the harassment, but this time she signed her name. The company's human resources attorney and outside counsel promptly commenced an investigation and decided to issue a written warning to Brandt, provide him with additional training, transfer and demote him with a $10,000 reduction in salary, and transfer Hill to prevent retaliation from her coworkers.

Hill complained that her transfer was to a high-crime area and claimed that the company was retaliating against her. She resigned and filed a claim for sexual and racial harassment under Title VII. The district court dismissed the case after finding both that the plaintiff had failed to take advantage of her employer's policies and procedures regarding harassment and that the company had promptly taken appropriate corrective action after learning of the harassment. Hill appealed.

**› ISSUE PRESENTED** What actions constitute reasonable care by an employer to prevent and correct sexually harassing behavior?

**› SUMMARY OF OPINION** The U.S. Court of Appeals for the Seventh Circuit began by stating that a defendant employer can raise an affirmative defense to a charge of harassment by establishing that (1) the employer exercised reasonable care to prevent and correct promptly any sexually harassing behavior, and (2) the plaintiff employee unreasonably failed to take advantage of any corrective or preventive opportunities provided by the employer.

With respect to the first prong of the defense, the court found that the company took immediate corrective action after receiving Hill's letter by launching an investigation regarding the allegations. As a result of this investigation, the company punished Brandt for his conduct and transferred him so that he could no longer harass Hill.

In determining whether the company took corrective action, the court also considered whether the company had policies or procedures to help employees deal with harassment. AGF had several policies in place at the time of these incidents. It had an equal employment policy and a sexual harassment policy. In addition, the company had established a complaint procedure with four levels. Employees could report to their immediate supervisor or manager. Alternatively, the employee could speak with the field relations consultant, the associate director of employee relations and benefits, or the director of human resources and systems management. The third level of a complaint was to the fair employment practices compliance officer. Employees were provided with a phone number so that they could communicate complaints. Finally, the fourth level was the Personnel Administration Committee through the director of human resources and system management.

Although Hill claimed that she did not receive AGF's policies, the policies were kept in a set of notebooks available to the public within each branch office. In addition, Hill testified that she knew that the human resources group in the company had the responsibility to prevent sexual and racial harassment. She testified that she knew that she could talk to that group or English about any complaints she had.

The court stated that Hill's signed letter reporting Brandt's conduct was a reasonable step taken to correct the situation, but it found that she did not notify the company of the harassment until sending this letter. The two previous letters signed with false names of customers were not a reasonable form of notice.

**› RESULT** The court of appeals affirmed the lower court's decision. The adequacy of AGF's policies and procedures and Hill's failure to take reasonable steps to notify the company of the harassment established a defense against her discrimination claims.

**Personal Liability** As a general rule, the U.S. courts of appeals have ruled that a supervisor cannot be held personally liable for discrimination in violation of Title VII against a subordinate employee.[40] There are exceptions to this rule, however. The U.S. Court of Appeals for the Second Circuit has held that supervisors may be held personally liable for harassment under other federal statutes.[41] In addition, supervisors may be held personally liable under some state antidiscrimination statutes.[42]

## Duty to Accommodate Religious Beliefs

The EEOC reported in 2003 that the number of religious discrimination claims under Title VII had increased 75 percent since 1993.[43] These claims include not just refusals to hire or promote based on religious prejudice, but also allegations that employers would not give employees flexible schedules so that they could attend religious ceremonies or flexibility in workplace dress codes to accommodate clothing mandated by the employee's religion.

A growing number of these religious discrimination cases involve Christian employees who bring their religious views into the workplace.[44] In the following case, the U.S. Court of Appeals for the Seventh Circuit considered whether an employer engaged in religious discrimination when it failed to reassign an employee whose job description violated his religious beliefs.

40. *E.g.*, Little v. BP Exploration & Oil Co., 265 F.3d 357 (6th Cir. 2001).
41. Patterson v. County of Oneida, New York, 375 F.3d 206 (2d Cir. 2004).
42. Dantz v. Apple Ohio, LLC, 277 F. Supp. 2d 794 (N.D. Ohio 2003).
43. EEOC, *Religion-Based Charges, at* http://www.eeoc.gov/stats/religion.html (last modified Mar. 4, 2004).

44. Jason Hoppin, *Cubicle Postings Merited Firing*, THE RECORDER, Jan. 7, 2004, at 1.

A CASE IN POINT

### Summary

**CASE 13.2**
**Endres v. Indiana State Police**
*United States Court of Appeals for the Seventh Circuit*
*349 F.3d 922 (7th Cir. 2003).*

**› FACTS** Endres was an officer in the Indiana State Police. Soon after Indiana began licensing casinos, Endres was assigned by lottery to a full-time position as a Gaming Commission agent at the Blue Chip Casino in Michigan City, Indiana. Gaming Commission agents certify gambling revenue, investigate complaints from the public about the gaming system, and conduct licensing investigations for the casinos and their employees. Endres, a Baptist, believed that he must neither gamble nor help others to do so because games of chance are sinful.

Endres told the State Police that he was willing to enforce general vice laws at casinos, but that providing the specialized services required of Gaming Commission agents would violate his religious beliefs because it would facilitate gambling. When the State Police refused his request for a different assignment, Endres refused to report for duty and was fired for insubordination.

Endres sued under Title VII, contending that the State of Indiana had discriminated against him on account of his religion by failing to reasonably accommodate his religious beliefs. The district court denied Indiana's motion to dismiss, and the State appealed. The U.S. Court of Appeals for the Seventh Circuit ruled for the State, and Endres moved for a rehearing en banc.

**› ISSUE** Is the State of Indiana required to reassign an employee who objects to working as a Gaming Commission agent on the basis that facilitating gambling violates his religious beliefs?

**› SUMMARY OF OPINION** The court began by stating that Section 701(j) of Title VII requires an employer to offer reasonable accommodations for an employee's religious beliefs unless doing so would cause "undue hardship on the conduct of the employer's business." Though Endres contended that Section 701(j) should give law enforcement

*(Continued)*

(Case 13.2 *continued*)

personnel a right to choose which laws they enforce and whom they will protect from crime, the court concluded that this argument was not practical:

> Many officers have religious scruples about particular activities: to give just a few examples, Baptists oppose liquor as well as gambling, Roman Catholics oppose abortion, Jews and Muslims oppose the consumption of pork, and a few faiths include hallucinogenic drugs in their worship and thus oppose legal prohibitions on these drugs. If Endres is right, all of these faiths . . . must be accommodated by assigning believers to duties compatible with their principles. Does Section 701(j) require the State Police to assign Unitarians to guard the abortion clinic, Catholics to prevent thefts from liquor stores, and Baptists to investigate claims that supermarkets misweigh bacon and shellfish? Must prostitutes be left exposed to slavery or murder at the hands of pimps because protecting them from crime would encourage them to ply their trade and thus offend almost every religious faith?

The court stated that juggling law enforcement assignments to make each compatible with the varying religious beliefs of a heterogeneous police force would be daunting to managers and difficult for other officers who would be called on to fill in for the objector. Even if it were possible to swap assignments on one occasion, another could arise when personnel were not available to cover for selective objectors, or when seniority systems or limits on overtime curtailed the options for shuffling personnel.

The court held that Title VII did not require the State Police to make an accommodation for Endres, stating that "Endres has made a demand that . . . would be unreasonable to require any police or fire department to tolerate."

**› RESULT** The court denied Endres's motion to rehear the case en banc, reversed the district court's decision, and remanded the case with instructions to enter judgment on the merits for the Indiana State Police.

## RETALIATION

Title VII states that it is unlawful for any employer to retaliate against an employee for complaining to the employer or the EEOC about discrimination banned by Title VII. To prove a case of retaliation, an employee must demonstrate that (1) the employee's activity was protected by Title VII; (2) the employer knew of the employee's exercise of protected rights; (3) the employer took some adverse employment action against the employee, or the employee was subjected to severe or pervasive retaliatory harassment by a supervisor; and (4) there was a causal connection between the protected activity and the adverse employment action or harassment. Generally, plaintiffs file a retaliation claim in conjunction with an underlying claim of discrimination. To succeed on a claim for retaliation, however, a plaintiff does not need to prevail on his or her Title VII discrimination claim.[45]

45. Fine v. Ryan Int'l Airlines, 305 F.3d 746 (7th Cir. 2002).

In *Fine v. Ryan International Airlines*,[46] the U.S. Court of Appeals for the Seventh Circuit found that Ryan retaliated against Fine by firing her a day after she submitted a letter outlining her multiple experiences of sexual discrimination at the company. In reaching its decision, the court noted that Ryan claimed Fine was fired because she "routinely missed work and was always hard to get along with." The court found that there were no written complaints about either Fine's attendance or her interpersonal skills in her personnel file, and thus Fine had adequately demonstrated that her dismissal was a retaliatory act by Ryan.

In contrast, in *Hill v. Lockheed Martin*,[47] Ethel Hill, an airline mechanic, was unable to prove that her employer terminated her in retaliation for reporting that Lockheed's safety inspector, Ed Fultz, often called her a "useless old lady" who needed to be retired. Hill claimed

46. *Id.*
47. Hill v. Lockheed Martin Logistics Mgmt., Inc., 354 F.3d 277 (4th Cir. 2004).

that after she complained about Fultz's comments, Fultz issued Hill several safety violations. The court found that although reporting evidence of discriminatory conduct is a protected activity, Hill's evidence was insufficient to establish a retaliation claim. Fultz held no disciplinary authority over Hill and he was neither the actual decision maker nor otherwise principally responsible for the decision to terminate Hill, which Lockheed claimed was predicated on Hill's shoddy performance.

Actions allegedly taken to prevent further harassment may be deemed a retaliation under Title VII if they harm the employee's employment situation. For example, in *White v. Burlington Northern & Santa Fe Railway Co.*,[48] the U.S. Court of Appeals for the Sixth Circuit found that transferring an employee from a forklift operator to a track laborer was an adverse employment action because the track laborer position, though involving equal pay, was more arduous than the forklift operator position, which was considered prestigious. Similarly, in *DiIenno v. Goodwill Industries of Mid-Eastern Pennsylvania*,[49] the Third Circuit found that transferring an employee to a job that the employer knew she could not perform was retaliation for her complaint that her manager was sexually harassing her. The plaintiff was transferred from her job of tagging and pricing clothing to a job requiring her to sort through clothes contributed to Goodwill. The employee's phobia of "critters," such as mice, insects, and bugs found in these bags of clothing, prevented her from performing the job. The court explained that "[i]t is important to take a plaintiff's job-related attributes into account when determining whether a lateral transfer was an adverse employment action."

In 1997, the U.S. Supreme Court unanimously ruled that both current and former employees can sue for retaliation. The case involved an employer who allegedly gave a former employee a negative reference because he had filed a claim of racial discrimination against the company.[50] In addition, the U.S. Court of Appeals for the Second Circuit has held that even involuntary participation in Title VII proceedings by an employee accused of sexual harassment qualifies as protected activity. As a result, it found that it would violate Title VII for an employer to retaliate against an employee who had successfully defended himself against harassment charges.[51]

48. 364 F.3d 789 (6th Cir. 2004).
49. 162 F.3d 235 (3d Cir. 1998).
50. Robinson v. Shell Oil Co., 519 U.S. 377 (1997).
51. Deravin v. Kerik, 335 F.3d 195 (2d Cir. 2003).

## Special Applications of Title VII

Civil rights legislation was founded on the fundamental premise that people should not be denied a job or an opportunity on the job because of their race, color, religion, national origin, or sex. The law has expanded beyond that basic premise to reach more subtle forms of discrimination.

### *Pregnancy Discrimination*

The Pregnancy Discrimination Act provides that discrimination on the basis of pregnancy is, on its face, a form of sex discrimination under Title VII.[52] For example, employers must provide the same compensation for disabilities related to pregnancy and childbirth as they provide for any other disability. Many states have enacted similar laws, and, as in other areas of discrimination law, these state laws provide greater protection than required under federal law.

These protections are not absolute, however. The U.S. Court of Appeals for the First Circuit, for example, ruled that an employer could discharge a manager who was on maternity leave when it realized that the company could function effectively without her.[53] The court reasoned that discharge is an ordinary risk of employment, whether or not one is pregnant, and it ruled that the employer had demonstrated that it would have eliminated her position regardless of her pregnancy. Likewise, the U.S. Court of Appeals for the Fifth Circuit held that an employer with a strict probationary attendance policy, which provided that any employee who was absent more than three days within the first ninety days of employment would be terminated, was not liable for pregnancy discrimination when it terminated a probationary employee who was absent for more than two weeks due to a miscarriage.[54] The court stated that the Pregnancy Discrimination Act does not require employers to treat pregnancy-related absences more leniently than other absences.

### *Fetal-Protection Policies*

Certain substances used in manufacturing are harmful to the fetus being carried by a pregnant woman. In an effort to avoid such harm, and related lawsuits for unsafe working environments, some companies adopted so-called fetal-protection policies. A *fetal-protection policy* bars a woman from certain jobs unless her inability to

52. 42 U.S.C. § 2000e(k).
53. Smith v. F.W. Morse & Co., 76 F.3d 413 (1st Cir. 1996); *accord* Rhett v. Carnegie Ctr. Assoc., 129 F.3d 290 (3d Cir. 1997).
54. Stout v. Baxter Healthcare Corp., 282 F.3d 856 (5th Cir. 2002).

bear children is medically documented. In *Automobile Workers v. Johnson Controls, Inc.*,[55] the Supreme Court struck down Johnson Controls' policy, which precluded women with childbearing capacity from working at jobs in which lead levels were defined as excessive.

The Court held that the fetal-protection policy was a facially discriminatory policy forbidden under Title VII and that women cannot be excluded from certain jobs because of their childbearing capacity. The Court stated that "[d]ecisions about the welfare of future children must be left to the parents who conceive, bear, support, and raise them rather than to the employers who hire those parents." The Court went on to say that "[i]t is no more appropriate for the courts than it is for individual employers to decide whether a woman's reproductive role is more important to herself and her family than her economic role."

In the wake of *Johnson Controls,* employers have been forced to walk a fine line between avoiding discrimination related to pregnancy and limiting or reducing potential workplace hazards. For example, in *Asad v. Continental Airlines,*[56] Asad sued Continental under state tort laws claiming that Continental was responsible for her newborn son's cerebral palsy. Asad had requested a job transfer for the duration of her pregnancy to escape exposure to carbon monoxide fumes. Continental refused the transfer, citing *Johnson Controls* and other cases holding that the Pregnancy Discrimination Act does not require employers to "accommodate" pregnant women.[57] The U.S. District Court for the Northern District of Ohio acknowledged the confusion caused by *Johnson Controls.*

> For the employer, the question involves whether compliance with the mandates of the Pregnancy Discrimination Act could potentially subject them to liability for fetal injuries. Pregnant women, on the other hand, face the uncertainty of their legal rights in a potentially hazardous workplace and the legal rights of their children who turn out to be born with injuries allegedly caused, at least in part, by employer negligence.

The court deviated from prior court rulings when it held that although *Johnson Controls* demonstrated that employers could not prevent women who are or who may become pregnant from working in an environment that may be hazardous to a fetus, "the PDA and Title VII should not prevent an employer from temporarily transferring a pregnant woman, at her request, for the protection of her fetus."

### *English-Only Laws*

The national origin provisions of Title VII have been used to challenge workplace rules that prohibit employees from speaking any language other than English at work. The EEOC has taken the position that language is closely linked with national origin, so English-only policies can have a disparate impact on Hispanic employees and others whose native language may not be English.[58] Federal courts have agreed with the EEOC. For example, in 2000, a federal court in Texas ruled that an employer's English-only policy barred Hispanic workers from speaking the language in which they were best able to communicate, causing them to face a disproportionate risk of termination for violating the policy.[59] The court concluded:

> [P]rohibiting employees at all times, in the workplace, from speaking their primary language or the language they speak most comfortably, disadvantages an individual's employment opportunities on the basis of national origin. It may also create an atmosphere of inferiority, isolation and intimidation based on national origin which could result in a discriminatory working environment.

### *Dress Codes*

Although employers have the right to enact and enforce dress codes, they can result in legal claims involving religious and sexual discrimination and harassment. The trend by employers to allow employees to wear casual clothing has the potential to further complicate this matter.

Employees have based claims of religious discrimination on their employer's refusal to let them wear turbans rather than protective headgear. In response, the Occupational Health and Safety Administration amended its regulations to exempt persons wearing turbans from its hard-hat requirements.

## DEFENSES UNDER TITLE VII

Title VII sets forth several statutory defenses to claims of discriminatory treatment. Of these defenses, the one most frequently cited is the defense of bona fide occupational qualification.

55. 499 U.S. 187 (1991).
56. 328 F. Supp. 2d 772 (N.D. Ohio 2004).
57. *See Johnson Controls,* 499 U.S. 187; Spivey v. Beverly Enters., Inc., 196 F.3d 1309 (11th Cir. 1999); Armstrong v. Flowers, 33 F.3d 1308 (11th Cir. 1994); Duncan v. Children's Nat'l Med. Ctr., 702 A.2d 207 (D.C. 1997).

58. *At Panel Discussion on National Origin Bias EEOC Says English-Only Challenges Are Rising,* 66 U.S.L.W. 2375 (Dec. 23, 1997).
59. EEOC v. Premier Operator Servs., Inc., 113 F. Supp. 2d 1066 (N.D. Tex. 2000).

### Bona Fide Occupational Qualification

Title VII provides that an employer may lawfully hire an individual on the basis of religion, sex, or national origin if religion, sex, or national origin is a *bona fide occupational qualification (BFOQ)* reasonably necessary to the normal operation of that particular business. This is known as the *BFOQ defense*. The BFOQ defense is not available when discriminatory treatment is based on a person's race or color. Because BFOQ is an affirmative defense, the employer has the burden of showing a reasonable basis for believing that the category of persons (for example, women) excluded from a particular job was unable to perform that job.

The BFOQ defense has been narrowly construed. EEOC regulations provide that gender will not qualify as a BFOQ where a gender-based restriction is based on (1) assumptions of the comparative employment characteristics of women in general (such as the assumption that women have a higher turnover rate than men); (2) stereotyped characterizations of the sexes (for example, that men are less capable of assembling intricate equipment than women); or (3) the preferences of coworkers, employers, or customers for one gender or the other.[60] Gender will be considered a BFOQ when physical attributes are important for authenticity (as with actors) or when a gender-based restriction is necessary to protect the rights of others to privacy (as with restroom attendants).

### Seniority and Merit Systems

Title VII states that it is not unlawful for employers to apply different standards of compensation, or different terms, conditions, or privileges of employment pursuant to a bona fide seniority or merit system, provided that such differences are not the result of an intention to discriminate because of race, color, religion, sex, or national origin. This is considered an exemption from Title VII rather than an affirmative defense. Consequently, the plaintiff has the burden of proving the employer had a discriminatory intent or illegal purpose in implementing the seniority or merit system. Moreover, although a disproportionate impact may be used as evidence of discriminatory intent, such an impact is not, in itself, sufficient to establish discriminatory intent.

### After-Acquired Evidence

When an employee initiates a suit under Title VII, sometimes over the course of discovery the employer will learn that the individual violated company rules. Under these circumstances, employers have argued that the plaintiff's discrimination claim should fail because, had the employer known of the employee misconduct, the employee would have been discharged anyway.

In *McKennon v. Nashville Banner Publishing Co.*,[61] the U.S. Supreme Court held that after-acquired evidence of misconduct does not bar a discrimination claim. But the employee misconduct is not ignored: remedies available to plaintiffs in cases involving misconduct should be limited to back pay and should not include reinstatement or front pay.

## Remedies Under Title VII

Remedies available under Title VII include compensation for lost salary and benefits ("back pay"), reinstatement or "front pay" equal to what the employee would have received had he or she not been discharged, and injunctive relief to stop prohibited discriminatory actions. Front pay is generally awarded when reinstatement is inappropriate because the position is unavailable or hostility raises a practical barrier.

The plaintiff may also recover compensatory damages for future pecuniary losses, emotional pain and suffering, inconvenience, mental anguish, loss of enjoyment of life, and other nonpecuniary losses. While front pay is limited in duration because it compensates for the immediate effects of discrimination, lost future earnings compensate an employee for a lifetime of diminished earnings resulting from the reputational harm suffered as a result of discrimination. Therefore, an employee may be awarded both front pay and damages for lost future earnings.[62]

### Punitive Damages

In *Kolstad v. American Dental Ass'n*,[63] the Supreme Court considered the circumstances under which punitive damages may be awarded under Title VII. The Court began by noting that punitive damages awards are available only in cases of "intentional discrimination," that is, cases that do not rely on the disparate impact theory of discrimination. To recover punitive damages, the complaining party must demonstrate that the employer engaged in a discriminatory practice or practices *with malice or with reckless indifference to the federally protected rights of an aggrieved individual.* (Punitive damages are not available in suits against a government, governmental agency, or political subdivision.) To prevail in obtaining punitive damages, the employee is not required to show

60. 29 C.F.R. pts. 1604.2(a)(1)(i)–1604.2(a)(1)(iii).

61. 513 U.S. 352 (1995).

62. Williams v. Pharmacia, Inc., 137 F.3d 944 (7th Cir. 1998).

63. 527 U.S. 526 (1999).

that the employer engaged in egregious misconduct. Rather, the employee must show that the employer had the requisite discriminatory mental state. Punitive damages are also available and can be awarded even if the jury awarded no compensatory damages.[64]

Even if the employee can show the requisite malice or indifference, the employer may still not be liable for punitive damages. The Court held that if the employer has engaged in "good-faith efforts" to comply with Title VII, then it is not vicariously liable for punitive damages based on discriminatory employment decisions by managerial agents when those decisions are contrary to those good faith efforts. To hold otherwise, the Court reasoned, would reduce the incentive for employers to implement antidiscrimination programs.

In *EEOC v. Wal-Mart Stores, Inc.*,[65] the U.S. Court of Appeals for the Tenth Circuit held that Wal-Mart's written antidiscrimination policy was not sufficient to establish a "good faith" defense preventing an award of punitive damages for discriminatory conduct prohibited under the Americans with Disabilities Act. The appeals court highlighted the language in *Kolstad* requiring employers both to adopt antidiscrimination policies and to educate employees on federal discrimination laws. Although Wal-Mart did establish a written policy, it did not "demonstrate an implemented good faith policy of educating employees on the Act's accommodation and nondiscrimination requirements."

### *Caps on Liability*

The compensatory and punitive damages available for discrimination based on sex or religion are capped by the Civil Rights Act of 1991 at $50,000 for employers of 100 or fewer employees, $100,000 for employers with 101 to 200 employees, $200,000 for employers with 201 to 500 employees, and $300,000 for employers with more than 500 employees.[66] However, the compensatory caps do not apply to intentional racial or ethnic discrimination. In addition, the Supreme Court has stated that front pay is not considered compensatory damages and thus is not subject to the cap on compensatory awards.[67]

64. Timm v. Progressive Steel Treating, Inc., 137 F.3d 1008 (7th Cir. 1998); Cush-Crawford v. Adchem Corp., 271 F.3d 352 (2d Cir. 2001); Corti v. Storage Tech. Corp., 304 F.3d 336 (4th Cir. 2002).
65. 187 F.3d 1241 (10th Cir. 1999).
66. Civil Rights Act of 1991, Pub. L. 102–106, § 1977(a)(b)(3), 105 Stat. 1071 (1991).
67. Pollard v. E.I. du Pont de Nemours & Co., 532 U.S. 843 (2001). *But see* Peyton v. diMario, 287 F.3d 1121 (D.C. Cir. 2002) (stating that awards of front pay may be considered too speculative, and thus reduced, if the length of time for which the front pay was awarded is considered too great).

Courts may also decide to limit the amount of compensatory damages awarded a plaintiff. For example, the Supreme Court of Michigan threw out a $21 million jury award to a sexual harassment plaintiff on the basis that it was excessive.[68] Employees claiming discrimination frequently sue under state employment-discrimination laws, which often do not include caps on damages.

## Age Discrimination

As the baby boomers, who comprise a substantial percentage of the American workforce, grow older, the issue of age discrimination in employment has become more visible. In fact, the number of workers above the age of fifty-five is expected to grow by more than 10.2 million by 2012, making this the fastest-growing age group in the workforce.[69] The Age Discrimination in Employment Act (ADEA) prohibits age discrimination in employment with respect to individuals aged forty years or older. Individuals under age forty have no protection from discrimination based on age. Courts have held that the employer, not the individual making the discriminatory decision, is liable for age discrimination.[70]

The substantive provisions of the ADEA are similar to those of Title VII. The ADEA generally prohibits age discrimination with respect to employee hiring, firing, and compensation, as well as with respect to the terms, conditions, and privileges of employment. As with Title VII, creation of a hostile environment because of age is a form of age discrimination.[71] The ADEA also prohibits retaliation against an individual aged forty or older because of the individual's opposition to unlawful age discrimination or because he or she has made a charge or testified or assisted in an investigation, proceeding, or litigation under the ADEA.

Although the ADEA protects individuals over the age of forty, a unanimous Supreme Court explained in *O'Connor v. Consolidated Coin Caterers Corp.*[72] that age discrimination cannot be inferred simply because the replacement employee is outside the protected class. In other words, replacing a 40-year-old employee with a 39-year-old employee does not give rise to a stronger infer-

68. Gilbert v. DaimlerChrysler, 685 N.W.2d 391 (Mich. 2004).
69. William C. Martucci & Carrie A. McAtee, *Is "Overqualified" a Pretext for Age Discrimination?*, NAT'L L.J., Sept. 20, 2004, at S3.
70. Stults v. Conoco, Inc., 76 F.3d 651 (5th Cir. 1996).
71. Crawford v. Medina Gen. Hosp., 96 F.3d 830 (6th Cir. 1996) (finding the hostile work environment claim a "relatively uncontroversial proposition").
72. 517 U.S. 308 (1996).

ence of discrimination than replacing a 52-year-old employee with a 40-year-old employee. Rather, "the fact that a replacement is substantially younger than the plaintiff is a far more reliable indicator of age discrimination."

Even so, the ADEA prohibits unlawful age discrimination among persons within the protected age group. Thus, for example, if two individuals aged 41 and 53 apply for the same position, the employer may not lawfully reject either applicant on the basis of age. On the other hand, an employer may still have engaged in age discrimination against the 53-year-old individual if it hires the 41-year-old applicant.

However, the U.S. Supreme Court has held that the ADEA does not protect younger workers over forty against older workers. In *General Dynamics Land Systems, Inc. v. Cline*,[73] a collective bargaining agreement between Land Systems and a union eliminated the company's obligation to provide health benefits to subsequently retired employees, except for then-current workers who were at least fifty years old. Employees who were at least forty and therefore protected under the ADEA, but under fifty, filed a complaint claiming that the agreement violated the ADEA because it discriminated against them because of their age. The district court dismissed the action, calling the claim one of "reverse age discrimination" on which no court had ever granted relief. The U.S. Court of Appeals for the Sixth Circuit reversed, but the Supreme Court held that "[w]e see the text, structure, purpose and history of the ADEA, along with its relationship to other federal statutes, as showing that the statute does not mean to stop an employer from favoring an older employee over a younger one."

To establish a *prima facie* case of age discrimination under the ADEA, the employee must prove that he or she (1) was within the protected age group, (2) was qualified for the position at issue, (3) suffered an adverse employment action, and (4) was replaced by a sufficiently younger person.[74]

In *Reeves v. Sanderson Plumbing Products, Inc.*,[75] the Supreme Court established that a finding of liability for intentional discrimination under the ADEA could be based solely on the plaintiff's *prima facie* case of discrimination together with sufficient evidence for a reasonable fact finder to reject the employer's nondiscriminatory explanation for its decision. In *Reeves,* a fifty-seven-year-old worker established a *prima facie* case and offered evidence showing that he had properly maintained attendance records to dispute the employer's claim that he was fired for failing to discipline late and absent employees due to shoddy record keeping. Reeves also introduced evidence that the supervisor responsible for his firing was motivated by age-based animus. The supervisor told Reeves that he was old enough to have come over on the *Mayflower* and said that he was just "too damn old" for the job. The Court found that this was sufficient evidence for the jury to conclude that the employer had intentionally discriminated and reinstated the jury verdict in favor of Reeves.

*"Do you think now that we're doing fewer illegal things we can scale back the legal department?"*



In contrast, the U.S. Court of Appeals for the First Circuit held that Ramon Suarez, the fifty-nine-year-old president of CaribAd (a subsidiary of Pueblo International), was not constructively discharged based on age when Pueblo was restructured and most of CaribAd's employees were relocated to corporate headquarters, leaving Suarez alone in an office with a receptionist.[76] Although Suarez was told that the in-house advertising for which he had been responsible was being transferred to someone else and that he would be responsible for bringing in new clients, he maintained his position as president and continued to be paid his salary of $190,000 a year. The court stated that "[i]n that rarified financial atmosphere . . . an increase in work

73. 124 S. Ct. 1236 (2004).
74. Anderson v. Consol. Rail Corp., 297 F.3d 242 (3d Cir. 2002).
75. 530 U.S. 133 (2000).
76. Suarez v. Pueblo Int'l, Inc., 229 F.3d 49 (1st Cir. 2000).

requirements that does not surpass reasonable expectations" cannot sustain a constructive discharge claim. Even if Pueblo was attempting to marginalize Suarez, the "unpleasantness, hurt feelings, and wounded pride" that resulted did not create working conditions that were "so onerous, abusive or unpleasant that a reasonable person in the employee's position would have felt compelled to resign." In short, the ADEA does not guarantee workplaces "free from the ordinary ebb and flow of power relations and inter-office politics."

In *Smith v. City of Jackson, Mississippi*,[77] the U.S. Supreme Court held that employer actions which on their face do not discriminate based on age may still violate the ADEA if they have a statistically significant impact on workers over forty. Nonetheless, the Court held that the scope of disparate-impact liability under the ADEA is narrower than under Title VII. Recognizing that "age, unlike race or other classifications protected by Title VII, not uncommonly has relevance to an individual's capacity to engage in certain types of employment," the Court ruled that employees must identify the specific test, requirement, or practice that is responsible for any observed statistical disparities. It is not enough to point to a generalized policy that leads to such an impact.[78] Moreover, even if the employee identifies the relevant practice, the employer has a defense if the employer bases its discussion on a "reasonable factor other than age" (the *RFOA defense*). The employer is not required to show business necessity.

## Older Workers' Benefit Protection Act

The Older Workers' Benefit Protection Act[79] (OWBPA) prohibits age discrimination in providing employee benefits. It also establishes minimum standards for employees who waive their rights under the ADEA.

To meet the minimum standards, the waiver must be "knowing and voluntary." The employee must be given at least twenty-one days to consider whether to enter into an agreement waiving rights under the ADEA. This period is extended to forty-five days when the waiver is in connection with an early retirement or exit-incentive plan offered to a group or class of employees. The agreement must also give the employee a period of at least seven days following execution of the agreement during which the employee may revoke it. An employee who has accepted a severance payment in exchange for waiving his or her rights under the ADEA can still sue the employer for violation of the ADEA without having to return the payment if the waiver was not made in accordance with the OWBPA.[80]

Employers may revoke a proposed early retirement agreement during the time frame that the OWBPA gives employees to act on it. For example, in *Ellison v. Premier Salons International, Inc.*,[81] the Eighth Circuit held that an employer could revoke a separation agreement containing a waiver of claims under the ADEA and provide a new, less valuable agreement, after learning that the employee had made defamatory statements about the company.

## Defenses

An employer faced with an age discrimination claim may assert in its defense that (1) age is a BFOQ reasonably necessary to the normal operation of the business (extremely difficult to prove); (2) the differential treatment is based on reasonable factors other than age; (3) the employer's action is based on a bona fide seniority system or employee benefit plan—such as a retirement, pension, or insurance plan—that is not invoked as a subterfuge to evade the purposes of the ADEA; or (4) the discharge or discipline of a protected individual was for good cause.[82] Although these defenses are set forth in the ADEA itself, employers should proceed with caution because the courts construe them strictly.

## Remedies Under the ADEA

Employees who bring successful claims under the ADEA are entitled to both equitable relief, which includes hiring, wage adjustments, promotion, or reinstatement, and monetary relief.[83] Monetary remedies include back pay, front pay, and liquidated damages. Back pay consists of wages, salary, and fringe benefits the employee would have earned during the period of discrimination. Front pay is awarded to restore employees to their "rightful place" and compensates the employees for anticipated future losses. Liquidated damages equal to the amounts owing to a person as a result of the violation are provided only in the event of willful violations by the employer. Compensatory damages and punitive damages are available under the ADEA.

77. 125 S. Ct. 1536 (2005).
78. This is the standard of proof the Supreme Court had imposed in *Wards Cove Packing Co. v. Atonio*, 490 U.S. 642 (1986), for disparate-impact cases under Title VII before Congress expanded the coverage of Title VII in the Civil Rights Act of 1991 (§ 2, 105 Stat. 1071 (1991).
79. 29 U.S.C. § 623(f) (1994).
80. Oubre v. Entergy Operations, Inc., 522 U.S. 422 (1998).
81. 164 F.3d 1111 (8th Cir. 1999).
82. 29 U.S.C. § 623(f) (1998).
83. EEOC, *When a Charge Is Filed Against My Company, at* http://www.eeoc.gov/employers/chargesfiled.html#if%20my%20company (last modified Dec. 17, 2001).

# Disability Discrimination

Title I of the Americans with Disabilities Act (ADA) prohibits employers from discriminating against a qualified individual because of a disability in regard to job-application procedures, hiring, advancement, discharge, compensation, job training, and other terms, conditions, and privileges of employment. Such discrimination includes the use of selection criteria to screen out individuals with disabilities unless the criteria are job related and consistent with business necessity. The employer may not exclude a disabled individual if that individual, with some "reasonable accommodation," could perform the essential functions of the position, unless the accommodation would impose an "undue hardship" upon the employer. The EEOC has indicated that employers may ask preemployment questions about reasonable accommodations but are barred from asking about disabilities.[84]

The employee must be able to attend work to be considered a "qualified individual" within the meaning of the ADA. In *Corder v. Lucent Technologies*,[85] the court found that an employee diagnosed with depression who was unable to attend work could not qualify for protection under the ADA.

The ADA also extends to employee benefit packages. In March 2000, however, the U.S. Court of Appeals for the Second Circuit agreed with six other federal circuits in holding that the ADA does not bar employers from providing less coverage for mental and emotional disabilities than for physical disabilities under long-term disability plans.[86] The court reasoned that "[s]o long as every employee is offered the same plan regardless of that employee's contemporary or future disability status, then no discrimination has occurred even if the plan offers different coverage for various disabilities."

## Impermissible Discrimination

Under the ADA, employers are prohibited from intentionally discriminating against disabled persons and from engaging in employment practices that are not intentionally discriminatory, but have the effect of discriminating against disabled persons or perpetuating the past effects of such discrimination. The term "discriminate" as construed by the ADA includes the following prohibited practices:

1. Limiting, segregating, or classifying an applicant or employee because of his or her disability so as to adversely affect his or her opportunities or status.
2. Entering into a contractual relationship with an employment or referral agency, union, or other organization that has the effect of subjecting employees or applicants with a disability to prohibited discrimination.
3. Utilizing standards, criteria, or methods of administration that have the effect of discriminating or perpetuating the effects of discrimination because of disability.
4. Denying equal job benefits to a qualified individual because of the known disability of a person with whom the qualified individual is known to have a relationship or association.
5. Not making reasonable accommodations to the known physical or mental limitations of an otherwise qualified employee or applicant with a disability unless to do so would impose undue hardship on the employer.
6. Denying job opportunities to an otherwise qualified employee or applicant with a disability in order to avoid having to make reasonable accommodations for that disability.
7. Using qualification standards or employment tests that tend to screen out individuals with disabilities, unless the qualification standards or employment tests are shown to be job related and are consistent with business necessity.
8. Failing to select and conduct job testing in such a way as to ensure that when the test is administered to an applicant or employee with a disability that impairs his or her sensory, manual, or speaking skills, the results of the test accurately reflect the skills or aptitude that test is designed to measure, rather than reflecting the sensory, manual, or speaking impairment.

Recently, the U.S. Courts of Appeals for the Fourth, Fifth, and Eighth Circuits have determined that employees can bring a claim for a hostile work environment under the ADA.[87]

## Definition of Disability

The ADA codifies existing law developed under the Vocational Rehabilitation Act of 1973 by defining a "person with a disability" as (1) a person with a physical

84. Asra Q. Nomani, *EEOC Eases Question Limits for Disabled*, WALL ST. J., Oct. 11, 1995, at A5.
85. 162 F.3d 924 (7th Cir. 1998).
86. EEOC v. Staten Island Sav. Bank, 207 F.3d 144 (2d Cir. 2000).

87. Fox v. Gen. Motors, 247 F.3d 169 (4th Cir. 2001); Flowers v. S. Reg'l Physician Servs., Inc., 247 F.3d 229 (5th Cir. 2001); Shaver v. Indep. Stave Co., 350 F.3d 716 (8th Cir. 2003).

or mental impairment that substantially limits one or more of that person's major life activities, (2) a person with a record of a physical or mental impairment that substantially limits one or more of that person's major life activities, or (3) a person who is regarded as having such an impairment.

## *Physical or Mental Impairment*

The first and second prongs of the ADA's definition of a disability focus on whether the individual has, or has a record of, a disability. The individual must have a physical or mental impairment. The Code of Federal Regulations defines a physical or mental impairment as:

> Any physiological disorder, or condition, cosmetic disfigurement, or anatomical loss affecting one or more of the following body systems: neurological, musculoskeletal, special sense organs, respiratory (including speech organs), cardiovascular, reproductive, digestive, genito-urinary, hemic and lymphatic, skin, and endocrine; or [a]ny mental or psychological disorder, such as mental retardation, organic brain syndrome, emotional or mental illness, and specific learning disabilities.[88]

Neither the ADA nor the Code of Federal Regulations lists all of the diseases or conditions that qualify as a "physical or mental" impairment. The ADA states generally, however, that an impairment is a physiological or mental disorder.[89] As a result, physical characteristics, such as skin color, weight, or height within the normal range, are not physical impairments, and personality traits like rudeness, irresponsible behavior, or a short temper are not themselves impairments either. In addition, environmental, cultural, or economic disadvantages, such as lack of education or a prison record, are not impairments. For example, a person who cannot read due to dyslexia, which is a learning disability, has an impairment and is thus disabled. In contrast, a person who cannot read because he or she did not go to school does not have a disability because failure to attend school is not an impairment.

**Substantially Limits a Major Life Activity** An impairment is a disability under the ADA only if it causes the individual to be unable to perform, or to be significantly limited in the ability to perform, an activity compared to an average person in the general population. Courts will consider the impairment's nature and severity, how long it will last or is expected to last, and its expected impact.[90]

A major life activity is one that an average person can perform with little or no difficulty. For example, the U.S. Supreme Court resolved a split in the circuits when it ruled in *Bragdon v. Abbott*[91] that reproduction is a major life activity. The Ninth Circuit ruled that an employee who took medication for an anxiety disorder that made him drowsy and sexually impotent was entitled to relief under the ADA on the grounds that sleeping, engaging in sexual relations, and interacting with others were major life activities.[92] In contrast, in *Furnish v. SVI Systems,*[93] the U.S. Court of Appeals for the Seventh Circuit held that an employee with cirrhosis of the liver caused by chronic hepatitis B had no claim under the ADA because lack of a fully functioning liver did not limit the ability to perform a "major life activity." Likewise, in *Pack v. Kmart Corp.,*[94] the U.S. Court of Appeals for the Tenth Circuit held that although a pharmacy technician's depression was a mental impairment that limited her ability to concentrate at work, concentration was not a "major life activity" under the ADA.

The U.S. Courts of Appeals for the Seventh, Eighth, and Ninth Circuits recently held that eating is considered a major life activity because it is integral to daily existence.[95] The U.S. Court of Appeals for the Seventh Circuit found that severe diabetes substantially limited an employee's major life activity of eating because he was required to perpetually and constantly monitor his food and sugar intake to avoid "debilitating, and potentially life-threatening, symptoms."[96]

In *Toyota Motor Manufacturing, Kentucky, Inc. v. Williams,*[97] an employee who claimed that she was unable to perform her automobile assembly-line job because she was disabled due to carpal tunnel syndrome and related impairments sued Toyota for failing to provide her with a reasonable accommodation as required by the ADA. The district court granted Toyota's motion for summary judgment, holding that the employee's impairment did not qualify as a "disability" under the

88. 29 C.F.R. pt. 1630.2.
89. ADA & IT Technical Assistance Centers, *What Is the ADA: Definition of Disability* (2004), *at* http://www.adata.org/whatsada-definition.html.

90. *Id.*
91. 524 U.S. 624 (1998).
92. McAlindin v. County of San Diego, 192 F.3d 1226 (9th Cir. 1999).
93. 270 F.3d 445 (7th Cir. 2001).
94. 166 F.3d 1300 (10th Cir. 1999).
95. *See* Lawson v. CSX Transp., Inc., 245 F.3d 916 (7th Cir. 2001); Land v. Baptist Med. Ctr., 164 F.3d 423 (8th Cir. 1999); Fraser v. Goodale, 342 F.3d 1032 (9th Cir. 2003).
96. *Lawson.*
97. 534 U.S. 184 (2001).

ADA because it had not "substantially limit[ed]" any "major life activit[y]." The U.S. Court of Appeals for the Sixth Circuit reversed, finding that her impairments substantially limited the employee in the major life activity of performing manual tasks. The Supreme Court faulted the appeals court for failing to ask whether the employee's impairments prevented or restricted her from performing tasks that were of central importance to most people's daily lives. The Court concluded that an employee is not considered to be substantially limited from performing manual tasks if he or she simply cannot perform tasks associated with his or her job. Accordingly, the Court reversed the Sixth Circuit's judgment and remanded the case for further proceedings.

Doctors can play a large role in deciding whether an impairment substantially limits a major life activity. For example, in *Blockel v. J.C. Penney Co.*,[98] the U.S. Court of Appeals for the First Circuit did not question whether an employee, who was fired after she was required to limit the number of hours she worked per week by her doctor due to a seizure disorder, depression, and post-traumatic stress disorder, was disabled. In contrast, in *McKenzie v. Dovala*,[99] the U.S. Court of Appeals for the Tenth Circuit stated that an employee, who had a prior record of a variety of psychological afflictions, including post-traumatic stress disorder related to childhood sexual abuse by her father, was not protected by the ADA because her doctors had cleared her for all work-related activities at the time her employment application was denied.

In the following case, the Supreme Court considered whether correctable myopia is a "disability" under the ADA.

98. 337 F.3d 17 (1st Cir. 2003).

99. 242 F.3d 967 (10th Cir. 2001).

A CASE IN POINT

## In the Language of the Court

**CASE 13.3**
**Sutton v. United Air Lines, Inc.**
*Supreme Court of the United States*
*527 U.S. 471 (1999).*

**› FACTS** Karen Sutton and Kimberly Hinton were twin sisters who had severe myopia. Although their myopia prevented them from conducting numerous activities, they could, with the help of glasses or contact lenses, function in the same way as individuals with normal vision. They applied to United Air Lines to become commercial airline pilots but were told that they did not meet the airline's minimum vision requirements (uncorrected vision of 20/100 or better). The sisters filed a suit, alleging that United had discriminated against them on the basis of their disability in violation of the ADA.

**› ISSUE PRESENTED** Is myopia that is correctable with glasses or contact lenses a "disability" under the ADA?

**› OPINION** O'CONNOR, J., writing for the U.S. Supreme Court:

A "disability" exists only where an impairment "substantially limits" a major life activity, not where it "might," "could," or "would" be substantially limiting if mitigating measures were not taken. A person whose physical or mental impairment is corrected by medication or other measures does not have an impairment that presently "substantially limits" a major life activity. To be sure, a person whose physical or mental impairment is corrected by mitigating measures still has an impairment, but if the impairment is corrected it does not "substantially limit" a major life activity.

. . .

. . . Had Congress intended to include all persons with corrected physical limitations among those covered by the Act, it undoubtedly would have cited a much higher number of disabled persons in the findings. That it did not is evidence that the ADA's coverage is restricted to only those whose impairments are not mitigated by corrective measures.

. . .

. . . Under subsection (C), individuals who are "regarded as" having a disability are disabled within the meaning of the ADA. . . .

. . .

*(Continued)*

(Case 13.3 *continued*)

Assuming without deciding that working is a major life activity and that the EEOC regulations interpreting the term "substantially limits" [to mean "unable to perform" or "significantly restricted"] are reasonable, petitioners have failed to allege adequately that their poor eyesight is regarded as an impairment that substantially limits them in the major life activity of working. They allege only that respondent regards their poor vision as precluding them from holding positions as a "global airline pilot." Because the position of global airline pilot is a single job, this allegation does not support the claim that respondent regards petitioners as having a *substantially limiting impairment.* Indeed, there are a number of other positions utilizing petitioners' skills, such as regional pilot and pilot instructor to name a few, that are available to them. Even under the EEOC's Interpretative Guidance, to which petitioners ask us to defer, "an individual who cannot be a commercial airline pilot because of a minor vision impairment, but who can be a commercial airline co-pilot or a pilot for a courier service, would not be substantially limited in the major life activity of working."

**› RESULT** The appeals court's decision dismissing the case was affirmed. The sisters were not disabled and therefore were not protected by the ADA.

**› CRITICAL THINKING QUESTIONS**

1. Would a person with diabetes that can be controlled with insulin be disabled if he or she elected not to take insulin and, as a result, could not work?
2. Could an employer terminate an employee with high cholesterol to avoid having to pay for expensive cholesterol-lowering drugs? Would the result be the same if the employee were HIV-positive and was taking very expensive drugs to control the condition?

---

## *Regarded as Disabled*

The third prong of the definition of a disability provides that a person is protected under the ADA if he or she is regarded as having an impairment that substantially limits one or more major life activities. This is based on the notion that societal stereotypes and prejudices may constrain individuals more than their actual limitations. As a result, the ADA prohibits an employer from discriminating against an individual based on its perception that the individual is disabled because the employer's reactions may be based on stereotypes, misinformation, and long-held misconceptions of handicapped individuals. In other words, an individual might be "regarded as" disabled even if he or she does not actually have a disability, if the employer treats him or her as if the condition constituted a disability.

## *Exclusions*

Although the definition of a disability under the ADA is relatively vague, the statute does clearly exclude many things. For example, the ADA specifically excludes homosexuality, bisexuality, sexual-behavior disorders, compulsive gambling, kleptomania, and pyromania from the definition of a disability.

Psychoactive-substance-use disorders resulting from current illegal use of drugs, including the use of alcohol in the workplace against the employer's policies, are also excluded from the ADA's definition of a disability. Although "current use" is not specifically defined in the statute, it has been interpreted to include drug use weeks or months before discharge.[100] However, an employee or applicant who no longer actively uses drugs or alcohol on the work site, but who is involved in or has completed a supervised rehabilitation program, may be regarded as a disabled person.[101] Also, although an individual may not be fired on the basis of his or her alcoholism, an employer may discharge the person based on behavior related to the alcoholism.[102] In 2000, the EEOC issued an informal guidance letter stating that an employer that

100. Shafer v. Preston Mem'l Hosp. Corp., 107 F.3d 274 (4th Cir. 1997).
101. *See* Brown v. Lucky Stores, Inc., 246 F.3d 1182 (9th Cir. 2001).
102. James Podgers, *Disability and DUIs: ADA Claims by Fired or Demoted Alcoholic Employees Fail,* A.B.A. J., Feb. 1996, at 46.

excludes injuries or diseases that result from chronic alcoholism or drug addiction from its disability retirement plan could be required to justify the exclusion by the risks or costs of coverage or as necessary for the viability of the plan.[103]

## Reasonable Accommodation

The ADA requires employers to make reasonable accommodations to an employee's disability, as long as doing so does not cause the employer "undue hardship." Thus, even if a disability precludes an individual from performing the essential functions of the position or presents a safety risk, the employer is required to assess whether there is a reasonable accommodation that will permit the individual to be employed despite the disability.

Title I sets forth a nonexhaustive list of what might constitute "reasonable accommodation." It includes (1) making work facilities accessible; (2) restructuring jobs or modifying work schedules; (3) reassigning the individual to another job; (4) acquiring or modifying equipment or devices; (5) modifying examinations, training materials, or policies; and (6) providing qualified readers or interpreters or other similar accommodations for individuals with disabilities.

To establish liability under the ADA, the employee must have requested an accommodation from the employer; it is the employee's initial request for an accommodation that triggers the employer's obligation to provide one.[104] An employee who fails to provide the employer with necessary medical information is precluded from claiming that the employer failed to provide reasonable accommodation.[105] Employers must train supervisors to recognize when a reasonable request for accommodation has been made.[106]

At least six federal appeals courts have found that once a request for accommodation is made, an employer must be proactive and make a reasonable effort to determine the appropriate accommodation.[107] A minimum requirement seems to be that the employer should discuss potential accommodations with the disabled employee and not make unilateral decisions regarding the adequacy of potential accommodations.[108] Courts have not been receptive to claims that a reasonable accommodation includes transferring the individual to a new supervisor.[109]

Reassignment, however, may be considered a reasonable accommodation. In *Smith v. Midland Brake, Inc.*,[110] the U.S. Court of Appeals for the Tenth Circuit found that the employer, Midland Brake, could have reassigned employee Robert Smith to another job within the company after he became unable to perform his job because of a chronic skin condition. The court argued that the ADA's reasonable accommodation requirement would be transformed into a "hollow promise" if it merely extended the right "to compete equally with the rest of the world for a vacant position" to disabled workers.

In contrast, in *EEOC v. Humiston-Keeling, Inc.*,[111] the U.S. Court of Appeals for the Seventh Circuit held that the employer did not violate the ADA by refusing to reassign a warehouse picker to a vacant clerical position for which she was minimally qualified when there were other applicants for the position who were better qualified. The court ruled that the ADA does not require an employer to reassign a disabled employee to a job for which a better qualified applicant exists, provided the employer's consistent and honest policy is to hire the best applicant for the job. The court rejected the argument that a disabled employee is entitled to more consideration than a nondisabled employee, saying that would amount to a policy of requiring employers to give bonus points to people with disabilities.

An employer does not have to accommodate a disabled employee if doing so would conflict with seniority rules under the employer's collective bargaining agreement.[112] In *U.S. Airways, Inc. v. Barnett*,[113] however, the Supreme Court held that an employer's unilaterally imposed seniority system (not embodied in a collective bargaining agreement) that conflicts with a reassignment that is a reasonable accommodation under the ADA will

103. *EEOC Says Alcohol-Related Disabilities May Not Be Excluded from Employer Plan*, 69 U.S.L.W. 2089 (Aug. 15, 2000).
104. Jovanovic v. In-Sink-Erator Div. of Emerson Elec. Co., 201 F.3d 894 (7th Cir. 2000).
105. Templeton v. Neodata Servs., 162 F.3d 617 (10th Cir. 1998).
106. *Employers Should Train Supervisors in ADA Accommodation Duty, EEOC Official Advises*, 69 U.S.L.W. 2254–5 (Oct. 31, 2000).
107. *See, e.g.*, Loulseged v. Akz. Nobel, Inc., 178 F.3d 731 (5th Cir. 1999) (an interactive process is a "means to the end of forging reasonable accommodation"); Mengine v. Runyon, 114 F.3d 415 (3d Cir. 1997) (an employer that fails to work with the employee requesting accommodation "may not discover a way in which the employee's disability could have been reasonably accommodated, thereby risking violation").
108. Bultemeyer v. Fort Wayne Cmty. Schs., 100 F.3d 1281 (7th Cir. 1996).
109. Frances A. McMorris, *Employee's Transfer Plea Rejected in Another Disabilities-Act Ruling*, WALL ST. J., Jan. 21, 1997, at B5.
110. 180 F.3d 1154 (10th Cir. 1999).
111. 227 F.3d 1024 (7th Cir. 2000).
112. *See, e.g.*, Davis v. Fla. Power & Light Co., 205 F.3d 1301 (11th Cir. 2000).
113. 535 U.S. 391 (2002).

not necessarily serve to bar the reassignment. In this case, an employee who suffered a serious back injury while working had asked his employer to reassign him to another job in the company's mail room. Two employees with greater seniority planned to exercise their seniority right to transfer to jobs in the mail room, thereby preventing the disabled employee from working there. The Court found that while a seniority system is ordinarily sufficient to show that accommodation is not reasonable under the ADA, the employee may present evidence of special circumstances that make exception to the seniority rule reasonable under particular facts. The Court stated that "the plaintiff might show, for example, that the employer, having retained the right to change the system unilaterally, exercises the right fairly frequently, reducing employee expectations that the system will be followed—to the point where the requested accommodation will not likely make a difference."

## Defenses Under the ADA

Defenses available to an employer under the ADA include undue hardship, business necessity, and permissible exclusion.

### *Undue Hardship*

A reasonable accommodation is not required if it would impose an undue hardship on the employer. The ADA defines "undue hardship" to mean an activity requiring significant difficulty or expense when considered in light of (1) the nature and cost of the accommodation needed; (2) the overall financial resources of the facility, the number of persons employed at the facility, the effect on expenses and resources, or any other impact of the accommodation on the facility; (3) the overall financial resources of the employer and the overall size of the business with respect to the number of employees and the type, number, and location of its facilities; and (4) the type of operation of the employer, including the composition, structure, and functions of the workforce, and the geographic separateness and administrative or fiscal relationship of the facility in question to the employer.

An example of an accommodation that was deemed unreasonable involved an employee with various mental impairments that made it impossible for him to work in an unduly stressful environment. The employee asked for a transfer out of the stressful work environment and later sued when the employer did not honor his request. The U.S. Court of Appeals for the Third Circuit ruled that transferring the employee away from the stressful work environment was not a reasonable accommodation because it would impose extraordinary administrative costs on the employer.[114]

### *Business Necessity*

Employers may also argue that they had to discriminate against an applicant or employee with a disability due to a business necessity. In *Belk v. Southwestern Bell Telephone Co.*,[115] the U.S. Court of Appeals for the Eighth Circuit ruled that employment tests, qualification standards, and other selection criteria are acceptable under the ADA if they are related to the job and consistent with business necessity. Southwestern Bell had argued that it had job-related reasons for not accommodating a worker who wore a leg brace during a physical performance test for a technician job.

In *EEOC v. Exxon Corp.*,[116] the U.S. Court of Appeals for the Fifth Circuit analyzed Exxon's policy, adopted in response to the 1989 *Exxon Valdez* oil spill disaster, of permanently removing any employee who had undergone treatment for substance abuse from certain safety-sensitive positions. The EEOC sued, arguing that Exxon had to prove that the class of individuals posed a "direct threat" to the health or safety of others. The court rejected this argument, stating that Exxon could justify its policy as a business necessity. Whereas the "direct threat" test focuses on the individual employee and the specific risk posed by the employee's disability, the "business necessity" defense concerns whether a safety policy is addressed to all employees of a given class. The court further ruled that in evaluating whether a safety policy constitutes a business necessity, both the magnitude of possible harm and the probability of harm must be evaluated.

In *Tice v. Centre Area Transportation Authority*,[117] the U.S. Court of Appeals for the Third Circuit held that a transportation authority did not violate the ADA by ordering a post-hiring physical examination of a bus driver who had repeatedly taken medical leave due to a back injury because the examination was job related and consistent with the business necessity of determining whether the employee was physically fit to perform his job.

### *Permissible Exclusion*

An applicant or employee who is disabled may be excluded from the employment opportunity only if, by reason of the disability, he or she (with or without rea-

114. Gaul v. Lucent Techs., Inc., 134 F.3d 576 (3d Cir. 1998).
115. 194 F.3d 946 (8th Cir. 1999).
116. 203 F.3d 871 (5th Cir. 2000).
117. 247 F.3d 506 (3d Cir. 2001).

sonable accommodation) cannot perform the essential functions of the job or if the employment of the individual poses a significant risk to the health or safety of others.

**Inability to Perform Essential Functions** In determining whether a job function is essential, the ADA requires that consideration be given to the employer's judgment as to which functions are essential, but it also looks to any written job description prepared *before* advertising or interviewing for the job commenced. The applicant or employee does not have to prove his or her ability to perform all the functions of the job, only the essential functions.[118]

**Direct Threat** An employer cannot deny a job due to risk of future injury unless, given the person's current condition, there is a probability of substantial harm. For example, the U.S. Court of Appeals for the Eleventh Circuit ruled that a dental office acted lawfully when it laid off an HIV-positive hygienist after concluding that he posed a direct threat to the health and safety of others. His job included engaging in invasive, exposure-prone activities, such as cleaning teeth, on a frequent basis.[119] The presence of sharp instruments on which the hygienist could prick his hand increased the risk of HIV transmission. Employers cannot rely on their own physician's opinion, however; risk of injury must be based upon generally accepted medical opinion.

In the following case, the Supreme Court considered whether the "direct threat" defense under the ADA applies to employees who pose a direct threat to their own health or safety, but not to other persons in the workplace.

118. Deane v. Pocono Med. Ctr., 142 F.3d 138 (3d Cir. 1998).

119. Waddell v. Valley Forge Dental Assoc., 276 F.3d 1275 (11th Cir. 2001).

A CASE IN POINT

**CASE 13.4**

**Echazabal v. Chevron USA, Inc.**

*Supreme Court of the United States*
*536 U.S. 73 (2002).*

## Summary

**› FACTS** Mario Echazabal worked for various maintenance contractors at Chevron's oil refinery in El Segundo, California. In 1992, he applied to work directly for Chevron. Chevron offered him a job contingent on his passing a physical examination. The exam revealed that Echazabal's liver was releasing certain enzymes at an abnormally high level. Chevron concluded that his liver might be damaged by exposure to solvents and chemicals in the refinery, so it rescinded the offer. Echazabal continued to work for a maintenance contractor operating at the refinery.

Subsequently, Echazabal was diagnosed with asymptomatic chronic active hepatitis C. His physicians did not advise him to stop working at the refinery because of his medical condition. In 1995, Echazabal applied again to Chevron for a position in the refinery. After making him an offer, Chevron again rescinded it after learning about Echazabal's liver disease. Chevron also wrote to the maintenance contractor who employed him and requested that it remove Echazabal from the refinery or place him in a position where he would not be exposed to solvents or chemicals. As a result, Echazabal could no longer work at the refinery. He filed a complaint against Chevron, alleging that it had violated the ADA. The district court dismissed his claim, and he appealed to the U.S. Court of Appeals for the Ninth Circuit, which reversed the summary judgment. Chevron then appealed to the U.S. Supreme Court.

**› ISSUE PRESENTED** Does the "direct threat" defense apply to employees who pose a direct threat to their own health or safety, but not to the health or safety of other persons?

**› SUMMARY OF OPINION** The U.S. Supreme Court began by examining the language of the ADA, which states that an employer's defense to alleged discrimination against a disabled individual may include denying employment to individuals who pose a "direct threat to the health or safety of *other* individuals in the workplace." The Court then pointed out that the EEOC expands upon this language by stating that an individual shall not pose a direct threat to the health or safety *of the individual* or others in the workplace.

*(Continued)*

(Case 13.4 *continued*)

The Supreme Court rejected Echazabal's argument that the EEOC's regulation is wrong in light of the language of the ADA. The Court pointed out that although Congress did not include a reference to individuals in the language of the ADA, the language does not specifically exclude individuals from the regulation either. Thus, it can be inferred that the EEOC was free to recognize threats to self in its regulations.

The Court further stated that employers can make a statutory defense against violations of the ADA by claiming that denying employment to threatened individuals was "job-related and consistent with business necessity." The Court found that Chevron's reasons for denying employment to Echazabal were reasonable: Chevron wished to avoid time lost to sickness, excessive turnover from medical retirement or death, litigation under state tort law, and the risk of violating the Occupational Safety and Health Act (OSHA). Even though Echazabal argued that there is no known instance of OSHA being enforced against an employer that relied on the ADA to hire a worker willing to accept a risk to himself from his disability on the job, the Court said that the text of OSHA itself mandates that employers provide a workplace free from recognized hazards to *each and every* worker. Hence, the Court stated, if an employer hires an individual who knowingly consents to the particular dangers the job would pose to him, "there is no denying that the employer would be asking for trouble." The employer's decision to hire "would put Congress's policy in the ADA, a disabled individual's right to operate on equal terms within the workplace, at loggerheads with the competing policy of OSHA, to ensure the safety of all workers."

**› RESULT** The Supreme Court reversed the judgment of the U.S. Court of Appeals for the Ninth Circuit, holding that the EEOC regulation authorizing an employer to refuse to hire an individual because his performance on the job would endanger his own health owing to a disability did not exceed the scope of permissible rulemaking under the ADA.

## HIV Discrimination

A major issue today is the employer's relationship with an employee who has HIV disease, that is, an individual who has been infected with the human immunodeficiency virus (HIV). Due to advances in drug treatments, more individuals are living healthy, productive lives while infected with HIV. This is called asymptomatic HIV disease. When an individual's immune system is compromised and the person becomes ill due to HIV-related complications, the individual is considered symptomatic. Acquired immune deficiency syndrome (AIDS) refers to the most serious stage of symptomatic HIV disease.

Although the ADA does not specifically list HIV disease as a disability, in *Bragdon v. Abbott*,[120] the Supreme Court held that asymptomatic HIV-positive individuals are disabled within the meaning of the ADA.[121] The Court concluded that infection with HIV constitutes a physiological disorder that substantially limits the major life activity of reproduction. Although the HIV infection did not make it impossible for Abbott to reproduce, it substantially limited her ability to reproduce by (1) imposing on the man a significant risk of becoming infected and (2) creating a risk that the child would be infected during gestation and childbirth. The Court rejected the defendant's attempt to limit the phrase "major life activity" to those aspects of a person's life that have a public, economic, or daily character.

Applying *Bragdon*, the U.S. Court of Appeals for the Fifth Circuit found that an HIV-positive employee was not disabled under the ADA because he and his wife did not want more children. Thus, his major life activity of reproduction was not substantially limited.[122]

In the context of HIV disease, courts have narrowly construed the direct threat defense in accordance with medical evidence that HIV cannot be transmitted through casual contact. Thus, only those professions that

120. 524 U.S. 624 (1998).

121. John Gibeaut, *Filling a Need*, A.B.A. J., July 1997, at 48.

122. Blanks v. Southwestern Bell Communications, 310 F.3d 398 (5th Cir. 2002).

could lead to the transmission of bodily fluids, such as health-care workers, are given closer analysis under the direct threat exception.

### *Dealing with HIV Disease in the Workplace*

An employer cannot justify discrimination against a person with AIDS on the basis of coworker or customer preference. Similarly, the fact that the employment of someone with AIDS will increase group health insurance costs or cause absenteeism does not make discrimination permissible.

Many states recognize either a common law or a constitutional right to privacy. This protects individuals from improper communication of their HIV status, even though the information is true and was properly obtained for a specific purpose. Communication of such personal information might be protected by the qualified-privilege defense as long as it is confined only to those people who have a legitimate need to know. General communication of someone's HIV status among coworkers is probably not protected by the privilege. Statutes prohibiting disclosure of medical information, specifically HIV-related information, may also be a source of employer liability. Thus, HIV-related information should be kept in confidence among individuals who need to know.

The employer also runs the risk of being sued for libel or slander if careless statements are made about employees. For example, falsely accusing an employee of having AIDS could be grounds for a defamation suit. Truth, however, is a complete defense.

### Genetic Discrimination

Approximately eighteen states have enacted laws banning genetic discrimination by insurers and employers. In 2000, President Clinton signed an executive order prohibiting federal departments and agencies from using genetic information in personnel decisions. In April 2000, the EEOC Commissioner announced that the ADA prohibits genetic discrimination pursuant to a 1995 policy guidance adopted by the EEOC. Although the ADA does not specifically refer to genetic discrimination, the statute's "regarded as disabled" prong includes discrimination on the basis of a diagnosed genetic predisposition toward an asymptomatic condition or illness.[123] Further information on genetic testing can be found in Chapter 12.

123. *EEOC Commissioner Says ADA Bans Genetic Discrimination*, Corp. Couns. Wkly., Apr. 12, 2000, at 7.

### Enforcement and Remedies

Title I of the ADA is enforced in the same manner as Title VII of the Civil Rights Act of 1964, and the same remedies are available. Compensatory and punitive damages are subject to the same caps as those applicable to discrimination based on sex or religion.

Claims of disability discrimination are frequently enforced. Disability-related claims now account for about 19 percent of all discrimination charges filed by the EEOC.[124] The EEOC received 15,377 charges of disability discrimination in 2003.[125] That same year, it collected $45 million from parties charged with such discrimination (not including awards from litigation).

## Family and Medical Leave Act of 1993

The Family and Medical Leave Act (FMLA) of 1993[126] states that eligible employees are entitled to twelve weeks of unpaid leave per year. An employee may use leave under the Act in four situations: (1) the birth of a child; (2) the placement of an adopted or foster-care child with the employee; (3) care of a child, a parent, or a spouse; or (4) a serious health condition that renders the employee unable to do his or her job.

The FMLA has a number of specific guidelines regarding employee eligibility and employer obligations. To be eligible for a family leave, the employee must have worked at the place of employment for at least twelve months and have completed at least 1,250 hours of service to the employer during that twelve-month period.

To vindicate rights under the FMLA, a plaintiff may sue both the employer and his or her supervisor individually.[127] This interpretation is distinctive because a supervisor generally cannot be sued in his or her individual capacity under Title VII, the ADEA, or the ADA. In addition, despite states' immunity from private actions under the Eleventh Amendment, the U.S. Supreme

124. EEOC, *EEOC Issues Fiscal Year 2003 Enforcement Data* (Mar. 8, 2004).

125. EEOC, *Disability Discrimination* (Dec. 10, 2004), *at* http://www.eeoc.gov/types/ada.html.

126. Pub. L. No. 103-3, 107 Stat. 6 (codified at 5 U.S.C. § 6381 *et seq.* and 29 U.S.C. § 2601 et seq.) (1993).

127. Freeman v. Foley, 911 F. Supp. 326 (N.D. Ill. 1995). *But see* Mitchell v. Chapman, 343 F.3d 811 (6th Cir. 2003) (holding that the FMLA does not impose individual liability on public agency employees).

Court has held that employees can sue state employers for FMLA violations.[128]

The FMLA's requirements should be considered a floor, not a ceiling, for what employers can provide their employees in terms of leave. Even if employers provide for more generous leave, however, they must give employees notice regarding the consequences of taking the extra leave.[129]

An employee cannot contract out of his or her right to leave time under the FMLA. But the employer may require, or an employee may choose, to substitute any or all accrued paid leave for the leave time that is provided for under the Act. Employers have no obligation to give employees advance notice that their paid leave will be counted toward the unpaid leave provided by the FMLA.[130]

In general, the employer is required to restore the employee to the same position, or one with equivalent benefits, pay, and other terms and conditions of employment, following the expiration of the leave. But the employer is not required to reinstate key employees to their previous position if the employer determines that "such denial is necessary to prevent substantial and grievous economic injury to the operations of the employer." "Key employee" is defined as a salaried employee who is among the highest-paid 10 percent of the employees located within seventy-five miles of the facility at which the subject employee is employed. The EEOC regulations require the employer to notify an employee, at the time the leave is requested, of his or her status as a key employee and of the consequence of taking a leave.[131]

In *O'Connor v. PCA Family Health Plan, Inc.*,[132] the U.S. Court of Appeals for the Eleventh Circuit held that an employee taking leave under the FMLA does not have an absolute right to reinstatement if his or her employment is terminated during the leave as part of a general reduction in force (RIF) by the employer. The court explained: "An employee has no greater right to reinstatement or to other benefits and conditions of employment than if the employee had been continuously employed during the FMLA leave period." The burden of proof is on the employer denying reinstatement to show that it would have discharged the employee even if he or she had not been on FMLA leave.

128. Nev. Dep't of Human Res. v. Hibbs, 538 U.S. 721 (2003).
129. *See* Kosakow v. New Rochelle Radiology Assocs., P.C., 274 F.3d 706 (2d Cir. 2001).
130. *See* Ragsdale v. Wolverine World Wide, Inc., 535 U.S. 81 (2002).
131. Panza v. Grappone Cos., Civil No. 99-221-M, Opinion No. 2000 DNH 224 (D.N.H. Oct. 20, 2000).
132. 200 F.3d 1349 (11th Cir. 2000).

Increasingly, employees are suing under the FMLA rather than the ADA to protect their rights.[133] The focus of the ADA is to demonstrate that an employee can work despite a disability, whereas one of the objectives of the FMLA is to provide time off to an employee who cannot work due to a serious health condition. In *Byrne v. Avon Products, Inc.*,[134] the U.S. Court of Appeals for the Seventh Circuit reinstated the FMLA claim of an employee who was terminated for repeatedly sleeping on the job after years of exemplary service. The court found that the ADA did not protect the employee because he could not do the job and was, as a result, not "qualified as an individual with a disability" who could "perform essential functions of the job." But, the court stated, Byrne's sudden behavior shift created a jury question as to whether he was entitled to FMLA leave.

## Affirmative Action

Affirmative-action programs are generally viewed as a means of remedying past acts of discrimination. Such programs are usually established pursuant to court orders, court-approved consent decrees, or federal and state laws that impose affirmative-action obligations on government contractors.

Executive Order 11246 requires federal government contractors to include in every government contract not exempted by the order provisions whereby the contractor agrees (1) not to discriminate in employment on the basis of race, color, religion, sex, or national origin; (2) to take affirmative steps to prevent discrimination; and (3) to file equal opportunity surveys every other year.[135] In some cases, a contractor's affirmative-action plan must be put in writing. Although individuals have no private right of action based on an alleged violation of the order, the Department of Labor, through its Office of Federal Contract Compliance Programs, can impose a wide range of sanctions, including terminating a government contract and disqualifying the contractor from entering into any future government contracts.[136] Government contractors are subject to affirmative-action obligations under other federal laws as well, including the Vocational Rehabilitation

133. David L. Hudson Jr., *Changing Act: Family Leave Law Taking Center Stage from Disabilities Act in Litigation*, A.B.A. J., Sept. 2003, at 15.
134. 328 F.3d 379 (7th Cir. 2003).
135. Exec. Order No. 11,246, 3 C.F.R. 339 (1964–1965), *reprinted in* 42 U.S.C. § 2000e (1994).
136. The Office of Federal Contract Compliance Programs' new regulations overhauling the thirty-year-old requirements for affirmative action under Executive Order 11,246 were published in the November 13, 2000 issue of the *Federal Register*, 65 Fed. Reg. 68,021, and took effect on December 13, 2000.

Act of 1973 and the Vietnam Era Veterans' Readjustment Assistance Act of 1972.

As explained in Chapter 2, the U.S. Supreme Court held in *Adarand Constructors, Inc. v. Peña*[137] that government-mandated affirmative-action plans are subject to strict scrutiny under the Equal Protection Clause. In reinstating a reverse-discrimination claim by a white-owned construction company that lost a contract to a minority-owned business, the Court held that benign and invidious racial classifications should be subject to the same standards. This ruling was significant because it required the government to show a specific history of discrimination in order to justify preferential treatment of minority-owned businesses in government contracts.

In 1998, in *Lutheran Church–Missouri Synod v. FCC,*[138] the U.S. Court of Appeals for the District of Columbia Circuit struck down the Federal Communications Commission's affirmative-action requirements for radio and television broadcast licenses. The court held that *Adarand's* requirement of strict scrutiny applied not just to racial preferences in hiring but to any race-conscious decision making that affects employment opportunities even if it does not establish preferences, quotas, or set-asides. The court explained:

> [W]e do not think it matters whether a government hiring program imposes hard quotas, soft quotas, or goals. Any one of these techniques induces an employer to hire with an eye toward meeting the numerical target. As such, they can and surely will result in individuals being granted a preference because of their race.

The court also held that the FCC's interest in fostering diverse programming was not compelling. Even if the diversity goal could be deemed a compelling state interest, the court concluded that the FCC's equal employment opportunity rules were not narrowly tailored to foster diverse programming.

In January 2000, in response to *Lutheran Church,* the FCC adopted new rules to promote employment of women and minorities in the broadcast and cable television industries.[139] The rules require broadcast licensees to disseminate information about job openings to all members of the community to ensure that all applicants have the opportunity to compete for jobs. The FCC chair stated that the rules were designed to advance the goals of prohibiting discrimination in hiring and promoting diversity in broadcasting.[140]

Although government programs have been struck down by the courts, some affirmative-action programs by private employers have been accepted. For example, the U.S. Supreme Court upheld a collective bargaining agreement containing an affirmative-action plan giving preference to African-American employees entering skilled-craft training positions.[141] Concluding that Title VII did not preclude all private, voluntary, race-conscious affirmative-action programs, the Court noted that the plan (1) like Title VII, was designed to break down patterns of racial segregation and hierarchy; (2) "did not unnecessarily trammel the interests of white employees"; and (3) was a temporary measure intended to attain rather than maintain racial balance. The EEOC has promulgated regulations regarding voluntary affirmative-action plans.[142]

In *Taxman v. Board of Education,*[143] the U.S. Court of Appeals for the Third Circuit struck down a school board's affirmative-action plan as a violation of Title VII. The plan gave preference to minority teachers over nonminority teachers in layoff decisions when teachers were equally qualified. The court read the Supreme Court's ruling in *United Steelworkers v. Weber* as permitting race-based employment decisions only when they are necessary to remedy past discrimination. A mere desire to promote diversity in education was not sufficient to warrant a discriminatory policy. The U.S. Supreme Court granted the petition for certiorari and heard oral arguments, but the parties settled the case before the Court ruled. Several civil rights groups feared that the Supreme Court would use this case as an occasion to ban all affirmative-action programs, so they contributed the bulk of the money paid in the settlement.[144]

The Civil Rights Act of 1991 limited the ability of persons to challenge affirmative-action litigated judgments and consent decrees. A person cannot challenge a judgment or consent decree if any of the following three conditions is applicable: (1) the person had actual notice of the proposed judgment or order sufficient to let that person know that the judgment or decree might adversely affect the interests and legal rights of that person and had an opportunity to present objections; (2) the person had a reasonable opportunity to present objections to the judgment or order; or (3) the person's interests were adequately represented by another person who had previously challenged the judgment or order on the same legal grounds and with a similar factual situation.

137. 515 U.S. 200 (1995).
138. 141 F.3d 344 (D.C. Cir. 1998).
139. 47 C.F.R. pt. 73.2080 (2000).
140. *FCC Votes to Adopt New Rule on Equal Employment Opportunity,* 68 U.S.L.W. 2443 (Feb. 1, 2000).
141. United Steelworkers of Am. v. Weber, 443 U.S. 193 (1979).
142. *See* 29 C.F.R. § 1608.1–12 (1997).
143. 91 F.3d 1547 (3d Cir. 1996).
144. Eva M. Rodriguez, *Rights Group's Settlement Settles Little,* WALL ST. J., Nov. 24, 1997, at A3.

### ETHICAL CONSIDERATION

In *Grutter v. Bollinger,*[a] the Supreme Court upheld the University of Michigan Law School's admission policy, which took race and ethnicity into account in an effort to achieve student body diversity. The Law School's policy did not define diversity solely in terms of racial and ethnic status, although it reaffirmed the Law School's commitment to diversity with reference to the inclusion of African-American, Hispanic, and Native American students. It did not use numerical quotas, however. The policy had been challenged by a white applicant who claimed that it discriminated against her on the basis of race in violation of the Fourteenth Amendment. In an amicus curiae brief submitted in support of the Law School, the U.S. military asserted that a racially diverse officer corps was essential to its national security mission. The Court ruled that, at least for law schools, diversity was a compelling state interest.

Yet, in a companion case,[b] the Supreme Court invalidated the University of Michigan's undergraduate admissions policy, which used mechanistic numerical formulas to admit more applicants of color. Unlike the Law School—which included race and ethnicity as just two of many factors used to make admissions decisions—the undergraduate programs specified one set of required grade point averages and board scores for whites granted automatic admission and another, lower set of grades and board scores for nonwhites granted automatic admission.

Many U.S. employers actively recruit and hire minority candidates. Is it ethical for employers to make hiring decisions based on race in order to promote workplace diversity? For example, should an employer choose a qualified minority candidate over a more qualified nonminority candidate to promote diversity? What if the two candidates are equally qualified for a particular job?

**a.** 539 U.S. 306 (2003) (Case 2.6).
**b.** Gratz v. Bollinger, 539 U.S. 244 (2003).

## Applicability of Civil Rights Laws to Temporary Workers

The EEOC has responded to the growth in the number of temporary or contingent workers by extending potential liability for discrimination against such workers to both the employment agencies or temporary staffing firms and their client-employers.[145] If both the staffing firm and its client have the right to control the worker, then they are treated as joint employers, and both are subject to liability for both back and front pay as well as compensatory and punitive damages.

If the staffing firm learns that one of its clients has discriminated against a temporary employee, the firm should not assign other workers to that work site unless the client has taken the necessary corrective and preventive measures to ensure that the discrimination will not recur. Otherwise, the staffing firm will be liable along with the client if a worker later assigned to that client is subjected to similar misconduct.

## The Extraterritorial Reach of American Law

In 1991, Congress amended Title VII to protect U.S. citizens employed in a foreign country by a U.S. employer or a U.S.-controlled employer. The ADEA and the ADA also apply extraterritorially to the same extent as Title VII.

The EEOC has provided guidance on how to determine whether an entity is a U.S. employer.[146] The nationality of an entity is determined on a case-by-case basis, taking into consideration the following factors: (1) the entity's place of incorporation, (2) the principal place of business, (3) contacts within the United States, (4) the nationality of dominant shareholders and/or those holding voting control, and (5) the nationality and location of management. An entity that is incorporated in the United States will generally be deemed a U.S. entity.

Even if a foreign entity is not deemed to be a U.S. entity, it will still be covered if it is "controlled by" a U.S. entity. Title VII provides that the determination of whether a U.S. employer controls an entity is based on the interrelation of the companies' operations, common management, centralized control of labor relations, and common ownership or financial control of the U.S. employer and the foreign entity.[147]

Section 109 makes it clear, however, that "it shall not be unlawful," under either Title VII or the ADA, for an employer to act in violation of either statute if compliance would cause the employer to violate the law of the foreign country in which the employee's workplace is located. For example, an employer may be permitted to deny employment to women in a country that prohibits women from working, even though this practice is in violation of Title VII.

145. The text of the EEOC's guidance on the application of the employment-discrimination laws to contingent workers is available at http://www.eeoc.gov/policy/docs/conting.html (last modified July 6, 2000).

146. EEOC, *Enforcement Guidance on Application of Title VII and the Americans with Disabilities Act, at* http://www.eeoc.gov/policy/docs/extraterritorial-vii-ada.html (last modified Apr. 24, 2003).
147. 42 U.S.C. § 2000e-1(c)(3).

ECONOMIC PERSPECTIVE

## GLOBALIZATION, CULTURAL NORMS, AND WORKPLACE DISCRIMINATION

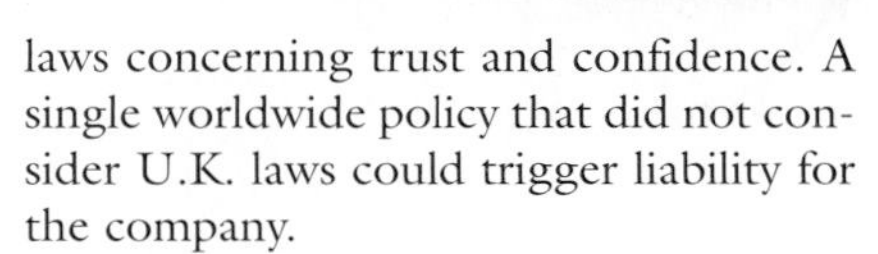

In 2004, Infosys Technologies, India's largest software exporter, settled its second sexual harassment lawsuit against one of its former officers and directors, Phaneesh Murthy. Murthy was accused of harassing two American women employed in Infosys's Fremont, California office. The suit sent shockwaves through Indian software companies with U.S. operations. In India, sexual harassment is widespread, but the Infosys suits caused Indian companies to realize that sexual harassment is taken seriously in the United States and that the possibility of lawsuits is very real.

In the current era of globalization, the interaction between the culture of a company's country of origin and the local culture and laws of its foreign branch offices is becoming more important. How multinational corporations should address this interaction as they create, implement, and maintain workplace diversity and antidiscrimination policies is the subject of much debate.

For example, many U.S. corporations, instilled with strong and well-established diversity and antidiscrimination views and practices, feel that it is important to implement a single global policy that applies to all employees in every country in order to create a corporate culture that clearly defines acceptable and unacceptable social norms. This worldwide approach may be based on the idea that certain sets of behaviors and practices are simply unacceptable for all people everywhere.

This global approach may encounter resistance from foreign employees who may view it as yet another way for Americans to impose their cultural standards on the rest of the world. For instance, kissing a work acquaintance may be the social norm in France and Italy. A corporate ban on displays of affection in the workplace could be viewed as offensive in these countries, even though its purpose is to prevent sexual harassment.

In Japan, it is generally acceptable to make distinctions based on such characteristics as age, gender, family, place of birth, ancestry, and education. Similarly, in Mexico, it is rare to find an indigenous Mexican manager or professional because individuals of European descent, who dominate the upper and middle classes, openly use family, social, and business ties to maintain advantages. As a result, a U.S.-mandated workplace policy that prohibits all decisions based on these characteristics may cause resentment and friction within the organization.

Because of these cultural differences, some companies have elected to create a single set of broad corporate values, but they implement these values differently at the local level based on the cultural norms and laws of each country in which the company operates. For example, a U.S. corporation could have a company-wide policy prohibiting sexual harassment and mandating investigation of all complaints. Yet this policy might be implemented differently in the United Kingdom, where an employer who questions employees and managers about alleged sexual harassment might violate laws concerning trust and confidence. A single worldwide policy that did not consider U.K. laws could trigger liability for the company.

In the wake of the Infosys lawsuits, Indian software companies have implemented this hybrid approach. For example, Indian multinational software giant Wipro, Ltd. instituted a company-wide discrimination policy including a sexual harassment policy, increased its focus on cross-cultural sensitivity training, and began to hire senior managers in its foreign offices to serve as workplace role models for Indian employees located there. "Today, geographic barriers are disappearing, and the way we do business is changing," said Nandan Nilekani, Infosys's chief executive. "Multicultural interaction is becoming a very important part of our work environment."

**Sources:** This discussion is based on *Discrimination Laws Vary from Country to Country,* CORP. COUNS. WKLY., Aug. 28, 2002, *at* http://pubs.bna.com/ip/bna/ccw.nsf/searchallviews/875e47bb58c936a085256c21007; Peggy Hazard, *Diversity: Think Locally for Global Success,* STRATEGIC HR REV., Aug. 2004, *available at* http://www.simonsassoc.com/html/new.html; Saritha Rai, *Harassment Suit in U.S. Shifts India's Work Culture,* N.Y. TIMES, Sept. 5, 2002, *available at* http://www.globalpolicy.org/globaliz/cultural/2002/0906india.htm.

# Global View

## DISCRIMINATION AND DIVERSITY

When engaging in business overseas, managers should familiarize themselves with the employment-discrimination laws of the foreign countries in which they are doing business.

### EUROPEAN UNION

In the early 2000s, the European Commission, Parliament, and Council of Ministers adopted various directives aimed at preventing workplace discrimination on the basis of sex, religion, age, race, national origin, disability, and sexual orientation.[a] One directive was also modified to ban harassment as a form of discrimination on any of these grounds.[b] Although many of the European Union (EU) member states already had legislation prohibiting some types of discrimination, the new directives brought all of the varying national antidiscrimination laws together to ensure that antidiscrimination law was applied evenly in all EU countries. The EU Commissioner for Employment and Social Affairs commented that the new directives send a strong signal that the EU is not concerned simply with economics but "is also a community of values."[c]

Under the new directives, EU member states are required to (1) ban all forms of discrimination by 2006, (2) establish judicial or administrative bodies to enforce equal treatment in the workplace, and (3) remove any caps on awards for discrimination cases (although each member state is permitted to establish its own system of remedies). Any EU citizen claiming to be the victim of discrimination can also file a claim in the European Court of Justice in Luxembourg.

In trying discrimination cases, EU member states are required to utilize a burden of proof mechanism similar to the U.S. concepts of disparate treatment and disparate impact. "Disparate treatment" is called "direct discrimination," and "disparate impact" is called "indirect discrimination" in the EU. Direct discrimination analysis ensures that the burden of proof shifts if the complainant establishes "facts [from] which it may be presumed that there has been direct or indirect evidence of discrimination." The burden of proof for indirect discrimination states that indirect discrimination occurs "where a provision, criterion, or practice would put persons of a racial or ethnic origin at a particular disadvantage compared with other persons, unless that provision, criterion, or practice is objectively justified by a particular aim." Like U.S. courts, European courts look at percentages to determine whether a protected class has been disadvantaged by a particular employment practice.

However, the Burden of Proof Directive, which became effective in October 2001, has caused the European system of analysis to differ from the U.S. system by shifting the burden of proof from employees to employers in cases of sex discrimination. Other European Commission directives have implemented similar rules regarding discrimination on the basis of race. For example, in the United Kingdom, if the facts indicate that there has been discrimination of some kind, then the employer is asked to give an explanation. Without a clear and specific explanation, unlawful discrimination will be inferred from the facts. If an employer hires a man, rather than a woman who is better qualified, then a tribunal can infer that the employer discriminated against the woman on grounds of gender unless the employer can show that its decision was based on other grounds. It might, for instance, have chosen the man because he appeared better motivated at the interview. This burden of proof method makes it easier for employees to prove direct discrimination in a court of law.

Even though the European Commission has mandated that all member states have uniform laws regarding employment discrimination, each member state implements and utilizes these directives in different ways.

### JAPAN

Article 14 of the Japanese Constitution provides that "all of the people are equal under the law and there shall be no discrimination in political, economic or social relations because of race, creed, sex, social status, or family origin."[d] Despite this provision, Japanese antidiscrimination law is not very developed. Japan has no statutes prohibiting discrimination on the basis of race or national origin (most likely because Japan is generally a racially homogeneous society), and its laws regarding age, disability, and sex discrimination do not contain substantial enforcement provisions.

For example, although Japanese employers are required to maintain a certain ratio of disabled employees in the workplace,[e]

**a.** Equal Treatment Directive, European Parliament and Council Directive 2002/73/EC, 2002 O.J. (L 269); Equal Treatment Framework Directive, Council Directive 2000/78/EC, 2000 O.J. (L 308) (Nov. 27); Race Equality Directive, Council Directive 2000/43/EC, 2000 O.J. (L 180) 22 (June 29).

**b.** Council Directive 2002/73/EC, 2002 O.J. (L 269) 15 (Oct. 5).

**c.** Vikram Dodd & Andrew Osborn, *New Laws for EU on Bias in Workplace,* GUARDIAN, Oct. 19, 2000.

**d.** *See generally* INTERNATIONAL LABOR AND EMPLOYMENT LAWS 32-50–32-52 (Timothy J. Dorby & William L. Keller eds., 2003).

**e.** Japanese law does protect disabled workers from discrimination in termination, hiring, or harassment, however.

*(Continued)*

(Global View *continued*)

employers who violate this law are simply required to pay a nominal penalty to the government. In addition, Japanese law prohibits age discrimination in hiring or recruiting (but not termination), but the punishment for a violation is limited to posting the employer's name in the local newspaper.

Laws regarding sex discrimination are the most highly developed discrimination laws in Japan. There was a surge in the number of sexual harassment claims in Japan in the 1990s. Most of these cases were tort claims resulting from physical contact or sexual assaults. One Japanese district court has held that a hostile work environment can also constitute an actionable tort because it infringes on the employee's human dignity and causes working conditions to deteriorate.

In June 1997, Japan's Equal Employment Opportunity Law of 1985 (EEOL) was drastically revised to provide more protection for women in the workplace. The 1997 amendment includes a provision imposing on employers a duty to prevent sexual harassment. The EEOL also prohibits discrimination against women in employment recruitment, hiring, assignment, promotion, training, education, fringe benefits, and termination. The 1997 amendment includes sanctions, which were not present in the original law, to enforce these new provisions. In addition, when an employer violates the EEOL, the Labor Minister can publicize that fact.

Although twelve women were successful in procuring a court order upholding a $1.6 million award against a company for systematically discriminating against them in pay and promotions, most recent Japanese job seekers, labor lawyers, economists, and women's rights advocates interviewed by the *New York Times* said that the new law has "had little real impact, and the old patterns of consignment of women to noncareer positions [has] continued unabated."[f]

## INDIA

Indian antidiscrimination law has developed slowly since the implementation of the Indian constitution in 1950. The constitution prohibits discrimination in employment on the basis of religion, race, caste, sex, descent, place of birth, or residence.[g]

Perhaps the greatest struggle for equal rights has involved members of the Dalit caste (formerly called "untouchables"). These people occupy India's lowest caste and are viewed as unclean by higher-caste Hindus. In an effort to end the caste system, India passed the Protection of Civil Rights Act, 1955.[h] One purpose of this Act was to enable Dalits to obtain jobs other than the low-paying and undesirable occupations to which they were traditionally relegated. As a result, the Indian government started an affirmative-action system for Dalits by implementing hiring quotas and special training programs in employment.[i] Christian Dalits, however, are not eligible for this program, although Buddhist and Sikh Dalits maintain eligibility. Some Indian states also reserve special government jobs for Muslim Dalits.[j]

The Indian government has started an affirmative-action program for citizens with disabilities as well. The Persons with Disabilities Act of 1995 mandates that 3 percent of government jobs be reserved for the disabled.[k]

The Indian government passed its first law regarding rights for women in the workplace in 1948. The law prohibited women from cleaning certain machinery in factories and granted female factory workers maternity leave for up to twelve weeks.[l] Since then, other laws mandating equal pay, maternity benefits, and equal opportunity in hiring have been passed. Sexual harassment is perhaps the most recent area of gender antidiscrimination law to be developed. In 1997, the Indian Supreme Court recognized sexual harassment in the workplace as not only a personal injury to the affected woman but also a violation of her fundamental human rights. In its ruling, the Supreme Court issued guidelines making employers responsible for both preventive and remedial measures to make the workplace safe for women.[m]

**f.** Howard W. French, *Diploma in Hand, Japanese Women Find Glass Ceiling Reinforced with Iron,* N.Y. TIMES, Jan. 1, 2001.

**g.** Unesco, *India—Constitution, available at* http://www.unesco.org/most/rr3indi.htm (last visited Jan. 16, 2005). Note that Indian law does not prohibit discrimination based on age.

**h.** Hillary Mayel, *India's "Untouchables" Face Violence, Discrimination,* NAT'L GEOGRAPHIC NEWS, July 2, 2003, http://news.nationalgeographic.com/news/2003/06/0602_030602_untouchables.html.

**i.** Andre Beteille, *Discrimination at Work,* THE HINDU, Nov. 7, 2002, http://www.thehindu.com/2002/07/11/stories/2002071100101000.htm.

**j.** Minority Rights Group, *India's Dalit Christians Face Caste Discrimination and Loss of Government Assistance* (Mar. 15, 2004), *at* http://www.minorityrights.org/news_detail.asp?ID=230.

**k.** Sugita Katyal, *India's Disabled Struggle for Survival* (Jan. 29, 2003), http://www.accessibility.com.au/news/articles/india.htm.

**l.** The Mines Act of 1952. *See* Ajmal Edappagath, *Gender Sensitive Legislative Legislation and Policies in India* (2001), http://www.unescap.org/esid/GAD/Events/EGMICT2001/edappagath.pdf.

**m.** Laxmi Murthy, *The Cost of Harassment,* INDIANEST.COM, Aug. 11, 2002, at http://www.boloji.com/wfs/wfs066.htm.

## THE RESPONSIBLE MANAGER

## HONORING EMPLOYEES' CIVIL RIGHTS

Managers must be diligent in preventing and correcting any unlawful discrimination either in the preemployment process or during employment. Management should develop a written policy, which (1) clearly outlines discriminatory acts prohibited by federal, state, and local statutes and (2) prohibits retaliation against employees who complain about discrimination. Employees should be advised that any form of discrimination is inappropriate. The policy should have an enforcement mechanism and should clearly state that violations of the policy will result in poor performance reviews or termination. Such a policy will not only curb discriminatory acts but will also demonstrate that management diligently attempted to prevent such behavior in the event that litigation should arise.

The firm should also create a working environment in which employees feel comfortable bringing complaints against fellow workers and supervisors. There should be at least two individuals in the company, a male and a female, to whom such complaints may be brought. Because supervisors are often the discriminators, an employee should not be required to first complain to his or her supervisor. Managers should not keep reports of harassment confidential, even if requested to do so by the employee. Each complaint should be thoroughly investigated, and, if necessary, the violator should be punished.

Although the establishment of a comprehensive policy is one way to prevent unlawful discriminatory practices, it is not sufficient in itself. Managers must also abide by the policy and comply with all federal, state, and local statutes prohibiting unlawful discrimination; supervisors should undergo training regarding such laws.[148] If management participates in discriminatory acts, the firm's employees will have little incentive to abide by its policy against discrimination and will hesitate to bring a claim for discriminatory treatment.

It is crucial that employers make sure that they do not retaliate against employees who have filed discrimination claims. Although employers often perceive discrimination claims by an employee as an act of disloyalty, retaliation for these claims will make it more likely that they will be found liable by a jury or judge even if the initial claim would not have supported liability.

Employers should also create nondiscriminatory policies and procedures for hiring new employees. The employer should avoid relying on word-of-mouth recruitment practices, which tend to reach a disproportionate number of persons of the same race or ethnicity as the employer's current employees and should utilize media designed to reach people in both minority and nonminority communities. When advertising vacant positions, employers should use a job posting system that allows for an open and fair application process. The job advertisements themselves should not express a preference or limitation based on race, color, religion, gender, national origin, or age, unless such specifications are based on bona fide occupational qualifications.

Employers should also train employees in interviewing to ensure that interviewers ask proper questions and use objective hiring criteria. Although federal laws do not expressly prohibit preemployment inquiries concerning an applicant's race, color, national origin, sex, marital status, religion, or age, such inquiries are disfavored because they create an inference that these factors will be used as selection criteria. These inquiries may also be expressly prohibited under state law. As a general rule, recruitment personnel should ask themselves, "What information do I really need to decide whether an applicant is qualified to perform this job?"

With respect to the ADA, employers should be proactive and engage in an interactive process with employees requesting accommodation. According to David Fram, director of equal employment opportunities and ADA services at the National Employment Law Institute, "Lack of communication is a big cause of lawsuits. If you share with someone how hard you're trying, he or she is likely to be less mad."[149] If an employer explores every option but still cannot find a way to provide an accom-

148. California codified this recommendation in 2004 by requiring that all supervisors employed in companies of more than fifty employees undergo harassment training every two years. CAL. GOV'T CODE § 12950.1 (West 2004).

149. *Interactive Process Helps Employers Prevail, but Isn't Required,* CORP. COUNS. WKLY., Jan. 10, 2001, at 12.

*(Continued)*

(The Responsible Manager *continued*)

modation, the employer should inform the individual and ask if he or she has any advice.[150] Employers should create a paper trail to document the actions they took to find an accommodation. While focusing on finding an accommodation, the employer should refrain from determining whether the employee is actually disabled and allow the courts to make that determination.

Employers may also want to purchase employment practice liability insurance (EPLI) to protect against discrimination claims. Although these insurance plans were expensive, did not have broad coverage, and excluded punitive damages when they were introduced in the early 1990s, by the late 1990s, more carriers had entered the market, resulting in lower prices and expanded coverage.

Dating and romantic relationships between employees at a company can lead to discrimination and sexual harassment claims, particularly when there is a significant power and age gap between partners. Such relationships are very perilous. If the parties have a falling out, the subordinate may claim that the relationship was not consensual and say that he or she feared adverse employment consequences for rebuffing the manager's advances. To address this problem, IBM instituted a policy that a manager may become involved with a subordinate as long as the manager transfers to another job within or outside the company so that he or she is not supervising or evaluating the performance of the subordinate involved.

150. *Id.*

INSIDE STORY

## FROM WALL STREET TO MAIN STREET, WOMEN DEMAND EQUAL OPPORTUNITY

In 1973, Helen O'Bannon, who had graduated with honors from Wellesley College and received a Master's degree in economics from Stanford University, applied for a job as a stockbroker at Merrill Lynch. The firm gave O'Bannon a test that included the question, "When you meet a woman, what interests you the most about her: (a) her beauty; (b) her intellect." She later learned that applicants received more points for choosing "beauty" than "intellect." When Merrill Lynch turned down her application, O'Bannon filed a class-action sex discrimination lawsuit against Merrill, which resulted in Merrill's 1976 agreement to comply with U.S. civil rights laws and to hire applicants based on their qualifications instead of their gender.[151]

Twenty-one years later, eight women filed another class-action sex discrimination lawsuit against Merrill. The women alleged that they received lower compensation and had fewer opportunities for advancement than men. The *Cremin v. Merrill Lynch* lawsuit was settled in 1998 when the class representatives accepted a dispute resolution process that, under certain circumstances, led to arbitration. Since that time, almost one thousand women have filed claims against Merrill, most of which were resolved privately through negotiation and mediation.

151. *Now ACTS: Join Us!, at* http://www.nownyc.org/news/julyaug00news/nowacts2.htm (last visited Feb. 16, 2005).

In April 2004, a panel of arbitrators found that Merrill had engaged in a "pattern and practice of discrimination" and ordered it to pay $2.2 million to Hydie Sumner, a broker who had worked in Merrill's San Antonio, Texas office.[152] This decision was the largest award to date stemming from the *Cremin* dispute resolution process.

In August 2004, the *New York Times* published an article about claims filed early on by Valery and Janine Craane, a high-revenue generating mother-daughter stockbroker team known as the Craane Group, that sex discrimination at Merrill had cost them tens of millions of dollars in lost compensation.[153] Valery Craane, who started at Merrill in the early 1970s, claims that she and Janine did not receive big accounts, were passed over when Merrill allotted shares of new stocks and initial public offering shares to brokers, and did not receive the same type of administrative and emotional support as their male colleagues. The Craanes asserted that sex

152. Susan Antilla, *Merrill's Woman Problem—What Men Didn't Know*, Nov. 29, 2004, *at* http://www.bloomberg.com/apps/news?pid=10000039&sid=aLk_rlImn86Y&refer=columnist_antilla.

153. Patrick McGreehan, *What Merrill's Women Want*, N.Y. TIMES, Aug. 22, 2004, available at http://www.nytimes.com/2004/08/02/business/yourmoney/22sex.html.

*(Continued)*

(Inside Story *continued*)

discrimination at Merrill continued because "it was like a fraternity," with Merrill managers regularly going to strip clubs with male brokers.[154] According to Janine Craane, "You have your boys, your soldiers, the guys that you trust. Whether they're not so talented is maybe not so important as their loyalty to the group."[155] The men simply feel that "women don't belong."[156]

The women at Merrill Lynch are not the only women on Wall Street who believe they have been treated unfairly by their employer. In the late 1990s, a class action was filed against Smith Barney on behalf of more than 20,000 current and former female employees who alleged that they were subjected to a hostile work environment. Smith Barney settled this action by agreeing to allow female employees to bring their claims before a selected arbitrator.[157] In July 2004, Morgan Stanley announced a $54 million settlement of a class-action sex discrimination lawsuit brought by its women employees.[158]

At about the same time, a federal district court judge in California certified a class of approximately 1.6 million current and former female Wal-Mart employees in a class-action lawsuit claiming that Wal-Mart failed to promote women to management and to pay them the same wages as similarly situated men.[159] This class action against the nation's largest employer is the largest workplace sex discrimination lawsuit in U.S. history.

The lawyers who brought the class-action lawsuit say their goal is to pressure Wal-Mart to change the way that it behaves toward its more than 700,000 female employees. Wal-Mart stores generally did not advertise openings for managerial trainees, and male managers frequently pinpointed men for "the management track."[160]

154. *Id.*
155. *Id.*
156. *Id.*
157. Richard H. Block & M. Alexis Pennotti, *Reducing Sex Bias Liability on Wall Street,* NAT'L L. J., Jan. 21, 2005, available at http://www.law.com/jsp/article.jsp?id=1105364095728.
158. Betsy Morris, *How Corporate America Is Betraying Women,* FORTUNE, Jan. 10, 2005, at 66, 67.
159. Associated Press, *Judge Approves Wal-Mart Class Action Case,* Forbes.com, June 22, 2004, *at* http://www.forbes.com/feeds/ap/2004/06/22/ap1426888.html.
160. Steven Greenhouse & Constance L. Hays, *Wal-Mart Sex-Bias Suit Given Class Action Status,* N.Y. TIMES, June 23, 2004, at A-1.

Although women comprise almost 90 percent of Wal-Mart's cashiers, only 15.5 percent of its store managers are women. In addition, men at all levels are generally paid more. Stephanie Odle, an assistant store manager in Riverside, California, was surprised to learn that a male assistant manager at the same store was making approximately $25,000 per year more than she did. When she confronted the district manager about the salary difference, he replied that the other "assistant manager has a family and two children to support."[161] Stephanie is a single mother.

Like the women of Wall Street, the Wal-Mart plaintiffs assert that the Wal-Mart culture "did not take them seriously" and included "visits to strip clubs for managers and clients."[162] A store manager told one plaintiff: "Men are here to make a career and women aren't. Retail is for housewives who just need to earn extra money."[163]

With such a large class, any settlement by Wal-Mart could cost the company billions of dollars, even if individual plaintiffs receive small awards. The day after the class was certified, shares of Wal-Mart's stock fell 1.8 percent on the New York Stock Exchange. Wal-Mart opposed the class-action certification, claiming that it does not have a "centralized employment policy and that individual stores and district managers, rather than headquarters, make decisions on pay and promotions."[164] The plaintiffs, however, disproved these claims. As Judge Jenkins, who certified the Wal-Mart class, noted:

> The plaintiffs' request for class certification is being ruled upon in a year that marks the 50th anniversary of the Supreme Court's decision in *Brown v. Board of Education.* This anniversary serves as a reminder of the importance of the courts in addressing the denial of equal treatment under the law wherever and by whomever it occurs.[165]

To help improve its image, Wal-Mart has spent millions of dollars on television advertisements showing that it treats women well. It also announced that all senior managers would lose 7.5 percent of their bonuses in the next year if women were not promoted in direct proportion to the numbers that applied for management jobs.

161. William Rodamor, *The Class of '04,* CAL. LAW., Sept. 2003, at 22.
162. Greenhouse and Hays, *supra* note 160.
163. *Id.*
164. *Id.*
165. Rodamor, *supra* note 161.

## KEY WORDS AND PHRASES

bona fide occupational qualification (BFOQ) 477
BFOQ defense 477
disparate impact 465
disparate treatment 464
fetal-protection policy 475
hostile environment harassment 466
*quid pro quo* harassment 466
reasonable factor other than age (RFOA) defense 480

## QUESTIONS AND CASE PROBLEMS

1. Hewlett-Packard launched a workplace diversity campaign that consisted of hanging posters entitled "Diversity Is Our Strength." Each poster depicted an HP employee above the caption "Black," "Blonde," "Old," "Gay," or "Hispanic." In response to the "Gay" posters, employee Richard Peterson, a self-described "devout Christian" who believes homosexual activities violate the commandments in the Bible, posted two biblical scriptures on an overhead bin in his work cubicle. One of these passages stated: "If a man also lie with mankind, as he lieth with a woman, both of them have committed an abomination; they shall surely be put to death; their blood shall be put upon them." Leviticus 20:13.

   Peterson's direct supervisor removed the scriptural passages after she determined that the posting of the verses violated HP's policy prohibiting harassment, which stated: "Any comments or conduct relating to a person's race, gender, religion, disability, age, sexual orientation, or ethnic background that fail to respect the dignity and feeling [sic] of the individual are unacceptable."

   Peterson informed management that HP's diversity campaign was an initiative to "target" heterosexual and fundamentalist Christian employees by condoning homosexuality. Peterson once again posted the scriptures in his cubicle and stated that he would not remove them unless HP removed the "Gay" posters. Peterson was subsequently terminated for insubordination. Does Peterson have a valid claim of religious discrimination against HP? Do Peterson's gay coworkers have a claim against HP for Peterson's postings? [*Peterson v. Hewlett-Packard*, 358 F.3d 599 (9th Cir. 2004).]

2. Marianne Stanley was hired as head coach of the University of Southern California's women's basketball team in 1989. She had a four-year contract that paid a salary of $62,000 and provided a $6,000 annual housing allowance. During negotiations to renew her contract in 1993, she sought a salary equivalent to the one paid to George Raveling, the men's basketball coach. USC refused to pay her this amount and terminated Stanley when she did not accept a lower salary.

   Stanley sued USC for sex discrimination and retaliatory discharge. USC argued that the men's coach received a higher salary because he had greater responsibility for generating revenues; generated more revenue for the university, and was placed under more pressure to win games by the fans and media. Stanley argued that this greater responsibility was due to the university's history of disparate treatment of the men's and women's teams: USC had invested more in the men's team and had promoted it more heavily than the women's team. Should this history be considered by the court in reaching a decision? [*Stanley v. University of Southern California*, 178 F.3d 1069 (9th Cir. 1999).]

3. Mary Lipphardt and Donald Knuth were employees of Durango Steakhouse. Lipphardt began dating Knuth, one of her supervisors, while they were both working at Durango. One month after they began living together, Lipphardt ended their relationship. Knuth consistently tried to convince Lipphardt to resume their intimate relationship. He called her at work and brushed up against her at the restaurant in a way that was sexual and made Lipphardt uncomfortable. At one point, Knuth blocked Lipphardt in a back office and propositioned her. He let her out after fifteen minutes, but he followed her to her car later that evening and asked her to resume their relationship.

   Lipphardt reported Knuth's actions to a manager, general manager, and a regional manager. While Lipphardt was on a previously scheduled vacation, the general manager told Knuth that his supervisor was considering firing both Lipphardt and Knuth. The general manager asked Knuth if he knew of anything that could get Lipphardt fired, as the restaurant would rather keep Knuth. Knuth told the general manager that Lipphardt was giving free food to employees at a tanning salon in exchange for free tanning services. Durango fired Lipphardt without verifying Knuth's information. Lipphardt sued Durango for hostile work environment sexual harassment and retaliation. What result? How should Lipphardt's general manager have responded to her complaints about Knuth? [*Lipphardt v. Durango Steakhouse of Brandon*, 267 F.3d 1183 (11th Cir. 2001).]

4. Rosalie Cullen was forty-nine years old and had worked as a manager of marketing administration for Olin Corporation for over twenty-five years. She was terminated in February 1996 because, according to Olin, they were downsizing due to an economic downturn. Cullen filed a suit against Olin under the ADEA, alleging that she was fired due to her age. She presented evidence that Doug Cahill, the president of

the Winchester Division of Olin, where Cullen worked, had remarked at a meeting that some employees were "old fashioned" and that "older people have trouble with change and that they were gonna have to learn to go with the change or conform or they were going to be out." In addition, she introduced evidence that after she was fired, all of her duties were taken over by employees ranging in age from thirty-two to forty-three years old. Olin argued that Cahill was so far removed from the selection process that his comments did not motivate the decision to discharge her. Cullen argued that Cahill was the person who decided that personnel cutbacks were necessary, set the parameters for the layoffs, and reviewed the vice president's personnel decisions. Did Olin violate the ADEA? [*Cullen v. Olin Corp.*, 195 F.3d 317 (7th Cir. 1999), *cert. denied*, 529 U.S. 1020 (2000).]

5. Amaani Lyle applied for the position of writers' assistant for *Friends*, a television show about the lives of young, sexually active adults. During her interview, she was told that one of the most important aspects of the job was taking very copious and detailed notes for the writers' meetings where story lines, jokes, and dialogue were discussed. She was also told that she must type incredibly fast. Four months after she was hired, the *Friends* producers fired Lyle because she consistently missed very important story lines and jokes during the writers' meetings and typed too slowly.

   Lyle subsequently filed a claim for sexual harassment. She claimed that during the writers' meetings, the writers constantly engaged in discussions about anal and oral sex, discussed their sexual exploits both real and fantasized, commented on the sexual nature of the female actors on the show, made and displayed crude drawings of women's breasts and vaginas, pretended to masturbate, and altered the words on the scripts and other documents to create new words such as "tits" and "penis."

   Warner Brothers defended on the basis that the writers' job was to create jokes, dialogue, and story lines for an adult-oriented situation comedy:

   > [B]ecause 'Friends' deals with sexual matters, intimate body parts and risqué humor, the writers of the show are required to have frank sexual discussions and tell colorful jokes and stories (and even make expressive gestures) as part of the creative process of developing story lines, dialogue, gags, and jokes for each episode. Lyle, as a writers' assistant, would reasonably be exposed to such discussions, jokes, and gestures.

   Who should prevail on Lyle's sexual harassment claim? [*Lyle v. Warner Brothers Television*, 12 Cal. Rptr. 3d 511 (Cal. Ct. App. 2004), *petition for review granted*, 94 P.3d 476 (Cal. 2004).]

6. Anthony Buie worked in the finishing department at Quad/Graphics. Buie's supervisors warned him about frequent absenteeism three times between March 1998 and September 1999. When providing the last warning, his supervisor gave him a written notice that continued attendance problems could result in termination. In October 1999, Buie called in sick again and told his supervisor that he had AIDS and that his absenteeism was due to the disease. This was the first time Quad/Graphics knew of Buie's condition. Several days later, Quad/Graphics told Buie not to return to work.

   Several days later, Buie met with Caroline Vrabel, Quad/Graphics' employee services manager, who told him that he could apply for FMLA leave for some of the absences when he had called in sick. She further told him not to report to work until he had completed the FMLA application and his attendance issue had been resolved. Buie complied, but after he returned to work, Frank Arndorfer, vice president of finishing operations, decided that Buie's leave would be considered a disciplinary suspension for excessive absenteeism.

   In November Buie met with Vrabel and Arndorfer. Vrabel told Buie that she had excused many of his absences, but that she had calculated that he still had accumulated fourteen unexcused absences during the preceding eleven months, including six no-call, no-show absences. When Buie met again with Vrabel and Arndorfer several days later, Arndorfer presented Buie with a last-chance agreement and offered him the choice between signing the agreement or being fired immediately. The agreement, which Buie signed, stated that he could be terminated for any violation of the employee services manual or the agreement itself. Several weeks later, Buie was terminated after a couple of confrontations with coworkers. His coworkers who were involved in the incidents were disciplined but not discharged.

   Did Quad/Graphics discriminate against Buie on the basis of his disability? Does Buie have a valid claim for retaliation under the FMLA? [*Buie v. Quad/Graphics, Inc.*, 366 F.3d 496 (7th Cir. 2004).]

7. In 1989, Audrey Jacques began working for DiMarzio, Inc., an electric guitar manufacturer. Jacques had been treated for psychiatric problems

for over forty years. Jacques's relations with her coworkers started to deteriorate after she took a two-week leave of absence to recover from a physical ailment. In 1993, she was diagnosed as having a "chronic" form of "Bipolar II Disorder." By 1996, her working relationship with her coworkers and managers had become poisonous. After a coworker complained that Jacque had harassed her, the plant manager terminated Jacques.

Jacques filed a lawsuit claiming that DiMarzio had fired her in violation of the Americans with Disabilities Act. DiMarzio conceded that Jacques's bipolar disorder is a "mental impairment" for purposes of the Act, but argued that "interacting with others" is not a major life activity protected under the ADA. Is "interacting with others" a major life activity? Why or why not? Assuming that it is a major life activity, what showing should be required for a plaintiff to be considered "substantially limited" in interacting with others? [*Audrey Jacques v. DiMarzio, Inc.*, 386 F.3d 192 (2d Cir. 2004).]

8. Rena Lockard worked as a waitress during the evening shift at a Pizza Hut in Atoka, Oklahoma. On November 6, 1993, two crude and rowdy male customers came into the restaurant. These two men had eaten at the restaurant several times in the past and had made offensive comments to Lockard, such as "I would like to get into your pants." Lockard had informed her manager, Micky Jack, that she did not like waiting on them but did not repeat the comments they had made. On November 6, Jack ordered Lockard to wait on the two men after other wait staff, including young men, argued over who would serve them because no one wanted to wait on them. While Lockard was waiting on them, one of the customers commented to Lockard that she smelled good and asked what kind of perfume she was wearing. When she responded that it was none of his business, he grabbed her by the hair. Lockard informed Jack of the incident and said that she did not want to continue waiting on them. Jack responded, "You wait on them. You were hired to be a waitress. You waitress." When Lockard returned to the table with a pitcher of beer, one of the customers pulled her to him by the hair, grabbed her breast, and put his mouth on it. Lockard told Jack that she was quitting and left.

   Lockard sued Pizza Hut, Inc., and its owner A&M Food Service, Inc., alleging sexual harassment under Title VII and intentional infliction of emotional distress. Should Pizza Hut be held responsible for its customers' actions? [*Lockard v. Pizza Hut, Inc.*, 162 F.3d 1062 (10th Cir. 1998).]

9. William West was a sixty-two-year-old engineer who had worked at Bechtel Corporation for thirty years. West was approached by Bechtel to work as manager of engineering on the Jubail Project, a two-year project constructing an industrial city in Saudi Arabia. The project was to be performed by Saudi Arabian Bechtel Company (SABCO), a Bechtel foreign subsidiary, for the Royal Commission, an organ of the Saudi government. The Royal Commission retained the right in its contract with SABCO to remove or replace any SABCO personnel at its sole discretion. West accepted the offer, viewing the position as the final "jewel in the crown" of a successful career. SABCO submitted West's résumé, which disclosed that he was sixty-two, to the Royal Commission, and he was approved for service.

   Before embarking for Saudi Arabia, West signed a "Recital of International Employment Conditions," which stated: "Your assignment is for an indefinite period; and, assuming your performance is satisfactory, the assignment will continue until Bechtel advises you that your services are no longer required, in which event you will be given a minimum of four weeks written notice of assignment completion."

   When West arrived in Saudi Arabia, he was informed by Norm Shotwell, SABCO's program director for the Jubail Project, that West was going to have a problem because his gray hair showed that he was over fifty, and people over fifty were "regarded with suspicion" in Saudi Arabia. (Saudi Arabian law does not prohibit employment discrimination on the basis of age.) Shortly after West's arrival, Shotwell received a letter from the deputy director of the Royal Commission stating that West did not satisfy the Commission's requirements and should be replaced as soon as possible. As a result, Shotwell immediately took West off the project.

   After he returned to the United States, West was depressed and withdrawn as a result of his dismissal. Bechtel offered him many other projects, but he turned them down. West then sued Bechtel Corporation, claiming that his employment on the SABCO project was terminated because of his age. How should the court rule on West's claim? Did SABCO act ethically when it terminated West? [*West v. Bechtel Corp.*, 96 Cal. App. 4th 966 (Cal. Ct. App. 2002).]

## MANAGER'S DILEMMA

**10.** Catherine Van Order is a manager at American Eagle's hangar at the Miami International Airport. The hangar's workforce consists of eighty mechanics, including a small number of African Americans, Latinos, and white ex-strikers from Eastern Air Lines who are earning half as much as they did at their old employer. American Eagle is struggling to regain the public's confidence after two of its planes suffered fatal crashes. Although the airline is downsizing in two other cities in the South, it wants to increase its business to Latin America and the Caribbean so it has hired more staff at the Miami airport. Workers were assigned heavy workloads at low pay and have to work with aging equipment in run-down facilities, leading to a great deal of tension at the Miami airport hangar.

Employees have tried to ease the tension by playing practical jokes on each other and making wisecracks. These jokes have included sexual and ethnic jokes along with comments about people's appearance, including weight, and their religion. Employees posted cartoons depicting black mechanics as gorillas or starving Somalis on the bulletin board. When Van Order suggested to one of the mechanics that the joking was getting out of control, he told her that people were just making fun of stereotypes and that nobody was trying to be personally offensive to their coworkers.

Although no employees complained to her about the joking, Van Order issued a memo setting forth the company's policy on discrimination and harassment. Several employees then told her that the memo had affected morale; without the joking, workers seemed tense and anxious and were less productive. Within several weeks, the joking commenced again and escalated when a poster of a black basketball player with a mop on his head and a watermelon in his hand was posted in the locker room. After this incident, Van Order spoke to several African-American workers about it, but they seemed reluctant to talk about it. She sensed that they were quiet for fear of either losing their jobs or becoming the victim of hostile treatment by their coworkers. What should Van Order do?

## INTERNET SOURCES

| | |
|---|---|
| Equal Employment Opportunity Commission | http://www.eeoc.gov |
| U.S. Department of Labor | http://www.dol.gov |
| The site for the International Labour Organization, a United Nations–sponsored agency, provides excellent reports on employment issues throughout the world. | http://www.ilo.org |
| This site, maintained by a nonprofit organization founded to disseminate information about disabilities in the workplace, provides a searchable guide, with links, to disability resources on the Internet and the Disability Resources Monthly reports. | http://www.disabilityresources.org/ |
| The Small Business Advisor maintains a searchable site with links to articles and sites concerning employment issues. | http://www.isquare.com/ |
| American Civil Liberties Union | http://www.aclu.org/ |
| This site, maintained by the National Employment Law Institute (a nonprofit organization providing training and information for human resources professionals and managers), provides articles and links relating to employment issues. | http://www.neli.org |
| The AHI Employment Law Resource Center publishes articles, provides links to government sites and other information, and offers free biweekly e-mail updates on employment law. | http://www.ahipubs.com/ |

# UNIT IV

# THE REGULATORY ENVIRONMENT

CHAPTER 14

# Criminal Law

## INTRODUCTION

### IMPACT ON CORPORATE BEHAVIOR

Criminal law is a powerful tool for controlling corporate behavior and ensuring ethical conduct. Companies devote significant resources to preventing and defending criminal law violations. Areas of concern for many managers include bribery, compliance with environmental laws, worker safety, government contracts, securities fraud, antitrust law compliance, and securities trading by officers and directors.

White-collar crime is rampant. According to a survey conducted in 2003, one-third of the companies in the world have engaged in criminal misconduct.[1] The most common U.S. crime was asset misappropriation, followed by cybercrime.[2] Criminal liability may be imposed in several ways. Individuals are always responsible for their own criminal acts, even if they are working under orders from top management. Supervisors may also be vicariously liable for the acts of their subordinates. Corporations (and other business entities) may also be found guilty of crimes based on the illegal conduct of their employees.

### CHAPTER OVERVIEW

This chapter defines the elements necessary to create criminal liability. It discusses the statutory sources of criminal law and then describes criminal procedure—the mechanics of a criminal action, the plea options, and the trial. Constitutional issues, including search warrant requirements and the privilege against self-incrimination, are explained. The chapter continues with a discussion of the Federal Sentencing Guidelines. Then it summarizes a variety of white-collar crimes, including violations of the Racketeer Influenced and Corrupt Organizations Act, wire and mail fraud, computer crime, and obstruction of justice. It concludes with a list of penalties and a description of three federal amnesty and leniency programs.

1. *Financial Misrepresentation Leads Concerns in New Corporate Economic Crime Survey*, CORP. COUNS. WKLY., July 23, 2003, at 227.
2. *Id.*

## Definition of a Crime

A *crime* is an offense against the public at large. It may be defined as any act that violates the duties owed to the community, for which the offender must make satisfaction to the public. An act is criminal only if it is defined as criminal in a federal or state statute or in a local ordinance enacted by a city or county.

Two elements are necessary to create criminal liability: (1) an act that violates an existing criminal statute, and (2) the requisite state of mind.

### THE CRIMINAL ACT

The term *actus reus* (guilty act or wrongful deed) is often used to describe the act in question. A crime is not committed unless some overt act has occurred. Merely thinking about a criminal activity is not criminal.

### THE STATE OF MIND

Generally, a crime is not committed unless the criminal act named in the statute is performed with the requisite state of mind, known as *mens rea* (guilty mind). Under some statutes, however, a person can be guilty regardless of his or her state of mind or degree of fault. This is known as *strict liability*.

### *Strict Liability*

Strict liability statutes are generally disfavored. Most courts will require clear legislative intent to impose strict liability before they will construe a statute as imposing strict liability. The U.S. Supreme Court has stated that the requirement of "a relation between some mental element and punishment for a harmful act is almost as instinctive as the child's familiar exculpatory 'But I didn't mean to.'"[3] Typically, strict liability statutes address issues of public health and safety. (Strict liability statutes that provide for vicarious criminal liability are discussed later in the chapter.)

### *Mens Rea*

The three forms of *mens rea* are negligence, recklessness, and intention to do wrong. Negligence is the least culpable state of mind, and intention to do wrong is the most culpable. The statute that defines the criminal act also defines the requisite state of mind. Generally speaking, crimes associated with a higher degree of culpability are punished more severely. Convictions for intentional homicide, for instance, bring penalties far more harsh than those for negligent homicide.

*Negligence* is the failure to see the possible negative consequences that a reasonable person would have seen. An individual may be negligent even if he or she did not know of the possible harm of his or her act. All that is necessary is that a reasonable person would have known of the possible harm. A reasonable person is often thought of as a rational person using ordinary care under the circumstances. *Recklessness* in the criminal context is conscious disregard of a substantial risk that the individual's actions will result in the harm prohibited by the statute. Recklessness is found when the individual knew of the possible harm of his or her act but ignored the risk. A person has an *intention to do wrong* when he or she consciously intends to cause the harm prohibited by the statute, or when he or she knows such harm is substantially certain to result from his or her conduct.

Merely being able to define these terms, however, often does not provide an answer to more complex questions of real-world guilt. Consider the intention-to-do-wrong requirement in the context of the federal false-statement statute.[4] The statute makes it a crime to "knowingly and willfully" make any false statement or representation "in any manner within the jurisdiction of any department or agency of the United States." Suppose that a defendant made a statement to a federal agent that she knew was false. However, she did not know that the person to whom she directed the statement was a federal agent. Would this defendant be convicted?

In *United States v. Yermian*,[5] the U.S. Supreme Court ruled that she would be. The Court applied the "intention-to-do-wrong" requirement only to the "false-statement" portion of the statute. In other words, it required only that the defendant knowingly lied to a person who was in fact a federal agent, rather than that she knowingly lied to a person who she knew was a federal agent.

A commonly invoked platitude is "ignorance of the law is no excuse." Although true as a general principle, this is an imprecise rule that, taken alone, does not tell courts how to apply the *mens rea* requirements of particular criminal statutes. There is often substantial room for interpretation and debate as to the meaning of certain statutes and the *mens rea* required under them. For example, in *Liparota v. United States*,[6] the Supreme Court addressed the *mens rea* required by the federal food stamp fraud statute, which provides that "whoever knowingly uses, transfers, acquires, alters or possesses coupons or authorization cards in any manner not authorized by [the statute] or the regulations" is subject to a fine and imprisonment. Acknowledging that it was unclear how far down the sentence the word "knowingly" traveled, the Court set forth the rule that when statutory language is ambiguous, the traditional assumption is that some *mens rea* is required. As a result, the Court held that the defendant could not be convicted under the statute unless he knew that he was acquiring food stamps in an unauthorized or illegal manner.

In *Bryan v. United States*,[7] the Supreme Court held that, as a general matter, a "willful" act is "one undertaken with a 'bad purpose.' In other words, in order to establish a 'willful' violation of a statute, 'the Government must prove that the defendant acted with knowledge that his conduct was unlawful.'" The defendant does not need to know which particular law he or she is breaking, however, only that some law is being violated. In contrast, the term "knowingly" merely requires proof of knowledge of the facts that constitute the offense, not knowledge of unlawfulness, unless (as in *Liparota*) the text of the statute dictates a different result.

3. Morissette v. United States, 342 U.S. 246, 250–51 (1952).
4. 18 U.S.C. § 1001.
5. 468 U.S. 63 (1984).
6. 471 U.S. 419 (1985).
7. 524 U.S. 184 (1998).

## Sources of Criminal Law

Conviction of a crime can lead to a substantial fine, a prison sentence, or even the death penalty. Because the results of a criminal conviction can be so serious, all criminal liability is specifically defined in statutes, which are binding on a court. In contrast, much of civil law was developed by the courts without applicable statutes.

A criminal charge and prosecution are brought by either the state or the federal government. Under most federal and state laws, crimes are divided into two categories. A *felony* is a crime punishable by death or by imprisonment for more than one year. A *misdemeanor* is a less serious crime, punishable by a fine or a jail sentence of one year or less.

### *The Model Penal Code*

The criminal statutes of the individual states and the federal government are similar but not exactly the same. This is because most states have adopted the Model Penal Code but have modified it to meet their own needs. The Model Penal Code is a set of criminal law statutes that were proposed by the National Conference of Commissioners on Uniform State Laws for adoption by the states.

## Criminal versus Civil Liability

Many regulatory statutes provide for both criminal and civil sanctions if they are violated. An individual or a corporation may therefore be sued under both criminal and civil law for a single act.

Civil law, particularly tort law (discussed in Chapter 9), compensates the victim for legal wrongs committed against the person or his or her property. Criminal law protects society by punishing the criminal. It does not compensate the victim. However, the victim of a crime may bring a civil suit for damages against the perpetrator. Violation of a criminal statute is *negligence per se;* this means that in a subsequent civil suit, the court will accept the criminal conviction as sufficient proof that the defendant was negligent, that is, that he or she did not act with the care a reasonably prudent person would have used under the same circumstances. Consequently, defendants must carefully review their criminal defense strategy in light of possible future civil litigation.

### *Burden of Proof*

Criminal trials differ from civil trials in imposing a much heavier *burden of proof.* Generally, to prevail in a civil trial, the plaintiff need only establish the facts by a *preponderance of the evidence.* If the evidence tips the scales only slightly in favor of the plaintiff, he or she wins. In a criminal case, the accused is presumed innocent until proved guilty beyond a reasonable doubt.

This difference in the degree of proof required is typical of the procedural and constitutional safeguards protecting defendants' rights throughout criminal proceedings. In a criminal case, the formidable resources of the state are focused on an individual. In this contest of unequal strength, it seems only fair to require the state to meet a higher standard of proof. Moreover, in a criminal prosecution, the accused faces the deprivation of personal liberty and the lifelong stigma of criminal conviction, whereas in a civil lawsuit only monetary damages are at stake.

# Criminal Procedure

A criminal action begins with the arrest of the person suspected of a crime and proceeds through a preliminary hearing to plea bargaining and trial.

## Arrest

After a person is *arrested* (taken into custody against his or her will for criminal prosecution or interrogation), he or she is taken to a police station and *booked;* that is, the charges against him or her are written in a register. The arresting police officer must then file a report with the prosecutor. Based on this report, the prosecutor decides whether to press charges against the arrested person. If charges are to be pressed, many states require that the accused be taken before a public judicial official, usually a justice of the peace or magistrate, to be informed of the charges. Bail is often determined during this initial appearance before the public official.

## Plea

If the charge is only a misdemeanor, the accused will be asked at this initial appearance whether he or she pleads guilty or not guilty. In the case of a felony, the next step in many states is a *preliminary hearing,* at which the prosecutor must present evidence demonstrating probable cause that the defendant committed the felony. Following this hearing, formal charges are usually filed either by the prosecutor through an *information,* a document filed with the court, or by a grand jury through an *indictment.* The accused is then arraigned before a trial court judge. At the arraignment, the accused is informed of the charges against him or her and asked to enter a *plea* of guilty or not guilty. If the defendant enters a plea of not guilty, the case is set for trial.

The accused can also plead *nolo contendere,* which means that he or she does not contest the charges. For the purpose of the criminal proceedings, this plea is equivalent to a guilty plea. Unlike a guilty plea, however, a plea of *nolo contendere* cannot be introduced at a subsequent civil trial. Therefore, a *nolo contendere* plea may be used by corporate defendants who anticipate civil suits based on the same activity for which they face criminal charges.

### *Plea Bargaining*

Very few cases ever reach trial. Most cases are resolved through plea bargaining between the accused and the prosecutor. *Plea bargaining* is the process whereby the prosecutor agrees to reduce the charges in exchange for a guilty plea from the accused.

Frequently, a lower-ranking member of a criminal conspiracy will "cop a plea," that is, provide the prosecutor with testimony incriminating his or her criminal superiors, in exchange for a reduced sentence or immunity from prosecution. The immunity granted may be either use immunity or transactional immunity. *Use immunity* prohibits the testimony of the witness from being used against him or her in any way. *Transactional immunity,* which is broader, prohibits any criminal prosecution of the witness that relates to any matter discussed in his or her testimony.

Some courts have challenged the offer of leniency in exchange for testimony as a violation of the federal statute forbidding the exchange of "anything of value" for testimony. However, a majority of U.S. courts of appeals allow the government to offer leniency.[8]

Consent decrees are common in the corporate context. A *consent decree* is a court order based on an agreement by the defendant corporation to take measures to remedy the problem that led to the criminal charges. Like a plea of *nolo contendere,* a consent decree cannot be introduced as evidence of guilt in a subsequent civil trial.

## TRIAL

A criminal trial proceeds in much the same way as civil trials, which were discussed in Chapter 3. There are opening statements, direct examination and cross-examination of witnesses, and closing arguments. The jury then deliberates to reach a verdict of guilty or not guilty.

8. *See, e.g.,* United States v. Singleton, 165 F.3d 1297 (10th Cir. 1999).

# Constitutional Protections

The U.S. Constitution affords criminal defendants a number of important rights and protections.

## EX POST FACTO CLAUSE

Under the *Ex Post Facto Clause* of the U.S. Constitution,[9] a person can be convicted of a crime only if his or her actions constituted a crime at the time they occurred. In *Lynce v. Mathis,*[10] the U.S. Supreme Court explained: "To fall within the ex post facto prohibition, a law must be retrospective—that is, it must apply to events occurring before its enactment—and it must disadvantage the offender affected by it, by altering the definition of criminal conduct or increasing the punishment for the crime."

The Ex Post Facto Clause also prevents a person from having to bear legal consequences for an act when such legal consequences did not exist at the time the act was committed. For example, in *Carmell v. Texas,*[11] Carmell was charged with several sexual offenses against his stepdaughter. At the time the offenses occurred, Texas law provided that a victim's testimony could serve as the basis for a conviction for sexual offenses only if supported by corroborating evidence. Prior to Carmell's trial, however, Texas law was amended to permit conviction for sexual offenses based solely on the victim's testimony. Carmell was convicted on the basis of his stepdaughter's testimony alone. The U.S. Supreme Court held that it was unconstitutional to apply the less strict proof requirements in the amended law to establish Carmell's conviction. Similarly, the U.S. Supreme Court struck down a California statute that permitted the resurrection of otherwise time-bound prosecutions for sex-related child abuse.[12] The U.S. Court of Appeals for the Tenth Circuit applied the Ex Post Facto Clause to an agency regulation that is legislative in nature but acknowledged that there was a split in the circuits over the applicability of the clause to administrative regulators.[13]

9. U.S. CONST. art. 1, § 10.
10. 519 U.S. 433, 441 (1997).
11. 529 U.S. 513 (2000).
12. Stogner v. California, 539 U.S. 607 (2003).
13. Smith v. Scott, 223 F.3d 1191 (10th Cir. 2000). *Accord* United States v. Bell, 991 F.2d 1445 (8th Cir. 1993) (subjecting Federal Sentencing Guidelines to ex post facto analysis). *Contra* Dominique v. Weld, 73 F.3d 1156 (1st Cir. 1996).

## FOURTH AMENDMENT PROTECTIONS

The Fourth Amendment to the U.S. Constitution provides:

> The right of the people to be secure in their persons, houses, papers, and effects, against unreasonable searches and seizures, shall not be violated, and no Warrants shall issue, but upon probable cause, supported by Oath or affirmation, and particularly describing the place to be searched, and the persons or things to be seized.

This provision was intended to prevent the arbitrary and intrusive searches that had characterized British rule during the American colonial period.

The Fourth Amendment applies only to actions by government officials, unless a private person is acting on behalf of the government. Courts have struggled to strike the appropriate balance between the individual's reasonable expectation of privacy and the government's legitimate need to secure evidence of wrongdoing to prevent criminal acts and apprehend criminals.

### *The Arrest Warrant Requirement*

An arrest is a Fourth Amendment seizure. No arrest is valid unless there is probable cause. *Probable cause* for arrest is defined as a reasonable belief that the suspect has committed a crime or is about to commit a crime. The Fourth Amendment does not require that a warrant be obtained prior to an arrest in a public place when the officer has reasonable suspicion to believe a felony has been committed by the individual or when a misdemeanor has been committed in the officer's presence. In general, an arrest warrant is required only for arrests in the suspect's own home or in another person's home. In determining what is "reasonable suspicion," the Supreme Court has deemed nervous, evasive behavior on the part of the suspect to be relevant. For example, in *Illinois v. Wardlow*,[14] the Court held that an arrest made by police officers patrolling a high-crime area was reasonable when the suspect fled after spotting the officers. Stating that headlong flight is a "consummate act of evasion," the Court reasoned that "determination of reasonable suspicion must be based on commonsense judgments and inferences about human behavior."

### *Searches and Seizures and Reasonable Expectations of Privacy*

The touchstone of the Supreme Court's analysis in Fourth Amendment search warrant cases has been whether the individual has a reasonable expectation of privacy under the circumstances. In the Court's landmark Fourth Amendment case, *United States v. Katz*,[15] Justice John Marshall Harlan's concurring opinion framed the issue as follows: Has government action intruded upon an individual's subjective expectation of privacy? If so, is that expectation one that society deems reasonable? If an individual does not have a subjective privacy expectation, or if he or she has an expectation that society would not deem reasonable, then the police are entitled to conduct a search without a warrant. Before conducting a search or seizure that would be deemed unreasonable under the Fourth Amendment, a law enforcement agent must obtain a warrant.

In applying this framework, courts have held that a citizen's interest in freedom from governmental intrusions is very strong in his or her private home—an expectation of privacy there is quite reasonable. In places open to the public (such as a business office), law enforcement has been given broader scope. For instance, the Supreme Court permitted warrantless searches of business offices when the government agent entered during business hours and observed whatever was visible to customers or the public from the public areas of the premises. Similarly, the Court permitted a warrantless search of garbage cans placed at curbside for collection where the garbage was readily accessible to animals and strangers, including the trash haulers who could have sorted through it before commingling it with garbage collected from other dwellings.

No search warrant is required for government officials to search an individual's bank deposit records. An individual lowers the expectation of privacy by revealing his or her affairs to the bank, and he or she assumes the risk that the information will be revealed to the government.

Some stops and searches may be justified without a showing of probable cause (e.g., brief questioning when police observe unusual conduct that leads to a reasonable suspicion of criminal activity). In fact, most police searches are not conducted pursuant to a warrant. These searches are permissible either because they are not deemed "searches" within the meaning of the Fourth Amendment[16] or because they are considered not "unreasonable searches" under the *Katz* test. There are six well-established exceptions to the search warrant requirement: (1) search incident to a lawful arrest; (2) search of an automobile if there is probable cause to believe evidence of a crime will be found;

14. 528 U.S. 119 (2000).

15. 389 U.S. 347 (1967).

16. *See* United States v. Karo, 468 U.S. 705, 712 (1984) (holding that a "search" occurs "when an expectation of privacy that society is prepared to consider reasonable is infringed").

(3) anything discovered by police in plain view if the officers are legitimately on the premises; (4) stop and frisk of a suspect if the officer reasonably believes the suspect is dangerous; (5) search when the owner or a person who appears to have authority voluntarily and intelligently consents to the search; and (6) instances when the police are in "hot pursuit" or when the evidence may disappear before a warrant can be obtained (e.g., blood samples containing alcohol). If a person is validly arrested, the officer has the authority to search the arrestee and the area immediately within the arrestee's control to protect the safety of the officer.

The Supreme Court has drawn a line between visual inspection and tactile examination. A border patrol officer cannot touch or squeeze a bus passenger's carry-on bag placed in the overhead rack, even though other passengers might also be expected to touch the bag.[17]

The Supreme Court has given police broad scope to stop motorists suspected of traffic violations. If a police officer makes a traffic stop that is objectively justified by probable cause to believe a traffic violation has occurred, then it is irrelevant that the police officer might have used the violation only as a pretext to stop the car.[18] Police officers need not inform detained drivers that they are "legally free to go" before asking for consent to search their vehicles.[19] A police officer may order passengers out of a vehicle during the course of a traffic stop,[20] but the police cannot conduct a full car search after issuing a routine traffic citation unless the driver consents.[21]

**Searches Employing New Technology** The framers of the Fourth Amendment protections could not have conceived of the technological tools at the disposal of today's law enforcement agencies. As a result, it has been the duty of the courts to apply those protections in a modern, technologically sophisticated context. The seminal *Katz* decision involved the government's use of an electronic bug on the outside of a pay-phone booth. The Supreme Court ruled this mode of surveillance unconstitutional without a warrant.

More than thirty years later, the Court ruled that police may not use infrared thermal-image scanners to scan homes without a warrant.[22] The scanners revealed artificial heat sources, such as heat being released from grow lights for hidden marijuana crops.

17. Bond v. United States, 529 U.S. 334 (2000).
18. Whren v. United States, 517 U.S. 806 (1996).
19. Ohio v. Robinette, 519 U.S. 33 (1996).
20. Maryland v. Wilson, 519 U.S. 408 (1997).
21. Knowles v. United States, 525 U.S. 113 (1998).
22. Kyllo v. United States, 533 U.S. 27 (2001).

The Court characterized "the right of a man to retreat into his own home and there be free from unreasonable governmental intrusion" as being at "the very core" of the Fourth Amendment. Thus, "[i]n the home . . . all details are intimate details, because the entire area is held safe from prying government eyes." Recognizing that future technology may make it possible to literally see through the walls of a dwelling and stressing the importance of drawing not only a firm but also a "bright" line at the entrance to the house, the Court ruled: "Where, as here, the Government uses a device that is not in general public use, to explore details of the home that would previously have been unknowable without physical intrusion, the surveillance is a 'search' and is presumptively unreasonable without a warrant."

The dissent argued that there is "a distinction of constitutional magnitude" between through-the-wall surveillance that gives the observer or listener direct access to information in a private area, on the one hand, and the thought processes used to draw inferences from information in the public domain obtained from off-the-wall surveillance on the other hand. The thermal-imaging device detected only the heat emitted from the exterior of the house, which could have been observed by a neighbor or passerby. As such, the dissent argued, it did not amount to a search and was "perfectly reasonable."

In a subsequent case, the Supreme Court held that a suspicionless search outside a car by a drug-detection dog during a lawful traffic stop for speeding that revealed the presence of marijuana was not a search subject to the Fourth Amendment.[23] Unlike the thermal-imaging device at issue in *Kyllo,* which could have detected lawful activity within the home—including "at what hour each night the lady of the house takes her daily sauna and bath"—a well-trained narcotics-detection dog's sniff and alert reveal "no information other than the location of a substance that no individual has any right to possess."

A more contested issue is whether police may obtain, without a warrant, the names and electronic addresses of the persons to whom a defendant has sent e-mail. Law enforcement personnel argue that this is equivalent to obtaining pen registers listing telephone calls, which are available without a warrant. Defense lawyers and privacy advocates claim that an e-mail list is far more intrusive and revealing because the names and addresses convey much more information than a series of telephone numbers.

**Suspicionless and Administrative Searches and Seizures** In general, a search or seizure is unreasonable "in the absence of individualized suspicion of

23. Illinois v. Caballes, 125 S. Ct. 834 (2005).

wrongdoing."[24] Nonetheless, the Supreme Court has upheld "certain regimes of suspicionless searches where the program was designed to serve 'special needs, beyond the normal need for law enforcement.'"[25] These include the random drug testing of student-athletes,[26] U.S. Customs Service employees seeking transfer or promotion to certain positions,[27] and railway employees involved in train accidents or found to be in violation of particular safety regulations.[28]

The Court has also upheld suspicionless searches for certain administrative purposes, including inspections of the premises of a "closely regulated" business,[29] fire-damaged structures to determine the cause of a blaze,[30] and buildings to ensure compliance with a city housing code.[31] A warrantless inspection of a closely regulated business will be reasonable only if (1) there is a "substantial" government interest that informs the regulatory scheme pursuant to which the inspection is made; (2) the warrantless inspections are necessary to further the regulatory scheme; and (3) the inspection program, in terms of the certainty and regularity of its application, provides a constitutionally adequate substitute for a warrant.[32]

Recognizing the government's interest in policing the nation's borders, the Court upheld brief, suspicionless seizures of motorists at two fixed Border Control checkpoints that were designed to intercept illegal aliens and were located on major U.S. highways less than one hundred miles from the Mexican border.[33] The Supreme Court also upheld highway sobriety checkpoints designed to detect signs of intoxication and to remove impaired drivers from the road.[34]

But the Court struck down highway checkpoints aimed at the discovery and interdiction of illegal narcotics: "When law enforcement authorities pursue primarily general crime control purposes at checkpoints . . . , stops can only be justified by some quantum of individualized suspicion."[35] The Court distinguished between sobriety checkpoints to protect the public from an "immediate, vehicle-bound threat of life and limb" and narcotics stops "justified only by the generalized and ever-present possibility that interrogation and inspection may reveal that any given motorist has committed a crime." The Court made it clear that sobriety checkpoints, border searches, searches at airports and government buildings, and "roadblocks set up to thwart imminent terrorist attack or to catch a dangerous criminal who is likely to flee by way of a particular route" were not prohibited. The Court left open the legality of a checkpoint program with the primary purpose of checking driver's licenses and a secondary purpose of interdicting narcotics.

**Obtaining a Search Warrant** When a law enforcement agent needs to obtain a search warrant, the agent must persuade a "neutral and detached" magistrate that a search is justified. The rights of private citizens are protected by the requirement that a magistrate, rather than a law enforcement agent, determine whether probable cause exists for a search.

A valid search warrant must (1) be based on probable cause, (2) be supported by an oath or affirmation, and (3) describe in specific detail (with particularity) what is to be searched or seized. Probable cause is to be determined by the totality of the circumstances, balancing the privacy rights of the individual against the government's law enforcement needs.

When government authorities obtain a warrant to conduct a physical search of a business, the scope of the search typically must have some limits. To obtain a broad warrant to conduct a sweeping raid of a company, the government must show that the company is "pervaded by fraud." The "pervaded by fraud" exception applies only to companies that are little more than "boiler room" sales operations engaged only negligibly in legitimate business activities.[36]

## The Exclusionary Rule

The *exclusionary rule* is virtually unique to the U.S. legal system. It prohibits, in many circumstances, the introduction in a criminal trial of evidence offered as proof of guilt that was obtained by an illegal search or seizure in violation of the Fourth Amendment (or in violation of the Fifth Amendment's ban on self-incrimination, discussed below). Illegal evidence includes evidence found when the search went beyond the scope of the warrant, evidence gathered without a warrant when a warrant was required, and evidence acquired directly or indirectly as a result of an illegal search or arrest or interrogation (called *fruit of the poisonous tree*).

24. City of Indianapolis v. Edmond, 531 U.S. 32 (2000).
25. *Id.*
26. Veronia Sch. Dist. 47J v. Acton, 515 U.S. 646 (1995).
27. Treasury Employees v. Von Raab, 489 U.S. 656 (1989).
28. Skinner v. Ry. Labor Executives' Ass'n, 489 U.S. 602 (1989).
29. New York v. Burger, 482 U.S. 691 (1987).
30. Michigan v. Tyler, 436 U.S. 499 (1978).
31. Camara v. Mun. Court of San Francisco, 387 U.S. 523 (1967).
32. United States v. Argent Chem. Labs., Inc., 93 F.3d 572 (9th Cir. 1996).
33. United States v. Martinez-Fuerta, 428 U.S. 543 (1976).
34. Michigan Dep't of State Police v. Sitz, 496 U.S. 444 (1990).
35. City of Indianapolis v. Edmonds, 531 U.S. 32 (2000).
36. *In re* Grand Jury Investigation Concerning Solid State Devices, Inc., 130 F.3d 853 (9th Cir. 1997).

The exclusionary rule is often criticized in the media as simply a device to set guilty criminals free on a technicality. Supporters of the rule argue that it is necessary to protect personal freedom.

### Exceptions to the Exclusionary Rule

After a shift in its composition during the 1980s, the U.S. Supreme Court began to sharply limit the application of the exclusionary rule. The two most important limitations the Court has elaborated are the good faith exception and the inevitable discovery exception.

The *good faith exception* provides that evidence obtained by police in good faith will not be excluded from trial, even if it was obtained in violation of the Fourth Amendment.[37] Because the exclusionary rule was designed to deter police misconduct, the Court reasoned that no deterrent purpose would be served by excluding evidence the police acquired while acting in good faith. The Court extended the good faith exception to cover errors made by court personnel. As a result, if police conduct an unconstitutional search relying on erroneous information from a court employee, the exclusionary rule will not apply.

The *inevitable discovery exception* provides that illegally obtained evidence can lawfully be introduced at trial if it can be shown that the evidence would inevitably have been found by other legal means.[38] For example, *United States v. Pimentel*[39] concerned Duroyd Manufacturing Company, a defense contractor that falsified documents and charges to the Defense Department. Evidence of this fraud was contained in a letter to Duroyd from one of its subcontractors, which the government obtained in an illegal search. Duroyd sought to exclude the letter from evidence. Because the contract gave the Defense Department's auditors the right to examine all "books, records, documents and other evidence . . . sufficient to reflect properly all direct and indirect costs . . . incurred for the performance of this contract," the court held that this letter would inevitably have been discovered and refused to apply the exclusionary rule.

37. United States v. Leon, 468 U.S. 897 (1984).
38. Nix v. Williams, 467 U.S. 431 (1984).
39. 810 F.2d 366 (2d Cir. 1987).

## Fifth Amendment Protections

The Fifth Amendment prohibits forced self-incrimination, double jeopardy, and criminal conviction without due process of law.

### Self-Incrimination

The Fifth Amendment provides that no person "shall be compelled in any criminal case to be a witness against himself." This protection against self-incrimination extends to the preliminary stages in the criminal process as well as the trial itself. In a landmark self-incrimination case, *Miranda v. Arizona*,[40] decided in 1966, the Supreme Court laid down what has become known as the *Miranda* rule: a statement made by a defendant in custody is admissible only if the defendant was informed prior to police interrogation of his or her constitutional right to remain silent and to have counsel present. These warnings are referred to as the *Miranda warnings*. In 2000, the Supreme Court invalidated a federal statute[41] that purported to overrule the *Miranda* rule,[42] reasoning that "Miranda's constitutional character prevailed against a federal statute that sought to restore the old regime of giving no warnings and litigating most statements' voluntariness."[43]

In the following case, the Supreme Court considered the constitutionality of the police practice of question first, warn later.

40. 384 U.S. 436 (1966).
41. 18 U.S.C. § 3501.
42. Dickerson v. United States, 530 U.S. 428 (2000).
43. Missouri v. Seibert, 124 S. Ct. 2601 (2004).

**A Case in Point**

## Summary

**CASE 14.1**
**Missouri v. Seibert**
*Supreme Court of the United States*
*124 S. Ct. 2601 (2004).*

**› FACTS** Patrice Seibert's son, who had cerebral palsy, died in his sleep. Concerned that Seibert would be accused of neglecting her son, Seibert's other sons and their friends plotted with her to burn down their mobile home in order to make it look as though her son had died in the fire. As part of the plan, Donald, an eighteen-year-old mentally challenged boy who was living with the Seiberts, was left in the mobile home when it was set on fire so that Seibert's son would not appear to have been alone. Donald died in the fire. An officer questioned Seibert for an estimated thirty to forty minutes before informing her of her rights. After she confessed, the officer read her the

*(Continued)*

(Case 14.1 *continued*)

*Miranda* warnings, which she signed; subsequently, she confessed again. Seibert was found guilty of second-degree murder in a Missouri state court that admitted the post-*Miranda* confession but not the pre-*Miranda* confession. The Missouri Supreme Court overturned the conviction, and the State of Missouri appealed.

**› ISSUE PRESENTED** Does purposefully waiting to provide a *Miranda* warning until the middle of an interrogation violate the accused's *Miranda* rights?

**› SUMMARY OF OPINION** The U.S. Supreme Court upheld the decision of the Missouri Supreme Court and ruled that Seibert's postwarning statements were inadmissible. The midstream recitation of warnings after an interrogation and unwarned confession did not comply with *Miranda*'s constitutional warning requirement.

The Supreme Court explained:

> Question-first's object . . . is to render Miranda warnings ineffective by waiting to give them until after the suspect has already confessed. The threshold question in this situation is whether it would be reasonable to find that the warnings could function "effectively" as Miranda requires. There is no doubt about the answer. By any objective measure, it is likely that warnings withheld until after interrogation and confession will be ineffective in preparing a suspect for successive interrogation, close in time and similar in content. The manifest purpose of question-first is to get a confession the suspect would not make if he understood his rights at the outset. When the warnings are inserted in the midst of coordinated and continuing interrogation, they are likely to mislead and deprive a defendant of knowledge essential to his ability to understand the nature of his rights and the consequences of abandoning them. And it would be unrealistic to treat two spates of integrated and proximately conducted questioning as independent interrogations subject to independent evaluation simply because Miranda warnings formally punctuate them in the middle.

Unlike the situation in *Oregon v. Elstad*,[44] when the police mistakenly forgot to read an accused his *Miranda* rights, the police in this case consciously chose to wait until the suspect had confessed before reading her her rights.

**› RESULT** Patrice Seibert's post-*Miranda* warning confession was inadmissible in court. Her conviction was overturned.

**› COMMENTS** Justice Breyer concurred with the majority decision, writing: "In my view, the following simple rule should apply to the two-stage interrogation technique: Courts should exclude the 'fruits' of the initial unwarned questioning unless the failure to warn was in good faith." Justices O'Connor, Scalia, and Thomas dissented.

44. 470 U.S. 298 (1985).

---

The Fifth Amendment privilege against self-incrimination applies only to compelled testimonial evidence. Requiring defendants to provide tangible evidence such as fingerprints, body fluids (urine and blood), or voice or handwriting samples does not violate the Fifth Amendment prohibition against self-incrimination. Requiring a person to appear in a lineup also does not violate the privilege.

**Business Records and Papers and the Collective Entity Doctrine** The Fifth Amendment protection for business records and papers is very limited. Corporations (and other business entities) enjoy no protection. Under the *collective entity doctrine*, the Supreme Court has held that the custodian of records for a collective entity (such as a corporation) may not resist a subpoena for such records on the ground that the act of production will incriminate him or her.[45] Nonetheless, the custodian cannot be compelled to testify as to the contents of the documents if that testimony would incriminate him or her personally.

The Fifth Amendment privilege may not be invoked to resist compliance with a regulatory regime, as long as that regime is designed with a public purpose unrelated to the enforcement of criminal laws.[46] Thus, when government regulations require a business to keep certain records, those records can be used against the reporting individual in a criminal prosecution.

The business records compiled by a sole proprietor may have some protection if the government cannot authenticate the documents without the proprietor. In that case, the act of furnishing the documents may have the qualities of self-incriminating testimony.[47] In short, although a person can be required to hand over specified documents, he or she cannot be required to assist in identifying sources of information.[48]

**Foreign Prosecutions** A witness in a U.S. proceeding who is not facing prosecution in the United States may not invoke the privilege to avoid having to give testimony that might incriminate the witness in another country, unless the sovereign that the witness fears will prosecute him or her is itself bound by the privilege.[49] The Supreme Court has left open the question of whether the privilege against self-incrimination may be asserted if the cooperation between the United States and another country has reached a point at which prosecution in the other country could not fairly be characterized as "foreign."

## *Double Jeopardy*

The *Double Jeopardy Clause* of the Fifth Amendment protects criminal defendants from multiple prosecutions for the same offense. If the defendant is found not guilty, the defendant is cleared of all charges, and the prosecutor may not appeal the verdict. If the defendant is found guilty, however, the defendant can appeal. Double jeopardy does not bar a second prosecution if the first proceeding ended with a hung jury.

There are important limitations on the protection against double jeopardy. A single criminal act may result in several statutory violations for which the defendant may be prosecuted even if each prosecution is based on the same set of facts. For example, if the defendant operated a securities scam, a prosecutor could bring criminal charges against him or her for securities law violations, wire and mail fraud, false statements, and tax evasion. The Double Jeopardy Clause also does not protect against prosecutions by different governments (such as state and federal) based on the same underlying facts. Thus, after two police officers who beat Rodney King in 1991 were acquitted on California state criminal charges, spawning the 1992 Los Angeles riots, they could still be tried and convicted one year later of federal charges of violating King's civil rights.

Finally, the prohibition against double jeopardy does not preclude a civil suit against a criminal defendant by the victim. Thus, although O.J. Simpson was acquitted on criminal murder charges in 1996, the families of his alleged victims were still able to secure multimillion-dollar monetary judgments against Simpson in a 1997 civil trial.

**Civil and Criminal Prosecutions by the Government** The government may often seek both civil sanctions (such as fines) and criminal punishment for the same illegal conduct. The Supreme Court emphasized that the Double Jeopardy Clause protects only against the imposition of multiple *criminal* punishments for the same offense. Legislative intent is the guiding factor in determining whether a particular penalty is "civil" or "criminal." When the legislature has indicated an intention to establish a civil sanction, courts should rarely transform it into a criminal penalty for double jeopardy purposes.[50]

## *Due Process and Voluntary Confessions*

When the conduct of law enforcement officials in obtaining a confession is outrageous or shocking, the *Due Process Clauses* of the Fifth and Fourteenth Amendments bar the government from using the involuntary confession, even if the *Miranda* warnings were given. For example, physical coercion or brutality invalidates a confession. However, the courts have usually held that misleading or false verbal statements that induce the suspect to confess are not grounds for invalidating the confession, unless the statements rise to the level of unduly coercive threats.

A Florida appeals court invalidated a confession elicited through the use of fabricated (and false) laboratory reports linking the defendant to the crime.[51] Other courts, however, have said that there is no "bright line" that dictates that all uses of false documents are unconstitutional. These courts have held that confessions

45. *See* Braswell v. United States, 487 U.S. 99 (1988).
46. *See* Shapiro v. United States, 335 U.S. 1 (1948).
47. *See* Fisher v. United States, 425 U.S. 391 (1976). *See also* Braswell v. United States, 487 U.S. 99 (1988).
48. United States v. Hubbell, 530 U.S. 27 (2000) (holding that "the constitutional privilege against self-incrimination protects the target of a grand jury investigation from being compelled to answer questions designed to elicit information about the existence of sources of potentially incriminating evidence").
49. United States v. Balsys, 524 U.S. 666 (1998).
50. Hudson v. United States, 522 U.S. 93 (1997).
51. Florida v. Cayward, 552 So. 2d 971 (Fla. App. 1989).

similarly obtained were in fact "voluntary," after considering the "totality of the circumstances."[52]

Before a confession of guilt will be admitted into evidence, the trial judge must determine whether the confession was voluntarily made, as required by the Due Process Clauses. Nonetheless, the erroneous admission at trial of a coerced confession will not always automatically require that the conviction be overturned.[53]

### SIXTH AMENDMENT PROTECTIONS

The Sixth Amendment grants the criminal defendant a number of procedural protections, including a right to counsel and to a trial by jury.

#### *Assistance of Counsel*

The defendant in most criminal prosecutions has the right "to have the Assistance of Counsel." This means, first, that the accused has the right to his or her own attorney. If the defendant cannot afford an attorney, he or she is entitled to a court-appointed attorney. Second, once taken into custody, the accused must be informed of his or her right to counsel as part of the *Miranda* warnings. Third, the assistance of counsel must be effective, that is, within the range of competence required of attorneys in criminal cases. In practice, counsel is presumed to be effective; only in outrageous cases is counsel considered ineffective. Fourth, an attorney must be appointed for an appeal of a verdict.

#### *Jury Trial*

Most defendants in criminal cases have the right to a jury trial. Jury trials are not required in cases in which the authorized punishment for the charged offense is six months or less. A jury is also not required in juvenile proceedings. State court juries consist of six to twelve individuals, with a minimum of six jurors. Federal courts have twelve jurors. To render a verdict in a federal criminal trial, the jury must reach a unanimous decision. Juries of six in state courts must also be unanimous in order to render a verdict in a criminal case, but the U.S. Supreme Court has not ruled on juries of seven or more. Application of the Sixth Amendment right to a jury trial to sentencing is discussed later in the chapter.

#### *Other Procedural Rights*

The Sixth Amendment also guarantees the right to a speedy trial and the right to confront and cross-examine witnesses.

52. *See, e.g.*, Sheriff, Washoe County v. Bessey, 914 P.2d 681 (Nev. 1996); Arthur v. Virginia, 480 S.E.2d 749 (Va. App. 1997).

53. *See* Arizona v. Fulminante, 499 U.S. 279 (1991) (holding that the harmless error test applies to determine whether conviction must be overturned).

## Nonconstitutional Protections

In a criminal prosecution, the prosecutor is obligated to show the defendant all evidence that the defendant specifically requests. In addition, certain items (such as any exculpatory evidence) must be turned over regardless of whether the defendant requests them. The accused may also be required to reveal certain information to the prosecutor, such as statements made by witnesses who have testified in a sworn statement.

More requirements to reveal evidence are imposed on the prosecutor than on the defendant. The rationale for this protection is the need to neutralize the natural advantage of the state against the individual defendant.

### ATTORNEY–CLIENT PRIVILEGE

When criminal charges are brought against a corporate employee who is represented by a lawyer paid by the corporation, it may be unclear to whom the attorney–client privilege belongs. Is the client the employee charged with the offense, the corporation that is paying the lawyer, or both? In general, a client must establish a relationship with the attorney for the attorney–client privilege to apply. Thus, if the employee wants to be treated as the client, the employee should obtain an engagement letter from the attorney that expressly states that the employee is the client even though the employer is paying the attorney's fees. In general, in-house counsel investigating possible violations of law represent the corporation, not the individual employees who might be questioned by counsel. (The attorney–client privilege is discussed in Chapter 3.)

## Sentencing

State and federal criminal statutes normally specify penalties that include both jail or prison time and monetary fines. The length of the sentence and the amount of the fine usually fall within a specified range. In a state court, if the defendant is found guilty, the judge generally has sentencing discretion within that range. Until the U.S. Supreme Court's decision in *United States v. Booker*,[54] discussed below, federal judges had considerably less discretion and were required to follow the Federal Sentencing Guidelines.

### FEDERAL SENTENCING GUIDELINES

Congress created the U.S. Sentencing Commission, an independent agency in the judicial branch, to provide an honest, fair, and effective federal sentencing system that

54. 125 S. Ct. 738 (2005) (Case 14.2).

would impose reasonably uniform sentences for similar criminal offenses committed by similar offenders. The Sentencing Commission established sentencing guidelines, which created categories of "offense behavior" and "offender characteristics." A sentencing court was required to select a sentence (up to the maximum authorized by statute for each federal crime) from within the guideline ranges specified by the combined categories. In unusual cases, a court was permitted to depart from the guidelines, but it had to specify reasons for the departure.

### *Individuals*

Congress abolished federal parole in 1984. Rather than permit a parole commission to decide how much of a sentence an offender actually serves, an offender serves the full sentence imposed by the court under the sentencing guidelines, less approximately 15 percent for good behavior.

Under the sentencing guidelines, individuals were sentenced to prison using offense levels and their criminal history. In addition to facing prison time, individuals could be fined. For example, if the defendant was convicted of garden-variety mail and wire fraud, the court would first consider the individual's criminal history. For a perpetrator with no history, the base offense level is 6. Then the offense level is increased depending on the amount of the loss. If the loss is more than $400 million, then an increase of 30 levels is applied to arrive at a base offense level of 36. An offense level of 36 would correspond to somewhere between 188 and 405 months in prison; perpetrators with extensive criminal history would receive sentences at the high end of the range. The fine for individuals convicted of this offense level would be between a minimum of $20,000 and a maximum of $200,000.

### *Organizations*

The Federal Sentencing Guidelines for Organizations, enacted in 1991, specify stiff fines for companies convicted of fraud, antitrust violations, and most types of corporate wrongdoing. According to the Sentencing Commission, the guidelines for organizations were "designed so that the sanctions imposed upon organizations and their agents . . . will provide just punishment, adequate deterrence, and incentives for organizations to maintain internal mechanisms for preventing, detecting and reporting criminal conduct."[55]

The guidelines take a carrot-and-stick approach. The "stick" is that organizations are held liable for the criminal actions of all their employees and agents. The "carrot" is that a company's maintenance of a meaningful voluntary compliance program is deemed a mitigating factor that will reduce otherwise applicable fines.[56] A company can also achieve significant mitigation of fines by cooperating with or self-reporting misconduct to authorities.

The guidelines apply to all companies with two or more members but recognize that for smaller organizations the compliance programs could be more informal. They "encourage larger organizations to promote adoption of compliance and ethics programs by smaller organizations, including those with which they conduct or seek to conduct business."[57] Exhibit 14.1 shows the steps involved in calculating corporate fines.

55. Itamar Sittenfeld, *Federal Sentencing Guidelines,* Internal Auditor, Apr. 1996, at 58.
56. Kathryn Keneally, *White Collar Crime: Corporate Compliance Programs: From the Sentencing Guidelines to the Thompson Memorandum—and Back Again,* Champion, June 2004.
57. U.S. Sentencing Guidelines Manual, Effective Compliance and Ethics Programs in Chapter 8, Synopsis of Amendment, at 109, *available at* http://www.ussc.gov/GUIDELIN.HTM.

**EXHIBIT 14.1 Determining the Fine for Non-Criminal-Purpose Organizations Under the Federal Sentencing Guidelines**

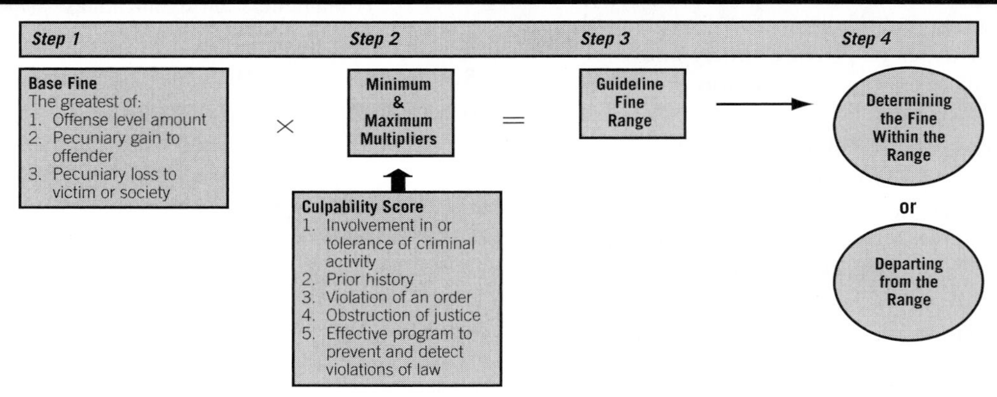


Source: Jennifer Moore, *Corporate Culpability Under the Federal Sentencing Guidelines,* 34 Ariz. L. Rev. 743, 783 (1992); U.S. Sentencing Guidelines Manual ch. 8 & appendices (2004).

The tables shown in Exhibit 14.2 are used to determine penalties for organizations convicted of a crime. Offense levels are determined by the type of crime committed, and base fines are specified by the Offense Level Table.

**Determining the Sentence** In determining the sentence for a particular crime, the first step is to determine the base fine, which depends on the severity of the crime. For instance, money laundering is considered a more serious offense than price-fixing; thus, the base fine for price-fixing is $20,000 (offense level 10), whereas the base fine for laundering money instruments (such as checks) is $1.6 million (offense level 23). If this base fine is exceeded by either the organization's gain or the victim's (or society's) loss from the crime, then that amount will supplant the base fine.

The second step is to adjust the base fine to reflect the culpability of the organization. The culpability score is used to determine minimum and maximum multipliers. The base fine is then multiplied by the minimum and maximum multipliers to determine the fine range. A culpability score starts at a baseline of five points out of ten. Points are then added or subtracted based on various criteria including whether (1) management condoned or willfully ignored the criminal misconduct, (2) management assisted authorities in their investigation, and (3) the organization had an effective compliance and ethics program in place at the time of the misconduct to not only prevent and detect criminal conduct but also facilitate compliance with all applicable laws. For example, the culpability score can be reduced by five points for timely and full cooperation and acceptance of responsibility.[58]

To receive full credit for cooperation, a firm may be required to waive attorney–client privilege and work-product protection. A waiver of protections is a prerequisite to a reduction in culpability score "when such waiver is necessary in order to provide timely and thorough disclosure of all pertinent information known to the organization."[59]

As mentioned earlier, the possibility of fine mitigation serves as a strong incentive for organizations to adopt and maintain effective compliance and ethics programs. Exhibit 14.3 sets forth the seven requirements that must be satisfied under the guidelines (as amended as of November 1, 2004) for mitigation due to the existence of an effective compliance and ethics program.[60]

58. Keneally, *supra* note 56.
59. *Id.*
60. U.S. SENTENCING GUIDELINES MANUAL, *supra* note 57.

**EXHIBIT 14.2 Determining Penalties for Organizations**

**Offense Level Fine Table for Organizations**

| Offense Level | Amount of Fine |
|---|---|
| 6 or less | $ 5,000 |
| 7 | 7,500 |
| 8 | 10,000 |
| 9 | 15,000 |
| 10 | 20,000 |
| 11 | 30,000 |
| 12 | 40,000 |
| 13 | 60,000 |
| 14 | 85,000 |
| 15 | 125,000 |
| 16 | 175,000 |
| 17 | 250,000 |
| 18 | 350,000 |
| 19 | 500,000 |
| 20 | 650,000 |
| 21 | 910,000 |
| 22 | 1,200,000 |
| 23 | 1,600,000 |
| 24 | 2,100,000 |
| 25 | 2,800,000 |
| 26 | 3,700,000 |
| 27 | 4,800,000 |
| 28 | 6,300,000 |
| 29 | 8,100,000 |
| 30 | 10,500,000 |
| 31 | 13,500,000 |
| 32 | 17,500,000 |
| 33 | 22,000,000 |
| 34 | 28,500,000 |
| 35 | 36,000,000 |
| 36 | 45,500,000 |
| 37 | 57,500,000 |
| 38 or more | 72,500,000 |

**Table of Minimum and Maximum Multipliers for Organizations**

| Culpability Score | Minimum Multiplier | Maximum Multiplier |
|---|---|---|
| 10 or more | 2.00 | 4.00 |
| 9 | 1.80 | 3.60 |
| 8 | 1.60 | 3.20 |
| 7 | 1.40 | 2.80 |
| 6 | 1.20 | 2.40 |
| 5 | 1.00 | 2.00 |
| 4 | 0.80 | 1.60 |
| 3 | 0.60 | 1.20 |
| 2 | 0.40 | 0.80 |
| 1 | 0.20 | 0.40 |
| 0 or less | 0.05 | 0.20 |

Source: U.S. SENTENCING GUIDELINES MANUAL ch. 8, pt. C, §§ 8C2.4 and 8C2.6 (2004).

**EXHIBIT 14.3 Key Components of Effective Corporate Compliance and Ethics Program**

To take advantage of the provisions in the Federal Sentencing Guidelines that reduce culpability for a company with an effective compliance and ethics program, a company must:

1. Establish compliance standards and procedures reasonably capable of reducing the prospect of criminal activity and otherwise promote an organizational culture that encourages ethical conduct and commitment to compliance with the law. A viable code of conduct is a good starting point.
2. Assign the board of directors the responsibility for overseeing the compliance effort. The company should assign a high-ranking person with adequate authority to be in charge of the program, to take "day-to-day operational responsibility," and to report on the program at least annually to the board of directors.
3. Use due care in delegating authority. The company must not delegate substantial discretionary authority to individuals who have previously engaged in any criminal or unethical misconduct. The fox can't guard the hen house.
4. Periodically, provide mandatory training to effectively communicate the standards to all employees and other agents. Training should include a discussion of the laws applicable to the business and focus on helping employees identify risk areas. A well-designed video can help ensure ongoing training about the standards. Good online training tools are available as well.
5. Adopt mechanisms for monitoring compliance with the standards and reporting criminal misconduct without fear of retribution. The company should provide an anonymous toll-free hotline or other mechanism for reporting that ensures anonymity or confidentiality to encourage reporting of misconduct.
6. Consistently enforce the standards through investigation and adequate discipline. The company must be willing to discipline violators through salary reduction, poor performance ratings, and termination of employment. When employees report misconduct, the company must take steps to respond. The company should also provide incentives to ensure compliance with the program.
7. Adopt procedures for feedback and correction. After an offense has been detected, the organization must take all reasonable steps to respond adequately to the offense and to prevent further offenses—including making any necessary modifications to its compliance program. Some sort of auditing or monitoring system should be in place to ensure the program is working.

**Letting Employees Take the Rap** When facing a criminal probe, corporations have increasingly responded to the guidelines' encouragement to cooperate with authorities by winning leniency for themselves at the expense of their employees. Because the guidelines call on corporations to apply "adequate discipline" to employees deemed responsible for criminal violations, a company has an incentive to isolate a small group of "fall guys," fire them, and cooperate with the federal government in their prosecution. This pattern frequently occurs even though it can often be difficult to determine who is really responsible for corporate crimes.[61]

Although it may be appropriate to let a true "rogue" employee take the rap, under certain circumstances, scapegoating raises fundamental questions of fairness. William S. Laufer warns that scapegoating is most likely to result in "self-deception, denial of responsibility, and lack of repentance" when top management is complicit or middle management tacitly encourages employees to engage in wrongdoing in spite of a comprehensive compliance program, when senior executives and managers condoned the commission of the offense or consciously disregarded knowledge of the illegality, when the person being blamed is far subordinate to those cooperating with the government, and when the firm "purchases" the trappings of compliance to impress regulators.[62]

### ETHICAL CONSIDERATION

Is it ethical for a corporation to turn in some but not all of the managers who may have participated in criminal wrongdoing?

## CONSTITUTIONAL CHALLENGE TO THE FEDERAL SENTENCING GUIDELINES

In the following case the U.S. Supreme Court considered whether the mandatory nature of the Federal Sentencing Guidelines violated defendants' right to a trial by jury under the Sixth Amendment.

61. See, e.g., Dean Starkman, *More Firms Let Employees Take the Rap,* WALL ST. J., Oct. 9, 1997, at B3.

62. William S. Laufer, *Corporate Prosecution, Cooperation, and the Trading of Favors,* 87 IOWA L. REV. 653, 659–60 (2002).

A CASE IN POINT

**CASE 14.2**

**United States v. Booker**

*Supreme Court of the United States*

*125 S. Ct. 738 (2005).*

## Summary

**› FACTS** In two separate cases, two defendants were convicted of distributing cocaine. The first defendant's sentence was increased under the Federal Sentencing Guidelines by more than eight years based on the judge's finding that the defendant possessed a greater quantity of drugs than was found by the jury. The Seventh Circuit reversed and ordered the trial judge to sentence the defendant within the sentencing range supported by the jury's findings or to hold a separate sentencing hearing before the jury. In the second case, the trial court did not follow the guidelines and imposed a sentence based solely on the jury's guilty verdict. The government appealed both cases.

**› ISSUE PRESENTED** Do the Federal Sentencing Guidelines violate the defendant's right to a trial by jury pursuant to the Sixth Amendment? If so, should the provision of the federal statute that makes the guidelines mandatory be severed and excised?

**› SUMMARY OF OPINION** In the part of the opinion written by Justice Stevens (in which Justices Scalia, Souter, Thomas, and Ginsburg joined), the U.S. Supreme Court held that the Federal Sentencing Guidelines, which were made mandatory by the Sentencing Reform Act of 1984, violated the Sixth Amendment right to be found guilty by a jury only upon proof beyond a reasonable doubt of all elements of the crime charged. In *Apprendi v. New Jersey,*[63] the Court set aside an enhanced sentence based on the trial judge's finding that the defendant, who had pled guilty to second-degree possession of a firearm for an illegal purpose, had committed a "hate crime." The Court ruled in *Apprendi* that any fact (other than the existence of a prior conviction) that increases the penalty for a crime beyond the prescribed statutory minimum must be submitted to a jury and proved beyond a reasonable doubt.[64]

In *Blakely v. Washington,*[65] the Court interpreted "statutory minimum" to mean "the maximum sentence a judge may impose solely on the basis of the facts reflected in the jury verdict or admitted by the defendant." Accordingly, the Court struck down a Washington state law that mandated a "standard" sentence of forty-nine to fifty-three months for kidnapping, a class B felony punishable by a term of not more than ten years, unless the judge found aggravating facts justifying a longer sentence. The Court rejected arguments that the jury verdict was sufficient to authorize a sentence within the general ten-year range for Class B felonies because the statute required the judge to impose a sentence longer than ninety months.

The Court concluded that there was "no distinction of constitutional significance" between the Federal Sentencing Guidelines and the Washington procedures at issue in *Blakely.* The fact that the guidelines were issued by an independent commission rather than Congress did not make the principles behind the right to a jury trial any less applicable.

The Court recognized "the authority of a judge to exercise broad discretion in imposing a sentence within a statutory range" and stated that "the defendant has no right to a jury determination of the facts that the judge deems relevant." Accordingly, "[i]f the guidelines as currently written could be read as merely advisory provisions that recommended, rather than required, the selection of particular sentences in response to different sets of facts, their use would not implicate the Sixth Amendment."

But the guidelines, as written, are not advisory: "they are mandatory and binding on all judges." Although judges may depart from the guidelines in the unusual case where

63. 530 U.S. 466 (2000).
64. *Id.* at 490.
65. 124 S. Ct. 2531 (2004).

*(Continued)*

(Case 14.2 *continued*)

there is an aggravating or mitigating circumstance not adequately taken into consideration by the Sentencing Commision, "[i]n most cases, as a matter of law, the Commission will have adequately taken all relevant factors into account, and no departure will be legally permissible. In those instances, the judge is bound to impose a sentence within the Guidelines range."

The Court acknowledged that in some cases requiring jury fact-finding may impair the most expedient and efficient sentencing, but explained that "the interest in fairness and reliability protected by the right to a jury trial—a common-law right that defendants enjoyed for centuries and that is now enshrined in the Sixth Amendment—has always outweighed the interest in concluding trials swiftly."

Justice Breyer delivered the next part of the Court's opinion dealing with the statutory provision that made the guidelines mandatory. He was joined by Chief Justice Rehnquist and Justices O'Connor, Kennedy, and Ginsburg. As a result, there was no one set of five justices who voted together on both issues.

The Court considered two approaches to modifying the guidelines to remedy the Sixth Amendment problems with the existing system. In his dissent, Justice Stevens recommended grafting onto the existing system a prohibition against sentencing judges' increasing a sentence on the basis of a fact that the jury did not find (or the offender did not admit). The Court rejected this approach, reasoning that delegating to juries the power to set sentences would "undermine the sentencing statute's basic aim of ensuring similar sentences for those who have committed similar crimes in similar ways."

The other approach, which the Court adopted, was to make the guidelines advisory. The Court considered the text of the Sentencing Reform Act and its legislative history and concluded that (1) Congress would likely have preferred the total invalidation of the Act to an Act with the Sixth Amendment requirement grafted onto it, and (2) Congress would likely have preferred the excision of some of the Act, namely the mandatory language, to the invalidation of the entire Act.

By severing and excising two provisions of the Sentencing Reform Act, the Court created a regime whereby sentencing courts are required to consider the guidelines' ranges but are permitted to tailor the sentence in light of other statutory concerns as well.

**› RESULT** Both sentences were vacated, and the cases were remanded to the trial courts for sentencing. A sentencing court is required to consider the ranges specified by the guidelines but has discretion to depart from them as the judge sees fit. If the sentence comes up for review on appeal, the court of appeals is instructed to determine whether the sentence is unreasonable in the light of a variety of mitigating and aggravating circumstances.

**› COMMENTS** Justice Breyer's opinion recognized that Congress would have the last word on this issue: "The ball now lies in Congress' court. The National Legislature is equipped to devise and install, long-term, the sentencing system, compatible with the Constitution, that Congress judges best for the overall system of justice."

A dissent written by Justice Stevens, with whom Justice Souter joined and in which Justices Scalia, Thomas, and Breyer joined in parts, characterized the Court's "creative remedy" as an inappropriate "exercise of legislative, rather than judicial, power." A dissent written by Justice Breyer (with whom Chief Justice Rehnquist and Justices O'Connor and Kennedy joined) rejected the Court's constitutional analysis in *Apprendi* and *Blakely,* maintaining that "[h]istory does not support a 'right to jury trial' in respect to sentencing facts."

# Liability for Criminal Actions

Liability may be imposed on the person who actually committed the crime, on that person's supervisors, and on the corporation (or entity) that employed the violator.

## INDIVIDUAL LIABILITY

Individuals may commit a criminal act for their own personal gain or on behalf of their employer.

### *Direct Liability*

If an officer, director, or employee commits a crime against the employer (such as theft, embezzlement, or forgery), that person will be prosecuted as an individual. Officers, directors, or employees who commit crimes will be prosecuted as individuals even if they were trying to benefit the corporation. As discussed below, that person's supervisor may also be held responsible.

If a supervisor asks an employee to commit an act that the employee suspects is criminal, the employee should bear two things in mind. First, if there is a criminal prosecution, it is not a valid defense for the employee to state that he or she was just following the orders of upper-level officers or directors of the corporation. Second, as discussed in Chapter 12, an employee cannot be terminated for refusing to commit a criminal act.

### *Vicarious Liability*

*Vicarious liability* (also called *imputed liability*) is the imposition of liability on one party for the wrongs of another. Under the theory of vicarious liability, officers, directors, and managers may be found guilty of a crime committed by employees under their supervision. Criminal statutes that provide for the vicarious liability of corporate officers usually require that the officer commit some wrongful act. Failure to provide adequate supervision or to satisfy a duty imposed by the statute is typically sufficient to fulfill this requirement.

The more delicate issue is what kind of *mens rea,* or mental state, is required to find a corporate officer vicariously liable for a crime. In cases involving criminal vicarious liability, the crucial questions are most often "How much did the manager know?" and "How much does the statute require that the manager know before he or she can be held criminally liable?"

**Responsible Corporate Officer Doctrine** The *responsible corporate officer doctrine* addresses these questions. In applying this doctrine, it is important to remember that two different but interwoven issues are involved. The first is a vicarious liability issue: whether an officer bears responsibility for the actions of his or her subordinates. The second is a *mens rea* issue: whether the officer must have known about or intended the violation before he or she can be held personally criminally liable.

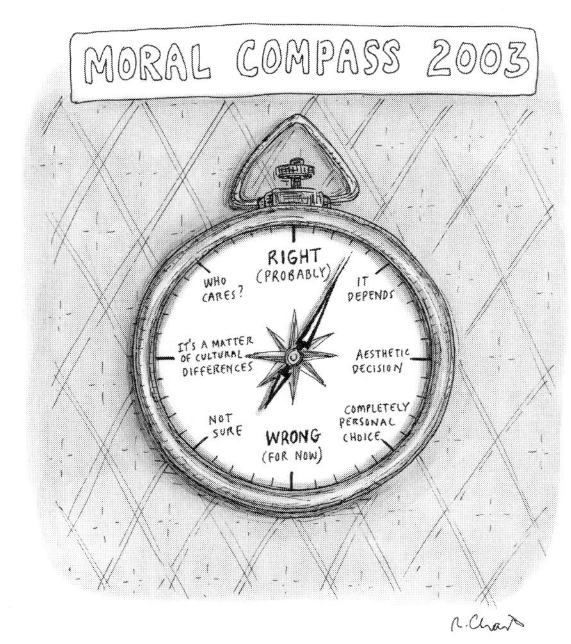




The Supreme Court applied the responsible corporate officer doctrine in *United States v. Park.*[66] John Park was the CEO of Acme Markets, a national retail food chain that employed 36,000 people and operated 874 retail outlets. On two separate occasions, the Food and Drug Administration (FDA) had advised Park that the company was storing food in rodent-infested warehouses. Although Park had been told by a vice president that the problem had been taken care of after the first FDA visit, he failed to personally investigate even after the FDA visited a second time and again complained of rats in the warehouses.

Despite Acme's enormous size and the multiple layers of authority between Park and the employees who had been instructed to eliminate the rodents in the warehouses, Park was found guilty as an individual of distributing "adulterated" food in violation of the Food, Drug and Cosmetic Act (FDCA). The Court noted that "Congress has seen fit to enforce the accountability of responsible corporate agents dealing with products which may affect the health of customers" by enacting

66. 421 U.S. 658 (1975). *See also* United States v. Dotterweich, 320 U.S. 277 (1943) (holding that criminal sanctions can be imposed on the corporate officers who have a "responsible relation" to the offending acts of the corporation even in the absence of proof that the officers were conscious of the wrongdoing).

"rigorous" penal sanctions. Corporate officers have a "duty to implement measures that will insure that violations will not occur"; in other words, the FDCA imposed "requirements of foresight and vigilance."

Under *Park,* a corporate officer may be found guilty of a crime if he or she bore a "responsible relation" to a violation of a statute dealing with "products which may affect the health of customers." Appellate courts have used the responsible corporate officer doctrine to impose fines under the Occupational Safety and Health Act (OSHA),[67] and the Radiation Control for Health and Safety Act[68] and to impose fines and imprisonment under the Clean Water Act and the Resource Conservation and Recovery Act (RCRA).[69]

When a statute requires that a defendant "knowingly" commit a wrongful act, courts have ruled that the responsible corporate officer doctrine cannot be used to convict officers absent direct or circumstantial proof of knowledge.[70] For example, the Federal Meat Inspection Act and environmental statutes such as the Comprehensive Environmental Response, Compensation, and Liability Act (CERCLA) and RCRA (discussed in Chapter 15) all require that defendants knowingly commit wrongful acts before being found guilty. Even though these statutes clearly concern public health and safety, the appellate courts refused to affirm convictions under the responsible corporate officer doctrine absent a showing of knowledge.[71]

Nonetheless, appellate courts have held that knowledge may be inferred for responsible corporate officers in appropriate circumstances.[72] For example, in *United States v. Self,*[73] the U.S. Court of Appeals for the Fifth Circuit stated: "[W]hile knowledge of prior illegal activity is not conclusive as to whether a defendant possessed the requisite knowledge of later illegal activity, it most certainly provides circumstantial evidence of the defendant's later knowledge from which the jury may draw the necessary inference."

**Impossibility Defense** A corporate officer may escape liability if he or she did everything possible to ensure legal compliance, but the company was still unable to comply with the applicable standards. In these circumstances, the officer can argue the defense of impossibility. According to the U.S. Court of Appeals for the Second Circuit: "To establish the ***impossibility defense,*** the corporate officer must introduce evidence that he exercised extraordinary care and still could not prevent violations of the Act."[74]

## Corporate Liability

Under the doctrine of ***respondeat superior,*** which means "let the superior give answer," a corporation (or other business entity) can be held liable for criminal offenses committed by its employees if the acts were committed within the scope of their employment (whether actual or apparent). (The application of *respondeat superior* in civil cases is discussed in Chapters 5 and 9.)

For example, the Pennsylvania Superior Court held a bus company criminally liable for homicide by vehicle when a low-level employee, the driver of a school bus owned by the corporation, ran over and killed a six-year-old who was crossing in front of the bus.[75] The bus driver could not see the child because mirrors that were required by state statute were missing.

In cases involving misdemeanor offenses or regulatory crimes, the well-established rule is that a corporation is criminally liable for all violations committed by any of its agents or employees.[76] Although a small minority of state courts have held that a corporation cannot be guilty of a non-strict liability crime—that is, a crime requiring a guilty mental state such as "knowledge" or "intent"—it is now the generally accepted rule that a corporation may be indicted for a crime (such as negligent homicide) for which a specific guilty mental state is essential. In such cases, the knowledge or intent of the corporation's

67. *See, e.g.,* United States v. Doig, 950 F.2d 411 (7th Cir. 1991).
68. *See, e.g.,* United States v. Hodges X-Ray, Inc., 759 F.2d 557 (6th Cir. 1985).
69. *See, e.g.,* Hansen v. United States, 262 F.3d 1217 (11th Cir. 2001), *cert. denied,* 535 U.S. 1111 (2002) (Case 15.5).
70. *See, e.g.,* United States v. MacDonald & Watson Waste Oil Co., 933 F.2d 35 (1st Cir. 1991) ("[I]n a crime having knowledge as an express element, a mere showing of official responsibility . . . is not an adequate substitute for direct or circumstantial proof of knowledge."). Similarly, the U.S. District Court for the Western District of Missouri held that "something more than a mere status should be required before civil penalties are assessed against corporate officers for knowing violations of the [Federal Hazardous Substances Act]." United States v. Shelton Wholesale, Inc., 1999 U.S. Dist. LEXIS 15980 (W.D. Mo. Sept. 21, 1999). *But see* United States v. Int'l Minerals & Chem. Corp., 402 U.S. 558 (1971) (holding that officers of chemical company were "under a species of absolute liability for violation of the regulations [proscribing knowing failure to record shipment of chemicals] despite the 'knowingly' requirement").
71. *See, e.g.,* United States v. Agnew, 931 F.2d 1397 (10th Cir. 1991).
72. *See, e.g.,* United States v. Johnson & Towers, Inc., 741 F.2d 662, 669–70 (3d Cir. 1984) (holding that "knowledge" in a RCRA criminal prosecution "may be inferred by the jury as to those individuals who hold the requisite responsible positions with the corporate defendant").
73. 2 F.3d 1071, 1087–88 (5th Cir. 1993).
74. United States v. Gel Spice Co., 773 F.2d 427 (2d Cir. 1985) (quoting United States v. New England Grocers Co., 488 F. Supp. 230 (D. Mass. 1980)) (emphasis added).
75. Commonwealth v. McIlwain Sch. Bus Lines, 423 A.2d 413 (Pa. Super. 1980).
76. *See* 18 Am. Jur. 2d *Corporations* § 2136 (1985).

**INTERNATIONAL SNAPSHOT**

Many European nations do not recognize corporate criminal liability because (1) the corporation does not possess a guilty mind, (2) the corporation is not viewed as the real offender when a crime is committed, and (3) the corporation is not considered well suited for either punishment or rehabilitation. For example, the German constitution prohibits imposition of criminal liability on corporations. These countries focus instead on identifying and punishing the individuals responsible for the criminal acts.

employees and agents is imputed to the corporation.[77] In many cases, the legislature has clearly indicated (either in the language of the statute or in legislative history) a desire to impose criminal liability on corporations; courts consistently enforce such legislative intent.[78]

The corporation will almost always be vicariously liable if upper management or the board of directors adopts a policy or issues instructions that cause an employee to violate the law. Even if an agent acted contrary to a corporate policy or express instructions, the corporation may still be criminally liable if the agent was acting within his or her apparent authority (and, in some states, at least in part for the benefit of the corporation).[79] As a practical matter, courts have been willing to impose liability upon the corporation if the agent's actions were at least "tolerated" by management.[80] Typically, courts make this determination based on the totality of the circumstances surrounding the agent's actions.

For example, one case[81] involved Edwin Clancy, the president of defendant Penn Valley Resorts, who agreed to provide dinner and an open bar for sixty undergraduate students from the State University of New York. A twenty-year-old minor became noticeably intoxicated, and en route back to the university, he caused an automobile accident in which he was killed. At the time of death, his blood alcohol content was .23; a level of .10 is normally considered sufficient to make a person intoxicated.

The Pennsylvania Superior Court held that a corporation could be found criminally liable even if the corporation's board of directors did not condone the action. If the illegal conduct is performed or tolerated by a high managerial agent acting on behalf of the corporation within the scope of his or her office or employment, the corporation can be held criminally liable. The corporation's conviction for criminal involuntary manslaughter, reckless endangerment, and furnishing liquor to minors and visibly intoxicated persons was upheld.

### *Deciding Whether to Prosecute: The Thompson Memorandum*

On January 20, 2003, Under Deputy Attorney General Larry D. Thompson issued revised "Principles of Federal Prosecution of Business Organizations" (the *Thompson*

77. *See, e.g.,* Boise Dodge v. United States, 51 F.3d 1390 (9th Cir. 1969); Vaughn & Sons, Inc. v. State, 737 S.W.2d 805 (Tex. Crim. App. 1987); 18 AM. JUR. 2D *Corporations* § 2137 (1985).
78. *See, e.g.,* Hanlester Network v. Shalala, 51 F.3d 1390 (9th Cir. 1995); People v. Mattiace, 568 N.E.2d 1189 (N.Y. 1990).
79. *See, e.g.,* United States v. Beusch, 596 F.2d 871 (9th Cir. 1979); State v. Hy Vee Food Stores, Inc., 533 N.W.2d 147 (S.D. 1995). *See also* State v. Pinarfville Athletic Club, 594 A.2d 1284 (N.H. 1991).
80. *See* Minnesota v. Christy Pontiac–GMC, Inc., 354 N.W.2d 17 (Minn. 1984).
81. Commonwealth v. Penn Valley Resorts, Inc., 494 A.2d 1139 (Pa. Super. 1985).

**EXHIBIT 14.4** **Factors Used by the Department of Justice to Decide Whether to Indict a Company**

The nine factors set out in the Thompson Memorandum for a prosecutor to consider in determining whether to charge a corporation are:

1. The nature and seriousness of the offense.
2. The pervasiveness of the wrongdoing within the corporation, including complicity or condonation by corporate management.
3. History of similar conduct.
4. Timely and voluntary disclosure of the wrongdoing and willingness to cooperate.
5. The existence and adequacy of a corporate compliance program.
6. Remedial actions, including efforts to implement or improve a compliance program, replace responsible management, discipline or terminate wrongdoers, pay restitution, and cooperate with relevant government agencies.
7. Collateral consequences of criminal liability, including disproportionate harm to nonculpable persons.
8. The adequacy of the prosecution of culpable individuals to effect law enforcement policies.
9. The adequacy of civil or regulatory remedies.

Source: Thompson Memorandum, cited in Kathryn Keneally, *White Collar Crime: Corporate Compliance Programs: From the Sentencing Guidelines to the Thompson Memorandum—and Back Again,* CHAMPION, June 2004.

*Memorandum*) to establish determinants of whether to prosecute a company. The nine factors used to make this determination are set forth in Exhibit 14.4.

One key factor that the Thompson Memorandum lists as appropriate to consider in determining whether the company cooperated is whether it waived its right to attorney–client privilege and work-product protection:

> Prosecutors may request a waiver in appropriate circumstances. The Department does not, however, consider a waiver of a corporation's attorney–client and work product protection an absolute requirement, and prosecutors should consider the willingness of a corporation to waive such protection when necessary to provide timely and complete information as one factor in evaluating the corporation's cooperation.[82]

**IN BRIEF**

**Liability for Criminal Actions**

| Type of Defendant | Standard for Liability |
|---|---|
| Individual | An individual can perpetrate a crime against the corporate employer (e.g., embezzlement) or for the benefit of the corporation (e.g., price-fixing). The individual must have performed *actus reus* (criminal act) with *mens rea* (guilty mind). |
| Corporate officers | Officers can be directly liable for failing to supervise subordinates. In addition to individual liability for their own acts, officers may be vicariously liable for crimes committed by other employees. Under the responsible corporate officer doctrine, officers can be liable for criminal actions of their subordinates if the officer bore a "responsible relation" to the violation of law. Typically, the doctrine is used to impose criminal liability only for violations of strict liability statutes involving public health where the officer is charged with a misdemeanor or the prosecution proves, through direct or circumstantial evidence, that the officer knew of the violation. |
| Corporations (and other business entities) | *Respondeat superior* liability. A corporation is criminally liable for (1) all misdemeanor offenses and regulatory crimes committed by any of its agents or employees; (2) all crimes committed pursuant to top management's corporate policy or express instructions; and (3) all crimes committed by employees if the acts were committed (a) within the scope of their employment (whether actual or apparent and, in some states, also in furtherance of the corporation's business interests) or (b) were tolerated by top management. |

As a result, corporations faced with significant criminal investigations are cooperating with the government by collecting and analyzing documents related to suspected criminal activity, interviewing employees, conducting costly and time-consuming internal investigations and forensic audits, and turning over the results of this work to the government.[83] In addition, companies are refusing to support employees or officers who are believed to be the architects of the underlying improper conduct.[84]

## White-Collar Crime

*White-collar crime* is violation of the law by a corporation (or other business entity) or one of its managers. Most white-collar crime is nonviolent.

White-collar employees—that is, managers or professionals—may be either the victims or the perpetrators of crime. W. Steven Albrecht, a professor of accountancy at Brigham Young University, estimated the cost of white-collar fraud to be more than $200 billion a year."[85] In contrast, the Federal Bureau of Investigation estimated that burglary and robbery combined cost only roughly $4 billion a year.[86]

Many white-collar criminal statutes do not have a *mens rea* requirement. It is, therefore, possible to commit a crime in the corporate setting without having the intention of breaking the law.

### Crime Against the Employer

Examples of crimes committed by an employee against his or her employer include theft, embezzlement, fraud, acceptance of a bribe, and certain computer-related crimes.

Theft, technically known as *larceny,* is simply the taking of property without the owner's consent. White-collar theft ranges from taking home pens and paper from the office to stealing money through the company's computer system.

82. Larry D. Thompson, "Principles of Federal Prosecution of Business Organizations," U.S. Department of Justice, Office of the Deputy Attorney General, Washington, D.C. (Jan. 20, 2003).
83. E. Lawrence Barcella Jr. et al., *Cooperation with Government Is a Growing Trend,* NAT'L L.J., July 19, 2004 at S2.
84. *Id.*
85. Eyal Press, *Look at the Cost of White-Collar Crime Too,* N.Y. TIMES, Apr. 7, 1996, at 1-22.
86. *Id.*

### ETHICAL CONSIDERATION

The line between accepting gifts and taking bribes is not always clear. For instance, if a data-processing manager will make the decision on the purchase of a mainframe computer, it is unethical or illegal for him or her to accept a percentage of the sales price of the computer from the seller. Some data-processing managers accept expensive meals, sports tickets, and other "perks" from computer salespersons. Is acceptance of such gifts ethical?

*Embezzlement* is the taking of money or property that is lawfully in the employee's possession by reason of his or her employment. For example, a company's treasurer who takes money that belongs to the company by writing checks to dummy accounts is guilty of embezzlement.

*Fraud* is any deception intended to induce someone to part with property or money. Fraud may involve a false representation of fact, whether by words or by conduct, or concealment of something that should have been disclosed. Examples of fraud include padding an expense account, submitting falsely inflated insurance reimbursement bills, and doctoring financial statements to influence the company's stock price.

Acceptance of a bribe may also be a crime against the employer. For example, a sales representative cannot legally accept a kickback from a purchaser of his or her employer's products. Similarly, a purchasing agent for a corporation must not accept a bribe from an outside salesperson.

Employees and outsiders may also commit a variety of computer crimes, including computer fraud, hacking, and transmitting viruses. These are discussed later in this chapter.

## CRIME BY THE CORPORATION AND ITS AGENTS

Examples of crimes perpetrated by corporations (and other business entities) and employees or agents acting on their behalf include consumer fraud, securities fraud, tax evasion, and environmental pollution. Corporations can also commit crimes against other corporations. Examples include price-fixing (discussed in Chapter 16) and misappropriation of trade secrets or violations of copyright or trade secret laws (discussed in Chapter 11).

The balance of this chapter is devoted to a description of the most common types of white-collar crimes. The maximum penalties for many of the most common types of white-collar crimes are listed in Exhibit 14.5. They are grouped by the public policies they further, as set out in Chapter 1.

### *Racketeering under the Racketeer Influenced and Corrupt Organizations Act (RICO)*

The Racketeer Influenced and Corrupt Organizations Act (RICO)[87] was originally designed to combat organized crime and to provide an enforcement mechanism against syndicate bosses and masterminds who might otherwise escape liability. Today, the criminal provisions of RICO are a prosecutor's most powerful weapon to fight classic white-collar crimes. RICO has proved particularly effective against groups of traders, brokers, and others who have developed a continuous relationship of passing and trading on inside information.

RICO prohibits (1) the investment in any enterprise of income derived from racketeering, (2) the acquisition of an interest in an enterprise through a pattern of racketeering activity, (3) participation in an enterprise through a pattern of racketeering activity involving at least two related predicate acts in a ten-year period, and (4) conspiring to engage in any of these activities.

**RICO Requirements** RICO broadly defines an *enterprise* as "any individual, partnership, corporation, association, or other legal entity, and any union or group of individuals associated in fact although not a legal entity." *Racketeering activity* is defined to include various state and federal offenses, specifically including mail and wire fraud and fraud in the sale of securities. Consequently, almost any business fraud can serve as the basis for a criminal RICO violation.

To demonstrate a pattern of racketeering activity, a plaintiff must show that at least two related predicate acts have occurred within a ten-year period. Two isolated acts are not considered sufficient.

**Limits on the Use of RICO** Although RICO is generally given a liberal construction to ensure that Congress's intent is not frustrated by an overly narrow reading of the statute, its reach is not unlimited. In *Reves v. Ernst & Young*,[88] purchasers of demand notes from a farmers' cooperative brought a securities fraud and RICO action against the cooperative's auditors. The U.S. Supreme Court held that the accountants hired to perform an audit of the cooperative's records did not exert control over the company and did not "participate in the operation or management" of the cooperative's affairs. Such a finding of participation would have been necessary to find the accountants liable under RICO for failing to inform the cooperative's board of directors that the cooperative was insolvent. As clarified by the U.S. Court of Appeals for the Seventh Circuit, "participation"

87. 18 U.S.C.A. §§ 1961–68.
88. 507 U.S. 170 (1993).

EXHIBIT 14.5 **Penalties for White-Collar Crime**

| Offense | Maximum Fine or Penalty | Maximum Sentence | Comments |
|---|---|---|---|
| | ***Promote Economic Growth by Facilitating Capital Markets*** | | |
| Failure to register nonexempt security offering (Securities Act of 1933) (15 U.S.C. § 77x) | $10,000 | 5 years | Purchasers can recover damages equal to the difference between purchase price and fair market value at time of suit or, if securities have been sold, difference between purchase price and sale price. |
| Insider trading of securities (Securities Exchange Act of 1934) (15 U.S.C. § 78ff) | $5 million for individuals and $25 million for corporations for willful violations. SEC can also recover a civil fine of up to three times profit gained or loss avoided. Brokerage firms can be fined up to $2.5 million if they "knew or recklessly disregarded" information that would indicate insider trading by employees. | 20 years | Contemporaneous traders can recover damages equal to the amount of profit gained or loss avoided. Tippers and all direct and remote tippees are jointly and severally liable. Individuals whose tips to prosecutors result in insider trading convictions can recover bounty payments as high as 10% of fines and penalties paid by the defendant. |
| Securities fraud (Securities Exchange Act of 1934 and Rule 10b-5) (15 U.S.C. § 78ff) | $5 million for individuals and $25 million for corporations for willful violations | 20 years | Private plaintiffs can recover damages equal to the difference between price paid to purchase or sell security and what would have been paid absent the fraud. |
| Public company securities fraud (Sarbanes–Oxley Act of 2002) (18 U.S.C. § 1348) | $5 million for individuals and $25 million for corporations for willful violations | 25 years | |
| False certification of SEC periodic reports or financial statements by CEO or CFO (Sarbanes–Oxley Act of 2002) (18 U.S.C. § 1350) | $1 million or $5 million if executive acted willfully | 10 years or 20 years if executive acted willfully | |
| Failure of accountants to keep audit documents and work papers for at least five years (Sarbanes–Oxley Act of 2002) (18 U.S.C. § 1520) | Greater of $250,000 fine per violation for individuals ($500,000 for organizations) and twice gain to violators or loss to victims for knowing and willful violations | 10 years for knowing and willful violations | |
| | ***Promote Economic Growth by Giving Incentives to Innovate*** | | |
| Copyright infringement (Copyright Act) (18 U.S.C. § 2319) | Greater of $250,000 fine per violation for individuals ($500,000 for organizations) and twice gain to violators or loss to victims | 5 years for first offense; 10 years for subsequent convictions | |

*(Continued)*

**EXHIBIT 14.5 Penalties for White-Collar Crime—continued**

| Offense | Maximum Fine or Penalty | Maximum Sentence | Comments |
|---|---|---|---|
| Patent infringement (Patent Act) (35 U.S.C. §§ 281, 283–285) | No criminal penalties | No criminal penalties | Civil remedies include injunctions to protect against infringement and damages to compensate for infringement. A court may triple the amount of damages and in exceptional cases award attorneys' fees to prevailing party. |
| Misappropriation of trade secrets (Economic Espionage Act) (18 U.S.C. § 1831) | $500,000 for an individual and $10 million for corporation for intentional and knowing violations | 15 years | |
| ***Protect Workers*** | | | |
| Willful violation of workplace safety laws resulting in death of an employee (Occupational Safety and Health Act or OSHA) (29 U.S.C. § 666) | $10,000 for first offender; $20,000 for subsequent convictions | 6 months for first offender; 12 months for subsequent convictions | |
| Willful violations of Employee Retirement Income Security Act (ERISA) (Sarbanes–Oxley Act of 2002) (29 U.S.C. § 1131) | $100,000 for individuals, $500,000 for organizations | 10 years | |
| Retaliation against whistleblowers who report securities law violations to government agencies (Sarbanes–Oxley Act of 2002) (18 U.S.C. § 1513) | Greater of $250,000 fine per violation for individuals ($500,000 for organizations) and twice gain to violators or loss to victims | 10 years | Whistleblower can also sue to recover damages resulting from retaliatory acts. |
| ***Promote Consumer Welfare by Ensuring Safe Products and Services*** | | | |
| Sale of adulterated or misbranded food or drug (Food, Drug and Cosmetic Act) (21 U.S.C. § 333) | $1,000 for first offenses without intent to defraud or mislead; $10,000 for subsequent convictions or first offenses with intent to defraud or mislead | 1 year for first offenses without intent to defraud or mislead; 3 years for subsequent convictions or first offenses with intent to defraud or mislead | |
| Sale of drug without required FDA approval (Food, Drug and Cosmetic Act) (21 U.S.C. § 333) | $250,000 per violation for knowing violations | 10 years for knowing violations | |

*(Continued)*

**EXHIBIT 14.5 Penalties for White-Collar Crime—continued**

| Offense | Maximum Fine or Penalty | Maximum Sentence | Comments |
|---|---|---|---|
| | ***Promote Consumer Welfare by Facilitating Low-Cost Goods and Services*** | | |
| Price-fixing and other antitrust violations (Sherman Act) (15 U.S.C. §§ 1–3) | $350,000 fine per violation for individuals; greater of $10 million per violation and twice gain to violators or loss to victims for corporate offenders | 3 years | |
| Payment of bribes or failure to have adequate internal accounting controls (Foreign Corrupt Practices Act) (15 U.S.C. §§ 78dd-2) | $100,000 for individuals and $2,000,000 for corporations; under the Alternative Fines Act, fines can be twice gross gain of corrupt bribe. | 5 years | |
| | ***Promote Consumer Welfare by Facilitating Innovative Products and Services*** | | |
| See "Promote Economic Growth by Giving Incentives to Innovate" above. | | | |
| | ***Promote Consumer Welfare by Preventing Deceptive Practices*** | | |
| Mail or wire fraud (Mail Fraud Act) (18 U.S.C. § 1341) (Wire Fraud Act) (18 U.S.C. § 1343) | Greater of $250,000 fine per violation for individuals ($500,000 for organizations) and twice gain to violators or loss to victims; $1 million for violations that affect financial institutions | 20 years; 30 years for violations that affect financial institutions | Violation of these acts can trigger civil and criminal liability under the Racketeer Influenced and Corrupt Organizations Act (RICO). |
| Money laundering (18 U.S.C. § 1956) | Greater of $250,000 for individuals ($500,000 for organizations) and twice the value of the property involved in the transaction | 20 years | |
| Computer fraud (Computer Fraud and Abuse Act) (18 U.S.C. § 1030) | Greater of $250,000 fine per violation for individuals ($500,000 for organizations) and twice gain to violators or less to victims | 10 years for first-time offenders; 20 years for subsequent offenders | |
| Racketeering (Racketeer Influenced and Corrupt Organizations Act or RICO) (18 U.S.C. § 1963) | Greater of $250,000 fine per violation for individuals ($500,000 for organizations) and two times the defendant's gain or the victim's loss; forfeiture of all property wrongfully acquired or maintained | Life | Any injured person may also sue to recover threefold the damages sustained and the cost of the suit except no private right of action based solely on securities fraud (18 U.S.C. § 1964). |
| Bribery (18 U.S.C. § 201) | Greater of $250,000 fine per violation for individuals ($500,000 for organizations) and twice gain to violators or loss to victims and three times the value of the bribe | 15 years | |

*(Continued)*

**EXHIBIT 14.5 Penalties for White-Collar Crime—continued**

| Offense | Maximum Fine or Penalty | Maximum Sentence | Comments |
|---|---|---|---|
| | ***Promote Public Welfare by Promoting Effective Administration of Justice*** | | |
| Obstruction of justice (18 U.S.C. §§ 1501–1520) | Greater of $250,000 fine per violation for individuals ($500,000 for organizations) and twice gain to violators or loss to victims | 20 years | Includes altering or destroying documents with intent to impair their use in an official proceeding; offering or promoting false testimony; and threatening or intimidating witnesses, jurors, or court officials. |
| Perjury (18 U.S.C. § 1621) | Greater of $250,000 fine per violation for individuals ($500,000 for organizations) and twice gain to violators or loss to victims | 5 years | Falsehood must be relevant to inquiry. |
| Tampering with a record or otherwise impeding an official proceeding (Sarbanes–Oxley Act of 2002) (18 U.S.C. § 1512) | Greater of $250,000 fine per violation for individuals ($500,000 for organizations) and twice gain to violators or loss to victims | 20 years | |
| | ***Promote Public Welfare by Collecting Taxes and Spending Money*** | | |
| False statements to U.S. Government (False Statements Act) (18 U.S.C. § 1001) | Greater of $250,000 fine per violation for individuals ($500,000 for organizations) and twice gain to violators or loss to victims for knowing and willful violations | 5 years for knowing and willful violations | |
| Tax fraud or evasion (Internal Revenue Code) (26 U.S.C. § 7201) | $100,000 for individuals ($500,000 for corporations) plus costs of prosecution | 5 years | Violations include willful attempts to evade any tax imposed under the code, including employee withholding requirements, false statements in a tax return, willful delivery of a fraudulent return to the secretary of the treasury, and any false statements in a tax return. |
| False claims for reimbursement to U.S. Government (False Claims Act) (18 U.S.C. § 287) | Greater of $250,000 fine per violation for individuals ($500,000 for organizations) and twice gain to violators or loss to victims for knowing and willful violations | 5 years | U.S. Government includes any individual or any agency in civil, military, or naval service. |

*(Continued)*

**EXHIBIT 14.5 Penalties for White-Collar Crime—continued**

| OFFENSE | MAXIMUM FINE OR PENALTY | MAXIMUM SENTENCE | COMMENTS |
|---|---|---|---|
| ***Promote Public Welfare by Protecting the Environment*** | | | |
| Unlawful transport or disposal of hazardous waste (Resource Conservation and Recovery Act) (42 U.S.C. § 6928) | $50,000 per day for first-time offenders and $100,000 per day for subsequent violations; $250,000 for knowingly endangering others and $1 million for organizations that knowingly endanger others | 2 years for first-time offenders and 4 years for subsequent violations; 15 years for knowingly endangering others | Imposes "cradle to the grave" responsibility for generators of hazardous waste and requires disposal in a licensed facility. |
| Unlawful disposal of hazardous materials in water (Clean Water Act) (33 U.S.C. § 1319) | Not less than $2,500 nor more than $25,000 per day for negligent first-time violations; $50,000 per day for subsequent violations; $250,000 for first-time knowing endangerment and $500,000 for subsequent knowing endangerment violations; $1 million for organizations that knowingly endanger others for the first time and $2 million for subsequent violations | 1 year for negligent first-time violations and 2 years for subsequent violations; 15 years for first-time knowing endangerment and 30 years for subsequent violations | |

requires that one "knowingly agree to perform the services of a kind which facilitate the activities of those who are operating the enterprise in an illegal manner."[89]

*Reves* is an important case for accountants, underwriters, attorneys, and others who work with a company issuing securities. Such persons can no longer be found liable under RICO just because they were involved in the offering process. Instead, some involvement in the management of the issuer of the securities is required.

**Private Civil Actions** In addition to criminal penalties, the statute grants a private right of action that permits individuals to recover treble damages (that is, three times their actual damages) and also their costs and attorneys' fees in a civil action. The private right of action was apparently intended as a tool against businesses fueled by funds generated through organized crime. The statute contains no explicit requirement that organized crime be involved, however, and RICO has been used in numerous civil suits against legitimate businesses.

To prevail in a civil case under RICO, the plaintiff must demonstrate that the defendant committed an "overt act . . . in furtherance of a RICO conspiracy."[90] Thus, a president fired for reporting activity that violated RICO did not have a private cause of action against his former employer because the termination of his employment was not a racketeering activity. In the Private Securities Litigation Reform Act of 1995,[91] Congress foreclosed the use of the RICO civil private right of action against alleged perpetrators of securities fraud. Denying the potential for RICO-based shareholder lawsuits was one of many measures in this statute that were designed to curb abusive shareholder litigation. Criminal RICO charges can still be based on securities fraud.

## *Mail and Wire Fraud*

Next to RICO, the Mail and Wire Fraud Acts[92] may be the prosecutor's most powerful weapon against the white-collar criminal defendant. Chief Justice Warren Burger characterized the Mail Fraud Act as a "stopgap"

89. Brouwer v. Raffensperger, 199 F.3d 961 (7th Cir. 2000).

90. Beck v. Prupis, 529 U.S. 494 (2000).

91. Pub. L. No. 104-67, § 107, 109 Stat. 737, 758 (codified at 18 U.S.C.A. § 1964(c)).

92. 18 U.S.C. §§ 1343, 1341.

### INTERNATIONAL SNAPSHOT

The inbred financial world of Japan has generated a series of scandals involving corporate extortion. By threatening to disclose unsavory information through magazines or shareholder meetings, elements of Japan's mobster class (referred to as the *sokaiya*) have squeezed payoffs from some of Japan's biggest companies, including Nomura Securities, retailer Ajinmoto, and Dai–Ichi Kangyo Bank. No other industrialized economy has lived with a comparable level of corporate blackmail. Extortion has thrived in Japan because in its corporate culture, public information is given out sparingly and a tight web of cross-shareholdings among companies excludes individual stockholders.

Official tolerance of corporate blackmail has been waning ever since the mob began taking a higher profile in the booming economy of the late 1980s. Moreover, the current Japanese government is cracking down on extortion as part of its broader effort to reform Japan's financial markets. The specter of mobster-backed blackmail cannot help Japan's attempts to woo global investors interested in trading securities or effecting mergers and other capital-raising transactions.

**Source:** The information in this feature is drawn from Brian Bremmer & Emily Thornton, *Blackmail!*, BUS.WK., July 21, 1997, at 42.

provision that criminalizes conduct that a court finds morally reprehensible but that is not mentioned in any other criminal statute.

To establish *mail fraud* or *wire fraud* under the Acts, the prosecutor must demonstrate (1) a scheme intended to defraud or to obtain money or property by fraudulent means and (2) the use of the mails or of interstate telephone lines in furtherance of the fraudulent scheme. The Supreme Court has broadly construed "fraud" to encompass "everything designed to defraud by representations as to the past or present, or suggestions and promises as to the future."[93]

Federal prosecutions under these acts have involved such diverse activities as defense procurement fraud, insurance fraud, false financial statements fraud, medical advertising fraud, tax fraud, divorce mill fraud, and securities fraud. In *Schmuck v. United States*,[94] the Supreme Court upheld an indictment for mail fraud although the actual mailings were merely incidental to the scheme to defraud. Wayne T. Schmuck, a used-car distributor, purchased used cars, rolled back their odometers, and sold them to Wisconsin retail dealers at prices artificially inflated by the low-mileage readings. The unwitting dealers, relying on the altered readings, resold the cars to customers at inflated prices. The dealers consummated these transactions by mailing title-application forms to the state authorities on behalf of the buyers. The U.S. Supreme Court held that the mailings at issue satisfied the mailing element of the crime of mail fraud.

A prosecution for wire and mail fraud can be brought in addition to other prosecutions based on the same events. Thus, the defendant may be charged with violation of the securities laws, the bankruptcy laws, the tax laws, or the Truth in Lending Act, as well as for wire or mail fraud. Indeed, it is rare for a white-collar criminal prosecution to be brought without alleging a violation of the Wire and Mail Fraud Acts.

This prosecutorial ability to bring charges under various statutes increases the plea-bargaining power of the government. By presenting multiple statutory violations to the jury, the prosecutor also increases the chances of conviction and the likelihood of a stiffer sentence.

Violation of the Wire and Mail Fraud Acts can also trigger RICO liability. As a result, wire and mail fraud and RICO prosecutions often proceed in tandem.

## *False Statements to the U.S. Government*

The False Statements Act provides:

> Whoever, in any manner within the jurisdiction of any department or agency of the United States knowingly and willfully
>
> (1) falsifies, conceals or covers up by any trick, scheme, or device a material fact;
> (2) makes any false, fictitious or fraudulent statements or representations; or
> (3) makes or uses any false writing or document knowing the same to contain any false, fictitious or fraudulent statement or entry, shall be fined or imprisoned . . . or both.[95]

Although not used as frequently as the Wire and Mail Fraud Acts, the False Statements Act has become an effective tool for criminal prosecutions of businesses and employees who deal dishonestly with governmental administrative agencies. For example, in *United States v. Yermian*,[96] an employee of Gulton Industries, a defense contractor, was convicted of making false statements to the Department of Defense in connection with his application for a security clearance.

93. Durland v. United States, 161 U.S. 306, 313 (1896).
94. 489 U.S. 705 (1989).
95. 18 U.S.C. § 1001.
96. 581 F.2d 595 (7th Cir. 1978).

HISTORICAL PERSPECTIVE

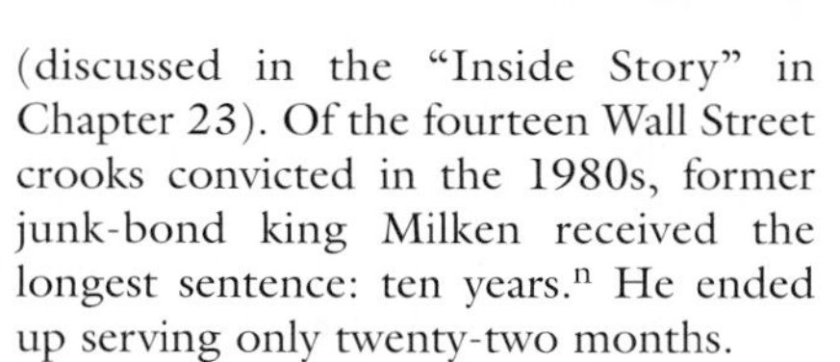

# WHITE-COLLAR CRIME

The term "white-collar crime" was first used in 1939 when Edwin Sutherland coined it in a speech about "crime in relation to business" that he was presenting to the American Sociological Society.[a] Sutherland defined white-collar crime as a "crime committed by a person of respectability and high social status in the course of his occupation."[b] Sutherland promoted the idea—revolutionary for his time—that wealthy or high-status individuals commit crimes, too. Prior to Sutherland's work, crime was viewed primarily as a reaction to poverty and thus endemic to the lower classes.

Sutherland asserted that "crime is not so highly concentrated in the lower class as the usual statistics indicate."[c] He further pointed out that the cost of white-collar crime was much higher than that of street crime: "The financial cost of white-collar crime is probably several times as great as the financial cost of all the crimes which are customarily regarded as the 'crime problem.'"[d] Sutherland went on to argue: "The financial loss from white-collar crime, great as it is, is less important than the damage to social relations. White-collar crimes violate trust and therefore create distrust, which lowers social morale and produces social disorganization on a large scale."[e] Nonetheless, white-collar criminals were not "regarded as real criminals."[f]

According to Sutherland, the "robber barons" of the late nineteenth and early twentieth centuries (including J.P. Morgan and John D. Rockefeller) were notorious examples of white-collar criminals.[g] These corporate titans openly exploited labor for their own gain and created monopolies violating the Sherman Antitrust Act of 1890, but they did not go to jail.[h]

After the stock market crash of 1929 and the ensuing Great Depression crippled the financial markets, Congress enacted the Securities Act of 1933 and the Securities Exchange Act of 1934 "to set limits on what people can do in the name of profit."[i] Yet it was not until 1961, seventy years after the passage of the Sherman Antitrust Act, that the first white-collar criminals were sent to jail.[j] Seven executives at major companies implicated in a price-fixing conspiracy, including General Electric and Westinghouse, were sentenced to thirty days, less time for good behavior.[k] During the first seventy years of the Sherman Act, the government had brought 1,580 antitrust cases against corporations, but all of them resulted in civil penalties.[l]

Prosecution of white-collar crime did not become commonplace until the mid-1970s. "[I]n the aftermath of the Watergate and foreign government bribery scandals, the federal government began targeting white collar crime as a high-priority prosecutorial area."[m]

By the mid-1980s and early 1990s, a number of high-profile corporate crime cases were making major headlines. These included a series of insider trading cases involving Ivan Boesky, Michael Milken, and Drexel Burnham Lambert (discussed in the "Inside Story" in Chapter 23). Of the fourteen Wall Street crooks convicted in the 1980s, former junk-bond king Milken received the longest sentence: ten years.[n] He ended up serving only twenty-two months.

Even before the Milken scandal was over, the government had a new target: the savings and loan industry. The most high-profile case involved Lincoln Savings & Loan headed by Charles Keating. Its collapse—dubbed "the largest public-finance scandal of the century"[o]—cost the U.S. taxpayers $2.5 billion.

In 1992, Keating was convicted of fraud, racketeering, and securities violations and sentenced to ten years in prison. He served four-and-one-half years before his sentence was overturned. In 1999, he pled guilty to defrauding investors and was sentenced to the four-and-one-half years he had already served.

One expert writing in 2002 commented that the "criminal sanction is generally reserved for the losers, the scamsters, the low-rent crime."[p] He compared the fate of "starched collar criminals" who loot companies of millions or billions of dollars with that of petty thieves:

> The starched-collar S&L crooks got an average of 36.4 months in the slammer. Those who committed burglary—generally swiping $300 or less—got 55.6 months; car thieves got 38 months; and first-time drug offenders, 64.9 months. Now compare the costs of the two kinds of crime: The losses from all bank robberies in the U.S. in 1992 *totaled* $35 million. That's about 1% of the estimated cost of Charles Keating's fraud at Lincoln Savings & Loan.[q]

**a.** This speech was later published as Edwin H. Sutherland, *White-Collar Criminality,* AM. SOC. REV. 1 (1940).
**b.** EDWIN H. SUTHERLAND, WHITE COLLAR CRIME: THE UNCUT VERSION (1983).
**c.** Sutherland, *supra* note a, at 4.
**d.** *Id.* at 4–5.
**e.** *Id.* at 8.
**f.** *Id.*
**g.** *Id.* at 2.
**h.** Leland Hazard, *Are Big Businessmen Crooks?* ATLANTIC MONTHLY, Nov. 1961.
**i.** Cynthia Crossen, *A Thirties Revelation: Rich People Who Steal Are Criminals, Too,* WALL ST. J., Oct. 15, 2003, at B1.
**j.** *Id.*
**k.** Hazard, *supra* note h.
**l.** *Id.*
**m.** Peter J. Henning, *Testing the Limits of Investigating and Prosecuting White Collar Crime: How Far Will the Courts Allow Prosecutors to Go?,* 54 U. PITTSBURGH L. REV. 405 (1993).
**n.** *Michael Milken; Junked,* ECONOMIST, Nov. 24, 1990, at 90.
**o.** *The S&L Mess,* U.S. NEWS & WORLD REP., Nov. 26, 1990, at 13.
**p.** Clifton Leaf, *White-Collar Criminals,* FORTUNE, Mar. 18, 2002, at 68.
**q.** *Id.* at 76.

## *False Claims to the U.S. Government and Health-Care Fraud*

Since the late 1980s, the U.S. government has used a civil statute, the False Claims Act (FCA),[97] to attack defense-contract and health-care fraud. Both the federal government and private parties (usually whistleblowers), acting on the government's behalf as *qui tam plaintiffs,* can bring civil suits to recover treble damages and penalties from persons who submit false claims for government funds knowingly or with recklessness or deliberate ignorance of their truth or falsity. In 2000, the U.S. Supreme Court rebuffed a challenge to the *qui tam* provisions when it held that whistleblowers have standing under Article III of the U.S. Constitution to sue on the government's behalf.[98] Often these civil suits lead to criminal prosecution under other federal statutes, such as the Mail and Wire Fraud Acts.

The *qui tam* plaintiffs receive up to 25 percent of the recovery. By February 2000, the United States had recovered more than $3.5 billion through FCA *qui tam* cases, of which $550 million was paid to the whistleblowers who brought the cases.[99]

The health-care industry is particularly susceptible to fraud. Companies often find it tempting to cheat rather than compete on price. The presence of third-party payors, such as private insurance companies and government programs, increases the opportunities and incentives to cheat. Despite continuing efforts to prevent health-care fraud, its cost increased from $10 billion a year in 1986[100] (roughly 2.5 percent of total health-care spending) to more than $50 billion in 1994 (roughly 5 percent).[101] By 2003, losses attributed to health-care fraud were estimated to be more than $150 billion, roughly 10 percent of total health-care spending.[102]

97. 31 U.S.C. §§ 3729 *et seq.*
98. Vt. Agency of Natural Res. v. United States *ex rel.* Stevens, 120 S. Ct. 1858 (2000).
99. Shelley R. Slade & Thomas A. Colhurst, *Health-Care Fraud and the False Claims Act: The Supreme Court Supports a Federal Weapon,* BUS. L. TODAY, Sept.–Oct. 2000, at 24, 26.
100. Michael A. Pollak, *Health Care Fraud Is Spreading Like the Flu,* BUS.WK., Dec. 1, 1986, at 125.
101. Jay Greene, *FBI Takes a Bite Out of Health Care Crime,* MOD. HEALTHCARE, Apr. 29, 1996, at 126.
102. *Health Care Fraud and Abuse Remains a Costly Challenge,* MANAGED HEALTHCARE EXECUTIVE, Oct. 1, 2004, *at* http://www.managedhealthcareexecutive.com/mhe/article/articleDetail.jsp?id=127451. See also GEN. ACCOUNTING OFFICE REP. TO BANKING MINORITY MEMBER, SUBCOMM. ON NAT'L SEC., INT'L AFFAIRS & CRIMINAL JUSTICE, HOUSE COMM. ON GOV'T REFORM & OVERSIGHT, HEALTH CARE FRAUD: INFORMATION-SHARING PROPOSALS TO IMPROVE ENFORCEMENT EFFORTS (May 1996), *at* http://www.securitymanagement.com/library/000187.html.

Since 1993, the Department of Justice has made fighting fraud and abuse in the health-care industry a top priority.[103] It focused first on the clinical laboratory industry, then on the major hospital chains, and most recently on pharmaceutical companies.[104]

In 1996, Congress created several new criminal offenses as part of the Health Insurance and Portability Account Act of 1996 (HIPAA).[105] These include health-care fraud,[106] theft or embezzlement in connection with a health-care offense,[107] false statements relating to a health-care offense,[108] and obstruction of a criminal investigation of a health-care offense.[109]

The number of federal criminal prosecutions of health-care companies and workers jumped 34 percent in 2002 to 333, nearly double the number ten years earlier.[110] Criminal convictions in health-care fraud cases increased from 59 in 1992 to 263 in 1999. Civil fines increased more than 50 percent from 1997 to 2000.[111]

The HIPAA makes firms convicted of felony health-care fraud after August 21, 1996, ineligible to participate in federal health-care programs. Nonetheless the government has been reluctant to use its power to bar major drug companies that have committed fraud from doing business with federal programs, such as Medicare or Medicaid, for fear of harming the 80 million elderly and poor clients who rely on the drugs the companies provide.[112]

Exhibit 14.6 shows health-care fraud settlements of $100 million or more in the period from 1994 to 2004. The government recouped $4.21 billion from health-care fraud cases in the three years ending in 2002, compared with $3.3 billion collected in the previous ten years.[113] Four companies alone—AstraZeneca, TAP Pharmaceuticals, Bayer, and Abbott Laboratories—paid more than $2 billion in penalties.[114]

103. Department of Justice, *Health Care Fraud Report, Fiscal Year 1998, at* http://www.usdoj.gov/dag/pubdoc/health98.htm.
104. Terry Carter, *Drug Wars,* A.B.A. J., Dec. 1, 2002, at 40; Bruce Japsen, *Targets Change in Drug Probes,* CHI. TRIB., Dec. 27, 2001, at 1.
105. Health Insurance and Portability Account Act, Pub. L. No. 104–191 (1996).
106. 18 U.S.C. § 1347.
107. 18 U.S.C. § 669.
108. 18 U.S.C. § 1035.
109. 18 U.S.C. § 1518.
110. Patricia Callahan, *Health Industry Sees a Surge in Fraud Fines,* WALL ST. J., Aug. 18, 2003, at B1.
111. Jennifer Steinhauer, *Justice Department Finds Success Chasing Health Care Fraud,* N.Y. TIMES, Jan. 23, 2001, at A5.
112. Julie Schmit, *Drug Companies Dodge Ban from Medicare, Medicaid,* USA TODAY, Aug. 16, 2004, at 3B.
113. Callahan, *supra* note 110.
114. Greg Garrell, *Pfizer Settles Fraud Case for $430M,* USA TODAY, May 14, 2004, at 1B.

**EXHIBIT 14.6** **Health-Care Fraud Settlements of $100 Million or More: 1994 to 2004**

| Company (Date of Settlement) | Crime | Settlement |
|---|---|---|
| National Medical Enterprises (June 1994) | The hospital chain pled guilty to seven criminal counts, including six counts of kickbacks in referral of Medicare patients and one count of conspiracy to make illegal payments. NME defrauded insurance programs by billing for unnecessary treatment, causing estimated losses of $100 million. | $379 million, including a $33 million criminal fine, a $324 million civil fine paid to the federal government, and $16.3 million divided among the states. The remainder of the settlement went to affected private parties. The company instituted a corporate integrity plan as part of the settlement and agreed to divest many of its hospitals. |
| Caremark International, Inc. (June 1995) | Pled guilty to two charges of mail fraud in two states and charges that the company defrauded the government through illegal kickbacks to doctors in exchange for referrals to use its products and services. | $161 million, including $29 million in criminal fines, $85.3 million in federal civil fines, and $44.6 million in state civil fines. The remaining $2 million was donated to treat AIDS. |
| SmithKline Beecham Labs (September 1996) | Settled charges that lab units committed insurance fraud by overcharging government insurance programs for unnecessary medical tests, fictitious tests, billing twice for the same test, and kickbacks to doctors to solicit patients. | $325 million in civil fines under False Claims Act and agreed to implement a corporate compliance agreement. |
| First American Healthcare of Georgia (October 1996) | Convicted of Medicare fraud for billing fraudulent costs to the program. | $255 million. |
| Corning (October 1996) | Pled guilty to one count of criminal conspiracy for defrauding Medicare by performing unnecessary medical testing. | $119 million, including a $35.3 million criminal fine and $83.7 million in civil fines. |
| LabCorp (November 1996) | Pled guilty to one count for defrauding Medicare for billing unnecessary medical tests. | $187 million, including $5 million in criminal fines and $182 million in civil fines. |
| Health Care Service Corp (July 1998) | Pled guilty to eight counts for false claims and obstruction of audits. The company submitted false reports to the Health Care Financing Administration to make its performance look better than it actually was. | $144 million, including $4 million in criminal fines and $140 million in civil fines under the False Claims Act. |
| Beverly Enterprises (December 1999) | Pled guilty to criminal fraud for overcharging Medicare by $460 million in phony cost reports. The nursing home chain billed the program for time not spent on Medicare patient care. | $175 million, including a $5 million criminal fine and a $170 million civil fine under the False Claims Act. The company agreed to implement a corporate integrity plan and divest ten nursing homes. |
| National Medical Care, Inc. (January 2000) | Pled guilty to charges that the company had engaged in a variety of illegal behavior, including giving kickbacks for referrals and submitting false claims to Medicare by charging for unnecessary testing. | $486 million, including criminal fines of $101 million and a $385 million civil fine under the False Claims Act. The company agreed to institute a corporate integrity agreement. |
| Vencor, Inc. (March 2001) | Settled claims alleging that the company submitted false claims to government insurance programs, including Medicare and Medicaid. | $244.5 million, including $104.5 million in civil fines under the False Claims Act, $25 million in fines for claims that were not fraudulent, $90 million to Medicare, and $25 million to the states. The company neither admitted nor denied wrongdoing. |

*(Continued)*

**EXHIBIT 14.6 Health-Care Fraud Settlements of $100 Million or More: 1994 to 2004—continued**

| Company (Date of Settlement) | Crime | Settlement |
|---|---|---|
| TAP Pharmaceuticals (September 2001) | Pled guilty to one count of criminal conspiracy to violate the Prescription Drug Marketing Act. The company used illegal kickbacks to doctors to induce them to prescribe its prostate cancer drug, Lupron, which was more expensive than other available drugs. Kickbacks included money as "educational grants" as well as expensive dinners, parties, golf and ski trips, and TVs/VCRs. The company gave doctors free samples with the understanding they would bill Medicare and Medicaid for the drugs. The company also ensured that doctors received profits by charging them substantially less than the federal government paid for the drug. Losses totaled an estimated $145 million. | $875 million, including a $290 million criminal fine under the Prescription Drug Marketing Act, a $559 million civil fine under the False Claims Act, and $25.5 million in civil fines to the states. TAP agreed to employ a corporate integrity agreement as part of its settlement. |
| Bristol–Myers Squibb (March 2003) | Settled charges that the company paid $72.5 million to competitors and illegally prolonged patents on its antidepressant, BuSpar, and cancer drugs, Taxol and Platinol, to prevent generic entry for these three drugs, which contributed $2 billion in annual revenues. | $670 million with $155 million going to state governments and the rest to affected private groups. The company agreed to a ten-year ban on its practice of filing patents to gain an automatic 30-month delay on the entry of generic versions of its off-patent drugs. |
| Bayer (April 2003) | Pled guilty to violating the Prescription Drug Marketing Act. Bayer also violated the law requiring drug companies to offer Medicaid the lowest prices. Bayer charged the federal program higher prices for its antibiotic, Cipro, and its hypertension drug, Adalat, than it charged HMOs. In a scheme referred to as "lick and stick," the company cheated the government by relabeling or repackaging the drugs to sell them at lower prices to HMOs. | $257 million, including $6 million in criminal fines and $251 million in civil fines for violating the Medicaid best-price statute. Of the civil fine, $108 million went to state Medicaid programs, and $143 million went to the federal government. Bayer also implemented an improved corporate integrity program to ensure accurate price reporting in the future. |
| AstraZeneca (June 2003) | Pled guilty to one count of health-care fraud for violating the Prescription Drug Marketing Act in promoting its prostate cancer drug, Zoladex. The company gave illegal kickbacks to doctors to induce them to prescribe the drug. The company gave doctors free samples with the understanding they would bill Medicare and Medicaid. The company also ensured that doctors received profits by charging them substantially less than the federal government paid for the drug. | $355 million, including a $64 million criminal fine, a $266 million civil fine under the False Claims Act, and $25 million to the states for Medicaid fraud. |
| HCA, Inc. (December 2000) (June 2003) | In 2000, pled guilty to fourteen criminal counts of defrauding government health insurance programs by an estimated $650 million. Additional claims against the company were settled in the spring of 2003. HCA defrauded Medicare and other federal programs by overcharging for services and provided kickbacks to doctors to induce them to refer patients to HCA hospitals. | $1.7 billion, including $631 million in civil fines, $250 million to Medicare, and $17.6 for state Medicaid programs. HCA agreed to increase the strength and scope of its compliance program. |

*(Continued)*

**EXHIBIT 14.6 Health-Care Fraud Settlements of $100 Million or More: 1994 to 2004—continued**

| Company (Date of Settlement) | Crime | Settlement |
|---|---|---|
| Abbott Laboratories CG Nutritionals Unit (July 2003) | Pled guilty to one count of obstructing a federal inquiry into allegations that the company sold or gave away its nutritional pumps to nursing homes and hospitals at discounted prices and charged Medicare and Medicaid higher prices. | $600 million, including $200 million in criminal fines and $400 million in civil fines. The company agreed to a corporate integrity agreement to monitor its marketing practices. |
| Pfizer/Warner–Lambert (May 2004) | Two criminal counts for violating the Federal Food, Drug and Cosmetic Act by marketing its epilepsy drug, Neurontin, for unapproved uses. The company also promoted its drug by giving kickbacks to physicians. | $430 million, including a $240 million criminal fine, $152 million in civil fines under the False Claims Act, and $38 million to consumer protection agencies. The company agreed to improve its corporate compliance program. |
| Schering–Plough (July 2004) | Pled guilty to one criminal count for fraud for violating the federal antikickback statute. Provided incentives to insurance companies to induce them to use Schering–Plough's allergy drug, Claritin, rather than a cheaper drug, Allegra. This scheme resulted in the private insurers receiving the drug at a discount, less than the federal government, a violation of a federal law that requires that Medicaid receive the lowest prices. | $345.5 million, including $52.5 million in criminal fines and $293 million in civil fines, with $117 million going to the states and $179 million to the federal government under the False Claims Act. |
| HealthSouth (December 2004) | Settled charges of fraudulent billing for Medicare and other federal insurance programs. | $325 million civil fine under the False Claims Act. |
| Gambro Healthcare (December 2004) | Pled guilty to health-care fraud. Cheated Medicare and Medicaid by charging the government insurance programs for unnecessary tests as well as setting up a phony subsidiary company to receive payments. Other crimes included paying kickbacks to doctors in exchange for referrals. | $350 million, including $25 million in criminal fines, $310.5 million in civil fines, and $15 million for the states. The company also agreed to institute a corporate integrity agreement. |

## *Computer Crime*

White-collar crime often involves computers. Many computer-related crimes are likely to go undetected because they generally involve little or no visible physical activity. The computer may be used not only to commit the offense but also to hide or destroy the evidence. Even if computer crime is detected, it often goes unreported. Most businesses, especially financial institutions, do not want it publicly known that an employee or an outsider used the company's computer system to steal from the company.

Despite efforts to thwart computer crime, it is flourishing. A 2001 survey showed that 47 percent of companies have had their computer systems illegally accessed, 90 percent have been vandalized, and 13 percent have had information stolen.[115]

115. Reid Skibell, *Cybercrimes & Misdemeanors: A Reevaluation of the Computer Fraud and Abuse Act*, 18 BERKELEY TECH. L.J. 909 (2003).

Computer crime can take several forms. *Computer fraud* is the use of a computer to steal company or government funds. This type of theft generally involves improper or unauthorized access to the computer system and the creation of false data or computer instructions. The computer system then generates fraudulent transfers of funds or bogus checks that are cashed by the wrongdoer.

More than forty different sections of the federal criminal code may apply to thefts by computer, ranging from embezzlement to wire fraud. Most computer-aided thefts can also be prosecuted under traditional state larceny laws. Other computer crimes can be prosecuted under a multitude of other laws that normally apply to non-computer-related crime.[116] Intellectual property

116. For a list of laws relevant to computer crime, see Computer Crime and Intellectual Property Section, U.S. Department of Justice, *Federal Code Related to Cybercrime, at* http://www.usdoj.gov/criminal/cybercrime/fedcode.htm.

violations, bootlegging, the Economic Espionage Act, child pornography statutes, and stalking laws are all applicable to computer crimes.

The ability of computer hackers to access protected financial and governmental records is one of the primary concerns spawned by increased use of the Internet. A 1996 study by the General Accounting Office estimated that, in 1995 alone, the two million computers on the 10,000 networks of the Defense Department were broken into as many as 250,000 times.[117] The private sector has been equally afflicted. Hackers have stolen credit card numbers, transmitted highly destructive viruses, and shut down popular online sites.[118]

**The Computer Fraud and Abuse Act** The Computer Fraud and Abuse Act[119] (CFAA) is the mainstay of federal computer fraud legislation. It prohibits (1) accessing a computer without authorization or exceeding authorized access; (2) knowingly transmitting a program, information, code, or command that results in intentionally causing "damage" without authorization to a protected computer; (3) knowingly and with intent to defraud trafficking in any password or similar information through which a computer may be accessed without authorization; and (4) threatening to cause damage to a protected computer. "Damage" is defined as "any impairment to the integrity or availability of data, a program, a system, or information."

The CFAA also makes illegal the knowing transmission of computer viruses. A *computer virus* is a computer program that can replicate itself into other programs without any subsequent instruction, human or mechanical. A computer virus may destroy data, programs, or files, or it may prevent user access to a computer (*denial-of-service attacks*). The proliferation of networks of personal computers has created millions of entry points for viruses. A virus can be concealed in any software and then passed on to other computers through attachments to electronic mail, information services, disks, or other means.

Although the CFAA originally applied only to "federal interest computers" (computers of the federal government and certain financial institutions), Congress amended the Act in 1996 to substitute the phrase "protected computer" in place of "federal interest computer." A *protected computer* is defined as a computer used in interstate or foreign commerce. Other amendments have created more crimes, lowered the required level of intent, and increased the penalties.[120]

The following case demonstrates how the 1996 amendments to the CFAA, together with the explosive growth in the use of the Internet, greatly expanded the types of activities covered by the Act. (Although this case involved civil claims, the sections of the CFAA the court analyzed also provide the basis for a criminal prosecution.)

117. See Jon Jefferson, *Deleting Cybercrooks,* A.B.A. J., Oct. 1997, at 68. See also Jon Swartz, *Hackers Hijack Federal Computers,* USA TODAY, Aug. 31, 2004, at 1B.
118. For an excellent discussion of the computer crime laws applicable to different types of cybercrime, see Eric J. Sinrod & William P. Reilly, *Hacking Your Way to Hard Time: Application of Computer Crime Laws to Specific Types of Hacking Attacks,* 4 J. INTERNET L. 1 (2000). See also Arthur J. Carter IV & Audrey Perry, *Computer Crimes,* 41 AM. CRIM. L. REV. 313 (2004).
119. 18 U.S.C. § 1030.
120. Skibell, *supra* note 115.

A CASE IN POINT

## In the Language of the Court

**CASE 14.3**

**Shurgard Storage Centers, Inc. v. Safeguard Self Storage, Inc.**

*United States District Court for the Western District of Washington*

*119 F. Supp. 2d 1121 (W.D. Wash. 2000).*

**› FACTS** Shurgard Storage Centers, the industry leader in full- and self-service storage facilities in both the United States and Europe, sued a competitor, Safeguard Self Storage, for allegedly embarking on a "systematic" scheme to hire away key employees for the purpose of obtaining trade secrets. Shurgard claimed that Eric Leland, one of its employees subsequently hired by Safeguard, used Shurgard's computers to access various trade secrets and proprietary information belonging to Shurgard and to send e-mails containing the information to Safeguard. Leland was still employed by Shurgard at the time he sent the e-mails.

Shurgard alleged misappropriation of trade secrets, conversion, unfair competition, tortious interference with a business expectancy, and violations of the Computer Fraud and Abuse Act. Safeguard moved to dismiss the CFAA claims.

**› ISSUE PRESENTED** Does the Computer Fraud and Abuse Act apply to an employee's use of his employer's computer to e-mail misappropriated trade secrets to a competitor?

*(Continued)*

(Case 14.3 *continued*)

**› OPINION** ZILLY, J., writing on behalf of the U.S. District Court for the Western District of Washington:

Under § 1030(a)(2)(C), "whoever . . . intentionally accesses a computer without authorization or exceeds authorized access, and thereby obtains . . . information from a protected computer if the conduct involved an interstate or foreign communication . . . shall be punished . . . . " [*Ed.:* Section 1030(g) creates a private right of action for persons who suffer damage or loss because of a violation.]

. . . [T]he defendant asserts that the plaintiff has not alleged that the employees in question accessed the trade secrets without authorization. . . .

. . .

The plaintiff responds by arguing that the authorization for its former employees ended when the employees began acting as agents for the defendant. . . .

. . .

Under the Restatement (Second) of Agency:

> Unless otherwise agreed, the authority of an agent terminates if, without knowledge of the principal, he acquires adverse interests or if he is otherwise guilty of a serious breach of loyalty to the principal.[121]

Under this rule, the authority of the plaintiff's former employees ended when they allegedly became agents of the defendant. . . .

. . .

. . . [T]he defendant maintains the CFAA is limited to those industries whose computers contain vast amounts of information, which if released, could significantly affect privacy interests in the public at large. The defendant also maintains the CFAA is limited to "outsiders" or "hackers," and not "insiders" (employees). Though the original scope of the CFAA was limited to the concerns addressed by the defendant, its subsequent amendments have broadened the scope sufficiently to cover the behavior alleged in this case.

. . .

. . . [T]he CFAA was intended to control interstate computer crime, and since the advent of the Internet, almost all computer use has become interstate in nature.

**› RESULT** The defendant's motion to dismiss was denied. Shurgard had stated valid claims under the CFAA.

**› COMMENTS** Section 1030(e)(8)(A) defines "damage" as "any impairment to the integrity or availability of data, a program, a system or information, that causes loss aggregating at least $5,000 in value during any one-year period to one or more individuals."[122] The court held that the defendant's collection and dissemination of confidential information was an impairment of its integrity even though no data were physically damaged or erased. The court also held that the plaintiff had stated a claim under 18 U.S.C. § 1030(a)(4), which prohibits any person from knowingly and with intent to defraud accessing a protected computer without authorization. The court held that a plaintiff need not prove the common law elements of fraud but only that the defendant engaged in wrongdoing or employed dishonest methods.

121. Restatement (Second) of Agency § 112 (1958).
122. United States v. Middleton, 231 F.3d 1207 (9th Cir. 2000) (holding that "individuals" includes corporations and other artificial entities).

*(Continued)*

(Case 14.3 *continued*)

**› CRITICAL THINKING QUESTIONS**

1. Is a computer or its information "damaged" within the meaning of the CFAA if intruders alter existing log-on programs to copy user passwords to a file that the hackers can retrieve later if, after retrieving the newly created password file, the intruders restore the altered log-in file to its original condition?
2. Does a computer user with authorized access to a computer and its programs act without authorization if he or she uses the program in an unauthorized way?

**Computer Piracy** *Computer piracy* is the theft or misuse of computer software. (With the increasing value and decreasing size of computer equipment, the theft of computer hardware is increasing. This is larceny, however, not computer piracy.)

Concerned with the increasing amount of computer software theft, Congress amended the Copyright Act in 1980 to cover computer software. (Copyright law is discussed further below and in Chapter 11.) Most states have also made the theft of computer software a crime. For example, Sections 156.30 and 156.35 of the New York Penal Law define six crimes related to computer misuse. The statute makes it a felony to duplicate a computer software program without authorization if the software has a value in excess of $2,500 or the duplication is done in connection with another felony. The legislation also prohibits the possession of unlawfully duplicated materials with a value in excess of $2,500.

**INTERNATIONAL SNAPSHOT**

The Tokyo High Court refused a request from the United States to extradict Takashi Okamoto, a Japanese scientist indicted under the Economic Espionage Act for stealing genetic materials related to Alzheimer's disease research conducted at the Cleveland Clinic Foundation.[a] The Court found insignificant evidence to show that Dr. Okamoto intended to benefit his employer, RIKEN, which is funded by the Japanese government, when he stole or destroyed the genetic materials. There was no evidence that RIKEN actually used the genetic materials at issue. This is apparently the first time the United States has requested the extradition of a Japanese national charged with a white-collar crime in the United States.

a. Tetsuya Morimoto, *First Japanese Denial of U.S. Extradition Request: Economic Espionage Case,* 20 INT'L ENFORCEMENT L. RPTR. 1 (2004).

## *Crimes Involving Intellectual Property*

U.S. companies lose more than $200 billion a year as a result of worldwide copyright, trademark, and trade secret infringement.[123] Chapter 11 discusses criminal liability under the Copyright Act, the No Electronic Theft Act, the Digital Millennium Copyright Act, and the Economic Espionage Act.

## *The Foreign Corrupt Practices Act*

The Foreign Corrupt Practices Act,[124] discussed further in Chapter 25, makes it a crime for any U.S. firm to make payments to an official of a foreign government in an attempt to influence the actions of the official. The Act also requires detailed record keeping and internal control measures by all public companies, whether international or purely domestic.

## *Antitrust Laws*

Criminal prosecutions under the antitrust laws occur most frequently in actions brought under Sections 1 and 2 of the Sherman Act.[125] As discussed in Chapter 16, Section 1 of the Sherman Act prohibits, among other things, all agreements in restraint of trade, including price-fixing. Section 2 prohibits monopolization, that is, the willful acquisition or maintenance of monopoly power coupled with the intent to monopolize.

Criminal prosecutions under the Sherman Act are initiated under the direction of the U.S. attorney general through the Antitrust Division of the Department of Justice or the appropriate U.S. attorney. Because the Sherman Act contains both criminal and civil sanctions, the government must always determine whether to bring a criminal action, a civil action, or both. In making this determination, the government continues to rely on a report issued by the U.S. attorney general in 1955,

123. *PBF Looks at What's Being Done to Arrest Cyberfraud,* PREVENTING BUS. FRAUD, Apr. 2000, at 1.
124. 15 U.S.C. § 78dd-2.
125. 15 U.S.C §§ 1–2.

## View from Cyberspace

### FIGHTING CYBERCRIME

From a criminal's viewpoint, cybercrime is appealing for a number of reasons. It is a nonviolent and often easy way to make money; it does not involve personal interaction with the victims; and it has only recently come to be regarded as a serious crime.

According to former U.S. Attorney General John Ashcroft, Internet-related fraud increased as a percentage of total reported consumer fraud from 31 percent in 2000 to more than 50 percent in 2002. The Federal Trade Commission (FTC) received more than 100,000 Internet-related fraud reports in 2002 alone.[a] Experts believe that cybercrime has become a multibillion-dollar underground enterprise: "Organized crime rings and petty thieves are flocking to the Internet like start-ups in the go-go '90s, federal authorities say—establishing a multibillion-dollar underground economy in just a few years."[b] Losses in the United States from cybercrime in 2003 were estimated at a minimum of $14 billion: $10 billion from spam, $2 billion from business fraud, and $2 billion from identity theft.[c]

The government's efforts to stop cybercrime may finally be paying off. In November 2004, Jeremy Jaynes became the first person in the United States to be sentenced to prison for violating Virginia's anti-spam statute. He received a nine-year sentence for e-mailing 10,000 messages to America Online customers. The severity of the sentence reflected the fact that "juries are now familiar with spam and are willing to impose tough sentences for the non-violent but annoying crime."[d]

Increasingly, the Department of Justice, the FBI, the FTC, the U.S. Postal Service, and state and local governments are working together to catch cybercrooks. In May 2003, "Operation E-Con" led to the recovery of $17 million and the arrest of 135 suspects for bilking 89,000 people out of $176 million.[e]

In August 2004, federal officials announced fifty-three convictions as part of "Operation Web Snare." Investigators targeted a variety of online crimes, including identity theft, fraud, counterfeit software, and computer intrusions. The crimes affected more than 150,000 victims and caused estimated losses of more than $215 million.[f] Dan Larkin, head of the Internet Crime Complaint Center, characterized Operation Web Snare as "not the end but rather the start of such investigations."[g]

The Department of Justice announced the first successful conviction in "Operation Fastlink" on December 22, 2004.[h] Jathan Desir pled guilty to three counts of copyright infringement and conspiracy to commit copyright infringement for pirating software, movies, videogames, and music. Desir faced up to fifteen years in prison. Investigators conducted more than 120 searches in twenty-seven states and eleven foreign countries and identified almost 100 individuals worldwide as leaders or high-level members of various international piracy organizations.[i] More arrests appeared likely.

a. Mike Keyser, *The Council of Europe Convention on Cybercrime,* 12 J. TRANSNAT'L L. & POL'Y 287 (Spring 2003); Aaron Burstein, *A Survey of Cybercrime in the United States,* 18 BERKELEY TECH. L.J. 313 (2003); *Federal Officials Announce Crackdown on Online Fraud,* U.S.L.W., Sept. 1, 2004, at 742.
b. Mark Helm, *135 Arrested in Cybercrime Cases,* MILWAUKEE J. SENTINEL, May 17, 2003, at 03A; Carlos Campos, *Internet Fraud Crackdown Leads to 130 Arrests in the U.S.,* ATLANTA-J. CONST., May 17, 2003, at 3F.
c. Jon Swartz, *Crooks Slither into Net's Shady Nooks and Crannies,* USA TODAY, Oct. 21, 2004, at B1; Jon Swartz, *Shhh, They're Hunting Cybercrooks,* USA TODAY, Sept. 21, 2004, at 4b; John Cox & Carolyn Duffy Marsan, *Is the Law's Arm Long Enough?* NETWORK WORLD, Nov. 29, 2004, at 50.
d. Wendy Leibowitz, *Nine-Year Sentence for Felony Spam Shows Jury Viewed E-mail Torrent as Serious Crime,* U.S.L.W. , Nov. 10, 2004, at 912.
e. *Federal Officials, supra* note a.
f. Jon Swartz, *Hackers Hijack Federal Computers,* USA TODAY, Aug. 31, 2004, at 1B; Thomas Claburn, *Feds Target Scofflaws and Spammers,* INFORMATIONWEEK, Aug. 30, 2004, at 22.
g. *Id.*
h. Department of Justice, *First "Operation Fastlink" Defendant Pleads Guilty to Online Software Piracy,* Dec. 22, 2004, *at* http://www.usdoj.gov/opa/pr/2004/December/04_crm_801.htm.
i. For a discussion of the Council of Europe Convention on Cybercrime, see Keyser, *supra* note a. See also Brian C. Lewis, *Prevention of Computer Crime Amidst International Anarchy,* 41 AM. CRIM. L. REV. 1353 (2004).

under which the criminal sanction has generally been limited to particularly egregious conduct, such as price-fixing or group boycotts, or has been applied to individuals previously convicted of an antitrust offense.

### Securities Law Violations

As explained further in Chapter 22, the offer and sale of securities are governed by a complex set of federal and state laws and regulations.

**Federal Securities Laws** Both the Securities Act of 1933[126] and the Securities Exchange Act of 1934[127] provide criminal penalties in addition to civil sanctions for offering and selling securities without an exemption, securities fraud, insider trading, and other violations. Although the Securities and Exchange Commission (SEC) administers both the 1933 Act and the 1934 Act, the U.S. attorney decides whether to bring criminal charges.

**State Blue Sky Laws** The states also impose criminal sanctions for violations of their *blue sky laws.* As demonstrated in the following case, state securities laws can be more restrictive than their federal counterparts.

126. 15 U.S.C.A. §§ 77a *et seq.*
127. 15 U.S.C.A. §§ 78a *et seq.*

A CASE IN POINT

**CASE 14.4**
**Mueller v. Sullivan**
*United States Court of Appeals for the Seventh Circuit 141 F.3d 1232 (7th Cir. 1998).*

## Summary

**› FACTS** Mark Mueller and James Stopple controlled Farm Loan Services, an auction house for the sale of securities. They persuaded their clients to accept payment for monies owed them in Farm Loan Services corporate notes rather than in cash, but they prohibited their staff from revealing that Farm Loan Services had significant debt and cash-flow problems and was unprofitable with no available assets.

Mueller and Stopple were charged with violating Wisconsin's version of the Uniform Securities Act, which provides that the willful omission of material facts in connection with the purchase or sale of securities is a crime. The trial judge instructed the jury that Mueller and Stopple could be convicted under the statute if the prosecution proved that they knew that the investors were not being told relevant information that was objectively material. Mueller and Stopple were subsequently convicted.

Mueller and Stopple challenged their convictions, claiming that the Due Process Clause of the Fourteenth Amendment required a more stringent showing of mental state, specifically, the intent to deceive, which is required in cases under Section 10(b) of the Securities Exchange Act of 1934 (1934 Act), on which many sections of the Uniform Securities Act were modeled.

**› ISSUE PRESENTED** Does the Due Process Clause permit conviction for violation of state securities laws when the defendants knew what they were doing but did not know that it was illegal?

**› SUMMARY OF OPINION** The U.S. Court of Appeals for the Seventh Circuit pointed out that few criminal statutes require proof that the defendant knew the wrongfulness of his or her acts. Rather, most statutes require only a showing that the defendant intended to bring about the forbidden consequence. The court concluded that states have a legitimate interest in penalizing conduct even if the defendant did not know that the conduct was unlawful:

> States are entitled to give corporate managers incentives to learn the law. No one with half a brain can offer "an opportunity to invest in our company" without knowing that there is a regulatory jungle out there. To say that the Constitution entitles entrepreneurs to propagate deceptive half-truths about their securities unless they have the same level of legal understanding as a practitioner of securities law . . . is to create a powerful incentive to go buccaneering. Regulatory statutes . . . serve to induce caution and consultation.

The court recognized that such a standard may have the effect of penalizing someone who had no idea the conduct was wrongful, but after weighing the relative hardships, it concluded that the burden should be placed on those who are engaging in the regulated activity, not on the innocent public.

**› RESULT** The convictions of Mueller and Stopple were upheld.

### *Obstruction of Justice, Perjury, and Related Offenses*

The Sarbanes–Oxley Act increased the penalties for existing obstruction-of-justice offenses, such as jury and witness tampering and destroying evidence while a government investigation or lawsuit is pending or imminent. It also created several new crimes, including (1) destroying corporate audit working papers, records, or analyses within five years after the completion of the audit;[128] (2) destroying, altering, or falsifying records relevant to potential future federal investigations or bankruptcy;[129] and (3) retaliating against an individual who provided a law enforcement officer any truthful information relating to the commission or possible commission of a federal offense.[130] (See Appendix N.)

If government prosecutors cannot get a conviction on a substantive crime, they are increasingly turning to related cover-up crimes like obstruction of justice and perjury. A person commits *perjury* when he or she takes an oath to tell the truth and willfully and contrary to such an oath states a material matter that he or she does not believe to be true.[131]

The conviction of Martha Stewart, chief executive of Martha Stewart Living Omnimedia, in 2004 is a prime example of this phenomenon. She was initially suspected of insider trading when she sold her ImClone stock after Samuel Waksal, ImClone's CEO, learned that the Food and Drug Administration had denied approval for ImClone's new cancer drug. She truthfully told investigators that Waksal had not tipped her to sell her shares, but she claimed that she had a preexisting agreement with her broker at Merrill Lynch to sell her shares if the price dropped below $60. She also told investigators that her broker had not told her that Waksal was selling ImClone stock. When her broker's assistant admitted that there was no prior sell agreement and testified that he had informed Stewart that Waksal was selling, Stewart was prosecuted for obstruction of justice. She was never indicted for insider trading, however, because it was not clear that knowing Waksal was selling was, by itself, material nonpublic information obtained in breach of a duty of trust or confidence. In short, she was convicted of lying about a crime for which she was never charged.[132]

Similarly, Frank Quattrone, the investment banker convicted of ordering employees to shred documents in the face of an SEC investigation of allocations of shares in initial public offerings, "was convicted for things he did to muck up a criminal investigation, not the acts that were actually being probed."[133] (This case is discussed further in Chapter 3.) According to a former federal prosecutor, Quattrone and Stewart's convictions send a message: "Jurors are saying, even if you're powerful and wealthy, don't even think about influencing the government's efforts to investigate."[134]

One of the first cases testing the revised obstruction-of-justice statutes involved Thomas Trauger, a former partner at the accounting firm Ernst & Young. Trauger was charged in September 2003 with obstruction of justice under 18 U.S.C. § 1519 for altering and destroying documents related to one of his audit clients, NextCard. After Trauger was notified that banking regulators had requested the accounting work papers relating to the audit of NextCard's 2000 fiscal year, Trauger allegedly told a fellow employee to "beef up" the work papers to make it appear as though the auditing team had been "right on the mark" all along. The men went into a computerized archive for the work papers and revised them, then deleted the original work papers from the system.[135] Trauger then proceeded to hand over the revised work papers to investigators.

In October 2004, Trauger pled guilty to obstruction of justice and was sentenced to five years in prison. His plea was viewed as a triumph of the new Sarbanes–Oxley provision. As one U.S. attorney explained, "This is one of the first cases in which an auditor has pled guilty to destroying key documents in an effort to obstruct a federal investigation."[136]

## Other Federal Regulatory and Tax Offenses

A large number of federal regulatory laws provide for criminal as well as civil penalties for their violation. Several of the more important are discussed in this section.

### THE ENVIRONMENTAL LAWS

As explained in Chapter 15, the federal environmental laws provide for criminal sanctions against both corporate and individual violators. For example, any person

128. 18 U.S.C. § 1520.
129. 18 U.S.C. § 1519.
130. 18 U.S.C. § 1513.
131. U.S.C. § 1621.
132. *The Trial of Martha*, WALL ST. J., Feb. 13, 2004, at A12.
133. Steven Syre, *The One That Didn't Get Away*, BOSTON GLOBE, Sept. 9, 2004, at D1.
134. Jonathan D. Glater, *On Wall Street Today, a Break from the Past*, N.Y. TIMES, May 4, 2004, at C1.
135. Kurt Eichenwald, *U.S. Charges Ernst & Young Ex-Partner in Audit Case*, N.Y. TIMES, Sept. 26, 2003, at C1.
136. Stephen Taub, *Auditor Pleads on Document Cover-Up*, CFO.COM, Nov. 2, 2004.

who knowingly falsifies any records required to be maintained under the Clean Water Act may be fined and imprisoned. Prison terms and fines are doubled for subsequent violations. The Resource Conservation and Recovery Act (RCRA)[137] imposes criminal penalties on both the corporation and individual employees who dispose of hazardous waste without the appropriate RCRA permit.

## WORKER SAFETY LAWS

### *The Occupational Safety and Health Act*

The Occupational Safety and Health Act (OSHA)[138] applies to all employers engaged in a business affecting interstate commerce. OSHA is discussed in Chapter 12.

Most violations of OSHA are punished by civil penalties. Civil penalties are mandatory when the employer receives a citation for a serious violation, discretionary when the violation is nonserious. More severe civil penalties are imposed for willful or repeated violations. The terms "serious," "nonserious," "willful," and "repeated" are all defined in the Act.

Section 666(e) of the Act provides for criminal penalties if the employer commits a willful violation that results in the death of an employee. In such a case, the employer may be fined, imprisoned, or both.

### *State Law Prosecutions of Workplace Safety Hazards*

As noted in Chapter 12, state prosecutors have taken an aggressive approach toward workplace safety hazards that result in injuries. Employers have tried to defend against such charges by claiming that OSHA preempts state prosecutions based on failure to maintain workplace safety. The U.S. Court of Appeals for the First Circuit rejected this argument,[139] and several other courts have adopted the First Circuit's reasoning.[140]

## TAX LAWS

Certain violations of the Internal Revenue Code are subject to criminal penalties. The strictest penalties are found in Section 7201,[141] which prohibits willful attempts to evade any tax imposed under the code, including employee withholding requirements. Section 7206 forbids any false statements in a tax return, and Section 7207 criminalizes the willful delivery of a fraudulent return to the secretary of the treasury.

A tax fraud prosecution must allege willful misconduct on the part of the accused. Consequently, prosecutors in tax fraud cases often add a mail fraud charge, which can result in a conviction even if willful misconduct is not proved. Moreover, mail fraud, unlike tax fraud, can be the basis for a RICO claim.

Section 6672 imposes civil liability for a penalty equal to the amount of a corporation's unpaid federal employment taxes on "those with the power and responsibility within the corporate structure for seeing that the taxes withheld from various sources are remitted to the Government."[142] The U.S. Court of Appeals for the Ninth Circuit has ruled that a person cannot be held liable for failure to pay over taxes unless the party (1) was the person required to collect, truthfully account for, and pay over the tax; and (2) willfully refused to pay the tax.[143]

# Amnesty and Leniency Programs

In an effort to promote self-policing and self-reporting, the federal government will provide amnesty or leniency to offenders who proactively report and remedy violations. Examples include the Department of Justice's amnesty for price-fixing cartels, the Environmental Protection Agency's reduction of penalties for self-reporting environmental violations, and the Occupational Safety and Health Administration's leniency for violations detected by voluntary self-audits. These policies work primarily by "making companies an offer they shouldn't refuse."[144]

## AMNESTY FOR CARTELS

The necessity of providing incentives to cooperate in price-fixing cases is particularly compelling given the nature of cartels: "Because cartel activities are hatched and

137. 42 U.S.C. §§ 6901 *et seq.*
138. 29 U.S.C. §§ 651 *et. seq.* & 29 U.S.C.A. §§ 651 *et. seq.*
139. *See* Pedraza v. Shell Oil Co., 942 F.2d 48 (1st Cir. 1991).
140. *See, e.g.,* Wickham v. Am. Tokyo Kasei, Inc., 927 F. Supp. 293 (N.D. Ill. 1996); Donovan v. Beloit Co., 655 N.E.2d 313 (Ill. App. Ct. 1995).
141. 26 U.S.C. § 7201.
142. Monday v. United States, 421 F.2d 1210, 1214 (7th Cir. 1970).
143. Teel v. United States, 529 F.2d 903 (9th Cir. 1976).
144. This phrase was the title of a speech given by Deputy Assistant Attorney General Gary Spratling in 1999 about the Department of Justice's amnesty policy. Gary R. Spratling, *Making Companies an Offer They Shouldn't Refuse: The Antitrust Division's Corporate Leniency Policy—An Update,* Address Presented at the Bar Association of the District of Columbia's 35th Annual Symposium on Associations and Antitrust, Washington D.C. (Feb. 16, 1999).

carried out in secret, obtaining the cooperation of insiders is the best, and often the only way to crack a cartel."[145]

The Department of Justice imposes six conditions for Type A amnesty from criminal prosecution:

1. The Antitrust Division of the U.S. Department of Justice has not yet received information from any other source about the conspiracy.
2. The applicant takes prompt and effective action to terminate its involvement in the conspiracy upon its discovery of the conspiracy.
3. The applicant reports the wrongdoing with candor and completeness and provides full, continuing, and complete cooperation throughout the investigation.
4. The applicant's confession is truly a corporate act as opposed to isolated confessions of individual executives or officials.
5. The applicant makes restitution to the injured parties.
6. The applicant did not coerce another party to participate in the cartel and was not the leader or originator of the cartel.[146]

Type B amnesty may be available, at the discretion of the Department of Justice, even after the investigation is under way if (1) the applicant is the first one to qualify for amnesty with respect to the cartel; (2) the Antitrust Division does not yet have evidence against the applicant that is likely to result in a sustainable conviction; (3) the applicant reports the cartel with candor and completeness and provides full, continuing, and complete cooperation that advances the Division's investigations; and (4) granting amnesty would not be unfair to others, considering the nature of the cartel, the applicant's role in it, and when the applicant comes forward.[147]

Another bonus to firms granted amnesty is the right to pay only actual damages, as opposed to treble damages, to private plaintiffs if the applicant cooperates with the plaintiffs in their efforts to recover joint and several treble damages from the other cartel members.[148]

**INTERNATIONAL SNAPSHOT**

The Antitrust Division of the U.S. Department of Justice realized over time that occasionally members of international cartels did not apply for amnesty in one jurisdiction because they had greater exposure in another jurisdiction that did not have a transparent and predictable amnesty policy. The recent convergence in amnesty policies in multiple jurisdictions has led to a number of simultaneous amnesty applications, which in turn facilitates coordinated raids, interviews, and service of subpoenas. The Antitrust Division has characterized its amnesty policy as "the cornerstone of our international anti-cartel enforcement program" and boasts that it has led "to the detection and prosecution of more international cartels than all of our search warrants, consensual monitoring, and FBI interrogations combined."[a] The convictions in the generic vitamin price-fixing case discussed in Chapter 16 were the direct result of the amnesty given the French participant in the cartel.

**a.** R. Hewitt Pate, *International Anti-Cartel Enforcement,* 2004 ICN Cartels Workshop, Sydney Australia (Nov. 21, 2004), at 5, *available at* http://www.usdoj.gov/atr/public/speeches/206428.pdf.

## EPA INCENTIVES FOR SELF-POLICING

The audit policy statement on self-policing issued by the Environmental Protection Agency (EPA) in 2000 is designed "to enhance protection of human health and the environment by encouraging regulated entities to voluntarily discover, promptly disclose and expeditiously correct violations of Federal environmental requirements." Parties that meet the terms of the audit policy are eligible for a substantial reduction in or the elimination of the gravity component of civil penalties[149] and a determination by the EPA not to recommend criminal prosecution of the disclosing entity.[150] A company must meet the nine conditions set forth in Exhibit 14.7 to receive leniency.[151]

If a company meets all of these conditions or all except the first one (that the discovery is made through systematic monitoring), the EPA will generally opt not to pursue criminal proceedings. Companies that meet all nine conditions are eligible for a substantial reduction in civil penalties. Companies that fulfill all the conditions except the first one can receive 75 percent mitigation of gravity-based penalties.[152] As an additional incentive, the EPA may "refrain from routine audits."[153]

145. R. Hewitt Pate, *International Anti-Cartel Enforcement,* 2004 ICN Cartels Workshop, Sydney Australia (Nov. 21, 2004), at 5–6, *available at* http://www.usdoj.gov/atr/public/speeches/206428.pdf.
146. *Id.* at 6–7.
147. *Id.*
148. *Id.*

149. The gravity component is that portion of the penalty over and above the violator's economic gain from noncompliance.
150. Environmental Protection Agency, *Incentives for Self-Policing: Discovery, Disclosure, Correction and Prevention of Violations, Final Policy Statement* (May 11, 2000), at 16–28.
151. *Id.*
152. *Id.*
153. *Id.*

**EXHIBIT 14.7** **Conditions for Leniency Under the EPA's Audit Policy Statement**

1. *Systematic discovery of the violation through an environmental audit or a compliance management system:* The violation must have been discovered through either (a) an environmental audit, or (b) a compliance management system that reflects due diligence in preventing, detecting, and correcting violations.
2. *Voluntary disclosure:* The violation must have been identified voluntarily, and not through a monitoring, sampling, or auditing procedure that is required by statute, regulation, permit, judicial or administrative order, or consent agreement.
3. *Prompt disclosure:* The entity must disclose the violation in writing to the EPA within twenty-one calendar days after discovery.
4. *Discovery and disclosure independent of government or third-party plaintiff:* The entity must discover the violation independently. That is, the violation must be discovered and identified before the EPA or another government agency likely would have identified the problem either through its own investigative work or from information received through a third party.
5. *Correction and remediation:* The entity must remedy any harm caused by the violation and expeditiously certify in writing to appropriate federal, state, and local authorities that it has corrected the violation.
6. *Prevent recurrence:* The regulated entity must agree to take steps to prevent a recurrence of the violation after it has been disclosed. Preventive steps may include, but are not limited to, improvements to the entity's environmental auditing efforts or compliance management system.
7. *No repeat violations:* Repeat offenders are not eligible to receive audit policy credit. Under the repeat violations exclusion, the same or a closely related violation must not have occurred at the same facility within the past three years.
8. *Other violations excluded:* Policy benefits are not available for violations that result in serious actual harm to the environment or that may have presented an imminent and substantial endangerment to public health or the environment. When events of such a consequential nature occur, violators are ineligible for penalty relief and other incentives under the audit policy.
9. *Cooperation:* The regulated entity must cooperate as required by the EPA and provide the EPA with the information it needs to determine policy applicability. The entity must not hide, destroy, or tamper with possible evidence following discovery of potential environmental violations.

Source: Environmental Protection Agency, *Incentives for Self-Policing-Discovery, Disclosure, Correction and Prevention of Violations, Final Policy Statement* (May 11, 2000), at 16–28.

## OSHA and Voluntary Self-Audits

In 2000, the Occupational Safety and Health Administration (OSHA) issued its final policy concerning its treatment of voluntary employer safety and health self-audits, which rewards companies that report violations of work safety and health laws. The stated purpose of the policy is "to develop and implement a policy that recognizes the value of voluntary self-audit programs that are designed to allow employers, or their agents, to identify and promptly correct hazardous conditions."[154] Under the policy:

> Where a voluntary self-audit identifies a hazardous condition, and the employer has corrected the violative condition prior to the initiation of an inspection (or a related accident, illness, or injury that triggers the OSHA inspection) and has taken appropriate steps to prevent the recurrence of the condition, the [Occupational Safety and Health] Agency will refrain from issuing a citation, even if the violative condition existed within the six month limitations period during which OSHA is authorized to issue citations. Where a voluntary self-audit identifies a hazardous condition, and the employer promptly undertakes appropriate measures to correct the violative condition and to provide interim employee protection, but has not completely corrected the violative condition when an OSHA inspection occurs, the Agency will treat the audit report as evidence of good faith, and not as evidence of a willful violation of the Act.[155]

154. Occupational Safety and Health Administration, *Final Policy Concerning the Occupational Safety and Health Administration's Treatment of Voluntary Employer Safety and Health Self-Audits* (July 28, 2000), *available at* http://www.osha.gov/pls/oshaweb/owadisp.show_document?p_id=16434&p_search_str=self-audit&p_search_type=CLOBTEXTPOLICY&p_table=FEDERAL_REGISTER.

155. *Id.*

## THE RESPONSIBLE MANAGER

### ENSURING CRIMINAL LAW COMPLIANCE

Senior management can take various actions to create a culture of "compliance-plus" that values both organizational integrity and compliance with the spirit and the letter of the law. First, the company should develop a code of ethics, as discussed in Chapter 1. All criminal acts should be outlawed by the code. The code of ethics should have an enforcement mechanism, and it should clearly state that violations of the code will result in sanctions, such as salary reductions, poor performance ratings, and, in extreme cases, termination of employment.

The corporation should develop a comprehensive program to ensure compliance with laws and regulations. The audit committee of the board of directors should oversee the program. A good reporting structure is crucial. Prosecutors and courts are more inclined to mitigate the punishment of a corporation if it consistently reports the criminal misconduct of its employees. The corporation should also have educational procedures to remind all employees about the provisions of the compliance program and to teach them the laws applicable to their areas of responsibility.

It should be clear throughout the company that ethical behavior is expected. A policy of honesty should be stressed. What top management does when it sees criminal law–related problems will influence all employees. It is much harder for employees to justify committing criminal acts against the corporation when they cannot claim that top management is also guilty of violating the law.

Criminal misconduct is often a function of goal-setting and performance measures that induce people to do what they should not do. Managers should be careful to avoid sending mixed signals that reward (or demand) performance at all costs regardless of compliance with the law.

Corporate in-house counsel should be independent and report directly to the board of directors. They should not succumb to pressure from division managers to give the go-ahead to an action that they believe may violate a criminal statute.

Outside firms can be hired to audit the corporation's methods of ensuring criminal law compliance. These firms can also make suggestions to improve the corporation's methods.

If the corporation is faced with a possible criminal investigation, quick action is important, as the corporation could be facing severe fines and harmful publicity that could prove damaging to future business. When there is some indication of possible criminal conduct by company employees, the corporation should seek the immediate advice of outside counsel and conduct an internal investigation prior to contacting the authorities. The fact of the internal investigation should not be widely publicized within the corporation. If employees are interviewed in connection with the investigation, outside counsel should make it clear that they are representing the company, and not the employee. Managers should be careful when turning over information about internal investigations to prosecutors because they may inadvertently waive the attorney–client privilege applicable to notes prepared by outside counsel.

Although companies may be reluctant to investigate and self-report violations, it is better to know about a problem and deal with it than to let it continue and get out of control. No corporate compliance program is foolproof, but an effective program can "prevent and detect most violations; reduce financial litigation, regulatory, and reputational harm; get mitigation credit under the Sentencing Guidelines; and help set a tone in investigations that shows the company cares about doing business the right way."[156] It can also help shield officers and directors from liability.

Corporate compliance may even be a source of competitive advantage.[157] According to the consulting firm Deloitte & Touche, "companies that follow both the letter and the spirit of the law by taking a 'values-based' approach to ethics and compliance will have a distinct advantage in the marketplace. Benefits of this approach can include improvements to a company's market performance, brand equity, and shareholder value."[158]

156. Karen L. Shapiro, *10 Steps to a Better Day*, BUS. L. TODAY, Sept.–Oct. 2003, at 43.
157. K. Schatterly, *Increasing Firm Value Through Detection and Prevention of White-Collar Crime*, 24 STRATEGIC MGMT. J. 587 (2003).
158. Deloitte & Touche, *Ethics and Corporate Compliance: The Advantages of a Value-Based Approach*, *at* http://www.deloitte.com/dtt/cda/doc/content/Ethics_Compliance%20final%20E.pdf.

## INSIDE STORY

# THE CEO AS FELON

In response to Enron, WorldCom, and other corporate scandals, President George W. Bush created the Corporate Fraud Task Force in July 2002 to promote prosecution of corporate criminals. In the ensuing two years, the Task Force charged more than fifty CEOs and corporate presidents with some form of corporate fraud.[159] Exhibit 14.8 summarizes a number of the high-profile cases that led to convictions or guilty pleas in the period from 2000 to 2004.

In June 2003, the former chief executive of Rite Aid, Martin Grass, was sentenced to eight years in prison for accounting fraud. One U.S. attorney commented, "This conviction . . . should serve as a warning for corporate executives: if you lie to the investing public, to grand juries, to investigators, regulators and prosecutors, you will be vigorously investigated and prosecuted."[160]

The case against former Tyco chief executive Dennis Kozlowski for using $600 million in company funds for personal expenditures resulted in a mistrial. A key issue for the jury in the first trial was whether Kozlowski thought he was committing a crime.[161] His retrial began in January 2005.

After the Kozlowski mistrial, John Rigas, the seventy-nine-year-old founder, former chair, and chief executive of Adelphia, was successfully convicted. This was the first time since Enron Corporation collapsed in December 2001 that a CEO of a bankrupt company took his case to a jury and lost.[162] Because the case against Tyco's Kozlowski foundered on whether he knew his personal use of Tyco's funds was against the law, the prosecutors took pains to show that John Rigas and his son had been warned that it was illegal to bill Adelphia for personal expenses and to use its credit to borrow money.[163]

By the end of 2004, the government had obtained felony charges against thirty Enron employees, including Jeffrey Skilling, the former chief executive, and Kenneth Lay, the former CEO and chair. The testimony of Andrew Fastow, former CFO of Enron, was crucial to obtaining indictments of Skilling and Lay. Fastow pled guilty to two counts of conspiracy to commit wire and securities fraud in early 2004 and will serve ten years of prison. Both Skilling and Lay pled not guilty.

WorldCom was forced to file bankruptcy in 2002 as a result of a record $11 billion accounting fraud. The former CFO Scott D. Sullivan pled guilty and was the key witness against his former boss former CEO Bernie Ebbers. Ebbers was convicted in March 2005 of securities fraud, conspiracy to commit securities fraud, and filing false reports with the Securities and Exchange Commission.[164] He had borrowed $400 million from WorldCom, secured by his WorldCom stock, and prosecutors claimed that he perpetuated the fraud to reverse the slide in WorldCom's stock price. Ebbers took the stand in his own defense and played down his expertise, testifying, "I don't know about technology and I don't know about finance and accounting."[165] Ebbers also testified that he was unaware of what the WorldCom CFO was doing. The jury didn't buy it. According to a posting by the father of juror Sarah Nulty, the jury "concluded that with his personal fortune evaporating and the company he built sinking, it was inconceivable that Ebbers was not paying attention" to WorldCom's finances.[166]

One source pointed out that without convictions of the top guys, little else matters: Bottom line: When it comes to restoring the public confidence in the courts and Wall Street, all the guilty pleas on earth won't amount to much if their purpose is to gain evidence against CEOs who nonetheless wind up tap-dancing their way to freedom on a smile and a handshake and the assurance that they're really, really stupid.[167] The Ebber's conviction, coupled with the CEO and CFO certification requirements imposed by the Sarbanes–Oxley Act of 2002, appear to spell the demise of the "Aw Shucks" or "It Wasn't Me" defense.[168]

159. Greg Farrell, *White-Collar Cases Become N.Y. Specialty,* USA Today, Sept. 20, 2004, at 4B.
160. Adrian Michaels, *Former Rite Aid Chief Jailed,* Fin. Times, May 28, 2004, at 32.
161. Kara Scannell & Mark Maremont, *Round 2 for Quattrone, in Post-Tyco World,* Wall St. J., Apr. 8, 2004, at C1. For a discussion of possible jury tampering in the Tyco case, see Mark Maremont & Kara Scannell, *Tyco Juror Denied to Rest of Panel That She Gave "OK",* Wall St. J., Apr. 7, 2004, at C1.
162. Brooke A. Masters & Ben White, *Adelphia Founder, Son Convicted of Fraud,* Wash. Post, July 9, 2004, at E01.
163. *Id.*
164. Jonathan D. Glater & Ken Belson, *Ebbers, on Witness Stand, May Have Lost His Case,* N.Y. Times, Mar. 16, 2005, at C1.
165. *Id.* at C8.
166. *Id.* at C9.
167. Christopher Byron, *The CEO Dunce Card,* N.Y. Post, July 26, 2004, at 37.
168. Joann S. Lublin & Christopher Rhoads, *It Better Not Be Lonely at the Top in the New World of Today's CEO,* Wall St. J., Mar. 16, 2005, at A10.

**EXHIBIT 14.8** **Executives on Trial**

| The CEO or CFO | The Crime | Conviction/Plea | The Outcome |
|---|---|---|---|
| Cosmo Corigliano, 40<br>Chief Financial Officer<br>*CUC*<br><br>Executive Vice President<br>*Cendant* | One count of conspiracy to commit mail and wire fraud and make false statements to the SEC and one count wire fraud | Pled guilty (June 2000) | Sentence pending with leniency expected based on his testimony at the trial of Walter Forbes and E. Kirk Shelton. |
| Diana D. Brooks, 50<br>Chief Executive<br>*Sotheby's Holdings* | Price-fixing conspiracy with rival Christie's | Pled guilty (October 2000) | Sentenced to three years probation with six months house arrest, fined $350,000, and ordered to perform 1,000 hours of community service. |
| Walter Forbes, 58<br>Chief Executive<br>*CUC*<br><br>Chairman<br>*Cendant* | Accused of a decade of wire, mail, and securities fraud; insider trading; and conspiracy resulting in investor losses of $19 billion. Also lying to the SEC. | Pled not guilty (April 2001) | Jury deliberating, with maximum sentence of forty years in prison. |
| Steven Madden, 44<br>Founder and Chief Executive<br>*Steven Madden, Ltd.* | Securities fraud and money laundering | Pled guilty (May 2001) | Serving forty-one months and ordered to pay $3.1 million in fines for restitution. |
| A. Alfred Taubman, 76<br>Chairman<br>*Sotheby's Holdings* | Six-year price-fixing conspiracy with rival Christie's | Convicted (December 2001) | Sentenced to one year and one day. Served ten months and ordered to pay for his incarceration as well as $7.5 million in fines. |
| Osamah S. Bakhit, 52<br>Chief Executive<br>*Aviation Distributors* | Eighteen counts, including conspiracy, securities fraud, falsifying documents, and making false statements | Pled guilty (February 2002) | Sentenced to three years in federal prison and fined $50,000. |
| Sam Waksal, 55<br>Founder and Chief Executive<br>*ImClone* | Six counts for fraud including securities fraud, conspiracy, insider trading, obstruction of justice, perjury, bank fraud, and a separate charge of tax evasion | Pled guilty (October 2002) | Serving seven years and three months in federal prison and fined $4.3 million. |
| Martin Grass, 49<br>Chief Executive<br>*Rite Aid* | Conspiracy to defraud and conspiracy to obstruct justice | Pled guilty (June 2003) | Serving eight years, fined $500,000, and ordered to forfeit $3 million. |
| Gholamreza Mikailli, 52<br>Chief Executive<br>*Unify Corporation* | Ten counts of conspiracy and securities fraud | Convicted (November 2003) | Sentenced to fifty-one months and ordered to pay $1 million in fines and restitution. |
| Richard M. Scrushy, 51<br>Chairman and Chief Executive<br>*HealthSouth Corporation* | Eighty-five counts, including conspiracy; mail, wire, and securities fraud; filing false statements and certifications; and money laundering. Engaged in $2.7 billion accounting fraud. | Pled not guilty (November 2003) | Trial in 2005. |

*(Continued)*

**EXHIBIT 14.8 Executives on Trial—continued**

| The CEO or CFO | The Crime | Conviction/Plea | The Outcome |
|---|---|---|---|
| Andrew Fastow, 42<br>Chief Financial Officer<br>*Enron* | Two counts of conspiracy to commit wire and securities fraud; dismissal of ninety-six other counts contingent on prosecutors' satisfaction with his cooperation against Skilling and Lay. | Pled guilty (January 2004) | Sentenced to ten years, to be followed by three years of supervised release. Agreed to forfeit more than $29 million. |
| Jeffrey Skilling, 50<br>Chief Executive<br>*Enron* | Thirty-six counts of fraud, including ten counts of insider trading, fifteen counts of securities fraud, four counts of wire fraud, six counts of making false statements, and one count of conspiracy to commit wire and securities fraud | Pled not guilty (February 2004) | Trial scheduled for January 2006 with life sentence possible if convicted on all counts. |
| Bernie Ebbers, 62<br>Founder and Chief Executive<br>*WorldCom* | Securities fraud, conspiracy to commit fraud, and filing false reports with the SEC | Pled not guilty (March 2004) | Convicted in 2005 with a maximum sentence of eighty-five years possible. |
| Scott Sullivan, 42<br>Chief Financial Officer<br>*WorldCom* | Three counts of securities fraud, conspiracy to commit securities fraud, and filing false reports with the SEC | Pled guilty (March 2004) | Sentence pending with maximum of twenty-five years possible. |
| Martha Stewart, 62<br>Founder and Chief Executive<br>*Martha Stewart Living Omnimedia* | Two counts of making false statements, one count of obstruction, and one count of conspiracy | Convicted (March 2004) | Served five months to be followed by five months home confinement. Also a fine of $30,000. |
| Oral Suer, 69<br>Chief Executive<br>*United Way* | Two counts for transporting stolen money across state lines, making false statements, and concealing facts about an employee retirement plan | Pled guilty (March 2004) | Serving twenty-seven months and fined $497,000 in restitution. |
| C. Gregory Earls, 59<br>Chairman and Chief Executive<br>*U.S. Technologies* | Twenty-two counts, including one count of securities fraud, two counts of mail fraud, and nineteen counts of wire fraud for defrauding the company of $13.8 million | Convicted (April 2004) | Sentenced to ten years and ordered to pay $21.9 million in restitution. |
| Dennis Kozlowski, 57<br>Chief Executive<br>*Tyco* | Conspiracy, grand larceny, tax evasion, and securities fraud for stealing more than $600 million from the company in unauthorized compensation and illicit stock sales | Mistrial (April 2004) | Retrial in 2005. |
| Mark Schwartz, 43<br>Chief Financial Officer<br>*Tyco* | Conspiracy, grand larceny, and securities fraud for stealing more than $600 million from the company in unauthorized compensation and illicit stock sales | Mistrial (April 2004) | Retrial in 2005. |

*(Continued)*

**EXHIBIT 14.8 Executives on Trial—continued**

| The CEO or CFO | The Crime | Conviction/Plea | The Outcome |
|---|---|---|---|
| Kenneth Lay, 62<br>Chairman and CEO<br>*Enron* | Eleven counts, including one count of bank fraud, three counts of making false statements to banks, one count of conspiracy, two of wire fraud, and four of securities fraud | Pled not guilty (July 2004) | Trial scheduled for January 2006 with life sentence possible if convicted on all counts. |
| Kenneth Rice, 45<br>Co-Chief Executive Officer<br>*Enron Broadband Services, Inc.* | One count of securities fraud for misrepresenting performance to inflate stock prices in the broadband unit | Pled guilty (July 2004) | Sentencing pending with a maximum of ten years possible. Agreed to forfeit $13.7 million. |
| John Rigas, 79<br>Chief Executive<br>*Adelphia Communications* | One count of conspiracy, two counts of bank fraud, and fifteen counts of securities fraud for looting the company of hundreds of millions, but acquitted of wire fraud charges | Convicted (July 2004) | Sentencing pending with the most serious charge, bank fraud, having a maximum sentence of thirty years. |
| Timothy Rigas, 47<br>Chief Financial Officer<br>*Adelphia Communications* | One count of conspiracy, two counts of bank fraud, and fifteen counts of securities fraud for looting the company of hundreds of millions, but acquitted of wire fraud charges | Convicted (July 2004) | Sentencing pending with the most serious charge, bank fraud, having a maximum sentence of thirty years. |
| David Wittig, 49<br>Chairman and Chief Executive<br>*Westar Energy* | Six counts of bank fraud including false bank entries and money laundering; another forty counts for looting the company of millions | Convicted (July 2004) | Sentenced to fifty-one months and fined $1 million for bank fraud; trial proceeding on another forty counts with minimum of ten years if convicted. |
| Enrique P. Fiallo, 52<br>Chief Executive<br>*Enterasys Network Systems* | Single count of conspiracy to commit wire, mail, and securities fraud | Pled guilty (September 2004) | Sentencing pending with a maximum of five years and a fine of $250,000 possible. |
| Sanjay Kumar, 42<br>Chief Executive<br>*Computer Associates International* | Ten counts, including securities fraud, conspiracy, and obstruction of justice | Pled not guilty (September 2004) | Trial date to be set in 2005. |

## KEY WORDS AND PHRASES

*actus reus* 504
arrest 506
blue sky laws 540
booked 506
burden of proof 506
collective entity doctrine 512
computer fraud 535
computer piracy 538
computer virus 536
consent decree 507
crime 504
denial-of-service attacks 536
Double Jeopardy Clause 513
Due Process Clauses 513
embezzlement 524
enterprise 524
exclusionary rule 510
Ex Post Facto Clause 507

felony 506
fraud 524
fruit of the poisonous tree 510
good faith exception 511
impossibility defense 521
imputed liability 520
indictment 506
inevitable discovery exception 511
information 506
intention to do wrong 505
larceny 523
mail fraud 530
*mens rea* 504
*Miranda* warnings 511
misdemeanor 506
negligence 505
negligence *per se* 506
*nolo contendere* 507
perjury 541
plea 507
plea bargaining 507
preliminary hearing 506
preponderance of the evidence 506
probable cause 508
protected computer 536
*qui tam* plaintiff 532
racketeering activity 524
recklessness 505
*respondeat superior* 521
responsible corporate officer doctrine 520
strict liability 505
Thompson Memorandum 522
transactional immunity 507
use immunity 507
vicarious liability 520
white-collar crime 523
wire fraud 530

## QUESTIONS AND CASE PROBLEMS

1. Argent Chemical Laboratories manufactures and repackages veterinary drugs. Food and Drug Administration (FDA) agents inspected Argent without a warrant several times between the summer of 1993 and May 1994 to ensure compliance with the Food, Drug and Cosmetic Act. The FDA cited Argent for certain deficiencies. Several months after the last inspection, FDA agents and U.S. marshals seized over $100,000 worth of veterinary drugs from Argent's premises. Did the seizure of Argent's veterinary drugs without a warrant violate the Fourth Amendment? [*United States v. Argent Chemical Laboratories, Inc.*, 93 F.3d 572 (9th Cir. 1996).]

2. Dow Chemical Company operated a 2,000-acre chemical-manufacturing facility with numerous covered buildings in Midland, Michigan. Dow maintained extensive security around the facility. Security measures around the perimeter of the facility prevent ground-level public viewing, and Dow also investigates any low-level aircraft flights over the facility.

   The Environmental Protection Agency (EPA) sought to inspect two of Dow's power plants in the facility for violations of federal air-quality standards. Without obtaining a search warrant to enter the property and despite Dow's refusal to voluntarily agree to a search, the EPA employed a commercial airplane with precision aerial-camera mapping equipment to photograph Dow's large manufacturing and research facilities from the air. The powerful equipment allowed power lines as small as 0.5 inch in diameter to be observed. Yet, at all times, the aircraft stayed within navigable airspace.

   Dow became aware of the EPA's actions and claimed that its Fourth Amendment rights had been violated. Did the EPA's photographs constitute an unreasonable search in violation of the Fourth Amendment? [*Dow Chemical Co. v. United States*, 476 U.S. 227 (1986).]

3. Rodney Stuart, CEO of NanoTech Corporation, was convicted of obstruction of justice after Regi Reardon, NanoTech's head of human resources, told police that Stuart had ordered her to delete all electronic files dealing with the hiring of twenty-seven former employees of NanoTech's main competitor. Reardon's statement to the police was read to the jury during Stuart's trial, but Reardon refused to testify on the grounds that it might incriminate her. Does Stuart have any constitutional grounds for appealing his conviction? [*Crawford v. Washington*, 541 U.S. 36 (2004).]

4. Bert's Sporting Goods, Inc., with stores located throughout the state of Lys, sells a wide variety of sporting goods, including guns. Section 123.45 of the Lys Penal Code requires sellers of guns to verify that the purchaser has not committed a felony within the last five years. If the purchaser has committed a felony within the last five years, the seller is not allowed to make the sale. "Willfully" selling a gun to a recent felon is considered a misdemeanor and is punishable by up to one year in jail and/or a maximum $10,000 fine.

   Jim Dandy, who was convicted of a felony under Lys's penal code four years ago, went to purchase a gun at one of the Bert's Sporting Goods stores. Joe Mountain, a salesman at Bert's, sold Dandy the gun without asking for identification or checking to see whether Dandy was a convicted felon.

   As a matter of fact, Mountain never checked whether any of the customers to whom he sold guns were felons. Mountain did not know of the Lys law requiring him to check on the customer's prior criminal history. However, Jay Lake, Mountain's supervisor, knew of the law and also knew that Mountain never checked whether a customer was a felon. Bert, the sole shareholder and director of Bert's Sporting Goods, Inc., knew about the law but did not know that Mountain did not check on his customers' prior criminal history.

Dandy used the gun in a robbery and shot two police officers during his getaway. He was never captured. Can Mountain be punished under Section 123.45 of the penal code? What about Lake? Bert? Bert's Sporting Goods, Inc.? What penalties should be assessed?

5. Barry Engel was president of Gel Spice Company, which imported, processed, and packaged spices. As president, he was responsible for the purchasing and storing of spices in the company's warehouse in Brooklyn, New York. In June 1972, the FDA inspected the Gel Spice warehouse and found widespread rodent infestation. Upon reinspection in August 1972, the FDA found evidence of continuing infestation. Following the two 1972 inspections, the FDA considered a criminal prosecution against Gel Spice. Before referring the case to the Department of Justice, however, the FDA conducted an additional inspection. At that July 1973 inspection, no evidence of rodent infestation was found, and the criminal prosecution was dropped. Three years later, in July 1976, the FDA inspected Gel Spice and again found active rodent infestation. Four additional inspections were performed from 1977 to 1979, each of which revealed continuing infestation. Thereafter, the government instituted criminal proceedings against Gel Spice and its president, Barry Engel. Under what theory of criminal liability could Engel be held liable for violating the Food, Drug and Cosmetic Act? Can Engel successfully assert any defense? [*United States v. Gel Spice Co.,* 773 F.2d 427 (2d Cir. 1985).]

6. An employee of Ladish Malting Company was killed when he fell from a dilapidated fire-escape platform that collapsed. Ladish was charged and indicted under a provision of the Occupational Safety and Health Act (OSHA) that imposes criminal penalties on any employer who "willfully violates" any occupational safety or health standard and thereby causes the death of an employee.

   At trial, the government did not prove that Ladish had actual knowledge that the fire-escape platform was hazardous. The trial judge's instruction to the jury permitted the conclusion that Ladish "willfully" violated the applicable regulation if it "should have known" that the fire escape was in disrepair. The jury found Ladish guilty of "willfully violating" a safety standard and thereby causing the death of an employee, and the judge imposed a $450,000 fine. On appeal, should the verdict be upheld? [*United States v. Ladish Malting Co.,* 135 F.3d 484 (7th Cir. 1998).]

7. Bermel Enterprises, Inc. is a supplier of computer programming consulting services to the federal government. In completing their time reports, Alex and Margot Frankel, two Bermel systems analysts, have consistently overstated the time they spent working on the government projects. These time reports determine how much money the government pays the company. Additionally, Michelle Laff, a manager at Bermel, has falsified the results of systems tests conducted on the computer systems installed for the government. As a result, the systems appear to be bug-free when, in fact, they contain many errors.

   What criminal charges may the government bring against the employees? Against Larry Bermel, owner of Bermel Enterprises, Inc.? Against Bermel Enterprises, Inc. itself?

8. Bradford C. Councilman was vice president of Interloc, an online rare and out-of-print book listing service. Interloc provided certain book dealer customers with an e-mail address and acted as the service provider. Councilman directed Interloc employees to write computer code to intercept and copy all incoming communications from Amazon.com to Interloc's subscriber dealers. The code intercepted, copied, and stored all incoming messages from Amazon.com before they were delivered to the members' e-mail server. The plan was to use the interrupted e-mails to develop a list of books, learn about competitors, and attain a competitive advantage for Interloc.

   Councilman was charged with violating the Wiretap Act (18 U.S.C. §§ 2510–2522). Section 2511 of Title 18 makes it a crime for any person to intentionally intercept any wire, oral, or electronic communication. At the time the messages were obtained by Interloc, they were in temporary storage in Interloc's computer systems. Councilman was not charged with violating the Stored Communications Act (18 U.S.C. §§ 2701–2711), which makes it illegal to (1) intentionally access without authorization a facility through which an electronic communication service is provided or (2) intentionally exceed an authorization to access that facility and thereby obtain, alter, or prevent authorized access to a wire or electronic communication while it is in electronic storage. Did Councilman violate either the Wiretap Act or the Stored Communications Act? [*United States v. Councilman,* 373 F.3d 197 (1st Cir. 2004), *vacated and reh'g en banc granted,* 385 F.3d 793 (1st Cir. 2004).]

9. Joseph Russo and Everett James Garner entered into an agreement to establish a building materials manufacturing business, Panel Building Systems, Inc. (PBS). To obtain capital to fund the development of the new company, Russo applied for a $630,000 loan from the U.S. Small Business Administration (SBA). On the loan application, Russo stated that he was the president and 100 percent owner of PBS. PBS subsequently defaulted on the loan, and the SBA suffered losses of about $474,000. During the SBA's investigation of the default, it was revealed that the actual president of PBS was Garner, not Russo, and that Garner had a poor financial record. Russo later admitted that he knew the information supplied on the loan application was false and that the false information was supplied in order to secure a loan from the SBA. Russo was sued for knowingly and willfully making a false statement to the federal government under 18 U.S.C. § 1001, which requires willful intent to deceive.

   Russo claimed that although he knew the information supplied on the loan application was false, he lacked willful intent to deceive the federal government because he always intended to be president and CEO of PBS. Russo also argued that he thought Garner was a wealthy man and did not know Garner had a poor financial record. Did Russo have willful intent to deceive the federal government? [*United States v. Russo,* 202 F.3d 283 (10th Cir. 2000).]

## MANAGER'S DILEMMA

10. You are the chief financial officer of X-Ray Corporation, the largest subsidiary of Medtech, a publicly traded medical-imaging firm. When you report to Medtech's CEO that X-Ray had better-than-expected earnings for the quarter ended June 30, 2005, the CEO asks you to "hold some of them back" as a cushion in case other subsidiaries report lower-than-expected earnings in future quarters. How would you respond? Suppose that you tell the CEO that you can't do that because this "cookie-jar reserve" would violate Generally Accepted Accounting Principles, but the CEO warns that failure to create the reserve would be a career-limiting move. What would you do?

    What if, instead of an earnings surplus over analyst projections, X-Ray Corporation had lower-than-expected earnings due to unforeseen bugs in the software for its new suite of imaging equipment? How would you respond to a request from the CEO to book sales in the quarter ending June 30, 2005, that would not actually be finalized until July 2005, which is when X-Ray's engineers predict that the bugs will be worked out? [This question is based, in part, on a scenario described in Carol J. Loomis, *Lies, Damned Lies, and Managed Earnings,* FORTUNE, Aug. 2, 1999, at 92.]

## INTERNET SOURCES

| | |
|---|---|
| U.S. Department of Justice | http://www.usdoj.gov |
| This site contains information about the Internet Fraud Complaint Center. | http://www.ifccfbi.gov |
| This site, maintained by the U.S. Department of Justice Criminal Division's Computer Crime and Intellectual Property Section, provides information about cybercrime. | http://www.cybercrime.gov |
| McConnell International, a computer security consulting firm in Washington, D.C., maintains a site that includes the text of its report, "Cyber Crime . . . and Punishment? Archaic Law Threatens Global Information." | http://www.mcconnellinternational.com |
| The U.S. Sentencing Commission site provides a copy of the sentencing guidelines and related information. | http://www.ussc.gov/ |
| This site for Corporate Compliance, Ltd. provides information on establishing and testing criminal compliance systems. | http://www.corporatecompliance.com |
| This FindLaw site, when searched using the word "criminal," provides links to a variety of cases and sites dealing with federal and state criminal law. | http://www.findlaw.com |

CHAPTER 15

# Environmental Law

## INTRODUCTION

### ROLE IN BUSINESS MANAGEMENT

*Environmental law* consists of numerous federal, state, and local laws with the common objective of protecting human health and the environment. These laws are of great concern to a variety of firms, many of which may not have considered environmental liability when they first went into business.

Some industries (such as petroleum, mining, and chemical manufacturing) are well accustomed to intense government regulation of the environmental effects of their operations. In the last thirty years, however, the scope and impact of environmental laws have grown steadily. Today, real estate owners and investors, developers, insurance companies, and financial institutions find that their operations, too, are often affected by laws and regulations intended to protect the environment.

For example, railroad yards have become one of the country's most serious pollution problems. Railroads began transporting and storing hazardous materials in the early twentieth century—long before environmental laws were enacted to regulate the transport and disposal of dangerous substances. As a result, toxic waste was routinely dumped at railroad sites.[1] More than 300 rail yards have been identified as contaminated, and more than $1.5 billion has been spent to clean them up.

Failure to comply with environmental laws can result in large judgments and punitive fines for companies, as well as criminal penalties (including imprisonment) for the corporate executives responsible for these violations. In 1999, an executive received a prison sentence of thirteen years, the longest sentence ever issued under federal environmental laws, after pleading guilty to felony charges that he ordered employees of his firm to illegally discharge hazardous waste into the city storm sewer system that emptied into a bay in Tampa, Florida.[2]

### CHAPTER OVERVIEW

This chapter introduces four federal environmental laws that illustrate the importance of environmental regulation for an expanding scope of business activities. The Clean Air Act, the Clean Water Act, and the Resource Conservation and Recovery Act are discussed as examples of environmental statutes that control the release of pollutants into the air, water, and land. The Comprehensive Environmental Response, Compensation, and Liability Act is discussed as an example of a remedial statute with broad application to all kinds of businesses and individuals. The chapter also addresses the potential liability under the environmental laws of shareholders, directors, officers, and managers, as well as affiliated companies and lenders. It outlines the key elements of effective compliance programs and audits, and it concludes with a discussion of international considerations.

## Environmental Laws

### COMMON LAW NUISANCE

Historically, public officials relied primarily on the common law theory of nuisance to control industrial and agricultural activities that interfered with the health or

1. Daniel Machalaba, *Local Ties, Decades of Mishandling Hazardous Cargo Leave Railroads a Toxic Legacy,* WALL ST. J., Feb. 3, 1999, at A1.

2. United States v. Benkovitz, 229 F.3d 1168 (11th Cir. 2000).

comfort of the community. Thus, industrial odors, noise, smoke, and pollutants of all kinds were the subjects of numerous lawsuits that attempted to balance the legitimate business interests of the polluter with the private interests of the surrounding community. But the need to file a lawsuit in each case and the complexity of the common law made nuisance a cumbersome way to control environmental pollution in an industrial society. Moreover, a lawsuit could not prevent pollution; it could only provide a remedy after the fact. Today, state and federal regulatory programs have largely replaced common law nuisance as a means of pollution control. Nonetheless, as discussed further in Chapter 9, a group of cities and states have invoked the tort of public nuisance in an effort to force power plants to reduce greenhouse gases.

## Statutes and Regulations

Environmental law consists of federal and state statutes, administrative regulations, and the administrative and judicial interpretations of their meaning. Environmental statutes establish policy, set goals, and authorize the executive branch or one of its administrative agencies to adopt regulations specifying how the law will be implemented. The statutes and regulations are interpreted and applied in administrative and judicial proceedings. In addition, administrative agencies, such as the Environmental Protection Agency, often issue policy statements and technical guidance, which do not have the force of law but guide enforcement efforts and provide assistance to the regulated community.

### *Three Categories*

There are three broad categories of environmental law. The largest category consists of laws that regulate the release of pollutants into the air, water, or ground. These laws usually authorize the government to issue and enforce permits for release of pollutants. They may also authorize emergency responses and remedial action if, for example, improper waste disposal or accidental chemical spills threaten human health or the environment. Statutes in this category include the Clean Air Act; the Federal Water Pollution Control Act, as amended by the Clean Water Act; the Solid Waste Disposal Act, as amended by the Resource Conservation and Recovery Act (RCRA); the Comprehensive Environmental Response, Compensation, and Liability Act (CERCLA or Superfund);[3] and similar state laws. These four federal pollution-control laws are discussed in this chapter.

3. As amended by the Superfund Amendments and Reauthorization Act of 1986, the Superfund Recycling Equity Act of 1999, and the Small Business Liability Relief and Brownfields Revitalization Act of 2002.

A second category includes laws that govern the manufacture, sale, distribution, and use of chemical substances as commercial products. This category includes (1) the Federal Insecticide, Fungicide and Rodenticide Act, which applies to pesticide products; and (2) the Toxic Substances Control Act, which applies to all chemical substances both manufactured in and imported into the United States, excluding certain substances that are regulated under other federal laws. The Safe Drinking Water Act, which governs the quality of drinking water served by public drinking-water systems, can also be included in this category.

A third category includes laws that require government decision makers to take into account the effects of their decisions on the quality of the environment. These include the National Environmental Policy Act of 1970 (NEPA)[4] and similar laws adopted by most states. As discussed in Chapters 6 and 18, NEPA affects all business activities that require governmental authorizations, permits, or licenses.[5]

## Natural Resources Laws

Although environmental law contributes to the protection of natural resources, it generally does not include wilderness preservation, wildlife protection,[6] coastal zone management, energy conservation, national park designation, and the like. Those laws are commonly referred to as *natural resources laws*. Nor does environmental law cover land-use regulation and zoning. Such laws, which are generally administered by local governments, are commonly referred to as land-use laws. They are discussed in Chapter 18.

4. Codified, as amended, at 42 U.S.C. §§ 7401–7671q.

5. The U.S. Supreme Court upheld the Federal Motor Carrier Safety Administration's proposed rules concerning Mexican motor carriers even though the agency did not consider the environmental impact of having more Mexican trucks after an executive order was issued allowing a larger number to cross the U.S. border. Dep't of Transp. v. Pub. Citizens, 541 U.S. 752 (2004). The Court reasoned that because the agency lacked discretion to prevent these cross-border operations, neither NEPA nor the Clear Air Act required an evaluation of their environmental effects.

6. The Ninth Circuit ruled that dolphins, whales, and other cetaceans did not have standing under the Endangered Species Act to sue to challenge the Navy's use of active sonar. Cetacean Cmty. v. Bush, 386 F.3d 1169 (9th Cir. 2004). The court dismissed as dicta its statement in *Palila v. Hawaii Department of Land & Natural Resources,* 852 F.2d 1106, 1107 (9th Cir. 1988), that the Hawaiian Palila bird "has legal status and wings its way into federal court as a plaintiff in its own right" to enforce the Endangered Species Act.

INTERNATIONAL SNAPSHOT

The National Environmental Policy Act was the first element of the new environmental regulatory regime in the United States. Other countries have also promulgated environmental policy acts. Central to each of these acts is the requirement that the government expressly consider environmental values in its decision making and that it document this consideration in written environmental impact reports that can be reviewed by the public. These requirements are especially important when the government itself is responsible for major development projects.

### Industry Participation

Environmental laws and regulations are constantly changing as new threats to human health and the environment become apparent and new ways are discovered to manage such threats safely and economically. Congressional or administrative agency staff may be unaware of how a proposed law or regulation may affect a particular industry and usually welcome constructive industry participation in the law- and rule-making process. This is particularly the case when a company can propose alternative ways to accomplish the same legislative goals.

## Administration of Environmental Laws

The Environmental Protection Agency (EPA) administers all the federal laws that set national goals and policies for environmental protection, except the National Environmental Policy Act, which is administered by the Council on Environmental Quality. State agencies administer state laws and, with the authorization of the EPA, federal laws as well.

#### Ethical Consideration

Environmental laws establish minimum standards to which companies must adhere. Companies also have fiduciary duties to their shareholders, and many labor activists argue that companies have similar duties to their employees. Is it ethical for a manager to adhere to stricter standards than mandated by law when such adherence will raise costs, reduce shareholder returns, and possibly jeopardize existing jobs? Is it more ethical, or less, to do so when the standards are to be implemented in a developing country with no environmental laws?

### The Environmental Protection Agency

The *Environmental Protection Agency (EPA)* was created in 1970 by an executive order and operates under the supervision of the President. The EPA administrator and assistant administrators are appointed by the President with the advice and consent of the Senate. The EPA is, however, neither an independent agency nor a cabinet-level department.

Several of the assistant administrators are responsible for administering the agency's regulatory programs; others have internal administrative functions. These national program managers share responsibility with the ten regional administrators who head each of the ten EPA regional offices. The national managers at headquarters develop policy and set goals for the regional offices. The regional administrators take responsibility for day-to-day program operation.

### State Programs

State environmental laws and programs often predate the comparable federal programs. Moreover, many states have laws that are more stringent and more comprehensive than the federal laws. For example, California's hazardous-waste-management laws, water-quality-control laws, underground-tank regulations, and ban on the land disposal of certain hazardous wastes all predate and, in some cases, provided the model for subsequent federal legislation.

In light of these preexisting state environmental programs and the need to reduce the EPA's administrative burden, Congress gave the EPA the authority to authorize or approve a state program in lieu of the federal program in that state. The EPA does not delegate its federal authority; it merely approves a state program as "equivalent to or more stringent than" the federal program and then refrains from implementing the federal program in that state. The EPA generally does provide oversight, however. It retains its enforcement authority and may revoke its authorization if the state program fails to meet federal requirements.

## The Clean Air Act

The Clean Air Act[7] sets four types of air quality goals. First, it requires the EPA to establish *national ambient air quality standards (NAAQS)*, that is, to establish the

7. 42 U.S.C. §§ 7401 *et seq.* The Fifth Circuit held that the Clean Air Act was a valid exercise of Congress's power under the Commerce Clause in *United States v. Ho*, 311 F.3d 589 (5th Cir. 2002), *cert. denied*, 539 U.S. 914 (2003).

maximum levels of pollutants in the outdoor air that, with adequate margins of safety, are compatible with public health.[8] Standards must be set without regard for cost considerations.[9] The EPA has set standards for six pollutants: (1) particulate matter, (2) sulfur dioxide, (3) ozone, (4) nitrogen dioxide, (5) carbon monoxide, and (6) lead. Every state and locality must seek to achieve and maintain these national air quality standards, which are revised periodically. If a nonattainment area fails to develop an adequate plan to attain the national standard, the federal government is required to impose penalties, such as bans on construction of new sources of pollution, limits on drinking-water hookups, withholding of federal air-pollution funds, and limits on the use of federal highway funds. By affecting decisions concerning land use and transportation, as well as imposing emission controls, the law helps determine which areas of the country and which industrial sectors will be able to grow.

Second, the Clean Air Act requires that air quality in those areas that already meet the NAAQS not be allowed to deteriorate. Third, the Act requires the preservation of natural visibility within the major national parks and wilderness areas. Fourth, it requires the EPA to establish emission standards that protect public health, with an ample margin of safety, from hazardous air pollutants.

The law also requires reductions in vehicle tail-pipe emissions of certain pollutants and the use of reformulated gasoline. It mandates that fleets use clean, low-emission fuels in some nonattainment areas. Major sources of some 200 hazardous air pollutants are required to meet emission limits based on maximum achievable control technology. Electric power plants must reduce emissions that lead to the formation of acid rain. Finally, the law phased out methylchloroform and chlorofluorocarbons and placed limitations on the production of certain substitute chemicals.

## The Clean Water Act

The Federal Water Pollution Control Act was adopted in 1972 and was substantially amended by the Clean Water Act of 1977 and by the Water Quality Act of 1987. The Act, as amended, is commonly referred to as the Clean Water Act.[10] The principal goal of the Clean Water Act is to eliminate the discharge of pollutants into the navigable waters of the United States.

*Navigable waters* are all "waters of the United States which are used in interstate commerce," including "all freshwater wetlands that are adjacent to all other covered waterways." In *Solid Waste Agency of Northern Cook County v. Army Corps of Engineers,*[11] the U.S. Supreme Court ruled that an abandoned sand and gravel pit in northern Illinois that provided habitat for migratory birds did not constitute "navigable waters" within the meaning of the Clean Water Act. The Court held that the Act does not apply to ponds that are not adjacent to open water. The Court reasoned that the term "navigable" in the statute reflected Congress's intention to limit application of the Clean Water Act to waters that are or had been navigable in fact or that could reasonably be made so. Permitting federal jurisdiction over ponds and mudflats would impinge on the states' traditional power over land and water use.

### National Pollutant Discharge Elimination System

The principal regulatory program established by the Clean Water Act is the *National Pollutant Discharge Elimination System (NPDES),* which requires permits for the discharge of pollutants from any point source to navigable waters. EPA regulations establish *national effluent limitations,* which impose increasingly stringent restrictions on pollutant discharges, based on the availability of economic treatment and recycling technologies. More stringent restrictions are imposed on new sources through the setting of national standards of performance. General and specific industry pretreatment standards are set for discharges to *publicly owned sewage treatment works (POTWs)*. The pretreatment standards are designed to ensure the effective operation of the POTW and to avoid the pass-through of pollutants. The POTW, in turn, must comply with its own NPDES permit for the discharge of treated waters. The NPDES program is administered largely through approved state programs, although the EPA maintains NPDES authority in areas not within the jurisdictions of states having EPA-approved programs.

8. The U.S. Supreme Court rejected claims that the Act constituted an unconstitutional delegation of legislative power because it arguably left the EPA free to set the NAAQS at any point between zero and concentrations that would yield a "killer fog." Whitman v. Am. Trucking Ass'ns, 531 U.S. 457 (2001).
9. *Id.*

10. 33 U.S.C. §§ 1251 *et seq.*
11. 531 U.S. 159 (2001).

### Individual Liability of Corporate Officers

A corporate officer can be held civilly liable under the Clean Water Act if he or she had the authority to exercise control over the activity that caused the unlawful discharge. A corporate officer can also be held criminally responsible if he or she knowingly violated the act.

In *United States v. Iverson*,[12] the U.S. Court of Appeals for the Ninth Circuit upheld a one-year prison sentence for the president and chairman of the board of CH20, Inc., a manufacturer of acid cleaners and alkaline compounds, after finding that he had actual authority to prevent the company's dumping of industrial waste into a sewer. The executive was also fined $75,000 and received an additional sentence of three years of supervised release.

Similarly, two business partners received criminal sentences after violating the Clean Water Act by illegally dumping sewage sludge on a California farm. One partner was sentenced to fifty-one months in prison after being convicted of violating the federal environmental law; the other served a six-month prison sentence after pleading guilty. The court justified the fifty-one-month sentence on the grounds that (1) the partner was a leader, manager, and supervisor in the offense; (2) he owned half of the company and oversaw its day-to-day operations; and (3) he found the farmer who agreed to accept the sludge.[13]

## The Resource Conservation and Recovery Act

The Solid Waste Disposal Act, as amended by the Resource Conservation and Recovery Act of 1976 and the Hazardous and Solid Waste Amendments of 1984 (RCRA),[14] governs the management of hazardous wastes. The Act authorizes the EPA to identify and list hazardous wastes, to develop standards for the management of hazardous wastes by generators and transporters of wastes, and to set standards for the construction and operation of hazardous-waste treatment, storage, and disposal facilities.

### Cradle-to-Grave Responsibility

RCRA imposes "cradle-to-grave" responsibility on generators of hazardous waste. Each generator must obtain an EPA identification number and use a transportation manifest when transporting wastes for treatment or disposal. This allows the EPA to track the transportation, treatment, and disposal of hazardous wastes from the generator's facility to the final disposal site. A manifest is also required to transport hazardous wastes to an authorized storage facility.

RCRA bans the disposal of hazardous wastes onto land without treatment to render them less hazardous. To comply with the EPA's requirements for disposal on land, companies that generate hazardous waste may have to make substantial capital investments in treatment systems or incur increased costs for having wastes treated elsewhere prior to disposal.

Generators of hazardous waste must certify that they have a program in place to reduce the quantity and toxicity of their wastes. They must also certify that they are disposing of their wastes in a manner that, to the extent practicable, minimizes future threats to human health and the environment.

Owners and operators of hazardous-waste facilities must obtain permits and comply with stringent standards for the construction and operation of their facilities. These standards include maintaining certain liability insurance coverage and providing financial assurances that show the owner/operator has the financial wherewithal to close the facility at the appropriate time and to maintain it properly after closure.

Even though hazardous-waste transporters and treatment and storage facilities are closely regulated, companies that generate hazardous wastes must carefully select treatment, transportation, and disposal facilities. Liability may be imposed not only on the persons who "own or operate" the facility but also on those who have used the facility for the storage, treatment, or disposal of wastes. Persons who "contributed" to the improper waste disposal are also potentially liable. This includes individuals, such as officers who had no direct involvement in the disposal but had the authority to control the corporation's actions and failed to do so.

In 2001, in an effort to recover part of the $60 million it paid to clean up a dump site in New Hampshire, the EPA sent bills, including one for only $1,663, to more than 2,000 small businesses that had sent waste to the site.[15] Among those forced to contribute was an auto dealer not even located in New Hampshire that had paid for the legal disposal of a few hundred gallons of antifreeze.

12. 162 F.3d 015 (9th Cir. 1998).

13. United States v. Cooper, 173 F.3d 192 (9th Cir. 1999).

14. 42 U.S.C. §§ 6901 *et seq.*

15. *A Super Pain*, BOSTON GLOBE, July 3, 2001, at B1.

ECONOMIC PERSPECTIVE

## STRATEGIC ENVIRONMENTAL MANAGEMENT

Although the use of laws, regulations, and standards, referred to as "command and control" policy, is still an important tool for ensuring that companies' operations do not pollute the environment, many corporations have gone beyond simply complying with the laws.[a] In response to the Union Carbide plant explosion in Bhopal, India, in 1984, which killed and injured thousands of people, the U.S. Chemical Manufacturers Association required its members to implement a program, called Responsible Care, to improve environmental performance.

Two years later, Congress enacted the Superfund Amendments and Reauthorization Act (SARA), which required companies to publish emission levels for hundreds of chemicals. This opened corporate books to public scrutiny and prompted many companies to try to reduce emissions. For example, in 1988, Monsanto announced a plan to reduce its emissions by 90 percent. Other companies, such as AT&T, made similar commitments to go beyond simply complying with the legal limits.

Corporations also broadened their focus to include the materials they used in production, as well as the pollutants they generated. After scrutinizing both their inputs and outputs, companies began to implement principles of "eco-efficiency" in their operations by using less energy, fewer new materials, and more reused and recycled materials. For example, Lockheed reduced the amount of energy it used in its 600,000-square-foot building by using sunlight rather than electrical lighting. This required an initial investment of $2 million, but saved the company $500,000 per year thereafter. Lockheed's use of sunlight also increased employee productivity.

During this period, corporations also began to look for pollution-prevention and eco-efficiency strategies that would produce economic savings, as well as environmental benefits. Michael E. Porter and Claas van der Linde maintained that firms could remain competitive and, in fact, gain competitive advantage through *innovation offsets,* technological advantages gained by companies that meet the challenge of environmental regulations and discover lower costs and better-quality products as a result.[b] Corporations started implementing the concept of *strategic environmental management,* which advocates placing environmental management on the profit side of the corporation rather than the cost side. This represented a profound shift in how companies viewed their relationship with the environment.

In the next era of corporate environmentalism that began in the 1990s and continues in the twenty-first century, companies are working not just to reduce waste but to eliminate it altogether. This process involves looking at whole systems rather than the individual parts to create designs that take advantage of feedback loops within the company's operations. Some companies have begun to sell services rather than products, for example, by providing a rug or copying machine to a corporation for a period of time and then recycling it for continued use.

Companies are also working with other firms for both economic and environmental benefit. For example, *industrial ecology* is an approach that advocates a systems approach to eco-efficiency and applies it to groups of corporations working together. The best-known application of this approach is in Kalundborg, Denmark, where a refinery, power plant, pharmaceutical company, and fish farm located next to each other reduce costs by using each other's waste as resource inputs. For example, heat generated from one operation is used in another company's manufacturing operations.

Finally, corporations have begun to exploit the opportunities created by environmental problems.[c] Honda and Toyota have introduced hybrid cars with reduced emissions and increased gas mileage and are racing to develop vehicles powered by fuel cells. Energy companies are also investing in developing alternative sources of energy, as reflected in BP's advertising that its corporate initials stand for "Beyond Petroleum."

Forest Reinhardt has identified five approaches that companies can take to incorporate environmental issues into their business model: (1) differentiate their products by making them environmentally friendly and, as a result, command high prices; (2) "manage" competitors by imposing a set of private regulations or helping government write rules; (3) cut costs by implementing environmental practices; (4) manage risk and reduce lawsuits and accidents; and (5) make systemic changes concerning environmental issues that will redefine competition in their markets.[d]

a. This "Economic Perspective" is based in part on CARL FRANKEL, IN EARTH'S COMPANY: BUSINESS, ENVIRONMENT, AND THE CHALLENGE OF SUSTAINABILITY (1998).

b. Michael E. Porter & Claas van der Linde, *Green and Competitive: Ending the Stalemate, in* MICHAEL E. PORTER, ON COMPETITION 351–75 (1980).

c. See C. Nehrt, *Maintainability of First Mover Advantages When Environmental Regulations Differ Between Countries,* 23 ACAD. MGMT. REV. 77 (1998); J. Alberto Aragon-Correa & Sanjay Sharma, *A Contingent Resource-Based View of Proactive Corporate Environmental Strategy,* 28 ACAD. MGMT. REV. 71 (2003).

d. FOREST REINHARDT, DOWN TO EARTH: APPLYING BUSINESS PRINCIPLES TO ENVIRONMENTAL MANAGEMENT (2000).

### CRIMINAL LIABILITY

Although RCRA imposes strict civil liability, a criminal violation requires some sort of knowledge. In particular, RCRA provides criminal sanctions for any person who "knowingly transports any hazardous waste identified or listed under this subchapter to a facility which does not have a permit."[16] As explained in Chapter 14, it is not always clear how far down the sentence the word "knowingly" travels.

In *United States v. Hayes International Corp.*,[17] the U.S. Court of Appeals for the Eleventh Circuit held that knowledge of the regulation banning transport of hazardous waste to an unlicensed facility is not an element of the offense. Furthermore, the defendants could be found guilty even if they did not know that the substance being disposed of (a mixture of paint and solvents) was a hazardous waste within the meaning of the regulations. It was enough that they knew that what was being disposed of was a mixture of paint and solvents. The court distinguished *Liparota v. United States*,[18] which required knowledge that the purchase of food stamps was illegal, on the grounds that (1) the food stamp law required "knowing violation of a regulation" and (2) RCRA, unlike the food stamp law, was a public welfare statute involving a heavily regulated area with great ramifications for the public health and safety. The court concluded that it was fair to charge those who chose to operate in such an area with knowledge of the regulatory provisions.

The court held, however, that the government did have to prove that the defendants knew that the facility to which the waste was sent did not have a permit. Thus, even if the transporters did not know a permit was required, as long as they knew the facility did not have one or knew that they had not inquired, that would be sufficient knowledge for a conviction. Such knowledge could be shown circumstantially. For example, given that it is common knowledge that properly disposing of wastes is an expensive task, if someone is willing to take away wastes at an unusually low price or under unusual circumstances, then a juror could infer that the transporter knew that the wastes were not being taken to a licensed facility.

The court did acknowledge that mistake of fact would be a defense if the defendants had had a good faith belief that the materials were being recycled. The regulations applicable at the time provided an exemption from the permit requirement for waste that was recycled. The court distinguished a case in which the U.S. Supreme Court had held that a person who believed in good faith that he was shipping distilled water, when in fact he was shipping dangerous acid, did not "knowingly" ship dangerous chemicals in violation of applicable regulations.[19] Unlike the defendant in that case, the defendants in *Hayes* knew what was being shipped—a combination of waste and solvents—and they did not have a good faith belief that the materials were being recycled. Therefore, the convictions were upheld.

## The Federal Superfund Law (CERCLA)

More than any other environmental law, the Comprehensive Environmental Response, Compensation, and Liability Act (CERCLA) of 1980, as amended,[20] has affected individuals and businesses that do not themselves produce environmental pollutants. CERCLA authorizes the federal government to investigate and take remedial action in response to a release or threatened release of hazardous substances to the environment. CERCLA established the *Hazardous Substance Superfund* to finance federal response activity. Since its creation, the Superfund has been replenished with tax revenue numerous times, for a total of more than $15 billion.

How federal Superfund money will be spent is determined in part by the EPA's National Priorities List, which identifies sites that may require remedial action. The EPA lists the sites in a rulemaking proceeding based on a *hazard ranking score*, which represents the degree of risk that the site presents to the environment and public health.

### STRICT LIABILITY

The courts have interpreted the liability provisions of CERCLA broadly in order to effectuate the statute's remedial policies. With few exceptions, CERCLA imposes strict liability, meaning that the responsible parties are liable regardless of fault. It is now well established, for example, that the present owner of the land is liable for the cleanup of hazardous substances disposed of on the land by another person (usually a previous owner or tenant), unless it can establish the third-party defense (also called the innocent landowner defense), discussed later in this chapter.

16. 42 U.S.C. § 6928(d)(1).
17. 786 F.2d 1499 (11th Cir. 1986).
18. 471 U.S. 419 (1985).
19. United States v. Int'l Minerals, 402 U.S. 558 (1971).
20. 42 U.S.C. §§ 9601 *et seq.*

## Potentially Responsible Parties

Under CERCLA, the EPA may undertake remedial action itself or require responsible parties to do so. If the EPA performs the remedial work, it can recover its costs from the responsible parties. The *potentially responsible parties (PRPs)* include (1) the present owner or operator of the facility, (2) the owner or operator at the time of disposal of the hazardous substance, (3) any person who arranged for treatment or disposal of hazardous substances at the facility, and (4) any person who transported hazardous substances to or selected the facility.[21] CERCLA allows recovery for cleanup costs but does not permit punitive damages unless recklessness is found.

### *Owner or Operator at Time of Disposal*

In the following case, the court considered whether a corporation should be treated as the owner at the time of disposal if the contamination was due to the passive movement of substances without any human intervention.

21. 42 U.S.C. § 9607.

**INTERNATIONAL SNAPSHOT**

A fundamental element of the U.S. environmental scheme is that the polluter pays. The European Union (EU) has also adopted this policy: "The cost of preventing and eliminating nuisances must, as a matter of principle, be borne by the polluter."[a] The EU's policy on the environment is designed to (1) preserve, protect, and improve the quality of the environment; (2) protect human health; (3) ensure prudent and rational utilization of natural resources; and (4) promote measures at the international level to deal with regional or worldwide environmental problems.

This concept is also being introduced in Asia. Taiwan, for example, has enacted an environmental law modeled, in part, on CERCLA, with modifications to address the local culture, issues, and concerns.

When the laws of other nations are closely patterned on U.S. laws, compliance may be easier for U.S. companies operating in those countries. U.S. companies must be careful, however, to note the differences between the U.S. laws and the laws of their host countries.

**a.** Objective 17, Restatement of the Objectives and Principles of a Community Environment Policy, 1977 O.J. (C 139).

**A CASE IN POINT**

**CASE 15.1**
**Carson Harbor Village, Ltd. v. Unocal Corp.**
*United States Court of Appeals for the Ninth Circuit 270 F.3d 863 (9th Cir. 2001), cert. denied sub nom. Carson Harbor Village v. Bradley, 535 U.S. 971 (2002).*

## Summary

**› FACTS** Carson Harbor Village, Ltd., the owner and operator of a mobile home park, sued the prior owner of the property, Unocal Corporation, for cleanup costs under CERCLA. Unocal had acquired the property from the petroleum producers that contaminated it, but Unocal did not contribute to the contamination. Carson claimed that Unocal was the owner of the property at the time of "disposal." Unocal countered that the contaminants had migrated over time through the soil. Unocal argued that the passive migration that occurred during the time it owned the property did not constitute a "disposal."

**› ISSUE PRESENTED** Does "disposal" of hazardous substances under CERCLA include passive movement of substances involving no human activity?

**› SUMMARY OF OPINION** The U.S. Court of Appeals for the Ninth Circuit began by noting that CERCLA refers to the Solid Waste Disposal Act for the definition of "disposal." That act provides that "the term 'disposal' means the discharge, deposit, injection, dumping, spilling, leaking, or placing of any solid waste or hazardous waste into or on any land or water."

Although several circuit courts have interpreted "disposal" to include passive movement of substances, several others have limited the term to spills caused by human interventions.[22] The Ninth Circuit characterized these holdings as a range, based largely on the facts of each case, rather than as a classic split in authority. All of the circuit

22. *See, e.g.,* United States v. 150 Acres of Land, 204 F.3d 698 (6th Cir. 2000).

*(Continued)*

(Case 15.1 *continued*)

court opinions define "disposal" on a continuum between "active-only" (requiring affirmative action by the landowner for liability) and "passive migration" (requiring no affirmative action as a basis for liability but only passive migration of hazardous substances).

The statute defined the word "release" to include passive migration and disposal. Thus, the court reasoned that if the writers of the statute intentionally used "disposal," not "release," in the definition of potentially responsible parties, then Congress must have meant to restrict the definition. But the court also noted that the overall purpose of CERCLA is to protect public health. The court concluded that allowing owners of property to escape liability by claiming passive migration would take away all incentives for owners to check on decaying containment tanks or any other facility that might leak hazardous materials into the ground. To preserve the meaning of the statute, the court held that in limited instances passive migration would be considered disposal if a finding to the contrary would allow landowners who were clearly negligent or should be held responsible in the spirit of CERCLA to escape liability.

› **RESULT** The court reversed the lower court's decision with respect to the issue of "disposal." Unocal could be held liable as the owner at the time of disposal because it owned the property at the time the hazardous waste migrated onto it.

**Lessee as Owner** Some courts have held lessees of contaminated property liable as "owners" under CERCLA, reasoning that site control is a sufficient indicator of ownership to impose owner liability on lessees or sublessors. The U.S. Court of Appeals for the Second Circuit rejected this approach, reasoning that site control confuses the two statutorily distinct categories of owner and operator under CERCLA.[23] Instead, the Second Circuit ruled, the critical question is whether the lessee's status is that of a de facto owner. In determining whether a lessee is an owner, important factors to consider are (1) the length of the lease and whether it allows the owner/lessor to determine how the property is used; (2) whether the owner has the power to terminate the lease before it expires; (3) whether the lessee can sublet the property without notifying the owner; (4) whether the lessee must pay taxes, insurance, assessments, and operation and maintenance costs; and (5) whether the lessee is responsible for making structural repairs.

## Joint and Several Liability

The law permits the imposition of joint and several liability, which means that any one responsible party can be held liable for the total amount of response (cleanup) costs and natural resource damage even though others may also be responsible for the release. A responsible party who incurs costs cleaning up a toxic-waste site can seek cost recovery or contribution from other responsible parties. In resolving contribution claims, the court may allocate response costs among liable parties using such equitable factors as the court determines are appropriate.[24] Of course, the right of contribution is of value only if the other parties are still in existence and able to pay. Many times, they are not. Thus, joint and several liability allows the government to select financially sound parties from whom to collect response costs and puts the burden of recovering these costs from other responsible parties on the selected defendants.

A party may escape joint and several liability if it can prove that it contributed to only a divisible portion of the harm or that it was the source of waste that, when mixed with other hazardous waste, did not contribute to the release and cleanup costs that followed. The party bears the burden of establishing a reasonable basis for apportioning liability.[25]

23. Commander Oil Corp. v. Barlo Equip. Corp., 215 F.3d 321 (2d Cir. 2000), *cert. denied,* 531 U.S. 979 (2000).

24. In *Browning-Ferris Industries of Illinois v. Ter Maat,* 195 F.3d 953 (7th Cir. 1999), the U.S. Court of Appeals for the Seventh Circuit held that if one party has been required to pay the entire cost of cleaning up a site to which several other parties also contributed hazardous waste, the other parties can be held jointly and severally liable for contribution.

25. United States v. Alcan Aluminum Corp., 990 F.2d 711 (2d Cir. 1993).

## Liability of Affiliated Companies and Piercing the Corporate Veil

Corporate relatives must also worry about CERCLA liability. In *United States v. Bestfoods,*[26] the U.S. Supreme Court outlined the responsibility a parent corporation has for the hazardous-waste disposal activities of a subsidiary. The Court held that there are two bases for imposing liability on parent corporations under CERCLA for operating facilities ostensibly under the control of their subsidiaries.

First, a parent corporation will have derivative CERCLA liability as an owner for its subsidiary's actions when (but only when) the corporate veil may be pierced. As explained more fully in Chapter 19, such a collapsing of the legal distinction between parent and subsidiary is appropriate only if the corporation is just a sham or if the distinction is a fiction meant simply to protect shareholders from illegal activity.

Second, a parent corporation may have direct liability as an operator for its own actions in operating a facility owned by its subsidiary. To be deemed an operator, the parent corporation "must manage, direct, or conduct operations specifically related to pollution, that is, operations having to do with the leakage or disposal of hazardous waste, or decisions about compliance with environmental regulations." Thus, the question is not whether the parent operates the subsidiary, but rather whether it operates the facility.

The Court acknowledged that it is common for directors of the parent to serve as directors of its subsidiary. Directors and officers holding positions with a parent and its subsidiary can and do "change hats" to represent the two corporations separately. Courts generally presume that the directors are wearing their "subsidiary hats," and not their "parent hats," when acting for the subsidiary. As a result, the parent is not liable just because dual officers and directors made policy decisions and supervised activities at the facility. But if an agent of the parent with only the parent's hat to wear manages or directs activities at the subsidiary's facility, then the parent company may be held directly liable.

The parent company may also be directly liable if (1) the parent operates the facility in the stead of its subsidiary or alongside the subsidiary in some sort of joint venture; or (2) a dual officer or director departs so far from the norms of parental influence exercised through dual officeholding as to serve the parent in operating the facility, even when ostensibly acting on behalf of the subsidiary. Activities involving the facility that are consistent with the parent's investor status (such as monitoring the subsidiary's performance, supervising the subsidiary's finance and capital budget decisions, and articulating general policies and procedures) should not give rise to direct operator liability for the parent.

In its initial ruling in *Bestfoods,* the U.S. Court of Appeals for the Sixth Circuit had turned to Michigan corporate law to decide whether to pierce the Michigan firm's corporate veil. Other courts have turned to federal common law, that is, the principles found in cases that the courts have developed for interpreting federal statutes like CERCLA. Under federal common law, courts may give less respect to the corporate form than under the common law of many states.

## Successor Liability

Another important issue is *successor liability,* that is, the responsibility an acquirer of corporate assets has for the liabilities of the seller. Ordinarily, a purchaser of corporate assets—as opposed to a purchaser of all the stock of a corporation—does not automatically assume any liabilities from the seller. The doctrine of successor liability arose out of attempts by companies to evade liability by selling the bulk of their business or assets and then distributing the proceeds to their shareholders, thereby leaving creditors with no assets to collect against. Although this aspect of corporate law is a province of state common law, several federal courts refer to a federal common law of successor liability for environmental cleanup under CERCLA.

The Third, Fourth, Seventh, and Eighth Circuits have taken the position that the doctrine of successor liability should be fashioned by reliance on federal common law. The Seventh Circuit reasoned that resort to federal common law was warranted to achieve national uniformity in interpreting CERCLA and to prevent parties from frustrating the statute's aims by incorporating under the laws of states that restrict successor liability.[27]

The Second Circuit read *Bestfoods*[28] to require reference to state corporate law to determine when there should be successor liability[29] and abandoned the substantial continuity test it had embraced in an earlier case.[30] The *substantial continuity test* (sometimes

26. 524 U.S. 51 (1998).

27. North Shore Gas Co. v. Salomon, Inc., 152 F.3d 642 (7th Cir. 1998).

28. 524 U.S. 51 (1998).

29. New York v. Nat'l Servs. Indus. 352 F.3d 682 (2d Cir. 2003). *Accord* Northeast Conn. Econ. Alliance, Inc. v. ATC P'ship, 861 A.2d 473 (Conn. 2004).

30. B.F. Goodrich v. Betkoski, 99 F.3d 505 (2d Cir. 1996).

referred to as the *continuity of enterprise approach*) imposes successor liability when the purchaser of assets "maintains the same business, with the same employees doing the same jobs, under the same supervisors, working conditions, and production process, and produces the same products for the same customers" as the seller corporation.[31] Although several states employ this test, the majority of states impose successor liability only when there is a single corporation after the transfer of assets with the same shareholders and directors before and after the acquisition.[32] Because most states apply this more stringent *mere continuation* or *identity test,* the Second Circuit concluded that the substantial continuity test was not part of the general federal common law. Instead, the Second Circuit applied the traditional common law rule, which states that a corporation acquiring the assets of another takes on its liabilities only when (1) the acquirer has expressly or implicitly agreed to assume them, (2) the transaction may be viewed as a de facto merger or consolidation,[33] (3) the successor is the mere continuation of the predecessor, or (4) the transaction is fraudulent. The First,[34] Sixth, and Eleventh Circuits have also relied on state common law to determine successor liability.

## Liability of Lenders and Fiduciaries

Lenders face potential liability under CERCLA because foreclosure of a contaminated property potentially makes a lender the owner and, therefore, liable. The Asset Conservation, Lender Liability, and Deposit Insurance Protection Act of 1996[35] excluded from the definition of "owner or operator" a lender that did not participate in the management of a facility prior to foreclosure. Participation in management means "actually participating in the management or operational affairs" of the facility. Mere capacity to influence management is not a sufficient basis for imposing operator liability on a lender.

Although a lender may take steps to sell the property and may even buy it at the foreclosure sale, to avoid liability the lender must attempt to sell or re-lease the property as soon as practicable for a commercially reasonable price. A lender may also hold "indicia of ownership," such as a deed of trust, to protect its security interest without facing liability.

The liability of a fiduciary, such as a trustee, is limited to the assets held in trust. There is also a safe harbor for fiduciaries that undertake lawful response actions, but the safe harbor does not protect against negligence that causes or contributes to the release or threatened release of hazardous substances.[36]

## Retroactive Application

In *United States v. Olin Corp.*,[37] the U.S. Court of Appeals for the Eleventh Circuit ruled that owners can be held liable for hazardous waste disposed of before CERCLA became law. The court reasoned that "Congress's twin goals of cleaning up pollution that occurred prior to December 11, 1980, and of assigning responsibility to culpable parties can be achieved only through retroactive application of CERCLA's response cost liability provisions."

Subsequent to the Eleventh Circuit's decision in this case, the U.S. Supreme Court held in *Eastern Enterprises v. Apfel*[38] that retroactive application of the Coal Industry Retiree Health Benefit Act of 1992 to a company that had abandoned its coal business in 1965 violated the Takings Clause of the Fifth Amendment to the U.S. Constitution. (This is discussed further in Chapter 2.) Although defendant firms have argued in several cases that *Eastern Enterprises* overrules all previous decisions holding that CERCLA could be constitutionally applied retroactively, three federal district courts (the Eastern District of Virginia, the Northern District of New York, and the Western District of Arkansas)[39] have rejected this argument and upheld the retroactive application of CERCLA.

In 2004, the U.S. Court of Appeals for the District of Columbia Circuit reversed a lower court decision denying General Electric's claims that CERCLA violated the Due Process Clause of the Fifth Amendment and remanded the case for consideration of GE's constitutional challenges.[40] The D.C. Circuit rejected the claim

31. United States v. Caroling Transformer Co., 978 F.2d 832 (4th Cir. 1992).
32. *Id.*
33. See Chapter 19 for a discussion of the de facto merger doctrine.
34. Cyr v. B. Offen & Co., 501 F.2d 1145 (1st Cir. 1974); United States v. Davis, 261 F.3d 1, 54 (1st Cir. 2001) (noting that *Bestfoods* "left little room" for the creation of a special federal rule of liability under CERCLA).
35. 42 U.S.C. § 9601(20).
36. 42 U.S.C. § 9607(n).
37. 107 F.3d 1506 (11th Cir. 1997).
38. 524 U.S. 498 (1998).
39. Combined Props./Greenbriar Ltd. P'ship v. Morrow, 58 F. Supp. 2d 675 (E.D. Va. 1999); United States v. Alcan Aluminum Corp., 49 F. Supp. 2d 96 (N.D.N.Y. 1999); United States v. Vertac Chem. Corp., 33 F. Supp. 2d 769 (W.D. Ark. 1998), *vacated on other grounds by* United States v. Hercules, Inc., 247 F.3d 706 (8th Cir. 1999).
40. Gen. Elec. Co. v. EPA, 360 F.3d 188 (D.C. Cir. 2004).

that adjudication of GE's preenforcement constitutional challenge would undermine Congress's goal of preventing delays in the cleanup of hazardous-waste sites.

## DEFENSES

There are four defenses to liability under CERCLA. The defendant must show that the release of hazardous substances was caused solely by (1) an act of God (that is, an unavoidable natural disaster, such as an earthquake); (2) an act of war; or (3) the act or omission of a third party, provided that certain other requirements are met. A fourth defense for purchasers of *brownfields*, contaminated sites that are eligible for cleaning and reclaiming with assistance from the Superfund,[41] was added by the Brownfields Reclamation Act.

### *Third-Party or Innocent Landowner Defense*

To assert the *third-party defense* (also referred to as the *innocent landowner defense*), a defendant must show that the third party responsible for the release was not an employee and had no contractual relationship with the person asserting the defense. If the facility was acquired from the third party, the written instrument of transfer is deemed to create a contractual relationship, unless the purchaser acquired the facility after the hazardous substances were disposed of and without any knowledge or reason to know that hazardous substances had previously been disposed of at the facility. To establish that the purchaser had no reason to know that hazardous substances were disposed of at the facility, the purchaser must show that, prior to the sale, it undertook "all appropriate inquiry into the previous ownership and uses of the property consistent with good commercial or customary practice in an effort to minimize liability."[42]

Until recently, the EPA declined to issue guidelines defining an "appropriate inquiry." In 2004, however, the EPA proposed standards for determining what constitutes "all appropriate inquiry."[43] If enacted, these regulations will give prospective purchasers definitive guidance on what is necessary to prove the appropriate inquiry required for the third-party defense.

In the following case, the court considered whether the current owners should be liable for the cow-eating acid pits left by a prior owner.

41. For a more in-depth look at brownfields, see the "Inside Story" in Chapter 18.

42. 42 U.S.C. § 9601(35)(B).

43. *EPA Proposes Standards for Conducting Superfund Protection Site Assessments*, 73 U.S.L.W. 2121 (2004).

A CASE IN POINT

## In the Language of the Court

**CASE 15.2**

**Western Properties Service Corp. v. Shell Oil Co.**

*United States Court of Appeals for the Ninth Circuit*

*358 F.3d 678*

*(9th Cir. 2004).*

**› FACTS** In the 1920s, a family sold the rights to dump a noxious by-product of oil petroleum production into large pits on their property (the Thomas Ranch). After the first pit was full, neighbors began to complain about the smell and the threat to their own water supplies. A town ordinance prohibited further dumping in the pits, but the sludge was still conspicuously present. One local paper reported that "as the years passed, a crust of varying thickness formed over the top. . . . Animals that ventured too far out upon this crust disappeared forever into the acid filled pits."

The property changed hands twice before 1986, when Western Properties, an arm of a failed bank, bought the land from its debtor. At this point, the Thomas Ranch was well known for the cow-eating pits. Western immediately entered into discussions with environmental officials in California regarding remediation. After an investigation, the officials labeled the land an immediate threat and ordered Western to clean up the site, which it did at a cost of $5 million. Western then brought a claim against the various oil companies that had dumped by-products in the pit to recover its remediation costs.

**› ISSUE PRESENTED** May a landowner who was aware of contamination when acquiring property, but in no way contributed to it, take advantage of the innocent landowner defense?

**› OPINION** KLEINFELD, J., writing for the U.S. Court of Appeals for the Ninth Circuit:

*(Continued)*

(Case 15.2 *continued*)

The oil companies argue that the district court erred in granting recovery against them jointly and severally for 100% of the cleanup expense, because Western Properties, as owner, was also a PRP (potentially responsible party) and must be required to share the loss. They argue that the most Western Properties can get is contribution. The current landowner argues that, because it did not have anything to do with dumping the sludge, it is therefore an innocent landowner entitled to full recovery of its cleanup expenses. . . .

On this issue, the oil companies have the better argument. CERCLA provides that persons who are liable or potentially liable [as a PRP] may seek contribution. Western Properties, as the owner of Thomas Ranch, is "potentially liable under § 107(a)" and is therefore a PRP from whom the oil companies may seek contribution. Western Properties knew about the acid sludge when it bought Thomas Ranch. A landowner that buys property with the knowledge that the property is contaminated with hazardous waste cannot establish any of the [innocent landowner] defenses to PRP liability. That knowledge prevents the landowner from being an innocent owner, which is statutorily restricted to those who "did not know and had no reason to know." Even if Western Properties had not known of the acid sludge pits, the statutory requirement that it "demonstrate to a court that . . . [it] carried out all appropriate inquiries" would prevent it from claiming it had no reason to know of the cow-eating pits. . . .

. . .

A non-innocent landowner cannot recover its costs jointly and severally from the polluters, nor can it recover them through indemnity, as distinct from contribution.

There is some attraction, in certain circumstances, to a broad innocent-landowner rule for non-polluting landowners who are not statutorily innocent under CERCLA. The attractiveness is equitable, not textual, and the contribution statute already allows for equity to be taken into account. Suppose a person bought a lot on which to build a home, not knowing that some years ago a truck had overturned and spilled hazardous substances into the ground, which had seeped down into the water table. Suppose further that by due diligence he could have found out and is deemed to have had reason to know, so he is not a statutory innocent owner. In such a case, the district court would be able to consider the equities, as between the almost-innocent PRP landowner and the company whose truck had overturned, using its authority granted under CERCLA to "allocate response costs among liable parties using such equitable factors as the court determines are appropriate."

**› RESULT** The court found that Western was not an innocent landowner and so was entitled only to contribution from the oil companies, not a complete shield to liability.

**› CRITICAL THINKING QUESTIONS**

1. What percentage of the cleanup costs should Western be required to pay?
2. If Western refused to pay the costs and instead sold the land to a third party, could that party later bring a claim against Western under CERCLA?

### *Recyclers*

The Superfund Recycling Equity Act of 1999 exempts recyclers from liability in private-party actions under CERCLA. They remain liable in suits brought by the state or federal government. Under the statute, a person "who arranged for recycling of a recyclable material shall not be liable under [CERCLA's cost recovery and contribution sections] with respect to such material." The term "recyclable material" includes lead-acid and nickel-cadmium used in batteries. The Act applies retroactively to private actions that were pending on its date of enactment, November 29, 1999.[44]

### *Brownfields and Ready for Reuse Certificates*

As discussed more fully in Chapter 18, the Brownfields Revitalization Act[45] makes it possible for acquirers of certain contaminated sites to avoid liability for legacy contamination on the site. Landowners must comply with all institutional controls and the guidelines issued by the EPA. Failure to comply with the guidelines exposes landowners to liability for the entire cleanup costs.[46] For example, a landowner must take "reasonable steps" to prevent future or continuing releases of hazardous materials onto the land. A full review of federal and state EPA guidelines is recommended to determine what constitutes "reasonable steps."

44. Gould Inc. v. A&M Battery & Tire Serv., 232 F.3d 162 (3d Cir. 2000).
45. Small Business Liability Relief and Brownfields Revitalization Act (2002); see also Robert Dahlquist & Tiffany Barzal, *Ah: Relief from CERCLA. But Where's the Relief?*, 12 BUS. LAW. 39 (May–June 2003), for an excellent discussion of the relief from Superfund liability granted to some small businesses. The Economic Development Administration Reauthorization Act of 2003, Pub. L. No. 108–373, 118 Stat. 1756 (2004), provided for a demonstration program to encourage the use of solar energy technologies at brownfields sites. Up to $5 million for each fiscal year from 2004 through 2008 is authorized to develop "brightfield" sites.
46. These guidelines are available at http://www.cfpub.epa.gov/compliance/resource/policies/cleanup/brownfields/index.cfm. See also *EPA Guidance Issued on Avoiding Liability for Properties Tainted by Contiguous Sites*, 72 U.S.L.W. 2448 (2003).

#### ETHICAL CONSIDERATION

An action that is cost-effective in the short term may not be in the long term, particularly when the environment and human health are concerned. Given the possibility of retroactive liability, managers should consider not just what the law requires of them at the time but also what effects their actions now might have on the environment in the future. Nevertheless, if there were no possibility of retroactive liability, would it be ethical for managers to ignore those possible but uncertain future effects?

To offer more certainty to acquirers of contaminated sites, the EPA has begun issuing certificates of reuse under RCRA. The EPA issued its first certificate of reuse to a steel plant in Oklahoma in 2002. This certificate "verifies that environmental conditions on this property are protective of its current use and anticipated future uses."[47] These reuse certificates are incentives to clean up formerly contaminated land.

## EXTRATERRITORIAL APPLICATION

In what appears to be the first application of CERCLA to activity outside the United States, the court in the following case permitted a case to proceed against a Canadian smelter that dumped hazardous waste in a river that ran into Washington State.

47. *First-Ever Certificate of Reuse Awarded Under RCRA to Oklahoma Steelmaking Plant*, 71 U.S.L.W. 2061 (2002).

A CASE IN POINT

## In the Language of the Court

**CASE 15.3**
**Pakootas v. Teck Cominco Metals, Ltd.**
*United States District Court for the Eastern District of Washington*
*2004 U.S. Dist. LEXIS 23041 (E.D. Wash. Nov. 8, 2004).*

**› FACTS** Plaintiffs Joseph A. Pakootas and Donald R. Michel, enrolled members of the Confederated Tribes of the Colville Reservation, sued to enforce a unilateral administration order (UAO) by the U.S. EPA requiring the defendant, Teck Cominco Metals, Ltd. (TCM), to investigate and determine the full nature of the contamination at the "Upper Columbia River Site" due to materials disposed of into the Columbia River from the defendant's smelter. TCM is a Canadian corporation that owned and operated a smelter in Trail, British Columbia, located approximately ten Columbia River miles north of the United States–Canada border. The State of Washington was also a plaintiff, having intervened in the litigation as a matter of right under CERCLA.

TCM moved to dismiss the action, contending that the U.S. court did not have subject matter or personal jurisdiction and that the plaintiffs' complaints failed to state claims upon which relief could be granted.

**› ISSUE PRESENTED** Does a U.S. court have the power to enforce the provisions of CERCLA against a Canadian corporation for actions taken by that corporation in Canada?

*(Continued)*

(Case 15.3 *continued*)

**› OPINION** MCDONALD, J., writing for the U.S. District Court for the Eastern District of Washington:

**A. Subject Matter Jurisdiction**

This case arises under CERCLA and, therefore, there is a federal question which confers subject matter jurisdiction on this court.

. . .

**B. Personal Jurisdiction**

. . .

Absent one of the traditional bases for personal jurisdiction—presence, domicile, or consent—due process requires a defendant have "certain minimum contracts with [the forum state] such that the maintenance of the suit does not offend traditional notions of fair play and substantial justice." *International Shoe Co. v. Washington*.[48] The forum state must have a sufficient relationship with the defendants and the litigation to make it reasonable to require them to defend the action in a federal court located in that state. . . .

The extent to which a federal court can exercise personal jurisdiction, absent the traditional bases of consent, domicile or physical presence, depends on the nature and quality of defendant's "contacts" with the forum state. . . .

If a non-resident, acting entirely outside of the forum state, intentionally causes injuries within the forum state, local jurisdiction is presumptively reasonable. Under such circumstances, the defendant must "reasonably anticipate" being haled into court in the forum state. Personal jurisdiction can be established based on: (1) intentional actions; (2) expressly aimed at the forum state; (3) causing harm, the brunt of which is suffered, and which defendant knows is likely to be suffered, in the forum state. . . .

The facts alleged in the individual plaintiffs' complaint and the State of Washington's complaint-in-intervention satisfy this three-part test. The complaints allege that from approximately 1906 to mid-1995, defendant generated and disposed of hazardous substances directly into the Columbia River and that these substances were carried downstream into the waters of the United States where they have eventually accumulated and cause continuing impacts to the surface water and ground water, sediments, and biological resources which comprise the Upper Columbia River and Franklin D. Roosevelt Lake. . . . This disposal causes harm which defendant knows is likely to be suffered downstream by the State of Washington and those individuals, such as Pakootas and Michel, who fish and recreate in the Upper Columbia River and Lake Roosevelt.

The burden is on the defendant to prove the forum's exercise of jurisdiction would not comport with "fair play and substantial justice.". . .

. . .

The exercise of jurisdiction over defendant TCM does not offend traditional notions of fair play and substantial justice. The burden on defendant in defending in this forum is not great. Trail, B.C. is located approximately 10 miles from the Eastern District of Washington. For reasons discussed below, the court finds the exercise of personal jurisdiction over defendant does not create any conflicts with Canadian sovereignty. It is obvious the State of Washington has a significant interest in adjudicating this dispute, as evidenced by its intervention as a plaintiff, and venue is proper here under CERCLA.

. . .

48. 326 U.S. 310 (1945).

*(Continued)*

(Case 15.3 *continued*)

**C. Failure to State a Claim**

A Rule 12(b)(6) dismissal is proper only where there is either a "lack of a cognizable legal theory" or "the absence of sufficient facts alleged under a cognizable legal theory.". . .

Defendant contends the UAO cannot be enforced against a Canadian corporation based on conduct which occurred in Canada. . . .

. . . CERCLA's definition of "environment" is limited to waters, land, and air under the management and authority of the United States, within the United States, or under the jurisdiction of the United States.

. . . The court . . . will assume this case involves an extraterritorial application of CERCLA to conduct occurring outside U.S. borders. In doing so, however, the court does not find that said application is an attempt to regulate the discharges at the Trail smelter, but rather simply to deal with the effects thereof in the United States.

Congress has the authority to enforce its laws beyond the territorial boundaries of the United States. It is, however, a longstanding principle of American law "that legislation of Congress, unless a contrary intent appears, is meant to apply only within the territorial jurisdiction of the United States.". . .

. . .

"[I]f Congressional intent concerning extraterritorial application cannot be divined, then courts will examine additional factors to determine whether the traditional presumption against extraterritorial application should be disregarded in a particular case." First, "the presumption is generally not applied where the failure to extend the scope of the statute to a foreign setting will result in adverse effects within the United States."

. . .

Here, defendant TCM contends the presumption against extraterritorial application is not defeated because CERCLA is "bare of any language affirmatively evidencing any intent to reach foreign sources." There is no dispute that CERCLA, its provisions and its "sparse" legislative history, do not clearly mention the liability of individuals and corporations located in foreign sovereign nations for contamination they cause within the U.S. At the same time, however, there is no doubt that CERCLA affirmatively expresses a clear intent by Congress to remedy "domestic conditions" within the territorial jurisdiction of the U.S. That clear intent, combined with the well established principle that the presumption is not applied where failure to extend the scope of the statute to a foreign setting will result in adverse effects within the United States, leads this court to conclude that extraterritorial application of CERCLA is appropriate in this case.

. . .

There is no direct evidence that Congress intended extraterritorial application of CERCLA to conduct occurring outside the United States. There is also no direct evidence that Congress did not intend such application. There is, however, no doubt that Congress intended CERCLA to clean up hazardous substances at sites within the jurisdiction of the United States. That fact, combined with the well-established principle that the presumption against extraterritorial application generally does not apply where conduct in a foreign country produces adverse effects within the United States, leads the court to conclude that extraterritorial application of CERCLA is not precluded in this case. The Upper Columbia River Site is a "domestic condition" over which the United States has sovereignty and legislative control. Extraterritorial application of CERCLA in this case does not create a conflict between U.S. laws and Canadian laws.

. . .

*(Continued)*

(Case 15.3 *continued*)

Because the fundamental purpose of CERCLA is to ensure the integrity of the domestic environment, we expect that Congress intended to proscribe conduct associated with the degradation of the environment, regardless of the location of the agents responsible for said conduct.

**› RESULT** The motion to dismiss was denied so that the case could proceed. But the district court certified the case for an immediate appeal to the Ninth Circuit to resolve "a controlling question of law as to whether there is a substantial ground for difference of opinion."

**› CRITICAL THINKING QUESTIONS**

1. Would the Canadian government be able to cite this case as precedent for holding U.S. companies liable under Canadian law for acid rain in Canada?
2. What public policy considerations are involved when deciding whether to apply U.S. environmental laws to conduct occurring outside the United States? Are they the same as those implicated when deciding whether to apply U.S. antitrust,[49] employment discrimination,[50] securities,[51] or copyright and trademark law[52] to conduct occurring outside the United States?

49. Envl. Def. Fund v. Massey, 986 F.2d 528 (D.C. Cir. 1993).
50. EEOC v. Arabian Am. Oil Co., 499 U.S. 244 (1991).
51. Tamari v. Bache & Co., 730 F.2d 1103 (7th Cir. 1984).
52. Suba Films v. MGM–Pathe Communications Co., 24 F.3d 1088 (9th Cir. 1994).

# Environmental Justice

In 1992, the EPA created the Office of Environmental Justice and began integrating environmental justice into the agency's policies, programs, and activities. *Environmental justice* refers to the belief that decisions with environmental consequences (such as where to locate incinerators, dumps, factories, and other sources of pollution) should not discriminate against poor and minority communities. Because such decisions usually require state or municipal permits, environmental justice concerns are often enforced by the federal government against states, cities, and counties.

# Enforcement of Environmental Laws

Enforcement of environmental laws includes the monitoring of regulated companies' compliance with the laws, remediation of problems, and the punishment of violators.

## Agency Inspections

The environmental laws give broad authority to the administering agencies to conduct on-site inspections of plant facilities and their records. Many laws authorize the agency to collect samples for analysis. Inspections may be conducted routinely or in response to reports or complaints from neighbors or employees. If criminal violations are suspected, the agency may choose to conduct an inspection under the authority of a search warrant. Violations observed during the inspection may be the subject of civil or criminal enforcement actions.

## Self-Reporting Requirements

Many statutes and regulations require regulated companies to report certain facts to the EPA, such as the concentrations and/or the amounts of pollutants discharged from a facility. These reports may indicate a violation and may therefore prompt an enforcement action by the agency. There are severe penalties for filing false reports, including criminal sanctions for knowingly providing false information to a government agency.

## Administrative and Civil Enforcement Actions

Because the environmental laws are intended to accomplish such important societal goals and violations of the laws may cause serious harm or injury, environmental regulatory agencies generally are given strong enforcement powers. For a first violation, the agency might issue a warning and impose a schedule for compliance. If the schedule is not met or the violations are repeated, more aggressive enforcement action will likely follow. Such action may take the form of an administrative order to take specified steps to achieve compliance or a formal administrative complaint containing an assessment of administrative penalties. The penalties vary. Because they can be assessed for each day of each violation, they can be substantial for repeated, multiple, or long-standing violations.

As discussed further in Chapter 14, the EPA may reduce or eliminate fines for civil or administrative violations by companies that discover such violations through their own systematic compliance reviews, report them to the EPA within twenty-one days of discovery by a responsible party, and remedy them.[53] A company may also qualify under the policy if, after having been found liable for violations at one facility, it discloses similar violations at others. The voluntary disclosure policy has been widely used. To date, more than 670 companies have made voluntary disclosures, resulting in the resolution of claims at more than 1,300 facilities.[54]

## Criminal Prosecution

In more egregious cases, the enforcing agency may refer the case to the U.S. Attorney's office or its state counterpart for criminal prosecution. In most instances, courts are authorized to impose penalties of $25,000 to $100,000 per day of violation and to sentence individuals to prison terms of one year or more.[55] In some cases, the agency may have authority to close down the violator's operations.

The following case has been described as the most expansive application to date of the responsible corporate officer doctrine in a criminal case.

53. In the spring of 2003, the EPA announced that it had waived $1.5 million in fines payable by East Coast–based companies after they self-reported violations occurring as far back as 1994 and as recently as 2001. The violations ranged from failing to file appropriate waste authorization forms to misreporting the qualities of dangerous chemicals being dumped by the companies. *EPA Waives $1.5 Million in Potential Fines Against Companies Reporting Own Violations,* 71 U.S.L.W. 2551 (2003).
54. Peyton Sturges, *Revisions to EPA Audit Policy Dovetail with Enforcement Initiatives, Official Says,* 68 U.S.L.W. 2576 (2000).
55. *See, e.g.,* 33 U.S.C. § 1319 & 42 U.S.C. § 6928.

### INTERNATIONAL SNAPSHOT

Although historically pollution laws were often not enforced in India, in November 1999, the Supreme Court of India ordered New Delhi authorities to comply with its 1996 order to close approximately 90,000 small factories that were polluting residential areas in the capital city or to relocate them to areas outside the city. The businesses at issue included leather, fertilizer, chemical, food processing, and paint plants that polluted the city's air and water sources. After the India Supreme Court issued the order, thousands of workers violently protested the closure of the factories by torching buses, blocking major roads, and throwing stones.[a] These protests essentially shut down the capital for a week. Opponents of the closures argued that shutting down the small factories, which provided employment to approximately one million people and generated business worth more than $1 billion annually, would cripple the city's economy.[b] The India Supreme Court argued that closure of the polluting factories was necessary for public health reasons and stated that it would not be influenced by the protests: "The court will not withdraw its orders just because hooligans have taken to the streets."[c] The governments of the rapidly industrializing states of Haryana and Uttar Pradesh, which are just north of New Delhi, ran advertisements encouraging factories to relocate there.[d]

**a.** Celia W. Dugger, *A Cruel Choice in New Delhi: Jobs vs. a Safer Environment,* N.Y. Times, Nov. 24, 2000.
**b.** Ranjit Devrai, *Development—India: Thousands of Jobless Question Green Concerns,* Inter Press Service, Dec. 29, 2000.
**c.** Dugger, *supra* note a.
**d.** Kartik Goyal, *India: Neighbouring States Gain As Delhi Shuts Polluting Units,* Reuters Eng. News Service, Dec. 29, 2000.

A Case in Point

## In the Language of the Court

**CASE 15.4**
**United States v. Hansen**
*United States Court of Appeals for the Eleventh Circuit*
*262 F.3d 1217*
*(11th Cir. 2001), cert. denied, 535 U.S. 1111 (2002).*

**› FACTS** Christian Hansen founded the Hanlin Group in 1972 and served as its CEO until April 1993. The Hanlin Group operated a chemical plant in Brunswick, Georgia, through its subsidiary, LCP Chemicals–Georgia (LCP). The plant employed about 150 workers. Hansen also served as the LCP plant manager for approximately two months in 1993. Before Hanlin acquired the Brunswick facility in 1979, the site had been occupied by other companies that had produced and dumped hazardous materials on the

*(Continued)*

(Case 15.4 *continued*)

land and the surrounding area. LCP constructed a wastewater treatment system and obtained a permit in 1990 to dump "treated" water into Purvis Creek, a nearby waterway. Although LCP had represented that its treatment facilities could process seventy gallons of water per minute, in fact, the facility could process only thirty-five gallons per minute. In August 1992, the Occupational Safety and Health Administration cited the plant for safety hazards associated with contaminated water on the cell room floors.

Hanlin filed for bankruptcy in 1991. Soon thereafter, Christian asked his son Randall to join LCP as an executive vice president to help turn the facility around.

In February 1992, James Johns, the Brunswick plant manager, informed Randall that, without "extensive work" on the wastewater treatment system, the plant could not operate for more than a few days without willfully violating environmental regulations. Randall attempted to raise additional funds by selling excess equipment and reducing the payroll, but the funds available for maintenance, repair, and environmental compliance remained limited. All major projects and all capital and extraordinary expenditures required the approval of the Hanlin board, the Hanlin bankruptcy creditors' committee, and the bankruptcy court. Although Randall requested funds to address the wastewater problems, the funds were usually not released.

Later that year, Randall visited the plant again after meeting with representatives from the EPA and was told by Alfred Taylor, the new plant manager, that the water treatment problem was growing even more serious. Taylor testified at trial that Randall was "just as concerned as they were" about the problems and authorized him to hire a task force to help solve the problem.

After a year and a half of more violations, which were duly reported to the state and federal EPA by Randall and LCP, Randall and his managers considered shutting down the facility either permanently or temporarily. But Randall told his managers, "They won't let me do that." In April 1993, the board removed Christian as CEO and elected Randall in his place. Randall also served as plant manager of the Brunswick facility from July through September 1993.

Randall searched for a suitable buyer with the resources and capital to fix the plant's problems. During this time, he received reports of the continuing violations at the plant.

In June 1993, the Georgia Environmental Protection Division (EPD) proposed a revocation of LCP's license to dump wastewater into Purvis Creek. In July and August 1993, Christian told employees to pump wastewater into drums containing oil, even though he knew that wastewater mixed with oil could not be run through the wastewater treatment system. He also advised employees not to dump any more water into Purvis Creek. Employees repeatedly told Randall, Christian, and Taylor that water was running out of the treatment facility's doors due to breaks in the beams. These employees were told that conditions would change as soon as the plant had a cash infusion from a buyer, but that nothing more could be done at that time.

During this period, Randall found a buyer that was willing to advance funds to help alleviate the releases of hazardous waste. Although conditions improved briefly, the deal fell through, and the Georgia EPD revoked LCP's license in September 1993, forcing LCP to close the plant entirely. Randall requested $1.5 million from the bankruptcy court to deal with the environmental impacts of a full plant closure, but his request was denied.

Following the closure, the facility was turned over to the U.S. EPA for cleanup, which cost approximately $50 million. Shortly thereafter, the U.S Attorney's office indicted Christian and Randall Hansen and Taylor for violating numerous environmental laws from 1984 through the plant's final shutdown in 1994. The government also indicted Douglas

*(Continued)*

(Case 15.4 *continued*)

Hanson, LCP's environmental and health and safety manager. Hanson pled guilty to violating CERCLA and the Endangered Species Act and testified against Christian, Randall, and Taylor.

Christian Hansen was convicted of violating the Clean Water Act (CWA), the Resource Conservation and Recovery Act (RCRA), and CERCLA, and he was sentenced to 108 months in prison. Randall was convicted of violating the CWA and RCRA and was sentenced to 46 months in prison. Taylor was convicted of violating the CWA, RCRA, and CERCLA and was sentenced to 78 months in prison. All three appealed their convictions.

**› ISSUE PRESENTED** When may corporate officers and plant managers be held individually guilty as operators of a hazardous-waste facility under the CWA, RCRA, and CERCLA?

**› OPINION** PER CURIAM, by the U.S. Court of Appeals for the Eleventh Circuit:

The indictment alleged that the defendants, "after learning that the Brunswick facility was disposing of hazardous wastes . . . without a RCRA permit, continued to operate the Brunswick facility in such a manner as to continue the disposal of these hazardous wastes without expending adequate funds . . . to prevent the disposal of such hazardous wastes into the environment." The jury was instructed that the defendants were responsible for the acts of others that they "willfully directed," "authorized," or aided and abetted by "willfully joining together with [another] person in the commission of a crime." . . .

**a. *Hansen***

. . .

The testimony at trial indicated that Christian Hansen was aware that wastewater was permitted to flow out the cell room back door in June 1993, and directed the use of the old Bunker C storage tanks for storage of wastewater, including the inadequately treated wastewater from the treatment system, from July through September 1993. Although the acts continued after Hansen left his decision-making position, the acts occurred at his direction. This evidence was sufficient for the jury to reasonably conclude beyond a reasonable doubt that his acts were in furtherance of the violations. . . .

**b. *Randall***

Randall claims that the government presented no evidence that he personally treated, stored, or disposed of a hazardous waste, personally effected a CWA violation, or instructed an agent to do so. He maintains that, under the laws of bankruptcy and corporate governance, he lacked the authority to close the plant or to allocate the funds for the needed capital improvements. He contends that LCP needed the bankruptcy court's approval to use the bankruptcy estate's assets, or to obtain a new debt, to perform the needed repairs at the Brunswick plant.

In February 1994, LCP applied to the bankruptcy court for the funds "to shutdown" the plant and for new equipment, but the motion was denied. . . . LCP Board of Directors member James Mathis testified that Randall was responsible for "running the day-to-day operations of the company" once he became the interim CEO and COO. . . .

LCP, as a debtor in possession, could use the property of the estate in the ordinary course of business, but needed court approval to use, sell, or lease, other than in the ordinary course of business, property of the estate. It could obtain secured credit . . . in the ordinary course of business, but needed court approval to obtain unsecured credit or to incur unsecured debt other than in the ordinary course of business. Bankruptcy does not insulate a debtor from environmental regulatory statutes. In

*(Continued)*

(Case 15.4 *continued*)

reviewing an injunction to clean up a hazardous waste site, the U.S. Supreme Court commented:

> We do not suggest that [the debtor's] discharge [in bankruptcy] will shield him from prosecution for having violated the environmental laws . . . or for criminal contempt for not performing his obligations under the injunction prior to bankruptcy. . . . We do not hold that the injunction . . . against any conduct that will contribute to the pollution of the site or the State's wasters is dischargeable in bankruptcy. . . . Finally, we do not question that anyone in possession of the site . . . must comply with the environmental laws. . . . Plainly, that person or firm may not maintain a nuisance, pollute the waters of the State, or refuse to remove the source of such conditions.[56]

Although Randall claims that his role as Executive Vice-President and acting CEO was limited to financial matters, he also received daily reports about the plant's operations and environmental problems, wrote and received memos regarding specific plant operational problems, received monthly written environmental reports, and oral environmental reports. He admitted that Hanlin's bankruptcy was not an excuse for violating environmental laws. There is no indication that he asked the Hanlin Board or the bankruptcy court to close the plant. The evidence indicates that he apparently misled them into believing that environmental compliance was not a problem. After the Georgia EPD attempted to revoke the plant's [dumping] permit in June 1993, Randall contested the revocation, explaining that the plant's CWA violations were due to a lightning strike and equipment failures, and asserted that "LCP has already taken steps to improve the situation." This evidence was sufficient for the jury to conclude that Randall's actions were in furtherance of the violations.

c. ***Taylor***

Taylor argues that he should not be held responsible for the environmental violations that occurred after he resigned as plant manager. Taylor resigned as plant manager on 16 July 1993, but returned shortly thereafter as a project engineer and continued in that position until the plant closed. . . .

Although Taylor left his managerial position, he continued to work in a position in which he directed or authorized acts of the employees on environmental and safety problems. . . . This evidence was sufficient for the jury to conclude beyond a reasonable doubt that these acts were in furtherance of the violations.

**› RESULT** The defendants' convictions were supported by the evidence and were, accordingly, upheld.

**› COMMENTS** The Justice Department has responded to criticism that environmental crime prosecutors are "overreaching by criminalizing what should be handled through the civil or regulatory process" with a resolute stance to continue to criminally pursue those it considers violators.

**› CRITICAL THINKING QUESTIONS**

1. Is it fair to hold an officer criminally liable for environmental problems when the officer lacks the funds to fix the problems or to shut the plant down properly to prevent further violations?
2. Is it fair to attribute corporate actions to the corporation's officers when they never instructed or encouraged their employees to violate the environmental laws?

56. Ohio v. Kovacs, 469 U.S. 274, 284–85 (1985).

### Ethical Consideration

Would it be a breach of fiduciary duty or unethical for top management to decide not to voluntarily disclose violations to the EPA due to fear of criminal prosecution of corporate employees? Who within the corporation should make the decision of whether to self-report?

As discussed further in Chapter 14, the EPA often recommends against criminal prosecution by the Department of Justice if the company self-reports and cooperates with the EPA.[57] Any protection against criminal prosecution gained by voluntary disclosures under the audit policy applies only to the company. Officers and employees may still be subject to criminal liability based on information disclosed by the company.

57. *EPA May Recommend Not Prosecuting Companies That Uncover, Report Crimes,* 66 U.S.L.W. 2520 (1998). The official EPA statement of its policy is available at http://es.epa.gov/compliance/index.html.

## Management of Environmental Compliance

Legally astute corporate officials recognize the need to adopt corporate policies and create management systems to ensure that company operations are protective of human health and the environment. These programs generally include several key elements.

### Corporate Policy

A strong corporate policy of environmental protection, adopted and supported at the highest levels of management, is usually the keystone of an effective program. Mere compliance with environmental laws may not be enough. A practice that is lawful today could nevertheless lead to environmental harm and future liability. For example, underground storage of flammable materials was once considered a sound practice and was actually required by many local fire codes. Little thought was given to the possibility of leaks or spillage around the tanks, with resulting harm to underground water supplies. If the risks had been

## *View from Cyberspace*

### The EPA Launches ECHO

In 2002, the EPA launched a pilot program called the Enforcement of Compliance History Online (ECHO).[a] The pilot was initially set to run for sixty days, but it proved so successful that it has operated ever since. The goal of ECHO is to provide everyone, from private citizen to government investigator, with instant and easy access to any company's record of compliance with environmental regulations. ECHO combines the following databases maintained by the EPA: (1) the Air Facility System, (2) the EPA's Permit Compliance System, (3) the Resource Conservation and Recovery Act Information System, (4) the Integrated Compliance Information System, and (5) the Facility Management System.

ECHO does not provide any new information on companies—its only function is to serve as an instant, single access point. In the past, individuals had to request records from multiple agencies and departments through the Freedom of Information Act.

ECHO is designed for simplicity. Users can search based on city, county, state, or zip code. By giving consumers easy access to each company's environmental history, the EPA hopes to increase the pressure on firms to comply fully with the environmental laws.

The only concern voiced over ECHO is that some data may be incomplete and therefore be misleading. ECHO receives its data from state-designed systems, and some states are providing less complete data than others. The EPA has committed a number of personnel to researching and correcting errors and has also posted caveats on the website warning, for example, that some data may be incomplete or missing. Though the system remains a work in progress and is subject to all the problems that accompany accessing important data on the Internet, it seems to be a prototype for a system to "out" violators that might otherwise be able to hide from the public eye.

a. This discussion is based heavily on *EPA Announces Pilot Program to Allow Public Access to Environmental Records,* 71 U.S.L.W. 2343 (2002). See also http://www.epa.gov/echo/.

perceived properly, double containment could have been provided when the tanks were first installed. This lack of foresight caused many companies to incur substantial costs for groundwater restoration.

The corporate policy should require every employee to comply with environmental laws. It should encourage management to consider more stringent measures than those required by law if such measures are necessary to protect human health and the environment. Finally, the policy should encourage a cooperative and constructive relationship with government agency personnel and should support active participation in legislative and administrative rule-making proceedings.

## Well-Defined Organizational Structure and Crisis-Management Plan

Management of environmental compliance requires a well-defined organizational structure with clearly delineated responsibilities and reporting relationships. The complex and technical nature of environmental laws and regulations requires a highly trained professional staff with legal and technical expertise.

A company should have policies and procedures for reporting environmental law violations to corporate management and for managing the company's reporting obligations to government agencies. Top management also needs to ensure that whistleblowers are not subject to retaliation.

Environmental problems are what Max Bazerman and Michael Watkins call "predictable surprises."[58] Therefore, every company should have a crisis-management plan in place that designates someone other than the CEO to coordinate the response. That response, in turn, should include immediate stabilization of the situation, objective inquiry into it, and some immediate action to assure the company's constituencies that things are being put under control. For that reason, constituencies must receive information as the response continues. To the extent that crises are at least foreseeable, more detailed plans should be developed ahead of time.[59]

## Education and Training

A corporation can be held liable for the malfeasance of its employees acting within the scope of employment, even if they acted contrary to company policies. At the same time, an employee involved in illegal conduct can be held personally criminally liable, even if he or she was just following orders from a supervisor. In addition, as explained in this chapter and in Chapter 14, under certain circumstances, the corporate executive officers responsible for operating or overseeing the operation of facilities or activities involving hazardous waste can be civilly and criminally liable for illegal conduct by the employees under their supervision.

The most essential component of good environmental management is comprehensive education and training. Every employee must know about and understand the company's environmental policy and recognize his or her responsibilities in carrying it out.

## Record Keeping, Accounting, and Disclosure

Good record-keeping and cost-accounting systems are also essential. Many environmental laws require certain records to be developed and maintained for specified periods of time. These laws should be consulted when a company develops a record-retention policy. The company should also develop cost-accounting procedures that will allow it to forecast and report the costs of environmental compliance.

Publicly traded companies must carefully evaluate the costs of complying with environmental law and potential environmental liabilities in order to meet the disclosure and reporting requirements of the Securities and Exchange Commission (SEC). The SEC requires disclosure of environmental enforcement proceedings and litigation, as well as estimated costs of environmental compliance, including capital expenditures and any effects of compliance on earnings and competitive position that may be material. The SEC uses information provided by the EPA in enforcing these reporting requirements.

Currently, companies are required under the Management's Discussion and Analysis of Financial Condition and Results of Operations (MD&A) section of Regulation S-K to discuss management's views on the company's financial condition, including any trends that might have an effect on the bottom line. Traditionally, this has been the only place management would theoretically be forced to divulge known environmental liabilities—as they pertain to the company's bottom line. However, these liabilities are subject to management's interpretation of how they affect the bottom line and thus are often severely underreported or not reported at all, according to some environmentalists. Environmental activists are pushing for specific SEC regulations requiring companies to

58. Max H. Bazerman & Michael D. Watkins, Predictable Surprises (2004).

59. Stanley Sporkin, *A Plan for Crisis Management and Avoidance*, Address at Nonprofit Risk Management Institute (Nov. 12, 1997).

disclose any environmental liabilities, regardless of their effect on firm profits.

## Periodic Environmental Audits

An important step in comprehensively managing environmental liability and reducing penalties for noncompliance is to conduct periodic environmental audits. Such candid, internal self-assessments document and measure (1) compliance with occupational health and safety requirements; (2) compliance with federal, state, and local emissions limits and other requirements of a company's licensing, if any; (3) current practices for the generation, storage, and disposal of hazardous wastes; and (4) potential liability for past disposal of hazardous substances. Audits should also test the effectiveness of the management system and ensure that all instances of noncompliance are corrected.

Although such programs can generate valuable information for management, they may also be self-incriminating. A thorough audit that reveals contaminated properties, shoddy disposal practices, and lax compliance with regulations will certainly aid a company seeking to improve its environmental compliance. If the results of such an audit were publicly available, however, plaintiffs in the discovery stage of litigation could use the audit results to further their case. For that reason, several states have enacted laws making such information privileged in order to encourage companies to produce and use it. At least one court has established a qualified privilege for certain self-critical analyses.[60]

60. Reichhold Chems., Inc. v. Textron, Inc., 157 F.R.D. 522 (N.D. Fla. 1994).

**INTERNATIONAL SNAPSHOT**

Although internal environmental audits in the United States may be protected through the attorney–client privilege, that may not be the case in other countries where the attorney–client privilege is either not recognized or provides less protection than in U.S. courts. For example, in many countries in Latin America, the attorney–client privilege does not extend to attorney memos that a company may have in its files. Internal environmental audit documents, including attorney memos, may be obtained in most Latin American countries through a court order. As a result, foreign citizens can use these documents to file claims in U.S. courts against domestic companies for their actions outside the United States.[a]

**a.** *U.S. Business Documents Can Be Used in Suits by Foreign Citizens, Attorney Says,* 69 U.S.L.W. 2251 (2000).

The more stringent governmental financial reporting required by the Sarbanes-Oxley Act of 2002 has prompted auditors to take a closer look at the actual procedures used by in-house environmental managers. The requirement that the CEO and CFO certify the accuracy of public-company financial statements provides yet another reason for companies to perform in-house environmental evaluations with diligence and foresight.[61]

Many businesses are complying with standards established by nongovernmental certification programs.[62] Environmental certification programs verify that the activities of certified firms are environmentally appropriate. The International Organization for Standardization (ISO) environmental management program and the chemical industry's Responsible Care program are two of the most widely used programs. Complying with these standards offers a number of benefits. The EPA has enacted a number of policies that promote certification, including the "Performance Track" program that gives special treatment to businesses meeting certification-like requirements. Among the prerequisites for qualifying for both ISO and Performance Track are (1) the adoption of an in-house environmental management system, (2) a commitment to improve environmental performance and open reporting to the public, and (3) a record of compliance with environmental requirements. Companies that meet the requirements enjoy streamlined monitoring, record keeping, and reporting under the Clean Air Act and Clean Water Act and greater flexibility in installing "best available control technology" under the Clean Air Act.[63] Furthermore, a number of major international banks have agreed to finance environmentally sensitive projects, such as power plants, dams, and pipelines, only if the projects also qualify under international environmental and social-impact standards.[64]

## Protocols for Agency Inspections

Government agencies may undertake inspections with little or no advance notice. The company should be prepared in advance for such an event by having a protocol for handling the inspection. Individuals trained in the company protocol should accompany the inspector to ensure that the inspection is conducted properly and within the inspector's authority. The person who accompanies the inspector should prepare a report to management and make sure that any instances of noncompliance identified during the inspection are corrected.

61. Goodwin and Procter, *Environmental Law Advisory,* June 2004.
62. Errol E. Meidinger, Environmental Certification and U.S. Environmental Law: Closer Than You May Think (2001).
63. *Id.*
64. Michael Phillips & Mitchell Pacelle, *Banks Accept Environmental Rules,* Wall St. J., June 4, 2003, at A2.

## Public and Community Relations

As popular sentiment increasingly favors environmental sensitivity and protection, companies must pay attention to the public relations consequences of their environment-affecting actions. Dissatisfaction with a company's environmental record can lead to adverse publicity, activist protests, consumer boycotts, and more stringent regulation.

The manner in which a company handles an environmental problem can also have an important impact on its relationship with the community where it is located, as well as on the economic damages it will suffer. A company can gain credibility and respect by handling an environmental accident in a proactive and fair manner.

For example, Eastman Kodak's response to an environmental problem increased its standing in the city of Rochester, New York, where it is headquartered. When the local newspaper reported that toxic chemicals from Kodak had seeped into the bedrock beneath the soil and were moving underground toward homes, panic erupted and the price of the homes plummeted. The company instituted a series of homeowner relief programs to assure homeowners that they would lose no money as a result of the decline in value of their homes. Kodak offered discounted refinanced mortgages and home improvement grants to encourage people to stay in their homes rather than sell them. For those who wanted to sell, the company agreed to pay the difference between the selling price and the home's market value before the environmental problem was discovered. If a house took longer than three months to sell, Kodak supplied interest-free bridge loans so that owners could move into their new homes before their old homes were sold. The president of the neighborhood association that represented 5,000 Rochester households commented, "The program was a perfect example of a company being proactive in their interactions with the community. Everyone I know [from the polluted area] felt they were given a good deal. I've not heard any objections."[65]

## Long-Term Strategies

The company should develop strategies for reducing the costs of compliance and the risk of liability over the long term. Corporate strategies might include minimizing the amounts and kinds of pollutants produced, developing ways to recycle waste products, and investing in new technologies to render wastes nonhazardous. If hazardous wastes are produced, the company should have procedures for evaluating and selecting well-managed and well-constructed treatment and disposal facilities.

65. *Uncivil Action*, 9 Treasury & Risk Mgmt. 25 (Jan.–Feb. 1999).

### IN BRIEF

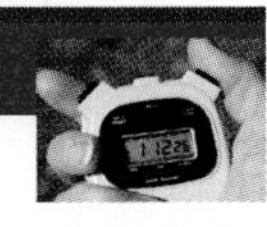

**Developing an Environmental Compliance Program**

In evaluating or developing an environmental program, a manager should consider the following areas and ask the following questions:

1. Achieving and maintaining compliance:
   - What laws and regulations affect the company's facilities?
   - What procedures effectively balance compliance costs with liability?
   - How can those procedures be communicated to those responsible for their implementation?
   - How can employees be persuaded they have a stake in the program's success?
2. Obtaining timely notice of new requirements:
   - What is being done to keep abreast of new requirements?
   - Will management receive notice early enough to make necessary changes cost-effectively?
3. Influencing future requirements:
   - What environmental laws and regulations are on the horizon?
   - How are they being tracked?
   - What is being done to influence their wording and enactment?
4. Monitoring compliance accurately:
   - What kind of monitoring is required?
   - Who will perform that monitoring?
   - How will the results be assessed?
5. Timely and accurate reporting:
   - When must a manager report information to regulators?
   - What procedures ensure that reportable incidents are brought to management's attention?
   - Does the company have databases for tracking chemical use and other technical information?
6. Responding to emergencies:
   - What systems are in place to respond to emergencies?
   - Are responsible employees trained to respond appropriately?
7. Maintaining community relations:
   - How strong is the company's relationship with the surrounding community?
   - What kind of programs are in place to maintain and expand that relationship?
   - How would management expect the community to respond to emergencies?

**Source:** Based on Steven J. Koorse, *When Less Is More—Trouble,* Bus. L. Today, Sept.–Oct. 1997, at 24.

# Global View

## SUSTAINABLE DEVELOPMENT, GLOBAL WARMING, AND THE KYOTO CLIMATE PROTOCOL

An environmental issue of increasing importance is the concept of sustainable development. *Sustainable development* "holds that future prosperity depends on preserving 'natural capital'—air, water, and other ecological treasures—and that doing so will require balancing human activity with nature's ability to renew itself. It also recognizes that growth is necessary to eliminate poverty, which leads to the plunder of resources."[a]

Sustainable development is politically controversial because it entails significant changes in national regulatory and economic policies. Increased cooperation among industrialized and developing nations, the possibility of industrialized nations scaling back their transformation of the world's resources into wealth, and the use of new technology to preserve the earth's environment and prevent pollution become very important.

One of the major obstacles to sustainable development is the world's continued production of greenhouse gases. The United States is the world's largest producer of these gases, producing more than 30 percent of all greenhouse gases. Experts estimate that if everybody on the planet lived like the average American, we would need at least three planets to live sustainably.[b]

As part of an international effort to curb greenhouse gases, the Kyoto Climate Protocol went into effect on February 16, 2005, after Russia became a signatory. It requires three dozen developed countries to cut their levels of greenhouse gas emissions by 5 percent, using 1990 emissions as the baseline, by 2012. The Kyoto Protocol's 128 signatories include Canada, Japan, and all of the European Union.[c] The United States and Australia are the only major developed countries that have refused to ratify the treaty.

In 2001, soon after taking office, President George W. Bush abandoned the Kyoto Protocol. He argued that it would retard U.S. economic growth and cost U.S. jobs by raising energy prices. Notwithstanding the scientific consensus regarding the role of greenhouse gases in global warming and the risks it poses, the Bush administration also questioned whether the emissions controls called for by the Kyoto Protocol were really necessary. Instead, Bush called for voluntary measures and additional research.[d] Senator John McCain, former chair of the Commerce, Service and Transportation Committee, called Bush's climate change policy "disgraceful."[e] In 2002, the Bush administration committed to reduce greenhouse emissions by 18 percent by 2012, subject to growth in gross domestic product. Even with these measures, U.S. officials concede that emissions will probably be 15 percent above 1990 levels, far higher than the levels mandated by the Kyoto treaty.[f] The Bush administration did, however, successfully develop a global plan to curb methane emissions by capturing this greenhouse gas (which comes primarily from decomposing trash in landfills) and using it as an energy source before it is released into the atmosphere.[g]

Under the Kyoto Protocol, industrialized countries are permitted to purchase unused quotas from other nations to meet their quotas. When the quotas were originally set in 1990, former members of the Soviet Union negotiated permissible emission levels comparable to those of other industrialized countries. After industrial production in these countries plummeted due to changes in their governments and economies, their actual emissions were only 40 percent of their levels at the time the quotas were set. As a result, these countries now have unused quotas that they can sell to other industrialized countries and reap huge profits. Analysts predict that Russia could potentially earn more than $12 billion annually (and Kazakstan $4 billion) by selling their rights to emit greenhouse gases to other countries.[h]

The European Climate Exchange, the first mandatory carbon emissions trading market, went live in February 2005. According to its founder Peter Koster, "It is the first time that you are rewarded for being an environmentally friendly manager."[i] By allowing plants to trade emission permits and giving companies the option of investing in emission-reduction projects in developing countries as a cheaper way to earn credits, the European Union is relying on the free markets to channel investment to the most energy-efficient technologies.

Ken Reiffing, the deputy director of the environmental directorate at the Organisation for Economic Cooperation and Development in Paris, predicts that forcing European businesses to pay more attention to their energy consumption will make

a. Emily T. Smith, *Growth vs. Environment,* BUS.WK., May 11, 1992, at 66.
b. MATHIS WACKERNAGEL & WILLIAM RESSE, OUR ECOLOGICAL FOOTPRINT, REDUCING HUMAN IMPACT ON THE EARTH (1996).
c.. Timothy E. Wirth & Mindy S. Lubber, *A Role for U.S. Firms in Energy Cleanup,* BOSTON GLOBE, Dec. 30, 2004, at A15.
d. Juliet Eilperin, *14 Nations to Participate in Plan to Reduce Methane,* WASH. POST, Nov. 17, 2004, at A24. For a summary of several key scientific papers on the effects of global warming, see William Kelly, *Global Warming,* L.A. WKLY., Dec. 24, 2004, at 30.
e. *Id.*
f. Hector Tobar, *U.S. Seen as Laggard at U.N. Climate Change Meeting,* L.A. TIMES, Dec. 12, 2004, at A3.
g. Eilperin, *supra* note d.
h. Steve LeVine, *Ex-Soviet States Sit on a Gold Mine of Greenhouse Gases,* WALL ST. J., Nov. 21, 2000, at A23.
i. Katrin Benhold, *New Limits on Pollution Herald Change in Europe,* N.Y. TIMES, Jan. 1, 2005, at C5.

*(Continued)*

(Global View *continued*)

them "leaner and more efficient, and that could turn into a long-term business advantage even if it's a bit painful in the short term."[j] Timothy E. Wirth, a former U.S. senator and the current president of the UN Foundation, and Mindy S. Lubber, executive director of CERES, called on U.S. companies to take the lead in developing and utilizing technologies to reduce greenhouse gases.[k] Although Cummins Engine and General Electric are taking advantage of new opportunities to sell climate-friendly products, such as compressed natural gas bus engines and windpower turbines, Wirth and Lubber assert that "most U.S. companies still lag far behind their worldwide competitors in facing the challenges posed by global warming."[l] They ask: "Is the United States going to lead the technological innovation and resulting job growth, as it did with the Internet? Or is it going to lag behind as Toyota and other foreign competitors develop and dominate clean technology markets?"[m]

j. *Id.*
k. Wirth & Lubber, *supra* note c.
l. *Id.*
m. *Id.*

As the experience with attempts to curb greenhouse gases demonstrates, efforts at negotiating international treaties and adopting national laws to implement them are insufficient to prevent the large and irreversible amount of destruction to the environment that is currently occurring. In an award-winning *Harvard Business Review* article, Professor Stuart Hart called on business leaders to step into the breach:

> Like it or not, the responsibility for ensuring a sustainable world falls largely on the shoulders of the world's enterprises, the economic engines of the future. Clearly, public policy innovations (at both the national and international levels) and changes in individual consumption patterns will be needed to move towards sustainability. But corporations can and should lead the way, helping to shape public policy and driving change in consumers' behavior. In the final analysis, it makes good business sense to pursue strategies for a sustainable world.[n]

n. Stuart L. Hart, *Beyond Greening: Strategies for a Sustainable World,* HARV. BUS. REV. (Jan.–Feb. 1997).

## THE RESPONSIBLE MANAGER

## MANAGING RISKS OF ENVIRONMENTAL LIABILITY

Several sources of potential environmental liability present risks to the parties in business transactions. In evaluating a company for purposes of acquisition, investment, or financing, a manager must consider that the company's earnings may be affected by the costs of compliance with environmental laws. The value of its equipment assets may be affected by regulatory limitations that make the equipment obsolete. Its ability to expand in existing locations may be impaired as a result of limitations on new sources of air emissions or the lack of nearby waste treatment or disposal facilities. A company's cash flow may be affected by additional capital investments or by increased operating costs necessitated by environmental regulations. Failure to comply with existing regulations may lead to the imposition of substantial penalties, also affecting cash flow. Small companies or companies that are highly leveraged may not be able to meet these additional demands for cash.

Similarly, a small company may not be able to survive the imposition of liability for response costs under CERCLA or similar state laws. Potential liabilities may not be properly reflected in the company's financial statements. Finally, a company's operations or the condition of its properties may present risks of injury to other persons and their property, giving rise to possible tort claims.

The most important element in managing the risk of these potential liabilities is *due diligence,* that is, a systematic and ongoing process for determining whether property contains or emits hazardous substances and whether the company is in compliance with environmental laws. The object of environmental due diligence investigations is to identify and characterize the risks associated with the properties and operations involved in the business transaction. Such investigations have become highly sophisticated undertakings, often requiring the use of technical consultants and legal counsel with special expertise. Although much of the effort focuses on the review of company documents and available public records, it may also involve physical inspections of the properties, including soil and groundwater sampling and analysis. Care should be taken to avoid

*(Continued)*

(The Responsible Manager *continued*)

negligent soil investigations, which can create liability for disposal of hazardous waste. Environmental due diligence may represent a significant cost of the transaction and may take much longer to complete than traditional due diligence efforts.

The scope of the due diligence effort will depend on the nature of the assets and the structure of the transaction. For example, if the transaction is a simple purchase and sale of real estate, then the due diligence can be limited to the property to be acquired and its surroundings. If the transaction involves the acquisition of a business with a long history of operations in many locations, however, then the due diligence investigation must cover not only the current operating locations but also prior operating locations and the sites used for off-site disposal of wastes. This is particularly true when a company is acquired by merger because the surviving company takes over all of the liabilities of the disappearing company.

Allocation of the risk of liability under CERCLA and other environmental laws has become a significant issue in the negotiation of business transactions. The parties can, by contract, allocate the identified risks of environmental liability by undertaking specified obligations, assuming and retaining contingent liabilities, adjusting the purchase price, making representations and warranties, giving indemnities, and the like. But care must be exercised when the identified risks are not yet quantifiable. For example, if liability for response costs is accepted in return for a reduction in the purchase price, it should be borne in mind that response costs often exceed by a wide margin the initial estimate provided by a consultant or government agency.

It is also important to remember that contractual arrangements to shift environmental liability are not binding on federal or state governments. Thus, even if the seller of a piece of property agrees to indemnify the purchaser for any environmental claims arising out of the seller's activities, the EPA can still recover response costs from the present owner. The present owner could sue the seller for indemnification and contribution, but the present owner will bear the entire cleanup cost if the previous owner is insolvent or has insufficient assets.

Under CERCLA, secured lenders, and in some cases equity investors, may be deemed liable for response costs as present operators if they participate in the day-to-day management of the borrower's facilities. If a lender takes title at foreclosure, it may also be deemed liable for response costs as a present owner unless it attempts to dispose of the property reasonably quickly. Thus, the risk of hazardous-substance releases on the subject property should be carefully evaluated in connection with the loan application. The operations of the borrower should also be carefully reviewed to evaluate the risks they present during the life of the loan. If a release of hazardous substances occurs on the property, its value as collateral is impaired. Upon default, the lender may not be able to recover the outstanding amount of the debt.

In trying to protect against diminishment of the value of collateral, a lender must be careful not to participate in management, however. Overly strict loan covenants that involve the lender in making operational decisions (such as approval of major capital expenditures) may create operator liability for the lender.

In addition, some states have adopted *superlien* provisions, which secure recovery of response costs incurred by state agencies. Where a superlien exists, it may take priority over existing security interests.

When an owner leases property, it must take care to evaluate the environmental risks of the tenant's operations. Use of the property should be carefully limited to prevent any unauthorized activities. If the tenant's activities present significant risks, financial assurances in the form of parent corporation guarantees, letters of credit, or performance bonds might be obtained to ensure that any damage caused by the tenant will be remedied. Tenants also should be cautious in taking possession of property formerly occupied by others. Many tenants perform *baseline assessments* to establish the environmental condition of the property at both the commencement and the termination of the lease. These assessments may provide some protection from liability for conditions caused by prior or succeeding tenants.

INSIDE STORY

## DREDGING UP THE HUDSON

The Hudson River, which runs through New York City, is known by locals as one of the dirtiest waterways in the area.[66] Its waters are brown or green at best. General Electric Company has been dumping its waste in the Hudson for decades. In 2001, despite GE CEO Jack Welch's strong and well-publicized political relationship with President George W. Bush, the EPA ordered GE to dredge the Hudson to clean it up after years of abuse. The cost of the cleanup is estimated at $460 million.

GE began dumping polychlorinated biphenyls, better known as PCBs, into the Hudson in the 1940s. At that time, the dumping of PCBs was legal. In 1977, GE stopped the dumping after PCBs were found to be dangerous and ultimately carcinogenic. Since the late 1970s, the river has rebounded remarkably well, with levels of PCBs in fish dropping by 90 percent.

In 1984, under the Reagan administration, the EPA agreed with GE and its scientists that the environmental benefits of dredging did not justify the economic costs. The EPA reversed its earlier decision during George H. W. Bush's administration and launched a ten-year investigation, which culminated in the controversial order.

GE has repeatedly pointed out that it did nothing illegal. It ran a massive media campaign to convince the public that the best way to heal the Hudson was to take no action at all.[67] The company claims that PCBs have fallen to acceptable levels and argues that dredging up the settled soil will only lead to spikes in levels, imposing an undue burden on its shareholders and exposing the people of the Hudson Valley to unnecessary health risks.[68]

66. This "Inside Story" is based largely on Jeffrey Kluger, *Here Comes the Dredge*, TIME (2001).
67. Associated Press, *EPA Vows to Clean Up Hudson River; GE Opposes Plan*, Dec. 6, 2000.
68. See GE's website devoted to the issue at http://www.hudsonvoice.com.

Another major problem facing the EPA is what to do with the dredged soil. Most likely, it will have to be relocated to landfills in the Hudson Valley, angering residents in whatever part of the region is saddled with the contaminated soil.

Many residents, including Representative John Sweeney of New York, violently oppose the dredging proposal. Sweeney claims that the dredging would "wreak havoc" on the affected areas and voiced his disappointment with the EPA.[69] Tim Havens, a spokesperson for CEASE (Citizen Environmentalists Against Sludge Encapsulation), stated unequivocally, "They are never going to dredge this river. We, the people of the upper Hudson River, will not let it be dredged."[70]

GE's efforts to use the courts to thwart the EPA's cleanup order got a boost in 2004 when the U.S. Court of Appeals for the D.C. Circuit ordered a trial court to hear GE's claim that the retroactive application of CERCLA to its operations was an unconstitutional violation of its right to due process.[71]

Nonetheless, EPA scientists are staunchly opposed to permitting any PCBs to remain in the river, and environmental groups hail the decision as a "triumph of public health over public relations." If the dredging of the Hudson is successful, many other large industrial companies that contributed to the destruction of some of the nation's most productive waterways may face similar suits of their own.

69. Julie Vorman, *GE Ordered to Dredge Hudson River*, REUTERS, 2001, *available at* http://espn.go.com/outdoors/fishing/news/2001/0808/1236869.html.
70. *Id.*
71. Gen. Elec. Co. v. EPA, 360 F.3d 188 (D.C. Cir. 2004).

## KEY WORDS AND PHRASES

baseline assessments 580
brownfields 564
continuity of enterprise approach 563
due diligence 579
environmental justice 569
environmental law 553
Environmental Protection Agency (EPA) 555
hazard ranking score 559

Hazardous Substance Superfund 559
industrial ecology 558
innocent landowner defense 564
innovation offsets 558
mere continuation (identity) test 563
national ambient air quality standards (NAAQS) 555
national effluent limitations 556
National Pollutant Discharge Elimination System (NPDES) 556
natural resources laws 554
navigable waters 556
potentially responsible parties (PRPs) 560
publicly owned sewage treatment works (POTWs) 556
strategic environmental management 558
substantial continuity test 562
successor liability 562
superlien 580
sustainable development 578
third-party defense 564

## QUESTIONS AND CASE PROBLEMS

1. Northeastern Pharmaceutical and Chemical Company (NEPACCO) had a manufacturing plant in Verona, Missouri, that produced various hazardous and toxic by-products. The company pumped the by-products into a holding tank, which a waste hauler periodically emptied. Michaels founded the company, was a major shareholder, and served as its president. In 1971, a waste hauler named Mills approached Ray, a chemical-plant manager employed by NEPACCO, and proposed disposing of some of the firm's wastes at a nearby farm. Ray visited the farm and, with the approval of Lee, the vice president and a shareholder of NEPACCO, arranged for disposal of wastes at the farm.

   Approximately eighty-five 55-gallon drums were dumped into a large trench on the farm. In 1976, NEPACCO was liquidated, and the assets remaining after payment to creditors were distributed to its shareholders. Three years later the EPA investigated the area and discovered dozens of badly deteriorated drums containing hazardous waste buried at the farm. The EPA took remedial action and then sought to recover its costs under RCRA and other statutes. From whom and on what basis can the government recover its costs? [*United States v. Northeastern Pharmaceutical and Chemical Co.*, 810 F.2d 726 (8th Cir. 1986), *cert. denied*, 484 U.S. 848 (1987).]

2. George Lu has been named the executive director of the Cornell University Foundation, a nonprofit association organized to support the university. As part of its efforts, the foundation has begun a program to preserve open-space land and ecologically sensitive environments near the university's campus in upstate New York. The foundation plans to buy or receive gifts of land, especially from alumni, and then sell the land to public entities for permanent preservation. The difference between the purchase price and the sale price will be used to finance the association's efforts and to support Cornell generally. One of Lu's first tasks is to develop a protocol and prepare model agreements for making acquisitions.
   a. As a nonprofit, educational organization, does the association have potential liability under the environmental laws?
   b. What procedures should Lu establish to protect the association from potential environmental law liabilities in connection with its acquisitions?
   c. What kinds of contractual arrangements should be considered to protect the association from environmental law liabilities? [*United States v. Alcan Aluminum Corp.*, 34 E.R.C. 1744 (N.D.N.Y. 1991).]

3. RCRA regulations defining solid waste state that a "solid waste is any discarded material." The EPA issued a new regulation classifying reclaimed mineral-processing materials destined for recycling as regulated "solid waste." These reclaimed materials are stored in tanks and containers before they are recycled. Industry groups representing most U.S. producers of steel, metal, and coal and most industrial miners challenged the new regulations. They argued that by allowing the materials stored before recycling to be considered waste, the rule conflicts with RCRA's definition of waste as discarded materials. How should the court rule? [*Ass'n of Battery Recyclers v. EPA*, 208 F.3d 1047 (D.C. Cir. 2000).]

4. The City of Florence, a municipal corporation organized under the laws of Alabama, purchased property for the purpose of encouraging industrial development within the county where the city is located. Florence leased the property to Stylon, a corporation that planned to construct and operate a ceramic tile manufacturing factory on the property. Florence issued bonds to finance the purchase of the property and mortgaged the property to First National Bank of Florence, pledging that Stylon's rent payments for the property would be used to secure the repayment on the bonds held by the bank.

Stylon operated a tile manufacturing facility on the property for approximately twenty years until it went bankrupt. During that time, it discharged hazardous substances, which contaminated the property. After Stylon went bankrupt, Monarch Tile, Inc. leased the property for fifteen years from the City of Florence, with the city retaining title. Subsequently, Monarch purchased the property from the city.

After Monarch discovered the contamination, it notified the EPA and was directed to remediate pursuant to CERCLA. Monarch brought suit against the City of Florence for contribution under CERCLA. The City of Florence argued that it was not liable because it held ownership of the property primarily to protect its security interest. How should the court rule? Should the National Bank of Florence or the former Stylon shareholders be forced to contribute to the cost of remediation? [*Monarch Tile Inc. v. City of Florence*, 212 F.3d 1219 (11th Cir. 2000).]

5. Johanna Landing has been hired by Newco Corporation to identify possible sites for construction of a major new manufacturing facility. Newco's operations will involve the production of substantial quantities of hazardous waste and constitute a major new source of air emissions.
   a. How will these facts affect Landing's consideration of possible construction sites?
   b. How will these facts and the location affect Newco's analysis of its costs of construction and operation?

6. Gregg Entrepreneur is organizing a small company to manufacture a new biotechnology product. Entrepreneur will be a principal shareholder and president of the company. What measures should Entrepreneur take to ensure that his company operates in compliance with environmental laws?

   Despite all the measures Entrepreneur has taken to ensure environmental law compliance, his vice president of operations reports that the production manager has been disposing of wastes into the sewer in violation of national pretreatment standards and that she has been submitting false reports to the publicly owned sewage treatment works (POTW) to cover up the violations. All of the reports have been signed by the vice president of operations, who had no knowledge that they contained false statements. What steps should Entrepreneur take? Should he report the violations to the POTW even if it could result in personal civil or criminal liability? What about the vice president? The production manager? What is Entrepreneur's ethical responsibility? [*United States v. Alley*, 755 F. Supp. 771 (N.D. Ill. 1990).]

7. A Colorado silver mine was owned by a company that went bankrupt. The three main creditors of the bankrupt firm formed the Raytheon Mine Company (RMI) as part of the plan of reorganization. RMI ran and operated the mine and gave each creditor a percentage of its stock commensurate with the original bankrupt company. Biller Company was one such minor creditor and never owned more than 20 percent of RMI. Years after the money owed Biller Company was repaid and Biller had sold its interest in the mine, the government assessed serious environmental cleanup costs under CERCLA. Biller's former partners in RMI brought a claim for contribution against Biller as a successor in interest to the tainted land to recover part of the cleanup costs. Will their claim be successful? [*Raytheon Construction Inc. v. Asarco Inc.*, 368 F.3d 1214 (10th Cir. 2003).]

8. In 1971, the owners of a landfill leased it to a predecessor of Browning-Ferris Industries, which operated it until 1975. Between 1975 and 1988, M.I.G. Investments, Inc. and AAA Disposal Systems, Inc. operated the landfill. Richard Ter Maat was the president and principal shareholder of these two corporations. In 1988, Ter Maat sold AAA and moved to Florida. M.I.G., an Illinois corporation, abandoned the site without properly covering it. M.I.G. had operated with little capital and, as a result, did not have funds to cover the landfill. Should Ter Maat be held individually liable for his actions? Or will the corporate veil shield him from personal liability? [*Browning-Ferris Industries of Illinois v. Ter Maat*, 195 F.3d 953 (7th Cir. 1999), *cert. denied*, 529 U.S. 1098 (2000); *United States v. Bestfoods*, 524 U.S. 51 (1998).]

9. In 1979, IBC Manufacturing Company purchased all of the outstanding stock of Chemwood Corporation. Chemwood had operated a wood-preservative blending site in Arlington, Tennessee, until 1976, three years before it was purchased by IBC. After IBC purchased it, Chemwood continued doing business at other locations until 1988, when it shut down. At that time, Chemwood's net worth was $282,000 in accounts receivables, primarily due from its parent corporation IBC. In 1983, the EPA began investigating contamination at the Arlington site. In 1993, the EPA ordered Chemwood to clean up the site. Chemwood agreed to contribute money for the cleanup, but by 1995, its assets were so depleted that it could no longer contribute to the remediation costs. IBC sought a court order declaring that it was

not liable for the costs to remediate the Arlington site. How should the court rule? [*IBC Manufacturing Co. v. Velsicol Chemical Corp.*, 187 F.3d 635 (6th Cir. 1999).]

### MANAGER'S DILEMMA

**10.** American Widgets is a manufacturing company that has gained a large share of the international widget market, largely because of its high quality and competitive pricing. The disposal of the company's wastes has become increasingly expensive, however. A new ban on land disposal will require the company to incinerate one of its largest waste streams. Plants of competitors located in Southeast Asia and South America are subject to increasing environmental regulation modeled after the laws in the United States, but they are not subject to a land-disposal ban and will have a significant competitive advantage over plants located in the United States. Jimmy Tsai, an American Widgets manager, is considering the possibility of locating a new plant in Southeast Asia. What factors should he take into account? What alternatives are there besides relocation?

## INTERNET SOURCES

| | |
|---|---|
| Environmental Protection Agency | http://www.epa.gov |
| ECHO is the EPA's website allowing virtually instant access to any company's environmental compliance records. | http://www.epa.gov/echo/ |
| The Chemical Scorecard website, developed by the Environmental Defense Fund, combines more than 150 government and university databases to allow users to locate polluters in their community, research the dangers of common household products, and compile sophisticated pollution rankings. | http://www.scorecard.org |
| This is the site for the Environmental Defense Fund, which has joined with the Pew Charitable Trusts to form the Alliance for Environmental Innovation, an organization that has worked with McDonald's, Starbucks, SC Johnson, and other large corporations to reduce the environmental impact of their operations. | http://www.edf.org |
| Sierra Club | http://www.sierraclub.org |
| The World Resources Institute website has reports and publications, including a library of business school case studies focusing on environmental issues, and information about its annual Bell Conference and other events. | http://www.wri.org |
| The World Business Council for Sustainable Development is a Geneva-based coalition of 150 international companies from thirty countries and twenty major industrial sectors (including Sony, Time Warner, Ford, and AT&T) united by a commitment to sustainable development. Its website includes publications and information about conferences addressing issues on business and the environment such as eco-efficiency. | http://www.wbcsd.org |
| The Global Environmental Management Initiative's website includes publications and tools to help companies assess and improve their environmental performance. GEMI sponsors a conference on business and environmental issues. | http://www.gemi.org |
| CERES is a U.S. coalition of environmental, investor, and advocacy groups. CERES has developed a ten-point code of environmental conduct. Its website includes information on environmental reporting. | http://www.ceres.org |
| General Electric's website provides information regarding the Hudson River Valley and PCBs. | http://www.ge.com/en/commitment/ehs/hudson/ |

CHAPTER 16

# Antitrust

## INTRODUCTION

### Firms Pay Record Fines

In 1996, the U.S. Justice Department fined Archer–Daniels–Midland (ADM—self-described "Supermarket to the World") $100 million for fixing prices in the markets for citric acid and lysine, a livestock-feed additive.[1] In 2000, the European Commission fined ADM and its four Asian co-conspirators $105 million, bringing ADM's total legal tab to more than $250 million in criminal fines and civil settlements.[2] Michael D. Andreas, former ADM executive vice president, was fined $350,000 and sentenced to three years in prison. ADM violated both U.S. and foreign *antitrust laws,* which prohibit unreasonable restraints on trade and competition, such as price-fixing among competitors, and also prohibit monopolies gained and maintained through predatory conduct.

The ADM fines were dwarfed by the $862 million fines levied in 1999 against five vitamin manufacturers (F. Hoffman-LaRoche of Switzerland, BASF AG of Germany, and Eisaid Company, Daichi Pharmaceuticals Company, and Takeda Chemical Industries Ltd. of Japan) for participating in a cartel to fix prices for wholesale vitamins. Hoffman-LaRoche alone paid a $500 million fine, the largest fine the U.S. Department of Justice had ever obtained in any criminal case. Two Swiss nationals and two German nationals, who were high-ranking officers at Hoffman-LaRoche or BASF, were sentenced to prison and fined a total of $625,000. The five companies, together with Rhone-Poulenc SA of France (which was not prosecuted because it provided key evidence against the other members of the cartel), agreed in November 1999 to pay $1.05 billion to settle the private class-action litigation brought in federal court on behalf of U.S. purchasers of vitamins and vitamin premix.[3] In November 2001, the European Union (EU) imposed record fines of 855.2 million euros against the same companies for colluding to fix the price of vitamins.[4]

The basic principle of antitrust law is that the economy functions best when firms are free to compete vigorously with one another. In a competitive economy, the consumer enjoys better goods at lower prices, or, as economists say, consumer welfare is maximized. If, however, competition is decreased or eliminated by firms seeking jointly or independently to wield monopoly power, consumers suffer and the performance of the economy declines.

Antitrust statutes contain certain very general prohibitions on business conduct. These general prohibitions often have little content until courts apply them to the particular facts of a case. Thus, bright lines that clearly separate lawful from unlawful conduct are rare in this field. A business practice that harms competition in one market setting might not harm competition in another. The courts and agencies that enforce the antitrust laws must distinguish between the pernicious and the benign.

As trade barriers continue to be broken down and the global market becomes more integrated, the antitrust laws of the major

1. Bryan Gruley, *ADM's $100 Million Price-Fixing Fine Blows Lid Off Usual Maximum Penalty,* WALL ST. J., Oct. 16, 1996, at A4.
2. Scott Kilman, *European Commission Sets ADM Fine,* WALL ST. J., June 8, 2000, at A4.
3. Harry First, *Antitrust at the Millennium (Part II): The Vitamins Case: Cartel Prosecutions and the Coming of International Competition Law,* 68 ANTITRUST L.J. 711 (2001).
4. *Vitamin Cartel Fined for Price-fixing,* THE GUARDIAN, Nov. 21, 2001, http://www.guardian.co.uk/print/0,3858,4304109,00.html.

commercial countries will need to be better harmonized or at least made more transparent through greater predictability as to which country's law applies. The EU's competition law, which is the foreign system most like the U.S. antitrust system, is quickly replacing U.S. antitrust law as the model for other countries as they develop their own competition laws.

## CHAPTER OVERVIEW

This chapter offers a general overview of the federal antitrust laws. It begins with a discussion of Sections 1 and 2 of the Sherman Act and then addresses the Clayton Act provisions relating to mergers and combinations. The chapter outlines the Robinson–Patman Act's prohibitions on price discrimination and briefly discusses the Federal Trade Commission Act. It concludes with a discussion of the extraterritorial application of the U.S. antitrust laws, the EU competition laws, and the extraterritorial effect of the EU laws.

# Agreements in Restraint of Trade: Section 1 of the Sherman Act

Section 1 of the Sherman Act provides that "[e]very contract, combination in the form of trust or otherwise, or conspiracy, in restraint of trade or commerce among the several States, or with foreign nations, is declared to be illegal."[5] On its face, Section 1 appears to prohibit all concerted activity that restrains trade. Yet almost every business transaction, even a contract for the purchase of goods or services, restrains trade to a certain extent. A contract, for example, restrains the parties from doing things that would constitute a breach, such as selling goods to someone else. Read literally, Section 1 would outlaw every type of business transaction involving more than one party. In order to avoid an unworkable construction of the Sherman Act, the courts have construed Section 1 to prohibit only those restraints of trade that *unreasonably* restrict competition.

## TRADE AND COMMERCE

The Sherman Act applies only to "trade or commerce" among states or with foreign nations. The phrase "commerce among the several States" extends the reach of the Act as far as constitutionally allowed under the Commerce Clause.[6] The resulting scope of antitrust jurisdiction therefore encompasses more than restraints on trade that are motivated by a desire to limit interstate commerce or that have their sole impact on interstate commerce. The commerce requirement is satisfied when the defendant's conduct (1) directly interferes with the flow of goods in the stream of commerce or (2) has a substantial effect on interstate commerce.

In 1997, a fraternity at Hamilton College in New York argued that the school's new policy of requiring all students to live in college-owned facilities and to purchase college-sponsored meal plans was an attempt to monopolize the housing and dining markets in that area, in violation of Section 2 of the Sherman Act (discussed below). Although the fraternity alleged substantial effects on interstate commerce, including Hamilton's out-of-state student population (56 percent) and its annual revenue for room and board from those students ($4 million), the district court dismissed the complaint on the grounds that the provision of residential services did not involve "trade or commerce." The appeals court reversed the dismissal, however, and ruled that such a question was suitable for trial.[7]

## PROVING A VIOLATION OF SECTION 1

For liability to attach under Section 1, a plaintiff must demonstrate that (1) there is a contract, combination, or conspiracy among separate entities; (2) it unreasonably restrains trade; (3) it affects interstate or foreign commerce; and (4) it causes an antitrust injury (the concept of antitrust injury is addressed later in this chapter).

## WHAT CONSTITUTES A CONTRACT, COMBINATION, OR CONSPIRACY?

Section 1 does not prohibit unilateral activity in restraint of trade. Acting by itself, an individual or firm may take any action, no matter how anticompetitive, and not violate Section 1. (In contrast, Section 2 of the Sherman Act, discussed later in this chapter, does prohibit some forms of unilateral conduct.)

This threshold requirement of concerted action is one of the most frequently litigated issues in antitrust cases. In 1984, the Supreme Court ruled that a parent corporation and its wholly owned subsidiary cannot "agree"

5. 15 U.S.C. § 1.

6. Summit Health, Ltd. v. Pinhas, 500 U.S. 322, 329 n.10 (1991).

7. Hamilton Chapter of Alpha Delta Phi, Inc. v. Hamilton Coll., 128 F.3d 59 (2d Cir. 1997).

## HISTORICAL PERSPECTIVE

# POLITICS AND ECONOMICS

The first U.S. antitrust law, the Sherman Act, was passed by Congress in 1890 as fear of corporate power grew during the Progressive Era. The Sherman Act was part of a populist movement to combat the rise of trusts in such basic industries as oil and steel. The *trusts* were powerful associations of companies with the intention and power to create a monopoly or otherwise interfere with the free course of trade. "You must heed [the voters'] appeal or be ready for the socialist, the communist, and the nihilist," Senator John Sherman declared during the debate over his bill. The Sherman Act's general prohibitions have evolved over the past hundred years through judicial decisions. This rather ad hoc development of the law has led to some seemingly confused results. For example, business practices forbidden by the Sherman Act in the early twentieth century are often permissible in today's changed economic environment.

More than a century after the enactment of the Sherman Act, the United States finds itself in the midst of a world economy in which firms in many industries compete on an international scale. Often the United States is no longer the dominant economic power. In this changed environment, a new generation of academics, lawyers, and judges has challenged their predecessors' conclusions that certain business practices or market conditions are inherently anticompetitive. This school of thought, known as the Chicago School, concludes that market forces defeat most anticompetitive practices. Its proponents question the efficacy of the government's regulation of commerce and markets, arguing that instead of promoting competition, attempts at regulation often decrease the competitiveness of markets.

As economics continues to inform legal decisions and market-based arguments are made and refined, antitrust law continues to evolve. To many, this evolutionary process is antitrust's greatest strength and the reason it has entered its second century.

within the concerted-action requirement of Section 1.[8] Whether a parent corporation and a less than wholly owned subsidiary can impermissibly agree remains an open issue.

Conspiracies are inherently secretive. Most price-fixers do not keep minutes of their meetings or send confirming letters. Consequently, requiring direct proof of a conspiracy would likely permit many companies that engage in these activities to escape Section 1 liability. On the other hand, because unilateral behavior is not a violation, courts must be careful in relaxing the requirement that conspiracy be proved. Courts have struggled to develop mechanisms that allow lawsuits under Section 1 to go forward without direct proof of a conspiracy or agreement while ensuring that defendants are not subjected to meritless lawsuits.

One such mechanism is the distinction between horizontal and vertical agreements. *Horizontal agreements* are those between firms that directly compete with each other, such as retailers selling the same range of products. *Vertical agreements* are those between firms at different levels of production or distribution, such as a retailer and its supplier.

### Proving a Horizontal Conspiracy

Because an agreement between horizontal competitors, such as Ford Motor Company and General Motors, almost invariably reduces interbrand competition, such agreements are generally disfavored under the antitrust laws. *Interbrand competition* is competition between companies producing the same type of product.

The classic definition of conspiracy, whether horizontal or vertical, focuses on whether the alleged conspirators had a meeting of the minds in a scheme that violates the law. The courts will not require evidence of an explicit agreement to violate the law. As the U.S. Court of Appeals for the Ninth Circuit stated with respect to a horizontal conspiracy, a "knowing wink can mean more than words."[9]

Plaintiffs often attempt to infer a horizontal conspiracy from evidence of parallel behavior by ostensibly independent firms, for example, by showing that they consistently

8. Copperweld Corp. v. Independence Tube Corp., 467 U.S. 752 (1984).

9. Esco Corp. v. United States, 340 F.2d 1000, 1007 (9th Cir. 1965).

## IN BRIEF

### Major Areas of Antitrust Concern

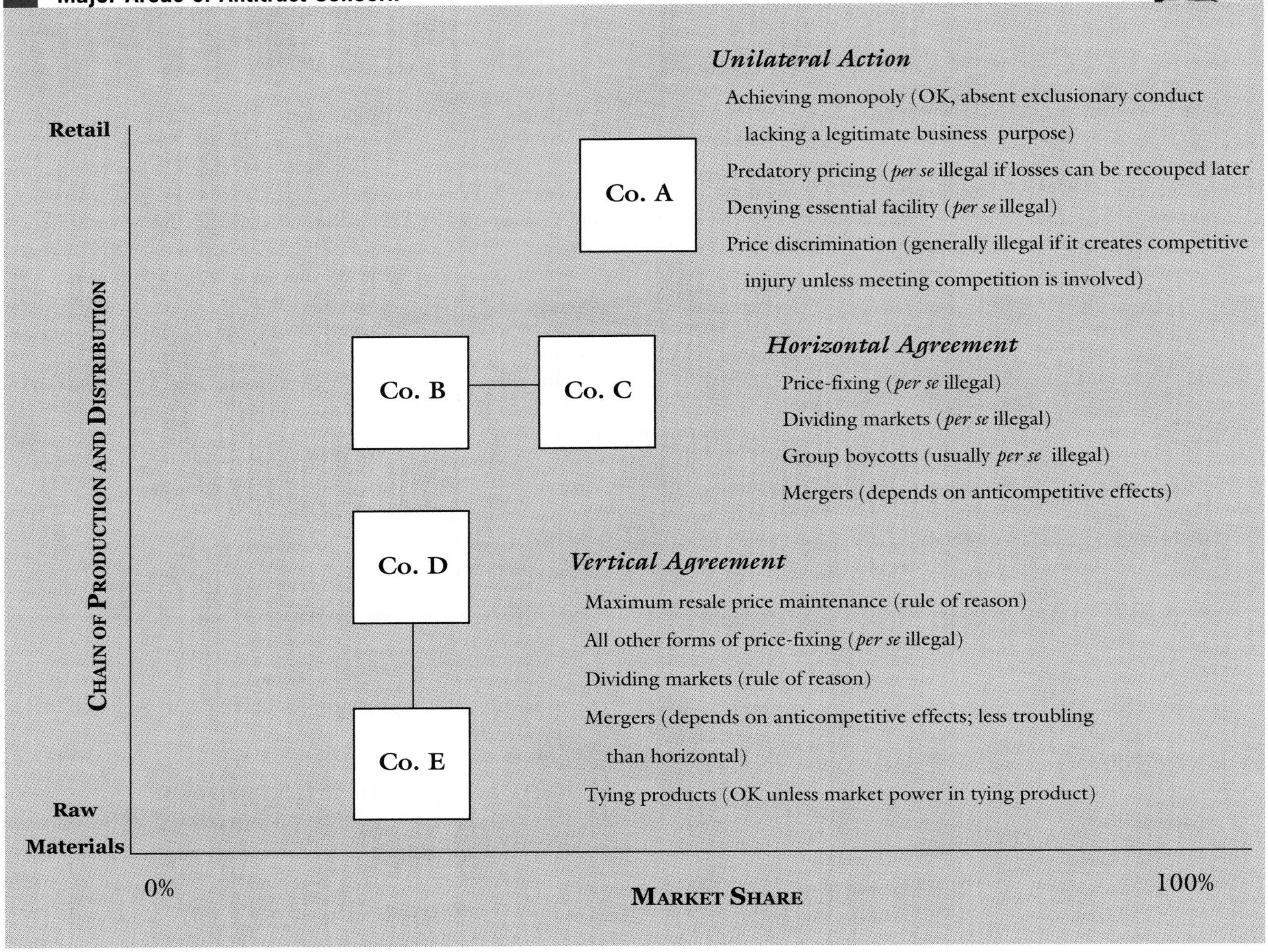

***Unilateral Action***

Achieving monopoly (OK, absent exclusionary conduct lacking a legitimate business purpose)

Predatory pricing (*per se* illegal if losses can be recouped later

Denying essential facility (*per se* illegal)

Price discrimination (generally illegal if it creates competitive injury unless meeting competition is involved)

***Horizontal Agreement***

Price-fixing (*per se* illegal)

Dividing markets (*per se* illegal)

Group boycotts (usually *per se* illegal)

Mergers (depends on anticompetitive effects)

***Vertical Agreement***

Maximum resale price maintenance (rule of reason)

All other forms of price-fixing (*per se* illegal)

Dividing markets (rule of reason)

Mergers (depends on anticompetitive effects; less troubling than horizontal)

Tying products (OK unless market power in tying product)

Retail

Co. A

Co. B — Co. C

Co. D | Co. E

CHAIN OF PRODUCTION AND DISTRIBUTION

Raw Materials

0%

MARKET SHARE

100%

set prices at the same levels and change prices at the same time *(conscious parallelism)*. The problem with this type of evidence (particularly when a homogeneous product or service is involved) is that it is ambiguous as an indicator of anticompetitive behavior. Parallel pricing of similar products or services can result either from illegal price-fixing or from vigorous competition.

The courts will not infer an agreement or conspiracy from parallel behavior unless the plaintiff shows additional facts or "plus factors." Parallel behavior that would appear to be contrary to the economic interests of the defendants, were they acting independently, supports an inference of conspiracy.[10] On the other hand, if the defendants can produce reasonable business explanations

### ETHICAL CONSIDERATION

You work in sales and are friendly with a sales representative from one of your employer's competitors. Your children are in the same class at school, so you see each other frequently. Recently, you talked about a new sales promotion that your company is offering. The promotion was the subject of an advertisement in the trade magazines. Is it ethical to have such a conversation?

10. Theatre Enters., Inc. v. Paramount Film Distrib. Corp., 346 U.S. 537 (1954).

for the behavior, a court will not infer a conspiracy. Other *circumstantial,* or indirect, *evidence* of an agreement, such as a meeting between two defendants, may be a plus factor. Increasing prices and persistent profits despite a decline in demand for the good or service may also be plus factors.

In the following case, the court considered whether tobacco companies had conspired to fix prices.

A CASE IN POINT

## In the Language of the Court

**CASE 16.1**

**Williamson Oil Co. v. Philip Morris USA**

*United States Court of Appeals for the Eleventh Circuit 346 F.3d 1287 (11th Cir. 2003).*

**› FACTS** Between 1993 and 2000, Philip Morris (PM), R.J. Reynolds (RJR), Brown & Williamson (B&W), and Lorillard (the manufacturers) produced more than 97 percent of the cigarettes sold in the United States. During the early 1990s, as a price gap widened between premium brands, such as Marlboro and Camel, and discount brands, such as Basic and Doral, some "premium smokers" began to shift to nonpremium brands. By 1993 nonpremium brands had captured over 40 percent of the U.S. market. Although this trend benefited RJR and B&W, it was undesirable for premium-intensive manufacturers, such as PM and Lorillard. PM then began to look for ways to reverse the trend toward discount cigarettes. In 1993, PM announced that it was cutting the retail price of Marlboro cigarettes, the single best-selling brand in America, by $.40 per pack and forgoing price increases on other premium brands "for the foreseeable future." This price cut was followed by price cuts to PM's other premium brands. PM's price cuts set off a price war, as RJR, B&W, and Lorillard matched PM's retail price reductions, which cut into the market share held by the discount brands.

Subsequently, however, RJR announced that it would no longer sacrifice profitability for market share and increased the price of its premium and discount brands. The other manufacturers matched the increase within a couple of weeks. Eleven more parallel increases occurred between May 1995 and January 2000.

A class of several hundred cigarette wholesalers sued the manufacturers, alleging that they had conspired between 1993 and 2000 to fix cigarette prices at unnaturally high levels, which resulted in wholesale list price overcharges of nearly $12 billion. The district court entered summary judgment in favor of the manufacturers after concluding that the wholesalers had failed to demonstrate the existence of a "plus factor." The court went on to state that even if the class had shown that a plus factor was present, the manufacturers had rebutted the inference of collusion because the economic realities of the 1990s cigarette market made the class's conspiracy theory untenable. The district court characterized the manufacturers' pricing behavior as nothing more than "conscious parallelism," a perfectly legal phenomenon often associated with oligopolistic industries. The wholesalers appealed.

**› ISSUE PRESENTED** What types of conduct may constitute "plus factors" necessary to create an inference of a price-fixing conspiracy?

**› OPINION** MARCUS, J., writing for the U.S. Court of Appeals for the Eleventh Circuit:

. . . "[T]he distinctive characteristic of oligopoly is recognized interdependence among the leading firms: the profit-maximizing choice of price and output for one depends on the choices made by others."

When they are the product of a rational, independent calculus by each member of the oligopoly, as opposed to collusion, these types of synchronous actions have become known as "conscious parallelism." The Court has defined this phenomenon

*(Continued)*

(Case 16.1 *continued*)

as "the process, not in itself unlawful, by which firms in a concentrated market might in effect share monopoly power, setting their prices at a profit-maximizing, supra-competitive level by recognizing their shared economic interests and their interdependence with respect to price and output decisions." . . .

. . .

As numerous courts have recognized, it often is difficult to determine which of these situations—illegal price fixing or conscious parallelism—is present in a given case. . . .

. . .

. . . [P]rice fixing plaintiffs are relegated to relying on indirect means of proof. The problem with this reliance on circumstantial evidence, however, is that such evidence is by its nature ambiguous, and necessarily requires the drawing of one or more inferences in order to substantiate claims of illegal conspiracy. . . .

. . .

. . . "[T]o survive a motion for summary judgment . . . a plaintiff seeking damages for [collusive price-fixing] . . . must present evidence that tends to exclude the possibility that the alleged conspirators acted independently." Evidence that does not support the existence of a price fixing conspiracy any more strongly than it supports conscious parallelism is insufficient to survive a defendant's summary judgment motion. . . .

. . .

In applying these principles, we have fashioned a test under which price fixing plaintiffs must demonstrate the existence of "plus factors" that remove their evidence from the realm of equipoise and render that evidence more probative of conspiracy than of conscious parallelism. . . .

. . .

. . . [T]he district court delineated . . . distinct factors that appellants had denominated "plus factors." These are: "(1) signaling of intentions; (2) permanent allocations programs; (3) monitoring of sales; (4) actions taken contrary to economic self-interest." . . .

. . . [W]e are satisfied that none of the actions on which appellants' arguments are based rise to the level of plus factors. . . . Indeed, when all of appellees' actions are considered together, the class has established nothing more than that the tobacco industry is a classic oligopoly, replete with consciously parallel pricing behavior, and that its members act as such.

**› RESULT** The appeals court affirmed the district court's grant of summary judgment for the defendants. The suit was dismissed.

**› COMMENTS** This case supports the strategy of "price leadership," whereby a firm with significant market share publicly announces its pricing policy, which other competitors elect to follow. As long as there is no explicit or implied agreement to act in concert, price leadership has withstood judicial scrutiny.

**› CRITICAL THINKING QUESTIONS**

1. The court stated that the plaintiffs in this case simply proved that the defendants acted as rational oligopolists. What sort of evidence would establish that the defendants actually were engaging in an illegal price-fixing scheme?
2. The court recognized that there are economic costs associated with using circumstantial evidence to distinguish between lawful conscious parallel decision making within an oligopoly and illegal collusive price-fixing. What are some of these economic costs?

### *Proving a Vertical Conspiracy*

Vertical agreements, such as those between an automaker and its local dealers, may reduce *intrabrand competition,* that is, price competition between local dealers selling the same manufacturer's products. But they often enhance interbrand competition, that is, competition between dealers selling different manufacturers' products. It is in the best interests of both the automaker and its dealers to provide the most marketable product so as to receive the greatest possible share of available consumer dollars. Courts look more favorably on reductions in intrabrand competition when there is vigorous interbrand competition that can prevent the reduction in intrabrand competition from harming consumers.

Since the mid-1980s, the courts have generally been unwilling to allow proof of vertical conspiracies by circumstantial evidence alone. The Supreme Court has held that firms in a vertical arrangement, unlike competitors, have many legitimate reasons to communicate with each other. Therefore, a plaintiff seeking to prove an unlawful conspiracy must introduce evidence that tends to exclude the possibility that the firms acted independently.[11] Evidence of action that could be either concerted or independent is insufficient to prove a Section 1 violation under this test.

## What Constitutes an Unreasonable Restraint of Trade?

There are two approaches to analyzing the reasonableness of a restraint: the *per se* rule and the rule of reason.

### Per se *Violations*

*Per se analysis* condemns practices that are considered completely void of redeeming competitive rationales. This is appropriate when the practice always or almost always tends to restrict competition and decrease output. Once identified as *illegal per se,* a practice will not be examined further for its impact on the market, and its procompetitive justifications will not be considered.

Scholars from the Chicago School have argued that very few practices are inherently anticompetitive. As many courts have accepted this scholarship, the number of truly *per se* violations of the antitrust laws has declined.

### *The Rule of Reason*

If the plaintiff has not proved a *per se* violation, the activity will be evaluated under the *rule of reason.* The objective of this rule is to determine whether, on balance, the activity promotes or restrains competition or, to put it differently, helps or harms consumers. In making this determination, the court will consider the structure of the market as well as the defendant's actions. The court will analyze the anticompetitive and procompetitive effects of the challenged practice. Activity that has a substantial net anticompetitive effect is deemed an unreasonable restraint of trade and is unlawful.

11. Monsanto Co. v. Spray-Rite Serv. Corp., 465 U.S. 752 (1984).

## Types of Horizontal Restraints

Restraints between direct competitors include price-fixing, market division, and some kinds of group boycotts. These horizontal restraints have traditionally been treated as *per se* violations of Section 1 of the Sherman Act. Trade associations may also be found to be acting unlawfully under the rule of reason in some circumstances.

Some products, such as sporting events, may require horizontal restraints in order to exist at all. Economists suggest that a sporting league comprising the different teams (such as the National Football League) should be viewed as a single firm in the business of providing competition. As a result, constraints on teams are simply attempts to put "departments" within the firm on an equal footing so that customers can enjoy balanced contests among them. Courts take a more formalistic view but make allowances for the needed horizontal constraints.

### *Horizontal Price-Fixing*

*Horizontal price-fixing,* such as an agreement between retailers to set a common price for a product, is the classic example of a *per se* violation of Section 1. Horizontal price-fixing agreements include (1) setting prices (including maximum prices); (2) setting the terms of sale, such as customer credit terms; (3) setting the quantity or quality of goods to be manufactured or made available for sale; or (4) rigging bids (agreements between or among competitors to fix contract bids).

The Justice Department views horizontal price-fixing as "hard crime," to be punished by prison sentences whenever possible. Many executives have been imprisoned for price-fixing. Indeed, under the Federal Sentencing Guidelines, some term of confinement is recommended for individuals convicted of horizontal price-fixing, bid rigging, or market-allocation agreements; in most cases, first-time offenders serve a minimum six- to twelve-month sentence.

Multimillion-dollar fines against corporations convicted of price-fixing are the rule rather than the exception. But civil actions, in particular class actions (which inevitably follow criminal prosecutions), can have even

INTERNATIONAL SNAPSHOT

During the 1990s, the world's leading auction houses, Christie's International PLC and Sotheby's Holding, colluded to set identical sliding-scale fee commission structures. Christie's and Sotheby's agreed to pay $537 million to settle civil suits by former buyers and sellers in the United States. The U.S. Justice Department fined Sotheby's $45 million, and the EU fined Sotheby's more than 20 million euros for operating the price-fixing cartel, but Christie's escaped criminal liability in both government proceedings because it was the first to come forward with information about the illegal activities.[a] Alfred Taubman, Sotheby's former chairman, was jailed for one year and fined another $7.5 million for his involvement in the scheme. Although the former chairman of Christie's, Sir Anthony J. Tennant, was indicted in May 2001 in the U.S. District Court for the Southern District of New York, Tennant refused to appear, prompting the judge to issue a bench warrant for his arrest.[b] Since that time, however, Tennant, an English citizen, has avoided prosecution by remaining in Britain, where only companies, not individuals, can be charged with price-fixing, and antitrust violations are not extraditable offenses.

**a.** *Sotheby's Fined £13m for Price-fixing,* BBC NEWS WORLD EDITION, Oct. 30, 2002.
**b.** *Sotheby's Ex-Chief Pleads Not Guilty,* N.Y. TIMES, May 5, 2001, at B12.

more drastic financial consequences. Liability for antitrust damages is joint and several among all of the conspirators, so each conspirator is potentially liable for treble damages for the losses caused by all of the defendants.

## *Horizontal Market Division and Nonprice Horizontal Restraints*

The U.S. Supreme Court considers market divisions so inherently anticompetitive as to constitute *per se* violations of Section 1. *Horizontal market division* can take various forms. For instance, competitors might divide up a market by class of customer or geographic territory or by restricting product output. In 1972, the Supreme Court considered the legality of an agreement among members of an association of supermarket chains to divide the grocery market.[12] The association's members, twenty-five small- and medium-sized independent supermarket chains, each agreed to sell a particular trademarked brand only in an assigned area. They also agreed not to sell the brand's products to other retailers. Although the association argued that exclusive territories were necessary to encourage local advertising of the fledgling brand, the Court ruled that market division is prohibited even if it is intended to enable small competitors to compete with larger companies and to foster interbrand competition. More recently, the Supreme Court has emphasized that horizontal market division by potential as well as actual competitors is *per se* illegal.[13]

Horizontal agreements among competitors not to compete on nonprice matters may also violate Section 1. For example, in the mid-1990s, as the volume of air travel grew, passengers increasingly tried to avoid checking luggage and began to carry more and more baggage onto commercial flights. United Airlines and a number of other airlines responded to the increase in carry-on baggage in various ways, including the use of baggage templates.[14] Continental Airlines rejected this approach, however, and opted instead to spend approximately $15 million to expand its overhead bins and provide more equipment and employees so that passengers could carry on or gate-check as much luggage as they wished. In late 1998, United sought to install templates at Dulles Airport but encountered a problem because Dulles is configured so that passengers for all airlines must use one of two common security checkpoints.[15] The airlines that serve Dulles are members of the Dulles Airport Airline Management Council (AMC), an unincorporated association mandated by the Federal Aviation Administration, which holds monthly meetings to resolve operating issues that affect more than one carrier at Dulles, including the installation, maintenance, and management of security checkpoints. When the AMC agreed to allow United to install templates on the X-ray screening devices at the Dulles security checkpoints to restrict the size of carry-on bags, Continental filed a lawsuit against United and the AMC, claiming that this agreement was a naked restraint on Continental's ability to engage in nonprice competition on the basis of carry-on luggage capacity. Continental argued that the agreement to restrict the size of carry-on bags had been adopted at the urging of United, which was the dominant carrier at Dulles and in charge of operating security checkpoints. Although the trial court ruled that the program consti-

12. United States v. Topco Assocs., Inc., 405 U.S. 596 (1972).

13. Palmer v. BRG of Ga., Inc., 498 U.S. 46 (1990).
14. Baggage templates are pieces of plastic or stainless steel, mounted on hinges, that cover the mouths of X-ray baggage screening machines. When the templates are down, they narrow the mouth of the machine, preventing oversize baggage from passing through.
15. Most other airports are configured so that airlines either have their own security checkpoints or share a checkpoint with at most only a few other airlines.

tuted a horizontal restraint on output with "manifest" anticompetitive impact and granted summary judgment in favor of Continental, the U.S. Court of Appeals for the Fourth Circuit subsequently vacated the judgment on the basis that the case should have been evaluated under the rule of reason analysis. The case was remanded to the trial court for further proceedings.[16]

## *Group Boycotts*

It is a fundamental principle of liberty and freedom of contract that an individual may choose to do business with whomever he or she wants. Nevertheless, an agreement among competitors to refuse to deal with another competitor—a *group boycott*—has traditionally been treated as a *per se* violation of Section 1. An agreement between or among competitors that deprives another competitor of something it needs to compete effectively is considered so inherently anticompetitive that no economic motivation for the action may be offered as a defense.

For example, the U.S. Supreme Court held that manufacturers of appliances could not agree with a distributor's competitors to refrain from selling to the distributor or to do so only at higher prices. Such an agreement was treated as a *per se* violation of Section 1 even though there was no agreement on the exact price, quantity, or quality of the appliances to be sold.[17]

More recently, the Supreme Court has begun to distinguish some forms of group boycotts that it believes are not so inherently anticompetitive as to merit *per se* treatment. In 1985, the Court refused to apply the *per se* rule when a wholesale purchasing cooperative of office-supply retailers expelled a member for violating a cooperative bylaw requiring notification of changes in ownership. The Court noted that there was no showing that the cooperative possessed market power or unique access to a business element necessary for effective competition.[18] (The concept of market power is addressed later in this chapter.) Applying the rule of reason analysis instead, the Court concluded that the decision of the cooperative members to expel the plaintiff was not an unreasonable restraint because cooperatives need to establish and enforce reasonable rules in order to function effectively. Furthermore, the expulsion did not completely exclude the plaintiff from access to the cooperative's wholesale operations.

16. Cont'l Airlines, Inc. v. United Airlines, Inc., 277 F.3d 499 (4th Cir. 2002).

17. Klor's, Inc. v. Broadway–Hale Stores, Inc., 359 U.S. 207 (1959).

18. Northwest Wholesale Stationers, Inc. v. Pacific Stationery & Printing Co., 472 U.S. 284 (1985).

**Trade Associations** Courts often do not look favorably upon attempts at self-regulation by trade and professional associations, particularly when such attempts result in group boycotts. For example, the U.S. Supreme Court struck down as a violation of the Sherman Act a minimum fee schedule for lawyers that was published by a county bar association and enforced through the prospect of professional discipline from the Virginia State Bar Association.[19]

Other types of self-regulation, however, will be upheld under the rule of reason if the presumptive economic benefits outweigh any potential economic harm. For example, the California Dental Association (CDA) adopted a code of ethics that included a section prohibiting dentists from soliciting patients with any false or misleading communication. The guidelines forbade advertising that referred to "low" or "reasonable" prices, offered volume discounts, or made any claims about quality of service, ostensibly because such statements could mislead consumers by implying unverifiable superiority over other dentists' services.

The U.S. Court of Appeals for the Ninth Circuit initially held that the CDA had violated Section 5 of the Federal Trade Commission Act because it prevented its members from engaging in truthful, nonmisleading advertising offering discounts or claims about service quality, but the U.S. Supreme Court held that the Ninth Circuit had erred by engaging in a *"quick look,"* or abbreviated, *rule of reason analysis* that failed to consider a number of theories under which the CDA restrictions on advertising might prove procompetitive. On remand, the Ninth Circuit found no antitrust violation, pointing out several ways in which the CDA's guidelines would have a net procompetitive effect: (1) the guidelines required dentists to disclose their regular and discounted rates, thereby allowing a price-conscious consumer to determine from the ads which dentist actually offered a lower fee; (2) restricting advertising in the dental market, where there is strong customer loyalty, was less detrimental than restricting advertising in markets where consumers are much more likely to switch brands; and (3) the restrictions did not amount to a complete ban on advertising.[20]

Trade and professional associations often disseminate information among their members. Association agreements rarely state goals that violate the Sherman Act, so courts must draw inferences about the probable effects of the information exchanged. Courts will consider the

19. Goldfarb v. Va. State Bar, 421 U.S. 773 (1975).

20. Cal. Dental Ass'n v. FTC, 224 F.3d 942 (9th Cir. 2000).

structure of the market and the type and timeliness of the information exchanged to ensure that the exchange of information does not facilitate anticompetitive behavior, such as price-fixing or market division.

A large *cartel,* or group of competitors that agrees to do something, is inherently unstable. Conversely, when a market has few competitors, they are more likely to be able to reach and enforce an agreement. Therefore, the more concentrated the industry, the more closely courts will scrutinize trade-association activity.

The type of information exchanged also plays a critical role in the analysis. For example, a weekly report disseminated by a hardwood manufacturers' trade association listed the names of companies that sold lumber and the prices at which they sold it. Additionally, monthly reports discussed future price trends and provided future estimates of production. The Supreme Court held that this exchange of information violated Section 1 of the Sherman Act, as members could use the information to police secret agreements setting uniform prices or terms.[21] Another manufacturers' association disseminated information on average costs and the terms of past transactions. It did not identify individual sellers or buyers and did not discuss future pricing. The Supreme Court found no violation of Section 1.[22]

Information that does not involve prices or terms of sale receives less scrutiny by the courts. Activities such as cooperative industrial research, market surveys, and joint advertising concerning the industry have been upheld. The exchange of information concerning contractors whose payments were two months in arrears was upheld as a reasonable way to help members avoid contractor fraud.[23]

The Supreme Court has recognized that standards-making activities by trade associations are generally procompetitive.[24] The availability of compatible products from different manufacturers can increase competition and make it easier for buyers to compare products. For example, DVD manufacturers compete only on price and features because all players will accept all DVDs. Standards also make it easier to introduce complementary new technologies by reducing buyers' concern that they will be left with incompatible products.

Companies with existing technologies, however, can also misuse standards in a way that stifles competition. For example, the U.S. Supreme Court found that the vice president of the dominant manufacturer of a safety device for heating boilers, who was also vice chairman of a trade association subcommittee that promulgated the standards for this device, had conspired with other members of the subcommittee to misrepresent the standards in order to discourage customers from buying a new manufacturer's products.[25]

Industry standards may also give rise to antitrust claims if they are structured to favor a specific company or technology. The Open Software Foundation (OSF) was formed in 1988 by eight computer manufacturers, including many of the major competitors in the market for computer systems, which competed with each other in two separate markets: (1) the purchasing of systems technology for independent developers, and (2) the sale of finished systems in the downstream market for operating systems. The OSF developed its first operating system, OS-1, by fusing existing technology through a competitive bidding process. When an OSF panel selected another vendor for the security program for OS-1, Addamax filed a lawsuit alleging that the entire OSF concept was an illegal buyers' cartel, designed to influence the market for operating systems technology. Although the district court found that the joint venture did not warrant *per se* scrutiny because joint purchasing agreements often produce legitimate economies of scale, it also found that Addamax had raised genuine issues of fact, which entitled it to further pursue its claims under a rule of reason analysis.[26]

## TYPES OF VERTICAL RESTRAINTS

Unlawful *vertical restraints,* that is, restraints between firms at different levels in the chain of distribution, include price-fixing, market division, tying arrangements, and some franchise agreements.

### *Vertical Price-Fixing*

Agreements on price between firms at different levels of production or distribution can be as anticompetitive as agreements between direct competitors at the same level of production or distribution. *Resale price maintenance (RPM),* an agreement that fixes minimum prices, is illegal *per se.*[27] RPM agreements have been challenged by

21. Am. Column & Lumber Co. v. United States, 257 U.S. 377 (1921).
22. Maple Flooring Mfrs. Ass'n v. United States, 268 U.S. 563 (1925).
23. Cement Mfrs. Protective Ass'n v. United States, 268 U.S. 588 (1925).
24. Radiant Burners v. Peoples Gas Co., 364 U.S. 656 (1961).
25. Am. Soc'y of Mech. Eng'rs v. Hydrolevel Corp., 456 U.S. 556 (1982).
26. Addamax Corp. v. Open Software Found., Inc., 888 F. Supp. 274 (D. Mass. 1995).
27. Dr. Miles Med. Co. v. John D. Park & Sons Co., 220 U.S. 373 (1911).

consumers claiming overcharges, by competitors claiming loss of sales, and by dealers or retailers terminated by the manufacturer for offering discounts from list or suggested prices. Some academics and jurists have challenged the treatment of RPM as a *per se* violation. They argue that most vertical price restrictions only affect competition among sellers of the supplier's products (intrabrand competition) and do not limit competition among sellers of various similar products (interbrand competition) or give them power to restrict output or raise prices. They contend that vertical price restrictions ensure economic efficiencies and maximize consumer welfare by preventing price competition that forces retailers to cut back on nonprice items such as customer service.

Although the U.S. Supreme Court has so far rejected these arguments with regard to maintenance of *minimum* prices, it has greatly increased the plaintiff's burden of proof by requiring evidence of an agreement on specific price levels. Many antitrust lawyers believe this change in the analysis has dealt a fatal blow to attempts by terminated discounters to invoke the *per se* rule in cases alleging RPM. Very few manufacturers are clumsy enough to insist that their dealers agree on specific minimum prices.

In contrast to *minimum* price restrictions, *maximum* price restrictions do not necessarily prevent price competition. Suppliers may sell their product at whatever price they choose, subject to a price cap that is arguably procompetitive, even though the maximum price restriction may effectively become the same as an agreement to set a particular price if all sellers tend to sell at the maximum price. Because of this difference, the Supreme Court has held that maximum price-fixing should be analyzed under a rule of reason to "identify those situations in which [it] amounts to anticompetitive conduct."[28] But the Court was careful to point out that vertical *minimum* price-fixing remains illegal *per se*.

As noted earlier, Section 1 of the Sherman Act addresses only concerted action. Because unilateral action is not prohibited, a manufacturer or distributor can announce list prices to dealers, and the dealers may decide independently to follow those suggestions. Similarly, manufacturers and distributors may advertise suggested retail prices. Indeed, a manufacturer or distributor may (absent any intent to create or maintain a monopoly) announce that it will terminate any dealer that does not charge its suggested list prices and then terminate those that do not do so (because the conduct is entirely unilateral).[29] Most manufacturers and distributors do not want to terminate dealers that violate the policy, however. They, therefore, frequently use termination as a threat to coerce agreement. Once there is agreement, there is a violation of Section 1. Any threats of sanctions that interfere with the retailer's freedom to set its own minimum price for the goods or services that it sells will constitute an unreasonable restraint of trade in violation of the Sherman Act. Similarly, if the manufacturer or distributor becomes a clearinghouse for complaints by dealers about another dealer's failure to charge the suggested list price, and the manufacturer or distributor agrees to police the prices charged by the other dealers, then concerted action has occurred.

## *Nonprice Vertical Restraints and Vertical Market Division*

*Vertical market division* is an arrangement imposed by a manufacturer on its distributors or dealers that limits the freedom of the dealer to market the manufacturer's product. Such an agreement may establish exclusive distributorships, territorial or customer restrictions, location clauses, areas of primary responsibility, and the like. These nonprice vertical restrictions are not illegal *per se*. Rather, they are judged under the rule of reason.

The central inquiry is whether the reduction in intrabrand competition is justified by interbrand competition. The higher the market share of a particular manufacturer's product, the greater the likelihood that a decline in intrabrand competition will violate the rule of reason. For example, suppose Pixel Unlimited controls 80 percent of the market for high-definition television (HDTV) screens in Atlanta, Georgia, and sells its products through five independent retail outlets. Pixel agrees with three of its dealers to terminate the other two. Although a reduction in competition among Pixel dealers might arguably increase interbrand HDTV competition, given Pixel's high market share, that increase may not offset the anticompetitive effect of the decrease in Pixel intrabrand competition. Accordingly, the reduction in the number of Pixel dealers might violate Section 1.

In the following case, the court considered whether a manufacturer's market share discount programs imposed an unreasonable restraint of trade in violation of Section 1.

28. State Oil Co. v. Khan, 522 U.S. 3 (1997).

29. United States v. Colgate & Co., 250 U.S. 300 (1919).

A CASE IN POINT

**CASE 16.2**

**Concord Boat Corp. v Brunswick Corp.**

*United States Court of Appeals for the Eighth Circuit 207 F.3d 1039 (8th Cir. 2000).*

## Summary

**› FACTS** Since the early 1980s, there have been a number of manufacturers of inboard and stern-drive marine engines for motorboats. Stern-drive engines are used primarily in recreational powerboats and in cruising boats, which together make up about 40 percent of all recreational powerboats. The manufacturers start with standard automobile engine blocks, "marinize" and equip them with a drive system, and then sell the engines to boat builders. The boat builders install the engines in their brand name boats and sell the completed boats to dealers.

In 1983, Brunswick had a 75 percent share of the stern-drive engine market. In 1984, Brunswick, along with several of its competitors, began to offer market share discounts to boat builders and dealers. Under the Brunswick programs, boat builders and dealers could agree to purchase a certain percentage of their engine requirements from Brunswick for a fixed period of time in exchange for a discount off the list price of the engine. From 1984 to 1994, Brunswick offered a 3 percent discount to boat builders who bought 80 percent of their engines from it; a 2 percent discount for 70 percent of all purchases; and a 1 percent discount for 60 percent of all purchases. From 1995 to 1997, the market share requirements were reduced so that the maximum 3 percent discount could be earned by buying 70 percent from Brunswick; 2 percent for 65 percent; and 1 percent for 60 percent. In 1989, Brunswick also offered long-term discounts of an additional 1 or 2 percent to anyone who signed a market share agreement for two or three years. These market share discounts were eliminated entirely in the middle of 1997.

In December 1986, Brunswick purchased two of the largest boat builders, U.S. Marine and Sea Ray Industries. Brunswick hoped this vertical integration would allow it to synthesize engine manufacturing and boat building, leading to a higher quality and less expensive product. Between 1986 and 1997, the price of Brunswick's stern-drive engine increased from $4,775 to $4,984, fluctuating both upward and downward in the interim.

In 1995, a number of boat builders filed an antitrust action, claiming that Brunswick had used its market share discounts, volume discounts, and long-term discounts and contracts, coupled with the market power it had achieved in purchasing U.S. Marine and Sea Ray Industries, to restrain trade and to monopolize the market in violation of Sections 1 and 2 of the Sherman Act. At the trial the boat builders relied heavily on expert testimony to the effect that Brunswick had monopoly power in the stern-drive market, which enabled it to use its market share discount programs to impose a "tax" on boat builders and dealers who chose to purchase engines from other manufacturers. The expert defined the "tax" as the discount these purchasers gave up by not buying from Brunswick. Other manufacturers could not easily enter into stern-drive engine manufacturing. This monopolization enabled Brunswick to charge supracompetitive high prices for its engines, driving other engine manufacturers out of business. Following judgment for the boat builders, the boat builders' damages were trebled by law to a total of $133 million. Brunswick appealed.

**› ISSUE PRESENTED** Did Brunswick's cost discounting and vertical integration violate the antitrust laws, or did it constitute competitive business behavior that should be encouraged because of the resulting benefits for consumers and purchasers?

**› SUMMARY OF OPINION** The U.S. Court of Appeals for the Eighth Circuit ruled that the expert witness's testimony should have been excluded because his model did not separate out any lawful acts and unrelated market events that might have contributed to

*(Continued)*

(Case 16.2 *continued*)

Brunswick's market share from any anticompetitive conduct. As a result, the jury had no basis for assigning damages for only the illegal actions taken by Brunswick. The court concluded that Brunswick did not violate Section 1 because the market share discounts were voluntary contracts that the boat builders accepted to receive the benefit of discounts if they bought large quantities of Brunswick engines. The court concluded: "The boat builders have not shown that a reasonable jury could have found that Brunswick's programs, which were not exclusionary, caused harm in the first instance, or that they were a 'material cause' of any harm allegedly suffered." The court also ruled that the plaintiffs had not established a Section 2 violation. Citing many other cases holding that cutting prices to increase business is the very essence of competition, the court stated that the plaintiffs had to overcome a strong presumption of legality by showing other factors that indicated that the price charged was anticompetitive. In this case, the boat builders were not able to show that Brunswick's superior market share was achieved or maintained by means other than competition on the merits. The fact that Brunswick's competitors also used the same types of programs to increase business confirmed that the practice was a normal competitive tool within the stern-drive manufacturing industry.

› **RESULT** The court reversed the judgment for the boat builders and found in favor of Brunswick.

› **COMMENTS** In contrast, the U.S. Justice Department successfully challenged Microsoft's practice of charging per processor royalties, whereby computer manufacturers agreed to pay Microsoft a discounted license fee for use of its Windows operating system based on the number of computers sold with a specific microprocessor regardless of whether the machines were shipped with Windows or another operating system. The arrangement made it highly unlikely that manufacturers would pay extra to install a competing operating system and enabled Microsoft to monopolize the market for Intel-compatible personal computers.

---

**Exclusive Distributorships** In an *exclusive distributorship*, a manufacturer limits itself to a single distributor in a given territory or, perhaps, line of business. A manufacturer may allocate different geographic areas to its distributors and refuse to sell to other potential distributors in those areas. Exclusive distributorships have been upheld under the rule of reason when there is some competitive pressure that limits the market power of the retailers holding them. Exclusive automobile dealerships for particular geographic regions are the classic example. This restriction on intrabrand competition is permissible because of the intense interbrand competition among U.S. and foreign automobile manufacturers.

**Territorial and Customer Restrictions** *Territorial* and *customer restrictions* prevent a dealer or distributor from selling outside a certain territory or to a certain class of customers. For example, a Dow representative selling industrial chemicals might be permitted to sell only to hardware stores, and only in a specified area. The Supreme Court has held that vertical territorial or customer restrictions are not *per se* violations of Section 1. Such restrictions often increase interbrand competition; thus, an accompanying reduction of intrabrand competition may be permissible.

A manufacturer cannot disguise an agreement to maintain minimum resale prices as a territorial restriction, however. A court will look beyond the form of the transaction to the substance and will use the *per se* rule to strike down what is in reality a vertical minimum price restraint. Similarly, where a number of retailers combine to force a manufacturer to impose an ostensibly vertical agreement on its retailers, the agreement is in reality horizontal and will be deemed a *per se* violation of Section 1.

**Dual Distributors** A manufacturer that sells its goods both wholesale and at retail is called a *dual distributor*. Early decisions held that such an arrangement was unlikely to create the efficiencies and increased competition created by permissible forms of vertical nonprice agreements.

Accordingly, restraints imposed by dual distributors were considered illegal *per se*. The trend in recent decisions, however, is to analyze such restraints under the rule of reason (as long as they originate with the manufacturer, not the retailers) because they can have beneficial economic effects.

## *Product Bundling and Other Tying Arrangements*

Tying arrangements can be challenged under Section 1 of the Sherman Act or Section 3 of the Clayton Act. In a *tying arrangement,* the seller will sell product A (the *tying,* or desired, product) to the customer only if the customer agrees to purchase product B (the *tied* product) from the seller. A tying arrangement is a way of forcing a buyer to purchase a product or service it would not buy on the product's or service's own merits.

For example, suppose Metro Cable expands its cable television service into a new town. The public utilities commission grants Metro the exclusive right to provide cable service in the new town. Metro is a subsidiary of Moviemax, a company that provides a cable television movie channel for subscribers. To improve Moviemax's profit margin, the marketing vice president decides to require all of Metro's customers to subscribe to Moviemax. In this example, the tying product is the basic cable service. The tied product is the Moviemax television channel.

Tying arrangements may unreasonably restrain trade by making it difficult for competitors to sell their goods to customers who are obliged to buy the tied product. In the Moviemax example, the tying arrangement would make it more difficult for other movie channels, such as HBO, to sell their product to cable customers in the new town. Tying arrangements also restrict the freedom of choice of purchasers who are forced to buy the tied product.

To establish a tying arrangement, a plaintiff must show that (1) the tying and tied products are separate products, (2) the availability of the tying product is conditioned upon the purchase of the tied product, (3) the party imposing the tie has enough market power in the tying product market to force the purchase of the tied product, and (4) a "not insubstantial" amount of commerce in the tied product is affected.

**Separate Products** Whether there are separate products may be difficult to determine. Firms often label or market a combination of goods and services as a single product. The courts attempt to determine whether there are two economically distinct products by ascertaining whether a separate demand exists for each product. For example, in one case the Supreme Court found that below-market financing that was provided to buyers of prefabricated metal homes was a separate product from the homes themselves. A key issue in the Justice Department's case against Microsoft Corporation, discussed in this chapter's "Inside Story," was whether Microsoft's Internet Explorer Web browser was a separate product from Microsoft's Windows operating system.

**Condition of Sale** If the tying product can be purchased on nondiscriminatory terms, without the tied product, there is no tie. It has been suggested that a manufacturer should not make a second product technologically interdependent with the purchased product such that technology, rather than contract terms, forces customers to buy both. To date, however, these technological ties have been found lawful as long as there is no separate demand for the products involved, or the interdependent products provide consumers with functionalities not available if the products are purchased separately.

**Market Power** The nature and extent of the market power required for a tying arrangement are frequently litigated. As the Supreme Court defines it, *market power* is "the power to force a purchaser to do something that he would not do in a competitive market."[30] Ordinarily, market power is inferred from a firm's predominant share of the market, but in tying cases the issue is how power in one market translates into power in another. A dispute between EchoStar and Viacom provides an example of how power in one market may translate into power in another. EchoStar, which provides programming to 9 million satellite television subscribers, sued Viacom in the U.S. District Court for the Northern District of California, claiming that the cable company was using its market power as the provider of CBS programming to force EchoStar to buy unrelated programming that it did not want as a condition for renewing its agreement to carry CBS programming. The complaint claimed that Viacom offered EchoStar the right to carry eighteen CBS-owned stations in fifteen big-city markets, but only if EchoStar also bought Viacom's MTV, Nickelodeon, and other cable channel programming. Because the dispute threatened to keep 1.6 million customers from watching the 2004 Super Bowl broadcast and thereby cause EchoStar immediate and irreparable injury, the district court issued a temporary restraining order that permitted EchoStar to keep transmitting CBS, MTV, and other Viacom channels to customers while the litigation proceeded.[31]

30. Eastman Kodak Co. v. Image Technical Servs., Inc., 504 U.S. 451 (1992).

31. *EchoStar Customers Will Get Super Bowl,* SEATTLE POST-INTELLIGENCER, Jan. 22, 2004, http://www.seattlepi.nwsource.com/printer/ap.asp?category=1310&slug=EchoStarpercent20Viacom. EchoStar and Viacom settled their dispute in March 2004 on undisclosed terms.

A firm's ability to translate power in one market to power in another is often a function of product complementarity. If one needs product B (for example, bicycle helmets) to use product A (bicycles), then the firm controlling the market for product A (bicycles) will have a good shot at forcing consumers to buy the complementary product (bicycle helmets) from it. Unfortunately, the courts have not fashioned any precise formula using market share and product complementarity by which firms can determine ahead of time the line between antitrust violation and shrewd business.

**Effect on Commerce** A "not insubstantial" amount of commerce is affected if more than a trifling dollar amount is involved.

**Business Justification** Although courts continue to say that tying arrangements are illegal *per se,* they now apply a flexible *per se* rule that considers market power and business justifications. As a result, tying arrangements are in effect judged under a type of rule of reason. For example, the U.S. Court of Appeals for the Ninth Circuit upheld Mercedes-Benz's policy of requiring its dealers to sell only factory-made parts.[32] The court ruled that this tying arrangement was justified by the assurance it provided to Mercedes that service on its automobiles, important in preserving its high-quality image, would not be performed with substandard parts.

Some lower courts have also allowed tying arrangements in fledgling industries. For example, one court upheld a tying arrangement whereby purchasers of cable television satellite antennas were required to purchase service contracts to ensure proper functioning of the antennas.[33] As discussed further in the "Inside Story," the U.S. Court of Appeals for the D.C. Circuit held that the rule of reason should be used to decide whether Microsoft had illegally tied its Internet Explorer browser to the Windows operating system.[34]

## *Franchise Agreements*

A *franchise* is a business relationship in which one party (the franchisor) grants to another party (the franchisee) the right to use the franchisor's name and logo and to distribute the franchisor's products from a specified locale. (Franchises are discussed further in Chapter 19.) The franchise agreement may provide that the franchisor will not grant another franchise within a specified distance of the franchisee's business location. The Supreme Court has held that under the rule of reason, vertical market division between a franchisor and a franchisee may be lawful when interbrand competition is enhanced by the limitation on intrabrand competition.[35] Such division may take the form of limits on the number of franchisees in a geographic region and restrictions on the sale of franchisor products to specifically franchised locations.

Antitrust issues are also raised when a franchisor, in an effort to promote uniformity and name recognition, imposes certain limitations on the franchisee. For example, McDonald's franchisees might be required to decorate their restaurants in an approved fashion and have all their employees wear approved uniforms.

Requirements for the franchisee to purchase goods or equipment from the franchisor have been challenged as illegal tying arrangements. In *Queen City Pizza, Inc. v. Domino's Pizza, Inc.,*[36] Domino's Pizza franchisees claimed that Domino's illegally tied the right to use its name and registered trademarks to a requirement that its franchisees purchase ingredients, materials, and supplies for use in their restaurants from Domino's or Domino's approved suppliers, thus forcing plaintiffs to pay above-market prices for their ingredients, materials, and supplies. Although the plaintiffs argued that the relevant market should be narrowly limited to pizza and ingredients approved by Domino's for sale to its franchisees, the U.S. Court of Appeals for the Third Circuit held that "ingredients, supplies, materials, and distribution services used by and in the operation of Domino's pizza stores" could not, as a matter of law, constitute a relevant market for antitrust purposes. The court appeared influenced by the fact that the alleged illegal tie of fresh dough to the purchase of other ingredients from Domino's was disclosed to the franchisees in the franchise agreement. As a result, the franchisees had the opportunity to evaluate these potential costs against Domino's competitors' costs before they purchased the Domino's franchise. The court concluded that if Domino's acted unreasonably in restricting franchisees' ability to purchase supplies from third parties, then the plaintiffs' remedy should be under contract, not antitrust, laws. This opinion has significantly reduced the ability of franchisees to use antitrust laws to attack restrictive terms in their franchise agreements. Unless the franchisor (1) has a high share of the relevant franchisor product or opportunity or, perhaps, (2) keeps the purchase requirement a secret from the would-be franchisee and makes it difficult for the franchisee to recoup its investment in the franchise, franchisee tying claims are likely to fail.

32. The Mozart Co. v. Mercedes-Benz of North Am., Inc., 833 F.2d 1342 (9th Cir. 1987), *cert. denied,* 488 U.S. 870 (1988).

33. United States v. Jerrold Elecs. Corp., 187 F. Supp. 545 (E.D. Pa. 1960), *aff'd,* 365 U.S. 567 (1961).

34. United States v. Microsoft Corp., 253 F.3d 34 (D.C. Cir. 2001).

35. Cont'l T.V., Inc. v. GTE Sylvania, Inc., 433 U.S. 36 (1977).

36. 124 F.3d 430 (3d Cir. 1997).

# Monopolies: Section 2 of the Sherman Act

Section 2 of the Sherman Act provides that "[e]very person who shall monopolize, or attempt to monopolize, or combine or conspire with any other person or persons, to monopolize any part of the trade or commerce among the several States, or with foreign nations, shall be deemed guilty of a felony."[37]

A firm that possesses monopoly power is able to set prices at noncompetitive levels, harming both consumers and competitors. Consequently, Section 2 condemns actual or attempted monopolization of any market. Unlike Section 1, Section 2 does not require an agreement or any other collective action; unilateral conduct may violate Section 2.

Section 2 does not, however, prohibit the mere possession of monopoly power. The offense of monopolization has two elements. The plaintiff must show first that the defendant has monopoly power in a relevant market and then that the defendant willfully acquired or maintained that power through anticompetitive acts. A firm that has monopoly power thrust upon it by circumstances or attains it by superior performance does not violate Section 2. Thus, there is a status element (the defendant must be an entity with monopoly power) and a conduct element (the defendant must commit anticompetitive acts).

## Market Power

Courts define *market power* (also called *monopoly power*) as the power to control prices or exclude competition in a relevant market. Market power is marked by supracompetitive prices (that is, prices that are higher than they would be in a competitive market) over an extended period of time and the unavailability of substitute goods or services. The determination of whether a particular corporation has market power usually requires complex economic analysis. Presumptions based on market share and other structural characteristics of markets are used to simplify the analysis; in practice, however, each case turns on its unique (and usually disputed) facts.

### *Defining the Relevant Market*

Competition takes place in discrete markets. Therefore, the existence of market power can be determined only after the relevant market for the product is determined. Markets have two components: a product component and a geographic component.

37. 15 U.S.C. § 2.

**Multiple-Brand Product Market** The *multiple-brand product market* is made up of product or service offerings by different manufacturers or sellers that are economically interchangeable and may therefore be said to compete. Sometimes it is easy to identify substitutes. No one would deny that Coca-Cola competes against Pepsi. Frequently, the question is more complex. Does Coca-Cola compete against Dr. Pepper? Maybe. Against powdered iced tea? That is harder to say.

These questions are important because the power of a seller to set prices above competitive levels is limited by the ability of purchasers to substitute other types of products. If purchasers are unable to substitute other goods in the face of a price increase, the seller can set prices at monopoly levels. The product market is that collection of goods or services that customers deem to be practically substitutable.

**Single-Brand Product Market** The Supreme Court in *Eastman Kodak Co. v. Image Technical Services, Inc.* held that "[b]ecause service and parts for Kodak equipment are not interchangeable with other manufacturers' service and parts, the relevant market from the Kodak-equipment owner's perspective is composed of only those companies that service Kodak machines."[38] The Court rejected Kodak's motion for summary judgment on the basis that the relevant market was all copy machines and that Kodak could not have market power as to Kodak parts and service for copy machines because it did not have market power in copy machines. Evidence in the case showed that Kodak controlled nearly 100 percent of the Kodak parts market and 80 to 95 percent of the Kodak service market, so Kodak-equipment owners had no readily available substitutes. Because of the high costs of switching to another brand, consumers could not readily change copy-machine manufacturers if Kodak unilaterally raised its service fees. Thus, in some cases, a single brand of a product or service may constitute a separate market in a Section 2 analysis.

38. 504 U.S. 451 (1992).

**INTERNATIONAL SNAPSHOT**

In a case brought in France by Orangina against Coca-Cola of France for abuse of dominant position, the French court ruled in 1997 that the relevant product market was all colas, not all soft drinks as Coca-Cola had asserted.[a]

a. David Buchan, *Orangina Takes Some Fizz Out of Coke*, FIN. TIMES, Jan. 30, 1997, at 2.

**Geographic Market** Competition is also affected by geographic restraints on product movement. If a firm in Michigan is the only maker of widgets in the Midwest, it has the potential to exercise market power unless widget makers from other parts of the country can profitably ship their products to that area. Some markets are national or even international in scope, for example, the markets for long-distance telephone service, supercomputer sales, and nuclear power plant–design services. Other markets are localized, for example, markets for products that are expensive to transport, such as wet cement. The contours of geographic markets may also be affected by government regulations that confine firms to certain regions.

By defining the geographic market, antitrust courts try to separate firms that affect competition in a given region from those that do not. The geographic market encompasses all firms that compete for sales in a given area at current prices or would compete in that area if prices rose by a modest amount.

### *Determining Market Share*

Once the relevant market is determined, the plaintiff must show that, within this market, the defendant possessed market, or monopoly, power. The Supreme Court has held that monopoly power may be inferred from a firm's predominant share of the market because a dominant share of the market often carries with it the power to control output across the market and thereby control prices. In determining market share, the initial definition of the relevant market is crucial. For example, if the relevant market is the market for imported mineral water, Perrier's competitors would include other imported mineral-water sellers like Pellegrino, and Perrier would hold a major share of that market. On the other hand, if the market is defined as all mineral water (including, for example, Calistoga and Poland Springs), then Perrier's market share would be considerably smaller. Consequently, how a relevant market is defined often determines whether a particular firm has a dominant share of the market.

In one case, the Supreme Court found that 87 percent of the market was a predominant share sufficient to create a presumption of market power. As a general proposition, firms with market shares in excess of 60 percent are especially vulnerable to Section 2 litigation. When a single brand of a product or service constitutes the relevant market, market share may be 100 percent.

### *Barriers to Entry*

Market shares do not, however, conclusively establish market power. Market share must be analyzed in the context of other characteristics of the market in question. The plaintiff must show that new competitors face high market barriers to entry and that current competitors lack the ability to expand their output to challenge a monopolist's high prices. Common entry barriers include patents, governmental licenses or approvals, control of essential or superior resources, entrenched buyer preferences, economies of scale, and, according to some authorities, high initial capital requirements. Courts will also look at profit levels, market trends, pricing patterns, product differentiation, and government regulation. Essentially, the court is trying to determine the likelihood that another company will become a viable competitor in the relevant market if there is a small but significant nontransitory increase in price levels.

**INTERNATIONAL SNAPSHOT**

The European Commission has taken an approach similar to that used in the *Eastman Kodak* case in deciding whether a nondominant manufacturer of a primary product can be dominant with respect to a secondary market consisting solely of replacement parts, consumables, and maintenance services that must be technically compatible with the primary product. Relevant factors include the price and life of the primary product, the transparency of prices of secondary products, the prices of secondary products as a proportion of the primary product value, and information costs.

Applying these factors, in 1995 the Commission rejected the complaint of Pelikan, a German manufacturer of toner cartridges for printers, against Kyocera, a Japanese manufacturer of computer printers, including toner cartridges for those printers. The Commission found that Kyocera did not have a dominant position in the market of printer consumables. Purchasers were well informed about the price charged for consumables and appeared to take it into account in making their decision to buy a printer. Life-cycle costs of consumables (mainly toner cartridges) represented a very high proportion of the value of a printer. Therefore, if the prices for consumables of a particular brand were raised, consumers were not locked into a particular brand of toner and would have a strong incentive to buy another brand of printer.[a]

**a.** European Commission, XXVth Report on Competition Policy 1995 (1996), at 41–42.

## MONOPOLISTIC INTENT

Once the presence of market power is established, the defendant's intent is relevant. Some cases hold that the plaintiff must prove that the defendant's conduct lacks a legitimate business purpose. Other cases hold that the

ECONOMIC PERSPECTIVE

## THE REGULATION OF NATURAL MONOPOLIES

In the imagined world of perfect competition, *productive efficiency* (an equilibrium in which only the lowest-cost producers of goods and services survive) and *allocative efficiency* (an equilibrium in which scarce societal resources are allocated to the production of various goods and services up to the point where the cost of the resources equals the benefit society reaps from their use) would go hand in hand. In the real world, however, this is not always so. For example, the most cost-efficient way to provide telephone connections to homes is to link all of the homes to one central station, using one set of lines. Competition would require duplication of this expensive infrastructure; productive efficiency is best served by a monopoly. But the pricing policy of a monopolist is not controlled by competition. Consequently, the unregulated price of local telephone service would rise above the socially efficient level, and allocative efficiency would be impaired (see Exhibit 16.1). This can be remedied only by regulation of such industries, which are known as natural monopolies.

For many years, the American Telephone and Telegraph Company (AT&T) enjoyed a regulated monopoly in both local and long-distance telecommunications. The provision of long-distance service is not a natural monopoly because more than one network of intercity telephone lines can be profitably operated. Nonetheless, there was no competition in long-distance service because AT&T controlled access to the lines to individual homes.

In 1974, the U.S. government brought an antitrust suit against AT&T, charging monopolization of the telecommunications industry in violation of Section 2 of the Sherman Act. The case was decided in 1983.[a] In 1984, AT&T signed a consent decree to enable competition to flourish in the long-distance market. The decree provided for (1) the breakup of AT&T's monopoly over local service by creating seven regional telecommunications companies, known as the Baby Bells, and (2) a complex set of rules to ensure that both AT&T and other companies providing long-distance service, such as MCI and Sprint, would have equal access to the local networks. The Baby Bells would, of course, be subject to regulation because each of them would still enjoy a monopoly in the provision of local telephone service.

a. United States v. Am. Tel. & Tel. Co., 552 F. Supp. 131 (D.D.C. 1982), *aff'd sub nom.* Maryland v. United States, 460 U.S. 1001 (1983).

---

initial burden is on the defendant to prove a legitimate business purpose; if it does so, the plaintiff must then prove a monopolistic intent. It is possible to prove intent through evidence of statements by the monopolist's executive expressing a desire to eliminate competition. Hostility between competitors is commonplace, however, and may even be beneficial to vigorous competition. Therefore, the courts often require that monopolistic intent be proved by evidence of conduct (not merely statements) that is inherently anticompetitive.

A defendant may rebut allegations of monopolistic intent by showing that its success in the marketplace is the result of "superior skill, foresight, and industry." A monopoly earned by superior performance is not unlawful. Indeed, the law recognizes that the possibility of attaining such a monopoly may be a powerful incentive to vigorous competition, which benefits consumers. Therefore, a key issue in Section 2 litigation is whether the defendant acquired or maintained its monopoly by procompetitive acts or by anticompetitive acts. Anticompetitive acts include predatory pricing and, under certain circumstances, refusals to deal.

### Predatory Pricing

The courts have not settled on a single definition of *predatory pricing*, that is, the attempt to eliminate rivals by undercutting their prices to the point where they lose money and go out of business, leaving the monopolist unrestrained by competition and thus able to raise its prices. The courts have struggled to develop principles that distinguish between such anticompetitive pricing and the procompetitive pricing that occurs when a more efficient firm competes vigorously yet fairly against its rivals. In the latter case, the more efficient firm could undercut its rivals, forcing them out of business, and a lawful monopoly would result.

Courts will usually find pricing legal when the prices are above average variable cost but below average total cost and the company has excess capacity. (*Variable cost* is the cost of producing the next incremental unit; *total cost* includes variable cost and fixed costs, such as rent and overhead.) If a company does not have excess capacity, the legality of the pricing depends on the company's intent; the cases are very fact-specific. Prices below average variable cost are presumptively illegal unless the business can

EXHIBIT 16.1 **Welfare Loss from Monopoly**

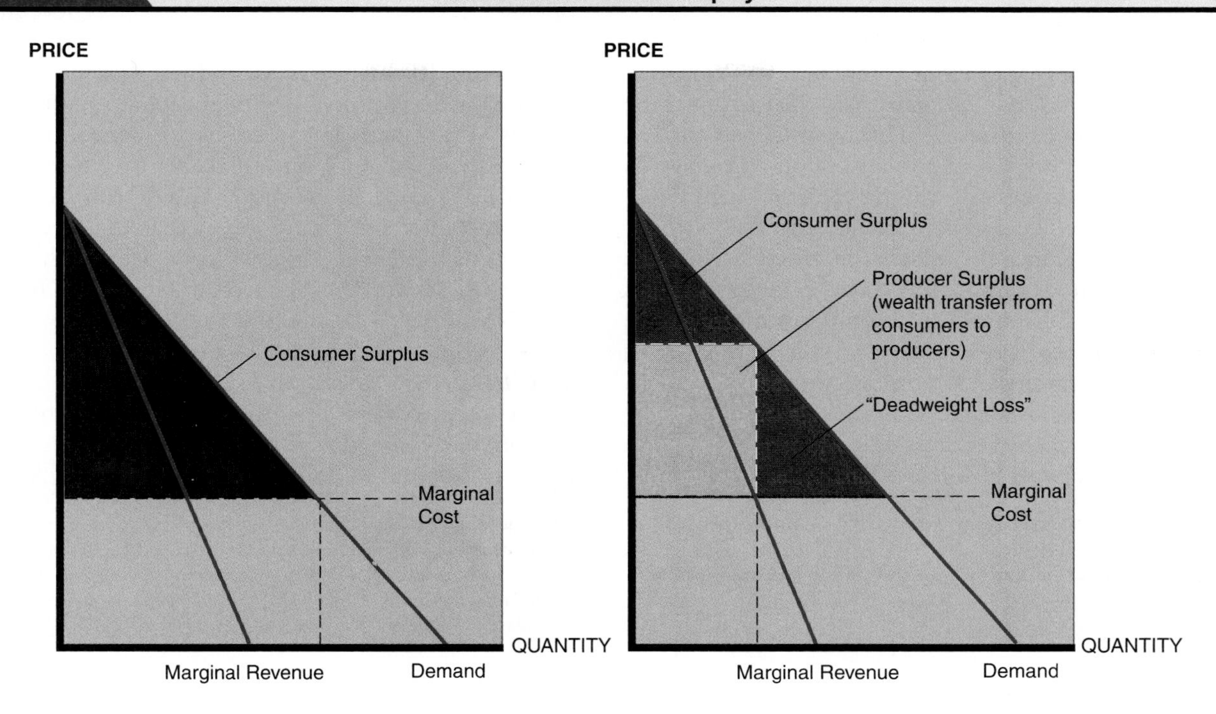


**DEFINITION OF TERMS**

**Consumer surplus** The difference between the value of a good to consumers (measured by the price they would be willing to pay for the good) and the price they actually must pay to obtain the good.

**Producer surplus** The difference between the cost to producers of producing a good (measured by the minimum price at which they would sell a given quantity of the good) and the price they actually receive in the market.

**Total surplus** The sum of producer and consumer surplus. Total surplus represents the difference between the cost to society of the inputs used to make a good, including raw materials and labor, and the value of the finished good to society. Total surplus measures the overall increase in societal wealth attributable to production of a good.

**Deadweight loss** The difference between total surplus in a competitive market and total surplus in a monopolized market.

demonstrate that the pricing is an introductory offer or that costs will fall dramatically as the company progresses along the learning curve. At some point, pricing below cost becomes economically irrational unless the predator is anticipating the long-term gains that would result from destroying its rivals.

Some academics have argued that predatory pricing is self-defeating in all but a few market scenarios. Having eliminated its rivals, the predator needs to keep its old rivals, and new entrants, out of the market when it raises its prices to recoup its losses. That will be difficult as the high prices—and high profits—can be expected to attract new entrants. Thus, predatory pricing is an irrational strategy unless the market, because of barriers to entry or other factors, is structurally conducive to monopolization.

The Supreme Court has accepted this argument. In 1986, the Court rejected a claim brought by U.S. television manufacturers against their Japanese counterparts.[39] It held that some allegations of predation are inherently implausible because the marketplace cannot be successfully monopolized. In such cases, there is no Sherman Act violation, whatever monopolistic intent the

39. *See, e.g.*, Matsushita Elec. Indus. Co. v. Zenith Radio Corp., 475 U.S. 574 (1986).

defendant may have had. This has been referred to as the *rule of impossibility*.[40]

In July 2003, the Wisconsin Supreme Court upheld a lower court ruling that dismissed a predatory pricing lawsuit that the *Waukesha Freeman* had filed against the *Milwaukee Journal Sentinel*.[41] The *Sentinel* had offered subscribers to its Sunday edition an option to receive its daily paper at no extra cost, causing the *Freeman*'s circulation to decline. The *Freeman* alleged that the *Sentinel* program offered papers below cost in an effort to drive the *Freeman* out of business. Although the lawsuit was brought under Wisconsin's predatory pricing law, the Wisconsin Supreme Court deferred to federal antitrust laws. It relied upon the U.S. Supreme Court's decision in *Brooke Group Ltd. v. Brown & Williamson Tobacco Corp.*,[42] the seminal federal case addressing predatory pricing. In that case, the Supreme Court held that a plaintiff must prove two conditions to succeed on a claim of predatory pricing: (1) that the prices and other direct revenues for the practice complained of are below an appropriate measure of the defendant's costs, and (2) that the defendant has a dangerous probability of recouping its investment "losses" by later raising prices above competitive levels. Noting that predatory pricing claims have rarely, if ever, prevailed under the *Brooke Group* standard,[43] the Wisconsin Supreme Court found that the *Freeman* had not met its burden of proof with respect to either part of the *Brooke Group* test. As a result, it upheld the lower court's summary judgment for the *Sentinel*.

### *Exclusionary Conduct*

The following case deals with the issue of whether above-cost pricing, coupled with exclusionary conduct, can give rise to a violation of Section 2 of the Sherman Act.

40. *See, e.g.,* Brooke Group Ltd. v. Brown & Williamson Tobacco Corp., 509 U.S. 209 (1993).
41. Conley Publ'g Group Ltd. v. Journal Communications, Inc., 665 N.W.2d 879 (Wis. 2003).
42. 509 U.S. 209 (1993).
43. Indeed, at least one commentator has stated that since the *Brooke Group* decision, no lawsuit alleging predatory pricing in the United States has succeeded. James Kogutkiewicz, *State Rejects Conley Anti-Trust Lawsuit,* GMTODAY.COM, July 17, 2003, *at* http://www.gmtoday.com/news/ local_stories/July_03/07172003_05.asp.

**A CASE IN POINT**

**CASE 16.3**
**LePage's, Inc. v. 3M**
*United States Court of Appeals for the Third Circuit*
*324 F.3d 141*
*(3d Cir. 2001).*

## Summary

**› FACTS** LePage's, founded in 1876, sold a variety of office products. In 1990, LePage's began selling a "second brand" and private label transparent tape. Private label tape is sold under the retailer's name, rather than the manufacturer's name, and sells at a lower price to the retailer and the end customer than branded tape. By 1992, LePage's was selling 88 percent of the private label tape sold in the United States, which represented a small portion of the overall transparent tape market. During this same period, the rapid growth of office superstores and mass merchandisers led to an increased demand for private label tape, resulting in a shift of some tape sales from branded tape to private label tape.

3M possesses monopoly power in the U.S. transparent tape market, with a 90 percent market share. In fact, the household penetration of 3M's Scotch-brand tape is virtually 100 percent. During the early 1990s, 3M also entered the private label business and sold its own second brand under the name "Highland." Through its rebate programs 3M offered many of LePage's major customers substantial rebates conditioned on purchases spanning six of 3M's diverse product lines: Health Care Products, Home Care Products, Home Improvement Products, Stationery Products (including transparent tape), Retail Auto Products, and Leisure Time Products. In addition to bundling the rebates, the program set customer-specific target growth rates in each product line. The size of the rebate was linked to the number of product lines in which targets were met, and the number of targets met by the buyer determined the rebate it would receive on all of its purchases. If a customer failed to meet the target for any one product, the failure resulted in loss of the rebate across the line. This created a substantial incentive for each customer to meet the targets across all product lines.

*(Continued)*

(Case 16.3 *continued*)

3M also entered into contracts with several large customers that conditioned discounts on exclusivity. Other contracts contained no express exclusive dealing provision but provided rebates and discounts that LePage's claimed were designed to induce the customers to award business only to 3M. For example, KMart, LePage's largest customer (accounting for 10 percent of its sales), entered into a contract with 3M that provided a $1 million "growth reward." After this contract was executed, a KMart buyer told LePage's, "I can't talk to you about tape products for the next three years."

LePage's brought an antitrust action against 3M claiming, among other things, that 3M's conduct violated Section 2 of the Sherman Act. After a jury trial, the district court entered judgment in favor of LePage's on its monopolization claim, and 3M appealed. The U.S. Court of Appeals for the Third Circuit reversed, and a rehearing *en banc* was granted.

**› ISSUE PRESENTED** Did 3M take steps to maintain its market, or monopoly, power in a manner that violated Section 2 of the Sherman Act?

**› SUMMARY OF OPINION** The U.S. Court of Appeals for the Third Circuit noted that 3M relied on the Supreme Court's decision in *Brooke Group Ltd. v. Brown & Williamson Tobacco Corp.* to support its position that "[a]bove-cost pricing cannot give rise to an antitrust offense as a matter of law, since it is the very conduct that the antitrust laws wish to promote in the interest of making consumers better off." Following an extensive review of the Supreme Court's Section 2 decisions, the court concluded that nothing in *Brooke Group* suggests that the decision applied to a monopolist with unconstrained market power.

Turning to the bundled rebates, the court stated that they should be compared with tying arrangements rather than predatory pricing because the foreclosure effects of both are similar. The court reasoned: "The principal anticompetitive effect of bundled rebates as offered by 3M is that when offered by a monopolist, they may foreclose portions of the market to a potential competitor who does not manufacture an equally diverse group of products and who therefore cannot make a comparable offer."

The court also concluded that the jury reasonably found that 3M's exclusionary conduct violated Section 2: "LePage's produced evidence that the foreclosure caused by exclusive dealing practices was magnified by 3M's discount practices, as some of 3M's rebates were 'all-or-nothing' discounts, leading customers to maximize their discounts by dealing exclusively with the dominant market player, 3M, to avoid being severely penalized."

**› RESULT** The court found that there was sufficient evidence to justify the jury's finding in favor of LePage's on its monopolization claim and let stand the judgment for trebled damages of $68,486,697, plus interest.

**› COMMENTS** In *Conwood Co. v. United States Tobacco Co.,*[44] the defendant, United States Tobacco Company (UST), had 75 percent of a niche market—U.S. moist snuff. Conwood claimed that UST engaged in tortious behavior against Conwood. For example, UST allegedly removed Conwood's critical "point of sale" displays without sufficient authorization, took advantage of "inattentive store clerks with various 'ruses' " (such as obtaining permission to "reorganize or neaten the section"), provided "misleading information to retailers," and entered "into exclusive agreements in an effort to exclude rival's products." UST argued that this conduct amounted to no more than "insignificant tortious activity" and that tortious activity alone could not form the basis for Section 2 liability. Although the U.S. Court of Appeals for the Sixth Circuit agreed that isolated tortious activity does not constitute exclusionary conduct for purposes of a Section 2 violation, it found that UST's pervasive pattern of tortious actions aimed at shutting out its competition constituted sufficient evidence for a jury to find willful maintenance of monopoly power.

44. 290 F.3d 768 (6th Cir. 2002), *cert. denied,* 537 U.S. 1148 (2003).

## *Refusal to Deal and the Essential Facilities Doctrine*

As a general proposition, the antitrust laws do not prevent a firm from deciding with whom it will or will not deal. Yet the courts have long recognized that there are circumstances in which a unilateral refusal to deal may allow a firm to acquire or maintain monopoly power.

A monopolist has a duty to deal with its rivals when it controls an *essential facility,* that is, some resource necessary to its rivals' survival that they cannot feasibly duplicate. A court considers four elements in an essential-facility case: (1) whether the defendant prevents would-be competitors from using the facility, (2) whether it is feasible for the defendant to permit access to the facility by its would-be competitors, (3) whether the defendant has monopoly power and control of the facility, and (4) whether the competitors are able to duplicate the essential facility. This approach was followed in the *AT&T*[45] case, which led to the breakup of the Bell Telephone System. The essential-facility doctrine does not require a firm to share resources that are merely useful, that would allow competitors to compete more effectively, or that the competitors could duplicate on their own.

In 1995, the Federal Trade Commission and the Department of Justice issued *Guidelines for Licensing Intellectual Property.* These guidelines set forth three core principles: (1) the standard antitrust analysis applies to intellectual property; (2) intellectual property rights do not necessarily confer market power; and (3) licensing is generally procompetitive and subject to rule of reason analysis.

On remand from the Supreme Court, the U.S. Court of Appeals for the Ninth Circuit upheld a jury verdict in favor of the independent service organizations in *Image Technical Services, Inc. v. Eastman Kodak Co.*[46] The court held that Section 2 of the Sherman Act prohibits refusal to deal in order to create or maintain a monopoly unless there is a legitimate business justification. The court acknowledged that intellectual property rights may create such a justification. In particular, a monopolist's desire to exclude others from its protected work is a presumptively valid business justification for any immediate harm to consumers caused by a monopolist's unilateral refusal to license a patent or copyright or to sell its patented or copyrighted work. That presumption may be rebutted, however, by evidence that the intellectual property protection was acquired unlawfully or that its use as a business justification was merely pretext.

The Ninth Circuit found that Kodak's refusal to sell replacement copier parts to independent service organizations was not justified by a desire to exploit its patents or copyrights. Although Kodak's equipment required thousands of parts, only sixty-five were patented, but Kodak refused to sell both patented and unpatented parts.

The Ninth Circuit noted the tension between antitrust law's concerns about monopoly as a threat to competition and copyright and patent law's goal of granting limited monopolies as an incentive to innovate. While acknowledging that patent and copyright holders may refuse to sell or license protected work, a monopolist that acquires a dominant position in one market through patents and copyrights may violate Section 2 if the monopolist exploits that dominant position to extend the lawful monopoly into a separate market.

In a subsequent case, the U.S. Court of Appeals for the Federal Circuit rejected the plaintiff's reliance on *Kodak* and upheld Xerox's policy of not selling or licensing its patented products and copyrighted software to independent service organizations.[47] Whereas the *Kodak* case was a tying case, the plaintiff in *Xerox* made no claims that Xerox had tied the sale of its patented parts to unpatented products. The Federal Circuit also declined to inquire into the subjective motivation behind Xerox's refusal to sell or license its patented and copyrighted works, finding that the antitrust defendant's subjective motivation is immaterial. The court held that in the absence of illegal tying, fraud on the Patent and Trademark Office or the Copyright Registrar, or sham litigation, Xerox's enforcement of its statutory intellectual property rights did not violate the antitrust laws. Yet in *United States v. Microsoft Corp.,*[48] the U.S. Court of Appeals for the D.C. Circuit ruled that Microsoft's assertion that its copyrights in the Windows operating system entitled it to dictate the terms on which the system was made available to original equipment manufacturers was "no more correct than the proposition that use of one's personal property, such as a baseball, cannot give rise to tort liability."[49]

45. United States v. Am. Tel. & Tel. Co., 552 F. Supp. 131 (D.D.C. 1982), *aff'd sub nom.* Maryland v. United States, 460 U.S. 1001 (1983).

46. 125 F.3d 1195 (9th Cir. 1997), *cert. denied,* 523 U.S. 1094 (1998).

47. CSU, LLC v. Xerox Corp., 203 F.3d 1322 (Fed. Cir. 2000), *cert. denied,* 531 U.S. 1143 (2001).

48. 253 F.3d 34 (D.C. Cir. 2001). See Constance E. Bagley & Gavin Clarkson, *Adverse Possession for Intellectual Property: Adopting an Ancient Concept to Resolve Conflicts Between Antitrust and Intellectual Property Laws in the Information Age,* 16 HARV. J. L. & TECH. 327 (2003), for a proposed standard to reconsider these approaches.

49. *Microsoft,* 253 F.3d at 63.

### *Other Anticompetitive Acts*

Other practices that have been held to indicate the presence of monopolistic intent include the allocation of markets and territories, price-fixing, fraudulently obtaining a patent, or engaging in sham litigation against a competitor. Firms can also incur Section 2 liability by acquiring or maintaining monopoly power through corporate mergers or acquisitions.

## DERIVATIVE MARKETS AND MONOPOLY LEVERAGING

Ordinarily, Section 2 liability is restricted to monopolistic behavior within the specific market in which the firm has market power. Through leveraging, however, a firm with monopoly power in one market can use that power to gain an advantage in a separate market. It is clear that when such an advantage amounts to monopoly power in the second market, the firm has violated Section 2. It is less clear whether a firm can use its monopoly power in one market to gain a competitive advantage, short of actual monopolization, in another market. In *Berkey Photo, Inc. v. Eastman Kodak Co.*,[50] the U.S. Court of Appeals for the Second Circuit suggested that the use of monopoly power in one market to obtain a competitive advantage in another market might violate Section 2. Recent Supreme Court decisions tend to undercut this suggestion, but they do not do so decisively. More specifically, in another case,[51] the Supreme Court held that the plaintiff in every Section 2 case involving unilateral conduct must prove a dangerous probability that the defendant's conduct will create or maintain monopoly power in a market. That holding seems to suggest that "leveraging" that confers only a "competitive advantage" in a market cannot violate Section 2.

The U.S. Court of Appeals for the Ninth Circuit adopted this approach when it found that two airlines that had developed the two largest proprietary computerized airline reservation systems did not violate Section 2 merely because the systems gave them a competitive advantage in the air-transportation market by listing their flights first.[52] The court held that unless the monopolist uses its power in the first market to acquire and maintain a monopoly in the second market, or to attempt to do so, there is no Section 2 violation. The plaintiffs had conceded that the two airlines did not have a monopoly in the leveraged, downstream air-transportation market and that there was no dangerous probability that either defendant would acquire such a monopoly. Therefore, their Section 2 claims were rejected.

50. 605 F.2d 263 (2d Cir. 1979), *cert. denied*, 444 U.S. 1093 (1980).
51. Spectrum Sports, Inc. v. McQuillan, 506 U.S. 447 (1993).
52. Alaska Airlines, Inc. v. United Airlines, Inc., 948 F.2d 536 (9th Cir. 1991).

# Price Discrimination: The Robinson–Patman Act

Section 2 of the Clayton Act, as amended by the Robinson–Patman Act, prohibits *price discrimination*, that is, selling the same tangible product to different purchasers at the same level of distribution at different prices. By outlawing price discrimination, Congress believed that it could protect independent businesses by preventing the formation of monopolies. The legislators assumed that price discrimination was the means by which trusts were built and that discriminatory price concessions were the means by which large retail chains expanded at the expense of smaller independent retailers.

## ELEMENTS OF A ROBINSON–PATMAN CASE

Six elements must be proved to establish a price-discrimination case under the Robinson–Patman Act: (1) there must be discrimination in price, that is, a difference in the price at which goods are sold, in the terms and conditions of sale, or in such items as freight allowances or rebates; (2) some part of the discrimination must involve sales in interstate commerce, that is, at least one sale must be across state lines; (3) the discrimination must involve sales for use, consumption, or resale within the United States; (4) there must be discrimination between different purchasers; (5) the discrimination must involve sales of tangible commodities of like grade and quality; and (6) there must be a probable injury to competition. The probable injury to competition is assessed at three levels: (1) the seller level, (2) the buyer level, and (3) the customer level.

## DEFENSES

Even if a plaintiff has shown the elements of a Robinson–Patman violation, the following defenses are available.

### *Availability*

The Robinson–Patman Act permits discrimination that arises from discounts and allowances that a company affirmatively offers to all competing customers. A customer who fails to take advantage of such an offer cannot claim an actionable injury.

### *Meeting the Competition*

Discriminatory prices are not prohibited if the seller acted in "good faith to meet an equally low price of a competitor."[53] As defined by the Federal Trade Commission (FTC), good faith is "a flexible and pragmatic, not a technical or doctrinaire, concept. The standard of good faith is simply the standard of the prudent businessman responding fairly to what he reasonably believes is a situation of competitive necessity."[54]

### *Cost Justification*

Price differentials that would otherwise be prohibited by the Robinson–Patman Act are not prohibited if the differentials "make only due allowance for differences in the cost of manufacture, sale or delivery resulting from the differing methods or quantities" in which the goods are sold and delivered (such as costs of billing; credit losses; costs of advertising, promotion, and selling; and freight and delivery charges).[55] To establish this defense and justify the price reduction, the defendant must show actual cost savings, not merely generalized assertions of cost savings. The FTC interprets this defense restrictively, and compiling the necessary paper trail is expensive.

### *Changing Conditions*

Section 2(a) does not prohibit price changes from time to time in response to changing conditions affecting the market for or the marketability of the goods concerned. Such conditions include but are not limited to actual or imminent deterioration of perishable goods, obsolescence of seasonal goods, distress sales under court process, or sales in good faith when the seller discontinues its business in the goods concerned.

In the few cases where this defense has been raised, the issue was whether the price discrimination was a response to one of the conditions listed in the statute. The changing-conditions defense has generally been confined to situations caused by the physical characteristics of the product, such as the perishable nature of fruit. For example, a court permitted price differentials on bananas from a single shipload because they reflected the perishable nature of bananas.

## Mergers: Section 7 of the Clayton Act

If a merger or acquisition unreasonably restrains trade, it violates Section 1 of the Sherman Act. If it results in monopolization, it violates Section 2. These statutes are, however, rarely invoked to challenge mergers. Dissatisfied with the ability of the government to attack mergers under the Sherman Act, Congress amended the Clayton Act in 1950 to prohibit mergers that threatened to harm competition. Section 7 of the Clayton Act provides:

> No person engaged in commerce or in any activity affecting commerce shall acquire, directly or indirectly, the whole or any part of the stock or other share capital and no person subject to the jurisdiction of the Federal Trade Commission shall acquire the whole or any part of the assets of another person engaged also in commerce or in any activity affecting commerce, where in any line of commerce or in any activity affecting commerce in any section of the country, the effect of such acquisition may be substantially to lessen competition, or to tend to create a monopoly.[56]

### HART–SCOTT–RODINO ANTITRUST IMPROVEMENTS ACT

The Hart–Scott–Rodino Antitrust Improvements Act amended Section 7 in 1976 to provide a premerger notification procedure whereby the FTC and the Justice Department can review the anticompetitive effects of proposed mergers meeting certain size-of-party and size-of-transaction tests. A premerger notification must be filed if (1) one party to the transaction has total assets or annual net sales of at least $100 million or more, and the other party has total assets or annual net sales of $10 million or more (the "size of persons test"); and (2) as a result of the acquisition, the acquiring person would hold an aggregate total amount of voting securities and assets of the acquired person in excess of $50 million (the "size of transaction test"). Even if the size of persons test is not met, a premerger notification must be filed if, as a result of the acquisition, the acquiring person would hold an aggregate total amount of voting securities and assets of the acquired person in excess of $200 million.

Parties to a merger must give the FTC and Justice Department thirty days to review their filings (fifteen days in the case of a tender offer). Either period can be extended if the government requests additional information. Requests for additional information should be avoided, if possible, because they cause further delays before the merging parties know whether the FTC or Justice Department will challenge the proposed merger.

53. 15 U.S.C. § 13(b).
54. Cont'l Baking Co., 63 F.T.C. 2071, 2163 (1963).
55. 15 U.S.C. § 13(a).
56. 15 U.S.C. § 18.

## MERGER GUIDELINES

In connection with their enforcement obligations, the FTC and the Justice Department have together developed a series of guidelines as to the kinds of transactions that are likely to be challenged as violations of the Clayton Act.

Under the 1992 merger guidelines, the FTC and Justice Department seek to determine whether a proposed corporate combination will more likely than not reduce competition; to make this determination, they use basically the same analysis as the courts use in applying Section 2 of the Sherman Act (discussed earlier in this chapter). The reviewing agency first determines the relevant geographic and product markets. Then it calculates the market shares of the companies proposing to merge. Finally, it determines the effect of the merger on the relevant market.

If the merger appears to increase concentration in the relevant market by a certain amount, the reviewing agency will ordinarily challenge the transaction. However, the question of whether to challenge a combination is left to the discretion of the agency.

As an aid to the interpretation of market data, the Justice Department uses the *Herfindahl–Hirschman Index (HHI)* of market concentration. The HHI is calculated by summing the squares of the individual market shares of all the firms in the market. For example, in a market with four competitors having market shares of 35 percent, 25 percent, 25 percent, and 15 percent, the HHI is 2,700 ($35^2 + 25^2 + 25^2 + 15^2 = 1{,}225 + 625 + 625 + 225 = 2{,}700$).

When the postmerger HHI is less than 1,000, the Justice Department characterizes the market as unconcentrated. In such cases, the department will not challenge the merger or other combination.

When the postmerger HHI is between 1,000 and 1,800 and the merger will produce an HHI increase of 100 points or more, the 1992 merger guidelines state that the merger will possibly raise significant competitive concerns.

When the postmerger HHI is above 1,800, the department considers the market to be highly concentrated. In such cases, an increase in the HHI of 100 points or more creates a rebuttable presumption of anticompetitive effects. For example, a merger between firms with market shares of 5 percent and 10 percent will result in a 100-point increase in the HHI ($15^2 = 225$, $5^2 + 10^2 = 125$), whereas a merger between firms with market shares of 7 percent and 8 percent will result in a 112-point increase ($15^2 = 225$, $7^2 + 8^2 = 113$).

When the increase in the HHI is less than 50 points, Justice Department action is unlikely. When the increase is between 50 and 100 points, the department will challenge the transaction if it determines, based on a broad-ranging analysis of the market, that the effect of the merger is "substantially to lessen competition." The department will consider such factors as changing market conditions, the relative strength or weakness of the firms in the market, and barriers to entry into the relevant market. It should be noted that even if the Justice Department or the FTC approves the merger, it may still be challenged in court by another party.

## LITIGATION UNDER SECTION 7

Although the Department of Justice's merger guidelines are of considerable persuasive value, the standards applied by the courts differ in several significant respects. A court's analysis may also vary depending on the type of merger or corporate combination that has been challenged.

### *Horizontal Mergers*

A *horizontal merger* is the combining of two or more competing companies at the same level in the chain of production and distribution. The first step in determining the lawfulness of such a merger is to identify the relevant product and geographic markets. The same standards discussed in connection with Section 2 of the Sherman Act are used.

Once the market is defined, the court will look primarily at three factors: (1) the market shares of the firms involved in the transaction, (2) the level of concentration in the market, and (3) whether the market is structurally conducive to anticompetitive behavior.

The case of *United States v. Philadelphia National Bank*[57] illustrates this method of analysis. In the early 1960s, Philadelphia National Bank (PNB) was the second largest bank in the Philadelphia market, which consisted of forty-two commercial banks in the metropolitan area of Philadelphia, Pennsylvania, and its three contiguous counties. After PNB signed a merger agreement with Girard Bank, the third largest bank in the same market, the United States sued to enjoin the merger on the grounds that it would violate Section 7 of the Clayton Act.

The merger would have resulted in PNB's controlling at least 30 percent of the commercial banking business in the four-county Philadelphia metropolitan area, a market share that the U.S. Supreme Court viewed as a threat to competition. After the merger, the two largest banks would control 59 percent of the market, whereas before the merger the two largest banks controlled only 44 percent. This increase in concentration also worried the Court. Neither the high level of government regulation of the banking business nor the banks' provision of services and intangible credit, rather than tangible products, made

57. 374 U.S. 321 (1963).

the banking industry immune from the anticompetitive effects of undue concentration. Because of these three elements, the Court directed the district court to enter judgment enjoining the merger. The Court explained:

> [A] merger which produces a firm controlling an undue percentage share of the relevant market, and results in a significant increase in the concentration of firms in that market is so inherently likely to lessen competition substantially that it must be enjoined in the absence of evidence clearly showing the merger is not likely to have such anticompetitive effects.

The 30 percent market share that the Court held to be excessive has been taken by many lower courts to create a presumption of illegality. The Supreme Court has insisted, however, that no single numerical standard can be applied to all markets. Most courts today require that, in the absence of a highly concentrated market, the merging firms have a combined market share of at least 30 percent before a Section 7 violation will be found.

In a more recent case, the FTC challenged the merger of office-supply retailers Office Depot, Inc. and Staples, Inc., the largest and second-largest operators of office-supply superstores, respectively. In 1996, the two firms agreed to merge their operations (with more than $8 billion in revenues), joining their more than 1,000 stores. Although Staples and Office Depot did not compete with each other in many geographic markets, the FTC contended that the merger would hurt consumers on balance by reducing competition in the markets in which the two companies did compete.

To satisfy the regulators, the companies negotiated a consent decree with the FTC staff to permit the merger on the condition that the companies sell sixty-three stores to OfficeMax, the third-largest office-supply superstore retailer, in those markets where the FTC most feared a reduction in competition. Nonetheless, the FTC commissioners again ruled against the merger and asked the district court to enjoin the companies from combining.

Defining the relevant product market as consumable office supplies sold through office-supply superstores, the court rejected the argument that Wal-Mart and other retailers compete in the same market with Staples, Office Depot, and OfficeMax. The court relied heavily on pricing data that indicated, among other things, that prices were on average 13 percent higher in geographic markets where Staples was the only office superstore than in markets where all three superstores competed, even though retail and discount chains selling consumable office supplies were present in both markets. Turning then to market concentration, the court noted that before the merger, the least concentrated market had an HHI of 3,597 and the most concentrated had an HHI of 6,944. After the proposed merger, those figures would rise to 5,003 and 10,000, respectively. Thus, these markets were already "highly concentrated" and would see an average increase of 2,715 HHI points. Furthermore, the industry's large economies of scale meant that new entrants would have to open many large stores nationally in order to compete. The large amount of capital necessary to do this would be a barrier to entry. Ultimately, the district court sided with the FTC and, in 1997, issued an injunction, killing the $3.4 billion deal.[58]

Even if a merger or combination is determined to be presumptively illegal on the basis of market shares, the defendants may still show that the transaction is not likely to decrease competition. For example, if there are no barriers to entry in the relevant market, any transitory increase in concentration will be quickly eroded by the entry of new competitors into the market. If one of the combined firms is failing, the proposed transaction may be the only alternative to that failure. In either of these cases, Section 7 liability can be avoided.

In the following case, the court considered whether the merger of Oracle Corporation and PeopleSoft, two large suppliers of enterprise application software, would violate Section 7 of the Clayton Act.

58. FTC v. Staples, Inc., 970 F. Supp. 1066 (D.D.C. 1997).

A CASE IN POINT

## In the Language of the Court

**CASE 16.4**

**United States v. Oracle Corp.**

*United States District Court for the Northern District of California*
*331 F. Supp. 2d 1098 (N.D. Cal. 2004).*

**› FACTS** Oracle Corporation initiated a tender offer for the shares of PeopleSoft, Inc. on June 6, 2003. The U.S. government, acting through the Antitrust Division of the Department of Justice, and the states of Connecticut, Hawaii, Maryland, Massachusetts, Michigan, Minnesota, New York, North Dakota, Ohio, and Texas (collectively, the plaintiffs) brought suit on February 26, 2004, seeking to enjoin Oracle from acquiring, directly or indirectly, all or any part of the stock of PeopleSoft.

*(Continued)*

(Case 16.4 *continued*)

Both Oracle and PeopleSoft license software applications that automate the overall data processing functions of businesses and similar entities. These applications are called "enterprise application software" (EAS). Oracle and PeopleSoft both develop, produce, market, and service enterprise resource planning (ERP) system software, which integrates most of an entity's data across all or most of the entity's activities. ERP software includes programs for human relations management (HRM), financial management systems (FMS), customer relations management (CRM), supply chain management (SCM), product life cycle management, and business intelligence (BI), among many others. These are called the pillars.

Although ERP encompasses many pillars, the plaintiffs asserted claims with respect to only two pillars: HRM and FMS. They defined the relevant product market as those HRM and FMS products able to meet the needs of large and complex enterprises with "high functional needs" and asserted that the only players in this market were Oracle, PeopleSoft, and SAP America. The plaintiffs also alleged that the relevant geographic market was confined to the United States. As a result, they argued that the proposed merger would constrict this highly concentrated oligopoly to a duopoly of SAP and a merged Oracle/PeopleSoft.

Oracle contended that the market definition was legally and practicably too narrow for a number of reasons, including (1) "high function" HRM and FMS software does not exist and is only a label created by the plaintiffs; (2) there is just one market for all HRM and FMS ERP products; (3) many firms besides the three compete in the larger HRM/FMS market; and (4) the geographic area of competition is worldwide or, at the very least, the United States and Europe.

**› ISSUE PRESENTED** What are the relevant product and geographic markets for purposes of determining the lawfulness of the proposed acquisition of PeopleSoft by Oracle Corporation?

**› OPINION** WALKER, C.J., writing for the U.S. District Court for the Northern District of California:

Section 7 of the Clayton Act prohibits a person "engaged in commerce or in any activity affecting commerce" from acquiring "the whole or any part" of a business' stock or assets if the effect of the acquisition "may be substantially to lessen competition, or to tend to create a monopoly." The United States is authorized to seek an injunction to block the acquisition, as are private parties and the several states. . . . Plaintiffs have the burden of proving a violation of section 7 by a preponderance of the evidence.

. . .

To establish a section 7 violation, plaintiffs must show that a pending acquisition is reasonably likely to cause anticompetitive effects. "Section 7 does not require proof that a merger or other acquisition [will] cause higher prices in the affected market. All that is necessary is that the merger create an appreciable danger of such consequences in the future." Substantial competitive harm is likely to result if a merger creates or enhances "market power," a term that has specific meaning in antitrust law.

. . .

In determining whether a transaction will create or enhance market power, courts historically have first defined the relevant product and geographic markets within which the competitive effects of the transaction are to be assessed. . . .

*(Continued)*

(Case 16.4 *continued*)

This is a "necessary predicate" to finding anticompetitive effects. Market definition under the case law proceeds by determining the market shares of the firms involved in the proposed transaction, the overall concentration level in the industry and the trends in the level of concentration. Significant trend toward concentration creates a presumption that the transaction violates section 7. In other words, plaintiffs establish a prima facie case of a section 7 violation by "showing that the merger would produce a 'firm controlling an undue percentage share of the relevant market, and [would] result in a significant increase in the concentration of firms in that market.'" Under Philadelphia Nat'l Bank,[59] a post-merger market share of 30 percent or higher unquestionably gives rise to the presumption of illegality.

. . .

The [Horizontal Merger] Guidelines view statistical and non-statistical factors as an integrated whole, avoiding the burden shifting presumptions of the case law. The Guidelines define market power as "the ability profitably to maintain prices above competitive levels for a significant period of time." Guidelines § 0.1. Five factors are relevant to the finding of market power: (1) whether the merger would significantly increase concentration and would result in a concentrated market, properly defined; (2) whether the merger raises concerns about potential adverse competitive effects; (3) whether timely and likely entry would deter or counteract anticompetitive effects; (4) whether the merger would realize efficiency gains that cannot otherwise be achieved; and (5) whether *either party would likely* fail in the absence of the merger Guidelines § 0.2.

. . .

Added together, plaintiffs propose a very restricted product market definition: HRM and FMS integrated suites sold to large complex enterprises ("high function FMS and HRM market"). Plaintiffs have defined the asserted relevant product market using a large number of factors. In sum, the competition between Oracle and PeopleSoft that plaintiffs claim will be impaired bears the following characteristics:

Product characteristics:

- Software licensing and maintenance;
- HRM and FMS (as separate markets);

Customer characteristics:

- High function needs;
- Oracle or PeopleSoft are major vendors in their software footprint;

Performance characteristics

- Scalable;
- Highly configurable;
- Seamlessly integratable;
- Able to accommodate rapid growth, acquisitions and reorganizations;
- Able to reflect actual units of business; and
- Able to adapt to industry specific requirements.

Plaintiffs contend that this product market does not include mid-market vendors, best-of-breed solutions, incumbent solutions or outsourcing.

. . .

59. United States v. Philadelphia Nat'l Bank, 374 U.S. 321, 364 (1963).

*(Continued)*

(Case 16.4 *continued*)

[Douglas Burgum, the senior vice president of Microsoft Business Solutions, testified that Microsoft competed with Oracle, PeopleSoft, and SAP only for mid-market customers and had "only the humblest of intentions" in entering into an alliance with BearingPoint, a consulting firm that recommends software to mid-market and high function customers. He also testified that Microsoft's proposal (which was ultimately abandoned) to acquire SAP was motivated not by a desire to enter the high function market for ERP and thereby start competing with Oracle or PeopleSoft, but rather by a desire to create "a better value for the customers who use Microsoft Office to work with and make decisions around the data that would come out of the SAP system." The court concluded that] Burgum's Uriah Heep like humility about Microsoft's intentions regarding the failed SAP alliance and the successful BearingPoint alliance was unconvincing. It strains credulity to believe that Microsoft would offer billions of dollars to acquire SAP merely to make data processing easier for customers who use both Microsoft Office and SAP ERP.

The test of market definition turns on reasonable substitutability. This requires the court to determine whether or not products have "reasonable interchangeability" based upon "price, use and qualities. . . ."

. . .

In order to sustain plaintiffs' product market definition the court must find, by a preponderance of the evidence, that plaintiffs have shown an articulable and distinct product market for HRM and FMS sold by Oracle, PeopleSoft and SAP only that does not include mid-market software, outsourcing solutions, best of breed solutions, legacy systems or the infrastructure layer.

Based upon a review of the law and the evidence, the court concludes that the plaintiffs have not met their burden of establishing that the relevant product market is limited to so-called high function FMS and HRM sold by Oracle, PeopleSoft and SAP. The equivocal and vague evidence presented by plaintiffs at trial does not permit the court to exclude mid-market vendors, outsourcing or best of breed solutions from any product market that includes ERP software sold by Oracle, PeopleSoft and SAP. . . .

. . .

Plaintiffs have proven that the relevant product market does not include incumbent systems or the integration layer. But plaintiffs failed to prove that outsourcing solutions, best of breed solutions and so-called mid-market vendors should be excluded from the relevant product market. Furthermore plaintiffs have failed to establish that the area of effective competition is limited to the United States. Accordingly, plaintiffs have failed to meet their burden of proving the relevant market for section 7 analysis.

Because plaintiffs have failed to meet this predictive burden, plaintiffs are not entitled to a presumption of illegality under *Philadelphia Nat'l Bank* or the Guidelines.

. . .

Because plaintiffs have not shown by a preponderance of the evidence that the merger of Oracle and PeopleSoft is likely substantially to lessen competition in a relevant product and geographic market in violation of 15 USC § 7, the court directs the entry of judgment against plaintiffs and in favor of defendant Oracle Corporation.

**› RESULT** The court entered judgment for Oracle Corporation. Its proposed acquisition of PeopleSoft did not violate Section 7 of the Clayton Act and thus could not be blocked on antitrust grounds.

*(Continued)*

(Case 16.4 *continued*)

**› CRITICAL THINKING QUESTIONS**

1. The court noted that although they were not alone in the ERP business, Oracle, PeopleSoft, and SAP had the "most comprehensive ERP software offerings." At the time of the tender offer, Oracle CEO Larry Ellison indicated that he planned to eliminate the PeopleSoft products after the merger. Even if the market is defined to include smaller players, outsourcing providers, and best-of-breed solutions, won't the elimination of one of the three key players in this larger market be anticompetitive?
2. What was the relevance of Douglas Burgum's testimony to the issue at hand? Would the result have been the same if Chief Judge Walker had believed Burgum?

## *Vertical Mergers*

A *vertical merger* is the acquisition by one company of another company at a higher or lower level in the chain of production and distribution. For example, the merger of an airplane manufacturer and an airplane-engine manufacturer would be a vertical merger. In vertical merger cases, courts tend to focus on whether the merger has excluded competitors from a significant sector of the market. For example, Section 7 was held to be violated when competing suppliers were denied access to approximately 25 percent of the highly concentrated automobile market. When the market is less concentrated, however, the courts will analyze the market more thoroughly to determine whether the transaction has any anticompetitive effects.

**INTERNATIONAL SNAPSHOT**

Invocation of another nation's antitrust laws can be an important strategy for international expansion. In recent years, Procter & Gamble (P&G) has successfully wielded antitrust laws against competitors to support its move into Latin America. After losing to Colgate–Palmolive in a bidding war to acquire a Brazilian toothpaste manufacturer with 52 percent market share, P&G contacted the Brazilian trade commission. P&G pointed out that Colgate already controlled 27 percent of the market, whereas P&G was simply trying to get its foot in the door. In 1996, after a two-year review, the agency ordered Colgate to pull the acquired Brazilian brand from the shelves for four years. Earlier that year, P&G complained to Mexican regulators about the likely effects of the merger between Kimberly–Clark and Scott Paper. Because the merger would give the new entity control over 90 percent of the Mexican tissue market, P&G supplied the Mexican officials with reams of data about the Mexican tissue business and pointed out that the earlier rulings on the merger by U.S. and European officials required Kimberly to sell off its worldwide baby-wipes operation. As a result, Mexican regulators required Kimberly to divest itself of a popular brand of tissue with 20 percent market share. P&G's use of similar tactics against Unilever Group in Argentina resulted in an investigation by Argentine officials into charges that Unilever used unfair trade practices in the market for laundry detergent.[a]

**a.** Tara Parker-Pope, *P&G Calls the Cops as It Strives to Expand Sales in Latin America,* WALL ST. J., Mar. 20, 1998, at A1.

## *Conglomerate Mergers*

In the 1960s and 1970s, many academics and government prosecutors favored expanding Section 7 prohibitions to cover mergers that were neither horizontal nor vertical in the traditional sense. The effort to prohibit *conglomerate mergers*—that is, the acquisition of a company by another company in a different line of business—has largely been abandoned. Because the merging companies are in different markets, there is no threat to competition.

One theory advanced during this period has endured, although it has rarely been applied. A merger between firms that are not competitors at the time of the acquisition but that might, without the merger, have become competitors may be held to violate Section 7. This is because potential competition is useful in keeping prices at competitive levels. When prices rise above competitive levels, potential competitors will have an incentive to enter the market and charge competitive prices. When there is no such potential entrant into the market, there is no pressure to keep prices at competitive levels. Monopoly pricing may result.

Consequently, it can be argued that a merger violates Section 7 if a plaintiff proves that (1) the market is highly concentrated; (2) one of the merging firms is an actual, substantial competitor in the market and the other is one of a small number of firms that might have entered the market; (3) entry of the latter firm would be reasonably likely to have procompetitive effects; and (4) without the merger, entry by the latter firm was likely. Some attorneys argue that a merger does not have to eliminate an actual potential entrant in order to violate Section 7. Under this theory, it is sufficient if the merger eliminates a perceived potential entrant.

## Unfair Methods of Competition: Section 5 of the Federal Trade Commission Act

Section 5 of the Federal Trade Commission Act (FTC Act) is broader than the other antitrust laws. It provides that "unfair methods of competition in or affecting commerce and unfair or deceptive acts or practices in or affecting commerce, are hereby declared unlawful." Congress did not define these terms; instead, it empowered the Federal Trade Commission, an independent administrative agency, to determine what practices violate Section 5 so that it can be adapted to changing business practices.

The FTC has the exclusive power to enforce the FTC Act. It can conduct investigations of suspected antitrust violations and issue interpretive rulings, general statements of policy, trade regulation rules, and guidelines defining unfair or deceptive practices. It can also issue cease-and-desist orders against violators, which can be appealed to a federal court.

## Antitrust Enforcement

Federal antitrust laws provide for both government and private lawsuits. The two federal agencies responsible for enforcing U.S. antitrust laws are the Justice Department, through its Antitrust Division, and the FTC.

### Ethical Consideration

False disparaging statements about a rival may rise to the level of antitrust violation only when they have significant and enduring anticompetitive effects.[a] Is it ethical to make such statements before they rise to the level of an antitrust violation? Is it ethical to threaten antitrust litigation to quiet a competitor's accurate but disparaging remarks about one's products?

**a.** Am. Prof'l Testing Serv., Inc. v. Harcourt Brace Jovanovich Legal & Prof'l Publ'g, Inc., 108 F.3d 1147 (9th Cir. 1997).

### Criminal Violations

Violations of the Sherman Act may be prosecuted by the Justice Department as felonies. The FTC routinely refers possible criminal violations of the antitrust laws to the Justice Department. Corporations can be fined up to $10 million for each violation, and the fines can be increased under other statutes to the greater of twice the gain to the competitors or twice the loss to the victims. Individuals can be fined up to $350,000 for each violation and imprisoned for up to three years. As a practical matter, however, criminal prosecution has been limited to violators of Section 1 who participate in bid rigging or price-fixing agreements between horizontal competitors.

### Civil Suits

The federal government may also bring civil actions to enforce the antitrust laws. The Justice Department enforces the Sherman and Clayton Acts through civil suits in the federal courts. The FTC enforces the Clayton Act and the FTC Act provisions on "unfair methods of competition" (but not the Sherman Act), primarily through administrative proceedings. The FTC also enforces provisions in the FTC Act that protect consumers against unfair or deceptive acts or practices (discussed further in Chapter 17). Pursuant to a liaison agreement, the Justice Department refers all civil Robinson–Patman Act matters to the FTC for action. Although enforcement of the Robinson–Patman Act is a low priority of the FTC,[60] private enforcement through civil litigation continues.

Private plaintiffs (sometimes called private attorneys general) are entitled to recover three times the damages they have sustained as a result of violations of the Sherman Act or the Clayton Act. (Enforcement of the FTC Act is reserved to the FTC.) The U.S. government can also sue for treble damages to recover for injury to its business or property resulting from an antitrust violation. These private actions can provide a powerful tool to fight anticompetitive conduct. For example, as of April 2004 Microsoft had agreed to pay $1.6 billion to settle a private antitrust suit and resolve intellectual property claims

60. In 1984, the FTC declared that the Robinson–Patman Act was protectionist legislation that has been costly to the consumer because its underlying goal is to protect individual competitors rather than competition in general. Since then it has initiated only two Robinson–Patman enforcement actions. Irving Scher, *Corporations Should Keep in Mind the Threat of Private Litigation When Ensuring Robinson–Patman Act Compliance,* CORP. COUNS. WKLY., Jan. 16, 2002, at 24.

brought by Sun Microsystems, a longtime rival. In addition, Microsoft has paid a total of $1.5 billion, including a $1.1 billion settlement in California, to settle class-action lawsuits brought in nine states and the District of Columbia, alleging that Microsoft competed unfairly and unlawfully monopolized markets for operating systems and certain software applications. A $1 billion antitrust action filed against Microsoft by Realnetworks in December 2003 was still pending in early 2005.[61]

Finally, state attorneys general may bring civil actions for injuries sustained by residents in their respective states. In these *parens patriae actions,* treble damages may also be recovered.

## Enforcement of Section 7 and the Hart–Scott–Rodino Antitrust Improvements Act

In the event of a violation of Section 7 of the Clayton Act, the Justice Department, through the courts, and the FTC, through its own administrative proceedings, may seek (1) divestiture of acquired stock or assets; (2) sale of particular subsidiaries, divisions, or lines of business; (3) compulsory sale of needed materials to a divested firm; (4) compulsory sharing of technology; or (5) temporary restrictions upon the defendant's own output or conduct. Justice Department or FTC action can delay, if not abort, a corporate merger or acquisition.

Private parties, such as competitors of the merging firms, may also bring actions for injunctive relief. Recently, however, some courts have come to look with disfavor upon such actions, fearing that they might halt mergers that would actually intensify competition. State attorneys general may enforce Section 7, and they have begun to do so with increasing frequency.

As mentioned earlier, the Hart–Scott–Rodino Antitrust Improvements Act (HSR) requires a premerger notification to be filed with the Justice Department and FTC under certain conditions. Item 4(c) of the HSR report form requires the reporting party to submit the following, as an exhibit to the filing:

> [All] studies, surveys, analyses and reports which were prepared by or for any officer(s) or director(s) (or, in the case of unincorporated entities, individuals exercising similar functions) for the purpose of evaluating or analyzing the acquisition with respect to market shares, competition, competitors, markets, potential for sales growth or expansion into product or geographic markets, and indicate (if not contained in the document itself) the date of preparation and the name and title of each individual who prepared the document.

The typical offering memorandum (whether prepared by investment advisers or in-house) and such documents as board books, slide presentations, and memos to senior managers or board members about a potential acquisition fall within the 4(c) definition and generally must be included in the HSR filing.

In 1999, the FTC filed an enforcement action against Blackstone Capital Partners, and one of Blackstone's partners who signed the HSR filing on behalf of Blackstone, for violating Item 4(c) by failing to include a document that should have been an exhibit to the HSR filing. Blackstone was required to pay $2.785 million in civil penalties, and the individual partner was required to pay $50,000, to settle the FTC suit. This was the first time in the history of the HSR premerger reporting program that the FTC named an individual in a civil penalty action for violation of the HSR rules. According to the FTC, the case was filed to emphasize the importance the FTC places on rigorous compliance with the mandatory disclosure requirements of the HSR report, especially the requirement for so-called 4(c) documents.[62]

In December 2001, the FTC announced a proposed settlement with Hearst Corporation, under which Hearst agreed to divest the Medi-Span integratable drug information database business, which Hearst had acquired as part of its acquisition of J.B. Laughery, Inc. The order also required Hearst to disgorge $19 million of profits obtained as a result of the acquisition to injured customers as part of the settlement of a private class-action suit alleging unlawful overcharges by Hearst. The FTC had alleged that Hearst illegally failed to include several high-level corporate documents prepared to evaluate the acquisition of Medi-Span and its competitive effects in violation of Item 4(c). This case marked the first time that the FTC sought either divestiture or disgorgement of profits in a federal court action for a consummated merger. In its statement, the FTC noted that while "the Commission should seek disgorgement as a remedy in competition cases only in exceptional circumstances, Hearst's conduct was suffi-

61. Laurie J. Flynn, *Preliminary Settlement Reached in Microsoft Case,* N.Y. Times, Apr. 20, 2004, http://www.nytimes.com/2004/04/20/technology/20soft.html.

62. Press Release, *Federal Trade Commission, Merchant Banking Firm, Partner Settle FTC Charges for Incomplete Premerger Report* (Mar. 30, 1999), *at* http://www.ftc.gov/opa/1999/03/blackst.htm.

ciently egregious to justify the extraordinary remedy of disgorgement."[63]

The settlements in the *Blackstone* and *Hearst* cases highlight the importance of ensuring that the HSR filings are accurate in all respects and include all required documents. The best way to deal with the 4(c) issue is for companies to limit the creation of such documents.

## Antitrust Injury

To recover damages, a plaintiff must establish that it sustained an *antitrust injury*, that is, a loss due to a competition-reducing aspect or effect of the defendant's violation of the antitrust laws. A plaintiff may not recover under the antitrust laws for losses that resulted from competition as such.

In 1990, the Supreme Court considered whether resale price maintenance gives rise to an antitrust injury in the absence of predatory pricing. USA Petroleum, an independent gasoline retailer, claimed that Atlantic Richfield Company (ARCO), an integrated oil company, conspired with retail service stations selling ARCO-brand gasoline to fix prices at below-market levels. USA Petroleum argued that this was an illegal maximum RPM scheme whereby the competition that would otherwise exist among ARCO-brand dealers was eliminated by agreement. As a result, the retail price of ARCO-brand gasoline was maintained at artificially low and uncompetitive levels. This allegedly drove many independents in California out of business.

The U.S. Supreme Court held that USA Petroleum could not recover damages for ARCO's RPM because there was no showing of predatory pricing, that is, pricing below cost designed to drive competitors out of the market.[64] The Court reasoned that when the prices under a RPM program are set at nonpredatory levels, there is generally no anticompetitive effect, even though such pricing may reduce the market share of competitors or the price that they may charge consumers. Without doubt, those competitors are injured as a result of the practice, but there is nothing anticompetitive about that in and of itself. Indeed, such a result benefits the consumer. In such a case, the Court held, the competitor may not recover damages under the antitrust laws. (The *ARCO* case was decided seven years before the Court's decision in *State Oil Co. v. Khan*[65] eliminating *per se* treatment of maximum RPM and in many ways laid the groundwork for that decision.)

63. Press Release, *Federal Trade Commission, Hearst Corp. to Disgorge $19 Million and Divest Business to Facts and Comparisons to Settle FTC Complaint* (Dec. 14, 2001), *at* http://www.ftc.gov/opa/2001/12/hearst.htm.

64. Atlantic Richfield Co. v. USA Petroleum Co., 495 U.S. 328 (1990).

## Limitations on Antitrust Enforcement

The courts have limited the private enforcement rights of individual citizens and states by invoking the doctrine of standing. They have also limited the liability of state governments by applying state-action exemptions.

### Standing

To prevent private parties from jumping on the treble-damages bandwagon, the Supreme Court requires that a private plaintiff have *standing* to sue; that is, the plaintiff must have suffered an injury from the defendant's violation of the antitrust law. For example, a consumer buying goods from an innocent middleman does not have standing to recover from the manufacturer who was a member of a price-fixing cartel.

### State-Action Exemption

More than fifty years ago, the Supreme Court declared that the antitrust laws apply to anticompetitive actions by private parties, not to anticompetitive actions by state legislatures or administrative bodies. Thus, state action is exempt as long as (1) there is a clear state purpose to displace competition, and (2) the state provides adequate public supervision. For example, the California legislature passed a law designed to limit the production, and consequently raise the price, of raisins. Given that California produced nearly one-half of the world's raisins, the effect of this statute on interstate commerce was substantial. Nevertheless, the U.S. Supreme Court enunciated and applied the state-action exemption in this case.[66]

The courts have refused to extend the exemption to local municipalities except in certain limited circumstances. The Local Government Antitrust Act of 1984, enacted to allay municipalities' fears of treble damages, eliminated local governments' liability for antitrust damages but preserved equitable remedies, such as injunctions. The act extended immunity from damages to all officials or employees acting in an official capacity.

65. 522 U.S. 3 (1997).

66. Parker v. Brown, 317 U.S. 341 (1943).

## The Extraterritorial Reach of U.S. Antitrust Law

Sections 1 and 2 of the Sherman Act expressly apply to "trade or commerce . . . with foreign nations," so they clearly have extraterritorial reach. Because Sections 2 and 3 of the Clayton Act apply to price discrimination, tying arrangements, and exclusive-dealing contracts for commodities sold "for use, consumption, or resale within the United States," they have no extraterritorial reach.

In 1995, the Antitrust Division of the Justice Department and the FTC published a new set of International Guidelines. They state that, in enforcing the antitrust laws, the agencies will take account of "international comity," defined as "respect among co-equal sovereign nations [that] plays a role in determining the recognition which one nation allows within its territory to the legislative, executive, or judicial acts of another nation." (The comity doctrine is discussed further in Chapter 25.) Section 3 of the guidelines lists the following factors that the agencies will consider: the significance to the violation of conduct within the United States versus conduct outside the United States; the nationality of the parties involved; the presence or absence of an intent to affect U.S. consumers, markets, or exporters; the significance and foreseeability of the effects on the United States versus the effects abroad; the existence of reasonable expectations that would be furthered or defeated by the action; the degree of conflict with foreign law and economic policies; the extent to which the enforcement actions of another country may be affected; and the effectiveness of foreign enforcement versus U.S. enforcement.

To avoid disputes with foreign governments, the U.S. courts apply a *sovereign immunity* doctrine. (This doctrine is discussed further in Chapter 25.) Much litigation turns on whether a foreign firm's anticompetitive activity was directed by the government or was merely tolerated. If the foreign government tolerates but does not require the anticompetitive acts, the U.S. antitrust laws apply.

The basic U.S. rule for evaluating conduct affecting U.S. imports (where the anticompetitive conduct occurs offshore, but the adverse impact is felt in the United States) is the purpose and effects test. In *Hartford Fire Insurance Co. v. California*,[67] the Supreme Court held that the Sherman Act will apply to conduct by foreign partners in a foreign nation when (1) the intent of the parties is to affect commerce within the United States and (2) their conduct actually affects commerce in the United States. Defendants cannot defend such conduct by arguing that applicable foreign law conflicts with U.S. law unless their compliance with the laws of both countries is impossible.

Most claims alleging that foreign conduct by foreign nationals has violated U.S. antitrust laws have arisen in civil lawsuits. The following case dealt with the question of whether conduct by a non-U.S. company outside the United States but having an effect on commerce in the United States could form the basis for a criminal antitrust case.

67. 509 U.S. 764 (1993).

**A CASE IN POINT**

**CASE 16.5**

**United States v. Nippon Paper Industries Co.**

*United States Court of Appeals for the First Circuit*
*109 F.3d 1 (1st Cir. 1997), cert. denied, 525 U.S. 1044 (1998).*

### In the Language of the Court

**› FACTS** In 1995, a federal grand jury indicted Nippon Paper Industries Company, Ltd. (NPI), a Japanese manufacturer of facsimile (fax) paper, for criminally violating Section 1 of the Sherman Act. The indictment alleged that in 1990 NPI and certain unnamed co-conspirators held meetings in Japan during which they agreed to fix the price of thermal fax paper throughout North America. To achieve this goal, NPI and other manufacturers purportedly sold the paper in Japan to unaffiliated trading houses on the condition that the houses charge inflated prices for the paper when they resold it in North America. The trading houses then shipped and sold the paper to their subsidiaries in the United States, which in turn sold it to American consumers at artificially high prices.

NPI moved to dismiss the indictment, in part because the alleged conduct took place entirely in Japan and was, therefore, beyond the reach of the Sherman Act in a criminal case. Accepting this argument, the district court dismissed the case. The government appealed.

**› ISSUE PRESENTED** May a criminal antitrust prosecution be based on conduct that took place entirely outside the United States?

*(Continued)*

(Case 16.5 *continued*)

**› OPINION** SELYA, J., writing for the U.S. Court of Appeals for the First Circuit:

Our law has long presumed that "legislation of Congress, unless a contrary intent appears, is meant to apply only within the territorial jurisdiction of the United States." . . .

. . . But a sovereign ordinarily can impose liability for conduct outside its borders that produces consequences within them. . . .

. . .

. . . [T]he case law now conclusively establishes that civil antitrust actions predicated on wholly foreign conduct which has an intended and substantial effect in the United States come within [Sherman Act] Section One's jurisdictional reach. . . .

. . . Were this case a civil case, our journey would be complete. But here the United States essays a criminal prosecution for solely extraterritorial conduct rather than a civil action. This is largely uncharted terrain. . . .

Be that as it may . . . in both criminal and civil cases, the claim that Section One applies extraterritorially is based on the same language in the same section of the same statute: "Every contract, combination in the form of trust or otherwise, or conspiracy, in restraint of trade or commerce among the several States, or with foreign nations, is declared to be illegal."

. . .

. . . It is a fundamental interpretive principle that identical words or terms used in different parts of the same act are intended to have the same meaning. . . .

. . .

NPI . . . make(s) much of the fact that this appears to be the first criminal case in which the United States endeavors to extend Section One to wholly foreign conduct. . . . There is a first time for everything, and the absence of earlier criminal actions is probably more a demonstration of the increasingly global nature of our economy than proof that Section One cannot cover wholly foreign conduct in the criminal milieu.

. . .

The next arrow which NPI yanks from its quiver is the rule of lenity. The rule . . . provides that, in the course of interpreting statutes in criminal cases, a reviewing court should resolve ambiguities affecting a statute's scope in the defendant's favor. . . . "[T]he rule of lenity applies only if, after seizing everything from which aid can be derived, [a court] can make no more than a guess as to what Congress intended." Put bluntly, the rule of lenity cannot be used to create ambiguity when the meaning of a law, even if not readily apparent, is upon inquiry, reasonably clear.

. . .

. . . [T]he rule of lenity plays no part in the instant case.

International comity is a doctrine that counsels voluntary forbearance when a sovereign which has a legitimate claim to jurisdiction concludes that a second sovereign also has a legitimate claim to jurisdiction under principles of international law. . . . In all events, [comity's] growth in the antitrust sphere has been stunted by *Hartford Fire*,[68] in which the Court suggested that comity concerns would operate to defeat the exercise of jurisdiction only in those few cases in which the law of the foreign sovereign required a defendant to act in a manner incompatible with the Sherman Act or in which full compliance with both statutory schemes was impossible. . . .

68. Hartford Fire Ins. Co. v. Cal., 509 U.S. 764 (1993).

*(Continued)*

(Case 16.5 *continued*)

In this case the defendant's comity-based argument is even more attenuated. The conduct with which NPI is charged is illegal under both Japanese and American laws, thereby alleviating any founded concern about NPI being whipsawed between separate sovereigns. . . . [T]he government charges that the defendant orchestrated a conspiracy with the object of rigging prices in the United States. If the government can prove these charges, we see no tenable reason why principles of comity should shield NPI from prosecution.

**› RESULT** The decision of the trial court was reversed, and the indictment reinstated. NPI could be criminally prosecuted in the United States for fixing prices of products sold in the United States even though the meetings to fix prices took place in Japan.

**› CRITICAL THINKING QUESTIONS**

1. Imagine that the court had ruled that Section 1 of the Sherman Act did not apply to criminal activity that occurred abroad. How would this ruling affect commerce? How would it affect other governments' roles in regulating commerce in the United States?
2. Should foreign plaintiffs who suffered antitrust injury as a result of conduct that occurred outside the United States be entitled to sue defendants in U.S. courts?

---

U.S. antitrust enforcement is less aggressive in dealing with conduct affecting U.S. exports where anticompetitive U.S. domestic conduct affects foreign markets. The Foreign Trade Antitrust Improvement Act of 1982 (FTAIA) expressly provides that Section 1 of the Sherman Act does not apply to conduct involving trade or commerce (other than import trade or commerce) with foreign nations unless:

> (1) such conduct has a direct, substantial and reasonably foreseeable effect: (a) on trade or commerce which is not trade or commerce with foreign nations, or (b) on export trade or export commerce with foreign nations, of a person engaged in such trade or commerce in the United States; [and] (2) such effect gives rise to a claim under the provisions of [the Sherman Act], other than this section.

The language of the FTAIA that is critical to coverage of U.S. exports is Subsection 1(b), which provides that antitrust conduct (whether by U.S. or foreign firms and whether occurring in the United States or elsewhere) can be regulated under the Sherman or FTC Acts if it has a "direct, substantial and reasonably foreseeable effect of restraining U.S. exports."

Section 4 of the Export Trading Act (also known as the Webb-Pomerene Export Act) exempts conduct affecting the export of goods by an association of U.S.-based firms that would otherwise violate the Sherman Act if the conduct does not (1) have an anticompetitive effect in the United States, (2) injure domestic competitors of the association members, or (3) "artificially or intentionally enhance or depress prices within" the United States. To gain and maintain this exemption, the association must file its articles of agreement and annual reports with the FTC.

Many countries do not accept treble damages as a remedy. For example, the United Kingdom does not allow any recovery in excess of single damages. Suppose a U.S. court awards a U.S. corporation, USCO, $15 million in damages, after trebling, in a suit against UKCO, a U.K. corporation. When USCO attempts to collect $15 million of UKCO's assets, the U.K. court will treat two-thirds of the $15 million award, or $10 million, as an illegal treble-damages award. Thus, USCO will be able to recover only $5 million in the U.K. court. Even when a U.S. court finds a foreign corporation in violation of the antitrust laws, any award of damages is meaningless without foreign enforcement of the award unless the foreign corporation has assets in the United States that can be attached to satisfy the judgment.

## U.S. Control over Offshore Mergers and Other Consolidations

The Justice Department and the FTC have generally required HSR reports for (1) U.S. acquisitions of foreign-based assets or securities and (2) foreign acquisitions of U.S.-based assets or securities that meet the size of persons and size of transaction tests. These requirements are actively enforced. For example, in 1997, the FTC fined German auto-parts maker Mahle GmbH $5.1 million for failing to alert the agencies to its $40 million purchase of 40.1 percent of a Brazilian rival's voting stock. The FTC found that it had authority to intervene because both companies had U.S. subsidiaries. In 1996, U.S.-based Sara Lee Corporation paid a fine of $3.1 million after the FTC challenged its failure to notify authorities in 1991 of its purchase of $26 million of assets from a company in the United Kingdom. Sara Lee had counted the deal as two transactions that were each separately exempt from the prenotification requirements as a result of their small size: $13.1 million for the company's U.S. assets and $12.7 million for its U.K. assets. The FTC determined that the transactions should have been aggregated and, in addition to imposing the fine, forced Sara Lee to sell one of the brands it had acquired from the U.K. company and another brand it had acquired previously.[69]

In April 2002, certain amendments to the Hart–Scott–Rodino Act became effective that relaxed the premerger filing requirements for foreign acquisitions by expanding the exemptions available to buyers of foreign assets and securities. However, these amendments also extended the scope of the Act to include some acquisitions of foreign assets by foreign companies for the first time, eliminating what had previously been an absolute exemption. Under the amendments, no HSR notification is required (1) if a U.S. or foreign person acquires foreign assets, unless those assets generated sales in or into the United States in excess of $50 million during the most recent fiscal year; (2) if a U.S. person acquires voting securities of a foreign issuer unless the issuer either (a) holds assets in the United States with an aggregate value in excess of $50 million or (b) made aggregate sales in or into the United States in excess of $50 million during the most recent fiscal year; or (3) if a foreign person acquires voting securities of a foreign issuer unless (a) the sale confers control of the issuer to the buyer and (b) the issuer either (i) holds assets in the United States with an aggregate value in excess of $50 million or (ii) made aggregate sales in or into the United States in excess of $50 million during the most recent fiscal year. Although the absolute exemption for foreign acquisitions of foreign assets has been eliminated, the amendments further provide that these transactions are still exempt if the size of the transaction is less than $200 million and (1) the aggregate sales of the acquiror and acquired person in or into the United States are less than $110 million, (2) the aggregate assets of the acquiror and acquired person located in the United States are less than $110 million, and (3) the size of persons test is not exceeded. This exemption protects small acquisitions by foreign buyers of foreign persons doing business with the United States.[70]

69. John R. Wilke & Bryan Gruley, *Fines Grow for Evading Antitrust Review*, WALL ST. J., Feb. 28, 1997, at A2.

70. 16 C.F.R. pts. 802.51, 802.52.

## *Global View*

### ANTITRUST LAWS IN THE EUROPEAN UNION

In the European Union, the principal rules of competition law are set forth in Articles 81 and 82 of the Treaty of Amsterdam and the Merger Control Regulation. Firms doing business in the EU must also comply with the various antitrust laws of member nations. However, to the extent EU law applies and conflicts with the laws of a member nation, EU law will prevail.

Article 81, which aims at conduct similar to that addressed in Section 1 of the Sherman Act ("concerted practices which have the object or effect of preventing, restraining or distorting competition with the Common Market"), includes a nonexclusive list of prohibited activities, which include price-fixing, output restrictions, market allocations, discriminatory practices, and tying arrangements. However, the European Commission has issued a number of "block" or group exemptions, which exempt whole categories of agreements. Even if a block exemption is not available, individual exemptions can be granted for specific agreements although the process for obtaining them is long and complex. Exemptions are binding on the EU, as well as on national authorities and the courts of member nations.

One of the major differences between U.S. and EU competition laws is the EU's approach to vertical territorial restraints. Although the EU generally prohibits horizontal agreements

*(Continued)*

(Global View *continued)*

between competitors in the same way as U.S. antitrust laws, the EU takes a stricter view of vertical arrangements because of their tendency to impede continent-wide market integration. As a result, whereas U.S. manufacturers are free to appoint exclusive distributors in each state, similar exclusive arrangements are suspect in the EU unless made pursuant to applicable block exemptions.

Article 82, which prohibits abuse of an entity's dominant position, is in some ways stricter than Section 2 of the Sherman Act because the definition of the relevant market is narrower and the degree of market power that makes a company dominant is less. The concept of what constitutes "abuse" is also broader than the U.S. concept of "monopolization." Unlike the broad language in Section 2 of the Sherman Act, Article 86 lists four types of conduct that constitute abuse of dominant position: imposing unfair pricing, limiting production, employing discriminatory trade practices, and imposing a tying arrangement.[a] The question of what constitutes a dominant position is complex and depends on a number of factors, such as the firm's market share in the relevant market, the competitive pressures it faces, its ability to control price, and barriers to entry to its market.

Although EU competition law shares the U.S. antitrust goal of preventing abuse of market power, there are substantive differences between the two laws. EU law is concerned with the effects of anticompetitive actions on competitors as well as consumers, whereas U.S. law focuses primarily on consumers. There are also material differences in enforcement. The European Commission has the primary responsibility for enforcing EU competition laws. Unlike U.S. law, EU law does not include a private right of action,[b] there is no criminal enforcement authority, and treble damages are not available.

### Extraterritorial Reach of EU Antitrust Law

EU competition law has an international component similar to the U.S. law announced in *Hartford Fire Insurance Co. v. California*. To date, antitrust enforcement in the EU has been predominantly government initiated and private enforcement has been very limited, so the problems associated with U.S. private enforcement do not arise in the EU. If U.S. or other firms engage in conduct outside the EU that, had it occurred within the EU, would have violated the antitrust laws of the Treaty of Amsterdam, and that conduct has the purpose and effect of distorting competition within the EU, then the conduct violates the treaty, and those provisions are enforceable against the violators, whether foreign or domestic. On the export side (i.e., can EU antitrust laws be used to protect U.S. markets?), there is no EU legislation that is equivalent to the Webb-Pomerene Export Act, but the language of the Treaty of Amsterdam does not appear to put EU export cartels in jeopardy unless they have impacts within the EU.

The EU and its predecessors have enforced its laws against U.S. companies doing business in Europe for many years. For example, in 1980, the European Commission opened a proceeding against IBM, the world's largest computer manufacturer. The Commission claimed that IBM had abused its dominant position in the supply of two key products (the central processing unit, CPU, and the operating system) for its most powerful range of computers, System/370, in an effort to control the markets for the supply of all products compatible with System/370. The alleged abuses included (1) failing to supply other manufacturers in sufficient time with the technical interface information needed to permit competitive products to be used with System/370, (2) not offering System/370 CPUs without main memory included in the price, (3) not offering System/370 CPUs without the basic software included in the price, and (4) refusing to supply certain software installation services to users of non-IBM CPUs.

In 1984, IBM agreed to offer its System/370 CPUs either without main memory or with only such capacity as was strictly required for testing and to disclose, in a timely manner, sufficient interface information to enable competitors to attach both their hardware and software products to System/370. IBM had previously advised the EC that it had taken steps to make installation services available to all users of its software and was in the course of unbundling all software.[c]

More recently, the EU challenged Microsoft on the basis that it was illegally leveraging its Windows operating system monopoly to gain unfair advantage in the server and audiovisual software markets. While the settlement struck by U.S. regulators with Microsoft allowed it to continue to freely bundle new technologies into its operating system (see the "Inside Story"), the EU ordered Microsoft to offer a version of its Windows operating system with its MediaPlayer software stripped out, in addition to requiring it to license certain of its proprietary code to its competitors so that their software could communicate more effectively with the Windows operating system. The EU also fined Microsoft more than $600 million for competing unfairly in the European software market (the EU had never fined a monopolist more than $75 million before). Microsoft announced that it will appeal the EU ruling in European courts.

### EU Control over Offshore Mergers and Other Consolidations

Although Articles 81 and 82 of the Treaty of Amsterdam appear to confer ample authority for the EU to control anticompetitive mergers, for a number of years mergers were not a focus of concern in EU competition law. In late 1989, however, the European Council passed the EC Merger Control Regulation, which became effective on September 21, 1990, and was amended in

a. MARK R. SANDSTROM & DAVID N. GOLDSWEIG, NEGOTIATING AND STRUCTURING INTERNATIONAL COMMERCIAL TRANSACTIONS 421 (2003).

b. Although EU competition law does not include a private right of action, many member states have a private right of action for violation of their local competition laws. Elizabeth Morony & Ingrid Cope, *Private Antitrust Remedies: Latest Developments*, GLOBAL COUNS. (Mar. 2003), *at* http://practicallaw/scripts/article.asp?Article_ID=28534.

c. Commission of the European Communities, Fourteenth Report on Competition Policy (1984).

*(Continued)*

(Global View *continued*)

1997. EU merger control has developed substantially over the past fifteen years, both in the volume of cases handled and in the greater substantive rigor with which the reviews are conducted. EU merger analysis is stricter than in the United States because of the EU's greater willingness to consider theories of competitive harm and its greater reliance on input from competitors. In addition, the fact that the EU can prohibit a merger without going to court gives the EU's Merger Task Force power and discretion that exceed that of its U.S. counterparts.

The Merger Control Regulation provides that in determining whether to challenge a merger within its jurisdiction, the EU must decide whether it is "compatible with the common market." The substantive test applied is whether a concentration will "create or strengthen a dominant position as a result of which effective competition would be significantly impeded in the common market or a substantial part of it." Although the analysis is similar to U.S. law, the outcome can be different. For example, even though the U.S. government had approved General Electric's $49 billion bid for Honeywell International, the European Commission vetoed the deal in January 2001, on the basis that GE might have been able to drive competitors out of the aerospace market by offering customers a complete package of GE engines, Honeywell avionics, and financing from GE Capital Aviation Services. The EU's decision was criticized in the United States, where regulators are inclined to allow businesses to pursue such synergies.[d] This was the first all-U.S. merger killed in the EU after having been approved by the U.S. antitrust authorities.

As the global economy becomes more of an economic reality, the antitrust analysis of the relevant market will have to take account of foreign goods produced but not sold in the United States. Another issue that must be resolved in the future is how the antitrust laws will apply to U.S. companies purchasing foreign entities that have potentially valuable national security or technology applications in highly concentrated markets.

**d.** *Q&A: GE's Failed Merger*, BBC NEWS, July 4, 2001, *at* http://bbc/co/uk/2/hi/business/1421879.stm.

THE RESPONSIBLE MANAGER

## AVOIDING ANTITRUST VIOLATIONS

Although a manager can never eliminate all possible antitrust violations, implementing a number of steps can help to avoid them. The underlying purpose of the antitrust statutes is to benefit consumers by promoting competition. The economy functions best when firms compete vigorously, but fairly, with one another. In antitrust, however, the line between legal and illegal conduct is often blurry. Consequently, there are few rules that a manager can give his or her employees. Rather, the manager must identify the activities or conditions that most often trigger antitrust liability, such as discussions with competitors, discussions with buyers about their future prices, and activities that may increase concentration in any market that is already highly concentrated.

Discussions among competitors receive the highest degree of antitrust scrutiny. Trade and professional associations are particularly vulnerable. If they disseminate information that identifies parties to individual transactions and the prices of even past or current individual transactions, the antitrust laws may be violated. Equally hazardous is the dissemination of information that may result in market division or output restriction. As a general rule, any trade association information concerning prices should be immediately forwarded to in-house or outside counsel to address potential antitrust concerns.

Antitrust scrutiny is also heightened whenever price is discussed, even between manufacturers and retailers. A corporation must make clear to its salespersons that they should not coerce the retailer regarding the minimum price it charges the end consumer. Such conduct may raise the specter of treble-damages liability.

Finally, antitrust scrutiny is heightened where markets are highly concentrated. The fewer the entities that compete in a particular market, the more likely that agreements among them can be effectuated and that mergers can lead to unlawful monopolies. Consequently, corporations operating in concentrated markets should be particularly cautious. A manager can obtain rough approximations of market concentration from company counsel.

Employees should be encouraged, through an appropriate award system, to inform the manager whenever any of the above "red flags" appear. A manager should not hesitate to seek assistance from counsel in analyzing any activity that might violate the antitrust laws. The manager should also be careful to avoid any situation that could be interpreted as evidence of illegal activity. If

*(Continued)*

(The Responsible Manager *continued*)

a manager attending a trade show, for example, hears competitors discussing price or other terms of sale, the manager should leave the room, preferably in a manner that calls attention to his or her departure, such as by spilling a drink while leaving a group of competitors having drinks at a bar.

Common sense and education are the keys. Actions that don't seem fair usually are not. Continuing education programs will keep corporate employees aware of potential antitrust problems. A manager should always stress that short-term gains through unethical or illegal behavior are always outweighed by longer-term losses, particularly in the area of antitrust with its treble-damages awards.

INSIDE STORY

## AN OPERATING SYSTEM BY ANY OTHER NAME WOULD BROWSE AS SWEETLY

In 1994, the U.S. Department of Justice's Antitrust Division charged Microsoft Corporation, the largest software company in the world, with unlawful monopoly and restraint of trade under Sections 1 and 2 of the Sherman Act. Among other things, the regulators alleged that Microsoft had engaged in anticompetitive marketing practices directed at personal computer (PC) manufacturers that preinstall operating system software on the PCs they produce for retail sale. These practices included charging per-processor royalties, whereby PC manufacturers were offered a discount if they agreed to pay a royalty to Microsoft for each computer processor sold, regardless of whether the unit was shipped with the Microsoft operating system or a competitor's operating system.

The government based its case on the notion of "network economics," a condition in which the value of owning a product rises as other consumers own the same product. Facsimile machines are an obvious example. Having the only fax machine in the world is worthless, but having one of a million fax machines is quite valuable because it allows one to communicate with 999,999 other fax-machine owners. Much of the value of the product arises from being part of the network. Networks can be physical, such as telephones and railroads, or virtual, such as most shared technologies and standards. For instance, software developers generally prefer to invest their resources in designing applications for operating systems in widespread, rather than limited, use. Once there are many applications for an operating system, that system becomes more attractive to consumers as well.

For this reason, Microsoft's stunning success in the market for PC operating system software worried the regulators. Because most PC owners used Microsoft's operating system, the regulators argued, Microsoft could coerce them into buying other products simply by tying the two together. For instance, Microsoft might condition the sale of Windows on the purchase of its word-processing software Word. By tying the products together, Microsoft would force PC users to combine, rather than separate, their choices for operating systems and word processors. As a result, consumers of PCs would end up buying Microsoft's operating system and its word processor even if they would prefer Microsoft's operating system and a non-Microsoft word processor. Of course, consumers could still purchase the non-Microsoft word processor, but the additional purchase price and switching costs would probably deter some.

Microsoft argued, however, that operating systems are dynamic and must respond to consumer demand and technological advances. Microsoft reasoned that operating systems initially did not include modules for data compression, memory management, file backup, or device driving. Such "extras" were provided separately. Over time, these functions were integrated into the operating system as consumers began to expect them as standard rather than options.

While the antitrust guardians were battling Microsoft and hammering out a consent decree,[71] the World Wide Web came into being and promised to give everyone

71. Microsoft signed a consent decree with the Department of Justice on August 21, 1995, pursuant to which Microsoft agreed not to charge per-processor royalties and not to condition the licensing of its operating system software to original equipment manufacturers (OEMs) on their agreement to license other Microsoft products. Microsoft retained the right to develop integrated products, however.

*(Continued)*

(Inside Story *continued*)

access to everything. In April 1994, Microsoft founder, chair, and CEO Bill Gates publicly announced Microsoft's intention to include Internet-browsing software in Windows 95. Soon after, Microsoft unveiled Internet Explorer (IE) to compete with Netscape Communications Corporation's wildly popular Navigator browser. By the time Microsoft signed the consent decree in 1995, Microsoft had already supplied to manufacturers a version of Windows 95 bundled with IE at no additional cost. OEMs were prohibited from disassembling the package.

Historically, PC operating systems have always served to coordinate a user's access to various sources of information, including internal hard drives, floppy disk drives, random access memory, and CD-ROM drives. With the birth of the Internet, Microsoft reasoned, it was time for operating systems to provide access to this next, great source of information. By its logic, integration of Web browsers was the natural next step in operating system evolution.

Within two years, Internet Explorer had garnered more than 40 percent of the Web browser market, largely at Netscape's expense. No doubt, IE's rapid success arose in part from Microsoft's provision of the browser with Windows for the same price. Its functionality, however, made it a worthy rival to Navigator. Many critics concluded that Internet Explorer 4.0, released in 1997, was a better product than Netscape Navigator.[72] Dell Computer Corporation chair Michael Dell claimed that his customers would demand Windows with IE even if the products were not bundled.[73]

On October 20, 1997, the Justice Department petitioned the U.S. District Court for the District of Columbia to find Microsoft in contempt of court for violating the 1995 consent decree and to fine the company $1 million per day until it complied by unbundling Windows and IE.

The case was assigned to Judge Thomas Penfield Jackson, a pro-business conservative Republican appointed by President Reagan. Although Judge Jackson did not find Microsoft in contempt, he did issue a preliminary injunction prohibiting Microsoft from further conditioning its licensing of PC operating system software (including Windows 95 or any successor version) on the licensing of any Microsoft browser pending development of the record.

On May 12, 1998, the U.S. Court of Appeals for the District of Columbia stayed the injunction insofar as it applied to Windows 98 (which further integrated IE into the operating system).[74] The court held that the United States had presented no evidence suggesting Windows 98 was not an integrated product and thus exempt from the prohibitions of the consent decree. The court ruled that, at least for purposes of deciding whether products were integrated within the meaning of the consent decree, the test was whether the integrated product provided functionalities and advantages that consumers could not themselves achieve by buying both products and using them together. The court also questioned the competency of judges to dictate what features should be included in an operating system.

Faced with the imminent launch of Windows 98 and perhaps believing that it was now or never, the Justice Department filed a wide-ranging complaint against Microsoft on May 18, 1998. The attorneys general of twenty states filed similar suits the same day. The Justice Department alleged that Microsoft's restrictive agreements with Internet and online service providers (such as America Online) and Internet content providers, whereby those companies agreed not to license, distribute, or promote non-Microsoft products (or to do so only on terms that materially disadvantaged such products), and Microsoft's agreements with OEMs restricting modification or customization of the PC boot-up sequence and screen, unreasonably restricted competition in violation of Section 1. The complaint also alleged that Microsoft had engaged in a series of anticompetitive practices (including tying and unreasonably exclusionary agreements) with the purpose and effect of maintaining its PC operating system monopoly and extending that monopoly to the Internet browser market in violation of Section 2. The case was assigned to Judge Jackson.

In February 1999, after a lengthy trial, the district court issued a 207-page finding of fact that strongly and clearly rejected Microsoft's version of the facts.[75] On April 3, 2000, the district court entered its conclusions of law. The court held that Microsoft had violated Section 1 by tying Internet Explorer to Windows and had attempted to monopolize the browser market in violation of Section 2. The court rejected the Justice Department's exclusive dealing claim under Section 1 on the grounds that Microsoft's promotion and distribution

72. For a list of product reviews, see http://www.microsoft.com/ie/press/.

73. David Bank, *Why Software and Antitrust Law Make an Uneasy Mix,* WALL ST. J., Oct. 22, 1997, at B1.

74. Microsoft Corp. v. United States, 147 F.3d 935 (D.C. Cir. 1998).

75. United States v. Microsoft Corp., 84 F. Supp. 2d 9 (D.D.C. 1999).

*(Continued)*

(Inside Story *continued*)

© Ingram Pinn/Financial Times, April 5, 2000.

agreements for Internet Explorer did not foreclose enough of the relevant market to constitute a violation.

On June 7, 2000, the district court ordered that Microsoft be split into two companies, with one selling the Window's operating system and the other selling Microsoft's Office suite of word-processing, spreadsheets, and other applications. Microsoft immediately appealed.

After issuing his decision, Judge Jackson agreed to be interviewed, an extremely unusual act by a sitting federal judge. During the interview, he made it clear that Microsoft's lack of credibility undermined its arguments. Quoting the Latin expression *"Falsus in uno, falsus in omnibus,"* which means "Untrue in one thing, untrue in everything," he commented, "I don't subscribe to that as absolutely true. But it does lead one to suspicion. It's a universal human experience. If someone lies to you once, how much else can you credit as the truth?"[76] The judge also referred to his lack of trust in Microsoft in his written decision explaining his order to break up the company.

In its appeal of the district court's decision, Microsoft criticized Judge Jackson's decision to speak to the press about the case. Microsoft also argued that the court's decision reflected a "profound misunderstanding" of antitrust laws. The company asserted that, contrary to the court's finding, its conduct was procompetitive and helped, rather than harmed, consumers.

On June 28, 2001, the U.S. Court of Appeals for the District of Columbia issued its opinion. It affirmed in part and reversed in part the district court's judgment that Microsoft had violated Section 2 of the Sherman Act by employing anticompetitive means to maintain a monopoly in the operating system market and reversed the district court's finding that Microsoft had violated Section 2 of the Sherman Act by illegally attempting to monopolize the Internet browser market. The court of appeals also reversed the finding that Microsoft had committed a *per se* violation of Section 1 by unlawfully tying its browser to its operating system and remanded this issue to the trial court for consideration under the rule of reason (the Justice Department subsequently elected not to pursue the tying issue). Most significantly, the court of appeals vacated the district court's final judgment on remedies and required that the case be assigned to a different trial judge on remand, noting:

> [W]e vacate the Final Judgment on remedies, because the trial judge engaged in impermissible ex parte contacts by holding secret interviews with members of the media and made numerous offensive comments about Microsoft officials in public statements outside of the courtroom, giving rise to an appearance of partiality. Although we find no evidence of actual bias, we hold that the actions of the trial judge seriously tainted the proceedings before the District Court and called into question the integrity of the judicial process.[77]

In November 2001, Microsoft, the Justice Department, and nine of the eighteen states that had joined in the litigation agreed to a settlement. The remaining nine states rejected the settlement and pressed for stiffer penalties in the penalty phase of the litigation, but Judge Colleen Kollar-Kotelly rejected most of the tougher penalties proposed by the states as overbroad and instead relied heavily on the earlier settlement proposal. Key elements of the remedy include the following:

- Microsoft must allow PC makers to add or substitute competitive products to handle popular tasks like Web browsing; Microsoft programs will remain on the machine, however, and Microsoft is allowed to offer

76. John R. Wilke, *For Antitrust Judge, Trust, or Lack of It, Really Was the Issue,* WALL ST. J., June 8, 2000, at A1.

77. United States v. Microsoft Corp., 253 F.3d 34 (D.C. Cir. 2001).

*(Continued)*

(Inside Story *continued*)

PC makers discounts if they agree to use all-Microsoft products on their desktop computers.

- There is no restriction on Microsoft's ability to develop and bundle new features into its operating system.
- Microsoft is required to disclose application program interfaces, along with related technical information, which Microsoft Middleware utilizes to interoperate with the Windows platform. In a small concession to the states, Judge Kollar-Kotelly expanded the definition of "Microsoft Middleware" to include server/network computing and interactive television software, although she refused to include handheld devices or Web services.
- Microsoft cannot enter into agreements with PC makers, independent service providers, and others to sell only Microsoft products, although Microsoft is allowed to provide financial incentives to them for promoting Microsoft products.
- The plaintiffs are required to appoint a committee to coordinate enforcement of the remedial decree. Plaintiffs may also select a compliance officer who will serve as a high-level Microsoft employee but retain a significant amount of autonomy and independence from the company.
- Judge Kollar-Kotelly retained jurisdiction over the implementation of the consent decree and asked Microsoft to designate a member of its board of directors to oversee its implementation.
- The agreement has a five-year minimum term and is subject to a two-year extension if the court finds that Microsoft engaged in a pattern of willful and systematic violation of the court's decree.

The U.S. Court of Appeals for the District of Columbia's July 2004 decision upheld Microsoft's settlement with the U.S. Department of Justice. An appeal by the attorney general of Massachusetts was denied in July 2004, marking the end of Microsoft's six-year antitrust case with the U.S. government. Microsoft faced continued litigation with regulators in Europe.

## KEY WORDS AND PHRASES

allocative efficiency 602
antitrust injury 617
antitrust laws 585
cartel 594
circumstantial evidence 589
conglomerate merger 614
conscious parallelism 588
customer restrictions 597
dual distributor 597
essential facility 606
exclusive distributorship 597
franchise 599
group boycott 593
Herfindahl–Hirschman Index (HHI) 609
horizontal agreement 587
horizontal market division 592
horizontal merger 609
horizontal price-fixing 591
illegal *per se* 591
interbrand competition 587
intrabrand competition 591
market power 598
monopoly power 600
multiple-brand product market 600
*parens patriae* action 616
*per se* analysis 591
predatory pricing 602
price discrimination 607
productive efficiency 602
"quick look" rule of reason analysis 593
resale price maintenance (RPM) 594
rule of impossibility 604
rule of reason 591
sovereign immunity 618
standing 617
territorial restrictions 597
total cost 602
trust 587
tying arrangement 598
variable cost 602
vertical agreement 587
vertical market division 595
vertical merger 614
vertical restraint 594

## QUESTIONS AND CASE PROBLEMS

1. Gerber, Heinz, and Beech-Nut, manufacturers of baby food, account for essentially the entire market in the United States. A number of retail stores filed an antitrust class action against the companies alleging that they violated Section 1 of the Sherman Act by engaging in an unlawful conspiracy to fix prices. The class presented evidence that sales representatives employed by the three companies exchanged price information about their products, including, on occasion, sending each other advance notice of

price increases. The class of store owners also introduced evidence of e-mails indicating that the companies were aware of anticipated price increases before they were announced in the market. One memo stated that Heinz would not try to secure a majority base of distribution in a sales area because it had agreed to a "truce" with Gerber. Did the companies violate the antitrust laws? Would you need any additional evidence to make this determination? [*In re Baby Food Antitrust Litigation,* 166 F.3d 112 (3d Cir. 1999).]

2. A manufacturer of electronics in New Orleans, Louisiana, authorized Hayman Electronics and Radio World to sell its products in the New Orleans area. Hayman had been a retailer of these products for several years; Radio World's relationship with the manufacturer was more recent. Hayman complained to the manufacturer that Radio World was price cutting and requested that the manufacturer terminate Radio World as a retailer. The manufacturer did so. Radio World comes to you, the company attorney, asking you what Radio World can do about the termination. What additional information would you like to know, and how will you respond?

3. U.S. manufacturers want to bring a suit against Japanese manufacturers, alleging a conspiracy to take over the U.S. automobile industry by exporting low-priced products to the United States while keeping the prices artificially high in Japan. The U.S. manufacturers tell you, their attorney, that the Japanese manufacturers have formed an association in which they discuss market conditions in the United States, potential or actual import restrictions, surcharges, and simplification of export procedures, as well as other topics.
   a. In light of these facts, what are the chances of successfully bringing an antitrust suit against these manufacturers? Assume that there are no conflict-of-law or other procedural problems due to the manufacturers being in another country.
   b. What if, instead of discussing the topics listed above, the manufacturers discussed the details of individual sales, production, inventories, current price lists, and future price trends?
   c. What if they discussed average costs, freight rates, and terms of past transactions without identifying buyers or sellers? [*Matsushita Electrical Industrial Co. v. Zenith Radio Corp.,* 475 U.S. 574 (1986).]

4. Every year since 1952, graduating medical school students wait anxiously for Match Day, when they receive the results of the National Resident Matching Program (NRMP), managed by the Association of American Colleges (which represents 125 accredited U.S. medical schools, 16 accredited Canadian medical schools, approximately 400 major teaching hospitals, and more than 105,000 faculty, 66,000 medical students, and 97,000 residents). Medical students submit ranked lists of their top hospital choices for residency programs, which are matched against similar lists submitted by the hospitals. On Match Day, each medical student receives one offer for a residency program, which the student agreed contractually to accept as a condition of enrolling in the match.

   The Association of American Medical Colleges, one of the sponsors of the NRMP, annually surveys its members regarding the anticipated compensation levels of their residents for the upcoming year and publishes this information in its *Survey of Housestaff Stipends, Benefits and Funding.* Medical colleges and hospitals also have access to resident physician compensation information through an electronic database maintained by the American Medical Association, another NRMP sponsor. The Accreditation Council for Graduate Medical Education, also an NRMP sponsor, encourages and/or requires medical schools to participate in the NRMP as a condition of accreditation, which is necessary to attract the best medical students.

   Almost all first-year residents make less than $40,000 per year and often work 100-hour weeks, meaning that they often make less than $10 per hour. Residents earn less than other hospital employees such as nurse practitioners and physician assistants, and their salary is substantially lower than the wages they can earn when moonlighting during off hours. With few exceptions, resident wages among the various hospitals are very close to the national average and very close to each other. Adjusted for inflation, the average first-year resident physician salary has remained virtually unchanged for more than thirty years, creeping up marginally each year to keep pace with inflation and little, if any, more.

   In May 2002, resident physicians filed a lawsuit against NRMP and its sponsors, alleging that the defendants had violated antitrust laws in several ways, resulting in low wages and poor working conditions. The defendants filed an answer in which they asserted that the match is primarily an educational endeavor and not a commercial activity subject to antitrust constraints. What antitrust laws would the plaintiffs claim the defendants have violated? How should the court rule? Could major consulting companies form a similar matching program for graduating MBA students who seek employment as consultants? [*Jung v. Ass'n of American Medical Colleges,* 2004 WL 1803198 (C.D.D.C. 2004).]

5. Digital Equipment Corporation (DEC) manufactured hardware ranging from personal computers to mainframes. In April 1994, DEC introduced a new line of mid-range servers that were more powerful and versatile than their predecessors and included a three-year warranty as part of the package. Although multiyear warranties for personal computers had become standard, a three-year warranty, rather than a one-year warranty, was uncommon in the mid-range server market. SMS Systems Maintenance Services is an independent service organization that specializes in servicing particular brands of equipment, including DEC equipment. SMS alleged that DEC's inclusion of a three-year warranty with its mid-range servers was anticompetitive and violated Section 2 of the Sherman Act. As a result, SMS alleged, the DEC warranty functioned as a vehicle for aftermarket monopolization by creating a disincentive for computer purchasers to consult service firms other than the manufacturer itself. How should the court rule? [*SMS Systems Maintenance Services, Inc. v. Digital Equipment Corp.,* 188 F.3d 11 (1st Cir. 1999), *cert. denied,* 528 U.S. 1188 (2000).]

6. U.S. purchasers of vitamin products filed an antitrust suit against Hoffman-LaRoche and certain foreign distributors and sellers of vitamins, claiming they operated a worldwide price-fixing cartel. Foreign purchasers of vitamin products joined the suit, claiming they were injured by the conspiracy and its effects on foreign commerce. The defendants filed a motion to dismiss the foreign plaintiffs' claim on the basis that the alleged conspiracy's effect on U.S. commerce did not cause the foreign plaintiffs' injury. Who wins? [*F. Hoffman-LaRoche Ltd. v. Empagran S.A.,* 124 S.Ct. 2359 (2004).]

7. You are the vice president for marketing at Lucky Liquor, a manufacturer of liquor. During a meeting with your staff, several pricing proposals are made with strong arguments to support each proposal.
   a. Lucky Liquor should set a minimum price per ounce that the wholesalers can charge.
   b. Lucky Liquor should set a maximum price per ounce that the wholesalers can charge.
   c. The wholesalers can charge any price they want within a certain range; if they charge a higher price, they must give the customer a rebate coupon for the differential.
   d. The wholesalers can charge any price they want, but if they advertise a price that is less than Lucky Liquor's specified minimum advertised price, the wholesalers are not entitled to receive the marketing funds that Lucky Liquor provides to wholesalers that do not advertise prices that are less than the specified minimum advertised price.

   After the meeting, you are considering the pros and cons of each plan so that you can make a recommendation to the president. Although each plan has different marketing advantages, your staff estimates that each will result in approximately the same level of sales. What other factors should you consider before making your recommendation? What are the legal pros and cons of each proposal? What else do you need to know before calculating the legal tradeoffs among the proposals?

8. The Aspen Skiing Company (Aspen Ski) owned three of the four mountain skiing facilities in Aspen, Colorado. The fourth facility was owned by the Aspen Highlands Skiing Corporation (Highlands). Between 1962 and 1977, Aspen Ski and Highlands jointly offered a six-day ticket providing skiers with unlimited access to all four facilities. Revenues from the "all-Aspen" ticket, which was very popular with skiers, were divided on the basis of usage. In 1976–1977, Aspen Ski's share of the market for downhill-skiing services in Aspen was approximately 80 percent.

   In the late 1970s, Aspen Ski's management came to believe that Aspen Ski could expand its market share if it discontinued the all-Aspen ticket. For the 1977–1978 season, Aspen Ski refused to market the all-Aspen ticket unless Highlands accepted a fixed share of the revenue, rather than a share based on usage. In 1978–1979, Aspen Ski refused to market the all-Aspen ticket unless Highlands accepted an extremely low fixed share of the revenue, which Highlands declined to do. An Aspen Ski official admitted that Aspen Ski intended to make Highlands an offer that it could not accept. In addition, Aspen Ski took affirmative steps to make it difficult for Highlands to market its own all-Aspen ticket. This included refusing to sell lift tickets for Aspen Ski's facilities to Highlands and refusing to accept guaranteed Highlands vouchers in exchange for lift tickets to Aspen Ski's facilities.

As a result of these actions, Highland's share of the market for downhill-skiing facilities in Aspen steadily declined, reaching 11 percent in 1980–1981. In 1979, Highlands sued Aspen Ski for monopolization of the downhill-skiing market in Aspen.

**a.** What elements are required to prove a charge of monopolization?

**b.** Did Aspen Ski enjoy market power in the relevant market?

**c.** Could the all-Aspen ticket be fairly characterized as an essential facility? If so, did Aspen Ski's refusal to provide Highlands with access to the all-Aspen ticket constitute evidence of intent to monopolize? [*Aspen Skiing Co. v. Aspen Highlands Skiing Corp.*, 472 U.S. 585 (1985).]

**9.** The two largest newspapers in Chicago are the *Chicago Tribune* and the *Sun Times,* and the two largest supplemental news providers are the New York Times News Service and the Los Angeles Times/Washington News Service. In addition to printing the work of its own staff, the *Tribune* has a contract with the New York Times News Service pursuant to which the Service provides news and other material of interest to the *Tribune* on an exclusive basis in the Chicago area. The *Sun Times* has a similar exclusive arrangement with the Los Angeles Times/Washington News Service. As a result of these exclusive contracts, Chicago's third largest newspaper, the *Daily Herald,* could not obtain newsfeed from either service, and it was also unable to obtain newsfeed from the third most popular provider because it was owned by the *Tribune,* which refused to license its stories to a competitor in its home market. The *Daily Herald* challenged this pattern of exclusive distributorships as a violation of Section 1 of the Sherman Act on the basis that it effectively denied the *Herald* the opportunity to subscribe to the best supplemental news services. Does a pattern of exclusive distributorships in a market violate the Sherman Act? In what way could the news services' practices harm consumers? What if the *Herald* could show that it had tried to outbid the *Tribune* or the *Sun Times* for their supplemental news service subscriptions? Would the *Herald*'s argument be stronger if the exclusive agreements were long-term agreements?

### MANAGER'S DILEMMA

**10.** DRAM (dynamic random access memory) is the most common form of computer memory in use today. Another form of memory is known as static random access memory, or SRAM. DRAM is an essential input for various downstream products, including a wide variety of computers, such as personal computers, workstations, and servers, as well as fax machines, printers, digital video recorders, and video game equipment. Rambus was founded in 1990 by two engineers who developed their own proprietary synchronous DRAM (or SDRAM) architecture. On April 18, 1990, Rambus filed its first DRAM-related patent application with the U.S. Patent and Trademark Office (the '898 patent). In March 1992, Rambus broke out portions of its '898 application into ten divisional patent applications. The original '898 application and these ten divisional applications gave rise to numerous other amended, divisional or continuation patent applications—all technically the "progeny" of the '898 application—and eventually resulted in the issuance of numerous Rambus patents.

The Joint Electron Device Engineering Council (JEDEC) is one of several standard-setting bodies affiliated with the Electronic Industries Alliance (EIA), a trade association representing all segments of the electronics industry. The EIA/JEDEC patent policy required members to disclose patents and patent applications "related to" the standardization work of the committees. During the period from 1992 through 1996, Rambus was a member of JEDEC and attended meetings of the JC-42.3 subcommittee on RAM devices, which was in the process of developing SDRAM standards. In 1993, Rambus disclosed its first issued Rambus DRAM (RDRAM) patent, a divisional application of the '898 application, to JEDEC during a meeting, but it did not disclose any other applications. In June 1996, shortly after the Federal Trade Commission announced its consent order in *In re Dell Computer, Inc.* (which involved allegations of anticompetitive unilateral conduct occurring within the context of an industry-wide standard-setting organization), Rambus formally withdrew from the JEDEC and wrote a letter to the council stating its intent to reserve all rights regarding its intellectual property. Rambus attached a list of twenty-three Rambus patents and made a vague reference to additional, unspecified patent applications, but it made no attempt to inform the JEDEC as to how, if at all, the patents or patent applications might relate to the work of the JC-42.3 subcommittee. After leaving the JEDEC, Rambus filed more divisional and continuation applications based on the '898 patent. In late 1999, Rambus began contacting major DRAM-related technology manufacturers worldwide to assert its patent rights.

In June 2002, the FTC accused Rambus of withholding information—namely, patent applications—that it claimed the company was required to disclose to the JEDEC subcommittee in which Rambus participated during the 1990s. [*In re Rambus, Inc.*, No. 932 (F.T.C. filed June 18, 2002).] What antitrust laws may have been violated by Rambus? In light of these facts, what are the chances of the FTC prevailing? What relief might the FTC seek? What defenses might be available to Rambus? Was Rambus's conduct ethical? Did it make good business sense?

## INTERNET SOURCES

| | |
|---|---|
| Department of Justice | http://www.usdoj.gov |
| Federal Trade Commission | http://www.ftc.gov |
| Microsoft Corporation | http://www.microsoft.com |
| The European Union On-Line | http://europa.eu.int |
| The Competition Online site, maintained by the editors of *Competition Journal* in Dublin, Ireland, is a gateway to numerous U.S., European, and other antitrust sites. | http://www.clubi.ie/competition/compframesite/index.htm |
| FindLaw—Antitrust and Trade Regulation | http://www.findlaw.com/01topics/01antitrust/index.html |

CHAPTER 17

# Consumer Protection

## INTRODUCTION

### Role of Consumer Protection Law in Business

Historically, consumers had little recourse in the event of a dispute with a vendor, manufacturer, producer, service provider, or creditor. The words commonly associated with consumer transactions were *caveat emptor* ("let the buyer beware"). Today, the standard has shifted closer to *venditur emptor* ("let the seller beware"). Federal and state laws protect consumers from unsafe or harmful consumer products, unfair and deceptive trade practices, fraud, and misleading or discriminatory credit requirements. Managers must, of course, comply with the law. In addition, by being proactive, working with administrative agencies, and promoting industry self-regulation, managers may be able to forestall burdensome new regulatory restrictions.

### Chapter Overview

This chapter examines four primary areas of consumer protection law and the agencies, departments, and commissions that administer and enforce them: (1) consumer health and safety (including the regulation of food, drugs, medical devices, alcohol, tobacco, smoking, gambling, firearms, automobiles, broadcasting, and the Internet); (2) consumer privacy; (3) unfairness, deception, and fraud (including the regulation of advertising, packaging and labeling, pricing, warranties, and certain sales practices); and (4) consumer credit. The discussion focuses primarily on federal legislation, although numerous state law topics are also discussed. In general, consumer protection law at the state level is more stringent than federal law. Consumer bankruptcy under Chapter 13 of the Bankruptcy Code is discussed in Chapter 24.

## Commissions and Agencies

Federal regulatory agencies involved in consumer protection are either independent commissions or executive branch agencies. Independent commissions include the Federal Trade Commission, the Federal Communications Commission, the Securities and Exchange Commission, the Federal Reserve Board, and the Consumer Product Safety Commission. The Federal Trade Commission, for example, has five commissioners appointed by the president and confirmed by the Senate for seven-year terms. No more than three of them can be from the same political party. The commissioners make decisions by majority vote and issue rules.

Executive branch regulatory agencies, on the other hand, are located in cabinet departments. Examples of executive branch regulatory agencies are the Food and Drug Administration (located within the U.S. Department of Health and Human Services), the Office of Interstate Land Sales Registration (U.S. Department of Housing and Urban Development), and the National Highway Traffic Safety Administration (U.S. Department of Transportation).

The "In Brief" identifies the key federal commissions and agencies charged with administering major consumer protection laws.

## Consumer Health and Safety

A number of federal, state, and local regulatory agencies protect consumers' health and safety, including the Food and Drug Administration (FDA), the Department of Agriculture, the Department of Transportation's National Highway Traffic Safety Administration, and the

## IN BRIEF

### Consumer Protection Laws and Their Administration

| Agency, Department, or Commission | Consumer Credit | Unfairness, Deception, and Fraud | Consumer Health and Safety |
|---|---|---|---|
| Federal Trade Commission<br>Established: 1914<br>Commissioners: 5 | Credit advertising; Fair Credit Reporting Act; Fair Debt Collection Practices Act | Advertising; sales practices | |
| Food and Drug Administration (U.S. Department of Health and Human Services)<br>Established: 1930<br>Commissioners: 1 | | | Labeling of food (except meat, poultry, and eggs), drugs, and cosmetics; adulterated food and cosmetics; approval of drugs and medical devices |
| U.S. Department of Agriculture<br>Established: 1862 | | | Labeling of meat, poultry, and eggs; inspection of meat, poultry, and egg processing facilities |
| National Highway Traffic Safety Administration (NHTSA) (U.S. Department of Transportation)<br>Established: 1970<br>Administrators: 1 | | | Automobile safety standards; driver safety |
| Consumer Product Safety Commission<br>Established: 1972<br>Commissioners: 3 | | | Consumer Product Safety Act (CPSA) |
| Federal Communications Commission<br>Established: 1934<br>Commissioners: 5 | | Telemarketing | Broadcast standards |
| U.S. Postal Service<br>Established: 1775<br>Reorganized: 1970 | | Sales practices | |
| Securities and Exchange Commission<br>Established: 1934<br>Commissioners: 5 | | Securities fraud | |
| Federal Reserve Board<br>Established: 1913<br>Governors: 7 | Truth in Lending Act (Regulation Z); Consumer Leasing Act (Regulation M); Equal Credit Opportunity Act (Regulation B); Electronic Fund Transfer Act (Regulation E) | | |
| U.S. Department of Labor<br>Established: 1913 | Garnishment of wages | | |
| Office of Interstate Land Sales Registration (U.S. Department of Housing and Urban Development)<br>Established: 1969 | | Interstate land sales | |
| Bankruptcy courts | Chapter 13 consumer bankruptcy | | |

Consumer Product Safety Commission. For example, under the Food, Drug and Cosmetic Act,[1] the FDA monitors the production and sale of more than $1 trillion of food and medical products each year. In addition to specifying the proper labeling of food, drugs, medical devices, and cosmetics to prevent *misbranding*, the FDA also regulates the new-drug approval process.

The Federal Trade Commission also regulates the packaging and labeling of some products. Numerous state laws cover such items as food, drugs, medical devices, cosmetics, clothing, tobacco, and alcohol.

Consumer protection law should not be confused with product liability law, discussed in Chapter 10. Product liability law provides a common law remedy enforced by private action, whereas consumer protection law provides a statutory remedy enforced by the government (and, in some cases, also by private parties). For example, in February 2005, the U.S. Court of Appeals for the District of Columbia Circuit ruled that the U.S. government had no basis for requiring the disgorgement of $289 billion in past profits from the major tobacco companies based on federal racketeering charges.[2] The government argued that the tobacco companies systematically deceived the public about the hazards of smoking for almost four decades. This is an example of the government attempting to enforce a statutory remedy.

At the state level, consumer health and safety laws cover a wide variety of areas, such as the availability of alcohol, tobacco, and gambling. State and local provisions also address no-smoking regulations, restaurant inspections, and the competency of professional workers through the granting of various occupational licenses.

# Food Safety and Labeling

## PRODUCT DEFINITION: FOOD OR DRUG?

*Drugs*, as defined by the Food, Drug and Cosmetic Act, include (1) articles intended for use in the diagnosis, cure, mitigation, treatment, or prevention of disease; and (2) articles (other than food) intended to affect the structure or any function of the body. Thus, many things that are, in fact, food may fit this definition. For example, orange juice might be used to prevent disease. Under the Act, *food* is defined as (1) articles used for food or drink, (2) chewing gum, and (3) articles used for components of either.

Because the distinction between drugs and food is important in the application of both the mislabeling and the adulteration provisions of the Act, as well as in the drug-approval process, the FDA must categorize each product. In general, the FDA looks at the intended use of a product in determining how to categorize it. Intent may be apparent from the manufacturer's purpose or from consumers' reasons for using the product, or it may be inferred from labels, promotional material, or advertisements.

## FDA STANDARDS FOR FOOD CONDEMNATION

The FDA protects consumer health and safety through the confiscation of contaminated or adulterated foods. Tainted food causes an estimated 9,000 or more deaths annually in the United States and millions of illnesses.

The standards for condemnation differ depending on whether the product is a natural food or contains additives. An *additive* is anything not inherent in the food product, including pesticide residue, unintended environmental contaminants, and substances unavoidably added from packaging. If an additive (in the quantity present in the food product) is injurious to any group in the general population, then the product will be deemed adulterated.

A natural food is *adulterated* if it "consist[s] in whole or in part of any filthy, putrid or decomposed substance, or if it is otherwise unfit for food." All foods contain some level of unavoidable natural defects, so the FDA sets minimum tolerance standards for defects that will be tolerated. Articles that exceed those minimum levels are deemed adulterated and seized by the FDA. In some cases, a seized product may be rehabilitated by a manufacturer and released by the FDA for sale.

In a hotly debated decision, the FDA allowed U.S. meat providers to sell "downed" cattle and other livestock.[3] Opponents claimed that these cattle, which were either too weak to walk or had collapsed entirely before slaughter, have a much greater chance of carrying a potentially fatal disease, known as mad cow disease. Nonetheless, the FDA concluded that as long as a postmortem inspection was performed by an official veterinarian, this food was safe for human consumption.

A chief executive officer of a food company may be held vicariously and strictly criminally liable for introducing adulterated articles into interstate commerce.[4] The CEO should ensure that the top managers have adequate policies and checks in place to ensure the proper handling

1. 21 U.S.C. §§ 321 *et seq.*
2. *Cigarette Makers Win Major Legal Fight in Racketeering Case*, BUS. J., Feb. 4, 2005.
3. Bauer v. Veneman, 352 F.3d 625 (2d Cir. 2003) (Case 6.6).
4. United States v. Park, 421 U.S. 658 (1975).

**INTERNATIONAL SNAPSHOT**

Free trade treaties have made the U.S. food market one of the most open in the world. Food imports now amount to more than 30 billion tons annually. The importation of fresh fruits and vegetables, gourmet cheeses, meats, and shellfish present new challenges for regulators. For example, raspberries imported from Guatemala carried a foodborne parasite that struck hundreds of people in 1996.

To allay concerns in the United States, authorities in Mexico (which ships 90 percent of its $4.5 billion in annual food exports to the United States) have encouraged produce exporters to have their operations certified by private U.S. laboratories that inspect the fields, irrigation water, packing conditions, and the bathrooms workers use. Mexican growers of mangoes destined for the United States employ sixty USDA inspectors. Still experts argue that the ultimate burden of ensuring safe food may fall on the globalized food industry.[a]

a. Paul Magnusson et al., *News: Analysis & Commentary,* Bus.Wk., Sept. 8, 1997, at 30–32.

and storage of food. If a problem is brought to a manager's attention, he or she should immediately report it to a supervisor and personally ensure that it is remedied.

## Role of the U.S. Department of Agriculture

The U.S. Department of Agriculture (USDA) also plays a major role in food safety. The USDA's primary consumer protection activities all involve food. They include inspecting facilities engaged in the slaughtering or processing of meat, poultry, and egg products; preventing the sale of mislabeled meat or poultry products; and offering producers a voluntary grading program for various agricultural products.

## Pesticides and Human-Made Bugs

Under the Food, Drug and Cosmetic Act, the FDA shares with the Environmental Protection Agency (EPA) the responsibility for regulating pesticide residues on food. The EPA registers pesticides and establishes tolerances under the Act. The FDA enforces the tolerance levels and deems a food to be adulterated if its residues exceed those levels.

Scientists are creating genetically engineered insects and microbes to fight pests, such as the glassy-winged sharpshooter, which has already destroyed $14 billion worth of grapes and other crops in California. In the absence of a clear framework for regulating bioengineered insects and pathogens, scientists are seeking approvals from the EPA, which regulates pesticides. According to the executive director of the nonprofit Pew Initiative on Food and Biotechnology, "The regulatory system is lagging well behind the science."[5]

## Genetically Modified Food

In April 2000, the National Academy of Science issued a report advising the federal government to increase its regulation of genetically modified foods. Although the report did not find that genetically modified food was unsafe, it urged scientists to develop better methods for identifying potential allergens and called on regulatory agencies to monitor the environmental impact of genetically modified organisms (GMOs). The report also concluded that the EPA, USDA, and FDA should do a better job of coordinating their work and informing the public about GMOs.[6]

European consumers have vehemently opposed the sale of genetically modified foods and launched a major campaign against efforts to market GMOs in European countries. In 2001, the European Parliament approved legislation that requires continuous monitoring of GMOs. The law calls for labeling and monitoring of genetically modified foods, seeds, feeds, and pharmaceuticals, and it requires governments to maintain a registry of where such plants are being grown.[7]

Opposition to GMOs has spread to the United States where consumers have protested GMOs because of both health safety and environmental concerns. In July 2003, the "Genetically Engineered Food Right to Know Act" was proposed in Congress.[8] As of 2004, it was still pending. Given the potentially enormous benefits of genetically modified foods, particularly for developing countries, the debate over regulating genetically engineered crops is far from over.

## Irradiated Foods

In December 1997, the FDA authorized the irradiation of fresh and frozen red meat as a means of killing foodborne bacteria (including *E. coli*) and lengthening shelf

5. Catherine Arnst, *Panacea—Or Pandora's Box?,* Bus.Wk., May 3, 2004, at 75.
6. Scott Kilman, *Government Is Advised to Tighten Regulation of Bioengineered Crops,* Wall St. J., Apr. 6, 2000, at B2.
7. *Genetic Engineering: Euro Parliament Approves Guidelines,* Feb. 14, 2001, *at* http://www.eenews.net.
8. H.R. 2916, 108th Cong. (2003).

life. During irradiation, food is passed through a sealed chamber, where it is exposed to gamma ray radiation from cobalt 60 or cesium 137 or to an electron beam. FDA regulations require irradiated foods to be prominently and conspicuously labeled with the radura symbol (a stylized green flower) and the words "Treated with Radiation" or "Treated by Irradiation."

For many consumers, irradiation conjures up images of mushroom clouds and the nuclear reactor meltdown in 1986 at Chernobyl in the Ukraine.[9] Some activists have threatened to organize consumer boycotts of companies selling irradiated foods and to launch media campaigns against irradiation. Nevertheless, experts predict that consumers will be won over by irradiation's safety and effectiveness in protecting consumers from bacteria and other microbes. Former FDA commissioner Dr. David Kessler drew parallels to the public's shunning of pasteurized milk in the early twentieth century and the initial distrust of microwave ovens in the 1970s.[10]

## Organic Foods

Sales of organic products in the United States amounted to approximately $10.8 billion in 2003.[11] Uniform standards for organic food promulgated by the USDA ban the use of pesticides, genetic engineering, growth hormones, and irradiation. They also require dairy cattle to have access to pasture. Foods grown and processed according to the standards may bear the seal "USDA Organic."[12]

## Food Labeling

The FDA has the primary responsibility for regulating the packaging and labeling of food (except meat, poultry, and eggs, which are under the jurisdiction of the USDA), drugs, medical devices, and cosmetics. The Fair Packaging and Labeling Act[13] requires prepackaged foods to bear labels containing the name and address of the manufacturer, packer, or distributor; the net quantity, placed in a uniform location on the frontpanel; the quantity in servings, with the net quantity of each serving stated; and the quantity listed in certain other ways, depending on how the product is classified. This last provision requires dual declarations of sizes (for example, one quart and thirty-two ounces) and forbids the use of terms such as "jumbo quart" and "super ounce." Many supermarkets now provide unit-pricing information so that consumers can more easily compare the prices of competing products. Manufacturers of goods that are to be exported also need to consider foreign labeling requirements, such as language translations, country of origin disclosures, and weight conversions.

### *Nutrition Facts*

The Nutrition Labeling and Education Act of 1990[14] (1) requires nutrition labeling of almost all foods through a nutrition panel entitled "Nutrition Facts," (2) requires expanded ingredient labeling, and (3) restricts nutrient content claims and health claims. The FDA has also issued regulations governing the use of nutrient claims, such as "light," "fat free," and "low calorie," and providing uniform definitions so that these terms mean the same for any product on which they appear. In 2004, the Illinois Appellate Court ruled that the Nutrition Labeling and Education Act preempted a suit against McDonald's Corporation for inadequate labeling of food intended for children between the ages of one and four brought under the Illinois consumer fraud and deceptive business practice laws.[15]

Approximately 90 percent of processed food must carry nutrition information. Exceptions include plain coffee and tea, delicatessen items, and bulk food. The Nutrition Facts panel must include the amount per serving of saturated fat, cholesterol, dietary fiber, sodium, and other nutrients. These panels also provide information on how the food fits into an overall daily diet. Point-of-purchase nutrition information is voluntary under the Act for many raw foods, including meat, poultry, raw fish, and fresh produce. The information may be shown in a poster or chart at a butcher's counter or a produce stand.

Recently, health experts have focused on the dangers of adding "trans fat," a form of partially hydrogenated oil, to foods and have called for trans fat labeling. Manufacturers use trans fats to improve the shelf life of products, many of which are marketed as "healthy" foods. The FDA has estimated that 2,100 to 5,600 lives are lost each year and that 6,300 to 17,100 cases of fatal and nonfatal coronary heart disease occur each year

9. Martha Groves, *Less-Than Glowing Image Hampers Food Irradiation*, L.A. TIMES, Mar. 15, 1998, at A1.
10. Joanna Ramey, *Food Industry Groups Near Start of Irradiation Campaign*, SUPERMARKET NEWS, Apr. 17, 1998, at 23.
11. Neal Haldane, *Better Health Touts All-Organic Produce,* DETROIT NEWS, Mar. 25, 2005.
12. Frederick J. Frommer, *Some Worry New USDA Label Will Change Organic Farming,* ASSOCIATED PRESS, Jan. 13, 2001.
13. 15 U.S.C. §§ 1451 *et seq.*
14. 21 U.S.C. §§ 301, 321, 337, 343, 371.
15. Cohen v. McDonald's Corp., 86 ANTITRUST & TRADE REG. REP. (BNA) 220 (Ill. App. Feb. 13, 2004).

because of the lack of trans fat labeling.[16] Mandatory labeling of these fats has been slow in coming, however. In 2003, the FDA announced that it was delaying plans to require labeling of trans fats until 2006 to give businesses time to phase out labels without trans fat listings. PepsiCo's Frito-Lay division has been proactive in eliminating trans fats from many of its products and including the trans fat information on labels.

### *Health Claims*

Prior to 1984, the FDA took the position that a statement that consumption of a food could prevent a particular disease was "tantamount to a claim that the food was a drug . . . and therefore that its sale was prohibited until a new drug application has been approved."[17] The Nutrition Labeling and Education Act of 1990 permits manufacturers to make health claims for foods on labels without FDA approval as a new drug, or the risk of sanctions for issuing a "misbranded" product, if the claim has been certified by the FDA as being supported by significant scientific agreement. The FDA has approved several health claims on foods, including the relationship between calcium and osteoporosis, fiber-containing products and cancer, fruits and vegetables and cancer, folate and neural tube defects, and soluble fiber and coronary heart disease.

# Drugs and Medical Devices

## FDA Standards for Drug Approval

The FDA has the authority to require that certain drugs be available only by prescription. If a drug authorized only for prescription use is sold over-the-counter, then it is misbranded and the FDA will halt its sale. In general, the FDA will require prescription use only when a drug is toxic, requires a physician's supervision for safe use, or is addictive.

The first step in the approval process for new drugs is their classification by the Drug Enforcement Administration (DEA) into one of five schedules based on potential for abuse and currently accepted medical use. Only Schedule I drugs, those with the highest potential for abuse and no currently accepted medical use, cannot be approved by the FDA.

The drug-approval process for non-Schedule I drugs begins with preclinical research (which includes animal testing) aimed at the discovery and identification of drugs that are sufficiently promising to study in humans. The drugmaker then submits this preclinical research, along with a document called "Claimed Exemption for Investigational New Drug," to the FDA. The FDA can then permit or deny continued research. If approved for investigational purposes, a drug will be tested in humans in three separate phases, with FDA review at the end of each phase. This framework is designed to protect the safety of the human subjects used in the study, to develop necessary data on the drug, and to ensure that all studies are done properly. Once all of the testing data are assembled, they are submitted to the FDA, which may approve or deny the application. Approval is based on a drug's safety and effectiveness; the approval may require marketing restrictions; and it can be contested by anyone. The FDA must also approve the description of a drug (for example, labels and package inserts).

Drugs with a high potential for therapeutic gain and no satisfactory alternative may be given priority (expedited) review by the FDA. In addition, through open protocols, such drugs may be available during the investigational stage to people not within the clinical test group. For example, people with AIDS may have access to new drugs under investigation if preliminary evidence of effectiveness exists.

Congress passed the Food and Drug Administration Modernization Act of 1997[18] to speed up the approval of new drugs and medical devices and to make it easier for seriously ill patients to obtain experimental drugs. The Act permits the FDA to use outside reviewers to evaluate certain drugs and medical devices. This Act also includes a safe harbor for the distribution by drug manufacturers of certain third-party materials concerning "off-label" uses of their drugs.[19] "Off-label" uses are uses of a drug other than those for which it was approved. A physician can prescribe a drug to serve any purpose that he or she thinks is appropriate regardless of whether the drug was

16. 64 Fed. Reg. 62,772 (Nov. 17, 1999).
17. H.R. Rep. No. 538, 101st Cong., 2d Sess. 9 (1990), *reprinted in* 1990 U.S.C.C.A.N. 3336, 3338.

18. 21 U.S.C. § 353a.
19. 21 U.S.C. §§ 360aaa *et seq.*

### Ethical Consideration

Drug companies provide financial support to academic researchers in the form of employment or consulting fees, research funds, money to attend symposiums, and speaking honoraria. Should scientists disclose their ties to drug companies when publishing articles about their research? Should drug companies disclose these financial ties?

initially approved for that use, but the FDA restricts companies' ability to promote off-label uses.[20]

In 2004, Pfizer, Inc. agreed to pay $430 million after pleading guilty to civil and criminal charges that Warner-Lambert (which it acquired in 2000) had illegally promoted off-label uses of its drug Neurontin.[21] The government calculated that the company's illegal promotions had brought it $150 million in ill-gotten gains. The fines include a $26.64 million whistleblower payment to Dr. David P. Franklin, a former medical adviser to Warner-Lambert's sales staff. Franklin quit after being asked to promote Neurontin for unapproved uses and then filed a federal whistleblower suit. The government may still file criminal charges against the former Warner-Lambert executives who apparently approved the marketing plans.

In *Thompson v. Western States Medical Center*,[22] the U.S. Supreme Court struck down the provisions of the Food and Drug Administration Modernization Act that exempted compounded drugs from the FDA's approval requirements only if the compounding pharmacy refrained from advertising particular compounded drugs. Compounding is a process whereby a pharmacist, pursuant to a physician's prescription, mixes ingredients to create a medication for a particular patient, usually because the patient is allergic to an ingredient in a mass-produced product. The Court held that the ban violated the Free Speech Clause of the First Amendment, as construed by the U.S. Supreme Court in *Central Hudson Gas & Electric Corp. v. Public Service Commission*.[23] The prohibited commercial speech was neither unlawful nor misleading. The Court recognized the importance of the government's interests in preserving the effectiveness and integrity of the FDA's new-drug approval process while also permitting compounding to create drugs produced on such a small scale that it would be prohibitively expensive to require them to undergo safety and efficiency testing. Nonetheless, the Court concluded that the speech restrictions were more extensive than necessary to serve these interests. The Court identified several non-speech-related means of drawing a line between compounding and large-scale manufacturing, which the government never even considered. The Court admonished Congress that "[i]f the First Amendment means anything, it means that regulating speech must be a last—not first—resort."

20. See 65 Fed. Reg. 14,286 (Mar. 16, 2000).

21. Gardiner Harris, *Pfizer to Pay $430 Million over Promoting Drug to Doctors*, N.Y. TIMES, May 14, 2004, at C5.

22. 535 U.S. 357 (2002).

23. 447 U.S. 557 (1980).

### LABELING OF MEDICAL DEVICES

The labeling of medical devices is also under the jurisdiction of the FDA. As noted in Chapter 10, even if a manufacturer provides the FDA-mandated warnings, it could still be found liable under state product liability law for failure to warn if reasonable manufacturers would have done more. For example, the U.S. Court of Appeals for the Tenth Circuit upheld a $10 million punitive damages award against International Playtex for failure to adequately warn users about the risk of fatal toxic shock syndrome from use of high-absorbing tampons.[24] The court concluded that Playtex had shown reckless indifference to consumer safety by deliberately disregarding studies and medical reports linking high-absorbency tampon fibers with increased risk of toxic shock at a time when other tampon manufacturers were responding to this information by modifying or withdrawing their high-absorbency products.

### DRUG ADVERTISING

In 1997, the FDA eased the restrictions on the advertising of prescription drugs on television and radio. Drug companies can now tout a drug's benefits without listing all of the side effects and explaining how to properly use the drug. Television ads must, however, warn of major risks and provide a quick way (such as a toll-free telephone number, Web address, or magazine advertisement) for consumers to obtain full information about the drug. The recall of the popular anti-inflamatory drug Vioxx by Merck in 2004 sparked further debate on the proper use of drug advertising.[25]

## Health Claims and Labeling of Dietary Supplements

Under the Dietary Supplement Health and Education Act of 1994,[26] the sale of dietary supplements is regulated only when the supplement contains a new dietary ingredient or poses a safety risk. Dietary supplements include products such as vitamins, minerals, herbs, and

24. Ogilvie v. Int'l Playtex, Inc., 821 F.2d 1438 (10th Cir. 1987), *cert. denied*, 486 U.S. 1032 (1988).

25. For an interesting article, coauthored by the Senior Corporate Counsel of Pfizer, Inc., promoting even less FDA regulation of drug advertising, see George W. Evans & Arnold I. Friede, *The Food and Drug Administration's Regulation of Prescription Drug Manufacturer Speech: A First Amendment Analysis*, 58 FOOD & DRUG L.J. 363 (2003).

26. 21 U.S.C. §§ 350b, 342(f).

amino acids. As with foods, however, health claims on dietary supplements can cause them to be characterized as drugs. The Nutrition Labeling and Education Act created a safe harbor for health claims on dietary supplements akin to that provided for food but delegated to the FDA the task of establishing a procedure and standard respecting the validity of health claims.

The FDA issued regulations providing that it would authorize a health claim only if there was substantial scientific agreement among experts that the claim was supported by the totality of publicly available scientific evidence.[27] In 1999, however, the U.S. Court of Appeals for the District of Columbia curtailed the FDA's right to ban health-related claims made by sellers of nutritional supplements.[28] The FDA published a final rule in 2000 clarifying the types of claims that manufacturers of dietary supplements may make without prior review by the FDA and identifying those that require prior authorization.[29]

27. 21 C.F.R. pt. 101.14(c) (1998).
28. Pearson v. Shalala, 164 F.3d 650 (D.C. Cir. 1999).
29. *FDA Regulates Statements Made on Effects of Dietary Supplements,* 68 U.S.L.W. 2392–93 (Jan. 11, 2000).

In early 2003, the FDA came under heavy fire when Steve Bechler, a twenty-three-year-old pitcher for the Baltimore Orioles baseball team, died suddenly during spring training workouts in Florida. Initially, Bechler's death was attributed to heat stroke, but a further medical examination found that Bechler had been taking Xenadrine, a legal over-the-counter drug containing a weight-loss supplement known as ephedra. The drug, which its makers liken to caffeine, was said to have strongly contributed to Bechler's death. Shortly thereafter, a young football player's sudden death was also linked to ephedra. Its makers claimed that improper use of the drug may have contributed to the deaths, but the FDA was blasted for allowing the drug to be marketed over-the-counter without significant warnings. In response, the FDA banned the use of ephedra in any dietary supplements and advised consumers to stop using any products containing ephedra.[30]

30. Available at http://my.webmd.com/content/article/81/97056.htm (accessed Aug. 17, 2004).

## HISTORICAL PERSPECTIVE
# FOOD AND DRUG REGULATION

### THALIDOMIDE TRAGEDY SPURS NEW LAWS, 1962

[T]he thalidomide tragedy of the 1960s, though Americans were spared its worst effects, produced the still-stronger drug-testing laws of 1962.

Thalidomide, developed in Germany, had been hailed as the greatest sleeping pill in history. After it became a bestseller in Germany, Britain and Canada, the century-old William Merrell Company asked the U.S. Food and Drug Administration in September 1960 for approval to sell it in the United States. The application, backed by four telephone-book-sized volumes of data, was assigned to Frances Kelsey, a Canadian-born physician and pharmacologist who had just joined the FDA.

Dr. Kelsey thought thalidomide looked "peculiar." For one thing, the sleeping pill didn't make test animals sleepy. Despite constant—and angry—pressure from Merrell, she blocked approval, asking Merrell for more and more data.

Meanwhile, German and other European doctors were puzzling over an epidemic of phocomelia, children born with flipper-like appendages instead of proper arms and legs. In November 1961, Widiking Lenz, a Hamburg pediatrician, discovered the link: Mothers of the deformed babies had been using thalidomide. The drug was withdrawn that month and Merrell dropped its application for FDA approval.

When the thalidomide story hit the United States, it caused shudders that had seismic effects in Congress. Sen. Estes Kefauver, whose tough drug-regulating bill had been gutted on Capitol Hill, now saw it revived, strengthened and sped on its way to President Kennedy's desk. He signed it into law in October 1962, two months after he had awarded Dr. Kelsey the Distinguished Federal Civilian Service Award.

**Source:** WALL ST. J., Sept. 6, 1989, at B1. Reprinted by permission of the *Wall Street Journal,* 

# Labeling of Other Products

## CLOTHING

The Federal Trade Commission (FTC) has the primary responsibility for regulating the packaging and labeling of commodities other than food, drugs, medical devices, and cosmetics. For example, numerous federal laws regulate the labeling of clothing. Among these are the Wool Products Labeling Act,[31] the Fur Products Labeling Act,[32] the Flammable Fabrics Act,[33] and the Textile Fiber Products Identification Act.[34] Each of these acts is intended to protect distributors and consumers against misbranding and false advertising.

## ALCOHOL

The Bureau of Alcohol and Tobacco Tax and Trade, a branch of the Treasury Department, regulates everything that appears on packages of alcoholic beverages and bottles of wine. The Bureau's regulations attach legal meanings to various statements made on wine labels, including the vintage year, grape variety, producer, and alcohol content. Warnings are also required to alert those who are allergic to sulfites that wine contains trace amounts of the substances, which may be used as a preservative and are also produced naturally during fermentation. In 1989, bottles, cans, and packages of wine, beer, and spirits began to carry a congressionally mandated warning label, which states that alcohol consumption increases the risks of birth defects, warns that consuming alcoholic beverages can impair one's ability to drive a car, and cautions against the use of alcohol when operating machinery.[35]

## MADE IN USA

The FTC has adopted guidelines specifying when manufacturers and marketers can label their products "Made in USA." Under the FTC's Made in USA policy, "all or virtually all" of the product must be made in the fifty states, the District of Columbia, or the U.S. territories and possessions. "All or virtually all" means that all significant parts and processing that go into the product must be of U.S. origin. A manufacturer or marketer must have a reasonable basis, based on competent and reliable evidence, to support its claim that the product was made in the USA.[36]

## STATE LABELING LAWS

Many states have enacted labeling laws aimed at protecting consumers from dangerous products. Historically, these laws have sought to protect consumers from risks that involved the danger of imminent bodily harm. Of particular note is California's Safe Drinking Water and Toxic Enforcement Act of 1986, better known as Proposition 65. Proposition 65 provides that "no person . . . shall knowingly and intentionally expose any individual to a chemical known to the state to cause cancer or reproductive toxicity without first giving clear and reasonable warning to such individual."[37] The law requires the governor to compile a list of the chemicals requiring warnings and to update the list annually. The current list includes ingredients such as alcohol and saccharin, as well as potential contaminants such as lead and mercury. The labeling requirements apply to manufacturers, producers, packagers, and retail sellers, and the warnings may be in the form of product labels, signs at retail outlets, or public advertising. An example of a Proposition 65 warning is: "Warning: This product contains a chemical known to the State of California to cause birth defects or other reproductive harm." The FDA has the authority to issue regulations that would preempt state labeling requirements, such as Proposition 65, but so far it has chosen not to do so.

# Broadcasting and the Internet

## BROADCASTING

Regulation of broadcasting by the Federal Communications Commission (FCC) seeks to ensure that broadcast media are competitive and operate for the public's benefit and use. During the 2003 Superbowl half-time performance, Janet Jackson "accidentally" revealed her breast on national television. Many people were outraged, and the National Football League and MTV (the group that sponsored and prepared the show)

31. 15 U.S.C. §§ 68 *et seq.*
32. 15 U.S.C. §§ 69 *et seq.*
33. 15 U.S.C. §§ 1191 *et seq.*
34. 15 U.S.C. § 70 *et seq.*
35. Dan Berger, *Modern Wine Industry Still Fears the "Feds" but for Labeling Reasons,* L.A. TIMES, Nov. 24, 1989, at H2; see generally, 27 C.F.R. pts. 4, 5, & 7 (Alcohol and Tobacco Tax and Trade Bureau, Department of the Treasury).

36. FTC Bureau of Consumer Protection, *Complying with the Made in the USA Standard, at* http://www.ftc.gov/os/1997/12/madeusa.pdf.
37. CAL. HEALTH & SAFETY CODE § 25,249.6.

were embarrassed. The incident prompted regulators to propose sharply higher penalties for indecent broadcasts.

Enforcement of the FCC's policies is achieved primarily through its ability to withhold license renewals, but a network as large as Fox or NBC is simply too large and too much a part of mainstream culture for its license to be withheld. Licenses cannot be transferred or assigned without the permission of the FCC and a finding that such a transfer will serve the public interest. In 2003, Congress invalidated FCC regulations that would have relaxed the limits on concentrated media ownership in the United States.[38]

As explained in Chapter 2, FCC regulation of the content of broadcast programming raises First Amendment issues. Controversial radio personalities like Howard Stern and Rush Limbaugh, called "shock jocks," are often involved in First Amendment battles with the FCC over their right to say things that many Americans find offensive.

### INTERNET

The Internet also raises free speech issues, as discussed in Chapter 2. As explained in Chapters 9 and 23, the Internet has spawned new types of fraudulent schemes, such as online auction fraud, pyramid schemes, and securities fraud. The FTC, the U.S. Department of Justice, and the Securities and Exchange Commission are active in prosecuting offenders. Finally, as discussed in Chapter 4, the FCC and the states are battling over the right to regulate the provision of phone service over the Internet.

## The Consumer Product Safety Commission

Congress created the Consumer Product Safety Commission (CPSC), an independent regulatory agency, in 1972. Its purposes include protection of the public against unreasonable risks of injury associated with consumer products and assistance to consumers in evaluating the comparative safety of such products. Under the Consumer Product Safety Act[39] (which created the CPSC), the CPSC is authorized to set consumer product safety standards, such as performance or product-labeling specifications.

Before implementing a mandatory safety standard, the CPSC must find that voluntary standards are inadequate. One obvious concern for the Commission is that producers motivated solely by short-term profits may not be willing or able to self-regulate. Any standards that the CPSC issues must also be reasonably necessary to eliminate an unreasonable risk of injury that the regulated product presents. To determine whether a standard is reasonably necessary, the Commission weighs the standard's effectiveness in preventing injury against its effect on the cost of the product.

The statute provides a detailed scheme governing the adoption of such a standard. Any interested person may petition the CPSC to adopt a standard and may resort to judicial remedies if the CPSC denies the petition. The CPSC itself can begin a proceeding to develop a standard by publishing a notice in the *Federal Register* inviting any person to submit an offer to do the development. Within a specified time limit, the CPSC can then accept such an offer, evaluate the suggestions submitted, and publish a proposed rule. The issuance of the final standard is subject to notice and comment by interested persons.

The penalty provisions of the Act make it unlawful to manufacture for sale, offer for sale, distribute in commerce, or import into the United States a consumer product that does not conform to an applicable standard. Violators are subject to civil penalties, criminal penalties, injunctive enforcement and seizure, private suits for damages, and private suits for injunctive relief. This means that if a product cannot be made free of unreasonable risk of personal injury, the CPSC may ban its manufacture, sale, or importation altogether. The supplier of any already-distributed products that pose a substantial risk of injury may be compelled by the CPSC to repair, modify, or replace the products, or refund the purchase price.

Goods produced in the United States that are manufactured for export only are exempt from compliance with U.S. product safety standards.[40] Goods declared "banned hazardous substances" by the CPSC are also exempt from regulation as long as they are intended for

### ETHICAL CONSIDERATION

On average, an American child sees about 8,000 murders on television before reaching high school. How should programming managers respond to scientific evidence that television violence leads to more violent behavior by children? Can content-based regulation of broadcasting protect consumer health and safety? What additional precautions (such as time, place, and manner restrictions), if any, should be taken to protect children?

38. S.J. Res. 17 (2003).

39. 15 U.S.C. §§ 2051 *et seq.*

40. 15 U.S.C. § 2067.

### ETHICAL CONSIDERATION

Should U.S. companies sell products determined to be hazardous by the CPSC or the FDA in countries where government regulations are less stringent? Consider silicone breast implants (regulated by the FDA, not the CPSC). In 1992, three of the four manufacturers of silicone-filled breast implants were continuing to export the devices, which were subject to a sales moratorium imposed in the United States earlier that year.[a] Is that more or less defensible than selling a heater without the extra safety features that would be required in the United States but would make the heater prohibitively expensive in some poorer countries?

a. Robert L. Rose, *Breast Implants Still Being Sold Outside U.S.*, WALL ST. J., Mar. 4, 1992, at B1.

export. Exporters of such goods must, however, file a notifying statement with the CPSC thirty days before shipping the product so that the CPSC can notify the government of the foreign country of the shipment and the basis for the applicable U.S. safety standard.

The CPSC administers several consumer protection acts, including the Flammable Fabrics Act, the Federal Hazardous Substances Act,[41] the Poison Prevention Packaging Act (which requires child-resistant bottle caps), and the Refrigerator Safety Act. The CPSC currently has no jurisdiction over tobacco products, firearms, pesticides, motor vehicles, food, drugs, medical devices, or cosmetics.[42] These matters are regulated by other entities, such as the FDA, or are unregulated. In addition to its other duties, the CPSC maintains an Injury Information Clearinghouse to collect and analyze information relating to the causes and prevention of death, injury, and illness associated with consumer products.

One of the CPSC's areas of responsibility is ensuring the safety of infant products and toys. In 1999, for example, consumers spent approximately $4.9 billion on cribs, car seats, high chairs, strollers, and other products for infants, but many of these products were dangerous. The CPSC recalled ninety-five toys and infant products in 1999, amounting to tens of millions of products. Despite these recalls, more than 65,000 children visited emergency rooms as a result of injuries associated with products for infants. Frequently, companies, reluctant to generate negative publicity about their product, try to negotiate with the CPSC to issue press releases that use language that minimizes the hazards. For example, the company may issue a press release that announces a "recall for repair" rather than a straight recall. These vaguely worded press releases are designed to attract less attention and, consequently, may not reach parents to inform them of potential dangers.[43]

In addition to the federal Consumer Product Safety Act, several states have enacted laws to protect children from dangerous products. Two University of Chicago professors, whose son died when his Playskool Travel-Lite portable crib collapsed while he was napping, initiated Illinois's Children's Product Safety Act, which was signed into law in August 1999. Michigan followed suit and enacted the same law in June 2000.[44]

41. This Act is a composite of three significant acts: the Hazardous Substances Labeling Act, the Child Protection Act, and the Child Protection and Toy Safety Act. 15 U.S.C. § 2052.
42. *Id.*

## Automobiles

Automobile safety has seen enormous gains since Ralph Nader first brought the issue to the nation's attention in the 1960s.[45] Air bags (for the driver and front passenger) and antilock brakes have become popular safety features and are standard equipment on many new cars.

The National Highway Traffic Safety Administration (NHTSA), created in 1970, is an agency of the U.S. Department of Transportation. By law, the NHTSA has

43. E. Marla Felcher, *Children's Products and Risk*, ATLANTIC MONTHLY (Nov. 2000).
44. *Id.*
45. RALPH NADER, UNSAFE AT ANY SPEED (1965) (criticizing in particular General Motors Corporation's Corvair model). For a critique of Ralph Nader's consumer activist activities, see DAN BURT, ABUSE OF TRUST (1982).

### ETHICAL CONSIDERATION

Suppose that you are the product manager for your company's portable infant playpen. Two infants suffocated after their caregiver failed to properly latch the sides open, permitting the unit to collapse. The CPSC orders a recall of the playpens but requires only minimal publicity about the recall. Should you do more than the CPSC requires to publicize the recall? What would you do if you knew that another three infants would die the same way if you did not publicize the recall? Suppose the parents of the third infant to die sue your company. Is it ethical to settle the case on the condition that the settlement be kept confidential?[a]

a. Thanks to Professor Michael Wheeler of the Harvard Business School for this hypothetical.

### Ethical Consideration

Adding new safety requirements for automobiles can increase product cost and shut some consumers out of the market. Should governments coerce individuals into paying for unwanted safety features, or should individual consumers be allowed to choose which features they are willing to pay for?

the power to establish motor vehicle safety standards,[46] establish a National Motor Vehicle Safety Advisory Council, engage in testing and development of motor vehicle safety, prohibit manufacture or importation of substandard vehicles, and develop tire safety.[47] In addition, the NHTSA is charged with developing national standards for driver safety performance, accident reporting, and vehicle registration and inspection. States refusing to comply with established federal standards are denied federal highway funds.[48]

## Privacy Protections

Technological developments, especially the Internet, have made it possible to amass large amounts of detailed personal information, causing Scott McNealy, CEO of Sun Microsystems, to quip, "You have zero privacy. . . . Get over it."[49] Concerned about identity theft (which is discussed in this chapter's "Inside Story") and other violations of privacy, the public has pressured state and federal governments to enact laws dealing with the collection and transmission of private data.

### State Legislation

The states have taken the lead in formulating consumer privacy policy in the United States. In 2000 alone, more than one hundred privacy bills were introduced in forty-one states.[50] The bills fell into three general categories: (1) bills to prohibit or limit the financial industry's use of account-related information; (2) bills to regulate the use of information collected by online service providers and websites; and (3) bills to prevent state agencies from selling information about people who do business with the state, including obtaining driver's licenses.[51] As noted in Chapter 2, Congress passed legislation banning the sale of driver's license information.

California has been particularly active, having enacted fifteen privacy laws in 2003 alone. In 1999, California passed a law that limits the information that supermarkets can demand from customers as a condition of signing up for grocery club discount cards. Supermarkets had been selling data about their customers' purchases of items such as liquor and tobacco to insurance companies.[52]

California created the first statewide Office of Privacy Protection in the nation in 2000. In 2004, California established an information security standard requiring businesses that own or license personal information about a California resident to implement and maintain "reasonable security measures" to protect that information; health-care providers, which are already regulated under the Health Insurance Portability and Accountability Act (HIPAA), discussed below, and other entities governed by the HIPAA privacy rules issued by the federal Department of Health and Human Services were excluded.[53] The statute defines "reasonable security measures" as "procedures and practices appropriate to the nature of the information to protect the personal information from unauthorized access destruction, use, modification or disclosure."[54] The law applies to any business, regardless of where it is located, that owns or licenses personal information about a California resident. For example, if a company based in Maine outsources warranties to a third party in New York, then the company will have to determine how that third party uses information about its California customers and ensure that it has adequate security measures in place.[55] California also requires firms to notify customers if their personal identifying information is improperly disclosed to third parties.

Opponents of states' efforts to protect consumers' privacy argue that the different states are creating a patchwork of conflicting rules, undermining efforts to enact federal legislation on privacy. But some consumer privacy advocates hope that enacting strong state privacy laws will put pressure on Congress to enact stronger federal privacy legislation.[56]

46. Boats are subject to safety regulation under the Federal Boat Safety Act of 1971 (46 U.S.C. §§ 4301 *et seq.*), and aircraft safety is regulated by the Federal Aviation Act of 1958 (49 U.S.C. §§ 1421 *et seq.*).
47. Motor Vehicle Safety Act of 1966, 15 U.S.C. §§ 1381 *et seq.*
48. Highway Safety Act of 1966, 23 U.S.C. §§ 401 *et seq.*
49. Adam Cohen, *Internet Insecurity,* TIME, July 2, 2001, at 47–51.
50. Rachel Zimmerman & Glenn R. Simpson, *Lobbyists Swarm to Stop Tough Privacy Bills in States,* WALL ST. J., Apr. 21, 2000, at A16.
51. *Id.*
52. James Glave, *The Safeway to Shop,* WIRED NEWS, Oct. 8, 1999.
53. Assembly Bill 1950 (2004).
54. *Id.*
55. *In 2004, California Again Leads States in Passage of Privacy-Related Legislation,* 9 ELECTRONIC COM. & L. REP. 843 (Oct. 13, 2004).
56. Michael Schroeder, *Business Targets State Privacy Initiatives,* WALL ST. J., Feb. 10, 2000, at A2.

## Federal Trade Commission Actions

For several years, the FTC has taken the position that it is an unfair or deceptive trade practice under Section 5(a) of the Federal Trade Commission Act[57] for firms to fail to honor their own privacy policies (see the "View from Cyberspace" below). The FTC went a step further in 2004 and warned that a company's failure to protect sensitive consumer information could itself be an "unfair" practice even if the company did not promise to keep the data secure.[58] This approach encourages businesses to report potential breaches to not only the individual affected but also other parties, such as credit

57. See Appendix H.

58. *Lax Security Could Bring FTC Enforcement Under 'Unfair' Practices Section of FTC Act*, 72 U.S.L.W. 2744 (June 8, 2004).

## *View from Cyberspace*

### Privacy in the Electronic Age: Eli Lilly's Prozac Website Is a Downer

From March 2000 through June 2001, Eli Lilly & Co. offered, through its Prozac.com website, a service called "Medi-Messenger," which enabled its subscribers to receive individualized e-mail messages from Lilly concerning their Prozac antidepressant medication or other matters. On June 27, 2001, Lilly sent subscribers to the service a form e-mail, which inadvertently disclosed all of the subscribers' e-mail addresses to each individual subscriber by including all of their addresses within the "To:" entry of the message.

The FTC sued Lilly, claiming that its representation that it employs measures and takes steps appropriate under the circumstances to maintain and protect the privacy and confidentiality of consumers' personal information obtained through its Prozac.com website was false or misleading and constituted an unfair or deceptive act or practice in violation of Section 5(a) of the Federal Trade Commission Act.[a] The FTC claimed that Lilly had not, in fact, employed such measures or taken such steps. For example, Lilly failed to (1) provide appropriate training for its employees regarding consumer privacy and information security; (2) provide appropriate oversight and assistance for the employee who sent out the e-mail, who had no prior experience in creating, testing, or implementing the computer program used; and (3) implement appropriate checks and controls on the process, such as reviewing the computer program with experienced personnel and pretesting the program internally before sending out the e-mail. Lilly's failure to implement appropriate measures also violated certain of its own written policies.

In January 2002, the FTC and Lilly agreed on a consent order that prohibited Lilly from misrepresenting the extent to which it maintains and protects the privacy or confidentiality of any personally identifiable information collected from or about consumers.[b] It also required Lilly to implement a four-stage information security program designed to establish and maintain reasonable safeguards to protect consumers' personal information and to guard against the unauthorized access, use, or disclosure of such information. In particular, Lilly agreed to:

1. Designate appropriate personnel to coordinate and oversee the information security program.
2. Identify reasonably foreseeable internal and external risks to the security, confidentiality, and integrity of personal information, including any such risks posed by lack of training, and address these risks in each relevant area of its operations, including (a) management and training of personnel; (b) information systems for the processing, storage, transmission, or disposal of personal information; and (c) prevention and response to attacks, intrusions, unauthorized access, or other information systems failures.
3. Conduct annual written reviews by qualified personnel to monitor and document compliance with the program, evaluate the program's effectiveness, and recommend changes to it.
4. Adjust the program in light of any findings and recommendations resulting from reviews or ongoing monitoring, and in light of any material change to Lilly's operations that affect the program.

Managers are well advised to review their company's privacy policies with counsel. Rather than waiting until there is a problem, they should work with their information technology staff to implement procedures of the sort Eli Lilly was required to put into place after its Prozac.com debacle.

a. Eli Lilly & Co., 67 Fed. Reg. 4963 (Feb. 1, 2002); *In re* Eli Lilly & Co., 2002 FTC LEXIS 3 (Feb. 1, 2002).

b. *Id.*

bureaus and banks. This would bring federal standards into line with California and other states that require businesses to notify individuals when their information has been revealed to third parties.[59] The FTC stressed that security is an ongoing process, not a static checklist. Therefore, companies must remain proactive in data protection.

In April 2004, the FTC proposed a rule (the Disposal Rule), pursuant to the Fair and Accurate Credit Transaction Act of 2003,[60] that would require consumer reporting agencies, resellers of consumer reports, lenders, insurers, employers, landlords, government agencies, mortgage brokers, arts dealers, and waste-disposal companies to "take reasonable measures to protect against unauthorized access to and use of [sensitive consumer] information in connection with its disposal."[61] The proposed rule calls for data destruction policies commensurate with the sensitivity of the data and the size of the business.

## Financial Information: Gramm-Leach-Bliley Act

In 1999, Congress enacted the Gramm-Leach-Bliley Financial Modernization Act of 1999,[62] which requires financial institutions to provide privacy protections to consumers. The law applies to banks, debt collectors, credit counselors, retailers, and travel agencies. Financial institutions must give notice to their customers before sharing personal information with other entities. Financial institutions must also disclose their privacy policy annually and give customers the right to opt out of disclosures to third parties. The Gramm-Leach-Bliley Act does not preempt states from implementing stricter privacy regulations, and as of 2004, a number of states had introduced or were planning to introduce their own financial privacy legislation.[63]

The Federal Trade Commission and seven other financial regulatory agencies (including the Federal Deposit Insurance Corporation, the Federal Reserve Board, and the Securities and Exchange Commission) have issued regulations that implement the privacy protections provided by the statute. The government has attempted to force businesses to better safeguard consumers' information through the Safeguard Rule contained in the Gramm-Leach-Bliley Act.

The Safeguard Rule requires financial services firms to (1) promulgate a written information security plan, (2) designate at least one employee to coordinate the plan, (3) identify and assess the risks to customer financial information, and (4) evaluate the safeguards for controlling these risks. To come within the Safeguard Rule, the firm must also (1) regularly monitor and test the plan, (2) select appropriate service providers and contract with them to implement the safeguards, and (3) evaluate and adjust the plan as material circumstances change. According to the FTC, its ultimate goal is to promote awareness among companies about the importance of protecting sensitive information while allowing the companies to tailor a plan based on their size, scope, and level of sensitive information.[64] Although some companies have called for stricter guidelines for determining whether a particular plan satisfies the rule,[65] the FTC claims that its requirements are simple and straightforward.

## Medical Information: The HIPAA

On April 14, 2001, the U.S. Department of Health and Human Services finalized its regulations, under the Health Insurance Portability and Accountability Act of 1996 (HIPAA), on maintaining the privacy of personal medical information.[66] At first blush, the regulations appear to apply only to health-care providers (such as doctors, hospitals, and nurses), group health plans (such as HMOs and self-insured plans that have fifty or more participants or are administered by an entity other than the employer that established and maintained the plan), and health-care clearinghouses that process claims. Yet, upon a closer reading, it becomes clear that, in fact, almost all employers that provide health-care coverage to their employees will be affected by the privacy regulations and required to develop privacy policies and procedures to safeguard protected health information.[67]

Protected health information includes any information relating to a person's health that (1) was created by a health-care provider, health plan, employer, or health-

59. *Id.*

60. 69 Fed. Reg. 21,387 (2004).

61. *Id.*

62. 15 U.S.C. §§ 6801–6809.

63. Eileen Canning, *States Legislating Financial Privacy Before Federal Regulators Even Issue Draft,* 68 U.S.L.W. 2453 (Feb. 8, 2000).

64. *Id.*

65. Michael Bologna, *Attorneys Claim That FTC Safeguards Rule Has Been Greeted with Confusion, Uncertainty,* 8 U.S.L.W. 746 (Aug. 6, 2003).

66. 42 U.S.C. §§ 1320d–1320d-8; *see also* 45 C.F.R. pts. 160, 164 (Final Rules for Administrative Data Standards and for Security and Privacy of Individually Identifiable Health Information) (2000).

67. *See, generally,* Linda Abdel-Malek, *HIPAA Privacy Rules Impact Employers,* N.Y. L.J., May 14, 2001, at 5.

care clearinghouse; and (2) identifies the person to whom the health information relates. For example, if, as is usually the case, the employer acts as the plan sponsor, then the employer must establish "firewalls" to ensure that private health information is used only for purposes of plan administration and not for any other employment-related decisions, such as termination of employment.

Any person who knowingly discloses individually identifiable health information to an unauthorized person can be fined up to $50,000 or imprisoned for up to one year or both.[68] If the defendant acted under false pretenses, the maximum sentences increase to not more than $100,000 and five years in prison; if the defendant acted with intent to "sell, transfer, or use individually identifiable health information for commercial advantage, personal gain, or malicious harm," they rise to not more than $250,000 and ten years in prison.

### Children's Online Privacy Protection Act

The Children's Online Privacy Protection Act of 1998 (COPPA)[69] prevents websites from collecting personal information from children under age thirteen without parental consent. Parental consent can be in the form of a note, credit card number, or e-mail with a password. Websites must disclose what personal information they collect from children and how they use it, including whether they share it with third parties. In 2004, the FTC fined UMG Recordings $400,000 and Bonzi Software $75,000 for violating COPPA.[70]

In *FTC v. Toysmart.com,*[71] the U.S. District Court for the District of Massachusetts precluded Toysmart.com, a Web toy vendor in dire financial straits, from selling the personal information it had collected from consumers. Toysmart had created family profiles with the names and birth dates of children, shopping preferences, names, addresses, and billing information. The company's privacy policy stated that the personal information collected would never be shared with third parties. The complaint filed by the FTC also alleged that the company had violated COPPA by collecting information from children under thirteen without obtaining parental consent. The court ordered Toysmart to delete or destroy any information collected in violation of COPPA.

In 2001, the FTC approved the self-regulatory program of the Children's Advertising Review Unit of the Council of Better Business Bureaus as the first "safe-harbor" program under COPPA. Companies that establish approved self-regulatory programs are deemed to have complied with COPPA.

## Junk Faxes, the Do-Not-Call List, and Spam

### Fax Blasts

The Telephone Consumer Protection Act of 1991 (TCPA)[72] bans unsolicited mass facsimile transmissions by telecopy (so-called *fax blasts*). In 2000, the Federal Communications Commission imposed a $5.379 million forfeiture, the largest of its kind, against Fax.com, a company that sends unsolicited fax advertisements to companies. "We're sending relief in the form of a simple message to junk faxers: violate our rules and you will pay the consequences," said FCC Chairman Michael Powell.[73]

### Telemarketing and the Do-Not-Call List

The TCPA also directed the FCC to adopt rules and regulations to curb telemarketing abuses. In general, the TCPA prohibits the use of either autodialers or simulated or prerecorded voice messages to deliver calls to emergency telephone lines, health-care facilities, radio telephone services, cell phones, and other services where the called party will incur some charge for the call. The only exception is for calls to a person who has given prior consent to such calls. The TCPA also prohibits the use of prerecorded messages when calling residential telephone numbers, except with the prior consent of the called party or in the case of an emergency. Consumers can recover $500 per infraction—triple that if they can prove that the marketer was aware of the law.[74]

68. 42 U.S.C. § 1320d-6.
69. 15 U.S.C. §§ 6501–6506. *See also* 16 C.F.R. pt. 312 (implementing regulations of Federal Trade Commission).
70. See http://www.ftc.gov/opa/2004/02/bonziumg.htm (FTC press release with links to complaints).
71. See Press Release, Federal Trade Commission, FTC Sues Failed Web Site, Toysmart.com, for Deceptively Offering for Sale Personal Information of Web Site Visitors (July 10, 2000), *at* http://www.ftc.gov/opa/2000/07/toysmart.htm.
72. 47 U.S.C. § 227. The provision was upheld in *Missouri ex rel. Nixon v. Am. Blast Fax, Inc.*, 323 F.3d 649 (8th Cir. 2003).
73. Statement of FCC Chairman Michael K. Powell regarding FCC Enforcement Action on Junk Faxes *at* http://hraunfoss.fcc.gov/edocs_public/attachmatch/DOC-242654A2.pdf (Jan. 5, 2004).
74. Riva Richmond, *Pre-Emptive Strike: Cellphone Spam Isn't a Huge Problem Yet. And Regulators Want to Make Sure It Never Is,* WALL ST. J., Sept. 13, 2004, at R13.

POLITICAL PERSPECTIVE

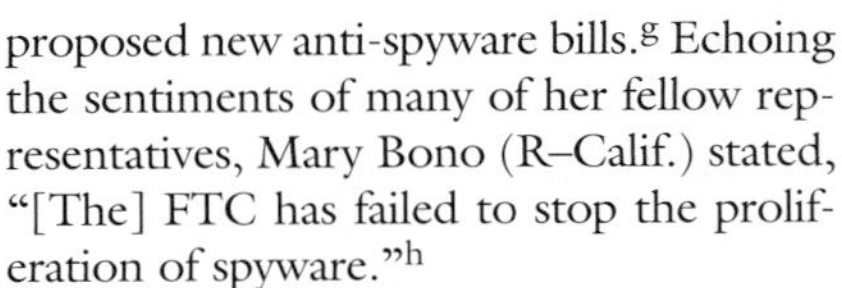

# STOPPING SPYWARE

*Spyware* consists of small computer software programs that are automatically inserted on the hard drive of a user's computer when the Internet is accessed.[a] Unbeknownst to the computer user, the programs collect and transmit data to a third party. Often spyware is included in programs or files. Because it operates from inside legitimate programs and makes calls out to the Internet, spyware can evade many virus protection programs and firewalls.

Some spyware is designed to steal credit card numbers, record keystrokes, relay passwords, change preference settings on the computer, or redirect the user to a completely different site than the user intended. In addition to raising privacy concerns and facilitating identity theft, spyware can also adversely affect the performance and stability of computer systems.

Certain types of spyware violate the Elecronic Communications Privacy Act,[b] which makes it illegal to intercept communications without a court order or permission from one of the parties. Programs that co-opt control of users' computers, exploit their Internet connection, or exploit security vulnerabilities in network software to steal passwords and other information may also violate the Computer Fraud and Abuse Act.[c] The installation of unwanted software without the user's consent may also constitute a deceptive or unfair trade practice under Section 5 of the Federal Trade Commission Act.[d]

The line between spyware and legitimate software can be blurred, however. For example, Microsoft Word is sold pursuant to an end-user license agreement that restricts the purchaser to installing the word processing software on only one computer at a time. MS Word has a built-in "feature" that searches all other computers on the computer network to which the host computer is attached for other copies of MS Word. If the serial numbers match, then MS Word will automatically shut itself down. Another common "feature" on many programs is the ability to check a given website for possible software updates, alert users of new programs, and display advertisements. Some people argue that any computer process running without the user's knowledge and often against the user's wishes is spyware.

In 2004, the FTC appealed to the software industry to regulate itself when it comes to spyware. The FTC commissioners concluded that this insidious problem could be dealt with most effectively through industry best practices, consumer education, and enforcement of existing legislation.[e] FTC Commissioner Mozelle Thompson stated, "[We] don't believe legislation is the answer at this time. [Self-regulation] may provide an efficient solution for problems spyware poses to both consumers and industry."[f]

At the same time the FTC made this appeal for self-regulation, it asked Congress not to pass new legislation directed at spyware. Its plea was ignored, however, as several members of Congress proposed new anti-spyware bills.[g] Echoing the sentiments of many of her fellow representatives, Mary Bono (R–Calif.) stated, "[The] FTC has failed to stop the proliferation of spyware."[h]

Following Utah's lead, California enacted the Consumer Protection Against Computer Spyware Act in the fall of 2004.[i] The Act prohibits the installation of software that (1) takes control of a computer; (2) modifies a consumer's interaction with the Internet; (3) collects personally identifiable information; (4) prevents without authorization a user's effort to block or disable such software; or (5) removes, disables, or renders inoperative security or antispy software.

Meanwhile, back in Washington D.C., on October 5, 2004, the House of Representatives passed, by a vote of 399 to 1, the "Securely Protect Yourself Against Cyber Trespass Act" or Spy Act (H.R. 2929).[j] The Spy Act would direct the FTC to require companies to provide notice before collecting any personally identifiable information. It would also prohibit certain deceptive practices associated with spyware, including hijacking a consumer's home page; sending advertisements that cannot be closed, except by shutting down the computer; and *phishing,* in which individuals attempt to attain personal information, including credit card numbers, using fake e-mails or websites that appear to come from a legitimate company.

**a.** See, generally, Paula J. Bruening & Michael Steffern, *"Spyware": Technologies, Issues and Policy Proposals,* 7 J. INTERNET L. 3 (2004); Christopher J. Volkmer, *Should Adware and Spyware Prompt Congressional Action?,* 7 J. INTERNET L. 1 (2004).
**b.** 18 U.S.C. §§ 2510–21, 2701–12.
**c.** 18 U.S.C. § 1030.
**d.** *See, e.g.,* FTC v. DSquared Solutions, No. 032-3223 (D. Md. filed Nov. 10, 2003).
**e.** Michael Warnecke & Alexei Alexis, *Developers Ratchet Up Anti-Spyware Efforts, but Legislators Won't Wait for Tech Solutions,* 9 U.S.L.W. 376–77 (Apr. 21, 2004).
**f.** Michael Warnecke, *Ubiquitous Spyware Propels New Bills, Drowns Out FTC's Plea for Self-Regulation,* 9 U.S.L.W. 418–19 (May 5, 2004).
**g.** H.R. 2929, 108th Cong. (1st Sess. 2003); S. 2145, 108th Cong. (1st Sess. 2004).
**h.** Warnecke, *supra* note f.
**i.** S.B. 1436, 9 ELECTRONIC COM. & L. REP. 820 (Oct. 6, 2004).
**j.** *House Passes Measure Targeting "Spyware" Programs,* 9 ELECTRONIC COM. & L. REP. 839 (Oct. 13, 2004).

*(Continued)*

(Political Perspective *continued*)

The Spy Act would also authorize the FTC to regulate spyware programs and seek civil penalties of up to $3 million per violation. Individuals would have no right to sue for violations of the act, however. The Spy Act would create a uniform national rule, preempting state regulation of spyware.

On October 7, 2004, the House of Representatives passed the Internet Spyware Prevention Act of 2004 (H.R. 4661) by a vote of 415 to 0.[k] It would amend the Computer Fraud and Abuse Act to make it a criminal offense, punishable by fines or up to five years in prison, to intentionally access a computer without authorization and cause a program or code to be copied onto the computer to (1) further the commission of another federal offense, (2) obtain or transmit the personal information of another person with the intent to defraud or injure or cause damage to a computer, or (3) intentionally impair the security protection of a computer. The act would preempt the states from creating private civil remedies for violations of the act. The Business Software Alliance praised the bill for imposing criminal penalties on "those persons who aim to harm innocent Internet users via spyware applications" without imposing new regulations on all technology companies.[l]

k. *House Passes Measure Providing Criminal Penalties for "Internet Spying,"* 9 ELECTRONIC COM. & L. REP. 838 (Oct. 13, 2004).

l. *Id.*

*"You know I'm not a telemarketer, Jimmy, and you are not going to fine me eleven thousand dollars. Now, for the last time, put your mother on."*



In 2003, the FTC created the *Do-Not-Call list,* a registry of names of persons not wanting to receive unsolicited telemarketer calls, pursuant to the Do-Not-Call Implementation Act.[75] Telemarketers are generally prohibited from calling persons who have added their names to the list. Charities, political parties, and companies with which the individual has done business recently are still permitted to call persons on the list. The Tenth Circuit upheld the constitutionality of the Do-Not-Call registry in 2004,[76] and by early 2005 more than 64 million telephone numbers were registered on the list.

75. Pub. L. No. 108–10, 117 Stat. 557 (2003), *to be codified at* 15 U.S.C. § 6101. More information is available at the official FTC website http://www.ftc.gov/donotcall.

76. Mainstream Mktg. Servs., Inc. v. FTC, 358 F.3d 1228 (10th Cir. 2004), *cert. denied,* 125 S. Ct. 47 (2004).

In 2004, the Federal Communications Commission adopted a rule prohibiting the sending of commercial messages to wireless phones without express prior authorization.[77] The FCC elected not to create a national wireless "do-not-spam" registry of individual e-mail addresses.[78] Instead, the FCC announced that it would create a "wireless domain name list" to help marketers distinguish wireless e-mail addresses from general e-mail addresses.[79]

## SPAM

It is estimated that more than 10 million unsolicited e-mails (so-called *spam*) are sent every *minute* worldwide.[80] The average consumer receives 1,466 unsolicited e-mails a year.[81] The spam epidemic has reached a point that goes beyond mere annoyance. It has begun to hinder business productivity.

The Controlling the Assault of Non-Solicited Pornography and Marketing Act of 2003 (the CAN-SPAM Act)[82] established national standards for sending unsolicited e-mail messages and preempted the state regulation of spam, which was often more stringent. The Act prohibits spammers from (1) disguising their identities by using false return addresses, (2) using misleading subject lines, and (3) gathering e-mail addresses from third-party websites.[83] Violators face up to five years in prison and up to $2 million in fines.[84] The U.S. Attorney's office secured its first conviction under the Act in September 2004 after a Los-Angeles-area resident pled guilty to driving around a neighborhood in a vehicle equipped with a wireless antenna attached to a laptop to find open, unencrypted access points and then send thousands of spam messages advertising pornographic websites.[85]

Congress and the Federal Trade Commission rejected calls for a national "do-not-spam" registry after concluding that it might become a target for unscrupulous marketers and would impose an undue burden on legitimate marketers. Meanwhile, lawmakers in California and other states with tough state spam legislation criticized CAN-SPAM for preempting more effective state protection. For example, CAN-SPAM would appear to preempt California legislation[86] that gave individuals, the California attorney general, and Internet service providers the right to recover damages of up to $1,000 per unsolicited e-mail (with a maximum of $1 million in damages per incident) sent to or from California without a valid e-mail address contact and the name and location of the sender.[87]

The sponsors of Canthespamact.com urge the repeal of the CAN-SPAM Act. They point out that the Act seeks only to control spam, not to ban it. Spam, they argue, costs everyone who gets it a small amount of time, effort, and money. Ultimately, these costs are borne by consumers. This group wants these costs shifted to the spammers. In 2003, 7 percent of U.S. Internet users polled reported purchasing something based on an unsolicited message.[88] With a return like this on a relatively cost-free form of advertising, spammers will persist unless a cost for their daily operation is imposed.

In 2003, AOL, Microsoft, and Yahoo announced a collective effort to reduce spam by encouraging one another to obtain "valid credentials" before permitting users to send mass e-mail. One year later, AOL, Microsoft, Yahoo, and Earthlink filed seven lawsuits in four states under CAN-SPAM to stop both spam and "spimming," the sending of unsolicited messages via instant messaging services and Internet chat rooms.[89] A marketing coalition of legitimate Internet marketers started project Lumos, which is designed to stop spam while allowing legitimate e-mail marketing to continue.[90] Private plans tend to focus on (1) forcing potential e-mailers to verify their identity so that they can be tracked down if they begin spamming and (2) stopping them from e-mailing entirely if they are not legitimate e-mail users.

## Unfairness, Deception, and Fraud

A number of regulatory agencies, both federal and state, are involved in the area of unfair and deceptive trade practices and consumer fraud. They include the Federal

77. The FCC order is available at http://hraunfoss.fcc.gov/edocs_public/attachmatch/FCC-04-194A1.doc.
78. *Id.*
79. *Id.*
80. Stephen Baker, *The Taming of the Internet,* BUS.WK., Dec. 15, 2003, at 78–82.
81. Suzanne Vranica, *You Have Mail,* WALL ST. J., Nov. 2, 2001, at B10.
82. CAN-SPAM Act, 17 U.S.C. §§ 7701–7713.
83. *Id.*
84. Cheryl Bolen, *Sentencing Commission Adds to Proposals, Seeks Comment on CAN-SPAM Act Provisions,* 9 U.S.L.W. 75–76 (Jan. 28, 2004).
85. United States v. Tombros, No. CR 04-1085 (C.D. Cal. filed Sept. 27, 2004), 9 ELECTRONIC COM. & L. REP. 829 (Oct. 6, 2004).
86. S.B. 1457.
87. *In 2004, California Again Leads States in Passage of Privacy-Related Legislation, supra* note 55.
88. Baker, *supra* note 80.
89. Laurie J. Flynn, *Internet Giants File 7 Suits Aimed at Stopping Spam,* N.Y. TIMES, Oct. 29, 2004.
90. *E-Mail Marketing Group Unveils Industry Solution to Spam Epidemic,* 71 U.S.L.W. 2687–88 (Apr. 29, 2003).

**INTERNATIONAL SNAPSHOT**

At the end of 1999, the Organisation for Economic Co-operation and Development issued Guidelines for Consumer Protection in Electronic Commerce reflecting agreement among twenty countries on general policies for protecting consumers shopping online. The guidelines describe fair business, marketing, and advertising practices and identify information that companies should disclose to consumers so that they can make informed choices. In addition, the guidelines point to the need for companies to establish procedures and mechanisms for confirming transactions and ensuring secure payment. The guidelines call for cooperation between countries on law enforcement, recognition of cross-border legal judgments, and development of alternative dispute resolution procedures.[a]

**a.** Bureau of Consumer Protection, FTC, *Consumer Protection in the Global Electronic Marketplace,* Sept. 2000, *at* http://www.ftc.gov/bcp/icpw/lookingahead/lookingahead.htm.

Trade Commission, the Food and Drug Administration, the Federal Communications Commission, the U.S. Postal Service, the U.S. Department of Housing and Urban Development, and the Securities and Exchange Commission. (Securities fraud is discussed in Chapter 23.) These federal agencies regulate advertising, packaging and labeling, pricing, warranties, and numerous sales practices. State attorneys general and state departments of consumer affairs are also involved on the state level in protecting consumers through their administration of various state labeling laws, state warranty provisions (such as "lemon laws"), state deceptive sales practices statutes, and state privacy laws.

## Deceptive Advertising and Warranties

Consumers are bombarded daily with the competing claims of various advertisers trying to generate new sales. From billboards to television to banner ads on websites and even the back of grocery receipts, advertisers vie for the consumer's attention. In this competitive environment, companies sometimes make claims that are deceptive or false. Legal solutions to this problem have historically involved three separate approaches: the common law, statutory law, and regulatory law. Regulatory law, enacted and enforced through the Federal Trade Commission, has proved to be the most effective vehicle for combating false advertisements.

**ETHICAL CONSIDERATION**

Should telemarketers use caller ID to identify and create a database of those individuals who call their 800 or 900 telephone numbers?

### Common Law

A traditional common law approach provides two remedies for a consumer who has been misled by false advertising. First, a consumer can sue for breach of contract. In this instance, however, it may be difficult to prove the existence of a contract because the courts usually consider advertisements to be only an offer to deal. A consumer might also sue for the tort of deceit. *Deceit* requires the proof of several elements, including knowledge by the seller that the misrepresentation is false. In addition, the misrepresentation must be one of fact and not opinion, a difficult distinction to make in the context of advertising. (Deceit, also called fraudulent misrepresentation, is discussed in Chapter 9.)

### Statutory Law

The Uniform Commercial Code (UCC) and the Lanham Trademark Act are two statutes that may protect consumers from false advertising. As noted in Chapter 8, under Section 2-313 of the UCC, any statement, sample, or model may constitute an *express warranty* if it is part of the basis of the bargain. Thus, an advertising term may be construed as an express warranty for a product. If the product does not conform to the representation made, the warranty is breached. Express warranties can be disclaimed in a sales contract, however, so the UCC generally does not provide a strong response to false advertising claims.

The Lanham Trademark Act forbids the use of any false "description or representation" in connection with any goods or services and provides a private cause of action for any competitor injured by any other competitor's false claims. The purpose of the Act is to ensure truthfulness in advertising and to eliminate misrepresentations of quality regarding one's own product or the product of a competitor. Neither consumers nor retailers have standing to sue for violations of the Lanham Act. Only direct commercial competitors or surrogates for direct commercial competitors have standing to pursue claims under the Lanham Act.[91]

91. Conte Bros. Auto., Inc. v. Quaker State, Inc., 165 F.3d 221 (3d Cir. 1998).

For example, the Coca-Cola Company, maker of Minute Maid orange juice, successfully sued Tropicana Products, Inc. in the early 1980s under the Lanham Trademark Act. At issue was a television commercial in which athlete Bruce Jenner squeezed an orange while saying, "It's pure, pasteurized juice as it comes from the orange," and then poured the juice into a Tropicana carton. Coca-Cola claimed that the commercial was false because it represented that Tropicana contains unprocessed, fresh-squeezed juice when in fact the juice is heated (pasteurized) and sometimes frozen before packaging. The court agreed that the representation was false because it suggested that pasteurized juice comes directly from oranges. The court enjoined Tropicana from continuing to use the advertisement.[92]

## *FTC Regulatory Law*

The Federal Trade Commission is charged with preventing unfair and deceptive trade practices, including false advertising. Among the areas that the FTC has addressed under Section 5 of the Federal Trade Commission Act are deceptive price and quality claims and false testimonials and mock-ups.

If the FTC believes a violation of Section 5 exists, it will attempt to negotiate a consent order with the alleged violator. A *consent order* is an agreement to stop the activity that the FTC has found illegal. If an agreement cannot be reached, the matter will be heard by an administrative law judge. The judge's decision can be appealed to the full commission, and the full commission's decision can be appealed to a U.S. court of appeals.

FTC remedies include civil damages, affirmative advertising (the advertiser is required to include specific information), counter or corrective advertising, and cease and desist orders. A *cease and desist order* instructs advertisers to stop using the methods deemed unfair or deceptive. In one case, the FTC required the maker of Listerine to cease and desist from making the claim that Listerine prevented colds and sore throats or lessened their severity. Testing performed by the FTC revealed that this claim, which the company had made for more than fifty years, was false. To counteract years of false claims, the FTC required the company to disclose in any future advertisements for Listerine that, contrary to prior advertising, Listerine did not help prevent colds or sore throats or lessen their severity. The order applied to the next $10 million of Listerine advertising.[93]

92. Coca-Cola Co. v. Tropicana Prods., Inc., 690 F.2d 312 (2d Cir. 1982).
93. Warner–Lambert Co. v. FTC, 562 F.2d 749 (D.C. Cir. 1977), *cert. denied*, 435 U.S. 950 (1978).

**Deceptive Price** One example of deceptive pricing practices involves the sale of advertised items at higher prices to customers unaware of the advertised price. In one case, a person purchased a blue 1986 Chevrolet Celebrity with 29,000 miles from an automobile dealer for $8,524.[94] Unbeknownst to the buyer, the dealership was currently advertising a blue 1986 Celebrity with 29,000 miles for $6,995 in a local newspaper. When he returned home, the man saw the ad and telephoned the dealership to demand that the deal be renegotiated. The salesman refused, claiming that the advertised car had been sent to auction. The customer sued under the Illinois Consumer Fraud Act, which forbids false misrepresentations as well as omission of material facts. The trial court held that the dealership had a duty to inform the customer of the advertised price and awarded him the difference in prices, plus costs.

Deceptive pricing practices also include offers of free merchandise with a purchase and two-for-one deals when the advertiser recovers the cost of the free merchandise by charging more than the regular price for the merchandise bought. Another example of deceptive pricing is bait and switch advertising. An advertiser violates the FTC *bait and switch advertising* rules if it refuses to show an advertised item, fails to have a reasonable quantity of the item in stock, fails to promise to deliver the item within a reasonable time, or discourages employees from selling the advertised item.

**Quality Claims** Advertisements often include quality claims. To determine whether an advertiser has made a deceptive quality claim, the FTC must first identify the

94. Affrunti v. Vill. Ford Sales, Inc., 597 N.E.2d 1242 (Ill. App. Ct. 1992).

### ETHICAL CONSIDERATION

A newspaper's publication of an article entitled "A Car Buyer's Guide to Sanity," which taught consumers how to negotiate lower prices, so angered car dealers that they pulled at least $1 million worth of advertising from the newspaper. The FTC challenged the dealers' actions under the antitrust laws, claiming that they had deprived consumers of essential price information in the form of newspaper advertising and had chilled the newspaper from publishing similar stories in the future.[a] Should the government become embroiled in an advertiser's decision to pull advertising from a news publication? Was the advertisers' conduct ethical?

**a.** Anthony Ramirez, *Car Dealers to Stop Ad Threat,* SAN FRANCISCO CHRON., Aug. 2, 1995, at B3.

claim and then determine whether the claim is substantiated. Quality claims made without any substantiation are considered deceptive. For example, the FTC concluded that the marketers of Doan's pills had disseminated false and deceptive statements when they claimed the pills were more effective at relieving back pain than other over-the-counter pain relievers without any reasonable basis for substantiating the representations.[95]

On the other hand, obvious exaggerations and vague generalities are considered *puffing* and are not considered deceptive because they are unlikely to mislead consumers. (Puffing is also discussed in Chapter 8.)

In the following case, a purchaser of the over-the-counter painkiller Aleve sued its distributor for false advertising in violation of California's Unfair Competition Law (UCL).

95. *In re* Novartis Corp., FTC Docket No. 9279 (Mar. 9, 1998), 66 U.S.L.W. 2582 (Mar. 31, 1998).

A CASE IN POINT

**CASE 17.1**
**Lavie v. Procter & Gamble Co.**
*California Court of Appeal*
*129 Cal. Rptr. 2d 486 (Cal. App. 2003).*

## In the Language of the Court

**› FACTS** Zion Lavie developed a stomach ulcer after using Aleve, an over-the-counter drug distributed by Procter & Gamble Company. He sued P&G, alleging that the company had engaged in false advertising. Aleve's advertising campaign explicitly claimed that Aleve was gentler on the stomach than aspirin. The plaintiff claimed that this implied that Aleve would not cause any stomach upset. The trial court granted summary judgment for P&G and dismissed all claims. Lavie appealed to the California Court of Appeal.

**› ISSUE PRESENTED** Should false advertising claims be based on what a reasonable consumer would understand, or should they be based on what the "least sophisticated consumer" would think about a product and its corresponding advertising?

**› OPINION** KLINE, J., writing on behalf of the California Court of Appeal:

The standard to be used in evaluating whether an advertisement is deceptive under the UCL is purely a question of law and certainly has important public policy implications for California consumers and businesses. Moreover, the Attorney General has a particular interest in the interpretation of [the provisions of the California Unfair Competition Law because they] are the basic tools of the Attorney General and the district attorneys in combating consumer fraud. . . . The Attorney General and district attorneys have an independent role in the enforcement of this state's false advertising laws. They are authorized to prosecute violations of the UCL criminally and may also seek redress through the bringing of civil law enforcement cases seeking equitable relief and civil penalties beyond those available to private parties. . . .

Asserting that an advertisement violates the law if it is false or if it has the capacity to mislead unwary, unsophisticated or the most gullible consumers, the Attorney General maintains, the "trial court's failure to apply the 'least sophisticated consumer' standard as the measure of deception and the court's imposition of responsibility on consumers to investigate the merits of advertising claims were error."

We disagree. California and federal courts applying the UCL have never applied a "least sophisticated consumer standard," absent evidence that the ad targeted particularly vulnerable customers. Rather, they have consistently applied a standard closer to an ordinary or "reasonable consumer" standard to evaluate unfair advertising claims. Nor do we view the court's application of the "reasonable consumer" standard as requiring consumers to investigate the merits of advertising claims.

. . .

*(Continued)*

(Case 17.1 *continued*)

As a necessary corollary to his argument, the Attorney General urges that we reject *Freeman v. Time, Inc.*[96] and *Haskell v. Time, Inc.*[97] as well as other federal decisions which have concluded that California employs the reasonable person or reasonable consumer standard in evaluating deceptive advertising. In *Freeman,* the Ninth Circuit agreed with the district court in *Haskell* that the "reasonable consumer" standard was the appropriate test for a violation of the UCL.

. . .

As *Haskell* observed, "[T]he reasonable person standard is well ensconced in the law in a variety of legal contexts in which a claim of deception is brought. It is the standard for false advertising and unfair competition under the Lanham Act; for securities fraud, for deceit and misrepresentation and for common law unfair competition."

. . .

*Haskell* also relied upon the FTC's interpretation of the Federal Trade Commission Act because of the relationship between the UCL and the federal act. "[T]he Unfair Business Practices Act is one 'of the so-called "little FTC Acts" of the 1930's, enacted by many states in the wake of amendments to the Federal Trade Commission Act enlarging the commission's regulatory jurisdiction to include unfair business practices that harmed, not merely the interests of business competitors, but of the general public as well.' Because of this relationship between the [UCL] and the Federal Trade Commission Act, judicial interpretations of the federal act have persuasive force. Since 1982 the FTC has interpreted 'deception' in Section 5 of the Federal Trade Commission Act to require a showing of 'potential deception of "consumers acting reasonably in the circumstances," not just any consumers.'"

. . .

Unless the advertisement targets a particular disadvantaged or vulnerable group, it is judged by the effect it would have on a reasonable consumer. As noted by the FTC many years ago: "Perhaps a few misguided souls believe, for example, that all 'Danish pastry' is made in Denmark. Is it, therefore, an actionable deception to advertise 'Danish pastry' when it is made in this country? Of course not. A representation does not become 'false and deceptive' merely because it will be unreasonably misunderstood by an insignificant and unrepresentative segment of the class of persons to whom the representation is addressed."

**› RESULT** The appeals court affirmed the dismissal of the complaint. P&G's ads were not misleading.

**› CRITICAL THINKING QUESTIONS**

1. Would you interpret the statement that Aleve is gentler on the stomach than aspirin to mean that it will not cause an ulcer?
2. Why shouldn't advertisers be required to ensure that their ads do not mislead the most gullible consumers?

96. 68 F.3d 285 (9th Cir. 1995).
97. 857 F. Supp. 1392 (E.D. Cal. 1994).

**Testimonials and Mock-ups** Testimonials and endorsements in which the person endorsing a product does not, in fact, use or prefer it are considered to be deceptive and therefore in violation of the FTC Act. It is also deceptive for the endorser to imply falsely that he or she has superior knowledge or experience.

In the mid-1960s, the FTC successfully challenged a series of three television commercials for Colgate–

Palmolive Company's Rapid Shave shaving cream. Each commercial featured a sandpaper test, in which Rapid Shave was applied to a substance that appeared to be sandpaper, and immediately thereafter a razor was shown shaving the substance clean. Meanwhile, an announcer informed the audience that "[t]o prove Rapid Shave's super-moisturizing power, we put it right from the can onto this tough, dry sandpaper. It was apply . . . soak . . . and off in a stroke." The FTC charged that the commercials were false and deceptive. Evidence disclosed that sandpaper of the type depicted in the commercials could not be shaved immediately following the application of Rapid Shave but required a soaking period of approximately eighty minutes. The evidence also showed that the substance resembling sandpaper was in fact a simulated prop, or "mock-up," made of plexiglass to which sand had been applied. Ultimately, the U.S. Supreme Court agreed with the FTC and decided that the commercials were unlawfully deceptive.[98]

### *Infomercials*

*Infomercials,* also known as long-form marketing programs or direct response television, are advertisements generally presented in the format of half-hour television talk shows or news programs. Their very format, however, may present problems by blurring the line between advertising and regular television programming.[99] The next trend in infomercials was the "sitcommercial," a full-length show resembling a family sitcom. For example,

98. FTC v. Colgate–Palmolive Co., 380 U.S. 374 (1965).
99. Karen Zagor & Gary Mead, *Illumination from the Stars: A Look at the New-Found Respectability of So-Called "Infomercials,"* FIN. TIMES, Nov. 5, 1992, at 18.

#### INTERNATIONAL SNAPSHOT

The Taiwan Fair Trade Law, adopted in 1991, bans false or misleading advertising. It imposes liability not only on the company advertising the product but also on the creator of the false or misleading advertisement and its medium of communication if they knew or should have known that the advertisement was misleading. The Enforcement Rules, adopted by the Taiwanese Fair Trade Commission in 1992, give the commission the authority to order the publication of corrective advertisements.[a]

a. For further discussion of the Fair Trade Law, see Monle Lee & Fred Naffziger, *The Taiwanese and American Legal Sea upon Which the Regulatory Ship of Deceptive Advertising Floats,* 1 PAN-PACIFIC MGMT. REV. 85 (1997).

#### ETHICAL CONSIDERATION

Should free-market, competitive forces determine the price of "essential" goods such as pharmaceuticals, or should their prices be regulated? What constitutes "reasonable" profits on a product such as AZT and the cocktail of protease inhibitors recommended for people with HIV or AIDS?[a]

a. For a complete discussion of the AZT controversy, see *Ethics, Pricing and the Pharmaceutical Industry,* J. BUS. ETHICS, Aug. 1992, at 617. See also Brian O'Reilly, *The Inside Story of the AIDS Drug,* FORTUNE, Nov. 5, 1990, at 112.

Bell Atlantic filmed "The Ringers," a sitcom intended to show off and sell telephone equipment.

In response to numerous complaints alleging deceptive advertising in infomercials, the infomercial industry established an internal watchdog agency, the National Infomercial Merchandising Association, in 1990. The association offers guidelines to combat deceptive practices, endorses legitimate infomercial producers, and reports violations to the FTC.

### *Magnuson–Moss Warranty Act*

As noted earlier, an advertisement may create an express warranty. Article 2 provides a buyer of goods with a remedy for a seller's breach of an express or implied warranty. UCC warranties are discussed in Chapter 8.

In addition to the statutory protections provided by the UCC, the federal government has passed a law that is designed to inform consumers about the products they buy. This law, which applies only when a seller offers a written warranty, is the Magnuson–Moss Warranty Act.[100] The Act does not require any seller to provide a written warranty, but if a seller does offer one, the Act requires certain disclosures. In addition, it restricts disclaimers for implied warranties and permits consumers to sue violators of the Act and to recover damages plus costs, including reasonable attorneys' fees.

A manufacturer or seller offering a written warranty on goods costing more than $15 must "fully and conspicuously disclose in simple and understandable language the terms and conditions of the warranty." The FTC has issued various rules relating to this provision, including one that requires consumer notification that some states do not allow certain manufacturer exclusions or limitations.

100. 15 U.S.C. §§ 2301 *et seq.*

A manufacturer or seller that offers a written warranty on goods costing more than $10 must also state whether the warranty is full or limited. Under the Act, for a warranty to be "full," it must meet the following minimum federal standards. First, a full warranty must give the consumer the right to free repair of the product within a reasonable time or, after a reasonable number of failed attempts to fix the product, permit the customer to elect a full refund or replacement. Second, the warrantor may not impose any time limit on the warranty's duration. Lastly, the warrantor may not exclude or limit damages for breach of warranty unless such exclusions are conspicuous on the face of the warranty. Any warranty that does not meet these minimum federal standards must be designated as "limited."

Also, under the Act, a seller that offers a written warranty may not disclaim *implied warranties*, such as the implied warranty of merchantability. These implied warranties may be limited to the duration of the written warranty, but then the written warranty must be designated as "limited." Still, a seller may disclaim all implied warranties by not offering any written warranty or service contract at all and selling a product "as is."

FTC rules allow a seller to establish an informal dispute resolution procedure and to require consumers to use this procedure before filing a lawsuit under the Act. Magnuson–Moss also requires that the warrantor be given an opportunity to remedy its noncompliance before a lawsuit is filed. In *Southern Energy Homes, Inc. v. Ard*,[101] an Alabama state court held that the Magnuson–Moss Warranty Act does not invalidate arbitration provisions in a written warranty. An Illinois state court reached the opposite conclusion.[102]

### State Lemon Laws

A majority of states have laws dealing with warranties on new cars and new mobile homes. These *lemon laws* are designed to protect consumers from defective products that cannot be adequately fixed. The statutes vary considerably from state to state, but there are several common features. In general, a new car must conform to the warranty given by the manufacturer. This means that if, after a reasonable number of attempts (usually four), the manufacturer or dealer is unable to remedy a defect that substantially impairs the value of the car, the car must be replaced or the purchase price refunded. Lemon laws also typically require replacement or refund if a new car has been out of service ("in the shop") for thirty days during the statutory warranty period.

101. 772 So. 2d 1131 (Ala. 2000).

102. Borowiec v. Gateway 2000, Inc., 772 N.E.2d 256 (Ill. App. Ct. 2002).

In addition to permitting the revocation of a new car sales contract, state lemon laws (like the Magnuson–Moss Warranty Act) are designed to encourage informal resolution of disputes concerning defective new cars. Lemon laws achieve this objective by requiring that a consumer use a manufacturer's arbitration program before litigating, as long as the manufacturer has established an informal dispute resolution program that complies with FTC regulations. Some states, including New York, have adopted their own standards for these dispute resolution programs.

## SALES PRACTICES

A number of state and federal agencies currently regulate sales practices, including the FTC, the FCC, the Postal Service, and the Department of Housing and Urban Development. Their regulations may apply to all industries or be industry specific, such as the FTC's rules for sellers of used cars or state insurance regulations.

Sometimes laws of general application can be invoked to protect consumers. For example, a lawyer in Washington, D.C., won two state court judgments totaling $11.6 million against affiliates of Tele-Communications, Inc. for charging excessive late fees on monthly cable television bills.[103] He successfully argued that the fees violated the general principle of contract law that damages assessed for breach of contract cannot be disproportionate to the actual harm caused by the breach.

By 2005, Prudential Insurance Company of America had paid approximately $2.7 billion to settle claims that its agents had engaged in illegal sales tactics, including tricking policyholders into cashing in old policies with accrued cash-surrender value to purchase new expensive ones with no surrender value, making false promises that dividends would build up quickly enough to pay for premiums, and disguising insurance policies as retirement programs.

103. Eben Shapiro, *Attorney Finds a Way to Battle Bills' Late Fees*, WALL ST. J., Oct. 6, 1997, at B1.

**INTERNATIONAL SNAPSHOT**

Taiwan adopted its Consumer Protection Law in 1994. The law covers consumer contracts, warranties, door-to-door sales, installment sales, product safety, and mechanisms for the resolution of consumer disputes.

### State Deceptive Practices Statutes

Most state consumer protection laws are directed at deceptive trade practices and prohibit sellers from providing false or misleading information to consumers. Although there is considerable variation among state laws, they often provide more stringent protections than federal laws.

### UCC Unconscionability Principle

Also on the state level, the Uniform Commercial Code protects consumers from unfair sales practices through the unconscionability principle contained in Section 2-302 of the UCC, as discussed in Chapter 8. This section prohibits the enforcement of any contracts for the sale of goods that are so unfair and one-sided that they shock the conscience of the court.

### Door-to-Door Sales

Door-to-door sales are initiated and concluded at a buyer's home. They pose special risks because individuals may feel more pressure to buy something from someone standing at their door, or they may make a purchase just to get rid of a persistent salesperson. As a result, the FTC has mandated a three-day cooling-off period during which a consumer may rescind a door-to-door purchase. Under FTC rules, the seller must also notify a buyer of the right to cancel. Laws in some states provide longer periods during which consumers can cancel a sale.

### Referral Sales and Pyramid Sales

A number of states have enacted legislation restricting referral and pyramid sales. In a *referral sale,* the seller offers the buyer a commission, rebate, or discount for furnishing the seller with a list of additional prospective customers. The discount, however, is usually contingent on the seller actually making later sales to the prospects provided by the original customer. In a *pyramid selling* scheme, a consumer is recruited as a product "distributor" and receives commissions based on the products he or she sells and on the recruitment of additional sellers (or even receives commissions on the sales of the recruits). The problem with both referral and pyramid sales is that unless the buyer or "distributor" becomes involved early in the chain, the supply of prospective recruits is quickly exhausted.

### Telemarketing

As discussed earlier, aggressive telemarketing sales practices, particularly the use of autodialers and "900" telephone numbers, have prompted congressional intervention. In 1997, the North American Securities Administrators Association and the FTC announced that their six-month "Field of Schemes" crackdown on investment-related telemarketing fraud had resulted in sixty-one enforcement actions. The schemes ranged from ostrich ranching in Idaho to digital fingerprint identification in Indiana and worthless oil and gas programs in Kentucky.

### Mail-Order Sales

Unscrupulous mail-order sales practices have led to a high incidence of consumer complaints with resultant state and federal regulation. Sellers must respond to consumer mail orders by shipping merchandise or offering refunds within a reasonable time. Unsolicited or unordered merchandise sent by U.S. mail may be kept or disposed of by the recipient without incurring any obligation to the sender. Book and record clubs are generally legal as long as they comply with state law provisions requiring sellers to provide consumers with forms or announcement cards that the consumer may use to instruct the seller not to send the offered merchandise. The U.S. Postal Service has authority to assess criminal and civil penalties for fraudulent mail schemes that injure consumers.

### Industry-Specific Sales Practices

Since the early 1980s, the FTC has become more involved in regulating the sales practices of specific industries. For example, in 1985 the FTC began to require used-car sellers to affix a Buyer's Guide label to the cars that they sell.[104] The Buyer's Guide is intended to disclose to potential buyers information about the car's warranty and any service contract provided by the dealer. If the car is sold without a warranty, the label must state that the car is being sold "as is."

A related and well-developed area of state and federal consumer law concerns restrictions on tampering with car odometers. Consumers purchasing a motor vehicle rely heavily on odometer readings as an indication of a car's safety and reliability. The Motor Vehicle Information and Cost Savings Act[105] makes it a crime to change car odometers.

On the state level, industry-specific regulation covers the insurance industry. State insurance commissioners both establish regulations regarding the disclosure of information to prospective policyholders and set maximum rates within a state.

104. 16 C.F.R. pt. 455 (Used Motor Vehicle Trade Regulation Rule).
105. 15 U.S.C. §§ 1901 *et seq.*

### *Real Estate Sales*

A number of state and federal laws, including the Federal Real Estate Settlement Procedures Act and the Interstate Land Sales Full Disclosure Act, protect consumers in real estate transactions. Certain disclosure requirements of the Truth-in-Lending Act apply to real estate credit transactions as well. In some transactions, real estate buyers have the right to cancel the purchase contract if certain information is not disclosed to them or if other procedures are not properly followed.

The Real Estate Settlement Procedures Act and revisions made to it in 1976 are designed to assist home buyers by requiring disclosure of any requirements for settlement proceedings, which may include title insurance, taxes, and fees for attorneys, appraisers, and brokers. In general, lenders must give an estimate of settlement costs, identify service providers the applicant is required to use, and provide a statement showing the annual percentage rate for the mortgage.

In response to fraudulent practices used in the sale of subdivided land for investment purposes or for second or retirement homes, Congress passed the Interstate Land Sales Full Disclosure Act[106] in 1968. It is administered by the secretary of the Department of Housing and Urban Development (HUD). Under the Act, the secretary created the Office of Interstate Land Sales Registration and imposed federal disclosure requirements on the sale of 100 or more lots of undeveloped subdivided land akin to those required for the offer of securities under the Securities Act of 1933. The Act gives the secretary of HUD the power to bring suit in federal district court to enjoin sales by developers who have not registered in accordance with the Act. Purchasers affected by a promoter's wrongdoing have a private cause of action and may cancel the purchase contract.

## State Occupational Licensing

State departments of consumer affairs protect the public by examining and licensing firms and individuals who possess the necessary education and demonstrated skills to perform their services competently. Among the occupations generally regulated are accountants, architects, barbers, contractors, cosmetologists, dentists, dry cleaners, marriage counselors, nurses, pharmacists, physical therapists, physicians, and social workers. Attorneys are regulated by state bar associations and the courts. As noted in Chapter 7, any person required to be licensed who is in fact not licensed cannot enforce a promise to pay for unlicensed work. State departments of consumer affairs also investigate and resolve consumer complaints and hold public hearings involving consumer matters.

106. 15 U.S.C. §§ 1701 *et seq.*

## Consumer Credit and the Consumer Credit Protection Act

Because credit plays an important role in many consumer transactions, a number of consumer protection laws address this area. Federal consumer credit law can be confusing because many of the acts have similar names. These complex acts and regulations are all part of the lengthy Consumer Credit Protection Act (CCPA),[107] which was initially passed by Congress in 1968. Since 1968, several additional acts (or titles) have been added to the original legislation. Exhibit 17.1 provides an overview of the CCPA and indicates the provisions that are omitted from the discussion in this chapter.

### TRUTH-IN-LENDING ACT

Title I, the Truth-in-Lending Act (TILA), is intended "to assure a meaningful disclosure of credit terms so that the consumer will be able to compare more readily the various credit terms available and avoid the uninformed use of credit."[108] In particular, the Act makes uniform

107. 15 U.S.C. §§ 1601 *et seq.*
108. 15 U.S.C. § 1601.

**EXHIBIT 17.1 Consumer Credit Protection Act (CCPA)**

| Title | Consumer Credit Protection Act |
|---|---|
| I. | Truth-in-Lending Act (TILA)<br>Chapter 1: General Provisions [omitted]<br>Chapter 2: Credit Transactions<br>Chapter 3: Credit Advertising<br>Chapter 4: Fair Credit Billing Act<br>Chapter 5: Consumer Leasing Act [omitted] |
| II. | Extortionate Credit Transactions |
| III. | Restrictions on Garnishment |
| IV. | National Commission on Consumer Finance [omitted] |
| V. | General Provisions [omitted] |
| VI. | Fair Credit Reporting Act |
| VII. | Equal Credit Opportunity Act |
| VIII. | Fair Debt Collection Practices Act |
| IX. | Electronic Fund Transfer Act |

the actuarial method for determining the rate of charge for consumer credit and requires certain disclosures. It is not a *usury statute,* however, and does not set maximum interest rates. TILA applies only to credit transactions between creditors and individual consumers, not to credit transactions between two consumers. Typical transactions covered by TILA include car loans, student loans, and home improvement loans; credit cards (such as Visa and MasterCard), which permit deferred payment over a period of time; charge cards (such as American Express), which require payment of the full balance upon receipt of the bill; and certain real estate loans in which the amount financed is less than $25,000.

Congress directed the Federal Reserve Board to issue regulations for the enforcement and interpretation of TILA. To that end, the Federal Reserve has produced model disclosure forms for use with credit sales and loans. The two most important terms in a TILA disclosure statement are the finance charge (interest over the life of the loan expressed as a dollar amount) and the annual percentage rate (interest expressed as a percentage), which are both defined in the Federal Reserve Board's *Regulation Z.*[109] Regulation Z also contains provisions dealing with disclosure of the terms of any credit or mortgage insurance offered in connection with a loan.

Regulation Z requires marketing materials for credit cards to prominently display a table that clearly states the annual percentage rate and other critical information (including the annual fee). The annual percentage rate for purchases and the variable rate information, grace period, minimum finance charge, method of computing the balance, cash advance fees, and over-limit fees, as well as any other fees that vary by state, must be printed in a box in at least eighteen-point type to prevent information from being hidden in the "fine print." In addition, the overall disclosure statement must be printed in at least twelve-point type and be in a reasonably understandable form.[110]

TILA draws a distinction between open-end credit and closed-end credit. *Open-end credit* occurs when the parties intend the creditor to make repeated extensions of credit (for example, Visa or MasterCard); *closed-end credit* involves only one transaction (for example, a car or house loan). Open-end consumer credit plans must make certain disclosures at three separate times: (1) in an initial disclosure statement when the account is opened, (2) in subsequent periodic billing statements, and (3) annually when a consumer must be notified of his or her rights under the Fair Credit Billing Act. In general, the required information includes finance and other charges, security interests (collateral), previous balance and credits, identification of transactions, closing date and new balance, and annual percentage rates and period rates.

Closed-end credit plans require disclosure of at least the following for each transaction: identity of creditor, amount financed, finance charge, annual percentage rate, variable rate, payment schedule, total of payments, total sale price, prepayment provisions, late payment fee, security interest, credit insurance, loan assumption policy, and required deposit. Special rules apply for certain residential mortgages and adjustable rate transactions.

In 2000, the FTC settled a claim against providers of short-term, high-interest-rate "payday loans" for alleged violations of TILA and the FTC's Telemarketing Sales Rule.[111] Two companies used direct mail and telemarketing to market the MoneyMarketCard. They offered consumers, regardless of their credit history, a credit line of $5,500 at a 14.99 percent interest rate. After consumers paid $149 to $169 to receive the MoneyMarketCard, they discovered that they could use the credit only to buy items from one of the company's catalogs and that the cash advance privileges were short-term payday loans of $20 to $40 with annual interest rates of 360 percent or more. The FTC alleged that although the companies collected membership fees of more than $12 million between 1996 and 1999, less than 8 percent of the customers ever purchased even one catalog product or took out a cash loan. The settlement required the companies to stop their deceptive practices, disgorge $350,000 received from consumers, and forgive $1.6 million in outstanding consumer debts.

Consumers can be required to arbitrate their claims if they agreed to do so when applying for or procuring credit. For example, in 2000, a federal district court ruled that a claim that a lender's consumer loan agreement violated TILA for failing to disclose the annual percentage rate, finance charge, and financing costs for rollover loans was subject to mandatory arbitration.[112] The loan agreement stated that any dispute regarding the loan was subject to arbitration. The court rejected the borrowers' argument that TILA gave them a statutory right to seek relief through a class action.

109. 12 C.F.R. pt. 226.

110. *Fed Issues Final Regulation Under TILA Requiring New Clarity for Card Disclosures,* 69 U.S.L.W. 2200 (Oct. 10, 2000).

111. FTC v. Consumer Money Mkts., Inc., No. CVS001071 (D. Nev. Sept. 6, 2000).

112. Thompson v. Ill. Title Loans, Inc., 2000 U.S. Dist. LEXIS 232 (N.D. Ill. Jan. 6, 2000).

TILA limits the liability of credit cardholders to $50 per card for unauthorized charges made before a card issuer is notified that the card has been lost or stolen. Once a card issuer has been notified, a cardholder incurs no liability from unauthorized use. In addition, a credit or charge card company cannot bill a consumer for unauthorized charges if the card was improperly issued by the card company.

### Home Equity Lending Plans and Predatory Lending

TILA provides specific protections for consumers who use their home as collateral for a second mortgage or an open-end line of credit. Because losing one's home has such significant consequences, Congress felt special disclosure requirements were in order. TILA provides consumers a *right of rescission* (that is, a right to cancel the contract) whenever their home is used as collateral except for original construction or acquisition. These cancellation rights are generally available for three days if all procedures are properly followed by the lender, three years if they are not. TILA also mandates disclosure of up-front costs, repayment schedules, and the annual percentage rate and its method of calculation.

Predatory lending involves mortgage loans secured by the borrower's house that are made at subprime interest rates. These loans tend to be concentrated in low-income communities and to be used for consumer debt rather than housing purposes. Because the loans are often based solely on the homeowner's equity in the home, without regard to the borrower's income and thus his or her ability to repay the loan, foreclosures are common. In 2004, the Federal Reserve Board fined Citigroup a record $75 million for violating regulations against predatory lending practices.

#### ETHICAL CONSIDERATION

Should businesses serving communities with a large non-English-speaking population provide written translations of written documents? Should businesses provide oral translations, perhaps on voice recording cassettes, of important terms in consumer transactions, such as home equity loans and door-to-door sales, so that illiterate consumers can understand what the transaction entails?

### Credit Advertising

TILA includes specific provisions that regulate credit advertising. The idea behind these provisions is that consumers equipped with complete and accurate credit information will be able to find the best terms. Regulation Z requires that any advertised specific credit terms actually be available and that any credit terms (for example, the finance charge or annual percentage rate) mentioned in the advertisement be explained fully. The FTC enforces the advertising provisions of Regulation Z. For example, all credit card advertising must have a "Schumer Box" (named after the congressman who championed the regulation) that contains all basic credit card information. Unlike the other sections of TILA, this provision does not give consumers a private cause of action to sue credit advertisers directly.

In the following case, the court considered whether a major credit card issuer had engaged in misleading or deceptive lending practices when it offered a no-fees credit card, and then changed the terms shortly thereafter.

A CASE IN POINT

## In the Language of the Court

**CASE 17.2**

**Rossman v. Fleet Bank (R.I.) National Association**

*United States Court of Appeals for the Third Circuit*
*280 F.3d 384*
*(3d Cir. 2002).*

**› FACTS** Paula Rossman sued Fleet Bank for misleading advertising under TILA. Rossman alleged that Fleet had advertised a credit card with no annual fees, but within a few months after issuing her a credit card, Fleet sent her a letter stating that the Federal Reserve had raised interest rates and that Fleet would begin charging a $35 annual fee. The trial judge dismissed Rossman's claim, and she appealed.

**› ISSUE PRESENTED** May a bank change the material terms of its original advertisement soon after it issues a credit card to a consumer who responded specifically to that ad?

**› OPINION** SCIRICA, J., writing on behalf of the U.S. Court of Appeals for the Third Circuit:

In this Truth in Lending Act case, we must interpret the "no annual fee" provision of a credit card solicitation. . . . The enclosure entitled "Consumer Information"

*(Continued)*

(Case 17.2 *continued*)

contained the "Schumer Box"—the table of basic credit card information that is required under the Truth in Lending Act, as amended by the Fair Credit and Charge Card Disclosure Act of 1988. Within the Schumer Box, there was a column with the heading "Annual Fee"; the box beneath that heading contained only the word "None." On the "Consumer Information" enclosure, but outside the Schumer box, Fleet listed other fees. Also in that location was the statement, "We reserve the right to change the benefit features associated with your Card at any time."

. . .

The stated purpose of the Truth in Lending Act, which took effect in 1969, is "to assure a meaningful disclosure of credit terms so that the consumer will be able to compare more readily the various credit terms available to him and avoid the uninformed use of credit, and to protect the consumer against inaccurate and unfair credit billing and credit card practices."

. . .

The disclosures are intended to make the terms of the contractual agreement accessible to the consumer. . . . Therefore, disclosures should reflect the contractual agreement itself. But the mere inclusion of these terms in the agreement is ordinarily insufficient to meet the disclosure requirements. The purpose of the disclosures is to present the significant terms of the agreement to the consumer in a consistent manner that is readily seen and easily understood, thereby "enabling consumers to shop around for the best cards.". . . Furthermore, the accuracy of the representations contained in the disclosures is measured at the time those representations are made. "The disclosures should reflect the credit terms to which the parties are legally bound at the time of giving the disclosures."

. . .

Fleet's statement that the card had "no annual fee" was lawful, therefore, only if it met two conditions. First, it must have disclosed all of the information required by the statute. And second, it must have been true—i.e., an accurate representation of the legal obligations of the parties at that time—when the relevant solicitation was mailed.

. . .

Rossman challenges the adequacy of the disclosures in Fleet's credit card solicitation on three related grounds. First, she contends the statute requires not only disclosure of presently imposed annual fees, but also any annual fee that might be imposed in the future. Second, she argues whether or not Fleet was required to disclose future fees, its disclosures failed to meet the requirements of the TILA because they misleadingly suggested there never would be an annual fee. Finally, she asserts Fleet used the disclosures as part of a bait-and-switch scheme, by which it attracted business with the offer for a no-annual-fee card, even though it intended to charge an annual fee on the card soon thereafter.

. . .

Fleet maintains that, assuming the facts as alleged by Rossman, the manipulation of the agreements may be wrongful, but the disclosures were accurate reflections of the substance of the agreements at the relevant times, which is all the TILA requires.

. . .

As noted, the TILA prohibits not only failures to disclose, but also false or misleading disclosures. Regardless of Fleet's disclosure obligations, it was not permitted to mislead the recipients of its credit card solicitations into believing that Fleet could not or would not impose such a fee.

*(Continued)*

(Case 17.2 *continued*)

. . .

[While Fleet is not bound to never charge an annual fee,] we believe a reasonable consumer would, at any rate, be entitled to assume upon reading Fleet's solicitation that the issuer was committed to refraining from imposing an annual fee for at least one year. The statement "no annual fee," in other words, is fairly understood to contain an implied term of a year. . . . In any event, the statement "no annual fee" is not a clear and conspicuous disclosure of a set of contract terms that permit the imposition of an annual fee within a year. Interpreting the statement with an implied annual term is at least as natural as interpreting it with no such term, so the statement is ambiguous at best. And because the TILA, which "should be construed liberally in favor of the consumer," is intended to provide clear information to consumers, such ambiguities should be resolved in favor of the consumer.

› **RESULT** The court found in favor of the plaintiff and ruled that she had stated a valid clam against Fleet. The case was remanded to the district court for trial.

› **COMMENTS** On September 14, 2004, the Office of the Comptroller of the Currency issued an advisory letter to national banks, which warned against (1) increasing the cost of credit to the cardholder without disclosing fully and prominently in promotional materials the circumstances under which the credit card agreement permits the bank to increase the consumer's annual percentage rate (APR), increase fees, or otherwise increase the cost of credit; (2) failing to disclose fully and prominently the bank's unilateral right to change the APR, fees, or other terms; (3) promoting credit limits up to a maximum amount that is seldom extended; or (4) advertising possible uses of the card when the initial available credit line is unlikely to cover such purchases.[113]

› **CRITICAL THINKING QUESTIONS**

1. If Fleet had no intention of charging an annual fee when it issued the card, why should Fleet have to wait a year before charging a fee?
2. Would the court have reached the same result if Fleet had included an asterisk next to "none" in the Schumer Box and added a note within the box saying, "Subject to change at Fleet's discretion"?

113. The OCC Advisory Letter (AL 2004-10) is available at http://www.occ.treas.gov/ftp/advisory/2004-10.txt.

## *Credit Billing*

The Fair Credit Billing Act requires creditors, such as credit card companies, to respond to consumer complaints with an acknowledgment of the complaint, followed by a reasonable investigation to determine whether the complaint is justified. Companies cannot evade this requirement by canceling a cardholder's account.

For example, in 1982, American Express Company canceled a cardholder's account during a dispute about incorrect billings. American Express argued that its contract with the cardholder allowed it to revoke a credit card at any time for any reason, but the U.S. Court of Appeals for the District of Columbia ruled that the Fair Credit Billing Act's protections could not be waived.[114] As the court explained:

> The rationale of consumer protection legislation is to even out the inequalities that consumers normally bring to the bargain. To allow such protection to be waived by boiler plate language of the contract puts the legislative process to a foolish and unproductive task. A court ought not impute such nonsense to a Congress intent on correcting abuses in the market place.

114. Gray v. Am. Express Co., 743 F.2d 10 (D.C. Cir. 1984).

Hence, the Fair Credit Billing Act protected the cardmember from the revocation of his account despite the provisions of the Cardmember Agreement purporting to permit American Express to cancel the account at any time.

## Extortionate Credit Transactions

The CCPA prohibits any *extortionate extension of credit,* that is, the extension of credit where the parties expect nonpayment to result in bodily harm.

## Restrictions on Garnishment

*Garnishment* is the legal procedure by which a creditor may collect a debt by attaching a portion of the debtor's weekly wages. The CCPA restricts the amount of a debtor's wages that is available for garnishment to the lesser of (1) 25 percent of the "disposable earnings" for that week (defined by the Act as the amount remaining after deductions required by law) or (2) the amount by which "disposable earnings" for that week exceed thirty times the current federal minimum hourly wage. The secretary of labor enforces the provisions of this title. Some states prohibit garnishment of wages altogether.

## Fair Credit Reporting Act

Almost everyone over the age of eighteen has a credit report on file somewhere. Lenders look to these various reporting agencies for information on an individual's creditworthiness. Because negative information in a credit report can make obtaining credit considerably more difficult, it is important for consumers to be able to access these credit reports and to correct any false information before it is reported to lenders or shared with another reporting agency's computer.

Under the Fair Credit Reporting Act of 1970 (FCRA), as amended by the Fair and Accurate Credit Transactions Act of 2003 (FACT Act), consumers can request all information (except medical information) on themselves, the source of the information, and any recent recipients of a report. The FCRA also gives consumers a right to have corrected copies of their credit reports sent to creditors. The FTC has the primary responsibility for the enforcement of the FCRA.

Credit bureaus must investigate disputed information in credit reports and resolve consumer complaints within thirty days. They must give consumers written notice of the results of the investigation within five days after it is completed. The credit-reporting agency must go beyond the original source of information to determine whether it is accurate. Thus, when a consumer notified the agency that she had never held the credit cards her report showed as being delinquent, the agency could not just rely on the credit card companies' statements that the applications for the cards had the correct information. Instead, the agency should have checked the handwriting on the credit applications and determined whether the applications were obtained by fraud.[115]

When a consumer tells a credit-reporting agency that he or she disputes a charge, the agency is required to notify the furnisher of the information that the information provided is in dispute. The creditor must then conduct a "reasonable" investigation and review all relevant information to determine whether it is accurate.[116] Any finding that information is inaccurate or incomplete must be reported to all national credit bureaus. Under certain circumstances, consumers can require the firm that furnished disputed information to the credit bureau to reinvestigate the accuracy of the information it passed on to the bureau. A furnisher is liable for providing inaccurate information if it "knows or has reasonable cause to believe that the information is inaccurate."[117]

As discussed more fully in the "Inside Story," the FACT Act gave consumers new tools to fight identity theft and to correct erroneous information resulting from the fraudulent use of credit cards and accounts. The FACT Act does not, however, contain an express private cause of action for consumers harmed by erroneous credit reports.

The Fair Credit Reporting Act also contains restrictions on *investigative consumer reporting,* that is, reports that contain information on character and reputation, not just credit history. In most cases, a consumer must be notified in writing that such a report may be made. This requirement applies to potential or current employers as well.

Before asking a credit bureau or private investigator for a report on a credit applicant or employee, the lender or employer must notify the individual in writing that a report may be used and obtain the individual's consent. Neither a lender nor an employer may rely on a credit or investigative consumer report to take adverse action (including denying credit or denying a job applicant a position, reassigning or terminating an employee, or denying a promotion), unless it first provides the individual with a "pre-adverse action disclosure," which

115. Cushman v. Trans Union Corp., 115 F.3d 220 (3d Cir. 1997).
116. Johnson v. MBNA Am. Bank NA, 357 F.3d 426 (4th Cir. 2004).
117. FACT Act § 312 (b).

includes a copy of the report and the FTC's "A Summary of Your Rights Under the Fair Credit Reporting Act." Lenders and employers who fail to obtain permission before requesting a credit or investigative report or to provide the pre-adverse action disclosures are subject to suits for damages (including punitive damages for deliberate violations) by individuals and civil penalties by the FTC.

After a lender or an employer has taken adverse action, it must give the individual notice—orally, in writing, or electronically—that the action has been taken. The notice must include (1) the name, address, and phone number of the credit bureau or private investigator that supplied the report; (2) a statement that the credit bureau or investigator did not make the decision to take adverse action and cannot give specific reasons for it; and (3) a notice of the individual's right to dispute the accuracy or completeness of any information the bureau or investigator furnished and the individual's right upon request to an additional free report from the credit bureau or investigator within sixty days.

Lenders that use risk-based pricing must provide notices to consumers who receive loans on "material terms that are materially less favorable than the most favorable terms available to a substantial portion of consumers . . . based in whole or in part on a consumer report."[118]

## EQUAL CREDIT OPPORTUNITY ACT

The Equal Credit Opportunity Act was originally intended to address the difficulty many women faced in obtaining credit, but it has since been expanded to prohibit discrimination against credit applicants on many other grounds. The current list of protected categories includes gender, marital status, race, color, religion, national origin, and age (except that older applicants may be given favorable treatment). The Act also prohibits discrimination against applicants who derive their income from public assistance or have exercised in good faith any right under the CCPA. The FACT Act generally prohibits lenders from using medical information about a consumer as a factor in decisions about credit eligibility.

Unlike most of the other acts covered so far, the Equal Credit Opportunity Act applies to business credit as well as consumer credit. In general, the rejection of an application for credit triggers the Act and various compliance steps, which include written notification of the reasons for denial. The regulations also establish methods for evaluating the creditworthiness of an applicant.

118. FACT Act § 311.

### ETHICAL CONSIDERATION

Is it ethical for a lender to call a friend in the police department to see whether a loan applicant has a criminal record? Should the applicant be notified of that investigation?

## FAIR DEBT COLLECTION PRACTICES ACT

The Fair Debt Collection Practices Act (FDCPA), which is enforced by the FTC, regulates debt collectors and debt collection practices and provides a civil remedy for anyone injured by a violation of the statute. In general, FTC guidelines require collectors to tell the truth and not to use any deceptive means to collect a debt or locate a debtor. For example, a collector sending a dunning letter must state very clearly and explicitly the amount owed.

The Act covers only third-party debt collectors (for example, collection agencies) or someone pretending to be a third-party collector. First-party debt collectors (for example, retail store collection departments) are not covered, although the FTC can reach these collectors under its duty to address "unfair and deceptive trade practices" under Section 5 of the Federal Trade Commission Act.

The U.S. Court of Appeals for the Seventh Circuit held that a letter from an attorney for a landlord demanding that a tenant pay back rent within three days or face eviction was subject to the FDCPA.[119] The court held that past due rent is a debt and that the lawyer's letter was a debt collection "communication" within the meaning of the statute.

People who write bad checks for goods and services are also protected from abusive debt collection practices by the FDCPA. The courts of appeals for the Seventh,[120]

119. Romea v. Helberger & Assocs., 163 F.3d 111 (2d Cir. 1998).
120. Bass v. Stolper, Koritzinsky, Brewer & Neider, 111 F.3d 1322 (7th Cir. 1997).

### ETHICAL CONSIDERATION

The FDCPA specifically forbids a debt collector to engage in certain practices, including contacting a debtor directly at any time if that debtor is represented by an attorney. What self-imposed limits, if any, might a debt collector adopt, and what role should a debtor's personal circumstances (for example, unemployment or terminal illness) play in how aggressive a debt collector chooses to be?

Eighth,[121] and Ninth Circuits[122] have each held that the payment obligation that arises from a bounced check is a "debt" within the meaning of the Act even though the transaction did not involve an offer or extension of credit.

121. Duffy v. Landberg, 133 F.3d 1120 (8th Cir. 1998), *cert. denied,* 525 U.S. 821 (1998).
122. Charles v. Lundgren & Assoc., P.C., 119 F.3d 739 (9th Cir. 1997), *cert. denied,* 522 U.S. 1028 (1997).

As the following case illustrates, debt collectors have serious obligations when attempting to collect a debt.

A CASE IN POINT

## In the Language of the Court

**CASE 17.3**

**Chuway v. National Action Financial Services Inc.**

*United States Court of Appeals for the Seventh Circuit 362 F.3d 944 (7th Cir. 2004).*

**› FACTS** Caldean Chuway received a letter from National Action Financial Services (NAFS), on behalf of a credit card company, stating that Chuway owed $367.42 to the card company. The letter notified Chuway that the account had been "assigned to our agency for collection." It went on to instruct the debtor, "Please remit the balance listed above in the return envelope provided." The letter further stated, "[T]o obtain your most current balance information, please call 1-800-916-9006. Our friendly and experienced representatives will be glad to assist you and answer any questions you may have." Chuway found the letter confusing. She was not sure whether the amount stated in the letter ($367.42) was the actual amount being sought or whether she needed to call NAFS for current balance information. She claimed that the letter violated the Fair Debt Collection Practices Act.

**› ISSUE PRESENTED** Does a dunning letter violate the FDCPA by stating an exact amount of debt owed, when that statement is followed by a message calling into question the current debt owed?

**› OPINION** POSNER, C.J., writing for the U.S. Court of Appeals for the Seventh Circuit:

The Fair Debt Collection Practices Act requires that any dunning letter by a debt collector as defined by the Act state "the amount of the debt" that the debt collector is trying to collect.

. . .

[I]f the letter had stopped after the "Please remit" sentence, the defendant would be in the clear. But the letter didn't stop there. It went on to instruct the recipient on how to obtain "your most current balance information." If this means that the defendant was dunning her for something more than $367.42, it's in trouble because the "something more" is not quantified.

. . .

It is not enough that the dunning letter state the amount of the debt that is due. It must state it clearly enough that the recipient is likely to understand it. Otherwise the collection agency could write the letter in Hittite and have a secure defense. The defendant concedes the principle but insists that to withstand summary judgment the plaintiff must always submit a survey or some other form of systematic empirical evidence demonstrating the propensity of the letter to confuse. There is no basis for so flat a rule. If it is apparent just from reading the letter that it is unclear . . . . and the plaintiff testifies credibly that she was indeed confused and that. . . she is representative of the type of people who received that or a similar letter, no further evidence is necessary to create a triable issue.

. . .

*(Continued)*

(Case 17.3 *continued*)

No survey was conducted here, but the entire bench was confused about the meaning of the letter until the defendant's lawyer explained it to us at the oral argument, and our confusion, coupled with the plaintiff's affidavit in which she plausibly attested that she had been confused by the letter, is enough to satisfy her burden of proof.

. . .

Our conclusion does not place debt collectors on a razor's edge, where if they say too little they violate the Act by failing to disclose the amount of the debt they are trying to collect and if they say too much they violate the Act by confusing the consumer. If the debt collector is trying to collect only the amount due on the date the letter is sent, then he complies with the Act by stating the "balance" due, stating that the creditor "has assigned your delinquent account to our agency for collection," and asking the recipient to remit the balance listed—and stopping there, without talk of the "current" balance. If, instead, the debt collector is trying to collect the listed balance plus the interest running on it or other charges, he should use the safe-harbor language of *Miller*:[123] "As of the date of this letter, you owe $___ [the exact amount due]. Because of interest, late charges, and other charges that may vary from day to day, the amount due on the day you pay may be greater. Hence, if you pay the amount shown above, an adjustment may be necessary after we receive your check, in which event we will inform you before depositing the check for collection. For further information, write the undersigned or call 1-800-[phone number]."

**› RESULT** The appeals court ordered judgment for the plaintiff and remanded the case to the trial court for the computation of statutory damages, costs, and attorneys' fees.

**› CRITICAL THINKING QUESTIONS**

1. Would you have understood the meaning of the dunning letter?
2. Does Judge Posner have the requisite knowledge to explain to NAFS, a business designed specifically to collect debts, how to do so?

123. Miller v. McCalla, Raymer, Padrick, Cobb, Nicholas & Clark, L.L.C., 214 F.3d 872, 875 (7th Cir. 2000).

## Electronic Fund Transfer Act: Debit Cards and Preauthorized Fund Transfers

The Electronic Fund Transfer Act, passed by Congress in 1978, covers online debit cards issued by banks for use with automatic teller machines (ATMs) and point-of-sale transactions, as well as preauthorized electronic fund transfers or automatic payments from a consumer's account. As with credit cards, banks are prohibited from sending out debit cards except in response to a consumer's request.

The Federal Reserve Board has issued regulations and model forms for banks to use to satisfy disclosure requirements under the Act. In general, the Federal Reserve forms ensure disclosure of contract terms, potential customer liability for unauthorized use (as with credit cards, customer liability is usually limited to no more than $50), and consumer complaint procedures. Banks are also required to issue receipts with every ATM transaction and to mail periodic statements showing electronic fund transfer activity on a consumer's account during the period. For preauthorized transfers or automatic payments, banks are required to provide either (1) written or oral notice within two days of the scheduled transaction date that the transaction did or did not occur or (2) a telephone line for consumers to call and ascertain whether the transfer occurred. Most financial institutions have adopted the latter approach.

Online debit cards are PIN-protected; that is, cash cannot be withdrawn from an ATM and a deduction cannot be made at a point-of-sale terminal unless the holder uses a personal identification number (PIN). In contrast, off-line debit cards (which may bear the Visa or

EXHIBIT 17.2 State Credit Laws

| Area Law Covers | Examples | Primary Goals |
|---|---|---|
| Installment sales | Legal interest rates, late charges, deferral charges, and other permissible charges | Place caps on late charges and limit remedies, attorneys' fees, and rights to assign sales contract |
| Consumer loans | Mortgages and private loans | Set maximum permissible interest rate, with exceptions available for special license holders |
| Credit cards | Credit card repayment rates, credit card fees | Stop exploitation by credit card companies |

MasterCard logo) have the characteristics of both an ATM card and a credit card, and they can be used without a PIN. For example, the holder of an off-line debit card can authorize a deduction from his or her bank account by signing a charge slip at a restaurant. Visa and MasterCard voluntarily agreed to impose a $50 cap on liability for their off-line debit cards.

## State Laws Regulating Consumer Credit

All states have statutes regulating consumer credit. Two types of consumer credit transactions are addressed primarily at the state level: installment sales and loans to consumers. State statutes vary widely, and an attempt to create uniform state laws on consumer credit through adoption of the Uniform Consumer Credit Code (UCCC, called the U–Triple C) has been largely unsuccessful. The UCCC is intended to replace a state's consumer credit laws, including those that regulate usury, installment sales, consumer loans, truth in lending, and garnishment. The UCCC has been adopted by only a handful of states, and in each of those it has been so significantly altered that little uniformity remains. Exhibit 17.2 summarizes common provisions in state credit laws.

Credit card companies have found a way around particularly stringent state credit card fee limits and usury laws by moving their operations to states with more lax laws. The Supreme Court ruled that the usury laws of the state in which the card company is located apply.[124] Thus, a bank with credit card operations in a state that permits high rates, such as South Dakota or Delaware, can charge a resident of Massachusetts the high rates of interest and fees permitted in that state even though they are in excess of the Massachusetts limits.

124. Marquette Nat'l Bank of Minneapolis v. First of Omaha Serv. Corp., 439 U.S. 299 (1978).

# Global View

## International Privacy Protection

Although generalizations are difficult, foreign privacy laws differ from U.S. privacy laws in two main respects. First, foreign laws tend to be comprehensive, meaning that they apply to classes of information regardless of the industry. Second, foreign laws are generally stronger than the U.S. equivalents and place more restrictions on the use and collection of information. These differences are due in part to a different perspective on ownership of personal information. The United States largely follows the view that companies own customer lists and other personal information. In Europe and elsewhere, this view is tempered with recognition that individuals have some ownership interest in their personal information.

### EUROPEAN UNION

In 1995, the European Union (EU) issued the Directive on the Protection of Individuals with Regard to the Processing of Personal Data and on the Free Movement of Such Data,[a] which

a. Council Directive 95/46/EC (Oct. 24, 1995).

(Continued)

(Global View *continued*)

required EU member states to enact legislation to protect personal data. The EU Directive, through each member state's implementing law, limits the ways in which a company may process the personal data of EU residents and requires companies intending to process[b] such personal data to register with the government data protection authority of the residents' state. The EU Directive applies to any company that collects EU personal data through offices based in the relevant member country or though equipment that is located in the relevant member country.

The EU Directive also prohibits companies from transmitting personal data concerning EU citizens to companies in non-EU countries unless the country provides "adequate protection" for the information or the non-EU company itself has agreed to provide adequate protection through special contractual provisions. To provide "adequate protection," the non-EU country must have privacy legislation with regulations that require, at a minimum, notice, consent, and resolution of disputes between people whose information is collected and the company collecting or using the information.

The response to the EU Directive has been mixed. Some countries, such as Canada and Australia, passed similar comprehensive privacy laws so that their citizens could continue to receive personal information concerning EU citizens. Other countries, including the United States, have continued to regulate information only for specific industries or certain groups, such as children, and therefore did not provide "adequate protection" as required by the EU Directive. After years of negotiations, the EU agreed in 2000 to a "safe-harbor" provision, which provides a set of guidelines that allow U.S. companies to collect data from EU citizens without concern that doing so will violate European privacy laws.

A U.S. company can come under the EU safe harbor in two ways: (1) it can join a self-regulatory program that adheres to the safe harbor's requirements and will certify adherence to the U.S. Department of Commerce on the organization's behalf,[c] or (2) it can develop its own self-regulatory privacy policy that conforms to the safe harbor and directly certify its adherence to the Department of Commerce. To take advantage of the safe harbor, a U.S. company must enact a privacy policy that complies with the safe-harbor principles and certify that it meets those standards. In particular, the privacy policy must provide that (1) the individual's consent must be obtained before data can be used, (2) data cannot be resold without the individual's prior consent, and (3) data will be destroyed when no longer needed. In addition, the U.S. company must provide individuals with notice and choice about the prospective uses of their information and access to it so that they can confirm its accuracy. The Federal Trade Commission, not the EU authorities, is responsible for enforcing violations of the safe-harbor guidelines under the Federal Trade Commission Act.[d] As of 2004, more than 500 U.S. firms had signed up to take advantage of the safe harbor.

In 2003, the European Court of Justice decided its first case interpreting the Directive. In *Bodil Lindqvist*,[e] a church volunteer created a Web page from her home computer that contained personal information about fellow parishioners including telephone numbers, names, and occupations. The volunteer was prosecuted criminally in Sweden and found guilty of mishandling personal information. The Swedish appellate court referred the case to the European Court of Justice, which interpreted the Directive very broadly and upheld the conviction. The court held that placing this information on the website qualified as processing personal information and constituted an unacceptably careless means of handling that data. The church volunteer's criminal conviction was upheld.

## JAPAN

Japan enacted privacy legislation in 2003. The Personal Information Protection Act protects individuals by regulating the use of personal information in personal information databases by private-sector businesses (known as "entities handling personal information"). The Act makes no distinction between transfers of personal information to third parties inside Japan and transfers to third parties outside Japan. This means that non-Japanese companies acquiring personal information from individuals residing in Japan will need to comply with the Act. The current schedule calls for those parts of the Act affecting the private sector to become effective in the spring of 2005.[f] Like the EU Directive, this Act is a comprehensive law.

Companies subject to the Personal Information Protection Act must comply with various requirements. Among other things, they must specify the purpose for collecting and using the information, promptly notify individuals protected by the Act of the purpose for which their personal information will be used, ensure that personal data are kept secure from loss and unauthorized access, refrain in most circumstances from supplying personal data to unaffiliated third parties without the prior consent of the affected individual, permit individuals to access and make corrections to their personal data, and respond to individual requests to cease using personal data altogether.

## INDIA

India does not have a comprehensive privacy law. Current Indian law provides penalties for unauthorized access and data theft but says nothing about data privacy itself. Unless a con-

**b.** "Process" includes a broad range of activities, such as collecting, recording, organizing, using, disclosing, combining, and destroying.
**c.** TRUSTe and the Better Business Bureau both administer self-regulatory programs, also called "seal" programs. Membership entitles the member to use a logo on its website indicating compliance. For more information on these programs, see http://www.truste.org or http://www.bbbonline.com.

**d.** John Reynolds & Amy Worlton, *Safe Harbor Agreement,* 5 ELECTRONIC COM. & L. REP. 1092 (Nov. 1, 2000).
**e.** European Court of Justice, Case C-101/01 (Nov. 6, 2003).
**f.** The Center for Social & Legal Research prepares regular reports on privacy law. A special issue of its newsletter, *Privacy & American Business,* concentrates on consumer privacy in Japan and the contours of the new privacy legislation. The report is available without charge at http://www.pandab.org or http://www.privacyexchange.com.

(Global View *continued*)

tract contains provisions that protect privacy, there is little recourse for breaches of privacy. Currently, however, the Indian government is under pressure to enact privacy legislation that satisfies the privacy concerns of EU and U.S. companies and provides, among other things, statutory penalties and specific requirements for security. This pressure is coming domestically from Indian providers of outsourced data processing services and internationally from their EU and U.S. customers who are concerned about the security of customer information they send to India for processing.

**CANADA**

Canada has two federal privacy laws, the Privacy Act[g] and the Personal Information Protection and Electronic Documents Act (PIPEDA).[h] The Privacy Act gives Canadians the right to access and correct information held by federal government agencies; PIPEDA sets ground rules for private-sector organizations. Phased in over a three-year period that concluded in early 2004, PIPEDA prohibits businesses from collecting, using, or disclosing personal information from a Canadian individual without first receiving informed consent. The Act applies to the collection, use, or disclosure of personal information in the course of any commercial activity within a province or between provinces.

g. Privacy Act, R.S.C, ch. P-21 (1985) (Can.).
h. Personal Information Protection and Electronic Documents Act, ch. 5, S.C. 2000 (Can.).

PIPEDA applies to businesses in all provinces with the exception of provinces that have passed and implemented privacy legislation determined to be "substantially similar." The provinces that have developed, or are in the process of developing, substantially similar privacy legislation include Quebec, British Columbia, and Alberta. Non-Canadian companies are only required to comply with PIPEDA if they have a physical presence or own assets in Canada.

**AUSTRALIA**

Australia enacted its Privacy Act in 1988, but amendments in 2000 added specific provisions directed at the private sector generally.[i] The private-sector provisions apply to organizations with an annual turnover of over AU$3 million and all health service providers. The states also have their own privacy legislation, which may impose additional restrictions. The Privacy Act sets out ten National Privacy Principles (NPP) that govern the way organizations subject to the Act must handle personal information. According to the NPP, Australian organizations may transfer personal information to someone in a foreign country if the organization transferring the information reasonably believes the recipient is subject to a law, binding scheme, or contract that is substantially similar and effectively upholds the NPP. Alternatively, transfer is allowed if the individual gives his or her consent to the transfer of personal information; it is allowed without consent if consent is too difficult to obtain and the transfer benefits the individual.

i. Privacy Act, 1988 (Austl.).

THE RESPONSIBLE MANAGER

## COMPLYING WITH CONSUMER PROTECTION LAWS

Managers have a responsibility to make sure that current and potential customers are treated fairly and in a manner that will not subject them to injury, economic or physical. Supervisors must take steps to ensure that employees are aware of, and in compliance with, various federal and state consumer protection regulations. Because both managers and employees can be held legally accountable for their actions (and criminally liable in some cases), specific procedures should be in place to educate employees about important consumer law topics.

In a competitive marketplace, managers often feel the need to be aggressive in their advertising of products or services. Nonetheless, managers must refrain from making claims that may be deceptive or false. The FTC and state attorneys general aggressively pursue companies that make false advertising claims. Remedies can include civil damages and corrective advertising campaigns, which can cost millions of dollars.

Volvo's ill-fated "Bear Foot" advertising campaign in 1990 almost destroyed thirty years of consistent brand messaging that equated Volvo with safety. The ad showed a Volvo suffering no damage after being driven over by a monster truck. The ad failed to disclose, however, that the internal structure of the Volvo had been reinforced and that the pillars in competing cars had been weakened for the commercial. According to five-time Clio award winner Mike Moser, "When people found out that the demonstration was rigged, the credibility of the brand was suddenly on shaky ground. People had bought into safety's being a core value of

*(Continued)*

(The Responsible Manager *continued*)

Volvo. . . . These same people didn't want to hear that Volvo didn't believe its own demonstration."[125]

The attorney general of Texas called the ads "a hoax and a sham"[126] and fined Volvo and its ad agency, Scali, McCabe, Sloves, $150,000 each for deceptive advertising. Volvo withdrew the spots and ran corrective ads in nineteen Texas newspapers, *USA Today,* and *The Wall Street Journal*. One month later, Scali, McCabe, Sloves resigned from the Volvo account. The incident cost the agency $40 million in annual revenues and the jobs of thirty-five to fifty staffers.[127]

Business leaders should not be satisfied merely to meet minimum government standards. Mere compliance may not be sufficient to release a manager or his or her company from liability when the manager has superior product information and should have taken additional precautions.

Managers whose companies extend credit to customers need to be aware that many discriminatory practices in the extension of credit are illegal under the Equal Credit Opportunity Act. Some states also prohibit discrimination in credit based on sexual orientation.

Companies should embrace the opportunity to self-regulate or, at least, work closely with a regulatory agency to establish industry standards that meet the concerns of both the agency and the company. A good example of a self-regulating industry is the infomercial industry. Faced with possible government regulation, the industry established its own watchdog agency. In doing so, it was able to avert government involvement and the possibility of more restrictive regulation.

125. MIKE MOSER, UNITED WE BRAND 16 (2001).
126. Bruce Horowitz, *Volvo, Agency Fined $150,000 Each for TV Ad Commercials,* L.A. TIMES, Aug. 22, 1991.
127. Joshua Levine, FORBES, May 27, 1991.

## INSIDE STORY

## WHAT'S IN A NAME? FIGHTING IDENTITY THEFT

*Identity theft* is the illegal practice of gaining access to other people's credit information and then using it to the thief's advantage. It has quickly become one of the most significant problems facing consumers today. More than 27 million Americans had their identities stolen from April 1998 to April 2003.[128] The FTC reported that businesses and financial institutions lost $48 billion in the twelve-month period ending in April 2003 as a result of identity theft and that victimized consumers paid more than $5 billion in out-of-pocket expenses to regain their financial identities.[129] Identity theft costs the average victim $15,500, requires thirty hours of time to deal with the problem, and results in a major blemish on the victim's credit report that remains indefinitely.[130] The financial services companies that are the keepers of a significant amount of individual personal data have already lost billions of dollars and stand to lose billions more as identity theft victims sue the companies for allowing the theft of their information.[131] The Financial Services Technology Consortium, a coalition of leading financial services firms and technology companies, has begun a three-phase effort to try to develop technology to battle phishing scams, in which fraudulent websites ask for credit card numbers.[132]

In the past, getting the personal information necessary to make identity theft profitable meant going through the garbage or stealing mail, both of which could easily be combated by potential victims. Now, however, doing business on the Internet often requires individuals to disclose sensitive information on the information superhighway, which is far less private than the U.S. mail or even the kitchen garbage can.

Personal credit information can be obtained on the Internet in many ways, ranging from phishing schemes to instant messages and e-mails purportedly from Internet providers or financial institutions asking for account information. Spyware (discussed in the "Political

128. Timothy L. O'Brien, *Identity Theft Is Epidemic: Can It Be Stopped?,* N.Y. TIMES, Oct. 24, 2004.
129. *Id.*
130. Andrea Chipman, *Stealing You,* WALL ST. J., Apr. 26, 2004, at R8.
131. TRW v. Andrews, 534 U.S. 19 (2001).
132. *Financial Consortium, Technology Firms Gird for Battle Against Phishing Scams,* 9 ELECTRONIC COM. & L. REP. 842 (Oct. 13, 2004). For more information, see http://www.fstc.org/projects/FSTC_Phishing_Prospectus_Final.pdf.

*(Continued)*

(Inside Story *continued*)

Perspective" earlier in the chapter) makes it possible for outsiders to see everything in a computer's memory.

The growing threat has spawned new legislation. Texas and California have enacted laws prohibiting businesses from printing Social Security numbers on health plan and employer ID cards and prohibiting banks from printing Social Security numbers on bank statements and other documents sent by mail. In 2004, Governor Arnold Schwarzenegger signed S.B. 1457, which gave Californians a private right of action to sue persons who send commercial e-mail that is false or misleading.

The Fair and Accurate Credit Transactions Act of 2003 (FACT Act)[133] made identity theft a federal offense and provides specific remedies for victims. It also made it a crime to post Social Security numbers on a website with the intent to aid and abet a crime.[134] In early 2004, a computer technician became the first person to be convicted under the federal statute.

Consumers seeking to bring suit against credit bureaus that made mistakes leading to identity theft must file these claims within two years of the actual mistake, regardless of whether the victim learned about the mistake in that time.[135] The FACT Act makes it possible for victims to work with creditors to block negative information from appearing on their reports if it occurred as a result of identity theft. In conjunction with the FACT Act, the FTC has proposed a number of measures that will give theft victims a right to place "fraud alerts" on their credit reports that tell credit-reporting agencies to contact the consumer directly because he or she may be an identity-theft victim.[136]

Those who suspect they are victims of identity theft should quickly place a fraud alert on all credit accounts with a credit bureau. The United States has three main credit agencies—GUS, Equifax, and Trans Union. Alerting one will effectively alert all three. Next, victims must fill out an FTC "ID Theft Affidavit." This form is akin to a police report, and it should be sent to any company that might have had unauthorized activity with a victimized account. Finally, an actual police report should be filled out as the credit bureaus will often take action only pursuant to an official police report.[137] Finally, victims should consult the ID Theft Data Clearinghouse, the government's database on all ID theft, which can help victims repair damage to their credit and their lives.[138]

The best way to protect against identity theft is by being proactive. Adam Cohen of *Time* recommends the following:[139]

1. Install a firewall and virus protection. A firewall acts like a gatekeeper to a network of computers so that there is one place that can deny any unauthorized access into the network (by hackers, for example) and out of the network (by employees surfing the Web, for example).
2. Do not download files from people you don't trust. Virtually all viruses are spread by innocuous looking files, including MP3 music files.
3. Many popular Web browsers store the user's name and address in their system. Security holes can allow other websites to obtain this information and make a permanent record of it. Users should make sure the preferences for their Web browser are secure and that the browser does not disclose this information.
4. Some websites reserve the right to share whatever information they obtain with third parties. However, they must usually offer the option of "opting out" of this at the website. Users should exercise their opt-out rights.
5. Users should not accept cookies unless they are aware of their origin. *Cookies* are bits of code sent by websites that identity the user to the site at a future visit. This is how websites, such as eBay and Amazon, know a particular user has returned. Usually, cookies are harmless, but they can interact with other computer processes. Most browsers permit users to decide whether or not to accept cookies. Users should only accept cookies from websites they trust.
6. All secure, reputable websites encrypt data. The browser will tell the user when data are being encrypted. Users should not send sensitive data unless the website indicates that they are encrypted. Otherwise anyone online can obtain this information.
7. Periodically clear the browser of cached data. A cache is a record the computer keeps of websites to allow faster access to them later. However, this acts like a roadmap to the websites the user has visited. Even if the websites visited are safe, virus software can transmit these data back to unauthorized users who can use the information.
8. To avoid exposing sensitive company or personal information to potential Internet thieves, promulgate a thorough and well-thought-out Internet policy that limits employees to job-related Internet use.

133. 18 U.S.C. § 10-28(A)(7).
134. U.S. Attorney's Office, Central District of California Press Release No. 03-052 (Apr. 16, 2004).
135. Amy Borrus, *To Catch an Identity Thief*, BUS.WK., Mar. 31, 2003, at 91.
136. *FACT Act Regulatory Plan Defines ID Theft, Requirements for Credit Report Fraud Alerts*, 72 U.S.L.W. 2652–53 (May 4, 2004).
137. Chipman, *supra* note 130.
138. For more information, see http://www.consumer.gov/idtheft.
139. Much of the following list is derived from Adam Cohen, *Internet Insecurity*, TIME, July 2, 2001, at 47–51.

## KEY WORDS AND PHRASES

additive 635
adulterated 635
bait and switch advertising 652
*caveat emptor* 633
cease and desist orders 652
closed-end credit 659
consent order 652
cookies 671
deceit 651
Do-Not-Call list 649
drug 635
express warranty 651
extortionate extension of credit 663
fax blast 647
food 635
garnishment 663
identity theft 670
implied warranties 656
infomercial 655
investigative consumer reporting 663
lemon laws 656
misbranding 635
open-end credit 659
phishing 648
puffing 653
pyramid selling 657
referral sale 657
Regulation Z 659
right of rescission 660
spam 650
spyware 648
usury statutes 659
*venditur emptor* 633

## QUESTIONS AND CASE PROBLEMS

1. On March 19, 1997, Gulender Ozkaya wrote a check for $1,041.55 to pay an automobile dealership for repairs to her car. When she realized that her car had not been properly repaired, Ozkaya stopped payment on the check. The canceled check was then purchased by Telecheck Services, Inc., which sent Ozkaya a form dunning letter attempting to collect payment. In the letter, Telecheck said, "Until this is resolved, we may not approve your checks or the opening of a checking account at over 90,000 merchants and banks who use Telecheck nationally." It also warned, "We have assigned your file to our Recovery Department where it will be given to a professional collection agent. Please be aware that we may take reasonable steps to contact you and secure payment of the balance in full." To resolve the issue and update her record quickly, Ozkaya was instructed to send a cashier's check or money order for the amount due in a return envelope that was provided. Telecheck added a $25 service charge, listed as a "fee" at the top of the letter, to the amount of the original check. Finally, it cautioned that "[a]ny delay, or attempt to avoid this debt, may affect your ability to use checks."

   At the bottom of the page, the reader was referred to the back "for important legal notice and corporate address." The reverse side of the letter contained a standard debt validation notice, which indicated that if the consumer disputed the debt, she should contact Telecheck in writing within thirty days.

   Ozkaya filed suit against Telecheck. What claims could she make against the company? What are Telecheck's strongest defenses? [*Ozkaya v. Telecheck Services, Inc.,* 982 F. Supp. 578 (N.D. Ill. 1997).]

2. Americans consume an estimated 80 billion aspirin tablets a year. More than fifty over-the-counter drugs contain aspirin as the principal active ingredient. Yet aspirin labeling intended for the general public does not discuss its use in arthritis or cardiovascular disease because treatment of these conditions—even with a common over-the-counter drug—has to be medically supervised. The consumer labeling contains only a general warning about excessive or inappropriate use of aspirin and specifically warns against using aspirin to treat children and teenagers who have chicken pox or the flu because of the risk of Reye's syndrome, a rare but sometimes fatal condition. In 1993, the FDA proposed a new label for aspirin products that would read: "IMPORTANT: See your doctor before taking this product for your heart or for other new uses of aspirin because serious side effects could occur with self treatment." As new uses for old drugs are discovered, how should the FDA respond to protect consumers from possible injury?

3. In 1989, John M. Stevenson began receiving phone calls from bill collectors regarding overdue accounts that were not his. After Stevenson obtained a copy of his credit report from TRW, Inc., a credit-reporting agency, he discovered numerous errors in the report. The report included information on accounts that belonged to another John Stevenson; it also included accounts belonging to his estranged son, John Stevenson, Jr., who had fraudulently obtained some of the disputed accounts by using the senior Stevenson's Social Security number. In all, Stevenson disputed sixteen accounts, seven inquiries, and much of the identifying information.

   TRW investigated the complaint. On February 9, 1990, it told Stevenson that all disputed accounts containing negative credit information had been removed. Inaccurate information, however, either continued to appear on Stevenson's reports or was reentered after TRW had deleted it. Stevenson then filed suit, alleging both common law libel and violations of the Fair Credit Reporting Act. Did TRW violate the Fair Credit Reporting Act in its handling of Stevenson's dispute? [*Stevenson v. TRW, Inc.*, 987 F.2d 288 (5th Cir. 1993).]

4. Rehavem and Eleanor Adiel entered into a contract with Lakeridge Associated, Ltd. to purchase a townhouse to be built by Lakeridge. Thereafter, Lakeridge executed and delivered a mortgage application to Chase Federal Savings & Loan Association. The loan was approved, and Lakeridge executed a promissory note payable to Chase. The funds were used by Lakeridge to construct the townhouse. Under the terms of the Adiels' purchase agreement, the Adiels were required to submit a mortgage loan application to Chase for the same amount as the Lakeridge loan. The Adiels' application to Chase was for a residential consumer loan. Once approved, the Adiels were to assume the Lakeridge loan.

   Chase did not provide a truth-in-lending statement in connection with the original loan to Lakeridge or later when the Adiels assumed the Lakeridge mortgage. Was the original loan a commercial loan or a consumer loan? Does the Truth-in-Lending Act apply to both? Can an argument successfully be made that if Chase was aware of the prearrangement it should have provided truth-in-lending documents with the original loan? [*Adiel v. Chase Federal Savings & Loan Ass'n*, 810 F.2d 1051 (11th Cir. 1987).]

5. You lose your wallet, which contains all of your credit cards, checkbook, automatic teller machine (ATM) card, Visa debit card, and numerous personal items. You later learn that someone found it and charged several thousand dollars on your credit cards before you had the opportunity to notify your credit card companies. He or she also forged a $500 check. This person used the Visa debit card to purchase a $10,000 home theater system, resulting in a $10,000 deduction from your checking account. In addition, he or she found your personal identification number (PIN) and was able to withdraw $400 from your checking account at an ATM. What are your liabilities to the credit card companies and your bank under the Truth-in-Lending Act and the Electronic Fund Transfer Act? Can you force your bank to return the $10,400 deducted from your checking account? Assume the finder uses your Social Security number to obtain new credit accounts in your name and then never pays the bills. What are your remedies under the Fair Credit Reporting Act?

6. You own a medium-sized California company that produces customizable teddy bears. Because the company takes direct orders, your employees take orders over the phone and from e-mails. Your employees all have e-mail addresses and telephones, and they communicate with each other and customers constantly through these media. You are concerned that some employees may be using their e-mail accounts and telephones inappropriately to send and receive personal e-mails and make personal calls. Because it is difficult to prove that any particular numbers they call or e-mails they send are "personal," you are considering asking your IT staff to listen in on phone calls and read e-mails that seem suspicious. Would this be legal? Ethical? [*United States v. Councilman*, 373 F.3d 197 (1st Cir., 2004), *vacated and hearing en banc granted*, 385 F.3d 793 (1st Cir. 2004).]

7. From 1934 to 1939, Charles of the Ritz Distributors sold more than $1 million worth of its "Rejuvenescence Cream." Advertisements for the cosmetic product typically referred to "a vital organic ingredient" and certain "essences and compounds" that the cream allegedly contained. Users were promised that the cream would restore their youthful appearance, regardless of the condition of their skin. How might the FTC analyze the representations made by Charles of the Ritz? What evidence might the FTC consider to determine whether the advertisements are deceptive? Is it important that consumers actually believe that the product will make them look younger? How might the product's name affect the FTC's analysis? [*Charles of the Ritz Distributors Corp. v. FTC*, 143 F.2d 676 (2d Cir. 1944).]

8. In a 1991 attempt to persuade soft drink bottlers to switch from 7UP to Sprite, Coca-Cola Company, the distributor of Sprite, developed a promotional campaign entitled "The Future Belongs to Sprite." In its presentation, Coca-Cola used charts and graphs to compare the two drinks' relative sales and market share during the previous decade. The campaign was especially targeted at seventy-four "cross-franchise" bottlers, which distribute 7UP along with Coca-Cola products other than Sprite. After Coca-Cola made the presentation to eleven of these cross-franchise bottlers, five decided to switch from 7UP to Sprite. In response, Seven-Up Company filed suit against Coca-Cola, alleging that the presentation violated the Lanham Act's prohibition on misrepresentations "in commercial advertising or promotion." Coca-Cola argued that its

presentation was not sufficiently disseminated to the public to constitute advertising under the statute. Was Coca-Cola's presentation "advertising" and therefore subject to the Lanham Act? [*Seven-Up Co. v. Coca-Cola Co.*, 86 F.3d 1379 (5th Cir. 1996).]

9. Mr. Begala obtained a sixty-month car loan from PNC Bank, which provided the disclosures required under the Truth-in-Lending Act. On nine occasions during the life of the loan, the bank sent him a letter offering him a payment holiday. During this holiday, he could pay a small fee, skip his monthly payment, and add that month onto the rest of the loan. The letters did not state that additional finance charges would be added to the loan as a result of his deferral of monthly payments. Begala took advantage of each of these payment holidays. When he made his final payment on the loan, PNC told him that he owed an additional $1,000 due to his deferrals of the monthly payments. He filed a class action, alleging that the bank violated its duty under TILA to disclose the additional finance charges assessed on his loan due to the payment holidays. How should the court rule? Did PNC act ethically? [*Begala v. PNC Bank*, 163 F.3d 948 (6th Cir. 1998), *cert. denied*, 528 U.S. 868 (1999).]

10. Windsor Pharmaceuticals manufactures a number of cutting-edge drugs. Due to its size, Windsor employs a number of researchers who are free to engage in whatever projects they feel merit their attention. In her most recent study, a researcher has collaborated with seven other doctors (all employed by a rival company) to determine whether Windsor's anti-inflammatory drug Quixx might be linked to heart attacks. The study concluded that users of Quixx had an increased risk of heart problems. When the article reporting these findings is published, it will undoubtedly lead to bad publicity and reduce Quixx sales. If you were the marketing manager at Windsor, would you ask the Windsor researcher to remove her name from the article? Is it ethical for Windsor to try to distance itself from these very real, and very valid, medical findings? Does it make good business sense?

## INTERNET SOURCES

| | |
|---|---|
| Federal Trade Commission | http://www.ftc.gov |
| This site, maintained by the FTC's Bureau of Consumer Protection, provides consumer news on product recalls, tips for avoiding scams, smart shopping suggestions, and contacts for lodging consumer complaints, as well as links to other websites containing consumer information. | http://www.consumer.gov |
| The Privacy Information page on the FTC's website contains information on how to protect personal information from public access, including sample "opt-out" letters for consumers to send to credit bureaus and the Direct Marketing Association requesting that their personal information not be sold, shared with third parties, or used for marketing purposes. | http://www.ftc.gov/privacy |
| This FTC site allows users to sign up online for the Do-Not-Call list to eliminate telemarketing phone calls. | http://www.ftc.gov/donotcall/ |
| Federal Communications Commission | http://www.fcc.gov |
| U.S. Postal Service | http://www.usps.gov |
| Securities and Exchange Commission | http://www.sec.gov |
| National Highway Traffic Safety Administration | http://www.nhtsa.dot.gov |
| Consumer Product Safety Commission | http://www.cpsc.gov |
| Alcohol and Tobacco Tax and Trade Bureau, U.S. Department of Treasury | http://www.ttb.gov |
| The *Georgia Institute of Technology Survey on Internet Privacy* is available at this site. | http://www.epic.org/privacy/survey |
| This site is dedicated to pressuring Congress to pass a bill aimed at forcing better labeling of genetically modified organisms. | http://www.thecampaign.org |

CHAPTER 18

# Real Property and Land Use

## INTRODUCTION

### IMPORTANCE

It is difficult to imagine any business enterprise that does not involve real property in some way. From the global company with factories or retail outlets on several continents to a mail-order business operated out of a rented apartment, real estate is important to the successful functioning of most businesses. In the past two decades, there has been an explosion in the commercial real estate field due to the securitization of mortgages and the public marketing of interests in commercial real estate. The real estate market is so ubiquitous that many fail to grasp its sheer size. The U.S. commercial real estate market has an estimated value of at least $11.2 trillion, and the U.S. housing market is worth $14.1 trillion.[1] By comparison, the entire U.S. gross domestic product for 2002 was $10.4 trillion.

Real estate law has its roots in both English common law and Spanish civil law. Many of the laws are determined by municipalities, others by the state. In recent years, the federal government has played an increasingly active role through tax policy and environmental regulations. The federal government is also interested in the safety of real estate (through the Occupational Safety and Health Administration), physical access to commercial facilities (under the Americans with Disabilities Act), foreign investment in U.S. real estate, and the preservation of parklands.

### CHAPTER OVERVIEW

This chapter discusses the forms of real estate ownership and the transfer of ownership, including the different types of deeds and the effect of recording statutes. It explains the role of brokers and the effect of express and implied warranties concerning the condition of real property. The chapter outlines the alternatives to acquiring real property for cash, including tax-deferred exchanges, sales and leasebacks, and real estate investment trusts. Certain types of preliminary agreements, including option contracts, rights of first refusal, and letters of intent, are then described. Methods of financing are also addressed, as are leasing and lease terms. Finally, the chapter outlines governmental regulation of the use of real property by the exercise of police and condemnation powers and the circumstances in which government restrictions on land use are deemed "takings," requiring compensation of the owner under the U.S. Constitution.

1. FLOW OF FUNDS ACCOUNTS OF THE UNITED STATES, BD. OF GOVERNORS OF THE FED. RESERVE SYS. (Sept. 9, 2003).

## Forms of Ownership

Real property can be held in a variety of ways. A business will normally own real estate in the name of the firm. Whether the firm is organized as a partnership (general or limited), a corporation, or a limited liability company will depend on tax, financial, securities, and liability factors. The choice of the proper entity for owning real estate is particularly important at the beginning of an investment or development. It may be difficult to make a change at a later date without adverse tax consequences. The issue of choice of entity is discussed further in Chapter 19.

### INDIVIDUAL OWNERSHIP

In the simplest type of ownership, property is owned by a single individual. From a business perspective, individual ownership is often undesirable because the individual owner may be liable in tort for any accidents occurring on the property. The risk of unlimited personal liability can, however, be reduced by obtaining liability insurance.

Ownership rights can also be shared by two or more individuals. Forms of co-ownership include tenancy in common, joint tenancy, tenancy by the entirety, and community property. Though not a form of co-ownership, a trust also involves more than one person.

### Tenancy in Common

*Tenants in common* each own an undivided fractional interest in a parcel of real property. Two or more persons can hold property as tenants in common. For example, one tenant in common may have a two-thirds interest and another a one-third interest. Regardless of the percentage ownership interest, each tenant in common has an equal right to possession of the property, and no co-tenant has the right of exclusive possession of the property against any other co-tenant. But a co-tenant does have the right to exclude any third party. Co-tenants share the income and burdens of ownership. The interest of a tenant in common is assignable and inheritable without the consent of any other co-tenant.

### Joint Tenancy

In a *joint tenancy*, property is owned in equal shares by two or more individuals. The key characteristic of a joint tenancy is the right of survivorship. If a joint tenant dies, his or her interest passes automatically to the remaining joint tenant or tenants. However, an attempt by a single joint tenant to convey separately his or her interest in the property will destroy the joint tenancy and convert it to a tenancy in common. Use of joint tenancy property in a business may also terminate the joint tenancy.[2]

### Tenancy by the Entirety

Historically, English common law recognized a special type of co-ownership of real property between husband and wife called *tenancy by the entirety*. Like joint tenancy, tenancy by the entirety includes a right of survivorship. Unlike a joint tenancy, however, neither spouse can convey an individual interest to a third party and thereby terminate the right of survivorship. Additionally, unlike joint tenancy, where joint tenants have equal rights to possession of the property, tenancy by the entirety entitled only the husband to possession, use, and enjoyment of the property. In effect, he acted as a guardian over the wife's interest.

Approximately twenty-two states recognize some form of tenancy by the entirety. Most states have retained the indestructible right of survivorship, but they give the husband and wife equal rights to the possession, use, and revenues of the property. Additionally, the modern view is that divorce converts a tenancy by the entirety to a tenancy in common.[3]

### Community Property

In Arizona, California, Idaho, Louisiana, Nevada, New Mexico, Texas, Washington, and Wisconsin, property acquired by either spouse during marriage is considered to be *community property;* that is, each spouse owns an undivided one-half interest in the property. Property acquired prior to the marriage or by gift or inheritance during the marriage is *separate property*, belonging solely to the spouse who acquired it before marriage or received it by gift or inheritance, unless the spouse owning the property has converted it to community property. Separate property is converted into community property when (1) one spouse gifts the separate property to the other spouse, (2) the parties treat the separate property in such a manner that a presumption of a gift arises, or (3) the separate and common property have been commingled, or mixed together.

**Conveyance** Community property cannot be conveyed unless both spouses execute the instrument by which the conveyance is effected. It should be noted, however, that when one spouse does not sign the instrument, but both spouses were present during negotiations and were fully aware of the terms and conditions, the nonsigning spouse may not claim that the transaction is void due to the absence of a signature.[4]

The community-property interest of a spouse may be separately willed upon death. In the absence of a will, community property passes to the other spouse.

**Divorce** Most of the cases interpreting what is or is not community property arise in the divorce context. Community-property laws vary from state to state. Complicated issues can arise, for example, when one spouse inherits land from his or her family (which is separate property at the date of inheritance), but subsequently one or both spouses improve or develop the property. In this case, some or all of the inherited property may turn into community property. Similarly, if one spouse uses separate property as seed capital for a busi-

2. Williams v. Dovell, 96 A.2d 484 (Md. 1953).

3. Markland v. Markland, 21 So. 2d 145 (Fla. 1945).

4. Calvin v. Salmon River Sheep Ranch, 658 P.2d 972 (Idaho 1983).

ness that he or she operates during the marriage, then part of the value of the business will be separate property and part will be community property.

### *Trust*

Property may be held in a *trust,* whereby the property is owned and controlled by one person, the *trustee,* for the benefit of another, the *beneficiary.* The duration of the trust, the powers of the trustee and the trustor (the person creating the trust), and the express rights of the beneficiary are set forth in a trust agreement.

### General Partnership

When property is held in a general partnership, the partners have rights similar to those of co-tenants, and each partner is liable for all the debts of the partnership. A general partner has no right to possess partnership property for other than partnership purposes. In addition, a general partner may not assign his or her individual interest in specific partnership property. On the other hand, a general partner can effectively convey the entire partnership property to a bona fide purchaser who has no knowledge of any restriction that might exist on the general partner's authority to convey partnership property.

### Limited Partnership

Real property may be held in a limited partnership, consisting of one or more general partners, who manage the property, and one or more limited partners. The liability of a limited partner is usually restricted to the amount of capital the limited partner has contributed or agreed to contribute to the partnership. Typically, limited partners will indemnify the general partners with the indemnity secured by the value of the real estate assets. The authority of the general partner to convey the property is determined by the limited partnership agreement and the jurisdiction's limited partnership law.

### Corporate Ownership

A corporation may own real property. Corporate authority to convey the property is governed by the corporation's certificate of incorporation and bylaws, as well as the jurisdiction's corporate law. The board of directors must authorize most transfers of real property.

### Limited Liability Company

Generally, the preferred form of ownership for real property is now the limited liability company or LLC (previously, limited partnerships were more popular). Authority to convey property is governed by the operating agreement as well as the jurisdiction's LLC law. The board of managers must authorize most transfers of real property.

## Transfer of Ownership

Ownership of land is normally transferred by a document known as a *deed,* which is recorded at a public office, typically the office of the county recorder in the county where the real property is located. Any document transferring an interest in real estate, such as a deed or a lease, is called a *conveyance.* The person conveying the property is the *grantor,* and the person to whom the property is conveyed is the *grantee.* Occasionally, but seldom in business, ownership is obtained through an installment sales contract, with the deed to follow when payment for the real estate has been completed. Ownership of property subject to probate is transferred by a court order from the probate court.

In most purchases of real estate, the interest conveyed is a *fee simple* interest, that is, absolute ownership of the property. However, many other transactions, such as a lease, convey less than an absolute ownership interest in the property.

### Title

A seller of real estate is generally required to convey *marketable title,* that is, an interest in the property free from defects. Defects that make a title unmarketable include any cloud on the title that would cause the buyer to receive less than a fee simple interest. For example, the existence of a lien on the property would constitute a defect of title sufficient to make the title unmarketable. In contrast, a fifty-year-old easement allowing neighbors to use a five-inch strip of the property for a fence probably is not sufficiently burdensome to render a title defective. If the title is found to be unmarketable prior to closing, the buyer may agree to purchase the property anyway or can elect to cancel the deal entirely.

The type of interest (usually fee simple) and the quality of title (that is, whether it is marketable) are set forth in a deed executed by the party conveying the property. The type of deed determines the scope of the warranties granted.

## Types of Deeds

An interest in real property can be conveyed only by a signed deed that specifically describes that interest and is delivered to and accepted by a named grantee. There are three basic types of deeds: grant deeds, quitclaim deeds, and warranty deeds. These differ in the specific express warranties they contain.

### Grant Deed

A *grant deed* contains implied warranties that (1) the grantor has not previously conveyed the same property or any interest in it to another person, and (2) the title is marketable. A grant deed also conveys *after-acquired title.* This means that if at the date the deed is executed the grantor does not have title to the real property referred to in the grant deed, but subsequently acquires it, the title will be automatically transferred to the grantee.

### Quitclaim Deed

A *quitclaim deed* contains no warranties, and the grantor conveys only whatever right, title, and interest the grantor holds, if any, at the time of execution. A quitclaim deed does not convey after-acquired title.

### Warranty Deed

A *warranty deed* contains the implied warranties of a grant deed; in addition, the grantor expressly warrants the title to and the quiet possession of the property. Warranty deeds may also contain other express warranties as well.

## Adverse Possession

In unusual circumstances, a person can acquire ownership of a piece of property by adverse possession. If a person adversely possesses a parcel of land for the period of time specified by the state statute (usually between fifteen and twenty-two years), then that person will become the legal owner of the parcel. To acquire a parcel of land by *adverse possession,* (1) a person must possess the land for the specified period of time; (2) the current owner of the land must have actual constructive notice of the adverse possession; (3) the possession must continue uninterrupted for the specified period; (4) the person must not have a legal right to be there (thus, the possession must be "adverse" to the current owner's rights); and (5) the possession must not be shared with another, such as the current owner or the general public. At first blush, adverse possession appears to reward illegal possession, yet the doctrine is designed to ensure that land is used in the most efficient, publicly beneficial manner. Landowners who have no use for their land are forced to give it to those who will put it to a more economic use. The grace period of fifteen-plus years offers ample time for a conscientious landowner to commence eviction proceedings, which would destroy the adverse possession.

## Representations and Implied Warranties

In the past, real estate transactions were governed by the traditional rule of *caveat emptor* ("let the buyer beware"). Under this rule, the seller of a house or other property made no warranties to the buyer other than those expressly included in the deed or written contract of sale. Current law is more protective of the buyer, especially when a person is buying a house.

### Implied Warranty of Habitability

A majority of the states impose on commercial builders of houses an implied warranty of habitability. As with the Uniform Commercial Code's implied warranty of merchantability for sales of goods (discussed in Chapter 8), under the *implied warranty of habitability* builders warrant that the house is in reasonable working order and is of reasonably sound construction. Because builders have a major hand in determining the overall fitness of a building, courts have deemed it appropriate to hold them responsible for its initial condition. This warranty applies only to the original builders, *not* to subsequent sellers. Thus, secondary sellers are not burdened by an implied warranty of habitability.

A number of courts have extended the warranty of habitability to protect individual lessees of residential property. The warranty of habitability has not yet been extended to commercial leases such as office space.

### Seller's Duty to Disclose

The traditional rule of *caveat emptor* is also giving way to a duty on sellers to disclose defects in real property. In most states, sellers have an obligation to disclose any known defect that (1) materially affects the value of the property and (2) could not reasonably be discovered by the buyer. As the following case illustrates, sellers—and their brokers (brokers' duties will be discussed in detail in a later section)—can be liable for nondisclosure of certain off-site conditions that materially affect the value of the property.

A CASE IN POINT

**CASE 18.1**
**Strawn v. Canuso**
*Supreme Court of New Jersey*
*657 A.2d 420 (N.J. 1995).*

## In the Language of the Court

**› FACTS** The plaintiffs comprised more than 150 families who purchased new homes in Voorhees Township. The homes were developed and marketed by companies controlled by the Canuso family. The home buyers sought damages against the Canusos and their companies because—unbeknownst to the buyers—the new homes they purchased had been constructed near the Buzby Landfill.

Between 1966 and 1978, large amounts of hazardous materials and chemicals were dumped at the Buzby Landfill. Toxic materials escaped, contaminating the groundwater and air. The federal Environmental Protection Agency recommended that the site be considered for a Superfund cleanup.

The home buyers alleged that the developers and brokers knew of the Buzby Landfill and its environmental hazards before they considered the site for residential development but failed to disclose those facts to the families when they purchased their homes. The representatives of the Canuso brokerage and development companies were instructed never to disclose the existence of the Buzby Landfill, even when asked about such conditions. The lower court found in favor of the home buyers.

**› ISSUE PRESENTED** Do the developers of new homes and the real estate brokers marketing those homes have a duty to disclose to prospective buyers that the homes were constructed near an abandoned hazardous-waste dump?

**› OPINION** O'HERN, J., writing for the New Jersey Supreme Court:

[A] seller of real estate or a broker representing the seller would be liable for nondisclosure of on-site defective conditions if those conditions were known to them and unknown and not readily observable by the buyer. Such conditions, for example, would include radon contamination and a polluted water supply. . . .

. . . [T]he principal factors shaping the duty to disclose have been the difference in bargaining power between the professional seller of residential real estate and the purchaser of such housing, and the difference in access to information between the seller and the buyer. Those principles guide our decision in this case.

The first factor causes us to limit our holding to professional sellers of residential housing (persons engaged in the business of building or developing residential housing) and the brokers representing them. . . . Hence, we believe that it is reasonable to extend to such professionals a similar duty to disclose off-site conditions that materially affect the value or desirability of the property.

. . . Defendants used sales-promotion brochures, newspaper advertisements, and a fact sheet to sell the homes in the development. That material portrayed the development as located in a peaceful, bucolic setting with an abundance of fresh air and clean lake waters. Although the literature mentioned how far the property was from malls, country clubs, and train stations, "neither the brochures, the newspaper advertisements nor any sales personnel mentioned that a landfill [was] located within half a mile of some of the homes.". . .

. . .

We hold that a builder-developer of residential real estate or a broker representing it is not only liable to a purchaser for affirmative and intentional misrepresentation, but is also liable for nondisclosure of off-site physical conditions known to it and unknown and not readily observable by the buyer if the existence of those conditions is of sufficient materiality to affect the habitability, use, or enjoyment of the property

*(Continued)*

(Case 18.1 *continued*)

and, therefore, render the property substantially less desirable or valuable to the objectively reasonable buyer.

**› RESULT** The verdict in favor of the home buyers was affirmed. The defendants had violated their duty to disclose the existence of the landfill.

**› CRITICAL THINKING QUESTIONS**

1. Would the court have reached a different result if the sellers had not touted the development's bucolic setting, fresh air, and clean lake waters?
2. Why should a seller of commercial property have a lesser obligation to disclose adverse off-site conditions than a seller of houses?

---

### *Contractual Protections and Due Diligence*

A skillful buyer will request express contractual representations and warranties from the seller as to the condition of the property. This is particularly important in commercial transactions, because courts are less willing to impose implied warranties and a duty to disclose when the buyer is a commercial entity, rather than an individual. From the seller's perspective, the representations and warranties are a potential source of liability. From the buyer's perspective, the representations and warranties provide some assurance that the buyer is getting what it expected. If nothing else, the negotiation of representations and warranties frequently leads to additional disclosures regarding the physical condition of the property.

The buyer should not rely on representations and warranties as an alternative to its own careful investigation of the condition of the property, however. Although the seller is generally required to indemnify the buyer against liability arising from the inaccuracy of any of its representations and warranties, the right to indemnification is not worth much if the seller does not have the resources to back it up. Perhaps more important, defects in the property can seriously disrupt the buyer's operations and business.

## Recording Statutes

Deeds and other instruments of conveyance must be recorded with a government official in a public office, where copies will be available to anyone. The documents must be in *recordable form*. The requirements vary from state to state, but they typically include legibility and some type of notarization by a notary public. The record in the public office is the principal basis for determining the state of title of real estate.

*Recording statutes* establish an orderly process by which claims to interests in real property can be resolved. There are three types of recording statutes: (1) race statutes, (2) pure notice statutes, and (3) race–notice statutes.[5] The applicable state statutes should always be checked before closing a transaction.

Under *race statutes*, recording is a race—the rule is "first in time is first in right." The first to record a deed has superior rights, even if he or she knew that someone else had already bought the property but had failed to record the deed.

Under *pure notice statutes*, a person who has notice that someone else has already bought the property cannot validate his or her deed by recording it first. Notice may be actual or constructive. Courts may find *constructive notice* if a reasonable inquiry (for instance, inspection of the property) would have disclosed the prior interest. A pure notice statute protects good faith subsequent purchasers. A *good faith subsequent purchaser* is one who purchases for value, in good faith, without knowledge of a prior outstanding interest. Thus, if a subsequent purchaser acquires a deed and has no notice (actual or constructive) of a prior deed at that time, then he or she will have superior rights. *Race–notice statutes* protect only those good faith subsequent purchasers who record their deed before the prior purchaser records its deed.

## Title Insurance

Despite the existence of recording statutes, the condition of title to a specific property and the priority of any claims against the property are often difficult to ascertain. In

5. Only two states (Delaware and North Carolina) use race statutes. Usage in other states is split about evenly between pure notice statutes and race–notice statutes.

some states, title is searched by attorneys, in others by title abstract companies on which attorneys rely, and in still others by title insurance companies. Title insurance companies may also insure the condition of title or the priority of one's interest. In some states, lawyers' opinions are still used rather than title insurance. Blindly relying on any title company's title abstract can be dangerous, however. The New Hampshire Supreme Court ruled that attorneys are not vicariously liable for relying on a faulty title report, unless they were negligent in choosing or supervising the title abstractor.[6] Thus, the buyer should make sure that the title company or the attorney issuing title insurance is reputable and competent.

## Extent of Coverage

A title insurance policy insures against loss as a result of (1) undisclosed liens or defects in title to the property or (2) errors in the abstraction of the title, that is, the summary of the relevant recorded deeds and liens. Generally, the policy limit is the purchase price of the property or the amount of the *encumbrance*, that is, the claim against the property.

It is important to review a title report or insurance policy carefully before acquiring title to property. The exceptions listed in the report may be defects in title.

6. Lawyers Title Ins. Corp. v. Groff, 808 A.2d 44 (N.H. 2002).

## Escrow

In addition to issuing title insurance policies, title companies often hold the purchase money in *escrow*, that is, in a special account, until the conditions for the sale have all been met. The money is then paid to the seller. If the sale does not go through, the money is returned to the would-be purchaser. Banks also perform this service, and in some jurisdictions there are separate escrow companies.

The *escrow agent* acts as a neutral stakeholder, allowing the parties to close the transaction without the physical difficulties of passing instruments and funds between the parties. Additionally, it is the duty of the escrow agent to coordinate the closing with the recording of documents, the issuance of title insurance, and other activities that take place concurrently with the closing.

### *Neutral Party*

As a neutral party, the escrow agent is an agent of all parties to the transaction and must follow their specific instructions. Because an escrow agent has a fiduciary duty to all of the parties, it cannot act when the parties have submitted conflicting instructions. Generally, if the parties fail to resolve conflicts between instructions, the escrow agent will go to court for a resolution of the conflict.

The following case addressed the scope of an escrow agent's fiduciary duty to one of its principals.

**A Case in Point**

**CASE 18.2**
**Schoepe v. Zions First National Bank**
*United States District Court for the District of Utah 750 F. Supp. 1084 (D. Utah 1990).*

## Summary

**› FACTS** In October 1980, Lion Hill, a Nevada partnership, contracted to sell Nevada mining property to Pacific Silver Corporation. In February 1981, Lion Hill and Pacific Silver signed an escrow agreement whereby Pacific Silver agreed to pay the purchase price in installments to Zions First National Bank, which, as escrow agent, would deliver the payments to Lion Hill.

In March 1984, Zions lent $1.6 million to Pacific Silver without the knowledge or consent of Lion Hill. In January 1985, again without the knowledge or consent of Lion Hill, Zions lent $700,000 to Pacific Silver.

Later in 1985, Lion Hill agreed to extend Pacific Silver's payment schedule by decreasing current payments and increasing later payments. This 1985 extension was also made part of the escrow agreement.

After making the 1986 payment on the loan, Pacific Silver defaulted. Lion Hill claimed that it would not have agreed to the 1985 extension had it known of the $2.3 million in loans that Zions had made to Pacific Silver. Lion Hill sued Zions, alleging that Zions, acting as escrow agent, breached its fiduciary duty to disclose these loans.

**› ISSUE PRESENTED** Does an escrow agent have a fiduciary duty to disclose dealings with principals that fall outside the scope of the escrow agreement?

*(Continued)*

(Case 18.2 *continued*)

**› SUMMARY OF OPINION** The U.S. District Court for the District of Utah first noted that the duties of an escrow agent do not rise to the level of common law agency. An escrow agent's fiduciary duty is limited by the terms of the escrow agreement. An escrow agent's primary obligation is to exercise reasonable skill and ordinary diligence in following the escrow instructions.

It was uncontested that Zions exercised reasonable skill and ordinary diligence in following the escrow instructions. It was also uncontested that the escrow agreement contained no language imposing a duty on Zions to disclose any information to its principals. Finally, Lion Hill did not allege that Zions was engaged in fraud or that it had knowledge of a third party committing a fraud upon Lion Hill.

Lion Hill argued that Zions' knowledge of the loans it made to Pacific Silver constituted "knowledge of material facts" that gave rise to a duty to disclose. The court disagreed, holding that, regardless of whether the existence of the loans was "material" to Lion Hill, Zions had no duty to disclose the loans because it did not acquire the knowledge "in the course of its agency." Instead, Zions was acting outside the scope of the escrow agreement when it made the loans to Pacific Silver.

**› RESULT** The court dismissed Lion Hill's claim.

**› COMMENTS** The court noted that Lion Hill could have avoided this result by requiring Pacific Silver to submit a financial statement before it agreed to extend the payments or by imposing a duty to disclose on the escrow agent in the escrow agreement.

**› QUERY** Was it ethical for Zions First National Bank to lend money to Pacific Silver without disclosing that fact to Lion Hill?

## Brokers

The market for real estate is imperfect, and brokers facilitate its operation by bringing buyers and sellers together.

### Compensation

Brokers are customarily retained by the seller through a listing agreement, which must be in writing to be enforceable. Generally, brokers receive a percentage of the gross selling price (or aggregate rental income) as compensation. To the extent that the buyer's or lessee's broker is compensated, it is usually by sharing the commission paid by the seller.

### Listing Agreements

There are several types of listing agreements: open, exclusive, and net.

#### *Open Listing*

In an *open listing*, the listing broker will receive a commission only if he or she procures a ready, willing, and able buyer. It is understood that the seller will be contracting with more than one broker, so the first broker to procure a buyer will receive the commission. Because of the uncertainty of earning a commission even if a buyer is found, it is hard to get a broker to work diligently to sell a commercial property with an open listing.

#### *Exclusive Listing*

An *exclusive listing* grants the broker the right to sell the property; any sale of the property during the term of the listing will entitle the broker to a commission. If a seller has dealt with particular potential buyers before signing an exclusive listing agreement, he or she may wish to exclude them from the agreement.

#### *Net Listing*

A *net listing* involves a completely different compensation scheme: the broker will receive any sales proceeds in excess of the net listing amount specified by the seller. Net listings are uncommon.

### Regulation of Brokers

In most states, real estate brokers are heavily regulated.

### *Licensing*

Real estate brokers are generally required to have a license to perform brokerage activities. Anyone who engages in brokerage activities without a license will not be able to sue successfully to recover his or her fee. Brokerage activities are broadly defined to include effecting or negotiating (1) any sale or offer to sell or purchase or offer to purchase real property or a business opportunity and (2) any leases, loans secured by real property, or real property sales contracts. A mere finder, who does nothing more than introduce two parties for a fee, does not need a broker's license.

In many states, real estate brokers must report and keep records of their transactions. Brokers may also be required to meet continuing education requirements and maintain up-to-date knowledge regarding the particulars of real estate loans.

### *Agency Relationship*

Brokers may also be subject to regulations concerning the disclosure of the agency relationship between the broker and the parties to the transaction. Brokers are fiduciaries. As a general rule, a broker may not act for more than one person in a transaction without the knowledge and consent of all parties to the transaction. When a broker acts for both the buyer and the seller, the relationship is characterized as a *dual agency.* In most instances, a dual agent is prohibited from disclosing to the buyer, without the consent of the seller, that the seller is willing to sell the property for less than the listing price. Similarly, a dual agent may not disclose to the seller that the buyer is willing to pay a price greater than the listing price. Agency issues are discussed further in Chapter 5.

# Acquisitions and Dispositions

Acquisitions and dispositions of real estate interests are contracted for in the same manner as most commercial transactions. Although standardized contracts are often used in relatively simple transactions (such as the conveyance of a single-family residence or a small commercial property), most large transactions require custom-drafted contracts.

Generally, contracts for the sale of an interest in real property are the result of protracted negotiations between the parties. In addition to essential terms such as price, time, and method of payment, common areas of negotiation include types of acceptable financing, the condition of title, the allocation of closing costs and taxes, and compliance with zoning laws, building codes, and environmental regulations. In many purchase and sale agreements, the most heavily negotiated provisions are the seller's representations and warranties concerning the condition of the property, as discussed earlier in this chapter.

## Tax-Deferred Exchanges

An alternative to acquiring real property for cash is a *tax-deferred exchange,* whereby the seller exchanges its property for another piece of property. Such transactions can have favorable tax consequences. In particular, the capital gains tax owed by the seller may be deferred if the seller (1) is disposing of a property held for investment or for productive use in a trade or business and (2) is acquiring a property that qualifies under the Internal Revenue Code. Tax-deferred exchanges take many forms. The most common is the three-party exchange, in which the buyer purchases a piece of property designated by the seller and exchanges it for the seller's property. Because these exchanges can be complex, it is prudent to consult an attorney specializing in tax and real estate issues when acquiring real property through a tax-deferred exchange.

## Sale and Leaseback

A *sale and leaseback* arrangement involves a simultaneous two-step transaction. In the first step, an institutional lender with funds to invest, such as a life insurance company or a pension fund, purchases real property from a corporation. In the second step, or often simultaneously, the property is leased back to the corporation for its use. The term of the lease is long, often ranging from twenty to forty years. The length of the term influences how the lease will be accounted for on the balance sheet. A longer-term lease may be capitalized as an asset on the balance sheet, whereas an *operating lease* (typically with a shorter term) will not appear on the balance sheet at all. The tenant may have the option of repurchasing the property on or before the termination date of the lease.

The amount of rent payable is structured so that during the term of the lease, the lessor will recoup the purchase price of the property and realize an acceptable return on its investment. The lessee pays all taxes and maintenance and operating costs.

## Synthetic Leases

Today, synthetic leases are commonly used to take advantage of the differences between the tax and accounting rules governing leases. In a *synthetic lease,* the transaction is treated as a conventional operating lease for accounting purposes, so it does not appear on the balance sheet. Payments under the lease are treated merely as rent. At the same time, for tax purposes, the lessee of the property treats the transaction as though it had purchased the property and obtained a loan from the seller. Thus, payments under the lease are treated as debt service on the loan, and the lessee may take favorable interest payment deductions as well as depreciation write-offs.[7]

## Real Estate Investment Trusts (REITs)

*Real estate investment trusts,* commonly referred to as *REITs,* can provide a good tax vehicle for investors seeking to invest in a portfolio of real property. REITs sell beneficial shares that are traded in the stock markets, and they permit small investors to invest in a diversified portfolio of real estate, similar to an investment in common stocks through a mutual fund.

As long as at least 95 percent of a REIT's net income is distributed to shareholder–beneficiaries, the REIT itself pays no income tax; taxes are paid at the shareholder–beneficiary level only. REITs are limited in the types of operations they may conduct. Ownership concentration is also limited: no five persons may own more than 50 percent of the REIT's beneficial interests; often the number of shares any shareholder may own is limited to 9.8 percent or less.[8]

### INTERNATIONAL SNAPSHOT

Many countries do not permit foreigners to own land. Therefore, in these countries, a foreigner must obtain a long-term lease on the property.

Mexico's laws restricting foreign ownership offer a complex example. Foreigners cannot obtain title to any property within thirty-one miles of the ocean or within sixty-two miles of the U.S. or Guatemalan borders. All a foreigner can legally acquire near a beach or border is the right to use the land for up to fifty years. This is obtained through a Mexican bank trust called a *fideicomiso translativo de dominio.*[a]

Even these trusts can be invalidated if the title to the land is not clear. Mexican title records are not thorough, and title insurance is rare. Public notaries in Mexico can search for liens against property title, but they rarely search back farther than a decade.[b]

In any country where foreign ownership is permitted, an investor should be cautious when purchasing property. Many countries do not have adequate means for searching the title of property. In addition, many countries allow for *squatter's rights,* whereby ownership of property that is not occupied by its owner for a certain period of time will be transferred to those who have been unlawfully occupying it. Such a transfer is usually not reflected in the official land records.

**a.** See Bob Ortega, *Quirky Laws for Americans Buying Mexican Property,* Wall St. J., Oct. 17, 1997, at B1.
**b.** See *id.*

## Transactions with Foreigners

Sales of real property interests to nonresident aliens are regulated by the federal government. Under the Foreign Investment in Real Property Tax Act (FIRPTA), the purchaser of a U.S. real property interest from a foreign person is required to withhold 10 percent of the purchase price to ensure that U.S. capital gains tax is paid on the sale. Additionally, the Agricultural Foreign Investment Disclosure Act requires foreign acquirers of U.S. agricultural land to file an informational report with the U.S. secretary of agriculture.

## Environmental Due Diligence

Due diligence before buying or leasing property is particularly necessary with respect to environmental issues (discussed more fully in Chapter 15). Because liability under federal and state environmental laws and regulations can be so large as to overshadow any other economic aspect of the property, the buyer should diligently investigate whether there are toxic or hazardous substances on or under the property.

Under the Comprehensive Environmental Response, Compensation, and Liability Act (CERCLA), the current owner or operator of a contaminated facility is potentially jointly and severally liable with the prior owner or the operator of the facility at the time of waste disposal for the costs associated with cleaning up the facility. If the prior owner is insolvent or nonexistent, the current owner may be responsible for the entire cleanup. (The "Inside Story" in this chapter discusses legislation designed to promote the reclaiming of *brownfields*—underutilized property with actual or suspected contaminants.) This liability attaches even if the current owner purchased the property with no knowledge of the prior contamination, unless it can show that it made all due inquiry and still had no reason to know about the contamination.

7. Gerard R. Boyce, *Synthetic Leases: The Hard Facts,* N.Y.L.J., Jan. 13, 2000.
8. David M. Einhorn et al., *REIT M&A Transactions—Peculiarities and Complications,* Bus. Law., Feb. 2000.

In addition, office workers and other tenants have successfully sued building owners and construction contractors for injury or fear of future injury due to asbestos on the premises.[9] Litigation related to potentially toxic mold is also increasing, causing some to call toxic mold "the new asbestos."[10]

## Preliminary Agreements

Often the parties to a real estate transaction are able to reach a general agreement on terms and conditions but need more time to negotiate specific representations and warranties or to investigate the property further. A number of alternatives to the traditional contract for the sale of real property have been developed. These include option contracts, rights of first refusal, and letters of intent.

### Option Contract

In an *option contract,* the potential buyer pays the seller for the right, but not the obligation, to purchase the property during a given time period. The option gives the buyer time to conduct investigations, determine whether the purchase of the property is economically feasible, and obtain financing. The seller receives payment for taking the property off the market for a specified period of time.

To be enforceable, an option contract must be in writing, and consideration must be paid to the seller. Additionally, the option contract must state the major terms of the proposed purchase agreement and must specify the manner in which the option may be exercised. It is also advisable to record the option to provide constructive notice to third parties and thereby prevent the sale of the property to a third party before the option has expired.

### Right of First Refusal

A *right of first refusal* is the right, conferred by a written contract, to purchase the property on the same terms offered by or to a third party. Perhaps its most frequent use is with a tenant of a leasehold interest. The holder of the right of first refusal should require that it be recorded.

A right of first refusal can chill the owner's ability to sell the property. Few buyers will want to start investigations and negotiations knowing that they could lose the deal if the party with the right of first refusal exercises its right.

Consequently, the owner will often want to modify the right of first refusal to give the holder only the right to negotiate the purchase of the property before the seller enters negotiations with another party. This is sometimes called a *right of first negotiation.* Another method of accommodating the needs of the seller is to provide for a very short time, such as seventy-two hours, for the holder to exercise its right of first refusal.

### Letter of Intent

A letter of intent may create the right to acquire an interest in a specific property. A *letter of intent* sets forth the general terms and conditions of a proposed purchase until a formal acquisition agreement can be signed. Although the parties often view letters of intent as unenforceable, courts have increasingly treated them as enforceable contracts. In one case, the court focused on the conduct of the parties to determine whether an enforceable agreement was intended despite express written statements to the contrary in the letter of intent.[11] Consequently, if the parties do not wish to be bound by their letters of intent, they must ensure that the terms and conditions are not set forth so specifically that a binding legal obligation is created; they must also conduct themselves consistently with the absence of a binding contract.

When properly utilized, letters of intent allow the parties to investigate the proposed transaction to determine whether it is worth pursuing. Although letters of intent are generally not as effective as options or rights of first refusal in removing property from the market, they can create an ethical commitment to consummate the transaction. In some states, the execution of a letter of intent creates an implied covenant of good faith and fair dealing between the parties, requiring good faith negotiation of a formal acquisition agreement.

## Financing

Financing the purchase of real estate may involve borrowing funds for a long or short term. The loan is usually secured by a lien on the property, known as a *mortgage* or a *deed of trust.* Although these two documents are virtually the same, the name usually varies

9. Susan Warren, *Asbestos Quagmire,* WALL ST. J., Jan. 27, 2003, at B1.
10. John M. Simon & Thomas J. Trautner Jr., *Mold: Should Your Client Be Worried?,* 13 BUS. L. TODAY 36–39 (2004).

11. Computer Sys. of Am. v. Int'l Bus. Machs. Corp., 795 F.2d 1086 (1st Cir. 1986).

from state to state. Generally, in the northeastern and southern states, the document conferring a security interest in real property is called a mortgage, whereas in the Midwest and on the West Coast, it is known as a deed of trust. Conceptually, a mortgage and a deed of trust secure a lien in different ways, but they operate to create the same end result.

Most large lenders use standard documents for loan agreements, although changes are sometimes made. In substantial transactions, it is essential that all documents be reviewed and negotiated by all parties to the transaction and their counsel.

The availability of financing depends on the intrinsic value of the property or on both its value and its potential for the production of income. The types of financing available are almost unlimited. Some of the more common forms are discussed in this section.

## Permanent Loans

The most common type of real estate loan is the *permanent loan*. This is usually a long-term loan, repaid over five, ten, or sometimes up to twenty years.

### Fixed-Interest Loans

Traditionally, permanent loans have had a fixed interest rate; that is, the rate of interest does not change over the term of the loan. The lender assumes the risk of losing the benefit of any increase in interest rates, and the borrower assumes the risk of losing the benefit of any decrease.

In order to benefit from any increases in market interest rates, many lenders reserve the right to call (that is, demand repayment of) fixed-interest loans after a specified period, often after five, ten, or fifteen years. Conversely, to prevent borrowers from refinancing their obligation when market interest rates fall below the fixed interest rate of the loan, some lenders insert a lock-in clause to prohibit prepayments of principal or impose a penalty, called a *prepayment penalty,* if the loan is paid off early. Usually, the penalty declines with time.

### Variable-Interest Loans

Variable-interest loans allow lenders to avoid the risk of fluctuating interest rates. In a *variable-interest loan,* the rate of interest is often set at a fixed number of percentage points over a specified standard or base rate (often the *prime rate,* i.e., the rate at which major financial institutions offer to lend to their most creditworthy customers). Over the term of the loan, the interest rate fluctuates with changes in the base rate or index. The interest rate is usually adjusted annually or semiannually. The total amount of the change over the term of the loan is generally subject to some cap or maximum top rate. A floor may also be established to ensure that the interest rate does not fall below a specified percentage.

### Points

In addition to interest, real estate lenders often charge a loan fee, called *points.* The fee is the amount funded, multiplied by a fixed percentage. Each 1 percent is a point. For example, a 2½-point fee on a $100,000 loan would be $2,500. Points are usually paid up front at the time the loan is made.

## Construction Loans

Construction loans generally have a term slightly longer than the estimated construction period. Upon completion of construction, the developer obtains either permanent (take-out) financing or interim (gap) financing and repays the construction lender. If the construction loan comes due before the permanent financing is available, the developer obtains *interim* or *gap financing* to pay off the loan. This financing is provided by someone other than the construction lender and is more long term. A *take-out commitment* is an agreement by a lender to replace the construction loan with a permanent loan, usually after certain conditions, such as the timely completion of the project, have been met.

## Development Loans

Developers use construction loans for the acquisition and improvement of commercial properties and *development loans* for the acquisition, subdivision, improvement, and sale of residential properties. Funds are advanced by the lender as development progresses. The lender normally requires that the developer obtain performance bonds and personal guaranties by its principals. From the lender's perspective, development loans are riskier than construction loans because repayment of a development loan depends on the developer's ability to sell parcels of the development.

## Equity Participation by Lender

Many lenders attempt to increase their yield from real estate projects by participating in the *equity,* or ownership, of the property. The developers can benefit from the higher loan-to-value ratio, lower interest rates, and slower repayment terms that a participating lender will accept.

Equity participation by lenders is a relatively recent phenomenon. Historically, federal and state statutes prohibited banks and other lenders from owning real estate. In recent years, however, these statutory restraints have been substantially relaxed. Lenders need to ensure that their equity participation does not result in an effective interest rate that is in excess of state usury limits.

## WRAPAROUND FINANCING

Occasionally, an owner will require financing in addition to an existing loan secured by a deed of trust or mortgage on the property. Unless the second lender is willing to take a position subordinate to the holder of the first loan with respect to rights to the property, the owner will need to obtain a second loan sufficient to satisfy (pay off) the first loan and still provide sufficient funds to meet its financing requirements.

Paying off the first loan may not be economically attractive, however, because of prepayment penalties or because the interest rate on the first loan may be lower than the rate available on a new loan. In such instances, wraparound financing can provide additional funds without requiring the owner to first pay off the original loan.

In a *wraparound financing* transaction, the second lender lends the owner the additional funds and agrees to take over the servicing of the first loan. In exchange, the owner executes a deed of trust or mortgage and an all-inclusive note, covering the combined amount of the first and second loans. The new lender benefits because the rate charged on the all-inclusive note is higher than the weighted-average interest rates of the first and second loans. The owner benefits because the interest rate on the all-inclusive note is lower than the rate it would have to pay if it paid off the first loan and took out a new loan to cover the entire amount.

## View from Cyberspace

### ELECTRONIC CLOSINGS

At one time, in the not so distant past, the typical real estate closing required lawyers and principals to sit down together in a conference room, to sign and exchange all the documents necessary to complete the transfer. This usually took an entire workday and involved significant costs for travel and attorneys' fees. Prior to closing, there was often a lengthy period of document drafting as the attorneys exchanged and re-exchanged different versions of the pertinent documents, often fifteen or more, until they reached agreement on all the provisions.

The Internet and e-mail have made the exchange of documents much easier, allowing for quicker, less expensive document revisions. Exchanging documents electronically has become so efficient that many large lenders, such as GMAC and Morgan Stanley, are now requesting an electronic copy, or e-copy, of all the closing documents, known as a closing package, in addition to a hard copy. Currently, the final documents are hand signed by both parties at the closing or are mailed to the necessary parties who countersign and return them. The executed documents are then scanned into a computer file to create a digital snapshot of each page. In contrast to the several inches of multiple volumes that make up a closing package, these e-copies take almost no storage space. They require almost no maintenance and can easily be retrieved when necessary. It is not hard to imagine a day when only the public recording office will have a hard copy of these documents. Still, the cumbersome task of meeting at a closing or the often expensive and time-consuming task of coordinating a massive overnight delivery remains.

The Electronic Signatures in Global and National Commerce Act (E-Sign Act) of 2000 could make the expensive, time-consuming "sit-down" closing a thing of the past. The Act makes it possible to "sign" and deliver documents electronically over the Internet. With the instantaneous exchange of documents, closings in cyberspace may soon be just a mouse click away. There are some practical barriers to overcome, however, including the inability of town recording offices to accept electronically signed documents and the lack of standardized regulations and procedures.[a] When finalized and if adopted by the states, the Uniform Real Property Electronic Recordation Act would standardize the recording of electronic real estate documents.[b]

a. Scott Brede, *An Idea Before Its Time*, CONN. L. TRIB., Feb. 26, 2002.
b. The current draft of the Act is available *at* http://www.law.upenn.edu/bll/ulc/urpera.htm.

### Foreclosure and Rights of Redemption

If the mortgagor fails to repay the loan, the lender—the mortgagee—may resort to foreclosure. *Foreclosure* is the legal process by which a mortgagee may put up a piece of property for sale in the public arena to raise cash in order to pay off a debt owed by the mortgagor to the mortgagee. The property is sold to the highest bidder; the proceeds are then first used to satisfy the debt obligation (plus interest) of the unpaid first mortgage and court costs. The proceeds are then used to pay any other secured creditors holding a mortgage or deed of trust on the property. The remainder, if any, is distributed to the mortgagor. The exact details of the foreclosure process differ from state to state. Generally, creditors will receive payment in the order in which they secured their debts. However, secondary creditors may condition a second mortgage or loan on the mortgagor getting prior creditors to waive their rights to first payment in the event of a foreclosure. The mortgagor receives nothing until all creditors with a security interest in the property are paid in full.

In some states, the lender can bid the amount of the outstanding indebtedness in the foreclosure sale. If the lender is the highest bidder, it acquires the property, and the debt is extinguished.

Some states provide *rights of redemption*, which give the mortgagor and certain other categories of interested persons the right to redeem (reacquire) the property within a statutory limited period, ranging from two months to two years after the sale. If the foreclosure amount plus interest is not paid by the expiration of the redemption period, the purchaser at the foreclosure sale receives the deed and clear ownership of the land.

## Appraisal Methods

The value of an income-producing property may be appraised by (1) the cost approach, which adds the cost of constructing a given improvement on the property to the value of the unimproved land; (2) the market approach, which looks at the selling prices in recent sales of properties with similar income-producing characteristics; or (3) the income approach, which establishes the present value of the estimated annual cash flow over the anticipated holding period. The income approach is generally favored because it provides a basis for comparison; the cost approach is rarely used.

The appraisal of property is an inexact science and is relatively unregulated by state governments. Because the funds available to a developer, and the financial institution's loan fees, are based upon the property's appraised value, the appraiser may be pressured to inflate the appraisal. Although increased loan fees and increased funds for development may provide short-term benefits, inflated appraisals can have disastrous long-term effects. For example, the savings and loan crisis in the 1980s (which cost taxpayers in excess of $300 billion) was in part caused by inflated appraisals that induced savings and loan associations to make reckless loans.

## Protective Laws for Borrowers

Every jurisdiction has laws that regulate the conduct of lenders and protect borrowers, especially in the areas of what interest rate can be charged *(usury laws)* and what remedies are available if a borrower fails to pay on time or is otherwise in default. Both sets of laws are designed primarily to protect individuals, not businesses. Many of the default laws originated during the Great Depression to protect farmers. Such laws include the rights of redemption discussed earlier.

In recent years, usury laws have tended to disappear because an out-of-date usury law (e.g., limiting the interest rate to 8 percent when the prevailing rate is 12 percent) will simply cause loan money to go to a more liberal jurisdiction. In some states, however, the usury laws still apply unless a corporation holds the title to the property. In other states, equity participation by a lender may result in an illegally high interest rate. The penalties for violating the usury laws can be severe, and treble damages are sometimes available. A borrower cannot effectively agree to waive the benefits of a usury law; such a waiver is considered contrary to public policy.

*Fair lending laws* prohibit racial discrimination in lending practices. The Department of Housing and Urban Development (HUD) actively enforces these laws.

## Commercial Leasing

A *commercial lease* is both (1) a conveyance of an interest in real property from the landlord (also called the *lessor*) to the tenant (also called the *lessee*) and (2) a contract that governs the respective rights and obligations of the parties during the lease term. Because most firms do not own the premises in which their business operations are conducted, the availability and the terms and conditions of commercial leasing can be crucial to the success or failure of the business.

## Types of Leases

There are four types of commercial leases: office leases, retail leases, industrial leases, and ground leases.

### Office Leases

Most office premises occupy only a portion of an office building. Unless the tenant is to occupy a substantial portion of the building, the landlord will ordinarily present a standard lease form used for all of the tenants of the building. Because the landlord is more interested in obtaining occupants than in obtaining any particular tenant as an occupant, it is often unwilling to negotiate each lease provision separately or to permit the tenant to prepare the lease. In a tight market for tenants, however, more negotiation is possible.

### Retail Leases

In the negotiation of retail leases, the focus is on the operation of the tenant's business. Retail leases frequently contain a *percentage rent clause* that requires the tenant to pay a percentage of its gross sales, in addition to a base monthly rent, to the landlord.

Environmental concerns are significant in retail leases. Having a paint store or a dry cleaner as a tenant can impose liability upon the landlord under federal and state environmental laws and regulations.

### Industrial Leases

Industrial leases tend to have a five-year term with renewal options. They usually contemplate substantial capital improvements by the tenant in the form of plant and equipment. Industrial leases are almost always *triple net,* which means the tenants pay all taxes, insurance, and operating maintenance expenses. Additionally, because the industrial use tends to be very site-specific, assignments of industrial leases are usually allowed only upon the sale of a tenant's business, and subleasing is usually strictly prohibited.

### Ground Leases

A *ground lease* is a very long-term lease, sometimes as long as ninety-nine years. Ground leases are used when a landowner desires to obtain a steady return of income from undeveloped commercial property without the expense of improving or managing the property. Alternatively, a ground lease may be proposed by a tenant that does not wish to invest its own funds in the land but is willing to erect improvements for its own use and at its own risk.

## Assignments and Subleases

If the premises fail to meet the tenant's needs, or if the tenant can no longer afford the lease, it may wish to assign or sublease the property. An *assignment* of a lease is a permanent transfer of the lease to a third party. The third party acquires the tenant's rights under the lease; however, the tenant remains liable for the rent if the third party defaults unless the lessor has agreed to look only to the third party. A *sublease* is a temporary transfer of the lease to a third party.

Landlords may be hesitant to grant the tenant the right to assign or sublease to a stranger, however. Moreover, landlords are often concerned about the financial wherewithal of any assignees or sublessees. Therefore, most leases require the landlord's written consent for an assignment or a sublease. Most landlords are willing to provide in the lease that they will not withhold consent unreasonably, and some leases allow for assignment without the landlord's consent if the assignee has the same credit rating as the assignor. In an escalating market, a lease may develop a substantial bonus value if market rents exceed the rent due under the lease. Therefore, the landlord may condition the assignment or sublease on the tenant's paying over any bonus value or splitting it with the landlord.

## Hidden Issues

Leases, especially commercial and retail leases, invariably contain a dizzying number of provisions and terms. Most of these terms are straightforward, but they should *always* be reviewed carefully to find any possible out clauses, also known as *early termination clauses.* Any provision that would allow the lessor or lessee to cancel the lease without completing the full term or paying the complete value of the lease is considered an *out clause.* Most leases contain a few standard out clauses involving complete destruction of the property, and all leases are subject to implied out clauses such as frustration of purpose.[12] Some leases, however, contain terms that

12. If a lessee enters into a lease with a lessor for a very specific purpose (for example, a reporter rents a room in London for a month to see a coronation), but that purpose is then frustrated by events over which the party wishing to terminate the lease had no control (the royal family announces they will move the coronation to Windsor Castle), then a court may void the lease because its purpose (to see the coronation) has been frustrated and release the lessee from its obligation to pay any further rent. *See* Krell v. Henry, 2 K.B. 740 (C.A. 1903).

ordinarily would not be grounds for invalidating the entire lease. For example, an owner of a mall may guarantee that it will maintain a certain percentage of occupancy. If occupancy drops below that percentage, the tenant may have the right to opt out of the lease. These clauses can easily be lost in a lease of twenty-five pages or more but can become very important if such circumstances ever come to pass.

## Government Regulation of Land Use

Land use is most heavily regulated at the local level, although several states regulate at least some aspects of land use on a regional or statewide level. For example, the state of Florida has preempted the authority of local jurisdictions to regulate land use. Federal and state laws concerning environmental matters, such as air and water quality and the protection of wetlands and endangered species, can also affect the permitted uses of property.

The discussion that follows first outlines federal and state regulations, then explains general principles of local land-use regulation. Each state has its own scheme for land-use regulation at the local level. Local regulatory systems operating under a state's scheme may vary from city to city, although some states require more uniformity than others ("city" is used here to refer to both cities and counties unless otherwise noted). The specific laws and regulations applicable in each state and local jurisdiction must be consulted to understand how land use in that jurisdiction is regulated.

### THE NATIONAL ENVIRONMENTAL POLICY ACT

The National Environmental Policy Act (NEPA)[13] requires all federal agencies to preserve and enhance the environment so that "man and nature can exist in productive harmony, and fulfill the social, economic, and other requirements of present and future generations of Americans." To implement this goal, NEPA requires all agencies of the federal government to consider the environmental consequences of their actions. As part of any proposal for legislation or other major federal action that may significantly affect the quality of the environment, the government must include an *environmental impact statement (EIS)*. The EIS considers (1) the environmental impact of the proposed action, (2) any adverse environmental effects that the proposed action would unavoidably have, (3) alternatives to the proposed action, (4) the relationship between the short-term uses of the environment and the maintenance and enhancement of long-term productivity, and (5) any irretrievable commitments of resources that the proposed action would involve.

13. 42 U.S.C. §§ 4321 *et seq.*

#### *EIS Requirement*

Some federal actions are categorically exempt from the EIS requirement because they do not have any environmental impact. If an action is not categorically exempt, the agency involved prepares an *environmental assessment (EA)*, which identifies any significant impact on the environment. If the EA indicates that the action will not have a significant impact on the environment, no EIS is prepared. If there may be a significant impact, an EIS is required. In some cases, courts have determined that an EIS may not be required when the agency proposing the action performs an environmental review substantially equivalent to an EIS.

#### *State Law Counterparts*

Most states have adopted environmental quality laws similar to NEPA, which require state and local agencies to consider the environmental impact of their decisions. NEPA and its state law counterparts are enforced mainly through litigation by persons who wish to challenge a governmental agency's decision. NEPA and state law complaints have been used extensively by groups opposing real estate developments and federal leases of public lands for private use. Such litigation can delay projects for many years.

#### *Planning*

Planning for compliance with NEPA or its state law counterparts is an important part of planning for any business project that requires state or federal decisions, approvals, or permits. This means not only preparing an EIS, if required, but also planning the project to minimize adverse effects on the environment.

### THE POLICE POWER

The legal basis for land-use planning and regulation is the *police power,* that is, the inherent authority of a city or county to protect the health, safety, and welfare of its residents. The courts have been giving the scope of the police power wider and wider interpretation. Its exercise is no longer limited to addressing immediate threats to the public health and safety, such as fires or unsanitary conditions. The U.S. Supreme Court explained:

> The concept of the public welfare is broad and inclusive. . . . The values it represents are spiritual as well as physical, aesthetic as well as monetary. It is within the power of the Legislature to determine that the community should be beautiful as well as healthy, spacious as well as clean, well-balanced as well as carefully patrolled.[14]

Under this broad reading of public welfare, regulations as varied as architectural review, rent control, limitations on condominium conversions, and restrictions on off-site advertising signs have all been upheld as being appropriate uses of a city's police power.

## Rent Control

In 1999, the California Supreme Court upheld the City of Santa Monica's rent control law, which, among other things, established maximum allowable rents, provided for adjustments of allowable rents, and prohibited evictions except in specified circumstances.[15] The law's stated purpose was to prevent owners from exploiting a growing shortage of affordable housing units by charging unreasonably high rents. A landlord challenged the rent control law, arguing that it did not accomplish its stated purpose but rather caused "gentrification" in Santa Monica.

The California Supreme Court "recogniz[ed] the well-established case law of the United States Supreme Court and of this court holding that ordinary rent control statutes are generally constitutionally permissible exercises of governmental authority," but the court also noted that particular decisions of public agencies charged with administering rent control may be deemed to be unconstitutional if they deprive landlords of a fair rate of return. In addition, rent control laws must possess certain structural features that safeguard against confiscatory results. The Fifth Amendment is violated when a land-use regulation "does not substantially advance legitimate state interests."

The court concluded that the prevention of "excessive and unreasonable rent increases" was a legitimate government interest, regardless of whether the primary beneficiaries of this protection were tenants with low income or merely moderate income. The court explained: "[W]ith rent control, as with most other such social and economic legislation, we leave to legislative bodies rather than the courts to evaluate whether the legislation has fallen so far short of its goals as to warrant repeal or amendment."

**INTERNATIONAL SNAPSHOT**

Nation-states have the right to expropriate or nationalize foreign property under the power of eminent domain. Western countries tend to consider expropriation or nationalization proper as long as (1) it is for a legitimate public purpose, (2) it does not discriminate against a particular class of foreigners, and (3) the state promptly pays fair compensation. Many emerging countries object to having to pay fair market value for expropriated property, citing, among other things, the history of European imperialism and colonialism.

## Regulatory Takings

Although the range of activities a city can engage in is broad, there are limitations to the police power. A land-use regulation will be upheld if it is reasonably related to the public welfare, but the city may not act arbitrarily or capriciously in enacting or applying land-use regulations. In addition, regulations are sometimes challenged on the ground that they amount to a taking of the property without just compensation, in violation of the Fifth Amendment to the U.S. Constitution (made applicable to the states by the Fourteenth Amendment).

The U.S. Supreme Court has stated that a *regulatory taking* (sometimes referred to as *inverse condemnation*) has occurred if the regulation either (1) does not substantially advance legitimate state interests or (2) denies the owner all economically viable use of its land.[16]

In *Penn Central Transportation Co. v. City of New York*,[17] the U.S. Supreme Court held that the City of New York did not effect a taking requiring just compensation when it denied Penn Central permission to build a fifty-story office building over Grand Central Terminal. New York City had designated Grand Central a landmark under the Landmarks Preservation Law, which restricted the owner's right to substantially alter the building. Although the application for the construction of the building met all local zoning requirements, Penn Central was denied permission under the landmarks law. Rejecting Penn Central's claim that the application of the landmarks law had deprived it of its property without

14. Berman v. Parker, 348 U.S. 26 (1954).

15. SMB, Ltd. v. Superior Court of Los Angeles County, 968 P.2d 993 (Cal. 1999), *cert. denied,* 526 U.S. 1131 (1999). Cf. Chevron USA, Inc. v. Lingle, 363 F.3d 846 (9th Cir. 2004), *cert. granted,* 125 S. Ct. 314 (2004) (rent cap on service station leases did not achieve state's goal of lowering retail gas prices and was therefore an unconstitutional regulatory taking).

16. Agins v. Tiburon, 447 U.S. 255, 260 (1980).

17. 438 U.S. 104 (1978).

just compensation, the Supreme Court emphasized that application of the law did not interfere with "Penn Central's primary expectation concerning the use of the parcel" or prevent Penn Central from earning a "reasonable return" on its investment.

In *Lucas v. South Carolina Coastal Council*,[18] the U.S. Supreme Court considered whether South Carolina's desire to prevent harmful or noxious uses justified its Beachfront Management Act. The Act effectively barred Lucas, the owner of two residential lots purchased in 1986 for $975,000, from erecting any permanent structure on his parcels. The Supreme Court held that if the Act did no more than duplicate the result under the state's common law nuisance law, then no compensation would be required. But, if the Act prohibited an activity not prohibited by common law nuisance and denied the owner all economically viable use of his land, then compensation may be required. The Court put the burden of proof on the state to show that its regulation was not a taking.

In *Palazzolo v. State of Rhode Island*, a thirty-year legal battle came to an end when the U.S. Supreme Court ruled that landowners may challenge regulations they consider to be takings requiring compensation even if the regulations were already in place at the time the property was purchased.[19] In the past, it was assumed that anyone purchasing property with regulatory restrictions on it was paying a lower price and purchasing the property with the understanding that its use was restricted. *Palazzolo* represented a major expansion extension of the rights theretofore generally reserved for owners who owned property that was later burdened by regulations.

In the following case, the U.S. Supreme Court considered whether a five-year moratorium on development constitutes a taking.

18. 505 U.S. 1003 (1992).

19. 533 U.S. 606 (2001).

A CASE IN POINT

**CASE 18.3**

**Tahoe-Sierra Preservation Council Inc. v. Tahoe Regional Planning Agency**

*Supreme Court of the United States*

*535 U.S. 302 (2002).*

## Summary

**› FACTS** The plaintiffs owned property in the Lake Tahoe Basin. Due to rapid development of the basin, nutrients were increasingly being washed into Lake Tahoe, where they encouraged the growth of algae, which caused the lake to become more and more green and opaque. To halt the increasing environmental damage, Congress approved the bistate Tahoe Regional Planning Compact in 1969. The Compact created the Tahoe Regional Planning Agency (TRPA) and set goals for preserving Lake Tahoe and the surrounding basin.

The 1969 Compact was amended in 1980 to provide for the adoption of a new regional plan. The 1980 Compact directed the TRPA to review all projects and to establish temporary restrictions on development in the basin pending formulation of a new regional land-use plan. To comply with the 1980 Compact, the TRPA enacted an ordinance that temporarily prohibited construction in several classes of land in the basin, with some possibility of exception. The moratorium continued for about thirty-two months between 1981 and 1984 until a new land-use plan was issued. Because that plan was challenged as too lenient, development permits were withheld for several more years.

The landowners whose rights to develop property were suspended during the moratorium sued the TRPA claiming, among other things, that the moratorium constituted a taking. They argued that because their use was limited, they were automatically entitled to compensation for that loss. The district court ruled that certain property owners in the basin were entitled to compensation, and the TRPA appealed.

**› ISSUE PRESENTED** Did the "temporary" moratorium on property development in the Lake Tahoe Basin constitute an unconstitutional taking of property?

**› SUMMARY OF OPINION** The U.S. Supreme Court began by noting the exceptional beauty and uniqueness of Lake Tahoe and then described the history that led to the

*(Continued)*

(Case 18.3 *continued*)

TRPA's creation. The Court then distinguished between a physical taking of property for public use and regulatory takings limiting the private use of land. The Fifth Amendment guarantees compensation for physical takings but is silent when it comes to regulatory takings. The Court concluded that prior rulings did not guarantee compensation in the absence of a physical taking. The owner is automatically entitled to compensation for a regulatory taking only when the regulation removes all the economic value of a piece of property. In all other cases, courts must look to see whether the "regulatory taking went too far," based on "essentially ad hoc, factual inquiries."

The Court then considered whether the regulations were in the interests of "fairness and justice." The temporary nature of the regulation weighed against a finding of a taking. More importantly, imposing strict compensation rules on future decision-making bodies like the TRPA might cause them to be less likely to make fair and just decisions out of fear that the costs might be prohibitive. The need to keep these bodies objective and focused on making the most socially beneficial decisions, despite the costs, was a major factor in the Court's decision.

**› RESULT** The temporary moratorium was not an unconstitutional taking, so the landowners were entitled to no compensation.

**› COMMENTS** Takings questions also arise when a regulatory agency imposes a condition that must be satisfied before a building permit or other land-use approval is granted. This is addressed later in this chapter as part of the discussion of regulatory schemes.

## Regulatory Schemes

The fundamental components of most land-use regulatory schemes are a general plan, a zoning ordinance, and a subdivision ordinance. Some jurisdictions also employ more specialized planning documents, often called specific plans or community plans, that function somewhere between the general plan and the zoning ordinances.

### The General Plan

Many cities have a general development plan, known variously as the general plan, city plan, master plan, or comprehensive plan. (All such plans are referred to in this chapter as the general plan.) A ***general plan*** is a long-range planning document that addresses the physical development and redevelopment of a city. It is comprehensive in that it addresses the entire city and a wide range of concerns, such as housing, natural resources, public facilities, transportation, and the permitted locations for various land uses. It includes goals, objectives, policies, and programs related to these concerns.

The practical effect of the general plan varies from state to state. In some states, a general plan is not required at all. In certain states, the general plan is strictly an advisory document that need not be adhered to when planning decisions are made. In other states, the plan functions as the "constitution" for development, and by law, planning decisions (such as zoning, subdivision approval, and road and sewer construction) must be consistent with it. When the general plan has this significance, anyone contemplating development of a specific piece of property should determine what the general plan says about the allowed uses for that property. The general plan may also provide important information about the city's policies regarding growth, where and when public services and facilities will be provided, and whether developers will be expected to provide or pay for needed infrastructure.

If development of the type contemplated is not authorized by the general plan, a general plan amendment will be required. The general plan may also be amended to preclude a contemplated development. Authorization of a type of development in the general plan is not, however, a guarantee that a specific development will be permitted. The development must also be authorized by the zoning ordinance, and other land-use approvals could be required.

## Other Planning Documents

Some jurisdictions employ other planning documents in addition to the general plan. Called *specific plans, special plans, community plans, area plans,* and a number of other names, these plans usually encompass just a portion of the city's geographic area. They may focus on areas in particular need of planning, such as a downtown area slated for redevelopment, an environmentally sensitive area, a transportation corridor, or an area facing unusual development pressure. Typically, these plans are more detailed than the general plan.

## Zoning

*Zoning* is the division of a city into districts and the application of specific land-use regulations in each district. Zoning regulations are divided into two classes: (1) regulations regarding the structural and architectural design of buildings (such as height or bulk limitations), and (2) regulations regarding the uses, such as commercial or residential, to which buildings within a particular district may be put. These types of regulations are employed both in traditional zoning systems and in more recently developed approaches to zoning.

### Traditional Zoning

Traditional zoning separates different land uses. For example, residential areas are separate from commercial and industrial areas, and residential areas of varying densities are separate. This approach to zoning finds its roots in the earliest land-use regulations, which promoted health and safety by separating residences from certain types of manufacturing and service industries. Early zoning also protected property values by preventing apartments from being built near more desirable single-family dwellings.

### Planned Unit Development

Although many cities still employ some form of traditional zoning, others have adopted different approaches. For example, under *planned unit development (PUD)* zoning, the land-use regulations for a given piece of property reflect the proposed development plans for that property. These plans may include a mixture of uses, such as residential, office, and retail commercial, which could not be accommodated under the separation of uses required by traditional zoning. Residential development may be clustered on a portion of the property, creating densities higher than those permitted under traditional zoning but also providing larger areas of open space. Planned offices or industrial parks may be subject to covenants and restrictions such as regulated setbacks or signage. Many feel that this more flexible approach to zoning allows more creativity and shows greater sensitivity to environmental and aesthetic concerns.

### Zoning Relief

Variances and conditional-use permits may create exceptions to a zoning ordinance. A *variance* allows a landowner to construct a structure or to carry on an activity not otherwise permitted under the zoning regulations. It allows the property owner to use the property in a manner basically consistent with the established regulations, with such minor variations as are necessary to avoid inflicting a unique hardship on that property owner. In some states, variances may be granted to allow uses not authorized by the zoning regulations. In other states, variances are limited to sanctioning deviations from regulations governing physical standards, such as minimum lot size, the maximum number of square feet that may be developed, and off-street parking requirements.

A *conditional-use permit* allows uses that are not permitted as a matter of right under the zoning ordinance. The permit imposes conditions to ensure that the use will be appropriate for the particular situation.

### Nonconforming Uses

A *nonconforming use* is an existing use that was originally lawful but does not comply with a later-enacted zoning ordinance. A zoning ordinance may not compel immediate discontinuance of a nonconforming use (unless it constitutes a public nuisance). A city can, however, require that nonconforming uses be eliminated within a reasonable time or upon application for a building permit to modify the premises.

## Subdivision

Frequently, development requires the division of land into separate parcels. This process is known as *subdivision.* It is a necessary step in residential development and often in industrial or commercial development.

The subdivision process allows the city to regulate new development and to limit harm, deterioration of water quality, soil erosion, and building in areas subject to earth movement. The subdivider may also be required to address, for example, the impact of the subdivision on views and other aesthetic concerns or on traffic circulation.

Frequently, to win approval for a subdivision, the subdivider must provide streets, utilities, sewers, drainage facilities, and other infrastructure to serve the subdivision. It may also be required to dedicate land for parks, schools, libraries, and fire stations and to pay impact fees to offset the increased burden on public facilities and services resulting from the subdivision. The conditions may include constructing on-site or off-site facilities or paying fees for purposes as varied as acquiring parkland or providing day-care centers, public art, or low-income housing.

## CONDITIONS

Conditions to a land-use approval will be upheld if they are reasonably related to the burdens on the community created by the development being approved. Thus, if the development will result in an influx of residents or employees, a fee to fund traffic improvements made necessary by that influx will be upheld. In the absence of the legally required relationship between a condition to an approval and the impacts of the development being approved (the *nexus*), the condition may be struck down as an unconstitutional taking.

For example, in the case of *Nollan v. California Coastal Commission,*[20] James and Marilyn Nollan sought a permit from the California Coastal Commission to demolish their existing single-story beachfront house and replace it with a two-story, three-bedroom house approximately three times larger than the existing structure. Public beaches were located within one-half mile to the north and south of the Nollans' property. Finding that the new house would further obstruct the ocean view, increase private use of the beach, and establish a "psychological barrier" to access to the nearby public beaches, the commission approved the construction subject to the condition that the Nollans dedicate an easement for public access across the portion of their property lying between the high-water mark and a sea wall approximately ten feet inland. The Nollans challenged this condition.

The U.S. Supreme Court held that the dedication condition amounted to an unconstitutional taking because it did not substantially advance a legitimate governmental interest. The Court found no nexus between the requirement of an easement for public access and the stated interest of reducing obstacles to the ocean view as well as "psychological barriers" to using the beach. The Court concluded by saying that if the government wanted an easement across the Nollans' property, "it must pay for it."

In *Dolan v. City of Tigard,*[21] the Supreme Court held that there has to be a showing of "rough proportionality" between the conditions imposed on a permit and the nature and extent of the proposed development's impact. The Court ruled that a city could not require Dolan to dedicate a portion of her property to a pedestrian/bicycle pathway as a condition to permitting the expansion of her retail sales facility. The Court acknowledged that the enlarged retail sales facility would increase traffic on the streets of the central business district by roughly 435 additional trips per day. The Court also noted that dedications for streets, sidewalks, and other public ways are generally reasonable exactions to avoid excessive congestion for a proposed property use. The Court concluded, however, that the city had not met its burden of demonstrating that the additional number of vehicle and bicycle trips generated by Dolan's development was reasonably related to the city's requirement for dedication of the pedestrian/bicycle easement. Thus, the exaction amounted to an unconstitutional taking.

In *Monterey v. Del Monte Dunes at Monterey, Ltd.,*[22] the U.S. Supreme Court held that *Dolan*'s rough proportionality test applied only to exactions and not to outright denials of permission to develop. The Court explained:

> Although in a general sense concerns for proportionality animate the Takings Clause, we have not extended the rough proportionality test of *Dolan* beyond the special context of exactions—land-use decisions conditioning approval of development on the dedication of property to public use. The rule applied in *Dolan* considers whether dedications demanded as conditions of development are proportional to the development's anticipated impacts. It was not designed to address, and is not readily applicable to, the much different questions arising where, as here, the landowner's challenge is based not on excessive exactions but on denial of development. We believe, accordingly, that the rough proportionality test of *Dolan* is inapposite to a case such as this one.

A city's imposition of a condition on the grant of a permit can also be evaluated under the Equal Protection Clause. In a case decided in 2000, the U.S. Supreme Court recognized that a valid claim for relief existed when a village "intentionally demanded a 33-foot easement as a condition to connecting [one property owner's] property to the municipal water supply where the village required only a 15-foot easement from similarly situated property owners."[23]

20. 483 U.S. 825 (1987).
21. 512 U.S. 374 (1994).
22. 526 U.S. 687 (1999).
23. Village of Willowbrook v. Olech, 528 U.S. 562 (2000).

POLITICAL PERSPECTIVE

## OREGON LAND-USE REFERENDUM COULD END THIRTY YEARS OF SMART GROWTH

On November 2, 2004, voters in Oregon passed by a 60-to-40 percent margin Measure 37, a ballot measure that requires fair compensation to landowners when environmental or zoning regulations reduce the value of their property. Four other states—Florida, Texas, Louisiana, and Mississippi—enacted similar laws in the wake of the 1994 Republican "Contract with America," but these laws require compensation for property owners only if newly enacted land-use regulations reduce the property value by at least 25 percent. In contrast, Measure 37 requires cities and counties to either (1) pay fair market compensation for *any* diminution in value due to land-use regulations enacted after the purchase of the property or (2) exempt the property owner from the regulation. Rules enacted to meet federal requirements or to protect the community from public nuisances and safety hazards will not trigger a right to compensation.

Proponents of Measure 37 ran a populist campaign with the slogan "Government should pay if it affects your property."[a] One advertisement depicted a woman penalized for "destroying a potential wildlife habitat" after she cut blackberry bushes in her backyard in Portland. Another featured a 92-year-old woman who bought land in the hills west of Portland in 1953 and was still fighting to get approval to sell several building lots out of the twenty acres she still owned.[b]

Property owners in rural areas were particularly critical of "urban policy makers and the urban elite," who established urban growth boundaries around cities and tried to keep development within them.[c] Houses could be built on farmland only under strict conditions; nonfarm dwellings were allowed only in areas with poor soil. Farmers complained that Oregon's 31-year-old land-use regulations left them with insignificant funds for retirement and unfairly forced property owners, rather than taxpayers, to pay the cost of socially imposed goals.[d]

The *Oregonian*, the state's largest newspaper, cautioned that cash-strapped local governments would not be able to afford to pay compensation so "most cities and counties would fold quickly [and waive the restrictions], and Oregon's land-use laws would crumple with them."[e] Others warned that the measure would result in "a blanket of subdivisions, 'ranchettes' and shopping centers sprawling over what was once Western Oregon's beautiful and fertile Williamette Valley."[f] Robert Liberty, a former president of 1,000 Friends of Oregon, an avid pro-planning group, who was just elected to the Portland regional planning agency board, argued: "Quality of life is something that is shared. A golf course is not. A four-car garage is not. One of the best things about the planning process is that it makes a better community for everyone, regardless of income."[g]

Former Maryland governor Parris N. Glendening called the implications of Measure 37 "devastating"[h] and predicted that property-rights activists would push similar initiatives in other states. "Oregon is still the premier state in terms of land-use issues," according to Gerrit Knaap, director of the National Center for Smart Growth Research and Education at the University of Maryland.[i] "If this happens in Oregon, it strikes fear into planners everywhere."[j]

a. Timothy B. Wheeler, *Md. Edgy as Ore. Eases Sprawl Curbs,* BALTIMORE SUN, Dec. 2, 2004, at 1B.

b. Felicity Barringer, *Property Right Law May Alter Oregon Landscape,* N.Y. TIMES, Nov. 26, 2004, at A3.

c. *Id.*

d. Thomas Bray, *Oregon Flashes Caution to Environmental Left,* DETROIT NEWS, Dec. 8, 2004, at 11A.

e. *Oregon Voters Deal Blow to Good Planning,* NEWS TRIBUNE (Tacoma, Washington), Nov. 28, 2004, at B10.

f. *Id.*

g. Barringer, *supra* note b.

h. Wheeler, *supra* note a.

i. *Id.*

j. *Id.*

## ENVIRONMENTAL ASSESSMENT

Some states, before approving a development project, require a detailed evaluation of the effects of the project on the environment. The state may also require the developer to discuss alternatives to the proposed project and identify measures that would mitigate adverse environmental effects.

## VESTED DEVELOPMENT RIGHTS

Until a developer obtains a *vested right*—that is, a fully guaranteed right—to develop a property, the regulations governing that property may be changed. In other words, a developer has no claim to the land-use regulations in effect when the property was acquired, when preliminary steps to development were taken, or at any

> **IN BRIEF**
>
> **Limits on Land-Use Regulation**
>
> 1. Regulation must be reasonably related to the public welfare.
> 2. Regulation cannot deny the owner all economically viable use of its land.
> 3. Regulation must substantially advance legitimate state interests.
> 4. Conditions to a land-use approval must be reasonably related to the burdens on the community created by the development being approved (nexus).
> 5. There must be rough proportionality between the conditions imposed and the nature and extent of the proposed development's impact.

other time prior to the vesting of the right to develop. A change in the land-use regulations prior to vesting may, therefore, preclude a development that would have been permissible under the regulations in force at the time the property was acquired.

In some states, the right to develop vests when substantial work is done and substantial liabilities are incurred in reliance on a building permit. In other states, vesting is tied to obtaining the "last discretionary approval" required for development. States differ on what constitutes the last discretionary approval.

### *Early Vesting*

Mechanisms to allow early vesting are available in several states. One such mechanism is a development agreement, which is authorized in Arizona, California, Colorado, Florida, Hawaii, and Nevada. The development project is governed by the land-use regulations in effect when the agreement is entered into and is immune from subsequent changes in the regulations.

## Physical Accessibility to Commercial Facilities

Under the Americans with Disabilities Act (ADA),[24] any new renovations or alterations to commercial facilities must be accessible to disabled persons, including those in wheelchairs. The Act defines "commercial facilities" as all structures except those intended for residential use. This accessibility rule applies only to the areas being renovated, and it requires compliance only to the extent feasible.

New construction, on the other hand, is subject to more complex accessibility rules. In building new structures, architects and builders must comply with regulations established by the U.S. attorney general regarding accessibility. In general, new structures must be designed and constructed so that they are "readily accessible to and usable by individuals with disabilities," unless it is structurally impossible to do so.

Violation of the physical-accessibility rules for renovations and new construction can result in a private lawsuit or action by the U.S. attorney general. Violators may be required to pay damages as well as civil penalties of up to $50,000 for a first violation and $100,000 for subsequent violations.

The ADA also requires minor physical changes to existing workplaces to accommodate disabled workers. For example, the ADA mandates removal of architectural barriers in existing stores, offices, and firms where the removal is "readily achievable." Modifications are readily achievable if they are easy to accomplish and can be done without significant expense. Readily achievable changes might include ramping a few steps or lowering a public telephone for wheelchair users, installing grab bars in rest rooms, putting raised letters and numerals on elevator controls, and rearranging office furniture to provide increased accessibility.

In addition, the ADA prohibits discrimination on the basis of disability in the enjoyment of "goods, services, facilities, privileges, advantages, or accommodations of any place of public accommodation." "Public accommodation" is defined to include, among other things, a restaurant, place of lodging, place of entertainment, place of public gathering, and place of exercise or recreation. The prohibited discrimination need not be at a physical location; screening or eligibility requirements imposed from a central location that the disabled person may never actually visit also qualifies under the ADA.[25] Similarly, some experts believe that the ADA will be applied to require certain websites to adopt special coding or features to provide access to the disabled.[26]

In *Stevens v. Premier Cruises,*[27] the plaintiff, who was confined to a wheelchair, sued Premier Cruises for failing

24. 42 U.S.C. §§ 12101 *et seq.*

25. Rendon v. Valleycrest Prods. Ltd., 294 F.3d 1279 (11th Cir. 2002) (automated telephone system to screen game show contestants may violate ADA).

26. *See Disabled Access Laws and Internet Web Sites—An Unsettled Area,* 72 U.S.L.W. 2371–73 (Jan. 6, 2004): Doe v. Mutual of Omaha Ins. Co., 179 F.3d 557 (7th Cir. 1999).

27. 215 F.3d 1237 (11th Cir. 2000).

to make all areas of the cruise ship wheelchair accessible. The U.S. Court of Appeals for the Eleventh Circuit ruled that "those portions of the cruise ship that come within the statutory definition of 'public accommodation' are subject to the public accommodation provisions" of the ADA. In contrast, the Third Circuit ruled that arenas subject to the ADA do not have to provide spectators in wheelchairs sight lines over standing spectators.[28] The Ninth Circuit took the opposite view in the following case.

28. Caruse v. Blockbuster–Sony Music Entm't Ctr. at the Waterfront, 193 F.3d 730 (3d Cir. 1999).

A CASE IN POINT

## In the Language of the Court

**CASE 18.4**

**Oregon Paralyzed Veterans of America v. Regal Cinemas Inc.**

*United States Court of Appeals for the Ninth Circuit 339 F.3d 1126 (9th Cir. 2003), cert. denied, 124 S. Ct. 2903 (2004).*

**› FACTS** The Oregon Paralyzed Veterans of America and three of its members brought suit under the ADA against two movie theater companies that owned and operated theaters in Oregon. The plaintiffs claimed that the cinemas did not provide wheelchair-bound patrons with "lines of sight" comparable to those provided to the general public who did not use wheelchairs. The lower court granted summary judgment to the movie theater companies, and the plaintiffs appealed.

**› ISSUE PRESENTED** Are theaters legally obligated to provide the same or comparable lines of sight for their handicapped patrons?

**› OPINION** FLETCHER, J., writing for the U.S. Court of Appeals for the Ninth Circuit:

In order to get to the seats in the stadium riser section, patrons must walk up stairs on either side of the seating section. The riser seats are not wheelchair-accessible. In all six theaters, seating for disabled patrons is located only in the first five rows; in five of the six theaters, wheelchair-accessible seating is located only on the sloped portion of the floor, not in the aisle or in the stadium seating, with over half of the accessible seats in the very front row. The result is that all patrons who require wheelchairs have no choice but to sit in the first few rows of the theater. . . . As the appellants [the Oregon Paralyzed Veterans and its members] point out, locating all of the wheelchair-accessible seating in the first few rows of the theaters creates significant disadvantages for wheelchair-bound patrons. Plaintiffs' experts, who visited the theaters and conducted research there, found that the vertical lines of sight for the wheelchair seating locations ranged from 24 to 60 degrees, with an average of approximately 42 degrees, as compared with the average median line of sight of 20 degrees in the non-wheelchair seating—a difference the experts termed a "tremendous disparity."

In its engineering guideline for movie theaters, the Society of Motion Picture and Television Engineers (SMPTE) concluded that, for most viewers, physical discomfort occurs when the vertical viewing angle to the top of the screen exceeds 35 degrees. . . .

In addition to ensuring that everyone will see well, seating in the effective cine theater must avoid physical discomfort, which occurs when the vertical viewing angle to the top of the screen image is excessive or the lateral viewing angle to the centerline of the screen requires uncomfortable head and/or body position. . . .

One of the central goals of Title III of the ADA is to ensure that people with disabilities have access to "the full and equal enjoyment of the goods, services, facilities, privileges, advantages, or accommodations of any place of public accommodation." In the theaters at issue in this case, wheelchair-bound movie theater patrons must sit in seats that are objectively uncomfortable, requiring them to crane their necks and twist their bodies in order to see the screen, while non-disabled patrons have a wide

*(Continued)*

(Case 18.4 *continued*)

range of comfortable viewing locations from which to choose. We find it simply inconceivable that this arrangement could constitute "full and equal enjoyment" of movie theater services by disabled patrons.

**› RESULT** The summary judgment for the defendants was reversed, and summary judgment was entered for the plaintiffs.

**› CRITICAL THINKING QUESTIONS**

1. The original case of this kind, *Lara v. Cinemark USA Inc.,*[29] found that the phrase "equal line of sight" meant an unobstructed view. To what extent, if at all, does *Regal Cinemas* require more than just an unobstructed view?
2. Would the ADA still apply if theater owners decided to classify their theaters as private clubs and allowed only "members" to watch movies?

29. 531 U.S. 944 (2000).

---

The ADA also prohibits discrimination on the basis of disability by public entities. In *MX Group Inc. v. Covington, Ky.,*[30] the U.S. Court of Appeals for the Sixth Circuit reviewed the denial of a permit to a group that sought to establish a methadone clinic for recovering drug addicts. The city of Covington, Kentucky, refused to grant the permit for the clinic due to concerns about a possible increase in crime and drug use if the clinic were located in the area. MX Group, Inc. brought an action to enjoin Covington to grant the permit on behalf of heroin addicts under the ADA and the Vocational Rehabilitation Act. The court held that the ADA's prohibitions against discrimination on the basis of disability apply to zoning and permits. The court emphasized that the goal of the ADA is to protect disabled individuals from deprivations based on prejudice, stereotypes, or unfounded fears and characterized the city's fears as based on just such assumptions.

If a significant risk is present, then to be qualified for protection under the ADA, a party must show that the risk can be ameliorated by reasonable modifications. If it cannot be ameliorated, ADA protections are unavailable.

Whether a significant risk exists turns on an individualized assessment of the nature, duration, and severity of the risk and the probability that the potential injury will actually occur.

Thus, when determining whether a significant risk exists, a court must distinguish legitimate concerns from mere expressions of prejudice, stereotypes, and unfounded fears.

30. 293 F.3d 326 (6th Cir. 2002).

## THE RESPONSIBLE MANAGER

## BUYING AND USING REAL ESTATE

The typical manager who does not deal with real estate full-time will probably find that there are more laws, administrative regulations, and governmental practices associated with real estate than with many other management activities. The manager will not always be able to rely on common sense in managing real estate because the laws and administrative practices can have surprising effects.

Before acquiring real estate, the manager should (1) determine whether the property is properly located for the company's operations; (2) determine whether the improvements, if already built, comply with applicable building codes and are suitable for the company; (3) determine whether the facility complies with physical-accessibility regulations under the Americans with

*(Continued)*

(The Responsible Manager *continued*)

Disabilities Act; (4) determine whether previous owners have fully complied with federal, state, and local environmental and hazardous-waste laws and confirm that the company will not be liable under any of those laws; (5) decide whether the company should lease or buy the property; (6) decide, if the property is rental property, for how long and under what terms it should be leased; (7) decide, if the property is for sale, how best to negotiate the purchase contract and finance the purchase; and (8) keep senior executives and/or the board of directors informed about the manager's actions and decisions throughout the process.

The magnitude of the investment and the permanence of the acquisition render these decisions some of the most important that a manager will make. Although large corporations generally have a department for facilities management, smaller organizations do not. The manager will need to have access to responsible professionals, including knowledgeable commercial/industrial real estate brokers, attorneys who specialize in real estate, environmental consultants, and attorneys specializing in environmental law. If the company is acquiring bare land and building its own improvements, the manager will also need to have available expertise in planning and land use. With the heavy use of outside consultants comes the responsibility of managing the consultants and controlling the costs.

Similar responsibilities accompany the occupancy of real estate. If a company occupies premises under a *full-service lease,* which requires the lessor to maintain the property, the tenant's responsibilities may be limited to seeing that the services provided are adequate. Most manufacturing companies, however, do not occupy leased premises on a full-service basis. Thus, management may be responsible for continuing maintenance, repairs, and compliance with laws, including environmental laws. In any type of occupancy, management must always plan ahead to ensure that the facilities will continue to be adequate for present and future operations. It is often difficult to anticipate future needs, and it is easy to overspend or, conversely, to fail to anticipate a new demand.

Finally, the manager is likely to find that he or she has less control than desired over real estate decisions. For example, building or other occupancy permits may need to be obtained from several agencies, such as building departments and fire departments. Those agencies may not be responsive to a company's urgent demands, and the officials involved may have a great deal of discretion in both the timing and the interpretation of the applicable laws. Delays beyond the company's control frequently try managers' patience and cause inconvenience and downtime. In either the acquisition or the disposition phase, a manager is well advised to allow considerable extra time for delay.

INSIDE STORY

## RECLAIMING BROWNFIELDS

For decades, so-called brownfields—such as dumps, landfills, and abandoned factory lots with actual or suspected hazardous contamination—have gone unused even though they are often in exceptional locations. In large part because of their often unique locations, these long neglected eyesores are now being reclaimed and are once again thriving.[31]

For example, a group of investors was willing to invest $30 million in the twenty-year-old town dump in Carteret, New Jersey.[32] It may seem odd that anyone would be willing to invest millions simply to clean up an old dump, but when one considers that Carteret is within ten minutes of Newark Liberty International Airport and fifteen minutes from New York City, has an exit on the most traveled road in the country, and is in the middle of the most densely populated state in America, then the venerable business mantra of "location, location, location" takes on a new meaning.

In the last two decades, regulations aimed at curbing suburban sprawl have severely limited new commercial development, making brownfields some of the last suburban and urban land that can be developed into lucrative commercial complexes. Success stories include the Jersey Gardens Mall, which was built on a former city

*(Continued)*

31. This discussion is based in part on John Holusha, *Town Dump #146's Buried Treasure: Location,* N.Y. TIMES, Apr. 4, 2004, at 1.
32. *Id.*

(Inside Story *continued*)
dump in Elizabeth, New Jersey, just to the north of Carteret.

A key incentive for investors is the limited cleanup responsibility provided by the Small Business Liability Relief and Brownfields Revitalization Act of 2002[33] and its state counterparts. For years, environmental groups have lobbied for strict cleanup laws. CERCLA generally holds current owners, as well as the owners who polluted the property originally, jointly and severally liable for the costs of remediation. Thus, if developers buy a piece of property that requires cleanup, they stand a good chance of having to pay the entire cost even if it is so prohibitive as to make their original investment a loss.

The Brownfields Revitalization Act and related state legislation have changed that. The Act encourages private groups to attempt to clean up brownfields by letting them off the hook for the entire cleanup cost. If the buyer is a "bona fide prospective purchaser" (BFPP), as defined in the Act, then it can avoid liability for so-called legacy contamination, that is, waste disposed of on the site prior to the acquisition. To qualify as a *bona fide prospective purchaser,* the buyer cannot have contributed to the contamination of the brownfield in the first place. In addition, the buyer must (1) conduct a diligent investigation of the property and report any contamination to the appropriate governmental authorities; (2) exercise appropriate care concerning the contamination to stop future or continuing release of contaminants; (3) cooperate with any authorized group, including the federal government, to conduct a cleanup of the property; and (4) obey any land-use restrictions on the property.[34]

Groups, such as the one attempting to build in Carteret, know that if their allocated costs for cleanup exceed what is profitable, then they have the option to stop the cleanup and walk away from the investment. Even if the entire site is not completely restored, Carteret and the public will receive at least a partial cleanup of an unsightly lot. If the cleanup is successful, everyone wins.

33. P.L. 107–118.

34. David Farer, *Brownfields Redevelopment Initiatives: Federal and Selected State Developments, in* American Law Institute–American Bar Association, THE IMPACT OF ENVIRONMENTAL LAW ON REAL ESTATE TRANSACTIONS, 501–90 (2003).

## KEY WORDS AND PHRASES

adverse possession 678
after-acquired title 678
area plan 694
assignment 689
beneficiary 677
bona fide prospective purchaser (BFPP) 701
brownfield 684
*caveat emptor* 678
commercial lease 688
community plan 694
community property 676
conditional-use permit 694
constructive notice 680
conveyance 677
deed 677
deed of trust 685
development loans 686
dual agency 683
early termination clauses 689
encumbrance 681
environmental assessment (EA) 690
environmental impact statement (EIS) 690
equity 686
escrow 681
escrow agent 681
exclusive listing 682
fair lending laws 688
fee simple 677
foreclosure 688
full-service lease 700
gap financing 686
general plan 693
good faith subsequent purchaser 680
grant deed 678
grantee 677
grantor 677
ground lease 689
implied warranty of habitability 678
interim financing 686
inverse condemnation 691
joint tenancy 676
lessee 688
lessor 688
letter of intent 685
marketable title 677
mortgage 685
net listing 682
nexus 695
nonconforming use 694
open listing 682
operating lease 683
option contract 685
out clause 689
percentage rent clause 689
permanent loan 686
planned unit development (PUD) 694
points 686
police power 690
prepayment penalty 686
prime rate 686
pure notice statutes 680
quitclaim deed 678
race–notice statutes 680
race statutes 680

## QUESTIONS AND CASE PROBLEMS

1. Miller granted his neighbor a *view easement,* that is, an interest in Miller's property that entitled the neighbor to an unobstructed view. The easement was recorded. Miller later contracted to sell the property and disclosed the existence of the view easement to the buyer, Gazzo. A preliminary title report issued by Fidelity National Title Insurance Company failed to disclose the existence of the easement. Gazzo then requested that Fidelity investigate the possible existence of the easement. Fidelity assured Gazzo that the easement did not exist and maintained that, except for those items set forth in Fidelity's title report, Miller had free title. Miller executed a grant deed conveying the property to Gazzo.

   Gazzo later found out that the easement had in fact been recorded, and he recovered $125,000 from Fidelity for the diminution in the property's value as a result of the easement. Gazzo assigned any claim that he had against Miller to Fidelity, and Fidelity sued Miller for breach of warranty. Fidelity claimed that by executing the grant deed Miller had implicitly warranted that title to the property was being conveyed free of any encumbrances. Does Miller's prior disclosure of a recorded encumbrance to Gazzo prevent Fidelity from relying on the warranty against encumbrances that is typically implied in a seller's grant deed? [*Fidelity National Title Insurance Co. v. Miller,* 264 Cal. Rptr. 17 (Cal. Ct. App. 1989).]

2. Ace owns Blueacre, a forty-acre parcel of unimproved real estate on the outskirts of a burgeoning city in the state of Calvada. In June 1992, the legislature of Calvada approved the construction of a freeway adjacent to Blueacre. Shortly after the completion of the freeway in 1999, Ace was approached by Greenhorn, who desired to construct an apartment building on Blueacre. Greenhorn is a licensed general contractor previously employed by several large apartment building developers. Although Greenhorn could not arrange financing to purchase Blueacre outright, he was able to negotiate a sixty-year ground lease from Ace on the express condition that Greenhorn complete construction of the apartment building before July 1, 2004. The lease was duly executed by both Ace and Greenhorn, and a memorandum of the lease was legally recorded.

   Greenhorn obtained a $10 million loan at 10 percent interest that was due and payable on or before July 1, 2004, from Construction Lender. To secure repayment of the construction loan, Greenhorn executed a leasehold mortgage in favor of Construction Lender and legally recorded it.

   Concurrently with the funding of the construction loan, Greenhorn obtained a standby commitment from Permanent Lender to advance $10 million at 7 percent interest contingent on (1) the issuance of certificates of occupancy for 80 percent of the apartment building and (2) the leasing of 60 percent of the total rentable space of the apartment building to tenants acceptable to Permanent Lender. Greenhorn contracted with various subcontractors for the construction of the apartment building. Certificates of occupancy for 80 percent of the apartment building were issued on or before May 31, 2004. Certificates of occupancy for the remaining units were not obtained until July 3, 2004. The leasing of units was hampered by the availability of apartments at a lower cost in competing complexes. As of May 31, 2004, Permanent Lender had approved leases for only 45 percent of the rentable space.

   Fearful of defaulting on the construction loan, Greenhorn approached both Construction Lender and Permanent Lender and was successful in negotiating a letter of intent between Greenhorn, Construction Lender, and Permanent Lender, whereby it was agreed in principle that the term of the construction note would be extended to December 31, 2004, subject to approval by counsel for both Construction Lender and Permanent Lender. Upon the execution of the letter of intent, the officer of Construction Lender negotiating it exclaimed that he was glad that an agreement had been reached to extend the construction loan. The officer representing Permanent Lender replied that he should receive a memento to mark the importance of the occasion.

Subsequently, the prime interest rate rose from 7 percent to 10 percent in a two-month period, the lending policies of Permanent Lender were scrutinized by the federal regulatory authorities, and its reserve requirements were substantially increased. Permanent Lender, unbeknownst to Greenhorn and Construction Lender, was not in a position to fund the permanent loan because of its increased reserve requirements.

Prior to December 31, 2004, Greenhorn submitted executed leases to Permanent Lender sufficient to meet the 60 percent lease contingency. The financial condition of the tenants who signed these leases was equal to or greater than that of the tenants previously approved by Permanent Lender. Recognizing the tight position that it was in, Permanent Lender's attorneys uncovered an ancient deed restriction that precluded the sale or lease of Blueacre or any portion thereof to any person of Chinese descent, and Permanent Lender refused to approve several leases to individuals with Chinese surnames. As a result, Greenhorn was unable to fulfill the 60 percent lease contingency prior to December 31, 2004, and Permanent Lender refused to fund the permanent loan.

On January 5, 2005, Construction Lender sent a notice of default to Greenhorn and announced its intent to foreclose the leasehold mortgage. What are the legal rights and obligations of Ace, Greenhorn, Construction Lender, and Permanent Lender? Has each of the parties acted ethically?

3. John Hardy, the general manager of a large retail home improvement chain, was seeking to expand into new locations. When Hardy learned that a large plot of land near a residential development was available for sale to commercial entities, he entered into negotiations with the property owner to purchase a majority of the land. Eventually, a letter of intent was signed, which set forth the general terms and conditions of the negotiated purchase. Although both parties intended to sign a formal acquisition agreement at the closing, neither expressed any doubt that the purchase would be successfully concluded. Moreover, it was well known that Hardy's company had the necessary financial backing to complete the transaction.

   A few days later, however, Hardy heard a rumor that the City Planning Commission was discussing the possible adoption of a new zoning ordinance that would reserve certain open lands for residential development. If passed, the ordinance would prevent Hardy from building a retail store on the tract of land that was the subject of the signed letter of intent. The proposed zoning ordinance had many opponents, but it was unclear how the Commission would ultimately resolve the issue. What should Hardy do?

4. Patricia and Bobby Star were married in New Mexico in July 1996. They had been living together since 1993. In July 2003, they separated. They had purchased a residence as joint tenants in April 1995. Bobby made the down payment from his separate funds. The mortgage payments were made out of commingled funds before and after marriage.

   In August 1997, Patricia founded BioGene Corporation, a biotechnology firm, with $20,000 that she received as an inheritance from her grandmother. All of the stock of BioGene was issued in Patricia's name, and Patricia worked full-time for BioGene. Bobby retained his job with another employer and was not involved in the operations of BioGene. Due to limited financial resources, Patricia did not draw a salary from BioGene until August 2003. In September 2003, BioGene's first product was approved by the Food and Drug Administration. Shortly thereafter, Patricia sold all of her BioGene stock to a large pharmaceutical concern for $30 million. Two days after the sale of the stock, Patricia filed for dissolution of the marriage.

   Is the residence that Patricia and Bobby acquired community property or property held in joint tenancy? Would it matter if after marriage they had written a document stating that they wanted to hold the property as community property? In joint tenancy? Does Bobby have any interest in the proceeds from the sale of the BioGene stock?

5. In 1984, Occidental Chemical Corporation sold a warehouse to BCW Associates, Ltd. The sales con-

tract provided that BCW would purchase the warehouse "as is." The contract also provided that BCW would have forty-five days to inspect the warehouse and could terminate the sale during this period. BCW formally waived this termination right and acquired the property. BCW subsequently leased the warehouse to Knoll International, Inc., which used the warehouse to store and distribute inventory from its office-furniture business.

Both BCW and Knoll had noticed a significant amount of dust present in the warehouse, but they viewed the dust as merely a nuisance. Three different consulting firms evaluated the warehouse and reported to BCW and Knoll that there were no environmental hazards at the facility. In addition, Occidental gave BCW comfort letters in which Occidental represented that no hazardous materials were stored in the warehouse.

In the fall of 1985, Knoll's activity in the warehouse caused dust to "rain down" from the rafters. When the dust was analyzed, Knoll learned that the dust showed dangerous levels of lead.

Firestone Tire and Rubber Company had owned and operated the warehouse before Occidental acquired it. The dust in the warehouse was created by the grinding phase of Firestone's production of white sidewall tires. Firestone conducted these operations throughout its occupation of the warehouse from 1952 to 1980.

Knoll and BCW jointly undertook a thorough cleaning of the warehouse. BCW paid for the cleanup of the warehouse structure, in part because Knoll's lease required BCW to indemnify Knoll for costs associated with cleaning the dust. Knoll paid for the cost of cleaning its inventory and equipment, and it incurred costs to provide its employees with personal protective equipment. Is the innocent landowner defense available to BCW and Knoll under the Comprehensive Environmental Response, Compensation, and Liability Act? [*BCW Associates, Ltd. v. Occidental Chemical Corp.,* 1988 WL 102641 (E.D. Pa. Sept. 29, 1988).]

6. Plaintiff owns a 150-acre tract of land in the town of Mamaroneck, which has been leased by a private country club since 1921. In 1922, the area where the country club was located became the subject of a zoning ordinance and was rezoned for residential use. The area around the private golf course has been subject to similar zoning rules. In 1994, the town of Mamaroneck enacted a local law that rezoned the area where the country club was located so that it could be developed only for recreational use. The purpose of the law was to slow down the process of urbanization, preserve recreational opportunities for the town, and prevent increased flooding in the area due to residential development. Just months prior to the passage of this law, plaintiff had submitted a plan for the property to be developed into 71 residential lots leaving 112 acres of standing open space. Because of the plan to rezone the area, the town denied plaintiff's development proposal. Did the local law effect an unconstitutional taking of plaintiff's property without just compensation? [*Bonnie Briar Syndicate, Inc. v. Town of Mamaroneck,* 721 N.E.2d 971 (N.Y. 1999).]

7. In 1978, California voters staged what has been described as a "property tax revolt" when they approved Proposition 13. This statewide ballot initiative amended the California state constitution and limited the rate at which real property was taxed within the state and the rate at which real property assessments were increased. Proposition 13 raised questions of equity and fairness because two very similar pieces of property could have drastically different tax consequences depending on when the property was last transferred. Property was reassessed when it was sold, so a new buyer often paid substantially more property tax than a neighbor with a comparable house who had owned the property for a number of years. Is Proposition 13's acquisition-value scheme for assessing property tax a violation of the Equal Protection Clause of the Fourteenth Amendment? [*Nordlinger v. Hahn,* 505 U.S. 1 (1992).]

8. Lucy Dunworth, developer of a shopping mall, entered into an easement and operating agreement with three major department stores. One of the covenants in the agreement was that each occupant promised to operate its store area as a first-class department store under its trade name for a twenty-year period. The occupants each purchased their commercial space in fee (that is, they actually purchased the land) from the developer. Kaufman–Straus Company, one of the tenants, sold its place to a discount store two years later. The other two first-class department stores bring an action against the discount store because it is not a first-class operation. What is the result? [*Net Realty Holding Trust v. Franconia Properties, Inc.,* 544 F. Supp. 759 (E.D. Va. 1982).]

9. In an effort to minimize the adverse effects on the supply of housing for low-income, elderly, and disabled persons caused by the conversion or demolition of hotel rooms, San Francisco passed the Residential Hotel Unit Conversion and Demolition Ordinance. The ordinance made it unlawful to eliminate a residential hotel without first obtaining a conversion permit.

   To obtain a permit, applicants were required to (1) construct new residential units comparable to the converted ones; (2) construct or rehabilitate housing for low-income, disabled, or elderly persons; or (3) pay an "in lieu fee" equal to the replacement site acquisition and construction costs.

   Owners of the San Remo Hotel sought to convert the hotel from mixed residential-tourist use to all tourist use. They paid an in lieu fee of $567,000 in return for the permit, then sued to recover the fee. They argued that the ordinance violated the California Constitution, which provides: "Private property may be taken or damaged for public use only when just compensation, ascertained by a jury unless waived, has first been paid to, or into court for, the owner." Was the conversion fee a compensable taking? [*San Remo Hotel LP v. San Francisco,* 41 P.3d 87 (Cal. 2002).]

## MANAGER'S DILEMMA

10. In 1986, Triple Five of Minnesota, Inc. secured the development rights for the land on which the Mall of America in Bloomington, Minnesota, was built. Teachers Insurance and Annuity Association provided $650 million in construction financing, which was converted into an equity interest in Mall of America Company LP (MOAC LP). MOAC LP was the managing partner and owner of 99 percent of the Mall of America Company (MOAC), which owned the Mall. MOAC LP was a partnership between Teachers, which owned 55 percent of MOAC LP, and Mall of America Associates (MOAA), which owned 45 percent. MOAA was a 50/50 partnership between Triple Five and a limited partnership controlled by the Melvin and Herbert Simon family (Si-Minn LP). Si-Minn LP became the managing partner of MOAA in 1987.

    Teachers had always received the entire income generated by the Mall, but MOAA was paid a management fee of 5 percent of the Mall's gross income per year. Si-Minn LP, the actual manager of the Mall, received 80 percent of this fee, and Triple Five, which had no day-to-day responsibility for managing the Mall, received 20 percent. In March of 1998, both Triple Five and Si-Minn LP became aware that Teachers was considering selling all or part of its interests in the Mall, which it had the right to do.

    A company controlled by the Simon family is considering acquiring 50 percent of Teacher's interests in the Mall. Are there any legal or ethical constraints on their ability to acquire Teacher's interests? [*Triple Five of Minnesota, Inc. v. Simon,* 280 F. Supp. 2d 895 (D. Minn. 2003).]

## INTERNET SOURCES

| | |
|---|---|
| The American Real Estate and Urban Economics Association site includes a biannual newsletter for professionals and academics interested in real estate and urban policy. | http://www.areuea.org |
| This site provides advice on buying and selling as well as home listings. | http://www.realty.com |
| The National Association of Real Estate Investment Trusts site includes information about legal issues affecting REITs. | http://www.nareit.com |
| The website for Case Shiller Weiss, a Cambridge, Massachusetts company mainly serving mortgage lenders and investors, offers an analysis of current value of a residential property, with a "confidence level" grade on its accuracy (one free sample, then $35/report). | http://www.cswcasa.com |
| This site, the oldest e-commerce residential site (created July 1998), is an all-purpose site with home listings, mortgages, and other tools. | http://homeadvisor.msn.com |
| This site uses Digital Handshake technology to transact home purchases online. | http://www.ilumin.com |
| This site provides free real estate legal forms and a dictionary of legal terms. | http://www.kaktus.com |
| This site provides natural hazard, environmental risk, and community information. | http://www.nearmyhome.com |
| This site provides information on pest control. | http://www.pestweb.com |
| This site provides market analysis reports, including information on neighborhoods. | http://www.RealEstate.com |
| This site offers closeyourdeal.com, which allows agents, lenders, and appraisers to collaborate and manage the transaction process online. | http://www.realtyplusonline.com |
| This site provides one of the largest databases of location-specific real estate, environmental, and underwriting information in the United States. | http://www.vistainfo.com |
| This site provides mortgage-market reports, mortgage calculators, and advice. | http://www.bankrate.com |
| This site provides a state-by-state comparison of mortgage rates and names of lenders. | http://www.HSH.com |
| The National Council on Disability site provides information concerning the application of the Americans with Disabilities Act to public accommodations and the Internet. | http://www.ncd.gov |
| This site includes home listings and information and offers a finance center with a featured lender (GMAC Mortgage). | http://www.realtor.com |

# UNIT V

# CORPORATE GOVERNANCE, OWNERSHIP, AND CONROL

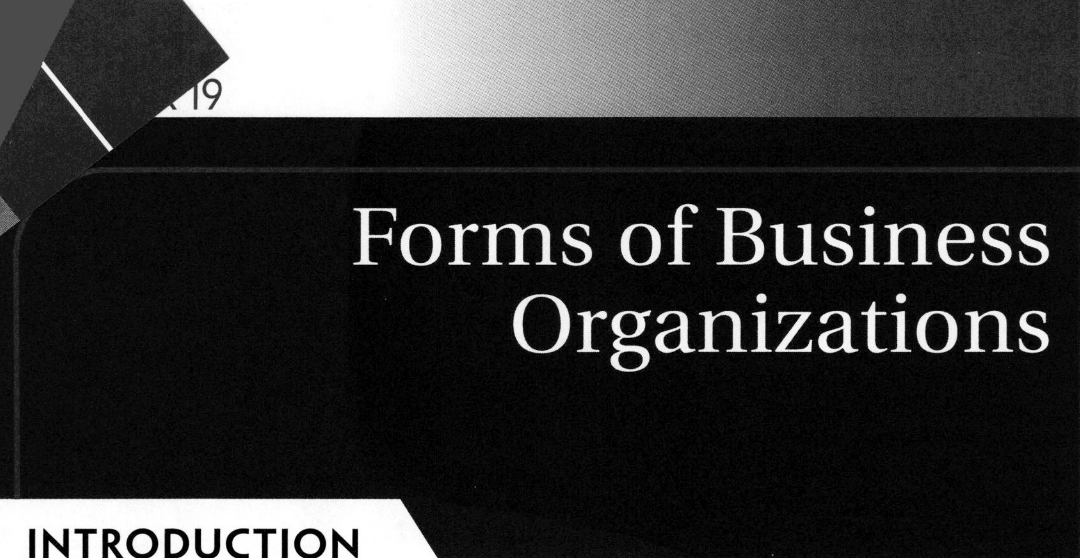


# Forms of Business Organizations

## INTRODUCTION

### CHOOSING THE PROPER FORM OF BUSINESS ENTITY

One of the first questions facing any entrepreneur wishing to start a business is which form of business organization will best suit the enterprise. In weighing the advantages and disadvantages associated with the various forms, four considerations take on primary importance. First, to what extent will the personal assets of the founders and investors be exposed to the liabilities of the business? Second, how can taxes be minimized? Third, which format will make the business most attractive to potential investors, lenders, and employees? Finally, what costs are associated with creating and maintaining the organization?

Founders enjoy a broad range of options. The decision on the entity form comes in the earliest stages in the life of a business, but it is nonetheless a crucial one. Changing the form of organization can be very costly. Not only will administrative and legal fees be incurred, but a change may also give rise to tax liability or cause a business opportunity to be lost. Thus, at the outset of their venture, entrepreneurs should carefully consider its expected evolution and choose the form of organization accordingly. In addition, once the form of entity is chosen, its managers must be diligent in complying with all statutory requirements.

### CHAPTER OVERVIEW

This chapter begins with an examination of the advantages and disadvantages of the most frequently used forms of business organizations: sole proprietorships, general and limited partnerships, limited liability partnerships, corporations (including S corporations), and limited liability companies. Next, the chapter summarizes the basic tax treatment of these different entities. The remainder of the chapter offers a more detailed discussion of how partnerships and corporations are structured and operated. It includes a discussion of the rules proposed by the Securities and Exchange Commission in 2003 to permit security holders of public companies to have their nominees for director included in management's proxy statement for the election of directors.

## Sole Proprietorship

The sole proprietorship is the simplest and most prevalent form of business enterprise in the United States. In a *sole proprietorship,* one individual owns all of the assets of the business and is solely and personally liable for all of its debts. In other words, the sole proprietor is the business. Any individual who conducts business without creating a separate organization is operating as a sole proprietorship.

There are no formal requirements for forming a sole proprietorship. However, if the business operates under a *fictitious business name*—that is, a name other than the name of the owner—that name must be registered with the state. A sole proprietorship ends upon either the discontinuation of the business or the death of the proprietor.

Advantages of a sole proprietorship include the flexibility afforded by having one person in complete control of the business. Also, because a sole proprietorship can be created without formal agreements or state filings, it is the easiest and least costly form of business organization to set up. Sole proprietorships pay only one level of income tax—the proprietor reports income and losses from the business on his or her personal tax returns. Finally, the proprietor receives all of the profits generated by the business.

If the business loses money, however, the proprietor alone bears liability for the losses. This element of risk is the major disadvantage of the sole proprietorship. In addition, it is more difficult for sole proprietorships to raise capital. A sole proprietor can only tap personal funds and borrow money.

## General Partnership

A *general partnership* is created when two or more persons agree to place their money, efforts, labor, or skills in a business and to share the profits and losses.[1] Their agreement can be express or implied, but they must share in real profits, not just receive wages or compensation.

Absent an express agreement to the contrary, each partner has some control over the business, and each may have the authority to bind the partnership with respect to third parties. In some respects, a partnership is like a marriage or a family. Its members share not only the benefits of the relationship but the burdens as well.

A partnership is treated as an entity separate from its partners and can acquire property in its own name. Property that is not acquired in the name of the partnership is nonetheless partnership property if the instrument transferring title refers to (1) the person taking title as a partner or (2) the existence of the partnership.

One of the key advantages of a partnership is that it allows for a wide variety of operational and profit-sharing arrangements. In essence, partners may agree to any terms in forming a partnership as long as they are not illegal or contrary to public policy. An example of this flexibility is that partners may contribute either capital or services to the partnership. Suppose Pro and Ron decide to form a partnership, called Rad Waves, to manufacture windsurfing equipment. Ron contributes the start-up and operating capital, and Pro contributes only his management services. Even though Pro has not contributed capital to the partnership, he is (unless agreed otherwise) an equal partner with Ron in Rad Waves.

Like a sole proprietorship, a partnership has the advantage of being subject to only one level of tax. Though it must file an informational return with the Internal Revenue Service (IRS), a partnerships does not pay income taxes as a separate entity. Instead, the profit earned (or loss incurred) by the partnership (whether distributed or not) "passes through" to the individual partners, who report it as income (or loss) on their individual returns. Thus, a partnership is a *pass-through entity*.

Unlike a sole proprietorship, which terminates upon the death of the owner, a partnership is not automatically dissolved upon a partner's death, bankruptcy, or withdrawal. Instead, the partners holding a majority of the partnership interests may elect to continue the general partnership within ninety days after the occurrence of such events.

General partnerships face a disadvantage similar to sole proprietorships in that individual partners are subject to personal liability for the obligations of the partnership. Thus, if the partnership is unable to pay its debts, creditors of the partnership have claims against the assets of individual partners.

### Joint Venture

A *joint venture* is a one-time partnership of two or more persons for a specific purpose, such as the construction of a hydroelectric dam or a cogeneration plant. Like a general partnership, a joint venture requires that the parties (1) share a community of interest; (2) have the mutual right to direct and govern; (3) share the partnership's profits and losses; and (4) combine their property, money, efforts, skill, or knowledge in the undertaking. Unlike a general partnership, a joint venture is not a continuing relationship; it terminates when the project is completed.

In a joint venture, the authority of one member to bind the partnership is more limited than in a general partnership. To avoid inadvertently conferring apparent authority to bind the other members, a joint venture should make it clear in its dealings with third parties that it is a joint venture and not a partnership. This distinction should be reflected in the entity's name and in the recitation of its legal status in its contracts.

## Limited Liability Partnerships

The *limited liability partnership (LLP)* is designed primarily for professionals who typically do business as a general partnership, such as law firms and accounting firms. LLPs are created by filing the appropriate forms with a central state agency. A major advantage of the

1. The Revised Uniform Partnership Act (RUPA) (1997) defines a partnership as "an association of two or more persons to carry on as co-owners a business for profit." This discussion is based on the RUPA, which has been adopted by a majority of the states.

LLP form for existing partnerships, such as law firms and accounting firms, is that they can attain LLP status without significant modification of the business's partnership agreement. Like other forms of partnerships, LLPs retain pass-through taxation treatment.

The main function of an LLP is to insulate its partners from *vicarious liability* for certain partnership obligations, such as liability arising from the malpractice of another partner. Partners in an LLP usually have unlimited liability for their own malpractice.

State LLP statutes are not uniform, however. Most statutes provide that liability will be limited at least for debts and obligations arising from the malpractice, or negligent or wrongful conduct, of other partners. However, a few states, such as Minnesota and New York, protect partners from commercial liabilities (such as trade debt) as well.[2] The trend in LLP statutes enacted since 1995 has been to provide the broader liability protection exemplified by Minnesota and New York.[3] This expanded protection further narrows the distinction between an LLP and a limited liability company.

The lawsuits against Arthur Andersen for its flawed audits of Enron are the most high profile test of the liability shield provided by the LLP structure to date. Andersen had reorganized into an Illinois LLP prior to the Enron audits. Because failure to supervise other partners may itself be a basis for liability, even those partners who did not work directly on the Enron audit may be personally liable. Although Andersen's conviction on obstruction of justice charges led to the firm's demise, the legal liability of its partners remained in question as of 2004.

Some scholars have suggested that the Andersen's partners' perception of protection from vicarious liability may have made them less critical of the risky Enron transactions that led to its downfall.[4] Unlike most other auditing firms, Andersen permitted the local engagement partner to overrule a decision by the central audit standards committee.

## Limited Partnership

A *limited partnership* is a special type of partnership consisting of general partners and limited partners. General partners of a limited partnership remain jointly and severally liable for partnership obligations (just like partners in a general partnership), and they are responsible for the management of the partnership. *Limited partners*, however, assume no liability for partnership debts beyond the amount of capital they have contributed, and they have no right to participate in the management of the partnership.

Limited partnerships are often used to raise capital—the limited liability for limited partners makes them attractive to investors. Returning to the Rad Waves example, suppose the general partners desire to raise capital to finance a sportswear line to promote their other products. To do so, they restructure their partnership as a limited partnership with Ron and Pro remaining as general partners. They can now offer an investor a limited partnership interest in the business, renamed Rad Waves, L.P. If Olivia contributes $1,000 to the partnership, she becomes a limited partner in Rad Waves (assuming compliance with the relevant state statute), and her personal liability for Rad Waves' obligations is limited to her $1,000 original investment.

This ability to attract investors with the assurance of limited liability is the main advantage of a limited partnership. A limited partnership is more difficult to create than a general partnership. Unlike a general partnership, a limited partnership does not come into existence until a certificate of limited partnership has been filed with the appropriate state agency. Moreover, courts generally take a strict approach to the formal requirements of limited partnership status. If a partnership runs afoul of those requirements, courts will treat it as a general partnership instead.

## Corporations

A *corporation* is an organization authorized by state law to act as a legal entity distinct from its owners. As a separate legal entity, the corporation has its own name and operates with limited powers to achieve specific purposes. Corporations are owned by shareholders, who have purchased an ownership stake in the business. The board of directors, which is elected by the shareholders, has central decision-making authority. The board of directors typically employs officers to manage the day-to-day operations of the business.

One of the most attractive features of the corporation is that the liability of its shareholders is limited to their investments. Only the corporation itself is responsible for its liabilities. (An important exception to this general rule, the piercing the corporate veil theory, is discussed later in this chapter.) This cap on liability permits entrepreneurs and investors to undertake risky ventures without the worry that they will lose personal assets if things go badly.

2. Elizabeth G. Hester, *Keeping Liability at Bay*, BUS. L. TODAY, Jan.–Feb. 1996, at 60.
3. *Id.*
4. Susan Saab Fortney, *High Drama and Hindsight*, BUS. L. TODAY, Jan. 2003, at 47–49.

**INTERNATIONAL SNAPSHOT**

*Salomon v. Salomon,*[a] decided by the British House of Lords in 1897, established the principle of corporations having a separate identity: "In the eyes of the law a company is a person capable of perpetual succession and quite distinct from the natural persons who are its members at any given time."

**a.** Salomon v. A. Salomon & Co. Ltd, [1897] A.C. 22 (H.L.).

Another benefit of a corporation is its ability to raise significant capital by selling ownership shares of corporate stock (also known as equity) to investors. Finally, corporations have the advantage of perpetual life. Thus, if a key investor dies or decides to sell his or her interest in the business, the corporation as an entity continues to exist and to conduct business.

## C Corporations

The main disadvantage of the corporate form of organization is that it is usually subject to two levels of taxation: both corporate and shareholder unless it is eligible for and elects S corporation status (discussed below). Any corporation not meeting the requirements for an S corporation is automatically a *C corporation* (so-named because it is taxed in accordance with the rules set forth in Subchapter C of the Internal Revenue Code). A C corporation pays tax on the income generated by the business, and the shareholders pay tax on that same income when it is distributed as dividends.

## S Corporations

Some closely held corporations can avoid this double taxation by electing to be treated as S corporations under Subchapter S of the Internal Revenue Code. An *S corporation* is taxed as a pass-through entity. In other words, the corporation itself is not taxed on its income; rather, the shareholders pay tax on their pro rata shares of the corporation's income. An election to be taxed under Subchapter S does not affect the status of the organization as a corporation for state corporate law purposes. Any corporation that has not elected to be an S corporation or that fails to continue to meet the requirements for an S corporation is automatically a C corporation.

To qualify for S corporation status, a corporation must satisfy the following requirements:

1. The corporation must have no more than 100 shareholders, all of whom must be individuals who are citizens of the United States or U.S. resident aliens, or certain types of tax-exempt organizations, trusts, or estates.
2. The corporation must have only one class of stock.
3. The corporation generally may not own 80 percent or more of any other corporation.
4. The corporation must file a timely election to be treated as an S corporation.

## Close Corporations

Some states have enacted laws that give close corporations extra operating flexibility. A *close corporation* is a corporation that (1) has elected in its charter to be treated as a close corporation and (2) has a "small" number of shareholders, typically thirty. A corporation must elect to become a close corporation by stating in its certificate of incorporation that it is a close corporation; otherwise, regardless of the number of shareholders, the corporation will not be treated as a close corporation.

State close corporation laws permit significant departures from the formalities required of traditional corporations.[5] Under some state statutes, if a close corporation's shareholders agree not to observe corporate formalities relating to meetings of directors or shareholders in connection with the management of its affairs, then the bypassing of these formalities may not be considered a factor in deciding whether to pierce the corporate veil and hold the shareholders personally liable. In addition, many statutes permit the shareholders of a close corporation to manage the corporation directly as long as a certain percentage of the shareholders agree to this in writing.

## Closely Held Corporations

It is important to distinguish between a close corporation—one that conforms to the rules set forth by the state of incorporation to legally qualify as such—and a closely held corporation. A *closely held corporation* may have any number of shareholders, but it is characterized by the absence of a market for its stock.[6] If a court characterizes a corporation as closely held, it will often impose a greater duty of loyalty and care upon the corporation's directors and majority shareholders. These impositions are *not* codified, however, and exist only in common law and traditional business practices.[7]

5. For an example of one such law, see CAL. GEN. CORP. § 300(e).
6. Donahue v. Rodd Electrotype Co., 328 N.E.2d 505 (Mass. 1975).
7. For more on closely held corporations and how they are operated, see American Bar Association Committee on Corporate Laws, *Managing Closely Held Corporations: A Legal Guidebook*, 58 BUS. LAW. 1077–126 (2003).

### ETHICAL CONSIDERATION

Edward Hall and Harry Hall were 50 percent owners of Hall Contractors and the corporation's only directors. Edward died, leaving all of his assets to his widow. Harry (the only surviving director at that point) appointed his own wife to fill the vacancy on the board. Initially, Harry and his wife refused to call a shareholder meeting. Even when one was called, Harry simply did not show up to vote. As a result, Edward's widow could never generate a quorum for a shareholder vote to replace Harry's wife with an impartial director. The corporation never paid dividends to Edward or his widow and did not intend to pay dividends in the future. As a result, Edward's widow's stock in the corporation became worthless. Did Harry and his wife have a legal right to do what they did?[a] Were they acting ethically? Would the answer be different if the case involved a corporation like IBM or McDonald's?

**a.** Hall v. Hall, 506 S.W.2d 42 (Mo. Ct. App. 1974).

## Limited Liability Companies

A *limited liability company (LLC)* combines the tax advantages of a pass-through entity with the limited liability advantages of a corporation. Like corporations and limited partnerships, the LLC is a creature of state law. To form an LLC, a charter document must be filed with the appropriate state agency (usually the office of the secretary of state). This LLC charter document is typically called the *articles of organization* (as in California) or the *certificate of formation* (as in Delaware). The name of the business must include the initials L.L.C. or the words Limited Liability Company.

The owners of an LLC are called *members.* The rights, obligations, and powers of the members, managers, and officers are set forth in an *operating agreement.* The members elect the *managers* who, like a board of directors, are responsible for managing the business, property, and affairs of the company. The managers appoint the officers of the company.

Unless a business is organized as a corporation under state law or is publicly held, the IRS's "check the box" regulations permit the founders to decide whether the entity is to be taxed as a corporation or a pass-through entity. State law corporations and publicly traded entities are always taxed as corporations. LLCs are not taxed at the firm level unless they elect to be taxed as corporations.

The LLC form of business organization offers the advantages of both the limited partnership and the S corporation without their respective drawbacks. Properly formed LLCs are taxed as partnerships, but unlike the general partners in limited partnerships, even the controlling persons in LLCs can limit their liability to the amount invested. Moreover, all owners of an LLC can participate fully in the management of the business. Like a partnership, an LLC can have flexible allocations of profits and losses. The main advantage of the LLC form over the S corporation is the lack of restrictions on shareholders and the ability to have more than one class of securities. Specifically, there is no limit on the number of members an LLC can have, and in contrast to an S corporation, its investors can be corporations, partnerships, and foreigners.

One disadvantage of the LLC form of business organization is the cost of preparing a customized operating agreement. As LLCs have become more common, however, standardized forms have started to emerge.[8] They provide a good starting point for drafting but must be tailored to the individual company and the needs of its members.

## Income Tax Considerations

The analysis that follows is concerned solely with federal income tax consequences under the Internal Revenue Code of 1986, as amended and in force as of January 1, 2005. Many state income tax provisions follow the federal rules. Because provisions in the tax laws change often, it is more important to understand the general issues than to strive for a detailed knowledge of the tax laws for any given year.

### COMPARING TAXABLE ENTITIES WITH PASS-THROUGH ENTITIES

The tax treatment of C corporations is different from that of pass-through entities (such as partnerships, S corporations, and LLCs) in several respects. Each may have favorable or unfavorable tax consequences, depending on the circumstances.

#### *Property Transfers*

Because a C corporation is a separate taxable entity, a transfer of cash or any other kind of property between the corporation and its owners is a taxable transaction unless

8. For example, see GUIDE TO ORGANIZING AND OPERATING A LIMITED LIABILITY COMPANY IN CALIFORNIA (Allan B. Dubott ed., 1995), published by the Partnerships and Unincorporated Business Organizations Committee of the Business Law Section of the State Bar of California. This guide includes annotated sample short-form and long-form operating agreements and other useful exemplars.

it comes within one of the statutory exceptions in Subchapter C. It is easier to transfer property to and from a partnership or an LLC on a tax-free basis than it is with either a C corporation or an S corporation. For example, a transfer of property to either type of corporation in exchange for stock is tax-free only if the persons transferring the property own, immediately after the transaction, 80 percent or more of the stock of the corporation to which the property is transferred. In contrast, an exchange of property for a share in a partnership is tax-free regardless of the transferor's percentage share in the partnership.

Similarly, property that has appreciated in value may be more easily distributed tax-free from a partnership or an LLC than from a corporation. Neither the partnership nor the LLC is subject to tax on the appreciated property, and the partner receiving the property is not taxed until he or she subsequently sells it. This can be particularly important for venture capital funds, which often make distributions of illiquid stock in the portfolio companies in which the fund has invested. If the fund is organized as a partnership or LLC, these securities can be distributed to the partners or members tax-free, with no tax due until the partner or member sells the securities. In contrast, a corporation will be taxed on the appreciation in value at the time of the transfer just as if it had sold the property for cash, and the shareholders will be taxed on the fair market value of the property they have received. Thus, with a C corporation there will be both a corporate-level tax and a shareholder-level tax on the distribution. For an S corporation, the taxable income is passed through and will be taxed only at the shareholder level.

### *Cash Distributions*

The income of a C corporation is taxed at the corporate level, and it is taxed again at the individual level when it is distributed. This double taxation does not occur with the other forms of business organizations. This difference alone may make a pass-through entity preferable to a C corporation as the chosen form of business organization. Qualified dividends are, however, taxed at a lower rate than ordinary income.

Double taxation can be reduced in two ways. First, the tax liability of the corporation can be reduced to the extent that corporate income can be offset by tax-deductible payments to shareholders. For example, if personal services are a major source of the corporation's income, payment of employee compensation to shareholders active in the business will reduce the corporation's taxable income. If capital investment is a major source of income, payment of interest or rent to shareholders may provide similar relief. Second, the tax liability of the shareholders can be reduced to the extent that the business income is retained by the corporation and not distributed to shareholders. However, the accumulated earnings of a corporation may be taxed if they are not being retained for a legitimate corporate business purpose.

Cash distributions from partnerships and S corporations are tax-free to the recipients, up to the amount of their previous capital contributions less any income previously passed through to them. Distributions from C corporations, on the other hand, generally result in taxable dividend income to the shareholders.

### *Operating Losses*

If the business operations of a C corporation produce a loss, as is frequently the case with start-up companies and real estate investments in their early years, the operating loss will be recognized at the corporate level. This means that the shareholders receive no tax benefits from the operating loss, and the corporation receives no benefit until it has operating income against which its prior losses can be deducted.

In contrast, if the same business is operated by a partnership, LLC, or S corporation, then the operating loss each year will be passed through to the individual partners or shareholders. They may, if certain tax law requirements are satisfied, deduct the operating loss from their other income. Under the limits on passive losses, only owners who materially participate in the business may deduct its losses from their other ordinary income (such as wages or interest). Passive investors may not deduct such losses from ordinary income, but they can use passive losses to offset passive gains (such as capital gains on the sale of stock).

### *Capitalization*

The tax laws impose no restrictions on a C corporation's capitalization. As business needs require, the corporation may issue common stock, preferred stock, bonds, notes, warrants, options, and other instruments. These instruments may confer the right to varying degrees of control and varying shares of earnings and may be convertible, redeemable, or callable. The tax treatment of each type of capital instrument may differ from its classification by the corporation, however. For example, shareholder debt may be treated as stock if the corporation has too little *equity capital,* that is, capital received in exchange for shares in the ownership of the corporation. As a consequence, tax-deductible "interest" payments may be recast as nondeductible "dividends" that are taxable to the shareholders.

## IN BRIEF

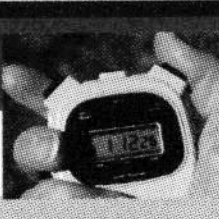

### Choice of Business Entity: Pros and Cons

The following chart lists the principal considerations in selecting the form of business entity and applies them to the general partnership, limited liability partnership, limited partnership, limited liability company, C corporation, and S corporation. The considerations are listed in no particular order, in part because their importance will vary depending on the nature of the business, its sources of financing, and the plan for providing financial returns to the owners (for example, distributions of operating income, a public offering, or a sale of the business). Other factors that are not listed will also influence the choice of entity. In addition, the "yes" or "no" format oversimplifies the applicability of certain attributes.

| | General Partnership | Limited Liability Partnership | Limited Partnership | Limited Liability Company | C Corporation | S Corporation |
|---|---|---|---|---|---|---|
| Limited liability | No | Yes[a] | Yes[b] | Yes | Yes | Yes |
| Flow-through taxation | Yes | Yes | Yes | Yes | No | Yes |
| Simplicity/low cost | No | No | No | No | Yes | Yes |
| Limitations on eligibility | No | No | No | No | No | Yes |
| Limitations on capital structure | No | No | No | No | No | Yes |
| Ability to raise venture capital | No | No | No | No | Yes | No |
| Ability to take public | No[c] | No[c] | No[c] | No[c] | Yes | Yes[d] |
| Flexible charter documents | Yes | Yes | Yes | Yes | No | No |
| Ability to change structure without tax | Yes | Yes | Yes | Yes | No | No |
| Favorable employee incentives (including incentive stock options) | No[e] | No[e] | No[e] | No[e] | Yes | Yes/No[f] |
| Qualified small business stock exclusion for gains | No | No | No | No | Yes[g] | No |
| Special allocations | Yes | Yes | Yes | Yes | No | No |
| Tax-free in-kind distributions | Yes | Yes | Yes | Yes | No | No |
| Ability to bring case in federal court based on diversity jurisdiction | Rarely[h] | Rarely[h] | Rarely[h] | Rarely[h] | Often[h] | Often[h] |

**a.** Partners in LLPs generally are protected from liability for malpractice and other wrongful conduct of fellow partners. States are split on whether LLP partners can be held individually liable for other partnership liabilities, such as commercial debt.
**b.** Limited liability for limited partners only; a limited partnership must have at least one general partner with unlimited liability.
**c.** Although the public markets are generally not available for partnership offerings, partnerships (including LLPs) and LLCs can be incorporated without tax and then taken public.
**d.** An S corporation would convert to a C corporation upon a public offering because of the number of shareholders.
**e.** Although partnership and LLC interests can be provided to employees, they are poorly understood by most employees. Moreover, tax-favored incentive stock options are not available.
**f.** Although an S corporation can issue incentive stock options, the inability to have two classes of stock limits favorable pricing of the common stock offered to employees.
**g.** A special low capital gains rate is available for stock of U.S. C corporations with not more than $50 million in gross assets at the time the stock is issued if the corporation is engaged in an active business and the taxpayer holds the stock for at least five years.
**h.** For purposes of deciding whether there is federal jurisdiction based on diversity of citizenship, a corporation is deemed a citizen of the state where it is incorporated and of the state where it has its principal place of business. A partnership partakes of the citizenship of each of its partners. Similarly, the citizenship of an LLC is the citizenship of each of its members.

## *Allocation of Losses*

Items of partnership (or LLC) income or loss generally can be allocated to specific partners (or members) at specific times as long as these allocations have a substantial economic effect apart from tax considerations. Thus, an LLC can allocate a disproportionate amount of losses or depreciation to a particular member in the early years and allocate a disproportionate amount of later income to the same member until the loss is recovered. This form of allocation may generate a valuable tax deferral for that member.

No comparable allocation can be made by a C corporation, except to a limited extent by capitalizing the corporation with different classes of stock and debt. An S corporation is even more limited in this respect. It may have only one class of stock, and all income and losses must be allocated strictly in proportion to stock ownership.

## Ability to Raise Venture Capital

Although pass-through entities (such as partnerships, LLCs, and S corporations) offer many tax advantages, they are rarely used for a business that intends to raise money from venture capitalists. Instead, the C corporation is usually used for two reasons. First, most venture capital firms raise money from large institutional investors, such as pension funds, university endowments, and the like. Nonprofit entities such as these can invest in securities and receive their income and capital gains tax-free only if the issuer of the securities is not a pass-through entity. Otherwise, the nonprofits will be deemed to have received unrelated business income, which is fully taxable. Second, most start-ups want the ability to sell securities to outside investors at a significantly higher price than was paid by the founders at the outset. To justify the price differential, and avoid having some of the value of the founders' shares treated as employee compensation, companies issue two classes of stock: common stock to the founders and preferred stock to the outside investors. Because an S corporation cannot have more than one class of stock, the C corporation is usually the easiest vehicle to use.

## Agency Law and Limited Liability

It is critical for individuals acting on behalf of any business entity to make it clear whether they are acting on their own or as agents of a separate legal entity. Failure to do this can result in personal liability for the manager involved. For example, if a person signs a contract in his or her own name, without indicating the name of the business entity on behalf of which he or she is acting, then the person is personally liable if the undisclosed principal fails to perform its obligations.

In addition, if the owners of a limited liability entity are active in the operation of the business, they can be held directly liable for their own tortious acts. This happened in the following case.

A CASE IN POINT

### In the Language of the Court

**CASE 19.1**

**Estate of Countryman v. Farmers Cooperative Association of Keota**

*Supreme Court of Iowa*

*679 N.W.2d 598*

*(Iowa 2004).*

**› FACTS** On Labor Day in 1999, an explosion caused by stray propane gas destroyed the home of Jerry Usovsky, killing seven people and seriously injuring several others. The survivors and the estates of the deceased filed a lawsuit based on several tort theories. Among those named in the complaint were Double Circle and Farmers Cooperative Association of Keota (Keota).

Double Circle, which delivered the propane prior to the accident, was a limited liability company and Keota was its 95 percent owner. Keota's executive board also served as Double Circle's executive board. An agreement between Double Circle and Keota stated that Keota was responsible for Double Circle's "human resource and management safety" activities.

The complaint alleged that Keota was personally liable for the accident. Keota moved for summary judgment, arguing that the structure of Double Circle as an LLC protected Keota from personal liability as long as Keota operated within its prescribed duties as a limited liability manager of Double Circle. The trial court granted summary judgment, and the plaintiffs appealed.

**› ISSUE PRESENTED** Can a member of an LLC be held personally liable in tort for its actions as a manager of the LLC?

*(Continued)*

(Case 19.1 *continued*)

**› OPINION** CADY, J., writing on behalf of the Supreme Court of Iowa:

The limited liability company, "LLC" as it is now known, is a hybrid business entity that is considered to have the attributes of a partnership for federal income tax purposes and the limited liability protections of a corporation. As such, it provides for the operational advantages of a partnership by allowing the owners, called members, to participate in the management of the business. Yet, the members and managers are protected from liability in the same manner shareholders, officers, and directors of a corporation are protected.

. . .

Sections 490A.601 and 490A.603 of the [Iowa Limited Liability Company] Act generally provide that a member or manager of a limited liability company is not personally liable for acts or debts of the company solely by reason of being a member or manager, except in the following situations: (1) the ILLCA expressly provides for the person's liability; (2) the articles of organization provide for the person's liability; (3) the person has agreed in writing to be personally liable; (4) the person participates in tortious conduct; or (5) a shareholder of a corporation would be personally liable in the same situation, except that the failure to hold meetings and related formalities shall not be considered.

While liability of members and managers is limited, the statute clearly imposes liability when they participate in tortious conduct. This approach is compatible with the longstanding approach to liability in corporate settings, where, under general agency principles, corporate officers and directors can be liable for their torts even when committed in their capacity as an officer. This approach has been explained as follows: Agency law generally, and Iowa law in particular, has long recognized that if a person commits a tort while acting for another person, the tortfeasor is personally liable for the tort, even if the person for whom he is acting is also vicariously liable for the same wrong. In other words, a person's status as an agent confers no immunity with respect to the person's own tort liability. Thus, if a member of a limited liability company injures another person while working in the course of the firm's business, the member is personally liable for that harm along with the company, just as the member would be if he worked for a firm organized as a corporation, a partnership, or any other business form.

Keota suggests that liability of an LLC member or manager for tortious conduct is limited to conduct committed outside the member or manager role. Yet, this approach is contrary to the corporate model and agency principles upon which the liability of LLC members and managers is based, and cannot be found in the language of the statute. We acknowledge that the "participation in tortious conduct" standard would not impose tort liability on a manager for merely performing a general administrative duty.

. . .

It is also important to recognize that this case is not about holding an officer, director, or shareholder of Keota personally liable for participating in tortious conduct. Plaintiffs have not sued individual members of Keota. Instead, the lawsuit filed by the plaintiffs seeks to hold Keota liable for participating in certain torts as the designated manager of an LLC. . . . While members and managers of an LLC are generally not personally liable for the acts of an LLC, Keota must also be viewed as a separate "legal" person.

. . .

*(Continued)*

(Case 19.1 *continued*)

We conclude that Keota is not protected from liability if it participated in tortious conduct in performing its duties as manager of Double Circle.

**› RESULT** The court found that Keota could potentially be liable and remanded the case back to the trial court.

**› CRITICAL THINKING QUESTIONS**

1. If Keota were owned in part by another LLC, Company X, could the plaintiffs also hold Company X liable for the accident?
2. Under what circumstances would the members of the Keota executive board who also sat on the Double Circle executive board be personally liable to the members of Double Circle? To third parties injured by the tortious conduct of Double Circle?

## Partnership Mechanics

This section describes in more detail how partnerships are formed, operated, and terminated.

### Formation of a General Partnership

A general partnership can be created with nothing more than a handshake and a general understanding between the partners. For example, students agree to work together on a business plan; a baker and a chef agree to open a restaurant together; an engineer and a mechanic agree to design bicycles together—in each case, a partnership is formed. The intention of one party alone, however, cannot create a partnership. There must be a meeting of the minds. Hence, in the Rad Waves example, if Ron viewed his agreement with Pro as forming a partnership, but Pro contemplated a mere employee–employer relationship, then there is no partnership.

A partnership does not require a minimum amount of capital in order to be formed. Partners usually contribute cash or property, or agree to provide personal services, to the partnership. In some instances, a partnership interest may be received as a gift. The partnership need not be given a name. There may or may not be a written partnership agreement.

#### *Without a Written Agreement*

If there is no written partnership agreement, the laws of the state where the parties are doing business will determine whether the relationship is to be treated as a partnership or some other relationship, such as an agency. If the relationship is recognized as a partnership, state partnership laws will govern the partnership and prescribe the rights of the partners if there is no written agreement. Some provisions of those laws could lead to undesirable business results.

In the Rad Waves example, Pro and Ron could form a partnership with a simple oral agreement. Under state partnership law, however, Pro and Ron will be required to share the profits and losses equally. Furthermore, until the partnership is terminated, neither partner may withdraw capital without the consent of the other. If there were a third partner, his or her death could terminate the partnership even if Pro and Ron preferred to continue it. These are just a few examples of the dangers of forming a partnership without a written partnership agreement.

In the following case, the Court of Appeal of California was asked to decide whether a partnership existed between two women who had never drafted documents expressly creating one.

A Case in Point

**In the Language of the Court**

**CASE 19.2**

**Holmes v. Lerner**

*Court of Appeal of California*
*88 Cal. Rptr. 2d 130*
*(Cal. App. 1999).*

**› FACTS** Sandra Lerner was a successful entrepreneur and an experienced businessperson. She and her husband were the original founders of Cisco Systems. When Lerner sold her interest in Cisco, she received a substantial amount of money, which she invested, in part, in a venture-capital limited partnership called "& Capital Partners."

*(Continued)*

(Case 19.2 *continued*)

Patricia Holmes met Lerner in late 1993, when Lerner visited Holmes's horse training facility to arrange for the training and boarding of two horses that Lerner was importing from England.

In 1995, Lerner and Holmes traveled to England to attend a horse show and to make arrangements to ship the horses to the United States. On this trip, Lerner decided that she wanted to celebrate her fortieth birthday by going pub crawling in Dublin. Lerner was wearing what Holmes termed "alternative clothes" and black nail polish, and she encouraged Holmes to do the same. Holmes did not like black nail polish, however, and was unable to find a suitable color in the English stores. At Lerner's mansion outside London, Lerner gave Holmes a manicure kit, telling her to see if she could find a color she would like to wear. Holmes looked through the kit, tried different colors, and eventually developed her own purple color by layering a raspberry color over black nail polish. Lerner also found the color attractive.

On July 31, 1995, the two women returned from England and stayed at Lerner's West Hollywood condominium while they waited for the horses to clear quarantine. While sitting at the kitchen table, they discussed nail polish colors. Len Bosack, Lerner's husband, was in and out of the room during the conversations. For approximately an hour and a half, Lerner and Holmes worked with the colors in a nail kit to try to re-create the purple color Holmes had made in England so that they could have the color in a liquid form, rather than having to layer two colors.

Lerner said to Holmes: "This seems like a good [thing], it's something that we both like, and isn't out there. Do you think we should start a company?" Holmes responded: "Yes, I think it's a great idea." Lerner told Holmes that they would have to do market research and determine how to have the polishes produced, and that there were many things they would have to do. Lerner said: "We will hire people to work for us. We will do everything we can to get the company going, and then we'll be creative, and other people will do the work, so we'll have time to continue riding the horses." Holmes agreed that they would do those things. They did not separate out which tasks each of them would do, but planned to do it all together.

Lerner then called David Soward, the general partner of & Capital and her personal business consultant. Holmes heard her say, "Please check for the name, Urban Decay, to see if it's available and if it is, get it for us." Holmes knew that Lerner did not joke about business and was certain, from the tone of her voice, that Lerner was serious about the new business. The telephone call to secure the trademark for Urban Decay confirmed in Holmes's mind that they were forming a business based on the concepts they had originated in England and at the kitchen table that day.

Holmes knew that she would be taking the risk of sharing in losses as well as potential success, but the two friends did not discuss the details at that time. Lerner's housekeeper heard Lerner tell Holmes: "It's going to be our baby, and we're going to work on it together." After Holmes left, the housekeeper asked Lerner what gave her the idea to go into the cosmetics business, given that her background was in computers. Lerner replied: "It was all Pat's idea over in England, but I've got the money to make it work." Lerner told her housekeeper that she hoped to sell Urban Decay to Estee Lauder for $50 million.

Although neither Lerner nor Holmes had any experience in the cosmetics business, they began work on their idea immediately. They met frequently in August and September at Lerner's home and experimented with nail colors.

*(Continued)*

(Case 19.2 *continued*)

Prior to the first scheduled August meeting, Holmes told Lerner she was concerned about financing the venture. Lerner told her not to worry because Lerner thought they could convince Soward that the nail polish business would be a good investment. Holmes and Lerner discussed their plans for the company and agreed that they would attempt to build it up and then sell it. Lerner and Holmes discussed the need to visit chemical companies and hire people to handle the daily operations of the company. However, the creative aspect, ideas, inspiration, and impetus for the company came from Holmes and Lerner.

The participants in these meetings referred to them as "board meetings," even though there was no formal organizational structure and, technically, no board. They discussed financing, and Soward reluctantly agreed to commit $500,000 toward the project. Urban Decay was financed entirely by & Capital, the venture-capital partnership composed of Soward as general partner and Lerner and her husband as the only limited partners. Neither Lerner nor Holmes invested any of their individual funds.

Lerner and Soward went to Kirker Chemical Company later in August 1995 and learned about mixing and manufacturing nail polish colors. Lerner discouraged Holmes from accompanying them. At the second board meeting, in late August, Soward introduced Wendy Zomnir, a friend of his former fiancée, as an advertising and marketing specialist. Holmes was enthusiastic about Zomnir, and they decided to hire her. At the conclusion of the September board meeting, after Holmes had left, Lerner and Soward secretly made Zomnir an offer of employment, which included a percentage ownership interest in Urban Decay. Holmes did not learn of the terms of the offer until a couple of meetings later, when Lerner or Soward referred to Zomnir as the "chief operating officer" of Urban Decay.

In early October, after Holmes learned of the secret offer to Zomnir, she asked Lerner to define her role at Urban Decay. Lerner responded, "Your role is anything you want it to be." When Holmes asked to discuss the issue in more detail, Lerner turned and walked away.

In December 1995, Urban Decay Cosmetics LLC was organized. Holmes asked for a copy of the articles of incorporation but was given only two pages showing the name and address of the company. On December 31, Holmes sent a fax to Lerner stating that it had been difficult to discuss her position in Urban Decay with Lerner. Holmes asked Lerner: "What are my responsibilities and obligations, and what are my rights or entitlements?" and "What are my current and potential liabilities and assets?" She requested that Lerner provide the information in writing. Soward intercepted the fax and called Holmes, asking: "What's going on?" Holmes explained that she wanted a written agreement, and Soward apologized, telling her that Lerner had asked him to get "something . . . in writing" to Holmes. Soward told Holmes that *no one* in the company had a written statement of their percentage interest in the company yet. Soward asked: "What do you want, 1 percent, 2 percent?" When Holmes did not respond, he told her that 5 percent was high for an idea. Holmes told him: "I'm not selling an idea. I'm a founder of this company." Soward exclaimed: "Surely you don't think you have 50 percent of this company?" Holmes told him that it was a matter between her and Lerner and that Soward should speak to Lerner. Soward agreed to talk to Lerner.

During January and February, an early press release stated: "The idea for Urban Decay was born after Lerner and her horse trainer, Pat Holmes, were sitting around in the English countryside." Lerner approved the press release. In February 1996, an article was printed in the *San Francisco Examiner* containing the following quotes from

*(Continued)*

(Case 19.2 *continued*)

Lerner. "Since we couldn't find good nail polish, in cool colors there must be a business opportunity here. Pat had the original idea. Urban Decay was my spin."

In March 1996, Holmes received a document from Soward offering her a 1 percent ownership interest in Urban Decay. Soward explained that Urban Decay had been formed as a limited liability company, which was owned by its members. For the first time, Holmes realized that she was now being asked to become a minor partner.

Holmes filed a complaint against Lerner and others claiming the existence of an oral contract making them partners. The trial court found in favor of Holmes, and Lerner appealed.

**› ISSUE PRESENTED** Can a general partnership be created through actions and words without any formal documentation?

**› OPINION** MARCHIANO, J., writing for the Court of Appeal of California:

Holmes testified that she and Lerner did not discuss sharing profits of the business during the July 31 "kitchen table" conversation. Throughout the case, Lerner and Soward have contended that without an agreement to share profits, there can be no partnership. . . .

[The] statutory predecessor of the Uniform Partnership Act (UPA) defined a partnership as: "the association of two or more persons, for the purpose of carrying on business together, and dividing its profits between them."[9]

The applicable version of the UPA omitted the language regarding division of profits and defined a partnership as: "an association of two or more persons to carry on as co-owners a business for profit." When the legislature enacts a new statute, replacing an existing one, and omits express language, it indicates an intent to change the original act. We can only conclude that the omission of the language regarding dividing profits from the definition of a partnership was an intentional change in the law.

. . .

Lerner and Soward argue that the agreement between Lerner and Holmes was too indefinite to be enforced. The cases they rely on do not support the argument. . . . The parties' outward manifestations must show that the parties all agreed "upon the same thing in the same sense." If there is no evidence establishing a manifestation of assent to the "same thing" by both parties, then there is no mutual consent to contract and no contract formation. The terms of a contract are reasonably certain if they provide a basis for determining the existence of a breach and for giving an appropriate remedy. There is no requirement, the intention to form a joint venture being otherwise present, that the parties must agree upon the post-acquisition management and operation of the property. In addition, there is nothing unusual about a partnership in which one party supplies an idea which the other party brings into a substantive form. Many businesses and great industrial organizations have sprouted from the germ of an idea in the mind of some man. When the idea is reduced to concrete form and put into action in the form of a business enterprise, an invention, a book, an opera or a theatrical production, the results of the idea are subject to private ownership. . . . The agreement between Holmes and Lerner was to take Holmes' idea and reduce it to concrete form. They decided to do it together, to form a company, to hire employees, and to engage in the entire process together.

. . .

9. CAL. CORP. CODE § 16001.

*(Continued)*

(Case 19.2 *continued*)

[T]he evidence is flatly and irreconcilably conflicting. A finding that no partnership had been formed, had one been made, would have had considerable evidentiary support. As the finding which was made of the formation and the existence of the partnership has ample support in evidence which was accepted by the trial judge as substantial and which was taken as true by him, we cannot disturb the judgment here.

**› RESULT** The Court of Appeal of California affirmed the trial court decision that an express agreement to divide profits is not a prerequisite to proving the existence of a partnership.

**› CRITICAL THINKING QUESTIONS**

1. How could Lerner and Holmes have avoided this dispute?
2. Did Lerner behave ethically?

### *With a Written Agreement*

A written partnership agreement can prevent future misunderstandings. It can also provide for a dispute resolution mechanism, such as arbitration. A written partnership agreement can override many of the provisions of partnership statutes that could turn out to be undesirable to the partners.

A partnership agreement usually includes (1) the term of the partnership's existence, (2) the capital characteristics of the partnership, (3) the division of profits and losses between the partners, (4) partnership salaries or withdrawals, (5) the duties of the partners, and (6) the consequences to the partnership if a partner decides to sell his or her interest in the partnership or becomes incapacitated or dies. Also included are the name of the partnership, the names and addresses of the partners, the type of business to be conducted, and the location of the business.

Drafting a partnership agreement focuses the partners' attention on matters that they might not consider if they made less formal arrangements.[10] For example, will all partners have an equal voice in management? What limits will be placed on the managing partners? How will disputes be settled? May a partner be expelled? May new partners be admitted? If so, by what process?

**INTERNATIONAL SNAPSHOT**

Before a business incorporates abroad, its management should consult a lawyer in the country in which the incorporation is to take place to be advised of the country's laws governing tax, labor, and corporate issues. Parties contemplating a partnership or joint venture should note that civil law jurisdictions usually do not recognize common law–style partnerships. Instead, they look through the partnership to the partners and view the partners as the legal owners.

## Operation of a General Partnership

Unlike a corporation, which has a centralized board of directors and a staff of hired executives for decision making, a general partnership is characterized by direct owner management and control of the business. Each partner's assets are vulnerable to the poor business decisions of the fellow partners. It is therefore important that each partner have a voice in the business decisions of the partnership.

A partnership may choose to cede managerial control of the business to one or more of its partners. Unless the partners expressly agree otherwise, partnership law requires unanimous agreement of all partners on all but the most ordinary matters. If the partners in an informal partnership cannot agree on a decision, they may disband the partnership, distribute its assets, and terminate it.

Each partner is an agent of the partnership for the purpose of its business unless the partnership has filed with the secretary of state a statement specifying which partners have authority for entering into certain transactions on behalf of the partnership, as specified in Sections 105 and 303 of the Revised Uniform Partnership Act (RUPA) (1997). Each partner in a general partnership is liable for the debts incurred by another partner acting in the name of the partnership if that partner had express

10. See Eleena de Lisser, *Partnership Prenuptials*, WALL ST. J., Sept. 25, 1999, at 12.

authority to incur the debt or was carrying on the business of the partnership in the usual way.

For example, if Pro and Ron form Rad Waves as a general partnership, they will each be responsible for the full amount of any liabilities incurred by the partnership or by either partner acting within the scope of his authority as a partner. Hence, Ron's personal assets can be seized if Rad Waves' partnership assets are insufficient to satisfy a judgment against Rad Waves. Ron's personal assets might also be seized if Rad Waves breaches a contract entered into by Pro on behalf of the partnership.

### *Fiduciary Duty*

Partners owe one another certain fiduciary duties, in particular, a duty of loyalty and a duty of care. Partners must also discharge their duties to the partnership and to one another in accordance with the obligation of good faith and fair dealing.

Among the duty of loyalty obligations listed in the RUPA are (1) accounting to the partnership and holding as trustee for it any property, profit, or benefit; (2) refraining from dealing with the partnership as or on behalf of a party having an interest adverse to the partnership; and (3) refraining from engaging in grossly negligent or reckless conduct, intentional misconduct, or a knowing violation of the law.

Be aware, however, that although some states, such as Delaware, have adopted the RUPA in its entirety, many states have chosen to tailor their own version, creating subtle differences that can be significant. For example, the California Uniform Partnership Act implies a higher fiduciary duty than the RUPA by analogizing partnership law with trust law rather than with corporate law.[11]

## DISSOLUTION, WINDING UP, AND TERMINATION OF A GENERAL PARTNERSHIP

*Dissolution* of a general partnership occurs when the partners no longer carry on the business together. A partnership may be dissolved for many reasons. The agreed term for the partnership may expire, or the partners may decide to dissolve the partnership prior to the expiration of the agreed term. A particular undertaking specified in the partnership agreement may be completed. One or more partners may desire to dissolve the partnership. (Unless there is an agreement to the contrary, withdrawal or death of a general partner results in the dissolution of the partnership.) A partner may be expelled, and the remaining partners may thereafter agree to terminate the partnership. A partner may die or go bankrupt, and the agreement may not provide for the partnership's continuation.

A partnership will also be dissolved if the business for which the partnership was formed becomes unlawful—for example, if there is a war between the countries of two or more of the partners. In such a case, the partnership will be dissolved regardless of the wishes of the partners. In other situations, a court may issue a decree of dissolution if a partner becomes disabled, insane, or otherwise unable to perform as a partner. Courts also have the power to dissolve a partnership when a partner willfully breaches the agreement or performs in such a manner as to make it impractical to carry on the partnership. Because the purpose of partnerships is to make a profit, a partnership may be dissolved by court decree if it becomes apparent that the partnership is unprofitable and lacks any real prospect of success. If the partnership has reasonable prospects of earning money in the future, however, it may not be dissolved by court decree despite recent losses.

Upon dissolution, all of the partners' authority ceases except their authority to complete transactions begun but not yet finished and to wind up the partnership. *Winding up* involves settling the accounts and liquidating the assets of the partnership for the purpose of making distributions and terminating the concern. The liabilities and obligations of the partners do not end at dissolution; the partnership continues throughout the winding-up period.

During the winding-up process, the partners' fiduciary duties to one another continue. The winding-up partners may not run the business for their own benefit but must account as trustees to the withdrawing partners or to the estate of a deceased partner.

*Termination* occurs when all the partnership affairs are wound up and the partners' authority to act for the partnership is completely extinguished. A dissolved partnership may terminate or may be continued by a new partnership formed by the remaining partners (including perhaps the estate or heirs of a deceased partner).

# Limited Partnership Requirements

The basic rules that govern formation, operation, and termination of general partnerships apply to limited partnerships as well. Some additional requirements placed on limited partnerships are discussed in this section.

11. Al Li, *Taking Care of Your Partners*, GRAYCARY, *at* http://www.graycary.com/gcc/GrayCary-C/News—Arti/newsletter/venture/030702.

### FORMAL REQUIREMENTS

In addition to the requirement that a certificate of limited partnership be filed with the appropriate state authority, most state statutes require that the partnership agreement clearly designate the limited partners as such. Any partnership that does not substantially meet this and other statutory requirements will be treated as a general partnership, with mutual liability and apparent authority attaching to each partner. A person who intended to be only a limited partner may face unlimited personal liability for all of the partnership's debts if there has not been substantial compliance in good faith with the formal requirements.

The Uniform Limited Partnership Act provides that persons who contributed capital to a business erroneously believing that they were becoming limited partners in a limited partnership will not be liable as general partners if, upon ascertaining the mistake, they promptly renounce their interest in the profits of the business.[12] A person who believed in good faith that he or she had become a limited partner is liable only to third parties that both transacted business with the purported limited partnership before the certificate of limited partnership was filed and reasonably believed that the person was a general partner at the time of the transaction.[13]

### LIMITED PARTICIPATION

A limited partner's liability is limited unless he or she takes part in the control of the business. Thus, if limited partners have a voice in the business decisions of the partnership, they are opening themselves up to the possibility of liability beyond their original capital investment. Furthermore, limited partners may contribute money or property to the partnership, but generally not services. Hence, in the Rad Waves example, if Olivia assists with the design of the sportswear line, in most states her liability could exceed her original $1,000 capital contribution. Therefore, limited partners should not take part in any partnership activity beyond monitoring the progress of their investment and exercising such statutory rights as the right to vote on the removal of a general partner. Moreover, the limited partner's name cannot appear in the name of the partnership without incurring unlimited liability.

12. If such a renunciation is not effectuated, the putative limited partners face liability in an individual capacity for debts of the partnership. Reiman v. Int'l Hospitality Group, Inc., 614 A.2d 925 (D.C. 1992).

13. *See, e.g.*, Section 15633 of the California Revised Limited Partnership Act.

## Incorporation

*Incorporation* is the process by which a corporation is formed. The corporate statutes of each state set forth the steps that must be taken to establish a corporation in that state. Many states' statutes are based in whole or in part on the Model Business Corporation Act, an annotated uniform statute prepared by academics and practitioners. The state under whose laws a corporation is formed is called the corporation's *corporate domicile*. A corporation is not limited to doing business in its corporate domicile. It can conduct business as a *foreign corporation* in other states. Typically, to do so, it must file a statement of foreign corporation with the appropriate secretary of state and state taxing authority.

### WHERE TO INCORPORATE

Corporations may incorporate in any state; it need not be the state in which most of their business is located. Two important factors affect the decision of where to incorporate: (1) the costs of incorporation in a given state, and (2) the relative advantages and disadvantages of that state's corporation laws. If the corporation is privately held and its business will be conducted largely within one state, incorporation in that state is probably the best choice. If the corporation will be large from the outset or will be engaged in substantial interstate business, however, then incorporation in a jurisdiction with the most advantageous corporate statutes and case law should be considered.

Corporation laws may be favorable either to management or to the shareholders. Some states, such as Delaware, are considered to be pro-management because their statutes and court decisions tend to give control on a wide range of issues to the officers and directors. Other states, such as California, make it difficult for corporate managers to do certain things without the approval and participation of the shareholders. These states are regarded as pro-shareholder.

Since the mid-1930s, Delaware has been considered the preeminent state for incorporation. Fifty percent of the companies on the New York and Nasdaq Stock Exchanges are incorporated in Delaware, and more than 65 percent of *Fortune* 500 companies are Delaware companies. Consequently, Delaware corporate law is considered the standard in America and much of the world.[14]

14. Cynthia Ribas, *California vs. Delaware: A Corporate Law Comparison*, BUS. L. NEWS, 2002, at 17–27.

The Delaware General Corporation Law is a dynamic statute designed to give corporations maximum flexibility in ordering their affairs. The Delaware Court of Chancery, established in 1792, hears (without juries) all cases involving corporate law issues and has rendered thousands of written opinions interpreting virtually every provision of the Delaware General Corporation Law.[15]

An examination of the Delaware statute helps highlight some of the key corporate governance choices. The power to elect the board of directors is the primary way in which shareholders exercise control, and all jurisdictions provide for it. Delaware permits, but does not require, cumulative voting (discussed further below), which allows a minority shareholder greater opportunity to elect someone to the board. Delaware also permits a *staggered* (or *classified*) *board*, whereby directors serve for specified terms, usually three years, with only a fraction of them up for reelection at any one time. A classified board makes it more difficult to replace the entire board at once. In Delaware, classified boards are the norm. Delaware prohibits the removal of directors on a classified board without cause, unless the certificate of incorporation provides otherwise. In contrast, all corporations incorporated in California, except publicly traded companies, must have cumulative voting and cannot have a staggered board. In addition, as explained further in Chapter 20, Delaware permits broader limitations on directors' personal monetary liability than California.

The primary reason a company would choose to incorporate in California, or any other state rather than Delaware, would be cost.[16] When deciding whether to incorporate in the local state or Delaware, entrepreneurs must weigh the advantages Delaware provides for managers against the expense of paying Delaware corporate franchise taxes, the expense of hiring lawyers familiar with Delaware law, and the possibility of having to defend a lawsuit in Delaware. Businesses incorporated in their local state often reincorporate in Delaware once they have grown large enough to justify the effort and expense of reincorporation.

## How to Incorporate

To create a corporation, one or more incorporators must prepare a document called the *certificate* or *articles of incorporation* (or the *corporate charter*). This document must be filed with the appropriate state governmental agency, usually the secretary of state for the jurisdiction that will become the corporate domicile.

The articles of incorporation are generally quite short. For example, the Pennsylvania Business Corporation Law specifies that the articles need only set forth the name of the corporation, the location and mailing address of the corporation's registered office in Pennsylvania, a brief statement of the purpose of the corporation, the term for which the corporation is to exist (which may be perpetual), the total number of shares that the corporation is authorized to issue, the name and mailing address of each of the incorporators, and a statement of the number of shares to be purchased by each.

Section 204 of the Pennsylvania Business Corporation Law, like most modern corporation statutes, goes on to provide that the purpose clause "may consist of or include a statement that the corporation shall have unlimited power to engage in and to do any lawful act concerning any or all lawful business for which corporations may be incorporated under this act." Pennsylvania's corporate law goes on to specify corporate powers, so there is no need to have a long purpose clause in the articles of incorporation. Indeed, to do so invites trouble because one might inadvertently exclude an activity in which the corporation may later want to engage.

After the articles of incorporation are filed, the incorporators adopt the *bylaws,* that is, the rules governing the corporation (including the number of authorized directors), and elect the initial board of directors. This can be done either at an organizational meeting or by unanimous written consent. The incorporators are exclusively empowered to place the directors in office. After electing the board of directors, the incorporators sign a written resignation. The directors then have an organizational meeting at which they (1) ratify the adoption of the bylaws by the incorporators or adopt new bylaws, (2) appoint officers, (3) designate a bank as depository for corporate funds, (4) authorize the sale of stock to the initial shareholders, and (5) determine the consideration to be received in exchange for such shares—cash, other property, or past (but not future) services rendered to the corporation.

Exhibit 19.1 outlines the steps required to form a corporation.

## Defective Incorporation

Because a corporation exists only by statute, not by common law, any defect in the incorporation process can have the effect of denying corporate status. A business

15 See Lewis S. Black, Jr., *Why Delaware? A Practitioner Gives Reasons for Incorporation,* CORP. COUNS. WKLY., Oct. 20, 1999, at 8.
16. Ribas, *supra* note 14.

**EXHIBIT 19.1 Steps Required to Form a Corporation**

- Select a corporate name and agent for service of process.
- File certificate of incorporation (also known as articles of incorporation or charter in some jurisdictions) signed by incorporator(s).
- Sign action by incorporator(s) that:
  - Adopts bylaws, and
  - Specifies initial directors.
- Obtain written resignation of incorporator(s).
- Hold first directors' meeting or take action by unanimous written consent of the directors. Among other items of business:
  - Ratify the adoption of the bylaws by the incorporator(s) or adopt new bylaws,
  - Elect officers,
  - Issue stock, and
  - Authorize corporate bank account.

organization that was intended to function as a corporation but has failed to comply with the statutory requirements is in fact a partnership or, if there is only one shareholder, a sole proprietorship. The owners will not enjoy the protection of limited liability and can be held personally responsible for all debts of the enterprise. The courts have, however, developed several doctrines to avoid this result if it would be unfair.

### De Jure Corporation

When incorporation has been done correctly, a *de jure corporation* is formed. This means that the entity is a corporation by right and cannot be challenged. Most jurisdictions will find de jure corporate status as long as the incorporators have substantially complied with the incorporation requirements. For example, substantial compliance will be found even if the incorporators failed to obtain a required signature or submitted an improper notarization.

### De Facto Corporation

If the incorporators cannot show substantial compliance, a court may treat the entity as a *de facto corporation,* that is, as a corporation in fact even though it is not technically a corporation by law. For the court to find a de facto corporation, the incorporators must demonstrate that they were unaware of the defect and that they made a good faith effort to incorporate correctly. For example, if a clerk for the secretary of state delayed filing the articles, the business would not be a corporation de jure, but it would probably be a corporation de facto.

### Corporation by Estoppel

An entity that is neither a de jure nor a de facto corporation may be a *corporation by estoppel.* If a third party, in all of its transactions with the enterprise, acts as if it were doing business with a corporation, the third party is prevented or *estopped* from claiming that the enterprise is not a corporation.[17] It is considered unfair to permit the third party to reach shareholders' personal assets when all along it believed it was dealing with a corporation whose shareholders had limited liability.

## Piercing the Corporate Veil

The corporation is built around the central premise of limited liability. Under certain circumstances, however, courts will deny this central premise and hold the shareholders liable for claims against the corporation. A court will *pierce the corporate veil* in this way if necessary to prevent the evasion of statutes, the perpetration of fraud, or other activities against public policy. The need to pierce arises only if the corporation is unable to pay its own debts.

Courts have used the same approach to decide whether to pierce the veil of a limited liability company and hold its members personally liable. For example, the Court of Appeal of Louisiana held that Insulation Sales and Service, Inc. (ISS), the majority owner of AAI Ventures, L.L.C., was liable for monies owed under a contract between AAI and Patrick Hamilton, an individual hired to provide general management services to AAI in connection with its subcontract to remove asbestos from a casino.[18] AAI, which was formed to do asbestos removal work at the casino, was undercapitalized; the separate corporate existence of AAI and its affiliated companies was disregarded; individuals associated with the casino project were unsure of coworkers' job titles or employers of record; employees of one organization were housed at the offices of other organizations; and AAI had no employees—its accounting was handled by employees of ISS.

There are two legal approaches to piercing the corporate veil. The *alter ego theory* applies when the owners of a corporation have so mingled their own affairs with those of the corporation that the corporation does not exist as a distinct entity—instead, it is an alter ego of its owners. The *undercapitalization theory* applies when the corporation is a separate entity, but its deliberate lack of

17. *See, e.g.,* Cranson v. Int'l Bus. Machs. Corp., 200 A.2d 33 (Md. 1964).

18. Hamilton v. AAI Ventures, L.L.C., 768 So. 2d 298 (La. Ct. App. 2000). *See also* Litchfield Asset Mgmt. v. Howell, 799 A.2d 298 (Conn. App. 2002).

adequate capital allows it to skirt potential liabilities. Such undercapitalization constitutes a fraud upon the public.

Courts usually apply some combination of these theories. If a court suspects wrongdoing or bad faith on the part of shareholders, it will be more inclined to pierce the corporate veil. Because a publicly traded corporation generally does not have one controlling shareholder, attempts to pierce the veil of such corporations are rare. Usually, the cases involve small, closely held corporations, including subsidiaries of larger corporations.

## Alter Ego Theory

A court will consider several factors when deciding whether a corporation is merely the alter ego of a shareholder.

### *Domination by Controlling Shareholder*

If an individual or another corporation owning most of the stock of the corporation exerts so much control that the standard corporate decision-making mechanisms are not in operation, the courts may find that the corporation has no separate mind, will, or existence of its own.

For example, following its acquisition of Atlanta-based HBO & Co. (HBOC), McKesson, a California-based health-care company, allowed HBOC to survive as its wholly owned subsidiary. Later that year McKesson announced that for several years prior to the merger HBOC had improperly recorded revenue amounting to over $50 million. The announcement prompted the value of the stock to plummet. Following the precipitous drop in value, McKesson brought a suit of unjust enrichment against former HBOC shareholders who had traded in their overvalued stock for equivalently valued McKesson stock. The judge denied the claim, finding it would be an unwarranted piercing of the corporate veil. Although the companies had not become completely merged, McKesson exercised such control over HBOC that its shareholders were, in effect, merely McKesson shareholders following their final approval of the merger agreement. McKesson argued that it had to sue the shareholders directly because suing its own subsidiary would harm itself, but the judge found that if suing HBOC would amount to suing itself, then the HBOC shareholders were protected as McKesson shareholders against such an attack.[19]

### *Commingling of Assets*

The courts will also examine whether the books and funds of the corporation and of the controlling shareholder have been commingled; for example, whether the shareholder uses company checks to make personal purchases or payments.

### *Bypassing Formalities*

If an action that requires approval by the board proceeds without a board meeting being held, or if other procedural rules (such as the requirement of an annual shareholders meeting) are consistently broken, the courts will be inclined to view the corporation as the instrument of the controlling shareholder unless the corporation qualifies as a statutory close corporation under the law of the state of incorporation. As noted earlier, the bypassing of these formalities is not a factor in deciding whether to pierce the veil of a close corporation.

## Undercapitalization Theory

In deciding whether a corporation is undercapitalized, a court will consider whether the founders should have reasonably anticipated that the corporation would be unable to pay the debts or liabilities it would incur. (Of course, the amount of capital invested does not have to guarantee business success—if it did, all failed businesses would be deemed undercapitalized.)

For example, assume a new corporation is formed to build airplanes, an activity that requires large expenditures and entails substantial risks of liability for third-party injury. The corporation has raised only $1,000 in capital. It is obvious that the corporation will run out of funds quickly and be unable to pay its bills. It will not have money to buy adequate product liability insurance or to self-insure against claims for injuries caused by defective airplanes. A court may, because of the undercapitalization, ignore the corporate form and hold the owners of the corporation personally liable for its debts and liabilities.

The above example is an exaggerated case. In reality, it is often difficult for a court to decide how much capital is enough. Two judges examining the same facts may come to different conclusions as to whether the owner should have reasonably anticipated that the corporation would need more capital. Judges may also disagree as to whether undercapitalization alone is sufficient grounds to pierce the corporate veil. In the following classic case, the majority opinion and the minority dissent reflect two sides of this issue.

### Ethical Consideration

Is it ethical for an entrepreneur to use the corporate form without ensuring that the corporation has sufficient funds to act in a socially responsible manner?

19. McKesson HBOC, Inc. v. New York State Common Ret., 339 F.3d 1087 (9th Cir. 2003).

A CASE IN POINT

**CASE 19.3**
**Walkovszky v. Carlton**
*Court of Appeals of New York*
*223 N.E.2d 6 (N.Y. 1966).*

## In the Language of the Court

**› FACTS** The plaintiff was severely injured in New York City when he was run down by a taxicab owned by the defendant, Seon Cab Corporation. The individual defendant, Carlton, was a shareholder of ten corporations, including Seon, each of which had two cabs registered in its name. Each cab was covered by only the minimum $10,000 per cab automobile liability insurance required by New York law.

Although seemingly independent of one another, these corporations were, according to the plaintiff, "operated . . . as a single entity, unit and enterprise" with regard to financing, supplies, repairs, employees, and garaging, and all were named as defendants. The plaintiff also asserted that the multiple corporate structure constituted an unlawful attempt "to defraud members of the general public" who might be injured by the cabs. He therefore sought to hold their sole shareholder personally liable for his injury.

**› ISSUE PRESENTED** May the corporate veil be pierced solely because the corporation is undercapitalized?

**› OPINION** FULD, J., writing for the New York Court of Appeals:

The law permits the incorporation of a business for the very purpose of enabling its proprietors to escape personal liability but, manifestly, the privilege is not without its limits. Broadly speaking, the courts will disregard the corporate form, or, to use accepted terminology, "pierce the corporate veil," whenever necessary "to prevent fraud or to achieve equity."

. . .

The individual defendant is charged with having "organized, managed, dominated and controlled" a fragmented corporate entity but there are no allegations that he was conducting business in his individual capacity. . . . The corporate form may not be disregarded merely because the assets of the corporation, together with the mandatory insurance coverage of the vehicle which struck the plaintiff, are insufficient to assure him the recovery sought. . . . [I]f the insurance coverage required by statute "is inadequate for the protection of the public, the remedy lies not with the courts but with the Legislature." It may very well be sound policy to require that certain corporations must take out liability insurance which will afford adequate compensation to their potential tort victims. However, the responsibility for imposing conditions on the privilege of incorporation has been committed by the Constitution to the Legislature and it may not be fairly implied, from any statute, that the Legislature intended, without the slightest discussion or debate, to require of taxi corporations that they carry automobile liability insurance over and above that mandated by the Vehicle and Traffic Law.

**› DISSENT** KEATING, J., dissenting from the majority opinion:

From their inception these corporations were intentionally undercapitalized for the purpose of avoiding responsibility for acts which were bound to arise as a result of the operation of a large taxi fleet having cars out on the street 24 hours a day and engaged in public transportation. And during the course of the corporations' existence all income was continually drained out of the corporations for the same purpose.

The issue presented by this action is whether the policy of this State, which affords those desiring to engage in a business enterprise the privilege of limited liability through the use of the corporate device, is so strong that it will permit that privilege

*(Continued)*

(Case 19.3 *continued*)

to continue no matter how much it is abused, no matter how irresponsibly the corporation is operated, no matter what the cost to the public. I do not believe that it is.

[Judge Keating then cited with approval a California Supreme Court case[20] holding that the corporate veil could be pierced based on undercapitalization alone.]

. . .

What I would merely hold is that a participating shareholder of a corporation vested with a public interest, organized with capital insufficient to meet liabilities which are certain to arise in the ordinary course of the corporation's business, may be held personally responsible for such liabilities. Where corporate income is not sufficient to cover the cost of insurance premiums above the statutory minimum or where initially adequate finances dwindle under the pressure of competition, bad times or extraordinary and unexpected liability, obviously the shareholder will not be held liable.

**› RESULT** In New York, the corporate veil may not be pierced solely because the corporation is undercapitalized. Accordingly, plaintiff Walkovszky cannot sue Carlton in his individual capacity unless the complaint is amended to allege alter ego.

**› COMMENTS** In *Walkovszky,* the court rejected the argument that undercapitalization alone constituted fraud. The court suggested, however, that the plaintiff amend the complaint to allege that the individual defendants were "shuttling . . . personal funds in and out of the corporation 'without regard to formality and to suit their immediate convenience,'" thus stating a valid cause of action under the alter ego theory.

In *Browning-Ferris Industries v. Ter Maat,*[21] the U.S. Court of Appeals for the Seventh Circuit held that undercapitalization alone did not justify piercing the corporate veil of an Illinois corporation operating a garbage dump.

**› CRITICAL THINKING QUESTIONS**

1. From a public policy standpoint, with which opinion do you agree, the majority or the dissent?
2. Would the result have been different if defendant Carlton's name had been conspicuously displayed on the sides of all of the taxis owned by the various corporations of which Carlton was the sole shareholder and if Carlton actually serviced, inspected, repaired, and dispatched the taxis?

20. Minton v. Cavaney, 364 P.2d 473 (Cal. 1961).
21. 195 F.3d 953 (7th Cir. 1999), *cert. denied,* 529 U.S. 1098 (2000).

## Tort versus Contract

A tort plaintiff's contact with the corporation (for example, being hit by a taxi) may be completely involuntary. Many courts are therefore more sympathetic to the tort victim who faces an undercapitalized corporate defendant than to a plaintiff seeking to pierce the corporate veil in a breach-of-contract case. Why should someone who voluntarily contracted to provide credit to a weakly capitalized corporation, perhaps charging a premium interest rate in so doing, later be entitled to reach the owner's personal assets? After all, the creditor had, or could have negotiated, access to the corporation's financial statements. The voluntary decision to do business with the undercapitalized company contrasts quite sharply with the plight of a party who is a victim of a tort committed by an officer or employee of the corporation. If, however, a shareholder misrepresents the financial condition of the corporation when negotiating a contract, then courts will pierce the corporate veil.

# Management of the Corporation

Corporate control is apportioned among the directors, officers, and shareholders. The directors are the overall managers and guardians of the corporation. The officers are the day-to-day managers. The shareholders, as the owners of the corporation, do not participate directly in management, but they elect the directors. The shareholders also must approve certain major transactions.

## DIRECTORS

Most state statutes provide that the business and the affairs of the corporation shall be managed, and all corporate powers shall be exercised, by or under the direction of the board of directors. The board may delegate the management of the day-to-day operations of the business of the corporation to a management company or to other persons, such as officers. A member of the board may also serve as an officer. Such a person is called an *inside director*. A director who is not also an officer is called an *outside director*. An understanding of the dynamics between the board and the officers is essential to comprehend the workings of a corporation.

## OFFICERS

The officers appointed by the board of directors are agents of the corporation and have the power to act on its behalf. A corporation will normally have a chief executive officer (often called president), a secretary, a chief financial officer, and other officers as designated in the bylaws or determined by the board.

Any number of offices may be held by the same person unless the articles or bylaws provide otherwise. Officers are chosen by the board and serve at the pleasure of the board. If an officer is terminated in violation of a contract of employment, the officer cannot sue to get his or her job back but can sue for damages. An officer may resign at any time upon written notice to the corporation. The corporation can sue for damages if an officer's resignation breaches his or her employment contract.

## SHAREHOLDERS

Shareholders are virtually never involved in the day-to-day operations of a corporation. Shareholders' main "power" in the corporation is their right to elect directors who will run the company in their stead. Exhibit 19.2 provides a graphic depiction of the relationship among the shareholders, directors, and officers of a corporation.

### *Voting Rights*

The shareholders elect the directors. The courts have held that directors have no inherent right to remain in office. In some states, directors can be removed by the shareholders with or without cause at any time. In other states, such as Delaware, a director who is elected to a staggered board (where directors serve for designated terms) may not be removed without cause, unless the certificate of incorporation provides otherwise. The shareholders might be able to accomplish the same result by first eliminating the charter or bylaw provision requiring the staggered board and then voting to remove the directors. In addition, certain transactions, such as a merger or the sale of substantially all of the corporation's assets, can be approved only by a vote of the shareholders.

Shareholders can act by voting at a meeting or by written consent. A shareholder who cannot be present at a meeting can vote by *proxy*, that is, by a written authorization for another person to vote on his or her behalf. Only *shareholders of record*, that is, persons whose names appear on the corporation's shareholder list on a specified date, are entitled to vote.

No action can be taken at a shareholder meeting unless there is a *quorum;* the quorum requirements are set forth in each state's corporate statute. In most jurisdictions, there is no quorum unless the holders of at least 50 percent of the outstanding shares are present in person or by proxy.

**Cumulative Voting Versus Straight Voting in the Election of Directors** Some states permit, and some require, *cumulative voting*, whereby each shareholder may cast all of his or her votes for one nominee or allocate them among the nominees as the shareholder sees fit. A shareholder's total number of votes is thus equal to the number of directors to be elected multiplied by the

## ETHICAL CONSIDERATION

Directors and officers are allowed to be shareholders in the corporation they manage. In fact, giving the managers an ownership stake is a standard strategy for increasing their motivation. A manager's duty is to act in the best interest of all of the shareholders. If there are conflicting interests among the shareholders, how should a director or officer who is also a shareholder resolve conflicts between his or her own interests and those of other shareholders?

EXHIBIT 19.2 The Corporate Governance Triangle

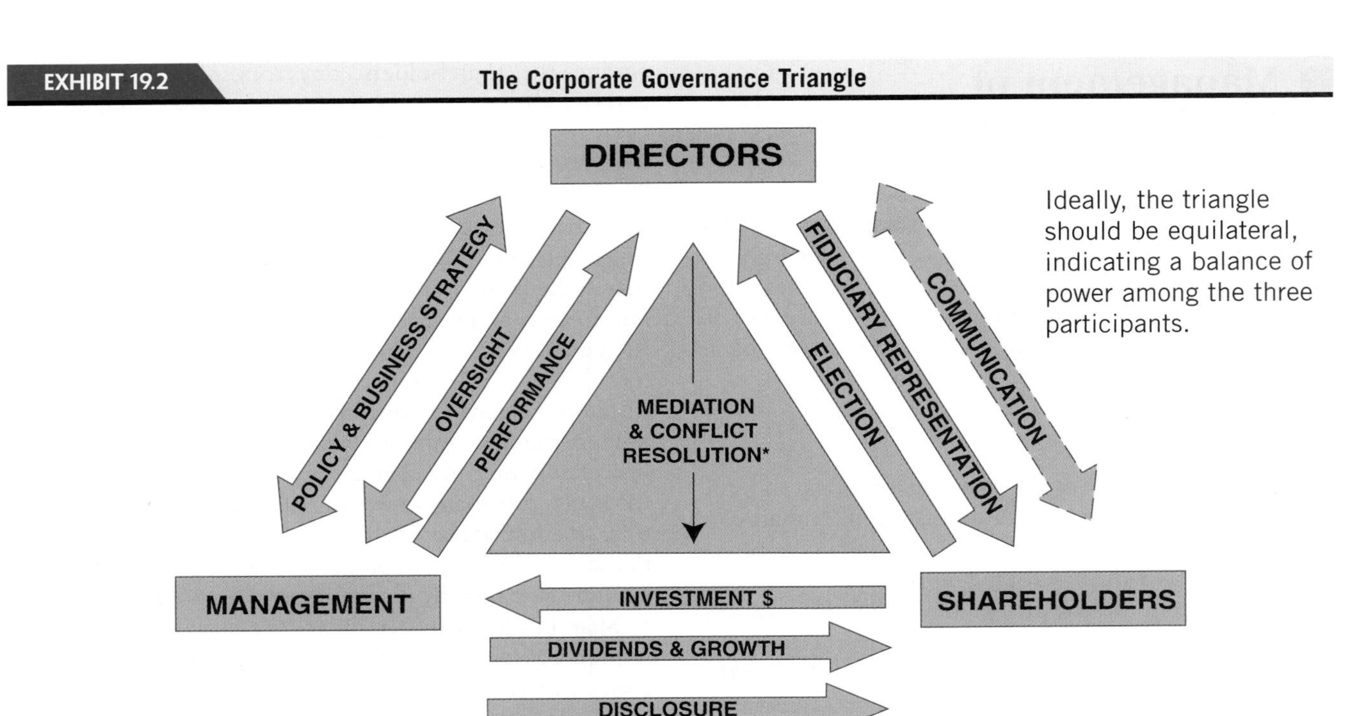


*The board is responsible for resolving the structural conflicts that arise between the conflicting but equally valid goals of management and shareholders on the following issues:

- Control
- Capital structure
- Compensation of senior management
- Nomination of directors
- Shareholders' rights

SOURCE: Georgeson Shareholder Communications Inc. Used by permission. All rights reserved.

number of shares owned by the shareholder. Cumulative voting gives minority shareholders a greater likelihood of electing at least one director.

In an election permitting cumulative voting, the number of shares, $x$, required to elect a given number of directors, $y$, may be calculated by the following formula:

$$x = \frac{y \times z}{1 + d} + 1$$

where $z$ is the total number of shares voting, and $d$ is the total number of directors to be elected.[22]

To illustrate, assume a shareholder wants to elect three directors ($y = 3$) to a board with five members up for election ($d = 5$). The corporation has 100 shares outstanding, and they are all voted ($z = 100$). Then

$$x = \frac{3 \times 100}{1 + 5} + 1$$
$$x = 51$$

With cumulative voting, a shareholder would need 51 shares to elect three directors.

In contrast, with *straight voting*, a shareholder can cast one vote for each share the shareholder owns for each nominee. Thus, a shareholder who owns 51 shares can cast 51 votes for each vacant director position. Consequently, a shareholder who controls more than half the voting stock of a corporation can effectively elect the entire board of directors.

22. CONSTANCE E. BAGLEY & DAVID J. BERGER, PROXY CONTESTS: STRATEGIC CONSIDERATIONS (1998).

**Class Voting** Class voting occurs when the charter or applicable corporate law requires one class of stock, usually preferred, to approve a given proposal while other classes of stock are excluded from the vote. For example, a charter might require all mergers and sales of substantially all of the assets to be approved by both a majority of the common shares voting as a class and a majority of the preferred shares voting as a class. Class voting is often sought by investors attempting to protect their control of certain key decisions even if they lose majority control of the corporation's voting equity.

Courts generally will enforce class-voting provisions but tend to construe them quite literally. In *Benchmark Capital Partners IV, L.P. v. Vague,*[23] the Delaware Court of Chancery reaffirmed its position that a class-voting provision should be narrowly construed even if it appears that a majority shareholder has crafted a transaction to avoid triggering the provision. Thus, a group of shareholders who were guaranteed the right to vote as a class on any change in the corporate charter that would dilute their rights or holdings in the corporation were held to have no right to a class vote on a merger that might dilute their equity interest.

## Including Shareholder Proposals in the Company's Proxy Statement

The Securities and Exchange Commission (SEC) requires publicly traded companies to include certain shareholder proposals in the proxy statement the board sends to shareholders to solicit proxies for the election of directors. Shareholder activists have used shareholder proposals extensively to raise social or political issues. Early examples included proposals for companies (1) to stop doing business in South Africa to protest the policy of apartheid (mandated segregation of blacks and whites) and (2) to adopt the CERES Principles, a ten-point code of environmental conduct.

More recently, shareholder proposals have focused more on corporate governance issues. In 2003, the SEC advised corporations that proposals involving any of the following could not be omitted from proxy materials: (1) requests that the board seek shareholder approval prior to adopting a "poison pill" antitakeover device, (2) limits on the compensation of nonemployee directors, (3) schemes for performance-based compensation for executives, (4) equity compensation plans, (5) compensation for senior officers, (6) a reduction in pension benefits, (7) requests that the company dissociate itself from any "offensive" advertising, (8) increased retirement benefits, and (9) a dividend increase.[24] Companies had unsuccessfully sought to exclude these proposals under SEC Rule 14a-8 under the Securities Exchange Act of 1934, which allows companies to exclude proposals that relate to the daily operations of the company.

## Shareholder Nomination of Directors

As discussed earlier, corporate law proceeds on the assumption that the shareholders will elect the directors who in turn are responsible for overseeing management. In practice, the CEO is often also the chair of the board and significantly influences both the selection of directors and the board's agenda.[25] As a result, the board may fail to exercise the necessary oversight.

The corporate excesses of the late twentieth century have led to renewed calls for greater director independence. In most public companies, a separate, independent committee of directors is charged with nominating directors for election. In 2003, the SEC adopted rules that require companies to disclose more information about the nomination process.[26] A public company must disclose (1) whether the company has a nominating committee at all and, if not, why not; (2) whether members of the committee satisfy independence requirements; (3) whether the company pays a third party to help find suitable directors; and (4) the company's minimum requirements for its director nominees. Commenting on the new rules, SEC Chairman William Donaldson stated:

> These rules are an important first step in improving the proxy process as it relates to the nomination and election of directors. The Commission believes that better information about the way board nominees are identified, evaluated and selected is critical for shareholder understanding of the proxy process regarding nomination and election of directors. We also believe that better information about the processes of shareholder communications with boards lies at the foundation of shareholder understanding of how

23. 2002 WL 1732423 (Del. Ch. 2002).

24. Michael Bologna, *Shareholder Proposals,* CORP. COUNS. WKLY., Feb. 20, 2003, at 60.

25. See Constance E. Bagley & Richard Koppes, *Leader of the Pack: A Proposal for Disclosure of Board Leadership Structure,* 34 SAN DIEGO L. REV. 1 (1997).

26. *Disclosure Regarding Nominating Committee Functions and Communications Between Security Holders and Boards of Directors,* Release No. 34–48825, 68 Fed. Reg. 69,204 (Dec. 11, 2003). For a more detailed discussion, see Task Force on Shareholder Proposals of the Committee on Federal Regulation of Securities of the Section of Business Law of the American Bar Association, *Report on Proposed Changes in Proxy Rules and Regulations Regarding Procedures for the Election of Corporate Directors,* 59 BUS. LAW. 109–25 (2003).

they can interact with directors and director processes. These are vital issues in strengthening the proxy process for the benefit of shareholders.[27]

In 2003, the SEC also made a highly contentious proposal to permit certain long-term significant shareholders to nominate candidates for the board without having to go through the considerable expense of commencing a proxy contest.[28] Proposed Rule 14a-11 would require publicly traded corporations to permit direct shareholder nominations of directors upon the occurrence of certain trigger events that suggest that security holders need such access to further an effective proxy process.[29] Under the proposed rule, only shareholders who have owned more than 5 percent of a company's voting securities for at least two years would be permitted to add director nominations to the company's proxy statements when a trigger event has occurred. Proposed triggers include a shareholder vote in which (1) 35 percent of the voting shares oppose management's slate of candidates or (2) more than 50 percent of the votes cast support a shareholder proposal requesting that the company be subject to the shareholder access procedure.

Although SEC Commissioner Roel Campos called the proposal "very, very modest," Martin Lipton of Wachtell, Lipton, Rosen & Katz characterized it as "an extreme overreaction to Enron and WorldCom."[30] The Business Roundtable, the National Association of Manufacturers, and other key business groups have publicly opposed the proposal, but public pension funds representing nearly $703 billion in assets have voiced their support.[31]

## *Shareholder Inspection Rights and Access to the Shareholder List*

Shareholders have a common law right to inspect the corporate books and records, including the stock register and/or shareholder list, the minutes of board meetings and shareholder meetings, the bylaws, and books of account. In making the examination, shareholders are permitted the assistance of an accountant, lawyer, or other expert.

In most states, the right of inspection is limited by the requirement that the inspection be conducted for a "proper purpose." States vary in their interpretation of this limit. Some jurisdictions construe "proper purpose" liberally, leaving shareholder inspection rights virtually unfettered. These states reason that inspection rights should be broad because everything that affects a corporation eventually has an effect on its shareholders. Other states, more concerned with the potential for the inspection right to be an abusive tool, protect against "fishing expeditions" by requiring more than a vague allegation of mismanagement to establish a proper purpose.

In one of the most famous cases in American corporate history, the Minnesota Supreme Court ruled that a shareholder of Honeywell, Inc., who opposed the Vietnam War and sought to persuade Honeywell to cease producing antipersonnel fragmentation bombs for use in the war, did not have a right to Honeywell's shareholder list or the corporate records dealing with weapons and munitions manufacture.[32] The court explained: "Considering the huge size of many modern corporations and the necessarily complicated nature of their bookkeeping, it is plain that to permit thousands of stockholders to roam at will through their records would render impossible . . . the proper carrying of their business." Because "the power to inspect may be the power to destroy," the court ruled that Delaware law (which governed the case because Honeywell was incorporated in Delaware) requires the shareholder to assert some concern with investment return. In this case, the shareholder's avowed purpose in buying Honeywell stock was to place himself in a position to try to impress his social and political opinions upon Honeywell's management and its other shareholders. Such an interest, the court concluded, could hardly be deemed a proper purpose germane to his economic interest as a shareholder.

Many of the most intense shareholder inspection battles involve access to the list of shareholders. Shareholders seeking to change a corporate policy or gain control of the board of directors want to identify and target their message to the holders of large blocks of stock. To do this, the insurgents need a copy of the shareholder list. Precisely because the list is so valuable to management's shareholder critics, incumbent managers are likely to resist efforts to obtain it.

Acknowledging that access to the shareholder list can be vital to a successful corporate power struggle, some jurisdictions allow such access without requiring a proper

27. See http://www.srimedia.com/artman/publish/article_681.shtml.

28. CONSTANCE E. BAGLEY & DAVID BERGER, PROXY CONTESTS: PREPARING FOR THE CAMPAIGN (1998).

29. *Security Holder Director Nominations,* Release No. 34–48626, 68 Fed. Reg. 60,784 (Oct. 23, 2003).

30. *Shareholder Access Proposal,* CORP. COUNS. WKLY., Mar. 17, 2004, at 84.

31. *SEC's Donaldson Condemns "Shrill" Critics of Proposal for Shareholders' Proxy Access,* CORP. COUNS. WKLY., June 30, 2004, at 193.

32. State *ex rel.* Pillsbury v. Honeywell, Inc., 191 N.W.2d 406 (Minn. 1971).

purpose, provided that the shareholder owns a substantial block of shares. For example, Section 1600(a) of the California Corporations Code provides that any 5 percent shareholder can inspect and copy the record of shareholders' names and addresses and shareholdings during usual business hours upon five business days' written notice.

*Proxy contests,* whereby insurgents propose their own slate of directors or rally to oppose a board proposal by sending out their own proxy statement and soliciting proxies for their candidates or position, continue to be an important technique for obtaining control of a publicly traded company or opposing a particular transaction proposed by the incumbent board of directors. Under the SEC's regulation for the solicitation of proxies, publicly traded companies must either mail the proxy materials for the insurgents seeking to elect their own directors or provide a shareholder list. Most companies elect to mail the materials, so insurgents often rely on state inspection statutes to gain access to shareholder lists.[33]

### *Shareholder Suits*

Shareholders generally have a right to sue individually and directly for specific harm done to them. However, shareholders alleging corporate mismanagement leading to harm to the corporation as a whole must usually sue derivatively in the name of the corporation in a shareholder derivative action. In such a case, the recovery is paid to the corporation, not any individual shareholder.

In *Tooley v. Donaldson, Lufkin & Jennette, Inc.,*[34] the Delaware Supreme Court articulated a more straightforward test for determining which type of claims must be brought derivatively. To determine whether a claim is direct or derivative, Delaware courts focus on "(1) who suffered the alleged harm (the corporation or the suing stockholders, individually); and (2) who would receive the benefit of any recovery or other remedy (the corporation or the stockholders, individually)?"[35] Also relevant is whether the plaintiffs have demonstrated that they can prevail without showing an injury to the corporation, which depends in part on the identity of the person or entity to whom a duty was owed. When a group of former shareholders sued the former chair of Syncor International Corporation for alleged misconduct that caused them to receive a lower price for their shares when the company was sold, the Delaware Court of Chancery applied this standard and concluded that the plaintiffs had stated a derivative claim that belonged to the corporation.[36] Because the plaintiffs were no longer Syncor shareholders, they had no standing to pursue the claim on Syncor's behalf. Their case was dismissed.

Before bringing a shareholder derivative action, the plaintiff shareholders must first demand that the directors bring suit on behalf of the corporation or prove that such a demand would be futile. Often companies will set up a special litigation committee to decide whether a suit is warranted. Because the would-be defendants are often fellow directors, the courts will not honor the committee's decision not to sue unless the committee was truly independent.[37]

33. See generally CONSTANCE E. BAGLEY & DAVID BERGER, PROXY CONTESTS: CONDUCTING THE CAMPAIGN (1998).

#### ETHICAL CONSIDERATION

In 2003, Hewlett-Packard (H-P) and Compaq were involved in the largest high-tech merger in history. Walter Hewlett, son of the company's founder and an H-P director, commenced a proxy contest to oppose the merger. On the day the stockholders were to vote, Deutsche Asset Management, a division of Deutsche Bank, suddenly changed most of its votes from against the merger to approval of the merger. The investment giant's sudden turnaround accounted for 17 million H-P shares, nearly 1 percent of the company's stock. What Walter Hewlett did not know at the time was that H-P's directors, who were in favor of the merger, had secretly hired Deutsche Bank and agreed to pay it $1 million to advise H-P concerning the merger. Deutsche Bank was to receive another $1 million upon the successful completion of the merger.[a] The merger was approved by a margin of roughly 2 percent of the company's stock. Was Deutsche Bank's conduct legal? Ethical?

**a.** *In re* Deutsche Asset Mgmt., Inc., SEC Admin. Proc. File No. 11226 (Aug. 19, 2003); also see Susan Beck, *Proxy Wars,* AM. LAW. NEWS GROUP, May 2002.

## Structural Changes in a Corporation

State laws establish mechanisms by which the fundamental structure of the corporation can be changed. These changes can range from a reorganization of the enterprise to the end of the corporation as a separate entity.

34. 845 A.2d 1031 (Del. 2004).
35. *Id.*
36. *In re* Syncor Int'l Corp. S'holders Litig., 857 A.2d 994 (Del. Ch. 2004).
37. *In re* Oracle Corp. Derivative Litig., 824 A.2d 917 (Del. Ch. 2003).

Because structural changes have far-reaching consequences, they cannot be made easily.

State corporation law prohibits certain changes, such as a merger or the sale of substantially all of the corporation's assets, unless they are approved by both the board of directors *and* the shareholders. Approval by the shareholders usually means approval by a simple majority of the outstanding shares, but the articles of incorporation may require approval by a larger majority, such as two-thirds of the shareholders. Such a requirement for supermajority approval reflects the importance of structural changes.

## MERGER

A *merger* is the combination of two or more corporations into one. The *disappearing corporation* no longer maintains its separate corporate existence but becomes part of the *surviving corporation*. The surviving corporation assumes, that is, becomes responsible for, all of the liabilities and debts of the disappearing corporation and automatically acquires all of its assets by operation of law. The new corporation may take on the name of one of the parties to the merger, or a new corporate name may be chosen.

An agreement of merger, negotiated between the two companies, will specify such crucial matters as who will comprise the management team of the new enterprise. A merger generally cannot occur unless the boards and the shareholders of both companies approve the transaction. Once the requisite approval is given, the agreement of merger is filed with the secretary of state.

In a noncash merger, the shares in the disappearing corporation are automatically converted into shares in the surviving corporation. Shareholders are required to surrender their old stock certificates for new certificates representing the stock of the surviving corporation. If a shareholder does not surrender the old certificate, it is deemed by operation of law to represent shares of the surviving corporation.

In a cash merger, some shareholders (usually the public shareholders) are required to surrender their shares in the disappearing corporation for cash. They retain no interest in the surviving corporation. Hence, such a merger is also called a *freeze-out merger*.

If a proposed merger meets certain size-of-party and size-of-transaction tests, a premerger notification must be filed with the Federal Trade Commission and the Department of Justice. This notification enables the federal agencies to review the anticompetitive effects of the proposed merger before the combination occurs. (Such Hart–Scott–Rodino filings and antitrust in general are covered in Chapter 16.)

## SALE OF ASSETS

A company may want to acquire the assets of another company but not its liabilities. To achieve this goal, it can purchase all or most of the other company's assets without merging with the other company. The proceeds of the asset sale can be distributed to the selling company's shareholders as part of a dissolution of the corporation. Alternatively, the selling company may choose to continue its corporate existence and invest the proceeds of the asset sale in a new business.

A sale of all or substantially all of the assets of a corporation must be approved by both the board and the shareholders of the selling company. Most states consider a sale of 50 percent or more of the assets of a company to be a sale of substantially all of the assets. On the theory that the acquisition of assets is a routine management decision, in which the shareholders should not be involved, some states do not require that the transaction be approved by the shareholders of the acquiring company.

A CASE IN POINT

### In the Language of the Court

**CASE 19.4**
**Cargo Partners AG v. Albatrans Inc.**
*U.S. Court of Appeals for the Second Circuit*
*352 F.3d 41 (2d Cir. 2003).*

**› FACTS** Albatrans Inc. entered into an agreement to purchase all the assets of Chase-Leavitt, a shipping company. In connection with the acquisition, Chase-Leavitt, which held a federal customs brokerage license allowing it to perform customs services for clients, agreed to provide its customs brokerage services exclusively to Albatrans until Albatrans (or one of its subsidiaries) acquired such a license. Chase-Leavitt was to operate as a distinct profit center within Albatrans during this interim period and use the assets it had sold to Albatrans for that purpose. Chase-Leavitt was also required to "accept the advice and direction" of managers hired by Albatrans in this arrangement.

*(Continued)*

(Case 19.4 *continued*)

The acquisition agreement also required Chase-Leavitt's sole shareholder Alison Leavitt to continue in Chase-Leavitt's employ until Albatrans obtained its license and gave Albatrans the option of continuing her employment for an additional five years on specified terms. Alison Leavitt agreed to indemnify Albatrans for any breach by Chase-Leavitt of its obligations under the agreement and for any liabilities Chase-Leavitt incurred before the agreement's execution. Her obligation was secured with a mortgage on her personal residence. In exchange, Chase-Leavitt was to be paid a declining percentage of profits generated by the "profit center" over the ensuing five years, with $250,000 paid in advance immediately upon the close of the transaction.

Before Albatrans and Chase-Leavitt entered into negotiations, Chase-Leavitt had incurred a debt to Cargo Partner AG for $240,000. Cargo Partner filed this suit against Albatrans, demanding that Albatrans pay Chase-Leavitt's debt on the theory that there had been a *de facto merger* of Albatrans and Chase-Leavitt.

**› ISSUE PRESENTED** Should a company that acquires all the assets of another be responsible for debts the acquired company incurred prior to the acquisition?

**› OPINION** SACK, J., writing for the U.S. Court of Appeals for the Second Circuit:

Under New York law, there are at least three ways in which a corporation can acquire the business of another: The purchaser can buy the seller's capital stock, it can buy the seller's assets, or it can merge with the seller to form a single corporation. In the first case, the purchaser does not become liable for the seller's debts unless the stringent requirements for piercing the corporate veil are met. Likewise, the purchaser of a corporation's assets does not, as a result of the purchase, ordinarily become liable for the seller's debts. The amount paid for the assets would ordinarily be available to satisfy those debts, at least in part.

So long as the buyer pays a bona fide, arms-length price for the assets, there is no unfairness to creditors in thus limiting recovery to the proceeds of the sale—cash or other consideration roughly equal to the value of the purchased assets would take the place of the purchased assets as a resource for satisfying the seller's debts. . . . [A]llowing creditors to collect against the purchasers of insolvent debtors' assets would "give the creditors a windfall by increasing the funds available compared to what would have been available if no sale had taken place." Only in the third case, when two corporations merge to become a single entity, is the successor corporation automatically liable for the debts of both predecessors; it is both predecessors.

New York recognizes four common-law exceptions to the rule that an asset purchaser is not liable for the seller's debts, applying to: (1) a buyer who formally assumes a seller's debts; (2) transactions undertaken to defraud creditors; (3) a buyer who de facto merged with a seller; and (4) a buyer that is a mere continuation of a seller. . . . A *de facto* merger occurs when a transaction, although not in form a merger, is in substance "a consolidation or merger of seller and purchaser." . . .

[We] conclud[e] that the hallmarks of a de facto merger include: [1] continuity of ownership; [2] cessation of ordinary business and dissolution of the acquired corporation as soon as possible; [3] assumption by the successor of the liabilities ordinarily necessary for the uninterrupted continuation of the business of the acquired corporation; and [4] continuity of management, personnel, physical location, assets and general business operation. But . . . [n]ot all of these elements are necessary to find a de facto merger. Cargo Partner argues that . . . a de facto merger may be found

*(Continued)*

(Case 19.4 *continued*)

without fulfillment of the last factor, continuity of ownership. We . . . are confident that the doctrine of de facto merger in New York does not make a corporation that purchases assets liable for the seller's contract debts absent continuity of ownership.

The purpose of the doctrine of de facto merger is to "avoid [the] patent injustice which might befall a party simply because a merger has been called something else."

**› RESULT** The arrangement did not constitute a de facto merger of Albatrans and Chase-Leavitt. Albatrans was not liable for Chase-Leavitt's debt to Cargo Partner.

**› CRITICAL THINKING QUESTIONS**

1. Whom is the doctrine of de facto merger meant to protect?
2. Would it have mattered if the members of Albatrans' board of directors had become the sole directors of Chase-Leavitt as well?

## Appraisal Rights

In a merger or a sale of assets, dissenting shareholders—those who voted against the transaction—are frequently granted *appraisal rights,* that is, the right to receive in cash the fair value of the shares they were forced to give up as a result of the transaction. This right is available only if the transaction was subject to shareholder approval and if the dissenting shareholder complies with certain statutory procedures.

In *M.P.M. Enterprises Inc. v. Gilbert,*[38] the Delaware Supreme Court held that for purposes of calculating the amount due shareholders exercising appraisal rights, "fair value" is "the value of the company to the stockholder as a going concern, rather than its value to a third party as an acquisition." Using projected revenue growth, terminal value in five years, and an appropriate discount rate, the court determined that the equity value of M.P.M. Enterprises was $156.33 million, even though Cookson Group PLC had agreed to buy M.P.M. for $65 million plus up to $73.6 million in subsequent payments, contingent upon earnings.

# Tender Offers and Stock Repurchases

One company may gain control of another by buying a majority of its voting shares, rather than by merging with it or purchasing its assets.

38. 731 A.2d 790 (Del. 1999).

## Tender Offers

A *tender offer* is a public offer to all the shareholders of a corporation to buy their shares at a stated price, usually higher than the market price. The party making the offer is called a *bidder* or sometimes a *raider* because of the hostile nature of the bid. The bidder may offer either cash or other securities in exchange for the stock it seeks to acquire. The bidder is often a new corporation formed for the purpose of making the offer.

The shareholders are free to reject or accept the tender offer without the approval of the board of the target. If shareholders sell sufficient stock to the bidder, it will acquire control of the *target corporation*. Hence, the term *takeover* is commonly used to describe this transaction. Because a takeover is almost certain to result in substantial changes in the corporate structure of the target, tender offers are the subject of much regulation by federal statutes, as well as by the laws of the individual states. (Takeovers and the defensive tactics that boards can use to thwart them are discussed more fully in Chapter 20.)

An example of a takeover that results in a major change in corporate structure is the *second-step back-end merger*. The bidder first acquires more than 50 percent of the shares of a company through a tender offer and replaces the target company's board of directors with its own people. The new board then approves the merger of the target company into a company owned by the bidder, with the shareholders of the target company receiving cash or securities for their stock. As the majority shareholder of the target company, the bidder can outvote any dissenters and provide the required shareholder approval. The remaining shareholders are thus frozen out of the new company, and the bidder ends up with all the equity.

## LEVERAGED BUYOUTS

Any tender offer or other stock purchase can be structured as a *leveraged buyout (LBO)*, that is, a stock purchase financed by debt. In many LBOs, the group of investors seeking to gain control of a corporation includes members of corporate management. The debt financing an LBO is typically secured by the assets of the target company (such as real estate or plant and equipment), and it may take the form of an issuance of bonds, a commercial bank loan, or a loan from an investment bank. An LBO often results in a high debt load, which requires the company to make a series of substantial interest payments.

## SELF-TENDER OFFERS AND GOING-PRIVATE TRANSACTIONS

A corporation can offer to repurchase its own shares, either in a privately negotiated transaction or through a tender offer available to the public shareholders. A large-scale repurchase can result in the corporation's *going private*, that is, having fewer than 300 shareholders and ceasing to be required to file public periodic reports under the Securities Exchange Act of 1934 (discussed further in Chapter 22). A host of SEC rules regulates share repurchases and going-private transactions.[39] A number of small public companies have elected to go private to avoid the expense of complying with the new record-keeping and certification requirements imposed by the Sarbanes-Oxley Act of 2002.

39. For a more detailed discussion of stock repurchases, see Matthew Haftner, *Stock Repurchases Can Provide Important Benefits to Corporations/Stockholders, but Care Needed to Avoid Pitfalls*, 29 U.S.L.W. 232 (July 25, 2001).

THE RESPONSIBLE MANAGER

## CHOOSING THE APPROPRIATE BUSINESS ORGANIZATION

The individuals who participate in the creation of a business organization will often go on to become its managers. These managers have a strong incentive to maximize the new enterprise's potential for success. To do this, several concerns must be addressed during the entity-selection process.

First, a founder should define and clarify the business goals of the enterprise in a business plan. For example, if the enterprise will need capital from a large number of individuals, it will be necessary to ensure limited liability for some or all of these investors. A general partnership would not be suitable, as there would be no limited liability for passive investors. A related concern is clarifying the goals of the individual participants in the enterprise. For example, experienced managers who have developed a new product that requires little capital outlay would probably want exclusive control of the new business. A general partnership might be best suited to their needs.

If a general partnership is chosen, there are additional concerns. For example, it is important to put the partnership agreement in writing. As we have seen, a written partnership agreement is not always absolutely necessary to form a partnership, but creating one forces people to think through their business objectives and relationships before they begin working together.

If several persons work together on an informal basis with a common business objective, and then one leaves, the *forgotten founder* problem can arise. The person who left may have ownership rights in the enterprise. Such rights can be based on the laws of intellectual property if the person leaving created a protectable piece of property, such as a patentable invention or computer software that is protected by copyright law. (Intellectual property is discussed in Chapter 11.) Even if a founder created no protectable intellectual property before leaving, he or she may have been a partner in an informal oral general partnership if the parties were sharing profits and losses. As such, that founder would be entitled to a share of the partnership assets.

One way to mitigate the forgotten founder problem is to incorporate early and issue shares that are subject to vesting over time. A common vesting schedule provides that if a person leaves in the first year, he or she forfeits all rights to any stock. Under this approach, called *cliff vesting*, one-quarter of the stock is often vested at the

*(Continued)*

(The Responsible Manager *continued*)
end of the first year. The remainder is vested monthly over the next three to four years.

If early incorporation is not feasible or is otherwise undesirable, it is important to spell out in writing at the beginning of a joint project what will happen if someone leaves. Otherwise, those who remain could find themselves sued years down the road for a share of the company that finally is formed, a partnership interest, or royalties for use of intellectual property.

Once the corporation has been established, the managers will oversee the process of capitalization. To decide what percentages of debt and equity are to be used in financing the operation, managers should have a realistic idea of the existing demand and the distinct markets for both types of financing. In addition, managers must be aware of the rates at which the corporation can borrow money and the terms that debt and equity holders will require. Tax considerations are crucial to this process.

The final capital structure can take a variety of forms, and much creativity can be employed in this area. Managers will often seek assistance from attorneys specializing in finance and tax law, as well as from accountants and investment bankers. The more a manager understands about capitalization, however, the better the manager can utilize the information provided by lawyers, bankers, and accountants to achieve a suitable capital structure.

Managers are often directors as well as officers. As board members, they should ensure that the board acts in accordance with the articles of incorporation and the applicable corporate law. Board actions are valid only if the directors act in their collective role and not in their individual capacity. The duties of board members to act in an informed manner and to make decisions based on the best interests of the corporation are discussed in Chapter 20.

INSIDE STORY

## FOCUS ON FRANCHISES

Although franchises are not a separate form of business entity in the traditional sense, they are a common business arrangement, subject to regulation by both the Federal Trade Commission (FTC) and the states. Well-known franchisors include McDonald's, The Southland Corporation (7 Eleven), Century 21, Avis Rent-a-Car, Realty World America, and Dunkin' Donuts.

The word *franchising* is commonly understood to refer to an arrangement whereby the franchisor receives cash up front, followed by monthly payments based on a reseller's gross receipts, in exchange for granting the franchisee the right to use the franchisor's trademarks and marketing plan. Yet some state statutes define the term far more broadly and may bring within their ambit product distribution arrangements between manufacturers and dealers that many managers would not have considered to be franchises.[40] Because franchise laws can override the parties' contractual arrangements (for example, by prohibiting termination of the relationship without good cause), manufacturers may find themselves constrained in their ability to alter their supply chains to take advantage of new distribution channels, such as the Internet.

### ADVANTAGES AND DISADVANTAGES OF FRANCHISING

A franchise offers people the opportunity to own their own business without having to start from scratch. Furthermore, a new franchisee can capitalize on the enormous capital inherent in large, established franchises. For example, a company like Best Buy or Circuit City can sell electronics at a considerably lower price because of the company's ability, in the aggregate, to stock expensive items that tend to become outdated quickly.[41]

On the other hand, the quality of customer service and the level of individual attention sometimes deteriorate as a result of the less flexible business plan imposed by the franchisor. Although there is a trend toward larger

40. Thomas J. Collin, *State Franchise Laws and the Small Business Franchise Act of 1999: Barriers to Efficient Distribution,* 55 BUS. LAW. 1699 (2000). This "Inside Story" is based in part on this article.

41. See Anne Field, *Your Ticket to a New Career?,* BUS.WK. INVESTOR, May 12, 2003, at 100.

*(Continued)*

(Inside Story *continued*)

franchises, some franchisees are finding niches by encouraging their employees to spend more time with customers, responding more promptly to problems, and empowering sales representatives to make decisions on the spot.[42]

## DEFINITION OF "FRANCHISE"

State franchise statutes tend to use either a marketing plan or a community of interest definition, with the marketing plan definition being more prevalent. The definition used by the FTC is broad enough to encompass relationships that would be included under either state definition.

### *Marketing Plan Definition*

The California Business and Professions Code, which is representative, defines a *franchise* as a contract or agreement, either expressed or implied, whether oral or written, between two or more persons by which:

> (a) A franchisee is granted the right to engage in the business of offering, selling, or distributing goods or services under a marketing plan or system prescribed in substantial part by a franchisor; and
> (b) The operation of the franchisee's business pursuant to that plan or system is substantially associated with the franchisor's trademark, service mark, trade name, logotype, advertising, or other commercial symbol designating the franchisor or its affiliate; and
> (c) The franchisee is required to pay, directly or indirectly, a franchise fee.[43]

The courts have construed the requirement for a marketing plan very liberally. It can be as little as a quota of copiers to sell in a specific territory, coupled with a requirement that the distributor's personnel participate in mandatory product training,[44] or an agreement with a boat manufacturer specifying that the dealer was to advertise intensively, conduct a variety of promotions, and carry the boat manufacturer's array of accessory sales devices.[45]

Similarly, it takes very little to satisfy the requirement for a franchise fee. Although many states exclude payments for goods at a bona fide wholesale price, payments for videocassettes, posters, and brochures to promote the manufacturer's product have been viewed as franchise fees when they were required by the manufacturer or recommended as essential for the successful operation of the business.

### *Community of Interest Definition*

The New Jersey definition of "franchise" is representative of state statutes using the community of interest definition:

> "Franchise" means a written arrangement for a definite or indefinite period, in which a person grants to another person a license to use a trade name, trade mark, service mark, or related characteristics, and in which there is a community of interest in the marketing of goods or services at wholesale, retail, by lease, agreement, or otherwise.[46]

Some states, including Hawaii and Minnesota, also require payment of a franchise fee.

The supplier is deemed to have given the requisite license if the distributor has the right to identify itself as an authorized dealer even if the distributor does not have the right to use the supplier's name as part of its own business name. A community of interest in the marketing of goods is also easily shown, and it is present in most supplier–dealer arrangements. For example, courts have found that a community of interest existed when (1) a "consultant" was required to pay an information services firm 1 percent of the proceeds received from each loan placed by the consultant using the information, and (2) a dealer made significant investments that were specific to the supplier's goods or services and therefore were not fully recoverable upon termination of the relationship.[47]

## VENUE FOR RESOLVING DISAGREEMENTS

One major difficulty inherent to franchises is determining where they actually are located and therefore where disputes should be resolved. Should a single Wendy's restaurant in Jersey City be considered to be located in New Jersey for purposes of lawsuits against the Wendy's Corporation? To decide where a franchise is located, the Wisconsin Supreme Court has developed a nine-point, nonexclusive test that concentrates on the "substance" rather than the physical "location" of the franchise, in this case, a dealership.[48] State public policy leans toward forcing franchisors to settle disputes that arise in the

42. Michael Selz, *Caring for Profits,* WALL ST. J., Sept. 25, 2000, at 8.
43. CAL. BUS. & PROF. CODE §§ 20001(a)–(c).
44. Wright-Moore Corp. v. Ricoh Corp., 908 F.2d 128 (7th Cir. 1990).
45. Boat & Motor Mart v. Sea Ray Boats, Inc., 825 F.2d 1285 (9th Cir. 1987).
46. N.J. STAT. ANN. § 56:10-3(a).
47. Collin, *supra* note 40, at 1722.
48. Baldewein Co. v. Tri-Clover, Inc., 606 N.W.2d 145 (Wis. 2000).

*(Continued)*

(Inside Story *continued*)

state's territory under the state's laws. In 2000, California invalidated all clauses in franchise agreements that mandated non-California venues for dispute resolution.[49] If states did not force franchises to obey their laws, franchisors could simply pick and choose which states to be "from" so as to take advantage of franchisor-friendly legislation.

#### STATE REGISTRATION AND DISCLOSURE REQUIREMENTS

Thirteen states (including California, Illinois, Indiana, Michigan, New York, and Wisconsin) require franchisors to register before they can sell franchises in that state and to provide presale disclosure to prospective franchisees in the form of a Uniform Franchise Offering Circular, which also satisfies the FTC Franchise Rule discussed below. Most of these states also have broad antifraud provisions, prohibiting any person from making any untrue statement of material fact, or a material omission, in connection with the offer or sale of a franchise in the state.

#### STATE FRANCHISE LAWS: NO TERMINATION WITHOUT GOOD CAUSE

In the 1960s and early 1970s, a number of state legislatures adopted laws to protect local businesses investing in franchises from the superior bargaining power of large franchisors. These statutes typically prohibit termination or nonrenewal except where there is good cause, such as (1) failure by the franchisee to comply with any material and reasonable obligation under the franchise agreement or (2) conduct by the franchisee that substantially impairs the franchisor's trademark or trade name.

Although manufacturers may feel justified in terminating a distribution arrangement if the franchisee's performance is "sub-par," according to Thomas J. Collin of Thompson Hine & Flory LLP, "Cases finding that sub-par performance constitutes good cause for termination are scarcer than hen's teeth . . . ."[50] As a result, a franchisor who seeks to terminate a dealer for lack of market penetration or performance "faces a steep uphill climb."[51] In some states, such as New Jersey and Indiana, the franchisor cannot terminate the franchise even if it has bona fide business reasons for doing so, such as a desire to eliminate distributors' exclusive territories or to terminate distributors in order to sell directly to end users.

49. GNC Franchising, Inc. v. Jones, 211 F.3d 495 (9th Cir. 2000), *cert. denied*, 531 U.S. 928 (2000).
50. Collin, *supra* note 40, at 1731–32.
51. *Id.* at 1732.

#### FTC'S FRANCHISE RULE

The Federal Trade Commission requires franchisors to give a prospective franchisee the detailed written disclosures specified in its Franchise Rule.[52] The Franchise Rule requires a franchisor to make material disclosures in five categories: (1) the nature of the franchisor and the franchise system, (2) the franchisor's financial viability, (3) the costs involved in purchasing and operating a franchised outlet, (4) the terms and conditions that govern the franchise relationship, and (5) the names and addresses of current franchisees who can share their experiences within the franchise system and thus help the prospective franchisee to verify independently the franchisor's claims. In addition, franchisors must have a reasonable basis and substantiation for any earnings claims made to prospective franchisees and must disclose the basis and assumptions underlying any such earnings claims.

Presale disclosure is intended to enable prospective franchisees to conduct their own due diligence investigations and to ensure that franchisees understand the relationships they are entering into, including any product source restrictions and any right to protected territories. The FTC enforces the rule, and there is no implied private right of action for its violation.

#### FRANCHISE RELATIONSHIP ISSUES

Many franchisees have criticized the FTC for not addressing what they consider to be the greatest problem in franchising today: postsale "abusive franchise relationships." They have urged the FTC to use its power under Section 5 of the Federal Trade Commission Act to ban unfair practices to prohibit postcontract covenants not to compete, obligations to purchase supplies or inventory from specified providers even though comparable items are available at cheaper prices from alternative suppliers, and encroachment on a franchisee's market territory. *Encroachment* occurs "when a franchisor sells a franchisee an outlet in a certain location, and then a few months later, sells another outlet a few blocks away to someone else."[53] The new establishment diverts customers and revenues away from the original franchisee, but the franchisor is often still better off because it is receiving its percentage royalty from two stores. According to Susan Kezios, president and founder of the

52. Disclosure Requirements and Prohibitions Concerning Franchising and Business Opportunity Ventures, 16 C.F.R. pt. 436 (2000).
53. Deidre Shesgreen, *Franchisees Seek Protection on the Hill*, LEGAL TIMES, Jan. 4, 1999, at 1.

*(Continued)*

(Inside Story *continued*)

American Franchisee Association, "McDonald's wants to have a Big Mac five minutes away from every man, woman, and child. . . . They don't give a rat's ass if they devalue your asset [in the process]."[54]

To date, the FTC has argued that it has no authority to address franchise relationship issues because (1) the benefits to consumers and existing franchises flowing from the franchisor's contractual terms may outweigh complaints or allegations of "oppression" by individual franchisees and (2) the contractual provisions that prospective franchisees voluntarily read, agree to, and sign are "reasonably avoidable."[55]

Matthew Shay, vice president and chief counsel of the International Franchise Association (which counts McDonald's and KFC among its members), sharply criticized proposed federal legislation—the Small Business Franchise Act of 1999[56]—that would have required good cause for termination, given franchisees more freedom in choosing where they buy their supplies, and prohibited encroachment. Shay claimed that the bill would "rewrite every condition and every term in a franchise agreement" and "impose such extreme restrictions on franchising that it would basically kill the business."[57] David J. Kaufman, a senior partner at Kaufman, Feiner, Yamin, Gilden & Robbins LLP, which represents some of the nation's largest franchise systems, has called for federal preemption of all state franchise relationship laws, which he called "pernicious in their impact upon the logistical and profitable operation of franchise networks, both the franchisor in question and all of its franchisees."[58] It appears unlikely that Congress would take such a dramatic step.

54. *Id.*

55. *Subcomm. on Commerce, Trade and Consumer Prot. of the House Comm. on Energy and Commerce,* 107th Cong. (June 25, 2002) (Testimony of J. Howard Beales III, Director of the Federal Trade Commission's Bureau of Consumer Protection), *at* http://ftc/gov.

56. H.R. 3308, 106th Cong. (1999), reproduced as Appendix I to the *Report of the American Bar Association Section of Antitrust Law on Proposed Small Business Franchise Act, at* http://www.abanet.org/antitrust/final.html.

57. *Id.*

58. Eryn Gable, *The Future of Franchise Laws: A Look Ahead at Franchise Legislation That Could Be Considered by the New Congress, at* http://www.entrepreneur.com/article/print/0,2361,286409,00.html.

## KEY WORDS AND PHRASES

alter ego theory 725
appraisal rights 736
articles of incorporation 724
articles of organization 712
bidder 736
bylaws 724
C corporation 711
certificate of formation 712
certificate of incorporation 724
classified board 724
cliff vesting 737
close corporation 711
closely held corporation 711
corporate charter 724
corporate domicile 723
corporation 710
corporation by estoppel 725
cumulative voting 729
de facto corporation 725
de facto merger 735
de jure corporation 725
disappearing corporation 734
dissolution 722
encroachment 740
equity capital 713
estopped 725
fictitious business name 708
foreign corporation 723
forgotten founder 737
franchise 739
franchising 738
freeze-out merger 734
general partnership 709
going private 737
incorporation 723
inside director 729
joint venture 709
leveraged buyout (LBO) 737
limited liability company (LLC) 712
limited liability partnership (LLP) 709
limited partner 710
limited partnership 710
managers 712
members 712
merger 734
operating agreement 712
outside director 729
pass-through entity 709
pierce the corporate veil 725
proxy 729
proxy contest 733
quorum 729
raider 736
S corporation 711
second-step back-end merger 736
shareholders of record 729
sole proprietorship 708
staggered board 724
straight voting 730
surviving corporation 734
takeover 736
target corporation 736
tender offer 736
termination 722
undercapitalization theory 725
vicarious liability 710
winding up 722

## QUESTIONS AND CASE PROBLEMS

1. Amy Rockwell was a brilliant but penniless electrical engineer. She had designed a new type of cogeneration plant that she believed had great commercial potential. On January 15, she approached Benjamin Furst, a successful and experienced manager in the energy field, with the idea of starting Cogen, Inc., a corporation devoted to building a plant based on this new design. Furst was enthusiastic. On January 28, he enlisted the support of Clyde Pfeffer, a well-known venture capitalist who had retired from venture-capital work but was looking to invest the proceeds of his past endeavors. On February 16, Pfeffer gave the green light to establish the new enterprise.

   Furst retained the law firm of Fumble & Botchem to handle the details of incorporation. Fumble, one of the partners, drafted the articles of incorporation, signed them as the incorporator, and filed them with the secretary of state on February 28. He then advised his clients that the articles had been filed. Because of a typographical error, the articles of incorporation filed with the secretary of state referred to the company as Cogene, not Cogen.

   Rockwell, Furst, and Pfeffer decided that they would save further expense by completing the incorporation process without any more assistance from Fumble & Botchem. On March 3, they held what they called the meeting of incorporators to elect the directors and proceeded to elect themselves to the board. As board members, they appointed themselves as the company's officers. They typed up the minutes of this meeting.

   On March 4, the daily operations of Cogen, Inc. commenced. In all of their transactions with third parties, the officers represented themselves as doing business for the corporation. One of these transactions was with Firstloan Bank, which lent the company \$5 million. The representations in the loan agreement stated that the corporation had been duly formed, that it existed as a valid corporation under Texas law, and that the shares of stock owned by the various shareholders had been duly authorized and were fully paid.

   On May 5, the corporation began building its cogeneration plant. Three months later, energy prices dropped drastically, and there was no longer a need for a cogeneration facility in that location. The corporation was forced to default on the bank loan.

   The lawyers for the bank, upon being informed that it would not receive any more loan payments, reviewed the original loan documents, the articles of incorporation, and the minutes of the first meeting of the incorporators. Upon reviewing these documents, they initiated an action directly against the three founders in their individual capacity for liability on the bank loan.

   a. Should the founders have done anything differently?
   b. Are the founders personally liable for the bank loan?

2. Roberto Martinez was the sole force behind In Over Our Heads, Inc., a corporation designed to run a year-round community swimming pool. The enterprise was incorporated in the correct manner in January, with Martinez as the sole director and shareholder. Martinez contributed \$100,000 of starting capital, which was just enough to purchase the pool, finance initial advertising, and leave a reserve of \$10,000. The corporation had no liability insurance.

   On March 10, the pool opened for business. The corporation operated with a profit over the next few months. In June, Martinez took a two-week vacation in Europe and used a check from the company bank account to purchase his airline ticket. In November, he decided to have the pool repainted. Because business had slowed and the corporation's bank account did not have sufficient funds, Martinez wrote a personal check for this job.

   Martinez feared he would not make enough money through the winter to turn a profit, so he decided to take a part-time job as a telephone salesperson for a real estate company. He used the swimming pool's office phone to make his calls and made a substantial profit.

   On February 11, a child drowned in the pool. The parents brought a suit for wrongful death against the corporation and against Martinez in his individual capacity as owner. At the time of the suit, the corporation had the \$10,000 reserve and less than \$1,000 in its bank account. Because of these limited funds, the child's parents hoped to recover most of their damages directly from Martinez.

   What arguments can be made to hold Martinez liable for any debt of the corporation arising from this death? Should they prevail? How could

Martinez have protected himself against such potential liability? Can an owner–manager of a small corporation guarantee that he or she will not be held liable for the corporation's debts?

3. Sullivan purchased an American Football League (AFL) franchise for a professional football team for $25,000. Several months later, he organized a corporation, the American League Professional Football Team of Boston. Sullivan contributed his AFL franchise, and nine other people contributed $25,000. In return, each of the ten investors received 10,000 shares of voting common stock in the corporation. Approximately four months later, the corporation sold 120,000 shares of nonvoting common stock to the public at $5 per share.

   In 1975, Sullivan obtained control of all 100,000 voting shares of the corporation. He immediately used his control to vote out the other directors and elect a friendly board. To finance the purchase of the voting shares, Sullivan borrowed approximately $5 million. As a condition of the loan, Sullivan was to use his best efforts to organize the corporation so that its income could be devoted to the payment of the personal loan and its assets pledged to secure the loan. To accomplish this goal, Sullivan had to eliminate the interests in the nonvoting shares.

   In 1976, Sullivan organized a new corporation. The boards of directors of the new and old companies executed a merger agreement for the two corporations, providing that after the merger the voting stock of the old corporation would be extinguished and the nonvoting stock would be exchanged for cash at $15 per share.

   David Coggins owned ten shares of nonvoting stock in the old corporation. He voted against the merger and brought suit against what he alleged was an unfair and illegal transaction. Was the transaction unfair to the nonvoting shareholders? Should Coggins be able to obtain an injunction to stop the merger? [*Coggins v. New England Patriots Football Club*, 492 N.E.2d 1112 (Mass. 1986).]

4. Craig Boulanger purchased three Dunkin' Donuts franchises in upstate New York. The franchise agreements restricted franchisees from owning or being employed by a competing business within five miles of any Dunkin' Donuts establishment for two years after expiration. In 2002, Boulanger sold his franchises and moved to New Hampshire. Before the expiration of the covenants, he approached Honey Dew Donuts and discussed the possibility of his working at or acquiring Honey Dew Donuts franchises in New Hampshire and Massachusetts. After Honey Dew became aware of the covenants with Dunkin' Donuts, it ceased discussions with Boulanger. Boulanger then requested that Dunkin' Donuts waive the covenants. Should Dunkin' Donuts agree to waive them? If not, does Boulanger have any legal basis for invalidating them? [*Boulanger v. Dunkin' Donuts, Inc.*, 815 N.E. 2d 572 (Mass. 2004).]

5. Francis McQuade was the manager of the New York Giants baseball team. Charles Stoneham (father of Horace Stoneham, who acquired the baseball franchise in 1936 and moved it from New York to San Francisco in 1958) owned a majority of the stock of the company that owned the Giants and sold shares in that company to McQuade and John McGraw. As part of this transaction, these three shareholders each agreed to use his best efforts to continue to keep each of the others as directors and officers of the company at their present salaries. Stoneham and McGraw subsequently failed to use their best efforts to continue to keep McQuade as a director and treasurer of the company. McQuade sued for specific performance of the agreement. What result? [*McQuade v. Stoneham*, 189 N.E. 234 (N.Y. 1934).]

6. Water, Waste, & Land, Inc. was a land development and engineering company doing business under the name "Westec." Donald Lanham and Larry Clark were managers and also members of Preferred Income Investors, L.L.C. (P.I.I.), a limited liability company organized under the Colorado Limited Liability Company Act (the LLC Act).

   In March 1995, Clark contacted Westec about the possibility of hiring Westec to perform engineering work in connection with the construction of a fast-food restaurant known as Taco Cabana. In the course of preliminary discussions, Clark gave his business card to representatives of Westec. The business card included Lanham's address, which was also the address listed as P.I.I.'s principal office and place of business in its articles of organization filed with the secretary of state. Section 7-80-208 of the LLC Act provides that the filing of the articles of organization serves as constructive notice of a company's status as an LLC.

   Although the name Preferred Income Investors, L.L.C. was not on the business card, the letters "P.I.I." appeared above the address on the card. There was, however, no indication as to what the acronym meant or that P.I.I. was an LLC.

Although Westec never received a signed contract from Lanham, in mid-August it did receive verbal authorization from Clark to begin work. Westec completed the engineering work and sent a bill for $9,183.40 to Lanham. No payments were made on the bill. Westec filed a claim in county court against Clark and Lanham individually as well as against P.I.I. Are Clark and Lanham personally liable to Westec? How might Clark, Lanham, and Westec have avoided this dispute?

7. Ernie Jameson is a design engineer with a proven track record in the field of electronic musical instruments. He recently designed a new VLSI (very large scale integrated) chip. This chip is meant to be the heart and soul of a digital sampling keyboard to be called Echo. Jameson believes the Echo will set a new industry standard. He wishes to organize a business enterprise to build and market it. He has a meeting with his lawyer and conveys to her the following bits of information:
   - **a.** It will take approximately two years to turn the VLSI chip into a marketable product.
   - **b.** Jameson has more than $200,000 in savings from previous ventures. He does not want any of that money at risk in this new venture. However, he wants a part of the ownership; he is unsure what percentage he wants.
   - **c.** Currently, five private investors are willing to put money into this venture. Only two of the five want to play an active role in the enterprise. Jameson is willing to give these two some limited control.
   - **d.** Jameson knows that he is not qualified to manage the new endeavor. Nonetheless, he wants a significant say in how it proceeds.
   - **e.** Five more investors could be attracted to this project, but only if they could be guaranteed some fixed return on their money or could realize immediate tax benefits from investing.
   - **f.** Jameson would like Bernie Lord, a manager much in demand in the electronics field, to be his CEO. It would take significant incentives to attract him to the enterprise.

   Jameson is not committed to using any particular type of business organization; he is interested in weighing the alternatives. What possible types of business organizations could accommodate the needs of the various players? What are the advantages and disadvantages of each alternative? Which one should Jameson choose?

8. Steckel Corporation, which was owned entirely by Faye Givler, owed Central Corporation more than $220,000. After Steckel became insolvent, Givler transferred all of her stock to Pemcor, Inc. for $1. In return, Pemcor agreed to allow her to continue to operate Steckel. Now Central wants to collect the debts owed by Steckel from Pemcor under a theory of de facto merger. Should Central be allowed to collect from Pemcor? [*Central National Gottesman v. Pemcor, Inc.*, 2001 WL 1198659 (E.D. Pa. 2001).]

9. William Ayres and Douglas Pickering entered into an operating agreement with AG Processing, Inc. to form AG Environmental Products, L.L.C. ("AEP LLC"), a Nebraska limited liability company formed to market methyl esters supplied by AG Processing. AG Processing owned 99 percent of AEP LLC, and Ayres and Pickering each owned one-half percent. Ayres and Pickering served as managers of the LLC along with three other managers—Reagan, Hoover, and Campbell—who were also corporate officers of AG Processing. The operating agreement provided that the business and affairs of the LLC shall be managed by its designated managers, acting as a group, with a majority vote required to take action.

   At some point Ayres and Pickering became concerned about certain actions taken by Reagan, Hoover, and Campbell, including investing in unsecured business investments, using AEP LLC funds for political lobbying, failing to hold annual meetings and to provide year-end financial disclosures on a timely basis, and failing to distribute equity bonuses to Ayres and Pickering. After Ayres and Pickering protested these actions and demanded that the operating agreement be followed and the unrelated business activities cease, they were terminated as managers, employees, and members of the AEP LLC. Did Reagan, Hoover, and Campbell act ethically? Do Ayres and Pickering have any valid legal claims against them? [*Ayres v. AG Processing, Inc.*, 345 F. Supp. 2d 1200 (D. Kan. 2004).]

## MANAGER'S DILEMMA

10. In February 1990, Collette Bohatch was named a partner in the Washington, D.C. office of Butler & Binion, a Houston-based law firm. John McDonald was then the managing partner of the firm's D.C. office, which worked almost exclusively for Pennzoil. Bohatch soon became privy to internal firm reports showing the

number of hours each attorney worked, billed, and collected. After reviewing such reports, she became concerned that McDonald was overbilling Pennzoil.

On July 15, 1990, Bohatch met with Louis Paine, Butler & Binion's managing partner, to report her concerns about McDonald's billing practices. Paine told Bohatch he would investigate. The following day, McDonald met with Bohatch and told her that Pennzoil was not satisfied with her work and wanted her work to be supervised. Bohatch later testified that this was the first time she had ever heard criticism of her work for Pennzoil.

After looking into Bohatch's complaint and discussing the allegations with Pennzoil's in-house counsel, who said that Pennzoil believed the firm's bills were reasonable, Paine informed Bohatch in August that he found no basis for her contentions. Paine also told her she should begin to look for other employment. In June 1991, she was informed that that month's partnership distribution would be her last. She was asked to leave by November.

Bohatch filed suit for breach of fiduciary duty and other claims in October 1991. The firm voted to expel her three days later. At trial, a jury found that the firm had breached its fiduciary duty to Bohatch. The court of appeals reversed, holding that the firm's only duty to Bohatch was not to expel her in bad faith. Bohatch appealed. Did Butler & Binion fulfill its legal obligations to Bohatch? Did it act ethically? Should it matter whether Bohatch was correct about the overbilling? [*Bohatch v. Butler*, 977 S.W.2d 543 (Tex. 1998).]

## INTERNET SOURCES

| | |
|---|---|
| The National Conference of Commissioners on Uniform State Laws, in association with the University of Pennsylvania Law School, makes available drafts and revisions to finalized versions of the Uniform Partnership Act, the Uniform Limited Partnership Act, the Uniform Limited Liability Partnership Act, and the Uniform Limited Liability Company Act. | http://www.law.upenn.edu/bll/ulc/ulcframe.htm |
| This site discusses the implications of California's Adopted Revised Uniform Partnership Act | http://www.taxlawsb.com/resources/BusTax/ptshp.htm |
| The Small Business Administration's site provides valuable information about starting and financing small businesses, a searchable online library, and links to other sites of interest (including the home pages for each state's department of corporations). | http://www.sba.gov/ |
| "A Consumer Guide to Buying a Franchise," prepared by the Federal Trade Commission, is available on the Small Business Administration's site. | http://www.sba.gov/starting_business/startup/consumerguide.html |
| The Federal Trade Commision's site provides information concerning its Franchise Rule, including proposal assessments. | http://www.ftc.gov |
| This site for Richards Layton & Finger, the largest law firm in Delaware, contains excellent articles on Delaware corporate and partnership law and provides links to other legal-related sites. | http://www.rlf.com/ |
| LLC-USA.com operates a website dedicated to issues surrounding limited liability companies. | http://www.llc-usa.com |
| The Harvard Business School Publishing site maintains a database of websites of interest to entrepreneurs. | http://www.hbsp.harvard.edu/ideasatwork/entrep/sites/html |

CHAPTER 20

# Directors, Officers, and Controlling Shareholders

## INTRODUCTION

### FIDUCIARY DUTIES

Directors and officers are agents of the corporation and owe a fiduciary duty to the corporation they serve. Under certain circumstances, a controlling shareholder owes a fiduciary duty to other shareholders as well.

These duties take two basic forms: a duty of care and a duty of loyalty. Generally, the *duty of care* requires fiduciaries to make informed and reasonable decisions and to exercise reasonable supervision of the business. The *duty of loyalty* mandates that fiduciaries act in good faith and in what they believe to be the best interest of the corporation, subordinating their personal interests to the welfare of the corporation. As then Judge Benjamin Cardozo stated, many forms of conduct permissible in the business world for those acting at arm's length are forbidden to those bound by fiduciary ties. A trustee, he said, is held to something stricter than the morals of the marketplace. Not mere honesty, but a "punctilio of honor the most sensitive" is the standard of behavior with which fiduciaries must comply.[1]

In certain cases, the Delaware Supreme Court has treated directors' duty to act in good faith as an independent duty, rather than subsuming it within the duty of loyalty. For example, in *McMullin v. Beran,*[2] the Delaware Supreme Court referred to the directors' "triad of fiduciary duties, loyalty, good faith, due care."[3]

### CHAPTER OVERVIEW

This chapter outlines the duties of directors, officers, and controlling shareholders. First, it analyzes the duty of care in terms of the most applicable judicial doctrine, the business judgment rule. Next, the chapter analyzes the duty of good faith and addresses issues arising under the duty of loyalty, including corporate opportunities. It discusses the fiduciary duties of directors that arise when the directors must decide whether to sell the company or resist a corporate takeover bid. Legislative responses to these issues are also described. Finally, the chapter looks at the duties of controlling shareholders in connection with sales of corporate control and squeeze-out mergers.

## The Business Judgment Rule and the Duty of Care

In cases challenging board decisions for breach of the duty of care, the courts generally defer to the business judgment of the directors, acknowledging that courts are ill equipped to second-guess directors' decisions at a

1. Meinhard v. Salmon, 164 N.E. 545, 546 (N.Y. 1928) (Case 1.2).
2. 765 A.2d 910, 917 (Del. 2000).
3. An article by former Delaware Chancellor William T. Allen, then Vice Chancellor and later Delaware Supreme Court Justice Jack B. Jacobs, and Vice Chancellor Leo E. Strine, Jr. suggested that good faith is a subsidiary requirement subsumed within the duty of loyalty and not "a compartmentally distinct fiduciary duty of equal dignity with the two bedrock fiduciary duties of loyalty and due care." *Function over Form: A Reassessment of Standards of Review in Delaware Corporate Law,* 56 BUS. LAW. 1287, 1305 n.69 (Aug. 2001), quoting Emerald Partners v. Berkin, 2001 Del. Ch. LEXIS 20, at *87 n.63 (Del. Ch. Feb. 7, 2001). For a discussion of the fiduciary duties of directors of a corporation near insolvency or in bankruptcy, see Myron M. Sheinfeld & Judy Harris Pippitt, *Fiduciary Duties of Directors of a Corporation in the Vicinity of Insolvency and After Initiation of a Bankruptcy Case,* 60 BUS. LAW. 79 (2004).

later date. Thus, under the *business judgment rule,* as long as certain standards are met, a court will presume that the directors have acted in good faith and in the honest belief that the action taken was in the best interest of the company. The court will not question whether the action was wise or whether the directors made an error of judgment or a business mistake.

To take advantage of the rule, the directors must have made an informed decision with no conflict between their personal interests and the interests of the corporation and its shareholders. If the business judgment rule does not apply to a transaction, courts generally shift to directors the burden of proving that their acts were not grossly negligent (or in cases involving transactions in which the directors are interested, that the transaction was fair and reasonable).

## INFORMED DECISION

The business judgment rule is applicable only if the directors make an informed decision. The general corporation law of most jurisdictions authorizes directors to rely on the reports of officers and certain outside experts. However, passive reliance on such reports may result in an insufficiently informed decision, as in the following case.

**A CASE IN POINT**

**CASE 20.1**
**Smith v. Van Gorkom**
*Supreme Court of Delaware*
*488 A.2d 858 (Del. 1985).*

### Summary

**› FACTS** Trans Union Corporation was a publicly traded, diversified holding company engaged in the railcar-leasing business. Its stock was undervalued, largely due to accumulated investment tax credits. Jerome W. Van Gorkom, the chairman of the board of Trans Union, was reaching retirement age. He asked the chief financial officer, Donald Romans, to work out the per-share price at which a leveraged buyout could be done, given current cash flow. Romans came up with $55, based on debt-servicing requirements. He did not attempt to determine the intrinsic value of the company. Van Gorkom later met with Jay Pritzker and worked out a merger at $55 per share. Trans Union stock was then trading at about $37 per share.

Van Gorkom called a board meeting for September 20, 1980, on one day's notice, to approve the merger. All of the directors were familiar with the company's operations as a going concern, but they were not apprised of the merger negotiations before the board meeting on September 20. They were also familiar with the current financial status of the company; a month earlier they had discussed a Boston Consulting Group strategy study. The ten-member board included five outside directors who were CEOs or board members of publicly held companies, as well as a former dean of the University of Chicago Business School.

Copies of the merger agreement were delivered to the directors, but too late for study before or during the meeting. The meeting began with a twenty-minute oral presentation by chairman Van Gorkom. The chief financial officer then described how he had arrived at the $55 figure. He stated that it was only a workable number, not an indication of a fair price. Trans Union's president stated that he thought the proposed merger was a good deal.

The board approved the merger after a two-hour meeting. Board members later testified that they had insisted that the merger agreement be amended to ensure that the company was free to consider other bids before the closing; however, neither the board minutes nor the merger documents clearly reflected this.

Plaintiff Smith sued to challenge the board's action, arguing that the merger price was too low. The Delaware Court of Chancery held that, given the premium over the market value of Trans Union stock, the business acumen of the board members, and the effect on the merger price of the prospect of other bids, the board was adequately informed and did not act recklessly in approving the Pritzker deal. In making its findings, the court relied in part upon actions taken by the board after the meeting on September 20, 1980, that were intended to cure defects in the directors' initial level of knowledge.

*(Continued)*

(Case 20.1 *continued*)

**› ISSUE PRESENTED** Were directors who accepted and submitted to the shareholders a proposed cash merger without determining the intrinsic value of the company grossly negligent in failing to inform themselves adequately before making their decision?

**› SUMMARY OF OPINION** The Delaware Supreme Court reversed the lower court and held that the directors were grossly negligent in failing to reach a properly informed decision. They were not protected by the business judgment rule even though there were no allegations of bad faith, fraud, or conflict of interest. The court found that the directors could not reasonably base their decision on the inadequate information presented to the board. They should have independently valued the company.

The court found that the directors had inadequate information as to (1) the role of Van Gorkom, Trans Union's chairman and chief executive officer, in initiating the transaction; (2) the basis for the proposed purchase price of $55 per share; and, most importantly, (3) the intrinsic value of Trans Union, as opposed to its current and historical stock price. The court held that in the absence of any apparent crisis or emergency, it was grossly negligent for the directors to approve the merger after a two-hour meeting, with eight of the ten directors having received no prior notice of the proposed merger.

The court stated:

> None of the directors, management or outside, were investment bankers or financial analysts. Yet the board did not consider recessing the meeting until a later hour that day (or requesting an extension of Pritzker's Sunday evening deadline) to give it time to elicit more information as to the sufficiency of the offer, either from inside management (in particular Romans) or from Trans Union's own investment banker, Salomon Brothers, whose Chicago specialist in mergers and acquisitions was known to the Board and familiar with Trans Union's affairs.
>
> Thus, the record compels the conclusion that on September 20 the Board lacked valuation information adequate to reach an informed business judgment as to the fairness of $55 per share for sale of the Company.

The court additionally held that the directors' subsequent efforts to find a bidder willing to pay more than Pritzker were inadequate to cure the infirmities of their uninformed exercise of judgment.

The court rejected the directors' argument that they properly relied on the officers' reports presented at the board meeting. The court stated that a pertinent report may be relied on in good faith, but not blindly. The directors were duty bound to make reasonable inquiry of Van Gorkom (the chief executive officer), and Romans (the chief financial officer). If they had done so, the inadequacy of those officers' reports would have been apparent. Van Gorkom's summary of the terms of the deal was inadequate because he had not reviewed the merger documents and was basically uninformed as to the essential terms. (Indeed, he had signed the merger agreement while at the opening of the Chicago Lyric Opera without first reading the document.) Romans's report on price was inadequate because it was just a cash flow–cash feasibility study, not a valuation study.

The court also held that the mere fact that a substantial premium over the market price was being offered did not justify board approval of the merger. A premium may be one reason to approve a merger, but sound information as to the company's intrinsic value is required to assess the fairness of an offer. In this case, there was no attempt to determine the company's intrinsic value.

**› RESULT** The Delaware Supreme Court held that the Trans Union directors were grossly negligent in making an uninformed decision regarding the proposed merger

*(Continued)*

(Case 20.1 *continued*)

agreement. Their decision was not protected by the business judgment rule. The case was remanded to the Delaware Court of Chancery for an evidentiary hearing to determine the fair value of the shares based on Trans Union's intrinsic value on September 20, 1980, the day when the board met to consider Pritzker's offer. If the chancellor found that value to be higher than $55 per share, the directors would be liable for the difference.

**› COMMENTS** The case was settled for $23.5 million—$13.5 million in excess of the directors' liability insurance coverage. Although the purchasers, the Pritzker family, ultimately paid the amount by which the settlement exceeded the directors' coverage, they were not legally obligated to do so.

*Smith v. Van Gorkom* is one of the most debated corporate law cases ever decided. Three years after the decision, one of the key defendants—Trans Union's CEO, Jerome W. Van Gorkom—wrote an article giving the defendants' side of the story. The article makes it clear that the defendants and the Delaware Supreme Court had very different views about what the directors actually did and what their options really were.

In his article, Van Gorkom stated that at the September 20 meeting:

> The directors, all broadly experienced executives, realized that an all-cash offer with a premium of almost 50 percent represented an unusual opportunity for the shareholders. They also knew, however, that $55 might not be the highest price obtainable. At the meeting, therefore, there was considerable discussion about seeking an outside "fairness opinion" that might shed further light on the ultimate value of the company.[4]

Furthermore, Van Gorkom explained:

> Acceptance of the offer was not a decision by the directors that the company should be sold for $55 a share. The acceptance was the only mechanism by which the offer could be preserved for the shareholders. *They* would make the ultimate decision as to the fairness of the price and they would do so only after the free market had had ample time in which to determine if $55 was the top value obtainable. The market's opinion would be definitive and worth infinitely more to the shareholders than any theoretical evaluation opinion that the directors could obtain in 39 hours or even longer. On this reasoning the offer was accepted.

Following the meeting, the Trans Union directors hired Salomon Brothers to conduct an intensive search for a higher bidder. In addition, Van Gorkom stated that once the $55 offer became a matter of public knowledge, an auction occurred in the market with Trans Union's stock sometimes selling above $56 on the New York Stock Exchange. After three months of the intensive search and the public auction, no higher bid was ever received. "[T]he market had proven beyond a shadow of a doubt that $55 was the highest price obtainable."

Van Gorkom believed that he and the other Trans Union directors wholeheartedly fulfilled their fiduciary obligations. He concluded that their actions clearly should have been protected under the business judgment rule.

## *Reliability of Officers' Reports*

As *Van Gorkom* underscores, not every statement of an officer can be relied on in good faith, and no statement is entitled to blind reliance. The passivity of the Trans Union directors in *Van Gorkom* unquestionably influenced the court's finding of gross negligence. When the chief financial officer, Romans, told the board that the $55 figure was within a "fair price range" for a leveraged buyout,

> no director sought any further information from Romans. No director asked him why he put $55 at the bottom of his range. No director asked Romans for any details as to his study, the reason why it had been undertaken or its depth. No director asked to see the study; and no director asked Romans whether Trans Union's finance department could do a fairness study within the remaining 36-hour period available under the Pritzker offer. . . . [If he had been asked,] Romans would have presumably . . . informed the Board of his view, and the widespread view of Senior Management, that the timing of the offer was wrong and the offer inadequate.[5]

4. J. W. Van Gorkom, *Van Gorkom's Response: The Defendant's Side of the Trans Union Case,* MERGERS & ACQUISITIONS, Jan.–Feb. 1988. Excerpts reprinted with permission.

5. Smith v. Van Gorkom, 488 A.2d 858, 876 (Del. 1985).

When the CEO, Van Gorkom, told the board that $55 per share was fair, no questions were asked.

> The Board thereby failed to discover that Van Gorkom had suggested the $55 price to [the bidder] Pritzker and, most crucially, that Van Gorkom had arrived at the $55 figure based on calculations designed solely to determine the feasibility of a leveraged buy-out. No questions were raised either as to the tax implications of a cash-out merger or how the price for the one million share option granted Pritzker was calculated.[6]

### Reliability of Experts' Reports

Two principles regarding the use of experts' reports emerge from the cases. First, a board should engage a reputable investment banking firm, aided if necessary by an outside appraiser, (1) to prepare a valuation study and (2) to give a written opinion as to the financial fairness of the transaction and of any related purchase of assets or options.

Second, directors have a duty to pursue reasonable inquiry and to exercise reasonable oversight in connection with their engagement of investment bankers and other advisers. A conclusory fairness opinion (that is, an opinion that merely states a conclusion without giving the factual grounds for that conclusion) of an investment banker, however expert, is not a sufficient basis for a board decision, particularly if the investment banker's conclusion is questionable in light of other information known to the directors. As the directors of SCM Corporation learned in *Hanson Trust PLC v. ML SCM Acquisition, Inc.*,[7] an expert's opinion must be in writing and be reasoned.

SCM was the subject of a hostile tender offer by a British conglomerate, Hanson Trust PLC. SCM's board negotiated a friendly management leveraged buyout led by "white knight" Merrill Lynch. As part of this agreement, SCM granted Merrill Lynch an *asset lock-up option* to purchase two of SCM's divisions, considered to be SCM's key assets or *crown jewels*. The option was exercisable if Merrill Lynch was not successful in acquiring control of SCM. A lock-up option is a kind of consolation prize for the loser in a bidding war; depending on how it is priced, a lock-up option can have the effect of deterring other bids. Merrill Lynch represented in negotiations that it would not proceed with its leveraged buyout offer without the lock-up.

SCM's investment banker, Goldman Sachs, issued a written fairness opinion on the overall deal, stating that the sale of SCM to Merrill Lynch was fair to the shareholders of SCM from a financial point of view. A partner at Goldman Sachs also orally advised SCM's directors that the option prices were "within the range of fair value." However, the directors did not inquire what the range of fair value was or how it was calculated. Unfortunately for the directors, the banker had not in fact calculated the fair value of the two divisions. Although the directors knew that the two divisions generated more than two-thirds of SCM's earnings, they never asked the investment banker why the divisions were being sold for less than half the total purchase price. The U.S. Court of Appeals for the Second Circuit held that the SCM directors' "paucity of information" and "their swiftness of decision-making" strongly suggested a breach of the duty of care. The asset lock-up was struck down. As in the case of officers' reports, blind reliance on the reports of experts creates a risk that the directors will not receive the protection of the business judgment rule.

## Reasonable Supervision

As fiduciaries, directors have a responsibility to exercise reasonable supervision over corporate operations. Because the prescribed role of the corporate directors is to establish broad policies and then rely on managers to implement them, the question of what constitutes reasonable supervision is necessarily one of degree. The outcome in reasonable supervision cases depends heavily on particular facts. The Delaware Court of Chancery refined and clarified the reasonable supervision doctrine in the following case.

6. *Id.*
7. 781 F.2d 264 (2d Cir. 1986).

A CASE IN POINT

**CASE 20.2**

***In re* Caremark International Derivative Litigation**

*Court of Chancery of Delaware*
*698 A.2d 959*
*(Del. Ch. 1996).*

## Summary

**› FACTS** After the Department of Health and Human Services and the Department of Justice conducted an extensive four-year investigation of alleged violations by Caremark employees of federal and state laws and regulations applicable to health-care providers, Caremark was charged with multiple felonies. It thereafter entered into a number of plea agreements in which it agreed to pay civil and criminal fines and to make payments to various private and public parties. In all, Caremark agreed to pay approximately $250 million.

*(Continued)*

(Case 20.2 *continued*)

A shareholder derivative suit was filed in 1994, in which the plaintiff initially sought to recover these losses from the individual members of Caremark's board of directors. The complaint charged that the directors had allowed a situation to develop and continue that exposed the corporation to enormous legal liability and, in so doing, they had violated a duty to be active monitors of corporate performance. The complaint did not charge the directors with either self-dealing or a breach of the duty of loyalty. The parties sought court approval of a proposed settlement that did not include any payment by individual board members; instead, it outlined a series of procedures the company would implement to promote future compliance with applicable laws and regulations.

**› ISSUE PRESENTED** What is the scope of a director's duty to exercise reasonable supervision over corporate operations?

**› SUMMARY OF OPINION** The Delaware Chancery Court began by noting that director liability for a breach of the duty to exercise appropriate attention may, in theory, arise in two distinct contexts. First, such liability may follow from a board decision that results in a loss because that decision was ill advised or negligent. Second, liability may arise from an unconsidered failure of the board to act in circumstances in which due attention would, arguably, have prevented a loss to the corporation.

Most of the decisions that a corporation, acting through its human agents, makes are not the subject of director attention. Legally, the board itself will be required only to authorize the most significant corporate acts or transactions: mergers, changes in capital structure, fundamental changes in business, appointment and compensation of the CEO, and the like. However, ordinary business decisions that are made by officers and employees deeper in the interior of the organization can vitally affect the welfare of the corporation and its ability to achieve its various strategic and financial goals. This raises the question: What is the board's responsibility with respect to the organization and monitoring of the enterprise to ensure that the corporation functions within the law to achieve its purposes?

The court noted an increasing tendency, especially under federal law, to employ the criminal law to ensure corporate compliance with external legal requirements, including environmental, financial, employee, and product safety regulations, as well as assorted other health and safety regulations. The federal Organizational Sentencing Guidelines offer powerful incentives for corporations to have in place compliance programs to detect violations of law, to promptly report violations to appropriate public officials when discovered, and to take prompt, voluntary remedial efforts.

In light of these developments, the court held that directors cannot satisfy their obligation to be reasonably informed concerning the corporation unless they assure themselves that appropriate information and reporting systems exist in the organization. These systems must be reasonably designed to provide senior management and the board itself with timely and accurate information sufficient to allow management and the board to reach informed judgments concerning both the corporation's compliance with the law and its business performance.

The level of detail that is appropriate for such an information system is a question of business judgment. The court acknowledged that no rationally designed information and reporting system will eliminate the possibility that the corporation will violate laws or regulations. But the board is required to exercise a good faith judgment that the corporation's information and reporting system is in concept and design adequate to assure the board that appropriate information will come to its attention in a timely manner as a matter of ordinary operations, so that it may satisfy its responsibility.

*(Continued)*

(Case 20.1 *continued*)

Thus, the court ruled that a director's obligation includes a duty to attempt in good faith to ensure that there is a corporate information and reporting system that the board concludes is adequate. Failure to do so under certain circumstances may, in theory at least, render a director liable for losses caused by noncompliance with applicable legal standards.

› **RESULT** The court concluded that the settlement was fair and reasonable and, therefore, approved it.

› **COMMENTS** The court noted that if the shareholders are not satisfied with the informed good faith judgment of the directors, their recourse is to elect different directors.

---

In 1997, the Securities and Exchange Commission (SEC) issued a release emphasizing the affirmative responsibility of officers and directors under the federal securities laws to ensure the accuracy and completeness of public company filings with the SEC, such as annual and quarterly reports and proxy statements.[8] The officers and directors are required to conduct a full and informed review of the information contained in the final draft of the filings. If an officer or director knows or should have known about an inaccuracy in a proposed filing, he or she has an obligation to correct it. An officer or director may rely on the company's procedures for determining what disclosure is required only if he or she has a reasonable basis for believing that those procedures are effective and have resulted in full consideration of those issues.

If a director or officer is aware of facts that might have to be disclosed, he or she must go beyond the established procedures to inquire into the reasons for nondisclosure. Officers and directors cannot blindly rely on legal counsel's conclusions about the need for disclosure if they are aware of facts that seem to suggest that disclosure is required. They must then discuss the issue specifically with disclosure counsel, telling counsel exactly what they know and asking specifically whether

8. Report of Investigation Pursuant to Section 21(a) of the Securities Exchange Act of 1934 concerning the Conduct of Certain Former Officers and Directors of W.R. Grace & Co., Exchange Act Release No. 39,157 (Sept. 30, 1997).

## *View from Cyberspace*

### SHAREHOLDER MEETINGS IN CYBERSPACE

On July 1, 2000, a number of amendments to the Delaware General Corporation Law that were designed to permit corporations to take advantage of evolving technology went into effect. Section 228(d), for example, permits a shareholder's written consent to be effected by electronic transmission (including e-mail), facsimiles (fax), or other reliable methods of reproducing a consent. Section 212(c) already authorized electronic transmission of proxies and the use of copies and faxes. New Section 232 permits the electronic delivery of notice to a shareholder if the shareholder has consented to delivery of notice in such form. A revamped Section 211(a) gives directors the power to authorize shareholders who are not physically present at a meeting to participate by means of remote communication, such as a conference call. Indeed, directors are given sole discretion to hold meetings either partially or totally by remote communication, without any physical location.

Amendments to Section 141 permit director action by unanimous consent that is effected by electronic transmission; previously, such consent had to be in writing. Although the drafters considered authorizing board meetings by remote communication, they determined that "considerations of collegiality precluded 'chat room' or similar formats, and that the current practice of holding meetings by telephone conference calls provided sufficient flexibility."[a]

a. Frederick H. Alexander, *Amendments to Delaware Corporation Law Allow for Evolving Technology*, 69 U.S.L.W. 2051, 2052 (Aug. 1, 2000).

disclosure is required. If they are not satisfied with the answers provided, they should insist that the documents be revised before they are filed with the SEC.

### DISINTERESTED DECISION

Even when the board makes an informed decision, the business judgment rule is not applicable if the directors have a financial or other personal interest in the transaction at issue. For example, if a board of inside directors (that is, directors who are also officers of the corporation) sets executive compensation, they can be required to prove to a court that the transaction was fair and reasonable. To be disinterested in the transaction normally means that the directors can neither have an interest on either side of the transaction nor expect to derive any personal financial benefit from the transaction (other than benefits that accrue to all shareholders of the corporation, which are not considered self-dealing).

Even if one or more individual directors have an interest in the transaction, the board's decision may still be entitled to the protection of the business judgment rule if the transaction is approved by a majority of the disinterested directors. If the board delegates too much of its authority or is too much influenced by an interested party, however, the entire board may be tainted with that individual's personal motivations and lose the protection of the business judgment rule.

In some jurisdictions, a relevant factor in determining whether a board is disinterested is whether the majority of the board consists of outside directors. The fact that outside directors receive directors' fees but not salaries is viewed as heightening the likelihood that the directors were not motivated by personal interest. Application of these rules in the context of takeovers, mergers, and acquisitions is discussed later in this chapter.

### THE DUTY OF CANDOR

When requesting shareholder action, directors have a duty to disclose all material facts. In *Malone v. Brincat*,[9] the Delaware Supreme Court went a step further and held that whenever directors disseminate information to shareholders, the fiduciary duties of care, loyalty, and good faith apply, even if no shareholder action is sought. As a result, the court held that "directors who knowingly disseminate false information that results in corporate injury or damage to an individual stockholder violate their fiduciary duty, and may be held accountable in a manner appropriate to the circumstances."

9. 722 A.2d 5 (Del. 1998).

## Statutory Limitations on Directors' Liability for Breach of Duty of Care

Cases such as *Van Gorkom* had a devastating impact on the market for directors' and officers' liability insurance and on the availability of qualified outside directors. In response, Delaware adopted legislation in 1986 to allow shareholders to limit the monetary liability of directors for breaches of the duty of care in any suit brought by the corporation or in a *shareholder derivative suit*, that is, a suit by a shareholder on behalf of the corporation. Most other states followed suit. Most statutes require that the limitation be contained in the original articles of incorporation or in an amendment approved by a majority of the shareholders.

The statutes do not affect directors' liability for suits brought by third parties; they merely allow the shareholders to agree that, under certain circumstances, they will not seek monetary recovery against the directors. The directors' liability for breach of the duty of loyalty may not be limited. Also, most states do not allow officers to be exonerated from liability for breach of the duty of care or the duty of loyalty.

### DELAWARE'S STATUTE

Section 102(b)(7) of the Delaware Corporation Code permits the certificate of incorporation to include a provision limiting or eliminating the personal liability of directors to the corporation or to its shareholders for monetary damages for breach of fiduciary duty. (Delaware law is especially relevant because many large public companies are incorporated there.) Such a provision cannot, however, eliminate or limit the liability of a director for (1) any breach of the director's duty of loyalty to the corporation or its shareholders, (2) acts or omissions that are not in good faith or that involve intentional misconduct or knowing violation of law, (3) unlawful payments of dividends or stock purchases, or (4) any transaction from which the director derived an improper personal benefit.

### CALIFORNIA'S STATUTE

Section 204(a)(10) of the California Corporation Code, which applies to corporations organized under California law, is more restrictive. In addition to the four exceptions contained in the Delaware statute, California prohibits the elimination or limitation of director liability for (1) acts or omissions that show a reckless disregard for the director's duty to the corporation or its shareholders in circumstances in which the director was aware, or should have been aware, of a risk of serious injury to the corporation or its shareholders; and (2) an unexcused pattern of inattention that amounts to an abdication of the director's duties to the corporation or its shareholders.

Although other states apply their corporate governance rules only to corporations incorporated there, California imposes its pro-shareholder provisions on so-called privately held *quasi-foreign corporations.* Such corporations are incorporated elsewhere but (1) have more than 50 percent of their stock owned by California residents and (2) derive more than 50 percent of their sales, payroll, and property tax from activities in California. As a result, a quasi-foreign corporation will be subject to California's more restrictive limits on monetary liability even though the state of incorporation (e.g., Delaware) is more permissive.

##  Duty of Good Faith

As noted earlier, the Delaware Supreme Court has characterized the duty of the directors to act in good faith as one of the directors' triad of fiduciary duties. Although arguably the duty of good faith is best understood as subsumed within the duty of loyalty,[10] failure to act in good faith takes on special significance in jurisdictions, such as Delaware, that permit corporations to eliminate directors' personal liability for breaches of the duty of care but not for breaches of the duty of loyalty or for acts or omissions not taken in good faith. Because the statutes authorizing such limitations on director liability list failures to act in good faith separately from breaches of the duty of loyalty, courts have started to focus more directly on good faith, especially when the directors had no personal interest in the transaction at hand.

At a minimum, the duty of good faith requires directors to at least try to fulfill their oversight responsibilities. They may not passively stand by or hide their heads in the sand when they become aware of potentially troubling developments. Instead, they must be proactive and intervene when they become aware of material risks or troublesome corporate behavior. As seen in the following case, directors who consciously ignore known risks of noncompliance risk losing the protection of both the business judgment rule and any exculpatory provisions in their corporate charter.

10. See Allen, Jacobs, & Strine, *supra* note 3.

A CASE IN POINT

**CASE 20.3**

***In re* Abbott Laboratories Derivative Shareholders Litigation**

*United States Court of Appeals for the Seventh Circuit*
*325 F.3d 795*
*(7th Cir. 2003).*

### In the Language of the Court

**› FACTS** In 1999, Abbott Laboratories, an Illinois corporation, entered into a consent decree that required it to pay a $100 million fine, at the time the largest penalty ever imposed for a civil violation of Food and Drug Administration (FDA) regulations. The FDA also required Abbott to withdraw 125 types of medical diagnostic test kits, destroy certain inventory, and make a number of corrective changes in its manufacturing procedures after six years of quality control violations. Abbott shareholders brought a shareholder derivative suit alleging that the directors breached their fiduciary duties when they failed to take necessary action to correct repeated noncompliance problems brought to Abbott's attention by the FDA in the period from 1993 until 1999.

Not only had the FDA sent Abbott a Form 483 noting deviations from the requirements set forth in the FDA's "Current Good Manufacturing Practice" after each of its thirteen inspections of Abbott's Abbott Park and North Chicago facilities, but the FDA had also sent four formal certified Warning Letters to Abbott. The first was sent to David Thompson, president of Abbott's Diagnostics Division (ADD), on October 20, 1993. The letter stated that the FDA had found adulterated in vitro diagnostic products and warned: "Failure to correct these deviations may result in regulatory action being initiated by the Food and Drug Administration without further notice. These actions include, but are not limited to, seizure, injunction, and/or civil penalties." A second Warning Letter was sent to Thompson on March 28, 1994, with a copy to Duane Burnham, Abbott's CEO and board chair.

*(Continued)*

(Case 20.3 *continued*)

On January 11, 1995, the *Wall Street Journal* reported that the FDA had uncovered a wide range of flaws in Abbott's quality assurance procedures used in assembling its diagnostic products. In July 1995, the FDA and Abbott entered into a Voluntary Compliance Plan to work together to correct Abbott's deficiencies. In February 1998, after finding continued deviations from the regulations, the FDA sent Abbott the equivalent of a Warning Letter closing out the plan. In 1999, the FDA sent the fourth and final Warning Letter to Miles White, a member of Abbott's board and the current CEO. White had replaced Burnham as CEO in April 1999.

The plaintiffs did not demand that the members of Abbott's board institute an action against themselves for breach of their fiduciary duties, arguing that such a demand would be futile. Under applicable law, such a demand is not required if the plaintiffs plead facts showing that the directors faced a substantial likelihood of liability for their actions. In particular, "demand can only be excused where facts are alleged with particularity which create a reasonable doubt that the directors' action was entitled to the protections of the business judgment rule."[11] The district court dismissed the complaint, and the plaintiffs appealed.

**› ISSUE PRESENTED** Is it a breach of directors' duty of good faith for them to fail to follow up on repeated notices of regulatory noncompliance?

**› OPINION** WOOD, J., writing on behalf of the U.S. Court of Appeals for the Seventh Circuit:

Plaintiffs in *Abbott* allege facts that the directors were aware of known violations, providing evidence that there was direct knowledge through the Warning Letters and as members of the Audit Committee. Under proper corporate governance procedures—the existence of which is not contested by either party in Abbott—information of the violations would have been shared at the board meetings. In addition, plaintiffs have alleged that, as fiduciaries, the directors all signed the annual SEC forms which specifically addressed government regulation of Abbott's products. The *Abbott* case is clearly distinguished from the "unconsidered" inaction in *In re Caremark*.[12]

. . .

The district court noted, correctly, that the plaintiffs did not allege that Abbott's reporting system was inadequate. . . . Where there is a corporate governance structure in place, we must then assume the corporate governance procedures were followed and that the board knew of the problems and decided no action was required. . . .

. . .

Delaware law states that director liability may arise from the breach of the duty to exercise appropriate attention to potentially illegal corporate activities or from "an *unconsidered failure of the board to act* in circumstances in which due attention would, arguably, have prevented the loss." *In re Caremark*. The court held that "a sustained or systematic failure of the board to exercise oversight . . . will establish the lack of good faith that is a necessary condition to [director] liability.". . .

Given the extensive paper trail in *Abbott* concerning the violations and the inferred awareness of the problems, the facts support a reasonable assumption that there was a "sustained and systematic failure of the board to exercise oversight," in this case

11. Aronson v. Lewis, 473 A.2d 805 (Del. 1984), *overruled on other grounds by* Brehm v. Eisner, 746 A.2d 244 (Del. 2000).
12. 698 A.2d 959, 967 (Del. Ch. 1996) (Case 20.2).

*(Continued)*

(Case 20.3 *continued*)

intentional in that the directors knew of the violations of law, took no steps in an effort to prevent or remedy the situation, and that failure to take any action for such an inordinate amount of time resulted in substantial corporate losses, establishing a lack of good faith. We find that six years of noncompliance, inspections, 483s, Warning Letters, and notice in the press, all of which then resulted in the largest civil fine ever imposed by the FDA and the destruction and suspension of products which accounted for approximately $250 million in corporate assets, indicate that the directors' decision to not act was not made in good faith and was contrary to the best interests of the company.

With respect to demand futility based on the directors' conscious inaction, we find that the plaintiffs have sufficiently pleaded allegations, if true, of a breach of the duty of good faith to reasonably conclude that the directors' actions fell outside the protection of the business judgment rule. . . .

The directors contend that they are not liable under Abbott's certificate of incorporation provision which exempts the directors from liability [for breach of the duty of care]. Directors are not protected by that provision when a complaint alleges facts that infer a breach of loyalty or good faith. [The burden of establishing good faith rests with the director seeking protection under the exculpatory provision.]

Plaintiffs in Abbott accused the directors not only of gross negligence, but of intentional conduct in failing to address the federal violation problems, alleging "a conscious disregard of known risks, which conduct, if proven, cannot have been undertaken in good faith."

**› RESULT** The plaintiffs pleaded sufficient facts to prove that the directors were not entitled to the protection of the business judgment rule. The plaintiffs' claims were also not precluded by Abbott's charter provision. The trial court's dismissal of the complaint was reversed. The plaintiffs could proceed with the derivative action.

**› COMMENTS** The directors were potentially liable even though a majority of the board was independent and there were no allegations of self-dealing.

**› CRITICAL THINKING QUESTIONS**

1. Would the independent directors have been liable if the CEO and board chair had not given them copies of the FDA Warning Letters?
2. If you had been an independent director on Abbott's board, how would you have responded upon receiving notice of the second FDA Warning Letter?

# Duty of Loyalty

To comply with their duty of loyalty, directors and managers must subordinate their own interests to those of the corporation and its shareholders. As a result, when a shareholder attacks a transaction in which managers or directors are engaged in self-dealing or have a self-interest other than that of a corporate fiduciary, courts will closely review the merits of the deal. Traditionally, such a transaction has been voidable unless its proponents could show that it was fair and reasonable to the corporation.

## Corporate Opportunities

One central corollary of the fiduciary duty of loyalty is that officers and directors may not take personal advantage of a business opportunity that rightfully belongs to the corporation. This is known as the *corporate opportunity doctrine*. For example, suppose that a copper-mining corporation is actively looking for mining sites. If an officer of the corporation learns of an attractive site in the course of his or her business for the corporation, the officer may not buy it for himself or herself. If the officer attempts to do so, a shareholder can block the sale or impose a *constructive trust* on any profits the officer makes from the acquisition, that is, force the officer to hold such profits for the benefit of the corporation and pay them over to the corporation on request.

The courts have devised several tests for determining whether an opportunity belongs to a corporation. Perhaps the most widely used is the *line-of-business test.* Under this test, if an officer, director, or controlling shareholder learns of an opportunity in the course of his or her business for the corporation and the opportunity is in the corporation's line of business, a court will not permit the officer, director, or controlling shareholder to keep the opportunity for himself or herself.

For example, the Delaware Supreme Court ruled in a classic case that the president and director of Loft, Inc., a company engaged in the manufacturing of candies, syrups, beverages, and foodstuffs, could not set up a new corporation to acquire the secret formula and trademarks of Pepsi Cola.[13] He had unsuccessfully sought a volume discount for Loft's purchases of syrup from the Coca-Cola Company and was contemplating substituting Pepsi for Coke.

If an officer or director develops an idea on company time using company resources, a court will be more likely to find a breach of fiduciary duty if the officer or director then leaves to pursue the idea. If the officer or director has signed an assignment of inventions, then the idea will usually belong to the company under the terms of that agreement. Even without such an agreement, use of company time or resources may restrict the ability of the officer or director to define the line of business narrowly.

Other courts have considered whether (1) it would be fair for the fiduciary to keep the opportunity, (2) the corporation has an expectancy or interest growing out of an existing right in the opportunity, or (3) the interference by the fiduciary will hinder the corporation's purposes. Because different states apply different tests, a corporate fiduciary should always consult local counsel if there is any question of the fiduciary's actions interfering with a corporate opportunity.

An officer or director presented with a corporate opportunity is expected to disclose it to disinterested directors, who may then accept or reject the opportunity. The adequate disclosure of a corporate opportunity will provide defendants with a safe harbor from liability for breach of fiduciary duty.

The Delaware Supreme Court held that corporate officers and directors who usurp a corporate opportunity must disgorge to the corporation any gains obtained through their breach of loyalty, even though they, acting in their capacity as controlling shareholders, could have prevented the corporation from taking advantage of the opportunity. In *Thorpe v. CERBCO Inc.,*[14] two brothers were officers, directors, and controlling shareholders of CERBCO. When a potential acquirer brought up the possibility of buying one of CERBCO's subsidiaries, the brothers instead proposed to sell their own shares to the acquirer. Because the brothers (in their capacity as shareholders) could have blocked every viable sale of the subsidiary, CERBCO was not in fact able to take advantage of the opportunity. Thus, CERBCO suffered no damages as a result of this lost opportunity because there was zero probability of the sale occurring (due to the brothers' lawful right to vote against it). Nevertheless, the brothers were fiduciaries of CERBCO and, as such, had the duty to present the sale opportunity to CERBCO. The court held that the brothers were not entitled to the profit gained by their breach of this duty. As a result, they were not entitled to keep the profit they had made on the sale of their stock to the potential acquirer of CERBCO's subsidiary.

## Duties in the Context of Takeovers, Mergers, and Acquisitions

In deciding whether to sell a company, directors should consider seven key factors: (1) the company's intrinsic value, (2) the appropriateness of delegating negotiating authority to management, (3) nonprice considerations, (4) the reliability of officers' reports to the board, (5) the reliability of experts' reports, (6) the investment banker's fee structure, and (7) the reasonableness of any defensive tactics. As explained earlier, the directors must act in good faith and be adequately informed.

### THE COMPANY'S INTRINSIC VALUE

The ability to make an informed decision as to the acceptability of a proposed buyout price requires knowledge of the company's intrinsic value. Determining intrinsic value entails more than an assessment of the premium of the offering price over the market price per share of the company's stock. When, as in *Van Gorkom,* it is believed that the market has consistently underval-

13. Guth v. Loft, Inc., 5 A.2d 503 (Del. 1939).

14. 703 A.2d 645 (Del. 1997).

ued the company's stock, evaluating the offered price by comparing it with the market price is, according to the Delaware Supreme Court, "faulty, indeed fallacious."

Thus, the directors must do more than assess the adequacy of the premium and compare it with the premiums paid in other takeovers in the same or similar industries. They must also assess the intrinsic or fair value of the company (or division) as a going concern and on a liquidation basis.

Practitioners have read *Van Gorkom* as virtually mandating participation by an investment banker if directors are to avoid personal liability. However, the *Van Gorkom* court expressly disclaimed such an intention:

> We do not imply that an outside valuation study is essential to support an informed business judgment; nor do we state that fairness opinions by independent investment bankers are required as a matter of law. Often insiders familiar with the business of a going concern are in a better position than are outsiders to gather relevant information; and under appropriate circumstances, such directors may be fully protected in relying in good faith upon the valuation reports of their management.[15]

For all practical purposes, however, directors should look to both internal and external sources for guidance. The most reliable valuation information will consist of financial data supplied by management and evaluated by investment bankers knowledgeable about the industry and recent merger and acquisition activity.

The *Hanson Trust* decision makes it clear, however, that the mere presence of investment bankers in the target's boardroom will not shield its directors from personal liability. In that case, the Goldman Sachs partner's oral opinion that the option prices were "within the range of fair value" did not withstand the scrutiny of the Second Circuit on appeal.

## Delegation of Negotiating Authority

If members of management are financial participants in the proposed transaction, the delegation of negotiation responsibilities to management or inside directors will expose the board to greater risks of liability. The Second Circuit observed in *Hanson Trust:*

> SCM's board delegated to management broad authority to work directly with Merrill to structure an LBO proposal, and then appears to have swiftly approved management's proposals. Such broad delegations of authority are not uncommon and generally are quite proper as conforming to the way that a Board acts in generating proposals for its own consideration. However, when management has a self-interest in consummating an LBO, standard post hoc review procedures may be insufficient. SCM's management and the Board's advisers presented the various agreements to the SCM directors more or less as faits accompli, which the Board quite hastily approved. In short, the Board appears to have failed to ensure that negotiations for alternative bids were conducted by those whose only loyalty was to the shareholders.[16]

## Nonprice Considerations

In evaluating a buyout proposal, directors have a fiduciary duty to familiarize themselves with any material nonprice provisions of the proposed agreement. Directors are duty bound to consider separately whether such provisions are in the best interest of the company and its shareholders or, if not, whether the proposal as a whole, notwithstanding such provisions, is in the best interest of their constituencies.

In *Van Gorkom,* for example, several outside directors maintained that Pritzker's merger proposal was approved with the understanding that "if we got a better deal, we had a right to take it." The directors also asserted that they had "insisted" upon an amendment reserving to Trans Union the right to disclose proprietary information to competing bidders. However, the court found that the merger agreement reserved neither of these rights to Trans Union. In the court's view, the directors had "no rational basis" for asserting that their acceptance of Pritzker's offer was conditioned upon a market test of the offer or that Trans Union had a right to withdraw from the agreement in order to accept a higher bid.

Directors should therefore ensure not only that they correctly understand the nonprice provisions of a proposed merger agreement but also that the provisions find their way into the definitive agreement. They should verify this by reading the documents prior to execution.

## Takeover Defenses

The business judgment rule creates a powerful presumption in favor of actions taken by the directors of a corporation. As noted earlier, the business judgment rule does not apply if the directors have an interest in the

15. Smith v. Van Gorkom, 488 A.2d 858, 876 (Del. 1985) (Case 20.1).

16. Hanson Trust PLC v. ML SCM Acquisition, Inc., 781 F.2d 264, 277 (2d Cir. 1986).

**INTERNATIONAL SNAPSHOT**

The laws of Germany and several Scandinavian countries require union and employee representation on the boards of directors of most public corporations. These representatives participate in all of the basic decisions related to investment policy, choice of product and technology, marketing, employee relations, and other matters of managerial concern. When Germany's Daimler-Benz AG merged with Chrysler Corporation in 1998, the combined entity, DaimlerChrysler, was organized under German law. As required by Germany's codetermination laws, half of the members of the supervisory board were elected by the employees and union leaders; half were elected by the shareholders. Under Germany's two-tier board system, the supervisory board consists solely of non-employee directors, and it is often chaired by a representative of the corporation's main bank. The supervisory board appoints the management board, which consists solely of inside directors and reports to the supervisory board.[a]

**a.** Greg Steinmetz & Gregory L. White, *Chrysler Pay Draws Fire Overseas*, WALL ST. J., May 26, 1998, at B1, B4.

transaction being acted upon. If a hostile raider is successful, it is probably going to replace the company's management and board of directors as its first step after assuming control. A successful defense against the takeover has the effect of preserving the positions of current management and directors. Thus, the directors arguably have a personal interest whenever a board opposes a hostile takeover.

## Unocal *Proportionality Test*

*Unocal Corp. v. Mesa Petroleum Co.*[17] established the principle that the business judgment rule applies to takeover defenses, provided that the directors can show that they had reasonable grounds for believing that the unwelcome suitor posed a threat to corporate policy and effectiveness and that the defense was a reasonable response to that threat. This enhanced judicial scrutiny is designed to guard against "the omnipresent specter that a board may be acting primarily in its own interests, rather than those of the corporation and its shareholders."

The Delaware Supreme Court further explained:

> If a defensive measure is to come within the ambit of the business judgment rule, it must be reasonable in relation to the threat posed. This entails an analysis by the directors of the nature of the takeover bid and its effect on the corporate enterprise. Examples of such concerns may include: inadequacy of the price offered, nature and timing of the offer, questions of illegality, the impact on "constituencies" other than shareholders (that is, creditors, customers, employees, and perhaps even the community generally), the risk of nonconsummation, and the quality of securities being offered in the exchange. While not a controlling factor, it also seems to us that a board may reasonably consider the basic stockholder interests at stake, including those of short term speculators, whose actions may have fueled the coercive aspect of the offer at the expense of the long term investor.

If the directors succeed in making this initial showing, then they are entitled to the protection of the business judgment rule. Under those circumstances, the Delaware Supreme Court stated:

> [U]nless it is shown by a preponderance of the evidence that the directors' decisions were primarily based on perpetuating themselves in office, or some other breach of fiduciary duty such as fraud, overreaching, lack of good faith, or being uninformed, a court will not substitute its judgment for that of the board.

Applying these standards to the hostile bid for Unocal by Mesa Petroleum and its CEO, T. Boone Pickens, the court upheld a discriminatory *self-tender* by Unocal for its own stock, whereby all of the shareholders, except Mesa Petroleum, Pickens, and their affiliates, could exchange their Unocal stock for debt securities worth $18 more per share than the $54 per share offered by Pickens in the first stage of his two-tier front-loaded tender offer. Pickens's offer was deemed coercive because he was acquiring just enough shares in the first stage to get control. Hence, even if shareholders considered the price inadequate, they might well feel coerced into tendering in the first stage for fear of receiving securities of even less value in the second stage, when Unocal was merged with a Mesa-controlled corporation. The Unocal board viewed the threat as a grossly inadequate two-tier coercive tender offer coupled with the threat of greenmail. (*Greenmail* occurs when a raider acquires stock in a target company and then threatens to commence a hostile takeover unless its stock is repurchased by the target at a premium over the market price.)

The strategy used in *Unocal* is no longer available because of the SEC's "all holders rule." According to the rule, a selective stock repurchase plan is deemed a tender offer in which all holders of securities of the same class must be allowed to participate. Nonetheless, this case

17. 493 A.2d 946 (Del. 1985).

remains a key Delaware precedent for the analysis of defensive tactics, including shareholder rights plans (also called poison pills), which can have much the same effect as a discriminatory self-tender.

## *Duty to Maximize Shareholder Value under* Revlon

Once the judgment is made that a sale or breakup of the corporation is in the best interests of the shareholders or is inevitable, directors have a fiduciary duty to obtain the best available price for the shareholders. This rule was first articulated in a case involving a hostile takeover bid for Revlon, Inc. by Pantry Pride.[18]

After initially resisting the takeover attempt, the Revlon board elected to go forward with a friendly buyout from another company at a lower price than that offered by the hostile bidder. The Revlon board sought to justify the lower price by pointing out the benefits of the friendly buyout for other corporate constituencies, such as the Revlon noteholders. The hostile bidder sued to enjoin the friendly buyout.

The Delaware Supreme Court required the Revlon board to seek the highest price for the shareholders. The court defined the duty of the directors as follows:

> The Revlon board's authorization permitting management to negotiate a merger or buyout with a third party was a recognition that the company was for sale. The duty of the board had thus changed from the preservation of Revlon as a corporate entity to the maximization of the company's value at a sale for the stockholders' benefit. . . . The directors' role changed from defenders of the corporate bastion to auctioneers charged with getting the best price for the stockholders at a sale of the company.

In *Barkan v. Amsted Industries*,[19] the Supreme Court of Delaware held that the basic teaching of cases such as *Revlon* is simply that directors of corporations must act in accordance with their fundamental duties of care and loyalty. The court ruled, however, that acting in accordance with these duties does not mean that every change of corporate control necessitates an auction. If fairness to shareholders and the minimizing of conflicts of interest can be demonstrated, the added burden of having an auction may not be necessary. The court in *Barkan* declined to make a specific rule for determining when a market test (or "market check") is required. The court simply stated: "[I]t must be clear that the board had sufficient knowledge of relevant markets to form the basis for its belief that it acted in the best interests of the shareholders."[20]

It is doubtful that a failure of directors to consider every conceivable alternative would in itself amount to a breach of fiduciary duty. Such a rule would be unduly harsh. In hindsight, a complaining shareholder could almost always conjure up at least one alternative that the directors failed to consider. On the other hand, the failure of a board to consider any alternatives at all, or the unwillingness of a board to negotiate with anyone other than its chosen white knight (or with the initial offeror), would be a breach of fiduciary duty unless there were special circumstances.

**When Is a Company in *Revlon* Mode?** The case of *Paramount Communications, Inc. v. Time Inc.*[21] examined the question of what constitutes an event triggering the *Revlon* duty to maximize shareholder value. (A company with such an obligation is deemed to be in *Revlon mode.*) Time had entered into a friendly stock-for-stock merger agreement with Warner Communications. Under that agreement, roughly 60 percent of the stock of the new combined entity Time–Warner would be held by former public shareholders of Warner. The merger agreement was subject to the approval of Time's shareholders.

Shortly before the Time shareholder vote was to take place, Paramount Communications made a hostile, unsolicited cash tender offer for all Time shares. In response, Time proceeded with its own highly leveraged cash tender offer to acquire 51 percent of Warner, to be followed by a back-end, second-step merger of the two companies. This tender offer, which would preclude acceptance of the Paramount tender offer, did not require approval by the Time shareholders. Paramount challenged the actions of Time's directors in opposing its offer, arguing that the Time board had put Time in the *Revlon* mode when it agreed to the stock merger with Warner.

The Delaware Supreme Court held that this transaction did not trigger *Revlon* duties because there was no change in control. Majority control shifted from one "fluid aggregation of unaffiliated shareholders" to another and remained in the hands of the public. As a result, the Time board could properly take into account such intangibles as the desire to preserve the Time culture and journalistic integrity in deciding to reject Paramount's hostile tender offer, which was arguably

18. Revlon, Inc. v. MacAndrews & Forbes Holdings, Inc., 506 A.2d 173 (Del. 1986).
19. 567 A.2d 1279 (Del. 1989).
20. *Id.* at 1288.
21. 571 A.2d 1140 (Del. 1990).

*"Before we discuss destroying the competition, screwing our customers, and laughing all the way to the bank, let's begin this meeting with a prayer."*



worth more to shareholders than the Time–Warner combination. The court considered this to be a strategic alliance, not a sale of Time to Warner, which would have triggered the *Revlon* duty to maximize shareholder value.

Relying heavily on the precedent established by the *Time–Warner* case, Paramount entered into a friendly merger agreement with Viacom Inc. in September 1993. At the time Paramount agreed to merge with Viacom, control of Paramount was vested in the "fluid aggregation of unaffiliated stockholders," and not in a single person, entity, or group. Sumner Redstone was the CEO, chair, and majority shareholder of Viacom. After the proposed merger, he would be the controlling shareholder of the combined Paramount–Viacom entity. When QVC Network, Inc. made a hostile unsolicited offer for Paramount that was worth $1.3 billion more than Viacom's offer, the Paramount board refused to negotiate with QVC and instead stood by its merger agreement with Viacom.

QVC then sued the Paramount directors, arguing that the Paramount board had put Paramount in the *Revlon* mode when it committed to a transaction that would shift control of Paramount from the public shareholders to Redstone. The Paramount board argued that it had no duty to maximize shareholder value because it was pursuing a strategic alliance with Viacom, not a breakup of the company. The Delaware Supreme Court rejected this argument and ruled that the Paramount directors had an obligation to continue their search for the best value reasonably available to the stockholders.[22]

The court ruled:

> [W]hen a corporation undertakes a transaction which will cause: (a) a change in corporate control; or (b) a break-up of the corporate entity, the directors' obligation is to seek the best value reasonably available to the stockholders. This obligation arises because the effect of the Viacom–Paramount transaction, if consummated, is to shift control of Paramount from the public stockholders to a controlling stockholder, Viacom.

Regardless of the present Paramount board's vision of a long-term strategic alliance with Viacom, once the Paramount–Viacom deal was consummated, Redstone

22. Paramount Communications, Inc., v. QVC Network, Inc., 637 A.2d 34 (Del. 1994).

would have the power to alter that vision. Furthermore, once control shifted, the current Paramount stockholders would have no leverage to demand another control premium in the future.

The Delaware Supreme Court was highly critical of the process the Paramount board followed:

> The directors' initial hope and expectation for a strategic alliance with Viacom was allowed to dominate their decisionmaking process to the point where the arsenal of defensive measures established at the outset was perpetuated (not modified or eliminated) when the situation was dramatically altered. QVC's unsolicited bid presented the opportunity for significantly greater value for the stockholders and enhanced negotiating leverage for the directors. Rather than seizing those opportunities, the Paramount directors chose to wall themselves off from material information which was reasonably available and to hide behind the defensive measures as a rationalization for refusing to negotiate with QVC or seeking other alternatives.

In *In re Lukens Inc. Shareholders Litigation*,[23] the Delaware Court of Chancery concluded that a merger of Lukens with Bethlehem Steel triggered *Revlon* duties even though more than 30 percent of the merger consideration consisted of shares of common stock of Bethlehem, a widely held company with no controlling stockholder. Because 62 percent of the consideration was cash, the court concluded that "for a substantial majority of the then-current shareholders, 'there is no long run.'"

The "In Brief" provides a decision tree for analyzing when the business judgment rule will apply to board decisions.

23. 757 A.2d 720 (Del. Ch. 1999), *aff'd*, 757 A.2d 1278 (Del. 2000).

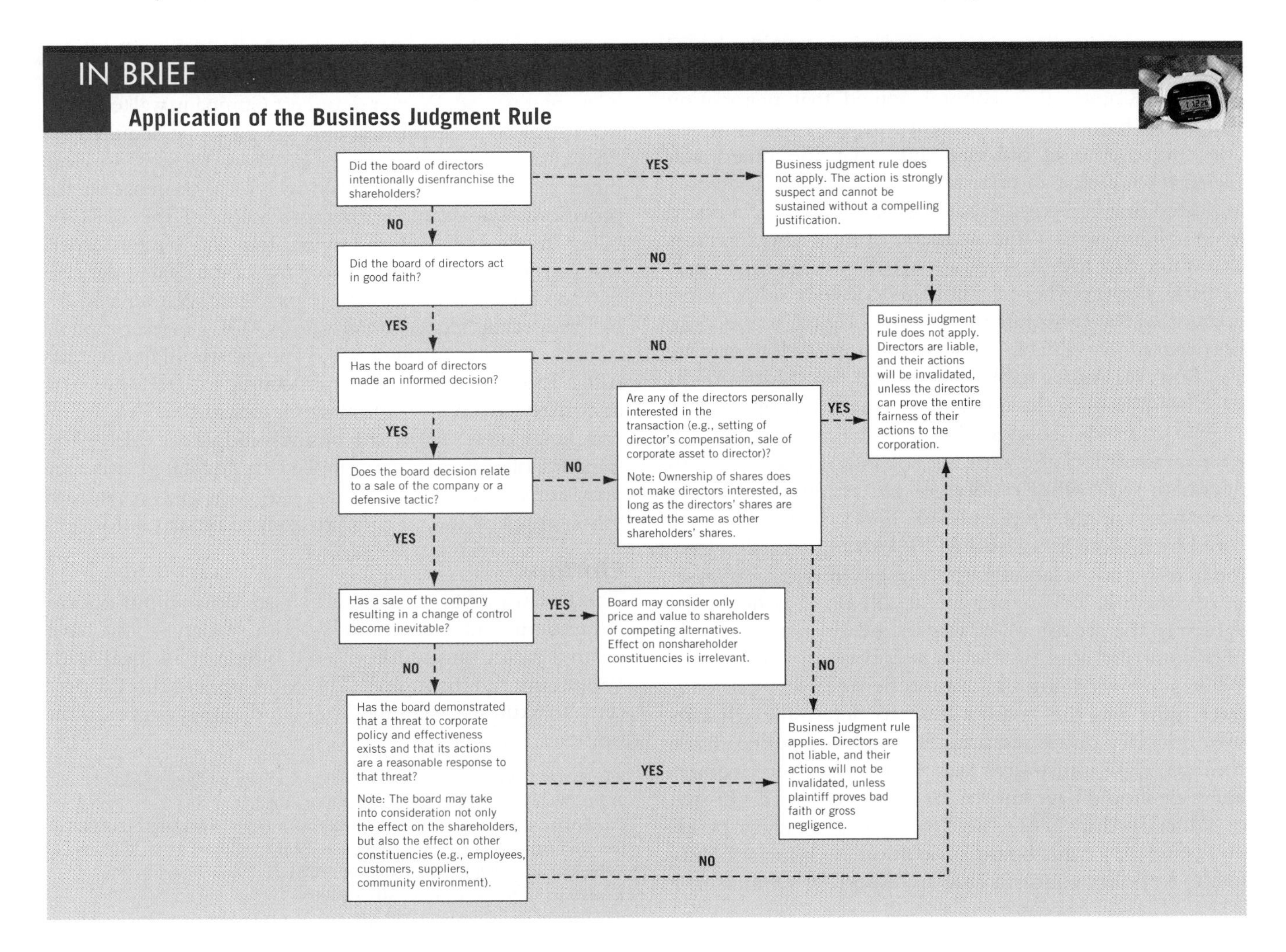

## Deal Protection Devices

Often the parties to a friendly merger will use *deal protection devices,* such as no-talk provisions, to dissuade other bidders and thereby protect the consummation of the friendly merger transaction. Defensive devices can be economic, structural, or both.

### No-Talk Provisions

Delaware courts are highly skeptical of agreements that purport to limit directors' ability to fulfill what they in good faith perceive their fiduciary duties to be. For example, the Court of Chancery refused to enforce a no-talk clause in a stock-for-stock merger agreement between Capital Re Corporation and Ace Limited. The *no-talk clause* permitted Capital Re Corporation to engage in discussions with and provide information to other bidders only if the board concluded, based on the written opinion of outside legal counsel, that engaging in discussions or providing information was required to prevent the board from breaching its fiduciary duties to its stockholders.[24] Although Capital Re's counsel opined that negotiating with other bidders was consistent with the board's fiduciary duties, counsel did not state that the board was *required* to discuss an offer by another bidder. The court indicated that a provision that purports to prevent a board from talking with other bidders, even if the directors determine that they have a fiduciary duty to do so, is "particularly suspect when a failure to consider other offers guarantees the consummation of the original transaction, however more valuable an alternate transaction may be and however less valuable the original transaction might have become since the merger agreement was signed."

The court did suggest that a no-talk clause with no *fiduciary out* (a clause allowing the board of directors to negotiate with other bidders or to terminate a merger agreement) might be permissible if (1) the stockholders could freely vote for or against the existing merger agreement and choose among the present merger, a subsequent merger, or no merger at all; or (2) the board agreed to the provision as a way to end an auction for sale of a company after a thorough canvass of the market. While acknowledging the tension between a vested contract right and the board's duty to determine what its own fiduciary duties require, the court concluded that a contract right must give way when (1) "the acquirer knew, or should have known, of the target board's breach of fiduciary duty"; (2) the "transaction remains pending"; and (3) "the board's violation of fiduciary duty relates to policy concerns that are especially significant."

24. Ace Ltd. v. Capital Re Corp., 747 A.2d 95 (Del. Ch. 1999).

On the other hand, courts are more likely to permit *no-shop agreements,* whereby the target agrees not to actively solicit other bidders but retains the right to negotiate with parties who submit unsolicited bids to the target. Once again, such devices are more likely to withstand attack when they are put into place after a canvass of the market and as a condition to a bidder's willingness to make a favorable bid.

### Breakup Fees

In exchange for providing a fiduciary out, a bidder will usually demand that some predetermined amount of money be paid to it if the deal fails to close because the target terminates the agreement. *Termination* or *breakup fees* are sometimes characterized as liquidated damages provisions, and they are often 2 to 3 percent of the value of the deal. They are usually intended to help make the bidder whole for its out-of-pocket expenses (for attorneys, investment bankers, and the like) and lost opportunity costs.

For example, in 2000, American Home Products Corporation received a termination fee of $1.8 billion when its merger partner Warner–Lambert Company walked away from their $72 billion deal and agreed to be acquired by Pfizer Inc. In mergers of equals, where there is no clear buyer or seller, there are often reciprocal termination fee provisions. For example, the agreement for the $131.49 billion merger of America Online, Inc. and Time–Warner, Inc. provided that if AOL backed out of the deal under certain conditions, it would have to pay Time–Warner a $5.37 billion breakup fee (2.75 percent of AOL's market capitalization); if Time–Warner walked away, it would have to pay AOL $3.9 billion.[25] Although courts in Delaware and elsewhere have upheld termination fees in the 1 to 3 percent range under either the business judgment rule or the standard of reasonableness applied to liquidated damages provisions, fees that are so large as to constitute "showstoppers" are much more likely to be struck down.[26]

### Options

The Delaware Supreme Court struck down a put option Paramount had granted to Viacom, which would have given Viacom an additional $1 billion if its deal with Paramount fell through.[27] The court upheld the 1.5 percent breakup fee as a valid liquidated damages provision, however.

25. Nikhil Deogun & Nick Wingfield, *Stock Drops Spur Questions on AOL Deal,* Wall St. J., Jan. 13, 2000, at A3.

26. For an interesting empirical analysis of deals involving breakup fees and other forms of lock-ups, see John C. Coates IV & Guhan Subramanian, *A Buy-Side Model of M&A Lockups: Theory and Evidence,* 53 Stan. L. Rev. 307 (2000).

27. Paramount Communications, Inc. v. QVC Network, Inc., 637 A.2d 34 (Del. 1994).

### *Other Devices*

In the following case, the Delaware Supreme Court considered whether the directors of an insolvent publicly traded corporation breached their fiduciary duty when they agreed to submit a merger agreement to a stockholder vote, knowing that the stockholders with a majority of the voting power had agreed unconditionally to vote all of their shares in favor of the inferior offer.

A CASE IN POINT

**CASE 20.4**

**Omnicare, Inc. v. NCS Healthcare, Inc.**

*Supreme Court of Delaware 818 A.2d 914 (Del. 2003).*

## Summary

**› FACTS** NCS Healthcare, Inc., a leading independent provider of pharmacy services to skilled nursing facilities and other long-term care institutions, became insolvent after changes in the timing and level of reimbursements by government and third-party payors adversely affected market conditions in the health-care industry. The price of its common stock dropped from about $20 in January 1999 to a range of $0.09 to $0.50 per share by early 2002 when Omnicare, Inc. offered to pay $313,750,000 for NCS's assets in a proposed asset sale in bankruptcy. Omnicare's offer was less than the amount of NCS's outstanding debt and would have resulted in no recovery for NCS's stockholders.

NCS's operating performance was improving by early 2002, when NCS contacted Genesis Health Ventures, Inc. in hopes of negotiating a transaction that would provide some recovery for NCS's stockholders. An independent committee of NCS board members, who were neither NCS employees nor major NCS stockholders, negotiated a transaction whereby Genesis agreed to repay the NCS senior debt in full, assume the trade debt, purchase the NCS notes or exchange them for cash and stock, and provide $24 million in value for the NCS common stock.

Genesis had previously lost a bidding war for another company when Omnicare made a last-minute overbid. Genesis told NCS that it was unwilling to be a stalking horse for a higher Omnicare bid and insisted on an exclusivity agreement that prevented NCS from negotiating with other bidders for a short period of time.

After NCS entered into the agreement, Omnicare concluded that NCS was negotiating a transaction with a competitor that would potentially present a competitive threat. In light of a run-up in the price of the NCS common stock, Omnicare also came to believe that whatever transaction NCS was negotiating probably included a payment for its stock. Omnicare then proposed a transaction that included $3 cash for the common shares but was conditioned on negotiating a merger agreement, obtaining certain third-party consents, and completing its due diligence. Although Omnicare's economic terms were attractive, the due diligence condition weakened its offer.

Genesis agreed to improve its offer by, among other things, increasing the payment to the stockholders by 80 percent but stipulated that the transaction had to be approved by midnight the next day or else it would terminate the discussions and withdraw its offer. After "balancing the potential loss of the Genesis deal against the uncertainty of Omnicare's letter," the NCS special committee and full board concluded that the only reasonable alternative was to approve the Genesis transaction. The NCS board authorized the voting agreements with the two majority stockholders, whereby they agreed to vote for the Genesis deal, and agreed to submit the merger agreement to the NCS stockholders regardless of whether the board continued to recommend the merger under Section 251(c) of the Delaware General Corporation Law.

Shortly thereafter Omnicare made an irrevocable offer to acquire the NCS stock for $3.50 per share in cash. The NCS board then withdrew its recommendation that the

*(Continued)*

(Case 20.4 *continued*)

stockholders vote in favor of the NCS–Genesis merger agreement, and NCS's financial adviser withdrew its fairness opinion. Nonetheless, the stockholder agreement ensured NCS stockholder approval of the Genesis merger. Omnicare then sued to prevent the consummation of the inferior Genesis transaction.

**› ISSUE PRESENTED** Did the directors of an insolvent publicly traded company violate their fiduciary duty when they entered into an agreement for a "bullet-proof" sale of the company to the "only game in town"?

**› SUMMARY OF OPINION** The Delaware Supreme Court began by explaining that a board's management decision to enter into and recommend a merger transaction can become final only when ownership action is taken by a vote of the stockholders. As a result, "a board of directors' decision to adopt defensive devices to protect a merger agreement may implicate the stockholders' right to effectively vote contrary to the initial recommendation of the board in favor of the transaction."

The court then reasoned that there is an "omnipresent specter" of conflicts of interest when a board of directors acts to prevent stockholders from effectively exercising their right to vote contrary to the will of the board. To be protected under the business judgment rule, defensive devices adopted by the board to protect the original merger transaction must withstand enhanced judicial scrutiny under the *Unocal* standard applied to antitakeover devices. The court explained that the board "does not have unbridled discretion to defeat perceived threats by any draconian means available." Defensive measures that are either preclusive or coercive are, by definition, considered draconian and invalid.

Enhanced judicial scrutiny requires (1) a "judicial determination regarding the adequacy of the decisionmaking process employed by the directors, including the information on which the directors based their decision," and (2) "a judicial examination of the reasonableness of the directors' action in light of the circumstances then existing." The directors have the burden of proving that they were adequately informed and acted reasonably. As long as the deal protection devices are not draconian and are within a range of reasonableness, a court will not substitute its judgment for that of the board.

The court first considered whether the NCS directors had demonstrated that they had reasonable grounds for believing that a danger to corporate policy and effectiveness existed. The threat identified by the NCS board was the possibility of losing the Genesis offer and being left with no comparable alternative transaction.

The court then applied the second stage of the *Unocal* test, which required the NCS directors to demonstrate that their defensive response was reasonable in relation to the threat posed. The court explained that this inquiry involves a two-step analysis. First, the NCS directors were required to establish that the merger deal protection devices adopted in response to the threat were not "coercive" or "preclusive." Second, they had to demonstrate that their response was within a "range of reasonable responses" to the threat perceived.

In this case, the court concluded that the deal protection devices the NCS board agreed to were *both* preclusive and coercive. The tripartite defensive measures—the Section 251(c) provision, the voting agreements, and the absence of an effective fiduciary out clause—made it "mathematically impossible" and "realistically unattainable" for the Omnicare transaction or any other proposal to succeed no matter how superior the proposal. Although the minority stockholders were not forced to vote for the Genesis merger, they were required to accept it because it was a *fait accompli.* The court

*(Continued)*

(Case 20.4 *continued*)

concluded that the NCS directors' defensive devices were not within a reasonable range of responses to the perceived threat of losing the Genesis offer because they were preclusive and coercive. As a result, the devices were unenforceable.

The court went on to hold that the deal protection devices were unenforceable for a second independent reason. Taken together, they completely prevented the board from discharging its fiduciary responsibilities to the minority stockholders.

Although the NCS board was seeking to ensure that the NCS creditors were paid in full and that the NCS stockholders received the highest value available for their stock, the NCS board did not have authority to accede to the Genesis demand for an absolute "lock-up." Because the directors of a Delaware corporation have a continuing obligation to discharge their fiduciary responsibilities, as future circumstances develop, after approving the merger with Genesis, the NCS board was required to negotiate a fiduciary out clause to protect the NCS stockholders if the Genesis transaction became an inferior offer. "By acceding to Genesis' ultimatum for complete protection in futuro, the NCS board disabled itself from exercising its own fiduciary obligations at a time when the board's own judgment is most important, i.e., receipt of a subsequent superior offer." Although the stockholders with majority voting power "had an absolute right to sell or exchange their shares with a third party at any price," the NCS directors had a supervening responsibility to discharge their fiduciary duties on a continuing basis.

The court explained:

> Any board has authority to give the proponent of a recommended merger agreement reasonable structural and economic defenses, incentives, and fair compensation if the transaction is not completed. To the extent that defensive measures are economic and reasonable, they may have become an increased cost to the proponent of any subsequent transaction. Just as defensive measures cannot be draconian, however, they cannot limit or circumscribe the directors' fiduciary duties.

**› RESULT** The provisions in the merger agreement requiring a stockholder vote on the Genesis deal were invalid, so the NCS board was not required to put the Genesis deal to a stockholder vote.

**› COMMENTS** This case resulted in a rare three–two split decision of the Delaware Supreme Court. The dissenting opinion by Chief Justice Veasey, with whom Justice Steele joined, pointed out that the merger agreement and the voting commitments of the majority stockholders concluded a lengthy search and intense negotiation process in the context of insolvency and creditor pressure where no other viable bid had emerged:

> Going into negotiations with Genesis, the NCS directors knew that, up until that time, NCS had found only one potential bidder, Omnicare. Omnicare had refused to buy NCS except at a fire sale price through an asset sale in bankruptcy. Omnicare's best proposal at that stage would not have paid off all creditors and would have provided nothing for stockholders. Genesis expressed interest that became increasingly attractive. Negotiations with Genesis led to an offer paying creditors off and conferring on NCS stockholders $24 million—an amount infinitely superior to the prior Omnicare proposals.
>
> But there was, understandably, a sine qua non. In exchange for offering the NCS stockholders a return on their equity and creditor payment, Genesis demanded certainty that the merger would close. If the NCS board would not have acceded to the

*(Continued)*

(Case 20.4 *continued*)

Section 251(c) provision, if [the majority shareholders] had not agreed to voting agreements and if NCS had insisted on a fiduciary out, there would have been no Genesis deal! Thus, the only value-enhancing transaction available would have disappeared.

The Majority invalidates the NCS board's action by announcing a new rule that represents an extension of our jurisprudence. That new rule can be narrowly stated as follows: A merger agreement entered into after a market search, before any prospect of a topping bid has emerged, which locks up stockholder approval and does not contain a "fiduciary out" provision, is per se invalid when a later significant topping bid emerges. As we have noted, this bright-line, per se rule would apply regardless of (1) the circumstances leading up to the agreement and (2) the fact that stockholders who control voting power had irrevocably committed themselves, *as stockholders,* to vote for the merger. Narrowly stated, this new rule is a judicially-created "third rail" that now becomes one of the given "rules of the game," to be taken into account by the negotiators and drafters of the given "rules of the game," to be taken into account by the negotiators and drafters of merger agreements. In our view, this new rule is an unwise extension of existing precedent.

The NCS board's actions—as the Vice Chancellor correctly held—were reasonable in relation to the threat because the Genesis deal was the "only game in town," the NCS directors got the best deal they could from Genesis and—but for the emergence of Genesis on the scene—there would have been no viable deal.

Because the deal protection measures were not adopted unilaterally by the board to fend off an existing hostile offer, the dissent argued that the majority's reliance on the discussion in an earlier case of "draconian" antitakeover devices measures was misplaced.

In a second dissenting opinion, Justice Steele chided the majority:

In effect, the majority has adopted the "duck" theory of contract interpretation. In my view, just as all ducks have their season and the wary hunter carefully scans the air to determine which duck may and which may not be shot at a given time on a certain day, the same holds true for distinguishing between contract provisions that could in another context be deemed truly defensive measures demanding enhanced scrutiny by a court. When certain, or when in doubt that the "duck" is not in season, courts, like prudent waterfowls, should defer.

## Allocation of Power Between the Directors and the Shareholders

A key issue that emerges from cases involving hostile takeovers and defensive tactics is who gets to decide whether the corporation should be sold—the board of directors or the shareholders. Theoretically, the board of directors is the guardian of the shareholders' interests, but the interests and obligations of the two groups sometimes conflict.

Frequently, a hostile takeover attempt presents such a conflict. Sometimes the proposed terms are attractive to the shareholders because the acquiring corporation offers to pay a substantial premium for their stock. The board of directors, however, may believe that the acquiring company's plans for the corporation are ultimately destructive, as in the case of a bust-up takeover, in which the acquired corporation is taken apart and its assets sold piecemeal. The directors may have legitimate concerns about the effect of such a takeover on the company's employees or on the community where the corporation is located. Or the directors might believe that the long-term value of the company is greater than the price being offered. Of course, directors might oppose a transaction just so they can remain on the corporation's board in violation of their legal obligation to put the corporation's interests before their own.

## Poison Pills

In one of the first cases addressing the allocation of power between the directors and the shareholders in deciding whether the corporation should be sold, a board of directors, without shareholder approval, had adopted a *poison pill* or *shareholder rights plan,* that is, a plan that would make any takeover not approved by the directors prohibitively expensive.[28] In 1984, the directors of Household International, fearing that Household might be taken over and busted up, adopted a poison pill in the form of a Preferred Share Purchase Rights Plan. This plan provided that, under certain triggering circumstances, common shareholders would receive a "right" for every common share of Household. In the event of a merger in which Household was not the surviving corporation, the holder of each common share of Household would have the right to purchase $200 of the common stock of the acquiring company for only $100. If these rights were triggered and exercised, they would dilute the value of the stock of the acquiring company, making a takeover prohibitively expensive for the acquirer.

The Delaware Supreme Court upheld the board's power to adopt the plan. The court found that the plan did not usurp the shareholders' ability to receive tender offers and to sell their shares to a bidder without board approval of the sale. Household's poison pill left "numerous methods to successfully launch a takeover." For example, a bidder could make a tender offer on the condition that the board redeem the rights, that is, buy them back for a nominal sum before they were triggered. A bidder could set a high minimum of shares and rights to be tendered; it could solicit consents to remove the board and replace it with one that would redeem the rights; or it could acquire 50 percent of the shares and cause Household to self-tender for the rights. In a self-tender, the company would agree to buy back the shareholders' rights for a fair price.

The court also found that the plan did not fundamentally restrict the shareholders' right to conduct a proxy contest. In a *proxy contest,* someone wishing to replace the board with his or her own candidates must acquire a sufficient number of shareholder votes to do so. Such votes are usually represented by *proxies,* or limited written powers of attorney entitling the proxy holder to vote the shares owned by the person giving the proxy. The court found that a proxy contest could be won with an insurgent ownership of less than 20 percent (the threshold for triggering distribution of the rights) and that the key to success in a proxy contest is the merit of the insurgent's arguments, not the size of his or her holdings.

The court concluded that the decision to adopt the poison-pill plan was within the board's authority. Moreover, because the directors "reasonably believed Household was vulnerable to coercive acquisition techniques and adopted a reasonable defensive mechanism to protect itself," the court held that the board had discharged its fiduciary duty appropriately under the business judgment rule. As of 2004, more than 2,000 poison-pill plans were in effect.

Although the Delaware Supreme Court upheld the adoption of a poison-pill plan in *Moran,* it reserved judgment on how such a plan would operate in practice. In particular, it left open the question of when directors must redeem the poison-pill rights to permit shareholders to tender their shares to a bidder.

The question of whether a board must redeem a pill is fact-specific—a court will look at all of the circumstances in making its decision. Certain factors will favor keeping the pill in place. These include (1) a tender offer that is only slightly above the market price of the stock; (2) a tender offer for less than all of the shares; (3) an active attempt by the board to solicit other offers; (4) a conscious effort by the board to allow its outside directors, deemed more disinterested, to make the decisions in this area; and (5) the fact that the tender offer is only in its early stages. The *Time–Warner* case made it clear that, under certain circumstances, a board faced with a hostile takeover bid can "Just Say No."

The Delaware Court of Chancery struck down a so-called dead-hand pill, which could be redeemed only by the directors in office before the hostile bidder gained control or their designated successors.[29] The court held that the dead-hand provision violated the requirement under Section 141 of the Delaware General Corporation Law that the directors manage the business and affairs of the corporation because it gave one category of directors distinctive voting rights that were not shared by the other directors. Although the Delaware statute permits different directors to be given distinctive voting rights, those rights must be set forth in the certificate of incorporation, which was not the case here.

The court also held that the dead-hand feature violated the directors' duty of loyalty for two reasons. First, the provision failed to meet the more exacting *Blasius*[30]

28. Moran v. Household Int'l, Inc., 500 A.2d 1346 (Del. 1985).

29. Carmody v. Toll Bros., Inc., 723 A.2d 1180 (Del. Ch. 1998).

30. Blasius Indus. v. Atlas Corp., 564 A.2d 651 (Del. Ch. 1988).

standard (after the case of the same name in which the Delaware Court of Chancery first articulated this standard) applicable to defensive tactics touching upon issues of control because it purposefully disenfranchised the company's shareholders without any compelling justification. In particular, "even in an election contest fought over the issue of the hostile bid, the shareholders will be powerless to elect a board that is both willing and able to accept the bid." Instead, the shareholders "may be forced to vote for [incumbent] directors whose policies they reject because only those directors have the power to change them." Second, the dead-hand provision failed to satisfy *Unocal's* requirement that the defense be proportionate to the threat because it was preclusive: it eliminated the use of a proxy contest as a possible means to gain control.

The Delaware Supreme Court also struck down a so-called no-hand pill, which could not be redeemed for six months even if the insurgent's slate of directors was elected and wanted to redeem it.[31] The delayed redemption provision in the plan would have prevented a new board of directors from redeeming the plan in order to facilitate a transaction that would serve the stockholders' best interests, even under circumstances where the board would be required to do so because of its fiduciary duty to the stockholders. Because the delayed redemption provision impermissibly circumscribed the board's statutory power under Section 141(a) to manage the business and affairs of the company and the directors' ability to fulfill their concomitant fiduciary duties, the delayed redemption provision was invalid.

## PROTECTING THE SHAREHOLDER FRANCHISE AND THE *BLASIUS* STANDARD OF REVIEW

A number of takeover cases have drawn a distinction between the exercise of two types of corporate power: (1) the power over the assets of the corporation, and (2) the power relationship between the board and the shareholders.[32] As explained earlier, directors have broad power over the assets of the corporation. Such decisions are generally protected by the business judgment rule or subjected to *Unocal's* proportionality analysis if they relate to defensive tactics. As Delaware Chancellor William Allen explained in *Paramount Communications, Inc. v. Time Inc.*, "The corporation law does not operate on the theory that directors, in exercising their powers to manage the firm, are obligated to follow the wishes of a majority of shares."[33] Thus, the Time directors had the power to acquire Warner Communications even though the holders of a majority of Time's stock would have preferred to take Paramount's offer.

If a board's unilateral decision to adopt a defensive measure touches on issues of voting control, however, then further judicial scrutiny is required to protect the shareholder franchise essential for corporate democracy. In particular, the court must decide whether the board purposefully disenfranchised its shareholders (that is, interfered with their right to elect the directors). If so, then under the *Blasius* standard, the action is strongly suspect and cannot be sustained without a compelling justification.[34]

Protecting the shareholder franchise is critical because the business judgment rule provides the directors and officers with great latitude in managing the day-to-day affairs of the corporation. As a result, shareholders who are displeased with the business performance generally have only two options: sell their shares or vote to replace the incumbent board members. The corporate governance system loses a key control if unhappy shareholders cannot vote the directors out of office.

For example, in *Chesapeake Corp. v. Shore*,[35] the Delaware Court of Chancery held that a supermajority bylaw provision adopted by the board of Shorewood Packing Corporation to thwart a hostile bid by Chesapeake Corporation was "a preclusive, unjustified impairment of the Shorewood stockholders' right to influence their company's policies through the ballot box." The provision increased from a simple majority to 60 percent of the number of Shorewood shares needed to amend the bylaws. Because Shorewood's management controlled almost 24 percent of its stock, the supermajority provision made it virtually impossible for Chesapeake to garner enough votes to amend the bylaws to eliminate the classified board so that it could unseat the current directors and install a new board amenable to its offer.

The Shorewood board claimed that Chesapeake's offer posed two threats: (1) the price was grossly inadequate, so Shorewood stockholders faced great harm if they sold their stock at that price; and (2) "there was a danger that Shorewood stockholders would be confused about the intrinsic value of the company, fail to understand manage-

31. Quickturn Design Sys., Inc. v. Shapiro, 721 A.2d 1281 (Del. 1998).

32. *See* Hilton Hotels Corp. v. ITT Corp., 978 F. Supp. 1342 (D. Nev. 1997).

33. Fed. Sec. L. Rep. (CCH) ¶ 94,514 (Del. Ch. July 14, 1989), *aff'd*, 571 A.2d 1140 (Del. 1990).

34. *See* Stroud v. Grace, 606 A.2d 75 (Del. 1992); Unitrin, Inc. v. Am. Gen. Corp., 651 A.2d 1361 (Del. 1995); Blasius Indus. v. Atlas Corp., 564 A.2d 651 (Del. Ch. 1988).

35. 2000 Del. Ch. LEXIS 20 (2000).

ment's explanation as to why the market was undervaluing their stock, and mistakenly tender consents to Chesapeake to facilitate its unfair offer." The court found the threat of confusion "at best quite a weak one" in light of (1) the fact that more than 80 percent of Shorewood's shares were held by management and institutional holders, (2) the ability of the board to engage in a more vigorous communications campaign, and (3) the fact that reputable analysts were already tracking the stock. Although the court acknowledged that the price offered might be inadequate, it held that the supermajority bylaw was "an extremely aggressive and overreaching response to a very mild threat." Instead, if the board truly believed that price inadequacy was the problem, it could have taken Chesapeake up on its offer to negotiate price and structure.

The court acknowledged that several cases have stated that a corporate board may consider a fully financed all-cash, all-shares, premium-to-market tender offer a threat to stockholders when "the board believes that the company's present strategic plan will deliver more value than the premium offer, the stock market has not yet bought that rationale, the board may be correct, and therefore there is a risk that 'stockholders might tender . . . in ignorance or based upon a mistaken belief.'" Yet the court noted that this threat of *substantive coercion*[36] can be invoked in almost every situation, seeing as how "[t]here is virtually no CEO in America who does not believe that the market is not valuing [his or] her company properly," so it called on courts to ensure that the threat is real and that the board is not imagining or exaggerating it.

The court also pointed out that:

> [O]ne of corporate management's functions is to ensure that the market recognizes the value of the company and that the stockholders are apprised of relevant information about the company. This informational responsibility would include, one would think, the duty to communicate the company's strategic plans and prospects to stockholders as clearly and understandably as possible.

## Duty of Directors to Disclose Preliminary Merger Negotiations

Directors can face a difficult decision when deciding whether they must disclose an offer to buy the company or the company's participation in merger negotiations. As is discussed more fully in Chapter 23, disclosure can be required even if the parties have not reached an agreement in principle on the price and structure of the transaction. The Supreme Court held in *Basic, Inc. v. Levinson*[37] that such "soft information" can be material.

Managers planning a management buyout (MBO) of a company face a real conflict of interest in deciding whether to disclose their offer to the public because disclosure will often bring forth competing bidders. Prudent directors, like the independent directors of RJR Nabisco when faced with CEO Ross Johnson's bid, will often require public announcement of the bid even if it puts the company "in play."

## Duties of Controlling Shareholders

A shareholder who owns sufficient shares to outvote the other shareholders, or to otherwise set corporate policy, and thus to control the corporation is known as a *controlling shareholder*. A person owning a majority of the outstanding shares is almost always a controlling shareholder, but persons owning a lower percentage (30 percent, for example) may still be deemed controlling if the shares are widely dispersed and there are no other large holders. In certain situations, controlling shareholders owe a fiduciary duty to the corporation and to its other shareholders. Generally, controlling shareholders have a responsibility to minority shareholders to control the corporation in a fair, just, and equitable manner. They may not engage in a bad faith scheme to drain off the corporation's earnings, thereby ensuring that minority shareholders are frozen out of all financial benefits.[38]

### SALE OF CONTROL

The obligation not to exercise control in a manner that intentionally harms the corporation and minority shareholders spills over into a sale of control. For instance, if a controlling shareholder knows or has reason to believe that the purchaser of its shares intends to use controlling power to the detriment of the corporation, the controlling shareholder has a duty not to transfer the power of management to such a purchaser.

A controlling interest in a corporation usually commands a higher price per share than a minority interest. Does this control premium belong to the corporation or

36. *See* Ronald J. Gilson & Reiner Kraakman, *Delaware's Standard for Defensive Tactics: Is There Substance to Proportionality Review?*, 44 BUS. LAW. 247, 267 (1989).

37. 485 U.S. 224 (1988).

38. Sugarman v. Sugarman, 797 F.2d 3 (1st Cir. 1986).

## POLITICAL PERSPECTIVE

# THE PENNSYLVANIA ANTITAKEOVER STATUTE

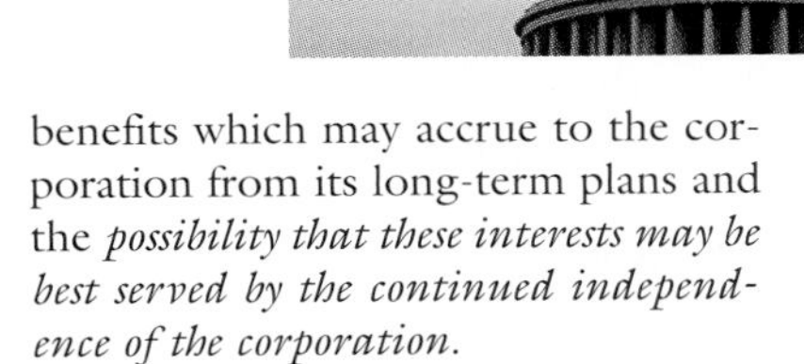

The nation's toughest state antitakeover statute, Pennsylvania Senate bill 1310, also known as Act 36, was signed into law by Governor Bob Casey (a Democrat) on April 27, 1990.[a] An examination of the events surrounding the enactment of this controversial statute highlights the ever-changing battle over defining, shaping, and reshaping the law in this area, as well as the role that politics can play in that process.

### Background

The impetus for drafting the statute came from the Belzberg family's hostile takeover bid for Armstrong World Industries, Inc., a *Fortune* 500 company specializing in flooring and furnishings, headquartered in Lancaster, Pennsylvania. After Armstrong's board rejected the Belzbergs' offer to buy the company, the Belzbergs' holding company, First City Financial Corporation, initiated a proxy fight for control of four directors' seats on the board. The shareholders' meeting, at which the results of the proxy fight were to be announced, was scheduled for April 30, 1990.

Noah W. Wenger (a Republican), the state senator from the Lancaster district, introduced a comprehensive antitakeover bill while the Belzbergs and Armstrong were in the midst of their conflict. The bill, drafted in part by the Pennsylvania Chamber of Business and Industry, was designed not only to throw a wrench into the plans of corporate raiders in general but perhaps also to impede the Belzberg bid in particular.

a. The independent sections are codified as 15 PA. CONS. STAT. ANN. §§ 511, 512, 1721, 2502 (1990); 15 PA. CONS. STAT. ANN. §§ 2561–2567, 2571–2574, 2581–2583, 2585–2588 (1990).

### The Statute

Pennsylvania's antitakeover statute attacks hostile bids for corporate control on three major fronts. First, it requires controlling persons (defined as those who own, or control proxies for, 20 percent of a company's stock) to disgorge—that is, give back to the company—any profits they make by selling stock of the company within eighteen months after becoming a controlling person. Such disgorgement is required if stock acquired within twenty-four months before or within eighteen months after becoming a controlling person is sold by the controlling person within eighteen months after becoming a controlling person.

This provision is aimed at those who, after failed takeover attempts, try to reap short-term profits by selling acquired stock at a premium. Institutional investors and other shareholders who launch proxy fights for purposes other than gaining control of a majority of the board are exempted from the disgorgement provision.

Second, the statute expands the directors' ability to consider other constituencies when making change-of-control decisions. Subsection (d) of Section 511 provides an expansive list of constituencies that a director may consider when exercising his or her duty to the corporation:

> In discharging the duties of their respective positions . . . directors may, in considering the best interests of the corporation, consider to the extent they deem appropriate:
> (1) The effects of any action upon *any or all groups affected by such action*, including shareholders, employees, suppliers, customers and creditors of the corporation, and upon communities in which offices or other establishments of the corporation are located.
> (2) The short-term and long-term interests of the corporation, including benefits which may accrue to the corporation from its long-term plans and the *possibility that these interests may be best served by the continued independence of the corporation.*
> (3) The resources, intent and conduct (past, stated and potential) of the person seeking to acquire control of the corporation.
> (4) *All other pertinent factors.* (Emphasis added.)

In addition, the directors are not required to regard any particular corporate interest or the interest of any group as "a dominant or controlling interest or factor." The implication is clear. A director's duty when considering a proposal for a change of control is not simply to maximize shareholder value.

Third, like some other states' antitakeover statutes, the Pennsylvania law deprives a shareholder of its voting rights when it crosses certain ownership lines, placed at 20 percent, 33 percent, and 50 percent of the company's stock. The voting rights can be regained only if the holders of a majority of the shares—excluding holders of shares acquired in the previous twelve months—give their approval at a special shareholders' meeting.

The statute also protects the employees of a company that is taken over. Existing labor contracts must be honored, and a successful bidder must pay severance benefits to employees who lose their jobs within two years of the takeover.

Corporations are allowed to opt out of various provisions of the antitakeover statute. As of 1992, more than 66 corporations (including Westinghouse Electric) of the estimated 200 corporations affected by the statute had opted out of at least one of its subchapters.[b]

b. Jeffrey L. Silberman, *How Do Pennsylvania Directors Spell Relief?* Act 36, 17 DEL. J. CORP. L. 115 (1992).

(Continued)

(Political Perspective *continued*)

In 1998, the Pennsylvania statute proved important in the successful effort by Mellon Bank (a Pennsylvania corporation) to thwart a hostile bid by the Bank of New York.[c] In rejecting Bank of New York's $23.6 billion offer (which represented a premium of 28 percent over Mellon's closing stock price the day before the offer was announced and a premium of 34 percent over Mellon's average closing stock price over the last thirty trading days), the chairman of Mellon's board seemed to be invoking the Pennsylvania statute when he criticized the proposed merger as not benefiting "our shareholders, employees, customers and—in particular—the communities we serve."[d]

c. See Bloomberg News, *In Pennsylvania, Watch Out What You Try to Take Over: Thanks to Tough Rules, Mellon Bank Is Able to Flatly Reject an Offer from Bank of New York*, L.A. TIMES, Apr. 23, 1998, at D7.

d. Associated Press, *Mellon Bank Sues Bank of New York to Avoid Takeover; $23 Billion Bid Was Rejected*, STAR TRIB. (Minneapolis), Apr. 24, 1998, at 1D.

to the majority shareholder? The widely accepted rule is that controlling shareholders normally have a right to derive a premium from the sale of a controlling block of stock.[39] For instance, in *Zetlin v. Hanson Holdings, Inc.*,[40] the New York Court of Appeals commented:

> In this action plaintiff Zetlin contends that minority stockholders are entitled to an opportunity to share equally in any premium paid for a controlling interest in the corporation. This rule would profoundly affect the manner in which controlling stock interests are now transferred. It would require, essentially, that a controlling interest be transferred only by means of an offer to all stockholders, that is, a tender offer. This would be contrary to existing law and if so radical a change is to be effected it would be best done by the Legislature.

In extreme circumstances, however, courts may be willing to characterize the control premium as a corporate asset, thus entitling minority shareholders to a portion. The U.S. Court of Appeals for the Second Circuit took such an approach in *Perlman v. Feldmann*.[41] *Perlman* involved Newport Steel Corporation, whose mills produced steel sheets for sale to manufacturers of steel products. C. Russell Feldmann was the chairman of the board of directors and president of the corporation; he was also the controlling shareholder. In August 1950, when the supply of steel was tight due to the Korean War, Feldmann and some other shareholders sold their stock to a syndicate of end users of steel who were interested in securing a source of supply.

Minority shareholders brought a shareholder derivative suit to compel the controlling shareholders to account for, and make restitution of, their gains from the sale. The court held that the consideration received by the defendants included compensation for the sale of a corporate asset, namely the ability of the board to control the allocation of the corporation's product in a time of short supply.

Note that the court did not seek to prohibit majority shareholders from ever selling their shares at a premium;

39. *See, e.g.*, Essex Universal Corp. v. Yates, 305 F.2d 572 (2d Cir. 1962).
40. 397 N.E.2d 387 (N.Y. 1979).
41. 219 F.2d 173 (2d Cir. 1955), *cert. denied*, 349 U.S. 952 (1955).

## INTERNATIONAL SNAPSHOT

Because European banks are not subject to the regulatory strictures applicable to U.S. banks, they are much more important institutional investors and exert a more powerful force on how a company is run than comparable U.S. banks. For example, German banks exercise extraordinary control over companies' access to capital. By law, the banks can represent shareholders who deposit their shares with the banks. Because only the banks are allowed to trade on the floor of the German stock exchanges and therefore have the best knowledge of stock performance, most shareholders take advantage of this service.

In 1986, German banks held proxies for an average of 65 percent of the shares present at the shareholder meetings at 100 of the largest German companies. For example, at the 1986 shareholder meeting of Siemens, approximately 61 percent of the outstanding shares were present at the meeting. Of the shares voted, Deutsche Bank voted 18 percent, Dresdner Bank 11 percent, and Commerzbank 4 percent. All banks taken as a group voted approximately 80 percent of the shares voted at the meeting.[a] Banks are also permitted to purchase directly up to 100 percent of the shares of a company, although it is considered imprudent for them to invest substantial portions of their capital in any single company.

a. Theodor Baums, *Corporate Governance in Germany: The Role of Banks*, 40 AM. J. COMP. L. 503, 524 (1992).

it was careful to circumscribe its holding with an emphasis on the extreme market conditions:

> We do not mean to suggest that a majority stockholder cannot dispose of his controlling block of stock to outsiders without having to account to his corporation for profits or even never do this with impunity when the buyer is an interested customer, actual or potential, for the corporation's product. But when the sale necessarily results in a sacrifice of this element of corporate good will and consequent unusual profit to the fiduciary who has caused the sacrifice, he should account for his gains. So when in a time of market shortage, where a call on a corporation's product commands an unusually large premium, in one form or another, we think it sound law that a fiduciary may not appropriate to himself the value of this premium.

The following classic case involved elements of abuse of control and sale of control. The dominant shareholders took a series of steps to ensure that they participated in the financial benefits of the company without letting the minority shareholders also participate.

A CASE IN POINT

**CASE 20.5**

**Jones v. H.F. Ahmanson & Co.**

*Supreme Court of California*
*460 P.2d 464 (Cal. 1969).*

## Summary

**› FACTS** The shares of the United Savings and Loan Association were not actively traded due to their high book value, the closely held nature of the association, and the failure of its management to provide information to shareholders, brokers, or the public.

In 1958, investor interest in shares of savings and loan associations and holding companies increased. Savings and loan stocks that were publicly marketed enjoyed a steady increase in market price. The controlling shareholders of the United Savings and Loan Association decided to create a mechanism by which the association, too, could attract investor interest. They did not, however, attempt to render the association's shares more readily marketable.

Instead, a holding company, the United Financial Corporation of California, was incorporated in Delaware on May 8, 1959. On May 14, pursuant to a prior agreement, certain association shareholders owning a majority of the association's stock exchanged their shares for those of United Financial.

After the exchange, United Financial held 85 percent of the association's outstanding stock. The former majority shareholders of the association had become the majority shareholders of United Financial and continued to control the association through the holding company. They did not offer the minority shareholders of the association an opportunity to exchange their shares.

The first public offering of United Financial stock was made in June 1960. An additional public offering in February 1961 included a secondary offering (that is, an offering by selling shareholders) of 600,000 shares. There was active trading in the United Financial shares. Sales of the association shares, however, decreased from 170 shares per year before the formation of United Financial to half that number by 1961. United Financial acquired 90 percent of the association's shares that were sold.

A shareholder of the association brought suit, on behalf of herself and all other similarly situated minority shareholders, against United Financial and the individuals and corporations that had set up the holding company. The plaintiff contended that the defendants' course of conduct constituted a breach of fiduciary duty owed by the majority shareholders to the minority. She alleged that they had used their control of the association for their own advantage and to the detriment of the minority when they created United Financial, made a public market for its shares that rendered the association's stock unmarketable except to United Financial, and then refused either to purchase the minority's association stock at a fair price or to exchange the stock on the same terms afforded to the majority. She further alleged that they had created a conflict of interest that might have been avoided had they offered all association shareholders the opportunity to participate in the initial exchange of shares.

*(Continued)*

(Case 20.5 *continued*)

**› ISSUE PRESENTED** Did majority shareholders who transferred their shares to a holding corporation, then took it public without allowing the minority to exchange their shares, breach their fiduciary duty to the minority shareholders?

**› SUMMARY OF OPINION** The California Supreme Court began its analysis by stating that the majority shareholders, acting either singly or in concert, have a fiduciary responsibility to the minority and to the corporation. They must use their ability to control the corporation fairly. They may not use it to benefit themselves alone or in a manner detrimental to the minority. Any use to which they put their power to control the corporation must benefit all shareholders proportionately and must not conflict with the proper conduct of the corporation's business. The court summarized the rule as one of "inherent fairness from the viewpoint of the corporation or those interested therein."

The court noted that the controlling shareholders of the association could have taken advantage of the bull market in savings and loan stock in two other ways. They could have caused the association to effect a stock split, thereby increasing the number of outstanding shares, or they could have created a holding company and permitted all shareholders to exchange their shares before offering the holding company's shares to the public. Either course would have benefited all of the shareholders alike, although the majority shareholders would have had to relinquish some of their control shares. Instead, the defendants chose to set up a holding company that they controlled and did not allow the minority shareholders to exchange their association shares for shares of the holding company. Moreover, the market created by the defendants for United Financial shares would have been available for association shares had the defendants chosen a stock split of the association's shares.

The court stated that when a controlling shareholder sells or exchanges its shares, the transaction is subject to close scrutiny, particularly if the majority receives a premium over market value for its shares. If the premium constitutes payment for what is properly a corporate asset, all shareholders are entitled to a proportionate share of the premium (citing *Perlman v. Feldmann*). The defendants' exchange of association stock for United Financial stock was an integral part of a scheme that the defendants could have reasonably foreseen would destroy the potential public market for association stock. The remaining association shareholders would thus be deprived of the opportunity to realize a profit from those intangible characteristics that attach to publicly marketed stock.

**› RESULT** The majority shareholders who transferred their shares to a holding corporation, then took it public without allowing the minority to exchange their shares, breached their fiduciary duty to the minority shareholders. The minority shareholders were awarded damages that would place them in a position at least as favorable as the majority shareholders had created for themselves.

## FREEZE-OUTS

The Delaware Supreme Court has held that a majority shareholder may *freeze out* the minority, that is, force the minority shareholders to convert their shares into cash, as long as the transaction is fair.[42] Sometimes a freeze-out is effected by merging a subsidiary into its parent, as in *Rosenblatt v. Getty Oil Co.*[43] In this case, Skelly Oil Company and Mission Corporation merged into Getty Oil Company, which was indirectly the majority shareholder of both Skelly and Mission. All three corporations were in the oil business. At issue was the fairness of the exchange ratio in the merger, that is, the ratio that would be used to convert the minority shareholders' stock into cash.

42. Weinberger v. UOP, Inc., 457 A.2d 701 (Del. 1983).

43. 493 A.2d 929 (Del. 1985).

The Delaware Supreme Court stated that the concept of fairness in parent–subsidiary mergers has two aspects: fair dealing and fair price. Both must be examined together in resolving the ultimate question of entire fairness.

As to fair dealing, a court will look at the timing of the transaction; how it was initiated, structured, negotiated, and disclosed to the board; and how director and shareholder approval was obtained. The court cited a number of factors leading to a conclusion of fair dealing by Getty, including the adversarial nature of the negotiations between the parties to the merger.

Regarding fair price, a court will look at such economic factors as asset value, market value, earnings, and future prospects, and at any other elements that affect the intrinsic value of a company's stock. Both Getty and Skelly believed that the real worth of an oil company is centered in its reserves. Therefore, the court was especially impressed with the fact that they had employed D & M, a petroleum consulting engineering firm with a worldwide reputation and with nearly thirty-seven years of experience, to estimate Getty's and Skelly's respective oil and natural gas reserves. The court concluded that Getty had dealt fairly with the Skelly minority shareholders in the merger.

Although the controlling shareholder may be permitted to negotiate a deal for the sale of the entire company, the board of directors of the target must still determine the intrinsic value of the company and the maximum shareholder value reasonably attainable so that it has an informed basis for recommending the proposed deal to the minority stockholders or for suggesting that the minority stockholders vote against the deal and exercise their appraisal rights.[44] The representatives of the controlling shareholder on the target board owe the target's minority shareholders "an uncompromising duty of loyalty."[45] This includes an obligation to provide the minority full and accurate information about the company even if the minority has no right to vote on the deal.

## Greenmail

Delaware courts analyze the payment of greenmail in the same way they analyze other defensive tactics under *Unocal*. Greenmail is a purchase of a dissident shareholder's stock by the issuer at a premium over market, often in exchange for a ***standstill agreement***, whereby the shareholder agrees not to commence a tender offer or proxy contest or to buy additional shares of the issuer for a period of time, often ten years. If the board demonstrates that the shareholder to be bought out poses a threat to corporate policy and effectiveness and the repurchase of shares at a premium is a reasonable response to that threat, then the payment will be protected by the business judgment rule.[46]

44. McMullin v. Beran, 765 A.2d 910 (Del. 2000).
45. *Id.* at 923.
46. *See also* Growbow v. Perot, 539 A.2d 180 (Del. 1988) (upholding repurchase by General Motors of GM stock and notes from H. Ross Perot at a "giant premium").

### THE RESPONSIBLE MANAGER

### CARRYING OUT FIDUCIARY DUTIES

Officers, directors, and controlling shareholders are fiduciaries. They owe their principal (the corporation and its shareholders) undivided loyalty. They must act in good faith. They may not put their own interests before those of the corporation and its shareholders. They cannot, for example, fight off a hostile takeover just to keep their jobs. They cannot use the company's confidential information for their personal gain.

Officers and directors also owe the corporation and its shareholders a duty of care. They should act with the care reasonable persons would use in the management of their own property. They have a duty to make only informed decisions. They cannot rely blindly on the advice of other people, even experts.

The duty to make informed decisions, which is a part of the duty of care, takes various forms. In the context of takeovers, board members cannot reject an offer without taking sufficient time to analyze its merit. Managers must be able to demonstrate that they made their decisions only after sufficient deliberation and after review of all relevant information. They should consider the possible effects of both the monetary and the nonmonetary aspects of the transaction.

*(Continued)*

(The Responsible Manager *continued*)

A manager should never sign a document without reading it first. Ideally, each director should read the document the board is asked to approve. If that is not practical, the directors should demand and read a written summary prepared by counsel. They should also make sure that the officers who are authorized to sign the agreement have read it before signing it.

A manager should be informed as to the rules regarding the duty of care in the company's state of incorporation. Some jurisdictions permit the shareholders to amend the articles of incorporation to relieve directors of any financial liability for violations of the duty of care. But even with such provisions in place, directors must still act in good faith and in what they honestly believe is the best interest of the corporation. Otherwise, they will breach their duty of loyalty. Such a breach can not only result in monetary liability but can also demoralize the shareholders and employees of the corporation, making it difficult to maintain a high level of ethical behavior among them.

In a situation involving a potential conflict of interest, a manager should excuse himself or herself and leave the decision to others who do not have a conflict. It is common, for example, to establish special independent committees of the board of directors, either to examine the fairness of a management offer to acquire the company or to review the merits of shareholder litigation against the directors or officers.

A repurchase of stock at a premium from a dissident (or unhappy) shareholder may violate both the directors' duty to the corporation and the shareholder's duty to the other shareholders. Different courts view such repurchases differently, and local counsel should always be consulted. It is often appropriate for the board not only to obtain a written opinion from counsel that such a repurchase is permissible but also to convene a special independent committee of directors to decide whether the consideration that will be paid for the stock is fair.

Any controlling shareholder engaging in a transaction such as a merger with the company it controls must be able to prove that the transaction is fair both procedurally and substantively. The use of independent committees, advised by independent financial consultants and counsel, helps show procedural fairness, as does a willingness to negotiate the proposed transaction with such a committee on an arm's length basis. Paying a fair price for corporate assets or for shares of a corporation shows substantive fairness. The fairness of a price can be demonstrated by evidence of competing offers or independent appraisals or evaluations. The form of compensation of the appraiser or investment banker should not give that person an interest in the outcome of the appraisal or of the transaction. It is often preferable to pay the appraiser or investment banker a flat fee regardless of whether the deal goes through, rather than an incentive fee based on the value of the deal struck.

Certain acts of directors, officers, and controlling shareholders are both illegal and unethical, such as the seizing of a corporate opportunity by an officer. Other conduct may be legal yet ethically questionable, such as the payment of greenmail.

Some situations present conflicting ethical concerns. The Delaware Supreme Court has held that the directors must maximize shareholder value, that is, get the best price available, if they decide to sell control of the corporation. Yet a sale to a bust-up artist who will sell the company's assets, or to a union buster, might adversely affect the corporation's other constituencies, such as employees, suppliers, and the community in which the corporation does business.[47] A manager should try to select a course of action that protects the corporation's constituencies without sacrificing the shareholders' right to the best price. If the management team itself bids for the company, the board may find itself forced to become an auctioneer whose sole goal is to get the best price for the shareholders.

A board of directors can use various defensive measures to prevent a hostile takeover, provided that the measures are reasonable in relation to the threat posed and that the board considers it in the best interests of the company and its constituencies for the company to remain independent. Any measures designed to interfere with the shareholder franchise require proof by the directors of a compelling justification.

Similarly, if the board adopts a strategy resulting in a change of control of a corporation, it cannot use defensive tactics such as no-shop provisions (whereby the board agrees not to consider other offers) or large asset or stock lock-ups to deter competing bidders. In short, if the board agrees to a change of control, it breaches its fiduciary duties if it makes competing offers impossible by adopting a scorched-earth policy that leaves the successful bidder with a depleted target. Although legal counsel will advise managers and directors in this area, a knowledge of the rules of the game is essential to good management.

47. See Constance E. Bagley & Karen Page, *The Devil Made Me Do It: Replacing Corporate Directors' Veil of Secrecy with the Mantle of Stewardship,* 36 SAN DIEGO L. REV. 4 (1999), for a discussion of the legal, economic, and organizational behavioral aspects of directors' consideration of factors other than simply shareholder return when acting on behalf of the corporation.

INSIDE STORY

## THE LONG TWILIGHT OF IMPERIAL CEOS

As a scandal involving the insurance industry unfolded in the fall of 2004, an article in the *Wall Street Journal* commented: "The long twilight of imperial CEOs—who run opaque giants that are granted unquestioning trust from shareholders—finally is coming to an end. True, the imperial CEO is harder to get rid of than Rasputin. But this seems to be it."[48]

On October 14, 2004, New York Attorney General Eliot Spitzer announced a civil suit against Marsh & McLennan Companies, the largest insurance brokerage firm in the United States. Spitzer charged the company with accepting kickbacks, price-fixing, and bid-rigging that forced corporate clients to pay higher prices for insurance coverage. The company practiced bid-rigging by prompting insurers to submit phony "B" quotes—bids that were too high to win but gave the appearance of competition.[49] In this way, executives at Marsh ensured that preferred insurers, the ones who paid the highest commissions, would win lucrative bids from corporate clients. An e-mail written by a Marsh executive to Ace Ltd., an insurer, was indicative of the coercive bid-rigging practice: "I do not want to hear that you are not doing 'B' quotes or we will not bind anything."[50]

Brokers who met volume or profitability targets on business they brought to the insurer were rewarded with contingent commissions, giving the brokers a financial incentive to place a client's business with insurers paying the most generous bonuses.[51] American International Group (AIG) was one of several firms facing investigation into its potential collaboration with Marsh. Two AIG executives pleaded guilty to illegal activities and agreed to cooperate with investigators against Marsh.

As the charges became public, Marsh's stock price halved, and its directors hastened to respond.[52] Board directors cooperated fully with the investigation to avoid Spitzer's biggest threat: a criminal indictment against the corporation itself.[53] Five executives implicated in the wrongdoing, including the chairman and CEO Jeffrey Greenberg, were dismissed. Upon Greenberg's departure, Spitzer announced he would not indict the company but would seek criminal charges against individuals. Michael G. Cherkasky, Marsh's new CEO and Spitzer's former boss, moved to implement a compliance program at Marsh. As part of its compliance effort, the board agreed to waive attorney–client privilege and submit the results of internal investigations to investigators. Cherkasky also ended the practice of offering contingent commissions, which comprised $843 million or 12 percent of the company's revenue in 2003.[54]

During roughly this same period, Michael D. Eisner, CEO of the Walt Disney Company, and his fellow directors were testifying in a Delaware courthouse, trying to defend their decision to pay $140 million in severance pay to former Disney officer Michael S. Ovitz.[55] The trial revealed a weak board whose members had personal ties to Eisner and were unwilling to stand up to him. The board even went so far as to agree to Eisner's request to nominate his wife Jane to the Disney board in the event of his untimely death or disability.[56]

Regardless of the ultimate outcome of the case, experts predicted that Chancellor William B. Chandler III, who presided over the case, would turn it into a primer of what not to do. Tom Wolzien, a media analyst at Sanford C. Bernstein & Co., remarked, "What this trial has shown is that even the bosses have a boss to answer to—in this case the board, and ultimately, shareholders."[57]

Roughly one year earlier, in August 2003, former SEC Commissioner Richard C. Breeden, corporate monitor of WorldCom during its bankruptcy proceed-

48. Jesse Eisinger, *AIG's Chief Shows Signs of Humility as Spitzer Probe Rattles the Industry,* WALL ST. J., Oct. 20, 2004, at C1.
49. See Ianthe Jeanne Dugan & Monica Langley, *Marsh Suspends Four Employees Amid Spitzer Probe,* WALL ST. J., Oct. 20, 2004, at A10.
50. *Id.*
51. Theo Francis & Vanessa Fuhrmans, *Class-Action Threat Added to Challenges Facing Insurers,* WALL ST. J., Oct. 20, 2004, at C6.
52. See Alex Berenson, *To Survive the Dance, Marsh Must Follow Spitzer's Lead,* N.Y. TIMES, Oct. 25, 2004, at A1.
53. *Id.* at C8.
54. Joseph B. Treaster, *Insurance Chief Quits in Inquiry Led by Spitzer,* N.Y. TIMES, Oct. 26, 2004, at A1.
55. *See In re* The Walt Disney Co. Derivative Litig., 825 A.2d 275 (Del. Ch. 2003) (Case 21.1) and *In re* The Walt Disney Co. Derivative Litig., 2004 Del. Ch. LEXIS 132 (Del. Ch. 2004) (denying motion to dismiss claims against Ovitz for corporate waste in connection with his receipt of nonfault termination benefits).
56. Laura M. Holson, *After the Ovitz Trial: Ushering in a New Era of Humility in Hollywood,* N.Y. TIMES, Dec. 20, 2004.
57. *Id.*

*(Continued)*

(Inside Story *continued*)

ings, proposed a series of corporate governance measures designed to prevent a recurrence of the massive fraud that destroyed roughly $200 billion in shareholder value, put tens of thousands of employees out of work, and wiped out the entire value of stock held in employee retirement accounts as well as the value of accumulated equity-based compensation.[58] According to Breeden, WorldCom's CEO Bernard J. Ebbers "was allowed nearly imperial reign over the affairs of the Company, without the board of directors exercising any apparent restraint on his actions, even though he did not appear to possess the experience or training to be remotely qualified for his position."[59] The board allowed "lavish compensation," including more than $400 million in "loans" to Ebbers, which were unlikely ever to be repaid. It also approved a $238 million "compensation slush fund" that Ebbers could allocate to favored executives or employees with no standards or supervision. Citing Lord Acton's remark in 1887 that, "power tends to corrupt and absolute power corrupts absolutely," Breeden said that " 'backbone' and 'fortitude' may be the most important qualities needed by a director of a public company."

As a condition to emerging from bankruptcy, WorldCom, which is now known as MCI, Inc., was required to convert its articles of incorporation into a governance constitution, which could be changed only with prior shareholder consent. MCI was required to:

- Give a group of shareholders the power to nominate their own candidates for inclusion in the management proxy statement if the group did not agree with the board's proposed candidates.
- Create the position of nonexecutive chair of the board.
- Ban the issuance of stock options without prior shareholder approval.
- Expense both stock options and restricted stock grants on its financial statements.
- Ban a staggered board, set ten-year term limits for directors, and restrict independent directors to a maximum of three boards, including the MCI board.
- Prohibit related-party transactions involving board members.
- Compensate directors solely with cash and require them to utilize not less than 25 percent of those fees to purchase MCI stock, which must be held until they leave the board.
- Have the board of directors meet at least eight times a year, hold an annual strategic review, and attend annual refresher training on topics relating to board responsibilities.
- Limit change-in-control devices, such as poison pills.

It remains to be seen whether the reports of the demise of the imperial CEO are premature.

58. Richard C. Breeden, *Restoring Trust,* filed with the U.S. District Court for the Southern District of New York (2003).
59. *Id.*

## KEY WORDS AND PHRASES

asset lock-up option 751
breakup fee 764
business judgment rule 748
constructive trust 757
controlling shareholder 771
corporate opportunity doctrine 757
crown jewels 751
deal protection devices 764
duty of care 747
duty of loyalty 747
fiduciary out 764
freeze out 775
greenmail 760
line-of-business test 758
no-shop agreement 764
no-talk clause 764
poison pill 769
proxy 769
proxy contest 769
quasi-foreign corporation 755
*Revlon* mode 761
self-tender 760
shareholder derivative suit 754
shareholder rights plan 769
standstill agreement 776
substantive coercion 771
termination fee 764

## QUESTIONS AND CASE PROBLEMS

1. Lee Gray was a director, president, and treasurer of HMG/Courtland Properties, Inc. (HMG), a publicly held real estate investment trust, and of its investment adviser Courtland Group, Inc. As such, he negotiated the terms of a joint venture with Norman Fieber, another HMG director, for the development of a

portfolio of properties located in the northeastern United States. During the course of the negotiations, Gray told Fieber that Martine Avenue Associates, a general partnership controlled by Gray and his sister, would be interested in co-investing with Fieber as a buyer of an interest in the properties. Neither Gray nor Fieber disclosed that possibility to HMG, but all parties agreed that the negotiated price was fair and reasonable. Martine did ultimately join a group of investors on Fieber's side of the transaction in May 1986, but HMG did not learn of Gray's economic interest in Martine until October 1996. Did either Gray or Fieber violate their fiduciary duties to HMG? [*HMG/Courtland Properties, Inc. v. Gray,* 749 A.2d 94 (Del. Ch. 1999).]

2. In 1997, General Cigar Holdings Inc., a family-owned business since 1906, went public at an offering price of $18 per share of class A stock. The founding Cullman family retained control with super-voting class B shares that were entitled to ten votes per share. Share prices for the class A stock rose as high as $33, but by 1999, they had sunk to $5.

   In 1999, tobacco giant Swedish Match AB offered to discuss acquiring a "significant stake" in General Cigar but indicated that it wanted Edgar Cullman Sr. and Edgar Cullman Jr. to remain in charge. General Cigar's board of directors formed a special committee of independent directors, which hired legal counsel and an investment bank to conduct a fairness review of any resulting offer. Swedish Match proposed a transaction whereby the public shareholders would be cashed out at $15.25 per share, Swedish Match would buy one-third of the Cullman family's equity interest at $15 per share, and General Cigar would be merged into a Swedish Match subsidiary. As a condition to continuing negotiations, Swedish Match required the Cullmans to enter into a lock-up arrangement or stockholders' voting agreement providing that if the proposed merger of Swedish Match and General Cigar failed, the Cullmans would not sell their shares in any other merger and would vote against any other merger for the next eighteen months. What legal and ethical considerations should the Cullmans take into account when deciding whether to sign such an agreement? Would it be enforceable if a higher bidder surfaced later?

   If the Cullmans did sign such an agreement and the independent committee decided in good faith, after informing itself about the value of General Cigar and unsuccessfully seeking higher bidders, that it was in the best interests of the public shareholders to enter into a merger agreement with Swedish Match, what, if any, nonprice terms would you recommend the board insist on including in the merger agreement? Should the General Cigar board agree to recommend the Swedish Match deal, to put it to a vote of the shareholders, or to use best efforts to consummate it? [*Orman v. Cullman,* No. Civ. A. 18039 (Del. Ch. Oct. 20, 2004).]

3. Missouri Fidelity Union Trust Life Insurance Company stock was trading at $2.63 per share. Eight directors sold their shares for $7.00 per share, conditioned on the resignation of eleven of the fifteen directors of the corporation and the provision that five nominees of the buyer be elected as a majority of the executive and investment committees. Did the directors violate their fiduciary duty? Would the answer be different if the directors had controlled a majority of the voting stock? [*Snyder v. Epstein,* 290 F. Supp. 652 (E.D. Wis. 1968).]

4. The After-School Care Corporation owned more than forty day-care centers specializing in providing care to elementary-school-aged children in the afternoons. The president of the company, Clark Holmes, received a phone call at work one day from Marney Stein, the owner and sole proprietor of Pro Providers, a firm that owned six nursery schools for children aged two to four. Stein indicated that she wanted to sell Pro Providers for $1 million and asked if After-School was interested. Holmes proposed the sale to the After-School board of directors. The directors were divided on the issue because they were not certain whether branching out into nursery care would be a smart move. As funds were not available, however, they saw no need to vote on the issue at that time.

   Holmes decided that he would try to purchase Pro Providers on his own. After securing a loan, Holmes entered into negotiations with Stein. They agreed on a price of $900,000, and the sale went through. Holmes did not inform the board of his activity until after the sale was completed.

   A shareholder is considering suing Holmes for breach of fiduciary duty. Does she have a valid claim? Should it matter whether Holmes plans to expand one of the Pro Provider nursery schools into a nursery/after-school center?

5. The Engulf Corporation is a large media and entertainment conglomerate with its stock trading on the New York Stock Exchange. Engulf is a major producer of films and videos and also publishes several magazines. The company has a shareholder rights

plan (that is, a poison pill), which would make any hostile takeover financially prohibitive unless the pill is redeemed by Engulf's board of directors. On January 10, the Megaclout Corporation, in a move designed to gain control of Engulf, announced a tender offer for 51 percent of Engulf's shares at $140, an $11 premium over the market price.

On January 14, in a meeting that lasted more than thirteen hours, the Engulf board of directors met to consider Megaclout's offer. Engulf's lawyers and investment bankers attended and made detailed presentations on the adequacy of the offer. The next day, the directors officially announced that they believed the Megaclout offer was unacceptable for two reasons: (1) the long-term value of the Engulf stock ranged from $160 to $170, so $140 was financially inadequate; and (2) Engulf had a distinct corporate culture that included special ways of doing business, an outstanding record of management–employee relations, and strong support of community projects in the towns in which Engulf businesses were located. Acceptance of Megaclout's tender offer would pose a direct threat to this corporate culture. For these reasons, the board refused to redeem the poison pill.

Megaclout brought suit as an Engulf shareholder against the Engulf board of directors, demanding that the board redeem the poison pill, which would allow all the shareholders to decide whether they wanted to accept the offer by tendering their shares.

- **a.** Must the Engulf board of directors redeem the poison pill at this time?
- **b.** The board argues that the offer, which is $11 over the market price of the stock, is financially inadequate. Is the argument convincing? Why or why not?
- **c.** Should managers be concerned about corporate constituencies other than shareholders, such as employees or communities in which businesses are located? What if these different concerns conflict?

**6.** Shlensky was a minority shareholder of Chicago National League Ball Club, Inc., which owned and operated the Chicago Cubs baseball team. The defendants were directors of the club. Shlensky alleged that since night baseball was first played in 1935, every major league team except the Cubs has scheduled most of its home games at night. This has allegedly been done for the specific purpose of maximizing attendance, thereby maximizing revenue and income.

The Cubs have sustained losses from their direct baseball operations. Shlensky attributed the losses to inadequate attendance at the Cubs' home games, which are played at Wrigley Field. He feels that if the directors continue to refuse to install lights at Wrigley Field and schedule night baseball games, the Cubs will continue to sustain similar losses.

Shlensky further alleged that Philip Wrigley, the president of the corporation, refused to install lights not, as Wrigley claims, for the welfare of the corporation, but because of his personal opinion that "baseball is a daytime sport." Shlensky charged the other directors with acquiescing in Wrigley's policy.

In his complaint, Shlensky claimed that the directors were acting for reasons contrary to the business interests of the corporation and wasting corporate assets. Have the directors failed to exercise reasonable care in the management of the corporation's affairs? Does the directors' decision fall within the scope of their business judgment? [*Shlensky v. Wrigley,* 237 N.E.2d 776 (Ill. App. Ct. 1968).]

**7.** McDonald, a potential buyer of financial institutions, visited Halbert at the Tulane Savings and Loan Association. Halbert was president, manager, and chairman of the board, and, along with his wife, the owner of 53 percent of the stock of the association. McDonald asked if the association was for sale. Halbert replied that it was not for sale but that he and his wife would sell their controlling stock for $1,548 per share. Halbert did not tell the association's board of directors or its shareholders about McDonald's interest in acquiring the association.

In addition to agreeing to sell his stock, Halbert also agreed to cause the association to withhold the payment of dividends. After Halbert's shares were purchased, Halbert, who had not yet relinquished his corporate offices, helped McDonald solicit the minority shareholders' shares and even advised them that, because McDonald was going to withhold dividends for ten to twenty years, they ought to take his offer of $300 per share. McDonald bought some of the minority shares at $300 and others for between $611 and $650.

Did Halbert owe the minority shareholders a fiduciary duty? If so, what was his duty in selling his minority stock position? Was his conduct ethical? [*Brown v. Halbert,* 76 Cal. Rptr. 781 (Cal. App. Ct. 1969).]

**8.** In early 1993, Joseph Bydalek and Robert M. Fox formed a corporation to buy and run the "Fill-Er-Up Club." Fox owned 51 percent of the stock and was the sole officer and director; Bydalek owned 49 percent.

On July 20, 1993, the day the club opened, Fox died in a car accident. Jeannine Willis, Fox's sister, became administrator. Five months later, she and two attorneys were elected officers and directors. Bydalek continued to run the club, and his wife Laura tended bar and kept the books until July 18, 1994, when Willis had the club's locks changed to lock them out of the premises. Prior to the lockout, the Bydaleks were salaried, at-will employees. Willis never took a salary. The club lost $10,000 in its first year, never generated a profit, and never paid dividends. Willis closed the club in February 1996 because it was losing money and could not renew its liquor license. In October 1995, the Bydaleks sued Willis for conversion, breach of fiduciary duty, and shareholder oppression. Result? [*Willis v. Bydalek*, 997 S.W.2d 798 (Tex. Ct. App. 1999).]

9. The board of directors of ITT Corporation adopted a reorganization plan to thwart a hostile tender offer bid and proxy contest by Hilton Hotels Corporation. The plan called for ITT to be broken up into three new entities, the largest of which (ITT Destinations) would hold more than 90 percent of ITT's current assets. The board of directors of ITT Destinations would consist of the current directors of ITT, but unlike the current ITT board, the ITT Destinations board would be classified or staggered. The board would be divided into three classes with each class of directors serving for a term of three years and with one class to be elected each year. A shareholder vote of 80 percent would be required to remove the directors without cause or to repeal the classified board.

   The ITT board proposed to implement this plan prior to ITT's annual meeting and without obtaining shareholder approval. The net effect of the plan was to make it impossible for the ITT shareholders at the 1997 annual meeting to elect a majority of the directors nominated under Hilton's proxy contest. Was ITT's adoption of the reorganization plan a valid exercise of business judgment? [*Hilton Hotels Corp. v. ITT Corp.*, 978 F. Supp. 1342 (D. Nev. 1997).]

### MANAGER'S DILEMMA

10. In March 1984, a group headed by Saul Steinberg purchased more than two million shares of stock of Walt Disney Productions, the owner of Disneyland. Disney responded by announcing that it would acquire the Arvida Corporation for $200 million in newly issued Disney stock and would assume Arvida's $190 million debt. The Steinberg group countered with a shareholder derivative suit in federal court, seeking to block the Arvida transaction. A shareholder derivative suit is a suit brought on behalf of the corporation by one or more of its shareholders. All of the proceeds of such a suit (less expenses) go to the corporation for the benefit of all of its shareholders.

    While the shareholder derivative suit was pending, the Steinberg group proceeded to acquire two million additional shares of Disney stock, increasing its ownership position to approximately 12 percent of the outstanding Disney shares. On June 8, 1984, the Steinberg group advised Disney's directors of its intention to make a tender offer for 49 percent of the outstanding shares at $67.50 a share and its intention to later tender for the balance at $72.50 a share.

    Should the Disney directors offer to repurchase all the Disney stock held by the Steinberg group at a premium and to reimburse the estimated cost incurred in preparing the tender offer in return for the Steinberg group's agreement not to purchase any more Disney stock and to drop the Arvida litigation? Is it legal or ethical for the Steinberg group to agree not to oppose a motion to dismiss the Arvida litigation? To sell its shares at a premium not offered other Disney shareholders? [*Heckman v. Ahmanson*, 214 Cal. Rptr. 177 (Cal. Ct. App. 1985).]

## INTERNET SOURCES

| | |
|---|---|
| This site for Richards, Layton & Finger, the largest law firm in Delaware, contains excellent articles on Delaware corporate and partnership law and provides links to other legal-related sites. | http://www.rlf.com |
| The California Public Employees Retirement System (CalPERS) is the largest public pension fund in the United States and is also a very active institutional investor. Its site contains detailed recommendations for corporate governance practices in the United States, Europe, and Japan. | http://www.calpers.ca.gov/site/invest.htm#CORPORATE |

CHAPTER 21

# Executive Compensation and Employee Benefits

## INTRODUCTION

### Compensation Excesses Lead to Corporate Reform

In 2002, Tyco International, Ltd. disclosed a pattern of improper and illegal activity by its former chief executive officer (CEO), Dennis Kozlowski, and a number of other executives, including its former chief financial officer and general counsel. Among the alleged abuses, Kozlowski reportedly received 200 loans from the company's key employee loan program, borrowing $274 million—of which $245 million was used for homes, yachts, furniture, and domestic help—forgave $25 million in corporate loans to himself; and created a special relocation program to obtain $29.7 million in interest-free loans to build a compound in Boca Raton, Florida, and then caused the company to forgive $100 million in loans pursuant to that program, including $32.6 million of loans to himself. Other alleged misuses of company funds included using corporate funds for a $1 million birthday party in Sardinia for his wife and a $700,000 investment in the movie *Endurance,* and charging $110,000 for corporate use of his yacht, *Endeavor.*[1] Numerous lawsuits followed, including a criminal case against Kozlowski and others relating to their staggering executive compensation arrangements.

Kozlowski and other executives like Gary Winnick of Global Crossing have also been criticized for attempting to keep stock prices high while they exercised their options and sold their stock at inflated prices. For example, insider sales from 1994 to 2001 by top executives and board members of high-flying Internet companies totaled approximately $66 billion.[2] Critics argue that at best, executive stock options promoted a short-term focus and, at worst, created an incentive for executives to inflate company earnings, make irresponsible forecasts, and, in some cases, even led to fraudulent activity by executives to manipulate earnings.[3]

While corporate executives were receiving rich compensation packages, including large, no-risk stock options, many rank-and-file employees were buying their company's stock for their 401(k) plans. When Enron, WorldCom, and other high-flying companies of the 1990s filed for bankruptcy, these employees suffered massive losses to their retirement plan savings.

Executive compensation and most employee benefits are regulated by state agency and employment laws, while pension plans and many other types of employee benefit plans are regulated by the federal Employee Retirement Income Security Act (ERISA). Until recently, the federal Securities and Exchange Commission (SEC) did not attempt to regulate executive compensation directly. In reaction to the corporate excesses of the 1990s, however, the federal Sarbanes-Oxley Act, passed in 2002, has intruded into state territory by, among other things, prohibiting loans to officers and directors. The National Association of Securities Dealers (NASD) and the New York Stock Exchange (NYSE) have also adopted new rules, including provisions on compensation committees, which have intruded even further into areas regulated by

1. Christopher Bowe & Andrew Hill, *Tyco Executives Treated Company "As If It Was Theirs,"* FIN. TIMES (London), Sept. 13, 2002, at 26.

2. Defined as companies that at one time had a market capitalization of at least $400 million.

3. Gretchen Morgenson, *When Options Rise to Top, Guess Who Pays,* N.Y. TIMES, Nov. 10, 2002, http://www.nytimes.com/2002/11/10/business/yourmoney/10OPTI.html?ei=5062+en=23.

state law. Large institutional shareholders have also turned up the heat on executive compensation issues. The 2003 annual meeting season generated a record 324 shareholder proposals related to executive compensation, triple the number filed in 2002.[4]

## CHAPTER OVERVIEW

This chapter offers a general overview of executive compensation and employee benefits laws. It describes state and federal securities laws governing executive compensation and stock options, the basic features of stock options and other stock ownership plans, ERISA, and other federally mandated employee benefits. It concludes with a discussion of international trends in executive and stock compensation.

4. John Gibeaut, *Stock Responses,* A.B.A. J., Sept. 2003, at 38, 40.

# Regulation of Executive Compensation

## STATE REGULATION

The board of directors of a corporation, either directly or through a compensation committee appointed by the board, is responsible for setting the compensation of corporate officers. The board's actions are governed by state agency laws. (The fiduciary obligations of officers and directors are discussed further in Chapter 20.)

In the following case, the Delaware Court of Chancery considered breach-of-fiduciary claims against the directors of the Walt Disney Company arising out of their approval of an employment agreement with Michael Ovitz, which included a severance package that wound up being worth $140 million.

A CASE IN POINT

**CASE 21.1**
***In re* The Walt Disney Company Derivative Litigation**
*Delaware Court of Chancery 825 A.2d 275 (Del. Ch. 2003).*

## In the Language of the Court

**› FACTS** In 1994, Michael Eisner, the CEO of the Walt Disney Company, unilaterally chose Michael Ovitz, a close friend for over twenty-five years, to become president. Ovitz was the founder and head of a talent agency but had never been an executive for a publicly owned entertainment company. Although Disney prepared a draft employment agreement that was sent to Ovitz's lawyers, only a rough summary of the agreement was provided to the Disney compensation committee. No spreadsheet or similar document showing the potential payout to Ovitz, or the possible cost of his severance package in the event of a nonfault termination, was presented, and the committee did not request or receive any comparative information or any presentations or analyses by experts. In a meeting lasting less than one hour, the committee approved the general terms of the agreement but did not condition its approval on being able to review the final agreement. Instead, the committee granted Eisner the authority to approve the final contract. The board of directors, which met immediately after the compensation committee, appointed Ovitz president and named Eisner as chief negotiator without any discussion about the details of Ovitz's salary, stock options, or possible termination.

Ovitz's tenure as Disney's president was unsuccessful. By December 1996, Ovitz had begun to seek other employment, but he had no contractual basis to terminate his employment. As a result, Eisner agreed to help Ovitz receive a nonfault termination so that he could leave Disney without sacrificing any of his benefits. Eisner finalized Ovitz's nonfault termination without consulting the compensation committee or obtaining its approval.

The plaintiffs filed a derivative action, alleging that the Disney directors breached their fiduciary duty when they approved the employment agreement and again when they failed to participate in Eisner's dealings with Ovitz regarding his nonfault termination. The plaintiffs sought rescission and/or money damages from the defendants or compensation for the damages allegedly sustained by Disney.

**› ISSUE PRESENTED** Should the directors of a public corporation be held personally liable if they abdicate their responsibility to appropriately consider the president's employment contract and subsequent termination?

*(Continued)*

(Case 21.1 *continued*)

**› OPINION** CHANDLER, C., writing for the Delaware Court of Chancery:

[*Eds.:* The matter came before the Delaware Chancery Court on a motion to dismiss the plaintiffs' second amended derivative complaint for failure to state a cause of action. The court found that the plaintiffs' complaint sufficiently pled a breach-of-fiduciary duty by the Disney board of directors to withstand the motion to dismiss.]

It is rare when a court imposes liability on directors of a corporation for breach of the duty of care, and this Court is hesitant to second-guess the business judgment of a disinterested and independent board of directors. But the facts alleged in the new complaint do not implicate merely negligent or grossly negligent decision making by corporate directors. Quite the contrary; plaintiffs' new complaint suggests that the Disney directors failed to exercise *any* business judgment and failed to make *any* good faith attempt to fulfill their fiduciary duties to Disney and its stockholders. . . . In short, the new complaint alleges facts implying that the Disney directors failed to "act in good faith and meet minimal proceduralist standards of attention." Based on the facts asserted in the new complaint, therefore, I believe plaintiffs have stated cognizable claims . . . .

. . .

[Defendants] . . . assert that even if the complaint states a breach of the directors' duty of care, Disney's charter provision, based on *8 Del. C.* § 102(b)(7), would apply and the individual directors would be protected from personal damages liability for any breach of their duty of care. A § 102(b)(7) provision in a corporation's charter does not "eliminate or limit the liability of a director: . . . (ii) for acts or omissions not in good faith . . . ." A fair reading of the new complaint . . . gives rise to a reason to doubt whether the board's actions were taken honestly and in good faith, as required. . . . Since acts or omissions not undertaken honestly and in good faith, or which involve intentional misconduct, do not fall within the protective ambit of § 102(b)(7), I cannot dismiss the complaint based on the exculpatory Disney charter provision.

. . .

These facts [alleged in the second amended complaint], if true, do more than portray directors who, in a negligent or grossly negligent manner, merely failed to inform themselves or to deliberate adequately about an issue of material importance to their corporation. Instead, the facts alleged . . . suggest that the defendant directors *consciously and intentionally disregarded their responsibilities,* adopting a "we don't care about the risks" attitude concerning a material corporate decision. . . . Viewed in this light, plaintiffs' new complaint sufficiently alleges a breach of the directors' obligation to act honestly and in good faith in the corporation's best interests for a Court to conclude, if the facts are true, that the defendant directors' conduct fell outside the protection of the business judgment rule.

**› RESULT** The court found that the plaintiffs' claims for relief concerning fiduciary duty breaches and waste survived the defendants' motion to dismiss. Therefore, the court required the defendants to answer the second amended complaint.

**› CRITICAL THINKING QUESTIONS**

1. The plaintiffs also named Michael Ovitz as a defendant in the lawsuit. Ovitz contended that the action against him should be dismissed because he had no fiduciary duty not to seek the best possible employment and severance agreement for himself. Do you agree with Ovitz's argument?
2. What actions could the board of directors have taken to minimize the risk of a derivative action like this?

The directors of privately held corporations are held to the same standards that are applied to the directors of public corporations. In a recent case,[5] the U.S. District Court for the Southern District of New York held that the directors of Trace, a privately held corporation, breached their fiduciary duty to the company when they ratified the excessive compensation that the CEO had paid to himself over a five-year period. The case originated after Trace filed for bankruptcy in 1998. The Chapter 7 trustee brought an action against Marshall Cogan, the CEO, controlling shareholder, and founder of Trace, and the other board members seeking to hold them personally liable for Cogan's excessive compensation. After a nonjury trial, the court found that Cogan had engaged in a series of self-dealing transactions from 1991 to 1996 that resulted in the payment of excessive compensation to him. The court held that not only had Cogan breached his fiduciary duties to Trace but that the directors had done so as well because the evidence did not establish that their action was a well-informed decision of a truly independent board of directors.

## FEDERAL REGULATION

The two principal federal acts that regulate securities transactions and issuers are the Securities Act of 1933 and the Securities Exchange Act of 1934. These Acts reflect three fundamental beliefs: (1) investors should be provided with full information prior to investing, (2) corporate insiders should not be allowed to use nonpublic information concerning their companies to their own financial advantage, and (3) investors who have been injured by misconduct should receive relief even in the absence of common law fraud. (The Securities Act and the Securities Exchange Act are discussed further in Chapter 22.)

Consistent with the beliefs reflected in the federal securities laws, the SEC has taken the position that although it does not have the power to regulate executive compensation directly, it can regulate such compensation indirectly by requiring companies to provide detailed information about executive compensation to their shareholders.[6] This position was reflected in former SEC Chairman Richard C. Breeden's statement that "the best protection against abuses in executive compensation is a simple weapon—the cleansing power of sunlight and the power of an informed shareholder base."[7] In addition to requiring disclosure, Congress has used federal tax laws to provide incentives to encourage certain types of executive compensation (such as options) and to discourage other types of executive compensation (such as excessive non-performance-based compensation and golden parachutes).

### *Disclosures and Shareholder Proposals*

In 1992, the structure of executive pay packages was one of the most visible and contentious issues facing U.S. corporations. This controversy triggered the SEC's adoption of rules that expanded the compensation and performance disclosures required in proxy statements. Under these new rules, the statements must include (1) a table showing the compensation of the company's five most highly paid executives, (2) a performance graph comparing the company's five-year cumulative total shareholder return with returns for the same period on both a broad market index and an industry or peer index, and (3) a report by the compensation committee presenting its rationale for its compensation philosophy and actual decisions for senior management and explaining how that philosophy is consistent with the actual compensation paid to the company's CEO. This information provides links between a firm's pay practices and its financial performance.

Shareholder proposals are submitted through SEC Rule 14a-8, which regulates the proposals that appear in a company's proxy statement and on the proxy ballot. This rule disallows any proposals that interfere with management's right to conduct the company's ordinary business. As public furor over executive compensation grew, the SEC announced late in 1992 that proposals regarding executive compensation would no longer be disallowed. The SEC also allows shareholder initiatives regarding approval of stock plans and option repricings. This ruling was made on the implicit assumption that the shareholder proposal mechanism could be used to initiate change when investors were unhappy with the compensation practices that were revealed in the proxy statement.[8] The alleged compensation abuses of the past few years have resulted in a significant rise in the number

5. Pereira v. Cogan, 294 B.R. 449 (S.D.N.Y. 2003).

6. Section 402 of the Sarbanes-Oxley Act is an exception to this general rule in that it prohibits loans to officers and directors. Sarbanes-Oxley Act of 2002, Pub. L. No. 107-204, 116 Stat. 745 (codified as amended in scattered sections of 11, 15, 18, 28, 29 U.S.C.A.).

7. MARILYN F. JOHNSON ET AL., RESEARCH PAPER NO. 1679: AN EMPIRICAL ANALYSIS OF THE SEC'S 1992 PROXY REFORMS ON EXECUTIVE COMPENSATION 4 (Feb. 2001), *at* http://gobi.stanford.edu/researchpapers/detail1.asp?Paper_No=1679.

8. *Id.* at 5. Note, however, that the SEC's position on these matters has been advisory only.

of shareholder proposals submitted for inclusion in the proxy materials of public companies. Limitations on lucrative compensation packages for executives and severance packages for departing officers, option expensing, and executive stock ownership requirements are some of the topics that have gained popularity in recent years.

### *Compensation Committees*

Executive compensation is generally set by a group of the company's board of directors known as the compensation committee. In theory, members of the compensation committee are supposed to be independent enough of the company's executives to deny them raises or force them to take pay cuts if the company is not doing well. In practice, however, a *New York Times* study of almost 2,000 of the country's largest corporations revealed that in 2001 more than 20 percent had compensation committees with members who had business ties or other relationships with the CEO or the company that could compromise their independence. Even the chair of the compensation committee had such ties at more than seventy of these companies.[9]

Although oversight groups like the National Association of Corporate Directors have called for independent compensation committees since the early 1990s, the Sarbanes-Oxley Act of 2002 did not address the makeup of the compensation committee, even though it set high standards of independence for audit committees. In November 2003, however, the SEC approved governance rules for the New York Stock Exchange and NASD that require independent compensation committees as part of their listing standards. These governance rules, which took effect for listed companies on the earlier of the date of the 2004 annual shareholders' meeting or October 31, 2004, require compensation committees to (1) approve and operate under a charter (NYSE only); (2) limit membership to independent directors (NYSE) or require a majority of independent directors (NASD); (3) review and approve corporate goals and objectives relevant to CEO performance (NYSE); (4) approve CEO compensation based on the goals and objectives used to evaluate the CEO's performance (NYSE) or determine CEO compensation without the CEO being present (NASD); (5) determine the CEO's long-term compensation based on the company's performance and relative shareholder returns, the value of awards to CEOs of comparable companies, and awards given to the company's CEO in prior years (NYSE); (6) make recommendations to the board about non-CEO compensation, incentive compensation plans, and equity-based plans (NYSE and NASD); and (7) prepare an annual report on executive compensation to be included in the company's annual meeting proxy statement or Form 10–K annual report (NYSE).

Although the NYSE and NASD requirements for compensation committees do not bind directors of non-public companies, they signal the standards to which courts may hold directors of all companies.[10]

## Stock Options

Stock option plans are a flexible way to share ownership with employees, reward them for performance, and attract and retain a motivated staff. For growth-oriented smaller companies, options are an effective way to preserve cash while giving employees a share in the company's future growth. They also make sense for publicly held companies that have well-established benefit plans but want to include employees in ownership. Options are not, however, a mechanism for existing owners to sell shares, and they are usually inappropriate for companies whose future growth is uncertain. They can also be less appealing in small, closely held companies that do not want to go public or be sold because these companies may find it difficult to create a market for the shares.

A *stock option* gives the person to whom it is granted (the *optionee*) the right to buy a certain number of shares at a fixed price for a fixed number of years, but usually no more than ten (the *exercise period*). The price at which the optionee can exercise the options by purchasing the stock is called the *grant price,* or the *strike price,* and is usually the market price of the stock at the time the options are granted. A company usually sets restrictions on when the options can be exercised. These restrictions, referred to as *vesting restrictions,* typically require that the optionee continue to work for the company for a minimum number of years before part or all of the options can be exercised.

9. Diana B. Henriques & Geraldine Fabrikant, *Deciding on Executive Pay: Lack of Independence Seen,* N.Y. TIMES, Dec. 18, 2002, http://www.nytimes.com/2002/12/18/business/18PAY.html?ei=5062&en=7aff406d2216573.

10. JOSEPH M. POERIO, *New Bearings for Compensation Committees: Five Steps for Getting Executive Compensation Right, Benefits Practice Center, Executive Compensation Library, Journal Reports: Law & Policy* (Feb. 2004), *at* http://www.bna.com/products/eb/bpcw.htm, *reprinted in* EXECUTIVE COMPENSATION & EMPLOYEE BENEFITS NEWSL. (Paul Hastings, Washington, DC), Feb. 2004, *at* http://www.xpay.net/CompComm2004NewBearings.htm.

## HISTORICAL PERSPECTIVE

# EFFECTS OF TAX LAWS ON STOCK OPTIONS

It is not clear exactly when U.S. corporations first issued stock options to employees. One of the earliest recorded examples involved the New England Norton Company, a manufacturer of grinding wheels, machines, and abrasives, that began to award options to its top employees in the late 1890s. Stock options did not gain general acceptance, however, until the advent of publicly traded corporations when shareholders, realizing that managers were no longer the principal owners of the corporations they managed, became concerned that the interests of nonowner managers might not be aligned with the interests of the shareholders. Stock options spread rapidly during the 1920s and 1930s.

Stock options became even more appealing to executives in 1950 when Congress enacted a law that allowed employees to pay the capital gains tax rate, then 25 percent, on profits from the sale of shares purchased with options; at the time, the top personal income tax rate was 91 percent. By 1952 one-third of the 1,084 companies on the New York Stock Exchange were using executive stock options.

During the 1960s, Congress enacted a number of restrictions on stock options that rendered them almost useless. When Congress removed capital gains treatment for option profits in 1976, stock options were virtually eliminated. Two developments in the 1970s, however, laid the groundwork for the explosion of stock options that occurred in the 1980s and 1990s. First, three economists came up with a way to value publicly traded options (the Black-Scholes method). Second, in 1973, the Chicago Board of Trade opened the first public market for stockholders to trade options on the shares of public companies.

Then, during the 1980s, Congress enacted new laws that created incentive stock options, restored capital gains treatment for option profits, and slashed the capital gains tax rate; companies soon began to offer increasingly large stock option grants to key executives instead of increasing their salaries.[a] In 1987, when Charles Lazarus earned an option payoff of $56 million, and other Toys "R" Us employees also became millionaires as a result of their options, CEOs began to realize that instead of earning a million or two from a traditional salary and bonus, they could earn millions of dollars through option grants. In 1992, the top five executives at the 1,500 largest U.S. corporations cashed in approximately $2.4 billion of options.

Changes to the tax laws in 1993 prevented companies from deducting non-performance-based compensation for a senior executive that was in excess of $1 million. Because stock options under shareholder-approved stock plans with an exercise price at fair market value or higher were treated as "performance-based compensation" that was exempt from the $1 million deduction limit, companies had an added incentive to shift CEO pay to options.[b]

During the 1990s, many U.S. corporations gradually began to extend options to a broader base of employees, although only 6 percent of large corporations came close to the high-tech companies' practice of awarding stock to most or all employees. As of 2002, between 20 percent and 25 percent of public companies made options available to most or all of their full-time employees.[c] The size of the stock option pool typically ranges from 10 to 20 percent of outstanding shares for public companies and from 15 to 25 percent of outstanding shares for private companies, although on occasion the reserve can be as high as 30 percent or more.

a. JOSEPH BLASI ET AL., IN THE COMPANY OF OWNERS: THE TRUTH ABOUT STOCK OPTIONS 72 (2003).

b. A growing number of companies do not seem to care about the effects of this law. For example, Archer Daniels Midland paid its chief executive a base salary of $2.4 million in 1999, which cost the company as much as $490,000 in deductions. In its proxy, the company noted that limiting pay to $1 million would be "inadvisable." David Leonhardt, *Order of Compensation Universe Reflects Pull of New Economy,* N.Y. TIMES, Apr. 2, 2000, http://www.nytimes.com/library/financial/sunday/040200biz-execs-options.html.

c. COREY ROSEN, REFORMING STOCK OPTIONS IN THE POST-ENRON, POST-WORLDCOM ERA (July 2002), *at* http://www.nceo.org/library/reforming_stock_options.html.

There are two principal kinds of stock options, each with different rules and tax consequences: *nonqualified stock options (NSOs)* and *incentive stock options (ISOs)*. In addition, many public companies also have *employee stock purchase plans (ESPPs)* that have optionlike features. ISOs are frequently used by privately held companies, whereas NSOs are more typically used by publicly held companies.

Optionees hope that the share price will go up and that they will be able to "cash in" by exercising their options at the lower grant price and selling the stock at the higher market price. When an employee exercises his or her option, the company must make that number of shares available, either by buying them from existing owners or by issuing new shares. Optionees can hold on to the stock after exercise, in the hope of higher returns, or sell it if there is a market or a private buyer. If the stock price falls after the option has been exercised, however, the optionee can lose money. Alternatively, the optionee can let the unexercised options expire if the stock price is lower than the grant price.

## EXEMPTION FROM FEDERAL REGISTRATION OF COMPENSATORY STOCK PLANS

Nonpublic companies that are not registered pursuant to the Securities Exchange Act of 1934 (the 1934 Act) often face a problem when instituting employee stock plans. If the company relies on Rule 504 of Regulation D issued pursuant to the Securities Act of 1933 (the Securities Act), it can issue only $1 million in stock in one twelve-month period. Because employee offerings are usually continuous, the issuer may face serious offering integration problems. It is seldom practical to shut a stock plan down for six months to take advantage of Regulation D's integration safe harbor. (The 1934 Act and Regulation D are discussed further in Chapter 22.)

In response to these problems, the SEC adopted Rule 701, which exempts offers and sales of securities made pursuant to either (1) a written compensatory benefit plan for employees, directors, general partners, trustees (if the issuer is a business trust), officers, consultants, or advisers or (2) a written contract relating to the compensation of such persons. If the benefit plan is for consultants or advisers, they must render bona fide services not connected with the offer and sale of securities in a capital-raising transaction. Exempt compensatory benefit plans include purchase, savings, option, bonus, stock appreciation, profit-sharing, thrift-incentive, and pension plans.

Under Rule 701, if total sales (not offerings) of stock[11] during a twelve-month period do not exceed the greater of (1) $1 million, (2) 15 percent of the total assets of the issuer, or (3) 15 percent of the outstanding securities of the class being offered and sold, the offerings are exempt from registration. If total sales during a twelve-month period to the specified class of persons above are more than $5 million, the issuer must disclose certain additional information, such as risk factors, and provide copies of plans under which the offerings are made and certain financial information. Other than providing a copy of the benefit plan or contract under which the options or securities are awarded, there are no specific disclosure requirements under Rule 701 for sales up to $5 million in a twelve-month period. Rule 701 provides additional integration relief for issuers who sell both under Rule 701 and under Rule 504, 505, or 506 of Regulation D or Section 4(2) of the Securities Act. Offerings under Rule 701 are not integrated with those under Regulation D or Section 4(2), and vice versa.

If a company has issued stock pursuant to Rule 701, employees and others holding such stock may sell it ninety days after its initial public offering without compliance with certain Rule 144 requirements.[12] Specifically, nonaffiliates may sell the shares through a broker without regard to any of the Rule 144 requirements, and affiliates may sell the shares without complying with the two-year holding period requirements of Rule 144(d).

## TAX AND ACCOUNTING TREATMENT OF STOCK OPTIONS

When an NSO is exercised, the company gets to deduct the spread from its earnings; the *spread* is the difference between the strike price of a stock option and the fair market value of the stock at the time that the optionee exercises the option. The spread is taxable to the optionee as ordinary income, whether or not the optionee actually sells the shares. The tax break the company receives is the amount it would have received if it had paid the employee the same amount in wages, but by using options the company doesn't have to part with cash to claim the deduction. According to one estimate, Microsoft received a $2.1 billion deduction from options in 2000.[13]

In contrast, with ISOs, the employee does not pay taxes at the time of exercise and pays only capital gains tax on the entire gain upon sale of the shares, but the company cannot deduct any of the spread or the gain from its earnings. Although the difference between the

11. In measuring sales, all options granted during the period are considered part of the aggregate sales, with the sales price defined as the option price as of the date of grant. Repriced options are treated as new grants. Shares issued pursuant to restricted stock or compensatory stock purchases are calculated as of the date of sale. For deferred compensation equity plans, measurements are based on the date of an irrevocable election to defer compensation. In calculating securities for the 15 percent rules, currently exercisable or convertible options, warrants, rights, and other securities are treated as outstanding. NAT'L CTR. FOR EMPLOYEE OWNERSHIP, EXEMPTION FROM SECURITIES REGISTRATION UNDER RULE 701 (2002), *at* http://www.nceo.org/library/rule701.html.

12. Subject to any contractual lockup provisions that may have been imposed on the stock.

13. JOSEPH BLASI ET AL., IN THE COMPANY OF OWNERS: THE TRUTH ABOUT STOCK OPTIONS 137 (2003).

strike price of an ISO and its fair market value on the date of exercise is not subject to ordinary income tax, it is a preference that must be included by the optionee when calculating *alternative minimum tax (AMT),* an extra tax that some taxpayers owe on top of the regular income tax. For optionees who hold large amounts of stock at inflated prices, the AMT can be huge, even if the stock price drops precipitously after exercise of the option. If this occurs, the only way for the optionee to avoid the AMT is to sell the stock in the same year that the option is exercised.[14]

Even though the company gets a deduction when employees exercise their NSOs, historically companies did not have to treat the ISOs or NSOs as an expense when it reported its profits to shareholders, although options had to be disclosed in footnotes. For example, if Microsoft gave its employees options worth 15 percent of its total outstanding stock in 2003, it could simply state its total profit figures without subtracting an estimate of the value of the 15 percent that its employees stand to earn if they exercise their options at a later date. With the collapse of Enron and Global Crossing, this lack of symmetry between the tax and accounting effects of stock options was criticized. Both of these corporations had issued huge option packages for their executives, who exercised these options and sold shares just before the stocks plummeted in value, leaving many other stockholders with huge losses.

In February 2004, the International Accounting Standards Board (IASB) issued a draft rule that requires companies using international accounting standards to expense stock options beginning on January 1, 2005. The IASB rule requires companies to set a value on stock options on the day of grant, treating it as an expense like salary. The IASB ruling affects about 7,000 publicly traded companies in ninety countries, excluding the United States, and it applies to all options issued after November 7, 2002, that have yet to mature. Companies reporting under the IASB rule will be able to choose the method they use for calculating the value of an option, provided that the model takes account of investment volatility.[15]

Although the IASB rules do not apply to U.S. companies, in December 2004 the Financial Accounting Standards Board (FASB) published Statement 123R, a revised standard that will impose similar rules on most U.S. companies by the middle of 2005. As of February 2004, at least 200[16] of the approximately 13,000 publicly traded U.S. companies had voluntarily started to expense options.[17] "If I put my pragmatic hat on, there are three chances of expensing not happening: slim chance, no chance and fat chance," quipped Mark Nebergall, president of the Software Finance and Tax Executives Council and a longtime opponent of expensing stock options.[18]

Some experts predict that if companies are required to expense options, top executives will get smaller grants, and many lower-level employees will no longer be eligible for options at all. There is already evidence to support their prediction. A 2003 survey by Mercer Human Resource Consulting found that 64 percent were reducing the number of options granted, and more than half were cutting the number of employees eligible to receive options.[19] Other companies are following the example of General Electric and Microsoft, which have eliminated their stock option programs in favor of stock grants. In addition to retaining some value in a low market, stock grants also allow companies to award fewer shares, reducing earnings dilution. Stock grant programs will receive the same accounting treatment as nonqualified options once option expensing begins. Exhibit 21.1 summarizes the characteristics of ISOs, NSOs, and other employee stock plans.

## IMPACT OF UNDERWATER STOCK OPTIONS

A stock option is *underwater* when its strike price is above the price at which the stock is trading. When the stock market fell in 2000, many employees wound up with underwater stock options.

Some companies such as Microsoft raised pay to offset employee option losses,[20] but most companies were

14. Consider the case of Jeff Chen, a former engineer at Cisco who owed AMT on $6.5 million in paper profits he never saw because the price of Cisco stock dropped after he exercised his options in 2000, and he failed to sell the stock before December 31, 2000. May Wong, *Stock Options Create Huge Tax Bills,* SEATTLE POST-INTELLIGENCER, Apr. 13, 2001, *at* http://seattlepi.nwsource.com/business/18470_optiontax13.shtml.

15. *Update 1—Accounting Watchdog Demands Stock Option Expensing,* FORBES, Feb. 19, 2004, *at* http://www.forbes.com/newswire/2004/02/19/rtr1267149.html.

16. Bruce Stanley, *Accounting Body Requires Firms to Treat Stock Options as an Expense,* SAN FRANCISCO CHRON., Feb. 19, 2004, *at* http://www.Californian.com/articles/2004/02/20/business/news/2_19_0421_41_15.txt.

17. Ellen Florian, *Don't Go Buying That Third House Just Yet,* FORTUNE, Nov. 18, 2002, at 30.

18. Mark Schwanhausser, *Domino Falls on Expensing Options,* SAN JOSE MERCURY NEWS, Nov. 8, 2002, *at* http://www.bayarea.com/mld/mercurynews/business/4470645.htm?template=center&mod.

19. Ruth Simon, *Companies Get Stingy with Stock Options,* WALL ST. J., July 30, 2003, http://online.wsj.com/PA2VJBNA4R/article_print/0,,SB105951151861758300,00.html.

20. Microsoft also granted additional options at lower prices to its employees.

**EXHIBIT 21.1 Broad-Based Equity Compensation Plans**

| | Incentive Stock Options (ISOs) | Nonqualified Stock Options (NSOs) | Section 423 Employee Stock Purchase Plans (423 ESPPs) | Restricted Stock Plans |
|---|---|---|---|---|
| **Technical Requirements** | • May be granted only to employees; must be in continuous employ from date of grant until no more than three months before date of exercise<br>• Maximum 10-year option term<br>• Exercise price cannot be less than fair market value (FMV) on date of grant (or 110 percent of FMV for ≥10 percent owner).<br>• $100,000 limit on value (value at date of grant) of options first exercisable in any one calendar year<br>• Nontransferable<br>• Shareholder approval and written plan meeting certain requirements<br>• Optionee must hold shares for at least two years after grant date and one year after exercise date. | • No limitations on who may be granted NSOs, terms of exercise, or holding periods<br>• Grant price of options can be less than FMV on date of grant. | • Purchase rights must be granted to all employees who have been working for at least two years, work at least 10 hours per week, and work a minimum of five months per year.<br>• Share price can be no less than 85 percent of FMV of stock.<br>• Employees with 5 percent or more of company stock are ineligible to participate.<br>• Shareholder approval, minimum purchase price, and limit on aggregate annual purchases | • No limitations on who may be granted restricted stock<br>• Price of stock can be less than FMV on date of grant. |
| **Tax Consequences to Employer** | • No tax consequences (deductions, withholding, or reporting) if employment and holding requirements are met<br>• If employee fails to meet employment and holding requirements, ISO becomes "disqualified," and tax treatment is essentially the same as NSOs, with no employment tax withholding. | • No tax consequences at grant (unless options are granted at far below FMV)<br>• At exercise, deduction is taken for spread between the FMV at date of exercise and the grant price.<br>• Employment taxes must be withheld. | • If holding conditions are met, employer cannot take a deduction for the ordinary income element.<br>• FICA must be withheld on the excess of grant price over FMV at time of exercise.<br>• If holding requirements are not met, employer may deduct the amount of ordinary income employee declares as a result of the disqualification. | • No tax consequences on issuance unless a Section 83(b) election was made, in which case compensation deduction equal to spread<br>• Compensation deduction on vesting of stock, unless an 83(b) election was made |

*(Continued)*

EXHIBIT 21.1 **Broad-Based Equity Compensation Plans—continued**

| | Incentive Stock Options (ISOs) | Nonqualified Stock Options (NSOs) | Section 423 Employee Stock Purchase Plans (423 ESPPs) | Restricted Stock Plans |
|---|---|---|---|---|
| **Tax Consequences to Employee** | • No tax consequences at grant or exercise except for AMT, at exercise<br>• For ISO tax treatment, employee must hold shares for two years from date of grant and one year from date of exercise.<br>• If employment and holding requirements are met, appreciation on shares (exercise price as basis) is taxed as long-term capital gain when stock is sold.<br>• If employment and holding requirements are not met, appreciation on shares is taxed as short-term capital gain when stock is sold. | • No tax consequences at grant (unless options are granted for far less than FMV)<br>• At exercise, ordinary income tax rates apply to spread between the FMV at the date of exercise and the grant price.<br>• At sale, capital gains tax rates apply to spread between sale price and exercise price. | • No tax consequences at grant or purchase<br>• For favorable tax treatment, employee must hold shares for at least two years from date of grant and one year from date of exercise.<br>• If holding requirements are met, employee pays ordinary income tax on the lesser of the purchase price discount or the actual gain at the time of sale; all additional gain is taxed as capital gain.<br>• If holding requirements are not met, employee pays ordinary income tax on the difference between the purchase price and the FMV on the date of purchase; the difference between FMV on the date of purchase and the FMV on the date of sale is taxed as capital gain. | • No tax consequence until shares vest, unless an 83(b) election is made, in which case employee recognizes ordinary income equal to FMV of shares at time of issuance minus price paid by employee<br>• Ordinary income equal to FMV of shares on date shares vest minus price paid by employee, unless an 83(b) election is made, in which case no tax is due on vesting |
| **Applications and Uses** | • Good for start-ups and companies without expected taxable income during the period when options will be exercised<br>• Preferred by employees with high personal income tax rates and for employees in companies without a market to sell their shares<br>• Less desirable for employers (unless options are disqualified); however, employees may be more motivated given the favorable tax treatment. | • Good for companies with ready market for selling shares (allows optionees more flexibility in exercising and selling shares) and companies with expected taxable income during period of exercise<br>• Design flexibility allows companies to structure plans in a variety of ways to meet their equity compensation strategies.<br>• Desired by employer for deductibility of spread on exercise | • Favored by employees who wish to purchase company stock, because all tax on appreciation of stock is deferred until sale<br>• Efficient and convenient method for employees to acquire stock through payroll deductions<br>• Employer can raise cash from "patient investors," avoid accounting charges (note FAS 123 reporting requirements), and increase employee ownership. | • Unlike stock options or stock appreciation rights, restricted stock retains some value for employees even if stock price goes down.<br>• Restricted stock requires fewer shares to provide a similar level of benefit compared to stock options (because awards have value even if share price declines).<br>• Design flexibility allows companies to structure plans in a variety of ways to meet equity compensation strategies. |

Source: From National Center for Employee Ownership, http://nceo.org. Used by permission.

not in a financial position to do this. Instead, most companies used their option programs in a variety of ways to compensate employees for their underwater options. In 2002, 200 of the largest companies awarded new options at lower strike prices in amounts approaching 3 percent of their outstanding shares every year, twice the run rate of ten years earlier. Investors have become concerned about this increased run rate in option grants, however. In 2001, they voted down a record 23.4 percent of option plans, according to the Investor Responsibility Research Center.[21]

Other companies such as Amazon exchanged old options for new options. Technically, Amazon allowed its workers to trade in older options with higher exercise prices for fewer options that carried strike prices at least 15 percent lower. Only a handful of companies used this repricing strategy, however, because guidelines issued by the FASB in 1998 require employers that reprice to subtract the gain employees get from the company's own earnings statement, thereby cutting profits by the value of the repricing.

To avoid problems with the FASB, many companies employed an exception to the FASB guidelines. The guidelines do not bar companies from canceling outstanding underwater options, and the FASB rule regarding an earnings charge is not triggered if the company waits six months and one day to issue new options at the then-current (hopefully lower) market price. This approach is known as a *slow-motion swap* or a *6&1 repricing*. Nearly half of the hundred largest public companies that derive more than half of their sales from the Internet did some version of a slow-motion swap in 2000. According to the authors of *In the Company of Owners:*

> Overall, the number of cancelled options jumped to 29 percent in 2000, from 11 percent the year before, as companies wiped out old high-priced options and replaced them with ones carrying strike prices at lower market levels. The practice accelerated dramatically in 2001 as the stock market continued its swoon. In fact, cancellations soared to a stunning 62 percent that year as employers struggled to cope with the morale impact of so many worthless options.[22]

In August 2002, Siebel Systems offered to trade underwater employee stock options for a combination of cash and stock. The offer applied to employee stock options priced at $40 or above. According to its SEC filing, Siebel agreed to pay $1.85 in cash and stock for each option that was exchanged. If the total was less than $5,000, employees received cash. Otherwise, they received Siebel stock. Siebel employees were able to cash in half the stock immediately and the rest over periods ranging from one to three years. Tom Siebel and members of the board of directors were excluded from the offer. Ken Goldman, Siebel's CFO, said that the company believed that the move would help retain employees and better align their interests with shareholder interests because they would become actual shareholders rather than holding worthless stock options.[23] Goldman also reported that the company would take a charge of nearly $64 million to pay for the new shares. Brett Trueman, director of the Center for Financial Reporting and Management at the Haas Business School, praised the move: "They are willing to suffer the accounting consequences. Most companies are not willing to do that. It makes you a little more confident in their other accounting numbers."[24]

Other companies have changed the other variable in the options equation—time—by awarding options with longer terms. For example, at Reebok the CEO held 500,000 underwater options that were about to expire, until Reebok's board extended their term by ten years. Coca-Cola and Procter & Gamble have issued options with fifteen-year terms, instead of ten-year terms.[25]

## Stock Option Litigation

As more employees have received stock options, litigation over them has increased. Stock options have become a key component of alleged damages in wrongful-termination lawsuits. In January 2001, John C. Fox, chair of the employment and labor law group at the Silicon Valley law firm Fenwick & West, reported that "[i]n about the last year or two years, wrongful termination suits in Northern California have been all about stock options. Every week $5 to 10 million [stock option] lawsuits cross my desk."[26] Although the

21. David Henry, *An Overdose of Options,* BUS.WK., July 15, 2002, at 112. The Investor Responsibility Research Center pointed out that, in contrast, investors voted down only 16.2 percent of the plans in 1996.

22. J. BLASI ET AL., *supra* note 13, at 120.

23. The exchange also helped to replenish Siebel's stock plan reserve in the face of tougher exchange listing requirements for shareholder approval of stock plans.

24. Elise Ackerman, *Options Traded for Cash,* SAN JOSE MERCURY NEWS, Aug. 30, 2002, at C-1.

25. David Leonhardt, *Order of Compensation Universe Reflects Pull of New Economy,* N.Y. TIMES, Apr. 2, 2000, http://www.nytimes.com/library/financial/sunday/040200biz-execs-options.html.

26. *Optional Illusions,* INFOWORLD, Jan. 8, 2001, *at* http://www.itworld.com/Career/1819/IW010108castock/pfindex.html.

pace of stock option litigation has slowed since 2001, it is still a significant issue in many wrongful-termination suits.

In *Fleming v. Parametric Technology Corp.*, the U.S. Court of Appeals for the Ninth Circuit found that Parametric had breached its duty of good faith and fair dealing when it fired Forrest Fleming to prevent him from exercising his options. The court held that "where an employee has earned a right to a benefit which is contingent upon his being employed at some later date, the employer cannot terminate him for the very purpose of depriving him of that benefit . . . ."[27] In *Benard v. Netegrity,* however, a New York federal district court dismissed a similar claim that Netegrity had wrongfully discharged Benard to prevent him from vesting in his stock options. The court found that Netegrity had not promised Benard any fixed term of employment and that there was no requirement of "good faith in an at-will employment relationship."[28]

Suits for stock option compensation often include allegations of discrimination and can result in much higher awards than the salary claims that are typically awarded in such cases. In *Greene v. Safeway Stores, Inc.,*[29] the U.S. Court of Appeals for the Tenth Circuit awarded Robert Greene the $4.4 million difference between the value of his stock options at the time he was forced to exercise them because his employment had been terminated in violation of the Age Discrimination in Employment Act and their value at the time he would otherwise have exercised them.

*Clawback provisions,* which give an employer the right to recoup some or all of an employee's stock option gain if he or she goes to work for a competitor within a certain period of time following exercise of the option, are also a significant source of litigation. The outcome may vary depending on which state law governs. In the following case, the U.S. Court of Appeals for the Ninth Circuit considered the validity of a noncompete agreement that included a clawback provision if a former employee went to work for a competitor within six months after exercising his options.

27. 187 F.3d 647 (9th Cir. 1999) (unpublished opinion).
28. 2000 WL 1760796 (S.D.N.Y. 2000).
29. 210 F.3d 1237 (10th Cir. 2000).

A CASE IN POINT

**CASE 21.2**

**International Business Machines Corporation v. Bajorek**

*United States Court of Appeals for the Ninth Circuit*
*191 F.3d 1033*
*(9th Cir. 1999).*

## Summary

**› FACTS** Dr. Bajorek worked for IBM for twenty-five years, mostly in California, but also in Minnesota and New York. IBM periodically issued stock options to selected employees, including Bajorek, to induce them to remain with IBM. Bajorek's stock option agreements provided that, upon exercise, he would certify that he was in compliance with a cancellation clause, which prohibited him from working for a competitor and provided that if he violated that clause during the six-month period after exercise, he had to pay back any profits from the options to IBM. Bajorek exercised stock options that were worth more than $900,000 at the time of exercise, but during his last week at IBM, he went to work part-time for Komag, an IBM competitor. Then, immediately upon leaving IBM, he went to work full-time with Komag as a senior executive. IBM therefore notified him that his stock options were canceled. Bajorek, a resident of California, sued IBM in California, seeking a declaratory judgment that he was in compliance with his agreements and that IBM was not entitled to cancel his stock options. IBM sued Bajorek in New York for breach of contract on the theory that he breached his promise not to go to work for a competitor for six months. The stock option agreements provided that all disputes were to be resolved according to the law of New York. The New York case was transferred to California and consolidated with the California case. The district court accepted Bajorek's argument that application of New York law would be contrary to California law and held that under California law the clawback provision in the stock option agreements was void.

**› ISSUE PRESENTED** Does application of the clawback provision in the IBM stock option agreements violate a fundamental California public policy, thereby negating the New York choice-of-law provision in the agreements and voiding the provision?

*(Continued)*

(Case 21.2 *continued*)

**› SUMMARY OF OPINION** The U.S. Court of Appeals for the Ninth Circuit first held that New York law governed the stock option agreements. The court rejected Bajorek's argument that application of New York law would be contrary to two fundamental public policies of California as established by California Labor Code Section 221, which prohibits recoupment of wages paid to employees, and California Business and Professions Code Section 16600, which limits anticompetition agreements.

The court held that stock options did not fall within the definition of "wages" in Labor Code Section 221. Because the stock options were not wages under the statute, the statute could not be treated as a fundamental policy of California, weighing against the parties' choice of New York law.

The court also rejected Bajorek's argument that, by conditioning his options on his not working for a competitor, IBM violated public policy expressed in Business and Professions Code Section 16600, which provides that "every contract by which anyone is restrained from engaging in a lawful profession, trade, or business of any kind is to that extent void." The court noted that it had previously held that Section 16600 does not make all restrictions unenforceable. The court distinguished *Muggill v. Reuben H. Donnelly Corp.,*[30] a 1965 California Supreme Court decision that invalidated a retirement plan that made an employee's pension forfeitable if the retired employee "at any time enters any occupation or does any act" in competition with the firm from which he retired. The court stated:

> It is one thing to tell a man that if he wants his pension, he cannot ever work in his trade again, as in *Muggill,* and quite another to tell him that if he wants a million dollars from his stock options, he has to refrain from going to work for a competitor for six months.

The court noted that New York law does not have provisions like those in California and it therefore appeared that the clawback provision is enforceable under New York law.

**› RESULT** The U.S. Court of Appeals for the Ninth Circuit vacated the district court's grant of judgment on the pleadings in favor of Bajorek and remanded the action for adjudication of IBM's suit for damages for breach of contract under New York law.

30. 62 Cal. 2d 239 (Cal. 1965).

## Other Types of Stock Ownership Plans

Although stock options gained popularity as a means of aligning the interests of executives with those of the shareholders of their companies, critics believe that options have backfired. They argue that at best, options have promoted a short-term focus, and at worst, they have created an incentive for executives to inflate company earnings and make irresponsible forecasts. In some cases, executives have even fraudulently manipulated earnings in an attempt to keep stock prices high while they exercised their options and sold their stock at inflated prices. Gary Winnick of Global Crossing and Dennis Kozlowski of Tyco were among the many executives who apparently used this *pump and dump* strategy to their personal advantage as the Internet bubble began to burst. Since 1999 insider sales by top executives and board members of high-flying Internet companies[31] have totaled approximately $66 billion.

Studies have also found an inverse relationship between the number of options that key executives hold and the success of their corporations. Interestingly, however, recent studies have also shown that broad-based employee stock ownership, coupled with ample opportunities to

31. Defined as companies that at one time had a market cap of at least $400 million and whose stock fell by at least 75 percent.

participate in decision making, motivates employees and positively affects corporate performance.[32]

A recent survey by Deloitte & Touche LLP of 165 of the Standard & Poor's 500 companies revealed that over 75 percent are planning to shift away from stock options, 29 percent have already made cuts in the most recent grant cycle, and 17 percent have eliminated stock options. Drivers for the change include the change in accounting treatment of stock options and institutional investor activism. The survey confirms that companies are cutting back on stock options due to running out of the shares needed to issue if the underlying options are exercised and institutional investors are increasingly voting against company proposals to increase these share reserves because of concerns about stock dilution.[33]

To replace stock options, companies consider many alternatives, including restricted stock, employee stock purchase plans, stock appreciation rights, and phantom stock.

*"Hastings—get rid of my lavish life style."*



## Restricted Stock Plans

Restricted stock plans are becoming a more popular way of compensating employees. In the past such plans were often used for key employees, but they are now being used more broadly. *Restricted stock* is stock whose sale or acquisition is subject to restrictions. For example, an employee might be given stock, or the right to purchase stock (sometimes at a discount from fair market value), but not be allowed to take possession of it until some later time when the restrictions have been removed (e.g., after the employee has worked for the company for a certain period of time or after certain performance goals have been met). If the employee does not meet these goals, then the stock will be forfeited. Some plans allow the restrictions to lapse gradually (e.g., an employee might be allowed to purchase 25 percent of his or her shares at the end of the first year of employment when the shares are 25 percent vested). Other plans provide that the restrictions do not lapse until the end of the period (e.g., an employee might not be allowed to purchase any shares of stock until he or she has worked for the company for the entire vesting period and the stock is 100 percent vested).

An employee who receives stock in connection with the performance of services is normally taxed at ordinary income tax rates to the extent that the value of the stock when received exceeds the amount paid. If an employee receives stock pursuant to a restricted stock plan, where the stock is subject to a substantial risk of forfeiture due to the restrictions placed on it, the taxable event (including the measurement of taxable income) is delayed until the restrictions lapse. (In general, a *substantial risk of forfeiture* exists if the recipient's right to full enjoyment of the stock is conditioned upon the future performance of substantial services.) This is true even when the employee pays full value for the stock at the time it is received.

As a result, if an employee is issued stock under a restricted stock plan that vests over a period of time, on each vesting date he or she will recognize taxable income equal to the difference (if any) between the fair market value of the stock on the date it becomes vested and the purchase price he or she actually paid for the stock. For example, assume an employee pays $25,000 for 10,000 shares of common stock ($2.50 per share) and one-fourth of the stock vests after one year with the balance vesting monthly thereafter for the next three years. Assume further that at the end of the first year, the value of the stock has increased to $5 per share. Unless the employee filed a timely *Section 83(b) election* at the end of the first year he or she will recognize ordinary taxable income equal to $6,250—the value of one-fourth of the stock ($12,500) minus one-fourth of the exercise price

32. See Nat'l Ctr. for Employee Ownership, The ESOP Reader: An Introduction to Employee Stock Ownership Plans 20–24 (2000). A recent study by Douglas Kruse and Joseph Blasi at Rutgers University found that over a three-year postplan period, companies that grant options to most or all employees show a 17 percent improvement in productivity over what would have been expected had they not set up such a plan. Corey Rosen, Reforming Stock Options in the Post-Enron, Post-WorldCom Era (July 2002), *at* http://www.nceo.org/library/reforming_stock_options.html.

33. *Deloitte's Michael Kesner Comments on Corporate Governance and Stock Option Reform,* SriMedia, Feb. 23, 2004, http://www.srimedia.com/artman/publish/article_759.shtml.

($6,250). This income will be recognized and the tax will be due even though the stock is still held by the employee and may be illiquid. Similarly, on each monthly vesting date thereafter, the employee will recognize additional ordinary taxable income measured by the then-current value of the shares that become vested minus the amount paid for those shares. This income is treated as if it were cash wages paid by the company to the employee, and it is subject to income and employment tax withholding from the employee's cash salary.

As an alternative to recognizing taxable income on each vesting date, the employee may file an election under Section 83(b) of the Internal Revenue Code within thirty days of the initial purchase of the shares, or the exercise of an option to acquire shares, pursuant to a restricted stock plan. By filing a timely 83(b) election, the employee elects to pay tax at the time the stock is purchased in an amount equal to what would be due if the stock were not subject to vesting. If the employee pays full market value at the time the restricted shares are purchased, no tax will be due because the value of the stock on that date does not exceed the purchase price. Once the employee has made a timely 83(b) election, subsequent vesting of the stock will not be taxable. Instead, the employee pays tax only when the stock is ultimately sold, and any gain recognized on the sale will be a capital gain.

Filing an 83(b) election is almost always advantageous when the differential between the value of the stock and the purchase price of the stock on the date of sale or exercise is zero or very small because it allows the employee to defer tax beyond the vesting dates and enables all appreciation in the stock's value to qualify for capital gains treatment. If the differential is larger, however, filing an 83(b) election can sometimes result in payment of tax for stock that is subsequently forfeited if the employee does not meet the vesting requirements.

## EMPLOYEE STOCK PURCHASE PLANS

Stock options granted under an employee stock purchase plan (ESPP), or a Section 423 plan, also receive special treatment under the Internal Revenue Code. By law, ESPPs must be broad based. Employers usually use purchase plan options as a way for rank-and-file employees to share in the growth of the company by purchasing stock, usually by way of payroll deductions. The discount from the fair market value of stock purchased via an ESPP that satisfies Internal Revenue Code Section 423 is deferred until the employee sells it, and a qualifying disposition receives capital gains treatment. A disqualifying disposition occurs if the employee disposes of the stock before the expiration of the statutory holding period, which is the later of two years after grant or one year from the date of purchase of stock pursuant to the option. At the time of the disqualifying disposition, the employee recognizes (1) ordinary income, measured by the difference between the option's exercise price and the fair market value of the stock at the time of option exercise, and (2) capital gain, measured by the difference between the fair market value of the stock on the date of exercise and the disposition proceeds. The granting employer may not take a tax deduction unless there is a disqualifying disposition by the employee.

The principal requirements of an ESPP are as follows: (1) the plan must include most groups of employees (excluding, if the company chooses, relatively new hires and part-time or seasonal employees); (2) the plan must be implemented after shareholder approval; and (3) the right to purchase stock under the plan must be non-transferable. The determination of the option exercise price, the payment provisions, and all other provisions must be uniform for all employees. The only exceptions are that the ESPP may limit the maximum amount of options that can be exercised under the plan and it may limit the amount of options that all employees may be granted to a specified relationship to total compensation, or to the base or regular rate of compensation.

To receive favorable tax treatment, an employee can own no more than 5 percent of the voting power of the employer or 5 percent of the value of all shares of stock of the employer. The ESPP must also provide that no employee can accrue the right at any time to purchase more than $25,000 of stock per calendar year, valued at the fair market value of such stock (determined at the time of the grant). In addition, the exercise price of the options must be no less than 85 percent of the stock's fair market value at the time the option is granted, or an amount that under the option's terms cannot be less than 85 percent of the stock's fair market value at the time the option is exercised. The maximum allowable option exercise is five years from the date of grant for an option that contains an exercise price at least 85 percent of the fair market value of the company's stock determined on the date of exercise. If the option exercise price is determined in any other manner, then the option must be exercised within twenty-seven months from the date of grant.

If the terms of an offering under a purchase plan do not meet the Section 423 requirements, all options granted under that offering will be treated as not having been granted under a Section 423 ESPP. Failure to meet the requirements results in the options being taxed upon exercise like nonqualified stock options, as discussed above.

## Phantom Stock and Stock Appreciation Rights

*Phantom stock* is a promise to pay a bonus in the form of the equivalent of the value of company shares or the increase in value of the company shares over a period of time. Unlike stock appreciation rights, phantom stock may reflect dividends and stock splits. Some phantom stock plans let an employee choose whether to take the bonus in the form of actual securities or in cash. Phantom stock plans are not tax qualified, so they are not subject to the same rules as employee stock ownership plans or 401(k) plans if they do not cover a broad group of employees. If they do cover a broad group of employees, however, they may be subject to ERISA rules.

*Stock appreciation rights (SARs)* can be used alone or with ISOs or NSOs to help finance the purchase of options or pay tax if any is due upon exercise of the options. A SAR gives an employee the right to obtain the future appreciation in the employer's stock without risking any capital. Like phantom stock, a SAR is normally paid in cash, but it could be paid in shares. SARs often can be exercised any time after they vest.

For both phantom stock and SARs, employees are taxed when the right to the benefit is exercised, and the employer is entitled to a deduction in the same amount.[34] If the award is settled in shares, the amount of the gain is taxable at exercise, even if the employee does not sell the shares. Any subsequent gain is taxable as capital gain. The company must record a compensation charge on its income statement as the employee's interest in a phantom stock award or a SAR increases. In each year, the value is adjusted to reflect the additional pro rata share of the award that the employee earns, with any adjustments to value arising from a rise or fall in the share price. The charge builds up during the vesting period. Then, after vesting, all additional stock price increases are taken as they occur, when the vesting is triggered by a performance event, such as a profit target. If vesting occurs gradually, the accounting treatment is more complicated and is usually based on incremental earnings of the award based on continued service.

## SEC Regulation of Equity Compensation Plans

Until 1996, stock plans had to be approved by stockholders in order for the exercise of an option to be exempted from potential short-swing trading profits liability under Section 16(b) of the 1934 Act. After receiving numerous no-action letter requests related to this rule, the SEC changed the rules in 1996 and eliminated the shareholder approval requirement. Although the NYSE and the NASD continued to require shareholder approval for listed companies, they did not require approval for plans granting only NSOs if at least 50 percent of the shares issued under the plan during a three-year period went to employees who were not officers or directors. As a result, many companies were able to avoid obtaining shareholder approval of all of their plans.

Shareholders and regulators, however, expressed concern that the lack of shareholder oversight of equity plans contributed to the wave of corporate executives who walked away with millions of dollars from stock sales that preceded the precipitous decline of their companies. In response, in 2002 the SEC began to require a new table in each reporting company's Form 10–K that increased disclosure of a company's equity compensation plans. In July 2003, the SEC approved new NYSE and NASD rules requiring shareholder approval of all stock option and other equity compensation plans.[35]

### Ethical Consideration

Do high-ranking executives have an ethical responsibility to think about the fairness of the transaction or the impact of the sale on the buyer when they sell stock at the top of the market? How far does this responsibility extend?

## ERISA

For several decades before 1974, the number of pension plans, the number of employees covered by those plans, and the annual benefits paid to retirees from these plans grew tremendously. Despite these increases, many employees who expected to receive pension payments upon retirement received either no benefits or far fewer benefits than they had anticipated. Plan officials made ill-advised investments; employees quit or were discharged with few or no vested benefits; or the employer terminated an underfunded plan with insufficient assets to cover its obligations. To help remedy these problems, Congress enacted the Employee Retirement Income Security Act of 1974 (ERISA).[36]

34. For phantom stock where no (or a very low) purchase price is paid, the amount of gain is generally taxable at vesting.

35. *See* Order Approving NYSE and Nasdaq Proposed Rule Changes, Release No. 34-48108 (June 20, 2003), http://www.sec.gov/rules/sro/34-48108.htm.

36. 29 U.S.C. §§ 1001–1461.

## COVERAGE

With few exceptions, ERISA applies to all pension plans, and to many other types of employee benefit plans, established by employers engaged in interstate commerce. With regard to pension plans, ERISA (1) establishes minimum funding requirements and participation and vesting standards; (2) imposes fiduciary obligations on pension plan administrators; (3) requires detailed disclosure and reporting of certain pension plan information; (4) imposes substantial restrictions on the investment of pension plan assets; and (5) calls for pension plan administrators to provide annual, audited financial statements to the government and participants. An employer must also maintain records of each employee's years of service and vesting percentage.

In the following case, the U.S. District Court for the Southern District of New York considered whether the officers of a corporate plan administrator are personally liable for a breach of fiduciary duty under ERISA.

**A CASE IN POINT**

**CASE 21.3**

***In re* WorldCom, Inc. ERISA Litigation**

*United States District Court for the Southern District of New York 263 F. Supp. 2d 745 (S.D.N.Y. 2003).*

## Summary

**› FACTS** The WorldCom 401(k) Salary Savings Plan (the Plan), an "employee pension benefit plan" as defined by ERISA, included a number of funds, among which was a fund invested in WorldCom stock. WorldCom was the sponsor, the fiduciary, the Plan Administrator, and the Investment Fiduciary of the Plan.

On June 25, 2002, WorldCom announced that it had improperly treated more than $3.8 billion in ordinary costs as capital expenditures in violation of generally accepted accounting principles and would have to restate its publicly reported financial results for 2001 and the first quarter of 2002. WorldCom later announced that its reported earnings for 1999 through the first quarter of 2002 had overstated earnings by $3.3 billion and that it would likely write off goodwill of $50 billion. These disclosures had a catastrophic effect on the price of WorldCom shares and the value of WorldCom notes. WorldCom stockholders and bondholders lost millions of dollars in investments.

On July 21, 2002, WorldCom filed for bankruptcy. Soon thereafter certain WorldCom employees who had invested in WorldCom stock through the company's Plan brought a class action alleging violations of ERISA against certain officers, directors, and employees of WorldCom, including Bernard Ebbers, CEO and president, and Dona Miller, WorldCom's employee benefits director. The defendants filed motions to dismiss the complaint. Among other things, the defendants contended that WorldCom alone was the ERISA fiduciary for the 401(k) plan and that ERISA claims for breach of fiduciary duty could be brought only against WorldCom. Ebbers and Miller also contended that the action sought improperly to extend the duties of disclosure created by the federal securities laws into the ERISA context.

**› ISSUE PRESENTED** Are the officers of a corporate plan administrator liable for breach of fiduciary duty under ERISA? Can an ERISA fiduciary be sued for failure to disclose items required by federal securities law?

**› SUMMARY OF OPINION** The U.S. District Court for the Southern District of New York acknowledged that Section 14.02 of the Plan provided that any WorldCom officer had authority to perform WorldCom's functions as Plan Administrator and Investment Fiduciary. However, it also provided that if WorldCom did not appoint an individual to carry out the duties, then "any officer" had "the authority to carry out, on behalf of WorldCom, the duties of the Administrator and the Investment Fiduciary." The court held that although an individual cannot be liable as an ERISA fiduciary solely by virtue of his or her position as a corporate officer, shareholder, or manager, that individual will be

*(Continued)*

(Case 21.3 *continued*)

held personally liable if he or she actually had and exercised discretionary authority and discretionary control over the administration and management of an ERISA plan. To the extent that the complaint alleged that certain officers, employees, and directors of WorldCom had and exercised discretionary authority and control over the Plan, the defendants' motion to dismiss was denied.

The court then rejected defendants Ebbers's and Miller's motion to dismiss the plaintiffs' claim that they had breached their fiduciary duties by failing to disclose fully and accurately infirmities in WorldCom's stock price. These misrepresentations were alleged to have been contained in WorldCom's SEC filings, which were attached as required to a prospectus given to WorldCom employees. The defendants argued that this would impose a continuous duty of disclosure on ERISA fiduciaries that would overwhelm the federal securities law disclosure requirements and compel fiduciaries to violate the prohibitions against insider trading. However, the court found that:

> The defendants have tried to describe a tension between the federal securities laws and ERISA that would require the dismissal of this claim. Their arguments, however, cannot undermine the soundness of the general principle . . . that ERISA fiduciaries cannot transmit false information to plan participants when a prudent fiduciary would understand that the information was false. . . . The difficulties that exist in the analysis of this claim arise principally from the facts that at least one of the defendants, Ebbers, is alleged to be both a corporate insider and an ERISA fiduciary, and that the alleged misrepresentations concern the company itself. . . . The Complaint alleges that WorldCom's SEC filings contained material misrepresentations regarding WorldCom's financial condition. Having spoken in its periodic SEC filings about the company's financial condition, WorldCom had a duty under the federal securities laws to correct any prior material misrepresentation when it became aware of the falsity. In any event, the existence of duties under one federal statute does not, absent express congressional intent to the contrary, preclude the imposition of overlapping duties under another federal statutory regime.

**› RESULT** The district court dismissed the ERISA claims against the directors and employees whom it found were not fiduciaries under ERISA but held that ERISA claims could be brought against defendants Ebbers and Miller on the basis that they transmitted materially false information to Plan participants in breach of their fiduciary duties.

---

*Nonpension benefit plans* (such as medical, dental, and disability plans) are also subject to ERISA's rules on reporting, disclosure, and fiduciary responsibility. For example, employees must be provided with documents such as a summary plan description, a summary annual report, and a summary of any material modifications to the plan. Further, the employer or plan administrator must maintain sufficient records, usually including the employee's age, hours worked, salary, and contributions, to calculate each employee's benefits.

Other employee benefits (which may not be part of a formal plan) are covered by ERISA if a reasonable person could determine from the surrounding circumstances the existence of the intended benefits, the beneficiaries, the financing for the benefits, and the procedures for receiving the benefits. Many types of group severance pay plans are deemed to be either welfare plans or, less commonly, pension plans and are thus regulated by ERISA. However, individually negotiated severance agreements generally are not.

## Employee Stock Ownership Plans

An *employee stock ownership plan (ESOP)* can provide numerous tax and other benefits for employees, the company, and shareholders. ESOPs are tax qualified, however, so they must meet many coverage, nondiscrimination, distribution, and other Tax Code requirements.

Among other things, ESOPs must not discriminate in favor of highly compensated employees, and the Code's distribution rules require the employer to repurchase the stock after an employee terminates employment at the election of the employee (if a market does not otherwise exist). An ESOP's assets must also be invested primarily in stock of the sponsoring employer, and an ESOP is the only plan that is allowed to borrow funds on the credit of the sponsoring company to acquire employer stock to hold as a plan asset in the ESOP trust.

Although public companies sponsor only about 10 percent of all ESOPs, these ESOPs have accounted for 80 percent of ESOP borrowing. Public company ESOPs also tend to differ from other ESOPs in several respects: (1) they tend to buy less of the company (5 to 15 percent), (2) they usually replace a company contribution to a 401(k) or profit-sharing plan, and (3) they are almost always leveraged.[37] ESOPs hold approximately $500 billion of company stock.[38]

*401(k) plans* let employees defer a portion of their salaries on a pretax basis into an investment fund set up by the company. By law, participation in 401(k) plans cannot be too heavily weighted in favor of higher compensated employees, so companies generally offer a partial match to encourage broad participation in these voluntary plans. The match can be in cash or any investment vehicle the company chooses, including company stock. The combined deduction that the company and the employees together can contribute to the plan on an annual basis is limited to 15 percent of taxable pay (in the aggregate, not by individual); this amount must be reduced by contributions to any other tax-qualified retirement-oriented benefit plans. At the end of 2003, 45 million workers had 401(k) plans with an estimated $1.795 trillion in assets.[39] Of this amount, 16 percent, or approximately $287 billion, was invested in employer stock.[40]

## PENSION PLANS

ERISA provides that officers and trustees of a pension plan are fiduciaries, required to act solely in the interest of the plan's participants and beneficiaries in providing benefits and defraying expenses.[41] ERISA expressly requires private pension plans to use the "prudent person" investment standard. This rule requires trustees to employ "the care, skill, prudence and diligence under the circumstances then prevailing that a prudent man acting in a like capacity and familiar with such matters would use in the conduct of an enterprise of a like character and with like aims."[42]

In *Hughes Aircraft Co. v. Jacobson*,[43] the U.S. Supreme Court held that Hughes Aircraft Company did not violate ERISA when it amended a contributory defined benefit pension plan and used the surplus assets in that plan to provide a new noncontributory plan and retirement program. In 1985, Hughes provided a defined benefit plan for employees to which both the company and employees made contributions. (In a *defined benefit pension plan*, the employer guarantees the employee a specific payment regardless of the total contributions made to the plan or the plan's investment performance. In contrast, in a *defined contribution pension plan*, the employer agrees only to make specific contributions, usually a percentage of salary, so the payout is dependent on both the total contributions and the plan's investment performance.) In 1987, when the plan had surplus assets of almost $1 billion, Hughes stopped making contributions to it. In 1989, Hughes amended the plan to include an early retirement program with additional benefits to certain eligible employees. Two years later, the company amended the plan to provide that new participants could not contribute to the plan and would receive fewer benefits. A class of retirees claimed that Hughes had violated ERISA by amending the plan.

The Supreme Court rejected the retirees' claim. The Court explained that a defined benefit plan consists of a general pool of assets rather than individual dedicated accounts. Although employees can contribute to the plan, the employer assumes the entire investment risk.

### ETHICAL CONSIDERATION

Is it ethical for company executives to urge employees to accumulate large holdings of the company's stock in their 401(k) retirement plans without telling them that the executives are considering selling large amounts of their own holdings in the company?

37. NAT'L CTR. FOR EMPLOYEE OWNERSHIP, *supra* note 32, at 16.
38. ESOP Facts and Figures, *at* http://www.esopassociation.org/pubs/stats.html (last visited Dec. 19, 2004).
39. Bull Market Boosts 401(k) Assets to Record Level, Apr. 19, 2004, *at* http://www.business-journal.com/archives/20040419BullMarket401k.asp.
40. Frequently Asked Questions About 401(k) Plans, *at* http://www.ici.org/funds/abt/faqs-401(k).html (last visited Dec. 18, 2004).
41. Richard H. Koppes & Maureen L. Reilly, *An Ounce of Prevention: Meeting the Fiduciary Duty to Monitor an Index Fund Through Relationship Investing*, 20 J. CORP. L. 413, 426 (1995).
42. *Id.* (citing 29 U.S.C. § 1104 (Supp. 1990)).
43. 525 U.S. 432 (1999).

The members of the plan have a right to their accrued benefits but not to any particular asset that is part of the plan's general asset pool. As a result, the plan's performance does not affect their statutory entitlement. The Court stated that "[s]ince a decline in the value of a plan's assets does not alter accrued benefits, members similarly have no entitlement to share in a plan's surplus—even if it is partially attributable to the investment growth of their contributions."[44] The Court also rejected the claims that Hughes had violated its fiduciary duties, finding that ERISA's fiduciary provisions did not apply to the amendments.

In *Bins v. Exxon Co. U.S.A.*,[45] the U.S. Court of Appeals for the Ninth Circuit addressed the issue of whether an employer considering a specific proposal to alter employee benefits presented by managers empowered to implement the changes has a fiduciary duty to disclose the proposed modification to the potentially affected employees. Ernest Bins, who had worked for Exxon for fifteen years, heard rumors in the months before his retirement that the company was considering offering a lump-sum retirement incentive under the employee benefit plan covered by ERISA. In response to his inquiries, a benefits counselor and human resources adviser told Bins that they knew nothing about whether the rumor was true. Less than two weeks after Bins retired, Exxon publicly announced the very retirement incentive about which he had inquired. Bins sued, claiming that the company had breached its duties as an ERISA fiduciary in not disclosing the potential change in ERISA benefits to all employees who might be affected. The appeals court agreed, ruling that an employer "seriously considering" a proposal to implement a change in ERISA benefits must disclose information about the proposal to all plan participants or beneficiaries to whom the employer knows, or has reason to know, the information is material. An employer "seriously considers" a proposal when (1) a specific proposal (2) is being discussed for purposes of implementation (3) by senior management with authority to implement the change. The U.S. courts of appeals are split on the issue of whether an ERISA fiduciary has an affirmative duty to disclose proposed changes in benefits in the absence of employee inquiries.

44. *Id.* at 440–41.
45. 189 F.3d 929 (9th Cir. 1999), *reh'g en banc*, 220 F.3d 1042 (9th Cir. 2000).

## HMOs

In the following case, the U.S. Supreme Court considered the fiduciary duties imposed by ERISA in the context of health maintenance organizations (HMOs) providing care pursuant to employer-sponsored health plans.

A CASE IN POINT

### In the Language of the Court

**CASE 21.4**
**Pegram v. Herdrich**
*Supreme Court of the United States*
*530 U.S. 211 (2000).*

› **FACTS** Carle Clinic Association P.C., Health Alliance Medical Plans, Inc., and Carle Health Insurance Management Company, Inc. (collectively Carle) constitute a health maintenance organization. Cynthia Herdrich was covered by Carle through State Farm Insurance Company, her husband's employer. In the course of a physical exam prompted by Herdrich's complaint of pain in her groin, Dr. Lori Pegram, a Carle doctor, discovered an inflamed mass in Herdrich's abdomen. Instead of ordering an immediate ultrasound at the local hospital, Dr. Pegram decided that she should wait eight more days for an ultrasound at a facility staffed by Carle. Prior to the scheduled ultrasound, Herdrich's appendix ruptured, causing peritonitis.

Herdrich sued Pegram and Carle in state court for medical malpractice and fraud. Carle and Pegram argued that ERISA preempted the fraud counts and removed the case to federal court. Herdrich argued that the provision of medical services under the Carle HMO, which rewarded its physicians for limiting medical care to cut costs, was a breach of Carle's fiduciary duty under ERISA because it created an incentive to make decisions in the physicians' self-interest rather than in the exclusive interests of patients. The district court dismissed the ERISA count on the grounds that Carle was not acting as an ERISA fiduciary in this situation. The appeal court reversed, and Carle appealed.

*(Continued)*

(Case 21.4 *continued*)

**› ISSUE PRESENTED** Are treatment decisions made by a physician employed by an HMO providing services pursuant to an employer-sponsored medical plan fiduciary acts within the meaning of ERISA?

**› OPINION** SOUTER, J., writing for the U.S. Supreme Court:

The nub of the claim . . . is that when State Farm contracted with Carle, Carle became a fiduciary under the plan, acting through its physicians. . . . The pleadings must . . . be parsed very carefully to understand what acts by physician owners acting on Carle's behalf are alleged to be fiduciary in nature. It will help to keep two sorts of arguably administrative acts in mind. What we will call pure "eligibility decisions" turn on the plan's coverage of a particular condition or medical procedure for its treatment. "Treatment decisions," by contrast, are choices about how to go about diagnosing and treating a patient's condition: given a patient's constellation of symptoms, what is the appropriate medical response?

These decisions are often practically inextricable from one another . . . . The kinds of decisions mentioned in Herdrich's ERISA count and claimed to be fiduciary in character are just such mixed eligibility and treatment decisions: physicians' conclusions about when to use diagnostic tests; about seeking consultations and making referrals to physicians and facilities other than Carle's; about proper standards of care, the experimental character of a proposed course of treatment, the reasonableness of a certain treatment, and the emergency character of a medical condition.

. . .

. . . [W]e think Congress did not intend Carle or any other HMO to be treated as a fiduciary to the extent that it makes mixed eligibility decisions acting through its physicians. . . . [T]he common law trustee's most defining concern historically has been the payment of money in the interest of the beneficiary.

Mixed eligibility decisions by an HMO acting through its physicians have, however, only a limited resemblance to the usual business of traditional trustees. To be sure, the physicians (like regular trustees) draw on resources held for others and make decisions to distribute them in accordance with entitlements expressed in a written instrument. . . . Traditional trustees administer a medical trust by paying out money to buy medical care, whereas physicians making mixed eligibility decisions consume the money as well. Private trustees do not make treatment judgments, whereas treatment judgments are what physicians reaching mixed decisions do make, by definition. . . . Thus, it is at least questionable whether Congress would have had mixed eligibility decisions in mind when it provided that decisions administering a plan were fiduciary in nature.

**› RESULT** The Supreme Court held that mixed eligibility decisions by HMO physicians are not fiduciary decisions under ERISA, so Herdrich could not sue Carle for breach of fiduciary duty under ERISA.

**› CRITICAL THINKING QUESTIONS**

1. Does an HMO have a duty under ERISA to disclose financial incentive arrangements between the HMO and doctors that cause doctors to keep testing, referrals, and use of health care to a minimum?[46]
2. Should an employer selecting an HMO for employees be required to disclose any financial incentives the HMO might have to restrict patient care?

46. *See* Ehlmann v. Kaiser Found. Health Plan of Tex., 198 F.3d 552 (5th Cir. 2000).

## *Federal Preemption*

Although patients can assert claims of medical malpractice against the physicians providing medical care through HMOs, most courts have prevented patients from suing the HMOs themselves for any state law claims, such as fraud. Instead, courts have held that ERISA provides the sole remedies for claims arising out of the administration of employee welfare plans. As a result, most courts have dismissed cases brought under state law against HMOs or their administrators based on the HMO's denial of benefits. The Supreme Court's decision in *Pegram v. Herdrich* dealt another blow to patients' rights activists because it precluded patients from suing HMOs for breach of fiduciary duty arising out of the denial of benefits. Although both houses of Congress have considered legislation that would amend ERISA to provide enrollees in health plans governed by ERISA with the right to sue plan administrators for injury or death caused by administrative decisions that denied or restricted health care, as of December 2004, none of the bills had been enacted into law.

In 2004 the U.S. Supreme Court strictly limited the ability of individuals to sue their HMO for damages for substandard medical care in state court in two Texas cases. In *Cigna Healthcare of Texas, Inc. v. Calad,*[47] Ruby Calad underwent a hysterectomy but was ordered to leave the hospital one day later. Despite her doctor's opposition, her HMO insisted on the discharge. Calad suffered complications and was rushed to the emergency room several days later. In the other case, *Aetna U.S. Healthcare Inc. v. Davila,*[48] Juan Davila nearly died of internal bleeding when his HMO refused to pay for a medication prescribed by his doctor and insisted he use a cheaper pain relief medication instead. The U.S. Court of Appeals for the Fifth Circuit held that the plaintiffs' claims were not preempted by ERISA because the HMOs were not acting as plan fiduciaries when denying them medical treatment and the plaintiffs were asserting tort claims, not claims for plan benefits. The court stated that "ERISA should not be interpreted to preempt state malpractice laws or to create a federal common law of medical malpractice."[49] The Supreme Court reversed the Fifth Circuit and held that Calad's and Davila's claims were completely preempted by ERISA. As a result, it appears that state tort claims resulting from plan coverage decisions will only be permitted when the plan administrator also serves as, or employs, the individual or entity that provides the medical treatment, such that the decisions are, in fact, mixed questions of treatment and eligibility. Justices Ginsburg and Breyer joined in a separate concurring opinion to join "the rising judicial chorus urging that Congress and [this] Court revisit what is an unjust and increasingly tangled ERISA scheme." They also referenced an amicus brief filed by the U.S. Solicitor General, which suggested that some form of "make whole" relief is available against a breaching fiduciary under ERISA.[50]

Although ERISA preempts many state laws, it does not preempt all of them. In *UNUM Life Insurance Co. of America v. Ward,*[51] UNUM had issued a long-term group disability policy to Management Analysis Company (MAC) as a benefit plan governed by ERISA. The policy provided that proof of claims must be furnished to UNUM within a certain limited period of time. Ward, a MAC employee, became disabled and qualified for state disability benefits. Upon inquiry, MAC informed Ward that its long-term disability plan covered his condition, and Ward submitted a benefits application. MAC processed the application and forwarded it to UNUM, which advised Ward that his claim was untimely. Under California's notice-prejudice rule, an insurer cannot avoid liability where proof of claim is untimely unless the insurer can show that it suffered actual prejudice from the delay. Under California's agency rule, a California employer that administers an insured group health plan should be deemed to act as the agent of the insurance company. Ward argued that under this rule, his notice to MAC, acting as UNUM's agent, sufficed to supply timely notice to the insurance company.

The issue before the U.S. Supreme Court was whether ERISA preempted the two California state law rules. The Court concluded that the notice-prejudice rule regulates insurance, an area traditionally governed by state law, and was not preempted by ERISA. By allowing a longer period to file than the minimum filing terms mandated by federal law, the state law complemented rather than contradicted ERISA. With respect to the agency rule, the Court ruled that it related to an employee benefit plan and was, therefore, preempted by ERISA.

47. Calad v. Cigna Healthcare of Tex., Inc., 2001 WL 705776 (N.D. Tex. 2001), *rev'd sub nom.* Roark v. Humana, Inc., 307 F.3d 298 (5th Cir. 2002), *cert. granted,* 124 S. Ct. 463 (2003).

48. Davila v. Aetna U.S. Healthcare, Inc., 2001 WL 34354948 (N.D. Tex. 2001), *rev'd sub nom.* Roark v. Humana, Inc., 307 F.3d 298 (5th Cir. 2002), *cert. granted,* 124 S. Ct. 462 (2003).

49. Roark v. Humana, Inc., 307 F.3d 298, 311 (5th Cir. 2002) (citing Pegram v. Herdrich, 530 U.S. 211, 236–37 (2000)).

50. Aetna Health Inc. v. Davila, 124 S. Ct. 2488 (2004).

51. 526 U.S. 358 (1999).

In an effort to avoid the HMOs' traditional defense that claims regarding quality of care should be filed under ERISA, a group of chronically ill and disabled patients, who claimed that they were denied quality medical care, filed a case alleging that two HMOs, Humana Health Plans of Texas and PacifiCare of Texas, and a physicians' group, HealthTexas Medical Group, violated the Americans with Disabilities Act (ADA) by limiting care for chronically ill patients because they are more costly to treat. Although the case was ultimately settled, a Texas federal court judge had held earlier that the ADA prevents HMOs from discriminating against patients with disabilities.[52]

### PENALTIES

ERISA imposes various penalties for failure to conform to requirements. Plan participants or beneficiaries may sue for lost benefits and for loss of the plan's tax benefits. Any fiduciary of a plan who breaches a duty is personally liable for the losses resulting from the breach. ERISA also provides for civil penalties for breach of its prohibited transaction rules (which bar many transactions between an ERISA plan and a fiduciary of that plan) of up to 100 percent of the amount of the prohibited transaction.[53]

To minimize costs and maximize benefit levels, many employers with union employees under collective bargaining agreements belong to multiemployer pension plans. Under the Multiemployer Pension Plan Amendments Act of 1980, withdrawal from such a plan may result in stiff penalties.

## Other Federal Laws Affecting the Employment Relationship

Federal legislation concerning employee benefits and layoffs indirectly affects employee relations. These laws, which apply regardless of whether employees belong to a union, are discussed below. The laws regulating minimum wage and collective bargaining are discussed in Chapter 12.

### CONSOLIDATED OMNIBUS BUDGET RECONCILIATION ACT

The Consolidated Omnibus Budget Reconciliation Act of 1985 (COBRA)[54] was enacted in 1986 to allow group health, dental, and visual benefits to continue for employees who are terminated voluntarily or involuntarily (unless the discharge was for gross misconduct) and for employees whose hours are reduced to the point that coverage would normally cease. COBRA applies to employers of twenty or more workers that sponsor a group health plan. Churches and federal government agencies are exempt. Employers must notify employees of their rights when they begin participation in a group health plan or when coverage has been threatened by an event such as termination or reduced hours. Under the Technical and Miscellaneous Revenue Act of 1988,[55] employers who fail to comply with COBRA's requirements are subject to adverse tax consequences.

Under COBRA, eligible employees must be given at least sixty days from the date their coverage ceases to elect to have their coverage continued for them and their covered spouse and dependents. If coverage continuation is elected, the employer is required to extend, for up to eighteen months, coverage identical to that provided under the plan for similarly situated employees. The eligible employee electing COBRA coverage is required to pay the entire premium, plus an administrative fee of up to an additional 2 percent of the cost of coverage. Disabled employees are eligible for continued coverage for up to twenty-nine months. If the employee declines to continue coverage, the employer has no further coverage obligations.

An employer may discontinue coverage for any one of five reasons: (1) the employer ceases to provide group health coverage to any of its employees; (2) the premium for the coverage is not paid; (3) the employee, or former employee, becomes insured under another group plan; (4) the employee, or former employee, becomes eligible for Medicare; or (5) a spouse of the employee, or former employee, is divorced, remarries, and becomes covered under the new spouse's plan.

### HEALTH INSURANCE PORTABILITY AND ACCOUNTABILITY ACT

The Health Insurance Portability and Accountability Act of 1996 (HIPAA)[56] is an employee health-care reform law that provides special protection for individuals with lifelong illnesses who change jobs. The principal provisions of the HIPAA cover all companies with fifty or more employees and went into effect on January 1, 1998.

52. Zamora-Quezada v. HealthTexas Med. Group of San Antonio, 34 F. Supp. 2d 433, 440 (W.D. Tex. 1998).
53. 29 U.S.C. §§ 1106, 1132.
54. Pub. L. No. 99-272, 100 Stat. 82 (1986) (codified as amended in scattered sections of 29 U.S.C.).
55. Pub. L. No. 100-647, 102 Stat. 3342 (1988) (codified as scattered sections of 26 U.S.C.).
56. Pub. L. No. 104-191, 110 Stat. 1936 (1996) (codified in scattered sections of 18, 26, 29, 42 U.S.C.).

### ETHICAL CONSIDERATION

The elimination or reduction of insurance agent commissions for sales to HIPAA-eligible individuals is a circumvention of the HIPAA, but it may not rise to the level of a failure to offer coverage under federal law. Is it ethical for a manager to adopt a policy of withholding commissions when it is not clearly illegal to do so?

The HIPAA requires that new employees and their dependents be eligible for health insurance coverage by the new employer without an exclusion (or higher premiums) for preexisting conditions if they had health insurance for at least eighteen months provided by the previous employer and joined the new company within sixty-three days of leaving the previous employer. The previous employer must provide a certificate to a leaving employee documenting the previous coverage.

The HIPAA also provides that the duration of an employee's previous coverage may be applied to fulfilling a new employer's waiting period. It also extended COBRA for up to twenty-nine months for individuals who leave work as a result of illness or disability, provided that they apply within sixty days of leaving. In addition, the HIPAA requires companies to offer the same health coverage whether the illness is physical or mental; it also provides greater health-related tax deductions for self-employed individuals.

Despite its multiple provisions, the HIPAA has not resolved all issues related to health insurance reform. For example, the HIPAA did not include insurance pools for small businesses nor did it raise the lifetime caps on insurance benefits.

## WORKER ADJUSTMENT AND RETRAINING NOTIFICATION ACT

The Worker Adjustment and Retraining Notification Act of 1988 (WARN Act)[57] requires an employer to provide timely notice to its employees of a proposal to close a plant or to reduce its workforce permanently. The Act applies to employers with 100 or more employees, either all working full-time or working an aggregate of at least 4,000 hours per week.

The WARN Act attempts to strike a balance between the employer's interest in maintaining employee productivity and efficiency and the employee's interest in being forewarned of a mass layoff or plant closing. It requires employers to give employees sixty days' advance notice of any plant closing that will result in a loss of employment during any thirty-day period for fifty or more employees. A shutdown of a product line or operation within a plant is included within the Act's definition of a plant closing. The Act also requires sixty days' notice for layoffs during any thirty-day period that affect at least 500 employees, or at least fifty employees if they comprise one-third of the workforce. Employers are required to give written notice of the plant closing or layoff to each representative of the affected employees or, if there is no representative, to each affected employee. Employers are also required to give written notice to the state and local governments where the layoff or plant closing will occur.

The WARN Act permits an employer to order the shutdown of a plant before the conclusion of the sixty-day notice period if (1) at the time notice would have been required, the employer was actively seeking capital or business that would enable it to avoid or postpone the shutdown, and the employer reasonably and in good faith believed that giving the required notice would preclude it from obtaining the needed business or capital; or (2) the plant closing or mass layoff was caused by a natural disaster or by business circumstances that were not reasonably foreseeable at the time notice would have been required. The terms "actively seeking capital" and "business circumstances that were not reasonably foreseeable" remain largely undefined.

The WARN Act does not apply to the closing of a temporary facility. It also does not apply to a closing or mass layoff that results from the completion of a particular project if the affected employees were hired with the understanding that their employment would not continue beyond the duration of the project. Finally, it does not apply to a closing or layoff that results from a strike or lockout that is not intended to evade the requirements of the Act.

The WARN Act includes several enforcement provisions. Aggrieved employees are entitled to receive back wages and benefits for each day that the employer is in violation. The court has discretion to award the prevailing party reasonable attorneys' fees. In addition, an employer who violates the Act may be subject to a civil penalty of up to $30,000, to be paid to the affected communities.

57. Pub. L. No. 100-379, 102 Stat. 890 (1988) (codified at 29 U.S.C. §§ 2101–2109).

# Global View

## International Trends in Stock Compensation

A recent survey of 100 U.S. multinationals showed that almost 70 percent had implemented stock plans within the previous eight-year period. As these companies have expanded in the global marketplace, stock ownership has become more common for employees in other countries, who are no longer satisfied with being paid in accordance with local practices. Compared to U.S. executives, European, Asian, and Latin American executives still have less of their total compensation tied to stock, but an increasing number of European companies are offering stock to executives and to a broader group of nonmanagement employees.

In addition, legislative activity aimed at encouraging and assisting in the implementation of employee stock plans outside the United States has increased. This legislative activity can be grouped into four categories: (1) laws aimed at leveling the playing field for the foreign country by bringing it into compliance with other countries, including improved tax treatment of stock compensation, relaxation of restrictions on the ability to grant equity, and preferential tax treatment for equity; (2) laws providing preferential tax treatment for stock plans for both domestic and foreign companies; (3) laws providing favorable tax treatment only for domestic companies; and (4) laws that facilitate the implementation of employee stock plans.

The stock option plan is the most commonly used stock plan among U.S. multinationals. Although the trend is toward more broad-based programs, most global stock option plans are still limited to executives. Performance-based option plans are very common among European multinationals but are seldom used by U.S. multinationals because of the adverse accounting consequences in the United States. The United Kingdom, Australia, Belgium, France, and Italy are among the foreign countries with specific legislation allowing companies to establish tax-effective stock option plans.

Stock-purchase or stock savings plans are most commonly used for broader employee groups. U.S. multinationals generally extend their plans to foreign employees in a program similar to plans qualifying under Code Section 423. Many foreign multinationals with U.S. employees take advantage of Section 423 in implementing their stock-purchase programs in the United States. In addition, many countries offer tax-effective, all-employee savings plans, but these plans are intended to promote short-term savings, rather than being retirement oriented (as they are in the United States).

Few U.S. multinationals extend their ESOPs to employees in foreign countries, and when they do, the plans tend to have a short-term orientation. However, many countries outside the United States encourage employees to share in the success of their companies through either mandatory or voluntary profit-sharing programs. A major disadvantage of this type of program is the lack of uniform global tax treatment.

Another global program used by U.S. multinationals is modeled after the U.S. 401(k) plans: U.S. participants in 401(k) plans can invest in company stock, employee contributions vest immediately, the employer match vests after a period of time, and the employee receives distributions from the plan on retirement. When this model is used globally, vesting and distribution generally occur at the same time because the plan is not intended to be retirement oriented. Non-U.S. multinationals offer an abundance of savings programs, but these programs tend to have a short-term orientation. This short-term focus probably occurs because European countries have had stronger publicly provided pension and social security benefits than the United States, so there is no need for longer-term corporate savings plans.[a]

a. Equity-Based Compensation for Multinational Corporations 7 (Scott S. Rodrick ed., 4th ed. 2001).

## THE RESPONSIBLE MANAGER

### SIX KEY PRINCIPLES RELATED TO COMPENSATION

Recent reports issued by the Conference Board Commission on Public Trust and Private Enterprise, the Business Roundtable, and the National Association of Corporate Directors' Blue Ribbon Commission on Executive Compensation and the Role of the Compensation Committee highlight six key principles relating to compensation.

First, a strong and independent compensation committee should oversee and understand the entire executive compensation package and engage its own advisers and consultants. In 2003, Institutional Shareholder Services, Inc. (ISS) updated its policy to require that all key committees be completely independent. An apparent erosion of the "business judgment rule" by Delaware courts will place more pressure on boards of directors to have a fully independent compensation committee and to make sure that the committee does its homework.

Second, executive compensation should have a significant performance-based component (some part of which can be equity incentives). Many institutional investors are also calling for a clearer link between pay and performance. For example, under its new policy, ISS will support shareholder proposals advocating the use of performance-based equity awards unless the proposal is overly restrictive or the company demonstrates that at least 50 percent of the shares awarded to the top five officers are already performance based. Now that there is a mandated change in option accounting, the pay-for-performance mandate is likely to spill over into stock option vesting. Companies may also respond by granting more performance-based restricted stock or restricted stock units.

Third, benchmarking should be discouraged because it facilitates what some refer to as the "Lake Woebegon Effect," where all executives (and as a result, their compensation) are above average. This leads to escalating executive compensation packages as companies seek to stay ahead of at least half of their peers. A report by former SEC Chairman Richard Breeden, the court-appointed monitor for MCI/WorldCom, suggests that a logical starting point for executive compensation might be the 25th percentile, rather than the 75th percentile. Clearly, benchmark data can be useful, but compensation committees need to examine competitive pay packages more carefully and sprinkle those packages with performance incentives.

Fourth, executive compensation decisions should be accounting neutral. In other words, options should be expensed and kept on a "level playing field" with other forms of equity compensation. The FASB's move toward a standard that mandates option accounting is being viewed as a "tidal wave" that cannot be stopped by congressional action, lobbying, or even logic. As mandated option expensing seems certain, shareholders continue to propose that companies adopt it now rather than wait.

Fifth, executives should be subject to acquire-and-hold policies that force them to retain a significant equity stake in their employers. Ownership guidelines have two purposes: (1) to align the long-term interests of executives and shareholders, and (2) to prevent executives from focusing on short-term increases in stock price at the expense of long-term performance. Presumably, these goals could be accomplished by option terms that prohibit option exercise for a substantial period of time; the leveraged nature of options would have a bigger financial impact on executives.

Sixth, executive compensation should be transparent and conspicuously disclosed. Disclosure of executive and director compensation is very important to institutional shareholders. Companies should clearly spell out, in terms that will be understood by investors, the company's compensation programs and philosophy, including the performance criteria upon which certain compensation will be paid and the rationale for the salary levels, incentive payments, and stock option grants of top executive officers.

Thoughtful companies will respond with well-constructed, well-communicated compensation programs that place greater emphasis on performance than has been the case in the past.

Source: Cooley Godward LLP, Compensation Issues in the 2004 Proxy Season: Stormy Weather Ahead?, Feb. 17, 2004, *at* http://www.cooley.com/news/alerts.aspx?id=38514520.

INSIDE STORY

## WHO IS WATCHING THE WATCHDOG?

The New York Stock Exchange, one of the largest stock exchanges in the world, is operated by New York Stock Exchange, Inc., a member-owned not-for-profit corporation. Its main function is to provide a market for its 1,336 members to trade securities. It is the principal source of corporate governance standards for its member organizations and is also the designated examining authority for the major securities firms in the United States, including more than 250 member organizations that deal with the public and account for 85 percent of the public customer accounts handled by U.S. broker dealers.

Coming from humble roots in Jackson Heights, Queens, Richard Grasso, a college dropout, joined the NYSE in 1968 as a clerk making $80 a week. In 1994, Grasso was appointed chairman and CEO of the NYSE. He became a hero in 2001 when he was able to reopen the U.S. stock market only six days after the September 11 terrorist attacks. As the months went by, however, attitudes toward Grasso began to change. Many exchange members were outraged when they learned that he had accepted a $5 million bonus for his work in the wake of September 11. By May 2003, reports of Grasso's "gargantuan pay package" were circulating.

Under pressure from the SEC, the NYSE announced in June 2003 that it would provide information about Grasso's compensation. It had earlier agreed to a broad reexamination of its own governance procedures. Until June, the NYSE compensation committee included a number of CEOs of the largest brokerage firms that the NYSE regulates. As a result of increased public scrutiny, several of these members resigned from the committee, including David Komansky of Merrill-Lynch, James Cayne of Bear Stearns, and Henry M. Paulson Jr. of Goldman Sachs. The chair of the compensation committee, Kenneth G. Langone, the director and founder of Home Depot, on whose board his longtime friend Richard Grasso sat, also stepped down. The reconstituted compensation committee appointed former New York State comptroller and unsuccessful Democratic candidate for governor, H. Carl McCall, as its new chairman.

The board of directors of the NYSE had a meeting scheduled for August 7, 2003. Henry Paulson, who had vigorously opposed Grasso's requests to withdraw his accumulated retirement and other benefits while he was still employed, informed Grasso that he would not attend the meeting due to a previously scheduled vacation. Although Paulson claims Grasso assured him on two occasions that his compensation would not be on the agenda for the August meeting, Grasso's compensation was added to the agenda on the morning of August 7. Paulson and several other members who were well versed in the details of the pay package were absent from the meeting (Laurance D. Fink, CEO of BlackRock, Inc., and Herbert M. Allison Jr., CEO of TIAA-CREF, both new members of the compensation committee). In addition, the compensation consultants who had been hired by the NYSE to help board members understand the more arcane aspects of Grasso's deal were not at the meeting. The directors who were at the meeting received a two-page summary of Grasso's compensation, and McCall informed the board that Grasso had accumulated $139.5 million in pension and deferred salary benefits. He also told the board that Grasso wanted the right to start withdrawing these benefits while he was still employed by the exchange. Although several board members questioned the size of the payout (including Phillip J. Purcell, the CEO of Morgan Stanley, and Madeleine K. Albright, former secretary of state), the board members in attendance voted to give Grasso the right to withdraw his pension and deferred salary benefits before he retired.

On August 27, the NYSE issued a statement disclosing that Grasso's annual salary was at least $2.4 million; that he had built up savings and retirement benefits of $139.5 million that the exchange had agreed he could withdraw immediately; and that it had extended his contract by two years, to May 2007. Many NYSE members were stunned. The exchange had imposed higher fees three times in the prior three-year period, claiming that the fee increases were needed to pay for regulatory costs and new technology. Now some of the members began to think that Grasso was also a prime beneficiary of the fee increase. The disclosure was also poorly received by the city of New York, where the NYSE was trying to win construction subsidies.

*(Continued)*

(Inside Story *continued*)

On September 2, William Donaldson, chairman of the SEC and Grasso's predecessor at the NYSE, wrote to the exchange, "The pay package raises serious questions regarding the effectiveness of the NYSE's current governance structure." He included a long list of questions about Grasso's pay package. He also asked for information about how the pay package affected the exchange's profits and how it was paid for, as well as minutes of the relevant meetings of the compensation committee, how the members were chosen, and whether any of them had financial relationships with Grasso.

A week later, during a telephonic board meeting to discuss when and how McCall should respond to the SEC's information request, McCall dropped a bombshell: Grasso was entitled to another $48 million in deferred pay. After a lengthy discussion in which board pressure was applied, Grasso reluctantly agreed to give up the $48 million. The NYSE announced the additional $48 million obligation on September 9, along with Grasso's decision to forgo it.

Additional details concerning Grasso's compensation were made available over the next several weeks. Beginning in 1998, Grasso's employment provided a guaranteed return on all of his deferred compensation. As market interest rates dropped, the 8 percent guarantee became highly advantageous, allowing Grasso to accumulate huge sums in his deferred compensation accounts. Also, during his tenure, the NYSE's executive compensation policy had changed from being on a par with other quasi-regulatory bodies to being comparable with the major brokerage houses. Grasso received salary and bonus of $15.1 million in 2001 and total compensation of $31.3 million. Although his compensation in 2002 went down to $8.5 million in salary and bonus, it was still larger than the pay and bonuses of eight CEOs at publicly held companies with whom Chicago law firm Vedder Price Kaufman & Kammholz compared Grasso after it was hired by the NYSE to conduct a review in 2002. His 2002 total compensation of about $12 million topped that of all but five of the CEOs.[58] Copies of Grasso's employment contract showed that the exchange also supplied him with a car and driver, use of a private plane and bodyguards, and paid memberships in various clubs. The contract also required the exchange to pay for his wife's "reasonable expenses" when she joined him on his travels.[59]

58. Gary Strauss, *Grasso's Pay Beat His Peers',* USA TODAY, Sept. 16, 2003, http://www.usatoday.com/money/markets/us/2003-09-16-grassopay_x.htm.

59. Greg Farrell et al., *Glasnost Puts Grasso Under Burning-Hot Spotlight,* USA TODAY, Sept. 11, 2003, http://www.usatoday.com/money/markets/us/2003-09-11-grasso_x.htm.

Outrage about Grasso's compensation continued to grow. Sean Harrigan, president of the California Public Employees Retirement System, the nation's largest public pension fund, stated, "We are absolutely incensed. At a time in our history when the N.Y.S.E. should be a model for best corporate behavior, we are shocked and dismayed." Alan G. Hevesi, comptroller of the State of New York and manager of the country's second largest pension fund, said, "Mr. Grasso is a regulator among other things. You create the perception of a conflict of interest when those that you regulate pay you $200 million over time."[60]

On September 17, the beleaguered NYSE board met in an emergency session and voted to ask for Grasso's resignation. When the meeting ended, Grasso announced that he had agreed to resign. Following Grasso's resignation, ten of the Wall Street executives on the twenty-five member board agreed to step down.

In February 2004, Acting Chair of the NYSE John Reed demanded that Grasso return $120 million to the exchange. Grasso refused, citing the approval that an "all star" team of corporate directors had given to his contract. His lawyer has also hinted that Grasso may sue for the rest of the money that is owed to him.[61]

Securities regulators who are trying to get back Grasso's millions are looking into what took place at the August 7, 2003 board meeting. During April 2004, investigators from the SEC questioned Kenneth G. Langone, chair of the compensation committee during the years that Grasso received his highest compensation, about his role in setting Grasso's pay. In May 2004, New York State Attorney General Eliot Spitzer filed a lawsuit against Grasso and Langone, demanding more than $100 million on the basis that the pay package was unreasonable and not commensurate with Grasso's duties under New York law on nonprofits.

Grasso has maintained that he never influenced the board's compensation decisions. Indeed, there is no evidence of any specific quid pro quo between Grasso and the executives on the board who set his compensation. Nevertheless, Grasso's compensation raises questions about why the NYSE played virtually no role in uncovering the Enron, WorldCom, and other scandals that shook many of the companies listed on the exchange.

60. Landon Thomas, *Officials in 2 States Urge Big Board Chief to Quit,* N.Y. TIMES, Sept. 17, 2003, at A1.

61. Landon Thomas Jr., *Regulators Said to Be Focusing on Board's Vote for Grasso Pay,* N.Y. TIMES, Mar. 26, 2004, at C1.

*(Continued)*

(Inside Story *continued*)

The NYSE also left it to state and federal authorities to pursue its broker members over various schemes to defraud investors. As Senator John Edwards stated at the time of Grasso's resignation:

> Dick Grasso's pay package is extraordinarily excessive, but the amount is just a symptom of the real problem. The real problem is that the board of the New York Stock Exchange has operated like a clubhouse, with no accountability to anybody except itself. Instead of setting an example for corporate America, the board has become a symbol of what's wrong at too many corporations.[62]

62. *Grasso Out As NYSE Chairman,* CNNMoney, Sept. 18, 2003, http://money.cnn.com/2003/09/17/markets/nyse_grasso/?cnn=yes.

## KEY WORDS AND PHRASES

alternative minimum tax (AMT) 790
clawback provision 794
defined benefit pension plan 801
defined contribution pension plan 801
employee stock ownership plan (ESOP) 800
employee stock purchase plan (ESPP) 788
exercise period 787
401(k) plan 801
grant price 787
incentive stock option (ISO) 788
nonpension benefit plan 800
nonqualified stock option (NSO) 788
optionee 787
phantom stock 798
pump and dump 795
restricted stock 796
Section 83(b) election 796
6&1 repricing 793
slow-motion swap 793
spread 789
stock appreciation rights (SARs) 798
stock option 787
strike price 787
substantial risk of forfeiture 796
underwater 790
vesting restrictions 787

## QUESTIONS AND CASE PROBLEMS

1. While attending Georgia Tech, Alan, Brian, and Diane conceived of an innovative design for a hospital management software system, but they did not actually write the code. At the time, they talked about starting a business after graduation, but there was no formal agreement. Four months after graduation, Alan and Brian formed a company to develop the system. They initially took the position that Diane was not entitled to share in the new enterprise because of the enormous amount of work that would be required to develop the code and make it commercially viable. Nevertheless, their lawyer suggested reaching an agreement with Diane, whereby she would receive a 5 percent equity interest in the new company in exchange for any rights she might have in the technology.

   Alan is a brilliant engineer. He prefers to speak machine language, rather than English. He has not been in a hospital since a week after his birth. As long as he has plenty of Diet Coke, he is happy to program computers 24/7. He will stick with a programming challenge until he has mastered it. Brian dropped out of medical school a semester before graduating. Although he was a brilliant student, he was searching for a way to cure people in a fashion that would enable him to leverage his ability to serve more than one patient at a time. Brian has great ideas, but he has a problem with commitment. He has already begun to wonder how soon he will leave this project and move on to something else.

   Will Alan and Brian react differently to their lawyer's advice? If so, how and why? Should Alan and Brian accept their lawyer's advice? What risks do they face if they do not accept the advice?

2. Anuj and Ying-Mei have formed a corporation to exploit a new software program conceived of, and written in large part by, Ying-Mei. Anuj and Ying-Mei met while Anuj was pursuing his MBA and Ying-Mei was obtaining a PhD in electrical engineering. During the two years that Anuj was in business school, he and Ying-Mei worked hard on their venture. Anuj engaged in extensive market research to validate the need for the software program and wrote a detailed set of functional specifications based on his

market research. Ying-Mei wrote design specifications based on the functional specifications and then wrote the code for the software. While Ying-Mei was writing the code, Anuj wrote the business plan for their company.

Anuj and Ying-Mei met with counsel during the summer after Anuj's first year of business school, and they agreed that they would each purchase 1 million shares of common stock in Nucorp at a price of $.01 per share. Because they agreed that they had already provided significant value to the venture, they also established that their stock would be 25 percent vested on the date of purchase and that another 25 percent would vest on the first anniversary, which would occur right after Anuj's graduation from business school. Ying-Mei wanted to be rewarded for her contribution of the program to the venture, and Anuj agreed to give her an additional 25 percent of vesting on the date that she contributed the software program to Nucorp.

As a result, when Anuj and Ying-Mei started talking to venture capitalists after Anuj's graduation, Anuj was 50 percent vested in his stock, and Ying-Mei was 75 percent vested. After several months of meetings, Enlightened Ventures presented Anuj and Ying-Mei with a term sheet, pursuant to which Enlightened Ventures agreed to provide Nucorp with the $5 million seed round of funding they were seeking, in exchange for preferred stock that would convert into 2.5 million shares of common stock. The term sheet provided that Anuj and Ying-Mei would have to revest in their vested stock. In other words, each of them would have to agree that their 1 million shares would be unvested, subject to 25 percent vesting on the first anniversary of the venture financing, with 2.08 percent vesting each month thereafter so that their stock would be fully vested four years after the venture financing.

Anuj and Ying-Mei are, of course, not happy about revesting their stock, especially because they believe they have already made significant contributions to the venture. Enlightened Ventures made it clear, however, that this condition is a "deal-breaker" and that they are lucky to have found a top tier venture-capital group that is willing to make a substantial investment in the company. Anuj and Ying-Mei are concerned that Enlightened Ventures may terminate them before they are vested in any of their stock. They are also concerned that if Nucorp is acquired before they are fully vested, the acquiring corporation will already have a CEO and a chief technical officer and, therefore, they may have no place in the merged company. What kinds of compromise positions might Anuj and Ying-Mei want to discuss with Enlightened Ventures regarding the vesting of their founders' stock?

3. In July 1996, Oracle signed a letter agreement with Pier Carlo Falotti to work from Geneva, Switzerland, as senior vice president for Europe, the Middle East, and Africa for $1 million in annual salary. The letter provided that Oracle would grant Falotti an initial option to purchase 600,000 shares of Oracle stock and that once Falotti accepted Oracle's offer, they would enter into an employment contract subject to Swiss law. Oracle and Falotti subsequently signed several additional letter agreements and an employment agreement, which were governed by Swiss law. There were no references to stock options in the subsequent letters or the agreement. During Falotti's employment, all stock option grants were governed by Oracle's 1991 Long-Term Equity Incentive Plan. This Plan, along with a Grant Agreement and an Exercise Notice Agreement, collectively formed Oracle's Stock Option Agreement and included a California choice-of-law provision. The Stock Option Agreement also provided that all disputes regarding stock option grants would be decided by Oracle's compensation committee and that the committee's decisions were binding on both Oracle and the employee.

   On May 31, 2000, four days before his options were to vest, Falotti was terminated. However, Falotti told Oracle's CEO that under Swiss law, he could not be fired because he was ill and unable to work. Oracle's compensation committee met and unanimously decided Falotti had "ceased to be employed" on May 31, 2000, and could not exercise any stock options after that date. Oracle filed a declaratory relief action seeking a declaration that Falotti could not exercise the $10 million of options that vested after May 31, 2000, and that he was not entitled to any stock option damages in lieu of the unexercised options. Falotti counterclaimed that Swiss law provided that before he could be terminated, there was a two-month notice period during which he was entitled to wages and benefits. What will Oracle argue? What will Falotti argue? Who wins? [*Oracle Corp. v Falotti*, 319 F.3d 1106 (9th Cir. 2003).]

4. In February 1998, Robert Phansalkar, a Wall Street executive, joined a small merchant banking firm,

Anderson Weinroth & Company (AWC). During his tenure, AWC sold Phansalkar more than 600,000 shares of its client, Millennium Cell, as part of an initial public offering. Phansalkar also represented AWC on the board of directors of several client companies, including Osicom Technologies, a public company, and Zip Global Network, a privately held company based in India. Both Osicom and Zip granted Phansalkar stock options. As required, Osicom described the stock options in a filing with the Securities and Exchange Commission, but privately held Zip was not required to make a public filing. In June 2000, Phansalkar left AWC to become president of Osicom. In September 2000, AWC filed a lawsuit against Phansalkar, claiming that he had failed to disclose the stock options he received as AWC's representative on the Osicom and Zip boards. A month later Phansalkar filed a counterclaim, arguing that AWC had illegally converted his Millennium shares, worth $4.4 million, so that they would become AWC property. Did Phansalkar have a legal or ethical obligation to disclose his stock option grants to AWC? If so, on what basis? [*Phansalkar v. Anderson Weinroth & Co.,* 344 F.3d 184 (2d Cir. 2003).]

5. Carmine Cicio received employer-sponsored health insurance coverage through Vytra Health Care, an HMO. In March 1997, Cicio was diagnosed with multiple myeloma. In January 1998, his doctor, Edward Samuel, asked Vytra to approve a double stem cell transplant, describing the procedure as medically necessary and possibly lifesaving. Vytra denied the request on the basis that the procedure was "experimental/investigational" and not covered under Cicio's policy. Cicio, through Dr. Samuel, appealed the decision. By the time Vytra approved a single stem cell transplant, the window for effective treatment had passed, and Cicio died about six weeks later. His widow sued Vytra in the New York Supreme Court, alleging eighteen causes of action, most of them under state law. The defendants first removed the case to the U.S. District Court for the Eastern District of New York, contending that Mrs. Cicio's claims were covered under ERISA, and then moved to dismiss based on the preemption doctrine. Does Mrs. Cicio have the right to sue Vytra under state tort law, or is her action preempted by ERISA? [*Cicio v. Vytra Healthcare,* 385 F.3d 156 (2d Cir. 2004).]

6. On January 1, 2001, Claudia Allen, an employee of BioGen, Inc., is granted an incentive stock option to purchase 100 shares of BioGen common stock at a strike price of $10 per share, the fair market value of BioGen stock at the time of the grant. On March 20, 2004, Claudia exercises her stock options when the price of BioGen stock is $15 per share. What are the consequences of Claudia's exercise if she sells the stock at $17 per share on or prior to March 20, 2005? What are the consequences of Claudia's exercise if she sells the stock at $17 per share after March 20, 2005?

7. Ray Friedman, the chief scientist and vice president of research & development, recently resigned from BKE Systems, Inc., a California corporation and developer of CRM software headquartered in San Carlos, California. While employed at BKE's California headquarters, Ray was in charge of the development of BKE's next generation wireless CRM software program, ZAPit, and he supervised a team of twenty engineers who were committed to the project. Five years ago, when hired by BKE, Ray had signed an employment proprietary information and inventions agreement with BKE. In his resignation letter, Ray indicated that he had accepted a position as chief scientist at IBM, which was not a direct competitor of BKE.

   At the time he left, Ray was holding a fully vested stock option for 200,000 shares of common stock, with a strike price of $1 per share. Ray exercised his options immediately prior to giving notice of his termination to the company, and the stock was trading at $12 per share on the date of exercise. Ray's stock option agreement provided that, upon exercise, he would certify that he was in compliance with a cancellation clause that prohibited him from working for a competitor and specified that he had to pay back to BKE his gains and payments from exercise of the options if he violated that clause during the two-year period after exercise. The stock option agreement also provided that the plan and all determinations made pursuant to it would be governed by the law of Massachusetts.

   Ray worked for IBM for fifteen months before joining Ceeboo Systems, one of BKE's principal competitors, eighteen months after terminating his employment with BKE. Ron Diehl, BKE's CEO, was not happy to lose Ray in the first place, but he is irate that Ray is going to work for Ceeboo. Ron wants to do everything that he can to stop Ray from working for Ceeboo. What can Ron do?

8. Chelsea Lamar joined Hitek, Inc., a venture-financed start-up, in 2000, immediately after graduating from

college. Her offer letter from Hitek states that her employment is "at will" and can be terminated by Hitek at any time, with or without cause. Chelsea turned down better paying consulting and investment banking opportunities to get in on the ground floor of a young, fast-growing company. As compensation, she received a nominal salary and stock options. Because the company's product required three years to bring to market, the options did not vest for three years. This meant that Chelsea would forfeit all of the stock options if she left the company before 2003.

In 2002, Hitek began having serious problems. Even though the project was on schedule and was expected to be a huge success, costs skyrocketed, and Hitek's investors demanded a significant reduction in operating expenses. As a result, Chelsea's employment was terminated. Although she had performed well, she was the most recent person hired. Chelsea has retained legal counsel. On what basis can Chelsea sue Hitek? Will she prevail? How could Hitek have structured the relationship to minimize this type of litigation?

9. Outboard Marine Corporation (OMC) filed a voluntary petition for Chapter 11 bankruptcy relief, shut down all of its facilities, and terminated the majority of its 6,500 employees without prior notice. Michael Vogt, on behalf of several employees terminated by OMC, brought an action under the WARN Act against OMC's eight investor companies, arguing that the investors were, together with OMC, joint employers of the plaintiffs. The investors moved to dismiss on the ground that they were not employers under WARN. Several of the investors in OMC (a) owned or controlled the majority of OMC's stock, (b) controlled all OMC transactions, (c) placed some of their members on OMC's board of directors, and (d) influenced OMC's decision to file for bankruptcy and carry out a mass layoff. As the agency delegated to establish regulations and administer the WARN Act, the U.S. Department of Labor has adopted regulations defining "employer" in relation to related entities and independent contractors. Such regulations state:

> Under existing legal rules, independent contractors and subsidiaries which are wholly or partially owned by a parent company are treated as separate employers or as part of the parent or contracting company depending upon the degree of their independence from the parent. Some of the factors to be considered in making this determination are (i) common ownership, (ii) common directors and/or officers, (iii) de facto exercise of control, (iv) unity of personnel policies emanating from a common source, and (v) the dependency of operations.

What arguments would Vogt make? What arguments would defendants make? Will the court grant defendant's motion to dismiss? [*Vogt v. Greenmarine Holding, LLC*, 318 F. Supp. 2d 136 (S.D.N.Y. 2004).]

## MANAGER'S DILEMMA

10. You are the president of Qualex, a publicly held company that was founded in 1990. Qualex is beginning to experience record growth and is having an excellent year. Each employment offer by Qualex includes language stating that "the employee will have an opportunity to acquire shares of Qualex stock through our Stock Option Plan." The letters also state: "We are convinced we have made an excellent decision in selecting you. We know your contributions will confirm our expectation that you will find yourself involved in many important ways in the future success of our company."

Qualex has a stock option plan pursuant to which it grants options to all employees. The terms and conditions of the plan are described in detail in a plan document drafted by Qualex management and approved by Qualex's directors and stockholders. The plan document is described in a plan prospectus that was created pursuant to federal securities laws and distributed to optionholders. The prospectus describes in lay terms all features of the stock option plan, including the participants' rights and obligations, vesting schedules, tax implications, and numerous other aspects of the plan. The vesting provisions typically provide for vesting over a five-year period. Only vested options can be exercised, and if the employee loses his or her position with Qualex for any reason, whether voluntarily or involuntarily, the employee also loses his or her right to exercise the unvested options.

The Qualex plan includes a "change of control" clause, which states that if there is a change in control of a majority of the company's stock without board approval, then all vesting schedules on the outstanding stock options accelerate and the options become immediately exercisable. The effect of this provision is to act as an antitakeover device. It forces an entity wanting to gain control of a corporation by acquiring a controlling interest in its stock to negotiate with the company's board to obtain its approval of any such takeover. Without such approval, all options would vest and be immediately exercised, adding more shares to the market and requiring a larger expenditure by the acquirer to purchase a controlling interest of stock.

About a year ago Qualex began discussions with a large German corporation, Henrikson, concerning a possible sale of its network equipment manufacturing division to Henrikson. During this period, Qualex continued its practice of granting its employees additional stock options with five-year vesting schedules in order to induce them to remain as Qualex employees. At no time did Qualex disclose to its employees that it was negotiating the possible sale of the network division to Henrikson. In fact, earlier this year, Qualex's CEO stated at an all-hands meeting of Qualex employees that the network division was not for sale and would not be sold. Since then the price of Qualex's stock has been rising and many Qualex employees have been becoming instant millionaires, on paper, from the stock options they were granted. Qualex is close to reaching an agreement in principle to sell the assets of the network division to Henrikson. Henrikson has also agreed to offer employment to the 1,000 Qualex employees employed by this division. Henrikson does not have a stock option plan for its employees and has not agreed to either assume the Qualex stock options or issue equivalent Henrikson stock options to the Qualex employees of the network division.

Qualex's CEO has asked you for input regarding how to deal with the employees of the network division. Will these employees have a cause of action against Qualex in the event that their stock options are terminated as a result of Henrikson's acquisition of the division? Does Qualex have an ethical obligation to the terminated employees? How might you be able to structure the acquisition to address the concerns of these employees? What, if anything, might you have done differently to avoid this situation?

## INTERNET SOURCES

| | |
|---|---|
| The National Center for Employee Ownership (NCEO) is a private, nonprofit membership and research organization that provides accurate, unbiased information on employee stock ownership plans, broadly granted stock options and related programs, and ownership culture. | http://www.nceo.org |
| Financial Accounting Standards Board | http://www.fasb.org |
| The Global Equity Organization is a member-founded and member-driven nonprofit organization that provides a forum for members to exchange information related to the use of equity-based compensation in the global community. | http://www.globalequity.org |
| BenefitsLink maintains a website to support people who design and run employee benefit plans in the United States, whether sponsored by private or governmental employers. | http://benefitslink.com |
| The ESOP Association is a national nonprofit association with a focus on ESOPs and employee ownership. The Association is a source of educational materials for the management of employee-owned companies. | http://www.esopassociation.org |
| The AFL–CIO website on executive pay—Executive PayWatch—tracks executive compensation, highlights shareholder proposals dealing with excessive executive compensation, and identifies directors on compensation committees who have conflicts of interest with the executives they are overseeing. | http://www.paywatch.org |

# UNIT VI

# SECURITIES AND FINANCIAL TRANSACTIONS

CHAPTER 22

# Public and Private Offerings of Securities

## INTRODUCTION

### Raising Capital Through Securities Offerings

Most businesses reach a certain point at which the founders' initial capital investment and ongoing bank loans are insufficient for continued growth. At this juncture, the directors and managers of the company must decide whether to rein in the company's growth consistent with its existing capital asset base or to sell an interest in the company to raise capital for continued expansion. Although entrepreneurs often turn first to family and friends and wealthy individual investors (*angels*), then to venture capitalists, many companies will eventually seek to raise capital through an initial public offering of the company's shares. Even those companies that can internally generate the cash flow for growth may decide to sell securities to spread the concentration of risk in the business venture and to give the founders and early investors liquidity.

Because registered public offerings are very expensive (often costing more than $900,000 in out-of-pocket expenses alone), sales of securities to private investors or venture capitalists are almost always structured to be exempt from the federal registration requirements. Whether the directors and managers of a company seek an exemption or go through the public offering process, they must understand and comply with federal and state securities laws. Penalties for noncompliance include damages, fines, and imprisonment.

### Chapter Overview

This chapter first provides an overview of the federal and state statutory schemes that regulate the offer and sale of securities. It then defines the key terms "security," "offer," and "sale" under the Securities Act of 1933 (the 1933 Act).

Next, the chapter describes the public offering process, including the registration of securities, the role of an underwriter, the importance of due diligence, and the preparation of the registration statement, and provides a managerial timeline for a public offering. Several of the most relied-on exemptions from registration for offerings by the issuer, including the private offering and small business exemptions, are then outlined. An exhibit listing the key elements of certain exemptions is also provided.

The chapter goes on to discuss exemptions for secondary offerings by shareholders, the restrictions on the resale of registered and unregistered securities, offerings outside the United States under Regulation S, and sales to qualified institutional buyers under Rule 144A. The periodic reporting and certain other requirements under the Securities Exchange Act of 1934 (the 1934 Act) are identified.

The chapter then highlights liability for failure to meet the registration and prospectus-delivery requirements under Section 12(a)(1) of the 1933 Act and for misstatements or omissions in the registration statement. The discussion focuses on Section 11, under which issuers are strictly liable for misstatements or omissions in a registration statement and certain officers, all directors, accountants, and underwriters are liable if they fail to act with due diligence. The chapter explains who may sue, who may be sued, the elements of liability, the available defenses, and the calculation of damages. It also provides guidelines for due diligence.

Then the discussion turns to Section 12(a)(2) of the 1933 Act, which provides a remedy for any person who purchases a registered or unregistered security in a public offering by means of a misleading prospectus or oral communication. The broader antifraud provisions contained in Section 10(b) of the 1934 Act and Rule 10b-5 (which apply to both registered and exempt offerings of securities) and the prohibitions against selective disclosure in Regulation FD are discussed in Chapter 23. This chapter concludes with a discussion of criminal penalties for violations of the 1933 Act.

## Federal Statutory Scheme

The two principal federal acts that regulate securities transactions and issuers, the Securities Act of 1933 and the Securities Exchange Act of 1934, were adopted during the depths of the Great Depression. These and subsequent acts embodied three beliefs: (1) investors should be provided with all essential information prior to investing in speculative ventures, (2) corporate insiders should not be allowed to abuse their position and use nonpublic information concerning their companies to their own financial advantage, and (3) misled investors should receive adequate relief even in the absence of common law fraud.

### The 1933 Act

In adopting the 1933 Act, the U.S. Congress sought to ensure adequate disclosure to investors of material information about the issuer and its business and the offering. The Act requires that promoters of securities offerings register them with the Securities and Exchange Commission (SEC), an agency of the U.S. government, and provide to prospective purchasers a prospectus containing material information about the issuer and the offering, unless the security or the type of transaction is exempt from registration.

Congress rejected suggestions that it also regulate the content or quality of securities offerings. As a result, investors are not protected from making highly speculative or foolish investments. The 1933 Act requires only that they be advised of all material facts before they invest their money.

In addition to requiring registration, the 1933 Act expressly creates private rights of action for certain violations of its provisions. This means that in addition to public enforcement by the SEC or criminal proceedings by the U.S. Attorney's Office, any investor can bring a private suit for damages.

### The 1934 Act

The 1934 Act sought to build upon the 1933 Act by implementing a policy of continuous disclosure. Companies of a certain size and with a certain number of shareholders or whose stock is traded on a national

HISTORICAL PERSPECTIVE

## GENESIS OF THE 1933 ACT

After the stock market crash of 1929, distrust of the nation's financial markets was widespread. Regulations governing securities offerings in the United States stem from the public and governmental outrage at the markets' excesses. According to Representative (later Speaker of the House) Sam Rayburn:

> Millions of citizens have been swindled into exchanging their savings for worthless stocks. The fraudulent promoter has taken an incredible toll from confiding people. . . .
>
> These hired officials of our great corporations who permitted, who promoted, who achieved the extravagant expansion of the financial structure of their respective companies today present a pitiable spectacle. Five years ago they arrogated to themselves the greatest privileges. They scorned the interference of the Government. They dealt with their stockholders in the most arbitrary fashion. They called upon the people to bow down to them as the real rulers of the country. Safe from the pitiless publicity of Government supervision, unrestrained by Federal statute, free from any formal control, these few men, proud, arrogant, and blind, drove the country to financial ruin. Some of them are fugitives from justice in foreign lands; some of them have committed suicide; some of them are under indictment; some of them are in prison; all of them are in terror of the consequences of their own deeds.[a]

a. House Consideration, Amendment and Passage of H.R. 5480, May 5, 1932, 77 CONG. REC. 2910, 2918 (1933), as reprinted in 1 FED. SEC. L. LEGIS. HIST. 1933–1982, at 2948 (1983).

securities exchange are required to file periodic reports with the SEC. The 1934 Act also contains stringent antifraud provisions and implements filing requirements for insiders dealing in their own company's stock. In addition, the 1934 Act established a framework for the self-regulation of the securities industry under the ultimate supervision of the SEC.

All of the securities acts have been amended numerous times since their adoption. Exhibit 22.1 briefly describes the main sections of the 1933 and 1934 Acts. More detailed excerpts from both acts and the SEC regulations adopted thereafter can be found in Appendices J and K of this book.

## The Private Securities Litigation Reform Act of 1995

The Private Securities Litigation Reform Act of 1995 (the Litigation Reform Act)[1] was designed to correct perceived abuses in private securities litigation, particularly class actions that coerced settlements and thereby increased the cost of raising capital and chilled corporate disclosure to investors. The Act included a variety of procedural provisions designed to prevent the filing of frivolous suits by so-called professional plaintiffs who often owned a limited number of shares in many companies and stood ready to lend their names to class-action complaints they often had not even read. The Act introduced the idea that the "most adequate plaintiff" should be the lead plaintiff and select counsel to represent the class. There is a rebuttable presumption that the plaintiff with the largest financial interest in the relief being sought by the class is the most adequate.

The Litigation Reform Act limited discovery to prevent "fishing expedition" lawsuits designed to force the defendants to settle frivolous claims to avoid the cost of discovery. Except in extraordinary circumstances, courts must stay discovery pending a ruling on a motion to dismiss the complaint.[2] Stricter and uniform pleading requirements require the investors to specify in the complaint each statement alleged to be misleading and the reason or reasons the statement is misleading. The plaintiffs also must plead and then prove that the misstatement or omission alleged in the complaint actually caused their loss. They must also specifically allege facts giving rise to a "strong inference" that the defendant acted with the required state of mind. Thus, in securities fraud cases under Section 10(b), which require *scienter*, the plaintiffs must allege facts giving rise to a strong inference of fraudulent intent on the part of the defendant. The combination of the stricter pleading requirements and the staying of discovery pending a decision on a motion to dismiss makes it more likely that defendants will be able to resolve frivolous claims more quickly and cheaply by winning motions to dismiss before incurring the time and expense of extensive discovery.

1. Pub. L. No. 104-67, 109 Stat. 737 (1995) (codified in scattered sections of 15 U.S.C.).

2. The Delaware Court of Chancery permitted a shareholder of a company defending a federal securities lawsuit to obtain access to corporate records and documents pursuant to Section 220 of the Delaware Corporation Law even though the shareholder might be part of the class ultimately certified to sue the corporation.

**EXHIBIT 22.1** **Important Sections of the 1933 and 1934 Acts**

**1933 Act**

- *Section 2*—defines terms, including security, offer, sale, and underwriter.
- *Sections 3 and 4*—list exempt securities and describe exempt transactions.
- *Section 5*—requires the registration of all securities offered and sold in the United States (unless an exemption from registration is available) and the delivery of a prospectus.
- *Sections 6–8 and 10*—outline the general procedures of the registration process and detail the guidelines for the registration statement and the accompanying prospectus.
- *Sections 11 and 12*—describe the penalties, elements of liability, damages, and parties held liable for violation of the 1933 Act.

**1934 Act**

- *Section 10*—prohibits the use of manipulative and deceptive devices in connection with the purchase or sale of securities.
- *Section 12*—lists the reporting requirements for registered public companies.
- *Section 16*—provides the reporting requirements for insiders (including directors, officers, and principal shareholders) and the limitations on insider transactions.

Rule 11 of the Federal Rules of Civil Procedure, which is designed to deter bad faith claims, provides for sanctions against an attorney who signs a complaint that the attorney does not reasonably believe has merit. The Litigation Reform Act gave Rule 11 new teeth by requiring courts to include in the record, at the conclusion of the action, specific findings as to whether all parties and all attorneys complied with each requirement of Rule 11(b). If the action was brought for an improper purpose, was not warranted by existing law, was legally frivolous, or was not supported by facts, then the Act creates a presumption that the appropriate sanction is an award to the prevailing party of all attorneys' fees and costs incurred in the case.

The Litigation Reform Act generally eliminated joint and several liability in cases under Section 10(b) of the 1934 Act for defendants who did not commit knowing violations and requires such defendants to pay only their "fair share" of the damages, that is, the portion attributable to their percentage of responsibility. Outside directors are given the same protection for suits under Section 11 of the 1933 Act as a way to encourage capable outsiders to serve on corporate boards.

The Litigation Reform Act also imposed new requirements for independent public accountants auditing the financial statements of publicly traded companies. These requirements, which are designed to result in early detection and disclosure of fraud, are discussed more fully in Chapter 23.

Finally, the Litigation Reform Act created a statutory safe harbor for written and oral forward-looking statements by issuers and certain persons retained by or acting on behalf of the issuer. This provision is discussed further in the sections dealing with liability under Sections 11 and 12(a)(2) of the 1933 Act. Its application to fraud cases under Section 10(b) of the 1934 Act and Rule 10b-5 is discussed in Chapter 23.

## The Securities Litigation Uniform Standards Act of 1998

In 1998, Congress passed the Securities Litigation Uniform Standards Act,[3] which limited plaintiffs' ability to bring securities fraud cases in state court by requiring removal of the cases to federal court in many circumstances. Parallel proceedings had become more prevalent since the passage of the Litigation Reform Act because most state laws do not provide companies and their officers and directors the protections afforded by that act. In the wake of the 1998 legislation, only state securities cases that are not class actions and do not involve more than fifty plaintiffs can be tried in state court. By limiting the availability of this end run around the Litigation Reform Act, Congress sought to create national standards for fraud cases brought against companies traded on the national securities exchanges (such as the New York Stock Exchange and the Nasdaq Stock Market).

The so-called *Delaware carve-out* permits shareholders to bring a state law class-action suit against a corporation and its directors for breach of preexisting common law fiduciary disclosure obligations. Because directors of a Delaware corporation have a fiduciary duty to disclose fully and fairly all material information within their control and to avoid misleading partial disclaimers, shareholders of USA Networks, Inc. were permitted to bring a class action in New York state court based on the allegation that the board had advised stockholders that it was going into television merchandising in Italy but failed to advise them of the risks involved.[4]

## The Sarbanes–Oxley Act of 2002

In the wake of Enron's collapse, Congress hastily, and by an impressive margin (99–0 in the Senate and 423–3 in the House), passed the most sweeping securities legislation since the 1934 Act. The Sarbanes–Oxley Act of 2002[5] (SOX) contains eleven titles, which attempt to eradicate specific problems that Congress believed caused numerous corporate debacles around the turn of the millennium.

Sarbanes–Oxley created the Public Company Accounting Oversight Board (PCAOB) to regulate and inspect the public accounting firms that provide audit reports for publicly traded companies that are (1) registered under Section 12 of the 1934 Act, (2) required to file reports under Section 15(d) of that act, or (3) have filed a registration statement under the 1933 Act. The PCAOB also has the authority to set auditing standards for public company audits and to adjudicate issues related thereto.

In an attempt to mitigate the conflicts of interest present when accounting firms provide auditing services to corporate clients for whom they also do consulting, tax planning, or other accounting work, SOX prohibits the

3. 15 U.S.C. § 77 p(d).

4. Lalondriz v. USA Networks, Inc., No. 99 Civ. 1711 (RO) (S.D.N.Y. June 30, 1999). *Accord* Gibson v. PS Group Holdings, Inc., No. 00-CV-0372 W (RBB) (S.D. Cal. Mar. 8, 2000).

5. Pub. L. No. 107-204, 116 Stat. 745 (codified in scattered sections of 15, 18, 28, & 29 U.S.C.).

provision of nonaudit services to audit clients in all but very limited circumstances (see Appendix N). It also makes it illegal for any person to attempt to improperly influence the auditors.

In the most sweeping federal regulation of corporate governance to date, Sarbanes–Oxley:

- Mandated the composition and authority of audit committees at public companies.
- Required corporations to disclose whether they have a financial expert on their audit committee.
- Prohibited many types of personal loans to executives.
- Ordered that CEOs and CFOs forfeit certain bonuses and profits if their employer is required to restate its financial statements due to material noncompliance with securities laws.
- Generally prohibited insiders from trading during pension fund blackout periods.
- Required corporations to disclose whether they have a code of ethics applicable to senior financial officers and, if not, to disclose why not.
- Gave the SEC the authority to indefinitely prohibit "unfit" persons from serving as officers or directors of a public company.
- Required management to maintain internal controls to facilitate accurate financial reporting and disclosure and to have the adequacy of those controls certified by the auditors.

Sarbanes–Oxley also:

- Mandated enhanced financial disclosures in periodic reports.
- Provided for enhanced SEC review of periodic reports.
- Mandated additional disclosures of transactions involving directors, officers, and principal stockholders.
- Required more rapid disclosure of material changes in a reporting company's financial conditions or operations.
- Required CEO and CFO certification of the accuracy and completeness of SEC periodic reports, including the financial statements contained therein.

In an effort to reduce securities analysts' conflicts of interest, Sarbanes–Oxley created new, severe criminal penalties for those who defraud shareholders of publicly held corporations. It delayed the running of the statute of limitations on certain actions brought by defrauded investors, and it provided that debts incurred from judgments or settlements relating to securities fraud are nondischargeable in bankruptcy. SOX also required that auditors retain records relevant to financial audits for seven years after the completion of the audit.

Sarbanes–Oxley increased maximum fines for securities and mail and wire fraud by tens of millions of dollars and increased the maximum duration of imprisonment by as much as tenfold. SOX created stiff criminal penalties (as much as twenty years' imprisonment and a $5 million fine) for officers who certify noncompliant financial reports, with similarly severe penalties for tampering with records relevant to an official proceeding or otherwise impeding such a proceeding. The Act strongly urged CEOs to sign federal income tax returns.

Two sections of SOX protect whistleblowers and informants. Discriminating against or discharging an informant was made a criminal offense punishable by a substantial fine or imprisonment for as long as ten years, or both.

## SEC Rules and Regulations

Since Congress enacted the 1934 Act, the SEC has used its power as an administrative agency to adopt a number of rules and regulations. The SEC uses these rules and regulations to address some of the ambiguity of the securities acts, make case-specific exemptions, carry out informal discretionary actions, and conduct investigations regarding compliance with the securities acts.

For instance, in 1972, the SEC adopted Rule 144 to clarify the definition of the term "underwriter." In 1982, the SEC adopted Regulation D with rules that outlined the requirements and limitations for exempt private offerings and offerings by small businesses. Subsequently, it adopted Rule 701 to exempt offers and sales of securities pursuant to employee benefit plans. Regulation A was revised to make it easier for small businesses to raise capital without going through a public offering.

**INTERNATIONAL SNAPSHOT**

On most U.S. stock exchanges, foreign securities are traded in the form of American Depository Receipts (ADRs). The securities themselves are held by a financial institution called a depository, which issues the ADRs traded by foreign investors and handles any foreign-exchange transactions. This structure allows the foreign securities to trade at a per-share price level customary in the U.S. market. In addition, it allows investors to trade interests in foreign securities in compliance with U.S. clearance and settlement requirements.

*"I was spreading some risk around, and apparently it all wound up in your portfolio."*



## State Blue Sky Laws

In addition to the federal securities laws, state statutes called *blue sky laws* also regulate offerings and sales of securities. These laws were the precursors to federal securities regulation and were "aimed at promoters who 'would sell building lots in the blue sky in fee simple.'"[6] An issuer selling securities must comply not only with the federal securities laws but also with the securities laws of all of the states in which the securities are offered or sold. This usually includes the state where the issuer is headquartered, the state from which any offering materials are dispatched or where any oral offers are made, the state where the offerees have their domicile, and the state to which offering materials are sent.

Fortunately, many states, the District of Columbia, and Puerto Rico have adopted the Uniform Securities Act, so there is some consistency among state laws. Other states, including New York and California, have retained their own versions of securities regulatory schemes. As explained in Chapter 14, in some respects the state laws are stricter than their federal counterparts, yet as the U.S. Court of Appeals for the Seventh Circuit noted in *Mueller v. Sullivan*,[7] ignorance of these laws is no excuse.

Like the federal statutes, the Uniform Securities Act emphasizes disclosure as the primary means of protecting investors. Some states, however, authorize the securities administrator to deny a securities selling permit unless he or she finds that the issuer's plan of business and the proposed issuance of securities are fair, just, and equitable. Even if the state statute does not specifically include this provision, a state securities commissioner can usually deny registration or qualification to sell in that state until he or she is satisfied that the offering is fair. This process is referred to as *merit review*.

6. SEC v. Edwards, 540 U.S. 389 (2004).

7. 141 F.3d 1232 (7th Cir. 1998).

Congress passed the Capital Markets Efficiency Act of 1996[8] in part to provide more uniformity between federal and state securities regulation. The Act precludes states from requiring pre-offer and pre-sale notice filings and from imposing merit review requirements in connection with transactions involving only accredited investors pursuant to Rule 506 under Regulation D. States may require only the type of filing required by the SEC (including any amendments), a consent to service of process, and a filing fee. The law similarly preempted state registration requirements and merit review in connection with most initial public offerings registered with the SEC. It also provided federal preemption for the issuance of securities to "qualified purchasers." The SEC has proposed that the definition of "qualified purchasers" be the same as the one for "accredited investors" under Regulation D.

## Definition of Terms

It is necessary to define three basic terms used in the 1933 Act—security, offer, and sale. Their meanings in a securities law context may be different from their everyday meanings.

### Security

The term *security* for purposes of the 1933 Act—and most other securities statutes—is much broader than the common conception of the term. Section 2(1) of the 1933 Act defines a security as:

> any note, stock, treasury stock, bond, debenture, evidence of indebtedness, certificate of interest or participation in any profit-sharing agreement, collateral-trust certificate, preorganization certificate or subscription, transferable share, investment contract, voting-trust certificate, certificate of deposit for a security, fractional undivided interest in oil, gas, or other mineral rights, any put, call, straddle, option, or privilege on any security, certificate of deposit, or group or index of securities (including any interest therein or based on the value thereof), or any put, call, straddle, option, or privilege entered into on a national securities exchange relating to foreign currency, or, in general, any interest or instrument commonly known as a "security," or any certificate of interest or participation in, temporary or interim certificate for, receipt for, guarantee of, or warrant or right to subscribe to or purchase, any of the foregoing.

Because "security" is defined so broadly, the circumstances of a particular transaction must be analyzed to determine whether it does, in fact, involve a security and is subject to regulation.

Certain investments that are commonly agreed to be securities include the stock and bonds of public and private companies. Yet some investments, which by their name fall into the definition of securities, are not necessarily considered securities. An example is the stock in a cooperative association owning an apartment building; an occupant of the building owns shares of stock that are inextricably linked to the lease of a particular unit of the building. In *United Housing Foundation v. Forman*,[9] the U.S. Supreme Court held that because the dwelling was used as a place of habitation, the inducement to purchase was solely to acquire living space and not to invest for profit. Consequently, the Court ruled that the shares of stock were not securities under the 1933 Act.

#### *Investment Contract*

An investment may be characterized as a security even if it involves the transfer of an interest in real property or another physical asset. Any transaction that involves an investment of money in a common enterprise with profits to come solely from the efforts of others is deemed to be an *investment contract* and thus a security. This test was first enunciated in *SEC v. W.J. Howey Co.*[10] The U.S. Supreme Court held that the offer and sale of parcels of land bearing citrus trees, coupled with optional management contracts pursuant to which the promoter cared for the trees, constituted an investment contract and hence a security under Section 2(1) of the 1933 Act. The following case further elaborated on this test.

8. Pub. L. No. 104-290, 110 Stat. 3416 (1996).

9. 421 U.S. 837 (1975).

10. 328 U.S. 293 (1946).

A CASE IN POINT

## In the Language of the Court

**CASE 22.1**
**SEC v. Edwards**
*Supreme Court of the United States*
*540 U.S. 389 (2004).*

> **FACTS** Charles Edwards was the chair, CEO, and sole shareholder of ETS Payphones, Inc. Acting partly through a subsidiary also controlled by Edwards, ETS sold payphones to the public. The payphones were offered in a variety of packages, but virtually all purchasers chose a package that included a site lease, a five-year leaseback and

*(Continued)*

(Case 22.1 *continued)*

management agreement, and a buyback agreement, at a total cost of around $7,000. ETS guaranteed $82 per month (a 14 percent annual return) to purchasers under the leaseback and management agreement. ETS also promised to refund the full purchase price of the package at the end of the lease or within 180 days of the purchaser's request.

ETS boasted in its brochure that "[v]ery few business opportunities can offer the potential for ongoing revenue generation that is available in today's pay telephone industry." Unfortunately, the payphones did not generate enough revenue for ETS to make its payments to purchasers under the leaseback agreements. ETS was forced to rely on funds from new investors to meet its obligations and, in 2000, the company filed for bankruptcy.

The SEC brought an action alleging that Edwards and ETS had sold securities in violation of various provisions of the 1933 and 1934 Acts. Edwards argued that schemes offering a fixed rate of return are not investment contracts because (1) they do not give the purchasers capital appreciation or the earnings of the enterprise and (2) the return is not "derived solely from the efforts of others," because the purchasers have a contractual entitlement to the return.

**› ISSUE PRESENTED** For purposes of the federal securities laws, does a moneymaking scheme fall outside the definition of an investment contract simply because the promised rate of return is fixed rather than variable?

**› OPINION** O'CONNOR, J., writing on behalf of a unanimous U.S. Supreme Court:

"Congress' purpose in enacting the securities laws was to regulate investments, in whatever form they are made and by whatever name they are called." To that end, it enacted a broad definition of "security," sufficient "to encompass virtually any instrument that might be sold as an investment."...

The test for whether a particular scheme is an investment contract was established in our decision in *SEC v .W.J. Howey Co.*[11] We look to "whether the scheme involves an investment of money in a common enterprise with profits to come solely from the efforts of others." This definition "embodies a flexible rather than a static principle, one that is capable of adaptation to meet the countless and variable schemes devised by those who seek the use of the money of others on the promise of profits."

In reaching that result, we first observed that when Congress included "investment contract" in the definition of security, it "was using a term the meaning of which had been crystallized" by state courts' interpretation of their "blue sky" laws. ... Thus, when we held that "profits" must "come solely from the efforts of others," we were speaking of the profits that investors seek on their investment, not the profits of the scheme in which they invest. We used "profits" in the sense of income or return, to include, for example, dividends, other periodic payments, or the increased value of the investment.

There is no reason to distinguish between promises of fixed returns and promises of variable returns for purposes of the test, so understood. In both cases, the investing public is attracted by representations of investment income, as purchasers were in this case by ETS' invitation to "watch the profits add up." Moreover, investments pitched as low-risk (such as those offering a "guaranteed" fixed return) are particularly attractive to

11. 328 U.S. 293 (1946).

*(Continued)*

(Case 22.1 *continued)*

individuals more vulnerable to investment fraud, including older and less sophisticated investors. Under the reading respondent advances, unscrupulous investments could evade the securities laws by picking a rate of return to promise. We will not read into the securities laws a limitation not compelled by the language that would so undermine the laws' purposes. . . .

The Eleventh Circuit's perfunctory alternative holding, that respondent's scheme falls outside the definition because purchasers had a contractual entitlement to a return, is incorrect and inconsistent with our precedent. We are considering investment contracts. The fact that investors have bargained for a return on their investment does not mean that the return is not also expected to come solely from the efforts of others.

**› RESULT** Edwards and ETS had offered and sold securities.

**› CRITICAL THINKING QUESTIONS**

1. Why was the Supreme Court unwilling to exclude contracts guaranteeing a fixed rate of return from the definition of security?
2. Are mortgage notes, sold with a package of management services and a promise to repurchase the notes in the event of default, securities?

---

There is a split in the circuits as to whether the "common enterprise" element of the *Howey* test can be met simply by showing "vertical commonality" between the promoter and the investor or whether there must be "horizontal commonality," that is, multiple investors who pool their funds and receive a pro rata share of the profits or buy very similar assets that are managed jointly.[12] The majority view is that horizontal commonality is required. A number of states, for purposes of their blue sky laws, define the term "investment contract" more broadly than the federal definition[13] and do not require commonality or sole reliance on the efforts of others.

Federal courts have also relaxed the sole reliance requirement. Although the *Howey* test required that the investor rely solely on the efforts of others for the expectation of profits, subsequent federal decisions have established that, under certain circumstances, there can be an investment contract, and thus a security, even if the investor participates in the generation of profits.[14] For example, an interest in a general partnership is generally held not to be a security because each partner by law has the right to exercise control in the operation of the partnership. But the courts have found a general partnership interest to be a security if it meets any of the following three tests:

1. The partnership agreement leaves so little power to the partners that the arrangement is tantamount to a limited partnership.
2. The investor is so inexperienced in business affairs that he or she is incapable of intelligently exercising his or her partnership powers.
3. The investor is so dependent on the unique management ability of the promoter or manager that he or she cannot replace the manager or exercise meaningful partnership powers.[15]

A limited partnership interest is almost always held to constitute a security because the limited partners, in order to protect their limited liability, are prohibited by law from taking part in the control of the partnership business. An interest in real estate is not in itself considered a security, though it may be a security if it is combined with a management contract, as in *Howey*.

The SEC and at least thirty-five state securities regulators have taken the position that interests in a limited liability company (LLC) are securities. Regulators base their conclusion on either of two theories: LLC interests

12. *See* SEC v. Unique Fin. Concepts, Inc., 196 F.3d 1195 (11th Cir. 1999) (vertical commonality sufficient) and the cases cited therein.
13. *See, e.g.*, King v. Pope, 91 S.W.3d 314, 321 (Tenn. 2002).
14. SEC v. Glenn W. Turner Enters., Inc., 474 F.2d 476 (9th Cir. 1973), *cert. denied*, 414 U.S. 821 (1973).
15. The test to determine whether a general partnership constitutes a security was set forth in *Williamson v. Tucker*, 645 F.2d 404 (5th Cir. 1981), *cert. denied*, 454 U.S. 897 (1981), and later applied in *Holden v. Hagopian*, 978 F.2d 1115 (9th Cir. 1992).

constitute an investment contract under *Howey* or they have all the characteristics of stock.

In *Robinson v. Glynn*,[16] the U.S. Court of Appeals for the Fourth Circuit ruled that an equity interest in an LLC was not a security. The court reasoned that the interest held by Robinson, a member of the LLC, was not an investment contract because he held 33,333 of the company's 133,333 shares, was treasurer of the company, took a seat on the board of managers, had the right to appoint two of the seven members of the board of managers, and was a member of the company's executive committee. As a result, Robinson was able to exercise control over his investment. The Fourth Circuit also rejected Robinson's argument that the membership certificates had all the characteristics of stock. The LLC members did not have a right to receive dividends based on their equity percentage as common shareholders typically do. Instead, Robinson received 100 percent of the LLC's net profits up to a certain amount, after which the funds were distributed pro rata to all equityholders. Common stock is typically negotiable, but Robinson's interest was not. Apparently, there was also some dispute as to whether Robinson's interest retained any voting rights if transferred. Because it was not an investment contract and did not have all the characteristics of stock, the LLC interest in *Robinson* did not qualify as a security. As of 2004, the U.S. Supreme Court had not ruled on this issue.

Until 1985 when the Supreme Court resolved the issue, there also was a controversy as to whether the sale of an entire business through the sale of its corporate stock involved the sale of a security. Under the *sale-of-business doctrine,* certain courts had held that compliance with federal securities laws was not necessary because the economic reality of the transaction was that a business, rather than securities, was being sold. The U.S. Supreme Court rejected this doctrine in *Landreth Timber Co. v. Landreth*,[17] holding that the sale of a business through a stock transaction is a securities transaction if the stock sold possesses all of the characteristics traditionally associated with common stock. This is the case even though the success of the venture going forward depends on the efforts of the buyer, not the seller.

### *Family Resemblance Test*

Promissory notes and other evidences of indebtedness may or may not constitute a security, depending on the factual context. In *Reves v. Ernst & Young*,[18] the U.S. Supreme Court set forth the *family resemblance test* for determining which types of notes are securities. Under this test, a promissory note is initially presumed to be a security based upon the literal language of the securities acts ("The term 'security' means any note . . ."). This presumption may be rebutted, however, by a showing that the note bears a "strong resemblance" (in terms of four specific factors) to an enumerated category of instruments commonly held not to constitute securities, such as notes delivered in connection with consumer financing, notes secured by a home mortgage, and short-term notes secured by accounts receivable. The four specific factors used in evaluating an instrument are:

1. The motivations that would prompt a reasonable seller and buyer to enter into the transaction.
2. The plan of distribution of the instrument.
3. The reasonable expectations of the investing public.
4. Whether some factor, such as the existence of another regulatory scheme, significantly reduces the risk of the instrument, thereby rendering application of the federal securities laws unnecessary.

The "In Brief" provides a decision tree for determining whether an instrument is a security and for analyzing the securities registration requirements discussed below.

### OFFER

Section 2(3) of the 1933 Act defines an *offer* as "every attempt or offer to dispose of, or solicitation of an offer to buy, a security or interest in a security, for value." This definition is much broader than that in contract law. An offer that is unacceptably vague for contract law purposes may still constitute an offer for federal securities law purposes. Section 2(3) expressly provides, however, that preliminary negotiations or agreements between an issuer and an underwriter or among underwriters do not constitute an offer to sell.

### SALE

A *sale* is defined by Section 2(3) to include "every contract of sale or disposition of a security or interest in a security, for *value*." The crucial term in this definition is value. The courts have defined "value" very broadly—more broadly, for example, than in state corporations statutes, which require that stock can be issued only for "value" in the form of cash, property, or compensation for past services.

## Registered Offerings

Once it is determined that an investment offering does, in fact, involve a security, the issue of registration must be addressed. On October, 26, 2004, the SEC proposed

16. 349 F.3d 166 (4th Cir. 2003).
17. 471 U.S. 681 (1985).
18. 494 U.S. 56 (1990).

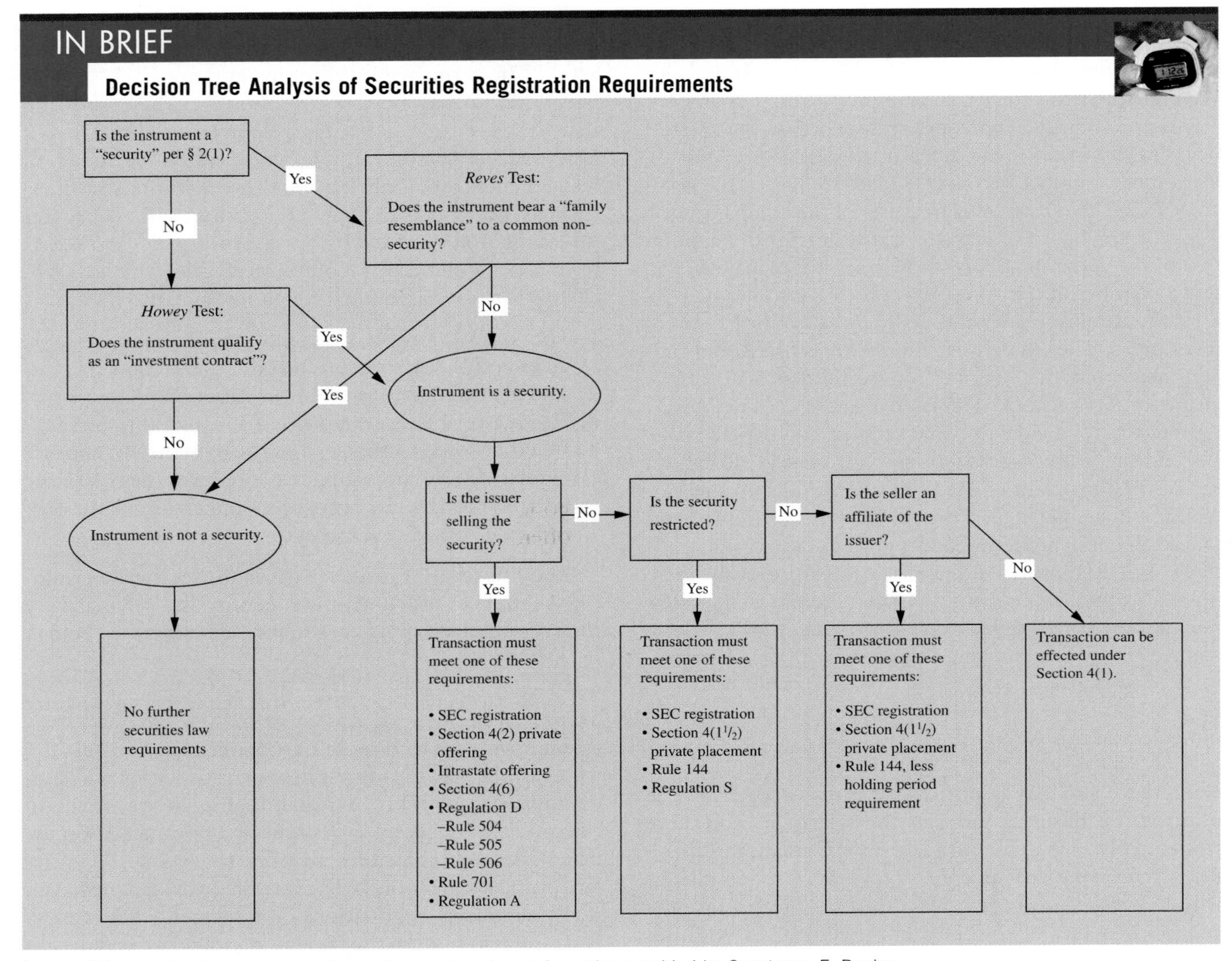


Source: This decision tree was created by John Lee based on information provided by Constance E. Bagley.

certain changes designed to update what Commissioner Cynthia Glassman dubbed an "outmoded" offering system. The proposed changes are discussed at the end of this section.

## Registration of Securities

Section 5 of the 1933 Act requires the registration of all securities offered and sold in the United States, unless an exemption from registration is available. Section 5 can be summarized as follows.

1. Section 5(a) prohibits the sale of a security before a registration statement has been filed with the SEC. The *registration statement* consists of filing forms and the *prospectus*, the disclosure document that an issuer of securities provides to prospective purchasers. Section 5(c) prohibits the use of any means of interstate commerce to offer to sell or buy any security during this time.
2. During the waiting period between the filing of the registration statement and the date the registration statement becomes effective with the SEC, written and oral offers to sell the security may be made, but all written offers must meet the standards required of a prospectus.
3. Once the registration statement becomes effective with the SEC (referred to as *going effective*), offers

and sales of securities may be made. However, Section 5(b) continues to require that any written offer or sale of a security made within forty days after the registration statement is declared effective be preceded or accompanied by a prospectus meeting the requirements of the 1933 Act.

In general, every public offering of securities must be registered with the SEC. The registration requirement is designed to ensure that certain information is filed with the SEC and distributed to potential investors by means of a prospectus. Unlike certain state securities authorities, the SEC does not have the statutory authority to approve or disapprove an offering on its merits. Instead, the registration process is designed to ensure that the information provided to investors is accurate and complete. The general procedures to be followed in the registration process are found in Sections 6 and 8 of the 1933 Act.

The registration of a public offering is an expensive and time-consuming affair. The process includes the preparation of the registration statement—that is, the document filed with the SEC—and of the prospectus, which must be included in the registration statement and provided to prospective investors. Securities lawyers, independent accountants, investment bankers, a printer, and an engraver all become involved in the process. The out-of-pocket fees and expenses for an initial public offering, excluding compensation for the investment bankers who underwrite the offering, can easily exceed $900,000. All such fees must be paid by the issuer of the securities (or in the case of offerings by persons other than the issuer, by the seller of the securities).[19]

A principal advantage of registering a securities offering with the SEC is that the securities may be traded relatively freely following the registered public offering. A *secondary offering*, that is, a subsequent offering by a person other than the issuer, must either be registered with the SEC or be exempt from registration. As discussed further below, if the secondary offering is of nonrestricted securities and is made by a nonaffiliate, then registration of the secondary offering is not required, regardless of the size of the offering or the number of offerees.

19. The process of doing an initial public offering is discussed in detail in CONSTANCE E. BAGLEY & CRAIG E. DAUCHY, THE ENTREPRENEUR'S GUIDE TO BUSINESS LAW 494–540 (2d ed. 2003).

## THE ROLE OF THE UNDERWRITERS

A public offering of securities is typically, though not necessarily, underwritten by one or more broker–dealers or investment banking firms.

### *Firm Commitment Underwriting*

In a *firm commitment underwriting*, the underwriters agree to purchase the entire offering, thus effectively shifting the risk of the offering from the issuer to the underwriters. The lead underwriter is responsible for negotiating with the issuer the terms of the offering and compensation and for putting together an underwriting group (the *syndicate*). Each member of the underwriting group agrees to purchase a certain number of securities once the offering is declared effective by the SEC.

In theory, such a commitment places the underwriters in a risky position. In practice, the lead underwriters will not go forward with the offering unless they have tentative offers from buyers for as much as five to ten times the number of shares being offered. Accordingly, the underwriting agreement between the issuer and the lead underwriter (as representative of the underwriting group) and the agreements among the members of the underwriting group are typically not signed until immediately before the offering is declared effective by the SEC. The price at which the securities will be offered and the underwriters' commission are usually not formally determined until the evening before the offering goes effective.

Once the offering becomes effective, the underwriters attempt to sell the securities that they are obligated to purchase. Most firm underwriting agreements are of short duration. Usually, the sale closes within two business days after the agreement is signed. As of the closing date, the underwriters are obligated to purchase any securities that remain unsold.

Because a firm commitment underwriting will provide the issuer with a predetermined amount of money within a specified period, it is attractive to issuers. A firm commitment underwriting is also attractive to investors because it implies that the underwriters themselves are willing to take a risk on the offering. Because it places the members of the underwriting group at risk for the amount of the offering, broker–dealers and investment bankers will usually agree to a firm underwriting only if they are certain that they will be able to sell the offered securities quickly. Such certainty will depend upon a variety of factors, including the amount of money being sought, the performance and prospects of the company, whether the company is seasoned or relatively new, and the condition of the public securities market.

### *Best-Efforts Underwriting*

In a *best-efforts underwriting,* the underwriters do not agree to purchase the securities being offered. Instead, they agree to use their best efforts to find buyers at an agreed-on price. Best-efforts underwritings are often used for initial public offerings or for companies that are unseasoned.

A best-efforts offering leaves the risks of the offering entirely with the issuer. Nevertheless, some established, successful companies may prefer a best-efforts offering because the cost of distribution is lower than for a firm commitment underwriting.

## THE REGISTRATION STATEMENT

Sections 7 and 10 of the 1933 Act, and the rules promulgated by the SEC under the Act, contain detailed guidelines as to what must be included in the registration statement and the accompanying prospectus. Regulations C and S–K, adopted by the SEC pursuant to the 1933 Act, list the general information required in connection with most public registrations.[20] In addition, the SEC has issued a variety of forms that list the information required in connection with particular types of transactions.

### *Forms*

Securities offered in an initial public offering are registered in a registration statement meeting the requirements of *Form S–1* or, if the issuer is a small business, *Form SB–1. Small business issuers* are defined as companies with revenues less than $25 million whose market value of publicly held securities (other than those held by affiliates) is less than $25 million.

The registration statement must include a complete description of the securities being offered, the business of the issuer, the risk factors, the management, and the major shareholders. It must also include audited financial statements.

Companies that have been filing periodic reports under the 1934 Act, but are not followed so widely that the SEC can be confident that information previously filed will be disseminated in the marketplace, file on *Form S–2* (or, if the issuer is a small business, on *Form SB–2*). Form S–2 allows these companies to present certain information in a streamlined form and to incorporate previous filings by reference so that investors can obtain more information if desired. This is part of the SEC's integrated disclosure system, which is designed to integrate the reporting requirements under the 1934 Act with the prospectus delivery requirement under the 1933 Act.

*Form S–3* is used by a category of companies that have filed periodic reports under the 1934 Act for at least three years and have a widespread following in the marketplace. An issuer can use Form S–3 for an offering of common stock only if the aggregate market value of the voting stock held by nonaffiliates is $150 million or more or, alternatively, if the aggregate market value of the voting stock held by nonaffiliates is $100 million or more and the issuer has an annual trading volume of three million shares or more. (*Affiliates* include officers, directors, and controlling shareholders. The SEC has a rebuttable presumption that any shareholder owning 10 percent or more of the issuer's stock is an affiliate.)

For companies filing on Form S–3, information about the registrant that has been reported in annual and quarterly reports filed under the 1934 Act need not be provided to investors in the prospectus, unless there has been a material change in the registrant's affairs or financial statements. Such reports are incorporated by reference and are deemed a part of the prospectus for liability purposes.

### *Prospectus*

The prospectus is the part of the registration statement that is provided to prospective purchasers of an issuer's securities.

The tone of a prospectus frequently strikes nonlawyers as dry, bleak, and confusing. Such a perception arises out of the conflicting purposes of the prospectus. On the one hand, it is a selling document, designed to present the best possible view of the investment and the issuing company. On the other hand, it is a disclosure document, an insurance policy against claims of securities fraud. This second function usually predominates. The prospectus usually contains only provable statements of fact, with numerous disclaimers regarding the future success of the issuer. Businesspeople, accustomed to presenting their company in the best possible light, frequently have difficulty adjusting to the somber tone of the prospectus.

Effective October 1, 1998, companies selling securities to the public in the United States were required to use plain English in the design and language of the cover page, summary, and risk factors sections of the prospectus. In these sections, companies must (1) use short sentences with everyday words, (2) avoid legal jargon and highly technical business terms, (3) use the active voice, (4) not use multiple negatives, and (5) use bulleted lists

20. 17 C.F.R. pts. 230.400 *et seq.*; 17 C.F.R. pt. 229.

for complex information, if possible. Companies are encouraged, but not required, to use plain English throughout the prospectus. On January 24, 2000, as part of Regulation M–A, the SEC extended the plain English requirements to the summary sheet for tender offers, mergers, and going-private transactions. The response to the plain English rules has been positive, as "most observers agree that prospectuses have become more understandable and useful documents."[21]

A sample cover page of a prospectus appears as Exhibit 22.2.

21. Pankaj K. Sinha & C. Grace Campnell, *'Plain English' Rules Have Generally Been Successful,* CORP. COUNS. WKLY., Mar. 14, 2001, at 88.

**EXHIBIT 22.2** **Sample Prospectus Cover Page**

Prospectus
August 18, 2004

**19,605,052 Shares**

**Class A Common Stock**

Google Inc. is offering 14,142,135 shares of Class A common stock and the selling stockholders are offering 5,462,917 shares of Class A common stock. We will not receive any proceeds from the sale of shares by the selling stockholders. This is our initial public offering and no public market currently exists for our shares. The initial public offering price is $85.00 per share.

Following this offering, we will have two classes of authorized common stock, Class A common stock and Class B common stock. The rights of the holders of Class A common stock and Class B common stock are identical, except with respect to voting and conversion. Each share of Class A common stock is entitled to one vote per share. Each share of Class B common stock is entitled to ten votes per share and is convertible at any time into one share of Class A common stock.

Our Class A common stock will be quoted on The Nasdaq National Market under the symbol "GOOG."

**Investing in our Class A common stock involves risks. See "Risk Factors" beginning on page 4.**

**Price $85.00 A Share**

| | Price to Public | Underwriting Discounts and Commissions | Proceeds to Google | Proceeds to Selling Stockholders |
|---|---|---|---|---|
| Per Share | $ 85.00 | $ 2.3839 | $ 82.6161 | $ 82.6161 |
| Total | $1,666,429,420 | $46,736,483 | $1,168,368,039 | $451,324,897 |

The selling stockholders have granted the underwriters the right to purchase up to an additional 2,940,757 shares to cover over-allotments.

The price to the public and allocation of shares were determined by an auction process. The minimum size for a bid in the auction was five shares of our Class A common stock. The method for submitting bids and a more detailed description of this auction process are included in "Auction Process" beginning on page 34. As part of this auction process, we attempted to assess the market demand for our Class A common stock and to set the size and price to the public of this offering to meet that demand. As a result, buyers should not expect to be able to sell their shares for a profit shortly after our Class A common stock begins trading. We determined the method for allocating shares to bidders who submitted successful bids following the closing of the auction.

The Securities and Exchange Commission and state securities regulators have not approved or disapproved of these securities, or determined if this prospectus is truthful or complete. Any representation to the contrary is a criminal offense.

It is expected that the shares will be delivered to purchasers on or about August 24, 2004.

**Morgan Stanley** **Credit Suisse First Boston**

**Goldman, Sachs & Co.**
**Lehman Brothers**
**JPMorgan**
**WR Hambrecht+Co**

**Citigroup**
**Allen & Company LLC**
**UBS Investment Bank**
**Thomas Weisel Partners LLC**

Source: Reprinted with permission from Google, Inc.

## DUE DILIGENCE

A key step in preparing the registration statement is the process of *due diligence*, whereby the company, the underwriters, and their respective counsel assemble and review the information about the company in the registration statement. The company must be prepared to back up every claim it makes in the prospectus. Even if the claim is stated as an opinion (such as "The company believes that it is the industry leader"), the company must be able to demonstrate the reasonableness of its belief.

Underwriters cannot simply rely on the representations of issuers or the officers of issuers but must perform their own independent due diligence investigation. They should go beyond the corporate documents provided by the issuer and examine information in press releases and news reports concerning key competitors and others important to the issuer's business. Underwriters should also monitor relevant websites and public agency filings. Exhibit 22.3 provides a long but useful list of tasks that should be undertaken by officers, directors, underwriters, and counsel engaged in the public offering of securities.

### EXHIBIT 22.3 Due Diligence Checklist

**The Product**

1. Examine and operate each product, particularly new products, to assess appearance, function, design, and so on.
2. Assess the threat of obsolescence for each significant product line.
3. Review new product and service plans and development progress.
4. Compare the product with those of competitors and assess the threat from new competitors.
5. Perform an analysis of unproven technology, using experts if necessary.

**The Industry**

1. Estimate the size of the industry, present and projected, in each significant product line and compare company growth projections with anticipated market size for consistency.
2. Review government and trade reports and trade literature regarding the company's market segments to check for consistency with the representations and unstated premises in the prospectus.
3. Analyze competitors' SEC filings and websites for unanticipated trends or developments.
4. Evaluate the importance of proprietary products, copyrights, and trademarks within the industry.
5. Interview trade association personnel concerning trends of relevance to the prospectus.
6. Assess the effect of macroeconomic trends (for example, interest rate fluctuations, inflation rates, and economic growth rates) on the issuer's prospects for success.
7. Assess the comparative strengths and weaknesses of competitors in terms of the dominant competitive factors in the industry (price, service, performance, and so on).
8. Compare the company's financial performance with that of its competitors.
9. Determine whether research and development (R&D) expenditures are consistent with industry practice.

**Marketing and Distribution**

1. Evaluate the importance of original equipment manufacturers (OEMs), present and future.
2. Interview principal customers regarding the company's products and services, complaints, anticipated future needs, and so on.
3. Analyze each significant contract regarding contingencies, extent of warranties and other service obligations, rights of cancellation, and so on. Check contracts with customers for completeness and to determine the existence of side written or oral commitments or other terms that materially vary company contracts. Evaluate the quality of the backlog.
4. Evaluate the adequacy of the distribution network, the degree of control over distribution, and the like.
5. Evaluate the effectiveness of marketing personnel.
6. For new products, estimate the cost of introduction, and determine whether the cost is adequately reflected in cash-flow projections.
7. Assess the likelihood of discontinuation of products or services and whether the prospectus should disclose this information.

*(Continued)*

**EXHIBIT 22.3** **Due Diligence Checklist—continued**

**Technology**

1. Review the company's R&D plans to determine whether any radical changes in product direction are anticipated and what cost burden will be imposed on the company in coming years.
2. Evaluate the effectiveness of R&D personnel and organization to assess the company's capacity for technological innovation.
3. Evaluate the company's patent position and the enforceability of its technology licenses.
4. Analyze any litigation regarding technology rights.
5. Review royalty contracts for contingencies and the like, and contact the licensees to determine the existence of any agreement or understanding that varies the terms of the contract.
6. With regard to government contracts, determine what interest, if any, the government asserts or may assert in company technology.
7. Review employee and independent contractor nondisclosure agreements, assignments of inventions, and noncompete agreements.
8. Evaluate other professional affiliations of management or R&D personnel (such as academic affiliations) to assess the likelihood of competing claims on company technology.
9. Evaluate the effectiveness of the company's efforts to police its patents, preserve its trade secrets, maintain its copyrights and marks, and other intellectual property; assess the company's resources to perform these tasks.
10. Evaluate the company's compliance with technology licenses, including those applicable to any open-source software used by the company or embedded in any of its products.
11. Determine whether the company's exports are consistent with export-control laws.

**Management**

1. Investigate the prior experience of management and directors in the same industry and the same size company, their experience with large firms, and so on. Also, investigate backgrounds of officers and directors (including any criminal complaints or lawsuits), standing in the community, reputation in the industry, and so on.
2. Evaluate the responsiveness of management to previous auditors' management letters.
3. Assess the effectiveness of management through interviews with outside customers and suppliers, bankers, auditors, and so on.
4. Review prior transactions between the company and insiders for fairness, propriety, full disclosure, and so on.
5. Assess the effectiveness of the board of directors and identify any gaps in expertise or independence.
6. Determine whether any significant defections from management or the board are imminent, and assess the effect on company competitiveness.

**Employees**

1. Compare the company's stock option plans, pension plans, salaries, and other executive compensation and benefit plans with those of competitors to assess the company's ability to attract and retain skilled employees.
2. Consider whether the public offering is likely to result in the loss of key employees to retirement.
3. Review employee contracts for terms, unrecorded benefit obligations, contingencies, and the like. Interview key employees to determine whether unrecorded written or oral commitments have been made to them.
4. Determine whether compensation obligations have been properly accounted for in the company's books.
5. Assess the adequacy of the labor supply for each operating division.
6. Evaluate the company's labor–relations history, union contracts, prospects of union activity, and so on.

**Production**

1. Assess the ability of production facilities to handle anticipated volumes and whether the cost of new plant and equipment is consistent with anticipated cash flow.
2. Evaluate product and process obsolescence, and compare production facilities to those of industry competitors to determine future competitiveness, both technical and economic.
3. Inquire into anticipated plant closings as well as plans for new facilities, and consider whether disclosure in the prospectus would be advisable.

*(Continued)*

**EXHIBIT 22.3 Due Diligence Checklist—continued**

4. Evaluate the adequacy of management information systems and inventory-control programs.
5. Assess the exposure from single-source suppliers, and evaluate the company's contingency plan for responding to an interruption to supplies.
6. Contact major suppliers to determine their satisfaction with the company and their plans to retire, reduce, or raise the price of key supplies and components.

**Accounting**

1. Determine whether intangible expenses, such as R&D expenditures, are being or should be expensed.
2. Analyze company finances, including supporting work papers where necessary, for prior years.
3. Review budgets and projections in order to determine material changes in the company's financial position, and compare past budgets and projections with actual experience in order to assess the accuracy of management's estimates.
4. Compare the company's revenue-recognition policy and other accounting conventions with those of the industry.
5. Evaluate the effect of customer financing practices on present and future revenues.
6. Evaluate the effect of changes in tax laws and the company's position with respect to open tax years.
7. Verify that the use of proceeds matches financial needs quantitatively and qualitatively.
8. Determine whether inventory turns are consistent with industry ratios.
9. Assess the accuracy of the inventory reported and the adequacy of the inventory obsolescence reserve, and determine the suitability of the mix of materials in inventory.
10. Review aging receivables for consideration of reserve or write-off, and assess the adequacy of the bad-debt reserve and other reserves against income.
11. Obtain a report as to the adequacy of the company's accounting controls.
12. Ascertain that the preeffective auditor's "cold comfort" letter is complete.

**Legal**

1. Identify and assess the effect of new and proposed governmental regulations on operations, expenses, and the like.
2. Check title, title insurance, encumbrances, liens, and the like on company property and equipment.
3. Review incorporation documents, bylaws, and minutes of all shareholder, board, and board committee meetings for several years, both to confirm regularity and to identify events that might require further investigation.
4. Review stock transfer records for regularity, and check for agreements affecting ownership or control of shares.
5. Evaluate pending litigation, review the terms of significant concluded litigation, and investigate the existence of threatened claims or future exposure for statutory or regulatory violations.
6. Determine whether any acquisitions, mergers, reorganizations, and the like are impending or likely and what effect they will have on the company.
7. Review all press releases, promotional literature, company reports, news accounts, websites, and the like for consistency with the prospectus.
8. Review company banking, leasing, factoring arrangements, and the like, and assess the likelihood and effect of disruption or termination.
9. Determine that all insurable risks have been adequately insured against and that policies do not have material adverse exclusions or omissions.

Source: Derived from Robert Alan Spanner, *Limiting Exposure in the Offering Process,* Rev. Sec. & Commodities Reg. 64–66 (Apr. 8, 1987). 

## Registration Procedure

The registration statement must be filed with the SEC. Section 8 of the 1933 Act provides that the registration statement automatically becomes effective on the twentieth day after filing, unless the SEC fixes an earlier date. Virtually all registrants file their registration statement with language stating that it will not become effective until declared effective by the SEC; this ensures that the SEC staff will have the necessary time (which usually exceeds the statutory twenty-day period) to review the filing.

Each amendment to the registration statement filed prior to the effective date starts the twenty-day period running again. If the SEC has consented to the amendment, the waiting period may be accelerated. If, however, the SEC finds that the registration statement is materially defective in some respect, it may, after notice and a hearing, issue a stop order suspending the effectiveness of the offering.

### *Review*

Registration statements received by the SEC are subject to review by the SEC staff. The extent of the review is usually affected by the nature of the offering and the number of filings that the SEC must review. In general, all first-time registrants will receive a complete review. Most repeat registrants will receive a more limited review, and some will receive no review.

Comments of the SEC staff are conveyed through a letter of comment, which is either read over the telephone to the issuer's counsel or, less often, mailed to counsel directly. Members of the SEC staff are usually available to discuss these letters of comment either by telephone or in person. Although the comment letters contain only suggestions without force of law, they generally result in the filing of an amendment to the registration statement. Acceding to the staff's reasonable suggestions is less expensive and less time-consuming than fighting an issue in an administrative hearing and in court. The amended registration statement is usually filed with a letter from counsel answering, item by item, the issues raised by the staff.

In 2000, the SEC staff required several companies seeking to go public to reduce their revenues by the value of warrants or cheap stock issued to customers that had placed large orders for the start-up's products. Dubbed a "unique marriage of convenience" by the *Wall Street Journal*,[22] the practice was particularly prevalent in the highly competitive telecommunications industry, where new companies sought an edge when battling industry giants such as Nortel Networks, Lucent Technologies, and Cisco Systems. In turn, the network operators had an incentive to buy the products because their firms could make far more on their investments in the start-up after it went public than they spent on the equipment. Brooke Seawell, a general partner at Technology Crossover Ventures, argued that the revenue from sales to warrant-holding customers should be offset by the value of the warrants.[23]

22. Scott Thurm, *SEC Questions Start-Ups' Cheap Stock Sales to Customers,* WALL ST. J., Sept. 26, 2000, at C1.
23. *Id.* at C18.

The SEC staff appears to have required CoSine Communications, Inc. to do just that. Cosine, which priced its initial public offering on September 26, 2000, amended its financial statements to reduce its revenues from $11.3 million to $7.6 million to reflect "non-cash charges related to equity" issuances. Six of CoSine's eight customers held stock or warrants.

The practice of issuing cheap stock or warrants in exchange for orders also raised the specter of a pyramid-type scheme. Purchasers were buying new equipment not because of their faith in the product but as a way to inflate the value of the start-up so that it could go public at an unrealistically high valuation. Public investors stood to get hurt when sales to nonaffiliated purchasers (i.e., purchasers that received neither the cheap stock nor warrants) failed to materialize.

### *Waiting Period*

The time between the filing of the registration statement and its becoming effective is called the *waiting period* or the *quiet period* because the law severely limits what the issuer and underwriters may say or publish during this time. No sale of securities can occur prior to the effectiveness of the registration statement; however, the underwriters may assemble selling groups, distribute copies of the preliminary prospectus, and even solicit offers to buy the securities.

The preliminary prospectus—sometimes referred to as a *red-herring prospectus* because a notice on the cover states in red ink that it is not final and is subject to revision—is an incomplete version of the final prospectus. It sets forth the proposed range for the selling price and omits the names of the underwriters except for the lead underwriters, whose names appear on the cover page. The preliminary prospectus usually is not distributed until all changes needed to respond to SEC staff comments are incorporated.

Selling efforts during the waiting period must be done in strict compliance with the securities laws. They usually include *roadshows,* that is, oral presentations to large institutional investors in key cities in the United States, Europe, and Asia.

Any offers to buy can be accepted only after the registration statement is declared effective by the SEC and only after each prospective investor is provided with a copy of the final prospectus. Notice of a proposed offer can be circulated by means of a *tombstone ad,* so named because of its appearance and somewhat somber tone.

The issuing company and its lead underwriter must be careful about the information they release to the public during the waiting period. Conditioning the market with a news article or press release about the company and its upcoming offering is referred to as *gun-jumping*. Gun-jumping may violate the 1933 Act, and the SEC may require the issuer to postpone the offering. For example, the SEC required Web Van, the Internet grocer, to postpone its initial public offering after it released significant information not contained in its prospectus during a conference call as part of its roadshow.

### *Going Effective*

Once a registration statement has been informally cleared by the SEC staff or the registrant has received notice that the registration statement will not be reviewed, a preeffective amendment will be filed with the SEC. This is typically accompanied by a request that the waiting period be accelerated so that the registration statement will become effective at a particular date and time. Without the request for acceleration, the registration statement would not become effective until the expiration of an additional twenty-day period.

Once an offering is declared effective, sales of the securities may be consummated, provided that each purchaser is given a copy of the final prospectus. Information concerning the price of the securities and underwriting arrangements is filed with the SEC as part of the final prospectus. Supplemental sales literature, which in most cases need not be reviewed by the SEC, may be provided to prospective purchasers. Such sales literature must be preceded or accompanied by the final prospectus. Often the underwriters will run a tombstone ad to publicize their involvement in the offering.

Exhibit 22.4 suggests a timeline for managers who are considering a public securities offering.

**EXHIBIT 22.4 Managerial Timeline for a Public Securities Offering**

| | |
|---|---|
| **Day 1** | Issuer decides upon a public offering of securities to raise capital and chooses the lead securities underwriting firm. |
| **Day 30–60** | With the aid of the underwriter, the issuer prepares the forms and prospectus for the registration statement. |
| **Day 61–90** | The issuer files the registration statement with the SEC for review and submits any amendments to the filing. |
| **Day 91–120** | During the quiet period, the underwriters may assemble selling groups, distribute copies of the preliminary prospectus, and solicit offers to sell the securities. |
| **Day 121 +** | Once the offering is declared effective and the pricing amendment is filed, the underwriters may commence sales of the company's securities. |

## SHELF REGISTRATION

Rule 415 under the 1933 Act provides for the *shelf registration* of securities, that is, the registration of a number of securities at one time for issuance later. The securities can then be issued over a period of time, for example, in connection with continuous acquisition programs or employee stock-benefit plans, or they can be issued at a later date, for example, when interest rates or market conditions are more favorable. Shelf registration can result in reduced legal, accounting, and printing expenses and increased competition among potential underwriters. Moreover, the issuer can respond more flexibly to rapidly changing market conditions by varying the structure and terms of the securities on short notice.

Registration is intended to ensure that current information is available to prospective underwriters and purchasers of securities. Accordingly, shelf registration is restricted to offerings in which the information contained in the registration statement will not become stale or inaccurate after some months or years.

Rule 415 limits the availability of shelf registration to ten types of offerings, which can be broken down into two basic categories: (1) traditional shelf offerings, and (2) offerings of securities of certain large, publicly traded companies that are eligible to use short-form registration procedures such as Form S-3.

*Traditional shelf offerings* include (1) securities offered pursuant to employee benefit plans; (2) securities offered or sold pursuant to dividend or interest reinvestment plans; (3) warrants, rights, or securities to be issued upon conversion of other outstanding securities; (4) mortgage-related securities; and (5) securities issued in connection with business combination transactions. With respect to offerings by certain large, publicly traded companies, the SEC has

### ETHICAL CONSIDERATION

During the roadshow, large institutional investors are frequently shown earnings projections by the lead underwriter, the assumptions underlying the company's business model, and industry comparisons. This information should not be provided in writing unless the underwriters gather it up after the meeting. Nonetheless, it sometimes finds its way into "cheat sheets" that are meant for the underwriters' internal use but are sometimes given to favored clients. Is it fair to give additional information—beyond that contained in the prospectus—to certain favored investors?

decided that because the market receives a steady stream of high-quality information concerning these issuers, the risks of stale information are minimal.

## Reorganizations and Combinations

When securities holders are asked to approve a corporate reorganization or combination—such as a reclassification of securities, a merger involving an exchange of securities, or a transfer of assets of one corporation in exchange for the securities of another—they are in effect faced with an investment decision. In recognition of this fact, the SEC adopted Rule 145, which expressly provides that the protections provided by the 1933 Act's registration requirements are applicable to certain types of business reorganizations and combinations. An offer, offer to sell, or sale of securities occurs when a plan of reorganization is submitted to the shareholders for approval. Transactions that fall within the guidelines specified in Rule 145 must be registered with the SEC in a combined registration statement and proxy statement on *Form S–4,* unless an exemption from registration is available. Because shareholder approval of mergers and other combinations necessarily involves communications between a corporation and its shareholders, Rule 145 also contains specific provisions concerning when such communications will be deemed to be a prospectus or an offer to sell for purposes of the 1933 Act.

Rule 145 also provides that under certain circumstances affiliates of the acquired company, such as officers, directors, or controlling shareholders, are deemed *underwriters,* that is, persons selling securities on behalf of the issuer or a person who controls or is under common control with the issuer. Such affiliates cannot resell their securities without compliance with certain resale restrictions, which include limitations on the amount of securities sold in a three-month period.

## SEC's Proposed Changes to the Registration Process

In October 2004, the SEC unanimously proposed a set of new rules and amendments designed to take advantage of advances in technology that make it possible to deliver more timely information to investors.[24] The proposed rules would define all methods of communications, other than oral communications, as "written communications" under the 1933 Act. Thus, any communication that is written, printed, broadcast, or embodied in any form of electronic media (such as audiotapes, videotapes, facsimiles, CD-ROM, electronic mail, Internet websites, computer networks, and other forms of computer data compilation) is treated as a written communication. A live telephone call would not be deemed a written communication even if it is carried over the Internet, but "blast" voice-mail messages would be.

### Gun-Jumping

The proposed rule would provide all issuers with a bright-line period ending thirty days prior to the filing of a registration statement, during which issuers may communicate (orally or in writing) without risk of violating the gun-jumping provisions as long as (1) the communication does not reference a securities offering, (2) the communication is made "by or on behalf of the issuer," and (3) the issuer takes reasonable steps within its control to prevent further distribution or publication of the information during the thirty-day period immediately before the issuer files the registration statement. The safe harbor would not be available to offerings by a blank check company, a shell company, an issuer offering penny stock, a registered investment company, or a business development company. (A *blank check company* is a development-stage company that has no specific business plan or has a business plan to acquire a currently unknown business.) Offerings in connection with business combinations and exchange offers would also be excluded.

### Free Writing Prospectuses

So-called *well-known seasoned issuers,* defined generally as firms eligible to use Form S–3 with $700 million of public common equity float, would also be permitted to make unrestricted oral and written offers before the registration statement is filed without violating the gun-jumping provisions. However, all written offers would have to meet the requirements set forth by the SEC in the proposed rules for a *free writing prospectus.* Any written offer would be a prospectus under Section 2(a)(10) of the 1933 Act, and both oral communications and free writing prospectuses would be subject to liability under Section 12(a)(2).

Issuers would be required to file all free writing propectuses with the SEC. They would not be deemed part of the registration statement, however, and therefore would not be subject to Section 11 liability, unless the issuer elected to include them in the registration statement.

The proposal would permit well-known seasoned issuers to use a free writing prospectus at any time. Other issuers would be able to use such a prospectus after a registration statement has been filed. In the case of unseasoned issuers, the free writing prospectus would have to

24. Securities Offering Reform, 69 Fed. Reg. 67,392 (Nov. 17, 2004).

be accompanied or preceded by the most recent statutory prospectus meeting the requirements of Section 10. A prospectus would be deemed to accompany an electronic free writing prospectus if the free writing prospectus contains a hyperlink to the statutory prospectus.

Eligible seasoned issuers and eligible well-known seasoned issuers would not be required to deliver a statutory prospectus. Instead, they would only be required to notify the recipient of the free writing prospectus, through a required legend, of where the recipient can access or hyperlink to the preliminary or base prospectus by using the URL provided for the prospectus.

Live roadshows would continue to be considered oral communications, but an electronic roadshow would be considered an issuer's free writing prospectus. As such, it would have to be made available electronically to unrestricted audiences. According to the SEC:

> This proposed treatment of roadshows would strike the appropriate balance between the need to market an issuer's securities to institutional investors and the desires of retail and other investors to have access to issuer information, such as management presentations, that are normally available only at roadshows that often have not been open to retail investors generally.

Given that Regulation FD's ban on selective disclosure (discussed in Chapter 23) does not apply to registered offerings, this proposal marks the first time the SEC has sought to ensure that individual investors who buy shares in a public offering have access to the same information provided to institutional investors.

### *Shelf Registration*

The proposed rules would also expand the availability of the shelf registration process and permit well-known seasoned issuers to make offerings, with automatic effectiveness, pursuant to an "automatic shelf registration." The special rules for such issuers reflect the SEC's belief that the ongoing information required by the 1934 Act is widely followed by investment professionals and provides adequate ongoing and current information about these firms.

## Exemptions for Offerings by the Issuer

In adopting the 1933 Act registration provisions, Congress provided exemptions from registration when there is no practical need for it or the costs would outweigh the public benefits. Exemptions from registration fall into two categories: exempt securities and exempt transactions.

*Exempt securities,* listed in Section 3 of the 1933 Act, include the following:

1. Any security issued or guaranteed by the United States or any state of the United States.
2. Any security issued or guaranteed by any national bank.
3. Any security issued by a charitable organization.
4. Any security that is part of an issue offered and sold only to persons residing within a single state or territory, if the issuer is a resident of the same state or territory. (*Note:* Even though the intrastate offering exemption is listed under Section 3, the SEC treats it as a transactional exemption under Section 4.)

*Exempt transactions* are described in Section 4 of the 1933 Act. They include the following:

1. "Transactions by any person other than an issuer, underwriter or dealer" (Section 4(1)).
2. "Transactions by an issuer not involving any public offering" (Section 4(2), the private-offering exemption).

Exemptions for offshore offerings are discussed later in this chapter. Most state blue sky laws have exemptions from registration that roughly correspond to the federal exemptions.

## Private Offerings Under Section 4(2)

Because of the expense and burdens of public offerings, companies trying to raise money usually attempt to qualify for an exemption from registration. They most frequently rely on the exemption for private offerings. A *private offering,* often called a *private placement,* is directed to selected qualified investors, rather than to the public. In 2000 alone, $400 billion was raised in private offerings in the United States—nearly a third of all funds raised in the U.S. capital markets that year.[25] A private offering can be consummated more quickly and with far less expense than a registered public offering.

Under Section 4(2), an offering is exempt from registration if it does not involve a "public offering." The SEC originally took the position that "under ordinary circumstances an offering to not more than twenty-five persons is not an offering to a substantial number and presumably does not involve a public offering."[26] This guideline was rejected by the Supreme Court in the following landmark case.

25. *Panel Seeks to Revamp Offering, Placement Processes,* Corp. Couns. Wkly., Sept. 12, 2001, at 275.
26. Securities Act Release No. 285 (1935).

A CASE IN POINT

**CASE 22.2**
**SEC v. Ralston Purina Co.**
*Supreme Court of the United States 346 U.S. 119 (1953).*

## Summary

**› FACTS** Ralston Purina, a feed and cereal company, offered common stock at market prices to its employees. Among those employees responding to the offer were artists, bake-shop foremen, chow-loading foremen, clerical assistants, clerks, stenographers, and at least one veterinarian. Between 1947 and 1951, the company sold a total of $2 million worth of stock to 2,000 of its employees. The employees lived in various locations throughout the United States. Ralston Purina took the position that because the stock was offered only to "key employees" of the company, it was a private offering exempt from registration under the 1933 Act.

**› ISSUE PRESENTED** Does the determination of whether a transaction is a public or private offering depend primarily on the number of offerees or the sophistication of the offerees?

**› SUMMARY OF OPINION** The U.S. Supreme Court held that the offering was not exempt from registration. The Court stated that absent a showing of special circumstances, employees are indistinguishable from other members of the investing public as far as the securities laws are concerned.

The Supreme Court also rejected a strict numerical test. Instead, the Court held that the critical consideration is whether the class of persons offered the securities needs the protection of the 1933 Act: "An offering to those who are shown to be able to fend for themselves is a transaction not involving any public offering." If, as in the present case, an offering is made to those who are not able to fend for themselves, the transaction is a public offering. The Court noted that an important factor affecting this determination is whether the offerees have access to the same kind of information that the 1933 Act would make available through a registration statement.

**› RESULT** Ralston Purina's offer of stock to its employees was not exempt from registration.

**› COMMENTS** The Supreme Court's ruling in *Ralston Purina* refocused attention under Section 4(2) from a strict numerical test to the sophistication of the offerees. The ruling did little to clarify the private-offering exemption, however, and reliance on Section 4(2) therefore remained an uncertain and somewhat risky proposition.

## REGULATION D: SAFE-HARBOR EXEMPTIONS

Responding to the need for greater certainty in connection with the private-offering exemption, the SEC adopted *Regulation D* in 1982. Regulation D offers a safe harbor for those seeking exemption from registration: An issuer that does not comply with all of the requirements of the applicable rule will not necessarily fail to have an exemption because the transaction may still meet the more general conditions of Section 4(2).

Regulation D contains three separate exemptions from registration, defined by Rules 504, 505, and 506. Rules 501–503 define terms and concepts applicable to one or more of the exemptions.

### *Accredited Investors*

The concept of an accredited investor, derived from earlier federal regulations and state securities laws, is based on the idea that certain investors are so financially sophisticated that they do not need all the protections afforded by the securities laws. Rule 501 defines an *accredited investor* as any one of the following:

1. Any national bank.
2. Any corporation, business trust, or charitable organization with total assets in excess of $5 million.
3. Any director, executive officer, or general partner of the issuer.
4. Any natural person who had individual income in

excess of $200,000 in each of the two most recent years, or joint income with that person's spouse in excess of $300,000 in each of those years, with a reasonable expectation of reaching the same income level in the current year.
5. Any natural person whose individual net worth, or joint net worth with that person's spouse, exceeds $1 million at the time of the purchase.
6. Any trust with assets greater than $5 million with the purchase directed by a sophisticated investor.
7. Any private development company.
8. Any entity in which all of the equity owners are accredited investors.

### *Rule 504*

Rule 504 exempts offerings of up to $1 million within a twelve-month period. There may be an unlimited number of purchasers under Rule 504. Rule 504 is not available to issuers registered under the 1934 Act—known as public companies—or to investment companies such as mutual funds. It is also not available to blank check companies. The issuer must file a notice on Form D with the SEC within fifteen days after the first sale of securities. Some relatively minor changes were made to Rule 504(b)(1) in 1999 with the intent of reducing the possibility of abuse in microchip and Internet offerings.

### *Rule 505*

Rule 505 exempts offerings of up to $5 million within a twelve-month period. General solicitations and advertising are not permitted in connection with a Rule 505 offering, and the issuer must reasonably believe that there are not more than thirty-five unaccredited investors. Rule 505 is not available to investment companies. Rule 505 requires that certain specified information be provided to purchasers (unless all are accredited investors). This information is generally compiled in a private-placement memorandum (described later) or offering circular. Rule 505 also requires that purchasers have the opportunity to ask questions and receive answers concerning the terms of the offering. A notice on Form D must be filed with the SEC within fifteen days of the first sale of securities.

### *Rule 506*

Rule 506, adopted by the SEC under Section 4(2), exempts offerings that in the issuer's reasonable belief are limited to no more than thirty-five unaccredited investors, provided that the issuer reasonably believes immediately prior to making any sale that each unaccredited investor, either alone or with his or her purchaser representative, has enough business experience to evaluate the merits and risks of the prospective investment. There can be an unlimited number of accredited investors. General solicitations and advertising are not permitted, however.

Like Rule 505, Rule 506 requires that certain specified information be provided to purchasers (unless all purchasers are accredited investors) and that purchasers have the opportunity to ask questions and receive answers concerning the terms of the offering. Unlike Rule 505, Rule 506 does not limit the aggregate offering price of the offering. A notice on Form D must be filed with the SEC within fifteen days of the first sale of securities.

### *Integration of Sales*

If an issuer makes successive sales within a limited period of time, the SEC may *integrate* the successive sales; that is, it may deem them to be part of a single sale. Integrating two or more offerings may increase the number of unaccredited investors beyond acceptable limits, resulting in the loss of a private-offering exemption. To determine whether offerings should be integrated, the SEC and the courts consider whether the offerings (1) are part of a single plan of financing, (2) involve the issuance of the same class of securities, (3) are made at or about the same time, (4) involve the same type of consideration, and (5) are made for the same general purpose.

Rule 502(a) provides an integration safe harbor for Regulation D offerings. Under Rule 502(a), offers and sales made more than six months before the start of a Regulation D offering or more than six months after its completion will almost never be considered part of the Regulation D offering, provided that the same issuer makes no offers or sales of a similar class of securities during those six-month periods.

If a company decides to abandon a proposed public offering due, for example, to a lack of investor interest, Rule 155(c) provides a way to shift to a private offering without having to wait the six months normally required to avoid integration of the two offerings. To qualify, issuers (1) may not sell any securities in the abandoned offering, (2) must wait thirty calendar days after withdrawal of the registration statement, and (3) must disclose to each offeree in the subsequent offering specific information related to the abandoned offering. There is also a private-to-registered safe harbor that permits a similar shift from a private offering to a registered public offering.

## Section 4(6) Exemption

Section 4(6) of the 1933 Act exempts offers and sales by any issuer to an unlimited number of accredited investors, provided that no offers or sales are made to any nonaccredited investors, the aggregate offering price does not exceed $5 million, and there is no public solicitation or advertising in connection with the offering. The Section 4(6) definition of "accredited investor" is almost identical to that of Regulation D. The availability of this exemption does not depend upon the use of any type of disclosure document, nor is the issuer required to make any filing with the SEC.

## *View from Cyberspace*

### OFFERINGS ON THE INTERNET

In 1995, Spring Street Brewing Company became the first company to conduct an initial public offering over the Internet.[a] Spring Street raised $1.6 million in an offering exempt under Regulation A. The securities were qualified under the blue sky laws of eighteen states, on the assumption that the majority of potential purchasers resided in those states.

Other small companies have done offerings of up to $1 million under Rule 504 of Regulation D, which does not prohibit general solicitation for offerings of up to $1 million. Rule 505 (with its $5 million limit) and Rule 506 (with no dollar limit) do prohibit general solicitation. The SEC has taken the position that offerings on the Internet violate that ban unless access to offering materials is restricted to prequalified, accredited investors. This is normally done by making the sites offering the securities accessible only by password and only to investors shown by questionnaire to be accredited.[b]

Companies doing registered offerings can post the registration statement on their website. In addition, NETRoadshow and other firms make audiovisual transmissions of live investor roadshows to authorized investors via the Internet. The transmission is not edited for content and contains the oral presentations by management, questions and answers, and charts and graphics presented at the roadshow.[c] Access to the online versions of the roadshow is generally password protected and limited to the analysts, securities professionals, institutional investors, and others typically invited to attend roadshows.[d] The SEC proposals discussed earlier would require firms to make electronic roadshows available to unrestricted audiences.

In April 2000, the SEC issued an interpretive release providing guidance on the electronic delivery of documents, website content, and online offerings.[e] The release made it clear that a hyperlink embedded within a prospectus causes the hyper-linked information to be treated as part of the prospectus.

But the fact that information on a website is close to the prospectus does not, by itself, make the information an offer within the meaning of the securities laws. For issuers in the process of registering, however, website contents qualify as communications subject to Section 5 of the 1933 Act and so can constitute gun-jumping if they condition the market.

All companies and individuals offering to sell or selling securities online must be registered brokers in accordance with Section 15(b) of the 1934 Act. At least as long as the broker solicits investors, the broker must be registered, even if the broker merely owns the required software and equipment and leases it to the issuer for purposes of an initial public offering.[f]

The SEC provides an Internet-based system called Electronic Data Gathering, Analysis and Retrieval (EDGAR). EDGAR provides companies that are required to file documents with the SEC an efficient and fair way to publicly present those documents. Collection, validation, indexing, acceptance, and forwarding are automated on the site.

Sometimes graphics, images, or audio material in a document cannot be easily reproduced in electronic form. According to Rule 304, electronic versions of the documents must include a fair and accurate narrative description, tabular representation, or transcript of the omitted material. Any graphic, image, or audio material in the version delivered to investors is deemed part of the electronic version delivered to the SEC. Thus, plaintiffs cannot seek rescissionary damages under Section 12(a) on the theory that they purchased securities relying on the printed prospectus and only the securities described in the electronic version (the one delivered to the SEC) were registered.[g] Plaintiffs can, however, seek relief under Section 11, alleging either that one version of the prospectus was misleading or that the different versions of the prospectus, taken together, were misleading.[h]

a. See Constance E. Bagley & John Arledge, *SEC Could Ease Offerings of Securities via the Web*, NAT'L L.J., Jan. 13, 1997, at B9.
b. See Constance E. Bagley & Robert J. Tomkinson, *Internet Is Seeing Its Share of Securities Offerings*, NAT'L L.J., Feb. 2, 1998, at C3.
c. *Id.* at C4.
d. *See, e.g.*, Activate.net corp., SEC No-Action Letter, available Sept. 21, 1999.
e. Available at http://www.sec.gov/rules/concindx.htm#int.
f. *See* In the Matter of Salvani and MainStreetIPO.com, Inc., *available at* http://www.sec.gov/litigation/admin/34-44590.htm.
g. *See* DeMaria v. Andersen, 318 F.3d 170, 175 (2d Cir. 2003).
h. *See id.* at 179.

## REGULATION A

The 1992 SEC Small Business Initiatives expanded the previously largely unused Regulation A exemption and included the adoption of a "testing the waters" provision, which permits issuers to solicit indications of interest before filing any required disclosure documents.

### *Size of Offering and Eligible Companies*

Under *Regulation A,* $5 million of securities can be offered and sold in a twelve-month period, of which up to $1.5 million may be sold by the selling security holders. Only U.S. and Canadian companies that are not required to report under the 1934 Act may use Regulation A. In addition, the regulation cannot be used by an investment company, a company issuing oil and gas rights, or a blank check company.

Under Rule 262, the "bad boy" provision, Regulation A is unavailable if the issuer or its officers, directors, principal shareholders, or affiliates have been subject to specified proceedings, convictions, injunctions, or disciplinary orders from the SEC or other regulatory agencies arising from the securities business or postal fraud. To disqualify the company from using Regulation A, the misconduct must have occurred within five years preceding the filing, or within ten years for officers, directors, and principal shareholders.

### *Testing the Waters*

Regulation A issuers can determine interest in a proposed offering prior to filing an offering statement. The issuer need only file a solicitation of interest document with the SEC, along with copies of any written or broadcast media ads. There is no prohibition on general solicitation or advertising. Radio and television broadcasts and newspaper ads are permitted to determine investor interest in the offering.

No sales may be made or payment received during the testing-the-waters period. To move forward, the company must file Form 1–A with the SEC, and the Regulation A offering statement must be qualified by the SEC. Once the offering statement is filed, testing-the-waters activity ceases. Sales can be made only after the passage of a required waiting period, usually twenty days from the time of the last solicitation of interest.

## OFFERINGS TO EMPLOYEES, DIRECTORS, CONSULTANTS, AND ADVISERS

As explained in Chapter 21, companies that are not registered pursuant to the 1934 Act often face a problem when instituting employee stock plans. If the company relies on Rule 504, it can issue only $1 million in any given twelve-month period. Because employee offerings are usually continuous, the issuer may face serious integration problems.

In response to these problems, the SEC adopted Rule 701, which exempts offers and sales of securities made pursuant to either (1) a written compensatory benefit plan for employees, directors, general partners, trustees (if the issuer is a business trust), officers, consultants, or advisers; or (2) a written contract relating to the compensation of such persons. If the benefit plan is for consultants or advisers, they must render bona fide services not connected with the offer and sale of securities in a capital-raising transaction. Exempt compensatory benefit plans include purchase, savings, option, bonus, stock appreciation, profit-sharing, thrift-incentive, and pension plans.

Rule 701 exempts total sales during a twelve-month period in an amount not more than the greatest of (1) $1 million, (2) 15 percent of the total assets of the issuer, and (3) 15 percent of the outstanding securities of the class being offered and sold.

Rule 701 provides additional integration relief for issuers who sell both under Rule 701 and under Rules 504, 505, or 506 of Regulation D or Section 4(2) of the 1933 Act. Offerings under Rule 701 are not integrated with those under Regulation D or Section 4(2), and vice versa.

Other than providing a copy of the benefit plan or contract under which the securities are awarded, there are no specific disclosure requirements under Rule 701 for sales up to $5 million in a twelve-month period. If total sales during a twelve-month period to the specified class of persons above are more than $5 million, the issuer must disclose certain additional information, such as risk factors, and provide certain financial information.

Exhibit 22.5 summarizes the key elements of certain exemptions from registration discussed in this chapter.

## THE PRIVATE-PLACEMENT MEMORANDUM

The *private-placement memorandum* (also called an *offering circular*) is the private offering counterpart to the prospectus. Like the prospectus, the private-placement memorandum is both a selling document and a disclosure document. The disclosure function is usually primary, so the memorandum may not be as upbeat as the issuer might like.

The content of the private-placement memorandum is determined by the exemption on which the issuer relies. For example, Rule 502(b) under Regulation D provides that if an issuer is selling securities under Rule 505 or 506 to any purchaser that is not an accredited investor, certain specified information must be provided

**EXHIBIT 22.5 Key Elements of Certain Federal Exemptions from Registration**

| Type of Exemption | Dollar Limit of the Offering | Limits on the Number of Purchasers | Purchaser Qualifications | Information Delivery Requirement | Issuer Qualifications |
|---|---|---|---|---|---|
| **Section 4(2)** | No limit | Generally limited to small number of sophisticated offerees able to understand and bear risk | Offerees and purchasers must have access to information and be sophisticated investors | No specific requirement but must answer questions from prospective investors and give access to information | No limitations |
| **Regulation D: Rule 504**[a] | Up to $1 million in twelve months | No limit | No requirements | None | Not a 1934 Act public-reporting company or an investment or blank check company |
| **Regulation D: Rule 505**[a] | Up to $5 million in twelve months | No limit on the number of accredited investors, but limited to thirty-five unaccredited investors and no general solicitation | No requirements for unaccredited investors | Private-placement memorandum meeting requirements of Regulation D if any purchasers are unaccredited investors | Not an investment company |
| **Regulation D: Rule 506**[a] | No limit | No limit on the number of accredited investors, but limited to thirty-five unaccredited investors and no general solicitation | Unaccredited investors must have sufficient experience to evaluate the investment | Private-placement memorandum meeting requirements of Regulation D if any purchasers are unaccredited investors | No limitations |
| **Section 4(6)** | Up to $5 million | No limit on the number of accredited investors | All purchasers must be accredited—no unaccredited investors allowed | None | No limitations |
| **Regulation A** | $5 million in twelve months, with a maximum of $1.5 million sold by the selling security holders | No limit | No requirements | Offering statement qualified by SEC | A U.S. or Canadian company, but not a 1934 Act public-reporting company, investment company, or blank check company, and not a company issuing oil/gas/mineral rights or disqualified under "bad boy" Rule 262 |
| **Rule 701**[b] | The greatest of $500,000, 15 percent of the total assets of the issuer, and 15 percent of the outstanding securities of the same class, up to a limit of $5 million over twelve months | No limit on the number of employees, directors, officers, advisers, or consultants | Advisory and consulting services must not be connected with the offer and sale of securities in a capital-raising transaction | None | Not a 1934 Act public-reporting company or an investment company |

**a.** All issuers relying on these exemptions are required to file a notice on Form D with the SEC within fifteen days after the first sale of securities.
**b.** The offering and sale must be pursuant to written compensatory benefit plans or written contracts relating to compensation, and all issuers relying on this exemption must file Form 701 with the SEC within thirty days after the sale of more than $100,000 worth of securities and annually thereafter.

to the purchaser, including audited financial statements. On the other hand, if the issuer is offering securities under Rule 504 or only to accredited investors, or in reliance upon the general Section 4(2) exemption, then the issuer is not required to provide any specific information. State blue sky laws may also influence the content and format of a private-placement memorandum.

In many circumstances, no private-placement memorandum is technically required. Nonetheless, an issuer is usually well advised to create such a document in order to clearly demonstrate the disclosure made to prospective investors. Such disclosure is important to rebut claims of securities fraud, a topic discussed in Chapter 23.

### ETHICAL CONSIDERATION

Because federal law only requires disclosure of all material information, who bears the responsibility for ensuring the quality and fairness of an offering? The managers and directors of the issuing company? The investment bankers? The securities lawyers?

## Exemptions for Secondary Offerings

A principal advantage of registering a securities offering with the SEC and the appropriate state securities authorities is that the securities may be traded relatively freely following the initial public offering. However, securities issued in a private placement cannot be sold in a *secondary offering*, that is, a subsequent offering by a person other than the issuer, unless they are either registered or exempt from registration. Securities issued in a private placement are thus called *restricted securities*.

Because securities offered in private offerings are unregistered, their subsequent transfer is restricted, and their price will be discounted accordingly. In addition, purchasers of privately offered securities may demand a greater voice in the operation of the business or sweeteners such as dividend preferences or mandatory redemption privileges, which force the company to repurchase the stock upon the occurrence of certain events.

Exhibit 22.6 summarizes certain key definitions and terms related to the resale of securities.

**EXHIBIT 22.6 Key Definitions and Terms Related to the Resale of Securities**

| | |
|---|---|
| **Restricted securities** | "Securities issued in a transaction not involving a public offering." [Rule 144] |
| **Issuer** | "Every person who issues or proposes to issue any security." [Section 2(4)] |
| **Affiliate** | Any officer, director, or major shareholder (generally presumed to include person owning at least 10 percent of issuer's stock). Someone who controls, or is controlled by, or co-controls the issuer. [Rule 144] |
| **Underwriter** | "Any person who has purchased from an issuer with a view to, or offers or sells for an issuer in connection with, the distribution of any security." For purposes of this definition, "issuer" includes "any person directly or indirectly controlling or controlled by the issuer, or any person under direct or indirect common control with the issuer." [Section 2(11)] |
| **"Not an underwriter"** | "Not an underwriter" safe-harbor requirements of Rule 144:<br>**1.** Adequate public information available<br>**2.** One-year holding period (unless affiliate sells unrestricted securities)<br>**3.** Sales limitations for any three-month period: the greater of 1 percent of the outstanding securities of the class and the average weekly trading volume for the preceding four weeks<br>**4.** Must sell through a broker or directly to a market maker<br>**5.** Form 144 filing if more than 500 shares or greater than $10,000 aggregate price in three months<br>**6.** Must have bona fide intention to sell within a reasonable amount of time after filing Form 144 |
| **Rule 144(k)** | A nonaffiliate who has held the security for more than two years may resell without restriction. |
| **Rule 144A** | A nonaffiliate may resell without restriction to a "qualified institutional buyer." |

## SECTION 4(1) EXEMPTION

Section 4(1) of the 1933 Act provides that "transactions by any person other than an issuer, underwriter, or dealer" are exempt from registration. Section 2 of the 1933 Act defines an *issuer* as any person "who issues or proposes to issue any security." A *dealer* is defined as "any person who engages either for all or part of his time, directly or indirectly, as agent, broker, or principal, in the business of offering, buying, selling, or otherwise dealing or trading in securities issued by another person."

An "underwriter" is defined as "any person who has purchased from an issuer with a view to, or offers or sells for an issuer in connection with, the distribution of any security." As used in the definition of an underwriter, the term "issuer" includes "any person directly or indirectly controlling or controlled by the issuer, or any person under direct or indirect common control with the issuer." For example, the sale of securities to the public by a controlling shareholder is a transaction involving an underwriter. Thus, the Section 4(1) exemption is unavailable.

If the person desiring to sell unrestricted securities is not an issuer, underwriter, or dealer, he or she may sell the securities without registration under Section 4(1). There is no limit on the size of the offering or the number of offerees. Section 4(1) is the exemption most often relied on by persons who sell securities in the secondary market in an ordinary transaction involving a broker.

## RULE 144

The SEC adopted *Rule 144* in 1972 to reduce the uncertainty associated with the definition of the term "underwriter." If the requirements of Rule 144 are met, then restricted securities may be sold publicly without registration. Rule 144 is intended merely to provide objective criteria for deciding whether a person is an underwriter; it is not meant to be the exclusive means through which restricted securities may be sold. Under Rule 144, a person is *not an underwriter* if the following conditions are met:

1. Adequate current public information must be available concerning the issuer. This requirement effectively means that the issuer must be a publicly traded company that has complied with the periodic reporting requirements imposed by the 1934 Act (discussed later in this chapter).
2. The securities must have been beneficially owned—with all economic rights belonging to the owner—and fully paid for at least one year prior to the date of sale.
3. In any three-month period, the seller must not sell more than the greater of (a) 1 percent of the outstanding securities of the class and (b) the average weekly trading volume in the securities during the four calendar weeks preceding the filing of the notice of sale on Form 144.
4. The securities must be sold in "broker's transactions," as defined in the 1933 Act, or directly to a "market maker," as defined in the 1934 Act. Solicitation of offers to buy is not permitted, and no commissions for the sale may be paid to any person other than the broker who executes the order of sale.
5. If the amount of the securities sold during any three-month period will exceed 500 shares or have an aggregate sale price in excess of $10,000, a notice on Form 144 must be filed with the SEC and with the principal stock exchange (if any) on which the securities are traded.
6. The person filing the Form 144 must have a bona fide intention to sell the securities within a reasonable time after the filing of the notice.

Rule 144(k) provides that a person who is not an affiliate of the issuer, and has not been an affiliate for three months preceding the sale, may sell restricted securities without regard to items 1, 3, 4, and 5 above if he or she has owned the securities for at least two years prior to their sale. This is of particular importance for shareholders of privately held companies that do not file 1934 Act reports. Affiliates include officers, directors, and major shareholders. The SEC has a rebuttable presumption that anyone owning at least 10 percent of the issuer's stock is an affiliate.

Usually, restricted securities are identified as such by legends appearing on the face or back of their stock certificates. Accordingly, an opinion from the issuer's attorney may be required before a broker-dealer or transfer agent is willing to consummate a transaction involving restricted securities. Certificates issued following a sale pursuant to Rule 144 may be issued without restrictive legends.

If an affiliate of the issuer wants to sell securities, then he or she must sell in accordance with Rule 144 (except for the one-year holding period requirement, which is inapplicable if the securities being sold were acquired in a registered offering) or use another available exemption. The most common is the *Section 4(1½) exemption* for private offerings by an affiliate. These offerings would qualify as private placements under Section 4(2) if made by the issuer. Thus, the securities can be offered only to persons who are capable of bearing and understanding the risk of the investment and who acquire the securities for investment purposes only and not with a view to distribution.

## RULE 144A

Rule 144A permits the resale of unregistered securities to *qualified institutional buyers*—that is, institutional investors holding and managing $100 million or more of securities—if the securities are not of the same class as any securities of the issuer listed on a U.S. securities exchange or quoted on an automated interdealer quotation system (such as the Nasdaq Stock Market). The rule creates a safe harbor for trading unregistered securities that are often issued to institutional investors in private placements and are generally subject to Rule 144's holding periods. The creation of a secondary market for eligible unregistered securities has increased their liquidity and value and reduced the private offering discount for them.

If a transaction meets the terms of Rule 144A, it is deemed not to be a distribution. Therefore, the seller is not an underwriter as defined in the 1933 Act. If the seller is also not an issuer or dealer, it may rely on the Section 4(1) exemption for transactions by persons who are not issuers, underwriters, or dealers, as long as it resells only to other qualified institutional buyers.

Dealers may also take advantage of Rule 144A. Under Section 4(3) of the 1933 Act, dealers are entitled to an exemption from registration, unless they are participants in a distribution or in a transaction taking place within a specified period after securities have been offered to the public. If a transaction complies with Rule 144A, the dealer will be deemed not to be a participant in a distribution, and the securities will be deemed not to have been offered to the public. Accordingly, the transaction will be exempt from registration.

Rule 144A is a nonexclusive exemption. If the requirements of Rule 144A cannot be met, the parties to the transaction may still rely on the facts-and-circumstances analysis commonly associated with nonpublic transfers of unregistered stock. For example, the so-called Section 4(1½) exemption for private resales of restricted securities may apply. In general, a Section 4(1½) offering is an offering by a person other than the issuer (usually either a control person or the holder of restricted unregistered stocks) that would, if it had been done by the issuer, be eligible for the Section 4(2) private offering exemption.

Exhibit 22.7 depicts the alternatives available for resales by affiliates and nonaffiliates.

**EXHIBIT 22.7 Exemptions for Resale**

| SECURITIES | SELLER: Affiliate | SELLER: Nonaffiliate |
|---|---|---|
| **Issued in public offering** | Register<br>Section 4(1½)<br>Rule 144 (without holding period requirement) | Section 4(1) |
| **Not issued in public offering** | Register<br>Section 4(1½)<br>Rule 144 (including holding period requirement) | Register<br>Rule 144 (including holding period requirement)<br>Rule 144(k)—if held for more than two years<br>Rule 144A |

# Offerings Offshore and Regulation S

*Regulation S* clarified the general rule that any offer or sale outside the United States is not subject to the federal registration requirements. The SEC had long taken the position that the Section 5 registration requirements do not apply to offers and sales effected in a manner that would result in the securities coming to rest abroad. Transactions meeting the requirements of certain safe harbors for the issuance and resale of securities set forth in Regulation S are deemed to occur outside the United States.

All offers and sales of any security under Regulation S must be made in *offshore transactions,* defined as transactions in which no offer is made to a person in the United States and either (1) the buyer is outside the United States at the time the buy order is originated; or (2) the transaction is one executed in, on, or through the facilities of a designated offshore securities market. No directed selling efforts may be made in the United States.

Regulation S has enabled U.S. companies to offer securities abroad with greater certainty that such securities are exempt from registration. Additionally, the combination of Rule 144A and Regulation S has expanded the private placement market by increasing the liquidity of privately placed securities.

Exhibit 22.8 provides a flow chart of the registration and exemption requirements applicable to primary and secondary offerings of securities.

**EXHIBIT 22.8 An Outline of Registration and Exemption Requirements**

**Initial Offerings of Securities**

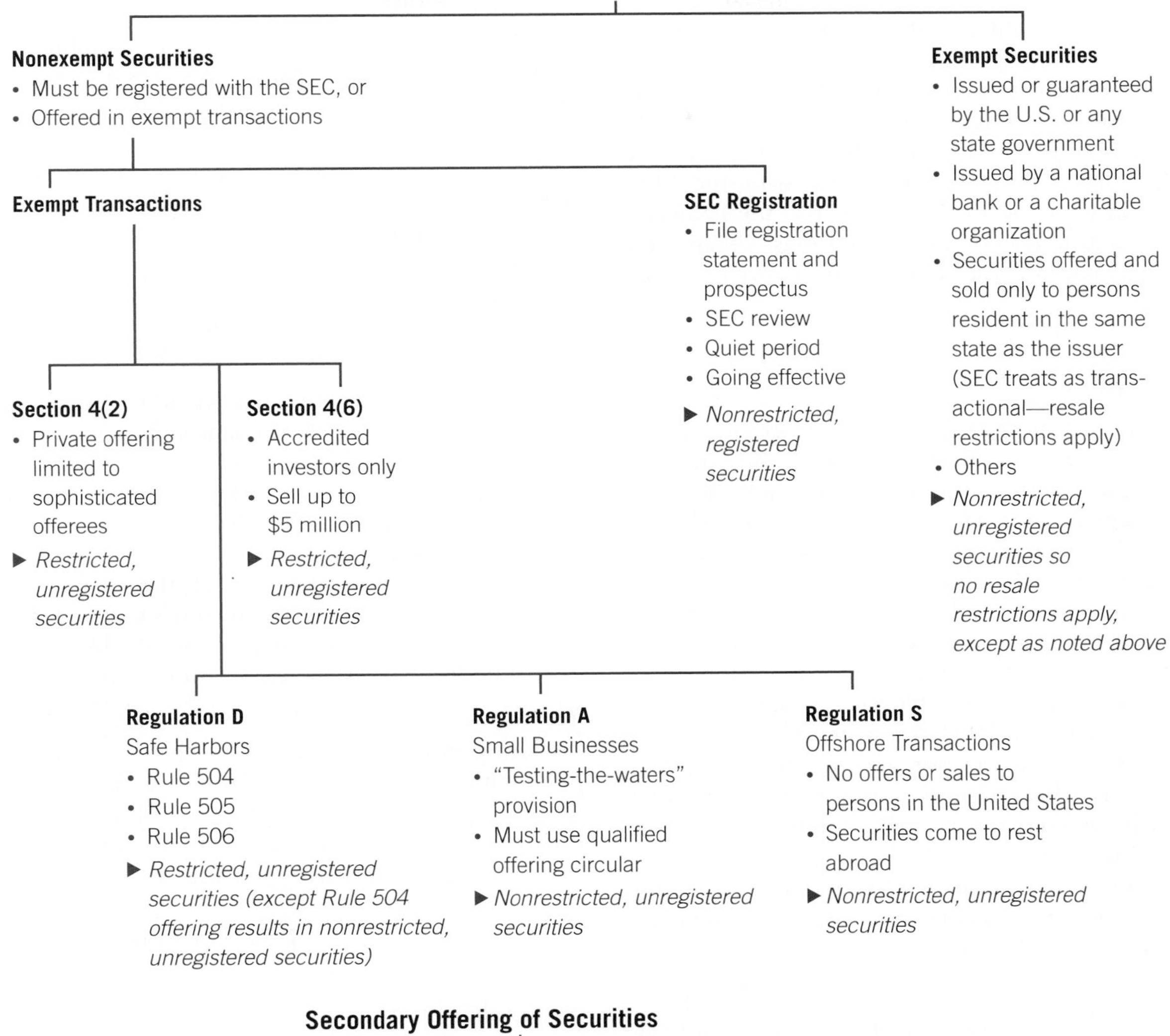

Nonexempt Securities
• Must be registered with the SEC, or
• Offered in exempt transactions
Exempt Securities
• Issued or guaranteed by the U.S. or any state government
• Issued by a national bank or a charitable organization
• Securities offered and sold only to persons resident in the same state as the issuer (SEC treats as transactional—resale restrictions apply)
• Others
▶ Nonrestricted, unregistered securities so no resale restrictions apply, except as noted above
Exempt Transactions
SEC Registration
• File registration statement and prospectus
• SEC review
• Quiet period
• Going effective
▶ Nonrestricted, registered securities
Section 4(2)
• Private offering limited to sophisticated offerees
▶ Restricted, unregistered securities
Section 4(6)
• Accredited investors only
• Sell up to $5 million
▶ Restricted, unregistered securities
Regulation D
Safe Harbors
• Rule 504
• Rule 505
• Rule 506
▶ Restricted, unregistered securities (except Rule 504 offering results in nonrestricted, unregistered securities)
Regulation A
Small Businesses
• "Testing-the-waters" provision
• Must use qualified offering circular
▶ Nonrestricted, unregistered securities
Regulation S
Offshore Transactions
• No offers or sales to persons in the United States
• Securities come to rest abroad
▶ Nonrestricted, unregistered securities
Secondary Offering of Securities

**Restricted Securities**
- SEC registration
- Section 4(1½) for private placements by affiliates
- Section 4(1) exemptions
  - Rule 144 "not an underwriter" safe harbor
  - Rule 144(k), not available to affiliates
  - Rule 144A for sales to qualified institutional buyers
  - Rule 145(d)
- Regulation S

**Nonrestricted Securities**
- Section 4(1) exemption for persons "other than an issuer, underwriter or dealer": no limitations on the size of offering or number of offerees, provided sale is by a nonaffiliate
- Affiliates must rely on Rule 144 or Section 4(1½)

# Reporting Requirements of Public Companies

The completion of a public offering does not terminate the issuer's relationship with the SEC. Under Section 15(d) of the 1934 Act, a company with registered securities in a public offering must file periodic reports. Usually, the company must also register the class of equity securities offered to the public with the SEC under Section 12 of the 1934 Act. Whereas the 1933 Act requires the registration of specific offerings of securities, the 1934 Act requires the registration of specific *classes* of securities.

## SECTION 12

Under Section 12 of the 1934 Act, an issuer engaged in interstate commerce and having total assets exceeding $5 million must register with the SEC each nonexempt class of security that (1) is listed on a national stock exchange or (2) is an equity security held of record by at least 500 persons. Registration subjects the issuer to various reporting requirements and to certain rules and regulations concerning proxies, tender offers, insider trading, and so on. A company registered under Section 12 is commonly referred to as a public or *reporting company.* Registration under the 1934 Act is intended to supplement the 1933 Act registration and to ensure that current information concerning the issuer is available to the public, enabling investors to make informed decisions about securities purchases and sales.

The following are some of the significant requirements associated with becoming a registered company under Section 12 of the 1934 Act:

- *10–Q* An unaudited quarterly statement of operations and financial condition must be filed with the SEC on Form 10–Q within thirty-five days after the end of each fiscal quarter.
- *10–K* An annual audited report must be filed with the SEC on Form 10–K within sixty days after the end of the issuer's fiscal year.
- *8–K* A special report on Form 8–K must be filed with the SEC within four days after certain events, including changes in control; acquisitions or dispositions of key assets; resignation of directors or auditors; entry into or termination of material agreements that are not made in the ordinary course of business; material impairments; specific issues affecting listing; determinations that past financial statements can no longer be relied on; creation of, or triggering events that accelerate or increase, obligations under off-balance-sheet arrangements; and costs associated with exit or disposal activities.

Small business issuers required to file periodic reports under the 1934 Act can do so with simplified forms under Regulation S–B. These abbreviated forms include Form 10–KSB for annual reports and Form 10–QSB for quarterly reports.

The periodic reports must include in narrative form Management's Discussion & Analysis of Financial Condition and Results of Operations (MD&A). Since its genesis in 1980, the MD&A has been clarified in numerous SEC releases. In December 2003, the SEC released further guidance on this requirement and identified three principal objectives of the MD&A:

- To provide a narrative explanation of a company's financial statements that enables investors to see the company through the eyes of management.
- To enhance the overall financial disclosure and provide the context within which financial information should be analyzed.
- To provide information about the quality of, and potential variability of, a company's earnings and cash flow so that investors can ascertain the likelihood that past performance is indicative of future performance.[27]

The release emphasized the need for clarity and material disclosure in the MD&A and, to that end, stressed the presentational aspects of the disclosure. Among the topics requiring disclosure within the MD&A are certain off-balance-sheet arrangements of the sort created by Enron, discussed further in Chapter 1.

## OTHER SECTIONS OF THE 1934 ACT

Other sections of the 1934 Act regulate such activities as proxy solicitations, insider trading, and tender offers.

### *Proxy Solicitations*

The proxy regulation provisions of Section 14 of the 1934 Act apply to all public companies. They govern the solicitation of written powers of attorney, or *proxies,* that give the proxy holder the right to vote the shares owned by the person who signs the proxy card. As explained in Chapter 19, proxy solicitations relate to management and shareholder proposals as well as to the election of the board of directors.

27. Interpretation: Commission Guidance Regarding MD&A, SEC Release Nos. 33-8350, 34-48960, 17 C.F.R. pts. 211, 231, 241 (Dec. 29, 2003).

### *Insider Trading Reports*

Section 16 of the 1934 Act requires executive officers, directors, and persons holding more than 10 percent of the equity securities of a public company to file ownership reports on Forms 4 and 5 with the SEC initially, when they acquire or dispose of securities, and on an annual basis. (These reports are described more fully in Chapter 23.) Purchases and sales of the public issuer's equity securities (including sales back to the issuer) must be reported within two business days. Insiders of companies not registered under the 1934 Act are not required to file regular reports with the SEC. Trading by insiders is also subject to Section 16(b)'s short-swing trading restrictions and Section 10(b)'s antifraud provisions, which are discussed in Chapter 23.

### *Tender Offers*

Any person making a *tender offer* to shareholders, whereby shareholders are asked to sell their shares to that person for a stated price, must comply with the tender offer rules found in Section 14 of the 1934 Act. Some rules, such as the requirement that a tender offer be left open for at least twenty business days, apply even if the company is not registered under the 1934 Act if it has a significant number of shareholders. Other rules, such as the rule giving shareholders the right to withdraw their shares once they are tendered and the rule requiring proration if the offer is oversubscribed, apply only if the company is registered under the 1934 Act.

### *Schedule 13D*

Under Section 13, any person acquiring more than 5 percent of the shares of a reporting company must file a Schedule 13D within ten days after crossing the 5 percent mark. The Schedule 13D must disclose the number of shares acquired and the intentions of the person acquiring them. Often the person acquiring the shares will state that it is buying the shares for investment purposes only. Sometimes, however, the company suspects an ulterior motive, such as preparation for a hostile takeover attempt.

# Violation of the Registration and Prospectus-Delivery Requirements: Section 12(a)(1) of the 1933 Act

As explained above, Section 5 of the 1933 Act provides that, absent an exemption, all securities must be registered and may be sold only after delivery of a prospectus meeting the requirements of the 1933 Act. The penalty for violation of Section 5 is simple and severe. Section 12(a)(1) provides that, absent an exemption, anyone who offers or sells a security without an effective registration statement or by means of a noncomplying prospectus is liable to the purchaser for recission or damages. In effect, the purchaser is given a put: if the investment proves successful, the investor can keep the shares, but if, within one year from the date of purchase, the investment proves unprofitable, the investor can get his or her money back.

## Elements of Liability

To establish a Section 12(a)(1) claim, the plaintiff must show that the defendant sold or offered securities without an effective registration statement, or by means of a noncomplying prospectus, through the use of interstate transportation or communication. A plaintiff typically satisfies the interstate transportation or communication requirement by proving that the mails, telephone, or other interstate means were used in the offer or sale to that particular plaintiff. The plaintiff must file suit within one year from the date the securities were offered or sold. Section 12(a)(1) imposes a standard of strict liability. The plaintiff need not show that the defendant acted willfully or negligently, only that the defendant committed the act of selling unregistered and nonexempt securities.

## Damages

If the plaintiff still owns the securities, he or she is entitled to rescind the purchase. To rescind, the plaintiff returns the securities, together with any income (such as dividends) he or she received from them, in exchange for the price paid for the securities, plus interest. If the plaintiff has sold the securities, he or she is entitled to recover damages—usually the difference between what was paid and what was received for the securities at sale.

## Who May Be Sued

The severity of the remedy under Section 12(a)(1) has led to questions about who may be considered to have offered or sold securities within the meaning of the statute. It clearly includes the issuer. But what about others involved in an unregistered securities transaction, such as attorneys, accountants, underwriters, and investment bankers?

Section 12(a)(1) provides that "any person who . . . offers or sells a security," in violation of the registration requirement, "shall be liable to the person purchasing such security from him." To be considered a seller, a nonowner must successfully solicit the purchase and be motivated at least in part by a desire to serve his or her own financial interests or those of the securities owner.[28] Thus, mere promotion of a security does not necessarily make a person a seller under Section 12(a)(1), even if that promotion is a substantial factor in inducing the purchase of the security.

### WHO MAY SUE

Anyone who purchases shares issued in violation of the registration requirements may bring suit. If the securities were sold to a number of persons, then a plaintiff could bring a class-action suit, which would be filed on behalf of all persons who purchased the illegally issued securities.

## Section 11 of the 1933 Act

Section 11 provides a remedy for a person who purchases a security pursuant to a misleading registration statement. Section 11 applies only to registered securities. The section is the longest and most detailed civil liability provision in the 1933 Act. It spells out who may sue, who may be sued, the elements of the offense, the permitted defenses, and the damages that may be awarded. Under Section 11, an issuer of securities is liable for its false statements or misleading omissions even if the issuer had no intent to defraud and was not even negligent in ascertaining the truth.

### WHO MAY SUE

#### *Tracing Requirement*

Any person who has purchased a registered security may sue under Section 11. But the purchaser must prove that the security at issue was actually one of those sold pursuant to the misleading registration statement.[29] Although this requirement does not present a problem for direct purchasers of an initial public offering, open-market purchasers may find it difficult to trace their securities back to a sale made under the defective registration statement.

#### *Class Actions*

Plaintiffs in a Section 11 case typically bring a class action, in which the named plaintiffs act on behalf of themselves and "all others similarly situated." The advantage to the plaintiffs (and their attorneys) of proceeding in this manner is that the individual plaintiffs' claims, worth only a few hundred or a few thousand dollars, together often amount to millions of dollars.

### WHO MAY BE SUED

Section 11 lists, and thereby limits, the entities and persons who may be sued: (1) the issuer offering the security; (2) the underwriters; (3) any member of the board of directors at the time of the offering; (4) persons who gave their consent to be named in the registration statement as future directors; (5) every person who signed the registration statement (under Section 6(a) of the 1933 Act, it must be signed by the issuer, its principal executive officer, its principal financing officer, and its principal accounting officer); and (6) experts who consented to give authority to the "expertized" portion of the registration statement, such as accountants who audited the financial statements contained in it. No person can be named in the registration statement as an expert unless that person has consented in writing to being named.

All defendants in a Section 11 case generally have joint and several liability for violations, meaning that one defendant can be held responsible for all the damages awarded to the plaintiff, even if that defendant was only partially responsible for the violation. The one exception is that outside directors who did not commit knowing violations are generally liable only for the portion of the damages attributable to their percentage of responsibility.

Plaintiffs often allege that persons or entities other than those specified in Section 11 are liable under a theory of secondary liability, such as aiding and abetting or conspiracy. Most (but not all) courts have rejected such attempts to expand liability under Section 11. The U.S. Supreme Court ruled in 1994 that a private plaintiff may not maintain an aiding and abetting suit under Section 10(b),[30] and it seems unlikely that the Court would extend Section 11 to include aiders and abettors.

### ELEMENTS OF LIABILITY

The elements of a Section 11 offense are straightforward. The plaintiff must show that, at the time the registration statement became effective, it (1) contained a false or

28. Pinter v. Dahl, 486 U.S. 622 (1988).

29. *See, e.g.*, Lee v. Ernst & Young LLP, 294 F.3d 969, 976–77 (8th Cir. 2002); De Maria v. Anderson, 318 F.3d 170 (2d Cir. 2003) (holding that after-market purchasers who can trace their shares to an allegedly misleading registration statement have standing to sue under Section 11).

30. Cent. Bank of Denver, N.A. v. First Interstate Bank of Denver, N.A., 511 U.S. 164 (1994).

misleading statement of a material fact or (2) omitted to state a material fact required to be stated in the registration statement or necessary to make the statements contained in the registration statement not misleading.

The Supreme Court has defined a *material fact* as one that a reasonable investor would most likely have considered important in deciding whether to buy or sell—that is, what a reasonable hypothetical investor would have considered important, not necessarily what the actual investor considered important. The Supreme Court has held that an omitted fact is material if there is "a substantial likelihood that the disclosure of the omitted fact would have been viewed by the reasonable investor as having significantly altered the 'total mix' of information made available."[31]

The following case further explored the definition of materiality.

31. TSC Indus. v. Northway, Inc., 426 U.S. 438, 449 (1976).

A CASE IN POINT

## Summary

**CASE 22.3**

**Rosenzweig v. Azurix Corp.**

*United States Court of Appeals for the Fifth Circuit*

*332 F.3d 854 (5th Cir. 2003).*

**› FACTS** In 1999, Enron Corporation formed Azurix, a global water and wastewater company. Azurix planned to take advantage of what appeared to be a trend toward privatization by acquiring and operating government-owned facilities. Azurix did an initial public offering in 1998 after securing a thirty-year concession from the province of Buenos Aires, Argentina. The offering price was around $20 per share. Enron took Azurix private in 2000 by buying all the public's shares at $8 per share.

Shareholders who had purchased Azurix stock in the secondary market brought this action, alleging, among other things, that the defendants had violated the federal securities laws by making misrepresentations and omissions in press releases and public filings. In particular, the plaintiffs alleged that the defendants knew that Azurix's business plan was fundamentally flawed and that the Buenos Aires concession was plagued with problems, but they nevertheless fraudulently inflated Azurix's stock price by making misleading optimistic representations and concealing the truth. The defendants challenged the materiality of the alleged misrepresentations and omissions.

**› ISSUE PRESENTED** What constitutes materiality for purposes of a Section 11 claim?

**› SUMMARY OF OPINION** The U.S. Court of Appeals for the Fifth Circuit declared that, "[t]he generalized, positive statements about the company's competitive strengths, experienced management, and future prospects" were not material, noting that "Azurix was under no duty to cast its business in a pejorative, rather than a positive light." More specific remarks were also found to be immaterial. In the prospectus, Azurix had stated, "We anticipate funding capital expenditures [for the Buenos Aires concession] through operating cash flows and long-term debt and equity at the concession level." The court focused on the word "anticipate" and the nine single-spaced pages of risk disclosures and concluded that this specific statement was immaterial.

The plaintiffs also claimed that the investing public was led to believe that the defendants had performed due diligence on the Buenos Aires concession, as well as others, which was either a material misrepresentation or an omission. The court agreed with the trial court that "a rational investor would not have relied on the due diligence statements contained in the prospectus," in light of the risk disclosures. The court described other, allegedly misleading, specific statements as "obviously immaterial puffery."

**› RESULT** The Fifth Circuit affirmed the dismissal of the plaintiffs' claims.

**› COMMENTS** The plaintiffs also brought claims under Section 12, but those claims were dismissed because the plaintiffs lacked standing. Additionally, the court pointed out that the claims were insufficiently particular and that the inferences of intent to deceive were weak.

The plaintiff does not have to establish that he or she read the prospectus or relied upon the misstatement or omission except in the following instance: A plaintiff who purchases a security on the open market after the issuing company has released its income statements for the year following the registration statement must show that the misrepresentation in the prospectus influenced his or her decision to buy.

## DEFENSES

Section 11 sets forth several defenses. The defenses of no reliance and no causation focus on the effects of the misstatements on the behavior of investors and the market, while the defense of due diligence looks to the culpability of the defendants.

### *No Reliance*

The defense of no reliance relates to the investor's knowledge. Investors who know that there was a misstatement or omission cannot claim to have relied on it; they are presumed to have acted despite the misstatement or omission. Thus, if the defendant can establish that the plaintiff actually knew that a statement was false or that there was an omission, there is no liability under Section 11. Again, note that investors need not prove that they actually relied on the misstatement or omission or even read the prospectus.

### *No Causation*

The defense of no causation focuses on the link between the misstatement and the investor's loss. Even if there was a misstatement or omission of a material fact, a defendant will not be liable if it can show that the misstatement or omission did not actually cause the plaintiff to suffer any loss. In other words, the plaintiff may have lost money on a trade, but that loss may not have been due to the defendant's conduct. This showing typically consists of an expert analysis of the various factors that influenced the price movements of the securities in question. Developments in this area are discussed in Chapter 23.

### *Due Diligence*

The defense of due diligence focuses on the behavior of the defendants. It is available to all defendants except the issuing company. A defendant is not liable for a misrepresentation or omission if it acted with due diligence, meaning that it (1) conducted a reasonable investigation and (2) reasonably believed (a) that the statements made were true and (b) that there were no omissions that made those statements misleading. A reasonable investigation is what a prudent person managing his or her own property would conduct.

The primary wrinkle in the due diligence defense arises in connection with the expertized portions of the registration statement, such as audit reports on the company's financial statements, appraisal reports, or engineering reports. The experts are, of course, responsible for their own reports, provided that the reports are identified as having been prepared by them and that the experts have given their consent to the use of their reports in the registration statement. The experts are generally not responsible under Section 11 for portions of the registration statement other than their reports.

Nonexpert defendants are generally entitled to rely on the experts. They can establish due diligence by showing that they had no reasonable basis to believe that the experts' reports were misleading and, in fact, did not believe them to be misleading. Significantly, the defendants need not show that they undertook any investigation of those reports.

The case that follows was the first to articulate the due diligence standards applicable to the various participants in the offering process and remains an accurate statement of the law.

A CASE IN POINT

**CASE 22.4**

**Escott v. BarChris Construction Corp.**

*United States District Court for the Southern District of New York 283 F. Supp. 643 (S.D.N.Y. 1968).*

## Summary

**› FACTS** BarChris was in the business of building bowling alleys. It obtained capital through a public offering in May 1961. Due to financial problems, the company filed for protection under the Bankruptcy Act in October 1962. A class action followed, alleging Section 11 claims against the company, its officers and directors, and its underwriters.

**› ISSUE PRESENTED** When is the due diligence defense available to the principal officers or the inside directors of the issuer? May a chief financial officer rely on the audited financial statements if he had reason to believe those statements were incorrect? Have outside directors and underwriters, who relied on management's statements and made no independent investigation, acted with due diligence?

*(Continued)*

(Case 22.4 *continued)*

**› SUMMARY OF OPINION** The U.S. District Court for the Southern District of New York first found that both the expertized and the nonexpertized portions of the registration statement were misleading. Every defendant raised the defense of due diligence except the issuer, to whom the defense was not available.

The court applied the most stringent standards to the company's principal officers and inside directors (that is, the directors who were also officers of the corporation). It first noted that principal officers and inside directors who sign a registration statement have a significant burden. Because of their extensive knowledge of the company's affairs, it is rare that they can successfully establish a due diligence defense. The court held that the chief financial officer was not entitled to rely on the outside auditors as to the accuracy of the financial statements because he had reason to believe that those statements were incorrect. The court concluded that the liability of principal officers and inside directors approaches that of the company itself. They cannot escape liability for the nonexpertized portions of the statement even if they did not read the statement, did not understand it, and relied on assistants and lawyers to make adequate disclosures.

The court then considered the liability of two outside directors who had become directors a month before the offering. Neither had read the registration statement in final form, and both had relied on assurances from the officers that everything was in order. The court ruled that Section 11 imposes liability on directors, no matter how new they are. Individuals are presumed to know their responsibility when they become directors. A director can escape liability only by using that degree of reasonable care to investigate the facts that a prudent person would employ in the management of his or her own property. The court concluded that a prudent person would not act in an important matter without any knowledge of the relevant facts, in sole reliance upon representations of persons who were comparative strangers, and upon general information that did not purport to cover the particular case.

The court then considered whether the underwriters had established the due diligence defense. The court concluded that the underwriters had made no effectual attempt at verification. The court ruled that it was not sufficient to ask management questions, obtain answers that, if true, would be thought satisfactory, and let the matter go at that without seeking to ascertain from the records whether the answers were, in fact, true and complete. The court explained:

> [I]n a sense, the positions of the underwriter and the company's officers are adverse. It is not unlikely that statements made by company officers to an underwriter to induce him to underwrite may be self-serving. They may be unduly enthusiastic. As in this case, they may, on occasion, be deliberately false.

The underwriters argued that the prospectus is the company's prospectus, not theirs. But the court ruled that the 1933 Act makes no such distinction. Prospective investors rely upon the reputation of the underwriters when deciding whether to purchase the securities. The court explained:

> The purpose of Section 11 is to protect investors. To that end the underwriters are made responsible for the truth of the prospectus. If they may escape that responsibility by taking at face value representations made to them by the company's management, then the inclusion of underwriters among those liable under Section 11 affords the investors no additional protection. To effectuate the statute's purpose, the phrase "reasonable investigation" must be construed to require more effort on the part of the

*(Continued)*

(Case 22.4 *continued)*

underwriters than the mere accurate reporting in the prospectus of "data presented" to them by the company. It should make no difference that this data is elicited by questions addressed to the company officers by the underwriters, or that the underwriters at the time believe that the company's officers are truthful and reliable. In order to make the underwriters' participation in this enterprise of any value to the investors, the underwriters must make some reasonable attempt to verify the data submitted to them. They may not rely solely on the company's officers or on the company's counsel. A prudent man in the management of his own property would not rely on them.

**› RESULT** None of the defendants could rely on the due diligence defense, except the outside directors, who were permitted to rely on the opinion of the auditors as to the audited financial statements.

**› COMMENTS** The degree of reliance a participating underwriter may place on a principal underwriter remains unclear. The court in *BarChris* summarily noted that the participating underwriters who relied solely on the primary underwriters did not establish due diligence. An SEC release has since suggested that a participating underwriter has met its due diligence requirements if it satisfies itself that the managing underwriter has made the kind of investigation the participant would have performed were it the manager.

### *Bespeaks Caution Doctrine*

According to another defense, the judicially created *bespeaks caution doctrine*, a court may determine that the inclusion of sufficient cautionary statements in a prospectus renders immaterial any misrepresentations and omissions contained therein. The doctrine is based on the proposition that a statement or omission must be considered in context, so accompanying statements may render it immaterial as a matter of law. The following case illustrates the doctrine in the context of an initial public offering.

A CASE IN POINT

**CASE 22.5**

**Steinberg v. PRT Group, Inc.**

*United States District Court for the Southern District of New York*

*88 F. Supp. 2d 294 (S.D.N.Y. 2000).*

## Summary

**› FACTS** PRT offered information technology (IT) services, primarily to Fortune 500 companies, on a proposal/bid basis. Clients would submit proposals; PRT and other IT firms would then prepare bids. Although PRT employed a number of full-time IT professionals, much of its talent pool comprised independent contractors hired for specific bids. In 1997, PRT commenced an initial public offering pursuant to a registration statement filed with the SEC. The offering price was $13 per share. When PRT released its fourth quarter and year-end financial results for 1997, the company reported that its revenues had increased 151 percent that year and that it earned $1.1 million in the fourth quarter. Yet within a month later, PRT announced that it expected a $3 million net loss in the first quarter of 1998. In the twenty-four hours following that announcement, PRT's price per share fell from $19.125 to $9.5625. The decline continued, and PRT's net losses for 1998 totaled $12 million. A class-action suit was brought alleging that the prospectus contained various false and misleading statements. PRT filed a motion to dismiss, arguing that the prospectus as a whole bespoke caution, that is, that the prospectus as a whole warned of precisely the risks that materialized.

**› ISSUE PRESENTED** Did the PRT prospectus bespeak caution?

*(Continued)*

(Case 22.5 *continued*)

**› SUMMARY OF OPINION** The U.S. District Court for the Southern District of New York first explained that under the "bespeaks caution" doctrine, a misrepresentation or nondisclosure will be deemed immaterial if it is surrounded by cautionary language sufficiently specific to render reliance on the misrepresentation unreasonable.

Furthermore, general statements of optimism are not actionable. Vague expressions of optimism constitute immaterial corporate "puffery," which cannot mislead the reasonable investor. The plaintiffs alleged that the prospectus falsely represented that PRT had developed proprietary software tools and processes. Yet the prospectus contained repeated disclosures about PRT's reliance on third-party software, technology, and expertise. As a result, this claim was "squarely contradicted by the disclosures in the prospectus" and therefore failed as a matter of law.

The plaintiffs also contended that because PRT hired IT professionals on a contract-by-contract basis, the prospectus falsely represented that PRT had built long-term relationships through its service offering, causing many clients to view PRT as an extension of their in-house IT organizations. The court concluded that the plaintiffs' allegations were contradicted by the prospectus itself. The prospectus revealed that in fact much of PRT's business in 1997 resulted from long-term relationships with clients.

The plaintiffs also asserted that the prospectus misrepresented the significance of PRT's "preferred vendor" status by implying that this status gave PRT a competitive advantage over other companies bidding for the same contracts. The court found the plaintiffs' contentions regarding PRT's statements about its "preferred vendor" status "similarly unavailing, in light of the actual representations contained in the prospectus." In fact, in the example of one of PRT's preferred vendor relationships, the prospectus stated that the client had designated seventeen preferred vendors.

The prospectus clearly and unequivocally warned investors that the IT business was highly competitive: "The Company experiences intense competition. The market for services such as PRT offers is very broad and such services are offered by a large number of private and public companies, many of which are significantly larger than, and have greater financial, technical and marketing resources than, PRT."

As for the plaintiffs' claim that PRT falsely represented that it held a "competitive advantage in attracting and retaining IT professionals," this statement was not actionable because it was a vague statement of optimism. With respect to PRT's alleged failure to disclose certain risks involved with recruiting IT personnel, the prospectus was "rife" with references to the extremely limited pool of qualified IT professionals. In light of these explicit risk disclosures, the plaintiffs' allegations of "undisclosed risks" in connection with PRT's recruitment of IT professionals failed as a matter of law.

In view of all of the disclosures in the prospectus concerning the recruitment of IT professionals, a reasonable investor would not attach any importance to alleged misstatements regarding PRT's recruiting and assessment tools in making the decision to invest in PRT. Accordingly, these statements were immaterial as a matter of law.

The plaintiffs alleged that the prospectus overstated fivefold the number of IT professionals PRT employed and subcontracted with just prior to the initial public offering. But the court concluded that no reasonable investor could find that PRT's inclusion of "temporary" employees was misleading, in view of the bid-based nature of the business, the industry practice of subcontracting IT professionals who worked for more than one IT company, and all the other disclosures in the prospectus.

The plaintiffs also claimed that the prospectus materially overstated PRT's ability to obtain Y2K business. The court concluded that even if the prospectus described PRT's

*(Continued)*

(Case 22.5 *continued)*

ability to generate Y2K business in highly positive terms, this rosy outlook was tempered by numerous specific risk disclosures about the potential pitfalls in the Y2K business.

In view of the foregoing, and looking at the prospectus as a whole, the court concluded that it could not reasonably conclude that the defendants' representations, taken together and in context, would have misled a reasonable investor about the nature of the investment in PRT. When read in its entirety, the prospectus was "not overly sanguine but instead bespeaks caution."

**› RESULT** The claims against PRT and its officers were dismissed.

Not all courts have adopted the bespeaks caution doctrine. Cautionary language will render an alleged omission or misrepresentation immaterial only if the cautionary statements are substantive and tailored to specific future projections, estimates, or opinions in the prospectus. In 1994, the Fifth Circuit stated:

> [C]autionary language is not necessarily sufficient, in and of itself, to render predictive statements immaterial as a matter of law. . . . The appropriate inquiry is whether, under all the circumstances, the omitted fact or the prediction without a reasonable basis "is one [that] a reasonable investor would consider significant in [making] the decision to invest, such that it alters the total mix of information available about the proposed investment." Inclusion of cautionary language . . . is, of course, relevant to the materiality inquiry. . . . Nevertheless, cautionary language as such is not dispositive of this inquiry.[32]

### *Litigation Reform Act Safe Harbor for Forward-Looking Statements*

The Litigation Reform Act provides a statutory safe harbor for certain forward-looking statements by issuers subject to the 1934 Act's reporting requirements and persons acting on their behalf. It is not available for initial public offerings or offerings by a blank check company, a partnership, a limited liability company, or a direct participation investment program, however. The safe harbor also does not apply to any forward-looking statement included in a financial statement prepared in accordance with generally accepted accounting principles.

The safe harbor provides two independent and alternative grounds for precluding liability. Under the first prong, liability for a written or oral forward-looking statement is precluded if it was identified by the speaker as a forward-looking statement and accompanied by meaningful cautionary statements that identify important factors that could cause actual results to differ materially from those in the statement. Even if the statement does not satisfy these criteria, a second prong precludes liability for a forward-looking statement unless the person who made the statement did so with actual knowledge that the statement was false or misleading. A company is not liable for a forward-looking statement it issues unless the plaintiff proves that the statement was made by, or with the approval of, an executive officer who had actual knowledge that the statement was false or misleading. This safe harbor is discussed further in Chapter 23.

### DAMAGES

Section 11 sets forth the damages recoverable for violation of its provisions. If the plaintiff has not sold the securities in question, the recoverable damages are the amount paid for each security minus its value at the time the plaintiff brings the claim. The value at the time the plaintiff brings the claim is usually the market price, unless the market price has been affected by the misrepresentation or omission. If the securities have been sold before the plaintiff brings the claim, the recoverable damages are the amount paid for the securities minus the amount received at sale.

## Section 12(a)(2) of the 1933 Act

Section 12(a)(2) provides a remedy for any person who purchases a security by means of a misleading prospectus or oral communication. To establish a Section 12(a)(2) claim, the plaintiff must prove that (1) through the mails or other means of interstate commerce, (2) the defendant offered or sold a security, (3) by means of a prospectus or oral communication, (4) that included a material misrepresentation or omission. Materiality

32. Rubinstein v. Collins, 20 F.3d 160 (5th Cir. 1994).

under Section 12(a)(2) is the same as materiality under Section 11.

The purchaser may rescind the purchase unless the defendant proves that the depreciation in the value of the security resulted from factors unrelated to the alleged misstatement or omission. If the purchaser has sold the security, he or she generally may recover damages equal to the difference between what was paid and what was received for the security. If the defendant demonstrates that part or all of the decline in the value of the security was caused by factors other than the misstatement or omission alleged in the complaint, then the plaintiff may not recover damages based on that portion of the decline.

Section 12(a)(2) does not require the plaintiff to prove that he or she relied on the misrepresentation or that the defendant acted with *scienter*, that is, an intent to deceive. On the other hand, Section 12(a)(2) applies only to those who offer or sell a security. Under Section 12(a)(2), the plaintiff must bring the action within one year from when he or she discovered or should have discovered the fraud, or three years after the sale, whichever is the shorter.

In *Gustafson v. Alloyd Co.*,[33] the Supreme Court limited Section 12(a)(2) to public offerings but did not define the term. The Court held that Section 12(a)(2) did not apply to a private placement exempt under Section 4(2). The Court reasoned that a stock-purchase agreement was not a prospectus under Section 10 and thus was not a prospectus for purposes of Section 12(a)(2) either.

*Gustafson* makes it clear that Section 12(a)(2) liability extends to fraudulent statements or omissions in statutory prospectuses used in a registered public offering, as well as in documents used to sell securities exempt under Section 3. It is not yet clear whether the term "public offering" applies to (1) all offerings not exempted under Section 4(2) or (2) only offerings that must be registered under Section 5 and offerings of securities exempted under Section 3. The latter reading would exclude offerings under Regulation D, Rule 144A, and Regulation S from Section 12(a)(2)'s reach. Several courts have held that Rule 144A or Regulation S offerings could be "public" for purposes of Section 12(a)(2).[34] Others have reached the opposite result.[35]

33. 513 U.S. 561 (1995).

34. *See, e.g.*, Newby v. Enron Corp., 310 F. Supp. 2d 819 (S.D. Tex. 2004); Sloane Overseas Fund v. Sapiens Int'l Corp., 941 F. Supp. 1369 (S.D.N.Y. 1996).

35. *See, e.g.*, *In re* Hayes Lemmerz Int'l, Inc. Equity Sec. Litig., 271 F. Supp. 2d 1007 (E.D. Mich. 2003).

Resales by affiliates under Rule 144 should not fall within the scope of Section 12(a)(2). However, resales by affiliates that would constitute a distribution under traditional Section 2(11) analysis are probably public offerings subject to Section 12(a)(2).[36]

Section 12(a)(2) clearly applies to oral communications made in connection with a registered public offering. It would also appear to extend to selling documents, such as a brochure sent to investors along with the statutory prospectus, used in connection with registered offerings.

## Who May Be Sued

Section 12(a)(2)'s language relating to who may be liable is identical to that of Section 12(a)(1): anyone who "offers or sells" a security by means of a misleading prospectus or oral communication. Accordingly, most courts treat Sections 12(a)(1) and 12(a)(2) as the same for the purposes of identifying potential defendants and limit the potential defendants to those in privity with the plaintiff or those who solicited the securities sale for financial gain. Those in privity would include underwriters, brokers, and dealers having a direct contractual relationship with the plaintiff.

## Reasonable Care Defense

Section 12(a)(2) provides a defense of reasonable care. A defendant (including the issuer) will not be liable for a Section 12(a)(2) violation if it can prove that it did not know, and in the exercise of reasonable care could not have known, about the misrepresentations or omissions. In contrast to the due diligence defense of Section 11, the defense of reasonable care is not spelled out in detail.

Commentators have suggested that reasonable care may require a defendant to undertake an investigation. In *Sanders v. John Nuveen & Co.*,[37] the U.S. Court of Appeals for the Seventh Circuit held that there is no difference between the duties imposed on an underwriter by Section 11, which requires a reasonable investigation, and Section 12(a)(2). An underwriter, the Seventh Circuit held, must look beyond published data and undertake some investigation of that part of the data that is verifiable. Because the underwriter in *Sanders* did not examine the issuing company's records, contracts, or tax returns, the underwriter did not act with reasonable care.

36. See Stephen M. Bainbridge, *Securities Act Section 12(2) After the Gustafson Debacle*, 50 Bus. Law. 1231, 1258 (1995).

37. 619 F.2d 1222 (7th Cir. 1980), *cert. denied*, 450 U.S. 1005 (1981).

## Liability of Controlling Persons

Section 15 of the 1933 Act imposes liability on anyone who "controls any person liable under Section 11 or 12." Section 15 of the 1933 Act deals only with civil liability for false registration statements and information contained in prospectuses and communications. Section 20(a) of the 1934 Act provides for broader *controlling-person liability,* although it does allow for a "good faith defense." Congress did not define the term "control" in either act but left it for the courts to decide:

> It was thought undesirable to attempt to define the term. It would be difficult if not impossible to enumerate or to anticipate the many ways in which actual control may be exerted. A few examples of these methods used are stock ownership, lease, contract, and agency. It is well known that actual control sometimes may be exerted through ownership of much less than a majority of the stock of a corporation either by the ownership of such stock alone or through such ownership in combination with other factors.[38]

Unfortunately, the courts do not agree as to when there is controlling-person liability. Some courts will find control if the defendant simply had the power to directly or indirectly control or influence corporate policy or the power to control the general affairs of an entity.[39] Others require that the defendant actually participated in the securities violation.[40] The majority of courts will find liability if a person merely possessed the power to control the specific activity that is the basis for the securities violation, regardless of whether that power was exercised, provided that the person did actually exercise some degree of general control or influence over the entity primarily liable.

A controlling person is usually an officer, director, or major shareholder of the company. The U.S. Court of Appeals for the Eleventh Circuit adopted a variation of the majority rule for establishing controlling-person liability in *Brown v. Enstar Group, Inc.*[41] In that case, Kinder-Care, Inc. (KCI) planned to spin off its wholly owned subsidiary, Kinder-Care Learning Centers, Inc. (KCLC). KCI's chair, Perry Mendel, was also the chair of KCLC. KCLC conducted a public offering, reducing KCI's holdings of KCLC to 87 percent. In preparation for a further restructuring plan that would completely separate the two entities, Mendel resigned as chair of KCI but stayed on as chair of KCLC. Instead of spinning off the subsidiary, KCI decided to offer KCI shareholders rights to purchase the KCI-owned shares of KCLC stock. KCI prepared and issued a prospectus to its shareholders to that end. After the restructuring was complete, KCI changed its name to The Enstar Group, Inc.

The issue in *Brown* was whether Mendel could be held liable as a controlling person of KCI for alleged omissions and fraud in the prospectus. The Eleventh Circuit held that the trial court correctly dismissed the complaints against Mendel because he "neither possessed nor exercised power over the entity primarily liable."[42] Mendel failed the first half of the following test:

> [A] defendant is liable as a controlling person if he or she had the power to control the general affairs of the entity primarily liable at the time the entity violated the securities laws. . . . [and] had the requisite power to directly or indirectly control or influence the specific corporate policy which resulted in the primary liability.[43]

Although the majority rule requires actual participation in the operations of the corporation in general, *Brown* requires only that the defendant have power over the corporation in general, whether or not that power is exercised. If Mendel had still been the chair of KCI's board, he probably would have been liable under the *Brown* rule, but perhaps not under the majority rule, depending on his level of participation in the operations of KCI in general. Notably, in the overwhelming majority of jurisdictions, a high-ranking official who simply signs a fraudulent document will be subject to controlling-person liability.

Neither Section 15 of the 1933 Act nor Section 20(a) of the 1934 Act imposes strict liability on controlling persons. Controlling persons are not liable under Section 15 if they had no knowledge of the facts giving rise to the controlled person's alleged liability and had no reasonable ground to believe in the existence of such facts. Controlling persons under Section 20(a) have a defense if they acted in good faith and did not directly or indirectly induce the violation. The majority view is that the defendant bears the burden of establishing the defenses of "no knowledge" and no "reasonable ground to believe," or "good faith" and lack of inducement. Generally, these defenses are established by proving that the defendant

38. H.R. Rep. No. 1383, 73rd Cong., 2d Sess. § 19 at 26 (1934).
39. *See, e.g.*, Abbott v. Equity Group, Inc., 2 F.3d 613 (5th Cir. 1993).
40. *See, e.g.*, Sharp v. Coopers & Lybrand, 649 F.2d 175 (3d Cir. 1981) (interpreting identical language in Section 20(a) of the 1934 Act to require culpable participation in the securities violation).
41. 84 F.3d 393 (11th Cir. 1996).
42. *Id.* at 397 n.6.
43. *Id.* at 396 (internal quotation marks omitted).

acted in good faith and took reasonable measures, in light of the situation, to prevent the securities violation.[44]

## Criminal Penalties

In addition to having to buy back the securities or pay damages, violators of state or federal securities laws also face criminal penalties, including fines and imprisonment. Under Section 24 of the 1933 Act, any person who willfully violates the provisions of the Act shall upon conviction be fined not more than $10,000 or imprisoned for up to five years, or both. A violation can be willful even if the defendant did not know that the transaction at issue involved securities or that the law was being violated. In cases claiming false statements or omissions of material facts, the government need show only that the defendant knew what investors were and were not being told, accompanied by proof that the statement or omissions were objectively material.[45] Penalties under the 1934 Act are set forth in Chapter 14.

44. See Lewis D. Lowenfels & Alan R. Bromberg, *Controlling Person Liability Under Section 20(a) of the Securities Exchange Act and Section 15 of the Securities Act,* 53 BUS. LAW. 1, 26–27 (1997).

45. United States v. English, 92 F.3d 909 (6th Cir. 1996).

THE RESPONSIBLE MANAGER

### COMPLYING WITH REGISTRATION REQUIREMENTS

Any person offering securities must comply with the registration requirements of the 1933 Act as well as any applicable blue sky laws. This includes start-up companies, as well as large, publicly traded companies. Failure to comply gives the purchaser of the security the right to keep the proceeds if the investment is successful or to return the security to the seller if the investment does not turn out as hoped. Moreover, as explained in Chapter 14, a willful failure to comply is a criminal offense. Even if a security is exempt from registration, it is not exempt from the antifraud provisions of the 1934 Act, as discussed in Chapter 23.

Managers, particularly those of small firms, should be familiar with the *Howey* test. They should be aware that certain arrangements that are not normally thought of as securities may run afoul of the 1933 and 1934 Acts.

Furthermore, securities held by officers, directors, and other affiliates cannot be freely resold. They must be sold under Rule 144, subject to its volume and public information requirements, or in a private offering to sophisticated, eligible buyers. Companies must put legends on affiliates' share certificates, issue stop-transfer orders to the transfer agent, or take other such steps as may be reasonable to ensure compliance with these rules.

The preparation of a private-placement memorandum is an involved process that requires an intimate knowledge of the statutory requirements. Managers face considerable liability for incorrect or misleading statements in these documents so should consult experienced counsel.

Any person involved in a public offering of securities has a legal and ethical duty to ensure that the prospectus contains no misleading statements or omissions. Experts, such as accountants, have a particularly heavy responsibility. The underwriters and outside directors cannot rely passively on the representations of management. Violations of these rules give rise to both civil and criminal liability.

Managers should work closely with counsel during the waiting period to ensure that there are no gun-jumping problems due to eagerness of the underwriter or the company's public relations department. It is very important that the company not issue an abnormal number of press releases or increase the amount of its advertising prior to the registration going effective. In other words, the manager should make sure that the company remains quiet and does not depart from its ordinary routine.

In addition, a manager should ensure that there are no material misstatements or omissions in any public disclosures (for example, Form 10–K or Form 10–Q). Even if there is no legal obligation to disclose a particular fact, once a disclosure is made, the statements contained in it must be truthful and complete.

## INSIDE STORY

## IMPROPER ALLOCATION OF "HOT" IPO SHARES

During the dot.com boom of the 1990s, shares of initial public offerings (IPOs)—*hot issues*—were in incredibly high demand and were often allocated to individuals by underwriters hoping to secure more investment banking business. A Credit Suisse First Boston analyst explained in a 1999 e-mail to someone less well versed in the workings of IPOs that some of the shares "are reserved not for friends of the company, but for friends of the investment bank."[46] She described the arrangement as "something of an 'if you scratch my back I will scratch yours.'"[47] Apparently, she was describing the practice of *spinning,* whereby underwriters would distribute IPO shares to a corporate executive in exchange for the investment banking business of the executive's corporation. Thanks to Salomon Smith Barney, Bernard J. Ebbers, former WorldCom CEO, received 869,000 shares in twenty-one companies between 1996 and 2000, pocketing around $11 million in profits.[48] Salomon maintained that the shares were allocated to Ebbers because he was a major brokerage customer, not because of his position at WorldCom.

Cristina Morgan, former managing director of investment banking at Hambrecht & Quist, defended the practice of allocating IPOs to the personal brokerage accounts of clients who also direct corporate-finance business to the firm, saying, "Is it appropriate? Well, yeah." She reasoned: "If you sell doughnuts, you do everything you can to enhance the image and service of your doughnut shop to customers. You're just doing your job. That's what we all are doing." Morgan asserted that the amounts involved, often 500 to 1,000 shares, were so small compared to the net worth of her clients that the IPO allocations could not have influenced the corporate decisions made by the executives who received them.[49]

Pursuant to another practice, called *laddering,* investment banks offered IPO shares to customers only if they promised to purchase more shares on the open market after the offering. One J.P. Morgan sales representative mentioned in an e-mail that she "was very aggressive in pushing [the customer] for after market action—stressing how important it was going to be for the process."[50] Laddering artificially affected the price of stocks. J.P. Morgan paid $25 million in 2003 to settle charges of laddering. Allegedly, investment banks also affected the market by inducing investors to purchase "cold" IPO shares with the understanding that they would be allocated stakes in upcoming "hot" offerings in exchange.

Sometimes investment banks charged customers who had received shares in "hot" IPOs unconscionably high commission fees on unrelated transactions. In 2003, J.P. Morgan Chase & Co. paid $6 million to settle claims that Hambrecht & Quist (which it acquired in 1999) charged commissions of up to $1.25 per share on unrelated trades by customers who had just been issued IPO stocks. Those customers usually paid a paltry six cents per share. In one e-mail, a sales broker wrote to a senior syndicate manager that one customer "has a consistent pattern of rewarding the firm with commissions when they are given [IPO] stock and I anticipate they will do the same here."[51] Credit Suisse First Boston paid $100 million to settle similar allegations.

Frank P. Quattrone, one of Wall Street's most prominent bankers during the 1990s, was convicted of obstructing federal investigations into "spinning" at Credit Suisse First Boston and sentenced to eighteen months in prison.[52] As of early 2005, the SEC was still considering new rules submitted by the National Association of Securities Dealers (NASD) that would ban spinning and quid pro quo allocations of IPO shares.[53]

46. Ben White, *Analyst's '99 E-Mail Details IPO Rewards; Credit Suisse Says She Got It Wrong,* WASH. POST, Sept. 6, 2002, at E1.
47. *Id.*
48. *Id.;* Gretchen Morgenson, *Ebbers Got Million Shares in Hot Deals,* N.Y. TIMES, Aug. 28, 2002, at C1.
49. Morgan is quoted in Michael Siconolfi, *Hambrecht & Quist Goes on Offensive on 'Spinning,'* WALL ST. J., Nov. 26, 1997, at C1, C20. See also Michael Siconolfi, *SEC, NASD Begin Probes of IPO 'Spin' Accounts,* WALL ST. J., Nov. 13, 1997, at A3.
50. Ben White, *J.P. Morgan, SEC Settle IPO Charges; Firm Allegedly Manipulated Market,* WASH. POST, Oct. 2, 2003, at E7.
51. Brooke A. Masters, *J.P. Morgan to Pay $6 Million to Settle Kickback Charges,* WASH. POST, Feb. 21, 2003, at E3. Fleet Boston Financial Corporation's Robertson Stephen's unit paid $28 million to settle similar charges.
52. Brooke A. Masters, *Banker's 2nd Trial Ends with Conviction; Jury Says Quattrone Obstructed Probes,* WASH. POST, May 4, 2004, at A1.
53. Exchange Act Release No. 34–50,896, 69 Fed. Reg. 77,804 (Dec. 28, 2004).

## KEY WORDS AND PHRASES

accredited investor 839
affiliate 830
angels 818
bespeaks caution doctrine 854
best-efforts underwriting 830
blank check companies 837
blue sky laws 823
controlling-person liability 858
dealer 845
Delaware carve-out 821
due diligence 832
exempt securities 838
exempt transactions 838
family resemblance test 827
firm commitment underwriting 829
Form S–1 830
Form S–2 830
Form S–3 830
Form S–4 837
Form SB–1 830
Form SB–2 830
free writing prospectus 837
going effective 828
gun-jumping 836
hot issues 860
integrate 840
investment contract 824
issuer 845
laddering 860
material fact 851
merit review 823
not an underwriter 845
offer 827
offering circular 842
offshore transactions 846
private offering 838
private placement 838
private-placement memorandum 842
prospectus 828
proxy 848
qualified institutional buyer 846
quiet period 835
red-herring prospectus 835
registration statement 828
Regulation A 842
Regulation D 839
Regulation S 846
reporting company 848
restricted securities 844
roadshow 835
Rule 144 845
sale 827
sale-of-business doctrine 827
*scienter* 820
secondary offering 829
Section 4(1½) exemption 845
security 824
shelf registration 836
small business issuers 830
spinning 860
syndicate 829
tender offer 849
tombstone ad 835
traditional shelf offerings 836
underwriter 837
value 827
waiting period 835
well-known seasoned issuers 837

## QUESTIONS AND CASE PROBLEMS

1. Life Partners, Inc. is the leading promoter of interests in viatical settlements, whereby investors purchase at a discount interests in a pool consisting of life insurance benefits of terminal AIDS patients. Is Life Partners engaged in the sale of securities? [*SEC v. Life Partners, Inc.*, 87 F.3d 536 (D.C. Cir. 1996).]

2. Rock Corporation proposes to merge with Quarry, Inc. Quarry will first obtain the approval of its shareholders; then, by operation of law, the Quarry shares will become shares of the survivor corporation, Rock Quarry, Inc. Is it necessary to register the Rock Quarry shares?

   Suppose that prior to the merger Felda Flintstone owned 30 percent of Quarry's stock that she had acquired three years before in a private placement. She will own only 2 percent of the Rock Quarry shares and will not be an officer or director of Rock Quarry. May she freely resell her Rock Quarry shares? Would it matter whether they were registered in connection with the merger?

3. LaserVision Technologies, Inc. developed a camera system to create souvenirs for fans at sporting events, then formed SurroundVision Advanced Imaging LLC (SAIL) to finance the marketing of the technology. Adrian Gluck was LaserVision's president and also served as CEO, president, and a director of SAIL. Donald Williams, a LaserVision director, served as a manager of SAIL, and Raymond Kelly had no connection to SAIL except through his role as a LaserVision outside director. In October 1997, Richmond Dellastatious purchased $261,000 in SAIL stock, relying at least in part on an offering memorandum provided by SAIL. SAIL ceased operations in 1998, and its shares are now worthless.

   Dellastatious and another investor sued SAIL, certain SAIL officers, LaserVision, and two of LaserVision's outside directors—Williams and Kelly. The plaintiffs alleged that the offering memorandum (1) materially misrepresented the closeness of the relationship between SAIL—essentially a shell corporation—and LaserVision and (2) grossly overstated SAIL's projected revenues and misrepresented the nature of its assets. The plaintiffs further alleged that Williams and Kelly were liable as "control persons" under Section 20 of the 1934 Act. The trial court granted Kelly and Williams's summary judgment motion, concluding that neither was a control person of any liable party and both lacked the requisite culpability for controlling person liability. What facts do the plaintiffs have to prove to hold Williams and Kelly liable? [*Dellastatious v. Williams,* 242 F.3d 191 (4th Cir. 2001).]

4. Susan Newton, thirty-eight, founded her own software firm at age fifteen and acquired her stock in an offering under Rule 505 of Regulation D. Newton grew her firm to $20 million in revenues before EBM Corporation purchased it in exchange for EBM common stock in a private placement under Section 4(2). Newton is no longer an officer of EBM or active in the day-to-day management, but she sits on the board of directors of EBM and owns 15 percent of its outstanding common stock. She proposes to sell all of her EBM stock to the public. The stock is actively traded on the Nasdaq Stock Market. Are there any restrictions on her ability to sell her EBM shares?

5. Security Pacific National Bank had extended a line of credit to Integrated Resources under which it obtained short-term loans from the bank. Participations in these loans were sold to various institutional investors under a master agreement containing a disclaimer stating that each investor participated in the loans without relying on Security Pacific. Integrated later defaulted on the loans and declared bankruptcy. Several investors sued Security Pacific, seeking to rescind their purchase agreement. They argued that the loan participations were securities under the 1933 Act. Did Security Pacific sell securities? [*Banco Español de Crédito v. Security Pacific National Bank,* 973 F.2d 51 (2d Cir. 1992), *cert. denied,* 509 U.S. 903 (1993).]

6. In January, Arbor Corporation, a paper company with annual sales of more than $2 billion and assets of more than $5 billion, issued 4 million registered common shares at an average price of $50 per share. In preparing the registration statement, Charles Controller relied on a report by Acme Appraisers, which stated that the company's woodlands were worth $900 million. Acme's report was not included in the registration statement, and Acme was not mentioned in the prospectus. Ollie Olson, the company's newly elected outside director (and Controller's brother-in-law) questioned whether the woodland estimate might be too high. Controller reassured him that "if the numbers are good enough for our CPAs, they're good enough for me."

   In February, the company discovered that the woodland appraisal was overstated by $150 million. Management and the directors were livid about the error. To add to Arbor's problems, a major competitor shocked the industry by announcing that it will double its paper production capacity. Arbor's stock price is now $20 per share.

   Do the shareholders have a basis for a suit? Who can they sue? What problems or defenses will they likely encounter? Assuming that the suit is otherwise successful, how will damages be determined?

7. Duke Distribution, Inc. recently had a public offering of its shares. The company's attorneys, its CPAs, and the underwriter's attorneys worked diligently to meet a tight deadline that management had imposed. Unfortunately, in its haste to meet the deadline, Duke's team failed to include several items in the registration statement. The prospectus failed to mention that while Duke's inventory-to-sales ratio was constant over the past few years, most competitors' ratios had declined significantly over the same period. It also failed to mention that the company leases warehouses from a partnership consisting of three of its directors. The leases require rent that is about 8 percent higher than the market rate for equivalent facilities. After the initial public offering, the company engaged in additional transactions with insiders.

   Now the economy has softened and competition has increased. The price of Duke stock has fallen from $15 to $10. Is there a cause of action? Against whom? What are the defenses?

8. SG Ltd., a Dominican corporation, operates a website called StockGeneration. The website's "virtual stock exchange" offers "players" the opportunity to invest real money in eleven "virtual companies," one of which is called the "privileged company." The privileged company, the website proclaims, is "supported by the owners of SG, this is why its value constantly rises; on average at a rate of 10% monthly (this is approximately 215% annually)." Is SG selling securities? [*SEC v. SG Ltd.,* 265 F.3d 42 (1st Cir. 2001).]

9. The price of an IPO is set jointly by the company and the lead underwriters. For at least five decades, studies have shown that IPOs generally trade on the open market at a price significantly higher than the offering price.

   Until the late 1990s, IPOs were underpriced by 5 to 20 percent, but in the "hot issues" market of 1998 to 2000, IPOs frequently surged to 100 to

200 percent of the offering price on the first day of trading. In the period from October 1982 to June 1998, the number of shares traded in the first five days after the IPO was on average equal to 85 percent of the shares offered. In the period from July 1998 to 2000, the number of shares traded in the first five days after IPOs increased to more than 350 percent of the shares issued.

Would an issuer have any basis for suing the lead underwriters if post-IPO it learned that the underwriter had signaled to potential purchasers that they would be allocated shares in high-demand IPOs only if they were willing to buy additional shares in the aftermarket? If so, how would the issuer prove that it had been damaged by such an undisclosed arrangement? If the arrangement had been disclosed to the issuer, would purchasers in the aftermarket have any claims against the issuer and its officers and directors or against the lead underwriters and their officers and directors? [*In re Initial Public Offering Securities Litigation*, 241 F. Supp. 2d 281 (S.D.N.Y. 2003); *Xpedior Creditor Trust v. Credit Suisse First Boston (USA), Inc.*, 309 F. Supp. 2d 459 (S.D.N.Y. 2003).]

## MANAGER'S DILEMMA

10. Interchange Corporation of Laguna Hills, California, operates a targeted search advertising network. Its primary competitors are Google and Yahoo. Last year, Interchange reported a $60,000 profit on sales of $8.7 million. The company's founders want to take Interchange public.

The IPO market is beginning to heat up again, and many companies in competitive industries need both the capital and the perception of credibility offered by being publicly held. A few relatively recent, high-profile offerings may provide ample coattails on which Interchange's stock could ride. On the other hand, the risks of taking a young company, particularly a technology company, public remain high. The demand for technology companies has not fully rebounded, and the prices of the sixty technology companies that offered stock between January 2003 and July 2004 suffered an average decline of 5 percent over the same period. Also, it is particularly difficult for investors to predict the success of young companies with inexperienced management teams.

If there is a market for the offering, should Interchange go ahead with the IPO? Should it matter whether Interchange is operating at a loss? Should companies offer their stock publicly simply because the public is willing to purchase it? What other factors should be taken into consideration?

Given that Interchange is short on cash, should it offer its outside counsel a 5 percent equity share in lieu of traditional hourly fees? [Robert C. Kahrl & Anthony T. Jacono, *"Rush to Riches": The Rules of Ethics and Greed Control in the Dot.Com World*, 2 MINN. INTELL. PROP. REV. 51 (2001), *available at* http://mipr.umn.edu/archive/v2n1/jacono.pdf.]

## INTERNET SOURCES

| | |
|---|---|
| This site for the Securities and Exchange Commission offers a broad range of information, including the SEC's guidance on how to comply with the plain English requirements—*A Plain English Handbook: How to Create Clear SEC Disclosure Documents.* | http://www.sec.gov |
| This site provides free access to electronic filings with the SEC. | http://www.freeedgar.com |
| Nasdaq Stock Market | http://www.nasdaq.com |
| New York Stock Exchange | http://www.nyse.com |
| This site maintained by Houlihan Smith & Co., a specialized investment banking firm, includes a helpful article on due diligence, entitled *The Investment Banker's Perspective on Due Diligence for Mergers, Acquisitions and Securities Offerings.* | http://www.houlihansmith.com |

CHAPTER 23

# Securities Fraud and Insider Trading

## INTRODUCTION

### MAINTAINING THE INTEGRITY OF THE SECURITIES MARKETS

Many attribute the size and success of the U.S. capital markets to the transparency and perceived fairness of the securities markets, which is a direct result of the registration requirements imposed by the Securities Act of 1933 (the 1933 Act), the periodic reporting requirements imposed by the Securities Exchange Act of 1934 (the 1934 Act), and the antifraud provisions in both acts. As the U.S. Supreme Court remarked in *Basic, Inc. v. Levinson*,[1] no one "would knowingly roll the dice in a crooked crap game."

Each company that takes advantage of the capital markets has a legal and ethical duty to ensure the integrity of those markets. Securities fraud, in any form, erodes investor confidence and makes it more difficult and expensive for honest businesses to raise capital.

The principal antifraud provisions of the federal securities laws are Sections 11 and 12(a)(2) of the 1933 Act, discussed in Chapter 22, and Section 10(b) of the 1934 Act. As explained in Chapter 22, Section 11 applies only to registered offerings, and Section 12(a)(2) applies only to public offerings not exempt from the 1933 Act's registration requirements. In contrast, Section 10(b) applies to all purchases and sales of securities, regardless of whether they are registered or exempt from registration.

Under Section 10(b) and Rule 10b–5, promulgated by the Securities and Exchange Commission (SEC) pursuant to the 1934 Act, it is unlawful for any person to use a fraudulent, manipulative, or deceptive device in connection with the purchase or sale of any security. Rule 10b–5 also prohibits *insider trading,* that is, trading securities based on material nonpublic information in violation of a duty to the corporation or its shareholders or the source of the information. SEC Rules 10b5–1 and 10b5–2 clarify certain aspects of insider trading.

Section 16(b) of the 1934 Act regulates "short-swing" trading by insiders. In particular, it allows a public corporation to recover the profits if any officer or director of the corporation or any person who owns more than 10 percent of the corporation's securities purchases and sells, or sells and purchases, securities of the corporation within a six-month period.

1. 485 U.S. 224 (1988).

### CHAPTER OVERVIEW

This chapter focuses on Section 10(b) and Rule 10b–5. It sets forth the seven elements necessary in a Rule 10b–5 securities fraud case and the fraud-on-the-market theory of liability. The safe harbor for certain forward-looking statements is discussed. Section 17(a) of the 1933 Act, under which the U.S. government can bring fraud claims, is briefly discussed along with the new securities fraud offense added by the Sarbanes–Oxley Act of 2002. The chapter discusses the legal elements of an insider trading case and SEC Regulation FD's ban on selective disclosure. The rules for calculating the recoverable profits from short-swing trading are discussed, as well as the requirements for reporting by insiders.

## Sections 10(b) and 20 of the 1934 Act and Rule 10b–5

Section 10(b) gives the SEC power to prohibit individuals or companies from engaging in securities fraud by authorizing the SEC to prescribe specific rules for the protection of investors. The SEC promulgated Rule 10b–5 to encourage disclosure of information relevant to the investing public, to protect investors, and to deter fraud in the securities industry. Rule 10b–5 states:

> It shall be unlawful for any person, directly or indirectly, by the use of any means or instrumentality of interstate commerce, or of the mails, or of any facility of any national securities exchange,
> (1) to employ any device, scheme, or artifice to defraud,
> (2) to make any untrue statement of a material fact or to omit to state a material fact necessary in order to make the statements made, in the light of the circumstances under which they were made, not misleading, or
> (3) to engage in any act, practice, or course of business which operates or would operate as a fraud or deceit upon any person, in connection with the purchase or sale of any security.

The SEC has broad power to investigate apparent violations of Rule 10b–5, to order that the violator stop its wrongful conduct, and to recommend criminal prosecution for willful violations.

More suits are brought under Rule 10b–5 than under any other provision of securities law, including those, such as Sections 11 and 12(a)(2) of the 1933 Act, that explicitly create private rights of action. Although there is some overlap, Rule 10b–5 extends to misconduct not covered by other securities laws. Under Rule 10b–5, managers could be liable for misleading statements contained in any document—such as a press release or a letter to shareholders—or even a speech to a trade association as long as the statements were made in a manner reasonably calculated to influence the investing public.

Since 1946, courts have held that Rule 10b–5 also creates an implicit private right of action, giving individual investors the right to sue a violator for damages. Although the Supreme Court has lately shown increasing hostility toward implied rights of action under other provisions of the securities laws, most commentators do not expect it to abrogate the private right of action under Rule 10b–5.

### AIDING AND ABETTING

In *Central Bank of Denver, N.A. v. First Interstate Bank of Denver, N.A.*,[2] the Supreme Court ruled that a private plaintiff may not maintain an aiding and abetting suit under Section 10(b). In that case, the plaintiff had attempted to hold the bank that was the indenture trustee for a municipal bond issue secondarily liable as an aider and abettor of the fraud perpetrated by the issuers of the bonds.

In reaching its decision, the Supreme Court noted the vexatious nature of Rule 10b–5 suits and the fact that such suits require secondary actors to expend large sums for pretrial defense and the negotiation of settlements. The Court went on to state:

> This uncertainty and excessive litigation can have ripple effects. For example, newer and smaller companies may find it difficult to obtain advice from professionals. A professional may fear that a newer or smaller company may not survive and that business failure would generate securities litigation against the professional, among others. In addition, the increased costs incurred by professionals because of the litigation and settlement costs under 10b–5 may be passed on to their client companies, and in turn incurred by the company's investors, the intended beneficiaries of the statute.

The SEC can still bring aider-and-abettor cases seeking injunctive relief or damages under Section 10(b). To prove that a person is an *aider and abettor*, it is necessary to show (1) the existence of a primary violation of Section 10(b) or Rule 10b–5, (2) the defendant's knowledge of (or recklessness as to) that primary violation, and (3) substantial assistance of the violation by the defendant.

### CONSPIRACY

In *Dinsmore v. Squadron, Ellenoff, Plesent, Sheinfeld & Sorkin*,[3] the U.S. Court of Appeals for the Second Circuit applied *Central Bank*'s reasoning to a claim of conspiracy to fraudulently buy or sell securities and held that there is no private implied cause of action for conspiracy under Section 10(b).

### PRIMARY LIABILITY FOR SECONDARY ACTORS

Both the Supreme Court in *Central Bank* and the Second Circuit in *Dinsmore* took pains to make it clear that secondary actors (such as an accountant, lawyer, or bank) can be liable in private suits if their conduct satisfies the requirements for primary liability, as happened in the following case.

2. 511 U.S. 167 (1994).
3. 135 F.3d 837 (2d Cir. 1998).

A CASE IN POINT

**CASE 23.1**

**McGann v. Ernst & Young**

*United States Court of Appeals for the Ninth Circuit 102 F.3d 390 (9th Cir. 1996), cert. denied, 520 U.S. 1181 (1997).*

## Summary

**› FACTS** Ernst & Young was the outside auditor for Community Psychiatric Centers (CPC), a publicly traded corporation. The plaintiffs alleged that Ernst & Young failed to disclose that CPC had a major accounts receivable problem and thereby issued a false and misleading audit opinion regarding CPC's financial statements for the fiscal year ending in November 1990.

Moreover, the plaintiffs alleged that Ernst & Young knew that CPC would include this audit opinion in its annual report on Form 10–K filed with the SEC. The plaintiffs claimed that the suppression of this information caused CPC's stock price to be artificially inflated. In September and November 1991, when CPC announced a major drop in earnings due to $37 million in uncollectible debts, the value of CPC's stock declined precipitously.

The plaintiffs were the class of persons who purchased CPC stock between the time Ernst & Young published its audit opinion for CPC's 1990 fiscal year and the time CPC announced its bad debts. They alleged that Ernst & Young, by producing a fraudulent audit report with the knowledge that its client would disseminate the report to the securities market, committed fraudulent acts "in connection with" the trading of securities and thus violated Section 10(b) of the 1934 Act. The district court dismissed the claim, and the plaintiffs appealed.

**› ISSUE PRESENTED** Is an accounting firm subject to primary liability under Section 10(b) of the 1934 Act when it prepares a fraudulent audit report that it knows its client will include in a Form 10–K?

**› SUMMARY OF OPINION** The U.S. Court of Appeals for the Ninth Circuit began by noting that accountants have no aider-and-abettor liability under Section 10(b) per *Central Bank of Denver.*[4] The court held, however, that *Central Bank* did not undercut *SEC v. Texas Gulf Sulphur Co.,*[5] which stands for the proposition that any false and misleading assertions made "in a manner reasonably calculated to influence the investing public" are made "in connection with" the purchase or sale of securities within the meaning of Section 10(b). The language of Section 10(b) does not limit liability to those who actually trade securities. One who "introduces fraudulent information into the securities market does no less damage to the public because that party did not trade stocks." Therefore, Ernst & Young could be liable for a primary violation of Section 10(b) if the plaintiff could prove that Ernst & Young made a misleading statement in the audit opinion, knowing that the opinion would be included in CPC's Form 10–K.

**› RESULT** The appeals court reversed the district court's judgment in favor of Ernst & Young and remanded the case to the district court. The allegations survived the motion to dismiss.

**› COMMENTS** Similarly, the Second Circuit held that a securities broker could be held primarily liable for market manipulation in violation of Section 10(b) and Rule 10b–5 when he followed a stock promoter's directions to execute stock trades designed to create the appearance of an actual market for a company's shares and thereby artificially raise the stock price.[6] The court stated that the broker would be liable if he knew, or was reckless in not knowing, that the trades were manipulative, even if he did not share the promoter's specific overall purpose of manipulating the market for the stock.

4. 511 U.S. 164 (1994).
5. 401 F.2d 833 (2d Cir. 1968).
6. SEC v. U.S. Envtl., Inc., 155 F.3d 107 (2d Cir. 1998).

*McGann* involved an alleged failure to disclose that caused the audit opinion to be false and misleading. Accountants are generally not responsible for misrepresentations or omissions in other parts of a document that they did not certify.[7] The Second Circuit applies a "bright-line" rule that a secondary actor will not have primary liability for a material misstatement unless (1) the person actually made the false or misleading statement; and (2) the misrepresentation was attributed to that specific person at the time of public dissemination, that is, in advance of the investment decision.[8] The Ninth Circuit uses a more lenient standard and will find a secondary actor liable for "substantial participation" in the misrepresentation.

Accountants must sign a written consent before their audited report can be included in a registration statement. Before doing so, they should do an *S–1 review,* which is a review of events subsequent to the date of the certified balance sheet in the registration statement to ascertain whether any material change has occurred in the company's financial position that should be disclosed to prevent the financial statements from being misleading. This review includes comparing recent financial statements to earlier ones, reading minutes of the shareholders' and directors' meetings, and investigating changes in material contracts, bad debts, and newly discovered liabilities.

7. *See* Shapiro v. Cantor, 123 F.3d 717 (2d Cir. 1997).

8. Winkler v. Wigley, 2000 U.S. App. LEXIS 31332 (2d Cir. Dec. 6, 2000). *See also* Wright v. Ernst & Young LLP, 152 F.3d 169 (2d Cir. 1998). *Accord* Anixter v. Home-Stake Prod. Co., 77 F.3d 1215 (10th Cir. 1996).

### Ethical Consideration

Suppose that, in the course of the S–1 review, the accountants learn that the company's earnings have dropped dramatically from earnings for the comparable periods included in the registration statement. Should the accountants refuse to sign the consent for inclusion of their opinion on the financial statements for the previous period unless the adverse results are disclosed in the prospectus?

## View from Cyberspace

### Securities Fraud Moves from the Boiler Room to the Internet

In early 2001, the SEC announced that it had filed charges against twenty-three companies and individuals who used phony Internet press releases, false message board postings, and spam e-mails to pump up stock prices and defraud investors. One case involved a company that used a promotional website and spam to promote an upcoming initial public offering (IPO) for its online eyewear sales business. In fact, the IPO was never registered and the company had no office, inventory, or products. The promoter used the investors' money to pay for trips to casinos and strip clubs and other personal expenses.[a]

Mark S. Jacobs, a twenty-three-year-old former community college student, pled guilty in December 2000 to one count of wire fraud and two counts of securities fraud in connection with his distribution of a bogus press release that caused Emulex shareholders to lose $110 million after trading on the phony news.[b] The press release falsely stated that Emulex was being investigated by the SEC, that it had overstated its reported earnings figures for the preceding quarter, and that its CEO had resigned. The plea agreement recommended that Jacobs be sentenced to thirty-seven to forty-six months in prison and pay $330 million in government fines and restitution to the Emulex shareholders.

The Massachusetts Securities Division launched an Internet securities fraud unit in 2000 to combat fraudulent securities trading using the Web. Secretary of State William F. Galvin reported "a continuing migration of bad brokers from the 'boiler room' to the Internet" and indicated that 25 percent of the division's cases now involved the Internet.[c]

a. Joanna Glasner, *SEC Attacks Online Scammers,* Wired News, Mar. 1, 2001.

b. Bloomberg News, *Guilty Plea Expected in Emulex Fraud Case,* CNET News.Com, Dec. 28, 2000.

c. Beth Healy, *State Launches Web Securities Fraud Unit,* Boston Globe, Apr. 20, 2000, at C4.

## STATUTE OF LIMITATIONS

Suits under Section 10(b) must be brought within one year of the date the plaintiff discovered or should have discovered the fraud or within three years of the date of the violation, whichever is shorter.[9]

## CONTROLLING PERSONS

Section 20(a) imposes joint and several liability on every person who, directly or indirectly, controls any person liable under the 1934 Act, unless the controlling person acted in good faith and did not directly or indirectly induce the acts constituting the violation. This provision is generally interpreted in the same way as Section 15 of the 1933 Act, which is discussed in Chapter 22.

# Elements of a Rule 10b–5 Cause of Action

To recover damages from a defendant under Rule 10b–5, a plaintiff must show each of the following elements:

1. The defendant used either an instrumentality of interstate commerce or the mails or a facility of a national securities exchange.
2. The defendant made a statement that either misrepresented or omitted a fact.
3. The fact was of material importance.
4. The misrepresentation or omission was made with *scienter* (culpable state of mind).
5. The statement or omission was made in connection with the purchase or sale of securities.
6. The plaintiff acted in reliance either on the defendant's misrepresentation or on the assumption that the market price of the stock accurately reflected its value.
7. The defendant's misrepresentation or omission caused the plaintiff to suffer losses.

Each of these seven elements is described in more detail below.

9. Lampf, Pleva, Lipkind, Prupis & Petigrow v. Gilbertson, 501 U.S. 350 (1991).

## INTERSTATE COMMERCE

The requirement that the defendant used interstate commerce, the mails, or a national securities exchange gives Congress the power to regulate the defendant's conduct under the Commerce Clause of the U.S. Constitution. The requirement is usually easy to satisfy. Use of interstate commerce includes use of a radio broadcast heard in more than one state; use of a newspaper advertisement in a newspaper delivered to more than one state; or use of a telephone wired for interstate calls, even if no interstate calls were actually made. Use of the mails includes sending a letter within a state because the mail is an instrumentality of interstate commerce. Use of a national securities exchange includes use of any facility of such an exchange.

## MISSTATEMENT OR OMISSION

A *misstatement* is a misrepresentation of a fact; in other words, a lie. An *omission* is a fact left out of a statement, such that the statement becomes misleading.

### *Misstatement*

In the following case, a company's attempts to dispel rumors were found to misrepresent the facts.

**A CASE IN POINT**

**CASE 23.2**

**SEC v. Texas Gulf Sulphur Co.**

*United States District Court for the Southern District of New York*

*312 F. Supp. 77 (S.D.N.Y. 1970), aff'd, 446 F.2d 1301 (2d Cir. 1971), cert. denied, 404 U.S. 1005 (1971).*

## Summary

**› FACTS** Texas Gulf Sulphur Company (TGS) drilled a test hole on November 12, 1963, which indicated the possible presence of copper. TGS did not immediately disclose the results of its drill hole or undertake further drilling because it wanted to acquire property in the surrounding area and did not want to drive up the price of the property.

On April 12, 1964, in response to rumors about the copper discovery, TGS issued a press release. By this time, the company had confirmed the presence of copper. Preliminary tests indicated that the amount was significant. The press release, however, minimized the importance of the discovery. It said (in part):

> For Immediate Release
>
> TEXAS GULF SULPHUR COMMENT ON TIMMINS, ONTARIO, EXPLORATION NEW YORK, April 12—The following statement was made today by Dr. Charles F. Fogarty,

*(Continued)*

(Case 23.2 *continued*)

executive vice president of Texas Gulf Sulphur Company, in regard to the company's drilling operations near Timmins, Ontario, Canada. Dr. Fogarty said:

> During the past few days, the exploration activities of Texas Gulf Sulphur in the area of Timmins, Ontario, have been widely reported in the press, coupled with rumors of a substantial copper discovery there. These reports exaggerate the scale of operations, and mention plans and statistics of size and grade of ore that are without factual basis and have evidently originated by speculation of people not connected with TGS.
>
> The facts are as follows. TGS has been exploring in the Timmins area for six years as part of its overall search in Canada and elsewhere for various minerals—lead, copper, zinc, etc. During the course of this work, in Timmins as well as in Eastern Canada, TGS has conducted exploration entirely on its own, without the participation by others. Numerous prospects have been investigated by geophysical means and a large number of selected ones have been core-drilled. These cores are sent to the United States for assay and detailed examination as a matter of routine and on advice of expert Canadian legal counsel. No inferences as to grade can be drawn from this procedure.
>
> Most of the areas drilled in Eastern Canada have revealed either barren pyrite or graphite without value; a few have resulted in discoveries of small or marginal sulfide ore bodies.
>
> Recent drilling on one property near Timmins has led to preliminary indications that more drilling would be required for proper evaluation of this prospect. The drilling done to date has not been conclusive, but the statements made by many outside quarters are unreliable and include information and figures that are not available to TGS.
>
> The work done to date has not been sufficient to reach definite conclusions and any statement as to size and grade of ore would be premature and possibly misleading. When we have progressed to the point where reasonable and logical conclusions can be made, TGS will issue a definite statement to its stockholders and to the public in order to clarify the Timmins project.

The SEC contended that TGS's April 12 release was a misstatement because it left investors with an impression that was contrary to the known facts at the time.

**› ISSUE PRESENTED** Does a press release giving a misleading impression about the results of a drilling operation violate Rule 10b–5?

**› SUMMARY OF OPINION** The U.S. District Court for the Southern District of New York acknowledged that the timing of disclosure is a matter for the business judgment of the corporate officers. When a company chooses to issue a press release to respond to spreading rumors regarding its activities, it must, however, describe the true picture at the time of the press release. This should include the basic facts known, or which reasonably should be known, to the drafters of the press release. Such facts are necessary to enable the investing public to make a reasonable appraisal of the existing situation.

Because the press release misled reasonable investors to believe either that there was no ore discovery or that any discovery was not a significant one, TGS violated Section 10(b) and Rule 10b–5.

**› RESULT** TGS violated Section 10(b) and Rule 10b–5.

**› COMMENTS** A company may have excellent reasons to attempt to dispel rumors. TGS, for example, had an interest in keeping the find quiet in order to keep down the

*(Continued)*

(Case 23.2 *continued*)

acquisition costs of land. Or consider a company involved in merger negotiations that is asked by the press whether there is any reason for unusual trading in its stock. The company may well want to keep the negotiations under wraps for a variety of legitimate reasons. Yet, if it says that it is unaware of any corporate developments, it runs the risk of Rule 10b–5 liability. The SEC has indicated that it considers such a statement in these circumstances to be a violation of Rule 10b–5. The Supreme Court addressed this issue in *Basic, Inc. v. Levinson,* discussed further below.

---

A prediction about the future can be a misstatement, but only if the person making the prediction does not believe it at the time. A prediction is not a guarantee, and it does not become a misstatement simply because the facts do not develop as predicted. If there is no reasonable basis for a prediction, however, then it is a misstatement because the person who made it could not honestly have believed it.[10] As discussed later in this chapter, the Private Securities Litigation Reform Act of 1995 (the Litigation Reform Act) contains a safe harbor for certain forward-looking statements.

## *Omission*

It is clear that a company must be careful if it chooses to speak. What if it chooses not to speak?

The general rule is that a company has no general duty under Rule 10b–5 to reveal corporate developments unless the company or its insiders (1) trade in its securities, (2) recommend trading to someone else, or (3) disclose the information as a *tip*—that is, a disclosure made to an individual and withheld from the general public. The fact that information is material does not, in itself, give rise to a duty to disclose.[11]

But the securities laws do require that certain information be disclosed in registration statements; annual, quarterly, and special reports; and proxy solicitations. In particular, Management's Discussion and Analysis of Financial Condition and Results of Operations must disclose any known material event or uncertainty that would cause reported financial information not to be necessarily indicative of future operating results or financial condition.[12] Stock exchange rules require that issuers promptly reveal material developments unless there is a business reason not to do so.

Silence or a "no comment" statement in response to rumors will not lead to liability if the company has not previously spoken on the subject and insiders are not trading or tipping. There is a caveat, however: A policy of not commenting on rumors must be adhered to in the face of both true and untrue rumors. If the company always says "no comment" when the rumor is true but provides facts to dispel untrue rumors, then the "no comment" acts as an admission that the rumor is true.

Although keeping silent may be safer under Rule 10b–5, in many cases that will be hard to do. If a corporation's stock is traded on rumors of some major development, silence may contribute to disorderly market activity, distrust of company management, and possible abuse by those with access to inside information. Moreover, a blanket "no comment" policy makes it impossible to dispel false but damaging rumors.

Once the company has said something about a particular topic, it has a duty to disclose enough relevant facts so that the statement is not inaccurate, incomplete, or

**INTERNATIONAL SNAPSHOT**

Under the London Stock Exchange rules, if a listed company's share price moves significantly on the basis of rumor and the rumor is true, the company must disclose the existence of the rumored event. For example, in January 1998, drug powerhouse SmithKline Beecham PLC was required to disclose that it was engaged in merger negotiations with American Home Products after rumors of a deal sent shares of both companies rising.[a] Although there is no numerical threshold for disclosure, a rule of thumb is that a 10 percent move in the stock triggers the duty to disclose the accuracy of truthful rumors. On the other hand, if the rumors are not true, then the company can continue to say "no comment."

**a.** Steven Lipin & Sara Calian, *Did U.K.'s Strict Rules Spur Deal?,* WALL ST. J., Feb. 2, 1998, at C1.

10. *See* Va. Bankshares v. Sandberg, 501 U.S. 1083 (1991) (holding that a statement as to beliefs or opinions may be actionable if the opinion is known by the speaker at the time it is expressed to be untrue or to have no reasonable basis in fact).
11. Backman v. Polaroid Corp., 893 F.2d 1405 (1st Cir. 1990).
12. *See* Item 303 of SEC Regulation S–K, Management's Discussion and Analysis of Financial Condition and Results of Operations, 17 C.F.R. § 229.303(a)(3)(ii).

misleading.[13] The statement may be an obligatory one. Or the statement may be voluntary; for example, a company may choose to publicize information about favorable new developments or to respond to unfavorable rumors. Whether the statement is obligatory or voluntary, the company's officials must tell the whole truth with respect to that topic or risk being sued later for a misleading omission.

The following case addressed the issue of whether a company has a duty to update or correct statements that have become misleading in light of subsequent events.

13. *See* Dale E. Barnes, Jr. & Constance E. Bagley, *Great Expectations: Risk Management Through Risk Disclosure,* 1 STAN. J.L., BUS. & FIN. 155 (1994).

A CASE IN POINT

## In the Language of the Court

**CASE 23.3**

**Weiner v. Quaker Oats Co.**

*United States Court of Appeals for the Third Circuit*
*129 F.3d 310*
*(3d Cir. 1997).*

**› FACTS** On November 2, 1994, the Quaker Oats Company and Snapple Beverage Corporation announced that Quaker would acquire Snapple in a tender offer and merger transaction for $1.7 billion in cash. The market disapproved of the deal. Subsequent to the announcement, Quaker's stock price fell $7.375 per share—approximately 10 percent of the stock's value.

To finance the acquisition, Quaker had obtained $2.4 billion of credit from a banking group led by NationsBank Corporation. The Snapple acquisition nearly tripled Quaker's debt, from approximately $1 billion to approximately $2.7 billion. The acquisition also increased Quaker's total debt-to-total capitalization ratio to approximately 80 percent.

Over the course of the year prior to its acquisition of Snapple, Quaker had announced in several public documents the company's guideline for debt-to-equity ratio and its expectations for earnings growth. The announcements formed the basis for the plaintiffs' action.

In its 1993 Annual Report (dated October 4, 1993), Quaker stated that "our debt-to-total capitalization ratio at June 30, 1993 was 59 percent, up from 49 percent in fiscal 1992. For the future, our guideline will be in the upper-60 percent range." Quaker's president reiterated this "guideline" in a letter contained in the same Annual Report. Quaker's Form 10–Q for the quarter ended September 30, 1993 (filed with the SEC in November 1993) repeated the total debt-to-total capitalization ratio guideline.

In its 1994 Annual Report (dated September 23, 1994), Quaker stated that "we are committed to achieving real earnings growth of at least 7 percent over time." In addition, the report noted that Quaker's total debt-to-total capitalization ratio was 68.8 percent, "in line with our guideline in the upper-60 percent range."

Negotiations between Quaker and Snapple apparently began in the spring of 1994. By early August 1994, Quaker had advised Snapple that it was interested in pursuing a merger of the two companies and had commenced a due diligence investigation. As noted, the merger was completed in November of that year.

The gist of the plaintiffs' complaint was that, even if Quaker's announcements about its total debt-to-total capitalization ratio and projected earnings growth were true at the time they were made, Quaker still had a duty to update or correct those statements if it knew they had become materially misleading in light of subsequent events. The plaintiffs alleged that (1) Quaker knew those statements were materially misleading as soon as it was reasonably certain the Snapple merger would be finalized, and (2) Quaker had such certainty at least sometime prior to its formal announcement of the merger on November 2, 1994.

The district court dismissed both portions of the plaintiffs' claim, on the basis that neither Quaker's statements relating to its total debt-to-total capitalization ratio nor its statements relating to its projected earnings growth were material. The plaintiffs appealed.

*(Continued)*

(Case 23.3 *continued*)

**› ISSUE PRESENTED** Under what circumstances do a corporation and its officers have a duty to update, or at least not to repeat, particular projections regarding the corporation's financial condition (for example, total debt-to-total capitalization ratio or earnings growth projections)?

**› OPINION** POLLAK, J., writing for the U.S. Court of Appeals for the Third Circuit:

Rule 10b–5, promulgated pursuant to § 10(b) of the [1934] Act, provides the framework for a private cause of action for violations involving false statements or omissions of material fact. To establish a valid claim of securities fraud under Rule 10b–5, plaintiffs must prove that the defendant: (1) made misstatements or omissions of material fact, (2) with *scienter,* (3) in connection with the purchase or sale of securities, (4) upon which plaintiffs relied, and (5) that plaintiffs' reliance was the proximate cause of their injury.

In the present litigation, the plaintiffs allege that . . . they purchased shares in reliance on statements made by Quaker . . . about (1) Quaker's guideline for the ratio of total debt-to-total capitalization (in the upper 60 percent range) governing the company's financial planning and (2) Quaker's expected earnings growth in fiscal 1995.

The statements about expected earnings growth were made in August and September of 1994 . . . and it is plaintiffs' contention that, at a point when Quaker was in active pursuit of Snapple, Quaker and Smithburg [Quaker's CEO] must have known that the projections were illusory.

Plaintiffs' central complaint with respect to [the statements regarding the guideline for the ratio of total debt-to-total capitalization] is that, when the Snapple negotiations went into high gear, Quaker . . . had to have known that a . . . ratio in the high 60 percent range was no longer a realistic possibility. At that point, plaintiffs contend, defendants had a duty publicly to set the guidelines record straight.

. . .

**A. The Total Debt-to-Total Capitalization Ratio Guideline**

. . .

Plaintiffs' claims under this heading are claims of nondisclosure. "When an allegation of fraud under Section 10(b) is based upon a nondisclosure, there can be no fraud absent a duty to speak." In general, Section 10(b) and Rule 10b–5 do not impose a duty on defendants to correct prior statements—particularly statements of intent—so long as those statements were true when made. However, "[t]here can be no doubt that a duty exists to correct prior statements, if the prior statements were true when made but misleading if left unrevised." To avoid liability in such circumstances, "notice of a change of intent [must] be disseminated in a timely fashion." Whether an amendment is sufficiently prompt is a question that "must be determined in each case based upon the particular facts and circumstances."

. . .

**1. Materiality**

. . .

In *Basic,* the Court adopted in the context of § 10(b) and Rule 10b–5 the standard of materiality set forth in *TSC Industries v. Northway, Inc.,* 426 U.S. 438 (1976). The *Basic* Court approved . . . the principle that "[a]n omitted fact is material if there is a substantial likelihood that a reasonable shareholder would consider it important in deciding how to [proceed]."

*(Continued)*

(Case 23.3 *continued*)

. . .

Therefore, "[o]nly if the alleged misrepresentations or omissions are so obviously unimportant to an investor that reasonable minds cannot differ on the question of materiality is it appropriate for the district court to rule that the allegations are inactionable as a matter of law."

. . .

In sum, in the present case, we find that a trier of fact could conclude that a reasonable investor reading the 1993 Annual Report published on October 4, 1993, and then the 1994 Annual Report published on September 23, 1994, would have no ground for anticipating that the total debt-to-total capitalization ratio would rise as significantly as it did in fiscal 1995. There was after all no abjuration of the "upper 60-percent range" guideline. The company had predicted the rise from 59 percent to the "upper 60-percent range" in the 1993 report and that rise had occurred by and was confirmed in the 1994 report. Therefore, it was reasonable for an investor to expect that the company would make another such prediction if it expected the ratio to change markedly in the ensuing year.

. . .

**B. Earnings Growth Projections**

. . .

Quaker's 1994 Annual Report—issued on September 23, 1994, more than five weeks prior to the November 2 merger announcement—contained the statement that "we are committed to achieving a real earnings growth of at least 7 percent over time." We conclude that the phrase "over time" in this second statement inoculates Quaker from any claims of fraud that point to a decline in earnings growth in the immediate aftermath of the Snapple acquisition. No reasonably careful investor would find material a prediction of seven-percent growth followed by the qualifier "over time." Therefore, we hold that no reasonable finder of fact could conclude that the projection influenced prudent investors.

**› RESULT** The claim relating to Quaker's total debt-to-total capitalization ratio guideline was reinstated and remanded to the district court; the dismissal of the claim relating to Quaker's earnings growth projections was affirmed.

**› CRITICAL THINKING QUESTIONS**

1. Given that a wealth of data compiled by market analysts demonstrates that, over the long run, stock prices follow corporate earnings, which piece of information would you find more important when deciding whether to buy or sell Quaker stock: (a) forecasts relating to the company's total debt-to-total capitalization ratio, or (b) forecasts relating to the company's real earnings growth?
2. Would an announcement by Quaker that it was contemplating increasing its total debt-to-total capitalization ratio have "tipped the market" to a pending acquisition?

An omission can occur when a company makes a statement that was true at the time it was made but becomes misleading in light of later events. There is a duty to correct when "a company makes a historical statement [of a material fact] that at the time made, the company believed to be true, but as revealed by subsequently discovered information actually was not."[14] In contrast, the duty to update—which may arise when a

14. Stransby v. Cummins Engine Co., 51 F.3d 1329 (7th Cir. 1995).

statement, reasonable at the time it is made, becomes misleading due to a subsequent event—is more limited.[15] There is no duty to update if the original statement was not material,[16] or "when the original statement was not forward looking and does not contain some factual representation that remains 'alive' in the minds of investors as a continuing representation."[17] On the other hand, if investors are reasonably relying on the previous statements, the company can be held liable for failing to disclose the new information. For example, a company incurs a duty to update its financial projections when a projection changes or the company discovers that the projection was incorrect from the outset.

There is a duty to disclose the results of product safety tests, if they make previously disclosed test results false. For example, A.H. Robins Company, a pharmaceutical manufacturer, reported in 1970 that its Dalkon Shield intrauterine contraceptive device was safe and effective. In 1972, internal studies indicated that the Dalkon Shield was not as safe or effective as originally reported.[18] The U.S. Court of Appeals for the Second Circuit held that Robins's omission of the new information rendered its earlier statements misleading. Because investors were still relying on the statement that the Dalkon Shield was safe, the company had a duty to correct that statement once it learned that it was inaccurate.

In contrast, in *Oran v. Stafford*,[19] the U.S. Court of Appeals for the Third Circuit held that reports that the diet pill combination fen-phen (made by American Home Products Corporation) caused heart-valve abnormalities were not material because they did not definitively establish a link between the two drugs and heart-valve disorders. As a result, AHP's failure to disclose this information did not render its statements about the inconclusiveness of the relationship materially misleading. The court also ruled that the data were not material because when they were eventually released, there was no adverse effect on AHP's stock price.

The Ninth Circuit took a different tack in *Broudo v. Dura Pharmaceuticals, Inc.*[20] and ruled that allegedly false and misleading statements about Dura Pharmaceuticals' Albuterol Spiros asthma medication delivery device could have caused the plaintiff investor's loss even though the market price of the stock did not decline after the corrective disclosure was made. The court reasoned that loss causation "merely requires pleading that the price at the time of purchase was overstated and sufficient identification of the cause." The U.S. Supreme Court agreed to review this decision to resolve the split in the circuits on whether investors must show that the stock price dropped following a corrective disclosure.[21]

### *Statements by Third Parties and Entanglement*

Even if the company itself did not publish the misleading projection, make the statement, or start the rumor, it may nevertheless have a duty to reveal all of the facts regarding the issue. This is the case when the company is so entangled with the third party's statement that the statement can be attributed to the company. The company is then responsible for making sure that the statement is accurate. For example, if a company makes it a practice to review and correct drafts of analysts' forecasts, then the company implicitly represents that the corrected forecast is in accord with the company's view, and it has a duty to reveal all facts necessary to ensure that the analyst's report is not misleading.[22] Similarly, a company's distribution of copies of an analyst's report to investors or other members of the public or the posting of an analyst's report on the company's website may be construed as an implied representation that the information in the report is accurate or reflects the company's views.

## MATERIAL FACT

A buyer or seller of stock cannot recover damages just because an executive misrepresented or omitted a fact about the company. The fact must be material. As

15. *See, e.g., In re* Time Warner, Inc. Sec. Litig., 9 F.3d 259 (2d Cir. 1993).
16. Hillson Partners Ltd. P'ship v. Adage, Inc., 42 F.3d 204 (4th Cir. 1994).
17. *In re* Int'l Bus. Machs. Corp. Sec. Litig., 163 F.3d 102 (2d Cir. 1998). *See also In re* Burlington Coat Factory Sec. Litig., 114 F.3d 1410 (3d Cir. 1997).
18. Ross v. A.H. Robins Co., 607 F.2d 545 (2d Cir. 1979), *cert. denied,* 446 U.S. 946 (1980).
19. 226 F.3d 275 (3d Cir. 2000).
20. 339 F.3d 933 (9th Cir. 2003), *cert. granted,* 124 S. Ct. 2904 (2004).
21. Both the Third and Eleventh Circuits require plaintiffs to allege a stock price drop after corrective disclosure. Semerenko v. Cendant Corp., 223 F.3d 165 (3d Cir. 2000); Robbins v. Koger Props., Inc. 116 F.3d 1441 (11th Cir. 1997).
22. *See, e.g.,* Stack v. Lobo, 903 F. Supp. 1361 (N.D. Cal. 1995).

**ETHICAL CONSIDERATION**

If there is no legal obligation to disclose bad news, is there ever an ethical duty to disclose it?

explained in Chapter 22, a fact is material if a reasonable investor would consider it important in deciding how to act. Materiality is judged at the time of the misstatement or omission. Materiality is not affected by the intent of the party making the statement. There can be liability even if the manager did not know the omitted or misrepresented fact came within the legal definition of a material fact.

Although it is not always possible to predict which facts a court will consider material, certain matters are nearly always considered material. For example, any statements about the earnings, distributions, or assets of a company (unless the misrepresentation is inadvertent and concerns a minor amount) are material. In August 1999, the SEC accounting staff cautioned companies and their auditors against using "rules of thumb" to determine whether errors in the financial statements are material.[23] Even if two errors net out to zero, they can still be material. For example, an overstatement of revenues can be material even if it is accompanied by an overstatement of cost of goods sold. The SEC staff also stated that any intentional misstatement of a number in the financial statements is, by definition, material.

Significant facts about a parent or a subsidiary are usually material. These include the discovery of embezzlement or falsification of financial statements, an impending tender offer, or the loss of a manufacturer's major customer. Other facts that are probably material include inability to obtain supplies, increased costs of supplies, a decision to close a plant, information regarding the outlook in the industry, an intention to market a new product or cease marketing an old one, potential liability for damages in a lawsuit, a major discovery or product development, cost overruns, a change in management or compensation of corporate officers, and an increase in real estate taxes. As this list illustrates, a material fact is any fact that is likely to affect the market value of the company's stock.

The Supreme Court has recognized that for contingent or speculative events, such as negotiations regarding a potential merger, it is difficult to tell whether a reasonable investor would consider the omitted fact material at the time. The Court has declined to adopt a bright-line rule, however; materiality is a fact-specific determination.[24] If a misstatement or omission concerns a future event, such as a potential merger, its materiality will depend upon a balancing of the probability that the event will occur and the anticipated magnitude of the event in light of the totality of the company's activity.

Thus, the materiality of preliminary merger discussions in any particular case depends on the facts. Generally, to assess the probability that the event will occur, a fact finder will look to indicia of interest in the transaction at the highest corporate levels. Without attempting to catalog all such possible factors, the Court noted by way of example that board resolutions, instructions to investment bankers, and actual negotiations between principals or other intermediaries may serve as indicia of interest. To assess the magnitude of the transaction to the issuer of the securities allegedly manipulated, a fact finder will consider such facts as the size of the two corporate entities and of the potential premiums over market value. No particular event or factor short of closing the transaction is either necessary or sufficient by itself to render merger discussions material.

Vague statements of corporate optimism that are not capable of objective verification and mere puffing are immaterial as a matter of law because reasonable investors do not rely on them in making investment decisions.[25] For example, the Second Circuit characterized a statement made on October 15, 1992, by Jim Clippard, the director of investor relations of International Business Machines Corporation (IBM), that "we're not—despite your anxiety—concerned about being able to cover the dividend for quite a foreseeable time" as an immaterial expression of optimism, not a guarantee, because he qualified it by noting that "this is a relatively short-term period of economic difficulty we're going through. And we think that we can ride through this with no problem [whatsoever] as far as [the] dividend is concerned."[26] The court held that there was no duty to *correct* the statement when the CFO concluded in late November 1992 that the dividend was likely to be cut because, at the time the statement was made (October 15, 1992), IBM did not have a plan or need to alter the dividend. The court also held that "there is no duty to *update* vague state-

23. Staff Accounting Bulletin No. 99, 1999 WL 1123073 (SEC Aug. 12, 1999).

24. Basic, Inc. v. Levinson, 485 U.S. 224 (1988).

25. *See, e.g.*, Raab v. Gen. Physics Corp., 4 F.3d 286 (4th Cir. 1993) (holding that statements in annual report that company expected 10 to 30 percent growth rate over the next several years and was "poised to carry the growth and success of 1991 well into the future" were immaterial puffing); San Leandro Emergency Med. Group Profit Sharing Plan v. Philip Morris Cos., 75 F.3d 801 (2d Cir. 1996) (holding that statement that company was "optimistic" about its earnings in 1993 and that it should deliver income growth consistent with its historically superior performance was mere puffery and lacked the sort of definite positive projections that might require later correction).

26. *In re* Int'l Bus. Machs. Corp. Sec. Litig., 163 F.3d 102 (2d Cir. 1998).

ments of optimism or expressions of opinion." (Emphasis added.) In another case, however, a prediction that the company "expects . . . a net income of approximately $1.00 a share" for the fiscal year to close in two months was held to be a material statement.[27]

### *Bespeaks Caution Doctrine*

As explained in Chapter 22, under the judicially developed *bespeaks caution doctrine,* a court may determine that the inclusion of sufficient cautionary statements in a document renders immaterial any misrepresentation and omission contained therein. The doctrine applies only to projections, estimates, and other forward-looking statements that are accompanied by precise cautionary language that adequately discloses the risks involved. The cautionary language must relate to the specific information that the plaintiffs allege is misleading[28] and reflect what the speaker knows or strongly suspects. As one judge commented, "The doctrine of bespeaks caution provides no protection to someone who warns his hiking companion to walk slowly because there might be a ditch ahead when he knows with near certainty that the Grand Canyon lies one foot away."[29]

27. Marx v. Computer Scis. Corp., 507 F.2d 485 (9th Cir. 1974).
28. *See, e.g.*, Kaplan v. Rose, 49 F.3d 1363 (9th Cir. 1994).
29. *In re* Prudential Sec., Inc. P'ships Litig., 930 F. Supp. 68, 72 (S.D.N.Y. 1996).

Unlike the safe harbor provided in the Litigation Reform Act, the bespeaks caution doctrine applies to forward-looking statements in any context, including initial public offerings. The legislative history of the Litigation Reform Act makes it clear that Congress did not intend its statutory safe-harbor provisions to replace the judicial bespeaks caution doctrine or to foreclose further development of that doctrine by the courts.

## *SCIENTER*

Rule 10b–5 does not impose liability for innocent misstatements or omissions. The misstatements or omissions must be made with *scienter,* that is, a mental state embracing the intent to deceive, manipulate, or defraud. Intent to deceive means that the defendant says something he or she believes is untrue with the expectation that others will rely on the statement, or that the defendant omits a fact in the hope that the omission will cause others to misunderstand what he or she does say. The Supreme Court has made clear that *scienter* is more than mere negligence or lack of care. The Litigation Reform Act requires the plaintiff to plead with particularity specific facts giving rise to a strong inference that the defendant acted with *scienter.*

As indicated in the following case, there is currently a split in the circuits as to whether the allegations of the defendant's motive and opportunity to commit fraud are sufficient to meet the strict pleading requirement.

A CASE IN POINT

**CASE 23.4**
**Kasaks v. Novak**
*United States Court of Appeals for the Second Circuit*
*216 F.3d 300 (2d Cir. 2000), cert. denied, 531 U.S. 1012 (2000).*

## In the Language of the Court

**› FACTS** The plaintiffs sued AnnTaylor Stores Corporation—which, through its wholly owned subsidiary, defendant AnnTaylor, Inc., is a specialty retailer of women's clothing, shoes, and accessories—and several of its top officers for violation of Section 10(b) and Rule 10b–5. They alleged that the defendants knowingly and intentionally issued financial statements that overstated AnnTaylor's financial condition by accounting for inventory that they knew to be obsolete and nearly worthless at inflated values and by deliberately failing to adhere to the company's publicly stated markdown policy. The plaintiffs focused on AnnTaylor's so-called Box and Hold practice, whereby a substantial and growing quantity of out-of-date inventory was stored in several warehouses without being marked down. Ultimately, the defendants were forced to publicly acknowledge serious inventory problems—i.e., that inventories were too high and liquidation would result in much lower fiscal 1995 earnings than expected—at which point AnnTaylor's stock price fell precipitously. The district court granted the defendants' motions to dismiss the complaint for failure to plead *scienter* and fraud with sufficient particularity. The plaintiffs appealed.

**› ISSUE PRESENTED** Are allegations of motive and opportunity sufficient to meet the heightened pleading standards for *scienter* under the Litigation Reform Act (the PSLRA)? Can fraud be pleaded with sufficient particularity if the plaintiff relies on unnamed confidential sources?

*(Continued)*

(Case 23.4 *continued*)

**› OPINION** WALKER, J., writing on behalf of the U.S. Court of Appeals for the Second Circuit:

In order "to curtail the filing of meritless lawsuits," the PSLRA imposed stringent procedural requirements on plaintiffs pursuing private securities fraud actions. . . .

**B. The Pleading Standard for Scienter**

**1. The Second Circuit's Pre-PSLRA Pleading Standard**

We can easily summarize the pleading standard for scienter that prevailed in this circuit prior to the PSLRA:

> Plaintiffs must allege facts that give rise to a strong inference of fraudulent intent. "The requisite 'strong inference' of fraud may be established either (a) by alleging facts to show that defendants had both motive and opportunity to commit fraud, or (b) by alleging facts that constitute strong circumstantial evidence of conscious misbehavior or recklessness."

. . .

. . . Plaintiffs could not proceed based on motives possessed by virtually all corporate insiders, including: (1) the desire to maintain a high corporate credit rating, or otherwise sustain "the appearance of corporate profitability, or of the success of an investment"; and (2) the desire to maintain a high stock price in order to increase executive compensation, or prolong the benefits of holding corporate office. Rather, plaintiffs had to allege that defendants benefited in some concrete and personal way from the purported fraud. This requirement was generally met when corporate insiders were alleged to have misrepresented to the public material facts about the corporation's performance or prospects in order to keep the stock price artificially high while they sold their own shares at a profit. Accordingly, in the ordinary case, adequate motive arose from the desire to profit from extensive insider sales.

. . .

**2. Implications of the PSLRA for the Pleading Standard for Scienter in This Circuit**

Courts have disagreed on the proper interpretation of the new pleading requirement imposed by . . . the PSLRA . . . . They have generally come to one of two conclusions:

(1) The statute effectively adopts the Second Circuit's pleading standard for *scienter* wholesale, and thus plaintiffs may continue to state a claim by pleading either motive and opportunity or strong circumstantial evidence of recklessness or conscious misbehavior.[30]

(2) The statute strengthens the Second Circuit's standard by rejecting the simple pleading of motive and opportunity.[31]

Our own review of the text and legislative history leads us to a middle ground. We conclude that the PSLRA effectively raised the nationwide pleading standard to that previously existing in this circuit and no higher (with the exception of the "with particularity" requirement). At the same time, however, we believe that Congress's failure to include language about motive and opportunity suggests that we need not be wedded to these concepts in articulating the prevailing standard. . . .

30. *See In re* Advanta Corp. Sec. Litig., 180 F.3d 525 (3d Cir. 1999).

31. *See* Bryant v. Avado Brands, Inc., 187 F.3d 1271 (11th Cir. 1999); *In re* Silicon Graphics, Inc. Sec. Litig., 183 F.3d 970 (9th Cir. 1999); *In re* Comshare, Inc. Sec. Litig., 183 F.3d 542 (6th Cir. 1999).

*(Continued)*

(Case 23.4 *continued*)

. . .

Accordingly, we hold that the PSLRA adopted our "strong inference" standard: In order to plead scienter, plaintiffs must "state with particularity facts giving rise to a strong inference that the defendant acted with the required state of mind." . . . Although litigants and lower courts need and should not employ or rely on magic words such as "motive and opportunity," we believe that our prior case law may be helpful in providing guidance as to how the "strong inference" standard may be met. . . . These cases suggest that the inference may arise where the complaint sufficiently alleges that the defendants: (1) benefited in a concrete and personal way from the purported fraud; (2) engaged in deliberately illegal behavior; (3) knew facts or had access to information suggesting that their public statements were not accurate; or (4) failed to check information they had a duty to monitor. . . .

**3. Strong Inference of Fraudulent Intent on the Part of the AnnTaylor Defendants**

. . .

By refusing to mark down inventory they knew to be "worthless," "obsolete," and "unsellable," the defendants acted "intentionally and deliberately" to artificially inflate AnnTaylor's reported financial results. They discussed the need to mark down inventory but refused to do so because that would damage the Company's financial prospects. Further, in approving the inventory management practices of "Box and Hold," the defendants knowingly sanctioned procedures that violated the Company's own markdown policy, as stated in the Company's public filings. . . . In short, the Complaint alleges that the defendants engaged in conscious misstatements with the intent to deceive. . . .

**C. Particularity of the Facts Pleaded**

. . .

In order to survive at this stage, the complaint must state with particularity sufficient facts to support the belief that the "Box and Hold" inventory was of limited value, and accordingly that the defendants' positive public statements concerning inventory growth were false and misleading. The district court concluded that the plaintiffs had failed to meet these particularity requirements, in substantial part because they failed to reveal their confidential sources for some of the facts on which their belief in the essential worthlessness of the "Box and Hold" inventory was based. . . .

. . .

[A] January 22, 1996 Weekly Report showed that even six months after the Class Period [February 3, 1994 to May 4, 1995], substantial amounts of "Box and Hold" inventory still dated from 1993 and 1994, which supports the inference that inventory during the Class Period was similarly dated.

Thus, the complaint identifies with particularity several documentary sources that support the plaintiffs' belief that serious inventory problems existed during the Class Period itself.

. . .

[T]here is nothing in the case law of this circuit that requires plaintiffs to reveal confidential sources at the pleading stage.

**› RESULT** The dismissal of the case was vacated. The case was remanded to the trial court with instructions that the plaintiffs be permitted to replead their claims in light of the Second Circuit's opinion.

*(Continued)*

(Case 23.4 *continued*)

**› CRITICAL THINKING QUESTIONS**

1. What weight, if any, should a jury give to the fact that a top executive sold a large block of stock shortly before a negative earnings announcement?
2. Why shouldn't the plaintiffs be required to disclose the names of their confidential sources in the complaint?

---

## *Recklessness*

There is a split in the circuits as to the effect, if any, of the Litigation Reform Act's heightened pleading standards on whether recklessness is sufficient for a finding of *scienter*. The Second Circuit made it clear in *Kasaks v. Novak*[32] that, in its view, recklessness continues to be sufficient for a showing of *scienter*. It defined reckless conduct as:

> conduct which is "highly unreasonable" and which represents "an extreme departure from the standards of ordinary care . . . to the extent that the danger was either known to the defendant or so obvious that the defendant must have been aware of it." . . . "[A]n egregious refusal to see the obvious, or to investigate the doubtful, may in some cases give rise to an inference of . . . recklessness."
>
> . . .
>
> [S]ecurities fraud claims typically have sufficed to state a claim based on recklessness when they have specifically alleged defendants' knowledge of facts or access to information contradicting their public statements. . . .
>
> Under certain circumstances, we have found allegations of recklessness to be sufficient where plaintiffs alleged facts demonstrating that defendants failed to review or check information that they had a duty to monitor, or ignored obvious signs of fraud. . . .
>
> At the same time, however, we have identified several important limitations on the scope of liability for securities fraud based on reckless conduct. First, we have refused to allow plaintiffs to proceed with allegations of "fraud by hindsight." . . . Corporate officials need not be clairvoyant; they are only responsible for revealing those material facts reasonably available to them. . . .
>
> Second, as long as the public statements are consistent with reasonably available data, corporate officials need not present an overly gloomy or cautious picture of current performance and future prospects. . . .
>
> Third, there are limits to the scope of liability for failure adequately to monitor the allegedly fraudulent behavior of others.

32. 216 F.3d 300 (2d Cir. 2000) (Case 23.4).

The Ninth Circuit reached a contrary conclusion in a case involving Silicon Graphics[33] and held that the Litigation Reform Act precludes liability under Section 10(b) for mere recklessness. Instead, a "heightened form of recklessness, i.e., deliberate or conscious recklessness, at a minimum, is required to establish a strong inference of intent."

The Sixth Circuit held that allegations giving rise to a strong inference of recklessness are sufficient to pass muster but that facts showing a mere motive and opportunity to commit fraud are not.[34] The court concluded that Congress changed the pleading, but not the state of mind, requirements applicable to Section 10(b) and Rule 10b–5 cases. The First Circuit also held that the Litigation Reform Act did not alter preexisting *scienter* requirements for securities fraud cases.[35]

To avoid liability, officers should, before making any statement, investigate what the facts are. Managers should make no statement unless they in good faith believe it to be true. The investigation must be fairly thorough. At least in the Second Circuit, an officer may be liable for misrepresenting facts that he or she should have been aware of, even if the officer was not in fact aware of them. For example, directors may be deemed to have knowledge of facts in the corporate books regardless of whether they have actually examined the books.

These tough pleading requirements make it more important than ever for insiders to avoid trading while in possession of material nonpublic information. Plaintiffs can be expected to claim that insiders who sold before the announcement of bad news knew of the impending negative developments and sold their stock while the market price was artificially high, thereby "cashing in" on their alleged misrepresentations and omissions.[36] This arguably creates an inference of fraud.

33. *In re* Silicon Graphics, Inc. Sec. Litig., 183 F.3d 970 (9th Cir. 1999).
34. *In re* Comshare, Inc. Sec. Litig., 183 F.3d 542 (6th Cir. 1999).
35. Greebel v. FTP Software, Inc., 194 F.3d 185 (1st Cir. 1999).
36. See Dale E. Barnes, Jr. & Karen Kennard, *Greater Expectations: Risk Disclosure Under the Private Securities Litigation Reform Act of 1995—An Update*, 2 STAN. J.L., BUS. & FIN. 331, 347–48 (1996).

The U.S. Court of Appeals for the Ninth Circuit rejected this argument in the *Silicon Graphics* case and held that the fact that company executives sold an unusually large amount of Silicon Graphics stock months before the announcement of disappointing news was insufficient to show fraud. In a later case, however, the Ninth Circuit characterized CEO Larry Ellison's sale of $900,000 of Oracle Corporation stock approximately one month prior to the announcement of lower-than-expected sales as "suspicious" and ruled that the unusual stock sales supported a strong inference of *scienter*.[37] Ellison had not sold any Oracle stock in the previous five years. Although Ellison sold only 2.1 percent of his Oracle stock, the court reasoned that "where, as here, stock sales result in a truly astronomical figure, less weight should be given to the fact that they may represent a small portion of the defendant's holdings." Although the sales, taken alone, may not have created a strong inference of *scienter*, when they were coupled with (1) evidence that Oracle maintained an internal database of sales that was monitored by top executives, (2) Oracle customers' billing and payment histories that were corroborated by a former Oracle senior manager and showed improper revenue accounting, and (3) the Oracle executives' detail-oriented management style, the plaintiffs had made allegations that in their totality created a strong inference that Oracle and its top three executives acted with *scienter*. Characterizing this as "far from a cookie-cutter complaint," the court concluded by stating: "The PSLRA was designed to eliminate frivolous or sham actions, but not actions of substance."

It is not yet clear how the U.S. Supreme Court will rule on this issue. Until there is a definitive ruling, managers and companies are well advised to assume that insider trading shortly before the announcement of bad news will create an inference of fraud sufficient to satisfy the Litigation Reform Act's pleading requirements.

## In Connection with the Purchase or Sale of Any Security

Rule 10b–5 requires that the conduct occur "in connection with the purchase or sale of any security." This requirement defines both those who can sue and those who can be sued under Rule 10b–5.

The Supreme Court has made it clear that only persons who actually purchase or sell securities can sue under Rule 10b–5. Persons who have not purchased (or sold) cannot sue on the theory that they would have purchased (or sold) had they known the true facts. Thus, liability under Rule 10b–5 does not extend to the whole world of potential investors but only to those who actually buy or sell stock after a misstatement or omission.

Parties that can be sued under Rule 10b–5 are those that make or are responsible for misstatements or omissions in connection with the purchase or sale of securities. Statements are made "in connection with" the purchase or sale of securities if they were made in a manner reasonably calculated to influence the investing public or if they were of the sort upon which the investing public might reasonably rely.

For example, the U.S. Court of Appeals for the Third Circuit held that fraudulent financial statements issued by Cendant during the course of its tender offer for American Bankers Insurance Group (ABI) were misrepresentations made "in connection with" the plaintiffs' purchase of ABI shares during Cendant's tender offer even though the plaintiffs had neither purchased any Cendant shares nor tendered shares of ABI stock to Cendant.[38] The plaintiffs had alleged that Cendant's misrepresentations artificially inflated the price at which they purchased their ABI shares, and that they suffered a loss when those misrepresentations were disclosed to the public and the merger agreement between Cendant and ABI was terminated.

In summary, a company must be careful to monitor its public statements, such as those made in periodic reports, press releases, proxy solicitations, and annual reports. Even when addressing noninvestors, such as creditors or labor union representatives, a manager should exercise caution if the statements can reasonably be expected to reach investors.

## Reliance

To establish liability under Rule 10b–5, investors must show that they relied either directly or indirectly on the misrepresentation or omission. If the investors did not rely on the misstatement or omission in deciding to buy or sell stock, then any loss they incurred cannot be blamed on the person that made the misrepresentation or omission.

### *Direct Reliance*

A plaintiff may show reliance by showing that he or she actually read the document, such as a press release or prospectus, that contained the misstatement. In the case of an omission, the U.S. Supreme Court has ruled that

37. Nursing Home Pension Fund v. Oracle Corp., 380 F.3d 1226 (9th Cir. 2004).

38. Semerenko v. Cendant Corp., 223 F.3d 165 (3d Cir. 2000).

the plaintiff will be presumed to have relied on the omission, if it was material. That presumption of reliance can be rebutted—that is, shown to be not true—by a showing that the plaintiff would have bought (or sold) the stock even if the omitted fact had been included.

In the following case, the seller of stock in a private placement sought to avoid liability for allegedly deceptive oral statements and omissions based on a nonreliance clause in the stock-purchase contract.

A CASE IN POINT

**CASE 23.5**

**Emergent Capital Investment Management, LLC v. Stonepath Group, Inc.**

*United States Court of Appeals for the Second Circuit 343 F.3d 189 (2d Cir. 2003).*

## Summary

**› FACTS** Emergent Capital Investment Management, LLC invested $2 million in Net Value Holdings, Inc. (NETV), now Stonepath Group, Inc. The investment arose out of a meeting set up by Lee Hansen, director and president of NETV and the former roommate and personal friend of Mark Waldron. Mark Waldron and Daniel Yun, the managing members of Emergent, owned 90 percent of Emergent's stock. Andrew Panzo, the chair and CEO of NETV, had a long history of collaborating with Howard Appel, who had been barred for life by the National Association of Securities Dealers from associating with any member of that organization in any capacity. In the negotiations leading up to the purchase, NETV executives represented, orally and in a brochure, that NETV's largest investment was a $14 million purchase of a 12 percent equity interest in Brightstreet.com. In fact, the Brightstreet.com investment amounted to only $4 million. NETV never mentioned any connection to Appel, who allegedly played a significant role in NETV's founding, financing, and control.

Emergent and NETV executed a stock-purchase agreement, in which NETV made extensive warranties and representations regarding its capital structure, indebtedness, involvement in litigation, ownership and leases of real and personal property, and other matters connected with its business. Further, the agreement contained a passage stating that the agreement and accompanying documents "contained the entire understanding and agreement among the parties . . . and superseded any prior understandings or agreements" between or among any of them.

Appel and Panzo apparently engaged in a number of investment schemes whereby Appel would acquire control of a public shell corporation and subsequently install Panzo as a director or senior officer. The company would transfer substantial quantities of stock to affiliates of Appel and Panzo, and the two men would, "through extraordinarily complex corporate legal maneuvers," end up with large amounts of stock. They would then sell the stock at a high price, leaving behind a virtually worthless company.

Between January and March 2000, the price of NETV's stock hovered between $10 and $30 per share. The stock subsequently fell to less than $1 per share. As the stock fell, Emergent demanded rescission of the agreement. NETV refused, prompting Emergent to sue for securities fraud under Rule 10b–5. Emergent alleged that NETV had misrepresented the size of the Brightstreet.com investment and had failed to disclose the company's connection to Appel.

**› ISSUE PRESENTED** Does a nonreliance clause in a stock-purchase agreement preclude liability in cases of misrepresentations or omissions?

**› SUMMARY OF OPINION** The U.S. Court of Appeals for the Second Circuit first laid out the substantive law, explaining that plaintiffs in such an action must establish reasonable reliance on the alleged misrepresentations or omissions. The reasonableness of the reliance is judged in light of the entire context of the transaction, including factors such as its complexity and magnitude, the sophistication of the parties, and the content of any agreements between them.

*(Continued)*

(Case 23.5 *continued*)

As for the misrepresentation of the Brightstreet.com investment, the court noted that the plaintiff had secured from the defendants extensive contractual representations concerning NETV's financial condition and operations. Because Emergent was a sophisticated investor, it should have protected itself by insisting that the representation regarding the Brightstreet.com investment be included in the stock-purchase agreement. The court ruled that Emergent's failure to require such a representation in the agreement precluded a finding of reasonable reliance on the misrepresentation.

Unlike the affirmative misrepresentation, the omission of Panzo's investment history and NETV's ties to Appel was not known by Emergent. As a result, Emergent could not have protected itself against them in the agreement. The court held that the plaintiff had sufficiently alleged that, but for the omission, the purchase would not have taken place. Further, the court found that the plaintiff had sufficiently asserted that Emergent's loss was a foreseeable consequence of the defendants' omissions, particularly in light of the drastic price declines that occurred in the shares of the other companies controlled by Panzo and Appel.

**› RESULT** The dismissal of Emergent's claim regarding the misstatement of the value of the Brightstreet.com investment was affirmed, but the dismissal of Emergent's claim regarding Panzo's investment history and NETV's connection to Appel was vacated. Emergent could pursue the latter claim.

**› COMMENTS** Given the "sophistication of the parties," the Second Circuit expected the buyer to include every material fact in the purchase agreement. In effect, the court reasoned that if a statement was important enough to be relied upon by a sophisticated investor, then it should have been included in the agreement.

The Seventh Circuit reached a similar result in *Rissman v. Rissman.*[39] As Judge Easterbrook noted, "Prudent people protect themselves against the limitations of memory (and the temptation to shade the truth) by limiting their dealings to those memorialized in writing, and promoting the primacy of the written word is a principal function of the federal securities laws." The Seventh Circuit also rejected the argument that the no-reliance clause should be ignored as mere "boilerplate." Judge Easterbrook explained that "the fact that language has been used before does not make it less binding when used again. Phrases become boilerplate when many parties find that the language serves their ends. That's a reason to enforce the promises, not to disregard them."

39. 213 F.3d 381 (7th Cir. 2000).

## *Fraud on the Market*

In the securities market, direct reliance is rare because transactions are usually not conducted on a face-to-face basis. The market is interposed between the parties, providing important information to them in the form of the market price. As the U.S. District Court for the Northern District of Texas said in the LTV Securities Litigation: "The market is acting as the unpaid agent of the investor, informing him that, given all the information available to it, the value of the stock is worth the market price."

The theory underlying this view is known to economists as the *efficient-market theory.* It holds that in an open and developed securities market, the price of a company's stock equals its true value. The market is said to evaluate information efficiently and to incorporate it into the price of a company's securities.

Against this background, the courts have approved the *fraud-on-the-market theory:* If the information available to the market is incorrect, then the market price will not reflect the true value of the stock. Under this theory, an investor who purchases or sells a security is presumed to have relied on the market, which has in turn relied on the misstatement or omission when it set the price of the security. In *Basic, Inc. v. Levinson,* the Supreme Court affirmed this theory. Quoting one of the earlier lower court decisions, the Supreme Court noted that "[i]t is hard to imagine that there ever is a buyer or seller who does not rely on market integrity. Who would knowingly roll the dice in a crooked crap game?"

Thus, plaintiffs do not have to show that they read or heard a defendant's misstatement in order to recover damages from that defendant. Instead, reliance is presumed if the investor shows that (1) the defendant made a public material misrepresentation that would have caused reasonable investors to misjudge the value of the defendant's stock and (2) the investor traded shares of the defendant's stock in an open securities market after the misrepresentations were made and before the truth was revealed.

A defendant can rebut the fraud-on-the-market presumption by showing that the plaintiff traded or would have traded despite knowing the statement was false. For example, an insider who is aware of nonpublic information that results in the stock being undervalued, but who sells for other reasons, cannot be said to have relied on the integrity of the market price.

Lower courts have declined to apply the fraud-on-the-market presumption in cases that do not involve an efficient, open, and developed market. The courts have identified at least five factors to consider in identifying an efficient market: (1) sufficient weekly trading volume, (2) sufficient reports and analyses by investment professionals, (3) the presence of market makers and arbitrageurs, (4) the existence of issuers eligible to file Form S–3 short-form registration statements, and (5) a historical showing of immediate price response to unexpected events or financial releases. In short, for a market to be open and developed, it must have a large number of buyers and sellers and a relatively high level of trading activity and frequency. It also must be a market where prices rapidly reflect new information.

**Truth on the Market** Defendants have also used the efficient-market theory to their advantage. For example, even if the defendant makes overly optimistic sales projections for a product, there is no fraud on the market if the market makers were privy to the truth. In such a case, an investor who did not directly rely on the misrepresentation (for example, by actually reading a misleading press release) could not successfully assert a securities fraud claim based on fraud on the market.

As the U.S. Court of Appeals for the Ninth Circuit explained, in a fraud-on-the-market case, a defendant's failure to disclose material information may be excused if that information has been made credibly available to the market by other sources: "[I]ndividuals who hear [only good news or only bad news] may receive a distorted impression . . . , and thus may have an actionable claim. But the market, and any individual who relies only on the price established by the market, will not be misled."[40]

A defendant is not relieved of its duty to disclose material information unless that information has been transmitted to the public with a degree of intensity and credibility sufficient to counterbalance any misleading impression created by the defendant. A brief mention of the omitted fact in a few poorly circulated or lightly regarded publications would be insufficient.

## CAUSATION

A plaintiff must prove that the defendant's misstatement or omission caused him or her to suffer losses. Increasingly, this is an economic question—what factors influence the price of a stock in the securities market?

In a securities case involving Nucorp Energy, for example, investors claimed that a misrepresentation by the company of the value of its oil reserves caused them to suffer losses. The claim was based on the contention that the stock price was maintained at an artificially high level as a result of the misrepresentation. The investors attributed the later drop in the stock price to the revelation of the true facts. At trial, the defendants presented the testimony of an economist that the drop in the stock price was caused by a drop in the price of oil and was not attributable to any misrepresentation of the value of the oil reserves. The jury found that the plaintiffs had failed to prove their claim.

In early 2005, the U.S. Court of Appeals for the Second Circuit dismissed securities fraud claims against Merrill Lynch & Co., its star analyst Henry M. Blodget, and other research analysts for allegedly issuing false and misleading analyst reports on two Internet companies—24/7 Media and Interliant.[41] Merrill Lynch had acted as lead under-

40. *In re* Apple Computer Sec. Litig., 886 F.2d 1109 (9th Cir. 1989), *cert. denied,* 496 U.S. 943 (1990).

41. Lentell v. Merrill Lynch & Co., 396 F.3d 161 (2d Cir. 2005).

### ETHICAL CONSIDERATION

Managers of companies frequently act as promoters, describing the company's products to the press and the public in an aggressive, upbeat manner. It is reasonable to expect them to engage in a certain amount of puffing and exaggeration. Are these exaggerations ethically justifiable as long as they do not violate the securities laws?

writer for two public offerings by 24/7 Media and as co-lead underwriter of Interliant's initial public offering. The plaintiffs alleged that Blodget and other research analysts issued knowingly or recklessly false bullish research reports to generate investment banking business for Merrill.

An earlier investigation of analyst conflicts of interest by New York Attorney General Eliot Spitzer had led to Merrill's agreement in 2002 to pay $100 million to settle New York's civil complaint and spawned more than 100 class-action complaints. Ultimately, ten investment banking firms paid more than $1 billion in a global settlement reached on April 28, 2003, to settle government investigations of the incestuous relationships between the firms' research groups—which purported to provide objective research reports—and their investment banking arms, which used favorable analyst coverage to garner more investment banking business. The scandal resulted in a new SEC regulation—Regulation Analyst Certification (Regulation AC)—that prohibits analysts from issuing reports that they do not personally believe to be true and require the disclosure of any analyst compensation arrangements related to the specific recommendation or views contained in the research report. [*See* Securities Exchange Act Release No. 47,384 (Feb. 20, 2003), 68 Fed. Reg. 9,482 (Feb. 27, 2003).]

The plaintiffs suing Merrill did not claim to have read Merrill's reports or to have bought 24/7 Media or Interliant shares through the firm. Instead, they asserted fraud on the market. To prevail, the plaintiffs had to show *loss causation,* that is, that "the misstatement or omission concealed something from the market that, when disclosed, negatively affected the value of the security." The plaintiffs did not allege that Merrill "doctored" the facts or hid the risks, the price volatility of the stocks, the negative earnings-per-share ratios, or the consistent quarterly losses. There was also no allegation that the market reacted negatively to a corrective disclosure regarding the falsity of Merrill's positive recommendations. The Second Circuit declared this "fatal" to the plaintiffs' case. The court also rejected the plaintiffs' efforts to characterize Merrill's actions as market manipulation in violation of Rule 10b–5(a) and (c).

As a result of these developments in the area of causation, proponents of the efficient-market theory may be right when they predict that an entire Rule 10b–5 case may boil down to one question: Did the misleading statement artificially affect the market price? The U.S. Supreme Court may provide more guidance on this issue when it decides the *Dura Pharmaceuticals* case discussed earlier.[42]

42. Broudo v. Dura Pharmaceuticals, Inc., 339 F.3d 933 (9th Cir. 2003), *cert. granted,* 124 S. Ct. 2904 (2004).

### Calculation of Damages

The measure of damages in a Rule 10b–5 case is typically the out-of-pocket loss, that is, the difference between what the investor paid (or received) and the fair value of the stock on the date of the transaction. Alternately, investors can elect to rescind the transaction, returning what they received and getting back what they gave. In the court's discretion, *prejudgment interest*—that is, interest on the amount of the award between the date the securities were purchased and the date of the judgment—may also be awarded. Punitive damages are not available.

In theory, damages must be proved with reasonable certainty. In practice, however, damages are awarded on the basis of expert testimony, which can be highly conjectural. For example, a claim that a company's failure to reveal negative information about its new product artificially inflated the price of its stock is quite difficult to evaluate with any scientific certainty because even the experts do not agree to what extent any particular piece of information affects the price of a company's securities.

In addition, the number of traders who can claim damage can only be estimated. For example, in-and-out traders' trades are included in the total volume of trading; but such traders who buy, then quickly sell, suffer no damage if they sell the securities before the price drop.

Evidence of damages is therefore often presented by comparing the stock's performance with the industry or market performance, on the assumption that the industry or the market was not subject to the same artificial inflation. This clearly remains a fertile field for argument and future litigation.

## Litigation Reform Act Safe Harbor for Forward-Looking Statements

The Private Securities Litigation Reform Act provides issuers subject to the 1934 Act's reporting requirements and persons acting on their behalf a two-prong safe harbor for certain forward-looking statements.[43] *Forward-looking statements* include (1) a statement containing a projection of revenues, income, earnings per share, capital expenditures, dividends, capital structure, or other financial items; (2) a statement of the plans and objectives of management for future operations, including plans relating to the issuer's products and services; (3) a statement of future economic performance, including any such statement in Management's Discussion and Analysis of Financial

43. 15 U.S.C.S. § 77z-2.

Condition and Results of Operations (MD & A) required to be included by the SEC; and (4) any statement of the assumptions underlying or relating to any such statement.

The safe harbor does not apply to forward-looking statements in connection with (1) an initial public offering; (2) an offering of securities by a blank check company; (3) a rollup or going-private transaction; (4) a tender offer; or (5) an offering by a partnership, limited liability company, or direct participation investment program. The safe harbor also does not apply to any forward-looking statement included in (1) a financial statement prepared in accordance with generally accepted accounting principles or (2) a report of beneficial ownership on Schedule 13D.

As explained in Chapter 22, the statutory safe harbor for forward-looking statements was designed to promote market efficiency by encouraging companies to disclose projections and other information about their future prospects. Anecdotal evidence indicated that corporate counsel were advising their clients to say as little as possible due to fear that if the company failed to satisfy its announced earning projections—perhaps due to an industry downturn or the timing of a large order or release of a new product—the company would automatically be sued.

Under the first prong of the safe harbor, a person is protected from liability for a misrepresentation or omission based on a written forward-looking statement as long as the statement (1) is identified as forward-looking and (2) is accompanied by meaningful cautionary statements identifying important factors that could cause actual results to differ materially from those projected in the statement. The safe harbor also protects forward-looking oral statements if the person making the statement (1) identifies the statement as forward-looking, (2) states that results may differ materially from those projected in the statement, and (3) identifies a readily available written document (such as a document filed with the SEC) that contains factors that could cause results to differ materially.

The stated factors must be relevant to the projection and of a nature that could actually affect whether the forward-looking statement is realized. Boilerplate warnings will not suffice. Failure to include the particular factor that ultimately causes the forward-looking statement not to come true will not mean that the statement automatically is not protected by the safe harbor. The company must disclose all important factors, not all factors. In this respect, the safe harbor provides greater protection than the bespeaks caution doctrine.

For example, in *Harris v. Ivax Corp.*,[44] the U.S. Court of Appeals for the Eleventh Circuit held that a generic drug manufacturer was not liable for securities fraud despite its failure to disclose the possibility of a $104 million reduction in the carrying value of goodwill for several of its businesses. The company's cautionary language was adequate even though it did not explicitly mention the factor that ultimately belied the forward-looking statement. The court explained: "When an investor has been warned of risks of a significance similar to that actually realized, she is sufficiently on notice of the danger of the investment to make an intelligent decision about it according to her own preferences for risk and reward."

When a court is ruling on a motion to dismiss based on this prong of the safe harbor, the state of mind of the person making the statement is not relevant. The court looks only at the cautionary language accompanying the forward-looking statement.

Even if a person cannot rely on this first prong, there is an independent prong based on the state of mind of the person making the statement. A person or business entity will not be liable in a private lawsuit involving a forward-looking statement unless the plaintiff proves that the person or business entity made a false or misleading forward-looking statement with actual knowledge that it was false or misleading. A statement by a business entity will come within the safe harbor unless it was made by or with the approval of an executive officer of the entity with actual knowledge by that officer that the statement was false or misleading.

## Section 17(a)

Section 17(a) of the 1933 Act prohibits fraud in connection with the sale of securities. It is similar in scope to Section 10(b) of the 1934 Act, which prohibits fraud in both the sale and the purchase of securities. Unlike Section 10(b), Section 17(a) does not require proof of *scienter*. The SEC and the U.S. Attorney's Office can use Section 17(a) to prosecute securities fraud, but private parties cannot sue based on it.

## Responsibility of Auditors to Detect and Report Illegalities

The Private Securities Litigation Reform Act added a new Section 10A to the 1934 Act to promote disclosure by independent public accountants of illegal acts committed by their publicly traded audit clients. Each audit must include, in accordance with generally accepted auditing standards, (1) procedures designed to provide reasonable assurance of detecting illegal acts that would

44. 182 F.3d 799 (11th Cir. 1999).

have a direct and material effect on the determination of financial statement amounts, (2) procedures designed to identify material related-party transactions (such as those involving officers, directors, and controlling shareholders of the company being audited), and (3) an evaluation of whether there is substantial doubt about the ability of the company to continue as a going concern during the ensuing fiscal year. The Sarbanes–Oxley Act of 2002 also requires auditors to report on the adequacy of the company's internal controls (see Appendix N).

If, in the course of the audit, the independent public accountant detects or otherwise becomes aware of information indicating that an illegal act has or may have occurred (regardless of whether it is perceived to have a material effect on the financial statements), then the accountant must (1) determine whether it is likely that an illegal act has occurred and, if so, determine and consider the possible effect on the financial statements; and (2) inform the appropriate level of the management of the company. The accountant must ensure that the audit committee, or the board of directors in the absence of such a committee, is adequately informed with respect to the illegal acts, unless the illegal act is clearly inconsequential. If after informing the audit committee or board, the accountant concludes that (1) the illegal act has a material effect on the financial statements of the company, (2) senior management has not taken timely and appropriate remedial actions with respect to the illegal act, and (3) the failure to take remedial action is reasonably expected to warrant departure from a standard audit report or resignation, then the accountant must, as soon as practicable, directly report its conclusions to the board of directors. The board is then required to notify the SEC within one business day after its receipt of the report. If the board fails to do so, the accountant must furnish the SEC a copy of its report (or the documentation of any oral report given).

## Sarbanes–Oxley Act of 2002

An unprecedented series of accounting scandals rocked the U.S. capital markets in the early years of the twenty-first century. Approximately 10 percent of publicly traded companies restated their financial statements between 1997 and 2001.[45] During roughly the same period, the analyst conflict-of-interest scandals discussed earlier further shook investor confidence.

45. REPORT TO THE CHAIRMAN, SENATE COMM. ON BANKING, HOUSING & URBAN AFFAIRS, U.S. GENERAL ACCOUNTING OFFICE, FINANCIAL STATEMENT RESTATEMENTS: TRENDS, MARKET IMPACTS, REGULATORY RESPONSES AND REMAINING CHALLENGES 15 (2002) (GAO–03–138).

*"The whole fun of accounting was that willingness to suspend disbelief."*



In addition to the reforms summarized in Chapter 22, the Sarbanes–Oxley Act of 2002 created a new crime, securities fraud involving a publicly traded company.[46] In particular, it is a felony to knowingly execute or attempt to execute a scheme or artifice (1) to defraud any person in connection with any security of a publicly traded company or (2) to obtain, by means of false or fraudulent pretenses, representations, or promises, any money or property in connection with the purchase or sale of any security of a publicly traded company. The provision applies to any security of an issuer with a class of securities registered under Section 12 of the Securities Exchange Act of 1934 or that is required to file reports under Section 15(d) of the Securities Exchange Act of 1934. Congress thereby made it clear that any fake or misleading statements reasonably calculated to affect the public securities markets—such as those made by Henry Blodget of Merrill Lynch, Jack Grubman of Citigroup, and other securities analysts who touted stocks they privately called "junk" or worse—constitute securities fraud.

## Definition of Insider Trading

Insider trading refers in general terms to trading by persons (often insiders, such as officers and directors) based on material nonpublic information. The Supreme Court has held, however, that not every trade while in possession of material nonpublic information violates Section 10(b). Because there is no statutory definition of insider trading, the law in this area has developed on a piecemeal basis. This lack of a clear definition has caused enforcement problems for the SEC and federal prosecutors. It can also make it difficult for investors to know whether their actions constitute prohibited insider trading.

46. 18 U.S.C. § 1348.

The safest course is never to trade while in possession of material nonpublic information; however, such a premise is unduly restrictive. The nature of insider trading can best be understood by examining the purposes underlying the laws that prohibit it.

Two fundamental goals of the securities laws in general are to protect the investing public and to maintain fairness in the securities markets. Allowing a party who knows that the market is incorrectly pricing a security to exploit another party's ignorance of that fact is fundamentally unfair. Yet, if an efficient market is to be maintained, market professionals, such as securities analysts, must be given an incentive to ferret out the truth about companies and their prospects. There would be no incentive if the persons who expended the time and effort to piece together the truth were precluded from either trading on that information or selling it to others in the form of a tip or analyst report.

In light of this need to promote an efficient market and the language of Section 10(b), which refers to fraudulent and manipulative practices, the Supreme Court has held that a trade based on material nonpublic information is illegal only if there is a breach of duty by the person trading; or if the person trading is the recipient of a tip—a piece of inside information—there must be a breach of duty by the person who gave the tip. The person giving the tip is known as the *tipper;* the person receiving it is known as the *tippee.*

Insider trading cases focus specifically on the duty to disclose, before trading, material information that is not publicly known (that is, not commonly available to the investing public). An insider must either disclose material nonpublic information in his or her possession or refrain from trading. The fundamental question in an insider trading case is whether this obligation should be imposed on a particular trader.

For example, corporate officers and directors have specific legal duties to the corporation and the shareholders they serve, which prohibit them from engaging in insider trading. As corporate fiduciaries, these individuals are required to subordinate their self-interests to the interests of the shareholders, as discussed in Chapter 20.

In 2000, the SEC sought to clarify several aspects of insider trading by promulgating Rules 10b5–1 and 10b5–2 (which are set forth in Appendix L). Rule 10b5–1 provides that any person who purchases or sells securities of any issuer on the basis of material nonpublic information about the security or issuer violates Section 10(b) if the purchase or sale was in breach of a duty of trust or confidence owed directly, indirectly, or derivatively to (1) the issuer or its security holders or (2) any other person who is the source of the material nonpublic information. A trade is "on the basis of" material nonpublic information if the person trading was aware of the information at the time of the trade, unless the person can demonstrate that:

1. Before becoming aware of the information, he or she (a) entered into a binding contract to purchase or sell, (b) gave instructions for the trade, or (c) adopted a written plan to trade; *and*
2. The contract, instruction, or plan either (a) specified the amount of securities to be traded and the price, or (b) included a written formula or algorithm for determining the amount and price, or (c) did not permit the person to exercise any subsequent influence over how, when, and whether to trade; *and*
3. The trade was pursuant to the contract, instruction, or plan.

Thus, Rule 10b5–1 creates a presumption that persons who trade while in possession of material nonpublic information trade on the basis of that information unless the trade is pursuant to a preexisting plan. The rule was adopted in response to several cases in which the court held that a person who trades while in possession of inside information violates Rule 10b–5 only if he or she decided to trade based on that information.[47]

The affirmative defense is designed to cover situations in which the person trading can demonstrate that the material nonpublic information was not a factor in the trading decision. It permits those who would like to plan securities transactions in advance, at a time when they are not aware of material nonpublic information, to carry out those preplanned transactions at a later time, even if they later become aware of material, nonpublic information. Rule 10b5–2, discussed further later, creates certain presumptions about the existence of a duty of trust or confidence in certain nonbusiness relationships, such as marriage.

## Classical Theory of Insider Trading

An *insider* is a person with access to confidential information and an obligation of disclosure to other traders in the marketplace. Insiders include not only traditional insiders—such as officers and directors—but also temporary insiders, such as outside counsel and financial consultants.

### *Traditional Insiders*

Traditionally, only persons closely allied with the corporation itself were considered insiders. They are true insiders because they acquire information by performing duties within or on behalf of the issuer corporation.

47. *See, e.g.,* SEC v. Adler, 137 F.3d 1325 (11th Cir. 1998).

Persons or entities traditionally considered insiders include (1) officers and directors, (2) employees, (3) controlling shareholders, and (4) the corporation itself. Even if an insider resigns before trading, he or she will still be liable for trading on the basis of material inside information learned while on the job.

**Officers and Directors** Officers and directors have a fiduciary obligation of loyalty and care to the corporate shareholders. They also have the greatest access to sensitive information regarding corporate events.

**Employees** As agents or servants of a corporation, employees have a duty of loyalty. They may not personally profit from confidential information that they receive in the course of their employment.

**Controlling Shareholders** Because of their majority stock ownership, controlling shareholders are generally in a position to control the activities of the corporation. They are therefore likely to be aware of impending corporate events.

**The Corporation** Often a corporation (or other issuer) will engage in the purchase or sale of its own securities. Under these circumstances, the corporation and those acting on its behalf are insiders and must not trade while in possession of material nonpublic information.

### *Temporary Insiders*

Outside attorneys, accountants, consultants, and investment bankers who are not directly employed by the corporation, but who acquire confidential information through the performance of professional services, are also considered insiders. The Supreme Court extended liability under Section 10(b) to such *temporary insiders* in footnote 14 to the *Dirks* case, which is presented as Case 23.6.

### *Tippees of Insiders*

Tippees—that is, persons who receive information from a traditional or temporary insider—may also be subject to liability under Rule 10b–5, but only if they can be considered derivative insiders. In most cases, a tippee has no independent duty to the shareholders of the corporation, whose shares the tippee is buying or selling and with which he or she may have little or no connection. A tippee will not be held liable as a *derivative insider* unless the insider's duty of disclosure can somehow be imposed upon the tippee. This rule was established in the following landmark case.

**A CASE IN POINT**

**CASE 23.6**
**Dirks v. SEC**
*Supreme Court of the United States*
*463 U.S. 646 (1983).*

## Summary

**› FACTS** Raymond Dirks, an officer of a New York broker–dealer firm, specialized in providing investment analysis of insurance company securities to institutional investors, was contacted by Ronald Secrist, a former employee of Equity Funding of America. Secrist was seeking aid in exposing fraudulent activities that had resulted in an overvaluation of Equity Funding's assets. Dirks was thus the potential tippee, with Secrist the tipper. After corroborating Secrist's story, Dirks advised certain clients that they should sell their shares in the company. When the corporate fraud was later revealed, the price of Equity Funding's stock went down.

The SEC brought proceedings against Dirks on the theory that he had constructively breached a fiduciary duty. In effect, the SEC maintained that anyone receiving information from an insider stands in the insider's shoes and should be held to the same standards and be subject to the same duties as that insider.

**› ISSUE PRESENTED** Is a tippee liable when the tipper has not violated a fiduciary duty?

**› SUMMARY OF OPINION** The U.S. Supreme Court rejected the argument that anyone receiving information from an insider should be held to the same standards as the insider. The Court held instead that a tippee is not liable unless the tippee and the tipper join in a co-venture to exploit the information. Only in such a case will the fiduciary duty of the tipper be derivatively imposed on the tippee. For the tippee to be liable, therefore, the tipper must have a duty to the corporation not to disclose the information and must breach this duty by seeking to benefit personally from the disclosure of the information. The benefit

*(Continued)*

(Case 23.6 *continued*)

sought by the tipper can be either tangible or intangible. Intangible benefits might include an enhanced reputation or the intangible benefit received through the giving of gifts.

In this case, the insider was motivated solely by a desire to expose fraudulent conduct. He did not breach any fiduciary duties because it was in the interests of the corporation that this information be disclosed.

**› RESULT** Without a breach of duty on the part of the insider/tipper, no derivative duty could be imposed on Dirks, the tippee. Dirks was not guilty of illegal insider trading.

---

The requirement that the tipper be seeking some benefit implies that the tipper must desire that the tippee trade on the information, but it is unclear whether such a showing is necessary. For example, the tipper could derive a benefit merely from impressing the tippee with his or her access to confidential information. Such a desire could stem from social or career aspirations of the tipper and could have nothing to do with the stock-trading ramifications of the information.

**Breach of Fiduciary Duty** In addition to seeking some benefit, the tipper must also be acting in breach of a fiduciary duty to the corporation (or to another under the misappropriation theory, discussed later in this chapter) by disclosing the information to the tippee. The information must be nonpublic at the time it is divulged, and it must be in the interests of the corporation (or the other party in a misappropriation case) to keep the information confidential.

In a classic case of illegal tipping, the former CEO of ImClone, Samuel D. Waksal, was convicted in 2003 of telling his daughter and father to sell their ImClone stock based on his nonpublic knowledge that the Food and Drug Administration (FDA) was denying approval of ImClone's anticancer drug Erbitex. In the course of sentencing Waksal to more than seven years in prison and ordering him to pay a $3 million fine, Judge William H. Pauley III stated:

> The harm that you wrought is truly incalculable. You abused your position of trust as chief executive officer of a major corporation and undermined the public's confidence in the integrity of the financial markets. Then you tried to lie your way out of it, showing a complete disregard for the firm administration of justice.[48]

Judge Pauley further rebuked Waksal, saying, "Your spectacular success in building ImClone into a company worthy of inclusion in the Nasdaq 100 led you to disconnect from reality and, most importantly, from the rule of law."[49]

The tippee is liable only if he or she knew or should have known that the tipper's disclosure of the confidential information constituted a fiduciary breach. If the tippee has reason to know that the insider's disclosure was wrong or against the interest of the corporation, the tippee's actual knowledge will be irrelevant.

Rule 10b5–2 creates a presumption that spouses, parents, children, and siblings are bound by fiduciary ties. The presumption can be rebutted only by a showing that their past dealings (with respect to securities or any other matter) did not involve an implied obligation of confidentiality.

The SEC sued Samuel Waksal's father in 2003 to recover the $7 million in profits he earned when he sold his ImClone shares before the public announcement of the FDA's rejection of the drug application. The complaint alleged that Samuel Waksal intended to bestow a gift of illegal profits or illegal loss avoidance on his father by telling him about the impending announcement of bad news and that his father knew that he should not have traded on that information.[50]

### *Remote Tippees*

*Remote tippees*—that is, the tippees of tippees—may be found to have violated Section 10(b) and Rule 10b–5 even if they are completely unacquainted with and removed from the original insider tipper. However, remote tippees are not liable unless they knew or should have known that the first-tier tipper was breaching a fiduciary duty in passing on the nonpublic information.[51] The phrase "should have known" is key to this formulation. It means that tippees cannot insulate themselves from liability merely by failing to inquire as to the source of the information. If a tippee has reason to sus-

48. Constance L. Hays, *Former Chief of ImClone Is Given 7-Year Term,* N.Y. Times, June 11, 2003, at C1.

49. *Id.*

50. Constance L. Hays, *Waksal's Father Named in S.E.C. Suit,* N.Y. Times, Oct. 11, 2003, at C3.

51. SEC v. Musella, 678 F. Supp. 1060 (S.D.N.Y. 1988).

pect that the information was wrongfully acquired, such conscious avoidance of knowledge will not prevent a finding of *scienter.*

## Misappropriation Theory of Insider Trading

From time to time, the SEC has unsuccessfully attempted to impose liability on anyone who trades while in possession of material nonpublic information. In *Chiarella v. United States,*[52] the Supreme Court rejected the argument that every trade based on material nonpublic information should be held to violate the securities laws.

52. 445 U.S. 222 (1980).

By embracing the misappropriation theory in the following case, the U.S. Supreme Court greatly expanded the class of potential defendants to include not only traditional and temporary insiders but also third parties unaffiliated with the company in whose securities they traded. Under the *misappropriation theory,* a Rule 10b–5 violation occurs if a person breaches a fiduciary duty to the source of the nonpublic information by trading on that information after misappropriating it for his or her own use. No independent duty of disclosure to the person from whom the securities were bought or sold or the issuer is required. Liability is imposed because the trader secretly converted the confidential information to his or her own use.

A Case in Point

**CASE 23.7**

**United States v. O'Hagan**

*Supreme Court of the United States*
*521 U.S. 642 (1997).*

## In the Language of the Court

› **FACTS** Attorney James Herman O'Hagan purchased stock and options for stock in Pillsbury Company prior to the public announcement of a tender offer for Pillsbury's stock by Grand Met PLC. O'Hagan possessed material nonpublic information about Grand Met's intentions, which he had obtained as a partner of the law firm representing Grand Met in connection with its acquisition of Pillsbury. O'Hagan realized a profit in excess of $4 million on his Pillsbury-related transactions.

O'Hagan was convicted of fifty-seven counts of securities fraud under Section 10(b), Rule 10b–5, and Rule 14e–3(a), mail fraud, and money laundering. Rule 14e–3 prohibits a person with nonpublic information about a pending tender offer that he or she knows or has reason to know has been acquired directly or indirectly from the offeror or the target or someone working on their behalf from trading on that information. (See Appendix M for the full text of Rule 14e–3.) The appeals court reversed, and the United States appealed.

› **ISSUE PRESENTED** Is a person who trades in securities for personal profit, using confidential information misappropriated in breach of a fiduciary duty to the source of the information, guilty of violating Section 10(b), Rule 10b–5, or Rule 14e–3?

› **OPINION** GINSBURG, J., writing for the U.S. Supreme Court:

In pertinent part, § 10(b) of the Exchange Act provides:

> It shall be unlawful for any person, directly or indirectly, by the use of any means or instrumentality of interstate commerce or of the mails, or of any facility of any national securities exchange—
>
> . . .
>
> **b.** To use or employ, in connection with the purchase or sale of any security registered on a national securities exchange or any security not so registered, any manipulative or deceptive device or contrivance in contravention of such rules and regulations as the [Securities and Exchange] Commission may prescribe as necessary or appropriate in the public interest or for the protection of investors.

The statute thus proscribes (1) using any deceptive device (2) in connection with the purchase or sale of securities, in contravention of rules prescribed by the Commission.

*(Continued)*

(Case 23.7 *continued*)

The provision, as written, does not confine its coverage to deception of a purchaser or seller of securities; rather, the statute reaches any deceptive device used "in connection with the purchase or sale of any security."

Pursuant to its § 10(b) rulemaking authority, the Commission has adopted Rule 10b–5, which, as relevant here, provides:

> It shall be unlawful for any person, directly or indirectly, by the use of any means or instrumentality of interstate commerce, or of the mails or of any facility of any national securities exchange,
>
> (a) To employ any device, scheme, or artifice to defraud, [or]
>
> . . .
>
> (c) To engage in any act, practice, or course of business which operates or would operate as a fraud or deceit upon any person, in connection with the purchase or sale of any security.

Liability under Rule 10b–5, our precedent indicates, does not extend beyond conduct encompassed by Section 10(b)'s prohibition.

Under the "traditional" or "classical theory" of insider trading liability, § 10(b) and Rule 10b–5 are violated when a corporate insider trades in the securities of his corporation on the basis of material, nonpublic information. . . .

The "misappropriation theory" holds that a person commits fraud "in connection with" a securities transaction, and thereby violates § 10(b) and Rule 10–5, when he misappropriates confidential information for securities trading purposes, in breach of a duty owed to the source of the information. Under this theory, a fiduciary's undisclosed, self-serving use of a principal's information to purchase or sell securities, in breach of a duty of loyalty and confidentiality, defrauds the principal of the exclusive use of that information. In lieu of premising liability on a fiduciary relationship between company insider and purchaser or seller of the company's stock, the misappropriation theory premises liability on a fiduciary turned trader's deception of those who entrusted him with access to confidential information.

. . .

**B.**

We agree with the Government that misappropriation, as just defined, satisfies § 10(b)'s requirement that chargeable conduct involve a "deceptive device or contrivance" used "in connection with" the purchase or sale of securities. We observe, first, that misappropriators, as the Government describes them, deal in deception. A fiduciary who "[pretends] loyalty to the principal while secretly converting the principal's information for personal gain" . . . defrauds the principal.

. . .

We turn next to the § 10(b) requirement that the misappropriator's deceptive use of information be "in connection with the purchase or sale of [a] security." This element is satisfied because the fiduciary's fraud is consummated, not when the fiduciary gains the confidential information, but when, without disclosure to his principal, he uses the information to purchase or sell securities. The securities transaction and the breach of duty thus coincide. This is so even though the person or entity defrauded is not the other party to the trade, but is, instead, the source of the nonpublic information. A misappropriator who trades on the basis of material, nonpublic information, in short, gains his advantageous market position through deception; he deceives the source of the information and simultaneously harms members of the investing public.

. . .

*(Continued)*

(Case 23.7 *continued*)

In sum, considering the inhibiting impact on market participation of trading on misappropriated information, and the congressional purposes underlying § 10(b), it makes scant sense to hold a lawyer like O'Hagan a § 10(b) violator if he works for a law firm representing the target of a tender offer, but not if he works for a law firm representing the bidder. The text of the statute requires no such result.

**› RESULT** O'Hagan's conviction was upheld. He violated Section 10(b) and Rule 10b–5 by trading on material nonpublic information in violation of his duty to his partners and the firm's client.

His conviction under Rule 14e–3, which applies regardless of whether the trader owed a preexisting duty to respect the confidentiality of the information concerning the pending tender offer, was also affirmed. The Supreme Court ruled that the SEC had not exceeded its powers under Section 14(e) when it adopted Rule 14e–3, which does not require proof that the trader breached any fiduciary duty.

**› CRITICAL THINKING QUESTIONS**

1. Would the misappropriation theory apply to a case in which a person defrauded a bank into giving him a loan or embezzled cash from another and then used the proceeds of the misdeed to purchase securities?
2. If the fiduciary disclosed to the source of the nonpublic information that she planned to trade on that information, would trading on that information constitute a Section 10(b) violation? Would it violate any other laws? Would it be ethical?

---

Liability under the misappropriation theory requires that the defendant's trading threaten some injury to the defrauded party or the source of information. Actual injury need not be demonstrated. The threatened injury need not be pecuniary; it may be reputational or intangible.

Rule 10b5–2 sets forth a nonexclusive list of three situations in which a person has a duty of trust or confidence for purposes of the misappropriation theory of insider trading. First, a duty of trust or confidence exists whenever a person agrees to maintain information in confidence. Second, a duty of trust or confidence exists when two people have a history, pattern, or practice of sharing confidences such that the recipient of the information knows or reasonably should know that the person communicating the material nonpublic information expects that the recipient will maintain its confidentiality. Third, as noted earlier, a duty of trust or confidence exists when a person receives or obtains material nonpublic information from a spouse, parent, child, or sibling unless the recipient of the information can demonstrate that, under the facts and circumstances of that family relationship, no duty of trust or confidence existed.

The misappropriation theory widens the class of persons who can be found liable for insider trading, but the requirement that there be a fiduciary duty remains a limiting factor. For instance, someone who merely overhears a conversation relating to confidential information has no fiduciary duty and therefore no liability. Similarly, someone who infers from the movements of corporate executives that an event will likely take place owes no duty to the corporation or its employees.

## MAIL AND WIRE FRAUD

The Supreme Court upheld the conviction of R. Foster Winans, author of the *Wall Street Journal* column "Heard on the Street," under the Mail and Wire Fraud Acts, thereby providing an additional way to prosecute insider trading.[53] Winans had misappropriated the content of his soon-to-be-published columns and tipped the information to two stockbrokers, who used the information to make trades based on the anticipated positive market response to the column's publication. The Court held that if a business generates confidential information and has the right to control the use of that information prior to public disclosure, then use of that information to trade can be prohibited under the wire and mail fraud statutes.

53. Carpenter v. United States, 484 U.S. 19 (1987).

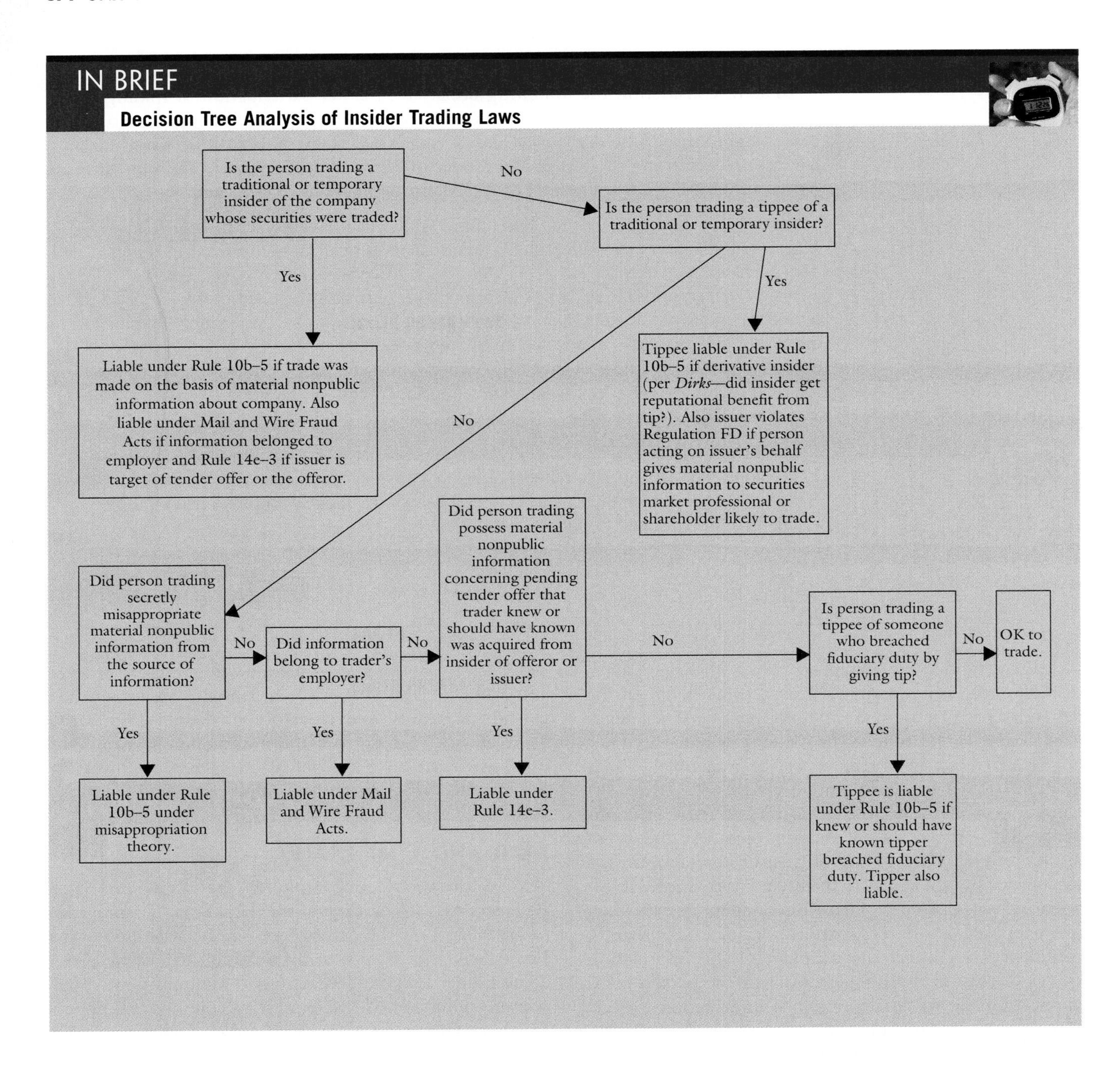


## RICO

A securities fraud claim cannot be used as a predicate act in a civil case under the Racketeer Influenced and Corrupt Organizations Act (RICO) (discussed in Chapter 14) unless the defendant has been criminally convicted in connection with the fraud. However, a criminal conviction under the Wire and Mail Fraud Acts for misappropriation of an employer's confidential information may, assuming other requirements are met, be the basis for a civil RICO case.

# Enforcement of Insider Trading Prohibitions

Persons who violate the insider trading provisions of the federal securities laws are subject to private suits for damages, civil enforcement actions by the SEC, and criminal prosecution.

## PRIVATE ACTIONS

In private actions the plaintiff must be an actual purchaser or seller of securities, and the plaintiff's loss must have been proximately caused by the acts of the defendant. All contemporaneous traders, that is, persons who purchased or sold securities of the same class at the same time the insider was trading, have standing to sue. The total amount of damages that may be recovered is limited to the amount of the profit gained or loss avoided in the unlawful transaction. Any amounts disgorged pursuant to court order or at the instance of the SEC will offset the amount of damages recoverable by contemporaneous traders. Tippers and all direct and remote tippees are jointly and severally liable. That means that any individual in the chain of information can be found liable for all of the profits gained or losses avoided in every transaction within the chain.

## CIVIL ENFORCEMENT

In an SEC civil enforcement action, violators and their firms may be liable for treble damages and disgorgement of profits and may be subject to an injunction prohibiting future trading.

The Insider Trading and Securities Fraud Enforcement Act of 1988, passed in the wake of insider trading charges against Michael Milken and Drexel Burnham Lambert in the late 1980s (discussed more fully in this chapter's "Inside Story"), provided strong encouragement to the brokerage industry to police itself. A brokerage house can be fined if it "knew or recklessly disregarded" information that would indicate insider trading activities on the part of its employees. Intended to force firms to police their employees, institute compliance systems, and monitor suspicious activities, the Act specifically requires registered brokers and dealers to maintain and enforce reasonably designed written policies and procedures to prevent the misuse of material nonpublic information. Although this legislation does not explicitly require it, many commentators have suggested that it is prudent for other companies not in the brokerage business to implement such policies and procedures in light of their potential liability.

### ETHICAL CONSIDERATION

A number of brokerage houses have investigated whether any of their employees were involved in insider trading. Most of these firms turned over their trading records to the New York Stock Exchange for computer analysis. Persons suspected of illicit activities could be subject to SEC enforcement actions and criminal prosecutions. Such investigations send a stern message to employees and encourage ethical behavior and compliance with the insider trading laws. They also improve the public's perception of the brokerage industry. How stringently should managers of brokerage houses follow these procedures?

## CRIMINAL PROSECUTIONS

The SEC itself has no criminal enforcement power. Criminal prosecutions are brought by the Department of Justice through the U.S. Attorney's Office, often on referral from the SEC. If criminally convicted, a defendant faces fines and/or imprisonment for willful violations. Willfulness has been interpreted as awareness by the defendant that he or she was committing a wrongful act; the defendant need not specifically know that he or she was violating a statute.

## BOUNTY PAYMENTS

Individuals whose tips result in insider trading prosecutions are entitled to receive bounties, similar to the payments provided by the Internal Revenue Service in tax cases. These bounties can be as high as 10 percent of any revenues recovered from a defendant through penalties or settlement.

# Selective Disclosure and Regulation FD

Effective October 23, 2000, the SEC adopted a broad prohibition on the practice of *selective disclosure,* whereby issuers of publicly traded securities disclosed material nonpublic information, such as advance warnings of earning results, to securities analysts or selected institutional investors before making full disclosure of the same information to the general public. Those privy to the information were able to make a profit or avoid a loss at the expense of those kept in the dark. According to the SEC, this led "to a loss of investor confidence in the integrity of our capital markets. Investors who see a security's price change dramatically and only later are given access to the information responsible for that move rightly question whether they are on a level playing field with market insiders."[54]

Selective disclosure also threatened the integrity of the securities markets by creating "the potential for corporate management to treat material information as a commodity to be used to gain or maintain favor with particular analysts or investors."[55] Analysts might feel pressure to report favorably about a company for fear of being excluded from calls and meetings to which other analysts are invited. Finally, the SEC reasoned, "Whereas issuers may once have had to rely on analysts to serve as information intermediaries, issuers now can use a variety of methods to communicate directly with the market." These include Internet webcasting and teleconferencing. Accordingly, the SEC concluded: "Technological limitations no longer provide an excuse for abiding the threats to market integrity that selective disclosure represents."[56]

*Regulation FD (Fair Disclosure)* provides that whenever an issuer, or a person acting on its behalf, discloses material nonpublic information to securities market professionals or holders of the issuer's securities who may well trade on the basis of the information, the issuer must publicly disclose that same information simultaneously (for intentional disclosures) or promptly (for nonintentional disclosures). A disclosure is considered intentional only if the person knows, or is reckless in not knowing, that the information he or she is communicating is both material and nonpublic. In cases of unintentional disclosure, the issuer must disclose the information to the public as soon as practical (but no later than twenty-four hours) after a senior official learns of the disclosure and knows (or is reckless in not knowing) that the information disclosed was both material and nonpublic. Market professionals include broker–dealers, investment advisers and investment managers, investment companies and hedge funds, and official persons thereof.

No public disclosure is required for communications (1) made to a person who owes the issuer a duty of trust or confidence (such as an investment banker, accountant, or attorney); (2) made to any person who expressly agrees to maintain the information in confidence; (3) with a credit-rating agency; or (4) made in connection with most offerings of securities registered under the 1933 Act.

Information is material if there is a substantial likelihood that a reasonable shareholder would consider it important in making an investment decision. Types of information or events likely to be considered material include (1) earnings information; (2) mergers, acquisitions, tender offers, or changes in assets; (3) new products or developments involving customers or suppliers; (4) changes in control or management; (5) changes in auditors; (6) defaults on senior securities, repurchase plans, or stock splits; and (7) bankruptcies. The SEC cautioned that an official who engages in a private discussion with an analyst seeking guidance about earnings estimates "takes on a high degree of risk under Regulation FD."[57] On the other hand, an issuer is not prohibited from disclosing nonmaterial information to an analyst even if, unbeknownst to the issuer, that piece of information helps the analyst complete a "mosaic" of information that, taken together, is material.

To avoid creating a chilling effect on issuers' willingness to communicate with outsiders, the SEC expressly provided that private parties cannot sue issuers for violations of Regulation FD. It is not an antifraud rule, and failure to make a public disclosure required solely by Regulation FD is not deemed to be a violation of Rule 10b–5. If an issuer fails to comply with Regulation FD, the SEC is empowered to bring an enforcement action and can seek an injunction and/or civil monetary penalties.

As of early 2005, the SEC had brought only six cases under Regulation FD since its enactment in 2000. Two involved Siebel Systems, Inc. The second complaint alleged that both Siebel's CFO and its senior vice president for investor relations had aided and abetted Siebel's violations.[58] The defendants responded by arguing that Regulation FD was an unconstitutional infringement of their right to free speech.[59] Critics charge that the SEC pursues only the most egregious violations under Regulation FD and claim that the rule seems to have done little to curb preferential treatment of analysts and well-placed investors.

54. Selective Disclosures and Insider Trading, SEC Release Nos. 33-7881, 34-43154, IC-24599, 17 C.F.R. pts. 240, 243, 249 (Aug. 15, 2000).
55. *Id.*
56. *Id.*
57. *Id.*
58. The SEC complaint is available at http://www.sec.gov/litigation/complaints/comp18766.pdf.
59. Marcia Coyle, *SEC's Fair Disclosure Regulation to Face Test,* 26 NAT'L L. J. 1 (2005).

# Other Restrictions on Trading by Officers, Directors, and Greater-than-10 Percent Shareholders

In addition to the prohibition against trading based on material nonpublic information, Section 16 of the 1934 Act imposes several additional requirements on officers, directors, and greater-than-10 percent shareholders of publicly traded firms.

## SHORT-SWING TRADING

Section 16(b) of the 1934 Act governs *short-swing trading*—the purchase and sale, or the sale and purchase, by officers, directors, and greater-than-10 percent shareholders of equity securities of a public company within a six-month period. Unlike Section 10(b), which requires *scienter* (that is, a showing of bad intent), liability is imposed under Section 16(b) regardless of the insider's state of mind.

Section 16(b) of the 1934 Act provides that each officer, director, and greater-than-10 percent shareholder of an issuer that has registered any class of its equity securities under the 1934 Act must surrender to the issuer "any profit realized by him from any purchase and sale, or any sale and purchase, of any equity security of such issuer (other than an exempted security) within any period of less than six months."

Although the purpose of Section 16(b) is to prevent insiders of publicly held companies from exploiting information not generally available to the public in order to secure quick profits, it need not be proved that the insider actually possessed any material nonpublic information at the time the insider traded in the securities. To establish liability under Section 16(b), it is sufficient to prove that an insider purchased and then sold, or sold and then purchased, equity securities within a period of six months.

### *Definition of an Equity Security*

An *equity security* includes (1) any stock or similar security; (2) any security that is convertible, with or without consideration, into such a security; (3) any security carrying any warrant or right to subscribe to or purchase such a security; (4) any such warrant or right; and (5) any other security that the SEC deems to be of a similar nature and that, for the protection of investors or in the public interest, the SEC considers appropriate to treat as an equity security. Thus, equity securities may include hybrids that ordinarily are not considered equity securities, such as convertible debt securities that have not been registered under the 1934 Act.

Special problems can arise in connection with the grant and exercise of stock options and other derivative securities. A set of complicated rules embodied largely in Rule 16b–3, adopted by the SEC under Section 16(b) of the 1934 Act, governs this area. Before becoming an officer or director, a person should consult counsel to avoid inadvertent Section 16(b) liability.

### *Persons Covered*

Section 16(b) applies to officers, directors, and greater-than-10 percent shareholders.

**Officer or Director** A person may be liable under Section 16(b) if he or she was an officer or director at the time of either the purchase or the sale. It is not necessary that both transactions occur during the person's tenure.

For example, if an officer purchased 100 shares of XYZ Corporation common stock at $10 per share on January 1, resigned as an officer on February 1, then sold 100 shares of XYZ common stock at $20 per share on March 1, she would be liable for $1,000 of short-swing profits because she was an officer when she made the January 1 purchase. Similarly, if a person purchased 100 shares of XYZ Corporation at $10 per share on January 1, became an officer of XYZ Corporation on February 1, and sold the shares at $20 on March 1, that person would be liable for $1,000 of short-swing profits because he was an officer at the time of the sale. On the other hand, if an officer who had not traded for more than six months before March 1 resigned on March 1, bought 100 shares of XYZ Corporation at $10 on April 1, then sold them at $20 on April 2, she would not have recoverable profits because she was not an officer or director at the time of either the purchase or the sale.

**Greater-than-10 Percent Shareholder** The rule is different for persons who are not officers or directors but are owners of more than 10 percent of the issuer's equity securities. Such persons are liable under Section 16(b) only if they hold more than 10 percent of the securities both at the time of the purchase and at the time of the sale. The transaction whereby the person becomes a 10 percent shareholder does not count.

For example, if a person purchased 10.5 percent of XYZ Corporation's common stock at $10 on January 1, then sold those shares at $20 on March 1, he would have no recoverable short-swing profits. However, if the same person had purchased another 2 percent of XYZ common stock in February, then the February purchase could be matched against the March sale because he owned more than 10 percent of the stock at the time of the February purchase and also at the time of the March sale.

### *Beneficial Ownership of Shares*

Officers, directors, and greater-than-10 percent shareholders can be liable for purchases and sales of shares they do not own of record but are deemed to own beneficially. Under Section 16(b), a person will be considered the *beneficial owner* of any securities held by his or her immediate family—his or her spouse, any minor children, or any other relative living in his or her household. There is a rebuttable presumption that a person is the beneficial owner of any securities over which he or she has the practical power to vest title in himself or herself, or from which he or she receives economic benefits (such as sales proceeds) substantially equal to those of ownership.

Purchases and sales of securities held beneficially by an officer, director, or greater-than-10 percent shareholder will be attributed to that person in determining his or her liability for short-swing trading. For example, the purchase of securities by an officer's husband could be matched under Section 16(b) with the sale of other securities by the officer herself within six months of her husband's purchase, thereby resulting in liability for short-swing profits. Thus, any officer, director, or greater-than-10 percent shareholder planning a purchase or sale must consider not only his or her own trading record but also the record of those persons whose securities he or she is deemed to own beneficially.

### *Purchase and Sale Within Six Months*

To result in recoverable short-swing profits, the purchase and sale, or sale and purchase, must have occurred "within any period of less than six months." That period commences on the day on which the first purchase or sale occurred and ends at midnight two days before the corresponding date in the sixth succeeding month. For example, for a transaction on January 1, the six-month period ends at midnight on June 29, two days before July 1.

### *Profit Calculation*

To calculate the profits recoverable under Section 16(b), the sale price is compared with the purchase price. If several purchases and sales occur within a six-month period, the lowest purchase price will be matched with the highest sale price; then the next lowest purchase price with the next highest sale price; and so on, regardless of the order in which the purchases and sales actually occurred. Matching purchases and sales in this manner maximizes the recoverable profit.

The shares that are sold need not be the same shares that were purchased. Any purchase and any sale will incur liability if they occur less than six months apart, regardless of whether the transactions involve the same shares. For example, if on January 1, an officer of XYZ Corporation sold 100 shares of XYZ common stock that he had held for ten years, then on February 1 purchased 200 shares of XYZ common stock at a lower price, he would be liable for the short-swing profits on 100 of the shares. The January 1 sale would be matched with the February 1 purchase, even though the officer had held the securities for ten years before he sold them.

Short-swing profits cannot be offset by trading losses that were incurred in the same period. Thus, there may be recoverable profits under Section 16(b) even though the officer or director suffered a net loss on the trading transactions.

The following example illustrates the "lowest-in, highest-out" matching principle just described. Assume that an officer made purchases and sales, each of 100 shares, as follows:

| Date | Transaction | Price |
|---|---|---|
| Jan. 1 | Purchase | $ 9 |
| Jan. 30 | Sale | 10 |
| Feb. 15 | Sale | 15 |
| Feb. 28 | Purchase | 12 |
| Mar. 15 | Purchase | 6 |
| Mar. 30 | Sale | 4 |

These transactions will result in a recoverable short-swing profit of $1,000, calculated as follows. The February 15 sale is matched with the March 15 purchase, for a profit of $15 − $6 = $9 per share, or $900. Then the January 30 sale is matched with the January 1 purchase, for a profit of $10 − $9 = $1 per share, or $100. Even though the March 15 purchase at $6 per share and the subsequent sale at $4 per share resulted in a loss of $2 per share, or $200, that loss will not be taken into account. The officer will have to surrender $900 + $100 = $1,000, even though she actually realized only $200 of net profit in the trading transactions (total sales of $2,900 less purchases of $2,700).

### *Unorthodox Transactions*

If a purchase or sale by an officer, director, or greater-than-10 percent shareholder that would otherwise result in recoverable short-swing profits was involuntary and did not involve the payment of cash, and if there was no possibility of speculative abuse of inside information, then a court may hold that it was an *unorthodox transaction* to which no liability will attach. These situations generally arise in the context of exchanges in mergers and other corporate reorganizations, stock conversions, stock reclassifications, and tender offers in which securities are sold or exchanged for consideration other than cash. On the other hand, in a tender offer or acquisition, an exchange of securities for cash by an officer, director, or greater-than-10 percent shareholder would almost certainly be deemed a sale for which the person receiving the cash could be liable under Section 16(b).

## FILING OF BENEFICIAL-OWNERSHIP REPORTS

Section 16(a) of the 1934 Act requires that officers, directors, and greater-than-10 percent shareholders of companies that have registered any class of equity securities under the 1934 Act file beneficial-ownership reports with the SEC and with any national securities exchange on which their company's equity securities are listed. Within ten days of becoming an officer or director, a person must file an initial ownership report on Form 3, even if the person does not beneficially own any securities of the company at that time. In the case of greater-than-10 percent shareholders, a Form 3 must be filed within ten days of the date they acquire a greater-than-10 percent interest. (In addition, as noted in Chapter 22, any person who acquires more than 5 percent of the voting securities of a public company must file a Schedule 13D within ten days after the date he or she acquired the more-than-5 percent stake. An amendment to the Schedule 13D must be filed promptly after any material change in beneficial ownership or investment purpose.)

Subsequently, an officer, director, or greater-than-10 percent shareholder must file a Form 4 within two business days after any transaction resulting in any change in beneficial ownership. For example, a transaction executed on Tuesday, September 3, would have to be reported to the SEC by the close of business (5:30 P.M. Eastern time) on Thursday, September 5. In the initial Form 4, an officer or director must report all purchases or sales that occurred within the previous six months, even if those transactions were effected before the person became an officer or director. A Form 5 showing changes in beneficial ownership during the preceding year must be filed annually within forty-five days after the issuer's fiscal year end.

Acquisitions and dispositions of shares acquired by officers or directors pursuant to employee benefit plans must also be reported within two business days on Form 4 even if the transactions are exempt from short-swing recovery under Rule 16b-3. A person who ceases to be an officer or director must continue to report any changes in beneficial ownership that occur within six months of the last reportable transaction while he or she was an officer or director.

## *Global View*

### INSIDER TRADING IN THE EUROPEAN UNION

The EU Market Abuse Directive[a] requires member states to enact national legislation punishing primary and secondary insiders who trade publicly held securities on the basis of "inside information," which is defined as nonpublic information "a reasonable investor would be likely to use as part of the basis of his investment decisions."[b] Primary insiders include officers, directors, employees, and shareholders of the issuer as well as persons who have access to inside information by virtue of their professional duties. Secondary insiders are those who obtain inside information from primary insiders, that is, tippees.

Issuers are required to maintain lists of persons working for them with access to inside information, and senior managers must report changes in beneficial ownership to the appropriate national authority within five business days.[c] In addition, the principle of "equal treatment" prohibits the selective disclosure of inside information.

Although the EU Directive does not on its face embrace the misappropriation theory, persons who obtain information as a result of their professional duties are deemed primary insiders even if they have no fiduciary duty to the issuer. Thus, trading by a person like O'Hagan[d] would violate European law.

a. European Parliament and Council Directive 2003/6/EC on Insider Dealing and Market Manipulation (Market Abuse), 2003 O.J. (L 96). This supersedes Commission Directive 89/592: Coordinating Regulations on Insider Dealing.
b. Commission Directive 2003/124/EC, 2003 O.J. (L 339).
c. Commission Directive 2004/72/EC, 2004 O.J. (L 162).
d. United States v. O'Hagan, 521 U.S. 642 (1997) (Case 23.7).

The SEC has brought enforcement actions to force executives to file these ownership reports within the required time frame. Publicly traded companies must disclose in their proxy statements and in their annual reports on Form 10–K whether their officers and directors have complied with their Section 16(a) reporting obligations.

## PROHIBITION ON SELLING SHORT

Section 16(c) of the 1934 Act prohibits officers or directors from *selling* any of their company's equity *securities short,* that is, from selling a security that the seller does not own. If the officer or director owns the security being sold, he or she must deliver it within twenty days after the sale or deposit it in the mails or other usual channels of delivery within five days. If the officer or director fails to do this, he or she will be liable under Section 16(c) unless (1) he or she acted in good faith and was unable to make the delivery or deposit within the specified time, or (2) he or she acted in good faith and satisfying the time requirements would have caused undue inconvenience or expense.

THE RESPONSIBLE MANAGER

## PREVENTING SECURITIES FRAUD AND INSIDER TRADING

Managers have an obligation not to mislead investors in company public announcements, periodic reports, or speeches. Although a company may remain silent about material developments if neither the company nor insiders are trading, early disclosure is often the better course. This gives all investors equal access to current information about the company. There is a trade-off here, however. Sometimes the company's business or transactions may be in a state of flux. For example, a party with no visible source of financing may have made an offer to buy the company's assets. In this case, it may be worse to disclose the offer and get the market's hopes up than to wait and see if the offer is real. Managers, together with their lawyers, must make these judgment calls.

Another reason for early disclosure is to avoid illegal insider trading. A company must make disclosure if it knows its insiders, such as officers or directors, are trading in the company's securities.

Any forward-looking statements should be identified as such and be accompanied by meaningful cautionary language identifying important factors that could cause actual results to differ materially from those in the forward-looking statement. It is often helpful to (1) prioritize the order of risk factors, (2) state the risk in the first sentence, (3) be specific, (4) convey the magnitude of the risk, and (5) focus risk factors on the negatives without softening them by including positives.

Trading by a manager while in possession of material nonpublic information is illegal. It violates the manager's fiduciary duty to subordinate his or her personal interests to the interests of the corporation and shareholders he or she serves. A manager is given access to nonpublic information not for the manager's own personal gain but to better enable the manager to serve his or her principal—the corporation and its shareholders. Violation of those rules erodes both shareholder confidence and the confidence of investors generally in the capital markets. It is also unethical.

A manager cannot give tips to others in exchange for money or even just to enhance his or her reputation as "someone in the know." A manager should carefully guard the information given in confidence by his or her employer or client. Managers must also instill these values in their subordinates. Everyone, from the person who empties the trash or runs the copy machine to the person who occupies the largest office in the executive suite, must be told to follow these rules or risk dismissal. This edict should be made clear in the corporation's code of ethics and in its personnel manual. All corporations, and especially brokerage firms, without adequate procedures in place to prevent illegal insider trading face potential liability for their insiders' illegal trades.

*(Continued)*

(The Responsible Manager *continued*)

A company cannot disclose material information only to certain favored analysts. This is unfair to the public investors and can result in liability for the company and for the manager who tips an analyst whose clients then trade based on the tip. It also violates Regulation FD.

A company's policy on insider trading[60] should prohibit any person associated with the company from trading in any security, regardless of whether it was issued by the company, based on material nonpublic information. The policy should also ban passing on material nonpublic information to outsiders who may trade (tipping). It should require persons who are likely to obtain material nonpublic information on a regular basis to pre-clear all purchases and sales of the company's securities. The policy should also (1) describe the legal penalties for insider trading and the company's potential liability for the insider trading violations of its employees and (2) provide that any employee who violates the policy may be terminated.

An officer or director of a public company who buys and sells securities within a six-month period has a legal and ethical responsibility to come forward and pay all profits over to the corporation. This is true even if the short-swing trade was inadvertent, as might happen if an officer sold securities not realizing that his or her spouse had bought securities less than six months before. A corporation that discovers a short-swing trade must try to persuade the insider to voluntarily turn the profits over to the corporation. If the insider refuses to do so, the corporation has an obligation to bring suit to recover the profits from the short-swing trading. If a corporation fails to bring suit, any shareholder has the right to sue on behalf of the corporation.

Officers and directors of public companies must report their security holdings and their trades in a timely manner. Disregard of these filing requirements breeds contempt for the law and encourages illegal or unethical behavior by others in the organization.

Each manager has a role to play in preventing securities fraud and insider trading. As with preventing the other types of criminal behavior described in Chapter 14, a manager leads by example. If the manager permits his or her company to engage in unlawful or unethical conduct, the manager exposes himself or herself and the company to considerable risk of civil and criminal liability. Such a manager is also likely to encourage illegal behavior by subordinates.

60. This discussion is drawn from *Effective Company Policy May Avoid Violations, ABA Told*, CORP. COUNS. WKLY., Aug. 11, 1999, at 2.

INSIDE STORY

## MICHAEL MILKEN AND THE INSIDER TRADING SCANDALS OF THE 1980s

Inquiries into insider trading tend to focus on high-volume trading that occurs before major corporate announcements. Enforcement agencies generally watch organized trading rings and well-known public figures because of their high profiles. However, ordinary investors and isolated violations are also detected and prosecuted. Surveillance groups monitor daily trading and investigate any suspicious activity.

### DENNIS LEVINE AND IVAN BOESKY

Prosecutors and enforcement agencies also rely heavily on information gathered from informers and persons already under indictment. For example, the arrest and prosecution of Dennis Levine and Ivan Boesky in 1986 set off the most comprehensive investigation of securities trading practices in the history of federal regulation.

Levine, a former managing director of Drexel Burnham Lambert, was initially charged with illegal trading in approximately fifty-four stocks. An investment banker, Ira B. Sokolow, then pled guilty to passing stolen information to Levine. As a result of cooperation by Levine, the SEC was able to bring insider trading charges against one of Wall Street's richest and most active speculators, Ivan Boesky.

Boesky, the son of an immigrant restaurateur, made his career and fortune as a risk arbitrageur who concentrated on the purchase and sale of stock in target corporations that were the subject of tender offers. Generally, the acquiring corporation pays a premium for the stock of the target corporation; thus, people who invest prior

*(Continued)*

(Inside Story *continued*)

to the announcement of the acquisition are in a position to make swift and substantial profits. The SEC alleged that Levine, who worked on mergers and acquisitions, passed on information to Boesky, who was able to purchase shares in the target prior to public announcement of the impending takeover. It is further believed that Boesky offered Levine a 5 percent commission for any information leading to an initial stock purchase and a 1 percent commission for information pertaining to stocks already owned by Boesky.

In 1985, Levine allegedly passed to Boesky information received from Sokolow regarding the merger of Nabisco and R.J. Reynolds. Use of this information resulted in approximately $4 million in profits for Boesky. In all, Boesky was alleged to have made approximately $50 million through these insider trading activities. Both Levine and Boesky pled guilty to criminal charges. Boesky settled the SEC's civil charges by agreeing to pay $100 million and to cooperate with the government in future prosecutions of others. Boesky was sentenced to three years in prison and ultimately served two years.

One commentator speculated on Boesky's motivation: "His need was not simply to be rich, but to be seen as richer and smarter than anyone else. He gambled less on stocks than on his ability to beat the cops."[61]

### DREXEL BURNHAM LAMBERT

Approximately two years later, with the cooperation of Ivan Boesky, the SEC brought dramatic charges against Drexel Burnham Lambert and four of its prominent employees, including the head of its junk-bond department, Michael Milken. According to the SEC, Drexel had entered into a secret agreement with Boesky to defraud its clients and drive up the price of target-company stocks. The complaint, filed in September 1988, alleged that Drexel utilized Boesky to engage in *stock parking*—the temporary sale of shares to another entity or individual so as to hide the true ownership of the shares in order to avoid tax-reporting requirements or the net-margin requirements of the securities laws applicable to brokerage firms. Drexel, which assisted companies interested in acquisitions, was also accused of advising Boesky to purchase massive amounts of shares in certain companies in order to give the appearance of active trading in them and to drive up the takeover price.

61. Robert J. Samuelson, *The Super Bowl of Scandal,* NEWSWEEK, Dec. 1, 1986, at 64.

In December 1988, Drexel agreed to plead guilty to six felony counts and to pay $650 million in fines and restitution—"by far the largest penalty ever paid in a securities case."[62] It agreed to pay an additional $30 million to settle civil charges in April 1989. As a condition to the settlement, Drexel was required to cooperate in the investigation of Milken and to fire him.

### MICHAEL MILKEN

In 1999, Milken pled guilty to six felony counts, ranging from securities and mail fraud to tax evasion and conspiracy.[63] He agreed to pay a fine of $200 million and to put $400 million into a fund for restitution to defrauded investors. The *Wall Street Journal* provided a vivid image of the courtroom scene when Milken pled guilty:

> He was almost at the end of a detailed confession when his voice faltered. Michael Milken bent forward, sobbing, as two of his lawyers rushed to support him. Suddenly, under the vast ceiling of Manhattan's largest federal courtroom, the world's once-most-powerful financier, the bigger-than-life commander of the X-shaped trading desk, seemed mortal, even frail.[64]

Milken was sentenced to ten years in prison but was released after serving only twenty-two months. He was also banned for life from acting as a securities broker or dealer.

U.S. Attorney General Richard Thornburgh characterized Milken's crimes as "some of the most serious efforts undertaken to manipulate and subvert Wall Street's securities markets."[65] But Thornburgh also observed that the case sends a strong message to those involved in "crime in the suites: those white-collar criminals are never so powerful or clever that they cannot be caught by diligent and persistent law enforcement efforts."[66] The convictions of Samuel Waksal (former CEO of ImClone), Bernie Ebbers (former CEO of WorldCom), John Rigas (former CEO of Adelphia Communications), and others convicted of securities fraud in the early twenty-first century suggest that they failed to take this message to heart.

62. Larry Reibstein & Carolyn Friday, *Nailing the Junk Kings,* NEWSWEEK, Jan. 2, 1989, at 44.

63. Laurie P. Cohen, *Public Confession: Milken Pleads Guilty to Six Felony Counts and Issues an Apology,* WALL ST. J., Apr. 25, 1990, at A1.

64. *Id.*

65. *Id.*

66. *Id.* For an excellent detailed account of the insider trading scandals of the 1980s, see JAMES B. STEWART, DEN OF THIEVES (1991).

## KEY WORDS AND PHRASES

aider and abettor 866
beneficial owner 898
bespeaks caution doctrine 877
derivative insider 889
efficient-market theory 883
equity security 897
forward-looking statement 885
fraud-on-the-market theory 883
insider 888
insider trading 865
loss causation 885
misappropriation theory 891
misstatement 869
omission 869
prejudgment interest 885
Regulation FD (Fair Disclosure) 896
remote tippees 890
S-1 review 868
*scienter* 869
selective disclosure 895
selling securities short 900
short-swing trading 897
stock parking 902
temporary insiders 889
tip 871
tippee 888
tipper 888
unorthodox transaction 899

## QUESTIONS AND CASE PROBLEMS

1. During a session with her psychiatrist, Dr. Robert Willis, Joan Weill mentioned in confidence the imminent merger of the company headed by her husband, Sanford Weill, with another company. Willis, upon hearing of the merger, communicated the information to Martin Sloate, who traded in the company's securities for his own account and for his customers' accounts.

   Did Weill, Willis or Sloate engage in illegal insider trading? Was the conduct of the parties ethical? [*SEC v. Willis*, 777 F. Supp. 1165 (S.D.N.Y. 1991).]

2. Gallop, Inc. is a toy manufacturer specializing in games for boys and girls aged eight to twelve. On March 30, Gallop had predicted first-quarter earnings of $.20 per share. On April 15, Gallop received a fax from its key distributor reporting a $10 million claim for personal injury of a nine-year-old child who was allegedly injured by a design defect in Gallop's most popular product line, the Spartan Warriors. Gallop's outside counsel was instructed to prepare a press release describing the claim. Before the press release was sent to the copy center at Gallop's executive office, the vice president of marketing, one director, and the outside counsel sold all of their Gallop shares at the prevailing market price of $25.25 per share.

   Collin Copier, who ran the photocopying machine at Gallop's executive office, saw the draft press release; called his broker, Barbara Broker; told her about the press release; and ordered her to sell the 500 shares of Gallop that Copier had acquired in Gallop's initial public offering. Broker then called her best client, Charleen Client, and suggested that she sell her 100,000 shares of Gallop stock but did not tell her why. Client agreed, and Broker sold Copier's and Client's stock at $25.25 a share right before the market closed on April 17.

   The press release was publicly announced and was reported on the Business Wire after the market closed on April 17. The next day, Gallop's stock dropped to $20.75 per share. A class-action suit has been brought, and the SEC has commenced enforcement proceedings. Criminal prosecution is threatened by the U.S. Attorney's Office.

   What are the bases on which each proceeding could be brought? Who is potentially liable? For how much?

3. Dow Chemical Company owned Destec Energy, Inc. (Destec), which owned Destec Engineering, Inc. (DEI). Dow decided to try to sell Destec. AES Corporation wanted to buy Destec's international assets, including DEI. DEI's sole asset was a contract to design and build a power plant in the Netherlands. Because Dow would not sell Destec's international assets alone, AES paired with NGC Corporation to make a joint bid. NGC bought all outstanding Destec stock from Dow through a merger agreement, and then AES bought all of Destec's international assets, including the DEI stock, from NGC under an asset purchase agreement. During the course of the negotiations, Dow and Destec orally represented what it would cost to build the power plant, but these representations were not reflected in the written documents.

   Most of the documents in the transaction contained nonreliance clauses, that is, clauses that attempted to limit the information on which the parties to the document could legally rely. For example, the merger agreement between NGC and Dow contained two pages of representations and warranties but stated that other than those, "neither Dow nor any other person makes any other express or implied representation or warranty on behalf of Dow." Unfortunately for AES, the Netherlands plant deal proved far more costly than represented, and AES lost $70 million on the plant.

Section 29(a) of the 1934 Act provides that "any condition, stipulation or provision binding any person to waive compliance with any provision of this title or of any rule or regulation thereunder, or of any rule of an exchange required thereby shall be void." Does AES have a valid claim under Section 10(b) and Rule 10b–5? [*AES Corp. v. Dow Chemical Co.*, 325 F.3d 174 (3d Cir. 2003).]

4. American Banknote Corporation (ABN) spun off its wholly owned subsidiary American Bank Note Holographics (ABNH) in an initial public offering. Morris Weissman was the founder of ABN and also the chair and CEO of both ABNH and ABN. Plaintiff purchasers of ABNH's stock sued Weissman, among others, for securities fraud under Sections 11, 12(a)(2), and 10(b). In two press releases, Weissman stated:

> Our most important goal in 1998 is to enhance shareholder value. We hope to prove to the market that inherent values of our underlying operating subsidiaries, not apparent when evaluating American Banknote on the basis of traditionally consolidated earnings per share, are indeed significant.
>
> This IPO is a win–win for both companies. . . . ABNH can now concentrate on continuing the profitable growth of its core security holography business as well as explore business and market expansion opportunities.

In fact, ABNH was neither a valuable company nor profitable. Is Weissman liable under Section 10(b) and Rule 10b–5? What would be the best argument in his defense? [*In re American Bank Note Holographics, Inc. Securities Litigation*, 93 F. Supp. 2d 424 (S.D.N.Y. 2000).]

5. National Industries acquired 34 percent of TSC Industries' voting stock from TSC's founder and principal shareholder and his family. After the sale, the TSC founder resigned from TSC's board of directors. Subsequently, five National nominees, including National's president and CEO, were placed on TSC's board. Several months later, TSC's board, with the National nominees abstaining, approved a proposal to liquidate and sell all of TSC's assets to National. One month later, the two companies issued a joint proxy statement to their shareholders, recommending approval of the proposal. The proxy solicitation was successful, TSC was liquidated, and the exchange of shares was effected.

A TSC shareholder brought an action against the two companies, claiming that their joint proxy statement was materially misleading. The basis of the claim was that the proxy statement omitted material facts relating to the degree of National's control over TSC. Were the omitted facts material? [*TSC Industries v. Northway, Inc.*, 426 U.S. 438 (1976).]

6. On November 8, 1990, the *Wall Street Journal* reported rumors of a possible merger of AT&T and NCR. AT&T declined to comment on the rumors. That same day, Charles Brumfield, vice president of labor relations for AT&T, called his friend Joseph Cusimano and told him that he believed the newspaper article was true and that "AT&T was going to be attempting to acquire NCR." Cusimano made a series of trades in NCR securities on November 9, 12, and 15 through 20. The AT&T board authorized the acquisition of NCR on November 14 and publicly announced its interest on December 2.

Did either Brumfield or Cusimano violate Section 10(b) and Rule 10b–5? On what theory? Was Brumfield's information nonpublic and material? [*United States v. Mylett,* 97 F.3d 663 (2d Cir. 1996); *United States v. Cusimano,* 123 F.3d 83 (2d Cir. 1997), *cert. denied,* 522 U.S. 1133 (1998).]

7. Texas International Speedway, Inc. (TIS) filed a registration statement for $4,398,900 in securities with the proceeds to be used to construct an automobile racetrack called the Texas International Speedway. The entire issue was sold on the offering date, October 30, 1969. On November 30, 1970, TIS filed for bankruptcy.

The prospectus stated that the speedway was under construction. It also included a pro forma balance sheet showing that, upon completion of the public offering and application of the proceeds to the construction costs of the speedway, TIS would have $93,870 in cash on hand on the speedway's opening date.

The TIS prospectus warned that "THESE SECURITIES INVOLVE A HIGH DEGREE OF RISK" and that the construction costs might be underestimated. If the plaintiff investors present evidence from which a jury could infer that, on the effective date of the registration statement, the two officers and directors of TIS and its accountant knew that the cost of construction was understated and that consequently TIS's working capital position would not be as favorable as the prospectus reflected, will the plaintiffs win a suit under Section 10(b) and Rule 10b–5? What would be the result if the Litigation Reform Act applied? [*Huddleston v. Herman & MacLean*, 640 F.2d 534 (5th Cir. 1981), *rev'd in part and aff'd in part*, 456 U.S. 914 (1982).]

**8.** In 1998, after working at two banks for about ten years, Bryan J. Mitchell helped found MCG Capital Corporation, a venture-capital firm that invested in the media, communications, and technology sectors. MCG went public in 2001, and Mitchell served as its CEO and chair of the board. Various documents filed with the SEC stated that Mitchell "earned a B.A. in economics from Syracuse University." In fact, he attended Syracuse for only three years and did not graduate. After being pressured by a journalist, Mitchell disclosed the misrepresentation to the MCG board. The same day, the company issued a press release correcting the statement. The board subsequently stripped Mitchell of his title as chair of the board and made him repay certain bonuses and loans.

The press responded negatively to "another CEO that lied about his résumé" and speculated about "what else might not be right." On the day the press release was issued, MCG's stock price dropped from $11.85 per share to $8.40 but fully recovered within a month.

Shareholders sued, alleging that the misrepresentation violated Section 11 of the 1933 Act, Section 10(b) of the 1934 Act, and Rule 10b–5. Was Mitchell's lie about having a college degree material? If you had been a member of the MCG board, would you have been comfortable keeping Mitchell as CEO? [*Greenhouse v. MCG Capital Corp.*, 392 F.3d 650 (4th Cir. 2004).]

**9.** EchoCath was a small New Jersey research and development company engaged in developing, manufacturing, and marketing medical devices to enhance and expand the use of ultrasound technology for medical applications and procedures. EchoCath consummated its initial public offering on January 17, 1996, and issued a lengthy prospectus, which cautioned that "an investment in the securities offered . . . is speculative in nature and involves a high degree of risk." It also set forth several pages of risk factors. In particular, EchoCath cautioned investors that the company "intended to pursue licensing, joint development and other collaborative arrangements with other strategic partners . . . but there can be no assurance . . . that the Company will be able to successfully reach agreements with any strategic partners, or that other strategic partners will ever devote sufficient resources to the Company's technologies."

More than six months after the public offering, MedSystems began to consider a sizable investment in EchoCath. Frank DeBernardis, the CEO of EchoCath, orally represented to MedSystems that EchoCath had engaged in lengthy negotiations to license its products and was on the verge of signing contracts with a number of prominent medical companies, which he identified as including UroHealth, Johnson & Johnson, Medtronic, and C.R. Bard, Inc., to develop and market EchoCath's women's health products. Throughout the negotiations and until the closing in February 1997, EchoCath's CEO continued to represent to MedSystems officials that the contracts with these companies to develop these products were "imminent." In the fifteen months after MedSystems made its investment, EchoCath failed to enter into a single contract.

MedSystems filed suit under Section 10(b) and Rule 10b–5, alleging that EchoCath intentionally or recklessly made misrepresentations to MedSystems in connection with the sale of securities in an effort to induce MedSystems to purchase its securities. MedSystems alleged that EchoCath was not on the verge of signing contracts with any company to develop its line of women's health products in August 1996, or any other time up to the closing on February 27, 1997. EchoCath moved to dismiss the complaint on the grounds that the CEO's statements were not material. Result? [*ER MedSystems v. EchoCath, Inc.*, 235 F.3d 865 (3d Cir. 2000).]

**MANAGER'S DILEMMA**

**10.** In 1984, several individuals (including David Greenberg) formed seven limited partnerships to develop and operate a chain of 100 "Video USA" video rental stores. One hundred and sixteen limited partners, who had invested $13 million in three private placements, sued accounting firm Touche Ross, among others, for securities fraud. They alleged that Touche Ross (1) had failed to disclose that David

Greenberg was a convicted felon; that his twelve-year-old son was the sole officer, director, and shareholder of one of the corporations that served as a general partner; and that the principals used fraudulent invoices and made fraudulent claims against insurance companies; and (2) had prepared the materially misleading financial projections attached as exhibits to the offering memoranda. Touche Ross did not issue an opinion or certification as to any part of the offering documents. Attached to each of the projections that Touche Ross issued was a letter stating that the projection was based on management's "knowledge and belief" and cautioning that the projection "does not include an evaluation of the support for the assumptions underlying the projections." Is Touche Ross liable under Section 10(b) to the limited partners? If you were the account manager at Touche Ross and learned about Greenberg's felony conviction and the existence of fraudulent invoices, what would you have done? [*Shapiro v. Cantor*, 123 F.3d 717 (2d Cir. 1997).]

## INTERNET SOURCES

| | |
|---|---|
| Securities and Exchange Commission | http://www.sec.gov |
| Milberg Weiss is perhaps the largest (and in Silicon Valley the most feared and hated) law firm specializing in representing plaintiffs in securities fraud suits and class actions. | http://www.milberg.com |
| This is the site for Lerach Coughlin et al., a securities litigation firm established by former Milberg Weiss partner Bill Lerach. | http://securities.lerachlaw.com |
| The brainchild of Stanford Law School professor (and former SEC commissioner) Joseph Grundfest, the Securities Class Action Clearinghouse site has been called the "Mecca for the securities lawyer." This is the first Designated Internet Site for required electronic posting of court documents in the United States. | http://securities.stanford.edu |
| The Securities Law Home Page provides access to many important securities law cases and useful links to other law-related sites. | http://www.seclaw.com |

CHAPTER 24

# Debtor–Creditor Relations and Bankruptcy

## INTRODUCTION

### Salvaging a Business in Financial Trouble

The reasons for borrowing money, and the uses to which the loan proceeds are applied, are many and varied. A business generally decides to borrow when it needs funds and believes it is in a position to pay interest for the use of such funds. Although lenders sometimes take equity positions in a borrower, whereby they receive returns based on the profits or losses of the borrower, lenders in a loan transaction are entitled only to interest at a stated rate on the amount borrowed (generally called the *principal*) and the return of the principal at the end of the term.

When a business is in trouble because of external events or internal miscalculations or misdeeds, it will inevitably run short of cash and fall behind in its payments. Creditors may be temporarily appeased; but those with collateral will ultimately pursue foreclosure, and others will file lawsuits in a race for the remaining assets. Defending against these actions can absorb resources and hamper management's ability to cure the company's underlying ills. Successful collection can cripple or kill the business.

Predatory dismemberment may destroy a company's real economic value. This loss in value will ultimately hurt creditors if there are not enough assets to go around. Even if all debts can be paid, the equity holders in the company will suffer. The collapse of a large enterprise could leave many unemployed and send disruptive waves through related industries.

The legal tools used to stem this potentially destructive tide are found mainly in the Bankruptcy Code.[1] The U.S. Constitution gives Congress the power to enact bankruptcy laws. A successful reorganization under Chapter 11 of the Bankruptcy Code results in the restructuring of financial relationships among the owners and creditors of a business and, ideally, the preservation of a viable going concern. Even when reorganization is not possible, the bankruptcy system is designed to realize the maximum value from the available assets, provide equitable distribution among claimants, and foster fair and efficient administration through a collective or multiparty process.

Corporate bankruptcies have increased dramatically in recent years, both in the number of individual cases filed and in the size of companies making such filings. Total bankruptcy filings were 1,492,129 in 2001, 1,577,651 in 2002, and 1,661,996 in 2003. The number of Chapter 11 business filings smashed records in 2002 for the second straight year.[2] In addition, the number of public companies filing bankruptcy set new records, with 186 public companies representing $368 billion in assets filing in 2003. Big bankruptcy cases have been common. In 2001, Enron Corporation's filing set the all-time record for assets in a bankruptcy case at $60 billion, but this was topped by WorldCom's 2002 filing, representing $104 billion in assets. Kmart's January 2002 bankruptcy was the all-time largest retail bankruptcy case; the 2002 filings by Global Crossing and WorldCom were the largest telecommunications bankruptcies; and the United Airlines filing in December 2002 was the largest aviation bankruptcy.[3]

1. Codified in scattered sections of 11 U.S.C.

2. The number of business Chapter 11 filings decreased slightly in 2003.

3. *Annual Review of Developments in Business and Corporate Litigation,* 2003 A.B.A. Sec. on Bus. L., Committee on Bus. & Corp. Litig. 93–94 (2003).

## CHAPTER OVERVIEW

This chapter summarizes the typical terms of a loan agreement. It then categorizes commercial loans according to the type of lender, the purposes to which the loan proceeds will be applied, and whether the loan is secured or unsecured. The terms of a typical security agreement, together with methods for perfecting a security interest under Article 9 of the Uniform Commercial Code, are discussed. Equipment leasing, guaranties, subordination, and lender liability are addressed. This is followed by a discussion of business bankruptcies under Chapters 11 and 7 of the Bankruptcy Code and consumer bankruptcies under Chapters 7 and 13. The chapter also includes a discussion of workouts. The chapter concludes with a discussion of recent efforts to coordinate insolvency proceedings with international implications.

# Loan Agreements

The basic structure of loan agreements is surprisingly standard. Lenders are concerned about the administration of the loan, their ongoing relationship with the borrowers, and the rights they have if the borrowers breach their promises. At times, these concerns must be addressed in specially tailored documentation; generally, however, banks use a collection of standard forms, which are distributed to loan officers along with instructions for their use. This section discusses the basic features common to all loan agreements.

## PARTIES TO THE AGREEMENT

The parties to a loan agreement are the lender and the borrower. There may be more than one lender and more than one borrower. If the lender is an insurance company, the loan agreement will be called a *note purchase agreement*.

### *Lenders*

When two or more lenders, usually banks, make a loan to a borrower together, it is called a syndicated loan. In a *syndicated loan,* the lenders enter into concurrent direct obligations with the borrower to make a loan, typically on a pro rata basis. The loan is coordinated by a lead lender that serves as agent for all of the lenders in disbursing the funds, collecting payments of interest and principal, and administering and enforcing the loan.

In a *participation loan,* the original lender sells shares to other parties, called participants. Each participant acquires an undivided interest in the loan. The sale may be made without the borrower's involvement.

### *Borrowers*

Multiple borrowers are usually related entities, such as a parent corporation and its subsidiaries. Corporate law recognizes each corporation as a separate entity. From the lender's perspective, the parent and its subsidiaries are one economic entity; but if each subsidiary is jointly and severally liable for the entire debt, a subsidiary's obligation may outweigh the economic benefit it receives from the loan. (To the extent the loan is used by the parent rather than the subsidiary, the transaction may be invalidated as to the subsidiary as a fraudulent transfer under state law and the federal Bankruptcy Code, as discussed below.)

### *Additional Parties*

In more complicated transactions, additional parties may become involved in the negotiations for a loan, even though they are not parties to the loan agreement. For example, in a leveraged buyout, the acquisition of a company is financed largely by debt secured by its assets. The lender will want assurances from the seller that the assets being sold to the borrower are free and clear of all liens, and this concern may affect the structure of the buyout; or, if the seller is taking a note from the buyer for part of the purchase price, the lender will want to negotiate an agreement with the seller setting forth their relative rights to repayment. In a construction loan, the construction lender will advance sufficient funds to complete the construction project with the expectation of being repaid when a permanent, long-term lender steps in. In such a situation, the construction lender will negotiate with the permanent lender as well as the borrower.

In certain types of project financings, a limited partnership may be formed for the sole purpose of constructing, say, a power plant. The general partner's liability is normally unlimited; however, for tax and other reasons, a lender may agree that it will look only to the partnership's assets for repayment of a loan. In such a case, the lender will need to assure itself that the limited partnership has sufficient resources to repay the loan. Thus, for example, if the partnership's primary resources are fees from the sale of goods or services, the lender will be concerned about the nature of the partnership's contracts for those sales.

In all of these examples, the lender has a legitimate interest in seeing that the borrower's relationships with third parties will not adversely affect the loan.

## Commitment to Make a Loan

A loan agreement may be preceded by a *term sheet,* which is a letter outlining the terms and conditions on which the lender will lend. A commitment to make a loan generally need not be in writing to be enforceable, but an oral promise may be difficult to enforce because reasonable people may honestly have different recollections of what was said. Nevertheless, a jury may award damages for breach of an oral loan commitment.[4]

Several state legislatures have proposed, and at least one has adopted, legislation specifically requiring loan commitments that exceed a threshold dollar amount to be in writing to be enforceable. Even in the absence of such legislation, a prudent lender will use a written term sheet or commitment letter to specify the terms of a proposed loan (including the amount, the interest rate, fees, and repayment provisions) and to disclaim any obligation to lend until additional investigation is completed, additional terms and conditions are negotiated, and formal documentation is signed.

## Description of the Loan

A loan agreement contains the lender's promise to lend a specified amount of money. Frequently, this will be the only promise that the lender will make in the loan agreement. The loan agreement also describes the mechanics by which funds will be disbursed, the rate of interest to be charged, the manner of computing such interest, and the repayment terms.

### *Mechanics of Funding*

The funds are usually sent by wire transfer to an account specified by the borrower. If timing is important, the borrower will want to discuss the logistical details of the loan agreement, such as the lender's deadline for sending wire transfers. The logistics may become critical if the lender and the borrower are in different time zones or if there are multiple lenders, as in a syndicated loan.

### *Interest Rates*

Interest rates may be fixed or *floating,* that is, fluctuating throughout the life of the loan according to the interest rate that the lender would pay if it borrowed the funds in order to relend them. Fixed-rate term loans are common from insurance companies; banks generally prefer a floating rate. The floating rate may be pegged to the bank's *prime rate,* that is, the lowest published rate of interest at which the bank lends to its best and most creditworthy commercial customers. Because a bank may lend money at a rate below its so-called prime rate, banks often use the terms *base rate* or *reference rate.* Some banks include an explicit statement that the prime (or base or reference) rate is not the bank's best or lowest rate. The floating rate may be expressed either as a percentage of the prime rate (such as 110 percent of the prime rate) or, more commonly, as the sum of the prime rate and a specified number of percentage points (such as the prime rate plus 10 percentage points).

Alternatively, the floating rate may be pegged to the London Interbank Offered Rate (LIBOR) or to the certificate of deposit (CD) rate. These rates are based on the theoretical cost that a bank incurs to obtain, for a given period of time, the funds it will lend. A *spread* (or margin) is added to this cost to arrive at the actual interest rate. Frequently, a loan agreement will offer prime-rate, LIBOR, and CD-rate options for the borrower to select during the life of the loan.

The *London Interbank Offered Rate (LIBOR)* interest rate is based on the cost of borrowing offshore U.S. dollars in the global interbank market, which today is centered in several locations in addition to London. Deposits made through the interbank offering market are generally for periods of one, two, three, six, nine, or twelve months; LIBOR loans are made for corresponding periods. At the end of an interest period, the borrower may elect to (1) roll over the LIBOR loan, that is, to continue it for another interest period; (2) repay the loan; or (3) convert it to a loan based on a different interest rate.

The *certificate of deposit (CD) rate* is based on the average of the bid rates quoted to the bank by dealers in the secondary market for the purchase at face value of the bank's CDs in a given amount and for a given term. CD-rate loans are commonly available for interest periods of 30, 60, 90, or 180 days.

4. *See, e.g.,* Landes Constr. Co. v. Royal Bank of Canada, 833 F.2d 1365 (9th Cir. 1987).

#### Ethical Consideration

Managers should be careful not to make oral promises that they cannot, or will not, perform. The business environment is always changing, and it is better to qualify one's statements than to make a strong commitment today that may be regretted tomorrow.

Managers should recognize that many types of oral contracts are binding. When there is no independent witness to an oral contract, a contracting party may be tempted to alter his or her version of the facts, leading to a contest of "your word against mine." This type of behavior is clearly unethical.

### *Computation of Interest*

Interest is generally computed on a daily basis according to one of several methods. Under the *365/360 method,* the nominal annual interest rate is divided by 360, and the resulting daily rate is then multiplied by the outstanding principal amount and the actual number of days in the payment period. Thus, for a year of 365 or 366 days, the actual rate of interest will be greater than the nominal annual rate.

Under the *365/365 method,* the daily rate is determined by dividing the nominal annual interest rate by 365 (or 366, in leap years); then this daily rate is multiplied by the outstanding principal amount and the actual number of days in the payment period. Under the *360/360 method,* it is assumed that all months have thirty days; thus, the monthly interest amounts are always the same.

The method used to compute interest is significant when large principal amounts are involved. It may also be significant if the lender or the loan is subject to state *usury* laws, which limit the maximum rate of interest that may be charged. National banks and other specified classes of lenders are subject to federal legislation that preempts state usury laws; and many states permit higher interest rates for exempt commercial transactions over a given dollar amount. Unless a state or federal exemption applies, lenders and borrowers should analyze whether a loan is usurious by virtue of its terms and conditions. For example, compensation paid for a loan, such as commitment fees, expenses, and prepayment penalties, may be treated as interest.

### *Repayment Terms*

A *revolving loan* may be repaid from time to time at the borrower's discretion, subject to a final maturity date when all sums outstanding become due and payable. In a *term loan,* the lender may require the entire principal to be repaid in one lump sum upon maturity or in equal or unequal installments.

Agreements for term or revolving loans may also call for mandatory prepayment when certain events occur. For example, in a receivables and inventory line of credit, a prepayment will be required if the level of receivables and/or inventory supporting the outstanding borrowings drops. A sale of assets outside the ordinary course of business or financial earnings below a specified level may also mandate a prepayment.

### *Asset-Based Loans*

In structuring a loan agreement, the fact that a loan is secured or unsecured is not particularly significant, except in certain types of asset-based financing in which the amount lent is determined according to the levels of assets available from time to time. One example of an asset-based loan is a revolving line of credit based on receivables, inventory, or both. Subject to certain criteria as to what inventory or receivables are eligible—that is, acceptable to the lender—the borrower borrows against such assets and repays the loans on a revolving basis out of collections of the receivables generated from the sale of inventory. Sometimes payments may be made directly to the lender through such mechanisms as a locked-box or blocked account, which allows the lender to take the outstanding loan repayments out of the collected proceeds before they are distributed to the borrower.

## Representations and Warranties

Before committing to make a loan, a lender will investigate the potential borrower's financial condition and creditworthiness. It will also require the borrower to make certain representations and warranties, including representations about the borrower's legal status and good standing; that all necessary actions have been taken to authorize the proposed borrowing; that regulatory and other approvals that might be required for the borrowing have been obtained; that the borrower has good and marketable title to all of its assets, including any assets that constitute collateral for the loan; that the loan agreement is legal, valid, and binding; and that no default has occurred or would result from entering into the loan agreement.

The purpose of these representations and warranties is to specify the assumptions on which the lender is willing to lend. The representations and warranties serve as a checklist of major areas of investigation by the lender. They also provide a framework for the borrower to examine its legal and financial position.

### *Qualifications*

Often a borrower will state that a representation is true to the best of its knowledge. The borrower will want to be held accountable only for what it knows, not for what it does not know. The lender will want the borrower to take steps to ascertain the accuracy of its representations. The risk that a representation will prove to be untrue is usually placed on the borrower rather than the lender. Any qualification based on the borrower's knowledge is therefore likely to be phrased in terms of what the borrower either knows or should know after diligent inquiry. It may include a definition of the appropriate standard of diligence.

In the loan agreement, the borrower states that the representations and warranties are true and complete as of the date of the loan agreement. They do not apply prospectively. However, the loan agreement may provide that if advances are to be made, the representations and warranties will be updated as of the time of the advances.

### *Truthfulness of Representations*

Before a disbursement is made under the loan agreement, the lender may require an opinion of counsel and a certification by an independent public accountant, confirming the representations made by the borrower. The lender's obligation to continue to lend will likewise be conditioned upon the continuing truthfulness of the representations in the loan agreement.

## CONDITIONS TO CLOSING

### *Authority to Approve the Loan*

The lender will require evidence that the borrower's internal requirements for approving the loan have been met. Thus, the lender may ask for copies of the relevant corporate resolutions, with a certification by the corporate secretary, and certification of the incumbency of the officers authorized to execute the loan agreement.

### *Completion of Documents*

The loan agreement is typically only one of several documents that must be signed in connection with a loan. The lender will also require a promissory note and, if the loan is secured, a security agreement and financing statements.

### *Payment of Fees*

Some fees, such as commitment fees, must be paid before any funds are disbursed.

### *Other Conditions*

Other conditions may apply in certain circumstances. For example, in the case of a term loan to finance a merger or acquisition, the lender will condition any disbursement on the consummation of the merger or acquisition.

Regulatory approval may be required because of the nature of the borrower's business. In such cases, the particular permits and approvals that must be obtained or issued before the lender is willing to disburse funds will be listed.

As explained in Chapter 15, lenders have become increasingly concerned about the liability they may face when real property held by them, either as security or outright after a foreclosure, is required to comply with environmental cleanup laws. The lender may, therefore, require an opinion of environmental counsel, an environmental audit by qualified consultants and engineers, and indemnity agreements with the borrower and with any third parties that may be responsible for the environmental condition of the property.

## CONDITIONS PRECEDENT

If the basic assumptions and facts upon which the lender has relied change materially after a commitment to lend has been made, the lender will reevaluate the loan. It may (1) refuse to advance the funds committed, (2) refuse to advance additional funds if some disbursements have already been made, or (3) accelerate the maturity of the loan. The loan agreement will specify the conditions that must be met before the lender's obligations arise under the agreement. These are known as *conditions precedent.*

## COVENANTS

*Covenants* are the borrower's promises that it will or will not take specific actions as long as either a commitment or a loan is outstanding. If a covenant is breached, the lender can terminate the loan. The list of covenants imposed upon the borrower can be quite lengthy.

The borrower's obligations may also affect nonparties to the loan agreement. For example, the lender may require that the borrower and its subsidiaries maintain a specified net worth, computed on a consolidated basis. The loan agreement cannot directly impose such an obligation on the subsidiaries because they are not parties to it, but the agreement can require the borrower to cause its subsidiaries to comply with the covenant. Such a covenant assumes that the borrower is in a position to influence the nonparties' actions.

### *Affirmative Covenants*

*Affirmative covenants* state the actions that the borrower will take, for example, maintain its corporate existence, pay taxes, maintain insurance, and comply with applicable laws.

The borrower is usually required to keep the lender informed of its financial condition and to submit unaudited financial reports monthly or quarterly and audited financial reports annually. Financial tests relating to income statement and balance sheet items may be imposed. A catchall covenant will require the borrower to inform the lender of any material adverse change in its operations or financial condition.

### *Negative Covenants*

*Negative covenants* state the actions that the borrower cannot take, for example, not to incur additional debt beyond a specified amount and not to grant liens other than those specifically enumerated or arising in the ordinary course of business. (A *lien* is a claim on property that secures a debt owed by the owner of the property.)

### Scope

Covenants are generally heavily negotiated. Because financial covenants are based on projections of future financial results, they require flexibility in long-term loans. A borrower will resist any covenants that appear to interfere with its control and operation of its business. A lender sensitive to borrowers' fears of lender control will draft its covenants carefully to impose the minimum control needed to protect its right to be repaid. For example, a provision that effectively gives the lender the right to select the borrower's management is difficult to justify. Lawsuits, some resulting in multimillion-dollar punitive judgments against unduly interfering lenders, have alerted lenders to the need for caution in drafting and enforcing such provisions.

## Events of Default

A loan agreement lists the events that will trigger the lender's right to terminate (or *call*) the loan, accelerate the repayment obligations, and, if the loan is secured, take possession of the property securing the loan. These events, known as the *events of default,* usually include (1) failure to pay on time the amounts due under the loan agreement, (2) making false or misleading representations or warranties in connection with the loan, and (3) failure to live up to any covenant in the loan agreement.

Some events of default may be outside the borrower's control. For example, if a loan is made to a corporation on the strength of the lender's confidence in a particular individual's management ability, the death of that individual may be included as an event of default. Similarly, involuntary liens or legal judgments against the borrower, although more or less outside the borrower's control, change the fundamental bases on which a loan was originally made.

### Cross-Default

A *cross-default* provision in a loan agreement provides that any breach by the borrower under any other loan agreement constitutes an event of default. A borrower will want the provision to apply only to a serious breach of a loan agreement covering a loan larger than a specified minimum. The borrower may also want the lender to agree that the borrower's breach of another agreement will not constitute an event of default under the loan agreement unless the other lender terminates its loan on account of the breach.

The lender, on the other hand, will want a broad definition of the events of default. It will want the right to join with other creditors to negotiate some form of protection for its position as soon as the borrower's financial condition deteriorates.

If the borrower does breach another agreement, the lender and borrower may renegotiate the terms and conditions on which the loan will remain outstanding. For example, the lender may agree to continue the loan in exchange for new or additional collateral, new guaranties, or a higher rate of interest. Such negotiations are a practical alternative to the more drastic measure of terminating the loan. Note, however, that if the borrower seeks bankruptcy, any efforts to restructure the loan will be subject to the jurisdiction of the bankruptcy court.

## Remedies for Default

The default section sets forth the lender's remedies for default. These remedies are optional. If the lender *waives* a default—that is, decides not to exercise any of its remedies—it may exact additional consideration from the borrower in the form of an increase in the interest rate or additional security.

It is prudent to set forth any waiver in writing to avoid any misunderstanding as to its scope or the terms and conditions on which it is being granted, including any additional obligations that the borrower will now be expected to satisfy. In lender liability lawsuits, express terms in a loan agreement have been found to be superseded by oral or written communications between the lender and the borrower or by the actions of the borrower or lender. Reducing understandings to writing and avoiding actions that may be inconsistent with the written documents will avoid surprises and failed expectations on both sides.

# Commercial Loan Categories

Commercial loans can be categorized by lender or by purpose.

## Loans Categorized by Lender

Commercial loans are most commonly made by banks, insurance companies, and purchasers of *commercial paper,* that is, short-term corporate indebtedness. Both banks and insurance companies are highly regulated. Extensive federal and state legislation prescribes the types of entities that may call themselves banks, who may own them, and what they may or may not do once they open for business. Similarly, insurance companies are restricted by state legislation in connection with their business of insuring against risk. The regulatory framework within which banks, insurance companies, and other types of lenders operate will affect their sources and availability of funds; these factors in turn will affect the terms on which they will offer to lend money. Banks generally are more flexible in the length of the terms of their loans, their interest rate formulas, and the mechanics of their loan administration. Insurance companies typically offer medium- to long-term loans at fixed interest rates. Whether a lender is a bank or an insurance company, it may have particular expertise in the industry in which the borrower does business or in making loans for particular purposes.

### LOANS CATEGORIZED BY PURPOSE

A borrower may require funds to meet everyday working capital needs, to finance an acquisition of assets or a business, or to finance a real estate construction project or an engineering project. Under regulations promulgated by the Board of Governors of the Federal Reserve System, lenders and borrowers may not enter into transactions whereby secured credit will be used to acquire stock, unless certain requirements are met. Apart from these basic restrictions and additional restrictions that apply to borrowers in regulated industries, borrowers may borrow money for a wide variety of reasons. These reasons dictate whether the loan will be a term loan or a revolving loan.

#### *Term Loans*

Funds required for a specific purpose, such as an acquisition or a construction project, are generally borrowed in the form of a term loan. A specified amount is borrowed, either in a lump sum or in installments, to be repaid on a specified date (known as the *maturity date*) or *amortized* (paid off over a period of time). For example, in an acquisition the buyer may be required to pay the purchase price up front and thus will require a lump-sum loan. By contrast, the owner of a construction project will require a loan to be disbursed in installments as scheduled progress payments become due. Amounts repaid under a term loan cannot be reborrowed.

#### *Revolving Loans*

A borrower may project its working capital needs for a given period but desire flexibility as to the exact amount of money borrowed at any given time. A revolving loan or *revolving line of credit* allows the borrower to borrow the amount it requires, up to a specified maximum. The borrower may also reborrow amounts it has repaid (hence the term "revolving"). The lender requires a *commitment fee* as consideration for its promise to keep the commitment available, as it receives no interest on amounts not borrowed.

## Secured Transactions Under the UCC

In making a loan, the lender relies on the borrower's cash flow, the borrower's assets, or the proceeds of another loan as sources of repayment. If the lender relies solely on the borrower's promise to repay the loan, the lender's recourse for nonpayment is limited to suing the borrower. Moreover, even if the lender sues the borrower, it stands in no better position than other general creditors of the borrower and has no special claim to any specific assets of the borrower as a source of repayment. Because of this risk, lenders often refuse to make loans without *collateral*, that is, property belonging to the borrower that becomes the lender's if the loan is not repaid. A loan backed up by collateral is known as a *secured loan*. Unsecured loans, if they are available, are priced at a higher rate to reflect the greater risk to the lender.

If the borrower fails to repay a secured loan, the lender, in addition to suing for return of the monies lent, may *foreclose* on—that is, take constructive or actual possession of—the collateral and either sell it to repay the debt or keep it in satisfaction of the debt. It should be noted that under some *antideficiency laws* and *one-form-of-action laws* lenders seeking remedies against real property security may be restricted from suing the borrower personally. In cases in which a lender has recourse to the borrower or to other property of the borrower and exercises such rights, the lender may be precluded from foreclosing on real estate mortgaged by the borrower. These laws, which date back to the Great Depression, are designed to protect borrowers from forfeiting their properties to overzealous lenders.

The mechanics of taking a security interest in personal property and fixtures, and the consequences of taking such a security interest, are governed by Article 9 of the Uniform Commercial Code (UCC). Before Article 9 was adopted, such common law security devices as the pledge, the chattel mortgage, the conditional sale, the trust receipt, and the factor's lien were all governed by different rules. Article 9 of the UCC was intended to provide a unified, comprehensive scheme for all types of *secured transactions,* that is, loans or other transactions secured by the borrower's collateral. Article 9 applies "to any transaction (regardless of its form) which is intended to create a security interest in personal property or fixtures including goods, documents, instruments, general intangibles, chattel paper or accounts."

Article 9 provides a single source of reference for most consensual security interests, but some security interests are outside its scope. For example, Article 9 does not apply to liens on real property, and various state and federal laws preempt the UCC in the areas of ship mortgages, mechanic's liens, and aircraft liens. Notices of security interests in trademarks are commonly filed in the Patent and Trademark Office, in addition to being perfected as general intangibles under the UCC. Article 9 does not apply to security interests subject to a landlord's lien, to a lien given by statute or other rule of law for services or materials, or to a right of setoff. (A *right of setoff* permits one party to automatically deduct amounts owed to it by the other party from the payments the first party makes to the second party.) Security interests in securities are governed by Article 8 of the UCC.

## Terminology

Part 1 of Article 9 defines terms. In place of the various common law security devices, the UCC uses the single term *security interest* to signify any interest in personal property or fixtures that is used as collateral to secure payment or the performance of an obligation. The parties to a secured transaction are (1) the *debtor,* that is, the person who owes payment or other performance of the obligation secured, whether or not that person owns or has rights in the collateral; and (2) the *secured party,* that is, the lender, seller, or other person in whose favor there is a security interest. A *security agreement* is an agreement that creates or provides for a security interest.

## Formal Requirements

Part 2 of Article 9 sets forth the formal requirements to create an enforceable security interest and describes the rights of the parties to a security agreement. If the secured party takes possession of the collateral, an oral agreement is sufficient to create a security interest; otherwise, a signed security agreement containing a description of the collateral is required. Under the UCC, for a security interest to be enforceable, value must have been given for it, and the debtor must have rights in the collateral. These requirements do not have to be fulfilled in any particular order. When all of the requirements have been met, a security interest is said to have *attached.*

## Rights and Remedies

The remainder of Article 9 sets forth the rights of the secured party against other creditors of the debtor; the rules for *perfecting* a security interest, that is, making it valid as against other creditors of the debtor; and the remedies available to a secured party when a debtor defaults.

## Security Agreements

A security agreement identifies the parties and the property to be used as collateral. It may also specify the debtor's obligations and the lender's remedies in case of default.

### Parties to the Agreement

Security agreements typically use the UCC terminology to identify the parties. In a loan transaction, the secured party is the lender. The debtor is the borrower, if it owns the collateral or if a third-party property owner has authorized it to use its property for collateral. If the third-party property owner acts as a guarantor of the borrower's obligation, it may also be referred to as the debtor. (Guaranties are discussed later in this chapter.)

### Granting Clause

Unless the security interest is a possessory interest (traditionally called a *pledge*), the security agreement must be signed by the debtor and must expressly grant a security interest in some specified property. The standard operative words are: "The debtor hereby grants to the secured party a security interest in . . . ." The UCC does not require a precise form, but the collateral must be described.

### Description of the Collateral

The description of the collateral does not have to be specific, as long as it reasonably identifies what is described. For example, a working capital loan may be secured by receivables and inventory, with the inventory described as "any and all goods, merchandise, and other personal property, wherever located or in transit, that are held for sale or lease, furnished under any contract of service, or held as raw materials, work in process, supplies, or materials used or consumed in the debtor's business." A secured party will frequently take a security interest in all of the debtor's assets—not only fixed assets, inventory, and receivables but also trademarks, trade names, goodwill, licenses, books, and records. In such cases, the collateral may be described

*"We're a day late and four hundred million dollars short."*



as all tangible and intangible property that, taken together, is intended to preserve the value of the debtor as a going concern. Loans to finance the purchase of specific property, such as an equipment loan, will typically be secured by the property purchased, and the security agreement will contain a description of that property.

### • *After-Acquired Property*

*After-acquired property* is property that the debtor acquires after it executes the security agreement. After-acquired assets may be included in the security agreement either in addition to, or as replacements of, currently owned assets. A security interest in after-acquired collateral will attach when the debtor acquires rights in the collateral, assuming that the other prerequisites for attachment have been met.

### • *Proceeds*

The UCC provides that, unless otherwise agreed, a security agreement gives the secured party a security interest in the proceeds if the collateral is sold, exchanged, collected, or otherwise disposed of. The security interest is equally effective against cash, accounts, or whatever else is received from the transaction. This feature makes a security interest created under Article 9 a *floating lien*.

## *Debtor's Obligations*

The debtor is obligated to repay the debt and to pay interest and related fees, charges, and expenses. In addition, the debtor will have nonmonetary obligations, such as obligations to maintain prescribed standards of financial well-being, measured by net worth, cash flow, and debt coverage (the ratio of debt to equity). These obligations are typically set forth in detail in a loan agreement or a promissory note, although occasionally they may be found in a security agreement.

## *Cross-Collateralization*

The collateral for one loan may be used to secure obligations under another loan. This is done by means of a *cross-collateralization* provision—sometimes called a *dragnet clause*—in the security agreement. For example, a lender extending an inventory and receivables line of credit to a borrower may insist that the line be secured not only by inventory and receivables but also by equipment owned by the borrower and already held by the lender as collateral for an equipment loan. Thus, if the lender forecloses on the equipment, any proceeds in excess of the amounts owed under the equipment loan will be available to pay down the inventory and receivables line of credit. Similarly, if the equipment loan is cross-collateralized with collateral for the inventory and receivables line of credit, any proceeds realized from foreclosure of the inventory and receivables will be available to pay down the equipment loan.

### *Remedies for Default of Security Agreement*

The remedies described in a security agreement track the rights and procedures set forth in Article 9. After default, the secured party has the right to take possession of the collateral without judicial process if this can be done without breach of the peace. The secured party may then dispose of the collateral at a public or private sale. If there is a surplus from the sale of the collateral, the secured party is required to return it to the debtor. If there is a deficiency, the debtor remains liable for that amount. The proceeds from the sale must be applied in this order: (1) to the reasonable expenses of foreclosure and, if provided for in the agreement, reasonable attorneys' fees and legal expenses; (2) to the satisfaction of the obligations secured; and (3) to the satisfaction of indebtedness secured by a subordinate security interest, if a written demand for such satisfaction is timely received. The secured party also has the option to retain the collateral (with the debtor's consent and after notice to, and with the consent of, any junior lienholders or other third parties claiming an interest in the collateral) in partial, as well as in full, satisfaction of the debt.

Although the UCC establishes a framework within which the lender may exercise its remedies, some details must be provided by contract. For example, the parties may agree to apply the proceeds of a foreclosure sale to attorneys' fees and legal expenses, or they may agree that the debtor will assemble the collateral and make it available to the secured party at a designated place. All such provisions are subject to the requirement that the secured party's disposition of the collateral must be commercially reasonable. This term is not defined in the UCC, but it is generally interpreted to require conformity with prevailing standards and to prevent one party from taking undue advantage of another. However, the secured party and the debtor are free to fashion a mutually acceptable standard of commercial reasonableness; and security agreements typically contain a description of such standards.

## Perfecting a Security Interest

To protect its rights in the collateral, a lender must ensure that its security interest is perfected, that is, valid against other creditors of the debtor and against a trustee in bankruptcy of the debtor. The UCC does not define perfection; instead, it describes the situations in which an unperfected security interest will be subordinated to the rights of third parties. For example, a security interest is subordinated to the rights of a person who becomes a lien creditor before the security interest is perfected. *Subordination* to lien creditors means in effect that the security interest is not valid against the debtor's trustee in bankruptcy.

### METHODS OF PERFECTION

Security interests can be perfected by (1) taking possession of the collateral, (2) taking control of the collateral, (3) filing a financing statement, or (4) automatically.

#### *By Possession*

A security interest in goods, instruments (other than certificated securities, which are covered by Article 8 of the UCC—see below), negotiable instruments, or tangible chattel paper may be perfected by the secured party's taking possession of the collateral. A security interest in money may be perfected only by possession. Although filing a financing statement perfects a security interest in negotiable instruments, possession is the preferred means of perfection, as a bona fide purchaser of a negotiable instrument will be senior to a secured party that perfects by filing.

#### *By Control*

A security interest in a deposit account or a letter-of-credit right may be perfected only by taking control of the collateral.

#### *By Filing*

For all types of collateral, including negotiable instruments such as promissory notes (but excluding money, deposit accounts, and letter-of-credit rights), perfection may be accomplished by filing a financing statement. Standard printed forms, known as *UCC-1 forms,* are widely available for this purpose.

#### *Automatic Perfection*

Some security interests require neither possession nor filing for perfection. For example, a *purchase-money security interest* in consumer goods (created when the seller of consumer goods lends the buyer the money with which to buy them) is automatically perfected. Under certain circumstances, a security interest in a certificated security or an instrument is temporarily perfected without filing or possession. Automatic perfection is of limited duration, however, and it must be followed by possession or filing if perfection is to survive for a longer period.

#### *Uncertificated Securities*

The once fundamental distinction between possessory and nonpossessory security interests became blurred by the introduction of uncertificated, or book-entry, securities. Article 8 of the UCC, which governs investment securities, was revised in 1977 to provide for the creation and perfection of security interests in certificated and uncertificated securities. These topics were then removed from Article 9, except for cross-references to the applicable sections of Article 8.

### Filing Procedure

The purpose of perfection by filing is to provide notice "to the world" that assets of one person are subject to the security interest of another. If a security interest is not perfected by possession, the collateral remains in the debtor's possession and control. This occurs, for example, when the collateral is intangible (such as accounts), or when possession by the secured party is impractical (as in the case of inventory). A centralized system gives effective public notice that property in the possession and under the apparent control of the debtor is actually subject to the rights of another. The filing system enables a prospective creditor to determine whether in claiming its rights to such assets it will be competing with other creditors or with a trustee in bankruptcy. It also enables a purchaser of goods to determine whether the seller's creditors have any claims against the goods. (Under certain circumstances, a purchaser of goods is protected from liens on the goods created by the seller; for example, consumers are protected from inventory liens on a seller's goods.)

#### *What to File*

To perfect a nonpossessory security interest in personal property, a financing statement must be filed. The financing statement merely gives notice that a financing transaction is being or is about to be entered into but does not describe the transaction. It needs to contain only the names of the debtor and secured party and an indication of the collateral in which a security interest has been or may be granted. If a financing statement covers crops grown or to be grown or goods that are or will become fixtures, the UCC also requires a legal description of the land concerned.

#### *Where to File*

For most debtors and in most cases, the proper place to file is in the office of the secretary of state in the state where the debtor is located. Location is determined based on the jurisdiction of organization for corporate-type debtors, including corporations, limited liability companies, and limited liability partnerships. A nonregistered organization is located at its place of business if it has only one place of business, and at its chief executive office if it has more than one place of business. Most foreign debtors are deemed to be located in the District of Columbia. A security interest in collateral closely associated with real property, such as fixtures, growing crops, timber, or minerals, must be filed in the state where the real property is located, in the office in which a mortgage on real estate would be recorded; this is usually the county recorder's office in the county where the real property is located.

#### *When to File*

A financing statement may be filed in advance of the transaction or the security agreement. This is important because, under the UCC, a security interest is perfected when the statement is filed. Thus, the first secured party to file has priority over other parties with security interests in the same debtor's property, unless special priority rules apply, as in the case of purchase-money security interests.

## Equipment Leasing

To conserve its working capital, a company may decide to lease needed equipment rather than purchase it. Leasing sometimes offers an attractive alternative to borrowing funds to purchase equipment because a leasing company may be willing to provide more lenient terms than a bank or other lender. A leasing company may also be willing to accept a greater credit risk than banks, but it will probably charge higher interest rates than a bank to accommodate the greater credit risk involved. A newer enterprise may sometimes be asked for a security deposit or personal guaranty in connection with an equipment lease.

When equipment is leased, three parties are involved: the seller of the equipment, the leasing company, and the user of the equipment. The user determines its needs and negotiates a purchase price for the equipment; then the user engages a leasing company to purchase the equipment and lease it to the user. The manufacturer or seller of the equipment may lease it to the user, either directly or through a leasing subsidiary, but third-party leasing companies are more frequently used.

### Differences from True Lease

An equipment lease that serves the purpose of financing is known as a *finance lease*. A finance-lease agreement differs from a true lease in several ways. First, it gives the lessor some degree of control over the use, alteration, and location of the equipment. It also prohibits major changes in the user's business operations without the consent of the lessor, unless the lessee first repays the lessor in full. The lessee is required to keep the equipment in good repair and to insure it against loss or damage. The lessor is given a security interest in the equipment, and it may foreclose and sell the equipment in the event of default by the user. Finally, in addition to the terms of the lease agreement, the rights and remedies of the lessor and lessee are governed by Articles 9 and 10 of the UCC.

For accounting purposes, a finance lease is treated as a long-term debt of the lessee, who is deemed to own the leased equipment; the lessee may therefore enjoy tax benefits such as depreciation deductions. If the lessee has the right to purchase the equipment at the end of the lease term, the lease will often provide that the purchase price shall be the fair market value of the equipment at that time.

## Guaranties

A *guaranty* is an undertaking by one person, the *guarantor*, to become liable for the obligation of another person, the *primary debtor*. A guaranty allows the party that is to receive payment to look to the guarantor in the event the primary debtor fails to pay. The guarantor can be an individual, a corporation, a partnership, a limited liability company, or any other type of entity willing to lend its credit support to another's obligation. The most common form of guaranty is that indebtedness or other payment obligations of another will be paid when due. A *guaranty of performance*, a less common form, assures that specified nonpayment obligations will be performed. The type of guaranty and the duties of the guarantor will be determined by the language of the guaranty instrument. The statute of frauds requires that a guaranty be in writing to be enforceable.

Lenders often require a guaranty when a credit analysis indicates that the borrower's credit is not sufficient to support the requested loan. The lender will then evaluate the credit of each guarantor and decide whether to make the loan based on the combined credit of the borrower and the guarantors. Also, a lender may require guaranties from officers, directors, or shareholders of a borrower, especially when the borrower is a closely held corporation. To protect its position under a guaranty, a lender may require that the guarantor refrain from incurring additional debt or granting liens on its assets.

### Payment Versus Collection

Under a *guaranty of payment*, the guarantor's obligation to pay the lender is triggered, immediately and automatically, when the primary debtor fails to make a payment when due. In contrast, under a *guaranty of collection*, the guarantor becomes obliged to pay only after the lender has attempted unsuccessfully to collect the amount due from the primary debtor. With a collection guaranty, the lender will generally have to file a lawsuit and take other steps to collect the debt before calling on the guarantor to pay (unless the primary debtor is insolvent or otherwise clearly unable to pay). This condition makes the enforcement of collection guaranties so cumbersome and expensive that lenders almost always require payment guaranties.

### Limited Versus Unlimited

A guarantor's liability under a guaranty may be either limited or unlimited. With a *limited guaranty*, the maximum amount of the guarantor's liability is expressly stated in the guaranty instrument. This maximum liability is usually a specific dollar amount, although it can be based on other criteria, such as a percentage of the primary debtor's total indebtedness to the lender.

### Restricted Versus Continuing

A *restricted guaranty* is enforceable only with respect to a specified transaction or series of transactions. A guaranty that covers all future obligations of the primary debtor to the lender is referred to as a *continuing guaranty*. The objective of the continuing guaranty is to make the guarantor liable for any debt incurred at any time by the primary debtor, regardless of whether the debt was contemplated at the time the guaranty was entered into. Lenders naturally favor continuing guaranties over restricted guaranties.

In many jurisdictions, a continuing guaranty may be revoked by the guarantor during his or her lifetime. Such a revocation prevents the guarantor from becoming liable for debts incurred by the primary debtor in connection with transactions entered into after the revocation date. The death of the guarantor also revokes a guaranty, but the guarantor's estate remains liable for debts incurred by the primary debtor prior to the guarantor's death.

## Discharging the Guarantor

A lender that makes a guaranteed loan must avoid any actions that would have the effect of discharging the guarantor, such as altering the terms of the agreement between the lender and the primary debtor (for example, increasing the interest rate on the loan or increasing the amount of the scheduled payments), extending the time for payment of the loan or renewing the indebtedness, or releasing or impairing the lender's rights with respect to collateral pledged by the primary debtor. A well-drafted guaranty can alleviate some of these potential pitfalls. The best approach, however, is for the lender to obtain the consent of the guarantor before making any material change to the arrangement between the lender and the primary debtor.

## Guaranties Versus Letters of Credit

As explained in Chapter 25, a standby letter of credit can often be used in place of a guaranty. Uniform standards for standby letters of credit can be incorporated into the letter of credit by reference to the International Chamber of Commerce's International Standby Practices (ISP98).[5]

## Fraudulent Conveyances

A guaranty may be attacked as a fraudulent conveyance under the federal Bankruptcy Code or state fraudulent transfer statutes. Under many fraudulent transfer statutes, assets may be recovered and transfers avoided under circumstances that constitute "actual fraud" or "constructive fraud." Fraud is actual when the assets are transferred with intent to hinder, delay, or defraud creditors by putting the assets out of the creditors' reach. Fraud is constructive when an asset is transferred for less than reasonably equivalent value and other factors, such as the insolvency of the debtor, are present.

5. ICC Publication No. 590 (1998).

A guaranty may be a fraudulent conveyance if it confers no benefit on the guarantor but makes the guarantor's assets unavailable to creditors other than the party receiving the guaranty. For example, if the guarantor did not receive fair value in exchange for giving its guaranty and was insolvent at the time it gave its guaranty, or if the guarantor was rendered insolvent or left with unreasonably small capital as a result of giving its guaranty, the party receiving the guaranty may have an unfair advantage over other creditors of the guarantor. In such a case, the other creditors would be able to invalidate the guaranty. A lender must carefully examine these issues before accepting a guaranty.

### *Upstream Guaranty*

With an *upstream guaranty*, subsidiaries guarantee the parent company's debt or pledge their assets as security for the parent's debt. An upstream guaranty may be found fraudulent if the guarantor received none of the loan proceeds or received an inadequate amount compared to the liability it incurred. Other creditors of the subsidiary (and the creditor's minority shareholders, if the subsidiary is less than wholly owned by the parent) may claim that the lender, as the beneficiary of the guaranty, received an unfair advantage at the other creditors' (or minority shareholders') expense.

### *Leveraged Buyouts*

Leveraged buyouts, in which the acquisition of a company is financed largely through debt, may be subject to attack as fraudulent conveyances. For example, if a leveraged buyout is structured so that a newly formed corporation will acquire the stock of the target company using proceeds from a loan, the lender's source of repayment will be dividends paid from the target company to the borrower. To ensure that such a source of repayment will be available, the lender may require the target company to give a guaranty, which may or may not be secured by the target's assets. Alternatively, the lender may require a merger between the target company and the borrower. Such guaranties or mergers will be invalidated if the target company both (1) failed to receive a reasonably equivalent value and (2) was left insolvent, with assets that were unreasonably small in relation to its business, or with insufficient working capital.

## Voidable Preferences

A transfer from a debtor to a creditor that results in a reduction in the guaranty liability of an insider may be a voidable preference if it occurs within one year of the date the debtor files bankruptcy.[6] For example, suppose that on February 1, 2004, ABC Corporation borrows $1 million from Friendly Bank and that Henri-Claude, a major shareholder of ABC Corporation, guarantees the loan. ABC Corporation makes a $100,000 payment to Friendly Bank on March 1, 2005. On October 1, 2005, ABC Corporation files bankruptcy. ABC Corporation's creditors will be able to set aside the $100,000 payment because it reduced Henri-Claude's guarantor liability dollar for dollar and thereby preferred an insider of ABC Corporation.

## Subordination

A *debt subordination* is an agreement whereby one or more creditors of a common debtor agree to defer payment of their claims until another creditor of the same debtor is fully paid. The indebtedness that is subordinated under the agreement is referred to as the subordinated or *junior debt*. The indebtedness that benefits from the subordination is called the *senior debt*.

The primary purpose of a debt subordination is to protect the senior creditor in the event of the debtor's insolvency. As long as the debtor is solvent, both the junior debt holder and the senior debt holder can expect to be paid. If the debtor becomes insolvent, there will be insufficient assets to satisfy all of its creditors. In such circumstances, creditors can expect to receive only a partial payment on their claims. In subordinating its claim, the holder of the junior debt agrees to yield its right of payment to the senior creditor until the senior creditor has been paid in full.

Corporations frequently use subordinated debt as a means of raising capital. The use of subordinated notes or subordinated debentures (long-term secured bonds) may have certain advantages over equity financing. For example, the interest payable on subordinated debt will be tax-deductible. In addition, the interest rate payable on subordinated debt is often less than the dividend rate that would have to be offered on comparable preferred stock.

### Indebtedness to Insiders

When a borrower seeks a short-term loan from a bank or other commercial lender, the lender will often require that the borrower's indebtedness to insiders, such as officers, directors, and shareholders, be subordinated. This is especially true when the borrower is a closely held corporation and the insider debt is significant in relation to the amount of the lender's loans.

### Lien Subordination

A *lien subordination* is an agreement between two secured creditors whose respective security interests, liens, or mortgages attach to the same property. The subordinating party agrees that the lien of the other creditor will have priority notwithstanding the relative priorities that the parties' liens would otherwise have under applicable law. Unlike debt subordination, a lien subordination does not limit the right of the subordinating party to accept payment from the debtor. Instead, the lien subordination has the effect of limiting the subordinating party's recourse to the collateral until the prior secured party's claim has been satisfied.

### Equitable Subordination

A creditor's claim may be involuntarily postponed through application of the doctrine of *equitable subordination*. This doctrine was developed in bankruptcy law to prevent one creditor, through fraud or other wrongful conduct, from increasing its recovery at the expense of other creditors of the same debtor. The court will order that the creditor that acted wrongfully shall receive no payment from the debtor until the claims of all other creditors have been fully paid.

## Lender Liability

As a series of court decisions have expanded the recoveries available to borrowers against lenders, lenders have become more aware of the risks of lender liability. This section describes several theories on which lender liability claims may be based.

### Breach of Contract

A breach of contract results from a lender's failure to act or to refrain from acting as required by the terms of a loan document or other agreement. As noted earlier, a lender's failure to honor a promise to make a loan may give rise to a breach-of-contract claim. Compensatory damages will be awarded to place the borrower in the same position it would have been in if the lender had properly performed the agreement.

6. *See, e.g.*, Levit v. Ingersoll Rand Fin. Corp. (*In re* V.N. Deprizio Constr. Co.), 874 F.2d 1186 (7th Cir. 1989).

## Breach of Duty of Good Faith

Some cases have imposed an implied obligation of good faith and fair dealing on lenders. This duty requires the lender to act reasonably and fairly in dealing with the borrower and in exercising its rights and remedies under the loan documents and under applicable law.

When there is a fiduciary relationship between the lender and the borrower or when the parties are of unequal bargaining strength, punitive damages may be recoverable for breach of the implied duty of good faith and fair dealing. For example, the U.S. Court of Appeals for the Sixth Circuit affirmed a judgment of $1.5 million compensatory damages and punitive damages against the Irving Trust Company. The company was found to have breached an implied covenant of good faith and fair dealing when it failed to give notice to the borrower before refusing to make further advances under a discretionary line of credit.[7]

## Fraudulent Misrepresentation

A lender may be liable for making false statements to a borrower if, for example, it represents that it will make a loan facility available to the borrower when, in fact, it has decided not to extend any credit to the borrower. If a fiduciary relationship exists between the lender and the borrower, the lender may have an additional duty to disclose information if nondisclosure would result in injury to the borrower. Both compensatory and punitive damages may be recovered for fraudulent misrepresentation.

## Economic Duress

*Economic duress* is the coercion of the borrower by threatening to do an unlawful act that might injure the borrower's business or property. If the lender pressures the borrower into doing something that the borrower is not required to do under the loan documents, a court may find the lender's action constitutes economic duress. For example, a threat by the lender to accelerate a loan unless the borrower provides additional collateral may constitute economic duress if there is no default under the loan documents. Compensatory and punitive damages may be recovered for economic duress.

## Tortious Interference

The lender was found liable for tortious interference with the borrower's corporate governance in *State National Bank of El Paso v. Farah Manufacturing Co.*,[8] which set a precedent for claims of this kind. In that case, the loan agreement between the bank lenders and the borrower prohibited any change in the borrower's management "which any two Banks shall consider, for any reason whatsoever, to be adverse to the interests of the Banks." The lenders threatened to accelerate the loan if the borrower reappointed a certain individual, of whom the lenders disapproved, as chief executive officer. In response to this threat, the borrower appointed a series of CEOs proposed by the lenders. After its financial position seriously deteriorated during the tenure of these chief executives, the borrower sued the banks for tortious interference.

The Texas Court of Appeals held that the banks had wrongfully interfered with the borrower's right to have its affairs managed by competent directors and officers who would maintain a high degree of undivided loyalty to the company. The interference compelled the election of directors and officers whose particular business judgment, inexperience, and divided loyalty proximately resulted in injury to the borrower. The banks were liable for the losses suffered by the borrower while under the bank-imposed management, resulting in a judgment in excess of $18 million against the banks.

## Intentional Infliction of Emotional Distress

A bank was found liable for intentional infliction of emotional distress when, after deciding not to make any additional advances to the borrower, bank officials publicly ridiculed him, pointing at him, using profanities, and laughing about his financial difficulties. To recover for intentional infliction of emotional distress, the lender's conduct must be extreme and outrageous and must intentionally or recklessly cause emotional distress to the borrower. Compensatory and punitive damages may be recovered.

## Negligence and General Tort Liability

Claims that do not fall into one of the other established categories may be characterized as negligence or general tort liability. Negligence is the failure to exercise reasonable care, resulting in injury to the borrower. General tort liability arises from conduct that intentionally causes injury to a borrower.

## Statutory Bases of Liability

A lender may be liable to the borrower if it violates a statutory standard of conduct. For example, the federal Racketeer Influenced and Corrupt Organizations Act (RICO) has been used by private litigants in lender

7. K.M.C. Co. v. Irving Trust Co., 757 F.2d 752 (6th Cir. 1985).
8. 678 S.W.2d 661 (Tex. App. 1984).

liability cases. Although RICO was enacted by Congress as a tool for fighting organized crime, the definition of a "pattern of racketeering activity" is arguably broad enough to encompass fraud or misrepresentation by banks or other lenders. The treble damages available under RICO provide an incentive for borrowers to claim RICO violations in their lender liability suits.

The federal antitying statutes prohibit banks and thrifts from conditioning a loan or other financial service on the borrower's purchase of an unrelated property or service from the lender or on the borrower's providing to the lender a product or service unrelated to the original loan. A lender may be subject to penalties in cases brought by the Securities and Exchange Commission (SEC) for aiding or abetting a borrower in violating federal securities laws if it knew, or should have known, that a violation was taking place or if it is found to be a controlling person with respect to the borrower.

Under the federal Comprehensive Environmental Response, Compensation and Liability Act (CERCLA, discussed in Chapter 15) and state law counterparts, if the lender falls within the statutory definition of an owner or operator of a site contaminated by hazardous wastes and does not come within the statutory safe harbor for lenders, it may find itself liable for all the costs of cleanup even if they exceed the amount of the loan.

## Special Defenses Available to the Federal Insurers of Failed Banks and Savings and Loans

When a bank or savings and loan has failed and federal banking agencies have taken control, a common law principle known as the *D'Oench, Duhme doctrine*[9] has been used by the Federal Deposit Insurance Corporation (FDIC)—and during the savings and loan debacle of the 1980s by the Resolution Trust Corporation (RTC)—to increase the value of the failed institution by easing the federal agencies' ability to collect on loans. *D'Oench, Duhme* bars many claims and defenses against conservators and receivers that might have been valid against the failed bank itself. In particular, the doctrine bars enforcement of any agreements (including secret agreements) unless those agreements are in writing and have been approved contemporaneously by the bank's board or loan committee and recorded in the bank's written records. This permits federal and state bank examiners to rely exclusively on the bank's written records in evaluating the worth of the bank's assets.[10] *D'Oench, Duhme* applies only to banking transactions engaged in by federally insured institutions. It does not apply to nonbanking transactions or to transactions engaged in by a bank's nonbank subsidiaries. Congress partially codified the holding of *D'Oench, Duhme* in the Federal Deposit Insurance Act of 1950, as modified by the Financial Institutions Reform, Recovery, and Enforcement Act (FIRREA).[11]

As a result of this doctrine, the federal agencies are often victorious over borrowers in cases in which a borrower asserts certain common law defenses to escape a loan obligation assumed by the FDIC or RTC. It has also been used as a defense to breach-of-contract and tort claims based on oral promises or arrangements.[12]

Support for the common law doctrine may be eroding, however. In 1995, the U.S. Court of Appeals for the District of Columbia Circuit held that the U.S. Supreme Court's reasoning in *O'Melveny & Myers v. FDIC*[13] leads "inelectably" to the conclusion that the common law *D'Oench, Duhme* doctrine has been preempted by the FIRREA.[14] The Ninth Circuit reached a similar conclusion in 1997 when it relied on the U.S. Supreme Court's decisions in *O'Melveny & Myers* and *Atherton v. FDIC*[15] to support its ruling that the *D'Oench, Duhme* doctrine does not protect the FDIC as a receiver of a failed bank.[16] In contrast, the Eleventh Circuit held in 1997 and again in 2000 that the FDIC, acting as receiver of a federal bank, was still protected by the common law doctrine.[17] The Eleventh Circuit discerned "no indications that *D'Oench* is ripe for overruling."

## Bankruptcy Law

Modern bankruptcy law in the United States began with the Bankruptcy Act of 1898. It was amended in 1938 by the Chandler Act, which was itself completely revised

9. From the Supreme Court case of the same name, *D'Oench, Duhme & Co. v. FDIC*, 315 U.S. 447 (1942).

10. Alexandria Assocs. v. Mitchell Co., 2 F.3d 598 (5th Cir. 1993).
11. 12 U.S.C.S. § 1823(e)(1).
12. *See, e.g.*, Murphy v. FDIC, 208 F.3d 959 (11th Cir. 2000), *cert. dismissed*, 531 U.S. 1107 (2001).
13. 512 U.S. 79 (1994).
14. Murphy v. FDIC, 61 F.3d 34 (D.C. Cir. 1995).
15. 519 U.S. 213 (1997).
16. Ledo Fin. Corp. v. Summers, 122 F.3d 825 (9th Cir. 1997). *Accord* DiVall Insured Income Fund Ltd. P'ship v. Boatmen's First Nat'l Bank, 69 F.3d 1398 (8th Cir. 1995).
17. Motorcity of Jacksonville, Ltd. v. Southeast Bank, N.A., 120 F.3d 1140 (11th Cir. 1997) (*en banc*), *cert. denied*, 523 U.S. 1093 (1998); Murphy v. FDIC, 208 F.3d 959 (11th Cir. 2000), *cert. dismissed*, 531 U.S. 1107 (2001). *Accord* Young v. FDIC, 103 F.3d 1180 (4th Cir. 1997), *cert. denied*, 522 U.S. 928 (1997).

by the Bankruptcy Reform Act of 1978. The 1978 Act changed—and substantially lessened—the requirements for filing bankruptcy. The 1978 Act, as amended, continues in effect today and is referred to in this chapter as the Bankruptcy Code.

In 1984, Congress enacted the Bankruptcy Amendments and Federal Judgeship Act of 1984, which made bankruptcy courts part of the federal district court system and attached a bankruptcy court to each federal district court. Bankruptcy judges, who are appointed by the President and serve for fourteen-year terms, decide *core proceedings* regarding bankruptcy cases (e.g., allowing creditor claims, deciding preferences, confirming plans of reorganization), and federal or state courts resolve *noncore proceedings* concerning the debtor (e.g., decisions on personal-injury and other civil proceedings).[18] Bankruptcy judges also have the power to adjudicate noncore proceedings, subject to *de novo* review by the federal district courts.

In 2000, Congress passed the Gekas–Grassley Bankruptcy Reform Act, which would have represented the most sweeping change in the Bankruptcy Code in twenty years. The Act was designed to reduce the number of individual bankruptcy filings and balance the needs of both debtors and creditors, in contrast to existing law, which favors debtors. However, President Clinton vetoed the law because he said it was unfair to moderate-income debtors while providing protection, such as homestead exemptions for lavish homes, for wealthy individuals.

In 2005, Congress passed, and President Bush signed, the Bankruptcy Abuse Prevention and Consumer Protection Act of 2005, the largest overhaul of bankruptcy laws in more than a quarter century. The 2005 Act creates an income-based test to determine whether individuals who file for bankruptcy should be required to repay some or all of their debts rather than receive a complete discharge of their debts.

18. The Bankruptcy Code was also amended in 1986 and 1994. In addition, certain sections have been revised in other amendments.

### ETHICAL CONSIDERATION

In many foreign countries, directors are personally liable if they allow a company to continue to conduct any business while it is insolvent. What are the reasons for imposing personal liability on the directors of an insolvent company? Although directors are not personally liable for all business conducted by an insolvent company in the United States, is it ethical for the directors of an insolvent company to allow the company to continue to transact business?

The Bankruptcy Code is divided into chapters. Chapters 1, 3, and 5 include definitions and provisions for the administration of bankruptcy proceedings that apply to all forms of bankruptcy. The most common forms of bankruptcy are liquidation under Chapter 7, reorganization under Chapter 11, and consumer debt readjustment under Chapter 13. Chapters 7 and 11 are available to individuals and most business organizations, but Chapter 13 is available only to individuals.[19] The remaining chapters govern bankruptcies of municipalities, stockbrokers, railroads, and farmers.

## MANAGEMENT DUTIES SHIFT WHEN COMPANY ENTERS INSOLVENCY ZONE

Generally, directors of a corporation owe their fiduciary duties to the shareholders (see Chapter 20). When a corporation enters the "zone of insolvency," however, the duties of the directors shift, and they now owe fiduciary duties to the corporation's creditors.[20] The majority of cases state that upon insolvency, fiduciary duties are owed to both creditors and stockholders, although certain duties to creditors may predominate under certain circumstances. Directors, as well as officers and, in most jurisdictions, those who aid, abet, or conspire with the directors or officers, may be personally liable to the bankrupt estate for breach of fiduciary duty.[21]

The Bankruptcy Court for the Northern District of Illinois explained the reason for this shift in duties:

> The economic rationale for the "insolvency exception" is that the value of creditors' contract claims against an insolvent corporation may be affected by the business decisions of managers. At the same time, the claims of the shareholders are (at least temporarily) worthless. As a result, it is the creditors who "now occupy the position of residual owners."[22]

Unfortunately, it is often not clear when a corporation becomes insolvent. Under fraudulent transfer law,

19. The Bankruptcy Code specifically authorizes the court to convert a case under Chapter 11 or 13 to a case under Chapter 7 or to dismiss a case for cause.
20. Geyer v. Ingersoll Publ'ns Co., 621 A.2d 784, 787 (Del. Ch. 1992).
21. *See In re* Healthco Int'l, Inc., 208 B.R. 288, 309–10 (Bankr. D. Mass. 1997); Crowthers McCall Pattern, Inc. v. Lewis, 129 B.R. 992, 999 (S.D.N.Y. 1991); Amerifirst Bank v. Bomar, 757 F. Supp. 1365, 1380 (S.D. Fla. 1991).
22. *In re* Ben Franklin Retail Stores, Inc., 225 B.R. 646, at 653 (Bankr. N.D. Ill. 1998), *aff'd in relevant part,* 2000 WL 282866 (N.D. Ill.).

insolvency is generally defined as an excess of liabilities over the value of assets. Under the principles of fiduciary obligations, however, insolvency is usually defined as an inability to pay debts as they mature. Even though not insolvent in the bankruptcy sense, a business is insolvent in the equity sense if its assets lack liquidity.

It is even less clear when a company enters the "zone of insolvency." There is no test or definition for the "zone of insolvency," although case law suggests that a company may enter the zone when there is a substantial risk that the company will be unable to pay its debts when they become due or the company is operating with unreasonably small capital that "connotes a condition of financial debility short of insolvency (in either the bankruptcy or equity sense) but which makes insolvency reasonably foreseeable."[23]

It is also unclear exactly what obligations management owes to the creditors of a company that is in the zone of insolvency. Minnesota courts have adopted a narrow view that management owes no duty of care to the creditors of an insolvent corporation and that management's fiduciary obligation consists solely of a prohibition against self-dealing and insider preferences.[24] New York,[25] Illinois,[26] and Florida[27] courts, on the other hand, have held that directors and officers owe a broader duty to creditors to minimize losses upon insolvency.

In *Credit Lyonnais Bank Nederland, N.V. v. Pathe Communications Corp.*,[28] the Delaware Court of Chancery took an even more expansive view of management's duties to creditors when a company is in the zone of insolvency. The case arose out of a leveraged buyout (LBO) of MGM–Pathe Communications Company (MGM) by Giancarlo Parretti. After the LBO, MGM's creditors forced MGM into bankruptcy. Credit Lyonnais financed MGM's emergence from Chapter 11 with substantial new debt and obtained significant governance restrictions that ceded control of MGM to a Credit Lyonnais–appointed executive committee as a part of that transaction. The governance contract provided that Parretti would regain control when MGM had paid down the debt to a specified amount. When MGM emerged from bankruptcy, Parretti demanded that the MGM executive committee sell certain assets to pay down enough of the loan to Credit Lyonnais to restore control to him. The executive committee rejected his demand because of concern about the adequacy of the price at which the assets were to be sold. Parretti alleged that the bank nominees on the executive committee had breached their fiduciary duty to the controlling shareholder. The chancellor ruled for Credit Lyonnais, finding that the executive committee's decisions were valid and did not represent a breach of duty. The court explained:

> In these circumstances where the company was in bankruptcy . . . and even thereafter the directors labored in the shadow of that prospect, [the executive committee members] were appropriately mindful of the potential differing interests between the corporation and its 98% shareholder [Parretti]. At least where a corporation is operating in the vicinity of insolvency, a board of directors is not merely the agent of the residue risk bearers, but owes its duty to the corporate enterprise.
>
> . . .
>
> [The executive committee] could reasonably suspect that he [Parretti] might be inclined to accept fire-sale prices. But the MGM board or its executive committee had an obligation to the community of interest that sustained the corporation, to exercise judgment in an informed, good faith effort to maximize the corporation's long-term wealth creating capacity.

The chancellor also emphasized the need to protect creditors: "The possibility of insolvency can do curious things to incentives, exposing creditors to risks of opportunistic behavior, and creating complexities for directors." The chancellor concluded that to the extent that their respective interests conflict, the interests of the shareholders should be subordinated to the interests of the creditors in an insolvency situation and that the directors of an insolvent corporation have an open-ended duty to "maximize the corporation's long-term wealth creating capacity."

## Initiation of a Bankruptcy Proceeding

### *Petition*

A bankruptcy filing begins when the debtor (in a *voluntary proceeding*, which is initiated by the debtor) or one or more of its creditors (in an *involuntary proceeding*, which is initiated by one or more creditors) files a petition with the bankruptcy court. On the filing of a bankruptcy petition, a new entity, called the *bankruptcy estate*, is created; it consists of all of the debtor's legal and equitable rights to the debtor's property.

23. *In re* Healthco Int'l, Inc., 208 B.R. 288, at 301–02.
24. St. James Capital Corp. v. Pallet Recycling Ass'n of North America, Inc., 589 N.W.2d 511 (Minn. Ct. App. 1999).
25. New York Credit Men's Adjustment Bureau v. Weiss, 110 N.E.2d 397 (N.Y. 1953); Pereira v. Cogan, 2001 WL 243537, at 9–10 (S.D.N.Y. Mar. 8, 2001).
26. *In re* Ben Franklin Retail Stores, Inc., *supra* note 22.
27. *In re* Toy King Distribs., Inc., 256 B.R. 1 (Bankr. M.D. Fla. 2000).
28. 1991 WL 277613 (Del. Ch. Dec. 30, 1991).

A voluntary petition must be signed and sworn under oath and must state that the debtor has debts; the debtor does not have to declare insolvency. The petition must include (1) a list of secured and unsecured creditors (including addresses and amount of debt); (2) a list of all property owned by the debtor, including any property claimed to be exempt; (3) a statement of the financial affairs of the debtor; and (4) a list of the debtor's current income and expenses.

An involuntary petition must allege that the debtor is not paying its debts as they come due. If the debtor has more than twelve creditors, the petition must be signed by at least three creditors. If there are twelve or fewer creditors, any creditor can sign. The signing creditor(s) must have valid unsecured claims of at least $10,000 in the aggregate. The debtor must file the same schedules filed by voluntary debtors.

### Order for Relief

The filing of the petition constitutes an *order for relief.* If the debtor challenges an involuntary petition for bankruptcy, a trial is held to determine whether an order for relief should be granted. If the order is granted, the case is accepted for further proceedings.

A meeting of creditors must be held within a reasonable period of time after the order for relief, but in no event earlier than twenty or later than forty days after entry. The bankruptcy judge cannot attend the meeting, but the debtor must appear and answer questions.

In Chapter 7 cases, an interim trustee is appointed by the court when an order for relief is entered. A permanent trustee is elected at the first meeting of the creditors. Once appointed, the *trustee* becomes the legal representative of the debtor's estate.

In most Chapter 11 cases, the debtor is left in place to operate the business and is referred to as the *debtor-in-possession (DIP)*. The DIP has the same powers as the trustee but also has the power to operate the business during the bankruptcy proceeding. The court may appoint a trustee in a Chapter 11 proceeding only upon a showing of cause (fraud, dishonesty, or gross mismanagement by the debtor or its managers). Even if a trustee is not appointed, however, the court may appoint an examiner to investigate the Chapter 11 debtor's financial affairs.

A CASE IN POINT

**CASE 24.1**

***In re* Marvel Entertainment Group, Inc.**

*United States Court of Appeals for the Third Circuit*
*140 F.3d 463*
*(3d Cir. 1998).*

## Summary

**› FACTS** After Marvel Entertainment Group filed for bankruptcy protection under Chapter 11, tensions arose between several of the creditors. Eventually, one creditor acquired control of Marvel, thereby assuming the roles of DIP and creditor. The new DIP and the other creditors attempted to settle their claims against the estate, but negotiations broke down. The new DIP then commenced adverse litigation against the other creditors. The other creditors petitioned for the appointment of a trustee, arguing that the new DIP was incapable of neutrality. The district court appointed a trustee, and the new DIP appealed.

**› ISSUE PRESENTED** Is acrimony between the DIP and certain creditors sufficient cause to justify appointment of a trustee?

**› SUMMARY OF OPINION** The U.S. Court of Appeals for the Third Circuit began by noting that appointment of a trustee should be the exception rather than the rule. Nonetheless, a court does have the power to appoint a trustee "for cause, including fraud, dishonesty, incompetence, or gross mismanagement of the affairs of the debtor by current management" or "if such an appointment is in the interests of the creditors, any equity security holders, and other interests of the estate." Because the new DIP's dual role had caused extreme acrimony, the court concluded that the appointment of a trustee was not an abuse of discretion by the district court.

The court explained that the determination of what kind of acrimony would rise to the level of cause was within the district court's discretion and should be made on a case-by-case basis "when the inherent conflicts extend beyond the healthy conflicts that always exist between debtor and creditor, or . . . when the parties 'begin working at cross purposes.'"

**› RESULT** The appointment of a trustee was affirmed.

## *Administration of Claims*

Unsecured creditors must file a *proof of claim* stating the amount of their claim in a form provided by the court within time periods established by the jurisdiction in which the case is filed. The proof of claim requirement in a Chapter 11 bankruptcy is deemed satisfied for claims listed in the debtor's schedules as uncontingent and undisputed (unless the creditor wishes to claim more than the debtor acknowledges is due).

A creditor's claim must be allowed by the court before a creditor is permitted to participate in the bankruptcy estate. Except for personal-injury or wrongful-death claims, which are triable to a jury in the district court, disputed claims are normally resolved through an abbreviated or expedited hearing before the bankruptcy judge. If resolution would unduly delay administration of the bankruptcy case (such as when a claim is contingent upon a future event), the bankruptcy court will estimate the allowable amount of certain claims.

Some claims are limited in bankruptcy. For example, a terminated employee's damages claim may not exceed one year's compensation. Unless the estate can pay all claims in a liquidation, postpetition interest is allowed only to secured creditors that can recover it from their collateral. Perhaps most significantly, Section 502(b)(6) of the Bankruptcy Code limits the amount of damages a landlord may collect from a bankrupt tenant (who rejects the lease) to the amount of unpaid back rent plus the greater of either (1) one year's rent or (2) 15 percent of the rent for the remaining term, not to exceed three years' rent. Many debtors holding a large number of unfavorable long-term leases have filed for bankruptcy to take advantage of this provision.

## *Bankruptcy Estate*

Because the primary role of the trustee is to collect and distribute the property of the estate, it is essential to know what constitutes that property. The basic rule is set forth in Section 541(a), which provides that the bankruptcy estate comprises "all legal or equitable interests of the debtor in property as of the commencement of the case."[29]

Exempt property, which is excluded from the bankruptcy estate, is intended to provide for the debtor's future needs and generally includes, among other things, an interest up to a specified amount in equity in property used as a residence and burial plots (the homestead exemption); one motor vehicle; certain household goods and personal items; some special deposits or cash; tools or books used in the debtor's trade; any unmatured life insurance policy; professionally prescribed health aids; a number of government benefits, including Social Security, veteran's, disability, unemployment compensation, and public assistance benefits; alimony or support payments; and personal-injury awards.

Subject to a cap on homestead exemptions in limited circumstances, which was added by the Bankruptcy Abuse Prevention and Consumer Protection Act of 2005 discussed later in this chapter, the Bankruptcy Code also allows states to enact their own exemptions. Some states give debtors the option of choosing between federal and state exemptions, while others require debtors to follow state law. State exemptions are frequently higher than under the federal exemption scheme. For example, Florida, Iowa, Kansas, South Dakota, Texas, and the District of Columbia have unlimited homestead exemptions.

The Bankruptcy Code permits debtors to nullify involuntary liens that impair their allowable exemptions. They can even invalidate consensual liens on most household items, tools of the trade, or health aids, unless the secured creditor financed the debtor's purchase of the property or was given possession of it. To take full advantage of the exemptions, debtors often convert assets from nonexempt to exempt forms before filing their bankruptcy cases. They must be careful not to take steps that could be considered fraudulent, however, because fraudulent conduct could jeopardize the right to discharge existing debts.

## *Distribution of Property*

A secured creditor's claim to the debtor's estate has priority over unsecured creditors' claims to the extent that the property of the estate consists of the creditor's collateral. The statutory priority of unsecured claims is as follows:

1. Alimony and child support.
2. Fees and expenses of administering the estate, including court costs, trustee fees, attorneys' fees, appraisal fees, and other administrative costs.
3. Claims arising in the ordinary course of business after the date of the filing of the petition but before (a) the appointment of the trustee or (b) the issuance of the order for relief, whichever is earlier.
4. Unsecured claims for a specified amount per employee in wages, salary, or commissions earned by each employee of the debtor within the ninety days immediately preceding the filing of the petition (all other salary claims are treated as a claim of a general unsecured creditor).
5. Unsecured claims for up to a specified amount per employee for contributions to employee benefit plans based on services performed within 180 days immediately preceding the filing of the petition.

29. 11 U.S.C. § 541(a)(1).

6. Claims up to a specified amount for each farmer or fisher against debtors who operate or own facilities for storing grain or processing fish.
7. Consumer claims up to a specified amount for deposits with or prepayments to the debtor for undelivered property or the purchase of services that were not delivered or provided by the debtor.
8. Certain tax obligations owed by the debtor.
9. Claims of general unsecured creditors.

Each class must be paid in full before any lower class is paid. If a class cannot be paid in full, the claims of that class are paid proportionately. If anything is left after all of the creditors above are paid in full, the balance is returned to the debtor.

# Principles Applicable to All Bankruptcies

## Good Faith Requirement

A debtor does not have to show that it is insolvent to file for bankruptcy. Some debtors may face a liquidity crisis that cannot be untangled without judicial intervention. A notable example of this is the bankruptcy filing by Texaco after a jury in Texas awarded Pennzoil more than $10 billion (see the "Inside Story" in Chapter 7).

On the other hand, courts have resisted the use of bankruptcy where they perceive that it is being used in bad faith. For example, in *In re SGL Carbon Corp.*, the officers of the debtor declared that the company was financially healthy and that they were filing solely to pressure the plaintiffs to settle some antitrust lawsuits. The U.S. Court of Appeals for the Third Circuit held that Section 1122 of the Bankruptcy Code implies a condition of good faith in filing and that the mere possibility that the debtor might need to file if it lost the lawsuits did not satisfy this condition.[30]

The following case addressed the propriety of a financially healthy company's decision to file for Chapter 11 protection solely to take advantage of the provision in the Bankruptcy Code that limits claims on long-term leases.

30. 200 F.3d 154 (3d Cir. 1999).

A Case in Point

## In the Language of the Court

**CASE 24.2**
***In re* Integrated Telecom Express, Inc.**
*United States Court of Appeals for the Third Circuit*
*384 F.3d 108 (3d Cir. 2004).*

› **FACTS** Within eighteen months after Integrated Telecom Express completed a successful initial public offering of its stock, the market for many of its products deteriorated, resulting in substantial net losses. Rather than expend all of its remaining assets, in about December 2001, the company began efforts to develop an alternative business model or to find a third-party acquiror. When it had experienced no success by April 2002, Integrated Telecom's board of directors approved a plan to liquidate the company's assets and dissolve the company so that it could maximize the portion of its more than $105 million in remaining cash available for distribution to its shareholders.

Before it could do so, however, the company had to dispose of its intellectual property and its continuing support and warranty obligations, resolve outstanding securities litigation, and dispose of its obligations under a long-term office lease. Integrated Telecom arranged a sale of its intellectual property for $1.5 million; the buyer also assumed Integrated Telecom's support and warranty obligations. It also had insurance to cover at least a portion of any liability associated with the securities litigation.

The term of the company's office lease was ten years, with monthly payments of $200,000 that were to increase at the rate of 5 percent each year. When the board approved its plan of dissolution in April 2002, almost nine years were remaining on the lease. Integrated Telecom sought to settle with the landlord for a payment of up to $8 million. The company's board of directors also authorized commencement of a Chapter 11 proceeding if negotiations with the landlord proved unsuccessful and authorized management to send the landlord a letter in which Integrated Telecom threatened to file a Chapter 11 bankruptcy case and to avail itself of the cap on lease claims under Section 502(b)(6) of the Bankruptcy Code if the landlord refused to settle.

*(Continued)*

(Case 24.2 *continued*)

When the landlord refused to settle on the offered terms, Integrated Telecom filed its Chapter 11 petition and moved to reject the lease. According to its schedules, Integrated Telecom had $105.4 million in cash, $20 million of insurance to cover potential securities liability, and other assets valued at $1.5 million. On the liability side, the landlord filed a proof of claim asserting that the present value of the company's remaining lease obligations (without applying the Section 502(b)(6) cap) was approximately $26 million; Integrated Telecom's bankruptcy schedule listed other liabilities totaling approximately $430,000. The class-action plaintiffs in the securities litigation sought a total of $93.24 million in damages, but Integrated Telecom disputed those claims and amounts.

**› ISSUE PRESENTED** Does a Chapter 11 petition filed by a financially healthy debtor solely to take advantage of a provision in the Bankruptcy Code that limits claims on long-term leases comply with the requirements of the Bankruptcy Code?

**› OPINION** SMITH, J., writing for the U.S. Court of Appeals for the Third Circuit:

Chapter 11 bankruptcy petitions are subject to dismissal under 11 U.S.C. § 1112(b) unless filed in good faith, and the burden is on the bankruptcy petitioner to establish that its petition has been filed in good faith. . . .

. . .

Our cases have accordingly focused on two inquiries that are particularly relevant to the question of good faith: (1) whether the petition serves a valid bankruptcy purpose, e.g., by preserving a going concern or maximizing the value of the debtor's estate, and (2) whether the petition is filed merely to obtain a tactical litigation advantage. . . .

. . .

Both the Bankruptcy Court and the District Court concluded that Integrated faced financial distress because it "was losing a lot of money," and "was experiencing a dramatic downward spiral" in September 2001, and that, as a result, Integrated had gone "out of business." We do not see how bankruptcy offers Integrated any relief from this sort of distress, which has no relation to any debt owed by Integrated. That is, we can identify no value for Integrated's assets that was threatened outside of bankruptcy by the collapse of Integrated's business model, but that could be preserved or maximized in an orderly liquidation under Chapter 11. Because Integrated's "dramatic downward spiral" does not establish that Integrated was suffering from financial distress, it does not, standing alone, establish that Integrated's petition was filed in good faith.

. . .

. . . [W]e turn to the [Official Committee of Equity Holders'] argument that Integrated's desire to take advantage of the cap on landlord claims provided by § 502(b)(6) establishes good faith in and of itself. . . .

The Bankruptcy Court did not hold that Integrated's desire to take advantage of the § 502(b)(6) cap established good faith. Instead, the Bankruptcy Court held that "it does not establish *bad* faith for a debtor to file a chapter [11] case for the purpose of taking advantage of provisions which alter pre-petition rights, including altering the rights of a landlord under State law." (Emphasis added). We agree. Indeed, we believe it to be a truism that it is not *bad* faith to seek to avail oneself of a particular protection in the Bankruptcy Code . . . .

The far more relevant question is whether a desire to take advantage of a particular provision in the Bankruptcy Code, standing alone, establishes good faith. We hold that it does not. . . .

*(Continued)*

(Case 24.2 *continued*)

**› RESULT** The court reversed the order of the district court affirming the bankruptcy court's denial of the landlord's motion to dismiss and remanded the case to the bankruptcy court with instructions to dismiss Integrated Telecom's Chapter 11 petition.

**› CRITICAL THINKING QUESTIONS**

1. The court in *Integrated Telecom* makes it clear that a Chapter 11 case must be filed by a debtor that is in financial distress that can be addressed in some manner by filing bankruptcy. But what qualifies as "financial distress"? Would the decision have been different if the debtor had claimed to be insolvent? If it had used Chapter 11 to maximize the value of its assets for its creditors, not its shareholders? If it was not clear at the outset that the debtor was solvent? Would pending litigation ever provide a good faith reason for filing bankruptcy?
2. Texaco filed for bankruptcy after a $10.5 billion judgment was rendered against it in litigation with Pennzoil over the acquisition of Getty Oil (this is the subject of the "Inside Story" in Chapter 7). What would the Third Circuit have done if presented with a good faith challenge to the Chapter 11 case filed by Texaco?

## AUTOMATIC STAY

The most immediate and dramatic advantage of any bankruptcy filing is the *automatic stay*, which instantly suspends most litigation and collection activities against the debtor, its property, or that of the bankruptcy estate. Many debtors file for bankruptcy on the eve of foreclosure to forestall the loss of crucial assets; others file primarily to stave off litigation or collection activities. The latter group includes such notable bankruptcy refugees as Dow Corning (facing 19,000 lawsuits involving 400,000 women claiming immune-system illness caused by silicon breast implants), Johns–Manville (sued for thousands of asbestos-related injuries), and Texaco (unable to post a bond while appealing the multibillion-dollar judgment against it for interfering with Pennzoil's efforts to acquire Getty Oil).

There are only a few exceptions to the automatic stay. Three of these are the most notable. First, several types of securities and similar financial transactions are not stayed. Second, the automatic stay does not stay the commencement or continuation of a criminal action against the debtor. Third, it does not stay any action to enforce a government's police or regulatory power. These exceptions are narrowly interpreted. For example, a federal bankruptcy judge in the Southern District of New York held that California was barred from pursuing its claims against Enron arising out of the state's energy crisis.[31] The court held that "[e]ven if a government action is a proper exercise of the police power, the collection of a money judgment is barred."

The U.S. Supreme Court has ruled that a bank could, without violating the automatic stay, put a temporary administrative hold on the portion of the bankrupt debtor's checking account that the bank claimed was subject to setoff.[32] The bank refused to pay withdrawals from the bankrupt's account that would reduce the balance below the sum the bank claimed was due on its loan to the bankrupt party. The bank then filed a motion for relief from the automatic stay in the bankruptcy court. The Court acknowledged that the bankruptcy filing gives rise to an automatic stay of various types of activities by creditors, including "the setoff of any debt owing to the debtor that arose before the commencement of the [bankruptcy case] against any claim against the debtor." The Court held that a setoff has not occurred, however, until three steps have been taken: (1) a decision to effectuate a setoff, (2) some action accomplishing the setoff, and (3) a recording of the setoff. Thus, there is no setoff unless the creditor intends to permanently settle accounts.

The Court reasoned that a bank account is not money belonging to the depositor but rather represents a promise by a bank to pay the depositor an amount equal to the money in the account. Therefore, by imposing an administrative hold, the bank does not exercise dominion over the bankrupt's property. Rather, the hold represents a temporary refusal of a creditor to pay a debt that is subject to setoff against a debt owed by the bankrupt.

31. *In re* Enron Corp., 302 B.R. 455 (Bankr. S.D.N.Y. 2003).

32. Citizens Bank of Maryland v. Strumpf, 516 U.S. 16 (1995).

## ETHICAL CONSIDERATION

Would it be ethical for the manager of company about to file bankruptcy to withdraw all company funds from accounts at banks to which the company owes money to avoid having an administrative hold imposed on the accounts?

The automatic stay prevents creditors from enforcing a clause in their agreements, referred to as an *ipso facto clause*, that expressly permits termination in the event of a bankruptcy filing. For example, in *In re Computer Communications, Inc.*,[33] Codex Corporation had entered into a joint marketing and development agreement with Computer Communications, Inc. (CCI), pursuant to which Codex agreed to make minimum quarterly purchases of equipment and software from CCI. After CCI filed a Chapter 11 petition, Codex notified CCI that it was terminating the agreement pursuant to an ipso facto clause in the agreement. CCI filed suit in bankruptcy court, alleging that Codex's termination of the agreement violated the automatic stay provision in the Bankruptcy Code. The bankruptcy court held that Codex had willfully violated the automatic stay and awarded general damages of $4,750,000 (apparently based on loss of projected profits), plus $250,000 in punitive damages, and the U.S. Court of Appeals for the Ninth Circuit affirmed.

Several recent decisions of the federal circuit courts have held that there is a private cause of action if a creditor violates the automatic stay,[34] although the Ninth Circuit concluded that a class action seeking injunctive relief for violation of the automatic stay was not appropriate.[35] In addition, willful violations of the automatic stay may also constitute contempt of court and warrant punitive damages.

33. 824 F.2d 725 (9th Cir. 1987).
34. Cox v. Zale Del., Inc., 239 F.3d 910 (7th Cir. 2001); Bessette v. AVCO Fin. Servs., Inc., 230 F.3d 439 (1st Cir. 2000); Pertus v. Ford Motor Credit Co., 233 F.3d 417 (6th Cir. 2000).
35. Walls v. Wells Fargo Bank, NA, 276 F.3d 502 (9th Cir. 2002).

## ETHICAL CONSIDERATION

In *In re Computer Communications, Inc.*, CCI extended its agreement with Codex only two days before filing for bankruptcy. It seems clear that Codex would not have renewed the agreement if it had known that CCI was going to declare bankruptcy. The managers of CCI locked in a favorable contract by concealing their intentions from Codex. Was the CCI managers' conduct unethical or just good business?

By stopping creditors in their tracks, the automatic stay provides a breathing spell that can enable a Chapter 11 debtor to focus on the operation of the business and the reorganization of its financial affairs. The stay is not a permanent shield, however. The court may authorize creditors to resume collection efforts, most often foreclosure on collateral, for cause—that is, if there is inadequate protection of the creditors' property interests, such as when the value of the collateral declines with use and no replacement security is provided. Relief from the stay will also be granted if the debtor has no equity in property and a stay is not necessary for effective reorganization. Such relief from the automatic stay becomes more likely as time passes without progress toward reorganization. The automatic stay is rarely lifted to permit garden-variety litigation against the debtor, however.

## EXECUTORY CONTRACTS AND LEASES

Under the Bankruptcy Code, the trustee (or debtor-in-possession in the case of a Chapter 11 reorganization) has the option of assuming or rejecting prebankruptcy *executory contracts*—that is, contracts that have not yet been fully performed—or unexpired leases. Assumption preserves the debtor's rights and duties under the existing relationship, whereas rejection terminates them.

In general, debtors will reject unfavorable contracts and assume favorable ones. For example, if an executory contract or unexpired lease is a valuable asset, the DIP will want to assume it so that it can be preserved for the reorganizing business or sold at a profit. Assumption is advantageous when it allows the debtor to sell or buy goods at a favorable price or to lease space or equipment at better-than-market rents. Even a contract or lease in default can be assumed, provided that the debtor cures and compensates for the breach and gives adequate assurance of future performance. Once assumed, the contract or lease obligations are allowable as administrative expenses, as with other authorized postpetition transactions. Even if a contract or lease contains contractual restrictions barring assignment, any assumed contract or lease can be sold and assigned intact if the prospective assignee's future performance is adequately assured.

On the other hand, by rejecting a disadvantageous contract or lease, the debtor can escape burdensome performance obligations. The nondebtor party to the contract or lease will be deemed to have a prepetition damages claim for breach and thus will be treated like others whose claims arose from prebankruptcy transactions.

The following case addressed the issue of whether an option to buy property is an executory contract.

A CASE IN POINT

**CASE 24.3**

**Unsecured Creditors Committee of Robert L. Helms Construction & Development Co. v. Southmark Corp. (*In re* Robert L. Helms Construction and Development Co., Inc.)**

*United States Court of Appeals for the Ninth Circuit*
*139 F.3d 702*
*(9th Cir. 1998)*
*(en banc).*

# In the Language of the Court

**› FACTS** Southmark, a Texas corporation, sold the Double Diamond Ranch in Nevada to the Double Diamond Ranch Limited Partnership (Double Diamond), retaining an option to buy back part of the ranch. Southmark later filed for bankruptcy in Texas. As part of its Chapter 11 reorganization plan, it assumed various executory contracts by filing a notice of assumption. The plan provided that all executory contracts not listed were deemed rejected. The notice did not list the option to buy back the ranch; therefore, it would have been deemed rejected if it was an executory contract.

Double Diamond then itself filed for bankruptcy in Nevada. The committee administering the Double Diamond bankruptcy decided to sell the ranch to South Meadows Properties Limited Partnership. The committee asked the bankruptcy court to allow sale of the ranch free and clear of Southmark's option. A free-and-clear sale was appropriate only if the option was no longer valid because it had been stripped away in the Texas bankruptcy proceeding. The Nevada bankruptcy court held that the option was an executory contract that had been rejected in Southmark's bankruptcy. Therefore, it allowed Double Diamond to sell the ranch to South Meadows free and clear of Southmark's option. Southmark appealed.

**› ISSUE PRESENTED** Is an option to buy property an executory contract?

**› OPINION** KOZINSKI, J., writing for the U.S. Court of Appeals for the Ninth Circuit:

An executory contract is one "on which performance remains due to some extent on both sides." More precisely, a contact is executory if "the obligations of both parties are so unperformed that the failure of either party to complete performance would constitute a material breach and thus excuse the performance of the other."

A paid-for but unexercised option presents a puzzle. Is it executory or isn't it? Each side may have unperformed obligations, but they are contingent on the optionee's decision to exercise the option. If it does, the optionor has a duty to deliver the property, and the optionee may have a duty to tender payment, depending on the mechanics of the option. But if the option is not exercised, nothing happens and neither party commits a breach. The contingent nature of the obligations has troubled courts. Some have said that these are contingent obligations, but obligations nonetheless, hence options are executory. Other courts have held that the optionee has fulfilled its only true obligation under the option by paying for it; the creation of further obligations lies within the optionee's sole discretion, so the contract isn't executory.

. . .

A better approach . . . is to ask whether the option requires further performance from each party at the time the petition is filed. Typically the answer is no, and the option is therefore not executory. The optionee need not exercise the option—if he does nothing, the option lapses without breach. The contingency which triggers potential obligations—exercising the option—is completely within the optionee's control. While some options may be executory, *Easebe*[36] is overboard in holding that they all are.

. . .

We therefore reject *Easebe's* broad rule that all options are executory contracts. Instead, we look to outstanding obligations at the time the petition for relief is filed and ask whether both sides must still perform. Performance due only if the optionee chooses at his discretion to exercise the option doesn't count unless he has chosen to

36. Gill v. Easebe Enters. (*In re* Easebe Enters.), 900 F.2d 1417 (9th Cir. 1990).

*(Continued)*

(Case 24.3 *continued*)

exercise it. An option may on occasion be an executory contract, for instance, where the optionee has announced that he is exercising the option, but not yet followed through with the payment at the option price.

The question thus becomes: At the time of filing, does each party have something it must do to avoid materially breaching the contract? Typically, the answer is no; the optionee commits no breach by doing nothing.

It appears likely that the option here wasn't executory when Southmark filed its petition, but the record is not entirely clear.

**› RESULT** The case was remanded to the bankruptcy court with instructions to determine the effect of the confirmed Southmark reorganization plan. If the plan did not resolve the question, the bankruptcy court was instructed to apply the legal test described above to determine whether the option contract was executory at the time of filing and to fashion a remedy if it found that the option was not an executory contract and remained an asset of the Southmark estate.

**› CRITICAL THINKING QUESTIONS**

1. If Southmark had given written notice of its intent to exercise the option, but had not yet paid the purchase price, before filing for bankruptcy, would the option have been an executory contract?
2. The option agreement expressly provided that the option was for a period of fifteen years "provided, however, that the option granted herein shall terminate in the event Southmark files for protection under Chapter 11 for the Bankruptcy Code." Why wasn't the option automatically terminated when Southmark filed under Chapter 11?

---

Section 365(c) provides an exception to the debtor's usual right to assume, assign, or reject executory contracts and unexpired leases. It provides that the debtor may not assume or assign an executory contract or unexpired lease if "applicable laws excuse a party . . . to such contract or lease from accepting performance from or rendering performance to an entity other than the debtor" unless the other party consents to the assignment or assumption. Bankruptcy courts have generally treated intellectual property licenses as executory contracts and have considered their assignability under Sections 365(a), which allows a debtor to assume an executory contract, and 365(f), which allows a debtor to assign an executory contract to a third party. A debtor may typically take either of these actions even if the executory contract expressly restricts assignment. In more recent decisions involving intellectual property licenses, however, courts have interpreted Section 365(c) as limiting the authority that Sections 365(a) and (f) grant to the debtor. Section 365(c) provides that a debtor may not "assume or assign" any executory contract if (1) applicable nonbankruptcy law excuses the nondebtor from accepting performance from or rendering performance to a third party and (2) the nondebtor does not consent to the assumption or assignment.

The U.S. Courts of Appeal for the Third,[37] Fourth,[38] Ninth,[39] and Eleventh[40] Circuits have held that a debtor may not assume an intellectual property license subject to Section 365(c) where applicable nonbankruptcy law prohibits assignment without consent, even if the debtor has no actual intention to assign its license. Once the license is assumed, these courts create a "hypothetical" third party to whom the license will be assigned. For this reason, the analysis is referred to as the "hypothetical test." On the other hand, the U.S. Court of Appeals for the First Circuit allows a debtor to assume an intellectual property license that is subject to Section 365(c), even over the objection of a nondebtor licensor, where the debtor licensee does not actually intend to assign the

37. *In re* West Elec., Inc., 852 F.2d 79 (3d Cir. 1988).
38. *In re* Catron, 158 B.R. 629 (E.D. Va. 1993), *aff'd without op.*, 25 F.3d 1038 (4th Cir. 1994).
39. *In re* Catapult Entm't, Inc., 165 F.3d 747 (9th Cir. 1999), *cert. dismissed*, 528 U.S. 924 (1999).
40. *In re* James Cable Partners, 27 F.3d 534 (11th Cir. 1994).

license to a third party. The First Circuit approach is called the "actual test."[41]

### Copyright Licenses

At least one court has held that an exclusive copyright license is freely assignable without the licensor's consent, notwithstanding a nonassignability provision, even though applicable nonbankruptcy law is unsettled with respect to the assignability of exclusive copyright licenses.[42] As a result, how a bankruptcy court will rule if a debtor seeks to assume and assign an exclusive copyright license will depend on which authority the court chooses to follow. One school of thought holds that exclusive copyright licenses are freely assignable; this would suggest that assignment is generally appropriate even if the copyright license expressly prohibits assignment.[43] On the other hand, *Nimmer* concludes that a copyright licensor may restrict assignment of even an exclusive copyright license by express contractual restrictions; this approach would suggest that assignment is appropriate unless there is an express contractual restriction to the contrary.[44] A third school of thought holds that Congress did not grant exclusive licensees the right to freely transfer their licenses. This approach would suggest that assignment should be prohibited unless consent is first obtained.

At least one bankruptcy court has held that a nonexclusive copyright license is nonassignable in a bankruptcy proceeding in the absence of consent by the licensor or express contractual provisions to the contrary.[45]

### Patent Licenses

Section 365(c) has not yet been applied to an exclusive patent license, so it is difficult to predict how a bankruptcy court will rule when presented with a debtor licensee who seeks to assume and assign an exclusive patent license. Bankruptcy courts have held that nonexclusive patent licenses are not assignable under Section 365(c) without the consent of the licensor.[46]

### Trademark Licenses

There do not appear to be any recent opinions that offer substantive analysis regarding the assignability of exclusive or nonexclusive trademark licenses under Section 365(c). However, case law appears to support the proposition that they are assignable without consent.[47]

### Know-How Licenses

There do not appear to be any cases that have applied Section 365 to the assignability of know-how licenses.[48]

## Sale of Property

Bankruptcy can facilitate favorable sales of assets other than contracts or leases. For example, if partition or division of property jointly owned by the debtor and another is impractical and a separate sale of the debtor's undivided interest would yield significantly less for the estate, the debtor can sell both interests and disburse the net proceeds proportionately, as long as the resulting benefit would outweigh the detriment to the other owner. Similarly, the debtor may sell property free and clear of liens or other interests (which normally will be shifted to the proceeds) if the price will exceed all encumbrances or if the nondebtor's interest is in bona fide dispute. Thus, although the debtor's sale before bankruptcy might be stymied, a bankruptcy proceeding can sometimes break the logjam and allow the debtor to pass clear title.

This cleansing power of bankruptcy extends beyond specific property. It can be the key to successful reorganization through the sale of the entire business or through new capital infusions. When a business is troubled and its future is in doubt, potential investors may shy away, despite the venture's intrinsic worth. Similarly, the price a prospective going-concern purchaser will pay may be seriously depressed by the fear that acquiring all of the assets will also subject the buyer to the debtor's obligations under doctrines of successor liability (discussed in Chapter 10). The same investors or buyers are often less jittery, and hence more willing to recognize the true value of the debtor's business, if the transaction proceeds under a confirmed plan or other court order that quantifies or cuts off preexisting claims. Subject to possible constitutional due process protections for unknown future claimants, bankruptcy can dispel uncertainties that would otherwise prevent the debtor from realizing the equity in its business.

## Avoiding Powers

The Bankruptcy Code provides trustees with certain *avoiding powers* that they can use to invalidate or reverse certain prebankruptcy transactions that would unfairly benefit the debtor or certain creditors.

41. Institut Pasteur v. Cambridge Biotech Corp., 104 F.3d 489 (1st Cir. 1997), *cert. denied,* 521 U.S. 1120 (1997).
42. *In re* Golden Books Family Entm't, Inc., 269 B.R. 300 (D. Del. 2001).
43. *In re* Patient Educ. Media, Inc., 210 B.R. 237 (S.D.N.Y. 1997).
44. *See* Nimmer on Copyright, 10.01[A] and [B][4] (2001).
45. *In re* Patient Educ. Media, 210 B.R. 237 (S.D.N.Y. 1997).
46. Everex Systems v. Cadtrak, 89 F.3d 673 (9th Cir. 1996).
47. *In re* Rooster, Inc., 100 B.R. 228 (Bankr. E.D. Pa. 1989).
48. Neil S. Hirshman et al., *Assignability of Intellectual Property Licenses in Bankruptcy,* IPL Newsl., Fall 2002, at 11–18.

### *Fraudulent Conveyances*

Section 548 of the Bankruptcy Code gives the court the power to avoid *fraudulent conveyances.* In general, these arise from transactions that occurred within a year before bankruptcy that (1) are actually intended to hinder, delay, or defraud creditors or (2) provide less than reasonably equivalent value in exchange and leave the debtor insolvent or without sufficient capital to engage in business or to pay expected debts. Thus, a leveraged buyout that leaves a company with insufficient capital and high debt leverage after the payouts to equity holders may be voidable as a fraudulent conveyance.[49] Most states have roughly parallel fraudulent transfer laws, but the Bankruptcy Code's version may be broader. For example, the state laws may be inapplicable to distressed foreclosure sales that are noncollusive and procedurally proper; bankruptcy law has been applied to invalidate such sales if the proceeds are less than 70 percent of the collateral's fair market value. However, in *BFP v. Resolution Trust Corp.*,[50] the U.S. Supreme Court affirmed the dismissal of a fraudulent transfer proceeding by a Chapter 11 debtor, holding that the price received at a mortgage foreclosure sale conclusively established the "reasonably equivalent value" of the mortgage property as long as the requirements of the state's foreclosure law were met. Thus, although a good faith buyer should have a lien for the value given (which is usually the amount of the secured debt), the bankruptcy trustee may be able to reverse the foreclosure and recapture equity.

### *Preferences*

*Preferences* are transfers to (or for the benefit of) creditors on account of antecedent debts that are made from an insolvent debtor's property within ninety days before bankruptcy and that enable the creditors to receive more than they would through a Chapter 7 liquidation. (The preference window is enlarged to a year before bankruptcy if the benefited creditor is an insider—that is, someone in a position to control the debtor's conduct, such as a relative, partner, director, officer, or substantial shareholder.) Preferences are made avoidable in bankruptcy both to discourage creditors from dismembering a troubled business in their race for its assets and to foster equal distribution among similarly situated claimants. Subject to limited exceptions, the bankruptcy court can recover voluntary or involuntary preferential payments and strip away preferential security interests or collection liens, all for the benefit of the bankruptcy estate.

A payment is a preference only if it is for an antecedent (or preexisting) debt. To avoid penalizing creditors that continue to deal in a customary fashion with the debtor during its slide into bankruptcy, current payments in the ordinary course of business cannot be recovered as preferences.[51] In *Union Bank v. Wolas*,[52] the U.S. Supreme Court held that payments on long-term debt, as well as payments on short-term debt, may qualify for the ordinary course of business exception to the trustee's power to avoid preferential transfers if (1) the loan was incurred in the ordinary course of the debtor's business and of the bank's business, (2) the payments were made in the ordinary course of business, and (3) the payments were made according to ordinary business terms.

The following case addressed the scope of the *earmarking doctrine*, whereby a payment to a preexisting creditor may not be recoverable as a preference if the funds for the repayment were provided by some other creditor and not by the debtor.

49. *See, e.g.*, United States v. Tabor Court Realty Corp., 803 F.2d 1288 (3d Cir. 1987), *cert. denied*, 483 U.S. 1005 (1987).
50. 511 U.S. 531 (1994).
51. 11 U.S.C. § 547(c)(2).
52. 502 U.S. 151 (1991).

A CASE IN POINT

## In the Language of the Court

**CASE 24.4**

**Adams v. Anderson (*In re* Superior Stamp & Coin Co.)**
*United States Court of Appeals for the Ninth Circuit*
*223 F.3d 1004*
*(9th Cir. 2000).*

**› FACTS** Superior Stamp & Coin operated as a full-service auction house specializing in the auction of coins, sports and Hollywood memorabilia, and related goods. In 1992, Carolyn Adams and Superior entered into an auction consignment agreement, whereby Superior agreed to auction Adams's coin collection and pay her the net proceeds within thirty days after receiving the funds. After Superior failed to remit the $374,125.57 of net proceeds, Superior negotiated a repayment schedule with Adams in April 1994, which called for Superior to remit the proceeds in six equal $62,355 payments.

*(Continued)*

(Case 24.4 *continued*)

In early 1994, Superior was under severe financial strain, and its largest creditor, the Bank of California, was actively involved in Superior's day-to-day management. In an effort to preserve Superior's business, the bank agreed to fund certain repayments, including the $62,355 installments owed to Adams.

Superior issued a $62,355 check to Adams on May 27, 1994. When the check was presented to the bank, it was subjected to a "special review" process and then approved by the bank. The bank then advanced to Superior's account the funds necessary to clear the check—in this case, the full amount of the $62,355 payment—and simultaneously electronically transferred the funds to Adams. Superior issued a second $62,355 check to Adams on July 7, 1994. The bank again approved the payment and advanced the funds necessary to cover the check. This time, because Superior's General Account already contained $42,439.10, the bank advanced only $19,915.90—the amount required to fund the shortfall.

In spite of the efforts to save Superior, the company failed. On August 26, 1994, Superior filed an involuntary petition for Chapter 11 bankruptcy. The trustee sought to recover the payments to Adams on the grounds that they were voidable preference transfers. Adams argued that the bankruptcy doctrine of earmarking immunized the transfers funded by the bank from avoidance.

**› ISSUE PRESENTED** Does the earmarking doctrine apply when a debtor requests a loan to pay a particular creditor, and the lender does not pay the creditor directly but advances the funds to the debtor for payment to the selected creditor?

**› OPINION** REINHARDT, J., writing for the U.S. Court of Appeals for the Ninth Circuit:

Under § 574(b) of the Bankruptcy Code, a trustee may recover certain transfers made by the debtor within ninety days before the bankruptcy petition was filed. A transfer by the debtor constitutes an avoidable preference if six elements are shown: (1) a transfer of an interest of the debtor in property; (2) to or for the benefit of a creditor; (3) for or on account of an antecedent debt; (4) made while the debtor was insolvent; (5) made on or within ninety days before the date of the filing of the petition; and (6) one that enables the creditor to receive more than such creditor would receive in a Chapter 7 liquidation of the estate. Adams concedes that five of those elements exist and disputes only the bankruptcy court's conclusion as to the first element. . . .

In order to determine whether property that is transferred belongs to the debtor for purposes of § 547, we apply the "diminution of estate" doctrine. Under this doctrine, a transfer of an interest of the debtor in property occurs where the transfer "diminishes directly or indirectly the fund to which creditors of the same class can legally resort for the payment of their debts, to such an extent that it is impossible for other creditors of the same class to obtain as great a percentage as the favored one." Adams concedes that, generally, transfers by a debtor of borrowed funds constitute transfers of the debtor's property because the borrowed funds, had they not been transferred, would have been available in bankruptcy to satisfy the claims of other creditors.

There is an exception (or perhaps a corollary) to this general rule, however, known as the earmarking doctrine. . . .

The earmarking doctrine applies "when a third party lends money to a debtor for the specific purpose of paying a selected creditor." . . .

*(Continued)*

(Case 24.4 *continued*)

If the debtor controls the disposition of the funds and designates the creditor to whom the monies will be paid independent of a third party whose funds are being used in . . . payment of the debt, then the payments made by the debtor to the creditor constitute a preferential transfer. . . .

The [bankruptcy] court suggested that Superior "controlled" the borrowed funds because the advances from the bank were deposited in Superior's account rather than paid directly to Adams by the bank. This gave Superior "control," the court stated, because possession of the funds gave it the power (though not the right) to divert the loan to another use. . . . The fact that Superior may have had the power to divert the loan after it was deposited into Superior's account does not amount to "control" of funds by Superior. . . .

Accordingly, the proper inquiry is not whether the funds entered the debtor's account, but whether the debtor had the right to disburse the funds to whomever it wished, or whether their disbursement was limited to a particular old creditor or creditors under the agreement with the new creditor. . . .

Here, the bank advanced the funds for the specific purpose of paying a specific creditor, namely Adams. The bank agreed to fund the payments to the extent necessary but only on the express condition that the amounts involved be paid to Adams. . . . Where there is an agreement between a new lender and the debtor that the funds will be used to pay a specified antecedent debt, a debtor has not exercised control over the funds by "designating the creditor to whom the monies will be paid independent of a third party whose funds are being used . . . in payment of the debt." Because the bank disbursed the funds pursuant to such an antecedent agreement, Superior did not exercise "control" over the money even though Superior requested the loan to pay Adams and the funds were placed in Superior's account rather than being paid directly to Adams by the bank.

**› RESULT** The $82,270.90 in payments made by the bank to fund the checks to Adams fell within the earmarking doctrine and were not voidable preferences.

**› CRITICAL THINKING QUESTIONS**

1. Was the $42,439.10 paid to Adams out of Superior's existing funds a voidable preference?
2. Why would a bank advance additional funds to a debtor already in financial trouble? How does the earmarking doctrine affect a bank's willingness to advance new funds?

### *Setoff Rights*

A creditor exercising a setoff right automatically deducts what the debtor owes the creditor from what the creditor owes the debtor. By analogy to the preference provision, creditors who exercise setoff rights within ninety days before bankruptcy can be required to disgorge such offsets to the extent that they decreased their obligations to the debtor within the ninety-day period.

### *Statutory Liens*

The bankruptcy court can avoid certain statutory liens, including those that first arise upon insolvency or that would not have been enforceable against a bona fide purchaser of the encumbered property when the bankruptcy was filed. This prevents state law from creating hidden priorities that would distort the federal bankruptcy distribution scheme.

### *Collective Bargaining Agreements*

The rules for avoiding collective bargaining agreements changed after Frank Lorenzo, the CEO of Continental Airlines, used Chapter 11 to avoid the company's collective bargaining agreements. In the early 1980s, when labor rejected his demands for sizable wage concessions, Lorenzo took Continental into a Chapter 11 proceeding and repudiated its collective bargaining agreements.

Continental emerged from bankruptcy as a nonunion carrier with a reduced wage structure.

Organized labor protested the use of the Bankruptcy Code by Lorenzo (and, increasingly, others) to break unions. In 1984, Congress responded, amending the Bankruptcy Code so that a debtor no longer has broad discretion to unilaterally abrogate its labor contracts. Instead, a debtor may reject collective bargaining agreements over the objection of its unions only if (1) it has presented labor with a proposal showing that rejection is economically necessary and fair to the affected parties; (2) it has bargained to an impasse; and (3) the bankruptcy court finds that, on balance, fairness clearly favors rejection.

# Chapter 11 Reorganizations

Chapter 11 is designed for reorganizing troubled businesses, from single-asset limited partnerships and joint ventures, such as Dow Corning, the manufacturer of silicon breast implants, to huge publicly held corporations, such as the oil giant Texaco, the pharmaceutical manufacturer A.H. Robins, the retailer Kmart, and United Airlines. Chapter 11 has two primary objectives: (1) to rehabilitate a troubled debtor, and (2) to maximize the return to creditors. It has the added benefit of maintaining jobs and preserving other economic benefits to the community. The goal of Chapter 11 is to reorganize the debtor with a new capital structure so that it can emerge from bankruptcy as a viable concern. Chapter 11 is available to individuals, partnerships, corporations, unincorporated associations, and railroads. It is not available to banks, savings and loan associations, credit unions, insurance companies, stockbrokers, or commodity brokers. The majority of Chapter 11 proceedings are filed by corporations.

The treatment of a Chapter 11 debtor's creditors and holders of ownership interests and the future of its business are set forth in a plan developed by one or more of the parties. If the plan meets the statutory requirements and is confirmed by the court, it becomes a master contract that redefines the legal relationships among all who have claims against (or interests in) the debtor; it binds even those who do not consent to its terms.

## Obtaining Credit

The DIP's first priority often is to stay in business and continue (or resume) providing goods and services to customers at a profit. Yet, as observed at the outset, poor cash flow often paves the way to Chapter 11. Although the bankruptcy system does not manufacture money, it may enhance or create some funding possibilities.

### *Customers' Payments*

The debtor's liquidity crisis sometimes stems from a secured lender's insistence that all encumbered customer payments be applied to the loan, leaving little or no cash to operate. If a bankruptcy petition is filed, customer payments on prebankruptcy accounts will remain the lender's cash collateral, but the court may authorize the DIP to use the funds if the lender's position is adequately protected. Such protection might be found in surplus collateral that gives the lender an ample equity cushion, or it might be provided by granting the lender a substitute lien on postpetition inventory and receivables. Of course, the court may underestimate the need for protection, and this risk often prods an otherwise recalcitrant lender to negotiate terms for use of its cash collateral.

### *Extension of Unsecured Credit*

Filing for reorganization may encourage suppliers (and perhaps other lenders) to extend unsecured credit. During the debtor's prebankruptcy decline, conventional trade terms (such as payment due thirty days after invoice) often become unavailable as the debtor falls behind on accounts payable and word of its shaky condition spreads. Fearful that they may recover only pennies on the dollar from credit sales if the debtor collapses, vendors typically begin requiring cash on delivery or even in advance. This only aggravates the debtor's problems. Ironically, the same suppliers, particularly those that are sophisticated and value the debtor's patronage most, may be willing to resume regular credit transactions with the DIP.

Flexibility returns because postpetition debts incurred in the ordinary course of doing business are allowable as administrative expenses, which are accorded priority over virtually all other unsecured claims. Thus, vendors that extend postpetition credit expect full payment on those transactions. In so doing, they may strengthen the debtor's business and promote a greater recovery on their prepetition claims.

### *Secured Borrowings*

The debtor's ability to borrow on a secured basis can be similarly enhanced in a Chapter 11 reorganization, mainly because collateral may be more available. For example, assets acquired after the bankruptcy petition is filed (other than those derived directly from prebankruptcy collateral) will not be subject to prepetition security agreements designed to cover such after-acquired property. Therefore, a debtor that can produce inventory or generate accounts receivable after the bankruptcy filing may have enough unencumbered property to support new secured loans. Moreover, if credit is not otherwise available, the court can authorize borrowing that is secured by a priming lien, provided that the preexisting lienholder is adequately protected. A *priming lien* is a lien that is senior to a previously granted security interest. Thus, for example, a first mortgage on raw land might be involuntarily subordinated to a new lien that will secure a DIP–developer's construction financing.

### Court Oversight

On occasion, the bankruptcy court's oversight alone may help the debtor arrange new secured loans. By obtaining court approval after giving appropriate notice to other creditors, lenders can virtually immunize their repayment rights and security interests from the attacks by other creditors that sometimes undermine prebankruptcy loans.

### Turnover of Debtor's Property

Though usually less expeditious than borrowing, other bankruptcy tools can also help the DIP obtain funds for operations and enhance the value of the estate. Almost anyone can be compelled to turn over property of the estate that could be used by the DIP. Thus, if adequate protection is provided, a lender that has frozen the debtor's deposit accounts at the banking institution or a taxing authority that has seized them may be required to relinquish these funds.

## The Plan

The debtor has the exclusive right to file a plan of reorganization with the bankruptcy court within the first 120 days after the date of the order for relief. The debtor also has the right to obtain creditor approval of the plan within the first 180 days after the date of the order. The court has discretion to extend these time periods in complex cases. After that, any party may propose a plan.

All plans divide claims and equity interests into separate classes according to their legal attributes. For example, lienholders' claims are classified by collateral and rank (often resulting in one claim per class, because each lien confers distinct rights and usually secures only one claim). Relevant priority claims (such as wages or consumer deposits) are put into discrete classes, separate from general unsecured claims. Holders of preferred shares are grouped separately from common shareholders.

A plan must also prescribe treatment for the claims and interests in each class. Some plans simply extend the time for repaying debts; others reduce the amounts payable. A reduction in the amount payable is known as a *composition*. In many cases, creditors exchange all or part of their claims for preferred or common stock or other ownership interests in the business, thereby diluting or extinguishing the rights of the prebankruptcy shareholders. Sometimes the entire business will be sold free of claims, with creditors dividing the sale proceeds. A plan can even call for liquidation and distribution comparable to the Chapter 7 process (to be discussed later in this chapter). Unless they agree otherwise, priority claimants usually are entitled to full payment when the plan becomes effective, except that prepetition unsecured taxes may be paid in installments over six years from the assessment date, with interest at the market rate.

In addition, the plan must explain the intended means for its execution. Plans often provide for payments from cash on hand, future earnings, asset sales, new capital contributions, or some combination of sources.

## Confirmation

To be confirmed, a plan must meet numerous statutory requirements. Some of the less technical requirements are discussed below.

### Feasibility

The plan must be feasible. There is no point in replacing the debtor's existing obligations with a new set of obligations that the debtor cannot meet.

### Best Interests of Creditors

Unless accepted unanimously, the plan must pass the *best interests of creditors test.* Dissenters must be given a bundle of rights with a current value at least as great as the distribution they would receive through a Chapter 7 liquidation.

### Disclosure Statement

Before deciding whether to accept the plan, creditors and shareholders are entitled to receive a disclosure statement that the court has found contains adequate information to enable them to make an informed judgment. This disclosure process largely displaces otherwise applicable laws and regulations governing the issuance and sale of securities, including the requirements of the Securities Act of 1933, described in Chapter 22.

### Acceptance

A creditor class accepts the plan if the affirmative ballots constitute a simple majority and represent two-thirds of the total claim amounts of those voting. An equity class accepts if the favorable ballots represent two-thirds of the voted interests.

### Impaired Claims

If a plan impairs any class of claims, it cannot be confirmed unless at least one impaired class accepts it (excluding favorable votes cast by insiders). Claims are considered *impaired* if the plan does not provide for full cash payment on its effective date and if it alters the creditors' legal, equitable, or contractual rights in any way (except by curing defaults and reinstating the maturity of the claim).

If the basic requirements discussed above are met and all impaired classes accept the plan, the plan should be confirmed.

### Cramdown Confirmation

Even though it is rejected by a class, the plan can still be confirmed by a *cramdown,* that is, confirmed over the objections of creditors. A cramdown can occur only if the court finds that the plan does not discriminate unfairly and is fair and if equitable and if at least one non-insider, impaired class has voted to accept the plan. Although the phrases "does not discriminate unfairly" and "fair and equitable" both have technical meanings that are open to interpretation, the phrase "fair and equitable" is more frequently the subject of debate. If the rejecting class consists of secured claims, the plan ordinarily can be found fair and equitable only if creditors will retain their liens until they receive full payment in cash of the secured claims. The cash payments must have a present value at least as great as the present value of the collateral. If the debtor elects to retain and use the creditor's collateral, the value of the collateral (and thus the secured claim) is the replacement value, that is, what the debtor would have to pay for comparable property.[53] For other creditors and equity holders, the plan will be considered fair and equitable only if no class junior to the naysayers will receive anything under the plan or if the rejecting class is to receive value equivalent to immediate payment in full.

Thus, to cram down a plan that would distribute stock in satisfaction of claims, the proponent must show that the stock will neither overpay nor underpay those who receive it. The value of the stock turns on the going-concern value of the business, which is often a controversial issue. When classes have not accepted a debt-for-stock plan, the confirmation hearing can easily become a battle among expert witnesses arguing over whether higher or lower multiples or multipliers should be used to capitalize the reorganized debtor's expected earnings, which are themselves subject to competing projections.

In the following case, the U.S. Supreme Court considered whether former equity holders could, upon payment of new value, be granted the exclusive right to buy equity in the reorganized venture.

53. Assocs. Commercial Corp. v. Rash, 520 U.S. 953 (1997).

A CASE IN POINT

**CASE 24.5**

**Bank of America National Trust & Savings Ass'n v. 203 North LaSalle Street Partnership**

*Supreme Court of the United States*

*526 U.S. 434 (1999).*

## Summary

**› FACTS** Bank of America National Trust and Savings Association was the major creditor of the debtor, 203 North LaSalle Street Partnership, an Illinois real estate limited partnership. The value of the partnership property mortgaged to the bank was less than the balance due, leaving the bank with an unsecured deficiency of $38.5 million. The partnership sought to cram down over the bank's objection a plan whereby (1) the bank's $38.5 million unsecured deficiency claim would be discharged for an estimated 16 percent of its present value; and (2) certain former partners of the partnership would contribute $6.125 million in new capital over the course of five years, in exchange for the partnership's entire ownership of the reorganized debtor. The old equity holders were the only ones given the right to contribute new capital in exchange for equity.

**› ISSUE PRESENTED** May a debtor's prebankruptcy equity holders, over the objection of a senior class of impaired creditors, contribute new capital and receive ownership interests in the reorganized entity, when that opportunity is given exclusively to the old equity holders under a plan adopted without consideration of alternatives?

**› SUMMARY OF OPINION** The U.S. Supreme Court began by explaining that the objection of an impaired creditor class may be overridden only if the plan is fair and

*(Continued)*

(Case 24.5 *continued*)

equitable. If the claims of the dissenting creditors are not paid in full, then a plan may be found to be "fair and equitable" only if the holder of any claim or interest that is junior to the claims of the impaired unsecured class will not receive or retain any property "on account of such junior claim or interest."[54] The Court characterized this requirement as the "core" of the *absolute priority rule.*

The Court rejected as "beset with troubles" the partnership's argument that property is received or retained "on account of" a junior interest only if the property was in exchange for the prior interest, without any significant new contribution. It instead concluded that "the better reading of subsection (b)(2)(b)(ii) recognizes that a causal relationship between holding the prior claim or interest and receiving or retaining property is what activates the absolute priority rule." At the same time, it criticized the "starchy position" advanced by the government, as *amicus curiae,* that an old equity holder simply cannot take any property under a plan if creditors are not paid in full, reasoning that a truly full-value transaction, whereby the old equity holders pay full value for the new property, would pose no threat to the bankruptcy estate not posed by any reorganization.

In this case, "the exclusiveness of the opportunity, with its protection against the market's scrutiny of the purchase price by means of competing bids or even competing plan proposals, rendered the partners' right a property interest extended 'on account of' the old equity position." The Court concluded:

> Whether a market test would require an opportunity to offer competing plans or would be satisfied by a right to bid for the same interest sought by old equity, is a question we do not decide here. It is enough to say, assuming a new value corollary, that plans providing junior interest holders with exclusive opportunities free from competition and without benefit of market valuation fall within the prohibitions of § 1129(b)(2)(B)(ii).

**› RESULT** The plan could not be approved over the objections of the bank.

**› COMMENT** The Supreme Court has yet to decide whether there is a new value exception to the absolute priority rule, whereby old equity can in effect buy back equity in the reorganized debtor via a contribution of new capital. Each year, bankruptcy courts confirm such plans, but the Court's decision in *Bank of America v. 203 North La Salle Street Partnership* left considerable uncertainty over these plans.

54. 11 U.S.C. § 1129(b)(2)(B)(ii).

### *Plan Negotiations*

Because confirmation by cramdown is both difficult and uncertain, plan proponents frequently try to draft terms that will encourage broad acceptance. For the first 120 days (or for a longer or shorter time that the court may fix), only the debtor can propose a plan. After this exclusivity period expires, any party may propose a plan. Thus, a debtor that does not bargain reasonably may be faced with a competing plan that might be threatened or proposed by a major secured creditor or by the official committee that is appointed in Chapter 11 cases to represent the interests of unsecured creditors. Even if the debtor is the only party proposing a plan, an endorsement from the creditors' committee can be essential to obtain the creditor support necessary to achieve confirmation without a cramdown. Taken together, these dynamics promote negotiation and accommodation among the interested parties. Most successful plans in large Chapter 11 cases reflect such compromises.

## DISCHARGE

Confirmation under Chapter 11 can give reorganized debtors a new financial beginning under the plan. Because entities such as corporations or partnerships are not eligible for a discharge under Chapter 7, they will similarly not be discharged under Chapter 11 in the event of a liquidation. If the business is rehabilitated, the debtor entity is liable for preconfirmation claims only insofar as they are expressly preserved by the plan. No bankruptcy discharge, whether under Chapter 11 or otherwise, protects the debtor's co-obligors, such as guarantors or joint tortfeasors. Increasingly, however, courts are enjoining collecting actions against nondebtor parties under the court's general equitable powers under Section 105(a) of the Bankruptcy Code in order to facilitate the debtor's reorganization. The most frequent example of this occurs in the mass tort bankruptcy. The use of these Section 105(a) injunctions is still the subject of much controversy. In addition, Section 524(g) affords the bankruptcy court the power to issue a channeling injunction in asbestos bankruptcies to provide similar injunctive relief to certain third parties, including insurance carriers, whose liability is derivative from the debtor's liability.

## WORKOUTS AND PREPACKAGED AND PRENEGOTIATED CHAPTER 11 CASES

### *Workouts*

Because the high transaction costs and adverse publicity of a Chapter 11 bankruptcy can be disadvantageous for debtors and creditors alike, the parties often try to negotiate an out-of-court settlement. Such an agreement, called a *workout,* restructures the debtor's financial affairs in much the same way that a confirmed plan would, but it can bind only those who expressly consent.

The foundation of any successful workout is trust. Creditors will not sign an agreement that leaves the business in the hands of managers they consider to be dishonest or incompetent. If the debtor has lost credibility by misleading creditors or evading their reasonable inquiries (a common problem), its management may need to recruit and defer to a turnaround specialist in order to restore confidence. Full disclosure and candor are especially important when creditors are agreeing to accept partial payment in full satisfaction of undisputed debts. The debtor's misrepresentation or concealment of material facts probably would invalidate an otherwise binding release.

Workouts are forged in the shadow of bankruptcy, and the parties measure their concessions against the obvious alternative. The debtor and major creditors may be willing to accept something less than unanimity (for example, to preclude dissenters from extorting preferred treatment), but the deal will unravel if there are too many holdouts. When this risk is apparent from the outset, the workout agreement can be drafted in the form of a Chapter 11 plan. If necessary, and provided the information disclosed in soliciting assent to the agreement was adequate, the debtor can then file for reorganization and use the prepetition votes to transform the workout into a prepackaged Chapter 11 bankruptcy (discussed below).

Regardless of its terms, a workout agreement cannot stop the debtor from taking refuge in Chapter 11 if the restructured obligations prove too great. The right to file bankruptcy cannot be waived. Sometimes, however, creditors have strategic reasons to defer the debtor's filing, perhaps to buttress their positions with new guaranties or to season transfers against the avoiding powers. In any event, if the debtor has broken faith with the workout pact, the court may consider previous creditor concessions in deciding whether to lift the stay, allow creditors to propose a plan at the outset, appoint a trustee, or convert the case to a Chapter 7 liquidation.

### *Prepackaged Chapter 11 Cases*

A prepackaged Chapter 11 case is a popular method for restructuring a troubled company. In a *prepackaged bankruptcy,* the company solicits votes on its plan of reorganization before filing for bankruptcy. Only after it has obtained the required votes in favor of the plan does it file for Chapter 11 protection. If the debtor is a publicly held company, the vote solicitation and the SEC filing are made promptly after the company and its creditors have agreed on the terms.

Although companies use prepackaged bankruptcies to implement many strategies, a company most commonly files a prepackaged Chapter 11 bankruptcy when it believes that the sale of its assets will exceed the costs of the bankruptcy because the Chapter 11 filing will allow it to sell the assets free and clear of liens. One of the reasons that buyers like these bankruptcy sales is that after competitive bidding and notice to all creditors, the sales are approved by the bankruptcy court. As a result, it is unlikely that the buyer of the assets of a company that has filed a prepackaged Chapter 11 case will be sued later for fraudulent conveyance.

In the following case, the U.S. Court of Appeals for the Third Circuit considered a corporate defendant's bid to resolve all of its outstanding asbestos claims in a prepackaged Chapter 11 filing.

A CASE IN POINT

**CASE 24.6**

***In re* Combustion Engineering**

*United States Court of Appeals for the Third Circuit 391 F.3d 190 (3d Cir. 2004), as amended (Feb. 23, 2005).*

## Summary

**› FACTS** Combustion Engineering defended asbestos-related litigation for nearly four decades, until growing personal-injury claims eventually brought it to the brink of insolvency. In the fall of 2002, Combustion attempted a final resolution of its asbestos problems through a prepackaged Chapter 11 bankruptcy reorganization. Combustion contributed half of its assets to a prepetition trust to pay asbestos claimants with pending lawsuits part of the amount of their claims. The remaining, unpaid portion of these claims (the "stub claims") provided prepetition trust participants with creditor status under the Bankruptcy Code. Combustion then filed a prepackaged Chapter 11 plan of reorganization, which included an injunction in favor of Combustion that would channel all of its asbestos claims into a post-confirmation trust created under Section 524(g) of the Bankruptcy Code, which was enacted in 1994 to codify the manner in which asbestos personal-injury claims were resolved in an earlier bankruptcy proceeding involving Johns–Manville. The law allows for the establishment of a trust to pay present and future asbestos claims, enjoins such claims from being asserted against the debtor, and discharges the debtor from all such liabilities.

The Combustion trust procedures split the pending asbestos claims into three categories based on the status of each claim as either settled (in which case, the trust paid 95 percent of the agreed value of the claim); resolved but without a documented settlement agreement (in which case, the trust paid 85 percent of the claim value); and all other claims (for which, the trust paid 75 percent of the claim value). As a result, each claimant was left with an unsecured stub claim that ultimately was impaired under Combustion's soon-to-be-filed bankruptcy plan. The plan was advanced with the support of the claimants' representative, who was appointed as required by Section 524(g). Under the plan, the trust was established to satisfy the stub claims from the prepetition settlement trust and all future asbestos claims. The plan met with significant opposition from a group of insurers and certain asbestos personal-injury claimants, but the bankruptcy court and the district court overruled their objections and approved the plan.

**› ISSUE PRESENTED** Was the process used to confirm the debtor's prepackaged Chapter 11 bankruptcy unfair?

**› SUMMARY OF OPINION** The U.S. Court of Appeals for the Third Circuit concluded that the process used to confirm the plan may have been unfair because it was approved by a group of asbestos claimants who had already been paid 95 percent of their claims, although the plan would provide as little as 18 percent recovery to some other claimants. The court found that Combustion "made a pre-petition side arrangement with a privileged group of asbestos claimants, who as a consequence represented a voting majority despite holding, in many cases, only slightly impaired 'stub claims.'" By winning approval from a group of creditors who had only a fragment of their claim remaining, the court held that Combustion may have violated Section 524(g) of the Bankruptcy Code. The court observed that "[t]his type of manipulation is especially problematic in the asbestos context, where a voting majority can be made to consist of nonmalignant claimants whose interests may be adverse to those of claimants with more severe injuries." However, the court reversed the confirmation on narrower grounds, saying that it lacked both (1) the jurisdiction to adjudicate nonderivative liabilities of certain nondebtor entities and (2) the power to issue a channeling injunction under Section 524(g) of the Bankruptcy Code to protect nondebtor entities from their own separate and independent asbestos liabilities.

**› RESULT** Although the appellate court did not close the door on possible future approval of the plan, it ordered extensive hearings and fact-finding on issues related to the plan's fairness.

### *Prenegotiated Chapter 11 Cases*

A prenegotiated Chapter 11 case combines the advantages of a prebankruptcy negotiation with creditors with the benefits of a postbankruptcy solicitation of votes on the plan of reorganization. In a *prenegotiated bankruptcy,* the debtor files its Chapter 11 petition as soon as it can after reaching agreement on the terms of the restructuring with its key creditors. Votes on the plan are not solicited until after the bankruptcy case is filed, however.

Companies and creditors may prefer a prenegotiated Chapter 11 to a prepackaged Chapter 11 for several reasons. First, complying with federal securities laws is easier in a prenegotiated Chapter 11 due to various provisions in the Bankruptcy Code and the federal securities laws. Second, a company filing a prenegotiated Chapter 11 does not have to publicly disclose its financial condition prior to the filing, which allows the company to run its operations as smoothly as possible during the prefiling period.

A prenegotiated Chapter 11 has one major disadvantage, however. If the debtor is a public company, the earliest the vote solicitation can begin is usually a month after the debtor files for bankruptcy. This means that creditors with nonpublic knowledge of the debtor's financial condition are unable to trade in the debtor's stock during this gap period.[55]

Another possible disadvantage of a prenegotiated Chapter 11 is that the debtor may not be able to obtain a binding postpetition commitment by the participating creditors to support a plan with certain specified terms. This commitment most often takes the form of a lockup. The Bankruptcy Code contains disclosure requirements that must be complied with as part of the plan confirmation process. In *In re Station Holdings Co.,*[56] the bankruptcy judge disallowed certain votes cast in favor of a prenegotiated Chapter 11 because the voters executed lockup agreements committing to support the plan after the debtor filed for bankruptcy, but before they were provided with the required, court-approved disclosure statement. The court found that the lockup violated the Bankruptcy Code's disclosure requirements, which specifically mandate that eligible voters be provided with a disclosure statement before being asked to vote.

## Chapter 7 Liquidations

In a Chapter 7 bankruptcy, sometimes called a *straight bankruptcy,* the trustee liquidates the estate and distributes the proceeds, first to secured creditors (to the extent of their collateral) and then in the prescribed order discussed earlier in the chapter and pro rata within each level.

Any persons, including individuals, partnerships, and corporations, may be debtors in a Chapter 7 proceeding, although certain types of businesses (including banks, savings and loan associations, credit unions, insurance companies, and railroads) cannot file a Chapter 7 proceeding.

### INDIVIDUAL DEBTORS

Individual debtors normally are *discharged*—that is, relieved—from bankruptcy (that is, prepetition) obligations, except for certain nondischargeable debts such as (1) taxes, (2) educational loans (unless repayment would constitute an undue hardship), (3) spousal or child support, (4) fines or penalties, (5) drunk-driving liabilities, and (6) claims arising from "willful and malicious injury by the debtor" under Section 523(a)(6) of the Bankruptcy Code. Punitive damages awarded on account of the debtor's fraudulent acquisition of money, property, services, or credit are also nondischargeable.[57] In *Kawaauhau v. Geiger,*[58] the U.S. Supreme Court found that a medical malpractice claim was discharged because there was no proof that the debtor's tortious conduct was intended to cause psychological or economic harm. Since then several bankruptcy courts have applied *Geiger* to Title VII discrimination cases, wrestling with whether sexual harassment is necessarily willful and malicious conduct, or whether a plaintiff must actually prove that the debtor intended harm. With conflicting trial court decisions and no appellate authority, it remains unclear whether sexual harassment is inherently a nondischargeable intentional tort.

In assessing whether repayment of a student loan would constitute an undue hardship, the most widely used criteria are whether the debtor, for most of the loan repayment period, can maintain a minimal standard of living on current income and expenses; whether the debtor has made good faith repayment efforts; the amount of the debt; the accumulation of interest; and the debtor's claimed expenses and current standard of living. A bankruptcy court may partially discharge student loans when full repayment would impose undue hardship on a debtor.

A Chapter 7 discharge is not available to debtors who have received a discharge in a bankruptcy filed in the preceding six years. It will also be denied if the debtor has mistreated his or her creditors or abused the system, such

55. Neil Cummings, *Smoothing the Way,* DAILY DEAL, Mar. 7, 2003.
56. No. 02-10822 (Bankr. D. Del. Sept. 28, 2002) (unpublished mem. decision).
57. Cohen v. de la Cruz, 523 U.S. 213 (1998).
58. 523 U.S. 57 (1998).

as by fraudulently transferring or concealing property, destroying or falsifying financial information, or disobeying lawful court orders. (Unlike in Chapter 7, a debtor's prior misconduct or discharge within the past six years will not bar Chapter 13 discharge.) The same debts that are nondischargeable under Chapter 7 are also excluded from a Chapter 11 discharge. Also, a Chapter 11 plan that calls for the liquidation and cessation of a business will only afford a discharge to individuals who would have been eligible for one in Chapter 7.

An individual who has filed under Chapter 7 can enter into a contract with a creditor (a *reaffirmation agreement*) whereby the debtor agrees to repay a debt even though the debt would otherwise be discharged in the debtor's bankruptcy case. The creditor must file the reaffirmation agreement with the bankruptcy court, which has the power to disapprove the agreement if the court finds that it is not in the debtor's best interests.

From 1985 to 1997, Sears, Roebuck & Co. unlawfully dunned more than 200,000 consumers who had outstanding debt on Sears credit cards and had filed for bankruptcy protection. Sears persuaded them to sign reaffirmation agreements but failed to file the agreements with the bankruptcy courts. In June 1997, Sears entered into a settlement with the Federal Trade Commission whereby it agreed to refund $100 million to consumers for its improper credit card collection practices.[59] Sears also agreed to write off the unpaid portion of the balances on the invalid reaffirmation agreements.[60]

There is a split in the circuit courts of appeals as to whether an individual debtor who has filed for protection under Chapter 7 may retain property that secures a loan if the debtor remains current on the loan payments without having to reaffirm the debt. The U.S. Court of Appeals for the Ninth Circuit held that a Chapter 7 debtor who was current on his car payments could retain a car financed by a credit union by making the loan payments specified in the loan agreement without having to reaffirm the debt.[61] The Second, Fourth, and Tenth Circuits reached the same result. In contrast, the Fifth, Seventh, and Eleventh Circuits have held that once a debtor decides to retain, rather than surrender, the property, the debtor must claim an exemption, redeem the property by paying off the debt, or reaffirm the debt.

## Bankruptcy Abuse Prevention and Consumer Protection Act of 2005

Prior to the Bankruptcy Abuse Prevention and Consumer Protection Act of 2005, a bankruptcy judge had discretion to determine whether Chapter 7 or Chapter 13 of the Bankruptcy Code was most appropriate for an individual seeking bankruptcy relief. The 2005 Act, however, established an objective income test that bankruptcy judges must use to determine a debtor's ability to pay. Under the 2005 Act, a debtor with income above his or her state's median income who can pay at least $6,000 over five years ($100 per month) is no longer eligible for Chapter 7 and will instead be forced into Chapter 13. (Chapter 13 bankruptcies are discussed below.) The 2005 Act also requires individuals who file for bankruptcy to pay for credit counseling; gives top priority to a spouse's claims for child support among creditors' claims against a debtor; provides special accommodations in the application of the new income test for active-duty members of the armed services, low-income veterans and those with serious medical conditions; and restricts the homestead exemption to $125,000 if the debtor bought his or her residence within three years and four months before filing. Wealthy individuals who file for bankruptcy may still keep their mansions if they bought them at least three years and four months before filing.

## Nonindividual Debtors

Chapter 7 does not provide a discharge for corporations, partnerships, or similar business entities. Once their assets are sold, these debtors essentially become defunct shells whose unpaid obligations have no significance. Thus, from the vantage point of the debtor firm's management, the only virtue of a liquidation may be that the task of selling

**INTERNATIONAL SNAPSHOT**

Winding-up proceedings in Australia are essentially *ex parte:* only the creditors appear before the court. As a result, debtors do not have the same recourse as under U.S. bankruptcy rules. Other countries, such as Germany, do not provide for the complete discharge of debts in bankruptcy; instead, they only arrange for the debts to be paid over time.

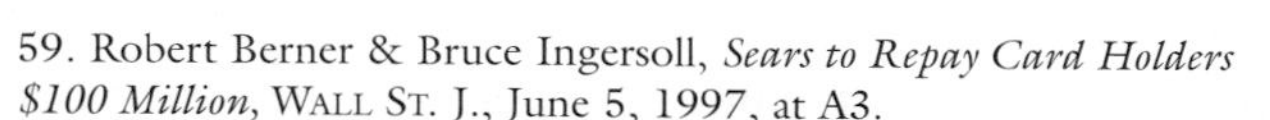

59. Robert Berner & Bruce Ingersoll, *Sears to Repay Card Holders $100 Million*, WALL ST. J., June 5, 1997, at A3.

60. The Seventh Circuit has held that there is no private right of action for damages for a creditor's failure to file debt discharge agreements with the bankruptcy court. Cox v. Zale Del., Inc., 239 F.3d 910 (7th Cir. 2001).

61. McClellan Fed. Credit Union v. Parker (*In re* Parker), 139 F.3d 668 (9th Cir. 1998).

HISTORICAL PERSPECTIVE

## FROM MOSAIC LAW TO VULTURE CAPITALISTS

The principle that debtors should be permitted to discharge certain debts has ancient roots. As early as 1400 B.C., Mosaic law required unconditional forgiveness of debts every seven years to encourage a proper focus on social relationships. The word "bankruptcy" is believed to have evolved from the Latin words "banca" and "rupta," referring to the broken bench or moneychangers' table left behind by failed merchants fleeing from their creditors. In 1542 A.D., during the reign of King Henry VIII, English lawmakers passed a Bankruptcy Act to regulate failing English merchants. Under this law, debtors were considered quasi criminals. Over the centuries, strong sanctions for insolvency, including imprisonment, generally made bankruptcy a remedy for creditors rather than a relief for debtors. For example, a 1604 amendment to the Bankruptcy Act permitted the debtor's ear to be cut off.

The roots of the American bankruptcy system can be traced to the experiences of colonists who were refugees from debtors' prisons in Europe. The drafters of the U.S. Constitution, recognizing the importance of debtor relief, gave Congress the exclusive right to establish national bankruptcy laws and thereby override the states' treatment of debtors and creditors. The first bankruptcy enactments, early in the nineteenth century, contained no provisions for voluntary bankruptcy. Not until 1898, when a severe depression forced many railroads into receivership, did Congress use its bankruptcy power to allow troubled enterprises to reorganize. The Bankruptcy Act of 1898 enabled failing railroads and other businesses to continue operating while reorganizing, generally stripping shareholders of their interests.

Financier J.P. Morgan reorganized so many busted railroads that his work in this area became known as "Morganization." Fifty years after Morgan, the trustee for the estate of Alfred I. du Pont obtained control of the Florida East Coast Railway by holding 56 percent of its defaulted mortgage bonds. Astute purchases of defaulted rail bonds in the 1940s provided the start for a number of Wall Street fortunes.[a]

The Bankruptcy Act of 1898 was overhauled in 1938, when Congress created the Chapter 13 consumer debt adjustment process. In 1978, Congress enacted the Bankruptcy Reform Act, which created the Bankruptcy Code that exists today. That legislation, the result of nearly a decade of intensive study and debate about problems in the bankruptcy system and proposed reforms, made sweeping changes in the law, most of them favorable to debtors.

In light of the massive defaults on junk bonds in 1989 and the early 1990s, some questioned whether Congress gave debtors too much relief under the Bankruptcy Code. The lead-in to a *Forbes* article on the subject summarizes the state of affairs as of 1990: "In the old days, a debt was an obligation and bankruptcy was a disgrace. Nowadays bond issuers concoct ever more ways to stiff investors."[b]

Matthew Schifrin compares the U.S. system with Australian law, which provides that a debtor's property will be auctioned off if the debtor can't pay its debts: "That's why Australian conglomerator Alan Bond is scrambling to save his highly leveraged empire. The bankruptcy laws in Australia have scant provision for reorganization. If you owe and you can't pay, your creditors can liquidate your company."[c]

Even in the United States, however, creditors are fighting back. A new breed, called vulture capitalists, has emerged. They buy up bonds at depressed prices and then seek to throw out existing management. Or as happened to Chapter 11 debtor R.H. Macy & Co. in 1994, a competitor—in this case, Federated Department Stores—can buy up senior debt and promise bondholders more than they might otherwise receive if the debtor stays independent. Then the competitor forces a merger of the two companies as part of the plan of reorganization needed for the debtor to emerge from bankruptcy.[d] The 2005 amendments to the Bankruptcy Code represent another favorable development for creditors.

**a.** Matthew Schifrin, *Enough Already!*, FORBES, May 28, 1990, at 126.

**b.** *Id.*

**c.** *Id.* at 128.

**d.** Patrick M. Reilly & Laura Jereski, *Macy, Federated Reach Accord in Merger Talks*, WALL ST. J., July 15, 1994, at A3.

property and paying creditors falls to a trustee. The principals of closely held companies are often better advised to avoid bankruptcy and to handle these chores themselves. Rather than adhering to the pro rata distribution model, they may wish to prefer some creditors by channeling funds first to those who are most likely to pursue them personally (such as holders of guaranties). Also, they may not want to expose earlier transactions (such as preferential payments) to scrutiny by a trustee, who can become a more troublesome foe than any of the company's creditors by invoking the avoiding powers discussed above.

# Consumer Bankruptcy Under Chapter 13

Chapter 13 (consumer bankruptcy) of the Bankruptcy Code deals with adjustments to the debt of an individual or a married couple with regular income. Although an individual may also be the subject of a Chapter 7 liquidation or a Chapter 11 reorganization, only individuals and small proprietorships are eligible under Chapter 13.

## CHAPTER 13 REQUIREMENTS

Individuals with regular income, including wage earners and individuals engaged in business, may qualify for Chapter 13 status if their unsecured debts do not exceed $307,657 and their secured debts do not exceed $922,975. Chapter 13 is similar to a reorganization in that it provides for a plan for repaying creditors.

Chapter 13 plans can be proposed only by debtors and usually are quite simple. The plan ordinarily allows

### IN BRIEF

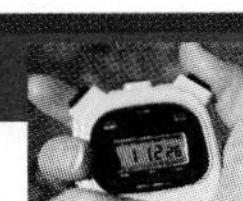

**Advantages and Disadvantages of Bankruptcy**

| Category | Advantages | Disadvantages |
|---|---|---|
| **Debtors** | *Automatic Stay*<br>• Instantly suspends most litigation and collection activities against the debtor, its property, or the bankruptcy estate.<br>*Control*<br>• Debtor retains possession of the bankruptcy estate (unless a trustee is appointed).<br>• Chapter 11 permits the debtor to operate in the ordinary course of business.<br>*Contracts, Leases, and Property*<br>• Debtor-in-possession (DIP) has option of assuming or rejecting prebankruptcy executory contracts or unexpired leases.<br>• DIP may (in certain circumstances) sell property free and clear of liens or other interests. | *Administrative Costs*<br>• Legal and accounting expenses.<br>• Official creditors' committee fees.<br>*Reduction in Autonomy.*<br>• Creditor oversight.<br>• Management's ability to make and implement decisions rapidly and autonomously is curtailed.<br>*Stigma of Bankruptcy*<br>• Morale or confidence problems among staff, vendors, or customers.<br>• Customer anxiety regarding future warranty claims or product support. |
| **Creditors** | *Enhanced Value and Participation*<br>• Preserves going-concern value of an insolvent business.<br>• DIP is more accountable due to bankruptcy reporting and notice requirements.<br>*Equitable Distribution*<br>• When inequitable conduct by any creditor (typically, an insider) has prejudiced others, bankruptcy court has authority to subordinate all or part of transgressor's claim to payment of other creditors.<br>*Involuntary Petitions*<br>• Creditors may file an involuntary petition for relief under Chapter 7 or (more rarely) Chapter 11 and force the debtor into bankruptcy. | *Suspension of Individual Remedies*<br>• Automatic stay stalls foreclosure.<br>• Nondebtor parties to executory contracts and unexpired leases are left in limbo.<br>*Unequal Effects*<br>• Some bankruptcy procedures affect various creditors unequally (e.g., avoiding actions, claim caps, equitable subordination).<br>*Reduced Distribution*<br>• Only a small fraction of Chapter 11 cases filed result in a successful reorganization. Continued operation results in less funds to distribute at liquidation. |

the debtor to retain all of his or her assets, not just those that would be exempt (exempt property was defined earlier in the chapter). However, his or her future disposable income (which would be the debtor's to keep in a Chapter 7 or Chapter 11 bankruptcy) must be paid to a disbursing trustee for the next three to five years. Creditors holding claims secured by a mortgage, deed of trust, or security interest are entitled to the equivalent of the present value of their lien rights, except that Chapter 13 plans cannot modify home mortgage loans unless they provide for payments to cure default. Unlike under Chapter 11, creditors do not vote on Chapter 13 plans. They can, however, object to confirmation if the plan is proposed in bad faith, is not feasible, or offers them less than they would get in a Chapter 7 liquidation.

A Chapter 13 plan may be either a composition plan or an extension plan. In a *composition plan,* creditors receive a percentage of the indebtedness, and the debtor is discharged of the remaining obligation. In an *extension plan,* creditors receive the entire indebtedness, but the period for payment is extended beyond the original due date.

After completing all plan payments, the debtor obtains a Chapter 13 discharge. An earlier discharge may be granted in hardship cases if the creditors have at least as much as they would have under Chapter 7. Apart from the hardship situation, this fresh start (sometimes called *super discharge*) will extinguish otherwise nondischargeable debts (such as claims for fraud, theft, willful and malicious injury, or drunk driving), but not spousal or child support.

### ETHICAL CONSIDERATION

When Italian food giant Parmalat's financial troubles were disclosed in 2003, the company was quickly pushed into bankruptcy proceedings in Italy. Section 304 of the U.S. Bankruptcy Code allows bankruptcy judges to stop creditors of bankruptcies filed abroad from pursuing their claims, or from obtaining discovery, in the United States. The intent of this provision is to encourage harmony among countries by having all creditors pursue their claims in one jurisdiction. Parmalat used Section 304 to enjoin its U.S. creditors. Several months later, however, Parmalat filed a number of lawsuits in the United States against several of these same companies, claiming that they had abetted Parmalat's fraud. Is it ethical for a foreign debtor to use a bankruptcy-related injunction to block counterclaims and discovery in U.S. suits that it initiates outside the bankruptcy proceeding?

## ADVANTAGES OF CHAPTER 13

Chapter 13 has many advantages for overextended consumers. For example, the filing of a bankruptcy petition stops all creditor collection activity other than the filing of a claim in the bankruptcy proceeding. In addition, unlike in a Chapter 7 liquidation, a Chapter 13 debtor does not surrender any assets. A good faith effort to pay creditors can preserve goodwill and future credit prospects. Unfortunately, Chapter 13 debtors are often unable to make the payments outlined in their plan and eventually convert from Chapter 13 to Chapter 7. After conversion, the debtor's nonexempt property is liquidated, and the debtor receives a Chapter 7 discharge.

## *Global View*

### HARMONIZATION OF INSOLVENCY LAWS

As a result of globalization, transnational insolvencies are becoming more common. High-profile international insolvency cases, such as *In re Maxwell Communications Corp.,*[a] which involved a media empire headquartered and managed in England with corporate entities and assets in the United Kingdom, the United States, and Canada, have highlighted the need for international harmonization of insolvency laws.[b] In

a. 93 F.3d 1036 (2d Cir. 1996). A detailed discussion of the Maxwell case is provided in Jay L. Westbrook, *The Lessons of Maxwell Communications,* 64 FORDHAM L. REV. 2531, 2534–40 (1996).

b. Samuel L. Bufford et al., *International Insolvency,* FED. JUD. CENTER (2001). The U.S. bankruptcy judge in *Maxwell* crafted a creative solution to these problems. He appointed an examiner to harmonize the British and U.S. proceedings to permit a reorganization under U.S. law that would maximize the return to creditors. The examiner succeeded in negotiating a joint plan of reorganization under U.S. law and a scheme of administration under British law that provided for the partial reorganization and partial liquidation of the Maxwell companies.

*(Continued)*

(Global View *continued*)

addition to dealing with failed and failing companies, international insolvency law is also an important consideration in international investment and the extension of international credit.

Cross-border insolvency problems are not limited to major multinational corporations. In its simplest form, a *transnational insolvency* involves an insolvency proceeding in one country, with a creditor located in a second country. More complex cases may involve subsidiaries, assets, creditors, and operations in many countries. In the absence of international laws to coordinate insolvency proceedings with transborder implications, multinational insolvency issues are addressed one nation at a time by applying the domestic insolvency laws of each affected country.

The two prevalent domestic models for addressing international insolvency problems are *universality* and *territoriality*. U.S. law is moving toward universality, which tracks international insolvency proceedings as a single case and treats the creditors equally, no matter where they are located. Under territoriality, each nation conducts its own proceeding with respect to the assets located in its jurisdiction and ignores any parallel proceedings in a foreign country.

The coordination of insolvency proceedings with international implications may be governed by at least four sources of international law. These sources represent only modest first steps to coordinate the administration of transnational insolvency proceedings. They do not attempt to harmonize domestic insolvency laws around the world, although efforts at such harmonization have also begun.[c]

## UNCITRAL MODEL LAW ON CROSS-BORDER INSOLVENCIES

The United Nations Commission on International Trade Law (UNCITRAL) has promulgated a Model Law on Cross-Border Insolvencies, which was approved by the UN General Assembly in 1997 but must be enacted by each country.[d] The model law is designed for cases involving a debtor, assets, creditors, operations, or transactions that are located in more than one country. It governs transnational insolvency problems between countries that have adopted the model law. Since 1997, several countries, including Japan, Mexico, South Africa, the United Kingdom, and Eritrea, have enacted or authorized legislation modeled after the law.

The model law provides for more timely and effective procedures for recognizing foreign insolvency proceedings. It also authorizes each accredited representative to participate in foreign courts in countries that have enacted the model law and mandates the cooperation of courts and estate representatives in all countries that have adopted the law.

Several features of the model law are beneficial for U.S. debtors. First, it recognizes debtors-in-possession as proper estate representatives. The domestic insolvency laws of many countries require the appointment of a trustee to represent a bankrupt estate and do not recognize the U.S. concept of DIP. The model law also contains an automatic stay that, as in U.S. bankruptcy law, applies to both unsecured and secured creditors even though the domestic insolvency laws of many countries have automatic stays that apply only to unsecured creditors. Finally, the model law promotes reorganization as a fundamental goal even though many foreign countries currently provide only for liquidation.

c. *Id.*

d. Model Law on Cross-Border Insolvencies, May 30, 1997, 36 I.L.M. 1386 (1997).

## EU REGULATION ON INSOLVENCY PROCEEDINGS

The European Union (EU) Council adopted a Regulation on Insolvency Proceedings effective May 2002. Instead of defining "insolvency," the EU Regulation lists the national laws of the corresponding member states. To promote a more efficient system of legal cooperation on insolvency matters within the EU, the EU Regulation focuses on the jurisdiction for opening and issuing binding judgments in a proceeding by recognizing both a main proceeding that may affect all creditors and property of a debtor and secondary proceedings that will affect only creditors and property of a debtor located in a country other than the country in which the main proceeding is conducted. It also attempts to deal with forum shopping by requiring that the main proceeding be opened in the member state where "the centre of main interests" of the debtor is located. The EU Regulation explains this concept as follows: "In the case of a company or legal person, the place of the registered office shall be presumed to be the centre of its main interests in the absence of proof to the contrary."[e] A main proceeding is generally governed by the internal laws of the member state where the proceeding is initiated. After the opening of the main insolvency proceeding, secondary proceedings may be brought by the liquidator in the main insolvency proceeding or by any party with standing under local law. In addition to protecting local creditors, a secondary proceeding may be useful if a case is too complex to be administered as a single unit. Although the EU Regulation governs the coordination of proceedings only within the EU, its underlying principles and approaches have been influential in the international community.

## ALI TRANSNATIONAL INSOLVENCY PROJECT

The Transnational Insolvency Project of the American Law Institute (ALI) is a source of international insolvency law for transnational insolvency cases that arise in member countries of the North American Free Trade Agreement (NAFTA). The ALI is seeking to encourage cooperation in the administration of bankruptcy cases involving more than one of the three NAFTA trading partners—the United States, Canada, and Mexico—beyond that envisioned under the UNCITRAL model law. Phase I of the project comprehensively reports on the domestic insolvency laws of these three countries, and Phase II identifies principles of cooperation in transnational bankruptcy cases among the members of NAFTA, including recommendations for legislation

e. See EU Reg., pmbl. art. 3(1), O.J. (L 160) (June 30, 2000).

*(Continued)*

(Global View *continued*)

or international agreements. The project proposes the following seven principles that are generally accepted among the three NAFTA countries: (1) courts and administrators should cooperate in transnational cases with a goal to maximizing the value of the debtor's worldwide assets and furthering the just administration of the case; (2) the bankruptcy of a debtor in one NAFTA country should be recognized in each of the other NAFTA countries; (3) bankruptcy cooperation requires a moratorium or stay at the earliest possible time in each country where a debtor has assets; (4) cooperation should include, at a minimum, a free exchange of information obtained in each case concerning assets and claims; (5) where a court has recognized the representative of a foreign proceeding in another NAFTA country, it should be prepared to approve the sharing of the value of the debtor's assets on a worldwide basis; (6) claimants should not be discriminated against based on nationality, residence, or domicile; and (7) a creditor should not be permitted to use distributions in multiple countries to recover in any country more than the percentage recovered by other creditors of the same class in that country.

The ALI project also includes twenty-seven procedural principles, representing either existing practice or a recommended best practice in the United States and at least one other NAFTA country, which it recommends be put into effect under existing law. The principles relate to the initiation of a bankruptcy and the consequences thereof, the administration of the domestic bankruptcy case, the coordination of parallel cases in different NAFTA countries, the treatment of entities within corporate groups, and the resolution of bankruptcy cases.

**CROSS-BORDER INSOLVENCY CONCORDAT**

The Cross-Border Insolvency Concordat, developed by Committee J of the Section on Business Law of the International Bar Association, also regulates and coordinates transnational insolvencies. The Concordat is a collection of general principles that are intended to assist courts and attorneys in coordinating and harmonizing insolvency proceedings that are pending in more than two countries. The Concordant is intended as an interim measure to be used by courts and counsel to guide transnational insolvencies until treaties or statutes are adopted by commercial nations. Because it is not binding law, courts may decide which Concordat principles to apply on a case-by-case basis.

The Concordat envisions that a single administrative forum will be the main forum for a transnational insolvency proceeding and that cases in other country's courts will be subsidiary to the main case. The main forum should coordinate the collection and administration of assets and receive all assets (after payment of secured and priority claims) from the other forums. If there is no main proceeding, the Concordat recommends using its protocol to coordinate the proceedings in the various countries. The Concordat also provides that all creditors in any forum should be able to appear in the other forums without being subject to personal jurisdiction in those forums on unrelated matters. Public information should be shared among creditors in all forums, and nonpublic information should be provided to the official representatives in each forum.

THE RESPONSIBLE MANAGER

## MANAGING DEBTOR-CREDITOR RELATIONS

A responsible manager must understand lender liability risks. The following steps will help lenders minimize those risks.

In negotiating loan terms, the lender should indicate clearly that any commitment must be in writing and approved by the loan committee or other appropriate officials of the lender. The lender's written communications to the borrower should disclaim any commitment if none is intended.

The lender should avoid provisions in loan documents giving it a broad right to control the borrower's management decisions or day-to-day business activities. The lender should refrain from using its financial leverage to influence such activities as the selection of management, the hiring or firing of employees, or the payment of other creditors.

The loan documents should contain a merger clause stating that the written loan documents supersede any prior oral understandings and that the borrower is not relying on any prior oral promise or representation by the lender. The loan documents should provide that any amendment, modification, or waiver of the terms of the documents or of the rights of the parties must be in writing and signed by both the lender and the borrower.

The lender may ask the borrower to insert in the loan documents a waiver of its right to a jury trial. Juries are often perceived as sympathetic to borrowers; a judge may

*(Continued)*

(The Responsible Manager *continued*)

be less likely to award large compensatory or punitive damages to the borrower. The lender may want to specify in the loan documents that any legal action by the borrower must be brought in a court in a specific state or city to avoid the possible disadvantage the lender may have as a defendant in a court in the borrower's home territory. The lender may want to add an arbitration clause to the loan documents, stating that any disputes arising under the loan documents will be resolved through binding arbitration instead of litigation in a court.

The lender should maintain accurate and complete credit files supporting all the actions it takes. Virtually all of the documents in the lender's files may be subject to legal discovery; it is wise to assume that any entry in the credit files may someday be read to a judge or jury in a lender liability case.

The lender should not threaten to take actions that are not yet authorized or that it does not actually intend to take. The lender should give reasonable warning and, if possible, written notice to the borrower before terminating a line of credit, changing an established course of conduct, accelerating a loan, or exercising any remedies. In a workout situation, when the borrower is trying to renegotiate a loan it cannot pay, or when it becomes apparent that the borrower may be preparing a lender liability suit, the lender should consult with legal counsel.

Except when acting as a trustee or other fiduciary, the lender should refrain from giving any legal, financial, or investment advice to the borrower that might create a fiduciary relationship between the lender and the borrower. The lender should be cautious about giving other creditors the borrower's financial history or opinions as to the borrower's creditworthiness.

At all times the lender's loan officers should behave professionally, regardless of their level of frustration with the borrower. Any personality conflicts with the borrower should be avoided. If a personality conflict does develop, the matter should be transferred to other loan officers.

It has become fashionable in some circles to view Chapter 11 as a strategic option for creative business planning. Apart from the fresh start granted to individual debtors, however, the bankruptcy system generally respects a debtor's obligations existing under state or other federal law; it merely provides a forum for dealing fairly, efficiently, and flexibly with the rights of all the creditors and equity holders. Thus, although insolvency is not a prerequisite for relief, a bankruptcy filing is generally not appropriate unless the business is in serious financial difficulties.

If those difficulties are present, the bankruptcy system can be an effective mechanism for overcoming them while preserving a productive enterprise. Yet for each celebrated success, there are countless failed Chapter 11 cases, in which no plan is confirmed and creditors are left with less than they would have received through prompt liquidation. This is partly the price of giving depressed businesses the chance to rebound, but it also reflects fundamental problems.

Many debtors, most of them single-asset or other small businesses, file Chapter 11 cases without any realistic prospect for reorganization. In some instances, the principals refuse to recognize and deal with financial ills until the business is too weak to survive. Continuing their ostrichlike pattern, they then file a Chapter 11 petition, awash in a sort of terminal euphoria and not recognizing that liquidation is inevitable. Other debtors see the writing on the wall but file to buy time, hoping for a miracle cure. Still others file merely to postpone management's impending unemployment.

Congress gave creditors the means to protect their interests, however. If management acts improperly, a trustee can be appointed; if reorganization is improbable, the case can be dismissed or converted to a Chapter 7 liquidation. Unfortunately, these remedies are rarely invoked before the creditors' interests are seriously prejudiced. Not surprisingly, individual unsecured creditors tend to be reluctant to throw good money after bad by policing the debtor's conduct. For the same reason (though with less justification), they frequently decline to serve or participate actively on the official creditors' committee, so this watchdog may be somnolent or nonexistent in smaller cases. Thus, unless a secured creditor is motivated to overcome this inertia, a Chapter 11 case may have a bleak outcome.

Unless prompted by an interested party, the bankruptcy judge ordinarily will not intervene until the situation becomes egregious, as when the DIP does not comply with the rules, such as those requiring regular financial and tax reporting. Because the court is not well equipped to investigate the progress of each Chapter 11 debtor, an abusive case can languish for a considerable time before the court itself initiates corrective action.

The effectiveness of the bankruptcy system depends largely upon knowledgeable and responsible conduct by the interested parties. In general, both debtors and creditors benefit by addressing financial problems early and pursuing a constructive workout. Because the charged emotional climate often makes this difficult, it is important to obtain objective and practical advice from counsel. If a workout is not possible, the debtor's management should consider whether a reorganization is plausible before filing for relief under Chapter 11. If

*(Continued)*

(The Responsible Manager *continued*)

the case is filed, creditors must recognize that meaningful participation, ideally through the official creditors' committee, is usually necessary to protect their interests.

Directors of a corporation in financial trouble assume new responsibilities to protect not only shareholders but the entire community of interests represented by creditors, employees, and other parties with a stake in the continued viability of the corporation. Once a corporation enters the zone of insolvency, the directors owe a fiduciary duty to creditors as well as shareholders.

INSIDE STORY

## RJR NABISCO LEVERAGED BUYOUT

From time to time, a company may incur long-term indebtedness in the form of bonds. The proceeds of such debt will generally be used for long-term purposes, such as the acquisition of machinery or the construction of a new plant. Bonds are usually negotiable and are available for purchase and sale by investors in the public market. The company that sells the bonds, called the issuer, will normally sell them to an underwriter that, in turn, will market them to the public.

The agreement governing a bond issue is contained in a written document called an *indenture*. Like a loan agreement or a note purchase agreement, an indenture contains a description of the terms, or characteristics, of the bonds. Such terms include the interest rate; the security, if any, for the bonds; and the terms for repayment of the principal and retirement of the bonds. In addition, the issuer will make certain representations and warranties about itself, the bonds, and certain promises (or covenants) with respect to what it will or will not do while the bonds are outstanding. Because a public market exists for bonds, many of the terms found in indentures have become standardized.

In the past, the standard indenture did not contain protections against changes in corporate structure, such as leveraged buyouts, mergers, or hostile takeovers. Such events, called *event risks,* cause the prices of high-grade investments to plummet. For example, in a leveraged buyout (LBO), in which the buyer acquires the stock or assets of a company by borrowing large sums of debt and using little equity, the company's assets must be pledged as security for the debt. Frequently, after the LBO is consummated, the acquired company's assets are sold off to reduce the debt burden.

The case of *Metropolitan Life Insurance Co. v. RJR Nabisco, Inc.*[62] arose when two institutional bondholders found themselves holding bonds whose values had declined after the issuer's LBO. They sued the issuer in the U.S. District Court for the Southern District of New York. Even though the indentures did not expressly prohibit an LBO, the bondholders argued that the issuer was required to repurchase the bonds because it had breached an implied covenant of good faith and fair dealing when it entered into the LBO. The court held that, because the written agreement did not contain an express LBO prohibition, to imply a covenant of good faith and fair dealing that prohibited the LBO would add to the indenture a term that was neither bargained for nor contemplated by the parties.

### BACKGROUND

On October 20, 1988, F. Ross Johnson, then the CEO of RJR Nabisco, Inc., proposed a $17 billion leveraged buyout of the company. A bidding war began, and Kohlberg Kravis Roberts & Co. (KKR) submitted the successful bid. KKR's proposal called for a $24 billion buyout valued at approximately $109 per share.

Even before the company had accepted KKR's proposal, the bondholders, Metropolitan Life Insurance Company (MetLife) and Jefferson Life Insurance Company, filed suit. They alleged that the company's actions drastically impaired the value of the bonds they held by "misappropriating" the value of those bonds to help finance the acquisition, thereby creating a windfall to the company's shareholders. The plaintiffs argued that the acquisition contradicted the understandings of the market on which the plaintiffs had relied. They also said that RJR had actively solicited, and received, investment-grade ratings for its bonds; because the ratings would be adversely affected by the LBO, the LBO contradicted a basic premise for their investment.

62. 716 F. Supp. 1504 (S.D.N.Y. 1989).

*(Continued)*

(Inside Story *continued*)

MetLife and Jefferson were sophisticated investors in the bond market, having held approximately $350 million in bonds issued by RJR between July 1975 and July 1988. MetLife had assets exceeding $88 billion and debt holdings exceeding $49 billion. Jefferson had more than $3 billion in total assets and $1.5 billion in debt securities. The court acknowledged that the plaintiffs, like other holders of public bond issues, had acquired the bonds after the indentures had been negotiated and memorialized. Nevertheless, the court noted, the underwriters that ordinarily negotiate the terms of the indentures with the issuers must then sell the bonds; thus, they must negotiate with the interests of the buyers in mind. Moreover, the plaintiffs presumably reviewed the indentures carefully before lending large sums to any company.

The indentures all contained the same basic provisions. None restricted the creation of unsecured debt or the payment of dividends by RJR. All permitted mergers as long as the surviving corporation assumed the existing debt. Two of the indentures had previously included restrictions on incurring the type of debt contemplated by the LBO, but these restrictions had been deleted in subsequent negotiations unrelated to the LBO. In one case, MetLife bargained for a guarantee from the parent of RJR's predecessor, R.J. Reynolds, in exchange for its agreement to delete the restrictive covenants. In the other case, MetLife had bargained for a new rate and different maturity in exchange for such deletion.

## THE COURT'S DECISION

The plaintiffs had argued that the company, explicitly or implicitly, had agreed with the bondholders' premise that the bonds would maintain their investment ratings. However, the court determined that the indentures contained no explicit prohibition against the LBO with KKR and that they unambiguously permitted the LBO. Because the indentures were unambiguous, the court said, the plaintiffs could not introduce extrinsic evidence—that is, evidence outside the indenture language—to show that the intention of the parties was to prohibit the LBO. Thus, documents indicating that MetLife had recognized the risk of an LBO to public debt (but had not taken any steps to protect against such risk) were inadmissible as evidence.

The court said that under certain circumstances, courts will consider extrinsic evidence to evaluate the scope of an implied covenant of good faith. However, the court noted that under applicable precedents, a different rule applied in interpreting boilerplate provisions of indentures used in the securities market. The court explained that boilerplate provisions do not result from the relationship of particular borrowers and lenders and thus do not depend upon the particularized intentions of the parties. Because the efficiency of capital markets relied upon uniform interpretation of indentures, the meaning of boilerplate provisions in such indentures was not subject to case-by-case determination.

The court noted that, even though the plaintiffs had not alleged that an express covenant had been breached, a covenant of good faith and fair dealing could be implied if the "fruits of the agreement" between the parties had been "spoiled." In this analysis, the court determined that the "fruits" guaranteed by the indentures included the periodic and regular payment of interest and the eventual repayment of principal. Yet interest payments had been continuing, and there was no indication that principal would not be paid when due. The court said that a restriction against incurring new debt would be an additional "fruit" or benefit that the parties had not bargained for. The court added that it had no reason to believe that the market, in evaluating bonds, did not discount for the possibility that the issuer might engage in a debt-financed buyout. Thus, the loss in bond value was a market risk that public bondholders accepted.

The court noted that the indentures contained provisions for adding new covenants on the mutual agreement of RJR and the bondholders, and it suggested that these provisions could be used to add restrictions against LBO debt. While acknowledging that huge, sophisticated companies like RJR might not accept such new covenants, the court said that multibillion-dollar investors like MetLife and Jefferson presumably had some say in the terms of the investments they make and continue to hold. If the issuers were to need new infusions of capital, for example, the bondholders would have an opportunity to impose new covenants. Because of the plaintiffs' and RJR's relatively equal bargaining positions, the court concluded that the contract between them was not inequitable.

## PROTECTING AGAINST EVENT RISK

In response to bond purchasers' concern about event risk, underwriters have begun to include new, express covenants. In one recent bond issue, the indenture included a provision granting bondholders the right to sell their bonds back to the issuer in the event of a change of control or LBO. Some lenders have devised debts in which the interest rate is adjusted if the issuer's debt rating is downgraded.

*(Continued)*

(Inside Story *continued*)

Standard & Poor Corporation responded by introducing a rating system called "event risk covenant rankings." Bonds are ranked on a scale of "E-l, strong protection" to "E-5, insignificant or no protection," based on the degree of covenant protection provided in a bond indenture.

## KEY WORDS AND PHRASES

absolute priority rule 940
affirmative covenants 911
after-acquired property 915
amortized 913
antideficiency laws 913
attached 914
automatic stay 929
avoiding powers 933
bankruptcy estate 924
base rate 909
best interests of creditors test 938
call 912
certificate of deposit (CD) rate 909
collateral 913
commercial paper 912
commitment fee 913
composition 938
composition plan 947
conditions precedent 911
continuing guaranty 918
core proceedings 923
covenants 911
cramdown 939
cross-collateralization 915
cross-default 912
debt subordination 920
debtor 914
debtor-in-possession (DIP) 925
discharged 943
*D'Oench, Duhme* doctrine 922
dragnet clause 915
earmarking doctrine 934
economic duress 921
equitable subordination 920
event risk 951
events of default 912
executory contract 930
extension plan 947
finance lease 918
floating 909
floating lien 915
foreclose 913
fraudulent conveyance 934
guarantor 918
guaranty 918
guaranty of collection 918
guaranty of payment 918
guaranty of performance 918
impaired 939
indenture 951
involuntary proceeding 924
ipso facto clause 930
junior debt 920
lien 912
lien subordination 920
limited guaranty 918
London Interbank Offered Rate (LIBOR) 909
maturity date 913
negative covenants 911
noncore proceedings 923
note purchase agreement 908
one-form-of-action laws 913
order for relief 925
participation loan 908
perfecting 914
pledge 914
preferences 934
prenegotiated bankruptcy 943
prepackaged bankruptcy 941
primary debtor 918
prime rate 909
priming lien 938
principal 907
proof of claim 926
purchase-money security interest 916
reaffirmation agreement 944
reference rate 909
restricted guaranty 918
revolving line of credit 913
revolving loan 910
right of setoff 914
secured loan 913
secured party 914
secured transactions 914
security agreement 914
security interest 914
senior debt 920
spread 909
straight bankruptcy 943
subordination 916
super discharge 947
syndicated loan 908
term loan 910
term sheet 909
territoriality 948
360/360 method 910
365/360 method 910
365/365 method 910
transnational insolvency 948
trustee 925
UCC-1 form 916
universality 948
upstream guaranty 919
usury 910
voluntary proceeding 924
waive 912
workout 941

## QUESTIONS AND CASE PROBLEMS

1. Filene's Basement, Inc. hired Kathleen Mason as president of Filene's Basement Division and chief merchandising officer in May 1999. Mason left a high-paying position as president of Home Goods, Inc. to join Filene's at a time when it was already experiencing financial difficulty. The parties signed

an employment agreement that provided, among other things, that Mason would receive three years' salary and other fringe benefits in the event she was terminated without cause. Filene's filed for relief under Chapter 11 in August 1999. After the filing, Mason continued to provide services pursuant to the prepetition employment agreement and received the salary and benefits specified in the agreement. According to Mason, she was induced to remain with the company by the DIP's postpetition promise that her employment agreement was in effect and would be honored. She also spoke with her attorney about the status of the agreement, and he recommended that the DIP seek formal bankruptcy approval of the agreement. Meanwhile, Filene's operations were quickly downsized: thirty-five of its fifty-five stores were closed shortly after the petition date, and on November 9, 1999, Mason was notified that she was being put on "administrative leave," with pay, pending a motion by the DIP to reject her employment agreement. In February 2000, the bankruptcy court granted the motion to reject the employment agreement; Mason was terminated four days later. Mason then filed a "Request for Payment of Chapter 11 Expenses," in which she claimed that her termination benefits specified in the employment agreement were entitled to first priority as administrative expenses because she was terminated after rendering postpetition services. The Official Committee of Unsecured Creditors opposed the request. What will Mason argue in support of her claim for termination benefits? What will the committee argue in opposition? Who wins and on what basis? What, if anything, could have been done to avoid this dispute? [*In re FBI Distribution Corp. v. Mason,* 330 F.3d 36 (1st Cir. 2003).]

2. ABC Food Corporation, a food company with annual sales of more than $1 billion, operated a paper division that supplied ABC with packaging for its food products. ABC's management determined that the company should concentrate on its core business of manufacturing food products and recommended to the board of directors that the assets of the paper division be sold.

   Newcorp, Inc. is a newly formed corporation with two shareholders who have experience in the timber industry. Those two shareholders also jointly own Lumber Corporation, which operates two lumber mills in the state of Washington. Newcorp was formed specifically to acquire the assets of ABC's paper division.

   On February 1, 2004, ABC and Newcorp signed a letter of intent specifying a closing no later than July 1, 2004, subject to Newcorp obtaining satisfactory financing. The letter of intent provided that ABC and Newcorp would enter into a long-term contract whereby Newcorp would supply specified quantities of paper packaging to ABC.

   On February 15, 2004, Newcorp approached the Bank of Hope to request a term loan to acquire the assets of ABC's paper division and a revolving line of credit to meet its day-to-day working capital requirements. On March 31, 2004, the Bank of Hope delivered to Newcorp a letter stating that it would agree to extend a credit facility to Newcorp on the terms and conditions described in a term sheet attached to the letter.

   Bank of Hope required, as a condition to its credit facility, that the credit be secured by all fixed and current assets of Newcorp. Carlos Banker, the account officer for the bank, took all steps necessary to give Bank of Hope a valid first-priority lien on all collateral.

   A major source of revenue for Newcorp will be the long-term supply contract with ABC. The Bank of Hope is requiring an assignment of the supply contract. The assignment would prohibit ABC and Newcorp from making any amendments to the contract without the bank's consent.

   **a.** You are a manager of Newcorp. What objections would you have to such an assignment?

   **b.** You are a manager of ABC. Any objections?

3. Assume the facts in Question 2. One of the terms of the Bank of Hope's loan is a guaranty from each shareholder and from Lumber Corporation.

   **a.** You are Sylvia Daily, president of Newcorp. As president, you will be involved in the day-to-day operations of Newcorp. What arguments might you make against giving such a guaranty?

   **b.** You are Joe Lucre. You own 51 percent of the stock of Newcorp, and you made loans to Newcorp during the initial stages of its existence. You have since left the running of Newcorp to Sylvia Daily and other managers. What arguments could you make against giving such a guaranty?

   **c.** You are the Bank of Hope's attorney. What advice would you give the bank about taking a guaranty from Lumber Corporation?

4. Assume the facts in Questions 2 and 3. On June 1, 2004, Revolving Credit Bank takes over the revolving line of credit from Bank of Hope and acquires

Bank of Hope's security interest in Newcorp's accounts receivable and inventory. Beginning in early 2005, due to a combination of internal and external conditions, Newcorp's business failed to generate sufficient revenue to meet its debt obligations. The loan agreement between Newcorp and Revolving Credit Bank contains an advance clause, which states that Revolving Credit Bank may, at its discretion, advance up to $2 million based on eligible accounts receivable and inventory. Revolving Credit Bank informed Newcorp that Newcorp has failed to maintain certain financial covenants contained in their credit agreement. Without declaring a default, Revolving Credit Bank then required Newcorp to establish a locked-box arrangement with the bank so that all payments made to Newcorp could be used first to repay any advances outstanding. On March 1, 2005, Newcorp's treasurer called Valerie Lender, Revolving Credit Bank's account officer, and asked for a $350,000 advance to cover checks that would be presented to the bank that day. Revolving Credit Bank refused to lend the full amount requested but did advance $200,000 to pay certain suppliers.

You are the manager of one of Newcorp's trade creditors that has not been paid. Do you have any rights against Revolving Credit Bank?

5. Assume the facts in Questions 2 through 4. In April 2005, Newcorp began to have difficulty meeting its monthly repayment obligations on the term loan from the Bank of Hope. Although Newcorp never missed a payment, the payments were all a few days late. In May 2005, Carlos Banker called the treasurer at Newcorp, assuring him that the Bank of Hope "would stand by the company" and that Newcorp should do whatever it could to keep the payments current. In September 2005, Revolving Credit Bank, concerned about continuing deteriorating conditions, decided to initiate foreclosure proceedings. The Bank of Hope followed suit only after Revolving Credit Bank began foreclosure proceedings. When the Bank of Hope began foreclosure proceedings against the paper plant, it discovered that the nearby Temecula River was polluted due to wastewater discharged from the plant.
   - **a.** You are a manager of Newcorp. What defenses would you raise against Revolving Credit Bank's foreclosure? Against the Bank of Hope's foreclosure?
   - **b.** You are a manager of Revolving Credit Bank. How would you respond to Newcorp's arguments?
   - **c.** You are a manager of the Bank of Hope. How would you respond to Newcorp's arguments? Should the Bank of Hope proceed to foreclose against the plant? Should it require Newcorp to clean up the river? What recourse does the Bank of Hope have against Newcorp if it does not foreclose? Does it have any recourse against any other party?
   - **d.** You are a manager of ABC and hold a junior deed of trust on the property. How would you react to the Bank of Hope's latest action?
   - **e.** Was the Bank of Hope's foreclosure ethical?
6. In August 1989, Bruce G. Murphy invested $515,672 in a limited partnership interest in Orchid Island Associates Limited Partnership, which was developing the Orchid Island Golf and Beach Club Project in Florida. The general partner had projected a 6.1 multiple return on investments. In the period from the fall of 1988 until the beginning of 1991, Southeast Bank provided loans for the project totaling $50 million. Orchid eventually defaulted on its loans, and Southeast foreclosed on the property. Southeast itself was declared insolvent in September 1991 and placed in FDIC receivership. Ultimately, after all of Southeast's creditors had been paid, there was a $150 million surplus available for distribution to its shareholders.

   In 1992, Murphy sued the FDIC, as receiver for Southeast, alleging that Southeast asserted extensive control over the project and that Southeast knew about and participated in the general partner's fraudulent misrepresentation that projections by Arthur Andersen & Co. reflected a "6.1 multiple return" on his investment. Murphy claimed that Southeast acted in concert with Orchid in making decisions pertaining to the Orchid development, and that these decisions were separate and apart from Southeast's role as a mere lender to Orchid. Murphy sued for breach of fiduciary duty, breach of contract, accounting deficiencies, fraud, negligent misrepresentation, and securities violations. What facts would Murphy have to prove to establish his claims against Southeast's receiver, the FDIC? What defenses are available to the FDIC? Who is likely to prevail? [*Murphy v. FDIC*, 208 F.3d 959 (11th Cir. 2000); *Murphy v. FDIC*, 61 F.3d 34 (D.C. Cir. 1995).]
7. Optimistic Enterprises, Inc. (OEI) has developed and patented a product for the home entertainment industry. Some industry experts predict that in two to five years the market for this technology could grow to $200 million in annual sales. Unfortunately,

due to a series of mistakes by management, the product has failed to gain traction in the marketplace. OEI is also being sued for patent infringement by its chief competitor. OEI has operated at a loss, and its current expenses exceed revenues by $250,000 on a quarterly basis. OEI has a revolving line of credit with BankOne; the credit facility is secured by a lien against all of the company's assets. OEI's balance sheet is as follows:

| Assets | |
|---|---|
| Cash | $1,000,000 |
| Accounts receivable | 5,000,000 |
| Inventory | 2,000,000 |
| Equipment | 1,000,000 |
| Total assets | $9,000,000 |

| Liabilities and Equity | |
|---|---|
| Accounts payable | $5,000,000 |
| Note payable to BankOne | 1,000,000 |
| Other liabilities | 1,000,000 |
| Total liabilities | $7,000,000 |
| Shareholders' equity | 2,000,000 |
| Total liabilities and equity | $9,000,000 |

OEI has exhausted all efforts to cut its operating expenses, including two rounds of employee layoffs. The company has stretched its accounts payables to ninety days or longer, except for key suppliers, and resorted to making partial rent payments for its manufacturing facility. Included within OEI's "other" liabilities are accrued, but unpaid, employee withholding taxes in the amount of $250,000.

Antonio Pardelli, a significant shareholder and director of OEI, has formed Pardelli Acquisitions Corporation (PAC) to acquire OEI's technology, inventory, and manufacturing equipment. He has presented OEI's board with PAC's offer to buy these assets for $3 million in cash. As part of the offer, PAC will acquire OEI's key engineers and attempt to renegotiate the lease to continue operating at the same location. PAC has also agreed to fund separate severance packages for OEI's senior executives upon closing of the sale. PAC will not assume any of OEI's debts. OEI will retain its cash and accounts receivables. PAC has waived any due diligence or other contingencies to the sale, provided that the sale closes in ten days. Is OEI in the zone of insolvency? Should the OEI board accept PAC's offer? What actions, if any, should OEI's board undertake before considering or accepting the offer? What actions, if any, could creditors take to challenge or threaten the sale? Should OEI consider filing for bankruptcy?

8. Venito, Inc. has just filed a voluntary petition under Chapter 11. Its primary asset was an unexpired lease for 9,000 square feet of office space in New York City at a rent of $27.50 per square foot (market rate in 2003). The lease was signed on January 31, 2003, and expires on January 31, 2011. Concurrent with execution of the lease Venito paid a $1 million security deposit ($500,000 in cash and $500,000 in the form of a letter of credit). The lease includes a provision stating that it terminates upon the lessee's insolvency or on the filing of either a voluntary or an involuntary petition in bankruptcy by the lessee. The lease also prohibits assignment or subletting without the landlord's consent. Venito had not paid rent for three months prior to the petition date, and it is currently in default on the lease. Prior to the petition date, the landlord had started eviction proceedings by serving a three-day notice to quit, but it had not yet retaken physical possession of the building.
   a. Assume that rental rates have increased to $50 per square foot. Venito has filed a motion with the bankruptcy court to approve assumption of the lease and assignment of it to Radical Media. Venito proposes to keep the $350,000 profit it will make on assignment of the lease. Is the lease an executory contract? Can Venito assume and assign the lease without the landlord's consent? Can the landlord file a motion to dismiss Venito's case for bad faith? Who will keep the profit on the lease assignment?
   b. Assume that rental rates have fallen to $10 per square foot, Venito does not pay the rent for two months after the petition date, and Venito files a motion to reject the lease. What rights/claims does the landlord have regarding the unpaid rent? Can Venito reject the lease? What are the landlord's rights to the cash and letter-of-credit security deposits?
9. Assume the facts in Question 8. Venito has a license from Langhorn, Inc. to make, use, and sell a patented product. The license provides that it terminates upon the licensee's insolvency or on the filing of a voluntary or involuntary bankruptcy proceeding by the licensee. It also provides that the license cannot be assigned without Langhorn's consent. At the

time that Venito filed its petition, it had not paid license fees for three months, but Langhorn had not yet sent a notice of default as required by the license. Subsequent to filing the petition, Venito filed a motion to assume the license and assign it to Radical Media. Does the license terminate upon the filing of the bankruptcy petition? Can it be assumed and/or assigned without Langhorn's consent? Can Langhorn terminate the license after the bankruptcy filing? What must Venito do to assume and assign the license?

### MANAGER'S DILEMMA

10. MNVA was a Minnesota corporation engaged in operating a short-line freight railroad. Larry and Diane Wood were officers and directors and major shareholders of MNVA, and DMVW was a wholly owned subsidiary of MNVA. In August 1994, MNVA agreed in principle to the terms of a letter of intent with Pioneer Railcorp under which Pioneer agreed to acquire MNVA's operating assets by purchasing MNVA's stock. MNVA decided to spin off DMVW to MNVA shareholders as part of the reorganization of MNVA in connection with the sale to Pioneer. In October 1994, the deal between MNVA and Pioneer was restructured as a sale of assets. On November 21, 1994, the MNVA board of directors determined that it would be able to pay its debts in the ordinary course of business after the proposed distribution of DMVW stock to MNVA shareholders and approved the distribution of DMVW stock to the existing MNVA shareholders in proportion to the percentage of stock they owned in MNVA. No consideration was paid to MNVA for the distribution of DMVW stock. DMVW became an independently operated entity after the distribution. In December 1994, MNVA sold its assets to Pioneer in exchange for $1 and the assumption of certain secured debts; it thereafter ceased operations.

    In May 1996, Helm Financial obtained a state court judgment against MNVA for railcar leasing fees in the amount of $96,028, plus interest and attorneys' fees and costs, but MNVA had insufficient assets to pay them. According to MNVA, during the course of winding up its affairs, it was unable to pay all of its creditors in full because it experienced an "unexpected shortfall" after losing several substantial claims, including one against the Minnesota Department of Transportation for reimbursement of track rehabilitation expenses.

    In June 1997, Helm sued MNVA, DMVW, and the individual officers and directors of MNVA, alleging that the distribution of DMVW stock to the MNVA shareholders defrauded MNVA's creditors in violation of the Minnesota Uniform Fraudulent Transfer Act and constituted an unlawful preference of the defendant officers, directors, and shareholders over MNVA's creditors in breach of their fiduciary duty to the creditors. Helm alleged that the spinoff left MNVA insolvent because DMVW was MNVA's most valuable asset.

    Was the distribution of the DMVW stock a fraudulent transfer? Did the Woods violate their fiduciary duty to creditors, such as Helm? Under the Minnesota corporation law, a distribution to shareholders is permitted only when "the corporation will be able to pay its debts in the ordinary course of business after making the distribution and the board does not know before the distribution is made that the determination was or has become erroneous." Did the Woods and their fellow officers and directors act ethically? Would your answer be any different if instead of distributing shares of a subsidiary as a dividend, the board had voted to repay preexisting loans from the Woods to MNVA? [*Helm Financial Corp. v. MNVA Railroad, Inc.*, 212 F.3d 1076 (11th Cir. 2000).]

## INTERNET SOURCES

| | |
|---|---|
| This site provides links to bankruptcy journals and publications and to law firm websites providing bankruptcy information. | http://findlaw.com/01topics/03bankruptcy |
| This site, maintained by the American Bankruptcy Institute, includes legislative updates. | http://www.abiworld.org |

*(Continued)*

(Internet Sources *continued*)

| | |
|---|---|
| The Bankruptcy Lawfinder site, maintained by the law offices of Warren E. Agin in Massachusetts, provides answers to frequently asked bankruptcy questions. | http://www.agin.com |
| This site, maintained by Cornell Law School, contains a full-text version of UCC Article 9. | http://www.law.cornell.edu/ucc/9 |
| This site is maintained by the Turnaround Management Association, the only international nonprofit association dedicated to corporate renewal and turnaround management. | http://www.turnaround.org |
| This site, maintained by LawResearch, Inc., contains a directory of international bankruptcy laws. | http://www.lawresearchservices.com |
| This site, maintained by Cornell University, contains a guide to world bankruptcy law. | http://www.lawcornell.edu/topics/bankruptcy.html |
| This site provides a unique guide to international bankruptcy laws. | http://www.hg.org/bankrpt.html |

# UNIT VII

# INTERNATIONAL BUSINESS

CHAPTER 25

# International Law and Transactions

## INTRODUCTION

### MANAGING IN A GLOBAL ECONOMY

A domestic company must follow the laws of its home country. A multinational company must obey the laws of its home country, but it also must follow the laws of all of the host countries in which it operates, as well as a variety of international treaties, customs, and trade practices. Unfortunately, these laws sometimes are in conflict with each other.

Understanding and applying these laws becomes more difficult if the countries involved use different legal systems. The United Kingdom and most of its former colonies, including the United States, use a common law system, which is based primarily on a collection of decisions rendered by judges in individual cases. Most other countries have adopted civil law systems, which are primarily based on comprehensive legal codes, often developed from a single drafting event. A few countries have adopted Islamic, Hindu, or Socialist legal systems.

The laws of the host countries in which a multinational company operates affect these companies in a variety of ways. Some of the laws, like labor, securities, banking, consumer protection, environmental, and intellectual property laws, are primarily designed to regulate the company's conduct within the host country and have been addressed in other chapters of this book.

A host country may also enact laws that are intended to regulate foreign-owned firms that are operating in its jurisdiction. On occasion, host countries have nationalized certain foreign-owned businesses. Some countries also regulate the percentage of foreign ownership of businesses that are incorporated within their borders. Many countries impose restraints on the ability of a multinational business to repatriate, or return to its home country, profits earned in the host country.

The laws of a multinational company's home country govern activities that occur within that country's borders. The home country may also have laws that attempt to regulate business activities of the company that are conducted outside the home country's borders. For example, the U.S. antitrust, foreign corrupt practices, and product safety laws purport to regulate certain offshore business activities of companies. Other laws, including sanctions, embargoes, and export laws, are designed to regulate the international trade activities of these companies.

The Asian financial crisis of the late 1990s and its impact on the U.S. economy underscored the existence of a global economy and the importance of international trade. Total U.S. trade in goods and services reached $2.5 trillion in 2003, representing $1 trillion in exports and $1.5 trillion in imports. In addition, there is a growing internationalization of production and service delivery. Whereas in the past U.S. companies mostly outsourced production jobs, now many service-sector jobs are also being moved overseas. Estimates of the number of jobs affected vary wildly. The McKinsey Global Institute suggests that offshore outsourcing may increase by 30 to 40 percent per year for the next five years, while Forrester Research predicts that 3.3 million white-collar jobs may be relocated overseas by 2015.[1]

International treaties and trade regimes, ranging from bilateral friendship, navigation, and commerce agreements to the regional

1. John McKay, *Outsourcing: Separating Fact from Hysteria*, Dec. 23, 2004, *at* http://www.techcentralstation.com/122304A.html.

North American Free Trade Agreement and the multilateral World Trade Organization, form a major part of the legal and economic environment in which multinational businesses operate. The most comprehensive effort to achieve regional integration is the European Union, which has an ultimate objective of complete economic, monetary, and political integration.

Managers in today's global economy can expect to engage in many types of international business transactions, including the sale and leasing of goods and services, transfers of technology, equity investments, and international lending. These transactions create a wealth of issues and risks, but they also provide opportunities that may not be seen in many domestic transactions. Because of the many overlapping laws and regimes, companies engaging in cross-border transactions rely heavily on contractual arrangements to address issues. In particular, contracts between companies located in different countries should address choice of law, choice of jurisdiction, and choice of a dispute resolution mechanism.

## CHAPTER OVERVIEW

This chapter begins with a discussion of the most common legal systems used by the world's countries. It discusses the various sources of international law, including treaties, customary practices, and decisions of international, national, and regional courts. It then discusses how national laws of both home and host countries are used to regulate the activities of multinational companies. The chapter then outlines the U.S. trade regime and certain international trade regimes such as the North American Free Trade Agreement and the World Trade Organization. It outlines the various types of regional trading alliances, focusing on the European Union, which is the most visible example of an economic union. The chapter then shifts to a review of some of the legal issues involved in international business transactions, as well as the laws governing doing business with and litigating against foreign governments.

# National Legal Systems

The legal systems used by the world's countries vary dramatically.

## COMMON LAW

Common law legal systems are used in countries that are or were British territories or colonies (with the exception of a few British colonies that had adopted civil law systems before they were taken over by the British). *Common law legal systems* primarily rely on case law and precedents. As a result, common law judges use accumulated past judicial decisions on a particular kind of dispute to form general rules (*precedents*) to serve as guidelines for similar cases in the future. A judge can depart from precedent and establish a new rule, however, if the case presents different or new considerations and facts. This new rule may itself become a precedent if it is accepted and subsequently used in other cases by different judges.

An important aspect of common law systems is the existence of different levels of courts to define and further refine the law, starting with the trial courts that normally consist of a single judge and a jury. To reach a judgment or verdict, the jury in a trial court applies the law, as stated by the judge, when determining the facts. Appellate courts form the next level in the judicial common law system. Appellate courts, which consist of judges, do not deal with the factual determinations made by the jury; instead, they only review whether the judge of the trial court applied the correct principles of law.

Statutes and codes exist in common law systems. They are created either through *codification*, a process in which existing common law positions are restated and laid down in a statute, or by enacting new *statutory law* that is not based on existing common law rules. Courts can declare statutory law unconstitutional in common law systems.

The principle of equity is unique to common law legal systems. The very formal character of the traditional English common law system, especially with regard to remedies, made exceptions necessary. As a result, the English common law system incorporated the royal prerogative to grant these exceptions, referred to as *equity*, in individual cases in the interest of justice. Initially, common law and equity were separate systems, each with its own courts. Later, these two systems were merged, but even today, the distinction between law and equity remains important. For example, the Seventh Amendment to the U.S. Constitution guarantees the right to a jury trial "in suits at common law," but no similar right is guaranteed in equity proceedings. As a result, it is necessary to ascertain whether a claim is legal or equitable in order to determine whether a jury trial is constitutionally guaranteed.

Although the U.S. legal system is undeniably rooted in the English common law legal system,[2] there are a number of differences between the current British and

2. The state of Louisiana, which was once a French, and later a Spanish, colony, is the only U.S. state that has a civil law system for matters that are not criminal in nature.

U.S. common law systems. Unlike the U.S. system, the British common law system does not use juries in civil cases. It allows for only limited *discovery* (the phase in a civil lawsuit before the trial, when each party can request documents and other evidence from the other party); has no *class-action lawsuits;* prohibits the payment of lawyers on a *contingency-fee* basis (in which the attorney receives a percentage of the judgment awarded to his or her client); and requires the losing party in a lawsuit to pay both its own attorneys' fees and those of the prevailing party. The British system has two types of lawyers: solicitors and barristers. A *solicitor* is allowed to perform legal services outside the court, but only *barristers* may argue in court.

## Civil Law

*Civil law legal systems* are based on Roman law as consolidated in the Corpus Juris Civilis (also called Justinian's Code after Justinian, the Roman emperor who initiated the consolidation) in A.D. 533 and 534. In the eighteenth century, stronger national systems were established all over Europe, and this led to the creation of separate national codes. The most prominent example was the French Napoleonic Code, which influenced the development of other national civil codes, especially in countries that were once under French control.

Civil law systems are found not only in Europe but also in countries that were once colonies of European countries. Several Asian countries have adopted civil law systems based on or modeled after European civil law systems. For example, Japan, South Korea, and Taiwan used the German Civil Code as the basis of their respective civil law regimes.

Civil law primarily relies on statutory laws that are embodied in a unified code. Lower courts usually cannot declare these statutes unconstitutional. Civil law systems generally draw a strong distinction between *private law* (the area of the law in which the sole function of government is the recognition and enforcement of private rights, e.g., civil and commercial codes) and *public law* (the area of the law that focuses on the effectuation of the public interest by state action, e.g., constitutional law, administrative law, and criminal law). Some civil law countries have different courts for private and public law.

Traditionally, civil law statutes and codes tend to be more abstract than codified common law to cover a wider range of facts. Civil law judges use analogies to apply the existing statutes and codes to new cases and discuss the underlying general principles at length. Judges also often use the work of legal scholars in reasoning and deciding the case at hand. Far less frequently, civil law judges use decisions in prior cases to further refine their decisions.

Judges play a different role in civil law systems than in common law systems. Common law judges are expected to be more creative when applying the law than civil law judges are. In addition to applying the law, common law judges also create law to balance the power of the legislature. In contrast, a civil law judge is bound by the existing statutes and codes as they were created by the legislature. In common law systems, the judge is a neutral party in the proceedings, whereas a civil law judge assumes many of the roles of a lawyer in a common law system, such as deciding what evidence needs to be developed or produced. Civil law systems make only very limited use of juries, if at all.

This discussion has focused on how common law and civil law systems differ, but increasingly there are also similarities. As case law has become more important in civil law systems and statutory law has become more important in common law systems, the differences between the two legal systems have become less distinct.

## Other Families of Law

Although common law and civil law systems predominate, some countries have adopted other forms of legal systems.

### Islamic

The traditional Islamic rules and laws that regulate Muslim life are called *Sharia* (also Shari'a or Shariah). Civil law in Islamic countries is interpreted in harmony with the Sharia. To honor agreements and observe good faith in commercial dealings is a central premise of Islamic law. Islamic trade and commerce is governed by the tenets of Riba and Gharar. *Riba* prohibits unearned or unjustified (illicit) profits and can therefore lead to problems when interest is charged on loans. *Gharar* refers to an event whose outcomes are unknown. Islamic law forbids Gharar if it will lead to exploitation. For example, an open-ended contract contains Gharar and therefore may be void. All gambling contracts have excessive Gharar that renders them void.

### Socialist

The term "Socialist law" is used for the legal systems in Communist states. Socialist law systems are based on civil law systems with changes and additions from the respective ideological background (mostly Marxist-Leninist). One of the most important aspects of a Socialist system is public ownership of property and the means of production. Today, only a relatively small number of states still have Socialist law systems. Some of them such as China have adapted their legal system to account for the market-oriented changes in their economic system.

IN BRIEF

**Comparison of Common Law and Civil Law**

| Common Law | Civil Law |
|---|---|
| Developed in Britain | Origins in Roman Republic |
| Adversarial | Inquisitional |
| Case based | Code based |
| Inductive (specific to general) | Deductive (general to specific) |
| Relies on precedent | Little reliance on precedent |
| Little distinction between public and private law | Distinguishes between public and private law |
| Equity courts/theories | Equitable doctrines, if any, must be written into the code |
| Judicial system usually drawn as a pyramid with the "highest" court at the top | Judicial system divided between private law courts and public law courts |
| Jury system | No or limited jury system |
| Strict rules of evidence | Looser rules of evidence |
| Pretrial discovery | Limited pretrial discovery |
| Integrated court system with courts of general jurisdiction that adjudicate criminal cases and most types of civil cases | Specialty court systems and specialty courts that deal with different areas of law (constitutional, criminal, administrative, commercial, and civil or private law) |
| A trial is a single event. | A trial is an extended process with a series of successive hearings and consultations. |
| Judges act as managers or referees of the lawyers acting in adversarial roles, and are secondary to the lawyers. | Judges use an inquisitorial process in which the judge is the principal interrogator of witnesses. |
| Judges search creatively for an answer to a question or issue among many potentially applicable judicial precedents. | Judges are appliers of the law. |
| Judges are selected as part of the political process for a specific judicial post that they hold for life or for a specified term; there is no system of advancement to higher courts as a reward for services. | Judges are usually part of the country's civil service. |

### *Hindu*

Classical Hindu law contained a set of rules, customs, and usages to guide the life and beliefs of Hindus. In today's India, Hindu law is applied only to very personal matters, namely marriage, divorce, and inheritance/succession questions, and is therefore referred to as "Personal law." Most other legal issues in India are governed by codified Indian law, which is a secular law based on English common law but tailored to the needs of Indian society.

## Sources of International Law

International law is often divided between public international law and private international law. *Public international law* governs the relationships between and the interactions of nations, whereas *private international law* governs the relationships between private parties engaged in transactions across national borders.

While national law normally is enacted by the legislative body of a country, there is no similar legislative body that creates international law. Therefore, in most cases,[3] at least two nations are involved in creating the legal rules that will be applied as international law.

### TREATIES

Most international rules of law are set forth in written agreements between or among two or more countries, called treaties, although they may also be referred to as conventions, pacts, protocols, or accords.[4] The Vienna Convention on the Law of Treaties defines a *treaty* as "an international agreement concluded between states in written form and governed by international law."[5] This Convention, which was signed but not ratified by the United States, sets the rules for all phases of a treaty, including negotiation, signature, ratification, entry into force, and termination.[6]

The sheer quantity of treaties—now more than 30,000—demonstrates their usefulness in defining international relations.[7] Each country must determine who is

3. In some instances, unilateral actions, like declarations of a state, can also be regarded as creating binding legal effects.

4. Treaties can bind two states bilaterally or more than two states multilaterally.

5. Vienna Convention, art. 2(1)(a). United Nations, Treaty Series, vol. 1155, p. 331.

6. See http://untreaty.un.org/english/bible/englishinternetbible/parti/chapter xxiii/treaty1.asp for a list of signatories.

7. While all treaties between 1648 and 1919 could be stored in 226 books, the treaties between 1920 and 1946 fill another 205 books and those between 1946 and 1999 an additional 2,039 volumes. MARK W. JANIS, AN INTRODUCTION TO INTERNATIONAL LAW 11 (3d ed. 1999).

POLITICAL PERSPECTIVE

## THE IMPORTANCE OF FAST-TRACK AUTHORITY FOR U.S. PRESIDENT

For the first time since President Franklin Delano Roosevelt began cutting tariffs in 1934, a U.S. president lost a significant vote in Congress for trade liberalization when Congress denied President Bill Clinton fast-track negotiating authority in 1997. The U.S. Constitution grants the president the power to enter into treaties, but he or she must obtain the consent of two-thirds of the senators present, a requirement that has almost always resulted in a renegotiation of any treaty presented to the Senate by the executive branch. *Fast-track negotiating authority* avoids renegotiation of treaties by allowing the president to negotiate trade agreements and then submit them for an up or down vote by Congress with no amendments permitted.[a]

Organized labor fought ferociously against granting President Clinton fast-track authority based on its belief that expanded trade undermines job security and wages in the United States. Unions have insisted that future trade agreements contain labor safeguards, enforceable by trade sanctions, a demand rejected by U.S. businesses and their Republican allies in Congress.

Since 1973, the wage gap between skilled and unskilled workers in the United States has widened. Trade has played a role in this widening of the wage gap, but there is no consensus as to how significant that role has been. William Cline, chief economist at the Institute of International Finance, an association of large financial services companies, estimates that 10.1 percent of wage inequality is due to trade, compared to 3.7 percent attributable to technological change, 4.4 percent to the decline of unions, and 2.9 percent to immigration.[b]

Since the North American Free Trade Agreement (NAFTA) took effect in January 1994, over 500,000 U.S. apparel and textile jobs have been lost, largely because of import competition from Mexico and other low-wage nations.[c] Free trade has also created jobs by increasing exports, however, so on balance, it appears to have been a wash.[d] Even so, a 1997 poll showed that a majority of Americans believed that trade agreements, such as NAFTA, destroy jobs in the United States.[e]

In September 1998, the thirty-four democratically elected governments of the Western Hemisphere initiated negotiations over the creation of a Free Trade Area of the Americas (FTAA) as a way to build on NAFTA. The ultimate goal of the FTAA was to achieve a comprehensive free trade agreement by 2005. According to some observers, the first step toward meeting this goal was for President George W. Bush to receive fast-track authority.

In August 2002, President Bush won a hard-fought battle when Congress narrowly approved the fast-track law, but only after the Democrats tacked on provisions that established or expanded a number of trade adjustment assistance programs designed to help U.S. workers who are displaced by foreign trade. These programs include providing displaced workers with health insurance, offering some displaced workers the option of wage insurance (including health benefits), providing health-care benefits to some retired steelworkers, and doubling the budget for retraining displaced workers. Supporters of the Bush administration stated that the president had compromised his free trade principles on both farm products and steel in order to win passage of this law, known officially as *Trade Promotion Authority.* "The passage of T.P.A. was essential," according to Matthew Baldwin, a senior policy adviser to Pascal Lamy, the European Union's top trade negotiator. He noted that no country wants to spend time hammering out a treaty with the executive branch, only to be forced to renegotiate it with Congress.[f] The *Trade Promotion Authority* granted in the T.P.A., which allows the president to negotiate trade agreements and then submit them for an up or down vote by Congress with no amendments permitted, expires on June 1, 2005, but it will be automatically extended if neither house of Congress adopts a resolution opposing the extension.

Since then, the Bush administration has entered into a number of bilateral free-trade deals, including treaties with Singapore, Australia, and Morocco. The administration is hoping to make progress toward the FTAA during President Bush's second term. According to President Bush, "[The FTAA] will make our hemisphere the largest free trade area in the world, encompassing 34 countries and 800 million people."[g] The Bush administration will need progress on two separate fronts before it can close the FTAA. First, countries throughout the Western Hemisphere will be closely watching the Central American Free Trade Agreement as it moves through Congress during 2005. This proposed treaty with Costa

a. Anthony DePalma, *Latin America Is Priority on Bush Trade Agenda,* N.Y. TIMES, Dec. 23, 2000, at C23.

b. Free Trade's Threat to California's Garment Workers, *at* http://www.industries.bnet.com/abstract.aspx?scname=Household&docid=103358.

c. *Id.*

d. Bob Davis, *At the Heart of the Trade Debate: Inequity,* WALL ST. J., Oct. 31, 1997, at A2.

e. *Id.*

f. Edmund L. Andrews, *Why Isn't Fast Track . . . Faster?,* N.Y. TIMES, Aug. 18, 2002, *at* http://www.nytimes.com/2002/08/18/business/yourmoney/18TRAD.html?todaysheadlines.

g. Nathan Victor, *Erasing America's Borders,* SIERRA TIMES, Jan. 21, 2005, *at* http://www.sierratimes.com/05/01/21/victor01212005.htm.

*(Continued)*

(Political Perspective *continued*)

Rica, El Salvador, Guatemala, Honduras, Nicaragua, and possibly the Dominican Republic faces strong opposition, and failure to pass it will damage the FTAA's prospects. The United States also needs to make progress on agricultural subsidies at the World Trade Organization. The Bush administration insists that U.S. farmers should accept reduced agricultural subsidies at the same pace as farmers in the European Union, Japan, and elsewhere. Making progress in this area will help the United States in negotiations related to the FTAA.[h]

**h.** Truth about Trade and Technology, *U.S., Brazil Eye Trade Area,* Jan. 6, 2005, *at* http://www.truthabouttrade.org/article.asp?id=3212.

---

authorized to enter into a treaty on its behalf; in most countries, the authorization is granted in the constitution. For example, the U.S. Constitution grants the president the power to enter into treaties "by and with the Advice and Consent of the Senate, . . . provided two-thirds of the Senators present concur."[8] Often the president delegates this constitutional power to negotiate treaties to other parts of the executive branch.

8. U.S. CONST., art. II, § 2.

The U.S. Constitution prohibits states from entering "into any Treaty, Alliance or Confederation,"[9] but the Supreme Court has allowed the states to enter into treaties that do not "encroach upon or impair the supremacy of the United States."[10] The following case makes it clear that the authority of states and localities in this area is very limited.

9. U.S. CONST., art. I, § 10.
10. Virginia v. Tennessee, 148 U.S. 503, 518 (1893).

A CASE IN POINT

**CASE 25.1**
**Crosby v. National Foreign Trade Council**
*Supreme Court of the United States*
*530 U.S. 363 (2000).*

## In the Language of the Court

**› FACTS** In 1996, the Commonwealth of Massachusetts passed a law barring governmental entities in Massachusetts from buying goods or services from companies doing business with Burma (Myanmar). Subsequently, the U.S. Congress enacted federal legislation imposing mandatory and conditional sanctions on Burma. The Massachusetts law was inconsistent with the new federal legislation. The National Foreign Trade Council sued on behalf of its several members, claiming that the Massachusetts law unconstitutionally infringed on federal foreign affairs power, violated the Foreign Commerce Clause of the U.S. Constitution, and was preempted by the subsequent federal legislation. The district and appeals courts ruled in favor of the Council, and the Commonwealth appealed.

**› ISSUE PRESENTED** Did Massachusetts exceed the scope of its authority by passing a law barring state entities from purchasing goods or services from companies doing business in Burma?

**› OPINION** SOUTER, J., writing for the U.S. Supreme Court:

The Massachusetts law is preempted, and its application unconstitutional under the Supremacy Clause of the U.S. Constitution. State law must yield to a congressional act if Congress intends to occupy the field, or to the extent of any conflict with a federal statute. This is the case even where the relevant congressional act lacks an express preemption provision. This Court will find preemption where it is impossible for a private party to comply with both state and federal law and where the state law is an obstacle to the accomplishment and execution of Congress's full purposes and objectives. In this case, the state Act is an obstacle to the federal Act's delegation of discretion to the President of the United States to control economic sanctions against Burma. Within the sphere defined by Congress, the statute has given the President

*(Continued)*

(Case 25.1 *continued*)

as much discretion to exercise economic leverage against Burma, with an eye toward national security, as law permits. It is implausible to think that Congress would have gone to such lengths to empower the President had it been willing to compromise his effectiveness by allowing state or local ordinances to blunt the consequences of his actions—exactly the effect of the state Act.

In addition, the Massachusetts law interferes with Congress's intention to limit economic pressure against the Burmese Government to a specific range. . . . Finally, the Massachusetts law conflicts with the President's authority to speak for the United States among the world's nations to develop a comprehensive, multilateral Burma strategy. In this respect, the state Act undermines the President's capacity for effective diplomacy.

**› RESULT** The Supreme Court affirmed the rulings of the lower courts. The Massachusetts law was struck down.

**› COMMENTS** By limiting the basis of its ruling to the theory of federal preemption and the Supremacy Clause doctrine, the Supreme Court did not address whether the Massachusetts law would have violated the Constitution in the absence of a federal law concerning Burma sanctions.

**› CRITICAL THINKING QUESTIONS**

1. Is it ever appropriate for states to adopt laws that affect international trade?
2. How should a manager of a U.S. company handle seemingly inconsistent state and federal laws related to federal trade?

---

The consent of a nation to enter into a treaty is expressed not by signing the treaty, but through the process of ratification or accession.[11] *Ratification* is a twofold process that occurs both on the national level, where it is governed by the laws of the nation that has to ratify the treaty, and on the international level, where it is often governed by the treaty itself. Although only a nation that is an original party to the treaty can ratify it, through the process of *accession* a nation that was not an original party can elect to participate in the treaty at a later time.

Treaties can be breached by one or more countries, and disputes can arise from these breaches or alleged breaches. These disputes can lead to adjudication in international courts, but more often these disputes are decided by national courts.

## Other Sources of International Law

### *Customary International Law*

Another form of international law is *customary practice*. Whereas treaties between nations are comparable to contracts between private parties in national legal systems, customary international law is analogous to "established practice" and "commercial usage" as they are known in the commercial laws of many nations. Customary practice arises from continuous practice, not from a legislative action. Thus, a state must give its express consent to be bound by a treaty, but it implicitly consents to customary practice through continuous observation of the practice.

Treaties and customary practice often complement each other. Customary practices are sometimes used to interpret treaties, and treaties often codify, clarify, or modify existing customary practices.

### *Decisions of International, National, and Regional Courts*

Although there are a number of international courts, these courts do not have exclusive jurisdiction over international disputes. For example, Article 34 of the statute creating the International Court of Justice dictates that "[o]nly States may be parties in cases before the Court."[12] The European Court of Justice at Luxembourg deals with cases brought by states, cases brought by European Union

11. Vienna Convention, art. 11.

12. Statute of the International Court of Justice, as annexed to the Charter of the United Nations, June 26, 1945, 59 Stat. 1031, T.S. No. 993, 3 Bevans 1153 (entered into force Oct. 24, 1945) [hereinafter ICJ Statute].

institutions, and cases brought by individuals or corporations against EU institutions. Similarly, the European Court of Human Rights is authorized to hear complaints filed by states or by individuals about violations of the human rights protected by the Human Rights Convention. Because of the limited authority of these international courts to hear disputes involving private parties, many international disputes must be resolved by national courts. As a result, courts on a national as well as an international level are also a source of international law.

##  National Laws

### National Laws Directed at Foreign-Owned Businesses

Some national laws are designed to limit foreign-owned businesses.

#### *Nationalization, Expropriation, Confiscation, and Privatization*

Host countries sometimes pass laws that directly affect foreign-owned business operations in their country. If a host country decides to assert ownership over some or all of a company's assets, *nationalization* takes place. If the host country compensates the company for its lost assets, this process of nationalization is referred to as *expropriation;* if no compensation is provided, it is called *confiscation.* The reverse situation in which property ownership is transferred from a nation to a private entity is called *privatization.*

The Overseas Private Investment Corporation (OPIC), a U.S. governmental agency, specializes in providing insurance for eligible U.S. investors against certain defined risks, including political risks such as expropriation. To be eligible for OPIC insurance, an investor must be (1) a U.S. citizen, (2) a U.S. partnership or corporation substantially owned by U.S. citizens, or (3) a foreign business at least 95 percent owned by a U.S. citizen or by a U.S. partnership or corporation. OPIC insures U.S. investors' interests only in "friendly" countries—that is, those that have investment-protection agreements (bilateral treaties of friendship, and navigation and commerce or FNCs, or bilateral investment treaties, or BITs) with the United States. Coverage is also available for inconvertibility of foreign-currency remittances and losses due to hostile action during civil unrest.[13]

13. OPIC publishes a number of handbooks that describe its programs and services. They are available from the Information Officer, Overseas Private Investment Corporation, 1129 20th Street, N.W., Washington, DC 20527.

#### *Constraints on Foreign Ownership*

Some governments try to protect what they regard as the key industries of their country, such as the energy and media industries, by limiting the allowed percentage of foreign ownership. Another constraint on foreign ownership is to restrict the profits that can be returned by a multinational company to its home country (*repatriation*).

### National Laws Directed at International Business Activities

Other national laws are designed to regulate international business activities.

#### *Sanctions*

*Sanctions* may be imposed by one country (or a group of countries) against the commerce of another country in an effort to influence that country's behavior, for example, with regard to international law. Sanctions can take very different forms and can include boycotts of goods, refusal to maintain commercial relationships, tariffs, quotas, and other penalties. Sanctions may lead to so-called trade wars, when a country retaliates by imposing tariffs on the goods of the country that imposed sanctions on it.

#### *Embargoes*

An *embargo* is a special kind of sanction against all commerce of one country that is declared by a country or, more frequently, a group of countries. As with other sanctions, the goal is to force the embargoed country to change its behavior or policies. An embargo often isolates the affected country and is intended to create economic suffering. Well-known examples of international embargoes are the embargo against goods coming out of or going into South Africa, which was imposed during the 1980s because of the country's apartheid politics, and the United Nations embargo imposed on Iraq after the invasion of Kuwait in 1990.

#### *Export Laws*

Export laws are another important form of sanction. Almost every country has its own export laws.[14] Thirty-three countries, among them the United States and most Western European countries, participate in the Wassenaar Arrangement.[15] The Wassenaar Arrangement was established in 1995 to promote greater transparency and

14. Sometimes the participation of a country in different international conventions may lead to various layers of export controls in the country.
15. The "Wassenaar Arrangement on Export Controls for Conventional Arms and Dual-Use Goods and Technologies" was adopted in 1996 and updated in 2001.

responsibility regarding the transfer of armaments and sensitive *dual-use* goods and technologies that have both military and nonmilitary applications. In December 2001, the Arrangement was extended in an effort to prevent terrorists and terrorist groups and organizations from acquiring armaments and sensitive dual-use items. The Arrangement facilitates the voluntary exchange of information among member states and creates a forum to assess the scope of coordination of national export control policies.

## National Laws with Extraterritorial Application

Increasingly, countries are asserting the right to regulate activities that occur beyond their borders, a practice known as *extraterritoriality*. For example, both the United States and the European Union have asserted the right to apply their antitrust laws to Microsoft's activities, on the basis that the company's activities have adversely affected competition within their respective markets. See the "Inside Story" in Chapter 16 for a discussion of the U.S. and EU antitrust actions against Microsoft.

Some product safety standards also have extraterritorial application. For example, pharmaceutical products exported to the United States must be produced in facilities that adhere to the manufacturing practices established by the U.S. Food and Drug Administration, and airplanes built overseas for use in U.S. airspace must be built according to Federal Aviation Administration (FAA) standards in FAA-certified facilities. Investment contracts for such export projects need to reflect the production standards required by U.S. law.

### Foreign Corrupt Practices Act

Another example of a national law with extraterritorial application is the Foreign Corrupt Practices Act. Following the discovery that more than 400 American corporations had paid bribes or made questionable payments abroad, the U.S. Congress enacted the Foreign Corrupt Practices Act (FCPA)[16] in 1977 as an amendment to the Securities Exchange Act of 1934 (the 1934 Act).

The FCPA prohibits any payment by a company, its employees, or its agents directly or indirectly to a foreign government official or a foreign political party for the purpose of improperly influencing government decisions in order to obtain business abroad. The statute is violated even if the bribe is only offered but never paid. It is also violated if the payment is made to a private company or individual with the knowledge that it will be funneled to the government.

*"Look! Stem cells and Lipitor from Uncle Henri in Quebec."*



An exception is made for payments to low-ranking officials who merely expedite the nondiscretionary granting of a permit or license. A second exception is made for payments to foreign businesses, as long as they are not acting as conduits for the money to pass to the foreign government.

Directors, officers, employees, or agents of the corporation who willfully violate the prohibited payments portion of the FCPA are subject to a $100,000 fine and up to five years in prison; the corporation can be fined up to $2 million or, if greater, twice its profits from the illegal activity.

The FCPA also imposes record-keeping requirements on all public companies that file periodic reports with the Securities and Exchange Commission under the 1934 Act. A purely domestic public company that is not engaged in foreign trade must still comply with the FCPA's record-keeping requirements.

Under these requirements, each corporation must keep records that accurately reflect the dispositions of its assets and must implement internal controls to ensure that its transactions are completed as authorized by management. Periodic reports must be filed.

Failure to maintain the appropriate records and procedures is a violation, whether or not there is payment of

16. 15 U.S.C. §§ 78a–78LLL.

a bribe. This portion of the FCPA was designed to prevent companies from developing a slush fund and then accounting for questionable payments as legitimate business expenses. The record-keeping provisions of the FCPA do not contain any specific penalties.

Since 1977, when the United States became the first major industrial country to ban bribes, it has encouraged other countries to adopt similar prohibitions. The United States scored a major victory when it helped persuade the Organisation for Economic Co-operation and Development (OECD) and its members to adopt the international convention on bribery, discussed in Chapter 1.

# U.S. Trade Regime

U.S. trade laws are enacted by Congress pursuant to the Commerce Clause of the U.S. Constitution, and they are administered by the federal government and its administrative agencies.

## THE ROLE OF GOVERNMENT BRANCHES AND AGENCIES IN TRADE RELATIONS

### *Congress*

Congress has the power to regulate all aspects of foreign commerce, including imports and exports, foreign investment, licensing of technology, and other commercial activities. International trade laws govern imports and exports. The trade laws may affect other aspects of foreign commerce as well.

Trade laws are generally designed to restrict or to facilitate imports and exports. Imports are restricted primarily by means of tariffs and quantitative limitations such as *quotas*. Conversely, imports may be facilitated through exemption from U.S. tariffs. Exports are controlled by means of *export licenses*. Exports may be facilitated by federal subsidies, tax breaks, and other legislation, including Section 301 of the Trade Act of 1974, discussed later in this chapter.

### *The Role of the President*

The president administers U.S. trade laws pursuant to the authority delegated to the president by Congress. As chief executive, the president has broad power to negotiate trade agreements, but the president cannot regulate trade without congressional delegation or approval.

**The President's Power to Restrict Trade** Over the years, Congress has authorized the president to regulate or restrict trade and other economic activity when necessary to protect the U.S. national security, foreign policy, or economy. The International Emergency Economic Powers Act,[17] passed in 1977, limited the president's authority to restrict trade and other commercial transactions to instances when a national emergency has been declared in response to an "unusual and extraordinary threat, which has its source in whole or substantial part outside the United States, to the national security, foreign policy or economy of the United States."

The economic sanctions imposed under these laws are administered by the Office of Foreign Assets Control in the Department of the Treasury, which issues appropriate regulations. To varying degrees, the regulations apply not only to transactions in the United States but also to transactions by foreign affiliates of U.S. companies and to transactions abroad involving U.S. property. The application of the regulations to foreign subsidiaries or operations of U.S. companies has caused considerable difficulty, particularly for companies subjected to conflicting requirements imposed by foreign governments on their foreign affiliates.[18]

**Trade Promotion Authority** Another way for the president to influence U.S. international trade is the so-called Trade Promotion Authority or fast-track negotiating authority. For more information about this authority, see the "Political Perspective" in this chapter.

### *Administrative Agencies*

The agencies primarily responsible for administration of the trade laws are the U.S. Trade Representative (USTR), the Department of Commerce, the Department of State, the Department of the Treasury, the U.S. International Trade Commission, and U.S. Customs and Border Protection (which is part of the Department of Homeland Security).

The USTR is responsible for the development of U.S. trade policy and the negotiation of trade agreements with other countries, with the assistance of the other agencies. The USTR makes all policy decisions concerning the operation of these agreements. The Department of Commerce is generally responsible for implementing U.S. trade policy, enforcing certain import relief laws and export controls, and promoting U.S. exports. The

17. 50 U.S.C. §§ 1701–06.

18. *See, e.g.*, Dresser Indus. v. Baldridge, 549 F. Supp. 108 (D.D.C. 1982) (French subsidiary of U.S. company unsuccessful in enjoining application of sanctions by U.S. Department of Commerce for failure to honor U.S. prohibition on exports of certain types of equipment to the Soviet Union even though French subsidiaries had been ordered by the French government to honor prior contractual commitments to ship the equipment).

Department of State administers controls on munitions exports and defends U.S. economic interests through U.S. embassies abroad.

The Department of the Treasury administers embargoes imposed on U.S. trade with countries such as Iran, Cuba, and North Korea. The International Trade Commission is an independent agency with a variety of responsibilities, including investigating the effect of imports on U.S. industries. U.S. Customs and Border Protection enforces all U.S. customs laws and import restrictions and collects U.S. tariffs. Other agencies, such as the U.S. Department of Agriculture, administer restrictions on U.S. trade falling in their particular areas of responsibility, with the assistance of Customs and Border Protection.

### *The Interagency Committee*

The president makes trade policy decisions based on the recommendations of an interagency committee, headed by the USTR. In addition to the agencies listed above, the committee includes members from the Department of Labor, the Council of Economic Advisers, and other agencies interested in trade policy. Private interests are typically given the opportunity to express their views to any of these agencies or to the interagency committee directly. For example, tariffs on a particular product are rarely changed without first consulting the affected industry. Government officials at all the agencies are generally receptive to requests and comments from U.S. companies. In many cases, public hearings are held before decisions are made.

### *Export-Import Bank*

The Export-Import Bank of the United States (Eximbank) was created to provide financing for the purchase of U.S. exports. The Eximbank is the U.S. government's response to foreign governments' export subsidies. By offering financing at below-market interest rates, the Eximbank allows U.S. exporters to compete with foreign companies.

## Laws Affecting Exports

Several U.S. laws serve to facilitate or, in some cases, control exports.

### *Export Administration Act*

The Export Administration Act of 1979[19] (EAA) is the primary restriction on U.S. exports. It authorizes the secretary of commerce to prohibit exports when necessary to protect national security, carry out U.S. foreign policy, enforce U.S. nuclear nonproliferation policy, or prevent the export of goods that are in short supply. Some controls are imposed unilaterally by the United States. Others, which are imposed jointly with U.S. allies on exports to Communist countries, are agreed on and administered through an informal arrangement known as *CoCom*. The EAA expired in 1990 but has remained in force by presidential executive order under the International Emergency Economics Powers Act (IEEPA). A new version was passed by the Senate in 2001, but the House blocked it because of concern that the new version weakened controls on potentially dangerous technologies.

The EAA's most significant restrictions are those that control high technology and its products. These restrictions have had serious adverse consequences for U.S. exporters competing for business abroad. The Omnibus Trade and Competitiveness Act of 1988, reflecting the importance attached to the trade deficit and the need to promote U.S. exports, removed many controls on exports, particularly to friendly countries.

U.S. export controls are enforced by a system of export licenses. Certain categories of commodities and technical data may not be exported without an export license from the Commerce Department's Bureau of Export Administration. It decides whether to grant an export license based on a number of factors, including the nature of the item to be exported, the country to which it is to be shipped, the foreign consignee, and the use to which the item will be put.

U.S. export restrictions apply to exports of technology (referred to as technical data) as well as goods. The restrictions apply not only to exports from the United States but also to many reexports of U.S.-origin goods and technology to third countries by other countries and to exports from other countries of certain foreign-made articles that are direct products of U.S. technology. In addition, the transfer of technical data to a foreign citizen in the United States is generally considered to be an export, which means that an export license is required. Such transfers include verbal exchanges of technology on U.S. soil and visits by foreign nationals to U.S. plants.

### *Export Administration Regulations (EARs)*

The Bureau of Industry and Security (BIS) in the Department of Commerce issues Export Administration Regulations (EARs) that apply to shipments of nonmilitary and dual-use goods and technology.[20]

19. 50 U.S.C.A. app. §§ 2401 *et seq.*

20. See the EAR website of the U.S. Government Printing Office *at* http://www.access.gpo.gov/bis/index.html for more information (last visited Jan. 2005).

### *The Arms Export Control Act*

The Arms Export Control Act,[21] which authorizes the U.S. secretary of state to prohibit exports of munitions and munitions technology from the United States, is administered by the Office of Munitions Control of the State Department, which issues the International Traffic in Arms Regulations (ITARs) and operates a licensing system similar to that of the Commerce Department, based on the United States Munitions List.[22] The Commerce and State Departments both issue advisory opinions to exporters concerning the applicability of export controls to specific transactions.

### *Penalties for Violations of Export Regulations*

There are substantial criminal and civil penalties for the violation of U.S. export regulations. For a violation, the penalty can be the greater of five times the value of the exports involved or $50,000, and up to five years in prison. If the violations are willful, the penalties can be even higher. Furthermore, a company that violates export regulations may be denied exporting privileges. The government can also impose sanctions or penalties under other legal regimes as well. In 2001 the Department of Commerce imposed a $2.12 million penalty against McDonnell Douglas, the second largest civil fine ever imposed by the Commerce Department in an export control case. This resulted from an investigation into exports of machine tools to China between 1994 and 1995. The Commerce Department claimed McDonnell Douglas submitted license applications containing false and misleading statements about the end use and end user of the machine tools and that the exports violated the terms of the U.S. export license issued to the company. The Commerce Department also imposed a $1.32 million civil penalty on the Chinese government-owned companies and their U.S. affiliates that received the machine tools and denied their export privileges.

### *Section 301*

Section 301 of the Trade Act of 1974 (*Section 301*)[23] is the principal U.S. statute addressing unfair foreign practices affecting U.S. exports of goods or services. It may be used to enforce U.S. rights under international trade agreements and to respond to unreasonable, unjustifiable, or discriminatory foreign government practices that burden or restrict U.S. commerce. Specifically, Section 301 authorizes the USTR to investigate alleged unfair practices of foreign governments that impede U.S. exports of goods and services. Subject to certain exceptions, the USTR must take action in response to foreign government practices that (1) violate trade agreements with the United States or (2) are unjustifiable (that is, in violation of the international legal rights of the United States) and burden or restrict U.S. commerce. The USTR has discretionary authority to take action if he or she determines that an act or policy of a foreign country is unreasonable or discriminatory and burdens or restricts U.S. commerce.

The Omnibus Trade and Competitiveness Act of 1988 created a program known as *Super 301,* which required the USTR to draw up a list of the foreign governments whose practices pose the most significant barriers to U.S. exports and to immediately commence Section 301 investigations with respect to these practices. Similarly, under the *Special 301 provisions* in U.S. trade law, the USTR identifies those countries that deny adequate and effective protection for intellectual property rights or deny fair and equitable market access for persons that rely on intellectual property protection. Countries that have the most onerous or egregious practices and whose practices have the greatest adverse impact on the relevant U.S. products are designated as "priority foreign countries" and are subject to Section 301 investigations. Other countries with less severe problems protecting intellectual property rights are placed on a "watch list" or "priority watch list" and are monitored closely.[24]

## LAWS AFFECTING IMPORTS

The United States has several laws limiting or otherwise regulating imports.

### *Tariffs*

*Tariffs* are the basic tool for limiting imports to protect domestic industries. Today, most tariffs are *ad valorem tariffs,* meaning that the importer must pay a percentage of the value of the imported merchandise. For instance, a 10 percent tariff on a shipment of imports valued at $10,000 will result in a *duty,* that is, a required payment, of $1,000.

U.S. tariffs are established by federal law and can be changed only by statute or by administrative action

21. 22 U.S.C. §§ 2751–96.
22. 22 C.F.R. pt. 121.
23. 19 U.S.C. § 2411.
24. *Id.*

authorized by statute. Congress frequently changes U.S. tariffs. In addition, Congress has periodically delegated to the president the authority to reduce U.S. tariffs in exchange for tariff concessions by other nations. Congress has also delegated to the president the power to increase tariffs temporarily in order to protect domestic industries in certain specified situations.

**The Harmonized Tariff Schedule** The United States has accepted an internationally harmonized tariff system. Current tariffs are found in a document entitled the *Harmonized Tariff Schedule of the United States (HTS)*.[25] The HTS lists the tariffs on goods imposed by Congress and by the president, based on their country of origin.

For each product category, there are two basic rates of duty. One column applies to most countries (column 1), and the second applies to several less favored countries, such as Cuba and North Korea (column 2). These columns reflect tariffs imposed by Congress or negotiated by the president. U.S. tariffs vary not only by the country of origin but also by the article's *tariff classification,* that is, where it is best described in the HTS.

The duty paid on an imported article depends on the value assigned to it by Customs and Border Protection, that is, on the *customs valuation* of the article. The lower the valuation, the lower the duty. The general rule of customs valuation in the United States is that the value of an article for customs purposes is the *transaction value,* which is the price indicated on the sales invoice.

U.S. customs laws are administered by Customs and Border Protection. Its headquarters are in Washington, D.C., but the agency has a district office at every U.S. port. Tariff rulings by the district offices can be appealed to headquarters and then to the U.S. Court of International Trade. Appeals from this court are to the U.S. Court of Appeals for the Federal Circuit and then to the U.S. Supreme Court.

**Tariff Preferences** Pursuant to authority delegated by Congress, the president has established preferential tariffs for imports from certain developing countries. The most important are embodied in the Generalized System of Preferences (GSP).

The GSP, which was agreed to multilaterally, is a program developed by the industrialized countries to assist developing nations by improving their ability to export. The GSP has been used to integrate developing countries into the international trade system and to encourage beneficiary countries to eliminate or reduce barriers to trade and to enforce intellectual property rights. Under the GSP, the president has designated certain products as eligible for duty-free treatment if they are produced in developing countries designated as eligible beneficiaries of the program.[26]

An eligible product receives duty-free treatment only if 35 percent or more of the value of the product was added in an eligible country. There are also limitations on the volume of eligible articles that may be imported from a single country. If the volume limitation is exceeded, the product is automatically removed from the category of eligible imports from that country.

If a country is found to be sufficiently competitive, the president can remove it from the program, either entirely or with respect to individual products. This process is referred to as "graduation." In 1989, Singapore, South Korea, and Taiwan were graduated from the program entirely. Countries can also be removed from the GSP program for policy reasons, such as failure to protect intellectual property rights. The program is reviewed annually to determine which countries and products should be removed from or added to the program. The program is administered for the president by the USTR.

## *Import Relief Laws*

In a series of laws, known collectively as the *import relief laws,* Congress has authorized the president to raise U.S. tariffs on specified products and to provide other forms of import protection to U.S. industries. These laws vary as to the nature of the unfair practice (if any) to which they are directed, the degree of injury required in order to obtain relief, the nature of the relief authorized, the agencies authorized to provide the relief, and the amount of discretion given to the president in determining whether to grant relief.

**Section 201** Section 201 of the Trade Act of 1974 (*Section 201*)[27] provides for temporary relief to domestic industries seriously injured by increasing imports, regardless of whether unfair practices are involved. It is sometimes called the *fair trade law.* The relief is designed to give the U.S. industry a few years (normally no more than five) to adjust to import competition.

The U.S. International Trade Commission (ITC) investigates petitions filed by U.S. industries. If the ITC makes an affirmative finding of injury from imports, it recommends specific import relief, such as higher duties or quantitative limits on imports. The president must

25. Published by the U.S. International Trade Commission.

26. 19 U.S.C. §§ 2461–66.

27. 19 U.S.C. § 2251.

provide the recommended relief unless he or she finds that it would not be in the national economic interest, as defined in the law. Because import relief always has economic costs, such as inflationary effects, the president may decide not to provide relief.

The Omnibus Trade and Competitiveness Act of 1988[28] encourages petitioning industries to submit plans illustrating how they would use Section 201 relief to adjust to import competition. It further provides that the ITC should recommend relief that not only addresses the injury caused by imports but also will facilitate the domestic industry's adjustment to import competition. As a complement to that, the law provides that the president can grant either import relief or other appropriate relief within his or her legal authority. Thus, the law encourages making relief conditional on the ability of the domestic industry to meet the competition or to transfer its resources elsewhere.

**Relationship Between WTO Dispute Settlement Process and U.S. Trade Laws** Whether U.S. trade laws like Sections 201 and 301 of the Trade Act of 1974 give the president (acting through the USTR) the ability to take unilateral action to penalize countries with trade practices that threaten American interests without going through the dispute settlement process established by the World Trade Organization (WTO) is a matter of some debate. (The WTO, which will be discussed in detail later in the chapter, is an international institution that regulates global trade.) On their face, the U.S. laws seem to allow for this result, and the legislative history of the U.S. statute implementing the Uruguay Round and creating the WTO suggests that Congress did not intend for the WTO dispute resolution process to displace the powers vested in the USTR. The implementing legislation includes the following language:

> Sec. 102(a) RELATIONSHIP OF AGREEMENTS TO UNITED STATES LAW—(1) UNITED STATES LAW TO PREVAIL IN CONFLICT—No provision of any of the Uruguay Round Agreements, nor the application of any such provision to any person or circumstance, that is inconsistent with any law of the United States shall have effect. (2) CONSTRUCTION.—Nothing in this Act shall be construed—(A) to amend or modify any law of the United States. . . . (B) to limit any authority conferred under any law of the United States.

On the other hand, the United States has generally attempted to use Trade Act powers after the WTO has authorized such actions. For example, the President's Statement of Administrative Action, issued by President Clinton, provided that the United States will use Section 301 only in a WTO "compliant manner."

Nonetheless, the United States has not always awaited WTO authorization before taking action under the Trade Act. For example, President George W. Bush was strongly criticized when he announced in January 2002 that he would use his authority under Section 201 to impose tariffs of up to 30 percent on foreign steel imports for three years to protect the U.S. steel sector. The tariffs were crafted to be in accord with the 1994 General Agreement on Tariffs and Trade, or GATT (GATT was the predecessor of the WTO and is discussed later in the chapter). The EU, however, responded that the tariffs protected inefficient U.S. steel producers from fair foreign competition, in clear breach of trade agreements. The tariffs were declared illegal by the WTO's Dispute Settlement Body and its Appellate Body in November 2003. The EU announced that it would impose $2.2 billion of sanctions on imports of U.S. textiles, shoes, fruit, and vegetables if the United States failed to lift its tariffs by December 15, 2003. Under the gun to remove the tariffs before the WTO formally approved the decision and the EU imposed sanctions, the White House averted a trade war by announcing that the tariffs had "now achieved their purpose and, as a result of changed economic circumstances, it is time to lift them."[29]

**The Antidumping Law** The antidumping law, codified in the Tariff Act of 1930, as amended,[30] is the most frequently used import relief law. If a U.S. industry is materially injured by imports of a product being *dumped* in the United States (that is, sold below the current selling price in the exporter's home market or below the exporter's cost of production), then the law imposes an antidumping duty on the dumped product. The amount of the duty is equal to the amount of the *dumping margin,* that is, the difference between the U.S. price and the price in the exporting country. If the ITC determines that dumping has occurred and caused material injury, the Commerce Department is required to impose duties on the imports sold at less than fair value.

**The Countervailing Duty Law** The countervailing duty law[31] provides that, if a U.S. industry is materially injured by imports of a product benefiting from a foreign subsidy, a *countervailing duty* (an import duty that

28. 15 U.S.C. §§ 78dd-1, 78dd-2, 78ff.

29. *EU Lifts Sanctions Threat After US Scraps Steel Tariffs,* Apr. 12, 2003, *at* http://www.eubusiness.com/afp/031204182808.wcpj0phr.

30. 19 U.S.C. §§ 1673–77.

31. 19 U.S.C. §§ 1303, 1671a–h.

offsets the amount of the benefit conferred by the subsidy) must be imposed on those imports.

**Section 337** Section 337 of the Tariff Act of 1930 (*Section 337*)[32] provides that if a U.S. industry is injured (or there is a restraint or monopolization of trade in the United States) by reason of unfair acts in the importation of articles into the United States, an order must be issued requiring the exporters and importers to cease the unfair acts or, if necessary, excluding imports of the offending articles from all sources. This law applies to unfair competition of all kinds not covered in other import relief laws, but it is most commonly used in cases involving patent or trademark infringement. Relief is mandatory unless the president disapproves the ITC decision, which seldom happens.

The Omnibus Trade and Competitiveness Act eliminated the requirement to show economic injury in cases involving intellectual property rights (infringement of patents, trademarks, and copyrights). The Act affected most Section 337 cases and made it significantly easier for U.S. companies to obtain relief under this statute.

**The Buy American Act** Under the Buy American Act,[33] federal agencies, in their procurement of supplies and equipment, must give a preference to products made in the United States unless their price is a certain percentage higher than the price of the equivalent foreign product. Products are deemed to be American made, and therefore eligible for the preference, if they are manufactured in the United States and at least 50 percent of the components are American made.

As explained later in this chapter, preferences to domestic industry in government procurement are a common form of nontariff barrier to imports that was addressed in one of the GATT codes. Pursuant to that code (the Agreement on Government Procurement),[34] many U.S. agencies have joined foreign agencies in eliminating this preference. Defense-related articles are not subject to the agreement, however, and still receive the Buy American Act preference.

## International Trade Regimes

In order to achieve its trade goals, both with respect to the regulation of imports and the facilitation of exports, the United States engages its trade partners in a wide array of bilateral, regional, and multilateral trade agreements. Bilateral agreements tend to be limited in subject matter, covering matters such as tariffs, taxes, and intellectual property rights. Several of the regional and multilateral agreements, such as the North American Free Trade Agreement and the World Trade Organization, have their own dispute settlement mechanisms, which were negotiated as part of each agreement.

### North American Free Trade Agreement

The trilateral North American Free Trade Agreement (NAFTA)[35] provides for the gradual elimination of all barriers to trade between the United States, Canada, and Mexico and for the free cross-border movement of goods and services between the territories of the three signatories. Designed to improve all three countries' economies and to benefit 390 million consumers with lower-priced goods and increased investment opportunities, NAFTA established the world's largest free trade zone. Congress approved the agreement on November 17, 1993, and it went into effect on January 1, 1994.

Under NAFTA, Mexico eliminated tariffs on U.S. capital goods in stages based on three categories: "A," "B," and "C." Tariffs on Category A goods, which include automobiles, were eliminated in January 1994. Category B goods, which include textile and apparel goods, became duty-free in 1998. Category C goods, which include the majority of capital goods, have been duty-free since 2003. The United States eliminated the majority of its tariffs on Mexican goods on January 1, 1994.

In addition to eliminating its custom duties, each country is required to accord national treatment to the goods of the other nations in accordance with Article III of GATT (discussed below). The agreement also substantially reduced the barriers to government procurement and has effectively resulted in totally open procurement.

NAFTA prohibits new restrictions on investment and on trade in services among the three countries. It includes major provisions relating to specific industries, such as agriculture, telecommunications, and energy. In addition, it established special rules of origin to ensure that only products originating in the United States, Canada, or Mexico enjoy duty-free treatment. Certificates of origin are required on all goods being exported between the three countries to certify that the good qualifies as an "originating" good.

The pact also provides for the adequate protection and enforcement of intellectual property rights and

32. 19 U.S.C. § 1337.
33. 41 U.S.C. §§ 10a–d.
34. 18 I.L.M. 1052 (1979).
35. North American Free Trade Agreement, Dec. 17, 1992, United States–Canada–Mexico, __ U.S.T. __, T.I.A.S. No. __, 32 I.L.M. 605 (1993).

attempts to ensure that these rights do not become barriers to trade. Each country was required to implement several international agreements regarding intellectual property rights, such as the Berne Convention for the Protection of Literary and Artistic Works (dealing with copyrights) and the Paris Convention for the Protection of Industrial Property Rights (dealing with patents).

NAFTA explicitly protects the continued enforceability of U.S. environmental regulations and includes a mechanism for sanctions if Mexico fails to enforce its own environmental laws. In addition, a side agreement set up a three-nation mechanism, the Commission on Environmental Cooperation, to address environmental disputes. Any country or private interest group that believes that a nation is not enforcing its environmental laws may complain. If the commission determines that a violation has occurred, it can impose a fine up to $20 million or impose trade sanctions on the offending country. Since 1992, Mexico has enacted a number of major environmental statutes and numerous regulations (often modeled on U.S. environmental laws) and has drastically improved its environmental enforcement regime.[36] Even so, some environmentalists have faulted the commission for not demanding more, especially in the area of transboundary cleanup and remediation.[37]

The North American Agreement on Labor Cooperation, a side agreement that established panels in the United States, Mexico, and Canada to hear complaints about worker abuse, has had little impact.[38] The panels have restricted themselves to fact-finding. They cannot levy fines or impose trade sanctions unless there is a persistent lack of enforcement of existing child labor, safety and health, or minimum employment standards.[39] Several U.S. unions have argued that violations relating to freedom of association, collective bargaining, and strikes should also give rise to fines and trade sanctions, not just the high-level ministerial consultations called for in the side agreement.[40] In the words of counsel for the International Labor Rights Fund, who litigated five cases filed in Mexico: "[I]n all of these cases workers are left with a piece of paper that says 'you were right.' Not a single worker was ever reinstated, not a single employer was sanctioned, no union was ever recognized."[41]

Primarily to protect fruit, vegetable, and sugarcane growers in Florida, NAFTA phases out U.S. agricultural tariffs over fifteen years. In addition, during that period, any dramatic increases in Mexican fruit and vegetable imports will trigger temporary "snap-back" tariffs to protect U.S. growers.

Efforts to build on NAFTA by creating a Free Trade Area of the Americas (FTAA) had stalled as of early 2005. See the "Political Perspective" in this chapter for more information about the FTAA.

## The World Trade Organization and the GATT

Besides negotiating bilateral and regional preferential agreements, the United States participates in the World Trade Organization (WTO), the successor to the General Agreement on Tariffs and Trade (GATT), entered into in 1994 (GATT 1994). The WTO came into existence on January 1, 1995,[42] after the conclusion of the Uruguay Round of GATT multilateral trade negotiations.

The WTO oversees all of the agreements reached in the Uruguay Round,[43] and it is the principal multilateral mechanism devoted to the regulation of international trade. As of 2004, the WTO had 148 members with at least another 30 countries (including Russia and Saudi Arabia) waiting to join.

The WTO is especially notable as an emerging international institution similar to, albeit less well funded than, the World Bank and the International Monetary Fund. It is this institutional aspect of the WTO, along with its large membership and broad scope, that draws attention to the organization, both positive and negative.

The GATT has had a profound effect on world trade.[44] Tariffs today are, on average, a small fraction of what they were when the GATT was formed in 1947. The Uruguay Round, the eighth in the history of the GATT, was the most ambitious GATT round ever held. The 117 nations represented at the Uruguay Round agreed to reduce their tariffs by an average of one-third over six years. In addition,

36. Richard H. Steinberg, *Trade-Environment Negotiations in the EU, NAFTA, and WTO: Regional Trajectories of Rule Development*, 91 Am. J. Int'l L. 231 (1997).
37. Joel Millman, *Nafta's Do-Gooder Side Deals Disappoint*, Wall St. J., Oct. 15, 1997, at A19.
38. *Id.*
39. Pamela M. Prah, *Labor, Business Say Labor Side Accord Misses the Mark; Suggest Major Changes*, U.S.L.W., Mar. 3, 1998, *available at* http://pubs.bna.com/IP/BNA/LAW2.NSF/e6da25ccbee90e3885256d09006981d3/aa8828a5dc9746ac852565b80080579d?OpenDocument.
40. *Id.*
41. Millman, *supra* note 37.
42. Agreement Establishing the World Trade Organization, Apr. 15, 1994, 33 I.L.M. 1132 (1994).
43. Final Act Embodying the Results of the Uruguay Round of Multilateral Trade Negotiations, Apr. 15, 1994, 33 I.L.M. 1140 (1994).
44. General Agreement on Tariffs and Trade, opened for signature Oct. 30, 1947, T.I.A.S. No. 1700, 55 U.N.T.S. 187.

agricultural tariffs were reduced by 36 percent in industrial nations and by 24 percent in developing nations. For the first time, agriculture, services, textiles, and investment services were covered by international rules of fair trade, as was the protection of intellectual property rights. The agreement, also for the first time, protected the right of service-sector companies to operate on foreign soil free of discriminatory laws.

The WTO agreement requires member states to participate in the Multilateral Trade Agreements, including (1) fourteen Agreements on Trade in Goods (including GATT 1994); (2) the General Agreement on Trade in Services (GATS); (3) the Agreement on Trade-Related Aspects of Intellectual Property Rights (TRIP); (4) the Understanding on Rules and Procedures Governing the Settlement of Disputes (DSU); and (5) the Trade Policy Review Mechanism (TPRM). These agreements are binding on all members of the WTO.

## BASIC PRINCIPLES OF THE WTO

Three basic principles undergird the GATT and its successor, the WTO: (1) most favored nation treatment, (2) bound tariffs, and (3) national treatment.

## View from Cyberspace

### WTO TACKLES ELECTRONIC COMMERCE

Though not regarded as one of the principal institutions that regulate electronic commerce, the WTO is involved indirectly through the establishment by its member states of trade policies related to the goods, services, and intellectual property that facilitate electronic commerce.[a] In May 1998, the WTO imposed a moratorium on customs duties applicable to electronic information sent over the Internet. In September 1998, the General Counsel of the WTO established a comprehensive work program to examine all trade-related issues arising from global electronic commerce; this program was continued by the WTO ministers at subsequent Ministerial Conferences.[b] Under the work program, issues related to electronic commerce have been examined by the Goods, Services, and TRIPS Councils and the Trade and Development Committee; the WTO Secretariat has produced a number of background notes summarizing the WTO's work on electronic commerce; and many member states have submitted documents in connection with the program's Dedicated Discussions on issues relevant to different Multilateral Trade Agreements.[c]

A Dedicated Discussion centered around two submissions. One submission, from the European Communities (EC), asserted that all products delivered electronically should be classified as services, as opposed to goods, and, therefore, should be governed by the WTO's General Agreement on Trade in Services. The second submission, from the United States, proposed general objectives. The U.S. submission called on governments to (1) adhere to an open trade environment by applying existing WTO agreements to electronic commerce; (2) commit to greater market access for goods and services sectors that will promote trade via electronic networks; (3) minimize domestic trade restrictions on electronic commerce, unless such restrictions are legitimate, transparent, and nondiscriminatory; (4) accept as permanent on a most favored nation basis the moratorium on imposing customs duties on electronic commerce; and (5) make electronic commerce accessible to developing countries through technical assistance and infrastructure improvements.[d]

At the Cancún Ministerial Conference in September 2003, however, the WTO member states failed to make formal decisions regarding continuation of the work program or the moratorium on the imposition of customs duties on electronic commerce, classification of digital products as goods or services, and confirmation of general electronic commerce objectives. Although the member states appear to generally agree that existing WTO trade agreements can address electronic commerce issues, the WTO is currently deadlocked on procedural issues related to the work program's structure and the classification of digital products, which determines the applicable rules governing trade in such products.[e]

a. Sacha Wunsch-Vincent, *WTO, E-commerce, and Information Technologies: From the Uruguay Round Through the Doha Development Agenda, A Report for the UNICT Task Force,* Oct. 20, 2004, at xi, *at* http://www.markle.org/downloadable_assets/wto_e_commerce_10.20.04.pdf.

b. World Trade Organization, Work Continues on Issues Needing Clarification, *at* http://www.wto.org/english/tratop_e/ecom_e/ecom_briefnote_e.htm.

c. *Id.*

d. General Counsel, Submission from the United States, Work Programme on Electronic Commerce, WT/GC/W/493/Rev.1 (July 8, 2003).

e. Wunsch-Vincent, *supra* note a, at 10–22.

### *Most Favored Nation Treatment*

The *most favored nation (MFN)* principle is the foundation of the current world trading system. Each member of the WTO must accord to all other member countries tariff treatment no less favorable than it provides to any other country. In other words, if the United States agrees to lower its tariff on imports of a product from a certain country, it must grant the same treatment to all other WTO members. (The Generalized System of Preferences and other preferential agreements discussed above are exceptions to the MFN principle and are authorized by the GATT.) The theory behind the MFN principle is that world trade will be enhanced if countries avoid discriminating among themselves and creating trading blocs that expand trade within the blocs but restrict trade between them.

The GATT encourages regional economic integration and participation in free trade areas and customs unions, however. A *free trade area* is created when a group of states reduce or eliminate tariffs between themselves but maintain their own individual tariffs as to other states. A *customs union* is similar but involves the establishment of a common tariff for all other states.

Once a free trade area or customs union is established, the GATT rules apply to the area or union as a whole and not to the constituent states. Members of the WTO may participate in free trade areas or customs unions only if the area or union does not establish higher duties or more restrictive commercial regulations for other WTO countries.

### *Bound Tariffs*

A second basic principle of the GATT is the concept of *bound tariffs*. Each time tariffs are reduced, they become bound; that is, they may not be raised again. If any country raises its bound tariffs, it must compensate the other WTO members, normally through other tariff concessions.

### *National Treatment*

A third basic principle is *national treatment*. WTO members may not discriminate against imported products in favor of domestically produced "like products." Thus, for example, special taxes on imported goods are illegal if not applied equally to domestic products. The determination of what is a "like product" is done on a case-by-case basis by examining such factors as (1) the product's end uses in a given market; (2) consumers' tastes and habits, which vary from country to country; and (3) the product's properties, nature, and quality.[45]

45. *See, e.g.*, World Trade Organization: Report of the Appellate Body in Japan—Taxes on Alcoholic Beverages, WTO Docs. WT/DS8/AB/R, WT/DS10/AB/R and WT/DS11/AB/4, 1997 BDIEL AD LEXIS 27 (Oct. 4, 1996) (shochu and vodka are like products, so Japan could not tax imported vodka at a higher rate than domestic shochu).

#### ETHICAL CONSIDERATION

France and other European countries have typically required a majority of television programming to be of European origin, thereby limiting American-made programs to less than 50 percent of the total television broadcasts. France also imposes a series of taxes on movie tickets, television movies, and videocassettes and uses the money generated from the taxes to underwrite French films.[a]

For years, Canada has been concerned that the U.S. media would turn the country into a mini–United States. In April 1998, federal regulators in Ottawa adopted a requirement that at least 35 percent of music played by commercial radio stations on weekdays between 6 A.M. and 6 P.M. must be Canadian selections played in their entirety.[b] In June 1999, similar restrictions were imposed on the distribution of movies in Canada by U.S. movie companies, as well as on ads in publications in order to bolster local Canadian magazines.[c] Liza Frulla, the Minister of Canadian Heritage, claimed that these measures were necessary because "Canadians must be able to find their own reflection in the music, films, television programs and literature created by our artists and distributed in our country."[d] Cultural policies were exempted in part from NAFTA.

An earlier attempt by Canada to impose an 80 percent excise tax on advertisements in split-run editions of periodicals was struck down by the WTO as a violation of Article III's requirement of national treatment.[e] A split-run edition of a magazine is one in which the publisher who is located in a foreign country inserts some domestic content as well as domestic advertising in the magazine that is originally targeted at the readership of the foreign country.

To what extent should media companies worry about protecting local culture? Should popular tastes prevail, or is it acceptable for governments to protect expressions of local culture by minimizing foreign competition through quotas?

**a.** Alan Riding, *Filmmakers Seek Protection from US Dominance*, N.Y. TIMES, Feb. 5, 2003, at E3.
**b.** Canadian Radio–Television & Telecommunications Commission, Fact Sheet: Commercial Radio—Content Issues, Apr. 26, 2002, *available at* http://www.crtc.gc.ca/eng/INFO_SHT/R3.HTM.
**c.** Department of Canadian Heritage, Backgrounder: Canada-U.S Agreement on Magazines, Jan. 8, 2004, *available at* http://www.canadianheritage.gc.ca/progs/ac-ca/pol/magazines/index_e.cfm.
**d.** News Release Communique, Department of Canadian Heritage, The Government of Canada Submits Its Comments Concerning the Preliminary Draft of the Convention on the Protection of the Diversity of Cultural Contents and Artistic Expressions (Nov. 19, 2004), *available at* http://www.canadianheritage.gc.ca/newsroom/news_e.cfm?Action=Display&code=4N0222E.
**e.** World Trade Organization: Report of the Appellate Body in Canada—Certain Measures Concerning Periodicals, WTO Doc. WT/DS31/AB/R, 1997 BDIEL AD LEXIS 12 (June 30, 1997).

## OTHER GATT AND WTO PRINCIPLES

### *Nontariff Barriers*

Tariffs are not the only barrier to trade. In some cases, countries have replaced tariffs with *nontariff barriers (NTBs)* as a means of protecting domestic industries threatened by import competition. For example, the preference often given to domestic products in government procurement can reduce the volume of imports. International codes designed to reduce nontariff barriers were negotiated during the Tokyo Round of the GATT (which occurred from 1973 to 1979). Further efforts to reduce NTBs, specifically those arising from regulatory measures that explicitly or effectively protect domestic industries, are reflected in the Agreement on Technical Barriers to Trade and the Agreement on the Application of Sanitary and Phytosanitary Measures.

### *Environmental and Health Exceptions and the SPS Agreement*

The GATT gives member states the right to adopt and enforce measures "relating to the conservation of exhaustible natural resources" as well as measures "necessary to protect human, animal or plant life or health." Such measures cannot be applied in an arbitrary or unjustifiably discriminatory manner, however; nor may they be used as a disguised restriction on trade.

This exception to national treatment has been construed very narrowly.[46] A GATT dispute resolution panel declared a U.S. embargo on tuna caught by fishing methods causing high dolphin mortality to be illegal.[47] Similarly, the U.S. reformulated gasoline standards (adopted as part of the Clean Air Act Amendments in 1990), which imposed tougher baselines for foreign producers and refiners, were successfully challenged by Venezuela and Brazil.[48] The Committee on Trade and Environment, established under the auspices of the WTO to make recommendations on the need for rules to enhance the positive interaction between trade and environmental measures for the promotion of sustainable development, has done little to date.

The Agreement on the Application of Sanitary and Phytosanitary Measures (SPS Agreement), adopted as part of the Uruguay Round, deals with additives, contaminants, toxins, and disease-carrying organisms in food. The SPS Agreement gives WTO member states the right to take sanitary and phytosanitary measures that are "necessary" for the protection of human, animal, or plant life and health. In addition to not being discriminatory or used as disguised restrictions on trade, the measures cannot be "more trade restrictive than required" to achieve their appropriate level of protection. A measure is more trade restrictive than required if there is a reasonably available and feasible alternative that would accomplish the same result.

The European Union unsuccessfully tried to defend its ban on hormone-treated imported meat as a health-related measure in the following case.

46. See Thomas J. Schoenbaum, *International Trade and Protection of the Environment: The Continuing Search for Reconciliation*, 91 AM. J. INT'L L. 268 (1997).
47. United States—Restrictions on Imports of Tuna, 30 I.L.M. 1598 (1992).
48. United States—Standards for Reformulated and Conventional Gasoline, 35 I.L.M. 274 (1996).

A CASE IN POINT

**CASE 25.2**
**EC Measure Concerning Meat and Meat Products (Hormones)**
*World Trade Organization Appellate Body*
*WTO Docs. WT/DS26/AB/R, WT/DS46/ABR (Jan. 16, 1998).*

## Summary

**› FACTS** The European Union banned the import of all meat from cattle treated with any of six growth hormones. The United States and Canada claimed that the hormone ban was not based on convincing scientific evidence and conflicted with the SPS Agreement.

**› ISSUE PRESENTED** Under what circumstances can a WTO member set a level of consumer protection higher than international health standards?

**› SUMMARY OF OPINION** The WTO Appellate Body held that WTO members have a sovereign and autonomous right to set a level of sanitary protection for their own consumers that exceeds international health standards, but only if the sanitary measures are based on a scientific risk assessment. The risk assessment for human health is not a quantitative scientific analysis, but it must cover risk in human societies as they actually exist. Responsible and representative governments may act in good faith on the basis of a divergent scientific view coming from qualified and respected scientists. But in this case, the EU scientific reports did not support the ban because the studies on which the reports were based did not focus specifically on the effects in humans of residues in meat from hormone-treated cattle.

*(Continued)*

(Case 25.2 *continued*)

**› RESULT** The EU ban was inconsistent with the requirements of the SPS Agreement.

**› COMMENTS** The deadline for compliance with the WTO ruling was set for May 13, 1999. When compliance was not reached by that date, the United States sought permission to retaliate by suspending tariff concessions on EU goods. Arbitrators determined that the amount of trade lost to the United States because of the EU's noncompliance was $116.8 million. The United States was given discretion as to which products from the EU would bear the significant increase in tariffs.

## WTO Dispute Settlement Procedures

The United States has used the WTO dispute settlement process both as a means of vindicating rights in particular cases and as a way to communicate to its trading partners that the United States expects them to take seriously compliance with the WTO rules. In fact, according to U.S. government figures, the United States has been an active user of the WTO dispute settlement process, having used it in seventy-five cases from January 1995 to January 2005.[49]

Although the United States has for the most part been successful in pursuing these matters, both by prevailing in cases it has brought and by negotiating settlement agreements, the United States has also lost its share of cases. The United States lost its first case before the WTO in December 1997, when the WTO rejected Eastman Kodak Company's claims that Fuji Photo Film and the Japanese government had erected internal barriers to trade in Japan. Until then, the United States had won outright or obtained concessions in all fourteen of the other cases it had brought at the WTO. The Kodak ruling sparked criticism of the WTO. In the words of then Senator John Ashcroft (R-Missouri), the ruling "raises serious questions about the credibility of this international body and of the U.S. trade representatives' capacity to secure and defend free-trade agreements."[50]

As of July 2004, the United States had lost twenty-three of the eighty-two proceedings initiated by other WTO member countries. In addition to the Kodak ruling, the losses included the WTO's decisions concerning reformulated gasoline, provisions of the U.S. tax code giving preferred treatment to U.S. foreign sales corporations (FSCs),[51] the operation of the U.S. Revenue Act of 1916,[52] and the U.S. imposition of tariffs on foreign steel imports discussed earlier in this chapter.[53]

A significant concern of the United States, as reflected in executive branch testimony before Congress and writings of academics and trade professionals,[54] involves the implementation of WTO decisions. Before the establishment of the WTO, the defendant in a GATT dispute could, in effect, block dispute settlement procedures because the GATT Council could only adopt a panel report unanimously. The WTO's Understanding on Rules and Procedures Governing the Settlement of Disputes improved that process. Under the WTO, a panel of experts will be established at the request of a complaining party. Panel reports will be adopted virtually automatically unless they are rejected by consensus

49. Office of the United States Trade Representative, Snapshot of WTO Cases Involving the United States (Jan. 14, 2005), *at* http://www.ustr.gov/assets/Trade_Agreements/Monitoring_Enforcement/Dispute_Settlement/WTO/asset_upload_file287_5696.pdf.
50. Robert S. Greenberger et al., *WTO's Kodak Ruling Heightens Trade Tensions,* WALL ST. J., Dec. 8, 1997, at A3.

51. FSCs are offshore corporations possessing special tax attributes allowing them to exempt from U.S. income taxation a portion of revenue earned on sales of U.S.-origin goods outside the United States. The WTO ruled in February 2000 that these exemption provisions constituted an illegal export subsidy under WTO rules. U.S.—Tax Treatment for "Foreign Sales Corporations," WTO Docs. WT/DS108/AB/R (WTO App. Body Feb. 24, 2000). The WTO Appellate Body affirmed this decision in 2002 and approved the EU's request for over $4 billion in retaliatory tariffs. As of the end of 2004, the EU had not implemented the sanctions.
52. In August 2000, a WTO Appellate Body upheld a dispute settlement panel finding that the U.S. Revenue Act of 1916 is inconsistent with WTO antidumping rules. The Appellate Body upheld the panel's findings that WTO antidumping rules are applicable to the 1916 Act and that the 1916 Act is inconsistent with these rules because the Act allows for treble damages and criminal penalties against importers of products sold below market value. In addition, according to the WTO, the 1916 Act impermissibly allows duties to be imposed against imports without first requiring a finding of material injury with respect to the import competing industry. The United States had argued that the 1916 Act was more akin to U.S. antitrust laws and, as such, should not be considered subject to WTO antidumping rules. The WTO ruling did not affect the antidumping law contained in the Tariff Act of 1930, which is consistent with the WTO Antidumping Agreement.
53. Office of the United States Trade Representative, *supra* note 49.
54. See, e.g., *Symposium on the First Three Years of the WTO Dispute Settlement System,* 32 INT'L LAW. (Fall 1998).

of the WTO members (including the member–complainant that filed the case in question).

The nature of the WTO as an international institution raises issues that do not arise in the context of implementing domestic judicial decisions. In the domestic setting, a court order has the force of law, and compliance with such orders is ultimately backed by the physical power of governmental authorities. By contrast, a WTO member can respond to losing a case before a panel or appellate body of the WTO by (1) implementing the recommendations and rulings, (2) providing compensation, or (3) accepting suspension of concessions by the winning party or parties. To date, the express preference of the United States has been for members to comply with WTO rulings and implement such changes to national law and policy as are necessary to achieve compliance with the applicable WTO agreement.

This strong preference—and the U.S. willingness to act on it—helps explain why the United States moved expeditiously in implementing a February 2000 WTO decision, compliance with which required a change in U.S. tax law relating to foreign sales corporations.[55] It also helps explain the strong trade tensions that erupted between the United States and the European Union over the EU's implementation of WTO decisions in the so-called bananas and beef hormone cases. In the "bananas case," the United States, along with Ecuador, Guatemala, Honduras, and Mexico, successfully challenged the EU banana regime in WTO dispute settlement proceedings.[56] The WTO panel found that the regime was designed, among other things, to take away a major part of the banana distribution business of U.S. companies. Nonetheless, on January 1, 1999, the EU adopted a regime that, from the U.S. perspective, perpetuated the WTO violations identified by the panel and the appellate body. Consequently, the United States sought WTO authorization to suspend concessions (i.e., retaliate) with respect to certain products from the EU, equivalent in value to the trade damage sustained by the United States. WTO arbitrators determined the level of damage to be $191.4 million. On April 19, 1999, the WTO authorized the United States to suspend concessions, and the United States imposed 100 percent *ad valorem* duties on a list of EU products with an annual trade value of $191.4 million.

The beef hormone case was presented earlier as Case 25.2. This case was important both as a test of the integrity of the WTO dispute settlement system and as the first completed WTO case interpreting the SPS Code. Notice that in response to the EU's position on implementation in these two cases, the United States sought and obtained WTO approval to retaliate by imposing duties on EU exports to the United States worth $308 million.

### *Timetable*

The WTO Understanding on Rules and Procedures Governing the Settlement of Disputes sets forth the procedures and the timetable for resolving disputes. The agreed limits are flexible, but normally a case should not take more than one year (fifteen months if the case is appealed) to run the full course from consultation among the countries involved in the dispute (with mediation by the WTO director–general if the parties cannot resolve the dispute themselves) to a ruling by the Dispute Settlement Body. Exhibit 25.1 presents the timetable for resolution of the reformulated gasoline cases brought by Venezuela and Brazil against the United States.

## Regional Economic Integration

Regional alliances play an important role in the promotion of international trade. More than one hundred regional alliance agreements are in existence. These regional trading alliances vary significantly, but they all achieve some amount of economic integration among the members. Regional alliances can be divided into five groups: free trade areas, customs unions, common markets, economic unions, and political unions. As explained earlier, a free trade area encourages trade among its members by eliminating trade barriers. NAFTA, which reduces tariffs and nontariff barriers among Canada, Mexico, and the United States, is an example of a free trade area.

A customs union not only eliminates internal trade barriers among its members but also adopts common external trade policies toward countries that are not members. The Mercosur Accord, an agreement among Argentina, Brazil, Paraguay, and Uruguay, is an example of a customs union.

55. See Press Release, United States Trade Representative (Sept. 30, 2000) (announcing that the United States and the European Union reached an agreement regarding procedures for reviewing whether replacement legislation for the then current FSC regime is WTO consistent and urging Congress to complete this action as expeditiously as possible).

56. European Communities—Regime for the Importation, Sale and Distribution of Bananas, WTO Doc. WT/DS27/15 (Jan. 7, 1998).

**EXHIBIT 25.1 Timetable for WTO Dispute Settlement Process in Practice: Reformulated Gasoline Decision**

On January 23, 1995, Venezuela complained to the WTO Dispute Settlement Body that, pursuant to amendments to the U.S. Clean Air Act adopted in 1990, the United States applied stricter rules on the chemical characteristics of imported gasoline than it did for domestically refined gasoline. Brazil joined the case in April 1996. The following chart shows the actual timetable for resolution of the dispute.[a]

| Time (0 = start of case) | Target Period | Date | Action |
|---|---|---|---|
| –5 years | | 1990 | U.S. Clean Air Act amended. |
| –4 months | | September 1994 | U.S. restricts gasoline imports under Clean Air Act. |
| 0 | | January 23, 1995 | Venezuela complains to Dispute Settlement Body, asks for consultation with U.S. |
| +1 month | 60 days | February 24, 1995 | Consultations take place. Fail. |
| +2 months | | March 25, 1995 | Venezuela asks Dispute Settlement Body for a panel. |
| +2½ months | 30 days | April 10, 1995 | Dispute Settlement Body agrees to appoint panel. U.S. does not block. (Brazil starts complaint, requests consultation with U.S.) |
| +3 months | | April 28, 1995 | Panel appointed. (On May 31, panel assigned to Brazilian complaint as well.) |
| +6 months | 6+ months | July 10–12 and 13–15, 1995 | Panel meets. |
| +11 months | (actual = 9 months) | December 11, 1995 | Panel gives interim report to U.S., Venezuela, and Brazil for comment. |
| +1 year | | January 29, 1996 | Panel circulates final report to Dispute Settlement Body. |
| +1 year, 1 month | 60 days | February 21, 1996 | U.S. appeals. |
| +1 year, 3 months | | April 29, 1996 | Appellate Body submits report. |
| +1 year, 4 months | 30 days | May 20, 1996 | Dispute Settlement Body adopts panel and appeal reports. |
| +1 year, 10½ months | | December 3, 1996 | U.S. and Venezuela agree on what U.S. should do (implementation period is 15 months from May 20). |
| +1 year, 11½ months | | January 9, 1997 | U.S. submits first monthly report to Dispute Settlement Body on status of implementation. |
| +2 years, 7 months | | August 19–20, 1997 | U.S. signs new regulation (19th). End of agreed implementation period (20th). |

**a.** *Settling Disputes; Case Study: The Timetable in Practice, at* http://www.wto.org/english/thewto_e/whatis_e/tif_e/disp3_e.htm (visited Mar. 13, 2001).

A *common market* has the features of a customs union, but it goes a step further by eliminating barriers that restrict the movement of labor, capital, and technology among the member nations. The European Economic Area, which is an agreement by EU members and several other European countries to promote the free movement of factors of production among them, is an example of a common market.

In an *economic union,* internal trade barriers are abolished, restrictions on mobility of factors of production among members are eliminated, and the economic policies of the member states (monetary, fiscal, taxation, and social welfare programs) are fully integrated so as to blend the member states' economies into a single entity. The European Union, discussed below, is the most visible example of an economic union.

A *political union* represents the complete political and economic integration of the member states. The integration of the thirteen separate colonies under the Articles of Confederation for the United States is an example of a political union.

## The European Union

The European Union (EU), formerly known and still often referred to as the European Community (EC), is an intergovernmental organization of twenty-five European states. The EC/EU was established through the following treaties: the European Coal and Steel Community (established in 1951); the European Atomic Energy Commission (Euratom, established in 1957); the Treaty of Rome, which established the European Economic Community (EEC) in 1957;[57] the Single European Act (1987); and the Treaty on European Union[58] (also known as the Maastricht Treaty), which established the European Union in 1993. From the beginning, the intention was to create a common market, which was formally established in 1993 and is now well down the path to economic, monetary, and political union. As of 2005, the member states were Austria, Belgium, Cyprus, Czech Republic, Denmark, Estonia, Finland, France, Germany, Greece, Hungary, Ireland, Italy, Latvia, Lithuania, Luxembourg, Malta, the Netherlands, Poland, Portugal, Slovakia, Slovenia, Spain, Sweden, and the United Kingdom. Romania and Bulgaria are expected to become members in 2007, and the EU decided at the end of 2004 to commence membership negotiations with Turkey.

Goods, services, people, and capital can move almost as freely within the EU as within one country. There are no tariff barriers between the states, and all states apply a single set of tariffs (called the *common customs tariff*) on goods imported from outside the EU.

The creation of the single EU market has had profound effects on U.S. businesses. It has facilitated the formation of larger European companies with a bigger home market and has increased large-scale research and development in Europe. At the same time, the single market has created a larger market for American goods and has made the EU a more attractive place in which to invest.

The EU negotiates international trade agreements on behalf of the member states, but all agreements (including negotiations with the WTO) must be approved by the individual states. The EU has the exclusive power to take action against dumping in the EU by companies in nonmember countries. Agriculture is centrally coordinated through the Common Agricultural Policy, which supports prices of agricultural products and promotes the modernization of agriculture throughout the EU.

EU competition law, based on U.S. antitrust principles, has been used to prevent companies from engaging in private restraints of trade affecting the member states. For example, the European Commission required Boeing to abandon certain exclusive contracts it had with American Airlines as a condition to obtaining European approval of its acquisition of McDonnell–Douglas. The contracts adversely affected the European aircraft company Airbus Industries. The EU also required America Online and Time–Warner to make certain concessions as a condition to approving their merger.

### *Principal EU Institutions*

Five main institutions have the responsibility for governing the EU: (1) the European Commission, (2) the Council of Ministers, (3) the European Parliament, (4) the European Court of Justice, and (5) the European Central Bank.

**The European Commission** The European Commission is the executive branch of the EU. It comprises twenty-five individuals appointed by the governments of the member states (with each member state appointing one member). Commissioners are expected to act independently of their national governments. With a staff of more than 15,000 civil servants, the Commission is at the heart of the EU's policy-making process.

The Commission formulates recommendations, addresses opinions to members, and may bring member states before the European Court of Justice for failure to carry out their obligations under the Maastricht and Rome Treaties.

**The Council of Ministers** The Council of Ministers, officially known as the Council of the European Union, is the legislative body of the EU. It enacts legislation based on proposals referred to it by the Commission. Members of the Council are appointed by the governments of the member states, but unlike the Commission members, they represent the interests of their respective states.

EU legislation may be in the form of *regulations,* which are directly applicable in the member states without the need for national measures to implement them. Legislation may also take two other forms. One is the *directive,* which is a law directing member states to enact certain laws or regulations. Directives are binding with

57. Treaty Establishing the European Economic Community, Mar. 25, 1957, 298 U.N.T.S. 11.
58. Treaty on European Union, Feb. 7, 1992, 1992 O.J. (C 224) 1, 31 I.L.M. 247 (1992).

respect to the objective to be achieved but allow national authorities to choose the form and means of implementation. The other form of legislation is the *decision,* which is an order directed at a specific person or member state.

**The European Parliament** The 732 members of the European Parliament (EP) are the only EU policymakers elected directly by the citizens of the member states, generally in proportion to the population of each state. The Parliament must be consulted twice on each legislative proposal. First, it considers the proposed law at the committee level; then it expresses its opinion by a vote in plenary session. If the EP rejects a proposal, the law can be enacted only by a unanimous vote of the Council of Ministers. The EP can also amend European Commission proposals. If the Commission supports the EP amendment, the amended proposal can be defeated only by a unanimous vote of the Council of Ministers. Finally, the Parliament has the power to dismiss the Commission with a two-thirds vote and to reject the Commission's annual budget.

**The European Court of Justice** The European Court of Justice (ECJ) is the judicial branch of the EU. Its role is to interpret the treaties establishing the EU and to determine whether national laws, as applied by the national courts, are consistent with those obligations. The ECJ has been a major force in affirming the powers of community institutions and the development of a single market.

The ECJ comprises up to fifteen judges and nine advocates general appointed by the national governments. In 2003, a total of 561 new cases came before the ECJ, bringing the number of pending cases to a total of 974. Of these, the ECJ decided 494. There are five primary avenues to the ECJ:[59]

1. *Failure to comply.* The Commission advises a company or a country that it has failed to comply with a directive or regulation. If the company or country contests the Commission's ruling, then the matter is brought before the ECJ.
2. *Annulment.* Any member state or EU institution (i.e., Commission, Council, or Parliament) may ask the ECJ to annul an EU decision as contrary to the Rome Treaty.
3. *Failure to act.* Member states or EU institutions may ask the ECJ to declare that a country, the Council of Ministers, or the Commission has failed to take a required action. Individuals who are personally and directly concerned may intercede in the proceeding.
4. *Civil liabilities.* National courts and individuals may ask the ECJ for a ruling that the EU or a national government is liable for damages for an act or failure to act.
5. *Preliminary rulings.* National courts can ask for an opinion as to whether a national law conflicts with one or more articles of the Rome or Maastricht Treaties and request guidance as to how EU law should be interpreted and applied to the matter at hand. Most of the ECJ's cases fall into this category.

59. The authors gratefully acknowledge the assistance of Professor Claude Mosseri-Marlio in the preparation of this discussion of the ECJ.

In an effort to reduce a two-year backlog, a junior court—the Court of First Instance—was created in 1989. It hears administrative cases, competition cases, dumping suits involving countries outside the EU, and intellectual property cases. Appeals from the Court of First Instance to the ECJ can be made only on matters of law, not matters of fact.

**The European Central Bank and the EMU** The Maastricht Treaty required all member states to converge their economic and monetary policies with the goal of creating a single European currency, the *euro.* The convergence criteria called for the member states to harmonize their budget deficits, inflation levels, public-sector debt, and long-term interest rates at specific target levels and to achieve exchange rate stability. These efforts culminated in the creation of the European Monetary Union (EMU) on January 1, 1999.

Eleven EU members qualified for initial participation in the euro: Austria, Belgium, Finland, France, Germany, Ireland, Italy, Luxembourg, the Netherlands, Portugal, and Spain. Greece was permitted to adopt the euro in 2001, after lowering its budget deficits and inflation. The United Kingdom, Sweden, and Denmark are eligible but have adopted a wait-and-see approach. By giving up their national currencies, members of the EMU have relinquished control of their exchange rates and monetary policies to the independent European Central Bank (ECB) based in Frankfurt, Germany, which came onstream on July 1, 1998. The ECB's primary duty is to maintain price stability, usually by lowering or raising interest rates.

On January 1, 1999, all currencies of participating member states were irrevocably locked together at a specified conversion rate, and the euro became the official currency. National currency units became denominations of the euro. Until June 30, 2002, national currencies remained legal tender in participating states, but both the euro and national banknotes were used simultaneously, with prices posted in both denominations. On June 30, 2002, the French franc, the German mark, the Dutch guilder, and the currencies of other members of the EMU ceased to exist, and the euro became the sole currency for much of Europe.

### *Challenges*

Notwithstanding the tremendous progress toward European integration, challenges remain. There is no European citizenship—a nonnational can vote in local but not national elections. There is no European company law or Europe-wide insurance. Rules for pension plans are not coordinated, and plans cannot hold nonnational shares of stock. There is still no tax harmonization; national varieties include value-added, income, company, capital gains, wealth, and inheritance taxes. In addition, the EU administrative structure is top-heavy and became even more unwieldy when the ten new members were added in 2004. The EU is in the process of adopting a constitution, which will modify certain aspects of the existing EU structure. See the "Inside Story" in this chapter for more information about these efforts.

# International Transactions

## Overseas Offices and Subsidiaries

U.S. businesses can establish a presence in a foreign country to supervise or manage sales with little or no investment by setting up a liaison, representative, or branch office in the host country. The scope of permissible activities, capital requirements, and tax liabilities of each of these forms of representation varies with the legal scheme of the host jurisdiction.

Typically, the greater the scope of permissible activities, the more stringent the capitalization and taxation rules. Thus, representative and liaison offices are generally limited to providing services on behalf of a home office. They cannot engage in manufacturing operations, and the nature of the sales support and marketing activities they can conduct typically is limited. In countries with very limited or no provision for such operations, companies may be forced to choose between use of an agent or distributor on the one hand and a branch or subsidiary on the other.

A branch office can perform certain kinds of services, such as import and export, provided it is formally capitalized, registers with local government authorities, and pays income and other required taxes. Legally, the lack of local limited liability protection is one reason not to use a branch office. Many companies have subsidiaries that are entirely separate legal entities, with their own capital structure, boards of directors, and officers. Different tax treatment is a second reason to favor a subsidiary rather than a foreign office when establishing an overseas presence. Another issue that should not be overlooked is the burden of disclosing and possibly restating company financials under local regulations.

## Contracting in an International Environment

An international contract, like a domestic one, may reallocate rights, obligations, and risks in a way different from what they would be in the absence of the contract under applicable law. In an international context, however, the practices common to the parties may be fewer, their assumptions and expectations more divergent, and the risks greater. There is, in short, more ground to be covered to ensure a true meeting of the minds—and more risk and uncertainty in proceeding without one.

## Payment and Letters of Credit

Because the parties to an international transaction may not be well known to each other, a very common payment mechanism for international transactions is the opening (that is, the establishment) of a documentary credit, commonly known as a letter of credit. The buyer or borrower (the *applicant*) enters into a contract with the issuing bank, which is usually in the buyer's or borrower's jurisdiction. The issuing bank issues a letter of credit in favor of the seller or lender (the *beneficiary*). The *documentary letter of credit (L/C)* provides for payment by the issuing bank to the beneficiary upon tender by the beneficiary (or its agent or assignee) of specified documents. The nature of these specified documents is based on the terms of the contract between the applicant and the beneficiary.

Two sets of rules can apply to L/Cs in international transactions. The first is Article 5 of the Uniform Commercial Code (UCC), which varies slightly from state to state. The second set of rules is set forth in the International Chamber of Commerce's Uniform Customs and Practice for Documentary Credits (UCP), the most recent version of which is contained in a document often cited in bank L/C forms as Uniform Customs and Practice for Documentary Credits, 1993 Revision, ICC Publication No. 500.

There are significant differences between UCC Article 5 and the UCP. For example, UCC Article 5, as interpreted by most U.S. courts, provides that, once established, an L/C is irrevocable unless otherwise agreed. The UCP, by its terms, establishes the opposite presumption: an L/C is revocable at the issuing bank's option and without prior notice to or agreement of the beneficiary unless the contract and the L/C expressly state that the L/C is irrevocable. These rules, as much as the terms of the underlying sales contract, can determine the outcome of a payment dispute.

The parties can elect to have their L/C governed by UCC Article 5 or by the UCP, and they should be specific about their choice.[60] It is also prudent to expressly specify in the L/C whether it is revocable or irrevocable.

## Guaranties and Standby Letters of Credit in Financing Transactions

Guaranties and standby letters of credit are also often used to provide security for those providing financing for a major construction project in another country. If the political or credit risks of a country are perceived to be especially great, an entity in the host country, often an instrumentality of the host country government, may be called upon to act as the guarantor. Under a *guaranty* arrangement, a local financial institution guarantees, for the benefit of the project owners, that the lender will be repaid if the project principals are unable to pay, as long as the parties to the project have adhered to the contracts.

U.S. law prohibits U.S. banks from issuing guaranties, so a standby letter of credit is sometimes used to provide payment or repayment comfort. Under a *standby letter of credit,* payment is usually conditioned upon a brief statement, in language previously agreed upon by the applicant and the beneficiary, that the applicant is in default or has failed to perform an obligation to the beneficiary under the construction or similar project and the beneficiary is therefore entitled to payment from the issuing bank. Unlike the common form of guaranty, the creditor only has to tender the specified document and is not required to establish that the debtor breached its obligations in the underlying contract. This means that a guarantor can raise any defenses that the primary debtor could have raised while a bank that issued a standby letter of credit cannot inquire into the underlying transaction or assert the defenses that the applicant has.

Although letters of credit are therefore more secure, they cost money, and, in an ongoing relationship, the buyer usually presses for more favorable payment terms. In the multinational-corporation context, having a well-known parent company guarantee a local affiliate's obligations is a fairly common cost-saving alternative to an L/C.

60. Certain provisions in revised Article 5 cannot be varied by agreement; as a practical matter, however, the nonvariable rules are unlikely to conflict with any UCP rule.

## Investment Abroad

Before investing outside the United States, U.S. firms should (1) assess their investment goals; (2) consider the economic, political, geographic, legal, and labor conditions in the host country; and (3) address any financial issues, such as currency considerations, project capitalization, and taxation.

### *Investment Goals*

A business plan for investing abroad must begin with an assessment of the investor's goals. The attractiveness of a prospective investment in a given host country can vary greatly, depending on these goals.

### *Local Market Penetration*

For legal or business reasons, some markets are almost inaccessible to U.S. manufacturers wishing to sell their products. Developing countries may lack hard currency—that is, convertible foreign exchange—and these shortages may limit their purchase of imports. Applicable laws may restrict imports of certain products but grant benefits to foreign investors wishing to manufacture those products locally. To penetrate these types of markets, the only practical approach may be to invest in a local manufacturing facility. Certain Asian countries permit only local companies to establish retail businesses—another example of how foreign companies may be prevented from competing in certain markets.

### *Regional Base*

U.S. businesses that wish to compete in Europe or Asia may need to establish manufacturing, marketing, and/or service centers in the relevant region to gain credibility with local customers. U.S. businesses may also need to be on-site to sustain their local sources of supplies for operations elsewhere. Regional bases can reduce transportation costs, enhance time-to-market responses, help avoid cultural difficulties, and generally help the home office monitor the business pulse of the region. They also avoid potential problems with distributors or agents not wholly committed to the products or not aligned with the foreign parent. The challenge of integrating an expatriate with the local business environment is the corollary of this issue of aligning locally hired managers with the overall corporate mission and goals.

### *Cheaper Production Costs*

Developing countries typically offer cheaper labor and raw materials than more industrialized countries. These lower costs are often the primary reason for U.S. business investment in foreign manufacturing operations. As discussed below, however, the assessment of true production costs is not limited to a line item comparison of the costs of each element of production. Intangible issues such as labor efficiency, reliability of supplies, local labor law requirements, and political stability can affect the true costs of production.

## Host Country Conditions

Prospective investors need to consider the economic, political, geographic, legal, and labor conditions in the host country.

### *Economic Conditions*

The host country's economic condition is usually a high-profile issue in the investment evaluation process. Per capita income, for example, may determine whether a particular country is a realistic market for a particular product or whether it is a likely source of inexpensive labor. Economic growth trends can suggest both a growing consumer market and increasing labor costs. The monetary system is also important because the existence of a readily convertible currency and the nature of the currency-exchange laws will determine whether profits can be easily repatriated (that is, transferred abroad). In a country with a high inflation rate, local suppliers may be reluctant to perform on long-term contracts, and capital and working loans may be more expensive.

The U.S. Department of Commerce, the U.S. Foreign Commercial Service, and the U.S. Department of State regularly publish reports on the economic condition of various countries. These agencies can offer a good introduction for a prospective foreign investor. The U.S. Foreign Commercial Service has a wide-ranging network of commercial officers stationed at U.S. embassies and consulates throughout the world. They collect and analyze economic data and are available on-site to U.S. businesses to interpret how that data may be relevant to an investment project.

### *Political Conditions*

Political instability inevitably leads to some degree of legal and economic instability. Generally, investors are mainly concerned with the reliability and stability of the local legal institutions that enforce contracts and protect property rights. Changes of government in Western democracies can lead to changes in the legal and policy environment that dramatically affect the economic results of foreign investments but do not undermine the rule of law. Other political systems may have a stable regime but with a corrupt judicial and legislative system that does not offer effective legal recourse for investors. At the outer extreme, violent political or civil divisions can lead to the complete collapse of the rule of law. Business can still be done in such an environment, but written contractual terms become insignificant next to practical considerations of power, possession, and protection.

A prospective foreign investor must, therefore, look beyond the reasonableness of the contract, the competence of its foreign business counterpart, and the desirability of the site to determine whether the existing government and its policies are aligned with the needs of the project and whether that government or its policies are likely to change in adverse ways. Managers should analyze both (1) political risks, such as expropriation, partial nationalization, and serious operational restrictions, which often stem from a change in the overall political orientation; and (2) legal risks, such as changes in tax, customs, employment, and other laws that do not represent an inherent shift against private ownership or foreign investment.

### *Geographic Conditions*

Climatic and geographic conditions can directly affect the production and transportation of products. Severe weather in certain seasons can affect delivery schedules. Consequently, it is important to ascertain the breadth and reliability of the transportation system and other infrastructure available.

The nature, cost, and development status of a prospective site are major considerations. In some countries (such as China, Indonesia, the Philippines, and Thailand), foreign investors are not permitted to own land but can, often with the assistance of a local partner, obtain long-term land-use rights. If the capital investment will be large relative to the parent company's assets, a foreign investor may want to consider investing only in countries that offer guaranties concerning expropriation or in friendly developing countries where U.S. investors are eligible for OPIC insurance (discussed earlier in the chapter). Sometimes a country may seek to attract investment to certain areas by offering attractive land-use terms and new infrastructure.

Mistaken assumptions about issues such as land rights and use, flood control, power supply, fire protection, utility service, legal and informal employee protections, and the like can present the most significant hidden operational hazard in foreign direct investment. It is critical for the investor and its legal and business advisers to probe these areas aggressively in their due diligence.

## Legal Conditions

Managers should ask whether local laws and courts offer predictability, uniformity, and evenhanded enforcement. Also, is the judicial system speedy, efficient, and inexpensive? Beyond the letter of the laws, their effectiveness depends on political conditions and the nature of the legal and administrative organs that interpret and enforce them. A reliable court system or comparable dispute resolution forum (such as an established arbitration system) is essential; without it, the investor will have little leverage to enforce contracts or invoke commercial laws.

Sources of necessary supplies should be secure, and their transportation and storage not subject to rampant theft. The existence of a reasonably diligent and fair law enforcement network is a factor to be considered in this regard.

Foreign investors must develop a working knowledge of the applicable host country laws and acceptable forums for dispute resolution, and they should obtain professional advice from local attorneys. These professionals can also assist in providing accurate contract translations where required. It is not uncommon for a country to require that the definitive text of a contract be in the local language (for example, Mexico requires contracts to be in Spanish), but an accurate English version is critical.

Many countries offer a variety of vehicles for foreign investment. A foreign investor can select the investment format most appropriate to its project in a foreign country, just as a U.S. business can choose to operate domestically as a sole proprietorship; a general, limited, or limited liability partnership; a limited liability company; or a corporation. Each form is subject to its own set of laws, which affect management structure, equity investment requirements, limitation of investor liabilities, and taxation.

Often, though, businesses have less structural flexibility in foreign jurisdictions. In contrast to the United States, in some countries more prestige is attached to specific forms (for example, in some European countries, the private limited company form may be perceived as a less serious commitment than the public limited company form). Country handbooks published by international accounting firms, local law firms, and the U.S. government contain useful information on such issues.

The licensing or contribution of technology by the U.S. business to the foreign business is often a component of an equity investment project. Some countries' investment laws or policies may limit the portion of the foreign party's equity investment that can be attributable to intellectual property as compared with cash or equipment, for example. Certain restrictions on technology use may be invalid under local technology licensing laws.

A would-be investor should also check for bilateral tax or investment treaties that grant reciprocal rights to businesses from the host and investor countries. These treaties may offer significant benefits, such as avoidance of double taxation (that is, taxation by both the host and investor countries) and guaranties against uncompensated expropriation by the host government.

The U.S. State Department compiles records of ratified treaties and their signatories. A quick review of this information can provide a sense of the relative involvement of various nations in international conventions that affect foreign investment.

## Labor Conditions

A leading reason for investing abroad is to take advantage of relatively low labor costs in a foreign country. The true cost of labor, however, is more than the hourly or daily wage. It includes labor efficiency, trainability, reliability, and adherence to quality control standards. In addition, the labor and foreign investment laws of some countries, particularly those with socialist economies, require employers to fund a wide range of employee benefits that are not expected by U.S. investors. These benefits include housing, travel, education, and food subsidies, as well as the more common retirement, health insurance, and maternity benefits. Many nations do not permit employers to terminate an employee without just cause, which can make it difficult to terminate inefficient or redundant workers. Local labor laws may limit the degree to which employees may be treated differently, thus restricting flexibility in incentive compensation.

## Financial Issues

Several common financial concerns for an equity investor in a foreign project include currency considerations, project funding and capitalization, and taxation.

**Currency Considerations** The currency in which the foreign entity does business and in which its assets and obligations are denominated can be a major concern for a U.S. investor in many developing countries. The ideal is an open economy (1) without currency and other monetary restrictions and (2) with a currency tied directly to the dollar or at least to another stable major currency such as the euro. This minimizes the fluctuations in investment results due solely to currency issues relative to those inherent in the fundamental economics of the business. In the second-best case, the prices of inputs and outputs are primarily denominated in hard currency, even though the local currency is the unit of account (a common requirement). This is most typical in export and processing operations. Often, however, the investor will find that local currency controls and financing restrictions are a significant issue. In that case, hedging contract commitments and planning capital allocation across currencies and in view of governmental restrictions will be an integral part of establishing and implementing a successful financial plan.

Local financial institutions are often restricted in offering foreign-currency loans. At the same time, foreign banks outside the host country may be reluctant to offer capital loans if local currency profits may not be freely convertible for loan repayment. Project proceeds, or even host country project properties, may not offer sufficient security for a loan from a foreign financial institution. Consequently, the foreign investor may be required to obtain and provide security entirely outside the host jurisdiction for any loans it desires.

The availability and cost of hard currency can be a major issue when the host country currency is not freely convertible. It may be of less concern to a foreign investor that expects to earn hard currency through exports of either the project's products or other local products purchased with its local currency profits. This latter arrangement is known as *countertrade*.

Cash-flow hedging methods are increasingly common in countries that maintain restrictive controls on foreign exchange. For example, a company with both import and export activities might structure import payments to match hard-currency inflows in order to reduce potential exchange rate losses. If the local currency is depreciating rapidly, inflows of hard-currency earnings may lag behind offsetting import payments. As a currency is devalued, import costs rise. Potential exchange rate losses can be avoided by delaying the conversion of export receivables into local currency until imported goods are paid for.

The currency denomination also affects the capitalization of an investment project. For example, a foreign partner in a joint venture may agree to contribute a specified amount of U.S. dollars over time, with the host country partner making an equal contribution in the local currency. If the local currency depreciates against the U.S. dollar, the foreign partner will end up making a greater than 50 percent contribution to the joint venture in local currency terms. Some reconciliation of paid-in capital and share pricing may be needed under local law. Unequal contributions may also arise where local law requires foreign-currency capital contributions to be valued at an official exchange rate that fails to reflect the local currency's true value. These currency risks can be addressed by careful contract drafting and, where possible, through currency swaps and hedging.

**Project Capitalization** The foreign business to which the investor is committing an investment typically requires fixed capital (often for construction costs) and working capital for daily operations. Local laws and practices may not permit the flexibility in capital structure available in the United States. The reliability and attractiveness of a host nation in this regard may be affected by factors such as political risk, currency-convertibility laws, profit-repatriation restrictions, local banking laws and practices, and the enforceability of guaranties or security agreements. As noted earlier, the lenders will usually require the borrower to secure its repayment obligations by providing a standby letter of credit or guaranty.

**Taxation** Careful tax planning can minimize the risk of withholding taxes and double income taxation and can enable the investor to take advantage of local tax benefits. One simple way of addressing tax risks is a *gross-up clause*, whereby the local party is obligated to pay all taxes other than those specifically allocated to the foreign party. In this way, the foreign party avoids the risk of tax increases or unknown taxes. Some countries prohibit such reallocation of responsibility for the payment of certain taxes, however, and will not recognize gross-ups. As a result, a gross-up, though simple in concept, often is not the most efficient way of addressing certain tax issues.

The United States has bilateral tax treaties with more than fifty countries. The treaties seek to avoid double taxation of U.S.-based businesses and individuals. Some treaties also impose tax ceilings on certain types of income; for example, one treaty imposes a 10 percent tax ceiling on passive income such as royalties from technology licenses or rental income. Bilateral tax treaties may not affect all the taxes applicable to a foreign investment project or to an individual expatriate employee's income; when a tax treaty provision is applicable, however, and offers more favorable tax treatment than the comparable domestic tax rule, the treaty rule will generally apply.

Tax credits may be available to U.S. businesses engaged in foreign projects that are taxed by the host country. Such credits are available for the amount of foreign taxes paid up to a certain limit, which is derived by dividing the foreign-source taxable income by the total taxable income (which includes all foreign- and domestic-source income) and multiplying that fraction by the U.S. tax liability on the total taxable income. (Thus, if foreign tax rates exceed U.S. rates, no credit is available for the excess in the current year.) Foreign tax credits for any one year cannot exceed the amount of foreign income taxes that have been paid or accrued, but taxes in excess of the limitation can be carried back two years and forward five years, subject to each year's tax credit limit.

### *Operational Concerns*

Many noncommercial issues can affect the desirability of operating a business abroad. Knowledge of the language and customs of the host country, or the use of proficient interpreters, is essential to the success of a business venture abroad. Stories abound concerning the gaffes of U.S. investors who, because of language difficulties or cultural misunderstandings, offended their foreign partners, misinterpreted contract negotiations, miscalculated the effect of their business operations, or simply could not maintain effective working relationships with their foreign counterparts. Contract terms, both legal and technical, require accurate translation to ensure effective implementation.

The business customs of a host country can have a substantial impact on local business operations on very basic levels. A frank and direct management style may be welcomed in some countries; in others, it may be viewed as arrogant and gauche. Gift giving may be appropriate, even expected, behavior in certain circumstances; in other situations, it may be regarded as unethical and possibly illegal.

International direct-dial land phones, cellular phones, fax machines, and electronic mail are common business tools in some regions but may not be available in some developing countries. Even postal or courier services may be unreliable. Such infrastructural deficiencies need to be reflected in contract provisions requiring timely notice or delivery of documents.

Developing countries may also lack reliable transportation, which can affect the delivery of raw materials within a host country. Inadequate port facilities can lead to delayed shipments abroad and lost sales. Inefficient or corrupt customs officials can have similar effects in delaying business transactions and increasing their cost.

In many developing countries, an expatriate manager and staff may be essential to provide needed skills and to proselytize the corporate culture and goals to local staff. To attract qualified personnel to hardship posts, a company usually must offer a compensation package that includes income premiums and benefits. If expatriate staff must pay considerable income tax to the host country, further additional compensation may have to be paid to counteract this disadvantage. Local managers may resent the higher compensation of their expatriate counterparts, however, and local laws may require that local managers receive comparable compensation.

Personal safety may be an issue in some countries, effectively precluding the assignment of personnel with families. It may also be difficult to extend comparable company health and life insurance benefits to expatriate employees.

## DISPUTE RESOLUTION IN INTERNATIONAL BUSINESS

As in domestic trade and transactions, disputes may arise in international trade and transactions, but the international environment often makes the resolution of disputes more difficult.

### *Dispute Resolution Mechanisms*

International law provides several possible methods for the resolution of disputes: negotiation, good offices, mediation, inquiry, conciliation, arbitration, and litigation.

Negotiation is a very informal process in which the goal is to reach a compromise. Often the parties try negotiation before resorting to other means of dispute resolution.

*Good offices* is a process used mainly in the area of public international law. A third party (often a disinterested government) brings the parties together by establishing communication and providing a site where the parties can meet, often in secret. Increasingly, international organizations are taking the role of the disinterested third party. Mediation is very similar to good offices and often is used in private international law disputes. In mediation, the third (disinterested) party is called the mediator and plays a more active role than the third party in good offices. The mediator facilitates the communications of the parties and may also intervene in a constructive way (for example, to propose a settlement). A mediator works to reconcile the opposing claims and to appease the feelings of resentment that may have arisen between the parties. Like good offices, mediation is generally nonbinding.

*Inquiry* is done by a commission of inquiry that is established ad hoc, often after a violation of international law. Two contending governments review the finding of the commission with the goal of achieving an acceptable solution to the dispute at hand. *Conciliation* is a more formalized method of dispute resolution. It is similar to inquiry but adds a "cooling-off" period. In addition, the parties agree in advance to accept the finding of the commission.

In arbitration, a legal process is carried out by a tribunal that is often very similar to a court. The parties must decide in advance whether the arbitration decision will be final and binding and not subject to review by any courts. Unless such a stipulation is made, the dispute may be reviewed by a court without reference to the arbitration (*de novo* review), rendering the arbitration decision unenforceable. Litigation, which is a legal proceeding conducted in the court system of a state or nation, is the most structured method of dispute resolution.

Arbitration can be preferable to litigation for several reasons. First, arbitration is potentially more flexible and allows the structure, formalities, and proceedings to be tailored to the specific case at hand. Second, international arbitral bodies often have more experience in dealing with international commercial disputes than their judicial counterparts. Another benefit is that arbitral bodies, unlike courts, can keep the nature and the outcome of the dispute confidential, and they may provide a more level playing field than some judicial systems. Finally, as discussed below, arbitral awards in many cases are enforceable in countries where a foreign court's judgment would not be.

## Choice of Law and Choice of Forum

Since most international transactions are conducted on a contract basis, most disputes involving international transactions relate to an alleged past or future contractual relationship. Crucial considerations in any dispute will be which law applies to the contract and which country's courts have jurisdiction over the dispute.

The substantive terms of a contract are typically subject to the laws of a single jurisdiction, which will clarify, modify, or even void the provisions of a contract. If a contract leaves an issue open, the applicable law may fill the gap, disregarding the parties' unwritten intentions. Certain provisions may be included to address requirements of laws of other jurisdictions (for example, U.S. export controls may affect non-U.S. contracts). Even if the written contract addresses an issue, that provision may be affected by what is allowed or required under the relevant local law. It is important, therefore, to understand not only what the parties wish to do but also what they are permitted to do. Achieving this understanding can be difficult. Familiar legal terms in one jurisdiction may have a different meaning and effect in another. Hence, it is often of utmost importance to have advisers in each jurisdiction who understand the relevant differences between that jurisdiction and others and can fully address the intricacies of cross-border transactions.

International contracts should generally include explicit choice-of-law and choice-of-forum provisions to avoid later disputes over which law applies and which country's courts (or other dispute resolution tribunal) have jurisdiction. It is important to remember, however, that under certain circumstances a court will not honor the parties' choice-of law-provision. As explained further in Chapter 3, this is most likely to occur when application of the chosen law would violate the public policy of the jurisdiction in which the lawsuit is brought. For example, an Indian court will not enforce a postemployment covenant not to compete against an Indian employee living in India even if the employer is based in Massachusetts and the employment contract specifies that the law of the Commonwealth of Massachusetts (which will enforce reasonable covenants not to compete) will govern the employment relationship. To enforce the covenant would violate India's strong public policy in favor of employees' right to ply their trade.

When jurisdiction and choice of law are not specified in the contract and are disputed, the court in which the suit is filed will apply *conflict-of-laws rules,* which usually focus on the significance of each country's relationship to the contract. These principles (sometimes referred to as principles of private international law) vary in some respects from country to country, and the process of litigating them can be extended and expensive. Consequently, it is prudent to address these issues in advance.

As explained in Chapter 8, if both parties to an international contract are nationals of countries that are signatories to the United Nations Convention on Contracts for the International Sale of Goods (CISG), the rules of that convention may apply, unless the parties opt out of the CISG rules. CISG rules also apply if the country whose law applies (as determined by the contract or by conflict-of-laws principles) is a signatory to CISG.

A contract party may be willing to accept the substantive law of the other party's country but prefer that any disputes be submitted to a neutral forum. In such a case, an international arbitral organization is commonly specified.

Commonly selected international arbitral forums include the International Chamber of Commerce (ICC) in Paris, the International Center for the Settlement of Investment Disputes (ICSID), the Arbitration Institute of the Stockholm Chamber of Commerce, and the Arbitration Institute of the Zurich Chamber of Commerce. Each international arbitral body has its own procedural rules. Internationally accepted arbitration rules, such as those adopted by the United Nations Commission on International Trade Law (UNCITRAL), may also be used in conjunction with the parties' own methods of selecting an arbitral panel. This latter type of arrangement is referred to as ad hoc arbitration. If there is no mutually convenient venue for the arbitration, the parties will often designate a place that is comparably distant and inconvenient for both parties.

### Enforcement of Awards

After a dispute has ended, the awards must be enforced, but enforcement across national borders can present additional problems. Under the principle of *comity,* a court will enforce another country's judgments under certain conditions. Usually, three conditions must be met: (1) reciprocity must be extended between the countries (i.e., the countries have agreed to mutually honor each other's court decisions, usually by way of a treaty); (2) proper notice is given to the defendant; and (3) the foreign court's judgment does not violate domestic statutes or treaty obligations. U.S. courts, however, generally do not require reciprocity in order to honor foreign judgments.[61]

Since 1993 thirty-five countries, including the United States, have been negotiating a Convention on Jurisdiction and Foreign Judgments in Civil and Commercial Matters under the auspices of the Hague Conference on Private International Law. Because the United States gives greater recognition and enforcement to foreign judgments than most foreign countries give to U.S. judgments, the United States has something to gain from the Convention; however, it may have to relinquish some of its present notions on jurisdiction in order to participate.

More than sixty countries, including the United States and most of the major trading nations, are parties to the 1958 United Nations Convention on the Recognition and Enforcement of Foreign Arbitral Awards (often referred to as the New York Convention). Its purpose is "to unify standards by which agreements to arbitrate are observed and arbitral awards are enforced in signatory countries." The New York Convention requires signatory countries to recognize and enforce foreign arbitration awards except in very limited circumstances. As a result, arbitration awards of another country can often be enforced more readily in a foreign court than foreign judgments.

### Forum Non Conveniens

Defendants in international disputes often invoke the doctrine of *forum non conveniens,* claiming that the forum chosen by the plaintiff is not convenient. To prevail on a motion to dismiss a case under this doctrine, the defendant must first show that an adequate alternative forum exists. On "rare occasions" the remedy available in the alternative forum may be so unsatisfactory that the forum is inadequate, but the "mere fact that the foreign and home fora have different laws does not ordinarily make the foreign forum inadequate."[62] Indeed, the U.S. Court of Appeals for the Second Circuit has explained:

> Even if particular causes of action or certain desirable remedies are not available in the foreign forum, that forum will usually be adequate so long as it permits litigation of the subject matter of the dispute, provides adequate procedural safeguards and the remedy available in the alternative forum is not so inadequate as to amount to no remedy at all.[63]

Thus, for example, England was deemed an adequate forum even though the Sherman Act and certain common law claims were not available and English courts had never awarded money damages in an antitrust case.[64] Trinidad was deemed adequate even though the plaintiff, who potentially could recover $8 million in the United States, was likely limited to $570,000 in Trinidad.[65]

After showing the adequacy of the alternative forum, the defendant must demonstrate that the ordinarily strong presumption favoring the plaintiff's chosen forum is countered by public and private interest factors identified by the U.S. Supreme Court in *Gulf Oil Corp. v. Gilbert.*[66] In *Gilbert,* the Supreme Court outlined four public interest factors for courts to weigh: (1) administrative difficulties associated with court congestion, (2) the unfairness of imposing jury duty on a community with no relation to the litigation, (3) the "local interest in having localized controversies decided at home," and (4) the interest in avoiding difficult problems in resolving conflict-of-law issues and applying foreign law. The private interest factors enumerated in *Gilbert* include (1) ease of access to evidence; (2) the availability of compulsory process to compel the attendance of unwilling witnesses; (3) the cost of willing witnesses' attendance; (4) if relevant, the possibility of a view of premises; and (5) all other factors that might make a trial quicker or less expensive.

### Suing Foreign Governments

Sovereign immunity and the act-of-state doctrine are international legal principles that affect the rights of private commercial parties when a government becomes

61. See Restatement (Second) of Conflict of Laws § 6 cmt. k, § 98 cmt. e (1971).

62. DiRienzo v. Philip Servs. Corp., 232 F.3d 49 (2d Cir. 2000).

63. *Id.* at 57.

64. Capital Currency Exch., N.V. v. Nat'l Westminster Bank PLC, 155 F.3d 603 (2d Cir. 1998), *cert. denied,* 526 U.S. 1067 (1999).

65. Alcoa S.S. Co. v. M/V Nordic Regent, 654 F.2d 147 (2d Cir. 1980) (*en banc*).

66. 330 U.S. 501 (1947).

involved in or interferes with an international commercial transaction.

**Sovereign Immunity** The doctrine of *sovereign immunity* prevents the courts of one country from hearing suits against the governments of other countries. The rationale underlying this rule is that all sovereign states are equal, and none may subject others to their laws.

The needs of commerce have gradually tempered this rule. Because private entities often enter into commercial transactions with foreign governments, it became apparent that allowing a government to have complete immunity from all suits was not desirable. Thus, the concept of absolute immunity has yielded to the restrictive theory of sovereign immunity, which allows immunity for a government's public activities but not for its commercial activities.

The Foreign Sovereign Immunities Act of 1976 (FSIA) is the U.S. codification of the restrictive theory of immunity. The FSIA was designed to eliminate the inconsistencies associated with politically initiated decisions to grant or withhold sovereign immunity in particular cases. It empowered the courts to determine when sovereign immunity applies, "by reference to the nature of the course of conduct or particular transaction or act."

The FSIA is the sole basis for obtaining jurisdiction over a foreign government in U.S. courts. The FSIA grants a blanket immunity to foreign states except in cases in which (1) the foreign state expressly or impliedly waives its immunity; (2) the foreign state engages in commercial activities; (3) the foreign state expropriates property in violation of international law (that is, seizes it without proper compensation); (4) property in the United States that is immovable or was acquired by gift or succession is at issue; (5) the foreign state commits certain noncommercial torts; (6) suit is brought to enforce a maritime lien under admiralty (maritime) law; or (7) the defendant wishes to file a counterclaim in a suit initiated by the foreign state.

The *commercial activity exception* to sovereign immunity provides that a foreign sovereign or its agencies and instrumentalities shall not be immune from the jurisdiction of the courts of the United States or of the states in any case in which the action is based upon an act (1) outside the territory of the United States in connection with a commercial activity of the foreign sovereign elsewhere (2) that causes a direct effect in the United States. As the U.S. Court of Appeals for the Second Circuit explained: "If the sovereign's activity is commercial in nature and has a direct effect in the United States, then the jurisdictional nexus is met, no immunity attaches, and a district court has the authority to adjudicate disputes based on that activity."[67] For example, in *Argentina v. Weltover*,[68] the U.S. Supreme Court held that Argentina's unilateral rescheduling of bond payments had a "direct effect" in the United States because New York was the place of payment.

The FSIA is particularly relevant to U.S. companies that do or intend to do business with state-owned or state-managed enterprises, such as those in China and Vietnam. The exception from immunity for the commercial activities of these entities may not always be clear, however. In addition, if the contract is between a foreign, wholly owned subsidiary of a U.S. company and a foreign, state-owned enterprise, the fact that the U.S. parent is affected by a breach of the contract may not give rise to any remedial rights under U.S. law. If the nature of the foreign party to a contract or the subject matter of a contract is not clearly commercial, it may be advisable to require the foreign government to waive sovereign immunity in the contract.

As the following Supreme Court case highlights, exceptions to sovereign immunity are narrowly interpreted.

67. Commercial Bank of Kuwait v. Rafidain Bank, 15 F.3d 238 (2d Cir. 1994).
68. 504 U.S. 607 (1992).

A CASE IN POINT

**CASE 25.3**
**Sosa v. Alvarez-Machain**
*Supreme Court of the United States*
*124 S. Ct. 2739 (2004).*

## Summary

**› FACTS** The Drug Enforcement Administration (DEA) approved using petitioner Sosa and other Mexican nationals to abduct Alvarez-Machain, also a Mexican national, from Mexico to stand trial in the United States for a DEA agent's torture and murder. After his acquittal, Alvarez sued the United States for false arrest under the Federal Tort Claims Act (FTCA), which waives sovereign immunity in suits "for . . . personal injury . . . caused by the negligent or wrongful act or omission of any [government] employees while acting within the scope of his office or employment." The U.S. district court dismissed the FTCA claim against the DEA, but the U.S. Court of Appeals for the Ninth Circuit reversed the district court's dismissal.

*(Continued)*

(Case 25.3 *continued)*

**› ISSUE PRESENTED** Does an individual have a right under the FTCA to sue the United States for injuries suffered in a foreign country, regardless of where the tortious act or omission occurred?

**› SUMMARY OF OPINION** The U.S. Supreme Court noted that the FTCA "was designed primarily to remove the sovereign immunity of the United States from suits in tort and, with certain specific exceptions, to render the Government liable in tort as a private individual would be under like circumstances." The Act gives federal district courts jurisdiction over claims against the United States for injury

> caused by the negligent or wrongful act or omission of any employee of the Government while acting within the scope of his office or employment, under circumstances where the United States, if a private person, would be liable to the claimant in accordance with the law of the place where the act or omission occurred.

But the Act also limits its waiver of sovereign immunity in a number of ways. The significant limitation on the waiver of immunity in this case involved the Act's exception for "[a]ny claim arising in a foreign country."

The Court noted that the exception to the waiver of sovereign immunity for claims "arising in a foreign country" seemed plainly applicable to the facts of this case. Alvarez's arrest was said to be "false," and thus tortious, only because, and to the extent that, it occurred in Mexico. Nevertheless the U.S. Court of Appeals for the Ninth Circuit allowed Alvarez's action to proceed under the "headquarters doctrine," concluding that his claim did not "aris[e] in" a foreign country because it was the direct result of wrongful planning and direction by DEA agents in California.

Two considerations led the Court to reject the headquarters doctrine. First, the Court concluded that even assuming the DEA officials' direction was a proximate cause of the abduction, so too were the actions of Sosa and others in Mexico. As a result, recognition of additional domestic causation left an open question as to whether the exception to sovereign immunity applied to Alvarez's claim. Second, the Court noted that there is good reason to think that Congress understood a claim "arising in" a foreign country to be a claim for injury or harm occurring in that country. When the FTCA was passed, courts generally applied the law of the place where the injury occurred in tort cases, which would have been foreign law for a plaintiff injured in a foreign country. However, Congress intended to avoid application of foreign substantive law with the foreign country exception. Applying the headquarters doctrine would therefore thwart the exception's objective by recasting foreign injury claims as claims not arising in a foreign country because of some domestic planning or negligence.

**› RESULT** The Court held that Alvarez was not entitled to a remedy under the FTCA because the doctrine of sovereign immunity prevented him from recovering against the United States.

---

## *Act-of-State Doctrine*

The *act-of-state doctrine* applies to the noncommercial acts of a government that affect foreign business interests within that government's territory. The doctrine was most clearly expressed by the U.S. Supreme Court in *Underhill v. Hernandez*,[69] when it stated that "the courts of one country will not sit in judgment on the acts of the government of another, done within its own territory." Pursuant to this doctrine, U.S. courts are extremely reluctant to provide a legal remedy under U.S. law for the public acts of a foreign government. As a result, U.S. businesses generally cannot look to the U.S. courts for protection from or compensation for acts such as expropriation unless there is a bilateral treaty between

69. 168 U.S. 250, 252 (1897).

the United States and the foreign country that specifies the procedural and substantive rights of a U.S. investor in that country. As mentioned earlier, however, OPIC (the Overseas Private Investment Corporation) will insure U.S. businesses against certain host government acts, such as expropriation or restrictions on the conversion of local currency earnings.

THE RESPONSIBLE MANAGER

## EXPANDING INTO INTERNATIONAL MARKETS

Before expanding into international markets, a firm must take into consideration not only market conditions but also the laws and mores of the foreign country. Examples of substantive laws that may affect a foreign business are import/export regulations, employment law, tax law, securities law, and antitrust law. A company that follows the correct form of doing business but fails to recognize or understand local law may reduce its profitability. A company considering foreign investments should therefore carefully analyze the sociopolitical and economic climate of the prospective host country, in addition to obtaining a clear understanding of the legal, regulatory, and administrative regimes and the foreseeable future changes to these.

One way in which companies typically expand into the international marketplace is through direct sales to customers. Direct sales may pose several problems for the company, however, including export regulations, international contract law, letters of credit, import regulations, and the use of local representatives.

If costs do not justify opening a local office, a firm will often retain a local representative to oversee the sale of its products. If the transaction is not correctly structured, however, the company may find that it has a dependent agent in the foreign country—that it has, under local law, opened an office in the foreign country. Transactions thought to be tax-free will, in fact, be subject to corporate tax, and the local agent may have acquired additional rights and protections under local employment law.

A company can also conduct business in a foreign country by acquiring an existing company. Such transactions are governed by the laws regulating foreign investment in the country. Tax issues will play a predominant role in determining the form of the acquisition and the method of future operation.

A firm may also choose to create a new entity distinct from the parent corporation. This entity could be a corporation with 100 percent foreign ownership or a joint venture in the form of a corporation or partnership. Local law will define the regulations and restrictions to be imposed on the firm. Common restrictions include requiring majority local ownership or that a majority of the board be resident directors. In many countries, investors may specify whether the entity is to be treated as a partnership or a corporation for U.S. tax purposes. Every jurisdiction seems to have some unique wrinkles in

### IN BRIEF

**Thinking Internationally**

**Market Conditions and Competition**
- Product/service market fundamentals
- Distribution/operational realities
- Personnel and management
- Location
- Currency
- Competitors
- Achieving "local touch"

**Legal Mores of Foreign Country**
- Rule of law
- Corruption
- Judicial integrity

**Substantive Foreign Law**
- Exchange controls
- Import/export costs and controls
- Employment law
- Taxes, both foreign and domestic
- Securities
- Antitrust
- Formation, governance, and dissolution of foreign entity

**Sociopolitical and Economic Climate of Host Country**
- Long-term economic stability
- Stable pro-market consensus
- Attitude toward foreign investors

*(Continued)*

(The Responsible Manager *continued*)

the areas of formation and administration; matters taken for granted by locals may occasion surprise and delays for foreign investors.

Local advisers experienced in dealing with foreign investors can help smooth the process and minimize surprises on both practical issues and matters of substantive and procedural law. Special attention should be paid to coordinating tax/accounting and legal advice within the context of the investor's business goals. The investor must recognize, though, that sometimes foreign lawyers and accountants take a compartmentalized rather than interdisciplinary approach—they may be accustomed to performing only a technical role and may not wish to act as general business advisers. It is important that the investor's point person, the transaction manager, actively set expectations and coordinate the advisory process.

This is perhaps nowhere more important than in the tax area. Even similar tax systems will differ in significant respects, and only rarely can one find a single individual who is thoroughly versed in the laws of two jurisdictions and their interrelations. It is important to coordinate carefully and start early in the planning stage to uncover potential problem areas. Obtaining tax credits is a relatively obvious issue. More subtle issues can appear in many contexts. An agreement, exchange of assets, or other transaction that creates no tax liability or is not deemed a tax event in one country may create income tax liability in another. For example, stock dividends and splits are not taxable in the United States and other major economies because there is no change of economic substance. Thus, it might not occur to a U.S. manager, tax lawyer, or accountant to inquire and discover that they may be taxable in other countries.

Corporate laws also vary by jurisdiction. The U.S. system of corporate law and procedure is relatively flexible. Most other jurisdictions have less permissive rules regarding capital structure, dissolution, corporate formalities, and officers and directors, as well as different penalties for noncompliance. An investor may not be able to form, operate, and close down the entity how and when it wants, and achieving the desired management structure may prove impossible or impractical.

If the company employs workers in the host country, it is subject to a system of employment laws, regulations, and customs that is, in most cases, more restrictive and more protective of workers than U.S. law. Employment laws are highly politicized and seek to protect local workers, particularly against foreign "exploitation." They need not make sense to U.S. managers. Restricted use of foreign personnel, required proportions of local workers, prescribed terms of employment, and difficulty in terminating unsatisfactory employees are all common issues. The foreign investor may have to compromise its employment policies to satisfy local requirements.

In some areas, such as environmental law, many developing countries are far less regulated than the United States, but the investor should expect to see these countries' legal regimes eventually catch up. Legal advantages, like business advantages, are often transitory. The investor needs to evaluate and understand both areas to develop the knowledge of and sensitivity to local conditions needed to make the right investment decision.

INSIDE STORY

## THE EUROPEAN UNION CONSTITUTION: UNITED IN DIVERSITY

The proposed constitution of the European Union establishes an official "motto" for the EU: "United in Diversity." This motto, like the proposed constitution itself, recognizes the equally prominent values of unity and diversity that exist among the member states of the EU and suggests the delicate balance between these two values that these states are attempting to strike. As one author put it, "The EU constitution is a compromise between the demands of those who want more integration and those who want to preserve the rights of the nation states."[70]

The EU constitution is not just a constitution; it is also an international treaty and a Charter of Fundamental Rights. Because the national states will not

70. Paul Reynolds, *Q&A: EU—Myths and Realities,* July 8, 2004, *at* http://newsvote.bbc.co.uk/2/hi/europe/3825521.stm.

*(Continued)*

(Inside Story *continued*)

disappear, there is still a need for an international treaty. On the other hand, many members of the EU community have recognized a need to create and define an entity above the member states by enacting a constitution that recognizes such an entity. In addition, like the Bill of Rights in the U.S. Constitution, the proposed Charter of Fundamental Rights included in the EU constitution guarantees that citizens of the EU have certain rights that every EU member nation will be required to respect. These rights, freedoms, and general principles include respect for human dignity; the right to life; the right to be free of torture and inhuman or degrading treatment; the right to liberty and security; respect for private and family life; freedom of thought, conscience, and religion; freedom of expression; the right to an education; freedom to conduct a business; the right to property; equality before the law; respect for cultural, religious, and linguistic diversity; equality between men and women; the integration of persons with disabilities; the right to access to justice and a fair trial; and the presumption of innocence and the right to a defense.

A draft constitution was published by the Convention on the Future of Europe in July 2003. However, EU leaders were unable to reach agreement on the constitution at their summit in Brussels in December 2003. Talks broke down over proposed changes to the voting rights assigned to the respective member countries. France and Germany refused to shift on their demand for a "double majority" voting system that would give greater clout to member countries with larger populations, while Poland and Spain insisted on maintaining the present system that gives each country an almost equal weight. Under the present system, Poland and Spain each get twenty-seven votes while France, Germany, the United Kingdom, and Italy (the four member states with the largest populations) each have twenty-nine. As a result, despite Germany's 80 million population, it can easily be outvoted by the combined votes of Poland and Spain, even though their total combined population is also 80 million.[71]

After several more months of wrangling, the European Parliament (EP), the only EU institution in which voters have a direct say, voted overwhelmingly in favor of a modified version of the constitution although a majority of Parliament members from three member states, including the United Kingdom, voted against the constitution. Approval by the EP is only the first step, however. The constitution will not become effective unless all twenty-five member nations ratify it, and approval in several countries, including France, the Netherlands, Denmark, the Czech Republic, Poland, and above all the United Kingdom, is far from certain. A January 2005 opinion poll showed that most Britons opposed the treaty.[72]

Critics of the constitution point out that it is very long, with about 265 pages and 60,000 words in the English text.[73] Still, the document is considerably shorter and less complicated than the set of treaties it is intended to replace. In addition, British businesses fear the constitution will enhance trade union power, while French socialists worry that it is too free market. Danes are worried that it undermines democracy; the Dutch are worried about their national identity; and Irish peace campaigners say that it turns the EU into a military power. Opinion polls indicate that the United Kingdom is most likely to reject the constitution, followed by Poland, the Czech Republic, and Denmark.[74]

For all the controversy, the EU will not be that much different if the constitution is ratified. One observer commented that "Henry Kissinger, the former U.S. Secretary of State, once complained that there was no single telephone number he could call in Europe. This constitution will not provide one number but there are perhaps fewer numbers his successor will have to call" if the constitution is ratified.[75] The major changes effected by the constitution include the following:

1. **Powers of the EU.** The constitution reconfirms that the EU derives its powers from the member states. The Union is subsidiary to the member states and can act only in the areas where "the objectives of the intended action cannot be sufficiently achieved by the member states but can rather . . . be better achieved at Union level."

   On the other hand, the EU will for the first time have a "legal personality," and in the areas where it is allowed to legislate, its laws will prevail over any

71. Chris Marsden, *National Tensions Sink Agreement on the European Union Constitution,* Dec. 17, 2003, *at* http://www.wsws.org/articles/2003/dec2003/euco-d17_prn.shtml.

72. *Voters 'Reject EU by two to one,'* Jan. 29, 2005, *at* http://news.bbc.co.uk/1/hi/uk_politics/4217949.stm.

73. The U.S. Constitution contains 4,600 words.

74. *Anti-EU Constitution Groups Join Forces,* Jan. 11, 2005, *at* http://washingtontimes.com/upi-breaking/20050111-105732-6603r.htm.

75. Paul Reynolds, *Constitution A Hard-Won Compromise, at* http://news.bbc.co.uk/2/hi/europe/3820557.stm.

*(Continued)*

(Inside Story *continued*)

national laws. By having a legal personality, the EU will be able to enter into international agreements for the first time.

2. **Division of Responsibilities.** The constitution extends the EU's right to legislate into some new areas, including justice policy, asylum, and immigration. This means that the EU will have a greater role in more aspects of the lives of the citizens of its member states.
3. **Qualified Majority Voting.** For about twenty-six decision-making areas, the requirement for unanimity in the Council has been changed to a requirement for a qualified majority. However, each country will have a veto in foreign policy, defense, and taxation, which means that each country will still be able to go its own way in these matters.
4. **President of the European Council.** Subject to approval of the European Parliament, the European Council will elect a President, by qualified majority, for a term of two and a half years, renewable once. Under existing law, the Council presidency rotates through the member states every six months. The new President will be a permanent figure, presumably with much greater influence and symbolism. The President will be the external representative of the EU.
5. **Union Minister of Foreign Affairs.** The constitution also creates the position of the Union Minister of Foreign Affairs, who will conduct the Union's common foreign and security policy. The Union Minister combines the present roles of the external affairs member of the European Commission and the High Representative on foreign policy, so it will be more prominent in negotiating trade and aid agreements. On the other hand, the Minister will only be able to speak on the EU's behalf when there is an agreed-on common policy.
6. **Reform of the European Commission.** The European Commission, which proposes and executes EU laws, "will consist of one national from each Member State" for its first five-year term, commencing November 2004, but after that it will be reduced to "a number of members . . . corresponding to two thirds of the number of Member States, unless the European Council, acting unanimously, decides to alter this." It is felt that the Commission is too big and should be downsized.
7. **Expansion of the Role of the EP.** The European Parliament has acquired real power over the years, and the constitution confirms this by providing that the EP will have powers of "co-decision" with the Council of Ministers for those policies requiring a decision by a qualified majority.
8. **Leaving the EU.** Although the constitution confirms the voluntary nature of the EU, it includes a new procedure that describes how a member would leave the EU. It has always been the case that a member state could leave by simply repealing its own legislation. Under the proposed constitution, however, "[a] member state which decides to withdraw shall notify the Council of its intention . . . . The Union shall negotiate and conclude an agreement with that state, setting out the arrangements for its withdrawal."

Paul Reynolds, world affairs correspondent for BBC News Online, has noted that:

> The constitution probably faces a bigger battle to get ratified than it did to get agreed. One of its major problems is that it is so complex that it is completely inaccessible to most EU citizens. They will rely on interpretation by others and probably misinterpretation. It is tempting to yearn for the simplicity of the US constitution. But that was and is doing a very different job. The European Union is a club which you join, not a family which you cannot leave.[76]

The battle for an EU constitution is just beginning. Many EU nations plan to hold popular votes on the treaty, and experts anticipate that the ratification process, if successful, will take at least two years. The United Kingdom has scheduled its critical vote for March 2006. The pro-constitution lobby is saying that a British "no" vote would mean expulsion from the EU—but there is no expulsion process in the treaties that created the EU, so the only way this could happen is if the United Kingdom itself votes to withdraw.

76. *Id.*

## KEY WORDS AND PHRASES

## QUESTIONS AND CASE PROBLEMS

**1.** A fast-growing U.S. beverage company wishes to import mineral water and has asked you, its vice president for purchasing, to recommend foreign sources. You know that sources exist in France, Canada, and Australia. What U.S. trade laws should you consider in choosing among these sources?

Suppose that you determine that the best source of mineral water for your purposes is France, but a tariff makes imports from that country noncompetitive. How could you seek a reduction in this tariff?

**2.** The New England Petroleum Corporation (NEPCO), a U.S. corporation, obtained refined oil from its wholly owned Bahamas subsidiary refinery, PETCO. In 1968, PETCO entered into a long-term contract to purchase crude oil from Chevron Oil Trading (Chevron), a branch of a petroleum company that held 50 percent of an oil concession in Libya. In 1973, Libya nationalized several foreign-owned oil concessions, including Chevron's. As a result, Chevron terminated its contract with PETCO.

PETCO then entered into a new contract with the National Oil Corporation, which was wholly owned by the Libyan government. One month after execution of the contract, Libya imposed an oil embargo on the United States, and National canceled its contract with PETCO. Three months later, after a dramatic increase in oil prices, PETCO executed a new contract with National. National allegedly breached that contract as well.

PETCO's assignee, Carey, brought suit against National, seeking to recover damages for National's breach of the two contracts. National raised the defense of sovereign immunity. Carey claimed that there was no sovereign immunity under the Foreign Sovereign Immunities Act because the breach of contract was an act outside the territory of the United States in connection with a commercial activity that caused a direct effect in the United States. Who should prevail? [*Carey v. National Oil Corp.*, 592 F.2d 673 (2d Cir. 1979).]

3. Optomagic, Inc. is a U.S. corporation that produces optomagic gizmos. Production of optomagic gizmos involves a confidential gizmo-processing technique (which is described in printed confidential Optomagic manuals), labor-intensive processing, and inclusion of an optomagic component for which Optomagic was granted a U.S. patent six months ago. The optomagic component has widespread uses in the space, aviation, and medical industries.

   Eight months ago, in the African country of Varoom, a relatively peaceful popular uprising resulted in the removal of the "old guard" leaders, who had favored a strong, centrally planned economy. The new provisional government called for free elections in one year, began taking immediate steps to reform the economy, and promised to liberalize foreign investment laws to attract foreign investors.

   Because the government bureaucracy is still in some disarray, it is extremely helpful, as a practical matter, to have close contacts with a government official who can speed the review and approval process for applications for foreign investment. In a recent official tour of the United States, Dr. Segun Ayantuga, the minister of health and welfare of Varoom, visited Optomagic's manufacturing facility in Boston, Massachusetts. Ayantuga is an eminent surgeon and a strong proponent of bringing advanced medical technology to his developing country so that the best medical care can be made available to the public. In addition, to earn badly needed foreign exchange for Varoom, he is interested in finding labor-intensive U.S. industries that may be able to produce products in Varoom for export to the more developed countries. Optomagic is very interested in the newly emerging markets of Africa, and in Varoom in particular. Optomagic would also like to obtain gizmonium, a raw material necessary for the production of optomagic gizmos, which is found in great abundance in the mountains of Varoom, but which, under Varoomian law, is available only to Varoomian enterprises.

   Two weeks after his visit to Optomagic, Ayantuga wrote to the CEO of Optomagic to make the following proposal. Ayantuga and a state-owned medical clinic, Varoom Medical, are interested in establishing a joint venture in Varoom with Optomagic. Current Varoomian law limits foreign investment interests in Varoomian enterprises to 50 percent of the total investment. Ayantuga states that, although under local law the Varoomian partners share equal responsibility for the management of the venture, they will in fact defer to Optomagic in all material matters related to the operation of the manufacturing facility. In addition, Ayantuga assures Optomagic that the foreign investment law is likely to be liberalized within the year. As his investment in the venture, Ayantuga offers to contribute his lease interest in certain property in Varoom and to ensure that all the necessary government permits for the construction and licensing of the facility are obtained. Ayantuga expresses his confidence in being able to obtain all the government approvals for the proposed project because "our government has recently issued a decree emphasizing the national importance of upgrading our health-care industries."

   The father of Optomagic's CEO emigrated from Varoom sixty years ago. He is excited about the developments in Varoom and finds Ayantuga to be a delightful, dynamic man. He is convinced that Optomagic should move into Varoom now, before its competitors do.

   Your assignment is to put together a business plan for the proposed joint venture, assuming that it's going to cost something up front but will be worth the expense in the long run. The CEO wants a preliminary report in two weeks to take to the board of directors, which will be considering establishing a wholly owned subsidiary in Cairo to operate prospective sales and manufacturing facilities in Africa. He also wants a comprehensive report to follow in another four weeks.

   a. You have full access to your expert in-house legal counsel, who has experience in international projects. How can you best use her to assist in putting your plan together? What issues of particular importance should be addressed by counsel for inclusion in the preliminary report?
   b. Given the uncertainty in the development of Varoom's foreign investment laws (and its government), what types of terms or conditions do you think should be included in the contract for the proposed joint venture to protect against unexpected changes in the laws or government policies? What is your evaluation of the desirability of other forms of protection?

4. Assume the facts in Question 3. Are there any legal problems with including Ayantuga as an investor in the project? As a paid consultant?

5. Upon further general inquiry on behalf of Optomagic, you learn the following facts in addition

to those set forth in Question 3. First, Varoom has a patent law and a trademark-registration law and is a signatory of the Paris and Madrid Conventions, but it has no copyright law. Second, Varoomian law provides that licenses of foreign technology cannot (1) unreasonably restrict the geographic market for such exports, (2) require that the Varoomian party purchase components or raw materials from the foreign party, or (3) restrict use of the technology by the Varoomian licensee beyond a term of ten years without approval from the supervising ministry (which in this case is the Ministry of Health).

What other information do you need to determine how best to protect Optomagic's intellectual property rights in the proposed venture? Based on what you do know, what steps should be taken to maximize the protection of Optomagic's intellectual property rights? What U.S. laws will apply to the contribution, licensing, or other transfer of optomagic gizmo components by Optomagic to the joint venture? What license and joint venture contract terms are important to obtain?

6. Assume the facts in Question 3. Varoom Medical is prepared to invest 950 million baninis (U.S. $1 = 1,000 baninis) over the first five years of the project. Its commitment will be backed by a standby letter of credit to be issued by the National People's Bank of Varoom, a state-owned bank.
   - **a.** What more do you need to know about the proposed capital contribution to be made by Varoom Medical and the standby letter of credit from the bank? Would you impose any additional conditions or requirements on the proposed contribution and the letter of credit?
   - **b.** What do you suggest that Optomagic contribute as its share of capital to the proposed joint venture? What factors do you need to consider to make that decision?

7. Assume the facts in Question 3. You begin to consider the labor force that the joint venture will need. Ayantuga suggests that the venture technicians should make regular technical training visits to Optomagic's facility in Boston, Massachusetts. Ayantuga also suggests that he can arrange to select the Varoomian technicians for the joint venture. Monthly salaries in Varoom for the relevant types of workers are 70 percent lower than in the United States. However, Varoom's labor laws require that all enterprises (1) provide employees with housing and health insurance subsidies equal to 50 percent of their salaries; (2) engage in mandatory arbitration with the local labor bureau prior to termination of any employee for any reason; and (3) in the case of foreign-invested enterprises, pay local managers salaries and benefits that are comparable to those of the expatriate management personnel of the foreign-invested enterprise.
   - **a.** How would you assess the legal and economic advantages and disadvantages of the employees that Ayantuga has proposed be hired?
   - **b.** Is there another way to structure the workforce?
   - **c.** What U.S. laws may apply to the training of joint venture technicians at Optomagic's U.S. facilities?
   - **d.** Would you recommend that resident expatriate management personnel, or just visiting technicians, be assigned to the prospective project? Why? What qualities do you think an expatriate employee in Varoom should have?

8. In addition to the facts covered in Questions 3 through 7, you learn that the banini is not freely convertible into dollars. The Varoom foreign-exchange and tax laws provide that a foreign-invested joint venture can repatriate up to 50 percent of its foreign-exchange earnings, subject to a repatriation tax of 15 percent (in addition to the tax imposed on the joint venture's income). Banini profits can be exchanged only upon prior approval by the supervising ministry (each ministry is allocated a quota of baninis for which it can approve an exchange into foreign currencies). In addition, Varoom's foreign investment law requires that foreign-invested enterprises export a minimum of 50 percent of their products.
   - **a.** What alternatives exist to repatriating foreign-currency earnings in the prospective venture?
   - **b.** What U.S. laws, if any, might apply to exports of optomagic gizmos to the United States from Varoom?

9. Union Carbide India Limited (UCIL) was incorporated under the laws of India. Union Carbide Corporation (UCC), a U.S. corporation, owned 50.9 percent of its stock; the government of India owned 22 percent; and the balance was held by approximately 23,500 Indian citizens. UCIL was engaged in the manufacture of a variety of products, including chemicals, plastics, fertilizers, and insecticides, at fourteen plants in India and employed over 9,000 Indian citizens. It was managed and operated

entirely by Indians in India. UCC had provided a summary "process design package" for construction of the UCIL Bhopal plant and the services of some of its technicians to monitor UCIL's progress in detailing the design and erecting the plant. However, the Indian government controlled the terms of the agreement and precluded UCC from exercising any authority to "detail design, erect and commission the plant," which was done independently by UCIL process engineers.

On December 2–3, 1984, winds blew deadly gas from UCIL's Bhopal plant into densely occupied parts of the city, resulting in the deaths of more than 2,000 persons and the injury of more than 200,000. No Americans had visited the plant for more than one year prior to the accident, and during the five-year period before the accident, communications between the plant and the United States were extremely limited. Four days after the Bhopal accident, the first of 145 purported class-action lawsuits on behalf of victims of the disaster was filed in federal district court in the United States. These actions were consolidated into a single complaint, which was filed in the Southern District of New York. Meanwhile, India had enacted the Bhopal Gas Leak Disaster Act (the Bhopal Act), which granted the government of India the exclusive right to represent the victims in India or elsewhere, and the Indian government also filed a lawsuit in the Southern District of New York on behalf of all victims of the disaster. In July 1985, UCC moved to dismiss the complaints on the basis of forum non conveniens.

The court granted defendant's motion to dismiss on the basis of forum non conveniens, and the government of India, acting pursuant to its authority under the Bhopal Act, then brought suit against UCC and UCIL in the District Court of Bhopal. In 1989, the Supreme Court of India approved a settlement of "all litigations, claims, rights and liabilities related to and arising out of the [Bhopal] disaster" pursuant to which UCC and UCIL agreed to pay $470 million to the government of India for the benefit of all victims of the disaster. After the settlement of the Indian lawsuit, two class actions were filed against UCC in the United States seeking compensation for injuries caused by the Bhopal disaster. The federal district court once again dismissed both actions on the basis of forum non conveniens. On appeal, however, the plaintiffs contended that they had standing to maintain their action in the courts of the United States despite the Bhopal Act's delegation to the government of India of the exclusive right to represent those injured in the Bhopal disaster. The plaintiffs argued that the Indian government had an unacceptable conflict of interest as part owner of UCIL, that most of the victims opposed the settlement as inadequate, and that their due process rights were violated because they received inadequate notice and inadequate representation in the proceedings and could not opt out of the settlement. The court concluded that the plaintiffs could not litigate their claims against the government of India in a U.S. court. Why would Indian citizens injured in the Bhopal disaster want to sue in the United States instead of India? What kinds of factors would argue in favor of dismissal of these cases on the basis of forum non conveniens? On what basis would the court have concluded that plaintiffs could not litigate their claims in a U.S. court, notwithstanding the Indian government's settlement with UCC and UCIL? [*In re Union Carbide Corp. Gas Plant Disaster at Bhopal, India, in December, 1984*, 408 F.2d 195 (2d Cir. 1987); *Bano Bi v. Union Carbide Chemicals & Plastics Co.*, 984 F.2d 582 (2d Cir. 1993).]

**MANAGER'S DILEMMA**

**10.** Domingo Castro Alfaro, a Costa Rican resident and employee of Standard Fruit Company, and eighty-one other Costa Rican employees and their wives brought suit against Dow Chemical Company and Shell Oil Company. The employees claimed that while they were working on a banana plantation in Costa Rica for Standard Fruit Company, they suffered personal injuries as a result of exposure to dibromochloropropane (DBCP). DBCP is a pesticide manufactured by Dow and Shell, which allegedly was furnished to Standard Fruit. Standard Fruit is an American subsidiary of Dole Fresh Fruit Company, headquartered in Boca Raton, Florida. The employees exposed to DBCP allegedly suffered several medical problems, including sterility.

After the U.S. Environmental Protection Agency (EPA) banned DBCP in the United States, Shell and Dow apparently shipped several hundred thousand gallons of the pesticide to Costa Rica for use by Standard Fruit. Alfaro sued Dow and Shell in Texas in April 1984, alleging that handling DBCP caused the employees serious personal injuries for which Shell and Dow were liable under the theories of product liability, strict liability, and breach of warranty. Under the doctrine of forum non conveniens, the defendants argued that Texas was not a convenient forum in which to litigate this case. Should the court grant the defendants' motion to dismiss? Was the conduct of Dow Chemical and Shell Oil ethical? Was Standard Fruit's use of the U.S.-banned pesticide ethical? Were the defendants arguing inconvenient forum to avoid a jury trial and Texas laws regarding personal injury and wrongful death? If so, is that ethical? If goods are not consistent with some sets of standards but are basically OK, is it ethical to sell them? If they are dangerous, how dangerous is too dangerous? Should it matter whether consumers in a developing country can afford products meeting higher but more expensive Western standards? [*Dow Chemical Co. v. Alfaro*, 786 S.W.2d 674 (Tex. 1990).]

## INTERNET SOURCES

| | |
|---|---|
| U.S. Department of Commerce | http://www.doc.gov |
| U.S. International Trade Commission | http://www.usitc.gov |
| U.S. Trade Representative | http://www.ustr.gov |
| World Trade Organization | http://www.wto.org |
| A Summary of the Final Act of the Uruguay Round is available at this site. | http://www.wto.org/wto/english/docs_e/legal_e/ursum_e.htm#Agreement |
| This site is maintained by Transparency International, a nongovenmental organization formed in 1993 to raise global awareness of corruption. It publishes an annual Corruption Index that measures perceptions of corruption around the world. | http://www.transparency.org |
| The WIPO includes the full text of the Berne Convention for the Protection of Literary and Artistic Works. | http://www.wipo.int/treaties/en/ip/berne/trtdocs_wo001.html |
| The World Intellectual Property Organization's website contains full-text versions of the WIPO Copyright Treaty and the WIPO Performances and Phonograms Treaty. | http://www.wipo.int/documents/en/diplconf/distrib/94dc.htm<br>http://www.wipo.int/documents/en/diplconf/distrib/95dc.htm |
| This site, maintained by C. Matthew Schulz of Baker & McKenzie, includes a "What's New?" link to information on visas and immigration. | http://www.schulzlaw.com |
| LawCrawler provides international law searching by country domains. | http://www.lawcrawler.com |
| The International Chamber of Commerce site provides information about doing business internationally and news alerts. | http://www.iccwbo.org/ |
| The law firm Baker & McKenzie offers weekly e-mail updates on legal developments throughout the world. | http://www.lawincontext.com |

# APPENDICES

## APPENDIX A The Constitution of the United States of America

### PREAMBLE

We the People of the United States, in Order to form a more perfect Union, establish Justice, insure domestic Tranquility, provide for the common defence, promote the general Welfare, and secure the Blessings of Liberty to ourselves and our Posterity, do ordain and establish this Constitution for the United States of America.

### ARTICLE 1

**Section 1.** All legislative Powers herein granted shall be vested in a Congress of the United States, which shall consist of a Senate and House of Representatives.

**Section 2.** The House of Representatives shall be composed of Members chosen every second Year by the People of the several States, and the Electors in each State shall have the Qualifications requisite for Electors of the most numerous Branch of the State Legislature.

No Person shall be a Representative who shall not have attained to the Age of twenty five Years, and been seven Years a Citizen of the United States, and who shall not, when elected, be an Inhabitant of that State in which he shall be chosen.

Representatives and direct Taxes shall be apportioned among the several States which may be included within this Union, according to their respective Numbers, which shall be determined by adding to the whole Number of free Persons, including those bound to Service for a Term of Years, and excluding Indians not taxed, three fifths of all other Persons. The actual Enumeration shall be made within three Years after the first Meeting of the Congress of the United States, and within every subsequent Term of ten Years, in such Manner as they shall by Law direct. The Number of Representatives shall not exceed one for every thirty Thousand, but each State shall have at Least one Representative; and until such enumeration shall be made, the State of New Hampshire shall be entitled to chuse three, Massachusetts eight, Rhode Island and Providence Plantations one, Connecticut five, New York six, New Jersey four, Pennsylvania eight, Delaware one, Maryland six, Virginia ten, North Carolina five, South Carolina five, and Georgia three.

When vacancies happen in the Representation from any State, the Executive Authority thereof shall issue Writs of Election to fill such Vacancies.

The House of Representatives shall chuse their Speaker and other Officers; and shall have the sole Power of Impeachment.

**Section 3.** The Senate of the United States shall be composed of two Senators from each State, chosen by the Legislature thereof, for six Years; and each Senator shall have one Vote.

Immediately after they shall be assembled in Consequence of the first Election, they shall be divided as equally as may be into three Classes. The Seats of the Senators of the first Class shall be vacated at the Expiration of the second Year, of the second Class at the Expiration of the fourth Year, and of the third Class at the Expiration of the sixth Year, so that one third may be chosen every second Year; and if Vacancies happen by Resignation, or otherwise, during the Recess of the Legislature of any State, the Executive thereof may make temporary Appointments until the next Meeting of the Legislature, which shall then fill such Vacancies.

No Person shall be a Senator who shall not have attained to the Age of thirty Years, and been nine Years a Citizen of the United States, and who shall not, when elected, be an Inhabitant of that State for which he shall be chosen.

The Vice President of the United States shall be President of the Senate, but shall have no Vote, unless they be equally divided.

The Senate shall chuse their other Officers, and also a President pro tempore, in the Absence of the Vice President, or when he shall exercise the Office of President of the United States.

The Senate shall have the sole Power to try all Impeachments. When sitting for that Purpose, they shall be on Oath or Affirmation. When the President of the United States is tried, the Chief Justice shall preside: And no Person shall be convicted without the Concurrence of two thirds of the Members present.

Judgment in Cases of Impeachment shall not extend further than to removal from Office, and disqualification to hold and enjoy any Office of honor, Trust, or Profit under the United States: but the Party convicted shall nevertheless be liable and subject to Indictment, Trial, Judgment, and Punishment, according to Law.

**Section 4.** The Times, Places and Manner of holding Elections for Senators and Representatives, shall be prescribed in each State by the Legislature thereof; but the Congress may at any time by Law make or alter such Regulations, except as to the Places of chusing Senators.

The Congress shall assemble at least once in every Year, and such Meeting shall be on the first Monday in December, unless they shall by Law appoint a different Day.

**Section 5.** Each House shall be the Judge of the Elections, Returns, and Qualifications of its own Members, and a Majority of each shall constitute a Quorum to do Business; but a smaller Number may adjourn from day to day, and may be authorized to compel the Attendance of absent Members, in such Manner, and under such Penalties as each House may provide.

Each House may determine the Rules of its Proceedings, punish its Members for disorderly Behavior, and, with the Concurrence of two thirds, expel a Member.

Each House shall keep a Journal of its Proceedings, and from time to time publish the same, excepting such Parts as may in their Judgment require Secrecy; and the Yeas and Nays of the Members of either House on any question shall, at the Desire of one fifth of those Present, be entered on the Journal.

Neither House, during the Session of Congress, shall, without the Consent of the other, adjourn for more than three days, nor to any other Place than that in which the two Houses shall be sitting.

**Section 6.** The Senators and Representatives shall receive a Compensation for their Services, to be ascertained by Law, and paid out of the Treasury of the United States. They shall in all Cases, except Treason, Felony and Breach of the Peace, be privileged from Arrest during their Attendance at the Session of their respective Houses, and in going to and returning from the same; and for any Speech or Debate in either House, they shall not be questioned in any other Place.

No Senator or Representative shall, during the Time for which he was elected, be appointed to any civil Office under the Authority of the United States, which shall have been created, or the Emoluments whereof shall have been increased during such time; and no Person holding any Office under the United States, shall be a Member of either House during his Continuance in Office.

**Section 7.** All Bills for raising Revenue shall originate in the House of Representatives; but the Senate may propose or concur with Amendments as on other Bills.

Every Bill which shall have passed the House of Representatives and the Senate, shall, before it become a Law, be presented to the President of the United States; If he approve he shall sign it, but if not he shall return it, with his Objections to the House in which it shall have originated, who shall enter the Objections at large on their Journal, and proceed to reconsider it. If after such Reconsideration two thirds of that House shall agree to pass the Bill, it shall be sent together with the Objections, to the other House, by which it shall likewise be reconsidered, and if approved by two thirds of that House, it shall become a Law. But in all such Cases the Votes of both Houses shall be determined by Yeas and Nays, and the Names of the Persons voting for and against the Bill shall be entered on the Journal of each House respectively. If any Bill shall not be returned by the President within ten Days (Sundays excepted) after it shall have been presented to him, the Same shall be a Law, in like Manner as if he had signed it, unless the Congress by their Adjournment prevent its Return in which Case it shall not be a Law.

Every Order, Resolution, or Vote to which the Concurrence of the Senate and House of Representatives may be necessary (except on a question of Adjournment) shall be presented to the President of the United States; and before the Same shall take Effect, shall be approved by him, or being disapproved by him, shall be repassed by two thirds of the Senate and House of Representatives, according to the Rules and Limitations prescribed in the Case of a Bill.

**Section 8.** The Congress shall have Power To lay and collect Taxes, Duties, Imposts and Excises, to pay the Debts and provide for the common Defence and general Welfare of the United States; but all Duties, Imposts and Excises shall be uniform throughout the United States;

To borrow Money on the credit of the United States;

To regulate Commerce with foreign Nations, and among the several States, and with the Indian Tribes;

To establish an uniform Rule of Naturalization, and uniform Laws on the subject of Bankruptcies throughout the United States;

To coin Money, regulate the Value thereof, and of foreign Coin, and fix the Standard of Weights and Measures;

To provide for the Punishment of counterfeiting the Securities and current Coin of the United States;

To establish Post Offices and post Roads;

To promote the Progress of Science and useful Arts, by securing for limited Times to Authors and Inventors the exclusive Right to their respective Writings and Discoveries;

To constitute Tribunals inferior to the supreme Court;

To define and punish Piracies and Felonies committed on the high Seas, and Offenses against the Law of Nations;

To declare War, grant Letters of Marque and Reprisal, and make Rules concerning Captures on Land and Water;

To raise and support Armies, but no Appropriation of Money to that Use shall be for a longer Term than two Years;

To provide and maintain a Navy;

To make Rules for the Government and Regulation of the land and naval Forces;

To provide for calling forth the Militia to execute the Laws of the Union, suppress Insurrections and repel Invasions;

To provide for organizing, arming, and disciplining, the Militia, and for governing such Part of them as may be employed in the Service of the United States, reserving to the States respectively, the Appointment of the Officers, and the Authority of training the Militia according to the discipline prescribed by Congress;

To exercise exclusive Legislation in all Cases whatsoever, over such District (not exceeding ten Miles square) as may, by Cession of particular States, and the Acceptance of Congress, become the Seat of the Government of the United States, and to exercise like Authority over all Places purchased by the Consent of the Legislature of the State in which the Same shall be, for the Erection of Forts, Magazines, Arsenals, dock-Yards, and other needful Buildings;—And

To make all Laws which shall be necessary and proper for carrying into Execution the foregoing Powers, and all other Powers vested by this Constitution in the Government of the United States, or in any Department or Officer thereof.

**Section 9.** The Migration or Importation of such Persons as any of the States now existing shall think proper to admit, shall not be prohibited by the Congress prior to the Year one thousand eight hundred and eight, but a Tax or duty may be imposed on such Importation, not exceeding ten dollars for each Person.

The privilege of the Writ of Habeas Corpus shall not be suspended, unless when in Cases of Rebellion or Invasion the public Safety may require it.

No Bill of Attainder or ex post facto Law shall be passed.

No Capitation, or other direct, Tax shall be laid, unless in Proportion to the Census or Enumeration herein before directed to be taken.

No Tax or Duty shall be laid on Articles exported from any State.

No Preference shall be given by any Regulation of Commerce or Revenue to the Ports of one State over those of another: nor shall Vessels bound to, or from, one State be obliged to enter, clear, or pay Duties in another.

No Money shall be drawn from the Treasury, but in Consequence of Appropriations made by Law; and a regular Statement and Account of the Receipts and Expenditures of all public Money shall be published from time to time.

No Title of Nobility shall be granted by the United States: And no Person holding any Office of Profit or Trust under them, shall, without the Consent of the Congress, accept of any present, Emolument, Office, or Title, of any kind whatever, from any King, Prince, or foreign State.

Section 10. No State shall enter into any Treaty, Alliance, or Confederation; grant Letters of Marque and Reprisal; coin Money; emit Bills of Credit; make any Thing but gold and silver Coin a Tender in Payment of Debts; pass any Bill of Attainder, ex post facto Law, or Law impairing the Obligation of Contracts, or grant any Title of Nobility.

No State shall, without the Consent of the Congress, lay any Imposts or Duties on Imports or Exports, except what may be absolutely necessary for executing its inspection Laws: and the net Produce of all Duties and Imposts, laid by any State on Imports or Exports, shall be for the Use of the Treasury of the United States; and all such Laws shall be subject to the Revision and Controul of the Congress.

No State shall, without the Consent of Congress, lay any Duty of Tonnage, keep Troops, or Ships of War in time of Peace, enter into any Agreement or Compact with another State, or with a foreign Power, or engage in War, unless actually invaded, or in such imminent Danger as will not admit of delay.

## ARTICLE II

**Section 1.** The executive Power shall be vested in a President of the United States of America. He shall hold his Office during the Term of four Years, and, together with the Vice President, chosen for the same Term, be elected, as follows:

Each State shall appoint, in such Manner as the Legislature thereof may direct, a Number of Electors, equal to the whole Number of Senators and Representatives to which the State may be entitled in the Congress; but no Senator or Representative, or Person holding an Office of Trust or Profit under the United States, shall be appointed an Elector.

The Electors shall meet in their respective States, and vote by Ballot for two Persons, of whom one at least shall not be an Inhabitant of the same State with themselves. And they shall make a List of all the Persons voted for, and of the Number of Votes for each; which List they shall sign and certify, and transmit sealed to the Seat of the Government of the United States, directed to the President of the Senate. The President of the Senate shall, in the Presence of the Senate and House of Representatives, open all the Certificates, and the Votes shall then be counted. The Person having the greatest Number of Votes shall be the President, if such Number be a Majority of the whole Number of Electors appointed; and if there be more than one who have such Majority, and have an equal Number of Votes, then the House of Representatives shall immediately chuse by Ballot one of them for President; and if no Person have a Majority, then from the five highest on the List the said House shall in like Manner chuse the President. But in chusing the President, the Votes shall be taken by States, the Representation from each State having one Vote; A quorum for this Purpose shall consist of a Member or Members from two thirds of the States, and a Majority of all the States shall be necessary to a Choice. In every Case, after the Choice of the President, the Person having the greater Number of Votes of the Electors shall be the Vice President. But if there should remain two or more who have equal Votes, the Senate shall chuse from them by Ballot the Vice President.

The Congress may determine the Time of chusing the Electors, and the Day on which they shall give their Votes; which Day shall be the same throughout the United States.

No person except a natural born Citizen, or a Citizen of the United States, at the time of the Adoption of this Constitution, shall be eligible to the Office of President; neither shall any Person be eligible to that Office who shall not have attained to the Age of thirty five Years, and been fourteen Years a Resident within the United States.

In Case of the Removal of the President from Office, or of his Death, Resignation or Inability to discharge the Powers and Duties of the said Office, the same shall devolve on the Vice President, and the Congress may by Law provide for the Case of Removal, Death, Resignation or Inability, both of the President and Vice President, declaring what Officer shall then act as President, and such Officer shall act accordingly, until the Disability be removed, or a President shall be elected.

The President shall, at stated Times, receive for his Services, a Compensation, which shall neither be increased nor diminished during the Period for which he shall have been elected, and he shall not receive within that Period any other Emolument from the United States, or any of them.

Before he enter on the Execution of his Office, he shall take the following Oath or Affirmation: "I do solemnly swear (or affirm) that I will faithfully execute the Office of President of the United States, and will to the best of my Ability, preserve, protect and defend the Constitution of the United States."

**Section 2.** The President shall be Commander in Chief of the Army and Navy of the United States, and of the Militia of the several States, when called into the actual Service of the United States; he may require the Opinion, in writing, of the principal Officer in each of the executive Departments, upon any Subject relating to the Duties of their respective Offices, and he shall have Power to grant Reprieves and Pardons for Offenses against the United States, except in Cases of Impeachment.

He shall have Power, by and with the Advice and Consent of the Senate to make Treaties, provided two thirds of the Senators present concur; and he shall nominate, and by and with the Advice and Consent of the Senate, shall appoint Ambassadors, other public Ministers and Consuls, Judges of the supreme Court, and all other Officers of the United States, whose Appointments are not herein otherwise provided for, and which shall be established by Law; but the Congress may by Law vest the Appointment of such inferior Officers, as they think proper, in the President alone, in the Courts of Law, or in the Heads of Departments.

The President shall have Power to fill up all Vacancies that may happen during the Recess of the Senate, by granting Commissions which shall expire at the End of their next Session.

**Section 3.** He shall from time to time give to the Congress Information of the State of the Union, and recommend to their Consideration such Measures as he shall judge necessary and expedient; he may, on extraordinary Occasions, convene both Houses, or either of them, and in Case of Disagreement between them, with Respect to the Time of Adjournment, he may adjourn them to such Time as he shall think proper; he shall receive Ambassadors and other public Ministers; he shall take Care that the Laws be faithfully executed, and shall Commission all the Officers of the United States.

**Section 4.** The President, Vice President and all civil Officers of the United States, shall be removed from Office on Impeachment for, and Conviction of, Treason, Bribery, or other high Crimes and Misdemeanors.

## ARTICLE III

**Section 1.** The judicial Power of the United States, shall be vested in one supreme Court, and in such inferior Courts as the Congress may from time to time ordain and establish. The Judges, both of the supreme and inferior Courts, shall hold their Offices during good Behaviour, and shall, at stated Times, receive for their Services a Compensation, which shall not be diminished during their Continuance in Office.

**Section 2.** The judicial Power shall extend to all Cases, in Law and Equity, arising under this Constitution, the Laws of the United States, and Treaties made, or which shall be made, under their Authority;—to all Cases affecting Ambassadors, other public Ministers and Consuls;—to all Cases of admiralty and maritime Jurisdiction;—to Controversies to which the United States shall be a Party;—to Controversies between two or more States;—between a State and Citizens of another State;—between Citizens of different States;—between Citizens of the same State claiming Lands under Grants of different States, and between a State, or the Citizens thereof, and foreign States, Citizens or Subjects.

In all Cases affecting Ambassadors, other public Ministers and Consuls, and those in which a State shall be a Party, the supreme Court shall have original Jurisdiction. In all the other Cases before mentioned, the supreme Court shall have appellate Jurisdiction, both as to Law and Fact, with such Exceptions, and under such Regulations as the Congress shall make.

The Trial of all Crimes, except in Cases of Impeachment, shall be by Jury; and such Trial shall be held in the State where the said Crimes shall have been committed; but when not committed within any State, the Trial shall be at such Place or Places as the Congress may by Law have directed.

**Section 3.** Treason against the United States, shall consist only in levying War against them, or, in adhering to their Enemies, giving them Aid and Comfort. No Person shall be convicted of Treason unless on the Testimony of two Witnesses to the same overt Act, or on Confession in open Court.

The Congress shall have Power to declare the Punishment of Treason, but no Attainder of Treason shall work Corruption of Blood, or Forfeiture except during the Life of the Person attainted.

## ARTICLE IV

**Section 1.** Full Faith and Credit shall be given in each State to the public Acts, Records, and judicial Proceedings of every other State. And the Congress may by general Laws prescribe the Manner in which such Acts, Records and Proceedings shall be proved, and the Effect thereof.

**Section 2.** The Citizens of each State shall be entitled to all Privileges and Immunities of Citizens in the several States.

A Person charged in any State with Treason, Felony, or other Crime, who shall flee from Justice, and be found in another State, shall on Demand of the executive Authority of the State from which he fled, be delivered up, to be removed to the State having Jurisdiction of the Crime.

No Person held to Service or Labour in one State, under the Laws thereof, escaping into another, shall, in Consequence of any Law or Regulation therein, be discharged from such Service or Labour, but shall be delivered up on Claim of the Party to whom such Service or Labour may be due.

**Section 3.** New States may be admitted by the Congress into this Union; but no new State shall be formed or erected within the Jurisdiction of any other State; nor any State be formed by the Junction of two or more States, or Parts of States, without the Consent of the Legislatures of the States concerned as well as of the Congress.

The Congress shall have Power to dispose of and make all needful Rules and Regulations respecting the Territory or other Property belonging to the United States; and nothing in this Constitution shall be so construed as to Prejudice any Claims of the United States, or of any particular State.

**Section 4.** The United States shall guarantee to every State in this Union a Republican Form of Government, and shall protect each of them against Invasion; and on Application of the Legislature, or of the Executive (when the Legislature cannot be convened) against domestic Violence.

## ARTICLE V

The Congress, whenever two thirds of both Houses shall deem it necessary, shall propose Amendments to this Constitution, or, on the Application of the Legislatures of two thirds of the several States, shall call a Convention for proposing Amendments, which, in either Case, shall be valid to all Intents and Purposes, as part of this Constitution, when ratified by the Legislatures of three fourths of the several States, or by Conventions in three fourths thereof, as the one or the other Mode of Ratification may be proposed by the Congress; Provided that no Amendment which may be made prior to the Year One thousand eight hundred and eight shall in any Manner affect the first and fourth Clauses in the Ninth Section of the first Article; and that no State, without its Consent, shall be deprived of its equal Suffrage in the Senate.

## ARTICLE VI

All Debts contracted and Engagements entered into, before the Adoption of this Constitution shall be as valid against the United States under this Constitution, as under the Confederation.

This Constitution, and the Laws of the United States which shall be made in Pursuance thereof; and all Treaties made, or which shall be made, under the Authority of the United States, shall be the supreme Law of the Land; and the Judges in every State shall be bound thereby, any Thing in the Constitution or Laws of any State to the Contrary notwithstanding.

The Senators and Representatives before mentioned, and the Members of the several State Legislatures, and all executive and judicial Officers, both of the United States and of the several States, shall be bound by Oath or Affirmation, to support this Constitution; but no religious Test shall ever be required as a Qualification to any Office or public Trust under the United States.

## ARTICLE VII

The Ratification of the Conventions of nine States shall be sufficient for the Establishment of this Constitution between the States so ratifying the Same.

## AMENDMENT I [1791]

Congress shall make no law respecting an establishment of religion, or prohibiting the free exercise thereof; or abridging the freedom of speech, or of the press; or the right of the people peaceably to assemble, and to petition the Government for a redress of grievances.

## AMENDMENT II [1791]

A well regulated Militia, being necessary to the security of a free State, the right of the people to keep and bear Arms, shall not be infringed.

## AMENDMENT III [1791]

No Soldier shall, in time of peace be quartered in any house, without the consent of the Owner, nor in time of war, but in a manner to be prescribed by law.

## AMENDMENT IV [1791]

The right of the people to be secure in their persons, houses, papers, and effects, against unreasonable searches and seizures, shall not be violated, and no Warrants shall issue, but upon probable cause, supported by Oath or affirmation, and particularly describing the place to be searched, and the persons or things to be seized.

## AMENDMENT V [1791]

No person shall be held to answer for a capital, or otherwise infamous crime, unless on a presentment or indictment of a Grand Jury, except in cases arising in the land or naval forces, or in the Militia, when in actual service in time of War or public danger; nor shall any person be subject for the same offence to be twice put in jeopardy of life or limb; nor shall be compelled in any criminal case to be a witness against himself, nor be deprived of life, liberty, or property, without due process of law; nor shall private property be taken for public use, without just compensation.

## AMENDMENT VI [1791]

In all criminal prosecutions, the accused shall enjoy the right to a speedy and public trial, by an impartial jury of the State and district wherein the crime shall have been committed, which district shall have been previously ascertained by law, and to be informed of the nature and cause of the accusation; to be confronted with the witnesses against him; to have compulsory process for obtaining witnesses in his favor, and to have the Assistance of Counsel for his defence.

## AMENDMENT VII [1791]

In Suits at common law, where the value in controversy shall exceed twenty dollars, the right of trial by jury shall be preserved, and no fact tried by jury, shall be otherwise re-examined in any Court of the United States, than according to the rules of the common law.

## AMENDMENT VIII [1791]

Excessive bail shall not be required, nor excessive fines imposed, nor cruel and unusual punishments inflicted.

## AMENDMENT IX [1791]

The enumeration in the Constitution, of certain rights, shall not be construed to deny or disparage others retained by the people.

## AMENDMENT X [1791]

The powers not delegated to the United States by the Constitution, nor prohibited by it to the States, are reserved to the States respectively, or to the people.

## AMENDMENT XI [1798]

The Judicial power of the United States shall not be construed to extend to any suit in law or equity, commenced or prosecuted against one of the United States by Citizens of another State, or by Citizens or Subjects of any Foreign State.

## AMENDMENT XII [1804]

The Electors shall meet in their respective states, and vote by ballot for President and Vice-President, one of whom, at least, shall not be an inhabitant of the same state with themselves; they shall name in their ballots the person voted for as President, and in distinct ballots the person voted for as Vice-President, and they shall make distinct lists of all persons voted for as President, and of all persons voted for as Vice-President, and of the number of votes for each, which lists they shall sign and certify, and transmit sealed to the seat of the government of the United States, directed to the President of the Senate;—The President of the Senate shall, in the presence of the Senate and House of Representatives, open all the certificates and the votes shall then be counted;— The person having the greatest number of votes for President, shall be the President, if such number be a majority of the whole number of Electors appointed; and if no person have such majority, then from the persons having the highest numbers not exceeding three on the list of those voted for as President, the House of Representatives shall choose immediately, by ballot, the President. But in choosing the President, the votes shall be taken by states, the representation from each state having one vote; a quorum for this purpose shall consist of a member or members from two-thirds of the states, and a majority of all states shall be necessary to a choice. And if the House of Representatives shall not choose a President whenever the right of choice shall devolve upon them, before the fourth day of March next following, then the Vice-President shall act as President, as in the case of the death or other constitutional disability of the President.—The person having the greatest number of votes as Vice-President, shall be the Vice-President, if such number be a majority of the whole number of Electors appointed, and if no person have a majority, then from the two highest numbers on the list, the Senate shall choose the Vice-President; a quorum for the purpose shall consist of two-thirds of the whole number of Senators, and a majority of the whole number shall be necessary to a choice. But no person constitutionally ineligible to the office of President shall be eligible to that of Vice-President of the United States.

## AMENDMENT XIII [1865]

**Section 1.** Neither slavery nor involuntary servitude, except as a punishment for crime whereof the party shall have been duly convicted, shall exist within the United States, or any place subject to their jurisdiction.

**Section 2.** Congress shall have power to enforce this article by appropriate legislation.

## AMENDMENT XIV [1868]

**Section 1.** All persons born or naturalized in the United States, and subject to the jurisdiction thereof, are citizens of the United States and of the State wherein they reside. No State shall make or enforce any law which shall abridge the privileges or immunities of citizens of the United States; nor shall any State deprive any person of life, liberty, or property, without due process of law; nor deny to any person within its jurisdiction the equal protection of the laws.

**Section 2.** Representatives shall be apportioned among the several States according to their respective numbers, counting the whole number of persons in each State, excluding Indians not taxed. But when the right to vote at any election for the choice of electors for President and Vice President of the United States, Representatives in Congress, the Executive and Judicial officers of a State, or the members of the Legislature thereof, is denied to any of the male inhabitants of such State, being twenty-one years of age, and citizens of the United States, or in any way abridged, except for participation in rebellion, or other crime, the basis of representation therein shall be reduced in the proportion which the number of such male citizens shall bear to the whole number of male citizens twenty-one years of age in such State.

**Section 3.** No person shall be a Senator or Representative in Congress, or elector of President and Vice President, or hold any office, civil or military, under the United States, or under any State, who having previously taken an oath, as a member of Congress, or as an officer of the United States, or as a member of any State legislature, or as an executive or judicial officer of any State, to support the Constitution of the United States, shall have engaged in insurrection or rebellion against the same, or given aid or comfort to the enemies thereof. But Congress may by a vote of two-thirds of each House, remove such disability.

**Section 4.** The validity of the public debt of the United States, authorized by law, including debts incurred for payment of pensions and bounties for services in suppressing insurrection or rebellion, shall not be questioned. But neither the United States nor any State shall assume or pay any debt or obligation incurred in aid of insurrection or rebellion against the United States, or any claim for the loss or emancipation of any slave; but all such debts, obligations and claims shall be held illegal and void.

**Section 5.** The Congress shall have power to enforce, by appropriate legislation, the provisions of this article.

## AMENDMENT XV [1870]

**Section 1.** The right of citizens of the United States to vote shall not be denied or abridged by the United States or by any State on account of race, color, or previous condition of servitude.

**Section 2.** The Congress shall have power to enforce this article by appropriate legislation.

## AMENDMENT XVI [1913]

The Congress shall have power to lay and collect taxes on incomes, from whatever source derived, without apportionment among the several States, and without regard to any census or enumeration.

## AMENDMENT XVII [1913]

**Section 1.** The Senate of the United States shall be composed of two Senators from each State, elected by the people thereof, for six years; and each Senator shall have one vote. The electors in each State shall have the qualifications requisite for electors of the most numerous branch of the State legislatures.

**Section 2.** When vacancies happen in the representation of any State in the Senate, the executive authority of such State shall issue writs of election to fill such vacancies: Provided, That the legislature of any State may empower the executive thereof to make temporary appointments until the people fill the vacancies by election as the legislature may direct.

**Section 3.** This amendment shall not be so construed as to affect the election or term of any Senator chosen before it becomes valid as part of the Constitution.

## AMENDMENT XVIII [1919]

**Section 1.** After one year from the ratification of this article the manufacture, sale, or transportation of intoxicating liquors within, the importation thereof into, or the exportation thereof from the United States and all territory subject to the jurisdiction thereof for beverage purposes is hereby prohibited.

**Section 2.** The Congress and the several States shall have concurrent power to enforce this article by appropriate legislation.

**Section 3.** This article shall be inoperative unless it shall have been ratified as an amendment to the Constitution by the legislatures of the several States, as provided in the Constitution, within seven years from the date of the submission hereof to the States by the Congress.

## AMENDMENT XIX [1920]

**Section 1.** The right of citizens of the United States to vote shall not be denied or abridged by the United States or by any State on account of sex.

**Section 2.** Congress shall have power to enforce this article by appropriate legislation.

## AMENDMENT XX [1933]

**Section 1.** The terms of the President and Vice President shall end at noon on the 20th day of January, and the terms of Senators and Representatives at noon on the 3d day of January, of the years in which such terms would have ended if this article had not been ratified; and the terms of their successors shall then begin.

**Section 2.** The Congress shall assemble at least once in every year, and such meeting shall begin at noon on the 3d day of January, unless they shall by law appoint a different day.

**Section 3.** If, at the time fixed for the beginning of the term of the President, the President elect shall have died, the Vice President elect shall become President. If the President shall not have been chosen before the time fixed for the beginning of his term, or if the President elect shall have failed to qualify, then the Vice President elect shall act as President until a President shall have qualified; and the Congress may by law provide for the case wherein neither a President elect nor a Vice President elect shall have qualified, declaring who shall then act as President, or the manner in which one who is to act shall be selected, and such person shall act accordingly until a President or Vice President shall have qualified.

**Section 4.** The Congress may by law provide for the case of the death of any of the persons from whom the House of Representatives may choose a President whenever the right of choice shall have devolved upon them, and for the case of the death of any of the persons from whom the Senate may choose a Vice President whenever the right of choice shall have devolved upon them.

**Section 5.** Sections 1 and 2 shall take effect on the 15th day of October following the ratification of this article.

**Section 6.** This article shall be inoperative unless it shall have been ratified as an amendment to the Constitution by the legislatures of three-fourths of the several States within seven years from the date of its submission.

## AMENDMENT XXI [1933]

**Section 1.** The eighteenth article of amendment to the Constitution of the United States is hereby repealed.

**Section 2.** The transportation or importation into any State, Territory, or possession of the United States for delivery or use therein of intoxicating liquors, in violation of the laws thereof, is hereby prohibited.

**Section 3.** This article shall be inoperative unless it shall have been ratified as an amendment to the Constitution by conventions in the several States, as provided in the Constitution, within seven years from the date of the submission hereof to the States by the Congress.

## AMENDMENT XXII [1951]

**Section 1.** No person shall be elected to the office of the President more than twice, and no person who has held the office of President, or acted as President, for more than two years of a term to which some other person was elected President shall be elected to the office of President more than once. But this Article shall not apply to any person holding the office of President when this Article was proposed by the Congress, and shall not prevent any person who may be holding the office of President, or acting as President, during the term within which this Article becomes operative from holding the office of President or acting as President during the remainder of such term.

**Section 2.** This article shall be inoperative unless it shall have been ratified as an amendment to the Constitution by the legislatures of three-fourths of the several States within seven years from the date of its submission to the States by the Congress.

## AMENDMENT XXIII [1961]

**Section 1.** The District constituting the seat of Government of the United States shall appoint in such manner as the Congress may direct:

A number of electors of President and Vice President equal to the whole number of Senators and Representatives in Congress to which the District would be entitled if it were a State, but in no event more than the least populous state; they shall be in addition to those appointed by the states, but they shall be considered, for the purposes of the election of President and Vice President, to be electors appointed by a state; and they shall meet in the District and perform such duties as provided by the twelfth article of amendment.

**Section 2.** The Congress shall have power to enforce this article by appropriate legislation.

## AMENDMENT XXIV [1964]

**Section 1.** The right of citizens of the United States to vote in any primary or other election for President or Vice President, for electors for President or Vice President, or for Senator or Representative in Congress, shall not be denied or abridged by the United States, or any State by reason of failure to pay any poll tax or other tax.

**Section 2.** The Congress shall have power to enforce this article by appropriate legislation.

## AMENDMENT XXV [1967]

**Section 1.** In case of the removal of the President from office or of his death or resignation, the Vice President shall become President.

**Section 2.** Whenever there is a vacancy in the office of the Vice President, the President shall nominate a Vice President who shall take office upon confirmation by a majority vote of both Houses of Congress.

**Section 3.** Whenever the President transmits to the President pro tempore of the Senate and the Speaker of the House of Representatives his written declaration that he is unable to discharge the powers and duties of his office, and until he transmits to them a written declaration to the contrary, such powers and duties shall be discharged by the Vice President as Acting President.

**Section 4.** Whenever the Vice President and a majority of either the principal officers of the executive departments or of such other body as Congress may by law provide, transmit to the President pro tempore of the Senate and the Speaker of the House of Representatives their written declaration that the President is unable to discharge the powers and duties of his office, the Vice President shall immediately assume the powers and duties of the office as Acting President.

Thereafter, when the President transmits to the President pro tempore of the Senate and the Speaker of the House of Representatives his written declaration that no inability exists, he shall resume the powers and duties of his office unless the Vice President and a majority of either the principal officers of the executive department or of such other body as Congress may by law provide, transmit within four days to the President pro tempore of the Senate and the Speaker of the House of Representatives their written declaration and the President is unable to discharge the powers and duties of his office. Thereupon Congress shall decide the issue, assembling within forty-eight hours for that purpose if not in session. If the Congress, within twenty-one days after receipt of the latter written declaration, or, if Congress is not in session, within twenty-one days after Congress is required to assemble, determines by two-thirds vote of both Houses that the President is unable to discharge the powers and duties of his office, the Vice President shall continue to discharge the same as Acting President; otherwise, the President shall resume the powers and duties of his office.

## AMENDMENT XXVI [1971]

**Section 1.** The right of citizens of the United States, who are eighteen years of age or older, to vote shall not be denied or abridged by the United States or by any State on account of age.

**Section 2.** The Congress shall have power to enforce this article by appropriate legislation.

## AMENDMENT XXVII [1992]

No law, varying the compensation for the services of the Senators and Representatives, shall take effect, until an election of Representatives shall have intervened.

# APPENDIX B The Uniform Electronic Transactions Act [Excerpts]

### Section 5. Use of Electronic Records and Electronic Signatures; Variation by Agreement.

(a) This [Act] does not require a record or signature to be created, generated, sent, communicated, received, stored, or otherwise processed or used by electronic means or in electronic form.

(b) This [Act] applies only to transactions between parties each of which has agreed to conduct transactions by electronic means. Whether the parties agree to conduct a transaction by electronic means is determined from the context and surrounding circumstances, including the parties' conduct.

(c) A party that agrees to conduct a transaction by electronic means may refuse to conduct other transactions by electronic means. The right granted by this subsection may not be waived by agreement.

(d) Except as otherwise provided in this [Act], the effect of any of its provisions may be varied by agreement. The presence in certain provisions of this [Act] of the words "unless otherwise agreed," or words of similar import, does not imply that the effect of other provisions may not be varied by agreement.

(e) Whether an electronic record or electronic signature has legal consequences is determined by this [Act] and other applicable law.

### Section 6. Construction and Application.

This [Act] must be construed and applied:

(1) to facilitate electronic transactions consistent with other applicable law;

(2) to be consistent with reasonable practices concerning electronic transactions and with the continued expansion of those practices; and

(3) to effectuate its general purpose to make uniform the law with respect to the subject of this [Act] among States enacting it.

### Section 7. Legal Recognition of Electronic Records, Electronic Signatures, and Electronic Contracts.

(a) A record or signature may not be denied legal effect or enforceability solely because it is in electronic form.

(b) A contract may not be denied legal effect or enforceability solely because an electronic record was used in its formation.

(c) If a law requires a record to be in writing, an electronic record satisfies the law.

(d) If a law requires a signature, an electronic signature satisfies the law.

. . .

### Section 10. Effect of Change or Error.

If a change or error in an electronic record occurs in a transmission between parties to a transaction, the following rules apply:

(1) If the parties have agreed to use a security procedure to detect changes or errors and one party has conformed to the procedure, but the other party has not, and the nonconforming party would have detected the change or error had that party also conformed, the conforming party may avoid the effect of the changed or erroneous electronic record.

(2) In an automated transaction involving an individual, the individual may avoid the effect of an electronic record that resulted from an error made by the individual in dealing with the electronic agent of another person if the electronic agent did not provide an opportunity for the prevention or correction of the error and, at the time the individual learns of the error, the individual:

(A) promptly notifies the other person of the error and that the individual did not intend to be bound by the electronic record received by the other person;

(B) takes reasonable steps, including steps that conform to the other person's reasonable instructions, to return to the other person or, if instructed by the other person, to destroy the consideration received, if any, as a result of the erroneous electronic record; and

(C) has not used or received any benefit or value from the consideration, if any, received from the other person.

(3) If neither paragraph (1) nor paragraph (2) applies, the change or error has the effect provided by other law, including the law of mistake, and the parties' contract, if any.

(4) Paragraphs (2) and (3) may not be varied by agreement.

# APPENDIX C Title VII of the Civil Rights Act of 1964 [Excerpts]

## Title VII of the Civil Rights Act of 1964—The Employment Discrimination Section

**Section 703. Unlawful Employment Practices.** (a) It shall be an unlawful employment practice for an employer—

(1) to fail or refuse to hire or to discharge any individual, or otherwise to discriminate against any individual with respect to his compensation, terms, conditions, or privileges of employment, because of such individual's race, color, religion, sex, or national origin; or

(2) to limit, segregate, or classify his employees or applicants for employment in any way which would deprive or tend to deprive any individual of employment opportunities or otherwise adversely affect his status as an employee, because of such individual's race, color, religion, sex, or national origin.

(b) It shall be an unlawful employment practice for an employment agency to fail or refuse to refer for employment, or otherwise to discriminate against, any individual because of his race, color, religion, sex, or national origin, or to classify or refer for employment any individual on the basis or his race, color, religion, sex, or national origin.

(c) It shall be an unlawful employment practice for a labor organization—

(1) to exclude or to expel from its membership, or otherwise to discriminate against, any individual because of his race, color, religion, sex, or national origin;

(2) to limit, segregate, or classify its membership or applicants for membership, or to classify or fail or refuse to refer for employment any individual, in any way which would deprive or tend to deprive any individual of employment opportunities, or would limit such employment opportunities or otherwise adversely affect his status as an employee or as an applicant for employment, because of such individual's race, color, religion, sex, or national origin; or

(3) to cause or attempt to cause an employer to discriminate against an individual in violation of this section.

(d) It shall be an unlawful employment practice for any employer, labor organization, or joint labor-management committee controlling apprenticeship or other training or retraining, including on-the-job training programs to discriminate against any individual because of his race, color, religion, sex, or national origin in admission to, or employment in, any program established to provide apprenticeship or other training.

(e) Notwithstanding any other provision of this subchapter—

(1) it shall not be an unlawful employment practice for an employer to hire and employ employees, for an employment agency to classify, or refer for employment any individual, for a labor organization to classify its membership or to classify or refer for employment any individual, or for an employer, labor organization, or joint labor-management committee controlling apprenticeship or other training or retraining programs to admit or employ any individual in any such program, on the basis of his religion, sex, or national origin in those certain instances where religion, sex, or national origin is a bona fide occupational qualification reasonably necessary to the normal operation of that particular business or enterprise, and

(2) it shall not be an unlawful employment practice for a school, college, university, or other educational institution or institution of learning to hire and employ employees of a particular religion if such school, college, university, or other educational institution or institution of learning is, in whole or in substantial part, owned, supported, controlled, or managed by a particular religion or by a particular religious corporation, association, or society, or if the curriculum of such school, college, university, or other educational institution or institution of learning is directed toward the propagation of a particular religion.

(f) As used in this subchapter, the phrase "unlawful employment practice" shall not be deemed to include any action or measure taken by an employer, labor organization, joint labor-management committee, or employment agency with respect to an individual who is a member of the Communist Party of the United States or of any other organization required to register as a Communist-action or Communist-front organization. . . .

(g) Notwithstanding any other provision of this subchapter, it shall not be an unlawful employment practice for an employer to fail or refuse to hire and employ any individual for any position, for an employer to discharge any individual from any position, or for an employment agency to fail or refuse to refer any individual for employment in any position, or for a labor organization to fail or refuse to refer any individual for employment in any position, if—

(1) the occupancy of such position, or access to the premises in or upon which any part of the duties of such position is performed or is to be performed, is subject to any requirement imposed in the interest of the national security of the United States . . . and

(2) such individual has not fulfilled or has ceased to fulfill that requirement.

(h) Notwithstanding any other provision of this subchapter, it shall not be an unlawful employment practice for an employer to apply different standards of compensation, or different terms, conditions, or privileges of employment pursuant to a bona fide seniority or merit system, or a system which measures earnings by quantity or quality of production or to employees who work in different locations, provided that such differences are not the result of an intention to discriminate because of race, color, religion, sex, or national origin, nor shall it be an unlawful employment practice for an employer to give and act upon the results of any professionally developed ability test provided that such test, its administration or action upon the results is not designed, intended or used to discriminate because of race, color, religion, sex, or national origin. . . .

(j) Nothing contained in this subchapter shall be interpreted to require any employer, employment agency, labor organization, or joint labor-management committee subject to this subchapter to grant preferential treatment to any individual or to any group because of the race, color, religion, sex, or national origin of such individual or group on account of an imbalance which may exist with respect to the total number or percentage of persons of any race, color, religion, sex, or national origin employed by any employer, referred or classified for employment by any employment agency or labor organization, or admitted to, or employed in, any apprenticeship or other training program, in comparison with the total number or percentage of persons of such race, color, religion, sex, or national origin in any community, State, section, or other area, or in the available work force in any community, State, section, or other area.

**Section 704. Other Unlawful Employment Practices.** (a) It shall be an unlawful employment practice for an employer to discriminate against any of his employees or applicants for employment, for an employment agency, or joint labor-management committee controlling apprenticeship or other training or retraining, including on-the-job training programs, to discriminate against any individual, or for a labor organization to discriminate against any member thereof or applicant for membership, because he has opposed any practice made an unlawful employment practice by this subchapter, or because he has made a charge, testified, assisted, or participated in any manner in an investigation, proceeding, or hearing under this subchapter.

(b) It shall be an unlawful employment practice for an employer, labor organization, employment agency, or joint labor-management committee controlling apprenticeship or other training or retraining, including on-the-job training programs, to print or publish or cause to be printed or published any notice or advertisement relating to employment by such an employer or membership or any classification or referral for employment by such a labor organization, or relating to any classification or referral for employment by such an employment agency, or relating to admission to, or employment in, any program established to provide apprenticeship or other training by such a joint-labor-management committee, indicating any preference, limitation, specification, or discrimination, based on race, color, religion, sex, or national origin, except that such a notice or advertisement may indicate a preference, limitation, specification, or discrimination based on religion, sex or national origin when religion, sex, or national origin is a bona fide occupational qualification for employment.

# APPENDIX D Americans with Disabilities Act of 1990 [Excerpts]

## *TITLE 1– EMPLOYMENT*

### Sec. 101. Definitions.

As used in this title: . . .

(8) Qualified individual with a disability. The term "qualified individual with a disability" means an individual with a disability who, with or without reasonable accommodation, can perform the essential functions of the employment position that such individual holds or desires. For the purposes of this title, consideration shall be given to the employer's judgment as to what functions of a job are essential, and if an employer has prepared a written description before advertising or interviewing applicants for the job, this description shall be considered evidence of the essential functions of the job.

(9) Reasonable accommodation. The term "reasonable accommodation" may include—

(A) making existing facilities used by employees readily accessible to and usable by individuals with disabilities; and (B) job restructuring, part-time or modified work schedules, reassignment to a vacant position, acquisition or modification of equipment or devices, appropriate adjustment or modifications of examinations, training materials or policies, the provision of qualified readers or interpreters, and other similar accommodations for individuals with disabilities.

(10) Undue Hardship.

**(A)** *In general.* The term "undue hardship" means an action requiring significant difficulty or expense, when considered in light of the factors set forth in subparagraph(B).

**(B)** *Factors to be considered.* In determining whether an accommodation would impose an undue hardship on a covered entity, factors to be considered include—

(i) the nature and cost of accommodation needed under this Act;

(ii) the overall financial resources of the facility or facilities involved in the provision of the reasonable accommodation; the number of persons employed at such facility; the effect on expenses and resources, or the impact otherwise of such accommodation upon the operation of the facility;

(iii) the overall financial resources of the covered entity; the overall size of the business of a covered entity with respect to the number of its employees; the number, type, and location of its facilities; and

(iv) the type of operation or operations of the covered entity, including the composition, structure, and functions of the workforce of such entity; the geographic separateness, administrative, or fiscal relationship of the facility or facilities in question to the covered entity.

### Sec. 102. Discrimination.

(a) General Rule. No covered entity shall discriminate against a qualified individual with a disability because of the disability of such individual in regard to job application procedures, the hiring, advancement, or discharge of employees, employee compensation, job training, and other terms, conditions, and privileges of employment.

(b) Construction. As used in subsection (a), the term "discriminate" includes—

(1) limiting, segregating, or classifying a job applicant or employee in a way that adversely affects the opportunities or status of such applicant or employee because of the disability of such applicant or employee;

(2) participating in a contractual or other arrangement or relationship that has the effect of subjecting a covered entity's qualified applicant or employee with a disability to the discrimination prohibited by this title (such relationship includes a relationship with an employment

or referral agency, labor union, an organization providing fringe benefits to an employee of the covered entity, or an organization providing training and apprenticeship programs);

(3) utilizing standards, criteria, or methods of administration—

(A) that have the effect of discrimination on the basis of disability; or

(B) that perpetuate the discrimination of others who are subject to common administrative control;

(4) excluding or otherwise denying equal jobs or benefits to a qualified individual because of the known disability of an individual with whom the qualified individual is known to have a relationship or association;

(5)(A) not making reasonable accommodations to the known physical or mental limitations of an otherwise qualified individual with a disability who is an applicant or employee, unless such covered entity can demonstrate that the accommodation would impose an undue hardship on the operation of the business of such covered entity; or

(B) denying employment opportunities to a job applicant or employee who is an otherwise qualified individual with a disability, if such denial is based on the need of such covered entity to make reasonable accommodation to the physical or mental impairments of the employee or applicant;

(6) using qualification standards, employment tests or other selection criteria that screen out or tend to screen out an individual with a disability or a class of individuals with disabilities unless the standard, test or other selection criteria, as used by the covered entity, is shown to be job-related for the position in question and is consistent with business necessity; and

(7) failing to select and administer tests concerning employment in the most effective manner to ensure that, when such test is administered to a job applicant or employee who has a disability that impairs sensory, manual, or speaking skills, such test results accurately reflect the skills, aptitude, or whatever other factor of such applicant or employee that such test purports to measure, rather than reflecting the impaired sensory, manual, or speaking skills of such employee or applicant (except where such skills are the factors that the test purports to measure). . . .

**Sec. 104. Illegal Use of Drugs and Alcohol.**

(b) Rules of Construction. Nothing in subsection (a) shall be construed to exclude as a qualified individual with a disability an individual who—

(1) has successfully completed a supervised drug rehabilitation program and is no longer engaging in the illegal use of drugs, or has otherwise been rehabilitated successfully and is no longer engaging in such use;

(2) is participating in a supervised rehabilitation program and is no longer engaging in such use; or

(3) is erroneously regarded as engaging in such use, but is not engaging in such use; except that it shall not be a violation of this Act for a covered entity to adopt or administer reasonable policies or procedures, including but not limited to drug testing, designed to ensure that an individual described in paragraph (1) or (2) is no longer engaging in the illegal use of drugs. . . .

**Sec. 107. Enforcement.**

(a) Powers, Remedies, and Procedures. The powers, remedies, and procedures set forth in sections 705, 706, 707, 709, and 710 of the Civil Rights Act of 1964 (42 U.S.C. 2000e-4, 2000e-5, 2000e-6, 2000e-8, and 2000e-9) shall be the powers, remedies, and procedures this title provides to the Commission, to the Attorney General, or to any person alleging discrimination on the basis of disability in violation of any provision of this Act, or regulations promulgated under section 106, concerning employment.

(b) Coordination. The agencies with enforcement authority for actions which allege employment discrimination under this title and under the Rehabilitation Act of 1973 shall develop procedures to ensure that administrative complaints filed under this title and under the Rehabilitation Act of 1973 are dealt with in a manner that avoids duplication of effort and prevents imposition of inconsistent or conflicting standards for the same requirements under this title and the Rehabilitation Act of 1973. The Commission, the Attorney General, and the Office of Federal Contract Compliance Programs shall establish such coordinating mechanisms (similar to provisions contained in the joint regulations promulgated by the Commission and the Attorney General at part 42 of title 28 and part 1691 of title 29, Code of Federal Regulations, and the Memorandum of Understanding between the Commission and the Office of Federal Contract Compliance Programs dated January 16, 1981 (46 Fed. Reg. 7435, January 23, 1981)) in regulations implementing this title and Rehabilitation Act of 1973 not later than 18 months after the date of enactment of this Act.

**Sec. 108. Effective Date.**

This title shall become effective 24 months after the date of enactment.

# APPENDIX E National Labor Relations Act [Excerpts]

**Section 3. National Labor Relations Board.** (a) The National Labor Relations Board (hereinafter called the "Board") . . . as an agency of the United States, shall consist of five . . . members, appointed by the President by and with advice and consent of the Senate . . . for terms of five years each. . . . The President shall designate one member to serve as Chairman of the Board. Any member of the Board may be removed by the President, upon notice and hearing, for neglect of duty or malfeasance in office, but for no other cause.

**Section 7. Rights of Employees.** Employees shall have the right to self-organization, to form, join, or assist labor organizations, to bargain collectively through representatives of their own choosing, and to engage in other concerted activities for the purpose of collective bargaining or other mutual aid or protection, and shall also have the right to refrain from any or all of such activities except to the extent that such right may be affected by an agreement requiring membership in a labor organization as a condition of employment as authorized in section 8(a) (3).

**Section 8. Unfair Labor Practice.** (a) It shall be an unfair labor practice for an employer—

(1) to interfere with, restrain, or coerce employees in the exercise of the rights guaranteed in section 7;

(2) to dominate or interfere with the formation or administration of any labor organization or contribute financial or other support to it: Provide, that subject to rules and regulations made and published by the Board pursuant to section 6, an employer shall not be prohibited from permitting employees to confer with him during working hours without loss of time or pay;

(3) by discrimination in regard to hire or tenure of employment or any term or condition of employment to encourage or discourage membership in any labor organization: Provided, that nothing in this Act . . . shall preclude an employer from making an agreement with a labor organization . . . to require as a condition of employment membership therein . . . Provided further, that no employer shall justify any discrimination against an employee for nonmembership in a labor organization (A) if he has reasonable grounds for believing that such membership was not available to the employee on the same terms and conditions generally applicable to other members, or (B) if he has reasonable grounds for believing that membership was denied or terminated for reasons other than the failure of the employee to tender periodic dues and initiation fees uniformly required as a condition of acquiring or retaining membership;

(4) to discharge or otherwise discriminate against an employee because he has filed charges or given testimony under this Act;

(5) to refuse to bargain collectively with the representatives of his employees, subject to the provisions of section 9(a).

(b) It shall be an unfair labor practice for a labor organization or its agents—

(1) to restrain or coerce (A) employees in the exercise of the rights guaranteed in section 7: Provided, that this paragraph shall not impair the right of a labor organization to prescribe its own rules with respect to the acquisition or retention of membership therein; or (B) an employer in the selection of his representatives for the purposes of collective bargaining or the adjustment of grievances;

(2) to cause or attempt to cause an employer to discriminate against an employee in violation of subsection (a) (3) or to discriminate against an employee with respect to whom membership in such organization has been denied or terminated on some ground other than his failure to tender the periodic dues and the initiation fees uniformly required as a condition of acquiring or retaining membership.

(3) to refuse to bargain collectively with an employer, provided it is the representative of his employees subject to the provisions of section 9 (a).

(4) (i) to engage in, or to induce or encourage any individual employed by any person engaged in commerce or in an industry affecting commerce to engage in, a strike or a refusal in the course of his employment to use, manufacture, process, transport, or otherwise handle or work on any goods, articles, materials, or commodities or to perform any services; or, (ii) to threaten, coerce, or restrain any person engaged in commerce or in an industry affecting commerce, where in either case an object thereof is:

(A) forcing or requiring any employer or self-employed person to join any labor or employer organization or to enter into any agreement which is prohibited by section 8 (e);

(B) forcing or requiring any person to cease using, selling, handling, transporting, or otherwise dealing in the products of any other producer, processor, or manufacturer, or to cease doing business with any other person, or forcing or requiring any other employer to recognize or bargain with a labor organization as the representative of his employees unless such labor organization has been certified as the representative of such employees . . . Provided, that nothing contained in this clause (B) shall be construed to make unlawful, where not otherwise unlawful, any primary strike or primary picketing;

(C) forcing or requiring any employer to recognize or bargain with a particular labor organization as the representative of his employees if another labor organization has been certified as the representative of such employees. . . .

(D) forcing or requiring any employer to assign particular work to employees in a particular labor organization or in a particular trade, craft, or class. . . .

Provided, that nothing contained in this subsection (b) shall be construed to make unlawful a refusal by any person to enter upon the premises of any employer (other than his own employer), if the employees of such employer are engaged in a strike ratified or approved by a representative of such employees whom such employer is required to recognize under this Act: Provided further, that for the purposes of this paragraph (4) only, nothing contained in such paragraph shall be construed to prohibit publicity, other than picketing, for the purpose of truthfully advising the public, including consumers and members of a labor organization, that a product or products are produced by an employer with whom the labor organization has a primary dispute and are distributed by another employer, as long as such publicity does not have an effect of inducing any individual employed by any person other than the primary employer in the course of his employment to pick up, deliver, or transport any goods, or not to perform any services, at the establishment of the employer engaged in such distribution;

(5) to require of employees covered by an agreement authorized under subsection (a) (3) the payment, as a condition precedent to becoming a member of such organization, of a fee in an amount which the Board finds excessive or discriminatory. . . .

(6) to cause or attempt to cause an employer to pay or deliver or agree to pay or deliver any money or other thing of value, in the nature of an exaction, for services which are not performed or not to be performed; and

(7) to picket or cause to be picketed, or threaten to picket or cause to be picketed, any employer where an object thereof is forcing or requiring an employer to recognize or bargain with a labor organization as the representative of his employees, or forcing or requiring the employees of an employer to accept or select such labor organization as their collective bargaining representative, unless such labor organization is currently certified as the representative of such employees:

(A) where the employer has lawfully recognized in accordance with this Act any other labor organization and a question concerning representation may not appropriately be raised under section 9(c) of this Act,

(B) where within the preceding 12 months a valid election under section 9(c) of this Act has been conducted, or

(C) where such picketing has been conducted without a petition under section 9(c) being filed within a reasonable period of time not to exceed 30 days from the commencement of such picketing:

Provided, that when such a petition has been filed the Board shall forthwith, without regard to the provisions of section 9(c) (1) or the absence of a showing of a substantial interest on the part of the labor organization, direct an election in such units as the Board finds to be appropriate and shall certify the results thereof: Provided further, that nothing in this subparagraph (C) shall be construed to prohibit any picketing or other publicity for the purpose of truthfully advising the public (including consumers) that an employer does not employ members of, or have a contract with, a labor organization, unless an effect of such picketing is to induce any individual employed by any other person in the course of his employment, not to pick up, deliver or transport any goods or not to perform any services.

Nothing in this paragraph (7) shall be construed to permit any act which would otherwise be an unfair labor practice under this section 8(b).

(c) The expressing of any views, argument, or opinion, or the dissemination thereof, whether in written, printed, graphic, or visual form, shall not constitute or be evidence of an unfair labor practice under any of the provisions of this Act, if such expression contains no threat of reprisal or force or promise of benefit.

(d) For the purposes of this section, to bargain collectively is the performance of the mutual obligation of the employer and the representative of the employees to meet at reasonable times and confer in good faith with respect to wages, hours, and other terms and conditions of employment, or the negotiation of an agreement, or any question arising thereunder, and the execution of a written contract incorporating any agreement reached if requested by either party, but such obligation does not compel either party to agree to a proposal or require the making of a concession: Provided, that where there is in effect a collective bargaining contract covering employees in an industry affecting commerce, the duty to bargain collectively shall also mean that no party to such contract shall terminate or modify such contract, unless the party desiring such termination or modification—

(1) serves a written notice upon the other party to the contract of the proposed termination or modification 60 days prior to the expiration date thereof, or in the event such contract contains no expiration date, 60 days prior to the time it is proposed to make such termination or modification;

(2) offers to meet and confer with the other party for the purpose of negotiating a new contract or a contract containing the proposed modifications;

(3) notifies the Federal Mediation and Conciliation Service within 30 days after such notice of the existence of a dispute . . .

(4) continues in full force and effect, without resorting to strike or lockout, all the terms and conditions of the existing contract for a period of 60 days after such notice is given or until the expiration date of such contract, whichever occurs later.

(e) It shall be an unfair labor practice for any labor organization and any employer to enter into any contract or agreement, express or implied, whereby such employer ceases or refrains or agrees to cease or refrain from handling, using, selling, transporting, or otherwise dealing in any of the products of any other employer, or to cease doing business with any other person, . . . Provided, that nothing in this subsection (e) shall apply to an agreement between a labor organization and an employer in the construction industry relating to the contracting or subcontracting of work to be done at the site. . . .

### Section 9. Representatives and Elections.

(a) Representatives designated or selected for the purposes of collective bargaining by the majority of the employees in a unit appropriate for such purposes, shall be the exclusive representatives of all the employees in such unit for the purposes of collective bargaining in respect to rates of pay, wages, hours of employment, or other conditions of employment: Provided, that any individual employee or a group of employees shall have the right at any time to present grievances to their employer and to have such grievance adjusted, without the intervention of the bargaining representative, as long as the adjustment is not inconsistent with the terms of a collective bargaining contract or agreement then in effect: Provided further, that the bargaining representative has been given opportunity to be present at such adjustment.

(b) The Board shall decide in each case whether, in order to assure to employees the fullest freedom in exercising the rights guaranteed by this Act, the unit appropriate for the purposes of collective bargaining shall be the employer unit, craft unit, plant unit, or subdivision thereof: Provided, that the Board shall not (1) decide that any unit is appropriate for such purposes if such unit includes both professional employees and employees who are not professional employees unless a majority of such professional employees vote for inclusion in such unit; or (2) decide that any craft unit is inappropriate for such purposes on the ground that a different unit has been established by a prior Board determination, unless a majority of the employees in the proposed craft unit vote against separate representation or (3) decide that any unit is appropriate for such purposes, if it includes, together with other employees, any individual employed as a guard to enforce against employees and other persons, rules to protect property of the employer or to protect the safety of persons on the employer's premises; but no labor organization shall be certified as the representative of employees in a bargaining unit of guards if such organization admits to membership, or is affiliated directly or indirectly with an organization which admits to membership, employees other than guards.

(c) (1) Wherever a petition shall have been filed, in accordance with such regulations as may be prescribed by the Board—

(A) by an employee or group of employees or any individual or labor organization acting in their behalf alleging that a substantial number of employees (i) wish to be represented for collective bargaining and that their employer declines to recognize their representative as the representative defined in section 9(a), or (ii) assert that the individual or labor organization, which has been certified or is being currently recognized by their employer as the bargaining representative as defined in section 9(a); or

(B) by an employer, alleging that one or more individuals or labor organizations have presented to him a claim to be recognized as the representative defined in section 9(a);

the Board shall investigate such petition and if it has reasonable cause to believe that a question of representation affecting commerce exists shall provide for an appropriate hearing upon due notice. Such hearing may be conducted by an officer or employee of the regional office, who shall not make any recommendations with respect thereto. If the Board finds upon the record of such hearing that such a question of representative exists, it shall direct an election by secret ballot and shall certify the results thereof.

(2) In determining whether or not a question of representation affecting commerce exists, the same regulations and rules of decision shall apply irrespective of the identity of the persons filing the petition or the kind of relief sought and in no case shall the Board deny a labor organization a place on the ballot by reason of an order with respect to such labor organization or its predecessor not issued in conformity with section 10(c).

(3) No election shall be directed in any bargaining unit or any subdivision within which, in the preceding twelve-month period, a valid election shall have been held. Employees engaged in an economic strike who are not entitled to reinstatement shall be eligible to vote under such regulations as the Board shall find are consistent with the purposes and provisions of this Act in any election conducted within twelve months after the commencement of the strike. In any election where none of the choices on the ballot receives a majority, a run-off shall be conducted, the ballot providing for a selection between the two choices receiving the largest and second largest number of valid votes cast in the election.

(4) Nothing in this section shall be construed to prohibit the waiving of hearings by stipulation for the purpose of a consent election in conformity with regulations and rules of decision of the Board.

(5) In determining whether a unit is appropriate for the purposes specified in subsection (b) the extent to which the employees have organized shall not be controlling.

(d) Whenever an order of the Board made pursuant to section 10(c) is based in whole or in part upon facts certified following an investigation pursuant to subsection (c) of this section and there is a petition for the enforcement or review of such order, such certification and the record of such investigation shall be included in the transcript of the entire record required to be filed under section 10(c) or 10(f), and thereupon the decree of the court enforcing modifying, or setting aside in whole or in part the order of the Board shall be made and entered upon the pleadings, testimony, and the proceedings set forth in such transcript.

(e)(1) Upon the filing with the Board, by 30 per centum or more of the employees in a bargaining unit covered by an agreement between their employer and a labor organization made pursuant to section 8(a)(3), of a petition alleging they desire that such authority be rescinded, the Board shall take a secret ballot of the employees in such unit, and shall certify the results thereof to such labor organization and to the employer.

(2) No election shall be conducted pursuant to this subsection in any bargaining unit or any subdivision within which, in the preceding twelve month period, a valid election shall have been held.

**Section 19. Individuals with Religious Convictions.**

Any employee who is a member of and adheres to established and traditional tenets or teachings of a bona fide religion, body, or sect which has historically held conscientious objections to joining or financially supporting labor organizations shall not be required to join or financially support any labor organization as a condition of employment; except that such employee may be required in a contract between such employee's employer and a labor organization in lieu of periodic dues and initiation fees, to pay sums equal to such dues and initiation fees to a nonreligious, nonlabor organization charitable fund exempt from taxation under section 501(c) (3) of title 26 of the Internal Revenue Code.

# APPENDIX F Sherman Antitrust Act [Excerpts]

**Section 1.** Every contract, combination in the form of trust or otherwise, or conspiracy, in restraint of trade or commerce among the several States, or with foreign nations, is hereby declared to be illegal. Every person who shall make any contract or engage in any such combination or conspiracy shall be deemed guilty of a felony, and, on conviction thereof, shall be punished by fine not exceeding $10,000,000 if a corporation, or, if any other person, $350,000 or by imprisonment not exceeding three years, or by both said punishments in the discretion of the court.

**Section 2.** Every person who shall monopolize, or attempt to monopolize, or conspire with any other person or persons, to monopolize any part of the trade or commerce among the several States, or with foreign nations, shall be deemed guilty of a felony, and, on conviction thereof, shall be punished by fine not exceeding $10,000,000 if a corporation, or, if any other person, $350,000 or by imprisonment not exceeding three years, or by both said punishments, in the discretion of the court.

# APPENDIX G Clayton Act of 1914 [Excerpts]

**Section 3.** That it shall be unlawful for any person engaged in commerce, in the course of such commerce, to lease or make a sale or contract for sale of goods, wares, merchandise, machinery, supplies, or other commodities, whether patented or unpatented, for use, consumption, or resale within the United States or . . . other place under the jurisdiction of the United States, or fix a price charged therefor, or discount from, or rebate upon, such price, on the condition, agreement, or understanding that the lessee or purchaser thereof shall not use or deal in the goods, wares, merchandise, machinery, supplies, or other commodities of a competitor or competitors of the lessor or seller, where the effect of such lease, sale, or contract for sale or such condition, agreement, or understanding may be to substantially lessen competition to tend to create a monopoly in any line of commerce.

**Section 4.** That any person who shall be injured in his business or property by reason of anything forbidden in the antitrust laws may sue therefor in any district court of the United States in the district in which the defendant resides or is found, or has an agent, without respect to the amount in controversy, and shall recover threefold the damages by him sustained, and the cost of suit, including a reasonable attorney's fee.

**Section 4A.** Whenever the United States is hereafter injured in its business or property by reason of anything forbidden in the antitrust laws it may sue therefor in the United States district court for the district in which the defendant resides or is found or has an agent, without respect to the amount in controversy, and shall recover actual damages by it sustained and the cost of suit.

**Section 4B.** Any action to enforce any cause of action under sections 4 or 4A shall be forever barred unless commenced within four years after the cause of action accrued. No cause of action barred under existing law on the effective date of this act shall be revived by this Act.

**Section 6.** That the labor of a human being is not a commodity or article of commerce. Nothing contained in the antitrust laws shall be construed to forbid the existence and operation of labor, agricultural or horticultural organizations, instituted for the purposes of mutual help, and not having capital stock or conducted for profit, or to forbid or restrain individual members of such organizations from lawfully carrying out the legitimate objects thereof; nor shall such organizations or the members thereof, be held or construed to be illegal combinations or conspiracies in restraint of trade, under the antitrust laws.

**Section 7.** That no person engaged in commerce shall acquire, directly or indirectly, the whole or any part of the stock or other share capital and no corporation subject to the jurisdiction of the Federal Trade Commission shall acquire the whole or any part of the assets of another corporation engaged also in commerce, where in any line of commerce in any section of the country, the effect of such acquisition may be substantially to lessen competition, or to tend to create a monopoly.

No person shall acquire, directly or indirectly, the whole or any part of the stock or other share capital and no corporation subject to the jurisdiction of the Federal Trade Commission shall acquire the whole or any part of the assets of one or more corporations engaged in commerce, where in any line of commerce in any section of the country, the effect of such acquisition, of such stocks or assets, or of the use of such stock by the voting or granting of proxies or otherwise, may be substantially to lessen competition, or to tend to create a monopoly.

This section shall not apply to persons purchasing such stock solely for investment and not using the same by voting or otherwise to bring about, or in attempting to bring about, the substantial lessening of competition . . . .

**Section 8.** . . . No person shall, at the same time, serve as a director or officer in any two or more corporations (other than banks, banking associations, and trust companies) that are—

(A) engaged in whole or in part in commerce; and

(B) by virtue of their business and location of operation, competitors, so that the elimination of competition by agreement between them would constitute a violation of any of the antitrust laws; if each of the corporations has capital, surplus, and undivided profits aggregating more than $10,000,000 as adjusted pursuant to paragraph (5) of this subsection.

# APPENDIX H Federal Trade Commission Act of 1914 [Excerpts]

## Unfair Methods of Competition Prohibited

### Section 5. Unfair methods of competition unlawful; prevention by Commission—declaration. Declaration of unlawfulness; power to prohibit unfair practices.

(a) (1) Unfair methods of competition in or affecting commerce, and unfair or deceptive acts or practices in or affecting commerce, are declared unlawful.

. . .

(b) Any person, partnership, or corporation who violates an order of the Commission to cease and desist after it has become final, and while such order is in effect, shall forfeit and pay to the United States a civil penalty of not more than $10,000 for each violation, which shall accrue to the United States and may be recovered in a civil action brought by the Attorney General of the United States. Each separate violation of such an order shall be a separate offense, except that in the case of a violation through continuing failure or neglect to obey a final order of the Commission, each day of continuance of such failure or neglect shall be deemed a separate offense.

# APPENDIX I Robinson-Patman Act [Excerpts]

## Price Discrimination; Cost Justification; Changing Conditions

### Section 2—Discrimination in price, services, or facilities. (a) Price; Selection of Customers.

It shall be unlawful for any person engaged in commerce, in the course of such commerce, either directly or indirectly, to discriminate in price between different purchases of commodities of like grade and quality, where either or any of the purchases involved in such discrimination are in commerce, where such commodities are sold for use, consumption, or resale within the United States or any Territory thereof or the District of Columbia or any insular possession or other place under the jurisdiction of the United States, and where the effect of such discrimination may be substantially to lessen competition or tend to create a monopoly in any line of commerce, or to injure, destroy, or prevent competition with any person who either grants or knowingly receives the benefit of such discrimination, or with customers of either of them; *Provided,* That nothing herein contained shall prevent differentials which make only due allowance for differences in the cost of manufacture, sale, or delivery resulting from the differing methods or quantities in which such commodities are to such purchasers sold or delivered: *Provided, however,* That the Federal Trade Commission may, after due investigation and hearing to all interested parties, fix and establish quantity limits, and revise the same as it finds necessary as to particular commodities or classes of commodities, where it finds that available purchasers in greater quantities are so few as to render differentials on account thereof unjustly discriminatory or promotive of monopoly in any line of commerce; and the foregoing shall then not be construed to permit differentials based on differences in quantities greater than those so fixed and established: *And provided further,* That nothing herein contained shall prevent persons engaged in selling goods, wares, or merchandise in commerce from selecting their own customers in bona fide transactions and not in restraint of trade: *And provided further,* That nothing herein contained shall prevent price changes from time to time where in response to changing conditions affecting the market for or the marketability of the goods concerned, such as but not limited to actual or imminent deterioration of perishable goods, obsolescence of seasonal goods, distress sales under court process, or sales in good faith in discontinuance of business in the goods concerned.

### Meeting Competition

**(b) Burden of rebutting prima-facie case of discrimination.**

Upon proof being made, at any hearing on a complaint under this section, that there has been discrimination in price or services or facilities furnished, the burden of rebutting the prima-facie case thus made by showing justification shall be upon the person charged with a violation of this section, and unless justification shall be affirmatively shown, the Commission is authorized to issue an order terminating the discrimination: *Provided, however,* That nothing herein contained shall prevent a seller rebutting the prima-facie case thus made by showing that his lower price or the furnishing of services or facilities to any purchaser or purchasers was made in good faith to meet an equally low price of a competitor, or the services or facilities furnished by a competitor.

### Brokerage Payments

**(c) Payment or acceptance of commission, brokerage or other compensation.**

It shall be unlawful for any person engaged in commerce, in the course of such commerce, to pay or grant, or to receive or accept, anything of value as a commission, brokerage, or other compensation, or any allowance or discount in lieu thereof, except for services rendered in connection with the sale or purchase of goods, wares, or merchandise, either to the other party to such transaction or to an agent, representative, or other intermediary therein where such intermediary is acting in fact for or in behalf, or is subject to the direct or indirect control, of any party to such transaction other than the person by whom such compensation is so granted or paid.

### Promotional Allowances

**(d) Payment for services or facilities for processing or sale.**

It shall be unlawful for any person engaged in commerce to pay or contract for the payment of anything of value to or for the benefit of a customer of such person in the course of such commerce as compensation or in consideration for any services or facilities furnished by or through such customer in connection with the processing, handling, sale or offering for sale of any products or commodities manufactured, sold, or offered for sale by such person, unless such payment of consideration is available on proportionally equal terms to all other customers competing in the distribution of such products or commodities.

### Promotional Services

**(e) Furnishing services or facilities for processing, handling, etc.**

It shall be unlawful for any person to discriminate in favor of one purchaser against another purchaser or purchasers of a commodity bought for resale, with or without processing, or by contracting to furnish or furnishing, or by contributing to the furnishing of, any services or facilities connected with the processing, handling, sale, or offering for sale of such commodity so purchased upon terms not accorded to all purchasers on proportionally equal terms.

### Buyer Discrimination

**(f) Knowingly inducing or receiving discriminatory price.**

It shall be unlawful for any person engaged in commerce, in the course of such commerce, knowingly to induce or receive a discrimination in price which is prohibited by this section.

### Predatory Practices

**Section 3—Discrimination in rebates, discounts, or advertising service charges; underselling in particular localities; penalties.** It shall be unlawful for any person engaged in commerce, in the course of such commerce, to be a party to, or assist in, any transaction of sale, or contract to sell, which discriminates to his knowledge against competitors of the purchaser, in that, any discount, rebate, allowance, or advertising service charge is granted to the purchaser over and above any discount, rebate, allowance, or advertising service charge available at the time of such transaction to said competitors in respect of a sale of goods of like grade, quality, and quantity; to sell, or contract to sell, goods in any part of the United States at prices lower than those exacted by said person elsewhere in the United States for the purpose of destroying competition, or eliminating a competitor in such part of the United States; or, to sell, or contract to sell, goods at unreasonably lower prices for the purpose of destroying competition or eliminating a competitor.

Any person violating any of the provisions of this section shall, upon conviction thereof, be fined not more than $5,000 or imprisoned not more than one year, or both.

# APPENDIX J Securities Act of 1933 [Excerpts]

### Prohibitions Relating to Interstate Commerce and the Mails

**Sec. 5.** (a) Unless a registration statement is in effect as to a security, it shall be unlawful for any person, directly or indirectly—

(1) to make use of any means or instruments of transportation or communication in interstate commerce or of the mails to sell such security through the use or medium of any prospectus or otherwise; or

(2) to carry or cause to be carried through the mails or in interstate commerce, by any means or instruments of transportation, any such security for the purpose of sale or for delivery after sale.

### [Prospectus Requirements]

(b) It shall be unlawful for any person, directly or indirectly—

(1) to make use of any means or instruments of transportation or communication in interstate commerce or of the mails to carry or transmit any prospectus relating to any security with respect to which a registration statement has been filed under this title, unless such prospectus meets the requirements of section 10, or

(2) to carry or to cause to be carried through the mails or in interstate commerce any such security for the purpose of sale or for delivery after sale, unless accompanied or preceded by a prospectus that meets the requirements of subsection (a) of section 10.

### [Prohibition Against Offers Prior to Registration]

(c) It shall be unlawful for any person, directly or indirectly, to make use of any means or instruments of transportation or communication in interstate commerce or of the mails to offer to sell or offer to buy through the use or medium of any prospectus or otherwise any security, unless a registration statement has been filed as to such security, or while the registration statement is the subject of a refusal order or stop order or (prior to the effective date of the registration statement) any public proceeding or examination under section 8.

### Civil Liabilities on Account of False Registration Statement

**Sec. 11.** (a) In case any part of the registration statement, when such part became effective, contained an untrue statement of a material fact or omitted to state a material fact required to be stated therein or necessary to make the statements therein not misleading, any person acquiring such security (unless it is proved that at the time of such acquisition he knew of such untruth or omission) may, either at law or in equity, in any court of competent jurisdiction, sue—

### [Signers of Registration Statement]

(1) every person who signed the registration statement;

### [Directors and Partners]

(2) every person who was a director of (or person performing similar functions), or partner in, the issuer at the time of the filing of the part of the registration statement with respect to which his liability is asserted;

### [Persons Named as Being, or About to Become, Directors or Partners]

(3) every person who, with his consent, is named in the registration statement as being or about to become a director, person performing similar functions, or partner;

### [Accountants, Engineers, Appraisers, and Other Professional Persons]

(4) every accountant engineer, or appraiser, or any person whose profession gives authority to a statement made by him, who has with his consent been named as having prepared or certified any part of the registration statement, or as having prepared or certified any report or valuation which is used in connection with the registration statement, with respect to the statement in such registration statement, report, or valuation, which purports to have been prepared or certified by him;

### [Underwriters]

(5) every underwriter with respect to such security.

### [Purchase after Publication of Earning Statement]

If such person acquired the security after the issuer has made generally available to its security holders an earning statement covering a period of at least twelve months beginning after the effective date of the registration statement, then the right of recovery under this subsection shall be conditioned on proof that such person acquired the securities relying on such untrue statement in the registration statement or relying upon the registration statement and not knowing of such omission, but such reliance may be established without proof of the reading of the registration statement by such person.

### [Defenses of Persons Other than Issuer]

(b) Notwithstanding the provisions of subsection (a) no person, other than the issuer, shall be liable as provided therein who shall sustain the burden of proof—

### [Resignation before Effective Date]

(1) that before the effective date of the part of the registration statement with respect to which his liability is asserted (A) he had resigned from or had taken such steps as are permitted by law to resign from, or ceased or refused to act in, every office, capacity or relationship in which he was described in the registration statement as acting or agreeing to act, and (B) he had advised the Commission and the issuer in writing, that he had taken such action and that he would not be responsible for such part of the registration statement; or

### [Statements Becoming Effective without Defendants Knowledge]

(2) that if such part of the registration statement became effective without his knowledge, upon becoming aware of such fact he forthwith acted and advised the Commission, in accordance with paragraph (1), and, in addition, gave reasonable public notice that such part of the registration statement had become effective without his knowledge; or

### [Belief on Reasonable Grounds that Statements Were True]

(3) that (A) as regards any part of the registration statement not purporting to be made on the authority of an expert, and not purporting to be a copy of or extract from a report or valuation of an expert and not purporting to be made on the authority of a public official document or statement, he had, after reasonable investigation, reasonable ground to believe and did believe, at the time such part of the registration statement became effective, that the statements therein were true and that there was no omission to state a material fact required to be stated therein or necessary to make the statements therein not misleading; and

### [Statement Made on Authority of Defendant as Expert]

(B) as regards any part of the registration statement purporting to be made upon his authority as an expert or purporting to be a copy of or extract from a report or valuation of himself as an expert, (i) he had, after reasonable investigation, reasonable ground to believe and did believe, at the time such part of the registration statement became effective, that the statements therein were true and that there was no omission to state a material fact required to be stated therein or necessary to make the statements therein not misleading, or (ii) such part of the registration statement did not fairly represent his statement as an expert or was not a fair copy of or extract from his report or valuation as an expert; and

### [Statement Made on Authority of Expert Other than Defendant]

(C) as regards any part of the registration statement purporting to be made on the authority of an expert (other than himself) or purporting to be a copy of or extract from a report or valuation of an expert (other than himself), he had no reasonable ground to believe and did not believe, at the time such part of the registration statement became effective, that the statements therein were untrue or that there was an omission to state a material fact required to be stated therein or necessary to make the statements therein not misleading, or that such part of the registration statement did not fairly represent the statement of the expert or was not a fair copy of or extract from the report or valuation of the expert; and

### [Statement Made by Official Person; Copy of Public Official Document]

(D) as regards any part of the registration statement purporting to be a statement made by an official person or purporting to be a copy of or extract from a public official document, he had no reasonable ground to believe and did not believe, at the time such part of the registration statement became effective, that the statements therein were untrue, or that there was an omission to state a material fact required to be stated therein or necessary to make the statements therein not misleading, or that such part of the registration statement did not fairly represent the statement made by the official person or was not a fair copy of or extract from the public official document.

### ["Reasonable" Investigation and "Reasonable" Grounds for Belief]

(c) In determining, for the purpose of paragraph (3) of subsection (b) of this section, what constitutes reasonable investigation and reasonable ground for belief, the standard of reasonableness shall be that required of a prudent man in the management of his own property.

### [Person Becoming Underwriter after Effectiveness of Registration Statement]

(d) If any person becomes an underwriter with respect to the security after the part of the registration statement with respect to which his liability is asserted has become effective, then for the purposes of paragraph (3) of subsection (b) of this section such part of the registration statement shall be considered as having become effective with respect to such person as of the time when he became an underwriter.

### [Amount of Damages; Bond for Costs of Suit]

(e) The suit authorized under subsection (a) may be to recover such damages as shall represent the difference between the amount paid for the security (not exceeding the price at which the security was offered to the public) and (1) the value thereof as of the time such suit was brought, or (2) the price at which such security shall have been disposed of in the market before suit, or (3) the price at which such security shall have been disposed of after suit but before judgment if such damages shall be less than the damages representing the difference between the amount paid for the security (not exceeding the price at which the security was offered to the public) and the value thereof as of the time such suit was brought: Provided, that if the defendant proves that any portion or all of such damages represents other than the depreciation in value of such security resulting from such part of the registration statement, with respect to which his liability is asserted, not being true or omitting to state a material fact required to be stated therein or necessary to make the statements therein not misleading, such portion of or all such damages shall not be recoverable. In no event shall any underwriter (unless such underwriter shall have knowingly received from the issuer for acting as an underwriter some benefit, directly or indirectly in which all other underwriters similarly situated did not share in proportion to their respective interests in the underwriting) be liable in any suit or as a consequence of suits authorized under subsection (a) of this section for damages in excess of the total price at which the securities underwritten by him and distributed to the public were offered to the public. In any suit under this or any other section of this title the court may, in its discretion, require an undertaking for the payment of the costs of such suit, including reasonable attorney's fees, and if judgment shall be rendered against a party litigant, upon the motion of the other party litigant, such costs may be assessed in favor of such party litigant (whether or not such undertaking has been required) if the court believes the suit or the defense to have been without merit, in an amount sufficient to reimburse him for the reasonable expenses incurred by him, in connection with such suit, such costs to be taxed in the manner usually provided for taxing of costs in the court in which the suit was heard.

### [Joint and Several Liability]

(f) (1) Except as provided in paragraph (2), All or any one or more of the persons specified in subsection (a) shall be jointly and severally liable, and every person who becomes liable to make any payment under this section may recover contribution as in cases of contract from any person who, if sued separately, would have been liable to make the same payment, unless the person who had become liable was, and the other was not, guilty of fraudulent misrepresentation.

(2)(A) The liability of an outside director under subsection (e) shall be determined in accordance with Section 21D(f) of the Securities Exchange Act of 1934.

[*Ed.*: Section 21D(f) provides that any person found liable shall be jointly and severally liable for all damages awarded the plaintiff only if the trier of fact specifically determines that the person knowingly committed a violation of the securities laws. Otherwise (except for uncollectible amounts, as described below), a person is liable solely for the portion of the judgment that corresponds to that person's percentage of responsibility (such percentage to be determined by considering both the nature of the person's conduct and the nature and extent of the causal relationship between the person's conduct and the damages incurred by the plaintiff). If part of the judgment owed by all defendants remains uncollectible, then each defendant has joint and several liability for the uncollectible share if the plaintiff is an individual with a net worth less than $200,000 and the recoverable damages represent more than 10 percent of that net worth. Otherwise, each defendant is liable for the uncollectible share in proportion to his or her percentage of responsibility up to a maximum of 50 percent of that person's proportionate share of liability.]

(B) For purpose of this paragraph, the term "outside director" shall have the meaning given such term by rule or regulation of the commission.

### [Limitation on Amount of Damages]

(g) In no case shall the amount recoverable under this section exceed the price at which the security was offered to the public.

### Civil Liabilities Arising in Connection with Prospectuses and Communications

**Sec. 12.** (a) *In General*—Any person who—

(1) offers or sells a security in violation of section 5, or

**Offers or Sells by Use of Interstate Communications or Transportation**

(2) offers or sells a security (whether or not exempted by the provisions of section 3, other than paragraph (2) of subsection (a) thereof), by the use of any means or instruments of transportation or communication in interstate commerce or of the mails, by means of a prospectus or oral communication, which includes an untrue statement of a material fact or omits to state a material fact necessary in order to make the statements, in the light of the circumstances under which they were made, not misleading (the purchaser not knowing of such untruth or omission), and who shall not sustain the burden of proof that he did not know, and in the exercise of reasonable care could not have known, of such untruth or omission, shall be liable, subject to subsection (b), to the person purchasing such security from him, who may sue either at law or in equity in any court of competent jurisdiction, to recover the consideration paid for such security with interest thereon, less the amount of any income received thereon, upon the tender of such security, or for damages if he no longer owns the security.

(b) *Loss Causation.*—In an action described in subsection (a)(2), if the person who offered or sold such security proves that any portion or all of the amount recoverable under subsection (a)(2) represents other than the depreciation in value of the subject security resulting from such part of the prospectus or oral communication, with respect to which the liability of that person is asserted, not being true or omitting to state a material fact required to be stated therein or necessary to make the statement not misleading, then such portion or amount, as the case may be, shall not be recoverable.

# APPENDIX K Securities Exchange Act of 1934 [Excerpts]

**Regulation of the Use of Manipulative and Deceptive Devices**

**Sec. 10.** It shall be unlawful for any person, directly or indirectly, by the use of any means or instrumentality of interstate commerce or of the mails, or of any facility of any national securities exchange—

. . .

**[Use or Employment of Manipulative or Deceptive Devices]**

(b) To use or employ, in connection with the purchase or sale of any security registered on a national securities exchange or any security not so registered, any manipulative or deceptive device or contrivance in contravention of such rules and regulations as the commission may prescribe as necessary or appropriate in the public interest or for the protection of investors.

. . .

**[Directors, Officers, and Principal Stockholders]**

**Sec. 16.** (a) Every person who is directly or indirectly the beneficial owner of more than 10 per centum of any class of any equity security (other than exempted security) which is registered pursuant to section 12 of this title, or who is a director or an officer of the issuer of such security, shall file, at the time of the registration of such security on a national securities exchange or by the effective date of a registration statement filed pursuant to section 12(g) of this title, or within ten days after he becomes such beneficial owner, director, or officer, a statement with the Commission (and, if such security is registered on a national securities exchange, also with the exchange) of the amount of all equity securities of such issuer of which he is the beneficial owner, and within ten days after the close of each calendar month thereafter, if there has been a change in such ownership during such month, shall file with the Commission (and if such security is registered on a national securities exchange, shall also file with the exchange), a statement indicating his ownership at the close of the calendar month and such changes in his ownership as have occurred during such calendar month.

**[Profits Realized from Purchase and Sales within Period of Less than Six Months]**

(b) For the purpose of preventing the unfair use of information which may have been obtained by such beneficial owner, director, or officer by reason of his relationship to the issuer, any profit realized by him from any purchase and sale, or any sale and purchase, of any equity security of such issuer (other than an exempted security) within any period of less than six months, unless such security was acquired in good faith in connection with a debt previously contracted, shall inure to and be recoverable by the issuer, irrespective of any intention on the part of such beneficial owner, director, or officer in entering into such transaction of holding the security purchased or of not repurchasing the security sold for a period exceeding six months. Suit to recover such profit may be instituted at law or in equity in any court of competent jurisdiction by the issuer, or by the owner of any security of the issuer in the name and in behalf of the issuer if the issuer shall fail or refuse to bring such suit within sixty days after request or shall fail diligently to prosecute the same thereafter; but no such suit shall be brought more than two years after the date such profit was realized. This subsection shall not be construed to cover any transaction where such beneficial owner was not such both at the time of the purchase and sale, or the sale and purchase, of the security involved, or any transaction or transactions which the Commission by rules and regulations may exempt as not comprehended within the purpose of this subsection.

# APPENDIX L Rules 10b-5, 10b5-1, and 10b5-2 from Code of Federal Regulations

**Regulations adopted by the Securities and Exchange Commission Pursuant to Section 10(b) of the Securities Exchange Act of 1934**

**§ 240.10b-5 Employment of manipulative and deceptive devices.**

It shall be unlawful for any person, directly or indirectly, by the use of any means or instrumentality of interstate commerce, or of the mails or of any facility of any national securities exchange,

(1) to employ any device, scheme, or artifice to defraud,

(2) to make any untrue statement of a material fact or to omit to

state a material fact necessary in order to make the statements made, in light of the circumstances under which they were made, not misleading, or

(3) to engage in any act, practice, or course of business which operates or would operate as a fraud or deceit upon any person, in connection with the purchase or sale of any security.

[13 Fed. Reg. 8, 183 (Dec. 22, 1948), as amended at 16 Fed. Reg. 7,928 (Aug. 11, 1951)]

### § 240.10b5-1 Trading "on the basis of" material nonpublic information in insider trading cases.

Preliminary Note to § 240.10b5-1: This provision defines when a purchase or sale constitutes trading "on the basis of" material nonpublic information in insider trading cases brought under Section 10(b) of the Act and Rule 10b-5 thereunder. The law of insider trading is otherwise defined by judicial opinions construing Rule 10b-5, and Rule 10b5-1 does not modify the scope of insider trading law in any other respect.

(a) General. The "manipulative and deceptive devices" prohibited by Section 10(b) of the Act (15 U.S.C. 78j) and § 240.10b-5 thereunder include, among other things, the purchase or sale of a security of any issuer, on the basis of material nonpublic information about that security or issuer, in breach of a duty of trust or confidence that is owed directly, indirectly, or derivatively, to the issuer of that security or the shareholders of that issuer, or to any other person who is the source of the material nonpublic information.

(b) Definition of "on the basis of." Subject to the affirmative defenses in paragraph (c) of this section, a purchase or sale of a security of an issuer is "on the basis of" material nonpublic information about that security or issuer if the person making the purchase or sale was aware of the material nonpublic information when the person made the purchase or sale.

(c) Affirmative defenses. (1)(i) Subject to paragraph (c) (1) (ii) of this section, a person's purchase or sale is not "on the basis of" material nonpublic information if the person making the purchase or sale demonstrates that:

(A) Before becoming aware of the information, the person had:

(1) Entered into a binding contract to purchase or sell the security,

(2) Instructed another person to purchase or sell the security for the instructing person's account, or

(3) Adopted a written plan for trading securities;

(B) The contract, instruction, or plan described in paragraph (c) (1) (i) (A) of this Section:

(1) Specified the amount of securities to be purchased or sold and the price at which and the date on which the securities were to be purchased or sold;

(2) Included a written formula or algorithm, or computer program, for determining the amount of securities to be purchased or sold and the price at which and the date on which the securities were to be purchased or sold; or

(3) Did not permit the person to exercise any subsequent influence over how, when, or whether to effect purchases or sales; provided, in addition, that any other person who, pursuant to the contract, instruction, or plan, did exercise such influence must not have been aware of the material nonpublic information when doing so; and

(C) The purchase or sale that occurred was pursuant to the contract, instruction, or plan. A purchase or sale is not "pursuant to a contract, instruction, or plan" if, among other things, the person who entered into the contract, instruction, or plan altered or deviated from the contract, instruction, or plan to purchase or sell securities (whether by changing the amount, price, or timing of the purchase or sale), or entered into or altered a corresponding or hedging transaction or position with respect to those securities.

(ii) Paragraph (c) (1) (i) of this section is applicable only when the contract, instruction, or plan to purchase or sell securities was given or entered into in good faith and not as part of a plan or scheme to evade the prohibitions of this section.

(iii) This paragraph (c) (1) (iii) defines certain terms as used in paragraph (c) of this Section.

(A) Amount. "Amount" means either a specified number of shares or other securities or a specified dollar value of securities.

(B) Price. "Price" means the market price on a particular date or a limit price, or a particular dollar price.

(C) Date. "Date" means, in the case of a market order, the specific day of the year on which the order is to be executed (or as soon thereafter as is practicable under ordinary principles of best execution). "Date" means, in the case of a limit order, a day of the year on which the limit order is in force.

(2) A person other than a natural person also may demonstrate that a purchase or sale of securities is not "on the basis of" material nonpublic information if the person demonstrates that:

(i) The individual making the investment decision on behalf of the person to purchase or sell the securities was not aware of the information; and

(ii) The person had implemented reasonable policies and procedures, taking into consideration the nature of the person's business, to ensure that individuals making investment decisions would not violate the laws prohibiting trading on the basis of material nonpublic information. These policies and procedures may include those that restrict any purchase, sale, and causing any purchase or sale of any security as to which the person has material nonpublic information, or those that prevent such individuals from becoming aware of such information.

[65 Fed. Reg. 51,716, 51,737 (Aug. 24, 2000)]

### § 240.10b5-2 Duties of trust or confidence in misappropriation insider trading cases.

**Preliminary Note to § 240.10b5-2:** This section provides a nonexclusive definition of circumstances in which a person has a duty of trust or confidence for purposes of the "misappropriation" theory of insider trading under Section 10(b) of the Act and Rule 10b-5. The law of insider trading is otherwise defined by judicial opinions construing Rule 10b-5, and Rule 10b5-2 does not modify the scope of insider trading law in any other respect.

(a) Scope of Rule. This section shall apply to any violation of Section 10(b) of the Act (15 U.S.C. 78j(b)) and § 240.10b-5 thereunder that is based on the purchase or sale of securities on the basis of, or the communication of, material nonpublic information misappropriated in breach of a duty of trust or confidence.

(b) Enumerated "duties of trust or confidence." For purposes of this section, a "duty of trust or confidence" exists in the following circumstances, among others:

(1) Whenever a person agrees to maintain information in confidence;

(2) Whenever the person communicating the material nonpublic information and the person to whom it is communicated have a history, pattern, or practice of sharing confidences, such that the recipient of the information knows or reasonably should know that the person communicating the material nonpublic information expects that the recipient will maintain its confidentiality; or

(3) Whenever a person receives or obtains material nonpublic information from his or her spouse, parent, child, or sibling; provided, however, that the person receiving or obtaining the information may demonstrate that no duty of trust or confidence existed with respect to the information, by establishing that he or she neither knew nor reasonably should have known that the person who was the source of the information expected that the person whould keep the information confidential, because of the parties' history, pattern, or practice of sharing and maintaining confidences, and because there was no agreement or understanding to maintain the confidentiality of the information.

**[65 Fed. Reg. 51,716, 51,738 (Aug. 24, 2000)]**

# APPENDIX M Rule 14e–3 from Code of Federal Regulations

**§ 240.14e-3 Transactions in securities on the basis of material, nonpublic information in the context of tender offers.** (a) If any person has taken a substantial step or steps to commence, or has commenced, a tender offer (the "offering person"), it shall constitute a fraudulent, deceptive or manipulative act or practice within the meaning of section 14(e) of the Act for any other person who is in possession of material information relating to such tender offer which information he knows or has reason to know is nonpublic and which he knows or has reason to know has been acquired directly or indirectly from:

(1) The offering person,

(2) The issuer of the securities sought or to be sought by such tender offer, or

(3) Any officer, director, partner or employee or any other person acting on behalf of the offering person or such issuer, to purchase or sell or cause to be purchased or sold any of such securities or any securities convertible into or exchangeable for any such securities or any option or right to obtain or dispose of any of the foregoing securities, unless within a reasonable time prior to any purchase or sale such information and its source are publicly disclosed by press release or otherwise.

(b) A person other than a natural person shall not violate paragraph (a) of this section if such person shows that:

(1) The individual(s) making the investment decision on behalf of such person to purchase or sell any security described in paragraph (a) of this section or to cause any such security to be purchased or sold by or on behalf of others did not know the material, nonpublic information; and

(2) Such person had implemented one or a combination of policies and procedures, reasonable under the circumstances, taking into consideration the nature of the person's business, to ensure that individual(s) making investment decision(s) would not violate paragraph (a) of this section, which policies and procedures may include, but are not limited to, (i) those which restrict any purchase, sale and causing any purchase and sale of any such security or (ii) those which prevent such individual(s) from knowing such information.

(c) Notwithstanding anything in paragraph (a) of this section to contrary, the following transactions shall not be violations of paragraph (a) of this section:

(1) Purchase(s) of any security described in paragraph (a) of this section by a broker or by another agent on behalf of an offering person; or

(2) Sale(s) by any person of any security described in paragraph (a) of this section to the offering person.

(d)(1) As a means reasonably designed to prevent fraudulent, deceptive or manipulative acts or practices within the meaning of section 14(e) of the Act, it shall be unlawful for any person described in paragraph (d)(2)) of this section to communicate material, nonpublic information relating to a tender offer to any other person under circumstances in which it is reasonably foreseeable that such communication is likely to result in a violation of this section except that this paragraph shall not apply to a communication made in good faith:

(i) To the officers, directors, partners or employees of the offering person, to its advisors or to other persons, involved in the planning, financing, preparation or execution of such tender offer;

(ii) To the issuer whose securities are sought or to be sought by such tender offer, to its officers, directors, partners, employees or advisors or to other persons, involved in the planning, financing, preparation or execution of the activities of the issuer with respect to such tender offer; or

(iii) To any person pursuant to a requirement of any statute or rule or regulation promulgated thereunder.

(2) The persons referred to in paragraph (d)(1) of this section are:

(i) The offering person or its officers, directors, partners, employees or advisors;

(ii) The issuer of the securities sought or to be sought by such tender offer or its officers, directors, partners, employees or advisors;

(iii) Anyone acting on behalf of the persons in paragraph (d)(2)(i) of this section or the issuer or persons in paragraph (d)(2)(ii) of this section; and

(iv) Any person in possession of material information relating to a tender offer which information he knows or has reason to know is nonpublic and which he knows or has reason to know has been acquired directly or indirectly from any of the above.

**[46 FR 60418 (SEPT. 12, 1980)]**

# APPENDIX N Sarbanes–Oxley Act of 2002 [Excerpts]

### Sec. 201. Services Outside the Scope of Practice of Auditors.

(g) ***Prohibited Activities.*** Except as provided in subsection (h), it shall be unlawful for a registered public accounting firm (and any associated person of that firm, to the extent determined appropriate by the [Securities and Exchange] Commission) that performs for any issuer any audit required by this title or the rules of the Commission under this title or . . . Board, the rules of the Public Company Accounting Oversight Board, to provide to that issuer, contemporaneously with the audit, any non-audit service, including—

(1) bookkeeping or other services related to the accounting records or financial statements of the audit client;

(2) financial information systems design and implementation;

(3) appraisal or valuation services, fairness opinions, or contribution-in-kind reports;

(4) actuarial services;

(5) internal audit outsourcing services;

(6) management functions or human resources;

(7) broker or dealer, investment adviser, or investment banking services;

(8) legal services and expert services unrelated to the audit; and

(9) any other service that the Board determines, by regulation, is impermissible.

(h) ***Preapproval Required for Non-Audit Services.*** A registered public accounting firm may engage in any non-audit service, including tax services, that is not described in any of paragraphs (1) through (9) of subsection (g) for an audit client, only if the activity is approved in advance by the audit committee of the issuer, in accordance with subsection (i).

[Codified at 15 U.S.C. § 78j-1.]

### Sec. 302. Corporate Responsibility for Financial Reports.

(a) ***Regulations Required.*** The Commission shall, by rule, require, for each company filing periodic reports under section 13(a) or 15(d) of the Securities Exchange Act of 1934, that the principal executive officer or officers and the principal financial officer or officers, or persons performing similar functions, certify in each annual or quarterly report filed or submitted under either such section of such Act that—

(1) the signing officer has reviewed the report;

(2) based on the officer's knowledge, the report does not contain any untrue statement of a material fact or omit to state a material fact necessary in order to make the statements made, in light of the circumstances under which such statements were made, not misleading;

(3) based on such officer's knowledge, the financial statements, and other financial information included in the report, fairly present in all material respects the financial condition and results of operations of the issuer as of, and for, the periods presented in the report;

(4) the signing officers—

(A) are responsible for establishing and maintaining internal controls;

(B) have designed such internal controls to ensure that material information relating to the issuer and its consolidated subsidiaries is made known to such officers by others within those entities, particularly during the period in which the periodic reports are being prepared;

(C) have evaluated the effectiveness of the issuer's internal controls as of a date within 90 days prior to the report; and

(D) have presented in the report their conclusions about the effectiveness of their internal controls based on their evaluation as of that date;

(5) the signing officers have disclosed to the issuer's auditors and the audit committee of the board of directors (or persons fulfilling the equivalent function)—

(A) all significant deficiencies in the design or operation of internal controls which could adversely affect the issuer's ability to record, process, summarize, and report financial data and have identified for the issuer's auditors any material weaknesses in internal controls; and

(B) any fraud, whether or not material, that involves management or other employees who have a significant role in the issuer's internal controls; and

(6) the signing officers have indicated in the report whether or not there were significant changes in internal controls or in other factors that could significantly affect internal controls subsequent to the date of their evaluation, including any corrective actions with regard to significant deficiencies and material weaknesses.

[Codified at 15 U.S.C. § 7241.]

### Sec. 404. Management Assessment of Internal Controls.

(a) ***Rules Required.*** The Commission shall prescribe rules requiring each annual report required by section 13(a) or 15(d) of the Securities Exchange Act of 1934 to contain an internal control report, which shall—

(1) state the responsibility of management for establishing and maintaining an adequate internal control structure and procedures for financial reporting; and

(2) contain an assessment, as of the end of the most recent fiscal year of the issuer, of the effectiveness of the internal control structure and procedures of the issuer for financial reporting.

(b) ***Internal Control Evaluation and Reporting.*** With respect to the internal control assessment required by subsection (a), each registered public accounting firm that prepares or issues the audit report for the issuer shall attest to, and report on, the assessment made by the management of the issuer. An attestation made under this subsection shall be made in accordance with standards for attestation engagements issued or adopted by the Board. Any such attestation shall not be the subject of a separate engagement.

[Codified at 15 U.S.C. § 7262.]

### Sec. 802. Criminal Penalties for Altering Documents.

Whoever knowingly alters, destroys, mutilates, conceals, covers up, falsifies, or makes a false entry in any record, document, or tangible object with the intent to impede, obstruct, or influence the investigation or proper administration of any matter within the jurisdiction of any department or agency of the United States or any [bankruptcy] case filed under title 11, or in relation to or contemplation of any such matter or case, shall be fined under this title, imprisoned not more than 20 years, or both.

[Codified at U.S.C. § 1519.]

# Glossary

## A

**abandonment (of a trademark)** The failure to use a mark after acquiring legal protection may result in the loss of rights, and such loss is known as abandonment.

**absolute priority rule** In a bankruptcy proceeding in which the claims of dissenting creditors are not paid in full, a plan may be found to be "fair and equitable" only if the holder of any claim or interest that is junior to the claims of the impaired unsecured class will not receive or retain any property "on account of such junior claim or interest."

**absolute privilege** In defamation cases, the right of the defendant to publish with impunity a statement known by the defendant to be false.

**acceptance** An agreement to the amount offered for certain services or products. Acceptance may be verbal, written, or implied by action.

**accession** A process whereby a nation that was not an original party to a treaty can elect to participate in the treaty at a later time.

**accord** *See* Accord and Satisfaction.

**accord and satisfaction** An agreement to accept performance that is different from what is called for in the contract.

**accredited investor** Certain investors who are so wealthy that they do not need all the protections afforded by the securities laws.

**act-of-state doctrine** The doctrine that states that the courts of one country will not sit in judgment on the acts of the government of another done within its own territory.

**actionable** Behavior that is the basis for a claim.

**actual abandonment** Loss of trademark rights that occurs when a trademark owner discontinues use of a mark with the intent not to resume use.

**actual authority** The express or implied power of an agent to act for and bind a principal to agreements entered into by an agent.

**actual cause** Proof that but for the defendant's negligent conduct the plaintiff would not have been harmed.

**actual damages** The amount required to repair or to replace an item or the decrease in market value caused by tortious conduct. Actual damages restore the injured party to the position it was in prior to the injury. Also called compensatory damages.

**actual intent** The subjective desire to cause the consequences of an act, or the belief that the consequences are substantially certain to result from it.

**actual malice** A statement made with the knowledge that it is false or with a reckless disregard for the truth.

**actual notice** Concerning claims on title, actual notice refers to a claimant actually knowing of a prior interest in the real property.

***actus reus* (guilty deed)** A crime; a criminal act.

**ad valorem** A condition of a tariff whereby the importer must pay a percentage of the value of the imported merchandise.

**additive** Anything not inherent in a food product—including pesticide residues, unintended environmental contaminants, and unavoidably added substances from packaging.

**adhesion contract** An unfair type of contract by which sellers offer goods or services on a take-it-or-leave-it basis, with no chance for consumers to negotiate for goods except by agreeing to the terms of said contract.

**administrative employee** An employee whose primary duty consists of nonmanual work directly related either to management policies or to the general business operations of the employer or the employer's customers.

**administrative law judge (ALJ)** The presiding official at an administrative proceeding who has the power to issue an order resolving the legal dispute.

**adulterated** Consisting in whole or in part of any filthy, putrid, or decomposed substance, or if it is otherwise unfit for food.

**adverse possession** Ownership of property that is not occupied by its owner for a certain period of time may be transferred to those who have been unlawfully occupying it and openly exercising rights of ownership. Such a transfer is usually not reflected in the official land records. Also called squatter's rights.

**affidavit** A written or printed declaration or statement of facts, made voluntarily, and confirmed by the oath or affirmation of the party making it, taken before a person having authority to administer such oath or affirmation.

**affiliate** Any person who controls an issuer of securities, or is controlled by the issuer, or is under common control. Includes officers, directors, and major shareholders of a corporation.

**affirmative covenant** The borrower's promise to do certain things under the loan agreement.

**affirmative defense** The admission in an answer to a complaint that defendant has acted as plaintiff alleges, but denies that defendant's conduct was the real or legal cause of harm to plaintiff.

**after-acquired property** The property a debtor acquires after the execution of a security agreement.

**after-acquired title** If, at the date of execution of a grant deed, the grantor does not have title to the real property referred to in the grant deed but subsequently acquires it, such after-acquired title is deemed automatically transferred to the grantee.

**agency** A relationship in which one person (the agent) acts for or represents another person (the principal).

**agency by estoppel** When the principal leads a third party to believe that a person is his or her agent, the principal is estopped (prevented) from denying that the person is his or her agent.

**agency by ratification** An agency formed when a principal approves or accepts the benefits of the actions of an otherwise unauthorized agent.

**agent** A person who manages a task delegated by another (the principal) and exercises whatever discretion is given to the agent by the principal.

**aided-in-the-agency doctrine** *See* Aided-in-the-Agency-Relation Doctrine.

**aided-in-the-agency-relation doctrine** An agency principle whereby the principal may be held vicariously liable for the wrongful acts of an agent acting outside of the scope of authority because the principal provided the instrumentability or created the circumstances that made it possible for the agent to commit the wrongful act.

**aider and abettor** A person with knowledge of (or recklessness as to) a primary criminal violation who provides substantial assistance to the primary violation.

**alter ego theory** When owners have so mingled their own affairs with those of a corporation that the corporation does not exist as a distinct entity, it is an alter ego (second self) of its owners, permitting the piercing of the corporate veil.

**alternative minimum tax (AMT)** A tax law that was passed to prevent higher income taxpayers from paying too little tax because they were able to take advantage of a variety of tax deductions or exclusions, including the spread on exercise of an incentive stock option. Taxpayers who may be subject to AMT must calculate their taxable income in two ways and pay whichever formula yields the higher tax.

**amortize** To pay the principal over a period of time.

**anchor tenant** A key tenant of a shopping center, such as a supermarket or department store.

**angels** Wealthy individual investors to whom entrepreneurs often turn for equity capital after exhausting the funds available from family and friends.

**answer** The instrument by which defendant admits or denies the various allegations stated in the complaint against the defendant.

**anticipatory repudiation** If a party indicates before performance is due that it will breach the contract, there is an anticipatory repudiation of the contract.

**antideficiency laws** Statutes that restrict lenders seeking remedies against real property security from suing the borrower personally. If a lender has recourse to the borrower or to other property of the borrower, and exercises such rights, the lender may be precluded from foreclosing on real estate mortgaged by the borrower. Alternatively, if the holder of a mortgage or deed of trust secured by real property forecloses on the property, the lender may be precluded from suing the borrower personally to recover whatever is still owing after a foreclosure sale. Also called one-form-of-action laws.

**antitrust injury** The damages sustained by a plaintiff in an antitrust suit as a result of the defendant's anticompetitive conduct.

**antitrust laws** The laws that seek to identify and forbid business practices that are anticompetitive. Also called competition laws.

***apartheid*** Prior to its abolition in the 1980s, an official policy of racial segregation in South Africa that relegated its black citizens to a second-class status in employment, housing, and opportunity.

**apex deposition** The deposition of the most senior executives of a corporation.

**apparent authority** A principal, by words or actions, causes a third party to reasonably believe that an agent has authority to act for or bind the principal.

**appellant** The person who is appealing a judgment or seeking a writ of certiorari. Also called a petitioner.

**appellate jurisdiction** The power of the Supreme Court and other courts of appeal to decide cases that have been tried in a lower court and appealed.

**appellee** The party in a case against whom an appeal is taken; that is, the party who has an interest adverse to setting aside or reversing the judgment. Also called respondent.

**applicant** Person (the buyer in a sales transaction) requesting an issuing bank to provide a letter of credit in favor of another party called the beneficiary (the seller in a sales transaction).

**appraisal rights** In a merger or sale of assets, shareholders who voted against the transaction have appraisal rights, that is, the right to receive the fair cash value of the shares they were forced to give up as a result of the transaction.

**appropriate collective bargaining unit** A collective bargaining unit in which the employees share a community of interest; that is, they have similar compensation, working conditions, and supervision, and they work under the same general employer policies.

**appropriation of a person's name or likeness** Unauthorized use of a person's name or likeness for financial gain.

**arbitrary and capricious standard** If an agency has a choice between several courses of action, the court will presume that the chosen course is valid unless the person challenging it shows that it lacks any rational basis.

**arbitrary marks** A real word whose ordinary meaning has nothing to do with the trademarked product.

**arbitration** The resolution of a dispute by a neutral third party.

**arbitration clause** A clause that specifies that in the event of a dispute arising out of a contract, the parties will arbitrate specific issues in a stated manner.

**arbitrator** The neutral third party who conducts an arbitration to resolve a dispute.

**arb-med** A shortened form of arbitration/mediation, a procedure whereby parties present their case to an arbitrator who makes an award but keeps it secret while the parties try to resolve the dispute through mediation. If the mediation fails, then the arbitrator's award is unsealed and becomes binding on the parties.

**area plan** A planning document that usually encompasses just a portion of the city's geographic area.

**arrest** To deprive a person of his or her liberty by legal authority. Taking, under real or assumed authority, custody of another for the purpose of holding or detaining him or her to answer a criminal charge or civil demand.

**articles of incorporation** The basic document filed with the appropriate governmental agency upon the incorporation of a business. The contents are prescribed in the general corporation statutes but generally include the name, purpose, agent for service of process, authorized number of shares, and classes of stock of a corporation. It is executed by the incorporator(s). Also called the charter or the certificate of incorporation.

**articles of organization** The charter document for a limited liability company. Also called certificate of formation.

**assault** An intent to create a well-grounded apprehension of an immediate harmful or offensive contact. Generally, assault also requires some act (such as a threatening gesture) and the ability to follow through immediately with the battery.

**assessment statute** A state statute that requires state and local governments to consider, before imposing conditions on development, whether the restriction will constitute a taking under federal or state constitutional law.

**asset lock-up option** A lock-up option relating to assets of the target company.

**assignment** The transfer by a tenant of all or a portion of rented premises.

**assumption of risk** The expressed or implied consent by plaintiff to defendant to take the chance of injury from a known and appreciated risk.

**asymmetric information** A problem that arises during discovery because each party has information not possessed by the other party.

**at-will contract** An employment relationship of indefinite duration.

**attach** If the three basic prerequisites of a security interest exist (agreement, value, and collateral), the security interest becomes enforceable between the parties and is said to attach. Also called attachment.

**attorney-client privilege** The common law rule that a court cannot force the disclosure of confidential communications between client and client's attorney.

**attorney work-product doctrine** A doctrine that protects information that an attorney prepares in the course of his or her work.

**attractive nuisance** Artificial conditions on land for which an owner is liable for physical injury to child trespassers if (1) the owner knew or should have known that children were likely to trespass; (2) the condition is one the owner would reasonably know involved an unreasonable risk of injury to such children; (3) the children, because of their youth, did not discover the condition or realize the risk involved; (4) the utility to the owner of maintaining the condition is not great; (5) the burden of eliminating the risk is slight compared with the magnitude of the risk to the children; and (6) the owner fails to exercise reasonable care to protect the children.

**attractive nuisance rule** The duty imposed on landowner for liability for physical injury to child trespassers caused by artificial conditions on the land.

**authoritative decision** A court decision that must be followed regardless of its persuasive power, by virtue of relationship between the court that made decision and the court to which decision is cited.

**automatic conversion** The exchange of preferred stock for common stock that is triggered by specified events at a specified ratio.

**automatic stay** Feature of bankruptcy filing that instantly suspends most litigation and collection activities against the debtor, its property, or property of the bankruptcy estate.

**avoiding powers** The powers bankruptcy trustees can use to invalidate or reverse certain prebankruptcy transactions.

## B

**back-to-back letter of credit** A seller uses the letter of credit in its favor provided by the buyer to finance its purchase of products or materials from its supplier.

**BACT (best available control technology)** *See* best available control technology.

**bait and switch advertising** An area of deceptive pricing in which an advertiser refuses to show an advertised item, fails to have a reasonable quantity of the item in stock, fails to promise to deliver the item within a reasonable time, or discourages employees from selling the item.

**bankruptcy estate** Virtually all of a debtor's existing assets, less exempt property.

**barristers** A type of lawyer in the British system who may argue in court.

**base rate** The lowest rate of interest publicly offered by major lending institutions to their most creditworthy customers. Also called reference rate or prime rate.

**baseline assessment** The appraisal performed by a tenant that establishes the environmental condition of leased property at the commencement and termination of the lease.

**battery** The intentional, non-consensual harmful or offensive contact with an individual's body or with those things in contact with or closely connected with it.

**beneficial owner** A person is considered to be a beneficial owner of any securities held by his or her immediate family, spouse, any minor children, and any other relative living in his or her household.

**beneficiary** An individual who is benefited by a trust or a will.

**bespeaks caution doctrine** A doctrine whereby a court may determine that the inclusion of sufficient cautionary statements in a prospectus or other document renders immaterial any misrepresentations and omissions contained therein.

**best alternative to a negotiated agreement (BATNA)** The outcome a person will choose if the negotiation fails.

**best available control technology (BACT)** An emission limitation that the permitting authority determines achieves the maximum reduction of pollutants, taking into account energy, environmental, and economic considerations.

**best available technology economically achievable (BAT)** For toxic pollutants, BAT represents the best economically achievable performance in the category.

**best conventional pollutant control technology (BCT)** For conventional pollutants, BCT is intended to prevent unnecessarily stringent treatment that might be required under BAT.

**best-efforts underwriting** A situation wherein the underwriters do not agree to purchase the securities being offered but instead agree to use their best efforts to find buyers at an agreed-on price. These underwritings are often used for initial public offerings or for companies that are unseasoned.

**best interests of creditors test** In a Chapter 11 bankruptcy case, dissenters must be given a bundle of rights the current value of which is at least as great as the distribution they would receive through a Chapter 7 liquidation.

**best mode** The best way the inventor knows of making an invention at the time of filing the patent application.

**best practicable control technology currently available (BPT)** The average of the best existing performances by industrial plants of various sizes and ages within a point source category.

**BFOQ defense** An affirmative defense wherein an employer may lawfully hire an individual on the basis of religion, sex, or national origin if religion, sex, or national origin is a bona fide occupational qualification (BFOQ).

**bicameralism** The state of being composed of two legislative chambers; in the case of the United States, the Congress consists of the House of Representatives and the Senate.

**bid rigging** An agreement between or among competitors to rig contract bids.

**bidder** The party who makes a tender offer.

**bilateral contract** A promise given in exchange for another promise.

**bill of attainder** A law enacted to punish individuals or an easily ascertainable member of a group. Prohibited by Article I, Section 9, of the U.S. Constitution.

**bill of lading** The document carrier issues to seller that indicates what goods the carrier has received from the seller, the loading location, the names of the carrying vessel, and the destination.

**Bill of Rights** The first ten amendments to the Constitution.

**blank check company** A development-stage company that has no specific business plan or whose business plan is to acquire a presently unknown business.

**blue sky laws** A popular name for the state statutes that regulate and supervise offerings and sales of securities to persons in that state.

**blurring** Dilution of a famous trademark that occurs when a non-famous mark reduces the strong association between the owner of the famous mark and its products.

**boilerplate clause** Nonnegotiable standardized text.

**bona fide occupational qualification (BFOQ)** A requirement that an employer places on certain jobs that actually requires that the person in that job has a certain gender, religion or national origin.

**bona fide prospective purchaser (BFPP)** A buyer who must do the following: (1) conduct a diligent investigation of the property and report any contamination to the appropriate governmental authorities; (2) exercise appropriate care concerning the contamination to stop future or continuing release of contaminants; (3) cooperate with any authorized group, including the federal government, to conduct a cleanup of the property; and (4) obey any land-use restrictions on the property.

**bond** Long-term corporate indebtedness.

**booked** Having criminal charges against someone who has been arrested written in a register at a police station.

**bound tariffs** The WTO principle that holds that each time tariffs are reduced, they may not be raised again.

**break-up fee** An amount agreed to in a merger agreement to be paid to a friendly suitor company if the agreement with the target company is not consummated through no fault of the friendly suitor company.

**brownfields** Contaminated sites that are eligible for cleaning and reclaiming with assistance from the Superfund.

**browse-wrap license** An online license agreement that appears on a website but does not require the user to take any action to express his or her consent to the agreement.

**burden of proof** The requirement of a prosecutor in a criminal case to establish a defendant's guilt beyond a reasonable doubt.

**business judgment rule** In a case challenging a board decision, this rule holds that as long as directors have made an informed decision and are not interested in the transaction being considered, a court will not question whether the directors' action was wise or whether they made an error of judgment or a business mistake.

**bust-up takeover** A takeover in which the corporation, upon acquisition, is taken apart and its assets sold.

**bylaws** The internal rules governing a corporation.

## C

**C corporation** A business organization that is taxed at both the entity level and the owner level.

**call a loan** To terminate a loan.

**capacity** The ability (requisite presence of mind) to enter into a binding contract.

**cartel** A group of competitors that agrees to set prices.

***caveat emptor* (let the buyer beware)** This maxim summarizes the rule that a purchaser must examine, judge, and test for himself or herself. It does not apply where strict liability, warranty, or other consumer protection laws protect consumer-buyers.

**cease and desist order** An order of an administrative agency or court prohibiting a person or business firm from continuing a particular course of conduct.

***cert. denied*** Indicates that a writ of certiorari was sought but denied by the Supreme Court.

**certificate of deposit (CD)** A bank deposit payable after a specified period of time.

**certificate of deposit (CD) rate** The CD rate is based on the average of the bid rates quoted to the bank by dealers in the secondary market for the purchase at face value of certificates of deposit of the bank in a given amount and for a given term.

**certificate of formation** The charter document for a limited liability company. Also called articles of organization.

**certificate of incorporation** *See* Articles of Incorporation.

**certification mark** A mark placed on a product or used in connection with a service that indicates that the product or service in question has met the standards of safety or quality that have been created and advertised by the certifier.

**certiorari** A writ of common law origin issued by a superior to an inferior court requiring the latter to produce a certified record of a particular case tried in the inferior court. The U.S. Supreme Court uses the writ as a discretionary device to choose the cases it wishes to hear.

**choice-of-forum clause** The clause in a contract wherein the parties agree in advance in which jurisdiction a dispute arising out of their agreement is to be litigated.

**choice-of-law provision** A provision that specifies which state's or country's laws will govern.

**churning** A practice whereby insurance agents write new policies for customers and pay for the new policies with the cash value of existing policies.

**circumstantial evidence** The indirect (not based on personal knowledge or observation) evidence of certain facts that, taken alone, do not prove a particular conclusion but, if taken as a whole, give a trier of fact a reasonable basis for asserting a certain conclusion is true.

**cite** The citation of a case.

**civil law legal system** Legal system based on the Roman law as consolidated by the Corpus Juris Civilis in 533 and 534 A.D.

**civil procedure** The methods, procedures, and practices that govern the processing of a civil lawsuit from start to finish.

**claims (under patent law)** The description of those elements of an invention that will be protected by the patent.

**class action suit** A suit filed on behalf of all persons who have allegedly been harmed by a defendant's conduct.

**classified board** A board on which directors serve for specified terms, usually three years, with only a fraction of them up for reelection at any one time. Also called staggered board.

**clawback provision** The right for an employer to recoup some or all of the employee's stock option gain if the employee goes to work for a competitor within a certain period of time following exercise of the option.

**clean bill of lading** Bill of lading that has no notations indicating defects or damage to the goods when they were received for transport.

**clear and present danger test** A phrase used to describe the circumstances under which the government may restrict or prohibit the constitutional guarantees of free speech and free press.

**click-wrap license** An online license agreement that presents the user with a notice on his or her computer screen that requires the user to agree to the terms of the license by clicking on an icon.

**cliff vesting** A common vesting schedule that provides that if a person granted stock options leaves within a certain period of time after employment (usually six months or a year), he or she forfeits all rights to any stock.

**close** To consummate a transaction.

**close corporation** A corporation owned by a limited number of shareholders, usually thirty, most of whom are actively involved in the management of the corporation, that elects close corporation status in its charter.

**closed-end credit** Credit that involves only one transaction, such as a car or house loan.

**closely held corporation** A corporation characterized by the absence of a market for its stock, though it may have any number of shareholders.

**CoCom** An informal arrangement between U.S. allies and Communist countries on how to administer and agree on exports.

**Code of Federal Regulations (CFR)** A multi-volume codification of federal regulations and rules.

**codify** To collect and arrange items, such as statutes or regulations, systematically.

**collaborative law** A quickly expanding breed of law that attempts to combine mediation and negotiation into a more efficient, more satisfying and ultimately more successful form of dispute resolution.

**collateral** The property belonging to a borrower that will become the lender's if the loan is not repaid.

**collective entity doctrine** Under this doctrine, the custodian of records for a collective entity (such as a corporation) may not resist a subpoena for such records on the ground that the act of production will incriminate him or her.

**comity** A situation whereby a court will enforce another country's judgments under certain conditions.

**commerce clause** The constitutional clause that gives Congress the power to regulate commerce with other nations, with Indian tribes, and between states.

**commercial activity exception** An exception to the blanket immunity from suits provided by the Foreign Sovereign Immunity Act for cases in which the foreign state was engaged in commercial activities.

**commercial impracticability** Section 2-615 of the Uniform Commercial Code states that unless the contract provides otherwise, a failure to perform is not a breach if performance is made impractical by an event unforeseen by the contract.

**commercial lease** A contract that conveys an interest in real property from the landlord to the tenant and governs the respective rights and obligations of the parties during the lease term.

**commercial paper** Short-term corporate indebtedness.

**commitment fee** The fee payable to a lender in connection with a revolving loan as consideration for its promise to keep the commitment available.

**common customs tariff** A single set of tariffs applied by all European Union (EU) member states on goods imported from outside the EU.

**common law legal system** A legal system that primarily relies on case law and precedents and is used in most countries that are or were British territories or colonies.

**common market** The customs union in which there are no tariffs on trade among its members, and a single set of tariffs applies to goods imported from outside the union.

**common stock** Stock that subjects all the shareholders to the same rights and restrictions.

**community plan** *See* Specific Plan.

**community property** The property acquired during marriage with assets earned by either spouse during the marriage.

**comp (compensatory) time** Extra paid vacation time granted instead of extra pay for overtime work.

**comparative fault** Reduced recovery for an injured party because of misuse or abuse of manufacturer's product.

**comparative negligence** The doctrine by which courts decide amount of award to be given a plaintiff based on the amount (percentage) of negligence plaintiff demonstrated when injured by defendant.

**compensation statute** A state statute that requires the government agency adopting a land use regulation to pay the landowner for the loss in property value if the regulation causes the value of the property to decline beyond a certain percentage.

**compensation trade** An international transaction in which a foreign party transfers use and/or eventual ownership of a good, usually equipment, to the local party, who then repays the foreign party with products produced using the foreign party's equipment.

**compensatory damages** In an action for breach of contract, the amount necessary to make up for the economic loss caused by the breach.

**compensatory justice** Aims at compensating people for the harm done by another.

**complaint** The statement of plaintiff's grievance that makes allegations of the particular facts giving rise to dispute and states the legal reason why plaintiff is entitled to a remedy, the request for relief, the explanation why the court applied to has jurisdiction over the dispute, and whether plaintiff requests a jury trial.

**composition** A reduction in the amount payable to creditors pursuant to a composition plan.

**composition plan** A composition plan in a Chapter 13 proceeding is a plan in which creditors receive a percentage of the indebtedness, and the debtor is discharged of the remaining obligation.

**computer employee** A computer systems analyst, computer programmer, software engineer and similarly skilled worker in the computer field.

**computer fraud** The unauthorized access of a computer used by the federal government, by various types of financial institutions, or in interstate commerce with the intent to alter, damage, or destroy information or to prevent authorized use of the such computers.

**computer piracy** The theft or misuse of computer software or hardware.

**computer virus** A computer program that can replicate itself into other programs without any subsequent instruction, human or mechanical.

**concerted activity** Under the National Labor Relations Act, the exercise by employees of their rights to band together for mutual aid and protection that is engaged in with or on the authority of other employees and not solely by and on behalf of one employee.

**conciliation** A more formalized method of dispute resolution that is similar to inquiry but adds the element of acceptance in advance of the result of the commission by the parties and a "cooling-off" period.

**condition precedent** A condition that must be met before a party's obligations to perform arise under a contract.

**condition subsequent** In contracts, a provision giving one party the right to divest itself of liability and obligation to perform further if the other party fails to meet the condition.

**conditional-use permit** A method of relief from the strict terms of a zoning ordinance that provides for other uses of real property that are not permitted as a matter of right, but for which a use permit must be obtained.

**conditions concurrent** Conditions that are mutually dependent and are to be performed at the same time or simultaneously.

**conduct test** A test for personal jurisdiction that asks in essence whether the fraudulent or wrongful conduct occurred in the United States.

**confirming bank** A bank located in the seller's jurisdiction that makes a legal commitment to the seller that it will honor the terms of the letter of credit issued by the issuing bank in the buyer's jurisdiction.

**confiscation** The process of nationalization when the host country does not compensate the company for its lost assets.

**conflict-of-laws rules** When choice of law is disputed, the court in which the suit is filed will apply conflict of laws principles to determine which state's or country's laws should govern the dispute. They usually focus on the significance of each state's or country's relationship to the parties and the contract.

**conflict resolution statute** A state statute that sets up formal procedures for negotiation between state agencies and property owners about land use.

**conglomerate merger** A combination of firms that were not competitors at the time of the acquisition, but that may, absent the merger, have become competitors.

**conscious parallelism** In business, the act of consistently setting prices at the same levels and changing prices at the same time as competitors.

**consent decree** A judgment entered by the consent of the parties whereby the defendant agrees to stop the alleged illegal activity without admitting guilt or wrongdoing. Also called consent order.

**consequential damages** Compensation for losses that occur as a foreseeable result of a breach of contract. Actual damages represent the damage, loss, or injury that flows directly and immediately from the act of the other party; in contrast, consequential damages refer to damage, loss or injury flowing from some of the consequences or results of such act.

**conscious parallelism** A business's undiscussed imitation of a competitor's activities, such as setting parallel prices.

**consideration** A thing of value (money, services, an object, a promise, forbearance, or giving up the right to do something) exchanged in a contract.

**construction (of a statute)** Interpretation.

**constructive abandonment** Loss of trademark rights that occurs when a trademark owner does something, or fails to do something, that causes the mark to lose its distinctiveness.

**constructive notice** Notice attributed by the existence of a properly recorded deed.

**constructive trust** A trust imposed on profits derived from an agent's breach of fiduciary duty.

**consumer contract** As defined in the 2003 amendments to Article 2 of the Uniform Commercial Code, a contract between a merchant seller and a natural person who enters into the contract primarily for personal, family or household purposes.

**contingency fee** A fee that is a percentage of the judgment awarded to the party that is represented by the attorney.

**continuation application** A patent application filed after the final office action on an earlier filed application that consists of the same disclosure; the claims may be the same or there may be a new set of claims directed to the same invention claimed in the prior application. Continuation applications must be filed before the earlier application is abandoned and must contain no new matter. A continuation application has the same filing date as the earlier filed application.

**continuing guaranty** A guaranty that covers all future obligations of the primary debtor to the lender.

**continuity of enterprise approach** *See* Substantial Continuity Test.

**contract** A legally enforceable promise or set of promises.

**contract of adhesion** *See* adhesion contract.

**contribution** The doctrine that provides for the distribution of loss among several defendants by requiring each to pay its proportionate share to one who has discharged the joint liability of the group.

**contributory copyright infringement** Inducing, causing, or materially contributing to the infringing conduct of another with knowledge of the infringing activity.

**contributory patent infringement** One party knowingly sells an item that has one specific use that will result in the infringement of another's patent.

**contributory negligence** Plaintiff was negligent in some manner when injured by defendant.

**controlling-person liability** A person (or other entity), usually an officer or director of a company, responsible and liable for a securities violation.

**controlling shareholder** A shareholder who owns sufficient shares to outvote the other shareholders, and thus to control the corporation.

**Convention on Cybercrime** The first international treaty to address various types of criminal behavior directed against computer systems, networks, or data, including computer-related fraud and forgery.

**conversion** The exercise of dominion and control over the personal property, rather than the real property (land), of another. Term includes any unauthorized act that deprives an owner of his or her personal property permanently or for an indefinite time.

**convertible debt instrument** The document that permits conversion of debt principal into stock.

**convertible preferred stock** Preferred stock that may be converted into common stock at a specified exchange ratio.

**conveyance** An instrument transferring an interest in real estate, such as a deed or lease.

**cookies** Bits of code sent by websites that identify the user to the site at a future visit.

**copyright** The legal right to prevent others from copying the expression embodied in a protected work.

**core proceedings** Proceedings of bankruptcy cases such as allowing creditor claims, deciding preferences, and confirming plans of reorganization.

**corporate charter** The document issued by a state agency or authority granting a corporation legal existence and the right to function as a corporation. Also called the articles or certificate of incorporation.

**corporate domicile** The state under whose laws a corporation is formed.

**corporate opportunity doctrine** The doctrine that holds that a business opportunity cannot legally be taken advantage of by an officer, director, or controlling shareholder if it is in the corporation's line of business.

**corporation** An organization authorized by state law to act as a legal entity distinct from its owners.

**corporation by estoppel** When a third party, in all its transactions with an enterprise, acts as if it were doing business with a corporation, the third party is prevented or estopped from claiming that the enterprise is not a corporation.

**counterclaim** A legal claim by defendant in opposition to or as a deduction from claim of plaintiff.

**counterfeit mark** A spurious trademark (1) that is used in combination with trafficking in goods or services, (2) that is identical to, or substantially indistinguishable from, a registered trademark, and (3) the use of which is likely to cause confusion or mistake or to deceive; or a spurious designation that is identical with, or substantially indistinguishable from, the holder of the right to use the designation.

**counteroffer** A new offer by the initial offeree that rejects and modifies the terms originally proposed by the offeror.

**countertrade** A foreign investor uses its local currency profits to purchase local products for sale abroad.

**countervailing duty law** The law that provides that if a U.S. industry is materially injured by imports of a product benefiting from a foreign subsidy, an import duty that offsets the amount of the benefit must be imposed on those imports.

**countervailing subsidy** The benefits provided by a government to stimulate exports.

**covenant** The borrower's promise to the lender that it will or will not take specific actions as long as either a commitment or a loan is outstanding.

**covenant not to compete** An agreement, generally part of a contract of employment or a contract to sell a business, in which the covenantor agrees for a specific period of time and within a particular area to refrain from competition with the convenantee. Also called a noncompete agreement.

**cover** In the case of a seller failing to make delivery of goods, cover refers to buyer's legal remedy of buying the goods elsewhere and recovering the difference between the cost of the substitute goods and the contract price.

**cramdown** A bankruptcy relief plan confirmed over the objections of creditors.

**creative personnel** A professional employee whose primary duty of performance of work requires invention, imagination, originality, or talent in a recognized field of artistic or creative endeavor.

**creditor beneficiary** Third party to a contract that the promisee enters into in order to discharge a duty to said third party.

**crime** An offense against the public at large; an act that violates the duties owed to the community, for which the offender must make satisfaction to the public.

**cross-default** Any breach by the borrower under any other loan agreement will constitute an event of default under the subject loan agreement.

**crown jewels** The most valuable assets or divisions of a target company in a takeover battle.

**cumulative voting** The process by which a shareholder can cast all its votes for one director nominee or allocate them among nominees as it sees fit.

**customary practice** A form of international law whereby treaties between nations can be compared to "established practice" or "commercial usage" as they are known in the commercial laws of many nations.

**customer restrictions** Restrictions that prevent a dealer or distributor from selling to a certain class of customer.

**customs union** A group of countries that reduce or eliminate tariffs between themselves, but establish a common tariff for trading with all other states.

**customs valuation** The value assigned to an imported article by the U.S. Customs Service.

**cybersquatting** The registration of a domain name that is confusingly similar or identical to a protected trademark, where the person registering the domain name has no legitimate interest in that particular domain name and registers and uses it in bad faith.

## D

***D'Oench, Duhme* doctrine** A doctrine that bars many claims and defenses against conservators and receivers that might have been valid against the failed bank or savings and loan itself. It bars enforcement of agreements unless those agreements are in writing and have been approved contemporaneously by the bank's board or loan committee and recorded in the bank's written records.

***de facto* (in fact) corporation** When incorporators cannot show substantial compliance with incorporation requirements, a court may find a corporation is a de facto corporation (corporation in fact), even though it is not technically a corporation by law, if the incorporators demonstrate that they were unaware of the defect and that they made a good faith effort to incorporate correctly.

***de facto* merger** A type of merger that occurs when a transaction, although not in form a merger, is in substance a consolidation or merger of seller and purchaser.

***de jure* (by law) corporation** When incorporators have substantially complied with incorporation requirements, the entity is a de jure corporation (a corporation by right).

***de novo*** Anew; a *de novo* proceeding takes place when a case has been successfully appealed and will be litigated again from the beginning.

**deal protection devices** These devices dissuade other bidders and thereby protect the consummation of the friendly merger transaction favored by the target.

**dealer** Under the Securities Act of 1933, any person who engages either for all or part of his or her time, directly or indirectly, as agent, broker, or principal, in the business of offering, buying, selling, or otherwise dealing or trading in securities issued by another person.

**debt securities** The documents indicating that a corporation has incurred a debt by borrowing money from the holder of the document.

**debt subordination** An agreement whereby one or more creditors of a common debtor agree to defer payment of their claims until another creditor of the same debtor is fully paid.

**debtor** Under the Uniform Commercial Code, the person who owes payment or other performance of the obligation secured, whether or not that person owns or has rights in the collateral.

**debtor-in-possession (DIP)** In most Chapter 11 bankruptcy cases the debtor is left in place to operate the business and is referred to as the debtor-in-possession (DIP). The DIP has the same powers as a trustee in bankruptcy, but also has the power to operate the debtor's business during the bankruptcy proceeding.

**deceit** *See* Fraudulent Misrepresentation.

**decision** A form of European Union legislation in which an order is directed at a specific person or member state.

**declaration by the inventor** Part of a patent application, the declaration by the inventor states that the inventor has reviewed the application and that he or she believes that he or she is the first inventor of the invention.

**declaratory judgment action** A lawsuit that seeks only a judicial order articulating the legal rights and responsibilities of the parties, rather than monetary damages.

**deed** A written document transferring an interest in real estate that is recorded at a public office where title documents are filed.

**deed of trust** A document evidencing a loan to buy real property secured by a lien on the real property. Also called a mortgage.

**defamation** The intentional communication to a third party of an untrue statement of fact that injures the plaintiff's reputation or good name, by exposing the plaintiff to hatred, ridicule or contempt.

**default judgment** A judgment that may be entered in favor of the plaintiff if the defendant does not file an answer within the time required.

**defendant** The person defending or denying; the party against whom relief or recovery is sought in an action or suit. The accused in a criminal case.

**defined benefit pension plan** A plan in which an employee's retirement benefit is expressed as a monthly annuity, the exact amount of which is calculated based on variables such as (1) number of years of service, (2) average compensation, (3) marital status, and (4) age at which benefits begin.

**defined contribution pension plan** A plan in which an employer agrees only to make specific contributions, usually a percentage of salary, so the payout is dependent on both the total contributions and the plan's investment performance.

**Delaware carve-out** Permits shareholders to bring a state law class-action suit against a corporation and its directors for breach of preexisting common law fiduciary disclosure obligations.

**Delaware Court of Chancery** The trial court in Delaware that hears corporate law cases.

**demand rights** An investor's right to require an issuer to register a stated portion of the investor's shares in a public offering.

**denial-of-service attacks** Computer viruses that prevent user access to an Internet site.

**deontological theory of ethics** An ethical theory that focuses on the motivation behind an action rather than the consequences of an action.

***depeçage*** A choice-of-law doctrine under which the court is permitted to apply the laws of different states to different issues when more than one state has an interest in the outcome of a case.

**deposition** The written or oral questioning of any person who may have helpful information about the facts of a case.

**derivative insider** A person, such as a tippee, upon whom the insider's duty of disclosure is imposed.

**descriptive mark** The identifying marks that directly describe (size, color, use of) the goods sold under the mark.

**design defect** A type of product defect that occurs when the product is manufactured according to specifications, but its inadequate design or poor choice of materials causes it to be defective.

**design patent** A patent that protects any novel, original, and ornamental design for an article of manufacture.

**detour** A temporary turning aside from a usual or regular route, course, or procedure, or from a task or employment. To be distinguished from a frolic, which is outside of an agent's scope of employment.

**detrimental reliance** Occurs when an offeree has changed his or her position because of justifiable reliance on an offer.

**development loans** Loans used for the acquisition, subdivision, improvement, and sale of residential properties.

**direct copyright infringement** Occurs when one party is alleged to have violated at least one of the five exclusive rights of the copyright holder by its own actions.

**direct patent infringement** The making, use, or sale of any patented invention in the jurisdiction where it is patented during the term of the patent.

**directed verdict** After the presentation of evidence in a trial before jury, either party may assert that other side has not produced enough evidence to support the legal claim or defense alleged. The moving party then requests that the judge take the case away from the jury and direct that a verdict be entered in favor of the moving party.

**directive** A form of European Union legislation that is a law directing member states to enact certain laws or regulations.

**disability** A physical or mental impairment that substantially limits one or more of a person's major life activities; having a history of such an impairment or being regarded as having one.

**disappearing corporation** In a merger of two corporations, the corporation that no longer maintains its separate corporate existence is the disappearing corporation.

**discharge** Relieve.

**discovery** The process through which parties to a lawsuit collect evidence to support their claims.

**discovery-of-injury statutes** Statutes that provide that the statute of limitations does not begin to run until the person discovers the injury.

**discovery rule** The statute of limitations period does not accrue until the injured party discovers or, by using reasonable diligence, should have discovered the injury.

**discriminate** To treat differently.

**disparagement** Untrue statements derogatory to the quality or ownership of a plaintiff's goods or services, that the defendant knows are false, or to the truth of which the defendant is consciously indifferent.

**disparate impact** The systematic exclusion of women, ethnic groups, or others in a protected class from employment through testing and other selection procedures.

**disparate treatment** Intentional discrimination against a person by employer by denying the person employment or a benefit or privilege of employment because of race, religion, sex, national origin, age, or disability.

**dispute negotiation** Backward looking negotiation that addresses past events that have caused disagreement.

**dissolution** The designation of the point in time when partners no longer carry on their business together.

**distributive justice** A theory of justice that looks to how the burden and benefits of a particular situation of a system are distributed.

**distributive negotiations** Negotiations in which the only issue is the distribution of the fixed pie. Also called zero-sum negotiations.

**diversity jurisdiction** The power of U.S. district courts to decide lawsuits between citizens of two different states when amount in controversy, exclusive of interest and all costs, exceeds $75,000.

**doctrine of equivalents** The doctrine that holds that a direct infringement of a patent has occurred when a patent is not literally copied, but is replicated to the extent that the infringer has created a product or process that works in substantially the same way and accomplishes substantially the same result as the patented invention.

**doctrine of self-publication** A doctrine that provides that a defamatory communication by an employer to an employee may constitute publication if the employer could foresee that the employee would be required to repeat the communication, for instance, to a prospective employer.

**documentary letter of credit (L/C)** A letter of credit issued by a bank that provides for payment by the bank to the beneficiary upon tender by the beneficiary (or its agent or assignee) of specified documents; frequently used to secure payment for goods and repayment of loans in international transactions.

**domain name** The unique name that identifies an Internet site. Domain names always have two or more parts, separated by dots. The part on the left is the most specific, and the part on the right is the most general.

**donee beneficiary** Third party to a contract to whom promisee does not owe an obligation, but rather wishes to confer a gift or a right of performance.

**Do-Not-Call-list** Created in 2003 by the FTC, a registry of names of persons not wanting to receive unsolicited telemarketer calls, pursuant to the Do-Not-Call Implementation Act.

**dormant commerce clause** An implied constitutional limitation on state action affecting interstate commerce even in the absence of preempting federal legislation.

**Double Jeopardy Clause** A clause of the Fifth Amendment that protects criminal defendants from multiple prosecutions for the same offense.

**dragnet clause** In a security agreement, a provision giving the secured party a security interest in all the debtor's property and in the proceeds from the sale of such property.

**dram shop act** A statute that makes a tavern liable for damage or injury caused by a drunk driver who was served drinks even though visibly intoxicated.

**drawings** The drawings (except in chemical cases) must show the claimed invention in a patent application in graphic form.

**drug** Defined by the Food, Drug and Cosmetic Act to include (1) articles intended for use in the diagnosis, cure, mitigation, treatment, or prevention of disease; and (2) articles (other than food) intended to affect the structure or any function of the body.

**dual agency** In a real estate transaction, a broker acts for both the buyer and the seller.

**dual distributor** A manufacturer that sells its goods both at wholesale and at retail.

**dual use** The state of goods and technologies that have both military and nonmilitary applications.

**due diligence** The identification and characterization of risks associated with property and operations involved in various business transactions. A defense available to a defendant (other than the issuer) in a securities violation case concerning a registration statement who (1) conducted a reasonable investigation, and (2) reasonably believed that (a) the statements made were true, and (b) that there were no omissions that made those statements misleading.

**due process clause** A clause in the Fourteen Amendment that provides that no state shall "deprive any person of life, liberty, or property without due process of law."

**due process clauses** Clauses of the Fifth and Fourteenth Amendments that bar the government from using involuntary confessions, even if the *Miranda* warnings were given, when the conduct of the law enforcement officials in obtaining a confession is deemed outrageous or shocking, among other things.

**dumping** Sale of imported products in the United States below the current selling price in the exporter's home market or below the exporter's cost of production.

**dumping margin** The difference between the U.S. price for foreign goods and the price of those goods in their country of origin.

**duress** Coercion.

**dutiable** Import articles subject to required payment.

**duty** (1) The obligation to act as a reasonably prudent person would act under the circumstances to prevent an unreasonable risk of harm to others. (2) The required payment on imports.

**duty of care** The fiduciary duty of agents, officers, and directors to act with the same care that a reasonably prudent person would exercise under similar circumstances. Sometimes expressed as the duty to use the same level of care a reasonably prudent person would use in the conduct of his or her own affairs.

**duty of loyalty** The fiduciary duty of agents, officers, and directors to act in good faith and in what they believe to be the best interest of the principal or the corporation.

**duty of obedience** The fiduciary duty of agents, officers, and directors to obey all reasonable orders of his or her principal.

## E

**early neutral evaluation (ENE)** A dispute resolution mechanism whereby a neutral attorney familiar with the law in the area reviews the case and offers each side his or her evaluation of the strengths and weaknesses.

**early termination clause** An out clause or provision that would allow the lessor or lessee to cancel the lease without completing the full term or paying the complete value of the lease.

**earmarking doctrine** A bankruptcy doctrine whereby a payment to a preexisting creditor may not be recoverable as a preference if the funds for the repayment were provided by some other creditor and not by the debtor.

**economic duress** The coercion of the borrower, threatening to do an unlawful act that might injure the borrower's business or property.

**economic strike** A union strikes employers when they are unable to extract acceptable terms and conditions of employment through collective bargaining.

**economic union** A union within which internal trade barriers are abolished, restrictions on mobility of factors of production among members are eliminated and the economic policies of the member states (monetary, fiscal, taxation and social welfare programs) are fully integrated in order to blend the member state economics into a single entity.

**effects test** A test for personal jurisdiction that asks whether conduct outside the United States has had a substantial adverse effect on American businesses, consumers, investors or securities markets.

**efficient-market theory** The theory that holds that in an open and developed securities market, the price of a company's stock equals its true value.

**effluent limitations** The regulations designed to impose increasingly stringent limitations on pollutant discharges based on the availability of economic treatment and recycling technologies.

**embargo** A special kind of sanction against all commerce of one country that is declared by a country, or more frequently, a group of countries.

**embezzlement** The acquisition by an employee of money or property by reason of some office or position, which money or property the employee takes for personal use.

**eminent domain** The power of state and federal governments to take private property for government uses for which property owners are entitled to just compensation.

**employee stock ownership plan (ESOP)** A type of qualified retirement plan that is governed by the tax qualification requirements of Internal Revenue Code Sections 401 (a), 408 and 4975 (e)(7) and which is invested primarily in stock of the employer.

**employee stock purchase plan (ESSP)** A plan structured under Internal Revenue Code Section 423 under which a company allows its employees to purchase stock at up to a 15 percent discount, and the employee-purchasers receive a favorable tax treatment.

**employer** One who employs the services of others; one for whom employees work, and who pays their wages or salaries.

***en banc* hearing** A hearing at which all the judges of a court of appeals sit together to hear and decide a particularly important or close case.

**encroachment** Occurs when a franchisor sells a franchisee an outlet and later sells another outlet nearby to another franchisee.

**encumbrance** A claim against real property.

**enterprise** Any individual, partnership, corporation, association, or other legal entity, and any union or group of individuals associated in fact although not a legal entity.

**entrenchment** Entrenchment occurs when a director opposes a transaction in order to maintain a place on the corporation's board.

**environmental assessment (EA)** A document that identifies any significant impact of a development on the environment.

**environmental impact statement (EIS)** A required document for any proposal for legislation or other major governmental action that may significantly affect the quality of the environment.

**environmental justice** The notion that decisions with environmental consequences (such as where to locate incinerators, dumps, factories, and other sources of pollution) should not discriminate against poor and minority communities.

**environmental laws** The numerous federal, state, and local laws with the common objective of protecting human health and the environment.

**Environmental Protection Agency (EPA)** Federal agency that administers all of the federal laws that set national goals and policies for environmental protection, except for the National Environmental Policy Act, which is administered by the Council on Environmental Quality.

**equal dignities rule** Under this rule if an agent acts on behalf of another (its principal) in signing an agreement of the type that must under the statute of frauds be in writing, the authority of the agent to act on behalf of the principal must also be in writing.

**equitable relief** An injunction issued by the court to prohibit a defendant from continuing in a certain course of activity or to require a defendant to perform a certain activity.

**equitable subordination** The doctrine that prevents one creditor, through fraud or other wrongful conduct, from increasing its recovery at the expense of other creditors of the same debtor.

**equity** The value of real property that exceeds the liens against it.

**equity capital** The cash or property contributed to an enterprise in exchange for an ownership interest.

**equity security** An equity security includes (1) any stock or similar security; (2) any security that is convertible, with or without consideration, into such a security; (3) any security carrying any warrant or right to purchase such a security; (4) any such warrant or right; and (5) any other security that the Securities and Exchange Commission (SEC) deems to be of a similar nature and that, for the protection of investors or in the public interest, the SEC considers appropriate to treat as an equity security.

***Erie* doctrine** In a diversity action in federal court, except as to matters governed by the U.S. Constitution and acts of Congress, the law to be applied in any case is the law of the state in which the federal court is situated.

**escrow** The system by which a neutral stakeholder (escrow agent) allows parties to a real property transaction to fulfill the various conditions of the closing of the transaction without the physical difficulties of passing instruments and funds between the parties.

**escrow agent** A neutral stakeholder who facilitates the transfer of real property between interested parties.

**essential facility** Some resource necessary to a company's rival's survival that they cannot economically or feasibly duplicate.

**Establishment Clause** A clause in the First Amendment that prohibits the establishment of a religion by the federal government.

**estopped** A defendant is legally barred from alleging or denying a certain fact when the defendant's words and/or actions have been to the contrary.

**Ethical Business Leader's Decision Tree** A guide for managers to use when deciding how to act.

**euro** The name of the currency for the European Monetary Union.

**event risks** Changes in the structure of a corporation such as leveraged buyouts, mergers, or hostile takeovers that affect the credit rating or riskiness of outstanding debt.

**events of default** The events contained in a loan agreement that will trigger the lender's right to terminate the loan, accelerate the repayment obligations, and, if the loan is secured, take possession of the property securing the loan.

***ex post facto* clause (after the fact)** The laws prohibited by the U.S. Constitution that punish actions that were not illegal when performed.

**exclusionary rule** The evidence obtained in an unlawful search or interrogation cannot be introduced into evidence at trial against a defendant.

**exclusive dealership (distributorship)** An agreement in which a manufacturer limits itself to a single dealer or distributor in a given territory.

**exclusive listing** A listing that grants the real estate broker the right to sell the property; any sale of the property during the term of the listing will entitle the broker to a commission.

**exclusivity clause** Limits or prevents the operation of a competing store in a shopping center.

**executive** An employee whose primary duty consists of the management of the enterprise where he or she is employed or of a customarily recognized department or subdivision of the enterprise.

**executive privilege** The type of immunity granted the president against the forced disclosure of presidential communications made in the exercise of executive power.

**executory contract** Contracts that have not yet been performed and involve an exchange of promises.

**exemplary damages** Damages awarded to a plaintiff over and above what will fairly compensate it for its loss. They are intended to punish the defendant and deter others from engaging in similar conduct. Also called punitive damages.

**exempt employee** An employee that is exempt from the minimum-wage and overtime requirements of the Federal Labor Standards Act; such an employee is generally paid a salary instead of an hourly wage.

**exempt property** Excluded from a bankruptcy estate, and intended to provide for the individual's future needs. Generally includes a homestead, motor vehicles, household or personal items, tools of the debtor's trade, health aids, personal injury awards, alimony or support payments, disability or retirement benefits (including IRAs), life insurance or annuities, and some special deposits of cash.

**exempt securities** Securities listed in Section 3 of the 1933 Act that include any security (1) issued or guaranteed by the United States or any state of the United States, (2) issued or guaranteed by any national bank, (3) issued by a charitable organization, and (4) that is part of an issue offered and sold only to persons residing within a single state or territory, if the issuer is a resident of the same state or territory.

**exempt transactions** Transactions described in Section 4 of the 1933 Act that include those (1) by any person other than an issuer, underwriter or dealer and (2) by an issuer not involving any public offering.

**exercise period** The fixed period during which a stock option may be exercised by the optionee, which is usually no longer than ten years.

**exhaustion of administrative remedies** A court will not entertain an appeal from the administrative process until an agency has had a chance to act and all possible avenues of relief before the agency have been fully pursued.

**exit vehicle** A way for investors to get their money back without liquidating a company, for example, through acquisition by a larger company or through an initial public offering of the company's securities.

**expectation damages** In the case of breach of contract, refers to remuneration that puts a plaintiff into the cash position the plaintiff would have been in if the contract had been fulfilled.

**export license** The control of exports.

**express authority** The power of an agent to act for a principal based on that agent's justifiable belief that the principal has authorized him or her to do so; may be given by the principal's actual words or by an action that indicates the principal's consent.

**express ratification** Express ratification occurs when the principal, through words or behavior, manifests an intent to be bound by the agent's act.

**express warranty** An explicit guarantee by the seller that the goods purchased by a buyer will have certain qualities.

**expropriation** The process of nationalization when the host country compensates the company for its lost assets.

**extension plan** A plan in a Chapter 13 bankruptcy proceeding in which creditors receive the entire indebtedness, but the period for payment is extended beyond the original due date.

**extortionate extension of credit** Making a loan for which violence is understood by the parties as likely to occur in the event of nonpayment.

**extraterritoriality** A practice whereby countries assert the right to regulate activities that occur beyond their borders.

## F

**failure to warn** Failure of a product to carry adequate warnings of the risks involved in the normal use of the product.

**fair lending laws** Laws that prohibit discrimination in lending practices.

**fair procedure** Common law doctrine that protects individuals from arbitrary exclusion or expulsion from private organizations that control important economic interests.

**fair trade law** A federal law providing for temporary relief to domestic industries seriously injured by increasing imports, regardless of whether unfair practices are involved.

**fair use doctrine** The doctrine that protects from liability a defendant who has infringed a copyright owner's exclusive rights when countervailing public policies predominate. Activities such as literary criticism, social comment, news reporting, educational activities, scholarship, or research are traditional fair use domains.

**false imprisonment** The confinement of an individual without that individual's consent and without lawful authority.

**family resemblance test** A test for determining whether an instrument is a security by asking whether it bears a family resemblance to any nonsecurity.

**fanciful mark** A coined term having no prior meaning until used as a trademark in connection with a particular product.

**fast-track negotiating authority** Legislation allowing the president to negotiate trade agreements and then submit them for an up or down vote by Congress with no amendments permitted.

**fax blasts** Unsolicited mass facsimile transmissions by telecopy, which are banned by the Telephone Consumer Protection Act of 1991.

**Federal Arbitration Act (FAA)** The federal law requiring courts to honor agreements to arbitrate and arbitration awards.

**federal common law** The judicial interpretations of federal statutes and administrative regulations.

**federal question** When a dispute concerns federal law, namely, a legal right arising under the U.S. Constitution, a federal statute, an administrative regulation issued by a federal government agency, federal common law, or a treaty of the United States, it is said to raise a federal question.

**Federal Rules of Civil Procedure (FRCP)** The procedural rules that govern civil litigation.

**Federal Rules of Evidence (FRE)** Federal rules governing the admissibility of evidence in litigation in federal court.

**federalism** The doctrine that serves to allocate power between the federal government and the various state governments.

**fee simple** Title to property that grants owner full right of disposition during his or her lifetime that may be passed on to owner's heirs and assigns forever.

**felony** An offense punishable by death or prison term exceeding one year.

**fetal-protection policy** A company policy that bars a woman from certain jobs unless her inability to bear children is medically documented.

**fictitious business name** The name of a business that is other than that of the owner.

**fiduciary** A person having a duty to act primarily for the benefit of another in matters connected with undertaking fiduciary responsibilities.

**fiduciary duty** The obligation of a trustee or other fiduciary to act for the benefit of the other party.

**file-wrapper estoppel** The doctrine that prevents a patent owner involved in infringement from introducing any evidence at odds with the information contained in the owner's application on file with the U.S. Patent and Trademark Office.

**final-offer arbitration** A form of arbitration used most notably in baseball salary disputes; each side submits its "best and final" offer to the arbitrator, who must choose one of the two proposals.

**financing lease** Under a financing lease (commonly used to finance the acquisition of expensive capital equipment and vehicles such as airplanes, locomotives, and ships), the parties expect the lessee to purchase the leased equipment at the end of the lease term at an agreed-upon residual value.

**firm commitment underwriting** The underwriters agree to purchase the entire offering, thus effectively shifting the risk of the offering from the issuer to the underwriters.

**firm offer** Under the Uniform Commercial Code, an offer signed by a merchant that indicates that the offer will be kept open and is not revocable, for lack of consideration, during the time stated, or for a reasonable period of time if none is stated, but in no event longer than three months.

**first sale doctrine** Once the copyright or trademark owner places a copyrighted or trademarked item in the stream of commerce by selling it, the owner has exhausted its exclusive statutory right to control its distribution.

**fixtures** The items of personal property that are attached to real property and that cannot be removed without substantial damage to the item.

**floating** Interest rates that fluctuate throughout the life of the loan according to the interest rate that the lender would pay if it borrowed the funds in order to relend them.

**floating lien** In a security interest, if the collateral is sold, exchanged, collected, or otherwise disposed of, the security interest is equally effective against cash, account, or whatever else is received from the transaction.

**food** Defined by the Food, Drug and Cosmetic Act as (1) articles used for food or drink; (2) chewing gum; and (3) articles used for components of either.

**foreclosure** The legal process by which a mortgagee may put up a piece of property for sale in the public arena to raise cash in order to pay off a debt owed by the mortgagor to the mortgagee.

**foreign corporation** A corporation doing business in one state though chartered or incorporated in another state is a foreign corporation as to the first state.

**foreign trade zone** A special area within or adjacent to U.S. ports of entry, where import duties on merchandise normally due upon entry into the United States are not due until the merchandise is withdrawn from the zone.

**forgotten founder** A problem that can arise when several persons work together on an informal basis with a common business objective, and then one leaves. The person who left (the forgotten founder) may have ownership rights in the enterprise.

**Form 8-K** A form on which companies registered with the Securities and Exchange Commission (SEC) must report certain events, including changes in control, acquisitions or dispositions of key assets, and resignation of directors or auditors, to the SEC.

**Form 10-K** A form on which companies registered with the Securities and Exchange Commission (SEC) must file their annual audited reports with the SEC.

**Form 10-KSB** A simplified form that small businesses required to file periodic reports to the Securities and Exchange Commission (SEC) may use to file annual reports.

**Form 10-Q** A form on which companies registered with the Securities and Exchange Commission (SEC) must file their unaudited quarterly statements of operations and financial condition with the SEC.

**Form 10-QSB** A simplified form that small businesses required to file periodic reports to the Securities and Exchange Commission (SEC) may use to file quarterly reports.

**Form S–1** The registration statement used in an initial public offering of securities.

**Form S–2** A form of registration statement that allows public companies to present certain information in a streamlined form and to incorporate previous filings by reference.

**Form S–3** An abbreviated form of registration statement that is available to companies that have filed periodic reports under the Securities Exchange Act of 1934 for at least three years and have a widespread following in the marketplace.

**Form S–4** A combined securities registration statement and proxy statement.

**Form SB–1** Allows nonreporting and transitional small business issuers to register up to $10 million of securities annually.

**Form SB–2** A form for registration of any amount of securities by small business issuers.

***forum non conveniens*** A doctrine whereby a suit is dismissed because an alternate, more convenient forum is available.

**forum shopping** A party to a lawsuit attempts to have a case tried in a particular court or jurisdiction where the party believes the most favorable judgment or verdict will be received.

**forward-looking statement** A statement by a publicly traded company (1) containing a projection of revenues, income, earnings per share, capital expenditures, dividends, capital structure, or other financial items; (2) of management's plans and objectives for future operations, including plans relating to the issuer's products and services; (3) of future economic performance, including any such statement in management's discussion and analysis of financial condition or in the results of operations required to be included by the SEC; and (4) of the assumptions underlying or relating to any such statement.

**franchise** A business relationship in which one party (the franchisor) grants to another party (the franchisee) the right to use the franchisor's name and logo and to distribute the franchisor's products from a specified locale.

**franchising** An arrangement whereby the franchisor receives cash up front, followed by monthly payments based on a reseller's gross receipts, in exchange for granting the franchisee the right to use the franchisor's trademarks and marketing plan.

**fraud** Any intentional deception that has the purpose of inducing another in reliance upon the deception to part with some property or money. Fraud may involve false representations of fact, whether by words or conduct; false allegations; omission (especially by fiduciary); or concealment of something that should have been disclosed.

**fraud in the factum** A type of fraud that occurs when a party is persuaded to sign one document thinking that it is another.

**fraud in the inducement** A type of fraud that occurs when a party makes a false statement to persuade the other party to enter into an agreement.

**fraud-on-the-market theory** The theory that holds that if the information about a company available to the market is incorrect, then the market price will not reflect the true value of the stock.

**fraudulent conveyance** The direct or indirect transfer of assets to a third party with actual intent to defraud or have inadequate consideration in circumstances when the transferor is insolvent.

**fraudulent misrepresentation** Deceit; intentionally misleading by making material misrepresentations of fact that the plaintiff relied on that cause injury to the plaintiff.

**Free Exercise Clause** A clause in the First Amendment that prohibits certain, but not all, restrictions on the practice of religion.

**free trade area** A free trade area is created when a group of countries reduce or eliminate tariffs among themselves, but maintain their own individual tariffs as to other states.

**free writing prospectus** Any written offer under Section 2(a)(10) of the 1933 Act and subject to liability under Section 12(a)(2).

**freeze-out merger** In a merger with a controlling shareholder, some shareholders (usually the public shareholders) are required to surrender their shares in the disappearing corporation for cash.

**frolic** An activity by an employee that is entirely outside the employer's purpose. To be distinguished from a detour, which is within the scope of employment.

**fruit of the poisonous tree** Evidence acquired directly or indirectly as a result of an illegal search or arrest is generally inadmissible.

**frustration of purpose** Frustration of purpose occurs when performance is possible, but changed circumstances have made the contract useless to one or both of the parties.

**full-service lease** A lease that requires the lessor to maintain the property that a company is occupying, which means, in turn, that the tenant's responsibilities may be limited to seeing that the services provided are adequate.

**full warranty** The warranty that gives the consumer the right to free repair or replacement of a defective product.

# G

**gap financing** Financing that a developer obtains to pay off a construction loan when it becomes due before the permanent financing is available. Also called interim financing.

**garnishment** The legal procedure by which a creditor may collect a debt by attaching a portion of a debtor's weekly wages.

**general partnership** A form of business organization between two or more persons in which the partners share in the profits or losses of a common business enterprise.

**general plan** A long-range planning document that addresses the physical development and redevelopment of a city.

**general release** An agreement by person engaging in a dangerous activity to assume all risks and hold the party offering access to said dangerous activity free of all liability.

**genericism** The use of a trademark as a generic name for the product, for example, "a Kleenex" for "tissue."

**geographic market** All firms that compete for sales in a given area at current prices, or would compete in that area if prices rose by a modest amount.

**Gharar** A tenet of Islamic trade and commerce that refers to an event where the outcomes are unknown.

**going effective** Culmination of the securities registration process with the Securities and Exchange Commission. Sales can be legally consummated as of this date and time.

**going private** A corporation that has fewer than 300 shareholders (or 500 if the corporation's assets total less than $10 million) and ceases to be required to file public periodic reports under the Securities Exchange Act of 1934.

**golden parachute** A termination agreement that gives extra salary and other benefits to an executive upon a corporate change in control.

**good faith exception** An exception to the exclusionary rule that provides that evidence obtained by police in good faith will not be excluded from trial, even if it was obtained in violation of the Fourth Amendment.

**good faith subsequent purchaser** A person who acquires real property for fair value without being aware of a disputed claim to the property.

**good offices** A process mainly used in the area of public international law, by which a third party (often a disinterested government) brings the parties together through establishing communication and providing a site where the parties can meet, often in secrecy.

**goods** As defined in Article 2 of the Uniform Commercial Code, all things (including specially manufactured goods) that are movable at the time of identification to the contract for sale.

**government-contractor defense** The limited immunity available for manufacturers that produce products to the specifications of government contracts.

**grant deed** A deed that contains implied warranties that the grantor has not previously conveyed the same property or any interest in it to another person and that the title is marketable.

**grant price** The price (which is generally the market price of the stock at the time the stock option is granted) at which an optionee can exercise his or her stock option by purchasing the stock. Also referred to as the strike price.

**grantee** A person to whom real property is conveyed.

**grantor** A person conveying real property.

**gray market** A market where products are sold outside the normal channel of distribution, often at a discounted price.

**greenmail** Payment by a target company to buy back shares owned by a potential acquiror at a premium over market. The acquiror in exchange agrees not to pursue its hostile takeover bid.

**gross-up clause** The clause in foreign investment contracts by which local partner or licensee is obligated to pay all taxes other than those specifically allocated to the foreign partner.

**ground lease** A lease for land on which a building will be built.

**group boycott** An agreement among competitors to refuse to deal with another competitor.

**guarantor** The person who agrees to be liable for the obligation of another person.

**guaranty** An undertaking by one person to become liable for the obligation of another person.

**guaranty of collection** Under a guaranty of collection, the guarantor becomes obliged to pay only after the lender has attempted unsuccessfully to collect the amount due from the primary debtor.

**guaranty of payment** A provision that holds guarantor's obligation to pay the lender is triggered, immediately and automatically, if the primary debtor fails to make a payment when due.

**guaranty of performance** A guaranty that specified nonpayment obligations will be performed.

**guardian *ad litem* (guardian for the suit)** A person authorized to bring suit for a minor.

**gun-jumping** A violation of the securities laws that occurs when an issuer or underwriter conditions the market with a news article, press release, or speech about a company engaged in the registration of its securities.

## H

**H-1B visa** A work authorization issued by the U.S. Citizenship and Immigration Services that is available only for foreign workers in professional and specialty occupations (generally those involving a bachelor's degree or its equivalent), such as computer programmers, engineers, doctors or fashion models, where the employer can show an inability to recruit qualified workers in the United States.

**harmonized tariff schedule (HTS)** A U.S. government document that lists the tariffs on goods imposed by Congress and by the president pursuant to the Trade Agreements Program, based on the country of origin.

**hazard ranking score** The Environmental Protection Agency ranking that represents the risks presented by certain sites to the environment and public health.

**hazardous substance superfund** Finances federal activity to investigate and take remedial action in response to a release or threatened release of hazardous substances to the environment.

**hearing** The phase of arbitration that is similar to a trial.

**Herfindahl-Hirschman Index (HHI)** An aid to the interpretation of market data when determining the anticompetitive effect of a merger; the HHI of market concentration is calculated by summing the squares of the individual market shares of all the firms in the market.

**horizontal agreement** A conspiracy agreement between firms that compete with each other on the same level of production or distribution.

**horizontal market division** An agreement among competitors to divide a market according to class of customer or geographic territory; it violates antitrust law.

**horizontal merger** A corporate combination of actual or prospective competitors.

**horizontal price-fixing** An agreement between competitors at the same level of distribution to set a common price for a product; it violates antitrust law.

**hostile environment harassment** The creation of a hostile working environment, such as continually subjecting an employee to ridicule and racial slurs, or unwanted sexual advances.

**hostile takeover** A transaction in which a third party (a raider) seeks to obtain control of a company (the target) over the objections of its management.

**hot issues** Shares of high-demand initial public offerings.

**hot news exception** A state law misappropriation claim that applies in cases where (a) the plaintiff generates or gathers information at its cost; (b) the information is time-sensitive; (c) the defendant's use of the information amounts to free-riding on the plaintiff's efforts; (d) the defendant is in direct competition with the plaintiff; and (e) the availability of other parties to free ride on the plaintiff's efforts would reduce the plaintiff's incentive to provide the product or service such that plaintiff's existence would be threatened.

**hushmail** A repurchase of shares at a premium over market to ensure silence from a shareholder who has been critical of management.

## I

**I-9** The Employment Eligibility and Verification Form that the U.S. government requires all employers to complete and keep on file to identify the identity and employment eligibility of all persons they hire.

**identification to the contract** Setting aside or otherwise designating the particular goods for sale under a contract.

**identity theft** Taking an individual's information (such as Social Security number and mother's maiden name) and using that information to fraudulently obtain credit or commit other financial crimes.

**illegal contract** A contract is illegal if its formation or performance is expressly forbidden by a civil or criminal statute, or if a penalty is imposed for doing the act agreed upon.

**illegal *per se*** A practice that is illegal regardless of its impact on the market or its procompetitive justifications.

**illusory promise** A promise that either does not in fact confer any benefit on the promisee or subject the promisor to any detriment.

**impaired** A characteristic of a claim when the plan does not provide for full cash payment on its effective date and if it alters the creditors' legal, equitable, or contractual rights in any way.

**impaired claim** A claim is considered impaired if the bankruptcy relief plan does not provide for full cash payment on its effective date and it alters the creditors' legal, equitable, or contractual rights in any way (except by curing defaults and reinstating the maturity of the claim).

**implied authority** The power of an agent to do whatever is reasonable to complete the task he or she has been instructed to undertake.

**implied contract** An employment agreement—implied from such facts as long-term employment; receipt of raises, bonuses and promotions; and assurance from management that the employee was doing a good job—that the employee would not be terminated except for good cause.

**implied covenant of good faith and fair dealing** An implied covenant in every contract that imposes on each party a duty not to do anything that will deprive the other party of the benefits of the agreement.

**implied intent** If a person does not intend a particular consequence of an act, but knew that the consequence of the act was certain, or substantially certain, and does the act anyway, intent to cause the consequence is implied.

**implied ratification** Implied ratification occurs when the principal, by his or her silence or failure to repudiate the agent's act, acquiesces in it.

**implied warranties** Representations about the quality or suitability of a product that are implied, not explicitly stated. *See also* Implied Warranty of Fitness for a Particular Purpose and Implied Warranty of Merchantability.

**implied warranty of fitness for a particular purpose** The warranty whereby goods involving the following elements are judged satisfactory for the buyer's purpose: (1) the buyer must have a particular purpose for the goods; (2) the seller must have known or have had reason to know of that purpose; (3) the seller must have known or had reason to know that the buyer was relying on the seller's expertise; and (4) the buyer must have relied upon the seller.

**implied warranty of habitability** A warranty made by a commercial seller of houses in which the seller warrants that the house is in reasonable working order and is of reasonably sound construction.

**implied warranty of merchantability** The warranty by which all goods sold by merchants in the normal course of business must meet following criteria: (l) pass without objection in the trade under the contract description; (2) be fit for the ordinary purposes for which such goods are used; (3) be within the variations permitted by the agreement, of even kind, quality and quantity within each unit and among all units involved; (4) be adequately contained, packaged, and labeled as the agreement may require; and (5) conform to the promises or affirmations of fact made on the container or label, if any.

**import relief laws** A series of laws through which Congress has authorized the president to raise U.S. tariffs on specified products and to provide other forms of import protection to U.S. industries.

**impossibility** An excuse for nonperformance based on the destruction of something vital to the performance of the contract or another unforeseen event that makes performance of the contract impossible.

**impossibility defense** A defense to strict liability in which a corporate officer might not be held strictly (and vicariously) liable if he or she did everything possible to ensure legal compliance to applicable standards, even though the company was still unable to comply.

**impracticability** A situation in which performance is possible but is commercially impractical.

**improper means** Deceitful actions through which party obtains trade secrets of another.

**imputed liability** The imposition of civil or criminal liability on one party for the wrongful acts of another. Also called vicarious liability.

**in loco parentis (in place of the parent)** Refers to actions of a custodian, guardian or other person acting in the parent's place.

***in personam* jurisdiction** Personal jurisdiction based upon the residence or activities of the person being sued. It is the power that a court has over the defendant itself, in contrast to the court's power over the defendant's interest in property (*quasi in rem* jurisdiction) or power over the property itself (*in rem* jurisdiction).

***in rem* jurisdiction** Jurisdiction over property based upon the location of the property at issue in the lawsuit.

**incentive stock option (ISO)** A stock option that qualifies for favorable tax treatment Internal Revenue Code section 422, granted to an employee of a corporation to buy stock at a specified price (at least 100% of fair market value on the date of grant) for a specified period of time (no more than ten years).

**incidental damages** In an action for breach of contract, the lesser and relatively minor damages that a nonbreaching party incurs, such as the charges, expenses and commissions incurred in stopping delivery; the cost of the transportation, care and custody of goods after a breach, the expenses incurred in connection with the return or subsequent disposition of goods that are the subject of the contract; or other expenses incurred in mitigating damages resulting from the breach.

**incorporation** The process by which a corporation is formed.

**indemnification** The doctrine that allows a defendant to recover its individual loss from a co-defendant whose relative blame is greater or who has contractually agreed to assume liability.

**indenture** The agreement governing a bond issue.

**independent contractor** A person is deemed to be an independent contractor only if the employer neither exercises control over the means of performing the work nor the end result of that work.

**indictment** Formal charges filed by a grand jury.

**indirect patent infringement** One party's active inducement of another party to infringe a patent.

**industrial ecology** A concept that advocates a systems approach to eco-efficiency and applies it to groups of corporations working together.

**inevitable disclosure doctrine** A doctrine that permits a former employer to prevent an employee from working for a competitor when the new position will require the employee to disclose or use the trade secrets of the former employer.

**inevitable discovery exception** An exception to the exclusionary rule that provides that illegally obtained evidence can lawfully be introduced at trial if it can be shown that the evidence would inevitably have been found by other legal means.

**infomercial** An advertisement generally presented in the format of half-hour television talk shows or news programs.

**informal discretionary action** The administrative agencies' decision-making process for repetitive actions that are inappropriate to litigate in courts.

**information** The formal charges filed with the court in a criminal case.

**initiative** A formal petition generated by a certain percentage of the electorate to introduce legislative change.

**injunction** A remedy granted by the court that requires defendant to perform or cease from performing some activity.

**injurious falsehood** False statements knowingly made that lead to economic loss for a plaintiff.

**innocent landowner defense** In a case under the Comprehensive Environmental Responsibility, Contribution, and Liability Act, a potentially responsible current owner can assert this defense if the release or disposal of hazardous materials was by a third party who was not an employee and with whom the current owner had no contractual relationship. Also called the third-party defense.

**innovation offsets** Technological advantages gained by companies that met the challenge of environmental regulations and discovered lower costs and better quality products as a result.

**inquiry** Done by a commission of inquiry that is established ad hoc, often after a violation of international law, it consists of two contending governments reviewing the finding of the commission with the goal to come to an acceptable solution for the dispute at hand.

**inquiry notice** Notice attributed when reasonable inquiry would have disclosed an adverse interest, for example, if inspection of a property would have revealed that some person other than the grantor was in possession or owned the property.

**inside director** A member of a board who is also an officer.

**insider** A person with access to confidential information and an obligation of disclosure to other traders in the marketplace.

**insider trading** Trading securities based on material nonpublic information, in violation of a duty to the corporation or its shareholders or others.

**integrated disclosure system** The system that seeks to eliminate duplicative or unnecessary disclosure requirements under the Securities Act of 1933 and the Securities Exchange Act of 1934.

**integration** When an issuer makes successive sales of securities within a limited period of time, the Securities and Exchange Commission may integrate the successive sales; that is, it may deem them to be part of a single sale for purposes of deciding whether there was an exemption from registration.

**integrative negotiations** Negotiations in which mutual gains are possible as parties trade lower valued resources for higher valued ones. Also called variable-sum negotiations.

**intellectual property** Any product or result of a mental process that is given legal protection against unauthorized use.

**intelligent agents** Semi-autonomous computer programs that can be dispatched by the user to execute certain tasks.

**intent** The actual, subjective desire to cause the consequences of an act, or the belief that the consequences are substantially certain to result from it.

**intent to be bound** The oral or written statement regarding intention of parties to enter into a contract.

**intention to do wrong** Subjective intent or desire to do wrong or intent to take action substantially certain to cause a wrong to occur.

**intentional infliction of emotional distress** Outrageous conduct by the individual inflicting the distress; intention to cause, or reckless disregard of the probability of causing, emotional distress; severe emotional suffering; and actual and proximate (or legal) causation of the emotional distress.

**interbrand competition** The price competition between a company and its competitors that sell a different brand of the same product.

**interference with contractual relations** A defendant intentionally induces another to breach a contract with a plaintiff.

**interference with prospective business advantage** Intentional interference by the defendant with a business relationship the plaintiff seeks to develop, which interference causes loss to the plaintiff.

**interim financing** Financing that a developer obtains to pay off a construction loan when it becomes due before the permanent financing is available. Also called gap financing.

**interlocutory** Something intervening between the commencement and the end of a suit that decides some point or matter, but is not a final decision regarding the whole controversy.

**interrogatory** Written question to a party to a lawsuit and its attorney.

**intrabrand competition** The price competition among the different dealers selling products produced by the same company.

**intrusion** Objectionable prying, such as eavesdropping or unauthorized rifling through files. It includes the act of wrongfully entering upon or taking possession of property of another.

**invasion of privacy** Prying or intrusion that would be objectionable or offensive to a reasonable person, including eavesdropping, rifling through files one has no authorization to see, public disclosure of private facts, or unauthorized use of an individual's picture in an advertisement or article with which that person has no connection.

**inverse condemnation** The taking of private real property for a public use; requires payment of just compensation.

**investigative consumer reporting** Report that contains information on character and reputation, not just credit history.

**investment contract** A type of security created by an investment of money in a common enterprise with profits to come solely from the efforts of others.

**investors** Persons putting up cash or property in exchange for an equity interest in an enterprise.

**invitee** A business visitor who enters premises for the purposes of the possessor's business.

**involuntary proceeding** An involuntary proceeding in bankruptcy that is initiated when one or more of the debtor's creditors files a bankruptcy petition with the bankruptcy court.

**involuntary redemption rights** The permission of a corporation, at its option, to redeem the shares for a specified price either after a given period of time or on the occurrence of a certain event.

***ipso facto* clause** A clause in a contract that expressly permits termination of the contract in the event of a bankruptcy filing by one or both parties to the contract.

**irrevocable letter of credit** A letter of credit that cannot be amended or canceled without the consent of the beneficiary and the issuing bank.

**irrevocable offer** Irrevocable offers arise in two circumstances: (1) when an option contract has been created, and (2) when an offeree has relied on an offer to its detriment.

**issuer** A company that offers or sells any security.

## J

**join** In cases in which more than one defendant is liable for damages, named defendant(s) may ask the court to join or add other defendants.

**joint and several liability** In a case in which the court determines that multiple defendants are at fault, the doctrine whereby a plaintiff may collect the entire judgment from any single defendant, regardless of the degree of that defendant's fault.

**joint tenancy** A specialized form of co-ownership involving real property owned in equal shares by two or more persons who have a right of survivorship if one joint tenant dies.

**joint venture** A one-time group of two or more persons in a single specific business enterprise or transaction.

**judgment notwithstanding the verdict (judgment N.O.V.)** Reverses the jury verdict on the ground that the evidence of the prevailing party was so weak that no reasonable jury could have resolved the dispute in that party's favor. Also called judgment n.o.v. (*non obstante veredicto*, notwithstanding the verdict).

**judicial review** The power of federal courts to review acts of the legislative and executive branches of government to determine whether they violate the Constitution.

**junior debt** Indebtedness that is subordinated under a debt subordination agreement.

**junk bond** A form of high yield, high risk unsecured corporate indebtedness that is not investment grade.

**juristic personality** The characteristic of a business entity, such as a corporation, whereby the entity is treated as a legal entity separate from its owners.

## K

**Kantian theory** An ethical theory that looks to the form of an action, rather than the intended result, in examining the ethical worth.

**kicker** A percentage of gross or net income in a real estate transaction payable to lender.

**know-how** Detailed information on how to make or do something.

## L

***laesio enormis*** A doctrine developed from language in the Code of Justinian that provided a remedy for those who sold land at less than half its just price.

**laddering** A practice whereby investment banks offer IPO shares to customers only if they promise to purchase more shares on the open market after the offering.

**larceny** Theft. The taking of property without the owner's consent.

**learned professional** A professional employee whose primary duty is the performance of work requiring advanced knowledge (defined as (1) work that is predominantly intellectual in character and (2) that includes work requiring the consistent exercise of discretion and judgment) in a field of science or learning customarily acquired by a prolonged course of intellectual instruction.

**legal duty** The requirement to act reasonably under the circumstances to avoid harming another person.

**lemon laws** Laws designed to protect consumers from defective products that cannot be adequately fixed, such as new cars and new mobile homes.

**lessee** A tenant or one to whom an interest in real property is conveyed.

**lessor** A landlord or one who conveys an interest in real property.

**letter of credit (L/C)** A payment mechanism for international sales transactions involving a bank in the buyer's jurisdiction that commits to pay the seller. Also called a documentary credit.

**letter of intent** An instrument entered into by the parties to a real estate or other transaction for the purpose of setting forth the general terms and conditions of a purchase and sale agreement until a formal legal commitment can be made through the execution of a formal acquisition agreement.

**leveraged buyout (LBO)** A takeover financed with loans secured by the acquired company's assets, in which groups of investors, often including management, use borrowed money along with some of their own money to buy back the company's stock from its current shareholders.

**libel** A written communication to a third party by a defendant of an untrue statement of fact that injures a plaintiff's reputation.

**licensee** Anyone who is privileged to enter upon land of another because the possessor has given expressed or implied consent.

**lien** A claim on a property that secures a debt owed by the owner of the property.

**lien notice** A written notice that property is subject to a claim by someone other than its owner for the payment of a debt.

**lien subordination** An agreement between two secured creditors whose respective security interest, liens, or mortgages attach to the same property. The subordinating party agrees that the lien of the other creditor shall have priority notwithstanding the relative priorities that the parties' liens would otherwise have under applicable law.

**limited fund class action** A class action in which the total of the aggregated liquidated claims exceeds the fund available to satisfy them.

**limited guaranty** A guaranty in which the maximum amount of the guarantor's liability is expressly stated in the guaranty instrument.

**limited liability company (LLC)** A form of business entity authorized by state law that is taxed like a limited partnership and provides its members with limited liability, but like a corporation gives its members the right to participate in management without incurring unlimited liability.

**limited liability partnership (LLP)** A form of limited partnership designed primarily for professionals who typically do business as a partnership that insulates its partners from vicarious liability for certain partnership obligations.

**limited partners** The participants in a limited partnership whose liability for partnership business is limited to their capital contribution.

**limited partnership** A form of business organization in which limited partners must refrain from actively participating in the management of the partnership but are liable for the debts of the partnership only up to the amount they personally contributed to the partnership.

**limited warranty** The warranty that limits the remedies available to the consumer for a defective product.

**line-item veto** Allowed the president to sign a bill into law and then cancel any dollar amounts that he or she believed to be fiscally irresponsible. Declared unconstitutional by the U.S. Supreme Court.

**line-of-business test** If an officer, director, or controlling shareholder learns of an opportunity in the course of business for the corporation, and if the opportunity is in the corporation's line of business, a court will not permit that person to keep the opportunity for personal gain.

**liquidated damages** The amount of money stipulated in a contract to be paid to non-breaching party should one of the parties breach the agreement.

**living wage ordinances** City laws that require employers to pay their employees wages that approximate the real cost of living in the locality, which is often significantly higher than the applicable state or federal minimum wage laws.

**lock-up option** An option to buy assets or stock of a target company; it is exercisable only if the recipient of the option is unsuccessful in acquiring control of the target company. Depending on how it is priced, a lock-up option can have the effect of deterring other bids.

**London Interbank Offered Rate (LIBOR)** An interest rate based on the cost of borrowing offshore U.S. dollars in the global interbank market, centered in several locations in addition to London.

**long-arm statute** A state statute that subjects an out-of-state defendant to jurisdiction when the defendant is doing business or commits a civil wrong in the state.

**loss causation** The misstatement or omission concealed something from the market that, when disclosed, negatively affected the value of the security.

**lost volume seller** A seller that can be put in as good a position as performance would have only by permitting the seller to recover the profit (including reasonable overhead) that it would have made from full performance by the buyer.

**lowest achievable emission rate (LAER)** The lowest achievable emission rate using best available technology.

## M

**mail fraud** A scheme intended to defraud or to obtain money or property by fraudulent means through use of the mails.

**malicious defense** A tort committed when a defendant creates false material evidence and gives false testimony advancing the evidence.

**malicious prosecution** A plaintiff can successfully sue for the tort of malicious prosecution if he or she shows that a prior proceeding was instituted against him or her maliciously and without probable cause or factual basis.

**malpractice** A claim of professional negligence.

**managers** Persons elected by the members (owners) of a limited liability company who, like a board of directors in a corporation, are responsible for managing the business, property, and affairs of the company.

**mandatory arbitration** One party will not do business with the other unless it agrees to arbitrate any future claims.

**manufacturing defect** A flaw in a product that occurs during production, such as a failure to meet the design specifications.

**market power** The power to control market prices or exclude competition in the relevant market. Also called monopoly power.

**market-share liability** The liability for damages caused by a manufacturer's products assessed based on a manufacturer's national market share.

**marketable title** Title to property that is fee simple and is free of liens or encumbrances.

**marshaling assets** Partnership creditors have first priority to partnership assets and, as to those assets, stand in front of creditors of individual partners themselves.

**material breach** A failure to perform a significant obligation under a contract, such as by not performing a service after receiving payment. A material breach discharges the nonbreaching party from its obligations and provides grounds to sue for damages.

**material fact** A fact that a reasonable investor would most likely have considered important in deciding whether to buy or sell his or her stock.

**maturity date** The date a term loan becomes due and payable.

**med-arb** The parties to a dispute enter mediation with the commitment to submit the dispute to binding arbitration if mediation fails to resolve the conflict.

**mediation** A form of dispute resolution whereby the parties agree to try to reach a solution themselves with the assistance of a neutral third party who helps them find a mutually satisfactory solution.

**mediator** The third party who helps the parties in mediation find a mutually satisfactory solution.

**members** The owners of a limited liability company.

***mens rea* (guilty state of mind)** Criminal intent.

**merchant** As defined in Article 2 of the Uniform Commercial Code, a person who deals in goods of the kind or otherwise by its occupation holds itself out as having knowledge or skill peculiar to the practices or goods involved in the transaction.

**merger** The combination of two or more corporations into one.

**merger agreement** An agreement between two companies to combine those companies into one.

**merger doctrine** If an idea and its expression are inseparable, the merger doctrine dictates that the expression is not copyrightable.

**merit review** A review by a state securities commissioner to determine whether the issuer's plan of business and the proposed issuance of securities are fair, just, and equitable.

**minimum contacts** As long as the person has sufficient minimum contacts with a state, such that it is fair to require him or her to appear in a court of that state, the state has personal jurisdiction over that person.

**minitrial** A cross between arbitration and negotiation, truncated presentation of evidence conducted by lawyers, usually with business persons present.

***Miranda* warnings** Once a person is placed in custody, he or she cannot be questioned by the police unless first advised of his or her constitutional rights to remain silent and to have counsel present.

**mirror image rule** A common law contract rule that requires acceptance to contain the exact same terms as the offer.

**misbranding** False or misleading labeling prohibited by federal and state statutes. Includes claiming unsubstantiated medicinal benefits for a food, inadequate labeling for a drug, or selling over-the-counter a drug for which a prescription is required.

**misdeameanor** An offense lower than a felony, punishable by fine or imprisonment for less than one year (not in a penitentiary).

**misrepresentation** A misleading or false representation of the facts intended to deceive another party.

**misstatement (Rule 10b–5)** A misrepresentation of a fact; a lie.

**mistake of fact** A mistake about an underlying fact that may make a contract voidable.

**mistake of judgment** A mistake of judgment occurs when the parties make an erroneous assessment about the value of what is bargained for.

**mitigate** Lessen.

**mitigation of damages** After a breach of contract, the non-breaching party has a duty to take any reasonable actions that will lessen the amount of the damages.

**monopoly power** The power to control market prices or exclude competition in the relevant market. Also called market power.

**mortgage** A loan to buy real property secured by a lien on the real property. Also called deed of trust.

**most favored nation (MFN)** The principle that holds that each member country of the World Trade Organization (WTO) must accord to all other

WTO members tariff treatment no less favorable than it provides to any other country.

**motion for judgment on the pleadings** A motion filed immediately after the complaint and answer have been filed. One party, usually the defendant, argues that the pleadings alone demonstrate that the action is futile.

**motion for summary judgment** A motion requesting the trial judge to decide a case as a matter of law, without a trial, when there are no material facts in dispute.

**motion to dismiss** The formal request that the court terminate lawsuit on the ground that plaintiff's claim is technically inadequate.

**multiple-brand product market** A market made up of product or service offerings by different manufacturers or sellers that are economically interchangeable and may therefore be said to compete.

**mutual rescission** An agreement by both parties to a contract to terminate the contract. A mutual recission is itself a type of contract.

**mutuality of obligation** Both parties in a bilateral contract are obligated to perform their side of the bargain.

# N

**national ambient air quality standards (NAAQS)** The permissible levels of pollutants in the ambient or outdoor air that, with adequate margins of safety, are required to protect public health; set forth in the Clean Air Act.

**national effluent limitations** Increasingly stringent Environmental Protection Agency restrictions on pollutant discharges, based on the availability of economic treatment and recycling technologies.

**national pollutant discharge elimination system (NPDES)** The principal regulatory program established by the Clean Water Act; requires permits for the discharge of pollutants from any point source to navigable waters.

**national treatment** The World Trade Organization principle that holds that WTO members must not discriminate against imported products in favor of domestically produced products.

**nationalization** When a host country decides to assert ownership over some or all of a company's assets.

**natural resource law** The laws that govern wilderness protection, wildlife protection, coastal zone management, energy conservation, and national park designation.

**navigable waters** The waters of the United States and the territorial seas, as well as lakes and streams that are capable of being used for purposes of navigation.

**negative commerce clause** *See* Dormant Commerce Clause.

**negative convenant** The borrower's promise of what it undertakes not to do under the loan agreement.

**negligence** A breach of the requirement that a person act with the care a reasonable person would use in the same circumstances.

**negligence *per se*** Violation of a statute that shifts the burden to the defendant to prove the defendant was not negligent once the plaintiff shows that the defendant violated a statute and the violation caused an injury.

**negligent-hiring theory** An employer is negligent if the employer hires an employee who endangers the health and safety of other employees.

**negligent infliction of emotional distress** A tort committed when the defendant negligently inflicts emotional distress that causes the plaintiff some form of physical injury.

**negotiation** The give and take people engage in when coming to terms with each other.

**net listing** A real estate listing in which the broker receives any sales proceeds in excess of the net listing amount specified by the seller.

**new source performance standards (NSPS)** Require use of technology chosen as BAT for new sources of pollutants.

**nexus** The legally required relationship between a condition to a land-use approval and the impacts of the development being approved.

***nolo contendere* (I will not contest it)** A plea that means the accused does not contest the charges.

**nominative use** A fair-use defense to a trademark infringement action that permits use of a trademark when necessary for purposes of identifying another producer's product, not the user's own product.

***non obstante veredicto*** Latin for "notwithstanding the verdict."

**nonbinding arbitration** Arbitration in which the parties are not bound by the arbitrator's decision.

**nonconforming use** An existing land use that was lawful but that does not comply with a later-enacted zoning ordinance.

**noncore proceedings** In bankruptcy cases, noncore proceedings are related actions concerning the debtor, such as decisions on personal injury and other civil proceedings. Federal or state courts have the power to adjudicate noncore proceedings. Bankruptcy judges may also adjudicate noncore proceedings, subject to de novo review by the federal district courts.

**nonexempt employee** An employee that is not exempt from the minimum-wage and overtime requirements of the Federal Labor Standards Act; such an employee is often paid an hourly wage.

**noninfringement** In a patent dispute, the defense of noninfringement asserts that the allegedly infringing matter does not fall within the claims of the issued patent.

**nonpension benefit plan** A benefit plan other than a pension plan, such as a medical, dental, or disability plan.

**nonqualified stock option (NSO)** A stock option that does not qualify for favorable tax treatment under Internal Revenue Code sections 422 or 423.

**nontariff barriers (NTBs)** Barriers to trade other than tariffs that have in some cases replaced tariffs as a means of protecting domestic industries threatened by import competition.

**no-shop agreement** An agreement whereby the target agrees not to actively solicit other bidders but retains the right to negotiate with parties who submit unsolicited bids to the target.

**not an underwriter** Under Rule 144, an affiliate or a person selling restricted securities is not an underwriter if certain conditions (e.g., holding period, volume limitations, manner of sale, filing of Form 144, and available public information) are met.

**no-talk clause** A clause permitting a corporation to engage in discussions with and provide information to other bidders only if the board has concluded, based on the written opinion of outside legal counsel, that engaging in discussions or providing information was required to prevent the board from breaching its fiduciary duties to its stockholders.

**note purchase agreement** The title of a loan agreement when the lender is an insurance company.

**novation** The method of contract modification by which the original contract is canceled and a new one is written with perhaps only one change, such as substitution of a new party.

**novel** An invention is novel if it was not anticipated; i.e., if it was not previously known or used by others in the United States and was not previously patented or described in a printed publication in any country.

**nuisance** A thing or activity that unreasonably and substantially interferes with an owner's use and enjoyment of owner's property.

## O

**obvious risk** If the use of a product carries an obvious risk, the manufacturer will not be held liable for injuries that result from ignoring the risk.

**offer (contracts)** A proposal to enter into a contract. Proposal may be verbal, written, or implied by action.

**offer (securities)** Every attempt or offer to dispose of, or solicitation of an offer to buy, a security or interest in a security, for value.

**offeree** A person to whom an offer is made.

**offering circular** Also known as a private placement memorandum, this circular is the private offering counterpart to the prospectus and is both a selling document and a disclosure document.

**offeror** A person making an offer.

**offshore transaction** A security transaction in which no offer is made to a person in the United States and either (1) at the time the buy order is originated, the buyer is outside the United States; or (2) the transaction is one executed in, on, or through the facilities of a designated offshore securities market.

**ombudsperson** A person who hears complaints, engages in fact finding, and generally promotes dispute resolution through information methods such as counseling or mediation.

**omission (Rule 10b–5)** A company or its managers fail to tell the whole truth about a fact to the investing public, and what the company does say makes it likely that reasonable investors will take away an impression contrary to the true facts.

**one-form-of-action laws** *See* Antideficiency Laws.

**open-end credit** Credit in which the creditor makes repeated extensions of credit (for example, Visa or MasterCard).

**open listing** A real estate listing in which the broker receives a commission only if he or she procures a ready, willing, and able buyer.

**operating agreement** A contract that sets forth the rights, obligations, and powers of the owners, managers, and officers of a limited liability company.

**operating lease** Typically a short-term lease that does not appear on the balance sheet.

**oppression** An inequality of bargaining power that results in no real negotiation and an absence of meaningful choice for one party to the contract.

**option contract** A contract in which the offeror promises to hold an offer open for a certain amount of time.

**optionee** The recipient of a stock option.

**order for relief** The filing of a bankruptcy petition constitutes an order for relief. If the debtor challenges an involuntary petition for bankruptcy, a trial is held to determine whether an order for relief should be granted.

**ordinary comparative negligence** In an ordinary comparative negligence jurisdiction, the plaintiff may recover only if it is less culpable than the defendant.

**organizational strike** An unlawful strike whose purpose is to organize employees.

**original jurisdiction** The power of the U.S. Supreme Court to take cognizance of a case at its inception, try it, and pass judgment upon the law and facts. Distinguished from appellate jurisdiction.

**out clause** A provision that would allow the lessor or lessee to cancel the lease without completing the full term or paying the complete value of the lease.

**output contract** A contract under which a buyer promises to buy all the products that the seller produces.

**outside director** A member of a board who is not also an officer.

**outside sales employee** An employee that has the primary duty of either making sales or obtaining orders or contracts for services or for the use of facilities and who is customarily and regularly engaged away from the employer's place of business in performing such duty.

**over-the-counter** A drug for which a prescription is not required.

**override** The ability of Congress to annul a president's veto by a two-thirds vote of both the House of Representatives and the Senate.

## P

***parens patriae* (parent of the country) action** Antitrust suits brought by state attorneys general for injuries sustained by residents of their respective states.

**parol evidence rule** If there is a written contract that the parties intended would encompass their entire agreement, oral evidence of prior or contemporaneous statements will not be permitted to vary or alter the terms of the contract.

**partial summary judgment** A summary judgment granted on some issues of a case while other issues proceed to trial.

**participation in a breach of fudiciary duty** A tort committed when the defendant induces another party to breach its fiduciary duty to the plaintiff.

**participation loan** A loan in which the original lender sells shares to other parties, called participants.

**pass-through entity** A business organization that is not a separate taxpayer; all its income and losses are passed through and taxed to its owner. S Corporations, partnerships, and limited liability companies are pass-through entities.

**passive investor** An investor in a business who does not materially participate in that business.

**passive-loss limitation** The rule enacted by the Tax Reform Act of 1986 under which only owners who materially participate in a business may deduct losses against their other ordinary income.

**patent** A government-granted right to exclude others for a stated period of time (usually 20 years) from making, using, or selling within the government's jurisdiction an invention that is the subject of the patent.

**patent misuse** In a patent dispute, a defense asserting that although the defendant has infringed a valid patent, the patent holder has abused its patent rights and therefore has lost, at least temporarily, its right to enforce them.

**pattern** An involvement in racketeering activity demonstrated by at least two predicate acts occurring within a ten-year period.

**payoff table** A diagram that illustrates the results the possible outcomes of various choices in game theory.

**penumbra** The peripheral rights that are implied by the specifically enumerated rights in the Bill of Rights.

***per se* analysis** A form of antitrust analysis that condemns practices that are completely void of redeeming competitive rationales.

**percentage rent clause** A clause frequently contained in retail leases that requires the tenant to pay, in addition to a base monthly rent, a percentage of its gross sales to the landlord.

**perfect tender rule** A Uniform Commercial Code rule that gives the buyer an absolute right to reject any goods not meeting all the contract requirements, including time of delivery.

**perfecting (under the UCC)** In connection with security interests, perfection refers to making the security interest valid as against other creditors of the debtor.

**perjury** An act by a person who takes an oath to tell the truth yet willingly and contrary to such oath states a material matter that he or she does not believe to be true.

**permanent loan** Usually a long-term loan used to acquire property that is repaid over five, ten, or sometimes up to twenty years.

**person (under environmental law)** A party who has contributed to imminent and substantial endangerment to human health or the environment and therefore is required in a civil action to take remedial action. Person in this sense includes companies, individual employees, and officers, as well as shareholders if state law would mandate piercing the corporate veil.

**personal jurisdiction** The power of state court to hear (decide) a civil case based upon residence or location of activities of the person being sued.

**persuasive decision** A well-reasoned court decision that another court, not bound by the first decision, would, when confronted with a similar dispute, probably follow.

**petitioner** The person who is appealing a judgment or seeking a writ of certiorari. Also called appellant.

**phantom stock** Promise to pay a bonus in the form of the equivalent of the value of company shares or the increase in value of the company shares over a period of time.

**phishing** Process by which individuals attempt to obtain personal information, including credit card numbers, using fake e-mails or websites that appear to come from a legitimate company.

**pierce the corporate veil** When a court denies limited liability to a corporation and holds shareholders personally responsible for claims against the corporation, the court has pierced the corporate veil.

**piggyback rights** An investor's right to request registration of that investor's shares in a public offering initiated by the company.

**placement agent** A broker-dealer who distributes the private placement memorandum to suitable persons and assists in private placement of securities.

**plaintiff** A person who brings an action; the party who complains or sues in a civil action and is so named on the record. The prosecution in a criminal case (i.e., the state or the United States in a federal case).

**planned unit development (PUD)** The land use regulations for a given piece of property that reflect the proposed development plans for that property. PUD allows for mixture of uses for property not possible under traditional zoning regulations.

**plant patent** A patent issued for new strains of asexually reproducing plants.

**plea** The response by a defendant in criminal case of guilty, not guilty, or nolo contendere.

**plea bargaining** The process by which the prosecutor agrees to reduce the charges in exchange for a guilty plea from the accused.

**pleadings** The formal allegations by the parties to a lawsuit of their respective claims and defenses.

**pledge** A type of security interest whereby the creditor or secured party takes possession of the collateral owned by the debtor.

**plenary** Complete, sufficient, unqualified.

**points** A one-time charge to a borrower buying real property (in addition to interest) computed by a lender by multiplying the amount funded by a fixed percentage.

**poison pill** A plan that would make any takeover of a corporation prohibitively expensive. Also called shareholder rights plan.

**police power** The general power granted state and city governments to protect the health, safety, welfare, or morals of its residents.

**political question** A conflict that should be decided by one of the political branches of government or by the electorate. A court will refuse to decide questions of a purely political character.

**political union** A union that represents the complete political and economic integration of the member states.

**posthearing** The final phase of arbitration in which the arbitrator renders his or her award after considering all the evidence presented in the prehearing and the hearing.

**potentially responsible parties (PRPs)** Parties potentially responsible for damages that include the present owner or operator of a facility, the owner or operator at the time of disposal of a hazardous substance, any person who arranged for treatment or disposal of hazardous substances at a facility, and any person who transported hazardous substances to or selected the facility.

**power of attorney** A written instrument that authorizes a person, called an attorney-in-fact (who need not be a lawyer), to sign documents or perform certain specific acts on behalf of another person.

**prayer** The request for relief in a complaint.

**precedents** General rules that are to be used as guidelines for similar cases in the future.

**precontractual liability** The claims by the disappointed party if contract negotiations fail before a contract has been finalized.

**predatory pricing** The act of pricing below the producer's actual cost with the intent of driving other competitors out of the market, thus enabling the person engaging in predatory pricing to raise prices later.

**preempt** A federal law takes precedence when state law conflicts with federal law.

**preemption defense (product liability)** The immunity granted manufacturers if they meet minimum standards of conduct under certain regulatory schemes.

**preferences** Transfers to (or for the benefit of) creditors on account of antecedent debts that are made from an insolvent debtor's property within ninety days before bankruptcy (one year if creditor is insider) and that enable the creditors to receive more than they would through a Chapter 7 liquidation.

**preferred return** The legal right to have distributions made to the person entitled to a preferred return before any distributions are made to any other equity holder.

**preferred stock** Stock that has priority over common stock in the payment of dividends (and in the distribution of assets if the corporation is dissolved).

**prehearing** The first stage in arbitration in which parties may submit trial-like briefs, supporting documents, and other written statements making their case.

**prejudgment interest** The interest on the amount of an award from the date of the injury to the date of judgment.

**preliminary hearing** A hearing in which the prosecutor presents evidence demonstrating probable cause that the defendant committed the crime.

**premises liability** A theory under which a building owner may be found liable for violating its general duty to manage the premises and warn of dangers, such as asbestos.

**prenegotiated bankruptcy** In a prenegotiated bankruptcy, the debtor files its Chapter 11 bankruptcy petition as soon as it can after it has reached agreement on the terms of the restructuring with its key creditors, but votes on the plan are not solicited until after the bankruptcy case is filed.

**prenuptial agreement** An agreement entered into before marriage that sets forth the manner in which the parties' assets will be distributed and the support to which each party will be entitled, in the event the parties get divorced.

**prepackaged bankruptcy** A workout plan approved by key creditors and the debtor before the debtor files bankruptcy; it becomes the plan of reorganization in a Chapter 11 bankruptcy.

**prepayment penalty** A clause whereby a lender imposes a penalty if the loan is paid off early.

**preponderance of the evidence** The evidence offered in a civil trial that is more convincing than the evidence presented in opposition to it.

**price amendment** Information concerning the price of securities and underwriting arrangement filed with the Securities and Exchange Commission once the registration statement has been informally cleared by the SEC staff, or the registrant receives notice that the registration statement will not be reviewed.

**price antidilution** A provision that prevents a corporation from diluting a shareholder's interests by simply issuing shares of common stock at a price below the conversion price.

**price discrimination** Sellers charge different prices to purchasers in interstate sales for commodities of like grade and quality.

**price fixing** The cooperative setting of price levels or ranges by competing firms.

***prima facie* (on its face)** A fact considered true until evidence is produced to the contrary.

**primary debtor** The person with an obligation for which the guarantor becomes liable.

**prime rate** The lowest rate of interest publicly offered by major lending institutions to their most creditworthy customers. Better practice dictates using the terms "base rate" or "reference rate" because sometimes lenders offer a loan below prime.

**priming lien** A lien that is senior to a previously granted security interest.

**principal** A person who delegates a portion of his or her tasks to another person who represents the principal as an agent.

**principal (of a loan)** The amount borrowed.

**prior art** Developments or pre-existing art that relates to a claimed invention.

**prior restraints** Prohibitions barring speech before it occurs.

**privalization** The transfer of property ownership from a nation to a private entity.

**private international law** Law that governs the relationships between private parties engaged in transactions across national borders.

**private law** The area of the law in which the sole function of government is recognition and enforcement of private rights, e.g., civil and commercial codes.

**private nuisance** Interference with a person's use and enjoyment of his or her land and water.

**private offering** An offering to selected individuals or entities who have the ability to evaluate and bear the risk of the investment; that is, they have the ability to fend for themselves. Also called private placement.

**private placement** *See* Private offering.

**private-placement memorandum** A booklet offered by entrepreneurs seeking financing from private individual investors that furnishes information about themselves and their enterprise.

**privately held corporation** A corporation whose shares are not bought and sold among the general public.

**Privileges and Immunities Clause** A clause in the Fourteen Amendment that provides that no state "shall make or enforce any law which shall abridge the privileges or immunities of citizens of the United States."

**privity of contract** The relationship which exists between the parties to a contract.

**probable cause** As applied to an arrest or a search warrant, a reasonable belief that the suspect has committed a crime or is about to commit a crime. Mere suspicion or belief, unsupported by facts or circumstances, is insufficient.

**procedural due process** The parties whose rights are to be affected are entitled to be heard and, in order that they may enjoy that right, they must be notified before adverse action is taken.

**procedural obligations** The rules that define the manner in which rights and duties are enforced.

**processing operation** In a compensation trade arrangement, a processing operation refers to the foreign party supplying the materials that are processed by the local party using the foreign party's equipment.

**product** A tangible item, as opposed to a service.

**product liability** The liability of a manufacturer or seller of a product that because of a defect, causes injury to a purchaser, user, or bystander.

**product market** A product or service offering made by different manufacturers or sellers that are economically interchangeable and may therefore be said to compete.

**professional corporation** An organization of professionals (such as doctors, lawyers, or architects) authorized by state law to act as a legal entity distinct from its owners.

**professional employee** An employee who holds a position requiring advanced knowledge in a field of science or learning customarily acquired by a prolonged course of specialized intellectual instruction and study.

**promisee** In contract law, the promisee is the person to whom the promise (contract) was made.

**promisor** In contract law, the promisor is the person who made the promise.

**promissory estoppel** A promise that the promisor should reasonably expect to induce action or forbearance on the part of the promisee or a third person and that does induce such action or forbearance can create liability for reliance damages if injustice can be avoided only by providing some relief when promise is broken.

**promissory fraud** A type of fraud that occurs when one party induces another to enter into a contract by promising to do something without having the intention to carry out the promise.

**proof of claim** A claim filed by creditors on uncontingent and undisputed debt.

**prospectus** Any document that is designed to produce orders for a security, whether or not the document purports on its face to offer the security for sale or otherwise to dispose of it for value. The descriptive document that an issuer of securities provides to prospective purchasers.

**protected computer** A computer used in interstate or foreign commerce.

**protected expression** The part of a work that is subject to copyright protection.

**proximate cause** A reasonably foreseeable consequence of the defendant's negligence, without which no injury would have occurred.

**proxy** A written authorization by a shareholder to another person to vote on the shareholder's behalf.

**proxy contest** A battle for corporate control whereby someone wishing to replace the board with its own candidates seeks to acquire a sufficient number of shareholder votes to do so.

**public disclosure of private facts** The publication of a private fact that is not newsworthy. The matter must be private, such that a reasonable person would find publication objectionable. Unlike in a defamation case, truth is not a defense.

**public figures** Individuals, who, by reason of their achievements or the vigor and success with which they seek the public's attention, are injected into the public eye.

**public international law** Law that governs the relationships between and the interactions of nations.

**public law** The area of the law that focuses on effectuation of the public interest by state action, e.g., constitutional law, administrative law and criminal law.

**public nuisance** Unreasonable and substantial interference with the public health, safety, peace, comfort, convenience, or utilization of land.

**public policy exception** An exception to the general employment at will doctrine that prohibits an employer from discharging an employee for a reason that violates public policy.

**publication** Communication to a third party.

**publicly held corporation** A corporation whose shares are traded on one of the national stock exchanges or the over-the-counter market.

**publicly owned sewage treatment works (POTWs)** General and specific industry pretreatment standards are set for discharges to publicly owned sewage treatment works (POTWs).

**puffing** The expression of opinion by a seller regarding goods; not a warranty.

**pump and dump** A term used to refer to situations where executives fraudulently manipulate their company's earnings in an attempt to keep stock prices high while they exercise their options and sell their stock at inflated prices.

**punitive damages** Damages awarded to a plaintiff over and above what will fairly compensate it for its loss. They are intended to punish the defendant and deter others from engaging in similar conduct. Also called exemplary damages.

**purchase-money security interest** A security interest created when a seller lends the buyer the money to buy the seller's goods.

**pure comparative negligence** A tort system in which the plaintiff may recover for the part of the injury due to the defendant's negligence, even if the plaintiff was the more negligent party.

**pure notice statutes** Under these statutes, a person who has notice that someone else has already bought the real property cannot validate his or her deed by recording it first.

**pyramid selling** A scheme whereby a consumer is recruited as a product "distributor" and receives commissions based on the products he or she sells and on the recruitment of additional sellers.

## Q

**qualified institutional buyer** Institutional investors holding and managing $100 million or more of securities.

**qualified privilege** In defamation cases, the right by a defendant to make statements to (1) protect one's own personal interests; (2) protect business interests, such as statements to a prospective employer; or (3) provide information for the public interest, such as credit reports.

***quantum meruit*** A basis for equitable relief by a court when there was no contract between the parties, but one party has received a benefit for which it has not paid.

**quash** To declare invalid.

**quasi-foreign corporation** A corporation incorporated outside of California but with more than 50 percent of its stock owned by California residents and with more than 50 percent of its sales, payroll, and property tax derived from activities in California.

***qui tam* plaintiff** A plaintiff suing on the government's behalf, often entitled to a share of the amount recovered.

**"quick look" rule of reason** The "quick look" rule of reason is used whenever the practice has obvious anticompetitive effects but is not illegal per se; it allows for immediate inquiry into procompetitive justifications.

***quid-pro-quo* (this for that) harassment** The specific, job-related adverse action, such as denial of a promotion, in retaliation for a worker's refusal to respond to a supervisor's sexual advances.

**quiet period** The time between filing of securities registration statement and the date the registration statement becomes effective. Also called the waiting period.

**quitclaim deed** A deed that contains no warranties; the grantor conveys only any right, title, and interest held by the grantor, if any, at the time of execution.

**quorum** The holders of more than 50 percent of the outstanding shares of a corporation.

**quotas** Tariffs and quantitative limitations that place restrictions on imports.

## R

**race norming of employment tests** A device designed to ensure that a minimum number of minorities and women are in an application pool by adjusting the scores or using different cutoff scores for employment related tests on the basis of race, color, religion, sex, or national origin.

**race statutes** Under these statutes, recording is a race—the rule is "first in time is first in right." The first to record a deed has superior rights, regardless of whether he or she knew that someone else had already bought or claimed an interest in the real property.

**race–notice statutes** These statutes protect only a good faith subsequent purchaser who recorded its deed before the prior purchaser recorded its deed.

**racketeering activity** The state and federal offenses involving a pattern of illegal acts, including mail and wire fraud.

**raider** In a hostile takeover, a third party who seeks to obtain control of a corporation, called the target, over the objections of its management.

**ratification** A principal affirms through words or actions a prior act of an agent that did not bind the principal.

**rational basis test** A test under which a discriminatory classification will be held valid if there is any conceivable basis upon which the classification might relate to a legitimate governmental interest; applies to all classifications that relate to matters of economics or social welfare.

**Rawlsian moral theory** A deontological line of thought that aims to maximize the utility of the worst off person in society.

**reaffirmation agreement** A contract with a creditor whereby an individual who has filed bankruptcy under Chapter 7 agrees to repay a debt even though the debt would otherwise be discharged in the debtor's bankruptcy case.

**real estate investment trust (REIT)** A tax-advantaged pool of real property.

**reasonable care under the circumstances** A standard requiring landowners to act in a reasonable manner with respect to entrants on their land, with liability hinging on the foreseeability of harm.

**recklessness** In the criminal context, conscious disregard of a substantial risk that an individual's actions would result in the harm prohibited by a statute.

**recognitional strike** An unlawful strike whose purpose is to force an employer to recognize the union as the collective bargaining agent for certain of its employees.

**recognized hazard** Under the Occupational Safety and Health Act, a workplace condition that is obviously dangerous or is regarded by an employer or other employers in the industry as dangerous.

**record** The oral and written evidence presented at an administrative hearing.

**recordable form** The requirements established by the state regarding how title to real estate is filed and recorded. Requirements generally include legibility and notarization.

**recording statutes** Statutes that establish an orderly process by which claims to interests in real property can be recorded as part of the public record and resolved.

**red-herring prospectus** Preliminary prospectus; incomplete version of the final prospectus.

**redemption** The buying back of shares by a corporation from a shareholder.

**reference rate** The lowest rate of interest publicly offered by major lending institutions to their most creditworthy customers.

**referral sale** The seller offers the buyer a commission, rebate, or discount for furnishing the seller with a list of additional prospective customers.

**registered mask work** Highly detailed transparencies that represent the topological layout of semiconductor chips.

**registration rights** An investor's right to require a company to register under applicable federal and state securities laws the shares of common stock into which the preferred stock is convertible.

**registration statement** The registration statement consists of filing forms and the prospectus, the disclosure document that an issuer of securities provides to prospective purchasers.

**Regulation A** A regulation whereby $5 million of securities can be offered and sold in a twelve-month period, of which up to $1.5 million may be sold by the selling security holders.

**Regulation D** A regulation adopted by the SEC in 1982 that offers a safe harbor for those seeking exemption from registration: An issuer that fails to comply with all of the requirements of the applicable rule will not necessarily have no exemption because the transaction may still meet the more general conditions of Section 4(2).

**Regulation FD (Fair Disclosure)** A regulation that provides that whenever an issuer, or a person acting on its behalf, discloses material nonpublic information to securities market professionals or holders of the issuer's securities who may well trade on the basis of the information, the issuer must publicly disclose that same information simultaneously or promptly.

**Regulation S** A regulation that has clarified the general rule that any offer or sale outside the United States is not subject to the federal registration requirements.

**Regulation Z** Regulations issued by the Federal Reserve Board to interpret and enforce the federal Truth-in-Lending Act.

**regulations** The rules of order prescribed by superior or competent authority relating to action of those under its control.

**regulatory negotiations (reg-neg)** A style of administrative rulemaking in which representatives of major groups convene with an administrative agency and work out a compromise through negotiation on the substance of new regulations.

**regulatory taking** The taking by the government of private real property for a public use; requires payment of just compensation.

**reliance damages** The awards made to a plaintiff for any expenditures made in reliance on a contract that was subsequently breached.

**remand** The power of a court of appeal to send a case back to a lower court for reconsideration.

**remedial promise** As defined in the 2003 amendments to Article 2 of the Uniform Commercial Code, a promise by the seller to repair or replace the goods or to refund all or part of the price of the goods upon the happening of a specified event.

**remote purchaser** As defined in the 2003 amendments to Article 2 of the Uniform Commercial Code, "a person that buys or leases goods from an immediate buyer or other person in the normal chain of distribution."

**remote tippee** Recipient of a tip from another tippee other than the original tippee.

**repatriation** A constraint on foreign ownership to restrict the profits that can be returned by a multinational company to its home country.

**reporter** The published volumes of case decisions by a particular court or group of courts.

**reporting company** A company registered under Section 12 of the Securities Exchange Act of 1934 that subjects issuers to various reporting requirements and to certain rules and regulations concerning proxies, tender offers, and insider trading.

**representation election** An election among employees to decide whether they want a union to represent them for collective bargaining.

**requests for production of documents** Requests for documents such as medical records and personal files to be produced as part of the discovery process before a trial.

**requirements contract** A contract under which the buyer agrees to buy all of a specified commodity the buyer needs from the seller and the seller agrees to provide that amount.

***res ipsa loquitur* (the thing speaks for itself)** The doctrine that allows a plaintiff to prove breach and causation indirectly.

**resale price maintenance (RPM)** An agreement on minimum price between firms at different levels of production or distribution that violates antitrust law.

**rescind** Void or make ineffective.

**reservation price** That price at which one is indifferent between the success and failure of the negotiation.

***respondeat superior* (let the master answer)** The doctrine under which an employer may be held vicariously or secondarily liable for the negligent or intentional conduct of the employee that is committed in the scope of the employee's employment.

**respondent** The party in a case against whom an appeal is taken; the party who has an interest adverse to setting aside or reversing the judgment.

**responsible corporate officer doctrine** A criminal law doctrine that, under certain circumstances, imposes vicarious liability on an officer responsible for compliance based on the actions of subordinates.

**responsible persons** The responsible persons from whom the Environmental Protection Agency can recover the costs of remedial work include (1) the present owner or operator of the facility; (2) the owner or operator at the time of disposal of the hazardous substance; (3) any person who arranged for treatment or disposal of hazardous substances at the facility; and (4) any person who transported hazardous substances to and selected the facility.

**restatement** Former common law rules in a particular subject area (e.g., contracts, torts) integrated into formal collections that a judge or legislature is free to adopt.

**restitution** An award made to a plaintiff of a benefit improperly obtained by the defendant.

**restricted guaranty** A guaranty in which the guarantor's liability is enforceable only with respect to a specified transaction or series of transactions.

**restricted securities** Securities issued in a private placement; they cannot be resold or transferred unless they are either registered or exempt from registration. The most common exemption is pursuant to Securities and Exchange Commission Rule 144.

**restricted stock** A conditional grant of shares of a company's stock, with vesting contingent upon continued employment for a specified period of time.

**retributive justice** A theory that states that every crime demands payment in the form of punishment.

**reversibility** An ethical theory that looks to whether one would want a rule applied to one's self.

**revival statutes** State and federal statutes that allow plaintiffs to file lawsuits that have been barred by the running of the statute of limitations.

***Revlon* mode** A company is said to be in *Revlon* mode when a change of control or breakup of the company has become inevitable.

**revoke** To annul an offer by recission.

**revolving line of credit** A line of credit that allows a borrower to borrow whatever sums it requires up to a specified maximum amount and reborrow amounts it has repaid.

**revolving loan** A loan that allows a borrower to borrow whatever sums it requires up to a specified maximum amount and to reborrow amounts it has repaid.

**Riba** A tenet of Islamic trade and commerce that prohibits unearned or unjustified (illicit) profits and can therefore lead to problems in the area of interest on loans.

**right of first negotiation** Gives the holder the right to negotiate the purchase of the property before the seller enters negotiations with another party.

**right of first refusal** A contract that provides the holder with the right to purchase property on the same terms and conditions offered by or to a third party.

**right of redemption** Gives the mortgagor and certain other categories of interested persons the right to redeem or get back foreclosed property within a statutorily limited period.

**right of rescission** A right to cancel a contract.

**right of setoff** Permits Party A to deduct automatically from payments due Party B amounts that are due from Party B to Party A.

**ripeness** A court will not hear agency cases if they are not ripe for decision, for example, after a rule is adopted but before the agency seeks to apply it to a particular case.

**roadshow** Oral presentations to large institutional investors in key cities in the United States, Europe, and Asia.

**rule of impossibility** The rule under which claims of predation are rejected because the marketplace in question cannot be successfully monopolized.

**rule of reason** The rule that takes into account a defendant's actions as well as the structure of the market to determine whether an activity promotes or restrains competition.

**Rule 144** Adopted by the SEC in 1972, it is meant to reduce the uncertainty associated with the definition of the term "underwriter" and to allow restricted securities to be sold publicly without registration if the Rule's requirements are met.

**rules** The regulatory enactments that serve as general principles and guidelines for sensitive issues not governed by law.

## S

**S–1 review** A review by the auditor of events subsequent to the date of the certified balance sheet in the registration statement to ascertain whether any material change has occurred in the company's financial position that should be disclosed to prevent the balance sheet figures from being misleading.

**S Corporation** A corporation meeting certain requirements that is taxed only at the owner level.

**sale (1933 Act)** Every contract of sale or disposition of a security or interest in a security, for value.

**sale and leaseback** A simultaneous two-step transaction, whereby an institutional lender purchases real property from a company, and the property is leased back to the company for its use.

**sale-of-business doctrine** A doctrine the U.S. Supreme Court rejected that held that compliance with federal securities laws was not necessary when 100 percent of the stock of a company was sold.

**salting** The practice of paying individuals to seek work with a nonunion employer with the intent of having them organize the other workers once hired.

**sanctions** Laws imposed by one country (or a group of countries) against the commerce of another country as an effort to influence that country's behavior, for example with regard to international law.

**satisfaction** *See* Accord and Satisfaction.

***scienter*** An intent to deceive.

**second-step back-end merger** The second step in a corporate takeover whereby the shareholders who did not tender their shares receive cash or securities in a subsequent merger.

**secondary boycott** A strike against an employer with whom a union has no quarrel in order to encourage it to stop doing business with an employer with whom it does have a dispute.

**secondary meaning** A descriptive trademark becomes protectable by acquiring secondary meaning, or sufficient consumer recognition through sufficient use and/or advertising of the goods under the mark.

**secondary offering** A securities offering by a person other than the issuer.

**Section 4(1½) exemption** An exemption for a private offering of securities by an affiliate that would qualify as a private placement under Section 4(2) of the Securities Act of 1933 if made by the issuer.

**Section 201** Provides for temporary relief to U.S. industries seriously injured by increasing imports, regardless of whether unfair practices are involved. It is sometimes called the fair trade law.

**Section 232** Provides for relief from imports threatening to impair U.S. national security.

**Section 301** Authorizes the U.S. Trade Representative to investigate alleged unfair practices of foreign governments that impede U.S. exports of both goods and services.

**Section 337** Provides that if a U.S. industry is injured (or there is a restraint or monopolization of trade in the United States) by reason of unfair acts in the importation of articles into the United States, an order must be issued requiring the exporters and importers to cease the unfair acts or, if necessary, excluding imports of the offending articles from all sources.

**Section 406** Provides for import relief if a U.S. industry is suffering material injury by reason of rapidly increasing imports from a communist country.

**secured loan** A loan backed up by collateral.

**secured party** The lender, seller, or other person in whose favor there is a security interest.

**secured transaction** A loan or other transaction secured by collateral put up by the borrower.

**security** Any note, stock, treasury stock, bond, debenture, evidence of indebtedness, certificate of interest or participation in any profit-sharing agreement, collateral trust certificate, pre-organization certificate or subscription, transferable share, investment contract, voting-trust certificate, certificate of deposit for a security, fractional undivided interest in oil, gas, or other mineral rights; any put, call, straddle, option, or privilege on any security, certificate of deposit, or group or index of securities (including any interest therein or based on the value thereof); or any put, call, straddle, option, or privilege entered into on a national securities exchange relating to foreign currency; or, in general, any interest or instrument commonly known as a "security," or any certificate of interest or participation in, temporary or interim certificate for, receipt for, guarantee, of, or warrant or right to subscribe to or purchase, any of the foregoing.

**security agreement** An agreement that creates or provides for a security interest.

**security interest** Any interest in personal property, fixtures or letters of credit and accounts that is used as collateral to secure payment or the performance of an obligation.

**selective disclosure** A practice whereby issuers of publicly traded securities disclose material nonpublic information, such as advance warnings of earnings results, to securities analysts or selected institutional investors before making full disclosure of the same information to the general public.

**self-financing** Generating capital by carefully managing a company's own funds.

**self-publication** A doctrine giving an employee a claim for defamation when the employer makes a false assertion in firing an employee, which the employer could reasonably expect the employee to repeat to a prospective employer.

**self-tender** An offer by a corporation to buy back its stock or shareholder rights for a fair price.

**selling securities short** The sale of securities the seller does not own.

**senior debt** Indebtedness that benefits from a debt subordination agreement.

**separate property** Property that belongs solely to the spouse who acquired it before marriage or received it by gift or inheritance.

**separation of powers** The distinct authority of governance granted the three branches of U.S. government (executive, legislative, and judicial) by the U.S. Constitution.

**sequestration order** A governmental order that requires spending levels to be reduced below the levels provided in the budget.

**service of process** Notifying a defendant of a claim.

**service mark** A legally protected identifying mark connected with services.

**settle** When parties to a lawsuit go over claims and ascertain and agree on the balance due one another prior to taking case to trial, they have settled the lawsuit.

**severability** The ability to separate a clause or provision in a contract from the remainder of the contract.

**shareholder** A holder of equity securities of a corporation. Also called stockholder.

**shareholder derivative suit** A lawsuit brought against directors or officers of a corporation by a shareholder on behalf of the corporation.

**shareholder of record** The persons whose names appear on a corporation's shareholder list on a specified date who are entitled to vote.

**shareholder primacy** Maximization of shareholder wealth, not legally mandated.

**shareholder rights plan** *See* Poison Pill.

**Sharia** The traditional Islamic rules and body of laws that regulate Muslim life.

**shelf registration** The registration of a number of securities at one time for issuance later.

**short-swing trading** The purchase and sale or sale and purchase by an officer, director, or greater-than-10 percent shareholders of securities of a public company within a six-month period.

**show-how** Nonsecret information used to teach someone how to make or do something; generally not legally protectable.

**shrink-wrap license** A license that customers cannot read when they purchase software but are deemed to have accepted when they open the wrapping around the envelope containing the discs.

**6 & 1 repricing** Occurs when a company cancels underwater stock options and waits at least six months and one day to issue new stock options at the then-current market price. Also referred to as a slow-motion swap.

**slander** A spoken communication to a third party by a defendant of an untrue statement of fact that injures a plaintiff's reputation.

**slander *per se*** Words that are slanderous in and of themselves. Only statements that a person has committed a serious crime, has a loathsome disease, is guilty of sexual misconduct, or is not fit to conduct business are slanderous *per se*.

**slow-motion swap** Occurs when a company cancels underwater stock options and waits at least six months and one day to issue new stock options at the then-current market price. Also referred to as a 6 & 1 repricing.

**small business issuers** Companies with revenues less than $25 million whose market value of publicly held securities (other than those held by affiliates) is less than $25 million.

**sole proprietorship** One person owns all the assets of the business, has complete control of the business, and is solely liable for all the debts of the business.

**solicitor** A type of lawyer in the British system who is allowed to perform legal services outside the court.

**sovereign acts doctrine** The government cannot be held liable for breach of contract due to legislative or executive acts of general application.

**sovereign immunity** The doctrine that prevents the courts of one country from hearing a suit against the government of another country.

**spam** Unsolicited e-mails.

**Special 301 Provisions** Provisions in U.S. trade law under which the U.S. Trade Representative identifies countries that deny adequate and effective protection for intellectual property rights or deny fair and equitable market access for persons who rely on intellectual property protection.

**special plan** *See* Specific Plan.

**specific performance** A court order to a breaching party to complete the contract as promised.

**specific plan** A planning document in addition to a general plan that usually encompasses just a portion of a city's geographic area; typically more detailed than the general plan.

**specifications** The description of an invention in a patent application in its best mode and the manner and process of making and using the invention so that a person skilled in the relevant field may make and use the invention.

**spinning** The practice whereby underwriters would distribute IPO shares to a corporate executive in exchange for the investment banking business of the executive's corporation.

**spoliation inference** Inference, as instructed to a jury, that missing or altered evidence should be presumed to have been unfavorable to the party causing its destruction or loss.

**sprawl** A condition that results from unchecked development; contributes to the decline of cities and inner suburbs as more people move away from the cities where they work.

**spread** (1) A margin which is added to the cost that a bank incurs to obtain, for a given period of time, the funds it will lend, in order to arrive at the actual interest rate for a loan. (2) The difference between the strike price of a stock option and the fair market value of the stock at the time the optionee exercises the option.

**spyware** Small computer software programs that are automatically inserted on the hard drive of a user's computer when the Internet is accessed.

**squatter's rights** *See* Adverse Possession.

**staggered board** A board on which directors serve for specified terms, usually three years, with only a fraction of them up for reelection at any one time. Also called classified board.

**standby letter of credit** A method of securing a party's performance, whereby an issuing bank undertakes to pay a sum of money to the person (the beneficiary) to which performance is due on presentation of certain documents specified in the letter of credit, usually a brief statement (in language agreed on by the two parties) that the other party is in default and the beneficiary is entitled to payment from the issuing bank.

**standing** A party to a lawsuit has standing if the person seeking relief is the proper party to advance the litigation, has a personal interest in the outcome of the suit, and will benefit from a favorable ruling.

**standstill agreement** An agreement whereby the shareholder agrees not to commence a tender offer or proxy contest or to buy additional shares of the issuer for a period of time, often ten years.

***stare decisis* (to abide by)** The doctrine that holds that once a court resolves a particular issue, other courts addressing a similar legal problem generally follow the initial court's decision.

**state implementation plans (SIPs)** The prescribed emission control measures for stationary sources existing prior to 1970 and on the use of motor vehicles as necessary to achieve national ambient air quality standards.

**state-of-the-art defense** A defense against claims based on a manufacturer's compliance with the best available technology (that may or may not be synonymous with the custom and practice of the industry).

**statute of frauds** A statute that requires that certain contracts, such as contracts conveying an interest in real property, must be in a signed writing to be enforceable in a court.

**statute of limitations** A time limit, defined by the statute, within which a lawsuit must be brought.

**statute of repose** A time limit that cuts off the right to assert a cause of action after a specified period of time from the date the product is sold.

**statutory bar** An inventor is denied patent protection in the event that prior to one year before the inventor's filing, the invention was (1) patented; (2) publicly used or sold in the United States; or (3) described in a printed publication in the United States or a foreign country.

**statutory law** Law that is based on statutes, not on existing common law rules.

**stock appreciation right (SAR)** A contractual right to receive an amount equal to the appreciation in stock price that occurs between the date the SAR is granted and the date of exercise. Payments of appreciation may be in the form of cash, stock, or both.

**stock lock-up option** A lock-up option relating to stock of the target company.

**stock option** A contract that allows an individual to buy a certain number of shares of a company's stock at a certain price (typically the fair market value of the stock at the time the option is granted) within a certain timeframe (typically five to ten years), but ending upon termination of employment.

**stock parking** The temporary sale of shares to another entity or individual to avoid tax reporting requirements or the net margin requirements of the securities laws applicable to brokerage firms.

**stockholder** A holder of equity securities of a corporation. Also called shareholder.

**straight bankruptcy** A Chapter 7 bankruptcy in which the trustee liquidates the estate and distributes the proceeds first to secured creditors (to the extent of their collateral) and then in a prescribed order, pro rata within each level.

**straight voting** A voting process whereby a shareholder can cast one vote for each share the shareholder owns for each nominee.

**strategic alliance** A source of financing by which a collaborative arrangement is entered into between an established company that has business needs or objectives complementary to another company.

**strategic environmental management** A concept that advocates placing environmental management on the profit side of the corporation rather than on the cost side.

**strict liability** Liability without fault. The concept that sellers are liable for all defective products. Also imposed for abnormally dangerous (or ultrahazardous) activities and toxic torts.

**strict scrutiny test** Under this test, a discriminatory classification will be held valid only if it is necessary to promote a compelling state interest and narrowly tailored; applies to classifications based on race or religion.

**strike price** The price (which is generally the market price of the stock at the time the stock option is granted) at which an optionee can exercise his or her stock option by purchasing the stock. Also referred to as the grant price.

**strong arm clause** The clause that grants a debtor in possession the rights of a hypothetical creditor who extended credit to the debtor at the time of bankruptcy and who, as a result, either obtained a judicial lien on all property in which the debtor has an interest or obtained an execution against the debtor that was returned unsatisfied.

**structural antidilution** A provision that adjusts the conversion ratio at which convertible preferred shares may be exchanged for shares of common stock, if the total number of shares of common stock is increased, for example, by a stock split.

**structural barriers** Barriers to negotiation that arise from the existing frameworks and institutions within which a manager operates.

**subdivision** A division of land into separate parcels for development purposes.

**subject matter jurisdiction** The specific types of cases enumerated under Article III of the U.S. Constitution to be decided by the Supreme Court and lower courts established by Congress.

**sublease** An act by a tenant of renting out all or a portion of property the tenant has rented from a landlord.

**subordinated debt instrument** The document providing that a holder's right to repayment is subordinate to that of other creditors of the debtor.

**subordination** Relegation to a lesser position, usually in respect to a right or security.

**subsequent remedial measures** A manufacturer's later fix of a dangerous condition or improvement of a design in a product that has been found to be inherently defective.

**substantial continuity test** A test that imposes successor liability when the purchaser of assets maintains the same business, with the same employees doing the same jobs, under the same supervisors, working conditions, and production process, and produces the same products for the same customers as the seller corporation. Also known as the continuity of enterprise approach.

**substantial evidence standard** Under this standard, the courts defer to an administrative agency's factual determinations in formal adjudications even if the record would support other factual conclusions.

**substantial risk of forfeiture** Stock is subject to a substantial risk of forfeiture if the recipient's right to full enjoyment of the stock is conditional upon the future performance of substantial service.

**substantially related test** A test under which a discriminatory classification will be held valid if it furthers a governmental interest that is "important" or "substantial" and it prevents real, not conjectural, harm "in a direct and material way"; applies to classifications such as gender and legitimacy of birth.

**substantive coercion** A threat that shareholders may agree to sell their shares in an otherwise noncoercive tender offer out of ignorance about the target company's true value.

**substantive due process** The constitutional guarantee that no person shall be arbitrarily deprived of life, liberty or property; the essence of substantive due process is protection from arbitrary and unreasonable action.

**substantive legal obligations** The legal rules that define the rights and duties of the agency and of persons dealing with it.

**successor liability** Individuals or entities who acquire an interest in a business or in real property may be held liable for personal injury and property or environmental damage resulting from acts (including sale of products) of the predecessor entity or previous owner.

**suggestive mark** A trademark that suggests something about a product without directly describing it.

**summary judgment** A procedural device available for disposition of a controversy without trial. A judge will grant summary judgment only if all of the written evidence before the court clearly establishes that there are no disputed issues of material fact and the party who requested the summary judgment is entitled to prevail as a matter of law.

**summary jury trial (SJT)** Parties to a dispute put their cases before a real jury, which renders a nonbinding decision.

**summons** The official notice to a defendant that a lawsuit is pending against the defendant in a particular court.

**Super 301** A provision of the Omnibus Trade Act of 1988 that required the U.S. Trade Representative to draw up a list of the foreign governments whose practices pose the most significant barriers to U.S. exports, and to immediately commence Section 301 investigations with respect to these practices.

**super discharge** After completing all payments in accordance with a Chapter 13 bankruptcy plan, the debtor obtains a Chapter 13 discharge (sometimes called a super discharge), which extinguishes otherwise nondischargeable debts (such as claims for fraud, theft, willful and malicious injury, or drunk driving), but not spousal or child support.

**superlien** An instrument that secures recovery of environmental cleanup response costs incurred by state agencies.

**supervening cause** An intervening cause that serves to separate an act of negligence from the resulting injury when it is (1) independent of the original act, (2) adequate to bring about the injury, and (3) not reasonably foreseeable.

**supervisor** Anyone possessing specified personnel functions if the exercise of that authority is not of a merely routine or clerical nature, but requires the use of independent judgment.

**suppress** To prevent the prosecution from introducing evidence.

**surprise** The extent to which the supposedly agreed on terms of the bargain are hidden in a densely printed form drafted by the party seeking to enforce the disputed terms.

**surviving corporation** In a merger of two corporations, the corporation that maintains its corporate existence is the surviving corporation.

**sustainable development** A theory that holds that future prosperity depends on preserving natural capital: air, water, and other ecological resources.

**syndicate** An underwriting group in a public offering; each member agrees to purchase a certain number of the securities of the issuer once the offering is declared effective by the Securities and Exchange Commission.

**syndicated loan** In a syndicated loan, the lenders enter into concurrent direct obligations with the borrower to make a loan, typically on a pro rata basis. The loan is coordinated by a lead lender that serves as agent for all the lenders in disbursing the funds, collecting payments of interest and principal, and administering and enforcing the loan.

**synthetic lease** A lease that is treated as a conventional operating lease for accounting purposes (so does not appear on the lessee's balance sheet) but is treated as if the lessee had purchased the property and obtained a loan from the seller for tax purposes.

## T

**take-out commitment** An agreement by a lender to replace the construction loan with a permanent loan, usually after certain conditions, such as the timely completion of the project, have been met.

**takeover** A bidder acquires sufficient stock from a corporation's shareholders to obtain control of the corporation.

**target corporation** A corporation that is the subject of a tender offer.

**tariff classification** The tariff on articles imported to the United States is determined by their description on the Harmonized Tariff Schedule.

**tariffs** The basic tool for limiting imports to protect domestic industries.

**tarnishment** Dilution of a famous trademark that occurs when use of the famous mark in connection with a particular category of goods or goods of an inferior quality reduces the positive image associated with the products bearing the famous mark.

**tax basis** The amount of cash or the fair market value of property exchanged for another asset, such as a general partnership interest.

**tax-deferred exchange** A transfer of real property for an alternative piece of real property meeting certain requirements.

**teleological theory** An ethical theory concerned with the consequences of something. The good of an action is to be judged by the effect of the action on others.

**temporary insiders** Outside attorneys, accountants, consultants, or investment bankers who are not directly employed by a corporation, but who acquire confidential information through performance of professional services.

**tenancy by the entirety** A special type of co-ownership of real property between husband and wife; like joint tenancy, it includes a right of survivorship.

**tenants in common** The individuals who own undivided interests in a parcel of real property.

**tender of delivery** Under Article 2 of the Uniform Commercial Code, when the seller notifies the buyer that it has the goods ready for delivery.

**tender offer** A public offer to all the shareholders of a corporation to buy their shares at a stated price, usually higher than the market price.

**term loan** A loan for a specified amount funded in a lump sum or in installments to be repaid on a specified maturity date or paid off over a period of time.

**term sheet** A letter that outlines the terms and conditions on which a lender will lend.

**termination** The point after the dissolution of a partnership when all the partnership affairs are wound up and partners' authority to act for the partnership is completely extinguished.

**termination fee** *See* Breakup Fee.

**territorial restrictions** Restrictions that prevent a dealer or distributor from selling outside a certain territory.

**territoriality** One of the two prevalent domestic models for addressing international insolvency problems, pursuant to which each nation conducts its own proceeding with respect to the assets located in its jurisdiction and ignores any parallel proceedings in a foreign country.

**third-party beneficiary** One who does not give consideration for a promise yet has legal rights to enforce the contract. A person is a third-party beneficiary with legal rights when the contracting parties intended to benefit that person.

**third-party defense** In a case under the Comprehensive Environmental Responsibility, Contribution, and Liability Act, a potentially responsible current owner can assert this defense if the release or disposal of hazardous materials was by a third party who was not an employee and with whom the current owner had no contractual relationship. Also called the innocent landowner defense.

**Thompson Memorandum** The revised "Principles of Federal Prosecution of Business Organizations" issued by Attorney General Larry D. Thompson to establish determinants of whether to prosecute a company.

**360/360 method** A method for calculating interest whereby it is assumed that all months have 30 days; thus the monthly interest amounts are always the same.

**365/360 method** A method for calculating interest whereby the nominal annual interest rate is divided by 360, and the resulting daily rate is then multiplied by the outstanding principal amount and the actual number of days in the payment period.

**365/365 method** A method for calculating interest whereby the daily rate is determined by dividing the nominal annual interest rate by 365 (or 366, in leap years), then this daily rate is multiplied by the outstanding principal amount and the actual number of days in the payment period.

**tip** Disclosure of a fact made to an individual and withheld from the general public.

**tippee** A person who receives inside information.

**tipper** A person who gives inside information.

**tombstone ad** A newspaper advertisement surrounded by bold black lines identifying the existence of a public offering and indicating where a prospectus may be obtained.

**tort** A civil wrong resulting in injury to a person or a person's property.

**tortious interference with contract** A wrongful interference with a contract by a third party when (1) there is a contract between the plaintiff and another; (2) the defendant has knowledge of the contract; (3) the defendant's actions cause the other party to breach that contract; (4) the plaintiff is damaged in some way; and (5) the defendant intentionally and wrongfully induces the other party to breach the contract.

**total-activity test** A combination of tests used to determine where a company engaged in multistate operations is domiciled; considers all aspects of the corporate entity, including the nature and scope of the company's activities.

**total cost** Variable cost plus fixed costs, such as rent and overhead.

**toxic tort** Any wrongful injury that is caused by exposure to a harmful, hazardous, or poisonous substance.

**trade dress** A manifestation of trademark law, the concept of trade dress is to protect the overall look of a product as opposed to just a particular design.

**trade name** A trade name or a corporate name identifies and symbolizes a business as a whole, as opposed to a trademark, which is used to identify and distinguish the various products and services sold by the business.

**Trade Promotion Authority** A law that allows the president to negotiate trade agreements and then submit them for an up or down vote by Congress with no amendments permitted; it expires on June 1, 2005, but will be automatically extended if neither house of Congress adopts a resolution opposing the extension.

**trade secret** Information that derives independent economic value from not being generally known and that is subject to reasonable efforts to maintain its secrecy.

**trademark** A word or symbol used on goods or with services that indicates their origin.

**traditional shelf offerings** The registration of (1) securities offered pursuant to employee benefit plans; (2) securities offered or sold pursuant to dividend or interest reinvestment plans; (3) warrants, rights, or securities to be issued upon conversion of other outstanding securities; (4) mortgage-related securities; and (5) securities issued in connection with business combination transactions.

**transaction value** The price of an imported article indicated on a sales invoice.

**transactional immunity** The prohibition from prosecution granted a witness that relates to any matter discussed in that person's testimony.

**transactional negotiation** Negotiation that is forward looking with concern for desired relationships.

**transnational insolvency** In its simplest form, an insolvency proceeding in one country, with a creditor located in a second country. More complex cases may involve subsidiaries, assets, creditors and operations in many countries.

**treaty** An international agreement concluded between states in written form and governed by international law.

**trespass to chattels** When personal property is interfered with but not taken, destroyed, or substantially altered (i.e., not converted), there is a trespass to chattels. Also called trespass to personal property.

**trespass to land** The intentional invasion of real property (below the surface or in the airspace above) without consent of the owner.

**trespass to personal property** When personal property is interfered with but not taken, destroyed, or substantially altered (i.e., not converted), there is said to be a trespass to personal property. Also called trespass to chattels.

**triple net lease** A type of industrial lease that requires the tenant to pay all taxes, insurance, and maintenance expenses.

**trust** (1) A combination of competitors who act together to fix prices, thereby stifling competition. (2) A manner of holding property that is controlled by a trustee for the benefit of a beneficiary.

**trustee** The legal representative of a bankrupt debtor's estate.

**tying arrangement** A business arrangement whereby a seller will sell product A (the tying or desired product) to the customer only if the customer purchases product B (the tied product) from the seller.

## U

**UCC-1 Form** In most states, this is the form a secured creditor uses for a financing statement under the Uniform Commercial Code.

**ultrahazardous activity** Activity that is so dangerous that no amount of care could protect others from the risk of harm.

**unavoidably unsafe product** A product, such as a vaccine, that is generally beneficial but is known to have harmful side effects in some cases.

**unconscionable** A contract term that is oppressive or fundamentally unfair.

**undercapitalization theory** A corporation is a separate entity, but its lack of adequate capital may constitute a fraud on the public. May be a basis for piercing corporate veil.

**underwater** A stock option is underwater when its strike price is above the price at which the stock is trading.

**underwriter** Any person who has purchased any security from an issuer with a view to, or offers or sells for an issuer in connection with, the distribution of any security.

**undisclosed principal** Use of an agent so that the third party to an agreement does not know or have reason to know of a principal's identity or existence.

**undue burden** Under the U.S. Constitution, a state regulation creates an undue burden when the regulatory burden on interstate commerce outweighs the state's interest in the legislation.

**undue influence** Sufficient influence and power over another as to make genuine assent impossible.

**unenforceable contract** A contract having no legal effect or force in a court action. A contract is unenforceable if it is (1) illegal or (2) unconscionable. A contract is also unenforceable if some public policy interest dictates that the agreement should not be upheld, regardless of the desire of one or more of the parties.

**unfair labor practice strike** A union strikes an employer for the employer's failure to bargain in good faith.

**unfair labor practices** Unlawful misconduct by an employer to employees exercising union rights.

**Uniform Customs and Practice for Documentary Credits (UCP)** A document that contains a set of rules that applies to letters of credit in international transactions; contrasts with the set of rules in Article 5 of the Uniform Commercial Code (UCC).

**unilateral contract** A promise given in exchange for an act. Offer can be accepted only by performing the act.

**universality** A domestic model for addressing international insolvency problems that tracks these proceedings as a single case and treats creditors equally, no matter where they are located.

**universalizability** An ethical theory that asks whether one would want everyone to perform in this manner.

**unjust enrichment** The unfair appropriation of the benefits of negotiation of contracts for the party's own use.

**unorthodox transaction** The purchase or sale by an officer, director, or greater-than-10 percent shareholder that would otherwise result in recoverable short-swing profits but is involuntary and does not involve the payment of cash, and there is no possibility of speculative abuse of insider information.

**unreasonable *per se*** Unreasonable no matter what the circumstances.

**upstream guaranty** A guaranty whereby subsidiaries guarantee the parent corporation's debt, or pledge their assets as security for the parent corporation's debt.

**use immunity** The prohibition on the use of the testimony of a witness against that witness in connection with the case in which that person is testifying or another case.

**useful article doctrine** The doctrine that holds that copyrightable pictorial, graphic, and sculptural works include works of artistic craftsmanship insofar as their form but not their mechanical or utilitarian aspects are concerned.

**usury** Charging an amount of interest on a loan that is in excess of the maximum specified by applicable law.

**usury laws** State statutes that set legal caps on what interest rates lenders may charge.

**utilitarianism** A major teleological system of ethics that stands for the proposition that the ideal is to maximize the total benefit for everyone involved.

**utility patent** A patent that protects any novel, useful, and nonobvious process, machine, manufacture, or composition of matter; or any novel, useful, and nonobvious improvement of such process, machine, manufacture, or composition of matter.

**utility requirement** A requirement that an invention must have a practical or real-world benefit in order for a utility patent to be issued.

## V

**vacate** The power of a court of appeal to nullify a previous court's ruling.

**value** Cash, property, or compensation for past services.

**variable cost** The cost of producing the next incremental unit.

**variable-interest loan** A loan in which the rate of interest is often set at a fixed number of percentage points over a specified standard or base rate (often the prime rate).

**variable-sum negotiations** Negotiations in which mutual gains are possible as parties trade lower valued resources for higher valued ones. Also called integrative negotiations.

**variance** A method of relief from the strict terms of a zoning ordinance that allows a landowner to construct a structure or carry on an activity not otherwise permitted under zoning regulations.

**venditur emptor** A phrase commonly associated with consumer transactions that means "let the seller beware."

**venture capital** Money managed by professional investors for investment in new enterprises.

**venue** The particular county or geographical area in which a court with jurisdiction may hear and determine a case.

**vertical agreement** An agreement between firms that operate at different levels of production or distribution.

**vertical market division** An agreement between a company and a dealer or distributor that prevents the dealer or the distributor from selling outside a certain territory or to a certain class of customer.

**vertical merger** A combination between firms at different points along the chain of distribution.

**vertical restraint** Unlawful restraint between firms at different levels in the chain of distribution, including price-fixing, market division, tying arrangements, and some franchise agreements.

**vested right** The right of a developer to develop property sometimes, but not always, obtained when a building permit is issued, substantial work is done, and substantial liabilities are incurred in reliance of that permit.

**vesting restrictions** Restrictions set by the company that grants a stock option on when the option can be exercised.

**veto power** The power of the president to prevent permanently or temporarily the enactment of a law created by Congress that does not meet his or her approval.

**vicarious copyright infringement** A doctrine that imposes liability on a third party for a direct copyright infringer's actions if the third party (a) has the right and ability to control the infringer's acts and (b) receives a direct financial benefit from the infringement.

**vicarious liability** The imposition of civil or criminal liability on one party (e.g., an employer) for the wrongful acts of another (e.g., an employee). Also called imputed liability.

**view easement** An interest in property owned by another by which an easement holder is guaranteed that a landowner will not obstruct the holder's view by making changes to said property.

**voidable** Unenforceable at the option of one party.

***voir dire*** Questioning of potential jurors to determine possible bias.

**voluntary conversion** The exchange by a holder of preferred stock for common stock on the occurrence of certain events.

**voluntary proceeding** A voluntary proceeding in bankruptcy filing begins when the debtor files a petition with the bankruptcy court.

**voluntary redemption rights** The requirement of a corporation to redeem an investor's shares for cash at a specified price, provided that the corporation is not prohibited by law from buying back stock or making distributions to its shareholders.

## W

**waiting period** The period between the filing of the registration statement and the date the registration statement becomes effective with the SEC. Also called the quiet period.

**waive** To refrain from exercising certain rights.

**warrant** A right, for a given period of time, to purchase a stated amount of a security (frequently, stock) at a stated price (often equal to the fair market value when the warrant is issued, permitting its holder to benefit from any increase in value of the securities).

**warranty deed** A warranty deed is similar to a grant deed. In addition to the implied warranties contained in a grant deed, the grantor of a warranty deed also expressly warrants the title to and the quiet possession of the property to grantee.

**web robots** Software programs that search and index the Internet for specific content by visiting websites, requesting documents based on certain criteria, and following up with requests for documents referenced in the documents already retrieved to identify illegal copying.

**well-known seasoned issuers** Firms eligible to use Form S-3 with $700 million of public common equity float and permitted to make unrestricted oral and written offers before the registration statement is filed without violating the gun-jumping provisions.

**whistleblower statutes** Federal and state statutes that prohibit employers from discharging or retaliating against an employee who has exercised the right to complain to a supervisor or government agency.

**white-collar crime** Nonviolent violations of the law by companies or their managers.

**winding up** The process of settling partnership affairs after dissolution.

**wire fraud** A scheme intended to defraud or to obtain money or property by fraudulent means through use of telephone systems.

**work letter agreement** An agreement between a tenant and a landlord, often an exhibit to a lease, that covers issues regarding tenant's improvements to rented space.

**work made for hire** A copyrightable work created by an employee within the scope of his or her employment, or a work in one of nine listed categories that is specially commissioned through a signed writing that states that the work is a "work made for hire."

**work-product doctrine** Protects information, including the private memoranda and personal thoughts of the attorney, created by the attorney while preparing a case for trial.

**workout** An out-of-court settlement between debtors and creditors that restructures the debtor's financial affairs in much the same way that a confirmed bankruptcy plan would, but it only binds those who expressly consent.

**wraparound financing** The transaction in which a new lender lends the owner of mortgaged real property additional funds and agrees to take over the servicing of the first loan. In exchange, the owner executes a deed of trust or mortgage and an all-inclusive note, covering the combined amount of the first and new loans.

**writ** An order in writing issued under seal in the name of a court or judicial officer commanding the person to whom it is directed to perform or refrain from performing an act specified therein.

**writ of certiorari** An order written by the U.S. Supreme Court when it decides to hear a case, ordering the lower court to certify the record of proceedings below and send it up to the U.S. Supreme Court.

**wrongful discharge** An employee termination without good cause that (1) violates public policy; (2) breaches an implied contract; or (3) violates the implied covenant of good faith and fair dealing.

## Z

**zero-sum negotiations** Negotiations in which the only issue is the distribution of the fixed pie. Also called distributive negotiations.

**zone of danger** The area in which an individual is physically close enough to a victim of an accident as to also be in personal danger.

**zone-of-danger test** A test of whether the consequences suffered by a plaintiff were foreseeable by the defendant and the plaintiff was foreseeably within the zone of danger caused by the defendant's careless conduct.

**zoning** The division of a city into districts and the application of specific land use regulations in each district.

# Index

Note: Page numbers followed by n. indicate footnotes.

## B

## C

## D

## E

## F

## J



## K

## N

## O



## P

## Q



## R

## T

## X



## Y



## Z